CASES AND MATERIALS

FAMILY LAW

SIXTH EDITION

by

JUDITH AREEN
Paul Regis Dean Professor of Law
Georgetown University Law Center

MARC SPINDELMAN
Professor of Law
Michael E. Moritz College of Law
The Ohio State University

PHILOMILA TSOUKALA
Associate Professor of Law
Georgetown University Law Center

FOUNDATION PRESS
2012

THOMSON REUTERS™

© 1978, 1985, 1992, 1999 FOUNDATION PRESS
© 2006 By FOUNDATION PRESS
© 2012 By THOMSON REUTERS/FOUNDATION PRESS

> 1 New York Plaza, 34th Floor
>
> New York, NY 10004
>
> Phone Toll Free 1–877–888–1330
>
> Fax 646–424–5201
>
> foundation–press.com

Printed in the United States of America

ISBN 978–1–60930–054–8

Mat #41181418

J.C.A.

For Rich and Jon and all the other members of our family.

M.S.

*For my mother, to the memory of my father,
and chosen families everywhere.*

P.T.

*For my family of origin, Maria, Ioannis, Victoria, Θεία Ελένη;
for Thani, who I will always miss, and Alvaro,
my family of destination.*

PREFACE TO THE SIXTH EDITION

This is the first edition of the casebook joined by Marc Spindelman and Philomila Tsoukala. As with earlier editions, this book is designed first and foremost for use in the classroom. It is structured to introduce students to the major issues in the field of family law with a particular emphasis on 21st century case law and statutes.

As previous editions have done, this book draws on a variety of sources in order to emphasize the powerful emotional and psychological dynamics of family life that the law must address. Material is provided on what occurred after a number of the included court decisions in order to illustrate the strengths and weaknesses of judicial intervention in family matters. Material from history and the social sciences is also included in order to provide students with a broader perspective on major issues. In addition to appellate opinions, the book includes other sources of law including a custody trial transcript, domestic abuse regulations, sample forms for parenting plans, and key sections from model acts. Finally, the casebook has been enriched with comparative and international materials that help to situate American family law in its global context.

Deletions from excerpted material are marked except when the omitted material consists only of citations or footnotes.

We are indebted to the many colleagues and students whose probing questions and suggestions over the years have helped to shape these materials. We are particular grateful to Milton C. Regan, Jr., for his many contributions to the Fifth Edition that continue to enrich the new edition. Georgetown law students Larkin Kittel, Kevin Lownds, Vanessa Nason, James Stanco, Tara Stearns, and Caroline Rose Van Wie together with Ohio State law students Aric Birdsell, Brookes Hammock, J.T. Larson, Richard Muniz, Sarah Rogers, Micah Tippie, and Joseph Wenger provided outstanding research assistance in preparing this edition. At Ohio State, Susan Edwards provided significant editorial assistance, and Katherine Hall gave indispensable help with both research and sources. At Georgetown, Anna Selden oversaw the entire manuscript and Jennifer Locke Davitt coordinated copyright permissions. Our thanks go to all of you and to our families for their inspiration and support.

JUDITH AREEN
MARC SPINDELMAN
PHILOMILA TSOUKALA

Washington D.C.
February, 2012

ACKNOWLEDGMENTS

We wish to thank the following authors and copyright holders for granting permission to reprint excerpts from the following copyrighted works:

CATHERINE R. ALBISTON, INSTITUTIONAL INEQUALITY AND THE MOBILIZATION OF THE FAMILY AND MEDICAL LEAVE ACT RIGHTS ON LEAVE ii–xi, 167–74, 181–86 (2010). Copyright 2010 by Catherine R. Albistan. Reprinted with the permission of the author and Cambridge University Press.

Anne L. Alstott, *Private Tragedies? Family Law as Social Insurance*, 4 HARV. L. & POL'Y REV. 3, 3–17 (2010). Copyright 2010. Reprinted with permission of the Harvard University Law School.

Paul R. Amato, *Good Enough Marriages: Parental Discord, Divorce, and Children's Long-Term Well-Being*, 9 VA. J. SOC. POL'Y & L. 71, 92–94 (2001).

AMERICAN LAW INSTITUTE, PRINCIPLES OF THE LAW OF FAMILY DISSOLUTION: ANALYSIS AND RECOMMENDATIONS (2002). Copyright 2002 by the American Law Institute. Reproduced by permission. All rights reserved.

Annette Ruth Appell, *Reflections on the Movement Toward a More Child-Center Adoption*, 32 W. NEW. ENG. L. REV. 1, 9–10 (2010).

Judith Areen, *Intervention Between Parent and Child: A Reappraisal of the State's Role in Child Neglect and Abuse Cases*, 63 GEO.L.J. 887 (1975). Reprinted with permission of the publisher; copyright 1975 by the Georgetown Law Journal.

R. Richard Banks, *The Color of Desire: Fulfilling Adoptive Parents' Racial Preferences Through Discriminatory State Action*, 107 YALE L. J. 875, 880–81, 934–44 (1998). Copyright 1998 by the Yale Law Journal Company, Inc. Reproduced with permission of Yale Law Journal Company, Inc.

Mary M. Beck, *Adoption of Children in Missouri*, 63 MO. L. REV. 423, 429–432 (1998).

Elizabeth F. Beyer, *A Pragmatic Look at Mediation and Collaborative Law as Alternatives to Family Law Litigation*, 40 ST. MARY'S L.J. 303 (2008).

Ben Barlow, *Divorce Child Custody Mediation: In Order to Form a More Perfect Disunion?*, 52 CLEV. ST. L. REV. 499 (2004–2005).

Brian Bix, *Private Ordering and Family Law*, 23 J. AM. ACAD. MATRIM. LAW 249, 249, 251–259 (2010). Reprinted with permission of the American Academy of Matrimonial Lawyers.

Sanford Braver, Ira Ellman & William Fabricus, *Relocation of Children After Divorce and Children's Best Interests: New Evidence and Legal Considerations*, 17 J. FAM. PSYCHOL. 206 (2003). Copyright 2003 by the American Psychological Association. Reproduced with permission.

Beth Burkstrand–Reid, *"Trophy Husbands" & "Opt-Out" Moms*, 34 SEATTLE U. L. REV. 663, 663–74 (2011).

Naomi R. Cahn & Jennifer M. Collins, *Eight is Enough*, 103 NW. U. L. REV. COLLOQUY 501 (2009). Reprinted by special permission of the Northwestern University School of Law, Northwestern University Law Review.

Mary Anne Case, *Feminist Fundamentalism on the Frontier Between Government and Family Responsibility for Children*, 11 J.L. & FAM. STUD. 333, 355–58 (2009).

ANDREW CHERLIN, THE MARRIAGE-GO-ROUND: THE STATE OF MARRIAGE AND THE FAMILY IN AMERICA TODAY 13–35 (2009). Reproduced with permission of Andrew Cherlin, Professor of Sociology and Public Policy at Johns Hopkins University.

NANCY F. COTT, PUBLIC VOWS: A HISTORY OF MARRIAGE AND THE NATION 1–2 (2002). Cambridge, Mass.: Harvard University Press. Copyright 2002 by Nancy F. Cott. Reprinted by permission of the publisher.

Nancy F. Cott, *Divorce and the Changing Status of Women in Eighteenth–Century Massachusetts*, 33 WM. & MARY Q. 586, 586–89 (1976).

Judith F. Daar, *Accessing Reproductive Technologies: Invisible Barriers, Indelible Harms*, 23 BERKELEY J. GENDER L. & JUST. 18, 35–46 (2008).

James Herbie Difonzo, *Customized Marriage*, 75 IND. L.J. 875, 885–928 (2000). Copyright 2000 by the Trustees of Indiana University. Reprinted with Permission.

Ariela R. Dubler, *From* McLaughlin v. Florida *to* Lawrence v. Texas: *Sexual Freedom and the Road to Marriage*, 106 COLUM. L. REV. 1165, 1170–72, 1177–78 (2006). Reproduced with permission of Columbia Law Review Association, Inc.

Lynne Duke, *Intermarriage Broken Up By Death*, WASH. POST, June 12, 1992, at A3.

Ira Mark Ellman & Stephen D. Sugarman, *Spousal Emotional Abuse as a Tort?*, 55 MD. L. REV. 1268, 1268, 1305–26 (1996).

Linda Elrod, *National and International Momentum Builds for More Child Focus in Relocation Disputes*, 44 FAM. L. Q. 341, 341–44, 351–57, 359–63 (2010). Reprinted with permission of the American Bar Association.

Jon Elster, *Solomonic Judgments: Against the Best Interest of the Child*, 54 U. CHI. L. REV. 1, 39–43 (1986). Copyright 1986. Reprinted with permission of the University of Chicago Law School.

Martha M. Ertman, *Telling*, 2009 UTAH L. REV. 531 (2009).

Laurie Essig & Lynn Owens, *What if Marriage Is Bad for Us?*, THE CHRON. OF HIGHER EDUC., Oct. 5, 2009, at B4–B5.

Melanie C. Falco, Comment, *The Road Not Taken: Using the Eighth Amendment to Strike Down Criminal Punishment for Engaging in Consensual Sexual Acts*, 82 N.C. L. REV. 723, 740–47 (2004).

LAWRENCE M. FRIEDMAN, A HISTORY OF AMERICAN LAW 142–45 (3d ed. 2005).

RICHARD FRY, THE REVERSAL OF THE COLLEGE MARRIAGE GAP 1–2 (2010), available at http://pewsocialtrends.org/2010/10/07/the-reversal-of-the-college-marriage-gap/. Copyright 2010 Pew Research Center.

Ruth Bader Ginsburg, *Some Thoughts on Autonomy and Equality in Relation to* Roe v. Wade, 63 N.C. L. REV. 375, 379–84 (1985).

Ruth Bader Ginsburg, *Gender and the Constitution*, 44 U. CIN. L. REV. 1–4 (1975).

Mary Ann Glendon, *Marriage and the State: The Withering Away of Marriage*, 62 VA. L. REV. 663, 677–82 (1976). Reprinted with permission of the Virginia Law Review Association.

Michele Goodwin, *Assisted Reproductive Technology and the Double Bind: The Illusory Choice of Motherhood*, 9 J. GENDER RACE & JUST. 1, 18–54 (2005).

Ronald S. Granberg & Sarah A. Cavassa, *Private Ordering and Alternative Dispute Resolution*, 23 J. AM. ACAD. MATRIM. LAW 287 (2010). Reprinted with permission of the American Academy of Matrimonial Lawyers.

Brandi Grissom, *Two El Paso Women Legally Married*, EL PASO TIMES (May 14, 2010).

Cheryl Hanna, *Because Breaking Up Is Hard To Do*, 116 YALE L.J. POCKET PART 92, 93–94 (2006).

Jill Hasday, *Contest and Consent: A Legal History of Marital Rape*, 88 CALIF. L. REV. 1373, 1482–1504 (2000). Copyright 2000 by the California Law Review. Reprinted by permission of the California Law Review and Jill Elaine Hasday.

Jennifer Meleana Hee, *How to Sell Your Body Parts . . . and Still Respect Yourself in the Morning*, HAW. WOMEN'S J., July–October 2010, at 29.

Rosabeth Moss Kanter, COMMITMENT AND COMMUNITY: COMMUNES AND UTOPIAS IN SOCIOLOGICAL PERSPECTIVE 1–4 (1972). (Cambridge, Mass.: Harvard University Press, 1972). Copyright 1972 by the President and Fellow of Harvard College. Reprinted by permission.

Pamela S. Karlan, *Foreward: Loving* Lawrence, 102 MICH. L. REV. 1447, 1449–50 (2004).

Pamela S. Karlan, *The Gay and the Angry: The Supreme Court and the Battles Surrounding Same–Sex Marriage*, 2010 SUP. CT. REV. 159, 159–62 (2011). Reprinted with permission of the University of Chicago Press.

Alicia Brokars Kelly, *Rehabilitating Partnership Marriage as a Theory of Wealth Distribution at Divorce: In Recognition of a Shared Life*, 19 WIS. WOMEN'S L.J. 141 (2004).

William M. Kephart, THE FAMILY, SOCIETY AND THE INDIVIDUAL 121–141 (1977). Reprinted with permission of Houghton Mifflin.

Mary Kay Kisthardt, *Re–Thinking Alimony: The AAML's Considerations for Calculating Alimony, Spousal Support, or Maintenance*, 21 J. AM. ACAD. MATRIM. LAW 61, 64–81 (2008). Reprinted with permission of the American Academy of Matrimonial Lawyers.

Kimberly D. Krawiec, *Altruism and Intermediation in the Market for Babies*, 66 Wash. & Lee L. Rev. 203 (2009).

Law Commission of Canada, Beyond Conjugality: Recognizing and Supporting Close Personal Adult Relationships, 1–7, 113–122 (2001). Reprinted with permission of the Minister of Public Works and Government Services Canada.

Claude Levi–Strauss, *The Family, in* Man, Culture, and Society 261, 276–78 (Shapiro ed. 1956). Copyright 1956, 1971 by Oxford University Press, Inc. Reprinted by permission.

Robert J. Levy, Custody Law and the ALI's Principles: A Little History, a Little Policy, and Some Very Tentative Judgments, in Reconceiving the Family 67–89 (Robin Fretwell Wilson ed., Cambridge University Press 2006).

Margaret M. Mahoney, *Forces Shaping the Law of Cohabitation for Opposite Sex Couples*, 7 J.L. & Fam. Stud. 135, 141–42 (2005). Originally published in the Utah Law Review and the Journal of Law & Family Studies, 2009 Utah L. Rev. 381; 7 J.L. & Fam. Stud. 135, 141–42 (2005).

Margaret Mead, *Anomalies in American Postdivorce Relationships in* Divorce and After 104–08, (Paul Bohannan ed., 1970). Copyright 1970 by Paul Bohannan. Used by permission of Doubleday & Company, Inc., a division of Random House, Inc.

Linda C. McClain, *Love, Marriage, and the Baby Carriage: Revisiting the Channelling Function of Family Law*, 28 Cardozo L. Rev. 2133, 2138–47, 2152, 2174–77 (2007).

S. M. Miller, *The Making of a Confused Middle–Class Husband*, 2 Soc. Pol'y 33, 34, 36–39 (July/August 1971). Reprinted by permission of the publisher, Social Policy Corporation , New York, N.Y. 10036.

Robert Mnookin, *Child–Custody Adjudication: Judicial Functions in the Face of Indeterminacy*, 39 Law & Contemp. Probs. 226, 289–91 (1975). Reprinted with permission from a symposium on children and law appearing in 9 Law and Contemporary Problems, Summer 1975, published by the Duke University School of Law, Durham North Carolina, Copyright 1975 by Duke University. Article copyright by the author.

Robert Mnookin & Lewis Kornhauser, *Bargaining in the Shadow of the Law: The Case of Divorce*, 88 Yale L.J. 950, 951, 954–57 (1979). Reprinted by permission of the Yale Law Journal Co. Fred B. Rothman & Co. from 88 Yale Law Journal 950.

Liza Mundy, *Fault Line*, Wash. Post Mag., Oct. 26, 1997, at W8. Copyright 1997, The Washington Post. Reprinted with permission.

National Conference of Commissioners on Uniform State Laws;

— The Uniform Adoption Act (1994);

— The Uniform Child Custody Jurisdiction and Enforcement Act (1997);

— The Uniform Marriage and Divorce Act (both 1971 and 1974 editions);

— The Uniform Premarital Agreement Act (1984);

— The Uniform Interstate Family Support Act (2008). Reprinted with permission.

Laura M. Padilla, *Single–Parent Latinas on the Margin: Seeking a Room With a View, Meals, and Built-in Community*, 13 WIS. WOMEN'S L.J. 179, 186–95 (1998).

Elizabeth G. Patterson, *Civil Contempt and the Indigent Child Support Obligor: The Silent Return of Debtor's Prison*, 18 CORNELL J.L. & PUB. POL'Y 95, 99–100 (2008).

PEW RESEARCH CENTER SOCIAL TRENDS STAFF, THE DECLINE OF MARRIAGE AND RISE OF NEW FAMILIES, Nov. 18, 2010, available at http://pewresearch.org/pubs/1802/decline-marriage-rise-new-families. Copyright 2010 Pew Research Center.

RICHARD POSNER, SEX AND REASON 409–16 (1992). Reprinted by permission of the publisher, Cambridge, Mass.: Harvard University Press, Copyright 1992 by President and Fellows of Harvard College. Reprinted by permission of the publisher.

Richard Posner, *Elite Universities and Women's Careers*—The Posner, Becker–Posner Blog (http://www.becker-posner-blog.com/2005/09/elite-universities-and-womens-careers—posner.html).

Radhika Rao, *Equal Liberty: Assisted Reproductive Technology and Reproductive Equality*, 76 GEO. WASH. L. REV. 1457, 1459–84 (2008).

Rosemary Ring, *Comment, Personal Jurisdiction and Child Support: Establishing the Parent–Child Relationship as Minimum Contacts*, 89 CALIF. L. REV. 1125, 1139–45 (2001). Copyright 2001 by the California Law Review, Inc. Reprinted from California Law Review volume 89, No. 4 by permission of California Law Review, Inc.

DOROTHY ROBERTS, KILLING THE BLACK BODY: RACE, REPRODUCTION AND THE MEANING OF LIBERTY 260–69 (1997). Copyright 1997 by Dorothy Roberts. Reprinted with permission of Pantheon Books, a division of Random House, Inc.

John A. Robertson, *Commerce and Regulation in the Assisted Reproduction Industry*, 85 TEX. L. REV. 665, 699–701 (2007). Copyright 2007 by the Texas Law Review Association.

Darren Rosenblum et al., *Pregnant Man?: A Conversation*, 22 YALE J.L. & FEMINISM 207, 209–17, 257–60 (2010).

Carl E. Schneider, *The Channeling Function in Family Law*, 20 HOFSTRA L. REV. 495, 496, 498, 500–04, 506–09, 511, 529–32 (1992).

Reva B. Siegel, *She the People: The Nineteenth Amendment, Sex Equality, Federalism, and the Family*, 115 HARV. L. REV. 947, 1005–09, 1012–19, 1022–24 (2002).

Mary Lyndon Shanley, *Collaboration and Commodification in Assisted Procreation: Reflections on an Open Market and Anonymous Donation in Human Sperm and Eggs*, 36 LAW & SOC'Y REV. 257, 271–73 (2002).

Pamela J. Smock & Wendy D. Manning, Population Studies Ctr., Living Together Unmarried in the United States: Demographic Perspectives and Implications for Family Policy 2–4, 7–9, 14–15 (2004) (Report No. 04–555).

Katherine Shaw Spaht, *Covenant Marriage Seven Years Later: Its As Yet Unfulfilled Promise*, 65 LA. L. REV. 605, 612–15 (2005). Reprinted by permission.

Marc Spindelman, *Surviving* Lawrence v. Texas, 102 MICH. L. REV. 1615, 1633–35 (2004). Reprinted with permission of the author.

Jeannie Suk, *Criminal Law Comes Home*, 116 YALE L.J. 2 (2006). Yale Law Journal Copyright 2006.

Pauline Tesler, *Collaborative Family Law*, 4 PEPP. DISP. RESOL. L.J. 317 (2004). Copyright 2004 by Pepperdine University School of Law. Reprinted by permission.

Lenore Weitzman, *Legal Regulation of Marriage: Tradition and Change*, 62 CAL. REV. 1169 (1974). Reprinted by permission of the author.

Jamil Zainaldin, *The Emergence of a Modern American Family Law: Child Custody, Adoption, and the Courts*, 1796–1851, 73 NW.U.L.REV. 1038, 1041–45 (1979). Reprinted by special permission of Northwestern University School of Law, Northwestern University Law Review.

SUMMARY OF CONTENTS

TABLE OF CONTENTS

TABLE OF CASES

The principal cases are in bold type. Cases cited or discussed in the text are in roman type. References are to pages. Cases cited in principal cases and within other quoted materials are not included.

FAMILY LAW

INTRODUCTION TO FAMILY LAW

Family law deals with "families," of course, but that explanation merely raises the question what constitutes a family? Most agree that two parents and their child or children are a family, but what of one parent and a child? A married couple with no children? An unmarried couple with no children? Two adult siblings? Three otherwise unrelated adults? Not only is there disagreement about what it takes to be considered a family, there is disagreement about which other intimate relationships the law should recognize, as well as about the rights, benefits, and obligations that should flow from recognition.

These controversies exist in large measure because there is often some distance between the relationships recognized by the legal system and the way people live. All areas of the law must struggle with the distance between legal form and substance to varying degrees, but the challenge in family law is especially acute. Perhaps more than in any other legal field, family law attempts to impose some measure of coherence and rationality upon an unruly, and often deeply irrational, domain of life. As people meet, become intimately involved, intertwine their lives, raise children, become estranged, attempt reconciliation, and decide to part, the legal forms and procedures available to address these experiences may be responsive and useful, or insensitive and even harmful. People act partly within the structures (such as marriage) that the law provides, but also may feel the need to ignore, transform, or destroy them in order to live their lives as they wish.

Many believe that the distance between form and substance in family law has widened considerably over the past several decades. Certainly marriage has become for some a less central legal form for organizing intimate relationships as shown by the increasing rates of unmarried cohabitation and of births outside of marriage. At the same time, marriage has acquired more legal and symbolic importance for some same-sex couples and some states. Advances in reproductive technology have called into question the relevance of traditional legal definitions of parenthood at the same time more families are crossing national boundaries to marry, to work, and to have and to adopt children. Some argue we should rely less on legal form, and more on the substance of relationships as the conceptual basis for family law. The concern is that in too many cases, adhering strictly to legal form leads to unfair results.

Rethinking family law in this way raises important and difficult questions. What characteristics should exist before it is said that a particular relationship is "in substance" a family relationship? Are those features the same across all types of relationships, or do they differ depending on whether adults, children, or some combination of the two are involved? What visions of "family" form the bases for these comparisons?

If state legislators (or other legal rule-makers) expand legal categories to encompass a wider range of relationships, how inclusive should they be?

Should the law permit anyone who wants it to assume a particular legal status, or should it impose certain requirements for being able to do so?

If legal form is of diminished significance, there are other issues to confront. Are we prepared for courts and agencies to conduct in-depth examinations of intimate relationships in order to identify those that have the essential characteristics of a family? At what level of government should these decisions be made? Would such case-by-case determinations provide enough predictability for the parties involved and those who deal with them? If legal form were no longer to play an important role in ordering intimate life, would society lose an important way of both shaping and expressing common values?

To guide your understanding of the field of family law, there are five significant trends to watch for in the cases and materials included in the Casebook and, indeed, throughout family law. There are other trends you may notice besides these five, of course, and some of the five have inspired counter-trends, thereby confirming how difficult it is to generalize in this diverse society about views on such charged topics as marriage, procreation, or the appropriate role of government. The five trends worth highlighting are (1) the movement from public to private ordering, exemplified by the increased acceptance by courts of premarital and separation contracts agreed to by the parties—which is partly offset by the counter-trend of increased government intervention in families to protect victims of domestic violence; (2) the expanding role of the federal government through constitutional law (for example, the decision of the Supreme Court in *Loving v. Virginia*, 388 U.S. 1 (1967) holding unconstitutional Virginia's antimiscegenation statute) and statutory law (such as the Parental Kidnapping Prevention Act of 1980); (3) the broadened commitment to equality, which has reduced discrimination on the basis of race, national origin, gender, illegitimacy, disabilities, sexual orientation, and gender identity in family matters; (4) the burgeoning number of transnational issues presented by families whose members live or hold citizenship in more than one country; and (5) a growing number of procedural innovations ranging from mediation and arbitration to collaborative divorce. Mastering these trends should equip you to understand this field in ferment and prepare you for the ways it may change in the future.

A. THE MODERN AMERICAN FAMILY

The Chapter begins with a look at the size and shape of families in the United States, with an emphasis on marriage and divorce patterns. Although many are concerned about the high rate of divorce in the United States, it is not a new problem. As early as 1816, Timothy Dwight, then president of Yale, complained that:

> At the present time, the progress of . . . evil is alarming and terrible. In this town, within five years, more than fifty divorces have been granted: at the average calculation, more than four hundred in the whole State during this period: that is one out of every hundred married pairs. What a flaming proof is here of the baleful influence of . . . corruption on a people.[1]

---

1. TIMOTHY DWIGHT, III THEOLOGY: EXPLAINED AND DEFENDED IN A SERIES OF SERMONS 433 (5th ed. Carvill 1828).

Imagine what Dwight would have thought of the current incidence of divorce when more than one out of three marriages ends in divorce.

In fact, the divorce rate actually has *declined* in the last few decades from its high in 1979, when it was 22.8 divorces per thousand married couples per year, to 16.7 divorces per thousand married couples in 2005.[2] The decline correlates with the level of education of the parties. Among college-educated women who married between 1975 and 1979, 29 percent were divorced within ten years. For those who married between 1990 and 1994, by contrast, only 16.5 percent were divorced. Among high-school graduates, the divorce rate rose from 35 percent for those who married in 1975–79, to 38 percent for those who married in 1990–94. These diverging divorce rates suggest that we are becoming "a nation of separate and unequal families."[3]

The United States may have a higher rate of divorce than most other nations, but we also have higher rates of marriage and remarriage. As you read the materials in this section, consider why this is so, and what the implications for family law and policy are.

ANDREW CHERLIN, THE MARRIAGE-GO-ROUND: THE STATE OF MARRIAGE AND THE FAMILY IN AMERICA TODAY

13–35 (2009).

On Valentine's Day in 2005, Governor Mike Huckabee of Arkansas, who would gain recognition in 2008 as a candidate for the Republican presidential nomination, and his wife, Janet, converted their marriage to a covenant marriage in front of a crowd of 6,400 at an arena in North Little Rock. The governor was aware that few Arkansas couples were choosing the covenant option—of the first hundred thousand or so marriages that had begun since it was introduced in 2001, about six hundred couples had chosen it. In Louisiana and Arizona, the other states that offered covenant marriages, the take-up rate wasn't much better. Advocates for covenant marriage claimed that many couples were unaware of it and that the laws had been poorly implemented. Even so, the numbers were far smaller than anyone expected. Those who chose Arkansas's option agreed to undergo premarital counseling. They also agreed that if either spouse ever requested a divorce, they would attend marital counseling before splitting up. And they agreed that neither spouse could obtain a quick divorce based on "no-fault" grounds such as incompatibility. Only if the other spouse had committed a serious transgression such as adultery or physical or sexual abuse could a covenant-married person ask for an immediate divorce. Otherwise, the person who wanted out had to wait at least two years for a divorce.[1]

. . .

Governor Huckabee's concern about the [high] divorce rate in Arkansas . . . was well-taken. In 2004, for instance, Arkansas had the second-highest

---

2. Tyler Cowen, *Matrimony Has Its Benefits, and Divorce Has a Lot to Do with That*, N.Y. TIMES, Apr. 19, 2007, at C3. Divorce statistics are not particularly reliable because the federal government has stopped collecting them. Estimates depend on state reporting, and some of the largest states, such as California, do not report them.

3. *The Frayed Knot*, THE ECONOMIST 23 (May 26, 2007) (quoting Kay Hymowitz).

1. My description of the rally draws upon [Laura] Kellams, [*Huckabees Say 'I Do" to Covenant Marriage*, ARK. DEMOCRAT-GAZETTE, Feb. 15] 2005. Governor Huckabee's radio address was aired on November 27, 2004; retrieved November 22, 2005, from http://www.arkansas.gov/governor/media/radio/text/r11272004.html.

number of divorces per person of any state (after Nevada, a divorce destination that does a brisk business with out-of-state visitors). But Governor Huckabee may not have known that Arkansas also had a large number of weddings. In 2004, it had the third-highest per capita rate of marriage (after Nevada and Hawaii, two popular wedding destinations). With much divorce *and* much marriage, Arkansas exemplifies the American pattern.

That a state in the Bible Belt—Arkansas is well above average in church membership—has a high rate of marriage may seem unremarkable; by contrast, its high divorce rate may seem odd. Yet six of the ten states with the highest divorce rates are in the South, and the other four are in the West.[2] George W. Bush carried all ten states in the 2004 presidential election, which suggests that having a socially conservative electorate does not insulate a state from divorce. It is true that people who are religious are less likely to divorce, but religious Americans still have high divorce rates by international standards. Moreover, people in high-divorce states tend to have less education, to marry earlier, and not to be Catholic—all of which are risk factors for divorce. That's why Arkansas stands out: it has one of the lowest percentages of high school graduates and of Catholics, and one of the lowest median ages at marriage, of any state.

Both marriage and divorce contribute to the larger picture of a country in which people partner, unpartner, and repartner faster than do people in any other Western nation. They form cohabiting relationships easily, but they end them after a shorter time than people in other nations. They tend to marry at younger ages. After a divorce, they tend to find a new partner more quickly. In other words, having several partnerships is more common in the United States not just because people exit intimate partnerships faster but also because they *enter* them faster and after a breakup *reenter* them faster. We know these facts from the work of demographers using the Fertility and Family Surveys, a remarkable set of surveys conducted between 1989 and 1997 in European countries, Canada, New Zealand, and the United States (as well as from other surveys in Great Britain and Australia, two countries that were not included). In each nation researchers asked a large, random sample of individuals comparable questions about their marriages, divorces, and cohabiting relationships.

Why, you might ask, did researchers go to the expense and trouble of conducting these surveys throughout Western Europe and non-European English-speaking countries? The answer is that enormous changes have occurred in family life not only in the United States but also throughout the Western world in the past half century (and, in much of the rest of the world, too, for that matter). People everywhere are concerned about the future of the family as they know it. In the Scandinavian countries and in France, cohabitation is even more common than in the United States, and a large proportion of all births occur to cohabiting couples—more than half of first births in Sweden. Divorce rates have increased, too, although not to the height seen in the United States. Yet what drives European concern is not the decline of marriage but rather the decline in births. It's hard for Americans to understand this concern because we don't share it. American women have enough children to maintain the size of our population, even ignoring immigration. In many European countries, in contrast, women are having fewer births. Countries such as France and Germany have long been

---

2. The ten states in order of divorces per person in 2004 are Nevada; Arkansas; Wyoming; Alabama and West Virginia (tied); Idaho; Kentucky, Oklahoma, and Tennessee (three-way tie); and New Mexico.

concerned with keeping their populations up so that they can field armies large enough to defend themselves. More recently, they have been concerned about having enough working-age adults to care for their growing elderly populations.

In the United States, however, the concern is about marriage, and the Fertility and Family Surveys have much to say about it. To compare, say, current divorce rates across countries, ideally we would interview a sample of people who get married this year in each country, follow them for the next several decades, and see how many become divorced. But no mere mortal has the time to wait that long. Instead, demographers use the "life table" method, so called because one of its first uses was to estimate how long people would live so that insurance companies could determine how much to charge them for life insurance policies.[3] It can be used to estimate the expected "survival" time of marriages, cohabiting relationships, or periods of singlehood. Its estimates will be inaccurate if conditions change greatly in the future. Essentially, the life table answers this question: If conditions stay the same as they have been recently, how long would we expect a marriage, a cohabiting relationship, or a spell of being single to last?

The American Difference

Here are some comparisons that can be made between women in the United States (the American survey did not include men) and in other Western nations in the mid–1990s, when most of the surveys were conducted:

Americans marry and cohabit for the first time sooner than people in most other Western nations. Half of all first marriages occurred by age twenty-five in the United States, compared to age twenty-nine in Italy, thirty in France, thirty-one in Sweden, and thirty-two in the former West Germany. In part, ages of marriage are older in Europe because in some countries more young adults cohabit prior to marrying. Yet even if we consider the age at which half of all first partnerships of either kind (marital or cohabiting) occur, American women were relatively young: age twenty-two, compared to twenty-one in Sweden, age twenty-three in France, twenty-six in West Germany, and twenty-eight in Italy.

A higher proportion of Americans marry at some point in their lives than in most other Western nations: 84 percent of American women are predicted to marry by age forty. In contrast, the forecast drops to 70 percent in Sweden and 68 percent in France. (For technical reasons, all of these forecasts are likely to be somewhat lower than the actual percentages who will ever marry.) If we consider both marital and cohabiting relationships, however, over 90 percent

---

3. Here's how the life table method works. Imagine a woman who marries this year. Suppose that every year in the future her risk of divorce will be the same as the risk of people who have been married for exactly that many years in the recent past. By calculating these annual risks from people's recent experience, demographers can obtain an estimate of her probability of getting a divorce in the future if (and this is the big if) her future experience is similar to that of married people in the recent past. For each FFS country, then, we identify all of the people in the survey who have ever married. Then we calculate the fraction who told the interviewer that they divorced in their first year of marriage. That's the divorce risk for year one. Then, for everyone whose marriage lasted at least one year, we calculate the fraction who told the interviewer they divorced during their second year. That's the risk for year two. We repeat that calculation for all those who made it through at least two years, then all who made it through at least three, then at least four, and so forth. Then we cumulate all of these risks in a mathematical formula and obtain the estimated lifetime risk of divorce for our imaginary newlywed. In practice, the procedure is a bit more complicated than this. . . .

of women in nearly all countries will eventually begin an intimate partnership.

So Americans begin to have partners at a relatively young age, whereas many Europeans wait longer. And Americans turn those partnerships into marriages—or marry without living together beforehand—much more quickly. In France and the Nordic countries, in contrast, young adults tend to live with partners for several years before marrying, if they marry at all. In some southern European countries, such as Spain and Italy, living together prior to marrying is less common, and many young adults live with their parents well into their twenties before marrying. Other English-speaking countries are more similar to the United States, but people there still marry at somewhat older ages and are less likely to ever marry over their lifetimes.

Marriages and cohabiting relationships in the United States are far more fragile than elsewhere. After only five years, more than one-fifth of Americans who married had separated or divorced, compared to half that many or even fewer in other Western nations. And among Americans who began a cohabiting relationship, over half had broken up five years later (as opposed to remaining together, whether they subsequently married or not), which is a substantially higher figure than in other nations. Whether they started a partnership by marrying or by living together, Americans were less likely to be living with that partner five years later.

Because of these fragile partnerships, American children born to married or cohabiting parents are more likely to see their parents' partnership break up than are children in most other countries. Forty percent experienced a breakup by age fifteen. About the same percentage experienced a breakup in New Zealand. In Sweden, the country with the next-highest rate, the comparable figure was 30 percent; it was in the high twenties in western Germany and Canada, and the low twenties in France and Australia. Children born to cohabiting parents in the United States and New Zealand faced exceptionally high risks of experiencing a breakup: about three-fourths no longer lived with both parents at age fifteen. But even if we look just at children born to married couples, American children were more likely to see their parents break up. In fact, children born to *married* parents in the United States were more likely to experience their parents' breakup than were children born to *cohabiting* parents in Sweden.

Without doubt, then, there are more breakups of married and cohabiting couples in the United States than in any other Western country with the possible exception of New Zealand. So not only do Americans marry more, they also divorce more. Further, they end their cohabiting relationships more quickly. So they start and end partnerships with a speed that is virtually unmatched.

After their breakups, American parents are more likely to repartner. Consequently, children in the United States who have seen their parents' partnership end are more likely to have another adult partner (cohabiting or married) enter their household than are children living elsewhere. In the United States, nearly half of children who had experienced the breakup of their parents' marriage or cohabiting relationship saw the entry of another partner into their household within three years, a much higher proportion than in Sweden (where one-third see a new partner within three years), West Germany (29 percent), France (23 percent), or Italy (8 percent). In fact, American children spent more of their childhoods in stepfamilies than did children in continental Europe, Canada, or New Zealand. As a result, American children experienced not only more breakups but also more new adults moving in with the biological parent who cared for them.

American women become parents at an earlier age and are much more likely to spend time as lone parents in their teens or twenties than are women in Western Europe. By age thirty, one-third of American women had spent time as lone mothers; in European countries such as France, Sweden, and the western part of Germany, the comparable percentages were half as large or even less. But children born to lone parents in the United States are also more likely to experience a parent's new partner moving into the household than in some other countries, including France, Sweden, and Germany. So more one-parent families started, and more ended.

What all these statistics mean is that family life in the United States involves more transitions than anywhere else. There is more marriage but also more divorce. There are more lone parents but also more repartnering. Cohabiting relationships are shorter. Over the course of people's adult lives, there is more movement into and out of marriages and cohabiting relationships than in other countries. The sheer number of partners people experience during their lives is greater. Jeffrey Timberlake has estimated the percentage of women in each country who had three or more live-in partners (married or cohabiting) by age thirty-five. These were women who may have lived with a man and then perhaps married him and had children, divorced him, lived with another man (partner number two), ended that relationship, and then lived with or married yet another man (partner number three). In most countries, the percentage of women who accomplished this feat by age thirty-five is negligible: almost no one in Italy or Spain, less than 2 percent in France or Canada, and 3 percent in Germany. The highest figures elsewhere were 4.5 percent in Sweden and 4 percent in New Zealand. But in the United States, 10 percent of women had three or more husbands or live-in partners by age thirty-five, more than twice the percentage in Sweden and New Zealand and several times the percentage anywhere else.

. . .

There are many similarities, of course, between the United States and other Western nations . . . but they won't help us to explain distinctive American family patterns. To do that, we have to look for differences, not similarities, between the United States and other countries.

One difference lies in the realm of culture: the contradictory emphases on marriage and individualism found only in the United States. . . .

. . .

The rise of individualism, historians and social commentators have argued, has been one of the master trends in the development of Western society over the past few centuries. And most would agree that an individualistic outlook on family and personal life has become more important since the mid-twentieth century. Robert Bellah and his colleagues, in an influential book on individualism and commitment in American life, distinguished between two types of individualism.[4] They called the older form "utilitarian individualism." Think of the utilitarian individualist as the self-reliant, independent entrepreneur pursuing material success, such as a high position in a corporation or a senior partnership in a law firm. The great German social

---

4. ROBERT BELLAH, RICHARD MADSEN, WILLIAM M. SULLIVAN, ANN SWINDLER, & STEVEN M. TIPTON, HABITS OF THE HEART: INDIVIDUALISM AND COMMITMENT IN AMERICA (1985).

theorist Max Weber, in a classic book, suggested that there is a link between a similar concept, which he called "the Protestant ethic," and the economic development of the West.[5] He noted that Calvinists (including the group that became known as the Puritans in England and America) believed that some individuals had been predestined by God for earthly success. This doctrine encouraged people to work hard so that they could prove to others (and themselves) that they were among the elect. Weber used the writings of Benjamin Franklin, a prototype of the utilitarian individualist, to illustrate this spirit of industriousness. "Early to bed and early to rise," Franklin advised in one of his famous aphorisms, "makes a man healthy, wealthy, and wise."

The newer form of individualism, which Bellah and his colleagues called "expressive individualism," germinated in the late nineteenth and early twentieth centuries and flowered in the second half of the twentieth. It is a view of life that emphasizes the development of one's sense of self, the pursuit of emotional satisfaction, and the expression of one's feelings. Until the past half century, individuals moved through a series of roles (student, spouse, parent, housewife or breadwinner) in a way that seemed more or less natural. Choices were constrained. In mill towns, two or three generations of kin might work at the same factory. Getting married was the only acceptable way to have children, except perhaps among the poor. Young people often chose their spouses from among a pool of acquaintances in their neighborhood, church, or school. But now you can't get a job in the factory where your father and grandfather worked because overseas competition has forced it to close, so you must choose another career. You get little help from relatives in finding a partner, so you sign on to an Internet dating service and review hundreds of personal profiles. As other lifestyles become more acceptable, you must choose whether to get married and whether to have children. You develop your own sense of self by continually examining your situation, reflecting on it, and deciding whether to alter your behavior as a result. People pay attention to their experiences and make changes in their lives if they are not satisfied. They want to continue to grow and change throughout adulthood.

This kind of expressive individualism has flourished as prosperity has given more Americans the time and money to develop their senses of self—to cultivate their own emotional gardens, as it were. It suggests a view of intimate partnerships as continually changing as the partners' inner selves develop. It encourages people to view the success of their partnerships in individualistic terms. And it suggests that commitments to spouses and partners are personal choices that can be, and perhaps should be, ended if they become unsatisfying.

The World Values Surveys asked about expressive individualism using a cluster of questions that contrast "survival versus self-expression" values. The answers to these questions suggest that the level of expressive individualism among Americans is high but not out of line for a wealthy Western nation: a little below that in Sweden and the Netherlands, comparable to the levels in Norway and West Germany, and greater than in Britain, Canada, or France. One question in this cluster asked people to place themselves on a scale of 1 to 10, where 1 means that they think the actions they take have no real effect on what happens to them (which indicates survival values) and 10 means they think they have completely free choice and control over their lives (self-expression values). More Americans placed themselves at the free choice end

---

5.   MAX WEBER, THE PROTESTANT ETHIC AND THE SPIRIT OF CAPITALISM (Routledge 2002) (1904).

than did people in any other Western country, but some of the other countries were close: 82 percent of Americans chose 7, 8, 9, or 10, compared to 77 percent of Canadians, 74 percent of Swedes, and 73 percent of Germans.

The cultural model of individualism, then, holds that self-development and personal satisfaction are the key rewards of an intimate partnership. Your partnership must provide you with the opportunity to develop your sense of who you are and to express that sense through your relations with your partner. If it does not, then you should end it.

. . .

In practice, few Americans use just the cultural tools of the marriage model or just the tools of the individualism model. Rather, most Americans draw upon both. As a result, our actual marriages and cohabiting relationships typically combine them. People may rely on both sets of tools at the same time, or they may move from one to the other over time as their assessment of their personal lives changes. Moreover, they may not realize that they are combining two inconsistent models.

For instance, [in] a national survey in which people were asked whether they thought marriage was a lifetime relationship that shouldn't be ended except under extreme circumstances, ... 76 percent agreed. The great majority, then, answered in a way consistent with the cultural model of marriage. Just a few pages farther along in the questionnaire they were asked whether they agreed or disagreed with this statement: "When a marriage is troubled and unhappy, it is generally better for the children if the couple stays together." It, too, reflects the marriage model, because the troubled and unhappy individual, by staying in the marriage, subordinates his or her personal satisfaction to the greater goal of raising the children well. It would seem logical, therefore, that most of the people who agreed that marriage is for life would also agree that it's better if the couple stays together. But they don't. Only 25 percent of the people who said marriage is for life also said that the couple should stay together. Forty percent disagreed and 35 percent said they neither agreed nor disagreed. How can it be that a few minutes after they all agreed that marriage is for life, only one-fourth agreed that unhappy people should stay in marriages for the sake of the children? These respondents, like many Americans, are drawing from two different cultural models simultaneously. When people think about the way marriage should be, they tend to say that it should be for life. But when people think about individual satisfaction, they tend to give others wide latitude to leave unhappy living arrangements. Cue them in one direction, and you get one picture; cue them in another, and you get a different picture. Both pictures, contradictory as they may be, are part of the way that Americans live their family lives. Together they spin the American merry-go-round of intimate partnerships.

NOTES

1. A recent study asked how the American public defines "family":

   By emphatic margins, the public does not see marriage as the only path to family formation. Fully 86% say a single parent and child constitute a family; nearly as many (80%) say an unmarried couple living together with a child is a family; and

63% say a gay or lesbian couple raising a child is a family. The presence of children clearly matters in these definitions. If a cohabiting couple has no children, a majority of the public says they are not a family. Marriage matters, too. If a childless couple is married, 88% consider them to be a family.

PEW RESEARCH CENTER SOCIAL TRENDS STAFF, THE DECLINE OF MARRIAGE AND RISE OF NEW FAMILIES, Nov. 18, 2010, *available at* http://pewresearch.org/pubs/1802/decline-marriage-rise-new-families.

The same study also describes how marriage rates have changed over the past five decades:

> Over the past 50 years, a quiet revolution has taken place in this country.... At the center of this transformation is the shrinking institution of marriage. In 1960, 72% of American adults were married. By 2008, that share had fallen to 52%.
>
> . . .
>
> Marriage rates are now more strongly linked to education than they have been in the past, with college graduates (64%) much more likely to be married than those who have never attended college (48%).
>
> The racial differences are even larger. Blacks (32%) are much less likely than whites (56%) to be married, and this gap has increased significantly over time. And black children (52%) are nearly three times as likely as white children (18%) and nearly twice as likely as Hispanic children (27%) to live with one parent.
>
> As the country shifts away from marriage, a smaller proportion of adults are experiencing the economic gains that typically accrue from marriage. In 2008, the median household income of married adults was 41% greater than that of unmarried adults, even after controlling for differences in household size. In 1960, this gap was only 12%. The widening of the gap is explained partly by the increased share of wives in the workforce (61% in 2008 versus 32% in 1960) and partly by the increased differential in the educational attainment of the married and the unmarried.
>
> The net result is that a marriage gap and a socio-economic gap have been growing side by side for the past half century, and each may be feeding off the other. Adults on the lower rungs of the socio-economic ladder (whether measured by income or education) are just as eager as other adults to marry. But they place a higher premium on economic security as a prerequisite for marriage than do those with higher levels of income and education. And this is a bar that they— and their pool of prospective spouses—may find increasingly difficult to meet, given the fact that, relative to other groups, they have experienced significant economic declines in recent decades.

Id.

2. Education correlates with the age at which people marry, as well as with the divorce rate:

> Throughout the 20th century, college-educated adults in the United States have been less likely than their less-educated counterparts to be married by age 30. In 1990, for example, 75% of all 30–year–olds who did not have a college degree were married or had been married, compared with just 69% of those with a college degree.
>
> In a reversal of long-standing marital patterns, college-educated young adults are more likely than young adults lacking a bachelor's degree to have married by the age of 30.
>
> In 2008, 62% of college-educated 30–year–olds were married or had been married, compared with 60% of 30–year–olds who did not have a college degree.

. . .

Among the possible explanations for this shift are the declining economic fortunes of young men without a college degree and their increasing tendency to cohabit with a partner rather than marry. From 1990 to 2008, the inflation-adjusted median annual earnings of college-educated men ages 24 to 34 rose by 5% (to $55,000 . . .) while the median annual earnings of those with only a high school diploma declined by 12% (to $32,000 . . .). During this same period, the number of cohabiting households (that is, partners of the opposite sex living together without being married) more than doubled. About half of all cohabitors are under age 35, and more than 80% do not have a college degree.

RICHARD FRY, THE REVERSAL OF THE COLLEGE MARRIAGE GAP 1–2 (2010), *available at* http://pewsocialtrends.org/2010/10/07/the-reversal-of-the-college-marriage-gap/.

3. There is also a link between marriage and social inequality:

[S]ocial inequality—the differences in standard of living and economic opportunity—is more pronounced in the United States than in other Western countries. The gap between high-income and low-income families is wider. Most other Western governments tax the wealthy more and provide more assistance to low- and moderate-income families. This is a major difference between the United States and other countries, and it matters for family life. Low- and moderate-income families in the United States have less protection against the vagaries of the labor market. And it is among low- and moderate-income Americans that we have seen the greatest increase in the number of people who have multiple partnerships.

ANDREW CHERLIN, THE MARRIAGE-GO-ROUND, 159–60 (2009).

B. THE AMERICAN FAMILY OVER TIME

Family law in America was different from the beginning. The original colonies varied in the approaches they took to the law on marriage and divorce depending on the religious background of the colonists. That pattern is still evident today in the state-by-state variations in marriage and divorce laws. By contrast, most nations have a single, national family law. Many of the colonies did not follow English law on marriage and divorce, moreover, although they did for most other areas of law. In Massachusetts Bay Colony, for example, Puritans permitted magistrates to perform marriages rather than ministers (in England, the church controlled access to marriages and required that they be performed by clergy), and divorce was available beginning in the 1640s. All of the New England colonies followed the Massachusetts Bay approach, as did some of the mid-Atlantic colonies. The southern colonies, by contrast, followed the Anglican tradition, which prohibited divorce. Indeed, divorce was not generally available in England (except for a small number granted by Parliament to aristocratic families) until 1857, more than two centuries after some American colonies began granting divorces.

Because they rejected English law on marriage and divorce, the colonists in Massachusetts Bay turned to their religious tradition to guide their handling of marriage and divorce. That tradition, which began during the Reformation, was shaped initially by the writings of Martin Luther. As early as 1525, the city of Zurich established a court to oversee its new marriage and divorce laws.

Nancy F. Cott, *Divorce and the Changing Status of Women in Eighteenth–Century Massachusetts*

33 WM. & MARY Q. 586, 586–89 (1976).

When a neighbor asked John Backus, silversmith of Great Barrington, Massachusetts, in 1784, why he kicked and struck his wife, John replied that "it was Partly owing to his Education for his father often treated his mother in the same manner." John's mother may have tolerated that abuse but his wife did not: she complained of his cruelty, desertion, and adultery, and obtained a divorce.

. . .

Massachusetts divorce proceedings between 1692 and 1786 can be fairly readily traced because they took place (with a few notable exceptions) before one body, a "court" composed of the governor and his Council. One hundred twenty-two wives and 101 husbands filed 229 petition in all (six wives petitioned twice). [T]he petitioners included the whole range of types in the population. Slightly more than a quarter of them lived in Boston, the others in all varieties of towns, from the smallest to the largest.... About 17 percent originated in families in which the husbands had the more prestigious status of gentlemen, merchants, professionals, ship captains, or militia officers; [about] 7 percent involved families at the lower end of the occupation scale—laborers, truckmen, and servants. [I]t is likely that the great majority—perhaps three-fourths—occupied the "middling ranks."

The petitioners had an easier time gaining divorce in provincial Massachusetts than they would have had in the mother country. In England marital controversies were judged by the ecclesiastical courts, and these courts applied canon law, under which a valid marriage was regarded as indissoluble. True divorce (*divorce a vinculo matrimonii*) was never granted unless a marriage was judged null to begin with on grounds such as ... bigamy or sexual incapacity. Such causes as adultery, desertion, or cruelty warranted only separation from bed and board (*divorce a mensa et thoro*), which ... did not allow either party to remarry....

[Massachusetts Bay Colony] divorce policies combined elements of English practice, Puritan divorce theory, ... and innovation. Opposing canon law, Puritan divorce theory held that marriage was a civil contract which could and should be dissolved for such breaches as adultery, long absence, or irremediable cruelty.

NOTE

Nancy Cott used divorce petitions to provide a revealing glimpse of what it was like to live in Massachusetts Bay Colony:

> Divorce petitioners successfully relied on the proximity and curiosity of neighbors, lodgers, and kin, and on their motives to preserve community norms, in order to obtain material to substantiate their cases. Mary Angel, for example, out walking in Boston with Abigail Calloway one day, saw through an open window her neighbor Adam Air "in the Act of Copulation" with a woman named Pamela Brichford. Nor did she stop there:
>
> > On Seeing this We went into the House, & stood behind them as they lay on the Floor, and after observing them some time, the said Abigail Galloway spoke, & asked him if he was not Ashamed to act so when he had a Wife at home, he got up & answered, one Woman was as good to him as another he then put up his nakedness before our faces, & went away and she on his getting off her, jumped up & ran away into another part of the House.

John Donnell used similar directness upon hearing suspicious noises from the house of Caleb Morey, a married man, in Brunswick. He took a light, "went into the House or Camp, & to the bedside, tuck [sic] hold of a persons hand" and ascertained that Caleb was in bed with Mary Knowles.

Nancy F. Cott, *Eighteenth–Century Family Law and Social Life Revealed in Massachusetts Divorce Records*, 10 J. OF SOCIAL HIST. 20, 22 (1976).

MARTIN LUTHER, SERMON ON THE ESTATE OF MARRIAGE

45 LUTHER WORKS: II THE CHRISTIAN IN SOCIETY 11, 30 (W. Brandt ed. & trans., Fortress Press 1962) (1533).

I know of three grounds for divorce. The first ... is the situation in which the husband or wife is not equipped for marriage because of bodily or natural deficiencies of any sort....

The second ground is adultery. The popes have kept silent about this; therefore we must hear Christ, *Matthew* 19[:3–9]. When the Jews asked him whether a husband might divorce his wife for any reason, he answered,

> "Have you not read that he who made them from the beginning made them male and female, and said, 'For this reason a man shall leave his father and mother and be joined to his wife, and the two shall become one'? What therefore God has joined together, let no man put asunder." They said to him, "Why then did Moses command one to give a certificate of divorce, and to put her away?" He said to them, "For your hardness of heart Moses allowed you to divorce your wives, but from the beginning it was not so. And I say to you: whoever divorces his wife, except for unchastity, and marries another, commits adultery; and he who marries a divorced woman commits adultery."

Here you see that in the case of adultery Christ permits the divorce of husband and wife, so that the innocent person may remarry....

. . .

But a public divorce, whereby one [the innocent party] is enabled to remarry, must take place through the investigation and decision of the civil authority so that the adultery may be manifest to all—or, if the civil authority refuses to act, with the knowledge of the congregation, again in order that it may not be left to each one to allege anything he pleases as a ground for divorce.

. . .

The third case for divorce is that in which one of the parties deprives and avoids the other, refusing to fulfill the conjugal duty or to live with the other person. For example, one finds many a stubborn wife like that who will not give in, and who cares not a whit whether her husband falls into the sin of unchastity ten times over. Here it is time for the husband to say, "If you will not, another will; the maid will come if the wife will not."? Only first the husband should admonish and warn his wife two or three times, and let the situation be known to others so that her stubbornness becomes a matter of common knowledge and is rebuked before the congregation. If she still refuses, get rid of her; take an Esther and let Vashti go, as King Ahasuerus did [*Esther* 1:12–2:17].

Here you should be guided by the words of St. Paul, *I Corinthians* 7[:4–5], "The husband does not rule over his own body, but the wife does; likewise the wife does not rule over her own body, but the husband does. Do not deprive each other, except by agreement," etc. Notice that St. Paul forbids either party to deprive the other, for by the marriage vow each submits his body to the other in conjugal duty. When one resists the other and refuses the conjugal duty she is robbing the other of the body she had bestowed upon him. This is really contrary to marriage, and dissolves the marriage. For this reason the civil government must compel the wife, or put her to death. If the government fails to act, the husband must reason that his wife has been stolen away and slain by robbers; he must seek another. We would certainly have to accept it if someone's life were taken from him. Why then should we not also accept it if a wife steals herself away from her husband, or is stolen away by others?

NOTES

1. Divorce was permitted under Roman law:

> By the time of Christ, Roman marriage had become a private partnership of the most intimate nature, in which the parties were equal, and shared in all rights. As marriage was founded on affection and consent, the parties had the right to dissolve it, when that affection had turned into aversion, either by consent or by one of them giving formal notice to the other, exactly like any other partnership.... The one spouse delivered to the other, through a messenger and in the presence of seven witnesses, a letter expressing the intention to put an end to the marriage, and saying that the other might in future keep his or her own property.... A judicial inquiry into the cause of the divorce was only necessary when the parties could not come to terms about the future of the children and the division of the property....

S.B. KITCHEN, A HISTORY OF DIVORCE 5–7 (1912).

2. George Howard contended that the views of the Roman Catholic Church on divorce developed in response to Roman law:

> [T]he founders of the Christian church ... regarded the laxity of the marriage bond as a sign, if not the primary cause, of the degradation of Roman society. From the beginning an earnest effort was made so far as possible to restrict the liberty of separation and to prohibit the persons separated on proper grounds from contracting further marriage....
>
>   . . .
>
> [W]ith Augustine, the strict doctrine of the early church takes a definite form.... He gave to the theory of indissolubility ... a "basis solid, in a measure scientific." He gave it a consistency forced from the sacrament of marriage. He set aside at one stroke all the causes of divorce admitted by the secular law: sickness, captivity, or prolonged absence.... According to Augustine, adultery is the only scriptural ground of separation; but even this does not dissolve the nuptial bond.

GEORGE ELLIOTT HOWARD, 2 A HISTORY OF MATRIMONIAL INSTITUTIONS CHIEFLY IN ENGLAND AND THE UNITED STATES 19, 26–27 (1904).

3. The Reformation not only led to changes in the laws on marriage and divorce, it was a major contributor to raising the status of the family. Both Protestant and Catholic reformers came to the view the family as the most important building block of society. Jeffrey R. Watt, *The Impact of the Reformation and Counter-Reformation in* 1 FAMILY LIFE IN EARLY MODERN TIMES: 1500–1789, 125 (David I. Kertzer and Marzio Barbagli eds., 2001).

Ordinance and Notice: How Matters Concerning Marriage Shall be Conducted in the City of Zurich

ULRICH ZWINGLI, SELECTED WORKS 118 (Samuel Macauley Jackson ed., Lawrence A. McLouth trans., 1901) (1525).[9]

We, the Mayor, Council and the Great Council, which they call the Two Hundred, of the city of Zurich, offer to each and all people's priests, pastors, those who have the care of souls, and preachers, also to all over-governors, under-governors, officials and any others who have livings, homes or seats in our cities, counties, principalities, high and low courts and territories, our greeting, favorable and affectionate good wishes. [We] call your attention to what each one of you has noticed and seen up to the present time, that many kinds of complaints and errors have arisen in matrimonial affairs. Since the parties have been summoned before the [ecclesiastical] court at Constance of or other foreign [ecclesiastical] courts again and again, and have been judged at considerable cost; since they, at that place, and in cases where the people were well off in temporal goods, have been detained without judgment, and, as far as we know, to their own danger, etc., and in order that such great cost, trouble and labor among you men and women having business with each other with regard to matrimony, and who live and are at home in our territories, high and low courts, may be put aside, done away with and avoided, and also in order that each may be properly judged with promptness, thus we have ordained the following common ordinances concerning marriage. . . .

And in order that such legal business may be attended to promptly, as necessity demands, we have chosen as judges six men, two from the people's priests in our city, who are taught in the Word of God, also two from the small, and two from the large council. Among these, each one shall serve two months as magistrate or judge, shall summon, order, collect, examine, practice, and execute such court business as necessity demands.

.   .   .

First, a general ordinance: That no one shall enter into matrimony in our city and county without the testimony and presence of at least two pious, honorable citizens in good standing.

.   .   .

What Can Nullify and Break Up a Marriage

It is proper for a pious married person, who has given no cause for such act, to put away from himself or herself the other who is caught in the open adultery, indeed to leave him or her, and to provide himself or herself with another spouse.

Thus we call and consider open adultery, which is discovered and proved, with sufficient public notice, before the matrimonial court. . . .

But in order that adultery may not be condoned, and that no one may seek a cause to secure a new marriage by means of adultery, it will be necessary that a severe punishment be placed upon adultery, for it was forbidden in the Old Testament on pain of stoning to death.

The preachers to whom the Word of God and superintendence (of morals) are commended shall ban and exclude such sinners from the

---

9. Translation revised by Martina Oertling, 2011.

Christian parish, but the corporal punishment and the matter of the property shall be referred to the civil authorities.

. . .

Since, now, marriage was instituted by God to avoid unchastity, and
since it often occurs that some, by nature or other shortcomings, are not
fitted for the partners they have chosen, they shall nevertheless live together
as friends for a year, to see if matters may not better themselves by the
prayers of themselves and of other honest people. If it does not grow better
in that time, they shall be separated and allowed to marry elsewhere.

Likewise, greater reasons than adultery, as destroying life, endangering
life, being mad or crazy, offending by whorishness, or leaving one's spouse
without permission, remaining abroad a long time, having leprosy, or other
such reasons, of which no rule can be made on account of their dissimilarity—these cases the judges can investigate, and proceed as God and the
character of the cases shall demand.

The ordinance shall be carefully and repeatedly announced by all
clergymen, and their parishes warned against trespassing them.

Given at Zurich on Wednesday, the 10th of May, in the year 1525.

NOTES

1. Half the divorces granted in the first six years of the Zurich marriage and divorce
court (*Ehegericht*) were granted to women. WALTHER KÖHLER, 1 ZURCHER EHEGERICHT
UND GENFER KONSISTORIUM 35–40 (1932) (Switz.).

2. In 1553, a commission headed by Thomas Cranmer, the Archbishop of Canter-
bury, proposed a series of changes to English canon law. Although their report,
Reformatio Legum Ecclesiasticarum, never became law, it is of importance because it
reflects what many religious and political leaders of the time wanted the law to be. It
would have abolished legal separation and provided five grounds for absolute
divorce: (1) adultery; (2) desertion; (3) two or three years of "unduly protracted
absence of the husband"; (4) "deadly hostility" which was defined as a situation in
which one spouse attacked the other "by treacherous means or by poison" with the
intent of taking his or her life; and (5) "ill treatment of a wife." TUDOR CHURCH
REFORM: THE HENRICIAN CANON OF 1535 AND THE *REFORMATIO LEGUM ECCLESIASTICARUM*
265–73 (Gerald Bray ed., 2000).

3. Alexis de Tocqueville was only twenty-five when he visited the United States in
1831, but he produced a penetrating analyses of the young nation and its inhabitants.
Consider his assessment of families in America:

> It has been universally remarked, that in our time the several members of a
> family stand upon an entirely new footing towards each other; that the distance
> which formerly separated a father from his sons has been lessened; and that
> paternal authority, if not destroyed, is at least impaired.

> Something analogous to this, but even more striking, may be observed in the
> United States. . . .

> . . .

> It may perhaps not be without utility to show how these changes which take
> place in family relations, are closely connected with the social and political
> revolution which is approaching its consummation under our own observation.

> . . .

> [I]n countries which are aristocratically constituted with all the gradations of
> rank, the government never makes a direct appeal to the mass of the governed:
> as men are united together, it is enough to lead the foremost,—the rest will
> follow. This is equally applicable to the family. . . .

> . . .

[I]n aristocracies, the father is not only the civil head of the family, but the oracle of its traditions, the expounder of its customs, the arbiter of its manners. He is listened to with deference, he is addressed with respect, and the love which is felt for him is always tempered with fear.

. . .

In a democratic family the father exercises no other power than that with which men love to invest the affection and the experience of age; his orders would perhaps be disobeyed, but his advice is for the most part authoritative. . . .

. . .

In aristocratic families, the eldest son, inheriting the greater part of the property, and almost all the rights of the family, becomes the chief, and to a certain extent, the master of his brothers. Greatness and power are for him,—for them, mediocrity and dependence. . . . [de Tocqueville had two older brothers].

Democracy also binds brothers to each other, but by very different means. Under democratic laws all the children are perfectly equal, and consequently independent: nothing brings them forcibly together, but nothing keeps them apart; . . . and as no peculiar privilege distinguishes or divides them, the affection and youthful intimacy of early years easily springs up between them. . . .

. . .

Amongst almost all Protestant nations young women are far more the mistresses of their own actions than they are in Catholic countries. This independence is still greater in Protestant countries like England, which have retained or acquired the right of self-government; the spirit of freedom is then infused into the domestic circle by political habits and by religious opinions. In the United States the doctrines of Protestantism are combined with great political freedom and a most democratic state of society; and nowhere are young women surrendered so early or so completely to their own guidance.

. . .

In a country in which a woman is always free to exercise her power of choosing, and in which education has prepared her to choose rightly, public opinion is inexorable to her faults. The rigour of the Americans arises in part from this cause. They consider marriages as a covenant which is often onerous, but every condition of which the parties are strictly bound to fulfill, because they knew all these conditions beforehand, and were perfectly free not to have contracted them.

. . .

In aristocratic countries the object of marriage is rather to unite property than persons; hence the husband is sometimes at school and the wife at nurse when they are betrothed. It cannot be wondered at if the conjugal tie which holds the fortunes of the pair united allows their hearts to rove; this is the natural result of the nature of the contract. . . .

ALEXIS DE TOCQUEVILE, 2 DEMOCRACY IN AMERICA, Third Book, Chapters VIII, IX, and XI (Henry Reeve trans., Schocken Books 1964) (1840).

C.   THE BURGEONING NUMBER OF TRANSNATIONAL DISPUTES

1.   TRANSNATIONAL FAMILIES

Aleem v. Aleem

Maryland Court of Special Appeals, 2007.
931 A.2d 1123.

■ RODOWSKY, J.

The appellant, Irfan Aleem (Husband), and the appellee, Farah Aleem (Wife), are nationals of the Islamic Republic of Pakistan. While Wife was suing Husband for divorce in the Circuit Court for Montgomery County, Husband divorced Wife by *talaq,* in accordance with Pakistani law. The controversy before us concerns the Maryland court's equitable division of marital property in the form of Husband's pension. Husband is aggrieved because the Maryland court did not give comity to Pakistani law under which his divorce by *talaq* did not include any equitable division of marital property titled in his name.

The Pakistani law of divorce was succinctly described by the House of Lords in *In re Fatima,* [1986] 2 W.L.R. 693, [1986] 2 All E.R. 32, [1986] A.C. 527, 1996 WL 406815 (HL) . . . :

> In Pakistan the law relating to divorce is the Islamic law as modified by the Muslim Family Laws Ordinance 1961. In traditional Islamic law the husband has the right unilaterally to repudiate his wife, without showing cause and without recourse to a court of law. Such divorce is effected by the announcement of the formula of repudiation, a talaq, and in traditional law a divorce by talaq would take the simple form of the husband announcing talaq three times. The divorce then becomes immediately effective and irrevocable. . . .

The background facts of this case are succinctly presented in the memorandum opinion of the circuit court (Pincus, J.).

> The parties were married on July 16, 1980 in Karachi, Pakistan after their families arranged their meeting. [Wife] was 18 years old and [Husband] was 29 years old. [Wife] had just finished high school and [Husband] was about to begin his doctoral studies at Oxford University in England.[1] A few weeks after the marriage, [Husband] moved to England. The parties never lived together in Pakistan. [Wife] eventually joined [Husband] in England and the two lived there together for four years. When [Husband] completed his studies, the parties moved to the United States. They have been living in Maryland for over twenty years. They have two children together, Zeeshan, born September 22, 1985 and Zoya, born September 12, 1988. Zeeshan is in college at George Washington University and Zoya is about to begin her senior year of high school in Washington, D.C. Both children were born in the United States and are U.S. citizens.
>
> [Wife] is 43 years old. She earned her high school diploma in Pakistan. Initially, she intended to study medicine immediately, however she was unable [to] attain placement in the local medical program. She had some educational training in England. After she moved to the United States, she began taking courses at Montgomery College in Maryland and later at American University in Washington, D.C. To date, she has earned 60 credits towards a bachelor's degree. She indicated a strong desire to complete her degree.
>
> During the marriage, [Wife] was a homemaker. Her responsibilities included caring for the children, the household, and [Husband]. [Husband] was employed at the World Bank during the marriage, from 1985 until his retirement in 2004. Due to her immigration status, [Wife's] ability to obtain employment was severely limited. World Bank and immigration policies required [Wife] to get [Husband's] written permis-

---

1. Husband holds a Ph.D. in economics. His expertise is the development of the economies of Third World countries.

sion before she could secure employment. [Husband] agreed to sign a work permit, and [Wife] began to work for Executive Office Suites in Virginia. She worked there for four and half years. [Wife's] immigration status has recently changed and she obtained her Green Card in January 2006. She is now a permanent resident of Maryland and she has no restrictions on employment. She currently works for Profitable Association in Washington, D.C. where she earns $2,894 net per month. She is responsible for her own medical insurance.

This litigation was commenced by Wife's bill of complaint filed March 3, 2003, which sought a limited divorce.... After numerous motions and hearings, the court, on October 31, 2003, ordered Husband to vacate the family home, and on November 20, 2003, the court entered judgment against the Husband in the amount of $10,800 for arrearage in *pendente lite* child support.... In February, Wife amended her complaint to seek an absolute divorce. On April 5, 2004, Husband moved to dismiss the divorce action on the ground that "all issues have already been decided in Pakistan[.]" Exhibits attached to that motion reflect what had transpired while the Maryland action was pending. The parties' marriage was pursuant to a contract ... which called for a deferred dowry of 51,000 Pakistani rupees, which Husband converts to $2,500 (U.S.).

The motion further informed the court that, four months after the divorce action was filed in Montgomery County, Husband presented at the Pakistani Embassy in Washington, D.C. There, before two witnesses, he signed and had notarized a "Divorce Deed," which in relevant part reads:

> Now this deed witnesses that I the said Irfan Aleem, do hereby divorce Farah Aleem, daughter of Mahmood Mirza, by pronouncing upon her Divorce/Talaq three times irrevocably and by severing all connections of husband and wife with her forever and for good.
>
> 1.   I Divorce thee Farah Aleem.
>
> 2.   I Divorce thee Farah Aleem.
>
> 3.   I Divorce thee Farah Aleem.
>
> .   .   .

Husband's position as to the legal effect of the above-described exhibits was presented in an affidavit of Ahsan Zahir Rizvi, an apparently highly regarded Pakistani lawyer. He affirmed that, under Pakistani law, the *talaq* pronounced by Husband on June 30, 2003, became effective ninety days after notice had been delivered to the "officer appointed for receiving the same."

With respect to property disposition on divorce under Pakistani law, that expert witness tendered by Husband would have opined:

> 5.   Under Pakistan law, a division of the properties, consequent upon termination of the marriage, takes place *ipso facto* upon such termination in the following manner:
>
> a) All property owned by the husband on the date of such termination of marriage remains the husband's property and the wife has [no] claim thereto.
>
> b) All property owned by the wife on the date of termination of the marriage remains the wife's property and the husband has no claim thereto.

Husband's motion to dismiss was heard on April 23, 2004, the first day of the first of three trials in this matter. The court (SUNDT, J.) denied the motion. In explanation of her ruling, she said:

The idea that in this case Mr. Aleem can apply for and on the basis of his declaration receive a divorce offends the notions of this Court in terms of how a divorce is granted. I am not, as a member of this bench, going to give comity to such an award.

The first trial terminated with a dismissal of the claim for divorce, without prejudice and with leave to amend, because Wife had not established the requisite duration of a voluntary separation as ground for an absolute divorce. . . .

At the second trial, on November 21, 2005, Husband appeared pro se. He submitted that the court was required to hold an evidentiary hearing on issues of comity under *Hosain v. Malik*, 671 A.2d 988 (Md. App. 1996). The court (SUNDT, J.) considered that the submission requested reconsideration of its previous determination. The court stood by its prior decision, i.e., "[t]hat the Pakistani divorce is not being given comity." That second trial also ended in a dismissal without prejudice, based on the lack of testimony as to the grounds for divorce and as to corroboration.

Husband, acting pro se and "in the spirit of justice," moved on March 9, 2006, for a "clarification from Judge Sundt on the possibility of judicial error underlying the court's decision not to grant comity to Pakistani divorce." He again relied on *Hosain v. Malik, supra.* The court (SUNDT, J.) denied that motion by an order signed June 6 and docketed June 27, 2006.

Trial number three, at which Husband again appeared pro se, commenced June 7, 2006. During that trial, on June 9, 2006, Husband complained that he had not received a ruling on his motion filed March 9, 2006, and he again began to argue that he should have been allowed an evidentiary hearing on Pakistani law. . . .

For the reasons stated in a memorandum opinion, the court entered a judgment granting Wife an absolute divorce, on the ground of a two-year separation, and the court signed an amended order for spousal support, docketed June 29, 2006. That order directed Husband to pay to Wife, until the death of either party, fifty percent of Husband's monthly benefit from the Staff Retirement Plan of the International Bank for Reconstruction and Development.

In response to the court's judgment, Husband moved to alter or amend it. . . .

The motion to alter was denied, and Husband noted this appeal. He presents two questions for review:

1. Whether The Trial Court Erred In Failing to Hold an Evidentiary Hearing to Determine If the Parties' Pakistani Divorce Should be Granted Comity.

2. Whether The Trial Court Erred In Refusing to Grant Comity to a Pakistani Divorce.

. . .

Husband contends that the Montgomery County court was required to receive evidence, via live testimony or deposition, in explanation of Pakistani law as it relates to the divorce by *talaq* obtained by him. As authority for this contention, he cites cases decided in this country, dealing with judgments rendered by courts in foreign countries. . . .

The litigation receiving principal emphasis by Husband is that reported in *Malik v. Malik*, 638 A.2d 1184 (Md. App. 1994) (*Malik I*), and *Hosain v. Malik*, 671 A.2d 988 (Md. App. 1996) (*Malik II*). The holdings of these cases, however, do not require that formal evidence of Pakistani law be admitted in the instant matter, as a preliminary to determining whether comity should be accorded the Pakistani divorce or its consequences under Pakistani law.

The *Malik* litigation was a child custody dispute. The parents, both citizens of Pakistan, were married in 1982. Their child was born in that country in 1983, where the family lived together until September 1990, when the mother moved to her parents' home, also in Pakistan, and took the child with her. The father sued for custody in a Pakistani judicial proceeding in which the wife was represented by counsel but in which she did not personally participate. After the Pakistani court awarded custody to the father, he spent two years trying to locate mother and child. They were found in Baltimore County. When the father sought enforcement of the Pakistani judgment in the Circuit Court for Baltimore County, that court concluded that it had jurisdiction, but refused to enforce the order for lack of comity. The reported opinion does not reflect whether, or, if so, how and to what extent, either party sought to present Pakistani law to the circuit court. In any event, this Court was not able to determine, on the record before it, whether Pakistani law lacked conformity with Maryland law.

The problem that this Court faced in *Malik I* was that the record did not even disclose whether a court in Pakistan, in a child custody dispute, applied the best interest of the child standard. In remanding for evidence and a determination as to Pakistani law, this Court stated that, unless the Pakistani court did not apply the best interest of the child standard, the circuit court should decline to exercise jurisdiction.

. . .

On remand, both parties elected to present their evidence through live witnesses at trial. *Malik II*, 671 A.2d at 991. The circuit court concluded that Pakistani law, as to custody, was in substantial conformity with Maryland law and declined to exercise jurisdiction. This Court affirmed, over a dissent. *Malik II* first considered the substantive issue and concluded, "[b]ased exclusively on the plain reading of the Pakistani court orders themselves, . . . that there was substantial competent evidence from which the circuit court could have concluded that the Pakistani courts applied the best interest standard." . . .

The issue presented in the instant matter is analogous to the question in *Malik* of whether the Pakistani law of child custody was based on a best-interest-of-the-child standard. That is a question of substantive law that does not involve the procedures in a particular case, or whether those procedures undermined confidence in the outcome. Here, Husband, on two occasions, tendered to the court in the form of affidavits from Pakistani counsel, evidence of what he contended was the substantive law of Pakistan with respect to divorce by *talaq*, and its consequences. We accept those tenders as accurate statements of Pakistani law. Thus, any error by the circuit court in not more formally receiving evidence concerning Pakistani law is harmless. This is because . . . the Pakistani law that Husband sought to prove is so contrary to Maryland public policy that it is not entitled to comity.

. . .

Husband's argument in support of recognizing and enforcing Pakistani law principally rests on *Chaudry v. Chaudry,* 388 A.2d 1000, *cert. denied,* 395 A.2d 204 (N.J. 1978). The Chaudrys were citizens and domiciliaries of Pakistan, where they were married and their children were born and raised. The husband went to New Jersey to practice psychiatry and became domiciled there, while his wife and children remained in Pakistan, except for a two year period ending seven years before the New Jersey action was filed. Alleging abandonment, the wife sued for divorce in New Jersey and claimed, *inter alia,* an equitable distribution. The defense was that, two years earlier, the husband had divorced the wife by *talaq,* pronounced at the Pakistani consulate in New York City, where the divorce deed was executed. When notice was sent to the wife, she contested the divorce in Pakistan and lost at the trial court and appellate levels.

The Appellate Division of the Superior Court of New Jersey, reversing a trial court grant of relief, rejected, *inter alia,* the wife's claim for an equitable distribution. It held that there was an insufficient nexus between the marriage and New Jersey, so that denial of that claim "cannot be said to offend [New Jersey] public policy." Alternatively, the court held that an ante-nuptial agreement negotiated by her parents, i.e., the marriage contract, barred an equitable distribution. The contract "could have lawfully provided for giving her an interest in her husband's property, but it contained no such provision." There was "no proof that the agreement was not fair and reasonable at the time it was made." The court saw "no reason of public policy that would justify refusing to interpret and enforce the agreement in accordance with the law of Pakistan, where it was freely negotiated and the marriage took place."

Conceptually, the New Jersey court performed both jurisdictional and choice-of-law analyses. Although they are interrelated, we shall consider these two grounds separately.

It is clear that this State has a sufficient nexus with the marriage to effect an equitable distribution of marital property. The parties resided in Maryland for over twenty years. Their children were born and raised here. In addition, Wife, who seeks the equitable relief, is now a permanent resident of the United States, in Maryland. Nor do we consider that the letter from Wife's counsel to the Cantonment Board Clifton to be the equivalent of a general appearance that conferred personal jurisdiction on that Board over the person of the Wife. The letter was a courteously phrased objection to jurisdiction, in the nature of a special appearance. Under these circumstances, this State would not be required to give preclusive effect, even under the Full Faith and Credit Clause of the United States Constitution, to the decision of the court of a sister state that purported to absolve one former spouse from any marital property obligation to the other former spouse. . . .

. . .

In the matter now before us, the actual controversy, in the sense of justiciability, concerns a matter of preclusive enforcement of the Pakistani divorce, i.e., as a bar to the equitable division of Husband's pension. Thus, it is unnecessary for us to decide whether Maryland would recognize the Pakistani divorce, as a divorce.[8] If . . . a court in another state of the United

---

8. A hypothetical will illustrate the distinction between recognition and enforcement. Assume two Pakistani citizens who were married in Pakistan and, after residing in Maryland for more than twenty years, divorced in Maryland in accordance with Pakistani law. The couple resolved property issues between themselves, and neither seeks a Maryland divorce in order to

States had adjudicated that Husband had no obligation equitably to divide marital property, that aspect of the foreign state's judgment would not be entitled to full faith and credit. *A fortiori*, a law of a foreign country that provides for the same result, does not require enforcement by comity. *See* Annot., "Conclusiveness as to merits of judgment of courts of foreign country," 46 A.L.R. 435, 440–41 (1927).

Husband argues that the circuit court erroneously rejected his request for "permission to present expert testimony regarding the legal effect of the marriage contract itself[.]" On this aspect of the case, we also accept, as accurate descriptions of Pakistani law, the opinions expressed by the Pakistani attorneys who were tendered as experts by Husband. In essence, their description is that, under Pakistani law, the distribution of property on divorce follows title, in the absence of a departure from the ordinary form of marriage contract, in order to include an express provision granting a wife some interest in property titled in the husband's name.

The marriage certificate/contract in the instant matter contains no such out of the ordinary provision. It consists of twenty-five items or questions. Questions eliciting information concerning the parties and other participants, the ceremony itself and the dower, were answered. All of the remaining items on the form, set forth below, were left blank. These were:

16. Whether any property was given in lieu of the whole or any part of the dower, with specification of the same and its valuation agreed to between the parties:

17. Special conditions, if any:

18. Whether the husband has delegated the power of divorce to the Wife, if so under what conditions:

19. Whether the husband's right of divorce in any way curtailed:

20. Whether any documents was [sic] drawn up at the time of marriage relating to dower and Maintenance, etc., if so contents thereof:

21. Whether the bridegroom has any existing wife, and if so, whether he has secured the Permission of Arbitration Council under the Muslim Family Ordinance, 1961 to contract another Marriage:

22. Number and date of the Communications conveying to the Bridegroom the permission of the Arbitration Council to contract another marriage[.]

The circuit court (Pincus, J.) made findings and conclusions concerning the marriage contract.

> According to the purported contract, each party had two witnesses and the [Wife] had a *Vakil*. [Husband] explained that the *Vakil* was a lawyer who was present to explain the terms of the contract to [Wife]. [Husband], however, was unable to prove to this Court that the *Vakil* was indeed an attorney or that he did advise [Wife] of her rights under the contract. [Wife] testified that the *Vakil* was her uncle who is a government officer. [Wife's] other witnesses to the contract were doctors. [Wife] contends that no lawyer explained the terms of the contract to

---

save money. Each former spouse then remarries in Maryland and resides with the new spouse in Maryland. Each former spouse is charged with bigamy in violation of Maryland Code (2002), § 10–502 of the Criminal Law Article. Each raises the Pakistani divorce as a defense.

In the instant matter, neither party objects to dissolution of their former marital status. The answer to the question of whether Pakistani law applies affects only enforcement of the Pakistani divorce on property rights under Maryland law.

her and she did not see the contract prior to that day. [Husband's] witness was unable to controvert [Wife's] testimony. Regardless, the contract only indicates that the Dower from the [Husband] to the [Wife] was deferred. There was no other agreement or waiver regarding any property in the contract.

This Court does not purport to be an expert on Pakistani contract law. [Husband] did not properly bring any expert to testify regarding Pakistani law. This Court examined the marriage certificate/contract and determined that, even if the contract is valid, it does not address most of the property at issue in this case. Further, [Wife] did not waive her right to any property. Under Maryland law, this Court does not find anything suspect about this contract. However, this Court similarly does not find anything of substance in this contract that would prohibit the Court from dividing the marital property.

Thus, the Pakistani marriage contract in the instant matter is not to be equated with a premarital or post-marital agreement that validly relinquished, under Maryland law, rights in marital property. If the Pakistani marriage contract is silent, Pakistani law does not recognize marital property. If a premarital or post-marital agreement in Maryland is silent with respect to marital property, those rights are recognized by Maryland law. In other words, the "default" under Pakistani law is that Wife has no rights to property titled in Husband's name, while the "default" under Maryland law is that the wife has marital property rights in property titled in the husband's name. We hold that this conflict is so substantial that applying Pakistani law in the instant matter would be contrary to Maryland public policy.

. . .

Further, the General Assembly of Maryland, when enacting the Property Disposition in Annulment and Divorce statute, FL §§ 8–201 through 8–214, expressly declared Maryland public policy. That legislation, Chapter 794 of the Acts of 1978, contains an uncodified preamble, which in relevant part states:

> The General Assembly declares further that it is the policy of this State that when a marriage is dissolved *the property interests of the spouses should be adjusted fairly and equitably,* with careful consideration being given to both monetary and nonmonetary contributions made by the respective spouses to the well-being of the family, and further, that if there are minor children in the family their interests must be given particular and favorable attention.

1978 Md. Laws at 2305 (emphasis added).

For all the foregoing reasons we hold that the Circuit Court for Montgomery County did not err in declining to apply, under principles of comity, the law of Pakistan in determining Wife's rights in marital property titled in Husband's name.

NOTES

1. Was the court correct to deny comity to Pakistani law on marital property?

2. If Mrs. Aleem had objected to the divorce, should the court have granted comity to Pakistani law on divorce?

2. RECOGNITION OF FOREIGN LEGAL SYSTEMS AND RELIGIOUS TRADITIONS

Awad v. Ziriax

United States District Court, Western District of Oklahoma, 2010.
754 F. Supp. 2d 1298.

■ MILES–LA GRANGE, C.J.

This order addresses issues that go to the very foundation of our country, our Constitution, and particularly, the Bill of Rights. Throughout the course of our country's history, the will of the "majority" has on occasion conflicted with the constitutional rights of individuals, an occurrence which our founders foresaw and provided for through the Bill of Rights. . . .

Before the Court is plaintiff's Complaint Seeking a Temporary Restraining Order and Preliminary Injunction, filed November 4, 2010. . . . Based upon the pleadings that have been filed and the evidence submitted at the hearing, the Court makes its determination.

State Question 755, which was on Oklahoma's November 2, 2010 ballot, provides:

> This measure amends the State Constitution. It changes a section that deals with the courts of this state. It would amend Article 7, Section 1. It makes courts rely on federal and state law when deciding cases. It forbids courts from considering or using international law. It forbids courts from considering or using Sharia Law.

> International law is also known as the law of nations. It deals with the conduct of international organizations and independent nations, such as countries, states and tribes. It deals with their relationship with each other. It also deals with some of their relationships with persons.

> The law of nations is formed by the general assent of civilized nations. Sources of international law also include international agreements, as well as treaties.

> Sharia Law is Islamic law. It is based on two principal sources, the Koran and the teaching of Mohammed.

State Question 755 was put on the ballot through the legislative adoption of Enrolled House Joint Resolution 1056. Said resolution proposes to amend section 1 of article VII of the Oklahoma constitution by adding the following section:

> C. The Courts provided for in subsection A of this section when exercising their judicial authority, shall uphold and adhere to the law as provided in the United States Constitution, the Oklahoma constitution, the United States Code, federal regulations promulgated pursuant thereto, established common law, the Oklahoma Statutes and rules promulgated pursuant thereto, and if necessary the law of another state of the United States provided the law of the other state does not include Sharia Law, in making judicial decisions. The courts shall not look to the legal precepts of other nations or cultures. Specifically, the courts shall not consider international law or Sharia Law. The provisions of this subsection shall apply to all cases before the respective courts including, but not limited to, cases of first impression.

. . .

Election results show that 70.08 per cent of the voters approved State Question 755. Once the Oklahoma State Board of Elections certifies the election results, the amendment set forth above will become a part of the Oklahoma constitution.

On November 4, 2010, plaintiff filed the instant action, challenging the constitutionality of State Question 755's amendment to the Oklahoma constitution. Specifically, plaintiff asserts that the ban on the state courts' use and consideration of Sharia Law violates the Establishment Clause and the Free Exercise Clause of the First Amendment to the United States Constitution. . . .

Under Article III, federal courts have jurisdiction only to decide "Cases" and "Controversies." U.S. CONST. art. III, § 2. An essential part of the case-or-controversy requirement is the concept that a plaintiff must have standing. . . .

. . .

Having carefully reviewed the briefs on this issue, and having heard the evidence and arguments presented at the hearing, the Court finds that plaintiff has shown that he will suffer an injury in fact, specifically, an invasion of his First Amendment rights which is concrete, particularized and imminent. . . .

[P]laintiff has sufficiently set forth a personal stake in this action by alleging that he lives in Oklahoma, is a Muslim, that the amendment conveys an official government message of disapproval and hostility toward his religious beliefs, that sends a clear message he is an outsider, not a full member of the political community, thereby chilling his access to the government and forcing him to curtail his political and religious activities. Further, the Court finds the consequences—the condemnation—that plaintiff believes will result from the amendment are objectively justified. Finally, the Court would note that it would be incomprehensible if, as plaintiff alleges, Oklahoma could condemn the religion of its Muslim citizens, yet one of those citizens could not defend himself in court against his government's preferment of other religious views.

. . .

A movant seeking a preliminary injunction must show: (1) a substantial likelihood of success on the merits; (2) irreparable injury to the movant if the injunction is denied; (3) the threatened injury to the movant outweighs the injury to the party opposing the preliminary injunction; and (4) the injunction would not be adverse to the public interest. . . .

. . .

When a claim asserting a violation of the Establishment Clause has been made, "[t]o pass constitutional muster, the governmental action (1) must have a secular legislative purpose, (2) its principal or primary effect must be one that neither advances nor inhibits religion, and (3) it must not foster an excessive government entanglement with religion." *Weinbaum v. City of Las Cruces, N.M.*, 541 F.3d 1017, 1030 (10th Cir. 2008). . . .

[T]he Court finds plaintiff has made a strong showing of a substantial likelihood of success on the merits of his claim asserting a violation of the Establishment Clause. Specifically, the Court finds that plaintiff has made a strong showing that State Question 755's amendment's primary effect inhibits religion and that the amendment fosters an excessive government entanglement with religion. While defendants contend that the amendment is merely a choice of law provision that bans state courts from applying the law of other nations and cultures, regardless of what faith they may be based on, if any, the actual language of the amendment reasonably, and perhaps more reasonably, may be viewed as specifically singling out Sharia Law, conveying a message of disapproval of plaintiff's faith. The amendment creates two independent restrictions on use/consideration of Sharia Law: (1) the amendment requires that Oklahoma courts "shall not consider ... Sharia Law", and (2) the amendment allows Oklahoma courts to use/consider the law of another state of the United States but only if "the other state does not include Sharia Law". No other "legal precepts of other nations or cultures" is similarly restricted with respect to the law of another state.

Furthermore, plaintiff has presented testimony that "Sharia Law" is not actually "law", but is religious traditions that provide guidance to plaintiff and other Muslims regarding the exercise of their faith. Plaintiff has presented testimony that the obligations that "Sharia Law" imposes are not legal obligations but are obligations of a personal and private nature dictated by faith. Plaintiff also testified that "Sharia Law" differs depending on the country in which the individual Muslim resides. For example, plaintiff stated that marrying more than one wife is permissible in Islam but in the United States, where that is illegal, Muslims do not marry more than one wife because Sharia in the United States mandates Muslims to abide by the law of the land and respect the law of their land. Based upon this testimony, the Court finds that plaintiff has shown "Sharia Law" lacks a legal character, and, thus, plaintiff's religious traditions and faith are the only non-legal content subject to the judicial exclusion set forth in the amendment. As a result, the Court finds plaintiff has made a strong showing that the amendment conveys a message of disapproval of plaintiff's faith and, consequently, has the effect of inhibiting plaintiff's religion.

Additionally, the Court finds that plaintiff has made a strong showing that the amendment will foster an excessive government entanglement with religion. Because, as set forth above, Sharia Law is not "law" but is religious traditions that differ among Muslims, the Court finds that plaintiff has shown that to comply with the amendment, Oklahoma courts will be faced with determining the content of Sharia Law, and, thus, the content of plaintiff's religious doctrines. The United States Supreme Court has held: "[i]t is well established ... that courts should refrain from trolling through a person's or institution's religious beliefs." *Mitchell v. Helms*, 530 U.S. 793, 828 (2000).

Plaintiff also asserts that State Question 755's amendment to the Oklahoma constitution violates the First Amendment's Free Exercise Clause. "At a minimum, the protections of the Free Exercise Clause pertain if the law at issue discriminates against some or all religious beliefs or regulates or prohibits conduct because it is undertaken for religious reasons." *Church of the Lukumi Babalu Aye, Inc. v. City of Hialeah*, 508 U.S. 520, 532 (1993). Further, "[a]lthough a law targeting religious beliefs as such is never permissible, if the object of a law is to infringe upon or restrict practices because of their religious motivation, the law is not neutral, and it is invalid unless it is justified by a compelling interest and is narrowly tailored to advance that interest." *Id.* at 533. However, "a law that is neutral and of general applicability need not be justified by a compelling governmental interest even if the law has the incidental effect of burdening a particular religious practice." *Id.* at 531.

Having carefully reviewed the briefs on this issue, and having heard the evidence and arguments presented at the hearing, the Court finds plaintiff has made a strong showing of a substantial likelihood of success on the merits of his claim asserting a violation of the Free Exercise Clause. As set forth above, plaintiff has shown that the actual language of the amendment reasonably, and perhaps more reasonably, may be viewed as specifically singling out Sharia Law (plaintiff's faith) and, thus, is not facially neutral. Additionally, as set forth above, the Court finds that plaintiff has shown that there is a reasonable probability that the amendment would prevent plaintiff's will from being fully probated by a state court in Oklahoma because it incorporates by reference specific elements of the Islamic prophetic traditions. Further, plaintiff has presented evidence that there is a reasonable probability that Muslims, including plaintiff, will be unable to bring actions in Oklahoma state courts for violations of the Oklahoma Religious Freedom Act and for violations of their rights under the United States Constitution if those violations are based upon their religion. Finally, the Court finds that defendants have presented no evidence which would show that the amendment is justified by any compelling interest or is narrowly tailored.

. . .

Therefore, for the reasons set forth above, the Court GRANTS plaintiff's request for a preliminary injunction and ENJOINS defendants from certifying the election results for State Question 755 until this Court rules on the merits of plaintiff's claims.

NOTE

In January 2006, David Yerushalmi founded the Society of Americans for National Existence, a nonprofit organization that likens Islamic law to sedition, and proposes making observing it a felony punishable by twenty years in prison. Andrea Elliott, *Behind an Anti–Shariah Push*, N.Y. TIMES, July 31, 2011, at 1. With funding from the Center for Security Policy in Washington, D.C., Mr. Yerushalmi drafted a model statute to restrict the use of foreign law by state judges. Early versions, which passed in Tennessee and Louisiana, made no mention of Shariah, in contrast to the law adopted in Oklahoma. In the fall of 2010, ACT for America, a group that describes itself as "opposed to the authoritarian values of radical Islam," spent $60,000 campaigning for the Oklahoma law, including 600,000 robocalls by James Woolsey, former director of the CIA. *Id.*

3.   MARRIAGE AND IMMIGRATION LAW

Contreras–Salinas v. Holder

United States Court of Appeals, Second Circuit, 2009.
585 F.3d 710.

■ PER CURIAM:

Petitioner Ysabel Contreras–Salinas ("petitioner" or "Contreras") seeks review of an August 22, 2008 decision of the Board of Immigration Appeals ("BIA") affirming the June 22, 2007 decision and order of an immigration judge ("IJ") denying petitioner's request for a "good faith marriage waiver" under 8 U.S.C. § 1186a(c)(4)(B) and ordering her removal. Petitioner argues that the IJ "failed to weigh" all material evidence showing that her first marriage was entered into in good faith. Because petitioner challenges a determination left to the sole discretion of the Attorney General, we lack jurisdiction to review her claims.

Petitioner is a native and citizen of Peru who came to the United States on October 15, 1994, as a nonimmigrant visitor. Shortly after her arrival she married Ramon Arroyo ("Arroyo"), a citizen of the United States, on December 17, 1994, in Hartford, Connecticut. On September 15, 1995, petitioner's status was adjusted to that of a conditional permanent resident. To obtain that adjustment she had to secure a waiver pursuant to 8 U.S.C. § 1182(i)(1) because her initial entry into the United States had been procured by fraud.[1]

As a conditional permanent resident, Contreras was required to petition for removal of her conditional status within 90 days of the second anniversary of obtaining permanent resident status and submit to a personal interview before immigration officials. 8 U.S.C. § 1186a(c)(1). In April 1997, prior to the time period during which she could petition for removal of conditional status, Contreras and Arroyo separated. In September 1997 Contreras and Arroyo filed a joint application for removal of conditional status as required by 8 U.S.C. § 1186a(c)(1)(A), but subsequently were divorced and failed to appear at the interview concerning the application. Her application was accordingly denied without objection on February 23, 1999.

Thereafter, on March 12, 1999, Contreras filed an application for a "good faith marriage waiver" of the § 1186a(c)(1) requirements pursuant to 8 U.S.C. § 1186a(c)(4)(B).[3] The Department of Homeland Security denied the waiver request on October 31, 2000, finding that Contreras failed to prove that her marriage to Arroyo was entered into in good faith, and thereafter commenced removal proceedings.

A hearing on the merits of petitioner's removal was held before an IJ on June 22, 2007, at which petitioner challenged the denial of her waiver application. In a decision and order entered on June 22, 2007, the IJ

---

1. This subsection provides, in relevant part:

The Attorney General may, in the discretion of the Attorney General, waive the [inadmissibility of an alien who fraudulently procures admission] in the case of an immigrant who is the spouse, son, or daughter of a United States citizen or of an alien lawfully admitted for permanent residence if it is established to the satisfaction of the Attorney General that the refusal of admission to the United States of such immigrant alien would result in extreme hardship to the citizen or lawfully resident spouse or parent of such an alien....

8 U.S.C. § 1182(i)(1). Contreras admitted to having misled immigration officials about her intention to reside in the United States and therefore required a waiver to obtain conditional permanent resident status.

3. This subsection provides, in relevant part:

The Attorney General, in the Attorney General's discretion, may remove the conditional basis of the permanent resident status for an alien who fails to meet the requirements of paragraph (1) if the alien demonstrates that

. . .

(B) the qualifying marriage was entered into in good faith by the alien spouse, but the qualifying marriage has been terminated (other than through the death of the spouse) and the alien was not at fault in failing to meet the requirements of paragraph (1),

. . .

. . . In acting on applications under this paragraph, the Attorney General shall consider any credible evidence relevant to the application. The determination of what evidence is credible and the weight to be given that evidence shall be within the sole discretion of the Attorney General.

8 U.S.C. § 1186a(c)(4).

concluded that petitioner had not established that her first marriage was bona fide. In particular, he expressed concern that some of the documents she submitted appeared to have been falsified and created in an attempt to "buttress her Immigration claim" and "mislead the Immigration authorities." Accordingly, the IJ affirmed the denial of the good faith marriage waiver and ordered petitioner removed to Peru. That decision was appealed to the BIA, which dismissed the appeal in a written decision on August 22, 2008.

This petition raises a threshold question of our jurisdiction to review the discretionary decision of the Attorney General to grant or deny a waiver under 8 U.S.C. § 1186a(c)(4). Pursuant to 8 U.S.C. § 1252(a)(2)(B)(ii), we lack jurisdiction to review a "decision or action of the Attorney General or the Secretary of Homeland Security the authority for which is specified *under this subchapter* to be in the discretion of the Attorney General or the Secretary of Homeland Security, other than the granting of [asylum]." The phrase "this subchapter" refers to subchapter II of chapter 12 of title 8 of the United States Code, which includes the waiver provisions of 8 U.S.C. § 1186a(c)(4). This jurisdiction-stripping provision is part of the Illegal Immigration Reform and Immigrant Responsibility Act of 1996 ("IIRIRA"), Pub. L. No. 104–208, 110 Stat. 3009–546, much of which, the Supreme Court has observed, is "aimed at protecting the Executive's discretion from the courts—indeed, that can fairly be said to be the theme of the legislation." *Reno v. Am.–Arab Anti–Discrimination Comm.*, 525 U.S. 471, 486 (1999).

Section 1186a(c)(4) explicitly provides that "[t]he Attorney General, *in the Attorney General's discretion*, may" waive the requirements of § 1186a(c)(1) for eligible aliens. The statute further provides that "[t]he determination of what evidence is credible and the weight to be given that evidence shall be within the *sole discretion of the Attorney General*." *Id.* (emphasis added). In *Atsilov v. Gonzales* [468 F.3d 112 (2d. Cir. 2006)] we held that we lack jurisdiction to review the decision to deny a good faith marriage waiver where eligibility for the waiver has been established but the agency nevertheless has exercised its discretion to deny relief. *Id.* at 116.

Here, unlike in *Atsilov*, petitioner was not deemed eligible for a waiver because her first marriage, the IJ concluded, was not entered into in good faith. She now challenges that determination of ineligibility. Whether such determinations are insulated from judicial review is an issue that has divided our sister Circuits. *Compare Assaad v. Ashcroft*, 378 F.3d 471, 475 (5th Cir. 2004) (holding that determination of eligibility for a waiver cannot be reviewed), *and Urena–Tavarez v. Ashcroft*, 367 F.3d 154, 159–60 (3d Cir. 2004) (same), *with Nguyen v. Mukasey*, 522 F.3d 853, 855 (8th Cir. 2008) (holding that determination of eligibility for a waiver is *not* discretionary and therefore is subject to review); *Oropeza–Wong v. Gonzales*, 406 F.3d 1135, 1142 (9th Cir. 2005) (same); *Cho v. Gonzales*, 404 F.3d 96, 101–02 (1st Cir. 2005) (same). We need not choose a side in this debate, however, because the specific nature of petitioner's claim clearly precludes judicial review.

Regardless of the disagreement among our sister Circuits on the Attorney General's discretion to determine eligibility for waivers under 8 U.S.C. § 1186a(c)(4), the statute does clearly commit to the Attorney General's "sole discretion" the determination of "what evidence is credible and the weight to be given that evidence." 8 U.S.C. § 1186a(c)(4); *see Cho*, 404 F.3d at 101 ("[W]e certainly have no quarrel with the conclusion that § 1252(a)(2)(B)(ii) precludes court review of petitions [directed at the Attorney General's credibility determinations and the weight he gave to the evidence that he credited]."). Because we conclude that petitioner's claims challenge only credibility determinations and the weight given to evidence by the IJ and BIA, we lack jurisdiction over her claims.

Petitioner claims that the IJ "failed to weigh the material evidence" showing that her marriage to Arroyo was entered into in good faith. In particular, she argues that the IJ failed to consider certain evidence, including (1) the § 1182(i) waiver she obtained in 1995, (2) evidence of a joint bank account in her name and her husband's, and (3) certain affidavits and testimony. . . .

Here, the record reveals that the agency considered all of petitioner's evidence but either found it lacking in credibility or outweighed by evidence suggesting petitioner's marriage was a sham. Although the IJ did not mention the § 1182(i) waiver, the BIA acknowledged this evidence. With respect to affidavits and testimony, the IJ explicitly acknowledged the "uncorroborated affidavits and testimony of [petitioner's] ex-sister-in-law" but found that they did "not overcome the overall lack of documentation, and the Court's concerns with the validity of [certain documentary evidence]." Finally, although neither the IJ nor the BIA explicitly mentioned evidence of petitioner's joint bank account, the IJ did note that "[i]n the record [ ] are some documents that the respondent provided" and that he "consider[ed] the evidence in the entirety" in reaching his conclusions. Although he may not have discussed all of petitioner's evidence purporting to show a good faith marriage, it is apparent from the IJ's decision that he found that evidence to be not credible and outweighed by documents that he found were "not . . . bona fide" and created to mislead immigration authorities.

Accordingly, regardless of how petitioner characterizes her claim, she is essentially challenging the agency's credibility determinations and the relative weight it accorded to evidence. Because such determinations are explicitly committed to the sole discretion of the Attorney General, we lack jurisdiction to review them.

NOTE

There are four categories of immigrants to the United States: family members of a U.S. citizen or resident; employees of a U.S. company; refugees; and those who win the "diversity lottery," a (somewhat) random allocation of a small percentage of immigration slots to residents of "underrepresented" countries. The largest category is immigrants to the United States who are related by marriage or birth to a U.S. citizen or resident. Kerry Abrams, *Immigration Law and the Regulation of Marriage*, 91 MINN. L. REV. 1625, 1635 (2007). In 2005, for example, of the 1,222,373 immigrants admitted on immigrant visas, 292,741 were spouses of U.S. citizens or residents and 186,304 were children of U.S. citizens or residents. *Id.*

The Immigration Marriage Fraud Amendments of 1986 subject couples married for less than twenty-four months to more searching scrutiny. Spouses who gain admission who have been married for less than twenty-four months must wait an additional two years before obtaining permanent residency, and are subject to deportation if it is determined during that two year period that the marriage was not bona fide. *Id.* at 1683.

4.   INTERNATIONAL STANDARDS V. DOMESTIC STANDARDS

Town of Castle Rock v. Gonzales

Supreme Court of the United States, 2005.
545 U.S. 748, 125 S.Ct. 2796, 162 L.Ed.2d 658.

■ JUSTICE SCALIA delivered the opinion of the Court.

We decide in this case whether an individual who has obtained a state-law restraining order has a constitutionally protected property interest in having the police enforce the restraining order when they have probable cause to believe it has been violated.

The horrible facts of this case are contained in the complaint that respondent Jessica Gonzales filed in Federal District Court. Respondent alleges that petitioner, the town of Castle Rock, Colorado, violated the Due Process Clause of the Fourteenth Amendment to the United States Constitution when its police officers, acting pursuant to official policy or custom, failed to respond properly to her repeated reports that her estranged husband was violating the terms of a restraining order.

The restraining order had been issued by a state trial court several weeks earlier in conjunction with respondent's divorce proceedings. The original form order, issued on May 21, 1999, and served on respondent's husband on June 4, 1999, commanded him not to "molest or disturb the peace of [respondent] or of any child," and to remain at least 100 yards from the family home at all times. 366 F.3d 1093, 1143 (10th Cir. 2004) (en banc) (appendix to dissenting opinion of O'Brien, J.). The bottom of the pre-printed form noted that the reverse side contained "IMPORTANT NOTICES FOR RESTRAINED PARTIES AND LAW ENFORCEMENT OFFICIALS." The preprinted text on the back of the form included the following "WARNING":

> "A KNOWING VIOLATION OF A RESTRAINING ORDER IS A CRIME.... A VIOLATION WILL ALSO CONSTITUTE CONTEMPT OF COURT. YOU MAY BE ARRESTED WITHOUT NOTICE IF A LAW ENFORCEMENT OFFICER HAS PROBABLE CAUSE TO BELIEVE THAT YOU HAVE KNOWINGLY VIOLATED THIS ORDER."

The preprinted text on the back of the form also included a "NOTICE TO LAW ENFORCEMENT OFFICIALS," which read in part:

> "YOU SHALL USE EVERY REASONABLE MEANS TO ENFORCE THIS RESTRAINING ORDER. YOU SHALL ARREST, OR, IF AN ARREST WOULD BE IMPRACTICAL UNDER THE CIRCUMSTANCES, SEEK A WARRANT FOR THE ARREST OF THE RESTRAINED PERSON WHEN YOU HAVE INFORMATION AMOUNTING TO PROBABLE CAUSE THAT THE RESTRAINED PERSON HAS VIOLATED OR ATTEMPTED TO VIOLATE ANY PROVISION OF THIS ORDER AND THE RESTRAINED PERSON HAS BEEN PROPERLY SERVED WITH A COPY OF THIS ORDER OR HAS RECEIVED ACTUAL NOTICE OF THE EXISTENCE OF THIS ORDER."

On June 4, 1999, the state trial court modified the terms of the restraining order and made it permanent. The modified order gave respondent's husband the right to spend time with his three daughters (ages 10, 9, and 7) on alternate weekends, for two weeks during the summer, and, "upon reasonable notice," for a mid-week dinner visit "arranged by the parties"; the modified order also allowed him to visit the home to collect the children for such "parenting time."

According to the complaint, at about 5 or 5:30 p.m. on Tuesday, June 22, 1999, respondent's husband took the three daughters while they were playing outside the family home. No advance arrangements had been made for him to see the daughters that evening. When respondent noticed the children were missing, she suspected her husband had taken them. At about 7:30 p.m., she called the Castle Rock Police Department, which dispatched two officers. The complaint continues: "When [the officers] arrived ..., she showed them a copy of the TRO and requested that it be enforced and the three children be returned to her immediately. [The officers] stated that there was nothing they could do about the TRO and suggested that [respondent] call the Police Department again if the three children did not return home by 10:00 p.m."

At approximately 8:30 p.m., respondent talked to her husband on his cellular telephone. He told her "he had the three children [at an] amusement park in Denver." She called the police again and asked them to "have someone check for" her husband or his vehicle at the amusement park and "put out an [all points bulletin]" for her husband, but the officer with whom she spoke "refused to do so," again telling her to "wait until 10:00 p.m. and see if" her husband returned the girls.

At approximately 10:10 p.m., respondent called the police and said her children were still missing, but she was now told to wait until midnight. She called at midnight and told the dispatcher her children were still missing. She went to her husband's apartment and, finding nobody there, called the police at 12:10 a.m.; she was told to wait for an officer to arrive. When none came, she went to the police station at 12:50 a.m. and submitted an incident report. The officer who took the report "made no reasonable effort to enforce the TRO or locate the three children. Instead, he went to dinner."

At approximately 3:20 a.m., respondent's husband arrived at the police station and opened fire with a semiautomatic handgun he had purchased earlier that evening. Police shot back, killing him. Inside the cab of his pickup truck, they found the bodies of all three daughters, whom he had already murdered.

On the basis of the foregoing factual allegations, respondent brought an action under REV. STAT. § 1979, 42 U.S.C. § 1983, claiming that the town violated the Due Process Clause because its police department had "an official policy or custom of failing to respond properly to complaints of restraining order violations" and "tolerate[d] the non-enforcement of restraining orders by its police officers." The complaint also alleged that the town's actions "were taken either willfully, recklessly or with such gross negligence as to indicate wanton disregard and deliberate indifference to" respondent's civil rights.

Before answering the complaint, the defendants filed a motion to dismiss under Federal Rule of Civil Procedure 12(b)(6). The District Court granted the motion, concluding that, whether construed as making a substantive due process or procedural due process claim, respondent's complaint failed to state a claim upon which relief could be granted.

A panel of the Court of Appeals affirmed the rejection of a substantive due process claim, but found that respondent had alleged a cognizable procedural due process claim. On rehearing en banc, a divided court reached the same disposition, concluding that respondent had a "protected property interest in the enforcement of the terms of her restraining order" and that the town had deprived her of due process because "the police never 'heard' nor seriously entertained her request to enforce and protect her interests in the restraining order." We granted certiorari.

The Fourteenth Amendment to the United States Constitution provides that a State shall not "deprive any person of life, liberty, or property, without due process of law." Congress has created a federal cause of action for "the deprivation of any rights, privileges, or immunities secured by the Constitution and laws." Respondent claims the benefit of this provision on the ground that she had a property interest in police enforcement of the restraining order against her husband; and that the town deprived her of this property without due process by having a policy that tolerated nonenforcement of restraining orders.

. . .

The procedural component of the Due Process Clause does not protect everything that might be described as a "benefit": "To have a property interest in a benefit, a person clearly must have more than an abstract need or desire" and "more than a unilateral expectation of it. He must, instead, have a legitimate claim of entitlement to it." *Board of Regents of State Colleges v. Roth*, 408 U.S. 564, 577 (1972). Such entitlements are "of course, . . . not created by the Constitution. Rather, they are created and their dimensions are defined by existing rules or understandings that stem from an independent source such as state law." *Paul v. Davis*, 424 U.S. 693, 709 (1976) (quoting *Roth, supra,* at 577).

Our cases recognize that a benefit is not a protected entitlement if government officials may grant or deny it in their discretion. The Court of Appeals in this case determined that Colorado law created an entitlement to enforcement of the restraining order because the "court-issued restraining order . . . specifically dictated that its terms must be enforced" and a "state statute commande[d]" enforcement of the order when certain objective conditions were met (probable cause to believe that the order had been violated and that the object of the order had received notice of its existence). Respondent contends that we are obliged "to give deference to the Tenth Circuit's analysis of Colorado law on" whether she had an entitlement to enforcement of the restraining order.

We will not, of course, defer to the Tenth Circuit on the ultimate issue: whether what Colorado law has given respondent constitutes a property interest for purposes of the Fourteenth Amendment. . . .

. . .

We do not believe that . . . provisions of Colorado law truly made enforcement of restraining orders *mandatory*. A well established tradition of police discretion has long coexisted with apparently mandatory arrest statutes.

> In each and every state there are long-standing statutes that, by their terms, seem to preclude nonenforcement by the police. . . . However, for a number of reasons, including their legislative history, insufficient resources, and sheer physical impossibility, it has been recognized that such statutes cannot be interpreted literally. . . . [T]hey clearly do not mean that a police officer may not lawfully decline . . . to make an arrest. As to third parties in these states, "the full-enforcement statutes simply have no effect, and their significance is further diminished." 1 ABA STANDARDS FOR CRIMINAL JUSTICE 1–4.5, commentary, pp. 1–124 to 1–125 (2d ed. 1980).

. . .

[A] true mandate of police action would require some stronger indication from the Colorado Legislature than "shall use every reasonable means to enforce a restraining order" (or even "shall arrest ... or ... seek a warrant"), 18–6–803.5(3)(a), (b). That language is not perceptibly more mandatory than the Colorado statute which has long told municipal chiefs of police that they "shall pursue and arrest any person fleeing from justice in any part of the state" and that they "shall apprehend any person in the act of committing any offense ... and, forthwith and without any warrant, bring such person before a ... competent authority for examination and trial." COLO. REV. STAT. § 31–4–112 (2004)....

The dissent correctly points out that, in the specific context of domestic violence, mandatory-arrest statutes have been found in some States to be more mandatory than traditional mandatory-arrest statutes. The Colorado statute mandating arrest for a domestic-violence offense is different from but related to the one at issue here, and it includes similar though not identical phrasing. *See* COLO. REV. STAT. § 18–6–803.6(1) (1999) ("When a peace officer determines that there is probable cause to believe that a crime or offense involving domestic violence ... has been committed, the officer shall, without undue delay, arrest the person suspected of its commission ..."). Even in the domestic-violence context, however, it is unclear how the mandatory-arrest paradigm applies to cases in which the offender is not present to be arrested. As the dissent explains, much of the impetus for mandatory-arrest statutes and policies derived from the idea that it is better for police officers to arrest the aggressor in a domestic-violence incident than to attempt to mediate the dispute or merely to ask the offender to leave the scene. Those other options are only available, of course, when the offender is present at the scene. *See* Hanna, *No Right to Choose: Mandated Victim Participation in Domestic Violence Prosecutions*, 109 HARV. L. REV. 1849, 1860 (1996) ("[T]he clear trend in police practice is to arrest the batterer *at the scene*...." (emphasis added)).

As one of the cases cited by the dissent recognized, "there will be situations when no arrest is possible, *such as when the alleged abuser is not in the home*." *Donaldson* [*v. City of Seattle*], 831 P. 2d 1098, 1105 (Wash. App. 1992) (emphasis added). That case held that Washington's mandatory-arrest statute required an arrest only in "cases where the offender is on the scene," and that it "d[id] not create an on-going mandatory duty to conduct an investigation" to locate the offender. *Id.* Colorado's restraining-order statute appears to contemplate a similar distinction, providing that when arrest is "impractical"—which was likely the case when the whereabouts of respondent's husband were unknown—the officers' statutory duty is to "seek a warrant" rather than "arrest." Section 18–6–803.5(3)(b).

Respondent does not specify the precise means of enforcement that the Colorado restraining-order statute assertedly mandated—whether her interest lay in having police arrest her husband, having them seek a warrant for his arrest, or having them "use every reasonable means, up to and including arrest, to enforce the order's terms." Such indeterminacy is not the hallmark of a duty that is mandatory. Nor can someone be safely deemed "entitled" to something when the identity of the alleged entitlement is vague.

Even if the statute could be said to have made enforcement of restraining orders "mandatory" because of the domestic-violence context of the underlying statute, that would not necessarily mean that state law gave *respondent* an entitlement to *enforcement* of the mandate. Making the actions of government employees obligatory can serve various legitimate ends other than the conferral of a benefit on a specific class of people. *See, e.g., Sandin v. Conner*, 515 U.S. 472, 482 (1995) (finding no constitutionally protected liberty interest in prison regulations phrased in mandatory terms, in part because "such guidelines are not set forth solely to benefit the prisoner"). The serving of public rather than private ends is the normal course of the criminal law because criminal acts, "besides the injury [they do] to individuals, . . . strike at the very being of society; which cannot possibly subsist, where actions of this sort are suffered to escape with impunity." 4 W. BLACKSTONE, COMMENTARIES ON THE LAWS OF ENGLAND 5 (1769). This principle underlies, for example, a Colorado district attorney's discretion to prosecute a domestic assault, even though the victim withdraws her charge. *See People v. Cunefare*, 102 P. 3d 302, 311–312 (Colo. 2004) (Bender, J., concurring in part, dissenting in part, and dissenting in part to the judgment).

· · ·

The creation of a personal entitlement to something as vague and novel as enforcement of restraining orders cannot "simply g[o] without saying." We conclude that Colorado has not created such an entitlement.

Even if we were to think otherwise concerning the creation of an entitlement by Colorado, it is by no means clear that an individual entitlement to enforcement of a restraining order could constitute a "property" interest for purposes of the Due Process Clause. Such a right would not, of course, resemble any traditional conception of property. Although that alone does not disqualify it from due process protection, as *Roth* and its progeny show, the right to have a restraining order enforced does not "have some ascertainable monetary value," as even our "*Roth*-type property-as-entitlement" cases have implicitly required. Merrill, *The Landscape of Constitutional Property*, 86 VA. L. REV. 885, 964 (2000). Perhaps most radically, the alleged property interest here arises *incidentally,* not out of some new species of government benefit or service, but out of a function that government actors have always performed—to wit, arresting people who they have probable cause to believe have committed a criminal offense.

The indirect nature of a benefit was fatal to the due process claim of the nursing-home residents in *O'Bannon v. Town Court Nursing Center*, 447 U.S. 773 (1980). We held that, while the withdrawal of "direct benefits" (financial payments under Medicaid for certain medical services) triggered due process protections, the same was not true for the "indirect benefits" conferred on Medicaid patients when the Government enforced "minimum standards of care" for nursing-home facilities. "[A]n indirect and incidental result of the Government's enforcement action . . . does not amount to a deprivation of any interest in life, liberty, or property." In this case, as in *O'Bannon,* "[t]he simple distinction between government action that directly affects a citizen's legal rights . . . and action that is directed against a third party and affects the citizen only indirectly or incidentally, provides a sufficient answer to" respondent's reliance on cases that found government-provided services to be entitlements. The *O'Bannon* Court expressly noted that the distinction between direct and indirect benefits distinguished *Memphis Light, Gas & Water Div. v. Craft*, 436 U.S. 1 (1978), one of the government-services cases on which the dissent relies.

We conclude, therefore, that respondent did not, for purposes of the Due Process Clause, have a property interest in police enforcement of the restraining order against her husband. It is accordingly unnecessary to address the Court of Appeals' determination that the town's custom or policy prevented the police from giving her due process when they deprived her of that alleged interest.

. . .

The judgment of the Court of Appeals is *Reversed*.

■ JUSTICE SOUTER, with whom JUSTICE BREYER joins, concurring.

I agree with the Court that Jessica Gonzales has shown no violation of an interest protected by the Fourteenth Amendment's Due Process Clause, and I join the Court's opinion. . . . Gonzales's claim of a property right thus runs up against police discretion in the face of an individual demand to enforce, and discretion to ignore an individual instruction not to enforce (because, say, of a domestic reconciliation); no one would argue that the beneficiary of a Colorado order like the one here would be authorized to control a court's contempt power or order the police to refrain from arresting. These considerations argue against inferring any guarantee of a level of protection or safety that could be understood as the object of a "legitimate claim of entitlement," *Board of Regents of State Colleges v. Roth*, 408 U.S. 564, 577 (1972), in the nature of property arising under Colorado law. Consequently, the classic predicate for federal due process protection of interests under state law is missing.

. . .

[I]n every instance of property recognized by this Court as calling for federal procedural protection, the property has been distinguishable from the procedural obligations imposed on state officials to protect it. Whether welfare benefits, *Goldberg v. Kelly*, 397 U.S. 254 (1970), attendance at public schools, *Goss v. Lopez*, 419 U.S. 565 (1975), utility services, *Memphis Light, Gas & Water Div. v. Craft*, 436 U.S. 1 (1978), public employment, *Perry v. Sindermann*, 408 U.S. 593 (1972), professional licenses, *Barry v. Barchi*, 443 U.S. 55 (1979), and so on, the property interest recognized in our cases has always existed apart from state procedural protection before the Court has recognized a constitutional claim to protection by federal process. To accede to Gonzales's argument would therefore work a sea change in the scope of federal due process, for she seeks federal process as a substitute simply for state process. (And she seeks damages under REV. STAT. § 1979, 42 U.S.C. § 1983, for denial of process to which she claimed a federal right.) There is no articulable distinction between the object of Gonzales's asserted entitlement and the process she desires in order to protect her entitlement; both amount to certain steps to be taken by the police to protect her family and herself. Gonzales's claim would thus take us beyond *Roth* or any other recognized theory of Fourteenth Amendment due process, by collapsing the distinction between property protected and the process that protects it[.] . . .

The procedural directions involved here are just that. They presuppose no enforceable substantive entitlement, and *Roth* does not raise them to federally enforceable status in the name of due process.

■ JUSTICE STEVENS, with whom JUSTICE GINSBURG joins, dissenting.

The issue presented to us is much narrower than is suggested by the far-ranging arguments of the parties and their *amici*. Neither the tragic facts of the case, nor the importance of according proper deference to law enforcement professionals, should divert our attention from that issue. That issue is whether the restraining order entered by the Colorado trial court on June 4, 1999, created a "property" interest that is protected from arbitrary deprivation by the Due Process Clause of the Fourteenth Amendment.

It is perfectly clear, on the one hand, that neither the Federal Constitution itself, nor any federal statute, granted respondent or her children any individual entitlement to police protection. *See DeShaney v. Winnebago County Dep't of Social Servs.*, 489 U.S. 189 (1989). Nor, I assume, does any Colorado statute create any such entitlement for the ordinary citizen. On the other hand, it is equally clear that federal law imposes no impediment to the creation of such an entitlement by Colorado law. Respondent certainly could have entered into a contract with a private security firm, obligating the firm to provide protection to respondent's family; respondent's interest in such a contract would unquestionably constitute "property" within the meaning of the Due Process Clause. If a Colorado statute enacted for her benefit, or a valid order entered by a Colorado judge, created the functional equivalent of such a private contract by granting respondent an entitlement to mandatory individual protection by the local police force, that state-created right would also qualify as "property" entitled to constitutional protection.

. . .

The central question in this case is therefore whether, as a matter of Colorado law, respondent had a right to police assistance comparable to the right she would have possessed to any other service the government or a private firm might have undertaken to provide. *See Board of Regents of State Colleges v. Roth*, 408 U.S. 564, 577 (1972) ("Property interests, of course, are not created by the Constitution. Rather, they are created and their dimensions are defined by existing rules or understandings that stem from an independent source such as state law—rules or understandings that secure certain benefits and that support claims of entitlement to those benefits").

. . .

Three flaws in the Court's rather superficial analysis of the merits highlight the unwisdom of its decision to answer the state-law question *de novo*. First, the Court places undue weight on the various statutes throughout the country that seemingly mandate police enforcement but are generally understood to preserve police discretion. As a result, the Court gives short shrift to the unique case of "mandatory arrest" statutes in the domestic violence context; States passed a wave of these statutes in the 1980's and 1990's with the unmistakable goal of eliminating police discretion in this area. Second, the Court's formalistic analysis fails to take seriously the fact that the Colorado statute at issue in this case was enacted for the benefit of the narrow class of persons who are beneficiaries of domestic restraining orders, and that the order at issue in this case was specifically intended to provide protection to respondent and her children. Finally, the Court is simply wrong to assert that a citizen's interest in the government's commitment to provide police enforcement in certain defined circumstances does not resemble any "traditional conception of property," *ante*, at 766; in fact, a citizen's property interest in such a commitment is just as concrete and worthy of protection as her interest in any other important service the government or a private firm has undertaken to provide.

. . .

[W]hen Colorado passed its statute in 1994, it joined the ranks of 15 States that mandated arrest for domestic violence offenses and 19 States that mandated arrest for domestic restraining order violations. *See Developments in the Law*, 106 HARV. L. REV. 1528, 1537, n. 68 (noting statutes in 1993); N. MILLER, INSTITUTE FOR LAW AND JUSTICE, A LAW ENFORCEMENT AND PROSECUTION PERSPECTIVE 7, and n. 74, 8, and n. 90 (2003), http://www.ilj.org/dv/dvvawa

2000.htm (as visited June 24, 2005, and available in Clerk of Court's case file) (listing Colorado among the many States that currently have mandatory arrest statutes).

Given the specific purpose of these statutes, there can be no doubt that the Colorado Legislature used the term "shall" advisedly in its domestic restraining order statute. While "shall" is probably best read to mean "may" in other Colorado statutes that seemingly mandate enforcement, *cf.* COLO. REV. STAT. § 31–4–112 (2004) (police "*shall suppress* all riots, disturbances or breaches of the peace, *shall apprehend* all disorderly persons in the city. . . ." (emphases added)), it is clear that the elimination of police discretion was integral to Colorado and its fellow States' solution to the problem of underenforcement in domestic violence cases. Since the text of Colorado's statute perfectly captures this legislative purpose, it is hard to imagine what the Court has in mind when it insists on "some stronger indication from the Colorado Legislature."

While Colorado case law does not speak to the question, it is instructive that other state courts interpreting their analogous statutes have not only held that they eliminate the police's traditional discretion to refuse enforcement, but have also recognized that they create rights enforceable against the police under state law. . . .

Indeed, the Court fails to come to terms with the wave of domestic violence statutes that provides the crucial context for understanding Colorado's law. The Court concedes that, "in the specific context of domestic violence, mandatory-arrest statutes have been found in some States to be more mandatory than traditional mandatory-arrest statutes," but that is a serious understatement. The difference is not a matter of degree, but of kind. Before this wave of statutes, the legal rule was one of discretion; as the Court shows, the "traditional," general mandatory arrest statutes have always been understood to be "mandatory" in name only. The innovation of the domestic violence statutes was to make police enforcement, not "more mandatory," but simply *mandatory*. If, as the Court says, the existence of a protected "entitlement" turns on whether "government officials may grant or deny it in their discretion," the new mandatory statutes undeniably create an entitlement to police enforcement of restraining orders.

Perhaps recognizing this point, the Court glosses over the dispositive question—whether the police enjoyed discretion to deny enforcement—and focuses on a different question—which "precise means of enforcement" were called for in this case. But that question is a red herring. The statute directs that, upon probable cause of a violation, "a peace officer shall arrest, or, if an arrest would be impractical under the circumstances, seek a warrant for the arrest of a restrained person." COLO. REV. STAT. § 18–6–803.5(3)(b) (1999). . . .

· · ·

Given that Colorado law has quite clearly eliminated the police's discretion to deny enforcement, respondent is correct that she had much more than a "unilateral expectation" that the restraining order would be enforced; rather, she had a "legitimate claim of entitlement" to enforcement. Recognizing respondent's property interest in the enforcement of her restraining order is fully consistent with our precedent. This Court has "made clear that the property interests protected by procedural due process extend well beyond actual ownership of real estate, chattels, or money." . . . Thus, our cases have found "property" interests in a number of state-conferred benefits and services, including welfare benefits, *Goldberg v. Kelly*, 397 U.S. 254 (1970); disability benefits, *Mathews v. Eldridge*, 424 U.S. 319 (1976); public education, *Goss v. Lopez*, 419 U.S. 565 (1975)....

Police enforcement of a restraining order is a government service that is no less concrete and no less valuable than other government services, such as education. The relative novelty of recognizing this type of property interest is explained by the relative novelty of the domestic violence statutes creating a mandatory arrest duty; before this innovation, the unfettered discretion that characterized police enforcement defeated any citizen's "legitimate claim of entitlement" to this service. Novel or not, respondent's claim finds strong support in the principles that underlie our due process jurisprudence. In this case, Colorado law *guaranteed* the provision of a certain service, in certain defined circumstances, to a certain class of beneficiaries, and respondent reasonably relied on that guarantee. As we observed in *Roth*, "[i]t is a purpose of the ancient institution of property to protect those claims upon which people rely in their daily lives, reliance that must not be arbitrarily undermined." Surely, if respondent had contracted with a private security firm to provide her and her daughters with protection from her husband, it would be apparent that she possessed a property interest in such a contract. Here, Colorado undertook a comparable obligation, and respondent—with restraining order in hand—justifiably relied on that undertaking. Respondent's claim of entitlement to this promised service is no less legitimate than the other claims our cases have upheld, and no less concrete than a hypothetical agreement with a private firm. The fact that it is based on a statutory enactment and a judicial order entered for her special protection, rather than on a formal contract, does not provide a principled basis for refusing to consider it "property" worthy of constitutional protection.

Because respondent had a property interest in the enforcement of the restraining order, state officials could not deprive her of that interest without observing fair procedures. Her description of the police behavior in this case and the department's callous policy of failing to respond properly to reports of restraining order violations clearly alleges a due process violation....

Accordingly, I respectfully dissent.

INTER–AMERICAN COMMISSION ON HUMAN RIGHTS, REPORT NO. 80/11: JESSICA LENAHAN (GONZALES) ET AL. V. UNITED STATES
1–2, 4, 8–13, 15–17, 21–22, 32–36, 40–43, 50–54, 56 (July 21, 2011).

This report concerns a petition presented to the Inter–American Commission on Human Rights (hereinafter the "Commission" or "IACHR") against the Government of the United States (hereinafter the "State" or the "United States") on December 27, 2005, by ... the American Civil Liberties Union.[1] The petition was presented on behalf of Ms. Jessica Lenahan, formerly Jessica Gonzales, and her deceased daughters Leslie (7), Katheryn (8) and Rebecca (10) Gonzales.

---

1. By note dated October 26, 2006, the Human Rights Clinic of Columbia University Law School was accredited as a co-petitioner, and on July 6, 2011 Peter Rosenblum was accredited as co-counsel and Director of said Clinic. By note dated October 15, 2007, Ms. Araceli Martínez–Olguín, from the Women's Rights Project of the American Civil Liberties Union, was also accredited as a representative. The University of Miami School of Law Human Rights Clinic was later added as co-petitioner, with Caroline Bettinger–Lopez as a representative of the Human Rights Clinic and lead counsel in the case. Sandra Park from the Women's Rights Project of the American Civil Liberties Union was also accredited later as co-counsel in the case.

The claimants assert in their petition that the United States violated ... the American Declaration by failing to exercise due diligence to protect Jessica Lenahan and her daughters from acts of domestic violence perpetrated by the ex-husband of the former and the father of the latter, even though Ms. Lenahan held a restraining order against him. They specifically allege that the police failed to adequately respond to Jessica Lenahan's repeated and urgent calls over several hours reporting that her estranged husband had taken their three minor daughters (ages 7, 8 and 10) in violation of the restraining order, and asking for help. The three girls were found shot to death in the back of their father's truck after the exchange of gunfire that resulted in the death of their father. The petitioners further contend that the State never duly investigated and clarified the circumstances of the death of Jessica Lenahan's daughters, and never provided her with an adequate remedy for the failures of the police. According to the petition, eleven years have passed and Jessica Lenahan still does not know the cause, time and place of her daughters' death.

The United States recognizes that the murders of Jessica Lenahan's daughters are "unmistakable tragedies." The State, however, asserts that any petition must be assessed on its merits, based on the evidentiary record and a cognizable basis in the American Declaration. The State claims that its authorities responded as required by law, and that the facts alleged by the petitioners are not supported by the evidentiary record and the information available to the Castle Rock Police Department at the time the events occurred. The State moreover claims that the petitioners cite no provision of the American Declaration that imposes on the United States an affirmative duty, such as the exercise of due diligence, to prevent the commission of individual crimes by private actors, such as the tragic and criminal murders of Jessica Lenahan's daughters.

In Report N° 52/07, adopted on July 24, 2007 during its 128th regular period of sessions, the Commission decided to admit the claims advanced by the petitioners ... and to proceed with consideration of the merits of the petition. At the merits stage, the petitioners added to their allegations that the failures of the United States to conduct a thorough investigation into the circumstances surrounding Leslie, Katheryn and Rebecca's deaths also breached Jessica Lenahan's and her family's right to truth in violation of Article IV of the American Declaration.

In the present report, having examined the evidence and arguments presented by the parties during the proceedings, the Commission concludes that the State failed to act with due diligence to protect Jessica Lenahan and Leslie, Katheryn and Rebecca Gonzales from domestic violence, which violated the State's obligation not to discriminate and to provide for equal protection before the law under Article II of the American Declaration. The State also failed to undertake reasonable measures to protect the life of Leslie, Katheryn and Rebecca Gonzales in violation of their right to life under Article I of the American Declaration, in conjunction with their right to special protection as girl-children under Article VII of the American Declaration. Finally, the Commission finds that the State violated the right to judicial protection of Jessica Lenahan and her next-of kin, under Article XVIII of the American Declaration. . . .

. . .

III. Positions of the Parties

A. Position of the Petitioners

[Petitioners allege that Simon Gonzales, Jessica Lenahan's estranged husband displayed erratic and unpredictable behavior, including several run-ins with the police department, and a domestic violence complaint initiated by Jessica Lenahan and followed by a restraining order against Simon Gonzales. This should have alerted the police to the fact that Jessica Lenahan considered him a potential danger to himself and his family. Police failed to enforce the restraining order against Simon Gonzales, despite Jessica Lenahan's repeated pleas to search for him because he had removed the children from their home without prior agreement. After the shootout the police failed to give her proper notice and there is still no in-depth investigation into the exact circumstances of her daughters deaths.]

Jessica Lenahan's case reached the Supreme Court, the highest court in the United States. On June 27, 2005, the Supreme Court rejected all of the claims presented by Jessica Lenahan, holding that her due process rights had not been violated. The Supreme Court held that despite Colorado's mandatory arrest law and the express and mandatory terms of her restraining order, Jessica Lenahan had no personal entitlement to police enforcement of the order under the due process clause.

The petitioners claim that, under the American Declaration, the judiciary had the obligation to provide a remedy for the police officers' failure to enforce the restraining order issued in favor of Jessica Lenahan in violation of state law and principles of international human rights law, which it failed to do. Moreover, the petitioners claim that the United States Supreme Court's decision in *Town of Castle Rock v. Gonzales* leaves Jessica Lenahan and countless other domestic violence victims in the United States without a judicial remedy by which to hold the police accountable for their failures to protect domestic violence victims and their children.

. . .

B.   Position of the State

... The State claims that the facts alleged by the petitioners are not supported by the evidentiary record and that the petition has not demonstrated a breach of duty by the United States under the American Declaration. The State claims that the evidentiary record demonstrates that throughout the evening of June 22, 1999 and the early hours of June 23, 1999, the Castle Rock Police Department responded professionally and reasonably to the information Jessica Lenahan provided and that the information available at the time revealed no indication that Simon Gonzales was likely to commit a crime against his own children.

[The State identifies three fundamental differences between the petitioners' claims and the actual record in this case. First, that, contrary to Jessica Lenahan's allegations, there was no evidence that the restraining order had been violated. Second, that there was no evidence that Simon Gonzales had actually abducted his daughters. And third, that there was no evidence that the police knew or should have known that the children were in real and imminent risk.]

The United States also notes the following about the Commission and its fact-finding capacity:

> ... with due respect to the Commission, it is not a formal judicial body that is fully equipped with a strong set of fact-finding authorities and tools. The Commission's petition and hearing process does not involve a discovery procedure, nor does it have formal rules of evidence or provisions for witness examination and cross-examination. In this context, we urge the Commission to exercise prudence and caution with

respect to its examination of the facts, and consider that the Petitioners bear the burden of establishing facts that constitute a breach of the Declaration.

. . .

The State alleges that the petitioners cite no provision of the American Declaration that imposes on the United States an affirmative duty, such as the exercise of due diligence, to prevent the commission of individual crimes by private parties. The petitioners cite case law of the Inter–American Court of Human Rights and of the Inter–American Commission on Human Rights, but these precedents cannot be interpreted to impose such a broad affirmative obligation upon the United States to prevent private crimes, such as the tragic and criminal murders of Leslie, Katheryn and Rebecca Gonzalez. The State moreover claims that the petitioners attempt unsuccessfully to argue that the entire corpus of international human right law and non-binding views of international bodies are embodied in obligations contained in the American Declaration, which in turn, are binding upon the United States. As a legal matter, the United States maintains that it is not bound by obligations contained in human rights treaties it has not joined and the substantive obligations enshrined in these instruments cannot be imported into the American Declaration.

IV. Analysis

. . .

After a comprehensive review of the arguments and evidence presented by the parties, the Commission concludes that the following facts have been proven:

. . .

Simon Gonzales' criminal history shows that he had several run-ins with the police in the three months preceding June 22, 1999. Jessica Lenahan called the Castle Rock Police Department on at least four occasions during those months to report domestic violence incidents. She reported that Simon Gonzales was stalking her, that he had broken into her house and stolen her wedding rings, that he had entered into her house unlawfully to change the locks on the doors, and that he had loosened the water valves on the sprinklers outside her house so that water flooded her yard and the surrounding neighborhood. Simon Gonzales also received a citation for road rage on April 18, 1999, while his daughters were in his car without seatbelts and his drivers' license had been suspended by June 23, 1999.

. . .

On Tuesday June 22, 1999 in the evening, Simon Gonzales purchased a Taurus 9mm handgun with 9 mm ammunition, from William George Palsulich, who held a Federal Firearms License since 1992. Simon Gonzales went to Palsulich's house at 7:10 p.m on June 22, 1999 with Leslie, Katheryn and Rebecca Gonzales. Simon Gonzales successfully passed a background check processed through the Federal Bureau of Investigations the evening of June 22nd, 1999, which was required to purchase the gun.

. . .

The Colorado Bureau of Investigations (hereinafter "CBI") undertook a detailed investigation of the crime scene . . . The report of this investigation does not contain any conclusions as to which bullets struck Leslie, Katheryn and Rebecca Gonzales or the time and place of their deaths.

A second investigation was undertaken at about 4:30 a.m. on June 23rd by the Critical Incident Team (hereinafter "CIT") of the 18th Judicial District, involving 18 members of the CIT, as well as a number of additional investigators. . . .

. . . Regarding the death of Leslie, Katheryn and Rebecca Gonzales, the CIT report solely concludes that the "autopsies revealed that the three girls were shot at extremely close range and were not struck by any rounds fired by the officers."

. . . The autopsy reports do not identify which bullets, those of the CRPD or Simon Gonzales, struck Leslie, Katheryn and Rebecca Gonzales.

. . .

a. Legal obligation to protect women from domestic violence under Article II of the American Declaration

The Commission begins analyzing this first question by underscoring its holding at the admissibility stage, that according to the well-established and long-standing jurisprudence and practice of the inter-American human rights system, the American Declaration is recognized as constituting a source of legal obligation for OAS member states, including those States that are not parties to the American Convention on Human Rights. These obligations are considered to flow from the human rights obligations of Member States under the OAS Charter. Member States have agreed that the content of the general principles of the OAS Charter is contained in and defined by the American Declaration, as well as the customary legal status of the rights protected under many of the Declaration's core provisions.

. . .

In light of these considerations, the Commission observes that States are obligated under the American Declaration to give legal effect to the obligations contained in Article II of the American Declaration. The obligations established in Article II extend to the prevention and eradication of violence against women, as a crucial component of the State's duty to eliminate both direct and indirect forms of discrimination. In accordance with this duty, State responsibility may be incurred for failures to protect women from domestic violence perpetrated by private actors in certain circumstances.

. . .

National law enforcement guidelines provided by the parties concerning the enforcement of restraining orders are instructive on the minimum measures that police authorities should have adopted to determine whether the order at issue had been violated. Guidelines from the International Association of Chiefs of Police, presented by the petitioners, provide that an officer must read an order in its entirety in determining its potential violation; that when a victim does not have a copy of her order, police officers should attempt to verify its existence; and that when missing, officers should attempt to locate and arrest the abuser and seize firearms subject to state, territorial, local or tribal prohibitions. There are some factors that police officers can weigh to determine the potential risk due to a restraining order violation, including threats of suicide from the aggressor; a history of domestic violence and violent criminal conduct; the separation of the parties; depression or other mental illness; obsessive attachment to the victim; and possession or access to weapons, among others. When an abuser has fled the scene, the guidelines instruct police officers to: determine whether the abuser's actions warrant arrest; and to follow departmental procedure for dealing with a criminal suspect who has fled the scene.

The Law Enforcement Training Manual published by the Colorado Coalition against Domestic Violence, mentioned by the State, offers similar guidelines to law enforcement officials when responding to potential restraining order violations in compliance with the Colorado Mandatory Arrest Statute....

Based on a thorough review of the record, the Commission considers that the CRPD failed to undertake the mentioned investigation actions with the required diligence and without delay. Its response can be at best characterized as fragmented, uncoordinated and unprepared; consisting of actions that did not produce a thorough determination of whether the terms of the restraining order at issue had been violated.

The Commission presents below some observations concerning the CRPD response from the evidence presented by the parties.

First, the Commission does not have any information indicating that the police officers who responded to Jessica Lenahan's calls and those who visited her house ever thoroughly reviewed the permanent restraining order to ascertain its terms and their enforcement obligations. Available information indicates that they took note of the existence of the order based on the information that Jessica Lenahan provided throughout the evening, and their conclusions and biases regarding this information, and not on the actual terms of the order....

. . .

Third, the file before the Commission also shows that the police officers never did a thorough check of Simon Gonzales' previous criminal background and contacts with the police. This history displayed a pattern of emotional issues, and unpredictable behavior that would have been important in understanding the risk of a violation of the protection order.

Fourth, the information before the Commission indicates there were apparently no protocols or directives in place guiding police officers on how to respond to reports of potential restraining order violations involving missing children, which contributed to delays in their response. For example, the undisputed facts show that it took a dispatcher an hour—between 2:15–3:25 a.m.—to find the guidelines to enter an "Attempt to Locate BOLO" for Simon Gonzales and his vehicle. She also reported having problems entering information into the screens for the "Attempt to Locate" because she was missing crucial information such as the physical descriptions of the children. This information was never requested from Jessica Lenahan despite her eight contacts with the police during that evening.

Fifth, the lack of training of the Castle Rock police officers throughout the evening of June 22nd and the morning of June 23rd was evident. The response of the Castle Rock police officers, when assessed as a whole throughout this time period, displays misunderstandings and misinformation regarding the problem of domestic violence. Even the State concedes in its pleadings that, from the point of view of the CRPD, this situation appeared to be a "misunderstanding" between Mr. and Ms. Gonzales, and the officers had a sense of relief that the children were at least in a known location with their father, even though he was subject to a restraining order.[248]

---

248. Reply by the Government of the United States of America to the Final Observations Regarding the Merits of the Case by the Petitioners, October 17, 2008, p. 7.

Some statements display that police officers did not understand the urgency or seriousness of the situation. When Jessica Lenahan called the CPRD for a third time at 9:57 p.m. to report that her children were still not home, the dispatcher asked her to call back on a "non-emergency line," and told her she wished that she and Simon Gonzales had made some arrangements since "that's a little ridiculous making us freak out and thinking the kids are gone."

Sixth, the Commission notes that the police officers throughout the evening evidence that they did not understand that they were the ones responsible for ascertaining whether the restraining order had been violated. They kept on asking Jessica Lenahan to call them back throughout the evening, and to contact Simon Gonzalez herself, even though they were aware that this was a domestic violence situation. The State itself in its pleadings has presented as a defense that Jessica Lenahan never reported to the police officers that the restraining order had been violated. The Commission has manifested its concern on how States mistakenly take the position that victims are themselves responsible for monitoring the preventive measures, which leaves them defenseless and in danger of becoming the victims of the assailant's reprisals.[250]

Seventh, the established facts also show systemic failures not only from the CRPD, but from the Federal Bureau of Investigations. On June 22, 1999, Simon Gonzales purchased a Taurus 9mm handgun with 9 mm ammunition, from William George Palsulich, who held a Federal Firearms License since 1992. Simon Gonzales contacted Palsulich at 6:00 p.m on June 22, 1999, in response to an advertisement Palsulich had placed in the newspaper concerning the sale of the gun, asking whether he could purchase the gun and ammunition. Simon Gonzales went to Palsulich's house at 7:10 p.m on June 22, 1999 with Leslie, Katheryn and Rebecca Gonzales to purchase this gun. The record before the Commission indicates that the seller processed a background check through the Federal Bureau of Investigations in order to make the sale to Simon Gonzalez. Palsulich initially had to decline the sale since the FBI refused the background check, but the FBI later called and informed Palsulich that the transaction had been approved. The State has not contested this point, nor it has indicated how the background check of a person, such as Simon Gonzales, subject to a restraining order and having a criminal history, could have been approved. The State has not explained either why the restraining order apparently did not show up in the review of data performed as part of the background check.

Based on these considerations, the Commission concludes that even though the State recognized the necessity to protect Jessica Lenahan and Leslie, Katheryn and Rebecca Gonzales from domestic violence, it failed to meet this duty with due diligence. The state apparatus was not duly organized, coordinated, and ready to protect these victims from domestic violence by adequately and effectively implementing the restraining order at issue; failures to protect which constituted a form of discrimination in violation of Article II of the American Declaration.

. . .

An expert report prepared by Peter Diaczuk, a forensic scientist, presented by the petitioners on July 16, 2009 and uncontested by the State, reviews in detail documentation related to these two investigations and

---

250. IACHR, *Access to Justice for Women Victims of Violence in the Americas*, OEA/Ser. L/V/II. doc. 68, January 20, 2007, para. 170.

identifies significant irregularities pertaining to the inquiry into Leslie, Katheryn and Rebecca's deaths. He notes that the "incomplete handling, documentation, and analysis of the evidence in this case resulted in unnecessary uncertainty surrounding the time, place, and circumstances of the three girls' deaths;" and that "while many answers appeared within reach, law enforcement officials simply did not take the steps necessary to fully uncover them."

Professor Diaczuk in his report notes key differences between the quality of the investigation of elements found outside of Simon Gonzales' pick-up truck, and the evidence found inside the truck, where the three bodies of the girl-children were found. For example, he observes that even though law enforcement used care in photographing and documenting the outside crime scene and evidence found at the street level, near Simon Gonzales' body, the bodies of the girls and the interior of the truck were photographed hastily, without use of the proper lighting equipment or measurements. Even though important items of physical evidence at the crime scene were recognized, photographed, documented and collected, most of the items collected from inside of the truck were not routed to the laboratory for analysis, as opposed to the items collected outside the truck, which were properly analyzed. Professor Diaczuk highlights as a particularly troubling aspect the Colorado authorities' analysis and accounting of the firearm evidence found inside of Simon Gonzales' truck, noting that pursuant to investigatory procedures, a laboratory examination of all cases, projectiles and fragments—including those found inside and outside of the truck—was critical; but was not performed in this case. He furthermore notes that the truck in which the bodies of the girl-children were found was disposed of quickly, before time, location and circumstances surrounding the deaths of Jessica Lenahan's children were even recorded on their death certificates, even though inquiries into the girl-children's deaths were still pending.

Professor Diaczuk concludes overall that even if circumstantial evidence may have suggested to the authorities that Simon Gonzales was responsible for the deaths of the girl-children, the forensic analyses he reviewed do not sustain this conclusion, instead showing that the investigation of their deaths was prematurely concluded. He indicated that the death of each victim should have been treated as a separate occurrence, and investigated in its own right.

The Commission notes that the State has not challenged the expert report presented by Professor Peter Diaczuk. The State has responded overall to the petitioners' claims by stating that if the petitioners considered the investigation of the girl-children's deaths inappropriate and incomplete, they should have availed themselves of the Citizen Complaint Procedure of the Castle Rock Police Department. Regarding this State claim, the Commission established at the admissibility stage that the State had not indicated how the alternative administrative remedy it mentions could have provided Jessica Lenahan with a different judicial redress for her pretentions, or how this could have been adequate and effective in remedying the violations alleged.

. . .

In light of the considerations presented, the Commission finds that the United States violated the right to judicial protection of Jessica Lenahan and her next-of-kin under Article XVIII, for omissions at two levels. First, the State failed to undertake a proper inquiry into systemic failures and the individual responsibilities for the non-enforcement of the protection order.

Second, the State did not perform a prompt, thorough, exhaustive and impartial investigation into the deaths of Leslie, Katheryn and Rebecca Gonzales, and failed to convey information to the family members related to the circumstances of their deaths.

VI.   Recommendations

Based on the analysis and conclusions pertaining to the instant case, the Inter–American Commission on Human Rights recommends to the United States:

1.   To undertake a serious, impartial and exhaustive investigation with the objective of ascertaining the cause, time and place of the deaths of Leslie, Katheryn and Rebecca Gonzales, and to duly inform their next-of-kin of the course of the investigation.

2.   To conduct a serious, impartial and exhaustive investigation into systemic failures that took place related to the enforcement of Jessica Lenahan's protection order as a guarantee of their non-repetition, including performing an inquiry to determine the responsibilities of public officials for violating state and/or federal laws, and holding those responsible accountable.

3.   To offer full reparations to Jessica Lenahan and her next-of-kin considering their perspective and specific needs.

4.   To adopt multifaceted legislation at the federal and state levels, or to reform existing legislation, making mandatory the enforcement of protection orders and other precautionary measures to protect women from imminent acts of violence, and to create effective implementation mechanisms. These measures should be accompanied by adequate resources destined to foster their implementation; regulations to ensure their enforcement; training programs for the law enforcement and justice system officials who will participate in their execution; and the design of model protocols and directives that can be followed by police departments throughout the country.

5.   To adopt multifaceted legislation at the federal and state levels, or reform existing legislation, including protection measures for children in the context of domestic violence. Such measures should be accompanied by adequate resources destined to foster their implementation; regulations to ensure their enforcement; training programs for the law enforcement and justice system officials who will participate in their execution; and the design of model protocols and directives that can be followed by police departments throughout the country.

6.   To continue adopting public policies and institutional programs aimed at restructuring the stereotypes of domestic violence victims, and to promote the eradication of discriminatory socio-cultural patterns that impede women and children's full protection from domestic violence acts, including programs to train public officials in all branches of the administration of justice and police, and comprehensive prevention programs.

7.   To design protocols at the federal and state levels specifying the proper components of the investigation by law enforcement officials of a report of missing children in the context of a report of a restraining order violation.

VII.   Actions Subsequent to Report No. 114/10

On October 21, 2010, the IACHR adopted Report No. 114/10 on the merits of this case. This report was sent to the State on November 15, 2010, with a time period of two months to inform the Inter–American Commission on the measures adopted to comply with its recommendations. On the same date, the petitioners were notified of the adoption of the report.

On January 14, 2011, the State requested an extension to present its response to the merits report. The Commission granted an extension to the State until March 15, 2011 to present its observations, in accordance with Article 37(2) of the IACHR's Rules of Procedure.

The petitioners presented their observations regarding the report on January 28, 2011, which were forwarded to the State on February 15, 2011, with a one-month period to send its observations. . . .

. . .

Given the lack of information from the State, the Commission must conclude that the recommendations issued have not been implemented, and that their compliance thus remains pending. The Commission is accordingly required to reiterate those recommendations and continue monitoring compliance.

. . .

In light of the above and in accordance with Article 47 of its Rules of Procedure, the IACHR decides to make this report public, and to include it in its Annual Report to the General Assembly of the Organization of American States. The Inter–American Commission, according to the norms contained in the instruments which govern its mandate, will continue evaluating the measures adopted by the United States with respect to the above recommendations until it determines there has been full compliance.

. . .

D. LEGAL FORM AND FAMILY LAW

Carl E. Schneider, *The Channelling Function in Family Law*

20 HOFSTRA L. REV. 495, 496, 498, 500–04, 506–09, 511, 529–32 (1992).

A. What is the Channelling Function?

[I] propose . . . to explor[e] a function of family law that I believe is basic, that underlies much of family law, that resonates with the deepest purposes of culture but that is rarely addressed expressly—namely, what I call the "channelling function." . . .

. . .

[I]n the channelling function the law creates or (more often) supports social institutions which are thought to serve desirable ends. "Social institution" I intend broadly: "In its formal sociological definition, an institution is a pattern of expected action of individuals or groups enforced by social sanctions, both positive and negative."[7] . . . Generally, the channelling function does not specifically require people to use these social institutions, although it may offer incentives and disincentives for their use. Primarily, rather, it is their very presence, the social currency they have, and the governmental support they receive which combine to make it seem reason-

---

7. ROBERT N. BELLAH, ET AL., THE GOOD SOCIETY 10 (1991).

able and even natural for people to use them. Thus people can be said to be channelled into them. . . .

.   .   .

[I] will . . . describe two broad social institutions which I will use to illustrate the working of family law's channelling function. These two institutions are "marriage" and "parenthood." . . . I have no doubt that both these institutions have somewhat different meanings for different people, that they have changed over time and are still changing, and that they do not monopolize intimate life in modern America. However, a legislator might plausibly identify a core of ideas which have enough social support to justify the term "institution" and which the legislator might conclude the law should try to support, to shape, and to channel people into.

Our legislator might, then, posit a normative model of "marriage" with several fundamental characteristics. It is monogamous, heterosexual, and permanent. It rests on love. Husbands and wives are to treat each other affectionately, considerately, and fairly. They should be animated by mutual concern and willing to sacrifice for each other. . . .

.   .   .

In the same way, our legislator might posit an institution of "parenthood" with several key normative characteristics. Parents should be married to each other. They are preferably the biological father and mother of their child. They have authority over their children and can make decisions for them. However, like spouses, parents are expected to love their children and to be affectionate, considerate, and fair. They should support and nurture their children during their minority. They should assure them a stable home, particularly by staying married to each other, so that the child lives with both parents and knows the comforts of security.

Obviously, these two normative models are not and never were descriptions of any universal empirical reality. . . . Nor are they the only models the channelling function might be recruited to serve. Nevertheless, they do describe ideals which have won and retained substantial allegiance in American life. I will thus use these models to illustrate how the channelling function can work. How, then, might our legislator interpret the law as supporting these two institutions and channelling people into them?

Our legislator might see family law as setting a framework of rules, one of whose effects is to shape, sponsor, and sustain the model of marriage I described above: it writes standards for entry into marriage, standards which prohibit polygamous, incestuous, and homosexual unions. It seeks to encourage marital stability by inhibiting divorce (although it pursues this goal much less vigorously than it once did). It tries to improve marital behavior both directly and indirectly: It imposes a few direct obligations during marriage, like the duty of support. Less directly, it has invented special categories of property . . . to reflect and reinforce the special relationship of marriage. It indirectly sets some standards for marital behavior through the law of divorce. Fault-based divorce does so by describing behavior so egregious that it justifies divorce. Marital-property law implicitly sets standards for the financial conduct of spouses. Finally, prohibitions against non-marital sexual activity and discouragements against quasi-marital arrangements in principle confine sexual life to marriage. . . .

Similarly, our legislator might see a framework of laws molding and promoting the institution of parenthood. Laws criminalizing fornication, cohabitation, adultery, and bigamy in principle limit parenthood to married couples, and those legal disadvantages that still attach to illegitimacy make it wise to confine parenthood to marriage. Laws restricting divorce make it likelier that a child will be raised by both parents. The law buttresses parents' authority over children. Parents may use reasonable force in disciplining their children. They may decide whether their children should have medical treatment. They may choose their child's school. Parents of "children in need of supervision" can summon up the state's coercive power. However, the law also tries, directly and indirectly, to shape parental behavior. It requires parents to support their children. It penalizes the "abuse" or "neglect" of children and obliges many kinds of people to report evidence of it. It obliges parents to send their children to school. Custody law obliquely sets standards for parental behavior and emphasizes the centrality of children's interests. Finally, some states further elaborate the relationship between parent and child by obliging adult children to support their indigent parents.

These sketches suggest how the law can be seen as performing the first task of the channelling function, namely, to create—or more often, to recruit—social institutions and to mold and sustain them. The function's second task is to channel people into institutions. It can perform these two tasks in several ways. First, it does so simply by recognizing and endorsing institutions, thus giving them some aura of legitimacy and permanence. Recognition may be extended, for instance, through formalized, routinized, and regulated entry and exit to an institution, as with marriage: "By the authority vested in me by the State of Michigan, I now pronounce you man and wife."

A second channelling technique is to reward participation in an institution. Tax law, for instance, may offer advantages—like the marital deduction—to married couples that it denies the unmarried. Similarly, Social Security offers spouses benefits it refuses lovers. These advantages are enhanced if private entities consult the legal institution in allocating benefits, as when private employers offer medical insurance only to "family members" as the law defines that term. In a somewhat different vein, the law of alimony and marital property offers spouses—but generally not "cohabitants"— protections on divorce.

Third, the law can channel by disfavoring competing institutions. Sometimes competitors are flatly outlawed, as by laws prohibiting sodomy, bigamy, adultery, and prostitution. Bans on fornication and cohabitation mean (in principle) that, to have sexual relations, one must marry. Sometimes competing institutions are merely disadvantaged. For instance, the rule making contracts for meretricious consideration unenforceable traditionally denied unmarried couples the law's help in resolving some disputes. Similarly, nonparents are presumptively disadvantaged in custody disputes with parents. Finally, restrictive divorce laws impede re-entry to the alternative institution of singleness.

. . .

By and large, then, the channelling function does not primarily use direct legal coercion. People are not forced to marry. One can contract out (formally or informally) of many of the rules underlying marriage. One need not have children, and one is not forced to treat them lovingly. Rather, the function forms and reinforces institutions which have significant social support and which, optimally, come to seem so natural that people use them almost unreflectively. It relies centrally but not exclusively on social approval of the institution, on social rewards for its use, and on social disfavor of its alternatives. . . .

. . .

B.   What Purposes Does the Channelling Function Serve?

. . .

[F]amily law's channelling function is partly a specialized way of performing its protective, facilitative, and arbitral functions. For instance, marriage variously serves the protective function. Law does not just (in conjunction with other social forces) create a shell of an institution; it builds (again with much help) institutions with norms. The institution of marriage which the law recruits and shapes attempts to induce in spouses a sense of an obligation to treat each other well—to love and honor each other. At the elemental level of physical violence, the law has tried to reinforce this socially imposed obligation by making cruelty a ground for divorce, by taking cruelty into account in settling the spouses' economic affairs, and by criminalizing and (increasingly aggressively in some jurisdictions) prosecuting spouse abuse. At the level of economic life, the law has tried to supervise the fairness of antenuptial agreements and the distribution of the spouses' assets on divorce. And marriage protects children by making it likelier that both parents will care for them throughout their minority.

. . .

But the channelling function is more than a specialized means of performing family law's other functions. Like the corporation, marriage and parenthood serve some broad social purposes. These are crucial, but they are also so familiar they hardly need elaboration. Sixty years ago Karl Llewellyn discerned thirteen such purposes in marriage. They included the regulation of sexual behavior, the reduction of sexual conflict, the orderly perpetuation of the species, the "building and reinforcement of an economic unit," the regulation of wealth, and the "development of individual personality."[26] And a large body of writing argues that the present happiness and future well-being of children depend on their growing up in something like the kind of institution I described above.

Less grandly . . . channelling's institutions spare people having to invent the forms of family life *de novo*. Imagine two nineteen-year-olds living in a state of nature who find themselves in love. Without established social institutions, they would have to work out afresh how to express that love, how to structure their relationship, and what to expect of each other. The same couple in, say, the United States of the mid-twentieth century would find a set of answers to those questions in the institution of marriage. To be sure, they would see other answers presented by other institutions. They would hear criticisms of marriage. They would not be compelled to marry. But marriage would seem natural to them because most of the adults they knew partook of it, because society and the law supported it, and because they had to some extent internalized its values . . . The institution, that is, would be part of a comfortable social vocabulary, a vocabulary that would save our lovers from having to invent their own language.

. . .

---

26.   Karl N. Llewellyn, *Behind the Law of Divorce: I*, 32 COLUM. L. REV. 1281, 1288–95 (1932).

More concretely, for example, the institution of marriage helps people to plan for the future even before becoming engaged and to reach easier understandings with their fiances and spouses about their married lives. People dealing with married couples benefit as well. Mundanely, they know that when they say, "Can you come for dinner on the sixteenth?," the invitation will be taken as including both husband and wife. Less banally and more consequentially, a wedding ring warns anyone attracted to its wearer not to contemplate an intimate relationship.

. . .

We can summarize these workings of the channelling function by imagining two people looking for recreation, who live in a world without tennis, and who are given three balls, two rackets, and one net. They could no doubt find some way of amusing themselves with these toys. But tennis is a good game partly because it developed over many centuries, and our couple could not easily invent as good a game. Further, where tennis is a social institution, the two will readily find people with whom to enjoy their recreation, to improve their game, to relish their successes, and to lament their failures. And part of the pleasure of tennis lies in knowing its past glories and following its current progress. Tennis, in other words, succeeds because it is a shared and well-established social institution. Marriage and parenthood benefit from that same fact.

. . .

[I]n discussions of the channelling function, I have found people most troubled by what I think is the sense that it violates the principle that the state should be neutral among visions of the good. The function's institutions necessarily have normative components and thus to some degree favor one such vision over the rest. More, the function seeks, however obliquely, to shape people's thoughts and acts in an area of life in which freedom is widely and properly prized.

. . .

[One] response to the claim that the channelling function is improper because it violates some visions of state neutrality is that, in an important sense, one *cannot* abolish the channelling function in family law. Family law's goals—particularly those goals represented by the protective, arbitral, and facilitative functions—are so central that they are unlikely to be abandoned. As long as we pursue those goals, we will be creating, building on, and shaping social institutions and channelling people into them. The most obvious way to try to escape doing so is by expanding the facilitative function, by turning family law into contract law. That venture could not entirely succeed, of course, if only because family law centrally involves children, and children (particularly the young children about whom we worry most) cannot make contracts. But even if the venture succeeded, it would create a new institution. Contract, after all, has its own social structures, its own assumptions, its own consequences. Indeed, these are at the heart of the resistance to contract law's incursion into the sphere of family life.

Channelling, then, cannot be escaped. It arises because we are social beings whose relations with those around us shape institutions that in turn shape us. It arises because we are imperfect people who without institutions behave in ways that injure our fellows. It arises because we see the faults of the institutions around us and seek to perfect them, because we value the aspirations those institutions embody and hope to achieve them. Channelling, like any social tool, may be and has been used badly and used to bad purposes. But it is also one of the ways we try to use law to soften the harshness of life.

NOTES

1. Why does Professor Schneider think that requiring compliance with legal form is likely to create more stable social institutions than a legal system in which the state simply ratifies whatever intimate arrangements people want to make?

2. Does the high divorce rate and growing incidence of unmarried cohabitation indicate that efforts to channel people toward marriage are becoming less effective?

3. Is it necessary to channel people into marriage in order to provide social support for the importance of "a sense of an obligation to treat each other well—to love and honor each other"? Is the long tradition and cultural resonance of marriage more likely to do this than unmarried cohabitation? Or does marriage have other less salutary connotations that make the meaning of the institution more mixed?

4. If it is appropriate for law to channel couples into marriage, what benefits, rights, or obligations that spouses have should be denied to unmarried partners in order to reinforce this social preference? For an exploration of the complex considerations that may inform decisions whether to treat married and unmarried couples alike in various circumstances, *see* Milton C. Regan, Jr., *Calibrated Commitment: The Legal Treatment of Marriage and Cohabitation*, 76 NOTRE DAME L. REV. 1435 (2001).

Linda C. McClain, *Love, Marriage, and the Baby Carriage: Revisiting the Channelling Function of Family Law*

28 CARDOZO L. REV. 2133, 2138–47, 2152, 2174–77 (2007).

This Article revisits a significant idea at the core of contemporary debates in family law: the channelling function of family law.... Family law scholar Carl Schneider helpfully invited attention to this familiar idea some years ago....

. . .

The childhood rhyme about love followed by marriage and the baby carriage might be said to reflect a conventional understanding of the proper sequence that men and women should follow in organizing their intimate lives. To put it in Schneider's terms, marriage and parenthood are social institutions into which men and women are—or should be—steered, with the help of family law. However, everyday life offers many examples of departures from this sequence; people skip steps or scramble the sequence (or bypass it entirely). For gay men and lesbians, excluded in [most states] from access to marriage, the sequence is simply not available and in their intimate lives, by necessity, they construct a different sequence.

In October 2006, a news headline in the *New York Times* declared: "It's Official: To Be Married Means to be Outnumbered." The article ... reported that, in 2005, "married couples, whose numbers have been declining for decades as a proportion of American households, have finally slipped into a minority"—49.7 percent of the nation's households. The article was quick to reassure that marriage is not "dead": "most Americans eventually marry," and "the total number of married couples is higher than ever." Why, then, the headline? Marriage is facing "more competition from other ways of living," to the extent that a tipping point may now be reached. The article mentions several alternative practices that have potentially "profound" economic and social implications, given the way in which marital status is used as a trigger for various economic and employment benefits. For example, (a) many Americans are marrying later in life than in earlier times, and some are not marrying at all; (b) more couples are cohabiting, either as a step to marriage (a "test drive" of the relationship) or instead of marriage; (c) more couples are parenting outside of marriage; and (d) some couples are bypassing both marriage and children. . . .

In this world in which marriage faces stiffer competition, there are fewer givens or certainties about life scripts. This suggests that for an increasing number of Americans, marrying is no longer an inevitable step in their own life plan and is not as universally a rite of passage on the way to mature adulthood. Instead of a predictable sequence, we might express it as: maybe love, or maybe not; perhaps marriage, but perhaps not, or at least not yet; and maybe the baby carriage, or maybe not. For example, interpreting survey data that the majority of American women are now living without a spouse, family historian Stephanie Coontz contends: "This is yet another of the inexorable signs that there is no going back to a world where we can assume that marriage is the main institution that organizes people's lives." . . .

The changing place of marriage in some life narratives must be seen in the context of a larger story about women's and men's changing expectations from marriage, as well as how economics and education shape one's access to marriage and one's "marriageability." A familiar story told about women stresses that they are less dependent than women in earlier eras on men or on the institution of marriage: younger women, realizing this, prepare to live "longer parts of their lives alone or with nonmarried partners"; at the same time, "for many older [baby] boomer and senior women, the institution of marriage did not hold the promise they might have hoped for," which may explain why divorced women delay remarriage more than divorced men.

Stories told about the place of marriage in men's lives more often stress disadvantage and obstacles to marriage. Illustrative of this point is another recent news story, *Facing Middle Age with No Degree, and No Wife* (part of a series on the "New Gender Divide" in America), with this lead-in: "Once, virtually all Americans had married by their mid–40s. Now, many American men without college degrees find themselves still single as they approach middle age."

Why do men "find themselves" single at middle age? Is it by chance or by choice? The answer seems to be: both. Some men do not marry because they fear divorce and losing money or property to a divorcing spouse. Another factor is the familiar one that, as women have become more economically independent, they do not need to marry for economic security. Those women who are not as economically secure are more likely to seek to "marry up" in order to improve their financial prospects. The comparative economic position of men—particularly blue-collar men—has worsened. Thus, "of the men remaining single, the greatest number are high school dropouts, especially blacks and unemployed men." But marriage is also declining among white men and men with jobs who lack college degrees.

This suggests that departures from the sequence love-marriage-baby carriage may not be wholly voluntary, but relate to forms of economic disadvantage and inequality. Indeed, some scholars and social commentators warn that there is a "marriage gap" in America linked to class and education: less educated and less affluent men and women marry at lower rates than the more educated and more affluent. Moreover, because people tend to seek marriage partners with similar educational achievement (and, hence, earning potential), this "assortative" marriage behavior leads—as married women's market participation has increased—to growing disparities between the household income of affluent and poor families, which appears to be a factor in the widening economic inequality in the United States.

At the same time, David Popenoe, Co–Director of the National Marriage Project, argues, [that] men are not marrying because they choose not to, preferring the more permissive social mores that make it acceptable to live together and raise children out of wedlock. A poster child for this lifestyle choice is a retired corrections officer profiled in the article, "a father of four, [who] has had long-term relationships with two women but has never married," one obstacle being his infidelity. This man explains: "Marriage, that's sacred to me; I'm committed to you for the rest of my life, my last breath. I'm not cheating, looking. Work, home, that's it. It's you and me against the world." Here we see an interesting example of someone who has internalized certain social messages about marriage as a social institution—a lifelong, exclusive commitment—but whose own life sequence has clearly resisted the script of love-marriage-baby carriage. A further explanation of the demographic changes in men's life patterns may be increased societal tolerance of openly homosexual lives, which may facilitate gay men resisting the heterosexual love-marriage-baby carriage script.

My second example of an altered, or scrambled, sequence is: baby carriage and motherhood first, and maybe later, love and marriage. A memorable cover story from the Sunday *New York Times* magazine, *Looking for Mr. Good Sperm*, featured a young woman in a bar with her arm around, and apparently entranced by, a giant test tube containing sperm. The cultural referent for the cover title and image, one assumes, is the novel and film from the 1970s, Looking for Mr. Goodbar, which chronicled a single woman's search, in the New York bar scene, for love and sex and did not end happily. This magazine story examines a very different world with more happy endings, that of unmarried women of a certain age—generally in their upper thirties and into their forties—who surf the web to identify their ideal sperm donor. A teaser for the story makes the unconventional sequence clear: "Shopping for a father doesn't have to mean shopping for a mate."
. . .

What these women shared in common was a strong desire to become a mother even though they had not yet become a wife. Many expressed an interest in marrying, but were not willing to sacrifice becoming a mother by waiting indefinitely to meet Mr. Right. Women in search of Mr. Good Sperm shared information and sometimes sperm with each other. The women profiled were, for the most part, well-educated and sufficiently secure in their careers to contemplate the economic, medical, and personal costs of taking on single motherhood by way of assisted reproductive technology.

This sequence of motherhood without marriage is not new, although advances in reproductive technology make it more viable. The organization Single Mothers by Choice dates back to 1981. In the early 1990s, Vice President Dan Quayle's criticism of the television show character Murphy Brown for having a baby outside of marriage drew attention to the growing trend of single motherhood among professional women in their thirties and forties. In the early twenty-first century, this trend continues to grow, as is evident from the subtitle of a new book by sociologist Rosanna Hertz: *Single by Chance, Mother by Choice: How Women Are Choosing Parenthood Without Marriage and Creating the New American Family.*

. . .

My third example of a scrambled sequence is reflected in the intimate and parenting relationships of some low-income, unmarried parents. Why low-income mothers and fathers separate marriage from parenthood has been a topic of keen interest for welfare policy makers. The year 2006 marked the tenth anniversary of the passage of the 1996 welfare law, the Personal Responsibility and Work Opportunity Reconciliation Act (PRWORA), which replaced the Aid to Families with Dependent Children program with the Temporary Assistance for Needy Families (TANF) block grant. This anniversary, along with the process of reauthorizing TANF, provided occasion for reflection upon progress made and challenges remaining for welfare policy. A common conviction voiced by lawmakers and policy analysts was that, although PRWORA included findings about the importance of marriage to society and the need to encourage two-parent families and discourage nonmarital pregnancy, states have done far more to move mothers from welfare to work than to promote marriage.

Promotion of "healthy marriage" and "responsible fatherhood" were features of President George W. Bush's welfare plans and various reauthorization proposals. The Department of Health and Human Services launched a healthy marriage initiative in 2002, spearheaded by Wade Horn, a major player in the responsible fatherhood movement. When Congress finally reauthorized the 1996 law, as part of a deficit reduction bill, included (as President Bush had requested) were governmental funds for the promotion of "healthy marriage" and "responsible fatherhood." As Dr. Horn explains: "for the first time, we have a dedicated funding stream at the federal level to focus exclusively on helping couples form and sustain healthy marriages."

A premise of marriage promotion is that it can help "fragile families," a term used by researchers to refer to the families formed by low-income, unmarried parents. Lawmakers rely on research showing that at the time of the birth of a child, a large percentage of low-income unmarried men and women are romantically involved with each other and say that there is a good chance they will later marry—but few actually do marry. Isn't this, politicians argue, a "magic moment" to offer marriage education and other incentives to help such couples go on to marry? Here, although couples have not followed the conventional love-marriage-baby carriage sequence, governmentally funded education might help them follow a sequence of love-baby carriage-marriage instead of no marriage at all.

In a speech on the occasion of PRWORA's tenth anniversary, conservative policy analyst Robert Rector praised the book, *Promises I Can Keep: Why Poor Women Put Motherhood Before Marriage*, by sociologists Kathryn Edin and Maria Kefalas, for teaching us that "these mothers have common goals with most other women in society. Most of them want to be married, to have a house in the suburbs, two kids, a dog, and a minivan." The authors report that low income mothers—white, black, and Latina—do value marriage as a social institution and hope to marry some day; precisely because they value marriage, they do not marry the fathers of their children. Economics are one reason—they believe that, to marry, one needs to be at a certain threshold level of economic well-being, and when this is elusive and their available marriage partner cannot contribute to this economic picture, they choose not to marry. A second set of reasons—not mentioned by Rector—relates to what we might call quality concerns and what has come to be called "gender distrust" in the literature. Low-income mothers, like women across the economic spectrum, expect a certain level of fairness and equity in marriage. They want a partnership of equals, and may avoid marriage if they believe their partner will try to dominate them, be violent or unfaithful, or not share in household responsibilities.

. . .

It may be evident that the "core of ideas" to which Schneider refers for [marriage and parenthood] has already been challenged significantly, particularly in the fifteen years since he published his article. [P]art of what is at issue in contemporary family law—as well as in the broader society—is debate over what the core of these institutions is. On one view, changes in the definition of marriage and parenthood will so alter these institutions that they can no longer serve their purposes and, worse, that society will no longer provide the necessary support for them. Schneider himself has argued that the advent of no fault divorce has challenged parts of the core of marriage, like permanence and willingness to sacrifice. Opponents of same-sex marriage contend that redefining marriage will so dilute the meaning of marriage that social support for marriage will diminish. And the core definition of parenthood—that it is marital—is already challenged by some of the social practices I mentioned, like looking for Mr. Good Sperm or having love and the baby carriage without marriage.

. . .

[Ira Ellman has written on] "why making family law is hard;"[229] one reason is that family law pursues different goals and these may take it in different directions. . . . Ellman points out that family law may be "instrumental, designed to affect people's behavior in some ways that policymakers believe desirable." But it may also pursue the goal of fairness: it may be "retrospective, concerned less with changing what might happen in the future, than with changing the consequences of what has already happened, to make the outcome more fair." Ellman argues that family law is hard because "it is difficult to formulate a family law rule that serves either purpose very well." For example, in addressing criticisms that the *ALI's Principles of the Law of Family Dissolution* (on which he was Chief Reporter) weakens the institution of marriage by turning to more functional definitions of family, he has noted the tension between pursuing the channelling and the fairness functions.

That family law may simultaneously pursue multiple purposes, some of which may be in conflict with each other or point in different policy directions, may offer one way to make sense of what may seem like contradictory movements within family law, sometimes even within the same state. Consider . . . *In re Elisa B.*, in which California's highest court interpreted the child support statutes to apply to a woman who had agreed to the conception of her lesbian partner's children, lived with them, supported them, and held out to the world that they were her children. Family law's protective function seems like a good explanation for this ruling: treating the lesbian partner like a father—or more precisely as a second mother—secures the child's well-being and provides the child with the support of two parents, thus reducing the state's public welfare burden and relying on the private welfare function of families. This rule helps to arbitrate a dispute between the adult partners; it facilitates the biological mother's care for her children,

---

229. Ira Ellman, *Why Making Family Law is Hard*, 35 ARIZ. ST. L. J. 699 (2003).

but one could not say it is facilitative for the nonbiological partner, who now resists further financial obligation.

.   .   .

It is useful, thus, to reflect on the different aims of family law and how they may be in alignment or in tension with each other. Perhaps, as Ellman suggests, we need to have some modesty about what family law can accomplish in terms of channelling people and even in achieving fairness. But at least recognizing how ends may conflict may help us grapple with the challenges posed by changing social norms and practices.

CHAPTER 2

MARRYING

Should society regulate marriage? If so, what restrictions are appropriate? In answering the basic questions posed in this Chapter, it is important to consider the purpose of marriage. Is it merely an institution to promote personal happiness and emotional well-being, or is it the very foundation of society? Does society have a stake in promoting marriages? In promoting sound marriages? If so, should there be any limits imposed on the power of society to regulate marriage? Is it appropriate, for example, to regulate the minimum age of the parties to a marriage? Their gender? Their wedding ceremony?

In evaluating restrictions, it is useful to consider their effects. If society lacks the ability to control fertility, for example, prohibiting some couples from marrying will not prevent them from having children out of wedlock. Marriage restrictions may also have the effect of denying to couples who are forbidden to marry some of the privileges and protections that are attached to marital status, such as income tax benefits. Are these results desirable? Harmful?

If it is decided that there should be restrictions placed on who may marry, which branch of government should be empowered to make the rules? The legislature? The judiciary? What if conflicts between states arise? If State A has fewer restrictions on marriage than State B, should State B have the ability to deny recognition to the marriage of two of its citizens who travel to State A to be married?

What limits are placed on the power of states to regulate marriage by the United States Constitution? By state constitutions?

Finally, who should enforce the rules? The clerk at the license bureau? The Internal Revenue Service? Parents? Potential heirs? If two individuals manage to marry despite restrictions designed to prohibit their liaison, and continue to live together happily, perhaps bearing children, should anyone have the power to void the marriage if the parties choose not to do so?

NANCY F. COTT, PUBLIC VOWS: A HISTORY OF MARRIAGE AND THE NATION

1–2 (2002).

Marriage is like the sphinx—a conspicuous and recognizable monument on the landscape, full of secrets. To newcomers the monument seems awesome, even marvelous, while those in the vicinity take its features for granted. In assessing matrimony's wonders or terrors, most people view it as a matter of private decision-making and domestic arrangements. The monumental public character of marriage is generally its least noticed aspect. Even Mae West's joke, "Marriage is a great institution ... but I ain't ready for an institution yet," likened it to a private asylum. Creating families and kinship networks and handing down private property, marriage certainly does design the architecture of private life. It influences individual identity and determines circles of intimacy. It can bring solace or misery—or both. . . .

At the same time that any marriage represents personal love and commitment, it participates in the public order. Marital status is just as important to one's standing in the community and state as it is to self-understanding. Radiating outward, the structure of marriage organizes community life and facilitates the government's grasp on the populace. To *be* marriage, the institution requires public affirmation. . . .

In the marriage ceremony, the public recognizes and supports the couple's reciprocal bond, and guarantees that this commitment (made in accord with the public's requirements) will be honored as something valuable not only to the pair but to the community at large. Their bond will be honored even by public force. This is what the public vows, when the couple take their own vows before public witnesses. . . .

Laurie Essig & Lynn Owens, *What if Marriage Is Bad for Us?*

CHRON. REV., at B4–B5 (2009).

. . .

Marriage as we imagine it today developed during the late 1800s, when it became "for love" and "companionate." Until that point, one married for material and social reasons, not romance. Women required marriage for survival; men did not. That left men free to behave as they wished: Prostitutes and buggery were part of many a married man's sexual repertoire. But then the Victorians (with their sexual prudishness) and first-wave feminists (with their sense that what's good for the goose is good for the gander) insisted that antiprostitution and antisodomy laws be enacted, and that married men confine their sexual impulses to the conjugal bed. The result was enforced lifelong sexual monogamy for both parties, at least in theory.

That might have seemed reasonable in 1900, when the average marriage lasted about 11 years, a consequence of high death rates. But these days, when a marriage can drag on for half a century, it can be a lot of work. Laura Kipnis calls marriage a "domestic gulag," a forced-labor camp where the inmates have to spend all their time outside of work working on their marriage.

And if the dyadic couple locked in lifelong monogamy was a radical new form, so was the family structure it spawned. The nuclear family is primarily a mutant product of the nuclear age. Before World War II, most Americans lived among extended family. The definition of family was not the couple and their offspring, but brothers, sisters, aunts, uncles, and grandparents as well. With the creation of suburbs for the middle classes, large numbers of white Americans began participating in the radical family formation of two married parents plus children in a detached house separated from extended family.

Although the nuclear family is idealized as "natural" and "normal" by our culture (*Leave It to Beaver*) and our government ("family values"), it has always been both a shockingly new way of living and a minority lifestyle. Even at its height, in the early 1970s, only about 40 percent of American families lived that way. Today that number is about 23 percent, including stepfamilies. The nuclear family is not only revolutionary; it is a revolution that has failed for most of us.

... According to the Centers for Disease Control and Prevention, married people have better health than those who are not married. A closer look at the data, however, reveals that married and never-married Americans are similar; it's the divorced who seem to suffer. The lesson might be to never divorce, but an even more obvious lesson to be drawn from the research might be to never marry.

Naomi Gerstel and Natalia Sarkisian's research shows that married couples are more isolated than their single counterparts. That is not a function just of their having children. Even empty-nesters and couples without children tend to have weak friendship networks. Marriage results in fewer rather than more social ties because it promises complete fulfillment through the claims of romance. We are instructed by movies, pop songs, state policy, and sociology to get married because "love is all you need." But actually we humans need more. We need both a sense of connection to larger networks—to community, to place—and a sense of purpose that is beyond our primary sexual relationships.

For those reasons, marriage has been self-destructing as a social form. The marriage rate in the United States is at an all-time low. In 1960[,] about two-thirds of adult Americans were married. Today only slightly more than half of Americans live in wedded bliss. Actually, even the bliss is declining, with fewer married Americans describing their unions as "very happy."

Maybe it's the decline in happiness that has caused an increasing number of Americans to say "I don't," despite Hollywood's presenting us with happy ending after happy ending and a government bent on distributing civil rights on the basis of marital status. Apparently no amount of propaganda or coercion can force humans to participate in a family form so out of sync with what we actually need.

With all that marriage supporters promise—wealth, health, stability, happiness, sustainability—our country finds itself confronted with a paradox: Those who would appear to gain the most from marriage are the same ones who prove most resistant to its charms. Study after study has found that it is the poor in the United States who are least likely to wed. The people who get married are the same ones who already benefit most from all our social institutions: the "haves." They benefit even more when they convince everyone that the benefits are evenly distributed.

Too often we are presented with the false choice between a lifelong, loving marriage and a lonely, unmarried life. But those are far from the only options. We should consider the way people actually live: serial monogamy, polyamory, even polygamy.

Instead of "blaming the victims" for failing to adopt the formative lifestyles of the white and middle class, we should consider that those avoiding marriage might know exactly what they are doing. Marriage is not necessarily good for all of us, and it might even be bad for most of us. When there is broad, seemingly unanimous support for an institution, and when the institution is propped up by such disparate ideas as love, civil rights, and wealth creation, we should wonder why so many different players seem to agree so strongly. Perhaps it's because they are supporting not just marriage but also the status quo.

We can dress up marriage in as many beautiful white wedding gowns as we like, but the fundamental fact remains: Marriage is a structure of rights and privileges for those who least need them and a culture of prestige for those who already have the highest levels of racial, economic, and educational capital.

So when you hear activists and advocates—gay, Christian, and otherwise—pushing to increase not only marriage rights but also marriage rates, remember these grouchy words of Marx: "Politics is the art of looking for trouble, finding it everywhere, diagnosing it incorrectly, and applying the wrong remedies." Marriage is trouble. Americans haven't failed at marriage. Marriage has failed us.

A.   RESTRICTIONS ON WHO MAY MARRY

1.   TRADITIONAL RESTRICTIONS

a.   INCEST

State v. Sharon H.

Superior Court of Delaware, New Castle County, 1981.
429 A.2d 1321.

■ STIFTEL, PRESIDENT JUDGE.

... Defendants, half-brother and half-sister, were charged with (1) engaging in a prohibited marriage in violation of 13 Del.C. § 102, and (2) perjury in the third degree in violation of 11 Del.C. § 1221, in that they swore falsely and contrary to the requirements of 13 Del.C. § 127.

The parties agree to the following facts:

> Sharon and Dennis H., appellees, are half-brother and half-sister by blood, born of the same mother, but of different fathers. Sharon, when approximately ten days old, was adopted by the W. family, by whom she was raised. Dennis became a ward of the State, and was raised in or by various State programs. After reaching maturity, Sharon discovered that she had a half-brother, Dennis. After locating him in the Smyrna Correctional institution, Sharon assisted Dennis in obtaining parole. They were married on July 11, 1979.

> On October 31, 1979, appellees were arrested and jailed for violations of 13 Del.C. § 102 and 11 Del.C. § 1221.

> In Municipal Court, appellees ... argued that even if they were half-brother and half-sister by blood, the provision of 13 Del.C. § 102 prohibiting marriages between brothers and sisters was inapplicable to the appellees' situation because under 13 Del.C. § 919, Sharon's adoption eliminated any tie between Sharon and Dennis as a matter of law. Appellees had also argued that the provisions of Chapter 9 of Title 13 prohibiting examination of the adoption records prohibited any inquiry into the matter of Sharon's adoption, which would be necessary for the State to prove its allegations.

The Municipal Court dismissed the information charging Sharon and Dennis with a violation of 13 Del.C. § 102, stating:

> [T]he Court concludes that the clear and unequivocal language used throughout Chapter 9 of Title 13 of the Code dictates that the State

cannot examine into relationships which as a matter of public policy and law are put at rest with adoption.

Since the perjury count was based on the denial under oath that Sharon and Dennis were related by blood, the Court held that inquiry would require the same type of prohibited inquiry, and so dismissed all charges.

The State appeals[.] . . .

[Appellees sought dismissal of the appeal on various procedural grounds, which the court rejected.]

Title 13 of the Delaware Code, § 101(a)(1) provides:

§ 101.   *Void and Voidable Marriages*

(a) A marriage is prohibited and void between:

(1) A person and his or her ancestor, descendant, brother, sister, uncle, aunt, niece, nephew or first cousin . . .

Title 13 of the Delaware Code, § 102 provides:

§ 102.   *Entering into a prohibited marriage; penalty*

The guilty party or parties to a marriage prohibited by § 101 of this title shall be fined $100, and in default of the payment of the fine shall be imprisoned not more than 30 days.

Title 13 of the Delaware Code, § 919 provides:

§ 919.   *General effect of adoption.*

(a) Upon the issuance of the decree of adoption, the adopted child shall be considered the child of the adopting parent or parents, entitled to the same rights and privileges and subject to the same duties and obligations as if he had been born in wedlock to the adopting parent or parents.

(b) Upon the issuance of the decree of adoption, the adopted child shall no longer be considered the child of his natural parent or parents and shall no longer be entitled to any of the rights or privileges or subject to any of the duties or obligations of a child with respect to the natural parent or parents; but, when a child is adopted by a stepparent his relationship to his natural parent who is married to the stepparent shall in no way be altered by reason of the adoption.

[Defendants] contend that 13 Del.C. § 919 must be read to end *all* relationships between the adopted child and its natural parents and kin, including the blood ties that the State asserts are the basis for the provision of 13 Del.C. § 101(a)(1). The State opposes such an interpretation[,] . . . contending that the Legislature did not intend such a result when it enacted 13 Del.C. § 919. The defendants seek to support their interpretation . . . with various cases holding . . . that, by adoption, a child is given the status of a natural child as to his or her adopted parents, and any legal relationship to the child's natural parents is ended. However, these cases deal exclusively with either the question of the child's right to inherit from the adopted parents, or the question of the effect of the adoption on the rights and duties of the natural parents as to the adopted child. The cases do not . . . address the issue presently before the Court, and so are irrelevant[.] . . . The cases cited by the State are similarly inappropriate, since they deal solely with the issue of whether a man may marry his *adopted* sister. It is clear that this issue may be resolved solely by an interpretation of the relevant statutes.

Section 101(a)(1) of Title 13 is what is commonly termed a consanguinity statute.... In general, a consanguinity statute prohibits marriages between blood relatives in the lineal, or ascending and descending lines. The historical basis for these statutes is rooted in English Canonical Law, which enforced what is considered to be a Biblical prohibition on incestuous relationships.

Another reason ... for ... incest and consanguinity statutes is a generally accepted theory that genetic inbreeding by close blood relatives tends to increase the chances that offspring ... will inherit certain unfavorable physical characteristics. Even if this theory is accepted, it is unlikely that it was the original basis for consanguinity statutes, given the relative newness of the theory and the ancient history of these statutes; however, it is possible that this theory served as an additional basis for the revision and reenactment of the various statutes.

In any case, ... consanguinity statutes were designed to prohibit marriages between blood relatives. The Delaware consanguinity statute is no exception....

The present version of Delaware's consanguinity statute, 13 Del.C. § 101(a)(1), expressly prohibits marriages between brother and sister. Although the Delaware Courts have never addressed the issue, other courts which have applied similar statutes have concluded that the policy behind the prohibition of marriages or sexual relations between blood relatives requires the Court to include relatives of half-blood in the prohibition. See *State v. Skinner*, 43 A.2d 76 [(Conn. 1945)]; *State v. Lamb*, 227 N.W. 830 [(Iowa 1929)]; *State v. Smith*, 85 S.E. 958 [(S.C. 1915)]. Given the obvious intent of 13 Del.C. § 101(a)(1) to prohibit marriages between blood relatives, it is clear that a reasonable interpretation of 13 Del.C. § 101(a)(1) would prohibit the marriage between the appellees.

However, appellees contend that 13 Del.C. § 101(a)(1) is a penal statute, insofar as it is applied through 13 Del.C. § 102 to criminally punish anyone who enters into a prohibited marriage. As a penal statute, it must be strictly construed in favor of the appellees. Thus, appellees argue, since 13 Del.C. § 101(a)(1) does not expressly prohibit marriages between a half-brother and half-sister, this Court must construe the statute so as to exclude a marriage between half-brother and half-sister from the reach of 13 Del.C. § 101(a)(1). I disagree.

In general, ... strict construction requires that ... any ambiguity [in a penal statute] must be resolved in favor of the defendant ... to insure that no individual is convicted unless a fair warning has been given to the public in understandable language what activities the statute prohibits. However, the doctrine of strict construction is not violated by allowing the language to have its full meaning where that construction is in harmony with the context and supports the policy and purposes of the Legislature.... If a statute can have two meanings, the principle of strict construction does not require the Court to accept automatically the meaning most favorable to the defendant; the Court's general objective is still to determine the general intent of the Legislature. Thus, strict construction does not require the Court to adopt an unreasonable construction, or one which results in an injustice which the Legislature should not be presumed to have intended.

Looking to the language of 13 Del.C. § 101(a)(1), I do not see that there is any reasonable ambiguity as to whether the marriage of the appellees was prohibited by that statute. The statute clearly prohibits marriages between brother and sister, as well as other blood relatives. No exception is made for relatives of the half-blood or blood relatives adopted by other families. To engraft such exceptions on the plain language of 13 Del.C. § 101(a)(1), because it does not expressly include such relations, requires an unreasonable interpretation of the statute which the doctrine of strict construction does not mandate.... [S]trict construction does not shield the appellees from 13 Del.C. §§ 101(a)(1) and 102.

Having concluded that 13 Del.C. § 101(a)(1) would normally prohibit marriage between the appellees, the question becomes whether the effect of 13 Del.C. § 919 is to destroy all ties between an adopted child and the child's natural relatives, including the ties of blood. As quoted earlier, 13 Del.C. § 919(b) states:

> (b) Upon the issuance of the decree of adoption, the adopted child shall no longer be considered the child of his natural parent or parents, and shall no longer be entitled to any of the rights or privileges or subject to any of the duties or obligations of a child with respect to the natural parent or parents....

Appellees contend that ... 13 Del.C. § 919 ends all relationships between an adopted child and its natural relatives, including blood relationships, and so the blood relationship prohibited by 13 Del.C. § 101(a)(1).... [T]he General Assembly did not intend that 13 Del.C. § 919 have such an effect.

Appellees would have this Court interpret the words "duties and obligations" to include compliance with criminal provisions such as 13 Del.C. § 101(a)(1), so that the language of 13 Del.C. § 919(b) stating that an adopted child "shall no longer be ... subject to any of the duties or obligations of a child with respect to his natural parent or parents ..." would legally eliminate the blood tie between an adopted child and its natural relative, barring prosecution under 13 Del.C. § 102 if these two later marry. However, such a literal interpretation of 13 Del.C. § 919 is clearly inconsistent with the obvious intent of the statute to eliminate such duties as the right to custody in the natural parents, and the reciprocal duties or obligations of the child and the natural parents to support one another.... To interpret 13 Del.C. § 919 as the appellees argue would require that I in effect amend 13 Del.C. § 101(a)(1) by implication. Such an interpretation would violate the general rules of statutory construction which require that a statutory ambiguity be interpreted in accordance with pre-existing law, unless there is an "irreconcilable inconsistency" between the statutes; and that amendment of existing law by implication is disfavored.

If 13 Del.C. § 919(b) is read to be limited to eliminating only the legal ties between the adopted child and its natural parents, there is no irreconcilable inconsistency between the two statutes, and 13 Del.C. § 101(a)(1) should not be considered to be impliedly amended by 13 Del.C. § 919. Thus, 13 Del.C. § 919 does not bar the application of 13 Del.C. §§ 101(a)(1) and 102 to the facts of the present case.

Appellees' last argument in support of the decision below contends that the strong public policy of maintaining the secrecy of adoption records as evidenced by 13 Del.C. §§ 923 and 924 bars *any* inquiry into the facts of the adoption, even where the information sought is not to be obtained from the adoption records....

· · ·

There is no indication that the provisions of 13 Del.C. §§ 923 and 924 were intended to eliminate any inquiry into the facts surrounding an adoption, including inquiry outside the adoption records.... [Thus,] 13 Del.C. §§ 923 and 924 do not prohibit the State from presenting its case against the appellees in the manner in which it intends to proceed.

For the reasons stated, ... the Municipal Court erred in dismissing the informations charging Sharon and Dennis H. with violations of 13 Del.C. § 102 and 11 Del.C. § 1221. The decision of the Municipal Court is reversed and the case is remanded ... for action that is consistent with this decision. IT IS SO ORDERED.

Back v. Back

Supreme Court of Iowa, 1910.
125 N.W. 1009.

■ McCLAIN, J.

... In 1890[,] William Back, the decedent, married a widow, one Mrs. Dirke, who then had living a daughter by her former husband, which child is the plaintiff in this case. In 1900, the wife obtained a divorce from said William Back, and four years later he married the plaintiff. No children were born to William Back by his first marriage, but as a result of his marriage to plaintiff four children were born, all of whom survive him. About two years after the second marriage, the divorced wife, mother of the plaintiff, died, and thereafter plaintiff and the decedent continued to live together as husband and wife until his death in 1906. The resistance of defendant to plaintiff's application as widow to have ... property set apart to her was on the ground that the marriage was incestuous and void under the provisions of Code, [§] 4936, which within the definition of "incest" includes marriage between a man and his wife's daughter, and prohibits such marriage. The trial court ruled ... that the marriage to plaintiff was void in its inception and continued to be void after the death of plaintiff's mother and until the death of decedent, and that, therefore, plaintiff is not the widow of decedent....

. . .

... [W]hether the marriage of plaintiff to decedent was within any of the prohibitions of Code, [§] 4936 ... depends upon the construction of the words "wife's daughter" in that section.... If the statute purported to be a definition only of degrees of relation within which marriage is prohibited, it might perhaps be argued with some plausibility that, as a man could not marry his wife's daughter while his wife was living and undivorced without committing bigamy, the object of including wife's daughter among those to whom a marriage is declared invalid was to prohibit such marriage after the death or divorce of the mother of such daughter; but, as the primary purpose of the statute apparent on its face is to punish carnal knowledge as between persons having the specified relationships as well as to punish marriage between them, it is quite evident that the enumeration of relationships is simply a method of stating more definitely what are the degrees of consanguinity or affinity rendering marriage or carnal knowledge between persons of the relationships named criminal....

We reach the conclusion, therefore, that the relationship of affinity between the decedent and plaintiff which existed during the continuance of the marriage relation between decedent and plaintiff's mother terminated when the latter procured a divorce from decedent, and after that time plaintiff was not the daughter of decedent's wife, and the marriage between them was valid.

. . .

Claude Levi–Strauss, *The Family, in* MAN, CULTURE AND SOCIETY

261, 276–78 (Shapiro ed., 1956).

. . . The universal prohibition of incest specifies, as a general rule, that people considered as parents and children, or brother and sister, even if only by name, cannot have sexual relations and even less marry each other. . . .

The space at our disposal is too short to demonstrate that . . . there is no natural ground for the custom. Geneticists have shown that while consanguineous marriages are likely to bring ill effects in a society which has consistently avoided them in the past, the danger would be much smaller if the prohibition had never existed, since this would have given ample opportunity for the harmful hereditary characters to become apparent and be automatically eliminated through selection: as a matter of fact this is the way breeders improve the quality of their subjects. Therefore, the dangers of consanguineous marriages are the outcome of the incest prohibition rather than actually explaining it. Furthermore, since very many primitive peoples do not share our belief in biological harm resulting from consanguineous marriages, but have entirely different theories, the reason should be sought elsewhere, in a way more consistent with the opinions generally held by mankind as a whole.

The true explanation should be looked for in a completely opposite direction, and what has been said concerning the sexual division of labor may help us to grasp it. This has been explained as a device to make the sexes mutually dependent on social and economic grounds, thus establishing clearly that marriage is better than celibacy. Now, exactly in the same way that the principle of sexual division of labor establishes a mutual dependency between the sexes, compelling them thereby to perpetuate themselves and to found a family, the prohibition of incest establishes a mutual dependency between families, compelling them in order to perpetuate themselves, to give rise to new families. . . .

We now understand why it is so wrong to try to explain the family on the purely natural grounds of procreation, motherly instinct, and psychological feelings between man and woman and between father and children. None of these would be sufficient to give rise to a family, and for a reason simple enough: for the whole of mankind, the absolute requirement for the creation of a family is the previous existence of two other families, one ready to provide a man, the other one a woman, who will through their marriage start a third one, and so on indefinitely. To put it in other words: what makes man really different from the animal is that, in mankind, a family could not exist if there were no society: i.e. a plurality of families ready to acknowledge that there are other links than consanguineous ones, and that the natural process of filiation can only be carried on through the social process of affinity.

How this interdependency of families has become recognized is another problem which we are in no position to solve because there is no reason to believe that man, since he emerged from his animal state, has not enjoyed a basic form of social organization, which, as regards the fundamental principles, could not be essentially different from our own. Indeed, it will never be sufficiently emphasized that, if social organization had a beginning, this could only have consisted in the incest prohibition since, as we have just shown, the incest prohibition is, in fact, a kind of remodeling of the biological conditions of mating and procreation (which know no rule, as can be seen from observing animal life) compelling them to become perpetuated only in an artificial framework of taboos and obligations. It is there, and only there, that we find a passage from nature to culture, from animal to human life, and that we are in a position to understand the very essence of their articulation.

. . . [T]he ultimate explanation is probably that mankind has understood very early that, in order to free itself from a wild struggle for existence, it was confronted with the very simple choice of "either marrying-out or being killed-out." The alternative was between biological families living in juxtaposition and endeavoring to remain closed, self-perpetuating units, over-ridden by their fears, hatreds, and ignorances, and the systematic establishment, through the incest prohibition, of links of intermarriage between them, thus succeeding to build, out of the artificial bonds of affinity, a true human society, despite, and even in contradiction with, the isolating influence of consanguinity. . . .

Margaret Mead, *Anomalies in American Post–Divorce Relationships, in* DIVORCE AND AFTER

104–08 (Bohannan ed., 1970).

Our present frequency of divorce has coincided with the development of a new set of attitudes and beliefs about incest. Incest taboos are among the essential mechanisms of human society, permitting the development of children within a setting where identification and affection can be separated from sexual exploitation, and a set of categories of permitted and forbidden sex can be established. Once these are established by the usually implicit but heavily charged learning of early childhood, the boy or girl is prepared to establish close relationships with others, of both a sexual and an asexual but affectional nature. The permissible sex partner, who may be one of a narrowly defined group of cousins, or any appropriately aged member of another village, or any age mate in the village who is not a relative, is sharply identified. The forbidden sex partners, a category which includes parents, aunts and uncles, brothers and sisters, nephews and nieces, and sometimes a wider group of all cousins, or all members of the clan or the community, are equally sharply distinguished. Close ties may be formed with forbidden sex partners without the intrusion of inappropriate sexuality; trust and affection, dependence and succorance, can exist independently of a sexual tie. Grown to manhood and womanhood, individuals are thus equipped to mate, and to continue strong, affectional ties with others than their own mates.

Where such incest categories are not developed, there are certain kinds of social consequences. Groups that can only absorb a non-member by establishing a sexual tie to a member, like the Kaingang of South America, have a limited capacity to form wider alliances. In parts of Eastern Europe, where the father-in-law may pre-empt the daughter-in-law in his son's absence, for example, on military service, certain inevitable suspicions and antagonisms exist between fathers and sons. The complications that may result from a mother-in-law's attraction to a young son-in-law—complications that were ruled out in the case of a juvenile own son, no matter how loved—are so ubiquitous, that mother-in-law taboos placing limitations on any social relationships between son-in-law and mother-in-law are the commonest and most stringent avoidance taboos in the world. The complementary taboo, between brother and sister, is also found in many parts of the world....

If the incest taboos are seen to make an essential contribution to the rearing of children within a situation where their own immature emotions are respected, and where they are at the same time prepared for both sexual and non-sexual relationships as adults, it is then obvious that the taboo must be extended to include all members of the household. No matter what the size of the household, sex relations must be rigorously limited to the sets of marital couples—parents, grandparents, married aunts and uncles—who live within its confines. When these rigorous limitations are maintained, the children of both sexes can wander freely, sitting on laps, pulling beards, and nestling their heads against comforting breasts—neither tempting nor being tempted beyond their years....

In England, until fairly recent times, the dangerous possibilities of attraction to the wife's sister, were considered so great that there was a compensatory legal rule which specifically forbade marriage with a deceased wife's sister. This device was designed to at least interrupt daydreaming and acting out during the wife's lifetime, since membership in the same household was possible after her death. In non-monogamous societies, marriage with the wife's sister is a common and often congenial type of marriage, especially in the cases where a sister may be given to complete a household into which her childless older sister is married.

Traditionally, within the Christian usages of the past, forbidden degrees of marriage have dealt more or less successfully with the problem of protecting those who live together in a single household. Stepbrotherhood and stepsisterhood are included within the impediments to marriage in the Roman Catholic Church.

However, imperceptibly and almost unremarked, the sanctions which protect members of a common household, regardless of their blood relationships, have been eroded in the United States. About all that remains today is the prohibition of sex in consanguineous relationships—a prohibition supported by the popular belief that the offspring of close relatives are defective. Stated baldly, people believe the reason that sex relationships between any close kin, father-daughter, mother-son, brother-sister, sometimes first cousins, uncle-niece and aunt-nephew, are forbidden, is simply that such unions would result in an inferior offspring—feeble-minded, deformed, handicapped in some way. This belief is a sufficient protection against incest so long as the two-generation nuclear family is the rule of residence, and the original marriage remains intact. In such households, neither aunts nor uncles are welcome as residents, cousins are members of other households, and even boarders and domestic servants are now regarded as undesirable. The small family, united by blood ties, can thus safely indulge in intimacy and warmth between biologically related parents and children. It can be pointed out that this sanction is based on a misunderstanding of the biological principles which govern the inheritance of specific genes which are more likely to appear in closely consanguineous matings. But a more serious limitation of this sanction is that it does not provide for a household which includes a stepparent, a stepchild, stepsiblings, or adopted children.

We rear both men and women to associate certain kinds of familiarity, in dress, bathing, and relaxation, with carefully defined incest taboos in which the biological family and the single household are treated as identical. We provide little protection when individuals are asked to live in close contact within a single, closed household, with members of the opposite sex to whom they have no consanguineous relationships. This leads to enormous abuses—girls are seduced by stepbrothers and stepfathers, men are seduced by precocious stepdaughters. It also leads to a kind of corruption of the possibilities of trust and affection, confusing the children's abilities to distinguish between mates and friends, whether of the same age, or among those of another generation. If the girl is below the age of consent, seduction which takes place between a stepfather and a stepdaughter, however initiated, is treated as a sex offense against a minor rather than as incest. Moreover, there is increasing evidence of the connivance of a consanguineous member of the family in such intrigues. The consenting minor may or may not be damaged psychologically, as she would be certain to be in a relationship with her own father or brother, which is experienced as incest. In fact, there is some evidence that where the biological mother connives in a sexual relationship between a father and daughter, the daughter has not been damaged psychologically. This finding may be interpreted as a sign that there is no natural or instinctive aversion to incest. But it may also be seen as a final weakening of incest taboos in our society, as the rationale has shifted from taboos governing the relationships of persons of opposite sex and different generations in close domestic contact, to a mere precaution against defective offspring, when offspring are not in any event the purpose of such liaisons.

As the number of divorces increases, there are more and more households in which minor children live with stepparents and stepsiblings, but where the inevitable domestic familiarity and intimacy are not counterbalanced by protective, deeply felt taboos. At the very least, this situation produces confusion in the minds of growing children; the stepfather, who is seen daily but is not a taboo object, is contrasted with the biological father, who is seen occasionally and so is endowed with a deeper aura of romance. The multiplication of such situations may be expected to magnify the difficulties young people experience in forming permanent-mating relationships, as well as in forming viable relationships with older people. They may also be expected to magnify the hazards of instructor-student intrigues, of patient-doctor complications, and of employer-employee exploitation. It may even be that the emergence of the very peculiar form of sex behavior in which couples unknown to each other, arrange to meet secretly and exchange sex partners may be an expression of the kind of object confusion that has grown up in our present much-divorced, much remarried society—a society in which, however, the ideal of the biologically related, two-generation, exclusive nuclear family is still preserved.

NOTES

1. All states and the District of Columbia prohibit marriages between parent and child, brother and sister, and aunt and nephew, or uncle and niece. As of 2011, twenty states and the District of Columbia permit marriages between first cousins.[1]

---

1. Alabama, California, Colorado, Connecticut, Florida, Georgia, Hawaii, Maine (Maine requires a certificate of genetic counseling for first cousins to marry), Maryland, Massachusetts, New Jersey, New Mexico, New York, North Carolina, Rhode Island, South Carolina, Tennessee, Texas, Vermont, and Virginia. In addition, Wisconsin permits such marriages if the woman is over 55 or if either party is sterile, Indiana allows them if both parties are over 65, Illinois does if both parties are over 50 or if either party is sterile, and Utah does if either both parties are 65 or older or both are 55 or older and either party is sterile.

One study reported that although married cousins are more likely than unrelated couples to have children with a birth defect, significant mental retardation, or serious genetic disease, the risk is smaller than many thought. For an unrelated couple, the risk of having a child with one of the listed problems is 3 to 4 percent. For close cousins, the risk increases between 1.7 and 2.8 percent. Robin Bennett et al., *Genetic Counseling and Screening of Consanguineous Couples and Their Offspring: Recommendations of the National Society of Genetic Counselors*, 11 J. GENET. COUNS. 97 (2002).

There is an organization working to overturn restrictions on cousin marriage: Cousins United to Defeat Discriminating Laws Through Education. *See* www.cousincouples.com. A recent news report described the difficulties faced by two cousins who married in March 2005. Although they were able to avoid a state prohibition on cousin marriage by traveling to another state, social sanctions were not as easily circumvented. Frederick Kunkle, *Pa. Cousins Try to Overcome Taboo of "I Do,"* WASH. POST, Apr. 25, 2005 at B1 (describing how wife's family "disowned her for a time," made clear she "was no longer welcome at Sunday dinner," and refused her calls, while friends "dredged up Bible passages to scold them.").

2. In light of the justifications for incest prohibitions advanced by Levi–Strauss and Mead, should statutory bars on marriages be held to apply to marriages between a parent and an adopted child? Consider *State v. Lee*, 196 Miss. 311, 17 So.2d 277 (1944) (father who married adopted daughter not guilty of incest), which was subsequently repudiated by the state legislature. MISS. CODE ANN. § 93–1–1. *Cf. Israel v. Allen*, 195 Colo. 263, 577 P.2d 762 (1978) (statute prohibiting marriage between brother and sister by adoption held unconstitutional). *But see In re MEW*, 4 Pa. D. & C.3d 51 (C.P. Allegheny 1977) (man may not marry sister by adoption).

As of 2011, the incestuous marriage bans of eight states specifically apply to adopted children: ALA. CODE § 13A–13–3; LA. CIV. CODE ANN. ART. 90; MASS. GEN. LAWS CH. 210 § 6; MISS. CODE ANN. § 93–1–1; MINN. STAT. ANN. § 517; OR. REV. CODE § 106.020; S.D. CODIFIED LAWS § 25–1–6; VERNON'S TEX. FAM. CODE ANN. § 2.21.

Compare Section 207 of the Uniform Marriage & Divorce Act:

(a) The following marriages are prohibited: . . .

(2) a marriage between an ancestor and a descendant, or between a brother and a sister, whether the relationship is by the half or the whole blood, or by adoption;

(3) a marriage between an uncle and a niece or between an aunt and a nephew, whether the relationship is by the half or the whole blood, except as to marriages permitted by the established customs of aboriginal cultures.

UNIFORM MARRIAGE & DIVORCE ACT § 207 PROHIBITED MARRIAGES (1973).

3. Most courts have reached the same conclusion as the court in *Back* that, in the absence of a contrary statutory provision, all affinity relationships cease upon termination of the marriages that produced them. As the opinion indicates, however, a few courts have exempted situations involving children of the original marriage.

b. AGE

In re J.M.N.

Tennessee Court of Appeals, 2008.
2008 WL 2415490.

■ KIRBY, J.

. . .

Plaintiff/Appellee Jerry Clyde Nix ("Father") and Defendant/Appellant Amy Nix Cantrell ("Mother"), both Mississippi residents, were married and had a daughter, Jacy Marie Nix ("Jacy"), born August 27, 1991. Mother and Father were divorced by final decree entered on August 22, 1995, in the

Chancery Court of Warren County, Mississippi. In the decree, Mother was designated the primary residential parent for Jacy.

Father later filed a petition for modification of the decree, seeking to be designated primary residential parent, based in part on Mother's mental illness. On August 26, 1999, the Mississippi chancery court entered an order granting Father's petition and appointing him as Jacy's primary residential parent. Mother was given the same visitation that had been awarded to Father in the original divorce decree.

At all pertinent times thereafter, Father has lived with Jacy ... in Winona, Montgomery County, Mississippi. Mother lived about three hours away from Father ... in Corinth, Alcorn County, Mississippi. Over the years, for Jacy's visitation, the parties met at a point in between their homes for the exchange.

On Friday, July 27, 2006, when Jacy was fourteen (14) years old, Father took Jacy for her regular visitation with Mother. Father was led to believe that Jacy would be going with Mother to vacation in Florida for the week. Instead, without notifying Father, Mother took Jacy across the Tennessee/Mississippi state line to the Juvenile Court in Selmer, McNairy County, Tennessee, to enable Jacy to marry her eighteen-year-old boyfriend, Kevin Brady Henry ("Henry"). When Mother, Jacy, and Henry arrived at the McNairy County Justice Center, Jacy and Henry sought to file an application for a marriage license. Because the legal age for marriage without parental consent in Tennessee is eighteen, and Jacy was only fourteen, Mother filled out a preprinted consent affidavit, acknowledging that she is Jacy's mother, that Jacy's birth date is August 27, 1991, and that she consented to and joined in the application for marriage between Jacy and Henry.

Thereafter, Wayne Bolton ("Bolton"), a youth services officer of the McNairy County Juvenile Court, met briefly with Jacy and Henry to ensure that they intended to be married. He then presented Mother's affidavit to Juvenile Court Judge Bob Gray. Along with Mother's affidavit, Bolton presented Judge Gray with a preprinted order finding that the marriage would be in Jacy's best interest, and that good cause was shown for the marriage. In addition, the pre-printed order suspended the three-day waiting period for the issuance of a marriage license, waived the age restriction to marriage, and authorized the County Court Clerk to issue a marriage license to Jacy and Henry. *See* T.C.A. § 36–3–107 (2005). Judge Gray signed the order proffered by the youth services officer. Mother, Jacy, and Henry did not appear before Judge Gray.

After obtaining Judge Gray's order, Mother, Jacy, and Henry went to the McNairy County Courthouse to apply with the County Court Clerk for a marriage license and to have the marriage ceremony performed. When Jacy and Henry applied for the license, a deputy clerk asked them for a copy of Jacy's birth certificate or some other record identifying her legal parents and her date of birth. Mother had no such records for Jacy with her. Instead, she showed the clerk the front page of a proposed Mississippi chancery court order drafted by her attorney, which indicated that she had primary custody of Jacy. This order had never been signed by a court; it had merely been proposed by Mother's attorney in the prior Mississippi chancery court proceedings between Mother and Father. In any event, the county clerk's office accepted the unsigned order in lieu of other forms of identification and issued the marriage license. Thereafter, Jacy and Henry were married by the County Court Clerk.

A few days later, Mother called Father and informed him that Jacy and Henry had married. She told him that, as a result of the marriage, Jacy was emancipated and that he no longer had custody of her under the Mississippi chancery court order.

On August 22, 2006, Father filed a motion in the McNairy County Juvenile Court asking the Juvenile Court to set aside Judge Gray's July 27, 2006 order authorizing the County Court Clerk to issue a marriage license to Jacy. As the basis for his motion, Father asserted fraud on the court by Mother. Father later modified his position, claiming that the prior order could be set aside based on "good cause being shown," regardless of any fraud.

Father's motion was filed as an adversarial proceeding under the same docket number as Judge Gray's Juvenile Court order, No. 8793, naming Mother as the respondent. Mother filed a response, claiming that no fraud had been committed on the court and that Father's motion to set aside should be denied.

Also on August 22, 2006, Father, on behalf of Jacy, filed a petition in the McNairy County General Sessions Court for annulment of the marriage.... In this petition ... Father named Henry as the defendant. On October 5, 2006, represented by the same attorney who represented Mother, Jacy filed an intervening petition in the McNairy County General Sessions action, asserting that she was legally married to Henry, that she was emancipated based on her marriage, and that she did not authorize Father to file the petition for annulment on her behalf. Jacy denied that fraud was committed in obtaining Judge Gray's Juvenile Court order, and she requested that Father's annulment petition be dismissed. On the same day, Henry filed an answer to Father's petition for annulment, claiming that he and Jacy were legally married and asking the General Sessions Court to dismiss Father's petition.

By this time, Judge Van McMahan ("Judge McMahan") had become both the Juvenile Court judge and the General Sessions judge for McNairy County. On October 9, 2006, Judge McMahan conducted a hearing on Father's Juvenile Court motion to set aside Judge Gray's order, as well as Father's General Sessions petition for annulment. Both matters were consolidated for purposes of the hearing "for the sake of judicial economy and based on the fact that the two separately filed cases arise from the same set of facts...."

Father, Mother, Henry, and Jacy all testified at the hearing. Father testified that, prior to Jacy's marriage, he and Jacy lived together at his home ... in Winona, Mississippi. He said that, ever since he was designated as Jacy's primary residential parent in 1999, he and Mother had been having trouble. On several occasions, Father stated, Mother refused to return Jacy to him after her regular visitation, requiring Father to go retrieve Jacy.

Father testified that on Friday, July 27, 2006, he took Jacy to visit Mother for an extended time because he understood that they planned to go on a vacation to Florida. Father had never met Henry, or even heard of him, prior to learning of the events of July 27, 2006. He did not find out that Jacy and Henry were married until a few days after the ceremony when Mother called and told him that Jacy was emancipated based on her marriage. Father viewed Mother's facilitation of Jacy's marriage as another one of Mother's "stunts" to get custody of Jacy. He said that he filed his petition for annulment because he did not believe that it was in Jacy's best interest to be married at only fourteen years old.

Mother also testified at the hearing. She admitted that she had a history of mental illness and said that she suffered from depression. Mother also admitted that she had tried to take Jacy from Father's custody on a prior occasion.

Mother said that, since late May 2006 when Jacy's school year ended, Jacy had lived with her in Alcorn County, Mississippi. Mother asserted that, during the time period between May 2006 and July 27, 2006, Jacy spent a total of about seven nights with Father.

Mother testified that, in July 2006, Jacy told Mother that she suspected that she was pregnant, and asked Mother's permission to marry the prospective father. Mother claimed that Jacy took a pregnancy test, with inconclusive results. She did not take Jacy to see a physician for a pregnancy test and, as it turned out, Jacy was not pregnant. Nevertheless, Mother explained, she consented to Jacy's marriage to Henry because she felt that marriage was in Jacy's best interest in light of the possibility that she was pregnant. Mother said that she did not discuss the decision with Father because she and Father "had a very hostile relationship." Although both Jacy and Henry lived in Mississippi, Mother took them to Tennessee to be married to avoid the waiting period associated with the blood test that was required in Mississippi. Mother said that Jacy and Henry planned for the trip to Florida to be their honeymoon.

Mother then described the events that took place. According to Mother, about a week prior to July 27, 2006, she called the Juvenile Court Clerk's office and asked whether a noncustodial parent could give consent for a minor to be married. She claimed that one of the Juvenile Court clerks, Jean Smith ("Smith"), assured her that either parent could give consent regardless of who had primary custody. On July 27, 2006, when she, Jacy, and Henry arrived at the McNairy County Juvenile Court, Mother claimed that no one asked her whether she was Jacy's custodial parent. Mother filled out all of the paperwork presented to her by Smith. After that, they were sent to youth services officer Bolton. In Bolton's office, he talked with Jacy and Henry about their decision to marry. Bolton then left the room and returned with an order signed by Judge Gray giving them permission to marry. Mother, Jacy, and Henry did not personally appear before Judge Gray. Mother denied showing anyone in the Juvenile Court office the proposed Mississippi chancery court order indicating that she had custody, and she asserted that she was not asked for such documentation by Juvenile Court personnel.

Once they obtained Judge Gray's order from Juvenile Court, Mother took Jacy and Henry to the McNairy County Clerk's office to obtain a marriage license and get married. In order to obtain a marriage license, Henry presented to the County Clerk's office his birth certificate and driver's license. Jacy was required to present a birth certificate or "something showing who her legal parents were and her date of birth." To fulfill this requirement, Mother gave the County Clerk's office the first page of her unsigned Mississippi proposed order, which recited Jacy's birth date and indicated that Mother was the primary custodian. Mother explained that she presented the first page of this order because it was all she had with her to show the identity of Jacy's parents. Once the marriage license was procured, the wedding ceremony took place there in the County Clerk's office.

A few days later, Mother called Father to tell him about Jacy's marriage. Mother testified that, at the time of the hearing, Jacy and Henry were living with her, and that Henry was not working.

Henry testified as well. He stated that he was not involved in the discussions with the clerks or with Judge Gray, but spoke only with Bolton, the Juvenile Court youth services officer, who interviewed the couple about their decision to marry. Henry testified that he told Bolton that he wanted to marry Jacy because he loved her and because marriage was what they believed was right. Henry refused to answer questions about whether he told Mother that Jacy was pregnant. At the time of the hearing, he said, he and Jacy were living with Mother. He planned to go into the National Guard. Henry testified that he did not wish to be divorced, and that divorce violated his religious beliefs.

Jacy also testified at the hearing. Prior to the marriage, she said, she lived primarily with Father and visited Mother. She acknowledged that there were substantial periods of time in which she did not visit Mother. Between May 24 and July 27, 2006, Jacy said, she stayed with Mother quite a bit. She corroborated Father's testimony that he took her to Mother's home on July 27, 2006, based on his understanding that she and Mother were going to go on vacation in Florida. Jacy said that it was her and Henry's idea to go to McNairy County to get married. A week before the three of them went to McNairy County, Jacy and Henry told Mother that they suspected that Jacy was pregnant. They told Mother that they loved each other and wanted to get married. Contrary to Mother's testimony, Jacy said that she did not take a pregnancy test. Jacy denied involvement in any misrepresentations to the Juvenile Court clerks, the Juvenile Court judge, or the County Court clerks in relation to this matter. She maintained that she wanted to remain married to Henry, and that she did not authorize Father to file the petition for annulment in General Sessions Court.

Over the objection of Mother's attorney, Judge Gray testified at the hearing. He said that he had no specific recollection of the matter involving Jacy and Henry, but that it was not uncommon for him to get requests for waiver of the age restriction for marriage. Judge Gray explained that it had been the Juvenile Court's "policy that a person ... that's requesting the child to be married to make this affidavit that you have here and have some supporting documentation that that person had custody of that child if mother and father both didn't sign the affidavit." Judge Gray said that "if both parents did not come in to show proof that they were parents of this child, then the policy was that the one parent would be required ... to provide proof that person had physical and legal custody of that child." He maintained that, without such documentation, he would not have signed the order permitting the marriage. Typically, he stated, he would not see the person making the affidavit because having the affidavit signed is "an administrative function done by one of the youth services officers." Judge Gray said that, in most cases, the youth services officer was the person who presented the petition to the court, and the judge signed the order.

At the conclusion of the hearing, Judge McMahan orally granted Father's motion to set aside the July 27, 2006 order. Judge McMahan determined from the evidence that it was inappropriate for Mother to make the decision to allow Jacy to get married at age fourteen without notifying Father:

> I think it's significant in this case that we're dealing with, at the time a 14–year–old. I think it's clear that the father, the person that has custody, I think both parents should have a say in that decision. That's a huge decision for parents to make in the lives of their children. And for

one parent to go and make it without notifying the other parent, that's just not right. You shouldn't do that.

I don't think the statute—I think based upon Judge Gray's testimony, the policy procedure of the Court in Juvenile Court has been that if both parents aren't there, then one parent's got to present evidence that they have custody. So . . . I don't think Judge Gray at that point would have granted this Motion had it not been—if he did not believe that Mrs. Cantrell had custody. Now, I believe the Court has basis to set this aside regardless of whether there's any fraud or not.

. . . And the Court concedes the best interest of the child as one of the grounds for overturning this motion.

I think it's in the best interest of this child that she not be married at age 14. At least not without the consent of both parents. So the Court finds that the Motion to Set Aside should be granted[.] . . .

After setting aside the July 27, 2006 order, Judge McMahan stated that doing so had the effect of rendering Jacy's marriage void and the petition for annulment moot.

On November 21, 2006, Judge McMahan entered a written order consistent with his oral ruling. . . . Judge McMahan's written order granted Father's . . . motion to set aside the July 27, 2006 Juvenile Court order and went on to state that "Jacy Marie Nix is not of legal age to be married in Tennessee, and . . . her marriage to Kevin Brady Henry is now void." Mother now appeals[.] . . .

On appeal, Mother contends that the trial court erred[,] . . . asserting that there was no evidence that she committed a fraud upon the court in obtaining the order. Mother claims that she had received assurances from Smith and Bolton that consent of the minor's custodial parent was not necessary, and she maintains that she did not hold herself out to the Juvenile Court to be Jacy's custodial parent. She notes that Bolton presented the affidavit and the preprinted order to Judge Gray, and that neither she, nor Jacy, nor Henry personally appeared before Judge Gray. Mother acknowledges that she showed the first page of the proposed Mississippi chancery court custody order to the county clerk's office, but maintains that she did so only for identification purposes, and asserts that she did not show the proposed order to either Smith or Bolton. Mother also argues that the trial court committed reversible error in permitting Judge Gray to testify in the proceeding below, asserting that his testimony was adduced in order to directly attack an order entered by him in the same proceeding and, as such, was improper pursuant to Tennessee Rule of Evidence 605.

. . .

. . . When . . . the trial court held a hearing[,] . . . [it] was presented with evidence that Father was Jacy's primary residential parent, that Mother did not have decision-making authority regarding Jacy, that Father was not notified of Mother's actions, and that Mother had a history of mental illness and of attempts to usurp Father's authority in decision-making matters involving Jacy. The evidence of these facts was not before Judge Gray when he signed the July 27, 2006 order. From this, Judge McMahan determined that setting aside the order giving Jacy permission to marry was warranted. The evidence adduced at the hearing before Judge McMahan is ample justification for granting relief from the order. Even if the admission of Judge Gray's testimony was erroneous, it is harmless error in light of the undisputed facts of this case. Therefore, we conclude that the Juvenile Court did not abuse its discretion in setting aside the July 27, 2006 order giving Jacy permission to marry.

As noted above, Judge McMahan . . . [declared] that the marriage between Jacy and Henry "is now void." Thus, we feel compelled to address the correctness of this comment.

The Juvenile Court's July 27, 2006 order legally removed the age restriction of marriage for Jacy and permitted her to legally obtain a marriage license. Setting aside this order vacated the court's waiver of the age restriction. Jacy was then relegated to the status of a minor who was not entitled to be married legally in Tennessee. This does not, however, change the fact that Jacy in fact obtained a marriage license and married Henry at the County Clerk's office.

In Tennessee, a marriage between and minor and an adult is voidable, not void. *Coulter v. Hendricks*, 918 S.W.2d 424, 426 (Tenn. Ct. App. 1995) (listing marriage of person who is under the age of consent as a voidable marriage). "A voidable marriage differs from a void marriage in that the former is treated as valid and binding until its nullity is ascertained and declared by a competent court." 18 TENN. JUR. *Marriage* § 4 (2005) (footnote omitted; citing *Brewer v. Miller,* 673 S.W.2d 530 (Tenn.Ct.App.1984)). If either party is under the age of consent at the time of the marriage, "the marriage is inchoate and voidable. Thus, a ceremonial marriage where a party is under [the age of consent] is valid until set aside." *Id.* (footnote omitted; citing *Warwick v. Cooper,* 37 Tenn. (5 Sneed) 659 (1858)). Indeed, the marriage of underage parties may be ratified or disaffirmed by them upon attaining the age of consent if the marriage is not annulled before that time. *See id.* "If the marriage is ratified, it is not necessary that it be again solemnized; a continuance of the relation after attaining the age of consent is a ratification of the voidable marriage." *Id.* Thus, until the marriage between Jacy and Henry is annulled or otherwise rendered void by a court of competent jurisdiction before Jacy reaches the age of consent, it remains valid, and Henry and Jacy remain husband and wife.

The decision of the Juvenile Court is affirmed. . . .

NOTES

1. According to the lawyer for the father in the case: "On September 18, 2009[,] I presented to the trial Court an Order of Annulment which the Court granted. The Order set out that the Court of Appeals had made the finding [it did] . . . and that the Court needed to make and additional specific finding that the marriage should be and is annulled. The order was presented on Notice[,] but no one from the opposing sides showed up." E-mail from Ken Seaton to M. Spindelman, Professor of Law, Ohio State Univ. Moritz College of Law (Sept. 22, 2011, 10:04 PDT) (on file with author).

2. At common law, children were considered capable of consenting to marriage at age seven, although the marriage was voidable by the underage party until he or she reached the "age of discretion," the presumptive age at which the marriage could be consummated, which was twelve for girls and fourteen for boys.

As of 2011, Mississippi and Nebraska are the only states that do not set 18 as the minimum age for marriage without parental consent. Mississippi requires parental permission only if the male is under 17 or the female is under 15, whereas Nebraska requires parental permission if either party is under 19–years–old. MISS. CODE ANN. §§ 93–1–5, 93–1–7, 1–3–27; NEB. REV. STAT. § 42–102. Mississippi law further allows any "interested party" (presumably including parents) three days to object to the issuance of a marriage license. A court must then order denial of the license if either of the parties is under 21, the age of majority in the state, and "not of mature discretion" or "not capable of assuming responsibilities of marriage."

Most states permit 16–or 17–year–olds to marry with parental consent. New Hampshire appears to have the lowest formal minimum: females may marry there with parental consent at age 13. N.H. REV. STAT. §§ 457:4, 457:5, 457:6. Many states also allow judges to override either parental consent or refusal to consent below the age of majority. *See, e.g.,* CAL. FAM. CODE § 302 (for persons under 18, court order permitting marriage required in addition to parental consent); 750 ILL. COMP. STAT. ANN. 5/208 (court can order issuance of marriage license to minor despite a lack of parental consent "if the court finds that the underaged party is capable of assuming the responsibilities of marriage and the marriage will serve his best interest."). In addition, statutory minimums need not be followed when certain exceptional circumstances exist, with pregnancy being the most common. *See, e.g.,* ARK. CODE ANN. § 9–11–103. *See generally* Lynn D. Wardle, *Rethinking Marital Age Restrictions,* 22 J. FAM. L. 1 (1983).

What should be the minimum age for marriage, if any? Would you make an exception, as some states do, if the wife-to-be is pregnant?

3. Child marriages are also discouraged through child neglect proceedings. *See People v. Benu,* 385 N.Y.S.2d 222 (1976) (father convicted of endangering the welfare of his 13–year–old daughter by arranging her marriage); *In Interest of Flynn,* 318 N.E.2d 105 (1974) (couple found unfit parents after they "sold" their 12–year–old daughter into marriage with a relative stranger for $28,000).

4. The divorce rate for teenage marriages is much higher than for other marriages. The 1970 census found that 25.2 percent of the white women married between the ages of 14 and 17 in the first half of the 1960s had their marriages dissolved by 1970. For women who married at 18 or 19, the figure was 17.3 percent. The rate fell to 10 percent for women who married in their twenties. For white men, the divorce rate for those married under age 19 was 20 percent, with a corresponding decrease as the age at marriage rose. Similar figures were recorded for non-whites, but the drop-off in divorces was not as dramatic. As many as half of these marriages were complicated by pre-marital pregnancy.

By 2005, the divorce rate within the first five years for women married between the ages of 15 and 17 was over 34 percent, and for women married at the ages of 18 or 19, the figure was over 28 percent. The divorce rate for all women within the first five years of marriage is just under 20 percent. *See* Anjani Chandra et al., *Fertility, Family Planning, and Women's Health, Data From the 2002 National Survey of Family Growth,* 23 VITAL HEALTH & STATISTICS 25, 90 (2005).

In the 1970s, most teenagers giving birth were married. Since 1990, most teenagers giving birth have been unmarried. By 2008, barely 17 percent of pregnant teens were married. JOYCE MARTIN ET AL., U.S. DEP'T OF HEALTH & HUMAN SERV., NO. 1, 59 NATIONAL VITAL STATISTICS REPORTS 46 (2010). By 2009, fewer than 4.5% of 15 to 19-year-olds were married. *See* ROSE M. KREIDER & RENEE ELLIS, U.S. CENSUS BUREAU, NUMBER, TIMING, AND DURATION OF MARRIAGES AND DIVORCES: 2009, at 16 (2011).

To combat the high divorce rate of young marriages, Arizona, California, and Utah require some premarital counseling. ARIZ. REV. STAT. ANN. § 25–102; CAL. FAM. CODE § 304; UTAH CODE ANN. §§ 30–1–30 to 39. Arizona requires both parties to undergo premarital counseling if one party is under 16 before a court can approve the marriage. California authorizes the courts to order premarital counseling for all couples in which one of the parties is under 18. Utah authorizes the county commissioners to require counseling for couples in which one partner is either under 19 or divorced. Should such barriers to "easy" marriage be encouraged? Are they constitutional? Does your answer depend on who is doing the counseling or how much is required?

c.   POLYGAMY

In re Steed

Texas Court of Appeals, Austin, 2008.
2008 WL 2132014.

■ PER CURIAM.

This original mandamus proceeding involves the temporary custody of a number of children who were removed from their homes on an emergency basis from the Yearning For Zion ranch outside of Eldorado, Texas.[1] The ranch is associated with the Fundamentalist Church of Jesus Christ of Latter–Day Saints (FLDS), and a number of families live there. Relators are thirty-eight women who were living at the ranch and had children taken into custody on an emergency basis by the Texas Department of Family and Protective Services based on allegations by the Department that there was immediate danger to the physical health or safety of the children.

Relators seek a writ of mandamus requiring the district court to vacate its temporary orders in which it named the Department the temporary sole managing conservator of their children. Relators complain that the Department failed to meet its burden under section 262.201 of the Texas Family Code to demonstrate (1) that there was a danger to the physical health or safety of their children, (2) that there was an urgent need for protection of the children that required the immediate removal of the children from their parents, or (3) that the Department made reasonable efforts to eliminate or prevent the children's removal from their parents. Tex. Fam. Code Ann. § 262.201 (West Supp. 2007). Without such proof, Relators argue, the district court was required to return the children to their parents and abused its discretion by failing to do so.

Removing children from their homes and parents on an emergency basis before fully litigating the issue of whether the parents should continue to have custody of the children is an extreme measure. It is, unfortunately, sometimes necessary for the protection of the children involved. However, it is a step that the legislature has provided may be taken only when the circumstances indicate a danger to the physical health and welfare of the children and the need for protection of the children is so urgent that immediate removal of the children from the home is necessary. *See id.*[4]

Section 262.201 further requires the Department, when it has taken children into custody on an emergency basis, to make a showing of specific circumstances that justify keeping the children in the Department's temporary custody pending full litigation of the question of permanent custody. Unless there is sufficient evidence to demonstrate the existence of each of the

---

1. The Department removed over 450 children from their homes on the Yearning For Zion ranch over the course of three days. This proceeding does not involve parents of all of the children removed.

4. Section 262.201 provides, in relevant part, as follows: [] (a) Unless the child has already been returned to the parent, managing conservator, possessory conservator, guardian, caretaker, or custodian entitled to possession and the temporary order, if any, has been dissolved, a full adversary hearing shall be held not later than the 14th day after the date the child was taken into possession by the governmental entity. [] (b) At the conclusion of the full adversary hearing, the court shall order the return of the child to the parent, managing conservator, possessory conservator, guardian, caretaker, or custodian entitled to possession unless the court finds sufficient evidence to satisfy a person of ordinary prudence and caution that: [] (1) there was a danger to the physical health or safety of the child which was caused by an act or failure to act of the person entitled to possession and for the child to remain in the home is contrary to the welfare of the child; [] (2) the urgent need for protection required the immediate removal of the child and reasonable efforts, consistent with the circumstances and providing for the safety of the child, were made to eliminate or prevent the child's removal; and [] (3) reasonable efforts have been made to enable the child to return home, but there is a substantial risk of a continuing danger if the child is returned home . . . . . [] (d) In determining whether there is a continuing danger to the physical health or safety of the child, the court may consider whether the household to which the child would be returned includes a person who: [] (1) has abused or neglected another child in a manner that caused serious injury to or the death of the other child; or [] (2) has sexually abused another child. [] Tex. Fam. Code Ann. § 262.201 (West Supp. 2007).

requirements of section 262.201(b), the court is required to return the children to the custody of their parents. Tex. Fam. Code Ann. § 262.201(b).

In this case, the Department relied on the following evidence with respect to the children taken into custody from the Yearning For Zion ranch to satisfy the requirements of section 262.201:

- Interviews with investigators revealed a pattern of girls reporting that "there was no age too young for girls to be married";

- Twenty females living at the ranch had become pregnant between the ages of thirteen and seventeen;

- Five of the twenty females identified as having become pregnant between the ages of thirteen and seventeen are alleged to be minors, the other fifteen are now adults;

- Of the five minors who became pregnant, four are seventeen and one is sixteen, and all five are alleged to have become pregnant at the age of fifteen or sixteen;[5]

- The Department's lead investigator was of the opinion that due to the "pervasive belief system" of the FLDS, the male children are groomed to be perpetrators of sexual abuse and the girls are raised to be victims of sexual abuse;

- All 468 children[6] were removed from the ranch under the theory that the ranch community was "essentially one household comprised of extended family subgroups" with a single, common belief system and there was reason to believe that a child had been sexually abused in the ranch "household"; and

- Department witnesses expressed the opinion that there is a "pervasive belief system" among the residents of the ranch that it is acceptable for girls to marry, engage in sex, and bear children as soon as they reach puberty, and that this "pervasive belief system" poses a danger to the children.

In addition, the record demonstrates the following facts, which are undisputed by the Department:

- The only danger to the male children or the female children who had not reached puberty identified by the Department was the Department's assertion that the "pervasive belief system" of the FLDS community groomed the males to be perpetrators of sexual abuse later in life and taught the girls to submit to sexual abuse after reaching puberty;

- There was no evidence that the male children, or the female children who had not reached puberty, were victims of sexual or other physical abuse or in danger of being victims of sexual or other physical abuse;

- While there was evidence that twenty females had become pregnant between the ages of thirteen and seventeen, there was no evidence regarding the marital status of these girls when they became pregnant or the circumstances under which they became pregnant other than the general allegation that the girls were living in an FLDS community with a belief system that condoned underage marriage and sex;[7]

---

5. One woman is alleged to have become pregnant at the age of thirteen. She is now twenty-two years old.

6. This number has fluctuated. It will likely continue to fluctuate somewhat as disputes regarding the age of certain persons taken into custody are resolved.

7. Under Texas law, it is not sexual assault to have consensual sexual intercourse with a minor spouse to whom one is legally married. Tex. Penal Code Ann. § 22.011(a), (c)(1), (2) (West

- There was no evidence that any of the female children other than the five identified as having become pregnant between the ages of fifteen and seventeen were victims or potential victims of sexual or other physical abuse;

- With the exception of the five female children identified as having become pregnant between the ages of fifteen and seventeen, there was no evidence of any physical abuse or harm to any other child;

- The Relators have identified their children among the 468 taken into custody by the Department, and none of the Relators' children are among the five the Department has identified as being pregnant minors; and

- The Department conceded at the hearing that teenage pregnancy, by itself, is not a reason to remove children from their home and parents, but took the position that immediate removal was necessary in this case because "there is a mindset that even the young girls report that they will marry at whatever age, and that it's the highest blessing they can have to have children."

The Department argues that the fact that there are five minor females living in the ranch community who became pregnant at ages fifteen and sixteen together with the FLDS belief system condoning underage marriage and pregnancy indicates that there is a danger to all of the children that warrants their immediate removal from their homes and parents, and that the need for protection of the children is urgent.[8] The Department also argues that the "household" to which the children would be returned includes persons who have sexually abused another child, because the entire Yearning For Zion ranch community is a "household." *See id.* § 262.201(d)(2).

The Department failed to carry its burden with respect to the requirements of section 262.201(b). Pursuant to section 262.201(b)(1), the danger must be to the *physical* health or safety of the child. The Department did not present any evidence of danger to the physical health or safety of any male children or any female children who had not reached puberty. Nor did the Department offer any evidence that any of Relators' pubescent female children were in physical danger other than that those children live at the ranch among a group of people who have a "pervasive system of belief" that condones polygamous marriage and underage females having children.[9] The existence of the FLDS belief system as described by the Department's witnesses, by itself, does not put children of FLDS parents in physical danger. It is the imposition of certain alleged tenets of that system on specific individuals that may put them in physical danger. The Department failed to offer any evidence that any of the pubescent female children of the Relators

---

Supp. 2007). Texas law allows minors to marry—as young as age sixteen with parental consent and younger than sixteen if pursuant to court order. TEX. FAM. CODE ANN. § 2.101 (West 2006), §§ 2.102–.103 (West Supp. 2007). A person may not be legally married to more than one person. TEX. PENAL CODE ANN. § 25.01 (West Supp. 2007).

8. The Department's position was stated succinctly by its lead investigator at the hearing. In response to an inquiry as to why the infants needed to be removed from their mothers, the investigator responded, "[W]hat I have found is that they're living under an umbrella of belief that having children at a young age is a blessing therefore any child in that environment would not be safe."

9. The Department's witnesses conceded that there are differences of opinion among the FLDS community as to what is an appropriate age to marry, how many spouses to have, and when to start having children—much as there are differences of opinion regarding the details of religious doctrine among other religious groups.

were in such physical danger. The record is silent as to whether the Relators or anyone in their households are likely to subject their pubescent female children to underage marriage or sex. The record is also silent as to how many of Relators' children are pubescent females and whether there is any risk to them other than that they live in a community where there is a "pervasive belief system" that condones marriage and child-rearing as soon as females reach puberty.

The Department also failed to establish that the need for protection of the Relators' children was urgent and required immediate removal of the children. As previously noted, none of the identified minors who are or have been pregnant are children of Relators. There is no evidence that any of the five pregnant minors live in the same household as the Relators' children.[10] There is no evidence that Relators have allowed or are going to allow any of their minor female children to be subjected to any sexual or physical abuse. There is simply no evidence specific to Relators' children at all except that they exist, they were taken into custody at the Yearning For Zion ranch, and they are living with people who share a "pervasive belief system" that condones underage marriage and underage pregnancy. Even if one views the FLDS belief system as creating a danger of sexual abuse by grooming boys to be perpetrators of sexual abuse and raising girls to be victims of sexual abuse as the Department contends, there is no evidence that this danger is "immediate" or "urgent" as contemplated by section 262.201 with respect to every child in the community. The legislature has required that there be evidence to support a finding that there is a danger to the physical health or safety of the children in question and that the need for protection is *urgent* and warrants *immediate* removal. *Id.* § 262.201(b). Evidence that children raised in this particular environment may someday have their physical health and safety threatened is not evidence that the danger is imminent enough to warrant invoking the extreme measure of immediate removal prior to full litigation of the issue as required by section 262.201.

Finally, there was no evidence that the Department made reasonable efforts to eliminate or prevent the removal of any of Relators' children. The evidence is that the Department went to the Yearning For Zion ranch to investigate a distress call from a sixteen year-old girl.[12] After interviewing a number of children, they concluded that there were five minors who were or had been pregnant and that the belief system of the community allowed minor females to marry and bear children. They then removed all of the children in the community (including infants) from their homes and ultimately separated the children from their parents. This record does not reflect any reasonable effort on the part of the Department to ascertain if some measure short of removal and/or separation from parents would have eliminated the risk the Department perceived with respect to any of the children of Relators.

---

10. The notion that the entire ranch community constitutes a "household" as contemplated by section 262.201 and justifies removing all children from the ranch community if there even is one incident of suspected child sexual abuse is contrary to the evidence. The Department's witnesses acknowledged that the ranch community was divided into separate family groups and separate households. While there was evidence that the living arrangements on the ranch are more communal than most typical neighborhoods, the evidence was not legally or factually sufficient to support a theory that the entire ranch community was a "household" under section 262.201.

12. The authenticity of this call is in doubt. Department investigators did not locate the caller on the ranch.

We find that the Department did not carry its burden of proof under section 262.201. The evidence adduced at the hearing held April 17–18, 2008, was legally and factually insufficient to support the findings required by section 262.201 to maintain custody of Relators' children with the Department. Consequently, the district court abused its discretion in failing to return the Relators' children to the Relators. The Relators' Petition for Writ of Mandamus is conditionally granted. The district court is directed to vacate its temporary orders granting sole managing conservatorship of the children of the Relators to the Department. The writ will issue only if the district court fails to comply with this opinion.

NOTES

1. In an opinion dated May 29, 2008, the Texas Supreme Court refused "to disturb the court of appeals' decision." *In re Texas Dep't of Family and Protective Servs.*, 255 S.W.3d 613, 615 (Tex. 2008) (per curiam); *see also In re Texas Department of Family and Protective Servs.*, 255 S.W.3d 618 (Tex. 2008) (per curiam). According to the concurring and dissenting opinion by Justice Harriett O'Neill:

> In this case, the Department of Family and Protective Services presented evidence that "there was a danger to the physical health or safety" of pubescent girls on the Yearning for Zion (YFZ) Ranch from a pattern or practice of sexual abuse, that "the urgent need for protection required the immediate removal" of those girls, and that the Department made reasonable efforts, considering the obstacles to information-gathering that were presented, to prevent removal and return those children home. Tex. Fam. Code § 262.201(b)(1)–(3). As to this endangered population, I do not agree with the Court that the trial court abused its discretion in allowing the Department to retain temporary conservatorship until such time as a permanency plan designed to ensure each girl's physical health and safety could be approved. *See id.* §§ 263.101–.102. On this record, however, I agree that there was no evidence of imminent "danger to the physical health or safety" of boys and pre-pubescent girls to justify their removal from the YFZ Ranch, and to this extent I join the Court's opinion. *Id.* § 262.201(b)(1).
>
> Evidence presented in the trial court indicated that the Department began its investigation of the YFZ Ranch on March 29th, when it received a report of sexual abuse of a sixteen-year-old girl on the property. On April 3rd, the Department entered the Ranch along with law-enforcement personnel and conducted nineteen interviews of girls aged seventeen or under, as well as fifteen to twenty interviews of adults. In the course of these interviews, the Department learned there were many polygamist families living on the Ranch; a number of girls under the age of eighteen living on the Ranch were pregnant or had given birth; both interviewed girls and adults considered no age too young for a girl to be "spiritually" married; and the Ranch's religious leader, "Uncle Merrill," had the unilateral power to decide when and to whom they would be married. Additionally, in the trial court, the Department presented "Bishop's Records"— documents seized from the Ranch—indicating the presence of several extremely young mothers or pregnant "wives"[1] on the Ranch: a sixteen-year-old "wife" with a child, a sixteen-year-old pregnant "wife," two pregnant fifteen-year-old "wives," and a thirteen-year-old who had conceived a child. The testimony of Dr. William John Walsh, the families' expert witness, confirmed that the Fundamentalist Church of Jesus Christ of Latter Day Saints accepts the age of "physical

---

1. Although referred to as "wives" in the Bishop's Records, these underage girls are not legally married; rather, the girls are "spiritually" married to their husbands, typically in polygamous households with multiple other "spiritual" wives. Subject to limited defenses, a person who "engages in sexual contact" with a child younger than seventeen who is not his *legal* spouse is guilty of a sexual offense under the TEXAS PENAL CODE. *See* TEX. PENAL CODE § 21.11(a)–(b). Those who promote or assist such sexual contact, *see id.* § 7.02(a)(2), or cause the child to engage in sexual contact, *see id.* § 21.11(a)(1), may also be criminally liable.

development" (that is, first menstruation) as the age of eligibility for "marriage." Finally, child psychologist Dr. Bruce Duncan Perry testified that the pregnancy of the underage children on the Ranch was the result of sexual abuse because children of the age of fourteen, fifteen, or sixteen are not sufficiently emotionally mature to enter a healthy consensual sexual relationship or a "marriage."

Evidence presented thus indicated a pattern or practice of sexual abuse of pubescent girls, and the condoning of such sexual abuse, on the Ranch[2]— evidence sufficient to satisfy a "person of ordinary prudence and caution" that other such girls were at risk of sexual abuse as well. *Id.* § 262.201(b). This evidence supports the trial court's finding that "there was a danger to the physical health or safety" of pubescent girls on the Ranch. *Id.* § 262.201(b)(1)[.] Thus, [as to these girls,] the trial court did not abuse its discretion in finding that the Department met section 262.201(b)(1)'s requirements.

In re Texas Dep't of Family and Protective Services, 255 S.W.3d at 616 (O'Neill, J., concurring in part and dissenting in part).

2. Consider Mary Anne Case's observations about *Steed*:

> As I see it, . . . court majorities [in *Steed*] were not only far too willing to be deferential to religious justifications, but also, in addition, far too unwilling to treat female subordination through traditional sex roles as something unusual and disturbing. . . .
>
> . . .
>
> A feminist fundamentalist take on the FLDS case, especially one informed by information available about the Yearning for Zion Ranch from sources in addition to those cited by the Texas courts, might instead see the case as an object lesson in what can go wrong when the constitutional mandate of equal protection on grounds of sex is not systematically and with full force applied in state regulation of the family and the education of children. A consistent story emerges from the autobiographies of Elissa Wall, whose court testimony about her forced marriage at age fourteen helped put FLDS leader Warren Jeffs in jail as an accomplice to rape; of Carolyn Jessop, who successfully challenged the FLDS elder whose fourth wife she became at age eighteen for sole custody of the eight children she ultimately bore him; and of the four former FLDS women among the eighteen "women who escaped" polygamy whose stories are told in *God's Brothel*. We read in each of these accounts of girls "treated like an indentured servant, forc[ed] to do all the cooking, cleaning, and babysitting," "condemned to a life of virtual slavery," and taught that " '[a] woman's role is to be obedient without question to her husband' " and that "[a] woman had no right to speak out . . . even if [her] goal was [to] protect [] her daughter." These women write, not only of being denied education they specifically longed for and requested, but of receiving education, not only in the home, but in FLDS controlled classrooms, into complete submission to the brutality young boys are simultaneously encouraged to perpetrate upon them. Thus, for example, according to Carolyn Jessop, Warren Jeffs, who served as a teacher at the FLDS school before he succeeded his father Rulon as the community's Prophet,
>
> > brought one of his wives into the auditorium, which was packed with boys. [She] had a long braid that fell past her knees. Warren grabbed the braid and twisted and twisted it until she was on her knees and he was ripping hair from her head. He told the boys that this was how obedient their wives had to be to them.

---

2. The Family Code defines "abuse" to include "sexual conduct harmful to a child's mental, emotional, or physical welfare"—including offenses under section 21.11 of the Penal Code—as well as "failure to make a reasonable effort to prevent sexual conduct harmful to a child." TEX. FAM. CODE § 261.001(1)(E)–(F). In determining whether there is a "continuing danger to the health or safety" of a child, the Family Code explicitly permits a court to consider "whether the household to which the child would be returned includes a person who . . . has sexually abused another child." Id. § 262.201(d).

These autobiographical accounts also give the lie to the FLDS claim that the state of Texas's seizure of the children was uniquely disruptive to the otherwise stable and secure home life the FLDS children had always known. Their authors tell of home life in the community repeatedly disrupted by order of the Prophet, who expelled boys and men from the community, reassigned the men's wives and children to other men in other households, frequently moved family members between and among enclaves in Texas, the Colorado/Utah border, and Canada, and then occasionally welcomed back those he had previously expelled from the community.

Unfortunately, however, so long as so many judges continue to underestimate the harm even extremely sexist parents such as those of the FLDS can do, and to undervalue the voices for women's equality raised against those parents, by, among others, some of their ex-wives and mothers of their children, our legal system will have failed to live up to its constitutional commitment to offer all persons, including the girls and boys whose education, adoption and custody the state regulates, the equal protection of the laws.

Mary Anne Case, *Feminist Fundamentalism on the Frontier Between Government and Family Responsibility for Children*, 11 L.J. & FAM. STUD. 333, 355–58 (2009).

3. For historical perspective on *Steed*, see Wiley S. Maloney, *Arizona Raided Short Creek—Why?* COLLIERS, Nov. 13, at 30–31 (1953); Ralph Nader, *The Law v. Plural Marriages*, 31 HARV. L. REC. 10 (1960); Lou Cannon, *Plural Marriages Flourish Out West*, WASH. POST, Aug. 8, 1977, at A14.

4. Cases challenging the constitutionality of laws against bigamy have been brought on various grounds urging that the practice is guaranteed by the U.S. Constitution. *See, e.g., Bronson v. Swensen*, 500 F.3d 1099, 1103–04 (10th Cir. 2007); *State v. Fischer*, 199 P.3d 663, 669 (Ariz. Ct. App. 2008); *State v. Holm*, 137 P.3d 726, 742 (Utah 2006). The decisive precedent repeatedly invoked in turning back these challenges is the U.S. Supreme Court's decision in *Reynolds v. United States*, 98 U.S. 145 (1878). Recent important sources on polygamy under law include Adrienne D. Davis, *Regulating Polygamy: Intimacy, Default Rules, and Bargaining for Equality*, 110 COLUM. L. REV. 1955 (2010), and Martha M. Ertman, *Race Treason: The Untold Story of America's Ban on Polygamy*, 19 COLUM. J. GENDER & L. 287 (2010).

5. In May of 2001, Tom Green, the first defendant charged with bigamy in Utah in almost fifty years, was convicted of four counts of bigamy and one count of criminal nonsupport. Green lived with five wives and twenty-five children, and publicized his arrangement in the media, stating that he chose to obey God rather than the law. Kevin Cantera & Michael Vigh, *Green Guilty on All Counts; Jury Takes Less Than Three Hours to Reach Verdict*, SALT LAKE TRIB., May 19, 2001, at A1. Green appealed his conviction, but lost and was then denied *certiorari* by the Supreme Court on his claim that his religious freedom was being denied. In 2002, Green was charged with the additional count of rape for impregnating one of his wives at the age of 13, convicted, and sentenced to from five years to life imprisonment (the minimum possible sentence). *See* Michael Janofsky, *Mormon Leader Is Survived by 33 Sons and a Void*, N.Y. TIMES, Sep. 15, 2002, at 22.

In 2007, Warren Jeffs was convicted by a jury as an accomplice to the rape of a fourteen-year-old girl. He was sentenced to two consecutive sentences of five years to life imprisonment. Citing deficiencies in the trial court's jury instructions, the Utah Supreme Court reversed and remanded for a new trial. *State v. Jeffs*, 243 P.3d 1250, 1254 (Utah 2010). *See also* Dan Frosch, *Polygamist's Rape Convictions Are Overturned in Utah*, N.Y. TIMES, July 28, 2010, at A11. In August 2011, in a different proceeding, Jeffs was convicted "for sexually assaulting an under-age follower he took as a bride in what his church deemed a 'spiritual marriage.'" *Texas: Polygamist Leader Gets Life Sentence*, N.Y. TIMES, Aug. 10, 2011, at A15. The jury also convicted Jeffs of a separate count of sexual assault of a different fifteen-year-old girl and sentenced him to twenty years imprisonment in addition to his life sentence. *Id.*

6. It has been estimated that a much larger proportion of American men and women have more than one spouse during a lifetime than adults in most polygamous societies, where typically not more than one out of ten or twenty can afford the polygamous state. *See* Paul Landis, *Sequential Marriage*, 42 J. HOME ECON. 625, 628 (1950). For a recent examination, see ANDREW J. CHERLIN, THE MARRIAGE-GO-ROUND (2009). Although polyandry (more than one husband) is much rarer than polygyny (more than one wife), American women—in theory—have as much freedom to remarry as do men. In practice, do they? *See* ROSE M. KREIDER, U.S. CENSUS BUREAU, REMARRIAGE IN THE UNITED STATES 2 (2006) (noting that, in the United States, men are 5 to 9 percent more likely than women to remarry within five years after divorce).

Is our "sequential polygamy" better or worse than concurrent polygamy? If the goal is to provide the best home life for children, would polygamy provide them with a more stable environment? Which is better for wives? For husbands? For parents?

d.   SAME-SEX MARRIAGE

Goodridge v. Department of Pub. Health

Supreme Judicial Court of Massachusetts, 2003.
798 N.E.2d 941.

■ MARSHALL, C.J.

Marriage is a vital social institution. The exclusive commitment of two individuals to each other nurtures love and mutual support; it brings stability to our society. For those who choose to marry, and for their children, marriage provides an abundance of legal, financial, and social benefits. In return it imposes weighty legal, financial, and social obligations. The question before us is whether, consistent with the Massachusetts Constitution, the Commonwealth may deny the protections, benefits, and obligations conferred by civil marriage to two individuals of the same sex who wish to marry. We conclude that it may not. The Massachusetts Constitution affirms the dignity and equality of all individuals. It forbids the creation of second-class citizens. In reaching our conclusion we have given full deference to the arguments made by the Commonwealth. But it has failed to identify any constitutionally adequate reason for denying civil marriage to same-sex couples.

We are mindful that our decision marks a change in the history of our marriage law. Many people hold deep-seated religious, moral, and ethical convictions that marriage should be limited to the union of one man and one woman, and that homosexual conduct is immoral. Many hold equally strong religious, moral, and ethical convictions that same-sex couples are entitled to be married, and that homosexual persons should be treated no differently than their heterosexual neighbors. Neither view answers the question before us. Our concern is with the Massachusetts Constitution as a charter of governance for every person properly within its reach....

Whether the Commonwealth may use its formidable regulatory authority to bar same-sex couples from civil marriage is a question not previously addressed by a Massachusetts appellate court. It is a question the United States Supreme Court left open as a matter of Federal law in *Lawrence* [*v. Texas*, 539 U.S. 558, 578 (2003),] where it was not an issue. There, the Court affirmed that the core concept of common human dignity protected by the Fourteenth Amendment to the United States Constitution precludes government intrusion into the deeply personal realms of consensual adult expressions of intimacy and one's choice of an intimate partner. The Court also reaffirmed the central role that decisions whether to marry or have children bear in shaping one's identity. The Massachusetts Constitution is, if anything, more protective of individual liberty and equality than the Federal Constitution; it may demand broader protection for fundamental rights; and it is less tolerant of government intrusion into the protected spheres of private life.

Barred access to the protections, benefits, and obligations of civil marriage, a person who enters into an intimate, exclusive union with another of the same sex is arbitrarily deprived of membership in one of our community's most rewarding and cherished institutions. That exclusion is incompatible with the constitutional principles of respect for individual autonomy and equality under law.

The plaintiffs are fourteen individuals from five Massachusetts counties. . . .

. . . Each plaintiff attests a desire to marry his or her partner in order to affirm publicly their commitment to each other and to secure the legal protections and benefits afforded to married couples and their children.

The Department of Public Health (department) is charged by statute with safeguarding public health. Among its responsibilities, the department oversees the registry of vital records and statistics (registry), which "enforce[s] all laws" relative to the issuance of marriage licenses and the keeping of marriage records. . . .

In March and April, 2001, each of the plaintiff couples attempted to obtain a marriage license from a city or town clerk's office. . . . In each case, the clerk either refused to accept the notice of intention to marry or denied a marriage license to the couple on the ground that Massachusetts does not recognize same-sex marriage. . . .

On April 11, 2001, the plaintiffs filed suit in the Superior Court against the department and the commissioner seeking a judgment that "the exclusion of the plaintiff couples and other qualified same-sex couples from access to marriage licenses, and the legal and social status of civil marriage, as well as the protections, benefits and obligations of marriage, violates Massachusetts law." *See* G. L. c. 231A. The plaintiffs alleged violation of the laws of the Commonwealth, including but not limited to their rights under arts. 1, 6, 7, 10, 12, and 16, and Part II, c. 1, § 1, art. 4, of the Massachusetts Constitution.[7] The department, represented by the Attorney General, admitted to a

---

7. Article 1, as amended by art. 106 of the Amendments to the Massachusetts Constitution, provides: "All people are born free and equal and have certain natural, essential and unalienable rights; among which may be reckoned the right of enjoying and defending their lives and liberties; that of acquiring, possessing and protecting property; in fine, that of seeking and obtaining their safety and happiness. Equality under the law shall not be denied or abridged because of sex, race, color, creed or national origin."

Article 6 provides: "No man, nor corporation, or association of men, have any other title to obtain advantages, or particular and exclusive privileges, distinct from those of the community, than what arises from the consideration of services rendered to the public. . . ."

Article 7 provides: "Government is instituted for the common good; for the protection, safety, prosperity, and happiness of the people; and not for the profit, honor, or private interest of any one man, family or class of men: Therefore the people alone have an incontestable, unalienable, and indefeasible right to institute government; and to reform, alter, or totally change the same, when their protection, safety, prosperity and happiness require it."

Article 10 provides, in relevant part: "Each individual of the society has a right to be protected by it in the enjoyment of his life, liberty and property, according to standing laws. . . ."

Article 12 provides, in relevant part: "[N]o subject shall be . . . deprived of his property, immunities, or privileges, put out of the protection of the law . . . or deprived of his life, liberty, or estate, but by the judgment of his peers, or the law of the land."

policy and practice of denying marriage licenses to same-sex couples. It denied that its actions violated any law or that the plaintiffs were entitled to relief. The parties filed cross motions for summary judgment.

A Superior Court judge ruled for the department....

... [T]he plaintiffs appealed. Both parties requested direct appellate review, which we granted.

Although the plaintiffs refer in passing to "the marriage statutes," they focus, quite properly, on G. L. c. 207, the marriage licensing statute, which controls entry into civil marriage....

. . .

... The plaintiffs argue that because nothing in that licensing law specifically prohibits marriages between persons of the same sex, we may interpret the statute to permit "qualified same sex couples" to obtain marriage licenses, thereby avoiding the question whether the law is constitutional. This claim lacks merit.

We interpret statutes to carry out the Legislature's intent, determined by the words of a statute interpreted according to "the ordinary and approved usage of the language." The everyday meaning of "marriage" is "the legal union of a man and woman as husband and wife," Black's Law Dictionary 986 (7th ed.1999), and the plaintiffs do not argue that the term "marriage" has ever had a different meaning under Massachusetts law. This definition of marriage, as both the department and the Superior Court judge point out, derives from the common law. Far from being ambiguous, the undefined word "marriage," as used in G. L. c. 207, confirms the General Court's intent to hew to the term's common-law and quotidian meaning concerning the genders of the marriage partners.

The intended scope of G. L. c. 207 is also evident in its consanguinity provisions. Sections 1 and 2 of G. L. c. 207 prohibit marriages between a man and certain female relatives and a woman and certain male relatives, but are silent as to the consanguinity of male-male or female-female marriage applicants. The only reasonable explanation is that the Legislature did not intend that same-sex couples be licensed to marry. We conclude, as did the judge, that G. L. c. 207 may not be construed to permit same-sex couples to marry.[11]

The larger question is whether, as the department claims, government action that bars same-sex couples from civil marriage constitutes a legitimate exercise of the State's authority to regulate conduct, or whether, as the plaintiffs claim, this categorical marriage exclusion violates the Massachusetts Constitution. We have recognized the long-standing statutory understanding, derived from the common law, that "marriage" means the lawful union

---

Article 16, as amended by art. 77 of the Amendments, provides, in relevant part: "The right of free speech shall not be abridged." Part II, c. 1, § 1, art. 4, as amended by art. 112, provides, in pertinent part, that "full power and authority are hereby given and granted to the said general court, from time to time, to make, ordain, and establish all manner of wholesome and reasonable orders, laws, statutes, and ordinances, directions and instructions, either with penalties or without; so as the same be not repugnant or contrary to this constitution, as they shall judge to be for the good and welfare of this Commonwealth."

11. We use the terms "same sex" and "opposite sex" when characterizing the couples in question, because these terms are more accurate in this context than the terms "homosexual" or "heterosexual," although at times we use those terms when we consider them appropriate. Nothing in our marriage law precludes people who identify themselves (or who are identified by others) as gay, lesbian, or bisexual from marrying persons of the opposite sex. See Baehr v. Lewin, 74 Haw. 530, 543 n.11, 547 n.14, 852 P.2d 44 (1993).

of a woman and a man. But that history cannot and does not foreclose the constitutional question.

The plaintiffs' claim that the marriage restriction violates the Massachusetts Constitution can be analyzed in two ways. Does it offend the Constitution's guarantees of equality before the law? Or do the liberty and due process provisions of the Massachusetts Constitution secure the plaintiffs' right to marry their chosen partner? . . . [T]he two constitutional concepts frequently overlap, as they do here. . . .

We begin by considering the nature of civil marriage itself. Simply put, the government creates civil marriage. In Massachusetts, civil marriage is, and since pre-Colonial days has been, precisely what its name implies: a wholly secular institution. No religious ceremony has ever been required to validate a Massachusetts marriage.

In a real sense, there are three partners to every civil marriage: two willing spouses and an approving State. While only the parties can mutually assent to marriage, the terms of the marriage—who may marry and what obligations, benefits, and liabilities attach to civil marriage—are set by the Commonwealth. Conversely, while only the parties can agree to end the marriage (absent the death of one of them or a marriage void ab initio), the Commonwealth defines the exit terms.

. . .

Without question, civil marriage enhances the "welfare of the community." It is a "social institution of the highest importance." Civil marriage anchors an ordered society by encouraging stable relationships over transient ones. It is central to the way the Commonwealth identifies individuals, provides for the orderly distribution of property, ensures that children and adults are cared for and supported whenever possible from private rather than public funds, and tracks important epidemiological and demographic data.

Marriage also bestows enormous private and social advantages on those who choose to marry. Civil marriage is at once a deeply personal commitment to another human being and a highly public celebration of the ideals of mutuality, companionship, intimacy, fidelity and family. . . . Because it fulfills yearnings for security, safe haven, and connection that express our common humanity, civil marriage is an esteemed institution, and the decision whether and whom to marry is among life's momentous acts of self-definition.

. . .

The benefits accessible only by way of a marriage license are enormous, touching nearly every aspect of life and death. . . . [W]e note that some of the statutory benefits conferred by the Legislature on those who enter civil marriage include, as to property: joint Massachusetts income tax filing, tenancy by the entirety . . .; extension of the benefits of the homestead protection (securing up to $300,000 in equity from creditors) to one's spouse and children; automatic right to inherit the property of a deceased spouse who does not leave a will; . . . the right to share the medical policy of one's spouse; . . . financial protections for the spouses of certain Commonwealth employees (fire fighters, police officers, prosecutors, among others) killed in the performance of duty; the equitable division of marital property on divorce; temporary and permanent alimony rights; . . . and the right to bring claims for wrongful death and loss of consortium, and for funeral and burial expenses....

. . .

Where a married couple has children, their children are also directly or indirectly, but no less auspiciously, the recipients of special legal and economic protections obtained by civil marriage. Notwithstanding the Commonwealth's strong public policy to abolish legal distinctions between marital and nonmarital children ..., the fact remains that marital children reap a measure of family stability and economic security based on their parents' legally privileged status that is largely inaccessible, or not as readily accessible, to nonmarital children. Some of these benefits are social, such as the enhanced approval that still attends the status of being a marital child. Others are material, such as the greater ease of access to family-based State and Federal benefits that attend the presumption of one's parentage.

It is undoubtedly for these concrete reasons, as well as for its intimately personal significance, that civil marriage has long been termed a "civil right." See, e.g., *Loving v. Virginia*, 388 U.S. 1 (1967). The United States Supreme Court has described the right to marry as "of fundamental importance for all individuals" and as "part of the fundamental 'right of privacy' implicit in the Fourteenth Amendment's Due Process Clause." *Zablocki v. Redhail*, 434 U.S. 374 (1978).

Without the right to marry—or more properly, the right to choose to marry—one is excluded from the full range of human experience and denied full protection of the laws for one's "avowed commitment to an intimate and lasting human relationship." *Baker v. State*, [744 A.2d 864, 889 (Vt. 1999)]. Because civil marriage is central to the lives of individuals and the welfare of the community, our laws assiduously protect the individual's right to marry against undue government incursion. Laws may not "interfere directly and substantially with the right to marry." *Zablocki v. Redhail, supra* at 387. See *Perez v. Sharp*, [198 P.2d 17, 19 (Cal. 1948)] ("There can be no prohibition of marriage except for an important social objective and reasonable means").[15]

Unquestionably, the regulatory power of the Commonwealth over civil marriage is broad, as is the Commonwealth's discretion to award public benefits. Individuals who have the choice to marry each other and nevertheless choose not to may properly be denied the legal benefits of marriage. But that same logic cannot hold for a qualified individual who would marry if she or he only could.

For decades, indeed centuries, in much of this country (including Massachusetts) no lawful marriage was possible between white and black Americans. That long history availed not when the Supreme Court of California held in 1948 that a legislative prohibition against interracial marriage violated the due process and equality guarantees of the Fourteenth

---

15. The department argues that this case concerns the rights of couples (same sex and opposite sex), not the rights of individuals. This is incorrect. The rights implicated in this case are at the core of individual privacy and autonomy. See, e.g., Loving v. Virginia, 388 U.S. 1 (1967) ("Under our Constitution, the freedom to marry or not marry, a person of another race resides with the individual and cannot be infringed by the State"); Perez v. Sharp, 198 P.2d 17[, 19 (Cal. 1948)] ("The right to marry is the right of individuals, not of racial groups"). See also A.Z. v. B.Z., 725 N.E.2d 1051[, 1059 (Mass. 2000)], quoting Moore v. East Cleveland, 431 U.S. 494, 499 (1977) (noting "freedom of personal choice in matters of marriage and family life"). While two individuals who wish to marry may be equally aggrieved by State action denying them that opportunity, they do not "share" the liberty and equality interests at stake.

Amendment, *Perez v. Sharp*, 198 P.2d 17[, 27 (Cal. 1948)], or when, nineteen years later, the United States Supreme Court also held that a statutory bar to interracial marriage violated the Fourteenth Amendment, *Loving v. Virginia*, 388 U.S. 1 (1967). As both *Perez* and *Loving* make clear the right to marry means little if it does not include the right to marry the person of one's choice, subject to appropriate government restrictions in the interests of public health, safety, and welfare. *See Perez v. Sharp, supra* at 20 ("the essence of the right to marry is freedom to join in marriage with the person of one's choice"). In this case, as in *Perez* and *Loving*, a statute deprives individuals of access to an institution of fundamental legal, personal, and social significance—the institution of marriage—because of a single trait: skin color in *Perez* and *Loving*, sexual orientation here. As it did in *Perez* and *Loving*, history must yield to a more fully developed understanding of the invidious quality of the discrimination.

The Massachusetts Constitution protects matters of personal liberty against government incursion as zealously, and often more so, than does the Federal Constitution, even where both Constitutions employ essentially the same language. . . .

     . . .

The Massachusetts Constitution requires, at a minimum, that the exercise of the State's regulatory authority not be "arbitrary or capricious." Under both the equality and liberty guarantees, regulatory authority must, at very least, serve "a legitimate purpose in a rational way"; a statute must "bear a reasonable relation to a permissible legislative objective." Any law failing to satisfy the basic standards of rationality is void.

     . . .

The department argues that no fundamental right or "suspect" class is at issue here, and rational basis is the appropriate standard of review. For the reasons we explain below, we conclude that the marriage ban does not meet the rational basis test for either due process or equal protection. Because the statute does not survive rational basis review, we do not consider the plaintiffs' arguments that this case merits strict judicial scrutiny.

The department posits three legislative rationales for prohibiting same-sex couples from marrying: (1) providing a "favorable setting for procreation"; (2) ensuring the optimal setting for child rearing, which the department defines as "a two-parent family with one parent of each sex"; and (3) preserving scarce State and private financial resources. We consider each in turn.

The judge in the Superior Court endorsed the first rationale, holding that "the state's interest in regulating marriage is based on the traditional concept that marriage's primary purpose is procreation." This is incorrect. Our laws of civil marriage do not privilege procreative heterosexual intercourse between married people above every other form of adult intimacy and every other means of creating a family. General Laws c. 207 contains no requirement that the applicants for a marriage license attest to their ability or intention to conceive children by coitus. Fertility is not a condition of marriage, nor is it grounds for divorce. People who have never consummated their marriage, and never plan to, may be and stay married. *See Franklin v. Franklin*, 28 N.E. 681 [(Mass. 1891)] ("The consummation of a marriage by coition is not necessary to its validity").[22] People who cannot stir from their

---

22. Our marriage law does recognize that the inability to participate in intimate relations may have a bearing on one of the central expectations of marriage. Since the earliest days of the

deathbed may marry. While it is certainly true that many, perhaps most, married couples have children together (assisted or unassisted), it is the exclusive and permanent commitment of the marriage partners to one another, not the begetting of children, that is the sine qua non of civil marriage.[23]

. . .

The "marriage is procreation" argument singles out the one unbridgeable difference between same-sex and opposite-sex couples, and transforms that difference into the essence of legal marriage. Like "Amendment 2" to the Constitution of Colorado, which effectively denied homosexual persons equality under the law and full access to the political process, the marriage restriction impermissibly "identifies persons by a single trait and then denies them protection across the board." *Romer v. Evans*, 517 U.S. 620, 633 (1996). In so doing, the State's action confers an official stamp of approval on the destructive stereotype that same-sex relationships are inherently unstable and inferior to opposite-sex relationships and are not worthy of respect.

The department's first stated rationale, equating marriage with unassisted heterosexual procreation, shades imperceptibly into its second: that confining marriage to opposite-sex couples ensures that children are raised in the "optimal" setting. Protecting the welfare of children is a paramount State policy. Restricting marriage to opposite-sex couples, however, cannot plausibly further this policy. "The demographic changes of the past century make it difficult to speak of an average American family. The composition of families varies greatly from household to household." *Troxel v. Granville*, 530 U.S. 57, 63 (2000). Massachusetts has responded supportively to "the changing realities of the American family," and has moved vigorously to strengthen the modern family in its many variations. Moreover, we have repudiated the common-law power of the State to provide varying levels of protection to children based on the circumstances of birth. The "best interests of the child" standard does not turn on a parent's sexual orientation or marital status. See e.g., *Doe v. Doe*, 452 N.E.2d 293 [(Mass. App. Ct. 1983)] (parent's sexual orientation insufficient ground to deny custody of child in divorce

---

Commonwealth, the divorce statutes have permitted (but not required) a spouse to choose to divorce his or her impotent mate. See St. 1785, c. 69, § 3. While infertility is not a ground to void or terminate a marriage, impotency (the inability to engage in sexual intercourse) is, at the election of the disaffected spouse. See G. L. c. 207, § 14 (annulment); G. L. c. 208, § 1 (divorce). Cf. Martin v. Otis, 233 Mass. 491, 495, 124 N.E. 294 (1919) ("impotency does not render a marriage void, but only voidable at the suit of the party conceiving himself or herself to be wronged"); Smith v. Smith, 50 N.E. 933 [(Mass. 1898)] (marriage nullified because husband's incurable syphilis "leaves him no foundation on which the marriage relation could properly rest"). See also G. L. c. 207, § 28A. However, in Hanson v. Hanson, 191 N.E. 673 [(Mass. 1934)], a decree of annulment for nonconsummation was reversed where the wife knew before the marriage that her husband had syphilis and voluntarily chose to marry him. We held that, given the circumstances of the wife's prior knowledge of the full extent of the disease and her consent to be married, the husband's condition did not go "to the essence" of the marriage. *Id.* at [675].

23. It is hardly surprising that civil marriage developed historically as a means to regulate heterosexual conduct and to promote child rearing, because until very recently unassisted heterosexual relations were the only means short of adoption by which children could come into the world, and the absence of widely available and effective contraceptives made the link between heterosexual sex and procreation very strong indeed. Punitive notions of illegitimacy, see Powers v. Wilkinson, 506 N.E.2d 842 [(Mass. 1987)], and of homosexual identity, see *Lawrence, supra* at [566–67], further cemented the common and legal understanding of marriage as an unquestionably heterosexual institution. But it is circular reasoning, not analysis, to maintain that marriage must remain a heterosexual institution because that is what it historically has been. As one dissent acknowledges, in "the modern age," "heterosexual intercourse,

action). See also *E.N.O. v. L.M.M.*, 711 N.E.2d 886 [891 (Mass. 1999)] (best interests of child determined by considering child's relationship with biological and de facto same-sex parents); *Silvia v. Silvia*, 400 N.E.2d 1330, 1331 & n.3 [(Mass. App. Ct. 1980)] (collecting support and custody statutes containing no gender distinction).

. . .

The third rationale advanced by the department is that limiting marriage to opposite-sex couples furthers the Legislature's interest in conserving scarce State and private financial resources. The marriage restriction is rational, it argues, because the General Court logically could assume that same-sex couples are more financially independent than married couples and thus less needy of public marital benefits, such as tax advantages, or private marital benefits, such as employer-financed health plans that include spouses in their coverage.

An absolute statutory ban on same-sex marriage bears no rational relationship to the goal of economy. First, the department's conclusory generalization—that same-sex couples are less financially dependent on each other than opposite-sex couples—ignores that many same-sex couples, such as many of the plaintiffs in this case, have children and other dependents (here, aged parents) in their care. The department does not contend, nor could it, that these dependents are less needy or deserving than the dependents of married couples. Second, Massachusetts marriage laws do not condition receipt of public and private financial benefits to married individuals on a demonstration of financial dependence on each other; the benefits are available to married couples regardless of whether they mingle their finances or actually depend on each other for support.

The department suggests additional rationales for prohibiting same-sex couples from marrying, which are developed by some amici. It argues that broadening civil marriage to include same-sex couples will trivialize or destroy the institution of marriage as it has historically been fashioned. Certainly our decision today marks a significant change in the definition of marriage as it has been inherited from the common law, and understood by many societies for centuries. But it does not disturb the fundamental value of marriage in our society.

Here, the plaintiffs seek only to be married, not to undermine the institution of civil marriage. They do not want marriage abolished. They do not attack the binary nature of marriage, the consanguinity provisions, or any of the other gate-keeping provisions of the marriage licensing law. Recognizing the right of an individual to marry a person of the same sex will not diminish the validity or dignity of opposite-sex marriage, any more than recognizing the right of an individual to marry a person of a different race devalues the marriage of a person who marries someone of her own race.[28] If anything, extending civil marriage to same-sex couples reinforces the importance of marriage to individuals and communities. That same-sex couples are willing to embrace marriage's solemn obligations of exclusivity, mutual

---

procreation, and childcare are not necessarily conjoined." 798 N.E. 2d at 995–96 (Cordy, J., dissenting).

28. Justice Cordy suggests that we have "transmuted the 'right' to marry into a right to change the institution of marriage itself," because marriage is intimately tied to the reproductive systems of the marriage partners and to the "optimal" mother and father setting for child rearing. *Post*, 789 N.E. 2d at 984 (Cordy, J., dissenting). That analysis hews perilously close to the argument, long repudiated by the Legislature and the courts, that men and women are so innately and fundamentally different that their respective "proper spheres" can be rigidly and universally delineated. An abundance of legislative enactments and decisions of this court negate any such stereotypical premises.

support, and commitment to one another is a testament to the enduring place of marriage in our laws and in the human spirit.[29]

It has been argued that, due to the State's strong interest in the institution of marriage as a stabilizing social structure, only the Legislature can control and define its boundaries.... The Massachusetts Constitution requires that legislation meet certain criteria and not extend beyond certain limits. It is the function of courts to determine whether these criteria are met and whether these limits are exceeded. In most instances, these limits are defined by whether a rational basis exists to conclude that legislation will bring about a rational result. The Legislature in the first instance, and the courts in the last instance, must ascertain whether such a rational basis exists. To label the court's role as usurping that of the Legislature is to misunderstand the nature and purpose of judicial review. We owe great deference to the Legislature to decide social and policy issues, but it is the traditional and settled role of courts to decide constitutional issues.

. . .

Several amici suggest that prohibiting marriage by same-sex couples reflects community consensus that homosexual conduct is immoral. Yet Massachusetts has a strong affirmative policy of preventing discrimination on the basis of sexual orientation. See G. L. c. 151B (employment, housing, credit, services); G. L. c. 265, § 39 (hate crimes); G. L. c. 272, § 98 (public accommodation); G. L. c. 76, § 5 (public education). See also, e.g., *Commonwealth v. Balthazar*, 318 N.E.2d 478 [(Mass. 1974)] (decriminalization of private consensual adult conduct); *Doe v. Doe*, 452 N.E.2d 293 [(Mass. App. Ct. 1983)] (custody to homosexual parent not per se prohibited).

. . .

The marriage ban works a deep and scarring hardship on a very real segment of the community for no rational reason. The absence of any reasonable relationship between, on the one hand, an absolute disqualification of same-sex couples who wish to enter into civil marriage and, on the other, protection of public health, safety, or general welfare, suggests that the marriage restriction is rooted in persistent prejudices against persons who are (or who are believed to be) homosexual. "The Constitution cannot control such prejudices but neither can it tolerate them. Private biases may be outside the reach of the law, but the law cannot, directly or indirectly, give them effect." *Palmore v. Sidoti*, 466 U.S. 429, 433 (1984). Limiting the protections, benefits, and obligations of civil marriage to opposite-sex couples violates the basic premises of individual liberty and equality under law protected by the Massachusetts Constitution.

. . .

In their complaint the plaintiffs request only a declaration that their exclusion and the exclusion of other qualified same-sex couples from access to civil marriage violates Massachusetts law. We declare that barring an individual from the protections, benefits, and obligations of civil marriage

---

29. We are concerned only with the withholding of the benefits, protections, and obligations of civil marriage from a certain class of persons for invalid reasons. Our decision in no way limits the rights of individuals to refuse to marry persons of the same sex for religious or any other reasons. It in no way limits the personal freedom to disapprove of, or to encourage others to disapprove of, same-sex marriage. Our concern, rather, is whether historical, cultural, religious, or other reasons permit the State to impose limits on personal beliefs concerning whom a person should marry.

solely because that person would marry a person of the same sex violates the Massachusetts Constitution. We vacate the summary judgment for the department. We remand this case to the Superior Court for entry of judgment consistent with this opinion. Entry of judgment shall be stayed for 180 days to permit the Legislature to take such action as it may deem appropriate in light of this opinion.

■ SPINA, J. (dissenting, with whom SOSMAN and CORDY, JJ., join).

What is at stake in this case is not the unequal treatment of individuals or whether individual rights have been impermissibly burdened, but the power of the Legislature to effectuate social change without interference from the courts.... The power to regulate marriage lies with the Legislature, not with the judiciary. Today, the court has transformed its role as protector of individual rights into the role of creator of rights, and I respectfully dissent.

. . .

Equal protection....

The court concludes ... that G. L. c. 207 unconstitutionally discriminates against the individual plaintiffs because it denies them the "right to marry the person of one's choice" where that person is of the same sex. To reach this result the court relies on *Loving v. Virginia*, 388 U.S. 1, 12 (1967), and transforms "choice" into the essential element of the institution of marriage. The *Loving* case did not use the word "choice" in this manner, and it did not point to the result that the court reaches today. In *Loving*, the Supreme Court struck down as unconstitutional a statute that prohibited Caucasians from marrying non-Caucasians. It concluded that the statute was intended to preserve white supremacy and invidiously discriminated against non-Caucasians because of their race. The "choice" to which the Supreme Court referred was the "choice to marry," and it concluded that with respect to the institution of marriage, the State had no compelling interest in limiting the choice to marry along racial lines. The Supreme Court did not imply the existence of a right to marry a person of the same sex. To the same effect is *Perez v. Sharp*, 198 P.2d 17 [(Cal. 1948)], on which the court also relies.

Unlike the *Loving* and *Sharp* cases, the Massachusetts Legislature has erected no barrier to marriage that intentionally discriminates against anyone. Within the institution of marriage, anyone is free to marry, with certain exceptions that are not challenged. In the absence of any discriminatory purpose, the State's marriage statutes do not violate principles of equal protection. This court should not have invoked even the most deferential standard of review within equal protection analysis because no individual was denied access to the institution of marriage.

Due process. The marriage statutes do not impermissibly burden a right protected by our constitutional guarantee of due process.... There is no restriction on the right of any plaintiff to enter into marriage. Each is free to marry a willing person of the opposite sex. Cf. *Zablocki v. Redhail*, 434 U.S. 374 (1978).

■ SOSMAN, J. (dissenting, with whom SPINA and CORDY, JJ., join).

Based on our own philosophy of child rearing, and on our observations of the children being raised by same-sex couples to whom we are personally close, we may be of the view that what matters to children is not the gender, or sexual orientation, or even the number of the adults who raise them, but rather whether those adults provide the children with a nurturing, stable, safe, consistent, and supportive environment in which to mature. Same-sex couples can provide their children with the requisite nurturing, stable, safe, consistent, and supportive environment in which to mature, just as opposite-sex couples do. It is therefore understandable that the court might view the traditional definition of marriage as an unnecessary anachronism, rooted in historical prejudices that modern society has in large measure rejected and biological limitations that modern science has overcome.

It is not, however, our assessment that matters. Conspicuously absent from the court's opinion today is any acknowledgment that the attempts at scientific study of the ramifications of raising children in same-sex couple households are themselves in their infancy and have so far produced inconclusive and conflicting results....

. . .

More importantly, it is not our confidence in the lack of adverse consequences that is at issue, or even whether that confidence is justifiable. The issue is whether it is rational to reserve judgment on whether this change can be made at this time without damaging the institution of marriage or adversely affecting the critical role it has played in our society. Absent consensus on the issue (which obviously does not exist), or unanimity amongst scientists studying the issue (which also does not exist), or a more prolonged period of observation of this new family structure (which has not yet been possible), it is rational for the Legislature to postpone any redefinition of marriage that would include same-sex couples until such time as it is certain that that redefinition will not have unintended and undesirable social consequences. Through the political process, the people may decide when the benefits of extending civil marriage to same-sex couples have been shown to outweigh whatever risks—be they palpable or ephemeral—are involved. However minimal the risks of that redefinition of marriage may seem to us from our vantage point, it is not up to us to decide what risks society must run, and it is inappropriate for us to arrogate that power to ourselves merely because we are confident that "it is the right thing to do."

. . .

NOTES

1. In 2003, the Massachusetts Senate submitted a bill that would have established civil unions instead of same-sex marriage for same-sex couples. In *Opinions of the Justices to the Senate*, 802 N.E.2d 565, 572 (2004), the court held that the bill, if enacted into law, would violate the equal protection and due process requirements of the Constitution of the Commonwealth and the Massachusetts Declaration of Rights. The court explained:

> The same defects of rationality evident in the marriage ban considered in *Goodridge* are evident in, if not exaggerated by, Senate No. 2175. Segregating same-sex unions from opposite sex unions cannot possibly be held rationally to advance or "preserve" what we stated in *Goodridge* were the Commonwealth's legitimate interests in procreation, child rearing, and the conservation of resources. Because the proposed law by its express terms forbids same-sex couples entry into civil marriage, it continues to relegate same-sex couples to a different status. The holdings in *Goodridge*, by which we are bound, is that group classification based on unsupportable distinctions, such as that embodied in the proposed bill, are invalid under the Massachusetts Constitution.

Id. at 569. A description of other developments in and around the *Goodridge* decision from one of the lawyers who argued it is found in Mary L. Bonauto, Goodridge *in Context*, 40 HARV. C.R.-C.L. L. REV. 1 (2005).

2. In November and December 2004, eleven states amended their constitutions to prohibit same-sex marriage.[1] As of 2011, the constitutions of twenty-nine states have been amended to prohibit same-sex marriage. In fifteen of these states, constitutional marriage amendments define marriage as the union of one man to one woman as husband and wife.[2] In the other fourteen states, constitutional marriage amendments define marriage as the union of one man to one woman as husband and wife and also go beyond that to address the legal status and recognition of other intimate relationships.[3] Additionally, thirty-four states ban same-sex marriage by statute.[4]

3. In *National Pride at Work v. Governor of Michigan*, 748 N.W.2d 524 (2008), the Michigan Supreme Court interpreted the state's constitutional marriage amendment as banning any state recognition of domestic partnership benefits afforded to state workers or their domestic partners because their relationships had some of the formal attributes of traditional marriage, the only such relationship to be recognized under state law. Concluding, the court observed:

> ... [G]iven that the marriage amendment prohibits the recognition of unions similar to marriage "for any purpose," the pertinent question is not whether these unions give rise to all of the same legal effects; rather, it is whether these unions are being recognized as unions similar to marriage "for any purpose." ... [W]e conclude that the marriage amendment, Const. 1963, art. 1, § 25, which states that "the union of one man and one woman in marriage shall be the only agreement recognized as a marriage or similar union for any purpose," prohibits public employers from providing health-insurance benefits to their employees' qualified same-sex domestic partners.

Id. at 543. The Ohio Supreme Court reached a different result when interpreting a similarly broad provision of the Ohio Constitution in *State v. Carswell*, 871 N.E.2d 547 (Ohio 2007). By its terms, Ohio's Marriage Amendment provides: "Only a union between one man and one woman may be a marriage valid in or recognized by this state and its political subdivisions. This state and its political subdivisions shall not create or recognize a legal status for relationships of unmarried individuals that intends to approximate the design, qualities, significance or effect of marriage." OHIO CONST. art. XV, § 11. Interpreting the amendment's second sentence, the *Carswell* court declared it "means that the state cannot create or recognize a legal status for unmarried persons that bears *all* of the attributes of marriage—a marriage substi-

---

1. ARK. CONST. AMEND. 83 §§ 1, 2, 3; GA. CONST. ART. 1, § 4; LA. CONST. ART. 12, § 15; MICH. CONST. ART. I, § 25; MISS. CONST. ART. 14, § 263A; MONT. CONST. ART. 13, § 7; OHIO CONST. ART. XV, § 11; OKLA CONST. ART. 2, § 35; OR. CONST. ART. XV, § 5A.

2. ALA. CONST. ART. I, § 36.03; ALASKA CONST. ART. 1, § 25; ARIZ. CONST. ART. 30 § 1; CAL. CONST. ART 1, § 7.5; COLO. CONST. ART. 2, § 31; GA. CONST. ART. 1, § 4; HAW. CONST. ART. 1, § 23; IDAHO CONST. ART. III, § 28; KAN. CONST. ART. 15, § 16; MISS. CONST. ART. 14, § 263A; MO. CONST. ART. 1, § 33; MONT. CONST. ART. 13, § 7; NEV. CONST. ART. 1 § 21; OR. CONST. ART. XV, § 5A; TENN. CONST. ART. 11, § 18.

3. ARK. CONST. AMEND. 83 §§ 1, 2, 3; KY. CONST. § 233A; LA. CONST. ART. 12, § 15; MICH. CONST. ART. I, § 25; NEB. CONST. ART. 1 § 29; N.D. CONST. ART. 11, § 28; OHIO CONST. ART. XV, § 11; OKLA CONST. ART. 2, § 35; S.C. CONST. ART. XVII, § 15; S.D. CONST. ART. 21, § 9; TEX. CONST. ART. 1, § 32; UTAH CONST. ART. 1, § 29; VA. CONST. ART. 1, § 15–A; WIS. CONST. ART. 13, § 13.

4. ALA. CODE § 30–1–19; ALASKA STAT. § 25.05.011; ARIZ. REV. STAT. §§ 25–101, 25–901; ARK. CODE ANN. §§ 9–11–109; 9–11–208; COLO. REV. STAT. ANN. § 14–2–104; DEL. CODE ANN. TIT. 13 § 101; FLA. STAT. ANN. § 741.04; GA. CODE ANN. § 19–3–3.1; HAW. REV. STAT. § 572–1; IDAHO CODE ANN. § 32–209; 750 ILL. COMP. STAT. ANN. 5/201; IND. CODE § 31–11–1–1; KAN. STAT. ANN. § 23–101; KY. REV. STAT. §§ 402.005; LA. CIV. CODE ANN. ART. 86; MD. CODE ANN., FAM. LAW § 2–201; MICH. COMP. LAWS ANN. §§ 551.1, 551.271; MINN. STAT. ANN. §§ 517.03, 518.01; MISS. CODE ANN. § 93–1–1; MO. REV. STAT. § 451.022; MONT. CODE ANN. §§ 40–1–103, 104; NEV. REV. STAT. ANN. § 122.020; N.C. GEN. STAT. § 51–1; N.D. CENT. CODE § 14–03–01; OHIO REV. CODE ANN. § 3101.01; 23 PA. CONS. STAT. ANN. § 1704; S.C. CODE ANN. § 20–1–15; TENN. CODE ANN. § 36–3–113; TEX. FAM. CODE ANN. § 2.001; UTAH CODE ANN. § 30–1–2; VA. CODE ANN. § 25–45; WASH. REV. CODE ANN. § 26.04.020; WIS. STAT. ANN. §§ 765.01, 765.04; WYO. STAT. ANN. § 20–1–101. CODE ANN. § 30–1–2; VA. CODE ANN. § 25–45; WASH. REV. CODE ANN. § 26.04.020; WIS. STAT. ANN. §§ 765.01, 765.04; WYO. STAT. ANN. § 20–1–101.

tute." *Carswell*, 871 N.E.2d, at 551. The court's only stated example of "a marriage substitute": civil unions. See *id.* & n.1.

4. As of 2011, six states—Connecticut, Iowa, Massachusetts, New Hampshire, New York, and Vermont—as well as the District of Columbia issue marriage licenses to same-sex couples.[5] Six states—California, Delaware, Hawaii, Illinois, New Jersey, and Rhode Island—afford same-sex couples the same rights, benefits, protections, and responsibilities as married couples under state law.[6] These relationships are often referred to as "civil unions." Seven states—Colorado, Maine, Maryland, Nevada, Oregon, Washington, and Wisconsin—recognize same-sex relationships but afford same-sex couples only some of the rights, benefits, protections, and responsibilities of civil unions or marriages.[7] These relationships are often referred to as "domestic partnerships."

5. A number of countries around the world recognize same-sex marriage. They include: Argentina, Belgium, Canada, Iceland, the Netherlands, Norway, Portugal, South Africa, Spain, and Sweden. Macarena Sáez, General Report, *Same–Sex Marriage, Same–Sex Cohabitation, and Same–Sex Families Around the World: Why "Same" Is So Different*, 19 AM. U. J. GENDER SOC. POL'Y & L. 1, 3–10 (2011). Additionally, "[s]ince 1989, several . . . countries have followed Denmark in successfully introducing civil union and/or registered domestic partnership laws. Same-sex civil union or domestic partnership status is also recognized in a number of regions and jurisdictions of other countries, though not at the federal or national level." Christy M. Glass, Nancy Kubasek & Elizabeth Kiester, *Toward a "European Model" of Same–Sex Marriage Rights: A Viable Pathway for the U.S.?*, 29 BERKELEY J. INT'L L. 132, 141 (2001) (footnotes omitted).

Perry v. Schwarzenegger

United States District Court, N.D. California, 2010.
704 F.Supp.2d 921.

■ WALKER, J.

Plaintiffs challenge a November 2008 voter-enacted amendment to the California Constitution ("Proposition 8" or "Prop 8"). Cal. Const. Art. I, § 7.5. In its entirety, Proposition 8 provides: "Only marriage between a man and a woman is valid or recognized in California." Plaintiffs allege that Proposition 8 deprives them of due process and of equal protection of the laws contrary to the Fourteenth Amendment and that its enforcement by state officials violates 42 USC § 1983.

Plaintiffs are two couples. Kristin Perry and Sandra Stier reside in Berkeley, California and raise four children together. Jeffrey Zarrillo and Paul Katami reside in Burbank, California. Plaintiffs seek to marry their partners and have been denied marriage licenses by their respective county authorities on the basis of Proposition 8. No party contended, and no evidence at trial suggested, that the county authorities had any ground to deny marriage licenses to plaintiffs other than Proposition 8.

---

5. CONN. GEN. STAT. ANN. § 46b–20; N.H. REV. STAT. § 457:1; N.Y. DOM. REL. §§ 10(a), (b); VT. STAT. ANN. tit. 15 § 8; D.C. CODE § 46–401. *See also* Varnum v. Brien, 763 N.W.2d 862, 907 (Iowa 2009); Goodridge v. Department of Public Health, 798 N.E.2d 941 (Mass. 2003).

6. CAL. FAM. CODE § 297.5(a); DEL. CODE ANN. TIT. 13, § 212(a); 2011 HAW. SESS. LAWS 1 (act takes effect January 1, 2012); 750 ILL. COMP. STAT. ANN. 75/5; N.J. STAT. ANN. § 26:8A–2(d); R.I. GEN. LAWS. § 15–3.1–6.

7. COLO. REV. STAT. ANN. § 15–22–101; ME. REV. STAT. ANN. tit. 22 § 2710; MD. CODE ANN., FAM. LAW §§ 6–201, 202; NEV. REV. STAT. ANN. § 122A.030; OR. REV. STAT. § 106.300; WASH. REV. CODE § 26.60.010; 2009 WISC. ACT 28.

Having considered the trial evidence and the arguments of counsel, the court pursuant to FRCP 52(a) finds that Proposition 8 is unconstitutional and that its enforcement must be enjoined.

BACKGROUND TO PROPOSITION 8

In November 2000, the voters of California adopted Proposition 22 through the state's initiative process. Entitled the California Defense of Marriage Act, Proposition 22 amended the state's Family Code by adding the following language: "Only marriage between a man and a woman is valid or recognized in California." Cal. Family Code § 308.5. This amendment further codified the existing definition of marriage as "a relationship between a man and a woman." *In re Marriage Cases*, 183 P.3d 384, 407 (Cal. 2008).

In February 2004, the mayor of San Francisco instructed county officials to issue marriage licenses to same-sex couples. The following month, the California Supreme Court ordered San Francisco to stop issuing such licenses and later nullified the marriage licenses that same-sex couples had received. See *Lockyer v. City & County of San Francisco*, 95 P.3d 459 (Cal. 2004). The court expressly avoided addressing whether Proposition 22 violated the California Constitution.

Shortly thereafter, San Francisco and various other parties filed state court actions challenging or defending California's exclusion of same-sex couples from marriage under the state constitution. These actions were consolidated in San Francisco superior court; the presiding judge determined that, as a matter of law, California's bar against marriage by same-sex couples violated the equal protection guarantee of Article I Section 7 of the California Constitution. *In re Coordination Proceeding, Special Title [Rule 1550(c)]*, 2005 WL 583129 (March 14, 2005). The court of appeal reversed, and the California Supreme Court granted review. In May 2008, the California Supreme Court invalidated Proposition 22 and held that all California counties were required to issue marriage licenses to same-sex couples. See *In re Marriage Cases*, 183 P.3d 384. From June 17, 2008 until the passage of Proposition 8 in November of that year, San Francisco and other California counties issued approximately 18,000 marriage licenses to same-sex couples.

After the November 2008 election, opponents of Proposition 8 challenged the initiative through an original writ of mandate in the California Supreme Court as violating the rules for amending the California Constitution and on other grounds; the California Supreme Court upheld Proposition 8 against those challenges. *Strauss v. Horton*, 207 P.3d 48 (Cal. 2009). *Strauss* leaves undisturbed the 18,000 marriages of same-sex couples performed in the four and a half months between the decision in *In re Marriage Cases* and the passage of Proposition 8. Since Proposition 8 passed, no same-sex couple has been permitted to marry in California.

PROCEDURAL HISTORY OF THIS ACTION

Plaintiffs challenge the constitutionality of Proposition 8 under the Fourteenth Amendment, an issue not raised during any prior state court proceeding. Plaintiffs filed their complaint on May 22, 2009, naming as defendants in their official capacities California's Governor, Attorney General and Director and Deputy Director of Public Health and the Alameda County Clerk–Recorder and the Los Angeles County Registrar–Recorder/County Clerk (collectively "the government defendants"). With the exception of the

Attorney General, who concedes that Proposition 8 is unconstitutional, the government defendants refused to take a position on the merits of plaintiffs' claims and declined to defend Proposition 8.

Defendant-intervenors, the official proponents of Proposition 8 under California election law ("proponents"), were granted leave in July 2009 to intervene to defend the constitutionality of Proposition 8. On January 8, 2010, Hak–Shing William Tam, an official proponent and defendant-intervenor, moved to withdraw as a defendant; Tam's motion is denied for the reasons stated in a separate order filed herewith. Plaintiff-intervenor City and County of San Francisco ("CCSF" or "San Francisco") was granted leave to intervene in August 2009.

The court denied plaintiffs' motion for a preliminary injunction on July 2, 2009 and denied proponents' motion for summary judgment on October 14, 2009. Proponents moved to realign the Attorney General as a plaintiff; the motion was denied on December 23, 2009. Imperial County, a political subdivision of California, sought to intervene as a party defendant on December 15, 2009; the motion is denied for the reasons addressed in a separate order filed herewith.

The parties disputed the factual premises underlying plaintiffs' claims and the court set the matter for trial. . . .

. . .

II FINDINGS OF FACT

[After "consider[ing] the evidence presented at trial, the credibility of the witnesses and the legal arguments presented by counsel, the court" went on to make extensive findings of fact relevant to its analysis of the constitutional issues presented by the case, adding a footnote to the entire "findings of fact" section indicating that, "[t]o the extent any of the findings of fact should more properly be considered conclusions of law, they shall be deemed as such." A few of the specific factual findings follow.]

. . .

32. California has eliminated marital obligations based on the gender of the spouse. Regardless of their sex or gender, marital partners share the same obligations to one another and to their dependents. As a result of Proposition 8, California nevertheless requires that a marriage consist of one man and one woman.

. . .

33. Eliminating gender and race restrictions in marriage has not deprived the institution of marriage of its vitality.

. . .

c. ([Historian Nancy] Cott: "[T]he primacy of the husband as the legal and economic representative of the couple, and the protector and provider for his wife, was seen as absolutely essential to what marriage was" in the nineteenth century. Gender restrictions were slowly removed from marriage, but "because there were such alarms about it and such resistance to change in this what had been seen as quite an essential characteristic of marriage, it took a very very long time before this trajectory of the removal of the state from prescribing these rigid spousal roles was complete." The removal of gender inequality in marriage is now complete "to no apparent damage to the institution. And, in fact, I think to the benefit of the institution.");

. . .

f. ([Historian Nancy] Cott: When racial restrictions on marriage across color lines were abolished, there was alarm and many people worried that the institution of marriage would be degraded and devalued. But "there has been no evidence that the institution of marriage has become less popular because * * * people can marry whoever they want.").

. . .

35. The state has many purposes in licensing and fostering marriage. Some of the state's purposes benefit the persons married while some benefit the state:

a. Facilitating governance and public order by organizing individuals into cohesive family units;

b. Developing a realm of liberty, intimacy and free decision-making by spouses;

c. Creating stable households;

d. Legitimating children;

e. Assigning individuals to care for one another and thus limiting the public's liability to care for the vulnerable;

f. Facilitating property ownership.

36. States and the federal government channel benefits, rights and responsibilities through marital status. Marital status affects immigration and citizenship, tax policy, property and inheritance rules and social benefit programs.

. . .

37. Marriage creates economic support obligations between consenting adults and for their dependents.

. . .

. . .

52. Domestic partnerships lack the social meaning associated with marriage, and marriage is widely regarded as the definitive expression of love and commitment in the United States.

. . .

53. Domestic partners are not married under California law. California domestic partnerships may not be recognized in other states and are not recognized by the federal government.

54. The availability of domestic partnership does not provide gays and lesbians with a status equivalent to marriage because the cultural meaning of marriage and its associated benefits are intentionally withheld from same-sex couples in domestic partnerships.

. . .

55. Permitting same-sex couples to marry will not affect the number of opposite-sex couples who marry, divorce, cohabit, have children outside of marriage or otherwise affect the stability of opposite-sex marriages.

a.   ([Psychologist Letitia] Peplau: Data from Massachusetts on the "annual rates for marriage and for divorce" for "the four years prior to same-sex marriage being legal and the four years after" show "that the rates of marriage and divorce are no different after [same-sex] marriage was permitted than they were before.");

. . .

f.   [Plaintiffs' Exhibit] PX0754 American Anthropological Association, *Statement on Marriage and the Family:* The viability of civilization or social order does not depend upon marriage as an exclusively heterosexual institution.

56.   The children of same-sex couples benefit when their parents can marry.

a.   ([Economist Lee] Badgett: Same-sex couples and their children are denied all of the economic benefits of marriage that are available to married couples.);

b.   [Plaintiffs' Exhibit] PX0787 Position Statement, American Psychiatric Association, *Support of Legal Recognition of Same–Sex Civil Marriage* at 1 (July 2005): "The children of unmarried gay and lesbian parents do not have the same protection that civil marriage affords the children of heterosexual couples.";

. . .

. . .

64.   Proposition 8 has had a negative fiscal impact on California and local governments.

a.   (Badgett: "Proposition 8 has imposed some economic losses on the State of California and on counties and municipalities.");

b.   (Badgett: Denying same-sex couples the right to marry imposes costs on local governments such as loss of tax revenue, higher usage of means-tested programs, higher costs for healthcare of uninsured same-sex partners and loss of skilled workers.);

c.   ([Economist Edmund] Egan: "What we're really talking about in the nonquantifiable impacts are the long-term advantages of marriage as an institution, and the long-term costs of discrimination as a way that weakens people's productivity and integration into the labor force. Whether it's weakening their education because they're discriminated against at school, or leading them to excessive reliance on behavioral and other health services, these are impacts that are hard to quantify, but they can wind up being extremely powerful. How much healthier you are over your lifetime. How much wealth you generate because you are in a partnership.");

. . .

65.   [City and County of San Francisco (CCSF)] would benefit economically if Proposition 8 were not in effect.

. . .

66.   Proposition 8 increases costs and decreases wealth for same-sex couples because of increased tax burdens, decreased availability of health insurance and higher transactions costs to secure rights and obligations typically associated with marriage. Domestic partnership reduces but does not eliminate these costs.

. . .

. . .

69. The factors that affect whether a child is well-adjusted are: (1) the quality of a child's relationship with his or her parents; (2) the quality of the relationship between a child's parents or significant adults in the child's life; and (3) the availability of economic and social resources.

70. The gender of a child's parent is not a factor in a child's adjustment. The sexual orientation of an individual does not determine whether that individual can be a good parent. Children raised by gay or lesbian parents are as likely as children raised by heterosexual parents to be healthy, successful and well-adjusted. The research supporting this conclusion is accepted beyond serious debate in the field of developmental psychology.

. . .

71. Children do not need to be raised by a male parent and a female parent to be well-adjusted, and having both a male and a female parent does not increase the likelihood that a child will be well-adjusted.

72. The genetic relationship between a parent and a child is not related to a child's adjustment outcomes.

73. Studies comparing outcomes for children raised by married opposite-sex parents to children raised by single or divorced parents do not inform conclusions about outcomes for children raised by same-sex parents in stable, long-term relationships.

. . .

78. Stereotypes and misinformation have resulted in social and legal disadvantages for gays and lesbians.

. . .

> j. [Plaintiffs' Exhibit] PX0619 The Williams Institute, *Chapter 14: Other Indicia of Animus against LGBT People by State and Local Officials, 1980–Present* at 9 (2009): The Williams Institute collected negative comments made by politicians about gays and lesbians in all fifty states. An Arizona state representative compared homosexuality to "bestiality, human sacrifice, and cannibalism." A California state senator described homosexuality as "a sickness * * * an uncontrolled passion similar to that which would cause someone to rape."

. . .

79. The Proposition 8 campaign relied on fears that children exposed to the concept of same-sex marriage may become gay or lesbian. The reason children need to be protected from same-sex marriage was never articulated in official campaign advertisements. Nevertheless, the advertisements insinuated that learning about same-sex marriage could make a child gay or lesbian and that parents should dread having a gay or lesbian child.

. . .

80. The campaign to pass Proposition 8 relied on stereotypes to show that same-sex relationships are inferior to opposite-sex relationships.

. . .

III   CONCLUSIONS OF LAW[3]

Plaintiffs challenge Proposition 8 under the Due Process and Equal Protection Clauses of the Fourteenth Amendment. Each challenge is inde-

---

3. To the extent any of the findings of fact should more properly be considered conclusions of law, they shall be deemed as such.

pendently meritorious, as Proposition 8 both unconstitutionally burdens the exercise of the fundamental right to marry and creates an irrational classification on the basis of sexual orientation.

DUE PROCESS

The Due Process Clause provides that no "State [shall] deprive any person of life, liberty, or property, without due process of law." US Const. Amend. XIV, § 1. Due process protects individuals against arbitrary governmental intrusion into life, liberty or property. See *Washington v. Glucksberg*, 521 U.S. 702, 719–720 (1997). When legislation burdens the exercise of a right deemed to be fundamental, the government must show that the intrusion withstands strict scrutiny. *Zablocki v. Redhail*, 434 U.S. 374, 388 (1978).

THE RIGHT TO MARRY PROTECTS AN INDIVIDUAL'S CHOICE OF MARITAL PARTNER REGARDLESS OF GENDER

The freedom to marry is recognized as a fundamental right protected by the Due Process Clause. See, for example, *Turner v. Safley*, 482 U.S. 78, 95 (1987); *Zablocki*, 434 U.S. at 384; *Cleveland Board of Education v. LaFleur*, 414 U.S. 632, 639–40 (1974); *Loving v. Virginia*, 388 U.S. 1, 12 (1967); *Griswold v. Connecticut*, 381 U.S. 479, 486 (1965).

The parties do not dispute that the right to marry is fundamental. The question presented here is whether plaintiffs seek to exercise the fundamental right to marry; or, because they are couples of the same sex, whether they seek recognition of a new right.

To determine whether a right is fundamental under the Due Process Clause, the court inquires into whether the right is rooted "in our Nation's history, legal traditions, and practices." *Glucksberg*, 521 U.S. at 710. Here, because the right to marry is fundamental, the court looks to the evidence presented at trial to determine: (1) the history, tradition and practice of marriage in the United States; and (2) whether plaintiffs seek to exercise their right to marry or seek to exercise some other right. *Id*.

Marriage has retained certain characteristics throughout the history of the United States. *See* FF 35. Marriage requires two parties to give their free consent to form a relationship, which then forms the foundation of a household. The spouses must consent to support each other and any dependents. FF 35, 37. The state regulates marriage because marriage creates stable households, which in turn form the basis of a stable, governable populace. FF 35, 37. The state respects an individual's choice to build a family with another and protects the relationship because it is so central a part of an individual's life. See *Bowers v. Hardwick*, 478 U.S. 186, 204–205 (1986) (Blackmun, J, dissenting).

Never has the state inquired into procreative capacity or intent before issuing a marriage license; indeed, a marriage license is more than a license to have procreative sexual intercourse. "[I]t would demean a married couple were it to be said marriage is simply about the right to have sexual intercourse." *Lawrence v. Texas*, 539 U.S. 558, 567 (2003). The Supreme Court recognizes that, wholly apart from procreation, choice and privacy play a pivotal role in the marital relationship. See *Griswold*, 381 U.S. at 485–486.

Race restrictions on marital partners were once common in most states but are now seen as archaic, shameful or even bizarre. When the Supreme Court invalidated race restrictions in *Loving*, the definition of the right to marry did not change. 388 U.S. at 12. Instead, the Court recognized that race restrictions, despite their historical prevalence, stood in stark contrast to the concepts of liberty and choice inherent in the right to marry. *Id.*

The marital bargain in California (along with other states) traditionally required that a woman's legal and economic identity be subsumed by her husband's upon marriage under the doctrine of coverture; this once-unquestioned aspect of marriage now is regarded as antithetical to the notion of marriage as a union of equals. FF 32 As states moved to recognize the equality of the sexes, they eliminated laws and practices like coverture that had made gender a proxy for a spouse's role within a marriage. [*Id.*] Marriage was thus transformed from a male-dominated institution into an institution recognizing men and women as equals. *Id.* Yet, individuals retained the right to marry; that right did not become different simply because the institution of marriage became compatible with gender equality.

The evidence at trial shows that marriage in the United States traditionally has not been open to same-sex couples. The evidence suggests many reasons for this tradition of exclusion, including gender roles mandated through coverture, social disapproval of same-sex relationships, and the reality that the vast majority of people are heterosexual and have had no reason to challenge the restriction. The evidence shows that the movement of marriage away from a gendered institution and toward an institution free from state-mandated gender roles reflects an evolution in the understanding of gender rather than a change in marriage. The evidence did not show any historical purpose for excluding same-sex couples from marriage, as states have never required spouses to have an ability or willingness to procreate in order to marry. Rather, the exclusion exists as an artifact of a time when the genders were seen as having distinct roles in society and in marriage. That time has passed.

The right to marry has been historically and remains the right to choose a spouse and, with mutual consent, join together and form a household. FF 35. Race and gender restrictions shaped marriage during eras of race and gender inequality, but such restrictions were never part of the historical core of the institution of marriage. FF 33. Today, gender is not relevant to the state in determining spouses' obligations to each other and to their dependents. Relative gender composition aside, same-sex couples are situated identically to opposite-sex couples in terms of their ability to perform the rights and obligations of marriage under California law. Gender no longer forms an essential part of marriage; marriage under law is a union of equals.

Plaintiffs seek to have the state recognize their committed relationships, and plaintiffs' relationships are consistent with the core of the history, tradition and practice of marriage in the United States. Perry and Stier seek to be spouses; they seek the mutual obligation and honor that attend marriage, FF 52. Zarrillo and Katami seek recognition from the state that their union is "a coming together for better or for worse, hopefully enduring, and intimate to the degree of being sacred." *Griswold*, 381 U.S. at 486. Plaintiffs' unions encompass the historical purpose and form of marriage. Only the plaintiffs' genders relative to one another prevent California from giving their relationships due recognition.

Plaintiffs do not seek recognition of a new right. To characterize plaintiffs' objective as "the right to same-sex marriage" would suggest that plaintiffs seek something different from what opposite-sex couples across the state enjoy-namely, marriage. Rather, plaintiffs ask California to recognize their relationships for what they are: marriages.

DOMESTIC PARTNERSHIPS DO NOT SATISFY CALIFORNIA'S OBLIGATION TO ALLOW PLAINTIFFS TO MARRY

Having determined that plaintiffs seek to exercise their fundamental right to marry under the Due Process Clause, the court must consider whether the availability of Registered Domestic Partnerships fulfills California's due process obligation to same-sex couples. The evidence shows that domestic partnerships were created as an alternative to marriage that distinguish same-sex from opposite-sex couples. FF 53–54; *In re Marriage Cases*, 183 P.3d 384, 434 (2008) (One of the "core elements of th[e] fundamental right [to marry] is the right of same-sex couples to have their official family relationship accorded the same dignity, respect, and stature as that accorded to all other officially recognized family relationships."); *id.* at 402, 434, 445 15 (By "reserving the historic and highly respected designation of marriage exclusively to opposite-sex couples while offering same-sex couples only the new and unfamiliar designation of domestic partnership," the state communicates the "official view that [same-sex couples'] committed relationships are of lesser stature than the comparable relationships of opposite-sex couples."). Proponents do not dispute the "significant symbolic disparity between domestic partnership and marriage."

California has created two separate and parallel institutions to provide couples with essentially the same rights and obligations. CAL. FAM. CODE § 297.5(a). Domestic partnerships are not open to opposite-sex couples unless one partner is at least sixty-two years old. CAL. FAM. CODE § 297(b)(5)(B). Apart from this limited exception—created expressly to benefit those eligible for benefits under the Social Security Act—the sole basis upon which California determines whether a couple receives the designation "married" or the designation "domestic partnership" is the sex of the spouses relative to one another. Compare CAL. FAM. CODE §§ 297–299.6 (domestic partnership) with §§ 300–536 (marriage). No further inquiry into the couple or the couple's relationship is required or permitted. Thus, California allows almost all opposite-sex couples only one option-marriage-and all same-sex couples only one option-domestic partnership. *See id.*, FF 53–54.

The evidence shows that domestic partnerships do not fulfill California's due process obligation to plaintiffs for two reasons. First, domestic partnerships are distinct from marriage and do not provide the same social meaning as marriage. FF 53–54. Second, domestic partnerships were created specifically so that California could offer same-sex couples rights and benefits while explicitly withholding marriage from same-sex couples. *Id.*; CAL. FAM. CODE § 297 (Gov. Davis 2001 signing statement: "In California, a legal marriage is between a man and a woman. * * * This [domestic partnership] legislation does nothing to contradict or undermine the definition of a legal marriage.").

The evidence at trial shows that domestic partnerships exist solely to differentiate same-sex unions from marriages. FF 53–54. A domestic partnership is not a marriage; while domestic partnerships offer same-sex couples almost all of the rights and responsibilities associated with marriage, the evidence shows that the withholding of the designation "marriage" significantly disadvantages plaintiffs. FF 52–54. The record reflects that marriage is a culturally superior status compared to a domestic partnership. FF 52. California does not meet its due process obligation to allow plaintiffs to marry by offering them a substitute and inferior institution that denies marriage to same-sex couples.

PROPOSITION 8 IS UNCONSTITUTIONAL BECAUSE IT DENIES PLAINTIFFS A FUNDAMENTAL RIGHT WITHOUT A LEGITIMATE (MUCH LESS COMPELLING) REASON

Because plaintiffs seek to exercise their fundamental right to marry, their claim is subject to strict scrutiny. *Zablocki*, 434 U.S. at 388. That the majority of California voters supported Proposition 8 is irrelevant, as "fundamental rights may not be submitted to [a] vote; they depend on the outcome of no elections." *West Virginia State Board of Education v. Barnette*, 319 U.S. 624, 638 (1943). Under strict scrutiny, the state bears the burden of producing evidence to show that Proposition 8 is narrowly tailored to a compelling government interest. *Carey v. Population Services International*, 431 U.S. 678, 686 (1977). Because the government defendants declined to advance such arguments, proponents seized the role of asserting the existence of a compelling California interest in Proposition 8.

As explained in detail in the equal protection analysis, Proposition 8 cannot withstand rational basis review. Still less can Proposition 8 survive the strict scrutiny required by plaintiffs' due process claim. The minimal evidentiary presentation made by proponents does not meet the heavy burden of production necessary to show that Proposition 8 is narrowly tailored to a compelling government interest. Proposition 8 cannot, therefore, withstand strict scrutiny. Moreover, proponents do not assert that the availability of domestic partnerships satisfies plaintiffs' fundamental right to marry; proponents stipulated that "[t]here is a significant symbolic disparity between domestic partnership and marriage." Accordingly, Proposition 8 violates the Due Process Clause of the Fourteenth Amendment.

EQUAL PROTECTION

The Equal Protection Clause of the Fourteenth Amendment provides that no state shall "deny to any person within its jurisdiction the equal protection of the laws." US Const. Amend. XIV, § 1. Equal protection is "a pledge of the protection of equal laws." *Yick Wo v. Hopkins*, 118 U.S. 356, 369 (1886). The guarantee of equal protection coexists, of course, with the reality that most legislation must classify for some purpose or another. See *Romer v. Evans*, 517 U.S. 620, 631 (1996). When a law creates a classification but neither targets a suspect class nor burdens a fundamental right, the court presumes the law is valid and will uphold it as long as it is rationally related to some legitimate government interest. See, for example, *Heller v. Doe*, 509 U.S. 312, 319–320 (1993).

The court defers to legislative (or in this case, popular) judgment if there is at least a debatable question whether the underlying basis for the classification is rational. *Minnesota v. Clover Leaf Creamery Co.*, 449 U.S. 456, 464 (1981). Even under the most deferential standard of review, however, the court must "insist on knowing the relation between the classification adopted and the object to be attained." *Romer*, 517 U.S. at 632; *Heller*, 509 U.S. at 321. The court may look to evidence to determine whether the basis for the underlying debate is rational. *Plyler v. Doe*, 457 U.S. 202, 228 (1982). The search for a rational relationship, while quite deferential, "ensure[s] that classifications are not drawn for the purpose of disadvantaging the group burdened by the law." *Romer*, 517 U.S. at 633. The classification itself must be related to the purported interest. *Plyler*, 457 U.S. at 220.

Most laws subject to rational basis easily survive equal protection review, because a legitimate reason can nearly always be found for treating different groups in an unequal manner. See *Romer*, 517 U.S. at 633. Yet, to survive rational basis review, a law must do more than disadvantage or otherwise harm a particular group. *United States Department of Agriculture v. Moreno*, 413 U.S. 528, 534 (1973).

SEXUAL ORIENTATION OR SEX DISCRIMINATION

Plaintiffs challenge Proposition 8 as violating the Equal Protection Clause because Proposition 8 discriminates both on the basis of sex and on the basis of sexual orientation. Sexual orientation discrimination can take the form of sex discrimination. Here, for example, Perry is prohibited from marrying Stier, a woman, because Perry is a woman. If Perry were a man, Proposition 8 would not prohibit the marriage. Thus, Proposition 8 operates to restrict Perry's choice of marital partner because of her sex. But Proposition 8 also operates to restrict Perry's choice of marital partner because of her sexual orientation; her desire to marry another woman arises only because she is a lesbian.

The evidence at trial shows that gays and lesbians experience discrimination based on unfounded stereotypes and prejudices specific to sexual orientation. Gays and lesbians have historically been targeted for discrimination because of their sexual orientation; that discrimination continues to the present. As the case of Perry and the other plaintiffs illustrates, sex and sexual orientation are necessarily interrelated, as an individual's choice of romantic or intimate partner based on sex is a large part of what defines an individual's sexual orientation. Sexual orientation discrimination is thus a phenomenon distinct from, but related to, sex discrimination.

Proponents argue that Proposition 8 does not target gays and lesbians because its language does not refer to them. In so arguing, proponents seek to mask their own initiative. Those who choose to marry someone of the opposite sex—heterosexuals—do not have their choice of marital partner restricted by Proposition 8. Those who would choose to marry someone of the same sex—homosexuals—have had their right to marry eliminated by an amendment to the state constitution. Homosexual conduct and identity together define what it means to be gay or lesbian. Indeed, homosexual conduct and attraction are constitutionally protected and integral parts of what makes someone gay or lesbian. *Lawrence*, 539 U.S. at 579; *see also Christian Legal Society v. Martinez*, 561 U.S. ___, 130 S.Ct. 2971, 2990, 177 L.Ed.2d 838 ("Our decisions have declined to distinguish between status and conduct in [the context of sexual orientation].") (June 28, 2010) (citing *Lawrence*, 539 U.S. at 583 (O'Connor, J, concurring)).

Proposition 8 targets gays and lesbians in a manner specific to their sexual orientation and, because of their relationship to one another, Proposition 8 targets them specifically due to sex. Having considered the evidence, the relationship between sex and sexual orientation and the fact that Proposition 8 eliminates a right only a gay man or a lesbian would exercise, the court determines that plaintiffs' equal protection claim is based on sexual orientation, but this claim is equivalent to a claim of discrimination based on sex.

STANDARD OF REVIEW

As presently explained in detail, the Equal Protection Clause renders Proposition 8 unconstitutional under any standard of review. Accordingly, the court need not address the question whether laws classifying on the basis of sexual orientation should be subject to a heightened standard of review.

Although Proposition 8 fails to possess even a rational basis, the evidence presented at trial shows that gays and lesbians are the type of minority strict scrutiny was designed to protect. *Massachusetts Board of Retirement v. Murgia*, 427 U.S. 307, 313 (1976) (noting that strict scrutiny may be appropriate where a group has experienced a " 'history of purposeful unequal treatment' or been subjected to unique disabilities on the basis of stereotyped characteristics not truly indicative of their abilities") (quoting *San Antonio Independent School District v. Rodriguez*, 411 U.S. 1, 28 (1973)). See FF 78. Proponents admit that "same-sex sexual orientation does not result in any impairment in judgment or general social and vocational capabilities." [Plaintiffs' Exhibit] PX0707 at RFA No 21.

The court asked the parties to identify a difference between heterosexuals and homosexuals that the government might fairly need to take into account when crafting legislation. Proponents pointed only to a difference between same-sex couples (who are incapable through sexual intercourse of producing offspring biologically related to both parties) and opposite-sex couples (some of whom are capable through sexual intercourse of producing such offspring). Proponents did not, however, advance any reason why the government may use sexual orientation as a proxy for fertility or why the government may need to take into account fertility when legislating. Consider, by contrast, *City of Cleburne v. Cleburne Living Center*, 473 U.S. 432, 444 (1985) (Legislation singling out a class for differential treatment hinges upon a demonstration of "real and undeniable differences" between the class and others); see also *United States v. Virginia*, 518 U.S. 515, 533 (1996) ("Physical differences between men and women * * * are enduring."). No evidence at trial illuminated distinctions among lesbians, gay men and heterosexuals amounting to "real and undeniable differences" that the government might need to take into account in legislating.

The trial record shows that strict scrutiny is the appropriate standard of review to apply to legislative classifications based on sexual orientation. All classifications based on sexual orientation appear suspect, as the evidence shows that California would rarely, if ever, have a reason to categorize individuals based on their sexual orientation. Here, however, strict scrutiny is unnecessary. Proposition 8 fails to survive even rational basis review.

PROPOSITION 8 DOES NOT SURVIVE RATIONAL BASIS

Proposition 8 cannot withstand any level of scrutiny under the Equal Protection Clause, as excluding same-sex couples from marriage is simply not rationally related to a legitimate state interest. One example of a legitimate state interest in not issuing marriage licenses to a particular group might be a scarcity of marriage licenses or county officials to issue them. But marriage licenses in California are not a limited commodity, and the existence of 18,000 same-sex married couples in California shows that the state has the resources to allow both same-sex and opposite-sex couples to wed. See Background to Proposition 8 above.

Proponents put forth several rationales for Proposition 8, which the court now examines in turn: (1) reserving marriage as a union between a man and a woman and excluding any other relationship from marriage; (2) proceeding with caution when implementing social changes; (3) promoting opposite-sex parenting over same-sex parenting; (4) protecting the freedom of those who oppose marriage for same-sex couples; (5) treating same-sex couples differently from opposite-sex couples; and (6) any other conceivable interest.

PURPORTED INTEREST #1: RESERVING MARRIAGE AS A UNION BETWEEN A MAN AND A WOMAN AND EXCLUDING ANY OTHER RELATIONSHIP

Proponents first argue that Proposition 8 is rational because it preserves: (1) "the traditional institution of marriage as the union of a man and a woman"; (2) "the traditional social and legal purposes, functions, and structure of marriage"; and (3) "the traditional meaning of marriage as it has always been defined in the English language." These interests relate to maintaining the definition of marriage as the union of a man and a woman for its own sake.

Tradition alone, however, cannot form a rational basis for a law. *Williams v. Illinois,* 399 U.S. 235, 239 (1970). The "ancient lineage" of a classification does not make it rational. *Heller,* 509 U.S. at 327. Rather, the state must have an interest apart from the fact of the tradition itself.

The evidence shows that the tradition of restricting an individual's choice of spouse based on gender does not rationally further a state interest despite its "ancient lineage." Instead, the evidence shows that the tradition of gender restrictions arose when spouses were legally required to adhere to specific gender roles. California has eliminated all legally-mandated gender roles except the requirement that a marriage consist of one man and one woman. FF 32. Proposition 8 thus enshrines in the California Constitution a gender restriction that the evidence shows to be nothing more than an artifact of a foregone notion that men and women fulfill different roles in civic life.

The tradition of restricting marriage to opposite-sex couples does not further any state interest. Rather, the evidence shows that Proposition 8 harms the state's interest in equality, because it mandates that men and women be treated differently based only on antiquated and discredited notions of gender.

Proponents' argument that tradition prefers opposite-sex couples to same-sex couples equates to the notion that opposite-sex relationships are simply better than same-sex relationships. Tradition alone cannot legitimate this purported interest. Plaintiffs presented evidence showing conclusively that the state has no interest in preferring opposite-sex couples to same-sex couples or in preferring heterosexuality to homosexuality. Moreover, the state cannot have an interest in disadvantaging an unpopular minority group simply because the group is unpopular. *Moreno,* 413 U.S. at 534.

The evidence shows that the state advances nothing when it adheres to the tradition of excluding same-sex couples from marriage. Proponents' asserted state interests in tradition are nothing more than tautologies and do not amount to rational bases for Proposition 8.

PURPORTED INTEREST #2: PROCEEDING WITH CAUTION WHEN IMPLEMENTING SOCIAL CHANGES

Proponents next argue that Proposition 8 is related to state interests in: (1) "[a]cting incrementally and with caution when considering a radical transformation to the fundamental nature of a bedrock social institution"; (2) "[d]ecreasing the probability of weakening the institution of marriage"; (3) "[d]ecreasing the probability of adverse consequences that could result from weakening the institution of marriage"; and (4) "[d]ecreasing the probability of the potential adverse consequences of same-sex marriage."

Plaintiffs presented evidence at trial sufficient to rebut any claim that marriage for same-sex couples amounts to a sweeping social change. See FF

55. Instead, the evidence shows beyond debate that allowing same-sex couples to marry has at least a neutral, if not a positive, effect on the institution of marriage and that same-sex couples' marriages would benefit the state. Id. Moreover, the evidence shows that the rights of those opposed to homosexuality or same-sex couples will remain unaffected if the state ceases to enforce Proposition 8. FF 55.

The contrary evidence proponents presented is not credible. Indeed, proponents presented no reliable evidence that allowing same-sex couples to marry will have any negative effects on society or on the institution of marriage. The process of allowing same-sex couples to marry is straightforward, and no evidence suggests that the state needs any significant lead time to integrate same-sex couples into marriage. See Background to Proposition 8 above. Consider, by contrast, *Cooper v. Aaron*, 358 U.S. 1, 7 (1958) (recognizing that a school district needed time to implement racial integration but nevertheless finding a delay unconstitutional because the school board's plan did not provide for "the earliest practicable completion of desegregation"). The evidence shows that allowing same-sex couples to marry will be simple for California to implement because it has already done so; no change need be phased in. California need not restructure any institution to allow same-sex couples to marry. See FF 55.

Because the evidence shows same-sex marriage has and will have no adverse effects on society or the institution of marriage, California has no interest in waiting and no practical need to wait to grant marriage licenses to same-sex couples. Proposition 8 is thus not rationally related to proponents' purported interests in proceeding with caution when implementing social change.

PURPORTED INTEREST #3: PROMOTING OPPOSITE–SEX PARENTING OVER SAME–SEX PARENTING

Proponents' largest group of purported state interests relates to opposite-sex parents. Proponents argue Proposition 8: (1) promotes "stability and responsibility in naturally procreative relationships"; (2) promotes "enduring and stable family structures for the responsible raising and care of children by their biological parents"; (3) increases "the probability that natural procreation will occur within stable, enduring, and supporting family structures"; (4) promotes "the natural and mutually beneficial bond between parents and their biological children"; (5) increases "the probability that each child will be raised by both of his or her biological parents"; (6) increases "the probability that each child will be raised by both a father and a mother"; and (7) increases "the probability that each child will have a legally recognized father and mother."

The evidence supports two points which together show Proposition 8 does not advance any of the identified interests: (1) same-sex parents and opposite-sex parents are of equal quality, FF 69–73, and (2) Proposition 8 does not make it more likely that opposite-sex couples will marry and raise offspring biologically related to both parents.

The evidence does not support a finding that California has an interest in preferring opposite-sex parents over same-sex parents. Indeed, the evidence shows beyond any doubt that parents' genders are irrelevant to children's developmental outcomes. FF 70. Moreover, Proposition 8 has nothing to do with children, as Proposition 8 simply prevents same-sex couples from marrying. Same-sex couples can have (or adopt) and raise children. When they do, they are treated identically to opposite-sex parents under California law. Even if California had an interest in preferring opposite-sex parents to same-sex parents—and the evidence plainly shows that California does not—Proposition 8 is not rationally related to that interest, because Proposition 8 does not affect who can or should become a parent under California law.

To the extent California has an interest in encouraging sexual activity to occur within marriage (a debatable proposition in light of *Lawrence*, 539 U.S. at 571) the evidence shows Proposition 8 to be detrimental to that interest. Because of Proposition 8, same-sex couples are not permitted to engage in sexual activity within marriage. FF 53. Domestic partnerships, in which sexual activity is apparently expected, are separate from marriage and thus codify California's encouragement of non-marital sexual activity. Cal. Fam. Code §§ 297–299.6. To the extent proponents seek to encourage a norm that sexual activity occur within marriage to ensure that reproduction occur within stable households, Proposition 8 discourages that norm because it requires some sexual activity and child-bearing and child-rearing to occur outside marriage.

Proponents argue Proposition 8 advances a state interest in encouraging the formation of stable households. Instead, the evidence shows that Proposition 8 undermines that state interest, because same-sex households have become less stable by the passage of Proposition 8. The inability to marry denies same-sex couples the benefits, including stability, attendant to marriage. Proponents failed to put forth any credible evidence that married opposite-sex households are made more stable through Proposition 8. FF 55. The only rational conclusion in light of the evidence is that Proposition 8 makes it less likely that California children will be raised in stable households. See FF 56.

None of the interests put forth by proponents relating to parents and children is advanced by Proposition 8; instead, the evidence shows Proposition 8 disadvantages families and their children.

PURPORTED INTEREST #4: PROTECTING THE FREEDOM OF THOSE WHO OPPOSE MARRIAGE FOR SAME–SEX COUPLES

Proponents next argue that Proposition 8 protects the First Amendment freedom of those who disagree with allowing marriage for couples of the same sex. Proponents argue that Proposition 8: (1) preserves "the prerogative and responsibility of parents to provide for the ethical and moral development and education of their own children"; and (2) accommodates "the First Amendment rights of individuals and institutions that oppose same-sex marriage on religious or moral grounds."

These purported interests fail as a matter of law. Proposition 8 does not affect any First Amendment right or responsibility of parents to educate their children. See *In re Marriage Cases*, 183 P.3d at 451–452. Californians are prevented from distinguishing between same-sex partners and opposite-sex spouses in public accommodations, as California antidiscrimination law requires identical treatment for same-sex unions and opposite-sex marriages. *Koebke v. Bernardo Heights Country Club*, 115 P.3d 1212, 1217–1218 (Cal. 2005). The evidence shows that Proposition 8 does nothing other than eliminate the right of same-sex couples to marry in California. Proposition 8 is not rationally related to an interest in protecting the rights of those opposed to same-sex couples because, as a matter of law, Proposition 8 does not affect the rights of those opposed to homosexuality or to marriage for couples of the same sex.

To the extent proponents argue that one of the rights of those morally opposed to same-sex unions is the right to prevent same-sex couples from marrying, as explained presently those individuals' moral views are an insufficient basis upon which to enact a legislative classification.

PURPORTED INTEREST #5: TREATING SAME–SEX COUPLES DIFFERENTLY FROM OPPOSITE–SEX COUPLES

Proponents argue that Proposition 8 advances a state interest in treating same-sex couples differently from opposite-sex couples by: (1) "[u]sing different names for different things"; (2) "[m]aintaining the flexibility to separately address the needs of different types of relationships"; (3) "[e]nsuring that California marriages are recognized in other jurisdictions"; and (4) "[c]onforming California's definition of marriage to federal law."

Here, proponents assume a premise that the evidence thoroughly rebutted: rather than being different, same-sex and opposite-sex unions are, for all purposes relevant to California law, exactly the same. The evidence shows conclusively that moral and religious views form the only basis for a belief that same-sex couples are different from opposite-sex couples. See FF 76–80. The evidence fatally undermines any purported state interest in treating couples differently; thus, these interests do not provide a rational basis supporting Proposition 8.

In addition, proponents appear to claim that Proposition 8 advances a state interest in easing administrative burdens associated with issuing and recognizing marriage licenses. Under precedents such as *Craig v. Boren,* "administrative ease and convenience" are not important government objectives. 429 U.S. 190, 198 (1976). Even assuming the state were to have an interest in administrative convenience, Proposition 8 actually creates an administrative burden on California because California must maintain a parallel institution for same-sex couples to provide the equivalent rights and benefits afforded to married couples. See FF 53. Domestic partnerships create an institutional scheme that must be regulated separately from marriage. Compare Cal. Fam. Code §§ 297–299.6 with Cal. Fam. Code §§ 300–536. California may determine whether to retain domestic partnerships or eliminate them in the absence of Proposition 8; the court presumes, however, that as long as Proposition 8 is in effect, domestic partnerships and the accompanying administrative burden will remain. Proposition 8 thus hinders rather than advances administrative convenience.

PURPORTED INTEREST #6: THE CATCHALL INTEREST

Finally, proponents assert that Proposition 8 advances "[a]ny other conceivable legitimate interests identified by the parties, amici, or the court at any stage of the proceedings." But proponents, amici and the court, despite ample opportunity and a full trial, have failed to identify any rational basis Proposition 8 could conceivably advance. Proponents, represented by able and energetic counsel, developed a full trial record in support of Proposition 8. The resulting evidence shows that Proposition 8 simply conflicts with the guarantees of the Fourteenth Amendment.

Many of the purported interests identified by proponents are nothing more than a fear or unarticulated dislike of same-sex couples. Those interests that are legitimate are unrelated to the classification drawn by Proposition 8. The evidence shows that, by every available metric, opposite-sex couples are not better than their same-sex counterparts; instead, as partners, parents and citizens, opposite-sex couples and same-sex couples are equal. Proposition 8 violates the Equal Protection Clause because it does not treat them equally.

A PRIVATE MORAL VIEW THAT SAME–SEX COUPLES ARE INFERIOR TO OPPOSITE–SEX COUPLES IS NOT A PROPER BASIS FOR LEGISLATION

In the absence of a rational basis, what remains of proponents' case is an inference, amply supported by evidence in the record, that Proposition 8 was premised on the belief that same-sex couples simply are not as good as opposite-sex couples. FF 78–80. Whether that belief is based on moral disapproval of homosexuality, animus towards gays and lesbians or simply a belief that a relationship between a man and a woman is inherently better than a relationship between two men or two women, this belief is not a proper basis on which to legislate. See *Romer*, 517 U.S. at 633; *Moreno*, 413 U.S. at 534; *Palmore v. Sidoti*, 466 U.S. 429, 433 (1984) ("[T]he Constitution cannot control [private biases] but neither can it tolerate them.").

The evidence shows that Proposition 8 was a hard-fought campaign and that the majority of California voters supported the initiative. See Background to Proposition 8 above, FF 79–80. The arguments surrounding Proposition 8 raise a question similar to that addressed in *Lawrence*, when the Court asked whether a majority of citizens could use the power of the state to enforce "profound and deep convictions accepted as ethical and moral principles" through the criminal code. 539 U.S. at 571. The question here is whether California voters can enforce those same principles through regulation of marriage licenses. They cannot. California's obligation is to treat its citizens equally, not to "mandate [its] own moral code." *Id.* (citing *Planned Parenthood of Southeastern Pa. v. Casey*, 505 U.S. 833 (1992)). "[M]oral disapproval, without any other asserted state interest," has never been a rational basis for legislation. *Lawrence*, 539 U.S. at 582 (O'Connor, J, concurring). Tradition alone cannot support legislation. See *Williams*, 399 U.S. at 239; *Romer*, 517 U.S. at 635; *Lawrence*, 539 U.S. at 579.

Proponents' purported rationales are nothing more than post-hoc justifications. While the Equal Protection Clause does not prohibit post-hoc rationales, they must connect to the classification drawn. Here, the purported state interests fit so poorly with Proposition 8 that they are irrational, as explained above. What is left is evidence that Proposition 8 enacts a moral view that there is something "wrong" with same-sex couples. See FF 78–80.

The evidence at trial regarding the campaign to pass Proposition 8 uncloaks the most likely explanation for its passage: a desire to advance the belief that opposite-sex couples are morally superior to same-sex couples. FF 79–80. The campaign relied heavily on negative stereotypes about gays and lesbians and focused on protecting children from inchoate threats vaguely associated with gays and lesbians. FF 79–80.

At trial, proponents' counsel attempted through cross-examination to show that the campaign wanted to protect children from learning about same-sex marriage in school. See [Plaintiffs' Exhibit] PX0390A Video, Ron Prentice Addressing Supporters of Proposition 8, Excerpt; (proponents' counsel to Katami: "But the fact is that what the Yes on 8 campaign was pointing at, is that kids would be taught about same-sex relationships in first and second grade; isn't that a fact, that that's what they were referring to?"). The evidence shows, however, that Proposition 8 played on a fear that exposure to homosexuality would turn children into homosexuals and that parents should dread having children who are not heterosexual. FF 79; [Plaintiffs' Exhibit] PX0099 Video, *It's Already Happened* (mother's expression of horror upon realizing her daughter now knows she can marry a princess).

The testimony of [historian] George Chauncey places the Protect Marriage campaign advertisements in historical context as echoing messages from previous campaigns to enact legal measures to disadvantage gays and lesbians. FF 77–80. The Protect Marriage campaign advertisements ensured California voters had these previous fear-inducing messages in mind. FF 80. The evidence at trial shows those fears to be completely unfounded. FF 68–73, 76–80.

Moral disapproval alone is an improper basis on which to deny rights to gay men and lesbians. The evidence shows conclusively that Proposition 8 enacts, without reason, a private moral view that same-sex couples are inferior to opposite-sex couples. FF 79–80; *Romer*, 517 U.S. at 634 ("[L]aws of the kind now before us raise the inevitable inference that the disadvantage imposed is born of animosity toward the class of persons affected."). Because Proposition 8 disadvantages gays and lesbians without any rational justification, Proposition 8 violates the Equal Protection Clause of the Fourteenth Amendment.

CONCLUSION

Proposition 8 fails to advance any rational basis in singling out gay men and lesbians for denial of a marriage license. Indeed, the evidence shows Proposition 8 does nothing more than enshrine in the California Constitution the notion that opposite-sex couples are superior to same-sex couples. Because California has no interest in discriminating against gay men and lesbians, and because Proposition 8 prevents California from fulfilling its constitutional obligation to provide marriages on an equal basis, the court concludes that Proposition 8 is unconstitutional.

REMEDIES

Plaintiffs have demonstrated by overwhelming evidence that Proposition 8 violates their due process and equal protection rights and that they will continue to suffer these constitutional violations until state officials cease enforcement of Proposition 8. California is able to issue marriage licenses to same-sex couples, as it has already issued 18,000 marriage licenses to same-sex couples and has not suffered any demonstrated harm as a result, see FF 64–66; moreover, California officials have chosen not to defend Proposition 8 in these proceedings.

Because Proposition 8 is unconstitutional under both the Due Process and Equal Protection Clauses, the court orders entry of judgment permanently enjoining its enforcement; prohibiting the official defendants from applying or enforcing Proposition 8 and directing the official defendants that all persons under their control or supervision shall not apply or enforce Proposition 8. The clerk is DIRECTED to enter judgment without bond in favor of plaintiffs and plaintiff-intervenors and against defendants and defendant-intervenors pursuant to FRCP 58.

IT IS SO ORDERED.

NOTES

1. In a highly unusual development, the state defendants involved in *Perry* refused to defend Proposition 8 on appeal to the Ninth Circuit, much as they had declined to defend its merits before the district court.[1] *See Perry v. Brown*, 52 Cal. 4th 1116, 1128–

---

1. Indeed, as the California Supreme Court noted in its recitation of the procedural history of the case, unlike the answers filed by other named state defendants in *Perry* that simply

32 (2011). Given that refusal, the defendant-intervenors who put on the substantive defense of Proposition 8 in the trial court maintained that they had standing under the U.S. Constitution to step into the shoes of the state parties to the case and challenge their loss on appeal. As part of its consideration of that question, the Ninth Circuit formally asked the California Supreme Court whether the proponents of Proposition 8 would have standing under state law to defend the measure when state officials whose responsibility it would ordinarily be to do so would not. *Perry v. Schwarzenegger*, 628 F.3d 1191, 1193 (9th Cir. 2011). Unanimously, the California Supreme Court said they do. *Perry v. Brown, supra.* The particularities of California's direct democracy rules aside, should the legal defense of a state's marriage laws be privatized this way? Are there circumstances—maybe these, maybe others—in which you would be concerned about private actors making decisions about the meaning and scope of family laws on behalf of the state? Do you think that allowing this defense might raise First Amendment or other concerns? What if the rule being defended were a state constitutional amendment recognizing a right to same-sex marriage?

2. Speaking generally, the trial court's opinion in *Perry* placed a great deal of emphasis on findings of fact, which it made after a trial, based on various forms of expert testimony. Consider the opinion's treatment of David Blankenhorn, one of the main witnesses supporting the constitutionality of Proposition 8.

> Proponents called David Blankenhorn as an expert on marriage, fatherhood and family structure. Blankenhorn received a BA in social studies from Harvard College and an MA in comparative social history from the University of Warwick in England.... [I]n 1987[,] [he] ... found[ed] the Institute for American Values, which he describes as "a nonpartisan think tank" that focuses primarily on "issues of marriage, family, and child well-being." ...

> Blankenhorn has published two books on the subjects of marriage, fatherhood and family structure: *Fatherless America: Confronting Our Most Urgent Social Problem* (HarperCollins 1995), and *The Future of Marriage* (Encounter Books 2006). Blankenhorn has edited four books about family structure and marriage, and has co-edited or co-authored several publications about marriage.

> Plaintiffs challenge Blankenhorn's qualifications as an expert because none of his relevant publications has been subject to a traditional peer-review process, has no degree in sociology, psychology or anthropology despite the importance of those fields to the subjects of marriage, fatherhood and family structure, and his study of the effects of same-sex marriage involved "reading articles and having conversations with people, and trying to be an informed person about it[.]" Plaintiffs argue that Blankenhorn's conclusions are not based on "objective data or discernible methodology," and that Blankenhorn's conclusions are instead based on his interpretation of selected quotations from articles and reports.

> The court permitted Blankenhorn to testify but reserved the question of the appropriate weight to give to Blankenhorn's opinions. The court now determines that Blankenhorn's testimony constitutes inadmissible opinion testimony that should be given essentially no weight.

> Federal Rule of Evidence 702 provides that a witness may be qualified as an expert "by knowledge, skill, experience, training, or education." The testimony may only be admitted if it "is based upon sufficient facts or data" and "is the product of reliable principles and methods." Id. Expert testimony must be both relevant and reliable, with a "basis in the knowledge and experience of the relevant discipline." *Kumho Tire Co. v. Carmichael*, 526 U.S. 137, 147, 149 (1999) (citing *Daubert v. Merrell Dow Pharm.*, 509 U.S. 579, 589, 592 (1993)).

"refused to take a position on the merits of plaintiffs' constitutional challenge and declined to defend the validity of Proposition 8," "[t]he answer filed by the [California] Attorney General" which "also declined to defend the initiative" "went further and affirmatively took the position that Proposition 8 is unconstitutional" under the federal Constitution. See Perry v. Brown, 52 Cal. 4th 1116, 1129 (2011).

While proponents correctly assert that formal training in the relevant disciplines and peer-reviewed publications are not dispositive of expertise, education is nevertheless important to ensure that "an expert, whether basing testimony upon professional studies or personal experience, employs in the courtroom the same level of intellectual rigor that characterizes the practice of an expert in the relevant field." *Kumho Tire* [*v. Carmichael*], 526 U.S. [137,] 152 [(1999)]. Formal training shows that a proposed expert adheres to the intellectual rigor that characterizes the field, while peer-reviewed publications demonstrate an acceptance by the field that the work of the proposed expert displays "at least the minimal criteria" of intellectual rigor required in that field. *Daubert v. Merrell Dow Pharm.*, 43 F.3d 1311, 1318 (9th Cir.1995) (on remand) ("*Daubert II*").

. . .

Blankenhorn offered opinions on the definition of marriage, the ideal family structure and potential consequences of state recognition of marriage for same-sex couples. None of Blankenhorn's opinions is reliable.

Blankenhorn's first opinion is that marriage is "a socially-approved sexual relationship between a man and a woman." According to Blankenhorn, the primary purpose of marriage is to "regulate filiation." Blankenhorn testified that the alternative and contradictory definition of marriage is that "marriage is fundamentally a private adult commitment." He described this definition as focused on "the tender feelings that spouses have for one another[.]" Blankenhorn agrees this "affective dimension" of marriage exists but asserts that marriage developed independently of affection.

Blankenhorn thus sets up a dichotomy for the definition of marriage: either marriage is defined as a socially approved sexual relationship between a man and a woman for the purpose of bearing and raising children biologically related to both spouses, or marriage is a private relationship between two consenting adults. Blankenhorn did not address the definition of marriage proposed by plaintiffs' expert [Historian Nancy] Cott, which subsumes Blankenhorn's dichotomy. Cott testified that marriage is "a couple's choice to live with each other, to remain committed to one another, and to form a household based on their own feelings about one another, and their agreement to join in an economic partnership and support one another in terms of the material needs of life." There is nothing in Cott's definition that limits marriage to its "affective dimension" as defined by Blankenhorn, and yet Cott's definition does not emphasize the biological relationship linking dependents to both spouses.

Blankenhorn relied on the quotations of others to define marriage and provided no explanation of the meaning of the passages he cited or their sources. Blankenhorn's mere recitation of text in evidence does not assist the court in understanding the evidence because reading, as much as hearing, "is within the ability and experience of the trier of fact." *Beech Aircraft Corp. v. United States*, 51 F.3d 834, 842 (9th Cir.1995).

Blankenhorn testified that his research has led him to conclude there are three universal rules that govern marriage: (1) the rule of opposites (the "man/woman" rule); (2) the rule of two; and (3) the rule of sex. Blankenhorn explained that there are "no or almost no exceptions" to the rule of opposites, despite some instances of ritualized same-sex relationships in some cultures. Blankenhorn explained that despite the widespread practice of polygamy across many cultures, the rule of two is rarely violated, because even within a polygamous marriage, "each marriage is separate." Finally, Blankenhorn could only hypothesize instances in which the rule of sex would be violated, including where "he's in prison for life, he's married, and he is not in a system in which any conjugal visitation is allowed."

Blankenhorn's interest and study on the subjects of marriage, fatherhood and family structure are evident from the record, but nothing in the record other than the "bald assurance" of Blankenhorn, *Daubert II*, 43 F.3d at 1316, suggests that Blankenhorn's investigation into marriage has been conducted to the "same level of intellectual rigor" characterizing the practice of anthropologists, sociologists or psychologists. See *Kumho Tire*, 526 U.S. at 152. Blankenhorn gave no explanation of the methodology that led him to his definition of marriage other than his review of others' work. The court concludes that Blankenhorn's proposed definition of marriage is "connected to existing data only by the *ipse dixit*" of Blankenhorn and accordingly rejects it.

Blankenhorn's second opinion is that a body of evidence supports the conclusion that children raised by their married, biological parents do better on average than children raised in other environments. The evidence Blankenhorn relied on to support his conclusion compares children raised by married, biological parents with children raised by single parents, unmarried mothers, step families and cohabiting parents.

Blankenhorn's conclusion that married biological parents provide a better family form than married non-biological parents is not supported by the evidence on which he relied because the evidence does not, and does not claim to, compare biological to non-biological parents. Blankenhorn did not in his testimony consider any study comparing children raised by their married biological parents to children raised by their married adoptive parents. Blankenhorn did not testify about a study comparing children raised by their married biological parents to children raised by their married parents who conceived using an egg or sperm donor. The studies Blankenhorn relied on compare various family structures and do not emphasize biology. The studies may well support a conclusion that parents' marital status may affect child outcomes. The studies do not, however, support a conclusion that the biological connection between a parent and his or her child is a significant variable for child outcomes. The court concludes that "there is simply too great an analytical gap between the data and the opinion proffered." Blankenhorn's reliance on biology is unsupported by evidence, and the court therefore rejects his conclusion that a biological link between parents and children influences children's outcomes.

Blankenhorn's third opinion is that recognizing same-sex marriage will lead to the deinstitutionalization of marriage. Blankenhorn described deinstitutionalization as a process through which previously stable patterns and rules forming an institution (like marriage) slowly erode or change. Blankenhorn identified several manifestations of deinstitutionalization: out-of-wedlock childbearing, rising divorce rates, the rise of non-marital cohabitation, increasing use of assistive reproductive technologies and marriage for same-sex couples. To the extent Blankenhorn believes that same-sex marriage is both a cause and a symptom of deinstitutionalization, his opinion is tautological. Moreover, no credible evidence supports Blankenhorn's conclusion that same-sex marriage could lead to the other manifestations of deinstitutionalization.

Blankenhorn relied on sociologist Andrew Cherlin and sociologist Norval Glen to support his opinion that same-sex marriage may speed the deinstitutionalization of marriage. Neither of these sources supports Blankenhorn's conclusion that same-sex marriage will further deinstitutionalize marriage, as neither source claims same-sex marriage as a cause of divorce or single parenthood....

. . .

Blankenhorn was unwilling to answer many questions directly on cross-examination and was defensive in his answers. Moreover, much of his testimony contradicted his opinions. Blankenhorn testified on cross-examination that studies show children of adoptive parents do as well or better than children of biological parents. Blankenhorn agreed that children raised by same-sex couples would benefit if their parents were permitted to marry. Blankenhorn also testified he wrote and agrees with the statement "I believe that today the principle of equal human dignity must apply to gay and lesbian persons. In that sense, insofar as we are a nation founded on this principle, we would be more American on the day we permitted same-sex marriage than we were the day before."

Blankenhorn stated he opposes marriage for same-sex couples because it will weaken the institution of marriage, despite his recognition that at least thirteen positive consequences would flow from state recognition of marriage for same-sex couples, including: (1) by increasing the number of married couples who might be interested in adoption and foster care, same-sex marriage might well lead to fewer children growing up in state institutions and more children growing up in loving adoptive and foster families; and (2) same-sex marriage would signify greater social acceptance of homosexual love and the worth and validity of same-sex intimate relationships.

Blankenhorn's opinions are not supported by reliable evidence or methodology and Blankenhorn failed to consider evidence contrary to his view in presenting his testimony. The court therefore finds the opinions of Blankenhorn to be unreliable and entitled to essentially no weight.

Perry v. Schwarzenegger, 704 F. Supp. 2d 921, 945–50 (N.D. Cal. 2010). Is peer review of scientific studies important? Is it fail-safe?

3. On February 23, 2011, U.S. Attorney General Eric H. Holder, Jr., informed Congressional leadership of the position that the Department of Justice would be taking in two then-pending cases, *Pedersen v. OPM*, 2011 WL 176764 (D. Conn. 2011), and *Windsor v. United States*, 797 F. Supp.2d 320 (S.D.N.Y. 2011), involving challenges to Section 3 of the federal Defense of Marriage Act (DOMA), 1 U.S.C. § 7, defining marriage as a union between a man and a woman for purposes of federal law. Letter from Eric J. Holder, Jr., Attorney Gen. of the United States, to John A. Boehner, Speaker of the U.S. House of Representatives (Feb. 23, 2011). Both cases, the Attorney General explained, called upon "the Department to take an affirmative position on the level of scrutiny that should be applied to DOMA Section 3 in a circuit without binding precedent on the issue." *Id.* at 2. He continued: "the President and I have concluded . . . classifications based on sexual orientation warrant heightened scrutiny and that, as applied to same-sex couples legally married under state law, Section 3 of DOMA is unconstitutional." *Id.*

In the course of explaining this action, the Attorney General described its implications for federal law this way:

Notwithstanding [the] determination [that "classifications based on sexual orientation should be subject to a heightened standard of scrutiny[,]" *id.* at 5, and also "that Section 3 of DOMA, as applied to legally married same-sex couples, fails to meet that standard and is therefore unconstitutional[,]" *id.*,] the President has informed me that Section 3 will continue to be enforced by the Executive Branch. To that end, the President has instructed Executive agencies to continue to comply with Section 3 of DOMA, consistent with the Executive's obligation to take care that the laws be faithfully executed, unless and until Congress repeals Section 3 or the judicial branch renders a definitive verdict against the law's constitutionality. This course of action respects the actions of the prior Congress that enacted DOMA, and it recognizes the judiciary as the final arbiter of the constitutional claims raised.

As you know, the Department has a longstanding practice of defending the constitutionality of duly-enacted statutes if reasonable arguments can be made in their defense, a practice that accords the respect appropriately due to a coequal branch of government. However, the Department in the past has declined to defend statutes despite the availability of professionally responsible arguments, in part because the Department does not consider every plausible argument to be a "reasonable" one. "[D]ifferent cases can raise very different issues with respect to statutes of doubtful constitutional validity," and thus there are "a variety of factors that bear on whether the Department will defend the constitutionality of a statute." Letter to Hon. Orrin G. Hatch from Assistant Attorney General Andrew Fois at 7 (Mar. 22, 1996). This is the rare case where the proper course is to forgo the defense of this statute. Moreover, the Department has declined to defend a statute "in cases in which it is manifest that the President has concluded that the statute is unconstitutional," as is the case here. Seth P. Waxman, *Defending Congress*, 79 N.C. L. Rev. 1073, 1083 (2001).

Letter from Eric J. Holder, Jr., Attorney Gen. of the United States, to John A. Boehner, Speaker of the U.S. House of Representatives 5 (Feb. 23, 2011). The President's decision to continue enforcing DOMA's definition of marriage as man and woman as husband and wife for purposes of federal law sits in an uneasy relation to his decision not to defend the federal law where he has decided not to, because of the conclusion that the law violates the federal constitution. In terms of the states' traditional authority to regulate marriage, how does the President's decision look? Does it respect that traditional authority? Undermine it? Both? How?

Several courts have already cited the Holder Memo with approval. *See In re* Balas, 449 B.R. 567, 576 (Bankr. C.D. Cal. 2011); *In re* Somers, 448 B.R. 677, 682 (Bankr. S.D.N.Y. 2011).

4. A summary of statistics released by the U.S. Census Bureau in September 2011 indicates that, based on "revised estimates from the 2010 Census, there were 131,729 same-sex married couple households and 514,735 same-sex unmarried partner households in the United States." Press Release, U.S. Census Bureau, Census Bureau Releases Estimates of Same–Sex Married Couples (Sept. 27, 2011), *available at* http://www.census.gov/newsroom/releases/archives/2010_census/cb11–cn181.html. The "technical paper" accompanying the summary additionally detailed:

The 2010 Census marks the first time that decennial census data will be shown for same-sex couple households by whether the couples reported themselves as living together as spouses or unmarried partners. . . .

Because of the relatively small number of same-sex marriages actually occurring in the United States (estimated at less than 50,000)[3] and the changes over the decade in state marriage laws, the data warrant careful analysis and evaluation. . . .

According to Census 2010, the total number of same-sex couple households was 901,997, representing less than 1 percent (0.773 percent) of all households in the United States. Data from Census 2000 tabulated 594,391 households or 0.564 percent of all households. Overall, census data show an increase of 52 percent in the number (307,606) of same-sex households over the past ten years.[5]

A greater percentage increase is observed among same-sex unmarried partner households (62 percent) than among same-sex spousal households (38 percent) since 2000. Unmarried partner households increased by 211,606 compared with an increase of 96,000 in spousal households. Overall, about 4 out of every 10 same-sex couple households both in 2000 and in 2010 were spousal households.

When examining these data, it should be noted that no state issued marriage licenses to same-sex couples in 2000. However, some households may have reported themselves as living together as spouses because they were in a civil union or domestic partnership, had made marriage-like commitments in a ceremony (although not sanctioned by state law), or had determined that this category best expressed their current household relationship. This count may have also included opposite-sex couples who were inadvertently included in the published Census 2000 tables as same-sex couples. . . .

By 2010, the population of same-sex spousal households also included those who were legally married either in the United States or foreign countries and were residents of the United States by the time of the April 2010 Census. It also may have included those couples in registered domestic partnerships or civil unions

---

3. By 2010, there were estimated to be as many as 50,000 same-sex marriages performed in the United States and possibly up another 30,000 performed in other countries to U.S. residents. In addition, there were possibly up to another 85,000 same-sex couples in civil unions or domestic partnerships according to estimates prepared by researchers in the Williams Institute of the UCLA School of Law. http://www3.law.ucla.edu/williamsinstitute/pdf/Pressrelease 2.24.pdf.

5. The data in this paper for Census 2000 represent the first time data for 2000 are shown for same-sex couple households separating the aggregate totals into unmarried partner households and spousal households for the Nation and individual states.

who found the relationship options limited on the form in describing their current living arrangements. . . .

Although same-sex couple households were less than one percent (0.773 percent) of households in the United States in 2010, distinct geographic patterns are evident. The pattern observed ... for all same-sex couple households shows states with above average percentages are found along the east and west coasts of the United States and in the southwestern part of the nation. When looking at state-level data for same-sex unmarried partner households, the geographic distribution for these households ... follows a similar pattern to the one found for all households. This is to be expected as 61 percent of same-sex couple households in 2010 were unmarried partner households.

A different pattern appears for same-sex spousal households. . . . [A] number of states reporting as same-sex spousal households with above average percentages are in the southern half of the nation ranging from Georgia to New Mexico. In addition, all of these states have explicit laws or state constitutions prohibiting same-sex marriages. None of these states have experienced legislative changes akin to those occurring in the east and west coasts of the United States in the past decade that would help explain the above average percentages of same-sex spousal households. . . .

. . .

Martin O'Connell & Sarah Feliz, *Same–Sex Couple Household Statistics from the 2010 Census* 3–8 (U.S. Census Bureau Soc., Econ & Hous. Statistics Div., Working Paper No. 2011–26, 2011), *available at* http://www.census.gov/hhes/samesex/files/ss-report. doc.

e. TRANSSEXUALS AND MARRIAGE

M.T. v. J.T.

Superior Court of New Jersey, Appellate Division, 1976.
140 N.J.Super. 77, 355 A.2d 204.

■ HANDLER, J.A.D.

The case started inauspiciously enough when plaintiff M.T. filed a simple complaint in the Juvenile and Domestic Relations Court for support and maintenance. The legal issue sharpened dramatically when defendant J.T. interposed the defense that M.T. was a male and that their marriage was void. Following a hearing the trial judge determined that plaintiff was a female and that defendant was her husband, and there being no fraud, ordered defendant to pay plaintiff $50 a week support. Notice of appeal was then filed by defendant.

. . . M.T. testified that she was born a male. While she knew that she had male sexual organs she did not know whether she also had female organs. As a youngster she did not participate in sports and at an early age became very interested in boys. At the age of 14 she began dressing in a feminine manner and later began dating men. She had no real adjustment to make because throughout her life she had always felt that she was a female.

Plaintiff first met defendant in 1964 and told him about her feelings about being a woman. Sometime after that she began to live with defendant. In 1970 she started to go to Dr. Charles L. Ihlenfeld to discuss the possibility of having an operation so that she could "be physically a woman." In 1971, upon the doctor's advice, she went to a surgeon who agreed to operate. In May of that year she underwent surgery for the removal of male sex organs and construction of a vagina. Defendant paid for the operation. Plaintiff then applied to the State of New York to have her birth certificate changed.

On August 11, 1972, over a year after the operation, plaintiff and defendant went through a ceremonial marriage in New York State and then moved to Hackensack. They lived as husband and wife and had intercourse. Defendant supported plaintiff for over two years when, in October 1974, he left their home. He has not supported plaintiff since.

Dr. Ihlenfeld, plaintiff's medical doctor with a specialty in gender identity, was accepted as an expert in the field of medicine and transsexualism. A transsexual, in the opinion of this expert, was "a person who discovers sometime, usually very early in life, that there is a great discrepancy between the physical genital anatomy and the person's sense of self-identity as a male or as a female.... [T]he transsexual is one who has a conflict between physical anatomy and psychological identity or psychological sex." Usually sexual anatomy was "normal" but for some reason transsexuals did not see themselves as members of the sex their anatomy seemed to indicate. According to Dr. Ihlenfeld, there are different theories to explain the origin of that conflict. There was, however, "very little disagreement" on the fact that gender identity generally is established "very, very firmly, almost immediately, by the age of 3 to 4 years." He defined gender identity as "a sense, a total sense of self as being masculine or female ..."; it "pervades one's entire concept of one's place in life, of one's place in society and in point of fact the actual facts of the anatomy are really secondary...."

... Dr. Ihlenfeld diagnosed [plaintiff] as a transsexual. He knew of no way to alter her sense of her own feminine gender identity in order to agree with her male body, and the only treatment available to her was to alter the body to conform with her sense of psych[ic] gender identity. That regimen consisted of hormone treatment and sex reassignment surgery. Dr. Ihlenfeld recommended such an operation and treated plaintiff both before and after it.

The examination of plaintiff before the operation showed that she had a penis, scrotum and testicles. After the operation she did not have those organs but had a vagina and labia which were "adequate for sexual intercourse" and could function as any female vagina, that is, for "traditional penile/vaginal intercourse." The "artificial vagina" constructed by such surgery was a cavity, the walls of which are lined initially by the skin of the penis, often later taking on the characteristics of normal vaginal mucosa; the vagina, though at a somewhat different angle, was not really different from a natural vagina in size, capacity and "the feeling of the walls around it." Plaintiff had no uterus or cervix, but her vagina had a "good cosmetic appearance" and was "the same as a normal female vagina after a hysterectomy." Dr. Ihlenfeld had seen plaintiff since the operation and she never complained to him that she had difficulty having intercourse. So far as he knew, no one had tested plaintiff to find out what chromosomes she had. He knew that plaintiff had had silicone injections in her breasts; he had treated her continuously with female hormones to demasculinize her body and to feminize it at the same time. In the doctor's opinion plaintiff was a female; he no longer considered plaintiff to be a male since she could not function as a male sexually either for purposes of "recreation or procreation."

. . .

Defendant called as an expert witness Dr. T, a medical doctor who was defendant's adoptive father. Over plaintiff's objection he was allowed to testify as an expert. Dr. T classified sex at birth according to sexual anatomy. He described a female as "a person who has female organs in an anatomical sense, who has a vagina and uterus and ovaries or at least has had them."

The witness had heard all of the prior testimony and he said that in his opinion plaintiff was still a male because she did not have female organs. . . .

The trial judge made careful findings of fact on this evidential record. . . .

. . . The judge ruled that plaintiff was of the female psychic gender all her life and that her anatomical change through surgery required the conclusion that she was a female at the time of the marriage ceremony. He stated:

> It is the opinion of the court that if the psychological choice of a person is medically sound, not a mere whim, and irreversible sex reassignment surgery has been performed, society has no right to prohibit the transsexual from leading a normal life. Are we to look upon this person as an exhibit in a circus side show? What harm has said person done to society? The entire area of transsexualism is repugnant to the nature of many persons within our society. However, this should not govern the legal acceptance of a fact. . . .

. . .

We accept—and it is not disputed—as the fundamental premise in this case that a lawful marriage requires the performance of a ceremonial marriage of two persons of the opposite sex, a male and a female. . . .

. . .

The issue must then be confronted whether the marriage between a male and a postoperative transsexual, who has surgically changed her external sexual anatomy from male to female, is to be regarded as a lawful marriage between a man and a woman.

An English case, *Corbett v. Corbett*, 2 W.L.R. 1306, 2 All E.R. 33 (P.D.A. 1970) appears to be the only reported decision involving the validity of marriage of a true postoperative transsexual and a male person. The judge there held that the transsexual had failed to prove that she had changed her sex from male to female. The court subscribed to the opinion of the medical witnesses that "the biological sexual constitution of an individual is fixed at birth (at the latest), and cannot be changed, either by the natural development of organs of the opposite sex, or by medical or surgical means. The respondent's operation, therefore, cannot affect her true sex." . . .

. . .

The English court believed, we feel incorrectly, that an anatomical change of genitalia in the case of a transsexual cannot "affect her true sex." Its conclusion was rooted in the premise that "true sex" was required to be ascertained even for marital purposes by biological criteria. In the case of a transsexual following surgery, however, according to the expert testimony presented here, the dual tests of anatomy and gender are more significant. On this evidential demonstration, therefore, we are impelled to the conclusion that for marital purposes if the anatomical or genital features of a genuine transsexual are made to conform to the person's gender, psyche or psychological sex, then identity by sex must be governed by the congruence of these standards.

Implicit in the reasoning underpinning our determination is the tacit but valid assumption of the lower court and the experts upon whom reliance was placed that for purposes of marriage under the circumstances of this case, it is the sexual capacity of the individual which must be scrutinized.

Sexual capacity or sexuality in this frame of reference requires the coalescence of both the physical ability and the psychological and emotional orientation to engage in sexual intercourse as either a male or a female.

Other decisions touching the marital status of a putative transsexual are not especially helpful. *Anonymous v. Anonymous*, 325 N.Y.S.2d 499 (Sup. Ct. 1971), cited by defendant, held a marriage a nullity, but there the two persons had never had sexual intercourse and had never lived together. Although it was claimed that respondent was a transsexual and had had an operation to remove his male organs after the marriage, there was no medical evidence of this. In *B. v. B.*, [355 N.Y.S.2d 712 (1974),] a female transsexual had had a hysterectomy and mastectomy but had not received any male organs and was incapable of performing sexually as a male. He had then married a normal female who later sued for an annulment on the ground that he had defrauded her by not informing her of his transsexualism and of the operation. The judge there held that even if defendant were a male and trapped in the body of a female, his attempted sex reassignment surgery had not successfully released him from that body.

Anonymous v. Weiner, 270 N.Y.S.2d 319 (Sup. Ct. 1966), sustained the refusal by the New York City Board of Health to amend a sex designation on a birth certificate. The court acquiesced in the view of the administrative agency that "male-to-female transsexuals are still chromosomally males while ostensibly females" and that the desire of the transsexual for "concealment of a change of sex . . . is outweighed by the public interest for protection against fraud." 270 N.Y.S.2d at 322. To reiterate, the chromosomal test of sex in this context is unhelpful. The potential for fraud, feared by the court, moreover, is effectively countered by the apt observation of the trial judge here: "The transsexual is not committing a fraud upon the public. In actuality she is doing her utmost to remove any false facade." Further, we note the *Weiner* case was sharply criticized in *In re Anonymous, supra*, which ordered a change to a female name for a postoperative transsexual. The court concluded that the chromosomal test recommended by the New York Academy of Medicine and adopted by the court in *Weiner* was unrealistic and inhumane. . . .

. . .

In sum, it has been established that an individual suffering from the condition of transsexualism is one with a disparity between his or her genitalia or anatomical sex and his or her gender, that is, the individual's strong and consistent emotional and psychological sense of sexual being. A transsexual in a proper case can be treated medically by certain supportive measures and through surgery to remove and replace existing genitalia with sex organs which will coincide with the person's gender. If such sex reassignment surgery is successful and the postoperative transsexual is, by virtue of medical treatment, thereby possessed of the full capacity to function sexually as a male or female, as the case may be, we perceive no legal barrier, cognizable social taboo, or reason grounded in public policy to prevent that person's identification at least for purposes of marriage to the sex finally indicated.

. . .

. . . The judgment of the court is therefore affirmed.

Brandi Grissom, *Two El Paso Women Legally Married*

Tex. Trib., May 14, 2010.*

Their love story started with fuschia fingernail polish and black leather.

Therese Bur got her first glimpse of Sabrina Hill—a tall, dark-haired woman decked out in leather gear and flashing those nails—at about 2 a.m. at an Arizona gas station.... One date later, their future was sealed.

That was 17 years ago. "Sabrina was the first person who just listened to who I was and accepted me for who I was," Bur says. "As strange as we are, that's important."

The two women are hardly the typical Texas married couple, yet their union has been blessed by the courts. That's because Hill is a transgender female: She was born with both male and female genitalia, and her father ordered surgery to make her a male. Three decades later, she would surgically reverse his decision. Today, Hill's driver's license and a judge's order say she's a woman—but her birth certificate and now her marriage license say she's a man. The county clerk in San Antonio gave Hill and Bur a license to wed, putting the couple at the center of a decade-long fight over whether unions like theirs are legal in a state that has overwhelmingly opposed same-sex marriage in polls and at the ballot box.

In a complex and ironic twist of Texas politics, a 1999 conservative court ruling actually sanctions unions like Hill and Bur's—though they are, by their own definition, a gay married couple. That's because the ruling, which sought to establish gender as unchangeable, established a person's birth certificate as the legal document that defines his or her gender, regardless of later sex-change operations. And so it had the odd side effect of allowing transgender homosexuals to legally marry. It's a conundrum that dismays social conservatives, confounds some county clerks and has advocates for gay and transgender rights calling for clarification. In perhaps their sole point of consensus on social issues, some conservatives and gay and transgender advocates agree, for different reasons, that people like Hill shouldn't be allowed to identify as one gender in daily life but another when getting married.

"It's all screwy, and the reason why it's screwy is because people are worried about same-sex marriage," says Houston lawyer Phyllis Randolph Frye, a transgender woman who represented the plaintiffs in the 1999 case.

For all the handwringing by politicians and courts over the anatomy and sexual orientation of married couples in Texas, the saga of Hill and Bur is infinitely more complicated and agonizing. Raised as a boy but never quite man enough for her father, Hill endured decades of abuse at the hands of those she expected to love and protect her. After discovering at age 28 that she had female internal organs, she came to terms with her identity and eventually found someone who accepted and loved her. That person happened to be a woman. In the ultimate irony of an arduous life, Hill is now legally married to a woman solely because of the gender on her birth certificate—the one she could never truly accept.

Frye, a female who was born a male, represented Christie Lee Littleton in the case that led to the court's 1999 ruling. After having sex-change surgery and legally changing her name from Lee Cavazos to Christie Lee

---

* The source can be found at: www.texastribune.org/texas-newspaper/texas-news/some-gay-marriages-legal-in-texas/.

Cavazos, she had married Jonathon Mark Littleton in 1989. He knew about her past, and Frye says the two were a happy couple until Mark died in 1996. Littleton filed a wrongful death suit against the doctors who attended to her husband, but the insurance company in the case argued Littleton could not sue as a surviving spouse because her birth certificate said she was a male. The Littletons' marriage, they argued, was invalid in Texas.

In the late 1990s, when Littleton came before the 4th Court of Appeals of Texas, there wasn't much case law to guide judges on transgender marriage, so the court looked to a 1970 case from England. . . . Once a male, always a male, the court ruled.

Chief Justice Phil Hardberger . . . wrote the appeals court's opinion in the Littleton case. The decision, he said, involved a deeper philosophical and legal question than simply determining when a man is a man and a woman is a woman: "Can a physician change the gender of a person with a scalpel, drugs and counseling, or is a person's gender immutably fixed by our Creator at birth?"

. . . Taking a cue from the English case, the court ruled that for purposes of marriage in Texas, a person's gender was determined at birth. No surgery could change that. "There are some things we cannot will into being. They just are," Hardberger wrote. "We hold, as a matter of law, that Christie Littleton is a male."

"The decision essentially said, for the purposes of marriage, Ms. Littleton is a vaginaed male. Stupid," Frye says. Frye believes the decision was predicated on the idea that homosexuals who wanted to get married would have sex-change operations so that they could get around laws prohibiting gay marriage. But what kind of crazy person, she asks, would have their body cut up just so they could get hitched? . . . [Frye] . . . appealed the Littleton decision first to the Texas Supreme Court and then to the U.S. Supreme Court. Both rejected the case, and so it stood. To get a marriage license in Texas, a couple would have to present one birth certificate with an "F" and one with an "M," no matter what surgical procedures or hormone treatments they'd had or what their driver's licenses said. The point seemed clear: Marriage in Texas should be between a man and a woman.

. . . Less than a year later, a Houston couple armed with "M" and "F" birth certificates and a copy of Hardberger's ruling went to the Harris County clerk for a marriage license. Robin and Jessica Wicks—the latter a male-to-female transsexual—were turned away by the court clerk. . . . [T]hey sought Frye's help[.] . . .

Frye and the Wickses held a press conference in front of the Bexar County clerk's office[.] . . . The clerk accepted the two women's birth certificates and gave them a marriage license. Newspapers across the state wrote about the legal gay nuptials. "Even though it looks like a duck and sounds like a duck and their genitals match, they're opposite sex for purposes of marriage," Frye says.

Since then, Bexar County Clerk Gerry Rickhoff has issued about two licenses per year to transgender couples, he says. "God has a sense of humor—you know what I mean? So I'm open to variations," Rickhoff says. As far as he's concerned, the Hardberger ruling makes granting transgender couples licenses to wed an unambiguous issue. "You are what you are by your birth, and so be it," he says.

State Rep. Warren Chisum, R–Pampa, the author of the 2005 constitutional amendment that banned same-sex marriage in Texas, believes, as many Texans do, that sinful men and woman choose homosexuality and God chooses gender. So the case of Hill and Bur presents something of a Hobson's choice. Prohibiting both gay marriage and legal recognition of sex changes means accepting something potentially even less acceptable: the gay marriage of transsexuals.

Although the Wicks and Hill–Bur unions follow the strict interpretation of the court's ruling, Chisum says it's clearly not what the justices had in mind. "You can't have it both ways, and I know that's what they're trying to do," he says. Hardberger, in his ruling, suggested legislators should specify in the law guidelines for transsexuals and marriage. But Chisum says the solution to preventing marriages that look like same-sex unions is not a legislative one. "I can't write the law for what everybody changes [themselves] to. That would be even more confusing," he says.

In Chisum's view, the fix is for judges to stop granting legal recognition to people who have sex-change operations, which would prevent them from getting documents like driver's licenses that identify them as a gender other than what's on their birth certificate. "You're either born as man or you're born as a woman, and you can't change that," he says. Because he doesn't believe medical procedures can change a person's gender, Chisum says he considers the Hill–Bur union a heterosexual one. "I'm pretty sure it won't last long," he says.

Conservatives like Chisum aren't the only ones with concerns about transgender marriages. Chuck Smith, director of Equality Texas, a gay rights advocacy group, says using the ruling as a loophole to get a same-sex marriage license is not entirely popular among transgender advocates. Many, he says, believe that people who have sex reassignment surgery should demand to be recognized as the man or woman they have become. "If the state allows us to change gender marker documents, then why don't we use the most current status as opposed to using that for some things and using an original birth certificate for other things?" Smith asks. Using more than one gender identity depending on the circumstance, he says, just confuses matters.

Confused is how Valerie Sanchez, the deputy clerk in El Paso County, felt when Hill and Bur came into the courthouse to apply for a marriage license in April. Hill presented a birth certificate with an "M." She also gave the clerk a driver's license that said "F" and a judge's order changing her name from Virgil to Sabrina. Bur's birth certificate and driver's license identified her as a woman, too. The state statute outlining identification documents that can be used to obtain a marriage license doesn't give priority to any of the numerous types of documentation, and it doesn't provide direction for clerks in cases in which the gender information on the various documents is conflicting. Could they legally issue a marriage license to two people who seemed to be women based on a birth certificate that indicated one of them was, at least initially, a male? "It's the first time we've come across this," Sanchez says.

At the request of Sanchez's boss, El Paso County Attorney Jo Anne Bernal asked Texas Attorney General Greg Abbott to weigh in and issue an opinion on which document should take precedence in decisions about granting marriage licenses. "Sometimes we get boring issues," says assistant county attorney Holly Lytle. "This was not a boring issue." Abbott hasn't yet issued an opinion.

Meanwhile, Hill and Bur found out from an El Paso television reporter about the county clerk in San Antonio who gives marriage licenses to transgender couples. "We said, 'You know what? We're going to get married, and they can't stop it,' " Hill says. They cooked up a roast for the road, packed up the car and headed east on Interstate 10. "Monday morning we were at the courthouse," Hill says. "They were the nicest people in the world." Not only did the clerks in Rickhoff's office grant the couple a marriage license, but they waived the 72–hour waiting period and the $40 fee.

For Hill and Bur, getting married was about more than a public declaration of their lifelong commitment to each other or making a statement about equal rights. The two have been living for years in poverty. They live in the house they've been building in rural Hudspeth County, just east of El Paso. They can't afford a hot water heater, and recently they've had trouble finding a way to pay Bur's medical bills. If they were legally married, though, Hill could draw more monthly benefits from the Veterans Administration (she served in the Army), and Bur could get health insurance. After the El Paso clerk turned down their request for a marriage license, Bur says she was despondent, ready to give up. "I thought maybe we should just continue on in poverty," she says. "It's not fun, but we can do this." Hill told her to have faith.

Hill knows about faith. That's what's kept her fighting through a lifetime of abuse because of her ambiguous gender identity. Hill wouldn't find out her true nature and history for three decades after her father ordered the surgery that aimed to make her a male. Her inability to live up to the role tormented her father, who in turn tormented her. . . . [S]he says[:] "This was a guy, so stereotypical, and if I didn't act like this growing up . . . then I was beaten within an inch of my life."

By age 4, Hill says, she knew what she felt inside her mind and body didn't match what was on the outside. In 1962, when she was 12, teachers at school started sending her to doctors and psychologists. They told her parents Hill might be more girl than boy. "I almost got killed over that one," she says. Her father was the first person to call her a faggot. Her mother often told her she wished that Hill had died in the car crash that took her younger sister's life. "There was a lot of abuse."

When she turned 18, Hill joined the Army. Though her father had died when she was 15, Hill says she remained on a mission to prove to him she could be the man he wanted—even tougher. It wasn't long, though, before her peers saw something different. In the shower, they could see the scar from her surgery as a baby. When she sang, her soprano voice rang out above the tenors and basses of her fellow soldiers. They harassed her and threatened her with "blanket parties" and gang rape. "I was more afraid of my buddies—[who] I was sworn to lay my life down for—than of going to war," she says. Hill was medically discharged in 1971, though she later returned as a reservist and directed a communications team.

After her discharge, Hill began seminary school to become a pastor in the Seventh-day Adventist Church. In 1978, during her first year of studies, doctors tested her for kidney stones. An ultrasound didn't show any, but it did reveal partially developed ovaries and fallopian tubes inside her abdomen. The discovery left her confused again, so she went to the college chaplain. "I said, 'What do I do here? I know how the Adventist Church feels about women—they're not supposed to preach at all. Now I've got these parts. What do I do?' I asked him to pray with me and pray for me for divine guidance." The chaplain told her she'd be kicked out of the missionary school, and she was told to leave within a week.

So she left for Germany to begin her transformation with hormones and therapy. A year later, she returned to the United States, looking much like a woman but still with male genitalia. Rather than having expensive sex reassignment surgery in the United States, Hill went to a Mexican doctor they called "The Butcher." She was so "sick and tired of looking at something that should not be there" that she told him to just lop off the offending appendage. She has been living as a woman since 1979.

When Bur walked into that Arizona gas station in 1993, Hill said she found her greatest defender and friend. In Hill, Bur found acceptance and faith. "Sabrina said, 'Don't let anyone tell you you're not a child of God,'" Bur says. "I was just lucky I had my very own preacher come and put that in my ear."

Hill and Bur realize they're not going to make everyone happy with their decision. They never have made everyone happy. "I suppose some people feel like we're sellouts—'Oh, you're taking easy way out,'" Bur says of the criticism from gay and transgender advocates. "There's nothing easy about living in Sabrina's shoes, because she has had prejudice from everyone, including from her parents. There's no easy way out."

They aren't the kind of couple who flaunt their love, Hill says, and they don't expect others to accept their lifestyle. But when they went into the San Antonio courtroom to exchange vows, Bur and Hill say they were greeted with graciousness. The judge who performed the ceremony even told Hill to kiss her bride. Hill calls it vindication. They spent another day in San Antonio and toured the Alamo before heading back to El Paso and presenting their marriage license to the Veterans Administration. "It lists me as the husband even though, believe me, with my clothes off, I don't look like a husband," Hill says. Officials there accepted the license, signed Bur up for benefits, and even congratulated the women. "It should help a lot," Bur says. "We can finish building our house, and we can put in a hot water heater."

NOTES

1. The opinion in *M.T. v. J.T.* indicates that plaintiff's capacity to perform sexually as a female was crucial to the court's decision. Does this mean that if a male is impotent or castrated, he should not be permitted to contract a valid marriage with a female?

2. All states except Ohio and Tennessee now recognize a change in legal sex status following a sex change operation based on a doctor's sworn statement. *See* TENN. CODE ANN. § 68–3–203(d); *In re Ladrach*, 513 N.E.2d 828 (Ohio Prob. Ct. 1987); *see also* John A. Fisher, *Sex Determination for Federal Purposes: Is Transsexual Immigration via Marriage Permissible Under the Defense of Marriage Act?*, 10 MICH. J. GENDER & L. 237 (2004). But not all states recognize the change for purposes of marriage. *See, e.g., Kantaras v. Kantaras*, 884 So. 2d 155, 161 (Fla. Dist. Ct. App. 2004); *In re Estate of Gardiner*, 42 P.3d 120, 135, 137 (Kan. 2002); *Littleton v. Prange*, 9 S.W.3d 223, 231 (Tex. App. 1999). For further reading about transgenderism and the law, see TRANSGENDER RIGHTS (Paisley Currah, Richard M. Juang & Shannon P. Minter eds., 2006); Julie Greenberg et al., *Beyond the Binary: What Can Feminists Learn from Intersex and Transgender Jurisprudence?*, 17 MICH. J. GENDER & L. 13 (2010); Julie A. Greenberg, *Intersex and Intrasex Debates: Building Alliances to Challenge Sex Discrimination*, 12 CARDOZO J.L. & GENDER 99 (2005); Dean Spade, *Documenting Gender*, 59 HASTINGS L.J. 731 (2008); Dean Spade, Keynote Address, *Trans Law & Politics on a Neoliberal Landscape*, 18 TEMP. POL. & CIV. RTS. L. REV. 353 (2009).

f. OTHER RESTRICTIONS ON MARRYING (OR NOT MARRYING)

Mental incapacity remains a widely accepted restriction on who may marry. As of 2011, thirty-nine states and the District of Columbia restrict marriage by people with mental retardation, although some states use cruder terms. *See, e.g.*, TENN. CODE ANN. § 36–3–109 (2011) (no marriage shall be granted to "drunk, insane, or an imbecile"); VT. STAT. ANN. tit. 15 § 514(2011) (marriage by "idiot" or "lunatic" is voidable). In twelve states and the District of Columbia, such marriages are void *ab initio*. In the other twenty-seven states, they are voidable if a court finds that one of the parties was either a person with mental retardation or lacked mental capacity to contract to marry. The legal standards for defining such disabilities, legal processes for voiding marriages, and the standing of particular individuals to seek to void a marriage (the person with mental retardation, their guardian, or their spouse usually) vary by state. *See, e.g.*, Brooke Pietrzak, *Marriage Laws and People With Mental Retardation: A Continuing History of Second Class Treatment*, 17 DEV. MENTAL HEALTH L. 1 (1997); Jonathan Matloff, *Idiocy, Lunacy, and Matrimony: Exploring Constitutional Challenges to State Restrictions on Marriage of Persons with Menial Disabilities*, 17 AM. U. J. GENDER SOC. POL'Y & L. 497 (2009). Could similar restrictions be placed on individuals with serious physical disabilities? Those with genetic disorders? Alcoholics?

NOTES

1. Lord Devlin, an English judge, observed that although it makes little sense to force partners who believe their marriage is over to stay together, it might be wise to limit the right to marry a second (or third) time. Specifically, he suggested that when a marriage has failed, society should "claim the right to demand proofs of sincerity before it licenses another." PATRICK DEVLIN, THE ENFORCEMENT OF MORALS 79 (1965). Do you agree? Would such a restriction be constitutional?

2. Private restraints on marriage in wills or contracts have been held to be illegal in some states, *see, e.g.*, CAL. CIV. CODE § 1669 ("Every contract in restraint of the marriage of any person, other than a minor, is void"), and, at least in theory, are disfavored by courts as being against public policy. Partial restraints are generally permitted, however, as long as they are not "unreasonable." *See, e.g., Gordon v. Gordon*, 124 N.E.2d 228 (Mass. 1955) (upholding will provision requiring children to marry a person of the "Hebrew faith"); *Shapira v. Union Nat'l Bank*, 315 N.E.2d 825 (Ohio Com. Pl. 1974) (accord).

3. This Chapter has focused primarily on state restrictions on who may marry. It is only fair to note that state laws also sometimes pressure unwilling parties to marry. It is clear that private citizens cannot force a marriage, because shotgun weddings have long been held voidable for want of consent.[1] But by making marriage a defense to prosecutions for fornication[2] or rape,[3] state policy has at times accomplished what a shotgun could not. As Professor Wadlington has observed, such decisions are conceptually at odds with a growing recognition in divorce proceedings that a marriage ended in fact should be terminable at law.[4]

---

1. *See, e.g.*, Burney v. State, 13 S.W.2d 375 (Tex. Crim. App. 1929). *See generally* Walter Wadlington, *Shotgun Marriage by Operation of Law*, 1 GA.L.REV. 183 (1967).

2. *See, e.g.*, IDAHO CODE ANN. § 18–6603; MASS. GEN. LAWS ch. 272 § 18; MINN. STAT. § 609.34; S.C. CODE ANN. § 16–15–60; UTAH CODE ANN. § 76–6–104.

3. Although many states have repealed the common law marital rape exemption in different ways, marriage can still be used as a defense to statutory rape in some jurisdictions. *See* Kelly C. Connerton, Comment, *The Resurgence of the Marital Rape Exemption: The Victimization of Teens By Their Statutory Rapists*, 61 ALB. L. REV. 237 (1997).

4. Wadlington, *supra* note 1, at 204.

4. Breach of promise actions once forced people into unwanted matrimony, but today they are no longer much of a threat.

The earliest breach of promise to marry suits were based on tort principles. The plaintiff sued to recover money paid in reliance on the (false) promise of marriage. Thus, in 1452 in England, Margaret and Alice Gardyner sued John Keche to recover the 22 marks they paid him to marry Alice. Sometime between 1504 and 1515, John James, a rebuffed law student, sought to recover in a slightly more ambitious suit not only the tokens of affection he had bestowed on Elizabeth Morgan, but also the expenses he had incurred in going to visit her. *Some Early Breach of Promise Cases*, 3 THE GREEN BAG 3, 5 (1891).

By the seventeenth century, the suits began to resemble contract actions, with breach of promise the injury, and only the tort measure of damages retained to indicate the earlier history. *See Stretch v. Parker*, Mich. 12 Car. Rot. 21 (1639); *Holcroft v. Dickenson*, Cart. 233, 124 Eng. Rep. 933 (C.P. 1672). Homer Clark has suggested that this change arose because marriage in seventeenth-century England was largely a property transaction, entered into for material reasons as much as for sentimental ones. Breach of promise to marry thus was recognized as a legal injury at roughly the same time as breach of commercial contracts. HOMER CLARK, DOMESTIC RELATIONS § 1.1 (1968).

The American colonies permitted recovery for breach of promise to marry as early as 1633, when a colonial court fined Joyce Bradwicke 20 shillings for not performing her promise to marry Alex Becke. RECORD OF THE COURT OF ASSISTANTS OF THE COLONY OF THE MASS. BAY 1630–1692, at 32 (John Noble ed., 1904). In 1661, John Sutton won 15 pounds plus costs when Mary Russell became engaged to another, and Richard Silvester collected 20 pounds for his daughter when John Palmer failed to marry her as promised. VII PLYMOUTH COLONY COURT RECORDS, 1636–92, JUDICIAL ACTS 101 (Nathaniel Shurtleff ed., 1857).

By 2011, twenty-six states and the District of Columbia had abolished the action of breach of promise to marry,[5] while several others had limited its use.[6] More significantly, in the twenty-four jurisdictions where such actions are still possible, only a handful have been reported in the last thirty-odd years.[7]

Breach of promise actions, in short, are almost extinct. Actions for damage to reputation or lost prospects are rarely successful, moreover, probably as a result of both the improving opportunities for rejected women, and the increase in divorce (and remarriage). With divorce such a likely outcome, breach of promise is generally viewed as a minor injury. *See generally* Jeffrey D. Kobar, Note, *Heartbalm Statutes and Deceit Actions*, 83 MICH. L. REV. 1770 (1985).

What remain are suits to recover gifts or money given in contemplation of the marriage. Plaintiffs have recovered on a number of legal theories ranging from

---

5. Alabama, California, Colorado, Connecticut, Delaware, District of Columbia, Florida, Indiana, Kentucky, Maine, Massachusetts, Michigan, Minnesota, Montana, Nevada, New Hampshire, New Jersey, New York, North Dakota, Ohio, Pennsylvania, Utah, Vermont, Virginia, West Virginia, Wisconsin, and Wyoming. *See, e.g.*, CAL. CIV. CODE § 43.4; IND. CODE ANN. § 34–12–2–1. Kentucky and Utah are the only states to abolish the action through judicial rulings. Gilbert v. Barkes, 987 S.W.2d 772, 776 (Ky. 1999); Jackson v. Brown, 904 P.2d 685 (Utah 1995).

6. *See, e.g.*, 740 ILL. COMP. STAT. ANN. 15/1 to 15/9 (limiting damages to actual damages and implementing strict time restrictions); MD. FAMILY LAW CODE ANN. § 3–102 (limiting use of breach of promise to marry actions to pregnant women who have corroboration for their claim).

7. *See e.g.*, Finch v. Dasgupta, 555 S.E.2d 22 (Ga. Ct. App. 2001); Menhusen v. Dake, 334 N.W.2d 435 (Neb. 1983); Phillips v. Blankenship, 554 S.E.2d 231 (Ga. Ct. App. 2001); Sanders v. Gore, 676 So.2d 866 (La. Ct. App. 1996); Schwalb v. Wood, 680 N.E.2d 773 (Ill. App. Ct. 1997); Wagener v. Papie, 609 N.E.2d 951 (Ill. App. Ct. 1993).

conditional gift[8] and fraud,[9] to unjust enrichment.[10] A few states even regulate the return of engagement gifts by statute.[11]

2. CONSTITUTIONALITY OF MARRIAGE RESTRICTIONS

Loving v. Virginia

Supreme Court of the United States, 1967.
388 U.S. 1, 87 S.Ct. 1817, 18 L.Ed.2d 1010.

■ CHIEF JUSTICE WARREN delivered the opinion of the Court.

This case presents a constitutional question never addressed by this Court: whether a statutory scheme adopted by the State of Virginia to prevent marriages between persons solely on the basis of racial classifications violates the Equal Protection and Due Process Clauses of the Fourteenth Amendment. . . .

In June 1958, two residents of Virginia, Mildred Jeter, a Negro woman, and Richard Loving, a white man, were married in the District of Columbia pursuant to its laws. Shortly after their marriage, the Lovings returned to Virginia and established their marital abode in Caroline County. At the October Term, 1958, of the Circuit Court of Caroline County, a grand jury issued an indictment charging the Lovings with violating Virginia's ban on interracial marriages. On January 6, 1959, the Lovings pleaded guilty to the charge and were sentenced to one year in jail; however, the trial judge suspended the sentence for a period of 25 years on the condition that the Lovings leave the State and not return to Virginia together for 25 years. He stated in an opinion that:

> "Almighty God created the races white, black, yellow, malay and red, and he placed them on separate continents. And but for the interference with his arrangement there would be no cause for such marriages. The fact that he separated the races shows that he did not intend for the races to mix."

After their convictions, the Lovings took up residence in the District of Columbia. On November 6, 1963, they filed a motion in the state trial court to vacate the judgment and set aside the sentence on the ground that the statutes which they had violated were repugnant to the Fourteenth Amendment. . . . On January 22, 1965, the state trial judge denied the motion to vacate the sentences, and the Lovings perfected an appeal to the Supreme Court of Appeals of Virginia. . . .

The Supreme Court of Appeals upheld the constitutionality of the antimiscegenation statutes and, after modifying the sentence, affirmed the convictions. The Lovings appealed this decision, and we noted probable jurisdiction on December 12, 1966, 385 U.S. 986.

The two statutes under which appellants were convicted and sentenced are part of a comprehensive statutory scheme aimed at prohibiting and punishing interracial marriages. The Lovings were convicted of violating § 20–58 of the Virginia Code:

---

8. *See, e.g.*, Glass v. Wiltz, 551 So. 2d 32 (La. App. 1989); Lindh v. Surman, 702 A.2d 560 (Pa. Super. 1997); Patterson v. Blanton, 109 Ohio App.3d 349, 672 N.E.2d 208 (1996). This theory has even worked in the case of an annulled marriage. LaVigne v. Wise, 43 Pa. D. & C. 4th 225 (1999).

9. Morgan v. Morgan, 193 Ga.App. 302, 388 S.E.2d 2 (1989); *see* Pine v. Price, 2002 WL 31168905.

10. *See, e.g.*, Bruno v. Guerra, 146 Misc.2d 206, 549 N.Y.S.2d 925 (1990); Dixon v. Smith, 119 Ohio App.3d 308, 695 N.E.2d 284 (3d 1997); Siegel v. Siegel, 1996 WL 222140 (Conn. Super.).

11. See Cal. Civ. Code § 1590; N.Y. CLS CIV. RTS. L. § 80–b.

"Leaving State to evade law.—If any white person and colored person shall go out of this State, for the purpose of being married, and with the intention of returning, and be married out of it, and afterwards return to and reside in it, cohabiting as man and wife, they shall be punished as provided in § 20–59, and the marriage shall be governed by the same law as if it had been solemnized in this State. The fact of their cohabitation here as man and wife shall be evidence of their marriage."

Section 20–59, which defines the penalty for miscegenation, provides:

"Punishment for marriage.—If any white person intermarry with a colored person, or any colored person intermarry with a white person, he shall be guilty of a felony and shall be punished by confinement in the penitentiary for not less than one nor more than five years."

Other central provisions in the Virginia statutory scheme are § 20–57, which automatically voids all marriages between "a white person and a colored person" without any judicial proceeding, and §§ 20–54 and 1–14 which, respectively, define "white persons" and "colored persons and Indians" for purposes of the statutory prohibitions.[4] The Lovings have never disputed in the course of this litigation that Mrs. Loving is a "colored person" or that Mr. Loving is a "white person" within the meanings given those terms by the Virginia statutes.

Virginia is now one of 16 States which prohibit and punish marriages on the basis of racial classifications.[5] Penalties for miscegenation arose as an incident to slavery and have been common in Virginia since the colonial

---

4. Section 20–54 of the Virginia Code provides:

"Intermarriage prohibited; meaning of term 'white persons.'—It shall hereafter be unlawful for any white person in this State to marry any save a white person, or a person with no other admixture of blood than white and American Indian. For the purpose of this Chapter, the term 'white person' shall apply only to such person as has no trace whatever of any blood other than Caucasian; but persons who have one-sixteenth or less of the blood of the American Indian and have no other non-Caucasic blood shall be deemed to be white persons. All laws heretofore passed and now in effect regarding the intermarriage of white and colored persons shall apply to marriages prohibited by this chapter." VA. CODE ANN. § 20–54 (1960 Repl. Vol.).

The exception for persons with less than one-sixteenth "of the blood of the American Indian" is apparently accounted for, in the words of a tract issued by the Registrar of the State Bureau of Vital Statistics, by "the desire of all to recognize as an integral and honored part of the white race the descendants of John Rolfe and Pocahontas...." Plecker, *The New Family and Race Improvement*, 17 VA. HEALTH BULL., Extra No. 12, at 25–26 (New Family Series No. 5, 1925), cited in Wadlington, The *Loving* Case: Virginia's Anti–Miscegenation Statute in Historical Perspective, 52 VA. L. REV. 1189, 1202, n. 93 (1966)....

5. After the initiation of this litigation, Maryland repealed its prohibitions against interracial marriage, Md. Laws 1967, c. 6, leaving Virginia and 15 other States with statutes outlawing interracial marriage: Alabama, ALA. CONST., art. 4, § 102, ALA. CODE, Tit. 14, § 360 (1958); Arkansas, ARK. STAT. ANN. § 55–104 (1947); Delaware, DEL. CODE ANN., Tit. 13, § 101 (1953); Florida, FLA. CONST., art. 16, § 24, Fla. Stat. § 741.11 (1965); Georgia, GA. CODE ANN. § 53–106 (1961); Kentucky, KY. REV. STAT. ANN. § 402.020 (Supp. 1966); Louisiana, LA. REV. STAT. § 14:79 (1950); Mississippi, MISS. CONST., art. 14, § 263, MISS. CODE ANN. § 459 (1956); Missouri, MO. REV. STAT. § 451.020 (Supp. 1966); North Carolina, N.C. CONST., art. XIV, § 8, N. C. Gen. Stat. § 14–181 (1953); Oklahoma, OKLA. STAT., Tit. 43, § 12 (Supp. 1965); South Carolina, S.C. CONST., art. 3, § 33, S.C. CODE ANN. § 20–7 (1962); Tennessee, TENN. CONST., art. 11, § 14, Tenn. Code Ann. § 36–402 (1955); TEXAS, Tex. Pen. Code, art. 492 (1952); West Virginia, W. VA. CODE ANN. § 4697 (1961).

Over the past 15 years, 14 States have repealed laws outlawing interracial marriages: Arizona, California, Colorado, Idaho, Indiana, Maryland, Montana, Nebraska, Nevada, North Dakota, Oregon, South Dakota, Utah, and Wyoming.

The first state court to recognize that miscegenation statutes violate the Equal Protection Clause was the Supreme Court of California. Perez v. Sharp, 198 P.2d 17 (Cal. 1948).

period.... The central features of ... current Virginia law[] are the absolute prohibition of a "white person" marrying other than another "white person," a prohibition against issuing marriage licenses until the issuing official is satisfied that the applicants' statements as to their race are correct, certificates of "racial composition" to be kept by both local and state registrars, and the carrying forward of earlier prohibitions against racial intermarriage.

In upholding the constitutionality of these provisions in the decision below, the Supreme Court of Appeals of Virginia referred to its 1955 decision in *Naim v. Naim*, 87 S.E.2d 749, as stating the reasons supporting the validity of these laws. In *Naim*, the state court concluded that the State's legitimate purposes were "to preserve the racial integrity of its citizens," and to prevent "the corruption of blood," "a mongrel breed of citizens," and "the obliteration of racial pride," obviously an endorsement of the doctrine of White Supremacy. The court also reasoned that marriage has traditionally been subject to state regulation without federal intervention, and, consequently, the regulation of marriage should be left to exclusive state control by the Tenth Amendment.

While the state court is no doubt correct in asserting that marriage is a social relation subject to the State's police power, *Maynard v. Hill*, 125 U.S. 190 (1888), the State does not contend in its argument before this Court that its powers to regulate marriage are unlimited notwithstanding the commands of the Fourteenth Amendment.... Instead, the State argues that the meaning of the Equal Protection Clause, as illuminated by the statements of the Framers, is only that state penal laws containing an interracial element as part of the definition of the offense must apply equally to whites and Negroes in the sense that members of each race are punished to the same degree. Thus, the State contends that, because its miscegenation statutes punish equally both the white and the Negro participants in an interracial marriage, these statutes, despite their reliance on racial classifications, do not constitute an invidious discrimination based upon race. The second argument advanced by the State assumes the validity of its equal application theory. The argument is that, if the Equal Protection Clause does not outlaw miscegenation statutes because of their reliance on racial classifications, the question of constitutionality would thus become whether there was any rational basis for a State to treat interracial marriages differently from other marriages. On this question, the State argues, the scientific evidence is substantially in doubt and, consequently, this Court should defer to the wisdom of the state legislature in adopting its policy of discouraging interracial marriages.

Because we reject the notion that the mere "equal application" of a statute containing racial classifications is enough to remove the classifications from the Fourteenth Amendment's proscription of all invidious racial discriminations, we do not accept the State's contention that these statutes should be upheld if there is any possible basis for concluding that they serve a rational purpose. The mere fact of equal application does not mean that our analysis of these statutes should follow the approach we have taken in cases involving no racial discrimination....

. . .

The State finds support for its "equal application" theory in the decision of the Court in *Pace v. Alabama*, 106 U.S. 583 (1883). In that case, the Court upheld a conviction under an Alabama statute forbidding adultery or fornication between a white person and a Negro which imposed a greater penalty than that of a statute proscribing similar conduct by members of the same race. The Court reasoned that the statute could not be said to discriminate against Negroes because the punishment for each participant in the offense was the same. However, as recently as the 1964 Term, in rejecting the reasoning of that case, we stated "*Pace* represents a limited view of the Equal Protection Clause which has not withstood analysis in the subsequent decisions of this Court." *McLaughlin v. Florida*, [379 U.S. 184, 188 (1964)]. As we there demonstrated, the Equal Protection Clause requires the consideration of whether the classifications drawn by any statute constitute an arbitrary and invidious discrimination. The clear and central purpose of the Fourteenth Amendment was to eliminate all official state sources of invidious racial discrimination in the States.

There can be no question but that Virginia's miscegenation statutes rest solely upon distinctions drawn according to race. The statutes proscribe generally accepted conduct if engaged in by members of different races. Over the years, this Court has consistently repudiated "[d]istinctions between citizens solely because of their ancestry" as being "odious to a free people whose institutions are founded upon the doctrine of equality." *Hirabayashi v. United States*, 320 U.S. 81, 100 (1943). At the very least, the Equal Protection Clause demands that racial classifications, especially suspect in criminal statutes, be subjected to the "most rigid scrutiny," *Korematsu v. United States*, 323 U.S. 214, 216 (1944), and, if they are ever to be upheld, they must be shown to be necessary to the accomplishment of some permissible state objective, independent of the racial discrimination which it was the object of the Fourteenth Amendment to eliminate. . . .

There is patently no legitimate overriding purpose independent of invidious racial discrimination which justifies this classification. The fact that Virginia prohibits only interracial marriages involving white persons demonstrates that the racial classifications must stand on their own justification, as measures designed to maintain White Supremacy. We have consistently denied the constitutionality of measures which restrict the rights of citizens on account of race. There can be no doubt that restricting the freedom to marry solely because of racial classifications violates the central meaning of the Equal Protection Clause.

These statutes also deprive the Lovings of liberty without due process of law in violation of the Due Process Clause of the Fourteenth Amendment. The freedom to marry has long been recognized as one of the vital personal rights essential to the orderly pursuit of happiness by free men.

Marriage is one of the "basic civil rights of man," fundamental to our very existence and survival. *Skinner v. Oklahoma*, 316 U.S. 535, 541 (1942). To deny this fundamental freedom on so unsupportable a basis as the racial classifications embodied in these statutes, classifications so directly subversive of the principle of equality at the heart of the Fourteenth Amendment, is surely to deprive all the State's citizens of liberty without due process of law. The Fourteenth Amendment requires that the freedom of choice to marry not be restricted by invidious racial discriminations. Under our Constitution, the freedom to marry, or not marry, a person of another race resides with the individual and cannot be infringed by the State.

These convictions must be reversed.

NOTES

1. As the Supreme Court's opinion in *Loving* makes clear, Virginia defended its miscegenation ban partly on the ground that it had a rational basis for treating "interracial marriages differently from other marriages." *Loving*, 388 U.S. 1, 8 (1967). According to the Court, "the State argue[d] [that] the scientific evidence [on the effects of miscegenation] is substantially in doubt and, consequently, this Court should defer to the wisdom of the state legislature in adopting its policy of discouraging interracial marriages." *Id.* Illuminating the point is the following exchange from the oral arguments before the Supreme Court, in which R.D. Mc Ilwaine III, Assistant Attorney General of the Commonwealth of Virginia, made the following arguments on behalf of the State:

MR. Mc ILWAINE: . . . Turning, then, to our . . . argument, which we say can only be reached if the legislative history of the Fourteenth Amendment is ignored, and the Fourteenth Amendment is deemed to reach the state power to enact laws relating to the marriage relationship, we say that the prevention of interracial marriage is a legitimate exercise of state power, that there is a rational classification, certainly so far as the Virginia population is concerned, for preventing marriages between white and colored people, who make up almost the entirety of the State's population; and that this is supported by the prevailing climate of scientific opinion. We take the position that while there is evidence on both sides of this question, when such a situation exists it is for the legislature to draw its conclusions, and that these conclusions are entitled to weight; and, that unless it can be clearly said that there is no debatable question, that a statute of this type cannot be declared unconstitutional.

We start with the proposition, on this connection, that it is the family which constitutes the structural element of society; and that marriage is the legal basis upon which families are formed. Consequently, this Court has held, in numerous decisions over the years, that society is structured on the institution of marriage; that it has more to do with the welfare and civilizations of a people than any other institution; and that out of the fruits of marriage spring relationships and responsibilities with which the state is necessarily required to deal. Text writers and judicial writers agree that the state has a natural, direct, and vital interest in maximizing the number of successful marriages which lead to stable homes and families, and in minimizing those which do not.

It is clear, from the most recent available evidence on the psycho-sociological aspect of this question that intermarried families are subjected to much greater pressures and problems than are those of the intramarried, and that the State's prohibition of racial intermarriage, for this reason, stands on the same footing as the prohibition of polygamous marriage, or incestuous marriage, or the prescription of minimum ages at which people may marry, and the prevention of the marriage of people who are mentally competent.

THE COURT: There are people who have the same feeling about interreligious marriages. But because that may be true, would you think that the State could prohibit people from having interreligious marriages?

MR. MC ILWAINE: I think that the evidence in support of the prohibition of interracial marriages is stronger than that for the prohibition of interreligious marriages; but I think that—

THE COURT: How can you say that? . . . Because you believe that?

MR. MC ILWAINE: No, sir. We say it principally on the basis of . . . a book by Dr. Albert I. Gordon, . . . which is characterized as the definitive book in intermarriage, and as the most careful, up-to-date, methodologically sound study of intermarriage in North America that exists. It is entitled *Intermarriage: Interfaith, Interracial, Interethnic* [(1964)].

Now, our proposition on the psycho-sociological aspects of the question is bottomed almost exclusively on this particular volume. This is the work of a Jewish rabbi who also has an M.A. in sociology and a Ph.D. in social anthropology. It is a statistical study of over 5,000 marriages which was made by the computers of the Harvard Laboratory of Social Relations and the MIT Computation Center. This book has given statistical form and basis to the proposition that, from a psycho-sociological point of view, interracial marriages are detrimental to the individual, to the family, and to the society.

I do not say that the author of the book would advocate the prohibition of such marriages by law, but we do say that he personally clearly expresses his view as a social scientist that interracial marriages are definitely undesirable; that they hold no promise for a bright and happy future for mankind; and that interracial marriages bequeath to the progeny of those marriages more psychological problems than parents have a right to bequeath to them.

... [T]his book has been widely accepted, and it was published in 1964 as being the definitive book on intermarriage in North America that exists.

THE COURT: Is he an Orthodox, or an Unorthodox Rabbi?

MR. MC ILWAINE: I have not been able to ascertain that, Your Honor, from any of the material that I've gotten here. He is the Rabbi of the Temple Emmanuel in Newton Center, Massachusetts. I do not understand that, certainly, the religious view of the Orthodox or the Conservative or the Reformed Jewish faiths disagree necessarily on this particular proposition. ...

I am more interested, of course, in his credentials as a scientist, for this purpose, ... than ... in his religious affiliation. ... [S]ome of the statements which are made in [Gordon's study] are based upon the demonstrably, statistically demonstrably greater, ratio of divorce/annulment in intermarried couples than in intramarried couples. Dr. Gordon has stated it, as his opinion, that "It is my conviction that intermarriage is definitely inadvisable; that they are wrong because they are most frequently, if not solely, entered into under present-day circumstances by people who have a rebellious attitude towards society, self-hatred, neurotic tendencies, immaturity, and other detrimental psychological factors."

THE COURT: You don't know what is cause, and what is effect. Presuming the validity of these statistics, I suppose it could be argued that one reason that marriages of this kind are sometimes unsuccessful is the existence of the kind of laws that are at issue here, and the attitudes that those laws reflect. Isn't that correct?

MR. MC ILWAINE: I think it is more the matter of the attitudes that, perhaps, the laws reflect. I don't find anywhere in this that the existence of the law does it. It is the attitude which society has toward interracial marriages, which in detailing his opposition, he says, "causes a child to have almost insuperable difficulties in identification," and that the problems which the child of an interracial marriage faces are those to which no child can come through without damages to himself.

Now, if the state has an interest in marriage, if it has an interest in maximizing the number of stable marriages, and in protecting the progeny of interracial marriages from these problems, then clearly there is scientific evidence available that this is so. It is not infrequent that the children of intermarried parents are referred to not merely as the children of intermarried parents, but as the victims of intermarried parents, but as the martyrs of their intermarried parents. These are direct quotes from the volume. ...

Transcript of Oral Argument, Loving v. Virginia, 388 U.S. 1 (1967) (No. 395), *reprinted in* 64 Landmark Briefs and Arguments of the Supreme Court of the United States: Constitutional Law 959, 986–89 (Philip B. Kurland & Gerhard Casper eds., 1975); *see also* Brief and Appendix on Behalf of Appellee, Loving v. Virginia, 388 U.S. 1 (1967) (No. 395), *reprinted in* 64 Landmark Briefs and Arguments of the Supreme Court of the United States: Constitutional Law 789, 831–43 (Philip B. Kurland & Gerhard Casper eds., 1975); *id.* at 834 ("If this Court (erroneously, we contend) should undertake such an inquiry [into the wisdom of Virginia's "statutory policy"] it would quickly find itself in a veritable Serbonian bog of conflicting scientific opinion upon the effects of interracial marriage, and the desirability of preventing such alliances, from the physical, biological, genetic, anthropological, cultural, psychological and sociological point[s] of view.").

2. Consider Derrick Bell, *The 1984 Term: Foreword: The Civil Rights Chronicles*, 99 HARV. L. REV. 4, 62 (1985):

> ... I will bet few law students know, and even fewer law scholars remember, that only a few months after *Brown*, the Court refused to review the conviction under an Alabama antimiscegenation law of a black man who married a white woman.[158] Many of us do remember, of course, and remember too the procedural contortions that the Court used one year after *Brown* to avoid deciding another challenge to a state law barring interracial marriages.[159]

Does this history shed light on the question of why the Supreme Court issued a full opinion in *Loving*? What, exactly, does *Loving* protect? Is it only "the freedom to marry"? What about the Court's observation that "[u]nder our Constitution, the freedom to marry, or not marry, a person of another race resides with the individual and cannot be infringed by the State?" Does *Loving* guarantee a private right to discriminate in the choice of one's intimate partners? For relevant discussion, see Elizabeth F. Emens, *Intimate Discrimination: The State's Role in the Accidents of Sex and Love*, 122 HARV. L. REV. 1307 (2009).

3. Mildred Loving was interviewed in 1992. A widow, with three grown children, her church had presented her with a plaque and compared her to Rosa Parks. "I don't feel like that. Not at all. What happened, we really didn't intend for it to happen. What we wanted, we wanted to come home." She was 17 when she married Richard, who was 24. She did not know the marriage was illegal. Their ordeal began at 2 a.m. one day in July, 1958, when a Caroline County, Va., sheriff roused the Lovings from sleep and took them to the Bowling Green jail. After they moved to the District, Mildred wrote for help to then-U.S. Attorney General Robert F. Kennedy. Bernard Cohen, an ACLU lawyer took on their case. Reflecting on the case, Cohen observed that it was full of ironies; ironic in the also tragic sense "that her husband was killed in an auto accident ... a few years after they finally got peace," and also in that the justice of the Virginia Supreme Court "who wrote the decision upholding the constitutionality of the law [became the chief justice of the court.]" Lynne Duke, *Intermarriage Broken Up By Death*, WASH. POST, June 12, 1992, at A3.

4. *Loving* was the first case in which the Supreme Court held unconstitutional a state restriction on marrying. In its wake, courts have overturned numerous other restrictions, as the next cases in this section illustrate. Indeed, now the question formally is whether *any* restrictions on marriage are constitutional. Could restrictions based on affinity or consanguinity be successfully challenged in light of *Loving* and its progeny? Age restrictions? Mandatory counseling restrictions?

Zablocki v. Redhail

Supreme Court of the United States, 1978.
434 U.S. 374, 98 S.Ct. 673, 54 L.Ed.2d 618.

■ JUSTICE MARSHALL delivered the opinion of the Court.

At issue in this case is the constitutionality of a Wisconsin statute, Wis. Stat. §§ 245.10(1), (4), (5) (1973), which provides that members of a certain class of Wisconsin residents may not marry, within the State or elsewhere, without first obtaining a court order granting permission to marry. The class

---

158. *See* Johnson v. [Alabama], 72 So. 2d 114 (Ala.Ct.App.) *cert. denied*, 348 U.S. 888 (1954).

159. In Naim v. Naim, 87 S.E.2d 749, *remanded*, 350 U.S. 891 (Va. 1955), *aff'd* 90 S.E.2d 849 (Va. 1956), *appeal dismissed*, 350 U.S. 985 (1956), the Supreme Court remanded the case after oral argument for development of the record regarding the parties' domicil. After the state court refused to comply with the mandate, claiming that no state procedure existed for reopening the case, the Supreme Court dismissed the appeal, finding that the state court ruling left the case devoid of a substantial federal question. Professor Wechsler remarked that this dismissal was "wholly without basis in law." [Herbert Wechsler, *Toward Neutral Principles of Constitutional Law*, 73 HARV. L. REV. 1, 34 (1959).]

is defined by the statute to include any "Wisconsin resident having minor issue not in his custody and which he is under obligation to support by any court order or judgment." The statute specifies that court permission cannot be granted unless the marriage applicant submits proof of compliance with the support obligation and, in addition, demonstrates that the children covered by the support order "are not then and are not likely thereafter to become public charges." No marriage license may lawfully be issued in Wisconsin to a person covered by the statute, except upon court order; any marriage entered into without compliance with § 245.10 is declared void; and persons acquiring marriage licenses in violation of the section are subject to criminal penalties.

After being denied a marriage license because of his failure to comply with § 245.10, appellee brought this class action . . . challenging the statute as violative of the Equal Protection and Due Process Clauses of the Fourteenth Amendment and seeking declaratory and injunctive relief. The United States District Court for the Eastern District of Wisconsin held the statute unconstitutional under the Equal Protection Clause and enjoined its enforcement. 418 F.Supp. 1061 (1976). We . . . now affirm.

Appellee Redhail is a Wisconsin resident who, under the terms of § 245.10, is unable to enter into a lawful marriage in Wisconsin or elsewhere so long as he maintains his Wisconsin residency. . . . In January 1972, when appellee was a minor and a high school student, a paternity action was instituted against him in Milwaukee County Court, alleging that he was the father of a baby girl born out of wedlock on July 5, 1971. After he appeared and admitted that he was the child's father, the court entered an order on May 12, 1972, adjudging appellee the father and ordering him to pay $109 per month as support for the child until she reached 18 years of age. From May 1972 until August 1974, appellee was unemployed and indigent, and consequently was unable to make any support payments.

On September 27, 1974, appellee filed an application for a marriage license with appellant Zablocki, the County Clerk of Milwaukee County, and a few days later the application was denied on the sole ground that appellee had not obtained a court order granting him permission to marry, as required by § 245.10. Although appellee did not petition a state court thereafter, it is stipulated that he would not have been able to satisfy either of the statutory prerequisites for an order granting permission to marry. First, he had not satisfied his support obligations to his illegitimate child, and as of December 1974 there was an arrearage in excess of $3,700. Second, the child had been a public charge since her birth, receiving benefits under the Aid to Families with Dependent Children program. It is stipulated that the child's benefit payments were such that she would have been a public charge even if appellee had been current in his support payments.

On December 24, 1974, appellee filed his complaint in the District Court, on behalf of himself and the class of all Wisconsin residents who had been refused a marriage license pursuant to § 245.10(1) by one of the county clerks in Wisconsin. . . . The complaint alleged, among other things, that appellee and the woman he desired to marry were expecting a child in March 1975 and wished to be lawfully married before that time. . . .

. . .

The leading decision of this Court on the right to marry is *Loving v. Virginia*, 388 U.S. 1 (1967). . . .

Although *Loving* arose in the context of racial discrimination, prior and subsequent decisions of this Court confirm that the right to marry is of fundamental importance for all individuals. Long ago, in *Maynard v. Hill*, 125 U.S. 190 (1888), the Court characterized marriage as "the most important relation in life," and as "the foundation of the family and of society, without which there would be neither civilization nor progress." ...

More recent decisions have established that the right to marry is part of the fundamental "right of privacy" implicit in the Fourteenth Amendment's Due Process Clause. *Griswold v. Connecticut*, [381 U.S. 479 (1965)].

. . .

It is not surprising that the decision to marry has been placed on the same level of importance as decisions relating to procreation, childbirth, child rearing, and family relationships. As the facts of this case illustrate, it would make little sense to recognize a right of privacy with respect to other matters of family life and not with respect to the decision to enter the relationship that is the foundation of the family in our society. The woman whom appellee desired to marry had a fundamental right to seek an abortion of their expected child, see *Roe v. Wade*, [410 U.S. 113 (1973),] or to bring the child into life to suffer the myriad social, if not economic, disabilities that the status of illegitimacy brings, see *Trimble v. Gordon*, 430 U.S. 762, 768–770, and n. 13 (1977); *Weber v. Aetna Casualty & Surety Co.*, 406 U.S. 164, 175–176 (1972). Surely, a decision to marry and raise the child in a traditional family setting must receive equivalent protection. And, if appellee's right to procreate means anything at all, it must imply some right to enter the only relationship in which the State of Wisconsin allows sexual relations legally to take place.

By reaffirming the fundamental character of the right to marry, we do not mean to suggest that every state regulation which relates in any way to the incidents of or prerequisites for marriage must be subjected to rigorous scrutiny. To the contrary, reasonable regulations that do not significantly interfere with decisions to enter into the marital relationship may legitimately be imposed. *See Califano v. Jobst*, [434 U.S. 47, 48 (1977)]. The statutory classification at issue here, however, clearly does interfere directly and substantially with the right to marry.

Under the challenged statute, no Wisconsin resident in the affected class may marry in Wisconsin or elsewhere without a court order, and marriages contracted in violation of the statute are both void and punishable as criminal offenses. Some of those in the affected class, like appellee, will never be able to obtain the necessary court order, because they either lack the financial means to meet their support obligations or cannot prove that their children will not become public charges. These persons are absolutely prevented from getting married. Many others, able in theory to satisfy the statute's requirements, will be sufficiently burdened by having to do so that they will in effect be coerced into forgoing their right to marry. And even those who can be persuaded to meet the statute's requirements suffer a serious intrusion into their freedom of choice in an area in which we have held such freedom to be fundamental.[12]

---

12. The directness and substantiality of the interference with the freedom to marry distinguish the instant case from Califano v. Jobst, [434 U.S. 47 (1977)]. In *Jobst*, we upheld sections of the Social Security Act providing, inter alia, for termination of a dependent child's benefits upon marriage to an individual not entitled to benefits under the Act. As the opinion for the Court expressly noted, the rule terminating benefits upon marriage was not "an attempt

When a statutory classification significantly interferes with the exercise of a fundamental right, it cannot be upheld unless it is supported by sufficiently important state interests and is closely tailored to effectuate only those interests. . . . Appellant asserts that two interests are served by the challenged statute: the permission-to-marry proceeding furnishes an opportunity to counsel the applicant as to the necessity of fulfilling his prior support obligations; and the welfare of the out-of-custody children is protected. We may accept for present purposes that these are legitimate and substantial interests, but, since the means selected by the State for achieving these interests unnecessarily impinge on the right to marry, the statute cannot be sustained.

There is evidence that the challenged statute, as originally introduced in the Wisconsin Legislature, was intended merely to establish a mechanism whereby persons with support obligations to children from prior marriages could be counseled before they entered into new marital relationships and incurred further support obligations. Court permission to marry was to be required, but apparently permission was automatically to be granted after counseling was completed. The statute actually enacted, however, does not expressly require or provide for any counseling whatsoever, nor for any automatic granting of permission to marry by the court, and thus it can hardly be justified as a means for ensuring counseling of the persons within its coverage. Even assuming that counseling does take place—a fact as to which there is no evidence in the record—this interest obviously cannot support the withholding of court permission to marry once counseling is completed.

With regard to safeguarding the welfare of the out-of-custody children, appellant's brief does not make clear the connection between the State's interest and the statute's requirements. At argument, appellant's counsel suggested that, since permission to marry cannot be granted unless the applicant shows that he has satisfied his court-determined support obligations to the prior children and that those children will not become public charges, the statute provides incentive for the applicant to make support payments to his children. This "collection device" rationale cannot justify the statute's broad infringement on the right to marry.

First, with respect to individuals who are unable to meet the statutory requirements, the statute merely prevents the applicant from getting married, without delivering any money at all into the hands of the applicant's prior children. More importantly, regardless of the applicant's ability or willingness to meet the statutory requirements, the State already has numerous other means for exacting compliance with support obligations, means that are at least as effective as the instant statute's and yet do not impinge upon the right to marry. Under Wisconsin law, whether the children are from a prior marriage or were born out of wedlock, court-determined support obligations may be enforced directly via wage assignments, civil contempt proceedings, and criminal penalties. And, if the State believes that parents of children out of their custody should be responsible for ensuring

---

to interfere with the individual's freedom to make a decision as important as marriage." [*Id.* at 54]. The Social Security provisions placed no direct legal obstacle in the path of persons desiring to get married, and . . . there was no evidence that the laws significantly discouraged, let alone made "practically impossible," any marriages. Indeed, the provisions had not deterred the individual who challenged the statute from getting married, even though he and his wife were both disabled. See [*id.* at 48]. See also [*id.* at 57 n. 17] (because of availability of other federal benefits, total payments to the Jobsts after marriage were only $20 per month less than they would have been had Mr. Jobst's child benefits not been terminated).

that those children do not become public charges, this interest can be achieved by adjusting the criteria used for determining the amounts to be paid under their support orders.

There is also some suggestion that § 245.10 protects the ability of marriage applicants to meet support obligations to prior children by preventing the applicants from incurring new support obligations. But the challenged provisions of § 245.10 are grossly underinclusive with respect to this purpose, since they do not limit in any way new financial commitments by the applicant other than those arising out of the contemplated marriage. The statutory classification is substantially overinclusive as well: Given the possibility that the new spouse will actually better the applicant's financial situation, by contributing income from a job or otherwise, the statute in many cases may prevent affected individuals from improving their ability to satisfy their prior support obligations. And, although it is true that the applicant will incur support obligations to any children born during the contemplated marriage, preventing the marriage may only result in the children being born out of wedlock, as in fact occurred in appellee's case. Since the support obligation is the same whether the child is born in or out of wedlock, the net result of preventing the marriage is simply more illegitimate children.

The statutory classification created by §§ 245.10(1), (4), (5) thus cannot be justified by the interests advanced in support of it. The judgment of the District Court is, accordingly,

Affirmed.

■ JUSTICE POWELL, concurring in the judgment.

I concur in the judgment of the Court that Wisconsin's restrictions on the exclusive means of creating the marital bond, erected by Wis. Stat. §§ 245.10(1), (4), and (5) (1973), cannot meet applicable constitutional standards. I write separately because the majority's rationale sweeps too broadly in an area which traditionally has been subject to pervasive state regulation. The Court apparently would subject all state regulation which "directly and substantially" interferes with the decision to marry in a traditional family setting to "critical examination" or "compelling state interest" analysis. Presumably, "reasonable regulations that do not significantly interfere with decisions to enter into the marital relationship may legitimately be imposed." The Court does not present, however, any principled means for distinguishing between the two types of regulations. Since state regulation in this area typically takes the form of a prerequisite or barrier to marriage or divorce, the degree of "direct" interference with the decision to marry or to divorce is unlikely to provide either guidance for state legislatures or a basis for judicial oversight.

On several occasions, the Court has acknowledged the importance of the marriage relationship to the maintenance of values essential to organized society....

Thus, it is fair to say that there is a right of marital and familial privacy which places some substantive limits on the regulatory power of government. But the Court has yet to hold that all regulation touching upon marriage implicates a "fundamental right" triggering the most exacting judicial scrutiny.[1]

---

1. Although the cases cited in the text indicate that there is a sphere of privacy or autonomy surrounding an existing marital relationship into which the State may not lightly intrude, they do not necessarily suggest that the same barrier of justification blocks regulation of

The principal authority cited by the majority is *Loving v. Virginia*, 388 U.S. 1 (1967).... [But] *Loving* involved a denial of a "fundamental freedom" on a wholly unsupportable basis—the use of classifications "directly subversive of the principle of equality at the heart of the Fourteenth Amendment...." It does not speak to the level of judicial scrutiny of, or governmental justification for, "supportable" restrictions on the "fundamental freedom" of individuals to marry or divorce.

In my view, analysis must start from the recognition of domestic relations as "an area that has long been regarded as a virtually exclusive province of the States." *Sosna v. Iowa*, 419 U.S. 393, 404 (1975). The marriage relation traditionally has been subject to regulation, initially by the ecclesiastical authorities, and later by the secular state. As early as *Pennoyer v. Neff*, 95 U.S. 714, 734–735 (1878), this Court noted that a State "has absolute right to prescribe the conditions upon which the marriage relation between its own citizens shall be created, and the causes for which it may be dissolved." The State, representing the collective expression of moral aspirations, has an undeniable interest in ensuring that its rules of domestic relations reflect the widely held values of its people.... State regulation has included bans on incest, bigamy, and homosexuality, as well as various preconditions to marriage, such as blood tests. Likewise, a showing of fault on the part of one of the partners traditionally has been a prerequisite to the dissolution of an unsuccessful union. A "compelling state purpose" inquiry would cast doubt on the network of restrictions that the States have fashioned to govern marriage and divorce.

State power over domestic relations is not without constitutional limits. The Due Process Clause requires a showing of justification "when the government intrudes on choices concerning family living arrangements" in a manner which is contrary to deeply rooted traditions. *Moore v. East Cleveland*, 431 U.S. 494, 499, 503–504 (1977) (plurality opinion). Due process constraints also limit the extent to which the State may monopolize the process of ordering certain human relationships while excluding the truly indigent from that process. *Boddie v. Connecticut*, 401 U.S. 371 (1971). Furthermore, under the Equal Protection Clause the means chosen by the State in this case must bear " 'a fair and substantial relation' " to the object of the legislation. *Reed v. Reed*, 404 U.S. 71, 76 (1971), quoting *Royster Guano Co. v. Virginia*, 253 U.S. 412, 415 (1920).

The Wisconsin measure in this case does not pass muster under either due process or equal protection standards. Appellant identifies three objectives which are supposedly furthered by the statute in question: (i) a counseling function; (ii) an incentive to satisfy outstanding support obligations; and (iii) a deterrent against incurring further obligations. The opinion of the Court amply demonstrates that the asserted counseling objective bears no relation to this statute....

The so-called "collection device" rationale presents a somewhat more difficult question. I do not agree with the suggestion in the Court's opinion that a State may never condition the right to marry on satisfaction of existing support obligations simply because the State has alternative methods of compelling such payments. To the extent this restriction applies to persons who are able to make the required support payments but simply wish to shirk their moral and legal obligation, the Constitution interposes no bar to this additional collection mechanism. The vice inheres, not in the collection

---

the conditions of entry into or the dissolution of the marital bond. See generally Henkin, *Privacy and Autonomy*, 74 Colum. L. Rev. 1410, 1429–1432 (1974).

concept, but in the failure to make provision for those without the means to comply with child support obligations. I draw support from Mr. Justice Harlan's opinion in *Boddie v. Connecticut*[, 401 U.S. 371 (1971)]. In that case, the Court struck down filing fees for divorce actions as applied to those wholly unable to pay, holding "that a State may not, consistent with the obligations imposed on it by the Due Process Clause of the Fourteenth Amendment, pre-empt the right to dissolve this legal relationship without affording all citizens access to the means it has prescribed for doing so." 401 U.S., at 383. The monopolization present in this case is total, for Wisconsin will not recognize foreign marriages that fail to conform to the requirements of § 245.10.

The third justification, only obliquely advanced by appellant, is that the statute preserves the ability of marriage applicants to support their prior issue by preventing them from incurring new obligations. The challenged provisions of § 245.10 are so grossly underinclusive with respect to this objective, given the many ways that additional financial obligations may be incurred by the applicant quite apart from a contemplated marriage, that the classification "does not bear a fair and substantial relation to the object of the legislation." *Craig v. Boren*, [429 U.S. 190, 211 (1976)] (Powell, J., concurring).

The marriage applicant is required by the Wisconsin statute not only to submit proof of compliance with his support obligation, but also to demonstrate—in some unspecified way—that his children "are not then and are not likely thereafter to become public charges." This statute does more than simply "fail to alleviate the consequences of differences in economic circumstances that exist wholly apart from any state action." *Griffin v. Illinois*, 351 U.S. 12, 34 (1956) (Harlan, J., dissenting). It tells the truly indigent, whether they have met their support obligations or not, that they may not marry so long as their children are public charges or there is a danger that their children might go on public assistance in the future. Apparently, no other jurisdiction has embraced this approach as a method of reducing the number of children on public assistance. Because the State has not established a justification for this unprecedented foreclosure of marriage to many of its citizens solely because of their indigency, I concur in the judgment of the Court.

■ JUSTICE STEVENS, concurring in the judgment.

. . .

When a State allocates benefits or burdens, it may have valid reasons for treating married and unmarried persons differently. Classification based on marital status has been an accepted characteristic of tax legislation, Selective Service rules, and Social Security regulations. As cases like *Jobst* demonstrate, such laws may "significantly interfere with decisions to enter into the marital relationship." That kind of interference, however, is not a sufficient reason for invalidating every law reflecting a legislative judgment that there are relevant differences between married persons as a class and unmarried persons as a class.[1]

---

1. In *Jobst*, we pointed out that "it was rational for Congress to assume that marital status is a relevant test of probable dependency. . . ." We had explained:

"Both tradition and common experience support the conclusion that marriage is an event which normally marks an important change in economic status. Traditionally, the event not only creates a new family with attendant new responsibilities, but also modifies the preexisting relationships between the bride and groom and their respective families. Frequent-

A classification based on marital status is fundamentally different from a classification which determines who may lawfully enter into the marriage relationship.[2] The individual's interest in making the marriage decision independently is sufficiently important to merit special constitutional protection. It is not, however, an interest which is constitutionally immune from evenhanded regulation. Thus, laws prohibiting marriage to a child, a close relative, or a person afflicted with venereal disease, are unchallenged even though they "interfere directly and substantially with the right to marry." This Wisconsin statute has a different character.

Under this statute, a person's economic status may determine his eligibility to enter into a lawful marriage. A noncustodial parent whose children are "public charges" may not marry even if he has met his court-ordered obligations. Thus, within the class of parents who have fulfilled their court-ordered obligations, the rich may marry and the poor may not. This type of statutory discrimination is, I believe, totally unprecedented,[4] as well as inconsistent with our tradition of administering justice equally to the rich and to the poor.

The statute appears to reflect a legislative judgment that persons who have demonstrated an inability to support their offspring should not be permitted to marry and thereafter to bring additional children into the world.[6] Even putting to one side the growing number of childless marriages and the burgeoning number of children born out of wedlock, that sort of reasoning cannot justify this deliberate discrimination against the poor.

The statute prevents impoverished parents from marrying even though their intended spouses are economically independent. Presumably, the Wisconsin Legislature assumed (a) that only fathers would be affected by the legislation, and (b) that they would never marry employed women. The first assumption ignores the fact that fathers are sometimes awarded custody,[7] and the second ignores the composition of today's work force. To the extent that the statute denies a hard-pressed parent any opportunity to prove that an intended marriage will ease rather than aggravate his financial straits, it not only rests on unreliable premises, but also defeats its own objectives.

These questionable assumptions also explain why this statutory blunderbuss is wide of the target in another respect. The prohibition on marriage

---

ly, of course, financial independence and marriage do not go hand in hand. Nevertheless, there can be no question about the validity of the assumption that a married person is less likely to be dependent on his parents for support than one who is unmarried."

[434 U.S. at 53.]

2. *Jobst* is in the former category; Loving v. Virginia, 388 U.S. 1, is in the latter.

4. The economic aspects of a prospective marriage are unquestionably relevant to almost every individual's marriage decision. But I know of no other state statute that denies the individual marriage partners the right to assess the financial consequences of their decision independently. I seriously question whether any limitation on the right to marry may be predicated on economic status, but that question need not be answered in this case.

6. The "public charge" provision, which falls on parents who have faithfully met their obligations, but who are unable to pay enough to remove their children from the welfare rolls, obviously cannot be justified by a state interest in assuring the payment of child support. And, of course, it would be absurd for the State to contend that an interest in providing paternalistic counseling supports a total ban on marriage.

7. The Wisconsin Legislature has itself provided:

"In determining the parent with whom a child shall remain, the court shall consider all facts in the best interest of the child and shall not prefer one parent over the other solely on the basis of the sex of the parent."

Wis.Stat. § 247.24(3) (1977).

applies to the noncustodial parent but allows the parent who has custody to marry without the State's leave. Yet the danger that new children will further strain an inadequate budget is equally great for custodial and noncustodial parents, unless one assumes (a) that only mothers will ever have custody and (b) that they will never marry unemployed men.

Characteristically, this law fails to regulate the marriages of those parents who are least likely to be able to afford another family, for it applies only to parents under a court order to support their children. § 245.10(1). The very poorest parents are unlikely to be the objects of support orders. If the State meant to prevent the marriage of those who have demonstrated their inability to provide for children, it overlooked the most obvious targets of legislative concern.

In sum, the public-charge provision is either futile or perverse insofar as it applies to childless couples, couples who will have illegitimate children if they are forbidden to marry, couples whose economic status will be improved by marriage, and couples who are so poor that the marriage will have no impact on the welfare status of their children in any event. Even assuming that the right to marry may sometimes be denied on economic grounds, this clumsy and deliberate legislative discrimination between the rich and the poor is irrational in so many ways that it cannot withstand scrutiny under the Equal Protection Clause of the Fourteenth Amendment.[10]

■ JUSTICE REHNQUIST, dissenting.

I substantially agree with my Brother Powell's reasons for rejecting the Court's conclusion that marriage is the sort of "fundamental right" which must invariably trigger the strictest judicial scrutiny. I disagree with his imposition of an "intermediate" standard of review, which leads him to conclude that the statute, though generally valid as an "additional collection mechanism" offends the Constitution by its "failure to make provision for those without the means to comply with child support obligations." For similar reasons, I disagree with my Brother Stewart's conclusion that the statute is invalid for its failure to exempt those persons who "simply cannot afford to meet the statute's financial requirements." I would view this legislative judgment in the light of the traditional presumption of validity. I think that under the Equal Protection Clause the statute need pass only the "rational basis test," and that under the Due Process Clause it need only be shown that it bears a rational relation to a constitutionally permissible objective. The statute so viewed is a permissible exercise of the State's power to regulate family life and to assure the support of minor children, despite its possible imprecision in the extreme cases envisioned in the concurring opinions.

. . .

. . . Because of the limited amount of funds available for the support of needy children, the State has an exceptionally strong interest in securing as much support as their parents are able to pay. Nor does the extent of the burden imposed by this statute so differentiate it from that considered in *Jobst* as to warrant a different result. In the case of some applicants, this

---

10. Neither the fact that the appellee's interest is constitutionally protected, nor the fact that the classification is based on economic status is sufficient to justify a "level of scrutiny" so strict that a holding of unconstitutionality is virtually foreordained. On the other hand, the presence of these factors precludes a holding that a rational expectation of occasional and random benefit is sufficient to demonstrate compliance with the constitutional command to govern impartially. See Craig v. Boren, 429 U.S. 190, 211 (STEVENS, J., concurring).

statute makes the proposed marriage legally impossible for financial reasons; in a similar number of extreme cases, the Social Security Act makes the proposed marriage practically impossible for the same reasons. I cannot conclude that such a difference justifies the application of a heightened standard of review to the statute in question here. In short, I conclude that the statute, despite its imperfections, is sufficiently rational to satisfy the demands of the Fourteenth Amendment.

NOTE

What is the constitutional status of marriage regulations after *Zablocki v. Redhail*? The majority opinion holds that "reasonable regulations that do not significantly interfere with decisions to enter into the marital relationship" are constitutional. But surely state laws barring incestuous marriages "significantly interfere" for couples who are so related. Does the majority opinion mean that such state laws are unconstitutional?

Justice Stevens in his concurring opinion asserts there is a difference between classifications based on marital status and those that determine who may lawfully marry. Is the asserted difference simply a reflection of the fact that restrictions on married couples are by definition "indirect" restrictions, and thus constitutional? *See Mapes v. United States*, 217 Ct.Cl. 115, 576 F.2d 896 (1978), *cert. denied*, 439 U.S. 1046 (1978) (upholding different income tax rates for married and single taxpayers resulting in a "marriage penalty"); *Druker v. Commissioner*, 697 F.2d 46 (2d Cir. 1982) (accord). The same constitutional rationale has been used to support marriage subsidies. *See also Peden v. State Dep't of Revenue*, 930 P.2d 1 (Kan. 1996) (upholding a tax schedule with individual rates higher than the highest possible rate for a married couple filing jointly). Do you think the *Zablocki* Court meant to cast marriage subsidies into doubt?

Turner v. Safley

Supreme Court of the United States, 1987.
482 U.S. 78, 107 S.Ct. 2254, 96 L.Ed.2d 64.

■ JUSTICE O'CONNOR delivered the opinion of the Court.

This case requires us to determine the constitutionality of regulations promulgated by the Missouri Division of Corrections relating to inmate marriages. . . .

. . .

The challenged marriage regulation, which was promulgated while this litigation was pending, permits an inmate to marry only with the permission of the superintendent of the prison, and provides that such approval should be given only "when there are compelling reasons to do so." The term "compelling" is not defined, but prison officials testified at trial that generally only a pregnancy or the birth of an illegitimate child would be considered a compelling reason. Prior to the promulgation of this rule, the applicable regulation did not obligate Missouri Division of Corrections officials to assist an inmate who wanted to get married, but it also did not specifically authorize the superintendent of an institution to prohibit inmates from getting married.

. . .

In support of the marriage regulation, petitioners first suggest that the rule does not deprive prisoners of a constitutionally protected right. They concede that the decision to marry is a fundamental right under *Zablocki v. Redhail* and *Loving v. Virginia*, but they imply that a different rule should obtain "in ... a prison forum." Petitioners then argue that even if the regulation burdens inmates' constitutional rights, the restriction should be tested under a reasonableness standard. They urge that the restriction is reasonably related to legitimate security and rehabilitation concerns.

We disagree with petitioners that *Zablocki* does not apply to prison inmates. It is settled that a prison inmate "retains those [constitutional] rights that are not inconsistent with his status as a prisoner or with the legitimate penological objectives of the corrections system." The right to marry, like many other rights, is subject to substantial restrictions as a result of incarceration. Many important attributes of marriage remain, however, after taking into account the limitations imposed by prison life. First, inmate marriages, like others, are expressions of emotional support and public commitment. These elements are an important and significant aspect of the marital relationship. In addition, many religions recognize marriage as having spiritual significance; for some inmates and their spouses, therefore, the commitment of marriage may be an exercise of religious faith as well as an expression of personal dedication. Third, most inmates eventually will be released by parole or commutation, and therefore most inmate marriages are formed in the expectation that they ultimately will be fully consummated. Finally, marital status often is a precondition to the receipt of government benefits (e.g., Social Security benefits), property rights (e.g., tenancy by the entirety, inheritance rights), and other, less tangible benefits (e.g., legitimation of children born out of wedlock). These incidents of marriage, like the religious and personal aspects of the marriage commitment are unaffected by the fact of confinement or the pursuit of legitimate corrections goals.

Taken together, we conclude that these remaining elements are sufficient to form a constitutionally protected marital relationship in the prison context. Our decision in *Butler v. Wilson*, 415 U.S. 953 (1974), summarily affirming *Johnson v. Rockefeller*, 365 F.Supp. 377 (S.D.N.Y.1973), is not to the contrary. That case involved a prohibition on marriage only for inmates sentenced to life imprisonment; and, importantly, denial of the right was part of the punishment for crime.

    . . .

Petitioners have identified both security and rehabilitation concerns in support of the marriage prohibition. The security concern emphasized by petitioners is that "love triangles" might lead to violent confrontations between inmates. With respect to rehabilitation, prison officials testified that female prisoners often were subject to abuse at home or were overly dependent on male figures, and that this dependence or abuse was connected to the crimes they had committed. The superintendent at Renz, petitioner William Turner, testified that in his view, these women prisoners needed to concentrate on developing skills of self-reliance, and that the prohibition on marriage furthered this rehabilitative goal. Petitioners emphasize that the prohibition on marriage should be understood in light of Superintendent Turner's experience with several ill-advised marriage requests from female inmates.

We conclude that on this record, the Missouri prison regulation, as written, is not reasonably related to these penological interests. No doubt legitimate security concerns may require placing reasonable restrictions upon an inmate's right to marry, and may justify requiring approval of the superintendent. The Missouri regulation, however, represents an exaggerated response to such security objectives. There are obvious, easy alternatives to the Missouri regulation that accommodate the right to marry while imposing a *de minimis* burden on the pursuit of security objectives. *See, e.g.,* 28 CFR § 551.10 (1986) (marriage by inmates in federal prison generally permitted, but not if warden finds that it presents a threat to security or order of institution, or to public safety). We are aware of no place in the record where prison officials testified that such ready alternatives would not fully satisfy their security concerns. Moreover, with respect to the security concern emphasized in petitioners' brief—the creation of "love triangles"— petitioners have pointed to nothing in the record suggesting that the marriage regulation was viewed as preventing such entanglements. Common sense likewise suggests that there is no logical connection between the marriage restriction and the formation of love triangles: surely in prisons housing both male and female prisoners, inmate rivalries are as likely to develop without a formal marriage ceremony as with one. Finally, this is not an instance where the "ripple effect" on the security of fellow inmates and prison staff justifies a broad restriction on inmates' rights—indeed, where the inmate wishes to marry a civilian, the decision to marry (apart from the logistics of the wedding ceremony) is a completely private one.

Nor, on this record, is the marriage restriction reasonably related to the articulated rehabilitation goal. First, in requiring refusal of permission absent a finding of a compelling reason to allow the marriage, the rule sweeps much more broadly than can be explained by petitioners' penological objectives. Missouri prison officials testified that generally they had experienced no problem with the marriage of male inmates, and the District Court found that such marriages had routinely been allowed as a matter of practice at Missouri correctional institutions prior to adoption of the rule. The proffered justification thus does not explain the adoption of a rule banning marriages by these inmates. Nor does it account for the prohibition on inmate marriages to civilians. Missouri prison officials testified that generally they had no objection to inmate-civilian marriages, and Superintendent Turner testified that he usually did not object to the marriage of either male or female prisoners to civilians. The rehabilitation concern appears from the record to have been centered almost exclusively on female inmates marrying other inmates or ex-felons; it does not account for the ban on inmate-civilian marriages.

Moreover, although not necessary to the disposition of this case, we note that on this record the rehabilitative objective asserted to support the regulation itself is suspect. Of the several female inmates whose marriage requests were discussed by prison officials at trial, only one was refused on the basis of fostering excessive dependency. The District Court found that the Missouri prison system operated on the basis of excessive paternalism in that the proposed marriages of *all* female inmates were scrutinized carefully even before adoption of the current regulation—only one was approved at Renz in the period from 1979–1983—whereas the marriages of male inmates during the same period were routinely approved. That kind of lopsided rehabilitation concern cannot provide a justification for the broad Missouri marriage rule.

It is undisputed that Missouri prison officials may regulate the time and circumstances under which the marriage ceremony itself takes place. On this record, however, the almost complete ban on the decision to marry is not reasonably related to legitimate penological objectives. We conclude, there-fore, that the Missouri marriage regulation is facially invalid.

NOTE

Does *Turner* stand for the broad proposition that prisoners have a constitutionally protected right to marry? *See, e.g. Akers v. McGinnis*, 352 F.3d 1030 (6th Cir. 2003); *Langone v. Couglin*, 712 F.Supp. 1061 (N.D.N.Y. 1989). How much is *Turner* a "right to marry" decision and how much is it animated by sex inequality concerns? *Cf. Keeney v. Heath*, 57 F.3d 579, 582 (7th Cir. 1995) (opinion by Posner, J.) (noting that "[s]ince the ratio of male prisoners to female guards is vastly higher than the ratio of female prisoners to male guards, there is no doubt that an anti-fraternization policy of the sort enforced [here] ... will impair the marital prospects of women far more than those of men[,]" though, "by relieving pressures to which women guards would otherwise be subjected, [they may] make women guards as a whole better off.").

Michael H. v. Gerald D.

Supreme Court of the United States, 1989.
491 U.S. 110, 109 S.Ct. 2333, 105 L.Ed.2d 91.

■ JUSTICE SCALIA announced the judgment of the Court and delivered an opinion, in which THE CHIEF JUSTICE joins, and in all but note 6 of which JUSTICE O'CONNOR and JUSTICE KENNEDY join.

. . .

The facts of this case are, we must hope, extraordinary. On May 9, 1976, in Las Vegas, Nevada, Carole D., an international model, and Gerald D., a top executive in a French oil company, were married. The couple established a home in Playa del Rey, California in which they resided as husband and wife when one or the other was not out of the country on business. In the summer of 1978, Carole became involved in an adulterous affair with a neighbor, Michael H. In September 1980, she conceived a child, Victoria D., who was born on May 11, 1981. Gerald was listed as father on the birth certificate and has always held Victoria out to the world as his daughter. Soon after delivery of the child, however, Carole informed Michael that she believed he might be the father.

In the first three years of her life, Victoria remained always with Carole, but found herself within a variety of quasi-family units. In October 1981, Gerald moved to New York City to pursue his business interests, but Carole chose to remain in California. The end of that month, Carole and Michael had blood tests of themselves and Victoria, which showed a 98.07% probability that Michael was Victoria's father. In January 1982, Carole visited Michael in St. Thomas, where his primary business interests were based. There Michael held Victoria out as his child. In March, however, Carole left Michael and returned to California, where she took up residence with yet another man, Scott K. Later that spring, and again in the summer, Carole and Victoria spent time with Gerald in New York City, as well as on vacation in Europe. In the fall, they returned to Scott in California.

In November 1982, rebuffed in his attempts to visit Victoria, Michael filed a filiation action in California Superior Court to establish his paternity and right to visitation. In March 1983, the court appointed an attorney and guardian ad litem to represent Victoria's interests. Victoria then filed a cross-complaint asserting that if she had more than one psychological or *de facto* father, she was entitled to maintain her filial relationship, with all of the attendant rights, duties, and obligations, with both. In May 1983, Carole filed a motion for summary judgment. During this period, from March through July of 1983, Carole was again living with Gerald in New York. In

August, however, she returned to California, became involved once again with Michael, and instructed her attorneys to remove the summary judgment motion from the calendar.

For the ensuing eight months, when Michael was not in St. Thomas he lived with Carole and Victoria in Carole's apartment in Los Angeles, and held Victoria out as his daughter. In April 1984, Carole and Michael signed a stipulation that Michael was Victoria's natural father. Carole left Michael the next month, however, and instructed her attorneys not to file the stipulation. In June 1984, Carole reconciled with Gerald and joined him in New York, where they now live with Victoria and two other children since born into the marriage.

In May 1984, Michael and Victoria, through her guardian ad litem, sought visitation rights for Michael *pendente lite*. To assist in determining whether visitation would be in Victoria's best interests, the Superior Court appointed a psychologist to evaluate Victoria, Gerald, Michael, and Carole. The psychologist recommended that Carole retain sole custody, but that Michael be allowed continued contact with Victoria pursuant to a restricted visitation schedule. The court concurred and ordered that Michael be provided with limited visitation privileges *pendente lite*.

On October 19, 1984, Gerald, who had intervened in the action, moved for summary judgment on the ground that under Cal. Evid. Code § 621 there were no triable issues of fact as to Victoria's paternity. This law provides that "the issue of a wife cohabiting with her husband, who is not impotent or sterile, is conclusively presumed to be a child of the marriage." The presumption may be rebutted by blood tests, but only if a motion for such tests is made, within two years from the date of the child's birth, either by the husband or, if the natural father has filed an affidavit acknowledging paternity, by the wife.

On January 28, 1985, having found that affidavits submitted by Carole and Gerald sufficed to demonstrate that the two were cohabiting at conception and birth and that Gerald was neither sterile nor impotent, the Superior Court granted Gerald's motion for summary judgment, rejecting Michael's and Victoria's challenges to the constitutionality of § 621. The court also denied their motions for continued visitation pending the appeal. . . . [T]he California Court of Appeal affirmed the judgment of the Superior Court and upheld the constitutionality of the statute. . . .

. . .

Michael contends as a matter of substantive due process that because he has established a parental relationship with Victoria, protection of Gerald's and Carole's marital union is an insufficient state interest to support termination of that relationship. This argument is, of course, predicated on the assertion that Michael has a constitutionally protected liberty interest in his relationship with Victoria.

. . . In an attempt to limit and guide interpretation of the [Due Process] Clause, we have insisted not merely that the interest denominated as a "liberty" be "fundamental" (a concept that, in isolation, is hard to objectify), but also that it be an interest traditionally protected by our society. As we have put it, the Due Process Clause affords only those protections "so rooted in the traditions and conscience of our people as to be ranked as fundamental." Our cases reflect "continual insistence upon respect for the teachings of history [and] solid recognition of the basic values that underlie our society...." *Griswold v. Connecticut*, 381 U.S. 479, 501 (1965) (HARLAN, J., concurring in judgment).

This insistence that the asserted liberty interest be rooted in history and tradition is evident, as elsewhere, in our cases according constitutional protection to certain parental rights. Michael reads the landmark case of *Stanley v. Illinois*, 405 U.S. 645 (1972), and the subsequent cases of *Quilloin v. Walcott*, 434 U.S. 246 (1978), *Caban v. Mohammed*, 441 U.S. 380 (1979), and *Lehr v. Robertson*, 463 U.S. 248 (1983), as establishing that a liberty interest is created by biological fatherhood plus an established parental relationship—factors that exist in the present case as well. We think that distorts the rationale of those cases. As we view them, they rest not upon such isolated factors but upon the historic respect—indeed, sanctity would not be too strong a term—traditionally accorded to the relationships that develop within the unitary family.[3] In *Stanley*, for example, we forbade the destruction of such a family when, upon the death of the mother, the state had sought to remove children from the custody of a father who had lived with and supported them and their mother for 18 years. As Justice Powell stated for the plurality in *Moore v. East Cleveland*, 431 U.S. 494, 503 (1977): "Our decisions establish that the Constitution protects the sanctity of the family precisely because the institution of the family is deeply rooted in this Nation's history and tradition."

Thus, the legal issue in the present case reduces to whether the relationship between persons in the situation of Michael and Victoria has been treated as a protected family unit under the historic practices of our society, or whether on any other basis it has been accorded special protection. We think it impossible to find that it has. In fact, quite to the contrary, our traditions have protected the marital family (Gerald, Carole, and the child they acknowledge to be theirs) against the sort of claim Michael asserts.

The presumption of legitimacy was a fundamental principle of the common law. Traditionally, that presumption could be rebutted only by proof that a husband was incapable of procreation or had had no access to his wife during the relevant period. As explained by Blackstone, nonaccess could only be proved "if the husband be out of the kingdom of England (or, as the law somewhat loosely phrases it, *extra quatuor maria* [beyond the four seas]) for above nine months...." 1 Blackstone's Commentaries 456 (Chitty ed. 1826). And, under the common law both in England and here, "neither husband nor wife [could] be a witness to prove access or nonaccess." The primary policy rationale underlying the common law's severe restrictions on rebuttal of the presumption appears to have been an aversion to declaring children illegitimate, thereby depriving them of rights of inheritance and succession, and likely making them wards of the state. A secondary policy concern was the interest in promoting the "peace and tranquility of States and families," a goal that is obviously impaired by facilitating suits against husband and wife asserting that their children are illegitimate. Even though,

---

3. JUSTICE BRENNAN asserts that only "a pinched conception of 'the family'" would exclude Michael, Carole and Victoria from protection. We disagree. The family unit accorded traditional respect in our society, which we have referred to as the "unitary family," is typified, of course, by the marital family, but also includes the household of unmarried parents and their children. Perhaps the concept can be expanded even beyond this, but it will bear no resemblance to traditionally respected relationships—and will thus cease to have any constitutional significance—if it is stretched so far as to include the relationship established between a married woman, her lover and their child, during a three-month sojourn in St. Thomas, or during a subsequent 8–month period when, if he happened to be in Los Angeles, he stayed with her and the child.

as bastardy laws became less harsh, "[j]udges in both [England and the United States] gradually widened the acceptable range of evidence that could be offered by spouses, and placed restraints on the 'four seas rule' . . . [,] the law retained a strong bias against ruling the children of married women illegitimate."

We have found nothing in the older sources, nor in the older cases, addressing specifically the power of the natural father to assert parental rights over a child born into a woman's existing marriage with another man. Since it is Michael's burden to establish that such a power (at least where the natural father has established a relationship with the child) is so deeply embedded within our traditions as to be a fundamental right, the lack of evidence alone might defeat his case. But the evidence shows that even in modern times—when, as we have noted, the rigid protection of the marital family has in other respects been relaxed—the ability of a person in Michael's position to claim paternity has not been generally acknowledged. . . .

Moreover, even if it were clear that one in Michael's position generally possesses, and has generally always possessed, standing to challenge the marital child's legitimacy, that would still not establish Michael's case. As noted earlier, what is at issue here is not entitlement to a state pronouncement that Victoria was begotten by Michael. It is no conceivable denial of constitutional right for a State to decline to declare facts unless some legal consequence hinges upon the requested declaration. What Michael asserts here is a right to have himself declared the natural father *and thereby to obtain parental prerogatives.* What he must establish, therefore, is not that our society has traditionally allowed a natural father in his circumstances to establish paternity, but that it has traditionally accorded such a father parental rights, or at least has not traditionally denied them. Even if the law in all States had always been that the entire world could challenge the marital presumption and obtain a declaration as to who was the natural father, that would not advance Michael's claim. Thus, it is ultimately irrelevant, even for purposes of determining *current* social attitudes towards the alleged substantive right Michael asserts, that the present law in a number of States appears to allow the natural father—including the natural father who has not established a relationship with the child—the theoretical power to rebut the marital presumption, see Note, *Rebutting the Marital Presumption: A Developed Relationship Test,* 88 COLUM. L. REV. 369, 373 (1988). What counts is whether the States in fact award substantive parental rights to the natural father of a child conceived within and born into an extant marital union that wishes to embrace the child. We are not aware of a single case, old or new, that has done so. This is not the stuff of which fundamental rights qualifying as liberty interests are made.[6]

        .   .   .

---

6. JUSTICE BRENNAN criticizes our methodology in using historical traditions specifically relating to the rights of an adulterous natural father, rather than inquiring more generally "whether parenthood is an interest that historically has received our attention and protection." There seems to us no basis for the contention that this methodology is "nove[l],". For example, in Bowers v. Hardwick, 478 U.S. 186 (1986), we noted that at the time the Fourteenth Amendment was ratified all but 5 of the 37 States had criminal sodomy laws, that all 50 of the States had such laws prior to 1961, and that 24 States and the District of Columbia continued to have them; and we concluded from that record, regarding that very specific aspect of sexual conduct, that "to claim that a right to engage in such conduct is 'deeply rooted in this Nation's history and tradition' or 'implicit in the concept of ordered liberty' is, at best, facetious." In Roe v. Wade, 410 U.S. 113 (1973), we spent about a fifth of our opinion negating the proposition that there was a long-standing tradition of laws proscribing abortion.

We do not accept JUSTICE BRENNAN's criticism that this result "squashes" the liberty that consists of "the freedom not to conform." It seems to us that reflects the erroneous view that there is only one side to this controversy— that one disposition can expand a "liberty" of sorts without contracting an equivalent "liberty" on the other side. Such a happy choice is rarely available. Here, to *provide* protection to an adulterous natural father is to *deny* protection to a marital father, and vice versa. If Michael has a "freedom not to conform" (whatever that means), Gerald must equivalently have a "freedom to conform." One of them will pay a price for asserting that "freedom"—Michael by being unable to act as father of the child he has adulterously begotten, or Gerald by being unable to preserve the integrity of the traditional family unit he and Victoria have established. Our disposition does not choose between these two "freedoms," but leaves that to the people of California. JUSTICE BRENNAN's approach chooses one of them as the constitutional imperative, on no apparent basis except that the unconventional is to be preferred.

We have never had occasion to decide whether a child has a liberty interest, symmetrical with that of her parent, in maintaining her filial relationship. We need not do so here because, even assuming that such a right exists, Victoria's claim must fail. Victoria's due process challenge is, if anything, weaker than Michael's. Her basic claim is not that California has erred in preventing her from establishing that Michael, not Gerald, should stand as her legal father. Rather, she claims a due process right to maintain filial relationships with both Michael and Gerald. This assertion merits little discussion, for, whatever the merits of the guardian ad litem's belief that such an arrangement can be of great psychological benefit to a child, the claim that a State must recognize multiple fatherhood has no support in the

---

We do not understand why, having rejected our focus upon the societal tradition regarding the natural father's rights vis-à-vis a child whose mother is married to another man, Justice Brennan would choose to focus instead upon "parenthood." Why should the relevant category not be even more general—perhaps "family relationships"; or "personal relationships"; or even "emotional attachments in general"? Though the dissent has no basis for the level of generality it would select, we do: We refer to the most specific level at which a relevant tradition protecting, or denying protection to, the asserted right can be identified. If, for example, there were no societal tradition, either way, regarding the rights of the natural father of a child adulterously conceived, we would have to consult, and (if possible) reason from, the traditions regarding natural fathers in general. But there is such a more specific tradition, and it unqualifiedly denies protection to such a parent.

One would think that Justice Brennan would appreciate the value of consulting the most specific tradition available, since he acknowledges that "[e]ven if we can agree ... that 'family' and 'parenthood' are part of the good life, it is absurd to assume that we can agree on the content of those terms and destructive to pretend that we do." Because such general traditions provide such imprecise guidance, they permit judges to dictate rather than discern the society's views. The need, if arbitrary decisionmaking is to be avoided, to adopt the most specific tradition as the point of reference—or at least to announce, as Justice Brennan declines to do, some other criterion for selecting among the innumerable relevant traditions that could be consulted—is well enough exemplified by the fact that in the present case Justice Brennan's opinion and Justice O'Connor's opinion, which disapproves this footnote, *both* appeal to tradition, but on the basis of the tradition they select reach opposite results. Although assuredly having the virtue (if it be that) of leaving judges free to decide as they think best when the unanticipated occurs, a rule of law that binds neither by text nor by any particular, identifiable tradition, is no rule of law at all.

Finally, we may note that this analysis is not inconsistent with the result in cases such as *Griswold v. Connecticut*, or Eisenstadt v. Baird, 405 U.S. 438 (1972). None of those cases acknowledged a longstanding and still extant societal tradition withholding the very right pronounced to be the subject of a liberty interest and then rejected it. Justice Brennan must do so here. In this case, the existence of such a tradition, continuing to the present day, refutes any possible contention that the alleged right is "so rooted in the traditions and conscience of our people as to be ranked as fundamental," or "implicit in the concept of ordered liberty."

history or traditions of this country. Moreover, even if we were to construe Victoria's argument as forwarding the lesser proposition that, whatever her status vis-à-vis Gerald, she has a liberty interest in maintaining a filial relationship with her natural father, Michael, we find that, at best, her claim is the obverse of Michael's and fails for the same reasons.

. . .

The judgment of the California Court of Appeal is

Affirmed.

■ JUSTICE O'CONNOR, with whom JUSTICE KENNEDY joins, concurring in part.

I concur in all but footnote 6 of JUSTICE SCALIA's opinion. This footnote sketches a mode of historical analysis to be used when identifying liberty interests protected by the Due Process Clause of the Fourteenth Amendment that may be somewhat inconsistent with our past decisions in this area. On occasion the Court has characterized relevant traditions protecting asserted rights at levels of generality that might not be "the most specific level" available. I would not foreclose the unanticipated by the prior imposition of a single mode of historical analysis.

■ [JUSTICE STEVENS concurred in the judgment.]

■ JUSTICE BRENNAN, with whom JUSTICE MARSHALL and JUSTICE BLACKMUN join, dissenting.

In a case that has yielded so many opinions as has this one, it is fruitful to begin by emphasizing the common ground shared by a majority of this Court. Five Members of the Court refuse to foreclose "the possibility that a natural father might ever have a constitutionally protected interest in his relationship with a child whose mother was married to and cohabiting with another man at the time of the child's conception and birth." (STEVENS, J., concurring in judgment). Five Justices agree that the flaw inhering in a conclusive presumption that terminates a constitutionally protected interest without any hearing whatsoever is a *procedural* one. See (WHITE, J., dissenting); (STEVENS, J., concurring in judgment). Four Members of the Court agree that Michael H. has a liberty interest in his relationship with Victoria, see (WHITE, J., dissenting), and one assumes for purposes of this case that he does, see (STEVENS, J., concurring in judgment).

In contrast, only one other Member of the Court fully endorse JUSTICE SCALIA's view of the proper method of analyzing questions arising under the Due Process Clause. See (O'CONNOR, J., concurring in part). Nevertheless, because the plurality opinion's exclusively historical analysis portends a significant and unfortunate departure from our prior cases and from sound constitutional decisionmaking, I devote a substantial portion of my discussion to it.

Once we recognized that the "liberty" protected by the Due Process Clause of the Fourteenth Amendment encompasses more than freedom from bodily restraint, today's plurality opinion emphasizes, the concept was cut loose from one natural limitation on its meaning. This innovation paved the way, so the plurality hints, for judges to substitute their own preferences for those of elected officials. Dissatisfied with this supposedly unbridled and uncertain state of affairs, the plurality casts about for another limitation on the concept of liberty.

It finds this limitation in "tradition." Apparently oblivious to the fact that this concept can be as malleable and as elusive as "liberty" itself, the plurality pretends that tradition places a discernible border around the Constitution. The pretense is seductive; it would be comforting to believe that a search for "tradition" involves nothing more idiosyncratic or complicated than pouring through dusty volumes on American history. Yet, as JUSTICE WHITE observed in his dissent in *Moore v. East Cleveland*: "What the deeply rooted traditions of the country are is arguable." Indeed, wherever I would begin to look for an interest "deeply rooted in the country's traditions," one thing is certain: I would not stop (as does the plurality) at Bracton, or Blackstone, or Kent, or even the American Law Reports in conducting my search. Because reasonable people can disagree about the content of particular traditions, and because they can disagree even about which traditions are relevant to the definition of "liberty," the plurality has not found the objective boundary that it seeks.

Even if we could agree, moreover, on the content and significance of particular traditions, we still would be forced to identify the point at which a tradition becomes firm enough to be relevant to our definition of liberty and the moment at which it becomes too obsolete to be relevant any longer. The plurality supplies no objective means by which we might make these determinations. Indeed, as soon as the plurality sees signs that the tradition upon which it bases its decision (the laws denying putative fathers like Michael standing to assert paternity) is crumbling, it shifts ground and says that the case has nothing to do with that tradition, after all. "What is at issue here," the plurality asserts after canvassing the law on paternity suits, "is not entitlement to a state pronouncement that Victoria was begotten by Michael." But that is precisely what is at issue here, and the plurality's last-minute denial of this fact dramatically illustrates the subjectivity of its own analysis.

It is ironic that an approach so utterly dependent on tradition is so indifferent to our precedents. Citing barely a handful of this Court's numerous decisions defining the scope of the liberty protected by the Due Process Clause to support its reliance on tradition, the plurality acts as though English legal treatises and the American Law Reports always have provided the sole source for our constitutional principles. They have not. Just as common-law notions no longer define the "property" that the Constitution protects, see *Goldberg v. Kelly*, 397 U.S. 254 (1970), neither do they circumscribe the "liberty" that it guarantees. On the contrary, " '[l]iberty' and 'property' are broad and majestic terms. They are among the '[g]reat [constitutional] concepts ... purposely left to gather meaning from experience.... [T]hey relate to the whole domain of social and economic fact, and the statesmen who founded this Nation knew too well that only a stagnant society remains unchanged.' "

It is not that tradition has been irrelevant to our prior decisions. Throughout our decisionmaking in this important area runs the theme that certain interests and practices—freedom from physical restraint, marriage, childbearing, childrearing, and others—form the core of our definition of "liberty." Our solicitude for these interests is partly the result of the fact that the Due Process Clause would seem an empty promise if it did not protect them, and partly the result of the historical and traditional importance of these interests in our society. In deciding cases arising under the Due Process Clause, therefore, we have considered whether the concrete limitation under consideration impermissibly impinges upon one of these more generalized interests.

Today's plurality, however, does not ask whether parenthood is an interest that historically has received our attention and protection; the answer to that question is too clear for dispute. Instead, the plurality asks whether the specific variety of parenthood under consideration—a natural father's relationship with a child whose mother is married to another man—has enjoyed such protection.

If we had looked to tradition with such specificity in past cases, many a decision would have reached a different result. Surely the use of contraceptives by unmarried couples, *Eisenstadt v. Baird*, or even by married couples, *Griswold v. Connecticut*, the freedom from corporal punishment in schools, *Ingraham v. Wright*, 430 U.S. 651 (1977), the freedom from an arbitrary transfer from a prison to a psychiatric institution, *Vitek v. Jones*, 445 U.S. 480 (1980), and even the right to raise one's natural but illegitimate children, *Stanley v. Illinois*, were not "interest[s] traditionally protected by our society," at the time of their consideration by this Court. If we had asked, therefore, in *Eisenstadt*, *Griswold*, *Ingraham*, *Vitek*, or *Stanley* itself whether the specific interest under consideration had been traditionally protected, the answer would have been a resounding "no." That we did not ask this question in those cases highlights the novelty of the interpretive method that the plurality opinion employs today.

The plurality's interpretive method is more than novel; it is misguided. It ignores the good reasons for limiting the role of "tradition" in interpreting the Constitution's deliberately capacious language. In the plurality's constitutional universe, we may not take notice of the fact that the original reasons for the conclusive presumption of paternity are out of place in a world in which blood tests can prove virtually beyond a shadow of a doubt who sired a particular child and in which the fact of illegitimacy no longer plays the burdensome and stigmatizing role it once did. Nor, in the plurality's world, may we deny "tradition" its full scope by pointing out that the rationale for the conventional rule has changed over the years, as has the rationale for CAL. EVID. CODE ANN. § 621 (West Supp. 1989); instead, our task is simply to identify a rule denying the asserted interest and not to ask whether the basis for that rule—which is the true reflection of the values undergirding it—has changed too often or too recently to call the rule embodying that rationale a "tradition." Moreover, by describing the decisive question as whether Michael and Victoria's interest is one that has been "traditionally *protected by* our society," rather than one that society traditionally has thought important (with or without protecting it), and by suggesting that our sole function is to "*discern* the society's views," the plurality acts as if the only purpose of the Due Process Clause is to confirm the importance of interests already protected by a majority of the States. Transforming the protection afforded by the Due Process Clause into a redundancy mocks those who, with care and purpose, wrote the Fourteenth Amendment.

In construing the Fourteenth Amendment to offer shelter only to those interests specifically protected by historical practice, moreover, the plurality ignores the kind of society in which our Constitution exists. We are not an assimilative, homogeneous society, but a facilitative, pluralistic one, in which we must be willing to abide someone else's unfamiliar or even repellant practice because the same tolerant impulse protects our own idiosyncracies. Even if we can agree, therefore, that "family" and "parenthood" are part of the good life, it is absurd to assume that we can agree on the content of those terms and destructive to pretend that we do. In a community such as ours, "liberty" must include the freedom not to conform. The plurality today squashes this freedom by requiring specific approval from history before protecting anything in the name of liberty.

. . .

The evidence is undisputed that Michael, Victoria, and Carole did live together as a family; that is, they shared the same household, Victoria called Michael "Daddy," Michael contributed to Victoria's support, and he is eager to continue his relationship with her. Yet they are not, in the plurality's view, a "unitary family," whereas Gerald, Carole, and Victoria do compose such a family. The only difference between these two sets of relationships, however, is the fact of marriage. The plurality, indeed, expressly recognizes that marriage is the critical fact in denying Michael a constitutionally protected stake in his relationship with Victoria: no fewer than six times, the plurality refers to Michael as the "*adulterous* natural father." ... However, the very premise of *Stanley* and the cases following it is that marriage is not decisive in answering the question whether the Constitution protects the parental relationship under consideration. These cases are, after all, important precisely because they involve the rights of *unwed* fathers. It is important to remember, moreover, that in *Quilloin, Caban,* and *Lehr,* the putative father's demands would have disrupted a "unitary family" as the plurality defines it; in each case, the husband of the child's mother sought to adopt the child over the objections of the natural father. Significantly, our decisions in those cases in no way relied on the need to protect the marital family. Hence the plurality's claim that *Stanley, Quilloin, Caban,* and *Lehr* were about the "unitary family," as that family is defined by today's plurality, is surprising indeed.

The plurality's exclusive rather than inclusive definition of the "unitary family" is out of step with other decisions as well. This pinched conception of "the family," crucial as it is in rejecting Michael and Victoria's claim of a liberty interest, is jarring in light of our many cases preventing the States from denying important interests or statuses to those whose situations do not fit the government's narrow view of the family. From *Loving v. Virginia,* 388 U.S. 1 (1967), to *Levy v. Louisiana,* 391 U.S. 68 (1968), and *Glona v. American Guarantee & Liability Ins. Co.,* 391 U.S. 73 (1968), and from *Gomez v. Perez,* 409 U.S. 535 (1973), to *Moore v. East Cleveland,* we have declined to respect a State's notion, as manifested in its allocation of privileges and burdens, of what the family should be. Today's rhapsody on the "unitary family" is out of tune with such decisions.

The plurality's focus on the "unitary family" is misdirected for another reason. It conflates the question whether a liberty interest exists with the question what procedures may be used to terminate or curtail it. It is no coincidence that we never before have looked at the relationship that the unwed father seeks to disrupt, rather than the one he seeks to preserve, in determining whether he has a liberty interest in his relationship with his child. To do otherwise is to allow the State's interest in terminating the relationship to play a role in defining the "liberty" that is protected by the Constitution. According to our established framework under the Due Process Clause, however, we first ask whether the person claiming constitutional protection has an interest that the Constitution recognizes; if we find that he or she does, we next consider the State's interest in limiting the extent of the procedures that will attend the deprivation of that interest. . . .

The plurality's premature consideration of California's interests is evident from its careful limitation of its holding to those cases in which "the mother is, at the time of the child's conception and birth, married to and cohabitating with another man, *both of whom wish to raise the child as the offspring of their union.*" . . . The highlighted language suggests that if Carole or Gerald alone wished to raise Victoria, or if both were dead and the State wished to raise her, Michael and Victoria might be found to have a liberty interest in their relationship with each other. But that would be to say that whether Michael and Victoria have a liberty interest varies with the State's interest in recognizing that interest for it is the State's interest in protecting the marital family—and not Michael and Victoria's interest in their relationship with each other—that varies with the status of Carole and Gerald's relationship. It is a bad day for due process when the State's interest in terminating a parent-child relationship is reason to conclude that that relationship is not part of the "liberty" protected by the Fourteenth Amendment.

The plurality has wedged itself between a rock and a hard place. If it limits its holding to those situations in which a wife and husband wish to raise the child together, then it necessarily takes the State's interest into account in defining "liberty"; yet if it extends that approach to circumstances in which the marital union already has been dissolved, then it may no longer rely on the State's asserted interest in protecting the "unitary family" in denying that Michael and Victoria have been deprived of liberty.

. . .

NOTES

1. After losing in the United States Supreme Court, Michael H. founded Equality Nationwide for Unwed Fathers (ENUF) and successfully lobbied (along with the California Joint Custody Association) to change California law so that an unwed father could petition the courts for visitation and joint or sole custody when the mother is married to another man. Marcia Coyle, *After the Gavel Comes Down*, The National Law Journal, Feb. 25, 1991, at 1.

2. If Michael H. does not have the constitutional right he believed and claimed he did, could the State ever impose parental obligations on him, including duties of child support? *Cf. Smith v. Cole*, 553 So. 2d 847 (La. 1989).

Pamela S. Karlan, *The Gay and the Angry: The Supreme Court and the Battles Surrounding Same–Sex Marriage*

2010 Sup. Ct. Rev. 159, 159–62 (2011).

Marriage is in the air at One First Street, N.E., and thoughts about it pop up in the oddest places. Like discussions over whether the Constitution confers a right to postconviction DNA testing.[1] Faced with that issue, a majority of the Court found no "freestanding, substantive due process right."[2] But in the course of his dissent, Justice David Souter, who was to leave the Court a fortnight later, included the following extraordinary passage about "the right moment for a court to decide whether substantive due process requires recognition of an individual right unsanctioned by tradition (or the invalidation of traditional law)":[3]

---

1.   District Attorney's Office v. Osborne, 557 U.S. 52, 129 S. Ct. 2308 (2009).

2.   *Id.* at 2312.

3.   *Id.* at 2340 (Souter, J, dissenting) (internal citations omitted).

[It is] essential to recognize how much time society needs in order to work through a given issue before it makes sense to ask whether a law or practice on the subject is beyond the pale of reasonable choice, and subject to being struck down as violating due process. . . .

Changes in societal understanding of the fundamental reasonableness of government actions work out in much the same way that individuals reconsider issues of fundamental belief. We can change our own inherited views just so fast, and a person is not labeled a stick-in-the-mud for refusing to endorse a new moral claim without having some time to work through it intellectually and emotionally. Just as attachment to the familiar and the limits of experience affect the capacity of an individual to see the potential legitimacy of a moral position, the broader society needs the chance to take part in the dialectic of public and political back and forth about a new liberty claim before it makes sense to declare unsympathetic state or national laws arbitrary to the point of being []unconstitutional.[4]

It is hard to read Justice Souter's observations as a commentary on whether convicted criminals should be able to gain access to physical evidence within the state's control for the purpose of running scientific tests designed to establish their innocence. What individual even *has* an "inherited view" on that question, let alone a view, however obtained, involving "issues of fundamental belief"? And postconviction DNA testing hardly seems the kind of question that society needs to "work through" in some therapeutic or "dialectic" way. It is a discrete, albeit important, issue of criminal justice policy.

But if the question is whether the Supreme Court should recognize a constitutional right to marriage for same-sex couples—well, then, this passage makes much more sense. That issue does involve moral claims, inherited views, societal understandings, and questions of timing. Social scientific evidence regarding changes in popular opinion and demography suggests that marriage equality is coming,[5] and coming more quickly than anyone might have hoped or feared eight years ago when the Supreme Court held, in *Lawrence v Texas*,[6] that "[t]he liberty protected by the Constitution" as a matter of substantive due process protects gay people's intimate sexual relationships. . . .[7]

The question whether the Constitution requires such recognition will, at some point in the foreseeable future, arrive at the Supreme Court, since it is unlikely that we will achieve national legal uniformity regarding same-sex marriage through the political process any time soon.[13] When the issue does

---

4.   *Id.* at 2340–41 (Souter, J, dissenting) (internal citations omitted).

5.   See Nathaniel Persily and Patrick J. Egan, *Court Decisions and Trends in Support for Same–Sex Marriage*, Polling Report (Aug 17, 2009), online at http://www.pollingreport.com/penp0908.htm; Pew Research Center, *Support For Same–Sex Marriage Edges Upward* (Oct 6, 2010), online at http://   pewforum.org/Gay–Marriage-and-Homosexuality/Support–For–Same–Sex–Marriage–Edges–Upward.aspx.

6.   539 U.S. 558 (2003).

7.   *Id.* at 567.

13.   In recent years, there has been a widespread reaction to the prospect of swift social change occasioned by the Supreme Court's decisions in Romer v. Evans, 517 U.S. 620 (1996), and Lawrence v. Texas, 539 U.S. 558 (2003), and the Massachusetts Supreme Judicial Court's decision in Goodridge v. Dep't of Public Health, 798 N.E.2d 941 (Mass 2003). *See* Jane S. Schacter, *Courts and the Politics of Backlash: Marriage Equality Then and Now*, 82 S. CAL. L. REV. 1153, 1155 (2009) ("In all, forty-one states and the U.S. Congress have enacted measures restricting the protections afforded same-sex couples since 1995, and twenty-six states have

arrive at the Court, the Justices will have to choose sides on an issue about which many Americans care passionately. They have, of course, done that before. In *Loving v Virginia*,[14] the Court recognized a constitutional right for interracial couples to marry even though sixteen states still forbade it. Yet there was nearly a generation between when the California Supreme Court became the first court to reach that conclusion[15] and when the United States Supreme Court so held. In the meantime, the Court dodged the issue for a decade, apparently because it feared that a decision striking down state bans on interracial marriage would imperil its recent decision in *Brown v Board of Education*.[16]

B.   RESTRICTIONS ON THE PROCEDURE FOR MARRYING

Rappaport v. Katz

United States District Court, Southern District of New York, 1974.
380 F.Supp. 808.

■ POLLACK, DISTRICT JUDGE.

This is an attempted federal suit against the City Clerk of the City of New York, cast in the mold of a suit for violation of Civil Rights, 42 U.S.C.A. § 1983[,] seeking an injunction and damages. Both sides have moved for summary judgment. . . .

The plaintiffs are two couples, one having been married by the defendant City Clerk on November 2, 1973 and one who has been planning marriage and is looking forward to a ceremony to be performed by the City Clerk. They complain that they were subjected (or are to be subjected) to dress guidelines promulgated by the City Clerk to be observed for wedding ceremonies at City Hall, including the exchange of a ring or rings. These guidelines are said to deprive them of due process of law in violation of their constitutional rights. . . .

The questioned guidelines are customarily handed to persons when they receive their marriage licenses if they request the City Clerk or his deputy to officiate at the wedding. Among other things the guidelines say that:

(9) Every couple should be properly attired, the bride must wear a dress or skirt and blouse—no slacks—and the groom must wear a coat and tie.

(10) One or two rings must be exchanged.

An office policy accepts in lieu of a tie, a turtleneck shirt or other shirts or jackets that do not require a tie. The ring requirement may be satisfied by the exchange of any other tangible item; the plaintiffs are not pressing any claim herein in regard to this requirement or its substitutes.

Plaintiff Rappaport wished to wear pants to her wedding but was told to present herself in a skirt. She did, but was unhappy that she did not wear her green velvet pants suit for her wedding. Plaintiff Dibbell states that she

---

passed constitutional bans just since the *Goodridge* decision in 2003."). In the states that have constitutionalized the nonrecognition of same-sex marriage, it seems plausible to assume that it may be harder to achieve marriage equality through the political process than would otherwise be the case.

14. 388 U.S. 1 (1967).

15. *See* Perez v. Sharp, 32 Cal. 2d 711 (1948).

16. 347 U.S. 483 (1954).

wishes to wear pants to her wedding, and she and her intended spouse say they do not wish to exchange either one or two rings as part of their wedding ceremony. The couple to be married are a free lance journalist and a music critic. The bride-to-be says: "I find dressing in pants . . . protects me from much of the sex-role stereotyping to which women continue to be subjected both professionally and socially." The groom-to-be says: "Because marriage has traditionally been an unequal yoke, it is essential to me that my marriage ceremony emphasize the equality of the partnership. For this reason, our dress at this ceremony must be virtually identical." The plaintiffs charge that defendant's guidelines put them to the choice between their statutory right to be married by the City Clerk and their fundamental right to marry free of unwarranted governmental intrusion on their privacy and with free expression.

. . .

The ruling herein, dismissing this suit, is not based upon or any reflection upon the merit of this complaint or the alleged justification for such guidelines and their relation to the statutory command to the Clerk—those have not been considered. While federal courts have accepted the case of a policeman's beard because "choice of personal appearance is an ingredient of an individual's personal liberty, and that any restriction on that right must be justified by a legitimate state interest reasonably related to the regulation," *Dwen v. Barry*, 483 F.2d 1126, 1130 (2d Cir. 1973), it does not seem to this Court that the institutional cases, the school and police cases, reach to the extent of federal cognizance of marriage decorum in City halls.

The threshold question here presented and decided is not the merit of the clothes guideline, but whether the federal courts should supervise marriage forms and procedures in City Clerk's offices. A line for acceptable issues must be drawn somewhere. The defendant's is a locally prescribed and directed function in an area fundamentally of state concern. Plaintiffs concede that some decorum is appropriate but draw the line at skirts, an accoutrement of diminishing use for many. Non constat, the forms and the degree of decorum at weddings in the City Clerk's office do not sufficiently justify provoking a federal-state conflict. Federal judges have too much to do to become involved in this type of dispute which is best and most appropriately resolved by the State of New York and the New York City Council to whom the defendant is responsible. This is a class of case where, certainly, "the state tribunals will afford full justice, subject, of course, to Supreme Court review." H.J. Friendly, Federal Jurisdiction: A General View (1973) p. 95.

Complaint dismissed.

NOTES

1. "The *Rappaport* case was appealed to the Second Circuit, but before the appeal was perfected, Herman Katz was indicted for padding the payroll. (The indictment was dismissed last week because the statute of limitations had run). The new City Clerk was more reasonable and the case was settled by stipulation. The new regulations suggest, but specifically do not require, any particular form of dress for marrying couples, and the exchange of rings requirement has been dropped." Letter from Eve Cary, attorney for the plaintiffs (Feb. 24, 1976).

2. Mary Ann Glendon, *Marriage and the State: The Withering Away of Marriage*, 62 VA. L. REV. 663, 677–82 (1976):

The preliminaries required by a legal system before marriage can take place are revealing indications of the degree to which the State is actively regulating marriage formation, as opposed to contenting itself with promulgating rules that describe ideal behavior but have no real sanctions....

. . .

All states and the Uniform [Marriage and Divorce] Act require a license before formal marriage, and the majority of states impose a waiting period (usually three days as in the UMDA) between the application for the license and its issuance. The licensing statutes usually require that the parties state under oath their names, ages, any relationship between them, whether they have been previously married, and if so how their marriages were terminated. If the statements of the parties do not reveal any irregularities, the license is issued. The licensing official need not make any investigation on his own. The Uniform Marriage and Divorce Act has followed this pattern. The UMDA draftsmen have stated that premarital regulation has been reduced to a minimum and that, as to this minimum, "substantial compliance" is enough. The UMDA does not require documentary evidence of eligibility to marry. In fact, it rejected the suggestion of the Family Law Section of the American Bar Association that, following the practice of some states, a copy of any divorce decree should be required in addition to the simple declaration of the parties regarding the termination of previous marriages. Many states require a physician's certificate stating that each party is free from venereal disease before a marriage license will be issued, but the requirement is easily evaded by marrying in another state, and a marriage contracted in violation of the requirement is not invalid. The draftsmen of the UMDA concluded that this requirement need not be preserved, but did include an optional section for those states that wanted to preserve their medical examination law.

A critical feature of this scheme of regulation is the fact that nearly every aspect of a particular state's plan of regulation can be avoided by going to another state whose law does not happen to include that aspect. There has been a great deal of sentiment in the United States in favor of a longer waiting period, but the ease of evading this or any other change making marriage more difficult has discouraged any such reforms. Compulsory counselling, waiting periods, restraints on remarriage, and consent requirements are being rejected or abandoned by the states at least as much out of despair as on principle or under the influence of recent constitutional interpretations. The law as a whole is not constructed to enforce effectively existing marriage impediments. For instance, the law lacks any system of registration that would facilitate checks on whether impediments exist in a given case.

State laws have, however, begun to manifest new and distinctively modern types of State interest in premarital preliminaries. This is apparent in the increasing number of states requiring that birth control information be dispensed to all applicants for marriage licenses. Another type of interest is manifested in requests on license application forms for information concerned not with revealing impediments to the marriage but with gathering data to study family life. This innovation poses a problem for reformers torn between the desire to protect privacy and the desire to have information in order to make better laws....

. . .

While the laws concerning marriage preliminaries are indicators of the degree to which various marriage restrictions are in fact policed, the laws establishing certain formalities for the actual celebration of the marriage reveal an entirely different aspect of State involvement in marriage regulation: the extent to which marriage rituals, usually religious or customary in origin, have been juridified and made uniform for all groups of the population....

The distinctive feature of American law, in contrast to that of England, France and West Germany, is that there are practically no required formalities for the celebration of marriage. In a few states a couple can form a legal marriage simply by agreeing to be husband and wife and holding themselves out as such.... Although every state requires marriage licenses and records marriage certificates, a wide variety of civil and religious officials are authorized to perform marriages, and states do not impose any particular form of ceremony.

... [I]t is not too much of an exaggeration to say that the present legal regulation of marriage in the United States is already just a matter of licensing and registration....

. . .

Accord In re Cantarella, 119 Cal.Rptr.3d 829, 924 (Cal. Ct. App. 2011) (declaring the failure of a couple to register their marriage after their 1991 wedding insufficient to find the marriage voidable or void, and contrasting the importance of licensing and solemnization with the relative insignificance of registering a marriage, which, the court said, does "little to ensure the parties ... validly consented to marriage, but rather serve[s] a record keeping function," hence is insufficient to negate the solemnized union); *see also In re Farraj*, 900 N.Y.S.2d 340 (N.Y. App. Div. 2010) (holding that because the parties had capacity to marry, celebrated a religious marriage, and were domiciled throughout their marriage in New York, their marriage was valid under New York law despite the failure ever to obtain a marriage license in New Jersey, where the couple held their Islamic wedding ceremony). *But see Betemariam v. Said*, 48 So. 3d 121 (Fla. Dist. Ct. App. 2010) (affirming a Florida trial court decision holding a man and woman were never legally married, hence that the woman's divorce petition should be denied, because they never obtained a valid marriage license or filed a marriage certificate with any clerk of court in Virginia, where their Islamic wedding ceremony was celebrated); *Pinkhasov v. Petocz*, 331 S.W.3d 285, 291 (Ky. Ct. App. 2011) (declaring no valid legal marriage where the parties "knowingly and intentionally evaded and disregarded statutory mandates for establishing a legally valid civil marriage, particularly including their duty to ... obtain a license to be civilly married within Kentucky" before the religious ceremony marrying them occurred).

3. Contrary to popular belief, the captain of a ship has no authority to marry a couple. Marriages performed on the high seas have been recognized, but only if the law of the state governing the marriage recognizes common law marriages. The real issue, therefore, is what state law governs. Courts have looked to the domicile of either the ship owner, *Fisher v. Fisher*, 250 N.Y. 313, 165 N.E. 460 (1929), or the parties, *Norman v. Norman*, 121 Cal. 620, 54 P. 143 (1898). Probably the best explanation of these seemingly disparate rulings is that the courts tend to bend over backwards to sustain such marriages if possible. Comment, *Law Governing Marriages on the High Seas*, 22 CAL. L. REV. 661 (1934). The exception to this pattern involves situations in which a couple attempts to circumvent the law of their domicile by marrying on the high seas, as was the case in *Norman*.

C. STATE OF MIND RESTRICTIONS

Lester v. Lester

Domestic Relations Court of New York, 1949.
195 Misc. 1034, 87 N.Y.S.2d 517.

■ PANKEN, JUSTICE.

. . .

A marriage procured in consequence of coercion or fraud will be regarded ab initio as if the marriage had not been entered into at all. Marriages procured by coercion or in consequence of fraud may in a court having jurisdiction be annulled. An annulment of a marriage is a determination that the conventional relationship of man and wife had not been established despite and in face of a marriage ceremony.

Marriage presumably is a relationship into which two individuals enter upon freely and voluntarily. Environmental influences, and that means education, conventions at a given time and in a given place, and economic status of the parties sometimes control the character of the freedom and the voluntary attitudes of the parties entering into the marriage relationship. To that extent the freedom exercised in a marriage contract is limited.

. . .

The state and the community are interested in and concerned with the institution which marriage creates. Man enters a marital relationship to perpetuate the species. The family is the result of marital relationship. It is the institution which determines in a large measure the environmental influences, cultural backgrounds, and even economic status of its members. It is the foundation upon which society rests and is the basis for the family and all of its benefits.

The character of the culture and civilization, the morals, conventions, law and relationship in the life of a community are what man develops. The community, man, has a vital interest in the marriage institution, for the present generation is father to the succeeding one, and that generation will be the determinant as to the advance of civilization, morals, law and relationships of the future. The character of the succeeding generation is influenced by the permanence and decency of the family institution. Public policy enlists and commands the need of regulation of marriage and the course that the family institution is to pursue. Though marriage is a free institution to be entered into freely and voluntarily because of the community's interest in that institution, the state has a right to regulate and insist upon decency and morals in its maintenance.

Agreements entered into ante-nuptially between parties which do violence to the accepted conventions and laws of the state and the community are unenforceable as a matter of public policy.

The petitioner and the respondent were married according to law. The respondent claims that no valid marriage was entered into; that it was never intended to be a real marriage. He introduced in evidence two documents bearing upon his claim. One exhibited in part reads, "Know all men by these presents that whereas C.L. can no longer bear to continue her relationship with N.C.L. in the same way as in the past, but at the same time is not willing to give him up; and whereas she is desirous of reestablishing herself in the good graces of her relatives and friends; and whereas, considering all things, this cannot be done unless said relatives and friends are given the impression that N.C.L. has married her; and whereas, for personal reasons, she can no longer continue staying with her sister, B.G., but must seek a place of her own; for these and other reasons important only to herself, . . ." and then the document proceeds to set forth that that was the reason and purpose for the marriage between the parties. Another portion of the same document reads, "N.C.L. hereby states, and C.L. hereby admits, that the pretended and spurious marriage contract and ceremonies, and simulated marriage relationship, is taking place against N.C.L.'s wishes, and only because of serious and dire threats of all types made against him and against herself by C.L.; and because of the understanding that the relationship being thus established is only for the benefit of C.L., and hence is not to be interpreted under any conditions as an actual marriage; and that the said relationship involves no obligations of any kind whatsoever, now or at any time in the future, on the part of N.C.L. . . ." Upon those grounds the respondent bases his claim that the marriage is not valid and the obligations which naturally flow from a marriage relationship in favor of the petitioner do not exist. He accepted the benefits of that relationship. He cannot blow hot and cold.

The other exhibit in part reads that both the petitioner and the respondent "do hereby declare that the marriage ceremony we went through at Elkton, Maryland, is in pursuance of our agreement and contract of August 27, 1938," (the date of the other exhibit) "and we therefore consider the marriage ceremony and contract performed between us at Elkton, Maryland, null and void in all its parts and implications whatsoever, ab initio."

. . .

Has the marriage contract entered into between the parties before me been the result of coercion, threat, force, fraud or other taint? . . .

. . .

The testimony as well as the documentary evidence submitted herein negatives the assertion that this marriage was entered upon as the result of threat or coercion.

Private individuals may not by agreement set aside the law of the land. They may not declare that which is valid in law null and void. . . . Persons may not enter upon a marital relationship in conformity with the law and then dissolve that marriage in violation of law. As a matter of public policy the regulation of divorce is as important as is that of marriage. The parties hereto did sign a paper which is in evidence that they both declared their marriage to be "null and void" in all its parts and implications whatsoever "ab initio". What they have signed and sealed after they have entered into a marriage relationship is not enforceable as a matter of law when the purport of that agreement runs counter to the established law and to the morals and mores and conventions of the society in which they live.

The respondent's claim of coercion or threat seems to be unfounded in the light of his relationship for about ten years with the petitioner subsequent to the agreements upon which he rests his claim to invalidity of the marital relationship.

. . .

In the course of the hearing before me it was testified by the respondent repeatedly that he had been under duress during the entire period of their marital relationship. He testified, for instance, that he had had intimate relations with her, sexually, under duress. In other words he was coerced by her to have sexual relations with her. His explanation when asked what the duress was which she exercised, was "The constant fear of committing suicide and leaving me, blackening my name at the College and blackening my name so that I would lose my employment." The respondent before me is a teacher in some college and oddly he teaches the law of family relations. Evidently he thought himself familiar with the law when he caused the petitioner to sign the two documents above referred to. It is quite odd. He prepared the documents in anticipation of a claim by him that the marriage was entered into by him because of coercion and threat.

I find as a matter of fact and as a matter of law for all purposes that the petitioner has established by fair preponderance the allegations in her petition [for support]. She is the wife of the respondent and continues to be such until the marriage is annulled by a court of competent jurisdiction, if at all. In this case the respondent claims that there has been no marriage and the only method in which he might be relieved of his obligation as the petitioner's husband is by an annulment of the marriage. It is very questionable indeed whether he could possibly prevail. Indeed, I think he could not.

. . .

NOTE

Duress and other causes of action to void a marriage on the ground that the partners lacked either the capacity or the intent to contract are rarely relied on now that it has become easier to obtain a divorce in most jurisdictions.

Insanity had been the most widely recognized basis for holding that one of the partners did not have the capacity to consent to marriage. Many states specifically provide that insanity is a ground for divorce or annulment, although a few have made it a defense to such actions. The statutes use a variety of undefined terms such as "idiocy" and "lunacy," which are applied to both people with mental retardation and people with mental illness. Courts in some jurisdictions construe such statutes quite strictly, however, in keeping with a general resistance to marriage dissolution. *See, e.g., Larson v. Larson*, 192 N.E.2d 594 (Ill. Ct. App. 1963) (annulment based on wife's insanity denied despite proof that she had a history of mental illness). Others have broadly construed such statutes in the pursuit of equity. *See, e.g., In re Acker*, 48 Pa. D. & C. 4th 489 (2000) (voiding the marriage of an elderly man with an unstable mental condition despite the fact that no party had sought an annulment).

Johnston v. Johnston

Court of Appeal, Fourth District, 1993.
18 Cal.App.4th 499, 22 Cal.Rptr.2d 253.

■ SONENSHINE, ASSOCIATE JUSTICE.

Donald R. Johnston appeals a judgment annulling his marriage to Brenda Johnston.

After a 20–month marriage, Brenda sought to have her marriage to Donald annulled. Donald agreed the marriage should be terminated but requested a judgment of dissolution be entered.

At the trial, Brenda testified she was unaware of Donald's severe drinking problem until after the marriage and she was upset to discover this and disappointed in his refusal to seek help. She knew before the nuptials that he was unemployed, but did not realize he would refuse to work thereafter. She stated their sex life after marriage was unsatisfactory and that he was dirty and unattractive. In short, he turned from a prince into a frog.

Donald testified to the contrary, but to no avail. The trial court believed Brenda. "There is a conflict in the testimony as to what happened in this marriage. But the court tends to believe [Brenda] has told the truth when she's described the events of the marriage and what occurred before."

The court found Brenda's consent had been fraudulently obtained and annulled the marriage. Donald appeals.

Donald complains the evidence is insufficient to support a finding of fraud. He is correct.

Civil Code section 4425, subdivision (d) delineates the grounds for a voidable marriage: "A marriage is voidable and may be adjudged a nullity if ... (d) The consent of either party was obtained by fraud, unless such party afterwards, with full knowledge of the facts constituting the fraud, freely cohabited with the other as husband or wife." There was no fraud.

Civil Code section 1710 defines deceit as "either: 1. The suggestion, as a fact, of that which is not true, by one who does not believe it to be true; 2. The assertion, as a fact, of that which is not true, by one who has no reasonable ground for believing it to be true; 3. The suppression of a fact, by one who is bound to disclose it, or who gives information of other facts which are likely to mislead for want of communication of that fact; or, 4. A promise, made without any intention of performing it."

Brenda testified Donald told her "he wanted to get a job and with my help in his life, maybe I could help him get himself back together and get his feet on the ground and go out and get a job. And he wanted to get married to me, to have a nice life with me." She also explained that prior to the marriage she saw him regularly and "he was just very polite. Very nice. Very respectful to me. Clean-shaven. Bathed. Just very nice." But after they were wed he "never treated me with respect after the marriage, that is correct. And on many occasions[,] unshaven."

Even if Brenda's testimony was believed by the trial court, she presented insufficient grounds for an annulment.[2] The concealment of "incontinence, temper, idleness, extravagance, coldness or fortune inadequate to representations" cannot be the basis for an annulment. *Marshall v. Marshall* 300 P. 816 (Cal. 1931). If a shoe salesman's false representation that he owned his own shoe store fell short of "fraud sufficient to annul a marriage" in *Mayer v. Mayer,* 279 P. 783 (Cal. 1929), or a future husband's statement that he was a "man of means" (when he was really "impecunious") was not enough in *Marshall v. Marshall, supra,* 300 P. at 817, how much less so are the grounds here, where the husband turned out to be, in the eyes of his wife, a lazy, unshaven disappointment with a drinking problem.[3] In California, fraud must go to the *very essence* of the marital relation before it is sufficient for an annulment. Thus, the trial court erred in granting the annulment.

Brenda testified that during the marriage she executed an interspousal deed, transferring title to real property she owned prior to the marriage to her name and Donald's. The trial judge, after finding the marriage void, declared the deed null and void based upon the failure of consideration. In

---

2. We therefore need not discuss whether Donald knew they were false when he made them or whether Brenda relied upon them in marrying him.

3. In *Mayer,* the Supreme Court reversed an annulment where the marriage had not even been consummated and the parties had never lived together as husband or wife. By contrast, here the court recognized the parties consummated their marriage but found Brenda's disappointment with the quantity and quality of the relationship as further grounds for the annulment. "Well, first of all, the court finds that especially in second marriages or in later in life marriages as opposed to early marriages, the parties are entitled to certain expectations. And foremost among them is a loving relationship, a loving, nurturing relationship. And that absent some very powerful financial considerations, which may be part of a lot of cases but are not a part of this case, is the basic reason for wanting to be married. In addition to that, any reasonably normal person, normal mature person, is entitled to be able to seek and have sexual satisfaction. And in the days where AIDS is a life threatening reality, people are certainly entitled to be able to look within a marriage for that satisfaction, both for fidelity and that type of satisfaction, because it's just too dangerous not to. Those things morally, theoretically have always been a consideration, but especially for the last 40 or 50 years, at least, that's not been a major item. I think it's a new ball game today, and I think that that's entirely within the expectations of a person in getting married."

other words, she deeded the property to Donald because they were married. If the marriage is void, then so is the deed. Because we find the court erred in declaring the marriage void, we must also conclude this portion of the judgment must be reversed.

Donald appealed only the judgment of nullity and the disposition of the real property. Brenda did not file a protective cross-appeal, although the judgment includes several other orders.[4] Moreover, we note the parties stipulated the value of the real property as of June 1992 was $139,000, the purchase price in January 1988 was $101,200 and Brenda's down payment was $19,400; the loan balance at the date of marriage was $82,459 and at the date of separation it was $81,392.56. The parties also stipulated "the negative on the property from October 1989 through June 1992 was $2,384."

Neither the reversal of the portion of the judgment regarding the real property nor the reversal of the judgment of nullity requires a reversal of the stipulation or other orders. Upon remand, the stipulation and the court's other orders shall remain.

The granting of a nullity of the marriage is reversed and a judgment of dissolution shall be entered. The parties' respective property rights in the real property shall be determined based on their previous stipulations. In all other respects, the judgment is affirmed. Donald shall receive his costs on appeal.

NOTES

1. As *Johnston* suggests, most courts have required a stronger showing of fraud to void a marriage contract than to void other contracts. What policy, if any, is served by this tradition?

2. Professor Max Rheinstein noted that "the tendency [of American courts] has been . . . to limit essentiality to those facts which relate to the sex aspects of the marriage, such as affliction with venereal disease, false representation by the woman that she is pregnant by her partner, concealed intent not to consummate the marriage or not to have intercourse likely to produce progeny, also concealed intent not to go through with a promise to follow the secular conclusion of the marriage with a religious ceremony considered by the other party essential to relieve intercourse from the stigma of sin. Annulments have rarely been granted for fraudulent misrepresentations of character, past life, or social standing and hardly ever for misrepresentations on matters of property or income." MAX RHEINSTEIN, MARRIAGE STABILITY, DIVORCE AND LAW 95 (1972). Case law supports this analysis. *See Stepp v. Stepp*, 2004 Ohio 1617 (disallowing annulment based on fraudulent portrayal of assets); *Adler v. Adler* 805 So.2d 952 (Fla. App. 2001) (lying about past marriages was not grounds for annulment). Even fraud concerning the sexual aspects of marriage will not make the marriage voidable once the marriage has been consummated. *See Blair v. Blair*, 147 S.W.3d 882 (Mo. App. 2004) (lying about paternity of children born during marriage did not support a claim for annulment). The primary—although not the only—exceptions to Rheinstein's observations are incest and bigamy, which render marriages void, not simply voidable, in most jurisdictions.

---

4. The court found the money that was in the bank and the tax refund to be Brenda's separate property. "The court also [found] that [Donald] paid $9,000 for the boat and that whether or not [Brenda's] name was on the title at one time, that the boat, . . . , [was Donald's] separate property. As to the check, as to the funds for the sale of the previous boat, the court [found] that there was a fair distribution at the time; that each party got what they put into it and is not going to rule further on that."

In re the Marriage of Farr

Colorado Court of Appeals, 2010.
228 P.3d 267.

■ GRAHAM, J.

Larry Allen Farr (husband) appeals from the judgment declaring his marriage to Joy Lynn Farr (wife) invalid[.] . . . We affirm.

I. Background

The parties' thirty-year marriage ended in dissolution in 1999. They remarried in 2004, and in 2007, husband filed for dissolution. Wife cross-petitioned to declare the second marriage invalid pursuant to section 14–10–111(1)(d), C.R.S.2009, asserting that she agreed to marry him based upon his representation that he had a terminal illness. A hearing was held, after which the trial court dismissed the petition for dissolution and declared the marriage invalid. Permanent orders regarding property, maintenance, and attorney fees were then entered pursuant to stipulation. Thereafter, husband appealed the order invalidating the marriage, and wife moved to dismiss his appeal as untimely.

. . .

III. Declaration of Invalidity

Husband contends that the trial court applied the wrong standard of proof in invalidating the parties' marriage and, further, that the court abused its discretion in finding that his representation concerning his illness was fraudulent and in neglecting to determine whether that representation went to the essence of the marriage. We disagree.

A. Standard of Proof

Whether the trial court applied the proper standard of proof is a question of law that we review de novo. *See McCallum Family L.L.C. v. Winger*, 221 P.3d 69, 72 (Colo. 2009).

For all civil actions accruing after July 1, 1972, the burden of proof shall be by a preponderance of the evidence, notwithstanding any contrary provision of law. § 13–25–127(1), (4), C.R.S.2009; *Gerner v. Sullivan*, 768 P.2d 701, 702–03 (Colo. 1989). The statute applies despite the existence of prior settled case law establishing a higher burden of proof. *Gerner*, 768 P.2d at 705. Pursuant to the statute, the preponderance of the evidence standard applies when a party seeks to avoid a transaction on equitable grounds alleging fraud, undue influence, or mistake. *See Page v. Clark*, 592 P.2d 792, 801 (Colo. 1979).

. . .

. . . Thus, . . . the trial court did not err in applying a preponderance of the evidence standard when determining wife's petition.

B. Findings in Support of Invalidity

We review for abuse of discretion the trial court's decision to invalidate a marriage. *See In re Marriage of Blietz*, 538 P.2d 114, 116 (Colo. App. 1975).

As relevant here, a court shall enter a decree declaring a marriage invalid if one party entered into the marriage in reliance on a fraudulent act or representation of the other party when the act or representation goes to the essence of the marriage. *See* § 14–10–111(1)(d).

Here, the trial court recited these statutory requirements and made the following findings: (1) that wife's testimony was more credible than husband's; (2) that wife believed husband's representation that his death was imminent; (3) that wife did not want husband to die alone; (4) that wife relied on husband's representation that he was suffering from myelodysplastic syndrome in deciding to remarry him; and (5) that such representation was fraudulent.

Because these findings are supported by the record, we reject husband's contention that the court abused its discretion in invalidating the parties' marriage. Wife testified that in 2003, before the parties remarried, husband told her that he had a serious illness and that he would die within a few years. Although the medical records husband brought to his meeting with her indicated that his disease had not progressed to a terminal form, wife testified that she was not familiar with the disease and believed what husband told her about his prognosis. She further testified, as did other witnesses, that she agreed to remarry because husband was dying and she did not want him to die alone.

Wife and the parties' son testified that after the parties remarried, husband did not appear to be ill and that they came to believe he had misled them into believing that he would die soon. Wife further testified that she reviewed husband's recent medical records and that they indicated to her that he was not ill. She also submitted a 2005 insurance application form, which was signed by husband and which indicated that he had no medical problems.

We recognize that there was contrary evidence presented regarding these issues. The evidence as to the nature and progression of husband's disease was particularly conflicting, and no expert testimony was presented. Nonetheless, it is the province of the trial court to determine the credibility of the witnesses and to resolve conflicting evidence. If the trial court's factual findings have support in the record, an appellate court may not substitute its own findings for those of the trial court. Thus, although the evidence sharply conflicted here and the court could have found, as husband suggests, that he made only an innocent misrepresentation, we may not disturb the court's findings because there is some evidence in the record to support them.

We reject husband's contention that the trial court bypassed the statutory requirement that his misrepresentation go to the essence of the marriage. Our review of the court's findings indicates that it first recognized that it had to find this element, and then found that wife relied on husband's representation in deciding to remarry and that husband made a sufficient fraudulent representation for the court to invalidate the marriage. We conclude that these findings, taken together, are adequate to imply that the court found that the misrepresentation went to the essence of the marriage, and we discern no basis for remand.

We also reject husband's contention that a misrepresentation about a spouse's prognosis and life expectancy cannot go to the essence of the marriage. Husband cites no case law specifically supporting this contention. Additionally, there was ample evidence that wife decided to remarry him *only* because she believed his death was imminent. Thus, the record supports the finding that, at least as to these parties, the misrepresentation did go to the essence of their remarriage.

· · ·

The judgment is affirmed.

D.   COMMON LAW MARRIAGE

Hargrave v. Duval–Couetil (In re Estate of Duval)

Supreme Court of South Dakota, 2010.
777 N.W.2d 380.

■ MEIERHENRY, JUSTICE.

Nathalie Duval–Couetil and Orielle Duval–Georgiades (Daughters) appeal the circuit court's judgment that Karen Hargrave (Hargrave) was the common-law wife of their father, Paul A. Duval (Duval). Daughters contend the circuit court erred when it held that Duval and Hargrave entered into a common-law marriage under the laws of Mexico and Oklahoma. We agree and reverse the circuit court.

FACTS AND BACKGROUND

Duval and Hargrave began living together in Massachusetts in 1994. In 1995, Duval acquired a home in Custer, South Dakota. Hargrave moved from Massachusetts to Duval's home in South Dakota in 1996. In 1997, Duval and Hargrave began a yearly routine of spending the summer months in Custer and the winter months in Mexico. In 1998, Duval and Hargrave bought a home together in Nuevo Leon, Mexico, as husband and wife.

In 2005, Duval was assaulted while in Mexico and placed in an intensive care unit for his injuries. Hargrave lived with Duval at the hospital while he was being treated. She later took Duval to Oklahoma for rehabilitation at a hospital in the Tulsa area and eventually to Rochester, Minnesota, for medical treatment at Mayo Clinic. Duval and Hargrave subsequently returned to Oklahoma for a period of time; and then, resumed their annual routine of spending winters in Mexico and summers in Custer. Duval was killed as a result of a rock climbing accident on June 24, 2008, in Custer County, South Dakota.

Duval and Hargrave never formally married. Hargrave testified that she and Duval had discussed a formal wedding ceremony, but mutually decided against it. She said they did not think they needed to marry because they held themselves out as husband and wife and felt like they were married. The circuit court specifically found that over the course of Duval and Hargrave's relationship, Duval referred to Hargrave as his wife on an income tax return form, designated her as the beneficiary on his VA health benefits application, and executed a general power of attorney in her favor.

The circuit court ultimately concluded that Hargrave had established that she and Duval met the requirements for a common-law marriage under the laws of both Mexico and Oklahoma. As such, Hargrave was treated as Duval's surviving spouse for inheritance purposes in South Dakota. Daughters appeal. Daughters' main issue on appeal is whether the circuit court erroneously recognized Hargrave as Duval's surviving spouse entitling her to inherit from his estate. They claim (1) that the South Dakota domicile of

Duval and Hargrave precluded them from entering into a common-law marriage in either Mexico or Oklahoma, (2) that South Dakota law does not recognize a Mexican concubinage as a marriage, and (3) that Hargrave and Duval had not entered into a common-law marriage under Oklahoma law.

ANALYSIS

The relevant facts are not in dispute. Because the issues involve questions of law, our review is de novo. *Sanford v. Sanford,* 694 N.W.2d 283, 287 (S.D. 2005). The first issue centers on whether South Dakota will give effect to a common-law marriage established by South Dakota domiciliaries while living in a jurisdiction that recognizes common-law marriage.

Common–Law Marriage

Common-law marriages were statutorily abrogated in South Dakota in 1959 by an amendment to SDCL 25–1–29. Notwithstanding, Hargrave contends that South Dakota continues to recognize valid common-law marriages entered into in other jurisdictions. Hargrave relies on SDCL 19–8–1, which provides that "[e]very court of this state shall take judicial notice of the common law and statutes of every state, territory, and other jurisdiction of the United States." *Id.* In addition to taking judicial notice of the common-law of other states, the South Dakota Legislature specifically addressed the validity of marriages entered into in other jurisdictions in SDCL 25–1–38. This statute provides that "[a]ny marriage contracted outside the jurisdiction of this state ... which is valid by the laws of the jurisdiction in which such marriage was contracted, is valid in this state." *Id.* In view of these statutes, we conclude that a common-law marriage validly entered into in another jurisdiction will be recognized in South Dakota.*

Daughters argue that the domicile of the couple controls their ability to enter into a common-law marriage. Daughters urge this Court to adopt a rule requiring parties to a common-law marriage to be domiciled in the state in which the marriage occurred. Thus, a couple domiciled in South Dakota could not be considered married merely by traveling to another state that recognizes common-law marriage and meeting that state's common-law marriage requirements. Daughters further allege that at all relevant times, Duval and Hargrave were domiciled in South Dakota, thereby precluding them from entering into a common-law marriage in either Mexico or Oklahoma. Daughters cite *Garcia v. Garcia* as authority for the domicile requirement. 127 N.W. 586 (S.D. 1910). In *Garcia,* we said that a marriage "valid in the state where it was contracted, is to be regarded as valid in [South Dakota]." *Id.* at 589. We do not interpret *Garcia* as requiring domicile in the state in which the marriage occurred.

This is consistent with other jurisdictions that do not require parties to establish domicile in the state where the common-law marriage occurred. Minnesota courts have recognized common-law marriages entered into in other jurisdictions. In *Pesina v. Anderson,* the court held it would "recognize a common-law marriage if the couple takes up residence (but not necessarily domicile) in another state that allows common-law marriages." 1995 WL 387752 *2 (Minn. Ct. App. 1995) (quoting *Laikola v. Engineered Concrete,* 277 N.W.2d 653, 658 (Minn. 1979)) (citations omitted). Similarly, in *Vandever v.*

---

* Notably, "a common law marriage contracted in a state of the United States that recognizes common law marriages is just as valid as a ceremonial marriage ... [and] is not a second-class sort of marriage [.]" Rosales v. Battle, 7 Cal.Rptr.3d 13, 17, 113 Cal.App.4th 1178, 1184 (2003) (citations and quotations omitted).

Indus. Comm'n of Ariz., the court stated that it "disagree[d] with the legal reasoning of cases which hold that the policy of the domicile disfavoring common-law marriages should govern unless the couple has subsequently established residence in a state recognizing such marriages." 714 P.2d 866, 870 (Ariz. 1985). The *Vandever* court went on to state, "[t]hese cases effectively read a requirement of residency into the law of all common-law marriage[] states which may or may not exist." *Id. See Grant v. Superior Court* in and for County of Pima, 555 P.2d 895, 897 (Ariz. Ct. App. 1976) ("Although Arizona does not authorize common law marriage, it will accord to such a marriage entered into in another state the same legal significances as if the marriage were effectively contracted in Arizona."). Mississippi has also recognized that "[t]he [domicile requirement] argument ignores the basic right of all persons to choose their place of marriage. As long as they follow the requirements of the law of the state of celebration, the marriage is valid in most jurisdictions." *George v. George*, 389 So.2d 1389, 1390 (Miss. 1980). Likewise, Maryland "has continuously held that a common-law marriage, valid where contracted, is recognized in [Maryland]." *Goldin v. Goldin*, 426 A.2d 410, 412 (Md. Ct. Spec. App. 1981).

In addition to *Garcia*, the plain meaning of SDCL 25–1–38 does not require domicile in the foreign jurisdiction in order for the marriage to be considered valid in South Dakota. Consequently, we hold that South Dakota does not require domicile in the foreign jurisdiction before recognizing that jurisdiction's common-law marriage scheme. All that is necessary for a marriage from another jurisdiction to be recognized in South Dakota is for the marriage to be valid under the law of that jurisdiction. *See* SDCL 25–1–38. Thus, the question in this case is whether Duval and Hargrave would be considered validly married under the laws of either Nuevo Leon, Mexico, or Oklahoma.

Concubinage in Mexico

.   .   .

We are persuaded by the reasoning of *Nevarez* [*v. Bailon*, 287 S.W.2d 521, 523 (Tex. Civ. App. 1956),] and *Rosales* [*v. Battle*, 7 Cal.Rptr.3d 13, 113 Cal.App.4th 1178 (2003)], and . . . conclude that a Mexican concubinage is not the legal equivalent of a common-law marriage in the United States. Consequently, the circuit court erred in concluding the concubinage between Duval and Hargrave, if one existed, had the same legal effect as a common-law marriage. Therefore, we reverse on this issue.

Common–Law Marriage in Oklahoma

The circuit court concluded that Duval and Hargrave entered into a valid common-law marriage while they lived in Oklahoma. The Oklahoma Court of Civil Appeals recently reaffirmed its recognition of common-law marriages and its requirements. The court stated:

> [T]his Court recognizes in accordance with established Oklahoma case law that, absent a marital impediment suffered by one of the parties to the common-law marriage, a common-law marriage occurs upon the happening of three events: a declaration by the parties of an intent to marry, cohabitation, and a holding out of themselves to the community of being husband and wife.

Brooks v. Sanders, 190 P.3d 357, 362 (Okla. Civ. App. 2008). In *Brooks*, the court referenced an earlier Oklahoma case that explained the requirements of Oklahoma's common-law marriage as follows:

> " 'To constitute a valid "common-law marriage," it is necessary that there should be an actual and mutual agreement to enter into a matrimonial relation, permanent and exclusive of all others, between parties capable in law of making such contract, consummated by their cohabitation as man and wife, or their mutual assumption openly of marital duties and obligations. A mere promise of future marriage, followed by illicit relations, is not, in itself, sufficient to constitute such marriage.' "

Id. at 358 n. 2 (quoting *D.P. Greenwood Trucking Co. v. State Indus. Comm'n*, 1954 OK 165, 271 P.2d 339, 342 (quoting *Cavanaugh v. Cavanaugh*, 275 P. 315 (Okla. 1929))). Based on the language of these two cases, it appears that Oklahoma requires (1) a mutual agreement or declaration of intent to marry, (2) consummation by cohabitation, and (3) publicly holding themselves out as husband and wife. Oklahoma law requires the party alleging a common-law marriage satisfy these elements by clear and convincing evidence. *Standefer v. Standefer*, 26 P.3d 104, 107 (Okla. 2001) (citing *Maxfield v. Maxfield*, 258 P.2d 915, 921 (Okla. 1953)).

Thus, the first requirement Hargrave had to satisfy by clear and convincing evidence was that she and Duval had mutually agreed and/or declared their intent to marry while in Oklahoma. *Brooks*, 190 P.3d at 362. "Some evidence of consent to enter into a common-law marriage are cohabitation, actions consistent with the relationship of spouses, recognition by the community of the marital relationship, and declarations of the parties." *Standefer*, 26 P.3d at 107 (citing *Reaves v. Reaves*, 82 P. 490 (Okla. 1905)). The circuit court made no finding on mutual agreement or declaration of intent to marry, yet concluded that Duval and Hargrave entered into a common-law marriage. We have said a circuit court "is not required to 'enter a finding of fact on every fact represented, but only those findings of fact essential to support its conclusions.' " *In re S.K.*, 587 N.W.2d 740, 742 (S.D. 1999) (quoting *Hanks v. Hanks*, 334 N.W.2d 856, 858–59 (S.D. 1983)). A finding on whether the couple mutually agreed or declared their intent to marry while in Oklahoma was essential to support the circuit court's conclusion that they entered into a common-law marriage. A review of the testimony may explain why the circuit court was unable to enter a finding of a mutual agreement or declaration of intent to enter into a marital relationship.

Hargrave testified that she and Duval entered into an "implicit agreement" to be married while they were in Oklahoma. She also testified that "nobody said, okay, so we should agree to be married and write it down and put the date on it." When asked on cross-examination if there was ever a point when she and Duval made an agreement to be married, Hargrave stated in the negative, and said the couple just decided "well, I guess we are [married]."

The Oklahoma Supreme Court addressed this issue under a similar situation and recognized the importance of establishing a clear intent to marry. *Standefer*, 26 P.3d at 107–08. In *Standefer*, the court stated the "evidence [wa]s clear and convincing that both parties assented to a marriage on Thanksgiving Day of 1988." Both the husband and wife in *Standefer* agreed that they were common-law spouses as a result of their mutual assent to marry on that day. Significantly, the couple was able to identify an instance where they mutually assented to a marriage. This fact stands in contrast to the present case where Hargrave's testimony established that no specific time existed when the couple mutually agreed or declared their intent to be married. To meet Oklahoma's requirements, their mutual agreement or declaration to marry would have to be more than an implicit agreement. This consent requirement is consistent with SDCL 25–1–38, which sets forth the requirement that a marriage must be "contracted" in the other jurisdiction before South Dakota will recognize the marriage as valid. SDCL 25–1–38 provides "[a]ny marriage *contracted* outside the jurisdiction of this state ... which is valid by the laws of the jurisdiction in which such marriage was *contracted*, is valid in this state." *Id.* (emphasis added). Failing to establish that mutual assent or a declaration to marry took place, Hargrave could not meet the first requirement for entering into a common-law marriage in Oklahoma as outlined by *Brooks*. 190 P.3d at 362.

The absence of a finding of fact on this issue, coupled with Hargrave's testimony, leads to a conclusion that as a matter of law Hargrave could not prove by clear and convincing evidence that the couple entered into a valid common-law marriage while in Oklahoma. Thus, no legal basis existed to support the circuit court's conclusion that the parties entered into a common-law marriage in Oklahoma.

. . .

We reverse and remand to the circuit court for proceedings consistent with this opinion.

NOTE

At the beginning of the twentieth century, two-thirds of the states recognized common law marriages. Today only nine states and the District of Columbia do.[1] This legal change in many respects reflects demographic changes. A practice that was almost a necessity when the population was scarce and scattered, and ministers or justices of the peace few and far between, became increasingly unacceptable as society grew and became more complex. Moral objections also grew. Otto E. Koegel, for example, argued that common law marriages "invite impulsive, impure and secret unions." OTTO E. KOEGEL, COMMON LAW MARRIAGE AND ITS DEVELOPMENT IN THE UNITED STATES 167 (1922). A growing concern with eugenics was a third factor in tightening the procedure for contracting a legal marriage. Blood tests and prohibitions on the marriage of mentally ill individuals also embodied this concern. For additional perspective, see Ariela R. Dubler, Note, *Governing Through Contract: Common Law Marriage in the Nineteenth Century*, 107 YALE L.J. 1885 (1998).

Recently, however, the trend toward abolishing common law marriage has abated somewhat. For one thing, it has been recognized that those jurisdictions that do not recognize common law marriage often have to resort to other devices to achieve the practically same end. Most jurisdictions, for example, have adopted a presumption in favor of the validity of a second marriage when one spouse was previously married (the burden of proving that the first marriage was still in existence lies with the party attacking the legitimacy of the second marriage).[2]

---

1. Alabama, Colorado, Iowa, Kansas, Montana, Oklahoma, Rhode Island, South Carolina, and Texas (called "informal marriage") plus the District of Columbia follow the traditional common law marriage requirements. Georgia, Idaho, Ohio, and Pennsylvania have grandfather clauses recognizing common law marriages prior to certain years (1997, 1996, 1991, 2005 respectively). New Hampshire recognizes common law marriages solely for purposes of probate (at the death of one spouse). Utah allows common law marriage of a sort, but has extra requirements beyond the traditional standard and adds a need for a court determination to validate the marriage.

2. It is consequently very difficult to tally exactly how many states recognize some form of common law marriage, particularly if a functional definition is used. Tennessee, for example,

There are three different situations to consider: (1) instances in which both parties believed in good faith they were formally married, but in fact they were not (e.g., the person who officiated had no authority to marry them, or there was a technical flaw in the license); (2) instances in which one party believed in good faith that he or she was formally married (e.g., one spouse lied and concealed the fact that he or she was still married to someone else); and (3) instances in which both knew they were not formally married, but believed they were nonetheless legally wed. Legal recognition of the marriage or other appropriate relief seems clearly justified for both spouses in instance one, and for the innocent spouse in example two. Any decision to abolish common law marriage in a jurisdiction should therefore at least consider adopting other forms of protection for innocent parties in instances one and two. California, for example, has adopted the putative spouse doctrine in its Family Code:

§ 2251.   Status of putative spouse; division of quasi-marital property

(a) If a determination is made that a marriage is void or voidable and the court finds that either party or both parties believed in good faith that the marriage was valid, the court shall:

(1) Declare the party or parties to have the status of a putative spouse.

(2) If the division of property is in issue, divide . . . that property acquired during the union. . . . This property is known as "quasi-marital property."

§ 2254.   Support of putative spouse

The court may, during the pendency of a proceeding for nullity of marriage or upon judgment of nullity of marriage, order a party to pay for the support of the other party in the same manner as if the marriage had not been void or voidable if the party for whose benefit the order is made is found to be a putative spouse.

It is important to note, however, that a putative marriage is not a marriage. For example, there is no need to seek an annulment or divorce to terminate a putative marriage. *See generally* Christopher Blakesley, *The Putative Marriage Doctrine*, 60 TUL. L. REV. 1 (1985); Raymond O'Brien, *Domestic Partnerships Recognition & Responsibility*, 32 SAN DIEGO L. REV. 163 (1995); Jennifer Robbennolt & Monica Johnson, *Legal Planning for Unmarried Committed Partners: Empirical Lessons for a Preventive and Therapeutic Approach*, 41 ARIZ. L. REV. 417 (1999).

---

has formally abolished common law marriage, but reachieved almost the same result by presumption. *See* Emmit v. Emmit, 174 S.W.3d 248 (Tenn.App. 2005); Richard T. Doughtie, Note, *Use of Presumptions in Proving the Existence of Marriage Relationships in Tennessee*, 5 MEM. ST. U. L. REV. 409 (1975).

CHAPTER 3

MARRIAGE

A. THE TRADITIONAL MODEL OF MARRIAGE

1. MARITAL PRIVACY

McGuire v. McGuire

Supreme Court of Nebraska, 1953.
157 Neb. 226, 59 N.W.2d 336.

■ MESSMORE, JUSTICE.

The plaintiff, Lydia McGuire, brought this action in equity in the district court for Wayne County against Charles W. McGuire, her husband, as defendant, to recover suitable maintenance and support money, and for costs and attorney's fees. Trial was had to the court and a decree was rendered in favor of the plaintiff.

The district court decreed that the plaintiff was legally entitled to use the credit of the defendant and obligate him to pay for certain items in the nature of improvements and repairs, furniture, and appliances for the household in the amount of several thousand dollars; required the defendant to purchase a new automobile with an effective heater within 30 days; ordered him to pay travel expenses of the plaintiff for a visit to each of her daughters at least once a year; that the plaintiff be entitled in the future to pledge the credit of the defendant for what may constitute necessaries of life; awarded a personal allowance to the plaintiff in the sum of $50 a month; awarded $800 for services for the plaintiff's attorney; and as an alternative to part of the award so made, defendant was permitted, in agreement with plaintiff, to purchase a modern home elsewhere.

. . .

The record shows that the plaintiff and defendant were married in Wayne, Nebraska, on August 11, 1919.... The plaintiff had been previously married. Her first husband died in October 1914, leaving surviving him the plaintiff and two daughters. He died intestate, leaving 80 acres of land in Dixon County. The plaintiff and each of the daughters inherited a one-third interest therein. At the time of the marriage of the plaintiff and defendant the plaintiff's daughters were 9 and 11 years of age. By working and receiving financial assistance from the parties to this action, the daughters received a high school education in Pender.... Both ... are married and have families of their own.

On April 12, 1939, the plaintiff transferred her interest in the 80–acre farm to her two daughters. The defendant signed the deed.

At the time of trial plaintiff was 66 years of age and the defendant nearly 80 years of age. No children were born to these parties. The defendant had no dependents except the plaintiff.

The plaintiff testified that she was a dutiful and obedient wife, worked and saved, and cohabited with the defendant until the last 2 or 3 years. She worked in the fields, did outside chores, cooked, and attended to her household duties such as cleaning the house and doing the washing. For a number of years she raised as high as 300 chickens, sold poultry and eggs, and used the money to buy clothing, things she wanted, and for groceries. She further testified that the defendant was the boss of the house and his word was law; that he would not tolerate any charge accounts and would not inform her as to his finances or business; and that he was a poor companion. The defendant did not complain of her work, but left the impression to her that she had not done enough. On several occasions the plaintiff asked the defendant for money. He would give her very small amounts, and for the last 3 or 4 years he had not given her any money nor provided her with clothing, except a coat about 4 years previous. The defendant had purchased the groceries the last 3 or 4 years, and permitted her to buy groceries, but he paid for them by check. There is apparently no complaint about the groceries the defendant furnished. The defendant had not taken her to a motion picture show during the past 12 years. They did not belong to any organizations or charitable institutions, nor did he give her money to make contributions to any charitable institutions. . . . For the past 4 years or more, the defendant had not given the plaintiff money to purchase furniture or other household necessities. Three years ago he did purchase an electric, wood-and-cob combination stove which was installed in the kitchen, also linoleum floor covering for the kitchen. The plaintiff further testified that the house is not equipped with a bathroom, bathing facilities, or inside toilet. The kitchen is not modern. She does not have a kitchen sink. Hard and soft water is obtained from a well and cistern. She has a mechanical Servel refrigerator, and the house is equipped with electricity. There is a pipeless furnace which she testified had not been in good working order for 5 or 6 years, and she testified she was tired of scooping coal and ashes. She had requested a new furnace but the defendant believed the one they had to be satisfactory. She related that the furniture was old and she would like to replenish it, at least to be comparable with some of her neighbors; that her silverware and dishes were old and were primarily gifts, outside of what she purchased; that one of her daughters was good about furnishing her clothing, at least a dress a year, or sometimes two; that the defendant owns a 1929 Ford coupe equipped with a heater which is not efficient, and on the average of every 2 weeks he drives the plaintiff to Wayne to visit her mother; and that he also owns a 1927 Chevrolet pickup which is used for different purposes on the farm. The plaintiff was privileged to use all of the rent money she wanted to from the 80–acre farm, and when she goes to see her daughters, which is not frequent, she uses part of the rent money for that purpose, the defendant providing no funds for such use. The defendant ordinarily raised hogs on his farm, but the last 4 or 5 years has leased his farm land to tenants, and he generally keeps up the fences and the buildings. At the present time the plaintiff is not able to raise chickens and sell eggs. She has about 25 chickens. The plaintiff has had three abdominal operations for which the defendant has paid. She selected her own doctor, and there were no restrictions placed in that respect. When she has requested various things for the home or personal effects, defendant has informed her on many occasions that he did not have the money to pay for the same. She would like to have a new car. She visited one daughter in Spokane, Washington, in March 1951 for 3 or 4 weeks, and visited the other daughter living in Fort Worth, Texas, on three occasions for 2 to 4 weeks at a time. She had visited one of her daughters when she was living in Sioux City some weekends. The plaintiff further testified that she had very little funds, possibly $1,500 in the bank which was chicken money and money which her father furnished her, he having departed this life a few years ago; and that use of the telephone was restricted, indicating that defendant did not desire that she make long distance calls, otherwise she had free access to the telephone.

It appears that the defendant owns 398 acres of land with 2 acres deeded to a church, the land being of the value of $83,960; that he has bank deposits in the sum of $12,786.81 and government bonds in the amount of $104,500; and that his income, including interest on the bonds and rental for his real estate, is $8,000 or $9,000 a year.... The plaintiff has a bank account of $5,960.22. This account includes deposits of some $200 and $100 which the court required the defendant to pay his wife as temporary allowance during the pendency of these proceedings. One hundred dollars was withdrawn on the date of each deposit.

The facts are not in dispute.

. . .

In the case of *Earle v. Earle*, 43 N.W. 118 [(Neb. 1889)], the plaintiff's petition alleged, in substance, the marriage of the parties, that one child was born of the marriage, and that the defendant sent his wife away from him, did not permit her to return, contributed to her support and maintenance separate and apart from him, and later refused and ceased to provide for her support and the support of his child. The wife instituted a suit in equity against her husband for maintenance and support without a prayer for divorce or from bed and board. The question presented was whether or not the wife should be compelled to resort to a proceedings [sic] for a divorce, which she did not desire to do, or from bed and board. On this question, in this state the statutes are substantially silent and at the present time there is no statute governing this matter. The court stated that it was a well-established rule of law that it is the duty of the husband to provide his family with support and means of living—the style of support, requisite lodging, food, clothing, etc., to be such as fit his means, position, and station in life—and for this purpose the wife has generally the right to use his credit for the purchase of necessaries. The court held that if a wife is abandoned by her husband, without means of support, a bill in equity will lie to compel the husband to support the wife without asking for a decree of divorce.

In the case of *Cochran v. Cochran*, 60 N.W. 942 [(Neb. 1894)], Mrs. Cochran was a school teacher in Wisconsin. Her husband came to Nebraska and decided to get a divorce. He did, secretly and fraudulently, on the theory that his wife abandoned him. The court held: "A court of equity will entertain an action brought for alimony alone, and will grant the same, although no divorce or other relief is sought, where the wife is separated from the husband without her fault."

. . .

In the case of *Brewer v. Brewer*, 113 N.W. 161 [(Neb. 1907)], the plaintiff lived with her husband and his mother. The mother dominated the household. The plaintiff went to her mother. She stated she would live in the same house with her husband and his mother if she could have control of her part of the house. The defendant did not offer to accede to these conditions. The court held that a wife may bring a suit in equity to secure support and alimony without reference to whether the action is for divorce or not; that every wife is entitled to a home corresponding to the circumstances and condition of her husband over which she may be permitted to preside as mistress; and that she does not forfeit her right to maintenance by refusing to live under the control of the husband's mother.

. . .

It becomes apparent that there are no cases cited by the plaintiff and relied upon by her from this jurisdiction or other jurisdictions that will sustain the action such as she has instituted in the instant case.

. . .

In the instant case the marital relation has continued for more than 33 years, and the wife has been supported in the same manner during this time without complaint on her part. The parties have not been separated or living apart from each other at any time. In the light of the cited cases it is clear, especially so in this jurisdiction, that to maintain an action such as the one at bar, the parties must be separated or living apart from each other.

The living standards of a family are a matter of concern to the household, and not for the courts to determine, even though the husband's attitude toward his wife, according to his wealth and circumstances, leaves little to be said in his behalf. As long as the home is maintained and the parties are living as husband and wife it may be said that the husband is legally supporting his wife and the purpose of the marriage relation is being carried out. Public policy requires such a holding. It appears that the plaintiff is not devoid of money in her own right. She has a fair-sized bank account and is entitled to use the rent from the 80 acres of land left by her first husband, if she so chooses.

. . .

Reversed and remanded with directions to dismiss.

■ YEAGER, JUSTICE (dissenting).

. . .

There is and can be no doubt that, independent of statutes relating to divorce, alimony, and separate maintenance, if this plaintiff were living apart from the defendant she could in equity and on the facts as outlined in the record be awarded appropriate relief.

. . .

In the light of what the decisions declare to be the basis of the right to maintain an action for support, is there any less reason for extending the right to a wife who is denied the right to maintenance in a home occupied with her husband than to one who has chosen to occupy a separate abode?

If the right is to be extended only to one who is separated from the husband equity and effective justice would be denied where a wealthy husband refused proper support and maintenance to a wife physically or mentally incapable of putting herself in a position where the rule could become available to her.

It is true that in all cases examined which uphold the right of a wife to maintain an action in equity for maintenance the parties were living apart, but no case has been cited or found which says that separation is a condition precedent to the right to maintain action in equity for maintenance. Likewise none has been cited or found which says that it is not.

In primary essence the rule contemplates the enforcement of an obligation within and not without the full marriage relationship. The reasoning contained in the opinions sustaining this right declare that purpose.

In *Earle v. Earle, supra,* it was said:

> The question is, whether or not the plaintiff shall be compelled to resort to a proceeding for a divorce, which she does not desire to do, and which probably she is unwilling to do, from conscientious convictions, or, in failing to do so, shall be deprived of that support which her husband is bound to give her.

. . .

If there may not be resort to equity in circumstances such as these then as pointed out in the following statement from *Earle v. Earle, supra,* a dim view must be taken of the powers of a court of equity: "As we have already said in substance, there is not much to commend an alleged principle of equity which would hold that the wife, with her family of one or more children to support, must be driven to going into court for a divorce when such a proceeding is abhorrent to her, or, in case of her refusal so to do, being compelled to submit to a deprivation of the rights which equity and humanity clearly give her; that, in order to obtain that to which she is clearly entitled, she must institute her action for a divorce, make her grievances public, which she would otherwise prefer to keep to herself, and finally liberate a husband from an obligation of which he is already tired, but from which he is not entitled to be relieved."

. . .

I conclude therefore that the conclusion of the decree that the district court had the power to entertain the action was not contrary to law.

I think however that the court was without proper power to make any of the awards contained in the decree for the support and maintenance of the plaintiff except the one of $50 a month.

. . .

I am of the opinion that the power of the court in such instances as this should not be extended beyond the allowance of sufficient money to provide adequate support and maintenance.

. . .

NOTES

1. "In my opinion, Mr. and Mrs. McGuire were very much alike, both being very cautious when it came to money. Mrs. McGuire was not poor in any respect, and of course, he was quite wealthy for those times. They never did separate, but continued to live together as husband and wife until Mr. McGuire's death. At the time the case was pending we had a number of motions to argue before the Court. They would come together in their old Model A car during the winter with no heater to the Courthouse. As soon as they got to the lobby of the Courthouse she would immediately meet with her attorney, Mr. H.D. Addison, and he would meet with me and we would discuss the various aspects of the case. After the hearings they would immediately get in their car and go back home.

Incidentally, while the case was pending in the Supreme Court, Mr. McGuire did comply with the District Court's orders and bought a used car with a heater and made some payments to her and if my memory serves me right, modernized the farm home, all of which he resented doing." Letter from Charles McDermott, attorney for the defendant (April 18, 1977).

2. Consider HENDRIK HARTOG, MAN & WIFE IN AMERICA: A HISTORY 11 (2000):

> To understand the decision in *McGuire*, we might begin by describing where and when the decision was made: the United States of America as it was between the 1790s and the last forty years of the twentieth century....

> The first thing to notice about the United States in this period ... was that the public officials, the authoritative legal voices, were all male. Judges, legislators, juries, treatise writers, all of them. By the early twentieth century, it was theoretically possible for a woman to become a lawyer, and by the 1920s there would be a sprinkling of women who were judges and a number of women who wrote texts (although not authoritative treatises) on family law. As late as the 1950s, however, women were a miniscule fraction of the lawmakers. One of the many "unique" aspects of *McGuire v. McGuire* was that the lower court judge who had recognized Lydia's right to a remedy, the judge reversed by the Nebraska Supreme Court, was a woman.

3. Does the doctrine of family privacy (which might also be termed the principle of not intervening in ongoing marriages) promote marital harmony? Does your answer depend, as the dissent in *McGuire* suggests, on whether or not the dispute at issue concerns only monetary support? Should a court, for example, attempt to enforce a wife's traditional duty of "services?" *Cf.* WILLIAM L. PROSSER, HANDBOOK OF THE LAW OF TORTS 888 (4th ed., 1971) ("[T]he 'services' of the wife were defined rather broadly to include her general usefulness, industry, frugality and attention in the home."). If not, is it appropriate to enforce the husband's traditional duty of support?

4. Third parties have long been entitled, in theory at least, to enforce a husband's duty of support by suing him for any "necessaries" sold to his wife. But due to the burden of litigating to enforce this duty, most merchants have not been willing to extend credit for the purchase of even obvious "necessaries" to a wife without the prior approval of her husband. Because a wife cannot enforce her right to support directly, as *McGuire* demonstrates, does a wife's alleged right to support in fact exist? Conversely does a husband really have a right to services? What kind of marital arrangements are promoted by the doctrine of "family privacy"?

2. GENDER ROLES

Graham v. Graham

United States District Court, Eastern District of Michigan, 1940.
33 F.Supp. 936.

■ TUTTLE, DISTRICT JUDGE.

This is a suit by a man against his former wife upon the following written agreement alleged to have been executed September 17, 1932, by the parties:

> This agreement made this 17th day of September, 1932, between Margrethe Graham and Sidney Graham, husband and wife. For valuable consideration Margrethe Graham hereby agrees to pay to Sidney Graham the sum of Three Hundred ($300.00) Dollars per month each and every month hereafter until the parties hereto no longer desire this arrangement to continue. Said Three Hundred ($300.00) Dollars per month to be paid to Sidney Graham by said Margrethe Graham directly to said Sidney Graham.

> This agreement is made to adjust financial matters between the parties hereto, so that in the future there will be no further arguments as to what money said Sidney Graham shall receive.

The parties were divorced on July 11, 1933. While the writing itself recites no consideration but merely states that it is made to prevent future arguments as to the amount of money the husband is to receive from his wife, the complaint alleges that the plaintiff had quit his job in a hotel at the solicitation of the defendant who wanted him to accompany her upon her travels, she paying his expenses, and that he was desirous of returning to work but that the defendant in order to induce him not to do so entered into this agreement. The total amount claimed until November 7, 1939, is $25,500, with interest at five per cent per annum from the time each monthly installment of $300 became due. . . .

. . .

A . . . question is presented as to whether the complaint sets forth any consideration for the alleged contract. . . . However, . . . it is unnecessary to decide this question, since I am convinced that even if the consideration is what counsel claims, and the plaintiff did agree to refrain from work and accompany his wife on her travels, the contract was not a competent one for married persons to enter into.

In the first place, it is highly doubtful if the alleged contract is within the capacity of a married woman to make under Michigan law. The degree of emancipation of married women with respect to contract and property rights varies widely in the different states. However, it has been repeatedly stated by the Michigan Supreme Court that under the Michigan statutes a married woman has no general power to contract, but can contract only in relation to her separate property. . . .

. . .

However, I do not rest my decision on this ground, but rather upon the broader ground that even if the contract is otherwise within the contractual power of the parties it is void because it contravenes public policy. Under the law, marriage is not merely a private contract between the parties, but creates a status in which the state is vitally interested and under which certain rights and duties incident to the relationship come into being, irrespective of the wishes of the parties. As a result of the marriage contract, for example, the husband has a duty to support and to live with his wife and the wife must contribute her services and society to the husband and follow him in his choice of domicile. The law is well settled that a private agreement between persons married or about to be married which attempts to change the essential obligations of the marriage contract as defined by the law is contrary to public policy and unenforceable. While there appears to be no Michigan decision directly in point, the principle is well stated in the Restatement of the Law of Contracts, as follows:

"Sec. 587. Bargain to Change Essential Obligations of Marriage

"A bargain between married persons or persons contemplating marriage to change the essential incidents of marriage is illegal.

"Illustrations:

"1. A and B who are about to marry agree to forego sexual intercourse. The bargain is illegal.

"2. In a state where the husband is entitled to determine the residence of a married couple, A and B who are about to marry agree that the wife shall not be required to leave the city where she then lives. The bargain is illegal."

Thus, it has been repeatedly held that a provision releasing the husband from his duty to support his wife in a contract between married persons, or those about to be married, except in connection with a pre-existing or contemplated immediate separation, makes the contract void. *Garlock v. Garlock*, 18 N.E.2d 521 [(N.Y. 1939)]; *French v. McAnarney*, 195 N.E. 714 [(Mass. 1935)].... Even in the states with the most liberal emancipation statutes with respect to married women, the law has not gone to the extent of permitting husbands and wives by agreement to change the essential incidents of the marriage contract.

The contract claimed to have been made by the plaintiff and defendant in the case at bar while married and living together falls within this prohibition. Under its terms, the husband becomes obligated to accompany his wife upon her travels; while under the law of marriage the wife is obliged to follow the husband's choice of domicile. Indeed, it is argued by the plaintiff's attorney that this relinquishment by the husband of his rights constitutes consideration for the promise of his wife; but, by the same token it makes the contract violative of public policy. The situation is virtually identical with that set forth in Illustration 2 of Section 587 of the Restatement quoted above. The contract, furthermore, would seem to suffer from a second defect by impliedly releasing the husband from his duty to support his wife, and thereby making it fall directly within the rule of the cases cited *supra* holding that a contract between married persons living together which contains such a release is void. The present contract does not expressly contain such a release, but if the husband can always call upon his wife for payments of $300 per month he is in practical effect getting rid of his obligation to support his wife. The plaintiff seems to place this construction on the contract since his claim makes no deduction from the promised $300 per month for support of his wife. It is unnecessary to consider in detail the second alleged basis of consideration, namely, the promise of the husband to refrain from working, but it would seem again that a married man should have the right to engage in such work as he sees fit to do, unrestrained by contract with his wife.

The law prohibiting married persons from altering by private agreement the personal relationships and obligations assumed upon marriage is based on sound foundations of public policy. If they were permitted to regulate by private contract where the parties are to live and whether the husband is to work or be supported by his wife, there would seem to be no reason why married persons could not contract as to the allowance the husband or wife may receive, the number of dresses she may have, the places where they will spend their evenings and vacations, and innumerable other aspects of their personal relationships. Such right would open an endless field for controversy and bickering and would destroy the element of flexibility needed in making adjustments to new conditions arising in marital life. There is no reason of course, why the wife cannot voluntarily pay her husband a monthly sum or the husband by mutual understanding quit his job and travel with his wife. The objection is to putting such conduct into a binding contract, tying the parties' hands in the future and inviting controversy and litigation between them. The time may come when it is desirable and necessary for the husband to cease work entirely, or to change to a different occupation, or move to a different city, or, if adversity overtakes the parties, to share a small income. It would be unfortunate if in making such adjustments the parties should find their hands tied by an agreement between them entered into years before.

It is important to note that the contract here was entered into between parties who were living together at the time and who obviously contemplated a continuance of that relationship. The case is to be distinguished in this respect from those cases which hold that a contract made after separation or in contemplation of an immediate separation which takes place as contemplated is legal, if the contract is a fair one, even though it contains a release of the husband's duty of support. . . .

NOTES

1. The court bases its holding in part on the view that allowing spouses to arrange their own marriage contract would "open an endless field for controversy." Is this correct? Is it not equally plausible that court enforcement of some private agreements might eliminate a major irritant, thereby heading off a divorce? A fascinating illustration of the possibilities (as legal actualities) is briefly discussed in Amy J. Cohen, *The Family, The Market, and ADR*, 2011 J. DISP. RESOL. 91, 110–11 (2011) (engaging LOUIS H. BURKE, WITH THIS RING 23 (1958)). Moreover, it is not likely that the mere *availability* of relief might deter conduct deleterious to otherwise harmonious marriages? *See generally* Note, *Litigation Between Husband and Wife*, 79 HARV. L. REV. 1650 (1966).

2. The traditional marriage model has been widely criticized for its adverse consequences for women. *See, e.g.*, KENNETH DAVIDSON, RUTH BADER GINSBURG & HERMA HILL KAY, CASES AND MATERIALS ON SEX-BASED DISCRIMINATION 140–42 (1974): "The support laws embody the legal view that a married woman is an economically nonproductive person dependent upon others for the necessities of life. . . . [The number of] women in the labor force . . . indicates the gross inaccuracy of this view. . . . [In addition] the wife's work in the home continues to be seen as a service she owes to the husband, rather than as a job deserving the dignity of economic return. . . ." For the larger discussion, see *id.* at 140–44.

Bradwell v. Illinois

Supreme Court of the United States, 1873.
83 U.S. (16 Wall.) 130, 21 L.Ed. 442.

■ MILLER, JUSTICE

[The petitioner, Myra Bradwell, sought admission to the bar of Illinois after being denied admission because she was a woman. The Supreme Court upheld the denial in a brief opinion. Justice Bradley, in his concurring opinion, explained:]

. . . [T]he civil law, as well as nature herself, has always recognized a wide difference in the respective spheres and destinies of man and woman. Man is, or should be, woman's protector and defender. The natural and proper timidity and delicacy which belongs to the female sex evidently unfits it for many of the occupations of civil life. The constitution of the family organization, which is founded in the divine ordinance, as well as in the nature of things, indicates the domestic sphere as that which properly belongs to the domain and functions of womanhood. The harmony, not to say identity, of interests and views which belong, or should belong, to the family institution is repugnant to the idea of a woman adopting a distinct and independent career from that of her husband. . . .

It is true that many women are unmarried and not affected by any of the duties, complications, and incapacities arising out of the married state, but these are exceptions to the general rule. The paramount destiny and mission of woman are to fulfill the noble and benign offices of wife and mother. This is the law of the Creator. And the rules of civil society must be adapted to the general constitution of things, and cannot be based upon exceptional cases.

. . .

B. CHALLENGES TO THE TRADITIONAL MARRIAGE MODEL

1. ECONOMIC AND SOCIAL CHANGES

NATIONAL COMMISSION ON CHILDREN, BEYOND RHETORIC: A NEW AMERICAN AGENDA FOR CHILDREN AND FAMILIES

21–23 (1991).

Perhaps the most dramatic social change of the past 20 years has been the steady march of mothers into the paid labor force. Between 1970 and 1990, the proportion of mothers with children under age six who were working or looking for work outside their homes rose from 32 percent to 58 percent. Today, approximately 10.9 million children under age six, including 1.7 million babies under one year and 9.2 million toddlers and preschoolers, have mothers in the paid labor force. Mothers of school-age children are even more likely to be in the labor force. In 1990 over 74 percent of women whose youngest child was between the ages of 6 and 13 were working or looking for paid work. Approximately 17.4 million children, more than 65 percent of all children in the latter age group, had working mothers in 1990. Among employed mothers, nearly 70 percent whose youngest child is under six and more than 74 percent whose youngest child is school age work full time.

Historically, unmarried mothers have been far more likely to work than married mothers. Yet the sharpest increase in labor force participation among mothers over the past 20 years has been among married mothers, especially those with very young children. More than 66 percent of married mothers are now working or looking for work outside their homes. In past generations, most of these women would have quit their jobs and stayed at home when they married or had children, but today they are remaining at work. Women who wait to have their first baby until after age 25 and women with four or more years of college are more likely to continue working than are younger mothers and those who fail to complete high school.

The reasons that individual mothers decide to go to work or stay in the labor force undoubtedly vary from one family to another. On an aggregate level, however, complex social, cultural, and economic factors have fueled this trend in the United States and most other developed countries. Increases in the number of available jobs, especially in the service sector; successful legal efforts to expand women's access to the workplace; the continued influence of the women's movement; and the mechanization of many household tasks have all undoubtedly contributed. The declining income and employment opportunities of young men, especially those who lack skills, and the difficulty of maintaining a secure standard of living on one income have also added momentum.

Changing patterns of mothers' employment represent more than a mere shift in American attitudes or fluctuations in short-term macroeconomic conditions, although these have clearly played a part. Over the past generation, the opportunity costs of staying at home, primarily in the form of foregone earnings, have increased for mothers. Some scholars call for a return to the single-earner "family wage" system of the 1940s. Others, however, suggest that the movement of mothers into the paid work force is likely to become even stronger in the future as projected labor shortages make women increasingly essential to the shrinking labor pool. To date, social adjustments—in the workplace, in communities, and even in families—have been rather slow to take root. Over the coming years, society's ability to adapt to the changing needs of working fathers, working mothers, and their children will be increasingly essential to the health and vitality of families and to the well-being of their children.

NOTES

1. In 2000, the labor force participation rate of women with children under 18 peaked at 72.9 percent, declining to 71.2 percent by 2008. Women with children under three years of age are less likely to participate in the labor force (59.6 percent) than women with children under 6 (63.6 percent) or women with children between 6 and 17 years of age (77.5 percent). Bureau of Labor Statistics, Dep't of Labor, Employment Status of Women by Presence and Age of Youngest Child (2009), *available at* http://www.bls.gov/cps/wlftable7.htm. Women continue to earn less than men, and the amount of the female-to-male earnings gap varies by race. Bureau of Labor Statistics, Dep't of Labor, Usual Weekly Earnings of Wage and Salary Workers (2d Quarter 2011), *available at* http://www.bls.gov/news.release/pdf/wkyeng.pdf.

2. In 2009, households with children under the age of 18 headed by women were more likely (26.6 percent) than households headed by men (18.2 percent) to live below the poverty line. Bureau of Labor Statistics, Dep't of Labor, A Profile of the Working Poor: 2009 (March 2011), *available at* http://www.bls.gov/cps/cpswp2009.pdf.

2.   Constitutional Limits on Sex Discrimination

a.   THE NINETEENTH AMENDMENT

Ratified on August 18, 1920, the Nineteenth Amendment provides:

The right of the citizens of the United States to vote shall not be denied or abridged by the United States or by any State on account of sex.

Congress shall have the power to enforce this article by appropriate legislation.

Reva B. Siegel, *She the People: The Nineteenth Amendment, Sex Equality, Federalism, and the Family*

115 Harv. L. Rev. 947, 1005–09, 1012–19, 1022–24 (2002).

. . .

Of the several cases that antisuffragists brought challenging the constitutionality of the Nineteenth Amendment, it was [William] Marbury's case, *Leser v. Garnett*,[179] that the Supreme Court decided on the merits. Marbury's brief in *Leser* . . . devoted considerable energy to the task of distinguishing the Fifteenth and Nineteenth Amendments, and it is here that Marbury presented the . . . arguments that the woman suffrage amendment inter-

---

179.   258 U.S. 130 (1922).

fered with local control over [family] matters.... There was a fundamental difference between race and sex discrimination, the brief argued. Race discrimination involved class discrimination of national concern, whereas the gender discrimination addressed by the Nineteenth Amendment involved matters concerning the family that the Constitution reserved to local control:

> The Nineteenth Amendment invades a totally new sphere from the constitutional point of view,—a sphere essentially belonging to municipal law and therefore to the States. It has no relation whatever to any national problem, past, present, or future. Women are not the "wards of the Nation." *The family is, however, the foundation of the State and if an arbitrary rule of suffrage is imposed upon the State that may break into and overthrow its whole domestic law it is plain that the State has lost "in a general sense the power over suffrage which has belonged to it from the beginning and without the possession of which power ... both the authority of the Nation and the State would fall to the ground."*
>
> Prohibiting race discrimination is a vitally different matter from imposing sexual equality. If any State can be coerced into rewriting its law of property or domestic relations so as to eliminate sex distinctions it has no independence in regard to legislation left.[183]

Justice Brandeis's opinion for the Court rejected the plaintiff's arguments in a passage remarkable for its terseness:

> This Amendment is in character and phraseology precisely similar to the Fifteenth. For each the same method of adoption was pursued. One cannot be valid and the other invalid. That the Fifteenth is valid ... has been recognized and acted on for half a century.... The suggestion that the Fifteenth was incorporated in the Constitution, not in accordance with law, but practically as a war measure which has been validated by acquiescence, cannot be entertained.[184]

With that abrupt assertion, the Court disposed of the states' rights argument against the woman suffrage amendment that had flourished for decades. It offered not a word affirming or negating the claims about the gendered structure of the federal system that opponents of the woman suffrage amendment had been advancing for decades.

. . .

The campaign for woman suffrage dramatically altered the conceptual framework within which Americans reasoned about the question of women voting. By the end of the campaign, the Nineteenth Amendment's supporters could appeal to forms of "common sense" that simply did not exist in the aftermath of the Civil War. In floor debate, congressmen argued, "Is it possible that any question could be more distinctly Federal than this? Is it possible that any question could go more directly to the source of the public

---

183. Brief for Plaintiffs in Error at 98–99 (emphasis added), Leser v. Garnett, 258 U.S. 130 (1922) (No. 533). The argument continues:

> The substantial difference then between the Fifteenth and Nineteenth Amendments is that one imposes conditions upon the exercise of the power over suffrage, while the other appropriates the power to itself, imposing upon the State and the Nation an arbitrary rule of sex uniformity from which there can be no relaxation or escape, creating a new electorate or body politic in all male suffrage states, and thus changing or depriving these States of their suffrage in the Senate, and making it impossible for them under their own laws to consent or refuse to consent to this or any other amendment whatever.

Id. at 99.

184. *Leser*, 258 U.S. at 136.

welfare than the right of one-half of its population to vote?" "There can be no logical objection to universal suffrage in a democracy. Indeed, a democracy is inconceivable without universal suffrage." As one congressman observed in the final debates over the Nineteenth Amendment, dramatic changes in the ways Americans understood women's position in the family in turn produced changes in the common sense application of democratic principles to the question of their voting:

> In the past the restriction of the right of suffrage to the male population was not contrary to democratic philosophy, because under the old order of civilization women derived their social status from their men and were economically dependent upon them. For the past half century a change in this regard has been taking place in the social structure, particularly in the last generation. The old conception of the place of woman in the scheme of existence was that she was the member of a household, which was ruled by a male head; that her place in the world was determined by the place held by this head; and that he was responsible for her economically. Among many this conception still obtains as a theory, and is still to an extent recognized in the law, but in reality has been substantially modified.[187]

Once inconceivable, women's enfranchisement was now understood by many as inevitable, reflecting and affirming important changes in the relations of the sexes and the role of the family in American life.

Of course, no major social change is experienced the same way by all who participate in it, and the ratification of the Nineteenth Amendment was no exception. Americans inside and outside the suffrage movement understood the Nineteenth Amendment to augur a shift in sex roles and family structure, but they understood and responded to this change in different ways.

This range of response is visible in the leadership of the women's movement itself. In the immediate aftermath of ratification, women activists turned to Congress for support in their campaign for progressive social reforms such as a federal maternal and infant health act, a child labor amendment, and the creation of federal agencies, including a Women's Bureau in the Department of Labor and a new Department of Education. Creation of the Women's Bureau in 1920 and the enactment of the Sheppard–Towner infant health act in 1921 and the child labor amendment in 1924 thus represented early and highly visible political successes for newly enfranchised women. Meanwhile, the National Woman's Party and the League of Women Voters identified sexually discriminatory legislation in states across the nation and targeted surviving elements of coverture in every jurisdiction for immediate statutory reform. The National Woman's Party circulated early drafts of a proposed equal rights amendment, while other organizations renewed proposals for a constitutional amendment that would give the federal government authority to enact uniform marriage and divorce legislation. In the early 1920s, an expanded electorate was inviting government to play a new role in shaping the lives of women, children, and the family itself.

But, as is often the case, moments of major social reform precipitate diverse forms of containment and backlash [which met with varying forms of success]. . . .

· · ·

---

187. 56 CONG. REC. 788 (1918) (statement of Rep. Lehlbach).

In the immediate wake of its adoption, there were signs that courts—including the United States Supreme Court—interpreted ratification of the Nineteenth Amendment as changing the foundational understandings of the American legal system. These courts viewed the Nineteenth Amendment as a constitutional amendment with normative implications for diverse bodies of law, including the law of marital status.

Yet judicial acknowledgment of women's enfranchisement as a break with traditional understandings of the family was short-lived. Soon after ratification, the judiciary moved to repress the structural significance of women's enfranchisement, by reading the Nineteenth Amendment as a rule concerning voting that had no normative significance for matters other than the franchise.

. . .

This process of domestication was not inevitable, as early cases such as *Adkins v. Children's Hospital*[199] illustrate. In *Adkins* we can see an alternative path of reception—one that views women's enfranchisement as a constitutional change of deep systemic significance, one that understands the ties between the constitutional law of suffrage and the common law of marital status.

. . .

In the opening decades of the twentieth century, the Court restricted state regulation of the employment relationship to protect employees' freedom of contract. But the Court reasoned about the contractual liberties of male and female employees differently. In *Lochner* [*v. New York*],[200] the Court struck down legislation restricting the number of hours a week employees could work, while in *Muller* [*v. Oregon*],[202] the Court held that states could validly impose such restrictions on female employees. To explain why states were constitutionally justified in regulating women's work as they could not regulate men's work, *Muller* pointed to women's role in bearing and rearing children. *Muller* presented this physiological justification for gender-differentiated treatment of women's contracts as carrying forward the traditions of coverture. The Court reasoned that even if the old coverture rules that restricted wives' capacity to contract were then being repealed, states were still justified in imposing special restrictions on women's employment because of women's childbearing role.

Adkins involved a challenge to the gendered framework of substantive due process law. Did a law requiring employers to pay their female employees a minimum wage interfere with the employees' liberty of contract, or was it a valid exercise of the police power recognized in *Muller*? The question divided the women's movement. Many in the suffrage movement had supported protective labor legislation for women as the only form of protective labor legislation viable under prevailing constitutional doctrine; but in the immediate aftermath of the Nineteenth Amendment's ratification, some in the movement were beginning to question the wisdom of supporting sex-differentiated legislation and to call for a general prohibition on sex distinctions in law. The critics of protective labor legislation who challenged the minimum wage law in *Adkins* drew on feminist criticism of sex-based legislation to attack the gendered assumptions on which substantive due process

---

199. 261 U.S. 525 (1923).

200. 198 U.S. 937 (1905).

202. 208 U.S. 412 (1908).

law rested. The lower court found their objections persuasive and tied the need for doctrinal reform to ratification of the Nineteenth Amendment, as did the Supreme Court.

Justice Sutherland, who had recently joined the Court, wrote the opinion in *Adkins* that struck down the sex-based minimum wage law on sex equality grounds. Before his appointment, Sutherland had counseled Alice Paul of the National Woman's Party on the suffrage amendment and, after its ratification, advised Paul about drafting an equal rights amendment. The opinion he wrote for the Court in *Adkins* pointed to the changes in women's status culminating in the ratification of the Nineteenth Amendment as a reason for distinguishing *Muller* and for analyzing the regulation of women's employment in the same constitutional framework the Court used to analyze the regulation of men's employment:

> But the ancient inequality of the sexes, otherwise than physical, as suggested in the *Muller* case . . ., has continued "with diminishing intensity." *In view of the great—not to say revolutionary—changes which have taken place since that utterance, in the contractual, political and civil status of women, culminating in the Nineteenth Amendment, it is not unreasonable to say that these differences have now come almost, if not quite, to the vanishing point.* In this aspect of the matter, while the physical differences must be recognized in appropriate cases, and legislation fixing hours or conditions of work may properly take them into account, *we cannot accept the doctrine that women of mature age,* sui juris, *require or may be subjected to restrictions upon their liberty of contract which could not lawfully be imposed in the case of men under similar circumstances.* To do so would be to ignore all the implications to be drawn from the present day trend of legislation, as well as that of common thought and usage, by which *woman is accorded emancipation from that old doctrine that she must be given special protection or be subjected to special restraint in her contractual and civil relationships.*[209]

The *Adkins* opinion is historically significant, not simply because it reads the Nineteenth Amendment as conferring equality on women, but because the opinion understands sex equality as freedom from traditions of reasoning about gender rooted in the common law of marital status: the Court describes the changes culminating in ratification of the Nineteenth Amendment as according woman "emancipation from that old doctrine" that subjects her to "special protection or . . . restraint in her contractual and civil relationships." Because *Adkins* views the gender-differentiated framework of substantive due process law as carrying forward the traditions of coverture and understands the Nineteenth Amendment as repudiating those same traditions, the opinion concludes that substantive due process law should be modified to reflect the changes in women's status expressed in the new constitutional amendment. With ratification of the Nineteenth Amendment, *Muller's* reasoning no longer controls, and women may not be "subjected to restrictions upon their liberty of contract which could not lawfully be imposed in the case of men under similar circumstances."

Many criticized the Court's reasoning in *Adkins*. Dissenters argued that the gender-differentiated framework of substantive due process law reflected differences in the physical and social roles of the sexes that were not eliminated by ratification of the Nineteenth Amendment. But *Adkins* remains historically significant, however one judges substantive due process law or the gender distinctions within it. The opinion demonstrates that in the

---

209.   Adkins v. Children's Hosp., 261 U.S. 525, 553 (1923) (emphasis added).

immediate aftermath of ratification, the Court interpreted the Amendment in light of the woman suffrage debates. In this period, the Court understood the Amendment to confer equality on women by breaking with traditional ways of reasoning about women's roles rooted in the family relationship.

Reasoning from this standpoint, *Adkins* interpreted the Amendment as a change in the Constitution with significance for other bodies of constitutional doctrine. The *Adkins* opinion pointed to shifts "in the contractual, political and civil status of women culminating in the Nineteenth Amendment," and treated this positive account of the ratification campaign normatively—as a reason for similarly transformative interpretation of the due process jurisprudence of the Fifth and Fourteenth Amendments. *Adkins* thus offers the first synthetic interpretation of the Nineteenth Amendment. The opinion understands the suffrage amendment as bringing about a major change in the terms of women's citizenship, a change having implications for the way the Court interprets diverse bodies of constitutional law.

The Supreme Court was not the only court to read the Nineteenth Amendment as embodying a sex equality norm that had implications for practices other than voting, or to suggest that the Amendment's ratification marked a break with the common law's marital status norms. For example, two years after the *Adkins* decision, a federal district court interpreted the suffrage amendment as abrogating coverture principles in federal law. Asked to apply the common law doctrine relieving a wife of liability for criminal conduct undertaken with her husband, the judge refused, observing that "since the adoption of the Nineteenth Amendment to the Constitution, it seems to me that the rule of common law has no application to crimes committed against the United States."[215] This same understanding of the Nineteenth Amendment moved a judge concurring in a federal tax case to reject the government's claim that, by marriage, a wife's tax domicile was her husband's.... Other courts ... invoked the suffrage amendment to authorize liberalizing interpretations of the common law. In these cases, courts invoked the Nineteenth Amendment as a reason for exercising their discretion in interpreting the common law so as to restrict the authority of traditional coverture concepts.

But these decisions were not common. More often, courts treated constitutional and common law regimes as juridically independent.... [W]hat ... shortly ... emerge[d] as the "common sense" view of the [Nineteenth] Amendment [was] ... that it had no direct bearing on marital status law. Indeed, soon after the Supreme Court invoked ratification of the Nineteenth Amendment as a reason for striking down the sex-based minimum wage law in *Adkins*, the Court upheld a law that prohibited women from working in restaurants at night, distinguishing *Adkins* and once again invoking the reasoning of *Muller*.[221]

[Federal and state] [l]egislatures responded to ratification of the Nineteenth Amendment in similar terms....

Thus, in the immediate aftermath of ratification, both the Supreme Court and Congress understood the Nineteenth Amendment to redefine citizenship for women in ways that broke with the marital status traditions of the common law. But neither the Court nor Congress acted consistently on this understanding. Some federal and state courts viewed ratification of the suffrage amendment as a reason to repudiate, or interpret restrictively,

---

215. United States v. Hinson, 3 F.2d 200, 200 (S.D. Fla. 1925).

221. *See* Radice v. New York, 264 U.S. 292, 295 (1924).

coverture concepts in various private law settings. But this understanding of constitutional reform never gathered significant momentum.

. . .

Modern sex discrimination doctrine is built on [a] "thin" conception of the Nineteenth Amendment—on the assumption that the Nineteenth Amendment is a nondiscrimination rule governing voting that has no bearing on questions of equal citizenship for women outside the franchise. In developing sex discrimination doctrine under the Fourteenth Amendment, the Court seems to have proceeded from the understanding that there is no constitutional history that would support a constitutional commitment to equal citizenship for women—that such a commitment is to be derived, to the extent it can be derived at all, by analogizing race and sex discrimination. These assumptions have given rise to a body of sex discrimination doctrine that is limited in legitimacy and acuity by the ahistorical manner in which it was derived from the law of race discrimination.

Erasure of the Nineteenth Amendment from our collective memory and constitutional canon has helped produce a body of sex discrimination law that lacks foundation in our constitutional history and that defines equal protection formalistically, as a constraint on state action that draws group-based distinctions between men and women. The Court's failure to ground sex discrimination jurisprudence in anything approximating constitutional or social history gives us a law of sex discrimination that begins by according heightened scrutiny to a statute regulating the sale of watered-down beer.

Of the twenty-nine equal protection cases involving sex discrimination that the Court has decided since *Reed v. Reed*, nineteen have involved laws that in some way regulated family relationships, but the sole question that the Court addressed in these cases was whether the state could distribute entitlements or obligations in a manner that employed group-based classifications. This question is not insignificant, but it is hardly the only question we might ask when considering whether a given state practice, especially one regulating family relations, accords women the equal protection of the law.

These omissions in equal protection law in turn have consequences in the law of federalism. Because sex discrimination doctrine does not identify the family as a historic site of status inequality for women, it exerts no constraints on federalism doctrines that identify the family as the paradigmatic site of state, rather than federal, jurisdiction. The interplay of equal protection and federalism doctrines can thus insulate state regulation of family life from Fourteenth Amendment scrutiny, thereby perpetuating traditional forms of status inequality between the sexes.

. . .

NOTE

For perspective on women's suffrage as history, see Neil MacFarquhar, *Saudi Monarch Grants Women Right to Vote*, N.Y. TIMES, Sept. 26, 2011, at A1 (reporting on the decision by King Abdullah of Saudi Arabia to grant "women the right to vote and run in future municipal elections," a right that is to apply to the " 'next' " election cycle which is not until 2015). *See also* Liam Stack, *Saudi Men Go to Polls; Women Wait*, N.Y. TIMES, Sept. 30, 2011, at A12.

b. THE FOURTEENTH AMENDMENT

Ratified on July 9, 1868, the Fourteenth Amendment provides:

Section 1. All persons born or naturalized in the United States, and subject to the jurisdiction thereof, are citizens of the United States and of the State wherein they reside. No State shall make or enforce any law which shall abridge the privileges or immunities of citizens of the United States; nor shall any State deprive any person of life, liberty, or property, without due process of law; nor deny to any person within its jurisdiction the equal protection of the laws.

Section 2. Representatives shall be apportioned among the several States according to their respective numbers, counting the whole number of persons in each State, excluding Indians not taxed. But when the right to vote at any election for the choice of electors for President and Vice–President of the United States, Representatives in Congress, the Executive and Judicial officers of a State, or the members of the Legislature thereof, is denied to any of the male inhabitants of such State, being twenty-one years of age, (*Note: Changed by section 1 of the Twenty–Sixth Amendment.*) and citizens of the United States, or in any way abridged, except for participation in rebellion, or other crime, the basis of representation therein shall be reduced in the proportion which the number of such male citizens shall bear to the whole number of male citizens twenty-one year of age in the State.

Section 3. No person shall be a Senator or Representative in Congress, or elector of President and Vice President, or hold any office, civil or military, under the United States, or under any State, who, having previously taken an oath, as a member of Congress, or as an officer of the United States, or as a member of any State legislature, or as an executive or judicial officer of any State, to support the Constitution of the United States, shall have engaged in insurrection or rebellion against the same, or given aid or comfort to the enemies thereof. But Congress may, by a vote of two-thirds of each House, remove such disability.

Section 4. The validity of the public debt of the United States, authorized by law, including debts incurred for payment of pensions and bounties for services in suppressing insurrection or rebellion, shall not be questioned. But neither the United States nor any State shall assume or pay any debt or obligation incurred in aid of insurrection or rebellion against the United States, or any claim for the loss or emancipation of any slave; but all such debts, obligations and claims shall be held illegal and void.

Section 5. The Congress shall have power to enforce, by appropriate legislation, the provisions of this article.

Ruth Bader Ginsburg, *Gender and the Constitution*

44 U. CIN. L. REV. 1, 1–4 (1975).

. . .

Two themes dominate Anglo–American literature and case reports. Their strains are echoed even to this day. First, women's place in a world controlled by men is divinely ordained; second, the law's differential treatment of the sexes operates benignly in women's favor. As to the first theme, Gunnar Myrdal, in his classic study of racism in the United States, noted:

> In the earlier common law, women and children were placed under the jurisdiction of the paternal power. When a legal status had to be found

for the imported Negro servants ... the nearest and most natural analogy was the status of women and children. The ninth commandment—linking together women, servants, mules and other property—could be invoked, as well as a great number of other passages of Holy Scripture.[7]

Discrimination as "benign preference" was Blackstone's justification for laws that denied the married woman legal capacity to hold property, contract or bring suit in her own name: "[T]he disabilities which the wife lies under are for the most part intended for her protection and benefit: so great a favourite is the female sex of the laws of England."[8]

During the long debate over women's suffrage the prevailing view of the natural subordination of women to men was rehearsed frequently in the press and in legislative chambers. For example, an 1852 New York Herald editorial asked:

How did women first become subject to man as she now is all over the world? By her nature, her sex, just as the negro, is and always will be, to the end of time, inferior to the white race, and therefore, doomed to subjection; but happier than she would be in any other condition, just because it is the law of her nature. The women themselves would not have this law reversed....[9]

Mid–19th century feminists, many of them diligent workers in the cause of abolition, looked to Congress after the Civil War for an express guarantee of equal rights for men and women. Viewed in historical perspective, their expectations appear unrealistic. A problem of far greater immediacy faced the nation. Overcoming the legacy of slavery was the burning issue of the day and it eclipsed all others. The text of the fourteenth amendment occasioned particular concern among feminists, for the second section of that amendment placed in the Constitution for the first time the word "male." Threefold use of the word "male," always in conjunction with the term "citizens,"[11] generated apprehension that the grand phrases of the first section of the fourteenth amendment—"privileges and immunities of citizens of the United States," guarantees to all persons of "due process of law" and "the equal protection of the laws"—would have, at best, qualified application to women.[12]

For more than a century after the adoption of the fourteenth amendment, the judiciary, with rare exception, demonstrated utmost deference to sex lines drawn by the legislature. In the nation's highest tribunal, until 1971, no legislatively drawn sex line, however sharp, failed to survive constitutional challenge.[13] ...

---

7. G. MYRDAL, AN AMERICAN DILEMMA 1073 (2d ed. 1962).

8. 1 W. BLACKSTONE, COMMENTARIES 445 (3d ed. 1768).

9. *The Woman's Rights Convention—The Last Act of the Drama*, N.Y. HERALD, Sept. 12, 1852, quoted in A. KRADITOR, UP FROM THE PEDESTAL 190 (1968).

11. The section provides for reduction of the number of Representatives where a state denies "male citizens" the right to vote. The intent was to assure the franchise to black men. *See also* 2 U.S.C. § 6 (1927).

12. *See* E. FLEXNER, CENTURY OF STRUGGLE 142–55 (1959).

13. The Court initially invalidated laws setting minimum wages for women, principally because the legislation interfered with liberty of contract, as that doctrine was then viewed. Adkins v. Children's Hosp., 261 U.S. 525 (1923), *overruled*, West Coast Hotel Co. v. Parrish, 300 U.S. 379 (1937)[.]

NOTE

"[T]o Pauli Murray, in particular, an intellectual debt was owed, for Murray had argued that sex classifications should be treated like race classifications, both in a report to the President's Commission on the Status of Women's Committee on Civil and Political Rights and in a 1965 law review article, thereby laying the foundation for Ginsburg's path breaking argument in *Moritz* [*v. Comm'r*, 469 F.3d 466 (10th Cir. 1972), *cert. denied*, 412 U.S. 906 (1973)] and *Reed* [*v. Reed*, 404 U.S. 71 (1971)]." Wendy Webster Williams, *Justice Ruth Bader Ginsburg's Rutgers Years: 1963–1972*, 31 Women's Rts. L. Rep. 229, 251 (2010) (making the observation and citing, among other sources, Margaret Mead & Frances Bagley Kaplan, American Women: The Report of the President's Commission on the Status of Women and Other Publications of the Commission 147–57 (1965), and Pauli Murray & Mary O. Eastwood, *Jane Crow and the Law: Sex Discrimination and Title VII*, 34 Geo.Wash.L. Rev. 232 (1965)).

Orr v. Orr

Supreme Court of the United States, 1979.
440 U.S. 268, 99 S.Ct. 1102, 59 L.Ed.2d 306.

■ Justice Brennan delivered the opinion of the Court.

The question presented is the constitutionality of Alabama alimony statutes which provide that husbands, but not wives, may be required to pay alimony upon divorce.

. . .

In authorizing the imposition of alimony obligations on husbands, but not on wives, the Alabama statutory scheme "provides that different treatment be accorded . . . on the basis of . . . sex; it thus establishes a classification subject to scrutiny under the Equal Protection Clause." *Reed v. Reed*, 404 U.S. 71, 75 (1971). The fact that the classification expressly discriminates against men rather than women does not protect it from scrutiny. *Craig v. Boren*, 429 U.S. 190 (1976). "To withstand scrutiny" under the equal protection clause, " 'classifications by gender must serve important governmental objectives and must be substantially related to achievement of those objectives.' " *Califano v. Webster*, 430 U.S. 313, 316–317 (1977). We shall, therefore, examine the three governmental objectives that might arguably be served by Alabama's statutory scheme.

Appellant views the Alabama alimony statutes as effectively announcing the State's preference for an allocation of family responsibilities under which the wife plays a dependent role, and as seeking for their objective the reinforcement of that model among the State's citizens. We agree, as he urges, that prior cases settle that this purpose cannot sustain the statutes. *Stanton v. Stanton*, 421 U.S. 7, 10 (1975), held that the "old notion" that "generally it is the man's primary responsibility to provide a home and its essentials," can no longer justify a statute that discriminates on the basis of gender. "No longer is the female destined solely for the home and the rearing of the family, and only the male for the marketplace and world of ideas," *id.*, at 14–15. See also *Craig v. Boren*, [429 U.S.,] at 198. If the statute is to survive constitutional attack, therefore, it must be validated on some other basis.

The opinion of the Alabama Court of Civil Appeals suggests other purposes that the statute may serve. Its opinion states that the Alabama statutes were "designed" for "the wife of a broken marriage who needs financial assistance," 351 So.2d, at 905. This may be read as asserting either of two legislative objectives. One is a legislative purpose to provide help for needy spouses, using sex as a proxy for need. The other is a goal of compensating women for past discrimination during marriage, which assertedly has left them unprepared to fend for themselves in the working world following divorce. We concede, of course, that assisting needy spouses is a legitimate and important governmental objective. We have also recognized "[r]eduction of the disparity in economic condition between men and women caused by the long history of discrimination against women ... as ... an important governmental objective," *Califano v. Webster*, [430 U.S.,] at 317. It only remains, therefore, to determine whether the classification at issue here is "substantially related to achievement of those objectives." Ibid.

Ordinarily, we would begin the analysis of the "needy spouse" objective by considering whether sex is a sufficiently "accurate proxy," *Craig v. Boren*, [429 U.S.,] at 204, for dependency to establish that the gender classification rests " 'upon some ground of difference having a fair and substantial relation to the object of the legislation,' " *Reed v. Reed*, [404 U.S.,] at 76. Similarly, we would initially approach the "compensation" rationale by asking whether women had in fact been significantly discriminated against in the sphere to which the statute applied a sex-based classification, leaving the sexes "*not similarly situated with respect to opportunities*" in that sphere. *Schlesinger v. Ballard*, 419 U.S. 498, 508 (1975).

But in this case, even if sex were a reliable proxy for need, and even if the institution of marriage did discriminate against women, these factors still would "not adequately justify the salient features of" Alabama's statutory scheme. Under the statute, individualized hearings at which the parties' relative financial circumstances are considered *already* occur. There is no reason, therefore, to use sex as a proxy for need. Needy males could be helped along with needy females with little if any additional burden on the State. In such circumstances, not even an administrative convenience rationale exists to justify operating by generalization or proxy. Similarly, since individualized hearings can determine which women were in fact discriminated against vis à vis their husbands, as well as which family units defied the stereotype and left the husband dependent on the wife, Alabama's alleged compensatory purpose may be effectuated without placing burdens solely on husbands. Progress toward fulfilling such a purpose would not be hampered, and it would cost the State nothing more, if it were to treat men and women equally by making alimony burdens independent of sex. "Thus, the gender-based distinction is gratuitous; without it the statutory scheme would only provide benefits to those men who are in fact similarly situated to the women the statute aids." *Weinberger v. Wiesenfeld*, [420 U.S.,] at 653, and the effort to help those women would not in any way be compromised.

Moreover, use of a gender classification actually produces perverse results in this case. As compared to a gender-neutral law placing alimony obligations on the spouse able to pay, the present Alabama statutes give an advantage only to the financially secure wife whose husband is in need. Although such a wife might have to pay alimony under a gender-neutral statute, the present statutes exempt her from that obligation. Thus, "[t]he [wives] who benefit from the disparate treatment are those who were ... nondependent on their husbands." *Califano v. Goldfarb*, 430 U.S. 199, 221 (1977) (Stevens, J., concurring). They are precisely those who are not "needy spouses" and who are "least likely to have been victims of ... discrimination," by the institution of marriage. A gender-based classification which, as compared to a gender-neutral one, generates additional benefits only for those it has no reason to prefer cannot survive equal protection scrutiny.

Legislative classifications which distribute benefits and burdens on the basis of gender carry the inherent risk of reinforcing stereotypes about the "proper place" of women and their need for special protection. Cf. *United Jewish Organizations v. Carey*, 430 U.S. 144, 173–174 (1977) (concurring opinion). Thus, even statutes purportedly designed to compensate for and ameliorate the effects of past discrimination must be carefully tailored. Where, as here, the State's compensatory and ameliorative purposes are as well served by a gender-neutral classification as one that gender classifies and therefore carries with it the baggage of sexual stereotypes, the State cannot be permitted to classify on the basis of sex. And this is doubly so where the choice made by the State appears to redound—if only indirectly—to the benefit of those without need for special solicitude.

. . .

Reversed and remanded.

NOTE

In *Kahn v. Shevin*, 416 U.S. 351 (1974), the Court upheld a state property tax exemption for widows that was intended to offset past economic discrimination against women. Is it possible to reconcile *Kahn* and *Orr* as asserted by Justice Blackmun? Consider the dissent of Justice Brennan, joined by Justice Marshall, in *Kahn*:

> I agree that, in providing special benefits for a needy segment of society long the victim of purposeful discrimination and neglect, the statute serves the compelling state interest of achieving equality for such groups. No one familiar with this country's history of pervasive sex discrimination against women can doubt the need for remedial measures to correct the resulting economic imbalances.... By providing a property tax exemption for widows, § 196.01(7) assists in reducing that disparity for a class of women particularly disadvantaged by the legacy of economic discrimination.... The statute nevertheless fails to satisfy the requirements of equal protection, since the State has not borne its burden of proving that its compelling interest could not be achieved by a more precisely tailored statute or by use of feasible, less drastic means. Section 196.191(7) is plainly overinclusive, for the $500 property tax exemption may be obtained by a financially independent heiress as well as by an unemployed widow with dependent children.

416 U.S. at 358–60 (Brennan, J., dissenting).

United States v. Virginia

Supreme Court of the United States, 1996.
518 U.S. 515, 116 S.Ct. 2264, 135 L.Ed.2d 735.

■ JUSTICE GINSBURG delivered the opinion of the Court.

Virginia's public institutions of higher learning include an incomparable military college, Virginia Military Institute (VMI). The United States maintains that the Constitution's equal protection guarantee precludes Virginia from reserving exclusively to men the unique educational opportunities VMI affords. We agree.

Founded in 1839, VMI is today the sole single-sex school among Virginia's 15 public institutions of higher learning. VMI's distinctive mission is to produce "citizen-soldiers," men prepared for leadership in civilian life and in military service. . . .

VMI has notably succeeded in its mission to produce leaders; among its alumni are military generals, Members of Congress, and business executives. The school's alumni overwhelmingly perceive that their VMI training helped them to realize their personal goals. VMI's endowment reflects the loyalty of its graduates; VMI has the largest per-student endowment of all public undergraduate institutions in the Nation.

. . .

VMI today enrolls about 1,300 men as cadets. . . . In contrast to the federal service academies, institutions maintained "to prepare cadets for career service in the armed forces," VMI's program "is directed at preparation for both military and civilian life"; "[o]nly about 15% of VMI cadets enter career military service."

VMI produces its "citizen-soldiers" through "an adversative, or doubting, model of education" which features "[p]hysical rigor, mental stress, absolute equality of treatment, absence of privacy, minute regulation of behavior, and indoctrination in desirable values." As one Commandant of Cadets described it, the adversative method "dissects the young student," and makes him aware of his "limits and capabilities," so that he knows "how far he can go with his anger, . . . how much he can take under stress, . . . exactly what he can do when he is physically exhausted."

VMI cadets live in spartan barracks where surveillance is constant and privacy nonexistent; they wear uniforms, eat together in the mess hall, and regularly participate in drills. Entering students are incessantly exposed to the rat line, "an extreme form of the adversative model," comparable in intensity to Marine Corps boot camp. Tormenting and punishing, the rat line bonds new cadets to their fellow sufferers and, when they have completed the 7–month experience, to their former tormentors.

VMI's "adversative model" is further characterized by a hierarchical "class system" of privileges and responsibilities, a "dyke system" for assigning a senior class mentor to each entering class "rat," and a stringently enforced "honor code," which prescribes that a cadet " 'does not lie, cheat, steal nor tolerate those who do.' "

VMI attracts some applicants because of its reputation as an extraordinarily challenging military school, and "because its alumni are exceptionally close to the school." "[W]omen have no opportunity anywhere to gain the benefits of [the system of education at VMI]."

In 1990, prompted by a complaint filed with the Attorney General by a female high-school student seeking admission to VMI, the United States sued the Commonwealth of Virginia and VMI, alleging that VMI's exclusively male admission policy violated the Equal Protection Clause of the Fourteenth Amendment. . . .

. . .

The District Court ruled in favor of VMI. . . .

. . .

The Court of Appeals for the Fourth Circuit disagreed and vacated the District Court's judgment. . . .

. . .

In response to the Fourth Circuit's ruling, Virginia proposed a parallel program for women: Virginia Women's Institute for Leadership (VWIL). The 4–year, state-sponsored undergraduate program would be located at Mary Baldwin College, a private liberal arts school for women, and would be open, initially, to about 25 to 30 students. Although VWIL would share VMI's mission—to produce "citizen-soldiers"—the VWIL program would differ, as does Mary Baldwin College, from VMI in academic offerings, methods of education, and financial resources.

. . .

Virginia returned to the District Court seeking approval of its proposed remedial plan, and the court decided the plan met the requirements of the Equal Protection Clause. . . .

A divided Court of Appeals affirmed the District Court's judgment. . . .

. . .

We note, . . . the core instruction of this Court's pathmarking decisions in *J.E.B. v. Alabama ex rel. T.B.*, 511 U.S. 127, 136–137, and n. 6 (1994), and *Mississippi Univ. for Women*, 458 U.S. [718, 724 (1982)]: Parties who seek to defend gender-based government action must demonstrate an "exceedingly persuasive justification" for that action.

Today's skeptical scrutiny of official action denying rights or opportunities based on sex responds to volumes of history. As a plurality of this Court acknowledged a generation ago, "our Nation has had a long and unfortunate history of sex discrimination." *Frontiero v. Richardson*, 411 U.S. 677, 684 (1973). Through a century plus three decades and more of that history, women did not count among voters composing "We the People";[5] not until 1920 did women gain a constitutional right to the franchise. And for a half century thereafter, it remained the prevailing doctrine that government, both federal and state, could withhold from women opportunities accorded men so long as any "basis in reason" could be conceived for the discrimination.

In 1971, for the first time in our Nation's history, this Court ruled in favor of a woman who complained that her State had denied her the equal protection of its laws. *Reed v. Reed*, 404 U.S. 71, 73 (holding unconstitutional Idaho Code prescription that, among " 'several persons claiming and equally entitled to administer [a decedent's estate], males must be preferred to females' "). Since *Reed*, the Court has repeatedly recognized that neither federal nor state government acts compatibly with the equal protection principle when a law or official policy denies to women, simply because they are women, full citizenship stature—equal opportunity to aspire, achieve, participate in and contribute to society based on their individual talents and capacities.

Without equating gender classifications, for all purposes, to classifications based on race or national origin, the Court, in post-*Reed* decisions, has carefully inspected official action that closes a door or denies opportunity to women (or to men). To summarize the Court's current directions for cases of

---

5. As Thomas Jefferson stated the view prevailing when the Constitution was new:

"Were our State a pure democracy . . . there would yet be excluded from their deliberations . . . [w]omen, who, to prevent depravation of morals and ambiguity of issue, should not mix promiscuously in the public meetings of men."

Letter from Thomas Jefferson to Samuel Kercheval (Sept. 5, 1816), *in* 10 WRITINGS OF THOMAS JEFFERSON 45–46, n. 1 (P. Ford ed. 1899).

official classification based on gender: Focusing on the differential treatment or denial of opportunity for which relief is sought, the reviewing court must determine whether the proffered justification is "exceedingly persuasive." The burden of justification is demanding and it rests entirely on the State. The State must show "at least that the [challenged] classification serves 'important governmental objectives and that the discriminatory means employed' are 'substantially related to the achievement of those objectives.'" The justification must be genuine, not hypothesized or invented *post hoc* in response to litigation. And it must not rely on overbroad generalizations about the different talents, capacities, or preferences of males and females.

The heightened review standard our precedent establishes does not make sex a proscribed classification. Supposed "inherent differences" are no longer accepted as a ground for race or national origin classifications. See *Loving v. Virginia*, 388 U.S. 1 (1967). Physical differences between men and women, however, are enduring: "[T]he two sexes are not fungible; a community made up exclusively of one [sex] is different from a community composed of both." *Ballard v. United States*, 329 U.S. 187, 193 (1946).

"Inherent differences" between men and women, we have come to appreciate, remain cause for celebration, but not for denigration of the members of either sex or for artificial constraints on an individual's opportunity. Sex classifications may be used to compensate women "for particular economic disabilities [they have] suffered," *Califano v. Webster*, 430 U.S. 313, 320 (1977) (*per curiam*), to "promot[e] equal employment opportunity," see *California Federal Sav. & Loan Assn. v. Guerra*, 479 U.S. 272, 289 (1987), to advance full development of the talent and capacities of our Nation's people.[7] But such classifications may not be used, as they once were, to create or perpetuate the legal, social, and economic inferiority of women.

Measuring the record in this case against the review standard just described, we conclude that Virginia has shown no "exceedingly persuasive justification" for excluding all women from the citizen-soldier training afforded by VMI. We therefore affirm the Fourth Circuit's initial judgment, which held that Virginia had violated the Fourteenth Amendment's Equal Protection Clause. Because the remedy proffered by Virginia—the Mary Baldwin VWIL program—does not cure the constitutional violation, *i.e.*, it does not provide equal opportunity, we reverse the Fourth Circuit's final judgment in this case.

... Virginia ... asserts two justifications in defense of VMI's exclusion of women. First, the Commonwealth contends, "single-sex education provides important educational benefits," and the option of single-sex education contributes to "diversity in educational approaches." Second, the Commonwealth argues, "the unique VMI method of character development and leadership training," the school's adversative approach, would have to be

---

7. Several *amici* have urged that diversity in educational opportunities is an altogether appropriate governmental pursuit and that single-sex schools can contribute importantly to such diversity. Indeed, it is the mission of some single-sex schools "to dissipate, rather than perpetuate, traditional gender classifications." See Brief for Twenty–Six Private Women's Colleges as *Amici Curiae* 5. We do not question the Commonwealth's prerogative evenhandedly to support diverse educational opportunities. We address specifically and only an educational opportunity recognized by the District Court and the Court of Appeals as "unique," an opportunity available only at Virginia's premier military institute, the Commonwealth's sole single-sex public university or college. Cf. Mississippi Univ. for Women v. Hogan, 458 U.S. 718, 720, n. 1 (1982) ("Mississippi maintains no other single-sex public university or college. Thus, we are not faced with the question of whether States can provide 'separate but equal' undergraduate institutions for males and females.").

modified were VMI to admit women. We consider these two justifications in turn.

· · ·

Neither recent nor distant history bears out Virginia's alleged pursuit of diversity through single-sex educational options. In 1839, when the State established VMI, a range of educational opportunities for men and women was scarcely contemplated. Higher education at the time was considered dangerous for women;[9] reflecting widely held views about women's proper place, the Nation's first universities and colleges—for example, Harvard in Massachusetts, William and Mary in Virginia—admitted only men. VMI was not at all novel in this respect: In admitting no women, VMI followed the lead of the State's flagship school, the University of Virginia, founded in 1819.

"[N]o struggle for the admission of women to a state university," a historian has recounted, "was longer drawn out, or developed more bitterness, than that at the University of Virginia." 2 T. Woody, *A History of Women's Education in the United States* 254 (1929) (History of Women's Education). In 1879, the State Senate resolved to look into the possibility of higher education for women, recognizing that Virginia " 'has never, at any period of her history,' " provided for the higher education of her daughters, though she " 'has liberally provided for the higher education of her sons.' " Despite this recognition, no new opportunities were instantly open to women.

· · ·

Ultimately, in 1970, "the most prestigious institution of higher education in Virginia," the University of Virginia, introduced coeducation and, in 1972, began to admit women on an equal basis with men. . . .

Virginia describes the current absence of public single-sex higher education for women as "an historical anomaly." But the historical record indicates action more deliberate than anomalous: First, protection of women against higher education; next, schools for women far from equal in resources and stature to schools for men; finally, conversion of the separate schools to coeducation. The state legislature, prior to the advent of this controversy, had repealed "[a]ll Virginia statutes requiring individual institutions to admit only men or women." And in 1990, an official commission, "legislatively established to chart the future goals of higher education in Virginia," reaffirmed the policy "of affording broad access" while maintaining "autonomy and diversity." Significantly, the Commission reported:

---

9. Dr. Edward H. Clarke of Harvard Medical School, whose influential book, Sex in Education, went through 17 editions, was perhaps the most well-known speaker from the medical community opposing higher education for women. He maintained that the physiological effects of hard study and academic competition with boys would interfere with the development of girls' reproductive organs. *See* E. CLARKE, SEX IN EDUCATION 38–39, 62–63 (1873); *id.*, at 127 ("identical education of the two sexes is a crime before God and humanity, that physiology protests against, and that experience weeps over"); *see also* H. MAUDSLEY, SEX IN MIND AND IN EDUCATION 17 (1874) ("It is not that girls have not ambition, nor that they fail generally to run the intellectual race [in coeducational settings], but it is asserted that they do it at a cost to their strength and health which entails life-long suffering, and even incapacitates them for the adequate performance of the natural functions of their sex."); C. MEIGS, FEMALES AND THEIR DISEASES 350 (1848) (after five or six weeks of "mental and educational discipline," a healthy woman would "lose ... the habit of menstruation" and suffer numerous ills as a result of depriving her body for the sake of her mind).

" 'Because colleges and universities provide opportunities for students to develop values and learn from role models, it is extremely important that they deal with faculty, staff, and students without regard to sex, race, or ethnic origin.' "

This statement, the Court of Appeals observed, "is the only explicit one that we have found in the record in which the Commonwealth has expressed itself with respect to gender distinctions."

Our 1982 decision in *Mississippi Univ. for Women* prompted VMI to reexamine its male-only admission policy. Virginia relies on that reexamination as a legitimate basis for maintaining VMI's single-sex character. A Mission Study Committee, appointed by the VMI Board of Visitors, studied the problem from October 1983 until May 1986, and in that month counseled against "change of VMI status as a single-sex college." Whatever internal purpose the Mission Study Committee served—and however well-meaning the framers of the report—we can hardly extract from that effort any state policy evenhandedly to advance diverse educational options. As the District Court observed, the Committee's analysis "primarily focuse[d] on anticipated difficulties in attracting females to VMI," and the report, overall, supplied "very little indication of how th[e] conclusion was reached."

In sum, we find no persuasive evidence in this record that VMI's male-only admission policy "is in furtherance of a state policy of 'diversity.' " No such policy, the Fourth Circuit observed, can be discerned from the movement of all other public colleges and universities in Virginia away from single-sex education. That court also questioned "how one institution with autonomy, but with no authority over any other state institution, can give effect to a state policy of diversity among institutions." A purpose genuinely to advance an array of educational options, as the Court of Appeals recognized, is not served by VMI's historic and constant plan—a plan to "affor[d] a unique educational benefit only to males." However "liberally" this plan serves the State's sons, it makes no provision whatever for her daughters. That is not *equal* protection.

Virginia next argues that VMI's adversative method of training provides educational benefits that cannot be made available, unmodified, to women. Alterations to accommodate women would necessarily be "radical," so "drastic," Virginia asserts, as to transform, indeed "destroy," VMI's program. Neither sex would be favored by the transformation, Virginia maintains: Men would be deprived of the unique opportunity currently available to them; women would not gain that opportunity because their participation would "eliminat[e] the very aspects of [the] program that distinguish [VMI] from . . . other institutions of higher education in Virginia."

The District Court forecast from expert witness testimony, and the Court of Appeals accepted, that coeducation would materially affect "at least these three aspects of VMI's program—physical training, the absence of privacy, and the adversative approach." And it is uncontested that women's admission would require accommodations, primarily in arranging housing assignments and physical training programs for female cadets. It is also undisputed, however, that "the VMI methodology could be used to educate women." The District Court even allowed that some women may prefer it to the methodology a women's college might pursue. "[S]ome women, at least, would want to attend [VMI] if they had the opportunity," the District Court recognized, and "some women," the expert testimony established, "are capable of all of the individual activities required of VMI cadets". The parties, furthermore, agree that "*some* women can meet the physical standards [VMI] now impose[s] on men." In sum, as the Court of Appeals stated, "neither the goal of producing citizen soldiers," VMI's *raison dêtre*, "nor VMI's implementing methodology is inherently unsuitable to women."

. . .

It may be assumed, for purposes of this decision, that most women would not choose VMI's adversative method. As Fourth Circuit Judge Motz observed, however, in her dissent from the Court of Appeals' denial of rehearing en banc, it is also probable that "many men would not want to be educated in such an environment." . . . Education, to be sure, is not a "one size fits all" business. The issue, however, is not whether "women—or men— should be forced to attend VMI"; rather, the question is whether the Commonwealth can constitutionally deny to women who have the will and capacity, the training and attendant opportunities that VMI uniquely affords.

The notion that admission of women would downgrade VMI's stature, destroy the adversative system and, with it, even the school, is a judgment hardly proved, a prediction hardly different from other "self-fulfilling prophec[ies]," once routinely used to deny rights or opportunities. When women first sought admission to the bar and access to legal education, concerns of the same order were expressed. For example, in 1876, the Court of Common Pleas of Hennepin County, Minnesota, explained why women were thought ineligible for the practice of law. Women train and educate the young, the court said, which

> forbids that they shall bestow that time (early and late) and labor, so essential in attaining to the eminence to which the true lawyer should ever aspire. It cannot therefore be said that the opposition of courts to the admission of females to practice . . . is to any extent the outgrowth of . . . 'old fogyism[.]' . . . [I]t arises rather from a comprehension of the magnitude of the responsibilities connected with the successful practice of law, and a desire to *grade up* the profession.

In re Application of Martha Angle Dorsett to Be Admitted to Practice as Attorney and Counselor at Law (Minn.C.P. Hennepin Cty., 1876), in The Syllabi, Oct. 21, 1876, pp. 5, 6 (emphasis added).

A like fear, according to a 1925 report, accounted for Columbia Law School's resistance to women's admission, although

> [t]he faculty . . . never maintained that women could not master legal learning. . . . No, its argument has been . . . more practical. If women were admitted to the Columbia Law School, [the faculty] said, then the choicer, more manly and red-blooded graduates of our great universities would go to the Harvard Law School!

The Nation, Feb. 18, 1925, p. 173.

. . .

Women's successful entry into the federal military academies, and their participation in the Nation's military forces, indicate that Virginia's fears for the future of VMI may not be solidly grounded.[15] The Commonwealth's justification for excluding all women from "citizen-soldier" training for

---

15. Inclusion of women in settings where, traditionally, they were not wanted inevitably entails a period of adjustment. As one West Point cadet squad leader recounted: "[T]he classes of '78 and '79 see the women as women, but the classes of '80 and '81 see them as classmates." U.S. Military Academy, A. Vitters, Report of Admission of Women (Project Athena II) 84 (1978).

which some are qualified, in any event, cannot rank as "exceedingly persuasive," as we have explained and applied that standard.

Virginia and VMI trained their argument on "means" rather than "end," and thus misperceived our precedent. Single-sex education at VMI serves an "important governmental objective," they maintained, and exclusion of women is not only "substantially related," it is essential to that objective. By this notably circular argument, the "straightforward" test *Mississippi Univ. for Women* described, was bent and bowed.

The Commonwealth's misunderstanding and, in turn, the District Court's, is apparent from VMI's mission: to produce "citizen-soldiers," individuals

> " 'imbued with love of learning, confident in the functions and attitudes of leadership, possessing a high sense of public service, advocates of the American democracy and free enterprise system, and ready ... to defend their country in time of national peril.' " 766 F.Supp., at 1425 (quoting Mission Study Committee of the VMI Board of Visitors, Report, May 16, 1986).

Surely that goal is great enough to accommodate women, who today count as citizens in our American democracy equal in stature to men. Just as surely, the Commonwealth's great goal is not substantially advanced by women's categorical exclusion, in total disregard of their individual merit, from the Commonwealth's premier "citizen-soldier" corps.[16] Virginia, in sum, "has fallen far short of establishing the 'exceedingly persuasive justification,' " that must be the solid base for any gender-defined classification.

. . .

Virginia chose not to eliminate, but to leave untouched, VMI's exclusionary policy. For women only, however, Virginia proposed a separate program, different in kind from VMI and unequal in tangible and intangible facilities. . . .

VWIL affords women no opportunity to experience the rigorous military training for which VMI is famed. . . .

VWIL students participate in ROTC and a "largely ceremonial" Virginia Corps of Cadets, but Virginia deliberately did not make VWIL a military institute. The VWIL House is not a military-style residence and VWIL students need not live together throughout the 4–year program, eat meals together, or wear uniforms during the school day. VWIL students thus do not experience the "barracks" life "crucial to the VMI experience," the spartan living arrangements designed to foster an "egalitarian ethic." "[T]he most important aspects of the VMI educational experience occur in the barracks," the District Court found, yet Virginia deemed that core experience nonessential, indeed inappropriate, for training its female citizen-soldiers.

VWIL students receive their "leadership training" in seminars, externships, and speaker series, episodes and encounters lacking the "[p]hysical

---

16. VMI has successfully managed another notable change. The school admitted its first African–American cadets in 1968. See The VMI Story 347–349 (students no longer sing "Dixie," salute the Confederate flag or the tomb of General Robert E. Lee at ceremonies and sports events). As the District Court noted, VMI established a Program on "retention of black cadets" designed to offer academic and social-cultural support to "minority members of a dominantly white and tradition-oriented student body." The school maintains a "special recruitment program for blacks" which the District Court found, "has had little, if any, effect on VMI's method of accomplishing its mission."

rigor, mental stress, . . . minute regulation of behavior, and indoctrination in desirable values" made hallmarks of VMI's citizen-soldier training. Kept away from the pressures, hazards, and psychological bonding characteristic of VMI's adversative training, VWIL students will not know the "feeling of tremendous accomplishment" commonly experienced by VMI's successful cadets.

Virginia maintains that these methodological differences are "justified pedagogically," based on "important differences between men and women in learning and developmental needs," "psychological and sociological differences" Virginia describes as "real" and "not stereotypes." The Task Force charged with developing the leadership program for women, drawn from the staff and faculty at Mary Baldwin College, "determined that a military model and, especially VMI's adversative method, would be wholly inappropriate for educating and training *most women*." The Commonwealth embraced the Task Force view, as did expert witnesses who testified for Virginia.

As earlier stated, generalizations about "the way women are," estimates of what is appropriate for *most women*, no longer justify denying opportunity to women whose talent and capacity place them outside the average description. Notably, Virginia never asserted that VMI's method of education suits *most men*. It is also revealing that Virginia accounted for its failure to make the VWIL experience "the entirely militaristic experience of VMI" on the ground that VWIL "is planned for women who do not necessarily expect to pursue military careers." By that reasoning, VMI's "entirely militaristic" program would be inappropriate for men in general or *as a group*, for "[o]nly about 15% of VMI cadets enter career military service."

In contrast to the generalizations about women on which Virginia rests, we note again these dispositive realities: VMI's "implementing methodology" is not "inherently unsuitable to women," 976 F.2d, at 899; "some women . . . do well under [the] adversative model," 766 F.Supp., at 1434 (internal quotation marks omitted); "some women, at least, would want to attend [VMI] if they had the opportunity," *id.*, at 1414; "some women are capable of all of the individual activities required of VMI cadets," *id.*, at 1412, and "can meet the physical standards [VMI] now impose[s] on men," 976 F.2d, at 896. It is on behalf of these women that the United States has instituted this suit, and it is for them that a remedy must be crafted,[19] a remedy that will end their exclusion from a state-supplied educational opportunity for which they are fit, a decree that will "bar like discrimination in the future." *Louisiana* [*v. U.S.*, 380 U.S. 145, 154 (1965)].

In myriad respects other than military training, VWIL does not qualify as VMI's equal. VWIL's student body, faculty, course offerings, and facilities hardly match VMI's. Nor can the VWIL graduate anticipate the benefits associated with VMI's 157–year history, the school's prestige, and its influential alumni network.

Mary Baldwin College, whose degree VWIL students will gain, enrolls first-year women with an average combined SAT score about 100 points

---

19. Admitting women to VMI would undoubtedly require alterations necessary to afford members of each sex privacy from the other sex in living arrangements, and to adjust aspects of the physical training programs. See Brief for Petitioner 27–29. Experience shows such adjustments are manageable. See U.S. Military Academy, A. Vitters, N. Kinzer, & J. Adams, Report of Admission of Women (Project Athena I–IV) (1977–1980) (4–year longitudinal study of the admission of women to West Point); Defense Advisory Committee on Women in the Services, Report on the Integration and Performance of Women at West Point 17–18 (1992).

lower than the average score for VMI freshmen. The Mary Baldwin faculty holds "significantly fewer Ph.D.'s," and receives substantially lower salaries.

Mary Baldwin does not offer a VWIL student the range of curricular choices available to a VMI cadet. VMI awards baccalaureate degrees in liberal arts, biology, chemistry, civil engineering, electrical and computer engineering, and mechanical engineering. VWIL students attend a school that "does not have a math and science focus," they cannot take at Mary Baldwin any courses in engineering or the advanced math and physics courses VMI offers.

For physical training, Mary Baldwin has "two multi-purpose fields" and "[o]ne gymnasium." VMI has "an NCAA competition level indoor track and field facility; a number of multi-purpose fields; baseball, soccer and lacrosse fields; an obstacle course; large boxing, wrestling and martial arts facilities; an 11–laps–to–the–mile indoor running course; an indoor pool; indoor and outdoor rifle ranges; and a football stadium that also contains a practice field and outdoor track."

Although Virginia has represented that it will provide equal financial support for in-state VWIL students and VMI cadets, and the VMI Foundation has agreed to endow VWIL with $5.4625 million, the difference between the two schools' financial reserves is pronounced. Mary Baldwin's endowment, currently about $19 million, will gain an additional $35 million based on future commitments; VMI's current endowment, $131 million—the largest per-student endowment in the Nation—will gain $220 million.

The VWIL student does not graduate with the advantage of a VMI degree. Her diploma does not unite her with the legions of VMI "graduates [who] have distinguished themselves" in military and civilian life. "[VMI] alumni are exceptionally close to the school," and that closeness accounts, in part, for VMI's success in attracting applicants. A VWIL graduate cannot assume that the "network of business owners, corporations, VMI graduates and non-graduate employers ... interested in hiring VMI graduates," will be equally responsive to her search for employment.

Virginia, in sum, while maintaining VMI for men only, has failed to provide any "comparable single-gender women's institution." Instead, the Commonwealth has created a VWIL program fairly appraised as a "pale shadow" of VMI in terms of the range of curricular choices and faculty stature, funding, prestige, alumni support and influence.

Virginia's VWIL solution is reminiscent of the remedy Texas proposed 50 years ago, in response to a state trial court's 1946 ruling that, given the equal protection guarantee, African Americans could not be denied a legal education at a state facility. See *Sweatt v. Painter*, 339 U.S. 629 (1950). Reluctant to admit African Americans to its flagship University of Texas Law School, the State set up a separate school for Herman Sweatt and other black law students. As originally opened, the new school had no independent faculty or library, and it lacked accreditation. Nevertheless, the state trial and appellate courts were satisfied that the new school offered Sweatt opportunities for the study of law "substantially equivalent to those offered by the State to white students at the University of Texas."

Before this Court considered the case, the new school had gained "a faculty of five full-time professors; a student body of 23; a library of some 16,500 volumes serviced by a full-time staff; a practice court and legal aid association; and one alumnus who ha[d] become a member of the Texas Bar." This Court contrasted resources at the new school with those at the school from which Sweatt had been excluded. The University of Texas Law School had a full-time faculty of 16, a student body of 850, a library containing over 65,000 volumes, scholarship funds, a law review, and moot court facilities.

More important than the tangible features, the Court emphasized, are "those qualities which are incapable of objective measurement but which make for greatness" in a school, including "reputation of the faculty, experience of the administration, position and influence of the alumni, standing in the community, traditions and prestige." Facing the marked differences reported in the *Sweatt* opinion, the Court unanimously ruled that Texas had not shown "substantial equality in the [separate] educational opportunities" the State offered. Accordingly, the Court held, the Equal Protection Clause required Texas to admit African–Americans to the University of Texas Law School. In line with *Sweatt,* we rule here that Virginia has not shown substantial equality in the separate educational opportunities the Commonwealth supports at VWIL and VMI.

. . .

The Fourth Circuit plainly erred in exposing Virginia's VWIL plan to a deferential analysis, for "all gender-based classifications today" warrant "heightened scrutiny." Valuable as VWIL may prove for students who seek the program offered, Virginia's remedy affords no cure at all for the opportunities and advantages withheld from women who want a VMI education and can make the grade. In sum, Virginia's remedy does not match the constitutional violation; the State has shown no "exceedingly persuasive justification" for withholding from women qualified for the experience premier training of the kind VMI affords.

. . .

For the reasons stated, the initial judgment of the Court of Appeals is affirmed, the final judgment of the Court of Appeals, is reversed, and the case is remanded for further proceedings consistent with this opinion.

It is so ordered.

■ JUSTICE THOMAS took no part in the consideration or decision of this case.

■ JUSTICE SCALIA, dissenting.

. . .

I shall devote most of my analysis to evaluating the Court's opinion on the basis of our current equal protection jurisprudence, which regards this Court as free to evaluate everything under the sun by applying one of three tests: "rational basis" scrutiny, intermediate scrutiny, or strict scrutiny. These tests are no more scientific than their names suggest, and a further element of randomness is added by the fact that it is largely up to us which test will be applied in each case. Strict scrutiny, we have said, is reserved for state "classifications based on race or national origin and classifications affecting fundamental rights," *Clark v. Jeter,* 486 U.S. 456, 461 (1988). It is my position that the term "fundamental rights" should be limited to "interest[s] traditionally protected by our society," but the Court has not accepted that view, so that strict scrutiny will be applied to the deprivation of whatever sort of right we consider "fundamental." We have no established criterion for "intermediate scrutiny" either, but essentially apply it when it seems like a good idea to load the dice. So far it has been applied to content-neutral restrictions that place an incidental burden on speech, to disabilities attend-

ant to illegitimacy, and to discrimination on the basis of sex. See, e.g., *Turner Broadcasting System, Inc. v. FCC*, 512 U.S. 622, 662 (1994); *Mills v. Habluetzel*, 456 U.S. 91, 98–99 (1982); *Craig v. Boren*, 429 U.S. 190, 197 (1976).
. . .

To reject the Court's disposition today, however, it is not necessary to accept my view that the Court's made-up tests cannot displace longstanding national traditions as the primary determinant of what the Constitution means. It is only necessary to apply honestly the test the Court has been applying to sex-based classifications for the past two decades. It is well settled, as JUSTICE O'CONNOR stated some time ago for a unanimous Court, that we evaluate a statutory classification based on sex under a standard that lies "[b]etween th[e] extremes of rational basis review and strict scrutiny." *Clark v. Jeter*, 486 U.S., at 461. We have denominated this standard "intermediate scrutiny" and under it have inquired whether the statutory classification is "substantially related to an important governmental objective."

. . . Notwithstanding our above-described precedents and their " 'firmly established principles,' " the United States urged us to hold in this litigation "that strict scrutiny is the correct constitutional standard for evaluating classifications that deny opportunities to individuals based on their sex." (This was in flat contradiction of the Government's position below, which was, in its own words, to "stat[e] *unequivocally* that the appropriate standard in this case is 'intermediate scrutiny.' ") The Court, while making no reference to the Government's argument, effectively accepts it.

Although the Court in two places recites the test as stated in *Hogan*, which asks whether the State has demonstrated "that the classification serves important governmental objectives and that the discriminatory means employed are substantially related to the achievement of those objectives," the Court never answers the question presented in anything resembling that form. When it engages in analysis, the Court instead prefers the phrase "exceedingly persuasive justification" from *Hogan*. The Court's nine invocations of that phrase, and even its fanciful description of that imponderable as "the core instruction" of the Court's decisions in *J.E.B. v. Alabama ex rel. T.B.*, [511 U.S. 127 (1994)], and *Hogan, supra*, would be unobjectionable if the Court acknowledged that *whether* a "justification" is "exceedingly persuasive" must be assessed by asking "[whether] the classification serves important governmental objectives and [whether] the discriminatory means employed are substantially related to the achievement of those objectives." Instead, however, the Court proceeds to interpret "exceedingly persuasive justification" in a fashion that contradicts the reasoning of *Hogan* and our other precedents.

That is essential to the Court's result, which can only be achieved by establishing that intermediate scrutiny is not survived if there are *some* women interested in attending VMI, capable of undertaking its activities, and able to meet its physical demands. . . .

. . . Intermediate scrutiny has never required a least-restrictive-means analysis, but only a "substantial relation" between the classification and the state interests that it serves. Thus, in *Califano v. Webster*, 430 U.S. 313 (1977) (*per curiam*), we upheld a congressional statute that provided higher Social Security benefits for women than for men. We reasoned that "women . . . as such have been unfairly hindered from earning as much as men," but we did not require proof that each woman so benefited had suffered discrimination or that each disadvantaged man had not; it was sufficient that even under the former congressional scheme "women *on the average* received lower retirement benefits than men." The reasoning in our other intermediate-scrutiny cases has similarly required only a substantial relation between end and means, not a perfect fit. In *Rostker v. Goldberg*, 453 U.S. 57 (1981), we held that selective-service registration could constitutionally exclude women, because even "assuming that a small number of women could be drafted for noncombat roles, Congress simply did not consider it worth the added burdens of including women in draft and registration plans." . . . There is simply no support in our cases for the notion that a sex-based classification is invalid unless it relates to characteristics that hold true in every instance.

Not content to execute a *de facto* abandonment of the intermediate scrutiny that has been our standard for sex-based classifications for some two decades, the Court purports to reserve the question whether, even in principle, a higher standard (*i.e.*, strict scrutiny) should apply. "The Court has," it says, "*thus far* reserved most stringent judicial scrutiny for classifications based on race or national origin . . .,"; and it describes our earlier cases as having done no more than decline to "equat[e] gender classifications, *for all purposes*, to classifications based on race or national origin." The wonderful thing about these statements is that they are not actually false—just as it would not be actually false to say that "our cases have thus far reserved the 'beyond a reasonable doubt' standard of proof for criminal cases," or that "we have not equated tort actions, for all purposes, to criminal prosecutions." But the statements are misleading, insofar as they suggest that we have not already categorically *held* strict scrutiny to be inapplicable to sex-based classifications. *See, e.g., Heckler v. Mathews*, 465 U.S. 728 (1984) (*upholding* state action after applying *only* intermediate scrutiny); *Michael M. v. Superior Court, Sonoma Cty.*, 450 U.S. 464 (1981) (same) (plurality and both concurring opinions); *Califano v. Webster*, [430 U.S. 313 (1977)] (same) (*per curiam*). And the statements are irresponsible, insofar as they are calculated to destabilize current law. Our task is to clarify the law—not to muddy the waters, and not to exact overcompliance by intimidation. The States and the Federal Government are entitled to know *before they act* the standard to which they will be held, rather than be compelled to guess about the outcome of Supreme Court peek-a-boo.

The Court's intimations are particularly out of place because it is perfectly clear that, if the question of the applicable standard of review for sex-based classifications were to be regarded as an appropriate subject for reconsideration, the stronger argument would be not for elevating the standard to strict scrutiny, but for reducing it to rational-basis review. The latter certainly has a firmer foundation in our past jurisprudence: Whereas no majority of the Court has ever applied strict scrutiny in a case involving sex-based classifications, we routinely applied rational-basis review until the 1970's, see, e.g., *Hoyt v. Florida*, 368 U.S. 57 (1961); *Goesaert v. Cleary*, 335 U.S. 464 (1948). And of course normal, rational-basis review of sex-based classifications would be much more in accord with the genesis of heightened standards of judicial review, the famous footnote in *United States v. Carolene Products Co.*, 304 U.S. 144 (1938), which said (intimatingly) that we did not have to inquire in the case at hand

> whether prejudice against discrete and insular minorities may be a special condition, which tends seriously to curtail the operation of those political processes ordinarily to be relied upon to protect minorities, and which may call for a correspondingly more searching judicial inquiry.

It is hard to consider women a "discrete and insular minorit[y]" unable to employ the "political processes ordinarily to be relied upon," when they constitute a majority of the electorate. And the suggestion that they are incapable of exerting that political power smacks of the same paternalism that the Court so roundly condemns. Moreover, a long list of legislation proves the proposition false. See, e.g., Equal Pay Act of 1963, 29 U.S.C. § 206(d); Title VII of the Civil Rights Act of 1964, 42 U.S.C. § 2000e–2; Title IX of the Education Amendments of 1972, 20 U.S.C. § 1681; Women's Business Ownership Act of 1988, Pub.L. 100–533, 102 Stat. 2689; Violence Against Women Act of 1994, Pub.L. 103–322, Title IV, 108 Stat. 1902.

With this explanation of how the Court has succeeded in making its analysis seem orthodox—and indeed, if intimations are to be believed, even overly generous to VMI—I now proceed to describe how the analysis should have been conducted. The question to be answered, I repeat, is whether the exclusion of women from VMI is "substantially related to an important governmental objective."

It is beyond question that Virginia has an important state interest in providing effective college education for its citizens. That single-sex instruction is an approach substantially related to that interest should be evident enough from the long and continuing history in this country of men's and women's colleges. But beyond that, as the Court of Appeals here stated: "That single-gender education at the college level is beneficial to both sexes is a *fact established in this case*." 44 F.3d 1229, 1238 (C.A.4 1995) (emphasis added).

The evidence establishing that fact was overwhelming—indeed, "virtually uncontradicted" in the words of the court that received the evidence. As an initial matter, Virginia demonstrated at trial that "[a] substantial body of contemporary scholarship and research supports the proposition that, although males and females have significant areas of developmental overlap, they also have differing developmental needs that are deep-seated." While no one questioned that for many students a coeducational environment was nonetheless not inappropriate, that could not obscure the demonstrated benefits of single-sex colleges. For example, the District Court stated as follows:

> One empirical study in evidence, not questioned by any expert, demonstrates that single-sex colleges provide better educational experiences than coeducational institutions. Students of both sexes become more academically involved, interact with faculty frequently, show larger increases in intellectual self-esteem and are more satisfied with practically all aspects of college experience (the sole exception is social life) compared with their counterparts in coeducational institutions. Attendance at an all-male college substantially increases the likelihood that a student will carry out career plans in law, business and college teaching, and also has a substantial positive effect on starting salaries in business. Women's colleges increase the chances that those who attend will obtain positions of leadership, complete the baccalaureate degree, and aspire to higher degrees.

> . . .

Virginia did not make this determination regarding the make-up of its public college system on the unrealistic assumption that no other colleges exist. Substantial evidence in the District Court demonstrated that the Commonwealth has long proceeded on the principle that " [h]igher education resources should be viewed as a whole—public and private' "—because such an approach enhances diversity and because " 'it is academic and economic waste to permit unwarranted duplication.' " *Id.*, at 1420–1421 (quoting 1974 Report of the General Assembly Commission on Higher Education to the General Assembly of Virginia). It is thus significant that, whereas there are "four all-female private [colleges] in Virginia," there is only "one private all-male college," which "indicates that the private sector is providing for th[e] [former] form of education to a much greater extent that it provides for all-male education." In these circumstances, Virginia's election to fund one public all-male institution and one on the adversative model—and to concentrate its resources in a single entity that serves both these interests in diversity—is substantially related to the Commonwealth's important educational interests.

. . .

In the course of this dissent, I have referred approvingly to the opinion of my former colleague, JUSTICE POWELL, in *Mississippi Univ. for Women v. Hogan*, 458 U.S. 718 (1982). Many of the points made in his dissent apply with equal force here—in particular, the criticism of judicial opinions that purport to be "narro[w]" but whose "logic" is "sweepin[g]." But there is one statement with which I cannot agree. JUSTICE POWELL observed that the Court's decision in *Hogan*, which struck down a single-sex program offered by the Mississippi University for Women, had thereby "[l]eft without honor . . . an element of diversity that has characterized much of American education and enriched much of American life." Today's decision does not leave VMI without honor; no court opinion can do that.

. . .

NOTE

Six members of the Court joined the majority opinion. Chief Justice Rehnquist concurred in the judgment. Only Justice Scalia dissented. Justice Thomas took no part in the decision.

United States v. Flores–Villar

United States Court of Appeals, Ninth Circuit, 2008.
536 F.3d 990.

■ RYMER, CIRCUIT JUDGE.

Ruben Flores–Villar raises a challenge under the equal protection component of the Fifth Amendment's due process clause on the basis of . . . gender to two former sections of the Immigration and Nationality Act, 8 U.S.C. §§ 1401(a)(7) and 1409 (1974), which impose a five-year residence requirement, after the age of fourteen, on United States citizen fathers—but not on United States citizen mothers—before they may transmit citizenship to a child born out of wedlock abroad to a non-citizen. This precise question has not been addressed before, but the answer follows from the Supreme Court's opinion in *Nguyen v. INS*, 533 U.S. 53 (2001). There the Court held that § 1409's legitimation requirements for citizen fathers, but not for citizen mothers, did not offend principles of equal protection [on sex equality grounds]. Assuming, as the Court did in *Nguyen*, that intermediate scrutiny applies to Flores–Villar's gender-based claim . . ., we conclude that the residence requirements of §§ 1401(a)(7) and 1409 survive. . . .

I

Flores–Villar was born in Tijuana, Mexico on October 7, 1974 to Ruben Trinidad Floresvillar–Sandez, his United States citizen biological father who was sixteen at the time, and Maria Mercedes Negrete, his non-United States citizen biological mother. Floresvillar–Sandez had been issued a Certificate of Citizenship on May 24, 1999 based on the fact that his mother-Flores Villar's paternal grandmother-is a United States citizen by birth.

His father and grandmother brought Flores–Villar to the United States for medical treatment when he was two months old. He grew up in San Diego with his grandmother and father. Floresvillar–Sandez is not listed on Flores–Villar's birth certificate, but he acknowledged Flores–Villar as his son by filing an acknowledgment of paternity with the Civil Registry in Mexico on June 2, 1985.

On March 17, 1997 Flores–Villar was convicted of importation of marijuana in violation of 21 U.S.C. §§ 952 and 960; and on June 16, 2003 he was convicted of two counts of illegal entry into the United States in violation of 8 U.S.C. § 1325. He was removed from the United States pursuant to removal orders on numerous occasions [from 1998 to 2005]....

He was arrested again on February 24, 2006, and this time was charged with being a deported alien found in the United States after deportation in violation of 8 U.S.C. § 1326(a) and (b). He sought to defend on the footing that he believed he was a United States citizen through his father. Meanwhile, Flores–Villar filed an N–600 application seeking a Certificate of Citizenship, which was denied on the ground that it was physically impossible for his father, who was sixteen when Flores–Villar was born, to have been present in the United States for five years after his fourteenth birthday as required by § 1401(a)(7). The government filed a motion in limine to exclude evidence of derivative citizenship for the same reason, which the district court granted. The court denied Flores–Villar's corresponding motion in limine, to be allowed to present evidence that he believed he was a United States citizen.

The district court found Flores–Villar guilty following a bench trial on stipulated facts. It denied his motion for judgment of acquittal. Flores–Villar timely appeals his conviction.

When Flores–Villar was born, § 1401(a)(7) provided, in relevant part:

(a) The following shall be nationals and citizens of the United States at birth:

. . .

(7) a person born outside the geographic limits of the United States and its outlying possessions of parents one of whom is an alien, and the other a citizen of the United States who, prior to the birth of such person, was physically present in the United States or its outlying possessions for a period or periods totaling not less than ten years, at least five of which were after attaining the age of fourteen years.

8 U.S.C. § 1401(a)(7) (1974). Section 1409 provided:

(a) The provisions of paragraphs (3) to (5) and (7) of section 1401(a) of this title, and of paragraph (2) of section 1408, of this title shall apply as of the date of birth to a child born out of wedlock . . . if the paternity of such child is established while such child is under the age of twenty-one years by legitimation.

. . .

(c) Notwithstanding the provision of subsection (a) of this section, a person born . . . outside the United States and out of wedlock shall be held to have acquired at birth the nationality status of his mother, if the mother had the nationality of the United States at the time of such person's birth, and if the mother had previously been physically present in the United States or one of its outlying possessions for a continuous period of one year.

8 U.S.C. § 1409(a), (c) (1974).

Thus, if a United States citizen father had a child out of wedlock abroad, with a non-United States citizen mother, the father must have resided in the United States for at least five years after his fourteenth birthday to confer citizenship on his child. But a United States citizen mother had to reside in the United States for a continuous period of only one year prior to the child's birth to pass on citizenship. It is this difference that Flores–Villar claims makes an impermissible classification on the basis of gender. . . .

In *Nguyen*, the United States citizen father of a child born in Vietnam to a Vietnamese mother challenged § 1409's imposition of different rules for obtaining citizenship depending upon whether the one parent with American citizenship is the mother or the father. There, the father complained about the affirmative steps a citizen father, but not a citizen mother, was required by § 1409(a)(4) to take: legitimation; a declaration of paternity under oath by the father; or a court order of paternity. Assuming, without deciding, that the intermediate level of scrutiny normally applied to a gender-based classification applies even when the statute is within Congress' immigration and naturalization power, 533 U.S. at 61, and drawing on Justice Stevens's prior opinion in *Miller v. Albright*, 523 U.S. 420 (1998), the Court identified two important governmental interests substantially furthered by § 1409's distinction between citizen fathers and citizen mothers. The first is "assuring that a biological parent-child relationship exists." *Id.* at 62. Mothers and fathers are not similarly situated in this respect; the relation is verifiable from the birth itself in the case of the mother, while a father's biological relationship to the child is not so easily established. The second interest is ensuring "that the child and the citizen parent have some demonstrated opportunity or potential to develop not just a relationship that is recognized, as a formal matter, by the law, but one that consists of the real, everyday ties that provide a connection between child and citizen parent and, in turn, the United States." *Id.* at 64–65. The mother knows that the child is in being and has immediate contact at birth such that an opportunity for a meaningful relationship exists, whereas, as the Court put it, "[t]he same opportunity does not result from the event of birth, as a matter of biological inevitability, in the case of the unwed father." *Id.* at 65. Unlike an unwed mother, there is no assurance that the father and his biological child will ever meet, or have the kind of contact from which there is a chance for a meaningful relationship to develop. The Court emphasized that Congress need not ignore these realities for purposes of equal protection, and found that the means chosen—additional requirements for an unwed citizen father to confer citizenship upon his child—are substantially related to the objective of a relationship between parent and child, and in turn, the United States. *Id.* at 66.

Although the means at issue are different in this case—an additional residence requirement for the unwed citizen father—the government's interests are no less important, and the particular means no less substantially related to those objectives, than in *Nguyen*.[2] The government argues that avoiding stateless children is an important objective that is substantially furthered by relaxing the residence requirement for women because many countries confer citizenship based on bloodline (*jus sanguinis*) rather than, as the United States does, on place of birth (*jus soli*). We explained the conundrum in *Runnett v. Shultz*:

> One obvious rational basis for a more lenient policy towards illegitimate children of U.S. citizen mothers is that illegitimate children are more likely to be "stateless" at birth. . . . As the government notes, if the U.S. citizen mother is not a dual national, and the illegitimate child is born in a country that does not recognize citizenship by *jus soli* (citizenship determined by place of birth) alone, the child can acquire no citizenship other than his mother's at birth. This policy clearly demonstrates a "rational basis" for Congress' more lenient policy towards illegitimate children born abroad to U.S. citizen mothers.

901 F.2d 782, 787 (9th Cir.1990). . . .

Avoiding statelessness, and assuring a link between an unwed citizen father, and this country, to a child born out of wedlock abroad who is to be a citizen, are important interests. The means chosen substantially further the objectives. Though the fit is not perfect, it is sufficiently persuasive in light of the virtually plenary power that Congress has to legislate in the area of immigration and citizenship. *See Nguyen*, 533 U.S. at 70 (noting the difficult context of conferring citizenship, and reiterating that an "exceedingly persuasive justification" is established "by showing at least that the classification serves 'important governmental objectives and that the discriminatory means employed' are 'substantially related to the achievement of those objectives.' ") (quoting *Miss. Univ. for Women v. Hogan*, 458 U.S. 718, 724 (1982)); *see also Fiallo*, 430 U.S. at 791–93, 799 n. 8 (indicating that congressional power is at its height with respect to immigration and citizenship, and that "legislative distinctions in the immigration area need not be as 'carefully tuned to alternative considerations' as those in the domestic area") (internal citations omitted).

Flores–Villar acknowledges that the prevention of stateless children is a legitimate goal, but contends that it cannot be furthered by penalizing fathers. In his view, the real purpose of the statute is to perpetuate the stereotypical notion that women should have custody of illegitimate children. Further, he suggests, the length of residence in the United States says nothing about the father-child relationship or the biological basis of that relationship. And understandably, Flores–Villar emphasizes that his father in fact had a custodial relationship with him. However, the Court rejected similar submissions by the father in *Nguyen*. As it explained:

> This line of argument misconceives the nature of both the governmental interest at issue and the manner in which we examine statutes alleged to

---

2. Like the Supreme Court in *Nguyen*, we will assume that intermediate scrutiny applies. The government makes a forceful argument that rational basis review should apply given Congress' broad authority under Article I, Section 8 of the Constitution in matters related to citizenship and immigration. *See* Fiallo v. Bell, 430 U.S. 787, 791–93 (1977). But we do not need to decide which level of review is the most appropriate, and we do not, for the equal protection challenge fails regardless of whether §§ 1401(a)(7) and 1409 are analyzed under intermediate scrutiny, a rational basis standard, or some other level of review in between.

violate equal protection. As to the former, Congress would of course be entitled to advance the interest of ensuring an actual, meaningful relationship in every case before citizenship is conferred. Or Congress could excuse compliance with the formal requirements when an actual father-child relationship is proved. It did neither here, perhaps because of the subjectivity, intrusiveness, and difficulties of proof that might attend an inquiry into any particular bond or tie. Instead, Congress enacted an easily administered scheme to promote the different but still substantial interest of ensuring at least an opportunity for a parent-child relationship to develop. Petitioners' argument confuses the means and ends of the equal protection inquiry; § 1409(a)(4) should not be invalidated because Congress elected to advance an interest that is less demanding to satisfy than some other alternative.

533 U.S. at 69, 121 S.Ct. 2053. The residence differential is directly related to statelessness; the one-year period applicable to unwed citizen mothers seeks to insure that the child will have a nationality at birth. Likewise, it furthers the objective of developing a tie between the child, his or her father, and this country. Accordingly, we conclude that even if intermediate scrutiny applies, §§ 1401(a)(7) and 1409 survive.

. . . Having passed intermediate scrutiny, the statutory scheme necessarily is rationally related to a legitimate government purpose. This follows from *Runnett.* There we held that it was rational to adopt a more lenient policy for illegitimate children of United States citizen mothers who satisfied a residence requirement than for legitimate children whose mothers failed to meet a higher residency requirement. 901 F.2d at 787.

Flores–Villar contends that there is no rational reason to entrust an eighteen year old male to vote and serve in the military, yet restrict his ability to confer citizenship on his child when a woman, who has greater ability to choose where a child is born, can transmit citizenship to her children without a lengthy residence requirement. However, it is not irrational to believe that residence in the United States advances the objective of a link between the citizen, this country, and a foreign-born child born out of wedlock, and that the children of citizen mothers born out of wedlock abroad run a greater risk of being stateless than the children of citizen fathers. *Wauchope v. United States Department of State,* 985 F.2d 1407 (9th Cir.1993), upon which Flores–Villar relies, does not suggest otherwise. There, we found no rational reason for § 1993 of the Revised Statutes of 1874, which accorded to American citizen males, but not American citizen females, the right to pass on citizenship to their foreign-born offspring. *Id.* at 1416. The statutory scheme at issue here is different, and is supported by a different rationale that is in accord with *Miller, Nguyen,* and *Runnett.*

. . .

Flores–Villar also argues that §§ 1401 and 1409 violate substantive due process because these provisions interfere with personal decisions relating to marriage, procreation, family relationships, child rearing, and education, as well as with the child's fundamental right to parental involvement. He lacks standing to pursue rights that belong to his father, however, as most of them do. Floresvillar–Sandez is not a party, and the record discloses no obstacle that would prevent him from asserting his own constitutional rights. *See Singleton v. Wulff,* 428 U.S. 106, 113–16 (1976); *United States v. $100,348.00 in U.S. Currency,* 354 F.3d 1110, 1127 (9th Cir.2004); *see also Barrows v. Jackson,* 346 U.S. 249, 257 (1953). The claimed right to parental involvement is personal to Flores–Villar, but he fails precisely to describe a right deeply rooted in the nation's history, as he must do in order to sustain a substantive due process violation. *Washington v. Glucksberg*, 521 U.S. 702, 720–21 (1997). In any event, we have already upheld similar requirements against similar challenges. *See, e.g., Runnett*, 901 F.2d at 787; *Uribe–Temblador v. Rosenberg*, 423 F.2d 717, 718 (9th Cir.1970).

. . .

NOTE

On June 13, 2011, the Supreme Court issued a per curiam affirming the judgment of the Ninth Circuit by an equally divided court. ___ U.S. ___, 131 S.Ct. 2313 (2011). Justice Elena Kagan took no part in the consideration of the case.

3. STATUTORY LIMITS ON SEX DISCRIMINATION

A series of positive law developments both at the federal and state level have sought to address discrimination on the basis of sex. As you read the materials in this section, consider some of their strengths and weaknesses.

a. TITLE VII

Hopkins v. Price Waterhouse

United States Court of Appeals, District of Columbia Circuit, 1990.
920 F.2d 967.

■ HARRY T. EDWARDS, CIRCUIT JUDGE:

This case, before this court for the second time, arises from a decision by appellant Price Waterhouse to deny partnership to one of its employees, appellee Ann B. Hopkins. We are again asked to review a finding by the District Court that Price Waterhouse's denial of partnership to Ms. Hopkins violated Title VII of the Civil Rights Act of 1964, 42 U.S.C. §§ 2000e *et seq.* (1988), and to assess its shaping of an appropriate remedy.

In *Hishon v. King & Spalding*, 467 U.S. 69 (1984), the Supreme Court clearly established that "partnership consideration may qualify as a term, condition, or privilege of a person's employment" such that Title VII will provide a cause of action if partnership is denied because of sex discrimination. . . .

It is undisputed that, for professional employees like Ms. Hopkins, Price Waterhouse held out the prospect of admission to partnership as a privilege of employment. . . . Moreover, decisions concerning admission to partnership were to be based exclusively on merit, taking into account a range of job-related considerations—"from practice development and technical expertise to interpersonal skills and participation in civic activities." The trial court found, however, that Ann Hopkins was denied partnership at Price Waterhouse in part because of sexual stereotyping, which is a form of sex discrimination under Title VII. We upheld that finding, as did the Supreme Court, *see* 490 U.S. at 250, 252 (plurality opinion); *id.* at 272, 275 (O'Connor, J., concurring in the judgment).

The Supreme Court, while agreeing that Price Waterhouse had been motivated in part by discriminatory stereotyping, remanded the case for reconsideration of Price Waterhouse's claim that the decision to deny partnership to Ms. Hopkins would have remained the same even in the absence of the proscribed discrimination. During the first trial before the District Court, Price Waterhouse was given an opportunity to show that it would have reached the same decision regarding Ms. Hopkins even absent any discrimination; however, both the trial court and this court required Price Waterhouse to make this showing by clear and convincing evidence. In reversing on this point, the Supreme Court ruled that the District Court must determine whether, on the record before it, Price Waterhouse had shown by a *preponderance of the evidence,* that it would have denied partnership to Ms. Hopkins in any event for nondiscriminatory reasons....

On remand, the District Court ... reviewed that evidence and found that Price Waterhouse failed to carry the burden placed upon it by the Supreme Court. Having found appellant liable under Title VII, the District Court ordered Price Waterhouse to admit Ann Hopkins into the firm's partnership and to pay her $371,000 in back pay. On this appeal, Price Waterhouse challenges both the District Court's finding of liability and its remedial order that Ms. Hopkins be made a partner. We can find no merit in either of these challenges.

Price Waterhouse's argument that Title VII does not authorize a court to order elevation to partnership rests ultimately upon the untenable suggestion that *Hishon* conferred only a cause of action for the discriminatory denial of partnership and never meant to imply a corresponding remedy. We find it inconceivable, however, that the Supreme Court intended to open up a partnership's admission decisions to judicial scrutiny while placing them beyond effective judicial remedy. On this point, it is important to note that this case involves only an employee's *elevation* to partnership; it does *not* involve a party's retention of partnership or the regulation of the relationship *among* partners. Thus, we are not confronted by the concerns expressed in Justice Powell's concurring opinion in *Hishon*, in which he emphasized that the Court in *Hishon* did not reach the question whether Title VII would protect employees after they became partners; we emphasize the same point today, for we have no occasion to decide this question.

Finding no error in either the trial court's finding of liability or in its shaping of an appropriate remedy, we affirm the judgment of the District Court.

Ann Hopkins joined Price Waterhouse in 1978, as a member of the professional staff in the firm's Office of Government Services ("OGS") in Washington, D.C. In this position, Ms. Hopkins was responsible for helping the firm to win and carry out management consulting contracts with federal agencies. She enjoyed a successful career in OGS and, in 1982, was proposed for partnership. In keeping with the firm's established personnel procedures, all partners who had worked with Ms. Hopkins were asked to submit written comments to the firm's Admissions Committee. These evaluations were written on so-called "long forms" by those partners who knew Ms. Hopkins well, and on "short forms" by those who had had only passing contact with her. The evaluations covered a range of considerations, including both technical skills and personal interactions. The Admissions Committee was then responsible for sorting through these forms, summarizing the various comments, and submitting recommendations to the firm's Policy Board. The Policy Board, in turn, was to decide whether to reject the candidate outright, "hold" her candidacy for another year or submit the candidate for a vote by the full partnership. *See* 618 F.Supp. at 1111–12 (recounting partnership review process).

Ms. Hopkins' record at the firm documented outstanding accomplishments as a senior manager. At the first trial in this case, the District Court found that Ms. Hopkins "played a key role in Price Waterhouse's successful effort to win a multi-million dollar contract with the Department of State." Moreover,

> she had no difficulty dealing with clients and her clients appear to have been very pleased with her work. None of the other partnership candidates at Price Waterhouse that year had a comparable record in terms of successfully securing major contracts for the partnership.... She was generally viewed as a highly competent project leader who worked long hours, pushed vigorously to meet deadlines and demanded much from the multidisciplinary staffs with which she worked.

A number of the comments submitted by partners, however, also criticized Ms. Hopkins' "interpersonal skills," suggesting that she was sometimes overbearing and abrasive. Some of these comments went further in suggesting that these defects were especially inappropriate because Hopkins was a woman. As the Supreme Court noted in its review of this case:

> One partner described her as "macho"; another suggested that she "overcompensated for being a woman"; a third advised her to take "a course at charm school." Several partners criticized her use of profanity; in response, one partner suggested that those partners objected to her swearing only "because it[']s a lady using foul language." Another supporter explained that Hopkins "ha[d] matured from a tough-talking somewhat masculine hard-nosed mgr to an authoritative, formidable, but much more appealing lady ptr candidate."

In March 1983, Price Waterhouse's Policy Board voted not to admit Ms. Hopkins as a partner. Rather than dismiss her outright, however, the Board decided to "hold" her candidacy, with the possibility that she might be reconsidered the following year. "When [Hopkins] consulted with the head partner at OGS, who was her strongest supporter and responsible for telling her what problems the Policy Board had identified with her candidacy, *she was advised to walk more femininely, talk more femininely, dress more femininely, wear make-up, have her hair styled, and wear jewelry.*"

Ms. Hopkins remained at Price Waterhouse but then ran into conflicts with some of the partners. Donald Epelbaum, one of the partners in appellee's home office, accused Ms. Hopkins of misrepresenting a conversation she had had with Price Waterhouse's managing partner concerning her partnership prospects. These conflicts culminated in a decision not to repropose Ms. Hopkins for partnership the following year. Ms. Hopkins then resigned and later brought this suit.

Following the first trial in 1985, the District Court held that Ms. Hopkins had proved that sex stereotyping had infected the decisionmaking process among Price Waterhouse's partners and that Price Waterhouse could avoid equitable relief only if it could show, by clear and convincing evidence, that it would have reached the same negative decision regarding Ms. Hopkins' candidacy even absent the sex stereotyping. The trial court went on, however, to hold that Price Waterhouse's subsequent decision not to renominate Ms. Hopkins was nondiscriminatory, and that Ms. Hopkins' resignation was not a constructive discharge. Consequently, the trial court held that Ms. Hopkins was not entitled to back pay for the period following her resignation.

. . . .

Following our initial review of this case, the Supreme Court granted certiorari and considered the case. The Court upheld the District Court's finding that sex discrimination had tainted Price Waterhouse's decisionmaking. *See* 490 U.S. at 250, 252 (plurality opinion); *id.* at 1802, 1805 (O'Connor, J., concurring in the judgment). It agreed that "a number of the partners' comments showed sex stereotyping at work," and stated forcefully that "we are beyond the day when an employer could evaluate employees by assuming or insisting that they matched the stereotype associated with their group." The Court then ruled that Price Waterhouse could avoid liability if it could show—by a preponderance of the evidence—that it would have reached the same decision absent any discrimination. Because the District Court had not evaluated the evidence by that standard, the Court remanded the case for reconsideration pursuant to the proper evidentiary standard.

.   .   .

Price Waterhouse raises two objections to the District Court's finding of liability. First, it asserts that the trial court did not carry out the Supreme Court's instruction that it reevaluate the evidence pursuant to the preponderance standard.... Second, it asserts that, even if the trial court did reweigh the evidence, it committed clear error in not being persuaded by Price Waterhouse's showing. We disagree on both counts.

... [A] fair reading of Judge Gesell's opinion shows that he *did* in fact "reweigh" the evidence and that he simply found it unpersuasive....

.   .   .

Price Waterhouse also asserts that the District Court had no authority to order admission to partnership to remedy a Title VII violation. Price Waterhouse's argument is apparently that while Title VII extends far enough to protect an employee against discrimination in partnership consideration, it comes to an abrupt halt once a violation has been found, leaving the employee with the promise of fair consideration for partnership but no effective means of enforcing it. This argument seems absurd in the light of the Supreme Court's decision in *Hishon v. King & Spalding*, 467 U.S. 69 (1984), in which the Court held that "nothing in the change in status that advancement to partnership might entail means that partnership consideration falls outside the terms of [Title VII]." Given the Court's judgment in *Hishon*, and after careful review of Title VII, its legislative history and the case law interpreting it, we find that the District Court clearly acted within the bounds of the remedial authority conferred by the statute.

.   .   .

It is also noteworthy that the EEOC, the agency to which we owe deference in construing Title VII, agrees with our construction of the remedial reach of Title VII. This is significant because Congress has recognized "the importance of administrative expertise relating to the resolution of problems of employment discrimination." S.Rep. No. 415, 92d Cong., 1st Sess. 18 (1971). In explaining Congress' decision to grant the EEOC administrative enforcement powers, the Senate Committee on Labor and Public Welfare observed that "[m]any of the Title VII proceedings involve complex labor relations and business operations issues *particularly in the fashioning of the remedies for eliminating discrimination*. The Equal Employment Opportunity Commission would be expected to develop an important reservoir of expertise in these matters, expertise which would not readily be available to a widespread court system."

The EEOC has applied its expertise to the question before us and has concluded that Title VII authorizes court-ordered elevation to partnership as a remedy for the discriminatory denial of partnership. The EEOC's view reinforces our own independent reading of the statute.

.   .   .

Although all signposts in the statute, its legislative history and the case law point strongly toward affirming the District Court's judgment to order partnership, thereby vindicating "[t]he 'make whole' purpose of Title VII," Price Waterhouse urges that there are several countervailing considerations weighing against this conclusion. We consider them in turn.

1. *Freedom of Association*

Price Waterhouse argues that a court order forcing it to accept Ann Hopkins as a partner would violate its partners' constitutional rights of free association. This argument is entirely unpersuasive. Even assuming *arguendo* that a large business partnership such as Price Waterhouse has cognizable associational rights, they must yield to the compelling national interest in eradicating discrimination. See, *e.g., New York State Club Ass'n v. City of New York*, 487 U.S. 1, 12–13 (1988); *Board of Directors of Rotary Int'l v. Rotary Club of Duarte*, 481 U.S. 537, 549 (1987) ("Even if [the forced admission of women members] does work some slight infringement on Rotary members' right of expressive association, that infringement is justified because it serves the State's compelling interest in eliminating discrimination against women."); *Roberts v. United States Jaycees*, 468 U.S. 609, 623 (1984); *Runyon v. McCrary*, 427 U.S. 160, 175–76 (1976).

It is difficult to differentiate between the constitutional argument Price Waterhouse advances here and the one rejected in a nearly identical setting in *Hishon*. There, King & Spalding, a large law partnership, had similarly insisted that "application of Title VII in [its] case would infringe constitutional rights of expression or association." 467 U.S. at 78. The Supreme Court brushed aside the argument, noting that " '[i]nvidious private discrimination may be characterized as a form of exercising freedom of association protected by the First Amendment, but it has never been accorded affirmative constitutional protections.' " *Id.*

On the basis of the foregoing authorities, we reject Price Waterhouse's suggestion that its claimed freedom of association precludes the court from ordering partnership as a Title VII remedy.

2. *Principles of Contract Law*

Price Waterhouse also points out that courts have traditionally been reluctant to order the creation of a partnership as an equitable remedy for breach of contract, and urges that this contract principle be carried over into the realm of antidiscrimination law. It is true that in common law contract cases the courts have hesitated to compel persons to work together or to enforce other ongoing human relationships, including partnerships. . . .

Title VII makes expressly clear, however, that this common law rule does not limit a court's power to fashion equitable remedies for employment discrimination in violation of the statute. Price Waterhouse concedes, as it must, that the "plain language" of Title VII contemplates judicial authority to order reinstatement and hiring of employees. Thus, even under appellant's analysis, it is plain that there is no merit to the argument that common law principles of contract law serve to limit Title VII's remedial reach.

3.   *The Equities of this Case*

Lastly, Price Waterhouse argues that even if the District Court was empowered under Title VII to order partnership as a remedy, it was an abuse of discretion for the court to do so on the facts of this case. Specifically, appellant argues that Ms. Hopkins' own alleged misconduct[13] following the March 1983 decision to defer her candidacy made her eventual elevation to partnership impossible and precludes the court from now making Ms. Hopkins a partner. We do not agree.

The misconduct to which Price Waterhouse refers occurred only after Price Waterhouse's own illegal sex discrimination had intervened to deny Ms. Hopkins her place in the partnership. Given the findings of sex discrimination committed by appellant's partners, there is a certain hint of irony in the moral indignation with which Price Waterhouse protests the prospect of having to offer partnership to a person who allegedly misstated the substance of a conversation. We also note that Price Waterhouse does *not* claim that, if Ms. Hopkins had been admitted to partnership in March 1983, her subsequent alleged misconduct would have justified her dismissal from partnership.

Yet, with these observations aside, we find that the District Court expressly considered Ms. Hopkins' alleged misconduct in the shaping of its equitable remedy, deducting from her back pay award any "claim for the fiscal year 1983–1984." We review this judgment under the highly deferential abuse-of-discretion standard, and, on the record before us, we can find no basis to overturn the trial court's decision. For us to reject the District Court's judgment on this issue would be a flagrant disregard of the obvious limits of the abuse-of-discretion standard.

Judge Gesell not only limited back pay, he was careful to consider whether there existed too much hostility between the parties to permit an effective working relationship; he found there did not. He also considered alternative remedies, such as front pay, and concluded that it would be impossible to tailor a prospective remedy so that Ms. Hopkins truly would be made whole. Finally, he considered and rejected Price Waterhouse's contention that Ms. Hopkins is entitled only to reconsideration for partnership by Price Waterhouse, finding that ordering reconsideration in this case would be "futile and unjust." We find no abuse of discretion by Judge Gesell in ordering a partnership based on the facts of the case before him.

E.   *Calculation of Back Pay*

Finally, we find no error or abuse of discretion in the District Court's calculation of Ms. Hopkins' back pay award. In particular, we find that Judge Gesell properly accounted for Ms. Hopkins' inadequate mitigation in formulating the award.

.   .   .

For all of the foregoing reasons, the judgment of the District Court is affirmed.

---

13.   The District Court found that Ms. Hopkins had "misstated the substance of a meeting ... between herself and Joseph E. Connor, the Chairman and Senior Partner of Price Waterhouse, regarding her partnership prospects. Ms. Hopkins misleadingly implied that Mr. Connor had disparaged certain partners who opposed her candidacy and that he had warned of the adverse consequences his partners might experience for opposing her the next year." 737 F.Supp. at 1213.

NOTE

A widely told story has it that Title VII's sex discrimination provision was added to the statutory language at the last minute as something of a joke. *See, e.g.*, Michael E. Gold, *A Tale of Two Amendments: The Reasons Congress Added Sex to Title VII and Their Implication for the Issue of Comparable Worth*, 19 Duq. L. Rev. 453 (1980) ("The Conventional view is that sex was added as a protected class to the employment discrimination title of the Civil Rights Act of 1964 for the purpose of defeating it by making it unacceptable to some of its supporters or by laughing it to death"). What do the following excerpts from the floor debate in the U.S. House of Representatives on the sex discrimination amendment to Title VII add to the conventional accounts?

110 Cong. Rec. H2577–83 (Feb. 8, 1964):

Amendment offered by Mr. Smith of Virginia

Mr. SMITH of Virginia. Mr. Chairman, this amendment is offered to the fair employment practices title of this bill to include within our desire to prevent discrimination against another minority group, the women, but a very essential minority group, in the absence of which the majority group would not be here today.

Now, I am very serious about this amendment.... I do not think it can do any harm to this legislation; maybe it can do some good. I think it will do some good for the minority sex.

... [A]ll throughout industry women are discriminated against in that just generally speaking they do not get as high compensation for their work as do the majority sex. Now, if that is true, I hope that the committee chairman will accept this amendment.

That is about all I have to say about it except ... to show you how some of the ladies feel about discrimination against them. I want to read you an extract from a letter that I received the other day. This lady has a real grievance on behalf of the minority sex. She said that she had seen that I was going to present an amendment to protect the most important sex, and she says:

I suggest that you might also favor an amendment or a bill to correct the present "imbalance" which exists between males and females in the United States.

Then she goes on to say—and she has her statistics, which is the reason why I am reading it to you, because this is serious—

The census of 1960 shows that we had 88,331,000 males living in this country, and 90,992,000 females, which leaves the country with an "imbalance" of 2,661,000 females.

Now, another paragraph:

Just why the Creator would set up such an imbalance of spinsters, shutting off the "right" of every female to have a husband of her own, is, of course, known only to nature.

But I am sure you will agree that this is a grave injustice—

And I do agree, and I am reading you the letter because I want all the rest of you to agree, you of the majority—

But I am sure you will agree that this is a grave injustice to womankind and something the Congress and President Johnson should take immediate steps to correct—

And you interrupted me just now before I could finish reading the sentence, which continues on:

Immediate steps to correct, especially in this election year.

Now, I just want to remind you here that in this election year it is pretty nearly half of the voters in this country that are affected, so you had better sit up and take notice.

She also says this, and this is a very cogent argument, too:

Up until now, instead of assisting these poor unfortunate females in obtaining their "right" to happiness, the Government has on several occasions engaged in wars which killed off a large number of eligible males, creating an "imbalance" in our male and female population that was even worse than before.

Would you have any suggestions as to what course our Government might pursue to protect our spinster friends in their "right" to a nice husband and family?

I read that letter just to illustrate that women have some real grievances and some real rights to be protected. I am serious about this thing. I just hope that the committee will accept it. Now, what harm can you do this bill that was so perfect yesterday and is so imperfect today—what harm will this do to the condition of the bill?

. . .

Mr. CELLER. You know, the French have a phrase for it when they speak of women and men. When they speak of the difference, they say "vive la difference."

I think the French are right.

Imagine the upheaval that would result from adoption of the blanket language requiring total equality. Would male citizens be justified in insisting that women share with them the burdens of compulsory military service? What would become of traditional family relationships? What about alimony? Who would have the obligation of supporting whom? Would fathers rank equally with mothers in the right of custody to children? What would become of the crimes of rape and statutory rape? Would the Mann Act be invalidated? Would the many State and local provisions regulating working conditions and hours of employment for women be struck down?

You know the biological differences between the sexes. In many States we have laws favorable to women. Are you going to strike those laws down? This is the entering wedge, an amendment of this sort. The list of foreseeable consequences, I will say to the committee, is unlimited.

. . .

Mr. BASS. Yes, now what I was leading up to is this. A young lady works for an airline company, and she is worried about discrimination against married women because she is about to get married. Then she will lose her job. So she wants something done to prevent discrimination against married women.

Mrs. FRANCES P. BOLTON. May I suggest to the gentleman that married women get along very well because they usually, after they have had their children and brought them to a certain age, go back into business to really protect the family against too little money.

Mr. BASS. I am for all women, I want the record to show that I am for both the unmarried and the married women.

. . .

Mrs. GRIFFITHS. Mr. Chairman, I move to strike out the last word and rise in support of the amendment.

Mr. Chairman, I presume that if there had been any necessity to have pointed out that women were a second-class sex, the laughter would have proved it.

Mr. Chairman, I rise in support of the amendment primarily because I feel as a white woman when this bill has passed this House and the Senate and has been signed by the President that white women will be the last at the hiring gate.

. . .

Now, Mr. Chairman, I would like to proceed to some of the arguments I have heard on this floor against adding the word "sex". In some of the arguments, I have heard the comment that . . . this makes it an equal rights bill. Of course it does not even approach making it an equal rights bill. This is equal employment rights. In one field only—employment. And if you do not add sex to this bill, I really do not believe there is a reasonable person sitting here who does not by now understand perfectly that you are going to have white men in one bracket, you are going to try to take colored men and colored women and give them equal employment rights, and down at the bottom of the list is going to be a white woman with no rights at all.

. . .

. . . Now, it has been suggested to me by one Member on the floor that if a job were repeatedly filled by colored women, that a white woman would be able to invoke the Federal Employment Practices Act. In my judgment, as long as a majority of the drivers in a haulaway concern were white drivers, as long as the majority of employees in [a] restaurant, in [a] university, were white people, no white woman could invoke the act. . . .

. . .

It would be incredible to me that white men would be willing to place white women at such a disadvantage except that white men have done this before. When the 14th amendment had become the law of the land, a brave woman named Virginia Minor, native-born, free, white citizen of the United States and the State of Missouri, read the amendment, and on the 15th of October 1872, appeared to register to vote. The registrar replied that the State of Missouri had a statute which said that only males could register to vote. Her reply, of course, was, "Why, the 14th amendment says 'No State shall make or enforce any law which shall abridge the privileges or immunities of citizens of the United States.' "

In October 1874 in 13 pages of tortured legal reasoning, the Supreme Court of the United States explained how the Missouri law prevailed, and finally said:

The amendment did not add to the privileges and immunities of a citizen. It simply furnished an additional guaranty for the protection of such as he already had.

So, Mr. Chairman, your great grand-fathers were willing as prisoners of their own prejudice to permit ex-slaves to vote, but not their own white wives.

. . .

Mr. Chairman, a vote against this amendment today by a white man is a vote against his wife, or his widow, or his daughter, or his sister.

If we are trying to establish equality in jobs, I am for it, but I am for making white women equal, also.

Mrs. ST. GEORGE. . . . Mr. Chairman, I was somewhat amazed when I came on the floor this afternoon to hear the very distinguished chairman of the Committee on the Judiciary make the remark that he considered the amendment at this point illogical. I can think of nothing more logical that this amendment at this point.

. . .

In support of this I would like to read a colloquy which was held not in executive session, certainly, but in open session of the Rules Committee, in which I asked the ranking member of the Committee on the Judiciary, the gentleman from Ohio [Mr. McCulloch], about this very thing. If you will bear with me a minute, I will read it:

Mrs. ST. GEORGE. Mr. Chairman, there is one question I would like to ask the gentleman from Ohio. Is it a fact that the law as now constituted in your State of Ohio and in my State of New York is, if anything, stronger than the law as it will be if this legislation passes?

Mr. McCULLOCH. The law of the State of New York and the law of the State of Ohio is much stronger in the affected fields than this legislation.

Mrs. ST. GEORGE. Another questions. There are 32 States, as I understand it, that already have civil rights legislation. Are those States also in most cases stronger in their civil rights legislation than they would be under this law?

Mr. McCULLOCH. Without having read every State statute, I would say the States with the large populations without exception have legislation in this field that is stronger than that which we propose.

Mrs. ST. GEORGE. Going on from there, in other words, there are 18 States that do not have such legislation, is that correct?

Mr. McCULLOCH. That is correct.

Mrs. ST. GEORGE. So, this is really being written for those 18 States, to all intents and purposes, because we already have this, so this will not make any very great difference to us, except if it supersedes the law of the State. Is it going to do that?

Mr. McCULLOCH. It is not intended to supersede the laws of the States, except when it is in conflict and grants or insures lesser rights than are provided for in this legislation.

Mrs. ST. GEORGE. Otherwise, as in my State of New York, we will continue to function under the law as it is now written in the State of New York, and in your State of Ohio it will be the same thing?

Mr. McCULLOCH. That is true.

Mrs. ST. GEORGE. So, when we come right back to brass tacks, this is legislation written for 18 States which do not have civil rights legislation at the present time.

Mr. McCULLOCH. I think that is an accurate statement, yes.

The reason I bring that up is that a great many gentlemen, the predominating membership of this House, have a facetious way of saying to any woman on the question of equality, equal rights under the law, and so forth, "But you have all that already."

Mr. Chairman, I am willing to admit that in a great many States we have got it already.

The CHAIRMAN. The time for the gentlewoman from New York has expired.

(By unanimous consent, Mrs. ST. GEORGE was allowed to proceed for 5 additional minutes.)

Mrs. ST. GEORGE. But there are still many States where ... equality does not exist.

There are still many States where women cannot serve on juries. There are still many States where women do not have equal educational opportunities. In most States and, in fact, I figure it would be safe to say, in all States—women do not get equal pay for equal work. That is a very well known fact.

Protective legislation prevents ... women from going into the higher salary brackets. Yes, it certainly does.

Women are protected—they cannot run an elevator late at night and that is when the pay is higher.

They cannot serve in restaurants and cabarets late at night—when the tips are higher—and the load, if you please, is lighter.

So it is not exactly helping them—oh, no, you have taken beautiful care of the women.

But what about the offices, gentlemen, that are cleaned every morning about 2 or 3 o'clock in the city of New York and the offices that are cleaned quite early here in Washington, D.C.? Does anybody worry about those women? I have never heard of anybody worrying about the women who do that work.

. . .

So you see the thing is completely unfair.

And to say that this is illogical. What is illogical about it? All you are doing is simply correcting something that goes back, frankly to the Dark Ages. Because what you are doing is to go back to the days of the revolution when women were chattels.

Of course, women were not mentioned in the Constitution. They belonged, first of all, to their fathers; then to their husbands or to their nearest male relative. They had no command over their own property. They were not supposed to be equal in any way, and certainly they were never expected to be or believed to be equal intellectually.

Well, I will admit from what I have seen very frequently here, I think the majority sex in the House of Representatives may not consider us mentally quite equal, but I think on the whole considering what a small minority we are here that we have not done altogether too badly.

I think for that reason, if for no other, we would like to be given more opportunities.

I can assure you we can take them.

I can assure you that we have fought our way a long way since those days of the Revolution. We have fought our way a long way even since the beginning of this century. Why should women be denied equality of opportunity? Why should women be denied equal pay for equal work? That is all we are asking.

We do not want special privileges. We do not need special privilege. We outlast you—we outlive you—we nag you to death. So why should we want special privileges?

I believe that we can hold our own. We are entitled to this little crumb of equality.

The addition of that little, terrifying word "s-e-x" will not hurt this legislation in any way. In fact, it will improve it. . . . It will make it logical. It will make it right.

. . .

Mrs. GREEN of Oregon. Mr. Chairman, in the spirit of American freedom and liberty, cruel discriminations cry out to be corrected in this Nation. Today, I repeat, let us not add any amendment that would place in jeopardy in any way our primary objective of ending that discrimination that is most serious, most urgent, most tragic, and most widespread against the Negroes of our country.

May I also say I am not in complete agreement with everything that has been said by my women colleagues. I think that I, as a white woman, have been discriminated against, yes—but for every discrimination that I have suffered, I firmly believe that the Negro woman has suffered 10 times that amount of discrimination. She has a double discrimination. She was born as a woman and she was born as a Negro. She has suffered 10 times as much discrimination as I have. If I have to wait for a few years to end this discrimination against me, and my women friends—then as far as I am concerned I am willing to do that if the rank discrimination against Negroes will be finally ended under the so-called protection of the law.

b.   FAMILY AND MEDICAL LEAVE

Knussman v. Maryland

United States Court of Appeals for the Fourth Circuit, 2001.
272 F.3d 625.

■ TRAXLER, CIRCUIT JUDGE:

Howard Kevin Knussman, a trooper in the Maryland State Police, brought an action alleging that the State of Maryland and several individual employees of the Maryland State Police (collectively "the defendants") unlawfully discriminated against him on the basis of his gender, for which he sought recourse under 42 U.S.C.A. § 1983 (West Supp. 2000); and that the defendants violated his rights under the Family and Medical Leave Act of 1993 (FMLA), see 29 U.S.C.A. §§ 2601–2654 (West 1999), for which he sought recourse under § 1983 and directly under the FMLA. Following a jury trial and various post-trial motions, judgment in the amount of

$375,000 was entered against only one of the defendants—Jill Mullineaux, a civilian employee of the Maryland State Police.

. . .

In 1994, Knussman learned that his wife Kimberly was pregnant. At the time, Knussman held the rank of trooper first class and served as a paramedic on medevac helicopters in the Aviation Division of the Maryland State Police ("MSP"). Unfortunately, Kim's pregnancy was difficult and ultimately resulted in her confinement to bed rest in the latter stages prior to delivery. In October 1994, Knussman submitted a written request to his supervisor asking that Knussman be permitted to take four to eight weeks of paid "family sick leave" to care for his wife and spend time with his family following the birth of his child.[1] Eventually, Knussman was informed by the MSP Director of Flight Operations, First Sergeant Ronnie P. Creel, that there was "no way" that he would be allowed more than two weeks. Creel testified that, at the time of Knussman's request, the Aviation Division was understaffed. According to Knussman, Creel misinformed him that if he wanted more leave, he would be forced to take unpaid leave because the FMLA did not entitle him to further paid leave. Knussman testified that he was unfamiliar with the FMLA because the MSP had failed to provide proper notice to its employees about their rights under the FMLA.

In early December, shortly before the Knussmans' daughter was born, Jill Mullineaux, manager of the medical leave and benefit section of the MSP Personnel Management Division, notified all MSP employees of a new Maryland statutory provision that allowed the use of paid sick leave by a state employee to care for a newborn. The statute permitted "[p]rimary care givers" to "use, without certification of illness or disability, up to 30 days of accrued sick leave to care for [a] child . . . immediately following . . . the birth of the employee's child." MD. CODE ANN., *State Pers. & Pens.* § 7–508(a)(1). A "[p]rimary care giver" was defined as "an employee who is primarily responsible for the care and nurturing of a child." By contrast, a "[s]econdary care giver," *i.e.*, "an employee who is secondarily responsible for the care and nurturing of a child," might use up to 10 days of accrued sick leave without providing proof of illness or disability.[2] In contrast to "family sick leave," which required an employee to provide verification of a family member's illness, the new "nurturing leave" provision permitted an employee to use paid sick leave without providing any medical documentation, since this type of leave was not actually related to the illness or disability of the employee or the employee's family.[3]

Believing that this "nurturing leave" might afford him more paid leave than he would receive from his request for "family sick leave," Knussman contacted Mullineaux for additional information about using his accrued sick leave under § 7–508. Specifically, he wanted to know whether he could

---

1.   Maryland law permitted a state employee to use paid sick leave for reasons other than the employee's own illness, including "for death, illness, or disability in the employee's immediate family." MD. CODE ANN., STATE PERS. & PENS. § 7–502(b)(2) (1994). The statute was later amended and reorganized; however, Maryland law still permits this particular use of a state employee's sick leave. *See* MD. CODE ANN., STATE PERS. & PENS. § 9–501(b)(2) (1996).

2.   Section 7–508 has been amended and recodified, and it now provides for the use of up to an aggregate of 40 days of accrued sick leave if two state employees are responsible for the care of a newborn. *See* MD. CODE ANN., STATE PERS. & PENS. § 9–505(b)(1) (1996). Section 7–508(b)(1), had it been in effect at the time, apparently would have applied to the Knussmans, who were both state employees.

3.   For ease of reference, we adopt the term "nurturing leave." This term, however, does not appear in the statute.

qualify as a primary care giver under § 7–508(a)(1) and take 30 days of paid sick leave. According to Knussman, Mullineaux informed him that only birth mothers could qualify as primary care givers; fathers would only be permitted to take leave as secondary care givers since they "couldn't breast feed a baby." Mullineaux, who testified that she was merely passing along the Maryland Department of Personnel's (DOP) view of "primary care giver," denied adopting such a categorical interpretation.[4] In any case, Knussman's superior officers in the Aviation Division, having consulted Mullineaux about the untested nurturing leave provision, granted him 10 days of paid sick leave as the secondary care giver under § 7–508(b).

The Knussmans' daughter was born on December 9, 1994. Kimberly Knussman, however, continued to experience health problems. Before his authorized 10–day leave expired, Knussman contacted Sergeant J.C. Collins, one of his supervisors, and inquired whether his status could be changed to that of primary care giver and his paid sick leave extended to 30 days under section 7–508(a). Knussman explained to Collins that he was the primary care giver for the child because, given his wife's condition following delivery, he was performing the majority of the essential functions such as diaper changing, feeding, bathing and taking the child to the doctor.

David Czorapinski, the Assistant Commander for the Aviation Division during this time, learned of Knussman's inquiry and, unable to reach Mullineaux, gathered some preliminary information on the new law himself. Czorapinski learned that the Maryland DOP intended to take the position that the mother was the primary care giver and the father was secondary. Czorapinski passed this information down the chain-of-command and Knussman was told that it was unlikely that his paid sick leave would be extended under section 7–508(a).

On the day before Knussman was scheduled to return to work, Knussman made a final attempt at obtaining additional sick leave. Sergeant Carl Lee, one of Knussman's immediate superiors, had earlier informed Knussman that although nurturing leave as a primary care giver was probably not an option, Knussman might be eligible for additional paid leave under the family sick leave provision as long as he could demonstrate that it was medically necessary for him to care for his wife. Knussman contacted Mullineaux to find out what information he needed to supply for family sick leave.[5] During this conversation, Knussman again discussed his eligibility for nurturing leave as a primary care provider under section 7–508(a) with Mullineaux, who explained that "God made women to have babies and, unless [he] could have a baby, there is no way [he] could be primary care [giver]" and that his wife had to be "in a coma or dead" for Knussman to qualify as the primary care giver.

---

4. Mullineaux testified that she never told Knussman that fathers were, as a class, ineligible for primary care giver status. Rather, Mullineaux's version was that she told Knussman, based on information provided by the state Department of Personnel, "that the birth mother was presumed to be the primary care giver and if he wanted to qualify as the primary care giver, he could, if he could provide [supporting] information."

5. Knussman subsequently submitted a letter from Kimberly Knussman's doctor in support of his request for family sick leave; however, Mullineaux concluded that the letter was insufficient to justify family sick leave because "it [did not] say what care [Knussman was] going to provide, and it [did not] say that [Knussman] needed to be home ... like it's [Knussman's] choice and not the doctor's requirement." Although Czorapinski suggested to Knussman that the deficiencies could be easily corrected, Knussman refused "to pursue this option any further."

Mullineaux denied Knussman's request for paid sick leave under § 7–508(a) as a primary care giver. Knussman returned to work as ordered and immediately filed an administrative grievance on the grounds that he had been improperly denied primary care giver status under § 7–508(a). He did not seek review of Mullineaux's denial of his request for family sick leave under section 7–502(b)(2). Once the grievance process was underway, Knussman's claim went up the MSP chain-of-command and Mullineaux's involvement ceased.

Knussman's grievance was denied at each stage of the four-level grievance procedure....

. . .

Essentially, Czorapinski believed that Kimberly Knussman, who was also a state employee, was enjoying the benefits of nurturing leave as a primary care giver because, following delivery, she took sick leave for a 30–day period—the same amount of time afforded a primary care giver under § 7–508(a). Thus, Czorapinski was concerned that both Knussmans were attempting to qualify as the primary care giver for their daughter when the statute indicated only one person could qualify. At trial, Knussman presented evidence that, prior to the step two grievance conference, Mullineaux and Czorapinski were made aware of the fact the Kimberly Knussman was, in fact, on sick leave for her own disability resulting from the difficult pregnancy. Following Czorapinski's decision, Knussman pursued his complaint through the two remaining steps of the internal grievance procedure without success.

Knussman then filed a three-count action in federal court. In Count I, Knussman sought relief under § 1983, claiming that his leave request under § 7–508(a) was denied as a result of gender discrimination in violation of the Equal Protection Clause of the Fourteenth Amendment to the United States Constitution.... He named as defendants the State of Maryland, the MSP, and several employees of the MSP, in both their individual and official capacities: Mullineaux, Czorapinski, Creel, and Colonel David B. Mitchell, Superintendent of the MSP.

. . .

After a period of discovery, the defendants moved for summary judgment on the grounds that they were entitled to qualified immunity and that Knussman could not prove an equal protection violation in the first place. With respect to Knussman's equal protection claim under § 1983 (Count I), the court concluded that the facts, viewed in the light most favorable to Knussman, indicated that the defendants applied a gender-based presumption that the birth mother was the primary care giver, which would amount to an equal protection violation. *See Knussman v. State of Maryland*, 16 F. Supp. 2d 601, 611–12 (D. Md. 1998). The district court further concluded that the defendants were not entitled to qualified immunity because it was well-established at the time that gender discrimination in employment was prohibited under the Fourteenth Amendment:

> Although the Maryland leave law had been amended effective less than one month before [Knussman] requested leave and the DOP had not issued any guidelines regarding application of the amended law, the right to equal protection is a well-established principle. It is also clear that gender discrimination violates the equal protection clause. Discrimi-

natory application of a gender neutral state law is patently illegal and defendants should have known at least this much.

. . .

Thus, the case went to trial on portions of both counts in the complaint. As for Count I, Knussman's § 1983 equal protection claim remained intact against the State of Maryland (but only for declaratory and injunctive relief) and the defendants in their individual capacities. At the close of the evidence, the court submitted the question of qualified immunity to the jury as well as the ultimate question of liability. . . . The jury concluded that each defendant denied Knussman's request for leave because of his gender; however, the jury also found that every defendant except Mullineaux was entitled to qualified immunity. Knussman does not challenge this conclusion on appeal. . . . The jury awarded Knussman the sum of $375,000 in damages.

. . .

On appeal, Mullineaux contends that she was entitled to qualified immunity on Knussman's equal protection claim under § 1983. She also challenges, on multiple grounds, the jury's verdict as well as the court's jury instructions.

. . .

We first consider the issue of whether the evidence adduced at trial is sufficient to establish that Mullineaux committed a constitutional violation under the law as it currently stands. In a nutshell, Knussman's contention is that Mullineaux applied a facially neutral statute unequally solely on the basis of a gender stereotype in violation of the Equal Protection Clause of the Fourteenth Amendment. The only distinction created by the statute was between "primary care givers" and "secondary care givers," the former being entitled to 30 days of accrued sick leave to care for a newborn and the latter being entitled to 10 days of accrued sick leave. The statute made no reference to gender. Rather, the gender classification was created in the application of § 7–508. Viewed in the light most favorable to Knussman, Mullineaux, based on the comments of an administrative assistant to the DOP's Director of Legislation, took the position that only mothers could qualify for additional paid leave as primary care givers under § 7–508(a). Essentially, Mullineaux applied an irrebutable presumption that the mother is the primary care giver, and therefore entitled to greater employment benefits.

We agree with Knussman that Mullineaux's conduct violated his rights under the Equal Protection Clause. Government classifications drawn on the basis of gender have been viewed with suspicion for three decades. . . .

In particular, justifications for gender-based distinctions that are rooted in "overbroad generalizations about the different talents, capacities, or preferences of males and females" will not suffice. [*U.S. v. Virginia*, 518 U.S. 515, 533 (1996).]. Thus, gender classifications that appear to rest on nothing more than conventional notions about the proper station in society for males and females have been declared invalid time and again by the Supreme Court. . . .

Gender classifications based upon generalizations about typical gender roles in the raising and nurturing of children have met a similar fate. . . .

. . .

The defendants have not even attempted to explain how an irrebuttable presumption in favor of the mother under § 7–508 relates to an important state interest. We conclude that the presumption employed by Mullineaux here was not substantially related to an important governmental interest and, therefore, was not permissible under the Equal Protection Clause.

We next must decide whether Mullineaux's actions contravened "clearly established statutory or constitutional rights of which a reasonable person would have known." *Harlow v. Fitzgerald*, 457 U.S. 800, 818 (1982)....

. . .

Mullineaux contends that the law was not clear because the Supreme Court had determined on a number of occasions that equal protection principles permit government officials to distribute employment-related benefits pursuant to gender-based classifications. In the decisions cited by Mullineaux, however, the gender-based classification was linked to something other than a sexual stereotype. For example, Mullineaux relies on *Geduldig v. Aiello*, 417 U.S. 484 [(1974)]. In our view, *Geduldig* does not cloud the issue. In *Geduldig*, the Court upheld a California insurance statute that excluded pregnancy-related disabilities from coverage against an equal protection challenge, observing that the exclusion of disabilities relating to normal childbirth (as well as other short-term disabilities not related to pregnancy) represented a permissible policy choice aimed at maintaining the solvency of the insurance program....

The authority cited by Mullineaux actually underscores our conclusion regarding the clarity of the law in December 1994. Mullineaux's distribution of sick leave benefits under § 7–508 was a by-product of traditional ideas about a woman's role in rearing a child, which was clearly impermissible under the Equal Protection Clause of the Fourteenth Amendment at the time in question.

. . .

In sum, we hold that Mullineaux was not entitled to qualified immunity against Knussman's equal protection claim under § 1983 and affirm the judgment as to liability, but we conclude that the jury's award of $375,000 was excessive. Accordingly, we vacate the jury's award and remand for a new trial on damages with respect to Knussman's equal protection claim (Count I). Knussman is entitled to be compensated for emotional distress caused by Mullineaux's constitutional violation but not for any emotional distress associated with the litigation of this action or his employer's general internal grievance process.

NOTES

1. Is *Knussman* a challenge to the traditional model of marriage or an affirmation of conservative "family values"? Both? *See* Eyal Press, *Family–Leave Values*, N.Y. TIMES MAG., July 29, 2007, at 36, *available at* http://www.nytimes.com/2007/07/29/magazine/29discrimination-t.html.

2. For some discussion of the traditional marriage model's adverse consequences for men, see SCOTT COLTRANE, FAMILY MAN: FATHERHOOD, HOUSEWORK, AND GENDER EQUITY (1996); NANCY E. DOWD, REDEFINING FATHERHOOD (2000); but also compare STEVEN L. NOCK, MARRIAGE IN MEN'S LIVES (1998).

CATHERINE R. ALBISTON, INSTITUTIONAL INEQUALITY AND THE MOBILIZATION OF THE FAMILY AND MEDICAL LEAVE ACT: RIGHTS ON LEAVE

vii–xi, 167–70, 174 (2010).

For many years the United States was virtually the only major industrialized country without a family and medical leave policy. Employers could legally fire a worker who needed time off to care for a seriously ill child, parent, or spouse. Employers had wide latitude to fire workers temporarily unable to work because of illnesses or injuries. Employers could legally fire women who needed time off for pregnancy and childbirth if they also denied time off to nonpregnant employees who were unable to work. And, although some employers provided parental leave after the birth of a new child, this discretionary leave was primarily available to professional or management employees and not to the rank and file. . . .

. . .

Family policy in the United States has begun to change, however. Since 1993 the federal Family and Medical Leave Act (FMLA) has provided some workers with a legal right of up to 12 weeks of unpaid, job-protected leave for family or medical crises.[1] Both men and women may take leave to care for a sick child, parent, or spouse. Workers may also use FMLA leave for pregnancy disability, and both men and women may take parental leave after the birth of a new child. The statute protects workers who take leave from retaliatory harassment, termination, and discrimination. Perhaps most importantly, FMLA leave is an entitlement for workers; the statute requires employers to provide FMLA leave even if they do not allow time off for any other reason. . . .

The FMLA represents a significant shift in American employment policy, and it challenges implicit, fundamental assumptions about the nature of work. It rejects unbroken attendance as the measure of a good worker and it takes away some of employers' unilateral control over the schedule of work. It changes the often-gendered division between the public life of employment and the private life of family by forcing work to accommodate family needs on a gender-neutral basis. . . . In short, the FMLA not only creates a new benefit for workers, it also challenges entrenched conceptions of what being a good worker means[,] . . . and creates an opportunity for social change.

But what will this new law mean in practice? FMLA rights are not self-enforcing; to enjoy their benefits, individual rights holders must actively claim or "mobilize" them in the workplace and in the courts. . . . [W]orkers do not mobilize their rights in a cultural vacuum. FMLA rights remain embedded within existing power relations, institutions, and culture, including deeply entrenched beliefs and practices associated with work, gender, and disability. Although the FMLA creates an opportunity for restructuring the workplace, what these new rights will mean in practice depends on the ways in which social institutions affect the rights mobilization process.

The existing empirical research paints a complicated and conflicting picture of rights to family and medical leave. Some empirical research

---

1. 29 U.S.C § 2612. Not all workers are covered by the FMLA. Workers who have worked for their employers for less than one year are not eligible for FMLA leave, nor are workers who work for companies with fewer than fifty employees. 29 U.S.C. § 2611.

indicates that the FMLA has significantly increased unpaid leave coverage for American workers, although class differences in leave coverage remain because low-wage workers tend to work for smaller employers who are not covered by the Act.... The vast majority of employers report that leave requirements have not been difficult to implement and have had little or no impact on productivity, profitability, or growth. The available evidence also indicates that employers have not shifted the costs, if any, of leave mandates to women in the form of lower wages or less employment. In short, most large-scale, policy-oriented studies indicate that the FMLA has substantially increased access to leave with little downside for either employers or employees.

Sociological research about the dynamics of family and medical leave in the context of the workplace, however, tells a somewhat different story. Both experimental and observational research indicate that workers who take leave or use family-friendly policies suffer penalties at work. Indeed, in a post-FMLA survey, 32 percent of eligible workers who chose not to take leave reported that they opted against taking leave because they feared they might lose their jobs.... Research also indicates that more powerful workers within organizations, in terms of pay or status, have more family and medical leave options and are more likely to use the options they have. In addition, managers retain significant control over how these policies are implemented, and in some instances implement them as discretionary benefits rather than as legal mandates.

The research makes clear that cultural norms about gender, work, and family also continue to matter. Despite gender-neutral legal reforms, men are generally less likely than women to take leave. Although this pattern may reflect gendered preferences, employers also expect gendered behavior from their employees in terms of taking leave and often resist leaves of more than a few days for male employees. Experimental research also indicates that men who took parental leave are perceived to be less likely to help their coworkers, be punctual, work overtime, or have good attendance than men who did not take parental leave, even when performance was held constant. Clearly the social meaning of taking leave is not the same as the entitlement created by the statute. Gendered cultural norms about the appropriate way to manage work and family continue to shape perceptions of leave, and may actively discourage some workers from taking leave.

. . .

Most respondents who took pregnancy or parental leave discovered that despite the law, family wage discourse framed the meaning of their leave. Indeed, many women found that taking leave changed perceptions of them at work because it seemed to signal that they were no longer committed to their jobs. For example, one respondent reported that even though her performance reviews had been very good, her supervisor's attitude changed after her leave to care for her ill daughter.

He's like, "Well she's having a problem with her kid." ... [Now] he makes me feel like I'm inadequate. Like I can't do the job, like I'm not bright enough.

Virtually all the female respondents initially had no difficulty taking leave. When they attempted to return, however, they encountered resistance and perceptions that they were less reliable and committed to their work after their leave.

. . .

The male respondents who took family leave had somewhat different experiences. In fact, both male and female respondents reported informal workplace norms against men taking all the parental leave legally available to them. For example, in one respondent's workplace, it was unthinkable that a new father would take more than a week or two of leave.

> [T]here was another guy who was having a baby and I think that they got more pressure to come back to work, okay, "It's okay for you to take a week off and maybe a week and a half off, but let's not go crazy here." And that wasn't, I don't think they would have been open for the FMLA for the men. At least the men I knew just took their vacation and didn't take, didn't use the FMLA when they could've. Because they were pressured to come back to work, like "Hey, *you* didn't have a baby."
>
> Interviewer: And there wasn't the same kind of pressure on women?
>
> No.

Although female respondents typically found that employers expected them to take leave to care for others, all the male respondents reported that their employers and coworkers were incredulous and even hostile when they decided to take family leave. Thus, the same family wage discourse constructed different social meanings for respondents' leaves depending upon their gender.[6]

. . .

As these examples illustrate, respondents who took family leave negotiated their rights within a web of meaning made up not only of law, but also of deeply entrenched assumptions about work and gender. Although these respondents negotiated rights within the same social context, the interpretations that flow from that context varied with gender. As the responses of their employers, friends, and families suggest, culturally, women are expected to quit work to care for new children, whereas men are expected to make work their first priority. By deploying this cultural frame, agents of transformation help define the meaning of leave, and sometimes identify a path of least resistance for resolving conflict over leave. In this way, institutions can shape workers' preferences and choices about rights mobilization by providing a graceful explanation for the first respondent to quit, by defining a compromise through which the second respondent justifies his decision to take leave, and by suggesting to the third respondent that quitting to care for others is the solution to her dispute. Because they reinforce gendered conceptions of work and family, however, these paths of least resistance help recreate the inequalities that FMLA rights were meant to change.

. . .

NOTES

1. In *Nevada Department of Human Resources v. Hibbs*, 538 U.S. 721 (2003), the U.S. Supreme Court upheld the FMLA against a constitutional challenge that Congress exceeded its constitutional powers under Section 5 of the 14th Amendment when it abrogated state sovereign immunity in the course of making the Act applicable to and enforceable against unwilling States.

---

6. Other studies have demonstrated consistent and widespread employer hostility toward male workers taking parenting leave. For example, one study found that 63 percent of large employers considered it unreasonable for a man to take any parental leave at all, and another 17 percent considered a reasonable leave to be no longer than two weeks (see Malin 1998: 39–40).

2. The protections of the FMLA do not presently extend to same-sex couples in virtue of the federal Defense of Marriage Act, 1 U.S.C. § 7 (2006) ("In determining the meaning of any Act of Congress . . . the word 'marriage' means only a legal union between one man and one woman as husband and wife, and the word 'spouse' refers only to a person of the opposite sex who is a husband or a wife.").

c. THE REALLOCATION AND PRESERVATION OF DUTIES WITHIN MARRIAGE

S.M. Miller, *The Making of a Confused Middle Class Husband*

2 Soc. Pol'y 33, 34, 36–39 (July/August 1971).

. . .

. . . In the left-wing ambience of New York City in the '40s and '50s, "male supremacy" and "male chauvinism" were frequently discussed. True, my male friends and I discussed the issues with our female friends and then often proceeded to exploit them, but a dextrous awareness we did have. (But I add, in order to avoid a reassuring self-debasement, that we did encourage our women friends and wives to think and to develop themselves; and I even believe that I was less exploitative than most.)

Yet I am dogged by the feeling expressed in the notion "If you're so smart, how come you're not rich?" Where is the egalitarian family life one would reasonably expect from my sophistication about women's issues and my personal experience with them in my younger manhood?

. . .

Probably the most important factor in accounting for the direction my wife and I took was our amazing naiveté about the impact of having children—a naiveté, incidentally, that I see today having a similarly devastating effect on many young parents. We just had no idea how much time and emotion children captured, how they simply changed a couple's lives, even when the wife's working made it possible, as it did in our case, to afford a housekeeper.

The early years of child rearing were very difficult. Our first son was superactive and did not sleep through the night. We were both exhausted. My wife insisted that I not leave everything to her; she fought with me to get me to participate in the care of our son and apartment. I took the 2 a.m. and 6 a.m. feedings and changings, for our ideology would not allow me just to help out occasionally: I had to "share," "really participate," in the whole thing. I resented that degree of involvement; it seemed to interfere terribly with the work I desperately wanted to achieve in. Indeed, I have always felt put upon because of that experience of many months.

To make matters worse, I did not know of other work-oriented husbands who were as involved as I with their children. True, I realized that my sons and I had become much attached to each other and that a lovely new element had entered my life; but I resented the time and exhaustion, particularly since I was struggling to find my way in my work. I did not consider myself productive and was in the middle of struggling to clarify my perspective. I looked at the problem largely in terms of the pressure of my job, which required a lot of effort, and, more importantly, in terms of my personality and my inability to work effectively. Although I wrote memoranda with great ease, I wasn't writing professional articles and books.

In retrospect, I think that it was the influence of the McCarthy and Eisenhower years that was more significant in my lack of development. My outlook and interests were not what social science and society were responding to. That changed later, and I was able to savor in the '60s that infrequent exhilaration of having my professional work and citizen concerns merge and of gaining both a social-science and a popular audience and constituency. But I did not know in the 1950s that this would unfold, and I felt resentment.

What I experienced was that, unlike my friends, I was working hard to make things easier for my wife, and I did not see rewards. Yes, she told me she appreciated my effort; but my activities were never enough, my sharing was never full, in the sense that I equally planned and took the initiative in the care of child and house. She was tired, too, and irritated by child care; and, in turn, I was irritated by what seemed to be her absorption in taking care of the children.

. . .

I guess what dismays me and makes me see my marriage and family as unfortunately typically upper-middle-class collegial, pseudo-egalitarian American—especially in light of my own continuing commitment to an egalitarian, participatory ethos—is that I assume no responsibility for major household tasks and family activities. True, my wife has always worked at her profession (she is a physician), even when our sons were only some weeks old. True, I help in many ways and feel responsible for her having time to work at her professional interests. But I do partial, limited things to free her to do her work. I don't do the basic thinking about the planning of meals and housekeeping, or the situation of the children. Sure, I will wash dishes and "spend time" with the children; I will often do the shopping, cook, make beds, "share" the burden of most household tasks; but that is not the same thing as direct and primary responsibility for planning and managing a household and meeting the day-to-day needs of children.

It is not that I object in principle to housekeeping and childrearing. I don't find such work demeaning or unmasculine—just a drain of my time, which could be devoted to other, "more rewarding" things. (Just as I don't like to shop for clothes for myself, even though I like clothes.) My energies are poised to help me work on my professional-political concerns, and I resist "wasting time" on other pursuits, even those basic to managing a day-to-day existence.

The more crucial issue, I now think, is not my specific omissions and commissions, but the atmosphere that I create. My wife does not expect much of me, which frees me for work and lessens the strain I produce when I feel blocked from working. Even our sons have always largely respected my efforts to work, feeling much freer to interrupt their mother at her work. The years have been less happy than they would have been if I had been more involved and attentive and my wife had not lowered her ambitions.

Outstanding academically from an early age, a "poor girl" scholarship winner to a prestige college and medical school, excelling in her beginning professional work, my wife expected, and was expected, to do great things. But with children, she immediately reduced her goals. Of course, medical schools don't pay much attention to faculty members who are part-time or female, and the combination of the two almost guarantees offhand treatment.

She is now realizing fuller professional development. I have always felt guilty about her not achieving more, so I have nagged her to publish, though I have not provided the circumstances and climate that would make serious work much easier. I have had the benefit of feeling relieved that I was "motivating" her by my emphasis on her doing more, but I have not suffered the demands on my time and emotions that making more useful time available to her would have required. In the long run, I have undoubtedly lost more by limited involvement, because she has been distressed by the obstacles to her professional work. But the long run is hard to consider when today's saved and protected time helps meet a deadline.

What are the lessons of this saga of a well-meaning male?

One is that equality or communality is not won once and for all, but must continually be striven for. Backsliding and easy accommodation to the male (because it is less troublesome) are likely to occur unless there is, at least occasionally, effort to bring about or maintain true communality rather than peaceful adjustment.

From this it follows that women must struggle for equality—that it will not easily be won or rewon. (A male is not likely to bestow it—in more than surface ways. Some women are arguing that it is not worth the effort to have equality with men in close personal relations and that they should not bother with men, but equality and communality among women will not be automatic, either.) The struggle does not necessarily mean nastiness, but it does require the perceptiveness and willingness to engage issues not only of prejudice and discrimination but also of subtle practices requiring female accommodation to males.

I know that the point I am about to make is often misused, and will open me to much criticism; but let me try to make it. A third lesson is that the bringing up of children must be changed, and that many women are lagging in this respect, although present day-care concerns suggest a possible change. For all of male reluctance, resistance and avoidance, many women, particularly when they have young children, end up structuring life so that it is difficult to achieve a collegial relationship. Indeed, the concentration on, nay absorption with, children makes even a low-level decent relationship, let alone an egalitarian one, difficult. Yes, I realize that the subordinate group is never the main source of difficulty, that men make women embrace the mother-housemother syndrome; but cultural and personal history are involved as well as direct or more covert husbandly pressure and unwillingness to be a full partner. Overinvolvement with children may operate to discourage many husbands from full participation because they do not accept the ideology of close attention to children.

... What is needed is a reconsideration of what is required in parenthood and in running a household.

Let me consider the household care first. The easy notion that in the right atmosphere housework is not so bad seems wrong to me. A lot of jobs can be stomached, treated as routine; that is the best one can say of them— that they are manageable, "do-able." But they are not exciting, stimulating or satisfying except to the extent that they are completed or "accomplished," i.e., gotten rid of for the moment. This is especially so when one's other interests are high, for then these tasks become highly competitive with other ways of using one's time and thus are dissatisfying. Housework can be a full-time job if it is not guarded against. Some agreement on a minimum, satisfactory level of household care and some efficiency and sharing in performing it are important for a couple.

I have mentioned, verbally at least, the desirability of ... "salutary neglect" (before Moynihan, incidentally). But it has been difficult for my generation, whose adolescence and early twenties were stirred by Freud and who have wallowed in the guilt of parental omniscience and ethnic parental concern, to erase the sense of responsibility and guilt for how our children develop. What if one's son doesn't graduate from college or becomes a bomb-thrower ... —isn't it the parents' fault? When a son or daughter is eighteen or twenty, it seems easier to deny the responsibility, since so many youths are also in troubled times that it is difficult to talk of Freudian acting-out rather than of a generational change in consciousness. But at earlier ages it is much more difficult to shake the feeling of responsibility for how a child is developing. Obviously I don't advocate callous neglect; but some less constraining and demanding views of parenthood—and probably some additional institutional aids like day care—are needed.

The problem is not always in the mothers' attitudes. Some studies show that working-class women are very interested in working, but that their husbands feel that it is important to the children for their mothers to be home. The issue is not so much that the mother or father is lagging but how to move toward new views on child development and new institutions to further these views.

　　.   .   .

But all these "implications" are minor, except for the importance of struggle. What strikes me as the crucial concern, at least for the occupationally striving family, is the male involvement in work, success and striving. This is the pressure that often molds the family. Accommodation to it is frequently the measure of being a "good wife"—moving when the male's "future" requires it, regulating activities so that the male is free to concentrate on his work or business. It isn't sexism or prejudice against women that is at work here—although they are contributing factors—but the compulsive concentration upon the objective of achievement and the relegating of other activities to secondary concern. Egalitarian relationships cannot survive if people are not somewhat equally involved with each other and if the major commitment is to things outside the relationship that inevitably intrude upon it.

So long as success or achievement burns bright for the male, it is going to be difficult to change drastically the situation of the family and the woman.

However, although I am strongly of the mind that success drives should be banked and other more humanitarian urges encouraged, I don't accept that all of the drive for success or achievement is pernicious or undesirable. This drive is exciting, and can be fulfilling. But it is a great danger to be avoided when it becomes all-embracing or when the success is without a content that is both personally and socially satisfying or beneficial.

To do interesting and useful things, to feel a sense of accomplishment, should be made easier. As in military strategy, a "sufficient level" of achievement rather than a "maximum level" of security or position should be sought. Being "number one" should not be the goal; rather, high competence should be enough for both men and women....

If women accept "success" to the same extent and in the same way that many men do, the problems will be enormous. If women simply adopt the "number-one-ism" that dominates the workplace, the drive for achievement will probably lead them into the same narrowing and unpromising obsessions that destroy many men.

A more egalitarian society in terms of the distribution of income and social respect would, of course, make it easier to escape "number-one-ism." But, meanwhile, we shall have to struggle with the values that surround us and corrode true equality in the home.

Finally, men have to feel some gain in the growing equality in their relationship with women. Over the long run there may well be greater satisfaction for males in egalitarian relationships, but in the short run the tensions and demands may not lead to enjoyment and satisfaction. Some short-term gains for males will be important in speeding up the road to equality. But such gains are not easily or automatically forthcoming. That is why I made the first points about the inevitability of struggle. Successful struggle requires modes of living and relationships to which the male can accommodate without total loss, which is hard to achieve without women's falling back again to accommodating to men.

I recognize that I concentrate upon the upper middle class and upon the experience of one male. I don't think either is the world—I really don't. But I do perceive that some of my experiences and interpretations are not solipsist pieces of life, that with things changing, others are experiencing similar shocks and stresses. I wonder whether the egalitarian changes I see in some young families will mean permanent changes, or "lapsed egalitarianism" once again. My hope is that the future will be different.

Beth A. Burkstrand–Reid, *"Trophy Husbands" & "Opt–Out" Moms*

34 SEATTLE U. L. REV. 663, 663–74 (2011).

Before women were "opting out" of the workforce . . . to stay at home with their children, a subset of fathers had already done so. The 2002 *Fortune* cover story titled *Trophy Husbands* documented the "dramatic shift afoot" of well-off, educated men leaving paid work in order to tend to the home and kids in support of their powerful wives' careers[.] . . . The article portrayed these men as taking one for the team: hitting a sacrifice fly so that their wives could advance.

> . . .

Any discussion of at-home fathers must start with two seemingly simple inquiries: (1) how is "at-home father" defined and (2) how many at-home fathers are there? The answers to these queries are far from clear. . . .

One might presume that, at a minimum, an at-home parent is one who has given up paid work. That . . . may be wrong. As *Fortune* shows, at-home fathers often keep at least a toe in the labor market by taking part-time consulting or other paid work. Some at-home mothers do as well. In other words, at-home parents, as portrayed by the media, may lack what we assume as the central characteristic of at-home parents: a singular focus on being a (unpaid) caregiver. Are parents who are both primary caregivers and part-time paid workers "at-home parents"? Are they "working parents"? Or are they a type of parent (and therefore part of a type of family) that has yet to be defined?

The . . . questions raised by media coverage of at-home parents are also unresolved by the government's definition of "at-home parents." . . . [T]he census [definition of "at-home parent"] ... exclud[es] many parents ... even though the[se] [parents] serve as primary family caregivers. According to the U.S. Census Bureau, an at-home father is a father "not in the labor force" for fifty-two weeks of the prior year and who is "caring for family" while his spouse works.[18] The definition of "not in the labor force" is complex, but it generally means that the father is not working *at all* and is not *looking* for paid work.[19] Some self-defined ... "at-home fathers," then, are excluded from the census count because (1) they work part-time (e.g., shift work or work on a freelance or contractual basis) or (2) they are seeking paid employment. For these reasons, the census definition of "at-home parents" may exclude a significant number of fathers. For example, one survey indicated that 37% of at-home fathers "were in transition between jobs or careers" and were therefore at home temporarily, presumably excluding them from the census definition. Moreover, depending on how long and how hard a father looks for paid work, he may be excluded from census numbers even if he is serving as the family's primary caregiver.

Because the definition of "at-home father" is unclear, the real number of at-home fathers is difficult to determine. In 2008 there were 158,000 at-home fathers, as compared with 5.1 million at-home mothers, according to the U.S. Census Bureau.[22] Men between forty and forty-four years old represented the highest number of at-home fathers.[23] But we also know that as of 2005, fathers served as primary caretakers for approximately 18% of all children four years old and younger—some two million children—who had an employed mother.[24] Unsurprisingly, households with the highest report-ed incomes had the greatest number of at-home fathers. These numbers, again, are based on census data and all of the potential problems that are implied.

Beyond their numbers, it is difficult not to essentialize at-home fathers based on the way they are portrayed in the media: as educationally and socioeconomically privileged men. For example, *Trophy Husbands* takes pains to emphasize that the at-home fathers featured are high-level professionals married to women executives at companies such as Charles Schwab, J.P. Morgan–Chase, Xerox, Sun, Verizon, and Coca–Cola. . . .

Undoubtedly, however, at-home parenting generally—and at-home fa-therhood specifically—is not homogenous. Many at-home-father families fall

---

18. U.S. CENSUS BUREAU, AMERICA'S FAMILIES AND LIVING ARRANGEMENTS: 2009 tbl.FG8 (2010) [hereinafter AMERICA'S FAMILIES AND LIVING ARRANGEMENTS], *available at* http://www.census.gov/ population/www/socdemo/hh-fam/cps2009.html. "Family" includes children only under fifteen years old. *Id.*

19. *Labor Force Statistics from the Current Population Survey: How the Government Measures Unemployment,* BUREAU OF LAB. STAT. (Oct. 16, 2009), http:// www.bls.gov/cps/cps_htgm.htm#nilf ("[T]he labor force is made up of the employed and the unemployed. The remainder—those who have no job and are not looking for one—are counted as 'not in the labor force.' Many who are not in the labor force are going to school or are retired. Family responsibilities keep others out of the labor force."). The criteria for at-home mothers and at-home fathers are the same. *Id.*

22. AMERICA'S FAMILIES AND LIVING ARRANGEMENTS, *supra* note 18. For the statistics on at-home fathers the year that *Trophy Husbands* was published, see U.S. CENSUS BUREAU, P20–547, U.S. CHILDREN'S LIVING ARRANGEMENTS AND CHARACTERISTICS: MARCH 2002, at 10 (2003) [hereinafter U.S. CHILDREN'S LIVING ARRANGEMENTS], *available at* http://www.census.gov/prod/2003pubs/p20–547.pdf.

23. *Id.*

24. These statistics don't add up: both come from census data, but the second statistic suggests that the number of at-home fathers may be significantly higher than the first statistic suggests. U.S. CENSUS BUREAU, P70–121, WHO'S MINDING THE KIDS? CHILD CARE ARRANGEMENTS: SPRING 2005 tbl.2B (2008), *available at* http://www.census.gov/population/www/socdemo/child/ppl–2005.html.

below the poverty line, are not heterosexual, or have varied cultural and geographic backgrounds—all facts which are often overlooked. At-home fathers with fewer financial resources are likely underrepresented in research: for example, they may have greater difficulty participating in research on their family structure or be less connected to the manner in which the research is conducted. Still, articles such as *Trophy Husbands* ... portray at-home parenthood as a province exclusively for the wealthy and a product of choice when, in fact, at-home fathers, for example, may be pushed out of paid work by economic realities beyond their control. If the parents in ... *Trophy Husbands* ... fall outside the privileged work-education-socioeconomic-status triad often depicted in the media, it is not apparent.

. . .

The men in *Trophy Husbands* ... suffer from troublesome representations in their opt-out stories. Though *Trophy Husbands* praises the at-home dad for his household contributions, he is also reduced to being a prize, a possession[.] ... Scratch ever-so-lightly beneath the surface and one will see that *Trophy Husbands* may not, in fact, show families subverting a dominant gender paradigm: gender roles may be merely swapped, rather than redefined.... As one child of an at-home father said, "*My dad has always been my mom.*" Just look at the photographs of the men in *Trophy Husbands*: the cover features a sneaker-clad, apron-covered dad holding two young girls, one clutching a baby doll. Another photograph features a man perched on a couch, folded towels in hand. A suit-clad corporate wife smiles at the camera while her husband stares at her longingly, a teddy bear dangling from his hand. These photographs—with an at-home wife, of course—could have appeared in a 1950s magazine.

It is not surprising, then, that one undercurrent of *Trophy Husbands* is how these men maintain their masculinity while at home. Sometimes the magazine itself heralds their masculinity. *Fortune* declared that these men "are not wimps." To the contrary, the story cites the fact that they left stereotypically masculine careers as scientists, lawyers, executives, and military men to be at home.... [H]ow could leaving such fabulous careers—a move that may threaten the very core of their masculinity—not be the product of choice? Any suggestion otherwise, regardless of its source, could undercut the very notion of a man's superior position in his family, whether he works at home or in an office. And as the men's masculinity is preserved, so too is the women's femininity.

. . .

Many "trophy husbands" note their wives' better earning capacity as a reason for staying at home. Implicit in these statements is that a wife's increased earning capacity is dependent on her ability to function as what [Joan] Williams terms an "ideal worker," or someone who can work full time (and overtime) with little or no time taken for childbearing or childrearing, and who can move if necessary. In this respect, men may be pushed out of the workforce for the same reasons women traditionally are pushed out: a family—especially one with children—can support only one ideal worker at a time because of the unrelenting employer expectations that the ideal worker may face. A "trophy husband," therefore, may not be able to function as an ideal worker because his wife is taking that role, thus necessitating that one spouse "choose" to leave paid work.

. . .

... [N]one of the men in *Fortune* [is] ... quoted as saying [he] ... chose to stay at home primarily to spend time with [his] ... children.... Men, it is presented, leave for money—either because they were laid off or because it would be economically advantageous to focus on their wives' careers. This justification may be a much more palatable reason for a man to proffer, as it does not threaten stereotypical notions of masculinity. This is not to say that at-home fathers did not leave in part out of a desire to spend time with their family, but that desire may not have been—or at least was not cited as—the motivation for their decision. Given that the men do not discuss a paternal pull toward home and their children, *if Fortune*'s representations are accurate, one could presume that some "trophy husbands" were, in fact, pushed out of the labor force because they made the "choice" to support their wives as the family's ideal worker.

. . .

NOTE

Consider STEVEN L. NOCK, MARRIAGE IN MEN'S LIVES 40 (1998):

> If husband and wives *are* economically rational, one might expect that wives would perform more housework if they are economically dependent on their husbands.... In general ... wives' housework time appears to vary with the degree of economic dependency on their husbands.... One researcher showed that a husband's dependency on his wife does *not* translate into greater shares of housework....
>
> Why would economically dependent husbands do *less* housework ... ? The answer is that housework and the time required to do it are more than simple economic commodities. The details of routine household life ... carry enormous symbolic meaning. "Men's" work means providing for the family and being the "breadwinner," whereas "women's" work means caring for the home and children. The associations are part of the culture and embedded in institutions. They are widely believed by American men and women and are reinforced by economic, religious, and educational institutional arrangements.... [A] dependent husband departs from traditional assumptions about marriage. Were he to respond by doing more housework he would deviate even more. When he does even *less* housework, therefore, he is compensating for his departure from normative associations by being more traditional in whatever ways he can.

Richard Posner, Elite Universities and Women's Careers

The Becker–Posner Blog (Sept. 25, 2005).*

An article in the *New York Times* of September 20 by Louise Story, entitled "Many Women at Elite Colleges Set Career Path to Motherhood," reports the results of surveys and interviews concerning career plans of women at the nation's most prestigious colleges, law schools, and business schools. Although not rigorously empirical, the article confirms—what everyone associated with such institutions has long known—that a vastly higher percentage of female than of male students will drop out of the work force to take care of their children. Some will resume full-time work at some point in the children's maturation; some will work part time; some will not work at all after their children are born, instead devoting their time to family and to civic activities. One survey of Yale alumni found that 90 percent of the male

---

* The source is available here: http://www.becker-posner-blog.com/2005/09/elite-universities-and-womens-careers—posner.html.

alumni in their 40s were still working, but only 56 percent of the female. A survey of Harvard Business School alumni found that 31 percent of the women who had graduated between 10 and 20 years earlier were no longer working at all, and another 31 percent were working part time. What appears to be new is that these earlier vintages did not expect to drop out of the workforce at such a high rate (though they did), whereas current students do expect this. That is not surprising, since the current students observe the career paths of their predecessors. So, contrary to the implication of the article, there is no evidence that the drop-out rate will rise. The article does not discuss the interesting policy issues presented by the disproportionate rate of exit of elite women from the workforce. Nor does it have much to say about why women drop out at the rate they do. The answer to the latter question seems pretty straightforward, however. Since like tend to marry like ("assortative mating"), women who attend elite educational institutions tend to marry men who attend such institutions (and for the further reason that marital search costs are at their minimum when the search is conducted within the same, coeducational institution). Those men have on average high expected incomes, probably higher than the expected incomes even of equally able women who have a full working career. Given diminishing marginal utility of income, a second, smaller income will often increase the welfare of a couple less than will the added household production if the person with the smaller income allocates all or most of her time to household production, freeing up more time for her spouse to work in the market. The reason that in most cases it is indeed the wife (hence my choice of pronoun) rather than the husband who gives up full-time work in favor of household production is not only that the husband is likely to have the higher expected earnings; it is also because, for reasons probably both biological and social, women on average have a greater taste and aptitude for taking care of children, and indeed for nonmarket activities generally, than men do. But it is at this point that policy questions arise. Even at the current very high tuition rates, there is excess demand for places at the elite colleges and professional schools, as shown by the high ratio of applications to acceptances at those schools. Demand is excess—supply and demand are not in balance—because the colleges and professional schools do not raise tuition to the market-clearing level but instead ration places in their entering classes on the basis (largely) of ability, as proxied by grades, performance on standardized tests, and extracurricular activities. Since women do as well on these measures as men, the student body of an elite educational institution is usually about 50 percent female. Suppose for simplicity that in an entering class at an elite law school of 100 students, split evenly among men and women, 45 of the men but only 30 of the women will have full-time careers in law. Then 5 of the men and 20 of the women will be taking places that would otherwise be occupied by men (and a few women) who would have more productive careers, assuming realistically that the difference in ability between those admitted and those just below the cut off for admission is small. While well-educated mothers contribute more to the human capital of their offspring than mothers who are not well educated, it is doubtful that a woman who graduates from Harvard College and goes on to get a law degree from Yale will be a better mother than one who stopped after graduating from Harvard. But I have to try to be precise about the meaning of "more productive" in this context. I mean only that if a man and woman of similar ability were competing for a place in the entering class of an elite professional school, the man would (on average) pay more for the place than the woman would; admission would create more "value added" for him than for her. The principal effect of professional education of women who are not going to have full working careers is to reduce the contribution of professional schools to the output of professional services. Not that the professional education the women who drop out of the workforce receive is worthless; if it were, such women would not enroll. Whether the benefit these women derive consists of satisfying their intellectual curiosity, reducing marital search costs, obtaining an expected income from part-time work, or obtaining a hedge against divorce or other economic misfortune, it will be on average a smaller benefit than the person (usually a man) whose place she took who would have a full working career would obtain from the same education. The professional schools worry about this phenomenon because the lower the aggregate lifetime incomes of their graduates, the lower the level of alumni donations the schools can expect to receive. (This is one reason medical schools are reluctant to admit applicants who are in their 40s or 50s.) The colleges worry for the same reason. But these particular worries have no significance for the welfare of society as a whole. In contrast, the fact that a significant percentage of places in the best professional schools are being occupied by individuals who are not going to obtain the maximum possible value from such an education is troubling from an overall economic standpoint. Education tends to confer external benefits, that is, benefits that the recipient of the education cannot fully capture in the higher income that the education enables him to obtain after graduation. This is true even of professional education, for while successful lawyers and businessmen command high incomes, those incomes often fall short of the contribution to economic welfare that such professionals make. This is clearest when the lawyer or businessman is an innovator, because producers of intellectual property are rarely able to appropriate the entire social gain from their production. Yet even noninnovative lawyers and businessmen, if successful— perhaps by virtue of the education they received at a top-flight professional school—do not capture their full social product in their income, at least if the income taxes they pay exceed the benefits they receive from government. Suppose a professional school wanted to correct the labor-market distortion that I have been discussing. (For I am not suggesting that the distortion is so serious as to warrant government intervention.) It would be unlawful discrimination to refuse admission to these schools to all women, for many women will have full working careers and some men will not. It would be rational but impracticable to impose a monetary penalty on the drop-outs (regardless of gender)—making them pay, say, additional tuition retroactively at the very moment that they were giving up a market income. It would also be infeasible to base admission on an individualized determination of whether the applicant was likely to have a full working career. A better idea, though counterintuitive, might be to raise tuition to all students but couple the raise with a program of rebates for graduates who work full time. For example, they might be rebated 1 percent of their tuition for each year they worked full time. Probably the graduates working full time at good jobs would not take the rebate but instead would convert it into a donation. The real significance of the plan would be the higher tuition, which would discourage applicants who were not planning to have full working careers (including applicants of advanced age and professional graduate students). This would open up places to applicants who will use their professional education more productively; they are the more deserving applicants. Although women continue to complain about discrimination, sometimes quite justly, the gender-neutral policies that govern admission to the elite professional schools illustrate discrimination in favor of women. Were admission to such schools based on a prediction of the social value of the education offered, fewer women would be admitted.

NOTE

For additional discussion of these themes, See Lisa Belkin, *The Opt–Out Revolution*, N.Y. TIMES, Oct. 26, 2003, § 6 (Magazine), at 42; Lisa Belkin, *When Mom and Dad Share It All*, N.Y. TIMES, June 15, 2008, § 6 (Magazine), at 44.

C. ENCROACHMENTS ON THE DOCTRINE OF FAMILY PRIVACY

1. PROPERTY DURING MARRIAGE

a. THE COMMON LAW SYSTEM

Most states follow common law principles when resolving property disputes between spouses. At common law, once a woman married, her personal property (except for paraphernalia or "pin money") became her husband's property and her real property became subject to his control,[1] at least for the duration of the marriage.[2] The harshness of this system was ameliorated somewhat in the 19th century with the passage of the Married Women's Property Acts.[3]

Mississippi passed the first such act in 1839. Apparently Mrs. T.J.D. Hadley, a Mississippi woman who had visited Louisiana and learned about their civil law system of marital property, played a major role in passing the legislation. While all the facts are not known, it is clear that she ran a boarding house that catered to many state senators and representatives, and that her husband was both a member of the state senate and spendthrift. The act that was passed read in pertinent part:

> Section 1. *Be it enacted, by the Legislature of the State of Mississippi,* That any married woman may become seized or possessed of any property, real or personal, by direct bequest, demise, gift, purchase, or distribution, in her own name, and as of her own property: *Provided,* the same does not come from her husband after coverture. Sec. 2. *And be it further enacted,* That hereafter when any woman possessed of a property in slaves, shall marry, her property in such slaves and their natural increase shall continue to her, notwithstanding her coverture; and she shall have, hold, and possess the same, as her separate property, exempt from any liability for the debts or contracts of the husband. Sec. 3. *And be it further enacted,* That when any woman, during coverture, shall become entitled to, or possessed of, slaves by conveyance, gift, inheritance, distribution, or otherwise, such slaves, together with their natural increase, shall enure and belong to the wife, in like manner as is above provided as to slaves which she may possess at the time of marriage. Sec. 4. *And be it further enacted,* That the control and management of all such slaves, the direction of their labor, and the receipt of the productions

---

1. His interest was termed an estate jure uxoris.

2. If the couple had a child, the husband also acquired "curtesy" or the right to control his wife's property until his death (if she died first, that is). The wife, by contrast was entitled to "dower," or an interest in 1/3 of his real property until her death if he died first, whether or not they had a child.

3. England did not give married women control of their earnings until 1870, Married Women's Property Act, 1870, 33 & 34 Vict., c. 93 (Eng.), probably because the wealthy had long used equity to arrange their affairs suitably. *See* Mary A. Glendon, *Matrimonial Property: A Comparative Study of Law and Social Change*, 49 TUL. L. REV. 21 (1974).

thereof, shall remain to the husband, agreeably to the laws heretofore in force.

This rather dubious "advance" in the property rights of women, marked the start of a trend that led eventually to the nearly universal acceptance of the right of a married woman (1) to her own earnings, (2) to contract and carry on a business and (3) to transfer property without her husband's consent. Because most married women did not work until well into the 20th century, however, the reforms of the 19th century were generally of theoretical importance only.

Southern New Hampshire Medical Center v. Hayes

Supreme Court of New Hampshire, 2010.
992 A.2d 596.

■ DUGGAN, J.

The defendant, Anthony Hayes, appeals: (1) an order of the Superior Court (*Brennan*, J.) granting summary judgment in favor of the plaintiff, Southern New Hampshire Medical Center (SNHMC), with respect to Karen Hayes' unpaid medical expenses; (2) an order of the Superior Court (*Nicolosi*, J.) granting SNHMC's motion *in limine* to exclude evidence that Karen Hayes "eloped" under the doctrine of necessaries; and (3) a ruling on the merits (*Smukler*, J.) finding Anthony Hayes liable under the doctrine of necessaries for Karen Hayes' medical bills. We affirm in part, reverse in part, and remand.

. . . Anthony and Karen Hayes married in 1977. In July, August, October and November 2006, Karen, who did not have health insurance, received emergency medical treatment at SNHMC for complications stemming from alcoholism, leaving a balance due of $85,238.88. The record contains conflicting evidence about the status of Karen and Anthony's marriage during this time. While Karen's medical records indicate that she was living with Anthony, Anthony disputes this, asserting that he and Karen "did not live as husband and wife for the past seven to eight years . . . when [the medical bills] were . . . incurred." For example, Anthony testified that sometimes Karen was admitted to SNHMC after being "taken out of hotels, motels, and other people's houses."

SNHMC filed suit against the Hayeses, and successfully sought a real estate attachment on two unencumbered parcels owned jointly by the[m]. . . . When SNHMC placed an attachment on the properties, Karen and Anthony were still married. The Hayeses were divorced in January 2007 pursuant to a stipulated agreement. Under the terms of the divorce, each party was responsible for his or her own medical expenses not covered by insurance. Specifically, "Karen [was] responsible for paying the debt to [SNHMC] as well as any other medical debts or bills." Karen received one automobile valued at $1,200, her bank account with a balance of $0.00, and all of her debts. Anthony received the marital properties subject to SNHMC's attachment.

Prior to trial, SNHMC moved *in limine* to prohibit Anthony "from introducing at trial any information, documentation or witnesses concerning or in any way referencing an alleged common law doctrine of elopement." SNHMC argued that elopement is an affirmative defense, and that Anthony failed to give adequate notice, pursuant to Superior Court Rule 28, that he intended to rely upon this doctrine. Anthony objected, contending that he gave adequate notice.

The trial court granted SNHMC's motion. It ruled that elopement is an affirmative defense, but that Anthony failed to properly raise it. The court found that it would be unfair to require SNHMC to counter this defense, given that "the legal fact of marriage was not in dispute."

The trial court granted summary judgment in favor of SNHMC against Karen, finding "no issue of material fact" that she was liable for the balance owed to SNHMC. The trial court, however, denied SNHMC's motion for summary judgment against Anthony, finding that genuine issues of material fact remained with respect to his liability for Karen's medical expenses. Following a bench trial on the merits, the trial court found that Anthony was liable, under the doctrine of necessaries, for Karen's medical debts to SNHMC. During the pendency of these proceedings, Karen passed away.

. . .

I. Summary Judgment: Karen Hayes

... We assume for the purposes of this appeal that Anthony has standing to attack the judgment against Karen.

. . .

II. The Doctrine of Necessaries

The ancient common law doctrine of necessaries imposed liability on husbands for "essential goods and services provided to [their wives] by third parties" if they failed to provide their wives "with such necessaries." *Cheshire Medical Center v. Holbrook*, 663 A.2d 1344 [(N.H. 1995)]. Necessaries included "necessary food, drink, washing, physic, instruction, and a suitable place of residence, with such necessary furniture as is suitable to her condition." *Ray v. Adden*, 50 N.H. 82, 83 (1870); *see Morrison v. Holt*, 42 N.H. 478, 480 (1861) (legal expenses not necessaries unless husband's conduct rendered expenses necessary to secure wife's personal protection or safety).

This doctrine originated as a result of draconian legal restrictions on the rights of married women to "contract, sue, or be sued individually" or exercise control over their property or financial affairs. A married woman's contracts " 'were absolutely void, not merely voidable, like those of infants and lunatics.' " *Holbrook*, 663 A.2d at 1346 (quoting *Dunlap v. Dunlap*, 150 A. 905 ([N.H.] 1930)). "[U]pon marriage a woman forfeited her legal existence and became the property of her husband," as, in the eyes of the law, a husband and wife were considered one legal entity. *Id.* In return for his responsibility for his wife's support and liability for her torts, a husband was entitled to her "society." *Drew's Appeal*, 57 N.H. 181, 183 (1876).

> "A man has as good a right to his wife, as to the property acquired under a marriage contract; and to divest him of that right without his default, and against his will, would be as flagrant a violation of the principles of justice as the confiscation of his estate." *Holbrook*, 663 A.2d 1346 (quoting *Drew's Appeal*, 57 N.H. at 183).

The husband was "the sole owner of the family wealth," and the wife was "viewed as little more than a chattel in the eyes of the law." *N.C. Baptist Hospitals, Inc. v. Harris*, 354 S.E.2d 471, 474 ([N.C.] 1987).

Accordingly, the law of necessaries "attempted to obviate some of the victimization which coverture would otherwise have permitted" by "providing a common-law mechanism by which the duty of support could be enforced." [*North Ottawa Cmty. Hosp. v.*] *Kieft*, 578 N.W.2d 267, 270 [(Mich. 1998)]. It reflected the sad reality that, "[b]ecause the wife could not contract for food, clothing, or medical needs, her husband was obligated to provide her with such necessaries." *Holbrook*, 663 A.2d 1346. To obtain compensation from a husband for goods or services provided to his wife, a creditor had to set forth a *prima facie* case that husband and wife were married, that the husband failed to provide his wife with necessaries, and that the articles or services in question were necessaries "according to the husband's situation in life." *Rumney v. Keyes*, 7 N.H. 571, 580 (1835). If the couple separated, the husband could nonetheless be liable under the necessaries doctrine if he caused the separation by abandoning his wife, evicting her without reason, or committing some other kind of misconduct that drove the wife out of the marital home. However, even if the husband and wife separated by consent, a husband could still be liable for his wife's necessaries.

Husbands could avoid liability under the necessaries doctrine under certain circumstances. For example, a husband whose wife "eloped" would not be liable for her necessaries. *Cogswell v. Tibbetts*, 3 N.H. 41, 42 (1824). A wife who voluntarily left her husband to live with an adulterer, or was removed forcibly from the marital home but chose to reside with the adulterer, "eloped" for the purposes of the doctrine. *Cogswell*, 3 N.H. at 42. Key to the determination of "elopement" was whether the wife had left her husband, committed adultery and also remained beyond his control. *Id.*

"In modern America, 'no longer is the female destined solely for the home and the rearing of the family, and only the male for the marketplace and the world of ideas.'" [*Medical Business Associates v.*] *Steiner*, 588 N.Y.S.2d [890,] 893 [(1992)] (quoting *Stanton v. Stanton*, 421 U.S. 7, 14–15 (1975)). "The modern marital relationship is viewed by law as a partnership of equality, an evolution from the nineteenth century relationship of dominance by a husband and submission by a wife who had little standing as an individual person or legal entity." *Forsyth Memorial Hosp., Inc. v. Chisholm*, 467 S.E.2d 88, 90 ([N.C.] 1996). Undoubtedly, married women today have an "unrestricted right to contract," and RSA 546–A:2 (2007) "imposes a gender-neutral obligation of spousal support." *Holbrook*, 663 A.2d 1346. The doctrine of necessaries has been characterized as "an anachronism that no longer fits contemporary society," *Steiner*, 588 N.Y.S.2d at 893 (quotation omitted), and some courts have abolished it. *See, e.g., Emanuel v. McGriff*, 596 So.2d 578, 580 (Ala.1992); *Condore v. Prince George's Cty.*, 425 A.2d 1011, 1019 ([MD] 1981). In New Hampshire, however, the doctrine endures: we extended it to apply to all married individuals, regardless of gender, *see Holbrook*, 663 A.2d 1347, and many courts have similarly extended the doctrine to apply to both husbands and wives. *See, e.g.,* Simons, Note, *Is the Doctrine of Necessaries Necessary in Florida: Should the Legislature Accept the Challenge of Connor v. Southwest Florida Regional Medical Center?*, 50 FLA. L. REV. 933, 939 (1998).

When considering the application of the doctrine in the modern day, some courts have outlined a *prima facie* case under the law of necessaries as follows:

> In order to establish a *prima facie* case against one spouse for the value of [services or goods] provided to the other spouse, the ... provider must show that (1) [services or goods] were provided to the receiving spouse, (2) [they] were necessary for the health and well-being of the receiving spouse, (3) the person against whom the action is

brought was married to the receiving spouse at the time the [services or goods] were provided, and (4) payment for the necessaries has not been made.

Wesley Long Nursing Center, Inc. v. Harper, No. COA06–1706, 2007 WL 4233643, at *2 (N.C.Ct.App. Dec.4, 2007) (unpublished opinion). This approach comports with our own common law on the necessaries doctrine. We note that, for the purposes of the necessaries doctrine, hospitals and other medical providers are uniquely situated and, therefore, uniquely likely to seek the application of this doctrine, as, unlike other creditors, medical providers may not turn away patients who require treatment.

A.   Elopement

. . . We conclude that "elopement" is no longer a defense to the doctrine of necessaries.

As noted above, the necessaries doctrine developed during a time when married women were severely restricted in their ability to contract, sue, or be sued, or to exercise control over their property, services, or earnings. To defend on the grounds of elopement, the non-debtor spouse had to prove that the debtor spouse left the non-debtor spouse, escaped his or her control and committed adultery. Such a defense does not comport with the modern status of marriage. . . .

Given that the "historical purposes underlying the [elopement] exception to the necessaries doctrine are incompatible with current mores and laws governing modern marital relationships in [New Hampshire]," we find that the elopement exception "has no place in the common law." [*Forsyth Mem'l. Hosp. v.*] *Chisholm*, 467 S.E.2d [88,] 91 [(N.C. 1996)]. Rather, we conclude that, under the third prong of the *prima facie* case that we have outlined above, the creditor—in this case, the hospital—must show more than the legal fact of marriage to demonstrate that the parties are "married" for the purposes of liability under the necessaries doctrine. "[P]roof of an undissolved marriage does not in itself provide the basis for liability to a creditor supplying a spouse with necessaries," as "in some circumstances a marriage will cease to [exist] for purposes of liability under" the necessaries doctrine. [*Nat'l Account Sys., Inc. v.*] *Mercado*, 481 A.2d 835, 837 [(N.J. Super. Ct. 1984)]. This is a fact-specific, and case-specific, inquiry.

The non-debtor spouse's liability under the necessaries doctrine depends on a mutual expectation that the spouses will share assets, expenses, and debts. Accordingly, factors to consider in determining whether the marriage is no longer viable for the purposes of the necessaries doctrine might include whether the parties were separated, when they separated, whether they are living apart, and whether they share their living expenses and debt. If a marriage has broken down to the extent that spouses are no longer sharing assets or debts, it makes little sense to hold a non-debtor spouse liable for the medical expenses of the other. *See id.* at 837. *But see* [*Queen's Medical Center v.*] *Kagawa*, 967 P.2d 686, 699–700 [(Haw. Ct. App. 1998)] (non-debtor spouse liable for necessaries until divorce finalized); *Bartrom* [*v. Adjustment Bureau, Inc.,*] 618 N.E.2d 1, 9 [(Ind. 1993)] (holding that "duty of spousal support continues at least until the marriage relationship is dissolved").

For the reasons described above, "elopement" is no longer a defense to the application of the necessaries doctrine; rather, the third party seeking to impose liability on the non-debtor spouse—in this case, SNHMC—retains the burden to demonstrate that the parties were "married" for the purposes of liability under the necessaries doctrine. Because we hold today that "elopement" is not an affirmative defense, we reverse and remand to the trial court for a new trial on the merits.

B.   Liability of Non–Debtor Spouse

We next consider Anthony's argument that SNHMC must determine that his wife could not satisfy her debt before seeking reimbursement from him. Anthony relies primarily upon *Holbrook*, 663 A.2d 1347. SNHMC argues that it must only seek payment from Karen before pursuing Anthony, relying upon language in *Holbrook* which states that "a medical provider must first seek payment from the spouse who received its services before pursuing collection from the other spouse." *Id.*

Under the doctrine of necessaries, "a husband or wife is not liable for necessary medical expenses incurred by his or her spouse unless the resources of the spouse who received the services are *insufficient* to satisfy the debt." *Holbrook*, 663 A.2d 1346 (emphasis added). Accordingly, "the spouse who receives the necessary goods or services is primarily liable for payment," and "the other spouse is secondarily liable." *Id.* at 188, 663 A.2d 1344. We have held that the doctrine of necessaries renders the non-debtor spouse "liable to the hospital to the extent [his or her spouse's] estate[ ] [is] *unable to pay* for the necessary medical services provided." *St. Joseph Hosp. of Nashua v. Rizzo*, 676 A.2d 98, 100 ([N.H.] 1996) (emphasis added).

The defendant argued before the trial court that SNHMC was required to demonstrate that Karen could not pay for her medical services before pursuing his assets. The trial court stated that it did "not necessarily agree with ... Mr. Hayes['] legal position," citing the language in *Holbrook* which states that the medical provider must "first seek payment from the spouse who received its services before pursuing collection from the other spouse." The trial court reasoned that the Holbrook "language is directed at collection efforts" and "does not necessarily restrict a finding of liability." However, the trial court, "[f]or the purposes of its analysis ... accept[ed] [without] deciding the defendant's legal position" and determined that, even under a standard requiring SNHMC to prove that Karen lacks the resources to pay her debts before pursuing Anthony, SNHMC demonstrated that Karen's estate could not satisfy the debt to SNHMC.

We clarify ... *Holbrook* by confirming that the trial court applied the correct standard when it determined that Karen could not satisfy her debt to SNHMC. On remand, the trial court should apply the standard set out above, that the non-debtor spouse is liable for his or her spouse's necessaries if the debtor spouse is unable to pay for his or her necessaries.

Affirmed in part; reversed in part; and remanded.

NOTES

1.   States with family expense statutes have taken different positions on the extent of a wife's liability. *Compare,* N.D. Cent. Code § 14–07–10 (imposing mutual liability on both spouses only for necessities provided to the other), *with* Neb. Rev. Stat. § 42–201 (exempting ninety percent of wife's wages from liability to necessity debts), *and* S.C. Code Ann. §§ 20–5–30; 20–5–60 (imposing liability for necessity support of wife and minor children on husband but no reciprocal obligation on wife).

2.   In the fall of 1979, the National Conference of Commissioners on Uniform State Laws established a committee to draft a proposed uniform act dealing with marital property. The Uniform Marital Property Act (UMPA) was promulgated in 1983 and approved by the ABA in August 1984. *See generally* William P. Cantwell, *The Uniform Marital Property Act: Origin and Intent*, 68 Marq. L. Rev. 383 (1985).

Professor William Reppy, Jr., has described the UMPA as "a community property act with a good premise: spouses should share extensively in property acquired during marriage." William A. Reppy, Jr., *The Uniform Marital Property Act: Some Suggested Revisions for a Basically Sound Act*, 21 Hous. L.Rev. 679 (1984). He adds:

> The Act does not, however, mimic the typical American community property regime. By directing that all of the rents and profits accrued during marriage from separate property, called "individual property" in the Act, be co-owned by the spouses, the Act provides for greater sharing by married persons than any other American community property scheme.

Id.

A version of the Act has been adopted only in Wisconsin. Wis. Stat. § 766.001 et seq. Marital Property Act, Nat'l Conf. of Commissioners on Uniform State Laws, http://www.nccusl.org/Act.aspx?title=Marital% 20Property% 20Act (last visited Oct. 2, 2011). *See also* Daniel Furrh, *Divorce and the Marital Property Act*, 62 Wis. Law, Jan. 1989, at 23. For a comparison between the WMPA and UMPA and a discussion of problems arising under the WMPA, see Howard S. Erlanger & June M. Weisberger, *From Common Law Property to Community Property: Wisconsin's Marital Property Act Four Years Later*, 1990 Wis. L. Rev. 769 (1990); and Palma Maria Forte, Comment, *The Wisconsin Marital Property Act: Sections in Need of Reform*, 79 Marq. L. Rev. 859 (1996).

b. COMMUNITY PROPERTY

The Evolution of Community Property

Nine states have community property systems: Arizona, California, Idaho, Louisiana, Nevada, New Mexico, Texas, Washington, and Wisconsin.[1]

The discussion that occurred at the California Constitutional Convention of 1849 on whether to retain the community property approach is particularly revealing of the debate. One delegate called upon his fellow bachelors to support community property on the theory that it would attract rich, marriageable women to California.[2] Another altruistically asked the convention not to impose the "despotic provisions" of the common law on wives. Delegate Lippit argued for the common law system by pointing to France where, he alleged, two thirds of the married couples were living apart because the civil law had turned the wife into an equal, raising her from being "head clerk to partner." Delegate Botts concurred, pointing out that the community property system was contrary to nature, and supported by the "mental hermaphrodites" who supported women's rights.

In fact, married women found they were not appreciably better situated in community property states than in common law jurisdictions because, at least until very recently, husbands were authorized to control all of the community property. Male control of community property has now been eliminated in all the community property states. In *Kirchberg v. Feenstra*, 450 U.S. 455 (1981), the Supreme Court held unconstitutional the Louisiana Code provision designating the husband as "head and master" of the community and giving him exclusive power to administer the community estate. The Court held that the provision violated the equal protection clause as interpreted in *Orr* and other cases. By the time the Court ruled, the

---

1. In 1998, Alaska, a common law state, enacted a statute that enables spouses to elect to hold their property as a community. Alaska Stat. § 34.77.030 (2011).

2. This discussion is drawn from Judith T. Younger, *Community Property, Women and the Law School Curriculum*, 48 N.Y.U. L. Rev. 211 (1973), and William Reppy & William Defuniak, Community Property in the United States (2d ed. 1982). For additional discussion see Chapter 9.

Louisiana legislature had in fact changed its law, but the change came too late to moot the issue in *Feenstra*.

Today, sole or individual management is the rule in Texas for community property derived from personal earnings, revenue from separate property, recoveries for personal injuries, and revenue from solely managed property. All other community property (including commingled separate property) is subject to dual management, requiring the concurrence of both spouses. *See* Tex. Fam. Code Ann. § 3.102 (West 2011).

The other community property states also provide for sole management of some property and joint management of some. But, in addition they provide for "equal" management of the rest. Consider for example:

New Mexico Stat. Ann. § 40–3–14:

A. Except as provided in Subsections B and C of this section, either spouse alone has full power to manage, control, dispose of and encumber the entire personal property.

B. Where only one spouse is:

(1) named in a document evidencing ownership of community personal property; or

(2) named or designated in a written agreement between that spouse and a third party as having sole authority to manage, control, dispose of or encumber the community personal property which is described in or which is the subject of the agreement, . . . only the spouse so named may manage, control, dispose of or encumber the community personal property described in such a document evidencing ownership or in such a written agreement.

C. Where both spouses are:

(1) named in a document evidencing ownership of community personal property; or

(2) named or designated in a written agreement with a third party as having joint authority to dispose of or encumber the community personal property which is described in or the subject of the agreement, . . . both spouses must join to dispose of or encumber such community personal property where the names of the spouses are joined by the word "and." Where the names of the spouses are joined by the word "or," or by the words "and/or," either spouse alone may dispose of or encumber such community personal property.

2.   The Constitutional Right to Privacy

Griswold v. Connecticut

Supreme Court of the United States, 1965.
381 U.S. 479, 85 S.Ct. 1678, 14 L.Ed.2d 510.

■ Justice Douglas delivered the opinion of the Court.

Appellant Griswold is Executive Director of the Planned Parenthood League of Connecticut. Appellant Buxton [was] . . . Medical Director for the League at its Center in New Haven—a center open . . . from November 1 to November 10, 1961, when appellants were arrested.

They gave information, instruction, and medical advice to *married persons* as to the means of preventing conception.... Fees were usually charged, although some couples were serviced free.

The statutes whose constitutionality is involved in this appeal are §§ 53–32 and 54–196 of the General Statutes of Connecticut (1958 rev.). The former provides:

Any person who uses any drug, medicinal article or instrument for the purpose of preventing conception shall be fined not less than fifty dollars or imprisoned not less than sixty days nor more than one year or be both fined and imprisoned.

Section 54–196 provides:

Any person who assists, abets, counsels, causes, hires or commands another to commit any offense may be prosecuted and punished as if he were the principal offender.

The appellants were found guilty as accessories and fined $100 each, against the claim that the accessory statute as so applied violated the Fourteenth Amendment....

. . .

Coming to the merits, we are met with a wide range of questions that implicate the Due Process Clause of the Fourteenth Amendment. Overtones of some arguments suggest that *Lochner v. New York*, 198 U.S. 45 [(1905)] should be our guide. But we decline that invitation.... We do not sit as a super-legislature to determine the wisdom, need, and propriety of laws that touch economic problems, business affairs, or social conditions. This law, however, operates directly on an intimate relation of husband and wife and their physician's role in one aspect of that relation.

The association of people is not mentioned in the Constitution nor in the Bill of Rights. The right to educate a child in a school of the parents' choice—whether public or private or parochial—is also not mentioned. Nor is the right to study any particular subject or any foreign language. Yet the First Amendment has been construed to include certain of those rights.

By *Pierce v. Society of Sisters*, [268 U.S. 510 (1925)], the right to educate one's children as one chooses is made applicable to the States by the force of the First and Fourteenth Amendments. By *Meyer v. Nebraska*, [262 U.S. 390], the same dignity is given the right to study the German language in a private school. In other words, the State may not, consistently with the spirit of the First Amendment, contract the spectrum of available knowledge....

In *NAACP v. Alabama*, 357 U.S. 449, 462 [(1958)] we protected the "freedom to associate and privacy in one's associations," noting that freedom of association was a peripheral First Amendment right.... In other words, the First Amendment has a penumbra where privacy is protected from governmental intrusion. In like context, we have protected forms of "association" that are not political in the customary sense but pertain to the social, legal, and economic benefit of the members. *NAACP v. Button*, 371 U.S. 415, 430–431 [(1963)]....

. . .

The foregoing cases suggest that specific guarantees in the Bill of Rights have penumbras, formed by emanations from those guarantees that help give them life and substance. Various guarantees create zones of privacy. The right of association contained in the penumbra of the First Amendment is one, as we have seen. The Third Amendment in its prohibition against the quartering of soldiers "in any house" in time of peace without the consent of the owner is another facet of that privacy. The Fourth Amendment explicitly affirms the "right of the people to be secure in their persons, houses, papers, and effects, against unreasonable searches and seizures." The Fifth Amendment in its Self–Incrimination Clause enables the citizen to create a zone of privacy which government may not force him to surrender to his detriment. The Ninth Amendment provides: "The enumeration in the Constitution, of certain rights, shall not be construed to deny or disparage others retained by the people."

. . .

The present case, then concerns a relationship lying within the zone of privacy created by several fundamental constitutional guarantees. And it concerns a law which, in forbidding the *use* of contraceptives rather than regulating their manufacture or sale, seeks to achieve its goals by means having a maximum destructive impact upon that relationship. Such a law cannot stand in light of the familiar principle . . . that a "governmental purpose to control or prevent activities constitutionally subject to state regulation may not be achieved by means which sweep unnecessarily broadly and thereby invade the area of protected freedoms." Would we allow the police to search the sacred precincts of marital bedrooms for telltale signs of the use of contraceptives? The very idea is repulsive to the notions of privacy surrounding the marriage relationship.

We deal with a right of privacy older than the Bill of Rights—older than our political parties, older than our school system. Marriage is a coming together for better or for worse, hopefully enduring, and intimate to the degree of being sacred. It is an association that promotes a way of life, not causes; a harmony in living, not political faiths; a bilateral loyalty, not commercial or social projects. Yet it is an association for as noble a purpose as any involved in our prior decisions.

Reversed.

■ JUSTICE GOLDBERG, whom THE CHIEF JUSTICE and JUSTICE BRENNAN join, concurring.

. . . I do agree that the concept of liberty protects those personal rights that are fundamental, and is not confined to the specific terms of the Bill of Rights. My conclusion . . . is supported both by numerous decisions of this Court . . . and by the language and history of the Ninth Amendment. . . .

. . .

This Court, in a series of decisions, has held that the Fourteenth Amendment absorbs and applies to the States those specifics of the first eight amendments which express fundamental personal rights. The language and history of the Ninth Amendment reveal that the Framers of the Constitution believed that there are additional fundamental rights, protected from governmental infringement, which exist alongside those fundamental rights specifically mentioned in the first eight constitutional amendments.

The Ninth Amendment reads, "The enumeration in the Constitution, of certain rights, shall not be construed to deny or disparage others retained by the people." The Amendment is almost entirely the work of James Madison. It was introduced in Congress by him and passed the House and Senate with little or no debate and virtually no change in language. It was proffered to quiet expressed fears that a bill of specifically enumerated rights could not be sufficiently broad to cover all essential rights and that the specific mention of certain rights would be interpreted as a denial that others were protected.

. . .

... To hold that a right so basic and fundamental and so deep-rooted in our society as the right of privacy in marriage may be infringed because that right is not guaranteed in so many words by the first eight amendments to the Constitution is to ignore the Ninth Amendment and to give it no effect whatsoever....

. . .

■ JUSTICE WHITE, concurring in the judgment.

In my view this Connecticut law as applied to married couples deprives them of "liberty" without due process of law....

. . .

... [T]he statute is said to serve the State's policy against all forms of promiscuous or illicit sexual relationships, be they premarital or extramarital, concededly a permissible and legitimate legislative goal.

Without taking issue with the premise that the fear of conception operates as a deterrent to such relationships in addition to the criminal proscriptions Connecticut has against such conduct, I wholly fail to see how the ban on the use of contraceptives by married couples in any way reinforces the State's ban on illicit sexual relationships....

. . .

... A statute limiting its prohibition on use to persons engaging in the prohibited relationship would serve the end posited by Connecticut.... I find nothing in this record justifying the sweeping scope of this statute....

■ JUSTICE BLACK, with whom JUSTICE STEWART joins, dissenting.

... I do not to any extent whatever base my view that this Connecticut law is constitutional on a belief that the law is wise or that its policy is a good one. In order that there may be no room at all to doubt why I vote as I do, I feel constrained to add that the law is every bit as offensive to me as it is my Brethren of the majority ... who ... hold it unconstitutional. There is no single one of the graphic and eloquent strictures and criticisms fired at the policy of this Connecticut law either by the Court's opinion or by those of my concurring Brethren to which I cannot subscribe—except their conclusion that the evil qualities they see in the law make it unconstitutional.

. . .

The Court talks about a constitutional "right of privacy" as though there is some constitutional provision or provisions forbidding any law ever to be passed which might abridge the "privacy" of individuals. But there is not. There are, of course, guarantees in certain specific constitutional provisions ... designed in part to protect privacy at certain times and places with respect to certain activities....

... For these reasons I get nowhere in this case by talk about a constitutional "right or privacy" as an emanation from one or more constitutional provisions.[1] I like my privacy as well as the next one, but I am

---

1. The phrase "right to privacy" appears first to have gained currency from an article written by Messrs. Warren and (later Mr. Justice) Brandeis in 1890 which urged that States

nevertheless compelled to admit that government has a right to invade it unless prohibited by some specific constitutional provision....

This brings me to the arguments [that] ... would invalidate it by reliance on the Due Process Clause of the Fourteenth Amendment [or] ... also [by reliance] on the Ninth Amendment.... [N]either the Due Process Clause nor the Ninth Amendment, nor both together, could under any circumstances be a proper basis for invalidating the Connecticut law....

The due process argument ... is based ... on the premise that this Court is vested with power to invalidate all state laws that it consider to be arbitrary, capricious, unreasonable, or oppressive, or on this Court's belief that a particular state law under scrutiny has no "rational or justifying" purpose, or is offensive to a "sense of fairness and justice." ... While I completely subscribe to the holding of *Marbury v. Madison*, 1 Cranch 137, and subsequent cases, that our Court has constitutional power to strike down statutes, state or federal, that violate commands of the Federal Constitution, I do not believe that we are granted power by the Due Process Clause or any other constitutional provision or provisions to measure constitutionality by our belief that legislation is arbitrary, capricious or unreasonable, or accomplishes no justifiable purpose, or is offensive to our own notions of "civilized standards of conduct." Such an appraisal of the wisdom of legislation is an attribute of the power to make laws, not of the power to interpret them. The use by federal courts of such a formula or doctrine or whatnot to veto federal or state laws simply takes away from Congress and States the power to make laws based on their own judgment of fairness and wisdom and transfers that power to this Court for ultimate determination—a power which was specifically denied to federal courts by the convention that framed the Constitution.

.   .   .

... [Considering the use of the Ninth Amendment] as authority to strike down all state legislation which this Court thinks violates "fundamental principles of liberty and justice," or is contrary to the "traditions and (collective) conscience of our people[,]" ... one would certainly have to look far beyond the language of the Ninth Amendment to find that the Framers vested in this Court any such awesome veto powers over lawmaking, either by the States or by the Congress. Nor does anything in the history of the Amendment offer any support for such a shocking doctrine. The whole history of the adoption of the Constitution and Bill of Rights points the other way[.] ... [T]he Ninth Amendment was intended to protect against the idea that "by enumerating particular exceptions to the grant of power" to the Federal Government, "those rights which were not singled out, were intend-

---

should give some form of tort relief to persons whose private affairs were exploited by others. *The Right to Privacy*, 4 Harv. L. Rev. 193. Largely as a result of this article, some States have passed statutes creating such a cause of action, and in others state courts have done the same thing by exercising their powers as courts of common law. See generally 41 Am.Jur. 926–27. Thus the Supreme Court of Georgia, in granting a cause of action for damages to a man whose picture had been used in a newspaper advertisement without his consent, said that "A right of privacy in matters purely private is * * * derived from natural law" and that "The conclusion reached by us seems to be * * * thoroughly in accord with natural justice, with the principles of the law of every civilized nation, and especially with the elastic principles of the common law * * *." Pavesich v. New England Life Ins. Co., 50 S.E. 68, 70, 80 [(Ga. 1905)]. Observing that "the right of privacy * * * presses for recognition here," today this Court, which I did not understand to have power to sit as a court of common law, now appears to be exalting a phrase which Warren and Brandeis used in discussing grounds for tort relief, to the level of a constitutional rule which prevents state legislatures from passing any law deemed by this Court to interfere with "privacy."

ed to be assigned into the hands of the General Government (the United States), and were consequently insecure." That Amendment was passed, not to broaden the powers of this Court or any other department of "the General Government," but, as every student of history knows, to assure the people that the Constitution in all its provisions was intended to limit the Federal Government to the powers granted expressly or by necessary implication. If any broad, unlimited power to hold laws unconstitutional because they offend what this Court conceives to be the "(collective) conscience of our people" is vested in this Court by the Ninth Amendment, the Fourteenth Amendment, or any other provision of the Constitution, it was not given by the Framers, but rather has been bestowed on the Court by the Court....

... [T]his Court does have power, which it should exercise, to hold laws unconstitutional where they are forbidden by the Federal Constitution. My point is that there is no provision of the Constitution which either expressly or impliedly vests power in this Court to sit as a supervisory agency over acts of duly constituted legislative bodies and set aside their laws because of the Court's belief that the legislative policies adopted are unreasonable, unwise, arbitrary, capricious or irrational. The adoption of such a loose, flexible, uncontrolled standard for holding laws unconstitutional, if ever it is finally achieved, will amount to a great unconstitutional shift of power to the courts which I believe and am constrained to say will be bad for the courts and worse for the country. Subjecting federal and state laws to such an unrestrained and unrestrainable judicial control as to the wisdom of legislative enactments would, I fear, jeopardize the separation of governmental powers that the Framers set up and at the same time threaten to take away much of the power of States to govern themselves which the Constitution plainly intended them to have.

... And so, I cannot rely on the Due Process Clause or the Ninth Amendment ... as a reason for striking down this state law....

. . .

So far as I am concerned, Connecticut's law as applied here is not forbidden by any provision of the Federal Constitution as that Constitution was written, and I would therefore affirm.

Eisenstadt v. Baird

Supreme Court of the United States, 1972.
405 U.S. 438, 92 S.Ct. 1029, 31 L.Ed.2d 349.

■ JUSTICE BRENNAN delivered the opinion of the Court.

Appellee William Baird was convicted at a bench trial in the Massachusetts Superior Court ... for exhibiting contraceptive articles in the course of delivering a lecture on contraception to a group of students at Boston University and ... for giving a young woman a package of Emko vaginal foam at the close of his address. The Massachusetts Supreme Judicial Court unanimously set aside the conviction for exhibiting contraceptives on the ground that it violated Baird's First Amendment rights, but by a four-to-three vote sustained the conviction for giving away the foam....

MASSACHUSETTS GENERAL LAWS ANN., c. 272, § 21, under which Baird was convicted, provides a maximum five-year term of imprisonment for "whoever ... gives away ... any drug, medicine, instrument or article whatever for the prevention of conception," except as authorized in § 21A. Under § 21A, "a registered physician may administer to or prescribe for any married person drugs or articles intended for the prevention of pregnancy or conception.... [A] registered pharmacist actually engaged in the business of pharmacy may furnish such drugs or articles to any married person presenting a prescription from a registered physician." ...

. . .

... The question for our determination in this case is whether there is some ground of difference that rationally explains the different treatment accorded married and unmarried persons under MASSACHUSETTS GENERAL LAWS ANN., c. 272, §§ 21 and 21A. For the reasons that follow, we conclude that no such ground exists.

First. ... It would be plainly unreasonable to assume that Massachusetts has prescribed pregnancy and the birth of an unwanted child as punishment for fornication, which is a misdemeanor under MASSACHUSETTS GENERAL LAWS ANN., c. 272, § 18. Aside from the scheme of values that assumption would attribute to the State, it is abundantly clear that the effect of the ban on distribution of contraceptives to unmarried persons has at best a marginal relation to the proffered objective....

. . .

Second.... If health were the rationale of § 21A, the statute would be both discriminatory and overbroad ... in view of the federal and state laws *already* regulating the distribution of harmful drugs. *See* Federal Food, Drug, and Cosmetic Act, § 503, 52 Stat. 1051, as amended, 21 U.S.C.A. § 353; MASS.GEN.LAWS ANN., c. 94, § 187A, as amended. We conclude, accordingly, that, despite the statute's superficial earmarks as a health measure, health, on the face of the statute, may no more reasonably be regarded as its purpose than the deterrence of premarital sexual relations.

Third. If the Massachusetts statute cannot be upheld as a deterrent to fornication or as a health measure, may it, nevertheless, be sustained simply as a prohibition on contraception? ... We need not and do not, however, decide that important question in this case because, whatever the rights of the individual to access to contraceptives may be, the rights must be the same for the unmarried and the married alike.

If under *Griswold* the distribution of contraceptives to married persons cannot be prohibited, a ban on distribution to unmarried persons would be equally impermissible. It is true that in *Griswold* the right of privacy in question inhered in the marital relationship. Yet the marital couple is not an independent entity with a mind and heart of its own, but an association of two individuals each with a separate intellectual and emotional makeup. If the right of privacy means anything, it is the right of the *individual,* married or single, to be free from unwarranted governmental intrusion into matters so fundamentally affecting a person as the decision whether to bear or beget a child. *See Stanley v. Georgia*, 394 U.S. 557 (1969). *See* also *Skinner v. Oklahoma ex rel. Williamson*, 316 U.S. 535 (1942); *Jacobson v. Massachusetts*, 197 U.S. 11, 29 (1905).

On the other hand, if *Griswold* is no bar to a prohibition on the distribution of contraceptives, the State could not, consistently with the Equal Protection Clause, outlaw distribution to unmarried but not to married persons. In each case the evil, as perceived by the State, would be identical, and the underinclusion would be invidious.... We hold that by providing dissimilar treatment for married and unmarried persons who are similarly situated, Massachusetts General Laws Ann., c. 272, §§ 21 and 21A, violate the Equal Protection Clause. The judgment of the Court of Appeals is affirmed.

. . .

NOTE

Does *Eisenstadt* make it unconstitutional for a state to favor married individuals over nonmarried? If so, consider the observations of John Noonan, Jr., *The Family and the Supreme Court*, 23 CATH. U. L. REV. 255, 273 (1973):

> [*Eisenstadt* and its progeny] are not justified by a principle of elementary justice. They are not explicable by the invocation of Equal Protection of the right of privacy. They cannot be explained by viewing marriage as an impermissible religious category, when marriage has social purpose in our society. They are, then, wrong—wrong in using the Equal Protection Clause on behalf of the unmarried parent and the unmarried spouse, wrong in extending the right of procreative privacy to the unmarried person. They are wrong in subverting the privileged status of marriage, contrary to the teaching of *Loving v. Virginia* . . . , contrary to the place of marriage in American experience. The vital personal right recognized by *Loving v. Virginia* is not the right to a piece of paper issued by a city clerk. It is not the right to exchange magical words before an agent authorized by the state. It is the right to be immune to the legal disabilities of the unmarried and to acquire the legal benefits accorded to the married. Lawful marriage in the society's hierarchy of values recognized by *Boddie v. Connecticut* and in the host of laws yet unchallenged—the tax law, the common law of property, the law of evidence—is a constellation of these immunities and privileges. To say that legal immunities and legal benefits may not depend upon marriage is to deny the vital right. To say that Equal Protection requires the equal treatment of the married and the unmarried in all respects is to deny the hierarchy of values of our society.

Is this too broad a reading of *Eisenstadt?* Even if it is, is there something to the point?

Roe v. Wade

Supreme Court of the United States, 1973.
410 U.S. 113, 93 S.Ct. 705, 35 L.Ed.2d 147.

■ JUSTICE BLACKMUN delivered the opinion of the Court.

This Texas federal appeal and its Georgia companion, *Doe v. Bolton,* present constitutional challenges to state criminal abortion legislation. . . .

. . .

The Texas statutes that concern us here . . . make it a crime to "procure an abortion," as therein defined, or to attempt one, except with respect to "an abortion procured or attempted by medical advice for the purpose of saving the life of the mother." Similar statutes are in existence in a majority of the States.

. . .

Three reasons have been advanced to explain historically the enactment of criminal abortion laws in the 19th century and to justify their continued existence.

It has been argued occasionally that these laws were the product of a Victorian social concern to discourage illicit sexual conduct. Texas, however, does not advance this justification in the present case....

A second reason is concerned with abortion as a medical procedure. When most criminal abortion laws were first enacted, the procedure was a hazardous one for the woman. This was particularly true prior to the development of antisepsis. Antiseptic techniques, of course, were based on discoveries by Lister, Pasteur, and others first announced in 1867, but were not generally accepted and employed until about the turn of the century. Abortion mortality was high. Even after 1900, and perhaps until as late as the development of antibiotics in the 1940's, standard modern techniques such as dilation and curettage were not nearly so safe as they are today. Thus it has been argued that a State's real concern in enacting a criminal abortion law was to protect the pregnant woman, that is, to restrain her from submitting to a procedure that placed her life in serious jeopardy.

Modern medical techniques have altered this situation. Appellants and various *amici* refer to medical data indicating that abortion in early pregnancy, that is, prior to the end of the first trimester, although not without its risk, is now relatively safe. Mortality rates for women undergoing early abortions, where the procedure is legal, appear to be as low as or lower than the rates for normal childbirth.... Of course, important state interests in the area of health and medical standards do remain. The State has a legitimate interest in seeing to it that abortion, like any other medical procedure, is performed under circumstances that insure maximum safety for the patient. This interest obviously extends at least to the performing physician and his staff, to the facilities involved, to the availability of after-care, and to adequate provision for any complication or emergency that might arise. The prevalence of high mortality rates at illegal "abortion mills" strengthens, rather than weakens, the State's interest in regulating the conditions under which abortions are performed. Moreover, the risk to the woman increases as her pregnancy continues. Thus the State retains a definite interest in protecting the woman's own health and safety when an abortion is proposed at a late stage of pregnancy.

The third reason is the State's interest—some phrase it in terms of duty—in protecting prenatal life. Some of the argument for this justification rests on the theory that a new human life is present from the moment of conception.... In assessing the State's interest, recognition may be given to the less rigid claim that as long as at least *potential* life is involved, the State may assert interests beyond the protection of the pregnant woman alone.

The Constitution does not explicitly mention any right of privacy ... [but] the Court has recognized that a right of personal privacy, or a guarantee of certain areas or zones of privacy, does exist under the Constitution....

   . . .

This right of privacy, whether it be founded in the Fourteenth Amendment's concept of personal liberty and restrictions upon state action, as we feel it is, or, as the District Court determined, in the Ninth Amendment's reservation of rights to the people, is broad enough to encompass a woman's decision whether or not to terminate her pregnancy. The detriment that the State would impose upon the pregnant woman by denying this choice altogether is apparent. Specific and direct harm medically diagnosable even in early pregnancy may be involved. Maternity, or additional offspring, may force upon the woman a distressful life and future. Psychological harm may be imminent. Mental and physical health may be taxed by child care. There is also the distress, for all concerned, associated with the unwanted child, and there is the problem of bringing a child into a family already unable, psychologically and otherwise, to care for it. In other cases, as in this one, the additional difficulties and continuing stigma of unwed motherhood may be involved. All these are factors the woman and her responsible physician necessarily will consider in consultation.

On the basis of elements such as these, appellants and some *amici* argue that the woman's right is absolute and that she is entitled to terminate her pregnancy at whatever time, in whatever way, and for whatever reason she alone chooses. With this we do not agree.... The Court's decisions recognizing a right of privacy also acknowledge that some state regulation in areas protected by that right is appropriate....

We therefore, conclude that the right of personal privacy includes the abortion decision, but that this right is not unqualified and must be considered against important state interests in regulation.

. . .

The appellee and certain *amici* argue that the fetus is a "person" within the language and meaning of the Fourteenth Amendment. In support of this they outline at length and in detail the well-known facts of fetal development. If this suggestion of personhood is established, the appellant's case, of course, collapses, for the fetus' right to life is then guaranteed specifically by the Amendment....

The Constitution does not define "person" in so many words. Section 1 of the Fourteenth Amendment contains three references to "person." The first, in defining "citizens," speaks of "persons born or naturalized in the United States." The word also appears both in the Due Process Clause and in the Equal Protection Clause. "Person" is used in other places in the Constitution: in the listing of qualifications for representatives and senators. Art. I, § 2, cl. 2, and § 3, cl. 3; in the Apportionment Clause, Art. I, § 2, cl. 3; in the Migration and Importation provision, Art. I, § 9, cl. 1; in the Emolument Clause, Art. I, § 9, cl. 8; in the Electors provisions, Art. II, § 1, cl. 2, and the superseded cl. 3; in the provision outlining qualifications for the office of President, Art. II, § 1, cl. 5; in the Extradition provisions, Art. IV, § 2, cl. 2, and the superseded Fugitive Slave cl. 3; and in the Fifth, Twelfth, and Twenty-second Amendments as well as in §§ 2 and 3 of the Fourteenth Amendment. But in nearly all these instances, the use of the word is such that it has application only postnatally. None indicates, with any assurance, that it has any possible pre-natal application.

All this, together with our observation that throughout the major portion of the 19th century prevailing legal abortion practices were far freer than they are today, persuades us that the word "person," as used in the Fourteenth Amendment, does not include the unborn....

. . .

The pregnant woman cannot be isolated in her privacy. She carries an embryo and, later, a fetus, if one accepts the medical definitions of the developing young in the human uterus. *See* Dorland's Illustrated Medical Dictionary, 478–479, 547 (24th ed. 1965). The situation therefore is inherently different from marital intimacy, or bedroom possession of obscene material, or marriage, or procreation, or education, with which *Eisenstadt* and

Griswold, Stanley, Loving, Skinner, and *Pierce* and *Meyer* were respectively concerned. As we have intimated above, it is reasonable and appropriate for a State to decide that at some point in time another interest, that of health of the mother or that of potential human life, becomes significantly involved. . . .

Texas urges that, apart from the Fourteenth Amendment, life begins at conception and is present throughout pregnancy, and that, therefore, the State has a compelling interest in protecting that life from and after conception. We need not resolve the difficult question of when life begins. When those trained in the respective disciplines of medicine, philosophy, and theology are unable to arrive at any consensus, the judiciary, at this point in the development of man's knowledge, is not in a position to speculate as to the answer.

It should be sufficient to note briefly the wide divergence of thinking on this most sensitive and difficult question. There has always been strong support for the view that life does not begin until live birth. This was the belief of the Stoics. It appears to be the predominant, though not the unanimous, attitude of the Jewish faith. It may be taken to represent also the position of a large segment of the Protestant community, insofar as that can be ascertained; organized groups that have taken a formal position on the abortion issue have generally regarded abortion as a matter for the conscience of the individual and her family. As we have noted, the common law found greater significance in quickening. Physicians and their scientific colleagues have regarded that event with less interest and have tended to focus either upon conception, upon live birth, or upon the interim point at which the fetus becomes "viable," that is, potentially able to live outside the mother's womb, albeit with artificial aid. Viability is usually placed at about seven months (28 weeks) but may occur earlier, even at 24 weeks. The Aristotelian theory of "mediate animation," that held sway throughout the Middle Ages and the Renaissance in Europe, continued to be official Roman Catholic dogma until the 19th century, despite opposition to this "ensoulement" theory from those in the Church who would recognize the existence of life from the moment of conception. The latter is now, of course, the official belief of the Catholic Church. . . .

In areas other than criminal abortion, [such as tort law and inheritance,] the law has been reluctant to endorse any theory that life, as we recognize it, begins before live birth or to accord legal rights to the unborn except in narrowly defined situations and except when the rights are contingent upon live birth. . . .

In view of all this, we do not agree that, by adopting one theory of life, Texas may override the rights of the pregnant woman that are at stake. We repeat, however, that the State does have an important and legitimate interest in preserving and protecting the health of the pregnant woman, whether she be a resident of the State or a nonresident who seeks medical consultation and treatment there, and that it has still *another* important and legitimate interest in protecting the potentiality of human life. These interests are separate and distinct. Each grows in substantiality as the woman approaches term and, at a point during pregnancy, each becomes "compelling."

With respect to the State's important and legitimate interest in the health of the mother, the "compelling" point, in the light of present medical knowledge, is at approximately the end of the first trimester. This is so because of the now-established medical fact that until the end of the first trimester mortality in abortion may be less than mortality in normal child-birth. It follows that, from and after this point, a State may regulate the abortion procedure to the extent that the regulation reasonably relates to the preservation and protection of maternal health. Examples of permissible State regulation in this area are requirements as to the qualifications of the person who is to perform the abortion; as to the licensure of that person; as to the facility in which the procedure is to be performed, that is, whether it must be a hospital or may be a clinic or some other place of less-than-hospital status; as to the licensing of the facility; and the like.

This means, on the other hand, that, for the period of pregnancy prior to this "compelling" point, the attending physician, in consultation with his patient, is free to determine, without regulation by the State, that in his medical judgment, the patient's pregnancy should be terminated. If that decision is reached, the judgment may be effectuated by an abortion free of interference by the State.

With respect to the State's important and legitimate interest in potential life, the "compelling" point is at viability. This is so because the fetus then presumably has the capability of meaningful life outside the mother's womb. State regulation protective of fetal life after viability thus has both logical and biological justifications. If the State is interested in protecting fetal life after viability, it may go so far as to proscribe abortion during that period except when it is necessary to preserve the life or health of the mother.

Measured against these standards, Art. 1196 of the TEXAS PENAL CODE, in restricting legal abortions to those "procured or attempted by medical advice for the purpose of saving the life of the mother," sweeps too broadly. The statute makes no distinction between abortions performed early in pregnancy and those performed later, and it limits to a single reason, "saving" the mother's life, the legal justification for the procedure. The statute, therefore, cannot survive the constitutional attack made upon it here.

. . .

To summarize and to repeat:

1. A state criminal abortion statute of the current Texas type, that excepts from criminality only a *life-saving* procedure on behalf of the mother, without regard to pregnancy stage and without recognition of the other interests involved, is violative of the Due Process Clause of the Fourteenth Amendment.

(a) For the stage prior to approximately the end of the first trimester, the abortion decision and its effectuation must be left to the medical judgment of the pregnant woman's attending physician.

(b) For the stage subsequent to approximately the end of the first trimester, the State, in promoting its interest in the health of the mother, may, if it chooses, regulate the abortion procedure in ways that are reasonably related to maternal health.

(c) For the stage subsequent to viability the State, in promoting its interest in the potentiality of human life, may, if it chooses, regulate, and even proscribe, abortion except where it is necessary, in appropriate medical judgment, for the preservation of the life or health of the mother.

2. The State may define the term "physician," as it has been employed in the preceding numbered paragraphs of this [part] of this opinion, to mean

only a physician currently licensed by the State, and may proscribe any abortion by a person who is not a physician as so defined.

. . .

This holding, we feel, is consistent with the relative weights of the respective interests involved, with the lessons and example of medical and legal history, with the lenity of the common law, and with the demands of the profound problems of the present day. . . .

■ [CHIEF JUSTICE BURGER and JUSTICES DOUGLAS and STEWART each filed a concurring opinion. JUSTICES REHNQUIST and WHITE each filed a dissenting opinion.]

NOTES

1. Consider the alternative rationale for *Roe* set forth by Ruth Bader Ginsburg, *Some Thoughts on Autonomy and Equality in Relation to* Roe v. Wade, 63 N.C. L. REV. 375, 379–84 (1985):

> *Roe v. Wade,* in contrast to decisions involving explicit male/female classification, has occasioned searing criticism of the Court, over a decade of demonstrations, a stream of vituperative mail addressed to Justice Blackmun (the author of the opinion), annual proposals for overruling *Roe* by constitutional amendment, and a variety of measures in Congress and state legislatures to contain or curtail the decision. In 1973, when *Roe* issued, abortion law was in a state of change across the nation. There was a distinct trend in the states, noted by the Court, "toward liberalization of abortion statutes." Several states had adopted the American Law Institute's Model Penal Code approach setting out grounds on which abortion could be justified at any stage of pregnancy; most significantly, the Code included as a permissible ground preservation of the woman's physical or mental health. Four states—New York, Washington, Alaska, and Hawaii—permitted physicians to perform first-trimester abortions with virtually no restrictions. This movement in legislative arenas bore some resemblance to the law revision activity that eventually swept through the states establishing no-fault divorce as the national pattern.
>
> . . .
>
> [I]n my judgment, *Roe* ventured too far in the change it ordered. The sweep and detail of the opinion stimulated the mobilization of a right-to-life movement and an attendant reaction in Congress and state legislatures. In place of the trend "toward liberalization of abortion statutes" noted in *Roe*, legislatures adopted measures aimed at minimizing the impact of the 1973 rulings, including notification and consent requirements, prescriptions for the protection of fetal life, and bans on public expenditures for poor women's abortions.
>
> Professor Paul Freund explained where he thought the Court went astray in *Roe*, and I agree with his statement. The Court properly invalidated the Texas proscription, he indicated, because "[a] law that absolutely made criminal all kinds and forms of abortion could not stand up; it is not a reasonable accommodation of interests." If *Roe* had left off at that point and not adopted what Professor Freund called a "medical approach," physicians might have been less pleased with the decision, but the legislative trend might have continued in the direction in which it was headed in the early 1970s. "[S]ome of the bitter debate on the issue might have been averted," Professor Freund believed; "[t]he animus against the Court might at least have been diverted to the legislative halls." Overall, he thought that the *Roe* distinctions turning on trimesters and viability of the fetus illustrated a troublesome tendency of the modern Supreme Court under Chief Justices Burger and Warren "to specify by a kind of legislative code the one alternative pattern that will satisfy the Constitution."

... Academic criticism of *Roe,* charging the Court with reading its own values into the due process clause, might have been less pointed had the Court placed the woman alone, rather than the woman tied to her physician, at the center of its attention. . . .

. . .

I do not pretend that, if the Court had added a distinct sex discrimination theme to its medically oriented opinion, the storm *Roe* generated would have been less furious. I appreciate the intense divisions of opinion on the moral question and recognize that abortion today cannot fairly be described as nothing more than birth control delayed. The conflict, however, is not simply one between a fetus' interests and a woman's interests, narrowly conceived, nor is the overriding issue state versus private control of a woman's body for a span of nine months. Also in the balance is a woman's autonomous charge of her full life's course—as Professor Karst put it [Foreword, *Equal Citizenship Under the Fourteenth Amendment*, 91 Harv. L. Rev. 1, 57–59 (1977)], her ability to stand in relation to man, society, and the state as an independent self sustaining, equal citizen.

See also, Ruth Bader Ginsburg, *Speaking in a Judicial Voice*, 67 N.Y.U.L. Rev. 1185, 1198–1209 (1992).

2. In *Planned Parenthood of Central Missouri v. Danforth,* 428 U.S. 52 (1976), the Court, in an opinion by Justice Blackmun, held unconstitutional a requirement that the father must consent to any abortion, explaining:

We recognize, of course, that when a woman, with the approval of her physician but without the approval of her husband, decides to terminate her pregnancy, it could be said that she is acting unilaterally. The obvious fact is that when the wife and the husband disagree on this decision, the view of only one of the two marriage partners can prevail. Since it is the woman who physically bears the child and who is more directly and immediately affected by the pregnancy, as between the two, the balance weighs in her favor.

Id. at 71.

Planned Parenthood v. Casey

Supreme Court of the United States, 1992.
505 U.S. 833, 112 S.Ct. 2791, 120 L.Ed.2d 674.

■ Justice O'Connor, Justice Kennedy and Justice Souter announced the judgment of the Court and delivered the opinion of the Court with respect to Parts I, II, III, V–A, V–C, and VI, an opinion with respect to Part V–E, in which Justice Stevens joins, and an opinion with respect to Parts IV, V–B, and V–D.

[This suit challenged five provisions of the Pennsylvania Abortion Control Act of 1982 on their face: § 3205, which requires that a woman seeking an abortion give her informed consent prior to the abortion procedure, and specifies that she be provided with certain information at least 24 hours before the abortion is performed; § 3206, which mandates the informed consent of one parent for a minor to obtain an abortion but provides for a judicial bypass option if the minor does not wish to or cannot obtain a parent's consent; § 3209, which requires that, unless certain exceptions apply, a married woman seeking an abortion must sign a statement indicating that she has notified her husband of her intended abortion; § 3203, which defines a "medical emergency" that will excuse compliance with the foregoing requirements; and §§ 3207(b), 3214(a), and 3214(f), which impose certain reporting requirements on facilities that provide abortion services. The trial court held all the provisions unconstitutional. The appeals court struck down the husband notification provision but upheld the others.]

I.

Liberty finds no refuge in a jurisprudence of doubt. Yet 19 years after our holding that the Constitution protects a woman's right to terminate her pregnancy in its early stages, *Roe v. Wade*, 410 U.S. 113 (1973), that definition of liberty is still questioned. Joining the respondents as *amicus curiae*, the United States, as it has done in five other cases in the last decade, again asks us to overrule *Roe*.

. . .

After considering the fundamental constitutional questions resolved by *Roe*, principles of institutional integrity, and the rule of *stare decisis*, we are led to conclude this: the essential holding of *Roe v. Wade* should be retained and once again reaffirmed.

It must be stated at the outset and with clarity that *Roe*'s essential holding, the holding we reaffirm, has three parts. First is a recognition of the right of the woman to choose to have an abortion before viability and to obtain it without undue interference from the State. Before viability, the State's interests are not strong enough to support a prohibition of abortion or the imposition of a substantial obstacle to the woman's effective right to elect the procedure. Second is a confirmation of the State's power to restrict abortions after fetal viability, if the law contains exceptions for pregnancies which endanger a woman's life or health. And third is the principle that the State has legitimate interests from the outset of the pregnancy in protecting the health of the woman and the life of the fetus that may become a child. These principles do not contradict one another; and we adhere to each.

II.

Constitutional protection of the woman's decision to terminate her pregnancy derives from the Due Process Clause of the Fourteenth Amendment. . . .

. . .

It is also tempting . . . to suppose that the Due Process Clause protects only those practices, defined at the most specific level, that were protected against government interference by other rules of law when the Fourteenth Amendment was ratified. *See Michael H. v. Gerald D.*, 491 U.S. 110, 127–128, n.6 (1989) (opinion of SCALIA, J.). But such a view would be inconsistent with our law. It is a promise of the Constitution that there is a realm of personal liberty which the government may not enter. We have vindicated this principle before. Marriage is mentioned nowhere in the Bill of Rights and interracial marriage was illegal in most States in the 19th century, but the Court was no doubt correct in finding it to be an aspect of liberty protected against state interference by the substantive component of the Due Process Clause in *Loving v. Virginia*, 388 U.S. 1, 12 (1967) (relying, in an opinion for eight Justices, on the Due Process Clause). . . .

Neither the Bill of Rights nor the specific practices of States at the time of the adoption of the Fourteenth Amendment marks the outer limits of the substantive sphere of liberty which the Fourteenth Amendment protects. . . .

. . .

Men and women of good conscience can disagree, and we suppose some always shall disagree, about the profound moral and spiritual implications of terminating a pregnancy, even in its earliest stage. Some of us as individuals find abortion offensive to our most basic principles of morality, but that cannot control our decision. Our obligation is to define the liberty of all, not to mandate our own moral code. The underlying constitutional issue is whether the State can resolve these philosophic questions in such a definitive way that a woman lacks all choice in the matter, except perhaps in those rare circumstances in which the pregnancy is itself a danger to her own life or health, or is the result of rape or incest.

. . .

These considerations begin our analysis of the woman's interest in terminating her pregnancy but cannot end it, for this reason: though the abortion decision may originate within the zone of conscience and belief, it is more than a philosophic exercise. Abortion is a unique act. It is an act fraught with consequences for others: for the woman who must live with the implications of her decision; for the persons who perform and assist in the procedure; for the spouse, family, and society which must confront the knowledge that these procedures exist, procedures some deem nothing short of an act of violence against innocent human life; and, depending on one's beliefs, for the life or potential life that is aborted. Though abortion is conduct, it does not follow that the State is entitled to proscribe it in all instances. That is because the liberty of the woman is at stake in a sense unique to the human condition and so unique to the law. The mother who carries a child to full term is subject to anxieties, to physical constraints, to pain that only she must bear. That these sacrifices have from the beginning of the human race been endured by woman with a pride that ennobles her in the eyes of others and gives to the infant a bond of love cannot alone be grounds for the State to insist she make the sacrifice. Her suffering is too intimate and personal for the State to insist, without more, upon its own vision of the woman's role, however dominant that vision has been in the course of our history and our culture. The destiny of the woman must be shaped to a large extent on her own conception of her spiritual imperatives and her place in society.

It should be recognized, moreover, that in some critical respects the abortion decision is of the same character as the decision to use contraception, to which *Griswold v. Connecticut, Eisenstadt v. Baird,* and *Carey v. Population Services International* afford constitutional protection. We have no doubt as to the correctness of those decisions. . . .

. . .

III.

. . .

Although *Roe* has engendered opposition, it has in no sense proven "unworkable," representing as it does a simple limitation beyond which a state law is unenforceable. . . .

. . .

No evolution of legal principle has left *Roe*'s doctrinal footings weaker than they were in 1973. No development of constitutional law since the case was decided has implicitly or explicitly left *Roe* behind as a mere survivor of obsolete constitutional thinking.

It will be recognized, of course, that *Roe* stands at an intersection of two lines of decisions, but in whichever doctrinal category one reads the case, the result for present purposes will be the same. The *Roe* Court itself placed its holding in the succession of cases most prominently exemplified by *Griswold v. Connecticut*, 381 U.S. 479 (1965). When it is so seen, *Roe* is clearly in no jeopardy, since subsequent constitutional developments have neither disturbed, nor do they threaten to diminish, the scope of recognized protection accorded to the liberty relating to intimate relationships, the family, and decisions about whether or not to beget or bear a child. *See, e.g., Carey v. Population Services International*, 431 U.S. 678 (1977); *Moore v. East Cleveland*, 431 U.S. 494 (1977).

Roe, however, may be seen not only as an exemplar of *Griswold* liberty but as a rule (whether or not mistaken) of personal autonomy and bodily integrity, with doctrinal affinity to cases recognizing limits on governmental power to mandate medical treatment or to bar its rejection. If so, our cases since *Roe* accord with *Roe*'s view that a State's interest in the protection of life falls short of justifying any plenary override of individual liberty claims. *Cruzan v. Director, Mo. Dept. of Health*, 497 U.S. 261, 278 (1990); *cf., e.g., Riggins v. Nevada*, 504 U.S. 127 (1992); *Washington v. Harper*, 494 U.S. 210 (1990); *see also, e.g., Rochin v. California*, 342 U.S. 165 (1952); *Jacobson v. Massachusetts*, 197 U.S. 11 (1905).

Finally, one could classify *Roe* as *sui generis*. If the case is so viewed, then there clearly has been no erosion of its central determination. . . .

We have seen how time has overtaken some of *Roe*'s factual assumptions: advances in maternal health care allow for abortions safe to the mother later in pregnancy than was true in 1973 and advances in neonatal care have advanced viability to a point somewhat earlier. But these facts go only to the scheme of time limits on the realization of competing interests, and the divergences from the factual premises of 1973 have no bearing on the validity of *Roe*'s central holding, that viability marks the earliest point at which the State's interest in fetal life is constitutionally adequate to justify a legislative ban on nontherapeutic abortions. The soundness or unsoundness of that constitutional judgment in no sense turns on whether viability occurs at approximately 28 weeks, as was usual at the time of *Roe*, at 23 to 24 weeks, as it sometimes does today, or at some moment even slightly earlier in pregnancy, as it may if fetal respiratory capacity can somehow be enhanced in the future. Whenever it may occur, the attainment of viability may continue to serve as the critical fact, just as it has done since *Roe* was decided; which is to say that no change in *Roe*'s factual underpinning has left its central holding obsolete, and none supports an argument for overruling it.

The sum of the precedential enquiry to this point shows *Roe*'s underpinnings unweakened in any way affecting its central holding. While it has engendered disapproval, it has not been unworkable. An entire generation has come of age free to assume *Roe*'s concept of liberty in defining the capacity of women to act in society, and to make reproductive decisions; no erosion of principle going to liberty or personal autonomy has left *Roe*'s central holding a doctrinal remnant; *Roe* portends no developments at odds with other precedent for the analysis of personal liberty; and no changes of fact have rendered viability more or less appropriate as the point at which the balance of interests tips. Within the bounds of normal *stare decisis* analysis, then, and subject to the considerations on which it customarily turns, the stronger argument is for affirming *Roe*'s central holding, with whatever degree of personal reluctance any of us may have, not for overruling it.

In a less significant case, *stare decisis* analysis could, and would, stop at the point we have reached. But the sustained and widespread debate *Roe* has provoked calls for some comparison between that case and others of comparable dimension that have responded to national controversies and taken on the impress of the controversies addressed. Only two such decisional lines from the past century present themselves for examination, and in each instance the result reached by the Court accorded with the principles we apply today.

The first example is that line of cases identified with *Lochner v. New York*, 198 U.S. 45(1905), which imposed substantive limitations on legislation limiting economic autonomy in favor of health and welfare regulation, adopting, in Justice Holmes's view, the theory of laissez-faire.... The *Lochner* decisions were exemplified by *Adkins v. Children's Hospital of District of Columbia*, 261 U.S. 525 (1923), in which this Court held it to be an infringement of constitutionally protected liberty of contract to require the employers of adult women to satisfy minimum wage standards. Fourteen years later, *West Coast Hotel Co. v. Parrish*, 300 U.S. 379 (1937), signaled the demise of *Lochner* by overruling *Adkins*. In the meantime, the Depression had come and, with it, the lesson that seemed unmistakable to most people by 1937, that the interpretation of contractual freedom protected in *Adkins* rested on fundamentally false factual assumptions about the capacity of a relatively unregulated market to satisfy minimal levels of human welfare. As Justice Jackson wrote of the constitutional crisis of 1937 shortly before he came on the bench: "The older world of *laissez faire* was recognized everywhere outside the Court to be dead." THE STRUGGLE FOR JUDICIAL SUPREMACY 85 (1941). The facts upon which the earlier case had premised a constitutional resolution of social controversy had proven to be untrue, and history's demonstration of their untruth not only justified but required the new choice of constitutional principle that *West Coast Hotel* announced. Of course, it was true that the Court lost something by its misperception, or its lack of prescience, and the Court-packing crisis only magnified the loss; but the clear demonstration that the facts of economic life were different from those previously assumed warranted the repudiation of the old law.

The second comparison that 20th century history invites is with the cases employing the separate-but-equal rule for applying the Fourteenth Amendment's equal protection guarantee. They began with *Plessy v. Ferguson*, 163 U.S. 537 (1896), holding that legislatively mandated racial segregation in public transportation works no denial of equal protection, rejecting the argument that racial separation enforced by the legal machinery of American society treats the black race as inferior. The *Plessy* Court considered "the underlying fallacy of the plaintiff's argument to consist in the assumption that the enforced separation of the two races stamps the colored race with a badge of inferiority. If this be so, it is not by reason of anything found in the act, but solely because the colored race chooses to put that construction upon it." Whether, as a matter of historical fact, the Justices in the *Plessy* majority believed this or not, this understanding of the implication of segregation was the stated justification for the Court's opinion. But this understanding of the facts and the rule it was stated to justify were repudiated in *Brown v. Board of Education*, 347 U.S. 483 (1954) (*Brown I*). As one commentator observed, the question before the Court in *Brown* was "whether discrimination inheres in that segregation which is imposed by law in the twentieth century in certain specific states in the American Union. And that question has meaning and can find an answer only on the ground of history and of common knowledge about the facts of life in the times and places aforesaid." Black, *The Lawfulness of the Segregation Decisions*, 69 YALE L. J. 421, 427 (1960).

The Court in *Brown* addressed these facts of life by observing that whatever may have been the understanding in *Plessy*'s time of the power of segregation to stigmatize those who were segregated with a "badge of inferiority," it was clear by 1954 that legally sanctioned segregation had just such an effect, to the point that racially separate public educational facilities were deemed inherently unequal. Society's understanding of the facts upon which a constitutional ruling was sought in 1954 was thus fundamentally different from the basis claimed for the decision in 1896. While we think *Plessy* was wrong the day it was decided, we must also recognize that the *Plessy* Court's explanation for its decision was so clearly at odds with the facts apparent to the Court in 1954 that the decision to reexamine *Plessy* was on this ground alone not only justified but required.

West Coast Hotel and *Brown* each rested on facts, or an understanding of facts, changed from those which furnished the claimed justifications for the earlier constitutional resolutions. Each case was comprehensible as the Court's response to facts that the country could understand, or had come to understand already, but which the Court of an earlier day, as its own declarations disclosed, had not been able to perceive. As the decisions were thus comprehensible they were also defensible, not merely as the victories of one doctrinal school over another by dint of numbers (victories though they were), but as applications of constitutional principle to facts as they had not been seen by the Court before. In constitutional adjudication as elsewhere in life, changed circumstances may impose new obligations, and the thoughtful part of the Nation could accept each decision to overrule a prior case as a response to the Court's constitutional duty.

Because the cases before us present no such occasion it could be seen as no such response. Because neither the factual underpinnings of *Roe*'s central holding nor our understanding of it has changed (and because no other indication of weakened precedent has been shown), the Court could not pretend to be reexamining the prior law with any justification beyond a present doctrinal disposition to come out differently from the Court of 1973. To overrule prior law for no other reason than that would run counter to the view repeated in our cases, that a decision to overrule should rest on some special reason over and above the belief that a prior case was wrongly decided....

The examination of the conditions justifying the repudiation of *Adkins* by *West Coast Hotel* and *Plessy* by *Brown* is enough to suggest the terrible price that would have been paid if the Court had not overruled as it did. In the present cases, however, as our analysis to this point makes clear, the terrible price would be paid for overruling. Our analysis would not be complete, however, without explaining why overruling *Roe*'s central holding would not only reach an unjustifiable result under principles of *stare decisis*, but would seriously weaken the Court's capacity to exercise the judicial power and to function as the Supreme Court of a Nation dedicated to the rule of law....

The root of American governmental power is revealed most clearly in the instance of the power conferred by the Constitution upon the Judiciary of the United States and specifically upon this Court. As Americans of each succeeding generation are rightly told, the Court cannot buy support for its decisions by spending money and, except to a minor degree, it cannot independently coerce obedience to its decrees. The Court's power lies, rather, in its legitimacy, a product of substance and perception that shows itself in the people's acceptance of the Judiciary as fit to determine what the Nation's law means and to declare what it demands.

. . .

... Where, in the performance of its judicial duties, the Court decides a case in such a way as to resolve the sort of intensely divisive controversy reflected in *Roe* and those rare, comparable cases, its decision has a dimension that the resolution of the normal case does not carry. It is the dimension present whenever the Court's interpretation of the Constitution calls the contending sides of a national controversy to end their national division by accepting a common mandate rooted in the Constitution.

The Court is not asked to do this very often, having thus addressed the Nation only twice in our lifetime, in the decisions of *Brown* and *Roe*. But when the Court does act in this way, its decision requires an equally rare precedential force to counter the inevitable efforts to overturn it and to thwart its implementation. Some of those efforts may be mere unprincipled emotional reactions; others may proceed from principles worthy of profound respect. But whatever the premises of opposition may be, only the most convincing justification under accepted standards of precedent could suffice to demonstrate that a later decision overruling the first was anything but a surrender to political pressure, and an unjustified repudiation of the principle on which the Court staked its authority in the first instance. So to overrule under fire in the absence of the most compelling reason to reexamine a watershed decision would subvert the Court's legitimacy beyond any serious question....

. . .

... A decision to overrule *Roe*'s essential holding under the existing circumstances would address error, if error there was, at the cost of both profound and unnecessary damage to the Court's legitimacy, and to the Nation's commitment to the rule of law. It is therefore imperative to adhere to the essence of *Roe*'s original decision, and we do so today.

IV.

... We conclude that the basic decision in *Roe* was based on a constitutional analysis which we cannot now repudiate. The woman's liberty is not so unlimited, however, that from the outset the State cannot show its concern for the life of the unborn, and at a later point in fetal development the State's interest in life has sufficient force so that the right of the woman to terminate the pregnancy can be restricted.

. . .

We conclude the line should be drawn at viability, so that before that time the woman has a right to choose to terminate her pregnancy. We adhere to this principle for two reasons. First, as we have said, is the doctrine of *stare decisis*. ...

The second reason is that the concept of viability, as we noted in *Roe*, is the time at which there is a realistic possibility of maintaining and nourishing a life outside the womb, so that the independent existence of the second life can in reason and all fairness be the object of state protection that now overrides the rights of the woman....

The woman's right to terminate her pregnancy before viability is the most central principle of *Roe v. Wade*. It is a rule of law and a component of liberty we cannot renounce.

On the other side of the equation is the interest of the State in the protection of potential life....

... [I]t must be remembered that *Roe v. Wade* speaks with clarity in establishing not only the woman's liberty but also the State's "important and legitimate interest in potential life." That portion of the decision in *Roe* has been given too little acknowledgement and implementation by the Court in its subsequent cases....

. . .

We reject the trimester framework, which we do not consider to be part of the essential holding of *Roe*. Measures aimed at ensuring that a woman's choice contemplates the consequences for the fetus do not necessarily interfere with the right recognized in *Roe*, although those measures have been found to be inconsistent with the rigid trimester framework announced in that case. A logical reading of the central holding in *Roe* itself, and a necessary reconciliation of the liberty of the woman and the interest of the State in promoting prenatal life, require, in our view, that we abandon the trimester framework as a rigid prohibition on all previability regulation aimed at the protection of fetal life. The trimester framework suffers from these basic flaws: in its formulation it misconceives the nature of the pregnant woman's interest; and in practice it undervalues the State's interest in potential life, as recognized in *Roe*.

As our jurisprudence relating to all liberties save perhaps abortion has recognized, not every law which makes a right more difficult to exercise is, *ipso facto*, an infringement of that right....

. . .

... Not all governmental intrusion is of necessity unwarranted; and that brings us to the other basic flaw in the trimester framework: even in *Roe*'s terms, in practice it undervalues the State's interest in the potential life within the woman.

. . .

... Not all burdens on the right to decide whether to terminate a pregnancy will be undue. In our view, the undue burden standard is the appropriate means of reconciling the State's interest with the woman's constitutionally protected liberty.

. . .

A finding of an undue burden is shorthand for the conclusion that a state regulation has the purpose or effect of placing a substantial obstacle in the path of a woman seeking an abortion of a nonviable fetus. A statute with this purpose is invalid because the means chosen by the State to further the interest in potential life must be calculated to inform the woman's free choice, not hinder it. And a statute which, while furthering the interest in potential life or some other valid state interest, has the effect of placing a substantial obstacle in the path of a woman's choice cannot be considered a permissible means of serving its legitimate ends.... Understood another way, we answer the question, left open in previous opinions discussing the undue burden formulation, whether a law designed to further the State's interest in fetal life which imposes an undue burden on the woman's decision before fetal viability could be constitutional. The answer is no.

Some guiding principles should emerge. What is at stake is the woman's right to make the ultimate decision, not a right to be insulated from all others in doing so. Regulations which do no more than create a structural mechanism by which the State, or the parent or guardian of a minor, may express profound respect for the life of the unborn are permitted, if they are not a substantial obstacle to the woman's exercise of the right to choose. Unless it has that effect on her right of choice, a state measure designed to persuade her to choose childbirth over abortion will be upheld if reasonably related to that goal. Regulations designed to foster the health of a woman seeking an abortion are valid if they do not constitute an undue burden.

Even when jurists reason from shared premises, some disagreement is inevitable. That is to be expected in the application of any legal standard which must accommodate life's complexity. We do not expect it to be otherwise with respect to the undue burden standard. We give this summary:

(a) To protect the central right recognized by *Roe v. Wade* while at the same time accommodating the State's profound interest in potential life, we will employ the undue burden analysis as explained in this opinion. An undue burden exists, and therefore a provision of law is invalid, if its purpose or effect is to place a substantial obstacle in the path of a woman seeking an abortion before the fetus attains viability.

(b) We reject the rigid trimester framework of *Roe v. Wade*. To promote the State's profound interest in potential life, throughout pregnancy the State may take measures to ensure that the woman's choice is informed, and measures designed to advance this interest will not be invalidated as long as their purpose is to persuade the woman to choose childbirth over abortion. These measures must not be an undue burden on the right.

(c) As with any medical procedure, the State may enact regulations to further the health or safety of a woman seeking an abortion. Unnecessary health regulations that have the purpose or effect of presenting a substantial obstacle to a woman seeking an abortion impose an undue burden on the right.

(d) Our adoption of the undue burden analysis does not disturb the central holding of *Roe v. Wade*, and we reaffirm that holding. Regardless of whether exceptions are made for particular circumstances, a State may not prohibit any woman from making the ultimate decision to terminate her pregnancy before viability.

(e) We also reaffirm *Roe*'s holding that "subsequent to viability, the State in promoting its interest in the potentiality of human life may, if it chooses, regulate, and even proscribe, abortion except where it is necessary, in appropriate medical judgment, for the preservation of the life or health of the mother." *Roe v. Wade*, 410 U.S., at 164–165.

These principles control our assessment of the Pennsylvania statute, and we now turn to the issue of the validity of its challenged provisions.

V.

. . .

A.

Because it is central to the operation of various other requirements, we begin with the statute's definition of medical emergency. Under the statute, a medical emergency is

> [t]hat condition which, on the basis of the physician's good faith clinical judgment, so complicates the medical condition of a pregnant woman as to necessitate the immediate abortion of her pregnancy to avert her

death or for which a delay will create serious risk of substantial and irreversible impairment of a major bodily function.

Petitioners argue that the definition is too narrow, contending that it forecloses the possibility of an immediate abortion despite some significant health risks. If the contention were correct, we would be required to invalidate the restrictive operation of the provision, for the essential holding of *Roe* forbids a State from interfering with a woman's choice to undergo an abortion procedure if continuing her pregnancy would constitute a threat to her health.

The District Court found that there were three serious conditions which would not be covered by the statute: preeclampsia, inevitable abortion, and premature ruptured membrane. Yet, as the Court of Appeals observed, it is undisputed that under some circumstances each of these conditions could lead to an illness with substantial and irreversible consequences. While the definition could be interpreted in an unconstitutional manner, the Court of Appeals construed the phrase "serious risk" to include those circumstances. It stated: "[W]e read the medical emergency exception as intended by the Pennsylvania legislature to assure that compliance with its abortion regulations would not in any way pose a significant threat to the life or health of a woman." . . . [W]e have said that we will defer to lower court interpretations of state law unless they amount to "plain" error. . . . We adhere to that course today, and conclude that, as construed by the Court of Appeals, the medical emergency definition imposes no undue burden on a woman's abortion right.

B.

We next consider the informed consent requirement. Except in a medical emergency, the statute requires that at least 24 hours before performing an abortion a physician inform the woman of the nature of the procedure, the health risks of the abortion and of childbirth, and the "probable gestational age of the unborn child." The physician or a qualified nonphysician must inform the woman of the availability of printed materials published by the State describing the fetus and providing information about medical assistance for childbirth, information about child support from the father, and a list of agencies which provide adoption and other services as alternatives to abortion. An abortion may not be performed unless the woman certifies in writing that she has been informed of the availability of these printed materials and has been provided them if she chooses to view them.

Our prior decisions establish that as with any medical procedure, the State may require a woman to give her written informed consent to an abortion. In this respect, the statute is unexceptional. Petitioners challenge the statute's definition of informed consent because it includes the provision of specific information by the doctor and the mandatory 24–hour waiting period. The conclusions reached by a majority of the Justices in the separate opinions filed today and the undue burden standard adopted in this opinion require us to overrule in part some of the Court's past decisions, decisions driven by the trimester framework's prohibition of all previability regulations designed to further the State's interest in fetal life.

In *Akron I*, 462 U.S. 416 (1983), we invalidated an ordinance which required that a woman seeking an abortion be provided by her physician with specific information "designed to influence the woman's informed choice between abortion or childbirth." *Id.*, at 444. As we later described the

Akron I holding in *Thornburgh v. American College of Obstetricians and Gynecologists*, 476 U.S. at 762, there were two purported flaws in the Akron ordinance: the information was designed to dissuade the woman from having an abortion and the ordinance imposed "a rigid requirement that a specific body of information be given in all cases, irrespective of the particular needs of the patient. . . ." *Ibid.*

To the extent *Akron I* and *Thornburgh* find a constitutional violation when the government requires, as it does here, the giving of truthful, nonmisleading information about the nature of the procedure, the attendant health risks and those of childbirth, and the "probable gestational age" of the fetus, those cases go too far, are inconsistent with *Roe*'s acknowledgment of an important interest in potential life, and are overruled. . . . [We have recognized] a substantial government interest justifying a requirement that a woman be apprised of the health risks of abortion and childbirth. It cannot be questioned that psychological well-being is a facet of health. Nor can it be doubted that most women considering an abortion would deem the impact on the fetus relevant, if not dispositive, to the decision. In attempting to ensure that a woman apprehend the full consequences of her decision, the State furthers the legitimate purpose of reducing the risk that a woman may elect an abortion, only to discover later, with devastating psychological consequences, that her decision was not fully informed. If the information the State requires to be made available to the woman is truthful and not misleading, the requirement may be permissible.

We also see no reason why the State may not require doctors to inform a woman seeking an abortion of the availability of materials relating to the consequences to the fetus, even when those consequences have no direct relation to her health. . . . We conclude . . . that informed choice need not be defined in such narrow terms that all considerations of the effect on the fetus are made irrelevant. As we have made clear, we depart from the holdings of *Akron I* and *Thornburgh* to the extent that we permit a State to further its legitimate goal of protecting the life of the unborn by enacting legislation aimed at ensuring a decision that is mature and informed, even when in so doing the State expresses a preference for childbirth over abortion. In short, requiring that the woman be informed of the availability of information relating to fetal development and the assistance available should she decide to carry the pregnancy to full term is a reasonable measure to ensure an informed choice, one which might cause the woman to choose childbirth over abortion. This requirement cannot be considered a substantial obstacle to obtaining an abortion, and, it follows, there is no undue burden.

.   .   .

Our analysis of Pennsylvania's 24–hour waiting period between the provision of the information deemed necessary to informed consent and the performance of an abortion under the undue burden standard requires us to reconsider the premise behind the decision in *Akron I* invalidating a parallel requirement. In *Akron I* we said: "Nor are we convinced that the State's legitimate concern that the woman's decision be informed is reasonably served by requiring a 24–hour delay as a matter of course." We consider that conclusion to be wrong. The idea that important decisions will be more informed and deliberate if they follow some period of reflection does not strike us as unreasonable, particularly where the statute directs that important information become part of the background of the decision. The statute, as construed by the Court of Appeals, permits avoidance of the waiting period in the event of a medical emergency and the record evidence shows that in the vast majority of cases, a 24–hour delay does not create any appreciable health risk. In theory, at least, the waiting period is a reasonable measure to implement the State's interest in protecting the life of the unborn, a measure that does not amount to an undue burden.

Whether the mandatory 24–hour waiting period is nonetheless invalid because in practice it is a substantial obstacle to a woman's choice to terminate her pregnancy is a closer question. The findings of fact by the District Court indicate that because of the distances many women must travel to reach an abortion provider, the practical effect will often be a delay of much more than a day because the waiting period requires that a woman seeking an abortion make at least two visits to the doctor. The District Court also found that in many instances this will increase the exposure of women seeking abortions to "the harassment and hostility of anti-abortion protestors demonstrating outside a clinic." As a result, the District Court found that for those women who have the fewest financial resources, those who must travel long distances, and those who have difficulty explaining their whereabouts to husbands, employers, or others, the 24–hour waiting period will be "particularly burdensome."

These findings are troubling in some respects, but they do not demonstrate that the waiting period constitutes an undue burden. We do not doubt that, as the District Court held, the waiting period has the effect of "increasing the cost and risk of delay of abortions," but the District Court did not conclude that the increased costs and potential delays amount to substantial obstacles. Rather, applying the trimester framework's strict prohibition of all regulation designed to promote the State's interest in potential life before viability, the District Court concluded that the waiting period does not further the State "interest in maternal health" and "infringes the physician's discretion to exercise sound medical judgment." Yet, as we have stated, under the undue burden standard a State is permitted to enact persuasive measures which favor childbirth over abortion, even if those measures do not further a health interest. And while the waiting period does limit a physician's discretion, that is not, standing alone, a reason to invalidate it. In light of the construction given the statute's definition of medical emergency by the Court of Appeals, and the District Court's findings, we cannot say that the waiting period imposes a real health risk.

We also disagree with the District Court's conclusion that the "particularly burdensome" effects of the waiting period on some women require its invalidation. A particular burden is not of necessity a substantial obstacle. Whether a burden falls on a particular group is a distinct inquiry from whether it is a substantial obstacle even as to the women in that group. And the District Court did not conclude that the waiting period is such an obstacle even for the women who are most burdened by it. Hence, on the record before us, and in the context of this facial challenge, we are not convinced that the 24–hour waiting period constitutes an undue burden.

We are left with the argument that the various aspects of the informed consent requirement are unconstitutional because they place barriers in the way of abortion on demand. Even the broadest reading of *Roe,* however, has not suggested that there is a constitutional right to abortion on demand. Rather, the right protected by *Roe* is a right to decide to terminate a pregnancy free of undue interference by the State. Because the informed consent requirement facilitates the wise exercise of that right it cannot be classified as an interference with the right *Roe* protects. The informed consent requirement is not an undue burden on that right.

C.

Section 3209 of Pennsylvania's abortion law provides, except in cases of medical emergency, that no physician shall perform an abortion on a married woman without receiving a signed statement from the woman that she has notified her spouse that she is about to undergo an abortion. The woman has the option of providing an alternative signed statement certifying that her husband is not the man who impregnated her; that her husband could not be located; that the pregnancy is the result of spousal sexual assault which she has reported; or that the woman believes that notifying her husband will cause him or someone else to inflict bodily injury upon her. A physician who performs an abortion on a married woman without receiving the appropriate signed statement will have his or her license revoked, and is liable to the husband for damages.

The District Court heard the testimony of numerous expert witnesses, and made detailed findings of fact regarding the effect of this statute....

. . .

... "Studies ... suggest that from one-fifth to one-third of all women will be physically assaulted by a partner or ex-partner during their lifetime." AMA COUNCIL ON SCIENTIFIC AFFAIRS, VIOLENCE AGAINST WOMEN 7 (1991). Thus on an average day in the United States, nearly 11,000 women are severely assaulted by their male partners. Many of these incidents involve sexual assault. In families where wife-beating takes place, moreover, child abuse is often present as well.

... Psychological abuse, particularly forced social and economic isolation of women, is also common. L. WALKER, THE BATTERED WOMAN SYNDROME 27–28 (1984). Many victims of domestic violence remain with their abusers, perhaps because they perceive no superior alternative. Many abused women who find temporary refuge in shelters return to their husbands, in large part because they have no other source of income. Returning to one's abuser can be dangerous. Recent Federal Bureau of Investigation statistics disclose that 8.8% of all homicide victims in the United States are killed by their spouse. Thirty percent of female homicide victims are killed by their male partners. *Domestic Violence: Terrorism in the Home, Hearing before the Subcommittee on Children, Family, Drugs and Alcoholism of the Senate Committee on Labor and Human Resources*, 101st Cong., 2d Sess., 3 (1990).

The limited research that has been conducted with respect to notifying one's husband about an abortion, although involving samples too small to be representative, also supports the District Court's findings of fact. The vast majority of women notify their male partners of their decision to obtain an abortion. In many cases in which married women do not notify their husbands, the pregnancy is the result of an extramarital affair. Where the husband is the father, the primary reason women do not notify their husbands is that the husband and wife are experiencing marital difficulties, often accompanied by incidents of violence. Ryan & Plutzer, *When Married Women Have Abortions: Spousal Notification and Marital Interaction*, 51 J. MARRIAGE & THE FAMILY 41, 44 (1989).

This information and the District Court's findings reinforce what common sense would suggest. In well-functioning marriages, spouses discuss important intimate decisions such as whether to bear a child. But there are millions of women in this country who are the victims of regular physical and psychological abuse at the hands of their husbands. Should these women become pregnant, they may have very good reasons for not wishing to inform their husbands of their decision to obtain an abortion. Many may have justifiable fears of physical abuse, but may be no less fearful of the consequences of reporting prior abuse to the Commonwealth of Pennsylvania. Many may have a reasonable fear that notifying their husbands will provoke further instances of child abuse; these women are not exempt from § 3209's notification requirement. Many may fear devastating forms of psychological abuse from their husbands, including verbal harassment, threats of future violence, the destruction of possessions, physical confinement to the home, the withdrawal of financial support, or the disclosure of the abortion to family and friends. These methods of psychological abuse may act as even more of a deterrent to notification than the possibility of physical violence, but women who are the victims of the abuse are not exempt from § 3209's notification requirement. And many women who are pregnant as a result of sexual assaults by their husbands will be unable to avail themselves of the exception for spousal sexual assault, § 3209(b)(3), because the exception requires that the women have notified law enforcement authorities within 90 days of the assault, and her husband will be notified of her report once an investigation begins. § 3128(c). If anything in this field is certain, it is that victims of spousal sexual assault are extremely reluctant to report the abuse to the government; hence, a great many spousal rape victims will not be exempt from the notification requirement imposed by § 3209.

The spousal notification requirement is thus likely to prevent a significant number of women from obtaining an abortion. It does not merely make abortions a little more difficult or expensive to obtain; for many women, it will impose a substantial obstacle. We must not blind ourselves to the fact that the significant number of women who fear for their safety and the safety of their children are likely to be deterred from procuring an abortion as surely as if the Commonwealth had outlawed abortion in all cases.

Respondents attempt to avoid the conclusion that § 3209 is invalid by pointing out that it imposes almost no burden at all for the vast majority of women seeking abortions. They begin by noting that only about 20 percent of the women who obtain abortions are married. They then note that of these women about 95 percent notify their husbands of their own volition. Thus, respondents argue, the effects of § 3209 are felt by only one percent of the women who obtain abortions. Respondents argue that since some of these women will be able to notify their husbands without adverse consequences or will qualify for one of the exceptions, the statute affects fewer than one percent of women seeking abortions. For this reason, it is asserted, the statute cannot be invalid on its face. We disagree with respondents' basic method of analysis.

The analysis does not end with the one percent of women upon whom the statute operates; it begins there. Legislation is measured for consistency with the Constitution by its impact on those whose conduct it affects.... The proper focus of constitutional inquiry is the group for whom the law is a restriction, not the group for whom the law is irrelevant.

... The unfortunate yet persisting conditions we document above will mean that in a large fraction of the cases in which § 3209 is relevant, it will operate as a substantial obstacle to a woman's choice to undergo an abortion. It is an undue burden, and therefore invalid.

This conclusion is in no way inconsistent with our decisions upholding parental notification or consent requirements. Those enactments, and our judgment that they are constitutional, are based on the quite reasonable assumption that minors will benefit from consultation with their parents and that children will often not realize that their parents have their best interests at heart. We cannot adopt a parallel assumption about adult women.

. . . If . . . [this case] concerned a State's ability to require the mother to notify the father before taking some action with respect to a living child raised by both, therefore, it would be reasonable to conclude as a general matter that the father's interest in the welfare of the child and the mother's interest are equal.

Before birth, however, the issue takes on a very different cast. It is an inescapable biological fact that state regulation with respect to the child a woman is carrying will have a far greater impact on the mother's liberty than on the father's. The effect of state regulation on a woman's protected liberty is doubly deserving of scrutiny in such a case, as the State has touched not only upon the private sphere of the family but upon the very bodily integrity of the pregnant woman. *Cf. Cruzan v. Director, Missouri Dept. of Health*, 497 U.S., at 281. The Court has held that "when the wife and the husband disagree on this decision, the view of only one of the two marriage partners can prevail. Inasmuch as it is the woman who physically bears the child and who is the more directly and immediately affected by the pregnancy, as between the two, the balance weighs in her favor." This conclusion rests upon the basic nature of marriage and the nature of our Constitution: "[T]he marital couple is not an independent entity with a mind and heart of its own, but an association of two individuals each with a separate intellectual and emotional makeup. If the right of privacy means anything, it is the right of the *individual*, married or single, to be free from unwarranted governmental intrusion into matters so fundamentally affecting a person as the decision whether to bear or beget a child." The Constitution protects individuals, men and women alike, from unjustified state interference, even when that interference is enacted into law for the benefit of their spouses.

. . .

. . . For the great many women who are victims of abuse inflicted by their husbands, or whose children are the victims of such abuse, a spousal notice requirement enables the husband to wield an effective veto over his wife's decision. Whether the prospect of notification itself deters such women from seeking abortions, or whether the husband, through physical force or psychological pressure or economic coercion, prevents his wife from obtaining an abortion until it is too late, the notice requirement will often be tantamount to the veto found unconstitutional in *Danforth*. The women most affected by this law—those who most reasonably fear the consequences of notifying their husbands that they are pregnant—are in the gravest danger.

The husband's interest in the life of the child his wife is carrying does not permit the State to empower him with this troubling degree of authority over his wife. . . . A State may not give to a man the kind of dominion over his wife that parents exercise over their children.

Section 3209 embodies a view of marriage consonant with the common-law status of married women but repugnant to our present understanding of marriage and of the nature of the rights secured by the Constitution. Women do not lose their constitutionally protected liberty when they marry. The Constitution protects all individuals, male or female, married or unmarried, from the abuse of governmental power, even where that power is employed for the supposed benefit of a member of the individual's family. These considerations confirm our conclusion that § 3209 is invalid.

D.

We next consider the parental consent provision. Except in a medical emergency, an unemancipated young woman under 18 may not obtain an abortion unless she and one of her parents (or guardian) provides informed consent as defined above. If neither a parent nor a guardian provides consent, a court may authorize the performance of an abortion upon a determination that the young woman is mature and capable of giving informed consent and has in fact given her informed consent, or that an abortion would be in her best interests.

. . . Our cases establish, and we reaffirm today, that a State may require a minor seeking an abortion to obtain the consent of a parent or guardian, provided that there is an adequate judicial bypass procedure. . . .

The only argument made by petitioners respecting this provision and to which our prior decisions do not speak is the contention that the parental consent requirement is invalid because it requires informed parental consent. For the most part, petitioners' argument is a reprise of their argument with respect to the informed consent requirement in general, and we reject it for the reasons given above. . . .

. . .

VI

Our Constitution is a covenant running from the first generation of Americans to us and then to future generations. It is a coherent succession. Each generation must learn anew that the Constitution's written terms embody ideas and aspirations that must survive more ages than one. We accept our responsibility not to retreat from interpreting the full meaning of the covenant in light of all of our precedents. We invoke it once again to define the freedom guaranteed by the Constitution's own promise, the promise of liberty.

. . .

■ Justice Blackmun, concurring in part, concurring in the judgment in part, and dissenting in part.

I join Parts I, II, III, V–A, V–C, and VI of the joint opinion of Justices O'Connor, Kennedy and Souter, *ante.*

Three years ago, in *Webster v. Reproductive Health Services*, 492 U.S. 490 (1989), four Members of this Court appeared poised to "cas[t] into darkness the hopes and visions of every woman in this country" who had come to believe that the Constitution guaranteed her the right to reproductive choice. See *id.*, at 499 (plurality opinion of Rehnquist, C. J., joined by White and Kennedy, JJ.); *id.*, at 532 (Scalia, J., concurring in part and concurring in judgment). All that remained between the promise of *Roe* and the darkness of the plurality was a single, flickering flame. Decisions since *Webster* gave little reason to hope that this flame would cast much light. *See, e. g., Ohio v. Akron Center for Reproductive Health*, 497 U.S. 502, 524 (1990) (Blackmun, J., dissenting). But now, just when so many expected the darkness to fall, the flame has grown bright.

I do not underestimate the significance of today's joint opinion. Yet I remain steadfast in my belief that the right to reproductive choice is entitled to the full protection afforded by this Court before *Webster*. And I fear for the darkness as four Justices anxiously await the single vote necessary to extinguish the light.

■ JUSTICE SCALIA, with whom THE CHIEF JUSTICE, JUSTICE WHITE, and JUSTICE THOMAS join, concurring in the judgment in part and dissenting in part.

... The States may, if they wish, permit abortion on demand, but the Constitution does not *require* them to do so. The permissibility of abortion, and the limitations upon it, are to be resolved like most important questions in our democracy: by citizens trying to persuade one another and then voting....

... I reach that conclusion not because of anything so exalted as my views concerning the "concept of existence, of meaning, of the universe, and of the mystery of human life." Rather, I reach it for the same reason I reach the conclusion that bigamy is not constitutionally protected—because of two simple facts: (1) the Constitution says absolutely nothing about it, and (2) the longstanding traditions of American society have permitted it to be legally proscribed.

· · ·

... [A]pplying the rational basis test, I would uphold the Pennsylvania statute in its entirety....

· · ·

The emptiness of the "reasoned judgment" that produced *Roe* is displayed in plain view by the fact that, after more than 19 years of effort by some of the brightest (and most determined) legal minds in the country, after more than 10 cases upholding abortion rights in this Court, and after dozens upon dozens of *amicus* briefs submitted in this and other cases, the best the Court can do to explain how it is that the word "liberty" *must* be thought to include the right to destroy human fetuses is to rattle off a collection of adjectives that simply decorate a value judgment and conceal a political choice. The right to abort, we are told, inheres in "liberty" because it is among "a person's most basic decisions"; it involves a "most intimate and personal choic[e]"; it is "central to personal dignity and autonomy"; it "originate[s] within the zone of conscience and belief"; it is "too intimate and personal" for state interference; it reflects "intimate views" of a "deep, personal character"; it involves "intimate relationships," and notions of "personal autonomy and bodily integrity"; and it concerns a particularly "'important decisio[n]'". But it is obvious to anyone applying "reasoned judgment" that the same adjectives can be applied to many forms of conduct that this Court ... has held are *not* entitled to constitutional protection—because, like abortion, they are forms of conduct that have long been criminalized in American society. Those adjectives might be applied, for example, to homosexual sodomy, polygamy, adult incest, and suicide, all of which are equally "intimate" and "deep[ly] personal" decisions involving "personal autonomy and bodily integrity," and all of which can constitutionally be proscribed because it is our unquestionable constitutional tradition that they are proscribable. It is not reasoned judgment that supports the Court's decision; only personal predilection....

· · ·

... [T]he joint opinion announces that "it is important to clarify what is meant by an undue burden." I certainly agree with that, but I do not agree that the joint opinion succeeds in the announced endeavor. To the contrary, its efforts at clarification make clear only that the standard is inherently manipulable and will prove hopelessly unworkable in practice.

The joint opinion explains that a state regulation imposes an "undue burden" if it "has the purpose or effect of placing a substantial obstacle in the path of a woman seeking an abortion of a nonviable fetus." An obstacle is "substantial," we are told, if it is "calculated[,] [not] to inform the woman's free choice, [but to] hinder it." This latter statement cannot possibly mean what it says. *Any* regulation of abortion that is intended to advance what the joint opinion concedes is the State's "substantial" interest in protecting unborn life will be "calculated [to] hinder" a decision to have an abortion. It thus seems more accurate to say that the joint opinion would uphold abortion regulations only if they do not *unduly* hinder the woman's decision. That, of course, brings us right back to square one: Defining an "undue burden" as an "undue hindrance" (or a "substantial obstacle") hardly "clarifies" the test. Consciously or not, the joint opinion's verbal shell game will conceal raw judicial policy choices concerning what is "appropriate" abortion legislation.

The ultimately standardless nature of the "undue burden" inquiry is a reflection of the underlying fact that the concept has no principled or coherent legal basis. As The Chief Justice points out, *Roe*'s strict-scrutiny standard "at least had a recognized basis in constitutional law at the time *Roe* was decided," while "[t]he same cannot be said for the 'undue burden' standard, which is created largely out of whole cloth by the authors of the joint opinion." The joint opinion is flatly wrong in asserting that "our jurisprudence relating to all liberties save perhaps abortion has recognized" the permissibility of laws that do not impose an "undue burden." It argues that the abortion right is similar to other rights in that a law "not designed to strike at the right itself, [but which] has the incidental effect of making it more difficult or more expensive to [exercise the right,]" is not invalid. I agree, indeed I have forcefully urged, that a law of general applicability which places only an incidental burden on a fundamental right does not infringe that right, but that principle does not establish the quite different (and quite dangerous) proposition that a law which *directly* regulates a fundamental right will not be found to violate the Constitution unless it imposes an "undue burden." It is that, of course, which is at issue here: Pennsylvania has *consciously and directly* regulated conduct that our cases have held is constitutionally protected. The appropriate analogy, therefore, is that of a state law requiring purchasers of religious books to endure a 24–hour waiting period, or to pay a nominal additional tax of 1 [cent]. The joint opinion cannot possibly be correct in suggesting that we would uphold such legislation on the ground that it does not impose a "substantial obstacle" to the exercise of First Amendment rights. The "undue burden" standard is not at all the generally applicable principle the joint opinion pretends it to be; rather, it is a unique concept created specially for this case, to preserve some judicial foothold in this ill-gotten territory. In claiming otherwise, the three Justices show their willingness to place all constitutional rights at risk in an effort to preserve what they deem the "central holding in *Roe*."

. . .

To the extent I can discern *any* meaningful content in the "undue burden" standard as applied in the joint opinion, it appears to be that a State may not regulate abortion in such a way as to reduce significantly its incidence. The joint opinion repeatedly emphasizes that an important factor in the "undue burden" analysis is whether the regulation "prevent[s] a significant number of women from obtaining an abortion," whether a "significant number of women . . . are likely to be deterred from procuring an abortion," and whether the regulation often "deters" women from seeking abortions. We are not told, however, what forms of "deterrence" are impermissible or what degree of success in deterrence is too much to be tolerated. For example, if a State required a woman to read a pamphlet describing, with illustrations, the facts of fetal development before she could obtain an abortion, the effect of such legislation might be to "deter" a "significant number of women" from procuring abortions, thereby seemingly allowing a district judge to invalidate it as an undue burden. Thus, despite flowery rhetoric about the State's "substantial" and "profound" interest in "potential human life," and criticism of *Roe* for undervaluing that interest, the joint opinion permits the State to pursue that interest only so long as it is not too successful....

. . .

I am certainly not in a good position to dispute that the Court *has saved* the "central holding" of *Roe*, since to do that effectively I would have to know what the Court has saved, which in turn would require me to understand (as I do not) what the "undue burden" test means. I must confess, however, that I have always thought, and I think a lot of other people have always thought, that the arbitrary trimester framework, which the Court today discards, was quite as central to *Roe* as the arbitrary viability test, which the Court today retains. It seems particularly ungrateful to carve the trimester framework out of the core of *Roe*, since its very rigidity (in sharp contrast to the utter indeterminability of the "undue burden" test) is probably the only reason the Court is able to say, in urging *stare decisis*, that *Roe* "has in no sense proven 'unworkable.'" I suppose the Court is entitled to call a "central holding" whatever it wants to call a "central holding"—which is, come to think of it, perhaps one of the difficulties with this modified version of *stare decisis*....

The Court's description of the place of *Roe* in the social history of the United States is unrecognizable. Not only did *Roe* not, as the Court suggests, *resolve* the deeply divisive issue of abortion; it did more than anything else to nourish it, by elevating it to the national level where it is infinitely more difficult to resolve. National politics were not plagued by abortion protests, national abortion lobbying, or abortion marches on Congress, before *Roe v. Wade* was decided. Profound disagreement existed among our citizens over the issue—as it does over other issues, such as the death penalty—but that disagreement was being worked out at the state level. As with many other issues, the division of sentiment within each State was not as closely balanced as it was among the population of the Nation as a whole, meaning not only that more people would be satisfied with the results of state-by-state resolution, but also that those results would be more stable. Pre–*Roe*, moreover, political compromise was possible.

Roe's mandate for abortion on demand destroyed the compromises of the past, rendered compromise impossible for the future, and required the entire issue to be resolved uniformly, at the national level. At the same time, *Roe* created a vast new class of abortion consumers and abortion proponents by eliminating the moral opprobrium that had attached to the act. ("If the Constitution *guarantees* abortion, how can it be bad?"—not an accurate line of thought, but a natural one.) Many favor all of those developments, and it is not for me to say that they are wrong. But to portray *Roe* as the statesman-like "settlement" of a divisive issue, a jurisprudential Peace of Westphalia that is worth preserving, is nothing less than Orwellian. *Roe* fanned into life an issue that has inflamed our national politics in general, and has obscured with its smoke the selection of Justices, to this Court in particular, ever since. And by keeping us in the abortion-umpiring business, it is the perpetuation of that disruption, rather than of any *pax Roeana,* that the Court's new majority decrees.

. . .

. . . I am as distressed as the Court is . . . about the "political pressure" directed to the Court: the marches, the mail, the protests aimed at inducing us to change our opinions. How upsetting it is, that so many of our citizens (good people, not lawless ones, on both sides of this abortion issue, and on various sides of other issues as well) think that we Justices should properly take into account their views, as though we were engaged not in ascertaining an objective law but in determining some kind of social consensus. The Court would profit, I think, from giving less attention to the *fact* of this distressing phenomenon, and more attention to the *cause* of it. That cause permeates today's opinion: a new mode of constitutional adjudication that relies not upon text and traditional practice to determine the law, but upon what the Court calls "reasoned judgment," which turns out to be nothing but philosophical predilection and moral intuition. . . .

What makes all this relevant to the bothersome application of "political pressure" against the Court are the twin facts that the American people love democracy and the American people are not fools. As long as this Court thought (and the people thought) that we Justices were doing essentially lawyers' work up here—reading text and discerning our society's traditional understanding of that text—the public pretty much left us alone. Texts and traditions are facts to study, not convictions to demonstrate about. But if in reality our process of constitutional adjudication consists primarily of making *value judgments;* if we can ignore a long and clear tradition clarifying an ambiguous text, as we did, for example, five days ago in declaring unconstitutional invocations and benedictions at public high school graduation ceremonies, *Lee v. Weisman,* 505 U.S. 577 (1992); if, as I say, our pronouncement of constitutional law rests primarily on value judgments, then a free and intelligent people's attitude towards us can be expected to be (*ought* to be) quite different. The people know that their value judgments are quite as good as those taught in any law school—maybe better. If, indeed, the "liberties" protected by the Constitution are, as the Court says, undefined and unbounded, then the people *should* demonstrate, to protest that we do not implement *their* values instead of *ours.* Not only that, but confirmation hearings for new Justices *should* deteriorate into question-and-answer sessions in which Senators go through a list of their constituents' most favored and most disfavored alleged constitutional rights, and seek the nominee's commitment to support or oppose them. Value judgments, after all, should be voted on, not dictated; and if our Constitution has somehow accidently committed them to the Supreme Court, at least we can have a sort of plebiscite each time a new nominee to that body is put forward. . . .

. . .

We should get out of this area, where we have no right to be, and where we do neither ourselves nor the country any good by remaining.

NOTE

Compare the partial concurrence and partial dissent below of then-Circuit Judge Samuel A. Alito:

. . . I do not believe that Section 3209 has been shown to impose an undue burden as that term is used in the relevant Supreme Court opinions[.] . . .

. . .

. . . First, as the district court found, the "vast majority" of married women voluntarily inform their husbands before seeking an abortion. Indeed, in the trial testimony on which the district court relied, the plaintiffs' witness stated that in her experience 95% of married women notify their husbands. Second, the overwhelming majority of abortions are sought by unmarried women. Thus, it is immediately apparent that Section 3209 cannot affect more than about 5% of married women seeking abortions or an even smaller percentage of all women desiring abortions.

The plaintiffs failed to show even roughly how many of the women in this small group would actually be adversely affected by Section 3209. . . . Section 3209 contains four significant exceptions. These exceptions apply if a woman certifies that she has not notified her husband because she believes that (1) he is not the father of the child, (2) he cannot be found after diligent effort, (3) the pregnancy is the result of a spousal sexual assault that has been reported to the authorities, or (4) she has reason to believe that notification is likely to result in the infliction of bodily injury upon her. If Section 3209 were allowed to take effect, it seems safe to assume that *some* percentage of the married women seeking abortions without notifying their husbands would qualify for and invoke these exceptions. The record, however, is devoid of evidence showing how many women could or could not invoke an exception.

Of the potentially affected women who could not invoke an exception, it seems safe to assume that *some* percentage, despite an initial inclination not to tell their husbands, would notify their husbands without suffering substantial ill effects. Again, however, the record lacks evidence showing how many women would or would not fall into this category. Thus, the plaintiffs did not even roughly substantiate how many women might be inhibited from obtaining an abortion or otherwise harmed by Section 3209. At best, the record shows that Section 3209 would inhibit abortions " 'to some degree' " or that "some women [would] be less likely to choose to have an abortion by virtue of the presence" of Section 3209. . . . Consequently, the plaintiffs failed to prove that Section 3209 would impose an undue burden.

Needless to say, the plight of any women, no matter how few, who may suffer physical abuse or other harm as a result of this provision is a matter of grave concern. It is apparent that the Pennsylvania legislature considered this problem and attempted to prevent Section 3209 from causing adverse effects by adopting the four exceptions noted above. Whether the legislature's approach represents sound public policy is not a question for us to decide. Our task here is simply to decide whether Section 3209 meets constitutional standards. The first step in this analysis is to determine whether Section 3209 has been shown to create an undue burden under Supreme Court precedent, and for the reasons just explained it seems clear that an undue burden has not been established.

Planned Parenthood of Southeastern Penn. v. Casey, 947 F.2d 682, 720–24 (3d. Cir. 1991) (Alito, J., concurring in part and dissenting in part) (footnotes omitted).

Gonzales v. Carhart

Supreme Court of the United States, 2007.
550 U.S. 124, 127 S.Ct. 1610, 167 L.Ed.2d 480.

■ JUSTICE KENNEDY delivered the opinion of the Court.

These cases require us to consider the validity of the Partial–Birth Abortion Ban Act of 2003 (Act), 18 U.S.C. § 1531 (2000 ed., Supp. IV), a federal statute regulating abortion procedures. . . . Compared to the state statute at issue in *Stenberg* [*v. Carhart*, 530 U.S. 914 (2000),] the Act is more specific concerning the instances to which it applies and in this respect more precise in its coverage. . . .

. . .

I.

. . .

. . . The operative provisions of the Act provide in relevant part:

(a) Any physician who, in or affecting interstate or foreign commerce, knowingly performs a partial-birth abortion and thereby kills a human fetus shall be fined under this title or imprisoned not more than 2 years, or both. This subsection does not apply to a partial-birth abortion that is necessary to save the life of a mother whose life is endangered by a physical disorder, physical illness, or physical injury, including a life-endangering physical condition caused by or arising from the pregnancy itself. This subsection takes effect 1 day after the enactment.

(b) As used in this section—

(1) the term 'partial-birth abortion' means an abortion in which the person performing the abortion—

(A) deliberately and intentionally vaginally delivers a living fetus until, in the case of a head-first presentation, the entire fetal head is outside the body of the mother, or, in the case of breech presentation, any part of the fetal trunk past the navel is outside the body of the mother, for the purpose of performing an overt act that the person knows will kill the fetus; and

(B) performs the overt act, other than completion of delivery, that kills the partially delivered living fetus; and

(2) the term 'physician' means a doctor of medicine or osteopathy legally authorized to practice medicine and surgery by the State in which the doctor performs such activity, or any other individual legally authorized by the State to perform abortions: *Provided, however,* That any individual who is not a physician or not otherwise legally authorized by the State to perform abortions, but who nevertheless directly performs a partial-birth abortion, shall be subject to the provisions of this section.

. . .

(d)(1) A defendant accused of an offense under this section may seek a hearing before the State Medical Board on whether the physician's conduct was necessary to save the life of the mother whose life was endangered by a physical disorder, physical illness, or physical injury, including a life-endangering physical condition caused by or arising from the pregnancy itself.

(2) The findings on that issue are admissible on that issue at the trial of the defendant. Upon a motion of the defendant, the court shall delay the beginning of the trial for not more than 30 days to permit such a hearing to take place.

(e) A woman upon whom a partial-birth abortion is performed may not be prosecuted under this section, for a conspiracy to violate this section, or for an offense under section 2, 3, or 4 of this title based on a violation of this section.

18 U.S.C. § 1531 (2000 ed., Supp. IV).

. . .

We assume the following principles for the purposes of this opinion. Before viability, a State "may not prohibit any woman from making the ultimate decision to terminate her pregnancy." [*Planned Parenthood of Southeastern Penn. v. Casey*, 947 F.2d 682, 719 (3d Cir. 1991) (Alito, J., concurring in part and dissenting in part), *rev'd,* 505 U.S. 833 (1992) (plurality opinion)]. It also may not impose upon this right an undue burden, which exists if a regulation's "purpose or effect is to place a substantial obstacle in the path of a woman seeking an abortion before the fetus attains viability." On the other hand, "[r]egulations which do no more than create a structural mechanism by which the State, or the parent or guardian of a minor, may express profound respect for the life of the unborn are permitted, if they are not a substantial obstacle to the woman's exercise of the right to choose."

III.

We begin with a determination of the Act's operation and effect. A straightforward reading of the Act's text demonstrates its purpose and the scope of its provisions: It regulates and proscribes, with exceptions or qualifications to be discussed, performing the intact [dilation of the cervix and evacuation, the usual abortion method in the second trimester, or] D & E procedure.

Respondents argue the Act encompasses intact D & E, but they contend its additional reach is both unclear and excessive. Respondents assert that, at the least, the Act is void for vagueness because its scope is indefinite. In the alternative, respondents argue the Act's text proscribes all D & Es. Because D & E is the most common second-trimester abortion method, respondents suggest the Act imposes an undue burden. In this litigation the Attorney General does not dispute that the Act would impose an undue burden if it covered standard D & E.

We conclude that the Act is not void for vagueness, does not impose an undue burden from any overbreadth, and is not invalid on its face.

The Act punishes "knowingly perform[ing]" a "partial-birth abortion." § 1531(a) (2000 ed., Supp. IV). It defines the unlawful abortion in explicit terms. § 1531(b)(1).

. . .

. . . "As generally stated, the void-for-vagueness doctrine requires that a penal statute define the criminal offense with sufficient definiteness that ordinary people can understand what conduct is prohibited and in a manner that does not encourage arbitrary and discriminatory enforcement." *Kolender v. Lawson,* 461 U.S. 352, 357 (1983). The Act satisfies both requirements.

. . . Doctors performing D & E will know that if they do not deliver a living fetus to an anatomical landmark they will not face criminal liability.

This conclusion is buttressed by the intent that must be proved to impose liability. . . . The Act requires the doctor deliberately to have delivered the fetus to an anatomical landmark. § 1531(b)(1)(A) (2000 ed., Supp. IV). Because a doctor performing a D & E will not face criminal liability if he or she delivers a fetus beyond the prohibited point by mistake, the Act cannot be described as "a trap for those who act in good faith." *Colautti* [*v. Franklin*, 439 U.S. 379, 395 (1979)] (internal quotation marks omitted).

Respondents likewise have failed to show that the Act should be invalidated on its face because it encourages arbitrary or discriminatory enforcement. *Kolender, supra*, at 357. Just as the Act's anatomical landmarks provide doctors with objective standards, they also "establish minimal guidelines to govern law enforcement." *Smith v. Goguen*, 415 U.S. 566, 574 (1974). The scienter requirements narrow the scope of the Act's prohibition and limit prosecutorial discretion. . . .

We next determine whether the Act imposes an undue burden, as a facial matter, because its restrictions on second-trimester abortions are too broad. A review of the statutory text discloses the limits of its reach. The Act prohibits intact D & E; and, notwithstanding respondents' arguments, it does not prohibit the D & E procedure in which the fetus is removed in parts.

The Act prohibits a doctor from intentionally performing an intact D & E. The dual prohibitions of the Act, both of which are necessary for criminal liability, correspond with the steps generally undertaken during this type of procedure. First, a doctor delivers the fetus until its head lodges in the cervix, which is usually past the anatomical landmark for a breech presentation. *See* 18 U.S.C. § 1531(b)(1)(A) (2000 ed., Supp. IV). Second, the doctor proceeds to pierce the fetal skull with scissors or crush it with forceps. This step satisfies the overt-act requirement because it kills the fetus and is distinct from delivery. *See* § 1531(b)(1)(B). The Act's intent requirements, however, limit its reach to those physicians who carry out the intact D & E after intending to undertake both steps at the outset.

The Act excludes most D & Es in which the fetus is removed in pieces, not intact. If the doctor intends to remove the fetus in parts from the outset, the doctor will not have the requisite intent to incur criminal liability. A doctor performing a standard D & E procedure can often "tak[e] about 10–15 'passes' through the uterus to remove the entire fetus." [*Planned Parenthood Fed'n of America v. Ashcroft*, 320 F. Supp. 2d 957, 962 (N.D. Cal. 2004).] Removing the fetus in this manner does not violate the Act because the doctor will not have delivered the living fetus to one of the anatomical landmarks or committed an additional overt act that kills the fetus after partial delivery. § 1531(b)(1) (2000 ed., Supp. IV).

. . .

By adding an overt-act requirement Congress sought further to meet the Court's objections to the state statute considered in *Stenberg*. Compare 18 U.S.C. § 1531(b)(1) (2000 ed., Supp. IV) with NEB. REV. STAT. ANN. § 28–326(9) (Supp. 1999). The Act makes the distinction the Nebraska statute failed to draw (but the Nebraska Attorney General advanced) by differentiating between the overall partial-birth abortion and the distinct overt act that kills the fetus. *See Stenberg*, 530 U.S., at 943–44. The fatal overt act must occur after delivery to an anatomical landmark, and it must be something "other than [the] completion of delivery." § 1531(b)(1)(B). This distinction matters because, unlike intact D & E, standard D & E does not involve a delivery followed by a fatal act.

The canon of constitutional avoidance, finally, extinguishes any lingering doubt as to whether the Act covers the prototypical D & E procedure. " '[T]he elementary rule is that every reasonable construction must be resorted to, in order to save a statute from unconstitutionality.' " It is true this longstanding maxim of statutory interpretation has, in the past, fallen by the wayside when the Court confronted a statute regulating abortion. The Court at times employed an antagonistic " 'canon of construction under which in cases involving abortion, a permissible reading of a statute [was] to be avoided at all costs.' " *Casey* put this novel statutory approach to rest. *Stenberg* need not be interpreted to have revived it. We read that decision instead to stand for the uncontroversial proposition that the canon of constitutional avoidance does not apply if a statute is not "genuinely susceptible to two constructions." In *Stenberg*, the Court found the statute covered D & E. Here, by contrast, interpreting the Act so that it does not prohibit standard D & E is the most reasonable reading and understanding of its terms.

> . . .

Under the principles accepted as controlling here, the Act, as we have interpreted it, would be unconstitutional "if its purpose or effect is to place a substantial obstacle in the path of a woman seeking an abortion before the fetus attains viability." *Casey*, 505 U.S., at 878 (plurality opinion). The abortions affected by the Act's regulations take place both previability and postviability; so the quoted language and the undue burden analysis it relies upon are applicable. The question is whether the Act, measured by its text in this facial attack, imposes a substantial obstacle to late-term, but previability, abortions. The Act does not on its face impose a substantial obstacle, and we reject this further facial challenge to its validity.

The Act's purposes are set forth in recitals preceding its operative provisions. A description of the prohibited abortion procedure demonstrates the rationale for the congressional enactment. . . . The Act expresses respect for the dignity of human life.

Congress was concerned, furthermore, with the effects on the medical community and on its reputation caused by the practice of partial-birth abortion. . . . There can be no doubt that government "has an interest in protecting the integrity and ethics of the medical profession." *Washington v. Glucksberg*, 521 U.S. 702, 731 (1997). . . .

Casey reaffirmed these governmental objectives. . . . Where it has a rational basis to act, and it does not impose an undue burden, the State may use its regulatory power to bar certain procedures and substitute others, all in furtherance of its legitimate interests in regulating the medical profession in order to promote respect for life, including life of the unborn.

The Act's ban on abortions that involve partial delivery of a living fetus furthers the Government's objectives. No one would dispute that, for many, D & E is a procedure itself laden with the power to devalue human life. Congress could nonetheless conclude that the type of abortion proscribed by the Act requires specific regulation because it implicates additional ethical and moral concerns that justify a special prohibition. Congress determined that the abortion methods it proscribed had a "disturbing similarity to the killing of a newborn infant," Congressional Findings (14)(L) [in notes following 18 U.S.C. § 1531 (2000 ed., Supp. IV), p. 769], and thus it was concerned with "draw[ing] a bright line that clearly distinguishes abortion and infanticide." Congressional Findings (14)(G). . . .

Respect for human life finds an ultimate expression in the bond of love the mother has for her child. The Act recognizes this reality as well. Whether to have an abortion requires a difficult and painful moral decision. While we find no reliable data to measure the phenomenon, it seems unexceptionable to conclude some women come to regret their choice to abort the infant life they once created and sustained. Severe depression and loss of esteem can follow.

In a decision so fraught with emotional consequence some doctors may prefer not to disclose precise details of the means that will be used, confining themselves to the required statement of risks the procedure entails. From one standpoint this ought not to be surprising. Any number of patients facing imminent surgical procedures would prefer not to hear all details, lest the usual anxiety preceding invasive medical procedures become the more intense. This is likely the case with the abortion procedures here in issue. *See, e.g., Nat'l Abortion Fed'n* [*v. Ashcroft*], 330 F. Supp. 2d [436,] 466 n.22 [(S.D.N.Y. 2004)] ("Most of [the plaintiffs'] experts acknowledged that they do not describe to their patients what [the D & E and intact D & E] procedures entail in clear and precise terms")[.]

It is, however, precisely this lack of information concerning the way in which the fetus will be killed that is of legitimate concern to the State. *Casey, supra,* at 873 (plurality opinion). The State has an interest in ensuring so grave a choice is well informed. It is self-evident that a mother who comes to regret her choice to abort must struggle with grief more anguished and sorrow more profound when she learns, only after the event, what she once did not know: that she allowed a doctor to pierce the skull and vacuum the fast-developing brain of her unborn child, a child assuming the human form.

It is a reasonable inference that a necessary effect of the regulation and the knowledge it conveys will be to encourage some women to carry the infant to full term, thus reducing the absolute number of late-term abortions. The medical profession, furthermore, may find different and less shocking methods to abort the fetus in the second trimester, thereby accommodating legislative demand. The State's interest in respect for life is advanced by the dialogue that better informs the political and legal systems, the medical profession, expectant mothers, and society as a whole of the consequences that follow from a decision to elect a late-term abortion.

It is objected that the standard D & E is in some respects as brutal, if not more, than the intact D & E, so that the legislation accomplishes little. What we have already said, however, shows ample justification for the regulation. Partial-birth abortion, as defined by the Act, differs from a standard D & E because the former occurs when the fetus is partially outside the mother to the point of one of the Act's anatomical landmarks. It was reasonable for Congress to think that partial-birth abortion, more than standard D & E, "undermines the public's perception of the appropriate role of a physician during the delivery process, and perverts a process during which life is brought into the world." Congressional Findings (14)(K) [in notes following 18 U.S.C. § 1531 (2000 ed., Supp. IV), p. 769]. There would be a flaw in this Court's logic, and an irony in its jurisprudence, were we first to conclude a ban on both D & E and intact D & E was overbroad and then to say it is irrational to ban only intact D & E because that does not proscribe both procedures. In sum, we reject the contention that the congressional purpose of the Act was "to place a substantial obstacle in the path of a woman seeking an abortion."

The Act's furtherance of legitimate government interests bears upon, but does not resolve, the next question: whether the Act has the effect of imposing an unconstitutional burden on the abortion right because it does not allow use of the barred procedure where " 'necessary, in appropriate medical judgment, for the preservation of the ... health of the mother.' " *Ayotte v.* [*Planned Parenthood of N. New England,* 546 U.S. 320, 327–328

(2006)] (quoting *Casey, supra*, at 879 (plurality opinion)). The prohibition in the Act would be unconstitutional, under precedents we here assume to be controlling, if it "subject[ed] [women] to significant health risks." In *Ayotte*[,] the parties agreed a health exception to the challenged parental-involvement statute was necessary "to avert serious and often irreversible damage to [a pregnant minor's] health." 546 U.S., at 328. Here, by contrast, whether the Act creates significant health risks for women has been a contested factual question. The evidence presented in the trial courts and before Congress demonstrates both sides have medical support for their position.

. . .

There is documented medical disagreement whether the Act's prohibition would ever impose significant health risks on women. *See, e.g.,* [*Planned Parenthood v. Ashcroft*, 320 F. Supp. 2d,] at 1033 ("[T]here continues to be a division of opinion among highly qualified experts regarding the necessity or safety of intact D & E") . . . .

The question becomes whether the Act can stand when this medical uncertainty persists. The Court's precedents instruct that the Act can survive this facial attack. The Court has given state and federal legislatures wide discretion to pass legislation in areas where there is medical and scientific uncertainty. *See Kansas v. Hendricks*, 521 U.S. 346, 360, n.3 (1997); *see also Stenberg, supra*, at 969–972 (Kennedy, J., dissenting); *Marshall v. United States*, 414 U.S. 417, 427 (1974) ("When Congress undertakes to act in areas fraught with medical and scientific uncertainties, legislative options must be especially broad").

This traditional rule is consistent with *Casey*, which confirms the State's interest in promoting respect for human life at all stages in the pregnancy. Physicians are not entitled to ignore regulations that direct them to use reasonable alternative procedures. The law need not give abortion doctors unfettered choice in the course of their medical practice, nor should it elevate their status above other physicians in the medical community . . . .

Medical uncertainty does not foreclose the exercise of legislative power in the abortion context any more than it does in other contexts. See *Hendricks, supra*, at 360, n. 3. The medical uncertainty over whether the Act's prohibition creates significant health risks provides a sufficient basis to conclude in this facial attack that the Act does not impose an undue burden.

The conclusion that the Act does not impose an undue burden is supported by other considerations. Alternatives are available to the prohibited procedure. As we have noted, the Act does not proscribe D & E . . . . In addition the Act's prohibition only applies to the delivery of "a living fetus." 18 U.S.C. § 1531(b)(1)(A) (2000 ed., Supp. IV). If the intact D & E procedure is truly necessary in some circumstances, it appears likely an injection that kills the fetus is an alternative under the Act that allows the doctor to perform the procedure.

. . .

. . . Considerations of marginal safety, including the balance of risks, are within the legislative competence when the regulation is rational and in pursuit of legitimate ends. When standard medical options are available, mere convenience does not suffice to displace them; and if some procedures have different risks than others, it does not follow that the State is altogether barred from imposing reasonable regulations. The Act is not invalid on its face where there is uncertainty over whether the barred procedure is ever necessary to preserve a woman's health, given the availability of other abortion procedures that are considered to be safe alternatives.

. . .

■ Justice Ginsburg, with whom Justice Stevens, Justice Souter, and Justice Breyer join, dissenting.

. . .

Today's decision is alarming. It refuses to take [*Planned Parenthood of Southeastern Pennsylvania v. Casey*, 505 U.S. 833 (1992)] and [*Stenberg v. Carhart*, 530 U.S. 914 (2000)] seriously. It tolerates, indeed applauds, federal intervention to ban nationwide a procedure found necessary and proper in certain cases by the American College of Obstetricians and Gynecologists (ACOG). It blurs the line, firmly drawn in *Casey*, between previability and postviability abortions. And, for the first time since *Roe*, the Court blesses a prohibition with no exception safeguarding a woman's health.

I dissent from the Court's disposition. Retreating from prior rulings that abortion restrictions cannot be imposed absent an exception safeguarding a woman's health, the Court upholds an Act that surely would not survive under the close scrutiny that previously attended state-decreed limitations on a woman's reproductive choices.

. . . Women, it is now acknowledged, have the talent, capacity, and right "to participate equally in the economic and social life of the Nation." Their ability to realize their full potential, the Court recognized, is intimately connected to "their ability to control their reproductive lives." Thus, legal challenges to undue restrictions on abortion procedures do not seek to vindicate some generalized notion of privacy; rather, they center on a woman's autonomy to determine her life's course, and thus to enjoy equal citizenship stature.

In keeping with this comprehension of the right to reproductive choice, the Court has consistently required that laws regulating abortion, at any stage of pregnancy and in all cases, safeguard a woman's health. *See, e.g., Ayotte* [*v. Planned Parenthood of N. New England*, 546 U.S. 320, 327–328 (2006)]; *Stenberg*, 530 U.S., at 930.

We have thus ruled that a State must avoid subjecting women to health risks not only where the pregnancy itself creates danger, but also where state regulation forces women to resort to less safe methods of abortion. See *Planned Parenthood of Central Mo. v. Danforth*, 428 U.S. 52, 79, (1976) (holding unconstitutional a ban on a method of abortion that "force[d] a woman . . . to terminate her pregnancy by methods more dangerous to her health"). Indeed, we have applied the rule that abortion regulation must safeguard a woman's health to the particular procedure at issue here—intact dilation and evacuation (D & E).[3]

In *Stenberg*, we expressly held that a statute banning intact D & E was unconstitutional in part because it lacked a health exception. 530 U.S., at 930, 937. We noted that there existed a "division of medical opinion" about the relative safety of intact D & E, *id*. at 937, but we made clear that as long as "substantial medical authority supports the proposition that banning a particular abortion procedure could endanger women's health," a health

---

3. . . . . Adolescents and indigent women, research suggests, are more likely than other women to have difficulty obtaining an abortion during the first trimester of pregnancy. Minors may be unaware they are pregnant until relatively late in pregnancy, while poor women's financial constraints are an obstacle to timely receipt of services. . . .

exception is required, *id.*, at 938.... Thus, we reasoned, division in medical opinion "at most means uncertainty, a factor that signals the presence of risk, not its absence." [*Id.*, at 937.] "[A] statute that altogether forbids [intact D & E] ... consequently must contain a health exception."

In 2003, a few years after our ruling in *Stenberg*, Congress passed the Partial–Birth Abortion Ban Act—without an exception for women's health. See 18 U.S.C. § 1531(a) (2000 ed., Supp. IV).[4] The congressional findings on which the Partial–Birth Abortion Ban Act rests do not withstand inspection....

Many of the Act's recitations are incorrect. For example, Congress determined that no medical schools provide instruction on intact D & E. But in fact, numerous leading medical schools teach the procedure.

More important, Congress claimed there was a medical consensus that the banned procedure is never necessary. But the evidence "very clearly demonstrate[d] the opposite." *Planned Parenthood Fed'n of Am.* [*v. Ashcroft*, 320 F. Supp. 2d 957, 1025 (N.D. Cal. 2004)]. See also [*Carhart v. Ashcroft*, 331 F. Supp. 2d 805, 1008–09 (D. Neb. 2004)]; *Nat'l Abortion Fed'n* [*v. Ashcroft*, 330 F. Supp. 2d 436, 488 (S.D.N.Y. 2004)].

Similarly, Congress found that "[t]here is no credible medical evidence that partial-birth abortions are safe or are safer than other abortion procedures." But the congressional record includes letters from numerous individual physicians stating that pregnant women's health would be jeopardized under the Act, as well as statements from nine professional associations, including ACOG, the American Public Health Association, and the California Medical Association, attesting that intact D & E carries meaningful safety advantages over other methods. No comparable medical groups supported the ban. In fact, "all of the government's own witnesses disagreed with many of the specific congressional findings." [*Planned Parenthood*, 320 F. Supp. 2d,] at 1024.

. . .

According to the expert testimony plaintiffs introduced, the safety advantages of intact D & E are marked for women with certain medical conditions, for example, uterine scarring, bleeding disorders, heart disease, or compromised immune systems. Further, plaintiffs' experts testified that intact D & E is significantly safer for women with certain pregnancy-related conditions, such as placenta previa and accreta, and for women carrying fetuses with certain abnormalities, such as severe hydrocephalus.

Intact D & E, plaintiffs' experts explained, provides safety benefits over D & E by dismemberment for several reasons: *First*, intact D & E minimizes the number of times a physician must insert instruments through the cervix and into the uterus, and thereby reduces the risk of trauma to, and perforation of, the cervix and uterus—the most serious complication associated with nonintact D & E. *Second*, removing the fetus intact, instead of dismembering it *in utero*, decreases the likelihood that fetal tissue will be retained in the uterus, a condition that can cause infection, hemorrhage, and infertility. *Third*, intact D & E diminishes the chances of exposing the patient's tissues to sharp bony fragments sometimes resulting from dismemberment of the fetus. *Fourth*, intact D & E takes less operating time than D &

---

4. The Act's sponsors left no doubt that their intention was to nullify our ruling in *Stenberg*.

E by dismemberment, and thus may reduce bleeding, the risk of infection, and complications relating to anesthesia.

Based on thoroughgoing review of the trial evidence and the congressional record, each of the District Courts to consider the issue rejected Congress' findings as unreasonable and not supported by the evidence. The trial courts concluded, in contrast to Congress' findings, that "significant medical authority supports the proposition that in some circumstances, [intact D & E] is the safest procedure."

The District Courts' findings merit this Court's respect. Today's opinion supplies no reason to reject those findings. Nevertheless, despite the District Courts' appraisal of the weight of the evidence, and in undisguised conflict with *Stenberg*, the Court asserts that the Partial–Birth Abortion Ban Act can survive "when … medical uncertainty persists." This assertion is bewildering. Not only does it defy the Court's longstanding precedent affirming the necessity of a health exception, with no carve-out for circumstances of medical uncertainty; it gives short shrift to the records before us, carefully canvassed by the District Courts. Those records indicate that "the majority of highly-qualified experts on the subject believe intact D & E to be the safest, most appropriate procedure under certain circumstances."

The Court acknowledges some of this evidence, but insists that [because of disagreement about the assessment of risk], the Act can stand. In this insistence, the Court brushes under the rug the District Courts' well-supported findings that the physicians who testified that intact D & E is never necessary to preserve the health of a woman had slim authority for their opinions. They had no training for, or personal experience with, the intact D & E procedure, and many performed abortions only on rare occasions. Even indulging the assumption that the Government witnesses were equally qualified to evaluate the relative risks of abortion procedures, their testimony could not erase the "significant medical authority support[ing] the proposition that in some circumstances, [intact D & E] would be the safest procedure."[6]

The Court offers flimsy and transparent justifications for upholding a nationwide ban on intact D & E *sans* any exception to safeguard a women's health. Today's ruling, the Court declares, advances "a premise central to [*Casey*'s] conclusion"—*i.e.*, the Government's "legitimate and substantial interest in preserving and promoting fetal life." But the Act scarcely furthers that interest: The law saves not a single fetus from destruction, for it targets only a *method* of performing abortion. And surely the statute was not designed to protect the lives or health of pregnant women. In short, the Court upholds a law that, while doing nothing to "preserv[e] … fetal life," bars a woman from choosing intact D & E although her doctor "reasonably believes [that procedure] will best protect [her]." *Stenberg*, 530 U.S., at 946 (Stevens, J., concurring).

---

6. The majority contends that "[i]f the intact D & E procedure is truly necessary in some circumstances, it appears likely an injection that kills the fetus is an alternative under the Act that allows the doctor to perform the procedure." But a "significant body of medical opinion believes that inducing fetal death by injection is almost always inappropriate to the preservation of the health of women undergoing abortion because it poses tangible risk and provides no benefit to the woman." Carhart v. Ashcroft, 331 F. Supp. 2d 805, 1028 (Neb. 2004), aff'd, 413 F. 3d 791 ([8th Cir.] 2005). In some circumstances, injections are "absolutely [medically] contraindicated." 331 F. Supp. 2d, at 1027. The Court also identifies medical induction of labor as an alternative. That procedure, however, requires a hospital stay, rendering it inaccessible to patients who lack financial resources, and it too is considered less safe for many women, and impermissible for others.

As another reason for upholding the ban, the Court emphasizes that the Act does not proscribe the nonintact D & E procedure. But why not, one might ask.... "[T]he notion that either of these two equally gruesome procedures ... is more akin to infanticide than the other, or that the State furthers any legitimate interest by banning one but not the other, is simply irrational." [*Id.*,] at 946–947.

Delivery of an intact, albeit nonviable, fetus warrants special condemnation, the Court maintains, because a fetus that is not dismembered resembles an infant. But so, too, does a fetus delivered intact after it is terminated by injection a day or two before the surgical evacuation, or a fetus delivered through medical induction or cesarean. Yet, the availability of those procedures—along with D & E by dismemberment—the Court says, saves the ban on intact D & E from a declaration of unconstitutionality. Never mind that the procedures deemed acceptable might put a woman's health at greater risk.

Ultimately, the Court admits that "moral concerns" are at work, concerns that could yield prohibitions on any abortion. *See ante,* at 158 ("Congress could ... conclude that the type of abortion proscribed by the Act requires specific regulation because it implicates additional ethical and moral concerns that justify a special prohibition."). Notably, the concerns expressed are untethered to any ground genuinely serving the Government's interest in preserving life. By allowing such concerns to carry the day and case, overriding fundamental rights, the Court dishonors our precedent. *See, e.g., Casey,* 505 U.S., at 850; *Lawrence v. Texas,* 539 U.S. 558, 571 (2003).

Revealing in this regard, the Court invokes an antiabortion shibboleth for which it concededly has no reliable evidence: Women who have abortions come to regret their choices, and consequently suffer from "[s]evere depression and loss of esteem." Because of women's fragile emotional state and because of the "bond of love the mother has for her child," the Court worries, doctors may withhold information about the nature of the intact D & E procedure. The solution the Court approves, then, is *not* to require doctors to inform women, accurately and adequately, of the different procedures and their attendant risks. Instead, the Court deprives women of the right to make an autonomous choice, even at the expense of their safety.

This way of thinking reflects ancient notions about women's place in the family and under the Constitution—ideas that have long since been discredited. *Compare, e.g., Muller v. Oregon,* 208 U.S. 412 (1908), [and] *Bradwell v. State,* 16 Wall. 130, 141 (1873) (Bradley, J., concurring), *with United States v. Virginia,* 518 U.S. 515, 533, 542, n. 12 (1996), [and] *Califano v. Goldfarb,* 430 U.S. 199 (1977).

Though today's majority may regard women's feelings on the matter as "self-evident," this Court has repeatedly confirmed that "[t]he destiny of the woman must be shaped ... on her own conception of her spiritual imperatives and her place in society." *Casey,* 505 U.S., at 852.

In cases on a "woman's liberty to determine whether to [continue] her pregnancy," this Court has identified viability as a critical consideration. See *Casey,* 505 U.S., at 869–870 (plurality opinion). "[T]here is no line [more workable] than viability," the Court explained in *Casey,* for viability is "the time at which there is a realistic possibility of maintaining and nourishing a life outside the womb, so that the independent existence of the second life can in reason and all fairness be the object of state protection that now overrides the rights of the woman.... In some broad sense it might be said that a woman who fails to act before viability has consented to the State's intervention on behalf of the developing child." *Id.*, at 870.

Today, the Court blurs that line, maintaining that "[t]he Act [legitimately] applies both previability and postviability because ... a fetus is a living organism while within the womb, whether or not it is viable outside the womb." Instead of drawing the line at viability, the Court refers to Congress' purpose to differentiate "abortion and infanticide" based not on whether a fetus can survive outside the womb, but on where a fetus is anatomically located when a particular medical procedure is performed.

One wonders how long a line that saves no fetus from destruction will hold in face of the Court's "moral concerns." The Court's hostility to the right *Roe* and *Casey* secured is not concealed. Throughout, the opinion refers to obstetrician-gynecologists and surgeons who perform abortions not by the titles of their medical specialties, but by the pejorative label "abortion doctor." A fetus is described as an "unborn child," and as a "baby;" second-trimester, previability abortions are referred to as "late-term;" and the reasoned medical judgments of highly trained doctors are dismissed as "preferences" motivated by "mere convenience." Instead of the heightened scrutiny we have previously applied, the Court determines that a "rational" ground is enough to uphold the Act. And, most troubling, *Casey*'s principles, confirming the continuing vitality of "the essential holding of *Roe*," are merely "assumed" for the moment, rather than "retained" or "reaffirmed," *Casey*, 505 U.S., at 846.

. . .

Without attempting to distinguish *Stenberg* and earlier decisions, the majority asserts that the Act survives review because respondents have not shown that the ban on intact D & E would be unconstitutional "in a large fraction of [relevant] cases." But *Casey* makes clear that, in determining whether any restriction poses an undue burden on a "large fraction" of women, the relevant class is *not* "all women," nor "all pregnant women," nor even all women "seeking abortions." [*Id.*] at 895. Rather, a provision restricting access to abortion, "must be judged by reference to those [women] for whom it is an actual rather than an irrelevant restriction." *Ibid.* Thus the absence of a health exception burdens *all* women for whom it is relevant— women who, in the judgment of their doctors, require an intact D & E because other procedures would place their health at risk.... The very purpose of a health *exception* is to protect women in *exceptional* cases.

. . .

[T]he notion that the Partial-Birth Abortion Ban Act furthers any legitimate governmental interest is, quite simply, irrational. The Court's defense of the statute provides no saving explanation. In candor, the Act, and the Court's defense of it, cannot be understood as anything other than an effort to chip away at a right declared again and again by this Court—and with increasing comprehension of its centrality to women's lives. When "a statute burdens constitutional rights and all that can be said on its behalf is that it is the vehicle that legislators have chosen for expressing their hostility to those rights, the burden is undue." *Stenberg*, 530 U.S., at 952 (Ginsburg, J., concurring) (quoting *Hope Clinic v. Ryan*, 195 F. 3d 857, 881 (7th Cir. 1999) (Posner, C. J., dissenting)).

NOTES

1.   In light of its ruling in *Gonzales v. Carhart*, 550 U.S. 124 (2007) (*Carhart II*), the Supreme Court vacated and remanded a Fourth Circuit decision involving a Virginia ban on what was statutorily described as "partial birth infanticide." *Herring v. Richmond Med. Ctr. for Women*, 550 U.S. 901 (2007). (For the earlier decision, see *Richmond Med. Ctr. for Women v. Hicks*, 409 F.3d 619 (4th Cir. 2005).) In a split decision, the Fourth Circuit declared the Virginia law unconstitutional for a second time. *Richmond Med. Ctr. for Women v. Herring*, 527 F.3d 128 (4th Cir. 2008). The majority opinion in the case explained that the Virginia statute outlawed "intact dilation and evacuation" without the same (kind of) *scienter* element that the *Carhart II* Court had held saved the federal "Partial–Birth Abortion Act" from constitutional demise. *Richmond Med. Ctr. for Women v. Herring*, 527 F.3d 128 (4th Cir. 2008). "[T]he Virginia Act has no provision requiring intent at the outset of the procedure[, and] . . . thus imposes criminal liability on a doctor who sets out to perform a standard D & E that by accident becomes an intact D & E." *Id.* at 131. The statute, the court continued, "thereby expos[es] all doctors who perform standard D & Es to prosecution, conviction, and imprisonment," *id.*, and, as a result, imposes " 'an undue burden upon a woman's right to make an abortion decision,' in violation of the Constitution." *Id.* at 135 (quoting *Stenberg v. Carhart*, 530 U.S. 914, 945–46 (2000), and citing *Gonzales v. Carhart*, 550 U.S. 124 (2007)). Sitting *en banc*, the Fourth Circuit vacated the panel decision, upholding the law as facially constitutional. *Richmond Med. Ctr. for Women v. Herring*, 570 F.3d 165 (4th Cir. 2009) (en banc). In doing so, the court explained: "[W]e read the Virginia Act intent requirement to require purpose, not mere knowledge, that a specific act—taken after emergence to the anatomical landmark—will result in fetal demise. Thus, the Virginia Act criminalizes both the intentional intact D & E and the accidental intact D & E, but only where the necessary *scienter* is present and no affirmative defense is presented." *Id.* at 176–77 (citation omitted). *See also Northland Family Planning Clinic, Inc. v. Cox*, 487 F.3d 323 (6th Cir. 2007) (declaring Michigan's Legal Birth Definition Act unconstitutional as an undue burden on D & E abortions).

2.   In the wake of *Gonzalez v. Carhart* there have been a series of legislative measures at the state level to restrict abortion in the name of protecting human life. According to Dahlia Lithwick's reporting, since the turn of the year, there have been "916 measures seeking to regulate reproductive health . . . introduced in 49 states." Dahlia Lithwick, *The Death of* Roe v. Wade, SLATE, Apr. 19, 2011, http://www.slate.com/id/2291596/. The Guttmacher Institute, a source Lithwick relies on, has found that: "[i]n the first sixth months of 2011, states enacted 162 new provisions related to reproductive health and rights. Fully 49% of these new laws seek to restrict access to abortion services[.]" *States Enact Record Number of Abortion Restrictions in First Half of 2011*, GUTTMACHER INST. (July 13, 2011), http://www.guttmacher.org/media/inthenews/2011/07/13/index.html. For other reports on developments, see N.C.. Aizenman, *Health-care Law Fuels Abortion Wars*, WASH. POST, Mar. 12, 2011, at A3; Erik Eckholm, *New Laws in 6 States Ban Abortions After 20 Weeks*, N.Y. TIMES, June 27, 2011, at A10; Erik Eckholm et al., *Across Country, Lawmakers Push Abortion Curbs*, N.Y. TIMES, Jan. 22, 2011, at A1; Rosalind S. Helderman, *Abortion Clinics in Virginia Will Face New Regulations*, WASH. POST, Feb. 25, 2011, at A1; A.G. Sulzberger & Monica Davey, *New Law in Kansas Seen as a Threat to Abortions*, N.Y. TIMES, June 25, 2011, at A11. One of the more noteworthy measures in this time frame has been an amendment to the Mississippi Constitution on the ballot in November 2011. It defined personhood under state law "to include every human being from the moment of fertilization, cloning or the functional equivalent thereof." *Elections: Initiatives—26 Definition of a Person*, MISS. SECRETARY OF STATE, http://www.sos.ms.gov/page.aspx?s=7&s1=1&s2=50 (last visited Nov. 15, 2011). Supporters of the measure "said it would have stopped the murder of innocent life and sent a clarion moral call to the world[,]" while opponents maintained it "would have outlawed all abortions, including in cases of rape and incest and when the mother's life was in danger; would have barred morning-after pills and certain contraception such as IUD's; and could have limited in vitro fertility procedures." Katherine Q. Seelye, *Voters Defeat Many G.O.P.-Sponsored Measures*, N.Y. TIMES, Nov. 8, 2011, at A20. The measure did not succeed in Mississippi, but similar proposals may soon be on the ballot in other states. *See, e.g.,* Tristan Navera, *Anti-Abortion Group Seeks 'Personhood' Amendment to Ohio Constitution,* COLUMBUS DISPATCH, Oct. 24, 2011.

Does Justice Kennedy's opinion in *Gonzalez v. Carhart* give reason to think some or all of these measures are (now) constitutional? For perspective, see David J. Garrow, *Significant Risks: Gonzales v Carhart and the Future of Abortion Law,* 2007 SUP. CT. REV. 1 (2007); Reva B. Siegel, *Dignity and the Politics of Protection: Abortion Restrictions Under* Casey/Carhart, 117 YALE L.J. 1694 (2008); Robin West, *From Choice to Reproductive Justice: De–Constitutionalizing Abortion Rights,* 118 YALE L.J. 1394 (2009)

Lawrence v. Texas

Supreme Court of the United States, 2003.
539 U.S. 558, 123 S.Ct. 2472, 156 L.Ed.2d 508.

■ JUSTICE KENNEDY delivered the opinion of the Court.

. . .

The question before the Court is the validity of a Texas statute making it a crime for two persons of the same sex to engage in certain intimate sexual conduct.

In Houston, Texas, officers of the Harris County Police Department were dispatched to a private residence in response to a reported weapons disturbance. They entered an apartment where one of the petitioners, John Geddes Lawrence, resided. The right of the police to enter does not seem to have been questioned. The officers observed Lawrence and another man, Tyron Garner, engaging in a sexual act. The two petitioners were arrested, held in custody over night, and charged and convicted before a Justice of the Peace.

The complaints described their crime as "deviate sexual intercourse, namely anal sex, with a member of the same sex (man)." The applicable state law is Tex. Penal Code Ann. § 21.06(a) (2003). It provides: "A person commits an offense if he engages in deviate sexual intercourse with another individual of the same sex." The statute defines "[d]eviate sexual intercourse" as follows:

"(A) any contact between any part of the genitals of one person and the mouth or anus of another person; or

"(B) the penetration of the genitals or the anus of another person with an object."

. . . The petitioners, having entered a plea of nolo contendere, were each fined $200 and assessed court costs of $141.25.

The Court of Appeals for the Texas Fourteenth District considered the petitioners' federal constitutional arguments under both the Equal Protection and Due Process Clauses of the Fourteenth Amendment. After hearing the case en banc the court, in a divided opinion, rejected the constitutional arguments and affirmed the convictions. The majority opinion indicates that the Court of Appeals considered our decision in *Bowers v. Hardwick,* 478 U.S. 186 (1986), to be controlling on the federal due process aspect of the case. *Bowers* then being authoritative, this was proper.

We granted certiorari to consider three questions:

"1. Whether petitioners' criminal convictions under the Texas 'Homosexual Conduct' law—which criminalizes sexual intimacy by same-sex couples, but not identical behavior by different-sex couples—violate the Fourteenth Amendment guarantee of equal protection of laws?

"2.   Whether petitioners' criminal convictions for adult consensual sexual intimacy in the home violate their vital interests in liberty and privacy protected by the Due Process Clause of the Fourteenth Amendment?

"3.   Whether *Bowers v. Hardwick*, [478 U.S. 186 (1986)] should be overruled?"

The petitioners were adults at the time of the alleged offense. Their conduct was in private and consensual.

We conclude the case should be resolved by determining whether the petitioners were free as adults to engage in the private conduct in the exercise of their liberty under the Due Process Clause of the Fourteenth Amendment to the Constitution. For this inquiry we deem it necessary to reconsider the Court's holding in *Bowers*.

.   .   .

The Court began its substantive discussion in *Bowers* as follows: "The issue presented is whether the Federal Constitution confers a fundamental right upon homosexuals to engage in sodomy and hence invalidates the laws of the many States that still make such conduct illegal and have done so for a very long time." That statement, we now conclude, discloses the Court's own failure to appreciate the extent of the liberty at stake. To say that the issue in *Bowers* was simply the right to engage in certain sexual conduct demeans the claim the individual put forward, just as it would demean a married couple were it to be said marriage is simply about the right to have sexual intercourse. The laws involved in *Bowers* and here are, to be sure, statutes that purport to do no more than prohibit a particular sexual act. Their penalties and purposes, though, have more far-reaching consequences, touching upon the most private human conduct, sexual behavior, and in the most private of places, the home. The statutes do seek to control a personal relationship that, whether or not entitled to formal recognition in the law, is within the liberty of persons to choose without being punished as criminals.

This, as a general rule, should counsel against attempts by the State, or a court, to define the meaning of the relationship or to set its boundaries absent injury to a person or abuse of an institution the law protects. It suffices for us to acknowledge that adults may choose to enter upon this relationship in the confines of their homes and their own private lives and still retain their dignity as free persons. When sexuality finds overt expression in intimate conduct with another person, the conduct can be but one element in a personal bond that is more enduring. The liberty protected by the Constitution allows homosexual persons the right to make this choice.

Having misapprehended the claim of liberty there presented to it, and thus stating the claim to be whether there is a fundamental right to engage in consensual sodomy, the *Bowers* Court said: "Proscriptions against that conduct have ancient roots." . . . [T]he following considerations counsel against adopting the definitive conclusions upon which *Bowers* placed such reliance.

At the outset it should be noted that there is no longstanding history in this country of laws directed at homosexual conduct as a distinct matter. Beginning in colonial times there were prohibitions of sodomy derived from the English criminal laws passed in the first instance by the Reformation

Parliament of 1533. The English prohibition was understood to include relations between men and women as well as relations between men and men. Nineteenth-century commentators similarly read American sodomy, buggery, and crime-against-nature statutes as criminalizing certain relations between men and women and between men and men.... Thus early American sodomy laws were not directed at homosexuals as such but instead sought to prohibit nonprocreative sexual activity more generally. This does not suggest approval of homosexual conduct. It does tend to show that this particular form of conduct was not thought of as a separate category from like conduct between heterosexual persons.

. . .

It was not until the 1970's that any State singled out same-sex relations for criminal prosecution, and only nine States have done so. Post–*Bowers* even some of these States did not adhere to the policy of suppressing homosexual conduct. Over the course of the last decades, States with same-sex prohibitions have moved toward abolishing them.

In summary, the historical grounds relied upon in *Bowers* are more complex than the majority opinion and the concurring opinion by Chief Justice Burger indicate. Their historical premises are not without doubt and, at the very least, are overstated.

It must be acknowledged, of course, that the Court in *Bowers* was making the broader point that for centuries there have been powerful voices to condemn homosexual conduct as immoral. The condemnation has been shaped by religious beliefs, conceptions of right and acceptable behavior, and respect for the traditional family. For many persons these are not trivial concerns but profound and deep convictions accepted as ethical and moral principles to which they aspire and which thus determine the course of their lives. These considerations do not answer the question before us, however. The issue is whether the majority may use the power of the State to enforce these views on the whole society through operation of the criminal law....

Chief Justice Burger joined the opinion for the Court in *Bowers* and further explained his views as follows: "Decisions of individuals relating to homosexual conduct have been subject to state intervention throughout the history of Western civilization. Condemnation of those practices is firmly rooted in Judeao–Christian moral and ethical standards." As with Justice White's assumptions about history, scholarship casts some doubt on the sweeping nature of the statement by Chief Justice Burger as it pertains to private homosexual conduct between consenting adults. In all events we think that our laws and traditions in the past half century are of most relevance here. These references show an emerging awareness that liberty gives substantial protection to adult persons in deciding how to conduct their private lives in matters pertaining to sex....

This emerging recognition should have been apparent when *Bowers* was decided. In 1955 the American Law Institute promulgated the MODEL PENAL CODE and made clear that it did not recommend or provide for "criminal penalties for consensual sexual relations conducted in private." ALI, Model Penal Code § 213.2, Comment 2, p. 372 (1980). It justified its decision on three grounds: (1) The prohibition undermined respect for the law by penalizing conduct many people engaged in; (2) the statutes regulated private conduct not harmful to others; and (3) the laws were arbitrarily enforced and thus invited the danger of blackmail. ALI, MODEL PENAL CODE,

Commentary 277–280 (Tent. Draft No. 4, 1955). In 1961 Illinois changed its laws to conform to the Model Penal Code. Other States soon followed.

. . .

The sweeping references by Chief Justice Burger to the history of Western civilization . . . did not take account of other authorities pointing in an opposite direction. A committee advising the British Parliament recommended in 1957 repeal of laws punishing homosexual conduct. The Wolfenden Report: Report of the Committee on Homosexual Offenses and Prostitution (1963). Parliament enacted the substance of those recommendations 10 years later.

Of even more importance, almost five years before *Bowers* was decided the European Court of Human Rights considered a case with parallels to *Bowers* and to today's case. An adult male resident in Northern Ireland alleged he was a practicing homosexual who desired to engage in consensual homosexual conduct. The laws of Northern Ireland forbade him that right. He alleged that he had been questioned, his home had been searched, and he feared criminal prosecution. The court held that the laws proscribing the conduct were invalid under the European Convention on Human Rights. *Dudgeon v. United Kingdom*, 45 Eur. Ct. H. R. (1981) ¶ 52. Authoritative in all countries that are members of the Council of Europe (21 nations then, 45 nations now) the decision is at odds with the premise in *Bowers* that the claim put forward was insubstantial in our Western civilization.

In our own constitutional system, the deficiencies in *Bowers* became even more apparent in the years following its announcement. The 25 States with laws prohibiting the relevant conduct referenced in the *Bowers* decision are reduced now to 13, of which 4 enforce their laws only against homosexual conduct. In those States where sodomy is still proscribed, whether for same-sex or heterosexual conduct, there is a pattern of nonenforcement with respect to consenting adults acting in private. . . .

. . .

As an alternative argument in this case, counsel for the petitioners and some *amici* contend that *Romer* [*v. Evans*, 517 U.S. 620 (1996)] provides the basis for declaring the Texas statute invalid under the Equal Protection Clause. That is a tenable argument, but we conclude the instant case requires us to address whether *Bowers* itself has continuing validity. Were we to hold the statute invalid under the Equal Protection Clause some might question whether a prohibition would be valid if drawn differently, say, to prohibit the conduct both between same-sex and different-sex participants.

Equality of treatment and the due process right to demand respect for conduct protected by the substantive guarantee of liberty are linked in important respects, and a decision on the latter point advances both interests. If protected conduct is made criminal and the law which does so remains unexamined for its substantive validity, its stigma might remain even if it were not enforceable as drawn for equal protection reasons. When homosexual conduct is made criminal by the law of the State, that declaration in and of itself is an invitation to subject homosexual persons to discrimination both in the public and in the private spheres. The central holding of *Bowers* has been brought in question by this case, and it should be addressed. Its continuance as precedent demeans the lives of homosexual persons.

. . .

... In his dissenting opinion in *Bowers* JUSTICE STEVENS came to these conclusions:

"Our prior cases make two propositions abundantly clear. First, the fact that the governing majority in a State has traditionally viewed a particular practice as immoral is not a sufficient reason for upholding a law prohibiting the practice; neither history nor tradition could save a law prohibiting miscegenation from constitutional attack. Second, individual decisions by married persons, concerning the intimacies of their physical relationship, even when not intended to produce offspring, are a form of 'liberty' protected by the Due Process Clause of the Fourteenth Amendment. Moreover, this protection extends to intimate choices by unmarried as well as married persons." 478 U. S., at 216 (footnotes and citations omitted).

JUSTICE STEVENS' analysis, in our view, should have been controlling in *Bowers* and should control here.

Bowers was not correct when it was decided, and it is not correct today. It ought not to remain binding precedent. *Bowers v. Hardwick* should be and now is overruled.

The present case does not involve minors. It does not involve persons who might be injured or coerced or who are situated in relationships where consent might not easily be refused. It does not involve public conduct or prostitution. It does not involve whether the government must give formal recognition to any relationship that homosexual persons seek to enter. The case does involve two adults who, with full and mutual consent from each other, engaged in sexual practices common to a homosexual lifestyle. The petitioners are entitled to respect for their private lives. The State cannot demean their existence or control their destiny by making their private sexual conduct a crime.... The Texas statute furthers no legitimate state interest which can justify its intrusion into the personal and private life of the individual.

■ JUSTICE O'CONNOR, concurring in the judgment:

The Court today overrules *Bowers v. Hardwick*. I joined *Bowers*, and do not join the Court in overruling it. Nevertheless, I agree with the Court that Texas' statute banning same-sex sodomy is unconstitutional. Rather than relying on the substantive component of the Fourteenth Amendment's Due Process Clause, as the Court does, I base my conclusion on the Fourteenth Amendment's Equal Protection Clause.

. . .

The statute at issue here makes sodomy a crime only if a person "engages in deviate sexual intercourse with another individual of the same sex." Tex. Penal Code Ann. § 21.06(a) (2003). Sodomy between opposite-sex partners, however, is not a crime in Texas. That is, Texas treats the same conduct differently based solely on the participants. Those harmed by this law are people who have a same-sex sexual orientation and thus are more likely to engage in behavior prohibited by § 21.06.

The Texas statute makes homosexuals unequal in the eyes of the law by making particular conduct—and only that conduct—subject to criminal sanction....

And the effect of Texas' sodomy law is not just limited to the threat of prosecution or consequence of conviction. Texas' sodomy law brands all homosexuals as criminals, thereby making it more difficult for homosexuals to be treated in the same manner as everyone else. . . .

Texas attempts to justify its law, and the effects of the law, by arguing that the statute satisfies rational basis review because it furthers the legitimate governmental interest of the promotion of morality. In *Bowers*, we held that a state law criminalizing sodomy as applied to homosexual couples did not violate substantive due process. We rejected the argument that no rational basis existed to justify the law, pointing to the government's interest in promoting morality. The only question in front of the Court in *Bowers* was whether the substantive component of the Due Process Clause protected a right to engage in homosexual sodomy. *Bowers* did not hold that moral disapproval of a group is a rational basis under the Equal Protection Clause to criminalize homosexual sodomy when heterosexual sodomy is not punished.

This case raises a different issue than *Bowers*: whether, under the Equal Protection Clause, moral disapproval is a legitimate state interest to justify by itself a statute that bans homosexual sodomy, but not heterosexual sodomy. It is not. Moral disapproval of this group, like a bare desire to harm the group, is an interest that is insufficient to satisfy rational basis review under the Equal Protection Clause. Indeed, we have never held that moral disapproval, without any other asserted state interest, is a sufficient rationale under the Equal Protection Clause to justify a law that discriminates among groups of persons.

Moral disapproval of a group cannot be a legitimate governmental interest under the Equal Protection Clause because legal classifications must not be "drawn for the purpose of disadvantaging the group burdened. . . ." Texas' invocation of moral disapproval as a legitimate state interest proves nothing more than Texas' desire to criminalize homosexual sodomy. But the Equal Protection Clause prevents a State from creating "a classification of persons undertaken for its own sake." And because Texas so rarely enforces its sodomy law as applied to private, consensual acts, the law serves more as a statement of dislike and disapproval against homosexuals than as a tool to stop criminal behavior. The Texas sodomy law "raises the inevitable inference that the disadvantage imposed is born of animosity toward the class of persons affected."

. . .

A State can of course assign certain consequences to a violation of its criminal law. But the State cannot single out one identifiable class of citizens for punishment that does not apply to everyone else, with moral disapproval as the only asserted state interest for the law. The Texas sodomy statute subjects homosexuals to "a lifelong penalty and stigma. A legislative classification that threatens the creation of an underclass . . . cannot be reconciled with" the Equal Protection Clause.

Whether a sodomy law that is neutral both in effect and application, would violate the substantive component of the Due Process Clause is an issue that need not be decided today. I am confident, however, that so long as the Equal Protection Clause requires a sodomy law to apply equally to the private consensual conduct of homosexuals and heterosexuals alike, such a law would not long stand in our democratic society. . . .

That this law as applied to private, consensual conduct is unconstitutional under the Equal Protection Clause does not mean that other laws distinguishing between heterosexuals and homosexuals would similarly fail under rational basis review. Texas cannot assert any legitimate state interest here, such as national security or preserving the traditional institution of marriage. Unlike the moral disapproval of same-sex relations—the asserted state interest in this case—other reasons exist to promote the institution of marriage beyond mere moral disapproval of an excluded group.

A law branding one class of persons as criminal solely based on the State's moral disapproval of that class and the conduct associated with that class runs contrary to the values of the Constitution and the Equal Protection Clause, under any standard of review. I therefore concur in the Court's judgment that Texas' sodomy law banning "deviate sexual intercourse" between consenting adults of the same sex, but not between consenting adults of different sexes, is unconstitutional.

■ JUSTICE SCALIA, with whom THE CHIEF JUSTICE and JUSTICE THOMAS join, dissenting:

. . .

I turn now to the ground on which the Court squarely rests its holding: the contention that there is no rational basis for the law here under attack. This proposition is so out of accord with our jurisprudence—indeed, with the jurisprudence of *any* society we know—that it requires little discussion.

The Texas statute undeniably seeks to further the belief of its citizens that certain forms of sexual behavior are "immoral and unacceptable,"—the same interest furthered by criminal laws against fornication, bigamy, adultery, adult incest, bestiality, and obscenity. *Bowers* held that this *was* a legitimate state interest. The Court today reaches the opposite conclusion. The Texas statute, it says, "furthers *no legitimate state interest* which can justify its intrusion into the personal and private life of the individual." ([E]mphasis added.) The Court embraces instead Justice Stevens' declaration in his *Bowers* dissent, that "the fact that the governing majority in a State has traditionally viewed a particular practice as immoral is not a sufficient reason for upholding a law prohibiting the practice." This effectively decrees the end of all morals legislation. If, as the Court asserts, the promotion of majoritarian sexual morality is not even a *legitimate* state interest, none of the above-mentioned laws can survive rational-basis review.

Finally, I turn to petitioners' equal-protection challenge, which no Member of the Court save JUSTICE O'CONNOR embraces: On its face § 21.06(a) applies equally to all persons. Men and women, heterosexuals and homosexuals, are all subject to its prohibition of deviate sexual intercourse with someone of the same sex. To be sure, § 21.06 does distinguish between the sexes insofar as concerns the partner with whom the sexual acts are performed: men can violate the law only with other men, and women only with other women. But this cannot itself be a denial of equal protection, since it is precisely the same distinction regarding partner that is drawn in state laws prohibiting marriage with someone of the same sex while permitting marriage with someone of the opposite sex.

The objection is made, however, that the antimiscegenation laws invalidated in *Loving v. Virginia*, 388 U.S. 1 (1967), similarly were applicable to whites and blacks alike, and only distinguished between the races insofar as the *partner* was concerned. In *Loving*, however, we correctly applied heightened scrutiny, rather than the usual rational-basis review, because the Virginia statute was "designed to maintain White Supremacy." A racially discriminatory purpose is always sufficient to subject a law to strict scrutiny, even a facially neutral law that makes no mention of race. See *Washington v.*

Davis, 426 U.S. 229 (1976). No purpose to discriminate against men or women as a class can be gleaned from the Texas law, so rational-basis review applies. That review is readily satisfied here by the same rational basis that satisfied it in *Bowers*—society's belief that certain forms of sexual behavior are "immoral and unacceptable," 478 U.S., at 196. This is the same justification that supports many other laws regulating sexual behavior that make a distinction based upon the identity of the partner—for example, laws against adultery, fornication, and adult incest, and laws refusing to recognize homosexual marriage.

Justice O'Connor argues that the discrimination in this law which must be justified is not its discrimination with regard to the sex of the partner but its discrimination with regard to the sexual proclivity of the principal actor.

> While it is true that the law applies only to conduct, the conduct targeted by this law is conduct that is closely correlated with being homosexual. Under such circumstances, Texas' sodomy law is targeted at more than conduct. It is instead directed toward gay persons as a class.

Of course the same could be said of any law. A law against public nudity targets "the conduct that is closely correlated with being a nudist," and hence "is targeted at more than conduct"; it is "directed toward nudists as a class." But be that as it may. Even if the Texas law *does* deny equal protection to "homosexuals as a class," that denial *still* does not need to be justified by anything more than a rational basis, which our cases show is satisfied by the enforcement of traditional notions of sexual morality.

Justice O'Connor simply decrees application of "a more searching form of rational basis review" to the Texas statute. The cases she cites do not recognize such a standard, and reach their conclusions only after finding, as required by conventional rational-basis analysis, that no conceivable legitimate state interest supports the classification at issue. See *Romer v. Evans*, 517 U.S., at 635; *Cleburne v. Cleburne Living Center, Inc.*, 473 U.S. 432, 448–450 (1985); *Department of Agriculture v. Moreno*, 413 U.S. 528, 534–538 (1973). Nor does Justice O'Connor explain precisely what her "more searching form" of rational-basis review consists of. It must at least mean, however, that laws exhibiting " 'a desire to harm a politically unpopular group,' " are invalid *even though* there may be a conceivable rational basis to support them.

This reasoning leaves on pretty shaky grounds state laws limiting marriage to opposite-sex couples. Justice O'Connor seeks to preserve them by the conclusory statement that "preserving the traditional institution of marriage" is a legitimate state interest. But "preserving the traditional institution of marriage" is just a kinder way of describing the State's *moral disapproval* of same-sex couples. Texas's interest in § 21.06 could be recast in similarly euphemistic terms: "preserving the traditional sexual mores of our society." In the jurisprudence Justice O'Connor has seemingly created, judges can validate laws by characterizing them as "preserving the traditions of society" (good); or invalidate them by characterizing them as "expressing moral disapproval" (bad).

. . .

Let me be clear that I have nothing against homosexuals, or any other group, promoting their agenda through normal democratic means. Social perceptions of sexual and other morality change over time, and every group has the right to persuade its fellow citizens that its view of such matters is the best. That homosexuals have achieved some success in that enterprise is attested to by the fact that Texas is one of the few remaining States that criminalize private, consensual homosexual acts. But persuading one's fellow citizens is one thing, and imposing one's views in absence of democratic majority will is something else. I would no more *require* a State to criminalize homosexual acts—or, for that matter, display *any* moral disapprobation of them—than I would *forbid* it to do so. What Texas has chosen to do is well within the range of traditional democratic action, and its hand should not be stayed through the invention of a brand-new "constitutional right" by a Court that is impatient of democratic change. It is indeed true that "later generations can see that laws once thought necessary and proper in fact serve only to oppress," and when that happens, later generations can repeal those laws. But it is the premise of our system that those judgments are to be made by the people, and not imposed by a governing caste that knows best.

NOTE

Consider Pamela S. Karlan, *Forward: Loving Lawrence*, 102 MICH. L. REV. 1447, 1449–50 (2004):

> *Loving* drew a clear distinction between rationality review and heightened scrutiny. *Lawrence*, by contrast, sidesteps this conventional doctrinal framework. *Loving* reflected the emergence of strict scrutiny under both the Equal Protection and the Due Process Clauses; *Lawrence*, however, does to due process analysis something very similar to what the Court's previous gay-rights decision, *Romer v. Evans*, did to equal protection analysis: it undermines the traditional tiers of scrutiny altogether. This approach reflects more than simply the fact that the two opinions share the same author. Both *Lawrence* and *Romer v. Evans* express an "analogical crisis." Gay rights cases "just can't be steered readily onto the strict scrutiny or the rationality track," let alone onto the due process/conduct or the equal protection/status track. Cases about race created the modern framework of heightened scrutiny; cases about sexual orientation may transform it.

Consider also Marc Spindelman, *Surviving* Lawrence v. Texas, 102 MICH. L. REV. 1615, 1633–35 (2004):

> Anyone who is seriously dedicated to equality between the sexes has to acknowledge the historic breakthrough for lesbian and gay rights that *Lawrence* represents. The elimination of discrimination against lesbians and gay men, integral to sexual hierarchy and the positioning of men and women within it, is indispensable to sexual equality's realization. As an affirmation of lesbian and gay rights, then, sex-equality theorists have some reason to be pleased about *Lawrence*. I, for one, am.
>
> But there is more to the evaluation of a judicial text than a simple assessment of, or reaction to, its ostensible ends. Looking beyond what seems to be *Lawrence*'s bottom line, its like-straight reasoning—especially its uncritical solicitude for heterosexuality, and the corresponding notion, reflected in its protection of a right to sexual intimacy, that heterosexuality is entitled to constitutional protections, in its intimacies above all—is cause for serious concern.
>
> To begin, empirical investigations into the conditions of sex inequality have demonstrated that heterosexuality is hardly as unproblematic as the Court's opinion in *Lawrence* may make it seem. These investigations have shown, for instance, that the institution of heterosexuality has largely been defined in male-supremacist terms—terms that include both the massive production and the massive denial of the sexual abuse and violence that women suffer at men's hands, along with the sexualized dimensions of the homophobic violence lesbians and gay men suffer at the hands of presumptively heterosexual men. The commonplace that sexual intimacy of the sort *Lawrence* approves should be heralded as the measure of non-violation has been uncovered as a myth, a way of ignoring and protecting the widespread abuses, including sexual assault, domes-

tic violence, and sexual abuse of children, by more powerful partners in intimate relationships, typically, though not exclusively, men. When sexual intimacy is thought to be normatively good, the basis for relationships "more enduring," as it is in *Lawrence*, how can it (also) be a prison of abuse? Can it be? What about when, not if, in actuality, it is?

See generally Symposium, *Equality, Privacy and Lesbian and Gay Rights After* Lawrence v. Texas, 65 OHIO ST. L.J. 1057 (2004); Symposium, *Gay Rights After* Lawrence v. Texas, 88 MINN. L. REV. 1021 (2004); Lawrence v. Texas *Symposium*, 46 S. TEX. L. REV. 245 (2004); Symposium, *Readings of* Lawrence v. Texas, 11 WIDENER L. REV. 171 (2005); *Standing in the Penumbras of Privacy: The Future of Privacy in the Wake of* Lawrence v. Texas *Symposium*, 8 RICH. J.L. & PUB. INT. 1 (2004); *Symposium on the Implications of* Lawrence *and* Goodridge *for the Recognition of Same–Sex Marriages and the Validity of DOMA*, 38 CREIGHTON L. REV. 233 (2004); *Symposium: Privacy Rights in a Post* Lawrence *World: Responses to* Lawrence v. Texas, 10 CARDOZO WOMEN'S L.J. 263 (2004).

3.   DOMESTIC VIOLENCE

a.   TRADITIONAL IMMUNITY AND EXEMPTION

The assumption of marital unity that characterized the traditional model of marriage for many years precluded states from "intervening" in a marriage to prevent or punish violence by one spouse against the other. In practical terms, this meant that husbands were not legally accountable for abusing their wives. The doctrine of interspousal tort immunity was one means by which this was accomplished, and the exemption of a husband from rape liability was another. Most states have now abolished interspousal tort immunity. This has enabled victims to bring actions against their abusers for such torts as assault, battery, intentional infliction of emotional distress, and even false imprisonment. *See generally* CLAIRE DALTON & ELIZABETH SCHNEIDER, BATTERED WOMEN AND THE LAW 816–45 (2001).

Elimination of the marital rape exemption has progressed more slowly. As you read the excerpt below, consider whether the asserted rationales for preserving some distinction between married and unmarried partners are distinguishable from those that underlay interspousal tort immunity.

Jill Elaine Hasday, *Contest and Consent: A Legal History of Marital Rape*

88 CALIF. L. REV. 1375, 1482–1504 (2000).

At common law, husbands were exempt from prosecution for raping their wives. Over the past quarter century, this law has been modified somewhat, but not entirely. A majority of states still retain some form of the common law regime: they criminalize a narrower range of offenses if committed within marriage, subject the marital rape they do recognize to less serious sanctions, and/or create special procedural hurdles for marital rape prosecutions. The current state of the law represents a confusing mix of victory and defeat for the exemption's contemporary feminist critics. Virtually every state legislature has revisited the marital rape exemption over the last twenty-five years, but most have chosen to preserve the exemption in some substantial manifestation. With rare exception, moreover, courts have not invalidated state laws protecting marital rape. Political protest and legislative action, rather than any clear judicial statement of constitutional norms, [have] driven the partial and uneven modification of the common law rule.

. . .

... The first sustained contest over marital rape was coterminous with the life span of the first woman's rights movement in the United States. Begun almost immediately upon the organization of nineteenth-century feminism, it dissipated when the movement disbanded. It was not until the last quarter of the twentieth century that the legal status of marital rape was again subject to significant attack, led this time by the second organized women's movement. Here too, however, the resulting reform has been partial and uneven.

. . .

... A majority of states still retain some form of the rule exempting a husband from prosecution for raping his wife. Some states require a couple to be separated at the time of the injury (and sometimes extend the exemption to cover unmarried cohabitants). Some only recognize marital rape if it involves physical force and/or serious physical harm. Some provide for vastly reduced penalties if a rape occurs in marriage, or create special procedural requirements for marital rape prosecutions. Almost all of this law, moreover, is the product of political advocacy and legislative action, rather than constitutional adjudication, so that the nature and continued path of change is insecure. Enforcement of the existing statutes recognizing some forms of marital rape has certainly been very infrequent.

. . .

The first prominent modern argument for the marital rape exemption, the claim from privacy, posits that there is something inherent in the nature of the relationship between husband and wife that makes legal intervention inappropriate, misguided, and ultimately self-defeating. It contends that the marital relation depends on intimacy protected from outside scrutiny, intimacy that could not survive if the law intervened to investigate and prosecute marital rape charges.

Contemporary defenders of the marital rape exemption do not articulate this privacy claim in sex-specific terms, or as a balancing test in which gains must be set against losses. They do not seek to explain why it is important to protect men's privacy in marriage through a marital rape exemption, even if women's interests may suffer. They make no mention of the possibility that marital rape or the absence of criminal remediation might inflict injury on wives. To the contrary, the exemption's modern defenders speak about protecting the privacy of the marital relationship that husband and wife share, of benefitting both. Consider, for instance, how a Florida state representative explained his support for a marital rape exemption: " 'The State of Florida has absolutely no business intervening into the sexual relationship between a husband and a wife.... We don't need Florida invading the sanctity and the intimacy *of a relationship.*' " The drafters of the Model Penal Code, who recommend an absolute marital rape exemption, similarly note that the exemption "avoids [an] unwarranted intrusion of the penal law into the life *of the family.*" Along the same lines, the Pennsylvania Superior Court interpreted a recent legislative modification of the exemption narrowly in order to stop the state from invading "the privacy of the marital bedroom for the purpose of supervising the manner in which *marital relationships* are consummated." The crucial claim of this privacy defense for the marital rape exemption is that keeping the judicial system away from disputes over marital rape serves the interests that a husband and wife *both* have in maintaining their joint privacy, that the exemption protects the intimacy that they have established with each other and from which each benefit unambiguously. Marriage here is envisioned as a necessarily harmonious relation, and legal intervention as the first, unwelcome introduction of antagonism and injury.

The other prominent modern claim articulated in favor of the marital rape exemption, that it facilitates marital reconciliation, similarly explains the exemption as promoting the shared interests of wives and husbands. Building on the proposition that marital intimacy is destroyed by outside observation, this argument contends that the legal system should not be able to investigate or prosecute marital rape because such intervention will make reconciliation between husband and wife significantly less likely. Once the state appears on the scene, the exemption's supporters suggest, the delicate shoots of love, trust, and closeness in a marriage will be trampled in a way unlikely ever to be undone. In contrast, if the exemption remains in place, this argument asserts that many married couples will be able to reconcile after what would otherwise be considered a marital rape.

. . .

A less prominent contemporary defense of the marital rape exemption might be called the "vindictive wife" argument. This claim contends that the exemption should be preserved in order to prevent wives from pursuing false charges of marital rape, especially to gain leverage in a divorce suit. The line of reasoning openly recognizes the possibility of marital antagonism (at least at the end of a relationship), placing it in some tension with the more prominent claims for the exemption from privacy and reconciliation. But there is a long, distinct tradition in Anglo–American law, traceable . . . to Hale's seminal treatise, advocating the particular disbelief of rape victims. Hale famously warned that rape was "an accusation easily to be made and hard to be proved, and harder to be defended by the party accused, tho never so innocent." The vindictive wife argument for preserving the marital rape exemption accords well with this tradition. There is, after all, no empirical evidence to support the proposition that wives are prone to make false charges of marital rape. To the contrary, the evidence available from states that allow marital rape prosecutions suggests that the incidents that women report to law enforcement officials tend to be very brutal, and relatively easy to prove.

More fundamentally, the vindictive wife defense of the marital rape exemption recognizes marital discord in a very particular, and limited, way. In this vision, the antagonistic and harmful act to be feared in marriage is not the possibility of an actual marital rape. The argument never suggests that the marital rape exemption may be shielding and facilitating injurious conduct inflicted by husbands on wives. To the contrary, it envisions the exemption as a check on self-interestedness within marriage, a legal rule that keeps one spouse from unjustifiably betraying the other (or, described more precisely, that keeps wives from betraying their husbands). As one state legislator explains the theory, "since society is already burdened with these kinds of women [vengeful wives], . . . the last thing we need is a law making it illegal for a husband to sexually assault his wife."

This mode of argument in defense of the marital rape exemption has been very successful. Granted, the law of marital rape has changed more notably in the late twentieth century than in the nineteenth. At the end of a half-century's effort by the first organized woman's rights movement, the only alteration apparent in the legal treatment of marital rape consisted of a marginal liberalization in the divorce law. In contrast, over the past quarter century, a minority of states have eliminated the exemption and many more have modified its reach. Yet the marital rape exemption survives in some substantial form in a majority of states, in an era in which almost every other aspect of women's legal subordination at common law (including a husband's right to assault his wife nonsexually) has been formally repudiated. The modern feminist campaign against marital rape, like its nineteenth-century predecessor, has encountered tremendous resistance and had much less of an impact on the law than it aimed for or achieved in other arenas.

Although not explicitly phrased this way, the contemporary feminist argument against the marital rape exemption, like that of the nineteenth-century woman's rights movement, is an effort to establish that marriage is a potentially antagonistic and dangerous relation, in which women need and deserve legal rights to protect themselves from the serious harms caused by unwanted sex in marriage. Modern feminists, for instance, have a radically different understanding of what privacy arguments for the marital rape exemption are safeguarding. In this view, the use of privacy rationales to justify nonintervention in cases of marital rape protects and exacerbates the current distribution of power within a marriage. Feminists take this distribution to be markedly imbalanced, noting that men are disproportionately richer, stronger, and bigger than their wives. They contend that privacy arguments for the marital rape exemption keep the state from acting to equalize relations in the wife's interest and add state sanction to the power that husbands exercise. On this account, the interests of husband and wife are very much unaligned on the question of legal remediation for marital rape, and the overriding function of the privacy defense of the exemption is not to shelter shared intimacy. Instead, the privacy claim gives husbands safety in committing highly injurious conduct that the law would otherwise consider felonious, while simultaneously disabling wives from summoning state resources for their own protection.

The feminist response to the marital reconciliation argument similarly stresses the divergent interests of husbands and wives, and the lasting harm that marital rape inflicts on married women. Feminists acknowledge that men who rape their wives will systematically favor a legal regime that permits them to avoid prosecution so that they can attempt to reconcile with their wives on private terms. But they contend that the exemption does not serve women's interests equally well. In this vision, what irreparably destroys marital harmony—from the wife's perspective—is not state prosecution, but the marital rape itself. Even with the exemption from prosecution firmly in place, a wife may have little interest in marital reconciliation after her husband has raped her. Marital rape causes women severe and abiding injury, feminists explain, and there is good reason for a wife to conclude that she will be better off if she does not reconcile with a husband who has raped her. Feminists argue that if a wife would be willing to cooperate in her husband's prosecution, the law should not second-guess her assessment of her own interests, even if that assessment diverges from her husband's preferred resolution.

In these feminist arguments, the injury ignored or denied by the exemption's modern defenders is presented in stark relief. The modern feminist rendering of the wound that marital rape inflicts upon women is somewhat different from the account that the nineteenth-century woman's rights movement provided, reflecting an evolving set of commitments. But contemporary feminists, like their nineteenth-century predecessors, empha-size that marital rape causes women serious harm.

First, modern feminists oppose marital rape on the ground that it deprives women of control over their reproductive capacity. This argument is the closest present-day equivalent to the nineteenth-century focus on control over the work of motherhood. Reproductive concerns, however, are far less prominent in modern feminist advocacy against marital rape, per-haps because contemporary feminism accepts contraception and abortion as alternate means of limiting fertility. Modern feminists also concentrate more on the physiological aspects of motherhood (like conception and gestation), than on the child rearing that occupied the nineteenth-century movement, a possible manifestation of the contemporary feminist decision to contest women's disproportionate responsibility for raising children.

More frequently, modern feminists argue that marital rape denies women the right to control their sexuality and their chances for sexual pleasure. . . . The first woman's rights movement, operating in an era that understood female sexuality to be weaker than its male counterpart, was more occupied by its effort to limit the downside risks of marital intercourse for women. Modern feminists, in contrast, tend (like contemporary Ameri-cans generally) to be more optimistic about and interested in the possibilities of sexual intercourse, which has implications for their understanding of the injury that marital rape inflicts. Their account of harm often notes that a marital rape victim loses the ability to determine her sexual "actions, pleasures, and desires free from external influence." From this perspective, "[t]he damage occasioned by [marital rape exemptions] is the subordination, and in many cases the annihilation, of the psychic, physical, emotional, and erotic female self." On a related note, modern feminists also attack marital rape as a violation of women's bodily integrity, never a focus of nineteenth-century feminism. The marital rape exemption, in these terms, "manifests disregard for women's bodily integrity and autonomy and, instead, sanctions their vulnerability in marriage."

The difficulties that the contemporary feminist campaign against marital rape has encountered are particularly remarkable because the modern empirical evidence on marital rape supports the feminists' sex-specific analy-sis in many ways, delineating how the interests of men and women differ and revealing the trauma that marital rape inflicts upon women. All available evidence, for instance, indicates that marital rape is virtually always commit-ted by husbands on wives. Indeed, I have been able to locate just a handful of cases in which women may have come to the attention of American law enforcement authorities for raping adult men. Only a few more examples of female-on-male rape have been reported in the psychiatric literature. It is possible to predict with almost perfect accuracy that marital rape cases will involve the husband as rapist and the wife as victim. The more lopsided the factual circumstances, the easier it is to differentiate the consequences that a marital rape exemption has for men as opposed to women. Within approxi-mately the past twenty-five years, almost all state exemptions have been revised in a gender-neutral idiom, so that they now regulate the rape of one "spouse" by the other. But it is not the case that wives routinely, or even occasionally, benefit from their immunity from prosecution. Just as a factual matter, husbands experience the marital rape exemption by enjoying immu-nity from prosecution. Wives experience the marital rape exemption as the person who does not receive the protection of the criminal law for acts that would otherwise be considered serious crimes.

Contemporary empirical research also casts valuable light on the extent and nature of the injury that marital rape causes wives, adding support to the feminist argument that marital rape and the exemption inflict serious harm on women. The best available evidence suggests that approximately one out of every seven or eight married women has been subject to what in the absence of the exemption would be considered to be rape or attempted rape by their husbands. Sociological studies of marital rape victims have concluded, moreover, that rape can be more traumatic within marriage than outside of it. As one research team explained, these "victims suffer from many of the same traumas as victims of other rape—the humiliation, the physical injuries, the guilt and self-reproach. But they suffer some special traumas, too—betrayal, entrapment, and isolation." "The kind of violation they have experienced is much harder to guard against [than rape by a stranger], short of a refusal to trust any man. It touches a woman's basic confidence in forming relationships and trusting intimates."

. . .

Despite the availability of [a] dramatic record of injury, the modern feminist attempt to explain the marital rape exemption in terms of the divergent, even antagonistic, interests of husbands and wives has not been particularly effective. . . .

. . . If the fate of the nineteenth-century campaign against a husband's conjugal prerogatives illuminates anything, it is that society's reluctance to acknowledge that marriage is a potentially antagonistic and dangerous relation by giving women legal rights against their husbands is long-standing, well-entrenched, and extremely resistant to feminist opposition, especially where marital sex and reproduction are directly implicated. Even the nineteenth-century prescriptive authors who expounded at length on the harm that marital rape was inflicting on wives were unwilling to translate that social recognition into support for granting women legal entitlements. Where feminists made a rights claim advancing women's interests as they were distinct from and defined in opposition to those of men, the prescriptive literature put forth a series of suggested strategies for marital harmony and happiness. Authoritative legal sources, in turn, absolutely refused to alter a husband's exemption from prosecution for raping his wife. After a half-century of writing and advocacy (feminist and otherwise) exploring sexual abuse in marriage, the only change in the legal status of marital rape consisted of a marginal amelioration in the terms on which divorce was available to (privileged) women.

Phrased another way, then, one reason that people are so attracted to the consensual account of the history of marital rape in the first place is that we greatly prefer to envision marital relations as loving, mutually supportive, and harmonious, rather than loathsome, abusive, and conflict-ridden—even though, as a practical matter, we encounter evidence all the time that the latter state of affairs characterizes some relationships. That cultural denial helps explain, for instance, the studies finding that even people who know current divorce rates believe that the possibility that they will divorce is negligible and fail to plan rationally for the contingency. . . .

The cultural need to understand marital relations as consensual and harmonious also helps explain another phenomenon of approximately the last quarter-century. During this period, dozens of states revisited their marital rape exemptions, but decided to retain them in substantial form nonetheless. One result of this review was that states modified the scope of their exemptions. Another result was that virtually every one of these states rewrote its marital rape exemption in gender-neutral terms, in contrast to the explicit and enthusiastic gender-specificity of the common law formulation. This latter, linguistic change has almost no practical consequences, given the accuracy with which one can predict that marital rapes will be committed by husbands on wives. But as a matter of modern equal protection doctrine, it is very important. Statutes that explicitly classify by sex are automatically subject to heightened scrutiny under the Equal Protection Clause, which relatively few statutes have managed to survive. Once a statute has been made formally gender-neutral, however, it is subject to heightened scrutiny only if a plaintiff can establish the equivalent of legislative malice: that the gender-neutral statute was enacted "at least in part 'because of,' not merely 'in spite of,' its adverse effects upon" women. This is precisely the sort of malignant motivation that is least likely to be uttered in the constitutionally conscious age in which we live. So, as a practical matter, modern marital rape exemptions are subject to rational basis review. Although a small number of state courts have found exemptions unconstitutional on a rational basis analysis, a marital rape exemption is likely to survive this relatively unrigorous level of constitutional scrutiny, which asks only whether the legislature has articulated one reason for the exemption that the court is willing to accept as rational.

> . . .

The effect of the current equal protection doctrine on gender-neutrality is to treat men and women as occupying interchangeable roles, in all cases except where the text of the statute or explicit legislative statements of malicious intent force the court to do otherwise. It is a doctrinal methodology for disregarding evidence about gender-specific consequences that suggests the possibility that the interests of men and women may be unaligned, differentially affected, even antagonistically opposed to one another, and not interchangeable at all. Marital rape exemptions are not the only statutes with disproportionate consequences for women to have undergone recent revision into a gender-neutral idiom. Child custody and alimony laws are now almost uniformly gender-neutral, and wife beating statutes now regulate "spousal abuse." Indeed, this impulse substantially predates modern equal protection law: State interspousal tort immunity doctrines, first developed when married women gained the right to sue in their own names in the middle of the nineteenth century, were phrased in gender-neutral terms from the outset. Yet the strength of the yearning to insist within the law that the interests of men and women always harmoniously coincide is nowhere more apparent than with the marital rape exemption, where the sex-specificity of the underlying conduct and injury is extraordinarily pronounced, but equal protection doctrine nonetheless treats husbands and wives as though they occupy unassigned positions.

... There is no easy path upon which contemporary feminists might proceed, given the profound and long-lived societal reluctance—particularly where marital intercourse and reproduction are at issue—to formulate women's legal rights around the understanding that marital relations are potentially antagonistic and dangerous. There is, however, a very pertinent difference between the arena in which the first organized woman's rights movement operated and the contemporary environment, which suggests that the future fate of the modern feminist campaign against marital rape need not track the historical record.

In the latter half of the nineteenth century, the proposition that marital rape inflicted severe harm upon married women was widely acknowledged.

The prescriptive literature described this harm in great detail. Authoritative legal sources, moreover, never denied the proposition, and courts occasionally remarked upon it themselves while deciding divorce cases later in the century.... [F]or instance, ... when a New Jersey court wanted to underscore the weakness of Abby English's divorce petition for sexual cruelty, it cited medical testimony that, "although there would be pain" whenever English was forced to have intercourse, "a large proportion of married women assent under exactly those circumstances." In an age that still accepted and endorsed a vast range of legal structures explicitly subordinating women to men, this recognition of injury was not enough to persuade either popular experts on marriage or lawmakers to repudiate a husband's legal right to rape his wife.

The modern defenders of the marital rape exemption, in contrast, submerge and deny the harm that the rule causes women. This has been good strategy for a reason. It is much more difficult to justify the harm that marital rape inflicts upon wives, and explain the absence of legal remediation, in a nation now formally committed to women's legal equality and the undoing of women's subjection at common law. The historical record helps make this harm concrete, revealing the ways in which it is buried by the contemporary defense of the marital rape exemption. If the injury that marital rape inflicts were more systematically put at issue, and arguments presuming that marital relations never cause women harm were more systematically resisted, it might be harder for the legal system to continue to shelter a husband's prerogatives.

b.   BATTERED WOMEN'S SYNDROME

People v. Humphrey

Supreme Court of California, 1996.
921 P.2d 1.

■ CHIN, J.

. . .

During the evening of March 28, 1992, defendant [Evelyn Humphrey] shot and killed Albert Hampton in their Fresno home. Officer Reagan was the first on the scene. A neighbor told Reagan that the couple in the house had been arguing all day. Defendant soon came outside appearing upset and with her hands raised as if surrendering. She told Officer Reagan, "I shot him. That's right, I shot him. I just couldn't take him beating on me no more." She led the officer into the house, showed him a .357 magnum revolver on a table, and said, "There's the gun." Hampton was on the kitchen floor, wounded but alive.

A short time later, defendant told Officer Reagan, "He deserved it. I just couldn't take it anymore. I told him to stop beating on me." "He was beating on me, so I shot him. I told him I'd shoot him if he ever beat on me again." A paramedic heard her say that she wanted to teach Hampton "a lesson." Defendant told another officer at the scene, Officer Terry, "I'm fed up. Yeah, I shot him. I'm just tired of him hitting me. He said, 'You're not going to do nothing about it.' I showed him, didn't I? I shot him good. He won't hit anybody else again. Hit me again; I shoot him again. I don't care if I go to jail. Push come to shove, I guess people gave it to him, and, kept hitting me. I warned him. I warned him not to hit me. He wouldn't listen."

Officer Terry took defendant to the police station, where she told the following story. The day before the shooting, Hampton had been drinking. He hit defendant while they were driving home in their truck and continued hitting her when they arrived. He told her, "I'll kill you," and shot at her. The bullet went through a bedroom window and struck a tree outside. The day of the shooting, Hampton "got drunk," swore at her, and started hitting her again. He walked into the kitchen. Defendant saw the gun in the living room and picked it up. Her jaw hurt, and she was in pain. She pointed the gun at Hampton and said, "You're not going to hit me anymore." Hampton said, "What are you doing?" Believing that Hampton was about to pick something up to hit her with, she shot him. She then put the gun down and went outside to wait for the police.

Hampton later died of a gunshot wound to his chest. The neighbor who spoke with Officer Reagan testified that shortly before the shooting, she heard defendant, but not Hampton, shouting. The evening before, the neighbor had heard a gunshot. Defendant's blood contained no drugs but had a blood-alcohol level of .17 percent. Hampton's blood contained no drugs or alcohol.

Defendant claimed she shot Hampton in self-defense. To support the claim, the defense presented first expert testimony and then nonexpert testimony, including that of defendant herself.

Dr. Lee Bowker testified as an expert on battered women's syndrome. The syndrome, he testified, "is not just a psychological construction, but it's a term for a wide variety of controlling mechanisms that the man or it can be a woman, but in general for this syndrome it's a man, uses against the woman, and for the effect that those control mechanisms have."

Dr. Bowker had studied about 1,000 battered women and found them often inaccurately portrayed "as cardboard figures, paper-thin punching bags who merely absorb the violence but didn't do anything about it." He found that battered women often employ strategies to stop the beatings, including hiding, running away, counter-violence, seeking the help of friends and family, going to a shelter, and contacting police. Nevertheless, many battered women remain in the relationship because of lack of money, social isolation, lack of self-confidence, inadequate police response, and a fear (often justified) of reprisals by the batterer. "The battering man will make the battered woman depend on him and generally succeed at least for a time." A battered woman often feels responsible for the abusive relationship, and "she just can't figure out a way to please him better so he'll stop beating her." In sum, "It really is the physical control of the woman through economics and through relative social isolation combined with the psychological techniques that make her so dependent."

Many battered women go from one abusive relationship to another and seek a strong man to protect them from the previous abuser. "[W]ith each successful victimization, the person becomes less able to avoid the next one." The violence can gradually escalate, as the batterer keeps control using ever more severe actions, including rape, torture, violence against the woman's loved ones or pets, and death threats. Battered women sense this escalation. In Dr. Bowker's "experience with battered women who kill in self-defense their abusers, it's always related to their perceived change of what's going on in a relationship. They become very sensitive to what sets off batterers. They watch for this stuff very carefully. . . . Anybody who is abused over a period of time becomes sensitive to the abuser's behavior and when she sees a change acceleration begin in that behavior, it tells them something is going to happen. . . ."

Dr. Bowker interviewed defendant for a full day. He believed she suffered not only from battered women's syndrome, but also from being the child of an alcoholic and an incest victim. He testified that all three of defendant's partners before Hampton were abusive and significantly older than she.

Dr. Bowker described defendant's relationship with Hampton. Hampton was a 49-year-old man who weighed almost twice as much as defendant. The two had a battering relationship that Dr. Bowker characterized as a "traditional cycle of violence." The cycle included phases of tension building, violence, and then forgiveness-seeking in which Hampton would promise not to batter defendant any more and she would believe him. During this period, there would be occasional good times. For example, defendant told Dr. Bowker that Hampton would give her a rose. "That's one of the things that hooks people in. Intermittent reinforcement is the key." But after a while, the violence would begin again. The violence would recur because "basically . . . the woman doesn't perfectly obey. That's the bottom line." For example, defendant would talk to another man, or fail to clean house "just so."

The situation worsened over time, especially when Hampton got off parole shortly before his death. He became more physically and emotionally abusive, repeatedly threatened defendant's life, and even shot at her the night before his death. Hampton often allowed defendant to go out, but she was afraid to flee because she felt he would find her as he had in the past. "He enforced her belief that she can never escape him." Dr. Bowker testified that unless her injuries were so severe that "something absolutely had to be treated," he would not expect her to seek medical treatment. "That's the pattern of her life. . . ."

Dr. Bowker believed defendant's description of her experiences. In his opinion, she suffered from battered women's syndrome in "about as extreme a pattern as you could find."

Defendant confirmed many of the details of her life and relationship with Hampton underlying Dr. Bowker's opinion. She testified that her father forcefully molested her from the time she was seven years old until she was fifteen. She described her relationship with another abusive man as being like "Nightmare on Elm Street." Regarding Hampton, she testified that they often argued and that he beat her regularly. Both were heavy drinkers. Hampton once threw a can of beer at her face, breaking her nose. Her dental plates hurt because Hampton hit her so often. He often kicked her, but usually hit her in the back of the head because, he told her, it "won't leave bruises." Hampton sometimes threatened to kill her, and often said she "would live to regret it." Matters got worse towards the end.

The evening before the shooting, March 27, 1992, Hampton arrived home "very drunk." He yelled at her and called her names. At one point when she was standing by the bedroom window, he fired his .357 magnum revolver at her. She testified, "He didn't miss me by much either." She was "real scared."

The next day, the two drove into the mountains. They argued, and Hampton continually hit her. While returning, he said that their location would be a good place to kill her because "they wouldn't find [her] for a while." She took it as a joke, although she feared him. When they returned, the arguing continued. He hit her again, then entered the kitchen. He threatened, "This time, bitch, when I shoot at you, I won't miss." He came from the kitchen and reached for the gun on the living room table. She grabbed it first, pointed it at him, and told him "that he wasn't going to hit [her]." She backed Hampton into the kitchen. He was saying something, but she did not know what. He reached for her hand and she shot him. She believed he was reaching for the gun and was going to shoot her.

Several other witnesses testified about defendant's relationship with Hampton, his abusive conduct in general, and his physical abuse of, and threats to, defendant in particular. This testimony generally corroborated defendant's. A neighbor testified that the night before the shooting, she heard a gunshot. The next morning, defendant told the neighbor that Hampton had shot at her, and that she was afraid of him. After the shooting, investigators found a bullet hole through the frame of the bedroom window and a bullet embedded in a tree in line with the window. Another neighbor testified that shortly before hearing the shot that killed Hampton, she heard defendant say, "Stop it, Albert. Stop it."

Defendant was charged with murder with personal use of a firearm. At the end of the prosecution's case-in-chief, the court granted defendant's motion under Penal Code section 1118.1 for acquittal of first degree murder.

The court instructed the jury on second degree murder and both voluntary and involuntary manslaughter. It also instructed on self-defense, explaining that an actual and reasonable belief that the killing was necessary was a complete defense; an actual but unreasonable belief was a defense to murder, but not to voluntary manslaughter. In determining reasonableness, the jury was to consider what "would appear to be necessary to a reasonable person in a similar situation and with similar knowledge."

The court also instructed:

> Evidence regarding Battered Women's Syndrome has been introduced in this case. Such evidence, if believed, may be considered by you only for the purpose of determining whether or not the defendant held the necessary subjective honest [belief] which is a requirement for both perfect and imperfect self-defense. However, that same evidence regarding Battered Women's Syndrome may not be considered or used by you in evaluating the objective reasonableness requirement for perfect self-defense.

> "Battered Women's Syndrome seeks to describe and explain common reactions of women to that experience. Thus, you may consider the evidence concerning the syndrome and its effects only for the limited purpose of showing, if it does show, that the defendant's reactions, as demonstrated by the evidence, are not inconsistent with her having been physically abused or the beliefs, perceptions, or behavior of victims of domestic violence."

During deliberations, the jury asked for and received clarification of the terms "subjectively honest and objectively unreasonable." It found defendant guilty of voluntary manslaughter with personal use of a firearm. The court sentenced defendant to prison for eight years, consisting of the lower term of three years for manslaughter, plus the upper term of five years for firearm use. The Court of Appeal remanded for resentencing on the use enhancement, but otherwise affirmed the judgment.

We granted defendant's petition for review.

. . . Evidence Code section 1107, subdivision (a), makes admissible in a criminal action expert testimony regarding "battered women's syndrome, including the physical, emotional, or mental effects upon the beliefs, perceptions, or behavior of victims of domestic violence...." ... Defendant presented the evidence to support her claim of self-defense. ... The only issue is to what extent defendant established its "relevancy." To resolve this question we must examine California law regarding self-defense.

For killing to be in self-defense, the defendant must actually and reasonably believe in the need to defend. If the belief subjectively exists but is objectively unreasonable, there is "imperfect self-defense," i.e., "the defendant is deemed to have acted without malice and cannot be convicted of murder," but can be convicted of manslaughter. *In re Christian S.*, [872 P.2d 574 (Cal. 1994)]. To constitute "perfect self-defense," i.e., to exonerate the person completely, the belief must also be objectively reasonable. As the Legislature has stated, "[T]he circumstances must be sufficient to excite the fears of a reasonable person...." PEN. CODE § 198. Moreover, for either perfect or imperfect self-defense, the fear must be of imminent harm. "Fear of future harm—no matter how great the fear and no matter how great the likelihood of the harm—will not suffice. The defendant's fear must be of *imminent* danger to life or great bodily injury."

Although the belief in the need to defend must be objectively reasonable, a jury must consider what "would appear to be necessary to a reasonable person in a similar situation and with similar knowledge...." CALJIC No. 5.50. It judges reasonableness "from the point of view of a reasonable person in the position of defendant...." To do this, it must consider all the " 'facts and circumstances ... in determining whether the defendant acted in a manner in which *a reasonable man* would act in protecting his own life or bodily safety.' " As we stated long ago, "... a defendant is entitled to have a jury take into consideration all the elements in the case which might be expected to operate on his mind...."

. . .

With these principles in mind, we now consider the relevance of evidence of battered women's syndrome to the elements of self-defense.

Battered women's syndrome "has been defined as 'a series of common characteristics that appear in women who are abused physically and psychologically over an extended period of time by the dominant male figure in their lives.' " *State v. Kelly,* [478 A.2d 364, 371 (N.J. 1984)].

The trial court allowed the jury to consider the battered women's syndrome evidence in deciding whether defendant actually believed she needed to kill in self-defense. The question here is whether the evidence was also relevant on the reasonableness of that belief. Two Court of Appeal decisions have considered the relevance of battered women's syndrome evidence to a claim of self-defense.

People v. Aris, [264 Cal. Rptr. 167 (Ct. App. 1989),] applied "the law of self-defense in the context of a battered woman killing the batterer while he slept after he had beaten the killer and threatened serious bodily injury and death when he awoke." There, unlike here, the trial court refused to instruct the jury on perfect self-defense, but it did instruct on imperfect self-defense. The appellate court upheld the refusal, finding that "defendant presented no substantial evidence that a reasonable person under the same circumstances would have perceived imminent danger and a need to kill in self-defense." ...

Although the trial court did not instruct on perfect self-defense, the appellate court first concluded that battered women's syndrome evidence is not relevant to the reasonableness element. "[T]he questions of the reasonableness of a defendant's belief that self-defense is necessary and of the reasonableness of the actions taken in self-defense do not call for an evaluation of the defendant's subjective *state of mind*, but for an objective evaluation of the defendant's assertedly defensive *acts*. California law expresses the criterion for this evaluation in the objective terms of whether *a reasonable person*, as opposed to the *defendant*, would have believed and acted as the defendant did. We hold that expert testimony about a defendant's state of mind is not relevant to the reasonableness of the defendant's self-defense."

The court then found the evidence "highly relevant to the first element of self-defense—defendant's actual, subjective perception that she was in danger and that she had to kill her husband to avoid that danger.... [¶] The relevance to the defendant's actual perception lies in the opinion's explanation of how such a perception would reasonably follow from the defendant's experience as a battered woman. This relates to the prosecution's argument that such a perception of imminent danger makes no sense when the victim is asleep and a way of escape open and, therefore, she did not actually have that perception." The trial court thus erred in not admitting the testimony to show "how the defendant's particular experiences as a battered woman affected her perceptions of danger, its imminence, and what actions were necessary to protect herself."

Concerned "that the jury in a particular case may misuse such evidence to establish the reasonableness requirement for perfect self-defense, for which purpose it is irrelevant," the *Aris* court stated that, "upon request whenever the jury is instructed on perfect self-defense, trial courts should instruct that such testimony is relevant only to prove the honest belief requirement for both perfect and imperfect self-defense, not to prove the reasonableness requirement for perfect self-defense." The trial court gave such an instruction here, thus creating the issue before us.

In *People v. Day*, [2 Cal. Rptr. 2d 916 (1992)], the defendant moved for a new trial following her conviction of involuntary manslaughter. Supported by an affidavit by Dr. Bowker, she argued that her attorney should have presented evidence of battered women's syndrome to aid her claim of self-defense. Relying on *Aris*, the appellate court first found that the evidence would not have been relevant to show the objective reasonableness of the defendant's actions. It also found, however, that the evidence would have been admissible to rehabilitate the defendant's credibility as a witness. Finding that counsel's failure to present the evidence was prejudicial, the court reversed the judgment.

The Attorney General argues that *Aris* and *Day* were correct that evidence of battered women's syndrome is irrelevant to reasonableness. We disagree. Those cases too narrowly interpreted the reasonableness element. *Aris* and *Day* failed to consider that the jury, in determining objective reasonableness, must view the situation from the *defendant's perspective*. Here, for example, Dr. Bowker testified that the violence can escalate and that a battered woman can become increasingly sensitive to the abuser's behavior, testimony relevant to determining whether defendant reasonably believed when she fired the gun that this time the threat to her life was imminent. Indeed, the prosecutor argued that, "from an objective, reasonable man's standard, there was no reason for her to go get that gun. This threat that she says he made was like so many threats before. There was no reason for her to react that way." Dr. Bowker's testimony supplied a response that the jury might not otherwise receive. As violence increases over time, and threats gain credibility, a battered person might become sensitized and thus able reasonably to discern when danger is real and when it is not. "[T]he expert's testimony might also enable the jury to find that the battered [woman] . . . is particularly able to predict accurately the likely extent of violence in any attack on her. That conclusion could significantly affect the jury's evaluation of the *reasonableness* of defendant's fear for her life." *State v. Kelly,* [478 A.2d 364, 378 (N.J. 1984)].

. . .

Contrary to the Attorney General's argument, we are not changing the standard from objective to subjective, or replacing the reasonable "person" standard with a reasonable "battered woman" standard. Our decision would not, in another context, compel adoption of a " 'reasonable gang member' standard." Evidence Code section 1107 states "a rule of evidence only" and makes "no substantive change." EVID. CODE, § 1107, subd. (d). The jury must consider defendant's situation and knowledge, which makes the evidence relevant, but the ultimate question is whether a reasonable *person*, not a reasonable battered woman, would believe in the need to kill to prevent imminent harm. Moreover, it is the *jury*, not the expert, that determines whether defendant's belief and, ultimately, her actions, were objectively reasonable.

Battered women's syndrome evidence was also relevant to defendant's credibility. It "would have assisted the jury in objectively analyzing [defendant's] claim of self-defense by dispelling many of the commonly held misconceptions about battered women." *People v. Day, supra.* For example, in urging the jury not to believe defendant's testimony that Hampton shot at her the night before the killing, the prosecutor argued that "if this defendant truly believed that [Hampton] had shot at her, on that night, I mean she would have left. . . . [¶] If she really believed that he had tried to shoot her, she would not have stayed." Dr. Bowker's testimony " 'would help dispel the ordinary lay person's perception that a woman in a battering relationship is free to leave at any time. The expert evidence would counter any "common sense" conclusions by the jury that if the beatings were really that bad the woman would have left her husband much earlier. Popular misconceptions about battered women would be put to rest. . . .' " *People v. Day, supra,* quoting *State v. Hodges,* [716 P.2d 563, 567 (Kan. 1986)].

. . .

We do not hold that Dr. Bowker's entire testimony was relevant to both prongs of perfect self-defense. Just as many types of evidence may be relevant to some disputed issues but not all, some of the expert evidence was no doubt relevant only to the subjective existence of defendant's belief. Evidence merely showing that a person's use of deadly force is scientifically explainable or empirically common does not, in itself, show it was objectively reasonable. To dispel any possible confusion, it might be appropriate for the court, on request, to clarify that, in assessing reasonableness, the question is whether a reasonable person in the defendant's circumstances would have perceived a threat of imminent injury or death, and not whether killing the abuser was reasonable in the sense of being an understandable response to ongoing abuse; and that, therefore, in making that assessment, the jury may not consider evidence merely showing that an abused person's use of force against the abuser is understandable.

We also emphasize that, as with any evidence, the jury may give this testimony whatever weight it deems appropriate in light of the evidence as a whole. The ultimate judgment of reasonableness is solely for the jury. We simply hold that evidence of battered women's syndrome is generally *relevant* to the reasonableness, as well as the subjective existence, of defendant's belief in the need to defend, and, to the extent it is relevant, the jury may *consider* it in deciding both questions. The court's contrary instruction was erroneous. We disapprove of *People v. Aris*, *supra*, and *People v. Day*, *supra*, to the extent they are inconsistent with this conclusion.

R. v. Malott

Supreme Court of Canada, 1998.
1 S.C.R. 123.

■ L'HEUREUX-DUBE, J. [concurring]:

I have read the reasons of my colleague Justice Major, and I concur with the result that he reaches. However, given that this Court has not had the opportunity to discuss the value of evidence of "battered woman syndrome" since *R. v. Lavallee*, [1990] 1 S.C.R. 852, and given the evolving discourse on "battered woman syndrome" in the legal community, I will make a few comments on the importance of this kind of evidence to the just adjudication of charges involving battered women.

. . .

. . . [T]he majority of the Court in *Lavallee* . . . implicitly accepted that women's experiences and perspectives may be different from the experiences and perspectives of men. It accepted that a woman's perception of what is reasonable is influenced by her gender, as well as by her individual experience, and both are relevant to the legal inquiry. This legal development was significant, because it demonstrated a willingness to look at the whole context of a woman's experience in order to inform the analysis of the particular events. But it is wrong to think of this development of the law as merely an example where an objective test—the requirement that an accused claiming self-defence must *reasonably* apprehend death or grievous bodily harm—has been modified to admit evidence of the subjective perceptions of a battered woman. More important, a majority of the Court accepted that the perspectives of women, which have historically been ignored, must now equally inform the "objective" standard of the reasonable person in relation to self-defence.

When interpreting and applying *Lavallee*, these broader principles should be kept in mind. In particular, they should be kept in mind in order to avoid a too rigid and restrictive approach to the admissibility and legal value of evidence of a battered woman's experiences. Concerns have been expressed that the treatment of expert evidence on battered women syndrome, which is itself admissible in order to combat the myths and stereotypes which society has about battered women, has led to a new stereotype of the "battered woman."

It is possible that those women who are unable to fit themselves within the stereotype of a victimized, passive, helpless, dependent, battered woman will not have their claims to self-defence fairly decided. For instance, women who have demonstrated too much strength or initiative, women of colour, women who are professionals, or women who might have fought back against their abusers on previous occasions, should not be penalized for failing to accord with the stereotypical image of the archetypal battered woman. Needless to say, women with these characteristics are still entitled to have their claims of self-defence fairly adjudicated, and they are also still entitled to have their experiences as battered women inform the analysis. Professor Grant warns against allowing the law to develop such that a woman accused of killing her abuser must either have been "reasonable 'like a man' or reasonable 'like a battered woman.'" I agree that this must be avoided. The "reasonable woman" must not be forgotten in the analysis, and deserves to be as much a part of the objective standard of the reasonable person as does the "reasonable man."

How should the courts combat the "syndromization," as Professor Grant refers to it, of battered women who act in self-defence? The legal inquiry into the moral culpability of a woman who is, for instance, claiming self-defence must focus on the *reasonableness* of her actions in the context of her personal experiences, and her experiences as a woman, not on her status as a battered woman and her entitlement to claim that she is suffering from "battered woman syndrome[.]" . . . By emphasizing a woman's "learned helplessness," her dependence, her victimization, and her low self-esteem. In order to establish that she suffers from "battered woman syndrome", the legal debate shifts from the objective rationality of her actions to preserve her own life to those personal inadequacies which apparently explain her failure to flee from her abuser. Such an emphasis comports too well with society's stereotypes about women. Therefore, it should be scrupulously avoided because it only serves to undermine the important advancements achieved by the decision in *Lavallee*.

There are other elements of a woman's social context which help to explain her inability to leave her abuser, and which do not focus on those characteristics most consistent with traditional stereotypes. As Wilson J. herself recognized in *Lavallee*, at p. 887, "environmental factors may also impair the woman's ability to leave—lack of job skills, the presence of children to care for, fear of retaliation by the man, etc. may each have a role to play in some cases." To this list of factors I would add a woman's need to protect her children from abuse, a fear of losing custody of her children, pressures to keep the family together, weaknesses of social and financial support for battered women, and no guarantee that the violence would cease simply because she left. These considerations necessarily inform the reasonableness of a woman's beliefs or perceptions of, for instance, her lack of an alternative to the use of deadly force to preserve herself from death or grievous bodily harm.

How should these principles be given practical effect in the context of a jury trial of a woman accused of murdering her abuser? To fully accord with the spirit of *Lavallee*, where the reasonableness of a battered woman's belief is at issue in a criminal case, a judge and jury should be made to appreciate that a battered woman's experiences are both individualized, based on her own history and relationships, as well as shared with other women, within the context of a society and a legal system which has historically undervalued women's experiences. A judge and jury should be told that a battered woman's experiences are generally outside the common understanding of the average judge and juror, and that they should seek to understand the evidence being presented to them in order to overcome the myths and stereotypes which we all share. Finally, all of this should be presented in such a way as to focus on the reasonableness of the woman's actions, without relying on old or new stereotypes about battered women.

NOTES

1. In *Nicholson v. Scoppetta*, 820 N.E.2d 840 (N.Y. 2004), the New York Court of Appeals considered whether a mother who is a victim of domestic violence fails to exercise a "minimum degree of care," and thus leaves her child neglected, if she fails to prevent the child from witnessing such violence. The court said that a determination of what constitutes minimum care under the circumstances must take into account:

> risks attendant to leaving, if the batterer has threatened to kill her if she does; risks attendant to staying and suffering continued abuse; risks attendant to seeking assistance through government channels, potentially increasing the danger to herself and her children; risks attendant to criminal prosecution against the abuser; and risks attendant to relocation. Whether a particular mother in these circumstances has actually failed to exercise a minimum degree of care is necessarily dependent on facts such as the severity and frequency of the violence, and the resources and options available to her.

Id. at 846.

2. Is it enough for legal actors "to appreciate that a battered woman's experiences are both individualized, based on her own history and relationships, as well as shared with other women, within the context of a society and a legal system which has historically undervalued women's experiences?" Does this view leave anything—or anyone—out? How, if at all, can one apply Justice L'Heureux–Dube's insights to the phenomenon of same-sex, including not only female-on-female but also male-on-male, domestic violence?

3. In addition to its implications for the criminal law, battered woman's syndrome has presented courts with challenges in the context of the law of torts, where no such tort—framed in terms of the syndrome—existed at common law. For one court's effort to address some of challenges, see *Giovine v. Giovine*, 284 N.J.Super. 3, 663 A.2d 109 (1995) (affirming the existence of a tort for battered woman's syndrome under a specified set of circumstances).

4. What should the legal system do with cases involving victims of domestic abuse convicted for crimes involving their perpetrators before the courts and other legal actors began recognizing the particular dimensions of the injuries they suffer? One approach is a law in California enacted in 2002 that entitles victims of domestic abuse to a new trial if "expert testimony relating to intimate partner battering and its effects, within the meaning of [a specified provision of the California] . . . Evidence Code, was not received in evidence at the trial court proceedings relating to the prisoner's incarceration," at least where that testimony "is of such substance that, had it been received in evidence, there is a reasonable probability, sufficient to undermine confidence in the judgment of conviction, that the result of the proceedings would have been different." CAL. PEN. CODE § 1474.5(a) (West 2012). One such case is the subject of a recent documentary: *Crime After Crime: The Battle to Free Debbie Peagler* (Life Sentence Films 2011).

c. LEGAL RESPONSES TO VIOLENCE

1. CIVIL PROTECTIVE ORDERS

Massachusetts Abuse Prevention Law

MASS. GEN. LAWS ch. 209A, §§ 1–4 (2005).

§ 1. Definitions.

As used in this chapter the following words shall have the following meanings:

"Abuse", the occurrence of one or more of the following acts between family or household members:

(a) attempting to cause or causing physical harm;

(b) placing another in fear of imminent serious physical harm;

(c) causing another to engage involuntarily in sexual relations by force, threat or duress.

. . .

"Family or household members", persons who:

(a) are or were married to one another;

(b) are or were residing together in the same household;

(c) are or were related by blood or marriage;

(d) having a child in common regardless of whether they have ever married or lived together; or

(e) are or have been in a substantive dating or engagement relationship, which shall be adjudged by district, probate or Boston municipal courts consideration of the following factors:

> (1) the length of time of the relationship; (2) the type of relationship; (3) the frequency of interaction between the parties; and (4) if the relationship has been terminated by either person, the length of time elapsed since the termination of the relationship.

. . .

"Vacate order", court order to leave and remain away from a premises and surrendering forthwith any keys to said premises to the plaintiff. The defendant shall not damage any of the plaintiff's belongings or those of any other occupant and shall not shut off or cause to be shut off any utilities or mail delivery to the plaintiff. In the case where the premises designated in the vacate order is a residence, so long as the plaintiff is living at said residence, the defendant shall not interfere in any way with the plaintiff's right to possess such residence, except by order or judgment of a court of competent jurisdiction pursuant to appropriate civil eviction proceedings, a petition to partition real estate, or a proceeding to divide marital property. A vacate order may include in its scope a household, a multiple family dwelling and the plaintiff's workplace. When issuing an order to vacate the plaintiff's workplace, the presiding justice must consider whether the plaintiff and defendant work in the same location or for the same employer.

. . .

§ 3. Remedies; periods of relief.

A person suffering from abuse from an adult or minor family or household member may file a complaint in the court requesting protection from such abuse, including, but not limited to, the following orders:

(a) ordering the defendant to refrain from abusing the plaintiff, whether the defendant is an adult or minor;

(b) ordering the defendant to refrain from contacting the plaintiff, unless authorized by the court, whether the defendant is an adult or minor;

(c) ordering the defendant to vacate forthwith and remain away from the household, multiple family dwelling, and workplace. . . . [A]n order to vacate shall be for a fixed period of time, not to exceed one year, at the expiration of which time the court may extend any such order upon motion of the plaintiff, with notice to the defendant, for such additional time as it deems necessary to protect the plaintiff from abuse;

(d) awarding the plaintiff temporary custody of a minor child; provided, however, that in any case brought in the probate and family court a finding by such court by a preponderance of the evidence that a pattern or serious incident of abuse . . . toward a parent or child has occurred shall create a rebuttable presumption that it is not in the best interests of the child to be placed in sole custody, shared legal custody or shared physical custody with the abusive parent. Such presumption may be rebutted by a preponderance of the evidence that such custody award is in the best interests of the child. For the purposes of this section, an "abusive parent" shall mean a parent who has committed a pattern of abuse or a serious incident of abuse.

. . .

§ 4. Temporary Orders; notice; hearing.

Upon the filing of a complaint under this chapter, the court may enter such temporary orders as it deems necessary to protect a plaintiff from abuse, including relief as provided in section three. Such relief shall not be contingent upon the filing of a complaint for divorce, separate support, or paternity action.

If the plaintiff demonstrates a substantial likelihood of immediate danger of abuse, the court may enter such temporary relief orders without notice as it deems necessary to protect the plaintiff from abuse and shall immediately thereafter notify the defendant that the temporary orders have been issued. The court shall give the defendant an opportunity to be heard on the question of continuing the temporary order and of granting other relief as requested by the plaintiff no later than ten court business days after such orders are entered.

Notice shall be made by the appropriate law enforcement agency as provided in section seven.

If the defendant does not appear at such subsequent hearing, the temporary orders shall continue in effect without further order of the court.

NOTE

Interpreting MASS. GEN. LAWS ch. 209A, §§ 1–4 (2005) in *Turner v. Lewis*, 749 N.E.2d 122 (Mass. 2001), the Massachusetts Supreme Judicial Court held that a paternal grandmother of a child and the child's biological mother were "family or household members" "related by blood or marriage" for purposes of the Abuse Prevention Act—even though there was no direct blood or biological tie between them, and the grandmother's son (the child's biological father) and the child's mother were never married. *See id.* at 123. The court reached this conclusion relying in part on the following line of reasoning:

[W]e conclude that the parties are "related by blood." The paternal grandmother, through her son, is "related by blood" to the child. Likewise, the child and her mother are "related by blood." Thus, the child is "related by blood" to both parties, making the mother and grandmother "related by blood" through that child.

Id. at 124–25. Importantly, the court bolstered its reading of the Abuse Prevention Act with the general suggestion that it should be given a liberal interpretation, *id.* at

124 ("We also bear in mind the importance of giv[ing] broad meaning to the words 'related by blood,'" and considering "whether the relationship puts the parties into contact with one another, even though they might not otherwise seek or wish for such contact." (quoting Commentary to § 3:02 of the GUIDELINES FOR JUDICIAL PRACTICE: ABUSE PREVENTION PROCEEDINGS (Dec. 2000))), backed up by a more particular argument that its interpretation "would be consistent with the Legislature's purpose in enacting c. 209A." *Id.* at 125. As the court remarked:

> Interpreting the term "related by blood" to include the relationship between the grandmother and the mother would be consistent with the Legislature's purpose in enacting c. 209A. We note first that, in light of the grandmother's custody of the child and the mother's visitation rights with the child, there will likely be significant, albeit unwanted, contact between the mother and the grandmother, a fact particularly evidenced by the events that precipitated this appeal. The "main object to be accomplished" by c. 209A, was the prevention of violence in the family setting. Violence brought on by, or exacerbated by, familial relationships was the "mischief or imperfection to be remedied" by c. 209A. Moreover, c. 209A has always reflected "[a] significant decision by the legislature ... to broaden the definition of persons eligible to seek protection from abuse and domestic violence beyond the 'family' and to also include other persons having some 'family-like' connection." C.P. KINDREGAN, JR., & M.L. INKER, FAMILY LAW AND PRACTICE, § 57.5 [(2d ed. 1996)].

Id. Additionally, in language the dissenting opinion in the case found very significant, the majority in *Turner* maintained:

> Our conclusion is supported by sound public policy. We take judicial notice of the social reality that the concept of "family" is varied and evolving and that, as a result, different types of "family" members will be forced into potentially unwanted contact with one another. The recent increases in both single parent and grandparent headed households are two examples of this trend.
>
> With respect to the increase in single parent headed households, "[c]hildren under age [eighteen] are considerably more likely to be living with only one parent today than two decades ago." Marital Status and Living Arrangements: March 1994, Bureau of the Census, United States Department of Commerce (Feb. 1996). See Marital Status and Living Arrangements: March 1998 (Update) Bureau of the Census (Dec. 1998) (between 1970 and 1998, proportion of children under age of eighteen years living with single parent grew from twelve per cent to 27.7 per cent). "High levels of divorce and postponement of first marriage are among the changes that have reshaped the living arrangements of children and adults since the 1970's." *Id.* In the majority of these cases, women are the head of the household. *Id.* (eighty-four per cent of children who lived with single parent in 1998 lived with mother). The often contentious nature of custody arrangements necessitates the protection of these single parents through legislation like G. L. c. 209A.
>
> Likewise, ... there has been a growing phenomenon of grandparents raising their grandchildren in the past thirty years:
>
>> Between 1992 and 1997, the greatest growth has occurred among grandchildren living with grandparents with no parents present. The increase in grandchildren in these 'skipped generation' living arrangements has been attributed to the growth in drug use among parents, teen pregnancy, divorce, the rapid rise of single-parent households, mental and physical illness, AIDS, crime, child abuse and neglect, and incarceration of parents.
>
> Coresident Grandparents and Grandchildren, Current Population Reports 1, Bureau of the Census, United States Department of Commerce (May, 1999) (75% increase in number of children residing in households headed by grandparents from 1970–1997).
>
> When grandparents are charged with the responsibility of caring for their grandchildren, they must often face "the biological parents' frequent resentment

of the grandparental custody, and/or their jealousy of the attention being paid by their parents to their offspring." Because of the parental hostility that may accompany grandparental custody, it is imperative that caregivers like the grandmother in this case be protected from such domestic abuse by c. 209A.

These trends require that "[d]omestic violence statutes [such as G. L. c. 209A] offer coverage to a wide range of extended family relationships to fully reflect the reality of American family life [and] . . . [t]he definition of 'family members' embraced by civil protection order statutes must be equally applicable to all concepts of family as they exist in the reality of our diverse family relationships." The relationship here meets the definition of "family," carrying with it all the risks and problems inherent in domestic violence. It is within that familial setting that this grandmother was exposed to violence and the threat of future violence.

Id. at 125–26.

Dissenting, Justice Corwin, joined by Justice Sosman commented, in part:

The court's decision ignores legislative history and bases its decision on social policy. General Laws c. 209A was enacted in 1978. St. 1978, c. 447, § 2. At that time a family or household member was defined as a "household member, a spouse, former spouse or their minor children or blood relative." *Id.* § 2. In 1986, the definition of a family or household member was amended to include a "blood relative *or* person who, though *unrelated by blood* or marriage, is the parent of the plaintiff's minor child" (emphasis supplied). St. 1986, c. 310, § 15. Pursuant to this change, two unmarried parents were considered family or household members because of their status as parents, not because of their blood connection to the child. By this definition, the Legislature expressly indicated that in its view the parents of a child were "*unrelated* by blood," despite any blood connection they have to their child (i.e., the father is related by blood to the child, and the mother is related by blood to the child, but, according to the statute, the father and mother are "unrelated by blood" to each other). Thus, if a father is "unrelated by blood" to the child's mother, then, *a fortiori*, a paternal grandmother also would be "unrelated by blood" to the child's mother.

In 1990, the definition of family or household member was amended again to its current version. The definition now includes, among others, persons "related by blood" and persons "having a child in common regardless of whether they have ever married or lived together." G. L. c. 209A, as appearing in St. 1990, c. 403, § 2, and as amended through St. 1996, c. 450, § 232. The statute continues to define unmarried parents as family members because of their status as parents, not because of a "blood" connection through their mutual child. Again, if the natural parents of a child would not be considered "related by blood," then the paternal grandmother is not "related by blood" to the child's mother.[1]

I recognize that each amendment of the definition of family or household member has broadened the categories of persons eligible for a protective order. However, the language and history of the statute do not support the court's interpretation on the present issue. Consequently, the court attempts to compensate by resorting to "the social reality that the concept of 'family' is varied and evolving." In identifying this "social reality," the court relies on reports from the United States Bureau of the Census as evidence of changes in family composition. These reports were issued subsequent to the 1990 amendment to the statute; there is no basis for concluding that the Legislature was aware of the

---

1. Additionally, although not addressed by the court, I do not believe that the paternal grandmother and mother in this case would fall within the category of persons "having a child in common." The phrase "having a child in common" is modified by the clause "regardless of whether they have ever married or lived together," which indicates that the Legislature contemplates this phrase to encompass persons who *could* have married or cohabited, but who did not do so.

information; or, if aware, that it would have based the Commonwealth's policy thereon.

Further, the court recognizes a "trend" in "single parent and grandparent headed households." According to the court, this trend "require[s]" that the protection offered under G. L. c. 209A extend to custodial grandparents, such as the grandmother here, in order "to fully reflect the reality of American family life." The role of the judiciary is to construe a statute "so that the enactment considered as a whole shall constitute a consistent and harmonious statutory provision capable of effectuating the presumed intention of the Legislature." The language of the statute "is the principal source of insight into the legislative purpose." I do not believe that it is the court's function to interpret a statute in accordance with the most recent "trend" or judicial perception of what "is best" as a matter of social policy, particularly when such interpretation is not consistent with the statutory language. "Whether a statute is wise or effective is not within the province of courts." *Commonwealth v. Leno*, 616 N.E.2d 453 (Mass. 1993). I recognize that the violence alleged in this case would, in common parlance, be viewed as a form of "domestic" violence, and that the unique remedies of G. L. c. 209A would seem suitable to the situation. However, it is not for this court to engraft G. L. c. 209A onto any dispute that is, in some sense, a "domestic" dispute. The appropriate procedure for protecting a person such as the paternal grandmother in this case is by legislative, not judicial, amendment to G. L. c. 209A.

Id. at 126–28 (Cowin, J., dissenting). Compare *Turner* with Justice Cowin's majority opinion for the same court in *C.O. v. M.M.*, 442 Mass. 648, 815 N.E.2d 582 (2004) (involving the meaning of a "substantive dating . . . relationship" under Mass. Gen. Laws ch. 209A).

Mitchell v. Mitchell

Appeals Court of Massachusetts, 2005.
62 Mass.App.Ct. 769, 821 N.E.2d 79.

■ Duffly, J.

Six months after Mary Mitchell obtained a G. L. c. 209A abuse prevention order against her husband, James Mitchell, a judge of the Probate Court vacated the order on the husband's motion seeking to reconsider or vacate it. We consider in this appeal by the wife the appropriate standard for deciding a motion to reconsider or vacate a c. 209A order, and whether the husband's evidence was sufficient to support the judge's decision. We conclude that it was not and, therefore, that it was error to vacate the order.

After suffering from more than ten years of verbal and physical abuse inflicted by the husband, the wife, on December 20, 2001, filed a complaint for protection from abuse under c. 209A, supported by her affidavit and three police reports.[1] An ex parte abuse prevention order was issued that same day directing the husband to (among other things) refrain from abusing or contacting the wife. The husband appeared pro se at a hearing on January 3, 2002, the date on which the initial order was fixed to expire, and after hearing, the order was extended for one year, to January 3, 2003. The husband did not appeal from the extended order.

On June 20, 2002, the husband filed a verified motion requesting the court "to reconsider or vacate" the order dated January 3, 2002; in the

---

1. We accept as fact the wife's averments in her affidavit, including that the husband had kicked and hit her, pulled her hair, and threatened to kill her if she attempted to "get anything" through separation or divorce or if she divulged to the court certain information concerning the parties' finances, and that she was terrified of the husband and feared for her life. . . .

motion he stated that the wife had contacted him repeatedly by telephone since the issuance of the order and had spent time with him in Los Angeles while attending the funeral of his mother.[2] In the husband's view, the wife's repeated "contact[s]" with him and her "successful requests" to spend time alone with him while they were in Los Angeles "clearly indicate that she does not fear physical or verbal abuse from [him] and did not fear such abuse in the past." The husband requested that the abuse prevention order be vacated retroactive to January 3, 2002.

A hearing, at which no testimony was taken, was conducted by the same judge who had issued the order of January 3, 2002. The judge had before her the husband's affidavit, the wife's verified opposition to the husband's motion,[3] and an affidavit of the husband's sister filed by the wife which, in large part, corroborated the wife's description of events and statements concerning her fear of the husband.[4]

. . .

The standard for extending a c. 209A order does not require a showing of new abuse. Were the wife to apply anew without the support of further incidents of abuse (and without the benefit of an appellate court decision concluding that the prior order should not have been vacated), a judge acting on her application would quite possibly feel bound by the findings implicit in the vacating of the prior order, that then-existing evidence did not warrant continuing it. Moreover, although relief on an initial c. 209A complaint is limited to one year, "at a renewal hearing, a judge's discretion is broad." *Crenshaw v. Macklin,* 722 N.E.2d 458 (Mass. 2000).

---

2. More specifically, the husband averred that he and the wife had engaged in numerous conversations which included both "chit chat" and discussions concerning the parties' pets (all of whom were in the husband's care and needed medical attention) and various civil litigation matters in which the parties were involved. The husband also averred that following the death of his mother in Los Angeles on May 15, 2002, the wife asked him if she could attend the funeral and proposed that they fly to California together; between May 18 and May 25, 2002, while in Los Angeles, he and the wife spent time alone (attending a movie and riding in an automobile) and with others (including at his mother's memorial service, burial, and a reception), often at the wife's request; he had dinner with the wife and his sister on May 19, 2002.

3. In her opposition, the wife denied or otherwise challenged the husband's averments or his characterizations of events and stated that she continued to be in fear of him. She said, among other things, that she had not voluntarily initiated contact with the husband other than to check on the medical condition of the parties' pets. As for the trip to Los Angeles following the death of the husband's mother, the wife stated that upon receiving an invitation from the husband to attend the services, she consulted with the husband's sister, brother-in-law, and father, who invited her to attend, as they considered her to be part of the family. The husband's family also assured the wife that steps would be taken to ensure her safety. This included paying for a separate flight for her to attend the funeral; arranging for the husband to stay at a hotel while she stayed with members of the husband's family; and attempting to keep the parties separated as much as possible within the circumstances of attending the funeral and related family events. Continuing, the wife stated that there were only two occasions when she was physically alone with the husband (at a movie she had planned to attend with the husband's sister, who backed out at the last moment, and during an automobile ride after the husband's sister sent the husband to pick her up) and that on neither occasion did she choose to be alone with him. The wife said that she was in fear of the husband during the movie and was afraid that the husband would harm her during the automobile ride because he blamed her for getting lost, drove at high rates of speed, and raised his voice at her.

4. In her affidavit, the husband's sister stated that the wife did not wish to be alone with the husband when she arrived in Los Angeles, that the wife asked that the husband be put up in a hotel so that he would not be in the same home with her, that the wife was "shaken" and "upset" after the two instances she was alone with the husband, and that she (the husband's sister) made sure that the wife was not alone with the husband during the remainder of the wife's stay. In addition, the husband's sister stated that, in her view, the wife's fears for her safety if the restraining order were lifted were "not unfounded."

"[P]reservation of the fundamental human right to be protected from the devastating impact of family violence" is the public policy of this Commonwealth, reflected in numerous statutes addressing the problem of domestic violence.

General Laws c. 209A sets out a statutory scheme intended to protect victims of abuse, as defined by the statute, through the issuance of abuse prevention orders....

Section 3 of c. 209A contemplates the possibility of modification of such orders "at any subsequent time upon motion of either party." It also refers to the vacating of orders, but provides that the fact abuse has not occurred during the pendency of an order shall not, in itself, constitute sufficient grounds for allowing an order to be vacated.

... The husband ... asserts in his motion that the wife's actions and conduct during the pendency of the c. 209A order indicate that she is not presently in fear of him, ... [showing] that there is no ongoing need for the order, which should, accordingly, be terminated. Such an assertion seeks *prospective* relief from the c. 209A order.

... CHAPTER 209A does not, however, articulate any standard relative to requests to modify, vacate, or terminate an abuse prevention order....

. . .

The husband's motion construed as a request for relief from prospective application of the abuse prevention order.... falls generally into that category of cases invoking the court's power to modify or prospectively to terminate an abuse prevention order. ... [T]hat power finds expression in c. 209A, § 3, and is also embodied in the last section of MASS.R.DOM.REL.P. 60(b)(5) (1975), which authorizes a judge to relieve a party from a final order if "it is no longer equitable that the [order] should have prospective application."

There is scant authority discussing the specific standard for modifying or terminating provisions of a c. 209A order. In determining the appropriate standard applicable to such determinations, we look to cases interpreting the statute and also seek guidance from the rules of procedure and statutes and decisions in related areas of the law.

We have said that "[i]n deciding whether to modify or renew an abuse prevention order, a judge's discretion is 'broad.'" In *Kraytsberg v. Kraytsberg*, 808 N.E.2d 1242 (Mass. 2004), the Supreme Judicial Court ... summarized an unpublished Rule 1:28 memorandum and order in which we said that the appellant "neither articulated any reasons why the [abuse prevention] order should be vacated nor suggested that anything of substance had occurred since the order was issued that would have allowed the District Court judge to decide to vacate her order."

Statutes governing divorce and children born out of wedlock provide that certain orders, including those pertaining to alimony and custody, may be modified upon a showing respectively, of a "substantial" or a "material and substantial" change in circumstances (and, in certain child-related matters, upon an additional finding that the modification will be in the child's best interests).

The provision in MASS.R.DOM.REL.P. 60(B)(5) authorizing a judge to relieve a party from a final judgment if it is "no longer equitable that the judgment have prospective application" is identical to that in Fed.R.Civ.P. 60(b)(5) and derives from the traditional power of a court of equity to modify its decree in light of changed circumstances. In *United States v. Swift & Co.*, 286 U.S. 106, 119 (1932) (a case predating the Federal Rules of Civil Procedure), the United States Supreme Court said, regarding a request to modify an injunction contained in a consent decree: "The inquiry for us is whether the changes are so important that dangers, once substantial, have become attenuated to a shadow.... Nothing less than a clear showing of grievous wrong evoked by new and unforeseen conditions should lead us to change what was decreed...." In the years after *Swift* was decided, the "grievous wrong" standard was frequently cited as the test for determining whether relief should be granted where "it is no longer equitable that the judgment should have prospective application."

More recently, the United States Supreme Court has indicated that the "grievous wrong" language in *Swift* "was not intended to take on a talismanic quality," *Rufo v. Inmates of Suffolk County Jail*, 502 U.S. 367, 380, (1992), and stated that Fed.R.Civ.P. 60(b)(5) permits a "less stringent, more flexible standard." The Court held that, under this flexible standard, "a party seeking modification of a consent decree must establish that a significant change in facts or law warrants revision of the decree...."

In *Alexis Lichine & Cie. v. Sacha A. Lichine Estates Selection, Ltd.*, 45 F.3d 582, 586 (1st Cir. 1995) the Court of Appeals for the First Circuit, commenting on *Swift* and *Rufo*, observed that the two cases distinguish between decrees protecting " 'rights fully accrued upon facts so nearly permanent as to be substantially impervious to change' and decrees [that] involve[e] 'the supervision of changing conduct or conditions and are thus provisional and tentative.' ... *Swift* illustrates the former and *Rufo* the latter. We view this not as a limited dualism but as polar opposites of a continuum...." The Federal Rule 60(b)(5), the court in *Alexis Lichine & Cie.* stated, "sets forth the umbrella concept of 'equitable' that both *Swift* and *Rufo* apply to particular, widely disparate fact situations."

We draw on the foregoing principles to reach our conclusion that the standard for determining whether prospective relief from a c. 209A order is warranted must be a flexible one. The level of impact on the underlying risk from harm that a c. 209A order seeks to protect against will vary from case to case; a flexible approach that incorporates the "continuum" paradigm set out in *Alexis Lichine & Cie.* is necessary to enable a court to deal effectively with the myriad circumstances that may arise during the pendency of an abuse prevention order. A request to modify a provision of the order that bears only tangentially on the safety of the protected party (e.g., certain orders for visitation or support) will fall at one end of the continuum, whereas a defendant's request to terminate an abuse prevention order *in its entirety* will fall at the other end. The greater the likelihood that the safety of the protected party may be put at risk by a modification, the more substantial the showing the party seeking relief must make.

In deciding whether to grant or deny a party's request for relief, the basis on which the order was initially issued is not subject to review or attack. Rather, the court must consider the nature of the relief sought keeping in mind the primary purpose of a c. 209A order: to protect a party from harm or the fear of imminent serious harm.

The husband's claims amounted to a collateral attack on an abuse prevention order that, at least for the one-year period of its duration, was final. Such an abuse prevention order, entered after a hearing that satisfies due process requirements, should be set aside only in the most extraordinary circumstances and where it has been clearly and convincingly established that the order is no longer needed to protect the victim from harm or the reasonable fear of serious harm. Furthermore, if the judge determines that it is appropriate to allow a motion to vacate or terminate a c. 209A order, the decision should be supported by findings of fact.

Taking as true the admissible averments of fact in the husband's verified motion, the evidence that the wife might have acquiesced in some contact with the husband (occasioned, in large part, by the unusual circumstance of the husband's mother's funeral) does not suffice to meet the husband's heavy burden of demonstrating that the order was no longer needed to protect the wife. Whether measured against a clear and convincing standard of proof, or proof by some lesser standard, the evidence was insufficient to establish that the order was no longer needed to protect the former wife from harm or reasonable fear of serious harm, and it was therefore error to terminate the order.

As we have stated, the abuse prevention order issued against the husband was to expire on January 3, 2003. Had the order not been vacated (erroneously) on July 11, 2002, the wife would have had the opportunity to seek an extension of the order on the date it was set to expire upon a showing of "continued need" for the order and without a showing of new abuse. She should be afforded the same opportunity now.

The order allowing the motion to reconsider and vacate the abuse prevention order is reversed. The wife may, within thirty days of the issuance of the rescript, seek a new order under c. 209A, the issuance of which shall be dependent upon the wife's sustaining her burden of demonstrating a continued need for the order. The judge may consider evidence subsequent to January 3, 2003.

So ordered.

Ba v. United States

D.C. Court of Appeals, 2002.
809 A.2d 1178.

■ REID, ASSOCIATE JUDGE:

Appellant Alassane Ba was convicted of violating a civil protection order (CPO) under D.C. CODE §§ 16–1004, –1005 (2001) at a bench trial. On June 9, 2002, this court issued an opinion affirming Mr. Ba's conviction. Subsequently, after receiving petitions for rehearing or rehearing en banc, the court vacated its opinion; granted rehearing; requested new briefing directed at the following issue: "Under the circumstances of appellant's case, was consent a defense to the Civil Protection Order"; and scheduled the matter for oral argument. On rehearing, Mr. Ba continues to contend that his reconciliation with the complainant after the issuance of the CPO effectively vacated that order and provided him with a valid defense, or at least precluded a finding that he wilfully violated the CPO.... We affirm appellant's conviction, holding that on the facts of this case, the government proved beyond a reasonable doubt that Mr. Ba wilfully violated the CPO.

The record before us reveals that in December 1999, Ms. Lashance Howard filed a petition and affidavit for a CPO against her ex-boyfriend of four years, Mr. Ba. On December 29, 1999, Mr. Ba signed a Consent CPO Without Admissions, which was effective for a twelve-month period. The CPO ordered Mr. Ba not to "assault, threaten, harass, or physically abuse [Ms. Howard] in any manner," to "stay at least 100 feet away from [Ms.

Howard], [her] home [and her] workplace[,]" and prohibited him from contacting her "in any manner." The CPO further explicitly warned that: "Any and every failure to comply with this order is punishable as criminal contempt and/or as a criminal misdemeanor and may result in imprisonment for up to six months, a fine of up to $1,000, or both."

Subsequently, Mr. Ba was charged with one count of violation of a CPO, which allegedly occurred on May 13, 2000. A hearing on this charge took place on July 14, 2000. . . .

Ms. Howard's direct, cross and redirect examination revealed that sometime after December 29, 1999, she and Mr. Ba lived together while the CPO still was in effect, and when they were attempting to work out problems in their relationship. During this period, Ms. Howard and Mr. Ba sometimes stayed at his place of residence and sometimes at Ms. Howard's home. The two continued to reside together until March 2000. Mr. Ba's testimony confirmed that he and Ms. Howard reconciled after the CPO took effect on December 29, 1999. He testified that he and Ms. Howard lived together, at times, from January 2000 to late March 2000.

Ms. Howard stated that: "As of March, the end of March, [Mr. Ba] knew [their relationship] was completely over." She also pinpointed the moment the relationship ended as "[m]id-March." . . .

Ms. Howard's testimony addressed the specific incident which led to the one count charge against Mr. Ba, alleging his violation of the CPO dated December 29, 1999. That event occurred on May 13, 2000. On that day, Ms. Howard received a phone call at approximately 2:20 a.m. The caller hung up without speaking. Ms. Howard's caller identification box informed her that the call came from a pay phone; she then "beeped" Officer Wayne David who had previously responded to her complaint about Mr. Ba. When Officer David returned her call, she "asked him if he would, on his way off duty, . . . stop by [her] home just to make sure everything was okay." While she was waiting for Officer David, she looked out of a window of her residence and observed a car that resembled Mr. Ba's; she "saw a male in the car."

Ms. Howard continued recounting the events of May 13, saying that: "[A]fter maybe 20 or 30 minutes had passed with nothing . . . well, I saw a black car drive up to the driveway. And I peered out of the window again, and the person just sat in the car." The person in the unmarked car was Officer David. Ms. Howard went outside when she recognized the officer as he illuminated his unmarked vehicle, and told him that she thought she saw Mr. Ba's car, but "had heard nothing from him for the last 20 minutes or so."

After Officer David left, and as Ms. Howard "was putting the key in the lock of the gate" to re-enter, Mr. Ba appeared, approached and came "within six feet" of Ms. Howard. As Ms. Howard "tried to get in the door," Officer David returned and inquired whether the man standing near Ms. Howard was Mr. Ba. When Ms. Howard "replied yes," the officer "pulled out his weapon." At that time, Mr. Ba was about "ten feet, twelve feet" from Ms. Howard. Officer David arrested him.

. . . Mr. Ba [testified that] . . . [h]e went to Ms. Howard's residence on May 13, 2000, "just to talk to her. . . ." When he "walked toward her . . . , and [said], how you can do this[,] . . . she started screaming." At that point, the officer intervened and arrested him.

The trial judge [found] Mr. Ba guilty beyond a reasonable doubt of violating the CPO [and sentenced him to 90 days in jail]. . . .

Mr. Ba primarily contends that Ms. Howard consented to the violation of the CPO when they reconciled shortly after the CPO was issued against him. Thus, he asserts, the CPO no longer had legal effect when he entered her property in May. Furthermore, he maintains that Ms. Howard's consent is a valid defense to all subsequent violations of the December 29, 1999, CPO. . . . The Public Defender Service ("PDS") as amicus . . . contends that in this case:

> Because the petitioner's consensual reconciliation over several months with Mr. Ba constructively and permanently modified the protection order, consent was available to Mr. Ba as a defense to the CPO violation charge regardless of whether he and the petitioner eventually broke off their relationship in March 2000.

The government argues that this court need not reach the "consent" issue essentially because Mr. Ba and Ms. Howard "could not, by their own conduct, void the CPO." However, the government asserts that if the court reaches the issue, "it should reject consent as a defense" to the CPO for a variety of reasons, including the need to "enforce the authority of the court that issued the order[,]" the difficulty of "determin[ing] whether consent to renewed contact has been freely given[,]" and "the incentive" that the subject of a CPO "would have . . . to contact the complainant indirectly or even to risk direct contact in the hope of gaining an agreement to reconcile."

Under D.C. CODE § 16–1005(f), violation of a CPO is punishable as criminal contempt. . . .

To establish the elements of a CPO violation, the government must present evidence proving . . . that defendant engaged in: (1) wilfull disobedience (2) of a protective court order. . . .

The purpose of the CPO proceeding is to protect the moving party, rather than to punish the offender. From this premise, as the trial court recognized, Mr. Ba arguably had a valid defense of consent when he and Ms. Howard reconciled between January and March 2000, particularly since Ms. Howard testified that there were times when she would stay at Mr. Ba's residence after the CPO was entered. The parties and amicus raise serious and complex issues regarding the consent defense and the frustration of the CPO by a party who seeks the order. We need not address those issues in this case, however, because we are satisfied that on the facts of this case, any consent by Ms. Howard during the January to March 2000 period would not establish her consent after late March 2000. Indeed, the evidence establishes, beyond a reasonable doubt, that Ms. Howard revoked her consent to violation of the CPO. As of late March, Ms. Howard and Mr. Ba had no consensual contact. In fact, according to the undisputed evidence, Mr. Ba tried to approach Ms. Howard at work and she reacted by calling the police. At this point, Ms. Howard's consent to the violation of the CPO, if such consent was possible, was effectively revoked. Moreover, Mr. Ba unsuccessfully sought to vacate the CPO in March. Thus, when he approached Ms. Howard on May 13, he clearly knew that the one-year CPO had not been vacated.

Finally, Mr. Ba's contention that there was insufficient evidence to establish his violation of the CPO is unpersuasive under the circumstances of this case. The trial court found that notwithstanding the earlier reconciliation from January to March, 2000, Mr. Ba's conduct in violation of the CPO in the early hours of May 13, 2000, was willful, and resulted in a violation of the CPO ... The CPO ordered Mr. Ba to "stay at least 100 feet away from [Ms. Howard], [her] home, [and her] workplace." In the early hours of May 13, 2000, Mr. Ba stood within at least ten or twelve feet of Ms. Howard, a clear violation of the CPO. In addition, even though the CPO ordered Mr. Ba not to contact Ms. Howard "in any manner," he went to her home and spoke with her on May 13, 2000, another clear violation of the CPO.

Accordingly, for the foregoing reasons, we affirm the judgment of the trial court.

NOTES

1. The *Ba* case raises several difficult issues. Should consent based on the behavior of the beneficiary of a Civil Protective Order be a defense to prosecution for violation of the order? Does this undercut the categorical force of the order and subject the behavior of the victim to unduly intrusive scrutiny? Or does the availability of such a defense take account of the complexity of intimate relationships and prevent unfairness to a party subject to the order? Should the order be deemed to be in force unless the victim officially requests that it be withdrawn? If the victim makes such a request, should the court scrutinize it to determine if it is genuinely voluntary?

2. If a victim allows someone subject to protective order to have contact with him or her, can he or she be liable for aiding and abetting the violation of the order? In *Henley v. District Court*, 533 N.W.2d 199 (Iowa 1995), the court said that she can, referring to authority holding that contempt orders may be enforced against anyone who acts with knowledge of the protective order and in concert with the person subject to it. By contrast, the court in *Ohio v. Lucas*, 100 Ohio St.3d 1, 795 N.E.2d 642 (2003), held that the beneficiary of an order cannot be prosecuted for aiding and abetting its violation. The court said, "If petitioners for protection orders were liable for criminal prosecution, a violator of a protection order could create a real chill on the reporting of the violation by simply threatening to claim that an illegal visit was the result of an illegal invitation." *Id.* at 647.

II. MANDATORY ARREST POLICY

Attorney General's Task Force on Family Violence

22–24 (1984).

Consistent with state law, the chief executive of every law enforcement agency should establish arrest as the preferred response in cases of family violence.

. . .

During the sixties, police trainers relied on the literature of psychologists and social scientists who believed that arrest was inappropriate because it exacerbated the violence, broke up families, and caused the abuser to lose his job. Consequently, mediation was the preferable solution to most family violence incidents. This method of response was based on assumptions that were neither closely examined nor adequately tested. Rather than emphasize the victim's right to safety and protection against future assaults, the mediation model moved away from law enforcement into social services. The shift to non-arrest was accepted by police officers who were attempting to provide help but did not have solid policy guidance. They welcomed this new intervention technique because it had the professional support and endorsement of the social scientists and did not, in and of itself, expose the officer to physical resistance.

Consequently, law enforcement officers have generally attempted to resolve incidents of family violence through the expeditious techniques of sending one party away from the home or superficially mediating the dispute. This arrest avoidance policy, based on incorrect social science assumptions, is emphasized by all segments of the criminal justice system. It starts with initial training in the police academy which teaches the officer that arrest is usually inadvisable. This is reenforced by the actions of the prosecuting attorney who generally does not issue criminal charges or routinely prosecute these cases. Many judges also act in ways to discourage arrest by setting low bail or releasing the assailant on his own recognizance, or upon conviction, failing to impose a meaningful sanction. Finally, the officers are confronted with anecdotal vignettes about victims themselves posting the assailant's bail, or refusing to appear to testify against the abuser, thereby frustrating the efforts of the most dedicated of officers.

Although called upon to stop the violence, law enforcement has not been encouraged by any component of the criminal justice or social service systems to intervene with a formal arrest. Clearly, officers regularly classify serious assaults between strangers as felonies and make appropriate arrests. Yet when the same level of injury occurs between family members, officers have been inclined to treat the crime as, at most, a misdemeanor and failed to make an arrest. They have instead tended to require the victim to initiate a citizen's arrest. By shifting the burden of arrest, police believe the credibility of the charges will be increased and their personal liability decreased. But it is precisely this burden of a citizen's arrest that often results in the victim's reluctant participation in mediation conducted by the responding officer.

However, mediation is most often an equally inappropriate law enforcement response in family violence incidents. Mediation may assume that the parties involved are of equal culpability in the assault even though one has a visible injury and the other does not, or it may assume that the underlying cause of violence can be resolved without arrest. But an abusive relationship is generally demonstrably one sided. The abuser is usually physically superior and the victim is injured and fearful of further harm.

Mediation not only fails to hold the offender accountable for his criminal actions but, worse yet, gives the abuser no incentive to change his behavior. Rather than stopping the violence and providing protection for the victim, mediation may inadvertently contribute to a dangerous escalation of violence.

The original shift by law enforcement to mediation was done for the most commendable reasons. They were responding to early assumptions of psychologists and sociologists and to signals from prosecutors and judges. But a recent research experiment is challenging these traditional beliefs that mediation is the appropriate law enforcement response. The results of the research demonstrated that arrest and overnight incarceration are the most effective interventions to reduce the likelihood of subsequent acts of family violence. A victim's chance of future assault was nearly two and a half times greater when officers did not make an arrest. Attempting to counsel both parties or sending the assailant away from home for several hours were found to be considerably less effective in deterring future violence. The research further indicated that the interaction between the officer and the victim also has significant impact on the likelihood that the abuser will commit further violence. When officers take time to listen to the victim, before making the arrest, and the offender is aware of this, the likelihood of recurring assaults declines significantly. Researchers suggest that the assaulter views the enhanced stature of the victim and subsequent arrest and overnight incarceration as a judgment that his behavior is criminal.

Because mediation is most often an inappropriate law enforcement response and because arrest and overnight incarceration have been shown to be an effective deterrent against household assault, arrest must be the presumed response in cases of family violence.... This policy of preferred arrest for household assaults puts the abuser on notice that family violence is a crime with serious consequences. It also helps the community appreciate the criminal nature of family violence.

NOTES

1. The conclusions of the Attorney General's Task Force have been called into question by more recent studies:

> The principal investigators in the original police arrest experiment concluded that their study "strongly suggest[ed] that police should use arrest in domestic violence cases," because arrest was most highly correlated with low recidivism rates. But when six replication studies were conducted in different jurisdictions, the findings ranged from arrest having no effect, to a deterrent effect, to an escalation effect. And even within the same jurisdiction, the effect of arrest often varied based on the length of detention and certain offender characteristics, such as employment and other ties to the community.

> What these studies ignored was the possibility that the procedures employed by the police might have affected the results. In 1997, researchers revisited the data from all seven studies to determine whether "the *manner* in which sanctions are imposed has an independent and more powerful effect on spouse assault than the sanction outcome itself." They found that perceptions of procedural justice have a statistically significant impact. The frequency of recidivist domestic abuse was lower for those perpetrators given only a warning than for those who were arrested, in cases where the arrested offenders perceived that they had been treated in a procedurally unfair manner. The frequency of subsequent abuse was far lower, however, when arrestees believed they had been treated fairly.

Deborah Epstein, *Effective Intervention in Domestic Violence Cases: Rethinking the Roles of Prosecutors, Judges, and the Court System*, 11 YALE J. L. & FEMINISM 3, 48 (1999).

2. The debate about mandatory arrest policies and their effect on escalation of violence and recidivism continues. Many jurisdictions have put such policies into effect. Mandatory arrest appears to be successful in some jurisdictions and harmful in others. There is nothing approaching a consensus on the topic. *See, e.g.*, Barbara Fedders, *Lobbying for Mandatory–Arrest Policies: Race, Class, and the Politics of the Battered Women's Movement*, 23 N.Y.U. REV. L. SOC. CHANGE 281 (1997); Erin L. Han, Note, *Mandatory Arrest and No–Drop Policies: Victim Empowerment in Domestic Violence Cases*, 23 B.C. THIRD WORLD L.J. 159 (2004).

3. One study of the impact of mandatory arrest policies in six cities concluded:

> *Arrest reduces domestic violence among employed people but increases it among unemployed people* (emphasis in original). Mandatory arrest policies thus protect working-class women but cause greater harm to those who are poor. Conversely, not making arrests may hurt working women but reduce violence against economically poor women. Similar trade-offs may exist on the basis of race, marriage, education and neighborhood. Thus, even in cities where arrest reduces domestic violence overall, as an unintended side effect it may increase violence against the poorest victims.

Janell D. Schmidt & Lawrence W. Sherman, *Does Arrest Deter Domestic Violence?*, *in* Do Arrests and Restraining Orders Work? 43, 49 (E.S. Buzawa & C.G. Buzawa, eds. 1996).

Liza Mundy, *Fault Line*

Wash. Post Mag., Oct. 26, 1997, at W8.

"This is not your decision. This is my decision," the thin young corn-blond cop is saying.

Early evening. A deserted parking lot in an office complex in Annandale. The humid aftermath of a rush-hour rainstorm. The cop stands talking to a middle-aged man of average height and average weight, a man who has sandy hair that's turning gray, and glasses, and a pink face, and a white shirt and blue pants and a diamond-patterned blue-and-white tie, and the glazed, unhappy look of a well-controlled professional in a situation that has spun horribly out of his control. Somewhere behind both of them, the man's wife is waiting in a second-floor office.

Domvio. Domestic violence. That's what the dispatcher's message said when it flashed on the computer screens of Fairfax County police squad cars. "Estranged wife has destroyed office/w/f/ . . . white T-shirt, pink shorts— hung up phone when I was talking," the message read, and now one, two, three cops have arrived to see what's going on, and one of them, Mike Tucker, is talking to the man, who was waiting on the sidewalk when they arrived, tucking his shirt into his pants. The man tells Tucker that earlier in the day his wife came to his office, bringing along a separation agreement for him to sign. He objected to some of the wording, and his wife got angry and pushed him. So, hoping a police report might be something he could use in a custody dispute, he called the cops.

Are you injured? Tucker asks.

No, says the man, whose name is Tom.

Tucker goes inside to talk to the wife, whose name is Judy. But Judy, still angry and combative, refuses to tell him anything. So Tucker talks to a witness who heard Tom say, "Stop pushing me!" and then goes outside to talk to Tom again.

All this is taking place a month after a domestic violence law went into effect throughout Virginia on July 1. The new law says that police must make an arrest whenever they have probable cause to believe a domestic assault has occurred. What constitutes probable cause? Tucker considers this question as he inspects a small tear in the breast pocket of Tom's shirt. Then, after consulting with another officer, he conveys the news to Tom: The pocket is enough. Judy must be arrested.

Tom is horrified. "Can I go on record that I don't want to press charges right now?" he asks, and Tucker says yes, he can go on record, but even so, pressing charges is not his decision, it is the decision of the commonwealth of Virginia, which is exactly what Tucker was just explaining, because that's what police are now trained to tell victims of domestic violence.

"Oh God, oh God!" Tom says while Tucker goes upstairs to make the arrest. Moments later he emerges from the doorway with a diminutive panicked woman in pink running shorts and a white "New York" T-shirt and, behind her back, handcuffs. The wife. Judy. Who has short soft brown hair, tied back, and a suntan. "Tom," she calls as she's led past her husband, "do you know they're arresting me? Tom, please! Tom, did I push you? Tom, please! Call my mother! Call our attorney!"

"Is this the Gestapo or what?" Tom says. "I just wanted documentation in a custody dispute. I certainly didn't want this!"

Tucker puts Judy in the back of his squad car and drives her to the Fairfax County Adult Detention Center, where she is charged with domestic assault and battery under Virginia's criminal code, section 18.2–57.2. The new law directs Tucker to request an emergency protective order to protect Tom from further acts of abuse, and so Tucker does, and the order is granted, directing Judy to stay away from her husband—specifically, his office—for three days, except for "incidental contact to assure welfare of children."

A $750 bond is set to guarantee she shows up for trial.

Her name is entered into the Virginia crime information network, so that if she violates the stay-away order, her existing criminal charge will be readily available.

She is fingerprinted and her mug shot is taken.

Asked if she has any scars, marks or tattoos, she says no.

Asked her occupation, she says, "Flutist."

Meanwhile, back at the office complex, the two remaining officers, T.J. Rogers and Ben Ferdinand, try to calm her husband—counseling the victim, as the new law also directs. "We don't have discretion," Ferdinand explains, gently, for the third time. "You're not pressing charges. It's Officer Tucker who's pressing charges." When Judy's court date comes up, they suggest, she probably won't get any jail time; more likely she'll be ordered to seek counseling. A good thing, perhaps. The two officers stand there in the suburban dusk, earnestly encouraging the man before them to look at the events of today, the argument and the pushing and the 911 call and the police arrival and the arrest and the handcuffs and the new law and the workings of Fairfax County's criminal justice system as, in Officer Ferdinand's words, a "positive step" for him and his family.

"There shall be an arrest. It's not may, if or should; it's shall, and in Virginia, 'shall' means there *will* be."

Fairfax County Police Chief M. Douglas Scott can be forgiven the pride he evinces when describing the language of Virginia's new domestic violence law, under which Judy and thousands of others have been arrested since it took effect. Variously known as "warrantless arrest," "pro-arrest" and "mandatory arrest," the law takes a single-minded approach to domestic violence, requiring that an arrest be made if there's any evidence an assault was committed. The law was fashioned by a commission that included Lt. Gov. Donald S. Beyer Jr. and James S. Gilmore III, the Democratic and Republican candidates in Virginia's gubernatorial election; it passed the General Assembly without a dissenting vote; and Scott is proud because the law was modeled, in part, on similar policies already in effect in Fairfax County and several urban Virginia jurisdictions.

"I can tell you that in my discussions with some of the rural chiefs and sheriffs, the mind set is still the old mind set: You know, old Charlie's a good guy, yeah, he got a little drunk Friday night, then he went home and slapped his wife around, so what's the problem here?" says Scott, who helped persuade cops around the state to change that Neanderthal way of thinking. He urged them to embrace the new law, convincing them that it wouldn't sap their resources or tie up their officers. What it would do, he told them, is cut down on a chronic law enforcement problem: the problem not only of domestic violence itself, but also of victims who out of love or fear or economic dependency or cultural isolation or all of the above are unwilling to press charges against their batterers, and batterers who, as a result, get away with their abuse.

"The goal is to send enough of a message to the violator that this behavior is not going to be tolerated, that it's serious, you can go to jail for it," is how Scott puts it.

The new approach represents a huge change, both practically and philosophically—and a huge victory for advocates on behalf of domestic violence victims. "We've done a fabulous job convincing the legislature that it is a highly criminal act to maim or abuse a spouse," says Judith Mueller of the Vienna-based Women's Center, who was among those lobbying for the bill. Similar victories have been won around the country: According to the Family Violence Project of the National Council of Juvenile and Family Court Judges, seven states plus the District of Columbia have mandatory arrest policies, and 26 others, including Maryland, have "presumptive arrest" policies that give officers a bit of discretion but still encourage them to make an arrest. Another 12 have laws that blend the two approaches. The thinking is that it's a lot easier on battered victims—and prosecutors—when the responsibility is taken off them and assumed by the state.

But a look at some of the arrests made in Fairfax County shortly after the law passed—arrests made by officers who are well trained and already familiar with an aggressive arrest policy—suggests that chronic abusers are by no means the only ones arrested under mandatory laws. As intended, the law has helped women—and men—who are in genuine danger from first-time and habitual batterers. But in other cases it may have created a new category of victim, indeed rendered the word so diffuse as to be meaningless.

"A lot of times, I think arrests are being made when they shouldn't be," says Kenneth E. Noyes, staff attorney and coordinator of the domestic violence project for Legal Services of Northern Virginia.

"I am stunned, quite frankly, because that was not the intention of the law. It was to protect people from predictable violent assaults, where a history occurred, and the victim was unable for whatever reason to press charges," says Mueller. "It's disheartening to think that it could be used punitively and frivolously. Frivolously being the operative word."

But in most cases, the police officers are not acting frivolously. They're acting conscientiously and in good faith, doing exactly what the law requires. And what the law requires is a rigid, inflexible response to a set of situations that are limitlessly vast. The river of human misery runs broad and deep; there are—as Tolstoy pointed out—all sorts of unhappy families, and all manner of domestic disputes. What do you do—for example—when a man calls 911 to report that his wife has destroyed his Mercedes with a ball-peen hammer and he would like her, please, arrested?

What do you do when a father calls to say that his son threw food at him, and now he would like the kid, please, arrested?

When a husband calls 911 to say that his wife slapped him with an open hand and he would like her, please, arrested?

What do you do when you have cast a net for sharks into waters that are brimming with all kinds of fish? "We didn't intend to catch minnows,"

Mueller says. "So, what do you do when the net brings in species or varieties for which you weren't casting?"

Alternatively: What do you do when a set of keys is flying through the air?

The keys belong to a dark-haired, dark-eyed, clear-skinned, soft-voiced young woman named Lora, who is 21. She has flung them out of fury and desperation and anger and disbelief. Her mother—her own mother!—has called the cops on Lora's boyfriend. Called the cops when her boyfriend wasn't even doing anything, in Lora's view; he just came over to visit on a Sunday morning, as he often does, except that Lora's mother, who doesn't much like him, wasn't in a visiting mood. Words were exchanged, there was an argument over a newspaper that somebody left on the floor, the argument escalated until Lora's mom threatened to call 911. Lora assumed she was kidding.

Of course she was kidding—she would never call the police.

Even so, her boyfriend thought it was a good idea to leave. Lora, too, was planning to go to a friend's house so everybody could cool off. As she was walking to the car, though, here came Officer M.A. Swain. Her mother had really done it, really called! Lora couldn't believe it—she lost her temper and flung an empty water bottle and her car keys. The water bottle, she's pretty sure, landed on the steps, but the officer said the keys went whizzing near her mother.

To Lora, the sight of the officer was shocking; to Swain, the sight of an angry mother and daughter must have been tediously familiar. Wife-beating—the old term for domestic violence—is still seen, dismayingly often, by cops. But it's by no means the only form of domestic violence or even the most common. In the fractious fractured families of the 1990s, domestic violence comprises so many kinds of behavior, and so many kinds of relationships, that it's more commonly known as "family violence," a term that embraces—to name a few—a fight between two lovers who live together, between the divorced parents of a child, between gay partners, between grandparents and grandchildren, between parents and kids.

In the course of two ordinary weekdays, for example, Fairfax County 911 dispatchers take calls from a Navy captain saying that his 21–year–old daughter is "kicking and hitting me," a woman saying that her 9–year–old daughter "hit me in the back with a shoe," a little girl complaining that her grandmother struck her on the hand and wrist with a kitchen strainer, and a woman who quickly retracts her complaint about "a little sister-to-sister fight over $50." Each call is coded as "domestic"—domestic dispute if there doesn't seem to be an assault taking place, domestic violence if there does—and the police are sent to investigate.

In other situations, cops have a great deal of discretion over how and whether to make an arrest. But in domestics—barring extraordinary circumstances such as an assailant who is quite young or mentally ill, or both—there's now just one thing that matters.

Was there an assault, or wasn't there?

In Lora's case, there really is no question. In the eyes of the law, you don't have to hit somebody to commit assault—all you have to do is *try* to hit them. Strictly speaking, assault is the attempt to commit "unwanted touching," while battery is the unwanted touching itself. In Fairfax, the two are treated as part of the same continuum; while the new domestic violence law says "assault and battery," this is not a distinction that the police, or the courts, stop to make. Before she knows it, Lora has handcuffs on her and is being led to a squad car and taken to the station, where she is fingerprinted and photographed.

"Is this your first time locked up?"

"Yes," Lora says.

"Have you ever tried to kill yourself?"

"No," Lora says.

"In the case of emergency, who should I contact?"

"My mom," Lora says, giving her mom's name and number. And now Swain is taking Lora before the magistrate, who says to Lora, "You're being charged with domestic assault.... When you threw the keys at your mother, that was the act of aggression that indicated your intent to assault her." The magistrate asks Lora where she works, and she gives the name of a firm where she was recently hired as a secretary, her first job, a job she loves. The magistrate asks how long Lora has lived at her current address, and she says 16 years. The magistrate asks whether there are ongoing problems between her mom and her boyfriend, whom, it turns out, Lora has been dating since high school, and who is not Lebanese, which, Lora suspects, is the main reason her mom doesn't like him, though her mom will later say that it's just that Lora is a sweet girl, a beautiful girl, who can do better than this particular guy.

Does this sort of argument happen a lot between you and your mother? the magistrate asks.

"Not that often."

"Once a month? Once every other week?"

"Sometimes when he comes over, she doesn't get mad," Lora says. "We go ahead and we eat and everything, and she doesn't get mad."

The magistrate sets a trial date and tells Lora that she's being released on her own recognizance—i.e., she's free to go. But she cannot have any contact with her mother for three days. Lora calls a friend to pick her up, and during the next three days her mom calls the friend's house, asking whether she's mad, whether she's going to move out. Last year Lora's dad died after an expensive and lingering bout with cancer, and if Lora moves out her mother will be alone and, probably, unable to afford the apartment. But Lora won't move out. "I would never leave my mom," she says, "until I get married."

Departing the station, Officer Mike Twomey, who assisted in the arrest, remarks that in the old days, the proper response would have been to say, hey, ladies, cool it. Now, arrest is the only option. For his part, Twomey sympathizes with the two women, but he doesn't think arrest is a bad thing, because sometimes it's the only way to help people figure out how to behave differently:

"Most of the time you feel you should drive around in one of the black-and-white shirts that referees wear, and stand in the middle, and yell, 'Foul! You're offsides!' "

Many officers, like Twomey, are comfortable with the law even as they understand the limits it places on them. That's because they know that arguments tend to recur in emotional relationships, particularly bad ones, and even if the first domestic call doesn't involve much injury—most don't—

the second is likely to be worse. That's the whole point of the law: Intervene early, because otherwise, you're going to be going back and back and back.

"I'd rather have it nol-prossed in court than have something else happen, and go back and find a dead body," says Officer John Vickery.

"It does give us less discretion," says Officer Ben Ferdinand, "but it takes some of the liability off us too." That's literally true. Thanks to mandatory arrest, police departments are less likely to face a lawsuit for false arrest, or for leaving a scene where violence breaks out again.

"Elaine," the man is saying into the telephone, while nearby a 3-year-old boy is saying, "Mommy! Mommy! Mommy!"

The man, Jesse, has opened the door of his apartment to see a police officer. He doesn't seem surprised, though he does seem a little dazed. He is a fit young dark-haired Navy man wearing khaki shorts and a purple shirt. Behind him is an Ansel Adams poster; in the living room is a television with Jesse's martial arts trophies atop it. The apartment is immaculate except for, on the kitchen floor, a half-empty jar of Jif.

Jesse is on the phone with his wife, Elaine, who has called him from the jail. Earlier that day, Jesse got home from his morning job and Elaine wanted to talk to him about day-care problems that were interfering with her new job at a hospital. But Jesse didn't want to talk; instead, he went to the kitchen and began making a peanut-butter-and-jelly sandwich for the boy. Elaine, frustrated by his silence, snatched the peanut butter jar and flung it toward the sink. Jesse called 911. When the officer arrived, Jesse said Elaine had tried to shove him away from the phone. Elaine said that it was Jesse who had shoved her away when he was talking to the dispatcher. There was no injury, no evidence of who was telling the truth.

Such mutual charges are common, and they are another reason domestics have traditionally been so hard for the law to handle. At the magistrate's office, for example, a sort of bad-checks list is kept containing the names of people who are known to swear out domestic warrants for reasons that seem less than legit: anger, perhaps, or jealousy, or revenge. "Warrant should NOT be issued to either of these individuals without a police investigation," one magistrate wrote on an application he denied, noting that the couple were cross-filing, or trying to have each other arrested. Recognizing the confusion of many domestic disputes, the new law contains a clause dealing with mutual accusation and mutual assault. When possible, officers are directed to identify the "primary aggressor" and arrest that person.

Some officers think this part of the law is weighted against men, since part of the definition of primary aggressor is the person who has the potential to commit greater violence. In this case, though, Officer Fred Kessel arrested Elaine, based solely on her angry demeanor and the fact that "I actually believed him more than her."

And now, two hours after the arrest, Elaine in jail, here is another officer, Mark Dale, waiting while Jesse hands the phone to the toddler. Dale presents Jesse with an emergency protective order that will give him even more protection from his wife. Under the new law, officers are required to seek an EPO, barring the assailant from contact with the victim for at least three days, to prevent acts of retaliation. Dale has brought a copy of the document to Jesse, to make sure he's aware of the stay-away directive. This is important because it's a sad fact of human relationships that often, after an arrest has been made, the victim lets the assailant right back in the door.

And indeed here is Jesse, taking the phone back from his son, standing in front of the police officer, talking to his wife.

"She is asking me to get her out," he says.

"She's not supposed to have any contact with you," Dale explains, and Jesse stands there looking at the piece of paper that explicitly forbids precisely the sort of contact that's going on now.

It's not the first time Jesse has had his wife arrested. Months earlier, before the new law went into effect, Jesse went to the magistrate and swore out a warrant against her, charging that she struck him during an argument in their car. When the case got to court, however, Jesse dropped charges. Subsequent to her own arrest, Elaine sought a Legal Services lawyer who helped her file a civil restraining order against Jesse—civil restraining orders being a way to get protection from somebody without having the person arrested. As she described it, Jesse was the one who struck her; when he forced her out of the car, she accidentally hit him in self-defense.

Since the couple met and married four years ago, they have had a tangled and unhappy history of breakups and reconciliation. "This is not me at all; my life totally changed when I met my husband," Elaine, a 27–year-old woman with long black hair, says in an interview later, pointing to a scar on her foot that she says she got when Jesse threw her into a couch during an argument. Jesse, who has a black belt in the martial art of kenpo, denies that he has hit Elaine, though he says he has "held onto her" to restrain her. She's the one who's always coming after him, he says; when she threw the peanut butter, he was afraid she'd pick up a knife. "I'm afraid of her," he says.

Who is the real victim? In arguing that Elaine is, counselors who have worked with her point to what they call classic abuse symptoms. A native of Hawaii whose first language is Tagalog, she is isolated from her family and culture, unemployed, without her own car, dependent on her husband for income. Kenneth Noyes, the Legal Services attorney who has helped her in a custody suit for her son, believes that her husband has learned to work the system against her. Jesse, for his part, says that Elaine has learned to use the system against him, specifically the Navy's family advocacy program, where she has sought counseling. Elaine and Jesse resolved their earlier charges, Noyes says, by signing an agreement that there would be no further acts of abuse by either.

But what, exactly, is abuse? Refusing to talk to your wife? Picking up the phone to have your spouse arrested? In the eyes of the law, the Jif jar is what matters. When the officer leaves, Jesse is still on the phone with Elaine, who spends the night in jail. She is released the next day and picked up—by Jesse.

Who later says that you'd think now, after all this, Elaine would be a little nicer to him.

"If she's there, I can't go there?" asks Carl, incredulous. "I own the place! Her name is not on anything! It's my house and I can't go there?"

It should be made clear that not all cases are murky and confusing. Despite all the permutations, all the amorphous forms that family violence can take, all the mutual squabbles and dubious 911 alarms and couples racing to beat each other to the telephone or the warrant office, there are plenty of cases that are both clear and egregious. Physical abuse does happen, real violence does happen, has just happened, in fact, late on a Sunday in Mount Vernon south of Alexandria. In the police station, a couple of sheriff's deputies and police officers are in the processing room, along with a middle-aged drunk wearing socks but no shoes. Also there is Carl, a truck driver who has just been arrested for hitting his girlfriend, bruising her arm and cutting her lip and breaking her eardrum.

The 911 call came from the victim's son, who was standing in the road waving the police down when they arrived. The son told the police that Carl had come home to find dirty dishes in the sink, and the dishes made him mad, and in his anger he woke up the boy's mother, Helen, and hit her, and kept hitting her. By the time the police showed up, Helen was bruised and cut on her face and feet. Even so, she begged the officer not to arrest Carl—a classic victim's reaction.

"Back off," the officer advised, telling her to step out the door or she might go to jail, too.

And now here is Carl, absorbing the unbelievable fact that not only has he been arrested but an emergency protective order has been issued, something he's never heard of, and thanks to this thing, he cannot return to his own trailer! Even though his name is on the lease! "Everything I own is there!" he says to the drunk beside him.

"I realize you are the one who purchased the home," the magistrate tells him when he is brought before her to be charged, "but you allowed her to move in, you and she are cohabiting, so I'm allowing her to use your trailer for 72 hours."

Meanwhile, Helen has been taken off in an ambulance. In the emergency room of Mount Vernon Hospital, she is having her jaw X-rayed and her foot swabbed. A doctor shoots a painkiller directly into a cut and asks her if it hurts. Helen politely says no. Helen is a tiny longhaired woman wearing a T-shirt and shorts. She now cannot hear out of one ear. Later, the doctor will give her an antibiotic to ward off infection and tell her that basically the eardrum is going to have to heal itself.

"Are you allergic to anything?"

"Codeine," Helen says. She is frank and friendly and, for somebody who has just been beaten up, calm. "I threw an antique chamber pot right through the front door," she says, explaining how the fight started. That was after Carl came home and started getting on her about the dishes. He's a finicky person, she says, constantly picking at her son in particular, getting on him when he flushes the toilet wrong or holds the refrigerator open. This time, when he started in on the dishes, Helen had just had it, and so she threw the chamber pot, she readily admits that. She threw the chamber pot, which was hers, part of a set. Then she upended a table. Then he really came at her, hitting her so hard that she doesn't remember what came afterward, just that now her head hurts and her backside hurts and she can't hear out of one ear.

She acknowledges that she tried to dissuade the arresting officer—"When you see them going off in handcuffs, it just seems so cruel"—but now she's glad the arrest has been made. She's glad the law exists.

Carl, presumably, is not. "I don't have my reading glasses," he says unhappily when presented with the EPO, an aging man with gray hair flying wildly above his head, and no shirt, and a crucifix around his neck, and black laceless loafer-type tennis shoes. The officer explains the EPO to him one more time, and with that, Carl sits down, predicts that Helen will steal his stuff and says, to the drunk beside him, "It's a strange world we live in, Master Jack."

Helen does not steal his stuff. What she does is, she shows up the next morning at the trailer with her son and her sister and cleans the trailer until it's spotless. Then she packs stuff into boxes, but only stuff she's sure is hers. She even leaves the pictures on the wall because, though they are her pictures, they are Carl's frames. While her sister and son carry out a mattress and dresser, she sits down at the table and thinks through the months ahead: storing her stuff, living with her sister, trying to find a place she can afford.

Because she is leaving. She is definitely leaving. She's been beaten before, not by Carl, she says, but by another man, and she's not going to be beaten again. The law has given her the time and space to make this decision. It's not an easy one, and the subsequent weeks aren't going to be easy, either. She's going to have to go to the doctor about her eardrum so many times that she finally must tell her boss what happened, and she's going to see Carl on the road while she's driving, and she's going to wonder how he's doing and why he hasn't called to say he loves her or, at the very least, that he's sorry. She's going to have to find out where the courthouse is and get the day off and meanwhile, she freely admits, she still has feelings for the man who cut her lip and broke her eardrum.

"Most of the time I feel like I'm doing fine, I don't need this jerk, then I think about the good times and how much I love him," she says. "But I don't like him anymore."

"Without," says Lora, whose car keys are safely stowed, this day, in her purse.

"Without," says a defendant named Crystal, who has a baby with her.

"I would like an attorney," says a defendant named Anna, and the next defendant, Debbie, says, "I don't wish to have an attorney," and a defendant named Richard rises and says, "No counsel."

The list of names goes on and on, names of people who have been arrested for domestic assault, names of women and men and sons and daughters and parents, people young and old, wealthy and poor. They are standing and sitting in a cavernous courtroom on the second floor of the Fairfax County juvenile and domestic relations court-house, a rambling two-story brick structure that, in its old-fashioned, restful, gracious, faintly Jeffersonian design, seems an incongruous contrast to the teeming chaos within. Here, every Thursday morning, assailants and victims gather precisely at 9 o'clock, showing up sometimes in their Sunday best, sometimes in sweats, sometimes separately, often together. They cram into benches while a bailiff tells them not to talk or chew gum or read. There are so many people—hundreds, each week—that latecomers inevitably have to stand against the wall.

When the cases are heard by judges, a number of things can happen. In Virginia, domestic assault is a misdemeanor, in the same class with trespassing, shoplifting an amount under $200, owning a still. The maximum penalty is 12 months in jail and a $2,500 fine, but cops often grumble that many cases result in "suspended disposition": Charges are dropped if the assailant commits no further violation for a set period of time. Often, if it's a first-time offense, the assailant is assigned to seek counseling in, say, a men's anger program. Sometimes assailants are fined. Less frequently, they're jailed.

All have the right to an attorney. At the outset of proceedings, the defendants' names are called out, and the presiding judge asks whether they have arrived with a private lawyer, whether they would like to request a public defender, or whether they waive their right to counsel. Once the entire list has been called—it takes quite a while—the cases are divvied up and heard in smaller courtrooms. On the day Lora's key-throwing case has come to trial, it's taken early, because judges handle the easier ones—the ones without lawyers—first. It's a curious fact of the Fairfax County system that *victims* do not, necessarily, have the right to an attorney. That's because, in Virginia, the commonwealth's attorney is not obliged to prosecute any misdemeanors, so the Fairfax office has fashioned a somewhat strange compromise: The state will prosecute if the defendant has a lawyer.

But if the defendant has waived the right to counsel—as defendants often do—then the victim doesn't get a lawyer either. Instead, the whole thing is sorted out before the judge based on the testimony of the two parties, the police officer, and witnesses if there are any. With the bizarre result that a daughter is sometimes obliged to cross-examine her own mother, a husband to field queries from his wife—assuming she has the nerve to ask them.

Only in Lora's case, nobody else has shown up: not her mother, not Officer Swain. "The case is dismissed and you're free to go," says the judge, and she leaves, looking miserable. Though she wasn't convicted, she will have an arrest permanently on her record.

Judy, the flutist, the pocket tearer, is lucky enough to get her case dismissed, too. Though she has hired a private lawyer, Tom requests that charges be dropped, and the commonwealth's attorney, somewhat uncharacteristically, agrees. Judy will also have an arrest record from now on.

Elaine is less fortunate. By the time her court date rolls around, Jesse is again willing to drop charges for the assault with the peanut butter jar. They are still living together, although they have just signed an agreement giving Elaine custody of their son for the next two years. She plans to leave Jesse and return to Hawaii, but first this case must be disposed of. When Jesse says he wants to drop charges, the commonwealth's attorney declines. Instead, he offers Elaine a plea bargain: If she agrees to plead guilty, he'll agree to a 60–day suspended jail sentence.

Elaine refuses. She doesn't want a conviction on her record. "It's his word against mine," she tells her public defender. "If a murder was committed, would they find a person guilty based on no evidence?" The day drags on until the case is called that afternoon. Jesse takes the stand; when Elaine's lawyer asks him if there was an argument going on, Jesse says just "the argument that's been going on for years." Then Elaine takes the stand and explains that she threw the peanut butter to get it out of the way and force her husband to talk to her. The kitchen is so small, she points out, that if she'd wanted to hit him, she easily could have. Under cross-examination, the commonwealth's attorney adroitly paints a picture of her as a hectoring wife, chasing her husband from room to room, picking a fight.

"It's an offensive touching; it's an assault," he says, and the judge agrees, and to her amazement Elaine is found guilty, and sits there, sobbing.

"What would you like the court to do?" the judge asks Jesse.

"Um," says Jesse. "I don't wish any jail time, or fine, or anything like that. I just don't wish it to happen again."

"Too bad there's not a women's anger program," the commonwealth's attorney remarks.

The judge fines her and suspends the fine. "Go back to Hawaii," he advises wearily. When they leave the courtroom together, Jesse complains that he's the one who has to pay the court fees.

Which leaves Carl and his now-ex-girlfriend, Helen, who still cannot hear well out of one ear. "She'll go back to him," one officer predicted after leaving Helen in the hospital. The cynicism is not gratuitous. Often, couples *have* reunited by the time an arrest comes to trial. Often the victim comes to court with the assailant, sits with him, tells the judge that she provoked the fight ("I'd thrown Coke on him the night before," one victim tells a judge one morning, rationalizing why her boyfriend threw a Buddha statue at her). Often victims say that things are better now that they're in counseling, often victims beg for mercy.

Equally often, victims don't show up at all.

Helen shows up. She doesn't beg for mercy. Although she has had thoughts about getting back together with Carl, she hasn't done so, not so far; in fact, she hasn't seen him since his arrest. She has gotten her hair cut, and she has put on a pink suit and sheer hose and white flats, and she has arrived early, flanked by her sister and her son and a victim counselor provided by the police department. She's freaked, a nervous wreck. After Carl's name is called in the courtroom, she goes into the bathroom to calm down. It has taken all her courage to show up and confront Carl, who is wearing jeans and cowboy boots and accompanied by a private lawyer.

Helen has done one other thing. On her own initiative, she has taken photos of her injuries. Armed with these, and with her hospital records, she tells her story to the commonwealth's attorney, who decides to make a plea offer. If Carl will plead guilty, he'll get a 180–day jail sentence, of which he will have to serve only five days, and a $100 fine, and he'll have to pay Helen's hospital costs of almost $600. Carl takes the plea, and then the plea agreement is presented to the judge, and this is done so quickly that in moments Carl is handcuffed and hustled out of the courtroom. Helen reaches out to comfort Carl's mother, and Carl's mother shrinks away.

And so Elaine, who threw the peanut butter, and Carl, who broke a woman's eardrum, are forever placed in the same category: convicted domestic abuser.

Both, when applying for jobs, will have to acknowledge the conviction.

Both, under a new federal domestic violence statute, are forbidden to possess or carry a firearm.

And maybe this is a good thing. Maybe it's a good thing to have a law so tough, so evenhanded, so inflexible that a relatively minor assault is treated much the same as a severe one. Maybe it's a good thing to have a law that tilts against a popular culture that embraces violence, celebrates violence, glamorizes violence. Certainly, the new law is a far cry from the days when husbands and wives regularly duked it out in sitcoms and Hollywood movies.

The law is a far cry, too, from the days when police officers either ignored domestic violence, or laughed it off, or were expected to solve it through touchy-feely sociological techniques. And there's no doubt that the law makes a difference. Since Fairfax County adopted the domestic violence policy that's now in effect throughout Virginia, arrests have soared. Back in 1988, only 8 percent of "family fights"—as they were quaintly known—resulted in arrest. By 1994, that number had climbed to 34 percent. And it keeps rising. In 1995, Fairfax County dispatchers received 3,105 domestic calls that resulted in 1,267 arrests. In 1996, there were 3,327 calls and 1,441 arrests, or 43 percent.

But every law can have unintended consequences. Despite the rise in arrests, some cops and dispatchers fear that some of the most serious cases may getting away from them—that mandatory arrest may fuel "underground abuse." That is, they worry that a zero-tolerance stance may make serious abuse victims more reluctant than ever to call, for the age-old reason that they don't want to see their assailant arrested.

"These situations are more complex than any of us would like to believe," says Harriet Russell, executive director of the Commission on Family Violence Prevention, which helped write the law. Russell says she understands that people are getting arrested for what appear to be minor assaults, that women are being arrested, and so are parents, and so, in some cases, are sons and daughters. But violence is violence. And so the solution that's been chosen, to these very complex situations, is a very simple law.

A good law?

A bad law?

A tough law.

A mercilessly consistent law.

"Let's assume that this is the first argument between these people that led to a violent act, and to everybody's surprise, the person who was violent is led away in handcuffs," says Russell. "The hope is there will never be a violent act between these people again. By either. That's the intent."

And this is the reality.

Another argument. Another public place. Not a parking lot, this time. A high school baseball diamond.

A 16-year-old boy comes to say hello to his dad, Rodney, who is in the dugout coaching a Babe Ruth All-Stars game. As will be explained later in court, Rodney can tell that the boy has been drinking, and the son—who *has* in fact consumed a couple of beers and some vodka—vehemently denies the accusation. Rodney, who is not fooled, asks his son to go sit in the bleachers until the game is over. The boy obeys, but the next inning he's back in the dugout, and Rodney confronts him again about his drinking, and this goes on and on until the son starts to leave and Rodney realizes that the son has the family car and is probably going to pick up Rodney's wife from work. So Rodney vaults over the dugout and runs to catch up with his son, and when he does, his son gets belligerent.

Leading up to this moment: Already this year, Rodney's son has driven the family car into a batting cage, and another time he and another kid were toilet-papering somebody's yard, and the homeowner came out with a gun and pumped some bullets into the car, and there has also been some unpleasant behavior toward the boy's mother, Rodney's wife. A difficult adolescence, in short, nothing extraordinary but nothing pleasant either, and now here the boy is drunk, in public, embarrassing them both, and suddenly Rodney, a military man practiced in self-control, in discipline, just snaps. He opens his hand and slaps his son once, twice, and his son falls to the ground.

Which is when he realizes that the game has stopped. The crowd's attention has shifted—to them. "There's been enough embarrassment," he tells his son quietly, and starts to walk away, but his son gets up and yells at Rodney and hits him in the back. Rodney keeps walking, he goes back to the dugout and gets his bag of baseballs and his fungo bat and starts to leave, but then he sees that his son has taken off running through the woods, and so Rodney takes off after him, both of them running and running, getting scratched by trees and brambles.

When Rodney finally catches his son, he cradles the boy's head between his own two hands, like a father holding a baby, and says all he can think to say: "Why are you doing this?"

What 16–year–old can explain why he does anything? Rodney returns to the ball field, where, by now, the police are waiting. Citizens have called 911. A man has struck his son!

"If the issue is did I strike my son, I did. I struck him this way and that way with an open hand," Rodney says to the officer, prepared to explain everything. But there's no need. The officer checks with his supervisor, and Rodney hears something about a new law, and suddenly Rodney learns that he must be arrested. "You're kidding," he says.

Down at the station, the officers take photos of the boy's face, which is slightly red, and of the scratches on his legs from the brambles. They take maybe 10 or 15 photos: from the front, from the side, photos of the chest, photos of the face, photos of the legs. Since the boy is a minor, the police call Fairfax County Child Protective Services, which launches an investigation into whether child abuse has occurred. Since Rodney works for the Marine Corps, Child Protective Services calls the Marines' family advocacy program, which launches its own investigation into what happened. And, since Rodney has a top-secret security clearance, a third inquiry is launched by the Marine Corps criminal investigation unit. On top of which, Rodney is barred from his home for the weekend.

"These are really hard cases for me," says Judge Sandra Havrilak after listening to Rodney's testimony in court. Havrilak is an attorney and substitute judge who often hears cases in juvenile and domestic relations court. She says later that she does not favor the mandatory arrest law, which, she believes, only forces officers to make more arrests.

But as long as an arrest was being made, she asks the officer, why wasn't the son arrested, too, since he clearly pushed his father?

"Our directives are to determine who the primary aggressor is and arrest that person," the officer replies.

Do you have anything to say? the judge asks the son.

"It was a one-time thing; it hasn't happened again," says the son, a tall youth who is dressed, like his father, in pants and a soft sports shirt and who admits to Judge Havrilak that he was in fact drinking that day, but now he doesn't drink anymore. He has sought counseling. His father has sought counseling. The incident at the ball field, he says, wasn't the big deal that everybody's making it out to be.

It's a big deal now, though. "I believe you're honest and sincere, I believe your son provoked you," the judge tells Rodney. "I'm not going to find you guilty, but I've got to continue the case for six months. If there are no further violations, it will be dismissed." So for the next six months Rodney will have a charge pending, and even if the charge is dismissed, the mere fact of arrest will cause him problems in his next security review, and, knowing this, Judge Havrilak urges him to try and have the arrest expunged from his record, something that in Virginia is very difficult to do.

Now Judge Havrilak turns her attention to the boy. "This could have cost your father his job," she tells him, and she repeats her opinion that he provoked his father into slapping him and suggests that "you give serious thought to what happened, because I believe you're just as culpable." Only the law doesn't permit her to do anything about the son's assault except just this, a stern lecture, and now the two men are leaving together, father and son, making their way through the crowded hallway of the courthouse, where scores of other victims and scores of other assailants are waiting, a hallway that's always so crowded, so teeming, more and more people showing up each week, that on another day in the same hallway, an astonished passerby, looking at all the faces, is moved to say, "Are all these domestic violence cases?"

"Yeah," says one officer, waiting for his arrest to come to trial. "They used to call it love."

NOTES

1. What impression does Mundy's reporting leave you with about laws against domestic violence? That they generally go too far? That only mandatory arrest policies do? Do you think that experiences with Virginia's mandatory arrest policy can or should be taken to constitute generalizable truths? In your estimation, does Mundy's reporting do enough to recognize other, ongoing realities of domestic violence? If not, which of those realities should be part of any conversation the story inspires?

2. In addition to mandatory arrest policies, "lethality assessments screening tools" are another device for combating domestic violence. An editorial in the *Washington Post* attributes a recent and dramatic drop in domestic violence-related deaths in Maryland and the District of Columbia "to a simple but effective tool that helps identify women most at risk of being killed by their husbands or boyfriends." Editorial, *Predicting and Preventing Murder*, WASH. POST, Oct. 29, 2011, at A14. According to the editorial, some of the questions in the "user-friendly, 11-question screening tool," *id.*, are predictable: "Has your husband or boyfriend ever used or threatened to use a weapon against you? Has he ever tried to choke you?" *Id.* Less obvious "questions . . . include whether the man is unemployed and whether there is a child in the household who is not the biological offspring of the potential perpetrator." *Id.* Currently, fourteen states and the District of Columbia "use some form of lethality assessment," but there is a movement afoot to increase the number through federal subsidies as part of the federal Violence Against Women Act. *Id.*

Town of Castle Rock v. Gonzales

Supreme Court of the United States, 2005.
545 U.S. 748, 125 S.Ct. 2796, 162 L.Ed.2d 658.

[The opinion is set forth on page 31 *supra*].

NOTES

1. For legal developments in *Castle Rock* following the Supreme Court's decision in the case, see Chapter 1, Section C(4). For a Fourth Amendment decision in which the needs and interests of victims and survivors of domestic abuse played a notable part, see *Georgia v. Randolph*, 547 U.S. 103 (2006).

2. Jeannie Suk has written about the ways in which domestic violence rules, as in New York County (Manhattan), a jurisdiction "that is considered to be 'in the forefront of efforts to combat domestic violence,'" are producing what she calls "de facto divorce." Jeannie Suk, *Criminal Law Comes Home*, 116 YALE L.J. 2 (2006). "[A] routine practice [in Manhattan] in the prosecution of misdemeanor [domestic violence] exemplifies the expanding criminal law control of the home: the prosecutorial use of criminal court protection orders to seek to end an intimate relationship. Prosecutors' deployment of protection orders in the normal course of misdemeanor domestic violence prosecution amounts in practice to state-imposed de facto divorce." *Id* at 42. Suk traces how temporary orders of protection in misdemeanor domestic violence cases—cases that "by definition ... do not involve serious physical injury," *id.* at 43—are subject to a "mandatory domestic violence protocol," *id.* at 44, an important dimension of which is "at the [defendant's] arraignment, ... the D.A.'s Office's mandatory practice involves asking the criminal court to issue a temporary order of protection (TOP). ... The order of protection ... normally prohibits any contact whatsoever with the victim, including phone, e-mail, voice-mail, or third-party contact. Contact with children is also banned. The order excludes the defendant from the victim's home, even if it is the defendant's home. ... Ascertaining that the victim wants the order is not part of the mandatory protocol. The prosecutor generally requests a full stay-away order even if the victim does not want it." *Id.* at 48. Elaborating, Suk writes:

> The criminal court routinely issues the order of protection at arraignment, the defendant's first court appearance. The brief, formulaic, and compressed nature of arraignments in criminal court, which run around the clock to ensure that all defendants are arraigned within twenty-four hours of arrest, means that courts often issue orders with little detailed consideration of the particular facts. DV orders are generally requested and issued as a matter of course.

> When the protection order goes into effect, the defendant cannot go home or have any contact with the victim (usually his wife) and his children. If the defendant does go home or contact the protected parties, he could be arrested, prosecuted, and punished for a fresh crime. This is so even if the victim initiates contact or invites the defendant to come home. Police officers then make routine unannounced visits to homes with a history of domestic violence. If a defendant subject to a protection order is present, he is arrested.

> Thus even when a DV case is destined ultimately to end in dismissal because the victim is uncooperative and there is insufficient evidence for conviction, keeping the case active for as long as possible enables the prosecutor and the court to monitor the defendant for months prior to dismissal. ... A violation of the order can lead to arrest and punishment for the more easily proven criminal charge. But in addition to the prospect of punishment for the proxy conduct of being present at home, the protection order shifts the very goal of pursuing criminal charges away from punishment toward control over the intimate relationship in the home.

> . . .

> The conventional wisdom is that the criminal court protection order practice is meant to safeguard the integrity of criminal proceedings by protecting the victim from violence and intimidation. But the practice of separating couples in DV cases by way of criminal protection orders extends beyond the needs of the judicial process. ... Court-ordered separation becomes a goal of prosecutors in bringing criminal charges—a substitute for, rather than a means of, increasing the likelihood of imprisonment. Punishment as a goal can be put on the backburner because separation is a more direct and achievable way to address or prevent violence. The practice that results amounts to what I term state-imposed de facto divorce, a phenomenon that is so routine in criminal court that it disappears in plain sight.

Id at 48–50, 53. According to Suk, in a number of cases prosecutors offer defendants plea bargains "consisting of little or no jail time (or time served) and a reduction of the charge, or even an adjournment in contemplation of a dismissal, in exchange for the defendant's acceptance of a final order of protection prohibiting his presence at home and contact with the victim. This is an attractive offer. It presents the opportunity to dispose of the criminal case immediately with little or no jail time, and in some cases, no criminal conviction or record." *Id.* at 54–55. When this happens, de facto divorces become, in effect, more or less permanent. But, as Suk goes on to observe:

> . . . The order of protection does not have the effect of ending formal marriage. And many intimate partners affected by orders are not married. Spouses can surely remain legally married even as they obey all the prohibitions of the order, but cannot live or act in substance as if they are in an intimate relationship. . . .
>
> Furthermore, the separation is not accompanied by the actual family law divorce regime of property division, alimony, child custody, and support. . . .
>
> But de facto divorce does entail de facto family arrangements regarding custody, visitation, and support—that is, no custody, no visitation, and no support. Thus in the imposition of de facto divorce, criminal law becomes a new family law regime. But because it is criminal law regulation, the parties cannot contract around the result except by risking the arrest and punishment of one of them.
>
> . . . Indeed, the order goes much further than would ordinary divorce, prohibiting any contact, even by express permission of the protected party. It is super-divorce. . . .
>
> The criminal law does not purport to give effect to private ordering, nor does it tolerate parties' contracting around default rules; rather, it regulates individuals' conduct through the threat of punishment to serve the public interest. . . .
>
> . . .
>
> . . . [s]tate-imposed de facto divorce is so class-contingent that it could be called poor man's divorce. The initial [domestic violence] arrest that sets the wheels into motion is much more likely to occur if people live in close quarters in buildings with thin walls, and neighbors can hear a disturbance and call the police. Those arraigned in New York County criminal court for DV crimes are by and large minorities who live in the poorest parts of Manhattan. . . .
>
> In practice, some, perhaps many, couples do remain together in disobedience of the criminal protection order. But couples who choose to continue their relationships do so in the shadow of the potential arrests and criminal prosecution of the person subject to the order. The enforcement of the order does not depend solely on the protected party's wishes, as the police do make surprise home visits and arrest people who are present in homes from which they are banned. . . .
>
> . . .
>
> . . . [This] means that the protected party is not simply the recipient of a strategic tool that shifts power from the abuser to her. . . .
>
> . . . Many of the parties protected by protection orders . . . [lack] sophistication about the operation of the enforcement protocol. They may not speak English well. They may be illegal immigrants for whom contact with government authorities is highly undesirable, frightening, and risky. Under these conditions, the overall effect of the protection order is not to confer power on victims, but rather to decide for them that they must discontinue their intimate relationship.
>
> . . .
>
> . . . [S]tate-imposed de facto divorce goes meaningfully beyond the prohibition and punishment of violence per se. It seeks to criminalize intimate relationships that adults have chosen for themselves and have not chosen to end. One would need to take a strong view of gendered coercion in intimate relationships generally to rationalize a world in which this kind of state control is regularly triggered by misdemeanor arrests not involving serious physical injury, particularly as the category of nonviolent conduct that constitutes DV expands.

Id. at 57–63, 68.

Jennifer Collins has challenged Suk's argument on the grounds that "New York City's aggressive approach to domestic violence cases is simply not representative of many—if not most—jurisdictions in this country." Jennifer Collins, *Criminal Law Comes Home to a Family*, *in* CRIMINAL LAW CONVERSATIONS 698 (Paul H. Robinson et al. eds., 2009). "[I]n another major metropolitan area," she writes:

> prosecutors typically do not ask for and judges do not impose, stay-away or no-contact orders at the time of sentencing if the victim objects. The defendant probably will be subject to an order directing him not to assault or harass the victim, but surely that kind of order does not result in the imposition of a "de facto divorce." In addition, even if a more aggressive stay-away order were to be imposed, it would not be enforced absent the cooperation of the victim, because the police simply do not have the time, resources, or inclination to make the kind of random, unannounced visits . . . that Suk describes. As a result, contempt charges would only be filed if the victim herself contacted the police to complain that the defendant violated the terms of a protection order.

Id. Collins also addresses Suk's emphasis on misdemeanor cases, which she says, "by definition do not allege any serious physical injury." *Id.* "[W]e must recognize," Collins urges:

> that serious physical injury is often involved even in cases that a prosecutor charges as a misdemeanor rather than as a felony. The reasons prosecutors elect to proceed with a misdemeanor charge even when faced with brutal injuries is plain: misdemeanor defendants facing a sentence of six months or less are not entitled to a jury trial. If a state must try a domestic violence case without the cooperation of the victim, as often happens, many prosecutors believe that it is easier to explain the victim's absence, and the dynamics of abusive relationships, to a judge rather than to a jury. . . . [T]he nature of the charge may not necessarily correspond with the seriousness of the particular offense being tried or the pattern and history of abuse in the relationship generally; use of protection orders in misdemeanor cases does not therefore by itself raise a normative . . . flag.

Id., at 698–99.

Along similar lines, Cheryl Hanna remarks:

> . . . Even in New York City, . . . only one-third of those arrested for domestic violence are convicted, and of those, fewer than twenty percent are sentenced to prison. Seventy-two percent receive a conditional discharge, which can include participation in a batterer treatment program or drug and alcohol counseling—interventions intended to help abusers and their partners have nonviolent relationships.
>
> Based on this data, I am more concerned about the under-enforcement of domestic violence laws throughout the country than the over-enforcement that troubles Suk. . . . The number of domestic homicides in the United States has decreased significantly since the 1970s, and one reason for that decline is our decision to treat domestic violence as a crime against the community.
>
> . . .
>
> . . . [U]nder-enforcement [remains] prevalent across the country. It can be incredibly difficult to get the criminal law to respond—even when a victim is clear and consistent about what she wants. I fear that contrary arguments like Suk's will undo the progress that we've made.
>
> That's not to say that the law can't do better. We should always rethink our strategies and avoid one-size-fits-all approaches. The criminalization of domestic violence is still in its infancy, and we have much to learn about what works best and for whom. As Suk notes, we need to be especially concerned about the impact of our policies on poor and minority communities, for whom the criminal law has often been an adversary rather than an ally.
>
> The goal, then, is to refine our practices, but not return to a time when the law and its officers were unable or unwilling to intervene when abuse happened behind closed doors.

Cheryl Hanna, *Because Breaking Up is Hard to Do*, 116 YALE L.J. POCKET PART 92, 93–94 (2006).

CHAPTER 4

PARENTING

A. THE LIMITS OF PARENTAL AUTHORITY

1. FAMILY PRIVACY

Kilgrow v. Kilgrow

Supreme Court of Alabama, 1958.
107 So.2d 885.

■ GOODWYN, J.

On August 29, 1957, Jack M. Kilgrow, appellee, filed a petition in the circuit court of Montgomery Country . . . against his wife, Christine B. Kilgrow, seeking a temporary injunction restraining her from interfering with petitioner's "right to carry the said Margaret Kilgrow [. . . the parties' 7–year old daughter] to Loretta School next Tuesday to resume her education" and also seeking . . . "a decree permanently enjoining the respondent from interfering or attempting to interfere and prevent the said Margaret Kilgrow from continuing her education at Loretta School." There is also a prayer for general relief.

The petition alleges that the parties are over 21 years of age, are bona fide residents of Montgomery, Alabama, and reside at 910 South Lawrence Street; that they were lawfully married in Montgomery County, Alabama, on May 19, 1948; that to this marriage was born one child, named Margaret Kilgrow, a girl now 7 years of age and who is residing with petitioner and respondent. The petition also contains the following allegations:

> 3. During the 1956–57 school year, the said minor child of petitioner and respondent, Margaret Kilgrow, entered the first grade at Loretta School in Montgomery, Alabama, and continued throughout the school year. That the said Margaret Kilgrow made an excellent scholastic record at Loretta. That all her friends and playmates go to school at Loretta and that the said Margaret Kilgrow had a happy school year at Loretta and took an active part in all the school activities. That last spring at the end of the 1956–57 school year, she was enrolled in the Loretta School to begin the fall term of the 1957–58 school year to begin on September 3, 1957. That last week your petitioner carried his minor daughter, Margaret Kilgrow, to Loretta School to ascertain what books and supplies would be required at the beginning of the new school term beginning next week.

> 4. That it would be to the best interest and welfare of the said Margaret Kilgrow that she return to Loretta School to resume her grade school education. That the respondent, Christine B. Kilgrow, mother of the said Margaret Kilgrow, is threatening to prevent petitioner from carrying his said minor daughter to Loretta and is threatening to interfere with the right of the petitioner to place his said minor daughter in Loretta School beginning Tuesday, September 3, 1957, and

has told petitioner that she will remain away from her job for the purpose of preventing the said Margaret Kilgrow from returning to Loretta School next week. That the threats and avowed purpose of the said respondent to prevent the said minor child from returning to Loretta School is inimical to the welfare and best interest of the said minor child.

. . .

5.   That since the filing of the original petition in this cause and on, to-wit, this date, September 3, 1957, your petitioner has gotten his minor daughter, Margaret Kilgrow, ready to carry her to Loretta School; that petitioner was going to carry his daughter down town to his place of business and wait the opening of Loretta School so that he could carry the child to the school; that petitioner drove his said minor child to town in the automobile with respondent and was intending to turn the automobile over to respondent so that she might go to work; that petitioner and respondent occupied the front seat and the child the back seat; that petitioner drove the automobile in front of his place of work and got out of the front seat and started to open the back door to get the child, whereupon respondent jumped under the steering wheel and drove the automobile away carrying the child with her, as a consequence of which the said child will not be able to enter Loretta School this morning and will not be able to enter the said school unless the respondent is enjoined and restrained from interfering with the placing of said child in the said school.

. . .

[O]n September 9th a hearing was had before the trial court and testimony taken on behalf of both petitioner and respondent. At the conclusion of the hearing a decree was rendered granting to petitioner the relief prayed for. To the extent here pertinent, the decree provides as follows:

Ordered, adjudged and decreed by the court that the said demurrer of the respondent to the petition as amended be and the same is hereby overruled.

And now coming to the merits of the matter the court is of opinion that it has jurisdiction of this matter. While it is true that the father of a minor child has in general the right to direct the education of his minor child, this right is subject to review and correction by the court if not exercised for the best welfare of the child. The decision of the father is prima facie correct, but subject to be rebutted by proper proof from the other parent.

The court has gone into the evidence in this case at length and has heard about ten witnesses all told, and upon a consideration of the same the court is of opinion that it is for the best interest of the minor child involved in these proceedings that she remain in the school where the father has placed her and that the mother refrain from interfering with the schooling of said minor child. It is, therefore,

Ordered, adjudged and decreed by the court

1) that it is for the best welfare of the child, Margaret Kilgrow, that she continue her studies where her father has placed her, in Loretta School.

2) That Mrs. Christine B. Kilgrow be and she is hereby enjoined and restrained from interfering with the schooling of the said child at

Loretta School, and that said child continue her schooling there until and unless this order be changed in proper proceedings.

. . .

From the pleadings and evidence it clearly appears that the dispute between the parents grows out of the fact that the father and mother are of different religious faiths. Loretta is a school operated by the church of the father's religious faith. He wants the child to attend that school while the mother wants her to attend a public school.

There was introduced in evidence an antenuptial agreement whereby the parties agreed that all the children of their marriage "shall be baptized and educated" in the "religion" of the father, whether he be "living or dead."

As we see it, the decisive question presented is whether a court of equity has inherent jurisdiction (there being no statute involved) to resolve a family dispute between parents as to the school their minor child should attend, when there is no question concerning the custody of the child incident to a separation (either voluntary or pursuant to a court order) or divorce of the parents, and to enforce its decision against one of the parents by injunction. In other words, should the jurisdiction of a court of equity extend to the settlement of a difference of opinion between parents as to what is best for their minor child when the parents and child are all living together as a family group?

This appears to be a case of first impression in Alabama and there seems to be little authority bearing on the question from other jurisdictions. In fact, no case has been cited to us, nor have we found any, which has dealt with the precise problem before us.

There can be no doubt that if this were a proceeding to determine the child's custody the equity court would have jurisdiction for that purpose. *Ex parte White*, 16 So. 2d 500, 502 (Ala. 1944); *State v. Black*, 196 So. 713, 717 (Ala. 1940); *Thomas v. Thomas*, 101 So. 738, 738 (Ala. 1924).... But that is not the situation before us. There is no issue as to the child's custody. Here, the injunctive process is employed at the instance of the father to restrain the mother, who continues to live with the father as a member of the family group and who also has natural custodial rights over her minor child.

It seems to us, if we should hold that equity has jurisdiction in this case such holding will open wide the gates for settlement in equity of all sorts and varieties of intimate family disputes concerning the upbringing of children. The absence of cases dealing with the question indicates a reluctance of the courts to assume jurisdiction in disputes arising out of the intimate family circle. It does not take much imagination to envision the extent to which explosive differences of opinion between parents as to the proper upbringing of their children could be brought into court for attempted solution.

In none of our cases has the court intervened to settle a controversy between unseparated parents as to some matter incident to the well-being of the child, where there was no question presented as to which parent should have custody. In all of our cases the real question has been which parent should properly be awarded custody. Never has the court put itself in the place of the parents and interposed its judgment as to the course which otherwise amicable parents should pursue in discharging their parental duty. Here, the sole difference between the parties is which school the child should attend. And, that difference seems not to have affected the conjugal attitude of the parents one to the other.

The inherent jurisdiction of courts of equity over infants is a matter of necessity, coming into exercise only where there has been a failure of that natural power and obligation which is the province of parenthood. It is a jurisdiction assumed by the courts only when it is forfeited by a natural custodian incident to a broken home or neglect, or as a result of a natural custodian's incapacity, unfitness or death. It is only for compelling reason[s] that a parent is deprived of the custody of his or her child. The court only interferes as between parents to the extent of awarding custody to the one or the other, with the welfare of the child in mind. And it is in awarding custody that the court invokes the principle that the welfare of the child is the controlling consideration. We do not think a court of equity should undertake to settle a dispute between parents as to what is best for their minor child when there is no question concerning the child's custody.

It would be anomalous to hold that a court of equity may sit in constant supervision over a household and see that either parent's will and determination in the upbringing of a child is obeyed, even though the parents' dispute might involve what is best for the child. Every difference of opinion between parents concerning their child's upbringing necessarily involves the question of the child's best interest.

. . .

It may well be suggested that a court of equity ought to interfere to prevent such a direful consequence as divorce or separation, rather than await the disruption of the marital relationship. Our answer to this is that intervention, rather than preventing or healing a disruption, would quite likely serve as the spark to a smoldering fire. A mandatory court decree supporting the position of one parent against the other would hardly be a composing situation for the unsuccessful parent to be confronted with daily. One spouse could scarcely be expected to entertain a tender, affectionate regard for the other spouse who brings him or her under restraint. The judicial mind and conscience is repelled by the thought of disruption of the sacred marital relationship, and usually voices the hope that the breach may somehow be healed by mutual understanding between the parents themselves.

The prenuptial agreement as to the child's religious education has no bearing on the question of the trial court's jurisdiction in this case. The bill does not even attempt to make that agreement a basis for relief.

It is argued that any apprehension about opening wide the jurisdiction of equity is not on sound footing because, in Alabama, a child is required by statute (§ 297, tit. 52, Code 1940, as amended by Act No. 117, § 3, approved April 14, 1956, Acts Spec. Sess.1956, p. 446), to attend school. Thus, it is argued, the instant case has for its purpose the fulfillment of this mandatory duty. But there is absolutely no question here concerning the neglect or failure of either parent to see that the child attends school. . . .

In view of what we have said it is unnecessary to decide whether the decree, in effect ordering that the child attend a school of a particular religious denomination which, according to the evidence, involves mandatory teaching of the religious doctrines of that denomination, would be giving preference by law to a particular religious sect contrary to the First and Fourteenth Amendments of the Constitution of the United States and § 3 of Article 1, Alabama Constitution of 1901.

The decree appealed from is ... reversed and one rendered here dismissing the petition.

NOTE

Compare the reasoning of the court in *Kilgrew* with the decision in *McGuire v. McGuire*, p. 179 *supra*. Is one opinion more persuasive than the other?

2.   EDUCATION

State-sponsored schools were the first serious intrusion on the right of parents to rear their own children. In 1647, the Puritans in Massachusetts Bay Colony provided:

> It being one chief project of that old deluder Satan to keep men from the knowledge of the Scriptures, [i]t is so at least the true sense and meaning therefore ordered, that every township in this jurisdiction, after the Lord increases them to the number of fifty householders, shall then forthwith appoint one within their town to teach all such children as shall resort to him to write and read....[1]

States first offered and later forced schooling on ever larger numbers of children for ever longer periods. Initially this effort was focused on poor children. In 1787, for example, Benjamin Rush proposed a plan for a system of free schools for the poor children of Philadelphia. By 1804, Washington, D.C., had established such a school system for its poor children with Thomas Jefferson as its first school board president.

The first publicly-funded high school was established in 1821. By 1890 about 7 percent of all 14– to 17–year–olds were enrolled; by 1930, 51 percent of that age group were in high school.

In the late 1800s there was a nation-wide shift from voluntary to compulsory schooling prompted in large part by a desire to Americanize the flood of immigrants:

> It is largely through immigration that the number of ignorant, vagrant, and criminal youth has recently multiplied to an extent truly alarming in some of our cities. Their depravity is sometimes defiant and their resistance to moral suasion is obstinate. When personal effort and persuasion and organized benevolence have utterly failed, let the law take them in hand, first to the public schools, and if there incorrigibly, then to the Reform School.[2]

Initially, parents were permitted a range of choice in schooling. The 1874 New York law, for example, provided that children aged 8–14 should attend some public or private school for at least fourteen weeks a year, or be instructed at home for the same period in spelling, reading, writing, English grammar, geography, and arithmetic. By 1909, however, New York required regular attendance of children aged 7–16 at a public school conducted in English, or equivalent instruction by a competent teacher for the same number of hours.

As the next case demonstrates, there are some limits on the power of states to force parents to send their children to public school.

---

1. Reprinted in ROBERT H. BREMNER, CHILDREN AND YOUTH IN AMERICA: A DOCUMENTARY HISTORY 81 (1970).

2. B.G. NORTHROP, REPORT OF THE SECRETARY OF THE BOARD OF EDUCATION OF THE STATE OF CONNECTICUT (1872).

Pierce v. Society of Sisters

Supreme Court of the United States, 1925.
268 U.S. 510, 45 S.Ct. 571, 69 L.Ed. 1070.

■ JUSTICE McREYNOLDS delivered the opinion of the Court.

The challenged Act, effective September 1, 1926, requires every parent, guardian or other person having control or charge or custody of a child between eight and sixteen years to send him "to a public school for the period of time a public school shall be held during the current year" in the district where the child resides; and failure so to do is declared a misdemeanor. There are exemptions—not specially important here—for children who are not normal, or who have completed the eighth grade, or who reside at considerable distances from any public school, or whose parents or guardians hold special permits from the County Superintendent. The manifest purpose is to compel general attendance at public schools by normal children, between eight and sixteen, who have not completed the eighth grade. And without doubt enforcement of the statute would seriously impair, perhaps destroy, the profitable features of appellees' business and greatly diminish the value of their property.

Appellee, the Society of Sisters, is an Oregon corporation, organized in 1880, with power to care for orphans, educate and instruct the youth, establish and maintain academies or schools, and acquire necessary real and personal property.... Systematic religious instruction and moral training according to the tenets of the Roman Catholic Church are also regularly provided....

    . . .

Appellee, Hill Military Academy, is a private corporation organized in 1908 under the laws of Oregon, engaged in owning, operating and conducting for profit an elementary, college preparatory and military training school for boys between the ages of five and twenty-one years....

No question is raised concerning the power of the State reasonably to regulate all schools, to inspect, supervise, and examine them, their teachers and pupils; to require that all children of proper age attend some school, that teachers shall be of good moral character and patriotic disposition, that certain studies plainly essential to good citizenship must be taught, and that nothing be taught which is manifestly inimical to the public welfare.

The inevitable practical result of enforcing the Act under consideration would be destruction of appellees' primary schools, and perhaps all other private primary schools for normal children within the State of Oregon. These parties are engaged in a kind of undertaking not inherently harmful, but long regarded as useful and meritorious. Certainly there is nothing in the present records to indicate that they have failed to discharge their obligations to patrons, students or the State. And there are no peculiar circumstances or present emergencies which demand extraordinary measures relative to primary education.

Under the doctrine of *Meyer v. Nebraska*, 262 U.S. 390 (1923), we think it entirely plain that the Act of 1922 unreasonably interferes with the liberty of parents and guardians to direct the upbringing and education of children under their control. As often heretofore pointed out, rights guaranteed by the Constitution may not be abridged by legislation which has no reasonable relation to some purpose within the competency of the State. The fundamental theory of liberty upon which all governments in this Union repose excludes any general power of the State to standardize its children by forcing them to accept instruction from public teachers only. The child is not the mere creature of the State; those who nurture him and direct his destiny have the right, coupled with the high duty, to recognize and prepare him for additional obligations.

Appellees are corporations and therefore, it is said, they cannot claim for themselves the liberty which the Fourteenth Amendment guarantees. Accepted in the proper sense, this is true. But they have business and property for which they claim protection. These are threatened with destruction through the unwarranted compulsion which appellants are exercising over present and prospective patrons of their schools. And this court has gone very far to protect against loss threatened by such action.

The courts of the State have not construed the Act, and we must determine its meaning for ourselves. Evidently it was expected to have general application and cannot be construed as though merely intended to amend the charters of certain private corporations, as in *Berea College v. Kentucky*, 211 U.S. 45 (1908). No argument in favor of such view has been advanced.

Generally it is entirely true, as urged by counsel, that no person in any business has such an interest in possible customers as to enable him to restrain exercise of proper power of the State upon the ground that he will be deprived of patronage. But the injunctions here sought are not against the exercise of any proper power. Plaintiffs asked protection against arbitrary, unreasonable and unlawful interference with their patrons and the consequent destruction of their business and property....

The suits were not premature. The injury to appellees was present and very real, not a mere possibility in the remote future. If no relief had been possible prior to the effective date of the Act, the injury would have become irreparable. Prevention of impending injury by unlawful action is a well recognized function of courts of equity.

The decrees below [restraining Oregon from enforcing the Act] are affirmed.

NOTES

1. Is *Pierce v. Society of Sisters* a First Amendment "freedom of religion" case? *Compare School Dist. of Abington v. Schempp*, 374 U.S. 203, 231 (1963) (Brennan, J., concurring) (*Pierce* decided no first amendment question) *with* 374 U.S. at 312 (Stewart, J. dissenting) (*Pierce* based ultimately on recognition of free exercise claim involved.) *See generally* Stephen Arons, *The Separation of School and State: Pierce Reconsidered*, 46 Harv. Educ. Rev. 76 (1976).

2. Justice McReynolds also authored *Meyer v. Nebraska*, 262 U.S. 390 (1923), which he cited in *Pierce* as precedent for recognizing "the liberty of parents and guardians to direct the upbringing and education of children under their control." *Meyer* involved a Nebraska statute that prohibited instruction in foreign languages before the eighth grade. Justice McReynolds summarized the reasons for finding the statute to be unconstitutional:

> It is said the purpose of the legislation was to promote civic development by inhibiting training and education of the immature in foreign tongues and ideals before they could learn English and acquire American ideals; and "that the English language should be and become the mother tongue of all children reared in this State." It is also affirmed that the foreign born population is very large, that certain communities commonly use foreign words, follow foreign

leaders, move in a foreign atmosphere, and that the children are thereby hindered from becoming citizens of the most useful type and the public safety is imperiled.

That the State may do much, go very far, indeed, in order to improve the quality of its citizens, physically, mentally and morally, is clear; but the individual has certain fundamental rights which must be respected. The protection of the Constitution extends to all, to those who speak other languages as well as to those born with English on the tongue. Perhaps it would be highly advantageous if all had ready understanding of our ordinary speech, but this cannot be coerced by methods which conflict with the Constitution—a desirable end cannot be promoted by prohibited means.

3. The *Meyer* Court held that the statute was an unconstitutional burden on the rights of teachers to work and of families to raise their children. Would the Supreme Court reach the same result today in *Pierce* and *Meyer*? On the same or different grounds?

3.   CHILD LABOR LAWS

Prince v. Massachusetts

Supreme Court of the United States, 1944.
321 U.S. 158, 64 S.Ct. 438, 88 L.Ed. 645.

■ JUSTICE RUTLEDGE delivered the opinion of the Court.

The case brings for review another episode in the conflict between Jehovah's Witnesses and state authority. This time Sarah Prince appeals from convictions for violating Massachusetts' child labor laws, by acts said to be a rightful exercise of her religious convictions.

When the offenses were committed she was the aunt and custodian of Betty M. Simmons, a girl nine years of age.... Mrs. Prince, living in Brockton, is the mother of two young sons. She also has legal custody of Betty Simmons, who lives with them. The children too are Jehovah's Witnesses and both Mrs. Prince and Betty testified they were ordained ministers. The former was accustomed to go each week on the streets of Brockton to distribute "Watchtower" and "Consolation," according to the usual plan. She had permitted the children to engage in this activity previously, and had been warned against doing so by the school attendance officer, Mr. Perkins. But, until December 18, 1941, she generally did not take them with her at night.

That evening, as Mrs. Prince was preparing to leave her home, the children asked to go. She at first refused. Childlike, they resorted to tears; and, motherlike, she yielded. Arriving downtown, Mrs. Prince permitted the children "to engage in the preaching work with her upon the sidewalks." That is, with specific reference to Betty, she and Mrs. Prince took positions about twenty feet apart near a street intersection. Betty held up in her hand, for passers-by to see, copies of "Watch Tower" and "Consolation." From her shoulder hung the usual canvas magazine bag, on which was printed: "Watchtower and Consolation 5¢ per copy." No one accepted a copy from Betty that evening and she received no money. Nor did her aunt. But on other occasions, Betty had received funds and given out copies.

Mrs. Prince and Betty remained until 8:45 p.m. A few minutes before this, Mr. Perkins approached Mrs. Prince. A discussion ensued. He inquired and she refused to give Betty's name. However, she stated the child attended the Shaw School. Mr. Perkins referred to his previous warnings and said he would allow five minutes for them to get off the street. Mrs. Prince admitted she supplied Betty with the magazines and said, "[N]either you nor anybody else can stop me.... This child is exercising her God-given right and her constitutional right to preach the gospel, and no creature has a right to interfere with God's commands." However, Mrs. Prince and Betty departed. She remarked as she went, "I'm not going through this any more. We've been through it time and time again. I'm going home and put the little girl to bed." It may be added that testimony, by Betty, her aunt and others, was offered at the trials, and was excluded, to show that Betty believed it was her religious duty to perform this work and failure would bring condemnation "to everlasting destruction at Armageddon."

[T]wo claimed liberties are at stake. One is the parent's, to bring up the child in the way he should go, which for appellant means to teach him the tenets and the practices of their faith. The other freedom is the child's, to observe these; and among them is "to preach the gospel ... by public distribution" of "Watchtower" and "Consolation," in conformity with the scripture: "A little child shall lead them."

. . .

The rights of children to exercise their religion, and of parents to give them religious training and to encourage them in the practice of religious belief, as against preponderant sentiment and assertion of state power voicing it, have had recognition here, most recently in *West Virginia State Board of Education v. Barnette*, 319 U.S. 624 (1943). Previously in *Pierce v. Society of Sisters*, 268 U.S. 510 (1925), this Court had sustained the parents' authority to provide religion with secular schooling, and the child's right to receive it, as against the state's requirement of attendance at public schools. And in *Meyer v. Nebraska*, 262 U.S. 390 (1923), children's rights to receive teaching in languages other than the nation's common tongue were guarded against the state's encroachment. It is cardinal with us that the custody, care and nurture of the child reside first in the parents, whose primary function and freedom include preparation for obligations the state can neither supply nor hinder. *Pierce v. Society of Sisters, supra* . . . .

But the family itself is not beyond regulation in the public interest, as against a claim of religious liberty. *Reynolds v. United States*, 98 U.S. 145 (1878); *Davis v. Beason*, 133 U.S. 333 (1890). And neither rights of religion nor rights of parenthood are beyond limitation. Acting to guard the general interest in youth's well being, the state as *parens patriae* may restrict the parent's control by requiring school attendance, regulating or prohibiting the child's labor and in many other ways.[3] Its authority is not nullified merely because the parent grounds his claim to control the child's course of conduct on religion or conscience. Thus, he cannot claim freedom from compulsory vaccination for the child more than for himself on religious grounds.[4] The right to practice religion freely does not include liberty to expose the community or the child to communicable disease or the latter to ill health or death. The catalogue need not be lengthened. It is sufficient to show what indeed appellant hardly disputes, that the state has a wide range of power for limiting parental freedom and authority in things affecting the child's welfare; and that this includes, to some extent, matters of conscience and religious conviction.

. . .

---

3. *Cf.* People v. Ewer, 36 N.E. 4 (N.Y. 1894).

4. Jacobson v. Massachusetts, 197 U.S. 11 (1905).

[T]he case reduces itself therefore to the question whether the presence of the child's guardian puts a limit to the state's power. That fact may lessen the likelihood that some evils the legislation seeks to avert will occur. But it cannot forestall all of them. The zealous though lawful exercise of the right to engage in propagandizing the community, whether in religious, political or other matters, may and at times does create situations difficult enough for adults to cope with and wholly inappropriate for children, especially of tender years, to face. Other harmful possibilities could be stated, of emotional excitement and psychological or physical injury. Parents may be free to become martyrs themselves. But it does not follow they are free, in identical circumstances, to make martyrs of their children before they have reached the age of full and legal discretion when they can make that choice for themselves. Massachusetts has determined that an absolute prohibition, though one limited to streets and public places and to the incidental uses proscribed, is necessary to accomplish its legitimate objectives. Its power to attain them is broad enough to reach these peripheral instances in which the parent's supervision may reduce but cannot eliminate entirely the ill effects of the prohibited conduct. We think that with reference to the public proclaiming of religion, upon the streets and in other similar public places, the power of the state to control the conduct of children reaches beyond the scope of its authority over adults, as is true in the case of other freedoms, and the rightful boundary of its power has not been crossed in this case.

The judgment is affirmed.

■ JUSTICE MURPHY, dissenting.

The state, in my opinion, has completely failed to sustain its burden of proving the existence of any grave or immediate danger to any interest which it may lawfully protect. There is no proof that Betty Simmons' mode of worship constituted a serious menace to the public. It was carried on in an orderly, lawful manner at a public street corner. And "one who is rightfully on a street which the state has left open to the public carries with him there as elsewhere the constitutional right to express his views in an orderly fashion. This right extends to the communication of ideas by handbills and literature as well as by the spoken word." The sidewalk, no less than the cathedral or the evangelist's tent, is a proper place, under the Constitution, for the orderly worship of God. Such use of the streets is as necessary to the Jehovah's Witnesses, the Salvation Army and others who practice religion without benefit of conventional shelters as is the use of the streets for purposes of passage.

It is claimed, however, that such activity was likely to affect adversely the health, morals and welfare of the child. Reference is made in the majority opinion to "the crippling effects of child employment, more especially in public places, and the possible harms arising from other activities subject to all the diverse influences of the street." To the extent that they flow from participation in ordinary commercial activities, these harms are irrelevant to this case. And the bare possibility that such harms might emanate from distribution of religious literature is not, standing alone, sufficient justification for restricting freedom of conscience and religion. Nor can parents or guardians be subjected to criminal liability because of vague possibilities that their religious teachings might cause injury to the child. The evils must be grave, immediate, substantial. Yet there is not the slightest indication in this record, or in sources subject to judicial notice, that children engaged in distributing literature pursuant to their religious beliefs have been or are likely to be subject to any of the harmful "diverse influences of the street."

Indeed, if probabilities are to be indulged in, the likelihood is that children engaged in serious religious endeavor are immune from such influences. Gambling, truancy, irregular eating and sleeping habits, and the more serious vices are not consistent with the high moral character ordinarily displayed by children fulfilling religious obligations. Moreover, Jehovah's Witness children invariably make their distributions in groups subject at all times to adult or parental control, as was done in this case. The dangers are thus exceedingly remote, to say the least. And the fact that the zealous exercise of the right to propagandize the community may result in violent or disorderly situations difficult for children to face is no excuse for prohibiting the exercise of that right.

NOTES

1. Congress adopted the Fair Labor Standards Act of 1938 (FLSA) to regulate child labor, but its provisions have been criticized for failing to protect children adequately from exploitation. *See, e.g.*, Seymour Moskowitz, *Save the Children: The Legal Abandonment of American Youth in the Workplace*, 43 Akron L. Rev. 107 (2010):

> The FLSA has not been significantly amended since its adoption in 1938. Many youth workers are not covered; penalties for violation of the act are extraordinarily lax. Unlike most federal civil rights statutes, the FLSA gives no private right of action. The most affected parties—aggrieved minor employees and their parents—are unable to sue. Enforcement is left entirely to administrative processes, and it is clear that the Department of Labor's (DOL) enforcement activities—both adjudicatory and rulemaking—are inadequate. The vast majority of state child labor laws and enforcement are also woefully weak. Children are de facto left without protection in the workplace, with disastrous consequences.
>
> . . .
>
> Many issues are not addressed by the act at all. There is no standardized reporting requirement of work-related injuries and deaths, an omission that leads to extraordinary difficulty in determining the incidence of those events. Nor are working youths required to have a work permit or certificate. Hours of employment are restricted only for minors 15 or younger; 16–and 17–year–olds may work any amount of time in any occupation not found to be "particularly hazardous." These older youths may thus be required to work long hours and during the night, with almost certain negative academic and other consequences. This statutory gap is even more egregious given that many of these working youths are already doing poorly in school. Many teenagers give work priority over their studies, despite the critical role education plays in achieving economic and other success in society. Moreover, even in jobs deemed "hazardous" by the DOL, if employers fall outside the jurisdiction of the FLSA, youth workers receive no protection from federal law. Despite the large number of workplace accidents, federal law does not require youth workers to be provided with safety training or adult supervision. Notably, 41 percent of workplace deaths occur while an adolescent is doing work prohibited by federal child labor laws.

Id. at 109, 138–39.

2. The outsourcing of manufacturing jobs overseas has led to concern about the use of child labor abroad by American companies. In *John Roe I v. Bridgestone Corporation*, 492 F.Supp.2d 988 (S.D. Ind. 2007), Firestone was sued by plantation workers in Liberia who alleged, among other claims, forced child labor in violation of international labor standards. *See id.* at 993.

3. In response to concerns about child labor safety and exploitation, on September 2, 2011, the Department of Labor proposed a series of new regulations under the FLSA. The regulations would "increase parity between the agricultural and nonagricultural child labor provisions . . . revise the exemptions which permit the employment of 14– and 15–year–olds to perform certain agricultural tasks that would otherwise be prohibited to that age group after they have successfully completed certain specified training ... [and] revise its civil money penalty [r]egulations." Child Labor Regulations, Orders and Statements of Interpretation; Child Labor Violations—Civil Money Penalties, 76 Fed. Reg. 54836 (proposed Sept. 2, 2011) (to be codified at 29 C.F.R. pts. 570, 579).

4. CHILD NEGLECT AND ABUSE

Roe v. Conn

United States District Court of Alabama, Northern Division, 1976.
417 F.Supp. 769.

■ Before RIVES, CIRCUIT JUDGE, JOHNSON, CHIEF DISTRICT JUDGE, AND VARNER, DISTRICT JUDGE.

[This is a class action challenging the constitutionality of Alabama's child neglect law.]

The investigation which led to termination of Plaintiff Wambles['] parental rights was prompted by Defendant Coppage. Mr. Coppage, who is white, lived intermittently with Plaintiff Wambles from 1970 until March, 1975, and claims to have fathered Richard Roe. On June 1, 1975, Mr. Coppage contacted the Montgomery Police Department and reported that Plaintiff Wambles might be neglecting Richard Roe, that she had been evicted from her former residence because she was keeping company with black males, and that she had moved to Highland Village (a black neighborhood) where she was living with a black man. On the basis of this information, Police Officer Conn initiated an investigation of Plaintiff Wambles. The records of the Montgomery Police Department were checked but revealed no previous complaints of child neglect against Plaintiff Wambles and no adult file on her. Meanwhile, on June 2, 1975, Defendant Coppage went to the office of Barbara Ward, Director of the Montgomery County Youth Facility, and told her that he was the father of Richard Roe; that he had once lived with Margaret Wambles, who was now living with a black man and entertaining other black men; that he had reported this to the Montgomery Police Department; that he wanted to get the child out of the house; and that he wanted custody of the child. Following Defendant Coppage's visit to her office, Defendant Ward conferred with Judge Thetford and then called the Montgomery Police Department. According to the police report prepared by Officer Conn, Defendant Ward advised the police to request a pick-up order if Margaret Wambles and Richard Roe were living with a man to whom Margaret Wambles was not married. Officer Conn went to the Wambles' residence, 1033–E Highland Village Drive, Montgomery, Alabama, at approximately 7:30 P.M. on June 2, 1975. Plaintiff Wambles permitted Officer Conn to enter and inspect her dwelling, which the officer found was a two-bedroom apartment, where Plaintiff Wambles and her son were living with a black man to whom she was not married. Richard Roe was clothed, clean, and in "fairly good" physical condition with no signs of physical abuse. The home was "relatively clean" and stocked with "adequate food." Upon completing his inspection, Defendant Conn left the home and called Defendant Ward and reported his findings. He was then instructed by Defendant Ward to go to the Youth Facility and get a pick-up order. The only facts about Margaret Wambles known to Judge Thetford before he issued the pick-up order were that she was unemployed and that she and her child are white and were living with a black man in a black neighborhood. Judge Thetford had no information as to how long Margaret Wambles had lived in Montgomery, where she had worked, or how long she had been unemployed.[5] He had no evidence that Richard Roe was being physically abused and no information as to the condition of the Wambles' home. Judge Thetford knew nothing about the man with whom Margaret Wambles was living, other than his race and the fact that he was not married to her. Judge Thetford testified that the race of the man with whom Plaintiff Wambles was living was relevant to his decision to order Richard Roe removed from his mother's custody, particularly because they were living in a black neighborhood. Judge Thetford concluded that this habitation in a black neighborhood could be dangerous for a child because it was his belief that "it was not a healthy thing for a white child to be the only [white] child in a black neighborhood."

At approximately 8:30 P.M. on June 2, 1975, after obtaining the pick-up order, Defendant Conn, accompanied by two other Montgomery police officers, returned to Plaintiff Wambles' home. When Defendant Conn announced that he had come to take Richard Roe, Plaintiff Wambles picked up her child and ran to the back of the apartment. After Defendant Conn showed Plaintiff Wambles the pick-up order, she still refused to surrender the child. Thereupon, with the child crying, "No, mama, don't let him take me," Defendant Conn grabbed Plaintiff Wambles by the arm and pulled her back into the living room, took Richard Roe from her arms, and left without leaving a copy of the pick-up order. After the seizure, Defendant Conn took Richard Roe to a DPS-licensed shelter home in Montgomery.

No hearing was scheduled or held following Richard Roe's removal until July 10, 1975. No attorney was requested or appointed to represent Richard Roe at the July 10 hearing. At the hearing in the Family Court of Montgomery County, both Defendant Coppage and Plaintiff Wambles were present and represented by counsel. Judge Thetford entered an order on July 11, 1975, wherein he awarded Defendant Coppage custody of Richard Roe after making a finding that he was the natural father of the child. The temporary custody order gave Margaret Wambles "the right to petition the court for custody of [Richard Roe] at any future date." Plaintiff Wambles' first petition for custody, filed on August 5, 1975, along with her motion for a new trial and motion for order for blood tests, was denied on August 14, 1975, by Judge Thetford as untimely filed. A second petition for custody was filed by Plaintiff Wambles in November and denied by Judge John W. Davis, III, on December 22, 1975. The denial of this last petition was affirmed by the Alabama Court of Civil Appeals.

. . .

Plaintiffs Wambles and Roe have submitted the testimony of witnesses Dr. Sally A. Provence and Dr. Albert J. Solnit as experts in the field of child care and development. Drs. Provence and Solnit summarized their views as follows:

1. Summary removal of a young child from a parent who has been his major caregiver is a severe threat to his development. It disrupts and grossly endangers what he most needs, that is, the continuity of affectionate care from those to whom he is attached through bonds of love.

2. Summary removal should be allowed only under conditions in which physical survival is at stake.

---

5. Plaintiff Wambles had lived in Montgomery, Alabama, since 1969 and had worked at Morrison's Cafeteria from 1969 to 1972 and again from August 1974 until May 1975.

3.   In situations in which some interference is indicated because parents are unable to take good care of their child, there are alternatives to summary removal which should be used either singly or in combination. Among these are the following: (a) the provision in the child's home of assistance to parents with child care and with managing a household; (b) the provision of counselling to parents about how to care for a child in ways that enhance his development and well-being; (c) the provision of a day care center or day care family in which assistance to child and parent can be provided which is addressed to their specific needs; (d) the provision of a residential facility or foster family in which both parent and child can receive the nurture and guidance they may need (in extended families, relatives often supply such benevolent help, and when they are unavailable, it is one of society's responsibilities to organize and make available such assistance); and (e) the provision of 24–hour substitute care for a child, which does not cut him off from contact with his parents.

    .   .   .

The Fundamental Right to Family Integrity: A district court in Iowa recently reviewed the long line of Supreme Court cases addressed to the constitutional interests at stake where various aspects of family life are threatened and concluded that there is a fundamental right to family integrity protected by the Fourteenth Amendment to the United States Constitution. *Alsager v. District Court of Polk County, Iowa*, 406 F. Supp. 10, 15 (S.D. Iowa 1975).... The seminal case in this constitutional development is *Meyer v. Nebraska*, 262 U.S. 390 (1923), where the Supreme Court held that the "liberty" guarantee of the Fourteenth Amendment "without doubt . . . denotes . . . the right of the individual . . . to marry, establish a home and bring up children." [I]n *Prince v. Massachusetts*, 321 U.S. 158[, 166] (1944), [the Supreme Court] said:

> It is cardinal with us that the custody, care and nurture of the child reside first in the parents, whose primary function and freedom include preparation for obligations the state can neither supply nor hinder . . . and it is in recognition of this that these decisions (*Meyer* and *Pierce*) have respected the private realm of family life which the state cannot enter.

    . . . Finally in *Stanley v. Illinois*, 405 U.S. 645 (1972), the Supreme Court declared unconstitutional the Illinois dependency statute that deprived an unmarried father of the care and custody of his natural children upon the death of their mother. In doing so, the Court held that the right to the integrity of the family unit was protected by the Fourteenth Amendment due process and equal protection clauses and by the Ninth Amendment.

    This Court is in full agreement with the conclusion of Chief Judge Hanson in *Alsager*, that the Constitution recognizes as fundamental the right of family integrity. This means that in our present case the state's severance of Plaintiff Wambles' parent-child relationship and of Plaintiff Roe's child-parent relationship will receive strict judicial scrutiny. Recognizing that fundamental right, this Court will now apply the pertinent constitutional principles to the facts of the present case.

    Summary Seizure: This Court holds that ALABAMA CODE, Title 13, § 352(4), which authorizes summary seizure of a child "if it appears that . . . the child is in such condition that its welfare requires," violates procedural due process under the Fourteenth Amendment of the United States Constitution.

To determine the nature of the procedural safeguards that the Constitution mandates, the administrative needs of the State must be carefully balanced against the interests of the affected citizens. There is no question that the family members will suffer a grievous loss if the State severs the parent-child relationship; an interest, we have held, that is part of the liberty concept of the Fourteenth Amendment. The State of Alabama, on the other hand, does have a legitimate interest in protecting children from harm as quickly as possible. Normally, before intrusion into the affairs of the family is allowed, the State should have reliable evidence that a child is in need of protective care. In the absence of exigent circumstances, this fact-finding process, as a matter of basic fairness, should provide notice to the parents and child of the evidence of abuse and provide them with an opportunity for rebuttal at a hearing before an impartial tribunal.

The facts of this case dispel any notion that the State was faced with an emergency situation. As we earlier found, Officer Conn's investigation revealed that Richard Roe was clothed, clean, and in "fairly good" physical condition with no signs of physical abuse. The Wambles' home was "relatively clean" and stocked with "adequate food." Without danger of immediate harm or threatened harm to the child, the State's interest in protecting the child is not sufficient to justify a removal of the child prior to notice and a hearing. Additionally, even in the event summary seizure had been justified, a hearing would have had to follow the seizure "as soon as practicable" and not six weeks later as it did in the present case. For these reasons, this Court is of the opinion that ALABAMA CODE Title 13, § 352(4) violates the procedural due process clause of the Fourteenth Amendment. We also hold that the statute's "welfare" standard is unconstitutionally vague and an unconstitutional infringement on the fundamental right to family integrity for reasons similar to those discussed, *infra*, concerning removal of the child after a hearing on the basis of a "neglect" finding.

Removal Upon a Finding of "Neglect": After the hearing on July 10, 1975, Judge Thetford ordered the termination of the parental rights of Plaintiff Wambles to Richard Roe on the basis that the child was "a dependent or neglected child as defined by the laws of Alabama." As mentioned earlier, ALABAMA CODE, Title 13, § 350, defines a "neglected child" as "any child, who, while under sixteen years of age has no proper parental care or guardianship or whose home, by reason of neglect, cruelty, or depravity, on the part of his parent or parents, guardian or other person in whose care he may be, is an unfit or improper place for such child." A co-ordinate provision in the Code authorizes a juvenile court to exercise the guardianship of the State over children who fit this description of "neglected."

[I]t is not disputed that the State of Alabama has a legitimate interest in the welfare of children. Minor intrusions into the affairs of the family may be permitted when the State has reason to believe that a child's best interest is at stake. In such cases, various options and alternatives are available to the State to achieve its objective of child protection. One possibility might be a requirement that the parents attend seminars and weekly counselling sessions on child care and the responsibilities of parenthood. Another situation might warrant supervision of the parents by a welfare counselor or the placing of a neutral person—such as an aunt—in the home to serve as a bridge between the parents and the child. The State's interest, however, would become "compelling" enough to sever entirely the parent-child relationship only when the child is subjected to real physical or emotional harm and less drastic measures would be unavailing.[6]

Here, the State offered no assistance to Plaintiff Wambles, who was faced with the troubling predicament of raising a young child without the aid of a husband, nor did it explore the possibility of accomplishing its objective of protecting Richard Roe's welfare by use of alternatives other than termination of custody.

. . .

In *Alsager*, the court held that "termination must only occur when more harm is likely to befall the child by staying with his parents than by being permanently separated from them." This standard appears to teach that the state's burden is not only to show that the child is being disadvantaged but also to show that the child is being harmed in a real and substantial way. Accordingly, this Court declares ALABAMA CODE, Title 13, §§ 350 and 352 unconstitutional, because it violates the family integrity of Margaret Wambles and all other mothers in the class represented by her and the family integrity of Richard Roe and all other children in the class represented by him.

This Court holds, as an alternative ground, that the challenged statutory provisions are unconstitutionally vague. We adopt the reasoning and the language of the district court in *Alsager v. District Court of Polk County, Iowa*, *supra*, which states that,

> Nevertheless, Due Process requires the state to clearly identify and define the evil from which the child needs protection and to specify what parental conduct so contributes to that evil that the state is justified in terminating the parent-child relationship.

In the present case, not only is the statutory definition of neglect circular (a neglected child is any child who has no proper parental care by reason of neglect), but it is couched in terms that have no common meaning. When is a home an "unfit" or "improper" place for a child? Obviously, this is a question about which men and women of ordinary intelligence would greatly disagree. Their answers would vary in large measure in relation to their differing social, ethical, and religious views. Because these terms are too subjective to denote a sufficient warning to those individuals who might be affected by their proscription, the statute is unconstitutionally vague.

NOTES

1.   Congress has become more involved in regulating interventions between parents and children in the years since *Roe v. Conn. See In re H.G.*, 757 N.E.2d 864 (Ill. 2001):

> In 1980, Congress enacted the Adoption Assistance and Child Welfare Act (AACWA). See 42 U.S.C. §§ 620 through 628, 670 through 679a (1994). AACWA created a program which authorizes the federal government to reimburse the states for certain expenses incurred by the states in the administration of foster care and adoption services. To be eligible for federal funds under AACWA, the states must have in place a plan which provides, in pertinent part, that "reasonable efforts" will be made to prevent the removal of children from their homes into foster care and, after removal, that "reasonable efforts" will be made to reunify the children with their parents. See 42 U.S.C. § 671(a)(15) (1994); *Suter v.*

---

6.   It must be emphasized that this standard does not apply to all custody proceedings but only those where the State seeks to assume custody. In proceedings where the parties have an arguably equal right to custody, such as pursuant to a divorce, a "best interest of the child" standard is entirely appropriate.

Artist M., 503 U.S. 347 (1992). Through the establishment of the reimbursement program under AACWA, Congress sought to prevent the unnecessary placement of children in foster care. *See generally* C. Kim, Note, *Putting Reason Back Into the Reasonable Efforts Requirement in Child Abuse and Neglect Cases*, 1999 U. ILL. L. REV. 287, 314 (1994).

Some time after the passage of AACWA, it became apparent to Congress that the courts and state agencies which were interpreting and implementing the "reasonable efforts" requirement of the Act were placing too great an emphasis on the goals of family preservation and reunification. As a result, a number of children were "languishing in foster care" and "remaining in limbo as to their permanency" while the states attempted to rehabilitate their parents. 1999 U. ILL. L. REV. at 293. In response to this and other problems, Congress passed the Adoption and Safe Families Act of 1997. Pub. L. No. 105–89, 111 Stat. 2115 (codified as amended in various sections of 42 U.S.C.).

Among other issues, the Adoption and Safe Families Act of 1997 (ASFA) addressed the question of how long the states must pursue the goal of family reunification under the "reasonable efforts" standard. ASFA mandates that, to retain eligibility for federal funding, and unless certain exceptions apply, the states "shall file a petition to terminate the parental rights of [a] child's parents" when the child "has been in foster care under the responsibility of the State for 15 of the most recent 22 months." 42 U.S.C. § 675(5)(E) (Supp. 1997). The exceptions to this rule requiring the filing of a petition to terminate parental rights are (1) the child is being cared for by a relative, (2) there is no compelling reason for filing such a petition, or (3) the state has not provided services necessary for the safe return of the child to the child's home.

2. Government intervention to protect children from neglect or abuse began in the seventeenth century, but only poor children were taken from their parents. The first intervention to protect a child from physical abuse rather than poverty did not take place until the late nineteenth century:

II. HISTORY OF NEGLECT INTERVENTION

A. FROM TUDOR TIMES TO THE NINETEENTH CENTURY

The sixteenth century was a period of economic transition and stress in England, during which bands of "sturdy beggars" began to fill the roads and to terrorize town and country. The number of poor mushroomed to the point that private charities no longer could provide adequate relief. As a result, Parliament began to provide for the relief of the poor and their children on a systematic basis. As early as 1535 a statute provided that "[c]hildren under fourteen years of age, and above five, that live in idleness, and be taken begging, may be put to serve by the governors of cities, towns, etc. to husbandry, or other crafts or labors." In 1601, the Elizabethan Poor Law consolidated similar early legislative efforts into a single, comprehensive program of poor relief that became the model for the next three centuries in the United States as well as England.

The Elizabethan system aided the poor in several ways. It provided for the establishment of tax-supported hospitals and poor houses, or almshouses, to shelter the poor who were too old or too ill to work. The employable poor were compelled to work or sent to houses of correction if they refused to work. Finally, children of the poor were put to work or apprenticed. . . .

It is impossible to determine exactly how many children were separated from their families under this legislation; hundreds were shipped to the American colonies beginning in 1617, and thousands were later impressed into the Merchant Marine. As distasteful as the cavalier separation of children from their parents may seem today, however, the conclusion that the statutes manifested only discriminatory attitudes toward the poor would be mistaken; the apparent harshness was more a product of cost consciousness than of discrimination. According to Professor tenBroek, "[o]nce the public agreed to pay the bill, it acquired a pressing concern about the size of the bill and an active interest in finding methods for reducing it." The system of "binding out" poor children reduced the costs; the children who were bound out could pay for part of their care through their own labor. Similarly, the decision to separate poor children from their families and to put them to work did not necessarily indicate class bias because in this pre-child labor law era, most children worked and upper class families of the time frequently sent their adolescents to other families for training. Indeed, the poor laws were quite humanitarian in their attempt to provide poor children with proper work attitudes as well as useful skills in an age when no public education or training was available.

The record of providing skills through apprenticeship, however, was poor almost from the start. "Rogues soon swarmed again," complained Lord Coke in 1624, and the cause allegedly was the failure of the overseers to apprentice children. The Privy Council for a time tried to correct the enforcement problems, but the outbreak of civil war soon made them worse. By mid-century, an increasingly harsh and repressive policy toward the poor emerged. Soon work houses for children were established, in sharp contrast with the earlier benevolent statutory scheme for training.

. . .

B.   REFORMS OF THE NINETEENTH CENTURY

Neglect proceedings in the nineteenth century continued to be primarily [a form of]poor relief, but they gradually were expanded to protect children from parental immorality and abuse. The first state intervention to protect a child from parental abuse occurred in 1874. According to the more dramatic versions of the episode, eight-year-old Mary Ellen Wilson was rescued only through the efforts of the recently formed New York Society for the Prevention of Cruelty to Animals, which argued that children were, after all, members of the animal kingdom. Within a few months the first Society for the Prevention of Cruelty to Children was formed in New York City by Elbridge Gerry, who had argued Mary Wilson's cause.

The Society's records demonstrate that poverty, rather than cruelty, continued to be the major justification for family interventions, despite the organization's professed dedication to protecting children from cruelty. Further, the Society focused on punishing cruel parents rather than on the provision of better environments for children. The Society's efforts facilitated passage of a neglect statute authorizing any New York court that convicted a parent for criminal abuse or neglect to commit their children to an orphanage or to effect any other disposition that was available for pauper children. The new statute focused principally on preventing the exploitation of children for commercial purposes rather than on enhancing their physical or emotional development.

. . .

C.   THE MODERN ERA

[T]wo major changes in the goals of neglect enforcement occurred in the beginning of the twentieth century. First, changes in the poor relief system, particularly the development of "mother's aid" and aid to dependent children made it possible for states to stop removing children from parents because of family poverty; for the first time poverty became a defense to rather than a ground for a neglect finding. This new distinction between neglect and destitution is highlighted by a 1930 New York statute which provided that destitute children were to be housed separately from those who were delinquent, neglected, or abandoned. Not until 1962, when poverty in theory became an absolute defense to state intervention in New York, was the change begun in 1922 made complete. The legislature abolished the destitute child category and redefined a neglected child as one "whose parent or other person legally responsible for his care does not adequately supply the child with food, clothing, shelter, education, or medical or surgical care, though financially able or offered financial means to do so." Unfortunately, a second section of the 1962 statute allowed its application to families who were simply poor or unconventional, for neglect was defined also to include "improper guardianship, including lack of moral supervision or guidance." The vagueness of this standard was tempered only slightly by a requirement that the state show that the child "suffers or is likely to suffer serious harm" from the improper guardianship and that the child "required the aid of the court," before the statute could be invoked.

The second major change in neglect practice in the twentieth century was the expansion of the *parens patriae* role of the states to encompass protection of children from emotional as well as physical harm. Often this change was accompanied by a revision of statutes that made parental immorality a basis for state intervention. In New York, for example, impairment of emotional health and impairment of mental or emotional condition were made grounds for intervention in 1970, while "lack of moral supervision" was eliminated. Similarly, in 1963 Idaho authorized intervention where a child was "emotionally maladjust-ed" or where a child who had been denied proper parental love or affectionate association "behaves unnaturally and unrealistically in relation to normal situations, objects, and other persons."

These changes undoubtedly reflect the influence of both Freud and a growing body of child development specialists, who documented the emotional needs of children and affirmed the importance of being raised in a family....

Judith Areen, *Intervention Between Parent and Child: A Reappraisal of the State's Role in Child Neglect and Abuse Cases*, 63 Geo. L.J. 887, 894–96, 903–04, 910–12 (1975).

B.   UNMARRIED FATHERS

Stanley v. Illinois

Supreme Court of the United States, 1972.
405 U.S. 645, 92 S.Ct. 1208, 31 L.Ed.2d 551.

■ JUSTICE WHITE delivered the opinion of the Court.

Joan Stanley lived with Peter Stanley intermittently for 18 years, during which time they had three children. When Joan Stanley died, Peter Stanley lost not only her but also his children. Under Illinois law, the children of unwed fathers become wards of the State upon the death of the mother. Accordingly, upon Joan Stanley's death, in a dependency proceeding instituted by the State of Illinois, Stanley's children were declared wards of the State and placed with court-appointed guardians. Stanley appealed, claiming that he had never been shown to be an unfit parent and that since married fathers and unwed mothers could not be deprived of their children without such a showing, he had been deprived of the equal protection of the laws guaranteed him by the Fourteenth Amendment.

. . .

[W]e are faced with a dependency statute that empowers state officials to circumvent neglect proceedings on the theory that an unwed father is not a "parent" whose existing relationship with his children must be considered. "Parents," says the State, "means the father and mother of a legitimate child, or the survivor of them, or the natural mother of an illegitimate child, and includes any adoptive parent," ILL. REV. STAT., c. 37, § 701–14, but the term does not include unwed fathers.

Under Illinois law, therefore, while the children of all parents can be taken from them in neglect proceedings, that is only after notice, hearing, and proof of such unfitness as a parent as amounts to neglect, an unwed father is uniquely subject to the more simplistic dependency proceeding. By use of this proceeding, the State, on showing that the father was not married to the mother, need not prove unfitness in fact, because it is presumed at law. Thus, the unwed father's claim of parental qualification is avoided as "irrelevant."

. . .

The private interest here, that of a man in the children he has sired and raised, undeniably warrants deference and, absent a powerful countervailing interest, protection. It is plain that the interest of a parent in the companionship, care, custody, and management of his or her children "come[s] to this Court with a momentum for respect lacking when appeal is made to liberties which derive merely from shifting economic arrangements." *Kovacs v. Cooper*, 336 U.S. 77, 95 (1949) (Frankfurter, J., concurring).

The Court has frequently emphasized the importance of the family. The rights to conceive and to raise one's children have been deemed "essential," *Meyer v. Nebraska*, 262 U.S. 390, 399 (1923), "basic civil rights of man," *Skinner v. Oklahoma*, 316 U.S. 535, 541 (1942), and "rights far more precious . . . than property rights," *May v. Anderson*, 345 U.S. 528, 533 (1953). "It is cardinal with us that the custody, care and nurture of the child reside first in the parents, whose primary function and freedom include preparation for obligations the state can neither supply nor hinder." *Prince v. Massachusetts*, 321 U.S. 158, 166 (1944). The integrity of the family unit has found protection in the Due Process Clause of the Fourteenth Amendment, *Meyer v. Nebraska, supra,* at 399, the Equal Protection Clause of the Fourteenth Amendment, *Skinner v. Oklahoma, supra,* at 541, and the Ninth Amendment, *Griswold v. Connecticut,* 381 U.S. 479, 496 (1965) (Goldberg, J., concurring).

Nor has the law refused to recognize those family relationships unlegitimized by a marriage ceremony. The Court has declared unconstitutional a state statute denying natural, but illegitimate, children a wrongful-death action for the death of their mother, emphasizing that such children cannot be denied the right of other children because familial bonds in such cases were often as warm, enduring, and important as those arising within a more formally organized family unit. *Levy v. Louisiana,* 391 U.S. 68, 71–72 (1968). "To say that the test of equal protection should be the 'legal' rather than the biological relationship is to avoid the issue. For the Equal Protection Clause necessarily limits the authority of a State to draw such 'legal' lines as it chooses." *Glona v. American Guarantee Co.,* 391 U.S. 73, 75–76 (1968).

These authorities make it clear that, at the least, Stanley's interest in retaining custody of his children is cognizable and substantial.

For its part, the State has made its interest quite plain: Illinois has declared that the aim of the Juvenile Court Act is to protect "the moral, emotional, mental, and physical welfare of the minor and the best interests of the community" and to "strengthen the minor's family ties whenever possible, removing him from the custody of his parents only when his welfare or safety or the protection of the public cannot be adequately safeguarded without removal...." Ill. Rev. Stat., c. 37, § 701–2. These are legitimate interests, well within the power of the State to implement. We do not question the assertion that neglectful parents may be separated from their children.

But we are here not asked to evaluate the legitimacy of the state ends, rather, to determine whether the means used to achieve these ends are constitutionally defensible. What is the state interest in separating children from fathers without a hearing designed to determine whether the father is unfit in a particular disputed case? We observe that the State registers no gain towards its declared goals when it separates children from the custody of fit parents. Indeed, if Stanley is a fit father, the State spites its own articulated goals when it needlessly separates him from his family.

. . .

It may be, as the State insists, that most unmarried fathers are unsuitable and neglectful parents. It may also be that Stanley is such a parent and that his children should be placed in other hands. But all unmarried fathers are not in this category; some are wholly suited to have custody of their children. This much the State readily concedes, and nothing in this record indicates that Stanley is or has been a neglectful father who has not cared for his children. Given the opportunity to make his case, Stanley may have been seen to be deserving of custody of his offspring. Had this been so, the State's statutory policy would have been furthered by leaving custody in him.

. . .

[I]t may be argued that unmarried fathers are so seldom fit that Illinois need not undergo the administrative inconvenience of inquiry in any case, including Stanley's. The establishment of prompt efficacious procedures to achieve legitimate state ends is a proper state interest worthy of cognizance in constitutional adjudication. But the Constitution recognizes higher values than speed and efficiency. Indeed, one might fairly say of the Bill of Rights in general, and the Due Process Clause in particular, that they were designed to protect the fragile values of a vulnerable citizenry from the overbearing concern for efficiency and efficacy that may characterize praiseworthy government officials no less, and perhaps more, than mediocre ones.

. . .

Procedure by presumption is always cheaper and easier than individualized determination. But when, as here, the procedure forecloses the determinative issues of competence and care, when it explicitly disdains present realities in deference to past formalities, it needlessly risks running roughshod over the important interests of both parent and child. It therefore cannot stand.

. . .

The State of Illinois assumes custody of the children of married parents, divorced parents, and unmarried mothers only after a hearing and proof of neglect. The children of unmarried fathers, however, are declared dependent children without a hearing on parental fitness and without proof of neglect. Stanley's claim in the state courts and here is that failure to afford him a hearing on his parental qualifications while extending it to other parents denied him equal protection of the laws. We have concluded that all Illinois parents are constitutionally entitled to a hearing on their fitness before their children are removed from their custody. It follows that denying such a hearing to Stanley and those like him while granting it to other Illinois parents is inescapably contrary to the Equal Protection Clause.

NOTES

1. "[A]fter the Supreme Court held in Stanley's favor, the state instituted child neglect proceedings. Since Peter was no longer indigent, we could not represent him. He lost the case and my former Legal Services Office did agree to represent him on appeal. The State subsequently returned the children and dismissed charges. They have been living with him for about a year." Letter from Patrick T. Murphy, attorney for Stanley (March 23, 1976).

2. The rationale of *Stanley* focuses on the interest of a parent in keeping his child, not on the interest of a child in staying with his parent. Why? Is this emphasis likely to advance the development of sound public policy?

Lehr v. Robertson

Supreme Court of the United States, 1983.
463 U.S. 248, 103 S.Ct. 2985, 77 L.Ed.2d 614.

■ JUSTICE STEVENS delivered the opinion of the Court.

The question presented is whether New York has sufficiently protected an unmarried father's inchoate relationship with a child whom he has never supported and rarely seen in the two years since her birth. The appellant, Jonathan Lehr, claims that the Due Process and Equal Protection Clauses of the Fourteenth Amendment, as interpreted in *Stanley v. Illinois*, 405 U.S. 645 (1972), and *Caban v. Mohammed*, 441 U.S. 380 (1979), give him an absolute right to notice and an opportunity to be heard before the child may be adopted. We disagree.

Jessica M. was born out of wedlock on November 9, 1976. Her mother, Lorraine Robertson, married Richard Robertson eight months after Jessica's birth. On December 21, 1978, when Jessica was over two years old, the Robertsons filed an adoption petition in the Family Court of Ulster County, New York. The court heard their testimony and received a favorable report from the Ulster County Department of Social Services. On March 7, 1979, the court entered an order of adoption. In this proceeding, appellant contends that the adoption order is invalid because he, Jessica's putative father, was not given advance notice of the adoption proceeding.

. . .

The State of New York maintains a "putative father registry." A man who files with that registry demonstrates his intent to claim paternity of a child born out of wedlock and is therefore entitled to receive notice of any proceeding to adopt that child. Before entering Jessica's adoption order, the Ulster County Family Court had the putative father registry examined. Although appellant claims to be Jessica's natural father, he had not entered his name in the registry.

In addition to the persons whose names are listed on the putative father registry, New York law requires that notice of an adoption proceeding be given to several other classes of possible fathers of children born out of wedlock—those who have been adjudicated to be the father, those who have been identified as the father on the child's birth certificate, those who live openly with the child and the child's mother and who hold themselves out to be the father, those who have been identified as the father by the mother in a sworn written statement, and those who were married to the child's mother before the child was six months old.[7] Appellant admittedly was not a member

---

7. At the time Jessica's adoption order was entered, N.Y. DOM. REL. LAW §§ 111–a (2) and (3) (McKinney 1977 and Supp. 1982–1983) provided:

2. Persons entitled to notice, pursuant to subdivision one of this section, shall include:

(a) any person adjudicated by a court in this state to be the father of the child;

(b) any person adjudicated by a court of another state or territory of the United States to be the father of the child, when a certified copy of the court order has been filed with the

of any of those classes. He had lived with appellee prior to Jessica's birth and visited her in the hospital when Jessica was born, but his name does not appear on Jessica's birth certificate. He did not live with appellee or Jessica after Jessica's birth, he has never provided them with any financial support, and he has never offered to marry appellee. Nevertheless, he contends that the following special circumstances gave him a constitutional right to notice and a hearing before Jessica was adopted.

On January 30, 1979, one month after the adoption proceeding was commenced in Ulster County, appellant filed a "visitation and paternity petition" in the Westchester County Family Court. In that petition, he asked for a determination of paternity, an order of support, and reasonable visitation privileges with Jessica. Notice of that proceeding was served on appellee on February 22, 1979. Four days later appellee's attorney informed the Ulster County Court that appellant had commenced a paternity proceeding in Westchester County; the Ulster County judge then entered an order staying appellant's paternity proceeding until he could rule on a motion to change the venue of that proceeding to Ulster County. On March 3, 1979, appellant received notice of the change of venue motion and, for the first time, learned that an adoption proceeding was pending in Ulster County.

On March 7, 1979, appellant's attorney telephoned the Ulster County judge to inform him that he planned to seek a stay of the adoption proceeding pending the determination of the paternity petition. In that telephone conversation, the judge advised the lawyer that he had already signed the adoption order earlier that day. According to appellant's attorney, the judge stated that he was aware of the pending paternity petition but did not believe he was required to give notice to appellant prior to the entry of the order of adoption.

Thereafter, the Family Court in Westchester County granted appellee's motion to dismiss the paternity petition, holding that the putative father's right to seek paternity "must be deemed severed so long as an order of adoption exists." Appellant did not appeal from that dismissal. On June 22, 1979, appellant filed a petition to vacate the order of adoption on the ground that it was obtained by fraud and in violation of his constitutional rights. The Ulster County Family Court received written and oral argument on the question whether it had "dropped the ball" by approving the adoption without giving appellant advance notice. After deliberating for several months, it denied the petition, explaining its decision in a thorough written opinion.

---

putative father registry, pursuant to section three hundred seventy-two-c of the social services law;

(c) any person who has timely filed an unrevoked notice of intent to claim paternity of the child, pursuant to section three hundred seventy-two of the social services law;

(d) any person who is recorded on the child's birth certificate as the child's father;

(e) any person who is openly living with the child and the child's mother at the time the proceeding is initiated and who is holding himself out to be the child's father;

(f) any person who has been identified as the child's father by the mother in written, sworn statement; and

(g) any person who was married to the child's mother within six months subsequent to the birth of the child and prior to the execution of a surrender instrument or the initiation of a proceeding pursuant to section three hundred eighty-four-b of the social services law.

3. The sole purpose of notice under this section shall be to enable the person served pursuant to subdivision two to present evidence to the court relevant to the best interests of the child.

The Appellate Division of the Supreme Court affirmed. . . .

. . .

Appellant has now invoked our appellate jurisdiction. He offers two alternative grounds for holding the New York statutory scheme unconstitutional. First, he contends that a putative father's actual or potential relationship with a child born out of wedlock is an interest in liberty which may not be destroyed without due process of law; he argues therefore that he had a constitutional right to prior notice and an opportunity to be heard before he was deprived of that interest. Second, he contends that the gender-based classification in the statute, which both denied him the right to consent to Jessica's adoption and accorded him fewer procedural rights than her mother, violated the Equal Protection Clause.

The Due Process Claim.

. . .

This Court has examined the extent to which a natural father's biological relationship with his child receives protection under the Due Process Clause in precisely three cases: *Stanley v. Illinois,* 405 U.S. 645 (1972), *Quilloin v. Walcott,* 434 U.S. 246 (1978), and *Caban v. Mohammed,* 441 U.S. 380 (1979).

. . .

Quilloin involved the constitutionality of a Georgia statute that authorized the adoption, over the objection of the natural father, of a child born out of wedlock. The father in that case had never legitimated the child. It was only after the mother had remarried and her new husband had filed an adoption petition that the natural father sought visitation rights and filed a petition for legitimation. The trial court found adoption by the new husband to be in the child's best interests, and we unanimously held that action to be consistent with the Due Process Clause.

Caban involved the conflicting claims of two natural parents who had maintained joint custody of their children from the time of their birth until they were respectively two and four years old. The father challenged the validity of an order authorizing the mother's new husband to adopt the children; he relied on both the Equal Protection Clause and the Due Process Clause. Because this Court upheld his equal protection claim, the majority did not address his due process challenge. The comments on the latter claim by the four dissenting Justices are nevertheless instructive, because they identify the clear distinction between a mere biological relationship and an actual relationship of parental responsibility.

JUSTICE STEWART correctly observed:

Even if it be assumed that each married parent after divorce has some substantive due process right to maintain his or her parental relationship, it by no means follows that each unwed parent has any such right. *Parental rights do not spring full-blown from the biological connection between parent and child. They require relationships more enduring.*

441 U.S. at 397 (emphasis added).

. . .

The difference between the developed parent-child relationship that was implicated in *Stanley* and *Caban*, and the potential relationship involved in *Quilloin* and this case, is both clear and significant. When an unwed father demonstrates a full commitment to the responsibilities of parenthood by "[coming] forward to participate in the rearing of his child," *Caban,* 441 U.S., at 392, his interest in personal contact with his child acquires substantial protection under the Due Process Clause. At that point it may be said that he "[acts] as a father toward his children." But the mere existence of a biological link does not merit equivalent constitutional protection. The actions of judges neither create nor sever genetic bonds. "[The] importance of the familial relationship, to the individuals involved and to the society, stems from the emotional attachments that derive from the intimacy of daily association, and from the role it plays in '[promoting] a way of life' through the instruction of children . . . as well as from the fact of blood relationship." *Smith v. Organization of Foster Families for Equality and Reform,* 431 U.S. 816, 844 (1977) (quoting *Wisconsin v. Yoder,* 406 U.S. 205, 231–33 (1972)).

. . .

In this case, we are not assessing the constitutional adequacy of New York's procedures for terminating a developed relationship. Appellant has never had any significant custodial, personal, or financial relationship with Jessica, and he did not seek to establish a legal tie until after she was two years old.[8] We are concerned only with whether New York has adequately protected his opportunity to form such a relationship.

. . .

After this Court's decision in *Stanley,* the New York Legislature appointed a special commission to recommend legislation that would accommodate both the interests of biological fathers in their children and the children's interest in prompt and certain adoption procedures. The commission recommended, and the legislature enacted, a statutory adoption scheme that automatically provides notice to seven categories of putative fathers who are likely to have assumed some responsibility for the care of their natural children. If this scheme were likely to omit many responsible fathers, and if qualification for notice were beyond the control of an interested putative father, it might be thought procedurally inadequate. Yet, as all of the New York courts that reviewed this matter observed, the right to receive notice was completely within appellant's control. By mailing a postcard to the putative father registry, he could have guaranteed that he would receive notice of any proceedings to adopt Jessica. The possibility that he may have failed to do so because of his ignorance of the law cannot be a sufficient reason for criticizing the law itself. The New York Legislature concluded that a more open-ended notice requirement would merely complicate the adoption process, threaten the privacy interests of unwed mothers, create the risk of unnecessary controversy, and impair the desired finality of adoption decrees. Regardless of whether we would have done likewise if we were legislators instead of judges, we surely cannot characterize the State's conclusion as arbitrary.

. . .

---

8. This case happens to involve an adoption by the husband of the natural mother, but we do not believe the natural father has any greater right to object to such an adoption than to an adoption by two total strangers. If anything, the balance of equities tips the opposite way in a case such as this. In denying the putative father relief in Quilloin v. Walcott, 434 U.S. 246 (1978), we made an observation equally applicable here:

> Nor is this a case in which the proposed adoption would place the child with a new set of parents with whom the child had never before lived. Rather, the result of the adoption in this case is to give full recognition to a family unit already in existence, a result desired by all concerned, except appellant. Whatever might be required in other situations, we cannot say that the State was required in this situation to find anything more than that the adoption, and denial of legitimation, were in the "best interests of the child."

Id. at 255.

The Equal Protection Claim.

.   .   .

The legislation at issue in this case is intended to establish procedures for adoptions. Those procedures are designed to promote the best interests of the child, to protect the rights of interested third parties, and to ensure promptness and finality. To serve those ends, the legislation guarantees to certain people the right to veto an adoption and the right to prior notice of any adoption proceeding. The mother of an illegitimate child is always within that favored class, but only certain putative fathers are included. Appellant contends that the gender-based distinction is invidious.

.   .   .

As we have already explained, the existence or nonexistence of a substantial relationship between parent and child is a relevant criterion in evaluating both the rights of the parent and the best interests of the child. . . . Because appellant, like the father in *Quilloin*, has never established a substantial relationship with his daughter, the New York statutes at issue in this case did not operate to deny appellant equal protection.

Michael H. v. Gerald D.

Supreme Court of the United States, 1989.
491 U.S. 110, 109 S.Ct. 2333, 105 L.Ed.2d 91.

[The opinion is printed at page 151, *supra*].

NOTES

1. Justice Scalia's plurality opinion, which did not recognize Michael H.'s parental rights as a protected liberty interest, has been criticized by some state court decisions. In *In re Adoption of B.G.S.*, 556 So. 2d 545 (La. 1990), the Louisiana Supreme Court observed:

> Four justices would hold that a protected liberty interest is created not by biological fatherhood plus an established parental relationship but is based on the historic respect traditionally accorded to the relationships that develop within the unitary family. Their departure from the previous analysis evidently was prompted by the extreme factual situation: Michael H. sought to establish his paternity and right to visitation with a child presumed to be Gerald D.'s daughter because Gerald was married to and living with the mother at the time of birth. An analysis of the various separate opinions, however, reveals that a majority of the court has not abandoned its traditional approach of focusing first upon the precise nature of the interest threatened by the state, i.e., the interest of the unwed father in his child. Moreover, even if the plurality's departure should become ascendant, it does not appear that it would lead to different results under the more normal factual pattern of the present case.

Id. at 550 n.2. Similarly, the Supreme Court of Appeals of West Virginia argued:

> We decline to follow *Michael H. v. Gerald D*, however, in construing our own Due Process Clause. We do so for two reasons. First, the split on the *Michael H. v. Gerald D.* Court weakened the case's precedential authority. The central holding of the plurality—that the putative father did not have an affected liberty interest—was joined in by only four justices. Four other justices expressly disagreed and insisted the putative father had a liberty interest in his relationship with the child in question. A fifth, Justice Stevens, cast the decisive vote, while concurring only in the judgment; he assumed the father could have a protected liberty interest in the child, even though the "mother was married to, and

cohabiting with, another man at the time of the child's conception and birth." Thus, even as a matter of federal constitutional law, *Michael H. v. Gerald D.* does not preclude recognition of a liberty interest in this case.

State ex rel. Roy Allen S., 474 S.E.2d 554, 561–62 (W. Va. 1996).

2. For a thoughtful discussion of the current status of the liberty interest of unwed fathers after *Michael H.*, consider Anthony Miller, *The Case for the Genetic Parent: Stanley, Quilloin, Caban, Lehr, and Michael H. Revisited*, 53 Loy. L. Rev. 395, 455 (2007):

> Even if the *Michael H.* decision had resulted in a majority, it would still remain very difficult to find a useful rule to apply in other cases despite the clear result in the case. If the rule is that the state can define a parent for constitutional purposes, then the case undermines all protections for parents afforded by the Constitution. If the plurality opinion stands for the principle stated by Justice Scalia that "our traditions [and, therefore, the Constitution] have protected the marital family (Gerald, Carole, and the child they acknowledge to be theirs) against the sort of claim Michael asserts," then the rule of Michael H. is absurdly narrow. If the rule is broader—that the constitution protects the family rather than the parent-child relationship—then the rule is vague and ambiguous to the point of being useless, for the case does not state any standard to establish who qualifies for the status of family. While Justice Scalia intimates that his definition of family may be broader than just a married mother and father and their child, he provides no guidance as to the intricacies of a broader definition other than to conclude that this definition does not include Michael and Victoria.

3. What are the implications of the *Michael H.* decision for constitutional recognition of rights in nontraditional families? Matthew Kavanagh argues that the decision rests on an assumption of exclusivity:

> Here, we have a case in which a child has two fathers and a mother—a reality that Victoria's guardian ad litem tried unsuccessfully to bring to the Court's attention. Both Gerald and Michael were known to Victoria as her father; each financially and emotionally supported the child; each lived with her for a significant amount of time. One was Victoria's biological progenitor; the other was her mother's husband and the man with whom she resided at the time.
>
> . . .
>
> The Court, however, was unable to translate this reality of Victoria's life into a de jure recognition of her essential parent-child relationships.
>
> . . .
>
> . . . Victoria, for her part, was deprived of a happy outcome by the Court. Through her guardian she sought to preserve her relationships with both of her fathers but, while the Court warred over which father's rights prevailed, her family structure was forced into a preconceived mold that required that Victoria lose one father. In the end, Michael was written out of the legal narrative of Victoria's life—he was not her father.

Matthew M. Kavanagh, *Rewriting the Legal Family: Beyond Exclusivity to a Care–Based Standard*, 16 Yale J.L. & Feminism 83, 103–04 (2004). Kavanagh proposes a new standard under which an "ethic of care" would be the paradigm in all custody cases, including those involving gay and lesbian families, grandparents, and other types of "familial" relations, such as surrogate parents. *See id.* at 104–14.

C.   THE EXTENDED FAMILY

Troxel v. Granville

Supreme Court of the United States, 2000.
530 U.S. 57, 120 S.Ct. 2054, 147 L.Ed.2d 49.

■ JUSTICE O'CONNOR announced the judgment of the Court and delivered an opinion, in which THE CHIEF JUSTICE, JUSTICE GINSBURG, and JUSTICE BREYER join.

Section 26.10.160(3) of the Revised Code of Washington permits "any person" to petition a superior court for visitation rights "at any time," and authorizes that court to grant such visitation rights whenever "visitation may serve the best interest of the child." Petitioners Jenifer and Gary Troxel petitioned a Washington Superior Court for the right to visit their grandchildren, Isabelle and Natalie Troxel. Respondent Tommie Granville, the mother of Isabelle and Natalie, opposed the petition. The case ultimately reached the Washington Supreme Court, which held that § 26.10.160(3) unconstitutionally interferes with the fundamental right of parents to rear their children.

. . .

Tommie Granville and Brad Troxel shared a relationship that ended in June 1991. The two never married, but they had two daughters, Isabelle and Natalie. Jenifer and Gary Troxel are Brad's parents, and thus the paternal grandparents of Isabelle and Natalie. After Tommie and Brad separated in 1991, Brad lived with his parents and regularly brought his daughters to his parents' home for weekend visitation. Brad committed suicide in May 1993. Although the Troxels at first continued to see Isabelle and Natalie on a regular basis after their son's death, Tommie Granville informed the Troxels in October 1993 that she wished to limit their visitation with her daughters to one short visit per month.

In December 1993, the Troxels commenced the present action by filing, in the Washington Superior Court for Skagit County, a petition to obtain visitation rights with Isabelle and Natalie. The Troxels filed their petition under two Washington statutes, WASH. REV. CODE §§ 26.09.240 and 26.10.160(3) (1994). Only the latter statute is at issue in this case. Section 26.10.160(3) provides: "Any person may petition the court for visitation rights at any time including, but not limited to, custody proceedings. The court may order visitation rights for any person when visitation may serve the best interest of the child whether or not there has been any change of circumstances." At trial, the Troxels requested two weekends of overnight visitation per month and two weeks of visitation each summer. Granville did not oppose visitation altogether, but instead asked the court to order one day of visitation per month with no overnight stay. In 1995, the Superior Court issued an oral ruling and entered a visitation decree ordering visitation one weekend per month, one week during the summer, and four hours on both of the petitioning grandparents' birthdays.

Granville appealed, during which time she married Kelly Wynn. Before addressing the merits of Granville's appeal, the Washington Court of Appeals remanded the case to the Superior Court for entry of written findings of fact and conclusions of law. On remand, the Superior Court found that visitation was in Isabelle and Natalie's best interests:

> The Petitioners [the Troxels] are part of a large, central, loving family, all located in this area, and the Petitioners can provide opportunities for the children in the areas of cousins and music.

> . . . The court took into consideration all factors regarding the best interest of the children and considered all the testimony before it. The children would be benefitted from spending quality time with the Petitioners, provided that that time is balanced with time with the childrens' [sic] nuclear family. The court finds that the childrens' [sic] best interests are served by spending time with their mother and stepfather's other six children.

Approximately nine months after the Superior Court entered its order on remand, Granville's husband formally adopted Isabelle and Natalie.

The Washington Court of Appeals reversed the lower court's visitation order and dismissed the Troxels' petition for visitation, holding that nonparents lack standing to seek visitation under § 26.10.160(3) unless a custody action is pending. In the Court of Appeals' view, that limitation on nonparental visitation actions was "consistent with the constitutional restrictions on state interference with parents' fundamental liberty interest in the care, custody, and management of their children...."

The Washington Supreme Court granted the Troxels' petition for review and, after consolidating their case with two other visitation cases, affirmed. The court disagreed with the Court of Appeals' decision on the statutory issue and found that the plain language of § 26.10.160(3) gave the Troxels standing to seek visitation, irrespective of whether a custody action was pending. The Washington Supreme Court nevertheless agreed with the Court of Appeals' ultimate conclusion that the Troxels could not obtain visitation of Isabelle and Natalie pursuant to § 26.10.160(3). The court rested its decision on the Federal Constitution, holding that § 26.10.160(3) unconstitutionally infringes on the fundamental right of parents to rear their children. In the court's view, there were at least two problems with the nonparental visitation statute. First, according to the Washington Supreme Court, the Constitution permits a State to interfere with the right of parents to rear their children only to prevent harm or potential harm to a child. Section 26.10.160(3) fails that standard because it requires no threshold showing of harm. Second, by allowing " 'any person' to petition for forced visitation of a child at 'any time' with the only requirement being that the visitation serves the best interest of the child," the Washington visitation statute sweeps too broadly. "It is not within the province of the state to make significant decisions concerning the custody of children merely because it could make a 'better' decision." The Washington Supreme Court held that "parents have a right to limit visitation of their children with third persons," and that between parents and judges, "the parents should be the ones to choose whether to expose their children to certain people or ideas." ...

We granted certiorari, 527 U.S. 1069 (1999), and now affirm the judgment.

. . .

The liberty interest at issue in this case—the interest of parents in the care, custody, and control of their children—is perhaps the oldest of the fundamental liberty interests recognized by this Court.

. . .

Section 26.10.160(3), as applied to Granville and her family in this case, unconstitutionally infringes on that fundamental parental right. The Washington nonparental visitation statute is breathtakingly broad. According to the statute's text, "any person may petition the court for visitation rights at any time," and the court may grant such visitation rights whenever "visitation may serve the best interest of the child." § 26.10.160(3). That language effectively permits any third party seeking visitation to subject any decision by a parent concerning visitation of the parent's children to state-court review. Once the visitation petition has been filed in court and the matter is placed before a judge, a parent's decision that visitation would not be in the child's best interest is accorded no deference. Section 26.10.160(3) contains no requirement that a court accord the parent's decision any presumption of validity or any weight whatsoever. Instead, the Washington statute places the best-interest determination solely in the hands of the judge. Should the judge disagree with the parent's estimation of the child's best interests, the judge's view necessarily prevails. Thus, in practical effect, in the State of Washington a court can disregard and overturn any decision by a fit custodial parent concerning visitation whenever a third party affected by the decision files a visitation petition, based solely on the judge's determination of the child's best interests.

. . .

The problem here is not that the Washington Superior Court intervened, but that when it did so, it gave no special weight at all to Granville's determination of her daughters' best interests.

. . .

The judge's comments suggest that he presumed the grandparents' request should be granted unless the children would be "impacted adversely." In effect, the judge placed on Granville, the fit custodial parent, the burden of disproving that visitation would be in the best interest of her daughters. The judge reiterated moments later: "I think [visitation with the Troxels] would be in the best interest of the children and I haven't been shown it is not in [the] best interest of the children."

The decisional framework employed by the Superior Court directly contravened the traditional presumption that a fit parent will act in the best interest of his or her child. In that respect, the court's presumption failed to provide any protection for Granville's fundamental constitutional right to make decisions concerning the rearing of her own daughters.

. . .

In an ideal world, parents might always seek to cultivate the bonds between grandparents and their grandchildren. Needless to say, however, our world is far from perfect, and in it the decision whether such an intergenerational relationship would be beneficial in any specific case is for the parent to make in the first instance. And, if a fit parent's decision of the kind at issue here becomes subject to judicial review, the court must accord at least some special weight to the parent's own determination.

. . .

Because we rest our decision on the sweeping breadth of § 26.10.160(3) and the application of that broad, unlimited power in this case, we do not consider the primary constitutional question passed on by the Washington Supreme Court—whether the Due Process Clause requires all nonparental visitation statutes to include a showing of harm or potential harm to the child as a condition precedent to granting visitation. We do not, and need not, define today the precise scope of the parental due process right in the visitation context.

. . .

■ JUSTICE SCALIA, dissenting.

In my view, a right of parents to direct the upbringing of their children is among the "unalienable Rights" with which the Declaration of Independence proclaims "all Men . . . are endowed by their Creator." And in my view that right is also among the "other [rights] retained by the people" which the Ninth Amendment says the Constitution's enumeration of rights "shall not be construed to deny or disparage." The Declaration of Independence, however, is not a legal prescription conferring powers upon the courts; and the Constitution's refusal to "deny or disparage" other rights is far removed from affirming any one of them, and even farther removed from authorizing judges to identify what they might be, and to enforce the judges' list against laws duly enacted by the people. Consequently, while I would think it entirely compatible with the commitment to representative democracy set forth in the founding documents to argue, in legislative chambers or in electoral campaigns, that the state has *no power* to interfere with parents' authority over the rearing of their children, I do not believe that the power which the Constitution confers upon me *as a judge* entitles me to deny legal effect to laws that (in my view) infringe upon what is (in my view) that unenumerated right.

Only three holdings of this Court rest in whole or in part upon a substantive constitutional right of parents to direct the upbringing of their children—two of them from an era rich in substantive due process holdings that have since been repudiated. *See Meyer v. Nebraska,* 262 U.S. 390, 399 (1923); *Pierce v. Society of Sisters,* 268 U.S. 510, 534–35 (1925); *Wisconsin v. Yoder,* 406 U.S. 205, 232–33 (1972). The sheer diversity of today's opinions persuades me that the theory of unenumerated parental rights underlying these three cases has small claim to *stare decisis* protection. A legal principle that can be thought to produce such diverse outcomes in the relatively simple case before us here is not a legal principle that has induced substantial reliance. While I would not now overrule those earlier cases (that has not been urged), neither would I extend the theory upon which they rested to this new context.

Judicial vindication of "parental rights" under a Constitution that does not even mention them requires (as JUSTICE KENNEDY's opinion rightly points out) not only a judicially crafted definition of parents, but also—unless, as no one believes, the parental rights are to be absolute—judicially approved assessments of "harm to the child" and judicially defined gradations of other persons (grandparents, extended family, adoptive family in an adoption later found to be invalid, long-term guardians, etc.) who may have some claim against the wishes of the parents. If we embrace this unenumerated right, I think it obvious—whether we affirm or reverse the judgment here, or remand as JUSTICE STEVENS or JUSTICE KENNEDY would do—that we will be ushering in a new regime of judicially prescribed, and federally prescribed, family law. I have no reason to believe that federal judges will be better at this than state legislatures; and state legislatures have the great advantages of doing harm in a more circumscribed area, of being able to correct their mistakes in a flash, and of being removable by the people.

For these reasons, I would reverse the judgment below.

■ JUSTICE KENNEDY, dissenting.

. . .

Turning to the question whether harm to the child must be the controlling standard in every visitation proceeding, there is a beginning point that commands general, perhaps unanimous, agreement in our separate opinions: As our case law has developed, the custodial parent has a constitutional right to determine, without undue interference by the state, how best to raise, nurture, and educate the child. The parental right stems from the liberty protected by the Due Process Clause of the Fourteenth Amendment. . . .

The State Supreme Court sought to give content to the parent's right by announcing a categorical rule that third parties who seek visitation must always prove the denial of visitation would harm the child. . . .

While it might be argued as an abstract matter that in some sense the child is always harmed if his or her best interests are not considered, the law of domestic relations, as it has evolved to this point, treats as distinct the two standards, one harm to the child and the other the best interests of the child. The judgment of the Supreme Court of Washington rests on that assumption, and I, too, shall assume that there are real and consequential differences between the two standards.

On the question whether one standard must always take precedence over the other in order to protect the right of the parent or parents, "our Nation's history, legal traditions, and practices" do not give us clear or definitive answers. *Washington v. Glucksberg*, 521 U.S. 702, 721 (1997). The consensus among courts and commentators is that at least through the 19th century there was no legal right of visitation; court-ordered visitation appears to be a 20th–century phenomenon. . . .

To say that third parties have had no historical right to petition for visitation does not necessarily imply, as the Supreme Court of Washington concluded, that a parent has a constitutional right to prevent visitation in all cases not involving harm. . . . The State Supreme Court's conclusion that the Constitution forbids the application of the best interests of the child standard in any visitation proceeding, however, appears to rest upon assumptions the Constitution does not require.

My principal concern is that the holding seems to proceed from the assumption that the parent or parents who resist visitation have always been the child's primary caregivers and that the third parties who seek visitation have no legitimate and established relationship with the child. That idea, in turn, appears influenced by the concept that the conventional nuclear family ought to establish the visitation standard for every domestic relations case. As we all know, this is simply not the structure or prevailing condition in many households. For many boys and girls a traditional family with two or even one permanent and caring parent is simply not the reality of their childhood. This may be so whether their childhood has been marked by tragedy or filled with considerable happiness and fulfillment.

Cases are sure to arise—perhaps a substantial number of cases—in which a third party, by acting in a caregiving role over a significant period of time, has developed a relationship with a child which is not necessarily subject to absolute parental veto. Some pre-existing relationships, then, serve to identify persons who have a strong attachment to the child with the concomitant motivation to act in a responsible way to ensure the child's welfare. As the State Supreme Court was correct to acknowledge, those relationships can be so enduring that "in certain circumstances where a child has enjoyed a substantial relationship with a third person, arbitrarily depriving the child of the relationship could cause severe psychological harm to the child," and harm to the adult may also ensue. In the design and elaboration of their visitation laws, States may be entitled to consider that certain relationships are such that to avoid the risk of harm, a best interests standard can be employed by their domestic relations courts in some circumstances.

. . .

In light of the inconclusive historical record and case law, as well as the almost universal adoption of the best interests standard for visitation disputes, I would be hard pressed to conclude the right to be free of such review in all cases is itself " 'implicit in the concept of ordered liberty.' " In my view, it would be more appropriate to conclude that the constitutionality of the application of the best interests standard depends on more specific factors. In short, a fit parent's right vis-a-vis a complete stranger is one thing; her right vis-a-vis another parent or a *de facto* parent may be another. The protection the Constitution requires, then, must be elaborated with care, using the discipline and instruction of the case law system. We must keep in mind that family courts in the fifty States confront these factual variations each day, and are best situated to consider the unpredictable, yet inevitable, issues that arise.

. . .

In my view the judgment under review should be vacated and the case remanded for further proceedings.

NOTE

Consider Kristine L. Roberts, *State Supreme Court Applications of Troxel v. Granville and the Courts' Reluctance to Declare Grandparent Visitation Statutes Unconstitutional*, 41 Fam. Ct. Rev. 14, 15 (2003):

> [Perhaps it should not be surprising, then, that the state courts that have examined nonparent visitation statutes since the *Troxel* decision] have been [similarly] reluctant to declare these statutes unconstitutional. For the most part . . . state courts either have endeavored to interpret their states' statutes to be facially constitutional or have held that specific applications of the statutes failed to meet the *Troxel* standard. To reach these results, some courts have construed the statutes to be stricter than written. Other courts have emphasized the ways in which their states' laws are distinguishable from the broadly sweeping Washington statute.

The element of a grandparent visitation scheme most often deemed essential to constitutionality is the presumption that a fit parent's decision concerning visitation is in the best interest of the child. *See, e.g., Santi v. Santi*, 633 N.W.2d 312 (Iowa 2001); *State Department of Social and Rehabilitation Services v. Paillet*, 16 P.3d 962 (Kan. 2001); *Lulay v. Lulay*, 739 N.E.2d 521 (Ill. 2000).

D. ADOPTION

1.   HISTORICAL BACKGROUND

Jamil Zainaldin, *The Emergence of a Modern American Family Law: Child Custody, Adoption, and the Courts*, 1796–1851

73 Nw. U. L. Rev. 1038, 1041–45 (1979).

Like many aspects of family law, the status of adoption can be traced back through early civilization. Adoption existed in ancient Greece and Rome, in portions of continental Europe that "received" Roman law in the fifteenth century, in the Middle East, in Asia, and in the tribal societies of Africa and Oceania. Adoption in history ordinarily served one or more purposes: preventing the extinction of a bloodline, preserving a sacred descent group, facilitating the generational transfer of a patrimony, providing for ancestral worship, or mending the ties between factious clans or tribes. In each case, the adoption of an individual, most often an adult male, fulfilled some kin, religious, or communal requirement.

Yet, unlike most historical phenomena, the first instance of departure from the traditional model of adoption can be isolated by location, day, and year. On April 2, 1847, the Massachusetts House of Representatives ordered that the Committee on the Judiciary consider the "expediency of providing by law for the adoption of children." On May 13, 1851, the Committee reported to the House "A Bill for the Adoption of Children." There seems to have been little or no opposition. Eleven days later the Massachusetts legislature passed the first general "Act to Provide for the Adoption of Children" in America.[9]

The Massachusetts adoption statute of 1851 was the first *modern* adoption law in history. It is notable for two reasons. First, it contradicted the most fundamental principles of English domestic relations law, and overruled centuries of English precedent and legislation which prohibited the absolute, permanent, and voluntary transfer of parental power to third persons. Second, the traditional status of adoption allocated benefits between the giver and the taker, while the Massachusetts statute distinguished the adoptee as the prime beneficiary. The heart of the adoption transaction became the judicially monitored transfer of rights with the due regard for the *welfare of the child* and the *parental qualifications* of the adopters.

Within the next twenty-five years, more than a score of states would enact some form of adoption law, and in most cases the Massachusetts statute served as the model. Strangely, it would seem, the passage of the first Massachusetts act attracted little public attention. Little or no debate over the issue occurred in the legislature, apparently no social reform movements advocated passage of the law, and, even when the law did appear, few newspapers bothered to take note of the event. And for several years after the passage of the statute, few adopters took advantage of the law. There is, then, no clear explanation for why the legislature passed the law when it did. Nor at first glance would there seem to be any explanation for the casual reception accorded such an apparently radical statute.

The new law may have been part of the larger legislative trend of substituting private enactments with general statutes. Private laws granting divorce, legitimacy, incorporation, and change of name were becoming particularly cumbersome in the 1840s. And there is ample evidence that children throughout the United States were being "adopted" through private acts, especially those concerning change of name. . . .

Just why the Massachusetts legislature moved in 1851 may never be known. Perhaps all of these reasons prompted the lawmakers to action. At once they endeavored to protect the child and to endow his standing in the family with status, while conferring upon adopters the rights and duties of

---

9. MASS. REV. STAT. ch. 324 (Supp. 1851). Under the novel 1851 Act, child adoption was to proceed by petition in the probate branch of the county court. The petitioners were required to notify and receive the consent of the natural parents to the adoption. If the child's parents or kin were not alive or could not be found, the judge was empowered to appoint some "discreet and suitable person" to act in the proceedings as the child's next friend. If satisfied that the adopters were of "sufficient ability to bring up the child, and furnish suitable nurture and education, having reference to the degree and condition of its parents, and that it is fit and proper that such adoption should take effect," the statute authorized the judge to issue a decree of adoption. The child was to stand toward the adopters as if born to them "in lawful wedlock" for the purposes of legitimacy, custody, support, obedience, inheritance, "and all other legal consequences and incidents of the natural relation of parents and children." All reciprocal rights and obligations between the child and the natural parents were terminated.

parents. The discretionary proceeding in the probate court was perceived as the soundest, most efficient method for effecting adoption.

2.   TYPES OF ADOPTION

Adoption creates a new, legally-recognized parent-child relationship. The child's birth parents must consent to the adoption unless they have been deemed unfit or certain other exceptions apply. In most, although not all, cases, adoption terminates all pre-existing parental rights.

There are two basic types of adoption: agency adoption and private adoption. Agency adoption involves either a governmental agency or an organization that has been licensed by the government. The latter often are affiliated with churches or other non-governmental social service entities.

In an agency adoption, the birth parents typically relinquish all parental rights to the agency, including the right to place the child themselves for adoption. When the surrender is to a public agency, the child may be placed in foster care for some period of time until suitable adoptive parents are found. The agency investigates potential adoptive parents and maintains a file to which it refers when a child becomes available to adopt. Most agency placements involve children older than infants and children with special needs such as physical disabilities and whose adoption may entitle the adoptive parents to financial assistance from the state.

In private adoptions, the birth parents make a child available to the adoptive parents, often with the aid of an intermediary. In most, but not all, states these intermediaries must be licensed. The major difference between private and agency adoptions is that in private adoptions, birth parents are more involved in selection of the adoptive parents. Most adoptions of infants are private adoptions.

As with agency adoptions, the adoptive parents in a private adoption generally must formalize the adoption in a court proceeding. As part of that process, the state must conduct an investigation into the suitability of the adoptive parents. Some observers suggest, however, that agency home study investigations in private placements are not as thorough as those conducted in agency adoptions.

a.   AGENCY ADOPTION

Vela v. Marywood

Court of Appeals of Texas, 2000.
17 S.W.3d 750.

■ LEE YEAKEL, J.

This case presents the question of how forthright a licensed child-placing agency must be with an unmarried, expectant mother who seeks its counsel prior to the birth of her child. The child's mother, Corina Vela, is an exemplary young woman who made a mistake. The district court held that the law compels the compounding of her error, terminated her parental rights, and appointed appellee Marywood managing conservator of her child. Corina appeals the district-court judgment.

. . .

In February 1998, this pregnant young woman sought counseling services from Marywood, a licensed child-placing agency. She met with a

Marywood counselor, Aundra Moore, several times in early March.[2] During these meetings, Corina informed Moore that she wanted to place her child for adoption. In Moore's view, Corina was adamant that her child have a future, be in a two-parent family, be safe, and have the security of a family. Moore observed that Corina wanted "the best for her child" and felt that adoption "was the place to go with that." Corina indicated to Moore that her parents could help but she didn't want to burden them. Moore told Corina that "the adoption process is very much at [Corina's] discretion" and that Corina's "wishes and requests" as to what type of family she would place her child with and what type of relationship she would have with her child after adoption would be "considered." At a meeting on March 16, Corina reported to Moore that she had bonded with her unborn child, and Moore noted that Corina "may be grasping the difficulty of her decision."

On March 25, Corina and Moore discussed what Marywood terms an "open adoption," a process by which the birth mother expresses her criteria for adoptive parents.... She also told Moore that "she wanted to visit with the child after the adoption." Moore informed Corina that "her relationship with the adoptive family would establish what type of ongoing relationship [with her child] she would have."

Moore first showed Corina an "Affidavit of Voluntary Relinquishment of Parental Rights" (the "relinquishment affidavit") on March 30.[4] Moore did not discuss the relinquishment affidavit with Corina and did not explain the meaning of the term "irrevocable"; rather, Moore simply "showed her the form" but did not give her a copy to take with her to study....

Corina selected an adoptive couple at her next counseling session with Moore and had a face-to-face meeting with them on April 8. The meeting lasted about an hour. The prospective adoptive parents met all of Corina's criteria and indicated their willingness to comply with post-adoption visits. Throughout Corina's counseling sessions, she and Moore discussed a "sharing plan," a standard practice of Marywood. A sharing plan ostensibly allows the birth mother to select the adoptive family, visit her child on a regular

---

2. Moore describes herself as "a maternity counselor ... responsible for working with birth parents and their families ... in finding options for an unplanned pregnancy."

4. In pertinent part, the relinquishment affidavit reads:

It is in the best interest of my child that the child be placed for adoption in a suitable home by an agency licensed by the Texas Department of Protective and Regulatory Services to place children for adoption. I therefore designate MARYWOOD, 510 West 26th Street, Austin, Texas, 78705 as managing conservator of the child. I have been informed of my parental rights, powers, duties and privileges. I freely, voluntarily, and permanently give and relinquish to the agency all my parental rights, privileges, powers and duties. I consent to the placement of the child for adoption by this agency.

I fully understand that a lawsuit will be promptly filed in the 126th District Court of Travis County, Texas, to terminate forever the parent-child relationship between me and my child. Termination of the parent-child relationship between me and my child is in the best interest of the child. I understand that by executing this affidavit, I make this termination possible. With this in mind, I hereby declare that this affidavit of relinquishment of parental rights is and shall be final, permanent, and irrevocable. I FULLY UNDERSTAND THAT IF I CHANGE MY MIND AT ANY TIME, I CAN NEVER FORCE THE AGENCY TO DESTROY, REVOKE, OR RETURN THIS AFFIDAVIT AND THAT I CANNOT TAKE BACK OR UNDO THIS AFFIDAVIT IN ANY WAY.

It is in the best interest of my child that this be my last parental act and deed. Not wishing to appear or be cited in the termination suit, I hereby waive the right to issuance, service and return of all process in any suit to terminate the parent-child relationship between me and the child. I agree to termination of the parent-child relationship between the child and me without further notice to me. I FULLY UNDERSTAND THAT I WILL NOT BE INFORMED FURTHER ABOUT THIS SUIT.

basis after the adoption, and exchange letters and pictures. The adoptive parents are aware of the plan prior to placement and agree in writing with Marywood to conform to this arrangement. Significantly, the birth mother does not sign this agreement; thus, neither Marywood nor the adoptive parents enter into any agreement with the birth mother. Marywood admits that aside from advocating that the adoptive parents abide by the plan, Marywood can do nothing if the adoptive parents decide, post-adoption, to disregard it. In fact, the executive director of Marywood admits that the sharing plan is an "empty promise." Clearly, the birth mother has no power to enforce such an agreement. Marywood never discussed the unenforceability of the sharing plan with Corina.

At Corina's last meeting with Moore before her child's birth, they discussed . . . the relinquishment affidavit with Corina. Moore read the affidavit to Corina and "talked about each paragraph, what each paragraph means, what it is saying." Moore also asked Corina if she had any questions. Although Moore did not first explain the word "irrevocable," she asked Corina if she knew what it meant. Corina replied that once the relinquishment is signed, it cannot be undone. Moore confirmed that meaning and also told Corina that once she signed the affidavit, she could not "take it back, undo it, or change it."

Corina gave birth to a son on April 24. Moore met with Corina at the hospital on April 26, and Corina signed a temporary foster-care request. Moore told Corina that she "would always be able to visit her baby" and that her baby would always know that Corina was his mother. Corina cried throughout the one-and-one-half-hour visit. Moore scheduled a subsequent meeting with Corina to complete the adoption process. The child was placed in foster care on April 27.

On April 28, Corina and her parents visited Marywood. Before the meeting, Corina was not aware that she was to sign the relinquishment affidavit then and was undecided as to whether she wanted to sign it. During the two-hour meeting, Corina, her parents, and Moore read and discussed the relinquishment affidavit in detail. Eventually, Corina signed the affidavit. During the meeting, and before Corina signed the relinquishment affidavit, Moore told Corina that she would "always be that child's birth mother and that with her sharing plan that she had with the adoptive family that she would have an opportunity to be in that child's life forever"; that she would "always have a relationship with [the adoptive] family and with [her] child"; that requests she made of the adoptive family would be "respected"; that the baby would have "two mothers," "both of whom would have input into his life"; that Corina "would be able to see her son grow up"; and that the birth family would be like the child's extended family. Corina specifically asked what the agency could do to guarantee that she would have continual, post-adoptive visits with the child. Moore responded by "assuring her that . . . the adoptive family has an adoption worker working with them and that they would encourage them to respect what she wished for in terms . . . of sharing and visits. And during their . . . face-to-face visit and even after that, they said that they would respect her wishes in . . . having that sharing plan." Moore repeated to Corina that she would always be a part of the baby's life. According to Corina and her mother, these promises are what convinced Corina to sign the relinquishment affidavit; the promises were "the only reason she signed."

[C]orina was crying when she signed the affidavit, but Moore testified that "it's very common to have tears." Moore asked Corina if signing the relinquishment affidavit "was what she wanted to do" and informed Corina that once she signed it, she "couldn't undo or take it back." Moore never told Corina that signing the relinquishment affidavit meant that she would "never have any legal rights to see [her] child." According to Corina, Moore told her that she would only be "giving up [her] guardianship of [the child]." Corina understood this to mean that she would not be the one "taking care of him and raising him." Corina was not aware and no one informed her that she could have signed a second foster-care agreement to allow herself more time to make the final decision. Moore was the only person who explained the relinquishment affidavit to Corina, and she never told Corina that she could seek legal counsel or another person's opinion. Marywood never revealed to Corina that the relinquishment affidavit could nullify the sharing plan that she believed would allow her a continuing role in her child's life. It is significant that the relinquishment affidavit was never mentioned to Corina until after she and Marywood had devised a sharing plan satisfactory to her. From that point forward, all of Corina's actions and decisions were founded on her belief in and reliance on the sharing plan.

The following day, April 29, Corina asked to visit her child. The same day Marywood filed a petition to terminate Corina's parental rights. On May 1, Corina was allowed to visit her son for one hour at Marywood. Later that day, Corina called Marywood. Exactly what was said in that phone call is disputed. Moore claims that although Corina was crying, in emotional pain, and "having a hard time," Corina never indicated that she wanted to terminate the adoption process. Corina claims that she told Moore that she "wanted [her] baby back" and that she "changed [her] mind." She asked if there was anything she could do, including hiring an attorney. Moore responded that there was nothing that could be done. Corina's mother also called on the afternoon of May 1 and according to Moore, asked if they "could undo the papers" because her daughter was in so much pain. Moore told Corina's mother that the relinquishment was "irrevocable and that it is signed and that there is no way to undo the document." Moore stated that there was nothing "in her conversation with Corina's mother on May 1st that would [have led her] to believe that Corina wanted the baby back" and that the conversation was "about documents." Yet Moore testified at trial that had Marywood known before the child was placed with the adoptive parents that Corina wanted to keep him, Marywood would have returned the child to Corina.

On May 12, an associate judge recommended termination of Corina's parental rights. In spite of the earlier conversations between Marywood, Corina, and Corina's mother, Marywood placed Corina's child with the prospective adoptive parents the day after the associate judge's decision. Corina immediately gave notice that she was appealing the associate judge's termination recommendation to the district court. . . . Even in the face of this clear and immediate assertion that Corina did not want to give up her child, Marywood continued its efforts to terminate Corina's parental rights.

On June 8, the district court conducted a *de novo* trial. . . . After hearing this testimony, the district court terminated Corina's parental rights and appointed Marywood managing conservator.

Corina brings this appeal, arguing that (1) there was not clear and convincing evidence that she knowingly and voluntarily executed the relinquishment affidavit, and in fact the evidence shows that she did *not* execute it voluntarily; and (2) there was not clear and convincing evidence that termination of Corina's parental rights was in the best interest of the child....

. . .

The Family Code provides that the court may order termination of the parent-child relationship if the court finds by clear and convincing evidence ... that the parent has ... executed before or after the suit is filed an unrevoked or irrevocable affidavit of relinquishment of parental rights as provided in this chapter; ...

. . .

[T]ermination proceedings must be strictly scrutinized, and termination statutes are strictly construed in favor of the parent. This oft-chanted mantra emphasizes that we must exercise the utmost care in reviewing the termination of parental rights to be certain that the child's interests are best served and that the parent's rights are acknowledged and protected.

It is undisputed that Marywood proved by clear and convincing evidence that the relinquishment affidavit was executed in conformity with section 161.001 of the Family Code. However, in her first issue, Corina argues that "no rational trier of fact could find ... that the Affidavit of Relinquishment was executed voluntarily and knowingly, rather than as the result of misrepresentation, fraud, overreaching, and coercion."

. . .

[A]t common law, the word "fraud" refers to an act, omission, or concealment in breach of a legal duty, trust, or confidence justly imposed, when the breach causes injury to another or the taking of an undue and unconscientious advantage.

. . .

Marywood, by its own admission, is more than an adoption agency. It provides extensive parental-counseling services and advertises these services to the public. Moore testified that she is given the discretion to counsel "openly, objectively, and honestly." Corina, in seeking counseling from Marywood, was reasonably entitled to rely fully and unconditionally on Marywood's representations. We hold that Marywood owed Corina a duty of complete disclosure when discussing adoption procedures, including any proposed post-adoption plan. Complete disclosure encompassed the obligation to tell Corina the entire truth about the ramifications of the sharing plan she had chosen with Marywood's help and to make her fully aware that it lacked legally binding effect. Marywood's duty springs from two sources. First, when Marywood made a partial disclosure to Corina about the post-adoption plan, it assumed the duty to tell the whole truth.... Second, the evidence conclusively establishes that Corina placed special confidence in Moore, who by virtue of the counseling relationship occupied a position of superiority and influence on behalf of Marywood; thus, Moore and Marywood became bound, in equity and good conscience, to act in good faith and with due regard to Corina's interests....

[M]arywood argues that it discharged any duty it owed Corina and that there is ample evidence that Corina fully understood the relinquishment affidavit and wanted to proceed with the adoption. Marywood points out that Moore read and explained the relinquishment affidavit to Corina on three separate occasions; that Corina and her mother both testified that Corina fully understood the relinquishment affidavit when she signed it; that the relinquishment affidavit itself says it was voluntary; and that after Marywood discussed with Corina her option to parent, Corina still wanted to place the child for adoption.

Although the face of the affidavit reflects it was signed knowingly and voluntarily, we must consider the surrounding circumstances to determine if Corina's signature on the document was procured by misrepresentation, fraud, or the like.... Corina neither signed nor understood the relinquishment affidavit in a vacuum. She signed and understood it in the context of and in reliance on the post-adoption plan that she and Marywood created, a plan that Marywood now admits is an "empty promise." The evidence conclusively establishes that Corina wanted to proceed with the adoption *only* if she could have post-adoption visits with her child; there is no evidence to the contrary.

There is no evidence in the record, however, that Corina was ever told that the post-adoption plan could not be legally enforced. Marywood's words to Corina were at worst deceptive and at best vague.... [I]n counseling Corina, Moore carefully selected her words and minced her explanation of the sharing plan with the result that Corina understood one thing while Moore meant another. Whether the incomplete disclosure was deliberate or inadvertent, it does not satisfy the duty of full disclosure that Marywood owed Corina.

. . .

[W]e hold that there is no evidence of probative value that supports the district court's finding that Corina voluntarily executed the relinquishment affidavit. Corina has surmounted the first hurdle.

We turn our attention now to [the] second hurdle: Has Corina established as a matter of law that the relinquishment affidavit was procured by fraud, coercion, overreaching, or misrepresentation?

We find no evidence in the record that Corina was compelled by force or threat to sign the relinquishment affidavit. We overrule Corina's issue to the extent that it complains that the affidavit was procured by coercion.

However, we find conclusive evidence in the record that the relinquishment affidavit was wrongfully procured. Considering only Marywood's version of events, we conclude as a matter of law that its statements and omissions to Corina constituted misrepresentation, fraud, or overreaching. Marywood admits that it told Corina that "with her sharing plan ... she would have an opportunity to be in that child's life forever"; that she would "always have a relationship with [the adoptive] family and with [her] child"; that requests she made of the adoptive family would be "respected"; that the baby would have "two mothers," "both of whom would have input into his life"; and that Corina "would be able to see her son grow up." Marywood never told Corina that she would not have any legal right to see her child after she signed the relinquishment affidavit, and even when Corina directly asked if Marywood could guarantee post-adoption visits, Marywood failed to give her a complete answer. Marywood's statements [were] misleading and stop short of complete disclosure. They are half-truths that would lead a reasonable person in Corina's circumstance to believe that she had a continuing right to see her child according to the terms of the sharing plan.... It is undisputed that Corina sought counseling from Marywood to aid her in the difficult decision of whether to keep her child. She was a young woman faced with a life-changing situation. She found comfort in and placed reliance on Marywood's counseling. We need not and do not determine whether Marywood deliberately misled Corina. At a minimum, Marywood's advice and counsel was incomplete. We hold that Corina conclusively established that the relinquishment affidavit was procured by misrepresentation, fraud, or overreaching and therefore was not voluntarily signed. We sustain Corina's first issue and hold that the relinquishment affidavit is void as a matter of law.

.   .   .

Because we hold that the evidence conclusively establishes that Corina did not voluntarily sign the relinquishment affidavit, we reverse the district court's judgment and render judgment in favor of Corina that her parental rights are not terminated.

UNIFORM ADOPTION ACT

Section 2–405.   Procedure for Execution of Consent or Relinquishment

.   .   .

(c) A parent who is a minor is competent to execute a consent or relinquishment if the parent has had access to counseling and has had the advice of a lawyer who is not representing an adoptive parent or the agency to which the parent's child is relinquished.

(d) An individual before whom a consent or relinquishment is signed or confirmed . . . shall certify in writing that he or she orally explained the contents and consequences of the consent or relinquishment, and to the best of his or her knowledge or belief, the individual executing the consent or relinquishment:

> (1) read or was read the consent or relinquishment and understood it;
>
> (2) signed the consent or relinquishment voluntarily and received or was offered a copy of it;
>
> .   .   .
>
> (4) received or was offered counseling services and information about adoption; and
>
> (5) if a parent who is a minor, was advised by a lawyer who is not representing an adoptive parent or the agency to which the parent's child is being relinquished, or, if an adult, was informed of the right to have a lawyer who is not representing an adoptive parent or an agency to which the parent's child is being relinquished.

Section 2–408. Revocation of Consent.

(a) In a direct placement of a minor for adoption by a parent or guardian, a consent is revoked if:

> (1) within 192 hours after the birth of the minor, a parent who executed the consent notifies in writing the prospective adoptive parent, or the adoptive parent's lawyer, that the parent revokes the consent, or the parent complies with any other instructions for revocation specified in the consent; or
>
> (2) the individual who executed the consent and the prospective adoptive parent named or described in the consent agree to its revocation.

(b) In a direct placement of a minor for adoption by a parent or guardian, the court shall set aside the consent if the individual who executed the consent establishes:

> (1) by clear and convincing evidence, before a decree of adoption is issued, that the consent was obtained by fraud or duress;

> . . .

(c) If the consent of an individual who had legal and physical custody of a minor when the minor was placed for adoption or when the consent was executed is revoked, the prospective adoptive parent shall immediately return the minor to the individual's custody and move to dismiss a proceeding for adoption or termination of the individual's parental relationship to the minor. If the minor is not returned immediately, the individual may petition the court named in the consent for appropriate relief. The court shall hear the petition expeditiously.

(d) If the consent of an individual who had legal and physical custody of a minor when the minor was placed for adoption or the consent was executed is set aside under subsection (b)(1), the court shall order the return of the minor to the custody of the individual and dismiss a proceeding for adoption.

b. INDEPENDENT ADOPTION

In re J.M.P.

Supreme Court of Louisiana, 1988.
528 So.2d 1002.

■ DENNIS, J.

The facts of this case follow a sadly familiar pattern. Dawn B., an eighteen year old unmarried woman, was employed in a grocery store but remained economically dependent on her mother and stepfather, Mr. & Mrs. B., with whom she resided. She became pregnant but concealed the fact from her mother for six months. At that time, with her mother's financial assistance, she traveled by bus from her home in Zachary to consult with a doctor at an abortion clinic in Metairie. The doctor informed her that her pregnancy was too far into its term to permit an abortion. Instead, he gave her the name and phone number of an anti-abortionist attorney, Perez, who would arrange for the placement of the child for private adoption free of charge. When she returned home Dawn placed a call to Perez but had to leave her number because he was out. When Perez returned the call, Dawn's mother, Mrs. B., answered and asked him to come to Zachary to discuss surrendering the expected child for private adoption. A few days later, Perez met with Dawn and Mr. and Mrs. B. in their home and explained what he was able to do: He could find a suitable couple to adopt the baby. He would have the couple pay the hospital, OBGYN, pediatrician, anesthesiologist, and drug bills. He explained that he would not charge a fee to them or the adoptive parents because his only interest was his personal cause of preventing abortions. Everything would be handled through him confidentially so that the identities of the two families would not be disclosed to each other. He told Dawn that she could change her mind and reclaim her child at any time up until the act of surrender was signed. Dawn, her mother and her stepfather agreed to the arrangement and asked him to proceed.

Between that meeting and the birth of the child Perez said he talked with Dawn on numerous occasions over the phone. On these occasions she called him to see if checks had been mailed for drug bills that she had sent him. During this period she gave him no indication of changing her mind with respect to the adoption.

After the birth of the child on November 30, 1985, Mr. Perez met with Dawn and Mr. & Mrs. B. at the hospital. Perez testified that he reminded them that his only interest was in seeing that the baby was born and told them that he would leave immediately if they wanted to keep the child. Dawn appeared to be sad about giving up the child, but this was not unusual, he said. At his request, she readily signed the hospital release form giving him permission to take the baby from the premises. Without any objection from Dawn he removed the baby from the hospital and took it to the prospective adoptive parents in Houma.

A week later, on December 7, 1985, Perez returned to Mr. & Mrs. B.'s house in Zachary to have Dawn execute the act of surrender. He brought along his law partner, Roberts, to act as Dawn's attorney and to advise her of her rights. Perez and the parents stepped out on the porch while Roberts and Dawn conferred in the house. Dawn testified that Roberts read the act of surrender to her, and that she did not ask any questions. She said that she told him to change the child's name in the act, and he said that he would do so later. The act of surrender which Dawn signed before a notary and two witnesses after conferring with Roberts, declares that it was fully explained to her by the attorney and that she understood she was surrendering the child for adoption and terminating her rights as a parent of the child. . . .

While they were on the porch, Perez again informed Mrs. B. that Dawn could still change her mind and he offered to undertake the six hour round trip to fetch the child if Dawn did not want to sign the act of surrender. Mrs. B. replied that Dawn would like to keep the child but that the only way she could raise it would be on welfare and that, since she, Mrs. B., had already raised five children, she was not going to raise another. Perez testified that he did not interpret this remark as an indication that Dawn had changed her mind.

After the act of surrender was signed, Perez continued to receive medical bills and calls about their payment from Dawn. Sometime prior to December 30, 1985, however, he received a letter from her revoking her consent to the adoption.[10]

The testimony of Dawn, Mrs. B. and Mr. B. reveals that the young natural mother signed the act and gave up her child although she knew that she had a right to refrain from doing so. Further, the record shows she surrendered the child not because of any improper act or omission by Perez or Roberts but primarily because she did not wish to undertake the hardship of caring for the child outside of her home and without her mother's assistance.

Dawn testified that early on the morning that the act of surrender was executed her mother and stepfather told her that if she refused to sign the instrument she could not bring the baby into their house. She expressed how this affected her decision to sign the act in several ways: she signed because it was what her mother wanted; her mother wanted her to start a new life. She couldn't bring the baby into the house and she had nowhere else to go with

---

10. The parties stipulated that the revocation was accomplished within the 30 day statutory period.

the baby. Although she could have gone to stay with her sister in Indiana, she would have had nowhere to go with the baby for the two days it would take for her to receive transportation fare from her sister or father in Indiana. This last explanation was inconsistent with other portions of her testimony in which she admitted that she had saved an unspecified sum of money before her child was born.

Dawn contradicted Perez on one point saying that he never told her that she had the right to refuse to surrender and reclaim her child. This disagreement is, however, without consequence because her testimony and that of her parents makes it clear that she fully understood her dilemma: she could either sign the act and lose her child or refuse to sign, keep her child, and lose her home and her mother's support.

Mr. & Mrs. B. admitted that they had caused Dawn to sign the act of surrender by telling her that she could not bring the child home. They testified that they had experienced a change of heart because of the suffering Dawn had endured, that they regretted their actions which had been intended only for her own welfare, and that they now stood ready to support Dawn financially and in every other way should she recover custody of the child.

Mrs. B. testified that after Perez received Dawn's revocation of consent he telephoned her and said that she and her husband would probably be "sued for financial responsibility." She testified that she had told Dawn about this conversation. Since the communication occurred after Dawn had signed the act of surrender and had revoked her consent, however, it is clear that this message could have had no effect upon her consent to surrender the child for adoption. Moreover, Perez testified several times that he had not threatened or pressured Dawn in any way.

At the conclusion of the hearing on the issue of the validity of the surrender, the trial judge ruled that because Perez was not acting as the adoptive parents' attorney, there was no conflict with his law partner's representation of Dawn; that Roberts was Dawn's attorney and that he provided her with adequate representation; that there was no coercion on the part of Perez or the adoptive parents; and that the pressure put on Dawn by her parents was not the type of coercion which would cause the act of surrender to be null and void. Therefore, the trial court concluded that the act of surrender was valid. Immediately after the trial judge's ruling, the hearing as to the best interests of the child was held.

James P., the adoptive father, testified that he had been married for approximately ten years to Laura P. and that they had a two and a half year old girl whom they had adopted. He further testified that he was a high school graduate, had attended trade school for two and a half years and had over the years attended schools in connection with his employment. In relation to his job, he said that he had been a mechanic for Halliburton for nearly ten years, earned about $41,000 a year, had around $44,000 in a profit sharing plan with Halliburton, that he rarely travels due to his work, and that he got three weeks of vacation every year. He also stated that he and his wife owned their four bedroom home that they only had $5,000 left to pay on it, that he owned three automobiles, a small boat and a three wheel motorcycle. He added that he had recently borrowed $10,000 to build a barn type structure in his backyard. According to him, they have had the child since December 7, 1985, she sleeps with a heart and respiratory monitor because she has been identified as a candidate for crib death, his wife takes care of the child during the day, and the child had developed an attachment to them.

Mr. P. testified that the child "responds" well to him and is "close" to his wife. However, in his explanation of these terms he spoke only of "starting to turn over and goo and laugh" and of physical resemblances. On the other hand, he did testify that the child stops crying more readily when picked up by his wife than by him.

Laura P. testified that she is a thirty year old high school graduate with two semesters at Nicholls State University in accounting and that she was a homemaker. She additionally testified that the child was doing fine, that the child's medical problem was being taken care of, that the child slept in their room with them, and that they had decided to adopt no more children. She testified that the child is responding to her "real good", that the child recognizes her, and that the child is progressing as well as their older adopted daughter.

Dawn stated that she was an eighteen year old high school graduate and that she worked at Winn Dixie about thirty-six hours a week making $110 a week. In response to a question about how she intended to care for the child, she answered that her parents had agreed to help take care of the baby both financially and by babysitting when she was not there, that someone would always be with the child, and that she was prepared to continue the precautions taken due to the child's medical condition. She also testified that she intended to improve her job situation by continuing her education, that she intended to pay the P.s back for the medical expenses they incurred, and that the father of the child, who was in Indiana, had agreed to help her out financially. She, however, admitted that she did not have any idea of how much day care, insurance, food or diapers for the baby would cost. In conclusion, Dawn said she loved the child very much and that she thought she would be able to raise the child responsibly.

Dawn's mother testified that she had raised five children, that she and her husband were willing and able to support Dawn and the baby financially, and that they would add Dawn and the child to their insurance. She added that she would do whatever was necessary to provide for the child's medical problems.

The trial court found that the adoption was in the child's best interest and entered an interlocutory decree of adoption. In his reasons for judgment the judge found it important that the P.s owned a large home on which they owed only $5,000, that James P., the main wage earner, made over $40,000 a year and had substantial savings, and that the P.s could provide the child a traditional family within which she could grow. He also thought it important that Dawn had originally sought an abortion, that she earned only minimum wage, that she was a single, working mother, who would have to rely on her parent's aid in raising the child and that the child would be raised in a trailer. In concluding that it would be in the best interests of the child to grant the adoption, the judge found that Dawn, as an unmarried eighteen year old, could not offer the child the stable and financially secure family unit the P.s could, and that the P.s were sincerely committed to providing for the welfare of the child and that they could offer the child a stable, supportive, and loving family unit. Dawn appealed the trial court's decision to the Court of Appeal, First Circuit, which affirmed for the reasons assigned by the trial court.

We granted Dawn's application for a writ of certiorari. . . .

ACT OF SURRENDER

The Private Adoption Act of 1979 applicable to this case provides that a parent of either a natural or legitimate child may execute a voluntary surrender of custody of the child for private adoption. LA. REV. STAT. 9:422.3 . . .

However, the surrendering parent may revoke her consent to the transfer and adoption by a written declaration within 30 days after executing the act of surrender. Nevertheless, the withdrawal of consent will not prevent the adoption if the adoption is found to be in the best interests of the child. Should an interlocutory decree have been entered without opposition, the child shall not be removed from the custody of the adopting parents nor adoption denied unless the department disapproves or the court finds the adopting parents unfit.

The Private Adoption Act of 1979 does not provide for any method whereby the act of surrender may be set aside because of vitiated consent. However, the executed act of surrender, although highly regulated and specialized, is in essence a contract, namely an agreement by two or more parties whereby obligations are created, modified, or extinguished. Accordingly, as in other agreements, the consent necessary to the surrender of a child for private adoption may be vitiated by error, fraud or duress.

. . .

The natural parent who asserts that the act of surrender is null, or that it has been modified or extinguished, must prove the facts or acts giving rise to the nullity, modification or extinction. Therefore, the burden of proof is upon the natural mother to prove that her consent was vitiated by error, fraud or duress.

. . .

The evidence does not establish that the plaintiff was subject to the type of duress which justifies vitiation of her consent. . . . Dawn's decision to surrender her child for adoption was induced principally by her own desire to do what was best for the child and by her mother's refusal to allow her to rear the child in her home. Mrs. B.'s decision to refuse assistance to her daughter in rearing the child did not pose a threat of considerable injury to Dawn's person, property or reputation. Furthermore, even if we were to assume that the mother's refusal could have caused a reasonable fear of considerable injury, the mother's action still could not have constituted unlawful duress. Mr. & Mrs. B. had a legal right to refuse to allow the adult natural mother to rear the child in their home. Therefore, their refusal was an exercise or threat to exercise a right and did not constitute duress.

. . .

Counsel for plaintiff in this court also argues that the act of surrender is null because the attorney who advised Dawn at that time had a conflict of interest. Nevertheless, she does not contend that the record reflects that the attorney gave Dawn bad or inadequate advice. Instead, plaintiff maintains that under the Adoption Act of 1979 the act of surrender is null if the natural parent was not represented by independent, conflict-free counsel, regardless of whether her interests were prejudiced by the representation. We do not think, however, this was the legislative aim.

At the time of the act of surrender, LA. REV. STAT. 9:422.7, in pertinent part, provided simply that "the surrendering parent or parents shall be represented by an attorney at the execution of the act of surrender." Subsequently, the Legislature amended this part of the statute to provide that:

> The surrendering parent or parents, and his, her, or their legal representative, if applicable, or the child's tutor, as provided in R.S. 9:422.3(A), shall be represented at the execution of the act by an attorney at law licensed to practice law in Louisiana; *provided, however, the attorney representing such person or persons shall not be the attorney who represents the person or persons who are the prospective adoptive parents, or an attorney who is a partner or employee of the attorney or law firm representing the prospective adoptive parents.*

LA. REV. STAT. 9:422.7(A) (Supp. 1988) (emphasis added). Thus, the requirement that the attorney advising the surrendering parent must be completely independent of the attorney representing the prospective adoptive parents did not become part of the law until after the act of surrender in the present case had been executed. Consequently, we conclude that the adoption statute at the time of the surrender herein required only that the surrendering parent be represented by an attorney providing adequate or reasonably effective legal service.

. . .

BEST INTERESTS OF THE CHILD

The natural parent in this case timely exercised her right to revoke her consent to the surrender and to oppose the adoption. However, her action does not bar a decree of adoption if the adoption is in "the best interests of the child." LA. REV. STAT. 9:422.11(A). Accordingly, in such a case there must be a best interest hearing to determine whether the adoption proceeding may go forward.

The statute does not allocate the burdens of proof with respect to the best interest of the child. But in our opinion both the burden of producing evidence and the burden of persuasion should be on the adoptive parents. The facts with regard to the crucial issue of the nature of the child's relationship with the adoptive parents lie peculiarly within their knowledge. Additionally, they are more apt to be able to produce expert witness testimony helpful to the court in deciding what is in the child's physical and emotional best interests.

The exact scope of the standard "best interest of the child" under the private adoption statute has not been detailed by the Legislature or this court. But the policy reflected in these words is firmly established in other statutes and in the law of virtually every American jurisdiction. The basic concept underlying this standard is nothing less than the dignity of the child as an individual human being. For this reason the words of the criterion cannot be precise and their scope cannot be static. "The best interests of the child" must draw its meaning from the evolving body of knowledge concerning child health, psychology and welfare that marks the progress of a maturing society.

Among modern legal and child psychological authorities, the consensus is that, of the multifarious considerations relevant to the best interests of a child in resolving a private custody dispute between the natural parent and the proposed adoptive parents, the most important factors are: (1) Whether each person seeking custody is fit to be the child's parent; (2) Whether either of the adoptive parents has a psychological relationship with the child; and (3) The natural parent's biological relationship with the child.[11]

Fitness

Custody should never be awarded to a claimant whose limitations or conduct would endanger the health of the child under minimum standards for child protection. The correct resolution of the dispute is obvious where one claimant poses an immediate and substantial threat to the child's physical health and the other does not. In such a case, there is no need to make longer-term predictions or more complicated psychological evaluations of what is likely to happen to the child's personality.

Psychological Relationship

The court should prefer a psychological parent (i.e., an adult who has a psychological relationship with the child from the *child's* perspective) over any claimant (including a natural parent) who, from the child's perspective, is not a psychological parent. To award custody to a person who is a "stranger" to the child would unnecessarily risk harming the child where the other claimant has, on a continuing, day-to-day basis, fulfilled the child's psychological needs for a parent as well as his physical need.

Whether any adult becomes the psychological parent of a child is based on day-to-day interaction, companionship, and shared experiences. J. GOLD-STEIN, A. FREUD, & A. SOLNIT, BEYOND THE BEST INTEREST OF THE CHILD 19 (2d ed. 1979); Robert H. Mnookin, *Foster Care—In Whose Best Interest?*, 43 HARV. EDUC. REV. 599 (1973). The role can be fulfilled either by a biological parent or by any other caring adult—but never by an absent, inactive adult, whatever his biological or legal relationship to the child. J. GOLDSTEIN, A. FREUD, & A. SOLNIT, *supra*, at 18; Martin F. Leonard & Sally Provence, *The Development of Parent Child Relationships and the Psychological Parent*, 53 CONN. B. J. 320 (1979). Thus, neither the biological relation nor the fact of legal adoption is any guarantee that an adult will become the psychological parent of a child.

The child's psychological tie to a parent figure is not the simple uncomplicated relationship that it may appear to be at first glance. It is rooted in the infant's ability to ensure his own survival, but a psychological interplay between adult and child is superimposed on the events of bodily care when the adult in charge is personally and emotionally involved. The child soon brings to this interaction not only his needs for bodily comfort and nourishment but also his emotional demand for affection, companionship, and stimulating intimacy. When these are answered reliably and regularly, the child-parent relationship becomes firm, with immensely productive effects on the child's intellectual and social development. J. BOWLBY, MATERNAL CARE AND MENTAL HEALTH 11 (1952). Continuity of parental affection and care provides the basis for the child's sense of self worth and security; parental discipline and example are essential for the child's development of values and ideals.

On the other hand, when parental care is inadequate, or when the child suffers a loss, change or other harmful interruption of the child-parent relationship, particularly in his early years, the child may experience serious

---

11. For a particularly insightful analysis of the authorities and helpful assessment of their priorities see Robert H. Mnookin, *Child–Custody Adjudication: Judicial Functions In The Face of Indeterminancy*, 39 L. & CONTEMP. PROBS. 226 (Summer 1975). We have relied extensively on this source in our own analysis.

deficits in his mental or emotional growth. J. GOLDSTEIN, A. FREUD, & A. SOLNIT, *supra*, at 31–32; ERIK ERIKSON, GROWTH AND CRISIS OF THE "HEALTHY PERSONALITY" IN PERSONALITY IN NATURE, SOCIETY AND CULTURE 190–97 (1955); Sigmund Freud, *Notes on Aggression*, 13 BULL. MENNINGER CLINIC 150–51 (1949). In such cases, the child may regress along the whole line of his affections, skills, achievements, and social adaptation.

There is little disagreement within the profession of child psychology as to the existence of the phenomenon of the child-psychological parent relationship and its importance to the development of the child. *Pikula v. Pikula*, 374 N.W.2d 705, 711 (Minn. 1985) (citing J. GOLDSTEIN, A. FREUD & A. SOLNIT, *supra*, at 31–35); Leonard & Provence, *supra*, 53 CONN. B.J. at 326. A substantial and impressive consensus exists among psychologists and psychiatrists that disruption of the parent-child relationship carries significant risks. A. FREUD & D. BURGLINGHAM, INFANTS WITHOUT FAMILIES: THE CASE FOR AND AGAINST RESIDENTIAL NURSERIES (1944); Harry Napier, *Success and Failure in Foster Care*, 2 BRIT. J. SOC. WORK 189 (1972); Phoebe C. Ellsworth & Robert J. Levy, *Legislative Reform of Child Custody Adjudication*, 4 LAW & SOC. REV. 167, 202–03 (1969)); John Bowlby, *Developmental Psychiatry Comes of Age*, 145: 1 AM.J. PSYCHIATRY 1 (Jan. 1988). The only disagreement among the experts appears to be over how great the significant risks are in comparison with other factors influencing a child's mental and emotional growth. *See* JEROME KAGAN, RICHARD B. KEARSLEY & PHILIP R. ZELAZO, INFANCY: ITS PLACE IN HUMAN DEVELOPMENT (1978); MICHAEL RUTTER, MATERNAL DEPRIVATION REASSESSED (1972); Alfred Kadushin, *Beyond The Best Interest of The Child: An Essay Review*, 48 SOC. SERV. REV. 508, 512 (1974); Michael Rutter, *Maternal Deprivation, 1972–78: New Findings, New Concepts, New Approaches*, 50 CHILD DEV. 283 (1979).

Biological Relationship

When the natural parent poses no danger to the child's physical health, and the child has not yet formed an attachment to and begun to view one of the adoptive parents as his psychological parent, the natural parent should be preferred over others. Under broadly shared social values the general rule is that the responsibility and opportunity of custody is assigned to a child's natural parents. The high value placed on family autonomy reflects a consensus that the natural parent-child relationship should be disturbed only if necessary to protect the child from physical or psychological harm. Moreover, preservation of the child's sense of lineage and access to his extended biological family can be important psychologically, as evidenced by the felt need of some adoptive children to search out their natural parents.

Guidelines Not Applicable to Other Types of Disputes

These guidelines are consistent with the best interests of the child principle and should dispose of most private adoption cases. They are not meant to be applied to other types of custody disputes, however, even though the best interests standard and the psychological parent phenomenon may have relevance to those cases. For example, these three guidelines would not be applicable to controversies between two natural parents, neither of whom would endanger a child's physical health, where both are psychological parents. Psychologists and psychiatrists can rather consistently differentiate between a situation where an adult and a child have a substantial psychological relationship and that where there is no relationship at all. But existing psychological theories do not provide the basis for choosing generally between two adults where the child has some relationship and psychological attachment to each. Furthermore, these private litigation guidelines certainly are not appropriate for use in public law proceedings such as actions under the child neglect or foster care laws. Legal standards in those types of cases must guide the courts in deciding when the state should intrude coercively on family autonomy and in making the bureaucracy purposeful and accountable, problems with which the private dispute guidelines discussed here are not concerned.

Application of the Best Interests Guidelines to This Case

The trial judge concluded that the adoption was in the best interests of the child. In its reasons the court compared wealth and earning capacities of the parties and concluded that Dawn, "an unmarried eighteen year old, cannot offer the child the stable and financially secure family unit that the [P.s] provide." The court did not determine whether there was a substantial psychological relationship (from the child's perspective) between the child and the adoptive parents and gave no apparent weight to the child's biological relationship to the natural mother. It is implicit that the court found the natural mother, as well as the adoptive parents, fit to have custody, because it did not declare any of them unfit and there is no warrant in the record for such a finding. The court of appeal merely adopted the trial court's reasons on the issue of the best interests of the child.

Applying the best interests guidelines we conclude that the trial court fell into error by omitting any consideration of two of the most important factors in a private adoption case, viz., the natural mother-child biological relationship and the possible psychological tie of the child to one or both of the adoptive parents. Instead, the trial court based its decision primarily on the relative wealth of the parties, a factor that can have little, if any, relevance in a case of this kind. If the natural mother is fit, the broad social policy of basing custody and responsibility on the biological relationship outweighs whatever material advantages might be provided by the adoptive parents, if neither of the adoptive parents is the child's psychological parent. On the other hand, if the adoptive parents are fit, and the child has formed a psychological attachment to one or both of them, the adoptive parents should be preferred so as to avoid the grave risk of mental and emotional harm to the child which would result from a change in custody, even if the natural parent is relatively affluent.

The record does not contain sufficient evidence from which we may determine whether the child had developed a substantial psychological relationship with one of the adoptive parents. There is no psychiatrist or psychologist testimony in the record and the adoptive parents' testimony is only sketchy on this subject. The child who was five months old at the time of the best interest hearing, is now approximately 2 1/2 years old. We can only speculate as to the child's psychological development at the time of the hearing and as to what has occurred since. It is quite possible that the child by now has acquired a strong and healthy psychological attachment to her adoptive parents. There is also the possibility that the child tragically has no psychological parent. More happily, it is possible that the child has developed a psychological tie with her natural mother if there has been regular contact between the two. We cannot decide what is in the best interest of this child on the basis of these speculations.

Accordingly, in the interest of justice we will vacate the adoption decree and remand the case for a new hearing on the best interest of the child. The trial court is directed to take steps, including the appointment of an expert by the court if necessary, to develop evidence as to the child's possible psychological attachment to the natural or adoptive parents. In order to expedite the completion of this case jurisdiction will be retained by this court. Any dissatisfied party may seek relief here upon the finality of the trial court's decision. The trial court is further instructed to conduct the new best interest hearing and render its decision with all possible dispatch.

NOTE

When John Bowlby began his work in the 1940s, the most widely-accepted explanation of a child's tie to his mother was that because she feeds the infant, "the pleasure experienced upon hunger drives satisfied comes to be associated with the mother's presence." Jude Cassidy, *The Nature of the Child's Ties*, Handbook of Attachment: Theory, Research, and Clinical Applications 3 (Jude Cassidy & Philip R. Shaver eds., 2008) (hereinafter Handbook of Attachment). But Bowlby became aware of evidence from animal studies by H.F. Harlow, K.E. Lorenz, and others that called the prevailing theory into question. Soon systematic observations of human infants confirmed that babies, too, became attached to people who did not feed them. *Id.*

By the 1950s, Bowlby used film to document how disruptions of children's bonds with their parents resulted in expressions of fear and angry protests that eventually gave way to sadness and despair. Roger Kobak & Stephanie Madsen, *Disruptions in Attachment Bonds: Implications for Theory, Research, and Clinical Intervention* 23 Handbook of Attachment. Unfortunately, the theory that feeding was the key implied that if a child was fed by a variety of caregivers, the relationship with the mother would have no special significance for the child. Some institutions followed this approach. Bowlby, by contrast, found that children who had been deprived of a close relationship to a parent developed into individuals "who lacked feeling, had superficial relationships, and exhibited hostile or antisocial tendencies." *Id.* at 25. Dorothy Burlingham and Anna Freud reached similar conclusions based on their work in a residential nursery for children whose parents had been unable to care for them during World War II. In Bowlby's words, "the provision of mothering is as important to a child's development as proper diet and nutrition." *Id.*

By the 1970s, Bowlby and others had documented that mere physical proximity was not enough; a child needs a parent who is not only accessible, but also responsive. *Id.* at 30. His work, and that of Anna Freud who together with law professor Joseph Goldstein and psychiatrist Albert Solnit produced a series of books on the best interests standard,[1] was relied on in a growing number of court decisions. Although attachment theory still occupies a central position in developmental psychology, legislatures and courts today more often use the term "continuity of care" rather than attachment in deciding what is in the best interests of a particular child.

In the Matter of Donna R. Hagedorn

Supreme Court of Indiana, 2000.
725 N.E.2d 397.

■ Per Curiam.

Attorney Donna R. Hagedorn neglected the legal affairs of three clients and, in certain instances, misrepresented to them the status of their case or

---

1. Joseph Goldstein, Anna Freud, & Albert Solnit, Beyond the Best Interests of the child (1973); Before the Best Interests of the Child (1979); and In the Best Interests of the Child (1986).

mismanaged funds she held in trust for them. For those acts, we find today that she should be suspended from the practice of law.

. . .

[Counts I and II, related to the commingling of funds, are omitted.]

Under Count III, we find that in March 1988 a couple contacted the respondent about handling a private adoption. Although she was not able to assist them at that time, the respondent indicated she might be able to assist with a private adoption in the future. In March of 1989, the respondent contacted the couple, indicating she knew of a woman who was due to deliver her child in April of 1989 and who wanted to make the child available for adoption. The respondent met with the couple and explained that they would be responsible for medical and legal expenses for the birth mother, and postpartum medical expenses for the child. The respondent indicated that her fee would be $1,200, with $500 of that due immediately. By check dated March 9, 1989, the couple paid the respondent $500. They paid an additional $500 to the respondent on April 6, 1989.

The child the couple sought to adopt was born April 21, 1989. The respondent did not prepare or file a petition for adoption. She did, however, obtain the birth mother's consent, and an order of the Vanderburgh Superior Court releasing the child to the couple's care on April 24, 1989. Before the child was released to the couple, the respondent failed to tell them that a pre-placement investigation was required, and the respondent did not arrange for such an investigation. Further, the respondent did not arrange for post-placement supervision as required by the Vanderburgh Superior Court.

As agreed, the couple, on July 19, 1989, paid to the respondent $3,001.70 for the medical expenses of the child and the birth mother. In turn, the respondent agreed to forward the bills for the child to the couple's employer for consideration of payment. Although the respondent failed to forward the bills as agreed, she did sign a personal guarantee of payment for the hospital expenses associated with the child's birth. The hospital later sued the respondent to recover these expenses, in the amount of $671.10, plus $223.70 in attorney fees. On May 14, 1991, the respondent entered into an agreed judgment with the hospital.

By the time the child was one year old, the respondent had still not filed a petition for the couple to adopt the child. On November 28, 1990, the respondent had the couple come to her office to sign a petition for adoption. The couple signed the petition, but the respondent failed to file the petition with the court. The respondent also told the couple that the birth mother's parental rights had been terminated in September 1990, when in fact respondent had no basis to believe that the parental rights of the birth mother had been terminated.

On April 21, 1991, the child's second birthday, the adoption still had not been filed. Nonetheless, the respondent informed the couple the adoption would be finalized on May 2, 1991. On May 1, 1991, the respondent informed them that finalization of the adoption would be postponed because the respondent was required to publish notice (to the putative father) of the adoption. On June 11, 1991, the respondent informed the couple that finalization of the adoption would once again be delayed, this time because the Vanderburgh County Welfare Department had allegedly lost a 1988 home study done in the couple's home. In fact, the home study was not a condition precedent to the adoption and the respondent misrepresented to the couple that the 1988 home study had been lost.

On July 1, 1991, the couple discharged the respondent as their attorney and instructed her to forward their files to another attorney. The respondent forwarded the files as requested.

By failing to arrange the required pre-placement evaluation, failing to terminate the parental rights of the birth mother and the putative father, and failing to prepare or file a petition for adoption, the respondent failed to provide competent representation in contravention of PROF. COND. R. 1.1.[1] The respondent's actions also reflected a disregard for the clients' decisions regarding their desire to obtain a private adoption, and thus violated PROF. COND. R. 1.2(a), which requires lawyers to abide by their clients' decisions regarding the objectives of representation.[2] By failing to begin formal adoption proceedings and thereby failing to act with reasonable diligence and promptness in representing the couple, the respondent violated PROF. COND. R. 1.3.[3] By failing to keep the couple reasonably advised about the status of the adoption, and failing to explain the matter to the extent reasonably necessary to allow the clients to make informed decisions about the representation, she violated PROF. COND. R. 1.4.[4] By purposefully misleading the couple about the course and status of the adoption proceedings, the respondent engaged in conduct involving dishonesty, fraud, deceit or misrepresentation in violation of PROF. COND. R. 8.4(c).[5]

. . .

Accordingly, the respondent, Donna R. Hagedorn, is hereby suspended from the practice of law for a period of six (6) months, beginning April 14, 2000, at the conclusion of which she shall be automatically reinstated.

Mary M. Beck, *Adoption of Children in Missouri*
63 Mo. L. Rev. 423, 429–32 (1998).

Adoptions fall into two categories—adoptions arranged by licensed child-placing agencies (agency adoption) and adoptions arranged independent of agency involvement (independent adoption). Agency adoption may

---

1.   Professional Conduct Rule 1.1 provides:

A lawyer shall provide competent representation to a client. Competent representation requires the legal knowledge, skill, thoroughness and preparation reasonably necessary for the representation.

2.   Professional Conduct Rule 1.2(a) provides:

A lawyer shall abide by a client's decisions concerning the objectives of representation, subject to paragraphs (c), (d) and (e), and shall consult with the client as to the means by which they are to be pursued. A lawyer shall abide by a client's decision whether to accept an offer of settlement of a matter.

3.   Professional Conduct Rule 1.3 provides:

A lawyer shall act with reasonable diligence and promptness in representing a client.

4.   Professional Conduct Rule 1.4 provides:

(a) A lawyer shall keep a client reasonably informed about the status of a matter and promptly comply with reasonable requests for information.

(b) A lawyer shall explain a matter to the extent reasonably necessary to permit the client to make informed decisions regarding the representation.

5.   Professional Conduct Rule 8.4(c) provides:

It is professional misconduct for a lawyer to engage in conduct involving dishonesty, fraud, deceit or misrepresentation.

be conducted by government or private agencies. Direct placement adoptions occur when the birth parents and the adoptive parents connect with each other without the assistance of an intermediary. Private placement adoptions occur when an adoption intermediary introduces the adoptive parents and the birth parents. Identified adoption occurs when an adoptive couple locates a birth mother who wishes to place her child with them, and an agency conducts the adoptive parent and birth parent investigations. Not all agencies will assist in identified adoptions. Public agencies handle 39.2% of adoptions; private agencies handle 29.4%; and independent adoptions account for 31.4% of adoptions. Twice as many birth mothers making a voluntary adoption plan choose independent adoption as those who choose agency adoption, and commentators indicate that independent adoptions have become the method of choice for birth mothers.

A tension exists between the proponents of agency adoptions and proponents of independent adoptions, but "(t)he majority of commentators support independent adoptions. . . ." Independent adoption is acclaimed for avoiding or minimizing foster care and making rapid placement of children with their adoptive parents, thus promoting the early parent-child bond. Independent adoption permits parents who might be excluded by agency policies to adopt. For example, agencies may implement policies pertaining to religion or age, whereas the criteria for independent adoption is a satisfactory home study.

The most distinguishing characteristic of independent adoptions is that the parties have more control. The birth parents personally select the adoptive parents from profiles or personal meetings, and the parties frequently develop relationships in person or over the phone. A birth parent's decision to make an adoption plan is typically an exquisitely painful and unselfish decision to further the interests of the child. The birth mother who controls the adoptive parent selection gains security in her decision and confidence in her choice by personalizing the adoption plan. Fewer birth mothers change their minds and cancel adoption plans in independent adoption than in agency adoption, presumably because of the comfort level derived from personal knowledge of the adoptive parents. Additionally, agencies have ranked independent adoptive placements as equally successful, if not more successful, than the placements of children made by agencies. Adoptive parents benefit in independent adoptions by developing a relationship with the birth parents so that they can gain perspective on the birth parents' decision to relinquish the child for adoption. Thus, the adoptive parents later can assure the adoptee of the love and devotion demonstrated by the birth parents in making the adoption plan and impart general information about the birth parents to the adoptee.

The National Committee for Adoption disfavors independent adoption and open adoption, citing two studies reporting that independent placements are less successful than independent adoptions. The National Committee cites various reasons for disfavoring independent adoptions, including: 1) the selling of babies on the black market, 2) open adoptions in which the parties know each other's identities, 3) failed adoptions in which adoptive parents return their child, 4) custody battles prior to finalization of the adoption, 5) couples who could not gain approval for adoption from an agency completing independent adoptions, 6) incomplete transmission of information on the health and history of the child, 7) failure to complete the legal process, and 8) inadequate counseling of the birth mother.

The studies cited by the National Committee to support its position, having been published in 1951 and 1963, are outdated. State laws have changed such that open adoption is a common option, black marketing in babies is, of course, prohibited, with exchange of all moneys in adoption typically disclosed to the court. The adoption laws of many states apply equally to independent and agency adoption, such that adoptive parents and birth parents must undergo home study in both independent and agency adoptions, and the information resulting from such studies increasingly is filed with the court. Additionally, counseling is routinely made available for birth mothers in independent adoptions and often is mandated in agency adoptions.

Comprehensive adoption law remedies the problems historically associated with independent adoptions. But no legislative amendments can eliminate outlaws who would take custody of children without complying with statutory procedures. States should build safeguards into their statutes to protect all parties to adoption and these safeguards should apply equally to independent and agency adoptions. The control available to the parties in independent adoption is desirable in that it provides more choices to biological and adoptive parents and ultimately promotes adoption. Independent adoption can be permitted without sacrificing security with carefully drafted legislation that: 1) identifies individuals who may act as intermediaries placing a child for adoption, 2) authorizes separate counsel for the birth parents at the adoptive parents' expense, 3) prohibits or exposes dual legal representation of birth parents and adoptive parents, 4) requires that the birth parents be offered counseling and that they sign a statement to that effect, 5) identifies the same requirements of adoptive parent home studies in both independent and agency adoptions, and 6) requires adoptive parents to file a financial accounting with the court.

c.   CHILDREN WITH SPECIAL NEEDS

Ferdinand v. Department for Children and Their Families

United States District Court, District of Rhode Island, 1991.
768 F.Supp. 401.

■ PETTINE, SENIOR UNITED STATES DISTRICT JUDGE.

Litigation in this case began when the plaintiff, Rose Ferdinand's request for an adoption subsidy under Title IV–E, 42 U.S.C. § 673(c) was denied by the defendants, Department for Children and Their Families of the State of Rhode Island *et al.* ("DCF"), in February of 1990. Ms. Ferdinand adopted her daughter, Nia, a black child, through Children's Friend and Service and DCF. At that time, Ms. Ferdinand was married, lived with her husband in Massachusetts and both she and her husband were employed at Dupont. As of 1990, the situation had changed. The Ferdinands were divorced. Rose Ferdinand received no child support and she was responsible for supporting not only herself and Nia but also a younger child born to the couple during the marriage. The defendants denied the "belated" request for adoption assistance contending that because the Ferdinands were offered and declined such at the time of the adoption, the present request could not even be considered. In other words, Nia Ferdinand's possible entitlement had been waived.

This matter first came before this Court on December 5, 1990 in response to the plaintiff's motion for preliminary injunction. At that time, I reviewed the case and decided to treat the motion as a request for a temporary restraining order ("TRO"). The TRO was granted and the defendants were ordered to "qualify plaintiff for adoption assistance payments and related available benefits, including medical insurance." The parties agreed that the TRO would remain in effect until this Court rendered a further opinion following the receipt of additional briefs. The TRO did not reach the issue of the plaintiff's requested effective date of eligibility. This court ordered payments to commence on December 15, 1990.

Based on the discussion that follows, plaintiff's motion for permanent injunction is now granted. I adopt the terms that were set out in the TRO: defendants shall continue to carry plaintiff as qualified plaintiff for adoption assistance payments and related available benefits, including medical insurance and shall continue to forward payments to the plaintiff. Such assistance shall continue in light of any changing circumstances pursuant to the periodic readjustment provisions of 42 U.S.C. § 673(a)(3) and the provision of 42 U.S.C. § 673(a)(4).

With the Adoption Assistance and Child Welfare Act of 1980, Congress "amended the Social Security Act to make needed improvements in the child welfare and social services programs . . . to establish a program of Federal support to encourage adoptions of children with special needs. . . ." 1980 U.S. Code Cong. and Admin. News at 1450. The subsidized adoption program provides federal matching once a state determines that a child in foster care would be eligible for such. Eligibility turns on whether the child has special needs which tend to discourage adoption. "Each State would be responsible for deciding which factors would ordinarily result in making it difficult to place certain children in adoptive homes." "The determination could be based on such factors as a physical or emotional handicap, the need to place members of a sibling group with a single adoptive family, difficulty in placing children of certain ages or ethnic backgrounds, or similar factors or combinations of factors." "If the State determines that adoption assistance is needed, it would be able to offer such assistance to parents who adopt the child, so long as their income does not exceed 125 percent of the median income of a family of four in the State, adjusted to reflect family size."[4]

---

4. The Adoption Assistance Program for children with special needs is set out at 42 U.S.C. § 673(a)(1)(C) and (c):

> (1) Each State with a plan approved under this part shall, directly through the State agency or through another public or nonprofit private agency, make adoption assistance payments pursuant to an adoption assistance agreement in amounts determined under paragraph (2) of this subsection to parents who, after June 17, 1980, adopt a child who—
>
> . . .
>
> (C) has been determined by the State, pursuant to subsection (c) of this section, to be a child with special needs.
>
> . . .
>
> (c) Children with special needs
>
> For the purposes of this section, a child shall not be considered a child with special needs unless—
>
> (1) the State has determined that the child cannot or should not be returned to the home of his parents; and
>
> (2) the State had first determined (A) that there exists with respect to the child a specific factor or condition (such as his ethnic background, age, or membership in a minority or sibling group, or the presence of factors such as medical conditions or physical, mental, or emotional handicaps) because of which it is reasonable to conclude that such child cannot be placed with adoptive parents without providing adoption assistance, and (B) that, except

To decide this case, this Court must first determine whether Nia Ferdinand is eligible for federal adoption assistance. This determination, in turn, focuses on 45 C.F.R. § 1356.40(b)(1). That section requires that the adoption assistance agreement "be signed and in effect at the time of or prior to the final decree of adoption." The defendants contend that because the Ferdinands did not enter into such an agreement, their right to adoption assistance was waived. Defendants argument, based on various policy interpretations issued by the Department of Health and Human Services including ACYF PIQ–83–5 (December 14, 1983), is that "if parents are apprised of the availability of a subsidy, decline such subsidy, and do not enter into *a nominal adoption assistance agreement*, they may not later receive any assistance as the child is no longer eligible as a child with special needs under the Act."

When the defendants denied adoption assistance to the Ferdinands in 1990, they noted that the "prior agreement" requirement could be "reviewed if there were extenuating circumstances at the time of the adoption. That is, if a subsidy was not offered, or proper benefits were not explained (i.e., SSI or SSA)." However, the defendants stated that with regard to the Ferdinands, "this was not the case."

Defendants contend and plaintiffs concede that there was some minimal discussion about adoption subsidies with the Ferdinands prior to Nia's adoption and that Ms. Ferdinand told Mr. deLong, Assistant Director of Children's Friend and Service, that "she hadn't needed a subsidy at that time." Inter–Office Memo to John Sinapi from Daniel Wheelan, Assistant Administrator, DCF (February 6, 1990). The fact that the discussion was nothing more than a minimal one is supported by a letter from Mr. deLong, dated February 4, 1991, stating that "we have found nothing in our records that indicates that Ms. Ferdinand or Mr. Ferdinand were ever offered a subsidy by our agency, nor any record that they either accepted or rejected an offer." Moreover, in a memorandum from Ted Keenaghan, Chief Social Services Policy and Systems Specialist, Children and Their Families, to Kevin Aucoin, Legal Counsel for the same, dated December 24, 1990, Mr. Keenaghan stated that he was "shocked to tell [Mr. Aucoin] that there is *no* mention in [the] records about a subsidy being offered to this family when the child was first adopted!!!" (emphasis in original). Even if the Ferdinands knew something about the program, the defendants' own interpretation of their mandate allows that if "proper benefits were not explained" the case may be re-opened based on the extenuating circumstances rationale.

What, therefore, would constitute a proper explanation of available benefits? This Court has no doubt that Congress intended to place the burden on the States to promote the adoption assistance program. The Code of Federal Regulations, 42 C.F.R. § 1356.40(f), states that "the State agency must actively seek ways to promote the adoption assistance program." Moreover, the United States Department of Health and Human Services, in Policy Announcement ACYF–PA–83–5, discussing various assistance programs available to adoptive parents stated:

> Because there are many complexities and financial implications for the States as well as the adoptive families, it is important for all parties to

___

where it would be against the best interest of the child because of such factors as the existence of significant emotional ties with prospective adoptive parents while in the care of such parents as a foster child, a reasonable, but unsuccessful, effort has been made to place the child with appropriate adoptive parents without providing adoption assistance under this section.

discuss all aspects of a combination of SSI and adoption assistance at the time the adoption assistance agreement is negotiated.

. . .

With full knowledge of the SSI and Adoption Assistance programs, the adoptive parents can then make an informed decision about application for or receipt of benefits from either or both programs for which they or the child are eligible. They should be advised, however, that if they decline Title IV–E adoption assistance and choose to receive only SSI for the child, and if they do not execute an adoption assistance agreement before the adoption is finalized and do not receive adoption assistance payments pursuant to such an agreement, they may not later receive Title IV–E adoption assistance payments, the child would no longer meet all of the eligibility requirements as a child with special needs (§ 473(c)(2)).

The clear implication is that the state has an affirmative duty to fully explain all available assistance programs so that potential adoptive parents can make an informed decision. The fact that Ms. Ferdinand was never made aware of the fact that even if she did not need a subsidy at that time she might still qualify for nominal assistance that would leave the door open for later recalculation constitutes an extenuating circumstance. In fact, the defendants' own procedures regarding adoption subsidies indicate that it is not the adoptive parents' needs, but rather the child's needs that determine eligibility for assistance.[5] Parents, therefore, should not be allowed to waive adoption assistance for their children without full information and knowledge of all possible benefits—present and future.

Reopening of the case, however, does not inevitably lead to the conclusion that the Ferdinands would have qualified for adoption assistance. The defendants argue that regardless of plaintiff's eligibility for federal adoption assistance, applicable federal law did not mandate that states provide Title IV–E adoption assistance subsidies to non-resident adoptive parents. Section 1356.40(3) of 45 C.F.R. states only that "[a] state may make an adoption assistance agreement with adopting parents who reside in another state." Because the defendants' own policies in effect at the time of Nia's adoption were mute on the issue of providing federal subsidies to non-resident parents, defendants contend that they have no obligation to the Ferdinands. Whether such obligation existed or not, however, is eclipsed by the fact that in Daniel Wheelan's memo to John Sinapi of February 6, 1990, he states that "after speaking with Camille Hardiman of Children's Friend and Service, Ted Keenaghan has determined that this child was probably IV–E eligible at the time of adoption." Mr. Keenaghan's statement is not *contrary* to the regulations which clearly allow subsidies for non-resident adoptive parents. My sense is that the residency issue is, as plaintiff contends, a mere post-hoc rationalization. I find that the Ferdinands' out of state residency did not and does not affect their eligibility for the Adoption Assistance Program.

Finally, the fact that Nia's special educational needs were not evident at the time of her adoption does not lead to the conclusion that she was not eligible for Title IV–E assistance as a "hard-to-place" special needs child. According to 42 U.S.C. § 673(c) race or minority status can enable a child to be classified as a "special needs" child for adoption assistance purposes.

---

5. . . . R.I. Department for Children and Their Families Adoption Procedures Manual states that a "worker meets with prospective adoptive parents to review the criteria for subsidy and makes them aware it is based on the needs of the child."

Again, Ted Keenaghan's statement comports with this understanding of Nia's eligibility at the time of her adoption.

In sum, plaintiffs have demonstrated that Nia was eligible for adoption assistance at the time of her adoption and that the Adoption Assistance Program was not adequately explained to the Ferdinands. Such lack of explanation was a violation by the defendants of their affirmative duty to inform clients of the program and provided the extenuating circumstances necessary to allow the reopening of the plaintiff's case and, finally, the grant of adoption assistance. The permanent injunction requested by the plaintiff is, therefore, granted.

NOTE

The Adoption Assistance and Child Welfare Act of 1980 authorized a federal adoption subsidy to be provided to states. Pub. L. No. 96–272. Congress later amended the law by passing the Adoption and Safe Families Act of 1997, which allowed children to retain eligibility for the adoption subsidy in a subsequent adoption if their adoptive parent died or the adoption was dissolved. Pub. L. No. 105–89. This law has been criticized by some academics, particularly for its "concurrent planning" provisions, which require the adoption agency to attempt to preserve the biological family and simultaneously prepare for a different permanent home if those efforts fail. *See, e.g.,* William Wesley Patton & Amy M. Pellman, *The Reality of Concurrent Planning: Juggling Multiple Family Plans Expeditiously without Sufficient Resources,* 9 U.C. Davis J. Juv. L. & Pol'y 171, 191–92 (2005); Deborah L. Sanders, *Toward Creating a Policy of Permanence for America's Disposable Children: The Evolution of Federal Foster Care Statutes from 1961 to Present,* 29 J. Legis. 51, 75 (2002). Patton & Pellman argue:

> Conceptually, concurrent planning with an emphasis on expedited permanency either through reunification with the biological family or in an alternative placement, such as adoption or relative guardianship, appears to be a wise policy that promotes the physical and psychological health of abused and/or neglected children. However, that policy, as implemented by the states under the mandate of the Adoption and Safe Families Act of 1997, is severely flawed for a number of reasons. First, one may question whether termination of parental rights was required in a significant number of cases because: (1) the expedited decision to terminate parental rights is often made in six months, and sometimes without the necessity of providing family rehabilitation and reunification; (2) necessary social services are often not readily available so while the termination clock ticks away, little reunification is possible; (3) social workers are so overloaded with cases, making it physically impossible for them to provide the quality of family and child monitoring and assistance necessary for the initial decision to seek court jurisdiction, adjudication fact-finding, or disposition-ordered periodic review; (4) parents' and children's counsel also have unmanageable case loads; (5) the ultimate fact-finder, juvenile dependency judges, have only a few minutes per case to determine the fate of families; and (6) the dictates of the Adoption and Safe Families Act are antagonistic to siblings' rights to association, with policies of expedited permanency and adoptive preference that often unreasonably split strongly bonded siblings.

Patton & Pellman, *supra,* at 191–92.

d. STEPPARENT ADOPTION

In the Matter of the Adoption of G.L.V. and M.J.V.

Supreme Court of Kansas, 2008.
190 P.3d 245.

■ Davis, J.

This case involves an appeal from the denial of a stepparent adoption. The Court of Appeals affirmed the district court's decision, holding that the natural father's consent was necessary since he had performed his parental duties during the 2 years preceding the adoption petition. We granted the stepfather's petition for review to examine the district court's and the Court of Appeals' interpretation and application of the recently amended stepparent adoption statute, K.S.A.2007 Supp. 59–2136(d), which now authorizes a court to consider the best interests of the child and the fitness of the nonconsenting parent in determining whether a stepparent adoption should be granted.

G.L.V. and M.J.V. are twin brothers, born on October 17, 1994. Their parents were never married and lived together only briefly prior to the time that the boys were born. In 1995, the mother filed a paternity action, resulting in a determination that the father was the natural father of the twins, and an order was issued requiring the father to pay child support. Three weeks after their birth, the father left the area and did not return until 1997.

Upon his return, the father filed an action to secure visitation rights to the twins and was awarded weekend visitation; however, he exercised his visitation rights only two or three times. During the instant adoption proceedings, the father testified he sought aid to enforce visitation from the sheriff but was advised his only remedy would be through court proceedings. Because he did not have funds to hire a lawyer, he did not pursue enforcement of his visitation rights.

Absent his two weekend visits, the father has had no direct contact with his twin sons since 1997. Nevertheless, the paternal grandparents and other members of the father's family have maintained a relationship with the twins.

Although the father was ordered by the district court to pay child support in 1994, his payments for the first several years were infrequent, leading to a significant arrearage. Since April 2003, however, the father has been regularly employed and has consistently made monthly child support payments of $366 through an income withholding order. From April 2003 until June 2006, he paid $21,003.86 in child support on an obligation of $14,274, with the overage applied toward the arrearage.

. . .

The natural mother of the twins married the petitioner stepfather in 2004. On June 13, 2006, the stepfather filed a petition to adopt the twins without obtaining the consent of the natural father. The stepfather requested the district court grant the adoption in light of the fact that father had not had any contact with the children for 9 years and had never voluntarily paid child support.

. . .

The stepfather advanced two alternative arguments before the Court of Appeals and now raises the same issues on petition for review: He contends that either (1) under the provisions of K.S.A.2007 Supp. 59–2136(d), the best interests of children involved in a contested stepparent adoption is an overriding factor in the determination; or, alternatively, (2) . . . the best interests of the child [is] entitled to equal weight and consideration in the stepparent adoption proceedings.

. . .

This court has ... explained in the specific area of adoption that adoption statutes are "strictly construed in favor of maintaining the rights of natural parents in those cases where it is claimed that, by reason of a parent's failure to fulfill parental obligations as prescribed by statute, consent to the adoption is not required." *Adoption of B.M.W.*, 2 P.3d 159, 166 (Kan. 2008).

The most recent version of the stepparent adoption statute, K.S.A.2007 Supp. 59–2136(d), states:

"[T]he consent of [the natural] father must be given to the adoption unless such father has failed or refused to assume the duties of a parent for two consecutive years next preceding the filing of the petition for adoption or is incapable of giving such consent. In determining whether a father's consent is required under this subsection, the court may disregard incidental visitations, contacts, communications or contributions. In determining whether the father has failed or refused to assume the duties of a parent for two consecutive years next preceding the filing of the petition for adoption, there shall be a rebuttable presumption that if the father, after having knowledge of the child's birth, has knowingly failed to provide a substantial portion of the child support as required by judicial decree, when financially able to do so, for a period of two years next preceding the filing of the petition for adoption, then such father has failed or refused to assume the duties of a parent. *The court may consider the best interests of the child and the fitness of the nonconsenting parent in determining whether a stepparent adoption should be granted.*"

(Emphasis added.) The final sentence in the stepparent adoption statute—that relating to the best interests of the child and the fitness of the nonconsenting parent—was added when the statute was amended in 2006....

Though the district court recognized that the amendment changed prior law by allowing the best interests of the child and the fitness of the nonconsenting parent to be considered in a stepparent adoption, the court had difficulty determining how these new considerations should be incorporated.

. . .

[W]e have consistently repeated that all surrounding circumstances are to be considered when determining whether a natural parent must consent to a stepparent adoption—that is, whether the natural parent has "assume[d] the duties of a parent for two consecutive years next preceding the filing of the petition for adoption or is incapable of giving such consent." *See* K.S.A.2007 Supp. 59–2136(d); *B.M.W.*, 2 P.3d at 162. This statement recognizes that there are numerous duties associated with being a parent to a child, and all such duties—even though not explicitly enumerated—may be considered. We have focused primarily on two very basic and important duties of parents—love and affection on one hand and financial support on the other—in the context of stepparent adoptions because these duties are contemplated by the statute....

Contrary to the findings by the district court and the Court of Appeals in this case, the legislative history behind the 2006 amendment in K.S.A. 2007 Supp. 59–2136(d) provides little guidance as to the legislative intent in enacting the new language. Nevertheless, it is clear that the legislature intended that courts in adoption cases at least have the option of considering the best interests of the child and the fitness of the nonconsenting parent....

The question before us, put simply, is whether the 2006 amendment in K.S.A.2007 Supp. 59–2136(d) permits a district court to override the statute's explicit requirement that a natural father who has assumed the duties of a parent give his consent to the stepparent adoption if it determines that the adoption is in the child's best interests. We hold that it does not.

Our decision is guided by two important considerations with reference to K.S.A.2007 Supp. 59–2136(d). First, a natural parent who has assumed his or her parental responsibilities has a fundamental right, protected by the United States and Kansas Constitutions, to raise his or her child, and the consent requirement in the stepparent adoption statute codifies these constitutional protections. Second, K.S.A.2007 Supp. 59–2136(d) expresses the public policy of Kansas by implicitly incorporating the determination that the best interests of the child is served by fostering the child's relationship with the natural parent in cases where the parent has assumed the duties of a parent toward the child. These two aspects of the statute have existed both before and after the 2006 amendment; the following discussion addresses each consideration in detail.

. . .

[*In re Guardianship* of] *Williams*[, 869 P.2d 661 (Kan. 1994)] makes it clear under state law, as *Quilloin* did under federal law, that a natural parent's right to raise his or her child is tempered by the extent that the parent has assumed his or her parental responsibilities. In this way ... K.S.A.2007 Supp. 59–2136(d) is completely in keeping with the Constitution's substantive protections of parental rights. If a parent has assumed his or her parental duties, then a stepparent adoption may not be granted without that parent's consent. If a parent has failed to assume those duties, the adoption does not require that parent's consent. The determination as to whether a parent has assumed his or her parental duties or has failed to do so does not itself involve a parent's constitutional rights, but instead acts as a threshold determination as to whether the Constitution is substantively involved at all. *See Quilloin*, 434 U.S. at 256. As this court noted in *B.M.W.*, the Constitution does not prohibit a stepparent adoption. 2 P.3d at 166.

The plain language of K.S.A. 59–2136(d)—both before and after the 2006 amendment—states that the consent of a known father must be given to a stepparent adoption unless such father "has failed or refused to assume the duties of a parent for two consecutive years next preceding the filing of the petition for adoption or is incapable of giving such consent." The statute then provides a guide for the court "[i]n determining whether a father's consent is required" in a stepparent adoption, stating: "The court may disregard incidental visitations, contacts, communications or contributions." The statute continues by providing a method for determining when a father has failed or refused to assume the duties of a parent relating to child support required by judicial decree.

Because the natural father in this case has assumed a sufficient level of parental responsibility under Kansas law, his rights as a parent are entitled to constitutional protection. K.S.A. 59–2136(d), both now and before the 2006 amendment, provides this protection by requiring the father's consent before a stepparent adoption can be granted. The father has not consented to the adoption in this case, and his decision to withhold his consent cannot be overridden absent compelling circumstances. *See Williams*, 869 P.2d at 667.

The stepfather argues on appeal that when the legislature amended K.S.A. 59–2136(d) in 2006 to include the best interests of the child as a consideration in stepparent adoptions, it intended the best interests to be either an overarching concern or, at a minimum, a concern on equal footing with the court's consideration of whether the nonconsenting parent assumed the parental duties of love and affection and financial support. Placed in the context of our previous discussion, the stepfather is essentially arguing that a court's determination of the best interests of the child may override a nonconsenting parent's fundamental rights even where that parent has assumed his or her parental responsibilities. We disagree with the stepfather's interpretation for two important reasons: First, this interpretation is inconsistent with the plain language of the statute, and second, this interpretation is inconsistent with the legislature's implicit recognition that the best interests of the child are protected in the usual case by protecting the natural parent-child relationship.

.   .   .

We note that the legislature, subject to the constitutional protection afforded a natural parent, could have expressly provided that best interests of the child be given overriding consideration by the court in a stepparent adoption. However, the legislature did not do so.

In this case, the district court found that the natural father had been making regular contributions to the court-ordered child support by way of an automatic garnishment of his wages. In fact, the father paid the entire amount of child support due during the 2–year period preceding the adoption and made significant payments toward his arrearage during that same period. These payments, when coupled with the father's expressed interest at the adoption hearing that he would like the children to continue to have contact with his extended family and to meet his other children at some time, demonstrate, considering all of the circumstances, that the father did not fail to assume his parental duties in the 2 years preceding the adoption. K.S.A.2007 Supp. 59–2136(d) therefore required his consent to the stepparent adoption. He did not give that consent, and the district court appropriately denied the adoption petition.

The decisions of the district court and Court of Appeals are affirmed.

Uniform Adoption Act, Article 4. Adoption of Minor Stepchild by Stepparent

(1994).

COMMENT

A stepparent who seeks to adopt a minor stepchild under this article has to deal with fewer as well as somewhat different legal requirements than does an individual who seeks to adopt an unrelated minor. These differences are justified because in the typical stepparent adoption, the minor has been living with the stepparent and the stepparent's spouse (the minor's custodial parent), and the adoption merely formalizes a de facto parent-child relationship.

.   .   .

Typically, the custodial parent is allowed to retain his or her parental status, the adoptive stepparent acquires the status of a legal parent, and the noncustodial parent's relationship to the child is cut off for most purposes. . . . For stepfamilies in which a child maintains emotional ties to a noncustodial parent or to the noncustodial parent's family, the traditional approach of completely severing all ties to the noncustodial parent and that parent's family is not necessarily beneficial for the child, and is not always preferred by the parents or the stepparent. . . .

. . . By allowing post-adoption visitation by noncustodial former parents, siblings, or grandparents, this article may encourage an increase in the number of stepparent adoptions in proportion to the total number of blended families. This would give more children the advantage of living in a household with two legal parents (custodial parent and adoptive stepparent), while not depriving these children of access to their noncustodial parent's family—assuming that such access would not be detrimental to the child. Moreover, if the traditional rule of "complete severance" between adoptive and biological families is subject to some exceptions in the context of stepparent adoptions, it might be possible to avoid the bitterness that is often attendant upon efforts to terminate the rights of noncustodial parents, and more consensual adoptions might result.

. . .

Section 4–103. Legal Consequences of Adoption of Stepchild.

(a) Except as otherwise provided in subsections (b) and (c), the legal consequences of an adoption of a stepchild by a stepparent are the same as [for other adoptions under the Act]

(b) An adoption by a stepparent does not affect:

(1) the relationship between the adoptee and the adoptee's parent who is the adoptive stepparent's spouse or deceased spouse;

(2) an existing court order for visitation or communication with a minor adoptee by an individual related to the adoptee through the parent who is the adoptive stepparent's spouse or deceased spouse; [or]

. . .

(4) A court order or agreement for visitation or communication with a minor adoptee which is approved by the court pursuant to Section 4–113.

. . .

COMMENT

Although the legal consequences of an adoption of a stepchild are generally the same as [for other adoptions under this Act], this section provides that the rights and duties of the adoptive parent's spouse—i.e., the child's custodial parent—are not terminated by the adoption. The child remains in all respects the child of the adoptive parent's spouse, even if the spouse is deceased, and becomes in all respects the child of the adoptive stepparent. . . . By contrast, except for child support arrearages, the rights and duties of the child's former noncustodial parent are terminated. . . .

Section 4–105. Content of Consent by Stepparent's Spouse.

. . .

(b) A consent . . . must state that:

(1) the parent executing the consent has legal and physical custody of the parent's minor child and voluntarily and unequivocally consents to the adoption of the minor by the stepparent;

. . .

Section 4–106. Content of Consent by Minor's Other Parent.

. . .

(b) A consent . . . must state that:

(1) the parent executing the consent voluntarily and unequivocally consents to the adoption of the minor by the stepparent and the transfer to the stepparent's spouse and the adoptive stepparent of any right the parent executing the consent has to legal or physical custody of the minor;

(2) the parent executing the consent understands and agrees that the adoption will terminate his or her parental relationship to the minor and will terminate any existing court order for custody, visitation, or communication with the minor, but:

. . .

(ii) a court order for visitation or communication with the minor by an individual related to the minor through the minor's other parent, or an agreement or order concerning another individual which is approved by the court . . . survives the decree of adoption

. . .

Section 4–113. Visitation Agreement and Order.

(a) Upon the request of the petitioner in a proceeding for adoption of a minor stepchild, the court shall review a written agreement that permits another individual to visit or communicate with the minor after the decree of adoption becomes final, which must be signed by the individual, the petitioner, the petitioner's spouse, the minor if 12 years of age or older, and, if an agency placed the minor for adoption, an authorized employee of the agency.

(b) The court may enter an order approving the agreement only upon determining that the agreement is in the best interest of the minor adoptee.

. . .

(c) In addition to any agreement approved pursuant to subsections (a) and (b), the court may approve the continuation of an existing order or issue a new order permitting the minor adoptee's former parent, grandparent, or sibling to visit or communicate with the minor. . . .

. . .

COMMENT

This section permits a petitioner in a proceeding to adopt under this article to ask the court to approve an agreement for post-adoption visitation or communication with the adoptee by another individual. . . . Subsection (c) permits an adoptee's former parent (i.e., the noncustodial parent), grandparent, or sibling to seek a court order for post-adoption visitation or communication with the adoptee over the objection of the custodial parent and the adoptive stepparent. The court cannot issue an order unless it . . . determines that, despite the objections, it would be in the best interests of the adoptee.

e. OPEN ADOPTION

Birth Mother v. Adoptive Parents and New Hope Child and Family Agency

Supreme Court of Nevada, 2002.
59 P.3d 1233.

■ SHEARING, J.

This case involves an agreement between the appellant, birth mother, and the respondents, adoptive parents and New Hope Child and Family Agency (New Hope), which allowed the birth mother continuing contact, after the adoption, with the adopted child. All parties consented to the agreement. After the birth mother attempted to terminate her relinquishment of the child for adoption, the adoptive parents refused to continue to allow the birth mother contact with the child.

The birth mother filed a complaint alleging several claims, including breach of contract, based on the adoptive parents' noncompliance with the communication agreement. The adoptive parents and New Hope filed a motion to dismiss, which the district court granted. The birth mother appealed.

Prior to relinquishing custody of her child, the birth mother executed a document with New Hope entitled "Agreement Regarding Communication With And/Or Contact Between Birth Parents, Child Adoptee, and Adoptive Parents" (communication agreement), which New Hope had prepared. The communication agreement stated that the birth mother, her ex-husband, and New Hope "entered into a post adoption communication and contact agreement which is in the child's best interests." With New Hope's assistance, the birth mother selected the adoptive parents, and after meeting them, she relinquished her parental rights and consented to the adoption. The adoptive parents signed the communication agreement, which required that any prospective adoptive parent of the child agree to and abide by its terms.

Pursuant to the communication agreement, the adoptive parents agreed to call the birth mother when they first got home with the child and then once a month for the first three months the child was in their custody. The adoptive parents further agreed to provide the birth mother with pictures of the child and letters detailing her progress. The adoptive parents agreed that the birth mother could request photos every six months. They also consented to allow the birth mother to visit the child on or near each of the child's first three birthdays and to send the birth mother a videotape when the child started walking.

The adoptive parents were complying with the communication agreement when they filed their petition to adopt the child. However, shortly thereafter, the birth mother filed a motion objecting to the adoption and demanding that the adoptive parents return the child to her. Thereafter, the adoptive parents no longer permitted the birth mother contact with the child. The district court denied the birth mother's motion and later granted the adoptive parents' petition to adopt the child.

Subsequently, the birth mother filed a complaint against the adoptive parents and New Hope seeking specific performance of the communication agreement or, in the alternative, monetary damages. She alleged breach of contract, unjust enrichment/quantum meruit, breach of the covenant of good faith and fair dealing, interference with contractual relations, emotional distress, and negligent or intentional misrepresentation. The adoptive parents and New Hope filed a motion to dismiss.

Without holding a hearing, the district court entered its order granting the motion to dismiss. The district court stated that "according to NRS 127.160 an adoption completely abrogates the legal relationship between a child and his natural parents." An adoption decree was entered for the adoption of the birth mother's child. The district court explained that the adoption decree is "the final and only document governing the terms of adoption," and therefore, the birth mother needed to seek relief under the adoption decree. Because the adoption decree did not refer to the communication agreement, and is the sole document governing the adoption, it provided no relief for the birth mother as to claims involving the communication agreement. Accordingly, the district court dismissed the birth mother's complaint for failure to state a claim upon which relief can be granted.

This court reviews a district court's conclusions of law, including statutory interpretations, de novo. Although Nevada does not have a statute that expressly addresses the issue of post-adoption contact, unlike a number of other states, NAC 127.210(4)(c) does state that a child-placing agency "may offer open adoptions in which ... contact between the adoptive family and biological parent may be arranged, if that contact is agreed upon by all persons involved." The regulation does not explicitly provide for post-adoption contact; however, it could be interpreted to permit agreements allowing such contact, especially because we conclude that these agreements do not per se violate Nevada's public policy of protecting a child's best interests. Yet, even if NAC 127.210(4)(c) encompasses these agreements, Nevada law fails to provide enforcement for such agreements. In other jurisdictions, agreements allowing post-adoption contact, while not prohibited, are also not enforceable absent specific statutory provisions. We conclude, therefore, that without such a specific Nevada statutory provision, the agreement between the birth mother and the adoptive parents is unenforceable.

Further, Nevada law makes it clear that an adoption decree terminates all rights of the natural parent and confers such rights upon the adoptive parents. NRS 127.160 addresses the rights and duties of adopted children and adoptive parents. It provides that:

> Upon the entry of an order of adoption, the child shall become the legal child of the persons adopting him, and they shall become his legal parents with all the rights and duties between them of natural parents and legitimate child.... After a decree of adoption is entered, the natural parents of an adopted child shall be relieved of all parental responsibilities for such child, and they shall not exercise or have any rights over such adopted child or his property.

We have previously determined that NRS 127.160 "establishes a new legal family for the adopted child and terminates the legal relationship between the child and her natural kindred." Thus, subsequent to an adoption decree, a natural parent has no rights to the child unless provided for in the decree. We conclude that while an agreement may grant a natural parent rights to post-adoption contact, enforcing it would be inconsistent with the Legislature's mandate that a natural parent may not exercise any right to the adopted child not incorporated in the adoption decree.

This decision leads to an unsatisfactory result in that natural parents may consent to an adoption because, pursuant to an agreement, they believe they have a right to post-adoption contact with the child.[9] However, what many of these natural parents fail to realize is that, if the agreement is not incorporated in the adoption decree, their rights as to the child are terminated upon adoption and any contact with the child may be had only upon the adoptive parents' permission, regardless of the agreement. Despite this unfortunate result, this court cannot enforce such an agreement until the Legislature mandates otherwise. Because this agreement is unenforceable under Nevada law and the adoption decree governs, the birth mother cannot seek relief based on the agreement. Accordingly, we affirm the judgment of the district court granting the motion to dismiss.

NOTE

Laws on post-adoption contact vary among the states. In about half the states, open adoption agreements are permitted and enforceable. *See, e.g., Loftin v. Smith*, 590 So. 2d 323 (Ala. Civ. App. 1991); AZ. REV. STAT. ANN. § 8–116.01 (2011); *Michaud v. Wawruck*, 551 A.2d 738, 741 (Conn. 1988); LA. CHILD. CODE art. 1269.2 (2011); *Weinschel v. Strople*, 466 A.2d 1301 (Md. App. 1983); *Groves v. Clark*, 920 P.2d 981 (Mont. 1996); R.I. GEN. LAWS § 15–7–14.1 (2011). In a few states, post-adoption contact is declared unenforceable. N.C. GEN. STAT. § 48–3–610 (2011); OHIO REV. CODE ANN. § 3107.65 (West 2011); S.C. CODE ANN. § 20–7–1770(D) (2011).

Some states explicitly prohibit post-adoption contact as a condition for consent to an adoption. N.C. GEN. STAT. § 48–3–610 (2011); *In the Matter of the Termination of the Parent–Child Relationship of M.B. and S.B.*, 921 N.E.2d 494 (Ind. 2009). Other states let decisions about contact and visitation with birth relatives be made by the adoptive parents. MO. ANN. STAT. § 453.080.4 (West 2011); S.D. CODIFIED LAWS § 25–6–17 (2011); TENN. CODE. ANN. § 36–1–121(f) (2011).

Consider Annette Ruth Appell, *Reflections on the Movement Toward a More Child-Centered Adoption*, 32 W. NEW. ENG. L. REV. 1, 9–10 (2010):

> These adoptions with contact statutes make clear that when open adoptions are entered into under such a statute, parties have rights and obligations. Those open adoption agreements entered into outside these mechanisms continue to be unregulated. Major factors motivating states to adopt such regulations were the desirability of providing procedures for these arrangements, the wisdom of clarifying when these arrangements are extralegal and when they are subject to enforcement, and, of course, the growing understanding of children's interest in openness. This codification, also known as cooperative adoption, models and accommodates family privacy and the existential facts of adoption: that the birth family and adoptive family are tied together through the child and that adopted children are "forever members of two families—the one that gave them life and the one that nurtured them through the process of adoption."
>
> These adoption with contact statutes, informed as much by the political process as academic research, apply only to some adoptions and to some family members and not others. For example, some statutes limit cooperative adoption to parents who have consented to the adoption and preclude parents whose parental rights were involuntarily terminated. Such statutes are inconsistent with research that suggests parents who contested the termination and adoption can be successful participants in post-adoption contact. Moreover, children's attachments to parents are not necessarily dependent on the way parental rights were terminated. A number of statutes confine the persons who can enter into

---

9. In such a situation, natural parents may attempt to contest the validity of their consent to an adoption by arguing mistake of fact. To avoid this issue in the future, agencies should inform natural parents of the need to incorporate the agreement into the adoption decree if their consent is conditioned upon post-adoption contact.

enforceable post-adoption-contact agreements to parents or relatives to whom children have a substantial relationship, even though research suggests that a number of relatives (especially grandparents) can be important participants in post-adoption contact and that many infant adoptions involve ongoing contact with them.

In addition, although the statutes are commendable for their respect for the adoptive kin network's autonomy, most do not provide for counseling or other mechanisms to help the participants understand their rights and responsibilities, the value and purpose of adoption with contact, or the special challenges of blending multiple families. In the end, though, these statutes signify an important message about the value and existence of adoptive kin networks, the endurance of biological kinship, and the status of post-adoption-contact agreements entered into pursuant to these statutes and those entered into without legal sanction.

f.   EQUITABLE ADOPTION

Lankford v. Wright

Supreme Court of North Carolina, 1997.
489 S.E.2d 604.

■ Frye, Justice.

The sole issue in this case is whether North Carolina recognizes the doctrine of equitable adoption. We hold that the doctrine should be recognized in this state, and therefore, we reverse the decision of the Court of Appeals.

. . .

Equitable adoption is a remedy to "protect the interest of a person who was supposed to have been adopted as a child but whose adoptive parents failed to undertake the legal steps necessary to formally accomplish the adoption." The doctrine is applied in an intestate estate to "give effect to the intent of the decedent to adopt and provide for the child."

. . .

Adoption did not exist at common law and is of purely statutory origin. Equitable adoption, however, does not confer the incidents of formal statutory adoption; rather, it merely confers rights of inheritance upon the foster child in the event of intestacy of the foster parents. In essence, the doctrine invokes the principle that equity regards that as done which ought to be done. The doctrine is not intended to replace statutory requirements or to create the parent-child relationship; it simply recognizes the foster child's right to inherit from the person or persons who contracted to adopt the child and who honored that contract in all respects except through formal statutory procedures. As an equitable matter, where the child in question has faithfully performed the duties of a natural child to the foster parents, that child is entitled to be placed in the position in which he would have been had he been adopted. Likewise, based on principles of estoppel, those claiming under and through the deceased are estopped to assert that the child was not legally adopted or did not occupy the status of an adopted child.

. . .

The elements necessary to establish the existence of an equitable adoption are:

(1) an express or implied agreement to adopt the child,

(2) reliance on that agreement,

(3) performance by the natural parents of the child in giving up custody,

(4) performance by the child in living in the home of the foster parents and acting as their child,

(5) partial performance by the foster parents in taking the child into their home and treating the child as their own, and

(6) the intestacy of the foster parents.

See 2 AM. JUR. 2D *Adoption* § 54 (1994).

. . .

The dissent points out that a minority of jurisdictions have declined to recognize the doctrine of equitable adoption. However, we again note that an overwhelming majority of states that have addressed the question have recognized and applied the doctrine. More importantly, it is the unique role of the courts to fashion equitable remedies to protect and promote the principles of equity such as those at issue in this case. We are convinced that acting in an equitable manner in this case does not interfere with the legislative scheme for adoption, contrary to the assertions of the dissent. Recognition of the doctrine of equitable adoption does not create a legal adoption, and therefore does not impair the statutory procedures for adoption.

In conclusion, a decree of equitable adoption should be granted where justice, equity, and good faith require it. The fairness of applying the doctrine once the prerequisite facts have been established is apparent. Accordingly, we reverse the Court of Appeals' decision which affirmed the trial court's entry of summary judgment for defendants and remand to the trial court for further proceedings not inconsistent with this opinion.

Reversed and remanded.

■ MITCHELL, C.J., dissenting:

In its opinion, the majority for the first time accepts the doctrine of equitable adoption for North Carolina. As applied by the majority in this case, the doctrine results in neither an adoption nor equity. Therefore, although I am convinced the majority is engaged in an honest but unfortunate attempt to do good in the present case, I must dissent.

. . .

One maxim of equity, as the majority explains, is that equity regards as done that which in fairness and good conscience ought to be done. A court's notion of what is good or desirable does not determine what "ought to be done" in applying equity. The maxim of equity upon which the majority relies must yield to other controlling and established rules or maxims. One such maxim is that a court of equity, however benevolent its motives, is "bound by any explicit statute or directly applicable rule of law, regardless of its view of the equities." Thus, no equitable remedy may properly be applied to disturb statutorily defined and established rights, such as those rights created by North Carolina statutes controlling intestate succession or those controlling legal adoption.

The North Carolina Intestate Succession Act provides a comprehensive and extensive legislative scheme controlling intestate succession by, through, and from adopted children. N.C.G.S. § 29–17(a) provides:

> A child, *adopted in accordance with Chapter 48 of the General Statutes* or in accordance with the applicable law of any other jurisdiction, and the heirs of such child, are entitled by succession to any property by, through and from his adoptive parents and their heirs the same as if he were the natural legitimate child of the adoptive parents.

N.C.G.S. § 29–17(a) (1995) (emphasis added). The extensive scheme created by the legislature is clear and unambiguous. It provides, in pertinent part, that only those children who are adopted *in compliance with chapter 48* or adopted according to the requirements of another jurisdiction are eligible to take by intestate succession. Therefore, the maxim relied upon by the majority may not properly be applied here.

> Equity will not interfere where a statute applies and dictates requirements for relief. Use of equitable principles to trump an apposite statute thus is legally indefensible. The disregard of an unambiguous law based on sympathy is unjustifiable under the rubric of equity.

27A Am. Jur. 2d *Equity* § 246. It is well established that "where an extensive legislative scheme governs, it is incumbent upon chancellors to restrain their equity powers." *Id.* The application of the doctrine of equitable adoption by the majority in this case violates this principle of equity requiring greater restraint when dealing with statutory law than when addressing the common law. . . .

. . .

Presently, all states recognize a parent-child relationship through adoption if the certain and unambiguous statutory procedures of each specific state are followed. A strong minority of courts that have reviewed the issue have declined to recognize the doctrine of equitable adoption. . . .

. . .

In the present case, the controlling maxims of equity clearly require that this Court restrain its equity powers so as not to overrule comprehensive statutory schemes and, thereby, do harm to innocents. For these reasons, I respectfully dissent from the decision of the majority and would affirm the holding of the Court of Appeals which affirmed the order of the trial court.

g. A MARKET FOR ADOPTIONS?

RICHARD A. POSNER, SEX AND REASON

409–16 (1992).

[W]hy is [adoption] so heavily regulated rather than being left, like other voluntary transactions, to the free market? And heavily regulated it is in the country—with the results predicted by economics. In most states, only adoption agencies may lawfully supply children for adoption. The agencies are private organizations, most of them nonprofit (often church-sponsored). Many states limit the fees that agencies may charge to the adoptive parents, but the essential regulation is the prohibition against the agencies' "buying" children. Buying is defined in this context as paying the biological mother more than the medical and maintenance costs (food, housing, and so forth) of pregnancy and childbirth. The nonprofit character of most adoption agencies, coupled with regulatory supervision, has generated a cost-plus system of adoption fees, with the result that the limitation on the payment to the biological mother is passed through to, and holds down, the adoption fee. Adoption agencies screen couples applying for a baby, excluding those couples whom the agency considers unfit to raise a child, for example because in the agency's opinion the couple is too old. Applicants who are not screened out often must wait years before the agency has a baby for them to adopt.

Some states permit independent adoption, that is, adoption not arranged through an adoption agency. Usually the arranger is a lawyer or an obstetrician. He is forbidden to charge a fee for the adoption beyond his usual professional fee for such incidental services as drawing up the necessary papers, in the case of a lawyer, or checking the health of the infant, in the case of an obstetrician. Thus, like the adoption agency, the arranger of an independent adoption is forbidden to "buy" children for adoption, defined as before. But because independent adoption is difficult to monitor (much more so than agency adoption), it often operates much as a free market in babies for adoption would, with payments to the biological mothers that exceed the mothers' medical and maintenance costs and that are recouped in high fees charged the adoptive parents. Independent adoption is therefore commonly referred to as the "gray market." Just as gray is a mixture of white and black, so independent adoption is a mixture of lawful adoption and "baby selling," the latter constituting an illegal (black) market.

The term *baby selling*, while inevitable, is misleading. A mother who surrenders her parental rights for a fee is not selling her baby; babies are not chattels, and cannot be bought and sold. She is selling her parental rights. Of course in like vein one might speak of a slaveowner's selling his rights over the slave. But those rights are rights of ownership; a parent's rights, in our society anyway, are not. So, sacrificing vividness to accuracy, I hereby rename "baby selling" "parental-right selling."

One of the best confirmed hypotheses of economics—confirmed daily, in fact, in eastern Europe and the Soviet Union—is that a ceiling on the price that may lawfully be charged for a good or service will created both queues (waiting periods) and a black market, provided, of course, that the ceiling is lower than the free market price (otherwise it is not a real ceiling). This is what we observe in the adoption market today. The price ceiling that results from limiting the amount that may be paid the biological mother to her medical and maintenance expenses has created a shortage of babies for adoption. The consequence is queuing by the clientele of adoption agencies and of other lawful suppliers, and a black market for the bolder demanders.

The imbalance between demand and supply is growing. It is true that advances in the treatment of infertility, which have reduced the number of childless couples, may have offset the rising age of marriage, which has increased the number of childless couples because infertility is a positive function of a woman's age. If so, the demand for children for adoption is not increasing. But the supply is decreasing. For even though the increase in the illegitimacy rate has exceeded the decrease in the birth rate, the resulting net increase in the number of illegitimate births has in turn been exceeded by the increase in the rate at which unmarried mothers decide to retain their child rather than put it up for adoption. There appear to be two reasons for this increase. Women's income has risen, making women less dependent on men to support them and their children and thereby reducing the cost of illegitimacy. And the availability of abortion has reduced the fraction of accidental pregnancies that result in unwanted births.

The diminished supply of babies for adoption, interacting with a demand that is not declining, has exacerbated the effects of the price ceiling. It has increased the queue for babies, increased the number of independent adoptions—many of them black market adoptions—at the expense of the adoption agencies, driven up the black market price of parental rights (to about $25,000 in the case of a healthy white infant, the type of baby most highly valued by the market), and increased the pressures from the adoption agencies for stronger laws against the sale of parental rights and against independent adoptions generally.

The straightforward way to deal with the problems created by a price ceiling is to remove the ceiling. Why has this not been done in the adoption market, now that the declining supply of babies for adoption has made the economic consequences of the price ceiling palpable? Usury laws, which are to lending as adoption law is to adoption, have been phased out for just this reason. The answer most students of adoption would give is that the social costs of a free market in babies for adoption would exceed those of the existing regulated market. All the arguments made in support of this proposition, however, either are bad ones or could easily be met by placing minor restrictions on an otherwise free market.

1. The rich will snap up all the good babies, and the cost of acquisition will deprive those few middle-income couples fortunate enough to obtain a good baby of the resources they require to raise it properly. Actually the rich do better under the present system than they would in a free market. The rich have connections, and connections are vital in maneuvering in a regulated system. Wealthy couples always manage to jump to the head of the adoption queue, thereby paying a lower real price—a price that includes the cost of waiting as well as the adoption fee—than the couple of modest means, who must wait years for their baby. (Granted this comparison ignores the cost to a wealthy person of using his connections.)

It is true that black market prices for adoption are high, though they are only a small fraction of the total cost of raising a child. But they are not a good predictor of what the price would be in a free, unregulated market. For they are high because the seller has to be compensated for bearing the risk of punishment and because illegal sellers incur high costs of operation by virtue of having to conceal their activities from the authorities. Competition among pregnant women to sell their parental rights would drive the price of those rights down to a level only slightly above the medical and maintenance costs of pregnancy. Since those costs are saved by a woman who does not become pregnant, the net additional cost of buying parental rights over an existing baby, versus making a baby, would be slight or even negative—as where a woman having high opportunity costs of pregnancy (maybe she has a high income) buys the parental rights of a woman whose opportunity costs of pregnancy are low.

What is probably true is that most women who sold their parental rights would be less prosperous than the women who bought them. But this means that parental-rights selling would be wealth-equalizing.

2. The sale of parental rights may be value-maximizing from the standpoint of pregnant women and infertile couples, but it is bad from the standpoint of the children. Of course the welfare of children as well as that of their natural and adoptive parents should be considered in the design of public policy, since neither set of parents can be relied on in their decision making to weight to child's welfare as highly as the child itself would do, if it could be consulted. Adoption agencies screen adoptive parents in the interest of the children, and this screening would not be an inherent feature of a market in parental rights, just as it is not a feature, at least a systematic feature, of independent adoption. But adoption agencies lack good information about the relative fitness of competing couples seeking children, and many of the rules that such agencies have employed—such as requiring that the adoptive parents be of the same religion as the infant's parents (for it is unrealistic to speak of the infant's religion), or automatically excluding all couples over 40 years of age—make a poor fit with the interests of the child. There is no evidence that children adopted independently—even those obtained through the black market—are less happy or successful or well adjusted than children adopted through agencies, though admittedly the question appears not to have been studied.

3. *What about the danger that pedophiles will buy parental rights over children in order to abuse the children sexually?* ... [T]his danger cannot be dismissed out of hand. But it can be minimized, perhaps eliminated, by forbidding the sale of rights over children who are no longer infants—say children more than six months old. Very few child abusers have a sexual interest in infants; very few would acquire an infant for the purpose of being able to abuse it five or ten or fifteen years later; and whereas a stepfather usually first encounters his stepchild after the latter has emerged from infancy, when it is too late for the stepfather to be expected to form a parental-type bond that will inhibit incest with the child, the adoptive father ordinarily meets his adopted child when the latter is an infant, and would do so only then if the sale of rights over noninfants was prohibited. The suggested restriction on sale would be a minor curtailment of the market because for reasons discussed earlier there is little demand—little legitimate demand, at least—to adopt children past infancy. Moreover, persons with a criminal record of child abuse, or even all men not living as part of a heterosexual couple, could be forbidden to buy parental rights.

4. *The sale of a human being in any circumstances and for any reason is morally repulsive, and if permitted could undermine the taboo against slavery.* A variant of this argument, made by Margaret Jane Radin, is that what she naturally terms baby selling promotes "commodification," which is the tendency, characteristic of capitalist societies, to view goods and services as things that can be exchanged in a market. Fair enough, but some of us believe that this and most societies could use more, not less, commodification and a more complete diffusion of the market-oriented ethical values that it promotes. If, for example, clean air were commodified, we would have less air pollution than we do.

A better answer, though, is that baby selling, when viewed as a method of adoption, is not at all like the sale of a person into slavery. The "purchasers" get no more power over the baby than natural parents have over their children. What is sold, in fact, is not the baby but the natural mother's rights to keep the baby—which is why I say that "baby selling" is misnamed. The term misled Radin.

5. *The sale of parental rights will encourage eugenic breeding, altering the human gene pool in potentially harmful ways.* Markets foster innovation; so should we not be concerned that eugenic entrepreneurs will try to breed a race of supermen and superwomen? Too great a disparity among human beings, owing to selective breeding of some, could create differences among persons in physical appearance and in physical and mental ability that would

undermine cooperation and foment conflict, exploitation, even genocide, and, much like selective breeding of domestic animals, could introduce harmful mutations or, like incest, reduce genetic diversity. There are three reasons to discount these dangers. The first is that the market is unlikely to attract fertile couples. The second (and related) reason is that most people want their baby, biological or adopted, to be like them, so only Superman and Superwoman will want to have Superbaby. There is a genetic explanation for this preference (which is gene-fooling when the baby is adopted)— the similarity increases the confidence that it is *your* baby, not someone else's—and in addition it reduces the potential for conflicts between parents and child. Third, long before the eugenicists create a master race, biological parents will be improving their babies by surgical intervention in the fertilized ovum.

The more plausible concern with the genetic effects of parental-rights selling is the opposite. The mothers are likely to be drawn from the lower strata of society; and, if poverty and intelligence are negatively related, the IQs of these mothers will be below average, and the average IQ in society will therefore fall, with possible detrimental effects—higher costs of public education, more crime, and so on. But the danger that IQs will fall hardly seems a serious one, even if there is a strong, and genetic rather than environmental, positive correlation between income and IQ. It's not so much that if infertile couples were willing to pay for rights over high-IQ babies, a supply would be forthcoming, for demand would be limited by price. It is that most of the babies who would be obtained in a free market in parental rights are not babies who would be aborted; they are babies who would be retained by unmarried mothers. There probably would be a net increase in the number of babies from this class of mothers, but a small one.

6.   *How would parental-rights selling work? Could the buyer return the baby if it was not as healthy and intelligent as the seller had warranted it to be? Does this question not show that such a market is simply too bizarre an intellectual construct to deserve serious consideration?* Contracts in which the thing contracted over is a human being do present unique difficulties in matters of remedy, although the usual response is to require modification of the remedy rather than abolition of the market. A contract for the exclusive services of a person for a specified period of time is lawful and enforceable—but not by deeming the person a slave of the other party or even by issuing an injunction commanding him to continue working for that party, as distinct from an injunction forbidding him to work for anyone else. Similar adjustments in the normal principles of contract remedies would be necessary if adoption were left to the market. Adjustments are necessary already for cases in which adoptive parents sue the adoption agency or the independent adoption middleman because the baby turns out to be defective. Maybe for the baby's sake the purchaser of parental rights should not be allowed the usual privilege of returning defective merchandise, any more than he should be allowed to destroy it, but should be limited to a remedy in damages against the seller for the breach of whatever warranty of quality the seller may have given. Intermediaries—successors to today's adoption agencies—would spring into existence to guarantee quality to buyers.

What is true is that this program *sounds* fantastic and weird, just as it seems fantastic to imagine these literal "bonus babies" bragging when they grow up of the tremendous prices their parents paid in the baby market, and just as it seems fantastic and sad to imagine what would undoubtedly be the pronounced racial element in baby pricing. The demand for babies for adoption is weaker among blacks than among whites, while the supply of such babies is vastly greater; so the price of acquiring parental rights over black babies would be lower unless white couples considered black babies a close substitute for white ones, which most white couples probably would not, even if white demand for black babies were not artificially depressed by opposition within the black community.

. . .

I have left for last Gary Becker and Kevin Murphy's criticism of parental-rights selling, a criticism of particular importance because it comes from within economics rather than from persons hostile to a market system or ignorant of its workings. They argue that the universal ban on this practice strongly suggests that the sale of children lowers social utility. Young unmarried women and poor parents who need money are the two groups most likely to sell their children. Some children sold to prosperous families who want them may consider themselves better off than if they had remained with their parents. But even children who would suffer greatly might be sold because they have no way to compensate their parents for keeping them. There actually are two arguments here rather than one. The argument from the universal ban on the practice is logically independent of the argument from the adverse effect on children. For one might think the existence of a universal ban against a practice a good reason for suspecting on Darwinian grounds that the practice was a bad one, even if one could not think of a convincing hypothesis as to why it was bad.

Neither of the arguments persuades me. First, the ban is not universal, even if we ignore Roman and Japanese adult adoptions—straightforward commercial exchanges—on the ground that an adult can protect his interests better than a child can. Not only was there adoption of children as well as adults among the Romans, but money changed hands frequently. And until the seventh century A.D. an Anglo–Saxon father was permitted to sell his child in a case of necessity, provided the child had not yet turned 7. What is true is that the sale of parental rights appears to be rare outside of the United States today (which is one reason the United States is the major importer of babies—from Romania, Korea, and elsewhere). But then adoption is rare outside of the United States, for reasons presumably independent of legal sanctions. As for the ban on such sales in the United States, it is extraordinarily porous, and parental-rights selling is therefore in fact common, to the despair of its critics. Do words speak louder than actions, or actions louder than words? Little effort is made to stamp out the sale of parental rights, so one may question the social commitment to the ban.

Becker and Murphy's second argument appears to envisage the sale of rights over children who are no longer infants. The picture is of parents who have decided they cannot afford to raise their child after all and therefore abandon it, to its intense distress, to strangers. In these circumstances the sale certainly has a serious third-party effect—that is an effect on the child—that the parties to the sale may not take fully into account. This is another reason for forbidding the sale of rights over children who are no longer infants, but it does not touch the sale of rights over infants. Here the only sellers are single mothers; and who can say whether the average infant would (if fully informed) prefer to be raised by an unmarried woman eager to unload it rather than by a couple from a higher social and economic stratum eager to raise it? Any loss of welfare to the child, moreover, would have to be compared to the gain to the transacting parties.

NOTE

Judge Posner's approach has stirred considerable controversy. For thoughtful criticisms, see Jane Maslow Cohen, *Posnerism, Pluralism, Pessimism*, 67 B.U. L. REV. 105 (1987); Robin West, *Submission, Choice, and Ethics: A Rejoinder to Judge Posner*, 99 HARV. L. REV. 1449 (1986).

h. TRANSNATIONAL ADOPTIONS

Eleanor P. v. California Department of Social Services

California Court of Appeal, 2010.
181 Cal. App. 4th 50.

■ SIMS, JUDGE.

This is a tragic case in which there can be no good ending for anyone.

Appellants Eleanor P. and Martin S. appeal from an order denying their petition to set aside their Ukrainian adoption of a Ukrainian girl, M.S. The petition was opposed by the California Department of Social Services (the Department or DSS).

. . .

In early 2003, appellants began the process to adopt a foreign-born child. Appellants engaged a California lawyer and a private California adoption agency, Heartsent Adoptions, Inc. (Heartsent), which was licensed by the Department to provide noncustodial intercountry adoption services.

In late 2003, appellants spent several weeks in Ukraine for the adoption. On December 15, 2003, by decree of a Ukrainian court, appellants adopted M.S., a three-year-old Ukrainian girl. The Ukrainian court decree stated in part: "It was found out from the case documents that the child's [biological] mother is mentally sick. She left the child at the hospital and never visited her. The place of father's residence was not identified. Since February 2002 the child has been made the ward of the government. The medical history of the girl says that she is almost healthy though psychologically delayed." A hospital record says the mother has epilepsy.

Appellants' declarations assert they believed M.S. was healthy, were not aware of this medical background information until after the adoption was finalized, and the documents were not translated for them until after the adoption was completed.

Appellants brought M.S. to live in their Davis home. They did not "readopt" M.S. in California, as authorized by section 8919.[1]

---

1. Undesignated statutory references are to the Family Code.

Section 8919 provides:

(a) Each state resident who adopts a child through an intercountry adoption that is finalized in a foreign country shall readopt the child in this state if it is required by the Department of Homeland Security. Except as provided in subdivision (c), the readoption shall include, but is not limited to, at least one postplacement in-home visit, the filing of the adoption petition, the intercountry adoption court report, accounting reports, the home study report, and the final adoption order. If the adoptive parents have already completed a home study as part of their adoption process, a copy of that study shall be submitted in lieu of a second home study. No readoption order shall be granted unless the court receives a copy of the home study report previously completed for the international finalized adoption by an adoption agency authorized to provide intercountry adoption services pursuant to Section 8900. The court shall consider the postplacement visit or visits and the

In California, various evaluations were performed due to M.S.'s low level of functioning. Healthcare professionals diagnosed her with spastic cerebral palsy, reactive attachment disorder, oppositional defiance disorder, moderate mental retardation, global development delay, ataxia, fetal alcohol syndrome or effect, microcephaly, and post-traumatic stress disorder. Appellants assert M.S. cannot live in a normal home environment, is unadoptable, and has been living in intensive foster care placement in Arizona since 2005.

On May 20, 2008, appellants filed in Yolo County Superior Court a "MOTION TO SET ASIDE ORDER OF ADOPTION UNDER FAMILY CODE SECTION 9100" (the petition). This petition was served on the Department, which filed an opposition. The opposition argued section 9100 is inapplicable to intercountry adoptions; the statutory remedy is not appropriate because the child could not be returned to Ukraine; the records gave notice of potential problems; and the Department did not have access to underlying investigative reports or documentation it would need to fulfill its obligation to make a full report to the court.

On October 31, 2008, after hearing oral argument, the superior court issued an "ORDER DENYING PETITION TO SET ASIDE INTERCOUNTRY ADOPTION PURSUANT TO FAMILY CODE SECTION 9100." The order denied the petition on the ground the court lacked jurisdiction to make a ruling on the matter.

. . .

---

previously completed home study when deciding whether to grant or deny the petition for readoption.

(b) Each state resident who adopts a child through an intercountry adoption that is finalized in a foreign country may readopt the child in this state. Except as provided in subdivision (c), the readoption shall meet the standards described in subdivision (a).

(c)(1) A state resident who adopts a child through an intercountry adoption that is finalized in a foreign country with adoption standards that meet or exceed those of this state, as certified by the State Department of Social Services, may readopt the child in this state according to this subdivision. The readoption shall include one postplacement in-home visit and the final adoption order.

(2) The petition to readopt may be granted if all of the following apply:

(A) The adoption was finalized in accordance with the laws of the foreign country.

(B) The resident has filed with the petition a copy of both of the following:

(i) The decree, order, or certificate of adoption that evidences finalization of the adoption in the foreign country.

(ii) The child's birth certificate and visa.

(C) A certified translation is included of all documents described in this paragraph that are not in English.

(3) If the court denies a petition for readoption, the court shall summarize its reasons for the denial on the record.

(d) The State Department of Social Services shall certify whether the adoption standards in the following countries meet or exceed those of this state:

(1) China

(2) Guatemala

(3) Kazakhstan

(4) Russia

(5) South Korea

(e) In addition to the requirement or option of the readoption process set forth in this section, each state resident who adopts a child through an intercountry adoption which is finalized in a foreign country may obtain a birth certificate in the State of California in accordance with the provisions of Section 102635 or 103450 of the Health and Safety Code.

Appellants contend the superior court erred in construing section 9100's language "pursuant to the law of this state" to mean that an adoption must have occurred within California's borders in order to be afforded section 9100 relief to vacate the adoption.

However, the language of section 9100 itself, plus the language of a companion statute-section 9101—clearly show that section 9100 is limited to un-doing adoptions that were granted by California state courts.

Thus, section 9100 says a petition under that section "may be filed with the court that granted the adoption petition." "It is a conceded principle that the laws of a state have no force, *proprio vigore*[8] beyond its territorial limits...." With this in mind, the California Legislature surely did not intend to legislate court filings in a Ukrainian court. We therefore infer "the court that granted the adoption petition" in section 9100 must be a California state court. Moreover, when two statutes touch upon a common subject, they are to be construed in reference to each other.... In the event an adoption is vacated under section 9100, section 9101 places responsibility for the support of the now unadopted child on "[t]he county in which the proceeding for adoption was had." In this case, there is no such county in California, and the California Legislature obviously has no power to order a Ukrainian county (if such even exists) to support the child. Where section 9100 requires the petition to be filed "with the court that granted the adoption petition," the reference is to a court within the state of California. In this case, the petition was not filed "with the court that granted the adoption petition." Accordingly, the Yolo County Superior Court correctly ruled that it had no authority to adjudicate the petition.

. . .

The sentence in which the word "may" occurs is as follows:

(a) If a child adopted pursuant to the law of this state shows evidence of a developmental disability or mental illness as a result of conditions existing before the adoption to an extent that the child cannot be relinquished to an adoption agency on the grounds that the child is considered unadoptable, and of which conditions the adoptive parent or parents had no knowledge or notice before the entry of the order of adoption, a petition setting forth those facts may be filed by the adoptive parents or parent with the court that granted the adoption petition. (§ 100.)

In this sentence, the word "may" is used in the permissive sense of giving a parent or parents discretion whether to file a petition under section 9100. This is in stark contrast to section 8919 ... which requires a readoption of a child adopted in a foreign country "if it is required by the Department of Homeland Security."

So, by its use of "may," section 9100 makes clear that the parent or parents have discretion whether to file a petition under that statute.

However, once the decision is made to file a petition, the petition must be filed "with the court that granted the adoption petition." This is the only construction that makes sense. No other court is designated as the proper place for the filing of a petition. If the petition could be filed in any court, then reference to "the court that granted the adoption petition" would be unnecessary. Moreover, since the petition seeks to unadopt a child, it is only reasonable to require the petition to be filed in the court that has the records

---

8. By its own strength.

of the original adoption. Thus, if a petition under section 9100 is filed, it must be filed "with the court that granted the adoption petition."

. . .

For these reasons, then, we conclude that section 9100 applies only to adoptions granted by a California state court. This is the law that must be applied in this difficult case. The trial court correctly found that section 9100 could not be used to undo the Ukrainian adoption.

The judgment (order) is affirmed.

NOTES

1. A seven-year-old child named Artyom adopted from Russia by a Tennessee woman was sent alone on a plane back to Russia with a note stating that the boy had violent and psychopathic tendencies. *See* Clifford J. Levy, *Adopted Boy, 7, Is Sent Back, Outraging Russia*, N.Y. TIMES, Apr. 10, 2010, at A1. Should adoptive parents be allowed to return children adopted from other countries? Should government agencies be required to warn prospective adoptive parents of the risks of transnational adoptions?

After Artyom was returned, Russia threatened to ban adoptions of Russian children by Americans. Michael Schwirtz, *Pact on Adoptions Ends a U.S.–Russian Dispute*, N.Y. TIMES, July 14, 2011, at A12. Russia is one of the largest sources of adopted foreign children in the United States, with more than 50,000 adopted since 1991. Although most adoptions have been successful, both countries have acknowledged some cases in which adopted children died from abuse in American homes. *Id.* On July 13, 2011, Secretary of State Hillary Rodham Clinton and her Russian counterpart, Foreign Minister Sergei V. Lavrov, signed an agreement that would allow such adoptions to proceed but under heightened scrutiny. The agreement gives the Russian government the authority to approve which adoption agencies operate in the country, and will provide mechanisms for monitoring families after adoptions. Prospective parents will be screened more thoroughly and be better informed about children's medical histories and upbringing. The agreement is awaiting ratification by the Russian Parliament. *Id.*

2. Consider Martin T. Stein, Scott Faber, Susan P. Berger, & Gilbert Kliman, *International Adoption: A 4–Year–Old Child With Unusual Behaviors Adopted at 6 Months of Age*, 114 PEDIATRICS 1425 (2004):

> The current generation of pediatricians have cared for thousands of children adopted from orphanages in Eastern Europe, Russia, and Asia. Medical, developmental, and behavioral conditions occur in these children with a higher frequency and greater severity compared with most children born in the United States. In many internationally adopted children, significant developmental delays in motor, language, and social skills associated with growth failure and malnutrition are seen when they arrive in the home of their adopted family. Remarkably, many of these children reveal a physical and psychological resiliency as age-appropriate neuromaturational milestones are achieved in a catch-up pattern. In addition, growth parameters are often expressed on growth charts as an accelerated velocity from adequate nutrition and nurturance. Other children in these circumstances do not catch up so dramatically. Failure to thrive, feeding problems, and behavioral disorders emerge in the first year after the adoption.

3. Should international law more tightly regulate intercountry adoptions? The Hague Convention on Protection of Children and Co-operation in Respect of Intercountry Adoption was signed by the United States in 1994 and came into force in April 2008. Seventy-five countries have signed the Convention. Article I states that the objectives are:

a) to establish safeguards to ensure that intercountry adoptions take place in the best interests of the child and with respect for his or her fundamental rights as recognized in international law;

b) to establish a system of co-operation amongst Contracting States to ensure that those safeguards are respected and thereby prevent the abduction, the sale of, or traffic in children;

c) to secure the recognition in Contracting States of adoptions made in accordance with the Convention.

For more information on intercountry adoptions by U.S. parents, see *Intercountry Adoption*, U.S. DEPARTMENT OF STATE BUREAU OF CONSULAR AFFAIRS, http://adoption.state. gov.

3. STANDARDS

a. CHILD'S BEST INTEREST

Sonet v. Unknown Father

Court of Appeals of Tennessee, 1990.
797 S.W.2d 1.

■ CANTRELL, J.

The appellant, Mary Elisabeth Sonet, appeals the trial court's dismissal of her petition to adopt Joseph Daniel Hasty, and the trial judge's finding that the adoption was not in the child's best interest.

Joseph Daniel Hasty was born on November 20, 1987 to an unmarried teen-aged daughter of a workman who did odd jobs for Mr. and Mrs. Sonet. The natural mother surrendered the child to Mr. and Mrs. Sonet on November 25, 1987. The Sonets filed a petition to adopt on April 7, 1988. After a hearing in the lower court in August of 1989, the trial judge denied the petition. For the reasons set out below, we affirm the judgment.

[Harry and Mary Elisabeth Sonet married in June of 1987. Mrs. Sonet was approximately sixty-five years old at the time of the marriage. Mr. Sonet was sixty-two. In November of 1987, the fourteen-year-old daughter of a man working for Mr. and Mrs. Sonet gave birth to a son, Joseph Daniel Hasty. The Sonets, who had previously discussed adopting a child, persuaded the mother to surrender the child to them. They filed a petition for adoption in April of 1988. Mr. and Mrs. Sonets' relationship became strained, and in February of 1989, Mrs. Sonet and the child had moved out of the home they had previously occupied. The Sonets have not lived together since that time. Mr. Sonet ceased to be a factor in this adoption. The petition has been pursued solely by Mrs. Sonet.]

Wanda Martin, a Protective Service worker assigned to the Sonet case, testified that the Department of Human Services had received five neglect referrals regarding this child. The first referral was received on June 27, 1988, and alleged that this child was not being properly cared for and was being carried awkwardly.... [A] second referral was received from Metro General Hospital on July 7, 1988 asserting that Joseph was a failure to thrive child. The failure to thrive was asserted to be caused by neglect due to a lack of knowledge in properly caring for an infant.

On September 30, 1988, the Department received two referrals alleging that Joseph was being neglected due to no electricity in the home among other concerns. An investigation revealed that although the home was without electricity, Ms. Sonet was making the necessary provisions for Joseph's food and care.

Another referral of neglect was made on January 4, 1989, alleging that Joseph was malnourished and developmentally delayed. An investigation by the Department of Human Services did not substantiate this allegation.

On March 31, 1989, Joseph was removed from the custody of Mrs. Sonet by the State of Florida Department of Health and Human Resources. Mrs. Sonet was in Florida taking care of some of her business interests. She stopped at a roadside park where the child allegedly ran into the road and climbed on the playground equipment unsupervised. When Mrs. Sonet asked a stranger in the park to watch the child for her, some bystanders became concerned and contacted the Florida Department of Human Services. Because of Mrs. Sonet's age, her out of state automobile registration, and the lack of any papers showing her right to custody of the child, the authorities were suspicious that the child was being kidnapped.

From March 31, 1989 until May 11, 1989, Joseph remained in the custody of the Florida Department of Health and Human Services and resided at the Lee County Children's Home. During that period of time Joseph contracted strep throat, scarlet fever, pink eye and ear infections. Joseph was placed in the temporary legal custody of the Tennessee Department of Human Services on May 11, 1989, and subsequently placed in a foster home in Tennessee for about one month until custody was returned to Ms. Sonet by court order on June 26, 1989. Ms. Sonet testified that when he was returned to her, Joseph had two fingernails missing and that one of his toes was raw and bleeding from wearing shoes that were too small and that he had another ear infection.

On June 23, 1989, the Tennessee Department of Human Services had Joseph evaluated at the Vanderbilt Child Development Center by Dr. Anna Baumgaertel. She found that Joseph had been environmentally deprived over a long period of time and that he was developmentally delayed as a result. At eighteen months, she found Joseph to have developed only to the extent of a thirteen month old. She advised against his being returned to the custody of Ms. Sonet.

On the other hand, Dr. Charlene Weisburg, the pediatrician at Metro Nashville General Hospital that treated Joseph for failure to thrive, feels strongly that Ms. Sonet should be allowed to adopt the child and does not attribute Joseph's slow development to environmental deprivation, but to the fact that Joseph's parents are short and small.

Ms. Sonet was evaluated by numerous doctors and social workers prior to the hearing. These evaluations resulted in both negative and positive recommendations....

Wanda Martin and Cindy Holton are the two social counselors from the Tennessee Department of Human Services assigned to the Sonet case. Wanda Martin testified that none of the five neglect referrals received prior to the Florida incident justified removal of Joseph from the Sonets' custody. Moreover, she testified that the Sonets were willing to work with the Department on any problem it found.

. . .

At the conclusion of the proof, the trial court dismissed the adoption petition and awarded custody of Joseph to the Tennessee Department of Human Services in order that Joseph be placed in a stable and permanent environment. The trial court found that due to the lack of Mrs. Sonet's parenting ability with no foreseeable improvement, her age and the child's failure to thrive, it is not in the best interest of Joseph to continue to live with or to be adopted by Mrs. Sonet.

. . .

It is well established that the best interest of the child is the paramount consideration in an adoption proceeding. . . . Moreover, when the interest of a child and those of an adult are in conflict, such conflict must be resolved in favor of the child. . . .

There was conflicting evidence presented at trial as to whether it was in the best interest of this child to be adopted by Mrs. Sonet. Mrs. Sonet testified that she loved Joseph and that she had been a good mother to him. There was no dispute that Joseph was bonded to Mrs. Sonet. However, for every positive evaluation of Mrs. Sonet as a parent, there is a negative evaluation to match it.

Mrs. Sonet's age was one factor mentioned by the trial court in its decision to dismiss the adoption petition. Age is a legitimate factor to be considered in adoptions especially if the petitioner could not be expected to be in good health until the child is emancipated. . . . Mrs. Sonet is now approximately seventy years old. Her only help in raising the child would come from the unrelated family living in her home. The child is now almost three. We agree that Mrs. Sonet's age is a factor to be considered. The other factors mentioned by the trial court were a lack of parenting ability with no foreseeable improvement and Joseph's failure to thrive in Ms. Sonet's care.

Our standard of review is "de novo upon the record of the trial court, accompanied by a presumption of the correctness of the finding, unless the preponderance of the evidence is otherwise." . . . Also, the findings of the trial court as to the credibility of the witnesses are entitled to great weight . . . After a careful review of the record in this case, we conclude that the judgment of the trial court is supported by a preponderance of the evidence.

b.   RACE AND ETHNICITY

Petition of R.M.G.

District of Columbia Court of Appeals, 1982.
454 A.2d 776.

■ FERREN, ASSOCIATE JUDGE:

In this case of competing petitions for adoption of a black child, we review a trial court decision granting the petition of the child's black grandparents and denying the petition of her white foster parents. Applying all relevant factors, the trial court found both families suitable to adopt the child, but concluded that the race factor tipped the scales in favor of the black grandparents.

Although race, among other factors, can be relevant in deciding between competing petitions for adoption, the statute expressly incorporating that factor, as well as the trial court's application of it, must survive "strict scrutiny," in order to comport with the equal protection requirement of the Constitution. I conclude that the statute on its face withstands constitutional challenge but that the trial court's application is not sufficiently precise to satisfy the Constitution. The judgment accordingly must be reversed and the case remanded for further proceedings.

. . .

D. was born September 22, 1977, to unwed, teenage, black parents. By that time, her father lived in Cleveland, Ohio; her mother, in Washington, D.C. In early January 1978, D.'s mother decided to give her up for adoption and signed papers relinquishing parental rights. She did not tell the natural father. Nor did she tell his mother and stepfather, appellees R.M.G. and E.M.G.

On January 6, 1978, the Department of Human Resources placed D. with foster parents, appellants J.H. and J.H., who are white. The foster mother realized almost immediately that D. was not healthy. D. was suffering from nausea and diarrhea and, although more than three months old, weighed only 10 pounds. D., moreover, was extremely lethargic and, according to Dr. Robert Ganter, a child psychiatrist, showed signs of mental retardation. During the next year, however, D.'s foster parents nurtured her to good physical and mental health.[1]

On April 26, 1978, a few months after D. came to live with them, J.H. and J.H. filed a petition for adoption. Initially, the Department of Human Resources recommended approval. At the foster mother's insistence, however, the Department notified the child's natural father of the proposed adoption. He objected. His own mother and stepfather, R.M.G. and E.M.G., then filed a petition to adopt D. The natural father consented. The Department of Human Resources studied the grandparents' home and, withdrawing its earlier support of the foster parents' petition, recommended approval of the grandparents' petition.

At the hearing on both petitions beginning on April 27, 1979, the court received the following evidence: [t]he foster parents have four other children—three natural and a fourth, a black male, by adoption. They are a military family, living on a racially integrated military base with racially integrated schools. When asked about the problems of raising a child of another race, the foster mother testified that she and her husband had begun "an affirmative program" with their adopted male child. For example, she had obtained pre-school black history and coloring books for their son. She testified, "I make sure he knows that he's not white. I don't care how long he lives with us, he's black, and he's beautiful, and he's ours."

The child's natural grandmother and her husband also testified at the hearing. The grandmother has eight children (all by a previous marriage) of whom the youngest was 14 at the time of the hearing. She also has nine grandchildren, two of whom reside at her home (one is a few months younger than D.). Although the grandmother is employed outside the home, she testified that she would take a leave of absence to be with the child. Both the grandmother and her husband added that they wanted to raise D., that they were able to care for her, and that they desired to show her their love.

Doris Kirksey, a social worker, testified on behalf of the Department of Human Resources. She recommended D.'s placement with her grandparents "based on the premise that the best place for a child is ... with blood relatives." Ms. Kirksey discounted any harm that might come to D. from

---

1. At the adoption hearing in April 1979, Dr. Ganter testified that D. had "bloomed enormously" and was of "high average to above average intelligence." The trial court concluded: "As a direct result of [the foster parents'] love, affection and special efforts, the child prospered to her present state of good health."

removal from her foster family. She based her assessment, in part, on the advice of her agency psychiatrist, Dr. Frances Welsing.

The trial court asked Dr. Welsing to testify in person. Her position, in a nutshell, was that cross-racial adoption always will be harmful to a child and—at the very least—should be discouraged. She emphasized that a non-white child would encounter particular difficulties in a white home upon reaching adolescence. Dr. Welsing made her recommendation to the Department of Human Resources without having met the J.H. family. Most of Dr. Welsing's testimony concerned the problems of cross-racial adoption in a broad social context.

In response to Dr. Welsing, the foster parents called their own expert, Dr. F. Jay Pepper. He identified several factors germane to adoption. He agreed that race should be considered, but only with respect to the attitudes of the particular family petitioning for adoption. Like Dr. Welsing, Dr. Pepper had not met J.H. and J.H.

. . .

The question of race is important.... However unpleasant, it would seem that race is a problem which must be considered and should not be ignored or minimized. Conversely, there are not conclusive absolutes to be drawn on the basis of race. It would seem, however, entirely reasonable that as a child grows older the ramifications of this problem would increase. At a later stage, notwithstanding love and affection, severe questions of identity arising from the adoption and race most probably would evolve. In the world at large, as the circle of contacts and routines widens, there are countless adjustments which must be made. Given the circumstances in this case, the child's present status is relatively secure and carefree. The future, in each of its stages—childhood, adolescence, young adulthood, etc.—would likely accentuate these vulnerable points. The Court does not conclude such a family could not sustain itself. Rather the question is, is there not a better alternative? ... The Court is concerned that, without fault, the H_____s stand to lose a beloved member of their family. However, our test remains the best interest of the child. It is believed that applying all of the factors to be considered, and evaluating the question in terms of past, present and future, that the appropriate alternative is adoption of the child by the G_____ family.

. . .

The cases I have found concerning the use of race in an adoption statute do not discuss whether advancement of a child's best interest is a "compelling" governmental interest. Implicitly, though, the courts treat it as such—and I agree. The critical question, then, is whether the particular use of race, as authorized and applied, is "necessary"—and thus precisely enough "tailored"—to achieve the child's best interest.

A. *Statutory Authorization of the Race Factor*

I turn, first, to statutory authorization. [The relevant statute] does not bar cross-racial adoption, which of course would be fatal. Thus, the racial classification is sustainable, if at all, only because it is one among a number of relevant factors.

. . .

The question thus becomes: whether statutory authority to consider race among the factors relevant to adoption, without preference for the race of any party, can ever be "necessary" for a determination of the child's best interest. Appellants say it cannot be, alleging that the "equal protection doctrine of the Constitution prohibits the use of skin color-defined race as a relevant issue in an adoption." I cannot agree with that unqualified statement.

Whether adopted by parents of their own or another race, adoptees often find it difficult to establish a sense of identity. "Identity," in this context, has at least three components: (1) a sense of "belonging" in a stable family and community; (2) a feeling of self-esteem and confidence; and (3) "survival skills" that enable the child to cope with the world outside the family. One's sense of identity, therefore, includes perceptions of oneself as both an individual and a social being. While adoptive parents' attitudes toward the adoption and their child are not the only influence on that child, these parental attitudes do affect, to a significant extent, whether the child will feel secure and confident in the family and community. Because race may be highly relevant to these parental attitudes—as the expert witnesses of both parties confirmed—it is relevant to the larger issue of the child's best interest.

I conclude, accordingly, that a significant number of instances where prospects for adoption are evaluated, those who are responsible for a recommendation and decision—social workers from the Department of Human Resources, expert witnesses at trial, and the trial court itself—will not be able to focus adequately on an adoptive child's sense of identity, and thus on the child's best interest, without considering race. Statutory authority for the court to take race into account, therefore, can be critically important in adoption proceedings. When considered among a number of factors, on the basis of evidence, without automatic or presumptive preference for an adoptive parent of a particular race, that criterion does not reflect a "racial slur or stigma" against any group. It is a criterion that markedly contrasts with the impermissible use of race both in facially discriminatory statutes and in facially neutral statutes—some referring to race, others not—masking invidious racial discrimination in the law either as enacted or as administered.

In sum, an inherently suspect, indeed presumptively invalid, racial classification in the adoption statute is, in a constitutional sense, necessary to advance a compelling governmental interest: the best interest of the child. It thus survives strict scrutiny—a result that is unusual, as racial classifications go, but not precluded.

B. *Judicial Application of the Race Factor*

The fact that the adoption statute does not per se reflect an unconstitutional denial of equal protection does not end our inquiry; for although—as a general proposition—the use of race, as one factor, may be necessary to serve the best interest of the child, there also is risk that this classification may be invoked in a racially discriminatory fashion. Thus, there remains the significant question whether the racial classification in the adoption statute, as applied in this particular case, is precisely enough tailored to the child's best interest to survive strict scrutiny, or suffers instead from a more generalized application that possibly reflects invidious discrimination.

. . .

[A] well-intentioned effort to protect a child against community prejudice [is not] a proper justification, in itself, for an adoption decision. This is not to suggest that such concerns motivated the trial court here. The point, rather, is to illustrate that there is a very real risk of misuse—of discriminatory application—of a racial classification in an adoption proceeding. We would be naive simply to ignore that possibility based on the commonly shared hope that times have changed. Thus, where race is a factor for the trial court to consider, appellate review of judicial discretion under the statute must be as exacting as our scrutiny of the statute itself.

. . .

When race is relevant in an adoption contest, the court must make a three-step evaluation: (1) how each family's race is likely to affect the child's development of a sense of identity, including racial identity; (2) how the families compare in this regard; and (3) how significant the racial differences between the families are when all the factors relevant to adoption are considered together.

In taking the first step concerning identity, the court must evaluate the probable effect of each family's race and related attitudes on the child's sense of belonging in the family and community, the child's self-esteem and confidence, and the child's ability to cope with problems outside the family.[37] Relevant questions bearing on one or more of these concerns, for example, would be: To what extent would the family expose the child to others of her own race through the immediate family? Through family friendships? Through the neighborhood? Through school? What other efforts will the family most likely make to foster the child's sense of identity—including racial and cultural identity—and self-esteem? To what extent has the family associated itself with efforts to enhance respect for the child's race and culture? To what extent has the family reflected any prejudice against the race of the child it proposes to adopt?

When the court takes the second step in the analysis—comparing the families—it hardly would be surprising if the answers to these questions favor prospective parents of the same race as the child.[38] But even when that is true, it is also possible that prospective parents of a different race may receive very positive ratings on these questions. If so, the third analytic step—how significant the racial differences are when all relevant factors are taken together—becomes especially important; for in that situation the racial factor may present such a close question that it will not have the significant, perhaps determinative, impact that it would if racial differences between parent and child simply were deemed a wholly negative factor.

. . .

In the present case, the trial court obviously was conscientious and thorough, properly treating race as only one of several relevant considerations. After reviewing the other concerns specified by statute, the court took the first analytic step as to race, beginning with the proposition—for which there was testimonial support—that "race is a problem which . . . should not be ignored or minimized." The court carefully noted, however, that, "[c]onversely, there are not conclusive absolutes to be drawn on the basis of

---

37. [A]ll black children, whether adopted or not, must be taught "survival skills"—that is, ways to cope with discrimination encountered in the world outside the family. To be capable of teaching survival skills, the family itself must be sturdy enough to stand up to any prejudice it may encounter.

38. Thus, contrary to our dissenting colleague's understanding of our opinion, I do not disagree with the proposition that there can be "a preference for intraracial adoption that is supported by evidence."

race. . . . The Court is concerned that little medical or scientific attention has been devoted to this problem." But the Court then found that generally "as a child grows older the ramifications of this problem would increase," and "severe questions of identity arising from the adoption and race most probably would evolve." As a consequence, the court concluded that racial differences between parent and child should be weighed as a negative factor in evaluating adoption.[39] The court then announced its decision, preceded by a rhetorical question: "The Court does not conclude such a[n interracial] family could not sustain itself. Rather, the question is, is there not a better alternative?" The Court answered in the affirmative. I understand the court to have concluded that although the other factors, taken together, may have slightly favored the white foster family, or at least given it equal standing to adopt, the race factor tipped the decision in favor of adoption by D.'s black grandparents.

The trial court . . . obviously was careful and concerned and did not necessarily reach an impermissible result. Nonetheless, while correctly beginning with the first analytical step as to race focusing on growth of the child's sense of identity, the court made no specific findings (reflecting the kinds of questions listed above) as to how race would be likely to affect this particular black child growing up, respectively, in the families of J.H. and J.H. and of E.M.G. and R.M.G. Furthermore, aside from reciting facts about the racial makeup of each family, the court did not articulate the comparative analysis required by steps two and three: how the families compare in their respective abilities to accommodate race, and how significant racial differences between the families are when all factors relevant to the adoption are considered together.

. . .

[A]ccordingly, we must reverse the judgment of the trial court and remand the case for further proceedings consistent with this opinion.

So ordered.

■ Mack, Associate Judge, concurring:

In joining the disposition ordered by Judge Ferren, I find it necessary to say in my own words what is, and is not, in issue here.

. . .

I think that reversal is required in this case because the trial court, unwittingly, employed the factor of race as an impermissible *presumption*. In *Bazemore v. Davis*, 394 A.2d 1377 (D.C. 1978) (en banc), we held that a presumption based upon the sex of a parent has no place in custody proceedings. Similarly, I suggest, a presumption based solely upon the race of competing sets of would-be parents has no place in adoption proceedings. In both instances the court is weighing the best interest of a particular child—Can interest in which the human factor of love is paramount. As we noted in *Bazemore*, a "norm is ill suited" for making that determination and it must be made "upon specific evidence relating to that child alone."

■ Newman, Chief Judge, dissenting:

. . .

---

39. The court was explicit in saying it would not rule out a cross-racial adoption if there were only the one petition at issue.

The hazards of interracial adoption should not be exaggerated, but neither should they be ignored. An inevitably imprecise prediction about the effects of an interracial placement must be made in the context of all relevant circumstances, including any mitigating efforts by the parents. But *when all other factors are in equipoise,* the *possibility* of an adverse effect, no matter how small or how unlikely, would suffice to permit the trial judge to tip the balance in the direction of the intraracial alternative.

The trial court found as facts that "[a]t a later stage, notwithstanding love and affection, severe questions of identity arising from the adoption and race most probably would evolve. In the world at large, as the circle of contacts and routines widens, there are countless adjustments which must be made." It concluded that the child's interests would probably be better served in the G. family. Given the equal balance of other factors, this conclusion is adequately supported if it is permissible to conclude that there is any potential adverse effect from the interracial alternative. That is indisputably the case here. Accordingly, the result below can be upset only if it is constitutionally impermissible to give any weight whatsoever to adverse effects on the child related to racial differences between herself and her parents.

NOTES

1. For more background on the controversy surrounding transracial adoptions, see generally Elizabeth Bartholet, *Where Do Black Children Belong?: The Politics of Race Matching in Adoption,* 139 U. Pa. L. Rev. 1163 (1991); Tavni Nagarsheth, Comment, *Crossing the Line of Color: Revisiting the Best Interest Standard on Transracial Adoptions,* 8 Scholar 45 (2005).

2. The three-part approach taken in *R.M.G.* was later criticized by a majority of the Court of Appeals of the District of Columbia "primarily because it effectuates a sharp departure from the flexible framework developed in our decisions for determining the best interests of the child." *In re Adoption of S.A.O.,* 494 A.2d 1316 (D.C. 1985). In *McLaughlin v. Pernsley,* 693 F.Supp. 318, 324 (E.D. Pa. 1988), the court explicitly found a compelling governmental interest in considering a child's "racial and cultural needs," but held race could not be the sole factor used in determining placement in a foster home.

3. In 1996, Congress passed legislation that prohibits states or any other entities that receive federal funds from denying or delaying a child's adoption because of the race, color, or national origin of the child or the person seeking to adopt the child. Pub. L. No. 104–188, Sec. 1808.

R. Richard Banks, *The Color of Desire: Fulfilling Adoptive Parents' Racial Preferences Through Discriminatory State Action*

107 Yale L.J. 875, 880–81, 943–44 (1998).

Both supporters and opponents of race matching often assume that putting an end to the practice would make adoption policy colorblind. The race-and-adoption debate, then, is framed as a contest between those who believe that race-conscious state action (race matching) furthers the interests of black children, and those who believe that colorblind state action (transracial adoption) does so. Contrary to the assumptions that underlie the debate, however, race matching is not the only form of race-based state action that structures the adoption process.

Adoption agencies' classification of children on the basis of race facilitates and promotes the exercise of racial preferences by prospective adoptive parents. I term this practice "facilitative accommodation." When engaged in by public agencies, facilitative accommodation, like race matching, is an instance of race-based state action. . . . Through facilitative accommodation, the state's racial classification promotes the race-based decisionmaking of prospective adoptive parents by framing the choice of a child in terms of race, encouraging parents to consider children based on the ascribed characteristic of race rather than individually. In both cases, a court, in finalizing the adoption, validates the actions of the adoption agency.

As a result of facilitative accommodation policies, most black children in need of adoption are categorically denied, on the basis of race, the opportunity to be considered individually for adoption by the majority of prospective adoptive parents. This could not occur were it not for current policies of facilitative accommodation.

. . .

My proposal is a simple one: Adoption agencies that receive any government funding should not accommodate adoptive parents' racial preferences. Beyond ceasing the classification of children by race in order to facilitate the satisfaction of adoptive parents' racial preferences, adoption agencies should make clear to prospective adoptive parents that their racial preferences are to play no role in the parents' selection of a child to adopt.

My vision of strict nonaccommodation consists of two elements. First, prospective adoptive parents would generally be prohibited from discriminating on the basis of race in their selection of a child to adopt, and birth parents who participate in the selection of adoptive parents would generally be prohibited from discriminating on the basis of race in doing so. Prospective adoptive parents and birth parents would be informed at the outset that the adoption process is not one in which racial discrimination is allowed. Parents would be encouraged to withdraw from the process if they did not think that they could abide by that rule, and adoption agency officials would have the authority to remove parents from the process if they determined that the parents in fact were discriminating on the basis of race. Parents could even be asked to sign a nondiscrimination agreement just as do other parties who do business with or enter a relationship with the government. Admittedly, this approach runs the risk of unintentionally underscoring the importance of race by constantly proclaiming that it must not matter. Nonetheless, the extent to which race currently matters in adoption suggests that mere governmental blindness to race would not decrease its significance.

Second, the general principle of nondiscrimination is qualified by my goal of promoting the maintenance of particular groups in the interest of cultural pluralism. Notwithstanding the law's focus on the rights of individuals and the primacy of the individual rather than the group in liberal political and social theory, our society has an important interest in maintaining cultural diversity. In American society, racial identity for minority groups is linked, though not identical, to a distinctive set of cultural characteristics, a nomos. To the extent the nomos is race-linked, racial minorities would be allowed to choose a child on the basis of race as a means of furthering that nomos. If one embraces cultural pluralism and accepts the inevitability of the state's either suppressing or promoting such communities (given the impossibility of neutrality), then such racially identified choices should be promoted in principle. The claim of contributing to the cultural pluralism of American society through their own race-consciousness is a claim that blacks and other racial minorities, but not whites, can make. The nomos of whiteness as a racial identity is nothing more than a historically generated and self-perpetuated set of privileges, expectations, and entitlements that are implemented through and reflected in the dominant norms, processes, rules, and structure of American society. There is no white race-based culture separate from mainstream American culture. In principle, then, strict nonaccommodation should allow fulfillment of the racial preferences of racial minorities, but not those of whites.

The demands of race politics, however, may make it difficult to enact a policy that allows blacks, but not whites, to choose a child of their own race. Whites might argue that such an asymmetry is unfair, perhaps even unconstitutional, a conclusion the Supreme Court might adopt as well. Even as it strives to undo the most pernicious race-consciousness, such a policy might itself be decried as a pernicious type of race-based treatment. More debate might ensue about the justice of the asymmetry than about the idea of nonaccommodation itself. If the merits of the policy were obscured by contentious debate about whether groups should be treated differently, I would advise the practical solution of not allowing any expression of same-race preference.

NOTE

For more on Professor Banks' proposal, see Elizabeth Bartholet, *Correspondence: Private Race Preferences in Family Formation*, 107 YALE L.J. 2351 (1998), and R. Richard Banks, *A Response to Elizabeth Bartholet*, 107 YALE L.J. 2357 (1998).

Mississippi Band of Choctaw Indians v. Holyfield

Supreme Court of the United States, 1989.
490 U.S. 30, 109 S.Ct. 1597, 104 L.Ed.2d 29.

■ JUSTICE BRENNAN delivered the opinion of the Court.

This appeal requires us to construe the provisions of the Indian Child Welfare Act that establish exclusive tribal jurisdiction over child custody proceedings involving Indian children domiciled on the tribe's reservation.

. . .

The Indian Child Welfare Act of 1978 (ICWA), was the product of rising concern in the mid–1970's over the consequences to Indian children, Indian families, and Indian tribes of abusive child welfare practices that resulted in the separation of large numbers of Indian children from their families and tribes through adoption or foster care placement, usually in non-Indian homes. Senate oversight hearings in 1974 yielded numerous examples, statistical data, and expert testimony documenting what one witness called "[t]he wholesale removal of Indian children from their homes, . . . the most tragic aspect of Indian life today." . . . Studies undertaken by the Association on American Indian Affairs in 1969 and 1974, and presented in the Senate hearings, showed that 25 to 35% of all Indian children had been separated from their families and placed in adoptive families, foster care, or institutions. . . . Adoptive placements counted significantly in this total: in the State of Minnesota, for example, one in eight Indian children under the age of 18 was in an adoptive home, and during the year 1971–1972 nearly one in every four infants under one year of age was placed for adoption. The adoption rate of Indian children was eight times that of non-Indian children.

Approximately 90% of the Indian placements were in non-Indian homes.... A number of witnesses also testified to the serious adjustment problems encountered by such children during adolescence, as well as the impact of the adoptions on Indian parents and the tribes themselves.

> . . .

At the heart of the ICWA are its provisions concerning jurisdiction over Indian child custody proceedings. Section 1911 lays out a dual jurisdictional scheme. Section 1911(a) establishes exclusive jurisdiction in the tribal courts for proceedings concerning an Indian child "who resides or is domiciled within the reservation of such tribe," as well as for wards of tribal courts regardless of domicile. Section 1911(b), on the other hand, creates concurrent but presumptively tribal jurisdiction in the case of children not domiciled on the reservation: on petition of either parent or the tribe, state-court proceedings for foster care placement or termination of parental rights are to be transferred to the tribal court, except in cases of "good cause," objection by either parent, or declination of jurisdiction by the tribal court.

Various other provisions of ICWA Title I set procedural and substantive standards for those child custody proceedings that do take place in state court. The procedural safeguards include requirements concerning notice and appointment of counsel; parental and tribal rights of intervention and petition for invalidation of illegal proceedings; procedures governing voluntary consent to termination of parental rights; and a full faith and credit obligation in respect to tribal court decisions.... The most important substantive requirement imposed on state courts is that of § 1915(a), which, absent "good cause" to the contrary, mandates that adoptive placements be made preferentially with (1) members of the child's extended family, (2) other members of the same tribe, or (3) other Indian families.

> . . .

This case involves the status of twin babies, known for our purposes as B. B. and G. B., who were born out of wedlock on December 29, 1985. Their mother, J. B., and father, W. J., were both enrolled members of appellant Mississippi Band of Choctaw Indians (Tribe), and were residents and domiciliaries of the Choctaw Reservation in Neshoba County, Mississippi. J. B. gave birth to the twins in Gulfport, Harrison County, Mississippi, some 200 miles from the reservation. On January 10, 1986, J. B. executed a consent-to-adoption form before the Chancery Court of Harrison County.... W. J. signed a similar form. On January 16, appellees Orrey and Vivian Holyfield filed a petition for adoption in the same court ... and the chancellor issued a Final Decree of Adoption on January 28.... Despite the court's apparent awareness of the ICWA, the adoption decree contained no reference to it, nor to the infants' Indian background.

Two months later the Tribe moved in the Chancery Court to vacate the adoption decree on the ground that under the ICWA exclusive jurisdiction was vested in the tribal court ... On July 14, 1986, the court overruled the motion, holding that the Tribe "never obtained exclusive jurisdiction over the children involved herein...." The court's one-page opinion relied on two facts in reaching that conclusion. The court noted first that the twins' mother "went to some efforts to see that they were born outside the confines of the Choctaw Indian Reservation" and that the parents had promptly arranged for the adoption by the Holyfields. Second, the court stated: "At no time from the birth of these children to the present date have either of them resided on or physically been on the Choctaw Indian Reservation." ...

The Supreme Court of Mississippi affirmed.... It rejected the Tribe's arguments that the state court lacked jurisdiction and that it, in any event, had not applied the standards laid out in the ICWA. The court recognized that the jurisdictional question turned on whether the twins were domiciled on the Choctaw Reservation....

[W]e now reverse.

. . .

[T]he sole issue in this case is, as the Supreme Court of Mississippi recognized, whether the twins were "domiciled" on the reservation.

The meaning of "domicile" in the ICWA is, of course, a matter of Congress' intent. The ICWA itself does not define it. The initial question we must confront is whether there is any reason to believe that Congress intended the ICWA definition of "domicile" to be a matter of state law....

First, and most fundamentally, the purpose of the ICWA gives no reason to believe that Congress intended to rely on state law for the definition of a critical term; quite the contrary. It is clear from the very text of the ICWA, not to mention its legislative history and the hearings that led to its enactment, that Congress was concerned with the rights of Indian families and Indian communities vis-a-vis state authorities. More specifically, its purpose was, in part, to make clear that in certain situations the state courts did *not* have jurisdiction over child custody proceedings. Indeed, the congressional findings that are a part of the statute demonstrate that Congress perceived the States and their courts as partly responsible for the problem it intended to correct.... Under these circumstances it is most improbable that Congress would have intended to leave the scope of the statute's key jurisdictional provision subject to definition by state courts as a matter of state law.

Second, Congress could hardly have intended the lack of nationwide uniformity that would result from state-law definitions of domicile....

We therefore think it beyond dispute that Congress intended a uniform federal law of domicile for the ICWA.

It remains to give content to the term "domicile" in the circumstances of the present case.... The question before us, therefore, is whether under the ICWA definition of "domicile" such facts suffice to render the twins nondomiciliaries of the reservation.

. . .

"Domicile" is, of course, a concept widely used in both federal and state courts for jurisdiction and conflict-of-laws purposes, and its meaning is generally uncontroverted.... "Domicile" is not necessarily synonymous with "residence," ... and one can reside in one place but be domiciled in another.... For adults, domicile is established by physical presence in a place in connection with a certain state of mind concerning one's intent to remain there.... One acquires a "domicile of origin" at birth, and that domicile continues until a new one (a "domicile of choice") is acquired.... Since most minors are legally incapable of forming the requisite intent to establish a domicile, their domicile is determined by that of their parents.... In the case of an illegitimate child, that has traditionally meant the domicile of its mother.... Under these principles, it is entirely logical that "[o]n occasion, a child's domicile of origin will be in a place where the child has never been." RESTATEMENT [(FOURTH) OF AMERICAN CONFLICTS LAW] § 14, Comment *b*.

It is undisputed in this case that the domicile of the mother (as well as the father) has been, at all relevant times, on the Choctaw Reservation.... Thus, it is clear that at their birth the twin babies were also domiciled on the reservation, even though they themselves had never been there. The statement of the Supreme Court of Mississippi that "[a]t no point in time can it be said the twins ... were domiciled within the territory set aside for the reservation," ... may be a correct statement of that State's law of domicile, but it is inconsistent with generally accepted doctrine in this country and cannot be what Congress had in mind when it used the term in the ICWA.

. . .

These congressional objectives make clear that a rule of domicile that would permit individual Indian parents to defeat the ICWA's jurisdictional scheme is inconsistent with what Congress intended.... The appellees in this case argue strenuously that the twins' mother went to great lengths to give birth off the reservation so that her children could be adopted by the Holyfields. But that was precisely part of Congress' concern. Permitting individual members of the tribe to avoid tribal exclusive jurisdiction by the simple expedient of giving birth off the reservation would, to a large extent, nullify the purpose the ICWA was intended to accomplish. The Supreme Court of Utah expressed this well in its scholarly and sensitive opinion in what has become a leading case on the ICWA:

> ... The protection of [the tribe's] interest [in its children] is at the core of the ICWA, which recognizes that the tribe has an interest in the child which is distinct from but on a parity with the interest of the parents. This relationship between Indian tribes and Indian children domiciled on the reservation finds no parallel in other ethnic cultures found in the United States. It is a relationship that many non-Indians find difficult to understand and that non-Indian courts are slow to recognize. It is precisely in recognition of this relationship, however, that the ICWA designates the tribal court as the exclusive forum for the determination of custody and adoption matters for reservation-domiciled Indian children, and the preferred forum for nondomiciliary Indian children.

We agree with the Supreme Court of Utah that the law of domicile Congress used in the ICWA cannot be one that permits individual reservation-domiciled tribal members to defeat the tribe's exclusive jurisdiction by the simple expedient of giving birth and placing the child for adoption off the reservation. Since, for purposes of the ICWA, the twin babies in this case were domiciled on the reservation when adoption proceedings were begun, the Choctaw tribal court possessed exclusive jurisdiction pursuant to 25 U.S.C. § 1911(a). The Chancery Court of Harrison County was, accordingly, without jurisdiction to enter a decree of adoption; ... its decree of January 28, 1986, must be vacated.

. . .

Whatever feelings we might have as to where the twins should live, however, it is not for us to decide that question. We have been asked to decide the legal question of *who* should make the custody determination concerning these children—not what the outcome of that determination should be. The law places that decision in the hands of the Choctaw tribal court. Had the mandate of the ICWA been followed in 1986, of course, much potential anguish might have been avoided, and in any case the law cannot be applied so as automatically to "reward those who obtain custody, whether lawfully or otherwise, and maintain it during any ensuing (and protracted) litigation." . . . It is not ours to say whether the trauma that might result from removing these children from their adoptive family should outweigh the interest of the Tribe—and perhaps the children themselves—in having them raised as part of the Choctaw community. Rather, "we must defer to the experience, wisdom, and compassion of the [Choctaw] tribal courts to fashion an appropriate remedy." . . .

The judgment of the Supreme Court of Mississippi is reversed, and the case is remanded for further proceedings not inconsistent with this opinion.

■ Justice Stevens, with whom The Chief Justice and Justice Kennedy join, dissenting.

The parents of these twin babies unquestionably expressed their intention to have the state court exercise jurisdiction over them. . . . Indeed, Appellee Vivian Holyfield appears before us today, urging that she be allowed to retain custody of B. B. and G. B.

Because J. B.'s domicile is on the reservation and the children are eligible for membership in the Tribe, the Court today closes the state courthouse door to her. I agree with the Court that Congress intended a uniform federal law of domicile for the Indian Child Welfare Act of 1978 (ICWA) . . . and that domicile should be defined with reference to the objectives of the congressional scheme. . . . I cannot agree, however, with the cramped definition the Court gives that term. To preclude parents domiciled on a reservation from deliberately invoking the adoption procedures of state court, the Court gives "domicile" a meaning that Congress could not have intended and distorts the delicate balance between individual rights and group rights recognized by the ICWA.

The ICWA was passed in 1978 in response to congressional findings that "an alarmingly high percentage of Indian families are broken up by the *removal*, often unwarranted, of their children from them by nontribal public and private agencies"

. . .

Although parents of Indian children are shielded from the exercise of state jurisdiction when they are temporarily off the reservation, the Act also reflects recognition that allowing the tribe to defeat the parents' deliberate choice of jurisdiction would be conducive neither to the best interests of the child nor to the stability and security of Indian tribes and families. . . .

. . .

When an Indian child is temporarily off the reservation, but has not been abandoned to a person off the reservation, the tribe has an interest in exclusive jurisdiction. . . . Similarly, when the child is abandoned by one parent to a person off the reservation, the tribe and the other parent domiciled on the reservation may still have an interest in the exercise of exclusive jurisdiction. That interest is protected by the rule that a child abandoned by one parent takes on the domicile of the other. But when an Indian child is deliberately abandoned by both parents to a person off the reservation, no purpose of the ICWA is served by closing the state court-house door to them. The interests of the parents, the Indian child, and the tribe in preventing the unwarranted removal of Indian children from their families and from the reservation are protected by the Act's substantive and procedural provisions. In addition, if both parents have intentionally invoked the jurisdiction of the state court in an action involving a non-Indian, no interest in tribal self-governance is implicated.

NOTE

On remand, the tribal court determined that it was in the best interest of the children to permit the Holyfields to adopt them. After the *Choctaw* ruling, some state courts created an "existing Indian family" exception to the ICWA that allows courts to rule that if the child was not part of an existing Indian family, the ICWA did not apply. This doctrine is losing favor; as of 2010, only six states still apply the exception: Alabama, Indiana, Missouri, Kentucky, Louisiana, and Tennessee. Several states first adopted the exception, then reversed themselves. *See, e.g., In re A.J.S.*, 204 P.3d 543, 549 (Kan. 2009). For more on the "existing Indian family" exception, see Dan Lewerenz & Padraic McCoy, *The End of "Existing Indian Family" Jurisprudence: Holyfield at 20, In the Matter of A.J.S., and the Last Gasps of a Dying Doctrine*, 36 Wm. Mitchell L. Rev. 684, 687 (2010).

Under the ICWA, the best interest of the child standard is considered in the context of the genetic continuity of a Native American tribe. *See, e.g., Quinn v. Walters*, 881 P.2d 795, 810 (Or. 1994):

> The ICWA is clearly concerned with the best interests of the "Indian child." However, the phrase "best interests of Indian children" in the context of the ICWA is different than the general Anglo–American "best-interest-of-the-child" standard applicable in adoption cases involving non-Indian children. Under the ICWA, what is best for the "Indian child" is to maintain ties with the Indian tribe, Indian culture, and Indian family. As one commentator states, "[i]n its strictest sense, the [ICWA] trades cultural protection for apparent economic and physical safety." Michael J. Dale, *State Court Jurisdiction Under the Indian Child Welfare Act and the Unstated Best Interest of the Child Test*, 27 Gonz. L. Rev. 353, 375 (1991–1992).

c.   SEXUAL ORIENTATION

Arkansas Department of Human Services v. Cole

Supreme Court of Arkansas, 2011.
2011 Ark. 145.

■ Brown, J.

Appellants, the Arkansas Department of Human Services and its Director and his successors, and the Arkansas Child Welfare Agency Review Board and its Chairman and his successors, appeal an Order and Judgment ruling Initiated Act 1 unconstitutional as a violation of fundamental privacy rights implicit in the Arkansas Constitution. . . .

On November 4, 2008, a ballot initiative entitled "An Act Providing That an Individual Who is Cohabiting Outside of a Valid Marriage May Not Adopt or Be a Foster Parent of a Child Less Than Eighteen Years Old" was approved by fifty-seven percent of Arkansas voters. The ballot initiative is known as the Arkansas Adoption and Foster Care Act of 2008 or "Act 1." Act 1 went into effect on January 1, 2009, and is now codified at Arkansas Code Annotated §§ 9–8–301 to –305.

Under Act 1, an individual is prohibited from adopting or serving as a foster parent if that individual is "cohabiting with a sexual partner outside of a marriage that is valid under the Arkansas Constitution and the laws of this state." Ark. Code Ann. § 9–8–304(a) (2009). This prohibition on adoption and foster parenting "applies equally to cohabiting opposite-sex and same-sex individuals." Act 1 further provides that the "public policy of the state is to favor marriage as defined by the constitution and laws of this state over unmarried cohabitation with regard to adoption and foster care." Act 1 also declares that "it is in the best interest of children in need of adoption or foster care to be reared in homes in which adoptive or foster parents are not cohabiting outside of marriage."

On December 30, 2008, appellees Sheila Cole and a group which includes unmarried adults who wish to foster or adopt children in Arkansas, adult parents who wish to direct the adoption of their biological children in the event of their incapacitation or death, and the biological children of those parents (collectively "Cole"), filed a complaint against the State of Arkansas, the Arkansas Attorney General, the Arkansas Department of Human Services (DHS) and its Director, and the Arkansas Child Welfare Agency Review Board (CWARB) and its Chairman (collectively "the State"). In her complaint, Cole pled ... (10) Act 1 burdens intimate relationships and thus violates their due process, equal protection, and privacy rights under articles 8 and 21 of the Arkansas Constitution and ARKANSAS CODE ANNOTATED § 16–123–101; (11) the ballot title of the initiative was materially misleading in violation of amendment 7 of the Arkansas Constitution; (12) Act 1 is unconstitutionally vague in violation of the Due Process Clause of the United States Constitution and the Civil Rights Act, 42 U.S.C. § 1983; and (13) Act 1 is unconstitutionally vague in violation of the Due Process Clause of the Arkansas Constitution and ARKANSAS CODE ANNOTATED § 16–123–101.

On January 16, 2009, the State moved to dismiss Cole's complaint for failure to state a claim upon which relief can be granted under Arkansas Rule of Civil Procedure 12(b)(6). On the same day, the Family Council Action Committee, a sponsor of Act 1, and its President Jerry Cox (collectively "FCAC"), moved to intervene as an additional party in support of Act 1. Following a hearing on March 6, 2009, the circuit court granted the motion to intervene, and FCAC filed a separate motion to dismiss adopting the State's motion to dismiss.

. . .

After conducting discovery, Cole, the State, and FCAC moved for summary judgment. The circuit court conducted a hearing, and in an order dated April 16, 2010, the circuit court granted Cole's motion for summary judgment on Count 10 and declared Act 1 unconstitutional under the Arkansas Constitution; granted the State's and FCAC's motions to dismiss and motions for summary judgment on all of the claims asserted under the United States Constitution (Counts 1, 3, 5, 7, 9, and 12); and dismissed the remaining claims under the Arkansas Constitution (Counts 2, 4, 6, 8, and 13), determining that it was not necessary to reach them. . . .

The circuit court further determined that because Act 1 burdens the fundamental right to privacy implicit in the Arkansas Constitution, as recognized by *Jegley v. Picado*, 80 S.W.3d 332 (Ark. 2002), the constitutionality of Act 1 must be analyzed under strict or heightened scrutiny, which means it cannot pass constitutional muster unless it provides the least restrictive method available that is narrowly tailored to accomplish a compelling state interest. The circuit court found that "Initiated Act 1 is facially invalid because it casts an unreasonably broad net over more people than is needed to serve the State's compelling interest. It is not narrowly tailored to the least restrictive means necessary to serve the State's interest in determining what is in the best interest of the child." Lastly, the circuit court concluded that "Due Process and Equal Protection are not hollow words without substance.

They are rights enumerated in our constitution that must not be construed in such a way as to deny or disparage other rights retained by the people." The circuit court, therefore, found Act 1 unconstitutional.

. . .

In *Jegley v. Picado,* this court considered a constitutional challenge to an Arkansas statute which criminalized acts of sodomy between homosexuals. The appellees in *Jegley* sought to have this sodomy statute declared unconstitutional insofar as it criminalized specific acts of private, consensual, sexual intimacy between persons of the same sex. The circuit court found the statute unconstitutional because Arkansas's fundamental right to privacy, which is implicit in the Arkansas Constitution, encompasses the right of people to engage in private, consensual, noncommercial, sexual conduct without the burden of government intrusions.

In considering the appellees' assertion in *Jegley* that the sodomy statute violated their right to privacy under the Arkansas Constitution, this court explored the rights granted to the citizens of Arkansas. We specifically found that no right to privacy is enumerated in the Arkansas Constitution. Nevertheless, we recognized that article 2, section 2 of the Arkansas Constitution does guarantee citizens certain inherent and inalienable rights, including the enjoyment of life and liberty and the pursuit of happiness, and section 15 guarantees the right of citizens to be secure in their own homes. *Jegley,* 80 S.W.3d at 347; Ark. Const. art. 2, §§ 2, 15. We further noted that privacy is mentioned in more than eighty statutes enacted by the Arkansas General Assembly, thereby establishing "a public policy of the General Assembly supporting a right to privacy."

In light of the language contained in the Arkansas Constitution, our statutes and rules, and our jurisprudence, this court concluded "that Arkansas has a rich and compelling tradition of protecting individual privacy and that a fundamental right to privacy is implicit in the Arkansas Constitution." We went on to hold that "the fundamental right to privacy implicit in our law protects all private, consensual, noncommercial acts of sexual intimacy between adults." Accordingly, because the sodomy statute burdened certain sexual conduct between members of the same sex, this court found that it impinged on the fundamental right to privacy guaranteed to all citizens of Arkansas. Furthermore, because the sodomy statute burdened a fundamental right, this court concluded that the constitutionality of the statute must be analyzed under strict or heightened scrutiny. The State conceded that it could offer no compelling State interest sufficient to justify criminalizing acts of sodomy. We held that the sodomy statute was unconstitutional as applied to private, consensual, noncommercial, same-sex sodomy.

The State and FCAC now contend in the case at hand that, unlike in *Jegley,* a fundamental right is not at issue in the instant case because Act 1 only proscribes cohabitation. That argument, however, is not altogether correct. The express language of Act 1 reads that "[a] minor may not be adopted or placed in a foster home if the individual seeking to adopt or to serve as a foster parent is *cohabiting with a sexual partner* outside of a marriage that is valid under the Arkansas Constitution and the laws of this state." Ark. Code Ann. § 9–8–304(a) (emphasis added). Those words clearly make the ability to become an adoptive or foster parent conditioned on the would-be parent's sexual relationship. Hence, Act 1 does not merely prohibit cohabitation. Instead, the act expressly prohibits those persons who cohabit *with a sexual partner* from becoming adoptive or foster parents.

The State and FCAC do not really contest the fact that cohabiting adults in Arkansas have a fundamental right under *Jegley* to engage in consensual, sexual acts within the privacy of their homes without government intrusion. Their bone of contention is whether this right is indeed burdened by Act 1, and they point to the fact that adopting and fostering children are privileges bestowed by state statutes and not rights in themselves.

The problem with the argument mounted by the State and FCAC is that under Act 1 the exercise of one's fundamental right to engage in private, consensual sexual activity is conditioned on foregoing the privilege of adopting or fostering children. The choice imposed on cohabiting sexual partners, whether heterosexual or homosexual, is dramatic. They must chose either to lead a life of private, sexual intimacy with a partner without the opportunity to adopt or foster children or forego sexual cohabitation and, thereby, attain eligibility to adopt or foster.

The United States Supreme Court has rejected the concept that constitutional rights turn on whether a government benefit is characterized as a "right" or as a "privilege." *See, e.g., Shapiro v. Thompson*, 394 U.S. 618, 627 n.6 (1969) (invalidating a law that conditioned receipt of welfare benefits on a residency requirement as an unconstitutional burden on right to interstate travel, and noting that "[t]his constitutional challenge cannot be answered by the argument that public assistance benefits are a 'privilege' and not a 'right.'"), *overruled in part on other grounds by Edelman v. Jordan*, 415 U.S. 651 (1974); *Sherbert v. Verner*, 374 U.S. 398, 404 (1963) ("[C]onstruction of the statute [cannot] be saved from constitutional infirmity on the ground that unemployment compensation benefits are not appellant's 'right' but merely a 'privilege.' It is too late in the day to doubt that the liberties of religion and expression may be infringed by the denial of or placing of conditions upon a benefit or privilege.")

. . .

Although the *Sherbert* case involved the First Amendment and the free exercise of religion, the underlying analysis used by the Court offers guidance in the instant case. Like the provision in the South Carolina Compensation Act, Act 1 exerts significant pressure on Cole to choose between exercising her fundamental right to engage in an intimate sexual relationship in the privacy of her home without being eligible to adopt or foster children, on the one hand, or refraining from exercising this fundamental right in order to be eligible to adopt or foster children, on the other. Similar to conditioning compensation benefits in *Sherbert* on foregoing religious rights, the condition placed on the privilege to foster or adopt thwarts the exercise of a fundamental right to sexual intimacy in the home free from government intrusion under the Arkansas Constitution.

The State and FCAC maintain that unlike the sodomy statute in *Jegley* and the DHS regulation preventing homosexuals from being foster parents in *Department of Human Services & Child Welfare Agency Review Board v. Howard*, 238 S.W.3d 1 (Ark. 2006), Act 1 does not penalize anyone for having sexual relations. And yet, this is precisely what Act 1 does. It penalizes those couples who cohabit and engage in sexual relations by foreclosing their eligibility to have children, either through adoption or by means of foster care.

. . .

We hold that a fundamental right to privacy is at issue in this case and that, under the Arkansas Constitution, sexual cohabitors have the right to engage in private, consensual, noncommercial intimacy in the privacy of their homes. We further hold that this right is jeopardized by Act 1 which precludes all sexual cohabitors, without exception, from eligibility for parenthood, whether by means of adoption or foster care. We quickly note that in certain instances, such as in custody, visitation, or dependency-neglect matters, the State and the circuit courts of this state have a duty to protect the best interest of the child. We will discuss this issue more fully below.

. . .

We strongly disagree with the State and FCAC's conclusion that if this court finds that the categorical ban on adoption and fostering for sexual cohabitors put in place by Act 1 violates an individual's fundamental right to sexual privacy in one's home, state courts and DHS will be prohibited henceforth from considering and enforcing non-cohabitation agreements and orders in deciding child-custody and visitation cases as well as dependency-neglect cases. That simply is not the case. The overriding concern in all of these situations is the best interest of the child. To arrive at what is in the child's best interest, the circuit courts and state agencies look at all the factors, including a non-cohabitation order if one exists, and make the best-interest determination on a case-by-case basis. Act 1's blanket ban provides for no such individualized consideration or case-by-case analysis in adoption or foster-care cases and makes the bald assumption that in *all* cases where adoption or foster care is the issue it is always against the best interest of the child to be placed in a home where an individual is cohabiting with a sexual partner outside of marriage.

But in addition to case-by-case analysis, there is another difference between cohabitation in the child-custody or dependency-neglect context and cohabiting sexual partners who wish to adopt or become foster parents. Third-party strangers who cohabit with a divorced parent are unknown in many cases to the circuit court and have not undergone the rigorous screening associated with foster care or adoption. By everyone's account, applicants for foster care must comply with a raft of DHS regulations that include criminal background checks, home studies, family histories, support systems, and the like. Adoption, under the auspices of the trial court, requires similar screening. Unsuitable and undesirable adoptive and foster parents are thereby weeded out in the screening process.[2] The same does not pertain to a third-party stranger who cohabits with a divorced or single parent.

The State and FCAC rely on the United States Supreme Court decision in *Lyng v. Castillo*, 477 U.S. 635 (1986), for the proposition that a law does not impinge on a fundamental right to a constitutional degree unless the infringement is direct and substantial. They urge that Act 1's infringement on a non-fundamental liberty interest—the right to cohabit with a sexual partner—is not constitutionally significant because Act 1 does not prohibit Cole from residing with whomever she chooses. It merely prohibits her from being eligible to adopt or foster children, if she cohabits with a sexual partner. They conclude that this infringement, at most, is only indirect and insubstantial.

We . . . disagree with the State and FCAC on the significance of the burden. The intrusion by the State into a couple's bedroom to enforce a

---

2. At oral argument counsel for the State made the point that the DHS screening process is not perfect. Yet, the fact remains, the process is rigorous for prospective adoptive or foster-care children.

sexual prohibition is exactly what was prohibited by this court in *Jegley v. Picado*. The same is at issue here under Act 1. State agencies must "police" couples seeking adoption or foster care to determine whether they are sexually involved in the event those couples represent that they are celibate. Compliance with Act 1 requires it.[3] The identical threat of intrusion into the bedroom to examine sexual behavior as was involved in *Jegley* is involved in the instant case.

In the case before us, the burden dispensed by the State is either to remove the ability to foster or adopt children, should sexual partners live together, or to intrude into the bedroom to assure that cohabitors who adopt or foster are celibate. We conclude that, in this case as in *Jegley,* the burden is direct and substantial.

. . .

Because Act 1 burdens a fundamental right, the circuit court applied heightened scrutiny rather than a rational-basis review in its analysis. We defined heightened scrutiny in *Jegley:* "When a statute infringes upon a fundamental right, it cannot survive unless 'a compelling state interest is advanced by the statute and the statute is the least restrictive method available to carry out [the] state interest.'" *Jegley*, 80 S.W.3d at 350 (quoting *Thompson v. Ark. Social Services*, 669 S.W.2d 878, 880 (Ark. 1984)).

According to the circuit court's April 16, 2010 order in the instant case, when viewed under this heightened-scrutiny standard, "Initiated Act 1 is facially invalid because it casts an unreasonably broad net over more people than is needed to serve the State's compelling interest. It is not narrowly tailored to the least restrictive means necessary to serve the State's interest in determining what is in the best interest of the child."

. . .

We have held in this case that a fundamental right of privacy is at issue and that the burden imposed by the State is direct and substantial. We now hold, as an additional matter, that because of the direct and substantial burden on a fundamental right, the standard to be applied is heightened scrutiny and not a rational-basis standard. Using the heightened-scrutiny standard, because Act 1 exacts a categorical ban against all cohabiting couples engaged in sexual conduct, we hold that it is not narrowly tailored or the least restrictive means available to serve the State's compelling interest of protecting the best interest of the child.

In holding as we do, we first note that Act 1 says "[t]he people of Arkansas find and declare that it is in the best interest of children in need of adoption or foster care to be reared in homes in which adoptive or foster parents are not cohabiting outside of marriage." Ark. Code Ann. § 9–8–301 (2009). Despite this statement in Act 1, several of the State's and FCAC's own witnesses testified that they did not believe Act 1 promoted the welfare interests of the child by its categorical ban.

. . .

Furthermore, the concerns raised by the State and FCAC and used as justification for Act 1's categorical ban of cohabiting adults, such as (1)

---

3. FCAC at oral argument contended that petitioners for foster care or adoption would reveal whether they were sexual partners as part of the process. That does not address the circumstance where the couples state they are celibate and the state agencies disbelieve them. Investigations into the privacy of the bedroom under Act I would necessarily have to ensue.

unmarried cohabiting relationships are less stable than married relationships, (2) they put children at a higher risk for domestic violence and abuse than married relationships, and (3) they have lower income levels, higher infidelity rates, and less social support than married relationships, can all be addressed by the individualized screening process currently in place in foster and adoption cases. The CWARB has Minimum Licensing Standards that require it to "select the home that is in the best interest of the child, the least restrictive possible, and is matched to the child's physical and emotional needs. The placement decision shall be based on an individualized assessment of the child's needs." Minimum Licensing Standards for Child Welfare Agencies § 200.1.

Prior to placing a child in foster care or in an adoptive home, DCFS conducts an individualized home assessment of each foster or adoptive family. The home assessment process is a mutual-selection process which involves several components including interviews, background checks, in-home consultation visits, preservice training, home studies, and ongoing consultations with prospective foster parents to ensure that all appropriate criteria related to compliance and quality are met. The home study, in particular, is conducted in order to evaluate the prospective foster family's dynamics, including the "motivation for wanting to foster, household composition, housing, safety hazards, income and expenses, health, education, childcare arrangements or plans, child rearing practices, daily schedules, social history, family activities, and support systems."

. . .

We conclude that the individualized assessments by DHS and our trial courts are effective in addressing issues such as relationship instability, abuse, lack of social support, and other factors that could potentially create a risk to the child or otherwise render the applicant unsuitable to be a foster or adoptive parent. These would be the least restrictive means for addressing the compelling state interest of protecting the welfare, safety, and best interest of Arkansas's children. By imposing a categorical ban on all persons who cohabit with a sexual partner, Act 1 removes the ability of the State and our courts to conduct these individualized assessments on these individuals, many of whom could qualify and be entirely suitable foster or adoptive parents. As a result, Act 1 fails to pass constitutional muster under a heightened-scrutiny analysis.

Florida Department of Children and Families v. Adoption of X.X.G. and N.R.G.

Florida Third District Court of Appeal, 2010.
45 So.3d 79.

■ Cope, J.

This is an appeal of a final judgment of adoption, under which F.G. became the adoptive father of two boys, X.X.G. and N.R.G. (collectively, "the children"). The trial court found, and all parties agree, that F.G. is a fit parent and that the adoption is in the best interest of the children.

The question in the case is whether the adoption should have been denied because F.G. is a homosexual. Under Florida law, a homosexual person is allowed to be a foster parent. F.G. has successfully served as a foster parent for the children since 2004. However, Florida law states, "No person eligible to adopt under this statute [the Florida Adoption Act] may adopt if that person is a homosexual." FLA. STAT. § 63.042(3) (2006). According to the judgment, "Florida is the only remaining state to expressly ban all gay adoptions without exception." Judge Cindy Lederman, after lengthy hearings, concluded that there is no rational basis for the statute. We agree and affirm the final judgment of adoption.

We begin with three observations. First, there does not appear to be any disagreement between the parties regarding the facts of the case. The parties entered into a lengthy list of stipulated facts.... Second, the parties agree that the father is a fit parent and that the adoption is in the best interest of the children. Third, the Department of Children and Families ["Department"] "agrees that gay people and heterosexuals make equally good parents."

Turning now to the facts of this case, in 2004 the Department removed X.X.G., then four years old, and N.R.G., then four months old, from their home based on allegations of abandonment and neglect. The Department contacted F.G., a licensed foster caregiver, and asked him to accept the children on a temporary basis until a more permanent placement could be found.[3]

The children arrived with medical problems and other needs. X.X.G. arrived wearing a dirty adult-sized t-shirt and sneakers four sizes too small. Both children were suffering from ringworm and the four-month-old suffered from an untreated ear infection. X.X.G., the four-year-old, did not speak and his main concern was changing, feeding and caring for his baby brother.

The children thrived in F.G.'s household. "It is clear to this Court that [F.G.] is an exceptional parent to [X.X.G. and N.R.G.] who have healed in his care and are now thriving."

Because of the natural parents' neglect of the two children, the Department filed a petition for termination of the natural parents' parental rights. In 2006, that petition was granted and the natural parents' parental rights were terminated. X.X.G. and N.R.G. became available for adoption.

F.G. applied to adopt the children. The Center for Family and Child Enrichment, Inc. ("The Family Center"), a private nonprofit corporation, had been monitoring the two boys during foster care and was assigned the duty of evaluating F.G.'s ability to provide a satisfactory adoptive placement. The Family Center reported that F.G.'s home presented a suitable environment and that he met all the criteria required to adopt the two boys. The parties stipulated that F.G. provides a safe, healthy, stable and nurturing home for the children meeting their physical, emotional, social and educational needs. The Family Center recommended against the application, though, because F.G. is a homosexual and is prohibited from adopting children under subsection FLA. STAT. § 63.042(3) (2006). The Department denied the application on that basis. The Department acknowledged that it would have approved the application if it had not been for the statute.

In 2007, F.G. filed a petition in the circuit court to adopt the children. F.G. asked the court to find subsection 63.042(3) unconstitutional because it violates his rights to equal protection, privacy, and due process. Independent counsel acting on behalf of the children asserted that the children's rights to

---

3. F.G. was an experienced foster parent who had previously served as a foster parent for seven other children.

equal protection and due process had also been violated. The Department filed a motion to dismiss, but the court only dismissed the privacy claim.

. . .

The trial court rendered a 53–page judgment declaring subsection 63.042(3) unconstitutional and granting the petition for adoption. The trial court found, among other things, that the statute violates the equal protection rights of F.G. and the children that are guaranteed by Article I, Section 2 of the Florida Constitution.

The Department has appealed.

The Department contends that the trial court erred by finding subsection 63.042(3) unconstitutional. The Department argues that there is a rational basis for the statute and that the trial court misinterpreted the law.

Under the Florida Constitution, each individual person has a right to equal protection of the laws. The constitutional provision states, in part:

> SECTION 2. Basic rights. All natural persons, female and male alike, are equal before the law and have inalienable rights, among which are the right to enjoy and defend life and liberty, to pursue happiness, to be rewarded for industry, and to acquire, possess and protect property. . . .

FLA. CONST. art. I, § 2. F.G. successfully argued in the trial court that the statute treated him unequally in violation of the constitutional provision because the statute creates an absolute prohibition on adoption by homosexual persons, while allowing all other persons—including those with criminal histories or histories of substance abuse—to be considered on a case-by-case basis.

. . .

Under the rational basis test, "a court must uphold a statute if the classification bears a rational relationship to a legitimate governmental objective." . . . The classification must be "based *on a real difference* which is reasonably related to the subject and purpose of the regulation." . . .

. . .

Given a total ban on adoption by homosexual persons, one might expect that this reflected a legislative judgment that homosexual persons are, as a group, unfit to be parents.

No one in this case has made, or even hinted at, any such argument. To the contrary, the parties agree "that gay people and heterosexuals make equally good parents." "The qualities that make a particular applicant the optimal match for a particular child could exist in a heterosexual or gay person."[8] Thus in this case no one attempts to justify the prohibition on homosexual adoption on any theory that homosexual persons are unfit to be parents.

Instead, the Department argues that there is a rational basis for the prohibition on homosexual adoption because children will have better role models, and face less discrimination, if they are placed in non-homosexual

---

8. There are, of course, homosexual persons who have their own biological children whom they raise. No one has suggested that such parents are unfit. As stated in the brief amicus curiae of the Family Law Section of The Florida Bar, "A parent's homosexuality is not a basis to terminate his or her parental rights. It is not a basis to deny that parent residential responsibility for his or her child or time-sharing with that child." Brief at 13.

households, preferably with a husband and wife as the parents. But that is not what the statute does.

As previously stated, the statute specifically allows adoption by an unmarried adult. FLA. STAT. § 63.042(2)(b). Single parent adoption has been allowed under the Florida Adoption Act, enacted in 1973, and predecessor statutes. FLA. STAT. § 63.042(2)(b) (1973); 1967 FLA. LAWS. 73–159; FLA. STAT. § 63.061 (1967); FLA. STAT. § 72.11 (1943). One-third of Florida's adoptions are by single adults. The Florida Statutes do not restrict adoption to heterosexual married couples.

The statute contains no prohibition on placing children with homosexual persons who are foster parents. The Department has placed children with homosexual foster parents in short-term placements, and long-term placements. The average length of stay in foster care before adoption is thirty months.

Florida also has a guardianship statute. FLA. STAT. Ch. 744. Homosexual persons "are not prohibited by any state law or regulation from being legal guardians of children in Florida." The Department has placed children in the legal guardianship of homosexual persons. This has included permanent guardianships in which the Department ceased supervision.

It is difficult to see any rational basis in utilizing homosexual persons as foster parents or guardians on a temporary or permanent basis, while imposing a blanket prohibition on adoption by those same persons. The Department contends, however, that the basis for this distinction can be found in the social science evidence.

The trial court heard extensive expert testimony in this case . . . [and concluded:]

> [I]n addition to the volume, the body of research is broad; comparing children raised by lesbian couples to children raised by married heterosexual couples; children raised by lesbian parents from birth to children raised by heterosexual married couples from birth; children raised by single homosexuals to children raised by single heterosexuals; and children adopted by homosexual parents to those raised by homosexual biological parents, to name a few. *These reports and studies find that there are no differences in the parenting of homosexuals or the adjustment of their children.* These conclusions have been accepted, adopted and ratified by the American Psychological Association, the American Psychiatry Association, the American Pediatric Association, the American Academy of Pediatrics, the Child Welfare League of America and the National Association of Social Workers. As a result, based on the robust nature of the evidence available in the field, *this Court is satisfied that the issue is so far beyond dispute that it would be irrational to hold otherwise*; the best interests of children are not preserved by prohibiting homosexual adoption.

This finding coincides with the Department's agreement "that gay people and heterosexuals make equally good parents."

. . .

The Department says that there are disturbingly high domestic violence rates among same-sex couples. However, the Department selectively quotes the testimony by Dr. Peplau. In reality, Dr. Peplau testified that gay people or gay couples do not have higher rates of domestic violence than heterosexual couples. In the population-based study cited by Dr. Peplau, "the highest rate of domestic violence, defined as physical assault or rape ... was 20 percent, and that was for women in heterosexual relationships being attacked by their male partner." The rates for all other groups were lower. This was consistent with a study by the Centers for Disease Control, which found that over an eighteen-year period, ninety-five percent of female homicide victims were women killed by a male domestic partner.

With regard to break-ups of relationships, the Department acknowledges Dr. Peplau's conclusion that unmarried heterosexual couples show break-up rates similar to homosexuals. The same predictors for divorce apply to evaluate the likelihood of break-up in unmarried or same-sex couples. The predictors include age at marriage, education, family income, race or ethnicity, and religion. Dr. Peplau concluded that sexual orientation is not the strongest predictor of break-up among all the different demographic characteristics. Other demographic factors "seem to have as strong or even stronger correlations with break-ups."

The Department claims that homosexual parents "support adolescent sexual activity and experimentations." The Department claims to draw this from the testimony of F.G.'s experts, but the experts did not say this. Dr. Lamb testified that research showed no difference between children of gay parents and heterosexual parents with respect to the age at which they initiated sexual activity.

Dr. Berlin testified that there is no evidence that the environment in which a child is raised, heterosexual or homosexual, would determine the sexual identity of the child who is raised in that environment. "[T]he overwhelming majority of homosexual individuals were raised in heterosexual households, suggesting that the environment in which they were raised in those instances certainly wasn't the determining factor of their development...." Similarly, the overwhelming majority of those children raised in a gay environment turned out to be heterosexual, a point with which Department expert Schumm agreed.

The Department argues that placement of children with homosexuals presents a risk of discrimination and societal stigma. Here, too, the argument is misplaced. Florida already allows placement of children in foster care and guardianships with homosexual persons. This factor does not provide an argument for allowing such placements while prohibiting adoption. We reject the Department's remaining arguments for the same reason: they do not provide a reasonable basis for allowing homosexual foster parenting or guardianships while imposing a prohibition on adoption.

In conclusion on the equal protection issue, the legislature is allowed to make classifications when it enacts statutes. [*State v.*]*Leicht*, 402 So. 2d [1153, 1155 (Fla. 1981)]. As a general proposition, a classification "will be upheld even if another classification or no classification might appear more reasonable." *Id.* The classifications must, however, be "based on a *real* difference which is reasonably related to the subject and purpose of the regulation." *Id.* (emphasis added). "The reason for the equal protection clause was to assure that there would be no second class citizens." *Osterndorf v. Turner*, 426 So. 2d 539, 545–46 (Fla. 1982).

Under Florida law, homosexual persons are allowed to serve as foster parents or guardians but are barred from being considered for adoptive parents. All other persons are eligible to be considered case-by-case to be adoptive parents, but not homosexual persons—even where, as here, the adoptive parent is a fit parent and the adoption is in the best interest of the children.

The Department has argued that evidence produced by its experts and F.G.'s experts supports a distinction wherein homosexual persons may serve as foster parents or guardians, but not adoptive parents. Respectfully, the portions of the record cited by the Department do not support the Department's position. We conclude that there is no rational basis for the statute.

. . .

We affirm the judgment of adoption, which holds subsection 63.042(3), Florida Statutes, violates the equal protection provision found in article I, section 2, of the Florida Constitution.

4. POST-ADOPTION ISSUES

a. AGENCY LIABILITY

Ann Marie N. v. City and County of San Francisco

Court of Appeal of California, First District, 2001.
2001 WL 1261958.

■ KAY, J.

Plaintiff Ann Marie N. sued the City and County of San Francisco (City) when she discovered the child she had adopted through the City's Department of Social Services was infected with HIV (human immunodeficiency virus). She alleged negligence, intentional misrepresentation, and intentional concealment. The trial court granted the City's motion for summary adjudication, eliminating the negligence and the intentional misrepresentation claims. The matter proceeded to trial on the intentional concealment claim, but after plaintiff presented her evidence, the trial court granted the City's motion for nonsuit.

Ann Marie N. contends she had ample evidence of negligent and intentional conduct and that all the claims she alleged should have been submitted to a jury. We find the trial court properly eliminated the negligence and intentional misrepresentation claims, but that the intentional concealment claim should have been submitted to the jury. We reverse the judgment with respect to that claim, but affirm the judgment in all other respects.

Mathew N. was born on August 7, 1986, with alcohol and cocaine in his system. His mother stated she regularly used cocaine and drank alcohol during her pregnancy. She was known to the City's Department of Social Services "because of her substance abuse, transient and unstable lifestyle, and involvement in prostitution."

Mathew was immediately removed from the custody of his mother and, on January 14, 1987, declared a dependent of the San Francisco County Juvenile Court. Later, the court terminated the parental rights of his birth parents and freed Mathew for adoption.

In October 1988, Ann Marie N. saw a television program on children waiting for adoption that featured Mathew. Ann Marie N. lived in Stockton and was a social worker for the County of San Joaquin. Ann Marie N. contacted the City's Department of Social Services, expressed interest in adopting Mathew, and began the adoption process. She filled out a questionnaire in which she indicated she did not want to adopt a child with a "blood disorder."

During the adoption process, Ann Marie N. learned Mathew had been a "drug exposed" infant. She was aware his mother had used alcohol and drugs during her pregnancy and that Mathew was born addicted to alcohol and drugs. She was not aware of the mother's involvement in prostitution.

. . .

Ann Marie N.'s adoption of Mathew became final on February 14, 1990.

In 1996, a social worker for the City called Ann Marie N. and told her that Mathew's birth mother had died of AIDS (acquired immunodeficiency syndrome). Ann Marie N. took Mathew to a medical clinic for testing, and, on September 18, 1996, learned Mathew was HIV positive. According to Ann Marie N., she would not have adopted Mathew if she knew he was HIV positive.

The City had begun developing procedures for HIV testing for children in dependency proceedings in 1987, but it did not implement any procedures until 1993.

Ann Marie N. sued both the City and the County of Stanislaus, which had assisted in the adoption process by evaluating Ann Marie N.'s suitability as an adoptive parent. In her claim for intentional misrepresentation of fact, Ann Marie N. alleged defendants had represented and assured her that Mathew was in good health and suitable for adoption, when in fact he was infected with HIV. In her claim for intentional concealment, she alleged defendants knew Mathew was infected with HIV and failed to reveal that fact. In her claim for negligence, she alleged: "As revealed in and reinforced by defendants' own internal polices [sic] and procedures, defendants owed a duty to prospective adoptive parents to identify whether or not children committed to their care were 'high risk' for HIV infection, to accurately screen and test such high risk children for HIV, and to accurately convey the results of such testing to prospective adoptive parents so that said prospective parents might make informed decisions as to any prospective adoption."

The City moved for summary judgment or, in the alternative, summary adjudication. The trial court granted the motion for summary adjudication on the negligence claim, finding as a matter of law that an adoption agency cannot be liable for mere negligence. The trial court also granted summary adjudication on the intentional misrepresentation claim, finding the defendants' statement that Mathew "is considered to be medically, socially, and psychologically a suitable subject for adoption" was not an actionable misrepresentation of fact. The trial court denied summary adjudication on the intentional concealment claim, finding a triable issue of material fact as to whether the City fraudulently failed to disclose that Mathew's natural mother was involved in prostitution.

The trial on the intentional concealment claim added few new facts. Ann Marie N. testified that two social workers, one from the City and one from the County of Stanislaus, were involved in handling the adoption of Mathew. Ann Marie N. remembered receiving some information regarding the health of Mathew and his birth mother from the Stanislaus social worker. She generally did not remember the substance of her conversations with the City's social worker, Bill Holman. She did not think that Holman gave her any information regarding Mathew's health before the completion of the adoption. Someone told her about Mathew's exposure to drugs and alcohol, but no one told her that Mathew's birth mother was involved in prostitution.

The City called Holman to testify out of order during Ann Marie N.'s case. He testified that he did not know Mathew was at risk for contracting

HIV or AIDS. He knew intravenous drug use was a risk factor, though he could not pinpoint exactly when he gained that knowledge. With regard to transmission of HIV from mothers to their babies, he was certain only that if the mother was HIV positive, her baby was at risk.

Ann Marie N. called Mildred Crear, the City's director of Children's Medical Services during the relevant time period, as an adverse witness pursuant to CAL. EVID. CODE § 776. She testified regarding the City's procedures for testing dependent children for HIV or AIDS. According to Crear, a committee composed of personnel from various City agencies considered HIV transmission to children. The risk factors considered by the committee included a mother who used drugs intravenously or who had sexual contact with persons with AIDS or HIV. A newborn baby testing positive for drugs abused intravenously was also considered a risk factor. Prostitution itself was not considered a risk. Because of their occupation, prostitutes "had better safe sex practices" than the general population. The testing guidelines were not completed and disseminated to the City's Department of Social Services personnel until 1993.

Finally, the parties stipulated that, if called, Lillian Johnson, the coordinator of a fragile infant special care program at St. Elizabeth's Hospital, would testify that in 1987 there were approximately 50 infants with AIDS in San Francisco. That number was expected to increase significantly. At St. Elizabeth's in 1987 and early 1988, one infant had died of AIDS, two had AIDS, and two others were HIV positive.

After Ann Marie N. presented her evidence, the City moved for nonsuit. In an order dated October 25, 2000, the trial court granted the motion, noting that Holman denied having any knowledge that Mathew was at risk for HIV, and that there was no evidence to the contrary. The trial court refused to impute the knowledge of Crear or Johnson to Holman.

. . .

Adoption agencies in this state are not liable for "mere negligence in providing information regarding the health of a prospective adoptee." *Michael J. v. Los Angeles County Dept. of Adoptions*, 201 Cal. App. 3d 859, 874–75 (1988); *Richard P. v. Vista Del Mar Child Care Service*, 106 Cal. App. 3d 860, 866–67 (1980). In both *Michael J.* and *Richard P.* the adoptive parents alleged the adoption agency possessed material information that it failed to convey. In *Michael J.*, the defendant allegedly knew or in the exercise of reasonable care should have known a birthmark on the adopted child was a manifestation of Sturge–Weber Syndrome. In *Richard P.*, the adoptive parents alleged the defendants were negligent in representing the child was healthy when it could have been predicted the child would suffer neurological damage in the future. For reasons of public policy, the Courts of Appeal in *Michael J.* and *Richard P.* rejected the negligence claims based on these allegations.

Ann Marie N. believes *Michael J.* and *Richard P.* are no longer good law, and that it is time for courts to impose a duty on adoption agencies to investigate a child's medical condition and to convey accurate information to adoptive parents. Ann Marie N. points to the trend in other states to recognize claims against adoption agencies for negligent misrepresentation, and the policy of this state to disclose an adoptee's background to adoptive parents. *See e.g.*, CAL. FAM. CODE §§ 8706, 8817 (requiring a written report on child's medical background and, if possible, medical background of biological parents); CAL. HEALTH AND SAFETY CODE § 121020 (permitting HIV testing of dependent children pursuant to court order).

We find no basis to depart from *Michael J.* and *Richard P.* in this case. The Legislature has not overruled *Michael J.* and *Richard P.* even as it has demonstrated an intent to provide prospective adoptive parents with as much information as possible. And though Ann Marie N. now relies on the FAMILY CODE § 8706, she did not allege a violation of then existing statutory requirement for delivery of a medical report, nor has she cited any evidence showing the City failed to comply with the requirement.

Ann Marie N., the City, and amicus curiae California State Association of Counties have advanced policies for and against imposing liability on adoption agencies for negligence. Those policies deserve consideration from a legislative body so that the issue can be resolved for the greatest good of children waiting for adoption and adoptive parents.

The trial court properly granted summary adjudication on the negligence claim.

At trial Ann Marie N. attempted to prove the City intentionally concealed the risk that Mathew was HIV positive. The only witnesses she presented on this issue were herself and Crear, who testified as an adverse witness. The stipulated offer of proof regarding the testimony of Lillian Johnson added some statistics regarding infants infected with HIV or AIDS. Other witnesses testified regarding damages. Holman testified out of order for the defense.

The trial court held Ann Marie N. had failed to present facts that were "(1) sufficient to establish the existence of a duty to disclose the material fact here at issue, or (2) sufficient to permit a jury to find an intentional concealment or suppression of that fact." The trial court noted the material fact at issue was whether Mathew was at risk for HIV infection based on his birth mother's health and lifestyle and Mathew's own health. The trial court relied on Holman's testimony regarding his knowledge of HIV transmission, stating in its order: "Mr. Holman, who is the person claimed to have intentionally withheld information, denied having any knowledge or information at or before the finalization of the adoption to the effect that Mathew was at risk for HIV-positive status."

Ann Marie N. argues a jury could have found Holman was lying when he disclaimed any knowledge that Mathew was at risk. She also advances a complex agency theory under which the knowledge of Crear would be imputed to Holman.

Holman's testimony should have been disregarded in connection with the motion for nonsuit. It was not favorable to Ann Marie N.'s case and he was not her witness. For purposes of the nonsuit motion, the only relevant evidence was Ann Marie N.'s own testimony, the stipulated testimony of Johnson, and the testimony of Crear favorable to Ann Marie N.'s case. *See Ashcraft v. King*, 228 Cal. App. 3d 604, 611 (1991) (testimony favorable to plaintiff adduced from an adverse witness under CAL. EVID. CODE § 776 must be taken as true and unfavorable portions disregarded).

Ann Marie N. testified that Holman did not give her any information regarding Mathew's health. According to Ann Marie N., she was not given Mathew's medical records until after the adoption was final. Nor was she told that a child born addicted to drugs was at risk for HIV, or that prostitution was a risk factor. She was not told Mathew's mother had a history of prostitution.

Crear testified that it was known by 1988 that intravenous drug use by a birth mother was a risk factor in HIV transmission to her baby. Crear also acknowledged that a baby born addicted to drugs abused intravenously by the mother was at risk. Prostitution was not a known risk factor, according to

Crear, but a mother who had sexual contact with persons infected with HIV or AIDS was a risk factor.

Though there was no direct evidence Holman concealed the fact that Mathew was at risk for HIV or that Mathew's birth mother was involved in prostitution, the jury could have inferred from his silence on Mathew's health and on the birth mother's history (according to Ann Marie N.), that he was concealing important facts in order to complete the adoption of Mathew. The nondisclosure of a significant fact may suggest fraud. However weak the evidence, it showed the existence of HIV risk factors known to City employees and not disclosed or discussed with Ann Marie N. Bearing in mind that Holman's testimony had to be disregarded in considering the motion for nonsuit, the state of the evidence was sufficient to require the City to offer evidence regarding Holman's discussions with Ann Marie N. and his knowledge of HIV risk factors, or evidence that Ann Marie N. would have adopted Mathew even if she had been told he was at risk.

We reverse the judgment with respect to the nonsuit on the intentional concealment claim. In all other respects the judgment is affirmed. The parties shall bear their own costs on appeal.

NOTE

Some states by statute provide for annulment of an adoption in certain circumstances. *E.g.*, CAL. FAM. CODE § 9100 (2011) provides:

(a) If a child adopted pursuant to the law of this state shows evidence of a developmental disability or mental illness as a result of conditions existing before the adoption to an extent that the child cannot be relinquished to an adoption agency on the grounds that the child is considered unadoptable, and of which conditions the adoptive parents or parent had no knowledge or notice before the entry of the decree or order of adoption, a petition setting forth those facts may be filed by the adoptive parents or parent with the court that granted the adoption petition. If these facts are proved to the satisfaction of the court, it may make an order setting aside the order of adoption.

(b) The petition shall be filed within five years after the entering of the decree or order of adoption.

Some states have held that courts may grant adoption annulments without a statutory basis. *See In re Lisa Diane G.*, 537 A.2d 131, 133 (R.I. 1988). Other states are more restrictive about which adoptions may be annulled. *See, e.g.*, MISS. CODE ANN. § 93–17–17 (2010) ("no adoption proceedings shall be permitted to be set aside except for jurisdictional defects and for failure to file and prosecute the same under the provisions of this chapter"). Additionally, states that limit adoption annulments to procedural defects often impose time limitations on such decrees. *See, e.g.*, ARIZ. REV. STAT. ANN. § 8–123 (2011) ("[a]fter one year from the date the adoption decree is entered, any irregularity in the proceeding shall be deemed cured and the validity of the decree shall not thereafter be subject to attack on any such ground in any collateral or direct proceeding"); D.C. CODE ANN. § 16–310 (2011) ("[a]n attempt to invalidate a final decree of adoption by reason of a jurisdictional or procedural defect may not be received by any court of the District, unless regularly filed with the court within one year following the date the final decree became effective").

b. ADOPTEE'S RIGHT TO KNOW IDENTITY OF BIOLOGICAL PARENTS

In the Matter of the Application of Victor M. I. I.

Surrogate's Court of New York, Nassau County, 2009.
881 N.Y.S.2d 367.

■ RIORDAN, J.

Before the court is the application of an adult who was adopted in 1968 at the age of eleven months, to unseal adoption records on the basis of alleged good cause pursuant to N.Y. Dom. Rel. Law § 114(2). Petitioner's application is supported by the affidavit of his biological mother, in which she consents to the unsealing of the adoption records. The biological father is unknown. Both adoptive parents are deceased. Petitioner has also submitted a copy of his original order of adoption, a copy of his post-adoption birth certificate, which reflects the names of his adoptive parents, and death certificates for petitioner's adoptive mother and father.

Petitioner has brought this application for the limited purpose of obtaining two certified copies of his original pre-adoption birth certificate in order to establish his Hungarian lineage. Petitioner avers that this will entitle him to become a citizen of Hungary, based upon the status of his biological mother, who is a Hungarian citizen. Petitioner would benefit from Hungarian citizenship because he frequently travels to Hungary for business and personal reasons and resides there on a part-time basis. Included with the petition are a photocopy and a verified translation of the birth certificate of petitioner's biological mother, and a photocopy of the passport of petitioner's maternal grandfather, which reflects Hungarian citizenship.

In New York State, the sealing of adoption records has been mandated for more than 60 years, although courts had the discretionary power to seal these records even before then. *Matter of Linda F.M.*, 418 N.E.2d 1302 (N.Y. 1981). Currently, adoption records are sealed pursuant to N.Y. Dom. Rel. Law § 114, to protect and insure confidentiality which is "vital to the adoption process" As expressed by the Court of Appeals, the purpose is to provide anonymity to the natural parents, enable the adoptive parents to form a close bond with their adopted child, protect the adopted child from possibly disturbing information that might be found in his records, and allow the state to foster an orderly and supervised adoption system. *Matter of Linda F.M.*, 418 N.E.2d 1302 (N.Y. 1981). There have been challenges to the power of New York State to seal adoption records, but the courts have determined that these statutes are not in violation of the [E]qual [P]rotection [C]lause of the 14th Amendment and are constitutional.

At the same time, the courts and the Legislature have recognized that circumstances may exist in which it is vital that an adopted child be provided with information regarding his background. When serious health issues arise, an adopted child or his adoptive parents may seek the medical history of the child's biological family pursuant to Dom. Rel. Law § 114(4). This statute permits interested parties seeking medical information to establish a prima facie case of good cause. It is also possible to petition the court for access to adoption records for other reasons pursuant to Dom. Rel. Law § 114(2). This section provides that adoption records may be unsealed upon a showing of "good cause." It further directs that there must be "due notice to the adoptive parents and to such additional persons as the court may direct." While it is unusual for adoption records to be unsealed for a non-medical reason, "[e]xceptions to the medical requirement are rare but do occur occasionally." The courts and the Legislature have attempted to strike a balance between the state's interest in maintaining sealed adoption records and the sometimes conflicting interests of all parties to an adoption, as further weighed against the justification underlying each particular request to unseal the records.

In weighing the opposing interests, courts may deny an adoptee's request to unseal his adoption record for lack of good cause. In a 2006 decision, the court denied adoptee's application where it determined that the request was based upon an "adoptee's general curiosity about her ancestry and background." Similarly, access to records was denied where petitioner wanted to give his children and grandchildren the opportunity to find out about their father's heritage. "By its very nature, good cause admits of no universal, black-letter definition." *Matter of Linda F.M.*, 418 N.E.2d 1302, 1304 (N.Y. 1981).

In cases in which good cause is found to exist, the court may require further steps to protect the parties to the adoption other than petitioner. In an application before this court, petitioner sought to unseal his adoption records for medical reasons, but failed to meet the specific statutory requirements of Dom. Rel. Law § 114(4) to establish good cause. The court advised petitioner that if he established good cause pursuant to Dom. Rel. Law § 114(2), he would also be required to furnish the court with consents signed by each of his adoptive parents, if they were living, or a death certificate for each deceased adoptive parent. In *Matter of Wilson*, [544 N.Y.S. 2d 886 (N.Y. App. Div. 1987)] the court found that petitioner, whose adoptive father was deceased and whose adoptive mother approved his petition, had established good cause to unseal his adoption records, but the court still required a hearing to protect the interests of the biological parents, who may have wished to remain anonymous.

The facts presented to the court on the application are highly unusual in that there are virtually no competing interests to weigh against petitioner's application. The court has been presented with the petition of an adult applicant who maintains that a substantive benefit will accrue to him if he is able to obtain certified copies of his original birth certificate, which is unavailable from any other source. As to the interests of his adoptive parents, the court has before it death certificates for both. The biological father is unknown and petitioner's biological mother has consented to the relief requested. The state's interest in maintaining confidentiality as part of a viable system of adoption is also not a factor in this case, as there is no information contained in the requested document which petitioner does not already possess, and petitioner is not requesting unfettered access to the entire adoption file. It is not information which petitioner seeks; it is the certified document necessary to acquire Hungarian citizenship.

"Whether [good cause] exists, and the extent of disclosure that is appropriate, must remain for the courts to decide on the facts of each case." *Matter of Linda F.M.*, 418 N.E.2d 1302 (N.Y. 1981). Under these unique circumstances, the court finds that petitioner has demonstrated good cause, and that the due notice requirement of Dom. Rel. Law § 114(2) may be dispensed with, on the grounds that petitioner's application is supported by his only known biological parent, and petitioner's adoptive parents are deceased.

The court's ruling today is limited to the unusual set of facts with which it is presented. The court is compelled to note that it is not opening the door for unsealing adoption records in every instance where an adopted child who has reached majority asserts that access to his adoption records would be beneficial. As noted earlier, in many cases, the assurance of confidentiality afforded by the Legislature to both biological and adoptive parents has been determined to outweigh the justification underlying an adoptee's request for access to adoption records.

NOTES

1. Some states permit adoptees to petition for a "confidential intermediary" who "shall search for and discreetly contact the birth parent ... [or] attempt to locate members of the birth parent or adopted person's family." WASH. REV. CODE § 26.33.343 (2011). *See also* N.C. GEN. STAT. § 48–9–104 (2010); OKL. STAT. tit. 10, § 7508–1.3 (2010). Other states employ an affidavit system whereby "[If] a biological parent has filed with the department or placement agency an affidavit objecting to such release, information regarding that biological parent shall not be released." GA. CODE ANN. § 19–8–23 (2011). *See also* HAW. REV. STAT. § 578–15 (2010); WIS. STAT. § 48.433 (2011). The majority of states, however, use a mutual consent registry. Consider New York's approach:

> 1.   There shall be established in the department an adoption information registry.... Access to all records and information in the registry shall be limited to ... designated employees and such records and information shall be kept strictly confidential except as specifically authorized by law. The commissioner shall establish rules and procedures designed to keep such records and information separate and apart from other records of the department and kept in a manner where access to such records and information is strictly limited to such designated employees and shall promulgate regulations designed to effectuate the purposes of this section....

> 2.   The registry shall accept, at any time, and maintain the verified registration transmitted by an agency pursuant to section [4138–d] of this title, or of the birth parents of an adoptee if such adoptee was born in this state. The registry shall not accept nor maintain the registration of an adoptee sooner than eighteen years after the adoptee's birth, or in the case of registration by a biological sibling of an adoptee, no sooner than the longer of eighteen years after the biological sibling's birth or eighteen years after the adoptee's birth; provided, however, that any person whose registration was accepted may withdraw such registration prior to the release of any identifying information. The adoptee registrant, and the biological sibling registrant, shall include as part of the registration the identification, including the name and address, of known biological siblings of the adoptee. The adoptee may upon registration or any time thereafter elect not to have release of information by the authorized agency involved in such adoption. The department shall establish an authorized agency fee schedule for search costs and registry costs and services provided by such agency in gathering and forwarding information pursuant to this section. The fee schedule may also include costs for disseminating information about the registry and the adoption medical information sub-registry to the public. Such publications or brochures may include information as to identifying and non-identifying information, how to register and fees charged to the registrants, and any other information deemed appropriate.

> 3.   For the purposes of this section, the term "non-identifying information" shall only include the following information, if known, concerning the adoptee, parents and biological siblings of an adoptee:

> (a) Age of the parents in years, at birth of such adoptee.

> (b) Heritage of the parents, which shall include nationality, ethnic background and race.

> (c) Education, which shall be the number of years of school completed by the parents at the time of birth of such adoptee.

> (d) General physical appearance of the parents at the time of the birth of such adoptee, which shall include height, weight, color of hair, eyes, skin and other information of similar nature.

> (e) Religion of parents.

> (f) Occupation of parents.

> (g) Health history of parents.

(h) Talents, hobbies and special interests of parents.

(i) Facts and circumstances relating to the nature and cause of the adoption.

(j) Name of the authorized agency involved in such adoption.

(k) The existence of any known biological siblings.

(l) The number, sex and age, at the time of the adoptee's adoption, of any known biological siblings.

4. Upon acceptance of a registration pursuant to this section, the department shall search the records of the department to determine whether the adoptee's adoption occurred within the state.

(a) If the department determines that the adoption occurred within the state, it shall notify the court wherein the adoption occurred to submit to the department non-identifying information as may be contained in the records of the court and the names of the birth parents of the adoptee. Notwithstanding any other provision of law to the contrary, the court shall thereupon transmit to the department non-identifying information as may be contained in the records of the court, and the names of the birth parents of the adoptee, provided that, if the court determines from its records that the adoption was from an authorized agency, the court shall submit to the department only the name and address of such authorized agency and the names of the birth parents of the adoptee. In such cases, unless the adoptee registrant shall have elected otherwise, the department shall notify the authorized agency whose name was provided by the court to release promptly to the adoptee all non-identifying information as may be contained in the agency records. Such agency shall thereafter promptly release the non-identifying information to the adoptee registrant. If the adoptee registrant shall have elected not to have the information released to him or her by the authorized agency, the agency shall submit promptly to the department all non-identifying information as may be contained in the agency records. In any case where the agency records are incomplete, no longer exist or are otherwise unavailable, the department shall so notify the court. The court shall thereupon promptly submit such non-identifying information as may be contained in their records. If no authorized agency was involved or if the adoptee registrant shall have elected not to have release of information by the authorized agency involved in such adoption, the department shall release the non-identifying information to the adoptee registrant. The department and/or an authorized agency may restrict the nature of the non-identifying information released pursuant to this section upon a reasonable determination that disclosure of such non-identifying information would not be in the adoptee's, biological sibling's, or parent's best interest.

(b) If the department determines that the adoption did not occur within the state, it shall notify the adoptee registrant that no record exists of the adoption occurring within the state.

5. Upon acceptance of a registration pursuant to this section, the department shall search the registry to determine whether the adoptee, any biological sibling of the adoptee, or birth parents of the adoptee is also registered.

(a) If the department determines the adoptee is not in contact with a biological sibling under the age of eighteen and that there is a corresponding registration for the adoptee, for either of the birth parents, and/or for the biological sibling registrant, it shall notify the court wherein the adoption occurred and the department shall notify all such persons that a corresponding match has been made and request such persons' final consent to the release of identifying information.

(b) If the department determines that there is no corresponding registration for the adoptee, for either of the birth parents, and/or for a biological sibling of the adoptee, it shall notify the registering person that no corresponding match has been made. The department shall not solicit or request the consent of the non-registered person or persons.

6. Upon receipt of a final consent by the adoptee, by either of the birth parents, and/or by a biological sibling of the adoptee, the department shall, unless the

adoptee or biological sibling registrant shall elect otherwise, if an authorized agency was involved in such adoption, release identifying information to such agency; such agency shall thereafter promptly release identifying information about the consenting registrants to the consenting registrants. If no authorized agency was involved, or if any registrant shall have elected not to have release of the information by the authorized agency involved in such adoption the department shall release identifying information to the consenting registrants. Such identifying information shall be limited to the names and addresses of the consenting registrants and shall not include any other information contained in the adoption or birth records. However, nothing in this section shall be construed to prevent the release of adoption records as otherwise permitted by law.

6–a.   (a) There shall be established in the registry an adoption medical information sub-registry. Access to all identifying records and information in the sub-registry shall be subject to the same restrictions as the adoption information registry.

(b) The department shall establish procedures by which a birth parent may provide medical information to the sub-registry, and by which an adoptee aged eighteen years or older or the adoptive parents of an adoptee who has not attained the age of eighteen years may access such medical information.

(c) A birth parent may provide the adoption medical information sub-registry with certified medical information. Such certified medical information must include other information sufficient to locate the adoptee's birth record.

(d) Upon receipt from the birth parent of certified medical information and other information needed to identify the adopted person, the department shall determine if the adoptee was born and adopted in New York state. If the adoptee was born and adopted in New York state, the department shall register such information and determine if the adoptee or adoptive parent of the adoptee is registered. Upon such determination, the department shall release the non-identifying medical information only to an adoptee, aged eighteen years or older, or adoptive parent of an adoptee who has not attained the age of eighteen years.

(e) Upon receipt from an adoptee aged eighteen years or older or the parent of an adoptee of a registration, the department shall determine if the adoptee was born and adopted in New York state. If the adoptee was born and adopted in New York state, the department shall search its records for medical information provided by the adoptee's birth parent. If such medical information is found, the department shall release the non-identifying medical information only, to an adoptee, aged eighteen years or older, or adoptive parent of an adoptee who has not attained the age of eighteen years.

(f) The department shall not solicit or request the provision of medical information from a birth parent or the registration by an adoptee or parent of an adoptee.

(g) A fee shall not be required from a birth parent for providing health information.

N.Y. Pub. Health L. § 4138–C (2011).

2.   Some states place conditions on the release of adoption records. In Texas, an adoptee seeking release of records must "participate in counseling for not less than one hour with a social worker or mental health professional with expertise in post-adoption counseling after the administrator has accepted the application for registration and before the release of confidential information." Tex. Fam. Code § 162.413 (2010).

c.   FRAUD

Joslyn v. Reynolds

Court of Appeals of Ohio, 2001.
2001 Ohio 1416.

■ Whitmore, J.

Robert B. Joslyn ("Appellant") and Michelle A. Reynolds ("Appellee") married on July 1, 1994. Appellee had three children from a prior marriage.

On November 8, 1994, Appellant adopted each of Appellee's three children. The parties divorced on August 14, 1998. Pursuant to the divorce decree, Appellant was ordered to pay child support for each of the three children.

On July 30, 1999, Appellant filed an action under R.C. 3107.16 to vacate the adoption decrees of Appellee's three children on the ground of fraud, and for compensatory damages, including all previously paid child support. Appellee filed a motion to dismiss, arguing that even if the allegations in Appellant's complaint were true, Appellant failed to state a claim upon which relief can be granted. The trial court found that Appellant's complaint was barred by the one-year statute of limitations found in R.C. 3107.16(B), and that Appellant could not be granted relief because his action endeavors to hold Appellee liable based upon a promise of marriage or upon an obligation dependent upon or growing out of a contract for marriage. The court granted the motion and dismissed the complaint.

From the dismissal of his complaint, Appellant has appealed and has assigned three errors for this Court's review. Appellant has asserted that the trial court erred in granting Appellee's motion to dismiss pursuant to Civ. R. 12(B)(6) because the court: (1) erred in ruling that he was required to file his action within one year of the entry of the adoption decrees; (2) erred in ruling that the one-year statute of limitations began to run in July 1997; and (3) erred in determining that the children's best interests prevented vacating the adoptions.

Appellant's complaint, filed nearly four and a half years after the decrees had been entered, sought vacation of the adoptions on the basis that Appellant had been fraudulently induced to marry Appellee and to adopt her children. Appellant asserts that Appellee's fraud had its origins in the early part of the parties' relationship—a relationship which began when Appellee was hired to care for Appellant, who is a quadriplegic. Appellant asserts that Appellee, who was married and had three children, began to ingratiate herself to Appellant, and began managing his money—which consisted of monthly annuity payments of over $10,000. Eventually, Appellee left her husband and she and her three children moved into Appellant's home. According to the complaint, Appellee immediately started spending large amounts of Appellant's money, and initiated a sexual relationship with him. Appellee told Appellant that she wanted to be married to him, that she, like he, believed marriage was a lifetime commitment, and that she wanted to spend her life with Appellant and her children as one family. Two years after Appellee and her children moved into Appellant's home, the couple married, and shortly thereafter, Appellant adopted Appellee's three children. However, Appellant says that it was not long before Appellee stopped providing Appellant the necessary care, and that she suddenly had no interest in a sexual relationship. She did, however, have a great interest in spending his money.

The relationship rapidly deteriorated. Appellee began engaging in adulterous affairs, and told Appellant's sister that she had married Appellant "only for her children and their security." The relationship became hostile, and Appellant feared for his life. Appellant's family intervened and transported Appellant to the hospital, while Appellee and one man with whom she was having an affair destroyed much of Appellant's property, including the wheelchair ramps at the house. Appellant went to live with his family. Appellee denied Appellant any contact with the children. The parties divorced and Appellant was ordered to pay $2,354.00 per month in child support. Appellant's complaint asserts that because Appellee "connived and plotted to get [him] to marry her and adopt her children and get his money, and falsely represented her intentions for the marriage and subsequent adoptions . . . inducing [him] to marry her and adopt her three children[,] . . . he has incurred damages including substantial financial damages for child support[.]"

While the allegations, which must be taken as true, are heart-wrenching, the issue, quite simply, is whether R.C. 3107.16(B) permits vacation of an adoption based on the facts as alleged in Appellant's complaint. This Court finds that it does not. We agree with the trial court's conclusion that "the nature of this action is one of the heart ... based upon a promise of marriage or upon an obligation dependent upon, or growing out of, a contract of marriage and [is] not cognizable by law[.]"

R.C 3107.16(B) provides:

Subject to the disposition of an appeal, *upon the expiration of one year after an adoption decree is issued, the decree cannot be questioned by any person,* including the petitioner, in any manner or upon any ground, including fraud, misrepresentation, failure to give any required notice, or lack of jurisdiction of the parties or of the subject matter, *unless,* in the case of the adoption of a minor, the petitioner has not taken custody of the minor, or, *in the case of the adoption of a minor by a stepparent, the adoption would not have been granted but for fraud perpetrated by the petitioner or the petitioner's spouse,* or, in the case of the adoption of an adult, the adult had no knowledge of the decree within the one-year period.

(Emphasis added.) Appellant has contended that the trial court erred in finding that his complaint is barred by the one-year statute of limitations. He has insisted that the language "the [stepparent] adoption would not have been granted but for fraud perpetrated by the.... petitioner's spouse[,]" expressly provides for his claim because "if the Court had known that [Appellee] had married [Appellant] and induced him to adopt her three children only because of his money with no intention of staying married to him, it certainly would not have granted the adoptions."

There is no case law interpreting what "fraud" means in the context of the particular provision "the [stepparent] adoption would not have been granted but for fraud perpetrated by the ... petitioner's spouse[.]" Courts have, however, permitted adoptions to be challenged on the basis of fraud in the general context. In those cases, the fraud has concerned either the consent of the birthparents, or the health or identity of the children.... We see no reason to expand the type of fraud permitted to challenge stepparent adoptions. This Court rejects Appellant's contention that the General Assembly intended to permit all stepparent adoptions to be challenged upon divorce of the adoptive parent(s). We also reject Appellant's assertion that a stepparent adoption can be vacated on the basis of fraud where the fraud goes to misrepresentations concerning the marriage. Therefore, we find that the trial court did not err in dismissing Appellant's complaint.

Because we have determined that Appellant has stated a claim for which there is no relief, this Court need not decide whether the trial court erred in finding that the statute of limitations began to run in July 1997, or whether the best interests of the children prevent vacating the adoption decrees.

In re Petition of Otakar Kirchner

Supreme Court of Illinois, 1995.
649 N.E.2d 324.

■ PER CURIAM

Otakar Kirchner was granted leave to file with this court a complaint for writ of *habeas corpus* on behalf of his son on November 15, 1994. The petition was premised upon this court's June 16, 1994, opinion invalidating the Does' adoption of Kirchner's son, herein identified as Richard.... The petition requested that this court order the Does to surrender custody of Richard to Kirchner.

. . .

Otakar Kirchner (Otto) and Daniella Janikova, both Czechoslovakian immigrants, started dating in September of 1989 and began living together later that year. Seven months later, Daniella became pregnant. She and Otto continued living together and planned to get married. They obtained two marriage licenses towards this end, though they did not marry prior to the birth of their child, now commonly known as "Baby Richard." Shortly before Richard's birth, Otto returned to his native Czechoslovakia for two weeks to visit a dying relative. While he was away, a relative from Czechoslovakia telephoned Daniella and told her that Otto had resumed a relationship there with a former girlfriend. Distraught upon hearing this report, Daniella tore up their current marriage license, gathered her belongings and moved into a women's shelter because she had nowhere else to go.

[While living at the shelter, and before Otto returned from his trip abroad, Daniella decided to place the baby up for adoption, and] the private adoption of not-yet-born Richard was arranged between Daniella and the Does.... At all relevant times, both the Does' lawyer and the Does were fully aware that Daniella knew who the father was and that she intended to tell the father that the child had died at birth....

Rather than insist that Daniella disclose the name of the father so that he could be properly notified and his consent to the adoption procured, the Does and their attorney acquiesced in Daniella's scheme to tell Otto that his child had died at birth, even arranging for Daniella to give birth in a different hospital than she and Otto had originally planned.

. . .

Unsuspecting, Otto returned to Chicago prior to Daniella's due date, whereupon he discovered that Daniella had left him. He learned through friends that she had gone to a women's shelter. He and Daniella then went through a period of reconciliation, during which time she did not inform him that she had arranged to place their child for adoption. When the birth took place on March 16, 1991, Otto's efforts to contact Daniella were rebuffed. He was told by Daniella's friends and relatives that his child had died at birth. We note that Otto and Daniella married in September of 1991.

In the weeks immediately following the birth, Otto, suspicious of the story that his child had died, attempted to discover the truth....

On May 12, 1991, or 57 days after the birth of Richard, Daniella confessed to Otto that she had given birth to a baby boy and had placed him in an adoptive home. At this juncture, Otto commenced his efforts to gain custody of his son.

[In May 1992, the trial court found that Kirchner's consent to Richard's adoption was not necessary because Kirchner was unfit pursuant to section 1(D)(*l*) of the Adoption Act, which provides that an unwed father is unfit where it is found by clear and convincing evidence that he has "failed to demonstrate a reasonable degree of interest, concern or responsibility as to the welfare of a new born child during the first 30 days after its birth." The appeals court affirmed, agreeing that Kirchner was an unfit parent. In addition, the court concentrated its discussion on the best-interests-of-the-child standard.]

... Otto then appealed to this court, which, in a unanimous decision on June 16, 1994, reversed the trial and appellate courts and vacated the adoption, holding that Otto was fit under section 8(a)(1) of the Adoption Act and, thus, that his parental rights had never been properly terminated....

. . .

Under Illinois law, parents may be divested of parental rights either through their voluntary consent or involuntarily due to a finding of abuse, abandonment, neglect or unfitness by clear and convincing evidence.... The adoption laws of Illinois ... intentionally place the burden of proof on the adoptive parents. In addition, Illinois law requires a good-faith effort to notify the natural father of the adoption proceedings.... We call this due process of law. In the case at hand, the Does and their lawyer knew that a real father existed whose name the birth mother knew. They also knew that the father, if contacted, would not consent to the adoption....

This court then observed that Otto, as the natural father of Richard, was statutorily entitled to receive notice of the adoption and statutorily required to consent in order for the adoption to be valid, absent a finding of unfitness. Examining the unfitness finding of the trial court, we concluded that the trial court's finding was against the manifest weight of the evidence....

The Does ... did not return Richard to Otto upon the issuance of this court's mandate. Subsequent to this court's opinion vacating the adoption, the General Assembly enacted an amendment to the Adoption Act which specified that it was to take effect immediately and apply to all cases pending at the time of the effective date.... This new legislation ... requires that upon the vacation of an adoption proceeding a custody hearing take place in order to determine who should have custody of the child based upon the child's best interests.

Armed with this new amendment to the Adoption Act, as well as their interpretation of section 601(b)(2) of the Illinois Marriage and Dissolution of Marriage Act ... the Does then petitioned for a custody hearing in the circuit court of Cook County. Richard's guardian *ad litem* joined that suit on Richard's behalf.

At this juncture, Otto filed the instant petition for writ of *habeas corpus* with our court, in essence arguing that upon the vacatur of Richard's adoption, he was legally vested with Richard's custody and that the Does and Richard's guardian *ad litem* were without standing to seek custody under either the Marriage and Dissolution of Marriage Act or the amendments to the Adoption Act. Insofar as Otto challenged the constitutionality of the Adoption Act, the Illinois Attorney General requested and was granted leave to intervene in support of the constitutionality of the amendment.

[T]his court concluded that the Does did not legally have standing to request a custody hearing. Consequently, we ordered the writ of *habeas corpus* to issue immediately.

. . .

Our decision of June 16, 1994, unanimously held that Otto had exhibited sufficient interest in his child during the first 30 days of his life and that the trial court had thus erred in finding him unfit pursuant to section 8(a)(1) of the Adoption Act. . . .

The Does assert that they have standing under section 601(b)(2) of the Marriage and Dissolution of Marriage Act to seek a custody hearing to determine who should have custody of Otto's son now that the adoption has been vacated. We disagree.

. . .

Moreover, without regard to Federal constitutional jurisprudence, Illinois law requires that Otto be granted the care, custody and control of his son. The Adoption Act . . . creates a framework which acknowledges the due process rights of unwed fathers and balances their rights to the care, custody and control of their children with the need to facilitate orderly and final adoptions which are not subject to collateral attack. Toward this end, the Adoption Act provides that where the birth mother is not married to the father, his consent to the adoption is essential except where he has been found unfit by clear and convincing evidence. . . . Among the statutory factors for finding unfitness, and the one asserted to be applicable to the instant case, is the provision finding unfitness where the father fails to "demonstrate a reasonable degree of interest, concern or responsibility as to the welfare of a new born child during the first 30 days after its birth."

Under the Adoption Act effective at the time this court invalidated the Does' adoption of Richard, an unwed father who was both fit and willing to take on the responsibility of raising his child had a right superior to all others except the birth mother to the care, custody and control of his child. Moreover, such a fit and willing father had the absolute right to block the adoption of his child, notwithstanding the birth mother's desire to place the child with an adoptive family. . . . In this manner, the statute safeguards the rights of unwed fathers who come forward and are willing and fit to raise their children.

. . .

Now that the invalid adoption of Richard has been vacated, the Does seek to use the Marriage and Dissolution of Marriage Act to obtain a custody hearing. However, it follows from the Adoption Act that the Does cannot, once an invalid adoption is vacated, attempt to circumvent the rights afforded fathers under the Adoption Act by seeking a custody hearing under the Marriage and Dissolution of Marriage Act, which, unlike the Adoption Act, could result in a father's being divested of his right to the care, custody and control of his child without being found unfit by clear and convincing evidence.

[W]e hold that where an unwed father is fit and willing to develop a relationship with and raise his child, but is prevented from doing so through deceit and an invalid adoption proceeding, that father is entitled to the care, custody and control of his child upon the subsequent vacatur of the invalid adoption. Under these facts, we hold that a section 601(b)(2) hearing under the Marriage and Dissolution of Marriage Act would be improper because it would contravene the safeguards afforded unwed fathers in the Adoption Act.

. . .

The final argument raised both by the Does and Richard's guardian *ad litem* is that Richard himself has a liberty interest in the familial relationship he has developed with the Does. In making this argument, the Does and the guardian *ad litem* fail to address the liberty interest Richard may have in being with his natural father. The United States Supreme Court has never decided whether a child has a liberty interest symmetrical with that of a natural parent in maintaining his current relationship. . . . Attempts to assert such a right on behalf of children who have become psychologically attached to a nonparent have not met with success. . . . We likewise hold that no such liberty interest exists as regards Richard's psychological attachment to the Does. To hold otherwise would be to overturn the entire jurisprudential history of parental rights in Illinois.

. . .

It would be a grave injustice not only to Otakar Kirchner, but to all mothers, fathers and children, to allow deceit, subterfuge and the erroneous rulings of two lower courts, together with the passage of time resulting from the Does' persistent and intransigent efforts to retain custody of Richard, to inure to the Does' benefit at the expense of the right of Otto and Richard to develop and maintain a family relationship. Moreover, the laws of Illinois, as hereinabove set forth, clearly compel us to order Richard delivered to his father, Otakar Kirchner. Accordingly, we ordered the writ of *habeas corpus* to issue on January 25, 1995, and we hereby reaffirm that order.

. . .

■ McMorrow, J., dissenting:

. . .

Today, by its total failure to recognize the rights of the child who has come to be known as "Baby Richard" and the rights of adoptive parents in the circumstances of this case, the majority grants Otakar Kirchner the unfettered right to remove Richard, almost four years old, from the only home and parents he has known. This ruling is extraordinary and in contravention of Illinois law and constitutional protections: the majority permits Richard to be taken by Kirchner from his home of the past four years, and be placed in the home occupied by a man and woman Richard has never seen or known. Significantly, the transfer into the home of these total strangers to Richard is ordered by the majority without any hearing to determine how and when such transfer should occur, and whether the home into which Richard is being placed is in his best interests. In abdication of its duty to minors, and irrespective of the fact that there has never at any time been a hearing at the trial court level at which a record would be developed, the majority issued the writ of *habeas corpus* to forthwith turn over the child to Kirchner.

The majority today sanctions the placement of this child into a home that is strange to him. The majority permits this transfer, although the court has little knowledge of the fitness of the occupants of that home or of the environment in that home.

. . .

The majority's summary decision to grant Kirchner's petition for a writ of *habeas corpus* violates Richard's right to procedural due process under the [F]ourteenth [A]mendment of the United States Constitution. [T]he issue of custody is different from the issues of adoption and the improper termination of parental rights. Unlike a termination of parental rights, which is concerned primarily with protecting the rights of parents, a change or modification of an existing custodial relationship is primarily concerned with protecting the child's interest in a healthy, stable environment. Under the Marriage Act and section 20 of the Adoption Act, the Illinois legislature created a constitutionally protected liberty interest in a child's emotional and psychological relationship with nonparent custodians, and has also provided the requisite procedures to prevent the summary or improper severing of this relationship in a way that would be harmful to the child.... By ignoring the child custody procedures provided by the Marriage Act and section 20 of the Adoption Act, the majority has arbitrarily deprived Richard of due process under the law by disregarding the intent of the legislature.

. . .

The granting of Kirchner's writ of *habeas corpus* effectively extinguished Richard's opportunity to receive a best-interests custody hearing. The trial court has jurisdiction under the Marriage Act and section 20 of the Adoption Act to adjudicate Richard's custody. The trial court is also the proper forum to conduct a fact finding hearing that would result in a custody determination in accord with Richard's best interests. Since this court found that Kirchner was a fit parent and that Kirchner's parental rights were improperly terminated, a valid adoption of Richard by the Does cannot be granted absent Kirchner's voluntary termination of his parental rights. [T]he proper termination of parental rights is the necessary prerequisite to granting a valid adoption.

However, in a custody dispute, the best interest of the child is of paramount importance. In dispensing with a custody hearing, the majority has placed the emotional and psychological well-being of a small child in danger.... One of the purposes of a custody hearing is to provide for an orderly change or modification in custody without exposing the child to risk of undue harm. At such a custody hearing, Kirchner's important rights will be considered along with the other relevant factors. The granting of the writ of *habeas corpus* to Kirchner, as the majority has done, ignores the State's valid interest in the psychological and emotional health of its children and unconstitutionally deprives Richard of a best-interests custody hearing, granted to him by the Illinois legislature.

. . .

By giving the constitutional protections afforded to a "natural" or "unitary" family to Kirchner, the majority has clouded the central question: [d]o the custody interests identified in the Marriage Act and the Adoption Act to prevent the summary, arbitrary or wrongful termination of Richard's emotional and psychological ties to the Does unconstitutionally impinge on the rights of Kirchner, the unwed, noncustodial, biological father who lacks any emotional or psychological ties to his offspring? A study of the five cases in which the U.S. Supreme Court has addressed the constitutional rights of unwed biological fathers indicates that Kirchner's rights as a biological father are not impinged upon by the allowance of the custody hearings sanctioned in the Marriage Act and the Adoption Act.

. . .

The majority asserts that the rationale underlying these five Supreme Court opinions entitles Kirchner to the highest degree of constitutional protection available to an unwed biological father because of the alleged deceit in the termination of Kirchner's parental rights.... This assertion is unfounded. The majority fails to understand that the Supreme Court, in these opinions, has afforded a biological father a high degree of due process protection to prevent improper *termination of his parental rights*.... These opinions do not afford the same protection to a biological father in a *custody proceeding*. Kirchner's parental rights were afforded complete protection under due process pursuant to *In re Petition of Doe*, 638 N.E.2d 181 (Ill. 1994), which reinstated Kirchner's improperly terminated parental rights. On the issue of Kirchner's improperly terminated rights, his due process rights have been vindicated. However, neither the United States Constitution nor Illinois law automatically vest custody in a noncustodial, biological father following the recognition of his parental rights. In sum, although Kirchner's right to develop a psychological father-son relationship was vindicated in the prior appeal, the State does not unconstitutionally impinge on that right by limiting or overseeing the way in which this relationship will develop under the circumstances of this case. That is the purpose of a custody determination. Custody will only be granted after a hearing on the child's best interests.

In defiance of established Illinois law and the constitutional rights of a small child under this law, the majority has given Kirchner the power to summarily terminate the only family relationship that Richard has ever known.

In denying Richard the protections the State has provided him, the majority places more importance on biology than on the importance of the nurturing, caring, and loving involved in raising a child....

Hopefully, someday children will be given their due process rights under the law, and also be given the same guarantees of their rights as are given to all other citizens. In its wisdom, this court should have examined its thinking, not only in the light of statutes and precedent, but also in the light of reality and human consequences. In both lights this court has failed Baby Richard. Accordingly, I dissent.

NOTES

1. Following the *Otakar Kirchner* decision, Baby Richard had no contact with his adoptive parents and was raised by his birth parents, who reported in 2003 that he was "in the 7th grade, getting straight A's, and ... doing fine." Jack Mabley, *Sad Case of "Baby Richard" Seems to Have a Happy Ending*, CHI. DAILY HERALD, Nov. 21, 2003. Otto and Daniella had more children, and reported that "Danny, his real name, is a normal, happy, emotionally unscarred kid living with his real parents and a couple of new siblings." *Id.* Does this apparently happy ending prove that the court made the right decision?

2. The decision has been heavily criticized by some. *See, e.g.*, Mary L. Shanley, *Unwed Fathers' Rights, Adoption, and Sex Equality: Gender–Neutrality and the Perpetuation of Patriarchy*, 95 COLUM. L. REV. 60 (1995); Anthony S. Zito, *Baby Richard and Beyond: The Future for Adopted Children*, 18 N. ILL. U. L. REV. 445 (1998); Deborah L. Forman, *Unwed Fathers and Adoption: A Theoretical Analysis in Context*, 72 TEX. L. REV. 967 (1994).

3. Consider Gregory Kelson's argument on the need to provide continuity of care for the children in such proceedings:

> Many children in the United States are very fortunate to be raised by their biological parents who give them love, encouragement, and will care for their

well-being and interests. However, problems frequently arise regarding the best interest of potentially adoptable children. For many of these children, foster care may be the only way to give them a stable home, although foster placements frequently do not result in permanent homes.

The aftermath of the . . . Baby Richard decision[] raised fear among adoptive parents, since the possibility arose that biological parents could change their minds at any time and regain custody of their children. Legislative and judicial action are needed to insure that once a child is placed for adoption, that adoption will not be disturbed in the future.

Children are not property. The manner in which a child grows up to become an adult will determine how productive he will be in society. To that end, it is important to provide the child with a stable home, free from distractions, where he can develop normally. Contrary to what courts have held throughout this nation, the best interest of the child should always prevail in adoption proceedings.

Gregory A. Kelson, *In the Best Interest of the Child: What Have We Learned from Baby Jessica and Baby Richard?*, 33 J. MARSHALL L. REV. 353, 381 (2000).

CHAPTER 5

THE NONTRADITIONAL FAMILY

A. UNMARRIED ADULTS

1. TRADITIONAL RULES

McLaughlin v. Florida

Supreme Court of the United States, 1964.
379 U.S. 184, 85 S.Ct. 283, 13 L.Ed.2d 222.

■ JUSTICE WHITE delivered the opinion of the Court.

At issue in this case is the validity of a conviction under § 798.05 of the Florida statutes, F.S.A., providing that:

Any negro man and white woman, or any white man and negro woman, who are not married to each other, who shall habitually live in and occupy in the nighttime the same room shall each be punished by imprisonment not exceeding twelve months, or by fine not exceeding five hundred dollars.

Because the section applies only to a white person and a Negro who commit the specified acts and because no couple other than one made up of a white and a Negro is subject to conviction upon proof of the elements comprising the offense it proscribes, we hold § 798.05 invalid as a denial of the equal protection of the laws guaranteed by the Fourteenth Amendment.

The challenged statute is a part of chapter 798 entitled "Adultery and Fornication."[1] Section 798.01 forbids living in adultery and § 798.02 pro-

---

1. Fla.Stat.Ann. § 798.01—Living in open adultery:

Whoever lives in an open state of adultery shall be punished by imprisonment in the state prison not exceeding two years, or in the county jail not exceeding one year, or by fine not exceeding five hundred dollars. Where either of the parties living in an open state of adultery is married, both parties so living shall be deemed to be guilty of the offense provided for in this section.

Fla.Stat.Ann. § 798.02—Lewd and lascivious behavior:

If any man and woman, not being married to each other, lewdly and lasciviously associate and cohabit together, or if any man or woman, married or unmarried, is guilty of open and gross lewdness and lascivious behavior, they shall be punished by imprisonment in the state prison not exceeding two years, or in the county jail not exceeding one year, or by fine not exceeding three hundred dollars.

Fla.Stat.Ann. § 798.03—Fornication:

If any man commits fornication with a woman, each of them shall be punished by imprisonment not exceeding three months, or by fine not exceeding thirty dollars.

Fla.Stat.Ann. § 798.04—White persons and Negroes living in adultery:

If any white person and negro, or mulatto, shall live in adultery or fornication with each other, each shall be punished by imprisonment not exceeding twelve months, or by fine not exceeding one thousand dollars.

Fla.Stat.Ann. § 798.05—Negro man and white woman or white man and Negro woman occupying same room:

scribes lewd cohabitation. Both sections are of general application, both require proof of intercourse to sustain a conviction, and both authorize imprisonment up to two years.[2] Section 798.03 also of general application, proscribes fornication[3] and authorizes a three-month jail sentence. The fourth section of the chapter, 798.04, makes criminal a white person and a Negro's living together in adultery or fornication. A one-year prison sentence is authorized. The conduct it reaches appears to be the same as is proscribed under the first two sections of the chapter.... Section 798.05, the section at issue in this case, applies only to a white person and a Negro who habitually occupy the same room at nighttime. This offense, however, is distinguishable from the other sections of the chapter in that it is the only one which does not require proof of intercourse along with the other elements of the crime.

Appellants were charged with a violation of § 798.05. The elements of the offense as described by the trial judge are the (1) habitual occupation of a room at night, (2) by a Negro and a white person (3) who are not married. The State presented evidence going to each factor, appellants' constitutional contentions were overruled and the jury returned a verdict of guilty. Solely on the authority of *Pace v. Alabama*, 106 U.S. 583 [(1883)], the Florida Supreme Court affirmed and sustained the validity of § 798.05 as against appellants' claims that the section denied them equal protection of the laws guaranteed by the Fourteenth Amendment.... We deal with the single issue of equal protection and on this basis set aside these convictions.[6]

It is readily apparent that § 798.05 treats the interracial couple made up of a white person and a Negro differently than it does any other couple. No couple other than a Negro and a white person can be convicted under § 798.05 and no other section proscribes the precise conduct banned by

---

Any negro man and white woman, or any white man and negro woman, who are not married to each other, who shall habitually live in and occupy in the nighttime the same room shall each be punished by imprisonment not exceeding twelve months, or by fine not exceeding five hundred dollars.

2. Section 798.02 proscribes two offenses: (1) open and gross lewdness and lascivious behavior by either a man or a woman; (2) lewd and lascivious association and cohabitation by a man and woman. The latter offense is identical to that proscribed by § 798.01, except that § 798.01 contains the additional requirement that one of the participants be married to a third party. Conviction under either section requires a showing that the parties lived together and maintained sexual relations over a period of time as in the conjugal relation between husband and wife. Braswell v. State, 88 Fla. 183, 101 So. 232 (1924); Lockhart v. State, 79 Fla. 824, 85 So. 153 (1920) (both cases involving what is now § 798.01); Wildman v. State, 157 Fla. 334, 25 So.2d 808 (1946); Penton v. State, 42 Fla. 560, 28 So. 774 (1900) (cases involving respectively, § 798.02 and what is now that statute).

3. Unlike all the other sections of chapter 798, § 798.03 does not relate only to habitual conduct. It proscribes single and occasional acts of fornication. See *Collins v. State*, 83 Fla. 458, 92 So. 681 (1922).

6. Appellants present two other contentions which it is unnecessary for us to consider in view of our disposition of their principal claim. First, they challenge the constitutionality of Fla.Stat.Ann. § 741.11—Marriages between white and Negro persons prohibited[.] ... Appellants' final claim is that their convictions violated due process either because there was no proof of appellant McLaughlin's race or because the Florida definition of "Negro" is unconstitutionally vague. Fla.Stat.Ann. § 1.01(6) provides: "The words 'negro,' 'colored,' 'colored persons,' 'mulatto' or 'persons of color,' when applied to persons, include every person having one-eighth or 03 more of African or negro blood." At the trial one of the arresting officers was permitted, over objection, to state his conclusion as to the race of each appellant based on his observation of their physical appearance. Appellants claim that the statutory definition is circular in that it provides no independent means of determining the race of a defendant's ancestors and that testimony based on appearance is impermissible because not related to any objective standard. Florida argues that under Florida appellate procedure this claim was abandoned when the appellants failed to argue it in the brief they presented to the Florida Supreme Court.

§ 798.05. Florida makes no claim to the contrary in this Court. However, all whites and Negroes who engage in the forbidden conduct are covered by the section and each member of the interracial couple is subject to the same penalty.

In this situation, *Pace v. Alabama*, *supra*, is relied upon as controlling authority. In our view, however, *Pace* represents a limited view of the Equal Protection Clause which has not withstood analysis in the subsequent decisions of this Court. In that case, the Court let stand a conviction under an Alabama statute forbidding adultery or fornication between a white person and a Negro and imposing a greater penalty than allowed under another Alabama statute of general application and proscribing the same conduct whatever the race of the participants. The opinion acknowledged that the purpose of the Equal Protection Clause "was to prevent hostile and discriminating state legislation against any person or class of persons" and that equality of protection under the laws implies that any person, "whatever his race * * * shall not be subjected, for the same offense, to any greater or different punishment." 106 U.S., at 584, 1 S.Ct., at 638. But taking quite literally its own words, "for the same *offence*" (emphasis supplied), the Court pointed out that Alabama had designated as a separate offense the commission by a white person and a Negro of the identical acts forbidden by the general provisions. There was, therefore, no impermissible discrimination because the difference in punishment was "directed against the offence designated" and because in the case of each offense all who committed it, white and Negro, were treated alike. Under *Pace*[,] the Alabama law regulating the conduct of both Negroes and whites satisfied the Equal Protection Clause since it applied equally to the among the members of the class which it reached without regard to the fact that the statute did not reach other types of couples performing the identical conduct and without any necessity to justify the difference in penalty established for the two offenses. Because each of the Alabama laws applied equally to those to whom it was applicable, the different treatment accorded interracial and intraracial couples was irrelevant.[8]

. . .

Judicial inquiry under the Equal Protection Clause ... does not end with a showing of equal application among the members of the class defined by the legislation. The courts must reach and determine the question whether the classifications drawn in a statute are reasonable in light of its purpose—in this case, whether there is an arbitrary or invidious discrimination between those classes covered by Florida's cohabitation law and those excluded. That question is what *Pace* ignored and what must be faced here.

Normally, the widest discretion is allowed the legislative judgment in determining whether to attack some, rather than all, of the manifestations of the evil aimed at; and normally that judgment is given the benefit of every

---

8. Had the Court been presented with a statute that, for example, prohibited any Negro male from having carnal knowledge of a white female and penalized only the Negro, such a statute would unquestionably have been held to deny equal protection even though it applied equally to all to whom it applied. See Strauder v. West Virginia, 100 U.S. 303, 306–08 [(1879)]; Ho Ah Kow v. Nunan, 12 Fed.Cas. p. 252 (No. 6546) (C.C.D.Cal.1879) (Field, J.) ("Chinese Pigtail" case). Because of the manifest inadequacy of any approach requiring only equal application to the class defined in the statute, one may conclude that in *Pace* the Court actually ruled *sub silentio* that the different treatment meted out to interracial and intraracial couples was based on a reasonable legislative purpose. If the Court did reach that conclusion it failed to articulate it or to give its reasons, and for the reasons stated *infra* we reject the contention presented here that the criminal statute presently under review is grounded in a reasonable legislative policy.

conceivable circumstance which might suffice to characterize the classification as reasonable rather than arbitrary and invidious. But we deal here with a classification based upon the race of the participants, which must be viewed in light of the historical fact that the central purpose of the Fourteenth Amendment was to eliminate racial discrimination emanating from official sources in the States. This strong policy renders racial classifications "constitutionally suspect," *Bolling v. Sharpe*, 347 U.S. 497, 499 [(1954)]; and subject to the "most rigid scrutiny," *Korematsu v. United States*, 323 U.S. 214, 216 [(1944)]; and "in most circumstances irrelevant" to any constitutionally acceptable legislative purpose, *Kiyoshi Hirabayashi v. United States*, 320 U.S. 81, 100 [(1943)]. Thus it is that racial classifications have been held invalid in a variety of contexts.

We deal here with a racial classification embodied in a criminal statute. In this context, where the power of the State weighs most heavily upon the individual or the group, we must be especially sensitive to the policies of the Equal Protection Clause which, as reflected in congressional enactments dating from 1870, were intended to secure "the full and equal benefit of all laws and proceedings for the security of persons and property" and to subject all persons "to like punishment, pains, penalties, taxes, licenses, and exactions of every kind, and to no other." R.S. § 1977, 42 U.S.C. § 1981 (1958 ed.).

Our inquiry, therefore, is whether there clearly appears in the relevant materials some overriding statutory purpose requiring the proscription of the specified conduct when engaged in by a white person and a Negro, but not otherwise. Without such justification the racial classification contained in § 798.05 is reduced to an invidious discrimination forbidden by the Equal Protection Clause.

The Florida Supreme Court, relying upon *Pace v. Alabama, supra*, found no legal discrimination at all and gave no consideration to statutory purpose. The State in its brief in this Court, however, says that the legislative purpose of § 798.05, like the other sections of chapter 798, was to prevent breaches of the basic concepts of sexual decency; and we see no reason to quarrel with the State's characterization of this statute, dealing as it does with illicit extramarital and premarital promiscuity.

We find nothing in this suggested legislative purpose, however, which makes it essential to punish promiscuity of one racial group and not that of another. There is no suggestion that a white person and a Negro are any more likely habitually to occupy the same room together than the white or the Negro couple or to engage in illicit intercourse if they do. Sections 798.01–798.05 indicate no legislative conviction that promiscuity by the interracial couple presents any particular problems requiring separate or different treatment if the suggested over-all policy of the chapter is to be adequately served. Sections 798.01–798.03 deal with adultery, lewd cohabitation and fornication, in that order. All are of general application. Section 798.04 prohibits a white and a Negro from living in a state of adultery or fornication and imposes a lesser period of imprisonment than does either § 798.01 or § 798.02, each of which is applicable to all persons. Simple fornication by the interracial couple is covered only by the general provision of § 798.03. This is not, therefore, a case where the class defined in the law is that from which "the evil mainly is to be feared," *Patsone v. Pennsylvania*, 232 U.S. 138, 144 [(1914)]; or where the "(e)vils in the same field may be of different dimensions and proportions, requiring different remedies," *Williamson v. Lee Optical*, 348 U.S. 483, 489 [(1955)]; or even one where the State has done as much as it can as fast as it can, *Buck v. Bell*, 274 U.S. 200, 208 [(1927)]. That a general evil will be partially corrected may at times, and without more, serve to justify the limited application of a criminal law; but legislative discretion to employ the piecemeal approach stops short of permitting a State to narrow statutory coverage to focus on a racial group. Such classifications bear a far heavier burden of justification. . . .

Florida's remaining argument is related to its law against interracial marriage, Fla.Stat.Ann. § 741.11, which, in the light of certain legislative history of the Fourteenth Amendment, is said to be immune from attack under the Equal Protection Clause. Its interracial cohabitation law, § 798.05, is likewise valid, it is argued, because it is ancillary to and serves the same purpose as the miscegenation law itself.

We reject this argument, without reaching the question of the validity of the State's prohibition against interracial marriage or the soundness of the arguments rooted in the history of the Amendment. For even if we posit the constitutionality of the ban against the marriage of a Negro and a white, it does not follow that the cohabitation law is not to be subjected to independent examination under the Fourteenth Amendment. "(A)ssuming, for purposes of argument only, that the basic prohibition is constitutional," in this case the law against interracial marriage, "it does not follow that there is no constitutional limit to the means which may be used to enforce it." *Oyama v. California*, 332 U.S. 633, 646–647 [(1948)]. Section 798.05 must therefore itself pass muster under the Fourteenth Amendment; and for reasons quite similar to those already given, we think it fails the test.

. . . Those provisions of chapter 798 which are neutral as to race express a general and strong state policy against promiscuous conduct, whether engaged in by those who are married, those who may marry or those who may not. These provisions, if enforced, would reach illicit relations of any kind and in this way protect the integrity of the marriage laws of the State, including what is claimed to be a valid ban on interracial marriage. These same provisions, moreover, punish premarital sexual relations as severely or more severely in some instances than do those provisions which focus on the interracial couple. Florida has offered no argument that the State's policy against interracial marriage cannot be as adequately served by the general, neutral, and existing ban on illicit behavior as by a provision such as § 798.05 which singles out the promiscuous interracial couple for special statutory treatment. In short, it has not been shown that § 798.05 is a necessary adjunct to the State's ban on interracial marriage. We accordingly invalidate § 798.05 without expressing any views about the State's prohibition of interracial marriage, and reverse these convictions.

Reversed.

■ MR. JUSTICE HARLAN, concurring.

I join the Court's opinion with the following comments.

I agree with the Court that the cohabitation statute has not been shown to be necessary to the integrity of the antimarriage law, assumed *arguendo* to be valid, and that necessity, not mere reasonable relationship, is the proper test.

The fact that these cases arose under the principles of the First Amendment does not make them inapplicable here. Principles of free speech are carried to the States only through the Fourteenth Amendment. The necessity test which developed to protect free speech against state infringement should be equally applicable in a case involving state racial discrimination—prohibition of which lies at the very heart of the Fourteenth Amendment. Nor does the fact that these cases all involved what the Court deemed to be a constitutionally excessive exercise of legislative power relating to a single state policy, whereas this case involves two legislative policies—prevention of extramarital relations and prevention of miscegenation—effectuated by separate statutes, serve to vitiate the soundness of the Court's conclusion that the validity of the State's antimarriage law need not be decided in this case. If the legitimacy of the cohabitation statute is considered to depend upon its being ancillary to the antimarriage statute, the former must be deemed "unnecessary" under the principle established by the cited cases in light of the nondiscriminatory extramarital relations statutes. If, however, the interracial cohabitation statute is considered to rest upon a discrete state interest, existing independently of the antimarriage law, it falls of its own weight.

■ MR. JUSTICE STEWART, with whom MR. JUSTICE DOUGLAS joins, concurring.

I concur in the judgment and agree with most of what is said in the Court's opinion. But the Court implies that a criminal law of the kind here involved might be constitutionally valid if a State could show "some overriding statutory purpose." This is an implication in which I cannot join, because I cannot conceive of a valid legislative purpose under our Constitution for a state law which makes the color of a person's skin the test of whether his conduct is a criminal offense. These appellants were convicted, fined, and imprisoned under a statute which made their conduct criminal only because they were of different races. So far as this statute goes, their conduct would not have been illegal had they both been white, or both Negroes. There might be limited room under the Equal Protection Clause for a civil law requiring the keeping of racially segregated public records for statistical or other valid public purposes. But we deal here with a criminal law which imposes criminal punishment. And I think it is simply not possible for a state law to be valid under our Constitution which makes the criminality of an act depend upon the race of the actor. Discrimination of that kind is invidious *per se.**

NOTE

Consider Ariela R. Dubler, *From* McLaughlin v. Florida *to* Lawrence v. Texas: *Sexual Freedom and the Road to Marriage*, 106 COLUM. L. REV. 1165, 1170–72, 1177–78 (2006):

> In April 1961, Connie Hoffman, a native Alabaman working as a waitress in Miami, moved into a one-room apartment owned by Dora Goodnick at 732 Second Street in Miami Beach, Florida. Sometime that fall, Dewey McLaughlin, a Honduran-born sometime hotel worker and sometime merchant seaman, moved in with Hoffman. Goodnick, it seems, watched the relationship between Hoffman and McLaughlin fairly closely. When called as a witness for the prosecution at Hoffman and McLaughlin's trial, Goodnick told the court that in both December 1961 and February 1962, she repeatedly saw Dewey McLaughlin enter the Second Street building at night and leave in the morning. Goodnick also claimed that she saw McLaughlin showering in Hoffman's apartment, saw his clothing hanging in the apartment, and heard him talking to Hoffman at night. According to Goodnick, when she inquired about McLaughlin's presence, Hoffman explained that he was her husband.

---

* Since I think this criminal law is clearly invalid under the Equal Protection Clause of the Fourteenth Amendment, I do not consider the impact of the Due Process Clause of that Amendment, nor of the Thirteenth and Fifteenth Amendments.

No matter how carefully she watched their comings and goings, Goodnick could not have known all the complications surrounding the legal status of the relationship between McLaughlin and Hoffman. When the nature of their relationship became a matter of formal legal dispute, people offered quite different accounts of McLaughlin's and Hoffman's respective marital situations at the time that they began cohabiting in Goodnick's building. McLaughlin was, apparently, legally married to someone other than Hoffman when he moved in to her apartment. In January 1961, when he was applying for a civilian registration card, McLaughlin told Joseph DeCesare, a city employee, that he was married but separated from his wife—not Connie Hoffman, but a woman named Willie McLaughlin. Likewise, at least one witness at McLaughlin and Hoffman's trial testified that Hoffman too was already married to someone other than McLaughlin when she moved into Goodnick's apartment. In fact, it seemed that she initially cohabited in the apartment with another man—a white man with the last name of Hoffman, presumably her legal husband. Moreover, in March 1962, Hoffman told a Florida child welfare worker that, although she had been living with McLaughlin since the fall of 1961, they had never formally married. Even as McLaughlin and Hoffman sought to bring themselves within the protective boundaries of the doctrine of common law marriage, their complicated lives would have made it difficult for them to argue that they had satisfied the central requirements of the doctrine—that is, that they had consistently acted as though they were married to each other and that they had been accepted by their community as husband and wife.

Dora Goodnick, no doubt, lacked all of this background information when she assessed the relationship between her legal tenant and McLaughlin. But Goodnick did know one thing: There was a black man spending a lot of time in the apartment of her white female tenant. In February 1962, Goodnick called the police. Based on information that Hoffman and McLaughlin were cohabiting illegally, as well as allegations that Hoffman's minor child was not receiving adequate care, Detectives Stanley Marcus and Nicolas Valeriana of the Miami Beach Police Department went to Hoffman's apartment on the evening of February 23, 1962. They found McLaughlin in the apartment and, in response to the detectives' queries, McLaughlin admitted that he lived there with Hoffman and had a sexual relationship with her. Shortly thereafter, Hoffman met McLaughlin at the police station and corroborated this story. Hoffman told the police that she lived with McLaughlin but that she did not think they were breaking any laws in doing so. Although neither McLaughlin nor Hoffman were charged with any unlawful conduct that day at the police station, less than a week later, when they were still living together in Goodnick's apartment, they were charged with violating section 798.05.

McLaughlin and Hoffman's trial began on June 27, 1962. The very next day the jury returned a guilty verdict, and McLaughlin and Hoffman were each sentenced to thirty days of hard labor in the county jail, and fined one hundred and fifty dollars. They served eighteen days before they were released on bond pending appeal. Following their release, with the assistance of the NAACP Legal Defense Fund, McLaughlin and Hoffman appealed their case, challenging the constitutionality of section 798.05 as well as the state's ban on interracial marriage....

   . . .

   ... [T]he Supreme Court's decision in *McLaughlin*, limited as it was in its revision of the category of illicit sex, represented a stark renunciation of the most basic premise of the interracial sex taboo: That is, that sexual unions between blacks and whites were uniquely threatening to the sociolegal fabric of the nation in a way that was different in kind from the threats posed by intraracial, nonmarital sexual relationships. Given that all discussions of civil rights, even outside the realm of laws regulating sex, had long been understood to implicate the constitutional status of state laws regulating interracial intimacy, the very acceptance of the idea that interracial relationships could be illicit in the same way as intraracial, nonmarital relationships constituted a radical break with the past.

Coming in 1964, therefore, *McLaughlin* deserves recognition for the substantial, albeit complicated, intervention it wielded in setting the constitutional parameters of the legal regulation of interracial sex and nonmarital intimacy. After all, *McLaughlin* marked the first time that the United States Supreme Court extended any measure of constitutional protection to interracial sex between blacks and whites. It was the first time, in other words, that the Court applied its race discrimination jurisprudence—developed in other areas—to the highly politically and socially sensitive area of interracial intimate relations. By targeting interracial couples, the Court unequivocally stated in *McLaughlin*, section 798.05 "trenche[d] upon the constitutionally protected freedom from invidious official discrimination based on race." It thus violated the Fourteenth Amendment of the Constitution for nonmarital sex between a white person and a black person to be singled out for particular criminal sanction because, from a constitutional perspective, interracial sex outside of marriage was no different then intraracial sex outside of marriage.

Margaret M. Mahoney, *Forces Shaping the Law of Cohabitation for Opposite Sex Couples*

7 J. L. & FAM. STUD. 135, 141–47 (2005).

I. Criminal Regulation of Unmarried Cohabitation

When the Model Penal Code [MPC] was published in 1962, most states in the United States criminalized nonmarital cohabitation. The traditional social norms, reflected in this type of criminal regulation, were in flux at that time. Following substantial debate, the ALI decided not to include the offense of cohabitation in the MPC. Most, but not all, U.S. jurisdictions subsequently repealed their unlawful cohabitation statutes. Nevertheless, the traditional perception of unacceptability and immorality associated with the private decisions of unmarried couples to live together has continuing resonance in the present day regulation of unmarried cohabitation.

A. The 2003 Debate in North Dakota

In April of 2003, the North Dakota Senate rejected a proposal to repeal the state statute making unmarried cohabitation a criminal offense. This was not the first repeal effort in North Dakota. . . .

The North Dakota unlawful cohabitation statute was first enacted during the state's inaugural legislative session in 1890. The current law provides that "[a] person is guilty of a . . . misdemeanor if he or she lives openly and notoriously with a person of the opposite sex as a married couple without being married to the other person." The maximum penalty for persons convicted of unlawful cohabitation is thirty days' imprisonment and a fine of $1000.

Lawmakers on both sides of the debate to repeal the North Dakota statute made familiar observations and arguments. . . .

Supporters of the recent repeal effort first pointed out that the North Dakota unlawful cohabitation statute was rarely enforced. . . . In fact, the last reported case involving a criminal prosecution for unlawful cohabitation in North Dakota was decided by the state supreme court in 1938. More recent cases in North Dakota actually involved prosecutorial decisions not to pursue violators of the unlawful cohabitation statute. In cases from 1999 and 2002, the state supreme court rejected the efforts of private citizens to compel the state to prosecute their unfaithful spouses for criminal cohabitation. Generally speaking, the failure to enforce existing criminal laws in this manner supports the case for their repeal, based on the theory that such widespread nonenforcement leads to disrespect for the legal system. . . .

The supporters of decriminalization also emphasized the disrespect for individual privacy interests inherent in the North Dakota criminal cohabitation law, and the inevitable intrusion into the private affairs of individual citizens required for its enforcement. . . . Other commentators pointed to specific examples of cohabitation which, they believed, demonstrated the wisdom of repealing the criminal regulation. Thus, one state representative asked whether "college students sharing apartments . . . and seniors sharing living arrangements in order to hang on to their maximum Social Security benefits . . . are . . . criminals." Another person spoke of her grandmother, who lived with her male companion of twenty-three years and believed, appropriately according to the granddaughter, that "what [she] was doing in the privacy of [her] own home . . . [was] none of your business."

The North Dakota senators who voted down the repeal bill responded to both the nonenforcement and privacy issues in predictable ways. First, according to the opponents, the legislature can and should take a position on moral issues, such as nonmarital cohabitation, even if the resulting legislation is not enforced. . . .

[O]pponents of repeal also attempted to identify more tangible benefits associated with the North Dakota unlawful cohabitation statute. Here, they took the position that the criminal proscription against cohabitation strengthened and stabilized families. To support this position, the lawmakers cited statistics indicating higher rates of domestic violence and instability in cohabiting families as compared to married families. They did not, however, attempt to demonstrate a causal connection between the decisions of couples not to marry and the violence and instability in their families. Nor did they attempt to demonstrate that the existence of a criminal law influenced marriage decisions by couples in North Dakota.

. . .

B. The Model Penal Code of 1962

The recent debate in North Dakota illustrated a broader ideological conflict about the merits of regulating sexual conduct between consenting adults within the criminal law system. A classic example of the conflict unfolded when the Model Penal Code of 1962 was promulgated by the American Law Institute as a model criminal code. The MPC advisory committee initially included the crimes of open and notorious fornication and illicit cohabitation in an early (1955) working draft of the Code. Illicit cohabitation was defined as living together with a person of the opposite sex other than a spouse in an open and notorious manner "under the representation or appearance of being married." The limitation involving an "appearance of being married" was a significant one, not contained in the majority of state unlawful cohabitation laws at that time. However, even this relatively narrow cohabitation provision, along with the proposed fornication regulation, was ultimately deleted by the ALI from the final version of the Code.

The commentary accompanying the 1955 draft of the MPC contains a summary of the arguments supporting the advisory committee's decision to define criminal cohabitation narrowly by including the "appearance of marriage" limitation. Ultimately, the same arguments supported the decision by the ALI to completely eliminate all regulation of unmarried cohabitation. Notably, the 1955 commentary contains many of the same arguments made by the proponents of the recent effort in North Dakota to repeal the state's criminal cohabitation statute.

First, the MPC advisory committee commented that the retention of widely unenforced criminal laws, such as the existing sex crime regulations, diluted the deterrent effect of other criminal laws. An additional concern raised about criminal laws that were not fully enforced involved the possibility of discriminatory enforcement. Here, the MPC commentary highlighted the selective enforcement of sex crime regulations based on race. The advisory committee's final concern relating to the nonenforcement of broad criminal cohabitation and fornication laws focused on their resulting use for purposes other than criminal regulation. As examples of this phenomenon, the MPC commentary cited and criticized the documented use of criminal laws as leverage against cohabiting adulterous spouses in divorce proceedings, and against unmarried cohabiting fathers in child support proceedings.

Next, the advisory committee took the position that most of the sexual activity historically regulated by broad criminal cohabitation and fornication statutes involved no victim and no harm beyond an affront to public morals. The committee stated that this type of harm was not the proper concern of the criminal justice system, as follows: "We deem it inappropriate for the government to attempt to control behavior that has no substantial significance except as to the morality of the actor. Such matters are best left to religious, educational and other social influences."

The final argument against broad regulation under the Model Penal Code focused on individual privacy rights. Here, the advisory committee emphasized the importance of respecting different viewpoints among citizens about the morality of various forms of sexual conduct, stating: "[I]n a heterogeneous community such as ours, different individuals and groups have widely divergent views of the seriousness of various moral derelictions." Of course, this same concern has come to figure prominently in more recent debates about sex crime regulation, including the 2003 legislative debate about the North Dakota unlawful cohabitation statute.

Having thus espoused a general position against legislating morality, the MPC advisory committee attempted to justify its 1955 proposal to criminalize cohabitation, narrowly defined with the "appearance of marriage" limitation, on other grounds. Here, the committee attempted to identify "secular aims" uniquely associated with the regulation of cohabitation taking place "under the representation or appearance of being married." The identified goals included promoting marriage and decreasing the opportunities for violence, the birth of children outside of marriage, and disease. Ultimately, the ALI membership voted down the advisory committee's proposal, apparently failing to see the uniqueness of these concerns to the "appearance of being married" context, or their association with the criminal regulation of cohabitation in any form. As in the recent North Dakota legislative debate, the proponents of criminal regulation set forth secular or utilitarian goals, but failed to establish that the criminal laws would further these purposes.

In the end, the MPC advisory committee reverted to a morality-based justification for including the narrowly-defined crime of cohabitation. Thus, their commentary stated that the behavior isolated for regulation, involving the appearance of being married, "not only contravenes the morals of others, but openly and provocatively flouts their standards...." The reference here to "provocatively flout[ing]" the standards of others emphasized the open, public nature of the conduct included in the draft proposal. Ultimately, the ALI found the proposed regulation of cohabitation, even with the limitation involving open and public conduct, to be unacceptable, and excluded unmarried cohabitation from regulation under the Model Penal Code of 1962.

C.   Summary of Current Law

When the Model Penal Code was drafted, unlawful cohabitation statutes appeared in the criminal codes of most states, along with proscriptions against other sex-based offenses such as adultery and fornication. The decision of the ALI to exclude sex crimes from the final version of the MPC in 1962 became a major factor influencing state lawmakers to repeal many of these state statutes in the decades that followed.

Currently, only a handful of jurisdictions, including North Dakota, continue the criminal ban on unmarried cohabitation. For example, the Michigan statute entitled "Cohabitation by Unmarried Men and Women," which appears in a chapter of the state criminal code entitled "Indecency and Immorality," provides that "[a]ny man or woman, not being married to each other, who lewdly and lasciviously associates and cohabits together, and any man or woman, married or unmarried, who is guilty of open and gross lewdness and lascivious behavior, is guilty of a misdemeanor...." The behavior of unmarried cohabitants involved in a sexual relationship may violate additional criminal laws, such as the fornication statutes which generally criminalize sexual conduct with a partner other than one's spouse. These regulations are more prevalent today than the unlawful cohabitation laws, and are also widely unenforced.

The remaining state laws that criminalize unmarried cohabitation are most likely unconstitutional, under the privacy doctrine established by the United States Supreme Court. Generally speaking, the Court has recognized a zone of individual privacy relating to sexuality and procreation that must be respected by the government. Neither the Supreme Court nor the lower courts have ruled on the validity of state cohabitation statutes under the privacy doctrine. However, the rulings in related cases involving the state regulation of private sexual activity, especially the 2003 decision of the Supreme Court in *Lawrence v. Texas*, could be easily extended to the criminal regulation of cohabitation.

. . .

NOTES

1. Like cohabitation, fornication and adultery (at least in their consensual varieties) were eliminated as offenses under the Model Penal Code § 213 (1962) (no provision for consensual fornication or adultery). MODEL PENAL CODE § 213, et seq. SEXUAL OFFENSES (1962). The decriminalization of these practices has been discussed this way:

> [T]he large number of states that have decriminalized fornication is evidence of a national consensus. Fornication and the related concept of cohabitation have been decriminalized by almost forty states[.] ... Additionally, the fornication laws that still are in existence in the United States are rarely enforced[.] ... Finally, within those states that continue to criminalize fornication, almost all classify the crime as only a misdemeanor.
>
> Public opinion also contributes to a national consensus with regard to fornication laws. There has been a strikingly clear direction of change whereby the public has expressed extreme dissatisfaction with the criminalization of fornication, and the legislatures of the states have responded. In opinion polls,

eighty-five percent of Americans indicated that they do not believe that the government should criminalize consensual fornication between adults.... Furthermore, many Americans engage in fornication and do so frequently.

Despite this public opinion data, American jurisdictions differ from most western European countries, "which do not use the criminal process to interfere with private behavior between consenting adults." Fornication is not a crime in England. Additionally, fornication has been legal in France since 1975. In Sweden, fornication is not only allowed, cohabitation is practiced by twenty-five percent of couples.

... Many religions still condemn fornication. However, such condemnation by religious groups may be more of a statement that the act is immoral than a view that such acts should be criminal....

... The states' decriminalization of fornication began in the late 1960s and continued to the present day....

. . .

2.   Adultery

Adultery is another consensual sexual act that is criminally punished in the United States. In *Griswold v. Connecticut*, the United States Supreme Court said, "marriage is a coming together for better or for worse, hopefully enduring and intimate to the point of being sacred." However, extramarital sex is widespread. Self-reported data on the prevalence of extramarital sex may be shocking to some. "Most American marriages include extramarital sex by at least one of the partners." In addition, five percent of Americans have had "open marriages," in which extramarital intercourse is explicitly permitted. Despite the lack of marital monogamy in our society, many states continue to demand monogamous marital relationships by retaining criminal adultery statutes.

Adultery was not a serious offense in England before monogamy became the norm. Once monogamy became the standard, adultery was characterized as a serious wrong that invaded a husband's "rights" with regard to his wife. As early as the year 565, illicit sex incurred pecuniary penalties under one of the first codified Anglo–Saxon codes. Historically, adultery was an ecclesiastical offense under the jurisdiction of the church. By the year 1650, adultery was a capital crime under canon law. The offense became less severely punished under canon law as the importance of the church declined; however, communal and criminal consequences remained.

Upon settling in the American colonies, the Puritans continued the English tradition and made adultery a crime. It soon became a crime in almost every jurisdiction. In colonial times, punishment for adultery included death, branding, whipping, and other types of social punishments. It was not until 1955, when the Model Penal Code decriminalized adultery, that many states followed suit. Today, adultery remains a crime in twenty-three states and the District of Columbia. Adultery is also a military crime in the United States.

As with the criminalization of fornication, states have adopted a wide variety of definitions and classifications of adultery. First, jurisdictions differ as to what acts constitute adultery. "[S]ome states require habitual relations, cohabitation, or open adultery." Other states require that to be valid, an adultery prosecution must be initiated by the non-adulterous spouse. Second, jurisdictions differ as to whether one must be actually married to commit the offense of adultery. Some jurisdictions limit criminal responsibility to those who are married when they commit adultery. Other jurisdictions specify that an unmarried person who has sexual intercourse with a married person is guilty of adultery. Finally, the states that do criminalize adultery differ as to whether it should be classified as a misdemeanor or a felony.

[A]lthough the statistics fall short of the almost forty states that have decriminalized fornication, a majority of the states in the United States currently do not have laws criminalizing adultery in any form.... The direction of change is moving towards the decriminalization of adultery. As with fornication, criminal adultery laws are rarely enforced, and when enforced the penalties are generally minor. Only four of the twenty-three states that criminalize adultery classify the offense as a felony. . . .

Public opinion polls show that Americans support this direction of change and suggest that while many believe that adultery is morally wrong, they do not feel it should be criminalized. The results of one poll indicate that seventy-eight percent of Americans believe that the military should not punish adultery as a crime. Another poll, conducted by CNN after the impeachment trial of President Clinton in 1999, indicated that sixty-four percent of American adults supported the Senate's decision not to punish by impeachment the admittedly adulterous Clinton. Furthermore, . . . many people engage in adultery.

With regard to the world view on adultery, there appears to be a split in direction, with most western countries decriminalizing the act. Adultery is a crime in South Korea and is actively prosecuted. Additionally, most Islamic countries still criminalize adultery. However, European attitudes towards adultery are more liberal. In Europe, particularly Italy and France, marriage historically has been a property transaction, so adultery has been more accepted. English common law has never classified adultery as a crime and it remains decriminalized in England today. Adultery is also not a crime in Germany or Sweden.

. . .

Melanie C. Falco, Comment, *The Road Not Taken: Using the Eighth Amendment to Strike Down Criminal Punishment for Engaging in Consensual Sexual Acts*, 82 N.C. L. Rev. 723, 740–47 (2004). Currently, five states ban fornication[1] and twenty-three states ban adultery[2] through criminal law. Of course, this does not mean that legal norms against the practices have been entirely disavowed. As the co-authors of one recent, important work on criminal justice and the family explain in relation to adultery:

> Although one might be tempted to dismiss the significance of adultery laws today, we are loathe to do so in light of the continued enforcement of such laws in some jurisdictions, especially the military. Indeed, although civilian courts have generally seen a decrease in adultery prosecutions, there is a steady flow of such prosecutions in the military courts. . . . Additionally, even though someone might not get prosecuted for the crime of adultery in a jurisdiction forbidding such misconduct, it bears mention that the fact that the criminal laws remain on the books has real consequences in civil contexts other than the military, such as child custody, adoption, and employment.

Dan Markel, Jennifer M. Collins & Ethan J. Lieb, Privilege or Punish: Criminal Justice and the Challenge of Family Ties 71–2 (2009) (footnotes omitted).

2.   The intensity of social and legal norms around illegitimacy has also diminished, as reflected in legal, including constitutional rules, against legal classifications based on this birth status, discussed below, see Section B. For a useful summary of the relevant constitutional doctrine, see Erwin Chemerinsky, Constitutional Law: Principles and Polices 777–82 (3d ed. 2006), and Laurence H. Tribe, American Constitutional Law 1553–58 (2d ed. 1988). A pertinent historical point is noted in William N.

---

1.   Idaho Code Ann. § 18–6603; Mass. Gen. Laws ch. 272 § 18; Minn. Stat. § 609.34; S.C. Code Ann. § 16–15–60; Utah Code Ann. § 76-6-104. Four other states—Illinois, Mississippi, North Dakota and Wisconsin—also ban fornication in select settings. 720 Ill. Comp. Stat. 5/11–40; Miss. Code Ann. § 97–29–1; N.D. Cent. Code § 12.1–20–08; Wis. Stat. § 944.15.

2.   Ala. Code § 13A–13–2; Ariz. Rev. Stat. Ann. § 13–1408; Colo. Rev. Stat. § 18-6-501; Fla. Stat. Ann. § 798.01; Ga. Code Ann. § 16–6–19; Idaho Code Ann. § 18–6601; 720 Ill. Comp. Stat. Ann. 5/11–7; Kan Stat. Ann. § 21–3507; Md Code Ann., Crim. Law § 10–501; Mass. Ann. Law ch. 272, § 14; Mich. Comp. Laws Ann. § 750.30; Minn. Stat. Ann. § 609.36; Miss. Code Ann. § 97–29–1; N.H. Rev. Stat. Ann. § 645:3; N.Y. Penal Law § 255.17; N.C. Gen. Laws § 14–184; N.D. Cent. Code § 12.1–20–09; Okla. Stat. Ann. Tit. 21, § 871; R.I. Gen. Laws § 11–6–2; S.C. Code Ann. § 16–15–60; Utah Code Ann. § 76-7-103; Va. Code Ann. § 18.2–365; Wis. Stat. Ann. § 944.16.

Eskridge, Jr., *Sexual and Gender Variation in American Public Law: From Malignant to Benign to Productive*, 57 UCLA L. REV. 1333, 1337–38 (2010):

> American law before 1861 pervasively reflected and provided normative confirmation for this natural law understanding [of sex, gender and sexuality]. State-supported marriage was the central regulatory institution: Free men and women were strongly encouraged to enter it, and within that institution they were governed by rigid rules. Thus, state criminal codes channeled sexual activities into procreative (penile-vaginal) intercourse within marriage by declaring fornication and adultery (intercourse outside of marriage), sodomy (nonprocreative anal intercourse), and seduction (intercourse with a minor incapable of marrying) to be serious felonies. Children born outside of marriage were subject to social disadvantages and legal exclusions.

3.   Although the Model Penal Code is not without its significance in relation to the legal status of the nontraditional family, other social and legal, including constitutional, developments have also contributed to the evolution of norms and rules involving cohabitation and extra-marital intimacies. For some relevant discussion, see DAVID J. GARROW, LIBERTY AND SEXUALITY: THE RIGHT TO PRIVACY AND THE MAKING OF *ROE v. WADE* (1998 ed.); Reva B. Siegel, *Constitutional Culture, Social Movement Conflict and Constitutional Change: The Case of the de facto ERA*, 94 CAL. L. REV. 1323 (2006); Robin West, *Constitutional Culture or Ordinary Politics: A Reply to Reva Siegel*, 94 CAL. L. REV. 1465 (2006). *See also* GEORGE CHAUNCEY, GAY NEW YORK: GENDER, URBAN CULTURE, AND THE MAKING OF THE GAY MALE WORLD 1890–1940 (1994); GEORGE CHAUNCEY, WHY MARRIAGE? THE HISTORY SHAPING TODAY'S DEBATE OVER GAY EQUALITY (2004).

2.   CONTEMPORARY PRACTICES

Pamela J. Smock & Wendy D. Manning, Population Studies Center, Institute for Social Research, *Living Together Unmarried in the United States: Demographic Perspectives and Implications for Family Policy*

2–4, 7–9, 14–15 (Report No. 04–555).

The last few decades have ushered in significant changes in family patterns—in union formation, union dissolution, childbearing and attitudes about a range of family issues. After a brief period characterized by early marriage and low levels of divorce after World War II (*i.e.*, the Baby Boom), recent decades have been marked by lower levels of childbearing, higher divorce rates, increases in the average age at marriage, rising nonmarital childbearing and ... rising levels of cohabitation.

Although most Americans still marry at some point and the vast majority express strong desires to marry, unmarried cohabitation has dramatically transformed the marriage process. Today, the majority of marriages and remarriages begin as cohabiting relationships. Most young men and women have cohabited or will cohabit, cohabitation has increased in all age groups and cohabitation is increasingly becoming a context for childbearing and childrearing; it is estimated that two-fifths of children born in the early 1990s will spend time in a cohabiting-parent family Clearly, cohabitation has become a widely-experienced, even normative, phenomenon in recent decades.

> . . .

One of the key changes in the union formation process has been a postponement in marriage since the Baby Boom (approximately 1947–1963). . . .

> . . .

[F]or women, age at marriage hovered around 21–22 years between 1890 and 1950, declined significantly during the Baby Boom, and began rising thereafter, reaching slightly over 25 years in 2000. Patterns for men are somewhat different, with a general decline in age at marriage between 1890 and the Baby Boom. Like women, however, age at marriage for men began rising after the Baby Boom, and, in the year 2000, is higher than at any time in the past century (nearly 27).

At the same time that marriage is being postponed, unmarried cohabitation has increased.... In 1960, the number [of opposite-sex cohabiting couples] was estimated at less than half a million; at the 2000 census, there were nearly five million such households. In fact, research suggests that this postponement in marriage has, by and large, been offset by the increase in cohabitation. In other words, while the pace of entering marriage has slowed, [one study has indicated] that unmarried cohabitation compensated for over 80% of the decline in marriage by age 25 over recent cohorts for Blacks and 61% for Whites.

Other indicators of the rapidly growing prominence of cohabitation are, first, that the percentage of marriages preceded by cohabitation rose from about 10% for those marrying between 1965 and 1974 to well over 50% for those marrying between 1990 and 1994. Second, the percentage of women in their late thirties who report having cohabited at least once rose from 30% in 1987 to 48% in 1995.

Cohabitations in general are of short duration with many ending as marriages (roughly 50%) and others dissolving without marriage. Moreover, over 50% of cohabiting unions in the U.S., whether or not they are eventually legalized by marriage, end by separation within five years compared to roughly 20% for marriages. In addition, research suggests that marriages that begin as cohabitations, a growing proportion of marriages, are more likely to dissolve than those that do not. In fact, one of the key distinctions between cohabitation and marriage is the duration of the relationship, with some arguing that the underlying "contract" of cohabitation is substantially more fragile than that of marriage.

The prominence of cohabitation is echoed in the beliefs of the American people. An ongoing survey of high school seniors asks whether living together is a good idea before marriage to determine compatibility; the percent of young women agreeing with this statement rose from 33% to 60% between the late 1970s and the late 1990s, and from 47% to 67% for young men. Another survey, this one focusing on a cohort of white children born in 1961 in the Detroit area, asked respondents in 1993 (when they were in their early 30s) whether living together is acceptable even if there are no plans to marry; 64% and 72% of women and men agreed, respectively. Moreover, 74% of the women and 78% explicitly *disagreed* with the statement "a young couple should not live together unless they are married." While it remains unclear precisely how these shifting attitudes are related to behavioral changes in cohabitation, the two are probably mutually reinforcing: changes in behavior may set the stage for changes in attitudes and shifts in attitudes may follow changes in behavior.

At the same time, while recently stabilizing, levels of union instability have increased over the past century or so, most studies suggest that the chance of marital disruption now stands at about 50%....

     . . .

... [C]ohabitation is intertwined with important changes in fertility and represents a family form increasingly experienced by children. This has made it of concern to a broader audience due to possible implications for child well-being.

. . .

As is by now well-known, a substantial proportion of births in the U.S., as well as Canada and many European countries, are now occurring outside of marriage: in the U.S. that proportion is approximately one-third. . . . [A] large share of these nonmarital births are occurring in the context of cohabitation. Recent estimates suggest that this percentage is almost 40% overall. . . .

In terms of trends, the percentage of children born in cohabiting unions doubled between 1980–84 and 1990–94, now accounting for nearly one in eight births. Further, the share of births to unmarried mothers who were cohabiting increased substantially more between the early 1980s and early 1990s than did the share to single mothers living without a partner. This pace of change is suggestive of a possible further increase in cohabitation as a setting for childbearing in the future.

. . .

Further, while earlier work demonstrated that in response to a pregnancy, single women rarely cohabited, nowadays single women who become pregnant are as likely to cohabit as to marry. Taken together, these results are suggestive that, for some couples, a cohabiting union is an acceptable context for childbearing and raising a family and this may be increasingly so.

. . .

While today cohabitation is common throughout the socioeconomic spectrum, there is evidence that its role may vary by social class. Overall, cohabitation appears to play a more prominent role in family life among those with fewer economic resources.

First, people with less education appear somewhat more likely to have experienced cohabitation at some point. [One study reports] that in 1995, nearly 60% of women ages 19–44 without high school degrees had ever cohabited compared to less than 40% among those with a college education. This is consistent with levels of educational attainment among currently cohabiting couples compared to married couples; in the year 2000, approximately 30% of husbands and 25% of wives were college graduates compared to 18% and 17% among cohabiting men and women, respectively.

Second, cohabitors tend to have lower incomes and higher poverty rates than married couples. In the year 2000, for example, approximately 27% of married men had earnings over $50,000 compared to 14.6% of cohabiting men. Conversely, only 6% of husbands had earnings of $10,000 or less compared to 12% of cohabiting men. . . . [R]oughly 30% of children in cohabiting families are poor compared to 9% for those in married couple households. Also, cohabitors' levels of unemployment are more than twice as high as those of married men and women.

Third, there is evidence that good economic prospects enhance the likelihood of marriage among cohabiting couples. Studies suggest that the male partners' economic well-being (e.g., as measured by indicators such as earnings, education, or employment) are positively associated with the transition to marriage among cohabitors. Consistent with this, there is some evidence that marriage is perceived as requiring better economic circumstances than cohabitation. . . .

. . .

. . . Marriage and childbearing . . . appear to be more "de-coupled" among Blacks than Whites, with roughly a third of first births among White women now occurring before marriage compared to 77% among Black women.

[The literature on racial and ethnic variation in cohabitation indicates first that] Whites, Blacks and Hispanics report similar *levels* of cohabitation experience, suggesting that cohabitation is commonplace in all these groups. Second, and however, there may be some differences in regard to the role played by cohabitation in family formation.

For example, while cohabitation has become an increasingly prominent feature of the lives of American children, this is especially so for minority children. . . . [C]hildren are more likely to be present in Black and Hispanic cohabiting couple households (54% and 59% respectively) than in White cohabiting households (35%). Further, estimates suggest that about half (55%) of Black children, two-fifths (40%) of Hispanic children and three-tenths (30%) of White children are expected to experience a cohabiting-parent family, with Black and Hispanic children expected to spend more time in such a family.

Correspondingly, there are racial and ethnic differentials in the proportion of children being born to cohabiting parents. Among Whites, only about one in ten children are now born into cohabiting-parent families compared to nearly one in five Black and Hispanic children. [Further, one study] shows that Hispanic and Black women are 77% and 69%, respectively, more likely than White women to conceive a child while cohabiting. Among those who do become pregnant, Hispanics are twice as likely and Blacks three times as likely to remain cohabiting with their partner, rather than marry, when their child is born. . . .

Other findings suggestive of racial and ethnic variation in the role of cohabitation include, first, that greater proportions of Hispanics and Blacks than Whites select cohabitation as their first union. In fact, the Black-White differential in union formation (including both cohabitation and marriage) is about half that of the gap in marriage. Second, Blacks more commonly separate from, rather than marry, their cohabiting partners, and cohabiting Whites move into marriage more quickly than Hispanics.

In sum, evidence suggests that cohabitation is less central to childbearing and family formation among Whites. However, it is very difficult to disentangle these patterns from economic status. In the U.S., there is a correlation between social class and race and ethnicity, with Whites being the most privileged economically. Non–Hispanic Whites enjoy, on average, the highest incomes and lowest levels of poverty. . . . [G]iven the correlation between race/ethnicity and economic status, and good economic prospects and marriage, it is not surprising that cohabitation appears to play a more prominent role in the family lives of the less advantaged, who are more likely to be people of color in the U.S. . . .

. . .

. . . In combination with concerns about its possible effects on child well-being, cohabitation is considered an important phenomenon to understand because it has been linked, directly or indirectly, to the more general issue of the decreasing centrality of marriage in the United States. In fact, arguably the first prominent debate about the significance of cohabitation was whether it represents a stage in the marriage process (i.e., a form of engagement that culminates in marriage) or is a substitute form of marriage. According to the first view, marriage as an institution is not threatened by cohabitation, and cohabitation plays much the same role as engagement. The second view— that cohabitation is an alternative kind of marriage—implies that marriage as an institution is threatened and losing its centrality in the United States. A third view ... is that cohabitation is more appropriately viewed as an alternative to singlehood than to marriage. This argument is that cohabitation represents an extension of dating and sexual relationships. Most recently, however, there has been recognition that cohabitation may represent all of these for different couples and at different points in the life course.

Our second observation is that the data suggest to us that cohabitation is not going away, and will most likely become a more prominent feature of family patterns, even among the advantaged. While the pace of growth in cohabiting households seems to have slowed during the 1990s, it is still growing.

Third, we think the proportion of children exposed to cohabitation (either by being born into one or by entering a quasi-stepfamily) will also continue to increase. As we noted earlier, this is a trend of great concern to policymakers due to its implications for child well-being, not least of which have to do with the effects of family structure instability on children.

Finally, our reading of the policy and social science research on family structure, economic well-being and child well-being, leads us to conclude that promoting or strengthening marriage will not go far over the long haul in alleviating poverty and improving child well-being unless equal attention is paid to improving access to other resources that undergird marriage (e.g., stable, well-paying jobs, good schools for children, safe communities). In this regard, we are struck by the economic and racial stratification in the likely impact of the "case for marriage" on individual lives. While in some respects the marriage movement has been a broad conversation, it is important to recognize that it is largely the disadvantaged (poor people, minorities) whose family lives are being interpreted as needing change.

3.   LEGAL DEVELOPMENTS

Marvin v. Marvin

Supreme Court of California, 1976.
557 P.2d 106.

■ TOBRINER, JUSTICE.

During the past 15 years, there has been a substantial increase in the number of couples living together without marrying. Such non-marital relationships lead to legal controversy when one partner dies or the couple separates....

. . .

In the instant case plaintiff and defendant lived together for seven years without marrying; all property acquired during this period was taken in defendant's name. When plaintiff sued to enforce a contract under which she was entitled to half the property and to support payments, the trial court granted judgment on the pleadings for defendant, thus leaving him with all property accumulated by the couple during their relationship....

Since the trial court rendered judgment for defendant on the pleadings, we must accept the allegations of plaintiff's complaint as true, determining whether such allegations state, or can be amended to state, a cause of action....

Plaintiff avers that in October of 1964 she and defendant "entered into an oral agreement" that while "the parties lived together they would combine their efforts and earnings and would share equally any and all property accumulated as a result of their efforts whether individual or combined." Furthermore, they agreed to "hold themselves out to the general public as husband and wife" and that "plaintiff would further render her services as a companion, homemaker, housekeeper and cook to . . . defendant."

Shortly thereafter plaintiff agreed to "give up her lucrative career as an entertainer [and] singer" in order to "devote her full time to defendant . . . as a companion, homemaker, housekeeper and cook;" in return defendant agreed to "provide for all of plaintiff's financial support and needs for the rest of her life."

Plaintiff alleges that she lived with defendant from October of 1964 through May of 1970 and fulfilled her obligations under the agreement. During this period the parties as a result of their efforts and earnings acquired in defendant's name substantial real and personal property, including motion picture rights worth over $1 million. In May of 1970, however, defendant compelled plaintiff to leave his household. He continued to support plaintiff until November of 1971, but thereafter refused to provide further support.

. . .

. . . Although that court did not specify the ground for its conclusion that plaintiff's contractual allegations stated no cause of action, defendant offers some four theories....

Defendant first and principally relies on the contention that the alleged contract is so closely related to the supposed "immoral" character of the relationship between plaintiff and himself that the enforcement of the contract would violate public policy. He points to cases asserting that a contract between nonmarital partners is unenforceable if it is "involved in" an illicit relationship.... A review of the numerous California decisions concerning contracts between nonmarital partners, however, reveals that the courts have not employed such broad and uncertain standards to strike down contracts....

. . .

Although the past decisions hover over the issue in the somewhat wispy form of the figures of a Chagall painting, we can abstract from those decisions a clear and simple rule. The fact that a man and woman live together without marriage, and engage in a sexual relationship, does not in itself invalidate agreements between them relating to their earnings, property, or expenses. Neither is such an agreement invalid merely because the parties may have contemplated the creation or continuation of a nonmarital relationship when they entered into it. Agreements between nonmarital partners fail only to the extent that they rest upon a consideration of meretricious sexual services. Thus the rule asserted by defendant, that a contract fails if it is "involved in" or made "in contemplation" of a nonmarital relationship, cannot be reconciled with the decisions.

The . . . cases cited by defendant which have *declined* to enforce contracts between nonmarital partners involved consideration that was expressly founded upon an illicit sexual service. In *Hill v. Estate of Westbrook*, 213 P.2d 727 [(Cal.App. 1950)], the woman promised to keep house for the man, to live with him as man and wife, and to bear his children; the man promised to provide for her in his will, but died without doing so. Reversing a judgment for the woman based on the reasonable value of her services, the Court of Appeal stated that "the action is predicated upon a claim which seeks, among other things, the reasonable value of living with decedent in meretricious relationship and bearing him two children. . . . The law does not award compensation for living with a man as a concubine and bearing him children. . . . As the judgment is, at least in part, for the value of the claimed services for which recovery cannot be had, it must be reversed." 213 P.2d at 730. Upon retrial, the trial court found that it could not sever the contract and place an independent value upon the legitimate services performed by claimant. We therefore affirmed a judgment for the estate.

In the only other cited decision refusing to enforce a contract, *Updeck v. Samuel*, 266 P.2d 822 [(Cal.App. 1954)], the contract "was based on the consideration that the parties live together as husband and wife." Viewing the contract as calling for adultery, the court held it illegal.

The decisions in the *Hill* and *Updeck* cases thus demonstrate that a contract between nonmarital partners, even if expressly made in contemplation of a common living arrangement, is invalid only if sexual acts form an inseparable part of the consideration for the agreement. In sum, a court will not enforce a contract for the pooling of property and earnings if it is explicitly and inseparably based upon services as a paramour. The Court of Appeal opinion in *Hill*, however, indicates that even if sexual services are part of the contractual consideration, any *severable* portion of the contract supported by independent consideration will still be enforced.

The principle that a contract between nonmarital partners will be enforced unless expressly and inseparably based upon an illicit consideration of sexual services not only represents the distillation of the decisional law, but also offers a far more precise and workable standard than that advocated by the defendant. . . .

Similarly, . . . a standard which inquires whether an agreement is "involved" in or "contemplates" a nonmarital relationship is vague and unworkable. Virtually all agreements between nonmarital partners can be said to be "involved" in some sense in the fact of their mutual sexual relationship, or to "contemplate" the existence of that relationship. Thus defendant's proposed standards, if taken literally, might invalidate all agreements between nonmarital partners, a result no one favors. Moreover, those standards offer no basis to distinguish between valid and invalid agreements. By looking not to such uncertain tests, but only to the consideration underlying the agreement, we provide the parties and the courts with a practical guide to determine when an agreement between nonmarital partners should be enforced.

. . .

In summary, we base our opinion on the principle that adults who voluntarily live together and engage in sexual relations are nonetheless as competent as any other persons to contract respecting their earnings and property rights. Of course, they cannot lawfully contract to pay for the performance of sexual services, for such a contract is, in essence, an agreement for prostitution and unlawful for that reason. But ... so long as the agreement does not rest upon illicit meretricious consideration, the parties may order their economic affairs as they choose, and no policy precludes the courts from enforcing such agreements.

In the present instance, plaintiff alleges that the parties agreed to pool their earnings, that they contracted to share equally in all property acquired, and that defendant agreed to support plaintiff. The terms of the contract as alleged do not rest upon any unlawful consideration. We therefore conclude that the complaint furnishes a suitable basis upon which the trial court can render declaratory relief. The trial court consequently erred in granting defendant's motion for judgment on the pleadings.

. . .

As we have noted, both causes of action in plaintiff's complaint allege an express contract; neither assert any basis for relief independent from the contract. In *In re Marriage of Cary,* [34 Cal.App.3d 345, 109 Cal.Rptr. 862 (1973),] however, the Court of Appeal held that, in view of the policy of the Family Law Act, property accumulated by nonmarital partners in an actual family relationship should be divided equally.... Although our conclusion that plaintiff's complaint states a cause of action based on an express contract alone compels us to reverse the judgment for defendant, resolution of the *Cary* issue will serve both to guide the parties upon retrial and to resolve a conflict presently manifest in published Court of appeal decisions.

. . .

... The classic opinion on this subject is *Vallera v. Vallera*, [134 P.2d 761 (Cal. 1943)]. Speaking for a four-member majority, Justice Traynor posed the question: "whether a woman living with a man as his wife but with no genuine belief that she is legally married to him acquires by reason of cohabitation alone the rights of a co-tenant in his earnings and accumulations during the period of their relationship." Citing *Flanagan v. Capital Nat. Bank*, 3 P.2d 307 [(Cal. 1931)] which held that a nonmarital "wife" could not claim that her husband's estate was community property, the majority answered that question "in the negative." ...

. . .

Consequently, when the issue of the rights of a nonmarital partner reached this court in *Keene v. Keene*, 371 P.2d 329 [(Cal. 1962)], the claimant forwent reliance upon theories of contract implied in law or fact. Asserting that she had worked on her partner's ranch and that her labor had enhanced its value, she confined her cause of action to the claim that the court should impress a resulting trust on the property derived from the sale of the ranch. The court limited its opinion accordingly, rejecting her argument on the ground that the rendition of services gives rise to a resulting trust only when the services aid in acquisition of the property, not in its subsequent improvement....

This failure of the courts to recognize an action by a nonmarital partner based upon implied contract, or to grant an equitable remedy, contrasts with the judicial treatment of the putative spouse. Prior to the enactment of the Family Law Act, no statute granted rights to a putative spouse. The courts accordingly fashioned a variety of remedies by judicial decision. Some cases permitted the putative spouse to recover half the property on a theory that the conduct of the parties implied an agreement of partnership or joint venture. Others permitted the spouse to recover the reasonable value of rendered services, less the value of support received. Finally, decisions affirmed the power of a court to employ equitable principles to achieve a fair division of property acquired during putative marriage.

Thus in summary, the cases prior to *Cary* exhibited a schizophrenic inconsistency. By enforcing an express contract between nonmarital partners unless it rested upon an unlawful consideration, the courts applied a common law principle as to contracts. Yet the courts disregarded the common law principle that holds that implied contracts can arise from the conduct of the parties. . . .

Justice Curtis noted this inconsistency in his dissenting opinion in *Vallera*, pointing out that "if an express agreement will be enforced, there is no legal or just reason why an implied agreement to share the property cannot be enforced." . . .

Still another inconsistency in the prior cases arises from their treatment of property accumulated through joint effort. To the extent that a partner has contributed *funds* or *property*, the cases held that the partner obtains a proportionate share in the acquisition, despite the lack of legal standing of the relationship. Yet courts have refused to recognize just such an interest based upon the contribution of *services*. As Justice Curtis points out "Unless it can be argued that a woman's services as cook, housekeeper, and homemaker are valueless, it would seem logical that if, when she contributes money to the purchase of property, her interest will be protected, then when she contributes her services in the home, her interest in property accumulated should be protected."

Thus as of 1973, the time of filing of *In re Marriage of Cary*, the cases apparently held that a nonmarital partner who rendered services in the absence of express contract could assert no right to property acquired during the relationship. The facts of *Cary* demonstrated the unfairness of that rule.

Janet and Paul Cary had lived together, unmarried, for more than eight years. They held themselves out to friends and family as husband and wife, reared four children, purchased a home and other property, obtained credit, filed joint income tax returns, and otherwise conducted themselves as though they were married. Paul worked outside the home, and Janet generally cared for the house and children.

In 1971 Paul petitioned for "nullity of the marriage." Following a hearing on that petition, the trial court awarded Janet half the property acquired during the relationship, although all such property was traceable to Paul's earnings. The Court of Appeal affirmed the award.

. . .

If *Cary* is interpreted as holding that the Family Law Act requires an equal division of property accumulated in nonmarital "actual family relationships," then we agree . . . that *Cary* distends the act. No language in the Family Law Act addresses the property rights of nonmarital partners, and nothing in the legislative history of the act suggests that the Legislature considered that subject. The delineation of the rights of nonmarital partners before 1970 had been fixed entirely by judicial decision; we see no reason to believe that the Legislature, by enacting the Family Law Act, intended to change that state of affairs.

But although we reject the reasoning of *Cary* ... we share the perception ... that the application of former precedent in the factual setting of those cases would work an unfair distribution of the property accumulated by the couple....

The principal reason why the pre-*Cary* decisions result in an unfair distribution of property inheres in the court's refusal to permit a nonmarital partner to assert rights based upon accepted principles of implied contract or equity. We have examined the reasons advanced to justify this denial of relief, and find that none have merit.

First, we note that the cases denying relief do not rest their refusal upon any theory of "punishing" a "guilty" partner. Indeed, to the extent that denial of relief "punishes" one partner, it necessarily rewards the other by permitting him to retain a disproportionate amount of the property. Concepts of "guilt" thus cannot justify an unequal division of property between two equally "guilty" persons.

Other reasons advanced in the decisions fare no better. The principal argument seems to be that "[e]quitable considerations arising from the reasonable expectation of ... benefits attending the statute of marriage ... are not present [in a nonmarital relationship]." But, although parties to a nonmarital relationship obviously cannot have based any expectations upon the belief that they were married, other expectations and equitable considerations remain. The parties may well expect that property will be divided in accord with the parties' own tacit understanding and that in the absence of such understanding the courts will fairly apportion property accumulated through mutual effort. We need not treat nonmarital partners as putatively married persons in order to apply principles of implied contract, or extend equitable remedies; we need to treat them only as we do any other unmarried persons.

The remaining arguments advanced from time to time to deny remedies to the nonmarital partners are of less moment. There is no more reason to presume that services are contributed as a gift than to presume that funds are contributed as a gift; in any event the better approach is to presume, as Justice Peters suggested, "that the parties intend to deal fairly with each other."

The argument that granting remedies to the nonmarital partners would discourage marriage must fail; as *Cary* pointed out, "with equal or greater force the point might be made that the pre–1970 rule was calculated to cause the income producing partner to avoid marriage and thus retain the benefit of all of his or her accumulated earnings." Although we recognize the well-established public policy to foster and promote the institution of marriage, perpetuation of judicial rules which result in an inequitable distribution of property accumulated during a nonmarital relationship is neither a just nor an effective way of carrying out that policy.

In summary, we believe that the prevalence of nonmarital relationships in modern society and the social acceptance of them, marks this as a time when our courts should by no means apply the doctrine of the unlawfulness of the so-called meretricious relationship to the instant case. As we have explained, the nonenforceability of agreements expressly providing for meretricious conduct rested upon the fact that such conduct, as the word suggests, pertained to and encompassed prostitution. To equate the nonmarital relationship of today to such a subject matter is to do violence to an accepted and wholly different practice.

We are aware that many young couples live together without the solemnization of marriage, in order to make sure that they can successfully later undertake marriage. This trial period, preliminary to marriage, serves as some assurance that the marriage will not subsequently end in dissolution to the harm of both parties. We are aware, as we have stated, of the pervasiveness of nonmarital relationships in other situations.

The mores of the society have indeed changed so radically in regard to cohabitation that we cannot impose a standard based on alleged moral considerations that have apparently been so widely abandoned by so many. Lest we be misunderstood, however, we take this occasion to point out that the structure of society itself largely depends upon the institution of marriage, and nothing we have said in this opinion should be taken to derogate from that institution. The joining of the man and woman in marriage is at once the most socially productive and individually fulfilling relationship that one can enjoy in the course of a lifetime.

We conclude that the judicial barriers that may stand in the way of a policy based upon the fulfillment of the reasonable expectations of the parties to a nonmarital relationship should be removed. As we have explained, the courts now hold that express agreements will be enforced unless they rest on an unlawful meretricious consideration. We add that in the absence of an express agreement, the courts may look to a variety of other remedies in order to protect the parties' lawful expectations.[24]

The courts may inquire into the conduct of the parties to determine whether that conduct demonstrates an implied contract or implied agreement of partnership or joint venture or some other tacit understanding between the parties. The courts may, when appropriate, employ principles of constructive trust or resulting trust. Finally, a nonmarital partner may recover in quantum meruit for the reasonable value of household services rendered less the reasonable value of support received if he can show that he rendered services with the expectation of monetary reward.

Since we have determined that plaintiff's complaint states a cause of action for breach of an express contract, and, as we have explained, can be amended to state a cause of action independent of allegations of express contract,[26] we must conclude that the trial court erred in granting defendant a judgment on the pleadings.

The judgment is reversed and the cause remanded for further proceedings consistent with the views expressed herein.

NOTES

1. On remand, plaintiff Michelle Marvin was awarded $104,000 for "her economic rehabilitation." This award was reversed on appeal, *Marvin v. Marvin*, 122 Cal.App.3d 871, 176 Cal.Rptr. 555 (1981), on the grounds that:

---

24. We do not seek to resurrect the doctrine of common law marriage, which was abolished in California by statute in 1895. Thus we do not hold that plaintiff and defendant were "married," nor do we extend to plaintiff the rights which the Family Law Act grants valid or putative spouses; we hold only that she has the same rights to enforce contracts and to assert her equitable interest in property acquired through her effort as does any other unmarried person.

26. We do not pass upon the question whether, in the absence of an express or implied contractual obligation, a party to a nonmarital relationship is entitled to support payments from the other party after the relationship terminates.

the trial court ... expressly found that defendant never had any obligation to pay plaintiff ... for her maintenance and that the defendant had not been unjustly enriched by reason of the relationship or its termination.... *Id.* at 876, 176 Cal.Rptr. at 558.

2. Compare David Chambers, *The "Legalization" of the Family: Toward a Policy of Supportive Neutrality*, 18 MICH. J. L. REF. 805, 826 (1985):

> [T]he California court would have been wiser to have fashioned a less expansive rule. It should have announced that, in cases of disputes between unmarried partners who are separating, courts are to honor express agreements if, but only if, they are in writing and that courts are neither to recognize implied contracts nor to create new equitable remedies. I regret that such a rule would prevent courts from giving relief to persons who make serious oral agreements and rely on them, and to persons, usually women, who have no formal agreement but who work for many years raising children, accumulate no assets in their own name, and come to regard themselves as in the same position as a married person. Despite this, a rule limiting judicial relief to written agreements would have the virtue of curtailing courts' opportunities to reframe the terms of private relationships and would reduce the number of acrimonious family disputes aired in public....

with Harry Prince, *Public Policy Limitations on Cohabitation Agreements: Unruly Horse or Circus Pony?*, 70 MINN. L. REV. 163, 207–08 (1985):

> [C]ohabitants should be allowed to prove an implied-in-fact agreement. Although it can hardly be doubted that cohabitants do not expect a weekly paycheck for their homemaking services, it is equally obvious that the parties do not expect the party contributing such services to derive nothing from their efforts. Some benefit or consideration, other than emotional satisfaction, is almost certainly contemplated by both parties in return for the pooling of their resources and concentration of their efforts. There may be, of course, some instances when both parties understand that a rendered service is gratuitous, but the cohabitants should at least have the opportunity to prove the contrary.

3. Under *Marvin*, support agreements between cohabitants are enforceable. Moreover, such support agreements are enforceable against an estate when one of the parties to the agreement dies. In *Byrne v. Laura*, 52 Cal.App.4th 1054, 60 Cal.Rptr.2d 908 (1997), the plaintiff sued the estate of the man with whom she had cohabited. On behalf of the estate, the administratrix contended that the alleged *Marvin* agreement between the plaintiff and the deceased man was void for uncertainty and thus was unenforceable. Relying primarily on the abundant testimony to the contrary of the plaintiff and of neighbors sympathetic to the plaintiff, the court disagreed.

4. In *Norton v. Hoyt*, 278 F. Supp. 2d 214 (D.R.I. 2003), a federal district court considered claims "aris[ing] out of an adulterous twenty-three year relationship between Plaintiff [Gail M. Norton] and Defendant [Russell L. Hoyt], during which time Defendant allegedly maintained that he would terminate his marriage, marry Plaintiff, and support her for the rest of her life." *Id.* at 217. Analyzing Norton's claims, the court reasoned:

> In Rhode Island, a promissory estoppel claim requires: "1) A clear and unambiguous promise; 2) Reasonable and justifiable reliance upon the promise; and 3) Detriment to the promisee, caused by his or her reliance on the promise."

> Norton avers that she relied to her detriment upon Hoyt's promise to divorce his wife, marry Norton and provide lifetime support to Norton. Alternatively, she frames the promise by Hoyt as one to provide lifetime support to her regardless of whether he divorced his wife or not. At oral argument Plaintiff's counsel represented that the latter promise, that Hoyt would take care of Norton for life, was the one on which she was basing her claim.

>   ...

> Even viewed most favorably to the Plaintiff, the record fails to reveal a clear, unconditional, and unambiguous promise.... [A]t the hearing on this motion,

counsel argued that Hoyt had simply promised to take care of Norton for life. However, there can be many interpretations of the phrase, "take care of for life". It could refer to care in a social, emotional, or financial context. As other courts have recognized, this is certainly not a clear and unambiguous promise.

. . .

By belatedly couching Hoyt's promise as one simply to take care of her for life, Norton actually undermines her claim, because she has represented in her answers to Defendant's Interrogatories that she would not have remained in the relationship if he had not promised to get divorced. Thus, any reliance on her part is definitively linked to Hoyt's promise to marry her, not simply the promise that Hoyt would support her for life. Thereby, she intertwines Hoyt's marital status back into the alleged promise.

Even assuming, *arguendo*, that there was a clear and unambiguous promise, Norton's reliance upon that promise was unreasonable. Though the couple had discussions about their life together and even discussed potential wedding plans, Plaintiff knew that Hoyt was married, and that he spent time at the marital domicile with his wife and children. Norton and Hoyt never openly associated as husband and wife, their friends and family knew that they were not married and they did not exclusively cohabitate. Furthermore, Norton knew that Hoyt had lied in the past, was in an adulterous relationship, and apparently had made little effort to fulfill the terms of the promise. Whatever detriment she suffered occurred with full knowledge that she was relying upon an adulterer; the law will not insure the decision to repose her confidence there. Reliance upon an unclear and ambiguous promise made by an apparently unreliable man was imprudent.

. . . Norton claims that she, in reliance on Hoyt's promises and, in fact, at his insistence, left gainful employment as a school teacher. She also claims that she gave up the opportunity to marry and have children at a younger age, and did not attempt to achieve her own financial security. Once again, however, Norton has stated that she remained in the relationship based solely upon Hoyt's promise to get a divorce. It is not clear that she relied to her detriment based on a promise for lifetime support. Any detrimental reliance flowed from the promise to remain together.

In any event, whatever form her reliance took, it is insufficient to overcome the other fatal flaws in her claim. Any promise for support that Hoyt made prior to the March 11, 1998 break-up is ambiguous at best, and, considering the source, was not a reasonable basis upon which to ground reliance. Sometime between year one and year twenty-three of the affair, it should have become clear to Norton that her reliance on Hoyt's promise to divorce his wife and marry her was misplaced

. . .

The doctrine of estoppel ". . . has no application to a contract or instrument which is void because it violates an express mandate of the law or the dictates of public policy." The public policy in favor of marriage militates against recognizing support claims arising from adulterous relationships. "The institution of marriage is so firmly established in the mores of Anglo–American society [that] agreements believed to be, 'in derogation of marriage' are held to be against public welfare and illegal." 15 Arthur Linton Corbin, Corbin on Contracts, § 1474 at 537 (1962). Therefore, an agreement in furtherance of facilitating divorce proceedings is illegal and contrary to public policy. . . .

Moreover, permitting a promissory estoppel claim based on a promise by Hoyt to divorce his wife, marry Norton and provide her with lifetime support would amount to re-instituting the breach of promise to marry claim that has already been dismissed. . . .

. . .

Here, Norton is essentially clothing a palimony claim in other robes. Rhode Island, however, has not recognized palimony as a cause of action and the Rhode Island Supreme Court has shown no inclination to do so. . . .

. . .

. . . Norton is seeking enforcement of a promise for future support payments: in a word, palimony. There was no property sharing agreement between Norton and Hoyt; no express agreement of any kind, merely an alleged, ambiguous promise to provide support.

. . .

For the foregoing reasons, the Court hereby grants Defendant's Motion for Summary Judgment. . . .

Id. at 223–28.

AMERICAN LAW INSTITUTE, PRINCIPLES OF THE LAW OF FAMILY DISSOLUTION

(2002).

Section 6.03.   Determination That Persons Are Domestic Partners

(1) For the purpose of defining relationships to which this Chapter applies, domestic partners are two persons of the same or opposite sex, not married to one another, who for a significant period of time share a primary residence and a life together as a couple.

(2) Persons are domestic partners when they have maintained a common household, as defined in Paragraph (4), with their common child, as defined in Paragraph (5), for a continuous period that equals or exceeds a duration, called the *cohabitation parenting period*, set in a rule of statewide application.

(3) Persons not related by blood or adoption are presumed to be domestic partners when they have maintained a common household, as defined in Paragraph (4), for a continuous period that equals or exceeds a duration, called the *cohabitation period*, set in a rule of statewide application. The presumption is rebuttable by evidence that the parties did not share life together as a couple, as defined by Paragraph (7).

(4) Persons *maintain a common household* when they share a primary residence only with each other and family members; or when, if they share a household with other unrelated persons, they act jointly, rather than as individuals, with respect to management of the household.

(5) Persons have a *common child* when each is either the child's legal parent or parent by estoppel. . . .

. . .

(7) Whether persons share a life together as a couple is determined by reference to all the circumstances, including:

(a) the oral or written statements or promises made to one another, or representations jointly made to third parties, regarding their relationship;

(b) the extent to which the parties intermingled their finances;

(c) the extent to which their relationship fostered the parties' economic interdependence, or the economic dependence of one party upon the other;

(d) the extent to which the parties engaged in conduct and assumed specialized or collaborative roles in furtherance of their life together;

(e) the extent to which the relationship wrought change in the life of either or both parties;

(f) the extent to which the parties acknowledged responsibilities to each other, as by naming the other the beneficiary of life insurance or of a testamentary instrument, or as eligible to receive benefits under an employee-benefit plan;

(g) the extent to which the parties' relationship was treated by the parties as qualitatively distinct from the relationship either party had with any other person;

(h) the emotional or physical intimacy of the parties' relationship;

(i) the parties' community reputation as a couple;

(j) the parties' participation in a commitment ceremony or registration as a domestic partnership;

(k) the parties' participation in a void or voidable marriage that, under applicable law, does not give rise to the economic incidents of marriage;

(l) the parties' procreation of, adoption of, or joint assumption of parental functions toward a child;

(m) the parties' maintenance of a common household, as defined by Paragraph (4).

COMMENT:

. . .

b. This section's relationship to existing law. In the United States, courts generally rely on contract law when they conclude that cohabiting parties may acquire financial obligations to one another that survive their relationship. The great majority of jurisdictions recognize express contracts, and only a handful of them require that the contract be written rather than oral. Jurisdictions split on whether to recognize implied contracts. Those that do recognize implied contracts differ in their inclination to infer contractual undertakings from any given set of facts. Some courts reach much further than others. In doing so, they appear to vindicate an equitable rather than a contractual principle. That is, having concluded that a particular set of facts demands a remedy, they may stretch ordinary contract principles to fit the remedy within a contractual rubric. This result is not surprising. Parties may share their lives for many years without having any clear agreement, express or implied, that sets out the financial consequences of terminating their relationship. To find such an agreement may therefore require filling many gaps with terms that flow more from the court's sense of fairness than from any mutual intentions inferable from the parties' conduct.

This section approaches the matter in a more straightforward manner. It identifies the circumstances that would typically lead such a court to find a contract, and defines those circumstances as giving rise to a domestic partnership. Remedies then follow unless the parties have made an enforceable contract to the contrary. In formulating a rubric combining expansive notions of contract with equitable remedies, one court observed that it is appropriate in these cases to presume "that the parties intend to deal fairly with each other." This suggests that, as in marriage, in the ordinary case the law should provide remedies at the dissolution of a domestic partnership that will ensure an equitable allocation of accumulated property and of the financial losses arising from the termination of the relationship. The result, in comparison with a narrow contract approach, is a system that places the burden of showing a contract on the party wishing to avoid such fairness-based remedies, rather than imposing it on the party seeking to claim them.

This section thus does not require, as a predicate to finding the existence of a domestic partnership, that the parties had an implied or express agreement, or even that the facts meet the standard requirements of a quantum meruit claim. It instead relies, as do the marriage laws, on a status classification: property claims and support obligations presumptively arise between persons who qualify as domestic partners, as they do between legal spouses, without inquiry into each couple's particular arrangement, except as the presumption is itself overcome by contract. This approach reflects a judgment that it is usually just to apply to both groups the property and support rules applicable to divorcing spouses, that individualized inquiries are usually impractical or unduly burdensome, and that it therefore makes more sense to require parties to contract out of these property and support rules than to contract into them. This approach, of course, demands careful attention to the factors required to establish a couple's status as domestic partners. . . .

. . .

Section 6.06.   Compensatory Payments

(1) Except as otherwise provided in this section,

(a) a domestic partner is entitled to compensatory payments on the same basis as a spouse under chapter 5, and

(b) wherever a rule implementing a Chapter 5 principle makes the duration of the marriage a relevant factor, the application of that principle in this Chapter should instead employ the duration of the domestic-partnership period. . . .

(2) No claim arises under this section against a domestic partner who is neither a legal parent nor a parent by estoppel . . . of a child whose care provides the basis of the claim.

COMMENT:

. . .

b.   Limitations on claims under this section. Paragraph (2) does not extend the application of 5.05 to claims by a domestic partner based upon the care of a child who is not a child of the other partner. By contrast, section 5.05 does permit claims by a married person for the care of a child who is not also the child of the other spouse, so long as the spouses shared a residence with each other and the child during the relevant child-care period. The rationale for recognizing this claim in the context of marriage depends in part upon the law's recognition of a stepparent's duty to support a child living with him during his marriage to the parent. There is no similar child-support duty for a person who lives in a nonmarital relationship with a child and that child's parent. . . .

NOTE

As the co-authors of a recent review of the general impact of the *ALI Principles of the Law of Family Dissolution* observe: "[T]he *Principles* took on the burning questions in family law[,] . . . [including:] Should individuals who cohabit be able to walk away with no obligation to the other and, if so under what circumstances? Unlike the ALI *Restatements of the Law*, which have been directed mainly at individual 'decision-makers,' courts, the *Principles* were directed largely to 'rule-makers,' state legislatures. This is so because much of what the *Principles* recommend would require legislative action to make them a reality." Michael R. Clisham & Robin Fretwell Wilson, *American Law Institute's Principles of the Law of Family Dissolution, Eight Years After Adoption: Guiding Principles or Obligatory Footnote*, 42 FAM. L.Q. 573, 575 (2008) (footnotes omitted). As Clisham and Wilson continue: "the *Principles* have not had the influence the ALI hoped for with legislators or courts[.] . . . Although one state, West Virginia, borrowed from the *Principles* in enacting child custody legislation, no other state code or legislation enacted since 1990 referencing the *Principles* was found[.] . . . While we cannot say definitively that the *Principles* have not had some legislative influence somewhere, if legislatures are borrowing from the *Principles*, they are certainly not tipping their hands." *Id.* at 576. Nevertheless, "while the *Principles* have had more success with individual decision-makers—courts—[as opposed to legislators,] the impact is nonetheless slight and mixed." *Id.* To the present point is the observation that: "[l]east influential was Chapter 6, recommending Domestic Partnerships. In only three instances was this chapter cited by courts in their decisions and in each, the courts treated this chapter negatively. This may be due in part to the *Principles'* approach to domestic partnership or because domestic partnerships have been eclipsed by same-sex marriage in recent years as a way to address the needs of same-sex partners." *Id.* at 600–01 (footnotes omitted).

Bashaway v. Cheney Bros., Inc.

District Court of Appeal of Florida, First District, 2008.
987 So.2d 93.

■ KAHN, J. gave the opinion of the Court

Appellant, Judith Bashaway, maintains a long-term committed relationship with her partner, Melinda Garrison. Melinda suffered injuries in an automobile accident and brought a civil action against appellees, Cheney Brothers, Inc., and Alex Roberts (collectively "Cheney"). Judith joined Melinda as a plaintiff in that suit. Count III of the suit concerned a claim made by Judith for loss of consortium. Cheney moved for dismissal of Judith's claim, setting out that Judith and Melinda were not legally married at the time of the injury and further that section 741.212, Florida Statutes (2006), prohibits recognition of marriage between persons of the same sex in any event. The circuit court granted the motion and entered final judgment against Judith as to Count III. We affirm because a consortium claim under Florida law is a derivative claim dependent upon legal status that does not exist in the present case.

On appeal, Judith makes two arguments. Initially, she contends that a claim for loss of consortium under the common law in Florida should turn on the seriousness of the relationship between the partners and not whether the partners are technically married. Alternatively, she asserts that Florida common law should recognize an exception to the marriage requirement for same-sex partners because they are prohibited in Florida from becoming legally married.

Cheney counters Judith's arguments by pointing out that, although the Florida Supreme Court has, over time, expanded and modified certain common law notions of consortium, the claim nevertheless enures only in favor of actual family members. This is so, Cheney asserts, because consortium claims compensate for loss within the family unit, and no Florida court has expanded such claims beyond the confines of the nuclear family. Such claims, then, derive solely from the relationship.

No dispute exists as to Judith's allegation that she and Melinda have a committed, exclusive, and intimate relationship. Accordingly, the question becomes whether a relationship such as that maintained by Judith and Melinda may, upon a case-by-case factual analysis, become the equivalent of a valid marriage for purposes of a consortium claim. We answer in the negative because this court does not have the authority to affirm that proposition.

Judith notes Florida cases expanding the scope of consortium rights. Before 1971, no woman in Florida could bring a claim for loss of consortium. *See Gates v. Foley,* 247 So.2d 40 (Fla. 1971). As recently as 1952, the Florida Supreme Court considered and rejected an argument that the claim for consortium should be extended to a wife where the husband has been permanently injured. *Ripley v. Ewell,* 61 So.2d 420 (Fla. 1952). The *Ripley* court declined to extend the right, finding that such an argument would be more appropriately made to the Legislature.

Nevertheless, and despite a period of legislative inaction, the Florida Supreme Court overruled *Ripley* in *Gates* some nineteen years later. Observing that under the then-extant 1968 state constitution, Florida recognized no distinction between married women and married men in holding, controlling, disposing, or encumbering of property, the *Gates* court could identify no valid reason to justify continued "disparity in the spouses' relative rights to secure damages for loss of consortium." 247 So.2d at 44. Although the Florida Supreme Court expanded the claim to include the wife, it did not change the underlying nature of the claim and, in fact, such expansion was necessary because the wife, as well as the husband, is apt to suffer "a real injury to the marital relationship." *Id.* Importantly, and difficult for Judith's position in the present case, the court squarely held that the right of action for loss of consortium "is a derivative right." *Id.* at 45. Under *Gates,* therefore, the right continues to derive from the legal relationship.

The Florida Supreme Court has also modified the common law with regard to a parent's claim for loss of consortium of a child, referred to as filial consortium. Under the common law, in the event of a child's disability, the father could recover for the economic loss of the child's services and earnings, but could not be compensated for loss of the child's companionship. *See United States v. Dempsey,* 635 So.2d 961, 962 (Fla. 1994). The common law had viewed the rights of a father to the services and earnings of a child as "valuable rights, constituting a species of property in the father." *Wilkie v. Roberts,* 109 So. 225, 227 ([Fla.] 1926). In 1994, the *Dempsey* court replaced this property-based notion with what it viewed as a more modern and just concept that "[r]ather than being valued merely for their services or earning capacity, children are valued for the love, affection, companionship and society they offer their parents." 635 So.2d at 964. Accordingly, the *Dempsey* court extended the loss of filial consortium to include loss of a child's companionship and society. *Id.* at 965. This claim derives, however, from the relationship between parent and child. Evidencing this conclusion, the *Dempsey* court observed, "[I]t is the policy of this state that familial relationships be protected and that recovery be had for losses occasioned because of wrongful injuries that adversely affect those relationships." *Id.* at 964–65.

Judith also attempts to draw a comparison with Florida's expanded recovery for the tort of negligent infliction of emotional distress. She cites such cases as *Champion v. Gray*, 478 So.2d 17 (Fla. 1985), and *Zell v. Meek*, 665 So.2d 1048 (Fla. 1995), for the proposition that the plaintiff in such a tort claim must only have a close personal relationship to the directly injured person. She acknowledges that certain Florida courts have concluded that a close personal relationship must, in fact, be a legal relationship such as marriage. *See Ferretti v. Weber*, 513 So.2d 1333 (Fla. 3d DCA), *rev. dismissed*, 519 So.2d 986 (Fla. 1987); *Reynolds v. State Farm Mut. Auto. Ins. Co.*, 611 So.2d 1294 (Fla. 4th DCA 1992), *rev. denied*, 623 So.2d 494 (Fla. 1993). Judith argues, however, that the First District has now adopted a case-by-case approach for determining whether a close personal relationship is sufficient, without requiring a legally recognized relationship. *See Watters v. Walgreen Co.*, 967 So.2d 930 (Fla. 1st DCA 2007).

This argument, in our view, ignores that the claim for negligent infliction of emotional distress is a direct tort claim rather than a derivative claim. Accordingly, the analysis in *Watters* turned upon such factors as whether the claimant was a reasonably foreseeable plaintiff. 967 So.2d at 932. As this court noted in *Watters*, "[T]he foreseeability question center[s] on the plaintiff's involvement in the incident giving rise to the cause of action, including the potentially dispositive question of whether the plaintiff suffered physical injury resulting from psychological impact, and his or her relationship to the directly injured person." *Id*. Such analysis was necessary because the tort of negligent infliction of emotional distress presumes that the plaintiff has suffered a physical, and not merely a psychological, injury, and moreover that the plaintiff was "involved in some way in the event causing the negligent injury to another." *Zell*, 665 So.2d at 1054.

Judith claims no personal involvement in the event causing her loss, nor does she claim physical injury. She thus recognizes that her claim derives from the injuries inflicted upon Melinda. In truth, we see no more than a vague and distant analogy between the negligent infliction cases and the present claim for consortium loss. No Florida case holds, or even suggests, the viability of a consortium claim independent of a legal relationship between the consortium claimant and the injured party.

Judith next asks that we create an exception to the marriage requirement because Florida law prohibits same-sex couples from marrying. *See* § 741.212, Fla. Stat. (2006). Having previously concluded that the loss-of-consortium claim is dependent upon a recognized legal relationship, we have little difficulty disposing of this argument. Florida has stated as its public policy that a legal relationship is simply unattainable for a couple such as Judith and Melinda. Although expressing no disrespect whatsoever concerning that relationship, we cannot see how a court in Florida could ignore the clear import of the Florida legislation. By prohibiting the establishment of a marital relationship between persons other than male and female, the Florida Legislature has left inescapable the conclusion that such legal rights as would flow from marriage will likewise not be recognized in Florida, absent some factor not present here.*

Contrary to Judith's implied assertion, many persons involved in close relationships find themselves without any possibility of a claim for loss of

---

* The present case, of course, has to do with the rights and liabilities of third persons. Florida law has long recognized that an agreement between unmarried, cohabiting parties, once proven, will be enforced by the courts. *See, e.g.* Posik v. Layton, 695 So.2d 759 (Fla. 5th DCA 1997); Crossen v. Feldman, 673 So.2d 903 (Fla. 2d DCA 1996).

consortium. This would be true for brothers and sisters, and perhaps even for close friends who have developed, over time, a living arrangement. The emotional injury, no matter how deeply felt, however, does not give rise to the claim; instead, the existence of the legal relationship fosters the claim. "There has to be a line drawn somewhere, and absent legislation it would be improvident for this court to extend it." *Tremblay v. Carter*, 390 So.2d 816, 818 (Fla. 2d DCA 1980); *accord Fullerton v. Hosp. Corp. of Am.*, 660 So.2d 389 (Fla. 5th DCA 1995).

AFFIRMED.

NOTE

Bashaway involves two issues that can be distinguished from one another. One is the extent to which the law should treat same-sex couples as conjugal family members; the other is whether law should extend such recognition to unmarried conjugal partners more generally.

The debate over same-sex marriage reflects consideration of the first issue. Chapter 2, Section A(1)(d) discusses this debate in some detail, as well as alternative forms of recognition for same-sex couples, such as civil unions and domestic partner registration programs.

The second issue requires that we decide whether the absence of marriage should preclude treating any conjugal couple as a family. Some of these couples will have deliberately chosen not to marry. Should that preclude recognizing any familial rights, benefits, or obligations? What if a couple is unable to marry because their state bans same-sex marriage? Is there a stronger or a weaker case for treating the partners as family members?

If we believe that formal marital status is not a prerequisite for treating conjugal partners as a family, which relationships are entitled to recognition and what benefits and responsibilities should result? Should we seek to determine whether the parties' relationship in substance resembles marriage? Does that risk imposing a conventional model of intimacy that a couple may not wish to adopt? If deference to individuals' preferences is our goal, should the law limit itself to enforcing any agreements that parties enter into about their rights and obligations? What about letting the couple choose from a "menu" of options and register as a domestic partnership?

These questions are especially salient in determining whether unmarried intimate partners should have any financial claims on one another when the relationship ends. For now, keep in mind the potential costs and benefits of recognizing unmarried partners as family members, and, if we choose to do so, the complex considerations that we must take into account in deciding which approach is the best way of accomplishing this.

LAW COMMISSION OF CANADA, BEYOND CONJUGALITY: RECOGNIZING AND SUPPORTING CLOSE PERSONAL ADULT RELATIONSHIPS

1–7, 113–22 (2001).

. . .

Chapter One: The Diversity of Personal Adult Relationships

Canadians have always formed a diverse range of adult personal relationships. Caring relationships are formed by married and common-law couples, relatives or friends sharing a household, and care recipients and caregivers, to name a few. Recognizing and supporting caring personal adult relationships is an important state objective. The diversity of personal adult relationships poses significant challenges to governments as they seek to align state policy with social facts. . . .

A majority of Canadian households have long consisted of married couples or other conjugal couples living together with or without children. Alongside the nuclear family centred on the conjugal couple, a variety of other living arrangements have been enduring features of Canadian society. There have always been, for example, significant numbers of adult siblings living together, widows and widowers forming blended families with new partners, adult children living with their parents and multi-generational households. In the past, because of shorter life expectancy and the loss of life during wartime, it was not uncommon for children to lose a parent or for spouses to become widowed. Often widows or widowers would form new relationships, and the new partner would become a parent to any dependent children living in the household.

Over the course of recent decades, particularly since the mid–1960s, a number of major, inter-related demographic shifts have occurred in the nature of Canadian adults' close personal relationships. As is the case in many other countries, domestic relationships in Canada appear to have become even more diverse in the past 30 years. . . .

. . .

Almost all adult Canadians form a conjugal union at some point in their lives. A clear majority of Canadians—over 60 percent—were married or cohabiting in a conjugal relationship at the time of the 1996 census.

It remains the case that a strong majority of opposite-sex conjugal unions are marital relationships. However, the marriage rate has declined steadily since 1971, while the number of opposite-sex couples choosing to live in common-law relationships outside of marriage has increased steadily since they were first recorded in 1981. Rates of opposite-sex cohabitation are highest among young never-married adults, although growth rates in non-marital cohabitation are highest among older adults, many of whom were previously married. Opposite-sex cohabitation—whether as an alternative to marriage, as a prelude to marriage, or as a sequel to marriage—is a growing phenomenon that now has widespread social acceptance.

There is as yet no census data or reliable studies on the number of lesbian and gay couples living together in Canada. While same-sex couples were included in the census questionnaire for the first time in 2001, it will take some time before the data is compiled and available for analysis. . . . A number of smaller-scale studies of the lesbian and gay population in urban Canada suggest that gays and lesbians form enduring conjugal relationships in numbers comparable to the population as a whole. Based on the available data, it appears that a significant minority of Canadian households consist of same-sex couples.

People today have more options in choosing whether to form a conjugal relationship and, if so, what type of conjugal relationship they wish to have. Once subject to punitive social and legal sanctions, both opposite-sex and same-sex common-law partners now enjoy much greater social acceptance and have many of the legal rights and obligations that attach to married spouses.

The ways in which individuals who form conjugal relationships are structuring their lives have also changed dramatically. The average age of marriage has increased. There are significant numbers of step-families, including blended families where children of different unions are raised in the same household. An increasing number of adults are delaying having children until their late twenties or early thirties, or are deciding not to have children at all. Those who decide to become parents are having fewer children than previous generations.

Women's participation in the paid labour force increased steadily from the 1950s to the 1990s. As a result, a declining minority of Canadian families rely on a sole male breadwinner for economic support. In 1996, the dual earnings of mothers and fathers supported 68 percent of married or opposite-sex common-law couples with children. Even when young children are in the home, both parents are employed in a strong majority of families. Women's participation in the labour force has become essential to the living standards of families. Indeed, economic necessity has been an important driving force behind the emergence of more dual earner families than ever before. . . .

Non–Conjugal Households and Non–Conjugal Relationships

While 60 percent of adult Canadians live in a conjugal relationship, and the majority of Canadian households consist of conjugal couples living with or without children, a substantial minority of households involve adults living alone, lone-parent families or adults living together in non-conjugal relationships. And within households centred around conjugal relationships, often other adults are present, having non-conjugal ties to other members of the household. Non-conjugal relationships may be with unrelated friends or they may be with relatives other than spouses or minor children.

Non–Conjugal Relationships Between Relatives

Adult children are remaining at home longer and also leaving home and then moving back in increasing numbers. As a result, it is now common for adult children to live with their middle-aged parents. It appears that adult children return home or stay at home mainly because of financial constraints imposed by difficulties in obtaining adequate employment or the need to complete their education; this allows them to benefit from the sharing of income and wealth within the household.

Many Canadians who are not defined by Statistics Canada as belonging to a census or nuclear family nevertheless live with relatives in what have been called "economic families". While a census family includes couples or parents with never-married children, an economic family is a broader concept that encompasses all relatives living in the same household, regardless of how they are related. For example, it would include an older woman living with her married children, or adult siblings sharing a home.

In 1996, 3 percent of the population in private households lived with relatives (other than a spouse or never-married children), a proportion that remained stable compared with the previous two decades. Domestic relationships between adult siblings form the largest component of economic families. There is reason to believe that sibling relationships will increase in importance in the future. The high birthrate of the 1950s and the aging population mean that within the next 20 to 30 years, older adults will have substantially more siblings alive as compared with older adults today. This may mean that in the future more siblings will care for each other in old age.

Non–Conjugal Relationships Between Non–Relatives

Another 3.5 percent of the population lived with non-relatives in 1996. Since same-sex couples were not counted in the census prior to 2001, by default they would have been included as households composed of non-relatives. Thus, same-sex conjugal relationships and non-conjugal relationships would together comprise unknown portions of this 3.5 percent of Canadians.

We know little about the characteristics of non-conjugal relationships between unrelated persons since it is a topic that has rarely been investigated. We do know that kinship relations between unrelated persons can be experienced as the equivalent of biological or legal ties. We also know that within gay and lesbian communities, individuals are more likely to form families of friends. If biological family members do not support an individual's sexual orientation or family decisions, then forming kinship relations with friends becomes a particularly important replacement or supplement to the family of origin.

"Families of friends" also appear to be particularly important to older adults. One recent study of older people in Ontario found that 4 percent of non-widowed and 8 percent of widowed individuals include a friend in their description of family. Friends are also particularly important in the lives of older women.

Caregiving Relationships

People with disabilities have the same range of close personal relationships as other Canadians. They are spouses, friends, lovers, parents, children, aunts, uncles, cousins, grandchildren, grandparents and so on. Many people with disabilities are also in close personal relationships that are characterized at least in part by personal care or support that is related to their disabilities. Caregiving relationships involve the provision or exchange of a number of different kinds of care necessary to maintain or enhance the care recipients' independence. The research suggests that there is frequently interdependence or reciprocity—an exchange of personal and social supports—in the personal relationships of people with disabilities. The kinds of care provided or exchanged include social and emotional support; assistance with the physical activities of daily living such as shopping, cleaning and cooking; and assistance with personal or medical aspects of daily living such as dressing, bathing and taking medications. The literature distinguishes between formal care provided by paid professionals and informal care provided without pay by family and friends.

Over 90 percent of persons with disabilities live in their own homes. The vast majority must develop relationships of support with paid and non-paid caregivers for their basic survival and well-being. In 1991, among the 1.8 million persons with disabilities residing in households and aged 15 or over who were in need of supports, almost 900,000 obtained those supports exclusively from family members. Almost 100,000 persons with disabilities rely on friends only for personal supports, while another 53,000 rely on friends in combination with family and an agency.

Persons with permanent disabilities are not the only Canadians whose relationships are characterized by the provision or exchange of personal care and supports. Everyone needs this kind of care at some point in their lives. The need for care, perhaps surprisingly, is not closely tied to age. Similar proportions of persons receive personal care across age groups. Over half of persons over the age of 65 say that they get some help with household chores and personal tasks. Half also say that they provide care to others.

The available data show that women continue to provide the bulk of caregiving on an unpaid basis and spend more time than men in providing care. For the most part, caregivers provide care willingly and as a reciprocal aspect of rewarding relationships. However, numerous studies have shown that supports to individuals with disabilities and their families are often insufficient. The demands placed on informal caregiving have been increased by an aging population, reductions in public services and deinstitutionalization. Many people are discharged from hospital while still requiring complex and skilled care. This situation puts stress on family members who are expected to compensate for gaps in formal care in their unpaid role as caregivers. The extent of their caregiving responsibilities can take a major toll on caregivers' economic security and physical, emotional and psychological health. Inadequate social support for caregiving has a negative impact on caregivers and care-receivers, and on the quality of their relationships.

Conclusion

Canadians have always formed a diverse array of personal adult relationships. While about half of the adult population is married, significant numbers of Canadians are choosing to form same-sex unions or non-marital opposite-sex conjugal unions. In addition, there are significant numbers of blended families, lone-parent families, non-conjugal domestic relationships and families with adult children living at home. Families with a sole male breadwinner are becoming rare. Large numbers of older adults and persons with disabilities rely on family and friends for personal care and support.

Recognizing and supporting personal adult relationships that involve caring and interdependence is an important state objective. In the past, many policies were framed to apply only to married persons. Governments have taken important steps forward in recent years by extending rights and obligations to persons who are living with same-sex partners or with a person of the opposite-sex outside of marriage. But this extension of rights and obligations has maintained the legal focus on conjugal relationships. A more principled and comprehensive approach is needed to consider not just the situation of spouses and common-law partners, but also the needs of persons in non-conjugal relationships, including caregiver relationships. . . .

. . .

Chapter Four: The Legal Organization of Personal Relationships

. . . What should the state's role be in relation to committed relationships? What is the nature of the state's obligation in providing legal mechanisms to support relationships and to assist in the legal organization of such relationships?

. . .

The Role of the State

Many people long for stability and certainty in their personal relationships just as they do in other areas of their lives, at work or in business. The state does have a role in providing legal mechanisms for people to be able to achieve such private understandings. It must provide an orderly framework in which people can express their commitment to each other and voluntarily assume a range of legal rights and obligations.

. . .

For a long time, the state has focused on marriage as the vehicle of choice for adults to express their commitment. Marriage provides parties with the ability to state publicly and officially their intentions toward one another. It is entered voluntarily. It also provides for certainty and stability since the marriage cannot be terminated without legal procedures. Marriage as a legal tool demonstrates characteristics of voluntariness, stability, certainty and publicity that made it attractive as a model to regulate relationships.

But it is no longer a sufficient model to respond to the variety of relationships that exist in Canada today. Whether we look at older people living with their adult children, adults with disabilities living with their caregivers, or siblings cohabiting in the same residence, the marriage model is inadequate. Some of these other relationships are also characterized by emotional and economic interdependence, mutual care and concern and the expectation of some duration. All of these personal adult relationships could also benefit from legal frameworks to support people's need for certainty and stability.

Throughout our consultations, it became clear that simply allowing people the option to enter into private contracts, such as cohabitation agreements or caregiving arrangements, was insufficient because it did not always have the official or public aspect that was needed, nor did it offer sufficient guarantee of certainty. In addition, the lack of official record of such private arrangements prevents the efficient administration of laws and programs where relationships could be relevant. . . .

We must therefore examine ways for the state to offer all Canadians appropriate legal frameworks that respond to their needs for certainty and stability in their personal relationships. This role of providing sufficient legal mechanisms for people to carry out their private and personal commitments is an important one. It is just as important as insuring that the corporate world has the legal tools to respond to its needs for stability and certainty. These legal frameworks must keep pace with the ways in which adults organize their lives.

It is in this context that one must look at the mechanisms currently developed to allow Canadians to organize their private lives.

Legal Frameworks for Personal Relationships

In this section, we review [different] . . . legal models of regulation of personal relationships. The first, the private law model, is one that operates by default. When governments do not provide any legal framework, parties resort to traditional private law concepts to organize their lives. This is the current case for non-conjugal relationships in Canada in which people may choose to be regulated privately. For conjugal relationships, there are [other] . . . models to regulate personal relationships that have been used around the world: ascription [i.e., treating unmarried cohabitants as if they were married, without their having taken any positive action to be legally recognized], registration and marriage. . . .

Private Law

People are always at liberty to express their commitments through contracts. Whether written or oral, contracts do regulate personal relationships. Expressly or implicitly, people who reside together, who help each other or who have an intimate relationship organize their lives around shared expectations that are more or less well defined. When such expectations are not fulfilled, they may seek remedy in court under various theories of private law, unjust enrichment, constructive trust, or the creation of an implicit partnership, to name a few.

Parties may choose to state explicitly in a written document their shared expectations and demand execution of such a contractual arrangement through the civil courts. The ability to forge one's own contractual regime and negotiate the terms of one's commitment is a valued tool in a free society and one which must always be available.

But it is a tool beyond the reach of many people. Leaving the parties to design their own contractual or private law arrangements imposes too high a burden on people who do not have time, energy or the requisite knowledge to do so. The possible involvement of a lawyer to design such arrangements is also too costly or inconvenient for the majority of people. Furthermore, there is also a concern that the stronger or wealthier party may impose unfavourable terms on the poorer or weaker party.

Although contracts will continue to remain an important method for individuals to determine their mutual rights and obligations, they are not a sufficient remedy in and of themselves....

.   .   .

Ascription

.   .   .

Ascription is generally heralded as a way for governments to prevent the risks of exploitation inherent in a contractual model. It imposes a set of obligations on people in conjugal relationships which are presumed to correspond to the expectations of the majority of people. It has hence allowed governments to respond to the changes in Canadian society, particularly with respect to the regulation of the relationships of unmarried conjugal relationships. It also supplies a default arrangement for couples who have not provided for any arrangements and who would otherwise have to resort to cumbersome traditional private law models.

However, ascription as a model has limits. First, it is a blunt policy tool in that it treats all conjugal relationships alike, irrespective of the level of emotional or economic interdependency that they may present. Second, it infringes upon the value of autonomy. Although people may opt out of certain statutory provisions governing their relationships, they are not always aware of this possibility. In addition, ascription is not the best way to respond to the needs of non-conjugal relationships. It would be inappropriate to presume that all older parents living with their adult children have the same needs or that adults with disabilities have equally similar patterns of caring and support. Although ascription may serve the particular purpose of preventing exploitation, it is a tool that must be used sparingly, where there is evidence of exploitation. Governments should continue to use the model of ascription but they should also provide Canadians with appropriate tools to define for themselves the terms of their relationships.

It is in that context that governments should look at a system that would affirm the capacity of people to establish for themselves the terms of their relationships while providing models for doing so. Registration models would serve that purpose.

Registration

Recently, there has been a move toward the creation of a new status, often called registered partnership (or Registered Domestic Partnership or RDP)....

The objective of . . . registration schemes is to provide an alternative way for the state to recognize and support close personal relationships. When people register their relationships, they are then included within a range of rights and responsibilities often similar to marriage. It is a regime that has begun to develop as a parallel to marriage, in which the state is promoting a similar set of objectives in the recognition and support of personal relationships. . . .

. . . [A] registration scheme is worthy of consideration because it would enable a broader range of relationships to be recognized. It would therefore provide both conjugal and non-conjugal unions with a way to formalize their relationship and to voluntarily assume rights and responsibilities toward each other. In this way, a registration system would promote the equality of non-conjugal relationships. The second major advantage of a registration scheme is that it affirms the autonomy and choices of Canadians in their close personal relationships. There is value in encouraging people to make their relationship commitments clear and in recognizing the choices that people make in their close personal relationships. A registration scheme provides a way in which a broad range of relationships, including non-conjugal relationships, can be recognized, while also promoting and respecting the value of autonomy. A registration scheme has a number of advantages specifically related to the value of autonomy and choice. In such a scheme, rights and responsibilities are based on the mutual and voluntary decisions of the individuals in the relationship. It thereby avoids many of the problems with functional definitions that impose relationship status on individuals whether or not they so desire.

A registration scheme could play an important role in broadening the range of options available for people (conjugal and non-conjugal alike) to voluntarily assume rights and responsibilities. The ability to formalize a relationship through a public declaration of commitment is important to Canadians. A registration scheme provides a way in which individuals in close personal relationships can choose to make such a public declaration of commitment, which would then be respected by government.

A registration system may also promote the values of equality and autonomy within relationships without compromising the value of privacy. The ascription model described above, if it were to use more functional definitions, would require that governments examine individual relationships to decide whether they fit the definition. It is an approach that necessarily involves some degree of invasion of privacy. A registration scheme, on the other hand, by leaving the choice entirely up to the individuals within relationships and then respecting that choice, provides a way of recognizing conjugal and non-conjugal relationships without . . . subject[ing] the relationship to [state] scrutiny. Ascription, however, should continue to be used where there is evidence of exploitation.

Designing a Registration Scheme

There are many challenging questions that governments will have to address in deciding how a registration scheme should be designed and implemented. In this section, we review some of these questions and, drawing on the insights that can be gleaned from developments in other jurisdictions, we suggest how a registration system should be designed.

Formal Attributes

The first question that must be addressed in designing a registration scheme involves its formal attributes, that is, who may register? Should there be any limits on who may register?

One of the greatest advantages of a registration scheme is that it provides an opportunity to recognize the formal commitment of individuals in any relationship. There is no reason for governments to restrict a registration scheme to conjugal couples or to same-sex couples or, indeed, only to couples. . . .

. . . [T]here [also] is no reason to impose a residential requirement on registrations. There is no similar restriction on marriage: married couples do not have to live together for the marriage to be valid. There is, then, no compelling reason to impose such a restriction on registered relationships.

Another question that governments will have to address is how registrations should be terminable; that is, how can partners decide to end their registration? In our view, registrations should be terminable by mutual agreement. Registered partners should be able to make a mutual declaration that their partnership has ended. Furthermore, given that married spouses can end their marriage unilaterally by making an application for divorce after living separate and apart for one year, it would not be justifiable to impose a more rigorous standard on domestic partners. Partners in a registered relationships should similarly be able to register a dissolution of their registration.

In addition, the regulation of the dissolution of registrations must ensure that the legal obligations between the registrants are respected upon relationship breakdown. Restructuring financial relationships on relationship breakdown remains an important state objective. The state should ensure that the reasonable expectations of partners are not undermined on the breakdown of the relationship.

Legal Implications of Registrations

. . .

Governments could enact a registration regime based on this model, whereby people could formally enter into a registration and then be entitled to predetermined rights and responsibilities. The possibility of choosing the same rights and responsibilities as spouses or common-law partners could be offered. It might also be possible to design more flexible arrangements that may respond better to the variety of caregiving relationships that exist. Models of caregiving arrangements could be proposed which parties could modify, if they so wish.

The legal consequences of registration might be limited to the private rights and responsibilities within the relationship. It could involve such issues as property and support obligations both during and after the relationship. It could involve determinations for care arrangements, consent to treatment or other aspects of the relationship. The commitment of entering into a registration would be about the voluntary assumption of mutual responsibilities. It would be about clarifying this commitment of mutual responsibility in law, both for the parties themselves and for potentially interested third parties.

. . .

Recommendation

Parliament and provincial/territorial legislatures should pass laws enabling adults to register their relationship.

Considerations:

—The registration should not be restricted only to conjugal relationships.

—It should provide for a set of commitments, which could include caring arrangements, consent to treatment dispositions, support and sharing in property from which the parties may opt out.

NOTE

At one point, the Law Commission's report suggests that registration may be a valuable way of promoting the state's objective of "recognizing and supporting personal adult relationships that involve caring and interdependence" outside of marriage. Should such a registration system displace marriage, so that the law recognizes a variety of relationships without privileging any one of them? For other prospects in these directions, see MARTHA A. FINEMAN, THE NEUTERED MOTHER, THE SEXUAL FAMILY, AND OTHER TWENTIETH-CENTURY TRAGEDIES (1995); Linda C. McClain, *Intimate Affiliation and Democracy*, 32 HOFSTRA L. REV. 397 (2003); Nancy D. Polikoff, *Ending Marriage As We Know It*, 32 HOFSTRA L. REV. 201 (2003); Elizabeth S. Scott, *Marriage, Cohabitation, and Collective Responsibility for Dependency*, 2004 U. CHI. LEGAL F. 225. Another important statement is in Beyond Same–Sex Marriage, A New Strategic Vision for All Our Families & Relationships, *available at* http://www.beyondmarriage. org/full_statement.html (July 26, 2006). For possible limitations, consider Pamela Karlan, *Let's Call the Whole Thing Off: Can States Abolish the Institution of Marriage*, 98 CALIF. L. REV. 697 (2010). *See also* Anita Bernstein, *For and Against Marriage: A Revision*, 102 MICH. L. REV. 131 (2003).

B.   THE CHILD BORN OUT OF WEDLOCK

Lalli v. Lalli

Supreme Court of the United States, 1978.
439 U.S. 259, 99 S.Ct. 518, 58 L.Ed.2d 503.

■ JUSTICE POWELL announced the judgment of the Court in an opinion, in which THE CHIEF JUSTICE and JUSTICE STEWART join.

This case presents a challenge to the constitutionality of § 4–1.2 of New York's Estates, Powers, and Trusts Law, which requires illegitimate children who would inherit from their fathers by intestate succession to provide a particular form of proof of paternity. Legitimate children are not subject to the same requirement.

Appellant Robert Lalli claims to be the illegitimate son of Mario Lalli who died intestate on January 7, 1973, in the State of New York. Appellant's mother, who died in 1968, never was married to Mario. After Mario's widow, Rosamond Lalli, was appointed administratrix of her husband's estate, appellant petitioned the Surrogate's Court for Westchester County for a compulsory accounting, claiming that he and his sister Maureen Lalli were entitled to inherit from Mario as his children. Rosamond Lalli opposed the petition. She argued that even if Robert and Maureen were Mario's children, they were not lawful distributees of the estate because they had failed to comply with § 4–1.2, which provides in part:

"An illegitimate child is the legitimate child of his father so that he and his issue inherit from his father if a court of competent jurisdiction has, during the lifetime of the father, made an order of filiation declaring paternity in a proceeding instituted during the pregnancy of the mother or within two years from the birth of the child."

Appellant conceded that he had not obtained an order of filiation during his putative father's lifetime. He contended, however, that § 4–1.2, by imposing this requirement, discriminated against him on the basis of his illegitimate birth in violation of the Equal Protection Clause of the Fourteenth Amendment. Appellant tendered certain evidence of his relationship with Mario Lalli, including a notarized document in which Lalli, in consenting to appellant's marriage, referred to him as "my son," and several affidavits by persons who stated that Lalli had acknowledged openly and often that Robert and Maureen were his children.

. . .

. . . After reviewing recent decisions of this Court concerning discrimination against illegitimate children . . . the [lower] court ruled that appellant was properly excluded as a distributee of Lalli's estate and therefore lacked status to petition for a compulsory accounting.

On direct appeal the New York Court of Appeals affirmed. . . .

. . .

. . . We now affirm.

We begin our analysis with *Trimble* [*v. Gordon*, 430 U.S. 762 (1977)]. At issue in that case was the constitutionality of an Illinois statute providing that a child born out of wedlock could inherit from his intestate father only if the father had "acknowledged" the child and the child had been legitimated by the intermarriage of the parents. The appellant in *Trimble* was a child born out of wedlock whose father had neither acknowledged her nor married her mother. He had, however, been found to be her father in a judicial decree ordering him to contribute to her support. When the father died intestate, the child was excluded as a distributee because the statutory requirements for inheritance had not been met.

We concluded that the Illinois statute discriminated against illegitimate children in a manner prohibited by the Equal Protection Clause. Although . . . classifications based on illegitimacy are not subject to "strict scrutiny," they nevertheless are invalid under the Fourteenth Amendment if they are not substantially related to permissible state interests. Upon examination, we found that the Illinois law failed that test.

Two state interests were proposed which the statute was said to foster: the encouragement of legitimate family relationships and the maintenance of an accurate and efficient method of disposing of an intestate decedent's property. Granting that the State was appropriately concerned with the integrity of the family unit, we viewed the statute as bearing "only the most attenuated relationship to the asserted goal." We again rejected the argument that "persons will shun illicit relations because the offspring may not one day reap the benefits" that would accrue to them were they legitimate. *Weber v. Aetna Casualty & Surety Co.*, 406 U.S. 164, 173 (1972). The statute therefore was not defensible as an incentive to enter legitimate family relationships.

Illinois' interest in safeguarding the orderly disposition of property at death was more relevant to the statutory classification. We recognized that devising "an appropriate legal framework" in the furtherance of that interest "is a matter particularly within the competence of the individual States." An important aspect of that framework is a response to the often difficult problem of proving the paternity of illegitimate children and the related danger of spurious claims against intestate estates. These difficulties, we said, "might justify a more demanding standard for illegitimate children claiming under their fathers' estates than that required either for illegitimate children claiming under their mothers' estates or for legitimate children generally."

. . .

Under § 4–1.2, by contrast, the marital status of the parents is irrelevant. The single requirement at issue here is an evidentiary one—that the paternity of the father be declared in a judicial proceeding sometime before his death.[5] The child need not have been legitimated in order to inherit from his father. Had the appellant in *Trimble* been governed by § 4–1.2, she would have been a distributee of her father's estate.

A related difference between the two provisions pertains to the state interests said to be served by them. The Illinois law was defended, in part, as a means of encouraging legitimate family relationships. No such justification has been offered in support of § 4–1.2. The Court of Appeals disclaimed that the purpose of the statute, "even in small part, was to discourage illegitimacy, to mold human conduct or to set societal norms." The absence in § 4–1.2 of any requirement that the parents intermarry or otherwise legitimate a child born out of wedlock and our review of the legislative history of the statute confirm this view.

Our inquiry, therefore, is focused narrowly. We are asked to decide whether the discrete procedural demands that § 4–1.2 places on illegitimate children bear an evident and substantial relation to the particular state interests this statute is designed to serve.

The primary state goal underlying the challenged aspects of § 4–1.2 is to provide for the just and orderly disposition of property at death. We long have recognized that this is an area with which the States have an interest of considerable magnitude.

This interest is directly implicated in paternal inheritance by illegitimate children because of the peculiar problems of proof that are involved. Establishing maternity is seldom difficult. As one New York Surrogate's Court has observed: "[T]he birth of the child is a recorded or registered event usually taking place in the presence of others. In most cases the child remains with the mother and for a time is necessarily reared by her. That the child is the child of a particular woman is rarely difficult to prove." *In re Ortiz*, 60 Misc.2d 756, 761, 303 N.Y.S.2d 806, 812 (1969). Proof of paternity, by contrast, frequently is difficult when the father is not part of a formal family unit. "The putative father often goes his way unconscious of the birth of a child. Even if conscious, he is very often totally unconcerned because of the absence of any ties to the mother. Indeed the mother may not know *who* is responsible for her pregnancy."

Thus, a number of problems arise that counsel against treating illegitimate children identically to all other heirs of an intestate father. These were

---

5. Section 4–1.2 requires not only that the order of filiation be made during the lifetime of the father, but that the proceeding in which it is sought be commenced "during the pregnancy of the mother or within two years from the birth of the child." . . . As the New York Court of Appeals has not passed upon the constitutionality of the two-year limitation, that question is not before us. Our decision today therefore sustains § 4–1.2 under the Equal Protection Clause only with respect to its requirement that a judicial order of filiation be issued during the lifetime of the father of an illegitimate child.

the subject of a comprehensive study by the Temporary State Commission on the Modernization, Revision and Simplification of the Law of Estates. This group, known as the Bennett Commission, consisted of individuals experienced in the practical problems of estate administration. The Commission issued its report and recommendations to the Legislature in 1965. See Fourth Report of the Temporary State Commission on the Modernization, Revision and Simplification of the Law of Estates, Legis.Doc. No. 19 (1965) (hereinafter Commission Report). The statute now codified as § 4–1.2 was included.

. . .

As the State's interests are substantial, we now consider the means adopted by New York to further these interests. In order to avoid the problems described above, the Commission recommended a requirement designed to ensure the accurate resolution of claims of paternity and to minimize the potential for disruption of estate administration. Accuracy is enhanced by placing paternity disputes in a judicial forum during the lifetime of the father. As the New York Court of Appeals observed in its first opinion in this case, the "availability [of the putative father] should be a substantial factor contributing to the reliability of the fact-finding process." In addition, requiring that the order be issued during the father's lifetime permits a man to defend his reputation against "unjust accusations in paternity claims," which was a secondary purpose of § 4–1.2. Commission Report 266.

The administration of an estate will be facilitated, and the possibility of delay and uncertainty minimized, where the entitlement of an illegitimate child to notice and participation is a matter of judicial record before the administration commences. Fraudulent assertions of paternity will be much less likely to succeed, or even to arise, where the proof is put before a court of law at a time when the putative father is available to respond, rather than first brought to light when the distribution of the assets of an estate is in the offing.[8]

Appellant contends that § 4–1.2, like the statute at issue in *Trimble*, excludes "significant categories of illegitimate children" who could be allowed to inherit "without jeopardizing the orderly settlement" of their intestate fathers' estates. He urges that those in his position—"known" illegitimate children who, despite the absence of an order of filiation obtained during their fathers' lifetimes, can present convincing proof of paternity—cannot rationally be denied inheritance as they post none of the risks § 4–1.2 was intended to minimize.

We do not question that there will be some illegitimate children who would be able to establish their relationship to their deceased fathers without serious disruption of the administration of estates and that, as applied to such individuals § 4–1.2 appears to operate unfairly. But few statutory classifications are entirely free from the criticism that they sometimes produce inequitable results. Our inquiry under the Equal Protection Clause does not focus on the abstract "fairness" of a state law, but on whether the

---

8. In affirming the judgment below, we do not, of course, restrict a State's freedom to require proof of paternity by means other than a judicial decree. Thus a State may prescribe any *formal* method of proof, whether it be similar to that provided by § 4–1.2 or some other regularized procedure that would assure the authenticity of the acknowledgment. As we noted in *Trimble*, 430 U.S., at 772 n. 14, such a procedure would be sufficient to satisfy the State's interests.

statute's relation to the state interests it is intended to promote is so tenuous that it lacks the rationality contemplated by the Fourteenth Amendment.

The Illinois statute in *Trimble* was constitutionally unacceptable because it effected a total statutory disinheritance of children born out of wedlock who were not legitimated by the subsequent marriage of their parents. The reach of the statute was far in excess of its justifiable purposes. Section 4–1.2 does not share this defect. Inheritance is barred only where there has been a failure to secure evidence of paternity during the father's lifetime in the manner prescribed by the State. This is not a requirement that inevitably disqualifies an unnecessarily large number of children born out of wedlock.

The New York courts have interpreted § 4–1.2 liberally and in such a way as to enhance its utility to both father and children without sacrificing its strength as a procedural prophylactic. For example, a father of illegitimate children who is willing to acknowledge paternity can waive his defenses in a paternity proceeding, or even institute such a proceeding himself.[10] In addition, the courts have excused "technical" failures by illegitimate children to comply with the statute in order to prevent unnecessary injustice.

. . .

Even if, as Justice Brennan believes, § 4–1.2 could have been written somewhat more equitably, it is not the function of a court "to hypothesize independently on the desirability or feasibility of any possible alternative[s]" to the statutory scheme formulated by New York. "These matters of practical judgment and empirical calculation are for [the State]. . . . In the end, the precise accuracy of [the State's] calculations is not a matter of specialized judicial competence; and we have no basis to question their detail beyond the evident consistency and substantiality."

We conclude that the requirement imposed by § 4–1.2 on illegitimate children who would inherit from their fathers is substantially related to the important state interests the statute is intended to promote. We therefore find no violation of the Equal Protection Clause.

The judgment of the New York Court of Appeals is

Affirmed.

Clark v. Jeter

Supreme Court of the United States, 1988.
486 U.S. 456, 108 S.Ct. 1910, 100 L.Ed.2d 465.

■ JUSTICE O'CONNOR delivered the opinion of the Court.

Under Pennsylvania law, an illegitimate child must prove paternity before seeking support from his or her father, and a suit to establish paternity ordinarily must be brought within six years of an illegitimate child's birth. By contrast, a legitimate child may seek support from his or her parents at any time. We granted certiorari to consider the constitutionality of this legislative scheme.

On September 22, 1983, petitioner Cherlyn Clark filed a support complaint in the Allegheny County Court of Common Pleas on behalf of her minor daughter, Tiffany, who was born out of wedlock on June 11, 1973.

---

10.   In addition to making intestate succession possible, of course, a father is always free to provide for his illegitimate child by will.

Clark named respondent Gene Jeter as Tiffany's father. The court ordered blood tests, which showed a 99.3% probability that Jeter is Tiffany's father.

Jeter moved to dismiss the complaint on the ground that it was barred by the 6–year statute of limitations for paternity actions. In her response, Clark contended that this statute is unconstitutional under the Equal Protection and Due Process Clauses of the Fourteenth Amendment....

. . .

In considering whether state legislation violates the Equal Protection Clause of the Fourteenth Amendment, U.S. Const., Amdt. 14, § 1, we apply different levels of scrutiny to different types of classifications. At a minimum, a statutory classification must be rationally related to a legitimate governmental purpose. Classifications based on race or national origin, and classifications affecting fundamental rights, are given the most exacting scrutiny. Between these extremes of rational basis review and strict scrutiny lies a level of intermediate scrutiny, which generally has been applied to discriminatory classifications based on sex or illegitimacy.

To withstand intermediate scrutiny, a statutory classification must be substantially related to an important governmental objective. Consequently we have invalidated classifications that burden illegitimate children for the sake of punishing the illicit relations of their parents, because "visiting this condemnation on the head of an infant is illogical and unjust." *Weber v. Aetna Casualty & Surety Co.*, 406 U.S. 164, 175 (1972). Yet, in the seminal case concerning the child's right to support, this Court acknowledged that it might be appropriate to treat illegitimate children differently in the support context because of "lurking problems with respect to proof of paternity." *Gomez v. Perez*, 409 U.S. 535, 538 (1973).

This Court has developed a particular framework for evaluating equal protection challenges to statutes of limitations that apply to suits to establish paternity, and thereby limit the ability of illegitimate children to obtain support.

"First, the period for obtaining support . . . must be sufficiently long in duration to present a reasonable opportunity for those with an interest in such children to assert claims on their behalf. Second, any time limitation placed on that opportunity must be substantially related to the State's interest in avoiding the litigation of stale or fraudulent claims." *Mills v. Habluetzel*, 456 U.S. 91, 99–100 (1982).

In *Mills*, we held that Texas' 1–year statute of limitations failed both steps of the analysis. We explained that paternity suits typically will be brought by the child's mother, who might not act swiftly amidst the emotional and financial complications of the child's first year. And, it is unlikely that the lapse of a mere 12 months will result in the loss of evidence or appreciably increase the likelihood of fraudulent claims. A concurring opinion in *Mills* explained why statutes of limitations longer than one year also may be unconstitutional. (O'CONNOR, J., joined by BURGER, C.J., BRENNAN and BLACKMUN, JJ., and joined as to Part I by POWELL, J., concurring). First, the State has a countervailing interest in ensuring that genuine claims for child support are satisfied. Second, the fact that Texas tolled most other causes of action during a child's minority suggested that proof problems do not become overwhelming during this period. Finally, the practical obstacles to filing a claim for support are likely to continue after the first year of the child's life.

In *Pickett v. Brown*, 462 U.S. 1 (1983), the Court unanimously struck down Tennessee's 2–year statute of limitations for paternity and child support actions brought on behalf of certain illegitimate children. Adhering to the analysis developed in *Mills*, the Court first considered whether two years afforded a reasonable opportunity to bring such suits. The Tennessee statute was relatively more generous than the Texas statute considered in *Mills* because it did not limit actions against a father who had acknowledged his paternity in writing or by furnishing support; nor did it apply if the child was likely to become a public charge. Nevertheless, the Court concluded that the 2–year period was too short in light of the persisting financial and emotional problems that are likely to afflict the child's mother. Proceeding to the second step of the analysis, the Court decided that the 2–year statute of limitations was not substantially related to Tennessee's asserted interest in preventing stale and fraudulent claims. The period during which suit could be brought was only a year longer than the period considered in *Mills*, and this incremental difference would not create substantially greater proof and fraud problems. Furthermore, Tennessee tolled most other actions during a child's minority, and even permitted a support action to be brought on behalf of a child up to 18 years of age if the child was or was likely to become a public charge. Finally, scientific advances in blood testing had alleviated some problems of proof in paternity actions. For these reasons, the Tennessee statute failed to survive heightened scrutiny under the Equal Protection Clause.

In light of this authority, we conclude that Pennsylvania's 6–year statute of limitations violates the Equal Protection Clause. Even six years does not necessarily provide a reasonable opportunity to assert a claim on behalf of an illegitimate child. "The unwillingness of the mother to file a paternity action on behalf of her child, which could stem from her relationship with the natural father or . . . from the emotional strain of having an illegitimate child, or even from the desire to avoid community and family disapproval, may continue years after the child is born. The problem may be exacerbated if, as often happens, the mother herself is a minor." *Mills, supra*, at 105, n. 4. (O'CONNOR, J., concurring). Not all of these difficulties are likely to abate in six years. A mother might realize only belatedly "a loss of income attributable to the need to care for the child," *Pickett, supra*, at 12. Furthermore, financial difficulties are likely to increase as the child matures and incurs expenses for clothing, school, and medical care. See, *e.g.*, *Moore v. McNamara*, 40 Conn. Supp. 6, 11, 12, 478 A.2d 634, 637 (1984) (invalidating a 3–year statute of limitations). Thus it is questionable whether a State acts reasonably when it requires most paternity and support actions to be brought within six years of an illegitimate child's birth.

We do not rest our decision on this ground, however, for it is not entirely evident that six years would necessarily be an unreasonable limitations period for child support actions involving illegitimate children. We are, however, confident that the 6–year statute of limitations is not substantially related to Pennsylvania's interest in avoiding the litigation of stale or fraudulent claims. In a number of circumstances, Pennsylvania permits the issue of paternity to be litigated more than six years after the birth of an illegitimate child. The statute itself permits a suit to be brought more than six years after the child's birth if it is brought within two years of a support payment made by the father. And in other types of suits, Pennsylvania places no limits on when the issue of paternity may be litigated. For example, the intestacy statute, 20 Pa.Cons.Stat. § 2107(3) (1982), permits a child born out of wedlock to establish paternity as long as "there is clear and convincing evidence that the man was the father of the child." Likewise, no statute of limitations applies to a father's action to establish paternity. Recently, the Pennsylvania Legislature enacted a statute that tolls most other civil actions during a child's minority. 42 Pa.Cons.Stat. § 5533(b) (Supp.1987). In *Pickett* and *Mills,* similar tolling statutes cast doubt on the State's purported interest in avoiding the litigation of stale or fraudulent claims. Pennsylvania's tolling statute has the same implications here.

A more recent indication that Pennsylvania does not consider proof problems insurmountable is the enactment by the Pennsylvania Legislature in 1985 of an 18–year statute of limitations for paternity and support actions. 23 Pa.Cons.Stat. § 4343(b) (1985). To be sure the legislature did not act spontaneously, but rather under the threat of losing some federal funds. Nevertheless, the new statute is a tacit concession that proof problems are not overwhelming. The legislative history of the federal Child Support Enforcement Amendments explains why Congress thought such statutes of limitations are reasonable. Congress adverted to the problem of stale and fraudulent claims, but recognized that increasingly sophisticated tests for genetic markers permit the exclusion of over 99% of those who might be accused of paternity, regardless of the age of the child. H.R.Rep. No. 98–527, p. 38 (1983). This scientific evidence is available throughout the child's minority, and it is an additional reason to doubt that Pennsylvania had a substantial reason for limiting the time within which paternity and support actions could be brought.

We conclude that the Pennsylvania statute does not withstand heightened scrutiny under the Equal Protection Clause.... The judgment of the Superior Court is reversed and the case is remanded for further proceedings not inconsistent with this opinion.

It is so ordered.

NOTE

Paternity litigation has been transformed by advancements in science. Although courts relied on HLA (human leucocyte antigen) tests for several decades to determine the likelihood of paternity, courts often expressed concern that the HLA test was not 100 percent accurate. *See, e.g., Brinkley v. King,* 549 Pa. 241, 254, 701 A.2d 176, 182 (1997) (Nigro, J., concurring and dissenting), citing *John M. v. Paula T.,* 524 Pa. 306, 316, 571 A.2d 1380, 1385 (1990), and *Smith v. Shaffer,* 511 Pa. 421, 515 A.2d 527 (1986).

With the development of DNA testing, accuracy has improved significantly, but there is still the problem of human error. In Las Vegas in 2001, a man spent a year in jail after being wrongly convicted of committing two sexual assaults. Investigators later determined that his DNA sample had been switched with another inmate's. Tom Jackman, *Paternity Suit Raises Doubts About DNA Tests,* WASH. POST, Aug. 21, 2005, at C1. *See generally* Mary R. Anderlik and Mark A. Rothstein, *The Genetics Revolution: Conflicts, Challenges and Conundra,* 28 AM. J.L. & MED. 215 (2002); Elizabeth Bartholet, *Guiding Principles for Picking Parents,* 27 HARV. WOMEN'S L.J. 323 (Spring 2004); Donald Hubin, *Daddy Dilemmas: Untangling the Puzzles of Paternity,* 12 CORNELL J.L. & PUB. POL'Y 29 (2003).

People in Interest of S.P.B.

Supreme Court of Colorado, 1982.
651 P.2d 1213.

■ DUBOFSKY, JUSTICE.

P.D.G., the natural father of S.P.B., appeals a child support order of the El Paso County District Court. P.D.G. questions whether the constitutional rights to due process and equal protection of the laws under the state and federal constitutions are violated by the Uniform Parentage Act (UPA), section 19–6–101, *et seq.*, C.R.S.1973 (1978 Repl.Vol. 8), which imposes the duty of child support upon both parents without according the father a right either to decide that the fetus should be aborted or to later avoid child support obligations by showing that he offered to pay for an abortion. . . .

The issue underlying this appeal arose in the course of a proceeding to determine the paternity of and support for S.P.B., a child. The respondent-appellant P.D.G. admitted to paternity of S.P.B. but denied any obligation to support the child. P.D.G. and the child's mother, C.F.B., have never married and are not presently living together. P.D.G. asserts that when C.F.B. informed him that she was pregnant, he responded that he did not want her to have the baby and offered to pay for an abortion. P.D.G. claims that this exchange took place within the first trimester of C.F.B.'s pregnancy. C.F.B. did not agree to an abortion and subsequently gave birth to S.P.B. C.F.B. has had custody of S.P.B. since birth.

. . . The district court . . . ordered P.D.G. to pay child support in the amount of $150 per month and one-half of the birth expenses of the child.

At the outset it is important to point out what is not at issue here. There is no question but that the duty to support a child falls upon both its parents. It is equally clear that this obligation of support extends to all parents, regardless of their marital status. Illegitimate children have the same judicially enforceable right to support as do legitimate children.

The crux of P.D.G.'s equal protection argument is that the UPA, while gender-neutral on its face, operates to deny him equal protection by implicitly accommodating the decision of C.F.B. to carry the fetus to term while ignoring his own express desire that the pregnancy be terminated.

Gender-based distinctions must serve important governmental objectives, and a discriminatory classification must be substantially related to the achievement of those objectives in order to withstand judicial scrutiny under the equal protection clause. *Mississippi University for Women v. Hogan*, 458 U.S. 718 (1982). The General Assembly articulated the state's objective in promulgating the UPA in section 19–1–102 of the Children's Code, of which the UPA is a part. The objective includes:

> (1)(a) To secure for each child subject to these provisions such care and guidance, preferably in his own home, as will best serve his welfare and the interests of society. . . .

We recognized the importance of the state's interest in promoting the welfare of the child in *R. McG. v. J.W.*, [200 Colo. 345, 615 P.2d 666 (1980)]. The appellant does not dispute the significance of the state's objective.

The state has little choice in the means employed to achieve its objective. The statute's tacit accommodation of the mother's decision not to terminate her pregnancy is the only constitutional course open to the state. A woman has a fundamental right to decide in conjunction with her physician whether to terminate her pregnancy. *Roe v. Wade*, 410 U.S. 113 (1973). Further, the United States Supreme Court declared in *Maher v. Roe*, 432 U.S. 464, 472, n. 7 (1977), "A woman has at least an equal right to choose to carry the fetus to term as to choose to abort it." In *Planned Parenthood of Missouri v. Danforth*, 428 U.S. 52, 69 (1976), the United States Supreme Court ruled that the "state cannot delegate to a spouse a veto power which the state itself is absolutely and totally prohibited from exercising during the first trimester of pregnancy." Here, the equal treatment which appellant seeks could only be achieved by according a father the right to compel the mother of his child to procure an abortion. This result is clearly foreclosed by *Roe, Maher,* and *Danforth.* As the Supreme Court noted in *Danforth,* 428 U.S. at 71, "The obvious fact is that when the wife and the husband disagree on this decision, the view of only one of the two partners can prevail. Inasmuch as it is the woman who bears the child and who is the more directly and immediately affected by the pregnancy, as between the two, the balance weighs in her favor."

Thus, at no stage does the appellant's right to be free from gender-based classifications outweigh the substantial and legitimate competing interest. The appellant's right is overridden prior to childbirth by the state's interest in protecting C.F.B.'s fundamental right to make decisions relating to her pregnancy, and thereafter by the state's interest in ensuring that children receive adequate support. We find no violation of equal protection in the statutory obligation of both parents to pay child support or in the denial to the appellant of the right to demand the termination of C.F.B.'s pregnancy.

The appellant claims that section 19–6–116 violates due process by creating an irrebuttable presumption that a father should share in the duty of child support.[10] He submits that so long as there existed an unalterable nexus between conception and childbirth, the presumption was valid, but contends that the current availability of legalized abortion creates the possibility of demonstrating that the nexus has been broken. In support of his position that he should not shoulder any of the responsibility for support of S.P.B., the appellant made an offer of proof in district court that he had promised to pay for an abortion within the first trimester of C.F.B.'s pregnancy. The appellant argues that the statute must, consistent with due process considerations, provide him an opportunity to rebut the presumption.

Statutes creating permanent irrebuttable presumptions have long been disfavored under the due process clauses of the Fifth and Fourteenth Amendments to the United States Constitution. *Vlandis v. Kline,* 412 U.S. 441 (1973)....

A statutory presumption can be invalidated only when a two-pronged test is met: when the presumption is not necessarily or universally true and when the state has reasonable alternative means of making the crucial determination. *Vlandis,* 412 U.S. at 452. Because the appellant's challenge to the child support statute fails to satisfy the second element of the *Vlandis* test, we need not examine the first.

The statutory presumption of a shared parental obligation of child support protects three critical interests: the interest of the child in receiving adequate support, the interest of the state in ensuring that children not become its wards, and the interest of the parents in being free from governmental intrusion into the intimate sphere of family life. In view of these critical functions, the state has no "reasonable alternative means of making the crucial determination" that a nexus exists between conception and childbirth. The alternative, which the appellant propounds, is a case-by-case determination of whether the presumed nexus was broken by the

---

10. Section 19–6–116(5) leaves open the possibility that either parent may demonstrate a financial inability to contribute to child support....

father's offer to pay for an abortion, by prior agreement between the parties, by a subsequent "release" of one party's obligation by another, or by any of a multitude of legal theories which ingenious litigants and their lawyers might advance. A judicial inquiry of this nature represents unconscionable governmental interference with privacy rights which the Supreme Court has deemed inviolate.

There are additional untoward consequences which lurk behind the establishment of a rule of law that fathers could avoid the obligation to support their children in the manner suggested by appellant. Once the criteria for proving a firm offer of an abortion had been enunciated, any man could forever escape this duty simply by making the offer in the prescribed manner. Taking this theory to its logical extreme, a woman could similarly avoid her obligation of support by proving that she had made a firm offer to procure an abortion and that the father, by declining it, assumed all responsibility for their child. The statutory presumption that parents who have participated in the conception of a child assume a joint responsibility for that child reflects the well-considered judgment of the legislature as to the only feasible means of achieving legitimate societal goals. The presumption embodied in section 19–6–116 furthers the substantial interests which the state has in protecting the respective rights of children, of parents, and of itself. Therefore, we conclude that the presumption contained in section 19–6–116 does not deny due process to the appellant.

. . .

NOTES

1. Consider the resolution in *In re Pamela P. v. Frank S.*, 110 Misc.2d 978, 443 N.Y.S.2d 343 (N.Y. Fam. Ct. 1981), where the court found clear and convincing evidence that petitioner falsely told respondent that she was "on the pill." The court concluded:

> . . . [S]ince it is consistent with the support rulings in this State to give weight to petitioner's deceit . . . it is in this court's opinion constitutional to deny her application for child support provided that the basic objective of satisfying the child's fair and reasonable needs nevertheless can be met. Accordingly, under a reasonable and valid accommodation of principles, a support order will be entered against respondent only if petitioner's means are insufficient to answer such need.

110 Misc.2d at 985, 443 N.Y.S.2d at 348. The holding was reversed on appeal, 88 A.D.2d 865, 451 N.Y.S.2d 766 (1982), and affirmed by 59 N.Y.2d 1, 462 N.Y.S.2d 819, 449 N.E.2d 713 (1983). *Accord Hughes v. Hutt*, 500 Pa. 209, 455 A.2d 623 (1983); *Linda D. v. Fritz C.*, 38 Wash.App. 288, 687 P.2d 223 (1984). *Cf. Stephen K. v. Roni L.*, 105 Cal.App.3d 640, 164 Cal.Rptr. 618 (1980) (plaintiff cannot sue defendant in tort for birth of child conceived when he relied on her false representation that contraceptive measures had been taken because "claims such as those presented . . . arise from conduct so intensely private that the courts should not be asked nor attempt to resolve such claims."). *See also Dubay v. Wells*, 506 F.3d 422 (6th Cir. 2007).

2. Concerns about children born out of wedlock have surfaced in the same-sex marriage debates in interesting ways. *See, e.g., Goodridge v. Department of Public Health*, 798 N.E.2d 941, 962–64 (Mass. 2003) (recognizing the constitutional impermissibility of the Commonwealth's exclusion of same-sex couples from marriage, in part, on the grounds of the impact of the exclusion on their children); *see also Morrision v. Sadler*, 2003 WL 23119998 at *6–8 (Ind.Super. 2003) (upholding the state's ban on same-sex marriage as justified, at least in part, on the grounds that heterosexual marriage is necessary to constrain heterosexual male sexuality, hence by extension to avoid illegitimacy). Does the principle that the rights, including the equality rights, of children should not be made to depend upon their parents' marital status imply a general autonomy of children's and adults' rights? Should the rights of same-sex couples to marry be affirmed, even in part, on the grounds of the rights of children to a marital, hence equal, family? Does that tend to undermine or reaffirm the traditional disapprobation against non-marital procreation? Both?

C.   THE EXTENDED FAMILY

Moore v. City of East Cleveland

Supreme Court of the United States, 1977.
431 U.S. 494, 97 S.Ct. 1932, 52 L.Ed.2d 531.

■ JUSTICE POWELL announced the judgment of the Court, and delivered an opinion in which JUSTICE BRENNAN, JUSTICE MARSHALL, and JUSTICE BLACKMUN joined.

East Cleveland's housing ordinance, like many throughout the country, limits occupancy of a dwelling unit to members of a single family. But the ordinance contains an unusual and complicated definitional section that recognizes as a "family" only a few categories of related individuals. § 1341.08.[2] Because her family, living together in her home, fits none of those categories, appellant stands convicted of a criminal offense. The question in this case is whether the ordinance violates the Due Process Clause of the Fourteenth Amendment.

Appellant, Mrs. Inez Moore, lives in her East Cleveland home together with her son, Dale Moore, Sr., and her two grandsons, Dale, Jr., and John Moore, Jr. The two boys are first cousins rather than brothers; we are told that John came to live with his grandmother and with the elder and younger Dale Moores after his mother's death.

In early 1973, Mrs. Moore received a notice of violation from the city, stating that John was an "illegal occupant" and directing her to comply with the ordinance. When she failed to remove him from her home, the city filed a criminal charge. Mrs. Moore moved to dismiss, claiming that the ordinance was constitutionally invalid on its face. Her motion was overruled, and upon conviction she was sentenced to five days in jail and a $25 fine. The Ohio Court of Appeals affirmed after giving full consideration to her constitutional claims, and the Ohio Supreme Court denied review. . . .

---

2.   Section 1341.08 (1966) provides:

" 'Family' means a number of individuals related to the nominal head of the household or to the spouse of the nominal head of the household living as a single housekeeping unit in a single dwelling unit, but limited to the following:

"(a) Husband or wife of the nominal head of the household.

"(b) Unmarried children of the nominal head of the household or of the spouse of the nominal head of the household, provided, however, that such unmarried children have no children residing with them.

"(c) Father or mother of the nominal head of the household or of the spouse of the nominal head of the household.

"(d) Notwithstanding the provisions of subsection (b) hereof, a family may include not more than one dependent married or unmarried child of the nominal head of the household or of the spouse of the nominal head of the household and the spouse and dependent children of such dependent child. For the purpose of this subsection, a dependent person is one who has more than fifty percent of his total support furnished for him by the nominal head of the household and the spouse of the nominal head of the household.

"(e) A family may consist of one individual."

The city argues that our decision in *Village of Belle Terre v. Boraas,* 416 U.S. 1 (1974), requires us to sustain the ordinance attacked here....

But ... [the] ordinance there affected only *unrelated* individuals. It expressly allowed all who were related by "blood, adoption, or marriage" to live together, and in sustaining the ordinance we were careful to note that it promoted "family needs" and "family values." East Cleveland, in contrast, has chosen to regulate the occupancy of its housing by slicing deeply into the family itself. This is no mere incidental result of the ordinance. On its face it selects certain categories of relatives who may live together and declares that others may not. In particular, it makes a crime of a grandmother's choice to live with her grandson in circumstances like those presented here.

When a city undertakes such intrusive regulation of the family, neither *Belle Terre* nor *Euclid* [*v. Amber Realty Co.* 272 U.S. 365 (1926)] governs; the usual judicial deference to the legislature is inappropriate. "This Court has long recognized that freedom of personal choice in matters of marriage and family life is one of the liberties protected by the Due Process Clause of the Fourteenth Amendment." A host of cases, tracing their lineage to *Meyer v. Nebraska,* 262 U.S. 390, 399–401 (1923), and *Pierce v. Society of Sisters,* 268 U.S. 510, 534–535 (1925), have consistently acknowledged a "private realm of family life which the state cannot enter." *Prince v. Massachusetts,* 321 U.S. 158, 166 (1944). Of course, the family is not beyond regulation. But when the government intrudes on choices concerning family living arrangements, this Court must examine carefully the importance of the governmental interests advanced and the extent to which they are served by the challenged regulation.

When thus examined, this ordinance cannot survive. The city seeks to justify it as a means of preventing overcrowding, minimizing traffic and parking congestion, and avoiding an undue financial burden on East Cleveland's school system. Although these are legitimate goals, the ordinance before us serves them marginally, at best.[7] For example, the ordinance permits any family consisting only of husband, wife, and unmarried children to live together, even if the family contains a half dozen licensed drivers, each with his or her own car. At the same time it forbids an adult brother and sister to share a household, even if both faithfully use public transportation. The ordinance would permit a grandmother to live with a single dependent son and children, even if his school-age children number a dozen, yet it forces Mrs. Moore to find another dwelling for her grandson John, simply because of the presence of his uncle and cousin in the same household. We need not labor the point. Section 1341.08 has but a tenuous relation to alleviation of the conditions mentioned by the city.

The city would distinguish the cases based on *Meyer* and *Pierce.* It points out that none of them "gives grandmothers any fundamental rights with respect to grandsons," ... and suggests that any constitutional right to live together as a family extends only to the nuclear family—essentially a couple and their dependent children.

To be sure, these cases did not expressly consider the family relationship presented here. They were immediately concerned with freedom of choice with respect to childbearing, or with the rights of parents to the custody and companionship of their own children, or with traditional parental authority

---

7. It is significant that East Cleveland has another ordinance specifically addressed to the problem of overcrowding. Section 1351.03 limits population density directly, tying the maximum permissible occupancy of a dwelling to the habitable floor area. Even if John, Jr., and his father both remain in Mrs. Moore's household, the family stays well within these limits.

in matters of child rearing and education. But unless we close our eyes to the basic reasons why certain rights associated with the family have been accorded shelter under the Fourteenth Amendment's Due Process Clause, we cannot avoid applying the force and rationale of these precedents to the family choice involved in this case.

. . .

Substantive due process has at times been a treacherous field for this Court. There *are* risks when the judicial branch gives enhanced protection to certain substantive liberties without the guidance of the more specific provisions of the Bill of Rights. As the history of the *Lochner* era demonstrates, there is reason for concern lest the only limits to such judicial intervention become the predilections of those who happen at the time to be Members of this Court. That history counsels caution and restraint. But it does not counsel abandonment, nor does it require what the city urges here: cutting off any protection of family rights at the first convenient, if arbitrary boundary—the boundary of the nuclear family.

Appropriate limits on substantive due process come not from drawing arbitrary lines but rather from careful "respect for the teachings of history [and] solid recognition of the basic values that underlie our society." Our decisions establish that the Constitution protects the sanctity of the family precisely because the institution of the family is deeply rooted in this Nation's history and tradition. It is through the family that we inculcate and pass down many of our most cherished values, moral and cultural.[13]

Ours is by no means a tradition limited to respect for the bonds uniting the members of the nuclear family. The tradition of uncles, aunts, cousins, and especially grandparents sharing a household along with parents and children has roots equally venerable and equally deserving of constitutional recognition.[14] Over the years millions of our citizens have grown up in just such an environment, and most, surely, have profited from it. Even if conditions of modern society have brought about a decline in extended family households, they have not erased the accumulated wisdom of civilization, gained over the centuries and honored throughout our history, that supports a larger conception of the family. Out of choice, necessity, or a sense of family responsibility, it has been common for close relatives to draw together and participate in the duties and the satisfactions of a common home. Decisions concerning child rearing, which [*Wisconsin v.*] *Yoder* [,406 U.S. 205 (1972)], *Meyer, Pierce* and other cases have recognized as entitled to constitutional protection, long have been shared with grandparents or other relatives who occupy the same household—indeed who may take on major responsibility for the rearing of the children. Especially in times of adversity, such as the death of a spouse or economic need, the broader family has tended to come together for mutual sustenance and to maintain or rebuild a secure home life. This is apparently what happened here.[16]

---

13. See generally Wilkinson & White, Constitutional Protection for Personal Lifestyles, 62 Cornell L. Rev. 563, 623–624 (1977).

14. See generally B. Yorburg, The Changing Family (1973); Bronfenbrenner, The Calamitous Decline of the American Family, WASH. POST, Jan. 2, 1977, p. C1. Recent census reports bear out the importance of family patterns other than the prototypical nuclear family. In 1970, 26.5% of all families contained one or more members over 18 years of age, other than the head of household and spouse....

16. We are told that the mother of John Moore, Jr., died when he was less than one year old. He, like uncounted others who have suffered a similar tragedy, then came to live with the

Whether or not such a household is established because of personal tragedy, the choice of relatives in this degree of kinship to live together may not lightly be denied by the State. *Pierce* struck down an Oregon law requiring all children to attend the State's public schools, holding that the Constitution "excludes any general power of the State to standardize its children by forcing them to accept instruction from public teachers only." By the same token the Constitution prevents East Cleveland from standardizing its children—and its adults—by forcing all to live in certain narrowly defined family patterns.

Reversed.

■ JUSTICE BRENNAN, with whom JUSTICE MARSHALL joins, concurring.

. . . I write only to underscore the cultural myopia of the arbitrary boundary drawn by the East Cleveland ordinance in the light of the tradition of the American home that has been a feature of our society since our beginning as a Nation—the "tradition" in the plurality's words, "of uncles, aunts, cousins, and especially grandparents sharing a household along with parents and children. . . ." The line drawn by this ordinance displays a depressing insensitivity toward the economic and emotional needs of a very large part of our society.

In today's America, the "nuclear family" is the pattern so often found in much of white suburbia. J. VANDER ZANDEN, SOCIOLOGY: A SYSTEMATIC APPROACH 322 (3d ed. 1975). The Constitution cannot be interpreted, however, to tolerate the imposition by government upon the rest of us of white suburbia's preference in patterns of family living. The "extended family" that provided generations of early Americans with social services and economic and emotional support in times of hardship, and was the beachhead for successive waves of immigrants who populated our cities, remains not merely still a pervasive living pattern, but under the goad of brutal economic necessity, a prominent pattern—virtually a means of survival—for large numbers of the poor and deprived minorities of our society. For them compelled pooling of scant resources requires compelled sharing of a household.

The "extended" form is especially familiar among black families. We may suppose that this reflects the truism that black citizens, like generations of white immigrants before them, have been victims of economic and other disadvantages that would worsen if they were compelled to abandon extended, for nuclear, living patterns. Even in husband and wife households, 13% of black families compared with 3% of white families include relatives under 18 years old, in addition to the couple's own children. In black households whose head is an elderly woman, as in this case, the contrast is even more striking: 48% of such black households, compared with 10% of counterpart white households, include related minor children not offspring of the head of the household.

I do not wish to be understood as implying that East Cleveland's enforcement of its ordinance is motivated by a racially discriminatory purpose: The record of this case would not support that implication. But the prominence of other than nuclear families among ethnic and racial minority groups, including our black citizens, surely demonstrates that the "extended family" pattern remains a vital tenet of our society. It suffices that in prohibiting this pattern of family living as a means of achieving its objectives,

---

grandmother to provide the infant with a substitute for his mother's care and to establish a more normal home environment.

appellee city has chosen a device that deeply intrudes into family association-al rights that historically have been central, and today remain central, to a large proportion of our population.

■ JUSTICE STEVENS, concurring in the judgment.

. . .

There appears to be no precedent for an ordinance which excludes any of an owner's relatives from the group of persons who may occupy his residence on a permanent basis. Nor does there appear to be any justification for such a restriction of an owner's use of his property. The city has failed totally to explain the need for a rule which would allow a homeowner to have two grandchildren live with her if they are brothers, but not if they are cousins. Since this ordinance has not been shown to have any "substantial relation to the public health, safety, morals, or general welfare" of the city of East Cleveland, and since it cuts so deeply into a fundamental right normally associated with the ownership of residential property—that of an owner to decide who may reside on his or her property—it must fall under the limited standard of review of zoning decisions which this Court preserved in *Euclid*. . . . Under that standard, East Cleveland's unprecedented ordinance constitutes a taking of property without due process and without just compensation.

For these reasons, I concur in the Court's judgment.

■ JUSTICE STEWART, with whom JUSTICE REHNQUIST joins, dissenting.

. . .

In my view, the appellant's claim that the ordinance in question invades constitutionally protected rights of association and privacy is in large part answered by the *Belle Terre* decision. The argument was made there that a municipality could not zone its land exclusively for single-family occupancy because to do so would interfere with protected rights of privacy or associa-tion. We rejected this contention, and held that the ordinance at issue "involve[d] no 'fundamental' right guaranteed by the Constitution, such as . . . the right of association, *NAACP v. Alabama*, 357 U.S. 449; . . . or any rights of privacy, cf. *Griswold v. Connecticut*, 381 U.S. 479; *Eisenstadt v. Baird*, 405 U.S. 438, 453–454." 416 U.S. at 7–8.

The *Belle Terre* decision thus disposes of the appellant's contentions to the extent they focus not on her blood relationships with her sons and grandsons but on more general notions about the "privacy of the home." Her suggestion that every person has a constitutional right permanently to share his residence with whomever he pleases, and that such choices are "beyond the province of legitimate governmental intrusion," amounts to the same argument that was made and found unpersuasive in *Belle Terre*.

To be sure, the ordinance involved in *Belle Terre* did not prevent blood relatives from occupying the same dwelling, and the Court's decision in that case does not, therefore, foreclose the appellant's arguments based specifical-ly on the ties of kinship present in this case. Nonetheless, I would hold, for the reasons that follow, that the existence of those ties does not elevate either the appellant's claim of associational freedom or her claim of privacy to a level invoking constitutional protection.

To suggest that the biological fact of common ancestry necessarily gives related persons constitutional rights of association superior to those of unrelated persons is to misunderstand the nature of the associational freedoms that the Constitution has been understood to protect. Freedom of association has been constitutionally recognized because it is often indispensable to effectuation of explicit First Amendment guarantees. But the scope of the associational right, until now, at least, has been limited to the constitutional need that created it; obviously not every "association" is for First Amendment purposes or serves to promote the ideological freedom that the First Amendment was designed to protect.

The "association" in this case is not for any purpose relating to the promotion of speech, assembly, the press, or religion. And wherever the outer boundaries of constitutional protection of freedom of association may eventually turn out to be, they surely do not extend to those who assert no interest other than the gratification, convenience, and economy of sharing the same residence.

The appellant is considerably closer to the constitutional mark in asserting that the East Cleveland ordinance intrudes upon "the private realm of family life which the state cannot enter." *Prince v. Massachusetts*, 321 U.S. 158, 166. Several decisions of the Court have identified specific aspects of what might broadly be termed "private family life" that are constitutionally protected against state interference.

Although the appellant's desire to share a single-dwelling unit also involves "private family life" in a sense, that desire can hardly be equated with any of the interests protected in the cases just cited. The ordinance about which the appellant complains did not impede her choice to have or not to have children, and it did not dictate to her how her own children were to be nurtured and reared. The ordinance clearly does not prevent parents from living together or living with their unemancipated offspring.

But even though the Court's previous cases are not directly in point, the appellant contends that the importance of the "extended family" in American society requires us to hold that her decision to share her residence with her grandsons may not be interfered with by the State. This decision, like the decisions involved in bearing and raising children, is said to be an aspect of "family life" also entitled to substantive protection under the Constitution. Without pausing to inquire how far under this argument an "extended family" might extend, I cannot agree.[7] When the Court has found that the Fourteenth Amendment placed a substantive limitation on a State's power to regulate, it has been in those rare cases in which the personal interests at issue have been deemed " 'implicit in the concept of ordered liberty.' " The interest that the appellant may have in permanently sharing a single kitchen and a suite of contiguous rooms with some of her relatives simply does not rise to that level. To equate this interest with the fundamental decisions to marry and to bear and raise children is to extend the limited substantive contours of the Due Process Clause beyond recognition.

NOTE

In *Moore*, the plurality opinion found constitutional protection for the extended family. Does this recognition mean that members of the extended family should be

---

7. The opinion of MR. JUSTICE POWELL and MR. JUSTICE BRENNAN's concurring opinion both emphasize the traditional importance of the extended family in American life. But I fail to understand why it follows that the residents of East Cleveland are constitutionally prevented from following what MR. JUSTICE BRENNAN calls the "pattern" of "white suburbia," even though that choice may reflect "cultural myopia." In point of fact, East Cleveland is a predominantly Negro community, with a Negro City Manager and City Commission.

given greater rights in intra-family disputes over such matters as custody disputes, placement of neglected children, or visitation claims?

Troxel v. Granville

Supreme Court of the United States, 2000.
530 U.S. 57, 120 S.Ct. 2054, 147 L.Ed.2d 49.

[The opinion is printed at page 384 *supra*].

Americana Healthcare Center v. Randall

Supreme Court of South Dakota, 1994.
513 N.W.2d 566.

■ AMUNDSON, JUSTICE.

. . .

Appellant Robert Randall (Robert) is the only child of Harry and Juanita Randall. Although he grew up in Aberdeen, Robert has not resided in South Dakota since in 1954. Robert is now a resident of the District of Columbia.

Robert's father died in 1981. Four years after his death, Robert's mother Juanita hired counsel to draft a trust document entitled "Juanita Randall Maintenance Trust Agreement." This irrevocable trust named Juanita as the income beneficiary and Robert as both trustee and residual beneficiary. The trust principal consisted of Juanita's house which was valued at approximately $30,000 and $100,000 in mutual funds. The trust did not grant the trustee authority to invade the principal for the benefit of Juanita. Juanita was ninety-two years old when she executed the trust document in 1985.

Following an accident which required Juanita's hospitalization, Robert came back to Aberdeen and checked into various nursing homes to place his mother. In the fall of 1990, Juanita was admitted to the Arcadia Unit of Americana Healthcare Center (Americana) in Aberdeen, South Dakota. The Arcadia Unit is specifically designed to deal with individuals who possess mental problems such as Alzheimer's disease. Robert completed and signed all the necessary documents under the power of attorney from his mother and made a two-month advance payment to Americana from his mother's checking account. He also listed himself as the person who should be sent the monthly statements from the nursing home.

At that time, in view of Juanita's limited income, Robert discussed the possibility of financial assistance from Medicaid with various Americana personnel. Later that month, Robert completed an application for long-term care medical assistance for Juanita. In November, the South Dakota Department of Social Services (DSS) denied this application because Juanita had not exhausted all of her assets.[1] At the time, Juanita's only assets were the house and mutual funds which had been conveyed to the trust.

Juanita's bill was two months delinquent at the time Americana learned of the rejected Medicaid application. Americana then contacted Robert about his mother's unpaid bills. Because of Juanita's financial position, Robert, as her legal guardian, filed a Chapter 11 bankruptcy on her behalf in the

---

1. In the November 30, 1990, letter of denial, Robert was advised as follows: "Therefore, until you can provide the Department with [more detailed financial information], the application will be rejected, and *you will be responsible for Private pay to the Nursing facility.*" (Emphasis added.)

District of Columbia. The District of Columbia court dismissed this bankruptcy proceeding after Americana refused resolution under bankruptcy. Robert then filed a Chapter 7 bankruptcy petition which was transferred to South Dakota and discharged the Americana bill for Juanita individually and Robert, as her guardian, on October 30, 1991. Meanwhile, Americana filed this suit to collect the unpaid bills.[2]

While Juanita stayed at Americana she received social security payments and income from the trust. While the amount of social security benefits is not shown in this record, Robert estimated that the trust produced about $5000–$6000 income per year. This income was used by Robert to pay legal fees incurred by forming the guardianship, the bankruptcy proceedings and the unsuccessful pursuit of Medicaid benefits.

In June of 1991, Robert was requested to remove his mother from Americana because of the unpaid bills. Despite this request, Juanita remained at Americana until her death on December 8, 1991. At the time of Juanita's death, the unpaid balance for her care was $36,772.30.

Americana notified Robert of his mother's unpaid bills on many occasions. Robert was named as a party to this suit in three capacities: individually, as trustee, and as guardian of the person and estate of Juanita Randall. Americana alleged that Robert had agreed to pay his mother's nursing home bill at the time of her admission to Americana's facility.

Prior to trial, the court granted Robert's motion for summary judgment as to Robert Randall as guardian of the person and estate of Juanita because of the discharge in bankruptcy, but denied summary judgment to Robert Randall individually and as trustee of the Juanita A. Randall Maintenance Trust. At the summary judgment hearing, Americana raised its claim under SDCL 25–7–27 for the first time.[3]

On September 3, 1992, Robert renewed his motion for summary judgment on the additional ground that SDCL 25–7–27 was unconstitutional and requested a continuance. Robert also notified the South Dakota Attorney General that the constitutionality of SDCL 25–7–27 was being challenged. The trial court stated that it was premature to rule on the constitutionality of the statute at that time and denied the continuance.

A court trial was held September 22, 1992. At the conclusion of Americana's case, Robert moved for directed verdict on the grounds that Americana had failed to establish either an oral or written contract to act as guarantor for his mother's nursing home bills. Additionally, Robert requested a directed verdict because Americana failed to submit any evidence regarding his financial ability to pay the nursing home bill pursuant to SDCL 25–7–27. The trial court granted Robert's motion for directed verdict on Americana's claims for liability based on an oral or written contract of guarantee. However, the court denied Robert's motion for directed verdict on the SDCL 25–7–27 claim and allowed Americana to orally amend their

---

2. During this entire time, Americana cared for Juanita without compensation.

3. SDCL 25–7–27 states:

    Every adult child, having the financial ability so to do shall provide necessary food, clothing, shelter or medical attendance for a parent who is unable to provide for himself; provided that no claim shall be made against such adult child until notice has been given such adult child that his parent is unable to provide for himself, and such adult child shall have refused to provide for his parent.

complaint to include the SDCL 25–7527 claim. The trial court found in favor of Americana on its SDCL 25–7–27 claim. This appeal followed.

.   .   .

Was Robert Randall liable for his mother's nursing home bill under SDCL 25–7–27?

.   .   .

At common law, an adult child was not required to support a parent. Such an obligation could only be created by statute. *McCook County v. Kammoss*, 64 N.W. 1123 ([S.D.] 1895); 67A C.J.S. "Parent & Child" '97 (1985). Such statutes trace their beginnings from the Elizabethan Poor Law of 1601 in England. *Swoap v. Superior Court*, 516 P.2d 840, 848 ([Cal.] 1973). South Dakota adopted the current version of SDCL 25–7–27 in 1963.

The North Dakota Supreme Court considered a claim premised on a similar statutory provision in *Bismarck Hospital & Deaconesses Home v. Harris*, 280 N.W. 423 ([N.D.] 1938). That court stated:

> If the person against whom liability is sought to be established refuses to pay for services rendered, an action may be brought against him by such third party. In such action, the plaintiff must establish the kinship of the parties, the financial ability of the person sought to be charged, the indigence of the person to whom relief was furnished, the reasonable value of the services, and that such relief was an immediate necessity.

Id. 280 N.W. at 426.

SDCL 25–7–27 requires an adult child to provide support only when they have the financial ability to do so. Robert claims that this is constitutionally defective because it is unclear when financial ability is to be determined. However, under the facts of this case, a fair reading of the statute shows that the financial ability of the adult child may be determined at any time there is an outstanding debt which has not been barred by the statute of limitations. This certainly seems appropriate where the parent continues to receive care while the child is in control of, and is expending, the parent's assets which are available to pay the debt.

Although Robert could not pay his mother's bills from his own funds, he certainly had the ability to pay after the trust assets had been distributed to him.[4] At trial, it was proven that Robert had received approximately $100,000 in mutual funds from the maintenance trust at his mother's death. Therefore, under the facts of this case, the trial court was correct in holding Robert liable under SDCL 25–7–27.

Does SDCL 25–7–27 deny Robert Randall equal protection of the law?

Robert claims SDCL 25–7–27 violates equal protection because it discriminates against adult children of indigent parents. The trial court held that it did not. Any legislative act is accorded a presumption in favor of constitutionality and that presumption is not overcome until the act is clearly and unmistakably shown beyond a reasonable doubt to violate fundamental constitutional principles. Since Robert challenges the constitutionality of the statute, he bears the burden of proving the act unconstitutional.

.   .   .

---

4. Approximately $30,000 of proceeds from sale of the house have been held in escrow pending disposition of this case.

Under the rational basis test, South Dakota uses a two-pronged analysis when determining whether a statute violates the constitutional right to equal protection under the laws. *Lyons v. Lederle Laboratories*, 440 N.W.2d 769, 771 (S.D.1989). First, does the statute set up arbitrary classifications among various persons subject to it and, second, whether there is a rational relationship between the classification and some legitimate legislative purpose.

When applying the first prong of the *Lyons* test, it is clear that SDCL 25–7–27 does not make an arbitrary classification. Rather, "it is the moral as well as the legal duty in this state, of every child, whether minor or adult, to assist in the support of their indigent aged parents." *Tobin v. Bruce*, 162 N.W. 933, 934 ([S.D.] 1917) (citing Section 118, Civil Code; *McCook County v. Kammoss*, 64 N.W. 1123 ([S.D.] 1895)). An adult child is liable under SDCL 25–7–27 upon the same principle that a parent is liable for necessary support furnished to their child. *Kammoss*, 64 N.W. 1123 [(S.D. 1895)].

Much like the plaintiffs in *Swoap v. Superior Court of Sacramento County*, Robert argues that the only support obligations which are rational are those arising out of a relationship voluntarily entered into. 516 P.2d 840, 851 ([Cal.] 1973). For instance, the obligation to support a child or spouse is at least initially voluntary, therefore, it is rationally based. Robert argues that, since children do not voluntarily enter into the relationship with their parents, it is arbitrary to force this obligation upon them. The fact that a child has no choice in the creation of a relationship with its parents does not per se make this an arbitrary classification. The fact that an indigent parent has supported and cared for a child during that child's minority provides an adequate basis for imposing a duty on the child to support that parent.

Robert also claims that this classification is unconstitutional because it is based on wealth. However, economic-based discrimination has been upheld by this court.

It is certainly reasonable to place a duty to support an indigent parent on that parent's adult child because they are direct lineal descendants who have received the support, care, comfort and guidance of that parent during their minority. If a parent does not qualify for public assistance, who is best suited to meet that parent's needs? It can reasonably be concluded that no other person has received a greater benefit from a parent than that parent's child and it logically follows that the adult child should bear the burden of reciprocating on that benefit in the event a parent needs support in their later years. *Swoap*, 516 P.2d at 851. Consequently, this statute does not establish an arbitrary classification.

The second prong of the test requires a rational relationship between this classification and some legitimate state interest. Clearly, this state has a legitimate interest in providing for the welfare and care of elderly citizens. SDCL 25–7–27 prevents a parent from being thrown out on the street when in need of specialized care. Placing this obligation for support on an adult child is as legitimate as those interests recognized by this court in the past when applying the rational basis test. We have found legitimate state interests to exist under constitutional challenges in the support of children, *Feltman*, 434 N.W.2d 590; balancing the treatment of debtors and creditors, *Accounts Management, Inc.*, 484 N.W.2d 297; education, *Birchfield v. Birchfield*, 417 N.W.2d 891 (S.D.1988); public safety, *Swanson v. Dept. of Commerce & Regulation*, 417 N.W.2d 385 (S.D.1987); preventing the adjudication of stale claims, *Janish v. Murtha*, 285 N.W.2d 708 (S.D.1979); and protecting the citizens from drunk drivers, *State v. Heinrich*, 449 N.W.2d 25 (S.D.1989).

The primary purpose of this statute is to place financial responsibility for indigent parents on their adult children when a parent requires such assistance. Although the legislature repealed similar laws in the past,[5] SDCL 25–7–27 has survived. Therefore, SDCL 25–7–27 serves a legitimate legislative interest, especially under the facts of this case, where indigency was voluntarily created by the trust and there would have been sufficient assets to pay for the parent's care had the trust not been created. Robert has not been denied his right to equal protection under the law.

Does SDCL 25–7–27 deny Robert Randall his right to due process?

Robert argues that SDCL 25–7–27 denies him of the right to due process. In support of his argument, he cites *Commonwealth v. Mong*, 117 N.E.2d 32 ([Ohio] 1954). *Mong* involved an Ohio resident who was not held responsible for the support of his father, a Pennsylvania resident. However, in *Mong*, the adult child was not liable for his indigent parent because Ohio law prohibited a parent who has abandoned their children to later assert their parental right to support from that child. *Id.* 117 N.E.2d at 33.

Robert, a resident of the District of Columbia, argues that Americana cannot enforce the South Dakota support statute against him because the District of Columbia has repealed its parental support statute. Robert has not been denied due process simply because the District of Columbia does not have a support statute similar to South Dakota's. Unlike the situation in *Mong*, District of Columbia does not prohibit an action for support of a parent, it has simply repealed the vehicle for such action in the District of Columbia.

Robert claims a violation of due process exists because the statute forces a nonresident to pay for a resident parent's expenses. Although Robert is not a resident of South Dakota, he has had numerous contacts with the state. He had a power of attorney pertaining to his mother's checking account in Aberdeen, South Dakota. He later became her legal guardian with her residency in South Dakota. As trustee, he held legal title to a house in South Dakota. He visited his mother on several occasions at Americana in Aberdeen. He also maintained a bankruptcy action in the State of South Dakota as guardian for his mother. With these contacts it is obvious that the South Dakota courts have properly asserted jurisdiction over this matter. Residency or, in this case, the lack thereof does not deprive Robert of due process.

Robert also argues that he was denied due process because he was not given notice that "his parent is unable to provide for herself" as required by SDCL 25–7–27. Where the statute contains a notice provision, failure to provide timely notice precludes any claim against an adult child for support of his parent on a due process basis. SDCL 25–7–27 does not specify the manner in which notice shall be given. Therefore, it should be assumed that it must be reasonable notice. . . .

In this case, the evidence indicates that Robert had complete control over his mother's financial affairs. He was notified by Americana on several occasions that his mother's bill remained unpaid. As his mother's guardian, it was Robert's responsibility to provide for his mother's needs including her nursing home bills. Robert's assertion that Americana's notices were given to him only as trustee or guardian and never individually does not withstand

---

5. *See* SDCL 25–7–6, Duty of parents and children to support poor person unable to work—Child's promise to pay for necessaries furnished to parent. Repealed by 1991 S.D.Sess.L. ch. 212. *See also* SDCL 25–7–29, Nonsupport of parent by adult child as misdemeanor—Notice required. Repealed by 1986 S.D.Sess.L. ch. 26, § 5.

scrutiny. Robert had sufficient notice even though Americana did not explicitly state that he was responsible for his mother's expenses. Surely, a sophisticated person such as Robert was aware that his mother's bills were delinquent and Americana was not in the business of providing services free of charge. This court concludes he received constitutionally adequate notice.

. . .

Under the circumstances, Americana furnished care to Juanita Randall relying on the representations made by her son, Robert. Therefore, it ought to be able to recover from the child who had control of the purse strings but chose to expend the assets to avoid the bill rather than pay for his mother's required care. Our conclusion is that given its plain and ordinary meaning, this statute is not unconstitutionally vague and was properly applied in this case.

NOTES

1. Roscoe Pound, *Individual Interests in the Domestic Relations*, 14 MICH. L. REV. 177, 185 (1916):

> In Roman law the duty of children to support parents in case of need, as a duty of gratitude and piety, was turned from a moral duty into a legal duty during the stage of equity and natural law. From the time of the empire this duty and the corresponding duty of the parent with respect to children, as duties of piety, were enforceable *extra ordinem* as legal duties. The principle of reciprocal duties of support on the part of ascendants and descendants passed from the civil law into the modern codes and is universally recognized in the Roman–law world. In the Anglo–American system the court of chancery did not take hold of this subject and it was left to modern legislation which is by no means universal.

2. "[The parents, grandparents, and the children of] everie poore olde blind lame and impotente person, or other poore person not able to worke, beinge of a sufficient abilitie, shall at their owne Chardges relieve and maintaine everie suche poore person, in that manner and according to that rate, as by the Justices of the Peace of that Countie where suche sufficient persons dwell, or the greater number of them, at their generall Quarter Sessions shall be assessed; upon paine that everie one of them shall forfeite twenty shillings for everie monthe which they shall faile therein." Jacobus tenBroek, *California's Dual System of Family Law: Its Origin, Development, and Present Status, Part I*, 16 STAN. L. REV. 257, 283 (1964) (quoting 43 Eliz. 1, c. 2, § VI (1601)). Similar statutes found ready acceptance in the American colonies. See generally, Stephan A. Riesenfeld, *The Formative Era of American Public Assistance Law*, 43 CAL. L. REV. 175 (1955).

3. As of 2011, twenty-eight states have filial responsibility statutes. Four states' laws carry criminal and civil penalties, sixteen only civil, and eight only criminal penalties.[1] For more discussion, see Shannon Frank Edelstone, *Filial Responsibility: Can The Legal Duty to Support Our Parents Be Legally Enforced?*, 36 FAM. L. Q. 501 (2002); Seymour

---

1. The four states with laws carrying criminal and civil penalties are: CAL. FAM. CODE § 4400; CONN. GEN. STAT. § 46B–215; IND. CODE § 31–16–17–1; MONT. CODE ANN. § 40–6–301. The sixteen states with laws that carry only civil penalties are: ALASKA STAT. §§ 25.20.030, 47.25.230; ARK. CODE ANN. § 20–47–106; DEL. CODE ANN. TIT. 13 § 503; GA. CODE ANN. § 36–12–3; IDAHO CODE ANN. § 32–1002; LA. REV. STAT. ANN. § 13:4731; LA. CIV. CODE ANN. ART. 229; MISS. CODE ANN. § 43–31–25; NEV. REV. STAT. § 428.070; N.H. REV. STAT. ANN. §§ 167:2, 546–A:2; N.D. CENT. CODE § 14–09–10; OR. REV. STAT. § 109.010; 23 PA. CONS. STAT. § 4603(C); S.D. COD. LAWS § 25–7–27; TENN. CODE ANN. § 71–5–115; UTAH CODE ANN. § 17–14–2; W.VA. CODE § 9–5–9. The eight states with laws that carry only criminal penalties are: KY. REV. STAT. ANN. § 530.050; MD. CODE ANN., FAM. LAW §§ 13–101; MASS. GEN. LAWS CH. 273, § 20; N.C. GEN. STAT. § 14–326.1; OHIO REV. CODE ANN. § 2919.2; R.I. GEN. LAWS §§ 15–10–1, 40–5–13; VT. STAT. ANN. TIT. 15, § 202; VA. CODE ANN. § 20–88.

Moskowitz, *Filial Responsibility Statutes: Legal and Policy Considerations*, 9 J.L. & POL'Y 709 (2001).

4. Does the legal treatment of the extended family offer a useful model for thinking about the legal treatment of domestic workers, or at least those who undertake significant caretaking, including child rearing, responsibilities? Are they part of the extended family in ways that might entitle them to the rights and privileges that status can afford? Does the fact they work for families suggest they should not receive the usual labor and employment rights that non-domestic workers are accorded, perhaps because of how those rights might disrupt familial privacy or repose? Should domestic workers be seen instead as workers who simply happen to work in someone else's home? How might the choice of legal rules applied to them—or not applied to them—impact their own families, and with what sorts of consequences? For some relevant materials, see 2010 N.Y. SESS. LAW CH. 481; Gabrielle Meagher, *Is It Wrong to Pay for Housework?*, 17 HYPATIA 55 (2002); Mary Romero, *Unraveling Privilege: Workers' Children and The Hidden Costs of Paid Childcare*, 76 CHI.-KENT L. REV. 1651 (2001); Katharine Silbaugh, *Turning Labor into Love: Housework and the Law*, 91 NW. U. L. REV. 1, 72–79 (1996).

D. GROUPS

Village of Belle Terre v. Boraas

Supreme Court of the United States, 1974.
416 U.S. 1, 94 S.Ct. 1536, 39 L.Ed.2d 797.

■ JUSTICE DOUGLAS delivered the opinion of the Court.

Belle Terre is a village on Long Island's north shore of about 220 homes inhabited by 700 people. Its total land area is less than one square mile. It has restricted land use to one-family dwellings excluding lodging houses, boarding houses, fraternity houses, or multiple-dwelling houses. The word "family" as used in the ordinance means "[o]ne or more persons related by blood, adoption, or marriage, living and cooking together as a single housekeeping unit, exclusive of household servants. A number of persons but not exceeding two (2) living and cooking together as a single housekeeping unit though not related by blood, adoption, or marriage shall be deemed to constitute a family."

Appellees (Dickmans) are owners of a house in the village and leased it in December, 1971 for a term of 18 months to Michael Truman. Later Bruce Boraas became a colessee. Then Anne Parish moved into the house along with three others. These six are students at nearby State University at Stony Brook and none is related to the other by blood, adoption, or marriage....

This case brings to this Court a different phase of local zoning regulations than we have previously reviewed. *Euclid v. Ambler Realty Co.,* 272 U.S. 365, involved a zoning ordinance classifying land use in a given area into six categories....

The Court sustained the zoning ordinance under the police power of the State, saying that the line "which in this field separates the legitimate from the illegitimate assumption of power is not capable of precise delimitation...."

The main thrust of the case in the mind of the Court was in the exclusion of industries and apartments and as respects that it commented on the desire to keep residential areas free of "disturbing noises"; "increased traffic"; the hazard of "moving and parked automobiles"; the "depriving children of the privilege of quiet and open spaces for play, enjoyed by those in more favored localities." *Id.* at 394. The ordinance was sanctioned because the validity of the legislative classification was "fairly debatable" and therefore could not be said to be wholly arbitrary.

. . .

The present ordinance is challenged on several grounds: that it interferes with a person's right to travel; that it interferes with the right to immigrate to and settle within a State; that it bars people who are uncongenial to the present residents; that it expresses the social preferences of the residents for groups that will be congenial to them; that social homogeneity is not a legitimate interest of government; that the restriction of those whom the neighbors do not like trenches on the newcomers' rights of privacy; that it is of no rightful concern to villagers whether the residents are married or unmarried; that the ordinance is antithetical to the Nation's experience, ideology and self-perception as an open, egalitarian, and integrated society.

We find none of these reasons in the record before us. It is not aimed at transients. It involves no procedural disparity inflicted on some but not on others. It involves no "fundamental" right guaranteed by the Constitution. . . . We deal with economic and social legislation where legislatures have historically drawn lines which we respect against the charge of violation of the Equal Protection Clause if the law be "reasonable, not arbitrary" and bears "a rational relationship to a [permissible] state objective." *Reed v. Reed,* 404 U.S. 71, 76.

It is said, however, that if two unmarried people can constitute a "family," there is no reason why three or four may not. But every line drawn by a legislature leaves some out that might well have been included. That exercise of discretion, however, is a legislative not a judicial function.

It is said that the Belle Terre ordinance reeks with an animosity to unmarried couples who live together. There is no evidence to support it; and the provision of the ordinance bringing within the definition of a "family" two unmarried people belies the charge.

The ordinance places no ban on other forms of association, for a "family" may, so far as the ordinance is concerned, entertain whomever they like.

The regimes of boarding houses, fraternity houses, and the like present urban problems. More people occupy a given space; more cars rather continuously pass by; more cars are parked; noise travels with crowds.

A quiet place where yards are wide, people few, and motor vehicles restricted are legitimate guidelines in a land use project addressed to family needs. . . . The police power is not confined to elimination of filth, stench, and unhealthy places. It is ample to lay out zones where family values, youth values, and the blessings of quiet seclusion, and clean air make the area a sanctuary for people.

. . .

Reversed.

■ JUSTICE MARSHALL, dissenting.

. . . In my view, the disputed classification burdens the students' fundamental rights of association and privacy guaranteed by the First and Fourteenth Amendments. Because the application of strict equal protection scrutiny is therefore required, I am at odds with my Brethren's conclusion that the ordinance may be sustained on a showing that it bears a rational relationship to the accomplishment of legitimate governmental objectives.

. . .

My disagreement with the Court today is based upon my view that the ordinance in this case unnecessarily burdens appellees' First Amendment freedom of association and their constitutionally guaranteed right to privacy. Our decisions establish that the First and Fourteenth Amendments protect the freedom to choose one's associates. Constitutional protection is extended not only to modes of association that are political in the usual sense, but also to those that pertain to the social and economic benefit of the members. The selection of one's living companions involves similar choices as to the emotional, social, or economic benefits to be derived from alternative living arrangements.

The freedom of association is often inextricably entwined with the constitutionally guaranteed right of privacy. The right to "establish a home" is an essential part of the liberty guaranteed by the Fourteenth Amendment. *Meyer v. Nebraska*, 262 U.S. 390, 399 (1923). And the Constitution secures to an individual a freedom "to satisfy his intellectual and emotional needs within the privacy of his own home." Constitutionally protected privacy is, in Mr. Justice Brandeis' words, "as against the government, the right to be let alone . . . the right most valued by civilized man." *Olmstead v. United States*, 277 U.S. 438, 478 (1928) (dissenting opinion). The choice of household companions—of whether a person's "intellectual and emotional needs" are best met by living with family, friends, professional associates or others—involves deeply personal considerations as to the kind and quality of intimate relationships within the home. . . .

The instant ordinance discriminates on the basis of just such a personal lifestyle choice as to household companions. It permits any number of persons related by blood or marriage, be it two or twenty, to live in a single household, but it limits to two the number of unrelated persons bound by profession, love, friendship, religious or political affiliation or mere economics who can occupy a single home. Belle Terre imposes upon those who deviate from the community norm in their choice of living companions significantly greater restrictions than are applied to residential groups who are related by blood or marriage, and comprise the established order with the community. The village has, in effect, acted to fence out those individuals whose choice of lifestyle differs from that of its current residents.

This is not a case where the Court is being asked to nullify a township's sincere efforts to maintain its residential character by preventing the operation of rooming houses, fraternity houses or other commercial or high-density residential uses. Unquestionably, a town is free to restrict such uses. Moreover, as a general proposition, I see no constitutional infirmity in a town's limiting the density of use in residential areas by zoning regulations which do not discriminate on the basis of constitutionally suspect criteria. This ordinance, however, limits the density of occupancy of only those homes occupied by unrelated persons. It thus reaches beyond control of the use of land or the density of population and undertakes to regulate the way people choose to associate with each other within the privacy of their own homes.

. . .

A variety of justifications have been proffered in support of the village's ordinance. It is claimed that the ordinance controls population density, prevents noise, traffic and parking problems, and preserves the rent structure of the community and its attractiveness to families. As I noted earlier, these are all legitimate and substantial interests of government. But I think it clear that the means chosen to accomplish these purposes are both overinclusive and underinclusive, and that the asserted goals could be as effectively achieved by means of an ordinance that did not discriminate on the basis of constitutionally protected choices of life style. The ordinance imposes no restriction whatsoever on the number of persons who may live in a house, as long as they are related by marital or sanguinary bonds—presumably no matter how distant their relationship. Nor does the ordinance restrict the number of income earners who may contribute to rent in such a household, or the number of automobiles that may be maintained by its occupants. In that sense the ordinance is underinclusive. On the other hand, the statute restricts the number of unrelated persons who may live in a home to no more than two. It would therefore prevent three unrelated people from occupying a dwelling even if among them they had but one income and no vehicles. While an extended family of a dozen or more might live in a small bungalow, three elderly and retired persons could not occupy the large manor house next door. Thus the statute is also grossly overinclusive to accomplish its intended purposes.

There are some 220 residences in Belle Terre occupied by about 700 persons. The density is therefore just above three per household. The village is justifiably concerned with density of population and the related problems of noise, traffic, and the like. It could deal with those problems by limiting each household to a specified number of adults, two or three perhaps, without limitation on the number of dependent children. The burden of such an ordinance would fall equally upon all segments of the community. It would surely be better tailored to the goals asserted by the township than the ordinance before us today, for it would more realistically restrict population density and growth and their attendant environmental costs. Various other statutory mechanisms also suggest themselves as solutions to Belle Terre's problems—rent control, limits on the number of vehicles per household, and so forth, but, of course, such schemes are matters of legislative judgment and not for this Court. Appellants also refer to the necessity of maintaining the family character of the village. There is not a shred of evidence in the record indicating that if Belle Terre permitted a limited number of unrelated persons living together, the residential, familial character of the community would be fundamentally affected.

By limiting unrelated households to two persons while placing no limitation on households of related individuals, the village has embarked upon its commendable course in a constitutionally faulty vessel. I would find the challenged ordinance unconstitutional. But I would not ask the village to abandon its goal of providing quiet streets, little traffic, and a pleasant and reasonably priced environment in which families might raise their children. Rather, I would commend the village to continue to pursue those purposes but by means of more carefully drawn and even-handed legislation.

NOTE

For discussion built on a more comprehensive theoretical framework that in important ways aligns with Justice Marshall's opinion, see John Rawls, *The Idea of Public Reason Revisited*, 73 U. CHI. L. REV. 765 (1997). *See also* SUSAN MOLLER OKIN, JUSTICE, GENDER, AND THE FAMILY (1991).

Penobscot Area Housing Development Corp. v. City of Brewer

Supreme Judicial Court of Maine, 1981.
434 A.2d 14.

■ NICHOLS, JUSTICE.

. . .

The Penobscot Area Housing Development Corporation is a private, nonprofit Maine corporation, recently organized to provide housing for retarded citizens. For that purpose it has negotiated a purchase and sale agreement to acquire a house and lot in a district of the City of Brewer which is zoned for low density single family residential use under the City's zoning ordinance. The Corporation applied to the City's code enforcement officer for an occupancy certificate and described the proposed use as "group home for six adults or older minors, which group home would be licensed as a Boarding Home by the State." The Corporation intended to use the property as a group home for six retarded persons who would be supervised by "approximately two" full-time employees. The Brewer Code Enforcement Officer, William L. Wetherbee, denied the occupancy permit because he concluded the Corporation's proposed use did "not meet the terms of the City of Brewer's zoning ordinance as a single family." ... [T]he Corporation appealed to the City's Board of Appeals. The Board of Appeals ... affirmed Wetherbee's decision that the proposed use could not be classified as a single family use under the ordinance.

From the Board of Appeal's decision, the Corporation sought review of that decision by the Superior Court (Kennebec County)....

. . .

The Plaintiffs ... challenge the Superior Court's affirmance of the Board's construction and application of a section of the Brewer Zoning Ordinance providing for districts in which low density, single family residential uses were favored. *Brewer Zoning Ordinance*, Art. 3, § 302. Another section of the ordinance explicitly defined family:

"FAMILY" is a single individual doing his own cooking, and living upon the premises as a separate housekeeping unit, or a collective body of persons doing their own cooking and living together upon the premises as a separate housekeeping unit in a domestic relationship based upon birth, marriage or other domestic bond as distinguished from a group occupying a boarding house, lodging house, club, fraternity or hotel.

Brewer Zoning Ordinance, Art. 1, § 101. After a hearing, the Brewer Board of Appeals concluded that the proposed group home for retarded persons did not meet the definition of family in the ordinance....

Construction of zoning ordinances is a legal determination. On appeal ..., the reviewing court's function is to determine only whether the decision of the Board of Appeals was unlawful, arbitrary, capricious, or unreasonable. In reviewing the ordinance before us, we note at the threshold that relationships other than those based on blood or law, i.e., founded on birth or marriage, are included in the definition of family. Relationships based upon "other domestic bond[s]" satisfy the ordinance as well.

The Plaintiffs' principal argument appears to be that the interpretation of the ordinance by the Board and its affirmance by the Superior Court placed undue emphasis on the role of the staff and ignored the fact that the plain purpose of the group home was to create a family environment for the residents. The requirement of a domestic bond, the Plaintiffs argue, would have been met by the relationship forged among the residents themselves as they lived and worked together. As authority for their position, the Plaintiffs cite several decisions from other jurisdictions in which similar definitions of family have been construed to include group homes. We reject the Plaintiffs' argument. Read in context with the definition as a whole, the concept of "domestic bond" implies the existence of a traditional family-like structure of household authority. Such a structure would include one or more resident authority figures charged with the responsibility of maintaining a separate housekeeping unit and regulating the activity and duties of the other residents. In so doing, this resident authority figure serves legitimate zoning interests of a community by stabilizing and coordinating household activity in a way that is consistent with family values and a family style of life.

Concerning the structure of authority at the proposed group home as it relates to the existence of a domestic bond, the Board found that although a staff would be employed by the Corporation for the purposes of maintaining a home for six retarded adults, staff members would not necessarily reside at the home; rather, the Board's findings suggested the staff would serve on a rotating basis. Thus, a central figure of authority residing on the premises similar to a parent or parents in a traditional family setting was clearly absent in the group home proposal tendered by these Plaintiffs.

As the Superior Court observed, the absence of a resident authority figure in the Corporation's proposal clearly distinguishes this case from cases cited by the Plaintiffs in which the definition of family was held to include group homes. See *Oliver v. Zoning Commission of Town of Chester,* [326 A.2d 841 (Conn.Super.Ct. 1974)] (resident houseparents for 10 retarded adolescents); *Group House of Port Washington, Inc. v. Board of Zoning,* [380 N.E.2d 207 (N.Y. 1978)] (resident surrogate parents for seven children). As such, evidence of a central component of the domestic bond concept was deficient. Indeed, where the domestic bond is not based on a biological or legal relationship among the residents, the importance of a relatively permanent, resident authority figure to the existence of a domestic bond may be particularly significant.

Like relationships founded on marriage or birth, the notion of domestic bond also connotes a quality of cohesiveness and permanence in the relationship of residents greater than that which typically exists among boarders, members of a fraternity or club, or hotel guests. The language of the definition itself clearly suggests the comparison is appropriate. Relevant to the potential for cohesiveness and permanence in the relationships developed at the home, the Board of Appeals found that the residents would not control "the choice of who the incoming residents would be nor when other residents would leave." Some residents would ultimately be transferred to foster homes. The Board of Appeals further found that the average stay of a resident would be one to one and one-half years. These facts are not consistent with the development of permanent and cohesive relationships among the residents, especially in the absence of a resident authority figure. Accordingly, the bond between the residents may well more resemble the relationship among boarders, club or fraternity members, whose exclusion from single family districts has been upheld in other jurisdictions.

Finally, the definition of family further specifies that the persons comprising the collective should not only be living together in a relationship founded on a domestic bond but should be "doing their *own* cooking and living together upon the premises as a *separate* housekeeping unit." *Brewer*

Zoning Ordinance, Art. 1 § 101 (emphasis supplied). The Board found that the Corporation and its rotating staff would plan and manage the activities of the residents. Further, staff members were to be responsible for preparing meals and providing "some cleaning and other services." The Board of Appeals could reasonably have concluded that such an arrangement would not comply with the requirement of the ordinance that the residents do their own cooking as a separate housekeeping unit. Indeed, as the decisions of other courts suggest, extensive outside aid in the management and operation of a household detracts from the family nature of the home.

In light of the definitional specifications of the Brewer ordinance reviewed above, we conclude that the decision rendered by the Board of Appeals and affirmed by the Superior Court was clearly reasonable and adequately supported by factual findings of record. The Board could reasonably have decided not only that the Corporation's proposal failed to meet the definitional criteria of a domestic bond but that it failed to satisfy more concrete specifications of the ordinance as well. While the purpose of such homes is laudable and, while the promise they hold for the retarded is heartening we decline to interpret and apply local zoning ordinances by abandoning relatively objective standards of evaluation in favor of a judicial approach that requires an intimate evaluation of a home's purpose and effect in each case. If, as these Plaintiffs contend, the problem of locating group homes is pervasive in this state, legislative, not judicial, action may be most appropriate.

Borough of Glassboro v. Vallorosi

Supreme Court of New Jersey, 1990.
568 A.2d 888.

■ PER CURIAM.

The narrow issue presented in this case is whether a group of ten unrelated college students living in defendants' home constitutes a "family" within the definition of a restrictive zoning ordinance. The Borough of Glassboro concedes that a primary purpose of the ordinance was to prevent groups of unrelated college students from living together in the Borough's residential districts. The ordinance limits residence in such districts to stable and permanent "single housekeeping units" that constitute either a "traditional family unit" or its functional equivalent. The Chancery Division concluded that the relationship among this group of students and their living arrangements within the home demonstrated the "generic character" of a family, and denied the Borough injunctive relief. The Appellate Division affirmed. We now affirm the judgment of the Appellate Division.

In July 1986, the Borough amended its zoning ordinance, apparently in response to a rowdy weekend celebration by Glassboro State College students. The amendment applied to the Borough's residential districts and limited the use and occupancy of "detached dwellings" and structures with "two dwelling units" to "families" only. The ordinance defined a "family" as

> one or more persons occupying a dwelling unit as a single non-profit housekeeping unit, who are living together as a stable and permanent living unit, being a traditional family unit or the functional equivalency [sic] thereof. [Glassboro, N.J., Code § 107–3 (1986).]

The amendment included a statement of purpose that plainly reflected the Borough's intention to confine college students either to the dormitories provided by Glassboro State College or to the other zoning districts that permit apartments and townhouses. . . .

In June 1986, defendants purchased a home located in the restricted residential zone. The purchase was intended to provide a college home for Peter Vallorosi, the brother of defendant Diane Vallorosi and the son of two partners in S & V Associates, a real-estate investment partnership. (Under the partnership agreement, S & V Associates acquired equitable title to the premises when defendants purchased the home.) It was contemplated that nine of Peter's friends would share the house with him while the group attended Glassboro State College. Seven of the ten students renting the house were sophomores at the time their lease took effect. They were all between the ages of eighteen and twenty. All ten students entered into separate, renewable leases for a semester-long period of four months. At the end of each semester, a student could renew the lease for another term "if the house is found to be in order at [the] end of [the preceding] term."

The students moved into their new home in early September 1986. The house had one large kitchen, which was shared by all ten students. The students often ate meals together in small groups, cooked for each other, and generally shared the household chores, grocery shopping, and yard work. A common checking account paid for food and other bills. They shared the use of a telephone. Although uncertain of living arrangements after graduation, the students intended to remain tenants as long as they were enrolled at Glassboro State College.

The Borough commenced this action in September 1986, seeking an injunction against the use and occupancy of the house by the students. The complaint alleged that the occupants did not constitute a "family" as defined in the Borough's ordinance. Defendants contended that the amendment to the zoning ordinance was not authorized by the Municipal Land Use Law, N.J.S.A. 40:55D–1 to –112, and violated the New Jersey Constitution in that it regulated a class of people rather than a use of property. . . .

The Chancery Division upheld the constitutionality of the ordinance, but . . . concluded that the relationship among the students "shows stability, permanency and can be described as the functional equivalent of a family." The Appellate Division affirmed on the basis of the trial court's analysis.

. . .

The legal principles determinative of this appeal are clear and well-settled. The courts of this state have consistently invalidated zoning ordinances intended "to cure or prevent . . . anti-social conduct in dwelling situations." *Kirsch Holding Co. v. Borough of Manasquan*, [281 A.2d 513, 519 (N.J. 1971)]. . . .

In *Kirsch Holding Co. v. Borough of Manasquan*, we invalidated ordinances in two shore communities that restrictively defined "family" and prohibited seasonal rentals by unrelated persons. We held that the challenged ordinances "preclude so many harmless dwelling uses . . . that they must be held to be so sweepingly excessive, and therefore legally unreasonable, that they must fall in their entirety." . . .

In *Berger v. State*, [364 A.2d 993 (N.J. 1976)], we expressed our agreement with the principle that "[t]he concept of a one family dwelling is based upon its character as a single housekeeping unit." A significant issue in *Berger* was the validity of a restrictive zoning ordinance limiting the definition of family to "persons related by blood, marriage or adoption. . . ." The challenged use was a group home for eight to twelve multi-handicapped, pre-school children who would reside in a twelve-room ocean-front house with a married couple experienced as foster parents. Staff hired by the New Jersey Department of Institutions and Agencies would provide support services but would not reside on the premises. We concluded that the State's proposed use of the premises was reasonable and thus immune from regulation by the local zoning ordinance. We also found the ordinance invalid by virtue of N.J.S.A. 40:55–33.2 (since repealed and replaced by N.J.S.A. 40:55D–66c), which prohibited municipalities from discriminating in zoning ordinances between children related to occupants of single-family dwellings by blood, marriage, or adoption, and children residing in such dwellings by virtue of placement in a "group home." Finally, we held that an ordinance limiting the term "family" to persons related by blood, marriage, or adoption cannot "satisfy the demands of due process." Such an ordinance

> so narrowly delimits the persons who may occupy a single family dwelling as to prohibit numerous potential occupants who pose no threat to the style of family living sought to be preserved.

Accordingly, we expressed our clear preference for zoning provisions that equated the term "single family" with a "single housekeeping unit."

. . .

Thus, our cases preclude municipalities from adopting zoning regulations that unreasonably distinguish between residential occupancy by unrelated persons in comparison with occupancy by individuals related by blood, marriage, or adoption. Our decisions permit zoning regulations to restrict uses in certain residential zones to single housekeeping units. But the standard for determining whether a use qualifies as a single housekeeping unit must be functional, and hence capable of being met by either related or unrelated persons.

. . .

Although the Public Advocate, as *amicus*, challenges the constitutionality of the Glassboro ordinance, we need not consider that issue, nor the issues raised in the cross-petition, in the context of this record. The narrow issue before us is whether there is sufficient credible evidence in this record to sustain the trial court's factual finding that the occupancy of defendants' dwelling by these ten college students constituted a single housekeeping unit as defined by the Glassboro ordinance.

In view of the unusual circumstances of this case, we find adequate evidence to uphold the Law Division's ruling. The uncontradicted testimony reflects a plan by ten sophomore college students to live together for three years under conditions that correspond substantially to the ordinance's requirement of a "stable and permanent living unit." To facilitate the plan, the house had been purchased by relatives of one of the students. The students ate together, shared household chores, and paid expenses from a common fund. Although the students signed four-month leases, the leases were renewable if the house was "in order" at the end of the term. Moreover, the students testified to their intention to remain in the house throughout college, and there was no significant evidence of defections up to the time of trial. As noted above, the students' occupancy ended in September 1988 because of Peter Vallorosi's post-trial withdrawal from college.

It is a matter of common experience that the costs of college and the variables characteristic of college life and student relationships do not readily lead to the formation of a household as stable and potentially durable as the one described in this record. On these facts, however, we cannot quarrel with the Law Division's conclusion that the occupancy at issue here "shows stability, permanency and can be described as the functional equivalent of a family."

It also bears repetition that noise and other socially disruptive behavior are best regulated outside the framework of municipal zoning. As we observed in *State v. Baker*, [405 A.2d 368 (N.J. 1979)]:

> Other legitimate municipal concerns can be dealt with similarly. Traffic congestion can appropriately be remedied by reasonable, evenhanded limitations upon the number of cars which may be maintained at a given residence. Moreover, area-related occupancy restrictions will, by decreasing density, tend by themselves to reduce traffic problems. Disruptive behavior—which, of course, is not limited to unrelated households—may properly be controlled through the use of the general police power. As we stated in *Kirsch v. Borough of Manasquan, supra*:

> > Ordinarily obnoxious personal behavior can best be dealt with officially by vigorous and persistent enforcement of general police power ordinances and criminal statutes.... Zoning ordinances are not intended and cannot be expected to cure or prevent most anti-social conduct in dwelling situations. [281 A.2d at 519.]

Judgment affirmed.

NOTES

1. What distinguished the ten college students from the *Penobscot* group home residents? Are any of these distinctions relevant to the purposes of the zoning statutes? The *Penobscot* court emphasized the lack of any permanent, resident authority figure in the community home who would act in the role of a parent. Do you think it should be relevant that a group is organized under a single "head?" That they are held together by a common purpose? Do most traditional families fit these descriptions? Consider *Crane Neck Association v. NYC/Long Island County Services Group*, 92 A.D.2d 119, 460 N.Y.S.2d 69 (1983), where the court ruled that the establishment of a community residence for mentally disabled adults living with a full-time staff who set up programs and taught basic skills, similar to the program in *Penobscot*, did not violate zoning provisions limiting use to single family dwellings.

2. The membership turnover in the *Penobscot* group home appears to have influenced the court's decision. Is the stability of a group arrangement relevant? If so, could a community exclude young couples because they have the highest rate of divorce?

3. In *Kirsch v. Prince George's County*, 331 Md. 89, 626 A.2d 372 (1993), the Court of Appeals of Maryland held that a zoning ordinance imposing stricter requirements on landlords renting to college students than to others denied the students equal protection of laws under the Fourteenth Amendment. The court's reasoning relied in part on the precedent provided by *Belle Terre*. Cf. also *Tyler v. College Park*, 415 Md. 475 (2010).

ROSABETH MOSS KANTER, COMMITMENT AND COMMUNITY: COMMUNES AND UTOPIAS IN SOCIOLOGICAL PERSPECTIVE

1–4 (2005).

Utopia is the imaginary society in which humankind's deepest yearnings, noblest dreams, and highest aspirations come to fulfillment, where all physical, social, and spiritual forces work together, in harmony, to permit the attainment of everything people find necessary and desirable. In the imagined utopia, people work and live together closely and cooperatively, in a social order that is self-created and self-chosen rather than externally imposed, yet one that also operates according to a higher order of natural and spiritual laws. Utopia is held together by commitment rather than coercion, for in utopia what people want to do is the same as what they have to do; the interests of the individuals are congruent with the interests of the group; and personal growth and freedom entail responsibility for others. Underlying the vision of utopia is the assumption that harmony, cooperation, and mutuality of interests are natural to human existence, rather than conflict, competition, and exploitation, which arise only in imperfect societies. By providing material and psychological safety and security, the utopian social order eliminates the need for divisive competition or self-serving actions which elevate some people to the disadvantage of others; it ensures instead the flowering of mutual responsibility and trust, to the advantage of all.

Utopia, then, represents an ideal of the good, to contrast with the evils and ills of existing societies. The idea of utopia suggests a refuge from the troubles of this world as well as a hope for a better one. Utopian plans are partly an escape, as critics maintain, and partly a new creation, partly a flight *from* and partly a seeking *for*; they criticize, challenge, and reject the established order, then depart from it to seek the perfect human existence.

At a number of times in history, groups of people have decided that the ideal can become reality, and they have banded together in communities to bring about the fulfillment of their own utopian aspirations. Generally the idea of utopia has involved a way of life shared with others—and shared in such a way that the benefit of all is ensured.

. . .

The ideal of social unity has led to the formation of numerous communes and utopian communities. These are voluntary, value-based, communal social orders. Because members choose to join and choose to remain, conformity within the community is based on commitment—on the individual's own desire to obey its rules—rather than force or coercion ... A commune seeks self-determination, often making its own laws and refusing to obey some of those set by the larger society. It is identifiable as an entity, for it has a physical location and a way of distinguishing between members and nonmembers. It intentionally implements a set of values, having been planned in order to bring about the attainment of certain ideals, and its operating decisions are made in terms of those values. All other goals are secondary and related to ends involving harmony, brotherhood, mutual support, and value expression. These ideals give rise to the key communal arrangement, the sharing of resources and finances.

. . .

The United States, in particular, has been the site for the founding of hundreds—possibly thousands—of utopian communities, from religious sects that retreated to the wilderness as early as 1680, to the vast numbers of communes today. . . .

The religious utopians criticized the evil and immorality of the surrounding society, which placed barriers between man and God, holding that a perfect society, in close touch with fundamental truths, was immediately possible for believers. . . . A major theme was the possibility of human perfection through conversion to the more spiritual life offered by the utopia. John Humphrey Noyes began a group in Putney, Vermont in the late 1830s dedicated to Perfectionist ideals, which were to be implemented through complete sharing of beliefs, property, and sexual life; this group grew into the Oneida Community (1848–1881) [in New York state]. He believed that the individual soul could come into direct contact with God and that through conversion it could free itself from the sins of the existing world.

WILLIAM M. KEPHART, THE FAMILY, SOCIETY AND THE INDIVIDUAL
121–41 (1977).

. . .

Starting ... as a small group—no more than 20 or 30 persons in all— the Oneida Colony was barely able to survive the first few winters. The original members were primarily farmers and mechanics, and while their collectivist economy had certain advantages, they found it difficult to support a growing community solely from their land yields. Fortunately, one of their members, Sewell Newhouse, invented a steel trap, which turned out to be peerless in design. Demand for the product grew, and soon the major part of the Oneida economy came to be based on the manufacture of the now-famous traps. Thereafter, the group was without financial worry.

SOCIAL ORGANIZATION

What was there, in terms of social organization, that held the Oneida Community together in the face of both internal problems and external pressures? One integrating element was the fact that practically the entire membership was housed under one roof. Although, over the years, there were six different branches and hundreds of members, the Perfectionists' home base was at Oneida, New York. It was there that the original communal home was built in 1849, to be replaced in 1862 by a spacious brick building known as the Mansion House. In subsequent years, as the membership grew, wings were added as needed. The building still stands, a striking architectural form internally as well as externally.

. . .

Although each adult had a small room of his or her own, the building was designed to encourage a feeling of togetherness, hence the inclusion of a communal dining hall, recreation rooms, library, concert hall, outdoor picnic area, etc. It was in the Big Hall of the Mansion House that John Humphrey Noyes gave his widely quoted home talks. It was here that musical concerts, dramas, readings, dances, and other forms of socializing were held. Community members were interested in the arts and were able to organize such activities as symphony concerts, glee club recitals, and Shakespearean plays, even though practically all the talent was drawn from the membership.

Occasionally, outside artists were invited, but on a day-to-day basis the Community was more or less a closed group, with members seldom straying very far from home. What might be called their reference behavior related entirely to the group. The outside community was, figuratively and literally, "outside" and was always referred to as The World. It was this system of *cultural enclosure,* sustained over several decades, that served as a primary solidifying force.

It should not be thought that life in the old Community was a continual round of entertainment. The Oneidans built their own home, raised their own food, made all their own clothes (including shoes!), did their own laundry, ran their own school, and performed countless other collective tasks. . . .

Additionally adults were subject to self-imposed deprivations whenever they felt the group welfare threatened, and by modern standards "group welfare" was given a most liberal interpretation. For example, although the Perfectionists ate well, meat was served sparingly, pork not at all. Alcoholic beverages were prohibited, as were tea and coffee. Smoking also came to be taboo. The reasoning behind these prohibitions is not always clear, but presumably the Oneidans were dead set against informal distractions of an "anti-family" nature. Thus, dancing was permitted, since it was a social activity, while coffee-drinking and smoking were condemned on the ground that they were individualistic and appetitive in nature. One of the descendants of the Oneida Community—in an interview with the writer—spoke as follows:

> I imagine the prohibitions were pretty well thought out. They didn't just spring up, but developed gradually. I know there were some differences of opinion, but the main thing was that certain practices were felt to be bad for group living.
>
> Remember, they were trying to create a spiritual and social brotherhood, and they spent much more time in the art of developing relationships than we do. They had to. After all, hundreds of them were living together as a family, and they worked at it day after day. They were successful, too, for they held together for almost two generations without a major quarrel.

Their unique social organization was not the only thing that held the Oneida Colony together. As the membership increased, three basic principles of Noyes' teaching combined to form the very heart of Perfectionist life style: (1) economic communism; (2) mutual criticism; and (3) complex marriage.

ECONOMIC COMMUNISM

Members of the Oneida Community held equal ownership of all property, their avowed aim being to eliminate competition for the possession of material things. The needs of individual members were taken care of, but there was simply no concept of private ownership, even in the realm of personal belongings such as clothes, trinkets, and children's toys.

Writing of his boyhood, Pierrepont Noyes, a son of John Humphrey, states that "throughout my childhood, the private ownership of anything seemed to me a crude artificiality to which an unenlightened Outside still clung. For instance, we were keen for our favorite sleds, but it never occurred to me that I could possess a sled to the exclusion of the other boys. So it was with all Children's House property." With respect to clothing, the same author writes that "going-away clothes for grown folks, as for children, were common property. Any man or woman preparing for a trip was fitted out with one of the suits kept in stock for that purpose."

In addition to the manufacture of traps, the Oneidans found a ready market for their crops, which they put up in glass jars and cans and which became known for their uniform quality. As their business know-how (and their prosperity!) increased, it became necessary to hire outside help, and eventually the Perfectionists were employing several hundred local workers.

Starting in 1877, the Oneidans embarked on the manufacture of silverware. This venture proved so successful that, when the Community was disbanded, the silverware component was perpetuated as a joint-stock company (Oneida Ltd.), whose product is still widely used today.

How much of the economic success of the group was due to the communistic methods employed, and how much was due to the fortuitous invention of the trap, is difficult to say. On the one hand, collectivist methods probably had certain advantages over competing private enterprise. In tracing the economic history of the Oneidans, for instance, Edmonds notes that "to meet the deadline on an order, the whole Community—including the children—turned out."

On the other hand, the fact remains that the Perfectionists were rapidly becoming bankrupt until Sewell Newhouse's trap, figuratively and literally, "caught on." . . .

It is debatable whether the subsequent Oneida industries—including that of silverware—would ever have developed had it not been for the financial windfall brought about by Sewell Newhouse's timely invention. Some idea of the magnitude of the business can be seen from the fact that, in a good year, the Community would turn out close to 300,000 traps!

The economic aspects of [the Oneidans has] been mentioned in some detail, since most of the other communistic experiments then under way in America (and there were scores of them) became defunct either partly or largely because of economic difficulties.

Insofar as possible, the various jobs within the Community were rotated from year to year in order to eliminate feelings of discrimination. Members were quick to point out that at one time or another almost everyone took a turn at the necessary menial tasks. Nevertheless, while the jobs were generally rotated, individual variations in ability were recognized, and members were not placed in positions beyond their innate capacities. At the same time, social differentiation by occupational status was played down. If people did their work well, they presumably had equal status whether they were farm laborers or plant superintendents. It was work, rather than a specific type of job, that was held in high regard. As a matter of fact, one of the Perfectionists' most successful innovations was their employment of the cooperative enterprise or *bee*. The latter was

> an ordinance exactly suited to Community life. A bee would be announced at dinner or perhaps on the bulletin board: "A bee in the kitchen to pare apples"; or "A bee to pick strawberries at five o'clock tomorrow morning"; or "A bee in the Upper Sitting Room to sew bags."

It should be mentioned that there was seldom any trouble with idlers. On the contrary, a major difficulty was to screen out most of those who made application to join the Community. Relatively few new members were admitted, and those who were accepted had to undergo a long and severe probationary period.

In their efforts to promote equality, all Perfectionists were required to eat the same kind of food, wear the same type of clothing, and live in the same home. For both sexes, dress was uniformly simple, with jewelry and adornments tabooed. . . .

MUTUAL CRITICISM

The Oneida Community had neither laws nor law-enforcing officers, and there was little need for them, major infractions being all but unknown. In any organization, however, no matter how closely knit, conduct problems are bound to occur, and while the Oneidans considered themselves to be

Perfectionists, they acknowledged that individual foibles did exist. "Mutual criticism" was the method by which such problems were handled. The system had its inception at Putney, where the original followers of Noyes would subject themselves periodically to a searching criticism by the rest of the group. At Oneida the system was perpetuated—with remarkably successful results.

Whenever a member was found to be deviating from group norms, or whenever a personality or character weakness manifested itself, a committee of peers would meet with the offender to discuss the matter. "The criticisms," according to Edmonds, "were administered in a purely clinical spirit. The subject sat in complete silence while each member of the committee in turn assessed his good points as well as his bad. In cases of unusual seriousness, perhaps involving the violation of a fundamental tenet of their common philosophy, the committee would be expanded to include the entire Community."

From the accounts of the individuals who had undergone criticism, it is evident that, while the experience itself was often an ordeal, the end result was that of a catharsis, or spiritual cleansing. The success of the system probably hinged on the subjects' willingness to accept analysis and also on the fact that, though the criticisms were penetrating, they were offered in a frank, impersonal manner.

. . .

Although the Perfectionists had their share of internal strife, as we shall see, the conflicts were over policy and had nothing to do with deviant behavior. The harmonious living enjoyed by the group and the virtual lack of pernicious behavior attest to the effectiveness of mutual criticism as an instrument of social control. In fact, as the Colony grew in membership, the technique of mutual criticism came to be employed not so much with errant members but with those who volunteered for purposes of self-improvement.

. . .

COMPLEX MARRIAGE

The world does not remember the Oneidans for their economic communism or their mutual criticism, but for their system of complex marriage. Rightly or wrongly, just as the term "Rappites" signifies celibacy, so the name "Oneida" conjures up thoughts about the unique sex practices of the Community. Noyes himself coined the term "free love," although he seems to have preferred the phrase "complex marriage," or occasionally "pantogamy." Realistically, the Oneida marital system can best be described as a combination of communitarian living and group marriage.

. . . John Humphrey Noyes had no time for romantic love or monogamous marriage. Such practices were to him manifestations of selfishness and personal possession. Romantic love, or "special love" as it was called in the Community, was believed to give rise to jealousy and hypocrisy and, according to Perfectionist doctrine, made spiritual love impossible to attain.

Accordingly, Noyes promulgated the idea of complex marriage: since it was natural for all men to love all women and all women to love all men, it followed that every adult should consider himself or herself married to every other adult of the opposite sex. This collective spiritual union of men and women also included the right to sexual intercourse.

The Perfectionist leader felt strongly that "men and women find universally that their susceptibility to love is not burnt out by one honeymoon, or satisfied by one lover. On the contrary, the secret history of the human heart will bear out the assertion that it is capable of loving any number of times and any number of persons. Variety is, in the nature of things, as beautiful and useful in love as in eating and drinking.... We need love as much as we need food and clothing; and if we trust God for those things, why not for love?"

John Humphrey Noyes was a devout person, and the Oneida Perfectionists were a deeply religious group; any assessment of their sexual practices must take these factors into consideration. Insofar as the available information indicates, the Community abided by the doctrine of complex marriage not for reasons of lust, as was sometimes charged, but because of the conviction that they were following God's word.

In practice, since most of the adult men and women lived in the Mansion House, sex relations were easy to manage. There was, however, one requirement that was adhered to: a man could not have sexual intercourse with a woman unless the latter gave her consent. Procedurally, if a man desired sex relations, he would transmit the message to a Central Committee, who would thereupon make his request known to the woman in question. The actual go-between was usually an older female member of the Committee.

The system was inaugurated, as Parker points out, so that the women members "might, without embarrassment, decline proposals that did not appeal to them. No member should be obliged to receive at any time, under any circumstances, the attention of those they had not learned to love.... Every woman was to be free to refuse any, or every, man's attention." Although the procedure varied somewhat over the years, if the Central Committee granted approval and the woman in question assented, then the man simply went to the woman's room at bedtime and spent an hour or so with her before retiring to his own quarters.

It must be admitted, apropos of complex marriage, that many of the operational details were never disclosed, and that some writers—both past and present—have taken a questioning look at the sex practices of the Oneidans. Webber, for instance, writes as follows:

> "It was commonly declared that a committee of men and women received applications from those desiring certain persons; that if they considered the pairing suitable they arranged the meetings or obtained a refusal which was relayed to the applicant.... Thus if there was a refusal there was less embarrassment than if the proposal were made directly.
>
> So much for the rule. One may suspect that it was honored largely, as it were, in the breach. Men and women constantly associated and were free to visit in each other's rooms. It seems unlikely that a burst of romantic feeling might be interrupted while someone trotted off to find a go-between.

Whether, in fact, the Central Committee or the go-between were frequently by-passed must remain a matter of conjecture. One should remember that the Oneidans were a devout group, and that their sexual practices were part of an overall religious system. It is difficult, therefore, for outsiders to assess the sexual motivations of individual Community members.

It is known that Oneidans were presumed to act like ladies and gentlemen at all times. Inappropriate behavior, suggestive language, overt displays of sexuality—such actions were not tolerated. As a matter of fact, sexual behavior was not openly discussed within the Community, and it is doubtful whether the subject of "Who was having relations with whom?" ever became common knowledge. One male member who became too inquisitive on this score was literally thrown out of the Community, an act which represented the only physical expulsion in the group's history.

ROLE OF WOMEN

There is no doubt that John Humphrey Noyes had a special place in his heart for the Oneida women—and in this respect he was years ahead of his time. He saw to it that they played an integral part in the day-to-day operations of the Community. The following remarks, made to the writer, provide a good example.

> One thing that most people have overlooked is that Noyes delegated a lot more responsibility to the women here than they ever would have received on the outside. Every committee had women on it. It made a difference, too. All the old folks will tell you it made both men and women respect each other.

In the sexual sphere, also, the Perfectionist leader had advanced ideas about the role of women. . . . [H]e rejected the idea that sex was simply a "wifely duty", that is, an act tolerated by the female at the pleasure of the male. Later on, he incorporated his beliefs in the Oneida *Handbook,* as the following passage indicates:

> "The liberty of monogamous marriage, as commonly understood, is the liberty of a man to sleep habitually with a woman, liberty to please himself alone in his dealings with her, liberty to expose her to child-bearing without care or consultation.

> The term Free Love, as understood by the Oneida Community, does *not* mean any such freedom of sexual proceedings. The theory of sexual interchange which governs all the general measures of the Community is that which in ordinary society governs the proceedings in *courtship.*

> It is the theory that love *after* marriage should be what it is *before* marriage—a glowing attraction on both sides, and not the odious obligation of one party, and the sensual selfishness of the other."

Although rumors a-plenty were carried by the outsiders, there is unfortunately no published record of the extent to which requested sexual liaisons were vetoed by the Central Committee or refused by the women themselves. All the evidence is fragmentary. Some individuals, naturally, were more in demand than others. Carden, who has done research on the subject, believes that the women often had more than four different sex partners a month.

> A physician who interviewed a number of ex-members after the break-up, reported that women had intercourse every two to four days. Another report, also by a physician, quoted an obviously discontented older woman who had left the Community. She complained that young girls would be called upon to have intercourse as often as seven times in a week and oftener.

On the other hand, that there was some rejection can be inferred from Parker's finding—based on a lengthy study—that "this entire freedom of the women to accept or reject the advances of their lovers kept men as alert as during more conventional courtships. Men sought, as always, to prove themselves worthy of the favor of their sweethearts; and that made their life, they confessed, one continuous courtship."

. . .

THE EUGENICS PROGRAM

Child-rearing occupied a special place in the Perfectionist scheme of things. Having familiarized himself with the principles of Charles Darwin and Francis Galton, Noyes was convinced of the feasibility of applying scientific methods to the propagation of the race. He felt that the only people who should have children were those who possessed superior physical and mental abilities. A clear statement of his position appeared in the Oneida Circular.

> Why should not beauty and noble grace of person and every other desirable quality of men and women, internal and external, be propagated and intensified beyond all former precedent—by the application of the same scientific principles of breeding that produce such desirable results in the case of sheep, cattle, and horses?

Although the term "eugenics" had not yet been coined, a eugenics program—in which specially chosen adults would be utilized for breeding purposes—was exactly what John Humphrey Noyes had in mind. And, of course, what more logical place to put eugenic principles into actual practice than the Oneida Community? Noyes called his program "stirpiculture" (from the Latin *stirps,* meaning root or stock), and it was not long before the scientific world was discussing the implications of the unique experiment being conducted in central New York State.

For 20 years after founding their Community, the Oneidans had largely refrained from bearing children. They reasoned that procreation should be delayed until such time as the group had the facilities for proper child care. The first two decades, so to speak, merely served the purpose of laying the groundwork for the future growth of the Colony. The birth control technique advocated by Noyes was *coitus reservatus,* i.e., sexual intercourse up to, but not including, ejaculation on the part of the male. Until they had learned the necessary coital control, younger males in the Community were required to limit their sex relations to women who had passed the menopause. Although the technique was claimed by many writers to be incapable of attainment, the record contradicts them.

In any case, by 1869 the group was ready to embark upon its pioneer eugenics program. Couples desirous of becoming parents (stirps) made formal application before a cabinet composed of key members of the Community, Noyes apparently holding the deciding vote. The cabinet, after assessing the physical and mental qualities of the applicants, would either approve or disapprove the requests. The stirpiculture program was in effect for about a decade before the Community disbanded, and during this 10–year period 58 children were born. Noyes himself fathered upwards of a dozen children, so that evidently he was not averse to self-selection.

Children remained in their mothers' care up to the age of 15 months, whereupon they were gradually transferred to a special section of the Mansion House. Henceforth they would spend most of their childhood in age-graded classes. Although the children were treated with kindness by their parents, sentimentalizing was frowned upon, the feeling being that under Perfectionism all adults should love all children and vice versa.

By their own reports, the children were evidently well adjusted. Recreation, schooling, medical care—all were provided in keeping with accepted child-rearing practices. As a group, the children were remarkably healthy. Mortality comparisons indicated that the products of stirpiculture had a significantly lower death rate than children born outside the Community.

That most of the youngsters had a happy childhood can be seen from the following comments, made to the writer:

> I was born in the old Community, and the times we used to have! I don't think kids today have the kind of fun we did. There was a ready-made play group all the time, with something always going on. There was some activity in the Big Hall almost every night—plays, musical concerts, entertainment of all kinds. As children, there was always something to look forward to.
>
> . . .
>
> ... You knew you were loved because it was like a big family. Also, there were so many activities for the youngsters, so many things to do, well—believe me—we were happy children....
>
> . . .
>
> We were happy youngsters, and we lived in a remarkable group. Unfortunately, they broke up when I was quite young. I wish I could have lived my whole life with them....
>
> . . .

In late 1879, after fearlessly defying public opinion for almost half a century, Noyes sent a message to the Community (from Canada) proposing that they abolish complex marriage and revert to the accepted marital practices. Soon afterward the group disbanded, many of the members becoming formally married. Economically, a joint-stock company was organized and the stock (worth about $600,000) was then divided among the members. Last-ditch efforts to salvage some communal type of family organization failed, thus ending—in rather pathetic fashion—what was probably the most radical social experiment in America.

NOTES

1. Spencer Klaw's book *Without Sin* explores the Oneida Community and the personal experiences of those who lived there. Through excerpts from the diaries and letters of many Oneida members, Klaw creates an intimate portrait of life in the community, and of the internal conflicts and external pressures that toppled the most successful utopian commune in American history. SPENCER KLAW, WITHOUT SIN (1993).

2. Was the Oneida community a family? If not, what characteristics was it missing? Could it be a family for some legal purposes but not others?

Laura M. Padilla, *Single–Parent Latinas on the Margin: Seeking a Room With a View, Meals, and Built-in Community.*

13 WIS. WOMEN'S L.J. 179, 186–95 (1998).

I. THE COHOUSING MODEL

. . .

A. *Anatomy of a Cohousing Community*

A cohousing community provides a unique housing experience. It combines elements of public space and privacy, with a goal of creating community. Most cohousing communities consist of twelve to thirty-six families.... [T]here are at least three consistent features among [cohousing developments]: common facilities, residential management and neighborhood design.

One feature of cohousing is its common facilities, generally including a common kitchen and dining area, laundry room, children's play room, outdoor play area, workshops, and a garden. The most prominent features of the "common house" are the kitchen and dining areas. Typically, a committee organizes kitchen-related responsibilities, and adults rotate dinner duties. Responsibility can be assigned or assumed in a variety of ways, but generally it is done on a voluntary basis. Common dinners are not necessarily prepared every night, leaving residents the choice of eating at home, elsewhere, or in the common house on an informal basis. Common house facilities can also be used by the surrounding neighborhood for organizational meetings concerning issues that affect the community at large.

A second characteristic common to most cohousing is residential management. This entails resident participation both in the planning and design of the development, and in the management of community concerns. Ideally, residents are involved in the development of their cohousing community from conception to construction. Numerous benefits derive from this type of extended participation. First, members who have been involved since the project's conception are more motivated to overcome the many obstacles which confront development without compromising their goals. Second, participating members, rather than developers, determine the physical layout of the communities, including how far the parking lot should be from the common house, how far the private houses should be from each other, et cetera. Third, members have a say in the geographic location of their community. Fourth, members may be able to choose their own housing style. Finally, and perhaps most importantly, members are involved in defining the intentions and goals of the group.

. . .

Regardless of a community's physical design, residents are involved in community management, which requires residents to work together as a group. This results in accountability because residents are responsible to each other for their decisions and must live with the results of their decisions for many years to come. In this respect, cohousing contrasts with a condominium homeowners' association form of management, which consists of a hierarchical governance structure and little accountability among neighbors.

In cohousing communities, even though there are legal relationships among members during the pre-site acquisition phase, the development partnership phase, and the post-construction phase, the nature of the legal relationships and the agreements governing those relationships are distinct from the relationships resulting through [homeowner's associations]. In this sense, cohousing promotes community and social development and encourages cooperation and personal contact when addressing conflicts. For example, at Southside Park Cohousing in Sacramento, residents meet twice a month to "catch up on news, discuss issues and try to reach consensus on decisions that affect the community." One Southside Park resident admitted that there are squabbles but said that cooperative living kept them together.

Decisions are made by consensus, and as one Southside Park cohousing resident noted, because of the extensive discussions that are involved in various proposals, a consensus is rarely blocked.

The third common characteristic of cohousing is a neighborhood design, which intentionally encourages interaction among neighbors. This is accomplished in a number of ways. First, the parking lot is usually placed at one end of the community or around the perimeter, which allows the rest of the development to be pedestrian-oriented. This layout increases social interaction because residents must walk from their cars to their homes. Second, the common house is strategically located to increase opportunities for social interaction. If residents must walk by the common house to get to their homes, they are more likely to stop in to check on activities. Similarly, if they can see the common house from their private residences, they are more likely to be aware of ongoing activities and therefore, more inclined to participate.

An important feature of cohousing's neighborhood design is its "child-friendly" environment. Most cohousing developments are designed around the safety, recreation and well-being of resident children. Common houses generally have either a children's room or complete day-care centers. Beyond the common house, children can play safely within most of the community because of the pedestrian-oriented design. Most kitchens face pedestrian walkways, so adults can keep an eye on children. Play areas are also set up so other community residents can see the children, even if the children's own parents cannot actually see them. This is beneficial because it encourages many adults beyond parents to be involved in children's lives. In turn, the relative degree of independence enjoyed by the children, coupled with the sense that many adults care about them, assists the children's development as it helps instill security and self-confidence. As one writer noted, "[m]ost people learn how to avoid emotional hijackings from the time they are infants. If they have supportive and caring adults around them, they pick up the social cues that enable them to develop self-discipline and empathy." Thus, cohousing's built-in interaction between adults and children is particularly beneficial for children because it can help them develop into self-assured and cooperative teenagers and adults.

Cohousing's neighborhood designs often have built-in flexibility. As the composition of the community changes, its members can modify the common facilities to adapt to the community's changing needs. For example, when children are younger, child care facilities are very important. However, as children get older, after-school care becomes more pressing and the common facilities can be adapted to meet those needs. As children get even older, there comes a point when independent supervision is no longer necessary, but it is still desirable to have activities, such as theatre, music or computer lessons, available to engage the children. These activities could take place in the common facilities.

While cohousing, by its own admission, has not been terribly successful in providing low-income housing, that has not been the primary focus; rather, it has been more concerned with building community. Cohousing has been about sharing, caring and community responsibility, and its main purpose and function is to develop a positive social living environment. It creates a community where children can live near their friends and where residents have a sense of belonging and can get to know others of all ages, thus fostering intergenerational interaction among community members. "Children thrive in the environment because they feel safe and appreciated by the adults around them, and elderly people enjoy the contact with other age groups." Intergenerational interaction "adds to the quality of life and broadens the individual." For example, such interaction allows residents to socialize with people from other age groups with whom they would not otherwise socialize, thereby learning from each other's experiences. Cohousing also:

> offers many role models of different ages. The easy, intergenerational social flow gives teens access to adults other than their parents—adults who can act as friends, mentors, even reality-checks. And in an age of smaller families, cohousing provides children with sibling relationships they might not otherwise have.

By encouraging social interaction, cohousing results in greater community participation. Since most residents are involved in the community, they get to know each other and this allows for a greater sense of acceptance, which in turn increases feelings of self-worth. Accordingly, cohousing provides general community support, which is good for individual residents, the cohousing community, and the broader community. Additional nuances of cohousing are best illustrated by examining the history of cohousing and its movement into America in the late 1980s.

B. *History of Cohousing*

Cohousing developed out of frustration with limited housing choices. The cohousing concept, known in Danish as *bofaellesskaber*, started in Denmark in 1964 when Jan Gudmand–Hoyer met with a group of friends to discuss alternative housing options. Mr. and Mrs. Gudmand–Hoyer planned to have children, but did not want to raise them in the city. The only housing option which countered the isolation of living in single-family homes, apartments and condominiums, was the row house option. Row houses, however, did not offer common facilities which contribute to the "sense of community" that the Gudmand–Hoyers sought.

Over several months, the Gudmand–Hoyers and friends considered their goals and desires. They wanted the "qualities of a country village," but also wished to remain accessible to "the professional and cultural opportunities" offered by the city. As originally conceived in the 1960s, cohousing residences would be large and private, with walls enclosing the front and back. Likewise, the common house would be virtually hidden from view. Focusing on the importance of cooperation in the home, they decided the housing community should be small enough to allow neighbors to get to know each other and to encourage social interaction.

In 1964, the group purchased some land outside Hareskov and proceeded with design plans. While city officials did not oppose the project, many neighbors did. The opposition's main concern was that the "increased number of children would bring excessive noise to their quiet neighborhood." Even though neighbors ultimately thwarted this project, the cohousing group did not quit. In 1968, Gudmand–Hoyer published an article on cohousing, which generated much interest and support. Times and attitudes had changed from four years earlier and an increasing number of people believed that a "more cooperative living environment would help build a more humane world." Society was certainly more accepting of cohousing and other alternative living arrangements such as "hippie communes."

That same year, Gudmand–Hoyer, Bodil Graae, and the remaining Hareskov families purchased property outside of Jonstrup and Hillerod. Planning and development proceeded and in 1972, twenty-seven families moved into Saettedammen. By 1980, twelve cohousing communities had been built in Denmark and cohousing had evolved into an established housing option.

Cohousing is not only popular in Denmark, it has exploded in the United States over the past several years. Most Americans still live in single-family residences, but these residences are not the best housing option for all family types.

> The modern single-family detached home, which makes up 67 percent of the American housing stock, was designed for a nuclear family consisting of a breadwinning father, a homemaking mother, and two to four children. Today, less than one-quarter of the population lives in such households. Rather, the family with two working parents predominates, while the single-parent household is the fastest-growing family type.

The rapid growth of single-parent families necessitates more housing options that are tailored to the needs of single-parent families. Other housing alternatives exist—condominiums, cooperatives, apartments and mobile homes. Yet none of these housing options intentionally attempt to provide anything but housing. Cohousing, on the other hand, provides a relatively new housing choice that as a bonus, comes with a built-in community.

In 1991, the first United States cohousing community opened in Davis, California. As of January 1997, there were at least twenty-four cohousing communities operating in the United States, with plans to build an additional 150 communities. This rapid growth is not surprising considering the loneliness of living in isolation, the need for community, and the many forms of today's families, which require more housing choices. As one cohousing architect stated,

> [W]e can no longer afford to push our old people aside and have them live apart from us. Old people need to be living in a place where they have a relationship with the young. We can no longer afford to isolate out single parents. Single parents need to be around traditional families with children.

Modern cohousing is an approach to housing that takes into consideration lifestyle, as well as a desire to live in community. Cohousing residents vary in occupation and background, and make a concerted effort to bring in residents from various income brackets, which leads to a more diverse environment for children, as well as adults. In spite of these efforts, not many cohousing developments have succeeded in providing low-income housing.

> Cohousing developments have not proved to be cheaper than traditional homes, because in building homes for the first time, people can get carried away in customizing it, which drives up the price. But money can be saved by pooling resources—buying food in bulk for group dinners, sharing child-care expenses and sharing costs on little-used household items, such as gardening equipment, tools and kitchen gadgets.

Although cohousing has not drawn many low-income residents, several cohousing communities are now placing a greater emphasis on affordability. If properly designed, cohousing may provide an affordable housing alternative. For example, one proposed housing project, Synergy Cohousing Community, received an award from the U.S. Department of Housing and Urban

Development for "design and promoting construction of affordable housing."

. . .

NOTES

1. Padilla suggests that "more and more families, [and] especially . . . single parents" could benefit from co-housing than already do if existing models for it were modified. Laura M. Padilla, *Single–Parent Latinas on the Margin: Seeking a Room with a View, Meals, and Built-in Community*, 13 Wis. Women's L.J. 179, 196 (1998). To illustrate, Padilla explores how co-housing could be used to address, in particular, the needs of low-income, single-parent families led by Latina women, emphasizing how co-housing might provide these women and their families not only housing, but also child-care, education, support, as well as nutrition and other health-care needs. Meanwhile, a growing number of older adults appear to be experimenting with co-housing as an alternative to nursing homes and other adult living communities, including assisted living facilities. *See, e.g.*, Sally Abrahms, *Elder Cohousing: A New Option for Retirement—or Sooner!*, AARP Bulletin, (Jan. 31, 2011), *available* http://at   www.aarp.org/home-garden/housing/info–01–2011/elder_cohousing.html; Sally Abrahms, *Intergenerational Cohousing: Clustered Homes and a Common House Foster a Community for Making Friends of All Ages*, AARP Bulletin, (Mar. 28, 2011), *available* at *http://www.aarp.org/home-garden/housing/info–03–2011/intergenerational-cohousing-for-all-ages.html; Sally Abrahms* Reinventing Home: Happy Together, *AARP Bulletin, Apr. 2011, at 10.* See also *Keith Wardrip*, Strategies to Meet the Housing Needs of Older Adults, *AARP Public Policy Institute (Mar. 2010). According to Keith Wardrip, Senior Research Associate at the Center for Housing Policy for AARP Public Policy Institute, there are now "roughly 115 cohousing communities in the United States [that] include nearly 2,700 households." Keith Wardrip*, Fact Sheet 175: Cohousing For Older Adults *1, AARP Public Policy Institute (Mar. 2010).*

2. Under what circumstances, if any, could or should co-housing communities be understood to constitute a "family" for legal purposes? Is "family" (ever) the right term to use? Would "kinship community" or "affinity community" be better terms to use? Is thinking of these living and interpersonal arrangements simply as "communities" missing something? Missing something that the legal system should try to capture and reflect? What?

CHAPTER 6

ASSISTED REPRODUCTIVE TECHNOLOGIES AND THE LAW

The term "Assisted Reproductive Technologies" (ART) denotes techniques for the biological reproduction of humans other than by sexual intercourse between a man and a woman. The Uniform Parentage Act, which was last amended in 2002, includes in its definition of assisted reproduction: "(A) intrauterine insemination; (B) donation of eggs; (C) donation of embryos; (D) in-vitro fertilization and transfer of embryos; and (E) intracytoplasmic sperm injection."[1]

The first of these techniques, also known as artificial insemination (AI), has been around at least since the nineteenth century and can be as low-tech as spurting semen into a woman's uterus with the help of a turkey baster. Use of sperm from a third party donor is commonly called Artificial Insemination by Donor (AID) and is contrasted to Artificial Insemination by Husband (AIH). Early use of AID by women married to infertile men gave rise to what were then considered tough legal cases of contested paternity. Intracytoplasmic sperm injection is a technique for treating male infertility, by which a single sperm is injected directly into an egg. Even the newer techniques of egg extraction and in vitro fertilization (IVF) are now more than thirty years old and can no longer be considered novel.

What remains novel in this domain is the host of legal and policy questions that keep arising as the desire for biological reproduction leads married and unmarried, homosexual and heterosexual couples and individuals to seek the help of a growing industry in the United States, but also increasingly abroad. In 2008, it was reported that 61,426 infants were born as a result of egg and sperm procedures, about double the number reported in 1999.[2] Annual estimates for children born as a result of artificial insemination are uncertain, but range from 4,000 to 30,000.[3] Currently, the federal government provides information about the success rates of fertility clinics, authorizes the use of fertility drugs and products commonly used in ART, oversees advertising by clinics, and mandates the screening of gamete (egg and sperm) donors for certain communicable diseases by ART clinics and laboratories.[4] States regulate the medical profession, which uses ART for the treatment of infertility. A few states even mandate insurance coverage for fertility treatment. Nonetheless, ART in the United States is mostly unregulated.

---

1. U.P.A § 102(4) (amended 2002).

2. CTRS. FOR DISEASE CONTROL & PREVENTION ET AL., DEP'T OF HEALTH & HUMAN SERVS., 2008 ASSISTED REPRODUCTIVE TECHNOLOGY SUCCESS RATES 65 (2008), *available at* http://www.cdc.gov/art/ART2008/PDF/ART_2008_Full.pdf.

3. *See, e.g.,* Kimberly D. Krawiec, *Altruism and Intermediation in the Market for Babies*, 66 WASH. & LEE L. REV. 203, 204 n. 5 (2009).

4. *See generally* David Adamson, *Regulation of Assisted Reproductive Technology in the United States*, 39 FAM. L.Q. 727 (2005).

From the point of view of family law, the ART industry operates in the shadow of legal norms that remain largely underdetermined. The use of IVF and gestational surrogacy, for example, has created the possibility of multiple contenders for parenthood. In some cases, there can be two intended parents, an egg and a sperm donor, a surrogate and her husband, all of whom have contributed in a direct or indirect way to the birth of a child. Even in the states that have addressed ART and parentage through statutes, questions of interpretation remain. The overall picture remains one of a legal patchwork at the state level that becomes even more complicated if participants move across state lines or international borders.

In studying the materials in this Chapter, consider what role the state currently plays in regulating ART. What are the interests at stake? How should the state adjudicate between them? Does ART give rise to new fundamental conceptualizations of kinship and family that call for new standards and legal concepts, or can the emerging practices fit into pre-existing discourses and doctrines of familial belonging?

A. SURROGACY CONTRACTS

1. THE LEGALITY AND ENFORCEABILITY OF SURROGACY CONTRACTS

D.C. CODE § 16–401

(2001).

(4) "Surrogate parenting contract" means any agreement, oral or written, in which:

(A) A woman agrees either to be artificially inseminated with the sperm of a man who is not her husband, or to be impregnated with an embryo that is the product of an ovum fertilization with the sperm of a man who is not her husband; and

(B) A woman agrees to, or intends to, relinquish all parental rights and responsibilities and to consent to the adoption of a child born as a result of insemination or in vitro fertilization as provided in this chapter.

THE BABY M CASE

In 1985, Mary Beth Whitehead made national headlines when she refused to abide by the terms of the surrogacy agreement she had signed with William Stern, the biological and intended father. She claimed custody of the baby, Melissa, who was her biological child, and the case led to a drawn-out court (and press) battle that alerted the nation to some of the legal and ethical dilemmas presented by surrogacy agreements.

Consider the terms of the Surrogate Parenting Agreement between Mary Beth Whitehead, her husband at the time, Richard Whitehead, and William Stern, and of the Agreement between William Stern and the Infertility Center of New York (ICNY):

SURROGATE PARENTING AGREEMENT

THIS AGREEMENT is made this 6th day of February, 1985, by and between MARY BETH WHITEHEAD, a married woman (herein referred to as Surrogate [sic]), RICHARD WHITEHEAD, her husband (herein referred to a "Husband" [sic]), and WILLIAM STERN, (herein referred to as "Natural Father").

THIS AGREEMENT is made with reference to the following facts:

(1) WILLIAM STERN, Natural Father, is an individual over the age of eighteen (18) years who is desirous of entering into this Agreement.

(2) The sole purpose of this Agreement is to enable WILLIAM STERN and his infertile wife to have a child which is biologically related to WILLIAM STERN.

(3) MARY BETH WHITEHEAD, Surrogate, and RICHARD WHITEHEAD, her husband, are over the age of eighteen (18) years and desirous of entering into this Agreement in consideration of the following:

NOW THEREFORE, in consideration of the mutual promises contained herein and the intentions of being legally bound hereby, the parties agree as follows:

1. MARY BETH WHITEHEAD, Surrogate, represents that she is capable of conceiving children. MARY BETH WHITEHEAD understands and agrees that in the best interest of the child, she will not form or attempt to form a parent-child relationship with any child or children she may conceive, carry to term and give birth to, pursuant to the provisions of this Agreement, and shall freely surrender custody to WILLIAM STERN, Natural Father, immediately upon birth of the child; and terminate all parental rights to said child pursuant to this Agreement.

2. ... RICHARD WHITEHEAD is in agreement with the purposes, intents and provisions of this Agreement and acknowledges that his wife, MARY BETH WHITEHEAD, Surrogate, shall be artificially inseminated pursuant to the provisions of this Agreement. RICHARD WHITEHEAD agrees that in the best interest of the child, he will not form or attempt to form a parent-child relationship with any child or children MARY BETH WHITEHEAD, Surrogate, may conceive by artificial insemination as described herein, and agrees to freely and readily surrender immediate custody of the child to WILLIAM STERN, Natural Father; and terminate his parental rights; RICHARD WHITEHEAD further acknowledges he will do all acts necessary to rebut the presumption of paternity of any offspring conceived and born pursuant to aforementioned agreement as provided by law, including blood testing and/or HLA testing.

3. WILLIAM STERN, Natural Father, does hereby enter into this written contractual Agreement with MARY BETH WHITEHEAD, Surrogate, where MARY BETH WHITEHEAD shall be artificially inseminated with the semen of WILLIAM STERN by a physician. MARY BETH WHITEHEAD, Surrogate, upon becoming pregnant, acknowledges that she will carry said embryo/fetus(s) until delivery. MARY BETH WHITEHEAD, Surrogate, and RICHARD WHITEHEAD, her husband, agree that they will cooperate with any background investigation into the Surrogate's medical, family and personal history and warrants the information to be accurate to the best of their knowledge. MARY BETH WHITEHEAD, Surrogate, and RICHARD WHITEHEAD, her husband, agree to surrender custody of the child to WILLIAM STERN, Natural Father, immediately upon birth, acknowledging that it is the intent of this Agreement in the best interests of the child to do so; as well as institute and cooperate in proceedings to terminate their respective parental rights to said child, and sign any and all necessary affidavits, documents, and the like, in order to further the intent and

purposes of this Agreement. It is understood by MARY BETH WHITE-HEAD, and RICHARD WHITEHEAD, that the child to be conceived is being done so for the sole purpose of giving said child to WILLIAM STERN, its natural and biological father. MARY BETH WHITEHEAD and RICHARD WHITEHEAD agree to sign all necessary affidavits prior to and after the birth of the child and voluntarily participate in any paternity proceedings necessary to have WILLIAM STERN'S name entered on said child's birth certificate as the natural or biological father.

4.   That the consideration for this Agreement, which is compensation for services and expenses, and in no way is to be construed as a fee for termination of parental rights or a payment in exchange for a consent to surrender the child for adoption, in addition to other provisions contained herein, shall be as follows:

(A) $10,000 shall be paid to MARY BETH WHITEHEAD, Surrogate, upon surrender of custody to WILLIAM STERN, the natural and biological father of the child born pursuant to the provisions of this Agreement for surrogate services and expenses in carrying out her obligations under this Agreement;

(B) The consideration to be paid to MARY BETH WHITEHEAD, Surrogate, shall be deposited with the Infertility Center of New York (hereinafter ICNY), the representative of WILLIAM STERN, at the time of the signing of this Agreement, and held in escrow until completion of the duties and obligations of MARY BETH WHITEHEAD, Surrogate . . . as herein described.

(C) WILLIAM STERN, Natural Father, shall pay the expenses incurred by MARY BETH WHITEHEAD, Surrogate, pursuant to her pregnancy, more specifically defined as follows:

(1) All medical, hospitalization, and pharmaceutical, laboratory and therapy expenses incurred as a result of MARY BETH WHITEHEAD'S pregnancy, not covered or allowed by her present health and major medical insurance, including all extraordinary medical expenses and all reasonable expenses for treatment of any emotional or mental conditions or problems related to said pregnancy, but in no case shall any such expenses be paid or reimbursed after a period of six (6) months have elapsed since the date of the termination of the pregnancy, and this Agreement specifically excludes any expenses for lost wages or other non-itemized incidentals . . . related to said pregnancy.

(2) WILLIAM STERN, Natural Father, shall not be responsible for any latent medical expenses occurring six (6) weeks subsequent to the birth of the child, unless the medical problem or abnormality incident thereto was known and treated by a physician prior to the expiration of said six (6) week period and in written notice of the same sent to ICNY, as representative of WILLIAM STERN by certified mail, return receipt requested, advising of this treatment.

(3) WILLIAM STERN, Natural Father, shall be responsible for the total costs of all paternity testing. Such paternity testing may, at the option of WILLIAM STERN, Natural Father, be required prior to release of the surrogate fee from escrow. In the event WILLIAM STERN, Natural Father, is conclusively determined not to be the biological father of the child as a result of an HLA test, this Agreement will be deemed breached and MARY BETH WHITE-

HEAD, Surrogate, shall not be entitled to any fee. WILLIAM STERN, Natural Father, shall be entitled to reimbursement of all medical and related expenses from MARY BETH WHITEHEAD, Surrogate, and RICHARD WHITEHEAD, her husband.

(4) MARY BETH WHITEHEAD'S reasonable travel expenses incurred at the request of WILLIAM STERN, pursuant to this Agreement.

5. MARY BETH WHITEHEAD, Surrogate, and RICHARD WHITE-HEAD, her husband, understand and agree to assume all risks, including the risk of death, which are incidental to conception, pregnancy, childbirth, including but not limited to, postpartum complications. A copy of said possible risks and/or complications is attached hereto and made a part hereof. . . .

6. MARY BETH WHITEHEAD, Surrogate, and RICHARD WHITE-HEAD, her husband, hereby agree to undergo psychiatric evaluation by JOAN EINWOHNER, a psychiatrist as designated by WILLIAM STERN or an agent thereof. WILLIAM STERN shall pay for the cost of said psychiatric evaluation. MARY BETH WHITEHEAD and RICHARD WHITEHEAD shall sign, prior to their evaluations, a medical release permitting dissemination of the report prepared as a result of said psychiatric evaluations to ICNY or WILLIAM STERN and his wife.

7. MARY BETH WHITEHEAD, Surrogate, and RICHARD WHITE-HEAD, her husband, hereby agree that it is the exclusive and sole right of WILLIAM STERN, Natural Father, to name said child.

8. "Child" as referred to in this Agreement shall include all children born simultaneously pursuant to the inseminations contemplated herein.

9. In the event of the death of WILLIAM STERN, prior or subsequent to the birth of said child, it is hereby understood and agreed by MARY BETH WHITEHEAD, Surrogate, and RICHARD WHITEHEAD, her husband, that the child will be placed in the custody of WILLIAM STERN'S wife.

10. In the event that the child is miscarried prior to the fifth (5th) month of pregnancy, no compensation, as enumerated in paragraph 4(A), shall be paid to MARY BETH WHITEHEAD, Surrogate. However, the expenses enumerated in paragraph 4(C) shall be paid or reimbursed to MARY BETH WHITEHEAD, Surrogate. In the event the child is miscarried, dies or is stillborn subsequent to the fourth (4th) month of pregnancy and said child does not survive, the Surrogate shall receive $1,000.00 in lieu of the compensation enumerated in paragraph 4(A). In the event of a miscarriage or stillbirth as described above, this Agreement shall terminate and neither MARY BETH WHITEHEAD, Surrogate, nor WILLIAM STERN, Natural Father, shall be under any further obligation under this Agreement.

11. MARY BETH WHITEHEAD, Surrogate, and WILLIAM STERN, Natural Father, shall have undergone complete physical and genetic evaluation, under the direction and supervision of a licensed physician, to determine whether the physical health and well-being of each is satisfactory. Said physical examination shall include testing for venereal diseases, specifically including but not limited to, syphilis, herpes and gonorrhea. Said venereal diseases testing shall be done prior to, but not limited to, each series of inseminations.

12. In the event that pregnancy has not occurred within a reasonable time, in the opinion of WILLIAM STERN, Natural Father, this Agreement shall terminate by written notice to MARY BETH WHITEHEAD, Surrogate, at the residence provided to the ICNY by the Surrogate, from ICNY, as representative of WILLIAM STERN, Natural Father.

13. MARY BETH WHITEHEAD, Surrogate, agrees that she will not abort the child conceived except, if in the professional medical opinion of the inseminating physician, such action is necessary for the physical health of MARY BETH WHITEHEAD or the child has been determined by said physician to be physiologically abnormal. MARY BETH WHITEHEAD further agrees, upon the request of said physician to undergo amniocentesis . . . or similar tests to detect genetic and congenital defects. In the event said test reveals that the fetus is genetically or congenitally abnormal, MARY BETH WHITEHEAD, Surrogate, agrees to abort the fetus upon demand of WILLIAM STERN, Natural Father, in which event, the fee paid to the Surrogate will be in accordance to Paragraph 10. If MARY BETH WHITEHEAD refuses to abort the fetus upon demand of WILLIAM STERN, his obligations as stated in this Agreement shall cease forthwith, except as to obligation of paternity imposed by statute.

14. Despite the provisions of Paragraph 13, WILLIAM STERN, Natural Father, recognizes that some genetic and congenital abnormalities may not be detected by amniocentesis or other tests, and therefore, if proven to be the biological father of the child, assumes the legal responsibility for any child who may possess genetic or congenital abnormalities. . . .

15. MARY BETH WHITEHEAD, Surrogate, further agrees to adhere to all medical instructions given to her by the inseminating physician as well as her independent obstetrician. MARY BETH WHITEHEAD also agrees not to smoke cigarettes, drink alcoholic beverages, use illegal drugs, or take non-prescription medications or prescribed medications without written consent from her physician. MARY BETH WHITEHEAD agrees to follow a prenatal medical examination schedule to consist of no fewer visits then: one visit per month during the first seven (7) months of pregnancy, two visits (each to occur at two-week intervals) during the eighth and ninth month of pregnancy.

. . .

17. Each party acknowledges that he or she fully understands this Agreement and its legal effect, and that they are signing the same freely and voluntarily and that neither party has any reason to believe that the other(s) did not freely and voluntarily execute said Agreement.

18. In the event any of the provisions of this Agreement are deemed to be invalid or unenforceable, the same shall be deemed severable from the remainder of this Agreement and shall not cause the invalidity or unenforceability of the remainder of this Agreement. If such provision shall be deemed invalid due to its scope or breadth, then said provision shall be deemed valid to the extent of the scope or breadth permitted by law.

19. The original of this Agreement, upon execution, shall be retained by the Infertility Center of New York, with photocopies being distributed to MARY BETH WHITEHEAD, Surrogate and WILLIAM STERN, Natural Father, having the same legal effect as the original.

. . .

AGREEMENT BETWEEN WILLIAM STERN AND ICNY

THIS AGREEMENT is made this Third day of December 1984, by and between William Stern hereinafter referred to as Natural Father, and the Primary Research Associates of United States, Inc., d/b/a Infertility Center of New York, (hereinafter referred to as "ICNY").

. . .

... [I]n consideration of the mutual promises contained herein, and with the intentions of being legally bound hereby, the parties mutually agree as follows:

(1) Natural Father hereby contracts with ICNY for the services offered by ICNY and ICNY agrees to contract with the Natural Father to use its best efforts to assist the Natural Father in the selection of a "surrogate mother" as hereinafter defined, it being understood that the final selection of the "surrogate mother" is solely within the discretion of the Natural Father....

(2) Natural Father agrees and understands that he must enter into an agreement with the selected surrogate mother whereby Natural Father agrees to the process of artificial insemination with the use of his semen for the purpose of impregnating the surrogate mother. Thereafter, the surrogate mother shall give birth to a child fathered by the Natural Father and voluntarily surrender custody of said child to the Natural Father.

(3) Natural Father hereby agrees to pay ICNY as compensation for the services provided by ICNY the sum of SEVEN THOUSAND FIVE HUNDRED DOLLARS ($7,500.00) incurred by ICNY on behalf of the Natural Father. The Natural Father understands and agrees that said sum is non-refundable....

The Natural Father agrees that ICNY shall act as escrow agent for the fee to be paid by the Natural Father to the selected surrogate mother.

. . .

(5) ICNY agrees to provide ... services including the offering, at the option of the Natural Father, of legal representation of the Natural Father in his negotiations and agreement with the surrogate mother. The Natural Father understands and acknowledges that ICNY offers these legal services through the law firm retained by ICNY but, ICNY makes no representations or warranties with respect to matters of law or the legality of surrogate parenting and is not rendering legal services or providing legal advice. However, the Natural Father has the absolute right to seek legal counsel of his own selection in his negotiations and agreement with the selected surrogate mother or her representative. In the event the Natural Father utilizes the legal services of counsel other than the law firm retained by ICNY, all legal fees and cost shall be borne by the Natural Father and such fees and costs shall be in addition to the fees and costs set forth in Paragraph 3 of this Agreement.

(6) Prior to signing this Agreement, each party has been given the opportunity to consult with an attorney of his own choice concerning the terms and legal significance of the Agreement, and the effect which it has upon any and all interests of the parties. Each party acknowledges that he fully understands the Agreement and its legal effect, and that he is signing the same freely and voluntarily and that neither party has any reason to believe that the other did not understand fully the terms and effects of this Agreement, or that he did not freely and voluntarily execute this Agreement.

(7) Natural Father warrants and represents the following to ICNY:

(a) That the Natural Father's semen is of sufficient nature both quantitatively and qualitatively to impregnate the selected surrogate mother.

(b) That the Natural Father is medically free from disease or other hereditary medical problems which could cause injury, defect, or disease to the surrogate mother or child.

(c) That the Natural Father will not make or attempt to make directly or through a representative, a subsequent agreement with the selected surrogate mother or any other surrogates introduced to the Natural Father by ICNY before or at any time after the birth of his child. In the event of a further arrangement with the surrogate for a child is made, the Natural Father agrees to pay to ICNY a second fee in the amount specified in Paragraph 3 of this Agreement.

(8) Natural Father agrees that breach of any of his warranties and representations shall cause this Agreement to immediately terminate but in no way relieve the Natural Father from his obligations under this Agreement. Further, the Natural Father agrees that his warranties and representations shall survive the termination of this Agreement.

(9) Natural Father hereby acknowledges that ICNY makes no representations or warranties with respect to any agreement or understanding which may be reached, or may have been reached, between himself and a prospective "surrogate mother." Natural Father further acknowledges that the nature of any such agreement or understanding as well as all ramifications, obligations and enforcement matters relating thereto are subject which he must seek advice from his attorney.

(10) It is expressly understood that ICNY does not guarantee or warrant that the "surrogate mother" will in fact conceive a child fathered by Natural Father; nor does ICNY guarantee or warrant that if a child is conceived, it will be a healthy child, free from all defects; nor does ICNY guarantee or warrant the "surrogate mother" (and her husband, if applicable) will comply with the terms and provisions of the separate agreement entered into between herself [sic] and Natural Father including but not limited to, the "surrogate mother's" refusal to surrender custody of the child upon birth.

(11) Natural Father hereby specifically releases ICNY and its officers, employees, agents and representatives from any and all liability and responsibility of any nature whatsoever except willful and gross negligence, which may result from complications, breaches, damages, losses, claims, actions, liabilities, whether actual or asserted of any kind, and all other costs or detriments of any kind, in any way related to or arising from any agreement or understanding between himself and a "surrogate mother" located through the services of ICNY. Moreover, the Natural Father understands the relationship between ICNY and the relationship of the doctors used in connection with insemination, monitoring and any other medical or psychiatric procedure or treatment of the surrogate or of the child is that of an independent contractor and that there is no other relationship between the parties.

. . .

(13) This Agreement has been drafted, negotiated and executed in New York, New York, and shall be governed by, continued and enforced in accordance with the laws of the State of New York.

(14) In the event any of the provisions of this Agreement are deemed to be invalid or unenforceable, the same shall be deemed severable from the remainder of this Agreement and shall not cause the invalidity or unenforceability of the remainder of this Agreement. If such provision(s) shall be deemed invalid due to its scope or breadth, then said provision(s) shall be deemed valid to the extent of the scope or breadth permitted by law.

. . .

NOTES

1. What obligations did the surrogate undertake in signing this agreement? What about the natural father? Why is the intended mother, Elizabeth Whitehead, not part of either contract? Is the Surrogate Parenting Agreement a contract for the sale of reproductive services, for the sale of the resulting baby, or for the sale of parenting rights?

2. What kinds of risks is the intermediary (ICNY) assuming here? What about the natural father? Why is it that the intermediary can command a fee that is three-quarters of the fee that the surrogate mother herself is to receive, if she successfully abides by the terms of the contract? Notice that the intermediary will receive the fee whether or not the attempt at insemination is successful.

In re Baby M

Supreme Court of New Jersey, 1988.
109 N.J. 396, 537 A.2d 1227.

■ WILENTZ, C.J.

In this matter the Court is asked to determine the validity of a contract that purports to provide a new way of bringing children into a family. For a fee of $10,000, a woman agrees to be artificially inseminated with the semen of another woman's husband; she is to conceive a child, carry it to term, and after its birth surrender it to the natural father and his wife. . . .

We invalidate the surrogacy contract because it conflicts with the law and public policy of this State. While we recognize the depth of the yearning of infertile couples to have their own children, we find the payment of money to a "surrogate" mother illegal, perhaps criminal, and potentially degrading to women. . . .

. . .

In February 1985, William Stern and Mary Beth Whitehead entered into a surrogacy contract. It recited that Stern's wife, Elizabeth, was infertile, that they wanted a child, and that Mrs. Whitehead was willing to provide that child as the mother with Mr. Stern as the father.

The contract provided that through artificial insemination using Mr. Stern's sperm, Mrs. Whitehead would become pregnant, carry the child to term, bear it, deliver it to the Sterns, and thereafter do whatever was necessary to terminate her maternal rights so that Mrs. Stern could thereafter adopt the child. Mrs. Whitehead's husband, Richard,[1] was also a party to

---

1. Subsequent to the trial court proceedings, Mr. and Mrs. Whitehead were divorced, and soon thereafter Mrs. Whitehead remarried. Nevertheless, in the course of this opinion we will

the contract; Mrs. Stern was not. Mr. Whitehead promised to do all acts necessary to rebut the presumption of paternity under the PARENTAGE ACT. Although Mrs. Stern was not a party to the surrogacy agreement, the contract gave her sole custody of the child in the event of Mr. Stern's death. Mrs. Stern's status as a nonparty to the surrogate parenting agreement presumably was to avoid the application of the baby-selling statute to this arrangement.

Mr. Stern, on his part, agreed to attempt the artificial insemination and to pay Mrs. Whitehead $10,000 after the child's birth, on its delivery to him. In a separate contract, Mr. Stern agreed to pay $7,500 to the Infertility Center of New York ("ICNY"). The Center's advertising campaigns solicit surrogate mothers and encourage infertile couples to consider surrogacy. ICNY arranged for the surrogacy contract by bringing the parties together, explaining the process to them, furnishing the contractual form, and providing legal counsel.

The history of the parties' involvement in this arrangement suggests their good faith. William and Elizabeth Stern were married in July 1974, having met at the University of Michigan, where both were Ph.D. candidates. Due to financial considerations and Mrs. Stern's pursuit of a medical degree and residency, they decided to defer starting a family until 1981. Before then, however, Mrs. Stern learned that she might have multiple sclerosis and that the disease in some cases renders pregnancy a serious health risk. Her anxiety appears to have exceeded the actual risk, which current medical authorities assess as minimal. Nonetheless that anxiety was evidently quite real, Mrs. Stern fearing that pregnancy might precipitate blindness, paraplegia, or other forms of debilitation. Based on the perceived risk, the Sterns decided to forego having their own children. The decision had a special significance for Mr. Stern. Most of his family had been destroyed in the Holocaust. As the family's only survivor, he very much wanted to continue his bloodline.

Initially the Sterns considered adoption, but were discouraged by the substantial delay apparently involved and by the potential problem they saw arising from their age and their differing religious backgrounds. They were most eager for some other means to start a family.

The paths of Mrs. Whitehead and the Sterns to surrogacy were similar. Both responded to advertising by ICNY. The Sterns' response, following their inquiries into adoption, was the result of their long-standing decision to have a child. Mrs. Whitehead's response apparently resulted from her sympathy with family members and others who could have no children (she stated that she wanted to give another couple the "gift of life"); she also wanted the $10,000 to help her family.

Both parties, undoubtedly because of their own self-interest, were less sensitive to the implications of the transaction than they might otherwise have been. Mrs. Whitehead, for instance, appears not to have been concerned about whether the Sterns would make good parents for her child; the Sterns, on their part, while conscious of the obvious possibility that surrendering the child might cause grief to Mrs. Whitehead, overcame their qualms because of their desire for a child. At any rate, both the Sterns and Mrs.

---

make reference almost exclusively to the facts as they existed at the time of trial, the facts on which the decision we now review was reached. We note moreover that Mr. Whitehead remains a party to this dispute. For these reasons, we continue to refer to appellants as Mr. and Mrs. Whitehead.

Whitehead were committed to the arrangement; both thought it right and constructive.

Mrs. Whitehead had reached her decision concerning surrogacy before the Sterns, and had actually been involved as a potential surrogate mother with another couple. After numerous unsuccessful artificial inseminations, that effort was abandoned. Thereafter, the Sterns learned of the Infertility Center, the possibilities of surrogacy, and of Mary Beth Whitehead. The two couples met to discuss the surrogacy arrangement and decided to go forward. On February 6, 1985, Mr. Stern and Mr. and Mrs. Whitehead executed the surrogate parenting agreement. After several artificial inseminations over a period of months, Mrs. Whitehead became pregnant. The pregnancy was uneventful and on March 27, 1986, Baby M was born.

... Her birth certificate indicated her name to be Sara Elizabeth Whitehead and her father to be Richard Whitehead. In accordance with Mrs. Whitehead's request, the Sterns visited the hospital unobtrusively to see the newborn child.

Mrs. Whitehead realized, almost from the moment of birth, that she could not part with this child. She had felt a bond with it even during pregnancy. Some indication of the attachment was conveyed to the Sterns at the hospital when they told Mrs. Whitehead what they were going to name the baby. She apparently broke into tears and indicated that she did not know if she could give up the child. She talked about how the baby looked like her daughter, and made it clear that she was experiencing great difficulty with the decision.

Nonetheless, Mrs. Whitehead was, for the moment, true to her word. Despite powerful inclinations to the contrary, she turned her child over to the Sterns on March 30 at the Whiteheads' home.

The Sterns were thrilled with their new child. They had planned extensively for its arrival, far beyond the practical furnishing of a room for her. It was a time of joyful celebration—not just for them but for their friends as well. The Sterns looked forward to raising their daughter, whom they named Melissa. While aware by then that Mrs. Whitehead was undergoing an emotional crisis, they were as yet not cognizant of the depth of that crisis and its implications for their newly-enlarged family.

Later in the evening of March 30, Mrs. Whitehead became deeply disturbed, disconsolate, stricken with unbearable sadness. She had to have her child. She could not eat, sleep, or concentrate on anything other than her need for her baby. The next day she went to the Sterns' home and told them how much she was suffering.

The depth of Mrs. Whitehead's despair surprised and frightened the Sterns. She told them that she could not live without her baby, that she must have her, even if only for one week, that thereafter she would surrender her child. The Sterns, concerned that Mrs. Whitehead might indeed commit suicide, not wanting under any circumstances to risk that, and in any event believing that Mrs. Whitehead would keep her word, turned the child over to her. It was not until four months later, after a series of attempts to regain possession of the child, that Melissa was returned to the Sterns, having been forcibly removed from the home where she was then living with Mr. and Mrs. Whitehead, the home in Florida owned by Mary Beth Whitehead's parents.

The struggle over Baby M began when it became apparent that Mrs. Whitehead could not return the child to Mr. Stern. Due to Mrs. Whitehead's refusal to relinquish the baby, Mr. Stern filed a complaint seeking enforcement of the surrogacy contract. He alleged, accurately, that Mrs. Whitehead had not only refused to comply with the surrogacy contract but had threatened to flee from New Jersey with the child in order to avoid even the possibility of his obtaining custody. The court papers asserted that if Mrs. Whitehead were to be given notice of the application for an order requiring her to relinquish custody, she would, prior to the hearing, leave the state with the baby. And that is precisely what she did. After the order was entered, *ex parte*, the process server, aided by the police, in the presence of the Sterns, entered Mrs. Whitehead's home to execute the order. Mr. Whitehead fled with the child, who had been handed to him through a window while those who came to enforce the order were thrown off balance by a dispute over the child's current name.

The Whiteheads immediately fled to Florida with Baby M....

Eventually the Sterns discovered where the Whiteheads were staying, commenced supplementary proceedings in Florida, and obtained an order requiring the Whiteheads to turn over the child. Police in Florida enforced the order, forcibly removing the child from her grandparents' home. She was soon thereafter brought to New Jersey and turned over to the Sterns. The prior order of the court, issued *ex parte*, awarding custody of the child to the Sterns *pendente lite*, was reaffirmed by the trial court after consideration of the certified representations of the parties (both represented by counsel) concerning the unusual sequence of events that had unfolded. Pending final judgment, Mrs. Whitehead was awarded limited visitation with Baby M.

The Sterns' complaint, in addition to seeking possession and ultimately custody of the child, sought enforcement of the surrogacy contract. Pursuant to the contract, it asked that the child be permanently placed in their custody, that Mrs. Whitehead's parental rights be terminated, and that Mrs. Stern be allowed to adopt the child, *i.e.*, that, for all purposes, Melissa become the Sterns' child.

The trial took thirty-two days over a period of more than two months.... [The trial court] held that the surrogacy contract was valid; ordered that Mrs. Whitehead's parental rights be terminated and that sole custody of the child be granted to Mr. Stern; and, after hearing brief testimony from Mrs. Stern, immediately entered an order allowing the adoption of Melissa by Mrs. Stern, all in accordance with the surrogacy contract. Pending the outcome of the appeal, we granted a continuation of visitation to Mrs. Whitehead, although slightly more limited than the visitation allowed during the trial.

· · ·

We have concluded that this surrogacy contract is invalid. Our conclusion has two bases: direct conflict with existing statutes and conflict with the public policies of this State, as expressed in its statutory and decisional law.

· · ·

(1) Our law prohibits paying or accepting money in connection with any placement of a child for adoption. Violation is a high misdemeanor. Excepted are fees of an approved agency (which must be a non-profit entity) and certain expenses in connection with childbirth.

Considerable care was taken in this case to structure the surrogacy arrangement so as not to violate this prohibition.... Nevertheless, it seems clear that the money was paid and accepted in connection with an adoption.

... The payment of the $10,000 occurs only on surrender of custody of the child and "completion of the duties and obligations" of Mrs. Whitehead, including termination of her parental rights to facilitate adoption by Mrs. Stern. As for the contention that the Sterns are paying only for services and not for an adoption, we need note only that they would pay nothing in the event the child died before the fourth month of pregnancy, and only $1,000 if the child were stillborn, even though the "services" had been fully rendered. Additionally, one of Mrs. Whitehead's estimated costs, to be assumed by Mr. Stern, was an "Adoption Fee," presumably for Mrs. Whitehead's incidental costs in connection with the adoption.

Mr. Stern knew he was paying for the adoption of a child; Mrs. Whitehead knew she was accepting money so that a child might be adopted; the Infertility Center knew that it was being paid for assisting in the adoption of a child. The actions of all three worked to frustrate the goals of the statute. It strains credulity to claim that these arrangements, touted by those in the surrogacy business as an attractive alternative to the usual route leading to an adoption, really amount to something other than a private placement adoption for money.

... The evils inherent in baby bartering are loathsome for a myriad of reasons. The child is sold without regard for whether the purchasers will be suitable parents. N. Baker, Baby Selling: The Scandal of Black Market Adoption 7 (1978). The natural mother does not receive the benefit of counseling and guidance to assist her in making a decision that may affect her for a lifetime. In fact, the monetary incentive to sell her child may, depending on her financial circumstances, make her decision less voluntary. . . .

... The negative consequences of baby buying are potentially present in the surrogacy context, especially the potential for placing and adopting a child without regard to the interest of the child or the natural mother.

(2) The termination of Mrs. Whitehead's parental rights, called for by the surrogacy contract and actually ordered by the court, fails to comply with the stringent requirements of New Jersey law. Our law, recognizing the finality of any termination of parental rights, provides for such termination only where there has been a voluntary surrender of a child to an approved agency or to the Division of Youth and Family Services ("DYFS"), accompanied by a formal document acknowledging termination of parental rights, or where there has been a showing of parental abandonment or unfitness. A termination may ordinarily take one of three forms: an action by an approved agency, an action by DYFS, or an action in connection with a private placement adoption. The three are governed by separate statutes, but the standards for termination are substantially the same, except that whereas a written surrender is effective when made to an approved agency or to DYFS, there is no provision for it in the private placement context.

. . .

Our statutes, and the cases interpreting them, leave no doubt that where there has been no written surrender to an approved agency or to DYFS, termination of parental rights will not be granted in this state absent a very strong showing of abandonment or neglect. That showing is required in every context in which termination of parental rights is sought, be it an action by an approved agency, an action by DYFS, or a private placement adoption proceeding, even where the petitioning adoptive parent is, as here, a stepparent. . . .

In this case a termination of parental rights was obtained not by proving the statutory prerequisites but by claiming the benefit of contractual provisions. From all that has been stated above, it is clear that a contractual agreement to abandon one's parental rights, or not to contest a termination action, will not be enforced in our courts. The Legislature would not have so carefully, so consistently, and so substantially restricted termination of parental rights if it had intended to allow termination to be achieved by one short sentence in a contract.

Since the termination was invalid, it follows, as noted above, that adoption of Melissa by Mrs. Stern could not properly be granted.

. . .

The surrogacy contract guarantees permanent separation of the child from one of its natural parents. Our policy, however, has long been that to the extent possible, children should remain with and be brought up by both of their natural parents. . . . This is not simply some theoretical ideal that in practice has no meaning. The impact of failure to follow that policy is nowhere better shown than in the results of this surrogacy contract. A child, instead of starting off its life with as much peace and security as possible, finds itself immediately in a tug-of-war between contending mother and father.

The surrogacy contract violates the policy of this State that the rights of natural parents are equal concerning their child, the father's right no greater than the mother's. . . . The whole purpose and effect of the surrogacy contract was to give the father the exclusive right to the child by destroying the rights of the mother.

The policies expressed in our comprehensive laws governing consent to the surrender of a child . . . stand in stark contrast to the surrogacy contract and what it implies. Here there is no counseling, independent or otherwise, of the natural mother, no evaluation, no warning.

The only legal advice Mary Beth Whitehead received regarding the surrogacy contract was provided in connection with the contract that she previously entered into with another couple. Mrs. Whitehead's lawyer was referred to her by the Infertility Center, with which he had an agreement to act as counsel for surrogate candidates. His services consisted of spending one hour going through the contract with the Whiteheads, section by section, and answering their questions. Mrs. Whitehead received no further legal advice prior to signing the contract with the Sterns.

Mrs. Whitehead was examined and psychologically evaluated, but if it was for her benefit, the record does not disclose that fact. The Sterns regarded the evaluation as important, particularly in connection with the question of whether she would change her mind. Yet they never asked to see it, and were content with the assumption that the Infertility Center had made an evaluation and had concluded that there was no danger that the surrogate mother would change her mind. From Mrs. Whitehead's point of view, all that she learned from the evaluation was that "she had passed." It is apparent that the profit motive got the better of the Infertility Center. Although the evaluation was made, it was not put to any use, and understandably so, for the psychologist warned that Mrs. Whitehead demonstrated certain traits that might make surrender of the child difficult and that there should be further inquiry into this issue in connection with her surrogacy. To inquire further, however, might have jeopardized the Infertility Center's fee. The record indicates that neither Mrs. Whitehead nor the Sterns were ever told of this fact, a fact that might have ended their surrogacy arrangement.

Under the contract, the natural mother is irrevocably committed before she knows the strength of her bond with her child. She never makes a totally voluntary, informed decision, for quite clearly any decision prior to the baby's birth is, in the most important sense, uninformed, and any decision after that, compelled by a pre-existing contractual commitment, the threat of a lawsuit, and the inducement of a $10,000 payment, is less than totally voluntary. Her interests are of little concern to those who controlled this transaction.

Although the interest of the natural father and adoptive mother is certainly the predominant interest, realistically the *only* interest served, even they are left with less than what public policy requires. They know little about the natural mother, her genetic makeup, and her psychological and medical history. Moreover, not even a superficial attempt is made to determine their awareness of their responsibilities as parents.

Worst of all, however, is the contract's total disregard of the best interests of the child. There is not the slightest suggestion that any inquiry will be made at any time to determine the fitness of the Sterns as custodial parents, of Mrs. Stern as an adoptive parent, their superiority to Mrs. Whitehead, or the effect on the child of not living with her natural mother.

This is the sale of a child, or, at the very least, the sale of a mother's right to her child, the only mitigating factor being that one of the purchasers is the father. Almost every evil that prompted the prohibition of the payment of money in connection with adoptions exists here.

The differences between an adoption and a surrogacy contract should be noted, since it is asserted that the use of money in connection with surrogacy does not pose the risks found where money buys an adoption. Katz, *Surrogate Motherhood and the Baby–Selling Laws*, 20 Colum. J.L. & Soc. Probs. 1 (1986).

First, and perhaps most important, all parties concede that it is unlikely that surrogacy will survive without money. Despite the alleged selfless motivation of surrogate mothers, if there is no payment, there will be no surrogates, or very few. That conclusion contrasts with adoption; for obvious reasons, there remains a steady supply, albeit insufficient, despite the prohibitions against payment. The adoption itself, relieving the natural mother of the financial burden of supporting an infant, is the equivalent of payment.

Second, the use of money in adoptions does not *produce* the problem—conception occurs, and usually the birth itself, before illicit funds are offered. With surrogacy, the "problem," if one views it as such, consisting of the purchase of a woman's procreative capacity, at the risk of her life, is caused by and originates with the offer of money.

Third, with the law prohibiting the use of money in connection with adoptions, the built-in financial pressure of the unwanted pregnancy and the consequent support obligation do not lead the mother to the highest paying, ill-suited, adoptive parents. She is just as well off surrendering the child to an approved agency. In surrogacy, the highest bidders will presumably become the adoptive parents regardless of suitability, so long as payment of money is permitted.

Fourth, the mother's consent to surrender her child in adoptions is revocable, even after surrender of the child, unless it be to an approved agency, where by regulation there are protections against an ill-advised surrender. In surrogacy, consent occurs so early that no amount of advice would satisfy the potential mother's need, yet the consent is irrevocable.

The main difference, that the plight of the unwanted pregnancy is unintended while the situation of the surrogate mother is voluntary and intended, is really not significant. Initially, it produces stronger reactions of sympathy for the mother whose pregnancy was unwanted than for the surrogate mother, who "went into this with her eyes wide open." On reflection, however, it appears that the essential evil is the same, taking advantage of a woman's circumstances (the unwanted pregnancy or the need for money) in order to take away her child, the difference being one of degree.

In the scheme contemplated by the surrogacy contract in this case, a middle man, propelled by profit, promotes the sale. Whatever idealism may have motivated any of the participants, the profit motive predominates, permeates, and ultimately governs the transaction. The demand for children is great and the supply small. The availability of contraception, abortion, and the greater willingness of single mothers to bring up their children has led to a shortage of babies offered for adoption. The situation is ripe for the entry of the middleman who will bring some equilibrium into the market by increasing the supply through the use of money.

Intimated, but disputed, is the assertion that surrogacy will be used for the benefit of the rich at the expense of the poor. *See, e.g.*, Radin, *Market Inalienability*, 100 Harv. L. Rev. 1849, 1930 (1987). In response it is noted that the Sterns are not rich and the Whiteheads not poor. Nevertheless, it is clear to us that it is unlikely that surrogate mothers will be as proportionately numerous among those women in the top twenty percent income bracket as among those in the bottom twenty percent. Put differently, we doubt that infertile couples in the low-income bracket will find upper income surrogates.

In any event, even in this case one should not pretend that disparate wealth does not play a part simply because the contrast is not the dramatic "rich versus poor." At the time of trial, the Whiteheads' net assets were probably negative—Mrs. Whitehead's own sister was foreclosing on a second mortgage. Their income derived from Mr. Whitehead's labors. Mrs. Whitehead is a homemaker, having previously held part-time jobs. The Sterns are both professionals, she a medical doctor, he a biochemist. Their combined income when both were working was about $89,500 a year and their assets sufficient to pay for the surrogacy contract arrangements.

The point is made that Mrs. Whitehead *agreed* to the surrogacy arrangement, supposedly fully understanding the consequences. Putting aside the issue of how compelling her need for money may have been, and how significant her understanding of the consequences, we suggest that her consent is irrelevant. There are, in a civilized society, some things that money cannot buy. In America, we decided long ago that merely because conduct purchased by money was "voluntary" did not mean that it was good or beyond regulation and prohibition. Employers can no longer buy labor at the lowest price they can bargain for, even though that labor is "voluntary," or buy women's labor for less money than paid to men for the same job, or purchase the agreement of children to perform oppressive labor, or purchase the agreement of workers to subject themselves to unsafe or unhealthful working conditions. There are, in short, values that society deems more important than granting to wealth whatever it can buy, be it labor, love, or life. Whether this principle recommends prohibition of surrogacy, which presumably sometimes results in great satisfaction to all of the parties, is not for us to say. We note here only that, under existing law, the fact that Mrs. Whitehead "agreed" to the arrangement is not dispositive.

The long-term effects of surrogacy contracts are not known, but feared—the impact on the child who learns her life was bought, that she is the offspring of someone who gave birth to her only to obtain money; the impact on the natural mother as the full weight of her isolation is felt along with the full reality of the sale of her body and her child; the impact on the natural father and adoptive mother once they realize the consequences of their conduct. Literature in related areas suggests these are substantial considerations, although, given the newness of surrogacy, there is little information.

The surrogacy contract creates, it is based upon, principles that are directly contrary to the objectives of our laws. It guarantees the separation of a child from its mother; it looks to adoption regardless of suitability; it totally ignores the child; it takes the child from the mother regardless of her wishes and her maternal fitness; and it does all of this, it accomplishes all of its goals, through the use of money.

Beyond that is the potential degradation of some women that may result from this arrangement. In many cases, of course, surrogacy may bring satisfaction, not only to the infertile couple, but to the surrogate mother herself. The fact, however, that many women may not perceive surrogacy negatively but rather see it as an opportunity does not diminish its potential for devastation to other women.

In sum, the harmful consequences of this surrogacy arrangement appear to us all too palpable. In New Jersey the surrogate mother's agreement to sell her child is void. Its irrevocability infects the entire contract, as does the money that purports to buy it.

We have already noted that under our laws termination of parental rights cannot be based on contract, but may be granted only on proof of the statutory requirements. That conclusion was one of the bases for invalidating the surrogacy contract. Although excluding the contract as a basis for parental termination, we did not explicitly deal with the question of whether the statutory bases for termination existed. We do so here.

. . .

Nothing in this record justifies a finding that would allow a court to terminate Mary Beth Whitehead's parental rights under the statutory standard. It is not simply that obviously there was no "intentional abandonment or very substantial neglect of parental duties without a reasonable expectation of reversal of that conduct in the future," *N.J.S.A.*9:3–48c(1), quite the contrary, but furthermore that the trial court never found Mrs. Whitehead an unfit mother and indeed affirmatively stated that Mary Beth Whitehead had been a good mother to her other children.

. . .

The right to procreate, as protected by the Constitution, has been ruled on directly only once by the United States Supreme Court. *See Skinner v. Oklahoma*, 316 U.S. 535 [(1942)] (forced sterilization of habitual criminals violates equal protection clause of fourteenth amendment). Although *Griswold v. Connecticut*, 381 U.S. 479 [(1965)], is obviously of a similar class, strictly speaking it involves the right *not* to procreate. The right to procreate very simply is the right to have natural children, whether through sexual intercourse or artificial insemination. It is no more than that. Mr. Stern has not been deprived of that right. Through artificial insemination of Mrs. Whitehead, Baby M is his child. The custody, care, companionship, and nurturing that follow birth are not parts of the right to procreation; they are rights that may also be constitutionally protected, but that involve many considerations other than the right of procreation. To assert that Mr. Stern's right of procreation gives him the right to the custody of Baby M would be to assert that Mrs. Whitehead's right of procreation does *not* give her the right to the custody of Baby M; it would be to assert that the constitutional right of procreation includes within it a constitutionally protected contractual right to destroy someone else's right of procreation.

. . .

Mr. Stern . . . contends that he has been denied equal protection of the laws by the State's statute granting full parental rights to a husband in relation to the child produced, with his consent, by the union of his wife with a sperm donor. The claim really is that of Mrs. Stern. It is that she is in precisely the same position as the husband in the statute: she is presumably infertile, as is the husband in the statute; her spouse by agreement with a third party procreates with the understanding that the child will be the couple's child. The alleged unequal protection is that the understanding is honored in the statute when the husband is the infertile party, but no similar understanding is honored when it is the wife who is infertile.

It is quite obvious that the situations are not parallel. A sperm donor simply cannot be equated with a surrogate mother. The State has more than a sufficient basis to distinguish the two situations—even if the only difference is between the time it takes to provide sperm for artificial insemination and the time invested in a nine-month pregnancy—so as to justify automatically divesting the sperm donor of his parental rights without automatically divesting a surrogate mother. Some basis for an equal protection argument might exist if Mary Beth Whitehead had contributed her egg to be implanted, fertilized or otherwise, in Mrs. Stern, resulting in the latter's pregnancy. That is not the case here, however.

Mrs. Whitehead, on the other hand, asserts a claim that falls within the scope of a recognized fundamental interest protected by the Constitution. As a mother, she claims the right to the companionship of her child. This is a fundamental interest, constitutionally protected. Furthermore, it was taken away from her by the action of the court below. Whether that action under these circumstances would constitute a constitutional deprivation, however, we need not and do not decide. By virtue of our decision Mrs. Whitehead's constitutional complaint—that her parental rights have been unconstitutionally terminated—is moot. . . .

. . .

. . . With the surrogacy contract disposed of, the legal framework becomes a dispute between two couples over the custody of a child produced by the artificial insemination of one couple's wife by the other's husband. Under the Parentage Act the claims of the natural father and the natural mother are entitled to equal weight. . . . The applicable rule given these circumstances is clear: the child's best interests determine custody.

. . .

The Whiteheads . . . contend that the award of custody to the Sterns *pendente lite* was erroneous and that the error should not be allowed to affect the final custody decision.... The Whiteheads' conclusion is that had the trial court not given initial custody to the Sterns during the litigation, Mrs. Whitehead not only would have demonstrated her perfectly acceptable personality—the general tenor of the opinion of experts was that her personality problems surfaced primarily in crises—but would also have been able to prove better her parental skills along with an even stronger bond than may now exist between her and Baby M. Had she not been limited to custody for four months, she could have proved all of these things much more persuasively through almost two years of custody.

The argument has considerable force. It is of course possible that the trial court was wrong in its initial award of custody. It is also possible that such error, if that is what it was, may have affected the outcome. We disagree with the premise, however, that in determining custody a court should decide what the child's best interests *would be* if some hypothetical state of facts had existed. Rather, we must look to what those best interests *are, today,* even if some of the facts may have resulted in part from legal error. The child's interests come first: we will not punish it for judicial errors, assuming any were made....

There were eleven experts who testified concerning the child's best interests, either directly or in connection with matters related to that issue. Our reading of the record persuades us that the trial court's decision awarding custody to the Sterns (technically to Mr. Stern) should be affirmed since "its findings ... could reasonably have been reached on sufficient credible evidence present in the record."...

Our custody conclusion is based on strongly persuasive testimony contrasting both the family life of the Whiteheads and the Sterns and the personalities and characters of the individuals. The stability of the Whitehead family life was doubtful at the time of trial. Their finances were in serious trouble (foreclosure by Mrs. Whitehead's sister on a second mortgage was in process). Mr. Whitehead's employment, though relatively steady, was always at risk because of his alcoholism, a condition that he seems not to have been able to confront effectively. Mrs. Whitehead had not worked for quite some time, her last two employments having been part-time. One of the Whiteheads' positive attributes was their ability to bring up two children, and apparently well, even in so vulnerable a household. Yet substantial question was raised even about that aspect of their home life. The expert testimony contained criticism of Mrs. Whitehead's handling of her son's educational difficulties. Certain of the experts noted that Mrs. Whitehead perceived herself as omnipotent and omniscient concerning her children. She knew what they were thinking, what they wanted, and she spoke for them. As to Melissa, Mrs. Whitehead expressed the view that she alone knew what that child's cries and sounds meant. Her inconsistent stories about various things engendered grave doubts about her ability to explain honestly and sensitively to Baby M—and at the right time—the nature of her origin. Although faith in professional counseling is not a *sine qua non* of parenting, several experts believed that Mrs. Whitehead's contempt for professional help, especially professional psychological help, coincided with her feelings of omnipotence in a way that could be devastating to a child who most likely will need such help. In short, while love and affection there would be, Baby M's life with the Whiteheads promised to be too closely controlled by Mrs. Whitehead. The prospects for a wholesome independent psychological growth and development would be at serious risk.

The Sterns have no other children, but all indications are that their household and their personalities promise a much more likely foundation for Melissa to grow and thrive. There *is* a track record of sorts—during the one-and-a-half years of custody Baby M has done very well, and the relationship between both Mr. and Mrs. Stern and the baby has become very strong. The household is stable, and likely to remain so. Their finances are more than adequate, their circle of friends supportive, and their marriage happy. Most important, they are loving, giving, nurturing, and open-minded people. They have demonstrated the wish and ability to nurture and protect Melissa, yet at the same time to encourage her independence. Their lack of experience is more than made up for by a willingness to learn and to listen, a willingness that is enhanced by their professional training, especially Mrs. Stern's experience as a pediatrician. They are honest; they can recognize error, deal with it, and learn from it. They will try to determine rationally the best way to cope with problems in their relationship with Melissa. When the time comes to tell her about her origins, they will probably have found a means of doing so that accords with the best interests of Baby M. All in all, Melissa's future appears solid, happy, and promising with them.

Based on all of this we have concluded, independent of the trial court's identical conclusion, that Melissa's best interests call for custody in the Sterns. Our above-mentioned disagreements with the trial court do not, as we have noted, in any way diminish our concurrence with its conclusions. We feel, however, that those disagreements are important enough to be stated. . . .

It seems to us that given her predicament, Mrs. Whitehead was rather harshly judged—both by the trial court and by some of the experts. She was guilty of a breach of contract, and indeed, she did break a very important promise, but we think it is expecting something well beyond normal human capabilities to suggest that this mother should have parted with her newly born infant without a struggle. Other than survival, what stronger force is there? We do not know of, and cannot conceive of, any other case where a perfectly fit mother was expected to surrender her newly born infant, perhaps forever, and was then told she was a bad mother because she did not. We know of no authority suggesting that the moral quality of her act in those circumstances should be judged by referring to a contract made before she became pregnant. We do not countenance, and would never countenance, violating a court order as Mrs. Whitehead did, even a court order that is wrong; but her resistance to an order that she surrender her infant, possibly forever, merits a measure of understanding. We do not find it so clear that her efforts to keep her infant, when measured against the Sterns' efforts to take her away, make one, rather than the other, the wrongdoer. The Sterns suffered, but so did she. And if we go beyond suffering to an evaluation of the human stakes involved in the struggle, how much weight should be given to her nine months of pregnancy, the labor of childbirth, the risk to her life, compared to the payment of money, the anticipation of a child and the donation of sperm?

There has emerged a portrait of Mrs. Whitehead, exposing her children to the media, engaging in negotiations to sell a book, granting interviews that seemed helpful to her, whether hurtful to Baby M or not, that suggests a selfish, grasping woman ready to sacrifice the interests of Baby M and her other children for fame and wealth. That portrait is a half-truth, for while it may accurately reflect what ultimately occurred, its implication, that this is what Mary Beth Whitehead wanted, is totally inaccurate, at least insofar as the record before us is concerned. There is not one word in that record to support a claim that had she been allowed to continue her possession of her newly born infant, Mrs. Whitehead would have ever been heard of again; not one word in the record suggests that her change of mind and her subsequent fight for her child was motivated by anything other than love— whatever complex underlying psychological motivations may have existed.

We have a further concern regarding the trial court's emphasis on the Sterns' interest in Melissa's education as compared to the Whiteheads'. That this difference is a legitimate factor to be considered we have no doubt. But it should not be overlooked that a best-interests test is designed to create not a new member of the intelligentsia but rather a well-integrated person who might reasonably be expected to be happy with life. "Best interests" does not contain within it any idealized lifestyle; the question boils down to a judgment, consisting of many factors, about the likely future happiness of a human being. Stability, love, family happiness, tolerance, and, ultimately, support of independence—all rank much higher in predicting future happiness than the likelihood of a college education. We do not mean to suggest that the trial court would disagree. We simply want to dispel any possible misunderstanding on the issue.

Even allowing for these differences, the facts, the experts' opinions, and the trial court's analysis of both argue strongly in favor of custody in the Sterns. Mary Beth Whitehead's family life, into which Baby M would be placed, was anything but secure—the quality Melissa needs most. And today it may be even less so. Furthermore, the evidence and expert opinion based on it reveal personality characteristics, mentioned above, that might threaten the child's best development. The Sterns promise a secure home, with an understanding relationship that allows nurturing and independent growth to develop together. Although there is no substitute for reading the entire record, including the review of every word of each experts' [sic] testimony and reports, a summary of their conclusions is revealing. Six experts testified for Mrs. Whitehead: one favored joint custody, clearly unwarranted in this case; one simply rebutted an opposing expert's claim that Mary Beth Whitehead had a recognized personality disorder; one testified to the adverse impact of separation on *Mrs. Whitehead*; one testified about the evils of adoption and, to him, the probable analogous evils of surrogacy; one spoke only on the question of whether Mrs. Whitehead's consent in the surrogacy agreement was "informed consent"; and one spelled out the strong bond between mother and child. None of them unequivocally stated, or even necessarily implied, an opinion that custody in the Whiteheads was in the best interests of Melissa—the ultimate issue. The Sterns' experts, both well qualified—as were the Whiteheads'—concluded that the best interests of Melissa required custody in Mr. Stern. Most convincingly, the three experts chosen by the court-appointed guardian *ad litem* of Baby M, each clearly free of all bias and interest, unanimously and persuasively recommended custody in the Sterns.

Some comment is required on the initial *ex parte* order awarding custody *pendente lite* to the Sterns (and the continuation of that order after a plenary hearing). The issue, although irrelevant to our disposition of this case, may recur; and when it does, it can be of crucial importance. When father and mother are separated and disagree, at birth, on custody, only in an extreme, truly rare, case should the child be taken from its mother *pendente lite, i.e.,* only in the most unusual case should the child be taken from its mother before the dispute is finally determined by the court on its merits. The probable bond between mother and child, and the child's need, not just the mother's, to strengthen that bond, along with the likelihood, in most cases, of a significantly lesser, if any, bond with the father—all counsel against temporary custody in the father. A substantial showing that the mother's continued custody would threaten the child's health or welfare would seem to be required.

In this case, the trial court, believing that the surrogacy contract might be valid, and faced with the probable flight from the jurisdiction by Mrs. Whitehead and the baby if *any* notice were served, ordered, *ex parte*, an immediate transfer of possession of the child, *i.e.*, it ordered that custody be transferred immediately to Mr. Stern, rather than order Mrs. Whitehead not to leave the State. We have ruled, however, that the surrogacy contract is unenforceable and illegal. It provides no basis for either an *ex parte*, a plenary, an interlocutory, or a final order requiring a mother to surrender custody to a father. Any application by the natural father in a surrogacy dispute for custody pending the outcome of the litigation will henceforth require proof of unfitness, of danger to the child, or the like, of so high a quality and persuasiveness as to make it unlikely that such application will succeed. Absent the required showing, all that a court should do is list the matter for argument on notice to the mother. Even her threats to flee should not suffice to warrant any other relief unless her unfitness is clearly shown. At most, it should result in an order enjoining such flight. The erroneous transfer of custody, as we view it, represents a greater risk to the child than removal to a foreign jurisdiction, unless parental unfitness is clearly proved. Furthermore, we deem it likely that, advised of the law and knowing that her custody cannot seriously be challenged at this stage of the litigation, surrogate mothers will obey any court order to remain in the jurisdiction.

... Our reversal of the trial court's order ... requires delineation of Mrs. Whitehead's rights to visitation.... We ... remand the visitation issue to the trial court for an abbreviated hearing and determination....

. . .

We also note the following for the trial court's consideration: First, this is not a divorce case where visitation is almost invariably granted to the non-custodial spouse. To some extent the facts here resemble cases where the non-custodial spouse has had practically no relationship with the child, but it only "resembles" those cases. In the instant case, Mrs. Whitehead spent the first four months of this child's life as her mother and has regularly visited the child since then. Second, she is not only the natural mother, but also the legal mother, and is not to be penalized one iota because of the surrogacy contract. Mrs. Whitehead, as the mother (indeed, as a mother who nurtured her child for its first four months—unquestionably a relevant consideration), is entitled to have her own interest in visitation considered....

In all of this, the trial court should recall the touchstones of visitation: that it is desirable for the child to have contact with both parents; that besides the child's interests, the parents' interests also must be considered; but that when all is said and done, the best interests of the child are paramount.

We have decided that Mrs. Whitehead is entitled to visitation at some point, and that question is not open to the trial court on this remand.... It also should be noted that the guardian's recommendation of a five-year delay is most unusual—one might argue that it begins to border on termination. Nevertheless, if the circumstances as further developed by appropriate proofs or as reconsidered on remand clearly call for that suspension under applicable legal principles of visitation, it should be so ordered.

. . .

The judgment is affirmed in part, reversed in part, and remanded for further proceedings consistent with this opinion.

NOTES

1. On remand, a New Jersey Superior Court held that Melissa's best interests would be served by unsupervised, liberal visitation with Mary Beth Whitehead–Gould. *In re Baby M*, 542 A.2d 52 (N.J. Super. Ct. Ch. Div. 1988). In 1994, it was reported that Melissa Stern, who called herself Sassy, was an active eight-year-old and still very much torn between her two families. She lived most of the year in New Jersey with the Sterns, but spent two days a week and every other weekend in Long Island with Mrs. Whitehead–Gould and her four half siblings. *Torn Between Two Moms: Baby M 8 Years Later*, REDBOOK, Jan. 1994, at 60. In 2007, upon turning eighteen, Ms. Stern reportedly terminated Mary Beth Whitehead–Gould's parental rights, in order to initiate the process of adoption by Elizabeth Stern. As a religion major at George Washington University, she reportedly found it strange to study the *Baby M* case in the context of a bioethics class. Jennifer Weiss, *Now it's Melissa's Time*, NEW JERSEY MONTHLY MAGAZINE, March, 2007, at 70–72. By 2010, Ms. Stern was pursuing graduate studies at King's College in London, and studying the policy issues raised by new reproductive technologies. *See* Melissa Kay Stern, Reviving Solomon: Modern Day Questions Regarding the Long–Term Implications for the Children of Surrogacy Arrangements (2010) (unpublished MSc thesis) (on file with the author).

2. *Baby M* was a case of "full surrogacy," meaning the surrogate contributed her own egg. Some commentators thought that the courts might not be as hostile to a contract for "gestational surrogacy," where the surrogate was not genetically related to the baby. This expectation proved unfounded. In *A.H.W. v. G.H.B.*, 772 A.2d 948 (N.J. Super. Ct. Ch. Div. 2000), a New Jersey superior court held that a gestational mother still had to follow adoption proceedings to legally relinquish parental rights in favor of the intended (and genetically-related) parents because the contract was unenforceable and could not confer parental rights. More recently, a different New Jersey superior court recognized a gestational surrogate as the legal mother of twins who were born to her using a donated egg and the semen of her brother's same-sex partner. The court affirmed that the principles in *Baby M* guided its ruling and that gestational surrogacy did not pose fundamentally different questions of public policy than traditional surrogacy. *A.G.R. v. D.R.H.*, No. FD–09–1838–07 (N.J. Super. Ct. Ch. Div. Dec. 23, 2009).

3. Approximately twenty states do not have either statutes or published case law directly addressing surrogacy. The states with statutes generally take one of five different approaches, with varying definitions of surrogacy that may or may not distinguish between traditional and gestational surrogacy: a) *general prohibition of surrogacy, see, e.g.*, ARIZ. REV. STAT. ANN. § 25–218(A) (2007); D.C. CODE § 16–402(a) (2001); IND. CODE ANN. §§ 31–20–1–1–3 (West 2008); MICH. COMP. LAWS ANN. § 722.855 (West 2011); N.Y. DOM. REL. LAW § 122 (McKinney 2010); N.D. CENT. CODE § 14–18–05 (2009); b) *civil or criminal punishment of surrogacy, e.g.*, D.C. CODE § 16–402(b) (2001); MICH. COMP. LAWS ANN. § 722.859 (West 2011); N.Y. DOM. REL. LAW § 123 (McKinney 2010); c) *prohibition of commercial surrogacy, see, e.g.*, KY. REV. STAT. ANN. § 199.590(4) (West 2006); LA. REV. STAT. ANN. § 9:2713 (West 2005); NEB. REV. STAT. § 25–21,200 (2008); WASH. REV. CODE §§ 26.26.230, 26.26.240 (2010); d) *direct regulation of surrogacy with approval requirements, e.g.*, FLA. STAT. ANN. §§ 742.15, 742.16 (West 2010); 750 ILL. COMP. STAT. 47/1–47/75 (2010); NEV. REV. STAT. § 126.045 (2009); N.H. REV. STAT. ANN. §§ 168–B:1–B:32 (LexisNexis 2010); TEX. FAM. CODE ANN. §§ 160.751–160.763 (Vernon 2008); UTAH CODE ANN. §§ 78B–15–801–809 (2008); VA. CODE ANN. §§ 20–156–165 (2008 & Supp. 2011); and e) *indirect acknowledgment of surrogacy*. States in this category do not have a surrogacy statute but instead contemplate surrogacy in their parentage, adoption or birth registration statutes. For example, in its statute on AI, Arkansas provides for the parentage in favor of biological or intended parents if a child is born to a surrogate mother, implicitly recognizing surrogacy but without offering further guidance. ARK. CODE ANN. § 9–10–201 (2009). Tennessee's statute on adoption denies that it authorizes surrogacy but also states that certain surrogate births are not subject to its surrender, termination, or adoption provisions. TENN. CODE ANN. § 36–1–102(48) (2010). Other states follow a similar pattern, not authorizing surrogacy per se but covering it in their birth registration statutes. *E.g.,* CONN. GEN. STAT. ANN. § 7–48(a) (West 2008); LA. REV. STAT. ANN. § 40:34 (West 2001 & Supp. 2011); WIS. STAT. § 69.14 (2009–10).

4. Some scholars suggest that the constitutional right to procreate includes an individual's right to have his or her own genetically-related descendents whether through sex or through ART. Among other things, this would mean that a state violates the right to procreate when it imposes a complete ban on surrogacy, or even when it heavily restricts its use. *See generally* JOHN A. ROBERTSON, CHILDREN OF CHOICE: FREEDOM AND THE NEW REPRODUCTIVE TECHNOLOGIES 119–45 (1994). Do you agree with this argument? For one court's examination of the state's interests in regulating surrogacy, *see Doe v. Attorney General,* 487 N.W.2d 484 (Mich. Ct. App. 1992).

5. Some states that permit surrogacy have developed requirements for the eligibility of the parties, terms of the contract, and procedures for validation and enforcement. For example, a section of Illinois' Gestational Surrogacy Act, 750 ILL. COMP. STAT. 47/20 (2010), provides:

§ 20. Eligibility.

(a) A gestational surrogate shall be deemed to have satisfied the requirements of this Act if she has met the following requirements at the time the gestational surrogacy contract is executed:

(1) she is at least 21 years of age; (2) she has given birth to at least one child; (3) she has completed a medical evaluation; (4) she has completed a mental health evaluation; (5) she has undergone legal consultation with independent legal counsel regarding the terms of the gestational surrogacy contract and the potential legal consequences of the gestational surrogacy; and (6) she has obtained a health insurance policy that covers major medical treatments and hospitalization and the health insurance policy has a term that extends throughout the duration of the expected pregnancy and for 8 weeks after the birth of the child; provided, however, that the policy may be procured by the intended parents on behalf of the gestational surrogate pursuant to the gestational surrogacy contract.

(b) The intended parent or parents shall be deemed to have satisfied the requirements of this Act if he, she, or they have met the following requirements at the time the gestational surrogacy contract is executed:

(1) he, she, or they contribute at least one of the gametes resulting in a pre-embryo that the gestational surrogate will attempt to carry to term; (2) he, she, or they have a medical need for the gestational surrogacy as evidenced by a qualified physician's affidavit attached to the gestational surrogacy contract and as required by the ILLINOIS PARENTAGE ACT of 1984; (3) he, she, or they have completed a mental health evaluation; and (4) he, she, or they have undergone legal consultation with independent legal counsel regarding the terms of the gestational surrogacy contract and the potential legal consequences of the gestational surrogacy.

Some states limit the category of intended parents to married couples. *E.g.,* FLA. STAT. ANN. § 742.15(1) (West 2010); N.H. REV. STAT. ANN. § 168–B:1(VII) (LexisNexis 2010); UTAH CODE ANN. § 78B–15–801(3) (2008); VA. CODE ANN. § 20–156 (2008); among those a number limit availability to married heterosexual couples. *E.g.,* NEV. REV. STAT. § 126.045 (2009); VA. CODE ANN. § 20–156 (2008). Several statutes require that at least one of the intended parents be genetically related to the child. *E.g.,* 750 ILL. COMP. STAT. 47/10, 47/20(b)(1) (2010). One state requires that the gestational carrier must be related to the child if the intended mother is not. N.H. REV. STAT.

ANN. § 168–B:17(IV) (LexisNexis 2010). In contrast, some statutes require that the gestational mother not make any genetic contribution to the child. *E.g.*, 750 ILL. COMP. STAT. 47/10 (2010); UTAH CODE ANN. § 78B–15–801(7) (2008); TEX. FAM. CODE ANN. § 160.754(c) (Vernon 2008). Some states prohibit any compensation beyond reasonable living, medical, legal, and other expenses related to the surrogacy. *E.g.*, FLA. STAT. ANN. § 742.15(4) (West 2010). A state may allow for additional compensation but may specify that it be reasonable. *E.g.*, UTAH CODE ANN. § 78B–15–803(2)(h) (2008). What kinds of policies are pursued by these requirements?

6.   The court in *Baby M* expressed concern about the motives and actions of the company that facilitated the arrangement: "It is apparent that the profit motive got the better of the Infertility Center." 537 A.2d at 1247. Some states have adopted prohibitions or regulations regarding the role that facilitators, intermediaries, or brokers play in surrogacy. New Hampshire, for example, provides, "No person or entity shall promote or in any other way solicit or induce for a fee, commission or other valuable consideration, or with intent or expectation of receiving the same, any party or parties to enter into a surrogacy arrangement." N.H. REV. STAT. ANN. § 168–B:16(IV) (LexisNexis 2010). What is lost and what is gained by prohibiting intermediaries in surrogacy contracts?

2.   THE LEGALITY AND ENFORCEABILITY OF TRANSNATIONAL SURROGACY CONTRACTS

Differences in regulation of the ART industry exist not only between states but also between countries. Many countries have banned surrogacy contracts altogether. On the other extreme, some countries have enacted laws that are very friendly to gestational surrogacy. Easier access to travel and information for middle class families in the developed world, along with dramatic differences in standards of living with countries of the developing world have spurred the emergence of a transnational medical-tourism industry. Transnational surrogacy is a relatively new but growing part of this industry. An American couple looking for a surrogate from a state that restricts commercial surrogacy might theoretically travel to California to evade those restrictions but they will be faced with steep costs. They might instead choose to become clients of one of the many medical tourism agencies specializing in transnational surrogacy. For a fraction of the price, they may be able to procure egg and sperm from Eastern Europe, fertilize them in a clinic in India, and transfer the pre-embryos to an Indian surrogate who agrees to carry the pregnancy to term.

In re X and [A]nother

Royal Courts of Justice, High Court of Justice, Family Division, 2008.
[2009] Fam. 71.

■ HEDLEY[,] J[.] handed down the following judgment.

Although the outcome of this case was in the end happy for all those involved, it provides a cautionary tale for any who contemplate parenthood by entering into a foreign surrogacy agreement. . . .

. . .

Surrogacy remains an ethically controversial area and different societies and different nations take radically different stances in their approach to it. Under some legal systems (e.g. Italy, Germany, Turkey) it is simply prohibited. In others, commercial surrogacy agreements are permitted (e.g. California, Ukraine, India) and perhaps sometimes even encouraged. The position in the United Kingdom lies between those extremes: whilst commercial surrogacy is unlawful, surrogacy itself is not but no surrogacy agreement is legally enforceable as such. Each sovereign state will have its own preferred approach and its own regulatory system. Those who enter into surrogacy agreements abroad will have to take account both of the law of that state and of the United Kingdom. As this case vividly demonstrates, not only may (and probably will) those laws be different but they may be incompatible to the point of mutual contradiction.

... After exploring many parenting options in this country and upon what appeared to be informed and responsible advice, the applicants decided to explore surrogacy in the Ukraine. Their inquiries revealed apparently admirable medical facilities, skilled English language advice and a readiness to assist. They were introduced to possible surrogate mothers. In the end they entered into an agreement with a married Ukrainian woman who had had her own children and had been interested in being a surrogate for her own sister. In the end the sister had become pregnant naturally and this woman had then decided to offer herself as a surrogate mother for another. Terms were discussed, to the details of which I will have to return. Suffice it to say at this stage that the terms agreed covered her expenses, compensated her for loss of earnings and would permit her to put down a deposit for the purchase of a flat in the place where she and her husband worked. The Ukrainian woman was implanted with embryos conceived with donor eggs (the donor being anonymous) and fertilised by the male applicant's sperm. The relationship between the parties ripened into friendship. In due course she conceived and gave birth to twins. Then the real trouble started, none of it caused by either the surrogate mother or the applicants.

[Court analyzes Section 27 of the U.K. Human Fertilisation and Embryology Act 1990, which provides that the surrogate mother is to be considered the legal mother of the child even if biologically unrelated. Section 28 of the Act similarly provides that if the surrogate mother is married then her consenting husband is to be treated as the legal father of the child.]

The court was provided with expert evidence of Ukrainian law. Consequent upon perusal of that evidence (and uncontroversially as between the parties), I find that the consequences of the application of Ukrainian law are that once the surrogate mother had given birth to the twins and delivered them to the applicants, she and her husband were free of all obligation to the children. They had neither the status nor the rights and duties of parents; indeed it seems that they could probably have been compelled under Ukrainian law to complete the surrogacy agreement once the children had been born. Moreover, the children had no rights of residence in or citizenship of the Ukraine and there was no obligation owed them by the state other than to accommodate them as an act of basic humanity in a state orphanage. The applicants became the parents for all purposes under Ukrainian law and were registered as such on the birth certificate. The children accordingly took their parents' nationality and were not therefore Ukrainian citizens.

The applicants had of course entered the Ukraine on a temporary visa and had no rights to remain (let alone work or reside) in the Ukraine beyond the period specified in the visa. The effect of all this was of course that these children were effectively legal orphans and, more seriously, stateless. Citizenship has sometimes been defined as "the right to have rights"; in the law of both the United Kingdom and the Ukraine they had indeed acquired certain rights. However, the children under English domestic law ... had no English parents or, at best, a putative father with no parental responsibility. Under Ukrainian law, however, the surrogate mother and her husband were not only relieved of but deprived of all rights, duties and status of parents, the applicants alone had them. Their legal position was the graver because under the law of the United Kingdom ... not only did these children have no right of entry of their own to the United Kingdom, for the applicants could not confer nationality on them, but the applicants had no right to bring them in; or at best the male applicant may have obtained leave to do so as a putative father or relative.

None of this was foreshadowed in any of the extensive inquiries the applicants had made before leaving this country, whether on Home Office websites or the information given by the bodies who advised them in the United Kingdom or the information given to them in and through the Ukrainian hospital. The effect was that the children were marooned stateless and parentless whilst the applicants could neither remain in the Ukraine nor bring the children home. In the end, having satisfied the immigration authorities by DNA tests (which had to be processed in this country, thus causing further delay) that the male applicant was the biological father of both children, the children were given discretionary leave to enter "outside the rules" to afford the applicants the opportunity to regularise their status under English law, hence the application for the parental order.... It was as well in this case that there was no pressing need for medical treatment. It may be worth adding that the grant of a parental order does not of itself confer citizenship although the evidence suggests that it is very unlikely to be denied if sought.

. . .

... The applicants contend that if [the surrogate's husband] is treated as the father two undesirable consequences follow. First, it will put a premium on making surrogacy agreements with unmarried women for were that the case here the male applicant would undoubtedly be treated as the father. In fact most surrogate mothers (so I have been informed in the evidence) tend to be married women at a more mature stage of their lives and there is encouragement to enter into these arrangements with such women. The unmarried surrogate mother may be more vulnerable, more prey to exploitation and be more likely to be motivated principally by material considerations. In my judgment that is a fair analysis of fact but whether it assists in statutory construction is more doubtful. Secondly it is said that a man, having no stake in the matter and no risk of responsibility might seek to abuse his position as, for example, by seeking further payment against his consent. Once again that may be so but it would be equally true of surrogate mothers after birth; that seems to me simply a risk inherent in foreign surrogacy agreements in jurisdictions whose domestic law imposes no responsibilities on surrogates after birth.

... The intention of Parliament was to recognise the particular relevance of marriage in surrogacy arrangements. I can see no reason why that should be affected by questions of domicile. The fact that the Ukrainian husband is relieved of responsibilities imposed on his English equivalent is not a valid reason given that the wife of each is in an identical position. This is a recognition of the particular position of the lawfully married husband and I see no reason why (given the statutory words) that should not be applied extra-territorially. It follows that in my view the Ukrainian husband's consent was required; as I have already indicated, I am satisfied that it has been lawfully given. . . .

. . . The evidence of the applicants, which I accept, was that they agreed to pay €235 per month to the surrogate mother during pregnancy and a lump sum of €25,000 on the live birth of the twins; 80% of that sum was payable on the surrogate mother's provision of a notarised consent to facilitate the applicants being registered on the Ukrainian birth certificate, the balance on the signing of written consent to the parental order application at six weeks. These are the figures actually paid, the payments being lawful under domestic Ukrainian law. They represented at the time rather lower sterling equivalents than they did at the time they were actually paid.

Clearly the surrogate mother would have incurred significant expense in terms of loss of earnings, medical care and so on. Nevertheless it was effectively conceded that the sums paid significantly exceeded "expenses reasonably incurred" however that might be construed. Such concession was really inevitable on the basis of the applicants' own evidence that the surrogate mother intended to use some of the money to put down a deposit for the purchase of a flat in a property economy not dissimilar to that then prevailing in this country. It follows that this application cannot succeed unless the court authorises these payments which exceed expenses and so offend English domestic law.

. . .

The statute affords no guidance as to the basis, however, of any such approval. It is clearly a policy decision that commercial surrogacy agreements should not be regarded as lawful; equally there is clearly a recognition that sometimes there may be reasons to do so. It is difficult to see what reason Parliament might have in mind other than the welfare of the child under consideration. . . . On the other hand, given that there is a wholly valid public policy justification lying behind Section 30(7), welfare considerations cannot be paramount but, of course, are important. . . .

. . .

In this case I am satisfied that the welfare of these children require that they be regarded as lifelong members of the applicants' family. Given my findings on the public policy considerations, I am able without great difficulty to conclude that I should in this particular case authorise the payments so made under Section 30(7) of the 1990 Act.

I feel bound to observe that I find this process of authorisation most uncomfortable. What the court is required to do is to balance two competing and potentially irreconcilably conflicting concepts. Parliament is clearly entitled to legislate against commercial surrogacy and is clearly entitled to expect that the courts should implement that policy consideration in its decisions. Yet it is also recognised that as the full rigour of that policy consideration will bear on one wholly unequipped to comprehend it let alone deal with its consequences (i.e. the child concerned) that rigour must be mitigated by the application of a consideration of that child's welfare. That approach is both humane and intellectually coherent. The difficulty is that it is almost impossible to imagine a set of circumstances in which by the time the case comes to court, the welfare of any child (particularly a foreign child) would not be gravely compromised (at the very least) by a refusal to make an order. . . . In relation to adoption this has been substantially addressed by rules surrounding the bringing of the child into the country and by the provisions of the Adoption with a Foreign Element Regulations 2005. The point of admission to this country is in some ways the final opportunity in reality to prevent the effective implementation of a commercial surrogacy agreement. . . .

. . .

As babies become less available for adoption and given the withdrawal of donor confidentiality (wholly justifiable, of course, from the child's perspective), more and more couples are likely to be tempted to follow the applicant's path to commercial surrogacy in those places where it is lawful, of which there may be many. This case may provide grounds for cautious reflection before that course is adopted. There are the obvious difficulties of inconvenience, delay, hardship and expense but there is more.

It will be readily apparent that many pitfalls confront the couple who consider commissioning a foreign surrogacy. First, the quality of the information currently available is variable and may, in what it omits, actually be misleading. Secondly, potentially difficult conflict of law issues arise which may (as in this case) have wholly unintended and unforeseen consequences as for example in payments made. Thirdly, serious immigration problems may arise having regard to the effect of Sections 27–29 of the 1990 Act, at least as understood by me. Children born to foreign surrogate mothers, especially to married women, may have no rights of entry nor may the law confer complementary rights on the commissioning couple. Fourthly, Section 30 is available only to a married couple, others may encounter even more significant difficulties in securing parental status to children born to a surrogate mother, and that is of importance since the Human Fertilisation and Embryology Act 2008 will by Section 54 open up parental orders to unmarried and same sex couples. Lastly, even if all other pitfalls are avoided, rights may depend both upon the unswerving commitment of the surrogate mother (and her husband if she has one) to supporting the surrogacy through to completion by Section 30 order and upon their honesty in not taking advantage of their absolute veto.

NOTES

1. In addition to the problems of recognition of the legal status of children born via transnational surrogacy, there are troubling questions about the degree of control exerted over foreign surrogates. In a recent piece about the Indian surrogacy industry on the Wall Street Journal's website, a same-sex couple was reported to have asked their two surrogates, who were both pregnant with twins and twelve weeks into their pregnancies, to each have a selective "reduction," as one of the fathers preferred to call the procedure, to reduce health risks to the children. The article quoted him discussing his feelings of responsibility for the children. Discussion of the surrogates' interests was conspicuously absent from the article. *See* Tamara Audi & Arlene Chang, *Assembling the Global Baby*, WALL ST. J. (Dec. 10, 2010), http://online.wsj.com/article/SB10001424052748703493504576007774155273928.html.

2. In some cases, possibly rare, traveling for reproduction may happen for reasons other than the reduced cost, such as avoiding the application of a national regulatory framework. The chief executive of a medical tourism business that includes surrogacy, is quoted in the same Wall Street Journal piece as saying that the business's ethics are neutral, but that they have in the past declined to accept certain clients. More specifically, he cites a case where he thought that the prospective client may have been trying to combine her own egg with her son's sperm. *See* Tamara Audi & Arlene Chang, *Assembling the Global Baby*, WALL ST. J.(Dec. 10, 2010), http://online.wsj.com/article/SB10001424052748703493504576007774155273928.html.

B. ASSISTED REPRODUCTIVE TECHNOLOGIES AND PARENTAGE

1. ART AND THE SPOUSE'S PARENTAL STATUS

Strnad v. Strnad

Supreme Court of New York, New York County, 1948.
78 N.Y.S.2d 390.

■ GREENBERG, JUSTICE.

The court has assumed . . . that the plaintiff was artificially inseminated with the consent of the defendant and that the child is not of the blood of the defendant. Predicated on that assumption the court concludes as follows:

(1) The defendant is entitled to rights of visitation. . . .

(2) The court holds that the child has been potentially adopted or semi-adopted by the defendant. In any event, in so far as this defendant is concerned and with particular reference to visitation, he is entitled to the same rights as those acquired by a foster parent who has formally adopted a child, if not the same rights as those to which a natural parent under the circumstances would be entitled.

(3) In the opinion of this court, assuming again that plaintiff was artificially inseminated with the consent of the defendant, this child is not an illegitimate child. Indeed, logically and realistically, the situation is no different than that pertaining in the case of a child born out of wedlock who by law is made legitimate upon the marriage of the interested parties.

(4) The court does not pass on the legal consequences in so far as property rights are concerned in a case of this character, nor does the court express an opinion on the propriety of procreation by the medium of artificial insemination. With such matters the court is not here concerned; the latter problem particularly is in the fields of sociology, morality and religion.

In re Marriage of Witbeck–Wildhagen

Appellate Court of Illinois, Fourth District, 1996.
281 Ill. App.3d 502, 217 Ill. Dec. 329, 667 N.E.2d 122.

■ JUSTICE KNECHT delivered the opinion of the court:

Petitioner, Marcia Witbeck–Wildhagen, filed a petition for dissolution of marriage on January 26, 1994. One issue raised during the dissolution action was whether respondent, Eric Wildhagen, was the legal father of a child conceived by artificial insemination and born during the marriage. The trial court determined respondent is not the legal father of the child because he did not consent to the artificial insemination of petitioner, as required by section 3 of the Illinois Parentage Act (Act) (750 ILCS 40/3 (West 1994)). Petitioner appeals and we affirm.

Petitioner and respondent were married in November 1990. In April 1992, petitioner and respondent consulted with a nurse clinician at Christie Clinic regarding the procedure of artificial insemination. At the consultation, respondent made it clear to petitioner and the nurse he did not want to participate in, nor did he consent to, petitioner's attempts to become pregnant. Petitioner acknowledges at the consultation respondent expressed his desire not to participate in her attempt to have a baby, but alleges respondent said it would be all right if she pursued the pregnancy alone. Whenever respondent had sexual relations with petitioner, he used a condom to prevent pregnancy. Following the initial consultation at Christie Clinic, petitioner underwent seven artificial insemination procedures. Respondent was not informed of this by Christie Clinic or by petitioner.

In approximately October 1993, petitioner became pregnant. In January 1994, she filed a petition for dissolution of marriage. The petition stated no children were born during the marriage but petitioner was pregnant. The complaint alleged petitioner did not have sufficient property and income to provide for her reasonable needs or those of her unborn child. Petitioner sought custody of the unborn child and asked the court to order respondent to pay reasonable sums for her maintenance, support of the unborn child, and prenatal and delivery expenses.

On July 2, 1994, petitioner gave birth to a son, M.W. In September 1994, respondent filed a motion for blood testing, which was allowed. Petitioner's attorney then notified respondent, in a letter dated September 14, 1994, of the seven artificial insemination procedures, the last of which, the letter stated, may have resulted in the conception of M.W. The parties and M.W. underwent blood testing in November 1994. Respondent was conclusively excluded as M.W.'s biological father.

. . .

The issue presented is whether, under section 3 of the Act, the lack of written consent by respondent to petitioner's artificial insemination precludes the establishment of a father-child relationship and the imposition of a support obligation.

Section 3(a) of the Act provides:

"(a) If, under the supervision of a licensed physician *and with the consent of her husband*, a wife is inseminated artificially with semen donated by a man not her husband, *the husband shall be treated in law as if he were the natural father* of a child thereby conceived. *The husband's consent must be in writing* executed and acknowledged by both the husband and wife. *The physician* who is to perform the technique *shall certify their signatures and the date of the insemination, and file the husband's consent* in the medical record where it shall be kept confidential and held by the patient's physician. However, *the physician's failure to do so shall not affect the legal relationship between father and child.* All papers and records pertaining to the insemination, whether part of the permanent medical record held by the physician or not, are subject to inspection only upon an order of the court for good cause shown." (Emphasis added.) 750 ILCS 40/3(a) (West 1994).

Only one Illinois case has analyzed this provision of the Act. In *In re Marriage of Adams*, 528 N.E.2d 1075, 1084 ([Ill. App. Ct.]1988), *rev'd on other grounds*, 551 N.E.2d 635 ([Ill.]1990), the Second District Appellate Court decided the failure to obtain the husband's *written* consent does not bar further inquiry into the circumstances surrounding the decision to use the artificial insemination procedure. The court examined the surrounding circumstances in the case and, although the husband had not executed a written consent to his wife's artificial insemination, agreed with the trial court's finding he had manifested his consent by his conduct before, during, and after the pregnancy. The court concluded nothing in section 3 bars the imposition of a support obligation on an estoppel or waiver theory where *written* consent is not obtained. Thus, the court imposed a support obligation on the husband, who had manifested actual consent to the procedure by his conduct. In *Adams* the court found the husband *consented* to the procedure. In this case respondent did not consent to the artificial insemination procedure, either in writing or in any other manner.

After the appellate court decision in *Adams*, the Supreme Court of Illinois reviewed the case but, because it determined Florida law was controlling and remanded the case, the court did not render a conclusive interpretation of section 3 of the Act. . . .

    . . .

We conclude the legislature intended a husband's written consent to be a prerequisite to the establishment of the legal father-child relationship and the imposition of a support obligation. The several provisions in section 3 of the Act which address the consent requirement would be superfluous if the failure to obtain the husband's written consent would not affect the legal status of the individuals involved.

In addition, because the statute requires the physician to certify the *date* of insemination, we conclude the husband's written consent is required *each time* his wife is to undergo the procedure. Such a requirement is not burdensome and it leaves no room for confusion on the part of the married couple or the physician regarding whether a consent previously given by the husband is still viable.

On the facts of this case, we need not decide whether the failure to obtain written consent would be an absolute bar to the establishment of a father-child relationship where the conduct of the father otherwise demonstrated his consent to the artificial insemination procedure. Such a situation was present in *Adams* and has also been addressed by commentators and the courts of other states.

Here, there is no evidence of consent by respondent to the artificial insemination procedure, written or otherwise. Petitioner filed for a dissolution of marriage within two or three months of becoming pregnant. She was impregnated by the sperm of a man other than respondent, without respondent's knowledge or consent, and apparently without any intention of raising the child with respondent. In her brief, petitioner admits she underwent the procedure relying on her doctor's written assurance respondent would be legally responsible for her child, even though it was not his wish she have a child. There is no evidence in the record of any contact or interaction between respondent and M.W., and petitioner had M.W.'s last name legally changed to her maiden name. Under the facts of this case, there is no statutory or equitable basis for concluding a father-child relationship exists between respondent and M.W.

Petitioner urges this court to impose a support obligation on respondent, even absent the existence of a father-child relationship, contending any other result would be contrary to public policy. The two primary policy considerations here are (1) M.W.'s right to support, and (2) respondent's right to choose not to be a parent.

Just as a woman has a constitutionally protected right not to bear a child (*see Roe v. Wade*, 410 U.S. 113 (1973)), a man has the right not to be deemed the parent of a child that he played *no* part in conceiving. Respondent made a choice not to parent a child. This choice was evidenced by not giving his consent to petitioner or any support to her choice to undergo artificial insemination. Petitioner underwent the procedure unbeknownst to respondent. Respondent was only informed of the manner in which M.W. was conceived *after* M.W. was born, by his attorney. This is not a case where respondent has changed his mind or is attempting to evade responsibility for his own actions in helping to conceive or encouraging the conception of a child. The facts of this case illustrate, and the trial court correctly determined, it would be inconsistent with public policy to force upon respondent parental obligations which he declined to undertake.

The second policy consideration here is M.W.'s right to support. The main purpose of the policy recognizing a child's right to support is to prevent minors from becoming dependent on the State. The trial court's order demonstrates it considered M.W.'s need for support and found that support would be forthcoming from his mother. The child's right to support cannot be met by requiring a nonparent to fulfill the obligation of a parent. Respondent has no financial obligation to this child.

It is the duty of the court to ensure the rights of the child are adequately protected. In this case, the trial court did so, and the balance it struck between the attendant interests of the parties was appropriate. It would be unjust to impose a support obligation on respondent where no father-child relationship exists between him and M.W. and he did not consent to the artificial insemination procedure. Accordingly, we affirm.

Miller–Jenkins v. Miller–Jenkins

Supreme Court of Vermont, 2006.
180 Vt. 441, 912 A.2d 951.

■ DOOLEY, J.

Lisa Miller–Jenkins appeals a family court decision finding her expartner [sic], Janet Miller–Jenkins, to be a parent of their three-year-old child conceived via artificial insemination. . . .

. . . We affirm the family court's determination that Janet is a parent of IMJ, the resulting visitation order, and the order of contempt issued against Lisa for her failure to abide by the visitation order.

Lisa and Janet lived together in Virginia for several years in the late 1990's. In December 2000, the parties traveled to Vermont and entered into a civil union. In 2001, while Lisa and Janet were still a couple, Lisa began to receive artificial insemination from sperm provided by an anonymous donor. Janet participated in the decision that Lisa become impregnated and helped select the anonymous donor. In April 2002, Lisa gave birth to IMJ, with Janet present in the delivery room. Lisa, Janet, and IMJ lived in Virginia until IMJ was approximately four months old and then moved together to Vermont around August of 2002. The parties lived together with IMJ in Vermont until the fall of 2003, when they decided to separate. After the separation, in September 2003, Lisa moved to Virginia with IMJ.

On November 24, 2003, Lisa filed a petition to dissolve the civil union in the Vermont family court in Rutland. In her complaint, Lisa listed IMJ as the "biological or adoptive child[ ]of the civil union." Lisa requested that the court award her custodial rights and award Janet parent-child contact. The family court issued a temporary order on parental rights and responsibilities on June 17, 2004. This order awarded Lisa temporary legal and physical responsibility for IMJ, and awarded Janet parent-child contact for two weekends in June, one weekend in July, and the third full week of each month, beginning in August 2004. The family court also ordered Lisa to permit Janet to have telephone contact with IMJ once daily.

Although Lisa permitted the first court ordered parent-child-contact weekend, she did not allow Janet to have parent-child contact after that date, nor did she allow Janet to have telephone contact with IMJ, as the family court had ordered. In fact, Lisa has not allowed Janet to have any contact with IMJ other than during that first weekend. Meanwhile, on July 1, 2004, after the Vermont court had already filed its temporary custody and visitation order and parentage decision, Lisa filed a petition in the Frederick County Virginia Circuit Court and asked that court to establish IMJ's parentage.

In response, on July 19, 2004, the Vermont court reaffirmed its "jurisdiction over this case including all parent-child contact issues," stated that it would not "defer to a different State that would preclude the parties from a remedy," and made clear that the temporary order for parent-child contact was to be followed. It added that "[f]ailure of the custodial parent to allow contact will result in an immediate hearing on the need to change custody."

... On October 15, the Virginia court followed with a parentage order finding Lisa to be the "sole biological and natural parent" of IMJ and holding that Janet has no "claims of parentage or visitation rights over" IMJ. That order is on appeal to the Virginia Court of Appeals.

On November 17, 2004, the Vermont court found that both Lisa and Janet had parental interests in IMJ and set the case for a final hearing on parental rights, property, and child support. Thereafter, on December 21, 2004, the Vermont court issued a ruling refusing to give full faith and credit to the Virginia parentage decision. Lisa appealed both of these decisions, as well as the decision finding her in contempt.

[The court affirms Vermont's jurisdiction over the case based on the Uniform Child Custody Jurisdiction Act and the Parental Kidnapping Prevention Act and refuses to enforce Virginia's order, which was in violation of these acts (part I). It declares that Lisa and Janet's civil union was valid (part II).]

III.   The Parentage Determination

Lisa's third argument attacks the temporary visitation order on the basis that Janet is not a parent of IMJ. She argues that Janet cannot be a parent of IMJ because she is not biologically connected to her. In making this argument, Lisa looks primarily to the Parentage Proceedings Act, 15 V.S.A. §§ 301–308. Under § 308(4):

> A person alleged to be a parent shall be rebuttably presumed to be the natural parent of a child if ... (4) the child is born while the husband and wife are legally married to each other.

This statute applies to civil unions by virtue of § 1204(f):

> (f) The rights of parties to a civil union, with respect to a child of whom either becomes the natural parent during the term of the civil union, shall be the same as those of a married couple, with respect to a child of whom either spouse becomes the natural parent during the marriage.

Lisa contends that because the Legislature used the word "natural" in § 308(4), it must have intended the presumption of parentage to apply only to a person who is biologically connected to the child. She argues, therefore, that because she is IMJ's biological mother, and Janet is not, Janet cannot be a parent of IMJ. If Janet is not IMJ's parent, Lisa continues, then the family court erred in awarding Janet visitation.

. . .

Ultimately, we have both a short and a long answer to Lisa's argument regarding the effect of § 308(4), and, because of the public interest in the issue, we provide both. The short answer is that the issue is controlled by this Court's decision in *Paquette v. Paquette*, 499 A.2d 23 ([Vt.]1985), under which the presumption of parentage contained in § 308 is irrelevant. In *Paquette*, the parties were involved in a divorce and the husband sought custody of both the child born of the marriage and another child born of the wife's prior marriage. The lower court ruled that custody could not be awarded to a stepfather and, on that basis, denied the husband custody of the older child. On appeal, this Court reversed, holding that where the stepparent has assumed the role of a parent with respect to the child—that is, had acted "in loco parentis"—the lower court can give custody to the stepparent, over the opposition of the biological parent, if it finds that it is in the best interest of the child to do so and "the natural parent is unfit or . . . extraordinary circumstances exist to warrant such a custodial order."

. . .

Under *Paquette*, regardless of the meaning of 15 V.S.A. § 308(4), Janet has at least the status of a stepparent of IMJ by virtue of § 1204(d) and (f). Assuming extraordinary circumstances are even required for a visitation order, we conclude that extraordinary circumstances are present in this case. The court's findings demonstrate that Janet acted in loco parentis with respect to IMJ as long as Janet and Lisa were together. Thus, our short answer to Lisa's argument is that the visitation order is supported by *Paquette* even if Janet is not considered IMJ's parent under § 308(4).

There is also a longer answer to Lisa's argument that biology must control the parentage issue. We find that Janet has status as a parent, even beyond her stepparent status under *Paquette*. If we were to accept Lisa's opposing position and conclude biology controlled, a child born from artificial insemination would have no second parent—whether that status is sought by a man married to the child's mother or by a woman or man in a civil union with the child's biological parent—unless the putative second parent adopted the child. In fact, the logical extension of Lisa's position that a biological connection is necessary for parentage is that the husband of a wife who bears an artificially inseminated child cannot be the father of that child, just like a civil union spouse cannot be a parent to the child. Such a holding would cause tremendous disruption and uncertainty to some exist-ing families who have conceived via artificial insemination or other means of reproductive technology, and we must tread carefully so that we incur such a consequence only if necessary. As a result, we reach the broader and longer answer to Lisa's argument and conclude that such a holding would be wrong.

. . .

The disruption that would be caused by requiring adoption of all children conceived by artificial insemination by nonbiological [sic] parents is particularly at variance with the legislative intent for civil unions. The Legislature's intent in enacting the civil union laws was to create legal equality between relationships based on civil unions and those based on marriage. The Legislature added a separate section on the construction of the civil union statutes that provides in part:

> Treating the benefits, protections and responsibilities of civil marriage differently from the benefits, protections and responsibilities of civil unions is permissible only when clearly necessary because the gender-based text of a statute, rule or judicial precedent would otherwise produce an unjust, unwarranted, or confusing result, and different treatment would promote or enhance, and would not diminish, the common benefits and protections that flow from marriage under Vermont law.

The result of Lisa's statutory argument would be to produce separate benefits and protections for couples in civil unions. Under her argument, no partner in a civil union could be the parent of a child conceived by the other partner without formally adopting that child.

> · · ·

We reach then the ultimate question—whether Janet is a parent within the meaning of the parentage act—without consideration of § 308, which is irrelevant to both sides of the argument in this case. We have held that the term "parent" is specific to the context of the family involved....

Many factors are present here that support a conclusion that Janet is a parent, including, first and foremost, that Janet and Lisa were in a valid legal union at the time of the child's birth. The other factors include the following. It was the expectation and intent of both Lisa and Janet that Janet would be IMJ's parent. Janet participated in the decision that Lisa would be artificially inseminated to bear a child and participated actively in the prenatal care and birth. Both Lisa and Janet treated Janet as IMJ's parent during the time they resided together, and Lisa identified Janet as a parent of IMJ in the dissolution petition. Finally, there is no other claimant to the status of parent, and, as a result, a negative decision would leave IMJ with only one parent. The sperm donor was anonymous and is making no claim to be IMJ's parent. If Janet had been Lisa's husband, these factors would make Janet the parent of the child born from the artificial insemination. Because of the equality of treatment of partners in civil unions, the same result applies to Lisa. 15 V.S.A. § 1204.

Virtually all modern decisions from other jurisdictions support this result, although the theories vary.... We adopt the result in this case as a matter of policy, and to implement the intent of the parties.

This is not a close case under the precedents from other states. Because so many factors are present in this case that allow us to hold that the nonbiologically-related [sic] partner is the child's parent, we need not address which factors may be dispositive on the issue in a closer case. We do note that, in accordance with the common law, the couple's legal union at the time of the child's birth is extremely persuasive evidence of joint parentage.

> · · ·

... The family court eventually ruled that Janet had parental status with respect to IMJ, a ruling we have affirmed.... The Commonwealth of Virginia's judgment regarding parentage is *not* entitled to full faith and credit.

NOTES

1. How does the court reach the conclusion in *Strnad* that the child is not illegitimate? After the judgment, the wife took the child to Oklahoma, where she once again challenged the ex-husband's visitation rights. The Oklahoma court ruled in her favor finding that the child was illegitimate and legally related only to its mother, the ex-husband having no rights. Charles E. Rice, *A.I.D.—An Heir of Controversy*, 34 NOTRE DAME L. REV. 510, 517 (1959). Other cases from around the same period sometimes even ruled that engaging in AID was akin to adultery. *See, e.g., id.* at 513–16 (discussing AID and adultery, including *Orford v. Orford*, 58 D.L.R. 251 (Ont. 1921) and *Doornbos v. Doornbos* from Illinois in 1954); Gaia Bernstein, *The Socio–Legal Acceptance of New Technologies: A Close Look at Artificial Insemination*, 77 WASH. L. REV. 1035, 1057–59 (2002) (discussing *Orford v. Orford*). *But see People v. Sorensen*, 437 P.2d 495, 501 (Cal. 1968) ("It has been suggested that the doctor and the wife commit adultery by the process of artificial insemination. [citation omitted]. Since the doctor may be a woman, or the husband himself may administer the insemination by a syringe, this is patently absurd; to consider it an act of adultery with the donor who at the time of insemination may be a thousand miles away or may even be dead, is equally absurd").

2. The *In re Marriage of Witbeck–Wildhagen* case is exceptional. Courts will often go a long way to discern implicit or de facto consent to artificial insemination or use contractual or equitable theories to justify an obligation of child support. *See, e.g., Brown v. Brown*, 125 S.W.3d 840, 844 (Ark. Ct. App. 2003) (where the elements of equitable estoppel were met, including that husband knew wife was using AID and accepted resulting children as his own, husband was estopped from denying fatherhood). In *R.S. v. R.S.*, the husband orally consented to artificial insemination of his wife, but the doctor never obtained his written consent per the relevant Kansas statute. 670 P.2d 923, 925 (Kan. Ct. App. 1983). However, the court ruled that the statute did not preclude the husband's oral consent from being grounds for an equitable estoppel or implied contract theory. *Id.* at 927–28. The court also held "that when a husband consents to heterologous insemination of his wife, that consent is presumed to continue through the time the wife becomes pregnant unless the husband establishes by clear and convincing evidence that such consent has been withdrawn." *Id.* at 928. How does this rule for consent compare to the *Witbeck–Wildhagen* court's interpretation of the Illinois statute's requirements?

3. After Vermont's decision in *Miller–Jenkins, supra*, a Virginia appeals court ruled that the Parental Kidnapping Prevention Act required the Virginia trial court "to give full faith and credit to the custody and visitation orders of the Vermont court." 637 S.E.2d 330, 337 (Va. Ct. App. 2006). For procedural reasons, that decision was never reviewed by the Virginia Supreme Court. *See* 661 S.E.2d 822, 825 (Va. 2008). Lisa subsequently challenged Janet's registration of the Vermont order in Virginia. *Id.* When that issue reached the Supreme Court of Virginia, it determined that it was barred from addressing the merits because of the "law of the case" doctrine: the issue had been settled by the earlier Virginia court of appeals decision. *Id.* at 827. Lisa was initially awarded sole physical and legal custody, with visitation by Janet. *See* 12 A.3d 768, 772 (Vt. 2010). But Lisa was held in contempt multiple times for violating parent-child contact orders, and a Vermont family court determined that custody should be transferred to Janet, an order that was upheld by the Vermont Supreme Court. *See id.* at 773, 778. However, Lisa and the child disappeared in 2009 before custody was transferred. There were insinuations in the press that Lisa fled to Nicaragua with the child under an assumed name with the help of a Christian organization. *See* Jessica Hopper, *Christian Network Implicated in Parental Kidnapping Involving Lesbian Partner*, ABC NEWS (Apr. 26, 2011), http://abcnews.go.com/US/christian-network-helped-woman-kidnap-girl-lesbian-partner/story?id=13452729.

4. In *Miller–Jenkins*, the court relied on the couple's civil union in holding that the same-sex partner of the biological mother was a parent within the meaning of Vermont's parentage act. The analogous application of the marital parental presumption to same-sex marriages, civil unions, or domestic partnerships is not necessarily followed in all states that recognize these unions. For more on the parental rights of same-sex partners, *see generally* Nancy D. Polikoff, *A Mother Should Not Have to Adopt Her Own Child: Parentage Laws for Children of Lesbian Couples in the Twenty–First Century*, 5 STAN J. CIV. RTS. & CIV. LIBERTIES 201 (2009). Even in *Miller–Jenkins*, the court pointed out that the civil union was only one among many factors that led it to conclude that the same-sex partner was a parent of a child born to her spouse via AID (the others included the parties' intent and expectations).

Even when the parental presumption applies, however, this may not be enough to provide protection throughout the country for the non-biologically related or non-gestating parent. In the case *In re Adoption of Sebastian*, a same-sex couple who had married abroad and whose marriage was recognized in New York sought a second-parent adoption for the child born during their marriage to one of the spouses via IVF. 879 N.Y.S.2d 677, 679, 682 (N.Y. Sur. Ct. 2009). The court granted the adoption petition noting that "although it is also true that an adoption should be unnecessary because Sebastian was born to parents whose marriage is legally recognized in this state, the best interests of this child require a judgment that will ensure recognition of both Ingrid and Mona as his legal parents throughout the entire United States." *Id.* at 692–93. Consider the court's observation as you read about the parental status of the unmarried partner.

2.   ART AND THE UNMARRIED PARTNER'S PARENTAL STATUS

Charisma R. v. Kristina S.

Court of Appeal of California, First District, Division 5, 2006.
44 Cal. Rptr. 3d 332.

■ GEMELLO, J.

Appellant Charisma R. appeals from denial of her petition to establish a parental relationship with a child born to her former partner, Kristina S. We reverse and remand for the trial court to reconsider the petition in light of the California Supreme Court decision *Elisa B. v. Superior Court*[,] 117 P.3d 660 [(Cal. 2005)] (*Elisa B.*).

Charisma R. and Kristina S. were a lesbian couple who began dating in July 1997, moved in together in August 1998, and registered as domestic partners with the State of California in January 2002. In 2002, Kristina became pregnant by artificial insemination from an anonymous donor, and Amalia Lynne was born in April 2003. Amalia was given a hyphenated last name, which was a combination of Charisma and Kristina's last names. In July 2003, Kristina moved out of the home she shared with Charisma, taking Amalia with her. Since then, Kristina has allowed Charisma to see Amalia on only two occasions.

In May 2004, Charisma filed a petition seeking to establish a parental relationship with Amalia. In an accompanying declaration, Charisma averred that she and Kristina decided to have a child together with the intention that they would both be the child's parents. The trial court denied the petition, holding that Charisma lacked standing to bring the action under the Uniform Parentage Act (FAM.CODE, § 7600 et seq.).

Under the Uniform Parentage Act, an "interested person" may bring an action to determine the existence or nonexistence of a mother and child relationship. (§ 7650.)

In concluding that Charisma lacks standing, the trial court followed three Court of Appeal decisions, each holding that a former lesbian partner lacking a biological tie to a child cannot establish a parent-child relationship under the Uniform Parentage Act. Subsequently, the California Supreme Court overruled those three decisions in *Elisa B.* The court held that a former lesbian partner may be able to establish parentage under the Uniform Parentage Act as a presumed parent under a gender-neutral application of section 7611, subdivision (d). That subdivision provides that a man is presumed to be a father if (1) he receives the child into his home and (2) openly holds out the child as his natural child.

In *Elisa B.* the El Dorado County District Attorney filed a complaint to establish that Elisa B. was the parent of twins born to her former lesbian partner, Emily B., and to order Elisa B. to pay child support. Elisa B. denied that she was the children's parent. It was undisputed that Elisa participated in the artificial insemination of her partner Emily with the understanding that they would raise the resulting child or children as coparents [sic], and they did in fact coparent [sic] the children in a common family home for over a year and a half. The court considered whether Elisa could be considered a presumed parent under section 7611, subdivision (d) and whether the case was "an appropriate action" to rebut the presumption of parenthood with evidence that there was no biological relationship between Elisa and the twins under section 7612, subdivision (a).

The court concluded that the court of appeal erred in relying in this context on language in *Johnson v. Calvert*[,] 851 P.2d 776 [(Cal. 1993)], to the effect that "for any child California law recognizes only one natural mother." The issue in *Johnson* was whether a wife whose ovum was fertilized in vitro by her husband's sperm and implanted in a surrogate mother was the mother of the child or whether the surrogate was the mother. The court held that only the wife was the child's mother. Whereas in *Johnson*, three people claimed to be a child's parents (the husband, the wife, and the surrogate), in *Elisa B.* the district attorney claimed that two people, both women, were a child's parents.

The court examined whether Elisa could be considered a presumed parent under section 7611, subdivision (d), providing that a man is presumed to be a parent of a child if "[h]e receives the child into his home and openly holds out the child as his natural child." The court pointed out that section 7650, subdivision (a) states that provisions applicable to determining a father and child relationship shall be used to determine a mother and child relationship " 'insofar as practicable.' " Accordingly, ... subdivision (d) of section 7611 applies equally in determining whether a man or a woman is a presumed parent.

As to the first part of the section 7611 test, it was undisputed that Elisa received the twins into her home. As to the second part, the court held that the circumstance that Elisa does not have a biological tie to the twins did not necessarily mean that she did not hold out the twins as her natural children. This conclusion followed from *In re Nicholas H.*[,] 46 P.3d 932 [(Cal. 2002)], in which a man sought parental rights even though he admitted that he was not the child's biological father. In *Nicholas H.*, the man, Thomas, met Nicholas' mother when she was pregnant; he was named as Nicholas' father on the birth certificate; and he lived with the mother and Nicholas for several years. After their separation, the mother tried to prevent Thomas from having any contact with Nicholas. Thomas sought parental rights when the county social services agency removed Nicholas from the mother's physical custody. The identity of the biological father had never been judicially determined and he had shown no interest in caring for Nicholas. The Supreme Court held that Thomas was Nicholas' presumed father under section 7611, subdivision (d).

The primary issue in *Nicholas H.* was actually whether the case was an appropriate one in which to rebut the section 7611 presumption, and *Elisa B.* relied heavily on *Nicholas H.* as it turned to an analysis of that issue. Section 7612, subdivision (a) provides that "a presumption under Section 7611 is a rebuttable presumption affecting the burden of proof and may be rebutted in an appropriate action only by clear and convincing evidence." *Nicholas H.* emphasized that section 7612 does not state that the presumption *is* rebutted by evidence that the presumed parent is not the child's biological father, but rather that it *may* be rebutted "in an appropriate action" by such evidence. In *Nicholas H.*, the court concluded that the Legislature, in permitting the section 7611 presumption to be rebutted in an appropriate action "had in mind an action in which another candidate is vying for parental rights and seeks to rebut a section 7611(d) presumption in order to perfect his claim. . . ." *Nicholas H.* held that the case was not an appropriate action to rebut the presumption because no one had raised a conflicting claim to being Nicholas' father. Permitting the presumption to be rebutted by Thomas' admission that he was not the biological father would leave Nicholas fatherless.

In *Elisa B.* the court held again that the action was not an appropriate one in which to rebut the parenthood presumption. The twins have no father because they were conceived by artificial insemination using an anonymous donor, and Elisa participated in and consented to that artificial insemination with the intention of coparenting [sic] any resulting children. Rebutting the presumption of Elisa's parenthood would leave the children with only one parent. That result would be contrary to the public policy favoring a child having two parents to provide emotional and financial support. Although whether an action is an appropriate one in which to rebut the parenthood presumption is normally a matter within the discretion of the trial court, no remand was necessary because on the facts it would have been an abuse of discretion for the trial court to permit the presumption to be rebutted. In other words, in *Elisa B.*, it would have been error to conclude that Elisa was not the twins' parent simply because she lacked a biological tie to them.

The court summarized: "We conclude, therefore, that Elisa is a presumed mother of the twins under section 7611, subdivision (d), because she received the children into her home and openly held them out as her natural children, and that this is not an appropriate action in which to rebut the presumption that Elisa is the twins' parent with proof that she is not the children's biological mother because she actively participated in causing the children to be conceived with the understanding that she would raise the children as her own together with the birth mother, she voluntarily accepted the rights and obligations of parenthood after the children were born, and there are no competing claims to her being the children's second parent."

Following *Elisa B.*, we remand to the trial court to determine first, whether Charisma is a presumed parent of Amalia under section 7611, subdivision (d), and then, whether this is an appropriate action in which to rebut the presumption that Charisma is Amalia's parent. Presumed parent status depends upon affirmative findings that Charisma (1) received Amalia into her home and (2) openly held Amalia out as her natural child. If the trial court finds that Charisma is a presumed parent, then it should determine whether the facts outlined in *Elisa B.* on the rebuttal issue are true, namely (1) whether Charisma actively participated in causing Amalia to be conceived with the understanding that she would raise Amalia as her own together with Kristina, (2) whether Charisma voluntarily accepted the rights and obligations of parenthood after Amalia was born, and (3) that there are no competing claims to being Amalia's second parent.

If the trial court finds that Charisma is a presumed parent and finds true all of the facts outlined in *Elisa B.* on the rebuttal issue, those findings support a conclusion that this is not an appropriate case to allow rebuttal of the presumption of Charisma's parenthood; in other words, the evidence that she has no biological tie to Amalia does not rebut the presumption. Absent other facts justifying rebuttal of the presumption, any other conclusion would be an abuse of discretion. If not all the facts outlined by *Elisa B.* are present, then the trial court should exercise its discretion with regard to the rebuttal issue based on the evidence and arguments. It may be that not all of the facts emphasized in *Elisa B.* are necessary to a finding that the presumption cannot be rebutted by the lack of a biological tie to the child. Or it may be that there are different facts that justify such a finding.

. . .

Because we remand for further factual findings, we need not address Kristina's claim that it would violate her federal constitutional rights were we to conclude that Charisma is Amalia's parent under the UNIFORM PARENTAGE ACT.

NOTES

1. On remand, the trial court found Charisma to be a presumed parent, a finding that the court of appeal found was supported by substantial evidence. 96 Cal. Rptr. 3d 26, 42 (Ct. App. 2009). Kristina challenged that finding based on the limited time that Charisma parented Amalia. *Id.* at 35. The court of appeal "conclude[d] that receipt of the child into the home must be sufficiently unambiguous as to constitute a clear declaration regarding the nature of the relationship, but it need not continue for any specific duration." *Id.* at 38–39. Although the court noted that duration may be relevant (though not required) in evaluating rebuttal of the parentage presumption, it was not applicable here where Kristina's actions, not Charisma's, prevented more parenting time. *Id.* at 44–45.

2. The 2002 version of the Uniform Parentage Act provides that consent by a man to the insemination of a woman with the intent to parent is sufficient to confer parental rights, but the consent needs to be in writing. U.P.A. (amended 2002) §§ 703–704. Only a few states and the District of Columbia have adopted such a provision for unmarried men, *e.g.*, DEL. CODE ANN. tit. 13, §§ 8–703, 8–704 (Supp. 2009); N.D. CENT. CODE §§ 14–20–61, 14–20–62 (2009); WYO. STAT. ANN. § 14–2–903, 14–2–904 (2011); with even fewer extending the right to unmarried female partners, *e.g.*, D.C. CODE § 16–909(e)(1) (2001 & Supp. 2010); N.M. STAT. §§ 40–11A–703, 40–11A–704 (Supp. 2011). Additionally, at least one state has extended its AI consent statute to apply to unmarried same-sex partners through case law. *See Shineovich v. Kemp*, 214 P.3d 29 (Or. Ct. App. 2009).

3. In states without a statutory mechanism for recognizing unmarried partners as legal parents of AID children, legal protection for these relationships is through either a second-parent adoption, if allowed, or reliance on doctrines of functional parenthood, such as psychological parent, de facto parent, or in loco parentis. *See, e.g.*, *Simons by & Through Simons v. Gisvold*, 519 N.W.2d 585 (N.D. 1994) reprinted *infra*, Chapter 8, Section H. These doctrines have been extended to same-sex unmarried partners in some court cases. In Maine, for example, a biological mother conceded that her former partner was a de facto parent to her child. *C.E.W. v. D.E.W.*, 845 A.2d 1146, 1151 (Me. 2004). De facto parent status allowed the court to consider an award of rights and responsibilities to the former partner based on the best interest standard. *Id.* at 1152. The Supreme Court of Pennsylvania affirmed a lower court finding that a biological mother's former partner stood *in loco parentis* to her child and therefore had standing to seek visitation. *T.B. v. L.R.M.*, 786 A.2d 913, 920 (Pa. 2001). The New Jersey Supreme Court granted a woman visitation with her former partner's biological children based on her standing as a psychological parent. *V.C. v. M.J.B.*, 748 A.2d 539, 552–55 (N.J. 2000). But former partners are not always successful in protecting their relationship with the child. *See, e.g., Wakeman v. Dixon*, 921 So.2d 669 (Fla. Dist. Ct. App. 2006).

4. In contested cases, it may become hard to distinguish between a gamete donor and an unmarried partner. In a recent Delaware case, a man whose former girlfriend was found to have lied about being pregnant with his child and about needing a semen sample to test for cystic fibrosis, but in reality used the sample for an AI procedure, was not the legal father of the child because he had not consented as required by the Uniform Parentage Act to the use of his sperm to become a father. *See Adams–Hall v. Adams*, 2010 WL 3489909 (Del. 2010). Because there was evidence that the man had not consented, *Adams–Hall* did not turn out to be such a difficult case. Sometimes, however, the evidence may be more ambiguous or its legal meaning contested, as in the following case.

3.   ART AND THE DONOR'S PARENTAL STATUS

In re K.M.H.

Supreme Court of Kansas, 2007.
285 Kan. 53, 169 P.3d 1025.

■ BEIER, J.:

This appeal from a consolidated child in need of care (CINC) case and a paternity action arises out of an artificial insemination leading to the birth of twins K.M.H. and K.C.H. We are called upon to decide the existence and extent of the parental rights of the known sperm donor, who alleges he had an agreement with the children's mother to act as the twins' father.

The twins' mother filed a CINC petition to establish that the donor had no parental rights under Kansas law. The donor sued for determination of his paternity. The district court sustained the mother's motion to dismiss, ruling that K.S.A. 38–1114(f) was controlling and constitutional. That statute provides:

> The donor of semen provided to a licensed physician for use in artificial insemination of a woman other than the donor's wife is treated in law as if he were not the birth father of a child thereby conceived, unless agreed to in writing by the donor and the woman.

Many of the underlying facts are undisputed. The mother, S.H., is an unmarried female lawyer who wanted to become a parent through artificial insemination from a known donor. She was a friend of the donor, D.H., an unmarried male nonlawyer [sic], who agreed to provide sperm for the insemination. Both S.H. and D.H. are Kansas residents, and their oral arrangements for the donation occurred in Kansas, but S.H. underwent two inseminations with D.H.'s sperm in Missouri.

D.H. accompanied S.H. to a Missouri clinic for the first procedure and provided the necessary sperm to medical personnel. The first procedure did not result in a pregnancy. D.H. did not accompany S.H. to Missouri for the second procedure. Instead, he provided the sperm to S.H., and she delivered it to the Missouri physician responsible for the insemination. The second procedure resulted in S.H.'s pregnancy and the birth of the twins.

There was no formal written contract between S.H. and D.H. concerning the donation of sperm, the artificial insemination, or the expectations of the parties with regard to D.H.'s parental rights or lack thereof.

The twins were born on May 18, 2005. The day after their birth, S.H. filed a CINC petition concerning the twins, seeking a determination that D.H. would have no parental rights. The petition identified D.H. as "[t]he minor children's father" and alleged that the twins were in need of care "as it relates to the father" and that "the [f]ather should be found unfit and his rights terminated." The petition continued to refer to D.H. throughout as the twins' father.

On May 31, 2005, D.H. filed an answer to the CINC petition and filed a separate paternity action acknowledging his financial responsibility for the children and claiming parental rights, including joint custody and visitation. The CINC and paternity actions were consolidated. S.H. filed a motion to dismiss the paternity action, invoking K.S.A. 38–1114(f). . . .

. . .

Given the relative newness of the medical procedure of artificial insemination, and thus the newness of K.S.A. 38–1114(f)'s attempt to regulate the relationships arising from it, it is not surprising that the issue raised by D.H. is one of first impression, not only in Kansas but nationally. We therefore begin our discussion of the constitutionality of the statute by surveying the landscape of various states' laws governing the rights of sperm donors for artificial insemination. This landscape and its ongoing evolution provide helpful context for our analysis of K.S.A. 38–1114(f).

The majority of states that have enacted statutes concerning artificial insemination state that the husband of a married woman bears all rights and obligations of paternity as to any child conceived by artificial insemination, whether the sperm used was his own or a donor's. Further, several of these states' statutes provide that a donor of semen used to inseminate a married woman will not be treated in law as the father of any child conceived, if he is not the woman's husband. . . .

The 1973 Uniform Parentage Act, promulgated by the National Conference of Commissioners on Uniform State Laws, 9B U.L.A. 377 (2001), provided the model for many of the state artificial insemination statutes that incorporate these two rules. Section 5 [addressed artificial insemination] . . . .

. . .

The wording of this original Act and statutes that imitated it did not address the determination of a sperm donor's paternity when an *unmarried* woman conceived a child through artificial insemination. . . .

. . .

Certain states . . . either anticipated the need for their original statutes to govern the relationship of a sperm donor to the child of an unmarried recipient as well as a married recipient or modified their original uniform Act-patterned statutes to remove the word "married" from the § 5(b) language. This meant these states' statutes contained complete bars to paternity for any sperm donor not married to the recipient, regardless of whether the recipient was married to someone else and regardless of whether the donor was known or anonymous. An example of such a provision reads: "The donor of semen provided to a licensed physician for use in artificial insemination of a woman other than the donor's wife is treated in law as if he were not the natural father of a child thereby conceived." *See, e.g.,* CAL. FAM.CODE § 7613(b) (West 2004).

Four cases interpreting one of these types of statutes covering both married and unmarried recipients and establishing an absolute bar to donor paternity were decided before a 2000 amendment to the uniform Act made it applicable to unmarried as well as married recipients of donor sperm. *See* UNIFORM PARENTAGE ACT (2000); 9B U.L.A. 295 (West 2001).

The first of the four arose in California in 1986. In that case, *Jhordan C. v. Mary K.,*224 Cal. Rptr. 530 ([Cal. Ct. App.]1986), a donor provided sperm to one of two unmarried women who had decided to raise a child together. California had adopted the language of the 1973 UNIFORM ACT with the exception that it had omitted the word "married" in the second subsection. As the court put it:

> [T]he California Legislature has afforded unmarried as well as married women a statutory vehicle for obtaining semen for artificial insemination without fear that the donor may claim paternity, and has likewise provided men with a statutory vehicle for donating semen to married and unmarried women alike without fear of liability for child support. Subdivision (b) states only one limitation on its application: the semen must be 'provided to a licensed physician.' Otherwise, whether impregnation occurs through artificial insemination or sexual intercourse, there can be a determination of paternity with the rights, duties and obligations such a determination entails.

Because the parties had no doctor involved in the donation or insemination and thus the sperm was never "provided to a licensed physician," the court ruled that the case before it fell outside the statute. It therefore affirmed the lower court's recognition of the donor's paternity. Although the court addressed its ruling's impact on the constitutional rights of the two women, it did not address any constitutional implications for the donor.

The second case, *In Interest of R.C.,* 775 P.2d 27 (Colo.[ ]1989), arose in Colorado in 1989. In that case, the district court had refused to admit proffered evidence of an agreement that the donor would act as a father based on relevance; it granted the unmarried mother's motion to dismiss the donor's paternity suit based on Colorado's statute. The Colorado provision, like that in California, applied to both married and unmarried recipients and contained a blanket bar to donor parental rights.

The Colorado Supreme Court reversed the district court and remanded for findings of fact. It explicitly rejected the idea that an unmarried recipient lost the protection of the statute "merely because she knows the donor." And it did not reach the equal protection and due process challenges raised by the donor. However, it concluded the statute was ambiguous and refused to apply its absolute bar to paternity because the known donor had produced evidence of an oral agreement that he would be treated as father of the child.

The next case, *McIntyre v. Crouch,* 780 P.2d 239 ([Or. Ct. App.]1989), *cert. denied* 495 U.S. 905 (1990), involved an unmarried woman who artificially inseminated herself with a known donor's semen. The donor sought recognition of his paternity, and both he and the woman sought summary judgment. The Oregon artificial insemination statute read:

> If the donor of semen used in artificial insemination is not the mother's husband: (1) Such donor shall have no right, obligation or interest with respect to a child born as a result of the artificial insemina-

tion; and (2) A child born as a result of the artificial insemination shall have no right, obligation or interest with respect to the donor.

The donor challenged this statute under equal protection and due process principles. He swore out an affidavit in support of summary judgment and argued he had relied on an agreement with the mother that he "would remain active" in the child's life and "participate in all important decisions concerning the child." He sought visitation and said that he was willing and able to accept the same level of responsibility for the support, education, maintenance, and care of the child and for pregnancy-related expenses that he would have had if the child had been born from his marriage to its mother. The district court ruled that the donor's paternity claim was barred by the Oregon statute.

. . .

The court [of appeal] . . . rebuffed the donor's due process challenge to the statute on its face. However, the donor also argued that the statute violated due process under the federal and state Constitutions as applied to him, a known donor who had an agreement with the mother to share the rights and responsibilities of parenthood. The court agreed the statute would violate the Due Process Clause of the Fourteenth Amendment as applied to the donor *if* such an agreement was proved.

On this point, the court looked to *Lehr v. Robertson*, 463 U.S. 248, 261 (1983), an adoption case. *Lehr* dealt with the necessity of notice of pending adoption proceedings to an unwed father who had not filed with New York's putative father registry and had never established a substantial relationship with the child. The Court stated:

> When an unwed father demonstrates a full commitment to the responsibilities of parenthood by 'com[ing] forward to participate in the rearing of his child,' [citation omitted], his interest in personal contact with his child acquires substantial protection under the Due Process Clause.... But the mere existence of a biological link does not merit equivalent constitutional protection.

The *Lehr* Court ultimately held that the State's failure to notify the father of adoption proceedings did not deny him due process of law. No substantive due process right to care, custody, and control of the child had vested in a man who could demonstrate nothing more than a biological link to his offspring. The *Lehr* Court noted, however, that an unwed father who demonstrated "a full commitment to the responsibilities of parenthood" could not be absolutely barred from asserting his parental rights without a violation of due process.

The *McIntyre* court reasoned that the Due Process Clause should afford no less protection to a sperm donor who had facilitated artificial insemination than an unwed father, "provided that [the sperm donor] could prove the facts" in his summary judgment affidavit that tended to support the existence of an agreement with the mother and his reliance upon it. Because the court concluded the constitutionality of the Oregon statute as applied to this donor would turn on whether he was given an opportunity to establish those facts, summary judgment in favor of the mother was reversed.

The last of the four cases, *C.O. v. W.S.*, 639 N.E.2d 523 ([Ohio Ct. App.]1994), also concluded, as the *McIntyre* court did, that a statute purporting to be an absolute bar to paternity of sperm donors, while constitutional in the absence of an agreement to the contrary, could be unconstitutional as applied when the donor can establish that an agreement to share parenting existed between him and the unmarried woman who was the recipient of the sperm.

In *C.O.*, the Ohio statute at issue stated: "If a woman is the subject of a non-spousal artificial insemination, a donor shall not be treated in law or regarded as the natural father of a child conceived as a result of the artificial insemination, and a child so conceived shall not be treated in law or regarded as the natural child of the donor." The statute also required artificial insemination to be conducted under the supervision of a physician. As in *Jhordan C.*, an unmarried woman had inseminated herself with a known donor's sperm. Although the court ultimately determined the statute was inapplicable because the mother had failed to comply with the physician involvement requirement, it further opined that the statute would violate due process if applied to the donor, because he and the mother, at the time of the procedure, had agreed there would be a relationship between the donor and the child.

Since the Uniform Act was amended in 2000 to state simply, "A donor is not a parent of a child conceived by means of assisted reproduction," two of our sister states have decided three additional cases addressing statutes with identical or substantively indistinguishable provisions governing sperm donors and unmarried recipients. *Steven S. v. Deborah D.*, 25 Cal. Rptr. 3d 482 ([Cal. Ct. App.]2005); *In re H.C.S.*, 219 S.W.3d 33 (Tex.App. 2006); *In re Sullivan*, 157 S.W.3d 911 (Tex.App.2005).

. . .

The third case, *Steven S.*, from California, involved an unmarried woman and a known sperm donor who tried artificial insemination; when that resulted in a miscarriage, they attempted to conceive through sexual intercourse, also without success. Finally, a second artificial insemination attempt resulted in conception. The donor initially was very involved with the pregnancy and the child, and he filed a paternity action when the child was 3 years old.

The district court noted that California's statute presented a bar to paternity for unmarried sperm donors, but ruled in favor of the donor based on equitable estoppel. The donor was known; he had engaged in sexual intercourse with the unwed mother; and she had acknowledged him as the child's father and had allowed him to participate in the pregnancy and celebrate the birth of the child. The California Court of Appeals reversed, holding that the "words of [CAL. FAM.CODE] section 7613, subdivision (b) are clear" and that, under such facts, "[t]here can be no paternity claim" because of the statute's absolute bar.

None of these three decisions raised or reached the equal protection or due process challenges raised by the donor here.

Where does our Kansas statute fit into this landscape and its ongoing evolution?

In 1985, Kansas became one of the states that adopted portions of the UNIFORM PARENTAGE ACT of 1973 regarding presumptions of paternity, but it did not adopt any provision relating to artificial insemination. *See* L.1985, ch. 114, sec. 5 (H.B.2012).

In 1994, Kansas amended its statute to incorporate the 1973 UNIFORM ACT's § 5(b) as K.S.A. 38–1114(f). It did not differentiate between known and unknown or anonymous donors, but it did make two notable changes in the uniform language.

As discussed above, although the 1973 Uniform Act governed the paternity of children born only to married women as a result of artificial insemination with donor sperm, the version adopted by Kansas omitted the word "married." This drafting decision demonstrates the legislature's intent that the bar to donor paternity apply regardless of whether the recipient was married or unmarried.

The other alteration in the 1973 Uniform Act's language is directly at issue here. The Kansas Legislature provided that a sperm donor and recipient could choose to opt out of the donor paternity bar by written agreement. The legislative record contains no explanation for this deviation from the 1973 Uniform Act's language.

This second drafting decision is critical and sets this case apart from all precedent. Our statute's allowance for a written agreement to grant a sperm donor parental rights and responsibilities means that, although we may concur with the *McIntyre* and *C.O.* courts in their constitutional analyses of absolute-bar statutes, we need not arrive at the same result. K.S.A. 38–1114(f) includes exactly the sort of escape clause the Oregon and Ohio courts found lacking—and unconstitutional—in their statutes.

Ultimately, in view of the requirement that we accept as true D.H.'s evidence supporting existence of an oral agreement, we are faced with a very precise question: Does our statute's requirement that any opt-out agreement between an unmarried mother and a known sperm donor be "in writing" result in an equal protection or due process violation? Although several other states have adopted statutes like K.S.A. 38–1114(f), including language permitting an unmarried woman and a sperm donor to avoid the statutory bar and provide for the paternity of the donor through an "agreement in writing"[,] none of the courts of these states has yet subjected such a statute to a constitutional crucible. We do so now, as K.S.A. 38–1114(f) is applied to D.H.

K.S.A. 38–1114(f) draws a gender-based line between a necessarily female sperm recipient and a necessarily male sperm donor for an artificial insemination. By operation of the statute, the female is a potential parent or actual parent under all circumstances; by operation of the same statute, the male will never be a potential parent or actual parent unless there is a written agreement to that effect with the female. As discussed with counsel for the parties at oral argument before this court, the male's ability to insist on father status effectively disappears once he donates sperm. Until that point, he can unilaterally refuse to participate unless a written agreement on his terms exists. After donation, the male cannot force the fatherhood issue. The female can unilaterally decide if and when to use the donation for artificial insemination and can unilaterally deny any wish of the male for parental rights by refusing to enter into a written agreement.

The guiding principle of equal protection analysis is that similarly situated individuals should be treated alike. . . .

Given the biological differences between females and males and the immutable role those differences play in conceiving and bearing a child, regardless of whether conception is achieved through sexual intercourse or artificial insemination, we are skeptical that S.H. and D.H. are truly similarly situated. However, assuming for purposes of argument that they are, we perceive several legitimate legislative purposes or important governmental objectives underlying K.S.A. 38–1114(f).

As the *McIntyre* Court observed about the Oregon statute, K.S.A. 38–1114(f) envisions that both married and unmarried women may become parents without engaging in sexual intercourse, either because of personal choice or because a husband or partner is infertile, impotent, or ill. It encourages men who are able and willing to donate sperm to such women by protecting the men from later unwanted claims for support from the mothers or the children. It protects women recipients as well, preventing potential claims of donors to parental rights and responsibilities, in the absence of an agreement. Its requirement that any such agreement be in writing enhances predictability, clarity, and enforceability. Although the timing of entry into a written agreement is not set out explicitly, the design of the statute implicitly encourages early resolution of the elemental question of whether a donor will have parental rights. Effectively, the parties must decide whether they will enter into a written agreement before any donation is made, while there is still balanced bargaining power on both sides of the parenting equation.

In our view, the statute's gender classification substantially furthers and is thus substantially related to these legitimate legislative purposes and important governmental objectives. K.S.A. 38–1114(f) establishes the clear default positions of parties to artificial insemination. If these parties desire an arrangement different from the statutory norm, they are free to provide for it, as long as they do so in writing. Encouraging careful consideration of entry into parenthood is admirable. Avoidance of the limbo in which D.H. finds himself is a worthy legislative goal. We therefore hold that the application of K.S.A. 38–1114(f) to D.H. does not violate equal protection.

. . .

We simply are not persuaded that the requirement of a writing transforms what is an otherwise constitutional statute into one that violates D.H.'s substantive due process rights. Although we agree with the [Washburn University School of Law's Children and Family Law] Center [as amicus curiae] that one goal of the Kansas Parentage Act as a whole is to encourage fathers to voluntarily acknowledge paternity and child support obligations, the obvious impact of the plain language of this particular provision in the Act is to prevent the creation of parental status where it is not desired or expected. To a certain extent, D.H. and the Center evidently misunderstand the statute's mechanism. It ensures no *attachment* of parental rights to sperm donors in the absence of a written agreement to the contrary; it does not *cut off* rights that have already arisen and attached.

We are confident this legislative design realizes the expectation of unknown or anonymous sperm donors, whether their motive for participation in artificial insemination is altruistic or financial. To the extent it does not realize the expectation of a known sperm donor, the statute tells him exactly how to opt out, how to become and remain a father. If, as the Center argues, genetic relationship must be destiny, then an anonymous donor with no intention to be a father would nevertheless automatically become one. It is evident to us the legislature chose an alternate arrangement. Neither D.H. nor the Center has convinced us there is a constitutional mandate for this court to make an independent policy choice.

We also reject the argument from D.H. and the Center that the statute inevitably makes the female the sole arbiter of whether a male can be a father to a child his sperm helps to conceive. This may be true, as we discussed above, once a donation is made, a recipient who becomes pregnant through artificial insemination using that donation can refuse to enter into an agreement to provide for donor paternity. This does not make the requirement of written agreement unconstitutional. Indeed, it is consistent with United States Supreme Court precedent making even a married pregnant woman the sole arbiter, regardless of her husband's wishes, of whether she continues a pregnancy to term. . . .

. . .

. . . K.S.A. 38–1114(f) does not require the donor *himself* to provide his sperm to the physician performing the insemination. It requires only that the donor's sperm be provided to the physician by *an unspecified someone or something*. The fact that S.H. was that someone here did not prevent application of the statute to this situation.

. . .

For the first time in his appellate reply brief, D.H. asserts that the district court must be reversed because S.H. has "unclean hands." In essence, he argues that he, a nonlawyer [sic], was tricked by lawyer S.H., who failed to inform him of the statute and failed to explain how the absence of independent legal advice or a written agreement could affect his legal rights. He asserts that he asked S.H. about whether he needed a lawyer or whether they should put their arrangement in writing and was told neither was necessary. This behavior, he alleges, may have constituted a violation of S.H.'s ethical duties as a licensed lawyer.

. . .

Generally speaking, mere ignorance of the law is no excuse for failing to abide by it. There may be a case in the future in which a donor can prove that the existence of K.S.A. 38–1114(f) was concealed, or that he was fraudulently induced *not* to obtain independent legal advice or *not* to enter into a written agreement to ensure creation and preservation of his parental rights to a child conceived through artificial insemination. This is not such a case.

Affirmed.

NOTES

1. How does the Kansas statute compare with the statutes in the other cases cited? How does the court distinguish between them?

2. The Uniform Parentage Act, as amended in 2000 and 2002, provides that a donor in assisted reproduction is not a parent of the child born through that process. *See* U.P.A. (amended 2002) § 702. It does not distinguish between donations to married or unmarried women. *Id.* § 702 cmt. This contrasts with standard family law doctrine when single women become mothers through sexual intercourse, which typically allows a biological father to seek to establish a father/child relationship and may impose upon him parental responsibilities, especially when there is no other contender. Does it make sense to distinguish between children born to unmarried women via AID and via sex? Commenting on the difference between sexual and non-sexual reproduction the court in a recent Pennsylvania case noted:

> In the case of traditional sexual reproduction, there simply is no question that the parties to any resultant conception and birth may not contract between themselves to deny the child the support he or she requires. In the institutional sperm donation case, however, there appears to be a growing consensus that clinical, institutional sperm donation neither imposes obligations nor confers privileges upon the sperm donor.

Ferguson v. McKiernan, 940 A.2d 1236, 1246 (Pa. 2007). The court observed that in-between these two extremes are a host of cases that require courts "to draw very fine lines." *Id.* In the specific case, the mother of twins asked the known sperm donor for child support. *Id.* at 1238. The court decided that the pre-existing agreement between the parties bore many of the hallmarks of an institutional arrangement, which the parties followed for five years. *Id.* at 1238, 1246. The court did not think that the mother's knowledge of the donor's identity justified treating this case differently than an institutional arrangement. *Id.* at 1246–47. The court further noted:

> This Court takes very seriously the best interests of the children of this Commonwealth, and we recognize that to rule in favor of Sperm Donor in this case denies a source of support to two children who did not ask to be born into this situation. Absent the parties' agreement, however, the twins would not have been born at all, or would have been born to a different and anonymous sperm donor, who neither party disputes would be safe from a support order.

Id. at 1248. Unmarried women comprise one-third of the clientele of sperm banks. However, it is unknown how many of them are single or partnered with a person of the same or the opposite sex. *See* Judith F. Daar, *Accessing Reproductive Technologies: Invisible Barriers, Indelible Harms*, 23 BERKELEY J. GENDER L. & JUST. 18, 25, n. 19, 27–28 (2008). Some countries, such as Italy, have adopted regulations that limit the use of AID to married women, which in most cases, by definition also excludes gays and lesbians from access to AID. For a discussion of the procreative rights of gays and lesbians, *see* John A. Robertson, *Gay and Lesbian Access to Assisted Reproductive Technology*, 55 CASE W. RES. L. REV. 323 (2004).

3. The man in *K.M.H.* argued that the statutory requirement of providing sperm to a physician had not been met, thereby preventing him from being considered a donor. This language was part of the 1973 version of the Uniform Parentage Act, variations of which were adopted by several states. Failure to adhere to the physician requirement may affect parental status. A court may strictly construe the requirements of the donor statute, finding that a man is a father when the procedure was done entirely without physician involvement. *See, e.g., Jhordan C. v. Mary K.*, 224 Cal. Rptr. 530 (App. 1986). Some states require AID to be performed by licensed physicians or by someone under their supervision. *See, e.g.,* ARK. CODE ANN. § 9–10–202 (2009); IDAHO CODE ANN. § 39–5402, 39–5407 (2011); OKLA. STAT. ANN. tit. 10, § 553 (West 2009). Why might states want physicians to be involved in the process? What arguments might women or donors make against the requirement? Even though the 2002 version of the Uniform Parentage Act dropped the physician requirement, *see* U.P.A. (amended 2002) § 702 cmt., relatively few states have adopted it so far.

4. The status of an egg donor may prove to be complicated. The 2002 Uniform Parentage Act makes no distinction between sperm and ovum donors. *See* U.P.A. (amended 2002) §§ 102(8), 7.02, 7.02 cmt. However, relatively few states have adopted this or a similar statute addressing egg donation. *E.g.,* FLA. STAT. ANN. § 742.14 (West 2010); N.D. CENT. CODE §§ 14–20–02, 14–20–60 (2009); OKLA. STAT. ANN. tit. 10, § 555 (West 2009); TEX. FAM. CODE ANN. §§ 160.102(6); 160.702 (Vernon 2008); UTAH CODE ANN. §§ 78B–15–102, 78B–15–702 (2008); VA. CODE ANN. §§ 20–156, 20–158 (2008); WYO. STAT. ANN. §§ 14–2–402, 14–2–902 (2011). This may leave courts with limited guidance to determine whether the person who provided the egg is a donor or a parent.

In 2005, the Supreme Court of California decided a case involving parental claims by a mother's former same-sex partner who had provided her ova for the children's conception. *K.M. v. E.G.*, 117 P.3d 673, 675 (Cal. 2005). The partner had signed an ovum donation agreement relinquishing all parental rights. *Id.* at 676. The trial court found that the parties' agreement was clear and the intent was that the ovum donor partner would not be considered a parent. *Id.* at 677. The Supreme Court reversed, holding that this was not a "true egg donation situation." *Id.* at 679. The court held that the Family Code section that excludes a sperm donor from paternity if he provides the sperm to a doctor for insemination of a woman not his wife does not apply in the situation where a woman provided her ova to impregnate her partner in a lesbian relationship "in order to produce children who would be raised in their joint home." *Id.* at 678. A dissenting opinion noted that the court was effectively changing the California statute to turn a gamete donor into a parent when the parties "intended that the resulting child would be raised in their joint home." *Id.* at 685 (Kennard, J., dissenting).

5. The parental status of the egg donor might also prove complicated in disputed gestational surrogacy cases, depending on how the specific state treats surrogacy. In *Rice v. Flynn*, the Ohio Court of Appeals examined whether a woman who had been compensated for providing her eggs to be used for gestational surrogacy might be a parent of the resulting triplets. Docket No. 22416, 2005 WL 2140576, at *1, *3 (Ohio Ct. App. 2005). The court declined to give full faith and credit to a previous Pennsylvania decision in the same case, which had not treated the egg donor as party to the parentage action before it, citing the Pennsylvania court's failure to properly notify her. *Id.* at *6–*7. In the Ohio proceedings, the trial court had relied on the first prong of the *Belsito* test, which stated that genetics is the primary means of determining a parent-child relationship. *Id.* at *3. As such, the trial court found a parent-child relationship between the egg donor and the children. *Id.* The court of appeals affirmed the use of the test, but noted that the trial court needed to determine whether the second prong of the test applied, namely whether the egg donor had waived her rights as natural mother. *Id.* at *9. *See In re C.K.G.*, 173 S.W.3d 714 (Tenn. 2005), *infra* Section B.4, for a review of the *Belsito* test.

4. ART AND THE GESTATIONAL MOTHER'S PARENTAL STATUS

In re C.K.G.

Supreme Court of Tennessee, 2005.
173 S.W.3d 714.

■ FRANK F. DROWOTA, III, C. J.

. . .

Dr. Charles K. G. and Ms. Cindy C. first met in 1993 while working at Vanderbilt University Medical Center in Nashville. Cindy was a nurse practitioner who managed a department through which Charles, then a medical resident, rotated. Charles and Cindy began dating in 1994. After an initial period of closeness, they maintained for several years an unsteady dating relationship which included an extended period of estrangement.

In 1999, Charles and Cindy not only reunited as an unmarried couple but also soon thereafter began discussing having a child together. By this time Cindy was forty-five years old and Charles was also in his mid-forties. Charles had never had children. He had not grown up in Tennessee, and a December 1999 visit to his birthplace influenced him; he wanted to be a father. Even though Cindy had at least two adult children from prior marriages as well as grandchildren, she was amenable to starting a family with Charles. However, given her age, Cindy was concerned about the viability of her ova, or eggs.

Having decided to have a child, Charles and Cindy pursued *in vitro* fertilization through the Nashville Fertility Center. On May 2, 2000, they jointly executed several agreements with the Fertility Center. Although Charles and Cindy were unmarried, they did not alter the boilerplate language that the Center frequently used in its agreements describing them as "husband" and "wife." Included among these agreements was a "RECIPIENT CONSENT FOR DONATION OF OOCYTES BY ANONYMOUS DONOR" ("Recipient Consent") which describes the fertilization procedure and its risks, waives the right of Charles and Cindy to know the egg donor's identity, and outlines the responsibilities of the parties to the agreement. The Recipient Consent further provides as follows:

> I, Cindy (wife), understand that the child(ren) conceived by this method will not have my genetic material, but will have that of the oocyte [egg] donor and my husband [sic]. However, regardless of the outcome, I will be the mother of any child(ren) born to me as a result of egg donation and hereby accept all the legal responsibilities required of such a parent.

This document was signed by Cindy as "wife" and by Charles as "husband" and was witnessed and signed by a physician who represented that he had fully explained the procedure to Charles and Cindy and had answered all their questions. However, Charles and Cindy executed no other agreements concerning their intentions as to parentage or surrogacy.

Shortly thereafter, Charles paid the Fertility Center $10,000 for the procedure of having two anonymously donated eggs fertilized with Charles's sperm and inserted in Cindy's uterus. Charles intended for them to conceive only one child (presumably two eggs were used to increase the procedure's odds of success). After fertilization, one of the eggs divided, resulting in the development of three embryos. All three embryos flourished; Cindy had become pregnant with triplets.

During Cindy's pregnancy, Charles began residing consistently at Cindy's home. Due to complications with the pregnancy, Cindy took an early leave from her job. When she was placed on bed rest, Charles maintained the household and cooked for her. On February 21, 2001, Cindy gave birth via caesarian section to three children: C.K.G., C.A.G., and C.L.G. Tennessee Department of Health birth certificates for the children identify Charles as the father and Cindy as the mother.

Although Charles had never promised to marry Cindy, he represented that he desired permanence and stability with her. Further, Cindy understood and expected that they would raise the children together as mother and father. In fact, Cindy even sought assurance from Charles that she would not have to rear them by herself. Cindy stayed home with the triplets on maternity leave until June 2001 when she returned to work four days per week. Having set aside money in anticipation of having a child, Charles took a one-year leave of absence (February 2001 to January 2002) from his position as an emergency room physician. For the first several months after the triplets' birth, Charles and Cindy lived together and shared parenting responsibilities. They each provided financially for the children's needs. Further, for some time they had discussed the need for a larger home, and they purchased a house in Brentwood together as tenants in common with the understanding that they would bear the cost equally. Cindy sold her prior residence, and she, Charles, and the triplets moved into the new house in August 2001.

After hiring a nanny, Charles and Cindy's relationship soon deteriorated. Cindy alleged that Charles began cultivating or renewing relationships with several other women; Charles admitted to having sex with another woman during a December 2001 trip to London, England. Cindy further alleged that once their relationship had begun to deteriorate, Charles not only became dramatically less involved with the children, but also began withholding financial support from them. In April 2002, after utility service to their home had been cut off, Cindy filed a petition in the juvenile court of Williamson County to establish parentage and to obtain custody and child support.

In response, Charles argued that because Cindy lacks genetic connection to the children, she fails to qualify as the children's "mother" under Tennessee's domestic relations statutes. Contending that Cindy thus lacks standing as a parent, Charles sought sole and exclusive custody of the triplets. Charles further denied that he had failed to support the children financially and also alleged that Cindy was often absent from home on account of her part-time pursuit of a master's degree in business administration. Cindy conceded that Charles increased his involvement with the children after she filed suit. A pendente lite order required Charles to pay Cindy $3,000 per month for child support. Charles and Cindy continued to live together pending trial.

In anticipation of trial, Charles and Cindy stipulated that: (1) eggs donated by an anonymous third-party female were fertilized with Charles's sperm and implanted in Cindy's uterus; (2) Cindy carried the resulting embryos to term and gave birth to triplets; (3) based on genetic testing, Charles is the biological father of all three children; (4) based on genetic testing, none of the children obtained genetic material from Cindy; and (5) the genetic testing was valid.

After a bench trial, the juvenile court ruled that Cindy had standing to bring a parentage action "as legal mother of these three (3) minor children with all the rights, privileges, and obligations as if she were their biological mother." The juvenile court reasoned that Cindy "is the birth mother and always had the intent to birth these children for herself and [Charles]." Having so decided, the juvenile court addressed the question of custody and support. The court concluded that in light of all the circumstances, Charles and Cindy were both good and caring parents. Based upon their "comparative fitness ... as that affects the best interests of the minor children," the court awarded joint custody with Cindy designated as the primary custodial parent. The court further ordered certain visitation rights in favor of Charles and required him to continue to pay Cindy child support in the amount of $3,000 per month. Charles appealed as of right.

The Court of Appeals affirmed the judgments of the juvenile court....

We granted Charles's application for permission to appeal.

In this case, an unmarried, heterosexual couple—Charles and Cindy—had children by obtaining eggs donated from an anonymous third-party female, fertilizing the eggs *in vitro* with Charles's sperm, and implanting the fertilized eggs in Cindy's uterus. Even though Cindy had no genetic connection to the three children to whom she eventually gave birth, she and Charles intended to rear the children together as mother and father. When the couple's relationship deteriorated, Cindy filed a parentage action seeking custody and child support from Charles. In response, Charles claimed that Cindy had no standing as a parent because, lacking genetic connection to the children, she failed to qualify as a parent under Tennessee parentage statutes. On this basis, Charles sought sole and exclusive custody. The facts of this case thus present us with a question of first impression in Tennessee: under such circumstances, who as a matter of law is the children's mother?
...

. . .

"Historically, gestation proved genetic parentage beyond doubt, so it was unnecessary to distinguish between gestational and genetic mothers." However, recent developments in reproductive technology have caused a tectonic shift in the realities which underlie our legal conceptions of parent-hood.

> With the technological development of a number of processes of procreation, most notably in vitro fertilization, the conceptive and gesta-tional phases of reproduction can now be separate. Thus, the genetic and gestational mothers of a child are no longer necessarily the same person, which can result in a child having several possible parents. These new reproductive technologies and arrangements give rise to the fundamental question of who should be recognized as the parents of a child born as a result of various parties making distinct contributions to the process of procreation.

Campbell, 77 A.L.R. 5th at 574, § 2[a].

This technological fragmentation of the procreative process, insofar as it includes techniques for egg and sperm donation and preservation, has engendered a bewildering variety of possibilities which are not easily recon-ciled with our traditional definitions of "mother," "father," and "parent."

> We now live in an era where a child may have as many as five different "parents." These include a sperm donor, an egg donor, a surrogate or gestational host, and two nonbiologically related individuals who intend to raise the child. Indeed, the process of procreation itself has become so fragmented by the variety and combinations of collabora-tive-reproductive methods that there are a total of sixteen different reproductive combinations, in addition to traditional conception and childbirth.

John Lawrence Hill, *What Does it Mean to Be a "Parent"? The Claims of Biology as the Basis for Parental Rights*, 66 N.Y.U. L. REV. 353, 355 (1991). The degree to which current statutory law governs or fails to govern these realities provides the initial framework for our analysis.

. . .

The [Tennessee] parentage statutes define "mother" as "the *biological* mother of a child born out of wedlock." TENN. CODE ANN. § 36–2–302(4) (2001) (emphasis added). Similarly, "parent" is defined as "the *biological* mother or *biological* father of a child, regardless of the marital status of the mother and father." TENN. CODE ANN. § 36–2–302(5) (emphasis added). The parentage statutes do not define "biological mother." Consequently, we adduce definitions provided by Tennessee's adoption statutes. Statutes *in pari materia*—that is, statutes relating to the same subject or having a common purpose—are to be construed together.

The adoption statutes define "biological parents" as "the woman and man who *physically or genetically conceived* the child." TENN. CODE ANN. § 36–1–102(10) (2001) (emphasis added). Code section 36–1–102(10) focuses solely on conception, making no reference to giving birth. The verb "conceived" is modified by two disjunctively related adverbs. On the one hand, "physically" is an adverb meaning "in a physical manner" and "in respect to the body," *Webster's Third New Int'l Dictionary of the English Language Unabridged* 1707, and which thus means in a manner which relates to or stands "in accordance with the laws of nature," *id.* at 1706 (defining "physical"). As used in the statute, "physically . . . conceived" therefore means having caused concep-tion through natural means (coitus) as opposed to artificial means.

On the other hand, "genetically conceived" means having caused con-ception in a manner pertaining to "genetic makeup and phenomena."

Genetic conception thus entails the contribution of one's genes to a child. By providing for genetic conception in addition to physical or natural conception, Code section 36–1–102(10) implicitly accounts for genetic procreation via technological assistance. If practicable, a statute is to be construed so that its component parts are reasonably consistent. *Marsh v. Henderson*, 424 S.W.2d 193, 196 (Tenn. 1968). "Every word used is presumed to have meaning and purpose, and should be given full effect if so doing does not violate the obvious intention of the Legislature." *Id.*

We agree with the Court of Appeals that Cindy falls outside the statutory scope of the parentage and adoption statutes, which do not expressly control the circumstances of this case....

. . .

... [T]he parentage statutes generally fail to contemplate dispute over maternity. For example, the rebuttable presumptions of parentage provided in TENNESSEE CODE ANNOTATED § 36–2–304 (2001) focus exclusively on establishing paternity. *See* TENN. CODE ANN. § 36–2–304(a) ("A *man* is rebuttably presumed to be the *father* of a child if....") (emphasis added). The statutes also employ the term "mother" in a way that assumes we already know who the "mother" is, *see, e.g.*[,] TENN. CODE ANN. §§ 36–2–303, 36–2–305(b)(1)(B) (2001), whereas references to "father" include such phrases as "a man claiming to be the child's father," TENN. CODE ANN. § 36–2–305(b)(1)(C), "alleged father," TENN. CODE ANN. § 36–2–305(b)(4), and "putative father," TENN. CODE ANN. § 36–2–318 (2001). Similarly, the statute providing for an order of parentage is concerned solely with the establishment of paternity. *See* TENN. CODE ANN. § 36–2–311(a) (2001) ("Upon establishing parentage, the court shall make an order declaring the *father* of the child.") (emphasis added). The statutes lack corresponding language concerning the establishment of maternity.

The legislative history of the parentage statutes reinforces our conclusion that they fail to contemplate or to control the circumstances of this case....

. . .

Significantly, the legislative history shows that the current parentage statutes were not designed to control questions of parentage where sperm or egg donation is involved. In response to the observation that the new parentage statutes could potentially allow a sperm donor to file a parentage claim, Mr. Steve Cobb stated as follows:

> I can tell you that the clear intention, discussed intention, of this [bill] was *not* to deal with sperm donors at all.... We wanted to put that off for another day.... The intent, and it should be stated by the sponsor in a colloquy on the floor if necessary, is not to affect that issue *at all*.

Tape S–Jud. #4 (Tennessee Senate Judiciary Committee May 13, 1997). Concerning the question of maternity where egg donation is involved, the legislative history contains no indication that this matter was ever contemplated as a potential issue.

In sum, we conclude that Tennessee's parentage and related statutes do not provide for or control the circumstances of this case. Contrary to the position taken by the dissent which would restrict the basis for legal maternity to genetic consanguinity alone, we determine that these statutes simply do not apply to all conceivable parentage determinations. In this regard, we agree with the Court of Appeals.

In the absence of express guidance from the legislature, the Court of Appeals looked to case law from other jurisdictions to resolve the dispute of maternity in this case. Among the few jurisdictions which have addressed cases like this one, where a gestational carrier implanted with donated eggs seeks parental status of the resulting children and where legislation does not clearly resolve the matter, two tests for maternity have arisen. Some courts have focused on intent, holding that under such circumstances the intended "mother" is to be deemed the legal mother. *See, e.g., Johnson v. Calvert*, 851 P.2d 776 ([Cal.]1993); *In re Marriage of Buzzanca*, 72 Cal. Rptr.2d 280 ([Cal. Ct. App.]1998); *McDonald v. McDonald*, 608 N.Y.S.2d 477 (N.Y. App. Div. 1994). Other courts have instead focused on genetics and gestation, holding that genetic connection to the children is of paramount importance in determining legal maternity. *See, e.g., Culliton v. Beth Israel Deaconess Med. Ctr.*, 756 N.E. 2d 1133 ([Mass.]2001); *Belsito v. Clark*, 67 Ohio Misc. 2d 54 ([Ohio Ct. Com. Pl.]1994).

The intent test has developed primarily in California. In *Johnson*, a married couple was unable to have children naturally because the wife had undergone a hysterectomy, yet the wife could still produce eggs. The couple entered into a surrogacy agreement with a third-party female who agreed to give birth to a child on their behalf in exchange for $10,000 and other consideration. One of the wife's eggs was fertilized with her husband's sperm and was successfully implanted in the surrogate's uterus. However, when the relationship between the couple and the surrogate deteriorated, litigation over maternity and custody ensued. Under California's version of the UNIFORM PARENTAGE ACT, both genetic consanguinity and giving birth were equally cognizable bases for establishing maternity. The Court declined to recognize two legal mothers. In order to break the tie, the California Supreme Court held that when gestation and genetic consanguinity "do not coincide in one woman, she who intended to procreate the child—that is, she who intended to bring about the birth of the child that she intended to raise as her own—is the natural mother under California law." The *Johnson* Court justified its holding in part by strongly affirming the validity of surrogacy contracts.

The genetic test has been set forth most thoroughly by the Ohio Court of Common Pleas in *Belsito*. In *Belsito*, a married couple wanted children, and the wife could produce eggs but could not sustain a pregnancy. By agreement, one of the wife's eggs was fertilized with the husband's sperm and then implanted in the uterus of a gestational surrogate (the wife's sister). Without objection from the surrogate, the couple sought a declaratory judgment of maternity and paternity. Like California, Ohio had adopted a version of the UNIFORM PARENTAGE ACT which provided that "maternity can be established by identifying the natural mother through the birth process or by other means, including DNA blood tests," as provided by statute. Also declining to recognize two legal mothers, the court applied a two-stage analysis for establishing maternity. First, if the male and female genetic providers have not waived parental rights, they must be declared the legal parents. Second, if the female genetic provider has waived her parental rights, then the gestator is the legal mother. On this basis, the court held that the married couple, as the child's genetic progenitors, were the legal parents.

Significantly, Tennessee's statutory framework for establishing maternity differs markedly from the California and Ohio statutes under consideration in *Johnson* and *Belsito. Compare* TENN. CODE ANN. § 36–2–302(4) (defining "mother" as "the biological mother of a child born out of wedlock") *and* TENN. CODE ANN. § 36–1–102(10) (defining "biological parents" as "the woman and man who physically or genetically conceived the child") *with* Cal. Civ. Code § 7003(1) (West 1983) ("The parent and child relationship may be established ... between a child and the natural mother ... by proof of her having given birth to the child, or under this part."), *repealed by* 1992 Cal. Stat. c. 162 (A.B. 2650), § 4 *and* Ohio Rev. Code Ann. § 3111.02 (West 1992) ("The parent and child relationship between a child and the child's natural mother may be established by proof of her having given birth to the child or pursuant to [other sections of the Ohio Revised Code]."). Consequently, neither California's intent test nor Ohio's genetic test is strictly apposite to our statutory scheme.

Further, both the intent test and the genetic test suffer from inadequacies. For example, in *Johnson* the California Supreme Court crafted an unnecessarily broad rule which could afford maternal status even to a woman who failed to qualify under either of California's two statutory bases for maternity. According to *Belsito*, the intent formulation of *Johnson* has "discarded both genetics and birth as the primary means of identifying the natural maternal parent," and provides for, "in effect, a private adoption process that is readily subject to all the defects and pressures of such a process." In Tennessee, unlicensed and unregulated adoption is statutorily prohibited and subject to criminal penalties. *See* Tenn. Code Ann. §§ 36–1–108 to–109 (2001).

However, the genetic test of *Belsito* also has significantly broad implications. In the event that a dispute were to arise between an intended mother who had obtained eggs from a third-party donor and a gestational surrogate in whom the eggs had been implanted, the genetic test would implicitly invalidate any surrogacy agreement. The genetic test could also have practical effects similar to the "adoption-default model" criticized by *In re Marriage of Buzzanca*, in that an intended "mother" who employs techniques for assisted reproduction including egg donation would by default have to submit to government-controlled adoption procedures to attain a secure legal status as "mother." Policy-wise, the requirement of such regulation may or may not be sound.

Consequently, we decline to adopt either the intent test or the genetic test as a general rule for resolving this case. We thus vacate the adoption of the intent test of *Johnson* by the courts below.

[The court then focuses on the particular facts of the case and examines the factors that it deems relevant to establishing maternity: (i) genetics, (ii) intent, (iii) gestation, and (iv) the absence of controversy between the gestator and the genetic mother.]

We conclude that Tennessee's parentage statutes neither provide for nor contemplate the circumstances of this case, where an unmarried couple has employed techniques for assisted reproduction involving third-party egg donation to produce children for their own benefit and where dispute has arisen over the genetically unrelated gestator's legal status as mother. Although in some jurisdictions courts have fashioned widely applicable tests for maternity where techniques for assisted reproduction are involved, we decline to adopt as a general rule either the intent test or the genetic test. Consequently, we vacate the adoption of the intent test by the courts below.

Instead we affirm on separate and narrower grounds the holding of the courts below that Cindy is the legal mother of the children C.K.G., C.A.G., and C.L.G. with all the rights and responsibilities of parenthood. Our holding in this regard depends on the following factors: (1) prior to the children's birth, both Cindy as gestator and Charles as the genetic father voluntarily demonstrated the bona fide intent that Cindy would be the children's legal mother and agreed that she would accept the legal responsibility as well as the legal rights of parenthood; (2) Cindy became pregnant, carried to term, and gave birth to the children as her own; and (3) this case does not involve a controversy between a gestator and a female genetic progenitor where the genetic and gestative roles have been separated and distributed among two women, nor does this case involve a controversy between a traditional or gestational surrogate and a genetically-unrelated intended mother. In our view, given the far-reaching, profoundly complex, and competing public policy considerations necessarily implicated by the present controversy, crafting a broadly applicable rule for the establishment of maternity where techniques for assisted human reproduction are involved is more appropriately addressed by the Tennessee General Assembly.

Having concluded that Cindy is the children's legal mother, the question of estoppel is moot, and we vacate the holding of the Court of Appeals that Charles is estopped to deny Cindy's maternal status. However, we affirm in full the judgments of the juvenile court and Court of Appeals concerning comparative fitness, custody, child support, and visitation. Costs of this appeal are taxed to the appellant, Charles, for which execution may issue if necessary.

■ ADOLPHO A. BIRCH, JR., dissenting.

Because my views differ from the majority opinion, I respectfully dissent. At the outset, I am convicted [sic] that any resolution reached in this case will be temporary only—a stop-gap solution usable for this case alone, pending legislative action, as the law accelerates to catch up with the rapidly evolving technology of reproduction and its consequences. Still, unless our legislature acts, I fear that this *narrowly tailored* solution designed for this specific case will be used as precedent for other cases involving reproductive technology.

My colleagues have, nevertheless, cobbled together a resolution which would appear at first glance to be just and reasonable. But in so doing, they have side-stepped a clear legislative mandate: the statutory definition of "parent."

The operative facts that this case presents are unusual, though not unique. In short, we have a biological father (hereinafter "Dr. G.") and a gestational host (hereinafter "Ms. C."). The children resulting from this procedure have the father's DNA, but have no DNA from the gestational host. Yet, she desires to be declared the children's legal mother and to receive child support from the children's father.

The majority has chosen to use a totality of the circumstances analysis to validate the plaintiff's status in this case. Although the majority declines to adopt either an intent test or a genetic test, they rely heavily upon intent as a primary factor. The intent test has been soundly criticized. Thus, I submit that using intent even as just a factor for establishing parentage, is unwieldy, subjective, and questionable. At least three reasons have been noted why a test based on intent should be rejected. These same criticisms also apply when intent is used solely as a factor. First, it is difficult to apply the "*Johnson* test," an intent test, because proof is hard to ascertain, especially when each party purports an intention to procreate and raise the child. Second, public policy areas of "procreation and parentage, which involve values that are basic to society," are not supported by this test in established areas such as "[the] surrender of parental rights [by agreement], the best interests of children, [and the] stability in the child-parent relationship." Third, this test does not completely recognize the right of the genetic-provider to decide whether or not to exercise fundamental rights—procreation and parental rights. Furthermore, a party's intent may change after conception, through gestation, and after birth.

. . .

The majority also places considerable weight on gestation, noting the historical link between gestation and genetics. Historically, there was no separation between the gestational host and the genetic provider; thus, the gestational host and genetic provider were one in the same. Now, technology has evolved as we can see in the instant case. It is because of this separation we now have this and other disputes regarding parentage. Therefore, because of the technological advances in reproduction I believe the majority's reliance on the historical binding of gestation to genetics is not applicable to this case and should not be used. Furthermore, the majority admits that gestation is conspicuously missing from the statutes. Therefore, we should conspicuously leave gestation out of consideration in determining parentage.

I would resolve this case through genetics. It is scientific, certain, and has found acceptance in several courts that have addressed the issue. Furthermore, it is easier to apply. Moreover, this is the test that our legislature has already ordained by providing that parentage may be established by either biology or adoption. Indeed, "courts have looked at genetics as the primary basis to determine who is the parent" based on the importance of historical precedence and common ancestry.

The plaintiff is, a fortiori, a non-parent, at least as is determined by the statutory definitions of "mother" and "parent" as one who has biological ties to the child(ren). *See* TENN. CODE ANN. §§ 36–2–302(4), 36–1–102(10), (28), (36) (2001 & Supp. 2004).

. . .

By inquiring—"Who is the mother of these children?"—the majority raises the specter of the "motherless child"; that is, the impression has been given that the children will have no mother unless we find a way to confer those rights upon Ms. C. Such is not the case. The children do indeed have a mother. It just happens that the mother's identity here is, as is sometimes the case, unknown. The real question which should have been considered and answered by this court is whether the plaintiff is the children's legal mother. The answer is apparently no.

The majority, in placing Ms. C. on equal legal footing with the children's biological and legal father, Dr. G., in my view, is an exercise of largesse gone too far awry. We are to apply the law, and in the process, we are neither to unduly restrict or expand statutes' coverage. In my view, the majority reached beyond existing law to produce a palatable result. This overreaching is not necessary in my opinion. Thus, this case should be resolved under the law as it currently exists today. Tennessee statutes do not use gestation or intent to confer parental status, instead genetics, marriage and adoption are the routes available. Therefore, by reviewing and analyzing the Tennessee statutes which are based on biology, Ms. C. is not the parent nor is she the legal mother of the children for purposes of this case, and she has no legal standing to sue for custody or support as a parent. Adoption, nevertheless, remains an option.

We, as interpreters of the law, not makers of the law, are powerless, in my view, to reach a different resolution. Accordingly, I would reverse the judgment of the Court of Appeals and remand the cause to the trial court where it would proceed as a contest between a parent and a non-parent under settled Tennessee authority.

In re Roberto d.B.

Court of Appeals of Maryland, 2007.
399 Md. 267, 923 A.2d 115.

■ Bell, C.J.

This case compels the Court to consider the ever-continuing development of artificial reproductive technologies. . . .

The law is being tested as these new techniques become more commonplace and accepted; this case represents the first challenge in Maryland. . . . [M]ust the name of a genetically unrelated gestational host of a fetus, with whom the appellant contracted to carry *in vitro* fertilized embryos to term, be listed as the mother on the birth certificate, when, as a result, children are born? The Circuit Court for Montgomery County held that it must. We shall reverse.

Because of the unusual procedural posture of this case, the facts are not disputed. The appellant, Roberto d.B., an unmarried male, initiated, on December 18, 2000, a medical procedure known as *in vitro* fertilization, with his sperm being used to fertilize eggs from an egg donor. The procedure resulted in two fertilized eggs.

The putative appellee in this case is the woman with whom the appellant contracted to act as a carrier for any embryo that might be created as a result of his fertilization efforts so that they might gestate in a womb. Fertilized eggs were implanted in the appellee on December 21, 2000, and she delivered twin children on August 23, 2001, at Holy Cross Hospital in Silver Spring, Maryland.

. . .

Neither the appellee nor the appellant, however, wanted the gestational carrier's name to be listed on the birth certificate as the "mother" of the children. It is the appellant's and the appellee's contention that the appellee was merely acting as a gestational carrier for children that were never intended, by either party, to be hers, and to whom she has no genetic relationship. The appellee does not wish to exercise parental rights to, or over, these two children, nor does the appellant desire that she do so. The appellee contends that, under her agreement, she had a reasonable expectation that her role in the lives of these children would terminate upon delivery of the children, and that the faithful performance of her duties under the agreement would not permanently impact her life, nor the lives of her family.

Thus, the appellee joined the appellant's petition to the Circuit Court for Montgomery County, asking it to issue an "accurate" birth certificate, i.e., one that did not list the gestational carrier as the children's mother. In the petition, they asked the court to declare that the appellant was the father of the children, and authorize the hospital to report only the name of the father to the MDVR [Maryland Division of Vital Records].

Despite the contentions of the appellant and appellee, the Circuit Court for Montgomery County refused to remove the appellee's name from the birth certificate and rejected the petition. The appellant noted an appeal to the Court of Special Appeals. On our own motion and prior to proceedings in that court, this Court granted certiorari.

The appellant is the genetic father of the twin children, having provided his sperm to fertilize donated eggs. The egg donor, not a party in this case, is the genetic provider of the egg. The appellee is the gestational carrier of the fertilized eggs that developed in her womb, despite contributing no genetic material to the fertilization process.

The Circuit Court's oral ruling is sparse, but outlines two primary reasons why the name of the gestational carrier should not be removed from the children's birth certificate. It first notes that no Maryland case law exists that would give a trial court the power to remove the mother's name from a birth certificate. Second, it notes that removing the name of the surrogate from the birth certificate is inconsistent with the "best interests of the child" standard ("BIC"), citing, generally, "health reasons."

The appellant's primary contention is that the parentage statutes in Maryland, as enforced by the trial court below, do not "afford equal protection of the law to men and women similarly situated." Maryland's Equal Rights Amendment (E.R.A.), Article 46 of the Maryland Declaration of Rights, specifies that "[e]quality of rights under the law shall not be abridged or denied because of sex." The appellant contends that because Maryland's parentage statutes allow a man to deny paternity, and do not, currently, allow a woman to deny maternity, these statutes, unless interpreted differently, are subject to an E.R.A. challenge.

The paternity statute in Maryland, codified as MARYLAND CODE (1999, 2006 Repl. Vol.) §§ 5–1001 *et seq.* of the Family Law Article, outlines the steps and processes through which the state can establish paternity, and thus hold alleged fathers responsible for parental duties, such as child support. It is also the statute that allows alleged fathers to deny paternity.

Section 5–1002 outlines the legislative purpose of the statute, providing that "this State has a duty to improve the deprived social and economic status of children born out of wedlock," and that its goals are "to promote the general welfare and best interests of children born out of wedlock by securing for them, as nearly as practicable, the same rights to support, care, and education as children born in wedlock," and "to impose on the mothers and fathers of children born out of wedlock the basic obligations and responsibilities of parenthood."

To establish paternity, a proceeding must be brought before a child's eighteenth birth day.... A blood test may be requested in conjunction with the proceeding, and, at trial, the burden is on the complainant to prove that the "alleged father is the father of the child." If, however, the trial court finds that the alleged father is the father, then it shall declare paternity.... If the trial court, however, finds that the alleged father is *not* the father, it can set aside or modify the declaration of paternity. Thus, the court has the power to declare that an alleged father has no parental status when no genetic connection is found.

The appellant argues that a woman has no equal opportunity to deny maternity based on genetic connection—in essence, that in a paternity action, if no genetic link between a man and a child is established, the man would not be found to be the parent, and the matter would end, but a woman, or a gestational carrier, as in this case, will be forced by the State to be the "legal" mother of the children, despite her lack of genetic connection.

.   .   .

The paternity statute was added to the Family Law Article in 1984. Judging from language the Legislature used in drafting the statute, the Legislature did not contemplate anything outside of traditional childbirth. For example, § 5–1027 of the Family Law Article provides, "[t]here is a rebuttable presumption that the child is the legitimate child of the man to whom its mother was married at the time of conception," and the legislative purpose of the statute purports to be to aid "children born out of wedlock." The statute does not provide for a situation where the potential parents are unmarried, much less a situation where children are conceived using an assisted reproductive technology.

. . . As it exists, the paternity statute serves to restrict, rather than protect, the relationships the intended parents wish to have with children conceived using these new processes.

Again, the paternity statute, as written, provides an opportunity for genetically unlinked males to avoid parentage, while genetically unlinked females do not have the same option. This Court has found that any action by the State, without a substantial basis, that imposes a burden on, or grants a benefit to one sex, and not to the other, violates the Maryland Equal Rights Amendment. . . .

. . .

Because Maryland's E.R.A. forbids the granting of more rights to one sex than to the other, in order to avoid an equal rights challenge, the paternity statutes in Maryland must be construed to apply equally to both males and females. . . .

The language of the paternity statute need not be rewritten. Interpreting the statute to extend the same rights to women and maternity as it applies—and works quite well—to men and paternity is all that is required.

Furthermore, for reasons discussed . . . *infra,* because there is sufficient evidence that the State would not object to the removal of the gestational carrier's name from the birth certificate, and because such a result would not be inconsistent with the current statutes controlling the issuance of birth certificates, we hold that it is within a trial court's power to order the MDVR to issue a birth certificate that contains only the father's name.

The Circuit Court opined that "it is not in the best interests of the minor child [to remove the surrogate mother's name from the birth certificate]." The only explanation it provides, however, is as follows:

> There are a lot of public policy reasons why it is not in the best interests of the child not to have the mother's name on the birth certificate.

> There are health reasons why you might want to have, and it would be good to have the mother's name on the birth certificate, and have that information available.

It is clear, however, that, the trial court's explanation aside, the best interests of the child ("BIC") standard does not apply to the unusual circumstance in the case *sub judice.* While we have noted previously that "the controlling factor in adoption and custody cases is . . . what best serves the interest of the child," it is clear that the context in which the issue arises is significant in determining the standard by which to evaluate the situation.

. . .

In the case *sub judice,* a third party desires to relinquish parental rights, not assert them. There simply is no contest over parental rights. There is no issue of unfitness on the part of the father. Moreover, there is nothing with which to measure the father's ability to be a parent against, in order for a trial court to rule that it is *not* in the best interests of the child to grant the father the relief he seeks. Accordingly, the implication by the trial court that the BIC standard should be used in the case *sub judice* is inappropriate, and its use by the trial court was error.

It requires noting that surrogacy contracts, that is, payment of money for a child, are illegal in Maryland. Two statutes, MARYLAND CODE (2002, 2006 Supp.) § 3–603 of the Criminal Law Article, entitled "Sale of minor" . . . and MARYLAND CODE (1999, 2006 Repl.Vol.) § 5–3B–32 of the Family Law Article, entitled "Prohibited payments" . . . so provide. We have enforced these statutes.

Finally, we reiterate that the Division of Vital Records has expressed no objection to the removal of the gestational carrier's name from the birth certificate in response to an order of the Court. . . .

[The dissenting opinion by Judge Cathell is printed at page 634 *infra.*]

NOTES

1. The Uniform Parentage Act (amended 2002) provides a framework for pre-conception judicial validation of gestational agreements and instructs courts to recognize the intended parents as the legal parents of the child born as a consequence of a validated gestational agreement. *See* U.P.A. Art. 8 (amended 2002). The ABA Model Act contains two alternatives. Like the Uniform Parentage Act, the first alternative provides for a judicial proceeding to validate the gestational agreement and determine parentage. *See* ABA MODEL ACT GOVERNING ASSISTED REPROD. TECH. Art. 7 Alt. A (2008). The second alternative provides for more direct recognition of parentage but only if the parties' attorneys certify that certain protective conditions have been fulfilled. *See id.* Art. 7 Alt. B. States that have accepted the legality of surrogacy under restrictive conditions usually provide a mechanism for recognizing the intended parents as legal parents. *E.g.,* FLA. STAT. ANN. § 742.16 (West 2010); 750 ILL. COMP. STAT. 47/15, 47/35 (2010); N.H. REV. STAT. ANN. § 168–B:23 (LexisNexis 2010); TEX. FAM. CODE ANN. §§ 160.756, 160.760 (Vernon 2008); UTAH CODE ANN. §§ 78B–15–803, 78B–15–807 (2008); VA. CODE ANN. §§ 20–160, 20–162 (2008 & Supp. 2011).

Even courts in states where no statute regulates parentage in surrogacy cases may be called upon to decide parentage questions. In *Raftopol v. Ramey,* the Supreme Court of Connecticut decided whether two same-sex partners who had contracted with a surrogate could be validly proclaimed the legal parents of the child, per the terms of their agreement. 12 A.3d 783, 785–86 (Conn. 2011). There was disagreement as to whether a statute that permitted a replacement birth certificate when the birth was subject to a valid gestational agreement conferred legal parentage upon intended parents. *Id.* at 793–99. The court ultimately held that such individuals do acquire parental status through this statute, without respect to their biological relationship to the children. *Id.* at 799. It also called upon the legislature to further define the conditions under which a gestational agreement would be considered valid. *Id.* at 800–04.

2. Even in states that have proclaimed surrogacy agreements void as against public policy, the question of parentage may have to be resolved. In Indiana, for instance, a surrogate agreement, as defined in the statute, is against public policy and void. IND. CODE ANN. §§ 31–20–1–1, 31–20–1–2 (West 2008). But in the case of *In re Paternity and Maternity of Infant R.,* the Indiana Court of Appeals reversed a decision of the trial court not to give relief to the intended and genetic mother of a child born to a surrogate and allowed her to rebut the surrogate's presumption of parentage by proving that she (the intended mother) was the biological mother. 922 N.E.2d 59, 60–62 (Ind. Ct. App. 2010). The court referred to equitable reasons for providing relief:

> Specifically, if equity ignores technological realities that the law has yet to recognize, a child born in the circumstances alleged herein would be denied the opportunity afforded to other children of this State, that is, to be legally linked to those with whom he or she shares DNA. Moreover, a woman who has carried a child but is not biologically related to that child would be denied a remedy available to putative, but not biological, fathers, that is, the removal of an incorrect designation on the birth certificate and the avoidance of legal responsibilities for another person's child.

Id. at 61. The court reversed with instructions for an evidentiary hearing on the child's genetic lineage. *Id.* at 62. The court did not discuss the state's public policy against surrogacy.

A Pennsylvania court has held that a surrogate with no biological connection to the children she carried did not have standing to challenge the biological father's custody. *See J.F. v. D.B.*, 897 A.2d 1261 (Pa. Super. Ct. 2006). Even more interestingly, an Ohio court granted an intended mother's petition to disestablish the gestational mother's parental rights where neither woman bore a genetic link to the child. *S.N. v. M.B.*, 935 N.E.2d 463, 464–67 (Ohio Ct. App. 2010). The court held that their surrogacy agreement was valid. *Id.* at 471. The agreement rebutted the gestational mother's presumption of parentage and established the intended mother as the legal mother. *Id.* at 471–72.

3. The parental status of a gestational mother can be further complicated when mistakes occur at the fertility clinic. In *Robert B. v. Susan B.*, for example, a couple used the husband's sperm and donor eggs to create embryos for implantation in the wife, which resulted in a child. 135 Cal.Rptr.2d 785, 786 (App. 2003). However, some of their embryos were also implanted in a woman who wanted to use anonymous donor gametes to have a child. *Id.* When the mistake was discovered and the couple sought parental rights to the resulting child, the court found that the husband was the father based on his genetic connection, that his wife, who had no genetic connection to the child, did not have a claim to parentage, and that the other woman was the legal mother because she gave birth to the child. *Id.* at 786, 789–90. *See also Perry–Rogers v. Fasano*, 715 N.Y.S.2d 19 (App. Div. 2000), *infra* Section D.2.

C. RIGHTS AND INTERESTS OF CHILDREN CONCEIVED THROUGH ART

1. HOW MANY PARENTS AT A MINIMUM OR MAXIMUM?

In re Roberto d.B.

Court of Appeals of Maryland, 2007.
399 Md. 267, 923 A.2d 115.

[The majority opinion is printed at page 630 *supra*]

■ CATHELL, J.

I dissent.

This case illustrates that the process of manufacturing children can lead to unusual situations that would have been virtually inconceivable decades ago when the relevant statutory scheme was enacted. I do not necessarily agree or disagree that the remedy for the present situation created by the majority is appropriate or otherwise. I think it is wrong for the majority to fashion, in the first instance, the public policy it is creating as a remedy. The issues present in this case, going as they do to the very heart of a society, are, in my view, a matter for the Legislative Branch of government and not initially for the courts.

It is important to note what this case is not. It is not about a woman, married or otherwise, wanting to be a mother, who has difficulty in conceiving through sexual intercourse or who does not want to conceive through sexual intercourse or direct artificial insemination, and thus wants to have her egg fertilized outside her body and then implanted back into her womb where she will, hopefully, be able to give natural birth to a child she will raise as the mother. This case has nothing to do with attempts to cope with female fertility problems of any kind. In this case (so far as the record reflects), there is no woman, genetic mother, birth mother, or otherwise, who wants to mother the resulting child or who wants her name on the birth certificate.

This is simply the case, apparently, of a man who wants to be a father and, recognizing that he could not do it by himself, went out and arranged for (perhaps hired) two different women and an assembler to help him manufacture a child—one woman to donate (or sell) the egg (a genetic mother), a technician (apparently paid) to fertilize the egg in a dish, and another woman (the birth mother) to carry the fetus through the gestation period and then to eject the child in what would normally be considered the birthing process. At the end of this manufacturing process, the result is a child who, according to the majority, is to have no mother at birth.

The hospital, having some familiarity with normal birthing processes, understandably perceives what happens to be a birth and places the name of the woman from whence the child has come (at least the child emerged from the birth canal of the woman), on the birth certificate as required by State law. Everybody, (except the child and the hospital) then claims foul because the law requires the naming of a mother on a birth certificate. Then the majority of this Court joins the clamor and decrees that the child has no mother at birth—a concept thought impossible for tens of thousands of years.

One supposes that under the aegis of what is occurring in this case, that if a source of sperm does not intend to be a father, he could assert that he was not the father, and under the theories of the majority, a child could come into the world with neither a mother nor a father at birth.

. . .

In the present case, what the majority does, is to establish as a matter of public policy that it is possible for there to be a denial of all maternity, i.e., that there is no mother at all at birth, not that a particular woman is not the mother. The majority, in essence, holds that if you do not intend to be the mother, you should not be responsible as a mother. There are probably tens, if not hundreds of thousands, of fathers (and certainly mothers as well) who did not intend to be parents at the time of the actions that led to conception, who have been judicially determined to be responsible for the support of the child they did not intend to conceive. With the majority's decision today, if a genetic and/or birth mother does not intend to act as a mother during this manufacturing process—they have no responsibility as a mother. Presumably, now both fathers and mothers (participating in invitro [sic] fertilization or sexual intercourse), if they enter into contracts or other writings or agreements, providing that neither intends to be a parent, or just engage in acts without any agreement, in which a child is conceived, the mother and the father (because he must be treated equally as well) can claim that no one should be responsible for the rearing and support of the child(ren). Presumably, under such circumstances the only responsibility for the rearing of children would be the State's.

If ever there was a strained interpretation of a statute, the majority's attempt to construe MARYLAND CODE (1982, 2005), § 4–211(a)(2)(ii), which allows the issuance of new birth certificates when a court enters "an order as to the parentage" of a child, as contemplating the issuance of certificates of birth showing that a child had no mother at birth, is it. . . .

I suggest, that the majority's decision today is not what was fathomed when the General Assembly enacted the relevant statute and also was not what the people of the State thought they were approving when they approved the Equal Rights Amendment (the writer amongst them). It simply defies common sense and all principles of logic to hold that the people of the State and their representatives thought at the time they were enacting and approving the statute and the Constitutional Amendment, that they were permitting the courts to create a procedure whereby children would end up not having any mothers, even at birth.

. . .

Additionally, the literature relating to families is replete with conclusions respecting the value of having fathers as a part of the process of family life— available from the birth of the child. Certainly there is similar, or even greater, value in having mothers involved in the rearing of children. Until now, I presume that it was not thought necessary to specifically relate such issues to females in that mothers obviously were going to be present at birth. But with this case, according to the majority, there is to be no mother—just a petridish [sic].

One only has to contemplate what might occur as the child matures, in order to believe that this issue is best left to the representatives of the people. What happens when a child is asked to present a birth certificate at a customs area in a foreign country (until recently that is all that was required of American citizens in many countries, and remains so in some) and a customs inspector sees that the birth certificate indicates that the person standing in front of him or her states that the person has no mother—or even no father *or* mother? What happens when the child presents such a birth certificate to authorities outside (or inside) this State in an attempt to acquire a passport? What happens when such a certificate is presented in the admission processes of colleges or presented when one wants to enlist in the armed services? How is the child going to be adversely affected throughout its minority when it has no mother from whom support can be obtained— and no mother at all? There are many reasons why the General Assembly might decide that it is in the best interests of children to have a surrogate or donor mother's name on a birth certificate and that, if afterwards she could establish that she should not have the obligations of a mother, she could seek the termination of her status in order to end her legal responsibility. But the Court assumes the policy mantle instead.

. . .

By its holding, the majority, in my view, under the circumstances of the issues presented here, has discarded the principle of judicial restraint in favor of one that improperly usurps the power of the General Assembly. Somewhere in this mad rush in which our society is engaged, at a time when increasing population contributes to many of the world's problems, even judges should occasionally pause and say, "What are we doing?"

I would affirm the finding of the trial court that the resolution of this issue does not lie within the Judicial Branch of government but within the Legislative Branch.

NOTE

In re Roberto d.B. creates the possibility of motherless children via the intent of the parties to a surrogacy contract. The same is true with AID statutes and cases that exclude the donors of eggs and semen from parenthood, while allowing single men and women to pursue parentage on their own. *See, e.g., In re K.M.H., supra.* The possibility of multiple parentage beyond the mother/father dyad has also become more visible through the use of ART. In *Jacob v. Shultz–Jacob*, a lesbian couple had entered into a civil union in Vermont and were raising four children, two of them adopted by one partner and two of them born to the same partner via AID with sperm from a known donor and friend. 923 A.2d 473, 476 (Pa. Super. Ct. 2007). The latter continued to be involved in the children's life throughout the duration of the couple's relationship. *Id.* When the couple's relationship ended, the trial court awarded shared legal custody of all children to both parties, with primary physical custody of three children to one of the partners and primary physical custody of one child to the other. *Id.* The biological father was also awarded partial physical custody of his children, but was not subject to any support obligations. *Id.* The non-biological mother of the children appealed the decision, claiming that the biological father's custodial right to his two children should obligate him for some child support. *Id.* at 479. The superior court rejected the trial court's argument that making three people financially responsible for the same children would be an unworkable situation unforeseen by Pennsylvania law, reversed the support part, and remanded for reconsideration. *Id.* at 482.

Of course, the possibility for multiple parentage does not arise only in AID situations. The same issues may arise in other "non-traditional" family patterns, which include marriage, dissolution, and remarriage. Some scholars have noted that certain family law concepts applicable to two-parent families may be suited to recognition of multiple parents. These include the ALI PRINCIPLES, notions of functional parenthood, parenting plans and statutory frameworks for allocating rights and responsibilities in divorces, and recognition of non-biological parents in ART cases. *See, e.g.,* Susan Frelich Appleton, *Parents by the Numbers*, 37 HOFSTRA L. REV. 11, 12–13, n. 7, 16–26 (2008); Melanie B. Jacobs, *Why Just Two? Disaggregating Traditional Parental Rights and Responsibilities to Recognize Multiple Parents*, 9 J.L. & FAM. STUD. 309, 318–323 (2006).

2.   ACCESS TO ONE'S GENETIC INFORMATION AND CONTACT WITH THE GAMETE DONOR

In re K.M.H.

Supreme Court of Kansas, 2007.
285 Kan. 53, 169 P.3d 1025.

■ BEIER, J.

[The following portion of the opinion was not included in the majority opinion reproduced *supra* Section B.3.]

. . .

All of this being said, we cannot close our discussion of the constitutionality of K.S.A. 38–1114(f) without observing that all that is constitutional is not necessarily wise. We are mindful of, and moved by, the Center's advocacy for public policy to maximize the chance of the availability of two parents—and two parents' resources—to Kansas children. We are also aware of continued evolution in regulation of artificial insemination in this and other countries. In particular, Britain and The Netherlands now ban anonymous sperm donations, near-perfect analogs to donations from known donors who will have no role beyond facilitating artificial insemination. These shifts formally recognize the understandable desires of at least some children conceived through artificial insemination to know the males from whom they have received half of their genes. The Human Fertilization [sic] and Embryology Authority Act of 1990, as amended by Disclosure of Donor Information, Regulations 2004 No. 1511 (requiring, effective April 2005, British donors' identities to be made available to donor-conceived children when children become 18); Netherlands Embryos Bill, Article 3 Dutch Ministry of Health, Welfare, and Sport (2004) *www.minvws.nl/en* (effective June 2004, child born using donated sperm have right to obtain information about biological father at age 16). As one such child recently wrote,

> [t]hose of us created with donated sperm won't stay bubbly babies forever. We're all going to grow into adults, and form opinions about the decision to bring us into the world in a way that deprives us of the basic right to know where we came from, what our history is and who both our parents are.

Clark, *My Father was an Anonymous Sperm Donor*, The WASH. POST, Dec. 17, 2006, at B01 (also currently available at http://www.washingtonpost.com/wp-dyn/content/article/2006/12/15/AR2006121501820.html). We sympathize. However, weighing of the interests of all involved in these procedures as well as the public policies that are furthered by favoring one or another in certain circumstances, is the charge of the Kansas Legislature, not of this court.

Johnson v. Superior Court

Court of Appeal, Second District, Division 2, California, 2000.
80 Cal. App. 4th 1050, 95 Cal. Rptr. 2d 864.

■ MALLANO, J.

Petitioners Diane L. Johnson and Ronald G. Johnson, along with their minor daughter Brittany L. Johnson, filed an action against real parties in interest, California Cryobank, Inc., Cappy Rothman, M.D., and Charles A. Sims, M.D., claiming that real parties failed to disclose that the sperm they sold came from a donor with a family history of kidney disease called Autosomal Dominant Polycystic Kidney Disease (ADPKD). That sperm was used to conceive Brittany who has been diagnosed with this serious kidney disease. When petitioners sought to take the deposition and obtain documents of John Doe, the person believed to be the anonymous sperm donor, real parties (including John Doe) filed motions to quash the deposition subpoena. At the same time, petitioners filed a motion to compel compliance with the deposition subpoena. The trial court denied petitioners' motion and granted the motions to quash the deposition subpoena. By their petition, petitioners seek a writ of mandate directing the superior court to vacate its order and issue a different order compelling John Doe's deposition and the production of records.

The novel issue presented here is whether parents and their child, conceived by the sperm of an anonymous sperm donor, may compel the donor's deposition and production of documents in order to discover information relevant to their action against the sperm bank for selling sperm that they alleged transmitted ADPKD to the child. As fully discussed below, we conclude that the alleged sperm donor in this case must submit to a deposition and answer questions, as well as produce documents, which are relevant to the issues in the pending action, but that his identity should remain undisclosed to the fullest extent possible.

. . .

In this case, the Johnsons promised in their contract with Cryobank that they would, among other things, "not now, nor at any time, require nor expect [Cryobank] to obtain or divulge ... the name of said donor, nor any other information concerning characteristics, qualities, or any other information whatsoever concerning said donor." The Johnsons further agreed "that, following the said insemination, [Cryobank] shall destroy all information and records which they may have as to the identity of said donor, it being the intention of all parties that the identity of said donor shall be and forever remain anonymous." The agreement bound the Johnsons as well as their heirs and assigns.

We conclude that the Cryobank agreement with the Johnsons expresses the clear intent of both the Johnsons and Cryobank that the donor's identity and related information would be kept confidential and that such intent was for the benefit of all parties, including the donor. Our conclusion is further supported by Diane Johnson's testimony at her deposition in this case where she stated it was her intent by executing the Cryobank agreement that the donor's identity would not be disclosed to her and that her identity would not be disclosed to the donor. While John Doe or Donor No. 276 are not specifically named in the agreement, it is clear that he belongs to the class of persons—Cryobank sperm donors—who are to benefit from the agreement's confidentiality provisions.

But, our analysis does not end here. We must determine whether the Cryobank agreement with the Johnsons is contrary to an express provision of law, the policy of express law, or public policy and, hence, unenforceable. We conclude for the reasons stated below, that the Cryobank agreement goes too far in precluding disclosure of the donor's identity and related information under *all* circumstances and thus conflicts with public policy.

. . .

The express terms of FAMILY CODE section 7613, subdivision (a) provide that a husband's written consent to the insemination must be retained by the physician "as part of the medical record." "All papers and records pertaining to the insemination" wherever located—which we construe as being broader than, and including, the "medical record" previously mentioned—are subject to being inspected "upon an order of the court for good cause." Such "papers and records pertaining to the insemination" would be expected in most cases to include the name and address and related information of the sperm donor whose sperm is used in the insemination, as is apparently the case here. Accordingly, we conclude that based on the policy expressed in FAMILY CODE section 7613, inspection of insemination records, including a sperm donor's identity and related information contained in those records, may be disclosed under certain circumstances. Thus, to prohibit disclosure of the donor's identity and related information in every situation and under all circumstances, as Cryobank and John Doe attempt to do here by the Johnsons' agreement with Cryobank, would be contrary to the policy expressed in the statute. We note that Cryobank has apparently recognized that disclosure of a donor's identity could be allowed under certain circumstances as its agreement with all of its donors provides that the donor's identity "will be kept in the strictest confidence unless a court orders disclosure for good cause."

. . .

And Donor No. 276's reasonable expectation of privacy in his identity was substantially diminished by his own conduct. This is not a case of a donor making isolated donations of his sperm in order to help one woman conceive a child. Rather, the record before us reveals that Donor No. 276 deposited over 320 specimens of his semen with Cryobank. Donor No. 276's 320 semen deposits earned him over $11,000. Thus, Donor No. 276's connection with Cryobank involved a substantial commercial transaction likely to affect the lives of many people.

We conclude that although Donor No. 276 does indeed have a limited privacy interest in his identity as a sperm donor and in his medical history, under the circumstances of this case, it would be unreasonable for Donor No. 276 to expect that his genetic and medical history, and possibly even his identity, would never be disclosed.

. . .

While Donor No. 276 has an interest in maintaining the confidentiality of his identity and medical history, we hold that in the context of the particular facts of this case the state's interests, as well as those of petitioners, outweigh Donor No. 276's interests. Accordingly, John Doe must appear at his deposition and answer all questions and produce documents that are relevant to the issues raised in the litigation. But this does not mean that John Doe's identity must automatically be disclosed if he indeed is Donor No. 276.

. . .

For example, an order could be fashioned which would allow John Doe's deposition to proceed and documents produced on matters relevant to the issues in the litigation but in a manner which maintains the confidentiality of John Doe's identity and that of his family. Attendance at the deposition could be limited to the parties' counsel and the deposition transcript might refer simply to "John Doe" as the deponent. But, we leave it to the trial court to craft the appropriate order.

NOTES

1. In *Doe v. XYZ Co., Inc.*, a mother sought the identity of an anonymous sperm donor in order to institute a paternity action and to obtain information relevant to her children's health. 914 N.E.2d 117, 119 (Mass. App. Ct. 2009). The trial judge dismissed her request relating to the paternity action. *Id.* at 120. The court allowed more latitude with respect to the medical need claim, but tailored the discovery to ensure that the alleged medical condition did exist and that the alleged donor was in fact the genetic father. *Id.* As in *Johnson*, there was a discussion about the donor's privacy, as well as how his rights would be affected by not being a party to the litigation. *Id.* at 122–23.

2. As noted in *K.M.H.,* many other countries have chosen to regulate ART in the direction of openness of information. Sweden, Austria, Switzerland, the Netherlands, Norway, the United Kingdom, New Zealand, Finland, and the Australian states of Victoria, Western Australia, and New South Wales have prohibited anonymous donation. *See, e.g.,* Gaia Bernstein, *Regulating Reproductive Technologies: Timing, Uncertainty, and Donor Anonymity,* 90 B.U. L. REV. 1189, 1205–16 (2010); Eric Blyth & Lucy Frith, *Donor–Conceived People's Access to Genetic and Biographical History: An Analysis of Provisions in Different Jurisdictions Permitting Disclosure of Donor Identity,* 23 INT'L J.L. POL'Y & FAM. 174 (2009). What other policies besides the protection of a descendant's health might be served by an open donation law? What could be some of the unintended consequences of such a policy?

3. There has been some market response to the demand for more information. Many clinics have started to offer gametes from donors who have agreed to be identified in the future. The price for such gametes is higher, as is the compensation for such gamete donors. *See* Michelle Dennison, *Revealing Your Sources: The Case for Non–Anonymous Gamete Donation,* 21 J.L. & HEALTH 1, 11–12 & 12n.82 (2008). About eighteen states have adopted legislation that would permit children of anonymous donors to obtain information by court order upon showing of good cause. The good cause standard can be found in UNIFORM PARENTAGE ACT § 5(a) (1973). But as demonstrated in *Johnson* and *Doe v. XYZ, supra,* this would not necessarily compel the revelation of a donor's identity.

4. Anonymity may be harder to maintain because of technological advances. Using basic information about the donor, the internet, and possibly the child's DNA, donor-conceived families may be able to find out the donor's identity. *See* Rachel Lehmann–Haupt, *Are Sperm Donors Really Anonymous Anymore?* SLATE (Mar. 1, 2010, 9:26 AM), http://www.slate.com/id/2243743/. An online effort to connect donor-conceived children with their half-siblings or donors was started by a mother and her son. *See* DONOR SIBLING REGISTRY, https://www.donorsiblingregistry.com/ (last visited Nov. 18, 2011). For a thoughtful discussion about donor-conceived children connecting with donors and half-siblings, *see* Naomi Cahn, *No Secrets: Openness and Donor–Conceived "Half Siblings,"* 39 CAP. U. L. REV. 313, 332–39 (2011).

3.   THE RIGHTS OF POSTHUMOUSLY CONCEIVED CHILDREN

UNIFORM PARENTAGE ACT

(amended 2002).

Section 707.   Parental Status of Deceased Individual

If an individual who consented in a record to be a parent by assisted reproduction dies before placement of eggs, sperm, or embryos, the deceased individual is not a parent of the resulting child unless the deceased spouse consented in a record that if assisted reproduction were to occur after death, the deceased individual would be a parent of the child.

NOTE

Inheritance rights of such children are regulated by the intestate laws of each state. For example, a Florida statute provides:

> [a] child conceived from the eggs or sperm of a person or persons who died before the transfer of their eggs, sperm, or preembryos to a woman's body shall not be eligible for a claim against the decedent's estate unless the child has been provided for by the decedent's will.

FLA. STAT. ANN. § 742.17(4) (West 2010). Louisiana allows for recognition and inheritance by a child that is posthumously conceived if certain conditions are met, including that the child is born within three years of the decedent's death. LA. REV. STAT. ANN. § 391.1.A (West 2008). Louisiana also allows heirs whose interest will be reduced by the birth of such child to contest paternity within a certain time frame. *Id.* § 391.1.B. California also recognizes posthumous conception under specified conditions and requires that the child be in utero within two years of the issuance of the death certificate or judgment of decedent's death. CAL. PROB. CODE § 249.5 (West Supp. 2011).

Schafer v. Astrue

United States Court of Appeals, Fourth Circuit, 2011.
641 F.3d 49.

■ WILKINSON, CIRCUIT JUDGE:

. . .

The sad facts giving rise to this case are not in real dispute. Janice and Don Schafer, Jr. were married in June 1992. Four months later he was diagnosed with cancer and informed that the chemotherapy he needed might render him sterile. In December 1992 he deposited sperm samples with a long-term storage facility, but in March 1993 he died of a heart attack. At the time Don was domiciled in Virginia.

In April 1999 Janice Schafer conceived a child through in vitro fertilization, and she gave birth to that child, W.M.S., on January 13, 2000 in Texas. There is significant evidence that W.M.S. is Don Schafer's biological child, born almost seven years after Don's death. There is also evidence that Don intended for Janice to use the stored semen to conceive a child after his anticipated death, though he never expressed consent in writing to be the legal father of a child resulting from post-humous [sic] in vitro fertilization. In 2001 a Texas court purported to declare Don Schafer W.M.S.'s father.

In 2004 Janice Schafer applied on W.M.S.'s behalf to the Social Security Administration ("SSA") for surviving child benefits under the Social Security Act ("the Act"), *see* 42 U.S.C. § 402(d). An administrative law judge initially awarded W.M.S. benefits, but the SSA's Appeals Council reversed, reasoning that W.M.S. was not Don Schafer's "child" within the meaning of the Act because W.M.S. could not inherit from him under Virginia intestacy law. Janice Schafer then sought review of the SSA's decision in federal district court, which upheld the SSA's denial of benefits. She now appeals.

Every child claiming survivorship benefits under the Act must meet a series of requirements. . . .

. . . [A]n applicant must establish something . . . fundamental: that he is the insured's "child" within the meaning of the Act. The Act's basic grant of benefits provides that "[e]very child (as defined in section 416(e) of this title) . . . of an individual who dies a fully or currently insured individual . . . shall be entitled to a child's insurance benefit. . . ." *Id.* § 402(d)(1). As relevant here, § 416(e) is sparse: "The term 'child' means (1) the child or legally adopted child of an individual." *Id.* § 416(e)(1).

Section 416(e)(1), however, is not the only provision of the Act that bears on the determination of child status. Section 416, titled "Additional definitions," also includes § 416(h), labeled "Determination of family status." That provision states:

> In determining whether an applicant is the child . . . of a fully or currently insured individual for purposes of this subchapter, the Secretary shall apply such law as would be applied in determining the devolution of intestate personal property by the courts of the State in

which such insured individual ... was domiciled at the time of his death.... Applicants who according to such law would have the same status relative to taking intestate personal property as a child ... shall be deemed such.

Id. § 416(h)(2)(A).

Section 416(h) also provides three additional gateways to child status for those who cannot establish it through § 416(h)(2)(A)'s intestacy provision. First, an applicant who "is a son or daughter of a fully or currently insured individual" but cannot inherit from that individual is deemed a child if his parents went through a marriage ceremony that turned out to be legally invalid. Second, a child who cannot inherit from a deceased insured individual under state intestacy law is a "child" under the Act where prior to death the decedent "had acknowledged [parentage] in writing," "had been decreed [the child's parent] by a court," or "had been ordered by a court to contribute to the support of the applicant because the applicant was [the insured individual's child]." Third, a child who cannot inherit is deemed a "child" if "such insured individual is shown by evidence satisfactory to the Secretary to have been the [parent] of the applicant, and such insured individual was living with or contributing to the support of the applicant at the time such insured individual died."

In addition, the Act gives the Commissioner of Social Security rulemaking authority. *See id.* § 405(a)

This case turns on the relationship between the brief definition of "child" in § 416(e)(1)—which is part of the only definition referred to in § 402(d)(1)'s basic grant of benefits—and § 416(h)'s more specific provisions....

The SSA has ... taken the view that posthumously conceived children such as W.M.S. can qualify as "children" under the Act only through the state intestacy provision. *See* Acquiescence Ruling, 70 Fed.Reg. at 55,657 ("[T]o meet the definition of 'child' under the Act, an after-conceived child must be able to inherit under State law."); Program Operations Manual System GN 00306.001(C)(1)(c), *available at* https://secure.ssa.gov/poms.nsf/lnx/0200306001 (same)....

On the SSA's view, then, W.M.S. is entitled to benefits only if he could inherit from Don Schafer under Virginia law. But Virginia law does not recognize any "child born more than ten months after the death of a parent" as that parent's child for intestacy purposes. VA.CODE ANN. § 20–164 (ten-month limitation); VA.CODE ANN. § 64.1–5.1(2) (incorporating the provisions of VA.CODE ANN. § 20–156 *et seq.* in determining the parentage of "a child resulting from assisted conception"). W.M.S., however, was born almost seven years after Don Schafer's death. The SSA therefore denied W.M.S.'s claim.

Schafer takes a very different view of the relationship between § 416(e)(1) and § 416(h). Adopting the view of *Gillett–Netting v. Barnhart*, 371 F.3d 593, 597 (9th Cir.2004), she argues that § 416(h)'s strictures do not apply to children whose "parentage ... is not disputed." ... It follows, she argues, that W.M.S.'s ability to inherit from Don Schafer under Virginia intestacy law is irrelevant to determining W.M.S.'s child status. Instead, as Don and Janice Schafer's undisputed biological child, W.M.S. must only show that he meets the other statutory conditions described above. The Third Circuit has recently joined *Gillett–Netting* in accepting Schafer's reading in posthumous conception cases, *see Capato ex rel. B.N.C. v. Comm'r of Soc.*

Sec., 631 F.3d 626 (3d Cir.2011), and the Eighth Circuit is currently facing the question, *see Beeler v. Astrue*, No. C09–0019 (N.D.Iowa Nov. 12, 2009), *appeal docketed*, No. 10–1092.

. . .

At first blush, Schafer's proposed course—rejecting the SSA's interpreta- tion . . . —is an alluring one. After all, . . . the plain meaning of "child" in § 416(e)(1) might seem necessarily to include the biological children of those who, because of tragic circumstances, could only become parents after their death. But . . ., we think this approach would be unsound. The "traditional tools of statutory construction," *Chevron*, [*U.S.A., Inc. v. NRDC*] 467 U.S. [437, 843 n. 9 (1984)] demonstrate that Congress intended the SSA to use state intestacy law, and even if it did not precisely speak to the question, the SSA's reasonable interpretation is entitled to deference.

We begin by examining the text of the Act. Section 416(e) itself is notably brief: "The term 'child' means (1) the child or legally adopted child of an individual. . . ." Although the "child" portion of this language does aim at natural children, other courts have noted that "this definitional tautology . . . does not provide much guidance" as to how the SSA should go about making that child status determination. *Conlon ex rel. Conlon v. Heckler*, 719 F.2d 788, 800 (5th Cir.1983).

This lack of guidance highlights the difficulty we have with the position of our colleagues on the Third and Ninth Circuits. Those courts have been willing to elevate the sparse definition found in § 416(e)(1) and to complete- ly de-emphasize the more extensive definition found in § 416(h)(2)(A), thereby treating Congress's more comprehensive efforts as a mere after- thought. . . .

. . .

It is clear, then, that § 416(e)(1) cannot provide all of the answers. But there is no need for us to join *Capato* and *Gillett–Netting* in crafting from whole cloth § 416(e)(1)'s meaning without reference to the Act's other provisions when the plain text of those provisions offers all of the guidance that is needed. Section 416(h)(2)(A) describes precisely how one ought to determine the meaning of "child" under § 416(e)(1): "*In determining whether an applicant is the child* . . . of a fully or currently insured individual *for purposes of this subchapter*"—that is, for the purposes of federal old-age, survivors, and disability insurance benefits—"the Secretary *shall apply* such [state] law as would be applied in determining the devolution of intestate personal property. . . ." 42 U.S.C. § 416(h)(2)(A) (emphasis added).

. . .

. . . Whether one looks at the instruction of § 416(h)(2)(A) individually or at the statute as a whole, the SSA's view is dutiful and faithful to Congress's intent.

. . .

Indeed, when considered in greater detail, the Act's legislative history demonstrates that Congress understood § 416(h)(2)(A)'s intestacy provisions to be the backbone of all child status determinations. The Senate Finance Committee's Report to the 1965 Amendments, which added § 416(h)(3)(C), stated that "[u]nder present law, whether a child meets the definition of a child for the purpose of getting child's insurance benefits . . . depends on the laws applied in determining the devolution of intestate personal property. . . ." S.Rep. No. 89–404, pt. 1, at 109 (1965), *reprinted in* 1965 U.S.C.C.A.N. 1943, 2049.

. . .

The Act's legislative history could hardly be clearer. Congress understood the Act's framework as requiring all natural children to pass through § 416(h) to claim child status, and it drafted in keeping with this view in adding § 416(h)(3)(C).

The SSA's interpretation also best comports with the Act's purposes. The Act is not a "welfare program generally benefiting needy persons," but rather an effort to "provide the . . . dependent members of [a wage earner's] family with protection against the hardship occasioned by his loss of earnings." *Califano v. Jobst*, 434 U.S. 47, 52 (1977). The Act thus creates a core beneficiary class: the children of deceased wage earners who relied on those earners for support.

. . .

By contrast, Schafer's interpretation contravenes the statute's purpose by threatening the core beneficiary class. She claims the Act provides child status to any undisputed biological child. But, as the Commissioner notes, the Act limits the total benefits payable from one employment record. *See* 42 U.S.C. § 403(a)(1). As a result, where an additional child claims benefits from a record, children already claiming from it could see a reduction in their benefits. Though the additional benefits would generally stay in the same family, it remains true that existing children, the Act's core intended beneficiaries, could receive proportionately less support. Congress designed the Act with those children in mind, and the SSA's interpretation best protects their interests.

. . .

The text, legislative history, purpose, and prior judicial approaches to the Act indicate that Congress wanted the SSA to apply § 416(h) in determining child status. . . .

. . .

As is often the case when applying the law, our decision is not without its costs. The tragedies of cancer and heart disease pulled the Schafer family's plans out from under them. While modern medicine allowed Janice Schafer to partially fulfill some of those plans years later, Virginia intestacy law, as incorporated by the Act, does render survivorship benefits unavailable here.

But if sad facts make hard cases, we cannot allow hard cases to make bad law. . . .

Affirmed.

■ DAVIS, CIRCUIT JUDGE, dissenting:

The majority contends that "the plain text of th[e]se provisions offers all of the guidance that is needed," and I agree. But where the majority believes that "Congress plainly intended" that 42 U.S.C. § 416(h)(2)'s definition of "child" control, I believe just the opposite: it could not be more clear that Congress instructed us to apply 42 U.S.C. § 416(e) in this case. And even if § 416(h) were to apply, proper consideration of § 416(h)(2)(B) would require that we reverse the district court.

. . .

In this case a husband, facing the prospect of sterility just four months after marrying, voluntarily left behind his sperm for a singular purpose: to produce a child with his wife. That the two of them achieved their joint purpose because she did exactly what they both contemplated provides scant justification to distort statutory meaning, structure, and purpose and thereby disqualify their offspring from his federal statutory entitlement. The majority is surely correct in its implied lament that we live in a "brave new world," one in which the law lags behind technology, as it ever has. But that truism has never defined a "hard case." What must be recalled is that judicial opinions, like the statutes they interpret, are not merely words arranged on paper. They have real effects on real people.

Respectfully, I dissent.

4. PROTECTION OF THE CHILD

In re Marriage of Buzzanca

Court of Appeal of California, Fourth District, Division 3, 1998.
61 Cal. App. 4th 1410, 72 Cal. Rptr. 2d 280.

■ SILLS, P. J.

Jaycee was born because Luanne and John Buzzanca agreed to have an embryo genetically unrelated to either of them implanted in a woman—a surrogate—who would carry and give birth to the child for them. After the fertilization, implantation and pregnancy, Luanne and John split up, and the question of who are Jaycee's lawful parents came before the trial court.

Luanne claimed that she and her erstwhile husband were the lawful parents, but John disclaimed any responsibility, financial or otherwise. The woman who gave birth also appeared in the case to make it clear that she made no claim to the child.

The trial court then reached an extraordinary conclusion: Jaycee had *no* lawful parents. First, the woman who gave birth to Jaycee was not the mother; the court had—astonishingly—already accepted a stipulation that neither she nor her husband were the "biological" parents. Second, Luanne was not the mother. According to the trial court, she could not be the mother because she had neither contributed the egg nor given birth. And John could not be the father, because, not having contributed the sperm, he had no biological relationship with the child.

We disagree. Let us get right to the point: Jaycee never would have been born had not Luanne and John both agreed to have a fertilized egg implanted in a surrogate.

The trial judge erred because he assumed that legal motherhood, under the relevant California statutes, could *only* be established in one of two ways, either by giving birth or by contributing an egg. He failed to consider the substantial and well-settled body of law holding that there are times when *fatherhood* can be established by conduct apart from giving birth or being genetically related to a child. The typical example is when an infertile husband consents to allowing his wife to be artificially inseminated. As our Supreme Court noted in such a situation over 30 years ago, the husband is the "lawful father" because he *consented* to the procreation of the child. (*See People v. Sorensen*[,] 437 P.2d 495 [(Cal. 1968)].)

The same rule which makes a husband the lawful father of a child born because of his consent to artificial insemination should be applied here—by the same parity of reasoning that guided our Supreme Court in the first surrogacy case, *Johnson v. Calvert*[,] 851 P.2d 776 [(Cal. 1993)]—to both husband and wife. Just as a husband is deemed to be the lawful father of a child unrelated to him when his wife gives birth after artificial insemination, so should a husband *and* wife be deemed the lawful parents of a child after a surrogate bears a biologically unrelated child on their behalf. In each instance, a child is procreated because a medical procedure was initiated and consented to by intended parents. The only difference is that in this case—unlike artificial insemination—there is no reason to distinguish between husband and wife. We therefore must reverse the trial court's judgment and direct that a new judgment be entered, declaring that both Luanne and John are the lawful parents of Jaycee.

. . .

Even though neither Luanne nor John are biologically related to Jaycee, they are still her lawful parents given their initiating role as the intended parents in her conception and birth. And, while the absence of a biological connection is what makes this case extraordinary, this court is hardly without statutory basis and legal precedent in so deciding. Indeed, . . . in our Supreme Court's *Johnson v. Calvert* decision, the court looked to *intent to parent* as the ultimate basis of its decision. Fortunately, as the *Johnson* court also noted, intent to parent " 'correlate[s] significantly' " with a child's best interests. That is far more than can be said for a model of the law that renders a child a legal orphan.

Again we must call on the Legislature to sort out the parental rights and responsibilities of those involved in artificial reproduction. No matter what one thinks of artificial insemination, traditional and gestational surrogacy (in all its permutations), and—as now appears in the not-too-distant future, cloning and even gene splicing—courts are still going to be faced with the problem of determining lawful parentage. A child cannot be ignored. Even if all means of artificial reproduction were outlawed with draconian criminal penalties visited on the doctors and parties involved, courts will still be called upon to decide who the lawful parents really are and who—other than the taxpayers—is obligated to provide maintenance and support for the child. These cases will not go away.

NOTES

1. In *Buzzanca*, the trial court reached the conclusion that Jaycee was a legal orphan despite the fact that Luanne Buzzanca wanted to be declared her legal mother. There have been other cases, seemingly rare, where the child remains "unclaimed." In one case, a prospective father, who had contracted for a surrogate to be inseminated with his sperm, contested his paternity of the child who was born with microcephaly. The surrogate was quoted as saying that she and her husband did not feel the baby was theirs, and that they felt pity for it but not a maternal or paternal connection. *See* Associated Press, *Surrogate Mother's Deformed Baby Rejected*, N.Y. TIMES (Jan. 23, 1983), http://www.nytimes.com/1983/01/23/us/surrogate-mother-s-deformed-baby-rejected.html. It turned out that the child was not the prospective father's but the surrogate's husband's, so the surrogate and her husband accepted the child. They still sued the broker, doctors, and a lawyer for negligence alleging that it was the prospective father's sperm that caused an infection in the mother, which in turn caused the child's pathology. *See Stiver v. Parker*, 975 F.2d 261 (6th Cir. 1992). Some legislatures have tried to prevent ART children from coming into the world un-claimed. Statutes regulating surrogacy arrangements may require the intended parents to take responsibility. Florida, for example, requires that the intended parents accept rights and responsibilities to the child, "regardless of any impairment of the child." FLA. STAT. ANN. § 742.15(3)(d) (West 2010). The next paragraph, however, provides that if neither of the intended parents are genetic parents, the surrogate is required to be responsible for the child. *Id.* § 742.15(3)(e).

2.   Some courts have attempted to protect children by finding that professionals may have a duty of protection to the children they help create. In one case, a surrogate filed a wrongful death action against the business that arranged the surrogacy after the resulting baby died as a consequence of abuse from the intended father. *Huddleston v. Infertility Center of America, Inc.*, 700 A.2d 453, 455–56 (Pa. Super. Ct. 1997). The court stated:

> In this case, we conclude that a business operating for the sole purpose of organizing and supervising the very delicate process of creating a child, which reaps handsome profits from such endeavor, must be held accountable for the foreseeable risks of the surrogacy undertaking because a "special relationship" exists between the surrogacy business, its client-participants and most especially, the child which the surrogacy undertaking creates. Such a special relationship existed between ICA, Appellant [the surrogate], and Jonathan [the baby] in this case and thus, ICA owed them an affirmative duty of protection.

Id. at 460. The court further noted that child abuse was not completely unforseeable in the surrogacy context and that a prima facie case of negligence had been established. *Id. See also Stiver v. Parker*, 975 F.2d 261, 272 (6th Cir. 1992).

D.   OTHER ISSUES

1.   DISPOSITION OF GAMETES AND EMBRYOS

In re Marriage of Witten

Supreme Court of Iowa, 2003.
672 N.W.2d 768.

■ TERNUS, JUSTICE.

. . .

The appellee, Arthur (Trip) Witten, and the appellant, Tamera Witten, had been married for approximately seven and one-half years when Trip sought to have their marriage dissolved in April 2002. One of the contested issues at trial was control of the parties' frozen embryos. During the parties' marriage they had tried to become parents through the process of in vitro fertilization. Because Tamera was unable to conceive children naturally, they had eggs taken from Tamera artificially fertilized with Trip's sperm. Tamera then underwent several unsuccessful embryo transfers in an attempt to become pregnant. At the time of trial seventeen fertilized eggs remained in storage at the University of Nebraska Medical Center (UNMC).

Prior to commencing the process for in vitro fertilization, the parties signed informed consent documents prepared by the medical center. These documents included an "Embryo Storage Agreement," which was signed by Tamera and Trip as well as by a representative of UNMC. It provided in part:

> <u>Release of Embryos.</u> The Client Depositors [Trip and Tamera] under-stand and agree that containers of embryos stored pursuant to this agreement will be used for transfer, release or disposition only with the signed approval of both Client Depositors. UNMC will release the

containers of embryos only to a licensed physician recipient of written authorization of the Client Depositors.

The agreement had one exception to the joint-approval requirement that governed the disposition of the embryos upon the death of one or both of the client depositors. Another provision of the contract provided for termination of UNMC's responsibility to store the embryos upon several contingencies: (1) the client depositors' written authorization to release the embryos or to destroy them; (2) the death of the client depositors; (3) the failure of the client depositors to pay the annual storage fee; or (4) the expiration of ten years from the date of the agreement.

. . .

The district court decided the dispute should be governed by the "embryo storage agreement" between the parties and UNMC, which required both parties' consent to any use or disposition of the embryos. Enforcing this agreement, the trial court enjoined both parties "from transferring, releasing or in any other way using or disposing of the embryos . . . without the written and signed approval and authorization" of the other party.

Tamera has appealed the trial court's order. . . .

Trip has filed a cross-appeal. . . .

. . .

We first consider Tamera's contention that the storage agreement does not address the situation at hand. As noted earlier, the agreement had a specific provision governing control of the embryos if one or both parties died, but did not explicitly deal with the possibility of divorce. Nonetheless, we think the present predicament falls within the general provision governing "release of embryos," in which the parties agreed that the embryos would not be transferred, released, or discarded without "the signed approval" of both Tamera and Trip. This provision is certainly broad enough to encompass the decision-making protocol when the parties are unmarried as well as when they are married.

The only question, then, is whether such agreements are enforceable when one of the parties later changes his or her mind with respect to the proper disposition of the embryos. In reviewing the scarce case law from other jurisdictions on this point, we have found differing views of how the parties' rights should be determined. There is, however, abundant literature that has scrutinized the approaches taken to date. Some writers have suggested refinements of the analytical framework employed by the courts thus far; some have proposed an entirely new model of analysis. From these various sources, we have identified three primary approaches to resolving disputes over the disposition of frozen embryos, which we have identified as (1) the contractual approach, (2) the contemporaneous mutual consent model, and (3) the balancing test.

. . .

. . . First, we note the purposes of the "best interest" standard . . . are to "assure the child the opportunity for the maximum continuing physical and emotional contact with both parents" and to "encourage parents to share the rights and responsibilities of raising the child." IOWA CODE § 598.41(1)(a). The principles developed under this statute are simply not suited to the resolution of disputes over the control of frozen embryos. Such disputes do not involve maximizing physical and emotional contact between both parents and the child; they involve the more fundamental decision of whether the parties will be parents at all. Moreover, it would be premature to consider which parent can most effectively raise the child when the "child" is still frozen in a storage facility.

... For these reasons, we conclude the legislature did not intend to include fertilized eggs or frozen embryos within the scope of section 598.41.

. . .

The currently prevailing view—expressed in three states—is that contracts entered into at the time of in vitro fertilization are enforceable so long as they do not violate public policy. The New York Court of Appeals expressed the following rationale for this contractual approach:

> [It is] particularly important that courts seek to honor the parties' expressions of choice, made before disputes erupt, with the parties' over-all direction always uppermost in the analysis. Knowing that advance agreements will be enforced underscores the seriousness and integrity of the consent process. Advance agreements as to disposition would have little purpose if they were enforceable only in the event the parties continued to agree. To the extent possible, it should be the progenitors—not the State and not the courts—who by their prior directive make this deeply personal life choice.

Kass[v. Kass], 696 N.E.2d [174]at 180[(N.Y. 1998)].

This approach has been criticized, however, because it "insufficiently protects the individual and societal interests at stake":

> First, decisions about the disposition of frozen embryos implicate rights central to individual identity. On matters of such fundamental personal importance, individuals are entitled to make decisions consistent with their contemporaneous wishes, values, and beliefs. Second, requiring couples to make binding decisions about the future use of their frozen embryos ignores the difficulty of predicting one's future response to life-altering events such as parenthood. Third, conditioning the provision of infertility treatment on the execution of binding disposition agreements is coercive and calls into question the authenticity of the couple's original choice. Finally, treating couples' decisions about the future use of their frozen embryos as binding contracts undermines important values about families, reproduction, and the strength of genetic ties.

[Carl H. Coleman, *Procreative Liberty and Contemporaneous Choice: An Inalienable Rights Approach to Frozen Embryo Disputes*, 84 MINN. L. REV. 55,] at 88–89[(1999)]. Another legal writer has echoed these concerns:

> Binding a couple to a prior disposition agreement has its roots in contract law. The primary advantage of treating the disposition of preembryos as a contract dispute is that it binds individuals to previous obligations, even if their priorities or values change. This advantage, while maximizing the efficiency of commercial transactions, is ill-suited to govern the disposition of human tissue with the potential to develop into a child. The potential of the embryo requires that couples be allowed to make contemporaneous decisions about the fate of the embryo that reflect their current values.

Christina C. Lawrence, Note, *Procreative Liberty and the Preembryo Problem: Developing a Medical and Legal Framework to Settle the Disposition of Frozen Embryos*, 52 CASE W. RES. L.REV. 721, 729 (2002) [hereinafter "Lawrence

Note"]; *accord J.B. v. M.B.*, 783 A.2d 707, 718–19 ([N.J.] 2001). In response to such concerns, one commentator has suggested an alternative model requiring contemporaneous mutual consent. We now examine that approach.

. . .

. . . [A]dvocates of the mutual-consent model propose "no embryo should be used by either partner, donated to another patient, used in research, or destroyed without the [contemporaneous] mutual consent of the couple that created the embryo." Under this alternate framework,

> advance instructions would not be treated as binding contracts. If either partner has a change of mind about disposition decisions made in advance, that person's current objection would take precedence over the prior consent. If one of the partners rescinds an advance disposition decision and the other does not, the mutual consent principle would not be satisfied and the previously agreed-upon disposition decision could not be carried out.

> . . .

> When the couple is unable to agree to any disposition decision, the most appropriate solution is to keep the embryos where they are—in frozen storage. Unlike the other possible disposition decisions—use by one partner, donation to another patient, donation to research, or destruction—keeping the embryos frozen is not final and irrevocable. By preserving the status quo, it makes it possible for the partners to reach an agreement at a later time.

[Coleman, 84 MINN. L. REV.] at 110–12. . . .

The New Jersey Supreme Court appears to have adopted an analysis regarding the disposition of frozen human embryos that incorporates the idea of contemporaneous decision-making, but not that of mutual consent. In *J.B.*, the New Jersey court rejected the *Kass* and *Davis* contractual approach, noting public policy concerns in "[e]nforcement of a contract that would allow the implantation of preembryos at some future date in a case where one party has reconsidered his or her earlier acquiescence." 783 A.2d at 718. The court stated:

> We believe that the better rule, and the one we adopt, is to enforce agreements entered into at the time in vitro fertilization is begun, *subject to the right of either party to change his or her mind about disposition up to the point of use or destruction of any stored preembryos.*

Id. at 719 (emphasis added). The court based its decision on "[t]he public policy concerns that underlie limitations on contracts involving family relationships." *Id.*; *see also A.Z.[v. B.Z]*, 725 N.E.2d [1051]at 1057–58 [(Mass. 2000)] (refusing, in light of the same public policy concerns, to enforce an agreement that allowed the wife, upon the parties' separation, to use the couple's preembryos for implantation).

The New Jersey court did not, however, adopt the requirement for mutual consent as a prerequisite for any use or disposition of the preembryos. Rather, that court stated that "if there is a disagreement between the parties as to disposition . . ., the interests of both parties must be evaluated" by the court. This balancing test was also the default analysis employed by the Tennessee Supreme Court in *Davis* where the parties had not executed a written agreement. *See Davis[v. Davis]*, 842 S.W.2d [588] at 604 [(Tenn. 1992)](holding in the absence of a prior agreement concerning disposition, "the relative interests of the parties in using or not using the preembryos must be weighed" by the court).

The obvious problem with the balancing test model is its internal inconsistency. Public policy concerns similar to those that prompt courts to refrain from enforcement of contracts addressing reproductive choice demand even more strongly that we not substitute the courts as decision makers in this highly emotional and personal area. Nonetheless, that is exactly what happens under the decisional framework based on the balancing test because the court must weigh the relative interests of the parties in deciding the disposition of embryos when the parties cannot agree.

. . .

We think judicial decisions and statutes in Iowa reflect respect for the right of individuals to make family and reproductive decisions based on their current views and values. They also reveal awareness that such decisions are highly emotional in nature and subject to a later change of heart. For this reason, we think judicial enforcement of an agreement *between a couple* regarding their future family and reproductive choices would be against the public policy of this state.

Our decision should not be construed, however, to mean that disposition agreements *between donors and fertility clinics* have no validity at all. We recognize a disposition or storage agreement serves an important purpose in defining and governing the relationship between the couple and the medical facility, ensuring that all parties understand their respective rights and obligations. In fact, it is this relationship, between the couple on the one side and the medical facility on the other, that dispositional contracts are intended to address. Within this context, the medical facility and the donors should be able to rely on the terms of the parties' contract.

In view of these competing needs, we reject the contractual approach and hold that agreements entered into at the time in vitro fertilization is commenced are enforceable and binding on the parties, "subject to the right of either party to change his or her mind about disposition up to the point of use or destruction of any stored embryo." *J.B.*, 783 A.2d at 719. This decisional model encourages prior agreements that can guide the actions of all parties, unless a later objection to any dispositional provision is asserted. It also recognizes that, *absent a change of heart by one of the partners*, an agreement governing disposition of embryos does not violate public policy. Only when one person makes known the agreement no longer reflects his or her current values or wishes is public policy implicated. Upon this occurrence, allowing either party to withdraw his or her agreement to a disposition that person no longer accepts acknowledges the public policy concerns inherent in enforcing prior decisions of a fundamentally personal nature. In fairness to the medical facility that is a party to the agreement, however, any change of intention must be communicated in writing to all parties in order to reopen the disposition issues covered by the agreement.

That brings us, then, to the dilemma presented when one or both partners change their minds and the parties cannot reach a mutual decision on disposition. We have already explained the grave public policy concerns we have with the balancing test, which simply substitutes the court as decision maker. A better principle to apply, we think, is the requirement of contemporaneous mutual consent. Under that model, no transfer, release, disposition, or use of the embryos can occur without the signed authorization of both donors. If a stalemate results, the status quo would be maintained.

The practical effect will be that the embryos are stored indefinitely unless both parties can agree to destroy the fertilized eggs. Thus, any expense associated with maintaining the status quo should logically be borne by the person opposing destruction. *See* Coleman, 84 MINN. L.REV. at 112 ("The right to insist on the continued storage of the embryos should be dependent on a willingness to pay the associated costs.").

Turning to the present case, we find a situation in which one party no longer concurs in the parties' prior agreement with respect to the disposition of their frozen embryos, but the parties have been unable to reach a new agreement that is mutually satisfactory. Based on this fact, under the principles we have set forth today, we hold there can be no use or disposition of the Wittens' embryos unless Trip and Tamera reach an agreement. Until then, the party or parties who oppose destruction shall be responsible for any storage fees. Therefore, we affirm the trial court's ruling enjoining both parties from transferring, releasing, or utilizing the embryos without the other's written consent.

NOTES

1.   Some statutes explicitly address the disposition of pre-embryos. Louisiana, for example, has a chapter devoted to human embryos. *See generally* LA. REV. STAT. ANN. §§ 9:121–133 (West 2008). One section provides that "[a] viable in vitro fertilized human ovum is a juridical person which shall not be intentionally destroyed by any natural or other juridical person or through the actions of any other such person." *Id.* § 9:129. Another section states that the in vitro patients owe the ovum a high duty of care and details the process for renouncing parental rights and adoption by a married couple. *Id.* § 9:130. "In disputes arising between any parties regarding the in vitro fertilized ovum, the judicial standard for resolving such disputes is to be in the best interest of the in vitro fertilized ovum." *Id.* § 9:131. Louisiana seems to be the only state to have adopted a best interests standard. Other states regulate embryo transfer or adoption. For example, Georgia includes an option for adoption of embryos in its general adoption statutes. GA. CODE ANN. §§ 19–8–40 to –43 (2010). Oklahoma provides a section in its chapter on artificial insemination addressing rights, obligations and interests with respect to embryo donation. OKLA. STAT. ANN. tit.10, § 556 (West 2009).

2.   As *Witten* notes, some courts have articulated a balancing test, which weighs the right of one individual to procreate against the other person's right not to procreate. *See, e.g., J.B. v. M.B.,* 783 A.2d 707 (N.J. 2001). One scholar has proposed that procreation be conceptualized as three rights, rather than only one, involving genetic, legal, and gestational parenthood. *See* I. Glenn Cohen, *The Right not to be a Genetic Parent*, 81 S. CAL. L. REV. 1115 (2008). If the right not to procreate is unbundled, as Professor Cohen suggests, how does this change the analysis in disputes over embryos?

3.   In *Evans v. United Kingdom*, (2008) 46 E.H.R.R. 34, the European Court of Human Rights ruled that the U.K. law which required consent by both parties for implantation of cryopreserved pre-embryos was well within the legislature's discretion and did not violate the European Convention on Human Rights' provisions on human dignity and liberty. A woman asked to have the pre-embryos implanted despite the fact that her former male partner withdrew his consent to implantation right after they broke up. The unique element in this situation was that the cryopreserved pre-embryos were the last chance for the woman to have genetically related children. In a case with similar facts, the Israeli Supreme Court allowed the wife to use the pre-embryos over her husband's objection. The majority argued that her rights to procreate under the circumstances trumped his objection because this was the last chance for her to procreate at all, whereas he was refusing to become a parent only with her specifically and had already become a biological father with his new partner. *See* Dalia Dorner, *Human Reproduction: Reflections on the Nachmani Case*, 35 TEX. INT'L L.J. 1, 7 (2000).

4. There are an estimated 400,000 frozen embryos in clinics. Deciding how to dispose of frozen embryos can also be difficult for couples not facing divorce. IVF treatments may result in a complete family and embryos to spare. A recent study in the Fertility and Sterility Journal and observation by practitioners demonstrate a variety of issues in couples' decision-making. For example, the choice of disposition may be limited by what is offered by the clinic, perhaps donation to another couple but not to research. Options may also be complicated by regulations, such as the ones relating to testing of gamete donors. Similar to the divorce cases, the partners may have divergent views on what to do. Couples may not feel comfortable with any of the choices and put off the decision by continuing to pay the storage fees indefinitely. *See* Denise Grady, *Parents Torn Over Fate of Frozen Embryos*, N.Y. TIMES (Dec. 4, 2008), http://www.nytimes.com/2008/12/04/us/04embryo.html?h.

5. Contrary to the disposition of frozen pre-embryos, courts have found that the disposition of cryopreserved sperm does not implicate both spouses' right to procreate. In the case of *In re Estate of Kievernagel*, the widow of a man who died in a helicopter crash wanted to use his cryopreserved sperm in order to procreate. 83 Cal. Rptr. 3d 311, 312 (App. 2008). The court held that "[t]he disposition of Joseph's frozen sperm does not implicate Iris's right to procreative autonomy. That would be so only if she could show that she could become pregnant only with Joseph's sperm." *Id.* at 318. The court therefore insisted that the sperm should be destroyed per the agreement that Joseph had signed with the clinic when he first deposited the vial because his intent was the only one that mattered as to the disposition of his own gametes. *Id.* at 316–17. Courts have also had to address posthumous retrieval of sperm. For example, in 2009, a court in Texas allowed the mother of a deceased son to harvest his sperm so that she could assure her son progeny even posthumously. *See Estate of Nikolas Colton Evans*, No. C–1–PB–09–000304, 2009 WL 7729555 (Tex. Prob. Ct. Apr. 7, 2009). The mother claimed her son had expressed the desire to have three sons and had even named them. *See* Tony Plohetski, *Judge OKs Collecting of Dead Son's Sperm*, STATESMAN.COM (Apr. 8, 2009), http://www.statesman.com/news/content/news/stories/local/04/08/0408evans.html. Similar cases have arisen in New York. *See* Hugh Collins, *NY Woman Allowed to Harvest Dead Husband's Sperm*, AOL NEWS (Oct. 16, 2010), http://www.aolnews.com/2010/10/16/new-york-woman-gets-permission-to-harvest-dead-mans-sperm/.

2. MISPLANTED EMBRYOS

Perry Rogers v. Fasano

Supreme Court of New York, Appellate Division, First Department, 2000.
276 A.D.2d 67, 715 N.Y.S.2d 19.

■ SAXE, J.

This appeal concerns a tragic mix-up at a fertility clinic through which a woman became a "gestational mother" to another couple's embryo, when the embryo was mistakenly implanted into the wrong woman's uterus. Since a determination of the issues presented may have far-ranging consequences, we attempt here to ensure that our holding is appropriately limited.

In April, 1998, plaintiffs Deborah Perry–Rogers and Robert Rogers began an in vitro fertilization and embryo transfer program with the In Vitro Fertility Center of New York. However, in the process, embryos consisting entirely of the Rogerses' genetic material were mistakenly implanted into the uterus of defendant Donna Fasano, along with embryos from Ms. Fasano's and her husband's genetic material. It is undisputed that on May 28, 1998 both couples were notified of the mistake and of the need for DNA and amniocentesis tests. The Rogerses further allege, and the Fasanos do not deny, that the Fasanos were unresponsive to the Rogerses' efforts to contact them.

On December 29, 1998, Donna Fasano gave birth to two male infants, of two different races. One, a white child, is concededly the Fasanos' biological child, named Vincent Fasano. The other, initially named Joseph Fasano, is a black child, who subsequent tests confirmed to be the Rogerses' biological son, now known as Akeil Richard Rogers.

The Fasanos took no action regarding the clinic's apparent error until the Rogerses, upon discovering that Ms. Fasano had given birth to a child who could be theirs, located and commenced an action against them.

[On March 12, 1999, the Rogerses requested a declaratory judgment of the rights and obligations to Akeil. DNA tests confirmed that the Rogerses were the genetic parents. The couples executed an agreement, which provided for visitation by the Fasanos. The Fasanos signed an affidavit that acknowledged the Rogerses' genetic connection to the child and consented to a custody order by the Rogerses. Custody of Akeil was turned over to the Rogerses on May 10, 1999.]

The Rogerses assert that over the next few months, the IAS court issued oral "visitation orders" in apparent reliance upon the visitation agreement, and directed that a full forensic psychological evaluation of the parties and their infants be conducted by two sets of mental health experts. On January 14, 2000, the IAS court granted the Fasanos visitation with the child every other weekend.

The Rogerses now challenge the court's January 14, 2000 visitation order....

. . .

The Rogerses suggest that the Supreme Court lacks subject matter jurisdiction over this dispute because the Fasanos are "genetic strangers" to Akeil. We decline to dispose of the Fasanos' claim on this basis alone. The Supreme Court of the State of New York has subject matter jurisdiction over petitions for custody and visitation pursuant to both the Domestic Relations Law and the Family Court Act.

This is not to say that the Fasanos necessarily have standing to seek visitation with Akeil. However, on this issue we will not simply adopt the Rogerses' suggestion that no gestational mother may ever claim visitation with the infant she carried, in view of her status as a "genetic stranger" to the infant. In recognition of current reproductive technology, the term "genetic stranger" alone can no longer be enough to end a discussion of this issue....

In referring to the rights and responsibilities of parents, the laws of this State, as well as the commentaries and case law, often use the term "natural parents," as distinguished from adoptive parents, stepparents, and foster parents. Until recently, there was no question as to who was a child's "natural" mother. It was the woman in whose uterus the child was conceived and borne.

. . .

In *Johnson v. Calvert*, 851 P.2d 776[(Cal. 1993)], *cert. denied* 510 U.S. 874, a surrogate mother, unrelated genetically to the child she had carried, declined to give the child to its genetic parents upon its birth, as had been agreed in a surrogacy contract. While "recogniz[ing] [both] genetic consanguinity and giving birth as a means of establishing a mother and child relationship," the California Supreme Court concluded that

> when the two means do not coincide in one woman, she who intended to procreate the child—that is, she who intended to bring about the birth of a child that she intended to raise as her own—is the natural mother under California law.

It therefore affirmed an award of custody to the genetic parents.

The Second Department applied this "intent" analysis to the converse situation, to recognize the parental rights of a gestational mother who had carried a fetus created from the egg of an anonymous donor which was fertilized with her husband's sperm (*see, McDonald v. McDonald*, 608 N.Y.S.2d 477[(N.Y. App. Div. 1994)]). The Court rejected the father's position, in the context of a divorce proceeding, that as "the only genetic and natural parent available," his claim to custody was superior to that of his wife, and held that the gestational mother was legally the mother of the child to whom she had given birth.

. . .

It is apparent from the foregoing cases that a "gestational mother" may possess enforceable rights under the law, despite her being a "genetic stranger" to the child. Given the complex possibilities in these kind of circumstances, it is simply inappropriate to render any determination solely as a consequence of genetics.

Parenthetically, it is worth noting that even if the Fasanos had claimed the right to custody of the child, application of the "intent" analysis . . . would—in our view—require that custody be awarded to the Rogerses. It was they who purposefully arranged for their genetic material to be taken and used in order to attempt to create their own child, whom they intended to rear.

To establish their claim that the Fasanos lack standing, the Rogerses focus upon the strict limits of New York statutory and case law regarding who may seek visitation. Under New York statutory law, the only people who have the right to seek visitation are parents, grandparents and siblings related by whole or half-blood. The Rogerses rely on the proposition that because the statutes must be strictly construed, they must be interpreted to preclude the Fasanos from within their framework. Specifically, they suggest that by their act of ceding Akeil to the Rogerses, the child's genetic parents, the Fasanos have surrendered any conceivable right to the parental status necessary to claim visitation rights.

We agree that under the circumstances presented, the Fasanos lack standing . . . to seek visitation as the child's parents. However, this is not because we necessarily accept the broad premise that in *any* situation where a parent, possessed of that status by virtue of having borne and given birth to the child, acknowledges another couple's entitlement to the status of parent by virtue of their having provided the genetic materials that created the child, the birth parent automatically gives up all parental rights.

Rather, we recognize that in these rather unique circumstances, where the Rogerses' embryo was implanted in Donna Fasano by mistake, and where the Fasanos knew of the error not long after it occurred, the happenstance of the Fasanos' nominal parenthood over Akeil should have been treated as a mistake to be corrected at soon as possible, *before the development of a parental relationship*. It bears more similarity to a mix-up at the time of a hospital's discharge of two newborn infants, which should simply be corrected at once, than to one where a gestational mother has arguably the same rights to claim parentage as the genetic mother. Under such circumstances, the Fasanos will not be heard to claim the status of parents, entitled to seek an award of visitation.

Additionally, the Fasanos' child, Vincent, is not a sibling "by whole or half-blood" ..., since the statute makes no reference to "gestational siblings."

. . .

... While there may well be occasions where a dispute between gestational and genetic parents requires a full evidentiary "best interests" hearing to ensure that the child's interests are fully protected, this is *not* such a case.

The only facts needed for this determination are those that are clearly established on this meager record: (1) plaintiffs are the genetic parents of the child, Akeil Rogers, and are concededly entitled to custody of him; (2) defendant Donna Fasano is the child's "gestational mother", having given birth to him after being implanted by mistake with the fertilized embryo of plaintiffs, (3) the parties were made aware of the mistake by the medical facility prior to the birth of the child, and (4) in the process of working out the transfer of Akeil to plaintiffs, the Fasanos and the Rogerses entered into an agreement providing for visitation.

In other circumstances, inquiry may be appropriate as to whether a psychological bond exists which should not be abruptly severed, and if so, what living arrangements would be in the child's best interests. For instance, when a child has been born into and raised as a part of a family for an extended period of time, a basis may be presented for directing custody with one family and visitation to another.

We are also cognizant that a bond may well develop between a gestational mother and the infant she carried, before, during and immediately after the birth, and that indeed, here, the parties' visitation agreement itself proclaimed the existence of a bond between the two infants. Nevertheless, the suggested existence of a bond is not enough under the present circumstances.

In the present case, any bonding on the part of Akeil to his gestational mother and her family was the direct result of the Fasanos' failure to take timely action upon being informed of the clinic's admitted error. Defendants cannot be permitted to purposefully act in such a way as to create a bond, and then rely upon it for their assertion of rights to which they would not otherwise be entitled.

Nor may the parties' visitation agreement form the basis for a court order of visitation. "[A] voluntary agreement ... will not of itself confer standing upon a person not related by blood to assert a legal claim to visitation or custody."

Finally, the circumstances presented, tragic as they are, do not form the basis for application of the doctrine of equitable estoppel to prevent the Rogerses from challenging the Fasanos' standing to seek visitation.

Accordingly, the order ..., which granted defendants visitation with the infant Joseph Fasano, now known as Akeil Richard Rogers, should be reversed, on the law, without costs, and the application for an order of visitation denied....

NOTE

What do you think of the outcome in *Perry–Rogers*? For one scholar's analysis of the decision, *see* Leslie Bender, *Genes, Parents, and Assisted Reproductive Technologies: ARTs, Mistakes, Sex, Race, & Law*, 12 COLUM. J. GENDER & L. 1 (2003).

3. REGULATION, ACCESS, AND INSURANCE COVERAGE

John A. Robertson, *Commerce and Regulation in the Assisted Reproduction Industry*

85 TEX. L. REV. 665, 699–701 (2007).

It has been a standard refrain in discussions of ART to bemoan the lack of regulation, and even call for a centralized system of regulatory control as occurs in the United Kingdom through the HFEA. . . .

In fact, a great deal of legal and professional self-regulation already exists. In addition to background tort, contract, and property doctrines and medical licensing laws, at least one state has laboratory and other regulations for ART. If gametes, embryos, stem cells, or tissue from others are involved, the lab must meet FDA requirements. There are also clinic-specific reporting requirements to the Centers for Disease Control. None of these are perfect. Gaps exist, but there are many avenues of information, control, and market discipline by patients and others. The problem is less with regulation than with particular issues of regulation, many of them having to do with moral conflicts over the status of embryos, eugenics, and family affiliation law.

An unusual indicator of the absence of major regulatory problems with ARTs was the difficulty that the conservative President's Council on Bioethics (PCB), under the direction of Dr. Leon Kass, a noted bioethicist and long-time opponent of reproductive technology, had in finding problems or ways to improve the delivery of ART services. After two years of study, it issued a report in 2004, *Reproduction & Responsibility: The Regulation of New Biotechnologies*. That report made some useful suggestions for increasing monitoring and information about these practices, but found none of the glaring problems said to exist in this "wild west" industry.

We can take the PCB's report as a benchmark for the state of the field and the lack of a compelling case for more extensive regulation. It found that much more research is needed before one can determine whether major changes in current practices and regulatory institutions are justified. Like many other commissions, it recommended that the federal government and relevant professional societies gather more information about present practices and their effects. These included such unglamorous steps as greater efficiency in reporting efficacy data, standardized consent forms, statistics on novel procedures like ICSI and PGD, and monitoring of the frequency of new practices, such as PGD and gamete sorting. It also wanted more studies of the long-term effect of ARTs on offspring. Recognizing that self-regulation plays a key role, it suggested a need for improving the enforcement of professional guidelines and for better methods for moving experimental procedures into clinical practice. Surprisingly, although it discussed commercial issues, it did not recommend against a market for reproductive services or for paying gamete donors and surrogates.

None of these recommendations are surprising or revolutionary. They are marginal improvements to a market-driven system that will continue to be so. They are also a reminder that calling assisted reproduction "the baby business" paints with too broad a brush to be meaningful. As we have seen, there are many "baby businesses," involving paid exchanges for some component of the complex of activities and factors brought together to make a child possible. The fact that doctors must be paid, and not everyone can afford it, is not surprising, much less shocking. Despite its moral-driven scrutiny of the field, the PCB ended up more concerned with protecting "the dignity of human reproduction" by banning animal-human gestation, chimeras, and the production of fetuses to obtain stem cells than with IVF or the use of donor genetics.

Radhika Rao, *Equal Liberty: Assisted Reproductive Technology and Reproductive Equality*

76 Geo. Wash. L. Rev. 1457, 1459–84 (2008).

Some scholars suggest that the U.S. Constitution confers a right to reproduce with the assistance of a wide variety of technologies, including in vitro fertilization ("IVF"), preimplantation genetic diagnosis of embryos ("PGD"), and even somatic cell nuclear transfer ("SCNT"), otherwise known as cloning. Under this expansive interpretation of reproductive liberty, almost every technology necessary to procreate would receive constitutional protection. Others contend that there is no such constitutional right at all, leaving the government completely free to regulate the field of fertility treatments. This Essay offers a novel approach that rejects both extremes. I argue that there is no general right to use ARTs as a matter of reproductive *autonomy*, but there may be a limited right to use ARTs as a matter of reproductive *equality*. Accordingly, the government could prohibit use of a particular reproductive technology across the board for everyone; however, once the state permits use in some contexts, it should not be able to forbid use of the same technology in other contexts. Hence, all persons must possess an *equal* right, even if no one retains an *absolute* right, to use ARTs.

. . .

Although there is no constitutional right to engage in assisted reproduction as a matter of reproductive autonomy, this does not mean that the government has free rein to permit ARTs in some situations but proscribe their use in others as a matter of reproductive equality. The government's decision to permit ARTs to be used by some persons may confer a relative right upon others. Hence, all persons must possess an *equal* right, even if no one retains an *absolute* right, to use ARTs.

This analysis finds support in *Skinner v. Oklahoma*, which perfectly exemplifies the principle of reproductive equality. . . .

A law that prohibits ARTs under some circumstances, but not others, must at the very least be based upon a legitimate governmental interest in order to be constitutional. Lines that are drawn based upon the status of the persons who seek to use ARTs are particularly troubling and likely unconstitutional under the reasoning of *Eisenstadt v. Baird*, which struck down a law that regulated the distribution of contraceptives because it discriminated between married and single persons, and *Lawrence v. Texas*, which invalidated a law that criminalized homosexual but not heterosexual sodomy. Hence, a law limiting ARTs to married persons or to heterosexual persons should fail because it would treat the very same act—the use of a particular technology—differently based upon the marital status or sexual preference of the persons involved, with no real basis for the distinction other than societal disapproval or prejudice.

. . .

What if a state enacts a law limiting ARTs to married persons based upon the justification that it is protecting the best interests of the children who may be born as a result of such technologies in being reared in the setting of a stable two-parent family? Some states restrict adoption to married persons, denying single persons and homosexuals the opportunity to become adoptive parents based upon precisely the same rationale. Yet such a justification appears to be unwarranted, at least as applied to married homosexuals, who exhibit as much stability and commitment as married heterosexuals. Moreover, many gay, lesbian, and single parents are currently raising their biological children. The state cannot simply presume that all of these parents are unfit; otherwise, it would be able to terminate their parental rights and take away their biological children. If a state seeks to restrict ARTs solely to those who prove themselves to be suitable parents and satisfy additional requirements, as in the adoption context, then these requirements must apply equally to all. . . .

What about . . . restriction upon the use of ARTs to infertile persons who are of the childbearing age? These provisions also limit ARTs based upon the status of the persons involved. Are they likewise unconstitutional? The distinction between fertile and infertile persons does not deny reproductive equality; instead, it provides special accommodations to those who possess a disability—infertility. Indeed, such provisions actually enhance equal liberty by leveling the field and affording everyone an equivalent opportunity to reproduce. Similarly, a line that separates those who are of childbearing age from those who are not does not contravene the right to reproductive equality if it is grounded in good reasons and applied equally to men as well as women. Age limits should be considered constitutional as long as they prevent both men and women above a certain age from using ARTs in order to promote a valid objective, such as ensuring that the children born of such technologies will have parents who are alive and able to care for them. But if the only justification for a law is that it replicates nature by allowing infertile men to procreate with the assistance of technology well into their eighties while denying infertile women the same opportunities, it should be judged unconstitutional.

Yet if infertility is a disability, why wouldn't it infringe reproductive equality to deny ARTs across the board to everyone? Although a prohibition upon the use of ARTs provides formal equality, its practical effect is to single out and prevent reproduction by only one particular class of persons—those who are infertile. If fertile persons possess a right to reproduce, shouldn't infertile persons be afforded equal liberty through the vehicle of ARTs?

The answer is no, because assisted reproduction does not involve the interests of a group that lacks political power. Although infertile persons cross racial and class lines, permeating all aspects of society, those who seek to use ARTs tend to be disproportionately white and wealthy. Moreover, fertility treatments have become a booming business; thus, all of those who profit from the infertility industry possess a vested interest in advocating access to ARTs on behalf of the infertile. For all these reasons, legislators are likely to be sufficiently sensitive to the concerns of the infertile.

Accordingly, a prohibition upon the use of ARTs is permissible as long as it is based upon a legitimate interest that goes beyond mere prejudice. The government could limit the use of ARTs in order to prevent physical, psychological, or social harms to the participants or the resulting children. Perhaps the government could prohibit IVF altogether if studies show that test-tube babies disproportionately suffer serious physical harms. Or the government could restrict the number of embryos that can be implanted at a single time in order to reduce the rate of multiple births, which typically result in premature babies who are born with dangerously low birth-weights. Such children are likely to suffer from a variety of health problems and could impose heavy costs upon all of society. Regulation of ARTs should be constitutional if it is grounded in good reasons such as these, but unconstitutional if it stems from nothing more than moral repugnance or prejudice against "unnatural" forms of reproduction.

. . .

Similarly, a law banning PGD under all circumstances would not violate the Constitution even if other forms of genetic selection—such as carrier testing and sperm and egg selection—are allowed. This is because PGD involves the selection of *embryos*, which raises quite different questions from the selection of *sperm and eggs*. Although embryos and fetuses are not constitutional persons for the purposes of the Fourteenth Amendment, the abortion cases make clear that the state may choose to safeguard them in other contexts.... Therefore, a law distinguishing between the genetic selection of eggs or sperm and the genetic selection of embryos probably would be deemed constitutional.

What about a law allowing PGD to prevent birth of a child afflicted with a genetic disease but not to select "cosmetic" traits? Such a law could be deemed constitutional for at least two reasons. First, such a law would permit *anyone*—married or single, heterosexual or homosexual—to use PGD to prevent disease. Accordingly, it would not treat the same act differently based upon the status of the persons involved. Second, the use of PGD to prevent disease is a different, arguably more worthy, act than the use of PGD for "cosmetic" purposes. Moreover, the distinction between these different uses of PGD goes beyond mere prejudice; it furthers the state's legitimate interest in advancing the welfare of children by allowing PGD to prevent serious harm but not for more speculative reasons, where the risks might outweigh the benefits. Of course, there are still difficulties in the interpretation and enforcement of such a line. If PGD is allowed only for the purpose of preventing disease, for example, what should count as a "disease"? Would this allow the use of PGD for the purpose of preventing obesity or even homosexuality? Moreover, how is the state to enforce this distinction and to ensure that PGD is being used only for disease prevention, and not for other rationales?

The issue of sex-selection raises even more difficult questions. A law prohibiting all PGD to select sex probably would be constitutional....

Some might argue that sex-selection for the purpose of "family balancing" is a qualitatively different act with different social consequences than sex-selection to achieve a "cultural preference" for males. Nevertheless, the fact that two families, both of whom seek to use PGD in precisely the same way, would receive different treatment based solely upon their personal circumstances or preferences appears to contradict this argument. In essence, such a law would grant the power to select sex to some persons (those who share the cultural preferences of the majority in the U.S.) while denying it to others (those who disproportionately come from certain minority groups). As a result, a law that permits sex-selection for the purpose of "family balancing," but not to achieve a "cultural preference" for males, should be viewed as drawing an unconstitutional line that is based upon the status of the persons involved.

. . .

If the Constitution guarantees equal liberty to use assisted reproductive technologies such as PGD, then the government must set forth some legitimate interest in order to justify any selective prohibition upon the use of PGD to select for or against certain traits but not others. On balance, it should be (a) relatively easy for the state to make the case for allowing PGD to select against a serious disease that would cause death, (b) more difficult but still possible to justify PGD to select against a "disability" that arguably decreases quality of life, such as deafness, but (c) much more difficult, and perhaps impossible, to defend PGD to select for traits such as sex, skin color, and sexual orientation that are disfavored solely because of negative societal attitudes and prejudice.

Judith F. Daar, *Accessing Reproductive Technologies: Invisible Barriers, Indelible Harms*

23 BERKELEY J. GENDER L. & JUST. 18, 35–46 (2008).

The steep trajectory accompanying the growing use and success of ART might at first glance suggest a market in reproductive services that is rational and largely free of restraints. Prospective patients who choose to enter the market, having assessed their ability to do so, can purchase lawful reproductive services from willing providers. If this loose description of a market system is accurate for the provision of medical services in general, does it also hold for the provision of highly specialized medical services that involve the conception and birth of a child? The answer is decidedly no. While the general medical market does impose at least two access barriers—the high of cost for services and providers' discretion in deciding whom to treat—these and a host of other barriers are magnified when the treatment involves assisted reproduction.

. . .

A.   Limitations Based on Cost

The most obvious barrier to ART access is cost. The cost of a single cycle of IVF hovers around $10,000 on average, and can reach as high as $20,000 at some clinics. The costs of IVF are generally paid directly by patients, as the vast majority of health insurance plans do not cover treatment for infertility. Logic and data suggest that a woman's inclination to access infertility treatment is directly related to her ability to access insurance to cover the costs of the expensive therapy. An international comparison of treatment-seeking behaviors among infertile individuals bears out this cause and effect relationship. In the United States, where insurance coverage for ART is extremely limited, only half of all women with infertility seek treatment. Compare this to that of Finland (sixty-seven percent), The Netherlands (86%), and the United Kingdom (72–95%), all developed countries with national health care systems that cover at least some forms of infertility treatment.

Disparities in treatment-seeking behavior based on access to health insurance suggest that an equalizing remedy would be to mandate insurance coverage for infertility care.... Today, ... a handful of state legislatures have addressed the issue of insurance coverage for infertility services. Just under a third of the states have some infertility insurance requirement—either that private insurers provide coverage or offer to provide coverage for those covered in the jurisdiction.

Logically mandated insurance coverage that reduces costs to individual patients should lead to greater utilization of infertility services. In fact, studies show that private insurance mandates for fertility treatment have little or no overall effect on the use of such treatments in the United States. Researchers postulate that the reason for the low impact of private insurance mandates on treatment utilization can be explained by examining the demographic characteristics of those who are affected by changes in health insurance coverage. Because insurance mandates only affect individuals who have access to private health insurance, this group is generally wealthier and more likely to be employed than the general population. These are often the same individuals who can access ART with their own resources; thus the marginal benefit from insurance coverage tends not to increase usage among the insured. In contrast, in countries where health insurance is not linked to wealth or employment, utilization would reflect actual medical need, not unrelated socioeconomic factors.

Thus, it appears that socioeconomic status, and to a lesser extent employment status, significantly affect one's ability to access ART services in the United States. For wealthy individuals who can afford to pay directly for these services, access, for the most part, appears to be wide open. For individuals covered by private health insurance that includes infertility benefits, access would again seem open, with limitations based on the patient's ability to afford co-payments or non-covered services. It must be noted, however, that insured individuals generally share another common attribute—the status of being employed. Most Americans under the age of sixty-five (when the federal benefit of Medicare becomes activated) receive health insurance coverage as an employer benefit—sixty-one percent in 2004. One part of the solution to unequal access to infertility treatment may rest in improving coverage by employer-sponsored insurance among those most likely to need ART services.

. . .

B.   Limitations Based on Race and Ethnicity

Racial and ethnic disparities in access to and quality of health care in the United States are well documented. In 2003, the Institute of Medicine ("IOM") released a report documenting differences in health status, available treatment, and clinical outcomes along racial and ethnic lines. The IOM report summarized data from over 100 studies addressing racial differences in health care, concluding that racial and ethnic disparities are consistent and extensive across a range of medical conditions and healthcare services. How these disparities affect access to and treatment by ART is only beginning to be seriously evaluated.

Over the last fifteen [sic] [years], commentators have highlighted disparities in the use of and access to ART services for women of color as compared to white women. Recent research confirms disparities in both the incidence of infertility and the utilization of fertility treatments among women of different races. Hispanic women, non-Hispanic black women, and other women of color are significantly more likely to be infertile than white women. Yet despite the documented higher incidence of infertility, women of color are far less likely to seek treatment than white women. Lower utilization relates to disparities in insurance coverage: thirty-three percent of Hispanics and twenty percent of African Americans lack health insurance, compared to eleven percent of whites. As a result of these insurance disparities, according to several public health researchers, "ART remains a private, fee-for-service form of health care delivery in the United States, accessible largely to white, middle-to upper-class infertile couples."

This "stratified reproduction" has been described as the "eugenic logic of IVF" because the cost barriers to ART services disparately impact low-income couples who are primarily of color. Social, structural, and ideological barriers to effective medical care may further aggravate the difficulties facing infertile, low-income individuals of color in accessing infertility treatment. Several recent studies shed light on these factors, documenting the experience of people of color in navigating the health care system in general, and ART services in particular. In one look at access to reproductive services by Arab and African Americans, researchers note that both communities regard the U.S. health system with a degree of suspicion and distrust, based on past experiences of racism and discrimination. Moreover, caricatures of these two groups perpetuate images of males as hypersexual and women as hyperfertile. Such stereotyping leads to "the convenient denial of their legitimate reproductive health needs."

One source of hope for reducing racial and ethnic disparities in access to ART can be found in state insurance mandates, which hold out the promise that at least one group of patients, those with private insurance, will have equal access to fertility treatments. However, this hope is dampened by studies showing that racial and ethnic disparities in utilization remain unchanged even when insurance coverage is mandated. . . .

. . .

The law's ability to respond to these internal and external factors is decidedly weak. Various federal and state civil rights statutes prohibit discrimination against potential patients on the basis of a host of factors, including race. Title VI of the federal Civil Rights Act of 1964 prohibits physicians and hospitals receiving federal funding from discriminating in the provision of health care on the basis of race, color, religion, or national origin. States also have enacted laws prohibiting racial discrimination in health care. But a review of case law confirms that attempts to address racial discrimination in health care via traditional civil rights litigation under existing statutory schemes have proved frustrating for private individuals, who often must show intentional discrimination on the part of the health care provider. . . .

. . . Instead of litigation, ART scholars suggest that the infertility industry become more patient-friendly to racial and ethnic minorities by, for example, lobbying to increase insurance coverage for ART services, locating fertility clinics in more diverse neighborhoods, and increasing public awareness in minority communities about infertility and its treatment. Whether these, or other measures will help lower racial and ethnic barriers to ART is an open question, but the seriousness of such reduced access cannot be overstated in a society that values equality and reproductive freedom for all.

C.   Limitations Based on Marital Status

Solid data about the percentage of ART patients who are unmarried is difficult to procure, as the national reporting system for assisted conception does not collect demographic information on ART users other than age. What we do know is that single women are giving birth in record numbers. According to the National Center for Health Statistics, 36.8% of all births in the U.S. were to unmarried women in 2005. Statistics regarding these unmarried women who sought infertility services is largely unavailable, with the exception of informal and anecdotal reports which peg the percentage of single women using one type of assisted conception—AID—at approximately one-third of all AID users.

... While access to treatment for unmarried individuals can be hampered by the same cost and racial barriers that plague ART access in general, single women and same-sex couples face reduced access from at least two additional sources: provider discrimination against single and lesbian women, and legislative efforts to ban access to unmarried individuals.

Documented cases of provider discrimination against single women and lesbian couples are few, but recent research suggests that such conduct is widespread. A University of Pennsylvania study reveals that one in five treatment providers refuses treatment to unmarried women. Whether such refusal is actionable as unlawful discrimination will likely depend upon the law of the state in which the treatment was refused....

. . .

In states in which medical antidiscrimination laws are either silent or ambiguous with respect to marital status or sexual orientation as protected categories, unmarried individuals may face impregnable barriers to access. Moreover, even if state law does prohibit discrimination on the basis of marital status or sexual orientation, presumably a provider could argue that ART services are not "medical services" as defined by the relevant statutes, and thus not covered services. We earlier noted the consensus among courts that infertility is a "medical illness" but it does not necessarily follow that its treatment will always be considered a medical service. This battle of the medicalization of ART services has been waged in the health insurance arena, with courts varying widely on whether infertility treatment should be considered medical treatment in the litigation context. Perhaps discrimination law should borrow from insurance law if these cases present in this fashion.

In addition to provider discrimination, unmarried individuals may be facing an increasingly hostile statutory environment, as lawmakers in several states attempt to limit ART to married individuals. In late 2005 and early 2006, legislators in Indiana and Virginia introduced legislation that would prohibit health care providers from offering and performing any medical procedure on an unmarried woman for the purpose of conception or procreation....

. . .

These proposed legislative restrictions on ART access based on marital status may have been dodged for now, but ART barriers based on marital status are already in place in several states. In two states, Texas and Florida, contracts for gestational surrogacy are enforceable only if the commissioning couple is legally married. Such a requirement translates into an automatic exclusion of single men and gay male couples from ART, who must turn to gestational surrogacy to achieve biological parenthood. Thus, the chief form of biological procreation for unmarried males is explicitly unavailable in two of our most populous states.

In addition to these specific ART exclusions based on marital status (and by extension sexual orientation), another recent bill would de facto reduce access to assisted conception for unmarried women. Another Virginia bill introduced in 2006 would require that all unrelated gamete donors be identified in a woman's medical chart. Though the proposed bill appears facially neutral in terms of the marital status of the woman patient, in fact it would have the most dramatic impact on single and lesbian women who are largely dependent on anonymous sperm donation to meet their procreational needs. Experience in other countries confirms that mandating donor identity significantly reduces the number of donors willing to provide gametes, because donors typically do not wish to be contacted by biological offspring in the future. Thus, a non-anonymous donor policy in the U.S. would reduce the availability of donor sperm for unmarried women, the vast majority of whom rely on commercial sperm banks to fulfill their procreative dreams.

Naomi R. Cahn & Jennifer M. Collins, *Eight is Enough*

103 Nw. U. L. Rev. Colloquy 501 (May 10, 2009).

On January 26, 2009, the nation's second set of live-born octuplets was delivered at a California hospital. The public fascination with this unusual event quickly turned ugly when the media revealed that the new mother was thirty-three-year-old Nadya Suleman, a single, unemployed woman already caring for six other children under the age of eight. As Ellen Goodman of the Boston Globe described it, upon discovery of Suleman's identity, the mood of the country went "from 'Gee whiz' to 'Are you kidding?' " in a matter of days.

.   .   .

The cultural backlash against Suleman has focused on three separate but related issues. The first set of concerns revolves around Suleman herself—specifically, her ability to parent fourteen young children. . . .

A second set of concerns revolves around the medical procedures that led to the octuplets' birth. The fertility clinic that treated Suleman agreed to implant her with at least six embryos during an in vitro fertilization (IVF) procedure. The leading fertility industry group asserts that this decision was contrary to its recommended guidelines that women under the age of thirty-five have no more than two embryos implanted during any single IVF attempt.

A final set of issues concerns more fundamental questions about screening parents. Many wonder how a clinic could agree to provide a single mother of six with a fertility treatment that might—and did—double her number of children. This particular debate echoes larger cultural concerns over the changing American family, including calls for two parents (one of each sex) for every child.

In response to these concerns, commentators and legislators are calling for new, more restrictive regulation of the fertility industry. . . .

Although the debate about whether and how to regulate the fertility industry is certainly not new, Suleman's story has thrown two kinds of proposals into particularly sharp relief. The first set of proposals seeks to increase regulation of assisted reproductive technologies ("ART") via the doctors that perform them. For example, some commentators urge the United States to adopt mandatory limits on the number of embryos that can be implanted, as other countries have done. Although the American Society of Reproductive Medicine has issued guidelines regarding the appropriate number of embryos to transfer, adherence is entirely voluntary and, quite obviously, not universal. The issues entwined with such restrictions are difficult and important, and the Suleman case has begun a conversation about more meaningful regulation of the medical procedures used by the fertility industry. . . .

We are far more troubled, however, by a second set of proposals arising out of the Suleman backlash: those that urge placing restrictions on which individuals may receive fertility treatment. . . . Some ART providers have already tried to impose access limitations on the basis of sexual orientation. Indeed, many ART clinicians say they would choose to reject patients based on their marital status or sexual orientation, and some states have laws that permit the use of reproductive technology only by married couples.

. . .

Perhaps the most difficult question raised by the Suleman case and other high-order births is whether government regulation can be justified *at all* in the context of ART. . . .

. . .

We begin with the question of patient autonomy, the idea that individuals ordinarily have the right to determine for themselves the most appropriate course of medical treatment. Doctors may not, for example, treat a patient without her consent, and patients have a right to be informed of the relevant risks and benefits of any medical procedure before undergoing it. But there have always been limitations to this core principle of autonomy. Patients do not have a right to receive medical procedures or medications that the Food and Drug Administration has deemed unsafe, and they do not have the right to compel others to undertake risks, such as submitting to bone marrow transplants, in order to further their own health agendas. Indeed, federal and state governments often cite the need to regulate risk in justifying limitations on individual autonomy. Better-known examples of such limitations include mandatory vaccinations, speed limits, and seatbelt and helmet laws. Autonomy has thus always been modified by risk, and we believe it is that principle that is relevant in the ART context.

When a patient undergoes an ART procedure that results in high-order multiples, two sets of health risks are created: one to the mother and one to the children. Mothers carrying high-order multiples face increased risks of pregnancy complications and even death. Children who are part of a multiple birth are far more likely to be born premature and at a low birth weight. Prematurity and low birth weight are associated with higher risks of infant death and a host of other impairments, including "cerebral palsy [,] vision and hearing problems[,] and long-term motor, cognitive, behavioral, social-emotional, health, and growth problems." Choices about the appropriate number of embryos to implant are therefore neither necessarily benign nor neutral—they carry the very real potential for adverse consequences. Importantly, these adverse consequences are not limited to the patient herself; rather, the ART patient's choices also create risk for third parties: the children who might be born as a result of the pregnancy attempt. It is this potential risk to third parties, against which any potential children are obviously unable to defend, that seems to outweigh concerns for patient autonomy and to justify at least minimal government intervention. In addition to patient autonomy, however, are other values that compete against the health risks to mother and children.

· · ·

Regulating the number of embryos that may be transferred during IVF procedures does not, of course, compel a woman to reproduce against her will, so that concern is not implicated by placing restrictions on ART. But embryo transfer restrictions may indeed reduce the likelihood that a woman will be able to *successfully* reproduce. This is an important and powerful counter-argument to ART regulation: if transferring more embryos increases the chance of a successful pregnancy, then perhaps government regulation should not stand in the way. Just as personal autonomy is modulated by risk, however, reproductive freedom is modulated by concerns for the rights and freedom of others. We do not allow individuals to become parents at any cost; an individual may quite obviously not appropriate another person's child in order to become a parent, nor force another woman to serve as a surrogate mother. Society has always been willing to draw some line that it will not cross in furthering any particular individual's quest to become a parent.

· · ·

... The risks posed to both patients and future children are too great, and the countervailing pressure for both doctors and patients to achieve a pregnancy too strong, to remain unaddressed. The American Society for Reproductive Medicine (ASRM) guidelines, developed by fertility practitioners, articulate the parameters of workable guidelines, and build in some flexibility to ensure that they are appropriately sensitive to the situation of each patient. For example, consider the current ASRM guideline that no more than two embryos should be transferred into a patient under the age of 35 "in the absence of extraordinary circumstances." A regulation that mirrors this directive leaves room for exemptions—a thirty-four-year-old woman might be able to establish, for example, that due to a repeated history of unsuccessful attempts or poor embryo quality, she should be allowed to transfer three embryos on her last ART attempt.

The need to reconcile generally binding guidelines with the potential for flexibility suggests that some sort of administrative agency may ultimately be the best mechanism for ART regulation. One possibility is to create an entity modeled on the British Human Fertilisation and Embryology Authority, a board-directed governmental organization whose members include representatives from various stakeholding constituencies. A second is Professor Marsha Garrison's suggestion that we look toward a "quasi-public regulatory system," like that in place in the organ transplant context. This quasi-public system could be responsible for reviewing appeals from patients who believe they warrant exceptions from the guidelines. Each of these alternatives involves creating a federal agency, which ensures that any new ART guidelines are national rather than state-based. This is critical, given the ease with which patients could travel between jurisdictions to circumvent unwelcome state restrictions. Such an agency could also implement enforcement mechanisms targeted at fertility clinics by imposing fines and handling de-accreditation proceedings.

· · ·

Ultimately, however, we cannot rely on doctors who perform ART to self-regulate. How can a doctor, who has treated a patient through repeatedly unsuccessful pregnancy attempts, be expected to resist a desperate plea to implant just one more embryo? Further, interference in the doctor-patient relationship is hardly unprecedented. Even if patients plead for them, doctors cannot legally prescribe medications that are not FDA-approved; nor can doctors enroll patients in medical studies without complying with informed consent guidelines. It is clear, moreover, that voluntary guidelines have not worked—statistics from 2006, the most recent available, show that almost 4% of ART pregnancies involved three fetuses or more. In sum, when procedures are deemed sufficiently risky, government regulation has traditionally intervened in the doctor-patient relationship, and we believe the risks here are sufficiently great to allow that imposition.

   . . .

June Carbone and Paige Gottheim suggest another potential problem with regulation: imposing limits on embryo transfers might cause us to "lose [] control of the activity altogether" by driving women underground to black market fertility clinics or overseas to doctors who will comply with their treatment preferences. These are legitimate concerns, but our proposal to increase insurance coverage will allay many of them. Most women are not seeking to transfer five embryos because they want quintuplets; they are transferring five embryos because they want a successful pregnancy. If women knew that multiple attempts with one or two embryos would be covered by insurance, they would feel less pressed to travel overseas or to engage in illegal fertility treatments.

Another powerful objection to regulation is the concern that opening the door to any kind of government interference in fertility treatments will also open the door to restrictions on ART access, issues that are surfacing in the wake of the Suleman case. We do not believe that any new government regulations should include rules that restrict access to fertility treatment by discriminating among potential patients. Clinics should not screen on the basis of preexisting family size, the financial resources available to care for any children born as a result of ART, or the marital status or sexual orientation of potential patients. Individuals able to conceive without reproductive technology are not subject to such restrictions before they expand their families. Indeed, we are confident that any general attempt to impose limits on family size, such as China's one-child policy, would be greeted with horror by the American public. For patients who are single or in a same-sex relationship, the state should not be in the position of barring access to parenthood. There is simply no rational basis for doing so. Virtually all states, for example, permit gay and lesbian parents to serve as foster parents and to adopt; allowing access to reproductive technology is entirely comparable.

Commentators might respond that ART is more like adoption than natural childbirth, and that while restrictions on family size have no place in the nation's bedrooms, they do have a place in the nation's medical labs and fertility clinics. . . .

   . . .

More fundamentally, we think families created via ART are not . . . truly analogous to families formed by adoption. Instead, the better comparison is to families created without physician intervention. Unlike ART, adoption is fundamentally concerned with actual children, not medical decisions. First, adoption inherently requires legal determinations that are solely within the power of the state—to grant an adoption, the state must terminate, and then reassign, parental rights. Second, adoptions increasingly involve the wishes of biological mothers.... Even when donors are involved in reproductive technology, that level of interaction between the parties is literally unheard-of. Third, adoption regulations necessarily focus on the best interests of a *living* child, and it is appropriate to consider the best alternatives for that particular child. In the ART context, we are obviously talking about potential children. Restricting a patient's access, by definition, means that the future children in question will never be born.

The possibility of regulation potentially raises complex morality-based issues concerning the scope of government control over families. We believe the government should focus on regulating *medical* procedures, not *family formation*.

E. BEYOND LEGAL REGULATION

1. ART PARTICIPANT VOICES

Jennifer Meleana Hee, *How to Sell your Body Parts . . . and Still Respect Yourself in the Morning*

HAWAII WOMEN'S JOURNAL, July–October 2010, at 29.

. . .

Things I have done for upwards of $10,000: Sell my eggs.

While I don't have a literary agent, an editorial assistant, or even a sycophantic friend, I do have an egg agent who is responsible for negotiating a decent sale of the most profitable commodity of my twenties—my genes, prepackaged in follicular bundles. By acquiring my eggs, future parents hope they'll end up with a me-like child: a Harvard graduate; Chinese and Caucasian; overachieving but existentially unsettled; athletic body type; passion for words; a history of social service and teaching professions; prefers the outdoors to the indoors; an introverted adventurer who loves travel; proficientish in music, artistic endeavors, and vegan baking. Thanks to egg donation, I no longer have to wonder, on the tops of isolated mountains, Buddhist temples, or in line at Target *how much am I worth?* I know exactly how much.

My egg agent works for an agency that specializes in Ivy League egg donors. We'll call her Trixie, because no one in real life has that name. Trixie has been a surrogate, and many women I met who work in various fertility centers have been surrogates or donors themselves. It's not just a day job—they are passionate about helping families who can't have babies, passionate enough to lend their bodies and give from their bodies. There is nothing black market about the fertility centers (or Trixie)—these doctors have the swankiest medical spaces my naked patient ass has ever seen. One reproductive endocrinologist said they have the reputation of being reproduction cowboys, experimenting on the wild, wild frontiers of baby making. What used to be "gifts from [insert deity of choice here]" are now gifts from doctors, nurses, embryologists, Gestational Carrier X, and Donor 6259. It used to take a village to raise a child, now it takes a village to create one.

. . .

Everyone's medications are slightly different, but during Donation Month—or, as I like to call it, "DoMo"—the job starts out pretty easy. I wake up and inject a synthetic hormone called Lupron into my abdomen. Lupron's the gateway hormone, which stops my ovaries from functioning. Scary? Yes. Profitable? You betcha.

After ten days on Lupron, the blood draws begin. Every few days, my blood is drawn and estradiol level checked until it is low enough to start taking the stimulation hormones. Throughout the entire egg-donation process, I'll have had my blood drawn at least ten times, and I hate blood draws more than I hate being honest with myself.

In a normal menstrual cycle, a woman's ovaries develop one follicle and mature egg. During DoMo, my count was 30. (*Thirty!*) I inject myself with the same hormones a woman who is having trouble conceiving would take. For me—as uberfertile as I already am—it causes the IVF doctor to say "HOLY GOD" . . . .

I also take antibiotics and a low-dose steroid . . . .

Three injections and three pills a day—a pretty intense regimen considering I won't eat white food because it has no nutritional personality. (Except tofu, obviously.) . . .

DoMo is long—it feels like it lasts longer than a month. . . . Indeed, while my ovaries are being stimulated, there's an extensive list of Do Nots:

Do not have sex. Do not have oral sex. Do not have anal sex. Do not use illegal drugs. Do not have sex with a man who's used heroin and had relations with a Mad Cow (without protection). Do not go swimming. Do not jump on trampolines. Whatever you are thinking—do not do that.

. . .

Here are a few examples from a "Potential Risks of Ovum Donation" form I signed, agreeing that I accept such risks:

Potential risks to ovum donor from ovum donation process:

- *Infection, requiring hospitalization or surgery or loss of fertility.*
- *Bleeding, requiring hospitalization or surgery or loss of fertility.*
- *Ovarian torsion, requiring surgery and possible loss of fertility.*
- *Ovarian follicle rupture, requiring hospitalization or surgery and possible loss of fertility.*
- *Potential, but as yet unknown, increased risks of ovarian or other types of cancer.*

. . .

Besides the minor discomforts of blood draws and injections and a month of Sybil-like behavior, egg donation and Jenn Hee were meant to be. I'm the friend who balks at the existence of baby showers because I don't understand what we're celebrating. . . . I'm 30—my desktop is cluttered with icons from downloaded photos of my friends' babies. Here's the zygotic sonogram! Negative five months! One month! Four! Eight! 48 months! Wow! *Can you believe it's been 48 months already?* I can't tell which baby/embryo belongs to whom, and I'm tempted to e-mail back photos of a dead rat with the message, *Can you believe it's been 48 months already?* But I don't, because I don't have a photo of a dead rat.

I am a bad person. The inner innerness of my head is dark and lonely.

If you are my friend, I will hold your baby and say *cute baby*, but inside I feel sad, and I do not judge you at all, nor do I feel superior—because you can't help wanting children with as much biological voracity as I do not want children, even though once they are here, I love them. I loved the kids whose happiness glowed through their malnourished yellow eyes in Sri Lanka. I love my six-year-old nephew, who cries when he surprise-attack kicks me in the crotch. He is full of small grievings; he doesn't mean to hurt. It's not the child's fault, but we yell at them anyway, try to make sure they know everything they cannot do. Welcome to life, the answer is no.

I have a few offspring in the world, who have perhaps already learned their bodies can break, who'll one day learn that love can fill and empty you faster than panic, who will feel the tight grasp of happiness and sadness arm wrestling in their hearts, the tension a reminder that every day is a game we can never win, not for long. So yes: I think having kids is wrong, but selling my eggs so that someone else can have kids and I can afford to go travel and hang out with orphans in the third world is my own kind of selfish survival.

I'm a pacifist who happens to be particularly gifted at constructing weapons, a factory farmer who doesn't eat meat. We don't always do the things that make us proud; we lock the doors of our dissonance so we can sleep at night. I realize it's not "sustainable" to stop having babies, but the sustainability of our kind is the least of my concerns.

. . .

. . . I've ended relationships because I can't date a man who wants to have a child—we just don't see sperm to ovum. I feel the strain of my own cognitive dissonance: my greatest guilt is knowing because of me, my selfish need for fast cash in order to escape, to avoid cubicles, to avoid committing to life—there is someone who will have to spend a lifetime avoiding pain.

In the end, what I learned from donating my eggs is how little I know my own body. The monitoring of hormone levels, counting and measuring of follicles, and gross manipulation of your reproductive system really gets you in touch with your inner innerness. My choices are surreal. I could: (a) take these little gobs and make a little me, (b) sell these little gobs and a stranger can make a little me, or (c) have my tubes tied, saving these little gobs from ever becoming a living thing that could know suffering.

The last thought in my head during the egg retrieval, before the prick of the IV sends me into a peaceful nowhere, is always: *sorry, baby.*

Darren Rosenblum with Noa Ben–Asher, Mary Anne Case, Elizabeth Emens, Berta E. Hernández–Truyol, Vivian M. Gutierrez, Lisa C. Ikemoto, Angela Onwuachi–Willig, Jacob Willig–Onwuachi, Kimberly Mutcherson, Peter Siegelman, Beth Jones, *Pregnant Man?: A Conversation*

22 YALE J.L. & FEMINISM 207, 209–17, 257–60 (2010).

Darren Rosenblum, *Prologue*

. . .

I'm pregnant. No, I can't say that—a person with a uterus is pregnant. But I'm expecting. Even that sounds strange for a man to say. Howard and I began this process a few years ago when we first met with an agency that helps (mostly gay) couples have children through gestational surrogacy (GS)....

. . .

When we first met with our surrogate, Beth, she shared with us her own path. She has a well-paid job and a life full of responsibilities met, including two amazing sons. She told us that a family member wanted to have a child but couldn't, and she was going to carry the baby instead. After that person changed her mind, Beth still wanted to help another family's development. Is money Beth's primary motivation, as some colleagues insist? I don't think so. Beth has enthused over every detail and shared every turn with us gleefully, snapping photos of herself in the bathroom during the day so we can see how pregnant she is, or sending us little videos of kicks viewed from the outside. She seems to enjoy identifying herself as a surrogate—when she first began showing a stranger remarked, "Oh you're pregnant, congratulations!" and Beth answered, "Thank you, but it's not mine," confounding the commentator. She was as thrilled to help us as we were to have her carry our baby. There is a contract, and money is exchanged, but this is a labor of love.

The creepy online shopping feel of our egg provider search was challenging. It felt strange at first, but we stuck with it—we conversed about our criteria, and then reviewed photos and stats of various providers. Our primary factors were intelligence and health. We had a minor preference for someone attractive, on the tall side, and with light eyes. But then we came across more than a few challenging choices. Intelligence of course is at best difficult to ascertain from a profile—in our graduate studies at respectable universities, we each knew many who were well-educated but not bright and the reverse. This was going to be a slightly informed guess, and we came across a tall, attractive provider with a great undergraduate affiliation. And she was black.

This drew some fairly careful thought. Was selecting a white provider giving into whiteness as an ideology? At first I thought yes, it was. I felt this way even more clearly after a white law professor asked me, "Why pay all that money for a black kid when you can adopt?"

I then thought that the white liberal solution, to go the other way and hire the black egg provider, would not solve the dilemma—any fork in this road will be racialized in some way. To get some context for the decision, I spoke with friends. Several commented on challenges they'd heard about for white parents with a mixed race child or a child of color. These friends (straight, if it matters) said that the child would have issues aplenty with two gay parents, and that adding racial difference might make the child even more of an outsider.... I imagined us, two white guys, grilled by border agents about what we were doing with this differently-raced child. Of course in my mind I look more like a big queen than a child trafficker, but I imagined all kinds of trauma every time we travel. This convinced us—we moved on. We first chose a partly-Native American provider, but she disappeared, and then we went with a white provider. Sometimes I think less of myself for perpetuating or at least falling into presumptions about whiteness. But I'm also learning that having a child involves problematic choices that can reconfigure, complicate, and even upend theoretical commitments.

. . .

. . . Beth was, from the very first moment, warm and sincere as well as implicitly nonconformist. The meeting was smooth as cheesecake and by the end of the day we were stroking one of their pet rats and on the floor, playing Twister with her then 9–year–old twin boys.

Time passed. I had a minor meltdown when my Skadden-trained mind contemplated an agreement governed by Oklahoma law, but the agency assured me it was the best option. Beth came to New York, stayed in Times Square, and met with the fertility clinic doctors and staff, and we all stopped for pizza at Arthur Avenue in the Bronx before dropping her off at LaGuardia. We were good to go. . . .

At a conference a few months later, I met another law professor who had tried surrogacy. He told me that their surrogate decided to abort at twenty weeks because she had fallen in love.

I was terrified, but the next morning, I got a Facebook message from the egg provider that she was ready. It was time. The next day we went to the clinic. In sequence, we each masturbated in a clinical room, which we had done before for testing purposes. The room was filled with mostly straight porn. We hung out and waited and then met the egg provider and her boyfriend. She was lovely and sweet even in her drugged state. She also had the good sense to wear mascara even for this procedure (this appealed to my inner drag queen).

We left. Each day, we received a report replete with numbers. Forty-three eggs. Thirty million sperm. Twenty-two eggs fertilized by one's sperm, twenty-one by the other's. Eleven three-day embryos. On the night of the fourth day, we had cocktails and sushi with our surrogate and her sister, indulging in soon-to-be forbidden fruit. On the fifth day, we went to the clinic, where nine five-day embryos awaited. The doctor showed us live video of the two most developed ones (one from each of us) and then implanted them. Our surrogate was quite simply a trooper. Not one complaint or even a glance that any of this was difficult, although we knew it was. We hung out with her and her sister a few more days in New York and then they went home.

We waited.

. . .

Am I a pregnant man? Feminists have said to me, "I hate it when men say they're pregnant." Clearly, I'm not actually pregnant, but I'm kind of pregnant the way gay people used to say that a committed couple was "married" and gay men would refer to a "husband," even though no marriage could have been performed. The difference, of course, is that a man cannot have a baby for biological reasons, while a gay couple could not marry for legal ones.

. . .

But when I tell people about the pregnancy, they say, "How exciting—you're going to be a father!" and I look around to see whom they're addressing. I don't feel like I'm about to become a father. I feel like I'm about to become a mother. I feel like Harvey Fierstein's Arnold Beckoff in *Torch Song Trilogy*, who adopts a teenage boy. Arnold, a Brooklyn Jew who works as a drag queen named "Virginia Ham," was perhaps the first media image of a gay parent I saw in 1989. Perhaps Harvey's tale inspired me, even as a young queen, to think about eventually becoming a parent. I especially enjoyed that his son called him "Ma," even though it was with some sarcasm.

. . .

The invisibility of "parent" has come to infuriate me. The person who congratulates me could say, "How exciting, you're going to be a parent!" and people could comment, "Are you excited to become a parent?" But somehow that term is used in a formal sense but not a real sense. Because I have a penis, society wills me into becoming a father. Parenting seems to be experienced as an almost entirely gendered phenomenon. I feel like I'm forced to become a father—a man—when I feel like a person and/or a parent-to-be.

. . .

Sometimes I think about this complex process. We've had to ask and answer really taxing questions like: 1) why and how badly do we want a child; 2) what would we do with a multiple birth; 3) how can we trust this [birth parent, agency, government official, egg provider, surrogate, lawyer, doctor, psychologist, social worker, etc.] to do what's best for us and for our potential child; 4) do we have the resources, both financial and psychological, to go through with this process? I know that my answers to these questions were exercises in practical ethics, decisions made in context, with reasoning full of blemishes. I hope the choices I made are ones with which I can live. My fantasy is that the fact of having to make these choices may lead me (and many LGBT parents) to better (more deliberate and mindful) parenting. More likely than a policy implication, this story runs in my head to reassure myself that, with all these complex decisions and shifts in my being, in the end I'm going to be a great mom.

Beth Jones, *Mutual Exploitation, A Response*

While this essay and the follow-up discussions present a vast array of topics and ideas, the most fascinating to me is the topic of exploitation. The obvious assumption is the possibility of exploitation by the intended parents towards the surrogate. However, the reverse is just as easily possible and likely much more prevalent than people realize. In fact, the process may work best when there is mutual exploitation, to a degree. Let me back up. From my perspective, I've known for years that I didn't want to raise another child. I have known since I was pregnant with my twins that two kids were all I would ever want. Unfortunately, that pregnancy was a hard one. I had complications many people have never known exist. Forty-five percent chance of survival one week, five percent the next. At nineteen years old, the pregnancy was a trial for which I was not prepared, culminating in the terrifying concept of labor. The best experience that I took away from my pregnancy—aside from the wonderful end result, of course—was survival.

Nine years later, I was more experienced and a lot less fearful. Motivations and altruisms aside, let me be completely selfish for a moment. Becoming a surrogate provided a way for me to experience a planned pregnancy at a time in my life when I could enjoy the experience. There would be no lifelong commitment to raising another child, and it was one of the rare chances so few people receive to do something over. Yes, there was the risk of twins, but so what? If I could survive it as a terrified nineteen-year-old, I could certainly handle it in my late twenties. Luckily for me, the experience was absolutely ideal. I had amazing people doting on me constantly, and I had the enjoyable pregnancy I had previously missed. It was a spiritual experience to be able to help create a life for two people who so desired a child, and I got to play the nurturing role, singing and talking to the little one growing inside me, doing all the things I wish I had done (or had been able to do) in my previous pregnancy. On top of all of this, I was compensated, and after it all, my life went back to being my life. So I can say, with absolute certainty, that any construed exploitation done "against" me was equally matched. Given the benignity of the exploitation, it seems incredibly mutually beneficial.

Outside of the surrogacy bubble, friends, family and perfect strangers all felt the obligation to provide "constructive criticism" regarding my surrogacy choices. One moment they'd say, "How can you give your baby away?" only to be followed by, "So how much are you getting?" For some people, no amount of explaining the concept of gestational surrogacy would convince them that it is not, in any way, my baby, and to take the child would be more akin to kidnapping than "keeping your baby." One example I have used when people start in that direction is comparing surrogacy to housing a foreign exchange student. No one questions families that have exchange students. A student will travel halfway around the world, and be completely dependent upon total strangers to be their surrogate family for up to a year at a time, yet no one expects a permanent parental bond with the kid. I care for Melina the same way I care for my nieces and nephews, and probably how I would care for a foreign exchange student. While there is much love involved, I would never decide that someone else's child was more rightfully mine than theirs, especially based on nothing more than spending one-on-one time with them.

. . .

My family's reactions were probably the most varied, from my unsurprised sisters to my unconvinced grandmother. I was cautioned by some to hide the fact that I was helping two gay dads, while others found that to be the best selling point. . . .

Also, an excellent point was made about subjugation, and the roles of surrogates. Surrogates can't be too motherly, too shrewd, too opinionated, or too distant. I've witnessed many surrogates agonize over contract decisions while constantly feeling they must explain their intentions at every turn. There is a fear of being seen as motivated by money, yet there is also the fear of being seen as too loving, too attached. Do you offer to breastfeed to encourage lactation, or will they think you want to steal their baby? Do you request specific fees for specific procedures, or will they think it's a way to "nickel and dime" them? It is unreal—and unfortunate—how heavily some surrogates agonize over each and every decision. While I am not much of a worrier, even I had my moments of hesitation and conflict for the sake of perception. I found it necessary to stop repeatedly in the process and analyze things from an imagined distanced perspective. What did the procedure involve? How would the choice impact my life? The practice helped me to stay centered and grounded, and not get carried away in one direction or another. I found a strange comfort in how thorough the standard contract was, though. If I had twins, would I need more recovery time? If my embryo transfer was cancelled, did I expect to be compensated for taking the full cycle of hormones? If I was put on bed rest, would a housekeeping expense or paid time off be more appropriate? While it brought up so many scenarios I had yet to envision, it was reassuring to know someone had thought of these details already.

... When my children were conceived, we weren't thinking about conception. There were no plans to conceive or not to conceive. We were simply enjoying ourselves like so many couples do. Conception resulted, but neither of us can pinpoint the day. There is no definite record, no moment memorialized as "that moment." By definition, that is completely selfish conception. My thoughts were on myself and my partner, not on what we might create. In surrogacy, it is the opposite. There isn't passionate reckless abandon; there is planning and there are huge financial, emotional, and practical decisions to be made. When the moment finally arrives, all thoughts are on the life being created and the possibilities ahead, not on you. Maybe I am overanalyzing, but traditional conception seems more enjoyable in the moment, while conception through surrogacy provides a more lasting, traceable timeline for later reminiscing. It is only with this experience— followed by the time to reflect and analyze the process—that I am able to change my perspective to view the situation from each side. I feel honored to be one of the very few people to experience both traditional pregnancy and gestational surrogacy.

Martha M. Ertman, *Telling*

2009 UTAH L. REV. 531 (2009).

Balancing the white plastic stick carefully on top of the toilet tank, I leave the bathroom. I feel a little crazy for wanting to take it with me for proof, good luck or an early demonstration of maternal dedication. . . . I walk slowly down the wood-paneled hall toward the living room. *What should I do?* I look around for a minute to memorize the look of this rattletrap living room, the 70s beige carpet, the rickety wooden coffee table, painted white like just about every other piece of furniture on Cape Cod, the couch where I lay . . . for an hour, reaching out to the gods, willing them to dispense new life into my life, out at the cape window whose blinds I lowered for privacy those three days I inseminated here, all alone.

I've been waiting for this result for so long. I examine my emotions for the standard-issue pregnancy responses. *Joy?* Check. *Excitement?* Yes. Also, crowding out the first, a hold back from these months of waiting. Worry. *What if I miscarry? What if the baby has Down syndrome? Whom do I tell?*

I want to tell Victor. He's in Seattle, teaching a summer class. Where he sent the sperm from two weeks ago. He's due to come here next week. I dial his number, anticipating the shared excitement of being the only ones who know. I get his voicemail.

"Hey Victor, it's Martha. Call me," I say. *Can he hear the glee in my voice?* I wonder *Why didn't he pick up?*

Annoyance joins the other emotions. I talked to him just before taking the pregnancy test. He said he was going out to dinner with Edsonya and would take his cell.

Maybe he just missed it by one ring will call right back.

Five minutes pass. He doesn't call.

What happened? He knew I was going to take the test.

Movies play in my head. Victor is walking out of the house—which I've never seen—with his cell phone in his pocket, but he can't hear it in the restaurant's din. I cut to a close-up of the phone falling out of his pocket as he gets out of the car. I flash back to his kitchen, watch him leave the cell phone on the table. *Negligent? Deliberate?* I wonder, watching the movie, what I think of Victor's character in this story.

I switch focus, eyes still a little narrow, and re-survey the living room. The rented room where I conceived all alone. Alone for the first time in eleven months of inseminations with friends, doctors, even just Victor and me a few times.... *All alone, how fitting,* I think raising one eyebrow, breathing deep. Now I finally have a positive result, and no-one to share it with. *How alone am I in this?* I wonder, and exhale.

I could call someone else. Lisa, another summer person here, ... friends in Salt Lake City. They're all in on it. But I want the story to be that I told Victor first.

I close my eyes to the shabbiness of this rattletrap cape rental, saying to myself. *If he's in the game, great. If not, it won't be because I left him out.*

At 1:00 a.m., 10:00 p.m. Seattle time, the phone wakes me up from a sound sleep.

"Hey, Martha, it's Victor." His voice is chipper, as usual.

"Victor . . ." I begin, coming out of my sleep a little confused, struggling to figure out why he's calling so late, where he is. Once I sit up I'm fully awake, happy to have the news and have him on the line.

"Victor, the test came back positive!" I tell him, loud and excited.

"What? I can't hear you." He replies through scratchy cell phone reception.

"Positive! It's positive. I'm pregnant. It worked!" I announce, pride swelling my voice.

Victor screams with delight, a high happy sound.

He tells me that he put the phone in the pocket of his camelhair blazer before leaving the house. Changed coats, but forgot to transfer the phone to his new coat. So he just got my message now. As he tells me, I close my eyes, rolling them inside my lids, the way I did when I was talking to him from Chicago the first time the sperm leaked out of the jar he sent it in. *Should I chide him?* I wonder, *What if I need to reach him in an emergency?* I don't. It's not a thought-out choice, if such a thing were possible at 1:00 in the morning of the first full day of knowing you are pregnant, figuring out your relationship with your gay friend who will also be a parent, six weeks before you turn forty, after nearly a year of trying. It's more like an intuition. If it had words, they might go something like:

> *Victor's your friend. He's not a partner. His voice is kind. You shouldn't demand that he take his phone with him. You don't want him to pinch you that way. You're getting away with something, being single, having a baby, with a kind, reliable, talented man who will be a father but not boss you around. Don't push it.*

I wonder if he knows I'm making this choice.

. . .

Alone in my bed, I don't know how alone I am. I don't know a month later, packing up to drive home to Salt Lake City. Lisa helps pack the car, and [another friend is] driving me as far as Chicago, where [yet another] will join me for the last leg. We probably took pictures of all of us on the porch that day, before driving away from the summer and toward the school year. But the one in the photo album is of Victor and me on the weathered gray front porch, standing in front of the screen door. I'm on the right, and his body is turned three-quarters toward me, almost coquettish, like a beauty queen. His head is a couple of inches higher than mine. His arms are circling my lower back and belly to clasp hands on my right hip. The folds of his sand-colored silk shirt flap a little in the breeze, as do the highlighted tips of my ear-length curls. We're both in shorts, laughing. Amazed, amused to be posing as a sort-of couple, in awe of the gift of being both coupled and not.

In that moment I realized what seems obvious now. That when I left my partner of twelve years because she didn't want to have a baby, I stepped off the tightrope of romantic love. After spending a year in something like freefall, finding a job and a house and friends in Salt Lake City, my world was no longer comprised of my partner and a small circle of intimate friends and family. In its place, or layered under and around it, was a net of various kinds of love. Each strand of rope a different kind of love. Friendship love, sexual love, co-parenting love, neighborly love, medical love, family love. All woven together tight enough to catch me on my way out of one family and into another. And loosely enough to allow unexpected freedom of movement. It would be years before I found a new home that was rooted in place in addition to people. But in this moment, on the porch of the Provincetown rental, Victor's arms playfully circled around my soon-to-expand waist, I have a human home.

NOTE

In a recent *New York Times Magazine* article, Melanie Thernstrom describes her travails with infertility. Having met her husband at forty-one, she underwent six unsuccessful cycles of IVF and thought about adoption before becoming a mother via double concurrent surrogacy using the same egg donor. The article seems to have coined the term "twiblings" for siblings who have been born almost concurrently to two different surrogates. *See* Melanie Thernstrom, *Meet the Twiblings*, N.Y. TIMES MAGAZINE (Dec. 29, 2010), http://www.nytimes.com/2011/01/02/magazine/02 babymaking-t.html?pagewanted=all. For audio clips with interviews of Melanie, her husband, and the two surrogates *see* Miki Meek, *The Futuristic Insta–Family*, N.Y. TIMES MAGAZINE (Dec. 28, 2010), http://www.nytimes.com/interactive/2010/12/22/magazine/20101222–twiblings-audio.html.

2.   COMMERCE, COMMODIFICATION, AND CRITIQUE

Kimberly D. Krawiec, *Altruism and Intermediation in the Market for Babies*

66 WASH. & LEE L. REV. 203 (2009).

Few proposals generate the moral outrage engendered by a suggestion that babies—or, more accurately but less vividly, parental rights—should be traded on the open market. More than anything else, baby selling flies in the face of our deeply held convictions that some items are too priceless to ever be bought and sold. Throughout the world, in fact, baby selling is formally prohibited. And throughout the world babies are bought and sold each day.

In the United States alone in 2001, roughly 41,000 children were born through assisted reproduction, 6,000 of whom were created through the use of "donated" eggs and 600 of whom were carried by surrogates. In 2003, Americans adopted 21,616 children through international adoptions and gave birth to thousands of babies using commercially purchased sperm. Each of these children was purchased, usually, at great cost. As will be demonstrated in this Article, the baby market is big business—a business in which parents pay, intermediaries profit, and surrogates, birth parents, and providers of egg and sperm "donate" their products and services for prices ranging from under one hundred to over one hundred thousand dollars.

Until recently, the most visible and contested debates regarding baby markets primarily addressed the normative desirability of an open-market baby exchange, largely assuming that formal bans against baby selling relegated the baby trade to the black and gray markets....

... Recent analyses persuasively document the legal, but highly imperfect, baby market, rendering (in some circles, at least) assertions regarding the existence of legal baby markets so widely accepted as to be almost mundane....

... [C]ommercial markets characterize all aspects of the distribution of parental rights, with one exception: Legal restrictions purport to limit the ability of surrogates, birth parents, and egg donors ("Baby Market Suppliers") to reap the full monetary benefits of their production. One of the defining characteristics of the baby market is thus the legal regime's formal exclusion of Baby Market Suppliers from the full profits of exchange. As a result, although Baby Market Suppliers charge for their services, they are expected to derive a substantial portion of their compensation from the utility associated with altruistic donation. Meanwhile, their monetary compensation frequently is characterized as a gift, donation, or reimbursement and may be well below market value. Not surprisingly then, supply in most sectors of the baby market falls far short of demand.

· · ·

To clarify, the recognition that the allocation of parental rights operates like other commercial markets in many significant respects does not imply that there are not important differences between the baby market and more traditional commercial markets. Needless to say, trafficking in human lives raises many public policy issues simply not implicated by the markets for cars, bonds, or janitorial services. Yet the failure to acknowledge the many ways in which the baby market operates like other commercial markets imposes severe costs on the market, its participants, the children and future children traded in the market, and society at large. Those costs include the forgone opportunities to develop legal policies designed to improve the functioning of the market and to further particular public policies unlikely to be advanced solely through the goal of profit-maximization. Perhaps the greatest cost imposed by the traditional romanticization of the baby market and its distribution networks, however, is the extent to which it masks attempts by politically and economically powerful market participants to cloak private wealth transfers as public-interested regulation in the form of "baby selling" restrictions and other laws dictating the allocation of parental rights.

· · ·

In the United States in 2004, fertility treatment constituted a $3 billion industry, serving one million customer-patients seeking a variety of services ranging from medical advice and fertility testing to sophisticated ART treatments. Today, assisted reproduction has become so ubiquitous that it is easy to forget the controversy and criticism surrounding the practice in its early years....

Such controversy notwithstanding, the fertility industry has enjoyed immense growth. In 1986, for example, there were only one hundred fertility clinics in the United States with revenues of roughly $41 million. By 2002, those numbers had grown to 428 clinics with revenues of nearly $3 billion. These figures don't include profits to other intermediary participants in the embryo industry, such as lawyers, consultants, equipment manufacturers and suppliers, and counselors of various sorts.

Infertile couples, of course, typically do not view themselves as purchasing a baby or, perhaps, even entering into a market transaction (despite charges averaging $12,400 per in vitro cycle in 2003, and total fees of as much as $100,000 before some couples conceive or give up). Consumer behavior in acquiring fertility services tends to reflect this, differing from consumer behavior in other types of transactions. Fertility customers, for example, do not engage in extensive price comparison or bargaining over fees; change fertility centers only reluctantly, even when faced with a lack of success through a given provider; and tend to blame themselves, rather than the provider, when they are unsuccessful in achieving pregnancy.

For their part, fertility centers do little to alter the perception that their relationship with infertile couples is a non-commercial one, highlighting instead their willingness and ability to help infertile couples realize their dreams of conception. As stated by doctors at Boston IVF, "our greatest honor is knowing that at least one of our patients fulfills their dream of becoming a parent every day of every year." . . .

. . . But profits are undeniably a—if not *the*—motivating factor in the industry as well. . . . Those fertility centers not affiliated with academic institutions are even more openly profit-centered and, like suppliers in any competitive industry, they engage in elaborate marketing efforts to attract customers. These efforts include hiring high-priced marketing consultants; advertising on billboards, the radio, newspapers, and magazines; and assiduously courting physician referrals by "wining and dining" doctors and hosting dinners and parties at medical meetings. Many clinics even offer "shared risk" or money-back guarantee programs and aggressive financing plans that, as advertised by the nation's largest network of fertility specialists, "make your fertility care less expensive than a second car."

. . .

Roughly one thousand children in the United States have been born through the use of PGD [preimplantation genetic diagnosis], but increasing numbers of customers seeking PGD do not carry genetic diseases—many are not even infertile. Instead, they are purchasing a custom-made baby that meets their genetic specifications, such as a particular gender. Decried by many ethicists, some specialists eschew PGD for non-medical reasons. . . . Jeffrey Steinberg, director of the Fertility Institute, which provides fertility services in Los Angeles and Las Vegas, reports that seventy percent of customers hire him specifically for the purpose of gender selection, paying as much as $18,000 for a comprehensive service that includes counseling, PGD, and IVF.

Finally, some clinics sell ready-made embryos, produced from the best eggs and sperm money can buy and then frozen until purchased. Unlike the excess embryos that often result after a successful fertility treatment, these embryos are specifically created for purchase. Fertility centers essentially create such embryos on speculation, allowing infertile couples to choose from a menu of donor genetic traits that include ethnic and educational background and appearance, such as hair and eye coloring.

Although Jennalee Ryan of the Abraham Center of Life recently caused an uproar by advertising "the world's first human embryo bank" online, contrary to the assumptions surrounding this debate, Ms. Ryan is not the first to offer such embryos for sale, but rather is the first third-party broker to advertise such services. But fertility centers across the country have quietly offered this service for nearly a decade to their customers for whom fertility treatments have failed. The centers have never advertised these services, however, and, consistent with this traditional secrecy, Ms. Ryan will not reveal the identities of the fertility centers that are her suppliers.

. . . [S]perm banking initially developed as a step in the artificial insemination process and relied almost exclusively on banking by men unable to inseminate their wives through natural means. When sperm banking by the husband was not possible, infertile couples sometimes turned to close friends and family members to provide sperm.

Eventually, however, fertility centers realized that a more impersonal, commercial system could increase both supply and quality. They began soliciting anonymous donors and offering a small fee for their sperm, choosing young men who offered specific physical and genetic characteristics such as a particular height, ethnicity, or hair color. In doing so, they also opened up the sperm market to other sources of demand: single women; lesbian couples; and heterosexual couples in which the man, while fertile, was older or carried genetic diseases.

. . .

Today, the sperm business consists almost entirely of free-standing banking centers unconnected to any specific fertility clinic, and offers services that include banking for men who want to freeze their sperm for later use, direct-order services to couples and single women in need of sperm, and commercial provision to fertility clinics. Although medical advances that address male infertility have caused a reduction in the demand for donor sperm among heterosexual couples over the past decade, demand from single women and lesbian couples has increased, resulting in significant industry growth. Moreover, a drop in supply in many other countries due to regulatory changes has increased the export market in the United States.

Sperm donors are actively solicited through the internet, newspaper ads, and college campus flyers, and receive $75 on average for each specimen. Each specimen yields three to six vials of sperm, which sell for an average of $250 to $400 each. Shipping costs an extra $100, and the sperm of donors with advanced degrees or who agree to reveal their identity to offspring command a premium.

Since the advent of AIDS awareness in the late 1980s, donor sperm is required by federal law to be washed, frozen, and quarantined for at least six months while the donor is tested for HIV, hepatitis, and other sexually-transmitted diseases. Although not required by law, most banks also test donors for the most common genetically-transmitted diseases, such as Tay–Sachs and cystic fibrosis, and collect extensive (but unverified) family medical histories. The costs of these storage and testing requirements are substantial, resulting in significant economies of scale. As a result, the sperm business has tended to be dominated by a small number of large, highly efficient producers.

Other than FDA attempts to control the spread of infectious disease through donor sperm, regulation of the sperm market is left largely to self-policing by individual banks, a fact increasingly met with sharp criticism. Although, compared to the egg market, the sperm market has operated for many years in the United States relatively free of controversy, calls for regulatory intervention are now increasing, driven by demand for more openness by single women and lesbian couples, advances in genetic testing, eugenics concerns, and recent sperm industry scandals.

... Like many other aspects of the baby business, the egg market was originally unprofitable, limited to gift exchanges between friends and family members, and used by a limited set of infertile women who suffered from ovarian failure. Today, however, the egg business enjoys a much broader market appeal, with such disparate sources as older women, women who carry genetic diseases, gay couples, and embryonic stem cell researchers contributing to demand.

In the market's early years, the term "egg donation" was a literal one. Women unable to produce their own eggs sometimes would seek the help of a close friend or family member who bore genetic characteristics (such as race, ethnicity, or hair or eye color) and other attributes (such as education levels) similar to their own. But so long as egg donation remained limited to altruistic transfers from known contributors, the market was fated to be undersupplied for a variety of reasons.

First, egg donation is a complicated process with some health risks. All egg donors must undergo a comprehensive medical screening, plus a three-week course of hormone injections to induce ovulation, during which period the donor cannot have unprotected sex, smoke, use illegal drugs or drink alcohol, and can take prescription and over-the-counter drugs only with permission. During this time, frequent doctor visits are required, at which the donor's hormone levels are checked through blood tests and her ovaries are examined through ultrasound to determine the extent of egg production.

The long-term risks of infertility treatments are unknown. Although the short-term side effects of ovarian stimulation are normally limited to mood swings, water retention, and ovarian swelling, fertility medications can cause ovarian hyperstimulation syndrome (OHSS), which in its severe form can cause serious medical problems, including kidney failure, fluid build-up in the lungs, and shock. Rarely, the condition can be life-threatening and necessitate removal of the ovaries.

When the eggs are ready for retrieval, they are surgically removed through a process that may cause bleeding and infection. During this process, the bowel, bladder, or nearby blood vessels may be punctured. Although this is a rare occurrence, if severe internal bleeding results, major abdominal surgery may be required.

These more serious risks are quite rare, and egg donation is normally little more than a time-consuming and physically uncomfortable inconvenience. It is easy to understand, however, why few women would undergo the process for a stranger without the inducement of financial compensation.

The second factor limiting egg supply relates to the fairly stringent qualifications required of egg donors. Donors must be in a certain age range, typically twenty-one to thirty-five. In addition, as previously noted, even in the early stages of the egg market, recipients desired egg donors with particular genetic characteristics to increase the chances that their offspring would bear a resemblance to the intended mother.

As the market has become more commercial, however, this demand for particular genetic characteristics has increased, resulting in greater price differentiation. Although the base-line rate for eggs in 1999 was $2,500 to $5,000, depending on geographic region, donors with traits that are particularly rare or desired commanded significantly higher prices. For example, East Asian and Jewish eggs command a price premium, because they are rarer, as do the eggs of Ivy League college students, women with high SAT scores, women with athletic ability, and women with extraordinary physical attractiveness.

... The luxury egg market has generated particular controversy. In 1999, to the horror of the mainstream fertility industry, a fashion photographer launched a scheme to auction off the eggs of models on the internet for prices as high as $150,000. The site is still up and running and claims sales of $39.2 million through 2004. "Donor" programs also have generated controversy—and profits—at Ivy League schools across the country through their aggressive advertising in student newspapers and on-campus flyers offering sums as high as $50,000 for egg donors. These fees are sometimes linked to specific qualifications, such as membership on a varsity athletic team, or a GPA or SAT score in a certain percentile.

... Historically, surrogates were induced into service through neither money nor altruism, but through coercion. Most were servants—for example, the maid of the intended mother or a concubine of the father. In this era, conception took place the old-fashioned way—through sexual intercourse—in contrast to today's more technologically advanced methods.

. . .

Today, surrogacy raises even more difficult legal issues due to technological innovations that permit gestational surrogacy, a process by which IVF is employed to implant the surrogate with an embryo created by an egg, donated by the intended mother or an egg donor, and sperm, from the intended father or a sperm donor. In the case of gestational surrogacy, therefore, the surrogate has no genetic relation to the child, an important distinction in determining parentage under many state laws. In the United States, ninety-five percent of all commercial surrogacy arrangements are for gestational surrogacy.

. . .

Freed by the advent of gestational surrogacy from the traditional constraints on the race or ethnicity of the surrogate, surrogacy is increasingly being outsourced overseas. Driving the push, in part, are concerns over the legal enforceability of commercial surrogacy contracts in the United States, as well as other considerations, including lower costs and the ability to supervise and control the behavior of the surrogate.

Since commercial surrogacy was legalized in India in 2002, for example, clinics have spread to nearly every major city, resulting in an industry estimated at $500 million. Indian surrogates typically earn less than their American counterparts (between six and ten thousand dollars, on average, plus room, board, and some educational or vocational training.) With some thirty-five percent of Indians surviving on less than one dollar per day, however, and a lack of similarly well-paying jobs for the uneducated (particularly women), there is no shortage of women willing to perform the task.

. . .

... [T]he baby market resembles other common markets in many important ways, including industry segmentation, price differentiation, the presence of powerful market intermediaries, and substantial industry profits. Given these similarities to other commercial markets, baby market participants should be expected to behave in at least some respects like participants in other commercial markets....

. . .

An intermediary has been defined as "an economic agent that purchases from suppliers for resale to buyers or that helps buyers and sellers meet and transact." Intermediation is an important—and profitable—function in developed economies, accounting for over twenty-five percent of the U.S. gross domestic product. Although the types of market imperfections associated with any given transaction ultimately will determine the types of intermediation services performed, intermediaries are generally thought to perform four general categories of services: (1) price setting and market clearing functions; (2) providing market liquidity; (3) coordinating buyers and sellers; and (4) performing monitoring and quality guarantee functions.

In the case of baby markets, a wide array of Baby Market Intermediaries performs these functions....

Coordinating buyers and sellers is another important role performed by Baby Market Intermediaries....

The baby market entails high search and matching costs, which various Baby Market Intermediaries seek to reduce. For example, prospective parents wishing to procure a child in the baby market face costs in identifying a prospective egg donor, surrogate, or birth parent. Prospective parents must determine who these women are, how they can be reached, and whether they have the desired characteristics. Baby Market Suppliers face similar search costs in finding a willing purchaser....

Perhaps the most important role played by Baby Market Intermediaries, however, involves the traditional intermediary functions of guarantee and monitoring. In markets where buyers and sellers have asymmetric information, intermediaries can capture gains from trade by reducing those asymmetries through, for example, certifying the quality of goods, monitoring the efforts of trading parties, and guaranteeing performance with warranties and contract terms.

. . .

Finally, the baby market is plagued with uncertainty.... Surrogate agencies and brokers reduce this uncertainty through contract drafting, and through careful psychological and other screening of surrogates and intended parents.

In sum, Baby Market Intermediaries perform an important role in reducing transaction costs in the baby market and likely would continue to do so even in a fully functioning, legalized baby market. These value adding functions, in part, explain the large intermediary fees in the baby market....

... [H]owever, these value-adding functions only partially explain the central role of intermediaries in the baby market and the resulting large profit opportunities. Instead, an asymmetric institutional framework—that is, a set of laws, legal and extra-legal institutions, and informal norms governing conduct—stymies full market access by Baby Market Suppliers, without similar restrictions on the activities of Baby Market Intermediaries. Moreover, in contrast to the institutional framework governing most markets, the institutional framework governing the baby market uniformly operates to increase, rather than reduce, transaction costs, increasing the dependency of both Baby Market Suppliers and consumers, and enhancing the role of Baby Market Intermediaries. This dichotomy contributes to the lopsided division of profits between Baby Market intermediaries and Baby Market Suppliers that many observers have criticized.

. . .

Formal and informal agreements to depress the price of eggs pervade the fertility industry....

. . .

Price-fixing attempts in the egg market take two basic forms: informal geographic-based and national. In 1998, for example, Dr. Paul Bergh of the St. Barnabas Medical Center decided—in violation of an apparent "community understanding" among fertility clinics in the New York Metropolitan area to pay no more than $2,500 for donated eggs—to double the center's egg donor fees, from $2,500 to $5,000. The move generated an enormous amount of media coverage and at least two essays in medical journals. During the ensuing debate, many fertility professionals openly discussed the need to control egg prices, lamenting that any increase in egg prices would have to be passed on to consumers.

Attempts at national price capping occur largely through professional standard-setting organizations. For example, the ASRM Ethics Committee has issued "compensation guidelines" of $5,000 per donation cycle, with an exception of up to $10,000 in special cases, such as an egg of very rare ancestry. Enforcement occurs through SART (the Society for Assisted Reproductive Technology), the primary member organization for assisted reproductive technology professionals in the United States, whose membership accounts for eighty-five percent of U.S. fertility clinics. SART requires both its members and all egg donation agencies doing business with a SART-affiliated fertility clinic to comply with the ASRM compensation guidelines. Surveys of SART member clinics and affiliated agencies suggest broad compliance.

. . .

Such openly anti-competitive behavior is largely impossible in other industries. Yet it has persisted in the egg industry for at least a decade, amidst the traditional romanticization of the baby market and the persistent dialogue of altruistic donation that pervades it.

An examination of recent egg industry controversy highlights the point. Although controversy over the egg market stems from several sources, one of the most common—as in other sectors of the baby market—is an objection to the commodification and commercialization of children, motherhood, or human organs.... In the absence of similar attempts to control the prices charged by providers of fertility goods and services to customers, anti-commodification objections boil down to assertions that the ultimate supplier of the good—the egg donor—should be the only party not fully profiting from the transaction. . . .

Moreover, despite the overwhelming evidence to the contrary, the egg market is characterized by an insistence that the primary motivation of egg donors—even those being paid—is, and should be, altruism. . . . Given such norms regarding the appropriate motivations of those who offer their eggs for use by others, it is perhaps not surprising that many egg donors report in surveys that helping infertile couples achieve parenthood was one of the primary concerns motivating their decision. Donors often are more forthcoming in informal interviews, however, explicitly discussing the motivating force of money in the decision to become an egg donor.

. . .

As stated by one commentator, "the implication that young women *should* desire to undergo a series of highly uncomfortable procedures that pose both short term and long term risks to their physical well-being for which they will not collect the market clearing price threatens to reinforce stereotypes of females as generous rather than self-interested." The true limits to women's altruistic nature are starkly revealed by the experience of countries, such as the United Kingdom, Japan, and Canada, that have banned paid egg donation. The egg supply in such countries is severely depressed, creating a lucrative export market and "reproductive tourism" trade in the United States.

This insistence on the altruistic nature of egg donation is in sharp contrast to the presumed motivations of sperm donors, who are exhorted through on-campus marketing campaigns that query, "why not get paid for it?" In fact, the presumption against altruistic sperm donation is so strong that men claiming such motives—as opposed to pure financial need—prompt skepticism and are suspected of hiding an egomaniacal desire to propagate the world with their sperm.

. . .

In the surrogacy market, the most obvious impediments to market access by Baby Market Suppliers are the uncertain legal enforceability of surrogacy contracts in many jurisdictions and the prohibition in some jurisdictions against paying surrogates amounts beyond necessary living and medical expenses. Many commentators have noted the fact that surrogates earn a relatively small share of the total price paid by intended parents, often less than the agency fee and typically much less than the total price paid, which includes medical and legal expenses and the agency placement fee.

. . .

Legal uncertainty surrounding surrogacy contracts enhances the role of intermediaries in the market, increasing their share of the surplus from any gains of trade in the surrogacy market. Restrictions on payments to surrogates—to the extent that they are effective—obviously would have the same impact. Critics of the current power structure between intermediaries and surrogates thus should support full enforceability of surrogacy contracts and the removal of restrictions designed to limit surrogate compensation rather than agitating for further restrictions on the surrogacy market.

. . .

As in the case of the egg market, formal attempts to cap surrogate compensation and the persistent dialogue of altruistic donation in the surrogacy market may further complicate the ability of surrogates to fully reap the value of their services. Surrendering a child that one has carried to term and given birth to is a profound disjuncture from our traditional societal notions of motherhood. Society insists that such a woman must be either crazy or venal. Prohibitions against, and limitations on, commercial surrogacy arrangements reinforce these norms.

As a result, the motivations of commercial surrogates are repackaged as altruistic and their compensation is defined as derived in large part from the enhanced utility that results from helping a childless couple. . . .

This altruistic rhetoric is not harmless and, indeed, may reduce the economic bargaining power of surrogates. By classifying money motivations as improper or, at best, secondary, in the surrogate context, surrogates may have a reduced ability to negotiate the financial terms of their arrangement, as open displays of monetary concerns are deemed socially unacceptable.

. . .

This Article . . . encourages recognition of the baby trade for what it is—a market, with similarities to and differences from, other markets. As with other markets, the legal regime may seek to improve competitive conditions, and should be suspicious of attempts to use the state's power to extract private benefits under the guise of public-interest regulation. Trafficking in human lives, however, poses public policy issues not implicated by the markets in other items. Pretending that legal baby markets do not exist accomplishes none of these objectives.

Mary Lyndon Shanley, *Collaboration and Commodification in Assisted Procreation: Reflections on an Open Market and Anonymous Donation in Human Sperm and Eggs*

36 LAW & SOC'Y REV. 257, 271–73 (2002).

In the United States, unlike many other countries, the mechanism by which gametes are transferred from one person to another has largely been the market. In market transactions, Marilyn Strathern declares, "an anonymously produced object becomes part of a store on which others draw. Preserving the social anonymity of market goods is . . . fundamental to the supposition that goods are available for all". Because gametes are separable from the provider they can appear to have certain characteristics of commodities, objects "produced" by the body that become part of a common store—as the term "sperm bank" suggests. Control over eggs or sperm can be transferred from provider to doctor or fertility clinic, and from these to the recipient. They can be treated as a generalized "resource" that can be traded in the market. Strathern believes that "the market analogy has already done its work: we think so freely of the providing and purchasing of goods and services that transactions in gametes is already a thought-of act of commerce". And once people conceptualize gametes as commodities, it becomes very difficult to argue against allowing a market in gametes.

The fact that it is appropriate for people to regard gametes as the possession of the provider in the sense that no one (including the government and medical research facilities) may commandeer them does not mean, however, that a gamete provider has a right to *sell* that material; the right to exclude others from use does not entail the right to sell. The liberal ideal of "self ownership" does not mean that we can do whatever we like with all our body parts, selling off what we don't need or want. The law allows people to sell hair, and sometimes blood, but prohibits the sale of body organs. Even someone willing and able to live with only one kidney or eye may not sell the other, nor may the kidney, eye, heart, or liver from a deceased person be sold. The distinction here is not simply that between renewable and nonrenewable material, or between material necessary and unnecessary to sustain life. It also involves a judgment that some parts of the body should not be for sale either because of the significance of reserving aspects of the human body from commodification, or because economic need might lead poor people to sell body parts. What kind of "body parts" are gametes, and how should we think about the ways in which they should be transferred from one person to another for purposes of procreation? To what extent should gametes be regarded as personal property, and providers as owners of those gametes?

Buying and selling gametes, whether by differential or uniform pricing, suggests that they are property and that the person in whose body they originate has rights of ownership until he or she transfers the gametes (and the rights of ownership) to someone else. Differential pricing of gametes based on characteristics like the provider's height, skin and hair color, athletic or academic achievement, and musical ability seems to validate the assumption that persons with such attributes—both providers and as-yet-unborn (indeed, as-yet-unconceived) children—are "worth more" than others. Certain characteristics people are born with are valued more than others: lighter-skinned people encounter less employment discrimination than darker-skinned individuals; men are paid more than women with comparable education. It is bad enough that these and other differences, which are accidents of birth, generate economic inequality in the labor market; it is far worse when these traits lead to differential compensation for the provider's gametes. When people know that the genetic material that made a particular child's existence possible was bought for a higher (or lower) price than that of some other child, such knowledge may undermine the proposition that all persons are of equal dignity regardless of their wealth or social status.

Some people believe that paying a flat rate to providers (higher for eggs than sperm donation because egg donation is much more difficult) avoids the affront to human dignity involved in an open market in eggs and sperm and is not improper. They point out that in gamete transfer, unlike adoption, there is no existing child and no social relationship between provider and gamete. Hence the prohibitions on baby-selling do not apply, and the gamete may be sold by the person from whom it is extracted. But treating gametes as property that can be sold, even for a uniform price, suggests that individuals "own" their gametes in the same way that they own other transferable property. This is the wrong way to conceptualize human beings' relationship to their genetic material. Donna Dickenson contends that "the kind of ownership which we can be said to possess in relation to our gametes is conditional: we are not allowed to do anything we like with them, because they are not unequivocally ours. They are held in common with past and future generations". A person's relationship to his or her genetic material is better thought of as a kind of stewardship than as ownership. To shape social practices to avoid conveying the idea that gametes are properly thought of as individually owned property, we must move either to a system of paying for the activities involved in providing gametes (not for gametes themselves), or to pure donation (gift)....

Dorothy Roberts, Killing the Black Body: Race, Reproduction and the Meaning of Liberty

260–69 (1997).

Blacks may also have an aversion to the genetic marketing aspect of the new reproduction. When infertile couples pay for the services of surrogate mothers and egg or sperm donors, they are purchasing the genetic material for their future children. When they undergo IVF, they are buying the assurance that their offspring will receive the parents' own genetic components. Black folks are skeptical about any obsession with genes. They know that their genes have been considered undesirable and that their alleged genetic inferiority has been used for centuries to justify their exclusion from the economic, political, and social mainstream.... In a society in which Black traits are consistently devalued, a focus on genetics will more likely be used to justify limiting Black reproduction rather than encouraging it.

Blacks have understandably resisted defining personal identity in biological terms. In America, whites have historically valued genetic linkages and controlled their official meaning. As the powerful class, they are the guardians of the privileges accorded to biology and they have a greater stake in maintaining the importance of genetics. The legal regulation of racial boundary lines during the slavery era, for example, concerned *whites*, not Blacks: "The statutes punishing voluntary interracial sex and marriage were directed only at whites; they alone were charged with the responsibility for maintaining racial purity."

Blacks by and large are more interested in escaping the constraints of racial ideology by defining themselves apart from inherited traits. They tend to see group membership as a political and cultural affiliation. Whites defined enslaved Africans as a biological race. Blacks in America have historically resisted this racial ideology by defining themselves as a political group. By the turn of the twentieth century, Black Americans had developed a race consciousness rooted in a sense of peoplehood that laid the foundation for later civil rights struggles. With the exception of an extreme version of Afrocentrism that links Africans' intellectual and cultural contributions to the genetic trait of melanin (the pigment in dark skin), "blackness" is gauged by one's commitment to Black people.

Black family ties have traditionally reached beyond the bounds of the nuclear family to include extended kin and non-kin relationships. Terms that connote genetic relationships—"brother," "sister," and "blood"—are used to refer to people linked together by racial solidarity. Black people's search for their ancestral roots has focused on cultural rather than genetic preservation. Their "ancestors" are not necessarily connected to them by a bloodline; they are all African people of a bygone era.

. . .

I have suggested that the suspicion of genetic marketing and the appreciation of self-definition in Black culture may help to explain Blacks' aversion to high-tech reproduction. Conversely, race may also influence the importance whites place on IVF's central aim—producing genetically related children. Using technology to create genetic ties focuses attention on the value placed on this particular form of connection.

. . .

Most scholarship on the new reproduction, however, fails to consider the tremendous impact that inheritability of race has had on the meaning of genetic relatedness in American culture. Although race is really a social construct, it has been treated as an inherited status for centuries. In this society, perhaps the most significant genetic trait passed from parent to child is race. How important is race to the desire to create genetically related children? It is impossible to tell: the decision to have children is influenced by a multitude of social, cultural, and biological factors. But surely the inheritability of race plays some role in the degree of importance whites invest in genetic ties with their children.

The social and legal meaning of the genetic tie helped to maintain a racial caste system that preserved white supremacy through a rule of racial purity. The colonists maintained a clear demarcation between Black slaves and white masters by a violently enforced legal system of racial classification and sexual taboos. The genetic tie to a slave mother not only made the child a slave and subject to white domination; it was also supposed to pass down a whole set of inferior traits.

.   .   .

The new reproduction also graphically discloses the disparate values placed on children of different races. By trading genes on the market, these technologies lay bare the high value placed on whiteness and the worthlessness accorded blackness. New reproductive technologies are so popular in American culture not simply because of the value placed on the genetic tie, but because of the value placed on the *white* genetic tie. The monumental effort, expense, and technological invention that goes into the new reproduction marks the children produced as especially valuable. It proclaims the unmistakable message that white children merit the spending of billions of dollars toward their creation. Black children, on the other hand, are the object of welfare reform measures designed to discourage poor women's procreation.

.   .   .

NOTE

Some of the race hierarchical problems analyzed by Roberts also seem to be present in the transnational ART context. PlanetHospital, for instance, advertises a broad range of medical tourism, of which fertility treatment is only one part. Within the category of fertility treatment, PlanetHospital offers anything from vasectomy, to IVF, to surrogacy. There are only two photos on the fertility webpage, both quite telling of race bias. The first one represents a beaming western looking pregnant woman next to the "tubal ligation reversal" category. Presumably she represents the best-case scenario: carrying her own genetic child after a minor mechanical correction. At the very bottom of the webpage, there is a photo of three pregnant bellies, one next to another, dark and faceless reproductive vessels exposed from the midst of a colorful symphony of saris. *See Fertility*, PLANETHOSPITAL http://www.planethospital. net/fertility.html (last visited Oct. 2, 2011). Surrogates for white parents are commonly impregnated with eggs from Eastern European donors unless these parents are on a budget, in which case they may choose an egg from India or Latin America. *See* Tamara Audi & Arlene Chang, *Assembling the Global Baby*, WALL ST. J. (Dec. 10, 2010), http://online.wsj.com/article/SB10001424052748703493504576007774155273928. html

Michele Goodwin, *Assisted Reproductive Technology and the Double Bind: The Illusory Choice of Motherhood*

9 J. GENDER RACE & JUST. 1, 18–54 (2005).

Researchers estimate that infertility rates may increase as more women delay childbearing until the years when reproductive fertility declines. For many infertile women, ART is perceived as more than a rational choice; it is a blessing. Accordingly, a growing number of women diagnosed as "infertile" are turning to ART in order to conceive.

. . .

Assisted conception technologies are medically complicated, painful for women, and expensive. Reproductive technology may offer "choice," but not all choices are equal, and some are more illusory than real. With incredibly low success rates, each attempt at these medical procedures is a financial gamble, yet the potential loss extends beyond the financial to the health of the mother, the surrogate (if one is used), and the potential fetus(es). Several surgeries with general anesthesia may be required with each fertility attempt or "cycle" that a woman undergoes. Thus, the complications associated with IVF are often distanced from the more glowing accounts about reproductive conception. . . .

. . .

ART techniques entail invasive, non-therapeutic procedures with the ovaries. Women endure a daily administration of drugs and hormone therapy. Each of these techniques within the ART family of procedures identified above, consist of several steps over the period of approximately two weeks. These steps are collectively known as *"cycles."* Cycles officially commence when a woman (the mother-to-be or donor) begins taking drugs to hyper-stimulate the production of eggs "or starts ovarian monitoring with the intent of having embryos transferred." If eggs are produced, the cycle proceeds to the next stage, *"egg retrieval."* Egg retrieval requires an abdominal surgery. First in this process, eggs are recovered from the woman's ovaries. Once retrieved, fertilization begins by clinically combining the sperm and the eggs, with the hope that viable embryos will result. If embryo selection occurs, the next step is *"transfer,"* which results in implantation into the uterus through the cervix (IVF) or directly into the fallopian tubes (GIFT or ZIFT). Not all cycles result in pregnancy; most do not. If one or more of the embryos implant successfully, the process then progresses to *"clinical pregnancy."* Because there is a low rate of successful implantation, most women undergo several cycles before pregnancy occurs or until they suspend the treatments.

Clinical pregnancies, however, do not indicate that fetuses will successfully carry to term, that children will be born "healthy," or that miscarriages will not result. *There are no guarantees in assisted reproduction and "success" is an elusive term in the reproductive industry.* This point cannot be overemphasized given the vulnerable and uninformed status of patients seeking fertility treatments. Instead, a "clinical pregnancy" simply indicates that a woman *achieved* or was pregnant at a certain time. To *diagnose* or monitor whether a fetus is actually healthy requires involvement with a separate group of physicians and necessitates more expensive, invasive procedures. To be sure, genetic diagnosis techniques are very helpful for women and couples seeking information about the health of their fetuses. Indeed, some of these fetal screening techniques are not new, including amniocentesis and fetal blood sampling, but the procedures have always posed health risks.

Nonetheless, while screening procedures provide diagnostic information about certain birth defects, they do not provide cures for the diagnosed defects. Thus, procedures to eliminate or reduce the risks of *birthing* ART children with congenital abnormalities are no less daunting, complicated, or expensive than the reproductive techniques to become pregnant. Yet, because ART pregnancies expose fetuses to greater health risks, parents are naturally motivated to screen for the very birth defects that result from or have a higher incidence of manifesting through reproductive technology. Herein a tragic medical and economic double bind unfolds. Given the strong correlation between ART and multiple births, certain health problems are bound to exist, such as low birth weight and cerebral palsy. Why would any woman voluntarily invite these challenges into her reproductive sphere?

. . .

Substantially low ART success rates deserve legal, social, and legislative scrutiny given the realities of patient manipulation and clinical misinformation guaranteeing pregnancy. ART failures affect only maternal health (although unhealthy uterine conditions could affect fetuses), while multiple gestations pose a serious health risk to fetuses. The health consequences are far more severe for infants than the consequences portrayed in ART advertisements. . . . Of the live pregnancies resulting from ART cycles, one third are multiple births. Consider the following: nearly 40% of ART live births to women under age 35 will produce multiple infants. For women aged 35 to 37, over 35% will produce multiple infants. Not only are these statistics uncharacteristic of typical pregnancies, but they result in added health harms to the fetuses.

. . .

What does reproductive liberty mean in the context of ART choice and these disquieting statistics? It is clear that women spend thousands of dollars on reproductive procedures with minimal possibility for success. Their engagement with the reproductive industry stimulates the growth and success of fertility clinics but does little in advancing women's maternal goals. For these reasons, we might question whether women's goals are not the only objectives valued in this process. In the battle for vigorous, innovative technology, perhaps a blind eye is turned to the mistakes along the way.

. . .

In the context of maternity, a woman choosing early childbearing over a career can be perceived as foolish and a less committed, intellectual or capable professional. For her, the glass ceiling is at shoulder-level. . . .

. . . ART accommodates the possibility of later childbearing while providing for early career entry. The technology provides an opportunity for parenting that would otherwise not be available to infertile couples. For thousands of women, the technology helps them avoid employment pitfalls and potentially uncomfortable confrontations in the workforce, including requesting maternity leave, a reduction in hours, or part-time employment in order to accommodate pregnancy and childrearing.

. . . A recent Defense Research Institute, DRI, survey, in which over 700 women attorneys participated, revealed that balancing family and work set back women's careers. . . . The majority of women surveyed (over 60%)

admitted that they seriously considered abandoning the practice of law because of "issues related to their gender, including work/life balance issues." Most persuasive and relevant to this article, however, is that 52% of those surveyed said that their jobs influenced "their personal decision on the timing of motherhood." The respondents confessed to postponing childbearing "so that they could meet the demands necessary to be considered for partnership." The women found those career demands to be in conflict with raising a family. . . .

. . .

Given the uphill battle for women to achieve equity in the workforce, even in the legal profession, it is perhaps little wonder that ART has such an incredibly seductive appeal. Career accommodation, at least, is part of ART's appeal. In this utopia, women can work longer and birth later. . . .

. . .

ART accommodates the very social inequities which limit women's opportunities to simultaneously pursue careers and families equal to their male counterparts. Thus it indirectly reifies problematic norms by providing a secondary "out" for the private sector by appearing to provide an unburdened utopian dream for women. This secondary option is not without its own murky socio-legal constructions and medical drawbacks. . . .

. . .

Feminists should avoid passive acceptance and complicity with the reproductive technology industry. The argument here is not against choice. The obvious benefits for some couples, such as gays and lesbians, cancer survivors, and others who otherwise have no biological options, are clear. Nor should highlighting the double bind in employment that leads to delayed childbearing be perceived as an indictment against reproductive technology. Reproductive technology serves a legitimate purpose and assists families in need.

Rather, the hope is to rethink what "choice" means among a number of real and impermissible or strained options. If, as studies suggest, women would prefer to bear children earlier, during optimal reproductive health, that should be part of a woman-focused agenda of "rights groups." This recommendation is not one strictly of gender accommodation in the workforce, although there might be laudable goals associated with that too. The value of such a position is indicated by the economic losses and health impairments experienced by women and their babies who as a last (and not best) option undergo aggressive reproductive treatments and bear the cost of raising more children than anticipated, including those suffering with disabilities. Such costs are not born exclusively by the parents. In the case of multiple birth babies requiring intensive medical treatment, states, private individuals, and corporations help to fill the financial gaps.

. . .

CHAPTER 7

DIVORCE

A. FAULT GROUNDS AND DEFENSES

1. HISTORICAL BACKGROUND

LAWRENCE M. FRIEDMAN, A HISTORY OF AMERICAN LAW

142–45 (3d ed. 2005).

England had been a "divorceless society," and remained that way until 1857. . . . The very wealthy might squeeze a rare private bill of divorce out of Parliament. . . . For the rest, unhappy husbands and wives had to be satisfied with annulment (no easy matter) or divorce from bed and board . . . , a form of legal separation. Separated couples had no right to remarry. No court before 1857 had authority to grant a divorce. The most common "solutions" when a marriage broke down were adultery and desertion.

In the colonial period, the South was generally faithful to English tradition. Absolute divorce was unknown, divorce from bed and board very rare. In New England, however, courts and legislatures occasionally granted a divorce. . . .

After Independence, the law and practice of divorce began to change; but regional differences remained quite strong. In the South, divorce continued to be unusual. The extreme case was South Carolina. . . . There was no such thing as absolute divorce in South Carolina throughout the nineteenth century. In other southern states, legislatures dissolved marriages by passing private divorce laws. . . .

North of the Mason–Dixon line, courtroom divorce replaced legislative divorce. Pennsylvania passed a general divorce law in 1785, Massachusetts one year later. Every New England state had a divorce law before 1800, along with New York, New Jersey, and Tennessee. In these states, divorce took the form of an ordinary lawsuit. An innocent spouse sued for divorce, which had to be based on legally acceptable "grounds." Grounds for divorce varied somewhat from state to state. New York's law of 1787 permitted absolute divorce only for adultery. Vermont, on the other hand, allowed divorce for impotence, adultery, intolerable severity, three years' willful desertion, and long absence with presumption of death (1798). . . .

This outbreak of divorce laws surely represented a real increase in the demand for legal divorce. More marriages seemed to be cracking under the strains of nineteenth century life. This increased the demand for divorce—or for legal separation. As the demand for divorce grew, private divorce bills became a nuisance—a pointless drain on the legislature's time. At the end of the period, some states still granted legislative divorce; but others had abolished them. Maryland passed a general divorce law in 1841; but for years, women still petitioned the legislature to set them free from odious or abusive husbands. Still, by the end of the century, private divorce laws had become extinct. The only road to divorce ran through the courtroom.

. . . Where did this growing demand for easy (or at least easier) divorce come from? The rate of divorce in the nineteenth century was the merest trickle compared to rates in later times. But it was noticeable. To many devout and respectable people, it was an alarming fire bell in the night, a symptom of moral dry rot and a cause in itself of further moral decay. President Timothy Dwight of Yale, in 1816, called the rise in divorces "dreadful beyond conception." . . . The "whole community," he warned, could be thrown "into a general prostitution."

This apocalyptic vision never really came to pass. The family, in any event, was not breaking down as badly as Dwight thought. Yes, the family was changing. There was a slow but real revolution in the way men and women related to each other. William O'Neill put it this way: "when families are large and loose, arouse few expectations, and make few demands, there is no need for divorce." That need arises when "families become the center of social organization." At this point, "their intimacy can become suffocating, their demands unbearable, and their expectations too high to be easily realizable. Divorce then becomes the safety valve that makes the whole system workable." . . .

. . . Easy divorce laws reflected changes in the nature of marriage; but they also grew out of the needs of the middle-class mass. The smallholder had to have some way to stabilize and legitimize relationships, to settle doubts about ownership of family property. It was the same general impulse that lay behind the common-law marriage. Divorce was simplest to obtain and divorce laws most advanced in those parts of the country—the West especially—least stratified by class. . . .

. . .

Since there was strong opinion on both sides, it was only natural that neither side got its way completely. Divorce laws were a kind of compromise. In general, the law never recognized full, free consensual divorce. It became simpler to get a divorce than in the past; but divorce was not routine or automatic. As we said, divorce was in form an adversary proceeding. An innocent and virtuous spouse sued an evil or neglectful partner. The defendant had to be at fault; there had to be "grounds" for the divorce. Otherwise, divorce was legally impossible. Later, the collusive or friendly divorce came to dominate the field. What went on in court was a show, a charade, an afterthought. The real issues were hammered out long beforehand. The law insisted that divorce by mutual consent was wrongful and impossible. But that was what in fact occurred.

NOTES

1. For accounts of divorce in the eighteenth and nineteenth centuries in the United States, *see* NORMA BASCH, FRAMING AMERICAN DIVORCE: FROM THE REVOLUTIONARY GENERATION TO THE VICTORIANS (1999); RICHARD H. CHUSED, PRIVATE ACTS IN PUBLIC PLACES: A SOCIAL HISTORY OF DIVORCE IN THE FORMATIVE ERA OF AMERICAN FAMILY LAW (1994).

2. As Judith Areen notes, Friedman "acknowledges that England was a 'divorceless society' until 1857 (except by Act of Parliament), yet never discusses the odd fact that this means divorce was available in some American colonies more than two centuries before it was accepted in England." Judith Areen, Assessing the Reformation Roots of American Marriage and Divorce Law 1 (June 16, 2011) (unpublished paper) (on file with the author). Areen argues that the true origins of the American law of divorce, custody, and alimony can be found in the Protestant doctrines of the Reformation. *Id.* at 2. This would explain why the New England colonies allowed divorce, while the Southern colonies, which were following Anglican tradition, did not. *Id.* at 5.

2. FAULT–BASED GROUNDS FOR DIVORCE

a. ADULTERY

Capone v. Capone

Court of Civil Appeals of Alabama, 2006.
962 So. 2d 835.

■ CRAWLEY, PRESIDING JUDGE.

John S. Capone, Jr. ("the husband"), and Beverly A. Capone ("the wife") were married in April 1984. In late December 2004, the parties separated and the husband sued the wife for a divorce; the wife counterclaimed for a divorce, alleging that the husband had committed adultery. After a trial, the trial court entered a judgment divorcing the parties on the grounds of adultery, incompatibility of temperament, and irretrievable breakdown of the marriage.

. . .

The wife testified that the husband [who was a sergeant major in the army] had had an affair with J.T., a mutual friend of the couple's and a coworker of the husband. According to the wife, J.T. and the husband would speak to each other regularly on the telephone and J.T. and the husband both lied to her about going on a temporary-duty assignment ("TDY") to Texas in November 2004. The wife said that she drove the husband to the Atlanta airport on November 13, 2004, and that he told her that he would be going to a TDY in Texas for a week. She also said that he told her that J.T. would also be on a TDY in Texas that week, but that she was taking a different flight. The wife further reported that the husband called her when his flight arrived and each day that week, reporting how hot it was and what activities he was engaging in. In addition, the wife stated that J.T. also called her during that week, likewise describing the TDY activities and how hot it was. She said that she believed that the husband and J.T. concocted the Texas TDY story as an elaborate scheme to cover up the husband's affair with J.T.

The wife also photographed the husband and his father's truck, which the husband was using, outside J.T.'s apartment on January 1, 2005. According to the wife, she arrived around 8:00 in the morning, central time, and that [sic] she watched J.T.'s apartment for approximately five hours. She said that she saw the husband go in and out of the apartment and load and unload boxes from J.T.'s vehicle; she also said that the husband left once and returned approximately 15 minutes later. The wife said that she later telephoned the husband on his cellular telephone and asked him what he was doing that day; according to the wife, the husband lied to her and told her he was with his father looking at old cars.

The husband denied having an affair with J.T., stating that they were friends. He said that he and J.T. had both attended a TDY in Texas in August, not November. He denied telling the wife that he was going to Texas in November because, he said, he attended a school in Stockbridge, Georgia, that week in November and, he testified, he had told his wife this.

He also admitted staying at J.T.'s apartment on certain nights after the parties' separation; however, he stated that he had always stayed in J.T.'s guest room.

The husband appeals the trial court's judgment, seeking reversal . . . .

The husband . . . argues that the wife failed to present sufficient evidence from which the trial court could have found that he had committed adultery with J.T.

> 'While it is difficult and somewhat rare to prove adultery by direct means, the charge of adultery in a divorce case may be proven by circumstantial evidence which creates more than a mere suspicion.' Proof to support the charge of adultery 'must be sufficiently strong to lead the guarded discretion of a reasonable and just mind to the conclusion of adultery as a necessary inference.'

The husband complains that the only evidence of adultery that the wife presented was her suspicion of an affair and the fact that the husband had visited and stayed at J.T.'s apartment at times after the parties' separation.

The evidence of adultery adduced in *Fowler* [*v. Fowler*, 636 So.2d 433, 435 (Ala. Civ. App. 1994)] consisted of the fact of the numerous telephone calls between the husband and a female coworker, some at very late hours and from public telephones, the fact that the husband and the coworker associated outside the office, the fact that the parties' marriage counselor considered the relationship between the husband and the coworker inappropriate, and the fact that the husband had rejected the wife during the period in which the telephone calls between the husband and the coworker had occurred. Those facts, while sufficient to create a suspicion of adultery, were not sufficient to " 'lead . . . to the conclusion of adultery as a necessary inference.' " *Id.* at 436. Likewise, the evidence in *Hooker* [*v. Hooker*, 593 So.2d 1023, 1025–26 (Ala.Civ.App.1991)], which consisted of late-night telephone calls and the alleged paramour's taking a job in the area and renting a room in the same building as the husband, was insufficient to create more than a suspicion of adultery.

Our supreme court has also had occasion to consider what degree of circumstantial evidence would "lead the guarded discretion of a reasonable and just mind to the conclusion of adultery as a necessary inference." In *Maddox* [*v. Maddox*, 281 Ala. 209, 212 (1967)], the husband presented the testimony of Jack Barbee, a friend of the husband's, who claimed to have seen the wife in a compromising situation. According to Barbee, while he was driving one day, he saw the wife stop her automobile near another automobile that an unidentified man was driving. Barbee said that the two automobiles then proceeded to drive to another location, at which time the wife and the man got into the same automobile. Once they were in the same automobile, said Barbee, the wife and the man drove to a motel. Barbee then explained that the wife and the man remained at the motel for at least an hour, based on the fact that Barbee, after concluding the business he had nearby in approximately one hour, drove through the motel parking lot and discovered the automobile still parked there.

In reversing the trial court's judgment insofar as it found that the wife had committed adultery, the court in *Maddox* stated:

> We are of the opinion that Barbee's testimony is wholly insufficient under our authorities to prove adultery. . . .

> We recognize the long-standing rule of presumption in favor of the correctness of the trial court's findings in a case where the evidence is

taken in the presence of the court. But in this case we are clear to the conclusion that the trial court's finding that the evidence showed that [the wife] was guilty of the charge of adultery is plainly and palpably wrong.

Id., 281 Ala. at 213.

The evidence at trial in this case indicated that both the wife and the husband had been friends with J.T. for a significant period of time. The wife had herself spent time with J.T., and the couple had often eaten dinner with J.T. when the husband and J.T. were required to travel on TDYs. The wife testified that she had been uncomfortable about the frequency of telephone calls between the husband and J.T.; she also said that she told her husband that his and J.T.'s frequent calls to each other might look inappropriate. The husband admitted that he and J.T. were friends and that he had stayed at J.T.'s apartment after the parties' separation; however, he denied having a romantic or sexual relationship with J.T.

The evidence concerning the husband's telephone contact with J.T. and his decision to stay overnight at her apartment on occasion after the parties' separation might lead one to suspect adultery. However, we agree with the husband that the evidence at trial was not a "sufficiently strong to lead the guarded discretion of a reasonable and just mind to the conclusion of adultery as a necessary inference." Thus, we must reverse the trial court's judgment insofar as it is based on a finding of adultery, and we instruct the court on remand to remove adultery as a ground for the divorce.

NOTES

1. What kind of evidence would have been sufficient to "lead the guarded discretion of a reasonable and just mind to the conclusion of adultery as a necessary inference"?

2. Some jurisdictions define adultery as "sexual intercourse between a married man and a woman not his wife, or a married woman and a man not her husband." *See, e.g., Marcotte v. Marcotte*, 886 So. 2d 671, 673 (La. Ct. App. 2004). A narrow definition of sexual intercourse led some courts in the past to conclude that non-coital, sexual acts were not sufficient to substantiate adultery. In a New Jersey case, the court held that "[e]ven actual proof of sex conduct with a third person other than intercourse is not tantamount to adultery." *W v. W*, 226 A.2d 860, 862 (N.J. Super. Ct. Ch. Div. 1967). Because the wife had proven through testimony of her gynecologist that her vagina had been completely occluded at the time of the alleged adultery due to cancer treatment, intercourse would have been impossible. *Id.* at 861. Adultery itself was therefore impossible, despite the fact that wife had been observed naked in a room with another man. *Id.* A later case abrogated this doctrine, observing that "[a]n extramarital relationship . . . is just as devastating to the spouse irrespective of the specific sexual act performed by the promiscuous spouse." *See S.B. v. S.J.B.*, 609 A.2d 124, 126 (N.J. Super. Ct. Ch. Div. 1992). Other courts have expanded their definition of adultery to non-coital sexual acts. *See, e.g., Menge v. Menge*, 491 So. 2d 700, 702 (La. Ct. App. 1986) (oral sex was within the definition of adultery). What are the different understandings of the harm of adultery underpinning these distinct approaches to its definition?

3. Because adultery was defined in many jurisdictions as nothing less than intercourse between a man and a woman, courts often held that a sexual relationship with a person of the same sex also did not constitute adultery. In a recent case, the Supreme Court of New Hampshire confirmed that adultery excluded sexual relations with a person of the same sex, based on the following reasoning:

> The plain and ordinary meaning of adultery is "voluntary sexual intercourse between a married man and someone other than his wife or between a married woman and someone other than her husband." *Webster's Third New International*

Dictionary 30 (unabridged ed.1961). Although the definition does not specifically state that the "someone" with whom one commits adultery must be of the opposite gender, it does require sexual intercourse.

The plain and ordinary meaning of sexual intercourse is "sexual connection esp. between humans: COITUS, COPULATION." *Webster's Third New International Dictionary* 2082. Coitus is defined to require "insertion of the penis in the vagina[ ]," *Webster's Third New International Dictionary* 441, which clearly can only take place between persons of the opposite gender.

In re Blanchflower, 834 A.2d 1010, 1011 (N.H. 2003). The court rejected the petitioner's argument that this distinction was against public policy because of its different treatment of people on the basis of sex or sexual orientation, noting that the basis for the decision was the non-coital nature of the act, regardless of the sex or sexual orientation of the person participating in it. *Id.* at 1012. Finally, the court engaged in a critique of the dissent's position:

The dissent defines adultery not as a specific act of intercourse, but as "extramarital intimate sexual activity with another." This standard would permit a hundred different judges and masters to decide just what individual acts are so sexually intimate as to meet the definition.

Id. Other courts have interpreted the term sexual intercourse more broadly. In the *Menge* case *supra*, which broadened the definition of adultery to non-coital sexual acts, the court also confirmed that adultery included homosexual sex. It cited a 1981 edition of Webster's Dictionary, which defined sexual intercourse to include acts of genital contact other than penetration. 491 So. 2d at 702. *See also RGM v. DEM*, 410 S.E.2d 564 (S.C. 1991). For a thorough discussion of the legal treatment of same-sex conduct under adultery laws (civil and criminal) *see* Peter Nicolas, *The Lavender Letter: Applying the Law of Adultery to Same–Sex Couples and Same–Sex Conduct*, 63 FLA. L. REV. 97 (2011).

4. A recently published study of 6,864 participants in 1975 and 2000, found significantly increased levels of monogamy in both homosexual and heterosexual couples. More specifically, the percentage of participants who had had sex with someone other than their partner since they had been a couple decreased across the board. For gay men it dropped from 82.6% to 59.4%, for lesbian women from 28.4% to 8.2%, for heterosexual men from 27. 6% to 10.1%. The least significant drop was in heterosexual females; their infidelity rate dropped from 22.9% to 14.2%, thus ending with more overall infidelity than heterosexual males. Gabrielle Gotta et al., *Heterosexual, Lesbian, and Gay Male Relationships: A Comparison of Couples in 1975 and 2000*, 50 FAM. PROCESS 353, 366 tbl.5 (2011).

b.   DESERTION

Jenkins v. Jenkins

Court of Appeal of Louisiana, Second Circuit, 2004.
882 So. 2d 705.

■ MOORE, J.

. . .

Frank Jenkins and Brenda Eldridge were married on September 16, 1983—his fourth and her first, although two of Frank's marriages were to the same woman. At the time Frank married Brenda, he had two sons, ages 19 and 17, and a daughter, Lindsey, age 2, from his previous marriage to Judy Bennett Jenkins. Frank had custody of Lindsey every other weekend.

. . .

The first signs of marital discord occurred near the end of the summer of 2000 when Brenda moved out of the house on August 29. She filed for a divorce on September 20, 2000, but the couple reconciled in January, 2001 after being separated for approximately five months.... One year later, on March 21, 2002, Brenda moved out again and filed for divorce on April 15, 2002. She sought interim and permanent spousal support.

. . .

Trial on all pending motions was held on October 8 and 10, 2003.... The judgment found that Brenda was without fault in the divorce and awarded her permanent periodic spousal support in the amount of $700 per month....

. . .

By his first assignment, Frank contends the trial court erred in finding that Brenda was free from fault. Frank alleges that Brenda abandoned him in March of 2002 when she moved out of the matrimonial domicile without lawful cause and refused to return. This abandonment, he argues, constitutes legal fault and precludes an award of permanent spousal support.

. . .

Abandonment was a ground for separation under former La. C.C. art. 138, and still constitutes legal fault for the purpose of preclusion of a party from permanent spousal support. The elements necessary to prove abandonment as provided in the former code articles are:

1.   the party has withdrawn from the common dwelling;

2.   the party left without lawful cause or justification; and

3.   the party has constantly refused to return to live with the other.

It is undisputed that Brenda moved out of the matrimonial domicile, and she had no plans to return. She testified as much. Frank testified that on one occasion he suggested that she return home and be a "decent wife." On the other hand, he also admitted at trial that he once told his former brother-in-law, whose wife (Brenda's sister) had also left him, that they may find that it's better that "the bitches are gone." Notwithstanding this remark, if we assume that Brenda refused to return, the sole question regarding the issue of abandonment is whether Brenda had lawful cause for leaving.

Brenda alleged in her petition and testified at trial that the cause of the physical separation and divorce was Frank's excessive drinking, which she said led to physical and verbal abuse directed at her. She testified his drinking began every afternoon around 2:00 o' clock at the trailer park with his brother L.C., and by the time Frank came home around 5:30 or 6:00, there was a personality change. He would have an additional three or four more drinks after he came home. She said when he was drinking, Frank verbally degraded her, accused her of infidelity, called her a "fucking bitch," and told her she could "carry her ass" if she did not like it. She testified that he pulled her hair and pinched her. On one occasion, she said he grabbed her hair and twisted her arm behind her back when she tried to walk away from him after they had been arguing about alcohol.

Brenda admitted that she sometimes drank two or three cocktails when they were at a party or holiday occasion, but denied that she drank excessively or ever became obnoxious from drinking. She said that she sometimes would go weeks without drinking, and has never drunk alcohol on a daily basis. She admitted that she received a DWI when she was a teenager.

Frank denied that he drank excessively or ever abused Brenda. He admitted that he drank two or three cocktails each evening during the marriage, but claimed that Brenda matched him drink for drink. Frank said that toward the end of the marriage, Brenda became very cold towards him and then left him without any reason. He says he was never physically or verbally abusive to Brenda.

Both parties tried to corroborate their testimony with testimony of friends and relatives.

.   .   .

To justify or establish lawful cause for leaving the common dwelling, the withdrawing spouse must make a showing which is substantially equivalent to a cause giving rise to grounds for separation under the former LSA–C.C. art. 138. Habitual intemperance or excesses, cruel treatment or outrages were included among the causes serving as "fault" grounds for separation under former Article 138.

It is well-settled that it is not the quantity of alcohol but rather the extent and habitualness of intoxication that constitutes "habitual intemperance" for purposes of "fault." Proof of intoxication on two or three occasions does not establish habitual intemperance. In *Broderick* [*v. Broderick*, 186 So. 5 (La. 1938)], Chief Justice O'Niell stated that

> habitual intemperance—like ill-treatment of one of the spouses toward the other—is not a just cause for a separation from bed and board unless such habitual intemperance, or such ill treatment, is of such a nature as to render their living together insupportable. And the question whether the habitual intemperance, or ill-treatment, in any given case, is of such a nature as to render the living together of the parties to the marriage unbearable,—or 'insupportable' . . .—is a question for the Court, and not for either of the parties to decide. In deciding that question, in any given case, the court must consider the habits of the complaining party, and his or her conduct towards the other party to the marriage. 186 So. at 6.

Regarding acts of cruelty, it has been held that where the conduct of a spouse is calculated permanently to destroy the peace of mind and happiness of the other so as to utterly destroy the objects of matrimony, a judgment of separation may be granted on grounds of cruelty.

The trial court in this case did not state for the record the factual determinations and credibility determinations upon which it based its conclusion that Brenda was not at fault and therefore implicitly finding that she was justified in leaving the house. Nevertheless, we conclude that the trial court must have found that Brenda had just cause for moving out of the matrimonial domicile based upon Frank's habitually excessive drinking and abusive language toward Brenda. The testimony supports a finding that Brenda drank on occasion with Frank, but not to excess and not with the same resultant personality change Frank underwent when he continued to drink. Brenda apparently complained to Frank about the excessive drinking to no avail, and it is obvious he does not believe he has a drinking problem. Frank's habitual, excessive consumption of alcohol followed by abusive language toward his wife seemed calculated to utterly destroy Brenda's peace of mind and happiness rendering the marriage unsupportable. For this reason, we conclude that the trial court did not err in finding that Brenda was without fault in the dissolution of the marriage.

NOTES

1. Desertion or abandonment was originally conceived of as the physical departure of a spouse from the marital home. However, if the departing spouse could establish a legitimate ground for divorce, then departing from the home was not considered desertion, as in this case. Because women were under a legal obligation to follow their spouses until roughly the last third of the twentieth century, a refusal to follow the husband could be construed as abandonment. Such constructions were later challenged on the basis of discrimination. *See Crosby v. Crosby*, 434 So.2d 162 (La. Ct. App. 1983).

2. Some jurisdictions have recognized constructive abandonment or desertion when a spouse refuses to engage in sexual relations. *See, e.g., Jacobs v. Jacobs*, 263 A.2d 155 (N.J. Super Ct. App. Div. 1970); *Ostriker v. Ostriker*, 609 N.Y.S.2d 922 (App. Div. 1994). This can lead courts into the dreaded domain of the marital bedroom. In *BM v. MM*, for example, the court had to decide whether a wife was under the obligation to continue her requests for sexual contact despite three previous occasions on which the husband allegedly had rebuffed her.

> The plaintiff testified that in July of 2003 her husband informed her that he wanted a divorce. She responded that she was not interested in getting a divorce and that she "would do anything to save our marriage." Because their sex life had been an issue between them she went on birth control pills to increase the spontaneity of sex. At this time the defendant had moved into the den and was sleeping there. She testified that [she] told him that [she] was anxious for sex and wanted a healthy sex life with him. When she was asked when she specifically remembered asking him for sex, she testified that in the winter of 2004 she purchased luxury sheets and she asked him to come to bed with her and he answered, "we'll see" but he did not sleep with her. In May of that year, 2004, after having gotten a letter from the defendant's attorney advising her of his desire for a divorce, the couple was away for their daughter's graduation weekend. She said that she asked him to come into her bed and he responded that he had gotten used to sleeping alone. The very next morning, while they were at a diner, she testified that she asked him if he "would like to use my toothbrush" which she said was their code for being intimate and she said that he did not answer her. Plaintiff testified under cross-examination that after this episode she did not believe she asked him to have sexual relations with her again. Beginning in May of 2004 and continuing through June of 2006 letters were exchanged between each party's counsel discussing future divorce proceedings and these were submitted into evidence. In fact, since that time the parties have continued to negotiate a divorce settlement to no avail and the plaintiff commenced the action November 20, 2008.
>
> . . .
>
> . . . The plaintiff's requests for sexual relations combined with the defendant's moving out of the marital bedroom and his advising her that he wanted a divorce by a lawyer's letter should relieve the plaintiff from continuing to ask for sexual relations.

880 N.Y.S.2d 850, 851–52 (2009).

3. Several trial courts in New York had expanded constructive abandonment to include the refusal to socially interact with a spouse. This interpretation, however, was struck down by the Appellate Division of the Supreme Court in *Davis v. Davis*, 889 N.Y.S.2d 611 (App. Div. 2009). The wife argued that her husband of forty-one years had constructively abandoned her because he refused to interact with her socially. *Id.* at 613. More specifically, she claimed that he would not celebrate important holidays with her including Valentine's Day, Christmas, Thanksgiving, or her birthday, and would not eat with her or attend any social events or services with her. *Id.* She alleged that he left while she was in the emergency room and expelled her possessions from the common bedroom. *Id.* While acknowledging that there was significant pressure from the matrimonial bench to expand constructive abandonment as a pragmatic way to deal with the lack of any no-fault ground for divorce in the state at the time, the court refused to do so. *Id.* at 620.

c. CRUELTY

Benscoter v. Benscoter

Superior Court of Pennsylvania, 1963.
200 Pa. Super. 251, 188 A.2d 859.

■ ERVIN, JUDGE.

In this case the husband filed a complaint in divorce . . . on the ground of indignities to the person. The master recommended that a divorce be granted; however the court below, after reviewing the matter, dismissed the complaint. . . .

. . . We . . . have arrived at an independent conclusion that the husband is not entitled to a divorce. . . .

The parties were married on August 21, 1946 in West Nanticoke, Pennsylvania. Four sons were born as a result of the marriage. . . . At the time of the hearing in January 1962 the plaintiff was 39 years of age and the defendant was 37 and she was suffering from multiple sclerosis.

The main indignity of which the husband complains is that the wife expressed her disappointment in failing to have a female child and that she verbally abused him and blamed him for this failure. The wife's alleged misconduct was sporadic in nature and did not constitute a course of conduct as required by law. It must be pointed out that the parties lived together for 15 years and it was not until August of 1961 that the plaintiff complained about the defendant. Therefore, the plaintiff's condition could not have been as intolerable nor his life so burdensome as he now alleges.

In August of 1958 the defendant-wife was stricken with the incurable disease, multiple sclerosis. As a result of this disease she has double vision, slurred speech, weakness of the muscles and she cannot walk without the assistance of another person or a cane. She falls down frequently. She lost weight and at the time of the hearing weighed only 86 pounds. She is subject to the frustrations that are attendant to this progressive disease. Even the plaintiff testified that in September of 1961 the defendant attempted to commit suicide three times. These circumstances cannot be blindly disregarded. Ill health both explains and excuses a wife's conduct and the acts of a spouse resulting from ill health do not furnish a ground for divorce.

During the summer of 1961 the defendant noticed that the plaintiff was taking more pride in his appearance, shaving every other day, using deodorants and changing clothes more frequently. Defendant's suspicions of another woman were aroused when she found prophylactics in the plaintiff's wallet and stains on his underclothes. Plaintiff offered a unique explanation of the presence of the prophylactics by stating that as game commissioner he used them for making turkey calls. The evidence clearly is that the plaintiff did accompany the other woman while trapping wild game and that he went swimming with her. We agree with the court below that plaintiff's interest in the other woman was above and beyond the call of duty. While the defendant was not able to prove adultery, certainly, under such circumstances, her suspicions were not unfounded. It was incumbent upon the plaintiff to show clearly and indubitably his status as the injured and innocent spouse. We do not believe that the plaintiff was the innocent and injured spouse.

The parties to a marriage take each other for better or for worse, in sickness and in health. The conclusion is inescapable that the plaintiff did not become dissatisfied with his wife until she became ill with multiple sclerosis. He cannot now discard her.

Hughes v. Hughes

Court of Appeal of Louisiana, Second Circuit, 1976.
326 So. 2d 877.

■ PRICE, JUDGE.

This appeal concerns the sufficiency of evidence presented to sustain a finding by the trial court that the defendant, Clifford Carey Hughes, was guilty of cruel treatment toward his wife, Marilyn Elizabeth Hughes, to entitle her to a separation from bed and board.

Mrs. Hughes filed this action in April 1974, alleging in her original and amended pleadings that defendant had treated her coldly and indifferently, was habitually intemperate, and that on an occasion in December 1971, he had ordered her from the family home and threatened to do her bodily harm. She further alleges they separated after this incident until November of 1972, at which time she returned to the domicile on defendant's promises to correct his behavior. Further allegations are made that after approximately one month, defendant returned to his general course of abusive treatment of plaintiff, including cursing and physical threats toward her, making it necessary that she again separate from defendant on December 18, 1973, and file this suit for a separation from bed and board.

Defendant denied plaintiff's accusations and reconvened for a separation in his favor contending the action of plaintiff in leaving the domicile on December 18th was without cause and constituted an abandonment.

. . .

In his reasons for judgment, the trial judge relied on the testimony of the only child of the marriage to resolve the conflicting testimony of the parties and to find plaintiff had proven her entitlement to a separation. This daughter who had married at the time of trial, was a college student during the troubled years of her parent's marriage but was present in the home on a number of occasions when there was discord between her parents. Her testimony confirmed her mother's allegations concerning the continuation of the cruel treatment by her father.

The trial judge construed her testimony to relate to the actions of defendant after the reconciliation in November 1972, and found the testimony sufficiently convincing to establish that defendant cursed his wife on many occasions and declared that he did not love either his wife or his daughter. The court found this conduct to constitute mental harassment sufficient to render the continued living together insupportable.

From our examination of the record, we find this conclusion to be supported by the evidence and to be in accord with the prior jurisprudence.

NOTES

1. How do you account for the difference in outcome in *Hughes* and *Benscoter*? If Mr. Benscoter came to your office to ask whether there was now any way for him to divorce Mrs. Benscoter, what would you advise? Should he move to Louisiana?

2. Cruelty originally was limited to bodily harm or a reasonable apprehension of bodily harm. *Evans v. Evans*, 1 Hagg.Cong.35, 161 Eng.Rep. 466 (Consistory Ct. of London, 1790). It gave the right to limited divorce; in other words, legal separation rather than the right to remarry. Today, most courts consider psychological harm sufficient to grant a divorce for cruelty or its statutory variant, indignities to the person. Even where "physical" harm is required, it may be met by such evidence as weight loss or nervousness. Nonetheless, a transitory psychological effect may not be enough. In *In re Guy*, the wife alleged that discovering her husband's suggestive e-mail communications with other women made her feel "angry, upset and distraught." 969 A.2d 373, 376 (N.H. 2009). The court held that this was not sufficient evidence of the injury required because it did not harm her physically, nor did it provoke the necessary "mental anguish." *Id.*

When there has been physical harm, most courts have held that one episode is not enough to justify a divorce, unless it was a particularly serious or shocking incident. This line of reasoning originates from the era before no-fault grounds were available and litigants were therefore trying to fit their factual circumstances into the available fault grounds. It also comes before widespread public consciousness about domestic violence (*see* Chapter 3, Section D.3). In *Das v. Das*, the Court of Special Appeals of Maryland observed the following:

> In reviewing these oft-cited cases on cruelty and excessively vicious conduct, we note that most are quite old and give victims little relief from their aggressive partners by modern standards. In part, we believe, the courts' reluctance to grant relief stems from the fact that cruelty and excessively vicious conduct were grounds for limited and not for absolute divorce, and Maryland courts have historically disfavored divorce from bed and board. . . .
>
>   . . .
>
> In the courts, we are now left holding a stack of cases–all "good law"–dating from the 1920's that no longer square with our modern understanding of appropriate family interaction. Verbal and physical abuse may have been tolerated in another era, and our predecessors at bar may have placed the continuity of the marital bond above the well-being of individual participants, but our values are different today.

754 A.2d 441, 459–61 (Md. Ct. Spec. App. 2000). The reluctance of courts to recognize one-time violent conduct as sufficient grounds on the basis of cruelty meant that if one left an abusive spouse after a violent incident, [one was] risking a counterclaim of desertion or abandonment by their abuser.

In some jurisdictions, the establishment of irreconcilable differences or other such no-fault grounds for divorce may have led courts to return to a more stringent standard of cruelty. In *Reed v. Reed*, the court explained that since incompatibility became available, the case law had returned to a more narrow definition of cruelty. 839 So.2d 565, 569 (Miss. Ct. App. 2003). Applying this stricter standard to the case, the court observed:

> In the course of a nineteen-year marriage, Gloria cites to one isolated physical attack [choking] and verbal threat. All of her other accusations such as Matthew's mean tricks, name-calling, and refusal to sleep with her, fall more in the categories of mere unkindness, rudeness, and incompatibility. The conduct alleged by Gloria, even if true, does not rise to the necessary level to prove cruelty.

Id. at 570–71.

3. In the jurisdictions that resisted characterizing homosexual sex as adultery, such conduct was sometimes categorized as cruel and inhuman treatment. *See, e.g., H. v. H.*, 157 A.2d 721, 726–27 (N.J. Super. Ct. App. Div. 1959) ("Added to the insult of sexual disloyalty Per se [sic] (which is present in ordinary adultery) is the natural revulsion arising from knowledge of the fact that the spouse's betrayal [sic] takes the form of a perversion. . . . Common sense and modern psychiatric knowledge concur as to the incompatibility of homosexuality and the subsistence of marriage between one so afflicted and a normal person."). *See also Thomas v. Thomas*, 1996 WL 679985

(Va. Ct. App. 1996). Do you think homosexual acts with a person other than a spouse should be considered cruelty for purposes of divorce? Could there be any problems with such state opprobrium of private sexual conduct after *Lawrence v. Texas*? Does your view change if a court includes any sexual act outside of marriage (homosexual or heterosexual) in the definition of cruelty?

3.   DEFENSES

Before the introduction of no-fault grounds, divorce was awarded on the basis of an allegation of fault on the part of the spouse and the law provided a series of defenses that the accused spouse could use against the divorce action. Many of these defenses still survive in jurisdictions that have retained fault grounds for divorce or that accord importance to marital misconduct for the purposes of equitable distribution or alimony. How does a defense against a fault ground operate when fault is the only available exit option, and how does it operate when there are no-fault grounds available as well?

a.   RECRIMINATION

Rankin v. Rankin

Superior Court of Pennsylvania, 1956.
181 Pa. Super. 414, 124 A.2d 639.

■ WRIGHT, JUDGE.

On February 3, 1953, Michael J. Rankin instituted an action in divorce against his wife, Edith L. Rankin. The parties were at that time aged 58 and 43 years, respectively. The complaint originally alleged cruel and barbarous treatment and indignities to the person, but was subsequently amended to include a charge of desertion. . . .

. . .

Considering first the question of cruel and barbarous treatment, we note that the master was "of the opinion that this ground has been established by clear and satisfactory evidence." However, the lower court said: "We have some doubt as to whether there is sufficient [evidence] in the case to sustain the cause of cruel and barbarous treatment." The term cruel and barbarous treatment comprises actual personal violence or a reasonable apprehension thereof, or such a course of treatment as endangers life or health and renders cohabitation unsafe. A single instance of cruelty may be so severe, and with such attending circumstances of atrocity, as to justify a divorce. The master bases his recommendation solely upon an incident which allegedly occurred when the parties were riding together in an automobile. As related in the master's report: "On one occasion while they were riding in a car with defendant driving, she stated: 'I am going to kill you, you son of a bitch', and proceeded to drive the car at a high rate of speed. On this occasion plaintiff succeeded in slowing down the car by turning the ignition key, following which he jumped from the car; thereupon defendant attempted to run him down." This circumstance was categorically denied by appellant, was entirely uncorroborated, and is utterly improbable in the light of appellee's testimony that he "jerked the key out to slow the car down," that he got out of the car, and that appellant then "turned the car" and endeavored "to get me along the road."

Next considering the question of indignities, the findings of the master which the lower court deemed important may be thus summarized: Appellant's "attitude toward plaintiff was one of marked antipathy; she called him vile and opprobrious names without provocation"; she refused to have children; she "had the furniture, with the exception of the box springs and mattress, removed from plaintiff's bedroom"; she "was frequently absent from the home without explanation . . . spit in his face and tried to strike him with a chair; that she threw hot water on plaintiff; and another time threatened him with a butcher knife." The lower court also considered the alleged incident in the automobile in connection with the charge of indignities, citing *Phipps v. Phipps*, 368 Pa. 291, 81 A.2d 523. Appellee testified that his wife had him arrested "a lot of times" for assault and battery. It should be here noted that much of appellee's testimony consisted of similar general expressions and was vague and indefinite throughout. Sidney A. Grubbs testified that, at the insistence of appellee, he went to see appellant in an effort to effect a reconciliation, but appellant said "there was no use to try to get along with that dumb hunky". Mollie M. Leathers testified that she frequently heard appellant use profanity and remark that she hated to see her husband come home. Harry Hickman testified concerning the removal of the bedroom furniture, and the use of profanity by appellant. Nora Stambaugh testified that appellant once took the keys to the truck, denied having them, but finally threw them on the floor.

As we pointed out in our opinion filed this day in *Moyer v. Moyer*, Pa.Super., 124 A.2d 632, 637: "In a proceeding for divorce on the grounds of indignities, it must clearly appear from the evidence that the plaintiff was the injured and innocent spouse". . . .

In her testimony appellant admitted using profanity and calling her husband names. By way of explanation, she alleged that she had acquired her knowledge of profanity from appellee, and that, in calling her husband "a dumb hunky", she was only repeating his own words. She flatly denied that she ever threw hot water on him, or threatened him with a butcher knife. With regard to the removal of the bedroom furniture, she testified that she and her husband had purchased a new bedroom suite. In anticipation of its delivery she and Mrs. Hickman removed the furniture, excepting the mattress and springs, from one bedroom. Before the suite could be delivered appellee cancelled the purchase. The outstanding incident about which appellant testified was a quarrel which took place while the Hickmans were living in the Rankin home. Appellant's story is that she fell to the floor, whereupon her husband stepped upon her, applying his full weight to her back. This is corroborated by Mrs. Hickman who testified that she was in the kitchen when she heard a commotion upstairs and appellant ran downstairs with her husband in pursuit. As appellant came into the kitchen she fell and appellee "kicked her and stepped on her." The witness went to call her husband and, when she returned, appellant was sitting on a chair and appellee was hitting her on the head with a belt. The master apparently chose to treat this entire incident as a fabrication, despite the fact that corroboration came, inter alia, from two unimpeachable sources. The one was James Morrison, the minister neighbor of the parties. The other was Dr. John A. Krosnoff, appellant's family physician, who testified that he treated appellant for multiple bruises, particularly of the left side of the face, a large swelling on the head, and bruises of the hip and back. When appellant's condition failed to improve, the doctor advised an x-ray examination which disclosed the herniated disc. A surgeon then performed an operation on appellant's spine which did not cure her condition. She is still undergoing treatment and is unable to work. On another occasion appellee pulled appellant from her chair and threw her out of the house. Appellant thereupon called the police and had appellee arrested for assault and battery. The charge was subsequently dropped. In answer to appellee's charge that she refused to have children, appellant testified that in 1949 it was necessary for her to undergo a hysterectomy. This was corroborated by Dr. Krosnoff, who referred appellant to Dr. Fisher for the operation. Catherine Reeves and Florence Mills, two other witnesses for appellant, testified that appellee frequently used vile language toward his wife. Both testified that appellant was a good cook and a good housekeeper, and that she tried to get along with her husband. As already noted, several witnesses testified that appellee threatened to kill his wife. When asked if he had not said that he "would like to shoot that God Damn Crummy," appellee's reply was: "I don't know if I did nor not."

The fact that married people do not get along well together does not justify a divorce. Testimony which proves merely an unhappy union, the parties being high strung temperamentally and unsuited to each other and neither being wholly innocent of the causes which resulted in the failure of their marriage, is insufficient to sustain a decree. If both are equally at fault, neither can clearly be said to be the innocent and injured spouse, and the law will leave them where they put themselves. At the very best, appellee's evidence might establish such a situation. A less favorable view of the evidence indicates that appellee was the principal offender, and that appellant was actually the innocent and injured spouse. In neither event has appellee established his right to a divorce on the ground of indignities.

NOTES

1. Although divorce proceedings are exclusively governed by statute in the United States, many courts resurrected defenses used by the ecclesiastical courts in England without statutory authorization. Some of these defenses were designed primarily to provide economic protection for wives in a society in which unattached women could not easily survive. They were never meant to bar divorce. Does use of the defense of recrimination make sense as a state policy today?

2. Recrimination as a bar to divorce has been expressly limited or abolished by statute or case law in most states. *See, e.g.,* MISS. CODE ANN. § 93–5–3 (2004); *Thomason v. Thomason*, 355 So. 2d 908, 910–11 (La. 1978) ("We do not understand that the doctrine of recrimination strengthens the institution of marriage or serves any useful social purpose.... If a divorce is possible where one party is guilty, there is all the more reason to grant a divorce where both are guilty. The judicially created doctrine of recrimination in divorce is therefore abrogated ...."). In other states the concept has been limited by: (1) granting a divorce to both spouses; (2) requiring that recrimination must be pleaded by a party rather than raised by the court; and (3) adopting the doctrine of comparative rectitude. *See Hendricks v. Hendricks*, 257 P.2d 366 (Utah 1953). The *Hendricks* court explained comparative rectitude as follows:

> [N]o good purpose, either social, moral, ethical or legal could be served by refusing to grant a divorce.... It would be but a mockery of the true concept of matrimony to thus purport to compel these two people, clearly ill-suited and maladjusted to each other to continue to retain the legal relationship of husband and wife.

> In view of the fact that neither spouse is accused of the commission of a felony, adultery or any other heinous offense but the reciprocal claims rest upon various acts and omissions alleged to constitute cruelty to the other, the trial court would best perform its function in the administration of justice by determining which party was least at fault, granting a divorce and adjusting their rights ....

Id. at 367.

3. Despite its diminished importance as a bar to divorce, recrimination might remain important when a jurisdiction attaches financial consequences to proof of marital misconduct, such as barring alimony. In *RGM v. DEM*, for instance, the Supreme Court of South Carolina ruled that recrimination was not a defense to the bar of alimony for the guilty spouse. 410 S.E.2d 564, 567 (S.C. 1991). In other words, if a spouse was guilty of marital misconduct (in this case adultery), the fact that the other spouse had also been guilty of marital misconduct did not block the operation of the alimony bar. Thus, the first spouse was prohibited from seeking alimony.

4. In terms of the evidence required, the spouse using recrimination as a defense can be subjected to the same standard of proof as the one required for establishing fault as a ground for divorce. *See Hunter v. Hunter*, 614 N.Y.S.2d 784 (App. Div. 1994) (defendant did not prove adultery, that is sexual intercourse or deviate sexual intercourse).

b. CONNIVANCE

Hollis v. Hollis

Court of Appeals of Virginia, 1993.
16 Va. App. 74, 427 S.E.2d 233.

■ Barrow, Judge.

In this appeal from a final decree of divorce, we address issues relating to the defense of connivance. We hold that a finding of connivance, the prior consent of one spouse to the misconduct of another, was sufficiently supported by the evidence. We further hold that the defense of connivance need not be expressly asserted in the pleadings.

Responding to the wife's allegation of the husband's adultery, the husband admitted that he was engaged in an adulterous relationship with another woman before the husband and wife separated. The wife asserted in her cross-bill for divorce that the husband's adultery began "on or about May 24, 1990." The husband acknowledged that he had lived together with another woman since March 22, 1990, and had had sexual relations with the other woman. The nature of the relationship was corroborated by the testimony of the other woman and the testimony of a private investigator.

The husband, however, asserted that his wife had urged him to date the other woman and that he had entered into a relationship only after his wife encouraged it. He introduced into evidence a handwritten letter from the wife dated February 4, 1990, which he received before an intimate relationship with the other woman began. The wife wrote that she wished to be free from her marriage but was afraid that the husband would "marry some bimbo." She wrote that she had seen the husband talking to the other woman at a Christmas party and hoped that the husband would fall in love with the other woman so that the wife could get out of her marriage. She said, "I want so badly for [the husband] to fall in love and share the rest of his life with someone who really loves him; someone like [the other woman], or even [the other woman]."

The wife wrote another letter dated February 22, 1990, which she gave to her husband in that month. She titled the letter, "Things I want [the husband and the other woman] to do before the divorce." In it she said that she wanted her husband and the other woman to "rent an apartment and live together for one year as man and wife everyday."

The husband and the other woman testified that they first had sexual relations at the Greenbrier Hotel the third weekend in February, 1990.

While there, they received flowers and a card from the wife. The card said, "My very best wishes to you both today, to your new beginning."

Finally, the husband and wife signed a document dated May 23, 1990, stating that the wife "consent[ed] to [the husband] moving out of our home." In it she also said that she was "aware that this could entail his moving in and living with another female." She agreed that she would not "use this against him as grounds for divorce or punitive action."

The trial court found that the husband's adultery resulted from the wife's "connivance and procurement" and granted the husband a divorce on no-fault grounds. The wife contends that the evidence does not support this finding and that the husband's failure to plead connivance barred his assertion of it.

. . .

Connivance is the consent, either expressed or implied, of one spouse to the proposed misconduct of the other spouse. One who consents to another's misconduct may not seek a divorce based on the misconduct.

The evidence supported the trial court's finding of the wife's connivance in the husband's misconduct. Her letters and the note accompanying the flowers amply support the finding that she encouraged, as well as consented to, the husband's adulterous relationship.

Furthermore, the husband was not barred from asserting this defense because he had not expressly pleaded the defense of connivance or condonation. His answer to the wife's cross-bill expressly denied her allegations that he had committed adultery that she had not procured or condoned. Furthermore, a court may, as with condonation, "deny a divorce where it appears from the record that the injured party has" connived to bring about the misconduct complained of.

For these reasons, we affirm the final decree of divorce.

Affirmed.

NOTES

1. Connivance may be thought of as a specific application of the clean hands doctrine. Since the conniving spouse has participated in bringing about the wrong complained of, she is barred from drawing legal benefit from it. Can it be said that one who suspects his spouse of adultery and hires a detective instead of stopping the contemplated adultery has connived to bring it about? If not, what is the relevant distinction with connivance? In *Wilson v. Wilson*, the husband saw the wife with a strange man, followed them to a hotel, stayed outside the room for about ten to fifteen minutes, and then burst in and caught them in bed together. 28 N.E. 167, 167 (Mass. 1891). The Supreme Judicial Court of Massachusetts held the following:

> Merely suffering, in a single case, a wife, whom he already suspects of having been guilty of adultery, to avail herself to the full extent of an opportunity to indulge her adulterous disposition, which she has arranged without his knowledge, does not constitute connivance on the part of the husband, even though he hopes he may obtain proof which will entitle him to a divorce . . . .

Id.

2. Courts will not always write a blank check to the suspecting spouse, however. In *Sargent v. Sargent*, the court thought that the husband should have dismissed the driver with whom he suspected his wife was cheating and should not have absented himself from the house on various nights, while employing detectives and servants to spy on her. 114 A. 428, 438 (N.J. Ch. 1920). The court noted that the husband "threw no protection around his wife." *Id.* He failed to protect her from the driver's "evil influence." *Id.* Note that courts would regularly hold that a husband's *positive* participation in bringing about his wife's suspected adultery was connivance. However, the holding in this case was influenced by racist considerations, quite common at the time. Consider the following paragraph from the court's decision:

> The thought of this cultured, refined, and modest appearing white woman in sexual relation with any negro is revolting to the senses. The acts and conduct with which she is charged by witnesses for petitioner are peculiarly contrary to the universal teachings and practice of the white society to which she belonged, which is absolutely opposed to any business or social alliance between the races and association of the nature charged against her with a black man, is repugnant to white women of her social standing, is unnatural, and rarely found to exist. So objectionable is it to the white race that in many states of our Union marriage between the races is prohibited. To convince me that defendant has departed from the traditions of her race and has fallen so low in the human scale and has been so grossly immoral as to place herself among the most debased of woman-kind the evidence must be so convincing and compelling as to leave no doubt whatever existing in my mind as to her guilt.

Id. at 429–30. The court spent several pages dismissing voluminous circumstantial evidence on various incidents of alleged adultery. The conclusion was that *if* one of them had indeed happened, the husband had connived to produce it. *Id.* at 439.

c. CONDONATION

Willan v. Willan

Court of Appeal for England and Wales, 1960.
2 All E.R. 463.

■ WILLMER, L.J.

... This is an appeal by a husband ... [whose] petition for dissolution of his marriage on the ground of cruelty ... [was] dismissed ... on the ground that the cruelty had been condoned.

The relevant facts lie within a comparatively small compass. The parties were married on June 2, 1925, and there are two children of the marriage, one born shortly after the marriage and the other born soon after the war in 1946. The husband was away on military service during the war, but cohabitation was resumed on his demobilisation, and he continued to live with his wife until the morning of Sept. 29, 1958.

The husband's case against the wife is that throughout the marriage, and more particularly in the latter part of it, she frequently and persistently assaulted him and showed violence to him and that she was immensely jealous of his relations with other women; and it was also said that she habitually used offensive and obscene language, calling him by horrible names and so forth. It is also alleged—and this is the real gravamen of the charge—that she frequently demanded sexual intercourse with him at times when he did not wish to have it, obliging him to conform to her wishes by indulging in various types of violence in order to bend his will to hers. In particular, it was said that she would pull his hair, catch hold of him by the ears, and shake his head violently to and fro; and, at any rate on one occasion, it was said that she kicked him on his injured leg, causing him great pain. She would also pester him far into the night to have sexual intercourse, so that eventually he was compelled to comply as the only means of getting his rest. That is the nature of the husband's case of cruelty which, as I have said, was found in his favour. I have referred to the details of it only because the alleged act of condonation is very largely bound up with the kind of conduct which is complained of by the husband as cruelty on the part of his wife.

It appears that for some time before the final separation the parties were on bad terms, although sexual intercourse was continuing in the circumstances which I have described. The husband at least was for some time in the hands of solicitors, and we know that on or about Aug. 13, 1958, the solicitors wrote on his behalf to his wife, complaining of her cruel conduct and informing her that the husband would be obliged to leave her. Even after that, however, life went on very much as before, the husband continuing to reside in the matrimonial home with his wife, and continuing to share the same bed with her. . . . It is not without significance, I think, that even after the solicitors' letter was written the husband is still found to be willingly and voluntarily having intercourse with his wife.

It is said (and this much is common ground between the parties) that, on the night of Sept. 28/29, i.e., the night before the husband left for the last time, an act of sexual intercourse took place between the parties. The husband says that that act, like many other acts previously, was induced by the wife pestering him far into the night, showing some degree of violence to him, pulling his hair and so forth and, finally, as I understand it, rolling on top of him, so that eventually, towards the small hours of the morning, and for the sake of peace, he did have intercourse with her. Thereafter, the parties appear to have gone straight to sleep, and the next thing that happened was the alarm clock going off at a quarter to six in the morning. The husband promptly got up, dressed and left the house at six o'clock in order to go to work. He kissed his wife and said goodbye, all in accordance with his usual procedure, the wife saying good-bye to him. I mention those facts as to what took place after the last act of intercourse because it was at one time suggested that, if that act of intercourse did amount to condonation, conduct subsequent thereto on the part of the wife was sufficient to bring about a revival. Clearly, however, on the evidence there never could have been any merit in that suggestion. . . .

When the case came on ultimately in this court . . . the first ground . . . was in the following terms:

> That the learned commissioner misdirected himself in law in that the last act of intercourse which occurred between the parties on the night of Sept. 28, 1958, could not have constituted condonation by reason of the fact that it constituted an important element of the cruelty complained of, and/or by reason of the fact that it took place when the petitioner was under duress and/or was not a free agent.

So stated, that ground of appeal runs two or three arguments together, and I will do my best to keep them separate. In the first place, it is said that this act of intercourse on the part of the husband could not be held to amount to condonation, because it was one and the same with an act which was of itself relied on as part of the cruelty alleged. . . . Certainly there is no finding by the learned commissioner that the last act of intercourse relied on as condonation was one with the cruelty alleged by the husband against the wife. Furthermore, as it seems to me, and as I indicated during the argument, the contention is really the result of muddled thinking, because it confuses the actual act of sexual intercourse, which constitutes the evidence of condonation, with the prior conduct complained of on the part of the wife, whereby she induced the act of intercourse. I can well understand that pestering in such circumstances on the part of the wife, in such a way as to deny the husband sleep, more particularly if accompanied by the pulling of his hair, might very well be capable of amounting to cruelty. But, whether that be so or not, I find it impossible to say that the subsequent action of the wife in submitting herself to an act of sexual intercourse could in any circumstances amount to an act of cruelty against the husband. . . .

Then it was said that this act of intercourse was induced by duress on the part of the wife, and that the husband was not to be regarded as a free agent. It is well established that, whatever may be the position of a wife, in the case of a husband the fact of having intercourse with the wife, with full knowledge of the matrimonial offence of which complaint is made, is conclusive evidence of condonation by the husband of the wife. It is conclusive evidence because it is the best possible way of showing that the wife has been reinstated as a wife. Only one exception to that rule was accepted by the House of Lords . . . and that is the case where the act of intercourse is induced by fraud on the part of the wife. Subject to that . . . intercourse by a husband with his wife after knowledge of the matters complained of is conclusive evidence of condonation.

. . .

All that has been proved in this case is that the wife used means, to which exception may well be taken, for the purpose of persuading her husband to have intercourse with her. He was free to submit or to resist. He was free, I suppose, to have run away, but in the end he decided that the best course to take was to submit to her wishes. I dare say he did show unwillingness, but to say that he showed unwillingness is not to say that he acted involuntarily. It might be otherwise in the case of a wife; but in the case of a husband who has sexual intercourse it can only be said of him that what he does he does on purpose, and that sexual intercourse with his wife must be a voluntary act on his part.

NOTES

1. Can this defense be squared with the interest society may have in encouraging attempts at reconciliation? This tension between condonation and reconciliation may explain why courts have differed so much as to what is required to establish condonation. *See, e.g., Bush v. Bush*, 205 S.W. 895 (Ark. 1918) (verbal forgiveness may suffice); *Lowensten v. Lowensten*, 190 A.2d 882 (N.J. Super. Ct. App. Div. 1963) (renewal of sexual relations is essential); *Seiferth v. Seiferth*, 132 So.2d 471 (Fla. Dist. Ct. App.1961) (while cohabitation may be evidence of condonation, forgiveness is still a necessary element). In *Hoffman v. Hoffman*, the Superior Court of Pennsylvania justified its choice of a single sexual act post-adultery as the standard for condonation in the following way:

> The resumption of sexual intercourse in this situation is an objective standard by which to judge the condonation of that behavior by the other spouse. The surrounding circumstances, such as the state of mind of that spouse, are subjective and cannot be accurately gauged. To find otherwise would require this Court to engage in a subjective review of the parties' marital relationship.

762 A.2d 766, 771 (Pa. Super. Ct. 2000). What do you think about this reasoning?

2. One court noted, " 'Condonation,' say the books, with respect to a woman, is held not to bear so strictly, 'because it is not improper she should for a time show a patient forbearance;' . . . [and] '[s]he may have no means of support except under his roof. . . .' " *Glass v. Glass*, 2 A.2d 443, 447 (Md. 1938) (quoting *Bowic v. Bowic*, 3 Md. Ch. 51, 55 (1850)). Could the *Glass* test today be successfully challenged as an unconstitutional gender-based standard?

d. COLLUSION

Fuchs v. Fuchs

Supreme Court of New York, Kings County, 1946.
64 N.Y.S.2d 487.

■ DALY, JUSTICE.

. . .

The final judgment of divorce was rendered on April 15, 1946, in favor of the plaintiff on defendant's default. Prior to the commencement of this action the plaintiff had commenced a previous action on August 30, 1945, in which action defendant appeared and denied the material allegations of the complaint. In a motion made in that action defendant alleged that the plaintiff was then living with a woman (whom he has married since the decree in this action became final) and had been having relations with her for four years prior thereto. Thereafter the first action for divorce was discontinued and this action was commenced on October 30, 1945. Defendant claims that the plaintiff stated he wanted a divorce and if she would permit him to obtain it he would give her full, absolute and complete custody of the child. Defendant states that she was interested only in the custody of her child and that on plaintiff's assurance that she would always have custody, she was willing to allow him the divorce he sought. She entered into an agreement with the plaintiff, by the terms of which the custody of the child was to remain with her and as soon as this agreement was made defendant advised her attorney not to contest the divorce action. She denies ever having committed adultery with anyone.

Where a party has deliberately and intentionally suffered a default, the motion to vacate will be denied. "It is deemed in such case that there is, in fact, no default, but an abandonment of the cause and a submission to the entry of judgment." Since a party cannot consent to the entry of a decree of divorce, it is obvious why the rule is different in divorce cases. As pointed out in 9 Carmody N.Y.Prac., Sec. 160, p. 242, "The strict rules relating to opening defaults is [sic] not applied to actions for divorce, because of the well-known vigilance of the courts to prevent collusion, and because of the general interest of the people of the state in the preservation of the matrimonial status of its citizens."

. . . This case is analogous to *Jacoby v. Jacoby*, 245 App.Div. 763, 280 N.Y.S. 611, 612, where it appeared "that defendant may have a good defense and was induced to refrain from answering the complaint by plaintiff's false promises to continue his payments of $40 a week during the life of the defendant, and by his threat to discontinue such payments if she defended the action." The Appellate Division, Second Department, reversed an order denying her motion to open her default and granted her leave to appear and answer. A threat to deprive a mother of her child would be an even more compelling inducement to persuade her to default in a divorce action. . . .

Even though the defendant may be tainted with fraud herself, in that she was willing to permit a fraud upon the court and thus does not come into court with clean hands, the state has an interest in the matrimonial status of its citizens and the two guilty spouses are not the only parties in interest.

The defendant's right to open the default and defend the action is not affected by the fact that the plaintiff has remarried. In each of the cited cases, the plaintiff had remarried but the court set aside the default and permitted the defendant to defend, allowing the decree to stand until the trial and determination of the issue between the plaintiff and defendant and providing in the order that, if the defense were sustained, the decree should be set aside and the complaint dismissed, but if the defendant were defeated, the decree should stand in full force for the protection of the second wife. The rights of all concerned will best be served by making a similar order in this case. Accordingly, defendant's motion to set aside her default is granted, and the defendant will be permitted to answer the complaint herein within ten days after the service of a copy of the order to be entered hereon with notice of entry. The decree may stand until the trial. If the defense be sustained, the decree shall be vacated and the complaint dismissed; but if plaintiff prevail, the decree shall remain in full force for the protection of plaintiff's second wife.

NOTES

1. *Compare Fuchs with Fender v. Crosby*, 76 S.E.2d 769 (Ga. 1953) (husband, who alleged he was induced to agree to a collusive divorce by wife who claimed she needed it for her health, was denied the chance to overturn the decree on grounds of estoppel, even though wife had allegedly lied and immediately married another man).

2. Before the introduction of no-fault grounds for divorce, spouses who mutually agreed to get divorced manufactured grounds or simply did not contest the other spouse's allegations. This led many courts to adopt heightened evidentiary requirements. Consider for example the court's observation in the following case:

> A petition for divorce will not be granted on the testimony of the complainant alone, even if the defendant admits the allegations. While I understand that corroboration is required to prevent collusion, I believe the law needs to be changed because the corroboration requirement seems to operate as an irrebuttable presumption of collusion. Courts should not presume collusion. Moreover, the corroborative testimony of a third party does not guarantee there will be no collusion. After all, the third party could be involved in the collusion.

Dee v. Dee, 258 S.W.3d 405, 407–08 (Ark. Ct. App. 2007) (Griffen, J., concurring). Extensive collusion and the manufacturing of grounds by the spouses led many judges and lawyers to support divorce reforms in order to spare spouses and the judicial system from the indignities of false allegations.

e. INSANITY

Anonymous v. Anonymous

Supreme Court of New York, Nassau County, 1962.
37 Misc. 2d 773, 236 N.Y.S.2d 288.

■ BERNARD S. MEYER, JUSTICE.

Involved in this divorce action is the question under what circumstances does the mental condition of an erring spouse constitute a defense.... [New York] has enacted no statute fixing criteria for responsibility for conduct in violation of marital obligations. New York case law has recognized that an insane wife is incapable of abandoning her husband and refused a divorce to a husband whose wife committed adultery while suffering from dementia praecox (*Laudo v. Laudo*, 188 App.Div. 699, 177 N.Y.S. 396). Some of those cases emphasize the marital obligation to provide support, including medical assistance, to an afflicted spouse; in none was it necessary to consider the degree of affliction that would excuse infidelity.

Should the standard be that advanced in M'Naghten's Case, 10 Cl. & F. 200, and now embodied in Penal Law, § 1120: ability to distinguish right from wrong or to understand the nature and quality of the act? ... Or should the criteria of responsibility be that suggested as a revision of the criminal rule in *Durham v. United States*, 94 U.S.App.D.C. 228, 214 F.2d 862, and expanded upon in *Carter v. United States*, 102 U.S.App.D.C. 227, 252 F.2d 608 under which the defense is established by showing (a) a mental disease or defect, and (b) that the act in question was the product or result of the disease or defect; that is—that the defendant would not have committed the act if he had not been diseased as he was.... While at first blush the conclusion of the American Bar Foundation's study of "The Mentally Disabled and the Law" appears contrary to use of Durham–Carter standards in matrimonial cases, its suggestion (at p. 203) that "serious thought should be given to the use [in divorce cases] of standards defining civil hospitalization" of necessity refers only to the presence of a mental disease or defect and is not understood as excluding causal relationship in matrimonial cases, although causal connection has no bearing on civil hospitalization.

... In the present case, however, it is not necessary for the court to choose between the possible standards, for whichever is applied, the Court's conclusion is that plaintiff is entitled to judgment of divorce.

The burden of proving mental condition relieving defendant of responsibility is on defendant. Her sanity is presumed and the presumption must be overcome by a contrary showing. To overcome the presumption defendant offered the testimony of her psychiatrist and the record of her hospitalization at Meadowbrook a few days after the incident which is the basis of this action. The psychiatrist testified that defendant had been under his care since September 1960; that she was even now highly unstable; that he had first diagnosed her as a character disorder, but later concluded that she was schizophrenic-affective type; ... that prior to the incident she was aware that she was being followed since plaintiff had told her in the presence of the psychiatrist that as a result of prior infidelities he intended to have her followed; that defendant had discussed the rendezvous with the witness three days before it occurred and told him that she had sought to dissuade her paramour from going through with it and had told the paramour that he might be involved in a lawsuit; that defendant nonetheless felt compelled to go ahead with the meeting; that she was motivated by emotionality rather than rational thinking and felt justified in what she was going to do; that she was unable to determine that it was a wrong act; that it was for her primarily a means of getting even with her father, and to a lesser degree with plaintiff, both of whom considered her a "bad" person; that in his opinion she was unable to control her actions and in poor contact with reality at the time of the incident, and was then unable to distinguish the true nature of the act she was committing or to differentiate right from wrong ....

On the other side of the scale is the testimony of plaintiff's psychiatrist that in his opinion while defendant has had psychiatric difficulty and was emotionally unstable and in need of treatment, she was sufficiently intact to be able to use the ordinary standards of right and wrong; that she behaved in a manner which indicated that she was aware of those factors; that she knew at the time of the incident that she was committing adultery and that it was wrong; that she is not schizophrenic and that her stating to him that she had no recollection of the incident but being able quickly and accurately to supply data unrelated to the incident indicated to him that she was lying in an attempt to evade discussion of the incident with him. . . .

The court concludes that defendant has not sustained the burden of proof. Had she testified the impressions gained by the court during her testimony would have supported the opinion of one or the other of the psychiatrists. At the base of the differing opinions of the experts is their differing views of her credibility. Her credibility is also the central issue in this case. Deprived of the opportunity of forming first hand impressions concerning defendant's credibility, the court can choose between the experts' views only on the basis of the consistency of those views with the evidence as a whole. The inconsistency between the conclusion that defendant was driven into acts of adultery by an irrational necessity to get even with her father and with plaintiff and, on the one hand, the homosexual overtures at the hospital, and, on the other, the implication in defendant's affidavit that the acts of adultery resulted from the necessity of proving herself a woman, suggests to the court that the hospital overtures and the affidavit's contention are afterthoughts contrived by defendant to escape the consequences of her act. That defendant went ahead with her tryst notwithstanding she had been warned she was being followed can be interpreted as irrational but might also indicate either disbelief that plaintiff would take action or a rational conclusion on her part that her relationship with plaintiff had so far deteriorated that she didn't care whether the marriage continued or not. While her statement to her psychiatrist that she tried to talk the paramour out of going ahead with their plans is consistent with irrationality, her actions when caught and thereafter, as demonstrated by word and deed, suggest a realization of the nature of her conduct and a desire to avoid its consequences. On all of the evidence the court concludes that defendant has not demonstrated by a preponderance of the credible evidence that she was, as pleaded in her separate defense, "suffering from mental and emotional disorders so as to make her incompetent and irresponsible for the acts charged against her in the complaint."

Plaintiff is, therefore, awarded judgment of divorce. . . .

NOTES

1. What policy, if any, is served by making insanity a defense to divorce actions?

2. In 1847, in *Matchin v. Matchin*, 6 Pa. 332 (1847), the Supreme Court of Pennsylvania held that insanity was not a defense to a divorce on adultery grounds, on the theory that allowing such a defense might result in imposing spurious offspring on the husband. In 1960, however, in *Manley v. Manley*, 164 A.2d 113, 120 (Pa. Super. Ct. 1960), the court declined to follow the *Matchin* rule explaining: "[T]here is authority for our ignoring an ancient higher court rule which is unreasonable and unjust by all known standards, and which has frequently been examined and universally rejected by legal authorities and by courts in other jurisdictions."

3. Even though insanity that temporarily precludes control over one's actions can constitute a defense against fault-based divorce allegations, long-term insanity can provide an independent ground for divorce in some jurisdictions. In Mississippi, for example, incurable mental illness is a ground for divorce.

> However, no divorce shall be granted upon this ground unless the party with mental illness has been under regular treatment for mental illness and causes thereof, confined in an institution for persons with mental illness for a period of at least three (3) years immediately preceding the commencement of the action. . . . No divorce shall be granted because of mental illness until after a

thorough examination of the person with mental illness by two (2) physicians who are recognized authorities on mental diseases.... Before incurable mental illness can be successfully proven as a ground for divorce, it shall be necessary that both of those physicians make affidavit that the patient is a person with mental illness at the time of the examination, and both affidavits shall be made a part of the permanent record of the divorce proceedings and shall create the prima facie presumption of incurable mental illness, such as would justify a divorce based on that ground.... [P]rocess shall be served upon the next blood relative and guardian, if any. If there is no legal guardian, the court shall appoint a guardian ad litem to represent the interest of the person with mental illness. The relative or guardian and superintendent of the hospital or institution shall be entitled to appear and be heard upon any and all issues. The status of the parties as to the support and maintenance of the person with mental illness shall not be altered in any way by the granting of the divorce.

MISS. CODE. ANN. § 93–5–1 (2004 & Supp. 2011). Why do you suppose there are such extensive procedural requirements for granting divorce on this basis?

4.   Should courts allow divorce actions filed on behalf of incapacitated spouses by their guardians? *See, e.g., Phillips v. Phillips,* 45 S.E.2d 621 (Ga. 1947) (divorce suit is a personal right that cannot be exercised by a guardian). *But see Broach v. Broach,* 895 N.E.2d 640 (Ohio Ct. App. 2008) (rules of civil procedure allow guardian to pursue law suits on behalf of incompetent person with no exception made, therefore divorce suit acceptable).

B.   NO FAULT GROUNDS

With California leading the way in 1969, every state by 1985 had adopted, at least in part, a "no-fault" approach to divorce. This section will examine how this transition from fault to no-fault unfolded and the main points of contention that have arisen in the adjudication and aftermath of no-fault divorce.

Contrary to the commonly held view that the advent of no-fault swept fault away, most states simply added a no-fault ground for divorce to their existing list of fault grounds. Today, only nineteen states and the District of Columbia provide for no-fault grounds as the exclusive means of exiting a marriage.[1] By contrast, thirty-one states simply added a no-fault ground to their existing list of fault grounds. Forty states provide for irreconcilable differences, irremediable breakdown, incompatibility of the spouses, or some such similar ground as their main no-fault ground, while a majority of states also allow a separation of a certain duration (six months to three years) to function as a ground for divorce.

In three states, Pennsylvania, Mississippi, and Washington, the no-fault ground of divorce can be asserted—at least initially—only when the spouses are filing jointly or by mutual consent. However, it is solely in Mississippi that contest of the ground by the other spouse leads to the rejection of that ground for divorce.[2] In both Pennsylvania and Washington, the court can accept irreconcilable differences, if the parties have lived separate and apart for more than two years in the former case[3] or if the court itself finds that

---

1.   *See* Linda D. Elrod & Robert G. Spector, *A Review of the Year in Family Law: Looking at Interjurisdictional Recognition,* 43 FAM. L.Q. 923, 796 chart 4 (2010). In the case of Arizona, fault is preserved for covenant marriages.

2.   MISS. CODE ANN. § 93–5–2 (2004 & Supp. 2011).

3.   23 PA. CONS. STAT. ANN. § 3301 (West 2010).

the marriage has been irretrievably broken in the latter.[4] It therefore seems that Mississippi is the only state not to establish a pure no-fault reason for divorce absent mutual consent.

Until recently, New York provided only for fault grounds, with the exception of a mutual consent to divorce on the basis of a separation. The state of the law in New York had come under increasing criticism over the past few years.[5] In October 2010, New York joined the rest of the country in adopting an independent no-fault ground (irretrievable breakdown for a period of six months). The divorce decree, however, cannot be finalized until all other ancillary issues have been settled by the parties or the court.[6]

Even in states where irreconcilable differences constitute the main ground for divorce, a contest by the other spouse can lead to significant delays and added costs. A characterization of no-fault divorce as automatic or unilateral is therefore a very partial description of the still burdensome process through which a marriage can be dissolved legally. In some countries, statutes have provided for expedient processes of exit, which can be as short as fifteen days, when the spouses agree and there are no children and no unresolved property issues involved.[7]

1.   THE CALIFORNIA REFORMS

California's reforms provided the impetus for the eventual adoption of no-fault grounds for divorce in every jurisdiction. Evidence indicates, however, that many supporters of the reforms saw no-fault divorce as a way to reduce the incidence of divorce, rather than simply as a means for spouses to walk away from their marriages easily. The material in this section discusses some of this evidence. Take note of how the California no-fault statute's failure to include lengthy separation as a ground for divorce arguably reflects this aim, and how it contrasts with the Uniform Marriage and Divorce Act's no-fault divorce provisions. Consider also how the California experience provides an example of how reforms can be adopted, understood, and implemented in ways that may be inconsistent with the aims of those who originally propose them.

REPORT OF THE [CALIFORNIA] GOVERNOR'S COMMISSION ON THE FAMILY

27–28 (1966).

. . .

. . . [T]he marital fault doctrine forces the Court to concentrate upon superficial aspects of the relationship of the parties before it, and it regards

---

4. WASH. REV. CODE § 26.09.030 (2010).

5. In her 2005 State of the Judiciary address, Chief Judge of the New York Court of Appeals Judith S. Kaye called on the state legislature to pass a no-fault provision that allows one party to invoke divorce unilaterally. Judge Kaye underlined that fault grounds heighten the already existing antagonisms between parties and waste judicial and human resources while not necessarily achieving the goal of preserving marriages. *See* Patrick D. Healey, *Chief Judge Asks Legislature to Consider No–Fault Divorce*, N.Y. TIMES, Feb. 8, 2005, at B8.

6. N.Y. DOM. REL. LAW § 170 (McKinney 2010).

7. For such a case in Mexico's Federal District *see* Sharilyn R. Payne, *A Comparative Study of the Divorce Laws of California and the Mexican Federal District*, 21 HASTINGS INT'L & COMP. L. REV. 979, 981–82 (1998).

each of the "grounds" and the acts or situations they represent as having precisely the same significance in each marriage. We have concluded that this is unrealistic.... As a recent study by a Church of England Commission put it, the retention of specific fault grounds leads to needless divorce and "invests with spurious objectivity acts [whose] real significance varies widely" with the varied marriage relationships that provide their setting.[17]

We believe that it is personally tragic and socially destructive that the Court should be absolutely required, upon proof of a single act of adultery or "extreme cruelty"—perhaps regretted as soon as committed—to end a marriage which may yet contain a spark of life. Under present law, the Court cannot go beyond this technical fault and reach the essential question: namely, has this particular marriage relationship so far broken down that the legitimate objects of matrimony have been destroyed and there remains no reasonable likelihood that this marriage can be saved?

It is precisely this question that we believe the Family Court must deal with, and our studies upon this point have led us to one conclusion: If the Family Court is to function at all, it must be by a procedure which permits and requires dissolution of a family only upon a finding of irremediable breakdown of the marriage. The marital relationship is a deep and complex one, and should not be sundered by the law unless the Court finds that the legitimate objects of the marriage have been irretrievably lost....

James Herbie Difonzo, *Customized Marriage*

75 IND. L.J. 875, 885–908 (2000).

Understanding our present divorce law conundrum requires a pointed look at the past. No-fault divorce's debut in 1969 was not entirely unprecedented. It came at the cusp of a rich history of marked changes in divorce law and practice, a palimpsest seemingly erased by the conversion—at one stroke—of divorce grounds from an assortment of multifaceted fault, "living apart," and even "temperamental incompatibility" statutes, into the touchstone of the no-fault revolution: "irreconcilable differences." In fact, however, the transformation of divorce grounds was far more complex, prolonged, and incomplete than this thumbnail sketch suggests. Beginning in the mid-nineteenth century many states added (and frequently later modified) a no-fault divorce provision onto the list of statutory marital dissolution grounds, while retaining a full menu of fault grounds. In 1866, for instance, Wisconsin added a provision allowing for divorce if the couple had lived apart for five years. An 1893 Rhode Island law similarly carved out an exception to the fault matrix for couples whose separation lasted ten years. At the beginning of the decade which gave birth to modern no-fault, Virginia added a provision allowing for divorce after three years living apart, but soon reduced the waiting period to two years. At present, the living apart period consists of one year. But if the couple have no minor children and have entered into a property settlement agreement, they need only live apart for six months. Similarly, when New Mexico added an incompatibility divorce ground in 1933, as when Oklahoma did two decades later, none of the statutory fault grounds were legislatively repealed. Through this incremental and tortuous fashion, more than half of American jurisdictions had enacted no-fault divorce grounds before 1970. Thus, what truly marks California's

---

17. REPORT OF THE MORTIMER COMMISSION OF THE CHURCH OF ENGLAND, PUTTING ASUNDER: A DIVORCE LAW FOR CONTEMPORARY SOCIETY 29 (1966).

divorce reform as revolutionary is not the creation of a no-fault ground, but rather the elimination of fault-based alternatives for divorce-minded spouses.

The "irreconcilable differences" standard minted in 1969 as the sole divorce criterion in California was designed to transform divorce litigation from an adversarial tempest to an amiable teapot. The routinization of divorce was intended to drain the anger from the process of family dissolution, thus ending the mutual flagellation thought to be endemic to divorce courtroom explosions. . . .

. . .

According to Herma Hill Kay, a leading figure in the no-fault movement, by the 1960s "it was impossible to make divorce easier in California than it already was." In typical ten minute court hearings, ninety-five percent of California divorce complainants recited accounts of their spouses' "extreme cruelty" destroying their marriage. This statutory requirement could be met by the wife's simple assertion that her husband was "cold and indifferent," which caused her to become "nervous and upset."

. . .

In the 1960s, California's executive and legislative branches combined forces to try to buttress family life through divorce reform. . . .

. . .

. . . Each stage of no-fault divorce litigation was designed to convert the divorce action into a conciliation procedure. A determined couple could, of course, dodge the persuasive machinations and endure the delays—eight months or longer in a busy urban court—until they were granted a "dissolution." But the very process of stalling divorce-minded partners was an integral component of therapeutic divorce, premised on its belief that slowing the divorce process would dissuade many couples from seeking to dissolve their marriages.

. . .

Upon signing into law the first modern no-fault divorce statute, California Governor Ronald Reagan affirmed that "[d]ivorce is a tragic thing." He hoped that the new law would "do much to remove the sideshow elements of many divorce cases . . . [and] the acrimony and bitterness between a couple that is harmful not only to their children but also to society as a whole." But the governor's message missed an important goal of the new statute. The Family Law Act of 1969 heralded the era of no-fault divorce, but it was intended to render divorce more difficult to obtain.

. . .

At the dawn of the no-fault divorce era, expectations were high that the process of marital dissolution had been transformed not only into a more rational process, but also into one focused on vouchsafing the traditional values of maintaining the American family. . . .

. . .

Even had trial judges been inclined, they were ill-equipped and understaffed to perform the inquests which the therapeutic divorce reformers prescribed. The California legislature had refused to enact state-wide family courts with the capacity to conduct social investigations. Concerns about unwarranted judicial probing into bedrooms merged with the steep price quoted for reconciliation-oriented divorce. As the former executive director of the Governor's Commission on the Family observed, the demise of the therapeutic family court was owed to "cost, concern that a family court structure would disrupt existing systems of court calendaring[,] and perhaps a fear that 'social work' would dilute 'hard legal process.'"

But "hard legal process" itself disappeared under the fire sale which divorce now became. By 1977, only three states (Illinois, Pennsylvania, and South Dakota) remained wedded to exclusively fault concepts in marital dissolutions. That same year, Riane Tennehaus Eisler reported that in the six years since the effective date of the irreconcilable differences standard in California, not a single divorce petition had been denied for failure to meet the standard of proof of irreconcilable differences. The appellate admonitions setting forth the statutory requirements for adequate proof turned out to have a nonexistent shelf life. Indeed, none of the forty-four California domestic relations judges interviewed by sociologist Lenore Weitzman in the "mid–1970's" could recall ever refusing a request for a divorce under the new dispensation. In 1975, the California legislature repealed the provision which had allowed proof of specific bad acts to show the existence of irreconcilable differences. The legislature thus removed one of the few remaining exemplars of the fault mentality as it recognized that irreconcilable differences were nothing more than a self-operated escape hatch from any marriage. Even in contested divorce cases, a "perfunctory judicial acknowledgment of marital breakdown replaced the parade of witnesses and staged courtroom battles."

The California story of legal and cultural transformation was quickly replicated. Reporting a "virtual unanimity as to the urgent need for basic reform," the National Conference of Commissioners on Uniform State Laws in 1970 proposed the Uniform Marriage and Divorce Act ("UMDA"). The UMDA specified that the sole ground for divorce should be an irretrievable breakdown of marriage. Six months after the effective date of California's divorce reforms, Iowa became the second state to completely gut its fault system and replace it with an "irretrievable breakdown" standard. A 1972 survey of twenty Iowa trial judges analyzed the 1810 divorce cases they had heard within the previous year. Of that total, 1599 had been uncontested, 211 contested, and in not one case had the prayer for a divorce been denied. Similarly, a Nebraska survey of nearly 10,000 dissolution cases in the mid–1970s "failed to reveal a single instance in which it could be said with certainty that a divorce which was desired by even one of the spouses was ultimately refused."

NOTE

Professor Herma Hill Kay, who participated in the California reforms observed that the Commission's proposed ground for divorce would have led to a much greater "factual inquiry" into the breakdown of the marriage than the finally adopted standard of "irreconcilable differences." *See* Herma Hill Kay, *Equality and Difference: A Perspective on No–Fault Divorce and Its Aftermath*, 56 U. Cin. L. Rev. 1, 35–36, 41–42 (1987). She also noted that the rejection of a special Family Court made it impossible to enforce the envisaged improvements consistently. *See id.* at 42.

California Family Code

(West, WestlawNext through ch. 285 of 2011 Reg. Sess. and ch. 8 of 2011–2012 1st Extraordinary Sess.).

§ 2310.   Grounds for dissolution or legal separation

Dissolution of the marriage or legal separation of the parties may be based on either of the following grounds, which shall be pleaded generally:

(a) Irreconcilable differences, which have caused the irremediable breakdown of the marriage.

(b) Incurable insanity.

§ 2311. Irreconcilable differences defined

Irreconcilable differences are those grounds which are determined by the court to be substantial reasons for not continuing the marriage and which make it appear that the marriage should be dissolved.

§ 2333. Irreconcilable differences; order for dissolution

Subject to Section 2334, if from the evidence at the hearing the court finds that there are irreconcilable differences which have caused the irremediable breakdown of the marriage, the court shall order the dissolution of the marriage or a legal separation of the parties.

§ 2334. Grounds for continuance; authority of court

(a) If it appears that there is a reasonable possibility of reconciliation, the court shall continue the proceeding for the dissolution of the marriage or for a legal separation of the parties for a period not to exceed 30 days.

(b) During the period of the continuance, the court may make orders for the support and maintenance of the parties, the custody of the minor children of the marriage, the support of children for whom support may be ordered, attorney's fees, and for the preservation of the property of the parties.

(c) At any time after the termination of the period of the continuance, either party may move for the dissolution of the marriage or a legal separation of the parties, and the court may enter a judgment of dissolution of the marriage or legal separation of the parties.

§ 2335. Misconduct; admissibility of specific acts of misconduct

Except as otherwise provided by statute, in a pleading or proceeding for dissolution of marriage or legal separation of the parties, including depositions and discovery proceedings, evidence of specific acts of misconduct is improper and inadmissible.

NOTE

If the proposed family court had been created by the California legislation as originally proposed, do you think it could have achieved the goals laid out for it?

2. THE UNIFORM MARRIAGE AND DIVORCE ACT

Section 302. Dissolution of Marriage; Legal Separation

(a) The court shall enter a decree of dissolution of marriage if:

(1) the court finds that one of the parties, at the time the action was commenced, was domiciled in this State, or was stationed in this State while a member of the armed services, and that the domicile or military presence has been maintained for 90 days next preceding the making of the findings;

(2) the court finds that the marriage is irretrievably broken, if the finding is supported by evidence that

(i) the parties have lived separate and apart for a period of more than 180 days next preceding the commencement of the proceeding, or

(ii) there is serious marital discord adversely affecting the attitude of one or both of the parties toward the marriage;

(3) the court finds that the conciliation provisions of Section 305 either do not apply or have been met;

(4) to the extent it has jurisdiction to do so, the court has considered, approved, or provided for child custody, the support of any child entitled to support, the maintenance of either spouse, and the disposition of property; or has provided for a separate later hearing to complete these matters.

(b) If a party requests a decree of legal separation rather than a decree of dissolution of marriage, the court shall grant the decree in that form unless the other party objects.

Section 305. Irretrievable Breakdown

(a) If both of the parties by petition or otherwise have stated under oath or affirmation that the marriage is irretrievably broken, or one of the parties has so stated and the other has not denied it, the court, after hearing, shall make a finding whether the marriage is irretrievably broken.

(b) If one of the parties has denied under oath or affirmation that the marriage is irretrievably broken, the court shall consider all relevant factors, including the circumstances that gave rise to filing the petition and the prospect of reconciliation, and shall:

(1) make a finding whether the marriage is irretrievably broken; or

(2) continue the matter for further hearing not fewer than 30 or more than 60 days later, or as soon thereafter as the matter may be reached on the court's calendar, and may suggest to the parties that they seek counseling. The court, at the request of either party shall, or on its own motion may, order a conciliation conference. At the adjourned hearing the court shall make a finding whether the marriage is irretrievably broken.

(c) A finding of irretrievable breakdown is a determination that there is no reasonable prospect of reconciliation.

3.   Adjudicating No-Fault

a.   WHAT CONSTITUTES SEPARATION?

In re Marriage of Dowd

Appellate Court of Illinois, Second District, 1991.
214 Ill. App. 3d 156, 573 N.E.2d 312.

■ Justice Unverzagt delivered the opinion of the court:

Respondent, Thomas Dowd, appeals from a judgment of dissolution of marriage entered by the circuit court of Kane County based on irreconcilable differences....

. . .

Respondent contends that the trial court erred in determining that the marriage between the parties should be dissolved on the basis of irreconcilable differences because the proof was insufficient to show that the parties lived separate and apart in excess of two years or that the marriage was irretrievably broken down, as required by the "no-fault" provision of the Illinois Marriage and Dissolution of Marriage Act (the Act) (Ill.Rev.Stat.1987, ch. 40, par. 401(a)(2)). It is respondent's position that the "living separate and apart" ground for dissolution set forth in section 401(a)(2) of the Act requires that spouses live physically separate and apart for two years. Respondent urges this court to reject the holding in *In re Marriage of Kenik* (1989), 181 Ill.App.3d 266, 129 Ill.Dec. 932, 536 N.E.2d 982, that the state of "living separate and apart" can be realized without a physical distance between the parties. We, however, are in agreement with the *Kenik* court's interpretation of the no-fault provision.

As pointed out in *Kenik*, the legislative debates surrounding the enactment of the no-fault provision disclose its sponsors intended an expansive reading of the statute and that it was not necessary for individuals in a marriage to live apart to make the provision applicable. State Senator William A. Marovitz, the senate sponsor of the bill, declared that it was up to the discretion of the trial court to determine whether parties exist "separate and apart." Marovitz explained:

> "If the judge determines that living separate and apart they have to be living in separate households, so be it. If the judge determines that living . . . apart . . . they can be living under the same roof but there is [sic] no conjugal visits, they . . . are living in separate bedrooms, they are doing . . . their own laundry, their own meals, whatever, that's up to the judge and that's . . . what the case law is today." 83d Ill.Gen. Assem., Senate Proceedings, November 3, 1983, at 60.

Testimony adduced in the *Kenik* case revealed that, although the parties resided in the same house until August or September of 1986, they had ended all marital relations a year before the husband filed for dissolution in May 1985. They used separate bedrooms, had no meaningful communication with each other, and shared the family's fundamental financial obligations. The *Kenik* court determined that under the no-fault statute, "dissolution is predicated upon a finding of 'irretrievable breakdown' of the marriage due to 'irreconcilable differences' " and that "this is a state which can be realized without physical distance between the parties." (*Kenik*, 181 Ill.App.3d at 274, 129 Ill.Dec. 932, 536 N.E.2d 982.) Based on the facts before it, the *Kenik* court found that no error arose from the trial court's finding that the parties lived "separate and apart" while residing in the same house.

In the instant case, the testimony established that the parties were married in 1970 and had one child, Adam, born in 1971. In November 1985 petitioner moved out of the marital home. She returned in May 1986 based on respondent's agreement to seek marital counseling with her. The parties, however, never went to counseling although, according to respondent, the parties had attended many marital counseling sessions in the past.

Following her return home in May 1986, petitioner returned to the marital bed for about two weeks. Thereafter, until she moved out again in July 1988, petitioner slept on the couch. In fact, by respondent's testimony, petitioner began sleeping on the couch in 1984 when the parties first moved into their house in St. Charles. By both parties' testimony the last time petitioner expressed her love for respondent was in 1986 and the last time the couple had sexual relations was during an attempted reconciliation trip to Jamaica in August 1987. Respondent stated that this was one of many reconciliation trips.

Petitioner filed for dissolution in June 1988; it was the third time during their marriage that she had begun dissolution proceedings. By the time petitioner again moved out of the marital home in July 1988, little conversation occurred between the parties. For the most part, the parties still did take dinner together, but it was done apparently for the sake of their son, and any dinner conversation was usually directed toward the son or about the son.

Based on these facts, it is apparent that irreconcilable differences existed in this case and that an irretrievable breakdown of the marriage occurred long ago. The evidence established that the legitimate objects of matrimony had been destroyed over the years, that the parties were unable to live together as husband and wife, and that no prospects of reconciliation existed. Although no physical separation of two years had occurred prior to the dissolution, the parties had been living "separate and apart" for more than two years. We conclude, therefore, that the trial court did not err in determining that the marriage between the parties should be dissolved under the no-fault provision of the Act.

Accordingly, the judgment of the circuit court of Kane County is affirmed.

NOTE

What are the costs and benefits of rejecting the bright-line rule of physical separation in favor of a standard that looks at the substance of the spouses' relations? Some courts have ruled that physical separation is necessary and that the interruption of normal marital relations is not enough. *See, e.g., Billac v. Billac*, 464 So. 2d 819 (La. Ct. App. 1985).

b.   WHAT CONSTITUTES IRRETRIEVABLE BREAKDOWN?

Grimm v. Grimm

Appellate Court of Connecticut, 2004.
82 Conn. App. 41, 844 A.2d 855.

■ SCHALLER, J.

"The tortured history of this case demonstrates the detrimental effect that procedural dysfunction in a marital dissolution action can have on the judicial process." . . .

The parties first separated in 1988, and the plaintiff, Beverly L. Grimm, commenced divorce proceedings in Ohio. The plaintiff subsequently withdrew the action after the defendant's repeated attempts to prolong the litigation by failing to appear or to plead except to contest the plaintiff's claim of irreconcilable differences. The plaintiff subsequently brought an action for dissolution of the marriage on the ground that she had lived separately and apart from the defendant for more than one year. She withdrew that action after the parties briefly resumed cohabitation. In 1992, the plaintiff brought another divorce proceeding. She withdrew that action after the defendant obtained employment in Connecticut where she was residing. In 1997, the plaintiff brought a divorce proceeding in the judicial district of Stamford–Norwalk, which she subsequently withdrew when she commenced the present action in Danbury seeking dissolution of her marriage on the ground of irretrievable breakdown. The defendant filed a motion to dismiss the action, or, in the alternative, to transfer the action to the judicial district of Stamford–Norwalk, arguing that the filing of the present action constituted forum shopping because the plaintiff had originally commenced a dissolution action in Stamford and later withdrew the action. The court denied the defendant's motion.

Documentary and testimonial evidence were presented to the court on approximately sixteen trial dates . . . . In January, 2003, the court dissolved the parties' marriage and entered various financial orders. . . .

The defendant first claims that § 46b–40(c)(1) violates the free exercise of religion clauses of the federal and state constitutions. The defendant argues that, as applied to him, § 46b–40(c)(1) violates his religious beliefs and liberties because his faith opposes divorce. We disagree.

The first amendment to the United States constitution provides that "Congress shall make no law respecting an establishment of religion, or prohibiting the free exercise thereof." The fundamental concept of liberty embraced in the first amendment applies to the states through the fourteenth amendment. The United States Supreme Court has "consistently held that the right of free exercise does not relieve an individual of the obligation to comply with a valid and neutral law of general applicability on the ground that the law proscribes (or prescribes) conduct that his religion prescribes (or proscribes)." General Statutes § 46b–40(c)(1) is a valid and neutral law of general applicability. The statute does not in any manner infringe on the defendant's right to exercise his religious beliefs merely because it permits the plaintiff to obtain a divorce from him against his wishes.

Our Supreme Court has held that § 46b–40(c)(1) is constitutional. "The legislature could rationally conclude that public policy requires an accommodation to the unfortunate reality that a marital relationship may terminate in fact without regard to the fault of either marital partner, and that such a relationship should therefore be dissoluble in law upon a judicial determination of irretrievable breakdown. Courts in other jurisdictions with similar statutes have unanimously upheld the constitutionality of no-fault divorce." Accordingly, we conclude that § 46b–40(c)(1) does not violate the defendant's right to exercise his religious beliefs.

. . .

The defendant argues that the court abused its discretion in finding that the marriage had broken down irretrievably.

The following additional facts are necessary to review the defendant's claim. At trial, the plaintiff testified that the marriage had irretrievably broken down. She testified that the defendant was very cold, distant, abusive, cruel, dishonest and controlling. She further testified that the defendant exposed himself in the presence of a child, committed larceny and made inappropriate and unwanted sexual advances. The defendant countered that he was willing to seek marriage counseling and that the plaintiff's pattern of behavior of commencing and withdrawing divorce proceedings demonstrated that she was mistaken in her belief that the marriage had broken down irretrievably. The plaintiff contended that her pattern of behavior was the result of the defendant's campaign to thwart her efforts to dissolve the marriage by prolonging the litigation. She cited the numerous continuances, stays, depositions, motions and other tactics that the defendant had utilized to delay the divorce proceedings. She also testified that the defendant had warned her that if she attempted to end the marriage, he would "drag out" the litigation and cause her to spend "$100,000" in counsel fees unless she agreed to give him 80 percent of the marital assets. Notably, the defendant has spent more than $1 million in counsel fees in relation to the divorce proceedings.

"The determination of whether a breakdown of a marriage is irretrievable is a question of fact to be determined by the trial court." ... "The fact that the defendant maintains hope for reconciliation will not support a finding that there are prospects for a reconciliation.... A difference, to be irreconcilable, need not necessarily be so viewed by both parties...."

"Factual findings, such as those determinations, are reviewed under the clearly erroneous standard of review. A factual finding is clearly erroneous when it is not supported by any evidence in the record or when there is evidence to support it, but the reviewing court is left with the definite and firm conviction that a mistake has been made.... Simply put, we give great deference to the findings of the trial court because of its function to weigh and interpret the evidence before it and to pass upon the credibility of witnesses." ...

... The allegations raised by the plaintiff concerning the difficulties in the marriage were serious and spanned almost the entire length of the marriage. The court was within its discretion to credit the plaintiff's version of the facts that the pattern of litigation was the result of the defendant's attempt to thwart the dissolution proceedings, not the plaintiff's lack of intent to end the marriage. Accordingly, we conclude that the court did not improperly find that the marriage had broken down irretrievably.

NOTES

1. Claims that no-fault divorce grounds are unconstitutional have been regularly rejected by courts. *See, e.g., Richter v. Richter*, 625 N.W.2d 490, 495 (Minn. Ct. App. 2001) ("marriage is not a contract for purposes of the Contract Clauses of the United States and Minnesota Constitutions").

2. How far should a court probe on the question of the existence of irreconcilable differences when the spouses are filing jointly? How far should it probe when the divorce is contested as in *Grimm*?

c.   CONTRACTING AROUND STATUTORY GROUNDS FOR DIVORCE

Massar v. Massar

Superior Court of New Jersey, Appellate Division, 1995.
279 N.J. Super. 89, 652 A.2d 219.

■ The opinion of the court was delivered by Cuff, J.S.C.

This appeal arises from an order enforcing an agreement between a husband and wife which limited the grounds for a complaint for divorce to eighteen months continuous separation.

This is the second marriage for both parties. Prior to their marriage on November 25, 1988, Jacqueline Massar and Cyril Massar signed a prenuptial agreement. In April 1993, the marriage had deteriorated to the point that the parties discussed separation and eventual divorce. In an agreement signed April 30, 1993, Mr. Massar agreed to vacate the marital home, and Mrs. Massar agreed not to seek termination of the marriage for any reason other than eighteen months continuous separation. Pursuant to this agreement, Mr. Massar moved out of the marital home.

However, contrary to the agreement, on October 1, 1993, Mrs. Massar filed a complaint for divorce on the grounds of extreme cruelty. Mr. Massar filed a motion to dismiss the complaint and to enforce the prenuptial agreement. After oral argument, Hon. Thomas Dilts, J.S.C. upheld the agreement and dismissed the complaint. He also denied without prejudice Mr. Massar's motion to enforce the prenuptial agreement citing the need for a plenary hearing. Finally, he ruled that Mrs. Massar could file a complaint for separate maintenance pursuant to *N.J.S.A.* 2A:34–24. . . . Mrs. Massar appeals from that portion of the order enforcing the agreement to seek a divorce solely on "no fault" grounds.

In enforcing this agreement, Judge Dilts found that the agreement was clear, unequivocal and supported by consideration. He also found that Mrs. Massar had failed to present facts which would lead him to conclude that the agreement was executed under duress. At most, she submitted facts to support that she wanted Mr. Massar out of the house. Furthermore, Mrs. Massar was represented by an attorney who was representing solely her interests. Moreover, Judge Dilts found that public policy did not prohibit such agreements. In fact, he concluded that public policy requires that agreements which restrict the grounds on which a divorce shall be obtained to the no-fault eighteen months continuous separation should be recognized. He reasoned that such an agreement should be encouraged by the State since it can give a couple a period of time to assess their relationship and determine whether a reconciliation is possible.

On appeal, Mrs. Massar argues that a complaint for divorce on the grounds of extreme cruelty does not violate the intent of the agreement. She further argues that the agreement violates public policy and is unenforceable. Finally, she argues that a plenary hearing was required. We disagree and affirm the order entered by Judge Dilts substantially for the reasons set forth in his oral decision of December 10, 1993 as supplemented by his letter opinion dated December 13, 1993. We add only the following comments.

This State has a strong public policy favoring enforcement of agreements. Marital agreements are essentially consensual and voluntary and as a result, they are approached with a predisposition in favor of their validity and enforceability. Marital agreements, however, are enforceable only if they are fair and equitable. Any marital agreement which is unconscionable or is the product of fraud or overreaching by a party with power to take advantage of a confidential relationship may be set aside. In fact, the law affords particular leniency to agreements made in the domestic arena and similarly allows judges greater discretion when interpreting these agreements. Such discretion is based on the premise that, although marital agreements are contractual in nature, "contract principles have little place in the law of domestic relations." Nevertheless, the contractual nature of such agreements has long been recognized and principles of contract interpretation have been invoked particularly to define the terms of the agreement and divine the intent of the parties. In interpreting the agreement, the court will not draft a new agreement for the parties.

In this case, Mr. Massar agreed to vacate the marital home. Mrs. Massar agreed as follows:

> [W]aives any claim that she may have against the husband in any action to dissolve, nullify, or terminate their marriage for desertion *or any other cause of action, except no-fault divorce based upon living separate and apart for a period of 18 months or more* based upon the husband's vacating the marital premises pursuant to this agreement. (emphasis added).

We agree with Judge Dilts that this language is clear and unequivocal and that Mrs. Massar surrendered her right to seek a divorce on any other than a no-fault basis. We also agree that the certifications submitted by Mrs. Massar establish nothing more than that she wished Mr. Massar out of the house; they certainly did not create a fact issue concerning duress. Similarly, we concur that this agreement is supported by consideration. Not only did Mr. Massar leave a house in which he had as much right to reside as Mrs. Massar, but also he had to undertake the additional expense of establishing a separate residence. Finally, we also agree with Judge Dilts that there is insufficient evidence to suggest that this waiver was not a knowing and voluntary act by Mrs. Massar, and a plenary hearing was not warranted.

Mrs. Massar urges us to adopt a per se rule that agreements confining a spouse to a particular cause of action for dissolution of a marriage are against public policy and are unenforceable. We have declined, however, to adopt a per se rule of enforceability of negotiated provisions in agreements between spouses. Rather, we have reviewed the enforceability of these provisions on a case-by-case basis to determine if the application of the provision is fair and just according to the circumstances of the particular case.

The State has certainly adopted a public policy through *N.J.S.A.* 2A:34–1 *et seq.* that the citizens of this state shall have liberal grounds to disengage themselves from marriages which are not viable. On the other hand, this State does not promote divorce and has always had a strong public interest in promoting marriage. Indeed, the no-fault provision requiring an eighteen-month continuous separation was adopted in part to allow divorcing spouses the time to reflect and discern if divorce is the appropriate action for them. As observed by Judge Dilts, there is good reason to encourage a cooling off period for spouses to assess their relationship and calmly reflect whether dissolution of their marriage is the course they wish to take.

Accordingly, we decline to adopt a per se rule. We can envision many circumstances where it may be in the best interests of the parties and any children born of the marriage to dissolve a marriage without the assertion of allegations of emotional or physical abandonment, substance abuse, or certain allegations that pass for extreme cruelty. Similarly, we can envision many instances in which such an agreement may not be enforceable because it may serve to hide from the court actions of an abusive spouse or substance-dependent spouse which may endanger the physical and emotional welfare of the other spouse and any children.

But that is not the situation in this case. Indeed, based on the certifications before Judge Dilts it appears that Mr. Massar realized that a physical separation was appropriate given the state of his marriage. However, he was concerned that such a separation might be interpreted as a financial abandonment of his wife. Similarly, he was concerned about his continuing ability to function as a deacon in his church. These concerns became real because upon the filing of the complaint for divorce alleging extreme cruelty he was temporarily suspended from his position in his church. Furthermore, the record before Judge Dilts suggests that Mrs. Massar filed the complaint for divorce only when her initial proposal for equitable distribution was not instantly embraced by Mr. Massar.

The parties entered this agreement presumably with full knowledge of the conduct of each during the marriage which could form the basis for a cause of action for divorce. We do not suggest that the parties could enter an agreement which would preclude seeking a judgment of divorce on a ground other than eighteen months separation based on conduct which occurred after the execution of the agreement.

We emphasize that there is no suggestion in this record of any physical or mental abuse. The certifications submitted by Mrs. Massar reveal no more than a couple engaging in verbal confrontations in the context of a disintegrating marriage. Two intelligent adults should be able to agree concerning the framework and timetable for the dissolution of their troubled marriage and have that agreement enforced, if that agreement is fair and equitable to both parties under the unique circumstances of their case.

Accordingly, the December 14, 1993 Order entered by Judge Dilts is affirmed.

In re Marriage of Cooper

Supreme Court of Iowa, 2009.
769 N.W.2d 582.

■ APPEL, JUSTICE.

In this case, we are called upon to consider the validity of a reconciliation agreement signed after the husband engaged in an extramarital affair. The wife sought to enforce the agreement in a subsequent dissolution action after discovering that the extramarital relationship had not ended. The district court found the postnuptial reconciliation agreement valid and considered its terms when equitably dividing the couple's property. The court of appeals reversed on the ground that the reconciliation agreement injected fault into the distribution of property contrary to established public policy. Upon further review, we conclude that the agreement is not enforceable under Iowa law.

Bernard and Vergestene Cooper were married in 1972....

In 2000, Vergestene discovered that Bernard was romantically involved with another woman. The discovery of the affair caused marital discord. Bernard wanted the marriage to continue, however, and was willing to make substantial promises regarding his future behavior in order to achieve reconciliation.

Some of the promises were reduced to writing and signed by both spouses on May 29. In the document, Bernard agreed that "if any of my indiscretions lead to and/or are cause of a separation or divorce ... I will accept full responsibilities [*sic*] of my action." In the event of a permanent breakdown in the marital relationship, Bernard further agreed to pay $2600 a month for household expenses, increased by a percentage of Bernard's annual raises, to maintain life insurance, retirement accounts, and family health insurance, to provide for the college expenses of their youngest daughter, and to pay one-half of all future retirement payments to Vergestene. On June 26, the reconciliation agreement was reformatted, re-signed by Bernard and Vergestene, and notarized.

In summer 2005, Bernard leased an apartment, gathered his belongings, and left the family residence without advising Vergestene of his plans. Vergestene and their daughters searched for Bernard, eventually learning from the bank that he had changed his address. Vergestene confronted her husband at his new apartment. She testified at trial that when she confronted Bernard, he admitted that he had continued his prior affair.

Vergestene filed for divorce in September 2005. She sought a temporary order of support and attached the notarized reconciliation agreement to her pleading. The district court granted temporary support in the amount of $2800 per month. Bernard filed a motion to reconsider. At the hearing, Bernard claimed not to remember whether he signed the reconciliation agreement, testimony which the district court discounted in declining to overrule the previous order.

. . .

The district court order, judgment, and decree found in favor of Vergestene on most issues of fact and law. The district court found that the terms of the reconciliation agreement, though generous to Vergestene, were not unconscionable, and that, despite Bernard's denials, the affair likely continued and caused the parties' separation, thereby triggering the terms of the reconciliation agreement. Other than spousal support, the district court's property distribution, including a $25,000 award of attorneys' fees, closely tracked the reconciliation agreement.

Bernard appealed both the temporary support order as well as the final property distribution. . . .

. . .

The thrust of Bernard's claim on appeal is that the parties' reconciliation agreement is unenforceable as it violates Iowa's public policy by considering fault in dissolution proceedings. . . .

There is no provision of Iowa statutory law that expressly authorizes or prohibits enforcement of reconciliation agreements between spouses. While IOWA CODE section 598.21(1)(k) states that any mutual agreement made by the parties *may* be considered by the court, this provision does not provide for enforcement of reconciliation agreements specifically, but only that mutual agreements may be considered, among other factors, in making property divisions. Likewise, section 598.21(1)(m) is a catch-all provision which allows the district court to consider any other relevant factor in equitably distributing property.

While statutory law is silent on the issue, there is dated Iowa case law related to the enforceability of reconciliation agreements. In *Miller v. Miller*, 78 Iowa 177, 35 N.W. 464 (1887) [hereinafter *Miller I*], we considered the validity of a written reconciliation agreement between married spouses. . . .

. . . The court found that the agreement was without consideration and against public policy. The court concluded that the contract bound Mrs. Miller only to do what she was already legally bound to do [i.e., keep house and not quarrel].

Two years later, this court agreed to rehear *Miller I*. *Miller v. Miller*, 78 Iowa 177, 179, 42 N.W. 641, 641 (1889) [hereinafter *Miller II*]. On rehearing, Mrs. Miller asserted that the contract was a postnuptial settlement sanctioned by law. The court again rejected enforcement of the contract. The court stated that the contract touched upon matters "pertaining so directly and exclusively to the home" that they are not to become matters of public concern or policy.

The reconciliation agreement in *Miller I & II*, of course, involved vague and ambiguous terms that would have made enforcement difficult under any circumstances. Subsequent case law, however, reinforced the notion that contracts between spouses which purported to govern their intimate relationships would not be enforced.... [I]n *Bohanan v. Maxwell*, 190 Iowa 1308, 1310, 1319–20, (1921), this court refused to enforce an agreement where a woman promised to marry and subsequently care for a man until his death in exchange for a generous property settlement. Finally, in *In re Straka's Estate*, 224 Iowa 109, 111–12, (1937), this court refused to enforce a contract between a husband and wife that provided compensation for the wife's domestic services because, among other things, the consideration for such an agreement violated public policy.

We note that this case does not involve a reconciliation agreement where the parties let go of the acrimonious past, agreed to continue their marriage, and chose to structure their financial relationship in the event of a future divorce with full disclosure and the assistance of independent counsel. Instead, this case involves a reconciliation agreement which has as a condition precedent the sexual conduct of the parties within the marital relationship. A unifying theme of our historic case law is that contracts which attempt to regulate the conduct of spouses during the marital relationship are not enforceable.

Although our precedents are relatively old, we see no reason to depart from them now. The relationship between spouses cannot be regulated by contracts that are plead [sic] and proved in the courts as if the matter involved the timely delivery of a crate of oranges. We do not wish to create a bargaining environment where sexual fidelity or harmonious relationships are key variables.

Further, like our predecessors, we reject the idea of injecting the courts into the complex web of interpersonal relationships and the inevitable he-said-she-said battles that would arise in contracts that can be enforced only through probing of the nature of the marital relationship. Indeed, our no-fault divorce law is designed to limit acrimonious proceedings. Further, a contrary approach would empower spouses to seek an end-run around our no-fault divorce laws through private contracts. *See Diosdado v. Diosdado*, 97 Cal.App.4th 470, 118 Cal.Rptr.2d 494, 496 (2002) (finding an agreement which provided for a $50,000 penalty upon infidelity contrary to the public policy of no-fault divorce laws).

As a result, we hold that the reconciliation agreement in this case is void. We further believe that as a void contract, it should be given no weight in the dissolution proceedings. We recognize that IOWA CODE section 598.21(1)(k) and (m) authorizes the court to consider any written agreements and other factors that the court determines to be relevant. We, nevertheless, conclude that these statutory provisions do not extend to agreements between spouses that are void, such as the one presented here, because they intrude on the intimacies of the marital relationship and inject fault back into dissolution proceedings. On remand, the district court should divide the property in an equitable fashion without regard to the reconciliation agreement.

d. IS THERE SPACE FOR INTERSPOUSAL TORTS IN NO-FAULT DIVORCE?

Twyman v. Twyman

Supreme Court of Texas, 1993.
855 S.W.2d 619.

■ CORNYN, JUSTICE.

In this case we decide whether a claim for infliction of emotional distress can be brought in a divorce proceeding. Because the judgment of the court of appeals is based on negligent infliction of emotional distress, and cannot be affirmed on that or any other basis, we reverse the judgment of that court and remand this cause for a new trial in the interest of justice. We deem a new trial appropriate because of our recent decision that no cause of action for negligent infliction of emotional distress exists in Texas. Today, however, we expressly adopt the tort of intentional infliction of emotional distress, and hold that such a claim can be brought in a divorce proceeding.

Sheila and William Twyman married in 1969. Sheila filed for divorce in 1985. She later amended her divorce petition to add a general claim for emotional harm without specifying whether the claim was based on negligent or intentional infliction of emotional distress. In her amended petition, Sheila alleged that William "intentionally and cruelly" attempted to engage her in "deviate sexual acts."[1] Following a bench trial, the court rendered judgment dissolving the marriage, dividing the marital estate, awarding conservatorship of the children to Sheila, ordering William to pay child support, and awarding Sheila $15,000 plus interest for her claim for emotional distress. William appealed that portion of the judgment based on emotional distress, contending that interspousal tort immunity precluded Sheila's recovery for negligent infliction of emotional distress. The court of appeals affirmed the judgment, holding that Sheila could recover for William's negligent infliction of emotional distress. 790 S.W.2d 819.

While this case has been pending, we have refused to adopt the tort of negligent infliction of emotional distress. *See Boyles v. Kerr*, 855 S.W.2d 593 (Tex.1993). Thus the judgment of the court of appeals cannot be affirmed. We consider, therefore, whether the court of appeals' judgment may be affirmed on alternative grounds. Because Sheila's pleadings alleging a general claim for emotional harm are broad enough to encompass a claim for intentional infliction of emotional distress, we consider whether the trial court's judgment may be sustained on that legal theory.

While this court has never expressly recognized the tort of intentional infliction of emotional distress, we found no reversible error in the court of appeals' opinion in *Tidelands Automobile Club v. Walters*, which did so. 699 S.W.2d 939 (Tex.App.—Beaumont 1985, writ ref'd n.r.e.). There, the court of appeals adopted the elements of the tort as expressed in the Restatement (Second) of Torts § 46 (1965). The Restatement elements of intentional infliction of emotional distress are: 1) the defendant acted intentionally or recklessly, 2) the conduct was extreme and outrageous, 3) the actions of the defendant caused the plaintiff emotional distress, and 4) the emotional distress suffered by the plaintiff was severe. *Id.* According to the Restatement, liability for outrageous conduct should be found "only where the conduct has been so outrageous in character, and so extreme in degree, as to go beyond all possible bounds of decency, and to be regarded as atrocious, and utterly intolerable in a civilized community." *Id.* cmt. d. Of the forty-six states that have recognized this tort, forty-three have adopted this Restatement formulation. The other three states, although not adopting the Restatement

---

1. At trial, Sheila testified that William pursued sadomasochistic bondage activities with her, even though he knew that she feared such activities because she had been raped at knife-point before their marriage. The trial court found that William "attempted to emotionally coerce [Sheila] in 'bondage' on an ongoing basis ..." and "engaged in a continuing course of conduct of attempting to coerce her to join in his practices of 'bondage' by continually asserting that their marriage could be saved only by [Sheila] participating with him in his practices of 'bondage.'"

definition, require the equivalent of "outrageous" conduct. Today we become the forty-seventh state to adopt the tort of intentional infliction of emotional distress as set out in § 46(1) of the Restatement (Second) of Torts.

We do not, however, adopt this tort only because of its broad acceptance in jurisdictions throughout the United States. As distinguished from the tort of negligent infliction of emotional distress, we believe the rigorous legal standards of the Restatement formulation of intentional infliction of emotional distress help to assure a meaningful delineation between inadvertence and intentionally or recklessly outrageous misconduct. The requirements of intent, extreme and outrageous conduct, and severe emotional distress before liability can be established will, we think, strike a proper balance between diverse interests in a free society. That balance, at minimum, must allow freedom of individual action while providing reasonable opportunity for redress for victims of conduct that is determined to be utterly intolerable in a civilized community.

.   .   .

We now consider whether the cause of action for intentional infliction of emotional distress may be brought in a divorce proceeding.[13] In *Bounds v. Caudle,* this court unanimously abolished the doctrine of interspousal immunity for intentional torts. 560 S.W.2d 925 (Tex.1977). Ten years later, we abrogated interspousal immunity "completely as to any cause of action," including negligence actions for personal injuries. *Price v. Price,* 732 S.W.2d 316, 319 (Tex.1987). Under the rules established in *Caudle* and *Price,* there appears to be no legal impediment to bringing a tort claim in a divorce action based on either negligence or an intentional act such as assault or battery.

The more difficult issue is when the tort claim must be brought and how the tort award should be considered when making a "just and right" division of the marital estate. *See* TEX.FAM.CODE § 3.63(b). Of the states that have answered this question, several have held that the tort case and the divorce case must be litigated separately.

We believe that the best approach lies between these two extremes. As in other civil actions, joinder of the tort cause of action should be permitted, but subject to the principles of res judicata.[17] Of course, how such claims are ultimately tried is within the sound discretion of the trial court. But joinder of tort claims with the divorce, when feasible, is encouraged. Resolving both the tort and divorce actions in the same proceeding avoids two trials based at least in part on the same facts, and settles in one suit "all matters existing between the parties."

When a tort action is tried with the divorce, however, it is imperative that the court avoid awarding a double recovery. When dividing the marital estate, the court may take into account several factors, including the fault of the parties if pleaded. The trial court may also consider "such factors as the

---

13. CHIEF JUSTICE PHILLIPS, and JUSTICES HECHT and ENOCH rue the court's decision to permit the tort of intentional infliction of emotional distress to be brought in divorce proceedings. But it appears that much of what they disapprove of is related to the consequences of recognizing *any* tort action between divorcing spouses. Their criticisms would seem to be better directed at the court's earlier decisions to abrogate the doctrine of interspousal tort immunity in Bounds v. Caudle, 560 S.W.2d 925 (Tex.1977), and Price v. Price, 732 S.W.2d 316 (Tex.1987).

17. We anticipate that most tort cases between spouses will be joined with the divorce proceeding, however, situations may exist in which the facts supporting the tort action will be different from those supporting a petition for divorce.

spouses' capacities and abilities, benefits which the party not at fault would have derived from continuation of the marriage, business opportunities, education, relative physical conditions, relative financial condition and obligations, disparity of ages, size of separate estates, and the nature of the property." *Id.* However, a spouse should not be allowed to recover tort damages and a disproportionate division of the community estate based on the same conduct. Therefore, when a factfinder awards tort damages to a divorcing spouse, the court may not consider the same tortious acts when dividing the marital estate. Contrary to CHIEF JUSTICE PHILLIPS' contention, an award for tortious conduct does not replace an analysis of the remaining factors to be considered when the trial court divides the marital estate. The court may still award a disproportionate division of property for reasons other than the tortious conduct. To avoid the potential problem of double recovery, the factfinder should consider the damages awarded in the tort action when dividing the parties' property. If a jury is used to render an advisory division of the parties' estate, the judge should limit, by appropriate instruction, the jury's consideration of the alleged tortious acts and later consider the award of damages in determining a just and right division of the marital estate.[20]

Sheila Twyman cannot recover based on the findings of fact made by the trial court in this case.[21] It is likely, however, that this case proceeded on a theory of negligent infliction of emotional distress in reliance on this court's holding in *St. Elizabeth Hospital v. Garrard*, 730 S.W.2d 649 (Tex.1987), which we recently overruled. *See Boyles v. Kerr*, 855 S.W.2d 593 (Tex.1993). As we noted in *Boyles*, this court has broad discretion to remand for a new trial in the interest of justice when it appears that a case proceeded under the wrong legal theory, and when it appears that the facts when developed on retrial may support recovery on an alternative theory. When, as here, a party presents her case in reliance on precedent that has been recently overruled, remand is appropriate. Therefore, in the interest of justice, we reverse the judgment of the court of appeals and remand this cause to the trial court for a new trial.

. . .

■ PHILLIPS, CHIEF JUSTICE, concurring and dissenting.

I join in the Court's recognition of the tort of intentional infliction of emotional distress. . . .

In recognizing this tort, however, I would not extend it to actions between spouses or former spouses for conduct occurring during their marriage. . . .

---

20.   In Texas, recovery for personal injuries of a spouse, including pain and suffering, is the separate property of that spouse. TEX.FAM.CODE § 5.01(a)(3); Graham v. Franco, 488 S.W.2d 390, 396 (Tex.1972). Therefore, an award to one spouse from the other does not add to the marital estate, and raises no possibility that the tort award becomes "self-offsetting." *See* Barbara H. Young, *Interspousal Torts and Divorce: Problems, Policies, Procedures*, 27 J.FAM.L. 489, 511 (1989).

21.   . . . The trial court made no findings of outrageous behavior or severe emotional distress, and the judgment was based specifically and exclusively on negligent infliction of emotional distress. The divorce decree recites:

> After considering the pleadings, the evidence, and the arguments of the attorneys, the Court finds the facts and law support judgment for Petition [sic] in her tort for negligent infliction of emotional distress upon Petitioner.

Additionally, the trial court made a disproportionate property division based on William's cruel treatment and adultery. It appears that such an award may allow Sheila a double recovery based on the same conduct. A new trial conducted in accordance with the principles announced in this decision should rectify this problem.

Married couples share an intensely personal and intimate relationship. When discord arises, it is inevitable that the parties will suffer emotional distress, often severe. In the present case, for example, Ms. Twyman testified that she suffered "utter despair" and "fell apart" upon learning that her husband was seeing another woman. She further testified that "[t]he mental anguish was unbelievable to realize, hoping every time, when he went off to Houston, that he was just going to fly and not be with her." Yet Ms. Twyman seeks no recovery for this distress, and apparently cannot do so under Texas law. In such circumstances, the fact finder is left to draw a virtually impossible distinction between recoverable and disallowed injuries.

Furthermore, recognition of this tort in the context of a divorce unnecessarily restricts the trial court's discretion in dividing the marital estate. Prior to today's opinion, the trial court could, but was not required to, consider fault in dividing the community property. The court had broad discretion to weigh any fault along with other appropriate factors, such as relative financial condition, disparity of ages, and the needs of the children. Now, however, where fault takes the form of "outrageous" conduct intentionally or recklessly inflicted, it becomes a dominant factor that must be considered at the expense of the other factors. Unlike battery, fraud, or other torts resting on more objective conduct, a colorable allegation of intentional infliction of emotional distress could arguably be raised by one or both parties in most intimate relationships. As the court noted in *Chiles v. Chiles*, 779 S.W.2d 127, 131 (Tex.App.—Houston [14th Dist.] 1989, writ denied):

> While we recognize the trial court may consider fault in the distribution of community property, we believe permitting such separate damages [for intentional infliction of emotional distress] in divorce actions would result in evils similar to those avoided by the legislature's abrogation of fault as a ground for divorce.

See also Henriksen v. Cameron, 622 A.2d 1135, 1151 (Me.1993) (Glassman, J., dissenting) (recognizing the common-law tort of intentional infliction of emotional distress in the marriage context skews "a carefully constructed scheme of legislation governing the marriage relationship").

Perhaps because of these difficulties, the tort of intentional infliction of emotional distress has not been generally recognized in the marital context. Although most states, like Texas, have abolished interspousal immunity, it appears that, until today, only two state supreme courts have expressly held that intentional infliction of emotional distress may be applied to marital conduct. *See Henriksen, supra*; *Davis v. Bostick*, 282 Or. 667, 580 P.2d 544 (1978). Moreover, these two decisions do not appear to represent typical actions for the recovery of emotional distress damages. In *Henriksen*, the husband inflicted on his wife not only verbal abuse but also physical attacks, including multiple assaults and rapes. 622 A.2d at 1139. Similarly in *Bostick*, the husband broke his wife's nose, choked her, and threatened her with a loaded pistol. 580 P.2d at 545–46. To the extent that emotional distress results from a physical attack or threat of attack, it is already compensable under tort theories previously recognized in Texas. The court in *Henriksen* apparently recognized the risk of spurious claims in the divorce context, noting that "to protect defendants from the possibility of long and intrusive trials on meritless claims, motions for summary judgment should ... be viewed sympathetically in interspousal cases." 622 A.2d at 1139. By contrast, it is far from clear that Texas' strict summary judgment standard will allow our trial courts to use this procedure in weeding out meritless or trivial claims.

. . .

Just as I join the Court's decision to recognize a tort now available in nearly every American jurisdiction, I depart from the Court's decision to extend that tort to a type of dispute where it is not generally applied in other states. I fail to understand how, lexigraphically or logically, it can be "medieval" or "archaic" to decline to adopt a position which has been expressly embraced by only two other state supreme courts. I therefore would reverse the judgment of the court of appeals and render judgment that Sheila Twyman take nothing on her tort claim.

■ Hecht, Justice, concurring and dissenting.

. . .

. . . The plurality opinion gives little indication that it has considered, or why it has rejected, the arguments against adopting this tort. It bases its decision solely on the fact that the high courts of almost all the other states have at one time or another recognized a tort of intentional infliction of emotional distress in some context, and on the conclusion that this tort is more manageable than negligent infliction of emotional distress. While a consensus of our sister courts on a proposition may be some indication of its merit, that circumstance alone has not always been, and should never be, reason enough to justify our concurrence. . . .

Slight though the foundation is for today's decision, its effects are far-reaching. There is little doubt that the new tort will be asserted in many if not most contested divorce cases. The Family Law Section of the State Bar of Texas has filed a brief as amicus curiae assessing the impact of spouses' suing one another for intentional infliction of emotional distress, discussing the arguments for and against allowing such an action without taking a position on the issue, and urging us to exercise caution in considering these arguments. The plurality opinion makes no mention of the family bar's arguments. . . . Nor has the Court considered the burden of additional jury trials in divorce cases on the judicial system. This Court, as steward of the common law, possesses the power to recognize new causes of action, but the mere existence of that power cannot justify its exercise. There must be well-considered, even compelling grounds for changing the law so significantly. Where, as here, no such grounds are given, the decision is more an exercise of will than of reason.

In my view, intentional or reckless infliction of emotional distress is too broad a rubric to describe actionable conduct, as this case illustrates. Accordingly, I dissent from the Court's decision to remand this case for trial on such a cause of action. I concur only in the reversal of the court of appeals' judgment allowing recovery for negligent infliction of emotional distress.

. . .

The standard of outrageousness is certainly no easier to apply in the marital context than in other contexts, as the facts of this case illustrate. Sheila Twyman's claim of intentional infliction of emotional distress is based upon the following testimony at trial, which was mostly undisputed. William, a Navy pilot, and Sheila, a college graduate with a degree in nursing, were married in 1969. In 1975, on two or three occasions at William's suggestion, the couple engaged in what they referred to as "light bondage"—tying each other to the bed with neckties during their sexual relations. Sheila testified that William did not force her to participate in these activities. After the last occasion Sheila told William she did not like this activity and did not want to participate in it further. She revealed to him that she associated the activities with the horrible experience of having been raped at knifepoint earlier in her life. William never again suggested that she engage in the activities, nor was the subject discussed again for ten years. In 1985 Sheila inadvertently discovered that William was consulting with a psychologist. When she asked him why, he told her that he was involved with another woman. William told Sheila that if she could only have done bondage, nothing else would have mattered. For the remainder of the year the couple sought counseling. At times during this period William made derogatory remarks to Sheila about her sexual ability, comparing her to his girl friend [sic]. On their counselor's advice, William and Sheila discussed William's bondage fantasies, and Sheila again tried to participate in bondage activities with William. But she found the activity so painful and humiliating that she could not continue it. Their last encounter, which did not include bondage activities, was so rough that she was injured to the point of bleeding. At one point Sheila was distressed to discover that their ten-year-old son had found magazines William kept hidden, which portrayed sadomasochistic activities. Eleven months after she first learned of William's affair, Sheila separated from him and filed for divorce. Throughout that period, Sheila testified, she experienced utter despair, devastation, pain, humiliation and weight loss because of William's affair and her feelings that the marriage could have survived if only she had engaged in bondage activities.

To recover damages Sheila must prove that William's conduct was outrageous—that is, "extreme," "beyond all possible bounds of decency," "atrocious," and "utterly intolerable in a civilized community." Although outrageousness is, according to the plurality opinion and the Restatement, a question for the court in the first instance, this Court refuses to say whether William's conduct was or was not outrageous. If it was not, as a matter of law, then there is no need to remand this case for further proceedings. If William's conduct was outrageous, or if that issue must be decided by a jury, then it is unclear what components of the conflict between Sheila and William were actionable. There is no question from the record that Sheila claims to have suffered bitterly, but there appear to have been three causes: William's affair, his interest in bondage, and the breakup of the marriage. If the first or last causes constitute outrageous behavior, then there a tort claim may be urged successfully in most divorces. Allowing recovery based upon the first cause of Sheila's emotional distress is simply to revive the old action for alienation of affections abolished by the Legislature. TEX.FAM.CODE § 4.06. I doubt whether the Court intends this result. If William's outrageous conduct was attempting to interest Sheila in sexual conduct which he considered enjoyable but she, in her words, "did not like," then again, this tort may be very broad indeed.

The sexual relationship is among the most intimate aspects of marriage. People's concepts of a beneficial sexual relationship vary widely, and spouses may expect that some accommodation of each other's feelings will be necessary for their mutual good. *Any* breach of such an intimate and essential part of marriage may be regarded as outrageous by the aggrieved spouse and will often be the cause of great distress. There are many other aspects of marriage which are likewise sensitive. How money is to be spent, how children are to be raised, and how time is to be allocated are only a few of the many areas of conflict in a marriage. Not infrequently disagreements over these matters are deep and contribute to the breakup of the marriage. If all are actionable, then tort claims will be commonplace in divorce cases, and judges and juries with their own deeply felt beliefs about what is proper in a marital relationship will face the hard task of deciding whether one spouse or another behaved outrageously with no standards but their own to guide.

The inquiry which must be made to determine whether a spouse's conduct is outrageous entails too great an intrusion into the marital relationship. Although courts are already called upon to consider fault in divorce actions, allowance of tort claims requires a more pervasive inspection of spouses' private lives than should be permissible. In this case the parties were called to testify in detail and at length about the most private moments of their marriage. If the court's only concern were the degree to which a spouse's fault had contributed to the demise of the marriage, the inquiry into each spouse's conduct need not have been so detailed. To recover damages, however, Sheila was required to testify at length before a jury, and to rebut her claim, William was obliged to answer in equal detail. The prospect of such testimony in many divorces is too great an invasion of spouses' interests in privacy, and promises to make divorce more acrimonious and injurious than it already is.

The plurality opinion's justification for allowing the tort of intentional infliction of emotional distress between spouses is that this represents a middle ground among the various positions taken by Members of this Court. But being in the middle does not equate to being right. Certainly the Court is not in the middle of the views of other state courts; rather, it is to one extreme.

. . .

For all the foregoing reasons, I dissent from the opinion and judgment of the Court.

. . .

■ SPECTOR, JUSTICE, dissenting.

Over five years ago, a trial court issued a divorce decree that included an award to Sheila Twyman of $15,000 for the years of abuse she had suffered at the hands of her husband. At the time, the award was consistent with prevailing Texas law. Today, the plurality sets aside the trial court's award and sends Sheila Twyman back to start the process over in a new trial. Because justice for Sheila Twyman has been both delayed and denied, I dissent.

. . .

The trial court found that William "engaged in a continuing course of conduct of attempting to coerce [Sheila] to join in his practices of 'bondage' by continually asserting that [their] marriage could be saved only by [Sheila] participating with [William] in his practices of 'bondage.' " The trial court also determined that Sheila's suffering was certainly foreseeable from William's continuing course of conduct, "in light of his existing knowledge of her long-existing emotional state, which was caused by her having been forcibly raped prior to their marriage." Finally, the trial court found that Sheila's mental anguish was a direct proximate result of William's sexual practices.

Based on the pleadings, evidence, and arguments, the trial court concluded that the facts and the law supported Sheila's recovery of $15,000 for William's negligent infliction of emotional distress. The court of appeals, in an opinion by Justice Gammage, affirmed the trial court's judgment under prevailing tort law and noted that this court had expressly approved the recovery of damages on a negligence claim in a divorce action.

This court, however, has now rejected Texas law established to provide redress for injuries of the kind inflicted by William Twyman. While allowing some tort claims to be brought in a divorce action, the plurality forbids recovery for negligent infliction of emotional distress, and insists that Sheila Twyman proceed on a theory of intentional infliction of emotional distress.

Today's decision is handed down contemporaneously with the overruling of the motion for rehearing in *Boyles v. Kerr*, 855 S.W.2d 593 (Tex.1993), in which this court reversed a judgment in favor of a woman who was surreptitiously videotaped during intercourse, then subjected to humiliation and ridicule when the tape was displayed to others. In *Boyles*, as in this case, a majority of this court has determined that severe, negligently-inflicted emotional distress does not warrant judicial relief—no matter how intolerable the injurious conduct. The reasoning originally articulated in *Boyles*, and now implied in this case, is that "[t]ort law cannot and should not attempt to provide redress for every instance of rude, insensitive, or distasteful behavior"; providing such relief, the *Boyles* majority explained, "would dignify most disputes far beyond their social importance." 36 Tex.S.Ct.J. 231, 233–234 (Dec. 2, 1992).[1]

Neither of these cases involves "rude, insensitive, or distasteful behavior"; they involve grossly offensive conduct that was appropriately found to warrant judicial relief. The decision in *Boyles* overturns well-reasoned case law, and I strongly agree with the dissenting opinion in that case. For the same reasons, I strongly disagree with the plurality here; the rule embodied in *Boyles* is no less objectionable when applied to the facts of this case. Sheila Twyman is entitled to recover the amount awarded by the trial court for the injuries inflicted by her husband.

It is no coincidence that both this cause and *Boyles* involve serious emotional distress claims asserted by women against men. From the beginning, tort recovery for infliction of emotional distress has developed primarily as a means of compensating women for injuries inflicted by men insensitive to the harm caused by their conduct. In "[t]he leading case which broke through the shackles,"[2] a man amused himself by falsely informing a woman that her husband had been gravely injured, causing a serious and permanent shock to her nervous system. *Wilkinson v. Downton*, 2 Q.B.D. 57 (1897). Similarly, in the watershed Texas case, a man severely beat two others in the presence of a pregnant woman, who suffered a miscarriage as a result of her emotional distress. *Hill v. Kimball*, 76 Tex. 210, 13 S.W. 59 (1890). By World War II, the pattern was well-established: one survey of psychic injury claims found that the ratio of female to male plaintiffs was five to one. Hubert Winston Smith, *Relation of Emotions to Injury and Disease: Legal Liability for Psychic Stimuli*, 30 Va.L.Rev. 193 (1944).

---

1. On rehearing, the *Boyles* majority has reworded slightly its discussion but reiterated its reasoning and result. The majority's overriding concern there has remained the avoidance of relief for "merely rude or insensitive behavior." 855 S.W.2d 593, 602.

2. William L. Prosser, *Insult and Outrage*, 44 Cal.L.Rev. 40, 42 (1956).

Even today, when emotional distress claims by both sexes have become more widely accepted, women's claims against men predominate. Of the thirty-four Texas cases cited by the plurality—all decided since 1987—women's claims outnumbered men's by a ratio of five to four; and only four of the thirty-four involved any female defendants. Of those cases involving relations between two individuals—with no corporations involved—five involved a woman's claim against a man; none involved a man's claim against a woman.

I do not argue that women alone have an interest in recovery for emotional distress. However, since the overwhelming majority of emotional distress claims have arisen from harmful conduct by men, rather than women, I do argue that men have had a disproportionate interest in downplaying such claims.

Like the struggle for women's rights, the movement toward recovery for emotional distress has been long and tortuous. *See* Peter A. Bell, *The Bell Tolls: Toward Full Tort Recovery for Psychic Injury*, 36 U.FLA.L.REV. 333, 336–40 (1984). In the judicial system dominated by men, emotional distress claims have historically been marginalized:

> The law of torts values physical security and property more highly than emotional security and human relationships. This apparently gender-neutral hierarchy of values has privileged men, as the traditional owners and managers of property, and has burdened women, to whom the emotional work of maintaining human relationships has commonly been assigned. The law has often failed to compensate women for recurring harms—serious though they may be in the lives of women—for which there is no precise masculine analogue.

Martha Chamallas and Linda K. Kerber, *Women, Mothers, and the Law of Fright: A History*, 88 MICH.L.REV. 814 (1990). Even Prosser recognizes the role of gender in the historical treatment of claims like that involved in *Hill v. Kimball*:

> It is not difficult to discover in the earlier opinions a distinctly masculine astonishment that any woman should ever allow herself to be frightened or shocked into a miscarriage.

W. Page Keeton et al., *Prosser and Keeton on the Law of Torts* § 12, at 55–56 (5th ed. 1984).

Displaying a comparable "masculine astonishment," the dissenting opinion by Justice Hecht insists that, with a few possible exceptions, women have played no distinct part in the development of tort recovery for emotional distress. As a general matter, Justice Hecht questions how a legal system dominated by men could develop a tort to compensate women even while marginalizing women's claims. The answer is amply illustrated by the present case: to provide some appearance of relief for Sheila Twyman, the court recognizes the tort of intentional infliction of emotional distress; but in doing so, it restricts her to a theory which, as Justice Hecht observes, is "seldom successful." 855 S.W.2d at 631.

Justice Hecht acknowledges that in the early cases, recovery for emotional distress "frequently involved female plaintiffs." 855 S.W.2d at 631. However, rather than viewing this phenomenon as an indication of actual, serious injuries, Justice Hecht suggests that it may have been due to a patronizing attitude on the part of the courts.

There is little doubt that some of the case law in this area, as in any other, reflects a patronizing view of women. More often, though, the case law reflects the logical application of existing law to a wide range of claims. For example, in the only case cited by Justice Hecht to illustrate an arguably patronizing view of women, there was evidence that men employed by a railroad had humiliated a man's ten-year-old daughter by subjecting her to obscene language; but there was no evidence that the language had humiliated the father. *Fort Worth & Rio Grande Ry. Co. v. Bryant*, 210 S.W. 556 (Tex.Civ.App.—Fort Worth 1918, writ ref'd). There is nothing patronizing about holding a railroad company responsible for the harm caused by its employees' conduct.

I would group *Bryant* with the many other common carrier cases that were decided, in Justice Hecht's terms, "without particular regard for gender." 855 S.W.2d at 639. Neither the Fort Worth Court of Appeals, nor any of the other courts at the time were primarily concerned with protecting women's rights. But in *Bryant*, as in so many of the other cases, the evolution of the law regarding emotional distress claims did enable a female to recover for emotional harm inflicted by men. This fact does not reflect a charitable desire to help women; it reflects the fact that the serious emotional distress claims usually involved injuries inflicted by men upon women.

Given this history, the plurality's emphatic rejection of infliction of emotional distress claims based on negligence is especially troubling. Today, when the widespread mistreatment of women is being documented throughout the country—for instance, in the areas of sexual harassment and domestic violence—a majority of this court takes a step backward and abolishes one way of righting this grievous wrong.

NOTES

1. The question of intentional infliction of emotional distress was not resolved because *Twyman* was never retried. Sheila and William Twyman settled rather than endure another trial. Telephone Interview with Douglas M. Becker, Counsel for William Twyman (Aug. 19, 1996); Telephone Interview with Edwin J. Terry, Counsel for Sheila Twyman (Aug. 19, 1996).

2. What if the claim of intentional infliction of emotional distress were tied to the spouse's adultery? Should they be allowed to recover damages in a no-fault era? Some courts have held that the abolition of the common law tort of alienation of affections bars a claim of intentional infliction of emotional distress claims on the basis of adultery because it shows the legislature's intent to take harm arising out of a spouse's sexual trespasses outside of the realm of the actionable. *See, e.g., Quinn v. Walsh*, 732 N.E.2d 330, 337 (Mass. App. Ct. 2000); *see also Doe v. Doe*, 747 A.2d 617 (Md. 2000). In addition, a majority of courts have held that the heightened standard required for intentional infliction of emotional distress cannot normally be met in cases of adultery. See, for example, the following reasoning:

> An affair of the sort alleged here would by most in our society be considered reprehensible and a cause for sadness, anger and distress; we do not condone the behavior which is alleged to have occurred. But an openly conducted affair, even one which is intended to, or which the actor should have known would, cause emotional harm, does not in our society constitute conduct which is " 'extreme and outrageous,' ... 'beyond all possible bounds of decency' and ... 'utterly intolerable in a civilized community.' "

Quinn, 732 N.E.2d at 339 (citations omitted). In the words of another court:

> We do not condone promiscuous sexual conduct. However, we do not find defendant's conduct in participating in a sexual relationship with a married woman, his friend's wife, who willingly continued the affair over an extended period, is atrocious and utterly intolerable conduct so extreme in degree as to go beyond all possible bounds of decency. The parties are residents of Iowa City, a

community of 50,000 and the home of the University of Iowa. A recitation of the facts of this case to an average member of the community would not lead him to exclaim, "Outrageous!"

Strauss v. Cilek, 418 N.W.2d 378, 380 (Iowa Ct. App. 1987).

Ira Mark Ellman & Stephen D. Sugarman, *Spousal Emotional Abuse as a Tort?*

55 MD. L. REV. 1268, 1269, 1305–26 (1996).

Introduction

Should "spousal emotional abuse" be a tort? More precisely, should states recognize a cause of action by one spouse against another for intentional infliction of emotional distress as set out in section 46 of the *Restatement (Second) of Torts*?[1] In recent years, courts have been asked to apply this tort of "outrageous" conduct to the marital setting in more than a handful of cases in which the plaintiff was not claiming a physical beating. Some judges have now allowed divorcing spouses to bring such fault-based tort suits, a remarkable development if one considers the historical trend toward no-fault divorce that is relentlessly squeezing out fault as a consideration in resolving family law disputes. Are such cases an aberration, or do they suggest a new and improved approach to considering fault in divorce? In this Article we describe and evaluate this new development.

. . .

V.   Is Spousal Emotional Abuse a Judicially Administrable Concept?

At several points in our discussion of the desirability of recognizing a tort of spousal emotional abuse, we have mentioned the importance of establishing a clear standard for what constitutes outrageous conduct. We now deal directly with this issue. . . .

. . .

B.   The New Section 46 Cases: The Standard Fact Patterns

We turn now to the decided IIED cases that have prompted our inquiry into whether there should be a tort action for spousal emotional abuse. . . .

. . .

1. *The Bully.*—Here we highlight two cases that we believe treated similar facts quite differently. In *Hakkila v. Hakkila*, the spouses separated in 1985 after ten years of marriage. When the husband filed a petition for dissolution, the wife, who had a history of depression, counterclaimed for IIED. It appears the divorce and tort cases were tried together before a

---

1. *Restatement (Second) of Torts 46* (1965). Section 46, titled "Outrageous Conduct Causing Severe Emotional Distress," states:

(1) One who by extreme and outrageous conduct intentionally or recklessly causes severe emotional distress to another is subject to liability for such emotional distress, and if bodily harm to the other results from it, for such bodily harm.

(2) Where such conduct is directed at a third person, the actor is subject to liability if he intentionally or recklessly causes severe emotional distress

(a) to a member of such person's immediate family who is present at the time, whether or not such distress results in bodily harm, or

(b) to any other person who is present at the time, if such distress results in bodily harm.

judge, who made factual findings to support his award of tort damages to the wife. Although apparently there was no separate claim for battery, the trial court supported the IIED verdict in part with a general finding that the husband had "assaulted and battered" the wife. The finding was supported in the record, according to the appeals court, by evidence of "several" incidents.

The New Mexico appellate court in *Hakkila* cautiously concluded that while spousal IIED claims might be valid in other settings, the facts of this case were inadequate as a matter of law to demonstrate such a tort. Hence it reversed the judgment for the wife. Indeed, the court expressed concern that the husband was subjected to a six-day trial on these claims, and urged trial courts to make more liberal use of summary judgments if similar IIED cases arise in the future.

In *Massey v. Massey*, the wife claimed that her husband, a bank president, denied her any independent access to funds and doled out money to her in small amounts, belittled her in front of others, had outbursts that sometimes included property destruction and that caused her to experience "intense anxiety and fear," and threatened to tell her children and friends of her extramarital affair and take custody of her youngest daughter from her. The wife's psychologist testified that the wife dealt with the husband by "walking on egg shells so as not to trigger [his] rage." The wife made no claim of personal physical violence, and the jury ultimately found that the husband "had not assaulted [the wife] by threat of imminent injury nor acted with malice." Although the husband portrayed most facts differently than his wife, he conceded that he often used threats in both his business and his marriage "to get his way." The husband claimed that the wife was an alcoholic, and that he had been devastated by her extramarital affair. The parties had been married for twenty-two years. The distress claim, tried with the divorce action, resulted in a judgment against the husband for $362,000 in compensatory damages, with no punitive damages award. A Texas appeals court affirmed the award.

. . .

Massey is troubling to us for two reasons. First, it seems wrongly decided and thereby portends further inappropriate decisions if the tort of spousal emotional abuse is unleashed. Second, the way the appellate court in *Massey* envisioned how "outrageousness" is to be determined in individual cases seems ultimately misguided.

In rejecting the arguments that the husband's conduct was outrageous as a matter of law, the appeals court in *Massey* approved the following instruction that the trial judge had given the jury:

> The bounds of decency vary from legal relationship to legal relationship. The marital relationship is highly subjective and constituted by mutual understandings and interchanges which are constantly in flux, and any number of which could be viewed by some segments of society as outrageous. Conduct considered extreme and outrageous in some relationships may be considered forgivable in other relationships. In your deliberation on the questions, definitions and instructions that follow, you shall consider them only in the context of the marital relationship of the parties to this case.

In short, by accepting the proposition that the "bounds of decency vary" among marital relationships, the court seemed thereby drawn to the conclusion that the same acts could be found "outrageous" in the context of one marriage but not in another. Put differently, the court approved a jury instruction that seeks to avoid imposing fixed societal standards of conduct on intimate personal relationships, asking the jury, in effect, to apply the couple's own standards. The instruction tells the jurors not to focus on what they would find outrageous in their own marriage, nor to search for some community consensus as to what marital behavior is completely out of bounds. Rather, they are to decide whether the complaining spouse can fairly label as "outrageous" the complained of acts in the setting of her own marriage.

The policy issue here—shall the outrageousness of spousal conduct be judged by external or internal standards—seems fundamental. The apparent justification for the choice expressed by the approved jury instruction is that the imposition of external standards on an intimate relationship may risk inappropriate, and possibly even unconstitutional intrusion on marital privacy. But while we agree that such intrusion should be avoided, we doubt that *Massey's* resort to internal standards offers a promising solution.

Presumably, any effort to judge a spouse's conduct by the couple's own standards must look for those standards in the parties' understanding at the time their marriage began, or as they mutually adjusted it at some later time, rather than in the unilateral expressions of one party after the marriage has fallen apart. Consider, then, some possible interpretations of the *Massey* facts. On the one hand, the opinion portrays the husband as an insensitive, domineering bully in his personal relations, a man whose conduct might be judged to fit precisely the classic fault-divorce standard of mental cruelty. Yet his marriage lasted over twenty years, and perhaps close scrutiny would have shown that during much of the marriage his wife enjoyed compensating benefits in her relationship with him. Possibly his behavior became more extreme during the course of the marriage. Or possibly when they first married both were poorly socialized and incapable of "normal" relationships, but later the wife matured. Still, their earlier understanding, even if "unhealthy," functioned for two decades or more, perhaps meeting each other's needs as well as either of them could. On this last understanding of the couple's marriage, the court's jury instruction would seem to require a verdict for the defendant.

Consider also the husband's claim in *Massey* that his wife was an alcoholic and that he had been devastated by her extramarital affair. Although *Ruprecht* tells us that the wife's affair would not give the husband an IIED action for *her* violation of her marital vows, under the approved jury instruction ought not the wife's adultery and excessive drinking in *Massey*, if proved, at least provide a context in which *his* behavior, even if still wrongful, should not be deemed outrageous? Indeed, on close examination, this couple's "mutual understanding" might well have condemned adultery more than the husband's behavior of which the wife complained.

What is going on here? In the first place, it appears that the kind of close examination of the couple's entire marriage history called for by the judge's instruction did not actually take place in *Massey*. Indeed, we find it highly questionable whether it is either realistic or desirable to ask the jury to make such an inquiry in order to determine exactly what standards the parties had set for themselves. To do so requires a great deal of nuanced detective work at a time when the parties have every incentive to cast earlier words and actions in an altogether false light. Moreover, to successfully make the inquiry requires a deep intrusion into the spouses' intimate affairs, thereby flying in the face of a central argument in favor of the internal standard in the first place—that it is supposed to respect their privacy by refraining from imposing outside standards on them.

It appears, then, that despite what both courts said, the jury and both levels of the judiciary are doing something different than what is called for by the appellate court's legal reasoning. Rather, it seems the jurors were permitted to deem the husband's conduct unacceptable for whatever reasons of their own they might have had, and, following the trial court, the reviewing court simply shrank from overturning that verdict as a matter of law. At the appellate level this means either that the court, applying its own values, decided that the husband's behavior was outrageous despite the wife's adultery and drinking, or that, by approving the internal standard, the court put itself in a position where appellate reversal of the jury determination becomes all but impossible.

The most disturbing implication for us is that standardless instructions combined with toothless appellate review add up to enormous jury discretion to impose on the couple just about any decision they wish. This not only threatens uneven justice and unpredictable outcomes, but also invites virtually all discontented, divorcing spouses to try their chance at the lottery.

．．．

Even if a jury wanted to be faithful to the *Massey* instruction, the implementation difficulties with internal standards seem irremediable. All too often it will be hopeless to derive internal marital standards from a postmarriage investigation of the typically informal and unarticulated understandings that once existed in the now-defunct relationship. . . .

．．．

We conclude, therefore, that the approach to these cases envisioned by the *Massey* appeals court is misguided, and that if section 46 of the *Restatement* were made applicable to interspousal claims, one would at least have to start with external standards. Yet we also agree that the *Massey* court was emphasizing an important consideration. Because marital understandings *do* vary, important privacy norms can be violated if tort law were to impose liability after the marriage for conduct that was within the bounds of the marriage as the spouses then understood it. This means that the external standard only should reach conduct that is highly unlikely to have been part of any couple's mutual understanding, or in any event is sufficiently malevolent to justify overriding these privacy norms. Indeed, one might argue that the outrage standard is meant to incorporate this very idea: marital conduct crosses the line into outrageousness at just the point when it becomes so extreme that it is not credible to think it was part of any reasonable couple's marital understanding.

The preeminent example of such conduct is battery. In holding spouses liable for the physical injuries they intentionally inflict on one another, a court has no occasion to remind the jury that "bounds of decency vary from marital relationship to marital relationship." We normally do not believe that couples meaningfully agree that one may batter the other in return for, say, providing financial support; and the social norm against spousal beating is sufficiently strong that we are prepared to condemn it anyway, notwithstanding any alleged mutual understanding of the couple.

This approach would serve, in addition, to exclude from recovery claims by spouses who had marital relationships that were extrasensitive to matters of sexual fidelity or honesty, as illustrated in the hypotheticals described earlier involving fundamentalist religious objections to adultery and written promises to tell the truth at all cost.

But what alleged spousal emotional abuse, if any, would be included? There's the rub. In contrast to battery, it is much more difficult to establish satisfactory standards to identify when emotional mistreatment is completely out of bounds. First of all, intimate relationships often involve complex emotional bargains that make no sense to third parties with different needs or perceptions. People often remain in marriages that look to others to be unhealthy. Although staying married is sometimes the result of coercion or delusion, often what may seem to outsiders as, say, intolerably extreme verbal harshness, is instead a feature of the particular relationship with which the parties, at least on balance, are content. In short, in many matters some couples arrive at solutions that depart from the social conventions that govern most of their acquaintances. Because those who sufficiently dislike their spouse's behavior can seek a divorce, it becomes more difficult to justify the conclusion that their marital relationship was so unacceptably uncivilized as to require tort damages when they wait many years to do so.

For example, was Mrs. Massey the victim of an extremely cruel husband who fiendishly exploited her personal insecurity in order to keep her trapped in an abusive relationship? Or was she someone who willingly accepted verbal unkindness and a loss of independence in return for relief from many ordinary responsibilities, who later changed her mind and wants compensation? ... The upshot is that while we are content to tell the batterer that he acts at his peril, we feel much less comfortable with a legal regime that says the same to Mr. Massey.

Turning away from the peculiarities of any specific couple, and looking generally at marital conduct that can be emotionally distressing, it is critical to recognize that by requiring "outrageous" conduct the *Restatement* clearly means to exclude from liability the common incivilities of everyday life. The idea is that such rude, insensitive, or mean-spirited behavior is better regulated, at least in the usual case, by social mechanisms or through self-help resort to divorce rather than through tort law. Although one reason for seeking to restrict recovery to extreme cases is to prevent a flood of litigation, surely another reason for a high threshold is the disparity between our aspirations and our conduct. Few if any of us consistently can avoid violating the norms of appropriate, sensitive social conduct that we endorse. The gap between societal aspiration and individual reality may be especially great in marital relations.

Yet, without clear guidelines as to what meets the threshold, the risk is that at least some juries will measure outrageousness against an ideal standard of marital relations—in effect lowering the threshold. This tendency is facilitated if outrageousness is left a flexible, open-ended concept. In this way, the outrage standard could yield liability for a much wider swath of marital conduct than for conduct by employers toward their employees, creditors toward their debtors, and landlords toward their tenants.

We concede that some commentators explicitly have urged the use of tort law as a tool for reforming intimate relations between the genders—by threatening to hold individuals to aspirational standards. But this strategy flies in the face of most modern family law reform that has acknowledged the need to conform the law to a social reality that traditional rules did not accept. Hence, applying tort law to claims of spousal emotional abuse risks a reprise of this very problem.

NOTE

Is the proposal by Professors Ellman and Sugarman the best way to ensure that marital tort claims are based on a relative consensus about the culpability of the behavior in question? Should tort law try to take account of the purely emotional or psychological injuries that spouses may inflict on one another?

C.   ACCESS TO DIVORCE

Boddie v. Connecticut

Supreme Court of the United States, 1971.
401 U.S. 371, 91 S.Ct. 780, 28 L.Ed.2d 113.

■ MR. JUSTICE HARLAN delivered the opinion of the Court.

Appellants, welfare recipients residing in the State of Connecticut, brought this action in the Federal District Court for the District of Connecticut on behalf of themselves and others similarly situated, challenging, as applied to them, certain state procedures for the commencement of litigation, including requirements for payment of court fees and costs for service of process, that restrict their access to the courts in their effort to bring an action for divorce.

It appears from the briefs and oral argument that the average cost to a litigant for bringing an action for divorce is $60. Section 52–259 of the CONNECTICUT GENERAL STATUTES provides: "There shall be paid to the clerks of the supreme court or the superior court, for entering each civil cause, forty-five dollars . . . ." An additional $15 is usually required for the service of process by the sheriff, although as much as $40 or $50 may be necessary where notice must be accomplished by publication.

There is no dispute as to the inability of the named appellants in the present case to pay either the court fees required by statute or the cost incurred for the service of process. . . .

. . .

. . . As this Court on more than one occasion has recognized, marriage involves interests of basic importance in our society. It is not surprising, then, that the States have seen fit to oversee many aspects of that institution. Without a prior judicial imprimatur, individuals may freely enter into and rescind commercial contracts, for example, but we are unaware of any jurisdiction where private citizens may covenant for or dissolve marriages without state approval. Even where all substantive requirements are concededly met, we know of no instance where two consenting adults may divorce and mutually liberate themselves from the constraints of legal obligations that go with marriage, and more fundamentally the prohibition against remarriage, without invoking the State's judicial machinery.

Thus, although they assert here due process rights as would-be plaintiffs, we think appellants' plight, because resort to the state courts is the only avenue to dissolution of their marriages, is akin to that of defendants faced with exclusion from the only forum effectively empowered to settle their disputes. Resort to the judicial process by these plaintiffs is no more voluntary in a realistic sense than that of the defendant called upon to defend his interests in court. For both groups this process is not only the paramount dispute-settlement technique, but, in fact, the only available one.

In this posture we think that this appeal is properly to be resolved in light of the principles enunciated in our due process decisions that delimit rights of defendants compelled to litigate their differences in the judicial forum.

. . .

Prior cases establish, first, that due process requires, at a minimum, that absent a countervailing state interest of overriding significance, persons forced to settle their claims of right and duty through the judicial process must be given a meaningful opportunity to be heard. . . .

. . .

Our cases further establish that a statute or a rule may be held constitutionally invalid as applied when it operates to deprive an individual of a protected right although its general validity as a measure enacted in the legitimate exercise of state power is beyond question. . . .

No less than these rights, the right to a meaningful opportunity to be heard within the limits of practicality, must be protected against denial by particular laws that operate to jeopardize it for particular individuals.

. . .

Just as a generally valid notice procedure may fail to satisfy due process because of the circumstances of the defendant, so too a cost requirement, valid on its face, may offend due process because it operates to foreclose a particular party's opportunity to be heard. The State's obligations under the Fourteenth Amendment are not simply generalized ones; rather, the State owes to each individual that process which, in light of the values of a free society, can be characterized as due.

Drawing upon the principles established by the cases just canvassed, we conclude that the State's refusal to admit these appellants to its courts, the sole means in Connecticut for obtaining a divorce, must be regarded as the equivalent of denying them an opportunity to be heard upon their claimed right to a dissolution of their marriages, and, in the absence of a sufficient countervailing justification for the State's action, a denial of due process.

The arguments for this kind of fee and cost requirement are that the State's interest in the prevention of frivolous litigation is substantial, its use of court fees and process costs to allocate scarce resources is rational, and its balance between the defendant's right to notice and the plaintiff's right to access is reasonable.

In our opinion, none of these considerations is sufficient to override the interest of these plaintiff-appellants in having access to the only avenue open for dissolving their allegedly untenable marriages. Not only is there no necessary connection between a litigant's assets and the seriousness of his motives in bringing suit, but it is here beyond present dispute that appellants bring these actions in good faith. Moreover, other alternatives exist to fees and cost requirements as a means for conserving the time of courts and protecting parties from frivolous litigation, such as penalties for false pleadings or affidavits, and actions for malicious prosecution or abuse of process, to mention only a few. In the same vein we think that reliable alternatives exist to service of process by a state-paid sheriff if the State is unwilling to assume the cost of official service. This is perforce true of service by publication which is the method of notice least calculated to bring to a potential defendant's attention the pendency of judicial proceedings. We think in this case service at defendant's last known address by mail and posted notice is equally effective as publication in a newspaper.

NOTE

Lee Lynk, while serving a life sentence in an Indiana prison, unsuccessfully filed for divorce in state court. Although conviction of a felony is a ground for divorce in Indiana, the state court refused to issue a writ of habeas corpus *ad testificandum* to enable Lynk to appear for the scheduled hearing. Lynk then filed suit in federal court under section 1 of the Civil Rights Act of 1871, 42 U.S.C. § 1983. On appeal, the Seventh Circuit held, in an opinion written by Judge Posner:

> It can hardly matter in this case whether the right to marry and the right to divorce stand on the same footing so far as the constitutional power of the states is concerned. We shall not try to add to the scholarly discussion of this question in *Murillo v. Bambrick*, 681 F.2d 898, 902–03 (3d Cir.1982), beyond noting the simple point that all civilized societies recognize a right to marry, and not all a right to divorce.... While ... there may be no constitutional right to divorce[,] ... if the right to marry and divorce is among the liberties encompassed by the due process clause the state can deprive a person of the right only if the state does so in accordance with due process of law. This conclusion was the necessary foundation of the *Boddie* decision, and survives, we believe, the *Sosna* decision.

Lynk v. LaPorte Superior Court No. 2, 789 F.2d 554, 566–67 (7th Cir.1986). The court directed Lynk to dismiss his divorce suit "voluntarily," and then refile the suit "in the hope that by refiling his petition for divorce he can clear the roadblocks to action on it." *Id.* at 568.

Sosna v. Iowa

Supreme Court of the United States, 1975.
419 U.S. 393, 95 S.Ct. 553, 42 L.Ed.2d 532.

■ Mr. Justice Rehnquist delivered the opinion of the Court.

Appellant Carol Sosna married Michael Sosna on September 5, 1964, in Michigan. They lived together in New York between October 1967 and August 1971, after which date they separated but continued to live in New York. In August 1972, appellant moved to Iowa with her three children, and the following month she petitioned the District Court of Jackson County, Iowa, for a dissolution of her marriage. Michael Sosna, who had been personally served with notice of the action when he came to Iowa to visit his children, made a special appearance to contest the jurisdiction of the Iowa court. The Iowa court dismissed the petition for lack of jurisdiction, finding that Michael Sosna was not a resident of Iowa and appellant had not been a resident of the State of Iowa for one year preceding the filing of her petition. In so doing the Iowa court applied the provisions of Iowa Code § 598.6 requiring that the petitioner in such an action be "for the last year a resident of the state."

. . .

The durational residency requirement under attack in this case is a part of Iowa's comprehensive statutory regulation of domestic relations, an area that has long been regarded as a virtually exclusive province of the States. Cases decided by this Court over a period of more than a century bear witness to this historical fact. In *Barber v. Barber*, 62 U.S. (21 How.) 582, 584 (1859), the Court said: "We disclaim altogether any jurisdiction in the courts of the United States upon the subject of divorce ...." In *Pennoyer v. Neff*, 95

U.S. 714, 734–735 (1877), the Court said: "The State ... has absolute right to prescribe the conditions upon which the marriage relation between its own citizens shall be created, and the causes for which it may be dissolved," and the same view was reaffirmed in *Simms v. Simms*, 175 U.S. 162, 167 (1899).

. . .

The imposition of a durational residency requirement for divorce is scarcely unique to Iowa, since 48 States impose such a requirement as a condition for maintaining an action for divorce.[15] As might be expected, the periods vary among the States and range from six weeks to two years. The one-year period selected by Iowa is the most common length of time prescribed.

Appellant contends that the Iowa requirement of one year's residence is unconstitutional ... because it establishes two classes of persons and discriminates against those who have recently exercised their right to travel to Iowa, thereby contravening the Court's holdings in *Shapiro v. Thompson*, 394 U.S. 618 (1969), *Dunn v. Blumstein*, 405 U.S. 330 (1972), and *Memorial Hospital v. Maricopa County*, 415 U.S. 250 (1974)....

State statutes imposing durational residency requirements were of course invalidated when imposed by States as a qualification for welfare payments, *Shapiro, supra*, for voting, *Dunn, supra*, and for medical care, *Maricopa County, supra*. But none of those cases intimated that the States might never impose durational residency requirements, and such a proposition was in fact expressly disclaimed. What those cases had in common was that the durational residency requirements they struck down were justified on the basis of budgetary or recordkeeping considerations which were held insufficient to outweigh the constitutional claims of the individuals. But Iowa's divorce residency requirement is of a different stripe. Appellant was not irretrievably foreclosed from obtaining some part of what she sought, as was the case with the welfare recipients in *Shapiro*, the voters in *Dunn*, or the indigent patient in *Maricopa County*. She would eventually qualify for the same sort of adjudication which she demanded virtually upon her arrival in the State. Iowa's requirement delayed her access to the courts, but, by fulfilling it, she could ultimately obtain the same opportunity for adjudication which she asserts ought to be hers at an earlier point in time.

... A decree of divorce is not a matter in which the only interested parties are the State as a sort of "grantor," and a plaintiff such as appellant in the role of "grantee." Both spouses are obviously interested in the proceedings, since it will affect their marital status and very likely their property rights. Where a married couple has minor children, a decree of divorce would usually include provisions for their custody and support. With consequences of such moment riding on a divorce decree issued by its courts, Iowa may insist that one seeking to initiate such a proceeding have the modicum of attachment to the State required here.

Such a requirement additionally furthers the State's parallel interests in both avoiding officious intermeddling in matters in which another State has a paramount interest, and in minimizing the susceptibility of its own divorce decrees to collateral attack. A State such as Iowa may quite reasonably decide that it does not wish to become a divorce mill for unhappy spouses who have

---

15. Louisiana and Washington are the exceptions....

lived there as short a time as appellant had when she commenced her action in the state court after having long resided elsewhere. . . .

· · ·

Affirmed.

· · ·

■ MR. JUSTICE MARSHALL, with whom MR. JUSTICE BRENNAN joins, dissenting.

· · ·

. . . Iowa's residency requirement, the Court says, merely forestalls access to the courts; applicants seeking welfare payments, medical aid, and the right to vote, on the other hand, suffer unrecoverable losses throughout the waiting period. This analysis, however, ignores the severity of the deprivation suffered by the divorce petitioner who is forced to wait a year for relief. The injury accompanying that delay is not directly measurable in money terms like the loss of welfare benefits, but it cannot reasonably be argued that when the year has elapsed, the petitioner is made whole. The year's wait prevents remarriage and locks both partners into what may be an intolerable, destructive relationship. Even applying the Court's argument on its own terms, I fail to see how the *Maricopa County* case can be distinguished. A potential patient may well need treatment for a single ailment. Under Arizona statutes he would have had to wait a year before he could be treated. Yet the majority's analysis would suggest that Mr. Evaro's claim for non-emergency medical aid is not cognizable because he would "eventually qualify for the same sort of (service)." The Court cannot mean that Mrs. Sosna has not suffered any injury by being foreclosed from seeking a divorce in Iowa for a year. It must instead mean that it does not regard that deprivation as being very severe.

D. DIVORCE AND OTHER NORMATIVE ORDERS

1. RELIGION

Aflalo v. Aflalo

Superior Court of New Jersey, Chancery Division, Family Part, Monmouth County, 1996.
295 N.J. Super. 527, 685 A.2d 523.

■ FISHER, J.S.C.

This case requires the court to visit an issue that has previously troubled our courts in matrimonial actions involving Orthodox Jews—a husband's refusal to provide a "get."[1]

Here, the parties were married on October 13, 1983 in Ramle, Israel, and have one child, Samantha. Plaintiff Sondra Faye Aflalo ("Sondra") has filed a complaint seeking a dissolution of the marriage. Defendant Henry Arik Aflalo ("Henry") has answered the complaint. The matter is on the court's active trial list and should be reached for trial in the very near future. Henry does not want a divorce and has taken action with The Union of

---

1. A "get" is a bill of divorce which the husband gives to his wife to free her to marry again. The word "get" apparently signifies the number 12, the "get" being a twelve-lined instrument. The word is a combination of "gimel" (which has a value of three) together with "tet" (which has a value of nine).

Orthodox Rabbis of the United States and Canada in New York City (the "Beth Din"[2]) to have a hearing on his attempts at reconciliation.

The issues at hand came to critical mass when the parties engaged in a settlement conference on February 14, 1996, while awaiting trial in this court. At that time the court was advised by counsel that the matter was "98% settled" but that Henry had placed what Sondra viewed as an insurmountable obstacle to a complete resolution: he refused to provide a "get." Unlike what the court faced in [related cases], Henry was not using his refusal to consent to the "get" as a means of securing a more favorable resolution of the issues before this court. That type of conduct the . . . court rightfully labelled "extortion". On the contrary, Henry's position (as conveyed during the settlement conference) was that regardless of what occurs in this court he will not consent to a Jewish divorce.

Henry's position spun off an unexpected problem; it caused his attorney to move to be relieved as counsel. Arguing that since he, too, is a practicing Orthodox Jew, Henry's counsel claims that he would "definitely have a religious problem representing a man who at the conclusion of a divorce proceeding refused, without reason, to give his wife a Get."

. . .

Henry opposed his attorney's motion. He stated under oath that he seeks a reconciliation and that Sondra had been summoned to appear before the Beth Din for this purpose. The court was also advised during oral argument that should reconciliation fail the Beth Din could recommend that Henry give Sondra a "get"; Henry stated under oath that while he desires a reconciliation he would follow the recommendations of the Beth Din and give the "get" if that was the end result of those proceedings. The court finds Henry both credible and sincere in this regard; his position clearly eliminates his counsel's stated concerns.

The problem, however, festers since Sondra appears unwilling to settle this case without a "get." Accordingly, this court must now lay to rest whether any order may be entered which would impact on Sondra's securing of a Jewish divorce.

Sondra claims that this court, as part of the judgment of divorce which may eventually be entered in this matter, may and should order Henry to cooperate with the obtaining of a Jewish divorce upon pain of Henry having limited or supervised visitation of Samantha or by any other coercive means. She claims that *Minkin v. Minkin*, 180 *N.J.Super.* 260, 434 A.2d 665 (Ch.Div. 1981) authorizes this court to order Henry to consent to the Jewish divorce. That trial court decision certainly supports her view. This court, however, believes that to enter such an order violates Henry's First Amendment rights and refuses to follow the course outlined in *Minkin*.

Prior to the adoption of our Nation's constitution, attempts were made in some colonies to legislate on matters of religion, including the governmental establishment of religion and the raising of taxes for the support of certain religions. Punishments were prescribed for the failure to attend religious services and for entertaining heretical opinions. In 1784 the Virginia legislature attempted to enact a bill "establishing provision for teachers of the Christian religion." This brought to bear the determined and eloquent opposition of Thomas Jefferson and James Madison. Madison responded in

---

2. The "Beth Din" is a rabbinical tribunal having authority to advise and pass upon matters of traditional Jewish law.

his "Memorial and Remonstrance" that "religion, or the duty we owe the Creator" was not within the cognizance of civil authority. The next session of the Virginia legislature led to the defeat of the aforementioned bill and the passage of a bill drafted by Jefferson which established "religious freedom" and declared that "to suffer the civil magistrate to intrude his powers into the field of opinion, and to restrain the profession or propagation of principles on supposition of their ill tendency, is a dangerous fallacy which at once destroys all religious liberty."

Not long after the adoption of the Constitution and the Bill of Rights, Jefferson made clear the meaning and intent of the First Amendment in his famous "reply" to the Danbury Baptist Association:

> Believing with you that religion is a matter which lies solely between man and his God; that he owes account to none other for his faith or his worship; that the legislative powers of the Government reach actions only, and not opinions, I contemplate with sovereign reverence that act of the whole American people which declared that their Legislature should "make no law respecting an establishment of religion or prohibiting the free exercise thereof," thus building a wall of separation between Church and State. Adhering to this expression of the supreme will of the Nation in behalf of the rights of conscience, I shall see, with sincere satisfaction, the progress of those sentiments which tend to restore man to all his natural rights, convinced he has no natural right in opposition to his social duties.

Since then the dimensions of this "wall of separation between Church and State" have been robustly debated and described frequently by our Nation's highest court.

The "Free Exercise Clause" of the First Amendment applies to the states through the Fourteenth Amendment's Due Process Clause. Not only does it bar a state's legislature from making a law which prohibits the free exercise of religion but it likewise inhibits a state's judiciary.

In the first instance, the Free Exercise Clause prohibits governmental regulation of religious beliefs but does not absolutely prohibit religious conduct. Second, to pass constitutional muster, a law must have both a secular purpose and a secular effect. That is, a law must not have a sectarian purpose; it must not be based upon a disagreement with a religious tenet or practice and must not be aimed at impeding religion.

Only when state action passes these threshold tests is there a need to balance the competing state and religious interests. The court is to engage in such balancing when the conduct or action sought to be regulated has "invariably posed some substantial threat to public safety, peace or order." Here, the relief Sondra seeks from this court so obviously runs afoul of the threshold tests of the Free Exercise Clause that the court need never reach the delicate balancing normally required in such cases.

The court will first endeavor to describe precisely what it is that Sondra seeks. And, while it seems beyond doubt, the court will then indicate why it cannot and certainly will not provide that relief.

"When a man takes a wife and possesses her, if she fails to please him because he finds something obnoxious about her, then he writes her a bill of divorcement, hands it to her, and sends her away from his house." *Deuteronomy* 24:1–4. From this biblical verse, the Jewish law and tradition that the "power of divorce rests exclusively with the husband" has its genesis. Wigoder, *The Encyclopedia of Judaism* (1989) 210.

The "get" is written almost entirely in Aramaic on parchment, and is drawn up by a "sofer" (a scribe), upon the husband's instruction to write "for him, for her, and for the purpose of a divorce," 6 *The Encyclopedia Judaica* (1971) 131. The materials used in the creation of the "get" must belong to the husband; the "sorer" presents them as a gift to the husband before the "get" is written. The spelling and the form of the document "are enumerated in minute detail in halakhic literature" and acknowledged by two witnesses. The rabbi who presides retains the "get"; he cuts it "in criss-cross fashion so that it cannot be used again," and to "avoid any later suspicion that it was not absolutely legal," *Encyclopedia Judaica, supra* at 132. The wife is given another document ("petor") which proves that she has been divorced and the "get" is filed away in its torn state. Wigoder, *supra* at 211.

Without such a divorce, the wife remains an "agunah" (a "tied" woman) and may not remarry in the eyes of Jewish law. Wigoder, *supra* at 211. If she remarries without a "get" she is considered to be an adulteress because she is still halakhically married to her first husband; any subsequent children are considered to be "mamzerim" (illegitimate) and may not marry other Jews. Himelstein, *The Jewish Primer* (1990) 161.

The court is not unsympathetic to Sondra's desire to have Henry's cooperation in the obtaining of a "get." She, too, is sincere in her religious beliefs. Her religion, at least in terms of divorce, does not profess gender equality. But does that mean that she can obtain the aid of this court of equity to alter this doctrine of her faith? That the question must be answered negatively seems so patently clear that the only surprising aspect of Sondra's argument is that it finds some support in the few cases on the subject.

In *Minkin*, the trial court requested the testimony of several distinguished rabbis. The court viewed the issue as whether a state court could order specific performance of the "ketubah." The "ketubah" is the marriage contract in which the couple is obligated to comply with the laws of Moses and Israel. It contains the promise of the husband "to honor and support thee and provide for thy needs, even as Jewish husbands are required to do *by our religious law* and tradition." *See, e.g., Avitzur v. Avitzur,* 58 N.Y.2d 108, 459 N.Y.S.2d 572, 576, 446 N.E.2d 136 (1983) (emphasis added), cert. denied 464 *U.S.* 817 (1983). The "ketubah" also contains the parties' agreement "to recognize the Beth Din . . . as having authority to counsel us in the light of Jewish tradition . . . and to summon either party at the request of the other. . . ." 459 N.Y.S.2d at 576, 446 N.E.2d at 140.

In determining that it could specifically enforce the "ketubah," *Minkin* relied on a New York decision which stated:

> Defendant has also contended that a decree of specific performance would interfere with his freedom of religion under the Constitution. Complying with his agreement would not compel the defendant to practice any religion, not even the Jewish faith to which he still admits adherence (paragraph Second of the complaint not denied in the answer). His appearance before the Rabbinate to answer questions and give evidence needed by them to make a decision is not a profession of faith. Specific performance herein would merely require the defendant to do what he voluntarily agreed to do.

[*Koeppel v. Koeppel,* 138 N.Y.S.2d 366, 373 (Sup.Ct.1954).] Analyzing the case against the test used to determine whether state action violates the Establishment Clause which is set forth in *Committee for Public Education and Religious Liberty v. Nyquist,* 413 U.S. 756, 772–773 (1973), the *Minkin* court said:

Relying upon credible expert testimony that the acquisition of a *get* is not a religious act, the court finds that the entry of an order compelling defendant to secure a *get* would have the clear secular purpose of completing a dissolution of the marriage. Its primary effect neither advances nor inhibits religion since it does not require the husband to participate in a religious ceremony or to do acts contrary to his religious beliefs. Nor would the order be an excessive entanglement with religion.

Also, in reliance upon the expert testimony found credible, the *Minkin* court concluded that an order compelling a husband to acquire a "get" is "not a religious act." *Id.* The court apparently relied on one of the rabbis who testified "that Jewish law cannot be equated with religious law, but instead is comprised of two components—one regulating a man's relationship with God and the other regulating the relationship between man and man. The *get*, which has no reference to God but which does affect the relationship between two parties, falls into the latter category and is, therefore, civil and not religious in nature." 180 *N.J.Super.* at 265–266, 434 A.2d 665.

Minkin's approach that the "ketubah" may be specifically enforced without violating the First Amendment is in accord with the decisional law of New York, Illinois, and Delaware, and at odds with Arizona, and, now, this court. *Minkin* and its followers (including the New Jersey trial court in *Burns*)[4] are not persuasive for a number of reasons.

First, it examined the problem against the backdrop of the Establishment Clause and not the Free Exercise Clause. The Establishment Clause prohibits government from placing its support behind a particular religious belief. The Free Exercise Clause, obviously implicated here, prohibits government from interfering or becoming entangled in the practice of religion by its citizens.

Second, the conclusion that an order requiring the husband to provide a "get" is not a religious act nor involves the court in the religious beliefs or practices of the parties is not at all convincing. It is interesting that the court was required to choose between the conflicting testimony of the various rabbis[7] to reach this conclusion. The one way in which a court may become entangled in religious affairs, which the court in *Minkin* did not recognize, was in becoming an arbiter of what is "religious." As Justice Brennan observed in *Serbian Eastern Orthodox Diocese v. Milivojevich*, 426 *U.S.* 696, 709 (1976):

> [W]here resolution of the disputes cannot be made without extensive inquiry by civil courts into religious law and polity, the First and Fourteenth Amendments mandate that civil courts shall not disturb the decisions of the highest ecclesiastical tribunal within a church of hierarchical polity, but must accept such decisions as binding on them, in their application to the religious issues of doctrine or polity before them.

---

4. *Burns* is equally unpersuasive, although the wife's position therein is even more sympathetic. There, the parties were divorced years earlier and the husband had remarried. However, he refused to provide his ex-wife with a "get" unless she invested $25,000 in an irrevocable trust for the benefit of their daughter. 223 N.J.Super. at 222, 538 A.2d 438. Relying upon *Minkin* and its broad equity powers, the court in *Burns* ordered the husband to "submit to the jurisdiction of the 'Bet Din' to initiate the proceedings for a 'get'." 223 N.J.Super. at 226, 538 A.2d 438. In the alternative, the court permitted the husband "to execute the prepared document, ... authorizing the preparation and presentation of the 'get' to the defendant by an agent on his behalf and forego the actual appearance before the 'Bet Din'." *Id.*

7. One rabbi testified that the acquisition of a "get" was a religious act. 180 N.J.Super. at 266, 434 A.2d 665.

Accordingly, civil courts may not override a decision of a religious tribunal or interpret religious law or canons. Of course, religious parties and organizations are entitled to the adjudication in our civil courts of "secular legal questions." But in doing so the civil court cannot decide any disputed questions of religious doctrine. That is exactly what the *Minkin* court did when it sifted among the rabbinical testimony to find the most credible version.

Third, the conclusion that its order concerned purely civil issues is equally unconvincing. In determining to specifically enforce the "ketubah," the court recognized that "[w]ithout compliance [the wife] cannot marry in accordance with her religious beliefs." 180 *N.J. Super.* at 263, 434 A.2d 665. As noted earlier the later children of a wife who remarries without a "get" are prohibited from marrying other Jews. No matter how one semantically phrases what was done in *Minkin*, the order directly affected the religious beliefs of the parties. By entering the order, the court empowered the wife to remarry in accordance with her religious beliefs and also similarly empowered any children later born to her. The mere fact that the "get" does not contain the word "God," which the *Minkin* court found significant, is hardly reason to conclude otherwise. Nor is it sound to argue that religion involves only one's relation to the creator and not one's relation to other persons, as may be obligated by religious traditions or teachings. *Minkin* might as well have said that a civil court may order a Christian to comply with the Second Great Commandment[8] but not the First.[9] The concept of "religion" certainly does have reference to one's relation to the creator but it also has relation to one's obedience to the will of the creator. In one's pursuit to comply with the creator's will one is certainly engaged in religious activity. While engaging in such conduct, one may also be subjected to civil authority but that does not remove that conduct from the scope of religious activity. *Minkin* draws too fine a line in its rejection of the latter as an area constituting "religion" to command this court's assent to its holding.

Fourth, *Minkin* fails to recognize that coercing the husband to provide the "get" would not have the effect sought. The "get" must be phrased and formulated in strict compliance with tradition, according to the wording given in the Talmud. 6 *Encyclopedia Judaica* (1971) 131. The precisely worded "get" states that the husband does "willingly consent, being under no restraint, to release, to set free, and put aside thee, my wife...." *Id.* Accordingly, in giving his wife a "get" a husband must "act without constraint." Wigoder, *supra* at 210. Indeed, during the proceeding the husband is asked "whether he ordered [the 'get'] of his own free will." Singer, *The Jewish Encyclopedia* at 647. What value then is a "get" when it is ordered by a civil court and when it places the husband at risk of being held in contempt should he follow his conscience and refuse to comply? Moreover, why should this court order such relief when that is something which the Beth Din will not do? If a "get" is something which can be coerced then it should be the Beth Din which does the coercing. In coercing the husband, the civil court is, in essence, overruling or superseding any judgment which the Beth Din can or will enter, contrary to accepted First Amendment principles.

Avitzur suggests a more indirect way of providing relief to the wife. A majority of the New York Court of Appeals found that the wording of the "ketubah" suggested an agreement of the marital partners to appear before

---

8. "Thou shalt love thy neighbor as thyself."

9. "Thou shalt love the Lord thy God with thy whole heart, and with thy whole soul, and with thy whole mind, and with thy whole strength."

the Beth Din and held that such an agreement could be enforced by the civil court without running afoul of First Amendment law. The majority was careful in recognizing that it was not called upon to order the husband to provide a "get," noting that "plaintiff is not attempting to compel defendant to obtain a Get or to enforce a religious practice arising solely out of principles of religious law." 459 N.Y.S.2d at 574, 446 N.E.2d at 138. An order requiring defendant to appear before the Beth Din was found to be available because the majority viewed the role of the civil court as enforcing "nothing more than an agreement to refer the matter of a religious divorce to a nonjudicial forum." *Id.* The three members of the court which dissented, however, in this court's view correctly ascertained that even the limited relief which the majority of four approved required "inquiry into and resolution of questions of Jewish religious law and tradition" and thus inappropriately entangled the civil court in the wife's attempts to obtain a religious divorce. *Id.* at 577–578, 446 N.E.2d at 141–142.

Even if the majority opinion in *Avitzur* were followed by this court, the circumstances of this case do not support the relief endorsed in *Avitzur.* The "ketubah" only states the parties' recognition of the Beth Din as "having authority to counsel" them and "to summon either party at the request of the other...." Here, Sondra has never sought relief in the Beth Din and in fact has not appeared in response to the summons forwarded to her by the Beth Din regarding Henry's pursuit of reconciliation. Even *Avitzur,* it is suspected, would not enforce any attempt by Sondra to compel Henry to appear before the Beth Din when she has not honored a similar request.[11]

Minkin ultimately conjures the unsettling vision of future enforcement proceedings. Should a civil court fine a husband for every day he does not comply or imprison him for contempt for following his conscience? Apparently so, according to New York law. Or, as suggested by Sondra, should visitation of Samantha be limited pending Henry's cooperation? That argument finds no support anywhere. Unlike *Minkin* (where a judgment of divorce had already been entered), Henry seeks the intervention of the Beth Din in order to effect a reconciliation with his wife.[12] Should this court enjoin Henry—no matter how imperfect he may be pursuing it—from moving for reconciliation in that forum and order other relief which the Beth Din apparently cannot give? This court should not, and will not, compel a course of conduct in the Beth Din no matter how unfair the consequences. The spectre of Henry being imprisoned or surrendering his religious freedoms because of action by a civil court is the very image which gave rise to the First Amendment.

It may seem "unfair" that Henry may ultimately refuse to provide a "get."[13] But the unfairness comes from Sondra's own sincerely-held religious beliefs. When she entered into the "ketubah" she agreed to be obligated to the laws of Moses and Israel. Those laws apparently include the tenet that if Henry does not provide her with a "get" she must remain an "agunah." That was Sondra's choice and one which can hardly be remedied by this court. This court has no authority—were it willing—to choose for these

---

11. During a brief hearing via telephone on February 22, 1996, Sondra's counsel indicated that Sondra had responded in writing to the summons from the Beth Din but has never provided a copy of that response to this court.

12. Apparently, however, Henry has not paid the necessary fee and the matter now sits moribund at the Beth Din level.

13. That Sondra has not cooperated with the summons of the Beth Din regarding Henry's attempts at reconciliation could also be viewed as "unfair."

parties which aspects of their religion may be embraced and which must be rejected. Those who founded this Nation knew too well the tyranny of religious persecution and the need for religious freedom. To engage even in a "well-intentioned" resolution of a religious dispute requires the making of a choice which accommodates one view and suppresses another. If that is permitted, it readily follows that less "well-intentioned" choices may be made in the future by those who, as Justice Jackson once observed, believe "that all thought is divinely classified into two kinds—that which is their own and that which is false and dangerous." *American Communications Ass'n v. Douds,* 339 *U.S.* 382, 438 (1950) (dissenting opinion).

The tenets of Sondra's religion would be debased by this court's crafting of a short-cut or loophole through the religious doctrines she adheres to; and the dignity and integrity of the court and its processes would be irreparably injured by such misuse. The First Amendment was designed to protect both institutions against such unwarranted, unwanted and unlawful steps over the "wall of separation between Church and State." This court will not assist Sondra in her attempts to lower that wall. As Justice Frankfurter said, "[i]f nowhere else, in the relation between Church and State, 'good fences make good neighbors.' " *McCollum v. Board of Education,* 333 *U.S.* 203, 232 (1948) (dissenting opinion).

For these reasons, the court has denied the motion to be relieved as counsel. Further, any relief sought by either party with respect to any proceedings either currently being maintained or contemplated in the Beth Din is denied. The parties are directed to engage in a four-way conference within seven (7) days of this date and attempt to amicably resolve the issues that are actually before this court. Thereafter, they will forthwith report any results back to the court.

Henry's consent, or refusal to consent, to the providing of a "get," and Sondra's consent, or refusal to consent, to appear before the Beth Din for proceedings relating to Henry's attempts at reconciliation, are matters which are not to be bargained for or against. *Accord, Segal, supra.* The parties are urged, having previously resolved "98%" of the case, to resolve the remaining 2% for their own sake and, most importantly, for Samantha's sake.

NOTES

1. As the court notes, other jurisdictions have agreed to compel spouses to comply with the terms of their Jewish religious contract. In fact, the precedential value of the *Aflalo* decision is unclear, given that it is only at trial court level. A later decision by a New Jersey appellate court observed the following about a trial court decision that was based on *Aflalo*:

> The trial court's determination that it should not compel defendant in regard to the *get* is correct, but for different reasons than those advanced. Plaintiff has not established the effect of this particular *ketubah* nor the mandate of Mosaic law, if applicable. Without such a record we lack the necessary factual context to determine whether a New Jersey court has power to compel cooperation in obtaining a get.

Mayer–Kolker v. Kolker, 819 A.2d 17, 21 (N.J. Super. Ct. App. Div. 2003). Does this mean that if the proper factual record was established the court *could* potentially force the spouse to give a *get* despite *Aflalo*?

2. It was rare in the past for a divorced Jewish woman to be made an "agunah," a chained woman unable to remarry within Orthodox Judaism because her former husband denied her a get. In recent years, however, it is estimated that there have been hundreds of cases in North America. *See* Annys Shin, *Man Who Won't Grant*

Religious Divorce is Given Rabbinical Sanction, WASH. POST, Sept. 30, 2011, at B1. Refusing to grant a *get* is considered so reprehensible in Israel that rabbinical courts keep an online record of intractable husbands with their photos. *Id.* In 2011, a Capitol Hill aide was sanctioned by the Union of Orthodox Rabbis of the United States and Canada for refusing to grant his former wife a *get*. The judgment makes him subject to shunning by members of his faith. He could also be denied a seat at his synagogue. *Id.*

3. Difficult interpretive issues have also arisen in regard to Islamic marriage contracts, which commonly include a sum of money to be paid to the bride in the event of divorce. This sum is called the mahr. Some courts have enforced mahr agreements applying the standard of review they would apply to any prenuptial agreement. *See, e.g., Aziz v. Aziz*, 488 N.Y.S.2d 123, 124 (Sup. Ct. 1985). Other jurisdictions, however, have found mahr agreements to be unenforceable. In *In re Marriage of Dajani*, 204 Cal. App. 3d 1387 (Ct. App. 1988), the court held that the mahr was a contract that would incentivize divorce, which was contrary to public policy. Courts in Europe and Canada have also had to struggle with the question of whether to enforce the mahr as a civil contract or a religious custom. The result has been a highly variable form of a legal transplant. Outcomes may depend on each court's interpretation of the mahr as either a civil contract or a religious or ethnic custom that may or may not conflict with a country's public policy. For a critical appraisal of these varying results *see generally*, PASCALE FOURNIER, MUSLIM MARRIAGE IN WESTERN COURTS: LOST IN TRANSPLANTATION (2010).

2.   FOREIGN DIVORCE DECISIONS

Aleem v. Aleem

Maryland Court of Special Appeals, 2007.
931 A.2d 1123.

[The opinion is printed at page 17, *supra*]

NOTE

On the enforcement of divorce decisions by other states see Chapter 10 on Jurisdiction.

E.   REVOLUTION AND COUNTER-REVOLUTION?

Katherine Shaw Spaht, *Covenant Marriage Seven Years Later: Its as Yet Unfulfilled Promise*

65 LA. L. REV. 605, 612–15 (2005).

A Louisiana covenant marriage differs in three principal respects from other legally recognized "standard" marriages: 1) mandatory pre-marital counseling; 2) the legal obligation to take all reasonable steps to preserve the couple's marriage if marital difficulties arise; and 3) restricted grounds for divorce consisting of *fault* on the part of the other spouse or two years living separate and apart. Each of the three components addresses John Witte's observation in *From Sacrament to Contract* that restricting exit rules of marriage by reforming divorce law requires complementary legal restrictions on entry into marriage. Covenant marriage restricts entry into and exit from marriage for those who choose it and attempts to strengthen the marriage itself by imposing a legal obligation upon the covenant spouses which they agree to in advance of their marriage—taking *reasonable* steps to preserve their marriage if difficulties arise.

The mandatory pre-marital counseling under the covenant marriage statute must contain counsel about the seriousness of marriage, the intent of the couple that it be lifelong, and the agreement that the couple will take all reasonable steps to preserve the marriage. Any minister, priest, rabbi, or the secular alternative of a professional marriage counselor is permitted to provide the counseling and sign an attestation form. Of course, many religious counselors require considerably more, especially if they have signed a Community Marriage Covenant (CMC) or Agreement. The CMC, signed by community clergy, ordinarily requires a minimum of counseling sessions with the minister (four, for example), a pre-marital inventory such as PREPARE or FOCCUS, and the guarantee of a mentoring couple assigned to the engaged couple. In those cities that now have Community Marriage Agreements, the clergy signatories provide counseling that is far more extensive than the covenant marriage legislation requires.

At the end of the mandatory pre-marital counseling, the prospective spouses sign a document called a Declaration of Intent that contains the content of their *covenant*, which includes the agreement to seek counseling if difficulties arise as well as their agreement to be bound by the Louisiana law of covenant marriage (choice of law clause). Both spouses sign the agreement and then execute an affidavit, signed by a notary, attesting to having had counseling as the law requires and having read the Covenant Marriage Act, the pamphlet prepared by the Attorney General that explains the differences between a covenant marriage and a standard marriage, including comparative grounds for divorce. The Declaration of Intent is in essence a special *contract* authorized by the state (Louisiana, Arizona, or Arkansas) that contains legal obligations similar to those in ordinary contracts. Most importantly, it is the agreement of the covenant spouses in advance to take reasonable steps to preserve their marriage which constitutes a legal obligation, the second distinguishing component of a covenant marriage. This obligation to take reasonable steps to preserve the marriage begins at the moment the marital difficulties arise and "should continue" until rendition of the judgment of divorce, the one exception being "when the other spouse has physically or sexually abused the spouse seeking the divorce or a child of one of the spouses."

Lastly, a spouse in a covenant marriage may obtain a divorce only if she can prove adultery, conviction of a felony, abandonment for one year, or physical or sexual abuse of her or a child of the parties. Otherwise, the spouses must live separate and apart for two years. A comparison of the grounds for divorce in a Louisiana "standard" marriage reveals that a covenant marriage commits the spouses in advance to a relinquishment of the easy exit rules in favor of more stringent, morally based exit rules. In a "standard" marriage a spouse may seek a divorce for adultery, conviction of a felony, or living separate and apart for *six months* either before *or* after a suit for divorce is filed. . . .

NOTES

1. Since Louisiana's adoption of covenant marriage, only two other states, Arkansas and Arizona, have enacted similar legislation. Approximately thirty other states have proposed covenant marriage statutes, but the bills have failed to become law. *See* Spaht, 65 La. L. Rev. at 605.

Louisiana's adoption of covenant marriage was, and continues to be, controversial. Proponents argue that it "bolster[s] the institution of marriage" by forcing couples to contemplate the seriousness of both marriage and divorce. Opponents of the law worry that it fails to protect victims of domestic violence and lacks provisions to ensure that participants understand the ramifications of entering into a covenant marriage. Some object to the role of clergy and other religious advisors in the premarital counseling stage. Still others have raised constitutional questions about the law's effect on individual liberty interests. For a thorough discussion of these and other viewpoints, *see* Joel A. Nichols, Comment, *Louisiana's Covenant Marriage Law: A First Step Toward a More Robust Pluralism in Marriage and Divorce Law?*, 47 EMORY L.J. 929 (1998).

Although covenant marriage is not statutorily available in most states, some couples have attempted to accomplish some of the same goals by developing agreements that limit the availability of divorce. In the event of divorce, courts are forced to decide whether or not they can enforce these agreements. *See supra* Section B.3.C. Contracting Around Statutory Grounds for Divorce.

2.   A recent study of covenant marriages in Louisiana suggests that only 1–2% of new marriages are covenant marriages. Steven L. Nock et. al., *Covenant Marriage Turns Five Years Old*, 10 MICH. J. GENDER & L. 169, 170 (2003). One reason for this may be that fewer than half the population in covenant marriage states are aware of this alternative. STEVEN L. NOCK ET AL., COVENANT MARRIAGE, THE MOVEMENT TO RECLAIM TRADITION IN AMERICA 43 (2008). The best estimate at this point is that covenant couples have about 55% the divorce rate of couples in standard marriages. *Id.* at 117. Researchers in this study concluded that it was the religiosity of the self-selected covenant spouses that affected the low divorce rate, rather than the institution itself. *Id.* One feature of covenant marriage that may have some positive effect on marital stability is the requirement of premarital counseling, which has been shown to reduce divorce rates. *Id.* at 132. Interestingly, marital counseling while a couple is already going through trouble has been shown to *increase* the chances that a couple will get divorced. *Id.* at 122.

James Herbie Difonzo, *Customized Marriage*

75 IND. L. J. 875, 905–28 (2000).

II.   The Divorce Counterrevolution

"On September 5, 1969, with a stroke of his pen, California governor Ronald Reagan wiped out the moral basis for marriage in America." Thus begins the revisionist history of the divorce counterrevolution. The mid to late 1960s have been described as the "cultural fault line, the B.C. and A.D. of American divorce." After that decade, the legal and social systems no longer considered divorce a concern involving "multiple stakeholders." Divorce abruptly became a solo voyage, often characterized as an immoral flight from responsibility. The legal system rejected the culpability-ground-turned-entitlement theory of divorce. But enacting the marital breakdown standard never resulted in a searching judicial inquiry into the state of each marriage, as many no-fault divorce reformers had hoped. Irreconcilable differences simply were not justiciable. As Mary Ann Glendon later reported, "the virtually universal understanding . . . is that the breakdown of a marriage is irretrievable if one spouse says it is." No-fault divorce became naked divorce.

. . .

But in the generation since the creation of no-fault divorce, a strong argument has emerged that the "happiness principle embedded in the no-fault ground has dealt a devastating blow to the durability of marriages."

Contemporary scholarly accounts are rife with calls for an end to a divorce process seen as facilitating individual irresponsibility at the expense of mutuality and the welfare of children. Many accounts in the popular press have also taken a cudgel to no-fault divorce, professing that "a whole generation . . . has placed its marital future in a [no-fault] law that favors the unfaithful, the uncommitted, the selfish and the immature. . . . 'Till death do us part' was replaced by 'as long as I'm happy.' "

. . .

B.   A Comeback for Culpability?

The campaign to reverse the perceived evils of the no-fault revolution has yielded a wide variety of counter-reform measures in legislatures, the academy, and the popular press. These proposals to eliminate or raise the threshold of no-fault divorce range from rewriting the constitution to enforcing pre-commitment restrictions on divorce, and include a variety of counseling and educational requirements, both mandatory and hortatory. The once-unthinkable return of a culpability hurdle for divorce has not only been thought, it has appeared in state house bills attempting to undo the no-fault revolution root and branch.

In 1991, social critic Christopher Lasch proposed the "most draconian proposal of the burgeoning divorce-buster movement," a constitutional amendment banning divorce for married couples with minor children:

> Marriage should be undertaken only by those who view it as a lifelong commitment and are prepared to accept the consequences, foreseeable and unforeseeable, of such a commitment. No state shall pass laws authorizing divorce for any but the weightiest reasons. In the case of couples with children under the age of twenty-one, divorce is hereby forbidden.

. . .

. . . [I]n articulating a difference between marriages based on the presence of children, Lasch anticipated another wing of counter-revolutionary thought. Grounded in the belief that divorce harms children, who are the innocent victims of their parents' quest for individualized happiness, reformers have called for treating marriages with children significantly different than those without. Many proposals to change our legal structure assert society's interest in preserving intact nuclear families and aim at deterring or delaying divorces in families with children.

C.   "Children First"

. . .

The 1990s have seen a growing legislative effort to focus on children of divorce. In the most widely discussed bid, Michigan State Representative Jessie F. Dalman introduced in 1995 an eleven-bill package heralded as "the state of the art on divorce policy." Dalman's proposals would have established a two-tier divorce system. In families without children, or in which the children were all emancipated, the couple could obtain a divorce upon mutual consent. But in families with minor children, or where one spouse objected to the dissolution, the divorce-seeking spouse would have to prove the marital fault of the other. The reinvigorated fault grounds were the historically familiar ones of adultery, desertion, and extreme cruelty, which would have to be established by a "preponderance of the evidence." Additionally, parents seeking divorce would be required to undergo counseling about the potential effects of divorce.

Other states have attempted similar measures. A 1997 Texas bill would have allowed divorce "without regard to fault" when the marriage becomes "insupportable because of discord or conflict of personalities that destroys the legitimate ends of the marriage relationship and prevents any reasonable expectation of reconciliation." But divorce on this ground would be available only to childless couples who had passed their first wedding anniversary. A measure introduced in Virginia in 1998 would have prohibited no-fault divorce if the parties have a minor child and either party files a written objection to the initial pleading within 21 days of service. A Hawaii bill would have required a one-year waiting period and mandatory counseling after a divorce filing in cases with minor children. Counseling sessions specifically including all children aged six to sixteen would have been mandated by a Pennsylvania measure. An Illinois bill would have limited no-fault divorce actions to couples who experienced a separation period, and—if the couple had a dependent child, the marriage were of ten or more years' duration, or the wife was pregnant—mutual consent. These laws were broadly aimed at authorizing courts " 'to consider what's best for the entire family, instead of being required to grant the desire of only one spouse who wants out.' "

Scholarly critics have kept pace with their legislative counterparts, and have often inspired or helped shape the reform proposals. William Galston has called for the elimination of unilateral no-fault divorce in marriages with minor children. Parents who seek divorce would, in Galston's scheme, either have to establish a fault ground against their spouse, or wait to get divorced until they had been separated for five years. . . .

NOTE

Would it be desirable to have a "two-tier" divorce system, in which it was more difficult for a couple to obtain a divorce if they have minor children?

Paul R. Amato, *Good Enough Marriages: Parental Discord, Divorce, and Children's Long–Term Well Being*

9 VA. J. SOC. POL'Y & L. 71, 92–94 (2001).

Some people may question the efficacy of marriage counseling for divorcing couples. After all, they might argue, by the time couples apply for divorce, the marriage has deteriorated to a point where it cannot be salvaged. But the research described here suggests otherwise. Many, perhaps most, divorces are *not* preceded by severe, chronic, destructive levels of discord. Indeed, some of these marriages seem to be functioning reasonably well as little as a year prior to divorce. There is much to build on in these marriages. Furthermore, the knowledge that children are more likely to be harmed than benefited when a "good enough" marriage ends in divorce could provide an additional incentive for these couples to attempt a reconciliation. These considerations suggest that screening for low-discord couples prior to marital dissolution and targeting this group for education and counseling could be useful strategies for preventing the divorces that are most damaging to children.

Rather than addressing the problem on a case-by-case basis, it would be easier to lower the divorce rate legislatively by making marital dissolution more difficult to obtain, perhaps by returning to fault-based grounds for divorce. The research described in this paper, however, does not support this idea. Although divorce harms some children, it benefits others. If we make divorce more difficult to obtain, then we are likely to benefit some children in low-discord marriages, but we also are likely to harm some children in high-discord marriages. These tradeoffs do not make this strategy appealing as a method for protecting children.

If we accept that it would be useful to lower the rate of divorce among low-discord couples, for the sake of the children, then this raises the question of whether we should try to do something for children living with parents in discordant but stable marriages. Should we attempt to *increase* the rate of divorce in these families? Although it seems like a harsh and unpopular policy to encourage some couples to divorce, it might be advisable in cases where violence or abuse is present in the marriage. More realistically, it would seem prudent not to put barriers in the way of these couples when they seek divorce, and to allow these dissolutions to occur as expeditiously as possible.

This line of reasoning raises another interesting question: If we could distribute a minimum number of divorces to couples every year in a way that maximizes children's well-being, then what effect would that have on the current level of divorce in our society? Would the overall divorce rate go down, go up, or remain unchanged? Although very speculative, one could use the data described above to provide a first step toward an answer. Currently, about 40% of marriages with children are projected to end in divorce. Further analysis of our data ... suggests that about half of children are harmed by divorce and about half of children are helped by divorce.

Cutting the divorce population in half would reduce projected divorces among couples with children from 40% to 20%. In addition, we might also want to facilitate divorce among truly troubled couples [estimated at 10% of all couples].... Encouraging these couples to end their marriages would increase the divorce projection to 26% (20% + [.10 × 60]). These admittedly simple calculations suggest that the current divorce rate is higher than it should be, and that a reduction of about 35% in the number of marriages ending in dissolution would provide an optimal level of divorce in American society, at least as far as children are concerned. Of course, this reasoning is based on the assumption of no increase in the availability or success of marriage education, counseling, and therapy. If we could find ways to lower the level of discord in marriages with children, then the divorce rate could be safely lowered even more.

CHAPTER 8

CUSTODY

Obtaining a divorce is often the easiest part of a marital dissolution. Contests over custody of children or over money, by contrast, which are the subject of this chapter and the next, are often not only more intensely fought but may continue for years after a divorce decree is granted. As you review the material in this chapter, consider what changes in the legal standards used or the process followed might reduce continued feuding between former spouses.

A. THE BEST INTEREST STANDARD

States typically direct courts to make custody decisions in accordance with the best interest of the child. The Uniform Marriage and Divorce Act § 402 provides a representative example of the considerations that courts take into account when deciding custody.

UNIFORM MARRIAGE AND DIVORCE ACT § 402.

Best Interest of the Child (1973)

The court shall determine custody in accordance with the best interest of the child. The court shall consider all relevant factors including:

(1) the wishes of the child's parent or parents as to his custody;

(2) the wishes of the child as to his custodian;

(3) the interaction and interrelationship of the child with his parent or parents, his siblings, and any other person who may significantly affect the child's best interest;

(4) the child's adjustment to his home, school, and community; and

(5) the mental and physical health of all individuals involved.

The court shall not consider conduct of a proposed custodian that does not affect his relationship to the child.

COMMENT

This section, excepting the last sentence, is designed to codify existing law in most jurisdictions. It simply states that the trial court must look to a variety of factors to determine what is in the child's best interest. The five factors mentioned specifically are those most commonly relied upon in appellate opinions; but the language of the section makes it clear that the judge need not be limited to the factors specified. Although none of the familiar presumptions developed by the case law are mentioned here, the language of the section is consistent with preserving such rules of thumb. The preference for the mother as custodian of young children when all things are equal, for example, is simply a shorthand method of expressing the best interest of children—and this section enjoins judges to decide custody cases according to that general standard. The same analysis is appropriate to the other common presumptions: a parent is usually preferred to a nonparent; the existing custodian is usually preferred to any new custodian because of the interest in assuring continuity for the child; preference is usually given to the custodian chosen by agreement of the parents. In the case of modification, there is also a specific provision designed to foster continuity of custodians and discourage change.

The last sentence of the section [would change] the law in those states which continue to use fault notions in custody adjudication. There is no reason to encourage parties to spy on each other in order to discover marital (most commonly, sexual) misconduct for use in a custody contest. This provision makes it clear that unless a contestant is able to prove that the parent's behavior in fact affects his relationship to the child (a standard which could seldom be met if the parent's behavior has been circumspect or unknown to the child), evidence of such behavior is irrelevant.

B.   ROSE V. ROSE

1.   THE TRIAL

DRAMATIS PERSONAE[1]

For the Plaintiff

Diane Winter Rose, plaintiff

Doctor Samuel Winter, her father

Amanda Winter, her mother

Polly Winter, her sister

Nancy Winter, her sister

Doug and Deborah Nathan, her friends and former neighbors

Mr. Fisk, her lawyer

For the Defendant

Steven Rose, defendant

Harold Rose, his father

Alice Rose, his mother

Keith Bennett, his friend

Mr. Mellon, his lawyer

SETTING

A Courtroom in the State of Washington, Spring, 1995

THE COURT: Okay, gentlemen, we're ready to proceed on the matter of Rose versus Rose, I understand.

MR. FISK: That's correct, Your Honor.

MR. MELLON: Yes, Your Honor.

---

1. This transcript is derived from an actual proceeding. Most names and identifying features have been changed to protect the privacy of participants.

THE COURT: Okay, you may proceed.

a. George Mitchell, M.D.—For the Plaintiff

(1). Direct Examination by Mr. Fisk.

Q. Doctor, are you a licensed physician? **A.** Yes, I'm licensed.

Q. In what state are you licensed? **A.** I'm licensed in the State of Maryland and in the State of Texas.

Q. Where do you practice? **A.** I practice in Kensington, Maryland.

[Dr. Mitchell next outlines his professional qualifications. He has board certification in psychiatry and neurology, and graduated from the Washington Psychoanalytic Institute. He has been a psychiatrist since 1972.]

Q. Can you tell the Court when you first saw Diane Rose and under what circumstances? **A.** Well, I first saw Diane on April the 7th, 1994.

Q. You were aware that she had made a suicide attempt? **A.** Yes, she had made a suicidal attempt by leaping from an eighth-story window, but had landed in a tree which had obstructed her fall and she survived it.

Q. Was she in the hospital when you first saw her? **A.** Yes, I saw her in the hospital on April the 7th. That was a Sunday morning, at about seven-thirty in the morning.

Q. Now, before you actually saw her did you have occasion to meet the husband, Steven Rose, or his mother, Alice Rose? **A.** I met them both. I met Steve and Alice at the—on the north end of the building on the first floor by the elevator.

Q. How did you happen to meet them there? **A.** Well, they were waiting there for me.

Q. Okay. Would you just tell the Court what happened? **A.** Well, they—I felt that they put me under great pressure to adopt their viewpoint of the case.

MR. MELLON: I'm going to object to that as a conclusion, Your Honor. He can state what happened. I move to strike that.

MR. FISK: Counsel would prefer you say what they told you and—

THE COURT: I'm going to overrule the objection at any rate.

A. They told me that Diane Rose was unable to love and, therefore, could not take care of her baby and was, therefore, too uncomfortable to live with the child. They told me that she was—that her mother was cold and that her father was far withdrawn from his children. I felt literally accosted. I tried to make some remarks that Diane Rose had to learn to take this responsibility and understand this move that she had made; and that I didn't think that anyone should be blamed right offhand. But I heard much blaming and—

Q. By the elevator you mean? **A.** Yes.

Q. Now, Doctor, is this a usual way that you interview one of your proposed patients, by the elevator, or do you usually go and interview the patients themselves—or herself? **A.** I usually see that patient first and then talk with the relatives, if they wish, and if the patient permits me to.

Q. All right. Then subsequent to being approached by Alice and Steve Rose, did you then go talk to Diane Rose? **A.** Yes, I talked to Diane Rose that morning of April the 7th.

Q. Who was there besides Diane, if anyone? **A.** Well, Diane had a nurse, and there was—the hospital—the ward nurse was there. And they very kindly provided me with a room where I could talk with Diane.

Q. In private? **A.** In private. And I talked with her in private for around an hour. And at this time Diane had some signs of organic brain damage. Her speech was somewhat garbled and her gait was scissory, and she seemed to be slow in her responses and to have an ironing-out of the facial musculature.

I tried to move slowly and find out about her psychological state. At that time she was not psychotic. She appeared very frightened and very tense and under great stress. She seemed to have only one thing in mind, and that was to whitewash her marital life, which I tried to ask her about and tried to find out what had obtained at the time in January of 1994. I didn't get very far and I tried not to pressure her for this information, but she did say that she loved her mother, she loved her father, she loved her sister, and she named each one; and that she loved Steve and she loved Alice and that she loved the baby. And it was—it was really a paucity of thought or a limitation of thought in her reporting to me, but I did find out that she didn't have loss of memory or sensory deficits that I could measure simply through an interview. I judged that she was guarding and the thoughts that she gave me were rather in direct opposition to the thoughts that I had had at the foot of the elevator when I first came into the building and that I had heard from Steve and Alice Rose.

When I left Diane, I arranged an appointment with her or told her that I would call her and arrange an appointment, I can't remember just how this came about.

Q. Anyway, a further appointment was arranged? **A.** Yes, a further appointment was arranged for three weeks later. I believe it was—April the 27th when I next saw her. But when I left the building, Steve and his mother were still waiting—

Q. And did they— **A.** —and still pressured me with the same kind of demand, that I listen to their theory of their case. I felt much disrespect to my professional stance and I felt this was a very hostile act toward the patient and her family to intercede in this way.

Q. Did they appear hostile towards Diane to you?

A. Well,—

MR. MELLON: I'm going to object—

A. —they said that Diane—

THE COURT: I'm sorry.

MR. MELLON: I object to that, Your Honor. I think—

MR. FISK: The doctor can testify.

THE COURT: I'm going to overrule it.

A. They said that—they said that Diane could not love; that Diane could not take care of the baby; and that it was for this reason that she jumped. And this was a—I felt that the force and insistence with which they brought these thoughts to me indicated that they had to have it that way.

Q. All right. Now, you saw her again three weeks later? **A.** Yes, I saw her again on April the 27th.

Q. Where did you see her at this time? **A.** I saw her in my office in Kensington, Maryland.

Q. And did someone bring her there? **A.** Yes. She was brought there by her nurse, who sat in the waiting room. And I understand that her husband drove them out there, but he went somewhere on his own business and came back and picked her up an hour later.

Q. Okay. Then did you see her on subsequent occasions? **A.** I saw her at that time, and I saw her eight more times during the month of May. During this time, she began to—slowly began to talk to me more freely about her marital life and premarital life with Steve and his mother, and she—I couldn't tell that she was making strides or improvements at that time, but she was—she did become more communicative. There was still—she would still block and become unable to say anything much more when it came to her marital life.

Q. And on each of these occasions did you find that she had some difficulty expressing herself about her marital relationship? **A.** Yes. She tended to deny the feeling side of her life at that time. She tended to call this suicidal attempt an accident and so on.

Q. Doctor, did you have any more contact with Steve Rose? **A.** Yes. There was a telephone call from Steve Rose in which he—he began by asking me how his wife was doing. And I told him that I didn't want to communicate with him about his wife. And he said, "Well, I'm her husband and I'm entitled to know."

And I said, "Yeah, well then, if she will bring you in, fine, but I'm not going to discuss this case with [you] behind her back." And I told him that he was too damned nosy about this, and that what Diane needed more than anything else was a place to express her own feelings, particularly about the people whom she loved, and that I was trying to provide this atmosphere.

The conversation ended with his telling me that I was sitting there on my fat ass collecting money at the expense of mental patients, and that the thing that was going on these days was family therapy, and that by and large I didn't know what the hell I was doing.

Q. He set himself up as a greater expert in this matter? **A.** Well,—

MR. MELLON: That's a conclusion,—

A. —that's what he told me.

MR. MELLON:—Your Honor.

THE COURT: I'll sustain the objection.

A. And before that there had been a similar call from his mother, a couple days before that, in which I refused to talk to her, but—

Q. What was Alice's reaction to that? **A.** She accepted it.

Q. Okay. In spite of his call, did you see Diane after that? **A.** I saw her on two more occasions. She remarked very candidly that I had been rude to her husband, and I thought that was true. And she didn't—I was—she didn't stop. And I asked her what was going on about that. And she said that her doctors, I believe it was Drs. Grant and Cooper, at the hospital had told her to keep coming, but the treatment was stopped on May the 28th.

Q. Now, did you see her a month or two or three later? **A.** Well, I next saw her—I next saw her late in October. I think that's the date. May I refer to my card?

THE COURT: Yes.

A.   (Pause—referring.) I saw her October the 27th. I sat with her for three hours at that time.

Q.   Did you take an interim history, what she had been doing and what all in the meantime? **A.** Yes. During that time she had been discharged from the hospital on June the 1st and had gone home to care for her baby, but she was very concerned at this time that she was being treated as though she were a bad influence on the baby; and she was never allowed to be alone with the baby, and was very much criticized, and was concerned about this. And she felt that her husband was quite dissatisfied with her care of the baby. And I asked her in what respect. And she told me that if—if she fed the baby when the baby cried, that this would—that she was breaking up the baby's schedule; but if the baby was allowed to cry, she said she was criticized by Alice and Steve for not loving the baby. And then she tried to somersault the baby and chuck him around, which children of that age find very helpful, and she was told she was being too rough; so if she stopped, then she was ignoring the child. And so it went. I mean, her mothering was picked to pieces and she was treated as though she was some kind of a noxious influence. This is the way she described it to me.

Q.   She advised you that she had since separated from her husband? **A.** Well, she said that in August—I think it was in August, maybe late in August, that she had—August 8th and 9th, she had moved out with the Nathans for a while and then tried to move back in; and then that Steve and Alice Rose had departed the house and moved to Silver Springs, which is another suburb of—adjacent to Bethesda, and adjacent to Kensington, too. They're all crowded in around there. But—

Q.   Where was the baby at this time? Did she tell you? **A.** The baby was with Steve and Alice. And she found it very difficult to visit the baby, that she—she was not—she didn't feel welcome and this concerned her. She was—she had made remarkable strides and improvement in her mental status. She was quite verbal and she seemed to be very, very occupied in the business of trying to exert herself as a mother. And I certainly thought that it would be good for her to do so, good for the baby and good for her. She seemed concerned that this child would grow up to regard its mother as a dangerous and bad influence. At no time during either of these sections of time at which she visited me did I find her to be psychotic.

Q.   Doctor, in people that have depression there are two general classifications, are there not? **A.** Yes.

Q.   You mentioned psychotic. That's one type, is it not? **A.** Well, there are a number of different types. The psychotic types are the psychotic depression and circular insanity. And then, there is a situational type or reactive type in which there are strong stress factors playing on the subject.

Q.   Now, in which category did you feel that Diane Rose was when she had made this suicide attempt? **A.** I didn't know. I didn't have enough information. I was trying to find out. It was very difficult to treat and diagnose her. You had the feeling like you're trying to take—to examine a fine Swiss watch, but somebody is stirring the parts around while you try to look at it. And I couldn't—I didn't know at that time what the situation was, but when October came and I saw her then, and I have talked on the telephone several times since, and I saw her last night for about three hours, and I find that she describes a situation which was very bleak, very critical of her in which multiple dissatisfactions were expressed with her behavior and her motives. And I think there are very, very strong situational factors in this case.

Q. Well, would you say then the depression that she was suffering was a situational type? **A.** Yes, I would diagnose it as a reactive depression.

Q. Now, since that situation has been removed, how do you find her? **A.** Well, she is very active and very involved in this case and very interested to be with her child. She made a significant remark to me in October. She said, "Well," she said, "I left in August and went to the Nathans' house." She said, "This time I did it legitimately," which I thought was a piece of growth. She didn't go out the window, but she walked out the door and removed herself from the marital discomfort.

Q. Doctor, on the basis of your examinations and treatment of Diane Rose, have you been able to form an opinion as to whether or not she is suicidal? **A.** I do not regard her as suicidal.

Q. And would you explain the basis on which you make that conclusion, Doctor? **A.** Well, I make that conclusion on the observations that I made in October and now, and on the basis that there are strong situational factors, and that she has improved markedly since removing herself from the marriage, and that she has improved markedly in the influence of her warm and gracious home here in Seattle since she moved here.

Q. Now Doctor,— **A.** I think she's also improved because she's exerting her energies toward the care of this child.

Q. —a claim is made in connection with this matter that she poses a danger to this child. I assume by that is meant she somehow threatens him. In your opinion, is there any danger whatsoever to this child for him to be— for her to have the care, custody, and control of him? **A.** None whatsoever.

Q. Now, in your opinion, would custody of the child be beneficial to Diane Rose herself? **A.** Yes, I think so.

Q. And conversely, would it be beneficial to the child? **A.** I think that the child should—yes, should have its mother.

(2). Cross Examination by Mr. Mellon.

Q. Dr. Mitchell, what experience have you had in treating suicidal patients? **A.** Oh, I've had really quite a bit.

Q. Have you ever had any occasion to treat a person, a highly—who had made a highly lethal attempt at suicide and was unsuccessful? **A.** Yes, I've worked on the program with many of these people at the—

Q. Well now, just specifically let me ask you this. Have you ever had occasion, Doctor, to treat a person who jumped out of a high-story window and survived, like the eighth floor or higher? **A.** No, I've never heard of such a case before.

Q. You never heard of such a case before? **A.** No, I haven't.

Q. It's rare, isn't it? **A.** I would think so.

Q. Doctor, before you came out here—Or first let me ask you this. Did you keep a record of all your consultations with Mrs. Rose? **A.** Yes, I have notes that I took.

Q. What type of notes did you take? **A.** Well, the type of notes that I take are a word here and there that I regard as a key word significant in her makeup.

Q. Did you take a history? **A.** Oh, yes, I took a history, best as I could get a history.

Q. Did you make tests? **A.** No, I made no tests.

Q. Now, you saw her on eight occasions, as I recall, in May of last year. **A.** That's right.

Q. Then you saw her again, you say, in October one time? **A.** Yes, I saw her for three hours in October. I had—

Q. Did you ever see her again after that? **A.** Yes, I saw her last night.

Q. All right. I mean in Washington, did you ever see her after October? **A.** No.

Q. And you never saw her again until last night? **A.** No, I didn't see her again.

Q. Did you get any information, Doctor, when you were attempting to get a history of this girl, of prior suicide attempts? **A.** There was not a prior suicide attempt. She thought of jumping from a window at a party in which she had smoked hash and she had felt very much out of place with a group of people. And she—I think she told me that she had mentioned this to her husband at that time.

Q. Doctor, this event that you have told us about that she told you about that happened at the University of Washington antedated her marriage, didn't it? **A.** Yes. That's what she said.

Q. And, thus, the feelings that caused her to consider suicide at that time had nothing to do, of course, with any marriage on her part. Do you consider that those feelings were the same feelings that she had when she did actually jump out the eighth-story window? **A.** I don't know that they are exactly the same feelings. They were related at the time. She told me, I recall, that she—that her husband chose her friends for her and that she felt was not given a voice, and she felt—

Q. Well, Doctor, you're not answering my question. I asked you if in your opinion the same feelings motivated her at the time she did jump out of the eighth-story window that motivated her when she was considering suicide at the University of Washington? **A.** I said, "not exactly," and I went ahead to tell you what the feelings were as she reported them to me then, and I think that my statements are germane to your question, sir.

Q. Did she ever tell you, Doctor, about a time that she was looking for sleeping pills that she could take in the house? **A.** She told me that she had taken some sleeping pills in January, I thought it was the 13th, but it's probably the 15th, which was the evening before she leapt from the window. That's the only story she told me. She didn't tell me that until in October or over the phone in November.

Q. That's the first time you heard about that she took some sleeping pills? **A.** Yes, the night before. It was not possible to get a history from her in—in a very orderly way. I didn't try to get it. I let her talk to me as best she could.

Q. How many sleeping pills did she say she took, Doctor? **A.** I don't remember. Something that was less than a bottle from when she had a preeclamptic condition. I think it was Phenobarbital.

Q. Was this in itself a suicide attempt? **A.** I don't know. She didn't say whether it was or not. She was very upset.

Q. Did you attempt to find out how many sleeping pills she took? **A.** I may have asked her. I don't remember how many.

Q. Did she indicate that she took anything else with the sleeping pills? **A.** I hadn't heard that, not yet.

Q. You didn't hear that she also took wine with it? **A.** No. I didn't hear that she took wine. Doesn't surprise me.

Q. What is the effect of taking alcohol or liquor with Phenobarbital? **A.** They enhance each other. They're very enhancing drugs, alcohol and Phenobarbital.

Q. In other words, if you take Phenobarbital and then add alcohol, like wine, to it, it takes less pills to kill you. Is that right? **A.** Yeah, and less wine.

Q. And less wine. So if she had taken wine along with the Phenobarbital, Doctor, that would be a further indication that she was attempting to commit suicide at that point, wouldn't it? **A.** Well, that depends on how much wine, and I didn't hear about any wine, not yet, not until you told me. May I speak to you about what I was trying to do with this woman?

Q. Well, we'll come to that, Doctor, but let me ask you this. Assuming that this girl did take wine or alcohol with the Phenobarbital, would that impress you as being a more serious attempt at suicide than even you had understood up to that time? **A.** It would depend on how much of either or both.

Q. And also in expressing an opinion at the present time, it would affect your opinion now as to what should be done regarding this girl, would it not? Wouldn't all that be important, the fact that she had done all of these things at that time? **A.** Its importance becomes less as it fades into the past. And as she works her level best to re-establish herself as a mother, and as she continues in therapy with Dr. Grant, and as she attempts to re-establish the relationships with her family, which were practically nil at the time I first saw her, that becomes less and less important and her recovery becomes more important.

Q. Now, Doctor, to what did you attribute or to what cause did you attribute as being the reason or reasons that Mrs. Rose made the suicide attempts that she did on the night of—in January of last year? **A.** I think it was because of her husband, and I think it was because of his attitude that he—the stance he took with her when he was her boyfriend. I don't think that that's absolutely all there is to it, but I think that's 99 percent of it. Now, I think that before they were married it was a disjunctive love relationship in which he was often dissatisfied with her, her performance and the friends she selected, and it was the same thing after the baby was born, only after the baby was born it was a very—very much more serious proposition.

Q. Well, do you blame— **A.** I mean, this hits a woman where it hurts, when she—

Q. Do you blame her husband for being the cause of her either attempting or seriously considering suicide at the University of Washington? She wasn't married at— **A.** I don't blame. I think he was deeply involved and he did not back off with his expression of dissatisfaction with her.

Q. Doctor, what did she tell you, if anything, about the relationship that she had with her family, that is, her own parental family? **A.** She told me the—just about the same thing, almost exactly word for word, what was said in the hall by Alice and Steve Rose, plus a statement that she loved all of them very dearly, which was much like her suicide note.

Q. Did Diane Rose say anything to you about having received a letter from her mother recently, prior to jumping out the window, that caused her great upset? **A.** No, she didn't describe a letter from her mother.

Q. Did she say anything about— **A.** She spoke of a camera, and she said that Alice Rose had become enraged with her family because the family didn't buy her a movie camera at Christmas to take pictures of the baby.

Q. Doctor, isn't it a fact that Mr. Rose wanted to buy a camera and the Winters didn't want him to because it cost too much money? Isn't that the fact of the matter? **A.** The Winters didn't buy the camera, the Roses did.

Q. Did she say anything to you about having received the letter from her mother within the past few weeks prior to the night she attempted suicide? **A.** She could tell me almost nothing for—really for the whole month—all—the only—for that first section of time in which I treated her, there was very little information. There was an attitude struck by her that her family had been depriving of her, but that she loved them anyway. This is essentially what she said over and over again. This is the paucity of thought that I referred to.

Q. Didn't she refer, in rather bitter terms, and blame her family for having deprived her of a great many things during the time she was growing up, and that this had caused her a great deal of unhappiness, and that this was what was bothering her? Did she ever indicate that to you? **A.** She indicated in a general sort of a way, without specification, which I tried to get from her and was not able to get at that time, that her family had deprived her. In October I went over that same area with her and it was no longer there.

Q. Are you a child psychiatrist, Doctor? **A.** No.

Q. Are you familiar with the book entitled "Beyond the Best Interests of the Child"— **A.** No.

Q. —written by Goldstein, Freud, and Solnit? **A.** No.

Q. Have you ever seen—You say you've never seen Mrs. Rose with the child. Have you ever seen Mr. Rose with the child? **A.** No, I have not.

Q. And, of course, you haven't seen both of them together with the child? **A.** No, I've had no occasion to see them.

Q. Do you feel under the circumstances—not having seen the child or having seen Mrs. Rose with the child and Mr. Rose with the child, how can you make an assessment as to what would be in the best interests of the child? **A.** I make my assessment on the best basis of what the patient told me. I make my assessment on the basis of a rather obvious and vast improvement in her condition since the end of May.

Q. You say that you're not a child psychiatrist, Doctor. Do you have any information concerning the desirability or the undesirability of continuity of care of a child under, say, two years of age? **A.** Oh, I think it's very important to have continuity of care. I think it's a very sad thing that this child has been kept away from its mother during a good part of its sixteenth to eighteenth month.

Q. What do you mean, Doctor, that he's been kept away from his mother? **A.** Well, the mother has been treated as an unwanted person, according to her statements to me. They moved out of the house and took the baby, and then they moved out here to the West Coast and she's followed them out here to the West Coast. The way she tells me is that she was unwanted, and that she was treated like a—I forget how she put it, a leper or a Nazi or something like that. So I think that the maternal care has been interrupted by herself and by her husband and mother-in-law.

b. Steven Rose—Defendant Called as Adverse Witness

MR. FISK: Your name is Steven Rose?

A. Yes.

Q. And you are the husband of Diane Winter Rose? **A.** Yes.

Q. And you are presently a medical student? **A.** Yes.

Q. Now, following the suicide attempt of your wife and following her release from the hospital, you insisted that your wife and all the relatives have a family-consultation session with a Dr. Bower, did you not? **A.** No. Dr. Bower insisted and I agreed.

Q. All right. In any event, you made the arrangements? **A.** Dr. Bower made the arrangements.

Q. Now, what was the purpose of this family get-together with Dr. Bower? **A.** The purpose was to explore the feelings, there were a lot of angry feelings expressed, and to explore these feelings amongst the members of the family.

Q. Who attended that conference? **A.** I attended the conference, Nancy, Diane, my mother, and Mr. and Mrs. Nathan and their child, Dr. Bower, and Dr. Grant, Diane's therapist.

Q. Now, was the purpose of that conference to try and commit your wife? **A.** No.

Q. Now, at that conference, I'm going to ask you if it isn't a fact that Dr. Bower stated that, "You are trying to commit her," meaning your wife, "but you are the most vicious people I've ever run into"? **A.** Yes, Dr. Bower said that about the group.

Q. Now, I'm talking about you and your mother. **A.** No. He said that including the group.

Q. Now, I'm going to ask you if Dr. Bower didn't say that there was a very unhealthy relationship between you and your mother. **A.** No, he didn't say that.

Q. He did not? **A.** No.

Q. You deny that? **A.** Yes.

Q. I'm going to ask you if he didn't say that your mother was mentally sleeping with you. **A.** Mentally sleeping with me?

Q. With you. **A.** With me?

Q. With you. **A.** I can't recall, though Diane did say I was sleeping with my mother.

Q. No, I'm talking about Dr. Bower. **A.** Yes.

Q. Let's answer the question. **A.** I'm trying to answer it as best I can. I don't recall her saying she was mentally sleeping with me. I don't recall.

Q. Is Dr. Bower a woman? **A.** No, Dr. Bower's a man.

Q. All right. I'm talking about a him, a man. **A.** Right. I don't recall if he said that.

Q. But he could have said it? **A.** I don't recall.

Q. Now, I'm going to ask you if he didn't say that you and your mother and the whole bunch of you needed treatment. **A.** Yes, he did say that.

Q. I want to ask you if he didn't say that your mother, Alice, should come back to Seattle and get out of your—the life of yourself and your wife. **A.** He said, "What are you doing here?"

Q. To Alice? **A.** To Alice. That's what he said, "What are you doing here?" He said, "Why don't you go back to Seattle?" He posed it as a question, as I remember.

Q. At this session did Alice, your mother, admit she had a poor husband-wife relationship with your father? **A.** I don't recall that. A poor husband-and-wife relationship with my father?

Q. Right, right. **A.** I believe she did say the relationship was strained. She had been living in Washington since Diane jumped out of the eight-story window, and my father had lived in Seattle and made a couple visits, and, yes, she said that it was—it was difficult.

Q. And I want to ask you if Dr. Bower didn't say to your mother that she had mentally castrated your father. **A.** I'm not sure if he said those words, but he did—

Q. Well, words to that effect? **A.** That she mentally castrated him? I believe when he spoke to us, he posed them in questions, if she did this. He said a lot of things at that session. He could have said that.

Q. He could have said that? **A.** Yes.

Q. And I want to ask you if it isn't a fact that he told her what she needed was a damned good lay. **A.** Yes. He said—that's what he did—that's what he said. I don't think he said it in that—quite that way. He didn't say "a damn good" one.

Q. Now, following these remarks to yourself and to your mother, even you refused to have any more sessions with Dr. Bower, did you not? **A.** Not so.

Q. Not so? **A.** No.

Q. Okay. **A.** I went to see Dr. Bower again.

Q. Did you ever take Diane to see him anymore? **A.** No, but he discussed Diane with me.

Q. I see. **A.** If you'd like to hear anything about that?

Q. We'll get to it a little bit more later. **A.** All right.

MR. FISK: That's all I wanted to ask of this witness at this time.

MR. MELLON: No questions.

c. Deborah Nathan—For the Plaintiff

(1). Direct Examination by Mr. Fisk

THE WITNESS: I just wanted to clarify one thing,—

MR. FISK: Just—Mrs. Nathan, now we'll give you a chance to clarify everything. I'll ask you some questions, okay?

THE WITNESS: I just want to tell you that he thinks—my husband and I weren't included as being vicious with Dr. Bower.

MR. FISK: We'll get to that.

Q. Your name is Deborah Nathan? **A.** Right.

Q. And, Mrs. Nathan, where do you live? **A.** In Washington, D.C.

Q. And are you acquainted with Diane Rose and her husband, Steven? **A.** Yes.

Q. How did you get acquainted with them? **A.** I met Diane through a mutual friend before Diane was pregnant, or she might have been pregnant and I didn't know that she was pregnant at the time. It might have—you know, it might have been the first or second month.

Q. All right. Were you and your husband friends of the Roses? **A.** I'd say casual acquaintances.

Q. Now, did there come an occasion when Diane Rose left the apartment where she was living with Steve and his mother following her release from the hospital and came to your home? **A.** Yes.

Q. How did she arrive at your home? **A.** Well, my husband picked her up. She called me up on the phone and she was very upset. She said she had to get out; she couldn't stay there and could she stay with us for a few days; could she come the next morning.

Q. Now, was there some reluctance on your part to let her come and stay with you? **A.** Yes. Well, Diane had just been released from the hospital in June and I had only seen her once during that time, and I had heard from people that I know through—this is just strictly hearsay, from not seeing her, that Diane had to be watched every minute, that she was a mental midget, you know, she was a vegetable. And it meant, since I have a baby, that meant me having two babies on my hands, Diane and my own baby.

Q. But nevertheless, you took her in on this occasion? **A.** Right.

Q. How long did she stay with you? **A.** I'd say about a month and a week.

Q. All right. Now, during the time she stayed with you, how did she get along? **A.** Very well. She—it turned out that she was a tremendous help. She took care of my baby. She did the cooking. She helped with the housework. She did everything.

Q. And within a few days did you find that she was competent to handle and take care of your own child? **A.** Yes. It was great having her there, 'cause it was less work for me.

Q. Now, during this month, I want to ask you whether she babysat for you on numerous occasions. **A.** Yes.

Q. And did you go away and leave your own child with her? **A.** Yes.

Q. And would she feed him, change him, bathe him,— **A.** Everything.

Q. —the whole bit? Did she cook, keep house? **A.** Yes.

Q. Did she appear perfectly competent to you to handle and take care of a child? **A.** More than competent. It was sad because she was giving my baby the love that she should have been giving her baby.

Q. How old was your child at that time? **A.** My baby, there's two months difference between them, so she was fourteen months.

Q. All right. Now then, were you asked to attend the conference with Dr. Bower? **A.** Well, I was threatened to it, but then Steve called up my husband and insulted him and told him that we had to go, seven o'clock in the morning we had to be there at Dr. Bower's, at a place that was an hour away, so it meant with our baby, because nobody would babysit for us at five o'clock in the morning, having to drag our baby and get her up, feed her, take her to this session where—expose her to all this viciousness, shouting, a very frightening experience for her.

Q. Well, the arrangements were made by Steve Rose. Is that what you're saying? **A.** For us it was.

Q. Now, by this time had Diane returned to the apartment or was she still with you? **A.** She was still with me. She couldn't return to the apartment.

Q. Now, who was at this session with Dr. Bower? **A.** Nancy, Steve, Diane, Mrs. Rose, Dr. Grant, my husband, Dr. Bower, and myself.

Q. Now,— **A.** And my daughter, Susan.

Q. Now, at this session, I want you to state whether or not Dr. Bower said that Steve and his mother were the most vicious people he'd ever seen, or words to that effect. **A.** It wasn't just Steve and his mother. It was Steve—

MR. MELLON: I'm going to object to this, your Honor, as being very leading.

MR. FISK: I'm going to—

MR. MELLON: She can tell what Dr. Bower said, but counsel is putting words in her mouth.

MR. FISK: I'll withdraw the question.

THE COURT: Agreed.

MR. FISK: I'll rephrase it.

Q. (Continuing) Would you state what, if anything, Dr. Bower said about the people there attending that conference, if he had anything specific to say with reference to any particular people? **A.** Well, he said about Nancy Winter, Steve Rose, and Alice Rose, that they were the most vicious people that he had ever seen; that they're the most self-righteous people and unforgiving people; and he couldn't blame Diane for doing what she had done; if she had lived—if he had lived in those circumstances, he'd probably do the same thing.

Q. And this was said in Steve Rose and Alice Rose's presence? **A.** Yes.

Q. And I'll ask you whether or not he told Alice Rose that she had an unhealthy relationship with—

MR. MELLON: I am going to object to this, Your Honor.

THE COURT: Sustained.

Q. What did she say— **A.** I can tell you what he said. The thing where Steve said—'cause I was listening carefully, that they were mentally sleeping together. He said they were literally sleeping together. He did mention that. He did say that they had an unhealthy relationship, because, you see, the way that whole meeting went, we thought they were out to commit Diane into an institution. The night before I had met with Dr. Grant and he said they were there to determine reality, Steve's reality, his mother's reality, and what was—what prescription as far as what was to be done with them. And he wanted Steve and his mother to go into therapy. He felt they both needed it. He thought Alice should go back home to Seattle to get help there; Steve should stay there and go see Dr. Bower. Nancy agreed to treatment with Dr. Bower, and I don't know what happened to them. It's really a shame she didn't continue with the treatment, because I worry for Nancy.

Q. Now, was anything said by Dr. Bower with reference to whether this was a kind of a commitment hearing?

MR. MELLON: I object again, Your Honor. Counsel is putting words in her mouth.

THE COURT: Overrule the objection.

A. We were sitting there with Dr. Grant the night—well, the night before we were there. Dr. Grant had thought we were all there for Diane's commitment. And I think, in a moment of anger, while they were screaming at each other, he said, "You know," that, "you want to commit her and look at the way you—" you know, "You are the ones." It was—I can't remember his exact words, but "You're the ones that need the treatment, not her. She's getting the therapy. She's still—"

THE COURT: Was this the night before?

THE WITNESS: No, this was in the group-therapy session. I had two sessions, one with Dr. Grant—

THE COURT: Where was that?

THE WITNESS: In Dr. Grant's office, Diane's psychiatrist.

THE COURT: Where is that?

THE WITNESS: In Washington, D.C.

THE COURT: Okay. Where is Dr. Bower's—

THE WITNESS: Dr. Bower, I think, is in Potomac, Maryland.

(2). Cross Examination by Mr. Mellon

Q. How many meetings did you have in Dr. Bower's office? **A.** One, and that was enough.

Q. About how long did it last? **A.** Well, we were there—we got there early and—'cause we thought it was going to take longer to get out there than it did. We got there around six-thirty and we left around twelve, one o'clock, and it was still going on.

Q. Dr. Bower apparently tends to strong language. **A.** Well, so do Steve and his mother.

Q. Well, I didn't ask you that. I said, "Dr. Bower tends to strong language," is that right? **A.** Well, not—well, you can say he tends to strong language and he also tends to soft-soap, so, you know, it depends on how you approach it. He was very sweet to my husband and myself.

Q. What do you mean "soft-soap"? **A.** Well, I meant, you know, he's soft, he's very nice and very gentle.

Q. But he can also get very rough? **A.** Well, so can Steve and his mother.

Q. I didn't ask you that. Are you out here to harpoon Steve and his mother? **A.** No, what I'm saying, you're trying to harpoon Dr. Bower. The thing is that Steve and his mother shouted at him and he shouted back to them. And when Steve and his mother were polite to him, then he was polite back to them.

Q. Did Dr. Bower also say—Well, first let me say: Were you there with Dr. Bower from seven o'clock in the morning until twelve-thirty? **A.** Uh-huh (affirmative response).

Q. Did Dr. Bower also say, as you left, "Now, don't you have compassion for Steve and his painful situation?" **A.** No.

Q. You didn't hear that? **A.** No.

Q. Well, you were gone, you left before the session ended? **A.** Right. Most of the time when we were there he just said that he wanted—he was mostly working out trying to get Steve and his mother and Nancy into therapy, trying to talk them into it.

Q. When did you come out here? **A.** Excuse me?

Q. When did you come to Seattle? **A.** Yesterday.

Q. Did you come out here just to testify in this case? **A.** Yes.

Q. Who's paying your expenses? **A.** Mr.—Dr. Winter.

Q. Did Dr. Winter contact you and ask you to come out here? **A.** Yes, he did.

d.   Steven Rose—Defendant As Adverse Witness II

(1).   Direct Examination by Mr. Fisk

Q. Mr. Rose, would you tell us when you first met your wife? **A.** I first met my wife when she came over to my house with a friend, Carrie Wallenberg, when I must have been in about the eighth grade.

Q. When did you first start going with her? **A.** I first dated Diane in 1986 in the summer. I didn't start going steady with her till about on her birthday when I pinned her with my college fraternity pin in May of—that would be '87.

Q. Okay. Now, were you both at college, University of Washington, at that time? **A.** Yes.

Q. Now, this would probably be a good time to discuss this so-called first suicide attempt. This occasion was in the room of Polly Winter, was it not? **A.** Yes.

Q. And you'd had a party or something? **A.** Well, it wasn't a party. It was a get-together between just a couple of people, one was her sister Polly, her sister's boyfriend John, Diane's roommate Anita, Diane, and myself. I don't—we just got together.

Q. Were you smoking hashish at that time? **A.** No.

Q. You weren't? **A.** No, I wasn't.

Q. Did you insist that Diane eat some hashish? **A.** No.

Q. You deny that? **A.** I deny that.

Q. Did she have some hashish? **A.** Yes.

Q. Where did she get it? **A.** She got it from her sister Polly, who had them baked in a brownie. I might say that I did have some hashish the night before. Her sister Polly gave me a brownie and said, "Here." And I—I put it in my mouth and then I spit some of it out in the sink because it tasted horrible. That night, the next night, Diane told me that she wanted to try some and she did.

Q. Now, did she become quite ill? **A.** Well, I don't know if you'd call it ill. She sat in the chair in this room. It was—it was in John Moss' room, Polly's boyfriend, and she sat in the chair and didn't move, occasionally looked up and smiled. I asked her what was wrong and she just smiled.

Q. Now, actually she was lying on the bed, wasn't she? **A.** No.

Q. She didn't lie on the bed? **A.** No, she sat in the chair in the corner.

Q. All right. What happened? **A.** She stayed that way for approximately an hour or two. I didn't know what was wrong, and then I finally said to her, "Diane, why don't you—why don't I escort you to Polly's room so you can lay down and go to sleep?"

Q. Oh, that's where she was on the bed? **A.** Right.

Q. Okay. Then she went to Polly's room? **A.** Right. When she laid down on the bed, I sat in one corner of the room and had one of the—one of the lamp lights on and was sitting in the chair. Then Diane opened the window—

Q. Well now, wait a minute. She's on the bed; the bed is by the window? **A.** The bed—right next to the window, yes.

Q. Okay. **A.** Diane opened the window and started to crawl out.

Q. What did you do? **A.** I went over and I had to grab her around the waist. Her head was already out the window. And I pulled her back in, slammed the window shut and stayed with her all night.

Q. Okay. Did she get okay the next day? **A.** She said—well, she said she was—felt a little funny. She said to me the next day, she says, "if you wouldn't have been there, I would have died." We talked about that incident many times.

Q. All right. Now then, what year was this that happened? **A.** Well, this was—I believe it was the winter term of 1989.

Q. So that is what? A year and a half before you got married? **A.** Sure. I was a senior in college and she was a junior.

Q. Now, you actually got married after she got out of college, did you not, she'd graduated from college? **A.** Right. We were engaged the spring before she graduated college.

Q. All right. What did you do when you first got out of college? **A.** Well, I had been accepted to Karl Franzen University in Graz, Austria, which was associated with the University of Vienna Medical School. Diane and I planned to go over there. I was going over to study medicine in Austria with two fellow dental students. I had been in dental school for one year.

Q. Mr. Rose, I think you're getting a little bit ahead of me. **A.** Okay. Well, we—

Q. You got out of college— **A.** Sure.

Q. —and you started dental school, didn't you? **A.** Right.

Q. Okay. Now then, you decided to go and try and go to medical school in Austria, right? **A.** Yes.

Q. Had you decided to get married at that time? **A.** No. Diane wanted to—Diane said to me, she said, "I would like to go with you to Austria." She says, "I think it's about time we got married." She said, "If you don't marry me, then I'll come over with you to live."

Q. Now, she was going to come and live with you whether you married her or not? **A.** Yes.

Q. And in effect she's the one that proposed to you, not the other way around? **A.** Well, it wasn't that I was opposed to being married to Diane, because I loved her very much.

Q. Well, originally hadn't you intended to go without her? **A.** We had set—we had talked about—

Q. Would you just answer my question? **A.** Okay. This is what I'm trying to say. We had talked about marriage and actually reserved the Synagogue in December before I was accepted. I had applied to the Austrian Medical School and we had reserved the Synagogue, but we had not been formally engaged when—for the—for the next few months, but she had the Synagogue date reserved.

Q. Now, when Diane suggested you ought to get married, did you have to seek some advice on that? **A.** No. I wanted to think about it.

Q. Well, isn't it a fact you told her you had to go home and ask your mother? **A.** No.

Q. Didn't you in fact go ask your mother and get her approval before you would say "yes" or "no"? **A.** No. My mother loved Diane. I knew that she—

Q. Now, just answer my question. Didn't you— **A.** No.

Q. —have to go and get Alice's approval? **A.** No.

Q. You didn't tell her that,— **A.** No.

Q. Now then, I want to ask you if one of the reasons that you thought you might marry Diane was that you thought that Dr. Winter's connections might help get you in medical school? **A.** There is no possible way I could have thought that. Do you want me to give you a reason?

Q. Yes. **A.** Dr. Winter has no academic standing at the University of Washington other than an associate clinical professor, which is—which is really the lowest person at the University.

Q. Lowest man on the totem pole there? **A.** Sort of.

Q. Now, Mr. Rose, you got married on July the 5th, 1990, right? **A.** Yes.

Q. And originally you had planned to go to the Winter's condominium for a honeymoon, had you not? **A.** Yes.

Q. And you changed those plans so you could be near your mother, did you not? **A.** No.

Q. No? **A.** No.

Q. Where did you stay on your wedding night? **A.** We stayed at Farley's.

Q. At Farley's? **A.** Yes.

Q. In Seattle? **A.** Yes.

Q. And the very next morning you got up and went to visit your mother, didn't you? **A.** Yes, the very next morning we had breakfast at Farley's. Mr. and Mrs. Martin Finch and their family—

Q. That isn't the question I asked you, Mr. Rose. **A.** The question is—

Q. Did you go visit your mother— **A.** Yes.

Q. —on the morning of July the 6th? **A.** We went over to our house, yes.

MR. MELLON: Now, Your Honor, Counsel should allow him to explain, if he desires.

MR. FISK: Well, I'll be happy to have him explain, but he should answer the question.

THE COURT: I think he is.

THE WITNESS: Yes. When we were having breakfast with Mr. and Mrs. Martin Finch at Farley's we saw these two people that came from New York who had come to our wedding. Diane had told me early in the morning that she didn't want to go down to the condominium at the beach. She said that we only had a couple more days until we were flying off to Austria and that she wanted to be close to her parents and the people that had come to see us.

Q. Now, as a medical student, you know the meaning of an Oedipal complex, do you not? **A.** Of course.

Q. And would you explain what it is? **A.** It's a fascination or desire to—love for your mother, not in a son-mother relationship, but in a lover relationship.

Q. Now, that's one of the things that Dr. Bower stated about your relationship with your mother, is it not, at this meeting that you had in Washington, D.C.? **A.** Dr. Bower did not mention that.

Q. He did not? **A.** He did not say "an Oedipal complex," no.

Q. You deny that? **A.** I deny that.

Q. Now, you went off to Austria, how long did you stay? **A.** We stayed in Austria, I believe, approximately six weeks.

Q. So that turned out to be an expensive fiasco, did it? **A.** Yes, it did, but there were circumstances surrounding that. We were taking German classes every day, twice a day. Diane refused to go to many of the German classes. Diane cried and became very depressed. She would not go with me, as the other wives did to these German classes. She told me she wanted to go home and she didn't want to live in Austria, that she hated Graz. I told her that this may be my last chance to be an M.D. She continued to cry. She wouldn't listen to me and we had an argument.

Q. Mr. Rose, during these German classes you repeatedly told your wife how stupid she was, did you not? **A.** No.

Q. You deny that? **A.** Yes.

Q. During all the time you went with her, as a matter of fact, you constantly told her she was stupid, didn't you, inadequate and (pause) **A.** Oh, when we got in arguments or something like that, she would call me something. I would say, "Oh you're so stupid," or something of that nature yes.

Q. Didn't you tell her on numerous occasions your friends couldn't understand why you did anything—had anything to do with her because you were so far above her intellectually? **A.** No.

Q. You didn't say that? **A.** No.

Q. Did you feel you were? **A.** Far above her intellectually?

Q. Yes. **A.** I thought—I thought I was more intelligent than she.

Q. And you didn't hesitate to tell her so? **A.** No, I didn't tell her so. Possibly in an argument I may say something, in—when you are in the heat of an emotional state, I may—you know, you may blurt out something that you—that you don't mean,—

Q. Well,— **A.** —but I don't recall.

Q. Okay. Finally you were admitted to George Washington University Medical School, were you not? **A.** Yes.

Q. Your wife worked at George Washington Hospital, did she not? **A.** Yes.

Q. And your wife and her earnings and what you got from the Winters is what financed your education. Isn't that true? **A.** No.

Q. Okay. Were you disturbed when Diane got pregnant? **A.** No. Happy.

Q. Did you have a feeling that this would interfere with her ability to work and send you to school? **A.** No.

Q. Didn't bother you? **A.** No.

Q. What was your wife doing at the hospital? **A.** She was a—she was a clerk-typist in Orthopedics my first—my first year, and the second year she was a typist for Radiology.

Q. In other words, she was what you would call a medical secretary? **A.** No. She was a clerk-typist. A medical secretary—she didn't answer a phone. What she did was type from the dictaphone. The doctors would read X-rays in Radiology and she was—she would just transcribe the tapes.

Q. Did she work for two different doctors? **A.** Well, she worked with— for many doctors, for Radiology, for whoever was the resident or the attendants who were reading the X-rays, and then in Orthopedics I think there were four people, four orthopedists in the clinic that she worked for.

Q. Jason was born April, 1993? **A.** Yes.

Q. That suddenly eliminated this source of income for you, didn't it? **A.** Yes.

Q. Did your wife work right up till the day of the delivery? **A.** Yes. Diane wasn't expected to deliver for at least another five weeks. Jason was born April—

Q. The answer to the question is "yes"? **A.** Yes. Jason wasn't expected until five weeks. In fact, May 25th was his due date. He was born April 21st.

Q. That suddenly put you in a position where you needed money, did it not? **A.** We had some money saved. We were going back to Seattle for the summer.

Q. Now, did you ask your father for money? **A.** I never had to ask my father for money.

Q. Well, let me ask you this. Did you go to the—or ask your wife to go to the Winters for money? **A.** No.

Q. Did she go to the Winters for money? **A.** In the summer of that year she did go to her father. She said for the first time in her life she was going to ask them for money for—for the following year.

Q. Now, if you were getting the support from your parents, why did she need to do that? **A.** She did—she said to me, she said, "I don't want your parents to carry the full burden of our—our money, the money that we need in Washington, D.C.," she said, "so I'm going to ask him for some of the money out of my trust fund that I have." She said, "So I won't be taking it really out of his pocket, but just taking it out of the trust fund." So, she said, "I'll ask him for $10,000."

Q. I want to ask you if it isn't a fact that you wanted her to ask for the entire trust fund. **A.** No.

Q. So you got a check from Dr. Winter for $10,000? **A.** Yes.

Q. Now, along about this time you were becoming extremely critical of the Winters, were you not? **A.** No.

Q. Specifically, weren't you upset with Dr. Winter because you thought he wasn't contributing enough? **A.** No.

Q. Weren't you upset with Dr. Winter because he was indiscreet enough on one occasion to mention what a nice young medical student Judge Green's son was; you took offense at that? **A.** No. What he did say, in front of my presence and to my face, I think after he gave the check or after Diane asked him, he said, "Mike Green's a wonderful guy." He says, "You know, he doesn't ask his dad for a penny," that, "He joined the service to finance his way through medical school and he worked through medical school."

Q. Now, shortly after that you decided, among other things, you needed a movie camera, did you not? **A.** No, not shortly after that, no.

Q. When? **A.** Before. What happened with that was, I wanted to get a movie camera because Jason was now starting to move around a little bit, roll on the ground, smile. I wanted to capture him in movies and so get an 8–millimeter movie camera. I had asked my mother-in-law if she would come back and visit us during my junior year, and she said—she refused because it cost too much money. So Diane and I thought that a good idea would be to have a movie camera and we could send the movie film to Seattle to show them pictures of Jason and also keep a good record of Jason.

Q. Who was going to buy this movie camera? **A.** We were.

Q. You and Polly—or, and Diane? I'm sorry. **A.** Yes, me and Diane. We had just thought about it. We weren't purchasing it.

Q. Okay. So what caused the big problem? **A.** Amanda got into a fight with my mother. She said, "You always run away from your troubles. We can't run away from our troubles." And she said, "Steve gets his spendthrift attitudes from you. Why, he even wants to buy a movie camera."

Q. And with that, your mother took her leave and— **A.** She says, "I'm—" yes. I think she said, "You've insulted me," and she left.

Q. After the baby was born there was nothing that his mother could do that suited you. Isn't that so? **A.** No. I told Diane many times that I thought she was doing a good job.

Q. I'll ask you if it isn't a fact that you criticized her about the way she fed the baby, how she bathed the baby, how she handled him; everything she did— **A.** No.

Q. —was incorrect? **A.** There were a couple episodes, and if I could illustrate that, I was not Diane's only critic at times. Her father was, too. One which upset me was when Diane would lie Jason, who was only a couple months old, on their living room floor.

Q. Would she lie with him there? **A.** No, she would lie Jason on the floor and go into the kitchen and do some cooking or something like that rather than put him in the crib. And her father made the observation and brought it to my attention that occasionally dogs got into their house when the door was open, namely, one that—the Frank's dog, which is a big black dog, and he said that—he's told her once, "Diane, that dog was sniffing at

Jason's head." He said, "All he'd have to do is make one lunge and he could dangerously harm Jason."

Q. But you deny that you generally criticized everything she did with the child? **A.** Of course I deny that.

Q. Now, your mother came back to Washington around Christmas or New Years, 1993, right? **A.** Yes.

Q. And how long did she stay? **A.** Two weeks, something like that.

Q. She was there up until about a week before the suicide attempt, wasn't she? **A.** No.

Q. How long? **A.** She was—she left a couple of weeks before.

Q. So she left around the first of the year? **A.** Before the first of the year.

Q. Now, during that period of time, isn't it true that your mother was very critical of your wife and the Winters? **A.** I'll tell you the truth, that I was on a clinical rotation in medicine at the hospital center in Washington, D.C.; that I didn't know what they talked about during the day, and Diane never told me. They seemed very happy and amicable when I got home and when I talked to them. So I don't know anything that went on.

Q. All right. After the suicide attempt you called Dr. Winter in Seattle, did you not? **A.** Yes, I called him. He was at, I believe, Hathaway Park Hospital. First—I called her mother first and told her what had happened, and she—her mother said she'd get in touch with my father-in-law, but I—I decided to call him anyway. I had some medical questions for him; Diane was very sick.

Q. And Amanda Winter came early in the day and Dr. Winter arrived there that evening. Is that true? **A.** No. Amanda Winter came later that evening. If I can tell you, I called up my parents first and told them what had happened. They told me immediately that they would come out in the first plane they could get. I called up my mother-in-law and told her, and she said, "Oh Steve" she says, "I just talked to Diane last night."

So I said,—I told her that she was in critical condition, and she says, "Oh,"—

Q. Mr. Rose, I hate to interrupt you,— **A.** I just want to tell—Okay, I just want to tell you the background.

Q. I know, you want to tell me everything I don't ask you. **A.** I told Amanda Winter to come out, yes, and she came out later that evening, I believe on the same plane as my mother and father.

Q. Okay. And when Dr. Winter arrived, you met him at the hospital, did you not? **A.** Yes.

Q. Now, at that time, that very night, I'm going to ask you if it isn't a fact you told Dr. Winter, "I've made some terrible mistakes for which I'm sorry and I just hope that I get a second chance." **A.** I told him, I said, "I pray for a second chance with Diane." I don't remember saying, "I've made terrible mistakes." I felt—I felt terrible about this. I had been up for—for now almost forty-eight—

Q. My question is if you made this statement to Dr. Winter. **A.** I remember him—

Q. Can you answer a question without making a speech? **A.** Yes. I remember—I remember saying that I wanted a second chance.

Q. Okay. That was the question. **A.** Diane was in critical condition at the time. She was decerebrate and her pupils were unequal.

Q. Now, is this in answer to whether you— **A.** Yes.

Q. —asked for a second chance? **A.** Yes. I was praying for a second chance. This was the most terrible time of my life.

Q. Okay. Now, within a couple days your whole attitude changed, had it not? **A.** No.

Q. No? **A.** No.

Q. Within a couple days it became suddenly all the Winters' fault. Isn't that true? **A.** No. In fact, my father-in-law, when he left five days later, hugged me and wished me good luck.

Q. But shortly thereafter you were telling Amanda Winter, "It's all your fault,"— **A.** No.

Q. —isn't that so? **A.** No.

Q. Now, you haven't lived with Diane since about September 9, 1994, correct? **A.** No, since August 12, 1994.

Q. All right, August 12,— **A.** Right. I did ask Diane to come back.

Q. Beg pardon? **A.** I did ask Diane to come back several times.

Q. Now, have you been having an affair with her sister? **A.** No.

Q. Are you sure of that? **A.** Positive.

Q. Do you know any reason why your suitcase would be in her apartment in Washington, D.C.? **A.** Yes. My—I had belongings—I had some of my things, my books at Nancy's where I stored it, and I have some at a former next-door neighbors where I stored it in her locker, too. She's about a 60–year old woman.

Q. When you were up at Silver Spring, Maryland, did Nancy come up there? **A.** Yes, she came over.

Q. Did she stay overnight? **A.** Yes.

Q. Numerous occasions? **A.** On weekends she would come over and stay, and I would sleep on the couch and my mom and—and Nancy would sleep in the two twin beds, and Jason had his own room.

Q. The night that Mr. Nathan came and got your wife and took her to his apartment— **A.** Yes.

Q. —there was an argument between Alice Rose and your wife, correct? **A.** Yes, there was.

Q. Now, at that time and in your presence did Alice Rose say to your wife, "Why do you think you should have this baby merely because you spread your legs?" **A.** I don't remember her saying that.

Q. You don't remember that? **A.** No.

Q. I see. And you deny that your wife said to you, "Are you going to let your mother talk to me like that?" and you said that you were not going to do anything or say anything about that? **A.** I deny that.

Q. You deny that. Now, at that same time in that same place do you deny that you told your wife you were going to have her committed? **A.** I deny that.

MR. MELLON: I'll reserve questioning until our case, Your Honor.

e. Samuel Winter, M.D.—For the Plaintiff

(1). Direct Examination by Mr. Fisk

Q. Your name is Samuel Winter? **A.** Yes, sir.

Q. And you are a licensed physician and surgeon in the State of Washington, are you? **A.** I am.

Q. And what is your specialty? **A.** Orthopedic surgery.

Q. How long have you been an orthopedic surgeon? **A.** Since 1959.

Q. Now, Doctor, you are the father of the respondent, Diane Rose, are you not? **A.** I am.

Q. And you also have two other children,— **A.** I do.

Q. —Polly and Nancy. Is that correct? **A.** Yes, sir.

Q. And in connection with these three children of yours, did they have everything so far as physical things that you can reasonably want? **A.** I think so. I think so. The girls were all sent to music school, music lessons. Most of them didn't want to continue it, but they went. They were given classes in skiing. They were—all of them were sent to take lessons in tennis, if they wanted. Some of them did, some of them didn't.

Q. Purchased ski equipment for them to go skiing? **A.** Yes.

Q. What was the atmosphere around your home? **A.** I thought it was good. My wife is a taciturn type of person. She's quiet, but—she certainly didn't belong to any organizations. She seldom left the house and she was always with the children. There was never a time—she never played bridge, never went out to play bridge. There was never any time I called that she wasn't there during the day. I think she was as good a wife as anybody could be.

Q. Okay. Now, did your girls all grow up and go to college? **A.** Yes. They all went to high school and went to college.

Q. And did Nancy go to the University of Washington? **A.** She did.

Q. And then she started going with Steve Rose the petitioner in this case? Is that correct? **A.** You're saying Diane, not Nancy.

Q. I'm sorry. Diane started going with Steve Rose? **A.** Yes, sir.

Q. And how long did they go together, to your knowledge? **A.** Well, I think Diane met him the first year in college. I'm—she may have met him with another girlfriend earlier. It's possible. I didn't know. She went out with several other boys and she went with Steve.

Q. Okay. And then they got married in 1990. Is that correct? **A.** That's right, sir.

Q. When did they go to Washington, D.C.? **A.** I think it was in 1991.

Q. And he was admitted there to medical school? **A.** Yes, sir.

Q. Were you approached by any member of his family in connection with a contribution to get him into school? **A.** Yes.

Q. By whom? **A.** By Mr. Harold Rose.

Q. Who is Mr. Harold Rose? **A.** Steve's father.

Q. And what was the story you got from him?

MR. MELLON: I'm going to object to this, Your Honor. I think that's pure hearsay, any conversation between Harold Rose and Mr.—and Dr. Winter.

MR. FISK: This is one of the parties that will end up with this child if it's left where it is, and I think—

MR. MELLON: That's not true.

THE COURT: Well, I don't know whether it's true or not, and that remains to be seen, I'm sure. I'm going to overrule the objection.

A. Mr. Rose told me he'd made a pledge to the University of $20,000, and that he needed some money and would I pay half of it.

Q. Did you do that? **A.** I did.

Q. And then did he later come back and change that story? **A.** Yes.

Q. What did he say the second time around? **A.** He said it wasn't $20,000, it was more than $20,000. I said to him, "Harold, how much was it?"

He said, "Oh it was a lot more than that." He said, "Can you give another $10,000?"

And I said, "I cannot give $10,000 at the moment, but I will give the—half of it now and half of it in a few months," which I did.

Q. Okay. And so how much total did you contribute on this pledge that Harold Rose had made to the University? **A.** $20,000.

Q. Did you know anything whatsoever about this pledge in advance? **A.** I did not.

Q. Now then, did your daughter go to work back in Washington, to your knowledge? **A.** She did.

Q. Did you give them any more money? **A.** Yes, I did.

Q. And can you tell us—give us an idea how much you gave them? **A.** I wrote to Steve and Diane—or in Diane's name or Steve and Diane's name $30,000 worth of checks.

Q. Over what period of time? **A.** Over a period of time from about 1991 to 1993 or '4. Then I—in '95 there were about $6,000 worth of checks—

Q. All right. Now, what was the first knowledge you had about her attempted suicide? **A.** I just had finished an operation. I was walking out of the Operating Room. I didn't even have my gloves off. And the Chief of Operating Service walked over to me and said, "Dr. Winter, there's a telephone—long-distance call." And on the other end of the line was Steve's voice crying, telling me something terrible had happened. I just didn't know what he meant. I said, "Who was it, for God's sake, Steve? Was it Jason?" He said—because someone fell.

He said, "No, it was Diane,"

And I said, "Where is she?"

He said, "She's in the Emergency Room at the Arlington Hospital." I think it was Arlington. And he said, "What can I do?"

I said, "Steve, do you have a neurosurgeon present?"

"Yes."

"Does she have an airway?" An "airway" means tracheal breathing.

"Yes."

I said then, "Did you get a urologist to be sure that she has kidney function?"

And he said, "Yes—no," he said, "No, I didn't get one, but that's a good suggestion."

I said, "Well, get that, please, Steve." I said, "I don't know what to— God, I don't know anything more to tell you now, Steve. I'm in the midst of an operation. There's a lady out in the hallway to go into the operating room. As soon as I finish it, I'll call you back."

Q. And did you do that? **A.** I did. No, I didn't call Steve back. I went over and, in between cases, I called Alice—rather, I called the Rose house. I didn't know whether I could do this operation, this next operation coming up, because the lady had already had her preoperative medication, the anesthetist was standing by, and she had been moved in the operating room. And I said—Alice answered the telephone. I said, "Alice, I am so sorry." She put the phone down and Harold picked up the phone and, in the distance— Harold said, "Hello." And I heard someone say, "Don't you talk to that son-of-a-bitch." And Harold said, "Alice, would you please get out of this room?"

And then I said, "Harold, it's the most critical situation," or, "a dire situation. I don't know what else to do at the moment."

He said to me, "Sam, she's your daughter. We're going right back."

I said, "Harold, I know very well she's my daughter and I intend to go back sometime today, but I can't go back when you go back."

Q. Well, you went back that evening? **A.** I did.

Q. Now, Doctor, who met you at the hospital? **A.** Well, he didn't meet me. I saw Steve at the hospital. He was sobbing and he said to me, "If I can only have another chance. I've made so many mistakes. If I can only have another chance."

I put my arm around him and I said, "Steve, I am sure we're going to do our best. Everything is being done that's possible. Don't castigate yourself."

Q. Okay. Now then, did that attitude change shortly? **A.** Well, I don't know, because that was Wednesday night and I—we all stayed up Wednesday night, all of us, I mean all of us who were at the—in the hospital. I slept—everybody slept on couches. I had a razor and shaving—

Q. Doctor,— **A.** But I left. I was there Wednesday night. Thursday, Friday, Saturday, Sunday. I left Monday morning. I rode in the ambulance from the Arlington Hospital to the George Washington University Intensive Care. I stayed there. I think she went over Saturday. I stayed Saturday, Sunday, and I left Monday morning back to Seattle. No, I didn't see any great difference.

Q. Now, while you were there, did you have a discussion the very next day or so with Harold Rose about the child? **A.** Yes.

Q. Proceed, Doctor. **A.** Harold said to me "Sam, you know Diane is in dangerous condition."

"And if anything happens to Diane, Alice would like to have the baby."

I said to him, "Harold,—I can't think of anything. The baby is being well taken care of. At the moment I can't think of anything but Diane's condition now." I said, "You know, if something happens to Diane, and God forbid that should take place, Amanda loves the baby, too, Harold." That was the extent of that conversation.

Q. Well, that's the main thing we want to develop. Now, how long were you here before you went back again, Doctor? **A.** One month, three-and-a-half weeks, something like that.

Q. Now, when you were back on this occasion, was there any change in Steve Rose's attitude towards yourself? **A.** Yes.

Q. In what way? **A.** He was more distant. He was irritated with me. He talked to me, but only in a perfunctory way.

(2). Cross Examination by Mr. Mellon

Q. Dr. Winter, you have three children, don't you? **A.** Yes, sir.

Q. They're three daughters; the oldest one is Diane, and then— **A.** Polly.

Q. —and then Nancy's the youngest? **A.** That's correct.

Q. Now then, when you saw Nancy in July, at some point along the line you said something about her being in love with Steve Rose? **A.** Yes.

Q. And what was her reply? **A.** "Yes, I am, but not the way you think."

Q. Is that all she said about it? **A.** Yes.

Q. Now, the way you thought was that it was love in the usual sense? **A.** I thought she was in love with him, that she wants to—she wants to marry Steve,—

Q. When she said,— **A.** —that she wants to—that she wants—she feels the baby isn't adequate in Diane's care, that she feels Steve is absolutely right about this whole thing.

Q. When she said "but not in the way you think," did you ask her what she meant by that? **A.** She didn't want to talk any more about it.

Q. I'm loath in a way to bring this up, Dr. Winter, but let me ask you this. Are you attempting to charge that your daughter, Nancy is having an improper—some kind of an improper relationship with Steve Rose? **A.** Yes, I am.

Q. Do you have any evidence to back up your statement? **A.** No, except for the feeling that I have.

Q. It's just a feeling? **A.** Nancy was always a loving daughter to me, I thought so. I thought we were close. I felt that we were together. She wrote letters to my wife and myself how much she loved us and how close she was to us. And then after this incident happened with Diane, Nancy began to drift away. And so this wasn't a—this wasn't anything that happened as you make it sound, on the day that she called me about Dr. Bower. This was mostly before that I couldn't communicate with Nancy no matter what I did or said. In fact, she berated me on my second visit to say to me, "How long have you practiced, Dad? Can't you give up your practice and stay here?"

And I said, "Nancy, I can't do that. I've got patients who are ill. I must go back. You've got your mother here, you've got your sister here." And this began to take place. She was supposed to have loved her sister, but she didn't seem to feel any closeness to Diane. It began to slip. Now, this—these are assumptions.

MR. MELLON: All right. I have nothing further, Doctor.

f.   Amanda Winter—For the Plaintiff

(1).   Direct Examination by Mr. Fisk

Q.   You're the wife of Dr. Samuel Winter? **A.** Yes.

Q.   And you are, of course, the mother of the three Winter girls? **A.** Yes.

Q.   Now, Mrs. Winter, did you go back to Washington, D.C., after your daughter Diane jumped from the— **A.** Yes.

Q.   And what day did you go back there? **A.** January 16th.

Q.   And what was your daughter's condition at that time? **A.** Diane was in the hospital, in intensive care in the Arlington Hospital, alive, but that's about all I knew.

Q.   Okay. And I assume that she was in no condition to be visited at that time. **A.** No.

Q.   How long were you in Washington, D.C.? **A.** From the time we moved to the apartment that I had found in Washington until about the middle of April.

Q.   Now, when did you get an apartment? **A.** After Diane was transferred to Washington, Polly and I went out to find an apartment there because the Arlington apartment was a one-bedroom apartment.

Q.   Where they'd been living you mean? **A.** Where Diane and Steve lived before Diane jumped from the window. I couldn't bear the thought of going to that apartment, so Polly and I went out and found a two-bedroom apartment in Washington, D.C., close to where Nancy lived. Nancy wanted it to be close to her, so we looked only in that neighborhood.

Q.   Now, did Steve Rose and his mother move into that apartment? **A.** Yes.

Q.   When? **A.** Must have been sometime toward the end of January when we moved over there. I'm not certain whether it was toward the end of January or the first of February. Dates were unimportant to me at that time. The only thing I was thinking of was Diane.

Q.   And who paid for that apartment? **A.** I did.

Q.   Okay. Where was the baby at that time? **A.** The baby was with Mrs. Rose in Arlington, in the Arlington apartment, until they moved over to Washington.

Q.   Okay. Now, who took care of the baby? **A.** Who took care of the baby? **Q.** Yes. **A.** I never saw the baby at all until they moved over to Washington, because I was with Diane and finding the apartment in Washington and cleaning that apartment to move into.

Q.   Now, did you take care of the baby when Alice would go to the hospital? **A.** Yes, after they moved to Washington, Alice went to the hospital almost every night and—and Polly and I took care of the baby until Polly left, and then I took care of the baby.

Q.   Now, when Alice was there, who took care of the baby? **A.** Alice took care of the baby when she was there.

Q.   And would she permit anyone else to take care of the baby? **A.** No, she made it very unpleasant for anyone else to take care of the baby. She went one time to get her hair done and came in when I was feeding the baby, and she immediately said, "He likes his bottle between bites."

And I said, "I've offered him the bottle and he has rejected it." And she snatched in front of my face and grabbed the bottle and she said, "He sometimes changes his mind." And he put the bottle in his mouth and then began to cry. And she said, "Oh, he doesn't want it now," and she put it down. And then she got toys and began dangling them in front of his face. So I got up and walked away. I didn't think it took two of us to feed the baby.

Q.   And did she get real physical if anyone else tried to take care of the baby?

MR. MELLON: This is leading.

A.   Yes.

MR. MELLON: This is leading, Your Honor.

A.   Yes.

THE COURT: Sustained.

A.   When I would change his diaper, she would come and push me aside and she would take over and I would just let her do it. Even when I slept in the room with the baby and he would wake in the night and I would get up to tend to him, she would come in and—and so I—I never tried very long to take care of the baby when she was there, because it took all the joy out of it. I enjoyed him thoroughly when she was not there.

Q.   Now, what was Steve's attitude toward you during the time you were there helping them? **A.** Steve was very hostile toward me all the time.

Q.   How would he— **A.** It was a—sort of a strained living-under-the-same-roof condition.

Q.   Well, in what way was he hostile? **A.** In the first family meeting with Dr. Grant which was, I think, when Diane was still in intensive care in Washington, he stated that I didn't even know what my—what my husband made. And said something about, "Did you folks think that when we—our son married the famous Dr. Winter's daughter that our financial problems with schooling were ended?" And there were many statements like that.

Q.   Eventually you came home in April, did you not? **A.** Yes, I came home in April.

Q.   And how did that come about? **A.** As I visited Diane daily during the day back there, she grew more and more hostile toward me and there were indications in family meetings that her father and I were to blame for all of her problems. And she was agreeing with this. And I would go to the hospital and visit her during the day and hear her reiterate to me things that she could not have known were happening unless Alice or Steve were telling them to her, that were more and more hostile toward her father and me. And finally I said, "Diane, do you think the pressure would be off if I went home?"

And she said, "Yes. I think you should go home."

Q.   As a result of that you did go home? **A.** I went home. And Dr. Cooper had asked that no one do anything until—without letting him know. So I went to Dr. Cooper and told him I was going home. He said, "Diane is more disturbed than she knows or you know at sending you home."

And I said, "I know that, Dr. Cooper but unless I go home and she can learn to hate us she doesn't have a snowball's chance in hell."

(2).   Cross Examination by Mr. Mellon

Q.   Now, just a couple of questions and then I'm through. Dr. Winter originally came from Baltimore, didn't he? **A.** Yes.

Q.   And you and he lived back there for awhile, did you not?

A.   Yes.

Q.   After you were married? **A.** Yes.

Q.   And did you leave your husband in Baltimore? **A.** Yes.

Q.   And was this—were you not accepted back there? **A.** I was accepted, but it was a very strained relationship and I decided if our marriage was going to survive, we had to live away and out of the influence of my husband's family. And he chose to leave his family and make our family ours and leave the other families out of it.

Q.   One of the difficulties back in Baltimore was the fact that you were non-Jewish. Isn't that it? **A.** Yes, they were—they were an Orthodox family and they had objected to him marrying a non-Jewish girl, however, I had converted.

Q.   Yes. **A.** That didn't make any difference to an Orthodox family.

Q.   Dr. Winter described you as taciturn. **A.** As what?

Q.   Taciturn. Do you know what that word means? **A.** Yes.

Q.   Would you say that that correctly describes you? **A.** I think so.

Q.   And your relationship with your daughters? **A.** I think so. I think— I always assumed that if anybody had anything to tell me, they'd tell me, and I never probed and questioned them a great deal.

MR. MELLON: That's all.

g.   Polly Winter—For the Plaintiff

(1).   Direct Examination by Mr. Fisk

Q.   Where do you live? **A.** I live with my folks.

Q.   And you are the sister, of course, of Diane and Nancy. **A.** Yes, I am.

Q.   Now, yesterday Steve Rose testified that when they were down at college and the time some of the youngsters were eating hashish, that you had baked the cookies. Is there any truth to that? **A.** No, there isn't.

Q.   Would you tell us what the facts are? **A.** Yes. A friend of my boyfriend at that time had baked the cookies and given them to my boyfriend. And Steve knew that they were there and he made arrangements with my boyfriend when they would take it, and he said that he would try it the night before, and that if he thought it was all right, Diane would try it the next night.

Q.   And did Steve take—eat the cookies both nights? **A.** Yes, he did.

Q.   You weren't in your room when this problem arose as to— **A.** No, I wasn't. Steve wanted to be alone with Diane and he wanted to stay with the— the night with her because she was in such physical pain.

Q.   Now, you were around Diane and Steve occasionally when they were going together before they were married? **A.** Yes, I was.

Q.   What was Steve's attitude toward Diane? **A.** Well, before they were married, once he told me that his friends had told him that Diane was not quite smart enough for him and below him.

Q.   What terminology did he use in describing her? **A.** Little dumb.

Q. Okay. You went back to Washington, D.C., after Diane attempted— or did jump— **A.** I went back on the 16th.

Q. That was that same day? **A.** Same day.

Q. For the most part, could you tell us who took care of Jason? **A.** There's not doubt about it. It was Alice Rose.

Q. Did Alice object to anyone else taking care of him if he was—if she was there? **A.** She sure did.

Q. How long did you stay? **A.** Until March.

Q. What was the attitude of Alice Rose towards your father? **A.** She hated him.

Q. Would you tell the Court what, if anything, she had to say about him? **A.** She told my mother and myself that he was dirt, and she would never consider him anything else. And at one time I overheard her talking with my little sister, Nancy, and my little sister was spilling her guts out to her, saying that she used to be able to laugh at my father, but now she couldn't it wasn't funny anymore. And Alice said, "I know, Nancy it's unforgivable."

Q. Did she ever use any epithets for him? **A.** She called him a son-of-a-bitch. She was talking to her brother on the telephone and she was saying "Diane is simply going to have to learn to live with the fact that her father is a son-of-a-bitch."

Q. What was Alice Rose's attitude toward yourself? **A.** She hated me.

Q. Now then, you are presently living at your parents' home, are you? **A.** Yes.

Q. Do you have any long-range plans? **A.** Yes, I do. When this whole matter is straightened out, my sister and I have plans of getting an apartment sooner or later.

h. Nancy Winter—For the Plaintiff

(1). Direct Examination by Mr. Fisk

Q. Where do you live, Nancy? **A.** I—well, I live—I presently am staying at the Roses'.

Q. Okay. Now, you attended some of those family sessions, [in Washington] did you not? **A.** Yes, I did.

Q. And at some of those family sessions did you express some hostility towards your parents? **A.** Yes, I did.

Q. And would you tell us what it was that brought out this—brought on this hostility? **A.** Well, it was a number of things. It was that—a lot of it had to do with the way we were brought up as children and the way that we—that Diane and I jointly—Diane and I had many discussions, the way we jointly felt that my parents did not—did not get involved with our childhood, and that they were never really there when we really needed them.

Q. Had there been some sudden change in your thinking? **A.** No. I always—I always understood my parents and I—and I did in fact search out for other—other—my other friends' families and I spent a lot of time at my other—at friends' families, because I didn't—I didn't particularly feel that—I have to say I didn't really have any—very many problems as a child, and I—and I didn't I hadn't really gone through the same things that my older sisters had gone through with—in dealing with my parents. I had a relationship with them, yes.

Q. Well, I want to ask you, Nancy, if up until about Christmastime, 1973, you thought you loved your parents very much and could hardly stand to be away from them. **A.** I did, yes. I really—I did love them.

Q. Nancy, apparently you feel somewhat estranged from your parents at the present time. **A.** Yes, I do.

Q. Now, would you tell the Court what your parents have done to you since the time of these letters, when you couldn't wait to get home for Christmas, that has caused you to take your present attitude towards your parents? **A.** All right. Well, since Diane's suicide attempt, I—it was a very distressing time for everybody, obviously, and I would—I had—I received a phone call from my father when he returned from Seattle—after about five days after he had come back, he returned to Seattle, he called me and he informed me that I must not stand on the sidelines any longer, that I must get involved in what my parents—in what my parents were disagreeing over and what—you know, this schism between the Roses and the Winters. I told him that I—I didn't want—I didn't want to get involved in this; I felt that it was—it was—you know, was completely irrelevant and that my mother was making a mountain out of a molehill about this idea about Mrs. Rose being very, very over—overly, you know, protective of the child.

Q. You didn't believe that? **A.** No, of course I didn't, because I was there.

i.   Diane Winter Rose, Plaintiff

(1).   Direct Examination by Mr. Fisk

Q. How old are you, Diane? **A.** Twenty-six.

Q. Would you tell us a little bit about your educational background? **A.** I am a graduate from college, graduated with a B.S. Degree.

Q. How did you do scholastically in college? **A.** 3–point.

Q. How about your high school grades? **A.** I graduated in the Honor Society. I'm not stupid.

Q. Now, when did you first start going with Steve Rose more or less steady? **A.** I was eighteen, right before I went to college.

Q. Did you go more less steadily with him up until the time you were married? **A.** Yes, four years.

Q. Now, you got married on July the 5th, 1990, did you not? **A.** Yes.

Q. At the time you got married did you have any honeymoon plans? **A.** Yes, we had planned to go to the beach for three days.

Q. Whereabouts at the beach now? **A.** At our condominium.

Q. You mean your parents' condominium? **A.** My parents' condominium, yes.

Q. Okay. Now, what happened to those plans? **A.** Steve didn't want to go, so we went to see his mother the next day.

Q. Where did you spend your wedding night then? **A.** Right near his home.

Q. Motel there? **A.** That was our honeymoon, so-called.

Q. Now, how did you come to get married to start with? **A.** Well, Steve was planning to go to Austria for medical school and it was two months before he was to leave, about two months. I didn't want to be separated from him for five or six years.

Q. Were you very much in love at that time? **A.** Very much, yes.

Q. Okay. And so what happened? **A.** I asked him to marry me, and he said he didn't know, that he had to ask his mother.

Q. And did he go ask his mother? **A.** Yes, he did. He came back the next day and he said, "She said it was okay," that she wanted him to marry me, so he said he thought that that was okay.

Q. And so then the wedding came off? **A.** Yes.

Q. Now, how was your trip to Europe financed? **A.** My father.

Q. Why did you return? **A.** Because Steve wanted to. We found that it was going to be eight or nine years and originally he had thought it was five or six. And he never dropped out of dental school.

Q. Now, during the time that you were going together and while you were in Germany, what was Steve's attitude towards you from an intellectual standpoint, if you can tell us? **A.** That I was stupid, that—German was a hard language, and whenever I didn't know an answer, he—he would laugh at me, and so I decided that I wouldn't try anymore because he was just laughing at me and saying I was stupid.

Q. Well, had he made remarks along those lines even before you were married? **A.** Yes, he sure did; I was stupid.

Q. How did you happen to marry him with that type of attitude on his part? **A.** I was in love with him and I was blind, and he did compliment me. He told me I was pretty.

Q. But stupid? **A.** But stupid, yes.

Q. Did you and Steve eventually go to Washington, D.C. then? **A.** Yes.

Q. Did you get a job there? **A.** Yes, I did.

Q. And would you tell Judge Hoover what the job was that you had? **A.** I was a medical secretary in Orthopedics and then in Radiology.

Q. And because of that fact, did Steve get a break in his tuition? **A.** He got it half off, and I paid for every monthly expense we had.

Q. Out of your salary? **A.** Yes.

Q. Did you get any money from home at that time from your parents. **A.** My father had helped us and we had come home for summers and he paid for that, of course.

Q. Now, when was the—you had been there, what, roughly a year and a half when the baby was born? **A.** Yes.

Q. Am I correct that his birthday is April 21st? **A.** 1993, uh-huh.

Q. Now, would you tell the Court whether or not you in truth and in fact worked right up to the day this boy was born? **A.** Yes, I did. It wasn't planned that way, but Jason was five weeks early, yeah.

Q. Now then, who took care of this baby? **A.** I did.

Q. You did? **A.** Yes.

Q. Did you have any babysitters? **A.** No. I loved doing it myself, yes.

Q. Well, and did you do it? **A.** Yes, I did.

Q. Now, is it true that you took care of the child from the time he was born right up until the time— **A.** Absolutely, yes.

Q. —until you— **A.** Yes.

Q. —jumped out the window? **A.** Yes. I loved doing it, m-hm.

Q. During all this time did Steve have really anything whatsoever to do with taking care of him? **A.** Absolutely nothing.

Q. Now, with your income cut off, was it necessary that you have some other money? **A.** Yes, it was.

Q. And how was that arranged then? What did you do? **A.** My father supported us.

Q. Now, during this period of time, would you tell the Court whether or not Steve was becoming increasingly critical of yourself? **A.** Yes, he certainly was.

MR. MELLON: If the Court please, counsel is assuming facts not in evidence. He can ask what the relationship was between she and Steve and so on, but—

THE COURT: Agreed.

Q. How was your relationship with Steve during this period of time? **A.** He was very critical of me. He had always told me how stupid I was, but— with the baby he said how I was inadequate. Quite a number of times he told me that a babysitter could do a better job than I could, and of course it upset me because I loved him very much.

Q. And was this a once-in-awhile or constant-daily thing? **A.** It was a daily thing.

Q. Did Alice Rose come back to visit you about— **A.** Yes, about December. I don't remember the exact date, but it was probably about the 15th, and she left a week prior to my suicide attempt.

Q. Okay. How long did she stay there? **A.** About three weeks.

Q. Now, during this period of time what was the relationship between yourself and Alice Rose? **A.** Well, she told—she would say to me that I couldn't feed the baby right, I couldn't change his diapers right, I couldn't dress him right, I couldn't bathe him right, I didn't put him down for his nap at the right time. And Steve was his mother's supporter.

Q. Now, was the baby healthy? **A.** Yes, he was.

Q. Was he getting along fine? **A.** Yes.

Q. Did Steve ever support you when his mother would criticize you? **A.** Never.

Q. Now, Diane, can you tell us the problems that—so far as how you reacted to the things that were bothering you that led up to this suicide attempt? What things were there that were—Were you depressed at that time? **A.** I was down. I don't know if you'd say I was depressed.

Q. Okay. **A.** I had been convinced that my parents did not love me by Steve and Alice. And Alice had just been back there telling me everything I was doing wrong. Steve was his mother's supporter. And he told me quite a few times that a babysitter could do a better job than I could. And I was very distraught, of course, because I loved him very much.

Q. You're talking about the baby or Steve or both? **A.** Both.

Q. All right. And before you made this suicide attempt what was the last thing that you did? **A.** I called down to the lobby for someone to come up and hold my baby.

Q. Now, of course, you don't remember too much that happened, I take it, during the first few weeks you were in the hospital. **A.** I remember nothing.

Q. Okay. About what's the first time that you began to remember? **A.** Oh, I'd say I started remembering spotty things in April, but didn't start to really remember from day to night until about, oh, June or July.

Q. You attended some—did you go to those early family sessions in March,— **A.** No.

Q. —late March? Or do you remember? **A.** When did I start? I can't remember if I started to go to them in March or April. I don't know.

Q. In the hospital records there's various quotes of your—what you had told the doctors and the nurses and so on. **A.** M-hm.

Q. For the most part, do you remember any of those for the first month or two, to say the least? **A.** No. No. Didn't even start to have a memory in late March or April or (pause)

Q. Okay. You were eventually released— **A.** June 1st.

Q. Okay. I'll ask you whether or not—Was there any pressure on you to leave the hospital actually before you left—before you did leave? **A.** Steve wanted me to come home because the problem was getting too close to home.

Q. And did Steve actually take you home from the hospital personally? **A.** He and Nancy did.

Q. Oh, Nancy was with him? **A.** Yes.

Q. Did Nancy visit you while you were in the hospital? **A.** Yes, daily.

Q. And did she come with Steve most of the time? **A.** Most of the time. And when she didn't come with Steve, she came with Alice or by herself and immediately called Steve up and had him come up.

Q. Now, when you got back to the apartment in Washington, D.C., who was living there? **A.** When do you mean? Oh, when—Okay.

Q. After the hospital. **A.** Steve, Alice. And I was going back to the same situation as Dr. Cooper didn't want me to.

Q. So you returned to Steve and Alice against his advice? **A.** Yes. I wanted to become reacquainted with my baby and I loved my husband.

Q. Now, what was the relationship after you got home from the hospital? **A.** Well, it was the same thing again. Everything that I was doing with Jason was wrong. I tried to do things, but Alice took over. And one of— the day I returned I was holding Jason and Steve said, "Diane, put him down. You will hurt him." So I could have no physical contact with him and it was terrible.

Q. Did Alice stay there all the time? **A.** She sure did.

Q. And was there anyone else there besides you three that were living there? **A.** Hm-m, hm-m (negative response).

Q. Did Nancy come over? **A.** Yes.

Q. How often did she come? **A.** Oh, two or three times a week. I really can't remember. She was close by, walking distance.

Q. All right. Now, you eventually left the apartment that you were sharing there in Washington, D.C., sometime in August. Is that correct? **A.** August 5th.

Q. So the Bower session was after you'd gone and were staying with the Nathans? **A.** Yes, uh-huh.

Q. All right. Can you tell us what led up to your leaving the apartment with Steve and Alice. **A.** That day I had seen Dr. Bower—Dr. Grant, I'm sorry, and he said to me, "Diane, how are you getting along with Alice."

And I said, "Well, she still grabs Jason away from me when he cries, and she won't let me do any—she won't let me finish anything."

And so he said to me, "Diane, you have to be consistent. You have to tell her off because Jason senses you are the child." So I returned home that day and I was bound and determined to be the only one to care for my child, and I was determined to give Jason his last bottle and put him to bed. Well, he wouldn't take it from me, and I had taken him in the bedroom away from anyone else, and I had tried out—tried to give him the bottle and he wouldn't take it. I had put him on my lap and things like that.

Alice walked into the room and she said to me, "Diane, he is not a doll." And she took him away. And I went to call the Nathans.

I said, "Debbie, I have to get away." And so she said that Doug would come and get me in about an hour or so.

Q. Was there an actual physical confrontation? **A.** Yes. Okay, I'll tell— I'll explain. In the meantime, Steve and I were talking and Alice had put Jason to bed. And Steve started to yell and woke Jason up. And Alice went to get him and Jason threw his arms out to me and I took him. I took him away from all the tension in the other room. Jason started to cry. Alice came in and grabbed Jason away from me and I was really mad. I scratched her arm. I have a maternal instinct.

And Steve came in the room and he said, "You're going to drive me crazy."

And Alice said to Steve, "She threw the baby to me."

And I said, "Quit arguing like Steve."

Q. So then you went to the Nathans? **A.** Yes. And I left Alice and Steve Rose. I was driven from my baby. I left this time legitimately.

Q. Now, Diane, how long did you stay at the— **A.** About a month.

Q. No, how long did you stay at the Nathans? **A.** About a month.

Q. Now, during the month that you were there, did you call Steve about some visitation with the baby? **A.** I called him every day and I begged him to bring Jason to see me.

Q. And did he bring him? **A.** He finally brought him three weeks later. No—well, two or three weeks later. Once he brought him with Nancy.

Q. Okay. Now, during the time that you lived with the Nathans did you care for the Nathan child? **A.** Always, yes.

Q. And what did you do for her child? **A.** Well, I fed her and I dressed her. I changed her diapers. I put her down for naps and bed and I loved her.

Q. What happened next? **A.** I returned to my—the apartment that I had left on September 9th. And I had said to Steve—Alice was gone with the baby and Steve returned a couple of hours later, was surprised to see me. And I said, "Steve, I'm back to stay."

And he said, "I'm leaving then." So he picked up a few clothes and a suitcase that I had later found in Nancy's room, and he said to me, "Diane, you're so inadequate. You couldn't even kill yourself." Then he called my doctor and told him I would be alone that night, and he said, "Fine."

Q. What doctor did he call? **A.** Grant. And he called my parents to tell them. And he said, "If anything happens to her, you are to blame."

Q. You heard this conversation? **A.** Yes, I did.

Q. When you came to Seattle, were you having difficulty with visitation then after you came here? **A.** I certainly was. I was to see the baby four times a week in Seattle without a Rose, and they wouldn't allow it, and this was for three weeks they wouldn't allow it, until I filed a custody hearing. Then they suddenly came up with a third neutral party, well, competent, and I could see Jason three times a week. Before it was two times a week and I could not see Jason without Steve.

Q. Now, the visitations you've had since this proceeding was started, how successful have they been? **A.** Well they have had not one but two and three watchdogs. They have them follow me from room to room. Everything I do with my baby is—I'm on display. Let's see. Many times I've gone there Jason has been very tired. They've said he missed his nap. And on one occasion he slept in my arms the whole night—the whole day, the whole visit. And they asked me to put him down for him to sleep and I said, "No, I want to hold my baby."

Q. Has he been—would you state whether or not he's been obviously tired on the occasions you've been there? **A.** Many times, yes.

Q. Where are you living now? **A.** At my parents.

Q. And your sister Polly lives there? **A.** Yes.

Q. Are you doing any work? **A.** Yes.

Q. What kind of work are you doing? **A.** I'm working at a church answering the phone. And when I'm not doing that, when I am free, I practice my typing, I'm a very good typist.

Q. Now, your mother has raised three children? **A.** M-hm.

Q. She knows how to wash a baby and feed him and that type of thing, does she? **A.** M-hm, yes.

Q. And if you're granted custody of this child, do you propose to keep him at the Winters temporarily? **A.** M-hm.

Q. And what are your long-range plans? **A.** Well, I am planning to move out in an apartment with my sister, and I will have a part-time job, and I'm going to put Jason in nursery school and work when he's in school, and that's what I'll do.

Q. Now, so far as the immediate future is concerned, do you have some money left in your trust account? **A.** Yes. I don't know how much, but yes.

Q. And your father is willing to help you financially? **A.** He has always been willing to help me.

Q. Do you have a good relationship with your parents at this time? **A.** Yes, I do.

(2).   Cross Examination by Mr. Mellon

Q.   You and Steve were happily married, weren't you? **A.** I thought so. I always hid my sad feelings. That's why I tried to commit suicide, because I had realized he didn't love me and I wouldn't admit it to myself.

Q.   When did you realize that? **A.** Well, I guess I—well, quite a few months it had been.

Q.   Pardon? **A.** Quite a few—quite a few—a few months, but I wouldn't bring it to my conscious.

Q.   You wouldn't do what? **A.** It was so conscious, I'm sorry. I wanted Steve to love me and—and he not only didn't love me, he wants me dead. That's what I found out when I went to find—I went to see Nancy and his suitcase was in her room. And he told me that I was so inadequate, I couldn't even kill myself.

Q.   Now, when did you find Steve's suitcase in your room—I mean in Nancy's room? **A.** About September 13th.

Q.   Yes. Well, you didn't know anything about any suitcase in Nancy's room at the time you jumped out the window, did you? **A.** No.

Q.   And you and Steve were living a happy, normal life at the time of— that you jumped out the window? **A.** I thought we were happy. I wanted—I hoped to God that we were happy. I was—I loved him. I wanted him to love me, but he didn't.

Q.   When you were in the hospital, Mrs. Rose, you didn't say one word against Alice Rose. **A.** I thought she was great.

Q.   You thought she was great? **A.** Yes, I was brainwashed, just like Nancy is now.

Q.   And you didn't say anything in the hospital against your husband, did you? **A.** No, I thought he was great, too.

Q.   But you didn't think he was great when you jumped? **A.** I wouldn't admit it to myself consciously. I wouldn't admit my sad feelings.

Q.   All during the time that you were in the hospital you never said anything derogatory about Steve or about his mother, did you? **A.** Not that I remember.

Q.   But you said a lot of derogatory things about your parents? **A.** I sure did. I was acting just like Alice.

Q.   What do you mean by that? **A.** I loved my husband, but I had to act just like Alice to keep him. That's what I mean.

Q.   You mean you had to act just like Alice to keep your husband? **A.** Yes, I had to hate my parents for her, uh-huh, and I tried to, believe me. I tried to.

Q.   And is that the only reason that you kept saying in the hospital how you blamed your parents— **A.** Yes.

Q.   —for what had happened? **A.** That is exactly right.

Q.   So that you could keep Steve? **A.** You hit it right on the nose.

Q.   And you felt in order to keep Steve that you had to say that you hated your parents, that you'd had a bad upbringing? **A.** That's right.

Q.   And that they were the ones that were responsible, because of the way they brought you up, for you being unhappy and depressed,— **A.** Yes, that's right.

Q. —and requiring and making you jump out the window? **A.** That's right. Yes.

Q. You did that just so you could keep Steve? **A.** Well, my mother is— yes. My mother is a very quiet woman. She never worked. She was always with the kids. And I began to misperceive her love for me.

Q. You say that you were very depressed at the time of the—that you jumped out of the window. And you say that—you say it wasn't because of your background and all that sort of thing. You say it was because of Steve. **A.** M-hm.

Q. Well, why didn't you just sue him for divorce? **A.** Because he would make me—made me feel so inferior, and I loved him and I thought that he was the best I could ever get. That's why.

Q. Well, you wanted your baby, didn't you? **A.** Yes, I did, but I thought that—I thought I was doing the best job I could as a mother, and I thought that it wasn't good enough. He made me feel that way, yes. I tried to kill myself for my baby actually.

Q. You tried to kill yourself for your baby? **A.** Because I felt I was a burden for him.

Q. For the baby? **A.** I felt I was a bad mother, yes.

Q. So you felt that divorce wouldn't be adequate, that you had to do away with yourself? **A.** I thought I couldn't do any better. Steve would not allow me to be myself and I—and I hadn't realized—I hadn't realized why. I loved him so much that I just thought there was nothing else I could do but to get rid of myself for him and my baby.

Q. Did you feel that by jumping out of the window you would in that way hurt Steve? **A.** Oh, no. No, I thought I was—I thought I was relieving him.

j. David Greenburg, M.D.—For the Plaintiff

(1). Direct Examination by Mr. Fisk

Q. And are you a licensed doctor? **A.** Yes. [The Doctor is qualified as an expert in psychiatry who has specialized in suicide.]

Q. All right. Now, Doctor, at my request, did you do a psychiatric examination of Diane Rose? **A.** Yes, I did.

Q. And when did you do that? **A.** June 8th, 1995.

Q. Okay. Now Doctor, when you examined her, were you able to form an opinion as to whether or not she was suicidal? **A.** Yes.

Q. What was your opinion? **A.** My opinion was that she was not suicidal at that time. I would put her in the lowest lethality group. And that is not to say that it would be absolutely impossible for her to make a suicide attempt, because in my way of thinking, I doubt that I would say that about any person that I have ever met. But that she certainly was in the low group.

Q. Now, do you know a suicidologist or psychiatrist, named Theodor Dorpat? **A.** Yes, I do know him, and I know of his work.

Q. And has he made a study of this same problem? **A.** Dr. Dorpat has written a number of articles and done some research, original research on suicide. He published an article in 1986 called "The Relationship Between Attempted Suicide and Committed Suicide." One of the points that he dealt with in this article was a list of thirteen factors which have been found to be associated with a high probability or risk of subsequent completed suicide, among those who have attempted suicide. Number one, age, older more than younger; number two, sex, men more than women; number three, serious suicide intent in the attempt; four, multiple prior suicide attempts; number five, unmarried marital status, unmarried could be single, widowed, divorced, or separated; number six, living alone; seven, poor physical health; eight, psychosis; nine, a lethal method used in the attempt of suicide; ten, a suicide note; number eleven, infrequent use of health agencies; number twelve—unemployed or retired; and number thirteen, from a broken home.

Q. (By Mr. Fisk) Now Doctor, of that list of thirteen, Diane Rose would fit in four categories, would she not?

MR. MELLON: I'm going to object to counsel testifying.

Q. (By Mr. Fisk) Well, how many would she fit in, Doctor? **A.** Out of this list of thirteen, I scored Diane Rose as pointing toward suicide on four of the thirteen issues. Now, there was one which I sort of have a question mark about, which is this: Number twelve says unemployed or retired. There is a question there, because although Diane Rose is not receiving any payment, it is my understanding that she has a regular agency at which she works, or a number of agencies at which she works. My prejudice would be to count that as against suicide, but it is a question.

Q. Well, assuming whether she's unemployed or not, now, assuming she fits four, is that in the low scale, or how would you rate that? **A.** That would put her at the, just speaking from this group, at four out of twelve, or four out of thirteen would, generally speaking, put her in the lower third of serious, in the spectrum of lethality.

Q. Now Doctor, up to now, we've been speaking of the statistical data, and I want to talk to you about Diane Rose as a person, and ask you, forgetting about all of those tables, how do you find her as a person, and how do you rate her? **A.** I rate Diane Rose as at the present time being of low lethality, and of continuing to move in a direction which will make her of lower lethality. Now I say this with all circumspection, that is, there are things that could happen to her. There are things that could happen to any one of us, which we cannot predict, and which turn us toward suicide or toward any other kind of untoward circumstance. But these are the reasons, as I see it, why I judge Diane Rose, at the present time, to be of low lethality.

In the first place, I think that one of the features of a suicidal person is the issue of their having a kind of an all-or-none philosophy; that is, there are one or two or whatever number of things that are very important to that person. And their feeling is—feelings of these extremely suicidal people are that if they cannot get that thing, then life is not worthwhile, and they will kill themselves.

Now, from this standpoint, I was unable to determine that there was that general kind of psychology in Diane Rose at this time. And I made a number of attempts, both to observe whether it was present, and even to ask her specific questions about it. Some of the specific questions that I remember were these: What will you do if you do not win custody of your child? Her answer, in essence, was that she would be disappointed and unhappy, but she had plans to do some other things. She was considering either going to school, or going to work, or a combination of both of them. So that seemed to me a striking thing.

Now, another issue—now I'll switch to another area, and that is, that the question of her passive personality is an extremely important one in my opinion in this case. And it is for this reason: My feeling is that the suicide attempt can best be described as a combination of an environmental stress with a particular kind of personality which tended to be subservient and to defer to authority, which also looked for authorities to whom to relate herself. Now, I think that she—a person in such a situation might have relatively good luck, and might get involved in a situation in which the authorities did not put her under stress, did not put her under states of extreme tension. That is a possibility. On the other hand, it is a possibility that the opposite could occur, and that is what I think happened in Diane Rose's case. So now, the problem, one of the problems with a passive personality is that they are caught in a severe kind of what you might call a double bind. That is, on the one hand, in order to get along with the authority who they fear and/or respect, and/or love, it is necessary for them to go along with whatever that person wants. However, at the same time, that person may be asking the passive person to do certain other things which the passive person doesn't want to do. For example, to—well, when I think of Mrs. Rose's case, to sever relations, or to have some—to decrease the intensity of her relationship with her parents, to give up her own opportunity, her own desire to treat her child as she wished. So—and there may be some other things, but I picked these as two examples that I think I remember from her history. So that in that kind of situation, the passive person's own passivity makes him vulnerable. Now, I think that Diane Rose, even prior to the time of the suicide attempt, was making some attempts to change this part of her personality. For example, I think that her marriage itself, and the resolve to utilize that as a way to move away from home, may have been part of that situation.

I believe that she is moving in that direction for some of the reasons that I cited, and I think that therefor makes the contribution to the possibility of suicide from her own passivity less. And it is for these reasons that I think that she is of less lethality, of low lethality, and that probably that this trend will continue. One other thing that I think I should add at this time is that Diane Rose, again in connection with the issue of turning—blaming herself for all kinds of things, now has changed in another way, and that is, that she has come to the conclusion that having someone, namely a professional person, namely a psychiatrist, work with her at times of stress, is a good idea. As far as I could tell, she has been working with a psychiatrist. She feels that, and I would concur, that she has made some advances. She feels that she has improved at this point, but that it is possible that she may have difficulties in the future. And that if she does, her intention is to resume more intense psychotherapeutic work. That, too, is something that I think is both an indication of less lethality, and an indication that should she have future difficulties, as all people are bound to have, that if she gets to the point where she feels it beyond her, she will seek help for them.

Q. Now, Doctor, all of this leads up to the question as to the care and custody and control of the minor child. Mr. Rose has testified that if he's awarded custody of the child, he intends to go to U.C.L.A. where he is starting a residency in internal medicine, where his hours will be eight or nine to five every day. With every fourth night, he'll have twenty-four-hour duty. I'll ask you to assume that for the past several months as you're aware, his mother has been largely responsible for taking care of the child while Mr. Rose has attended the University of Washington Medical School.

I'll ask you to assume that Diane Rose, and for the first eight months of the child's life, or thereabouts, before the suicide attempt, was, of course, a person that cared for him mostly, and his father, the child's father, was going to medical school at George Washington at that time. That since they've been out here in Washington, she did not have much visitation up until February or—January or February of this year, at which time the Court ordered visitation of four hours twice weekly, plus every other weekend, which she's enjoyed since that time.

Ask you to assume that the child views both his father and his mother as psychological as well as biological parents. Ask you to assume that either of them could provide an adequate physical facility; that if Diane gets the custody of the child, she will live with her parents, and she will devote full time to the child until he's old enough at least to be put in a nursery school or something of that kind, at which time she will probably work short hours while he was in the nursery school.

If Mr. Rose gets custody of the child, he proposes to take the child to Los Angeles; his mother proposes to go with him and stay there indefinitely until such time as he can get what is thought to be a suitable live-in person to take care of the child when he's not available.

Now, with those alternatives, and considering the welfare of the child, I'll ask you who, in your opinion, should be awarded the permanent care and custody of this child. **A.** I would say that with the knowledge that I now have, and given the particular question, that I would say that Mrs. Rose would be a superior parent to Mr. Rose. And I base that statement, I believe, on two ideas. The first one is that it is a general postulate in Western society that the mother is a more important parent than the father. And the second one is that I think at this young time in a child's life, a time when a child traditionally needs more intimate and attentive care from a parent, it also—it is possible for Mrs. Rose to supply this intimate and constant attention to a greater degree than Mr. Rose. That's my answer.

(2).   Cross Examination by Mr. Mellon

Q. You feel that the mother is a more important parent than the father, even with the male child with the father? **A.** Yes.

Q. Are you familiar with the law [of this State] on this subject? **A.** No.

Q. Are you familiar with the fact that the Washington law is that no parent shall be favored by reason of the fact that that parent happens to be the mother? **A.** No.

Q. Do you agree with that? **A.** No.

Q. You do not agree with the Washington law? **A.** No.

Q. As I understand it, Doctor, you have never seen this child, or have you? **A.** I have never seen the child.

Q. And you've never seen Steve Rose, you assume he's sitting on my left, but that's the only time you've ever seen him? **A.** That is correct.

Q. And you saw Diane Rose down in Los Angeles—was it in Los Angeles? **A.** Yes, it was.

Q. For how long? **A.** An hour and fifteen minutes.

Q. And is that the only time you saw her until you came up here today? **A.** That's correct.

Q. Did you see her prior to coming to the courtroom today? **A.** No.

Q. And you feel comfortable in making the assertion, Doctor, that with what you know about your visit of an hour and fifteen minutes, with never having seen the child, and never having seen Steve Rose with the child, never having observed Steve Rose with child, and how they get along, and never having observed Diane with the child, and how they get along, you feel comfortable in sitting up there and saying that you think she should have the custody of this child? **A.** Yes, I do. And I did want to remind you that I did say that I thought those issues were important ones, and that I was making—I was giving my impression without having that kind of information available.

Q. Now, are you familiar with the work of Goldstein, Freud, and Solnit, Beyond the Best Interests of the Child? **A.** No, I am not.

Q. Have you ever heard of it? **A.** I've heard of Solnit. Is the "Freud," Anna Freud?

Q. Yes. **A.** Yes. I've heard of those two people.

Q. Those are well-known people who enjoy excellent reputations, are they not? **A.** Yes.

Q. Are you familiar with the fact that their work has been cited with approval by the appellate courts in California? **A.** No, I am not.

(3). Redirect Examination by Mr. Fisk

Q. [D]octor, counsel asked you some questions about the Winter family, and placing the child there, and so on; now, I want you to assume this: In this case, there is evidence and testimony that in some of these family sessions, the doctor who was conducting the session, indicated that Steve Rose and his mother both needed psychiatric treatment; that Alice Rose, the mother, was mentally sleeping with her son, Steve; that she had emasculated her own husband, mentally; that both she and Steve were in need of psychiatric treatment. He went so far as to say that what Alice Rose needed was a "good lay."

Now, with that background, would that buttress the opinion you have previously expressed? **A.** Well, of course, I can't pass—

Q. Assuming that's the facts. **A.** If that were the fact, then I think that would be further supportive of the position that I stated.

MR. FISK: Thank you, Doctor. That's all.

(4). Re-cross by Mr. Mellon

Q. If you want to enter into that type of speculation, Doctor, assume that this same doctor told Diane Rose that her father was a stuffy son of a bitch; and that he should have thrown her out of the window a long time ago. Is that the sort of thing that is going to alter your opinion one way or the other? **A.** If it is true, then it mitigates against the recommendation that I made.

MR. MELLON: That's all.

MR. FISK: Thank you, Doctor.

THE COURT: Thank you. You may step down.

k. Constance Howe, Psychologist—For the Plaintiff

(1). Direct Examination by Mr. Fisk

Q. Now, your name is Constance Howe? **A.** That's correct.

[Dr. Howe is qualified as a clinical psychologist who has specialized in child development].

Q. Will you describe your current work? **A.** What I do is both in a service sense to the citizens of the State and in a research sense, I'm attempting to conduct a program that takes parents who have extreme difficulties in dealing and interacting with their children, and then apply an approach to this pair, call it a "parent-child pair," that entails observation of parent and child interacting in what we call a "standardized," if you will, laboratory, playroom setting.

One circumstance is what might best be known as an absence of parent control. We call it the "Child's Game." The mother is instructed to just go along and play with the child. It's his game, his activity, his time to do as he wishes. You just go play along with him until we communicate with you again. We'll tap on the one-way mirror.

That used to go on for thirty minutes at a time, although now, we don't have to observe that long. At the end of ten minutes, we'll rap on the window, and instructions are now reversed, and we have the necessity for a parent-control time. We call it "Mother's Game." The instructions are somewhat the same, with just one variation, "All right, Mrs. Rose, now it's time for your game, and your rules. You get Jason to play in whatever game or activity you wish. It's your game, your rules, and you keep him at it." And we will observe again for ten minutes. We also, just to wind this up, we also should we not observe the problem behavior in either of those two circumstances, which is very rare, but should we not observe the behavior, we then have other circumstances that we have the child and mother engage in. Perhaps we have had reports that the child is out of control or unmanageable when the parents have company. We would proceed to put several people in the room with the mother, for example, to try to simulate mother occupied with other people, or father occupied with other people, and watch, and observe again how a child will function.

Q. Well, before we get to this, now for a moment—you referred to "we," you are talking about yourself, or— **A.** All right. I train students. I train psychiatric residents, I train medical students, and when I say "we," we have a team of people who are lined up to receive training in this very approach.

Q. How many students do you have under you? **A.** I would have as many as seven at a time.

Q. Is this the type of thing you've been doing for the last thirteen years? **A.** I developed this approach, yes. It took me about five years to develop it. And then—I have been doing it for thirteen years.

Q. Now Doctor, what can you say with reference to whether or not this is something unique and different than has been put forward in the past, at the time you were taking training, for example? **A.** The contribution, I hope, which will come over time with this, to all kinds of community agencies, is that it will assist in the decision-making process, based on the giving of relatively solid, reliable information, observed or obtained standardly over time. In contrast to opinion-giving, based perhaps on one encounter where the conditions aren't even defined, you might—for example, you might say— my own colleagues do this, it's still in the field—where a person says, "Well, I saw Mrs. Smith, Johnny Jones"—whoever it is—"I saw them in my office, and we had a discussion, and I came to a conclusion based on that. I'm a competent person."

The problem is ... we know that clinical inference-making is very unreliable unless we have relatively repeatable data that we can bring to bear on that. We can't replicate what went on. The kinds of circumstances I've tried to describe in these observation sessions could be replicated in Atlanta, Georgia, or in Ottawa, Ontario.

Q. In other words, you've tried to standardize these? **A.** That's right.

Q. All right. Now, Doctor, I'll ask you if you were requested to do some of your specialized testing on Diane Rose and her son Jason. **A.** Yes, I was.

Q. And specifically, would you tell the Court, what were you to find out? **A.** The referral question that was posed to me was, "would you be willing to help us determine the competency of a young mother to mother her child? Would you be willing to do this?"

Q. When was the first date that you saw her? **A.** May I look at my—I don't remember all these dates.

Q. Sure. If you need to refer to your notes, please do so. **A.** Yes. I just have the initial interview. The first date—2–25.

Q. How did she do? **A.** All right. Supposing we keep in mind three categories. Diane and Jason as one category. Another category, a sample of twenty excellent moms, moms judged to be excellent by professional people, physicians, social workers, occupational therapists, psychiatrists, they all helped get the sample of good mothers.

So Diane is being compared with twenty mothers who are good moms, and twenty mothers who are poor moms. And then average moms, those who are in the middle. So we have the categories. Diane, if you take a look— if I give you numbers, it's just like trying to remember numbers, nobody is going to remember them.

First, on these mother behaviors, Diane scored in—Now, I'm going to try not to be technical, this is going to be a problem. I don't want to make it cloudy for people. When a child is doing his own thing, if you could think in terms of any human beings, when any two people want to be, or are together, just to enjoy each other, the goal there is that—neither of them, or certainly one of them, doesn't take over and command or control. That it's a kind of enjoyable thing.

And in the mother-child circumstance, it would be a condition where the mother wouldn't do what all poor mothers do. They tend to teach. "What's this, what's that, what are you doing," that's poor behavior in that circumstance. But Diane and the good moms do not—or did not do that. In other words, we have what we call a behavior called "attending," where you can just note what's going on, and what another person is doing, and make comments about it. Appreciative comments.

Q. Yes. And how did she score? **A.** The average for the three sessions, for the good mother sample, those mothers would attend to their child for 49 out of a possible 60 seconds. Diane attended for 36 seconds, and poor moms attend for 15.

Q. Okay. **A.** 15, 36, 49. Average moms attended for 38 seconds, and the 2 points, one way or the other, makes no difference. I mean you don't fix it exactly.

Q. Now, did I understand you correctly that in this particular category she came out high? **A.** She came out with the good moms.

Q. Okay. **A.** Now, the second test gives us a clue in a way, how it goes between a mother and a child when there is no need for the mother to force the child to come to me, or to do this or that.

In the good moms sample, their children interacted with that mother out of a possible 50 seconds a minute, their children interacted 46.8, forty-seven seconds a minute. Diane—or Jason, interacted 38 seconds a minute, and poor moms' children interacted 26.9—make it 27 seconds a minute. And the average mom's 39, so again, on their children interaction with them, Diane and the average moms are absolutely together, and certainly nowhere near, you know, poor parenting.

Q. Taking into consideration your own observations of Diane interacting with the child, and I'm going to ask you if you have an opinion as to the—considering the welfare of the child, who should be awarded the custody? **A.** My opinion is that Diane should be awarded custody, period. I don't know if you want reasons.

Q. All right. Now, if she's awarded custody, and do you see some plusses for the child, looking at it from the child's standpoint? **A.** In terms of the hypothetical—

Q. Psychological development of a child? **A.** In terms of the hypothetical points that you've put to me, it would seem that there is a continuing stable relationship provided in the mother-child situation. Not because she's just the mother, but because of the one-to-one, and absence of other individuals. There's a stability in that situation that I think—and given the fact that she has the competencies to do it, which is my—I'm satisfied with that data. I would see no reason why she should not be awarded the custody of this child.

(2).   Cross Examination by Mr. Mellon

Q. Now Dr. Howe, you testified yesterday, as I understand it, that you'd had no M.D. training? **A.** No, I do not. I'm a Ph.D. psychologist.

Q. You say that you have a Master's in education and psychology. And you had a Ph.D in what? **A.** Psychology.

Q. Now, your training that you had was not with children, was it? **A.** Absolutely it was, yes.

Q. Pardon? **A.** It was. It's with both, but with a good bit of emphasis on work with children.

Q. When did you get this training? **A.** The City College in New York, and also at the—

Q. That was your Master's Degree? **A.** That was at the Master's level, and then at the Ph.D., not only in the practicum work that went on, but in the post-doctoral work I took here at the University of Washington Medical School, it's another level of training, I forgot that one, beyond the Ph.D., I took a year's post-doctoral work with children.

Q. Ph.D. was obtained where? **A.** Pennsylvania State University.

Q. Incidentally, Dr. Howe, are you married? **A.** I'm not.

Q. Have you ever been? **A.** I have not been.

Q. And have you—not going to ask if you've had any children, naturally, but have you had occasion to raise any children, have you adopted any children? **A.** No. I haven't, and that brings a very interesting point that I would like to discuss with you, and that is, that at one point in my life, this is my own personal matter, but at one point in my life, I made a decision, Mr. Mellon, that I could not carry out the kind of what I hoped would be competent professional life and rear a child and conduct a family the way I thought it should be done. I could not personally do both of those things, so you ought to know that I made that decision.

Q. Now, I also understand all of your reference was to the good moms and the average moms and the poor moms, and I believe you said that your dealing is almost primarily with mothers; is that right? **A.** Yes. For the data collection, because we can't get enough fathers to come. But whenever in our work a father can come, we work directly with him. We'll stay until six and seven at night to do so.

Q. Do I understand your testimony is, though, that the great bulk of your work is with mothers, and not fathers? **A.** Yes. I would say that has to be the case.

Q. Now Dr. Howe, have you in connection with the work that you've been doing, do I understand that you have had no publications that have been printed in any of the periodicals? **A.** That is correct. And it's correct as I tried to indicate yesterday, because I wanted to wait until we had the followup work as well, which we do now have.

Q. So, go ahead. **A.** We have parents who have participated in the program between five and seven years. You see, it's easy to get followup data after two months, for example, and then you can rapidly publish, and say, "You see, our findings show that the same thing prevails, or it doesn't," but five or seven years later, to me, seemed to be a far better time. That's what I wanted to do.

Q. You've written no texts on the subject? **A.** No, I have not.

Q. And you've had no publications? **A.** That's right.

Q. And so the data that you have, or the system that you use, that you have developed yourself, has not been submitted in any of the periodicals? **A.** Or has not been subject to peer review, your thinking?

Q. Yes. **A.** In the formal sense of periodicals, no; in the sense of national requests to do what I do because it is working, that would not be the case; but for formal publications, you are correct.

l.   Harvey Pyle, M.D.—For the Defense

(1).   Direct Examination by Mr. Mellon

Q. Dr. Pyle, where do you come from? **A.** Washington, D.C., Metropolitan area.

Q. And what is your occupation? **A.** I'm a psychiatrist.

Q. Do you practice in Washington or in Maryland or in both? **A.** I'm licensed to practice in Washington and Maryland. [Dr. Pyle is next qualified as an expert on suicide.]

Q. And have you had occasion, Dr. Pyle, at my suggestion to read over the hospital records, of Diane Rose? **A.** I have.

Q. Do you have an opinion as to what this young lady was suffering from at the time of her attempted suicide? **A.** I do.

Q. Would you explain it, please? **A.** I feel that this young lady was suffering from a severe depressive reaction.

Q. Now, could you explain that? **A.** By "severe" I mean it was out of her ability to control her feelings, her reactions, and her behaviors.

Q. Now, do you have, Doctor, any opinion as to what the likelihood is of a repeat as far as this young lady is concerned in the future? **A.** Yes, I do.

Q. What is your opinion? **A.** My opinion is that it will be likely that this lady will make another suicidal attempt.

Q. Now, how do you arrive at that conclusion, Doctor? **A.** I arrive at that conclusion from several sources. My first source is my clinical experience in which I have treated over a hundred patients who have made highly lethal attempts from which they have survived only by chance. This young lady survived by the chance of having a shrub break her fall, but there are any number of lethal overdoses that you can survive by chance. These people, by definition, have been followed in our Suicide Study Unit at the National Institute of Mental Health and we've studied them in depth, and we find that they are depressed, seriously depressed and chronically depressed; that their ability to handle stress is very, very greatly impaired; that they are subject to going into precipitous and somewhat unpredictable depressive episodes from which they are likely to have great difficulty to emerge without adequate professional help or adequate support systems, support-system help, too.

Q. Now, do you have an opinion, Doctor, based upon what you've seen and heard concerning the—and your experience and learning, on what—whether or not the child in this case would be in any danger.—

A. I do.

Q. —if she were given custody of the child? **A.** I do.

Q. What is your opinion? **A.** I believe that the child is at risk of sustaining both psychological trauma and physical trauma, and that the psychological trauma could be considered both as an immediate trauma and also considered as a future trauma. By that I mean to say that the psychological trauma that happens to a child when it is separated from its mother by any forceful circumstances, by a suicidal attempt, as this was, has indeed affected that child. The circumstances, I believe, are likely to occur again, thus exposing this child to another psychological separation and trauma.

There is a psychological phenomenon involving children who tend to personalize or who feel that there is something wrong with them when a parent abandons them. The future implication is that people who go to make suicidal attempts themselves have often been exposed to suicidal behavior, so that by continuing the child in an environment where suicidal behavior is likely, there is more exposure.

The second aspect of my answer has to do with physical.

Q. With the physical, yes. **A.** A study by—by Reznick, who reviewed the infanticides in this country, show that there were two characteristics of the mothers who killed their children that were very significant. Seventy-one percent of the mothers who killed their children has a history of diagnosed depression. A third of the mothers who killed their children had a history of prior suicide attempt. I find these both present.

(2). Cross Examination by Mr. Fisk

Q. Now, you put Diane in the high risk category in part because she had chronic depression? **A.** Yes.

Q. And yet all the people who have seen her, all experts and colleagues of yours, have stated that she is not depressed at this time. You heard that testimony? **A.** Yes.

Q. And yet you placed her in the chronic depressive category. **A.** I did.

Q. Now, all of your testimony is based just upon some statistical studies and has nothing to do with any examination of this particular person? **A.** It's not based on solely statistical studies. It's also based on my review of the record,—

Q. All right. **A.** —the information and my having sat in this courtroom today.

Q. But not involving any examination of Diana Rose? **A.** That's correct.

Q. Now, Doctor, as a psychiatrist, do you feel that rearing a child in the Rose home, Steve Rose and Alice Rose, in view of the admissions by Steve Rose, is healthy for this child? **A.** Excuse me. In view of the what by—

Q. All right. I'll ask you to assume that Dr. Bower is correct in his assessment that they needed therapy. **A.** Are you going to ask me to assume that Dr. Bower is a competent practitioner of psychiatry?

Q. Right. **A.** I will not assume that.

Q. You will not assume that? Well, I will ask the Court to instruct you to assume it.

THE COURT: This is a hypothetical question he's asking.

THE WITNESS: M-hm.

MR. MELLON: Could I ask the witness one question, Your Honor?

THE COURT: All right, go ahead.

MR. MELLON: Do you know Dr. Bower?

THE WITNESS: I do not know Dr. Bower. I've only heard about his practices in the treatment of this—

MR. MELLON: Now, this is a Dr. Bower in Washington, D.C., not Dr. Bower here in Seattle we're talking about.

THE WITNESS: Oh. Oh. I know Dr. Bower by reputation in Washington, D.C.

MR. FISK: But you don't know him personally?

THE WITNESS: I do not know him personally.

Q. Does he enjoy a good reputation? **A.** Not amongst the people that I've talked with.

Q. Doctor, I'll ask you to assume that Dr. Bower was correct in his assessment that Alice Rose, Nancy Winter, and Steve Rose all needed psychotherapy, and ask you if under those circumstances you think that is the type of home that this child should be reared in. **A.** I think that people can undergo psychotherapy and have psychotherapy, many people do, and still have proper and appropriate homes in which to rear children.

Q. So you wouldn't think there was anything that was contraindicated so far as custody of the child concerned? **A.** No, no. I don't think that psychotherapy and custody are incompatible.

Q. Doctor, who's paying your expenses for coming here and testifying? **A.** My arrangements are with counsel.

Q. And what are your arrangements? **A.** My arrangements are my expenses, my transportation, and my fee for testifying.

Q. Now then, your fee for coming out and reciting these statistics is several thousand dollars, is it not? **A.** I think it will come to that.

Q. And specifically, it's in the area of seven—or $8,000, is it not? **A.** I don't believe so.

Q. Well now, you know what it is. You've made the arrangements. Will you tell the Court what you're being paid to recite these statistics?

MR. MELLON: I'm going to object to the form of the question. He isn't being paid anything to come out and recite statistics, Your Honor.

THE COURT: Sustained.

Q. Would you tell the Court what you're being paid to come here and testify? What's your professional fee? What has Mr. Mellon agreed that his clients would pay you? Now, that's clear enough, isn't it? **A.** Right. A thousand dollars a day.

Q. A thousand dollars a day. And does that include your travel time here and back? **A.** Yes, yes.

Q. And when did you come? **A.** I arrived last night at nine p.m.

Q. Last night at nine p.m. And so you'll have at least two days or three days, depending when you get back? **A.** No, I'm leaving tonight at ten-thirty p.m. I had to make extensive rearrangements to be able to do this.

Q. Are you sure it isn't more than that, Doctor? **A.** More than what?

Q. More than a thousand dollars a day. **A.** For my testimony here?

Q. No, that isn't what I asked you. I'm asking you if you're testifying under oath that all you're getting for testifying here is $1,000. Now, you recognize the penalty for perjury, do you not?

MR. MELLON: I object to that, Your Honor. There's no point—

MR. FISK: I'm just simply—

MR. MELLON:—in making it appear as though he's going to be up for perjury. He's—

MR. FISK: I think we ought to have the truth and I just want to be sure we're getting it.

MR. MELLON: You're getting the truth.

THE COURT: Well, I understand, and you can go ahead and answer the question. Overrule the objection.

A. In addition to this, I am being paid for the compensatory time that I have had to cancel my patients in my office schedule.

Q. Are you being paid also for consultation with Mr. Mellon and Mr. Rose and so on? **A.** I am.

Q. Now, can you give us an idea what all of this amounts to, how many thousand dollars? **A.** About $4,000.

Q. Plus your travel time— **A.** M-hm (affirmative response).

Q. —or traveling expenses? **A.** M-hm, around—in that neighborhood.

MR. FISK: Thank you very much, Doctor.

m.   Kenneth Piller, M.D.—For the Defense

(1).   Direct Examination by Mr. Mellon

Q. Doctor, you have already stated that you are an M.D. What is your specialty? **A.** Psychiatry.

Q. And are you in the general practice of psychiatry in Seattle? **A.** I am.

Q. All right. Now, in connection with your practice of psychiatry, Doctor, did you have occasion to talk to Steve Rose in the recent past? **A.** I did.

Q. All right, Doctor, would you go ahead and tell us what happened with Mr. Rose. **A.** Yes. Now, in going to the biologic or the biologic-medical area, I was the one who directed the entire interview by asking specific questions to get information, such as, he told me that his birth was normal. I asked him about family history of illness, both psychiatric and medical. He told me his grandmother had cancer. Continuing, he told me that he had no significant childhood illnesses, but as an adult had infectious mononucleosis. He practically drinks no alcohol now, but in college he did. He doesn't smoke. And he denied use of marijuana and hallucinogenic agents.

The only major accident was in the fourth grade, a skating accident, with a fracture of the right forearm.

His weight is 145 and stable. Appetite: good. Sleeps without difficulty. That led me to the next area, which is the social. He was born in Seattle, Washington, and raised in this general area. I asked him about his mother, age forty-six. His feeling about her, quote, "I respect her and I love her, and I often disagree with her. She's giving, she's honest. She's opinionated." Later I asked him about her health and he said that she's in good health. And then he said, quote, "She's been a strong influence on my life morally and spiritually."

Father is fifty, Vice President of a tool and dye company. Good health except for some bile stones. Quote, the feeling was "I love him very much. He's very warm, intelligent, and forceful," unquote.

Sisters: Julie, nineteen. And perhaps you might notice that I definitely asked for feelings, because I'm searching to see if an individual uses feelings, such as glad, sad, warm, good, versus opinions, such as, "I feel that so-and-so," because I need to know if a patient can distinguish feelings from opinions as they talk in interpersonal communication.

"How do you feel towards your sister Julie?"

"I love Julie very much." Diane, twenty-three, feeling—

Q. That's his sister Diane? **A.** Diane, another sister, twenty-three, married, who lives in Ashland. His feeling: With love.

Then, "How were you raised?"

He said, "Jewish."

"How do you feel about being raised Jewish?"

Answer: "Good." Conservative synagogue he attends.

Then I got on to his marriage. He described his wife Diane, as 26, having been pregnant once and having given birth to one living child or fetus. They were together for under four years prior to marriage. He said, quote, "I loved her. She was an honest—or is an honest and loving person." Sex was okay. He told me that she worked as an orthopedic secretary and a radiology secretary the first and second years of his attendance at medical school. They've been married about four-and-a-half years. The baby is about twenty-and-a-half months old. She has a Bachelor of Science Degree from Seattle State University. He commented that there were two suicide attempts. One he thought was about 1979, the other January of 1994. I asked him if he knew why the second attempt, and he said, "One, feelings of inadequacy with the child; and, two, feeling of abandonment by her parents."

Now she lives with her parents in Seattle. The two families are about eight minutes apart by car. He has some relatives, three aunts and three uncles, and he is distant toward them.

The next area is the vocational area. He worked for his father-in-law, the first and second summers of medical school. At age sixteen he worked in a supermarket. In college he worked for a pipe and casing company. One summer he sold insurance. He's never been fired. And for the future, he would like to go into academic internal medicine.

The next area is the avocation or the recreational area. He reads for pleasure. He enjoys basketball, plays the piano. He likes movies and television.

The fifth area is the learning area. He graduated high school, graduated four years of college, had two years of dental school. Now, I could slip back to the social area in this sense, although it still relates to the learning area, that in 1990, after one year of dental school, he and his wife went to Austria, and spent some days in England also, because he wanted to see about the possibility of attending medical school in Austria. He told me that his wife was with him, but was upset because of not being near her parents. He returned and finished his second year of dental school and was accepted to George Washington School of Medicine, currently is in his fourth year, taking an elective here in Seattle and can graduate without necessarily returning to Washington, D.C. He would like to go into oncology, which is the study of cancer and diseases of that nature.

The sixth area is the emotional area. In this case it is how an individual might handle his or her major emotions. With anger to his wife he at times was sarcastic and at times he would express it straightforwardly, with anger to community personnel, such as clerks, gas station attendants, and so forth, he would be open. With depression he replied, quote, "I try physical exercise and I also will tell people."

There was no history of suicidal ideation. I asked him how he handled anxiety, and it was similar to the above, physical exercise or telling friends that he was anxious.

I gave him a brief IQ test. He knew the date. He told me his birthdate as June 25th, 1967. He knew the current President, current Vice President, he knew the first Vice President, the number of colonies, the current number of states, the capitals of Oregon, China. He got the wrong answer for Spain, saying it was Barcelona. He knew the three largest cities in the United States. I had him do serial 7 subtractions and made him go the whole way and he got them all right. He knew the difference between "idle" i-d-l-e, and "lazy." And he had recent recall for three unrelated words: "Table, red" and "Broadway" after a few minutes. And I asked him to interpret two fairly difficult proverbs: "A rolling stone gathers no moss," and "The golden hammer opens the iron door," and both were abstract, were interpreted in an abstract, correct manner. My impression then would be above average IQ, no evidence of organic brain damage, and no evidence from this of schizophrenic process. So that my final diagnosis was: no mental disorder.

Q. What is your opinion as to whether or not then Mr. Rose is what you would call a normal human being? **A.** My opinion is that he is.

Q. And did you observe any possible reason why he could not make a good father to a young son? **A.** I did not.

MR. MELLON: That's it, thank you.

(2). Cross Examination by Mr. Fisk

Q. You knew that Steve Rose was a smart medical student and you found him to be such, did you not? **A.** Correct.

Q. Now, you specifically inquired of him about his mother, and he told you he loved his mother, often disagreed with her? **A.** Correct.

Q. Now, suppose that you were advised that that was an out-and-out fabrication, that he never disagrees with her. How would that affect your judgment? **A.** Well, I wouldn't get that information—

Q. No, just—if you—I'm asking you a question. If you found that the statement that he often disagrees with his mother was not true,— **A.** If I were told that he were dominated by his mother, after having done a complete evaluation, I would ask his mother to come in to see me, because it doesn't jibe.

Q. I see. Now, have you ever examined his mother? **A.** I have not.

Q. Now then, did Mr. Rose advise you that he had attended some family counseling sessions in Washington, D.C.? **A.** I believe so. And I was just looking at my notes from the first session. (Pause—referring.) I don't see a note on here specifically relating to your question.

Q. Now, I'm still not quite clear in my own mind whether or not Steve Rose told you that in the late fall of '94 he'd been to a family counseling session with a psychiatrist in Washington, D.C. **A.** Well, my notes do not indicate that.

Q. Well, do you know a Dr. Bower in New York—or excuse me, in Washington, D.C., a psychiatrist there? **A.** I know a Dr. Bower, a psychiatrist in Seattle, but not in Washington, D.C.

Q. You don't know—I think the one in Washington is a brother. You don't know him? **A.** No.

Q. Doctor, if you were advised that Dr. Bower saw Steve Rose, Alice Rose, and a bunch of relatives in a family session, and told Steve Rose that his mother was emotionally sleeping with him, would that surprise you? **A.** I would be surprised. I'd be curious.

Q. You have a medical term for that, do you not? **A.** Yes.

Q. Would you tell us what it is? **A.** The Oedipus complex.

Q. And would you be surprised to find out that Dr. Bower said that's what the problem was in Steve Rose's case? **A.** Yes, I would be surprised.

Q. Now, Doctor, if in truth and in fact Alice Rose is caring for this child, as distinguished from its natural mother, and she has an Oedipus complex for her son, and she is vicious person, would that—and that she dominates her son, would that contraindicate her caring for this child. **A.** Well, in using—

Q. No, Doctor. Would you answer my question? Explain it any way you want. **A.** I'd like to answer your question.

Q. All right. **A.** In using my review of areas, I would have to make an assumption. Physically meaning the biomedical area Mrs. Rose is competent and intact physically because she's in the role of mother to a grandson.

Q. Right. **A.** Okay. Socially you're talking about an Oedipal complex toward her son.

Q. Right. **A.** And jumping over to the emotional area, you're saying that she handles her emotions viciously. I don't know—

Q. I'm asking you to assume that. **A.** But I don't know if you mean viciously with her mouth, viciously with her hands,—

Q. Both. **A.** I would want the grandmother in the role of motherhoodery to have some psychotherapy as soon as possible, if she's handling her feelings viciously and has an Oedipus complex.

Q. You'd want some psychotherapy for her? **A.** Yes, I would.

Q. And why would you want that, Doctor? **A.** Because if she were to physically strike a twenty-and-a-half-month-old baby, it might lead to damage physically; and if she has outbursts emotionally, that could also create a shy, withdrawn little baby.

Q. You know Dr. Samuel Winter, do you not, Doctor? **A.** On an impersonal basis.

Q. Well, I don't mean you're social friends, but you know who he is? **A.** Yes.

Q. And he's a highly-respected member of the medical community, isn't he, as far as you know?

MR. MELLON: I'm going to object to that, Your Honor. That has nothing to do with the issues in this case.

THE COURT: I don't know whether it does or not. I'll allow him to answer.

A. He has a good reputation and he is highly respected in the community.

MR. FISK: Thank you, Doctor.

(3). Re-direct by Mr. Mellon

Q. Doctor, do you know anything about Alice Rose at all? **A.** I do not.

Q. Have you ever seen her? **A.** I don't think I have. I hope this isn't "Candid Camera."

(Laughter.)

Q. Do you have any evidence of any kind of viciousness on the part of Steve Rose? **A.** Nothing came through to me on the evaluation that Mr. Rose had a vicious handling of his emotions.

(4). Re-cross by Mr. Fisk

Q. Just one further question: Did Steve Rose tell you that his mother considered her own father a psychopath? **A.** This was not told to me.

Q. Did he tell you that at one time his mother beat the hell out of her father with a belt? **A.** This was not told to me.

Q. Did Steve tell you that during married life every time there was a family argument, he would say, quote, "I attack and she withdraws"? **A.** His marriage or his parents' marriage?

Q. No, his own marriage, his relationship with his wife. **A.** This information was not given to me.

Q. So the things that were given to you were pretty much what we might call ginger and spice? **A.** Is that a question?

Q. Yes. **A.** The things which were given to me were what I told the Court.

Q. But none of these things that I have mentioned were told to you? **A.** Correct.

MR. FISK: Thank you, Doctor.

n. Steven Rose—Defendant

(1). Direct Examination by Mr. Mellon

Q. Now, Mr. Rose, there's been testimony in this case, about you going to Austria as a medical student and that, of course, you returned after a relatively short period of time. Was that because you wanted to return or was there some other reason? **A.** Not at all. I—I acquiesced to my wife's desire to come home.

Q. What was the problem? **A.** When we went to Austria, we had planned to stay for the—the five to six years. And we knew that it was going to be hard, that we were going to take German classes twice a day and to study the language. In fact, the German classes, there were—there was no English spoken, only German, and it was very difficult. There were two dental students who had applied along with me to Karl Franzen University in Graz, Austria, to attend medical school.

THE COURT: I'll sustain the objection.

Q. Well, what I, of course, want you to tell us, Mr. Rose, is—and I think that's what you were doing, is as to why you gave up your chance to go to medical school in Austria. Was it your idea or was it—

MR. FISK: He's already said it was Diane's idea.

MR. MELLON: It was hers, and now he's explaining, which I think he's entitled to do. I think he's entitled to tell exactly what happened, because—

MR. FISK: I object to any more testimony on this point. Your Honor.

THE COURT: Is that the question you want to ask him?

MR. MELLON: Yes.

THE COURT: Okay.

A. And Diane cried and said that she wanted to go home. There was another—we had other people there and we talked back and forth whether to go home. And I—I wanted to stay. And I told Diane that, "This may be my last chance for medical school." I had applied before and was not accepted in the United States. And I said that all I had was dental school, which I did not tell them that I was going to leave dental school. And so after—after awhile and after the pressure, I told her we'd come back. I had ambivalent feelings about leaving Austria, but finally I—I left. Diane and I left and we went to London for a week and New York for a few days and then went home.

Q. So when you left Austria, did you have at that time any hope of ever getting into any other medical school? **A.** Well, I always had the hope of getting into medical school, and I—

Q. Did you have any knowledge of any place you could possibly get into? **A.** No, because if there was, medical school took six years over there, it would be a lot easier to go to dental school and then—then four years to medical school, if I had a shoo-in.

Q. Well, did you know of any medical school in the United States at the time you left Austria that you could possibly get into? **A.** None.

Q. Had you attempted, exhausted the possibilities before you went over there? **A.** Yes, yes. I—well, there's over a hundred medical schools. I'd applied at a number of them and was not accepted, so my—you know, my hopes weren't high.

Q. And now do you recall a letter Diane received from her mother just before her suicide attempt? **A.** Generally I do.

Q. All right. Would you just—First, let me ask you: How long a letter was it? **A.** It was maybe ten pages typed.

Q. Would you, as best you can recall, state what the content of that letter was? **A.** Well, it was a very castigating letter against myself, both my parents and Diane, and told how we were like little children and that I—how we didn't need a car, that they never had a car when they were first married, that I should have taken the bus; and that I didn't need a camera; that I—we should not have lived in—in Virginia, we should have lived in Washington, D.C. And it talked about all the terrible times that she went through with my father-in-law; and that—that since they went through it, we should—we should go through it, too.

And one thing, what I thought was probably the lowest blow and really hurt me the most, is a reference in the letter to a physician in Seattle who had recently passed away by an unknown cause. It was Dr. Fall, and he was a very renowned thoracic surgeon. I used to have political discussions and we would argue. . . . And she said in the letter, she said, "Charley Fall now lies dead in his grave and it was you who argued with him."

And the whole letter was that she was—she said that my parents were—were like children, that they spent too much money on luxuries; the camera was just their inbreeding on me, and I was doing this to Diane; and that then she talked about Diane being like a child and she shouldn't be acting this way. And that was the general attitude of the letter.

Q. All right. Now,— **A.** She also said that we could never come home again; and to never tell Daddy, she said, that she never wrote the letter because she would be so upset.

Q. Because he would be so upset? **A.** Because he would be so upset with her.

Q. Oh. Well, did you say that she said you could never come home again? **A.** Right.

Q. Well, what effect did this have on your wife, if any? **A.** I read the letter first and I said, "Diane, we got a letter from your mother."

And she looked at it and she said, "I don't want to read it." So I read it. Then she sat at the kitchen—at the dining room table and started to read it. And she was totally fractured after she read the letter.

She—she just said, "I can't believe it. I can't believe she's saying these things to me." She said, "I don't—I don't know what's wrong."

Q. All right. What, if anything, did she do about this after that? Did she contact her mother, anything— **A.** Well, we talked—we talked about it that evening, and then she said she was going to call her father and tell him. She—she then called her father.

Q. The day you got the letter, the evening you got the letter? **A.** I really can't remember the time sequence, but she called him shortly after she got the letter.

Q. And were you present during the conversation? **A.** Yes.

Q. What did you hear as far as the conversation was concerned? **A.** Well, my conversation was only one-sided, because I only heard Diane, and I—I did not talk to my father-in-law.

Q. How long did the conversation last? **A.** Oh, forty-five minutes to an hour.

Q. Forty-five minutes to an hour? **A.** Yes.

Q. And did you discuss the conversation after it was over with— **A.** Oh, yes.

Q. —with your wife? **A.** Diane—Diane would intermittently yell and get upset, and she—

Q. You mean during the conversation— **A.** Yes.

Q. —with her father? **A.** Yes. And I was—I was holding Jason at the time and would walk out of the room. I didn't listen to all of the conversation. I'd walk out of the room and back in the room with him. And she—and she was very upset, and she said "Don't you believe me? Don't you believe me that she wrote that?"

And afterwards she told me that he said, "Your mother couldn't write something like this. I can't believe she would write it." And Diane said, "She wrote it. I would—I have it here. I would like you to see it. I'm telling you what's in the letter."

Q. Did she report anything further to you after the conversation was over that her father had said to her? **A.** Just that he couldn't believe that my mother-in-law would write such a thing.

Q. On the night of the 15th of January, 1994, were you home at the apartment? **A.** No.

Q. Where were you? **A.** I was at the Veterans Hospital in Washington, D.C. I'd been on twenty-four—I was on twenty-four hour duty starting Tuesday morning and was on all night.

Q. When did you leave—when did you last see your wife? **A.** I last actually saw my—I last talked to my wife Monday evening. I last saw her Tuesday. She was sleeping when I—when I left the apartment.

Q. Now, between that time and the next time you saw her in the hospital, did you have any occasion to talk to her by telephone? **A.** Yes.

Q. When did you talk to her? **A.** I spoke to her at, oh, six or seven o'clock in the evening.

Q. Is that on the 15th? **A.** Yes.

Q. All right. **A.** I called her up, and she knew I was—I was a little upset because I—I really didn't like the Veterans Hospital. There was a lot of work there. And she—she sounded a little funny to me, because she said— she told me, "Don't call back because I'm very tired and I'm going to go to bed early." She never said that to me.

I said, "Well, what if I get a little depressed? Can I call you?"

She said, "Sure." But she mentioned to me that she was going to call her folks and then go to sleep.

Q. Is that the last time then that you talked to her? **A.** Yes.

Q. When you were away from home like that on duty, did you or did you not attempt to call her usually during the course of the day or the evening? **A.** I always called Diane. I called her in the day and I called her in the evening. And she had my phone number if she ever needed me.

Q. How did you hear—how did you get the word that she had jumped out the window? **A.** I was on the ward at the Veterans Hospital, having been up the full twenty-four hours. I was just going in to see a patient who was in sickle-cell crisis, and they said, "There's a phone call for Steve Rose." I thought it was just somebody saying it was a library book overdue, and I got to the telephone and it was a Mrs. Jenkins who was our—our landlady. And she said, "I have some bad news for you."

And so I said, "What is it?"

And she said, "Your wife jumped out of the window." And I—I—a nurse must have seen my expression or something and she grabbed me and she—and then Mrs. Jenkins said, "What do you want me to do with your baby?"

And I started to cry, and I said, "Hold him there." I said, "Where is she?"

She said, "She's alive and she's at Arlington Hospital."

Q. Arlington Hospital? **A.** Yes.

Q. That's Arlington, Virginia, Hospital? **A.** Yes.

Q. What did you do then? **A.** I—well, there were a lot of people around me at that time, and then people would—one guy wanted to give me an injection of Valium, and I remember throwing a chair across the—the hallway. And another medical student of mine who—friend of mine said he was going to take me, because he worked at Arlington on the weekends and he—he could get me there. So that's how I found out.

Q. Well, what did you do then after that? **A.** Well, we drove through every red light and every stop sign to get to Arlington. It took about a half an hour. And I went right to the Emergency Room where Diane was lying.

Q. And what was being done for her at that time? **A.** At that time nothing had been done. They said that X-rays had been taken and they were awaiting the results. I said, "Is there a neurosurgeon or a neurologist?"

And they said, "There's a neurosurgeon who has been called."

And I said, "Where is—"

Q. Was she actually in the— **A.** She was in the—

Q. —Emergency Room? **A.** She was in the Emergency Room on the table when I saw her there, and she was decerebrate, and she was—she was barely moving. And I went in and saw her just lying there in this decerebrate posture, and emotionally I was just destroyed.

Q. So what did you do? **A.** Well, they escorted me out of her room and said the neurosurgeon was coming. And then I—I called my parents and told them. Then they said that they'd—they would come on the—the next plane. They were very upset as well. And then I called my mother-in-law and said that, "Something terrible has happened," that, "Diane—Diane jumped out the window and she's in critical—critical condition at the hospital," and I really didn't know what to do and it looked just terrible to me.

And she said, "Oh my." She said, "What shall I do?" She said, "Are your parents coming back?"

And I said, "Yes."

So then she said, "Well, at least you'll have your parents." And then she said, "I'll call—I'll call Father. He's at the hospital."

But I didn't wait for her to call him. I—well, I—I didn't call him immediately, but I went up to the Intensive Care Unit, where they said they were going to be bringing her up. I talked to her neurosurgeon, Dr. Bortnik, and he said, "I've seen a case like this, something like this before;" that, "There was a girl in an automobile accident that was decerebrate and comatose for six months and now she's riding horses in England."

So I said, "Well, what are the chances? Does she have any real chance?"

So he said, "Well, I've seen it before. It's happened once before." He said, "It can happen again."

I said, "But does it look bad?"

He said, "Well, of course, it's bad." He says, "I'm going to start her on Asmatrol drip," that's to relieve the edema from the brain.

And I called—tried to get in touch with a neurologist who I'd been working with just a month previously.

Then I called my father-in-law after Diane had come up to the floor and I saw her, and—in a special room, just right outside the main room of the Intensive Care Unit. I was very upset. I called him and—

MR. FISK: Is this witness answering some question, Your Honor? I've lost track, it's been so long.

MR. MELLON: I asked him what he did, Your Honor, and I think he's entitled to tell what he did.

THE COURT: Go ahead.

A.   I called him on the phone and I said—and I told him—I guessed he had not got the message. And he said, "Hello." And I told him that—that Diane had attempted suicide, she'd jumped out the window, and I didn't know what to do. And I said, "What—" I said, "What do you think I can do?" And he asked me if I had a neurosurgeon. And then he said, "Well,—" I told him that she had taken Phenobarbital, that the police had found Phenobarbital there. And he said, "Well, get a urologist and maybe we should have the urine alkalinized because that would get rid of more Phenobarb in the blood stream." And I told him that was a good idea, and I said, "I don't know what to do;" he said, "Neither do I." I said, "I've got to go back in."

He said, "I'll call you back." So he called me back. I went in to see Diane. By this time the whole right side of her face was swollen. I thought she had a broken jaw. I called the neurosurgeon who had left the hospital, and I told him about this, and I said, "Did you realize that her face was swollen?" And he said, "No." So I ordered ice packs on her face. The Asmatrol drip had not started, so I got the nurses to—to start an I.V. They called one of the residents to start an I.V. She was not being cardiovas—did not have a cardiovascular monitor, so I ordered a monitor on her. And I asked her to be moved out of this room where they came in every 15 minutes, to be moved to the main room where she could be seen at all times by the staff, by the nursing staff.

Q. She wasn't in Intensive Care then? **A.** She was in Intensive Care, but she was in a room right next to the main room of the Intensive Care Unit. The Intensive Care Unit had about eight beds, but there was one room that was right next to it which had a door and Diane was in that room, and the nurses would come in every fifteen minutes to watch her and take vital signs.

Q. So you had her moved to the main room? **A.** Yes.

Q. Now, as a medical student, were you entitled to give any orders in that hospital? **A.** No.

Q. But you did anyhow? **A.** Yes, because she—Dr. Bortnik told me that she was going to have the Asmatrol drip. Her orders hadn't come up from the—from the Emergency Room. Diane was decerebrate, which showed that this may be fatal. Her pupils weren't equal. Her pulse was irregular and I honestly thought that she was going to die at any time.

Q. All right. Now, did her condition improve any or did it get worse, or what? **A.** Her condition stabilized that—that evening, and in the morning, on Thursday, Dr. Bortnik had his associate come. And he said, "Well, she looks better than yesterday." On Friday morning she took a turn for the worse. Her pulse became irregular. She started with Cheyne–Stokes respirations. She—her pupils became unequal again and one was not reacting to light, and she became decerebrate again. Her respirations became irregular, as the Cheyne–Stokes respirations, and her heart rate dropped to around forty, showing that there was possible herniation of her brain into the spinal canal, and this scared the hell out of me.

And I—I called—I wanted Dr. Bortnik to know and start this Asmatrol drip again, he did over the phone, but we couldn't get—we didn't see him in person. Diane did not seem to be improving, so I—I really panicked. My Dean had called the hospital before. I had not talked to him, someone else did. So I called up the Dean, to ask him for help. He told me that the best neurosurgeon in the city, Washington, D.C., was Dr. Raymond. So they gave me Dr. Raymond's number. I called him and they said Dr. Raymond was in a meeting and couldn't be reached at that time.

Q. Now, did you have any discussion with Dr. Winter at that time or about that time concerning getting Dr. Raymond? **A.** Yes. I remember that we were—he knew I wanted to get Dr. Raymond and I—I was—I left a message for him to call, to come over to Arlington Hospital. And we were in the Intensive Care Unit with one of the nurses, and he said to me, "Don't you think that this is the best, all we can do?"

And I told him, "I don't know." I said, "Dr. Raymond is supposed to be the best." I said, "If Diane dies and I don't get the best man over here, I'll blame myself forever, if there's something he could do."

Dr. Bortnik had been a student of Dr. Raymond I later found. Dr. Raymond—Dr. Bortnik was not at the hospital at that time and we couldn't reach him on the phone.

Q. And did you get Dr. Raymond over there? **A.** Yes.

Q. Did you ever have any discussion with Dr. Winter concerning the measures that you had taken that you described the first day—or the first—yes, the first day that she jumped? **A.** No, the only discussion that we had is—was—we were in the hall and I—I said I wanted another chance with Diane. I told him I shouldn't have gone to medical school, that it may have been too much of a strain on her for me to be away; that I knew Diane wanted me to be home more. And I—I told him that if she came through, that I would think about quitting. And I—I didn't want to have anything more to do, I was so upset. I told the other medical students who came later that, "I just don't think that I can go on," and that, "I should have stayed in dental school and not tried to be an M.D."

Q.   Did Dr. Winter ever commend you for the emergency measures that you had taken in Diane's behalf? **A.** A few days later, at Howard Johnson's Motel—Hotel across from the Watergate, we were—we were—we went to bed—we went to sleep in the same bed and we were talking about the first day and the circumstances, and he said—and I told him what happened and—Diane's you know,—the ice packs and everything. He said, "Well, Steve if Diane pulls through," he says, "you'll be—you're to be a great part of her help."

Q.   What kind of a person is Dr. Bower? **A.** Oh, he's very hostile sometimes, very affectionate other times. He—he's sort of like a Don Rickles, I think, of psychiatry. He hits you with a shock before you even mention a word and then will sort of make up to you at the end, and then he'll hit you with a few more shocks, then will walk out of the room saying he refuses to talk to you people anymore, then come back in and sort of smile and then say, "I'm going to present you my bill right now. I'm finished talking to you people." Then he'll—he'll sit—he'll laugh a little bit and then talk to you in a—with respect. And it's—it's a different—I've never experienced anybody like him. He'll hit you with everything. So he brought up things about everybody.

Q.   All right. Now, did he in any way—he did accuse you of certain things, did he not? **Q.** Oh, yes.

Q.   Did he say to the effect—to the group as a whole something to the effect that, "You're the most—"

MR. FISK: I'll object to counsel's leading questions, Your Honor.

MR. MELLON: Well, Your Honor, these questions—these things have been brought out by counsel.

THE COURT: You can refer him to the incident.

Q.   Well, this was a five-hour get-together, wasn't it? **A.** Yes.

Q.   —would you tell us everything that was said? **A.** I can't tell you everything that was said, but I can tell you some things. He said, "You're the most vicious group of people I've ever met." This is before we had a chance to even speak. Then he—then he said about me, he said I needed therapy. He said—he said my mother needed therapy. He said, "Nancy needs therapy." He needs—he said, "Diane, if I—if I were her husband, I would have thrown her out the window." He says, "She's a spook. She scares the hell out of me. She's incompetent." She said—he said to Nancy—these are the castigating things he said. He said to Nan—about my father-in-law, he says, "I talked to him on the phone and I know what an s.o.b. he is." He says, "Nancy, you're worse than—than fatherless." He says, "Anybody who would have a man like that," he said, "this man's in medicine," and he went on and said things of that flavor. Then he asked me a little later to explain myself and my feelings, and which he did let me have a chance to expound.

Q.   Your feelings about what? **A.** About what I went through during this tragedy. And I told him—I told him how I felt. And then he came over and put his arm around me, and Diane's therapist, Dr. Grant shook my hand. And before Doug Nathan left he also shook my hand and—and told me he misjudged me. Everybody in the room at that time was crying except Diane.

Q. Was there anything said about any relationship between you and your mother? **A.** No.

Q. By Dr. Bower or anyone else? **A.** No.

Q. There was something said about your mother needing certain type of treatment? **A.** Yes.

Q. Could you give the context in which that statement was made? **A.** Well, he said—he said it on two different planes of thought. Once—once he said, "You need treatment." He says, "God, how can you take this?" He said, "This is just a terrible situation that you're in. You're not getting any support from anybody." So then he said—then at the end, I know what you're referring to, he said,—this is as he closed the meeting, he says—he sat back in his chair, he says, "What you need, Alice," he says, "you need a lay," he says, "not that I'm offering my services." So that—that sort of ended the meeting. He said to the four of us that we should go out—he says, "There's been enough things said on this day. Go out and have an outing together," he says, "do something nice." And I told him that was a very good idea. We all said that was a good idea and we left to plan an outing.

Q. Wasn't anything said about what your mother had done to your father supposedly? **A.** Certain things were said. I—I'm not sure of the specifics. He mentioned everybody and he said everybody was sick at one time, but I'm not—I'm not sure what specifically was said.

Q. Now, after the Bower incident Diane was still living away from— **A.** Yes.

Q. —the apartment, wasn't she? **A.** Yes.

Q. Did she ever come back? **A.** Well, I asked Diane to come back on several occasions. I told Diane that I wanted her to see Jason and I wanted to see her. And I told her at one time that I would pick her up, bring her over; my mother wouldn't be around and just the three of us would be there, and she refused. Diane rarely called. And then finally I talked her into—to coming over. And so on several occasions I picked her up and we visited with Jason on a couple—I think the Nathan's dropped her off one or two times.

Q. Now, what comes next as far as your progress in the medical field is concerned? **A.** I have been accepted by the matching program to the University of California at Los Angeles, and a residency program in internal medicine for the upcoming year, to commence on June 23rd.

Q. I believe that the testimony before was that you had stated your preferences for your residency program prior to the trouble that has arisen, that gave rise to this case? **A.** Yes, I did. And then after this case in Seattle, I notified my dean, and the matching program, which takes care of the residencies in the United States for the American hospitals—and placed the University of Washington—the number one position—was not chosen by the University of Washington in the match, and was chosen—I was taken by my second choice, U.C.L.A.

Q. Incidentally, you say you're graduating from George Washington? **A.** Yes.

Q. Is it with honors? **A.** Yes.

Q. What's the meaning of that? **A.** Well, a certain amount of people are chosen out of a class of a hundred and thirty who graduate with distinction, and nine this year graduated with distinction, and I'm one of those. The minimum criteria that they set is to have half of all courses to be honors, we are on honors, pass-fail system.

Q. Is that the highest you can graduate with, with distinction? **A.** Yes.

Q. All right. Now, when are you due to go to U.C.L.A.? **A.** I'm to start—our orientation is on June 23rd.

Q. Have you been down there and looked over the situation? **A.** Yes. I went down to U.C.L.A. twice. Once to talk to Dr. Richards, who is the head of the house staff training, that's all the residents, all the people training at the hospital, and talked to him and discussed my difficulties with him. And then I went down on another occasion and secured an apartment and furniture that was four blocks away from U.C.L.A. Hospital.

Q. Now, you say you've discussed your situation with Dr. Richards? **A.** Yes.

Q. And what situation are you talking about? **A.** I informed Dr. Richards that I had received temporary custody of my son, Jason; that I would be coming down to U.C.L.A., and would be the only parent; so I asked him for special privileges, to grant me special privileges, so that I would be able to spend as much time as possible with my son. And he responded by giving me the easiest rotation at U.C.L.A. in internal medicine, of the twenty-seven that they give. He also said he would do everything in his power—

MR. FISK: Just a moment, your Honor. This is all hearsay; it's self-serving, and I'm going to object to it.

THE COURT: Sustain the objection.

MR. MELLON: Well, your Honor, could I be heard just a moment on that?

THE COURT: Go ahead.

MR. MELLON: I think this is vital as far as—or maybe not vital, but I think it's important as to what arrangements he's going to make down there, what arrangements he is able to make. I don't know how else he can get it before the Court, unless he reports to the Court what arrangements have been made, and what he's been informed as to what the situation will be, and what hours he'll have to work, and so on. It's the only way that the information can be gotten to the Court.

MR. FISK: I would suggest counsel can secure a sworn affidavit that Mr. Rose is getting these special privileges. We might be willing to let that go in evidence.

THE COURT: Maybe, Mr. Mellon, you could then, on that suggestions, if you wish to take it up, maybe you could make a call to Mr. Richards and arrange for that, but I still sustain the objection. The fact that it would be helpful doesn't get it over the evidentiary objection. It makes alternate means more attractive, is all.

Q. (By Mr. Mellon) All right. Have you checked, Mr. Rose, generally what your duties will be at U.C.L.A.? **A.** Yes.

Q. And would you just tell the Court what you will be doing? **A.** Okay. The on-call schedule is usually every fourth night. What we do is we rotate through different services. I have chosen to rotate through the emergency room for three months, which is a twelve-hour on shift, and will be able to take nights, seven to seven. So I'll be working at night for three months, seven to seven, and be home in the day.

The rest of the months will be one month of vacation, one month of adolescent medicine, two months of what they call the Wilson Pavillion, which is their private service, and also one of the easier services.

Q. What do you mean, "their private service?" **A.** Private service is they already have their private doctor who has already seen to it that they have their diagnosis. It's their private service—the residents don't do all the work. The private doctor is the one that's in charge of taking care of the patient. We just act as ancillary help there; and then the respiratory care, and cardiac care unit. And that's more or less what my duties will be, and one month of elective time. So what generally is the case, is I will be on every fourth night.

Q. From when to when? **A.** Well, for the twenty-four hours that you're on, and you come in the morning, and then you go from eight to eight. I might add that if you live close by, you can take night call from home.

Q. In other words, you just sit there in the house, and if the phone rings, then— **A.** Right. They call you, yes.

Q. Then you go over there? **A.** Yes.

Q. Approximately how many hours a week would you be working? **A.** On the days that I am not on duty, I'll be home from five o'clock on. The days that I am on duty, you're allowed to leave in the afternoon and come back and be on call from six o'clock till the next morning, so you're able to go home in the afternoon. So I'd be able to go home for three or four hours in the afternoon, and come on call at night again. Take calls from home. It all depends on the emergencies at the hospital, how much I would have to be there, living right next to the campus, next to the hospital.

Q. Now, what arrangements have you made as far as the actual physical care of Jason is concerned? **A.** Immediately, I have contacted Dr. Kenneth Talbot, through Dr. Bower, from Seattle who is the head of the in-patient child psychiatry unit at U.C.L.A. He said that he will work with me—he said that—

MR. FISK: Just a moment. Object to all of this hearsay testimony, your Honor.

THE COURT: Sustained.

Q. (By Mr. Mellon) Have you made any advances, or have you made any inquiries to determine whether or not competent people are available to act as housekeepers, in-housekeepers? **A.** I have.

Q. And what's the situation? **A.** Situation is that they're available.

Q. And is it your intention to have this woman there part time or full time? **A.** Full time.

Q. And what would be her duties? **A.** To take care of Jason while I'm at the hospital.

Q. What are your intentions when you go down to Los Angeles the end of this month, or within ten days or so, with Jason, if the Court awards you the care, custody, and control of Jason? **A.** My intentions are to take Jason with me, and my mother, and for her—for me to screen available women to live in, and to have them live in, and then my mother to go home after a certain period of time, when Jason feels comfortable and adjusts to another face.

Q. You said "them." Are you talking about getting more than one woman? **A.** No. Just one woman.

Q. And is it your intention to have this woman there part time or full time? **A.** Full time.

Q. And what would be her duties? **A.** To take care of Jason while I'm at the hospital, to see that he gets his recreation, and his sleep, and his meals, when I'm not there. And to provide affection and care for him.

Q. Do you have any doubt at all, Mr. Rose, as to whether or not you will be able to provide good and adequate care for Jason while you're down there? **A.** I have no doubt that I can.

(2). Cross examination by Mr. Fisk.

MR. FISK: Now, the person that's been taking care of this child for the most part continues to be your mother, isn't that right? **A.** Incorrect.

Q. Oh? **A.** Myself.

Q. Yourself? **A.** Yes.

Q. You've been carrying on full-time duties at the hospital, and doing most of the care yourself? **A.** I've been—during Jason's waking hours, I've been there approximately five and a half—on the weekdays—five and a half hours of his nine hours awake-time, and during that time, which is almost two-thirds, I have been the one who takes care of Jason.

Q. Now, if you are permitted to take the child to California, your mother is going to go with you, just the same as she spent eight months back in Washington with you, or six, or whatever it was? **A.** She's going to go with me for a certain length of time for adjustment.

Q. Well, if you were the one that's been taking care of him, why does he need to be adjusted away from your mother? **A.** Well, because number one, he's known my mother for a year and a half. She lives at our house; she's a familiar face, and she has taken care of Jason when I'm not there.

Now, I don't know how much study you've done on the subject of a child in a separation anxiety—

MR. FISK: Just a moment, your Honor. I didn't ask for any lectures from this witness. I'm just asking him questions.

THE COURT: That's correct. I'm not sure that's an answer. That's going quite a bit further than what he called for.

A. (Continuing) The reason is that Jason has known my mother for a year and a half, is going to get a new caretaker, and I want to have her broken in slowly. You don't suddenly throw a child against somebody new to take care of them for a prolonged period of time.

Q. Well, I take it this is going to be a dramatic change for the child if this happens? **A.** No. Not a dramatic change.

Q. I didn't say "traumatic," dramatic. **A.** I said not a dramatic change. But there would be a change in any child's life; this change to them is more dramatic than to you or I, and I want to smooth the change for Jason's sake.

Q. Now, how long is your intern or residency program? **A.** Your first year is—you sign a year contract, then you're able to practice medicine in general medicine anywhere, if you pass the national boards. I've taken two parts of three parts of the national boards, and then you can practice medicine as a general practitioner.

Q. Now, some of those residency programs last as much as four years, don't they? **A.** Not my residency program. Surgery lasts five years. If you want to be a thoracic surgeon, then you go seven years. You can go ad infinitum, what you want to do, subspecialize, and then sub-subspecialize.

Q. I understand. But on internal medicine, now, is it your testimony that your program, you can be a specialist in internal medicine in one year? **A.** No. I didn't say that. I said you could be a G.P. in one year.

Q. I beg your pardon? **A.** You can be a general practitioner in one year.

Q. But you said you wanted to be an internist. **A.** I want to do internal medicine, practice internal medicine, yes.

Q. I gather you want to be a specialist in internal medicine? **A.** That takes three years.

Q. Three years? **A.** Yes. Takes three years of training, doesn't make any difference when you do it.

Q. Now, Mr. Rose, where did you propose to practice medicine at the end of three years, or have you thought that far ahead? **A.** No. I haven't.

Q. I beg your pardon? **A.** I haven't thought that far ahead. I have always thought to come back to Seattle.

Q. But if you get down in California and like it, you might stay? **A.** I haven't thought that far ahead. I will be applying to the University of Washington for my second year of residency next year.

Q. Well now, if the Court should permit you to take that child to California, then I assume that it would be a physical impossibility for Diane to continue on anywhere near her present visitation. **A.** Of the way we have it set up now, yes. That would be impossible to fly him up or fly her down on Tuesday and Thursday for four hours, that would be very difficult.

Q. Well now, what would be your solution to that?—assuming for the moment that you were awarded the custody of the child. **A.** There could be a couple of solutions to that. One is I have a vacation which consists of a month length of time. My home base will still be Seattle, Washington; this is the town that—this is the city that I was raised in and born in. I'll be up here visiting, probably in two-week blocks.

Q. Two-week blocks, you say? **A.** Yeah, during that time. Also, provide the money for Diane to fly down to Los Angeles to visit.

Q. How many times, once a week? **A.** No. Whatever the Court felt would be proper.

o.   Keith Bennett—For the Defense

(1).   Direct Examination by Mr. Mellon

Q. Your name is Keith Bennett. Where do you live? **A.** I live in Bloomington, Indiana.

Q. Are you acquainted with and a friend of both Mr. and Mrs. Rose? **A.** Yes.

Q. Where did you first meet them? **A.** In Graz, Austria.

Q. Were you a beginning medical student over there as well as Mr. Rose? **A.** Technically I wasn't—I was there to go to the medical school program, yes.

Q. Did you actually go to medical school there? **A.** No, I did not.

Q. Now, you've seen Mr. Rose with Jason, have you not? **A.** Yes, yes.

Q. Would you just describe how—what you've observed about how he and Jason get along? **A.** Well, I think they get along famously. Steve's always—oh, he's taught Jason a couple little dance things that he does. He's taught him how to slap 5, like basketball players do. When Steve comes in, he says, "Hey, Jason, give me five," and he slaps his hand. He's taught Jason to pretend he's dribbling down the floor and stuffing a basketball. Steve's a basketball fan. They're very entertaining together and they get along very well.

Q. Did Steve visit you in Indiana? **A.** Yeah, yeah.

Q. When was that? **A.** That was, I think,—I believe it was just before Thanksgiving.

Q. What, if anything, did he say about Jason? **A.** Well, Steve called Jason "Little Man" a lot, and it seemed whenever Steve and I had ran out of things to say or—or when we'd just—there's a lull in the conversation or anything like that, Steve would always say, "Man, I can't wait to get out to Seattle and see the little man again, 'cause, God, I miss the little—Jason so much." He was very anxious to get back out. He mentioned that—I can't remember exactly how long he'd left Jason, but I think it was seven days or something like that, and he said, "It's only been seven days and I miss my little man so much." So he appeared very anxious to see him.

MR. MELLON: I believe that's all.

p.   Joseph Goldstein, Professor of Law—For the Defense

(1).   Direct Examination by Mr. Mellon

Q. Your name is Joseph Goldstein? **A.** Yes.

Q. You come from the state of Connecticut, do you not? **A.** Yes, sir.

Q. What is your present occupation? **A.** I'm a professor of law at Yale Law School.

Q. How long have you been connected with Yale Law School? **A.** Let's see, I think I joined the faculty in 1966 or seven, something like that, not quite certain of that date.

Q. Now, perhaps you could give the Court a little bit of your educational background. **A.** I hold a bachelor's degree from Dartmouth College, and a doctoral degree from the London School of Economics and Political Science, and a law degree from Yale Law School, and I'm a graduate of the Western New England Psychoanalytic Institute, which is a credited institute of the American Psychoanalytic Association.

Q. All right, sir. Now, do I call you Professor Goldstein, or Mr.— **A.** Mr. is fine with me. I think that's easiest.

Q. Perhaps you could give the Court, so the Court will have an idea of your knowledge and qualifications, a little bit of your background and experience, Mr. Goldstein. **A.** Well, if I focus primarily on work with regard to families and children, I have been the Yale Law School Professor of Family Law, for, oh, I guess fifteen of those seventeen or eighteen years that I've been there.

During that time, I developed a course with a psychoanalyst, Dr. Jay Katz, which focused primarily on the relationship of the law to children, and which resulted in a casebook which is called The Family and the Law, which has been out for about ten years. And in the preparation of that casebook and in giving seminars, we did, over a period of years, invite Anna Freud, from England, to join us in the presentation of work to the students in the law school, and then ultimately with joint seminars in the medical school for residents in child psychiatry and for social workers who were doing related work.

And during that period, I've spent periods up to three months at the Hampstead Child Therapy Clinic in London, working with Anna Freud, and over the years met with her three to four times a year for periods of a week, working on materials and writing together, which resulted in the book Beyond the Best Interests of the Child, which was done also in collaboration with Dr. Albert Solnit, who's the head of our children's center, Child Study Center, at Yale University, and the former president of the American Psychoanalytic Association.

Q. Are you a married man? **A.** Yes, I am.

Q. How long have you been married? **A.** Twenty-seven or twenty-eight years.

Q. To the same wife? **A.** To the same wife.

Q. And you have children? **A.** Four children, three will be in college next fall.

Q. Three boys and a girl? **A.** Three boys and a girl, that's right.

Q. Referring to this book Beyond the Best Interests of the Child, has that been cited as authority by any courts in the United States? **A.** It has. I've not done a survey, but there's come to my attention cases from the Appellate Court of this State, from the State of Connecticut, Pennsylvania, and I know of at least one case in California—and I don't know, did I say New York State?

Q. I don't think you mentioned New York. **A.** I think New York State. I know there's at least one case that's cited the volume.

Q. When was the book first published? **A.** I believe it was the late fall of '93, but I would have to look. I'm terrible on dates, I'm quick to acknowledge that.

Q. Now, Mr. Goldstein, you have a fair idea what this case is about, do you not? **A.** Yes, I have.

Q. You understand that this case involves primarily—the reason you're testifying, or we asked you to testify in this case is it involves—or this is a dissolution of marriage case that involves—particularly the matter that we're talking to you about, involves the care, custody, and control of a boy who was born to this couple in April of 1993, so at the present time, he's about twenty-six months old.

The evidence in the case shows ... [Mr. Mellon here recapitulates the defendant's case.]

Now, Mr. Goldstein, with the background of information, which I'll ask you to assume is correct, I assume counsel will ask you to assume other things, but this Court will be determining at the end of the case which parent, Mr. or Mrs. Rose, should have the care, custody, and control of this child, Jason. I'm going to ask you what, in your opinion, should the Court do in this regard. **A.** Accepting the facts as you've presented them, and focusing on certain ones which I think are critical, as opposed to a number of details which I don't think are particularly relevant to my answer, I would say for a child of Jason's age, which I gather is two years plus—

Q. Two years, two months. **A.** —two years and two months, who at the age of what was it, six months, that in effect he lost contact with his mother for a period of almost six months—

Q. He was about eight months old. **A.** Eight and a half months old. And for a child of that age who's had a continuing relationship with his father, it would be my expectation that that child has begun to internalize and incorporate as a psychological parent in a very substantial sense, the father, and in a much less substantial sense, the mother.

Clearly the first six or eight months of the child's life, and the visits, have contributed to what might be called a psychological parent-child tie. But it's one that's been substantially, I would expect, though I have not examined the child, substantially damaged and bruised by the very long separation, from the child's point of view, from a child's sense of time, that took place after the unpleasant events that you describe, and also by the separations that occur weekly between visits, so that I would say that the child has been substantially scarred. And a child of that age who doesn't know the reasons for absences, clearly has experienced a sense of what might be called abandonment, not in legal terms, but in psychological terms. A sense of rejection and distrust about the external world that's represented by mother, and at the same time, has experienced a sense of continuing and growing security of the tie between himself and the father.

And from the facts as you give them, and in terms just of the passage of time for a child as young as Jason and it's much more significant for a youngster that age than it is for older children, but even for older children, this would be, I think, a separation that would strain dramatically the tie between parent and child, unless extraordinary efforts are made to keep those relationships viable. That from the child's vantage point, which is the only way I can really look at this, I would say it would be least harmful—we say least detrimental to the child—to allow the child to continue in the custody of his father, and his father making whatever arrangements he feels are necessary in order to protect the child's well-being during his absences.

By "psychological parent," we're talking about a person who has assumed responsibility and continuity of care on a daily basis. That doesn't mean an hour-to-hour or minute-by-minute basis, but it means someone to whom the child can turn in times of need and frustration, someone whom the child can find a source of affection and a source of control. And that in terms of the prior experience of this youngster, it seems clear from the facts as you've stated them that the only person with whom Jason has had a chance to develop that relationship is his father, but stressed, I think by the tie that must have begun to develop between Jason and his paternal grandmother, if I understand the facts correctly.

So I would conclude that custody should remain with the father because to do otherwise, and that's really what one is thinking about, what the alternative is, is only to subject the child to another shattering experience. It would mean, I gather, since the father will be going to leave the city for study, it would mean breaking the continuous tie with the father, it would mean interrupting what apparently is a nourishing and meaningful tie with the grandmother, and can only make the child, to the extent one can put oneself inside the child, who's two, feel that the external environment doesn't offer him the security which allows him over time to develop a sense of trust in himself, because he's been let down.

He will have been let down more than once at a crucial time in which he's coming to terms with his own impulses, with the internal struggle that helps develop his identity, and all of that internal turmoil requires as much stability as is possible from the external world, and that's what we're talking about when we say maintaining a continuity of relationship.

But we're also recognizing that there's no perfect solution here. This is a family that is torn apart, so you're looking for the least harmful, or at least from our vantage point, looking for the least harmful alternative for the child. Now I think one—

MR. FISK: Your Honor, he asked him a question ten minutes ago. Are we going to have a lecture all day?

THE COURT: I'm going to overrule the objection. Implicit in the question is an explanation of why he feels the way he does, which I think he's got a right to do.

A.   (Continuing) I'll try and be more brief.

The only thing I would like to add at this time, had the child Jason been placed with some third party at this length of time, at his age, and separated from both parents, except for the visits, I would expect that sufficiently new ties were developing that it would be a terrible thing to break those ties, assuming that there's nothing like abuse or neglect in the current situation, and that the child is doing well.

We originally were going to call the book, as a kind of advice, to the legal system, "Leave Well Enough Alone." We start with very strong presumption that if a child is thriving or developing well in a family constellation, whether it's a total unit or one that's been partially interrupted, that that child should not be moved.

Now, I am not saying that to move the child would necessarily bring the world to an end for that child, but it would be as if one intentionally broke a child's arm with the knowledge that certainly we have ways of putting arms in casts and expecting them to be healed. I have no question that to move the child now, just on the basis of short-term expectations, could only scar the child doubly, both in terms of the very substantial tie with the father, and what I expect is a very meaningful tie with the grandmother.

Q.   When you say "move," you're talking about moving custody, not moving physically from— **A.** No. I'm not talking about a geographical move. I think they're more for older children who begin to establish very meaningful ties with playmates and peers and elementary school and high school. There is a substantial part of the continuity concept which favors leaving the child, if possible, all of the things being equal, in the geographical area in which it finds itself, but to weigh that against the very complex and delicate fabric of the psychological relationships that exist, that it's far more important that the child's ties be made continuously viable. A child and an adult, too, can cope with moves better if there's the security of the external support that comes from having a parent present with the move, then if it's a complete move without those ties.

If I were a parent in a situation like this, I would try to mitigate the extent of the impact of the move by carrying with me the kinds of items the child associates with his room, his crib, his blankets, favorite toys, maybe his potty, whatever it is, I would try and keep the continuity of objects that exist here, available there. And in the same way, I would anticipate that the father must ultimately judge when it is that a phasing out of the relationship with the grandmother and child can take place without too much difficulty for the child; hopefully those relationships being kept alive by visits and the like so the child doesn't feel there's been a rejection.

Q. Assume that Diane Rose, that's the wife, was available at all times. Now, the hypothesis I stated to you, or the facts as I stated them to you, indicated that she intended to work, or be away from the home a substantial period of time. But let's just assume that she was available all the time to care for this child, as contrasted with Dr. Rose and his medical-training schedule, as I generally indicated it to you. Would that change your view any at all, Mr. Goldstein? **A.** No. Even assuming the mother could spend full time and was in perfect health, it would be like saying, "Well, all right, let's give the child a handicap and see if he can make it during those first six or eight crucial years," because what you will be doing, I would anticipate, is making the child, in his own docile, incoherent way, suffer the idea that the world out there can't take care of him, that familiar objects can disappear at will without his understanding, and, that over time, he will find it difficult to establish a new relationship.

Each time you break a tie abruptly, you make it more difficult for the next relationship. This is an experience we've had with foster care children. They move them from one family to another, and then it becomes harder and harder for those children to have enough confidence in themselves to establish meaningful relationships. So even to move the child to a setting that is ideal by any standard, would put the child, at this stage, at a disadvantage because it would be much more difficult the next time around to establish new and meaningful relationships. It casts another very dark shadow on that child's sense of what adults have to offer him, so I would be very reluctant.

Q. You have taken into consideration, I assume, in answering as you have, that Mr. Rose will be by necessity away from the child during periods of time when he's going to have to be on training at the school, and that during those periods of time, that he will be under the care of a competent woman, or possibly even a babysitter at times, or some child-care center. You realize that, do you not? **A.** Yes. I realize that no parent can spend every minute with a child, and in fact, I think it probably would be detrimental to the well-being of the child if every minute was spent with the child.

One of the things that we're talking about when we talk about psychological parent is what is beginning to be internalized by the child about the outside world and its reliability. That's how kids are able to go to school and go to nursery school and spend time away from their parents; they begin to internalize the parent. The parent becomes a part of them, because there's an experience that the child grows on of the parent always coming back. And so the experience as you've described it that Jason has had, is that his father is always coming back, even though he's out of the house from time to time. And that he's there night after night after night, or day after day, even though it's not every hour or every minute. So it's that inner strength that's being built, which permits a child over time to develop the independence that we all want for each of our kids, to be able to walk alone in the world, but that they're carrying within them, if the relationship has been substantial, a rather substantial hunk of what their parents had to offer.

Q. What would you anticipate would be the effect on Jason if custody were transferred from his father to his mother? **A.** Well, as I tried to say, it would be putting him at an enormous handicap. It wouldn't be out of his best interests. It might be out of the best interests of the parent who wants the child, to do that. And it may be that, in fact, I would hope and would want everyone to give as much assistance as possible for a child to survive that experience, but it would be as I suggested, like doing some damage to a child to establish that medicine somehow can do a half-way decent repair job.

I just find it hard to contemplate, under the facts as you present them and the length of time of prior separations and the age of this particular child, to contemplate submitting him to that kind of abrupt termination of a relationship. I would think unless one could establish that the child is not thriving, not doing well, or has been abused or neglected by his current custodians, that one should be very reluctant to make a move or to break those relationships.

Q. Assume, Mr. Goldstein, that you have a parent, I'm just asking you to make this assumption, not based particularly on the facts of this case, but assume that you have a parent that for some reason is not everything a parent should be, he may be a drinker or have some sort of defect of some sort, but you have the situation where he has had or she has had a continuous relationship with the child, and the child seems to be getting along well. And on the other hand, you have the other parent who has not had the care, custody, and control, who doesn't have these defects. What would be your attitude on a change of custody in that situation? **A.** If we keep as given the statement of facts about the length of time?

Q. Yes. **A.** I without hesitancy would say that there's no reason to move the child. One of the problems that we try to confront in examining these issues generally is the absence of what I think a lot of us attribute to law, a kind of magic that this is an opportunity to make things perfect and beautiful and give a guarantee for the child. It's just not in the cards. I don't know of any perfect parent. In fact, a perfect parent might be an impossible one for a child to live with.

But I would say unless there are indications which justify moving that constitute neglect or abuse, that there must be in that relationship that you hypothesize, some very important strengths that are communicated between that parent, the custodial parent, and the child, which ought not to be tampered with, because you don't know what the next situation has to offer. You have a prior experience to build on that has proved reliable for the child, and you are speculating about a new experience, if everything were as perfect as the model that you describe as the alternative.

(2). Cross Examination by Mr. Fisk

Q. Mr. Goldstein, you were given a little background about this case, and I want you to assume that the reason for this suicide attempt in the first place was because of pressure put upon Diane Rose by her husband and his mother, specifically with reference to permitting her to care for her own child, things of that nature. Now, assuming that to be a fact, would that make any difference in what you're testifying today? **A.** Not really.

Q. You think that's okay? **A.** If you're asking me to make a judgment about that kind of interpersonal relationship, it isn't something that I would favor, but if you're asking me in terms of how that event can be perceived or digested by the child, whatever the reason for the suicide attempt, whatever the reason for the period of absence for by the child, even if it were for the best of reasons.

Q. All right. Now, you place great emphasis, I take it, on what you refer to as "continuity of care"? **A.** Yes, continuity of relationships, yes.

Q. Now, let's take a situation. Suppose people are always snatching up a child and taking off with him. And let's assume that that happens, and a person takes the child and disappears with him, has him for several months before anybody locates him, or so on, and during the interim, the child gets a real attachment to the person that has him. **A.** Yes.

Q. Now, under that kind of a situation, do you think the person doing that should profit by their own wrong? **A.** No. I don't think the person doing that should profit by his own wrong, nor do I think that the reward or punishment should be translated in the terms of altering the custodial relationship of the child. We do have, when people are harmed in our society, a form of responding either in terms of money damages, or if there's been a violation of the criminal law, to invoke the criminal law. While I do not condone the kidnapping that you're describing, I would ultimately not want to use the child, which is always the object that's looked at, as the reward or punishment.

Q. Well, that's not what I'm asking you. Under the situation I've described, I'm asking you if you think a court under that situation ought to leave the child with the parent who stole him away, on the theory that it would be bad to give him back to the proper person. **A.** If a new and meaningful relationship had developed over a sufficient period of time, I would be very reluctant, from the child's point of view, to move that child, and I think I am responding to your question, because to move the child in order to protect the State's policy with regard to kidnapping, is to use the child as chattel, which is what we're moving away from.

Q. So if I understand you, you'd leave him there? **A.** If the facts were as you suggest, that he's thriving under those circumstances. If I may, I could give you a—

Q. Just answer the question, if you will. **A.** All right, certainly.

Q. And your answer is that you would leave him there? **A.** My answer is if the child is thriving, and a substantial period of time has gone by where the old ties have begun to dissolve or break down, and new meaningful ties have developed, that I would, from the child's vantage point, I would leave him there.

Q. Now, you have no information whatsoever as to the relationship of this child with his real mother, do you? **A.** With the biological mother?

Q. Yes. **A.** Right.

Q. Now, I'm going to ask you to assume that in the period of roughly six months since we established the visitation arrangement of four hours twice a week, plus every other weekend, that the mother has had this child, and this child is extremely fond of her, will hardly let her out of his sight when she has visitation privileges, that so far as the child is concerned, this is not only the biological mother, but the psychological mother, and that he enjoys himself. **A.** What I would take it as is evidence that there must be a very healthy relationship that exists in the regular day to day caring for the child, so that the child is able to manage these visits successfully. And so my answer would be the same in the sense, to the extent the observation or the facts you give are in fact correct, it would support my expectation that a more meaningful relationship could develop with the mother over time, if the child continued in a setting where it's thriving.

Q. Now, Professor Goldstein, I'm going to ask you to assume that the father has—by evidence on official records and by other evidence which we have—has a very hostile attitude toward the parents of the mother, and against Mrs. Rose herself, and that he has done everything that's possible that he can think of to attempt to influence or alienate the child away from the mother. And I'll ask you if you think that is a good thing from the standpoint of the child? **A.** If the child is being alienated from the mother at the, I guess, instigation, you're saying—

Q. That's right, right. **A.** —of the father, it's not something that I think is particularly beneficial for the child.

Q. To put it another way, it's detrimental, isn't it? **A.** Well, we're talking about alternatives, unfortunately, because we don't have a whole family here. Ultimately, from the child's interest as far as we're concerned, the custodial parent has to deal with the child and the child's relationships with others in a way that is comfortable for that parent. That's the only way that a strong and meaningful tie can develop with the parent. We want to at least preserve one for this child's well-being.

From the vantage point of continuity, which is what we were stressing, if the father came to me for counseling, I would urge him to try to come to terms with his antagonism, and to work out in a flexible way . . . opportunities for the child to see the absent parent. But I'd say it's much more significant that that kind of relationship be encouraged for children who are much older, where there was a real tie. Say the family had remained together for ten years, and we're talking about children nine and eight, there you have a long-standing relationship—

Q. Professor— **A.** —that might be more significant.

Q. Excuse me for interrupting you. You've written so many articles it takes you all day to answer a simple question.

MR. MELLON: I object to counsel's remarks.

THE WITNESS: I apologize, I'm sorry.

THE COURT: I'm going to sustain the objection. If you ask him a question, I think you'll have to wait until he finishes answering, or—

MR. FISK: I'm willing to do that, your Honor.

THE COURT:—or object to his answer without trying to cover him over. It's going to be difficult for the court reporter to report that, among other things.

Q. (By Mr. Fisk) Now, let me ask you again, Professor. **A.** Yes, sir.

Q. The question was whether it was good for the child, or detrimental, or what, for one parent to attempt to alienate the child from another. That's a simple thing, I would think, as much experience as you've had, you ought to be able to answer it. **A.** Well, one of the problems is we're talking about very complex and delicate interpersonal relationships, and that it's not as easy to say an answer as I guess you would like. We're talking about alternatives.

Q. Is it yes or no? **A.** It's neither yes or no.

Q. Well, when I ask you this way— **A.** Certainly.

Q. —that you condone that sort of thing? **A.** As a parent, I don't condone one parent playing another parent against the other, to the child.

Q. That's detrimental, is it not? **A.** It can be very harmful to the child, yes.

Q. Now, I want you to assume that almost all of the care of this child, since Mr. Rose took off with the child—has been by Mr. Rose's mother. I want you to assume that. **A.** Okay.

Q. And now, then, he's testified here today that he's going to, if he gets the child in this custody hearing, he's going to take him to Los Angeles, and he's going to have a babysitter or a live-in housekeeper to take care of the child, in place of his mother.

Now, if that happens, then there's going to be an interruption in this continuity of care that you've referred to, isn't there? **A.** There's going to be an interruption with regard to part of the continuity of care that I was talking about. I relied very substantially, unless you alter the facts—

Q. I did alter the facts. **A.** —well, on the continuity of the relationship with the father. See—

Q. I ask you to assume that the paternal grandmother, for all practical purposes, has had the care of this child. Now she's, according to the present plans, she's not going to do that anymore, except for a transition period. Now, if that happens, you don't have this continuity of care that you've been talking about, do you? **A.** You have to the extent you haven't taken away the responsibility of the father to make arrangements for the child during the periods when he's at work. To the extent that that still remains, you have the continuity of the tie with the father. To the extent that you break both ties between father and grandmother, in order to place the child with the "absent parent," you're just scarring the child twice over.

Now, the expectation, as I heard it, was that this was not to be an abrupt change, but to be something that was done over time.

Q. I understand. But you're not going to have a continuity of the same care? **A.** Oh, one never has the continuity of the same care. One has the continuity of the relationship with primarily one, and hopefully, two, parents. So, yes, there is going to be for the child some transition which that child can manage better if it's got a father that it can rely on continuously, as there's a shift from the grandmother to someone else.

Q. Well, why couldn't the child rely on its mother? **A.** Well, I gather the child could; had the facts been reversed, and the child been with the mother all this time, and not with the father, clearly that would be the way it ought to be. But to break and scar the child by terminating in an abrupt fashion, a relationship with both grandmother and father, is probably as harsh a thing as you can conceive of, and as great a handicap as you can impose on that child, other than that both of those parties die unfortunately in a tragic airplane accident.

Q. Professor, you don't claim to be a child psychiatrist, do you? **A.** No, I don't. I'm not a psychiatrist. I'm a psychoanalyst.

Q. Well, isn't that a kind of a subspecialty of psychiatry? **A.** No, I think you'll find that most psychiatrists are required to have a medical degree. I have no medical degree. And my training is primarily in psychoanalysis.

Q. Now, earlier in this case, we had a child psychologist, and he testified that as between giving the custody to a babysitter and to the mother, there's no question the best interest of the child was to go to the mother; do you agree with that?

MR. MELLON: No, just a moment, your Honor. I'm going to object. He was not a child psychologist.

THE COURT: Psychiatrist, I think.

MR. MELLON: He was a psychiatrist.

MR. FISK: I'm sorry. I meant "psychiatrist," if I had inadvertently used "psychologist."

MR. MELLON: And in the second place, counsel is stating that this individual testified so and so. I recall no such testimony. He's stating it as a fact that that's the way he testified.

THE COURT: I'll overrule the objection. He was a psychiatrist, however.

MR. FISK: That's right.

THE WITNESS: Could you just restate your question, please?

Q. (By Mr. Fisk) A child psychiatrist was here to testify, right where you are and he testified in response to a direct question that as between giving the custody of this child to a new babysitter or housekeeper, whatever term you want to use, on the one hand, and giving it to the mother on the other, that there wasn't any question. The child would be better off with the mother.

MR. MELLON: I'm going to object to that, because that was assuming also that the father would be completely out of the picture.

THE WITNESS: I'd be willing to answer that if you want.

THE COURT: Overruled.

A. If by "custody", you mean give the custody to some unknown figure that hasn't yet been identified, or to the mother who currently has some relationship, no matter how tenuous, with the child, if those are your only choices, then certainly you would favor giving the custody, which I gather is the control and care of the child, to the mother. That isn't what I understand the facts to be.

Q. Now, we've got a practical consideration, Mr. Goldstein. If custody was to go to the father, and he carries out his plans to go to Los Angeles, obviously it's going to be impractical for the mother to see the child except on rare occasions. Now, isn't that in and of itself detrimental to the child? **A.** To the extent they're meaningful ties, it's detrimental. To the extent of choosing between what is the least detrimental, it's less detrimental to tamper with those tenuous ties than it is with the real ties that have developed over a two-year plus period with the one adult the child has been able to rely on.

MR. FISK: Thank you.

(3). Redirect by Mr. Mellon

Q. Let me ask you just one other question. When you are faced with a problem like we've been discussing here this morning, from whose standpoint do you attempt to always solve that problem, from the parents' standpoint, the father's standpoint, the mother's standpoint, or the child's standpoint? **A.** I try to examine the question from the child's vantage point, and if I am allowed to elaborate—

Q. Yes, please do. **A.** —I would give an illustration how time often alters a position that we take. In a case in Connecticut, where a group of us, including Dr. Solnit and some—

MR. FISK: I'm going to object to this, your Honor. We don't care about his Connecticut case. I object to it.

THE COURT: I'll overrule it, because I think it explains his position.

A. (Continuing) I'll try to be very brief.

It involved a child who had been placed with a foster mother fairly early in its life, something like three or four months old, and remained with the foster mother for almost two years, at which time the court abruptly took the child, literally, the court official moved the child from the arms of the mother while sleeping in the courtroom, that is the foster mother, and returned it to the natural biological mother.

The court—and this was over the objection of all of the psychiatrists in the Child Study Center, which said that so many ties had developed with this foster parent, who wanted to adopt, that the child shouldn't be moved.

The case was in litigation for almost, I think, two years, and by the time the court again had to consider the factual issue, we felt that the new relationship that the child had begun to develop after this trauma, was such that it would be terribly damaging to move the child once again, to have it develop a sense that there isn't anything permanent in his life. That our staff had to conclude otherwise and advise the judge, "Now, look, you have to leave the child where it is," even though we thought at the time we made the judgment, it was a mistake. And it clearly was, it scarred the child. But to do it again after a two-years' lapse, we felt was terribly harmful for the child.

Now, we're constantly confronted with having to deal with our own blind spots, and it's just that kind of case, it makes us force into view for ourselves, but it's the child's interests we're concerned about, not any particular adult party, and that's the way we had to respond in that case.

q. Alice Rose—For the Defense

(1). Direct Examination by Mr. Mellon

Q. You're the mother of Steve Rose, are you not? **A.** Yes.

Q. Mrs. Rose, as soon as you heard about the events of a year ago, that is, when Diane jumped out of the window, did you go right back to Washington? **A.** Right.

Q. And what, if anything, did you try to do about that situation? **A.** Well, we more or less almost started to panic. Everything, her heart rate, everything, all her vital signs looked like this was going to be it. And I felt that I wanted to do everything she—you know, that was possible, because otherwise you'd never forgive yourself. And so I called Dr. Allen, a friend and distinguished surgeon in town, and I told him in desperation, I said I—I just didn't want to hear about professional ethics, I wanted to—and I compared her with the Kennedys or Wallace when they were shot, that teams of doctors forgot about professional ethics and with just one thought in mind, to save the patient. And I felt that I wanted this for Diane and I felt that Washington, D.C., was an area that had so many medical facilities and experts that they don't have anywhere else in the country that there had to be someone there that was a top neurosurgeon that we could call in. And so he said to me—I called him from a pay phone at the—in the Waiting Room, and he said, "I'll get right back to you." And then he called in five minutes and he said, "I'm taking Dr. Hugo Raymond out of a meeting and I'll be right over." And they came over within a half an hour.

Q. Dr. Allen and Dr. Raymond. **A.** M-hm.

Q.   Now, at about this time, Mrs. Rose, did you make any statement to the effect that if Diane died, that you wanted to have—that you wanted to raise Jason, or that you wanted to have his custody. **A.** That is so ridiculous.

Q.   —or something like that? **A.** That is—that is—in the first place, I have raised my family.

Q.   Well, did you have any—or was there any conversation with Dr. Mitchell at the hospital before you went up to see Diane the next morning? **A.** Well, Steve spent a few minutes trying to give him some background inasmuch as just—just the pertinent facts that—you know, that they were married and they had a small child, and that she had taken an overdose of Phenobarbital and gone out an eight-story window, and that she was alive. And he gave her physical condition and that he wanted to have him possibly as a therapist.

Q.   All right. And did you get a chance to go up and see Diane that morning? **A.** No, they wouldn't let us up there.

Q.   So then did you see Dr. Mitchell? **A.** Yes.

Q.   —when he left the hospital also? **A.** Yes. He came down and he mentioned that Diane was—all she could talk about was how she hated her parents. And he said, "I'd like to try to tone that down."

And so I said, "Thank you very much," because nobody had ever told us how to talk to her. You know, she was constantly berating them and we didn't know what to say to her, because we didn't know whether to just let her talk or say—you know, quiet her up or—or what.

Q.   Did you attempt to follow his advice? **A.** Yes. In fact, many times after that I—I would bring up the point that, "Diane, you are a parent now and it's more important for you to think of getting well and being a mother to Jason."

Q.   Now, when Diane came home from the hospital, you were, of course, still there, were you not? **A.** Yes.

Q.   And now, Mrs. Rose, let me go back a little bit here. How long have you known Diane? Do you recall approximately? **A.** Well, she went with Steve for four years before they were married.

Q.   They were married in 1990, so you've known her about eight years— **A.** Yes.

Q.   And what sort of relationship did you have with Diane? **A.** Well, it was unusual for a mother-in-law and daughter-in-law.

Q.   I mean, even before, even before she became your daughter-in-law, what type of relationship did you have? **A.** All right. Well, like, for the first three years she was just a real sweet girl that my son went with, and then for the year before they were married we became very close and it was like a mother-and-daughter relationship. She brought her problems to me. I don't think that I would have given her a "no" in the world unless it was just totally impossible.

Q.   Would she stay weekends at your place? **A.** Oh yes, yes. In fact, it was—it was the opposite. Usually when a boy goes with a girl, the boy's always at the girl's house and in this case she was always at our house.

(2).   Cross Examination by Mr. Fisk

Q. Now, Mrs. Rose, I'm going to ask you a few questions about this problem at the Winters' in September, October, whatever it was, of 1993. You remember that well, I take it. **A.** Yes.

Q. Well, what led to a discussion of money where—with reference to the camera incident then, if you can tell us? **A.** That was brought up by Amanda out of the blue.

Q. But if I understand correctly, she stated that (quoting Amanda Winter) that, "They're just spendthrifts like your kids," or something like that. **A.** Well, like our family.

Q. Yes. **A.** Actually she said like me. She was more specific, yes.

Q. Like you? **A.** "Your son—your son gets his spendthrift habits from you."

Q. Okay. And with that you flew into a rage, said that you and your son had been insulted, and stormed out of the house? **A.** No. She went on to explain that my son that summer had talked about buying a movie camera. That's when I said, "I'm highly insulted," and I left.

Q. Now, what we just talked about is all that occurred that made you feel that you were so highly insulted? **A.** No. There were a few more remarks—

Q. All right. **A.** —that were made.

Q. Would you tell us everything there that caused you to feel that you were insulted? **A.** Well, she started out by saying that, when I mentioned that—she, "That's the way you handle your problems. When you have a problem, you get out of town." And I asked her to explain herself, and she mentioned that when Steve and Diane and Jason went back to Washington, D.C., I left that same day for Las Vegas. That started it.

Q. Well, was there any truth in that statement? **A.** Yeah, I went to Las Vegas. I can't see the similarity. I don't—wasn't running away from problems.

Q. Were you a compulsive gambler? **A.** You want an answer?

Q. Well, if you can answer it. **A.** I'm not a compulsive gambler. (Laughing.)

Q. But you don't go down to Las Vegas by yourself? **A.** I met a—girl from New York.

Q. All right. Now, the very next day is when you called Dr. Winter. Is that right? **A.** No.

Q. All right. When did you call him? **A.** Well, I waited several days because I felt that possibly there would be some acknowledgment of the unfairness of—of any type of a misunderstanding and that I would get a call. Well, when I didn't, I felt really that I was entitled to some explanation, and so I called Dr. Winter at his office.

Q. You told him he was no better than his goddamn brother, didn't you? **A.** No, I didn't say that at all. No.

Q. Did you tell him you should have beat the shit out of Amanda before you left? **A.** No.

r. Jonathan Bower, M.D.—For the Defense

(1). Direct Examination by Mr. Mellon

Q. And you are a licensed physician in the State of Washington are you? **A.** I am.

Q. What is your specialty, Doctor? **A.** I'm considered to have perhaps three or four.

Q. Well, that's fine. Tell us about all of them. **A.** I'm a pediatrician and I'm a professor of Pediatrics at the University of Washington Medical School. I'm a general psychiatrist and I'm a professor of Psychiatry at the University of Washington Medical School. I'm a child psychiatrist and that is the major work I do at the Medical School right now.

Q. Child psychiatry? **A.** That's right, a psychiatrist for children. And I'm a psychoanalyst.

Q. Now, Dr. Bower, there's been talk in this courtroom or testimony in this courtroom about another Dr. Bower, David Bower, in Washington, D.C. He's your brother, is he not? **A.** Yes, we are brothers.

Q. Now, have you had occasion to examine Diane Rose? **A.** Yes. I examined Diane.

Q. All right. Now, did you also have occasion to examine Jason Rose? **A.** I examined Jason Rose on perhaps five different occasions in my office, in the company of his father, and I examined Jason Rose once again in the Rose home, when Mrs. Rose and Steve Rose were present.

Q. Which Mrs. Rose? **A.** I'm sorry, Mrs. Harold Rose. And then I did still another examination of Jason in my office last week, in the presence of his mother, Mrs. Diane Rose.

Q. All right. And then you've had—did you examine Steve Rose also? **A.** I can't say that I've done a precise, formal psychiatric evaluation on Steve Rose, but I think I can venture a psychiatric opinion about him, since I've seen him in about eight different times in different circumstances.

Q. Now, I'm going to ask you, Dr. Bower, if you would just tell the Court, or give the Court the results of your examination of these three people. **A.** I'll have to take a moment to organize my thinking about that. In the first place, with Steve Rose, there was never a formal psychiatric examination, since that was never requested. I have seen him alone several times, in discussing the issues of care and custody of Jason, and in the planning for some of the examinations and my testimony here. I have also seen him in his home. My psychiatric opinion about him is that he is an intelligent, ordinary, aggressive, young man who has capable powers of organization, who is distraught and preoccupied by what I consider distressing circumstances.

THE COURT: Are you referring to the circumstances of this case?

THE WITNESS: Yes, I am.

THE COURT: Okay.

A. (Continuing) My opinion about his intellectual functioning is that he's at least of normal intelligence. My opinion about his so-called emotional or mental functioning, his ability to manage severe stresses under less than optimum conditions, is that he is of at least ordinary capability. So I would call him a psychologically normal person.

Q. (By Mr. Mellon) All right. Now— **A.** You want me to go ahead?

Q. Yes, go ahead. **A.** I examined Diane Rose last week in a one-hour psychiatric examination. I had some knowledge of Diane's condition ahead of time, because I had reviewed page by page the hospital record of her hospitalization, and my opinion—some of this may be distressing to Mrs. Rose, but my opinion is that she does not function in an ordinary, intact, normal manner. Without—

Q. How did you arrive at that? **A.** Well, by doing a rather formal, orthodox, clear psychiatric examination, which is rather standard. The procedure that I follow is most closely described in one of the standard textbooks, Daniel Freedman's Textbook of Psychiatry. The stimulus during the examination is the office, the physical setting, the psychiatrist in person, and in addition, questions and comments which ordinary enough, by themselves, are brought in mainly to attempt to determine the patient's mode of thinking, their response to ordinary human events. Through this, it's possible to make a professional guess about the patient's ability to withstand stresses of various kinds, the ability to follow a straight line of thinking, the ability to be aware of the world around them. That's how I do it.

Q. All right. Now, did you give her a mental status examination? **A.** I did.

Q. Do you have one called the "proverbs"? **A.** Yes. In an ordinary psychiatric examination, there is one section called the proverb test. The usual mode of administering it is to ask the patient what the people ordinarily mean when they say, and then you ask a proverb such as, "What do people ordinarily mean when they say, 'Don't close the barn door after the horses are out,' or, 'People in glass houses should not throw stones.'" It's a stimulus somewhat like an ink blot. There is no exact proper answer. But one can make a guess, an educated guess, by watching how a patient's thinking can stay anchored in reality, can remain unconfused, and can remain relevant to the task at hand.

Mrs. Rose's performance on the proverb test leads me to believe that under pressure, and under continued pressure, not of a terribly severe type, she becomes confused in her—her thinking becomes loose and loses the point.

Q. I don't believe you told us what your actual conclusions are. **A.** My conclusion is that from her behavior, which was not limited to watching her response to the proverb test, but watching her behavior in what is a standard setting, that is, my office, by watching and thinking about her responses to the questioning, by watching her ability to reconstitute herself after she has some difficulty in thinking, my conclusion is that she does have a disturbance in her thinking. I cannot be crystal clear at this point, since I don't have my own information of her thinking and her behavior before the suicide. So my conclusion at this point, must be that it's consistent with a personality disorder, and I use that word in the sense of the standard psychiatric nomenclature. It is also consistent with evidence of brain damage, and that comes from the manner in which she thinks and the kinds of stresses which will disorganize her, as well as observations of actual physical behavior and neurological functioning, such as the difficulty she has using her tongue and controlling her mouth movements.

THE COURT: You're going to have to tell me what personality disorder is, because I've heard over the years a lot of definitions of that.

THE WITNESS: Well, your Honor, the problem in psychiatric diagnosis is that we don't have a blueprint, and yet we have a need to communicate with others about what we see in something less than verbatim accounts, or— of our observations.

Sometime after World War II, the World Health Organization attempt-ed to develop a world-wide diagnostic scheme. Recognizing the difficulties in that, and nevertheless trying to make—feeling that any scheme that could be agreed to by everyone, even though it was a bad one, would be preferable to no scheme. And so the standard psychiatric nomenclature was developed and was made part of an international classification scheme of diseases.

This standard nomenclature was developed in part by the American Psychiatric Association, under the World Health Organization's auspices. It's basically a very simple scheme. The major tasks are between separating the organic illnesses from the so-called psychogenic illnesses, and the major task within those is an attempt to separate the so-called psychoses from the so-called neuroses, and that's like separating ice and water. Because in real life, with real people, you add one degree of heat with one degree of lack of heat, and you suddenly have ice, or you suddenly have water. And so often, even in the best category, the best scheme, you end up with having slush.

The scheme is really very simple. It makes certain assumptions, right or wrong. It assumes that for the psychogenic diseases, they are expressions, as of this moment, of a human being's ability to manage stress, large or small. They attempt to say very little about the past or the future. The other assumption they make, which is terribly important, is that there are only four ways open to human beings to respond to stress. Psychological stress, I'm talking about, not stress of the everyday world, but the stress that's per-ceived.

One is to transmute it psychologically, and displace it onto a body part, usually the so-called autonomic nervous system. And those are called psycho-somatic disorders, and the common everyday representatives of this are gastrointestinal disorders like stomach ulcers, although there are other kinds, migraine headaches, in the olden days, hysterical paralysis, but again the notion is, one way is to take the stress and pretend it's not a psychological stress, but one that belongs to your body.

Another way to deal with the psychological stress is to transmute it through the ordinary, normal mechanisms of thinking. That is, denial, identification, repression, sublimation, introjection, reaction formation, and that's—one example of that is seen every day with adolescents. With the stress of being an adolescent, one adolescent might identify with the ordinary stress of adolescence, being, you don't know who in the world you are at the moment, and you don't know where you're going. One adolescent might identify with a hero, a positive hero, one might identify with a negative hero.

Some of these psychological mechanisms are more adaptive to reality and to continued functioning in the rest of life, and some aren't. A surgeon who does things to people, draws blood, and things like that, that's a much more adaptive mechanism than simply destroying things. These are the so-called neuroses, and they use the ordinary so-called neurotic mechanisms of dealing with life stresses, severe or mild.

One is to displace it onto a body part, one is to deal with it purely psychologically, and to use ordinary neurotic mechanisms. The third method is to take action, to do things, to move. Sometimes this is adaptive and sometimes it isn't.

In that category, the so-called character disorders and the so-called personality disorders. The character disorders take actions that seem or prove to be more adaptive through one's life. The personality disorders are those that have a lifetime history of being maladaptive and being exceedingly brittle. They follow quite rapidly, and they reconstitute rapidly. And they are pulled into play under ordinary life stresses, rather than severe stresses.

The fourth method is a pattern of regression, disorganization, and denial of reality. Those are called the psychoses. In a proper psychiatric diagnosis, one is really not allowed to use a name alone, because that's like a swear word. One is supposed to say something about the stress that called the defense into play. And therefore, you have some idea of the severity of what that human being is dealing with at the moment. You have an idea of the stress, you have an idea of the responses of which they're capable.

You're also supposed to say something, if at all possible, about the predominant life pattern. I named these, except for the psychophysiologic reactions, in order of decreasing adaptability and capability with an ordinary human life. That is, the neuroses are generally less debilitating, and the psychoses are most debilitating. A personality disturbance is a descriptive term that applies to a human being, who for most of their life, responds to even minimal stresses with a pattern of action for behavior, attempting to get away from what's happening, rather than actually dealing with it head on.

Some of the personality disturbances are the psychopath, the sociopath, the borderline psychotic; but you must recognize that in this scheme, there are lots of borders and combinations.

That's a long answer, and I hope it helped.

Q. (By Mr. Mellon) What, Dr. Bower, is the treatment for a personality disorder, or a borderline personality?—particularly a borderline personality. **A.** You have to—you have to do a careful examination first. You have to decide—

Q. First, could I interrupt you just a minute. What is the meaning of the word "borderline," borderline with what, between what? **A.** It's generally used as a borderline between a psychosis and something that is not a psychosis, that is in touch with reality, but not functioning so well, or out of touch with reality and functioning in a very unadaptive way. You have to do a careful evaluation of what the patient's present functioning is reacting to at that moment, because they can change in time.

If the stress is an internal one, that comes from associations, memories, things, or one's own actual physical state, then you attempt to provide reality to that, as well as support to that, through providing a reliable, trustworthy listener; or, if there's a physical state that's involved, by attempting to moderate the physical disease that's causing the stress, such as a diabetic who's out of diabetic control.

So you attempt to provide internal support. If the stresses seem to be coming from outside the thinking of that human being, you attempt to provide support and strength and regularities and predictabilities in that person's world. If the stress seems to be of anxiety, it is possible nowadays to moderate or ameliorate or take the edge off anxiety, using the so-called tranquilizer. You tend then to modify the importance or the hierarchy of your treatment scheme according to where you think your patient is.

Q. Are borderline personality problems ever—or usually cleared up, or do they last throughout the person's lifetime? **A.** Borderline personality, or if we can stick to one diagnostic scheme, and I prefer, although I don't like the scheme, I find fault with it, it's the best one around, I prefer to stick with the standard psychiatric nomenclature, that is, that personality disorders are never cured. They are like a diabetic. They are like my own myopia, my nearsightedness. One doesn't cure them, one manages them. They are subject to disturbance throughout one's life, depending on both the severity of the stress perceived by the patient, and the state of their own defenses, both internal and external defenses.

For instance, if one moves away from home, certain external supports are withdrawn. For instance, if one's body changes through illness, there are other kinds of stresses. It's difficult to predict then, exactly what will happen to the so-called personality disorder, because you can't predict life's accidents. All you can do is attempt to provide a relatively benign, ordinary existence, that pays attention only to the external events.

It's almost impossible to predict what will go on internally. A more direct answer to your question, it is a disturbance, or a deficiency, or a style of thinking which is never cured, only managed.

Q. Is a manic-depressive illness a psychosis? **A.** Well, that's one of those slush items in that darn diagnostic manual.

Q. Now, Dr. Bower, let me ask you first, you are a board certified child psychiatrist, among other things, are you not? Did you find anything wrong at all with Jason this time, or when you examined him? **A.** Well, when you ask the question, did I find anything wrong, I prefer to say what I found right. Jason, in my opinion, is an ordinarily well-functioning child, a toddler who is extraordinarily susceptible to the feelings and the confusions and the intentions of the adults around him. He is exquisitely tuned to the wishes of the grownups with whom he is with at that time.

Q. Now, Doctor, do you have an opinion as to who should have the—between these two parents, who should have the care, custody, and control over Jason? **A.** Yes, I do.

Q. And what is your opinion? **A.** I came to the opinion last week after examining Mrs. Rose, and after examining her with Jason in my office. My—in my opinion, the custody should go to Mr. Steven Rose.

Q. All right. Now then, I'll ask you to explain why you have come to that conclusion. **A.** At the simplest level, I came to that conclusion because Mr. Rose manages stresses in an adaptive, continuously functioning way.

During my examination, Mrs. Rose did not. As tension would mount, as it became more and more necessary for her to provide decisions based on her own thinking, her thinking collapsed and became confused.

In part, my decision is based upon the history as I know it, that is a suicide attempt, and a history of brain damage. In my examination of Mrs. Rose, the brain damage also was interfering with her ability to think and to continue to force her thinking past the mere simple responses. As she attempted to do that, her thinking collapsed.

And then finally, my opinion is based upon my observations of Mr. Rose tending his son, compared with my observations of Mrs. Rose tending her son in the same examining situation.

Q. Do you want to go into— **A.** I can if you wish.

Q. Is there anything in particular—I don't want you to go into any great detail, but can you explain that just a little bit? **A.** I can touch on the predominant themes. I might have to explain them in more detail.

Q. Well, I don't want to take too much time doing this. **A.** The predominant theme is that Mrs. Rose was unable to continue dealing with stressful incidents of ordinary life with a child beyond a certain point.

Secondly, during the examination, she tended more to her own needs, to her own thinking, rather than those of the child.

For example, at one point during the interview, I asked Mrs. Rose to direct Jason to a large uncomfortable wooden chair. It's an inappropriate chair for a child. It was purposely a stress-inducing instruction on my part. She was unable to give Jason, in my opinion, clear direct instructions. Rather, she begged, she cajoled, she offered rewards. I continued my insistence that she make Jason comply. Obviously, Jason did not want to comply. Mrs. Rose then attempted to lift Jason up by the seat of his pants, head first into a large chair, which is a terribly inappropriate way to deal with the child. Most people turn a child around, lift him up by the armpits, and put him down.

After I released both of them from this obviously unhappy situation, Jason went about his business, Mrs. Rose relaxed into what was her characteristic posture during both her examination alone with me, as well as with Jason, what would at first sight be a modest, naive, attentive attention, was really a relatively wooden, immobile, introspective posture. There was little recognition of the rather intense discomfort that Jason had gone through.

This was one example. There were others. It confirmed Mrs. Rose's behavior during the hour-long examination that I had with her alone.

Q. Are you familiar with the term "psychological parent"? **A.** I am.

Q. In your opinion, from what you've observed, seen, and so on, in this matter, who is the psychological parent of this child? **A.** Well, I wish you wouldn't put the question that way, because it's possible to have—

Q. All right. Is there— **A.** —many important people in one's life.

Q. Yes. All right. Let me put it this way: Does the child, in your opinion, have at least one psychological parent? **A.** The child has indeed at least one psychological parent, that is, one adult to whom the child turns to for care, for restitution from pain, for love, yes.

Q. All right. Does Jason have one or more psychological parents? **A.** Jason has at least two: Steve Rose; he has Mrs. Harold Rose; and to some, but much less a degree he has a third, and that is Mrs. Diane Rose.

Q. Are you familiar with the book by Goldstein, Freud, and Solnit, Beyond the Best Interests of the Child? **A.** I am.

Q. Do you consider it to be authoritative in the field? **A.** Yes. Although I don't—the book—book's primary intent was not to provide a final authority. The book intended to raise questions, provide discussion and close examination of important issues; but when it does touch on issues where authority is important, it is authoritative.

Q. Now, are you familiar with the fact that Steve Rose is going to be leaving the end of this month to take up his residency at U.C.L.A. Medical Center? **A.** He has told me that.

Q. Did you take that into consideration when you were expressing the opinion to the Court as to who should have the care, custody, and control of Jason, the fact that he's going to be leaving for U.C.L.A.? **A.** I suppose I did, but not at a very high level of priority.

Q. Who do you mean by that? **A.** The highest level of priority of my considerations was the present mental functioning of the two parties whom I examined. My assumption then being that given ordinary powers of thinking and pursuing problem-solving, and reacting to stress without confusion or breakdown, one will make the best of life's situations.

Q. Just one more question, Dr. Bower. There has been testimony concerning your brother in Washington, D.C., and a visit that—or two that he had with members of both families some time back. Are you and your brother considerably different or are you about the same? **A.** I said we are brothers.

(Laughter.)

We shared the same parents, I believe.

(Laughter.)

He is ten years older than I am, ten years and one month older than I am. I'm the baby of the family. So we share many things and then there are many things we do not share. Some of these are by virtue of the different genetic basket that we got from our parents. Some of these have to do with different lives. The infant of the family does not live the same life that the firstborn does. He came into our family at a time of prosperity. I came into our family at a time of depression. So there are these accidents of life. Then in addition there are those things that people do to themselves.

So in many ways I constructed my life in a different way, almost as a reaction to my own brother much—sometimes the way some people do in reaction to their fathers. And looking back on it, I think some of my wandering around, avoiding a certain career, had to do with avoiding confusion created in my mind and my parents' mind and my brother's mind between my brother and myself.

We're also different not only personally, we are different psychologically and we are different professionally. I'm a psychoanalyst. People have strong feelings positively and negatively about psychoanalysts. My brother is not. I feel strongly about institutions, certifications, all that kind of proper thing; my brother does not. In my professional life I tend to find some pleasure and some usefulness in zeroing in on things with precision; my brother, and I think validly, tries to deal with things globally. My brother tends to do things like family therapy, group therapy; I don't, because it's invalid. We are different people and yet we're quite close.

THE WITNESS: Does that answer your question, Mr. Mellon?

MR. MELLON: I think so. Thank you, Doctor.

NOTES

1. If you were representing Steven Rose, the defendant, how would you have presented his case to the court?

2. If you were the judge who had presided over the Rose hearing, to which parent would you grant custody? As you read the material in the next section on how courts have applied the best interest standard, consider how useful a guide for making custody decisions. Is there a better standard?

2.   THE TRIAL COURT DECIDES

■ SANGSTER, J.

This case has taken us quite a long time to complete, and it took me quite a bit of time last night to wrestle around with it and come up with what I wanted to say. I don't think it will be too long, but I have several things that need to be said. I appreciate, of course, all those of you who have been witnesses, and friends and family, who have been here to give your support, and of course, Steve and Diane have gone through a lot; and the lawyers, I want to thank you for your preparation and presentation. Those people who hired you I think can be pleased with your work. You presented the best case that I've ever heard, on the bench or off of it.

Now, we've had sixteen days of trial, and so it shouldn't surprise anybody that I have found that there are irreconcilable differences which have arisen and have caused the irremediable breakdown of the marriage relation, and I'm therefore going to decree the dissolution of the marriage.

Now, the thing that you are all concerned with has to do with what's going to happen to Jason. Of the . . . factors mentioned in the relevant case law, I found that really only two are relevant here, the others either don't apply or they weigh equally on both parties, obviously. The two things that I think that we have questions about are number one . . . the moral, emotional, and physical fitness of the parties; and the second one that applies here is the desirability of continuing an existing relationship and environment.

I find some substantial changes in circumstances from the hearing [I held in January to make a temporary decision on custody.] I now find that Diane is not suicidal. I was not convinced of this in January, and that played a large part in my judgment at that point. I find that Diane is now much improved physically and mentally. In January, I didn't feel that she was quite ready for the possibility of full-time care. Now, if she is given custody, she would be able to handle it.

Diane is now viewed as a psychological parent to some degree. This was certainly not true in January. And I've found that she has now proven that she can take care of the child. In January I felt I was taking a justifiable risk, nonetheless, in allowing the frequent visitation, or at least more frequent and different kind of visitation than had been the case previously. She's now demonstrated her ability to care for Jason: in short, my reason for awarding Steve temporary custody in January was that Steve was able to care for Jason, and I felt that Diane was not. I now find that they are both fit physically and mentally to care for Jason.

Now the testimony from January and from June, taken together, has convinced me that Diane had a passive-dependent personality disorder, which, when combined with what some people have described as a demeaning husband, meddling in-laws, and parents trying to push independence on her, created a situation where she, in her depressed state, jumped from that eighth-story window. I believe that she was mentally ill at the time she was attempting suicide. I think her depression can best be described as a reaction to the situation in which she found herself. I think she's now free of that situation; I'm mindful that she meets some of the criteria for potential future suicides; however, it's now clear to me that these factors only consider past events and do not consider the person as we find her today. The mere fact that renowned psychiatrists have appeared here in this case, that those psychiatrists, even in the sub-speciality of suicidology, have disagreed as to her potential, should be enough to bring us back to more of a human consideration. I find she is not now suicidal, and not likely to be a significant risk in the future.

To the . . . factors of moral, emotional, and physical fitness, I've added, as you have seen, kind of a special consideration for this case, of mental fitness to care for the child. They're both, of course, morally fit to care for Jason. I will return to the relative emotional fitness of the parties, as it appears, and to the best interests of Jason, but first I want to talk about continuity of care. A great deal has been made of this during this trial, and rightfully so. We have all been subjected to a good deal of testimony concerning continuity of care and how it applies here. Does it apply in favor of Steve because he has had the major custody the past year and a half? Or does it apply toward Diane because she would have more time to give to Jason in the future? Or does it mean I should favor Steve because he's viewed as a primary psychological parent? Or should I go in favor of Diane because she will be here in Jason's home area with continued contact with her, her parents, Steve's parents, and Jason's playmates?

Now, I've read and reviewed all of the testimony from both hearings concerning continuity of care, and I find that both parents have valid and favorable and reasonable claims which would favor them in that consideration. I guess I gave a slight edge to Diane here, as I feel she would be continually available, and on a long-term basis. Mr. Fisk's suggestion that medicine is a consuming mistress has some merit here.

I would like finally, then, to return to the emotional factors mentioned previously. This is possibly the most difficult for me to verbalize in this case. Diane is still a bit immature, and certainly tending to excessive sarcasm, though I noticed this much less now than I did in January. Steve has progressed much faster academically than socially and emotionally. It's obvious to me that he is able to apply himself to the science of medicine and do superior work.

So, I come now to the part that's difficult to, for me, to really put into words. I'm going to give my impressions, because I think it's important for you all to know the basis for my judgments in this particular area. I have heard a great deal about Steve Rose from him and a great many witnesses, but I've also had the opportunity to watch him on the witness stand here, and down there at counsel table, for almost sixteen days now. It appears to me that he's a very demeaning person; he's prone to criticize and quick to demonstrate some kind of intellectual superiority. I got the impression that he felt that he was smarter than a good many of the experts who testified here. And in considering the emotional makeup of the parties, the things they will pass on to their child, and in subtle ways, I have given a large preference here to Diane.

Accordingly, I find that the best interests of Jason lie in his care, custody, and control by Diane Rose, subject to the reasonable and seasonable visitation by his father. I will enter an order requiring the petitioner to contribute $150 per month to the support of Jason. Further, the Court will make no award of alimony, attorneys' fees, or costs to either party. I feel that each party is able to handle these from existing assets or resources. Counsel are requested to discuss the transfer of custody and provisions for visitation, and report to me as soon as you've either agreed or find that you can't reach an agreement. And if there are any matters that I've not ruled on that I should, or any matters upon which you are unclear, I'll be able to talk with you about that today, also, or at any other time. I'll be on a jury trial, but I'll have some recesses, and I'll be glad to take up any of these matters at that time.

NOTE

If you were Steve Rose's attorney, on what grounds would you argue for reversal on appeal?

3. THE APPEALS COURT DECIDES

■ THORNTON, J.

Husband appeals from that portion of a dissolution of marriage decree which awarded custody of the couple's only child, a two and one-half year old boy, to the wife.

Husband alleges error on two bases. First, that the trial court erred in not awarding him custody since he, contends husband, is the sole psychological parent of the child, the mother having little contact with the child since her unsuccessful suicide attempt of January 1994. Secondly, that the wife should not have been awarded custody because of her suicidal tendencies and because of the brain damage incurred in the suicide attempt.

The trial lasted sixteen days and the record contains nearly 2,500 pages of testimony. Both the husband and the wife called an imposing array of expert witnesses to the stand to testify on behalf of each party. They could agree on very little. Additionally, there was a tremendous amount of lay testimony regarding the conduct of each party and the fitness of each for custody. This testimony, too, was in hopeless conflict.

Considering the first basis, we do not agree that the husband is the sole psychological parent; both the husband and wife are psychological parents. The record reveals that even while in the hospital recovering from her attempted suicide the wife remained in frequent contact with her child. And after her release from the hospital in June of 1994 we find that she has spent a great deal of time with her son. At all times she has remained a psychological parent.

After reviewing all the medical testimony we agree with the trial judge that the wife is not now or prospectively suicidal and that she is a fit person, both physically and psychologically, to be awarded custody. Regarding the question of her possible brain damage, we conclude that she has no significant damage.

Where, as here, the issues are ones of fact and the testimony conflicts, the believability of the witnesses becomes crucial and the decision of the trial court must be given great weight.

Having considered the entire record de novo, we believe that the trial court reached the correct result.

Affirmed. Costs to respondent-wife.

NOTE

Consider the assessment of Judge Sangster set forth in JOSEPH GOLDSTEIN, ANNA FREUD, ALBERT SOLNIT, & SONJA GOLDSTEIN, IN THE BEST INTERESTS OF THE CHILD 23–26 (1986):

> The judge assumed a professional role for which he was not qualified. He acted as a psychologist by using his own courtroom observations to determine the emotional makeup of Steven and Diane. As a judge he was authorized to take into account his personal observations of the witnesses' behavior on the stand for purposes of evaluating the veracity of their testimony. Here, however, he used these observations not for such an authorized purpose but to assess the emotional and social maturity of two adults. He assumed the role of expert in child development by relating his findings about "the emotional makeup of the parties" to "the things they will pass on to their child ... in subtle ways." Presumably deciding that Steven would "pass on" detrimental traits to Jason, he

gave "a large preference" to Diane as the better parent. He reached this conclusion despite guidance from statutory and case law that "continuing an existing relationship and environment" is usually in the child's best interest and despite uncontroverted expert evidence that Jason had thrived in Steven's custody.

. . .

Had the judge in the Rose case realized that he was about to venture beyond what ordinary knowledge, his own training, the statutory guides or the testimony of the experts in the case qualified him to do, he might have acted differently. He might have asked counsel for both parties to present evidence on whether Steven's personality would be harmful to Jason's development and, if so, whether that harm would be greater than the harm that would result from uprooting the child and disrupting his relationship with his father. But the judge made his finding without explicitly posing such questions. He thus denied himself the opportunity to learn from experts that they cannot make subtle comparisons between two fit parents and that they are unable to assess the relevance of a parent's "arrogance" or "immaturity" to a child's future well-being.

C. APPLYING THE BEST INTEREST STANDARD

1. FITNESS

In re Marriage of Carney

Supreme Court of California, 1979.
598 P.2d 36.

■ MOSK, J., for a unanimous court.

Appellant father (William) appeals from that portion of an interlocutory decree of dissolution which transfers custody of the two minor children of the marriage from himself to respondent mother (Ellen).

In this case of first impression we are called upon to resolve an apparent conflict between two strong public policies: the requirement that a custody award serve the best interests of the child, and the moral and legal obligation of society to respect the civil rights of its physically handicapped members, including their right not to be deprived of their children because of their disability. As will appear, we hold that upon a realistic appraisal of the present-day capabilities of the physically handicapped, these policies can both be accommodated. The trial court herein failed to make such an appraisal, and instead premised its ruling on outdated stereotypes of both the parental role and the ability of the handicapped to fill that role. Such stereotypes have no place in our law. Accordingly, the order changing custody on this ground must be set aside as an abuse of discretion.

William and Ellen were married in New York in December 1968. Both were teenagers. Two sons were soon born of the union, the first in November 1969 and the second in January 1971. The parties separated shortly afterwards, and by written agreement executed in November 1972 Ellen relinquished custody of the boys to William. For reasons of employment he eventually moved to the West Coast. In September 1973 he began living with a young woman named Lori Rivera, and she acted as stepmother to the boys. In the following year William had a daughter by Lori, and she proceeded to raise all three children as their own.

In August 1976, while serving in the military reserve, William was injured in a jeep accident. The accident left him a quadriplegic, i.e., with paralyzed legs and impaired use of his arms and hands. He spent the next year recuperating in a veterans' hospital; his children visited him several times each week, and he came home nearly every weekend.[1] He also bought a van, and it was being fitted with a wheelchair lift and hand controls to permit him to drive.

In May 1977, William filed the present action for dissolution of his marriage. Ellen moved for an order awarding her immediate custody of both boys. It was undisputed that from the date of separation (Nov. 1972) until a few days before the hearing (Aug. 1977) Ellen did not once visit her young sons or make any contribution to their support. Throughout this period of almost five years her sole contact with the boys consisted of some telephone calls and a few letters and packages. Nevertheless the court ordered that the boys be taken from the custody of their father, and that Ellen be allowed to remove them forthwith to New York State.[2] Pursuant to stipulation of the parties, an interlocutory judgment of dissolution was entered at the same time. William appeals from that portion of the decree transferring custody of the children to Ellen.

William contends the trial court abused its discretion in making the award of custody. Several principles are here applicable. First, since it was amended in 1972, the Code no longer requires or permits the trial courts to favor the mother in determining proper custody of a child "of tender years." Civil Code section 4600 now declares that custody should be awarded "To either parent according to the best interests of the child." Regardless of the age of the minor, therefore, fathers now have equal custody rights with mothers; the sole concern, as it should be, is "the best interests of the child."

Next, those "best interests" are at issue here in a special way: this is not the usual case in which the parents have just separated and the choice of custody is being made for the first time. In such instances the trial court rightly has a broad discretion. Here, although this is the first actual court order on the issue, we deal in effect with a complete *change* in custody: after the children had lived with William for almost five years—virtually all their lives up to that point—Ellen sought to remove them abruptly from the only home they could remember to a wholly new environment some 3,000 miles away.

It is settled that to justify ordering a change in custody there must generally be a persuasive showing of changed circumstances affecting the child. And that change must be substantial: a child will not be removed from the prior custody of one parent and given to the other "unless the material facts and circumstances occurring subsequently are of a kind to render it essential or expedient for the welfare of the child that there be a change." The reasons for the rule are clear: "It is well established that the courts are reluctant to order a change of custody and will not do so except for imperative reasons; that it is desirable that there be an end of litigation and undesirable to change the child's established mode of living."

Moreover, although a request for a change of custody is also addressed in the first instance to the sound discretion of the trial judge, he must

---

1. He was scheduled to be discharged shortly after the trial proceedings herein.

2. The court also imposed substantial financial obligations on William. He was ordered to pay all future costs of transporting his sons back to California to visit him, plus $400 a month for child support, $1,000 for Ellen's attorney's fees, $800 for her travel and hotel expenses, and $750 for her court costs.

exercise that discretion in light of the important policy considerations just mentioned. For this reason appellate courts have been less reluctant to find an abuse of discretion when custody is changed than when it is originally awarded, and reversals of such orders have not been uncommon.

Finally, the burden of showing a sufficient change in circumstances is on the party seeking the change of custody. In attempting to carry that burden Ellen relied on several items of testimony given at the hearing; even when these circumstances are viewed in their totality, however, they are insufficient for the purpose.

First, Ellen showed that although she had been unemployed when William was given custody in 1972, at the time of trial she had a job as a medical records clerk in a New York hospital. But her gross income from that job was barely $500 per month, and she admitted she would not be able to support the boys without substantial financial assistance from William. By contrast, at the time of the hearing William's monthly income from a combination of veteran's disability compensation payments and social security benefits had risen to more than $1,750 per month, all tax-free.

Ellen next pointed to the fact that William's relationship with Lori might be in the process of terminating. From this evidence Ellen argued that if Lori were to leave, William would have to hire a baby-sitter to take care of the children. On cross-examination, however, Ellen admitted that if custody were transferred to her she would likewise be compelled because of her job to place the children "in a child care center under a baby-sitter nine hours a day," and she intended to do so. During that period, of course, the children would not be under her supervision; by contrast, William explained that because he is not employed he is able to remain at home "to see to their upbringing during the day as well as the night."

Additional claims lacked support in the record. Thus Ellen impliedly criticized William's living arrangements for the boys, and testified that if she were given custody she intended to move out of her one-bedroom apartment into an apartment with "at least" two bedrooms. Yet it was undisputed that the boys were presently residing in a private house containing in effect four bedrooms, with a large living room and a spacious enclosed back yard; despite additional residents, there was no showing that the accommodations were inadequate for the family's needs. Ellen further stated that in her opinion the older boy should be seen by a dentist; there was no expert testimony to this effect, however, and no evidence that the child was not receiving normal dental care. She also remarked that the younger boy seemed to have a problem with wetting his bed but had not been taken to a doctor about it; again there was no evidence that medical intervention in this matter was either necessary or desirable. We obviously cannot take judicial notice of the cause of, or currently recommended cure for, childhood enuresis.

In short, if the trial court had based its change of custody order on the foregoing circumstances alone, it would in effect have revived the "mother's preference" rule abrogated by the Legislature in 1972. The record discloses, however, that the court gave great weight to another factor—William's physical handicap and its presumed adverse effect on his capacity to be a good father to the boys. Whether that factor will support the reliance placed upon it is a difficult question to which we now turn.

Ellen first raised the issue in her declaration accompanying her request for a change of custody, asserting that because of William's handicap "it is almost impossible for [him] to actually care for the minor children," and "since [he] is confined to a hospital bed, he is never with the minor children and thus can no longer effectively care for the minor children or see to their physical and emotional needs." When asked at the hearing why she believed she should be given custody, she replied *inter alia*, "Bill's physical condition." Thereafter she testified that according to her observations William is not capable of feeding himself or helping the boys prepare meals or get dressed; and she summed up by agreeing that he is not able to do "anything" for himself.

The trial judge echoed this line of reasoning throughout the proceedings. Virtually the only questions he asked of any witness revolved around William's handicap and its physical consequences, real or imagined. Thus although William testified at length about his present family life and his future plans, the judge inquired only where he sat when he got out of his wheelchair, whether he had lost the use of his arms, and what his medical prognosis was. Again, when Lori took the stand and testified to William's good relationship with his boys and their various activities together, the judge interrupted to ask her in detail whether it was true that she had to bathe, dress, undress, cook for and feed William. Indeed, he seemed interested in little else.

The final witness was Dr. Jack Share, a licensed clinical psychologist specializing in child development, who had visited William's home and studied his family. Dr. Share testified that William had an IQ of 127, was a man of superior intelligence, excellent judgment and ability to plan, and had adapted well to his handicap. He observed good interaction between William and his boys, and described the latter as self-disciplined, sociable, and outgoing. On the basis of his tests and observations, Dr. Share gave as his professional opinion that neither of the children appeared threatened by William's physical condition; the condition did not in any way hinder William's ability to be a father to them, and would not be a detriment to them if they remained in his home; the present family situation in his home was a healthy environment for the children; and even if Lori were to leave, William could still fulfill his functions as father with appropriate domestic help.

Ellen made no effort on cross-examination to dispute any of the foregoing observations or conclusions, and offered no expert testimony to the contrary. The judge then took up the questioning, however, and focused on what appears to have been one of his main concerns in the case—i.e., that because of the handicap William would not be able to participate with his sons in sports and other physical activities. Thus the court asked Dr. Share, "It's very unfortunate that he's in this condition, but when these boys get another two, three years older, would it be better, in your opinion, if they had a parent that was able to actively go places with them, take them places, play Little League baseball, go fishing? Wouldn't that be advantageous to two young boys?" Dr. Share replied that "the commitment, the long-range planning, the dedication" of William to his sons were more important, and stated that from his observations William was "the more consistent, stable part of this family regardless of his physical condition at this point." The judge nevertheless persisted in stressing that William "is limited in what he can do for the boys," and demanded an answer to his question as to "the other activities that two growing boys should have with a natural parent." Dr. Share acknowledged William's obvious physical limitations, but once more asserted that "On the side dealing with what I have called the stability of the youngsters, which I put personally higher value on, I would say the father is very strong in this area." Finally, when asked on redirect examination what effect William's ability to drive will have, Dr. Share explained, "this opens up more vistas, greater alternatives when he's more mobile such as having his own van to take them places. . . ."

We need not speculate on the reasons for the judge's ensuing decision to order the change of custody, as he candidly stated them for the record. First he distinguished a case cited by William, emphasizing "There was no father there or mother that was unable to care for the children because of physical disabilities. . . ." Next he found William and Ellen to be "both good, loving parents," although he strongly chided the latter for failing to visit her sons for five years, saying "She should have crawled on her hands and knees out here if she had to to get the children. . . ." The judge then returned to the theme of William's physical inability to personally take care of the children: speculating on Lori's departure, the judge stressed that in such event "a housekeeper or a nursery" would have to be hired—overlooking the admitted fact that Ellen would be compelled to do exactly the same herself for nine hours a day. And he further assumed "There would have to be pick up and probably delivery of the children even though [William] drives his van"—a non sequitur revealing his misunderstanding of the purpose and capabilities of that vehicle.

More importantly, the judge conceded that Dr. Share "saw a nice, loving relationship, and that's absolutely true. There's a great relationship between [William] and the boys. . . ." Yet despite this relationship the judge concluded "I think it would be detrimental to the boys to grow up until age 18 in the custody of their father. *It wouldn't be a normal relationship between father and boys.*" And what he meant by "normal" was quickly revealed: "It's unfortunate [William] has to have help bathing and dressing and undressing. *He can't do anything for the boys himself except maybe talk to them and teach them, be a tutor, which is good, but it's not enough.* I feel that it's in the best interests of the two boys to be with the mother even though she hasn't had them for five years." (Italics added).

Such a record approaches perilously close to the showing in *Adoption of Richardson*, 59 Cal. Rptr. 323 (Cal. Ct. App. 1967). There the trial court denied a petition to adopt an infant boy because of the physical handicap of the proposed adoptive parents, who were deaf-mutes. As here, professional opinions were introduced—and remained uncontradicted—stating that the petitioners had adjusted well to their handicap and had a good relationship with the child, and that their disability would have no adverse effects on his physical or emotional development. Nevertheless, in language strangely similar to that of the judge herein, the trial court reasoned: "Is this a normally happy home? There is no question about it, it is a happy home, but is it a normal home? I don't think the Court could make a finding that it is a normal home when these poor unfortunate people, they are handicapped, and what can they do in the way of bringing this child up to be the type of citizen we all want him to be." The Court of Appeal there concluded from this and other evidence that the trial judge was prejudiced by a belief that no deaf-mute could ever be a good parent to a "normal" child. While recognizing the rule that the granting or denial of a petition for adoption rests in the discretion of the judge, the appellate court held that such discretion had been abused and accordingly reversed the judgment.

While it is clear the judge herein did not have the totally closed mind exhibited in *Richardson*, it is equally plain that his judgment was affected by serious misconceptions as to the importance of the involvement of parents in the purely physical aspects of their children's lives. We do not mean, of course, that the health or physical condition of the parents may not be taken into account in determining whose custody would best serve the child's interests. In relation to the issues at stake, however, this factor is ordinarily of minor importance; and whenever it is raised—whether in awarding custody originally or changing it later—it is essential that the court weigh the matter with an informed and open mind.

In particular, if a person has a physical handicap it is impermissible for the court simply to rely on that condition as prima facie evidence of the person's unfitness as a parent or of probable detriment to the child; rather, in all cases the court must view the handicapped person as an individual and the family as a whole. To achieve this, the court should inquire into the person's actual and potential physical capabilities, learn how he or she has adapted to the disability and manages its problems, consider how the other members of the household have adjusted thereto, and take into account the special contributions the person may make to the family despite—or even because of—the handicap. Weighing these and all other relevant factors together, the court should then carefully determine whether the parent's condition will in fact have a substantial and lasting adverse effect on the best interests of the child.

The record shows the contrary occurred in the case at bar. To begin with, the court's belief that there could be no "normal relationship between father and boys" unless William engaged in vigorous sporting activities with his sons is a further example of the conventional sex-stereotypical thinking that we condemned in another context in *Sail'er Inn v. Kirby*, 485 P.2d 529 (Cal. 1971).... For some, the court's emphasis on the importance of a father's "playing baseball" or "going fishing" with his sons may evoke nostalgic memories of a Norman Rockwell cover on the old Saturday Evening Post. But it has at last been understood that a boy need not prove his masculinity on the playing fields of Eton, nor must a man compete with his son in athletics in order to be a good father: their relationship is no less "normal" if it is built on shared experiences in such fields of interest as science, music, arts and crafts, history or travel, or in pursuing such classic hobbies as stamp or coin collecting. In short, an afternoon that a father and son spend together at a museum or the zoo is surely no less enriching than an equivalent amount of time spent catching either balls or fish.

Even more damaging is the fact that the court's preconception herein, wholly apart from its outdated presumption of proper gender roles, also stereotypes William as a person deemed forever unable to be a good parent simply because he is physically handicapped. Like most stereotypes, this is both false and demeaning. On one level it is false because it assumes that William will never make any significant recovery from his disability. There was no evidence whatever to this effect. On the contrary, it did appear that the hearing was being held only one year after the accident, that William had not yet begun the process of rehabilitation in a home environment, and that he was still a young man in his twenties. In these circumstances the court could not presume that modern medicine, helped by time, patience, and determination, would be powerless to restore at least some of William's former capabilities for active life.

Even if William's prognosis were poor, however, the stereotype indulged in by the court is false for an additional reason: it mistakenly assumes that the parent's handicap inevitably handicaps the child. But children are more adaptable than the court gives them credit for; if one path to their enjoyment of physical activities is closed, they will soon find another. Indeed, having a handicapped parent often stimulates the growth of a child's imagination, independence, and self-reliance. Today's urban youngster, moreover, has many more opportunities for formal and informal instruction than his isolated rural predecessor. It is true that William may not be able to play tennis or swim, ride a bicycle or do gymnastics; but it does not follow that his children cannot learn and enjoy such skills, with the guidance not only of family and friends but also the professional instructors available through schools, church groups, playgrounds, camps, the Red Cross, the YMCA, the Boy Scouts, and numerous service organizations. As Dr. Share pointed out in his testimony, ample community resources now supplement the home in these circumstances.

In addition, it is erroneous to presume that a parent in a wheelchair cannot share to a meaningful degree in the physical activities of his child, should both desire it. On the one hand, modern technology has made the handicapped increasingly mobile, as demonstrated by William's purchase of a van and his plans to drive it by means of hand controls. In the past decade the widespread availability of such vans, together with sophisticated and reliable wheelchair lifts and driving control systems, have brought about a quiet revolution in the mobility of the severely handicapped. No longer are they confined to home or institution, unable to travel except by special vehicle or with the assistance of others; today such persons use the streets and highways in ever-growing numbers for both business and pleasure. Again as Dr. Share explained, the capacity to drive such a vehicle "opens more vistas, greater alternatives" for the handicapped person.

. . .

[A]lthough William cannot actually play on his children's baseball team, he may nevertheless be able to take them to the game, participate as a fan, a coach, or even an umpire—and treat them to ice cream on the way home. Nor is this companionship limited to athletic events: such a parent is no less capable of accompanying his children to theaters or libraries, shops or restaurants, schools or churches, afternoon picnics, or long vacation trips. Thus it is not true that, as the court herein assumed, William will be unable "to actively go places with [his children], take them places. . . ."

On a deeper level, finally, the stereotype is false because it fails to reach the heart of the parent-child relationship. Contemporary psychology confirms what wise families have perhaps always known—that the essence of parenting is not to be found in the harried rounds of daily carpooling endemic to modern suburban life, or even in the doggedly dutiful acts of "togetherness" committed every weekend by well-meaning fathers and mothers across America. Rather, its essence lies in the ethical, emotional, and intellectual guidance the parent gives to the child throughout his formative years, and often beyond. The source of this guidance is the adult's own experience of life; its motive power is parental love and concern for the child's well-being; and its teachings deal with such fundamental matters as the child's feelings about himself, his relationships with others, his system of values, his standards of conduct, and his goals and priorities in life. Even if it were true, as the court herein asserted, that William cannot do "anything" for his sons except "talk to them and teach them, be a tutor," that would not only be "enough"—contrary to the court's conclusion—it would be the most valuable service a parent can render. Yet his capacity to do so is entirely unrelated to his physical prowess: however limited his bodily strength may be, a handicapped parent is a whole person to the child who needs his affection, sympathy, and wisdom to deal with the problems of growing up.

Indeed, in such matters his handicap may well be an asset: few can pass through the crucible of a severe physical disability without learning enduring lessons in patience and tolerance.

No expert testimony was necessary to establish these facts. As the Court of Appeal correctly observed in a somewhat different context, "It requires no detailed discussion to demonstrate that the support and, even more, the control of the child is primarily a mental function to which soundness of mind is a crucial prerequisite. It is also well known that physical handicaps generally have no adverse effect upon mental functions. . . . It is also a matter of common knowledge that many persons with physical handicaps have demonstrated their ability to adequately support and control their children and to give them the benefits of stability and security through love and attention."

We agree, and conclude that a physical handicap that affects a parent's ability to participate with his children in purely physical activities is not a changed circumstance of sufficient relevance and materiality to render it either "essential or expedient" for their welfare that they be taken from his custody. This conclusion would be obvious if the handicap were heart dysfunction, emphysema, arthritis, hernia, or slipped disc; it should be no less obvious when it is the natural consequence of an impaired nervous system. Accordingly, pursuant to the authorities cited above the order changing the custody of the minor children herein from William to Ellen must be set aside as an abuse of discretion.

Both the state and federal governments now pursue the commendable goal of total integration of handicapped persons into the mainstream of society: the Legislature declares that "It is the policy of this State to encourage and enable disabled persons to participate fully in the social and economic life of the state. . . ." Thus far these efforts have focused primarily on such critical areas as employment, housing, education, transportation, and public access. No less important to this policy is the integration of the handicapped into the responsibilities and satisfactions of family life, cornerstone of our social system. Yet as more and more physically disabled persons marry and bear or adopt children—or, as in the case at bar, previously nonhandicapped parents become disabled through accident or illness—custody disputes similar to that now before us may well recur. In discharging their admittedly difficult duty in such proceedings, the trial courts must avoid impairing or defeating the foregoing public policy. With the assistance of the considerations discussed herein, we are confident of their ability to do so.

. . .

The portion of the interlocutory decree of dissolution transferring custody of appellant's minor children to respondent is reversed.

NOTES

1. When the case was retried, the father was awarded custody of the children. Telephone conversation with Lawrence Buchanan, attorney for Ellen Carney (Mar. 18, 1985).

2. If the case had involved an initial award of custody rather than a request to modify an existing award, would the result have been the same?

2. WEIGHING MULTIPLE FACTORS

Hollon v. Hollon

Supreme Court of Mississippi, 2001.
784 So. 2d 943.

■ DIAZ, JUSTICE.

This matter arises from a divorce action decided by the Chancery Court of Jackson County, wherein Timothy Paul Hollon (Tim) and Dorothy Elisabeth Hollon (Beth) were granted a divorce on the grounds of irreconcilable differences. The only disputed issues argued before the trial court involved child custody, child support, and the assessment of court costs....

On December 20, 1999, a final judgment *nunc pro tunc* was entered granting Tim and Beth a divorce. The chancellor also granted Tim custody of Zach, but reserved visitation rights for Beth.... Beth appeals the chancellor's decision to award custody of their son to Tim....

Tim and Beth were married on April 9, 1994, in Jackson, County, Mississippi. During the course of the marriage, Zachary Thomas Hollon was born on July, 16, 1996. In addition to Zach, Tyler Watson, Beth's child from a previous marriage lived with Tim and Beth. The family resided in Bonaparte Square Apartment complex in Pascagoula, where Beth served as the on-site manager. The apartment complex owners provided Beth and Tim with a rent-free apartment as part of her compensation package. Tim served the City of Moss Point as a police officer.

Soon after Zach's birth, Tim and Beth's marriage began to deteriorate. They separated in January of 1997, for approximately eight weeks. After reconciling, their marriage again drifted into troubled waters leading to a second separation on January 11, 1998. Tim moved out of the marital apartment and into his parents' home, leaving Zach and Tyler in Beth's care. In an effort to alleviate the financial strain placed upon her during her separation, Beth took in a roommate, Beth Dukes (Dukes). Prior to this arrangement, Bonaparte Square Apartment complex also provided Dukes, an officer with the Pascagoula Police department, with a rent-free apartment in exchange for her service as a "courtesy officer." Dukes performed minimal security duties and fulfilled much of her obligation to the owners by simply serving as a police officer while residing at the apartment complex. Dukes lived with her son, Seth Holder, a child from her previous marriage.

[A]t the time, five people inhabited Beth's three-bedroom apartment; Beth and her two children, Tyler and Zach, as well as Dukes and her son Seth. Tyler, a teenager, was given his own bedroom, while Seth and Zach shared a bedroom as they were both under the age of five. Beth and Dukes shared the third bedroom.

At trial, Beth freely admitted that she and Dukes slept in the same bed. However, she vehemently denied any sexual relationship existed between her and Dukes, continually characterizing their relationship as platonic. Donna Mauldin, a friend of Beth's, testified that Beth told her that she and Dukes were engaged in a sexual relationship. Mauldin further testified that Beth wanted her to deny, if asked, that she ever admitted having a sexual relationship with Dukes. Mauldin refused to do so.

During the separation, while Beth and Dukes were sharing the apartment at Bonaparte Square, Tim heard the surfacing allegations surrounding Beth and Dukes' relationship. In order to investigate, Tim borrowed a key to the apartment, his former marital residence, from Donna Mauldin. While Beth and Dukes were away, Tim and Calvin Hutchins entered the apartment without permission and made a photographic record of things Tim felt were "inappropriate." These photographs and rumors led him to become concerned with "the environment that [Zach] would be raised in." Among other things, Tim took photographs of Dukes' clothing and police equipment in the shared bedroom, beer bottles in the refrigerator and wastebasket, liquor bottles on the counter, and one red light bulb in a ceiling fixture. These photographs were admitted into evidence over Beth's objection.

. . .

Tim and Beth each testified that the other was a good parent and had only Zach's best interests at heart. Both testified that their parents would serve as supplemental care givers to Zach when they were at work or unable to fulfill their parental obligations. Tim admitted that the only problem he had with Beth retaining permanent custody of Zach was his belief that she engaged in homosexual activity.

Tim lives with his parents in their four-bedroom house and pays them fifty dollars a month in rent. During the trial, Beth moved out of the apartment complex with her two children and into her parents' five-bedroom house. She initiated this move during the break in the trial because she felt the judge disapproved of her living situation. Beth's plan to reside with her parents is temporary. She and Tyler will move into a newly remodeled three bedroom house provided, in part, by her new job as the rental property manager for R.J. Homes. Beth no longer lives with Dukes and her son, although they remain friends.

Our familiar standard holds that, absent an abuse of discretion, we will uphold the decision of the chancellor. . . .

. . .

The polestar consideration in child custody cases is the best interest and welfare of the child. *Albright* v. *Albright*, 437 So. 2d 1003, 1005 (Miss. 1983). The *Albright* factors used to determine what is, in fact, in the "best interests" of a child in regard to custody are as follows: 1) age, health and sex of the child; 2) determination of the parent that had the continuity of care prior to the separation; 3) which has the best parenting skills and which has the willingness and capacity to provide primary child care; 4) the employment of the parent and responsibilities of that employment; 5) physical and mental health and age of the parents; 6) emotional ties of parent and child; 7) moral fitness of parents; 8) the home, school and community record of the child; 9) the preference of the child at the age sufficient to express a preference by law; 10) stability of home environment and employment of each parent; and 11) other factors relevant to the parent-child relationship. It should further be noted that marital fault should not be used as a sanction in custody awards, nor should differences in religion, personal values and lifestyles be the sole basis for custody decisions.

In order to determine whether or not the chancellor was manifestly wrong, clearly erroneous or abused his discretion in applying the *Albright* factors, we review the evidence and testimony presented at trial under each factor to ensure his ruling was supported by record.

1) The age, health and sex of the child

Although this Court has weakened the "tender years" doctrine in recent years, there is still a presumption that a mother is generally better suited to raise a young child. Chancellor Watts began his analysis of the case with the statement that the child was barely three years old at the time the trial ended. He pointed out that the tender years doctrine had been weakened and found Zach to be a healthy male child, with no physical or mental impairments who could be cared for equally well by both parties. The chancellor did not explicitly say that this factor favored one party over another. This factor favors Beth because the legal presumption, although weakened, still favors the mother to raise a very small child.

2) The determination of which parent had continuous care of the child prior to the separation

Chancellor Watts was mindful of the fact that since the parties separated, the mother retained primary care of the child, with the father retaining visitation privileges. The chancellor failed to note that Tim did not have custody of Zach during the previous separation, nor express any interest in becoming the custodial parent until the allegations of homosexuality arose. The chancellor did not point out that Tim rarely exercised his visitation rights, nor did he make a specific finding that this favored one parent over the other. Clearly, this factor weighs in favor of Beth.

3) The determination of which parent has the best parenting skills as well as the willingness and capacity to provide primary child care

[T]he chancellor found that

[B]oth parties cared equally for the child prior to their separation, and that both parties are found to have contributed equally to the continuity of care of the child prior to their separation.... [T]he Court finds that either party—that neither parties [sic] parenting skills, willingness and capacity to take care of the child, is greater than the other.

This finding is not entirely supported by Tim's testimony and is directly contradicted by Beth's testimony. Tim admitted that he had not paid his child support obligations regularly, forcing Beth to garnish his wages. He also admitted not visiting Zach for approximately two months during the final separation. Beth further testified that Tim failed to pay any child support for Zach for four months during the separation.

Prior to the separation, Beth testified that she had the primary responsibility of caring for her two children. She estimated that she provided approximately ninety percent of the direct care for Zach, such as changing, feeding, and supervising him, as well as doing laundry and other housework. Beth shared cooking duties with Tim. Tim testified that he helped change and feed Zach, but qualified his testimony adding that he provided said care in the evenings or on his days off. Tim's work schedule prohibits consistent, in-depth care of the child.

The chancellor found that neither parent held an advantage over the other here. From the entirety of the record, it is clear that Beth provided primary child care and if from familiarity or practice alone, holds an advantage over Tim in this area.

4) The employment of the parent and responsibilities of that employment

[A]lthough [the chancellor] did not cite a preference for either parent in the record, it is obvious that Beth's working situation is far more conducive to caring for a young child. Tim serves the public as a police officer and thus logs eighty-four hours on duty during his two-week shift. The schedule follows a two days on, two days off, three days on, two days off, two days on, three days off pattern with Tim on duty twelve hours each working day, rotating from a day shift to a night shift every twenty-eight days.

Beth works approximately thirty-five hours a week as a rental property manager in an office environment. Her position requires her to work only during the day, never on weekends and never during the holidays. This is in stark contrast to the regimented schedule that Tim must adhere to, regardless of weekends, holidays, or the hour of the day. . . . Without question, this factor weighs heavily in Beth's favor.

5) The physical and mental health and age of the parents

[A]lthough not specifically stated by the trial judge, this factor balances equally between Beth and Tim.

6) The emotional ties of parent and child

[T]he trial court held that no testimony was presented that showed Zach exhibited a stronger attachment to one parent over the other. Despite this finding, the trial court noted that Zach has been in Beth's continual care throughout both separations and subsequent divorce proceedings. The trial court implied that this factor also balanced equally between Tim and Beth, again never specifying for the record who, if anyone, benefitted from this factor.

7) The moral fitness of the parents

The seventh factor, moral fitness, took the lion's share of the chancellor's attention and is essentially what Beth argues dealt the fatal blow to her attempt to retain custody of Zach. Chancellor Watts noted that neither parent attended church regularly, which was "disturbing to the Court to some degree". . . .

The chancellor then dove into the allegations of the homosexual affair. Chancellor Watts found Beth's testimony regarding this issue to be untrustworthy. In fact, because Beth's testimony denying her relationship with Dukes directly contradicted Donna Mauldin's testimony confirming it, he asked the District Attorney's office to consider conducting an investigation into whether or not Beth committed perjury by denying she had a homosexual relationship with Dukes. The chancellor further noted that he ought to have confidence that the custodial parent is a truthful, forthright person, and he stated that he lacked that confidence in Beth. Accordingly, he found that this factor weighed heavily in Tim's favor.

Chancellor Watts also noted that evidence of a homosexual relationship is not, per se, a basis to determine that child custody should be denied.[7] He then went on to rehash, in detail, all of the testimony regarding Beth's alleged sexual relationship with Dukes. This Court has held that:

> In divorce actions, as distinguished from proceedings for modification of custody, sexual misconduct on the part of the wife is not per se grounds for denial of custody. A husband may upon proof of his wife's adultery be granted an absolute divorce on that grounds and yet in the same case custody of the children may be awarded to the mother. Our cases well recognize that it may be in the best interest of a child to remain with its mother even though she may have been guilty of adultery.

Cheek v. Ricker, 431 So. 2d 1139, 1144–45 n. 3 (Miss. 1983).

. . .

---

7. This Court has held that it is of no consequence that a mother was having an affair with a woman rather than a man. Plaxico v. Michael, 735 So. 2d 1036, 1039–40 (Miss. 1999).

The trial court never found the mother unfit to care for Zach, and no evidence was presented regarding any detrimental effects the child may have suffered as a result of living with his mother. The chancellor failed to mention that Tim admitted drinking a couple of beers every other day, that he drank to the point of being under the influence in the past, and formerly gambled every other week, but had not gambled recently because he did not have the money to do so. Beth also admitted to drinking to the point of intoxication in the past, but admitted that she gambled only once every six months.

While this factor is as important as any other and should be given its due consideration, it appears that the allegations offered under this heading were far and away the most scrutinized among the evidence reviewed at trial.

. . .

10) The stability of home environment and employment of each parent

The chancellor found, after considering the stability of the home environment and employment of each parent, that this factor favored Tim. This reasoning is inexplicable. Beth's current employment situation, discussed above, is clearly more favorable to child-rearing than Tim's schedule.

By the time the second day of the trial arrived, both Tim and Beth lived with their parents, although Beth stated her intention to move into a house of her own. The trial court seemed to hold this relocation and change in employment against her, although a less than subtle warning offered by the chancellor was the sole reason that Beth initiated the change in living situations.

. . .

11) Other factors relevant to the parent-child relationship

[T]he trial judge noted that the pictures submitted as evidence portrayed a messy house with empty beer bottles on the counter. The court acknowledged that Tim admitted taking clothes out of the closet and rearranging them in the bedroom to take the picture, and that drinking is "done almost everyday by everyone." Again, no reference was made to Tim's admitted drinking.

After considering all of the evidence and weighing the enumerated factors, the trial judge found that it would be in the best interest of the child to be relocated to Tim's care. A cursory glance at the above analysis reveals that the evidence supports a finding that more factors weigh in favor of Beth than Tim. The chancellor found otherwise. While the chancellor did cover each ... factor, he rarely did anything but restate some of the pertinent evidence to be considered under each factor, only once or twice actually ruling that a factor favored one party over the other.

This Court has held that although it could not be said that the chancellor's conclusion regarding the application of the ... factors was so lacking in evidentiary support as to be manifest error, the absence of specific findings prevented affirming the lower court with the confidence. A similar situation presents itself today. While the chancellor analyzed the applicable factors, he did not do so with specificity, assigning very few to a particular parent. If ... one factor should not outweigh another, the chancellor erred by determining the case on the basis of Beth's moral fitness, when upon review, Beth clearly wound up with more factors weighing in her favor.

[I]t is clear from the record that the chancellor's defining consideration in determining custody of Zach centered on the allegations of Beth's homosexual affair. In doing so, the chancellor committed reversible error.

. . .

Within his analysis of the . . . factors, the chancellor abused his discretion by placing too much weight upon the "moral fitness" factor and ignoring the voluminous evidence presented under the remaining factors supporting Beth as the preferred custodial parent. Therefore, we reverse the decision of the Chancery Court of Jackson County and award Beth custody of Zach and remand the case for a determination of Tim's visitation rights and further proceedings not inconsistent with the dictates of this opinion.

3. RACE AND ETHNICITY

Palmore v. Sidoti

Supreme Court of the United States, 1984.
466 U.S. 429, 104 S.Ct. 1879, 80 L.Ed.2d 421.

■ CHIEF JUSTICE BURGER delivered the opinion of the Court.

We granted certiorari to review a judgment of a state court divesting a natural mother of the custody of her infant child because of her remarriage to a person of a different race.

When petitioner Linda Sidoti Palmore and respondent Anthony J. Sidoti, both Caucasians, were divorced in May 1980 in Florida, the mother was awarded custody of their three-year-old daughter.

In September 1981 the father sought custody of the child by filing a petition to modify the prior judgment because of changed conditions. The change was that the child's mother was then cohabiting with a Negro, Clarence Palmore, Jr., whom she married two months later. Additionally, the father made several allegations of instances in which the mother had not properly cared for the child.

After hearing testimony from both parties and considering a court counselor's investigative report, the court noted that the father had made allegations about the child's care, but the court made no findings with respect to these allegations. On the contrary, the court made a finding that "there is no issue as to either party's devotion to the child, adequacy of housing facilities, or respect[a]bility of the new spouse of either parent."

The court then addressed the recommendations of the court counselor, who had made an earlier report "in [another] case coming out of this circuit also involving the social consequences of an interracial marriage. *Niles v. Niles*, 299 So. 2d 162 (Fla. Dist. Ct. App. 1974)." From this vague reference to that earlier case, the court turned to the present case and noted the counselor's recommendation for a change in custody because "[t]he wife [petitioner] has chosen for herself and for her child, a life-style unacceptable to her father *and to society*.... The child ... is, or at school age will be, subject to environmental pressures not of choice."

The court then concluded that the best interests of the child would be served by awarding custody to the father. The court's rationale is contained in the following:

The father's evident resentment of the mother's choice of a black partner is not sufficient to wrest custody from the mother. It is of some significance, however, that the mother did see fit to bring a man into her home and carry on a sexual relationship with him without being married to him. Such action tended to place gratification of her own desires ahead of her concern for the child's future welfare. *This Court feels that despite the strides that have been made in bettering relations between the races in this country, it is inevitable that Melanie will, if allowed to remain in her present situation and attains school age and thus more vulnerable to peer pressures, suffer from the social stigmatization that is sure to come.*

. . .

The judgment of a state court determining or reviewing a child custody decision is not ordinarily a likely candidate for review by this Court. However, the court's opinion, after stating that the "father's evident resentment of the mother's choice of a black partner is not sufficient" to deprive her of custody, then turns to what it regarded as the damaging impact on the child from remaining in a racially-mixed household. This raises important federal concerns arising from the Constitution's commitment to eradicating discrimination based on race.

The Florida court did not focus directly on the parental qualifications of the natural mother or her present husband, or indeed on the father's qualifications to have custody of the child. The court found that "there is no issue as to either party's devotion to the child, adequacy of housing facilities, or respect[a]bility of the new spouse of either parent." This, taken with the absence of any negative finding as to the quality of the care provided by the mother, constitutes a rejection of any claim of petitioner's unfitness to continue the custody of her child.

The court correctly stated that the child's welfare was the controlling factor. But that court was entirely candid and made no effort to place its holding on any ground other than race. Taking the court's findings and rationale at face value, it is clear that the outcome would have been different had petitioner married a Caucasian male of similar respectability.

A core purpose of the Fourteenth Amendment was to do away with all governmentally-imposed[2] discrimination based on race. Classifying persons according to their race is more likely to reflect racial prejudice than legitimate public concerns; the race, not the person, dictates the category. Such classifications are subject to the most exacting scrutiny; to pass constitutional muster, they must be justified by a compelling governmental interest and must be "necessary . . . to the accomplishment" of its legitimate purpose, *McLaughlin v. Florida*, 379 U.S. 184, 196 (1964).

The State, of course, has a duty of the highest order to protect the interests of minor children, particularly those of tender years. In common with most states, Florida law mandates that custody determinations be made in the best interests of the children involved. FLA. STAT. § 61.13(2)(b)(1) (1983). The goal of granting custody based on the best interests of the child is indisputably a substantial governmental interest for purposes of the Equal Protection Clause.

It would ignore reality to suggest that racial and ethnic prejudices do not exist or that all manifestations of those prejudices have been eliminated. There is a risk that a child living with a step-parent of a different race may

---

2. The actions of state courts and judicial officers in their official capacity have long been held to be state action governed by the Fourteenth Amendment. Shelley v. Kraemer, 334 U.S. 1 (1948); *Ex parte* Virginia, 100 U.S. 339, 346–347 (1880).

be subject to a variety of pressures and stresses not present if the child were living with parents of the same racial or ethnic origin.

The question, however, is whether the reality of private biases and the possible injury they might inflict are permissible considerations for removal of an infant child from the custody of its natural mother. We have little difficulty concluding that they are not. The Constitution cannot control such prejudices but neither can it tolerate them. Private biases may be outside the reach of the law, but the law cannot, directly or indirectly, give them effect. "Public officials sworn to uphold the Constitution may not avoid a constitutional duty by bowing to the hypothetical effects of private racial prejudice that they assume to be both widely and deeply held." *Palmer v. Thompson*, 403 U.S. 217, 260–261 (1971) (White, J., dissenting).

This is by no means the first time that acknowledged racial prejudice has been invoked to justify racial classifications. In *Buchanan v. Warley*, 245 U.S. 60 (1917), for example, this Court invalidated a Kentucky law forbidding Negroes from buying homes in white neighborhoods.

> It is urged that this proposed segregation will promote the public peace by preventing race conflicts. Desirable as this is, and important as is the preservation of the public peace, this aim cannot be accomplished by laws or ordinances which deny rights created or protected by the Federal Constitution.

Id. at 81.

Whatever problems racially-mixed households may pose for children in 1984 can no more support a denial of constitutional rights than could the stresses that residential integration was thought to entail in 1917. The effects of racial prejudice, however real, cannot justify a racial classification removing an infant child from the custody of its natural mother found to be an appropriate person to have such custody.

The judgment of the District Court of Appeal is reversed.

NOTE

By the time the Supreme Court announced its decision, the father and his new wife had moved with Melanie to Texas. He immediately initiated proceedings in Texas to obtain custody. Noting that the Supreme Court did not direct a reinstatement of the original custody degree, the Florida Court of Appeals in 1985 upheld the decision of a Florida trial court to decline jurisdiction in favor of Texas. *Palmore v. Sidoti*, 472 So. 2d 843 (Fla. Dist. Ct. App. 1985). The court explained:

> The eight-year-old child appears to have had substantial upheavals of her life, and we find no compelling reason at this point to add a further upheaval. The record indicates that Melanie lived with both her parents until they separated when she was about two and one-half years old. She then lived with her mother for about two years until her father was awarded custody. After only two months with her father, Melanie was returned to her mother by court order. She stayed with her mother for about eight months, and then was ordered to her father's custody, where she has remained for about two and one-half years except for a ten-day visit with her mother in August 1984. We cannot disagree that it appears to be in the best interests of Melanie that she continue in the status quo at least for the time being. . . .

Id. at 846–47. What should a court do when a particular child's need for continuity of care conflicts with society's views about the proper use of race in child custody disputes?

Jones v. Jones

Supreme Court of South Dakota, 1996.
542 N.W.2d 119.

■ JOHNS, CIRCUIT JUDGE.

Dawn R. Jones (Dawn) appeals from a decree of divorce awarding custody of the parties' three minor children to Kevin Mark Jones (Kevin). Dawn also appeals the amount of rehabilitative alimony awarded. We affirm.

Dawn and Kevin Jones were married on March 11, 1989 in Britton, South Dakota. Kevin was thirty years old at time of trial and is an enrolled member of the Sisseton–Wahpeton Dakota Nation. He was adopted at age seven by Maurice and Dorothy Jones. Dawn was twenty-five years old at time of trial and is Caucasian. The parties have three children, Lyndra, Elias and Desiree. Lyndra was born to Dawn prior to her marriage to Kevin.[1] She was subsequently adopted by Kevin.

During the marriage, the parties resided in a trailer house on the farm of Kevin's parents. Kevin is a minority shareholder in and works for Penrhos Farms. Penrhos is a close family farm corporation, owned primarily by Kevin's father and his three uncles. The Jones are an extremely close-knit and supportive family. In fact, Kevin often takes the children to work with him, as this is a family tradition. However, farm safety is very important and is stressed by all members of the family.

Kevin works predominantly in construction and in the feeding of the cattle on the Penrhos farm. His net earnings for child support purposes are approximately $1,880.00 a month. During the marriage, Dawn was a home-maker for a time and also held various jobs. She is currently enrolled in a nursing program at the Sisseton–Wahpeton Community College.

Kevin is a recovering alcoholic who, while drinking, exhibited a behavior of violence towards Dawn and a somewhat casual indifference to the children. He has been sober since December 1992 and regularly attends and presents Alcoholics Anonymous meetings.[2] Dawn suffers from depression and low self-esteem but is seeking counseling at this time.

Deterioration of the marriage is attributed to Kevin's alcoholism, Dawn's depression, financial problems and a lack of communication. Both parties were granted a divorce based upon mental cruelty. They were also granted joint legal custody of the children with primary physical custody being awarded to Kevin.[3] The court awarded Dawn rehabilitative alimony to allow her to finish the nursing program. She was awarded the cost of two years tuition, $10,680.00, with a monthly payment of $445.00, to commence when she returns to school.

. . .

Dawn argues that the trial court awarded the children to Kevin for the principal reason that, as a Native American, he has suffered prejudice and will therefore be able to better deal with the needs of the children when they are discriminated against because, although they are biracial, they have Native American features. She contends that the trial court impermissibly

---

1. Lyndra's natural father is also of Native American descent.

2. The trial court stressed the importance of Kevin remaining alcohol-free in its decision to award him custody.

3. The trial court granted Kevin primary physical custody of the children during the pendency of the action after hearing the testimony of the parties.

considered the matter of race when determining the custody of the children and thereby violated her right to equal protection of the laws as found in Section One of the Fourteenth Amendment to the United States Constitution.

In support of her arguments, Dawn cites to the decision of the United States Supreme Court in *Palmore v. Sidoti*, 466 U.S. 429 (1984).... [In *Palmore*, the Court] recognized that, while the child may well experience prejudice because she lived in a biracial home and that her best interests might be served by a change of custody, "the effects of racial prejudice, however real, cannot justify a racial classification removing an infant child from the custody of its natural mother found to be an appropriate person to have such custody." The rationale for this holding was that although the Constitution cannot control racial and other ethnic prejudices, "neither can it tolerate them. Private biases may be outside the reach of the law, but the law cannot, directly or indirectly, give them effect."

Albeit the trial court did not cite to *Palmore* in either its memorandum opinion (which was incorporated into its findings and conclusions) or in the findings of fact and conclusions of law, the court was apparently aware of its holding and scrupulously honored it. The trial court wrote in the memorandum opinion:

> Plaintiff addressed the issue of racial discrimination and Native American culture in his testimony. He states that all three children would be discriminated against as Native Americans if they left Penrhos farm to live. He wants for them the same loving, non-discriminatory upbringing that he received as a child at Penrhos. Plaintiff also wants to continue to make the children aware of their culture and heritage and participate in Tribal functions.
>
> This is an example of the Plaintiff's concern for the totality of the upbringing of his children. However, this Court's determination of custody must be made on a racially neutral basis as far as concerning itself with the effects of any potential discrimination....

Also in finding number 27 of the findings of fact and conclusions of law prepared by Kevin's counsel, the trial court deleted the portion that stated that the children would be subject to discrimination if they were raised away from Penrhos Farms and handwrote that "custody determinations are to be made on a racially neutral basis." ...

While the trial court was not blind to the racial backgrounds of the children, we are satisfied that it did not impermissibly award custody on the basis of race. As noted, Kevin showed a sensitivity to the need for his children to be exposed to their ethnic heritage. All of us form our own personal identities, based in part, on our religious racial and cultural backgrounds. To say, as Dawn argues, that a court should never consider whether a parent is willing and able to expose to and educate children on their heritage, is to say that society is not interested in whether children ever learn who they are. *Palmore* does not require this, nor do the constitutions of the United States or the State of South Dakota. We hold that it is proper for a trial court, when determining the best interests of a child in the context of a custody dispute between parents, to consider the matter of race as it relates to a child's ethnic heritage and which parent is more prepared to expose the child to it.

Furthermore we refuse to second guess, as Dawn argues, the trial court's mental processes. The trial court said it decided custody on a racially neutral basis and we accept its statements as the record does not clearly impel us to do otherwise.

In summary, the trial court's decision is not clearly against the laws of this country or state. There was no abuse of discretion.

4.   Religion

Kendall v. Kendall

Supreme Judicial Court of Massachusetts, 1997.
687 N.E.2d 1228.

■ Lynch, Justice.

This appeal arises out of a judgment of divorce nisi issued on August 20, 1996. Jeffrey P. Kendall, the defendant, appeals from provisions of the divorce judgment and a temporary order issued after Barbara Zeitler Kendall, the plaintiff, filed a complaint against him in the Probate Court for contempt of the divorce judgment. The plaintiff also filed a cross appeal, requesting an award of attorney's fees and reversal of the joint custody order and disposition of the marital home. . . .

The parties professed to hold different religious beliefs when they were married in 1988, the plaintiff being Jewish, and the defendant, Catholic. The parties' fundamental religious differences would be unremarkable but for their controversial effect on their three minor children[4] caught in the crossfire generated by their parents. Before the parties were married, they discussed the religious upbringing of any children, and agreed that children would be raised in the Jewish faith.[5]

In 1991, the defendant became a member of the Boston Church of Christ, a fundamentalist Christian faith. The defendant believes in Jesus Christ and that those who do not accept the Boston Church of Christ faith are "damned to go to hell" where there will be "weeping and gnashing of teeth." The defendant testified that he would like his children to accept Jesus Christ and that he "will never stop trying to save his children."

The parties' divergent views polarized in 1994 when the plaintiff adopted Orthodox Judaism.[6] Ariel also began studying and adhering to principles of Orthodox Judaism. Soon after the parties' beliefs drifted to opposite doctrinal extremes, the plaintiff filed for divorce in November, 1994, based on an irretrievable breakdown of the marriage, pursuant to G.L. c. 208, § 1B.

At the outset the plaintiff sought to limit the children's exposure to the defendant's religion, and the defendant objected to any limitation on his ability to share his religious beliefs with the children. On October 18, 1995,

---

4.   The children are Ariel (born October 10, 1988) Moriah (born May 19, 1991), and Rebekah (born April 21, 1993).

5.   The majority of courts adhere to the view that predivorce agreements are unconstitutionally unenforceable. *See* C.P. Kindregan & M.L. Inker, Family Law and Practice § 20.5, at 647 (2d ed. 1996). We note, however, that the judge found the children had primary familiarity with the Jewish faith. The judge concluded the children had a "Jewish identity" based on evidence that: the parties were married in a traditional Jewish wedding ceremony; Ariel was circumcised in accordance with Jewish tradition; both Moriah and Rebekah had traditional Jewish naming ceremonies; the parties agreed the children would attend a Jewish school; and all three children are so enrolled.

6.   Orthodox Judaism is considered the most strictly doctrinal of the three Jewish movements (Reform, Conservative, and Orthodox).

the judge granted the plaintiff's request for the appointment of a guardian ad litem (GAL) to "address the inter-religious conflict between the parties in particular."

In *Felton v. Felton*, 418 N.E.2d 606 (1981), this court addressed the question of accommodating diverse religious practices of parents, living apart, in the upbringing of minor children. The court held that the over-riding goal in any such inquiry is to serve the best interests of the children even where "the attainment of that purpose . . . involve[s] some limitation of the liberties of one or other of the parents." *Id.* at 607.

The judge found it substantially damaging to the children to leave each parent free to expose the children, as he or she wishes, to his or her religion. The resulting judgment of divorce contained the following paragraphs:[9]

> 5.   *RESTRICTIONS UPON RELIGIOUS EXPOSURE:* Each parent shall be entitled to share his/her religious beliefs with the children with restrictions as follows: neither may indoctrinate the children in a manner which substantially promotes their . . . alienation from either parent or their rejection of either parent. The [defendant] shall not take the children to his church (whether to church services or Sunday School or church educational programs); nor engage them in prayer or bible study if it promotes rejection rather than acceptance, of their mother or their own Jewish self-identity. The [defendant] shall not share his religious beliefs with the children if those beliefs cause the children significant emotional distress or worry about their mother or about themselves. Thus, for example, [the defendant] may have pictures of Jesus Christ hanging on the walls of his residence, and that will not serve as any basis for restricting his visitation with his children. But, [the defendant] may not take the children to religious services where they receive the message that adults or children who do not accept Jesus Christ as their lord and savior are destined to burn in hell. By way of further example, [the defendant] may not shave off [Ariel's] payes. This provision shall not be construed so as to prevent [the defendant] from having the children with him at events involving family traditions at Christmas and Easter.
>
> In the event that there is a disagreement between the parents as to whether one or more of the children could be exposed to the religious belief(s) of [the defendant] *without* substantial negative impact upon their emotional health, the parents shall engage the services of Michael Goldberg, Ph.D., to act as G.A.L./ investigator/evaluator on such issues and disputes. . . . In the event that Dr. Goldberg is unable to serve in this capacity, then the parties shall agree upon an alternate child psychologist, or an alternate shall be selected by the Court. . . .
>
> 6.   *EXPLANATION TO CHILDREN.* Neither party shall initially discuss with the children the terms and conditions of this Judgment. Within two (2) days of the date of receipt of this Judgment, the Plaintiff shall contact the Court-appointed Guardian Ad Litem, Dr. Michael Goldberg, to arrange for a meeting with the children. Dr. Goldberg shall explain to the children, in a developmentally appropriate manner, the Court's decision, with the goal being to help the children understand that they are being raised in the way they are because the Court believes that it is

---

9. The judgment also ordered that the plaintiff retain sole physical custody of the children, and awarded the parties joint legal custody. . . .

in their best interest. It is intended by the Court that this intervention may help the children avoid blaming themselves.

The defendant argues in this appeal that the judge's findings did not demonstrate "substantial harm" to the children so as to warrant the limitations imposed on his liberty interest in educating his children in the tenets of his religion. He challenges both the judge's factual findings of harm and the legal conclusions based on that evidence.

. . .

The determinative issue is whether the harm found to exist in this case to be so substantial so as to warrant a limitation on the defendant's religious freedom. In *Felton v. Felton,* this court suggested that a "likely source [ ]" of proof of substantial harm "by implication" could be derived from testimony as to the child's general demeanor, attitude, school work, appetite, health or outlook. The court also opined that the "wholly uncorroborated testimony" of a parent was insufficient to demonstrate harm. By implication, the court suggested that a plaintiff should consult "church, school, medical or psychiatric authorities" to support a charge that a child has been harmed by exposure to the parent's religious beliefs. *Id.* Moreover, the court specifically recommended the appointment of "a qualified investigator whether called a guardian (or some other title) who would look into the facts, render a report, and be subject to examination by the parties." *Id.*

Other states have struggled to define what constitutes substantial harm. Very few have actually ruled that substantial harm had been demonstrated.

We adhere to the line of cases requiring clear evidence of substantial harm. Application of the strict requirements in those cases comports with the protections of religious freedoms historically preserved under the Massachusetts Constitution.

The harm found to exist in this case presents more than the generalized fears criticized in *Felton v. Felton, supra.* The judge afforded substantial weight to the GAL's report.[16] The judge considered the report so "comprehensive" that it should be considered in its entirety on any appellate review. Among the factors the judge cited to support her conclusion that substantial harm to the children had been demonstrated are the following findings:

20.   I find that, in early 1995, the [defendant] threatened to cut the fringe off Ariel's tzitzitz if he did not tuck it inside his pants. This greatly upset Ariel and the [plaintiff], and the [defendant] later apologized.

21.   I also find that, in the summer of 1995, the [defendant] cut off Ariel's payes. I do not find credible the [defendant's] explanation that he did so at Ariel's request.

. . .

24.   I find that the Boston Church of Christ services to which [the defendant] has taken his children have included teachings that those who do not accept the Boston Church of Christ faith are damned to go to hell where there will be "weeping and gnashing of teeth."

---

16. The GAL's report was based on interviews with the parents, the children, and the children's teachers, psychological tests, and observations of the children interacting with both parents.

25. I find that the oldest child, Ari, has drawn from the above teaching the conclusion that [the plaintiff] may go to hell, and that this causes him substantial worry and upset.

. . .

56. [The defendant's] behavior toward his children fosters negative and distorted images of the Jewish culture. . . . [The defendant] opposes his children being taught the history of the Holocaust. Further, [the defendant's] cutting off of Ari's religiously meaningful side burns (payes), and his threats to cut off his clothing fringes (tzitzitz) show that he does not refrain from inducing guilt in the child for having the beliefs that he does.

57. I find that Ari has a strong Jewish self-identity. I am persuaded by the report of the G.A.L. that Ari "clearly identified himself and his siblings as being Jewish and provided a rationale based on Jewish law for his belief that he is Jewish," and that the child's "behavior in which he ascribes his Jewish identity to Jewish law and theology is indicative of his attainment of a formal self-identification of himself as a Jew." Indeed, [the defendant] himself reluctantly concedes that if asked, Ari would unquestionably say he is Jewish.

58. [The defendant] understands that Ari perceives himself as Jewish, and that having a Jewish identity is akin to having an ethnic identity. But the matter goes further. Ari perceives his Jewishness as being part of his "soul." For Ari, efforts to convince him that his religion is wrong are logically equated with convincing him that his "soul" is damaged or inadequate. . . .

59. I credit the G.A.L.'s report and testimony that Ari "may experience choosing a religion as choosing between his parents, a task that is likely to cause him significant emotional distress." In fact, the G.A.L. specifically concludes, and I credit his conclusion, that the children are now in a position where they are perilously close to being forced to choose between their parents, and to reject one.

60. I find, based upon the G.A.L.'s report as well as his testimony, that the oldest child Ari ". . . is emotionally distressed by the conflict between his strong desire for affection and approval from [the defendant] and his desire to maintain his Jewish religious practice," and that as a direct result ". . . there has been a decline in his motivation and academic performance."

. . .

62. I find that Ari is understandably uncomfortable and unhappy when he "has to do the stuff [he's] not supposed to do on Shabbas," and that precisely as the G.A.L. indicates, Ari then has the no-win dilemma of pleasing and obeying [the defendant] (while displeasing and disobeying [the plaintiff] and his own internalized beliefs about how the world is "supposed" to function on the Sabbath) or the reverse. Poor Ari: he told [the defendant] that he "wants to celebrate the Sabbath and not do stuff that I'm not supposed to do," and [the defendant's] response was "we'll discuss that with the lawyers."

. . .

64. I credit the G.A.L.'s report that "Moriah is experiencing emotional distress related to the parental conflict. . . ." I find that Moriah has a

very solid understanding of who she is and who her family is: "I'm not Christian. I'm Jewish. Mom is Jewish. My dad is Christian. My brother is Jewish and my sister is Jewish." Moriah's straightforward description is comfortable and age-appropriate. More importantly, it is accurate. And most important of all, it shows that she can tolerate the knowledge of her parents' religious differences.

. . .

66.   I find, based upon the G.A.L.'s report that Rebekah is likely to experience "... a sense of not belonging in her own home" by "... anything that serves to promote her identity as fundamentally different from that of her mother and siblings." I find this would be substantially to her detriment.

67.   I credit the report of the G.A.L. that "should the children come to accept the religious beliefs that [the defendant] reports he wants them to accept, they are likely to come to view their mother negatively and as a person who will be punished for her sins ..." resulting in a "... negative impact on their relationship with their mother ... and difficulty accepting guidance and nurturance from her." I find this would be to the children's substantial detriment.

68.   For children of tender years (and it seems to me that this likely means at least up to age 12), I find directly contradictory messages from trusted adults to be solidly contrary to their best interests.

Whether the harm found to exist amounts to the "substantial harm" required to justify interference with the defendant's liberty interest is a close question, especially because there is considerable value in "frequent and continuing contact" between the child and both parents, and "contact with the parents' separate religious preferences." *Felton v. Felton, supra* at 607. In this regard the judge ruled:

There is surface appeal to the [defendant's] argument that the [plaintiff] has not met her burden of establishing substantial present harm to the children from exposure to [the defendant's] religious beliefs and practices, for the G.A.L. found only a few instances of concrete present harm to the children. I am mindful that the G.A.L. has not found current damage to the children so severe that it has caused them to suffer a psychotic break, or to have a "formal psychiatric diagnosis".... The case law does not require the court to wait for formal psychiatric breakdown and the evidence paints a strong picture of the reasonably projected course if the children continue to be caught in the cross-fire of their parents' religious difference: [the defendant's] religion may alienate the children from their custodial parent (she is bad, she will burn in hell), and may diminish their own sense of self-worth and self-identity (Jews are bad, Jews will burn in hell). At minimum they will be called upon to "choose" between their parents, in itself a detrimental result. The G.A.L. predicts damaging consequences of the children's exposure to two vastly different, and on some points directly contradictory religious views. "Sometimes ... a diversity of religious experience is itself a sound stimulant for a child ... the question that comes to the courts is whether, in particular circumstances, such exposures are disturbing a child to its substantial injury, physical or emotional, and will have a like harmful tendency for the future." (*Felton, [supra]* at 608). Applying that standard to the facts of this particular case, I see substantial evidence of current and imminent harm, to these 7, 5, and 3–year–old children.

In balancing these conflicting interests, fully aware of the complexities and nuances involved, we conclude that the judge's findings support her order in paragraph 5 of the judgment.

Where, as here, the judge has found demonstrable evidence of substantial harm to the children, we reject the defendant's arguments that the divorce judgment burdens his right to practice religion under the free exercise clauses of the Massachusetts and United States Constitution. . . .

Judgment affirmed.

Elk Grove Unified School District v. Newdow

Supreme Court of the United States, 2004.
542 U.S. 1, 124 S.Ct. 2301, 159 L.Ed.2d 98.

■ JUSTICE STEVENS delivered the opinion of the Court, in which JUSTICES KENNEDY, SOUTER, GINSBURG, and BREYER joined.

Each day elementary school teachers in the Elk Grove Unified School District (School District) lead their classes in a group recitation of the Pledge of Allegiance. Respondent, Michael A. Newdow, is an atheist whose daughter participates in that daily exercise. Because the Pledge contains the words "under God," he views the School District's policy as a religious indoctrination of his child that violates the First Amendment. A divided panel of the Court of Appeals for the Ninth Circuit agreed with Newdow. In light of the obvious importance of that decision, we granted certiorari to review the First Amendment issue and, preliminarily, the question whether Newdow has standing to invoke the jurisdiction of the federal courts. We conclude that Newdow lacks standing and therefore reverse the Court of Appeals' decision.

"The very purpose of a national flag is to serve as a symbol of our country," *Texas* v. *Johnson,* 491 U.S. 397 (1989), and of its proud traditions "of freedom, of equal opportunity, of religious tolerance, and of good will for other peoples who share our aspirations," *id.,* at 437 (STEVENS, J., dissenting). As its history illustrates, the Pledge of Allegiance evolved as a common public acknowledgment of the ideals that our flag symbolizes. Its recitation is a patriotic exercise designed to foster national unity and pride in those principles.

The Pledge of Allegiance was initially conceived more than a century ago. As part of the nationwide interest in commemorating the 400th anniversary of Christopher Columbus' discovery of America, a widely circulated national magazine for youth proposed in 1892 that pupils recite the following affirmation: "I pledge allegiance to my Flag and the Republic for which it stands: one Nation indivisible, with Liberty and Justice for all." In the 1920's, the National Flag Conferences replaced the phrase "my Flag" with "the flag of the United States of America."

Congress [in 1954] amended the text to add the words "under God."
. . .

Under California law, "every public elementary school" must begin each day with "appropriate patriotic exercises." CAL. EDUC. CODE ANN. § 52720 (West 1989). The statute provides that "[t]he giving of the Pledge of Allegiance to the Flag of the United States of America shall satisfy" this requirement. The Elk Grove Unified School District has implemented the state law by requiring that "[e]ach elementary school class recite the pledge of allegiance to the flag once each day." Consistent with our case law, the

School District permits students who object on religious grounds to abstain from the recitation. *See West Virginia Bd. of Ed. v. Barnette*, 319 U.S. 624 (1943).

In March 2000, Newdow filed suit in the United States District Court for the Eastern District of California against the United States Congress, the President of the United States, the State of California, and the School District and its superintendent. At the time of filing, Newdow's daughter was enrolled in kindergarten in the School District and participated in the daily recitation of the Pledge. Styled as a mandamus action, the complaint explains that Newdow is an atheist who was ordained more than 20 years ago in a ministry that "espouses the religious philosophy that the true and eternal bonds of righteousness and virtue stem from reason rather than mythology." The complaint seeks a declaration that the 1954 Act's addition of the words "under God" violated the Establishment and Free Exercise Clauses of the United States Constitution, as well as an injunction against the School District's policy requiring daily recitation of the Pledge. . . .

In its first opinion the appeals court unanimously held that Newdow has standing "as a parent to challenge a practice that interferes with his right to direct the religious education of his daughter." That holding sustained Newdow's standing to challenge not only the policy of the School District, where his daughter still is enrolled, but also the 1954 Act of Congress that had amended the Pledge, because his "injury in fact" was "fairly traceable" to its enactment. On the merits, over the dissent of one judge, the court held that both the 1954 Act and the School District's policy violate the Establishment Clause of the First Amendment.

After the Court of Appeals' initial opinion was announced, Sandra Banning, the mother of Newdow's daughter, filed a motion for leave to intervene, or alternatively to dismiss the complaint. She declared that although she and Newdow shared "physical custody" of their daughter, a state-court order granted her "exclusive legal custody" of the child, "including the sole right to represent [the daughter's] legal interests and make all decision[s] about her education" and welfare. Banning further stated that her daughter is a Christian who believes in God and has no objection either to reciting or hearing others recite the Pledge of Allegiance, or to its reference to God. Banning expressed the belief that her daughter would be harmed if the litigation were permitted to proceed, because others might incorrectly perceive the child as sharing her father's atheist views. Banning accordingly concluded, as her daughter's sole legal custodian, that it was not in the child's interest to be a party to Newdow's lawsuit. On September 25, 2002, the California Superior Court entered an order enjoining Newdow from including his daughter as an unnamed party or suing as her "next friend." That order did not purport to answer the question of Newdow's Article III standing.

In a second published opinion, the Court of Appeals reconsidered Newdow's standing in light of Banning's motion. The court noted that Newdow no longer claimed to represent his daughter, but unanimously concluded that "the grant of sole legal custody to Banning" did not deprive Newdow, "as a noncustodial parent, of Article III standing to object to unconstitutional government action affecting his child." The court held that under California law Newdow retains the right to expose his child to his particular religious views even if those views contradict the mother's, and that Banning's objections as sole legal custodian do not defeat Newdow's right to seek redress for an alleged injury to his own parental interests.

. . .

In every federal case, the party bringing the suit must establish standing to prosecute the action. . . .

[O]ur standing jurisprudence contains two strands: Article III standing, which enforces the Constitution's case-or-controversy requirement; and prudential standing, which embodies "judicially self-imposed limits on the exercise of federal jurisdiction." . . . "Without such limitations—closely related to Art. III concerns but essentially matters of judicial self-governance—the courts would be called upon to decide abstract questions of wide public significance even though other governmental institutions may be more competent to address the questions and even though judicial intervention may be unnecessary to protect individual rights."

One of the principal areas in which this Court has customarily declined to intervene is the realm of domestic relations. Long ago we observed that "[t]he whole subject of the domestic relations of husband and wife, parent and child, belongs to the laws of the States and not to the laws of the United States." *In re Burrus,* 136 U.S. 586, 593 (1890). So strong is our deference to state law in this area that we have recognized a "domestic relations exception" that "divests the federal courts of power to issue divorce, alimony, and child custody decrees." *Ankenbrandt* v. *Richards,* 504 U.S. 689, 703 (1992). . . .

Thus, while rare instances arise in which it is necessary to answer a substantial federal question that transcends or exists apart from the family law issue, *see, e.g., Palmore* v. *Sidoti,* 466 U.S. 429, 432–434 (1984), in general it is appropriate for the federal courts to leave delicate issues of domestic relations to the state courts.

[T]he extent of the standing problem raised by the domestic relations issues in this case was not apparent until August 5, 2002, when Banning filed her motion for leave to intervene or dismiss the complaint following the Court of Appeals' initial decision. At that time, the child's custody was governed by a February 6, 2002, order of the California Superior Court. That order provided that Banning had "*sole* legal custody as to the rights and responsibilities to make decisions relating to the health, education and welfare of" her daughter. The order stated that the two parents should "consult with one another on substantial decisions relating to" the child's "psychological and educational needs," but it authorized Banning to "exercise legal control" if the parents could not reach "mutual agreement."

[A]fter the Court of Appeals ruled, however, the Superior Court held another conference regarding the child's custody. At a hearing on September 11, 2003, the Superior Court announced that the parents have "joint legal custody," but that Banning "makes the final decisions if the two . . . disagree."

Newdow contends that despite Banning's final authority, he retains "an unrestricted right to inculcate in his daughter—free from governmental interference—the atheistic beliefs he finds persuasive." The difficulty with that argument is that Newdow's rights, as in many cases touching upon family relations, cannot be viewed in isolation. This case concerns not merely Newdow's interest in inculcating his child with his views on religion, but also the rights of the child's mother as a parent generally and under the Superior Court orders specifically. And most important, it implicates the interests of a young child who finds herself at the center of a highly public debate over her custody, the propriety of a widespread national ritual, and the meaning of our Constitution.

The interests of the affected persons in this case are in many respects antagonistic. Of course, legal disharmony in family relations is not uncommon, and in many instances that disharmony poses no bar to federal-court adjudication of proper federal questions. What makes this case different is that Newdow's standing derives entirely from his relationship with his daughter, but he lacks the right to litigate as her next friend. In marked contrast to our case law on *jus tertii, see, e.g., Singleton* v. *Wulff,* 428 U.S. 106, 113–118 (1976) (plurality opinion), the interests of this parent and this child are not parallel and, indeed, are potentially in conflict.

Newdow's parental status is defined by California's domestic relations law. Our custom on questions of state law ordinarily is to defer to the interpretation of the Court of Appeals for the Circuit in which the State is located. In this case, the Court of Appeals, which possesses greater familiarity with California law, concluded that state law vests in Newdow a cognizable right to influence his daughter's religious upbringing. The court based its ruling on two intermediate state appellate cases holding that "while the custodial parent undoubtedly has the right to make ultimate decisions concerning the child's religious upbringing, a court will not enjoin the noncustodial parent from discussing religion with the child or involving the child in his or her religious activities in the absence of a showing that the child will be thereby harmed." *In re Marriage of Murga,* 163 Cal.Rptr. 79, 82 (Ct. App. 1980). *See also In re Marriage of Mentry,* 190 Cal.Rptr. 843, 849–50 (Ct. App. 1983) (relying on *Murga* to invalidate portion of restraining order barring noncustodial father from engaging children in religious activity or discussion without custodial parent's consent). Animated by a conception of "family privacy" that includes "not simply a policy of minimum state intervention but also a presumption of parental autonomy," 190 Cal.Rptr., at 848, the state cases create a zone of private authority within which each parent, whether custodial or noncustodial, remains free to impart to the child his or her religious perspective.

Nothing that either Banning or the School Board has done, however, impairs Newdow's right to instruct his daughter in his religious views. Instead, Newdow requests relief that is more ambitious than that sought in *Mentry* and *Murga.* He wishes to forestall his daughter's exposure to religious ideas that her mother, who wields a form of veto power, endorses, and to use his parental status to challenge the influences to which his daughter may be exposed in school when he and Banning disagree. The California cases simply do not stand for the proposition that Newdow has a right to dictate to others what they may and may not say to his child respecting religion. *Mentry* and *Murga* are concerned with protecting "the fragile, complex interpersonal bonds between child and parent," 190 Cal.Rptr., at 848, and with permitting divorced parents to expose their children to the "diversity of religious experiences [that] is itself a sound stimulant for a child," 190 Cal.Rptr., at 847. The cases speak not at all to the problem of a parent seeking to reach outside the private parent-child sphere to restrain the acts of a third party. A next friend surely could exercise such a right, but the Superior Court's order has deprived Newdow of that status.

In our view, it is improper for the federal courts to entertain a claim by a plaintiff whose standing to sue is founded on family law rights that are in dispute when prosecution of the lawsuit may have an adverse effect on the person who is the source of the plaintiff's claimed standing. When hard questions of domestic relations are sure to affect the outcome, the prudent course is for the federal court to stay its hand rather than reach out to resolve a weighty question of federal constitutional law. There is a vast difference between Newdow's right to communicate with his child—which both California law and the First Amendment recognize—and his claimed right to shield his daughter from influences to which she is exposed in school despite the terms of the custody order. We conclude that, having been deprived under California law of the right to sue as next friend, Newdow lacks prudential standing to bring this suit in federal court.

The judgment of the Court of Appeals is reversed.

■ CHIEF JUSTICE REHNQUIST, with whom JUSTICE O'CONNOR joins, and with whom JUSTICE THOMAS joins as to Part I, concurring in the judgment.

The Court today erects a novel prudential standing principle in order to avoid reaching the merits of the constitutional claim. I dissent from that ruling. On the merits, I conclude that the Elk Grove Unified School District (School District) policy that requires teachers to lead willing students in reciting the Pledge of Allegiance, which includes the words "under God," does not violate the Establishment Clause of the First Amendment.

5.   THE CHILD'S PREFERENCE

Johns v. Cioci

Superior Court of Pennsylvania, 2004.
865 A.2d 931.

■ BECK, JUSTICE.

This is a custody dispute involving the twelve-year-old daughter of divorced parents who was in the primary physical custody of her mother for approximately a decade. After Father petitioned for modification of custody and Mother petitioned for relocation, the trial court held a consolidated hearing. The trial court then denied Mother's petition for relocation and granted Father primary physical custody. We affirm the court's denial of Mother's petition for relocation; however, we reverse the court's order granting primary physical custody to Father and remand for further proceedings.

Appellant Mother and Appellee Father were divorced in Delaware in 1994 after approximately four years of marriage and the birth, in April 1992, of one child. By orders of a Delaware court in 1996 and 2000, parents shared legal custody, Mother had primary physical custody, and Father had partial physical custody. Both parties have remarried. Mother moved to Pennsylvania with permission of the Delaware court, but Father has continued to reside in Delaware. In September 2003, the Court of Common Pleas of Chester County entered an order, by agreement of the parties, that retained the structure of the custody arrangement originally ordered in Delaware. Mother had primary physical custody of the child, and Father had custody every other weekend and one afternoon during the week. The parties' relationship has been characterized by poor communication, frequent disagreements, and numerous court appearances.

. . .

The court subsequently received a letter signed by the child and dated April 12, 2004, expressing her desire to live with her mother. The court returned the letter to the child, advising her that such information, being *ex parte*, could not appropriately be seen by the judge and that any other correspondence should be directed to her mother's attorney. We note that neither Mother nor Father introduced this letter into evidence at any proceeding, and the circumstances surrounding its writing are unclear. . . .

On May 26, 2004, the court entered a detailed custody order that transferred primary physical custody to Father, granted Mother partial physical custody, and provided for shared legal custody.

The child started classes in her new school near Father's residence in Delaware in late summer 2004. Shortly thereafter, in mid-September, Mother filed an emergency application for stay of enforcement of the custody orders of May 26 and June 11, 2004, and Father filed an emergency petition seeking sole legal custody so that he could immediately take the child to a counselor without Mother's consent. In their petitions, both parties similarly recounted several recent events of concern involving the child. Specifically, the child was performing poorly in school, in contrast to her excellent academic performance in previous years. In addition, she had run away from Father's home, ending up in a scuffle at the local police station. We note that no documents or testimony in support of these allegations has been admitted into evidence in any proceeding. However, we also note that after a hearing on September 27, 2004, the trial judge agreed that the child's problems were sufficiently serious to warrant immediate counseling.

. . .

With any child custody case, including petitions for modification or relocation, the paramount concern is the best interests of the child. This standard requires a case by case determination of all the factors that may legitimately affect the "physical, intellectual, moral and spiritual well-being" of the child.

. . .

A party seeking modification of custody arrangements has the burden to show that modification is in the child's best interest. *McMillen v. McMillen*, 602 A.2d 845, 847 (Pa. 1992). In evaluating whether a modification of custody is in a child's best interest, the court "has an obligation to consider all relevant factors that could affect the child's well-being." One substantial factor, although not the sole one, is the role that one parent has assumed as the primary caretaker of the child. "[W]hen both parents are otherwise fit, one parent's role as the primary caretaker may be given weight as the determining factor in a custody determination." The court must give attention to the benefits of continuity and stability in custody arrangements and to the possibility of harm arising from disruption of long-standing patterns of care.

. . .

We turn now to Father's petition for modification, which the trial court granted, transferring primary physical custody of the child from Mother to him. Mother contends that the trial court abused its discretion in transferring primary physical custody to Father, apparently disregarding the fact that Mother has been the primary care-giver for almost all of the child's life; in not ordering a full custody evaluation; in not directly inquiring as to the child's preference during the court's first interview with the child; and in not affording significant weight to the preference stated by the child in the court's second interview with her.

We hold that the trial court abused its discretion in transferring primary physical custody to Father without directly assessing the benefits of stability in custody arrangements and the potential harm to the child from disruption of her long-standing patterns of care. In addition, we hold that the trial court's factual conclusion that the parental households are not equally suitable was unreasonable and thus an abuse of discretion. Finally, we hold that the trial court did not give adequate consideration to the child's expressed preference to live with her Mother. We discuss each trial court error in turn below.

First, the trial court erred in not directly and thoroughly considering the potential deleterious effect on the child of a change in primary physical custody . . . The child in this case has lived with Mother for her whole life. She was two years old when her parents divorced in 1994, and Mother has had primary physical custody since that time. The loving relationship and emotional bond between Mother and child are not in dispute. The child has developed into an articulate, intelligent, academically successful young person while in the primary care of her Mother. However compelling Father's case for modification may be, any benefits of a change in custody must be weighed against the benefits of stability and the potential harm of an abrupt switch in primary caregiver. The trial court abused its discretion by giving virtually no consideration to Mother's historical role as caregiver.

. . .

The second trial court error is the factual conclusion that Father's household is more suitable for the child. There is no competent evidence to support this conclusion. The households are clearly different, as explained by the child in her testimony:

> Court: One of the things I want to try to understand is that the difference is [sic] between what goes on in your mom's house and what goes on in your dad's house. Can you explain how things are different there?
>
> Child: Well, my dad's house, there's more people.
>
> Court: Okay.
>
> Child: There's always a lot more going on with a lot more people.
>
> Court: I see you smile when you say that.
>
> Child: Yeah.
>
> Court: Do you like that or not like that?
>
> Child: I like both houses.
>
> Court: Okay.
>
> Child: At my mom's house, I'm the only child so I get a lot of attention.
>
> Court: Do you like that? I see you smiling about that, too.
>
> Child: Yeah, I like a lot of—I like having siblings and I like being the only child. I like both.

. . .

The trial court found Father's household more suitable because it was more stable and family-oriented, allowing the child to reside with other children and to interact frequently with Father's extended family. In contrast, the trial court viewed Mother's household as less suitable because it was less stable and Mother's living arrangements for the future were uncertain;

she was presently living apart from her husband, . . . and she has little if any contact with her extended family. Based on the facts of record, the trial court's conclusions with regard to the superiority of Father's household were unreasonable and thus an abuse of discretion.

. . .

The question of suitability of the households is particularly important because, when the households are equally suitable, the preference of the child can tip the scales in favor of one or the other. Even when the trial court gives little weight to a child's preference, that preference may still be determinative if the households are equally suitable. . . .

Even if the households are not equivalently suitable for rearing the child, the child's preference is a factor that must be carefully considered in custody decisions, keeping in mind the child's maturity and intelligence, as well as the reasons that the child offers for the preference. We are mindful that the child's preference is not controlling and that the trial judge is in the best position to determine the weight to be given to the child's preference.

In this case, the trial court interviewed the child three times, once on March 19, 2004 and twice on June 9, 2004. In the first interview, the court did not directly ask the child her preference, but tried to elicit information about her feelings for both parents and their households. The court concluded, and based on the record, we must agree, that the child was hesitant to decide between her parents and did not like being in the middle of their dispute. However, in June, after custody had been transferred to her Father, her testimony was more definitive, as shown by the following two examples:

> Question (by Mother's attorney): Meghan, what—why was June 1st, the day that you wrote 'This is the worst day of my life,' why that day?
>
> Child: Because I just hurt my dad's feelings, but I wanted to stay with my mom.
>
> Court: Is there something else you wanted to tell me now?
>
> Child: Yes
>
> Court: What is that?
>
> Child: I want to live with my mom.
>
> Court: Can you tell me why?
>
> Child: Because I like the school—
>
> Court: You like what? I can't hear. You dropped your voice.
>
> Child: I like the school, and I've always lived with her and I like living with her.

The child gave two good reasons—school and continuity—for wanting to stay with her Mother. Her young age does not preclude careful consideration of her preference and her reasons. Our case law has ample precedent in which the custody preference of eleven or twelve year old children was honored. The child in the present case is an intelligent and articulate twelve-year-old girl, who is academically gifted and excels in school. In essentially dismissing her testimony because of her youth or because it was deemed as not based on good or consistent reason, the trial court acted unreasonably and abused its discretion.

Because the trial court's factual conclusions are unreasonable based on the evidence of record, we vacate the order that granted Father's petition for modification. We remand for a new custody hearing under a different trial judge. Pending the order from the new hearing, the present custody arrangements shall remain in effect.

NOTES

1. Should a child who is the subject of a custody battle be asked his or her preference? The growing trend toward recognizing the rights of children might suggest that the best answer is yes. Certainly in a situation where the parents are equally fit to assume custody, and both want custody, then the temptation to maximize happiness by allowing the child's preference to control seems almost irresistible. Turning to the child's preference may be a way to avoid making a difficult decision, however, as much as it is an objective way to decide what is best for the child. How is a child to know, for example, which parent is more "fit"? The parent who is more permissive may be better liked, but is not necessarily the "better" parent. In addition, even if a child prefers one parent to another, it may place a terrible responsibility on the shoulders of the child to be asked to reveal that preference to his parents—or to the world.

One way of at least reducing the burden assumed by the child would be to make his preference only one factor in the court's decision, and for the court to make this clear to the child.

2. Should all children be consulted or only children above a particular age? The Uniform Probate Code, § 5–206 gives a minor of fourteen or more years the right to "nominate" his guardian unless his choice is "clearly contrary to the best interest of the minor." Would a test of maturity be preferable to this kind of chronological test?

3. Who should ask the child and where? Consider the caution of Anna Freud on having the judge ask the question, even in the privacy of the judge's chamber:

> What each [child] has to contribute to the picture is limited inevitably to what they know about themselves. To face up to one's real emotions and to probe into one's real motives is not a capacity which we expect to find in children. On the contrary, children of all ages have a natural tendency to deceive themselves about their motivations, to rationalize their actions, and to shy back from full awareness of their feelings, especially where conflicts of loyalty come into question. To pierce through these defenses demands more than usual skill from the investigator. Verbal and non-verbal communications (attitudes, behavior) have to be scrutinized, assessed, and translated into their underlying meaning.

Joseph Goldstein & Jay Katz, The Family and the Law 262 (1965).

4. Even if it is decided that the preference of the child should be given some weight, the question remains whether the "best interests" of the child should be viewed from a long-term or a short-term perspective. The conditions that make a person happy at age seven may have adverse consequences at age thirty. Should the judge decide by thinking what the child as an adult looking back will think? How should a judge weigh happiness at one age against happiness at another age? *See generally* Robert Mnookin, *Child Custody Adjudication: Judicial Functions in the Face of Indeterminacy*, 39 Law and Contemp. Probs. 226 (1975).

6. Reliance on Mental Health Experts

K.J.B. v. C.M.B.

Court of Appeals of Missouri, Eastern District, 1989.
779 S.W.2d 36.

■ Karohl, J.

Husband-father appeals from modification of divorce decree which terminated his rights of visitation and temporary custody with the parties' two minor children.... In 1987, mother withheld father's custody and visitation rights. She alleged the children, now ages seven and eight, were being physically, psychologically and sexually abused during their visits with father or his parents. Mother instituted a motion to modify by petitioning the trial court for modification of custody order.

[O]n October 27, 1987, by agreement of the parties the hearing was suspended and ordered continued until January 22, 1988. The court ordered, pending further hearing, that the parties undergo counseling with a therapist, to be selected by mutual agreement of the parties. Father was ordered to undergo separate, individual counseling preparatory to joint counseling with his two children. The joint counseling was to commence when the therapist deemed it reasonably safe for the children. The parties, pursuant to the consent order, stipulated in open court that the therapist's written report would be admissible in future proceedings on the pending motions.

After only two sessions, the therapist decided any contact between the father and the children would be dangerous. The therapist discontinued the sessions because he felt father was simply showing up for therapy and not really working to cure the problems.

The hearing resumed on April 21, 1988. The court issued findings of fact and law, and awarded mother sole custody of the two children and terminated any further contact between father and the two children.

Father's principal complaint is there was no substantial evidence to support modification of the decree awarding sole custody to mother or to terminate all contact between father and children.... Specifically, father contends the trial court's fifth and sixth findings of fact are erroneous. In the court's fifth finding of fact the court found father refused to cooperate in the psychological evaluation process and indicated an unwillingness to comply with court orders. The sixth finding of fact was father intentionally undermined the mother's authority as primary custodian and did not intend to change this behavior.

. . .

The testimony which supports the trial court's custody findings and order is substantial. Mother offered testimony from three witnesses concerning the effect of joint custody and the relationship currently existing between the children, father and paternal grandparents. Dr. Joel Ray, a clinical psychologist diagnosed the children as being emotionally disturbed and found their behavior to be consistent with abuse but he could not say abuse was the cause of the disturbance in these children. Dr. A.E. Daniel, a physician and psychiatrist, testified the children had been subjected to physical abuse by their grandfather, grandmother and father in the environment in Montgomery County. His conclusions were based upon facts reported to be several years old and he was not aware of any current physical abuse beyond suspicion. He refused to recommend father not be allowed to see the children. When asked about visitation rights he responded, "Certainly,", "no problem [with that]." Dr. Ann Dell Duncan, a clinical psychologist, testified the boys gave descriptive indication that they had been traumatized at the hands of both the father and the grandparents. She suggested supervised visitation followed by unsupervised visitation for the father only, none for his parents.

Dr. Corrales and Dr. Ro–Trock evaluated father, mother, children, stepfather, and paternal grandparents. Both recommended mother be given primary custody of the children. Even father's expert witness psychologist,

Dr. James Hall, testified: "there's a lot of anxiety in the boys ... there's something wrong in the relationship between them and their father and grandparents on father's side." This evidence was sufficient to support the award of sole custody to the mother. We cannot say the trial court abused its discretion and we defer to the trial court and its opportunity to judge the credibility of the witnesses.

. . .

Father contends he did not have the same opportunity as mother to obtain expert testimony. Father claims he was prejudiced because he was unable to develop evidence of the children's inter-relationship with him and the paternal grandparents. Father claims this prejudiced his ability to prepare and develop his case.

The Rules allow the court to order the mother to submit the children to physical or mental examinations. Mo. Rev. Stat. § 60.01 (1986). Here the court did not abuse its discretion by denying father's requests for examination. The court found father, both before and after the dissolution, physically and psychologically abused his children. Father's requests for physical examination of the children were honored in part. Mother testified the children had received bruises during their visits with their father. Father requested physical examinations in September 1987, although he had not been allowed unsupervised visitation with the children after May, 1987. Any evidence of bruises would have disappeared by September. Hence, the request came too late to support a claim of error directed to the relief the court denied.

In October, 1987, at father's request a psychologist, Dr. James Hall, met with the children, mother, father, paternal grandparents, and mother's husband. Although Dr. Hall testified he did not know if it would be dangerous for the children to see their father or paternal grandparents, he did say there is "something wrong" in the relationship between the children and their father and paternal grandparents. Dr. Hall recommended the court not sever the relationship between the children and father. Father also chose Dr. Bill Graham, a psychologist, jointly with mother in connection with an agreement between the parties and pursuant to the court's order. Dr. Graham testified it was dangerous for the children to have further contact with their father and paternal grandparents. The children saw psychologists, Dr. Ramon Corrales and Dr. Larry Ro–Trock, during the interim agreement. These doctors recommended mother be given custody. They did not oppose children's "safe contact" with father. Father had three opportunities to have the children psychologically evaluated, while the mother had expert testimony from four witnesses: Dr. Joel Ray, Dr. A.E. Daniel, Dr. Ann Duncan and Dr. Bill Graham.

The record reflects each expert found, at a minimum, the children, father and paternal grandparents had an abnormal relationship and more counseling was needed. The welfare of the children is the court's primary concern. Father had already been accused of physical and psychological abuse of the children. Also, Dr. Graham testified that in his opinion the children have seen enough professional people and forcing the children to see more professionals would be detrimental to the children. After considering the number of experts each party was able to obtain, the testimony of the experts, and the welfare of the children, we find the trial court did not err in denying father's motion for additional discovery.

. . .

We next review the complete termination of father's visitation rights with the minor children. . . .

There was general agreement by the psychologists who testified at the hearing, that reestablishing a father's relationship with his children is a desirable goal. Dr. Hall, father's expert witness, testified "the father not seeing the kids anymore would be the worst outcome." No expert testified specifically that visitation at the home of the children would be detrimental.

The trial court agreed some form of visitation by the father was in the children's best interest provided the visitation would not endanger the children's physical health or impair their emotional development. This was the purpose of the consent order of October 27, 1987. . . .

The temporary consent order of October 27, 1987 provided for father to receive counseling to reestablish visitation and insure that father's visits would not endanger the children's physical health or impair their emotional stability. The parties mutually agreed upon Dr. Graham as the therapist. . . .

Father attended both counseling sessions scheduled with Dr. Graham, and has not refused to attend any other sessions. However, no further sessions were scheduled, because Dr. Graham felt the father was uncooperative. . . . Dr. Graham testified concerning father, "generally he was friendly towards me. There was no behavior of animosity or any anger outbursts, [he] appeared to want to be cooperative with me during both sessions."

Dr. Graham's reason for asserting father was uncooperative was that he was merely showing up for therapy but not working on problems honestly, and was unwilling to admit any of the allegations against him or his parents. Significantly, these counseling sessions took place while the modification motions were pending, albeit suspended.

The third condition in the temporary consent order of October 27, 1987, which provided for counseling of father and others and for eventual visitation was: "The parties stipulate in open court that the therapist's written report shall be admissible in future proceedings on the pending motions."

In effect, Dr. Graham required the father, as a precondition to seeing his children, to confess to child abuse and testify that his parents had physically and sexually abused the children, even though these allegations were at issue in the pending case. Further, many of the alleged abusive acts by the grandparents could only have occurred while the father was in Germany. Consequently, father had no personal knowledge and could not admit that these acts occurred. Moreover, the trial court subsequently found the allegations against the grandparents to be unproven.

[D]r. Graham's impressions and conclusions are not conclusive on the matter of visitation. Dr. Graham assumed the allegations made against father and paternal grandparents were true. When asked whether he would reevaluate and change his opinion if some of the assumed facts were not true, Dr. Graham replied, "I don't know." Significantly, the court found many of the allegations unproven.

. . .

Father has not refused to comply with a single court order to date, and has complied with those orders issued. Also, subsequent to the counseling sessions, father testified he would do whatever he had to do concerning supervised visitation.

Dr. Graham was asked what change would have to take place in father in order for beneficial contacts to be possible between the father and the minor children. Graham responded that father would have to come, internally, to an awareness of his behavior, accept that damage has been done, and be willing to work on these problems honestly. Given the fact that the therapist selected pursuant to the consent order, Dr. Graham, felt the ultimate issues in dispute had to be discussed before safe contact could occur between the father and children, it appears that counseling was attempted prematurely.

We affirm the modification decree in all respects except the denial of visitation of father with his children and they with him. We remand solely for an order allowing visitation as determined by the court.

7. COUNSEL FOR THE CHILD

Schult v. Schult

Supreme Court of Connecticut, 1997.
699 A.2d 134.

■ BORDEN, ASSOCIATE JUSTICE.

The sole issue in this . . . appeal is whether an attorney representing a minor child in connection with a custody dispute may advocate a position that is contrary to that of the child's guardian ad litem. The plaintiff, Cheryl Schult, brought this dissolution of marriage action against the defendant, Jeffrey Scot Schult, seeking, *inter alia*, custody of their only child. The child's maternal grandmother, Joan Radin, intervened in the dissolution action pursuant to General Statutes § 46b–57. The trial court appointed both an attorney and a guardian ad litem for the child. The guardian ad litem appeals from the judgment of the Appellate Court, which affirmed the judgment of the trial court granting sole custody to the intervenor and visitation rights to the plaintiff and the defendant. . . .

The plaintiff and the defendant were married on February 14, 1986. Their only child was born approximately two and one-half years later, and has a history of emotional, psychological and developmental problems. On March 7, 1991, the plaintiff brought the present dissolution action against the defendant seeking, *inter alia*, custody of their child. The defendant filed a cross complaint in which he, too, sought custody of the child.

On April 18, 1991, the defendant moved out of the family home. On that same date, Steve Norman moved into the family home as a boarder. The plaintiff and Norman have resided together since that time and now have plans to marry. On August 16, 1991, upon motion by the defendant, the trial court, Jones, J., appointed Colette Griffin as the child's attorney.

The following additional facts are set forth in the Appellate Court opinion.

> On the evening of November 19, 1991, Norman was baby-sitting while the plaintiff, a licensed nurse practitioner, was at work. The child was three years old at the time. Norman testified that about five minutes after the child had gone to bed, he came out of the bedroom and was crying. Norman observed that the child had a mark above his eye and treated the injury with an ice pack. After fifteen to twenty minutes, the child stopped crying and went back to bed. The following morning, Norman noticed that the child was limping and would not put any

pressure on his leg. When the plaintiff returned home at 7:30 a.m., Norman told her that "we've got a problem."

The plaintiff called Karen Laugel, their pediatrician.... After examining the child, Laugel stated that "it looks like a broken leg." Feeling that the child's injury was "very worrisome for the possibility of abuse" and that the child's injury could not "be explained by falling out of the bed," Laugel instructed the plaintiff and Norman to bring the child to Bridgeport Hospital where the child could be treated for his injury and where an investigation would be initiated for child abuse. Laugel also told the plaintiff and Norman that she would meet them at the hospital shortly.

The plaintiff and Norman then took the child to the University of Connecticut Health Center, John Dempsey Hospital (Dempsey Hospital), where the child was admitted on November 20, 1991.... The doctors at Dempsey Hospital did not conclude that the child had been abused and released the child to the plaintiff on November 25. The child's discharge diagnosis stated that he had suffered a fractured leg.

At the request of Laugel, the department of children and family services [department] conducted an investigation for abuse. After meeting with the child, the plaintiff, Norman, and several doctors at Dempsey Hospital, [the department] concluded that the origin of the child's injury was unknown and that abuse could not be confirmed.

On January 3, 1992, Radin intervened in the dissolution action, and the trial court, Sequino, J., ordered that temporary joint custody be awarded to the plaintiff and the intervenor, with physical residence with the intervenor. The child has resided with the intervenor since January 3, 1992. On December 4, 1992, upon motion by the plaintiff, the trial court, Jones, J., appointed Elizabeth Gleason as the child's guardian ad litem.

The trial began on November 1, 1993, before Hon. Thomas J. O'Sullivan, judge trial referee. At the trial, the guardian ad litem was called as a witness during the plaintiff's case-in-chief and testified that custody should be awarded to the plaintiff. The guardian ad litem was the only witness, other than the plaintiff and Norman, to testify that the child's safety would not be endangered by awarding custody to the plaintiff. Allen Rubin the family relations officer who conducted a review of the case, testified that it was in the child's best interest that custody be awarded to the intervenor. Sidney Horowitz, the child's and plaintiff's treating psychologist who conducted a court-ordered evaluation of the child, expressed serious concerns for the child's safety in Norman's presence and recommended that custody be awarded to the intervenor. Laugel testified that the child was not safe in the plaintiff's custody. Margaret Kunsch, the child's clinical social worker at the Parent Child Resource Center, testified that it would be detrimental to the child to remove him from the intervenor's custody. Kunsch also testified that the child considered "home" to be with the intervenor and had made "remarkable progress" within the past three months.

The child's attorney did not testify; rather, she participated in the trial by calling witnesses and conducting direct and cross-examination. The guardian ad litem and the plaintiff objected during the trial to the line of questioning by the child's attorney and requested that the trial court order her to ask the witnesses questions prepared by the guardian. The trial court, however, overruled their objections.

At the conclusion of the evidence, the trial court heard final arguments from all of the attorneys in the case, including the child's attorney, who argued that custody should be awarded to the intervenor. Both the plaintiff and the guardian ad litem objected to the closing argument by the child's attorney. The trial court overruled their objections.

The trial court rendered judgment granting sole custody to the intervenor pursuant to General Statutes § 46b–56b,[3] with visitation rights to the plaintiff and the defendant. In its memorandum of decision, the trial court found

> [A]s a fact that [the child's] leg was broken by [Norman], that [Norman] told [the plaintiff] when she came home what he had done and they both decided to tell the story that [the child's] leg was broken while [he] was alone in the bedroom in bed. When they told [Laugel] they did not know what happened to [the child], [Laugel] told them that she felt there was some abuse involved and that an investigation would be made for child abuse. They did not follow the doctor's order to go to Bridgeport Hospital but went eventually to [Dempsey Hospital] in Farmington. [Norman] left that hospital as soon as he could and testified that he wanted to get away, that he did not know what was going to happen to him. Under these circumstances, it is clear that it would not be in the best interest of [the child] for him to be given into [the plaintiff's] custody with [Norman] there, knowing that he got away with breaking [the child's] leg as the court has found and with the opportunity to abuse [the child] further. The court cannot conceive of a situation more detrimental to [the child] than to permit [the plaintiff] to have custody of [the child] now. Under the above circumstances, [the plaintiff] sided with [Norman] against [the child]. She should not be given the opportunity to do that again.

In her appeal from the judgment of the trial court to the Appellate Court, the plaintiff claimed, *inter alia*, that the trial court abused its discretion by allowing the child's attorney to argue against the recommendation of the child's guardian ad litem. The guardian ad litem filed a brief in support of the plaintiff's position, and argued that the trial court's decision to permit the child's attorney to make a recommendation contrary to that of the guardian ad litem prevented a fair trial on the question of custody. The Appellate Court concluded that the trial court did not abuse its discretion in allowing the attorney for the child to offer her recommendation concerning the custody of the child because there was no indication in the record that the attorney's recommendation was without a basis in fact or that the court relied solely on it.

The guardian ad litem filed a petition for certification to appeal from the judgment of the Appellate Court to this court. We granted certification limited to the following issue: "In an action for dissolution of a marriage, if a child is represented by both a guardian ad litem and an attorney, does the attorney for the child have the authority to express an opinion on behalf of the child that differs from the opinion of the guardian ad litem?" After reviewing the record and the parties' briefs, however, we rephrase the issue as follows: "In an action for dissolution of a marriage, if a child is represent-

---

3. General Statutes § 46b–56b provides: "Presumption re best interest of child to be in custody of parent. In any dispute as to the custody of a minor child involving a parent and a nonparent, there shall be a presumption that it is in the best interest of the child to be in the custody of the parent, which presumption may be rebutted by showing that it would be detrimental to the child to permit the parent to have custody."

ed by both a guardian ad litem and an attorney, may the trial court allow the child's attorney to advocate a position that is different than that recommended by the guardian ad litem?" We answer the reformulated certified question in the affirmative. Accordingly, we affirm the judgment of the Appellate Court, although we do so on a different rationale.

The certified question presents an issue of first impression for this court. The guardian ad litem, plaintiff and amicus curiae urge us to adopt a bright line rule that prohibits a child's attorney from advocating a position that is contrary to that of the guardian ad litem. They argue that when a child is represented by both an attorney and a guardian ad litem in a custody dispute, the guardian ad litem becomes the attorney's "client," and that, as the client, the guardian ad litem makes the decisions on behalf of the child, and the attorney must advocate those decisions.

[W]e reject a rule that would unduly restrict the trial court's ability to receive information that might aid it in determining where the best interests of a child lie. Therefore, we decline to adopt the bright line rule requested by the guardian ad litem, plaintiff and amicus, and, instead, hold that it is within the trial court's discretion to determine, on a case-by-case basis, whether such dual, conflicting advocacy of position is in the best interests of the child.

The guiding principle in determining custody is the best interests of the child. The best interests of the child include the child's interests in sustained growth, development, well-being, and continuity and stability of its environment.

This principle also governs the appointment of counsel for a minor child in a marriage dissolution action. "The court may appoint counsel for any minor child ... if the court deems it to be in the best interests of the child...." General Statutes § 46b–54(a). The appointment of counsel lies firmly within the trial court's discretion in the best interests of the child. Counsel may also be appointed "when the court finds that the custody, care, education, visitation or support of a minor child is in actual controversy...." General Statutes § 46b–54(b). The statute further provides that "[c]ounsel for the child or children shall be heard on all matters pertaining to the interests of any child, including the custody, care, support, education and visitation of the child, so long as the court deems such representation to be in the best interests of the child." General Statutes § 46b–54(c). The purpose of appointing counsel for a minor child in a dissolution action is to ensure independent representation of the child's interests, and such representation must be entrusted to the professional judgment of appointed counsel within the usual constraints applicable to such representation.

The appointment of a guardian ad litem is neither required nor specifically authorized in chapter 815j of the General Statutes, which governs the resolution of custody disputes. The appointment of a guardian ad litem is authorized, however, pursuant to General Statutes § 45a–132(a), which provides that the court may appoint a guardian ad litem for a minor or incompetent "[i]n any proceeding before a court of probate or the Superior Court including the Family Support Magistrate Division...." The appointment of a guardian ad litem lies within the discretion of the trial court. General Statutes § 45a–132(b). Likewise, the guardian ad litem may be removed by the trial court whenever it appears to the court to be in the best interests of the child to do so. General Statutes § 45a–132(f).

Although this Court has not previously delineated the exact roles of the attorney for the child and the guardian ad litem, we have recognized the potential for conflict between these roles when both are appointed by the court. *See Newman v. Newman*, 663 A.2d 980, 990 (Conn. 1995) ("there may be instances in which the functions of counsel for minor children differ fundamentally from those of a guardian ad litem"); *Knock v. Knock*, 621 A.2d 267, 276 (Conn. 1993) ("[t]he legislature has not delineated, nor has this court yet been presented with the opportunity to delineate, the obligations and limitations of the role of counsel for a minor child").

. . .

[W]e conclude that, where the court has appointed both an attorney and a guardian ad litem to represent a child in a dissolution action, the attorney for the child may advocate a position different from that of the guardian ad litem so long as the trial court determines that it is in the best interests of the child to permit such dual, conflicting advocacy. Leaving the determination to the sound discretion of the trial court is particularly important in those difficult cases, such as the present one, in which the child is unable to state a preference directly, there is an allegation of child abuse, and the parties present drastically differing views of the events. In such situations, it may be particularly difficult for the trial court to determine where the best interests of the child lie. To aid the court in its duty to determine the best interests of the child for purposes of custody, it may be helpful to the trial court to hear the contradictory positions of the attorney and the guardian ad litem. The trial court is in the best position to evaluate the child's needs for representation as the case and the evidence unfold.

In the present case, it is important to note the context in which the attorney and the guardian ad litem were appointed. The minor child suffers from emotional, psychological and developmental problems. Custody of the child was initially contested by the plaintiff and the defendant. At the request of the defendant, the court appointed the attorney for the child pursuant to § 46b–54. Following the intervention by Radin, custody became bitterly contested between the plaintiff and the intervenor, with the defendant siding with the intervenor. The custody battle centered largely around whether the child would be safe in the plaintiff's custody in light of allegations of abuse against the plaintiff's live-in boyfriend. At the request of the plaintiff, the court then appointed the guardian ad litem for the child.

During the course of the trial, the trial referee frequently stated that the case was a very difficult one and that he intended to "hear everyone" on the issues. The guardian ad litem was heard on the issues relating to the child's custody. She was called as a witness in the plaintiff's case-in-chief and testified that she saw no danger in the child being in the plaintiff's custody. Furthermore, she was not the only actor to present that position, which was the same as that advocated by the plaintiff. In addition, there was adequate evidence in the record to support the position of the child's attorney that custody should be awarded to the intervenor. Several experts testified that they had serious reservations about returning the child to the plaintiff's care in light of unanswered questions surrounding the incident of alleged abuse. In fact, the trial court specifically found that Norman had broken the child's leg and that the plaintiff had cooperated in the cover-up of that serious abuse. Finally, the position advocated by the child's attorney was the same as that taken by the attorneys for the intervenor and the defendant. In such circumstances, we cannot conclude that the trial court abused its discretion in hearing from the child's attorney and the guardian ad litem, despite their contrary positions, in making its decision regarding the best interests of the child concerning custody.

The guardian ad litem, plaintiff and amicus nonetheless argue that the Connecticut Rules of Professional Conduct require counsel to advocate for the position of the guardian ad litem. In support of this argument, they point to Rules 1.2 and 1.14 of the Connecticut Rules of Professional Conduct. Rule 1.2 requires an attorney to abide by a client's decision with respect to the objectives of the representation. Rule 1.14 requires the attorney representing a client under a disability, which includes minority, to maintain a lawyer-client relationship that is as normal as possible. When the client cannot act in his or her own interest, Rule 1.14 permits, but does not require, the attorney to seek the appointment of a guardian. The official comment to Rule 1.14 provides that, where the client has a legal representative, such as a guardian ad litem, "the lawyer should ordinarily look to the representative for decisions on behalf of the client." Rules of Professional Conduct 1.14, comment (1995). The guardian ad litem argues that, because she was appointed as the legal representative of the child, the child's attorney was ethically bound to follow her recommended position.

Our review of the rules, however, does not lead us ineluctably to the result advocated by the guardian ad litem. At the most, the rules merely recognize that there will be situations in which the positions of the child's attorney and the guardian may differ. At the least, the Rules neither contemplate nor answer the problem posed in the present case. Although we agree that *ordinarily* the attorney should look to the guardian, we do not agree that the rules require such action in every case. This case is one of those unusual situations. There was no evidence that the child's attorney had been unable to determine the child's interests from her review of the expert reports, medical records and school records. Furthermore, the guardian ad litem was appointed by the court at the request of the plaintiff, not at the request of the child's attorney. In light of the trial court's finding that the plaintiff's boyfriend had abused the child, and that the plaintiff had sided with the boyfriend against the safety of the child, we cannot conclude that the attorney for the child should have been prevented from advocating that custody not be awarded to the plaintiff.

The judgment of the Appellate Court is affirmed.

D.   ALTERNATIVE APPROACHES

1.   TENDER YEARS PRESUMPTION

Pusey v. Pusey

Supreme Court of Utah, 1986.
728 P.2d 117.

■ DURHAM, J.

The parties were married twelve years and had two sons, ages twelve and nine at the time of trial in 1984. . . .

The trial court conversed with the parties' two minor children in chambers and learned that the older boy expressed a marked preference for living with his father, whereas the younger boy indicated equal attachment to both parents. In spite of recommendations by a social worker that the parties be awarded joint custody and by plaintiff's brother, who had given the family professional counseling, that plaintiff would be the better parent to have custody of both children, the trial court awarded custody of the older boy to defendant and custody of the younger to plaintiff, with reasonable visitation rights in both parties.

. . .

Plaintiff cross-appeals from that portion of the divorce decree awarding custody of the older son of the marriage to defendant and requests that both children be awarded to her. This Court's judicial preference for the mother, reaffirmed in *Nilson v. Nilson,* 652 P.2d 1323 (Utah 1982), and *Lembach v. Cox,* 639 P.2d 197 (Utah 1981), is cited in support. We acknowledged in dictum the continued vitality of that preference in *Jorgensen v. Jorgensen,* 599 P.2d 510, 511 (Utah 1979), "all other things being equal." We believe the time has come to discontinue our support, even in dictum, for the notion of gender-based preferences in child custody cases. A review of the cases cited by plaintiff shows that "all other things" are rarely equal, and therefore this Court has not treated a direct challenge to the maternal preference rule in over five years. In the unlikely event that a case with absolute equality "of all things" concerning custody is presented to us, the provisions of article IV, section 1 of the Utah Constitution and of the Fourteenth Amendment of the United States Constitution would preclude us from relying on gender as a determining factor.

Several courts have declared the maternal preference, or "tender years presumption," unconstitutional. *See, e.g., State ex rel. Watts v. Watts,* 350 N.Y.S.2d 285, 290 (1973). . . . Although *Watts* used a strict scrutiny test, it is equally doubtful that the maternal preference can be sustained on an intermediate level of review. This is particularly true when the tender years doctrine is used as a "tie-breaker," as it is in Utah, because in that situation the Court is "denying custody to all fathers who . . . *are as capable as the mother.* . . . While over inclusiveness [sic] is tolerable at the rational basis level of review, it becomes problematic at the heightened level of scrutiny recognized in gender discrimination cases."

Even ignoring the constitutional infirmities of the maternal preference, the rule lacks validity because it is unnecessary and perpetuates outdated stereotypes. The development of the tender years doctrine was perhaps useful in a society in which fathers traditionally worked outside the home and mothers did not; however, since that pattern is no longer prevalent, particularly in post-separation single-parent households, the tender years doctrine is equally anachronistic. Further, "by arbitrarily applying a presumption in favor of the mother and awarding custody to her on that basis, a court is not truly evaluating what is in the child's best interests."

We believe that the choice in competing child custody claims should instead be based on function-related factors. Prominent among these, though not exclusive, is the identity of the primary caretaker during the marriage. Other factors should include the identity of the parent with greater flexibility to provide personal care for the child and the identity of the parent with whom the child has spent most of his or her time pending custody determination if that period has been lengthy. Another important factor should be the stability of the environment provided by each parent.

In accord with those guidelines, we disavow today those cases that continue to approve, even indirectly, an arbitrary maternal preference, thereby encouraging arguments such as those made by the cross-appellant in this case. . . .

Although the trial court in this case found both parties to be fit custodial parents, its ultimate judgment on custody required an assessment of the complex situation before it. The court did not follow the recommendations made by the social worker or the plaintiff's brother. As child custody determination turns on numerous factors, however, that choice was within its discretion. The evidence indicated that the twelve-year-old son manifested a strong preference for his father, which had caused friction and ill feelings between him and his mother. The father also appeared to show a preference for the older son, which fact supports the trial court's decision to split the custody of the children between the parents. Certainly these were factors dictating the course of action taken by the trial court. We find no abuse of discretion in the custody award.

NOTE

A study of 238 randomly selected cases in urban Ohio found that approximately 13 percent of sole and joint custody awards went to men. The study found that the age of the child still plays a significant role in custody determinations; only 23 percent of custodial fathers were awarded custody of a child under the age of five. Wendy Reiboldt and Sharon Seiling, *Factors Related to Men's Award of Custody*, 15 FAM. ADV. 42 (1992). *See generally*, TERRY ARENDELL, FATHERS AND DIVORCE (1995); ROBERT E. EMERY, RENEGOTIATING FAMILY RELATIONSHIPS: DIVORCE, CHILD CUSTODY AND MEDIATION (1994); DEMIE KURZ, FOR RICHER, FOR POORER: MOTHERS CONFRONT DIVORCE (1995).

2.   PRIMARY CARETAKER PRESUMPTION

Garska v. McCoy

Supreme Court of Appeals of West Virginia, 1981.
278 S.E.2d 357.

■ NEELY, JUSTICE.

The appellant, Gwendolyn McCoy, appeals from an order of the Circuit Court of Logan County which gave the custody of her son, Jonathan Conway McCoy, to the appellee, Michael Garska, the natural father. While in many regards this is a confusing case procedurally, since the mother and father were never married, nonetheless it squarely presents the issue of the proper interaction between the 1980 legislative amendment to W. VA. CODE, 48–2–15 which eliminates any gender based presumption in awarding custody and our case of *J.B. v. A.B.*, 242 S.E.2d 248 (W. Va. 1978) which established a strong maternal presumption with regard to children of tender years.

In February, 1978 the appellant moved from her grandparents' house in Logan County, where she had been raised, to Charlotte, North Carolina to live with her mother. At that time appellant was 15 years old and her mother shared a trailer with appellee, Michael Garska. In March, Gwendolyn McCoy became pregnant by Michael Garska and in June, she returned to her grandparents' home in West Virginia.

The appellant received no support from the appellee during her pregnancy, but after she gave birth to baby Jonathan the appellee sent a package of baby food and diapers. In subsequent months the baby developed a chronic respiratory infection which required hospitalization and considerable medical attention. Gwendolyn's grandfather, Stergil Altizer, a retired coal miner, attempted to have his great-grandson's hospitalization and medical care paid by the United Mine Workers' medical insurance but he was informed that the baby was ineligible unless legally adopted by the Altizers.

In October, 1979 Gwendolyn McCoy signed a consent in which she agreed to the adoption of Jonathan by her grandparents, the Altizers. Upon learning of the adoption plan, the appellee visited the baby for the first time and began sending weekly money orders for $15. The Altizers filed a petition for adoption in the Logan County Circuit Court on 9 November 1979 and on 7 January 1980 the appellee filed a petition for writ of habeas corpus to secure custody of his son.

Both the adoption and the habeas corpus proceedings were consolidated for hearing ... and the circuit court awarded custody of Jonathan McCoy to the appellee based upon the following findings of fact:

(a) The petitioner, Michael Garska, is the natural father of the infant child, Jonathan Conway McCoy;

(b) The petitioner, Michael Garska, is better educated than the natural mother and her alleged fiance;

(c) The petitioner, Michael Garska, is more intelligent than the natural mother;

(d) The petitioner, Michael Garska, is better able to provide financial support and maintenance than the natural mother;

(e) The petitioner, Michael Garska, can provide a better social and economic environment than the natural mother;

(f) The petitioner, Michael Garska, has a somewhat better command of the English language than the natural mother;

(g) The petitioner, Michael Garska, has a better appearance and demeanor than the natural mother;

(h) The petitioner, Michael Garska, is very highly motivated in his desire to have custody of the infant child, and the natural mother had previously executed an adoption consent, for said child.

. . .

While the issue of adoption by the Altizers does, indeed, enter into this case, in the final analysis the entire dispute comes down to a custody fight between the natural father and the natural mother....

In the case before us the father, by providing fifteen dollars a week child support, probably showed sufficient parental interest to give him standing to object to an adoption. However, there is no evidence before us to indicate that the mother was an unfit parent and, consequently, no justification for the trial court to remove custody from the primary caretaker parent and vest it in a parent who had had no previous emotional interaction with the child.

. . .

The loss of children is a terrifying specter to concerned and loving parents; however, it is particularly terrifying to the primary caretaker parent who, by virtue of the caretaking function, was closest to the child before the divorce or other proceedings were initiated. While the primary caretaker parent in most cases in West Virginia is still the mother, nonetheless, now that sex roles are becoming more flexible and high-income jobs are opening to women, it is conceivable that the primary caretaker parent may also be the father. If the primary caretaker parent is, indeed, the father, then under W.

Va. Code, 48–2–15 [1980] he will be entitled to the alimony and support payments exactly as a woman would be in similar circumstances.

Since the parent who is not the primary caretaker is usually in the superior financial position, the subsequent welfare of the child depends to a substantial degree upon the level of support payments which are awarded in the course of a divorce. Our experience instructs us that uncertainty about the outcome of custody disputes leads to the irresistible temptation to trade the custody of the child in return for lower alimony and child support payments. Since trial court judges generally approve consensual agreements on child support, underlying economic data which bear upon the equity of settlements are seldom investigated at the time an order is entered. While Code, 48–2–15 [1980] speaks in terms of "the best interest of the children" in every case, the one enormously important function of legal rules is to inspire rational and equitable settlements in cases which never reach adversary status in court.

If every controversy which arose in this society required court resolution, the under-staffed judiciary would topple like a house of cards. It is only voluntary compliance with the criminal law and the orderly settlement of private affairs in the civil law which permits the system to function at all. Consequently, anytime a new statute is passed or a new rule of common law developed, both legislators and judges must pay careful attention to interpreting it in a way which is consonant with equity in the area of private settlements.

[*J.*]*B. v. A.B.*, *supra*, attempted to remove from most run-of-the-mill divorce cases the entire issue of child custody. Certainly if we believed from our experience that full-blown hearings on child custody between two fit parents would afford more intelligent child placement than an arbitrary rule, we would not have adopted an arbitrary rule. However, it is emphatically the case that hearings do not enhance justice, particularly since custody fights are highly destructive to the emotional health of children. Furthermore, our mechanical rule was really quite narrowly drawn to apply only to those cases where voluminous evidence would inevitably be unenlightening. We limited the mechanical rule to the custody of children who are too young to formulate an opinion concerning their own custody and, further, we limited it to cases where an initial determination had been made that the mother was, indeed, a fit parent. While in *J.B. v. A.B.*, *supra*, we expressed ourselves in terms of the traditional maternal preference, the Legislature has instructed us that such a gender based standard is unacceptable. However, we are convinced that the best interests of the children are best served in awarding them to the primary caretaker parent, regardless of sex.

Since trial courts almost always award custody to the primary caretaker parent anyway, establishment of certainty in this regard permits the issues of alimony and support to stand upon their own legs and to be litigated or settled upon the merits of relevant financial criteria, without introducing into the equation the terrifying prospect of loss to the primary caretaker of the children. As we noted in *J.B. v. A.B.*, *supra*, "empirical findings directly or indirectly relevant to questions for which judges deciding difficult [custody] cases need answers are virtually nonexistent." The 1980 Amendment to Code, 48–2–15 was not intended to disturb our determination that in most instances the issue of child custody between two competent parents cannot be litigated effectively. Its intent was merely to correct the inherent unfairness of establishing a gender-based, maternal presumption which would defeat the just claims of a father if he had, in fact, been the primary caretaker parent.

In setting the child custody law in domestic relations cases we are concerned with three practical considerations. First, we are concerned to prevent the issue of custody from being used in an abusive way as a coercive weapon to affect the level of support payments and the outcome of other issues in the underlying divorce proceeding. Where a custody fight emanates from this reprehensible motive the children inevitably become pawns to be sacrificed in what ultimately becomes a very cynical game. Second, in the average divorce proceeding intelligent determination of relative degrees of fitness requires a precision of measurement which is not possible given the tools available to judges. Certainly it is no more reprehensible for judges to admit that they cannot measure minute gradations of psychological capacity between two fit parents than it is for a physicist to concede that it is impossible for him to measure the speed of an electron. Third, there is an urgent need in contemporary divorce law for a legal structure upon which a divorcing couple may rely in reaching a settlement.

While recent statutory changes encourage private ordering of divorce upon the "no-fault" ground of "irreconcilable differences," W. VA. CODE, 48–2–4(a)(10) [1977], our legal structure has not simultaneously been tightened to provide a reliable framework within which the divorcing couple can bargain intelligently. Nowhere is the lack of certainty greater than in child custody. Not very long ago, the courts were often intimately involved with all aspects of a divorce. Even an estranged couple who had reached an amicable settlement had to undergo "play-acting" before the court in order to obtain a divorce. Now, however, when divorces are numerous, easy, and routinely concluded out of court intelligible, reliable rules upon which out-of-court bargaining can be based must be an important consideration in the formulation of our rules.

Since the Legislature has concluded that private ordering by divorcing couples is preferable to judicial ordering, we must insure that each spouse is adequately protected during the out-of-court bargaining. Uncertainty of outcome is very destructive of the position of the primary caretaker parent because he or she will be willing to sacrifice everything else in order to avoid the terrible prospect of losing the child in the unpredictable process of litigation.

This phenomenon may be denominated the "Solomon syndrome", that is that the parent who is most attached to the child will be most willing to accept an inferior bargain. In the court of Solomon, the "harlot" who was willing to give up her child in order to save him from being cleaved in half so that he could be equally divided, was rewarded for her sacrifice, but in the big world out there the sacrificing parent generally loses necessary support or alimony payments. This then must also be compensated for "in the best interests of the children." Moreover, it is likely that the primary caretaker will have less financial security than the nonprimary caretaker and, consequently, will be unable to sustain the expense of custody litigation, requiring as is so often the case these days, the payments for expert psychological witnesses.

Therefore, in the interest of removing the issue of child custody from the type of acrimonious and counter-productive litigation which a procedure inviting exhaustive evidence will inevitably create, we hold today that there is a presumption in favor of the primary caretaker parent, if he or she meets the minimum, objective standard for being a fit parent as articulated in *J.B.*

v. A.B., supra[9] regardless of sex. Therefore, in any custody dispute involving children of tender years it is incumbent upon the circuit court to determine as a threshold question which parent was the primary caretaker parent before the domestic strife giving rise to the proceeding began.

While it is difficult to enumerate all of the factors which will contribute to a conclusion that one or the other parent was the primary caretaker parent, nonetheless, there are certain obvious criteria to which a court must initially look. In establishing which natural or adoptive parent is the primary caretaker, the trial court shall determine which parent has taken primary responsibility for, *inter alia*, the performance of the following caring and nurturing duties of a parent: (1) preparing and planning of meals; (2) bathing, grooming and dressing; (3) purchasing, cleaning, and care of clothes; (4) medical care, including nursing and trips to physicians; (5) arranging for social interaction among peers after school, i.e. transporting to friends' houses or, for example, to girl or boy scout meetings; (6) arranging alternative care, i.e. babysitting, day-care, etc.; (7) putting child to bed at night, attending to child in the middle of the night, waking child in the morning; (8) disciplining, i.e. teaching general manners and toilet training; (9) educating, i.e. religious, cultural, social, etc.; and, (10) teaching elementary skills, i.e., reading, writing and arithmetic.

In those custody disputes where the facts demonstrate that child care and custody were shared in an entirely equal way, then indeed no presumption arises and the court must proceed to inquire further into relative degrees of parental competence. However, where one parent can demonstrate with regard to a child of tender years that he or she is clearly the primary caretaker parent, then the court must further determine only whether the primary caretaker parent is a fit parent. Where the primary caretaker parent achieves the minimum, objective standard of behavior which qualifies him or her as a fit parent, the trial court must award the child to the primary caretaker parent.

Consequently, all of the principles enunciated in *J.B. v. A.B., supra*, are reaffirmed today except that wherever the words "mother," "maternal," or "maternal preference" are used in that case, some variation of the term "primary caretaker parent," as defined by this case should be substituted. In this regard we should point out that the absolute presumption in favor of a fit primary caretaker parent applies only to children of tender years. Where a child is old enough to formulate an opinion about his or her own custody the trial court is entitled to receive such opinion and accord it such weight as he feels appropriate. When, in the opinion of the trial court, a child old enough to formulate an opinion but under the age of 14 has indicated a justified desire to live with the parent who is not the primary caretaker, the court may award the child to such parent.

. . .

In the case before us it is obvious that the petitioner was the primary caretaker parent before the proceedings under consideration in this case arose, and there is no finding on the part of the trial court judge that she is an unfit parent. In fact, all of the evidence indicates that she mobilized all of the resources at her command, namely the solicitous regard of her grandparents, in the interest of this child and that she went to extraordinary lengths to provide for him adequate medical attention and financial support.

---

9. As we said in J.B. v. A.B., *supra*, where the primary caretaker fails to provide: emotional support; routine cleanliness; or nourishing food, the presumption shall not apply.

While, as the trial court found, the educational and economic position of the father is superior to that of the mother, nonetheless, those factors alone pale in comparison to love, affection, concern, tolerance, and the willingness to sacrifice—factors above which conclusions can be made for the future most intelligently upon a course of conduct in the past. At least with regard to the primary caretaker parent there is a track record to which a court can look and where that parent is fit he or she should be awarded continued custody.

Certainly the record in the case before us does not demonstrate any intent by the mother to abandon the child through permitting him to be adopted by the grandparents; it is well recognized that mothers in penurious circumstances often resort to adoption in order to make the child eligible for social security or union welfare benefits, all of which significantly enhance the child's opportunities in life. Absent an explicit finding of intent to abandon we cannot construe manipulation of the welfare system to direct maximum benefits towards this child as anything other than a solicitous concern for his welfare.

Reversed and remanded.

NOTE

How does a "primary caretaker" differ from a "psychological parent," which is defined as "one who, on a continuing, day-to-day basis, through interaction, companionship, interplay, and mutuality, fulfills the child's psychological needs?" JOSEPH GOLDSTEIN, ANNA FREUD, & ALBERT J. SOLNIT, BEYOND THE BEST INTERESTS OF THE CHILD 98 (1978).

As the Rose transcript indicates, in many divorces both parents may be "psychological parents." The term "primary caretaker," by contrast, suggests only one parent qualifies. Is this appropriate?

The court in *Garska* justifies the new presumption as necessary to eliminate the use of custody challenges as a weapon in the economic bargaining between the divorcing couple. But there may be other ways to avoid emotional blackmail, such as clarifying the standards courts will follow in awarding property or alimony, a subject covered in Chapter 9. The primary caretaker presumption appears to operate at the expense of a spouse who works outside the home. Is that fair? Is the quantity of time spent with a child, as opposed to the quality, the best basis for determining custody? A fair basis? *See* MINN. STAT. ANN. § 518.17(a) (West 2011) (stating that "[t]he primary caretaker factor may not be used as a presumption in determining the best interests of the child").

3.   JOINT CUSTODY

Rivero v. Rivero

Supreme Court of Nevada, 2009.
216 P.3d 213.

■ GIBBONS, J.

[M]s. Rivero filed a complaint for divorce, and the parties eventually reached a settlement. The district court entered a divorce decree incorporating the parties' agreement. The parties agreed to joint physical custody of the child, with Ms. Rivero having physical custody five days each week and Mr. Rivero having physical custody for the remaining two days. The divorce decree also reflected the parties' agreement that neither party was obligated to pay child support.

Less than two months after entry of the divorce decree, Ms. Rivero moved the court to modify the decree by awarding her child support. The district court dismissed her motion. Less than one year later, Ms. Rivero moved the district court for primary physical custody and child support. She alleged that Mr. Rivero did not spend time with the child, that instead his elderly mother took care of the child, and that he did not have suitable living accommodations for the child. Ms. Rivero also argued that she had de facto primary custody because she cared for the child most of the time. Mr. Rivero countered that Ms. Rivero denied him visitation unless he provided food, clothes, and money and denied him overnight visitation once he became engaged to another woman. Mr. Rivero requested that the district court enforce the 5/2 timeshare in the divorce decree, or, alternatively, order a 50/50 timeshare.

The district court held a custody hearing, during which the parties presented contradictory testimony regarding how much time Mr. Rivero actually spent with the child. The district court ruled that the matter did not warrant an evidentiary hearing. The district court further found that the use of the term joint physical custody in the divorce decree did not accurately reflect the timeshare arrangement that the parties were actually practicing, in which Ms. Rivero seemed to have physical custody most of the time. As a result, the court denied Ms. Rivero's motion for child support, found that the parties had joint physical custody, and ordered the parties to mediation to establish a more equal timeshare plan to reflect a joint physical custody arrangement.

. . .

At a subsequent hearing . . . the district court addressed the custody timeshare arrangement because the parties had been unable to reach an agreement in mediation. Although the divorce decree provided Ms. Rivero with custody five days each week and Mr. Rivero with custody two days each week, the district court concluded that the parties actually intended an equal timeshare. The district court noted that it was "just trying to find a middle ground" between what the divorce decree provided and what the parties actually wanted regarding a custody timeshare. Further, the court found that the decree's order for joint physical custody was inconsistent with the decree's timeshare arrangement because the decree's five-day, two-day time-share did not constitute joint physical custody. In its order, the district court concluded that the parties intended joint physical custody and ordered an equal timeshare.

The district court found that Ms. Rivero did not have de facto primary physical custody. Therefore, the court determined that an evidentiary hearing was unnecessary because it was not changing primary custody to joint custody, but was modifying a joint physical custody arrangement.

Ms. Rivero appeals, challenging . . . the order modifying the custody timeshare.

. . .

In order to clarify the definition of joint physical custody, we first address the definition of legal custody. Physical and legal custody involve separate legal rights and control separate factual scenarios. . . .

. . .

Legal custody involves having basic legal responsibility for a child and making major decisions regarding the child, including the child's health, education, and religious upbringing. Sole legal custody vests this right with one parent, while joint legal custody vests this right with both parents. Joint legal custody requires that the parents be able to cooperate, communicate, and compromise to act in the best interest of the child. In a joint legal custody situation, the parents must consult with each other to make major decisions regarding the child's upbringing, while the parent with whom the child is residing at that time usually makes minor day-to-day decisions.

. . .

Joint legal custody can exist regardless of the physical custody arrangements of the parties. Also, the parents need not have equal decision-making power in a joint legal custody situation. For example, one parent may have decisionmaking authority regarding certain areas or activities of the child's life, such as education or healthcare. If the parents in a joint legal custody situation reach an impasse and are unable to agree on a decision, then the parties may appear before the court "on an equal footing" to have the court decide what is in the best interest of the child.

Physical custody involves the time that a child physically spends in the care of a parent. During this time, the child resides with the parent and that parent provides supervision for the child and makes the day-to-day decisions regarding the child. Parents can share joint physical custody, or one parent may have primary physical custody while the other parent may have visitation rights.

The type of physical custody arrangement is particularly important in three situations. First, it determines the standard for modifying physical custody. Second, it requires a specific procedure if a parent wants to move out of state with the child. Third, the type of physical custody arrangement affects the child support award. Because the physical custody arrangement is crucial in making these determinations, the district courts need clear custody definitions in order to evaluate the true nature of parties' agreements. Absent direction from the Legislature, we define joint physical custody and primary physical custody in light of existing Nevada law.

Ms. Rivero and the Family Law Section assert that this court should clarify the definition of joint physical custody to determine whether it requires a specific timeshare agreement. The Family Law Section suggests that we define joint physical custody by requiring that each parent have physical custody of the child at least 40 percent of the time. In accordance with this suggestion, and for the reasons set forth below, we clarify Nevada's definition of joint physical custody pursuant to Nevada statutes and caselaw and create parameters to clarify which timeshare arrangements qualify as joint physical custody.

Although Nevada law suggests that joint physical custody approximates an equal timeshare, to date, neither the Nevada Legislature nor this court have explicitly defined joint physical custody or specified whether a specific timeshare is required for a joint physical custody arrangement. In fact, even the terminology is inconsistent. This court has used the following phrases to describe situations where both parents have physical custody: shared custodial arrangements, joint physical custody, equal physical custody, shared physical custody, and joint and shared custody. Given the various terms used to describe joint physical custody and the lack of a precise definition and timeshare requirement, we now define joint physical custody and the time-share required for such arrangements.

. . .

Although NRS Chapter 125 does not contain a definition of joint physical custody, the legislative history regarding NRS 125.490 reveals the Legislature's understanding of its meaning. Joint physical custody is "[a]warding custody of the minor child or children to BOTH PARENTS and providing that physical custody shall be shared by the parents in such a way to ensure the child or children of frequent associations and a continuing relationship with both parents." Hearing on S.B. 188 Before the Assembly Judiciary Comm., 61st Leg. (Nev., Apr. 2, 1981) (summary of supporting information). This does not include divided or alternating custody, where each parent acts as a sole custodial parent at different times, or split custody, where one parent is awarded sole custody of one or more of the children and the other parent is awarded sole custody of one or more of the children. *Id.*

The question then remains, what constitutes joint physical custody to ensure the child frequent associations and a continuing relationship with both parents? Our law presumes that joint physical custody approximates a 50/50 timeshare. *See Wesley* [*v. Foster*], 65 P.3d at 252–53 [Nev. 2005] (discussing shared custody arrangements and equal timeshare); *Wright* [*v. Osburn*], 970 P.2d [1071,] 1071–72 [Nev. 1998] (discussing joint physical custody and equal timeshare). This court has noted that the public policy, as stated in NRS 125.490, is that joint custody is presumably in the best interest of the child if the parents agree to it and that this policy encourages equally shared parental responsibilities.

Although joint physical custody must approximate an equal timeshare, given the variations inherent in child rearing, such as school schedules, sports, vacations, and parents' work schedules, to name a few, an exactly equal timeshare is not always possible. Therefore, there must be some flexibility in the timeshare requirement. The question then becomes, when does a timeshare become so unequal that it is no longer joint physical custody? Courts have grappled with this question and come to different conclusions. For example, this court has described a situation where the children live with one parent and the other parent has every-other-weekend visitation as primary physical custody with visitation, even when primary custody was changed for one month out of the year and the other parent would revert back to weekend visitations. In *Wright*, 970 P.2d at 1071, this court described an arrangement where the parents had the children on a rotating weekly basis as joint physical custody.

. . .

We conclude that, consistent with legislative intent and our caselaw, in joint physical custody arrangements, the timeshare must be approximately 50/50. However, absent legislative direction regarding how far removed from 50/50 a timeshare may be and still constitute joint physical custody, the law remains unclear. Therefore, to approximate an equal timeshare but allow for necessary flexibility, we hold that each parent must have physical custody of the child at least 40 percent of the time to constitute joint physical custody. We acknowledge that the Legislature is free to alter the timeshare required for joint physical custody, but we adopt this guideline to provide needed clarity for the district courts. This guideline ensures frequent associations and a continuing relationship with both parents. If a parent does not have physical custody of the child at least 40 percent of the time, then the arrangement is one of primary physical custody with visitation. We now address how the courts should calculate the 40–percent timeshare.

. . .

Our dissenting colleague ... argues that the Legislature should be creating the custody definitions set out in this opinion. The issues in this case and the Family Law Section's amicus curiae brief demonstrate that there are gaps in the law. However, despite these gaps, attorneys must still advise their clients, public policy still favors settlement, and parties are still entitled to consistent and fair resolution of their disputes. To resolve the issues on appeal and ensure consistent and fair application of the law by district courts, this court has attempted to fill some of these gaps by defining the various types of child custody.

. . .

The district court should calculate the time during which a party has physical custody of a child over one calendar year. Each parent must have physical custody of the child at least 40 percent of the time, which is 146 days per year. Calculating the timeshare over a one-year period allows the court to consider weekly arrangements as well as any deviations from those arrangements such as emergencies, holidays, and summer vacation. In calculating the time during which a party has physical custody of the child, the district court should look at the number of days during which a party provided supervision of the child, the child resided with the party, and during which the party made the day-to-day decisions regarding the child. The district court should not focus on, for example, the exact number of hours the child was in the care of the parent, whether the child was sleeping, or whether the child was in the care of a third-party caregiver or spent time with a friend or relative during the period of time in question.

Therefore, absent evidence that joint physical custody is not in the best interest of the child, if each parent has physical custody of the child at least 40 percent of the time, then the arrangement is one of joint physical custody.

[A] parent has primary physical custody when he or she has physical custody of the child subject to the district court's power to award the other parent visitation rights. The focus of primary physical custody is the child's residence. The party with primary physical custody is the party that has the primary responsibility for maintaining a home for the child and providing for the child's basic needs.

Primary physical custody arrangements may encompass a wide array of circumstances. As discussed above, if a parent has physical custody less than 40 percent of the time, then that parent has visitation rights and the other parent has primary physical custody. Likewise, a primary physical custody arrangement could also encompass a situation where one party has primary physical custody and the other party has limited or no visitation.

Having determined what constitutes joint physical custody and primary physical custody, we now consider whether the district court abused its discretion in determining that the parties had joint physical custody when their divorce decree described a 5/2 custodial timeshare but labeled the arrangement as joint physical custody.

. . .

We conclude that the district court properly disregarded the parties' definition of joint physical custody because the district court must apply Nevada's physical custody definition—not the parties' definition. We also conclude that the district court abused its discretion by not making specific findings of fact to support its decision that the custody arrangement constituted joint physical custody and that modification of the divorce decree was in the best interest of the child.

We now address the modification of custody agreements. We conclude that the terms of the parties' custody agreement will control except when the parties move the court to modify the custody arrangement. In custody modification cases, the court must use the terms and definitions provided under Nevada law.

Parties are free to contract, and the courts will enforce their contracts if they are not unconscionable, illegal, or in violation of public policy. Therefore, parties are free to agree to child custody arrangements and those agreements are enforceable if they are not unconscionable, illegal, or in violation of public policy. However, when modifying child custody, the district courts must apply Nevada child custody law, including NRS Chapter 125C and caselaw. Therefore, once parties move the court to modify an existing child custody agreement, the court must use the terms and definitions provided under Nevada law, and the parties' definitions no longer control. In this case, Ms. Rivero moved the district court to modify the decree. Therefore, the district court properly disregarded the parties' definition of joint physical custody.

. . .

Under the definition of joint physical custody discussed above, each parent must have physical custody of the child at least 40 percent of the time. This would be approximately three days each week. Therefore, the district court properly found that the 5/2 timeshare included in the parties' divorce decree does not constitute joint physical custody. The district court must then look at the actual physical custody timeshare that the parties were exercising to determine what custody arrangement is in effect.

The district court summarily determined that Mr. and Ms. Rivero shared custody on approximately an equal time basis. Based on this finding, the district court determined that it was modifying a joint physical custody arrangement, and therefore, Ms. Rivero, as the moving party, had the burden to show that modifying the custody arrangement was in the child's best interest. However, the district court did not make findings of fact supported by substantial evidence to support its determination that the custody arrangement was, in fact, joint physical custody. Therefore, this decision was an abuse of discretion.

Moreover, the district court abused its discretion by modifying the custody agreement to reflect a 50/50 timeshare without making specific findings of fact demonstrating that the modification was in the best interest of the child.

Specific factual findings are crucial to enforce or modify a custody order and for appellate review. Accordingly, on remand, the district court must evaluate the true nature of the custodial arrangement, pursuant to the definition of joint physical custody described above, by evaluating the arrangement the parties are exercising in practice, regardless of any contrary language in the divorce decree. The district court shall then apply the appropriate test for determining whether to modify the custody arrangement and make express findings supporting its determination.

We conclude that the district court abused its discretion when it determined, without making specific findings of fact, that the parties had joint physical custody and when it modified the custody arrangement set forth in the divorce decree. We therefore reverse and remand this matter to the district court for further proceedings, including a new custody determination pursuant to the definition of joint physical custody clarified in this opinion.

NOTE

Robert H. Mnookin and Eleanor Maccoby oppose a presumption in favor of joint physical custody, particularly in cases where there is substantial conflict between parents. Robert H. Mnookin & Eleanor Maccoby, Dividing the Child 284–85 (1992). *See also*, Robert H. Mnookin & Eleanor Maccoby, *Facing the Dilemmas of Child Custody*, 10 Va. J. Soc. Pol'y & L. 54, 62, 74, 75 (2002), a study of 1,100 post-divorce families in California:

> Our most disturbing finding with respect to legal conflict concerns the frequency with which joint physical custody decrees are being used by high-conflict families to resolve disputes. About a third of the 166 cases in our study in which the decree provided for joint custody involved substantial or intense legal conflict. In about half of these cases, the children in fact resided with the mother—the legal label did not reflect the social reality. Nevertheless, we did find some 25 joint physical custody cases in which the children were in fact dividing their residential time fairly equally between parents who had substantial legal conflict. Moreover, we found a strong relationship between the intensity of legal conflict and the ability of parents to develop cooperative co-parental relations following the divorce: a much higher proportion of those families with substantial or intense legal conflict had conflicted co-parenting styles, and many fewer were able to develop cooperative co-parenting relationships.

> . . .

> Although our study has not examined the impact of co-parental conflict on children, follow-up work in the context of the Stanford Child Custody Study as well as the research of others strongly suggests that such conflict can create grave risks for children. True, some intensely hostile parents manage not to draw the children into their conflict. But many do. We do not think it good for children to feel caught in the middle of parental conflict, and in those cases where the parents are involved in bitter dispute, we believe a presumption for joint custody would do harm. Our study suggests that in a number of cases in which families today adopt joint physical custody, there has been substantial legal conflict. To the extent that this custody arrangement is the result of encouragement by mediators, or judges for that matter, we think it is unwise. We wish to note, however, that joint custody can work very well when parents are able to cooperate. Thus we are by no means recommending that joint custody be denied to parents who want to try it.

Do you agree with Mnookin and Maccoby?

4.   Past Care or the "Approximate the Time" Standard

Young v. Hector

Court of Appeal of Florida, Third District, 1998.
740 So. 2d 1153.

■ Green, J.

Upon our rehearing en banc of this cause, we withdraw the prior panel opinion issued on June 24, 1998, and substitute the following opinion in its stead.

The former husband/father (Robert Young) appeals from the final judgment of dissolution of marriage. We affirm the trial court's decision designating the former wife/mother (Alice Hector) as the primary custodial parent of the two minor children. . . .

The father's main contention on this appeal is that the trial court abused its discretion when it awarded custody of the minor children to the mother. We do not agree. . . . [W]e conclude that there was substantial competent evidence to support the trial court's discretionary call in this regard. Thus, there is no basis for us to overturn the lower court's decision.

As we see it, the child custody issue in this case, with all its attendant notoriety, centers only around our standard of review as an appellate court. The simple issue for our consideration is whether the trial court abused its discretion when it determined that the best interests of the two minor children dictated that their mother be designated their primary custodial parent.

At the outset, it is important to emphasize that both the mother and father are very loving and capable parents. Nobody disputes this fact. . . . What then tilted the scales in favor of awarding custody to the mother? The father suggests that it was gender bias. The record evidence, however, simply does not support this suggestion.

· · ·

At the time of their marriage in 1982, both the father and mother were successful professionals in New Mexico. He was an architectural designer with his own home design firm as well as an entrepreneur with a publishing company. She was an attorney in private practice at her own firm. Their marriage was a second for both. He had no children from his first marriage. She had custody of her two minor children (now grown) from her first marriage, which she successfully reared while simultaneously juggling the demands of her law practice.

· · ·

Hector and Young became the parents of two daughters born in 1985 and 1988. After the birth of their children, both parents continued to work outside of the home and pursued their respective professional endeavors with the assistance of a live-in nanny, au pair, or housekeeper. As typical working parents, they would both arrive home between the hours of 5:30 and 6:00 each evening. Both contributed to and shared in the household expenditures at all times.

Sometime in late 1987, the father's business ventures began to suffer certain financial reversals and the mother became bored with her practice in New Mexico. Both parties agreed to relocate to Miami. Although there is a complete conflict in the record between the parties as to who broached the subject of the couple's relocation to Miami and the circumstances under which they would relocate in terms of their respective careers, it is significant that neither of these parties ever testified that they ever agreed or expected the mother to pursue her legal career while the father remained at home as the full-time caregiver to their minor children. To the contrary, the father actively pursued job leads in the Miami area prior to the couple's relocation.

In June 1989, the mother and her two minor daughters arrived in Miami first. During that summer, she studied for and took the Florida Bar exam and landed a position with a mid-sized law firm. The father stayed behind in New Mexico until October 1989 in order to complete the construction of a new house and to remodel the couple's New Mexico home in order to enhance its resale potential.

After the father's move to Miami in the fall of 1989, he studied for and passed the Florida contractor's examination. Thereafter, during the spring and summer of 1990, the father spent his time repairing the couple's first marital residence in Miami. Thereafter, he renovated the home, which ultimately became the couple's second marital residence.... [I]t is undisputed that from the time the minor children were brought to Miami in 1989 until the fall of 1993, the needs of the minor children were attended to by a live-in housekeeper when they were not in school during the day and by the mother upon her arrival from work in the evenings.

After the father's renovations to the couple's second Miami residence were completed and the family moved in, the mother testified that she began to have serious discussions (which eventually escalated into arguments) about the father's need to find gainful employment. Although the mother was earning a very decent income as an attorney at the time, it was undisputed that this family was operating with a negative cash flow.

Rather than pursue gainful employment to financially assist the household and his minor children, the father turned his attentions elsewhere. During the remainder of 1990 through 1993, the father left the state and was frequently away from the mother and minor children for months at a time. During this time, he returned to New Mexico to attend to lingering matters involving his prior businesses there and to make preparations for an upcoming treasure hunt. He also visited his sick brother in Arkansas and later handled his brother's estate matters upon his brother's demise.... [T]he father spent approximately fourteen months away from his family pursuing buried gold in New Mexico on a treasure hunt. The minor children were continuously being cared for by the housekeeper/baby-sitter during the day and the mother after work. The father saw his family during this fourteen-month period once every five weeks and according to the mother, only at her insistence and pursuant to her arrangements for such family reunions.

When the father finally returned to South Florida, in the fall of 1993, the mother had accepted a partnership position with a large Florida law firm at a salary of approximately $300,000 annually. Even with the mother's salary increase, the family remained steep in debt. At that time, the couple no longer had a live-in nanny or baby-sitter for the children. The children were in a public school full-time between the hours of 8:30 a.m. and 2:00–3:00 p.m. The mother had employed a housekeeper ("Hattie") who came to the house each weekday between the hours of noon and 8:00 p.m. to clean, pickup and baby-sit the children after school. The mother's time with the children during the weekdays consisted of her awakening, dressing, and having breakfast with them prior to transporting them to school, and spending the early evening hours with them prior to their bedtime. The mother engaged in activities with the children on a full-time basis on the weekends. When the children became ill or distressed during the middle of the night, the mother was always the parent they looked to for assistance or solace.

. . .

Approximately one month after the father's return to the household in 1993, the mother asked the father for a divorce because of his continued refusal to seek gainful employment and due to his extramarital affair in New Mexico. It must be re-emphasized that at no time did the mother and father have any mutually expressed or tacit agreement for the father to remain unemployed. The father candidly conceded as much at trial. Consequently, this case simply did not involve the typical scenario where two spouses, by mutual agreement, agreed for one to remain at home to care for the children and the other spouse to work outside of the home.

. . .

Once the mother announced to the father that she wanted a divorce, the father began to spend less of his time away from Miami. Although he steadfastly refused to make any efforts to obtain employment, he did become more involved in the activities of his two daughters, who by that time, were 8 and 5. Since both girls were in school full-time at this time, the father's involvement with the girls' activities occurred primarily Mondays through Fridays between the hours of 3:00 p.m. and 6:30 p.m., prior to the mother's arrival from work. Upon the mother's arrival at the home, the father generally absented himself.

. . .

The father nevertheless maintained that he was the "primary caretaker" or "Mr. Mom" of these two children in the three years preceding this dissolution proceeding. The trial court viewed this contention with some degree of skepticism as it was entitled. The trial court's skepticism or disbelief was not at all unreasonable, given the father's admission that the nanny, Hattie, had taken care of these children in large part during the afternoon hours until their mother's arrival at home. The father's concession is what prompted the court to ultimately make inquiry as to why the father did not seek employment or alternatively, why there was a need for a full-time nanny:

[Father's attorney]: Who picks the kids up?

[Father]: Either Hattie or I. Typically, it's me. If I am tied up, whether it's a meeting or whatever, or if I go somewhere like your office, way up in North Miami Beach, and I don't get back in time and I thought I would, I can call Hattie and say, "Hattie, please pick up the children." She does. She picks them up frequently.

[The Court]: Is Hattie there five days a week?

[Father]: Yes sir. She comes at noon every day. She cleans the house in the afternoons. She prepares the dinners. The kids eat. We eat. I eat with the children every day typically at 6:30. She cleans up after that.

She'll draw a bath for Avery and she leaves at eight o'clock in the evening five days a week.

[The Court]: Maybe I'm missing something. Why don't you get a job?

[Father]: Well, because my background is architecture. That's my degree, but when I graduated, they did not have computers. Today, it's computer dominated and I'm computer illiterate.

. . .

I've gone on interviews. They like me. They like what I have to offer but their offices are basically all computerized.

Previously, because of the number of hours Ms. Hector worked, I filled in. Ms. Hector has a secretary that handles her whole life at the office and in a sense I was the secretary that handled her whole life at home and took care of the children.

[The Court]: But you've got a nanny doing that.

[Father]: No sir, I don't believe you can buy parents. Nannies can pick up. They can drop off.

[The Court]: Why [sic] do you need the nanny for, if you're there doing it?

[Father]: She cooks. She cleans. I could do a lot of that. Typically, people that have incomes of over a quarter of a million dollars or $300,000 can afford the luxury of having help, hired help.

I am not the kind of person that sits around and watches soap operas. I try to do meaningful, worthwhile things.

. . .

Contrary to the father's suggestion on appeal, this inquiry by the court is not evidence of gender bias. Given the undisputed large financial indebtedness of this couple, the trial court's inquiry about the need to employ a full-time nanny was both logical and practical under these circumstances and certainly could have also been appropriately posed to the mother if she had been recalcitrant about seeking gainful employment to assist the family's financial situation.

. . .

Apart from this evidence, the court also had the report and recommendations of the guardian ad litem upon which to rely. In recommending that the mother be named the primary custodial parent, the guardian ad litem cited three factors, all of which we find are supported by competent substantial evidence in the record. First of all, the guardian noted that the mother had been the more economically stable of the two parents throughout the marriage. We do not believe that the guardian gave the mother the edge simply because she earned a large salary. We believe, that what the guardian was attempting to convey was that the mother had shown a proclivity to remain steadily employed, unlike the father who unilaterally removed himself from the job market, although he was employable and the family needed the additional income. The trial court concluded that the father was "where he is largely because of his own choice." ... Given a choice between the mother, who maintained constant steady employment throughout the marriage to support the children (regardless of the amount of her income), and the father who unilaterally and steadfastly refused to do the same, the trial court's designation of the mother as custodial parent cannot be deemed an abuse of discretion.

. . .

The second factor relied upon by the guardian ad litem in recommending that the mother be declared the primary custodial parent was the fact that the mother had been a constant factor and dominant influence in the children's lives and the father had not. The guardian ad litem observed:

There have been times in the children's life [sic] when Bob has been, for whatever reasons, away from the home for substantial periods of time and Alice has been the dominant influence.

More recently, while she has been working, he has been available at home more hours of the day than she has been, but over a continuum of time, I believe that her presence has been a more steady presence in the sense of available almost the same time for the kids throughout the relationship, whereas Bob has been intensely absent and intensely present.

In its determination as to the best interests of the minor children, the trial court obviously deemed it more important to assess the children's time spent with each of the parents throughout the course of the marriage and not merely focus on the years immediately preceding the announcement of the dissolution action. That is, the trial court, in an effort to maintain continuity, could have legitimately determined that the children's best interests dictate that they remain with the parent who had continuously been there to care for their needs throughout their young lives rather than the parent who had devoted a substantial amount of time with them perhaps only when it was convenient and/or opportunistic to do so. The record evidence clearly supports the trial court's conclusion that the mother had been the constant parent throughout the children's lives. Thus, there was no basis for the panel to overturn the trial court's finding in this regard.

The last factor cited by the guardian ad litem, which tilted the scale in favor of the mother, was the mother's superior ability to control her anger around the children. The guardian ad litem testified that he personally witnessed one of the father's outbursts of anger in the presence of the children. For that reason, the guardian, who is also a retired circuit court judge, went so far as to recommend that the father receive anger control counseling.

Given this substantial competent evidence in the record, we cannot conclude that the trial court abused its discretion when it awarded custody of the minor children to their mother. Nor can we conclude that the court's determination was impermissibly influenced by gender bias against the father.

As long as the trial court's decision is supported by substantial competent evidence and is not based upon legally impermissible factors such as gender bias, it must be affirmed on appeal. For this reason, we affirm the order awarding primary residential custody of the minor children to the mother. However, on remand, the trial court should grant the father liberal and frequent access to the children.

. . .

■ SCHWARTZ, C.J., dissenting.

I remain convinced by the panel decision and by the dissent of . . . Judge Goderich that the trial court's "award" of the children's primary physical residence to the mother is unsupported by any cognizable, equitable consideration presented by the record. As the panel opinion, which has not in my view been successfully challenged by any of the contrary briefs or opinions, demonstrates, the children's parents, who know and care most about their welfare, had themselves established an arrangement prior to the dissolution as a part of which, upon any fair assessment, the father was the primary caretaker. As everyone agrees, under that regime, if not because of it, their girls have turned out to be well-behaved, well-adjusted, and accomplished young women who love both their parents: just what we all devoutly wish for and from our children. There is simply no reason for a court to tamper with what has worked so well. *See* PRINCIPLES OF THE LAW OF FAMILY

DISSOLUTION: ANALYSIS AND RECOMMENDATIONS (Am. Law Inst. 1998) (Tentative Draft No. 3, Part I) § 2.09(1). This is not only because it is almost always better to preserve a known good rather than to risk what the unknown future may bring, but, much more important, because the children are themselves entitled to stability in their lives and routine which would be compromised by any purposeless change in their caregiver. In many areas, the law properly recognizes the undesirability of disrupting the children's circumstances any more than is already necessarily required by their parents' separation and divorce. FLA. STAT. § 61.13(3)(d) (1995). *See Mize v. Mize*, 621 So. 2d 417 (Fla. 1993) (relocation of custodial parent); *Pino v. Pino*, 418 So. 2d 311 (Fla. Dist. Ct. App. 1982) (importance of children's remaining in home). This principle finds special application in the rule that modifications of the custody provisions of a final judgment may be made only when there has been a change of circumstances adversely affecting the welfare of the children.... When, as here, the children have manifestly benefitted from an arrangement established before the judgment, the same rule should apply.

. . .

Unless otherwise resolved by agreement of the parents ... or unless manifestly harmful to the child, the court should allocate custodial responsibility so that the proportion of custodial time the child spends with each parent approximates the proportion of time each parent spent performing caretaking functions for the child prior to the parents' separation.

. . .

What happens when that rule is not applied is illustrated by the result in this very case, in which it was necessary below and has been found necessary on appeal to resort to other, inadmissible, factors to justify the so-called exercise of discretion by the trial court and the affirmance of that result by this one.

. . .

In my opinion, there is no question whatever that the result below was dictated by the gender of the competing parties. It is usually extremely difficult to gauge the underlying motivations of any human being and one resists even more the assignment of an unworthy or impermissible reason to any judge's exercise of her judicial functions. This case, however, permits no other conclusion. I believe that this is shown by contemplating a situation in which the genders of the hard working and high earning lawyer and the stay at home architect were reversed, but everything else remained the same. The male attorney's claim for custody would have been virtually laughed out of court, and there is no realistic possibility that the mother architect would have actually "lost her children." (The fact, so heavily emphasized by members of the majority, that the hypothetical mother architect might have sought employment after the dissolution, as usually occurs, and that her time with the children would have therefore diminished, would have made no difference either.) It is, at best, naive in the extreme to suggest, let alone find, that the result below was not dictated by the evil of gender bias.

. . .

By rejecting the obvious but unacceptable in its search for a basis for the result below, the majority ... bases its determination that the discretion of the trial court was properly exercised upon the belief that the record shows (or that the trial court might have properly believed) that Mr. Young is less sincere, less well motivated, less admirable and generally a worse person and a worse parent than Ms. Hector. As I might do myself, one may agree with this assessment of the parties while profoundly disagreeing, as I certainly do, with the idea that any such consideration is a proper basis for decision-making in this field.

It is of course true, as the majority repeatedly emphasizes, that a "custody" decision is one within the discretion of the trial court. But judicial discretion may properly be exercised only on the basis of factors which are legally pertinent to the issue involved.... In this area, that issue is the children's best interests. Its resolution, in turn, cannot be based on a subjective assessment of the worth of the contending parties so long as, as was conclusively demonstrated in this case, the conduct and character traits referred to have not impacted upon the children. We had, I thought, come a long way from the time when a parent could be denied her parental rights—or, more properly stated, when the children could be deprived of their rights to having only their interests considered—merely because a judge may disapprove of her standards of conduct, much less of her character. Apparently, I was mistaken.

. . .

■ GODERICH, J., dissenting:

[T]he majority opinion focuses on the fact that the parties did not mutually agree that the father would stay at home to care for the children. Although it may be true that the mother did not expressly agree, the record demonstrates that the mother nonetheless acquiesced to this arrangement by allowing it to continue for three years. For example, although the parties had "separated," the mother permitted the husband to live in the marital home and to continue his role as a stay-at-home parent. Moreover, there is no doubt that the mother benefited from this arrangement (and possibly that is why she allowed it to continue). As a result of this caretaking arrangement, the mother was free to dedicate herself to her legal career by working extremely long hours without having to worry about whether the minor children's emotional needs were being met. Also, the record indicates that the children also benefited from their father's role as the primary caretaker since he was actively involved in their school and after-school activities.

. . .

Further, I believe that gender played a role in the trial court's decision, and continues to play a role in this Court's decision. At one point, the trial court, while questioning the father as to the nanny's role, stated to the father: "Maybe I'm missing something. Why don't you get a job." Shortly thereafter, the trial court also stated: "Why [sic] do you need the nanny for, if you're there doing it?"

. . .

I do not agree with the majority's observation that these statements had nothing to do with gender bias, but rather was a result of the parties' financial condition. During the trial court's exchange with the husband, there is nothing that would indicate that the trial court was concerned with the parties' financial condition. Further, I find it extremely hard to believe that if the roles were reversed any trial judge would question a mother's lack of employment or the employment of a nanny when the father earns over $300,000 per year. Moreover, the record indicates that it was the mother, not the father, who employed the nanny.

The majority opinion also suggests that the father should have obtained gainful employment in order to financially assist the household and minor children in light of the parties' financial condition. The record clearly demonstrates that with the husband's present skills, he did not have the ability to earn a substantial amount of money.... The record clearly establishes that the minor children's basic necessities were more than taken care of. There are certain things that money cannot buy and that a nanny cannot provide, such as the attention of caring parents. Once again, I do not believe that if the roles were reversed (a father who earns over $300,000 per year and a non-working mother), the majority would have suggested that the children would have been better off if the mother would have attained employment when her earning potential is limited and the father already makes over $300,000 per year. Instead, the majority would have probably suggested that the father restructure his debt, sell assets, and/or cut down on expenses so that the mother could continue the caretaking role that was established during the marriage.

The majority opinion also addresses the three "determinative factors" that the guardian ad litem looked at in recommending that the mother be named the primary residential parent. First, the guardian focused on the fact that the mother has been more economically stable throughout the marriage. Once again, if the roles were reversed, I believe that the guardian ad litem would not have considered economical stability as a "determinative factor." Further, in light of the child support guidelines, a parent's financial resources should never be considered as a "determinative factor" in deciding which parent should be awarded primary residential custody of the minor children.

The second "determinative factor" was that the mother has been "the more constant factor throughout the entire relationship." The guardian ad litem focused on the fact that the father had been "away from the home for substantial periods of time...." I feel that it is important to explain why the father had been away from the home. First, when the parties decided to move to Miami, the father stayed in New Mexico for approximately three months in order to move the family's possessions to Miami and to make improvements to the marital home so that the parties could sell the home at its highest possible price. Second, the husband, was away for three to four weeks to be with his ill brother, who died shortly after he arrived, and to help settle his brother's estate. Finally, the father was in New Mexico from June 1992 to September 1993 in order to direct a treasure hunt project. The majority relies on the "treasure hunt" to make it appear as if the treasure hunt was a crazy or weird notion. However, what the majority has failed to state is that it may not have been so strange since the mother's parents and trial counsel also invested in this project. Therefore, the reasons for the father's absence from the home were valid. Further, the fact that the father had been away from the family should not be a "determinative factor" when taking into consideration that the father has been the primary caretaker since the fall of 1993.

Finally, the third determinative factor was that the mother "controls her anger better around the kids." The guardian ad litem testified that the father "would say things in the presence of the children that indicated to me his anger and his displeasure at what he perceives to be the financial inequities of the situation...." I agree with the guardian ad litem that being able to control anger is an important factor in deciding child custody issues. However, the father's anger was based on the "financial inequities of the situation," a problem that should be completely resolved based on the majority's decision to reverse and remand all financial determinations made by the trial court, including the insufficient award of alimony to the father and the inequitable distribution of the marital assets and liabilities.

NOTES

1. Would the decision in this case have been the same if the mother were the architect and the father the lawyer? Would the court have inquired of the mother, "Maybe I'm missing something. Why don't you get a job?"

2. One interpretation of the facts is that the father in *Hector* became more involved with the children once a divorce began to seem likely. If that is so, should it reduce the weight the court gives to the father's caregiving activities?

AMERICAN LAW INSTITUTE, PRINCIPLES OF THE LAW OF FAMILY DISSOLUTION

(2002).

Section 2.08 Allocation of Custodial Responsibility

(1) Unless otherwise resolved by agreement of the parents ..., the court should allocate custodial responsibility so that the proportion of custodial time the child spends with each parent approximates the proportion of time each parent spent performing caretaking functions for the child prior to the parents' separation or, if the parents never lived together, before the filing of the action, except to the extent ... necessary to achieve one or more of the following objectives:

(a) to permit the child to have a relationship with each parent which, in the case of a legal parent or a parent by estoppel who has performed a reasonable share of parenting functions, should be not less than a presumptive amount of custodial time set by a uniform rule of statewide application;

(b) to accommodate the firm and reasonable preferences of a child who has reached a specific age, set by a uniform rule of statewide application;

(c) to keep siblings together when the court finds that doing so is necessary to their welfare;

(d) to protect the child's welfare when the presumptive allocation under this section would harm the child because of the gross disparity in the quality of the emotional attachment between each parent and the child or in each parent's demonstrated ability or availability to meet the child's needs;

(e) to take into account any prior agreement ...;

(f) to avoid an allocation of custodial responsibility that would be extremely impractical or that would interfere substantially with the child's need for stability in light of economic, physical, or other circumstances, including the distance between the parents' residences, the cost and difficulty of transporting the child, each parent's and the child's daily schedules, and the ability of the parents to cooperate in the arrangement;

. . .

(h) to avoid substantial and almost certain harm to the child.

COMMENTS:

a. In general. This section states the criteria for allocating custodial responsibility between parents when they have not reached their own agreement about this allocation. These criteria also establish the bargaining context for parents seeking agreement.

Custodial responsibility refers to physical control of and access to the child, or what traditionally has been called child custody. This term refers to the child's living arrangements, including with whom the child lives and when, and any periods of time during which another person is scheduled by the court to have caretaking responsibility for the child . . .

b. Rationale for reliance on past caretaking. The ideal standard for determining a child's custodial arrangements is one that both yields predictable and easily adjudicated results and also consistently serves the child's best interests. While the best-interests-of-the-child test may appear well suited to this objective, the test is too subjective to produce predictable results. Its unpredictability encourages strategic bargaining and prolonged litigation. The indeterminacy of the test also draws the court into comparisons between parenting styles and values that are matters of parental autonomy not appropriate for judicial resolution.

The allocation of custodial responsibility presumed in Paragraph (1) yields more predictable and more easily adjudicated results, thereby advancing the best interests of children in most cases without infringing on parental autonomy. It assumes that the division of past caretaking functions correlates well with other factors associated with the child's best interests, such as the quality of each parent's emotional attachment to the child and the parents' respective parenting abilities. It requires factfinding that is less likely than the traditional best-interests test to require expert testimony about such matters as the child's emotional state or developmental needs, the parents' relative abilities, and the strength of their emotional relationships to the child. Avoiding expert testimony is desirable because such testimony, within an adversarial context, tends to focus on the weaknesses of each parent and thus undermines the spirit of cooperation and compromise necessary to successful post-divorce custodial arrangements; therapists are better used in the divorce context to assist parents in making plans to deal constructively with each other and their children at separation.

Some parents will disagree over how caretaking roles were previously divided, making the past division of caretaking functions itself a potential litigation issue. The difficulties in applying the standard, however, must be evaluated in light of the available alternatives. While each parent's share of past caretaking will in some cases be disputed, these functions encompass specific tasks and responsibilities about which concrete evidence is available and thus offer greater determinacy than more qualitative standards, such as parental competence, the strength of the parent-child emotional bond or—as the general standard simply puts it—the child's best interests. These qualitative criteria are future-oriented and highly subjective, whereas how the parents divided caretaking responsibilities in the past is a concrete question of historical fact, like other questions courts are accustomed to resolving.

Section 2.09   Allocation of Significant Decisionmaking Responsibility

(1) Unless otherwise resolved by agreement of the parents . . . the court should allocate responsibility for making significant life decisions on behalf of the child, including decisions regarding the child's education and health

care, to one parent or to two parents jointly, in accordance with the child's best interests, in light of the following:

> (a) the allocation of custodial responsibility under § 2.08;
>
> (b) the level of each parent's participation in past decisionmaking on behalf of the child;
>
> (c) the wishes of the parents;
>
> (d) the level of ability and cooperation the parents have demonstrated in past decisionmaking on behalf of the child;
>
> * * *

(2) The court should presume that an allocation of decisionmaking responsibility jointly to each legal parent or parent by estoppel who has been exercising a reasonable share of parenting functions is in the child's best interests. The presumption is overcome if there is a history of domestic violence or child abuse, or if it is shown that joint allocation of decisionmaking responsibility is not in the child's best interests.

> . . .

COMMENTS:

a. In general. [D]ecisionmaking responsibility ... refers to authority to make decisions with respect to significant areas in the child's life. The most common decisionmaking issues covered by this section are education and health care, but other issues may arise, such as permission to enlist in the military, drive a car, work, participate in school sports, and sign a contract.

NOTES

1. The AMERICAN LAW INSTITUTE'S PRINCIPLES focus on the parties' prior division of parental responsibilities bears some resemblance to the primary caretaker presumption. It is important, however, to appreciate the difference. The primary caretaker presumption is used to determine which parent will be designated the sole custodian, with a right of physical custody superior to that of the noncustodian, and a right of legal custody—the authority to make major decisions regarding the child—equal to or greater than that of the noncustodian.

By contrast, the ALI PRINCIPLES deliberately avoid the terms "custodian" and "noncustodian," because these terms imply that there is a winner and a loser in the custody proceeding. Instead, § 2.08 seeks to allocate shares of "custodial responsibility"—physical custody—in accordance with the preexisting pattern. Consistent with the Principles' ostensibly non-adversarial focus, § 2.09 presumes that joint "decisionmaking responsibility"—legal custody—is in the best interest of the child.

2. Consider the argument of Professor Carl Schneider that critics of the best interest standard have overlooked the advantages of vesting some discretion in custody decisionmakers:

> Discretion can lead to better decisions because they can be tailored to the particular circumstances of each case. Discretion gives the decisionmaker flexibility to do justice. It does so not just by allowing a decisionmaker to heed all the individual facts that ought to affect a decision but that could not be listed by rules. It also does so by allowing a decisionmaker to see over time how well a decision worked and to adjust future decisions accordingly. Discretion may also conduce to better decisions by discouraging overly bureaucratic ways of thinking, since they often are born of too rigid an insistence on writing elaborate rules and on following them with too mechanical a regularity. Finally, endowing decisionmakers with discretion may make their jobs more interesting and more powerful and thus more attractive to able people.

Discretion has within its fold another, subtler advantage. Discretion sometimes permits the decisionmaker to conceal the basis for his ruling. In custody
decisions, for example, a choice commonly must be made between two parents,
both of whom have virtues, both of whom have faults, and both of whom will (or
should) continue to see their child. It may unnecessarily damage the loser's
feelings (and his feelings for his child) to point out to him his faults and the other
parent's virtues. This may be true even where the choice involves no moral
judgements about the parties. For instance, a parent might not like to hear
detailed all the reasons he was not a child's "psychological parent."

Carl Schneider, *Discretion, Rules and Law: Child Custody and the UMDA's Best–
Interest Standard*, 89 MICH. L. REV. 2215, 2247–48. Schneider concludes "it is worth
considering the possibility that, at its best, the present system provides as reasonable a
framework for balancing the advantages of rules and discretion as we are likely to
find." *Id.* at 2291. Do you agree?

3. The American Law Institute was founded in 1923 after a committee of American
judges, lawyers, and teachers concluded that the uncertainty and complexity of
American law had produced "general dissatisfaction with the administration of
justice." The institute's mission is "to promote the clarification and simplifaction of
the law and its better adaptation to social needs, to secure the better administration of
justice, and to encourage and carry on scholarly and scientific legal work." American
Law Institute, http://www.ali.org/index.cfm?fuseaction=about.creation. Some of the
restatements the Institute has produced over the years have been adopted by many
state legislatures and courts. Others have not. There were high hopes for the
PRINCIPLES when they were adopted in 2000 and published in 2002 after eleven years
of work and four successive drafts. By 2008, however, only West Virginia had
adopted the "approximate the time" custody standard, and no legislature had
adopted the *Principles'* concept of parent by estoppel. Only 100 cases had cited the
principles, and most would have been reached the same result without the *Principles.*
They were cited simply to bolster the court's own conclusion. Michael R. Clisham and
Robin Fretwell Wilson, *American Law Institute's Principles of the Law of Family Dissolution,
Eight Years AfterAdoption: Guiding Principles or Obligatory Footnote?*, 42 FAM. L.Q. 573,
573–76 (2008). Why do you think the *Principles* have not been more widely embraced?

Robert J. Levy, *Custody Law and the ALI's Principles: A Little History, a Little Policy, and Some Very Tentative Judgments,*

in RECONCEIVING THE FAMILY 67–89 (Robin Fretwell Wilson ed., 2006).

[J]udges, divorce practitioners, forensically sophisticated mental health
experts, as well as academic commentators agree about very little. But there
does seem to be a consensus that the standards governing judicial determinations of post-divorce custody of children pose a most difficult and unresolved
legal policy conundrum. . . .

. . .

Legal scholars of almost every intellectual persuasion and from almost
every place on the political compass have tried to formulate doctrinal
standards for custody litigation. Professor Mary Becker argued for a "maternal deference" standard under which judges would acquiesce to the mother's
wishes as to custody in order to protect the greater commitment of mothers
to the children of their marriages.[11] This proposal has gained no legislative
or policy group's support. Professor Andrew Schepard recommended that
custody be determined by the spouses themselves with the aid of a media-

---

11. Mary E. Becker, *Maternal Feelings: Myth, Taboo, and Child Custody*, 1 REV. L. & WOMEN'S
STUD. 133 (1992).

tor;[12] but Professor Trina Grillo warned that mediation poses grave risks to those many divorcing women who are subservient to their husbands in the marriage relationship.[13]

The "joint custody" movement, although separable from mediation, has often been associated with it. Joint custody enjoyed substantial legislative popularity for a time because its advocates claimed it kept noncustodial fathers involved in the post-divorce parenting of their children. The theory is that if divorce fathers are not deprived of authority over their children they will continue to support them and stay emotionally attached to them, to the children's developmental advantage. Although quite a few legislatures have passed joint custody statutes, most legal observers believe that only "joint legal custody" (sharing of legal decision-making authority) rather than "joint physical custody" (some kind of shared parenting) has or should become common. Moreover, many lawyers and mental health experts believe that joint legal custody is often used more as a sop to fathers' egos than as an effective inducement to paternal participation in parenting. The doctrine has attracted substantial opposition. . . .

Mental health professionals have produced equally varied and inconsistent proposals for solving the enormous complexities of custody law. Some psychologists and psychiatrists, many lawyers believe, would be satisfied only by a standard that refers all custody disputes to a mental health expert. Thus, a psychiatrist recommended "the psychological best interests of the child" as the appropriate dispositional standard, believing that the standard's indeterminate qualities could be controlled with lavish advice from mental health experts.[20] A group of mental health professionals recommended that custody be awarded to "the psychological parent"—the adult whom the child identifies as his or her parent. This proposal and its implications were rigorously criticized in the literature.

In recent years, influenced by mental health professionals, a number of legislatures have sought to obviate the "winner/loser" mentality that sometimes results when parents view custody disposition as a zero-sum game. In some states the terms "custody" and "custodian" as well as "visitation" have been abolished and replaced with a concept of actual and shared parenting. The Washington statute has become the model for what is now often called the "Parenting Plan" formula: a post-dissolution care and management plan for children of the marriage is conceived and executed primarily by the parents themselves with the aid of their choice of a mediator, a mental health specialist, or some other neutral, such as the judge. The plan is intended to make parents deal cooperatively with every aspect of the child's postdivorce life without requiring a choice between a "winning" and a "losing" parent.

. . .

The PRINCIPLES' "Approximate the Time" Standard

Professor Elizabeth Scott . . . suggested that custody and visitation be awarded so as to approximate the time each parent spent with the child during the marriage.[40] Although the notion attracted few adherents initially,

12. Andrew I. Schepard, *Taking Children Seriously: Promoting Cooperative Custody After Divorce*, 64 TEX. L. REV. 726 (1983).

13. Tina Grillo, *The Mediation Alternative: Process Danger's for Women*, 100 YALE L.J. 1545 (1991).

20. Andrew S. Watson, *The Children of Armageddon: Problems of Custody Following Divorce*, 21 SYRACUSE L. REV. 55 (1969).

40. Elizabeth S. Scott, *Pluralism, Parental Preference, and Child Custody*, 80 CAL. L. REV. 615 (1992).

it has received substantially more attention since the drafters [of the ALI PRINCIPLES] adopted the proposal. This effort to give substantial and determinate substantive content to the "best interests" test gained traction when the West Virginia legislature surprised most commentators by adopting the approximation standard.[42] . . .

The drafters claim that their analysis "is a refinement and rationalization of the elastic 'best interests of the child' standard set forth in the relevant statutes of every state, and may therefore be relied upon by courts in interpreting and applying their statutes."[44] The dispositive provisions construct an extremely complex and integrated policy designed to replace all previous law—changing doctrinal denominations like "custody" and "visitation" and "deconstructing" the several aspects of parenting responsibilities. The PRINCIPLES break down traditional post-divorce parental powers and responsibilities into two sources of authority, "Allocation of Custodial Responsibility," and "Allocation of Significant Decision-making Responsibility." The former standard requires that "the proportion of time the child spends with each parent [approximate] the proportion of time each parent spent performing caretaking functions for the child prior to the parents' separation. Exceptions to the rule are designed to protect the child and one of the parents from the other parent's neglect or abuse, domestic violence, drug or alcohol abuse, or persistent interference with the child's access to that parent. Additional indeterminate exceptions to the "approximate the time" rule include allocations designed: to "permit the child to have a relationship with each parent;" to accommodate the "firm and reasonable preferences" of a child who has reached a certain (but unspecified) age; to keep the siblings together if necessary for their welfare; to protect the child's welfare from harm due to operation of the rule "because of a gross disparity in the quality of the emotional attachment between each parent and the child or in each parent's demonstrated ability or availability to meet the child's need" to avoid allocations that "would be extremely impractical or that would interfere substantially with the child's need for stability. . . .," and to accomplish the relocation objectives of the PRINCIPLES.

Decision-making responsibility pertains to "significant life decisions on behalf of the child, including decisions regarding the child's education and health care." The provision includes a presumption of a joint allocation to each parent, overcome by a history of domestic violence or child abuse, or "if it is shown that joint allocation of decision-making responsibility is not in the child's best interests." The "approximate the time" provisions are tempered by separate sections supporting parental autonomy in custodial decision-making. The PRINCIPLES require that the parent file, separately or jointly, a "Parenting Plan" making the allocations the doctrine requires, and that courts order provisions of a Parenting Plan agreed to by the spouses. According to Dean Katherine Bartlett, one of the PRINCIPLES' drafters, these provisions differ from the "primary caretaker" presumption in both theory and practice:

> The primary caretaker presumption assumes as a fact that a primary caretaker existed, and then assumes as a state norm that one parent should have primary custody at divorce. The PRINCIPLES' pastcaretaking standard makes no such factual or normative assumption; in fact, it is indifferent to the nature of the past-caretaking arrangements. If parents equally shared caretaking responsibilities, that fact will be

---

42. *See* W. VA. CODE §§ 48—11—101 (2001).

44. PRINCIPLES, Chief Reporter's Foreward, at xviii.

reflected in the custodial allocations; if there was a clear primary caretaker, that will also be reflected, as well as everything else in between. Under the PRINCIPLES' approach, past arrangements—whatever they were—are to guide post-divorce arrangements. To the extent the courts adopt this approach, they are taking their cue not from some state-selected preference in favor of a certain custody ideal, but from the parents themselves. As the law moves in this direction, more weight is given to parental decision-making—in this case decision-making during the marriage—and less to the state itself.

These provisions reflect the drafters' belief that the "best interests" test is a "policy goal and not an administrable legal standard." Past caretaking has become an important factor for judges applying the best interests test; and a number of state statutes specifically direct courts to make past caretaking an important factor in custody decision-making—although the extant statutes seldom prioritize among a great variety of factors.

It is certainly true that what might be called a "pure" "approximate the time" standard is less indeterminate than "best interests," and the standard, if administered rigorously, would more effectively channel and limit judicial discretion than the traditional rule. But like the "primary caretaker" rule, the standard denies either spouse the opportunity without the other's permission, to expand contacts and his or her relationship with the child by changing roles when the marriage has factually terminated. Such role changes commonly occur long before the divorce action is filed and even longer before a judge must decide to whom custody should be awarded. Role changing spouses are gravely disadvantaged in divorce negotiations and the pre-divorce homemaker spouse is given as a great a tactical advantage as the maternal presumption gave mothers. Nor does this rigorous standard recognize that comparative time spent with the children may not reflect each parent's emotional relationship with them.

For parents and for those anxious to increase doctrinal determinacy, the PRINCIPLES pose even more troubling problems. The exceptions to the rigid "approximate the time spent" doctrine seem to give judges as much discretion as the "best interests" test does. How many trial judges, committed to "individualizing" justice and caring about the healthy development of the children, would ignore the discretion authorized by Section 2.09? Consider the provision which requires the judge to vary the custody award to "protect the child's welfare when the presumptive allocation ... would harm the child because of a gross disparity in the quality of the emotional attachment between each parent and the child or in each parent's demonstrated ability or availability to meet the child's needs." What good trial judge would not be able to reach any outcome consistent with the judge's view of the facts and beliefs as to the child's "best interests?" How many judges could or would resist the siren call to avoid allocations that "would be extremely impractical or that would interfere substantially with the child's need for stability?"

The drafters designed these exceptions as "escape hatches" to the rigorous commands of the "approximate the time" standard. And the exceptions were drafted carefully in an effort to limit their scope and use— with the inclusion of such limiting language as "harm the child because of a gross disparity," "extremely impractical," and "interfere substantially." The important questions cannot be answered empirically now and probably never will be: To what extent will trial judges confronting an entirely new doctrinal custody regime, one which compels them to focus on "narrow" "escape hatches" to a determinate principle, change their habitual decision-making assumptions and styles? To what extent, under traditional doctrinal regimes, did judges decide custody disputes by masking their personal value preferences in the vague language of "best interests?" In how large a percentage of such decisions were the child's "best interests" in fact undermined? Even if these questions were subject to inquiry, varying hunches about the answers by scholars, lawyers, and judges would inevitably be based upon their own personal, familial, and legal backgrounds and political preferences. On the other hand, the law itself requires us to presume that judges will follow the legislature's command. On the other hand, academics and legislators have sought a more determinate standard for years for a reason. These efforts, outlined above, suggest the belief that "best interests" alone—or supplemented by the standard traditional presumptions—has been utilized by judges to introduce more individualized and personalized justice in the custody determinations than may be morally appropriate or good for families.

It may well be true that a strict "approximate the time" standard is too rigid and difficult to allow fair administration. It may also be true that with its "escape hatches" the standard is as determinate as legislative compromise and precatory statutory language can achieve. In fact, it is much easier to criticize the indeterminacy of the PRINCIPLES' "escape hatches" than it is to draft a fair, administrable, and determinate standard to replace them. Nonetheless, it cannot be denied that the PRINCIPLES allow judges considerable discretion to accomplish the child's "best interests" as they perceive them.

. . .

The three great public policy issues of custody law and practice are not difficult to identify. The first, of course, is how to construct the substantive standard. It is not clear that we have a social consensus on this subject. Are we willing to rely on judges' discretionary administration of an indeterminate standard? If not, what standard can we agree to and what value would that standard reinforce? Or is the endeavor a waste of time because parents, lawyers, and judges will—in a variety of ways and for a variety of inconsistent reasons in individual cases—undermine any feasible expression of an compromise?

A second, also contested, issue is whether the value to children of more shared parenting than most parents apparently adopt on their own is worth the cost of doctrinal and practice modification that accomplishing the change would require. A subsidiary issue is whether any proposed legal change would increase shared parenting or if, instead, doctrinal change would impose great transaction costs in lawyers' fees and judicial resources, and still be undermined by lawyers' and parents' resistance to change.

A third great public policy issue is the extent to which legislatures or judges should modify the traditional American commitment to "private ordering"—that is, to the acceptance of parental autonomy in determining post-dissolution custodial arrangements for children. It is true that judges have always had the authority to reject any custody and visitation arrangement agreed to by parents and their lawyers. But parentally arranged custody—as occurs with more than 90 percent of the custody awards from year to year—takes place with almost no judicial interference. These practice policies have been adopted and maintained despite their obvious cost—that is, in some unknown proportion of the cases, one spouse will obtain an agreement from the other that was in some fashion coerced or might not have been the decision imposed by a judge if the case had been contested. The common policy response has been to prefer parental decision-making on grounds of efficiency—that judicial resources would be overwhelmed if all dissolution custody arrangements were to be subjected to real judicial oversight—and parental autonomy, which is prized as an independent value in a free society. The notion is that the benefit to children of legal representation and more active judicial undermining the countervailing values.

Answers to these basic questions are not likely to be discovered easily. In any event, it is likely that custody law and procedure doctrines and practices will change, if at all, as legal doctrine in general does—in modest ways and with glacial slowness. Yet personal, parental, and marital values do seem to be changing, slowly, but in important ways. Only unscientific and unrepresentative examples are available: many airport men's rooms have added changing tables from infants to their décor during the last five years; expectations (and therefore values) about fathers' roles with young children are changing. In recent years, moreover, a number of authors have complained that judges too frequently deny women custody of their children for inadequate or inappropriate reasons. And there have been many new custody proposals—the "primary caretaker," the "maternal deference," the "approximate the time spent" standards—which seem to route the law implicitly in the direction of the maternal presumption of earlier days. There are few signs that at least some judges' practices may be changing; but the extant empirical research seems to indicate that parents' practices (how parents actually allocate their children when they separate and divorce) have not changed all that much from earlier times. These circumstances suggest that we may have entered a transitional period during which disputes about legal doctrines engage not only litigants, lawyers, and judges, but political and pressure groups, as well. One of the most interesting aspects of a potential shift in social mores is that the law may change in fact without any formal or overt change in the legal standard. The "best interests" test, with all its indeterminacy and lack of legal guidance, might provide cover for a basic sea-change in American social values and practices. Substantial legal doctrinal stability may be purchased at the cost of continued substantial discretion for judges during a period of slowly changing judicial values. The winners will be the judges who prize discretion, the lawyers who will be paid to litigate more contested cases, an those who favor doctrinal stability for its own sake; the losers will be those who value predictability and litigants' bank accounts.

5. PARENTING PLANS

Huelskamp v. Huelskamp

Court of Appeals of Ohio, 2009.
925 N.E.2d 167.

■ WILLIAMOWSKI, JUDGE.

Defendant-appellant, Timothy Huelskamp, appeals the judgment of the Auglaize County Court of Common Pleas, Domestic Relations Division, granting a divorce from plaintiff-appellee, Amy Huelskamp. Timothy contends that the trial court erred ... in awarding custody of the children to Amy....

Timothy and Amy were married on May 20, 2000. Two children were born as issue of the marriage. The parties separated in April 2007, and Amy filed for divorce in November 2007. Trial was first set for September 30, 2008, but was rescheduled for May 27 and 28, 2009, after the trial court ordered the joinder of third parties who shared property interests in the parties' real estate and hog-finishing business. The trial court granted the divorce and issued its final judgment entry on June 30, 2009.

At trial, the parties stipulated that the grounds for the divorce would be incompatibility and that they had reached an agreement concerning the division of personal property....

Timothy and Amy have two children, Dalton, age 9, and Gabrielle, age 5. In 2008, both parties originally filed shared-parenting plans with differing divisions of time. However, at trial, Amy requested that she be named the residential parent and that the visitation schedule that had been in effect for the past year be continued. There was considerable testimony indicating that the parties' relationship with each other was very acrimonious. The guardian ad litem recommended shared parenting, but suggested that the children should be exchanged in a public location to avoid confrontation between the parents. The trial court rejected any shared-parenting plan, due to the parties' inability to cooperate, and designated Amy as the residential parent and legal custodian. The trial court granted Timothy expanded visitation times, in excess of the standard orders, and ordered him to pay child support, with credit given for the extra time that the children would be spending with him.

. . .

It is from this judgment that Timothy appeals, presenting [several] assignments of error for our review.

. . .

Eighth Assignment of Error

The Trial Court erred and committed an abuse of discretion in finding that the shared parenting plan is not in the best interest of the minor children.

[I]n his final assignment of error, Timothy claims that the trial court abused its discretion in finding that a shared-parenting plan was not in the best interest of the children. Timothy argues that because he and Amy filed shared-parenting plans and the guardian ad litem recommended shared parenting, the trial court erred in not adopting any of the plans.

A trial court has broad discretion in determining whether to order shared parenting. *Lopez v. Coleson*, 2006–Ohio–5389 (Ohio Ct. App. 2006); OHIO REV. CODE ANN. § 3109.04(D)(1)(b). An appellate court will presume that a trial court's decision regarding child custody is correct and will not reverse the decision absent an abuse of discretion. *Bechtol v. Bechtol*, 550 N.E.2d 178 (Ohio 1990).

OHIO REV. CODE ANN. § 3109.04(D) sets forth standards and procedures for allocation of parental rights and responsibilities using a shared-parenting plan. Under OHIO REV. CODE ANN. § 3109.04(D)(1)(a)(i), the trial court may deny a motion for shared parenting and proceed as if the motion had not been made if it determines that such a plan is not in the best interest of the children. In further discussing shared-parenting plans, the statute states:

> The approval of a plan under division (D)(1)(a)(ii) or (iii) of this section is discretionary with the court. The court shall not approve more than one plan under either division and shall not approve a plan under either division unless it determines that the plan is in the best interest of the children. *If the court, under either division, does not determine that any*

filed plan or any filed plan with submitted changes is in the best interest of the children, the court shall not approve any plan.

(Emphasis added.) OHIO REV. CODE ANN. § 3109.04(D)(1)(b).

Although both Timothy and Amy filed shared-parenting plans, Amy made it very clear at trial that she did not feel shared parenting was appropriate. The parties' plans were very different, and Amy's plan, although labeled a "shared-parenting plan," more closely followed the typical plan associated with the allocation of a residential parent and traditional visitation schedule.

The testimony at trial indicated that the parties had great difficulty cooperating with each other. There was considerable testimony about the derogatory and demeaning language that Timothy used in reference to Amy in the presence of the children. Amy had been the children's primary caretaker ever since their birth. It was only recently that Timothy began to take a more active role in the children's lives.

Although the guardian ad litem recommended shared parenting, the primary rationale for that recommendation was to allow the children to spend time with each parent. The guardian ad litem's report also stated, "I am not confident Tim and Amy are at a point emotionally they can work together," and "the parents' disparate emotional states ... will make Shared Parenting difficult." The guardian ad litem even recommended exchanges at a public place due to the relationship of the parties.

The trial court found:

The very crux of shared parenting requires the parties to cooperate with one another in the daily lives of the children. The Court does not believe that these parties can cooperate to the extent necessary to implement any type of shared parenting plan. Such a forced cooperation would not be in the best interests of the children. Accordingly, the Court rejects the shared parenting plans of the parties.

Although the trial court designated Amy as the residential parent and legal custodian, it addressed the guardian ad litem's concerns and awarded Timothy more time with the children than normally allotted under standard visitation orders. Based upon the testimony and evidence before the trial court, we do not find that the court abused its discretion when it declined to order a shared-parenting plan. Timothy's eighth assignment of error is overruled.

Based on the foregoing, we find that ... Timothy's assignments of error are overruled and the judgment of the trial court pertaining to those assignments of error is affirmed. [T]he matter is remanded to the trial court for further consideration consistent with this opinion.

In re the Custody of Halls

Court of Appeals of Washington, Division 2, 2005.
109 P.3d 15.

■ ARMSTRONG, J.

June Arden appeals two permanent parenting plan modifications granting sole custody of her children to their father, Jeffrey Halls. . . .

June Arden and Jeffrey Halls have three minor children, Trina Halls (age 12), Jeffrey Halls, Jr. (age 11), and Selma Halls (age 8). The court entered a final parenting plan (Original Parenting Plan) on February 4, 2003; both Arden and Halls were represented by counsel in that proceeding. Under the plan, during the school year, the children resided with Arden and had residential time with Halls on the first and third Saturday and Sunday of each month and on certain holidays every other year. The summer schedule remained the same except Halls would have the children for the month of July. Arden and Halls had joint decision-making power.

In April 2003, Arden was evicted from her home. On April 7, 2003, she took the children to Red Wing, Minnesota, where she could stay in a family home. Arden and the children arrived in Minnesota on or around April 12. A few days later, Arden called Halls and told him she was in Red Wing with the children. Arden did not deliver the children to Halls for their next scheduled weekend visit. At the time, Halls was not in Washington; he was visiting his mother in Wisconsin.

On April 22, Halls moved for a contempt order, alleging that Arden violated the Original Parenting Plan by failing to give notice of her move to Minnesota and by failing to make the children available for Halls's scheduled weekend visit. Halls asked the court to sanction Arden with jail time.

At the first contempt hearing on May 9, 2003, Arden represented herself, appearing by telephone. The trial court found her in contempt of the Original Parenting Plan and ordered her confined in the Jefferson County jail. . . .

On May 12, 2003, the trial court ordered Arden's release and set a show cause hearing on May 30, 2003, for Arden to appear and show cause why Halls should not have primary residential care of the children. . . . Halls had still not petitioned to modify the parenting plan.

Arden again represented herself at the May 30 hearing. At that hearing, the court stated that if the children were not delivered to Halls in 24 hours, he would incarcerate Arden. The court also set a review hearing for June 13, and explained to Arden that it would appoint counsel for her at that hearing because she faced possible jail time if it found her in contempt. On May 30, the court found her in contempt of the parenting plan. And, although Halls had not yet petitioned to modify the plan, the court granted him sole custody of the children.

At the June 13, 2003 hearing, Arden was not present but a public defender appeared on her behalf. By then, Halls had custody of the children, and Arden had been visiting them on weekends. The court asked Halls, "Want me to put her in jail or are you satisfied?" Report of Proceedings (RP) (June 13, 2003) at 33. Halls stated that he was not asking the court to incarcerate Arden. Instead, his attorney asked the court "to enter a new Parenting Plan that reflects what's going on now."

[T]he court . . . entered a final judgment and modified parenting plan (First Modified Parenting Plan).

The First Modified Parenting Plan changed the children's primary residence from Arden to Halls. The parties retained joint decision making authority. Nothing in the record shows that Halls petitioned to modify the Original Parenting Plan.

Arden asked the court to reconsider the first parenting plan modification. . . . The court denied the motions on July 21, ruling that because "it was not in the children's best interest to be denied visitation with their father, the Court changed their residence. It's up to the father's lawyer to straighten out the paperwork."

Arden appealed to this court on August 19, 2003. On August 22, while the appeal was pending, Halls petitioned to modify the Original Parenting Plan. Appearing *pro se*, Arden opposed the petition.

On September 5, 2003, the trial court heard Halls's motion for an order finding Arden in contempt of the First Modified Parenting Plan and for entry of a new parenting plan "that doesn't leave any room for error." Halls alleged that Arden failed to return the children on time. Arden, again representing herself, denied that she had failed to comply with the parenting plan.

The trial court found Arden in contempt, entered a new final parenting plan (Second Modified Parenting Plan), and entered a temporary order (Temporary Order) restraining Arden from (1) molesting or disturbing the peace of Halls or any child; (2) entering Halls's home, the grounds of his home, or his workplace; or (3) entering the children's schools. The order also restrained her from removing the children from Jefferson County. While labeled "[t]emporary," the order does not expire until 2013 (10 years from the date of the order).

As to this last ruling, the court reasoned: "All it takes is two contempts and the Court can change the Parenting Plan without further findings." The Second Modified Parenting Plan ordered that the children reside with Halls; it allowed Arden visitation for two weekends a month, two blocks of two weeks each during the summer, and certain holidays every other year. It also delegated major decision making authority to Halls.

On October 3, 2003, Arden appealed a second time, challenging the most recent contempt order, the Second Modified Parenting Plan, and the Temporary Order. We consolidated the appeals. Due to Halls repeated failure to file a brief or make a motion to extend time, we precluded him from filing a brief or presenting oral argument.

Halls failed to file a response brief by March 15, 2004, as required. We repeatedly informed Halls that he must file a brief or face sanctions. Because Halls nevertheless failed to timely file a brief, we precluded him from arguing. RAP 11.2(a).

Arden argues that the trial court entered a series of orders that violated the substantive and procedural rules governing the modification of final parenting plans. Specifically, she argues that the court modified a final parenting plan without a pending petition for modification, an adequate cause hearing, or adequate consideration of the statutory criteria. We agree.

Generally, we review a trial court's rulings about the provisions of a parenting plan for abuse of discretion. . . .

. . .

Under WASH. REV. CODE § 26.09.260, the court may modify a parenting plan only if it finds "a substantial change has occurred in the circumstances of the child or the nonmoving party and . . . the modification is in the best interest of the child and is necessary to serve the best interests of the child." WASH. REV. CODE § 26.09.260(1). These findings must be based on "facts that have arisen since the prior decree or plan or that were unknown to the court at the time of the prior decree or plan." We employ a strong presumption against modification because changes in residences are highly disruptive to children. [*In re Parentage of*] *Schroeder*, 22 P.3d 1280 (citing *In re Marriage of McDole*, 859 P.2d 1239, 1242 (Wash. Ct. App. 1993)). Thus, the moving party must prove that a modification is appropriate. *Schroeder*, 22 P.3d at 1284 (citing *George v. Helliar*, 814 P.2d 238, 241 (Wash. Ct. App. 1991)).

A substantial change has occurred when "[t]he court has found the nonmoving parent in contempt of court at least twice within three years because the parent failed to comply with the residential time provisions in the court-ordered parenting plan." *Schroeder*, 22 P.3d at 1284 (citing WASH. REV. CODE § 26.09.260(2)(d)). Thus, when one parent prevents another from having contact with a child in violation of the parenting plan, a court may consider these violations in deciding whether to change the children's residence. But absent a finding that modification is in the best interests of a child, the court may not modify for mere violations of the parenting plan.

WASH. REV. CODE § 26.09.181 requires a petitioning party to file and serve his motion to modify with a proposed parenting plan. Further, under WASH. REV. CODE § 26.09.270, a party seeking to modify a parenting plan must submit with his motion "an affidavit setting forth facts supporting the requested . . . modification and shall give notice, together with a copy of his affidavit, to other parties to the proceedings, who may file opposing affidavits." And the court must deny the motion unless it finds adequate cause from the affidavits to hear the motion. WASH. REV. CODE § 26.09.270. Jefferson County's local rules also require a petition and the "affidavits as required by WASH. REV. CODE § 26.09. 270." J.C.L.R. 94.

Halls filed only a motion for contempt. And the motion complied with none of the requirements of WASH. REV. CODE § 26.09.270. It did not ask for a modification of the parenting plan; it provided no basis for an adequate cause finding (and the court did not find adequate cause); and it gave Arden no notice that Halls sought to modify the parenting plan. Because of these basic procedural flaws, the court lacked authority to modify the parties' parenting plan.

In addition, the First Modified Parenting Plan states that it was entered following an "order entered on May 30, 2003." The only order appearing in the record entered on May 30, 2003, is a contempt order. In the section of the order reserved for allocating additional residential or make-up time, the court wrote "[Halls] is granted sole custody" of the children "pending further order." This grant of sole custody was an improper exercise of the court's contempt power, deviating from the contempt remedies WASH. REV. CODE § 26.09.160 provides.

Moreover, the court never found that a modification was in the children's best interests. Rather, the court found "that it was not in the children's best interest to be denied visitation with their father." This does not meet the statutory best interests requirement. Finding that it was not in the children's best interest to be denied visitation with their father is not the same as a finding that a changed primary residential parent was in their best interests. Specifically, the court did not find that living with their father or removing them from their mother's care was in their "best interests."

The Second Modified Parenting Plan suffers from some of the same defects as the first. Again, the court held no adequate cause threshold hearing as WASH. REV. CODE § 26.09.270 and Jefferson County Local Rule 94 requires. And the court concluded that "[a]ll it takes is two contempts and the Court can change the Parenting Plan without further findings." But the court cannot modify a parenting plan solely on the basis of "two contempts." WASH. REV. CODE § 26.09.260(1) requires, in addition to contempt findings, a finding that the proposed change is in the children's best interests. Thus, we reverse the order granting the Second Modified Parenting Plan.

. . .

Arden argues that entry of the 10–year Temporary Order was actually an impermissible, permanent parenting plan modification. Again we agree.

In *In re Marriage of Christel and Blanchard*, 1 P.3d 600, 606 (Wash. Ct. App. 2000), the court held that a temporary order amounted to an impermissible modification. The court found that the trial courts order establishing a new dispute resolution procedure for matters affecting the parties' child had a permanent effect on the parenting plan, and because no petition to modify had been submitted, the modification was impermissible. Accordingly, the court vacated the trial court's "Temporary Order," finding an abuse of discretion.

The Temporary Order here has the same permanent effect. It restricts Arden's right to travel with her children outside of Jefferson County and prohibits her from going to the children's residence or schools for 10 years. By the time the order expires, all of Arden's and Halls's children will have reached the age of majority and the parenting plan will no longer apply to them. And Halls submitted no petition to modify and no adequate cause affidavits, and the court did not find facts sufficient to modify the parenting plan. Thus, we vacate the order.

. . .

Arden argues that under the due process clause of the Fourteenth Amendment to the United States Constitution and article 1, sections 10 and 32 of the Washington State Constitution, she is entitled to appointed counsel in the modification proceedings. She asks that we direct the trial court to appoint counsel to represent her on remand. But the issue is not before us yet.

No Washington case has held that a party to a child custody dispute is entitled to representation at State expense.

Although not part of the appeal record, counsel advised us during oral argument that the children are back living with Arden. In addition, Halls has not participated in the appeal process, ignoring our letters and order concerning his right to file a brief and argue the case. Given this history, we question whether a real dispute still exists between the parties.

In addition, if there is a dispute on remand, we do not know whether Arden would now qualify as indigent. Moreover, Halls asked to modify the parenting plans only because of Arden's alleged contempts. But as we have discussed, contempt findings alone will not support a parenting plan modification. If Halls still seeks modification, he must file a new petition alleging more than contempt. We do not know what such allegations might be or whether the contempt proceedings would necessarily threaten Arden with incarceration. Yet Arden asks for an attorney on the modification because it is so interwoven with the contempt issues. In short, without knowing whether the parties still have a dispute and the parameters of the dispute, we are unwilling to issue an advisory opinion.

We reverse and vacate the May 9, May 30, and September 8, 2003 contempt orders; we also vacate the First and Second Modified Parenting Plans and the Temporary Order. We remand to the trial court for further proceedings.

SUPERIOR COURT OF THE DISTRICT OF COLUMBIA
FAMILY COURT
Domestic Relations Branch

PRINT PLAINTIFF'S NAME

STREET ADDRESS

CITY, STATE AND ZIP CODE

☐ SUBSTITUTE ADDRESS: CHECK BOX IF YOU
HAVE WRITTEN SOMEONE ELSE'S ADDRESS BECAUSE
YOU FEAR HARASSMENT OR HARM.

DR _____

Related Cases:

PLAINTIFF,

V.

PRINT DEFENDANT'S NAME

STREET ADDRESS

CITY, STATE AND ZIP CODE

☐ SUBSTITUTE ADDRESS: CHECK BOX IF YOU
HAVE WRITTEN SOMEONE ELSE'S ADDRESS BECAUSE
YOU FEAR HARASSMENT OR HARM.

DEFENDANT.

PARENTING PLAN

THE PURPOSE OF A PARENTING PLAN IS TO HELP YOU THINK CAREFULLY ABOUT THE DETAILS OF
YOUR CUSTODY ORDER. YOU CAN DECIDE:

WHO WILL MAKE WHAT DECISIONS ABOUT THE CHILD(REN)?
WHO THE CHILD(REN) WILL STAY WITH AND WHEN?
WHAT FINANCIAL CONTRIBUTIONS SHOULD BE MADE TO SUPPORT THE CHILD(REN)?

IF YOU WANT, YOU CAN ASK THE JUDGE IN YOUR CASE TO INCORPORATE THIS PARENTING PLAN
INTO A COURT ORDER.

NOTE:
IF THE PARENTING ARRANGEMENTS ARE DIFFERENT FOR SOME OF YOUR CHILDREN,
YOU SHOULD WRITE UP A SEPARATE PARENTING PLAN FOR EACH CHILD.

THIS PARENTING PLAN INVOLVES THE FOLLOWING CHILD(REN):

Child's Name	Age	Where does this child live?

IF YOU HAVE CHILDREN NOT ADDRESSED BY THIS PARENTING PLAN, NAME HERE:

Child's Name	Age	Where does this child live?

LEGAL CUSTODY (who makes decisions about certain things)

Diet	☐ Both parents decide together	☐ Plaintiff	☐ Defendant
Religion	☐ Both parents decide together	☐ Plaintiff	☐ Defendant
Medical Care	☐ Both parents decide together	☐ Plaintiff	☐ Defendant
Mental Health Care	☐ Both parents decide together	☐ Plaintiff	☐ Defendant
Discipline	☐ Both parents decide together	☐ Plaintiff	☐ Defendant
Choice of School	☐ Both parents decide together	☐ Plaintiff	☐ Defendant
Choice of Study	☐ Both parents decide together	☐ Plaintiff	☐ Defendant
School Activities	☐ Both parents decide together	☐ Plaintiff	☐ Defendant
Sports Activities	☐ Both parents decide together	☐ Plaintiff	☐ Defendant
_____	☐ Both parents decide together	☐ Plaintiff	☐ Defendant
_____	☐ Both parents decide together	☐ Plaintiff	☐ Defendant
_____	☐ Both parents decide together	☐ Plaintiff	☐ Defendant

What process will you use to make decisions?

FOR EXAMPLE – THE PARENT CONFRONTED WITH OR ANTICIPATING THE CHOICE WILL CALL THE OTHER PARENT WHEN THE CHOICE PRESENTS ITSELF AND THE OTHER PARENT MUST AGREE OR DISAGREE WITHIN 24 HOURS OF ANY DEADLINE OR IF IN LESS TIME, THEN BEFORE ANY DEADLINE)

If you cannot agree, which of you will make the final decision?

_____

PHYSICAL CUSTODY (where the child(ren) live)

The child(ren)'s residence is with _____

Describe which days and which times of day the child(ren) will be with each person:

Sunday	Monday	Tuesday	Wednesday	Thursday	Friday	Saturday

This schedule is ☐ every week   ☐ every two weeks   ☐ other _____

If not weekly, which of you has the child(ren) the rest of the time? _____

Drop-off
Where? _____

When? (time and day) _____

Pick-up
Where? _____

When? (time and day) _____

If one of you doesn't show up, how long will the other wait? _____

If there are extraordinary costs (taxi, train, plane, etc.) who will pay for which costs?

HOLIDAY VISITATION

HOLIDAY	Where will the child stay in...		
	Year A	Year B	Every Year
Martin Luther King Day			
President's Day			
Easter			
Memorial Day			
4th of July			
Labor Day			
Yom Kippur			
Rosh Hashanah			
Thanksgiving			
Vacation after Thanksgiving			
Christmas Vacation			
Christmas Day			
Kwanza			
New Year's Eve/Day			
Spring Vacation			
Easter Sunday			
Child's Birthday			
Mother's Day			
Father's Day			
Other holiday: (Chanukah, Passover, Ramadan, etc)			

Summer Vacation:

SPECIAL ACTIVITIES OR SCHOOL ACTIVITIES

Name of Child	Activity	Will both of you attend? If not, which of you will attend?

TEMPORARY CHANGES TO THIS PARENTING SCHEDULE

FROM TIME TO TIME, ONE OF YOU MIGHT WANT OR NEED TO REARRANGE THE PARENTING TIME SCHEDULE DUE TO WORK, FAMILY OR OTHER EVENTS. YOU CAN ATTEMPT TO AGREE ON THESE CHANGES, IF YOU CANNOT AGREE, THE PARENT RECEIVING THE REQUEST WILL MAKE THE FINAL DECISION.

The parent asking for the change will ask

☐ in person ☐ by letter/email ☐ by phone ☐ _____

no later than ☐ 12 hours ☐ 24 hours ☐ 1 week ☐ 1 month ☐ _____

The parent being asked for a change will reply

☐ in person ☐ by letter/email ☐ by phone ☐ _____

no later than ☐ 12 hours ☐ 24 hours ☐ 1 week ☐ 1 month ☐ _____

COMMUNICATION

May parents contact one another? _____

When the child(ren) is/are with the one of you, how may they contact the other parent?
_____
_____

When and how may _____ contact the child?_____
_____
_____

When and how may _____ contact the child, when the child is visiting? _____
_____
_____

CHILD(REN)'S EXPENSES

Expense	Mother - amount or %	Father – amount or %
Health Insurance Coverage		
Medical Care (including co-pays)		
Dental (braces, fillings, etc.)		
Vision (eyeglasses, contacts, etc.)		
Other Health Care		
Mental Health Care		
Education (tuition, books, fees, etc.)		
Childcare (work-related)		
Other (music lessons, sports equipment, car insurance, etc.)		
Other		
Other		
Other		
Other		
Unexpected Expenses not anticipated at the time of this agreement		

CHILD SUPPORT GUIDELINES

Child support will be paid by ☐ Plaintiff ☐ Defendant

Amount $_____ ☐ every week ☐ every two weeks
☐ once a month ☐ other _____

TAXES (who can take the income tax deduction for the child(ren) each year)

Plaintiff can take the deduction ☐ in Year A ☐ in Year B ☐ Every Year

Defendant can take the deduction ☐ in Year A ☐ in Year B ☐ Every Year

Other

COLLEGE (if you send your child(ren) to college)

☐ **Plaintiff** will pay all college tuition, room and board, and books.

☐ **Defendant** will pay all college tuition, room and board, and books.

☐ **Plaintiff and Defendant will share** expenses for college tuition, room and board, and books.
Plaintiff will pay _____ % of the total expenses.
Defendant will pay _____ % of the total expenses.
* these must add up to 100%

☐ **Other**

OTHER (anything else you want to agree on)

Date _____   Signature of Mother _____

Date _____   Signature of Father _____

Date _____   Signature of Witness _____

AMERICAN LAW INSTITUTE, PRINCIPLES OF THE LAW OF FAMILY DISSOLUTION

(2002).

Section 2.05   Parenting Plan

(1) An individual seeking a judicial allocation of custodial responsibility or decisionmaking responsibility under this Chapter should be required to file with the court a proposed parenting plan containing proposals for each of the provisions specified in Paragraph (5). Individuals should be allowed to file a joint plan.

. . .

(3) The court should have a process to identify cases in which there is credible information that child abuse, as defined by state law, or domestic violence . . . has occurred. The process should include assistance for possible victims of domestic violence . . . referral to appropriate resources for safe shelter, counseling, safety planning, information regarding the potential impact of domestic violence on children, and information regarding civil and criminal remedies for domestic violence. The process should include a system for ensuring . . . court review . . . when there is credible information that child abuse or domestic violence has occurred.

(4) Prior to a decision on a final parenting plan and upon motion of a party, the court may order a temporary allocation of custodial responsibility or decisionmaking responsibility as the court determines is in the child's best interests, considering the factors in §§ 2.08 and 2.09. A temporary allocation order ordinarily should not preclude access to the child by a parent who has been exercising a reasonable share of parenting functions. Upon credible information of one or more of the circumstances set forth in § 2.11(1) and pending adjudication of the underlying facts, the court should issue a temporary order limiting or denying access to the child as required by that section, in order to protect the child or other family member.

(5) After consideration of any proposed parenting plans submitted in the case and any evidence presented in support thereof, the court should order a parenting plan that is consistent with the provisions of §§ 2.08–2.12 and contains the following provisions:

(a) a provision for the child's living arrangements and for each parent's custodial responsibility, which should include either

(i) a custodial schedule that designates in which parent's home each minor child will reside on given days of the year; or

(ii) a formula or method for determining such a schedule in sufficient detail that, if necessary, the schedule can be enforced in a subsequent proceeding.

(b) an allocation of decisionmaking responsibility as to significant matters reasonably likely to arise with respect to the child; and

(c) a provision consistent with § 2.07 for resolution of disputes that arise under the plan, and a provision establishing remedies for violations of the plan.

(6) The court may provide in the parenting plan for how issues relating to a party's future relocation will be resolved, and it may provide for future modifications of the parenting plan if specified contingencies occur.

(7) Expedited procedures should facilitate the prompt issuance of a parenting plan.

COMMENTS:

a. In general. [T]his section requires parents to file a parenting plan in order to encourage them to anticipate their children's needs and make arrangements for them. Although courts will still be called upon to resolve conflicts between some parents, the parenting-plan requirement locates responsibility for the welfare of the child in the first instance in parents rather than in courts. If the parents reach agreement on how their children's needs will be met, § 2.06 requires the court ordinarily to accept and order that plan. Even when the parents cannot agree, the requirement that courts consider each of their proposed plans gives each of the parents an incentive to produce a thoughtful and rational plan.

The parenting-plan concept presupposes a diverse range of childrearing arrangements, and rejects any pre-established set of statutory choices about what arrangements are best for children. Rules that favor sole custody with visitation, joint custody, or some other specified arrangement express particular preferences about what is best for children, but they do not reflect the preferences, experiences, or welfare of all families. The parenting-plan requirement allows parents to customize their arrangements to take account of the family's own actual circumstances; if they cannot agree, other rules in the Chapter retain the focus on the family's actual experience, through its patterns of past caretaking. *See* § 2.08(1).

b. Filing. Individuals seeking responsibility for a child under this Chapter may jointly file a single plan, or they may file separate plans. A proposed plan should be viewed as a potential draft of the court plan, containing all of the features required of parenting plans under Paragraph (5). . . .

Although the filing requirements of this section ask more of parents than is traditionally required in custody cases, these requirements should not be overly onerous. The information required ordinarily will be accessible to the parents, and will not require research of difficult factual determinations. In many cases forms can be made available by the court that will enable parents to check boxes and fill in blanks without the need for lawyers. When one parent has been providing virtually all of the caretaking for the child, when the case is uncontested, or when the proposed plans are not complicated, the reporting requirements will be correspondingly easy to comply with. For more complicated cases, other court-based assistance may also be made available to parents. For example, the screening process required under Paragraph (3) might well include advisers who can help parents fill out the forms.

c. Child abuse and domestic violence. Specific provisions in the section are directed toward addressing the issues of child abuse and domestic violence. . . .

Since parents often are not forthcoming about the existence of child abuse and domestic abuse, Paragraph (3) also requires that the court develop a process to identify cases in which such abuse or violence has occurred. The purpose of the screening process is to determine if various cautions are required. For example, the Chapter assumes that parents ordinarily are capable of freely consenting to agreements, participating in mediation, and otherwise protecting their own interests. But under § 2.06, when there is credible information that domestic violence has occurred, the court must take a more active role in ensuring that parental agreements are voluntary.

Information about child abuse and domestic violence also gives rise to obligations on the part of mediators, who must under § 2.07(2), take steps to ensure the voluntariness of the mediation and to protect the safety of the victim.

The process established by the court under Paragraph (3) must take account of the barriers to reporting that often silence victims of domestic violence. A parent may be reluctant to provide information about violence, for example, if that parent fears retaliation by the abuser, or if the parent believes he or she will be disbelieved, or have his or her credibility reduced in later proceedings with the court. A parent may be especially reluctant to disclose information about violence if resources are not available to help secure the child's or the parent's safety. A routine process that gives information about violence, its significance in the legal process, and resources for addressing it will be more effective than a process that needs to be triggered affirmatively by the victim. Thus, Paragraph (3) requires not only a process for identifying cases in which child abuse and domestic violence has occurred, but also the availability of information to parents regarding the potential impact of domestic violence on children and the available civil and criminal remedies for domestic violence. In addition, Paragraph (3) requires referrals to assist victims in obtaining safe shelter, counseling, and safety planning.

If feasible, the screening process should include a process for review of policy and court records to check for prior complaints of violence, convictions for crimes including acts of violence, and domestic-violence civil-protection orders involving the parties to the proceedings.

. . .

d. Temporary plan. Paragraph (4) allows temporary orders pending adjudication of the issues necessary to establish the final parenting plan. . . .

. . .

e. Order allocating custodial responsibility. Paragraph (5)(a) requires that a court-ordered parenting plan allocate custodial responsibility for the child. . . . The custodial arrangements should include either a schedule for each parent's access to the child or a method for determining such a schedule, with sufficient specificity that the court or third-party decisionmaker can enforce the order if necessary. A method may involve decisionmaking by a third party or another nonjudicial mechanism for dispute resolution. *See also* Comment *g* and § 2.10. An order for "reasonable" access is not specific enough unless a method is specified for interpreting the provision in the event of future disputes.

f. Order allocating decisionmaking responsibility. Paragraph (5)(b) requires an allocation of decisionmaking responsibility relating to significant matters the parents or the court reasonably anticipate arising with respect to the child, such as the child's health and education. . . .

Not all potential issues of decisionmaking responsibility must be resolved in the parenting plan. Some assessment must be made of those likely to arise, which should be resolved, and those that are not likely to arise. Efforts to resolve detailed hypothetical questions in advance may provoke unnecessary parental conflict. The parents, of course, are free to settle any issues they wish on their own, in a jointly submitted parenting plan. A court, however, should not address potentially inflammatory issues that appear unlikely to arise. It may also defer unresolved issues that may arise to a mechanism for dispute resolution specified in the parenting plan.

   g.   Provisions for resolving future disputes. Paragraph (5)(c) requires that a parenting plan address how disputes that may arise under the plan will be resolved. Such provisions should minimize the need for future judicial involvement. They may entail mediation or a designated arbitrator or decisionmaker who has the authority, when the parents disagree, to assess a child's circumstances and resolve the disagreement. Such provisions may also provide a mechanism for periodic review of the child's circumstances to anticipate and prevent future disputes. . . .

6.   RANDOM SELECTION

Robert Mnookin, *Child–Custody Adjudication: Judicial Functions in the Face of Indeterminacy*

39 L. & CONTEMP. PROBS. 226, 289–91 (1975).

   [A]n inquiry about what is best for a child often yields indeterminate results because of the problems of having adequate information, making the necessary predictions, and finding an integrated set of values by which to choose. But some custody cases may still be comparatively easy to decide. While there is no consensus about what is best for a child, there is much consensus about what is very bad (e.g., physical abuse); some short-term predictions about human behavior can be reliably made (e.g., chronic alcoholism or psychosis is difficult quickly to modify). Asking which alternative is in the best interests of a child may have a rather clear-cut answer in situations where one claimant exposes the child to substantial risks of immediate harm and the other claimant already has a substantial personal relationship with the child and poses no such risk. In a private dispute between two parents, for example, if a judge could predict that one parent's conduct would seriously endanger the child's health, it would not be difficult to conclude that the child's expected utility would be higher if he went with the other parent, whose conduct did not, even without the necessity of defining utility carefully. More generally, where one alternative plainly risks irreversible effects on the child that are bad and the other does not, there is no need to make longer-term predictions or more complicated psychological evaluations of what is likely to happen to the child's personality.

   But to be easy, a case must involve only one claimant who is well known to the child and whose conduct does not endanger the child. If there are two such claimants or none, difficult choices remain. Most custody disputes pose difficult choices.

   .   .   .

   Assuming that an "intimate" acceptable to both parents cannot be found to make an individualized decision, would not a random process of decision be fairer and more efficient than adjudication under a best-interests principle? Individualized adjudication means that the result will often turn on a largely intuitive evaluation based on unspoken values and unproven predictions. We would more frankly acknowledge both our ignorance and the presumed equality of the natural parents were we to flip a coin. Whether one had a separate flip for each child or one flip for all the children, the process would certainly be cheaper and quicker. It would avoid the pain associated with an adversary proceeding that requires an open exploration of the intimate aspects of family life and an ultimate judgment that one parent is preferable to the other. And it might have beneficial effects on private negotiations.[254]

Resolving a custody dispute by state-administered coin-flip would probably be viewed as unacceptable by most in our society. Perhaps this reaction reflects an abiding faith, despite the absence of an empirical basis for it, that letting a judge choose produces better results for the child. Alternatively, flipping a coin might be unacceptable for some because it represents an abdication of the search for wisdom. While judgments about what is best for the child may be currently beyond our capacity in many cases, this need not be true in fifty years. Movement towards better judgments implies, however, that judges and decision-makers as a group learn from the process of decision. In the absence of systematic feedback, this is not likely. Indeed, adopting a coin-flip now means neither that at a time when more were known and a consensus existed an adjudicatory system might not be adopted, nor that efforts to discover an adjudicatory standard would cease.

Deciding a child's future by flipping a coin might be viewed as callous. Is it more callous, however, than drafting for the military by lottery? In the same way that a lottery is a social affirmation of equality among those upon whom the government might impose the risks of war, a coin-flip would be a government affirmation of the equality of the parents. In a custody case, however, a coin-flip also symbolically abdicates government responsibility for the child and symbolically denies the importance of human differences and distinctiveness. Moreover, flipping a coin would deprive the parents of a process and a forum where their anger and aspirations might be expressed. In all, these symbolic and participatory values of adjudication would be lost by a random process.

While forceful arguments can be made in favor of the abandonment of adjudication and the adoption of an openly random process, the repulsion many would probably feel towards this suggestion may reflect an intuitive appreciation of the importance of the educational, participatory, and symbolic values of adjudication as a mode of dispute settlement. Adjudication under the indeterminate best-interests principle may yield something close to a random pattern of outcomes, while at the same time serving these values, affirming parental equality, and expressing a social concern for the child. Insofar as judges as a group may have value preferences that systematically bias the process and make the pattern less than random, these value preferences may reflect widespread values that have not been acknowledged openly in the form of legal rules.

---

254. The effect on negotiation would depend on each parent's risk preferences and on how much each wanted the child. Because each parent would face a 50 percent chance of losing, this might encourage private compromise if both wanted the child and were very risk-averse. But because a coin-flip would be less painful than an adversary proceeding the threat of holding out for such a resolution might be more frequently and credibly used than the threat of litigation is today by a party who did not much want the child but who was bargaining for advantage with regard to other elements of the marriage dissolution. To avoid these bargaining problems, the state might insist that the coin-flip occur at the time of the marriage. Through a state-supervised random process, one of the parents could then be designated as the parent who would have custody (absent a showing of neglect) if the parents should later separate and be unable themselves to decide who should have custody. For children of unmarried parents, the rule of maternal preference might be kept. The winner of the coin-flip would, of course, have an enormous negotiating advantage. It is interesting to speculate whether such a rule would affect the loser's emotional commitment to the child or willingness to stay married to avoid losing custody of the child.

Jon Elster, *Solomonic Judgments: Against the Best Interest of the Child*

54 U. Chi. L. Rev. 1, 39–43 (1986).

[R]obert Mnookin's argument that coin flipping [to determine custody when both parents are fit] would deprive the parents of a forum where their angers and aspirations might be expressed does not seem well-founded. Social psychology research does not confirm the view that aggression can be relieved by being expressed, through some form of catharsis. If anything, acting out leads to more aggression. Nor do I agree with Mnookin's contention that symbolic and participatory values of adjudication would be lost in a random choice mechanism. One could imagine a cointossing procedure coming to symbolize the equal worth of the parents, as well as the child's right to a speedy decision. It may well be true that "[l]aw, after all, is for the happiness of men, and some men will always be happier with the appearance of justice"[127]—happier, presumably, than with the reality of justice. A legal procedure is not viable if it strongly offends the sense of justice of a large part of the population, whatever else might be said for it. Yet if there *is* something to be said for it, one ought to think seriously about how it could be implemented, perhaps gradually, partially, or optionally, in ways that would not give offense. The cart of procedural justice should not be set before the horse of substantive justice.

Many people seem to think the proposal is inhuman, frivolous, or both. They argue that a decision with such far-reaching consequences must be made by appeal to reason and argument, not by an arbitrary choice. Coin tossing may be acceptable in trivial decisions, but not in matters of such momentous importance. On the other hand, it has been argued that "[r]andom selection is most favoured when the outcome is either of very *small* or very *great* importance to the recipients."[130] This may well be so. Examples of randomly made decisions of great importance to the recipients include draft lotteries, random allocation of kidney machines, and choices by lot of persons to be thrown overboard in an overcrowded life boat or to be eaten by the other passengers.

One central rationale for randomization in these cases seems to be that random choice is appropriate when other criteria would force us to compare the intrinsic worth of persons. This argument also applies to custody decisions. Although the best interest analysis ostensibly scrutinizes the mother and the father only with respect to their fitness for custody, it is easily understood as a judgment on their worth more generally. But the essential point is that randomizing in custody decisions recommends itself because it has good consequences for a person other than the potential recipients—for the child.

In sum: tossing a coin to decide custody disputes shares the advantages of any automatic decision rule, in minimizing the harm done to children by protracted litigation. With regard to parents, it appeals to intuitions about equal treatment and equal worth, whereas it can violate rights-based and needs-based considerations. It shares a drawback with the best interest principle, in creating uncertainty about the final outcome ... [As a result,]

---

127. John E. Coons, *Approaches to Court–Imposed Compromise—The Uses of Doubt and Reason*, 58 Nw. Univ. L. Rev. 750, 771 (1964).

130. Torstein E. Eckhoff, Justice, Its Determinants in Social Interaction 305 (1974) (emphasis in original).

the more risk-averse parent, usually the one for whom the child matters most, is punished by loss of bargaining power over other matters.

E. MODIFICATION

In theory, most courts will modify a custody decision only if there is a "substantial change in circumstances." If "substantial change" were construed narrowly to mean proof sufficient to declare the child neglected there would be little incentive to challenge most custody decisions once made. Some courts, however, have construed the modification standard rather loosely, so that parents who lose the initial custody decision can fairly easily find a basis for relitigating the issue, particularly in a different jurisdiction. Although the laudable desire to provide the "best" possible home for children may have created this body of law, consider whether the pursuit of the "best" may be self-defeating in some instances because of the disruption resulting from a change in custody.

1. CHANGE IN CIRCUMSTANCES

UNIFORM MARRIAGE AND DIVORCE ACT

(1973).

Section 409   Modification

a) No motion to modify a custody decree may be made earlier than 2 years after its date, unless the court permits it to be made on the basis of affidavits that there is reason to believe the child's present environment may endanger seriously his physical, mental, moral, or emotional health.

(b) If a court of this State has jurisdiction pursuant to the Uniform Child Custody Jurisdiction Act, the court shall not modify a prior custody decree unless it finds, upon the basis of facts that have arisen since the prior decree or that were unknown to the court at the time of entry of the prior decree, that a change has occurred in the circumstances of the child or his custodian, and that the modification is necessary to serve the best interest of the child. In applying these standards the court shall retain the custodian appointed pursuant to the prior decree unless:

(1) the custodian agrees to the modification;

(2) the child has been integrated into the family of the petitioner with consent of the custodian; or

(3) the child's present environment endangers seriously his physical, mental, moral, or emotional health, and the harm likely to be caused by a change of environment is outweighed by its advantages to him.

(c) Attorney fees and costs shall be assessed against a party seeking modification if the court finds that the modification action is vexatious and constitutes harassment.

COMMENT

Most experts who have spoken to the problems of post-divorce adjustment of children believe that insuring the decree's finality is more important than determining which parent should be the custodian. This section is designed to maximize finality (and thus assure continuity for the child) without jeopardizing the child's interest. Because any emergency which poses an immediate threat to the child's physical safety usually can be handled by the juvenile court, subsection (a) prohibits modification petitions until at least two years have passed following the initial decree, with a "safety valve" for emergency situations. To discourage the noncustodial parent who tries to punish a former spouse by frequent motions to modify, the subsection includes a two-year waiting period following each modification decree. During that two-year period, a contestant can get a hearing only if he can make an initial showing, by affidavit only, that there is some greater urgency for the change than that the child's "best interest" requires it. During the two-year period the judge should deny a motion to modify, without a hearing, unless the moving party carries the onerous burden of showing that the child's present environment may endanger his physical, mental, moral, or emotional health.

Subsection (b) in effect asserts a presumption that the present custodian is entitled to continue as the child's custodian. It does authorize modifications which serve the child's "best interest;" but this standard is to be applied under the principle that modification should be made only in three situations: where the custodian agrees to the change; where the child, although formally in the custody of one parent, has in fact been integrated into the family of the petitioning parent (to avoid encouraging noncustodial kidnapping, this ground requires the consent of the custodial parent); or where the noncustodial parent can prove both that the child's present environment is dangerous to physical, mental, moral, or emotional health and that the risks of harm from change of environment are outweighed by the advantage of such a change to the child. The last phrase of subsection (b) (3) is especially important because it compels attention to the real issue in modification cases. Any change in the child's environment may have an adverse effect, even if the noncustodial parent would better serve the child's interest. Subsection (b) (3) focuses the issue clearly and demands that presentation of evidence relevant to the resolution of that issue.

Hassenstab v. Hassenstab

Nebraska Court of Appeals, 1997.
570 N.W.2d 368.

■ INBODY, JUDGE.

Thomas Kelly Hassenstab appeals from an order entered by the Douglas County District Court denying his application to modify custody from Carol Marie Hassenstab to him. For the reasons set forth herein, we affirm the order of the district court.

Thomas and Carol were married on September 13, 1986. One child was born of this marriage, Jacqueline A. Hassenstab, on March 28, 1986. On May 24, 1990, the Douglas County District Court entered an order dissolving the parties' marriage and awarding custody of Jacqueline to Carol with reasonable rights of visitation to Thomas.

On June 13, 1995, Thomas filed an "Application to Modify Decree of Dissolution of Marriage" requesting, among other things, that the court modify the prior custody determination by awarding custody of Jacqueline to Thomas. Carol filed an answer, which generally denied the allegations contained in Thomas' application to modify. . . .

A trial on the application to modify ... was held on March 22, 1996. The evidence adduced at trial established that following the parties' divorce, Carol had been involved in a homosexual relationship. Additionally, Thomas testified to Carol's alleged suicide attempts, which he contends occurred prior to and during the marriage. Carol testified that she attempted suicide on one occasion, which was 7 years prior to the modification hearing and prior to the time that the dissolution decree became final. In describing the suicide attempt, Carol stated she "fell" out of a car traveling approximately 40 miles per hour. Additionally, the evidence did establish that Carol has sought counseling for several reasons, including her confusion over her sexual identity, but that she was not in counseling at the time of the modification hearing.

The trial judge met with Jacqueline in the court's chambers prior to submission of the case for determination. During the meeting, Jacqueline expressed a desire to remain in her mother's custody.

The district court subsequently entered an order dismissing Thomas' application to modify.... Thomas timely appealed to this court....

On appeal, Thomas contends that the district court erred in finding that no substantial and material change in circumstances had taken place since the entry of the dissolution decree showing that Carol was unfit to retain custody of Jacqueline or that Jacqueline's best interests required a modification of her custody to Thomas....

. . .

Thomas contends that the district court erred in finding that no substantial and material change in circumstances had taken place since the entry of the dissolution decree that showed that Carol was unfit to retain custody of Jacqueline or that Jacqueline's best interests required a modification of her custody to Thomas.

Ordinarily, custody of a minor child will not be modified unless there has been a material change of circumstances showing that the custodial parent is unfit or that the best interests of the minor child require such action. *Smith–Helstrom v. Yonker*, 544 N.W.2d 93 (Neb. 1996); *Krohn v. Krohn*, 347 N.W. 2d 869 (Neb. 1984). The party seeking modification of child custody bears the burden of showing that a material change in circumstances has occurred.

In determining a child's best interests in custody and visitation matters, NEB. REV. STAT. § 42–364(2) (Cum. Supp. 1994), provides that the factors to be considered shall include, but not be limited to, the following:

(a) The relationship of the minor child to each parent prior to the commencement of the action or any subsequent hearing;

(b) The desires and wishes of the minor child if of an age of comprehension regardless of chronological age, when such desires and wishes are based on sound reasoning;

(c) The general health, welfare, and social behavior of the minor child; and

(d) Credible evidence of abuse inflicted on any family or household member.

Additionally, a court may consider other factors in determining a child's best interests in custody matters, including the moral fitness of the child's parents and the parents' sexual conduct. *Helgenberger v. Helgenberger*, 306

N.W.2d 867 (Neb. 1981). However, the best interests of the minor child remain the court's paramount concern in deciding custody issues. *Smith–Helstrom, supra.*

First, we address Thomas' contentions that Carol is an unfit mother by reason of her alleged suicide attempts, alcohol consumption, and other psychological difficulties as well as her failure to provide a stable home environment.

. . .

The evidence was that a suicide attempt occurred 7 years prior to the modification hearing and prior to the time that the dissolution decree became final in which Carol "fell" out of a car traveling approximately 40 miles per hour. Additionally, the evidence did establish that Carol has sought counseling for several reasons, including her confusion over her sexual identity, but that she was not in counseling at the time of the modification hearing.

With regard to Carol's alcohol consumption and throwing loud parties, the record contains no evidence that Jacqueline has ever observed Carol in an intoxicated state or that Carol's alcohol consumption has adversely affected Jacqueline or endangered the child in any way. Furthermore, although Carol and Jacqueline have changed residences approximately four times and Carol has had several different roommates since the divorce decree was entered in 1990, there is no evidence that the change of residences has been harmful to Jacqueline. To the contrary, Carol testified that each move resulted in improved living conditions and that Jacqueline has never had to change schools because of the moves. Thus, based upon the evidence, Thomas has not shown that the above factors were a material change in circumstances requiring a change of custody.

Second, we address Thomas's concerns over the effect that Carol's homosexuality has on Jacqueline. The Nebraska Supreme Court has repeatedly held, albeit not in the context of a homosexual relationship, that a parent's sexual activity is insufficient to establish a material change in circumstances justifying a change in custody absent a showing that the minor child or children were exposed to such activity or were adversely affected or damaged by reason of such activity. *Smith–Helstrom, supra; Kennedy, supra; Krohn, supra* (where there was no showing that children were exposed to sexual activity or otherwise damaged, mother could retain custody of children). Thus, the issue is whether this rule is to be applied in the context of a homosexual parent.

The South Dakota Supreme Court, in *Van Driel v. Van Driel*, 525 N.W.2d 37 (S.D. 1994), held that a custodial parent's homosexual relationship does not render that parent unfit or require an award of custody to the other parent absent a showing that the custodial parent's conduct has had some harmful effect on the children and that a change of custody is in the child's or children's best interests. We agree that sexual activity by a parent, whether it is heterosexual or homosexual, is governed by the rule that to establish a material change in circumstances justifying a change in custody there must be a showing that the minor child or children were exposed to such activity or were adversely affected or damaged by reason of such activity and that a change of custody is in the child or children's best interests.

In some cases, courts of other jurisdictions have denied custody and liberal visitation to a homosexual parent. However, these cases involved situations where the children have been exposed to the parent's homosexual activity or where, for other reasons, placing the children in the homosexual parent's custody was not in the children's best interests. For example, in *Hall v Hall*, 291 N.W.2d 143, 144 (Mich. 1980), the appellate court affirmed the trial court's placement of the minor children with the father rather than with the homosexual mother where the evidence established that, given a conflict, the mother would "unquestionably choose the [homosexual] relationship over the children."

In *In re Marriage of Wiarda*, 505 N.W.2d 506, 508 (Iowa App. 1993), the appellate court affirmed the trial court's grant of custody of the minor child to the father where "it appears from the record that [the mother's] relationship with her [female] friend has not had a calming effect upon either the children or upon the difficult problems of the breakup of this marriage" and "it is certain that [the mother's] friend's presence in this matter has caused twelve-year-old Sarah certain anxieties and, from Sarah's viewpoint, has contributed to the continued breakdown of the relationship between [the mother and father]."

. . .

The case at bar is distinguishable from the aforementioned cases because, although there was evidence that Carol and her partner would engage in sexual activity at times when Jacqueline was in Carol's residence and that Jacqueline was generally aware of her mother's homosexual relationship, there was no showing that the daughter was directly exposed to the sexual activity or that she was in any way harmed by the homosexual relationship between Carol and her partner. Because the evidence in the case at bar simply does not establish any harmful effect on Jacqueline because of Carol's homosexual relationship, there has been no showing of a material change of circumstances.

Furthermore, the evidence does not establish that Jacqueline's best interests require a change of custody. At the trial, Jacqueline was described as a happy, self-assured, and confident child. Thomas characterized Jacqueline as "a very loving, fun, special daughter." He further stated that she is "very, very happy, very joyful, very spirited." Other witnesses testified that Jacqueline is dressed in clean clothes, which are appropriate for the weather, she is well-kept, and her hair is combed. The record further reflects that Jacqueline is a "B" student and has few discipline problems.

. . .

In sum, Thomas has failed to meet his burden of proving a material change of circumstances necessitating a change of Jacqueline's custody. Therefore, the order of the district court is affirmed.

NOTE

Hassenstab involved a modification of custody rather than an initial award. If the challenged actions had occurred before the initial custody hearing, would the mother have won?

Rose v. Rose Revisited: The Court Changes Its Position

June 6, 1999.

■ SANGSTER, J.

This case had its origin late in 1994 when the Dissolution Petition was first filed. The temporary custody hearing consumed seven trial days and saw the presentation of an impressive array of expert witnesses. This Court at that time indicated a reluctance to grant custody to the father because of what might be termed an arrogant, overprotective and super critical attitude. However, the mother showed some observable residual effects from her suicide attempt (jumping from an eighth story window) and subsequent medical treatment. This court noted that because of some fear and uncertainty as to the mother's ability to care for an almost two-year-old child, the father would continue as the primary custodian. The mother, however, was granted extensive and exclusive visitation privileges, something she had been denied since her hospitalization a year previous.

Trial on the dissolution itself covered nine trial days in mid-June of 1995. By stipulation the Court was urged to read all notes and exhibits from the January hearing and authorized to consider them at the June dissolution trial. In return counsel agreed to present only evidence which had not been given in the earlier hearing. In effect, the trial lasted 16 full days. Literally dozens of expert witnesses testified, many being flown in from the East Coast and other distant points.

The Court was persuaded that the father's attitude had not changed but the mother's condition had improved substantially. Accordingly, the mother was granted permanent custody. In the decree, the father was given frequent and liberal visitation rights. In retrospect, this may have had the effect of causing some emotional damage to the child, as will be later pointed out.

The continuing saga of the *Rose* case resumed in November of 1998, with the mother filing a request to eliminate some of the authorized visitation periods. By January 1999, the father had by affidavit and motion resisted the mother's modification motion and filed for a change of custody to himself.

The motions were heard for 14 trial days in April 1999. Again, a number of expert witnesses testified. In substance, the evidence covered two periods since the decree: a time when the mother lived in an apartment in her parents' home, and later when she found her own residence in Northwest Seattle.

The Court finds that the testimony is overwhelming that there has been a substantial change of circumstances since the 1995 Decree. Whatever the custody arrangements are to be, the visitation schedule must be changed to restrict the out of custody parent's visitation rights. It is obvious that there has been an excess of shifting the child from one parent to the other.

The change in circumstances found here is sufficient to bring the Court back into the arena of a custody decision. Some general conclusions as they apply to the parents and child may be relevant here. The child may have some emotional depression at times, he has suffered some possibility of a lowered growth rate, and may have a problem with proper sexual identification. The mother has undergone some emotional traumas since leaving her parents' home for her own apartment, has at times been too dependent on her child and at other times has given him more independence than may have been necessary. The father has mellowed some in his previous poor attitudes, possibly because of his remarriage, has sometimes exhibited poor judgment during the visitation transfers with his ex-wife and has continued to be somewhat overprotective and reactionary.

Having found that the circumstances have substantially changed, the Court now turns to the difficult decision as to which parent is better suited to be the primary custodian and which would be the least detrimental alternative for the child. While our judicial terminology calls for an "award" of custody, this Court cautions the parties that any grant of custody is not an "award" but a responsibility and an awesome obligation. This child has become an emotional pawn between two well meaning parents. He has suffered damage because they could not trust each other and often resorted to tactics of inflicting emotional pain on the other. Without a shadow of a doubt, both parents have, at times, put the child's best interests aside for their own purposes in "getting back" at the other.

Unfortunately, a decision of this kind must be based upon what one or the other parent has done to demonstrate in some small way their disqualification to be the primary custodian. On the brighter side, both parents have shown their love for the child and for the most part been good parents.

As to the child, Jason, the Court has little concern as to his rate of growth. I assume that will accelerate after a decision in this case, if it is somehow connected to something other than simply being the offspring of small parents who themselves come from a long line of small people. I also assume that his diagnosed depression, unhappiness and mood swings can be improved in time, given a better visitation schedule and more consistency in authority figures.

I do find that Jason is emotionally unstable and depressed beyond that to be expected from a child his age. It appears that this condition resulted in large part from frequent contact with two parents who gave their love in vastly differing ways.

After leaving her parents' home for her own apartment, Ms. Rose's emotional stability suffered. She became inclined toward periods of wide emotional swings. At times she would become enraged. Though this was probably not directed at Jason in a physical sense, he did have to experience it. She sometimes sank into depression, at other times acted more like the child's friend than mother, and then could swing into an aggressive mood. It is apparent that while she lived with her parents and when they later visited at her apartment she was able to keep her moods at a consistent level and react normally. Without their steadying influence she became unstable. I think Jason suffered from this inconsistency as much as from the frequent visitations.

The Court finds that the father was more consistent in his parenting of Jason. While he appeared to retain some of his arrogant, overprotective and super-critical attitudes, he has moderated. He is now somewhat established both in his profession and his new marital life. Above all, he has been a good father to Jason on a consistent basis.

Generally, courts give great weight to the primary custodian in motions to modify custody. It is generally thought that continuity of care, stability and psychological parenthood go hand in hand with the in-custody parent. These factors deserve less weight here, however, because of the frequent visitations and the history of the relationship. There is less continuity to be disturbed, little stability and no single psychological parent.

There would be little point to an extensive discussion of each of the numerous points raised by the parties. Suffice it to say, that I have had the opportunity to listen to tens of thousands of words, view hundreds of pages of exhibits, and sit through three hearings covering about thirty full trial days. While the testimony at the 1995 hearings cannot be considered as directly bearing on this instant custody decision, it does lend an important factor by demonstrating changes and causal relationships. I have had the opportunity to compare now with then and see the changes and growth or regression made by the parents and child.

The Court concludes that Jason's best interests lie with his father as primary custodian. He is more stable and offers Jason the best chance to make progress toward normalcy.

As mentioned earlier, the frequent and liberal visitation schedule has been a problem not only to Jason but also to his parents as they confront each other. Accordingly, the Court will set visitation as follows: 30 days in the summer with 30 days notice; one weekend a month (5 p.m. Friday until 5 p.m. Sunday); in alternating fashion: 5 p.m. the day before until 5 p.m. the day of Jason's birthday, Thanksgiving and New Years; and each Mother's Day.

Because of the present difference in the income-producing abilities of the parents, there will be no provision for child support. In that these motions were brought on behalf of Jason and in their roles as parents, no costs or attorney fees will be awarded.

NOTE

For an excellent overview of custody modification, see Joan G. Wexler, *Rethinking the Modification of Child Custody Decrees*, 94 YALE L.J. 757 (1985). In addition to summarizing social science data that suggest custody modifications can be damaging to the emotional needs of the children, Professor Wexler raises constitutional objections to most custody modifications:

> First, the justification for the state's initial intrusion—that the parents could not agree on custody—no longer applies. No decision is being thrust upon the courts; custody has already been allocated, and the matter between the two parents no longer stands in equilibrium. The state may not, simply because a divorce once took place, rely upon a "shattered family" rationale forever to justify its intervention and continuing jurisdiction over the new family unit.... The implications of a rule that authorizes the state to have continuing jurisdiction over [the estimated one third of this nation's children who will during their minority experience the divorce of their parents] based on a change of circumstances or best interests standard are Orwellian. Under the traditional standard of custody modification, the behavior of the custodial parent is examined under a microscope, with the noncustodial parent and the family court in the role of Big Brother. Has she nurtured her child sufficiently in a manner acceptable to the court? Has she done anything else that in the court's eye constitutes less than acceptable parenting? ... Any rule of law that puts the government in a position to oversee the most private of matters and sensitive of interests raises serious constitutional questions.

Id. at 817. Do you agree with her argument?

2.   RELOCATION

Morgan v. Morgan

Supreme Court of New Jersey, 2011.
12 A.3d 192.

■ LONG, J.

After a divorce, applications by a custodial parent to relocate with the children are fairly common. For all their ubiquity, however, such requests present us with difficult and often heart-wrenching decisions.

Inevitably, upon objection by a noncustodial parent, there is a clash between the custodial parent's interest in self-determination and the noncustodial parent's interest in the companionship of the child. . . .

Our evolving case law has attempted to balance those competing interests. Most recently, in *Baures v. Lewis*, 770 A.2d 214 (N.J. 2001), we clarified the two-pronged standard for resolving such a matter: a custodial parent will be permitted to move if (1) that party has a good faith reason to do so, and (2) the children will not suffer from the move. To aid in that analysis, we set forth a metric consisting of twelve relevant considerations. Here, a mother sought to move with her children to another state where her fiancé and her extended family were located. The father objected. In 2006, the trial judge blocked the move, declaring that the mother did not have a valid reason to go and that the children would be harmed thereby.

In 2007, both parties appealed and in 2010 the Appellate Division reversed the denial of relocation because the trial court's conclusions were not supported by the record, permitted relocation, and remanded solely for proceedings to expedite the move. We granted the father's petition for certification and now affirm and modify. We agree with the appellate panel that the trial judge's analysis was seriously flawed and warranted reversal. However, the scope of the Appellate Division's remand order was too narrow. Enormous changes in the lives of the parties and their children have occurred over the four years since the trial court's decision. Thus, we hold the remand requires an assessment of the *Baures* factors in light of present-day realities.

Paul Morgan and Kristin Leary were married on April 11, 1992. Two daughters were born of the marriage—Anna on November 22, 1998, and Greta on June 29, 2001. Morgan and Leary divorced on August 16, 2005. The final judgment of divorce incorporated a March 2005 Property Settlement Agreement (PSA), which provided for joint legal custody of the children, indicated that Leary would be the "parent of primary residence," and detailed a parenting-time schedule. The schedule provided that Morgan would have the girls on alternate weekends beginning Friday evening and ending Monday evening, every Thursday night until Friday morning, and every Tuesday evening for dinner. Holidays would be alternated and each parent would have the children for one week of vacation during the school year and one during the summer.

On November 23, 2005, in anticipation of an application by Leary to move with the children to Massachusetts, Morgan filed a motion seeking a re-determination of custody based on "a substantial change in circumstances. . . ."

On January 11, 2006, Leary opposed Morgan's motion and filed a cross-motion seeking permission to move with their daughters to Massachusetts or, alternatively, a plenary hearing. In support of her request to relocate, Leary pointed to the fact that Massachusetts is her home state; her entire family resides there; she was by then engaged to Mambro, a Massachusetts resident; that her marriage would enable her to forego employment and become a "stay-at-home" mother; and that the PSA was not based on her promise to remain in New Jersey. Morgan filed a reply certification disputing Leary's assertions and underscoring her emotional volatility which he claimed would render the proposed relocation away from him harmful to their children.

The trial judge denied Morgan's motion to re-determine custody because there was no change in circumstances from the time of the divorce.... In ruling, the judge declared Leary to be the parent of primary residence, warranting application of the relocation principles of *Baures;* denied Leary permission to move the children to Massachusetts, but granted her request for a plenary hearing; and appointed a forensic psychologist, Dr. Edwin Rosenberg, to perform the relocation evaluation. Morgan retained a clinical psychologist, Dr. Amie Wolf–Mehlman, to evaluate the issues.

Both experts interviewed the parties, the children, and Mambro, and observed each of the parties with the children. They also reviewed relevant records and conferred with collateral sources, including two therapists whom the parties saw at times from 2000 to 2004. Additionally, Dr. Rosenberg administered psychological tests to the parties and Mambro, the results of which were reviewed by Dr. Wolf–Mehlman.

Dr. Rosenberg's August 26, 2006 report concluded that Leary did not suffer from any significant emotional problems and that she was sincere in her desire to be closer to her family and to spend more time with the girls, which would be facilitated by her marriage to Mambro. The report, which recommended approval of the move, proposed an extensive parenting-time schedule that would foster Morgan's bond with the children, which Dr. Rosenberg recognized as an important one.

Morgan argues that he and Leary shared *de facto* custody of the girls and that the courts below erred in ruling otherwise without a plenary hearing specifically addressing that subject; that he established Leary's move would harm the children; and that, in no event should Leary now be permitted to move without a full hearing on presently existing circumstances.

Leary counters that she is the girls' custodial parent and the primary caretaker; that she satisfied the removal standards set forth in *Baures;* and that she should be permitted to move forthwith.

An analysis of New Jersey's removal scheme begins with N.J. STAT. ANN. § 9:2–2:

> When the Superior Court has jurisdiction over the custody and maintenance of the minor children of parents divorced, separated or living separate, and such children are natives of this State, or have resided five years within its limits, they shall not be removed out of its jurisdiction against their own consent, if of suitable age to signify the same, nor while under that age without the consent of both parents, unless the court, upon cause shown, shall otherwise order.

The purpose of N.J. STAT. ANN. § 9:2–2 must be effectuated within the realities of post-divorce life:

> [T]he family unity which is lost as a consequence of the divorce is lost irrevocably, and there is no point in judicial insistence on maintaining a wholly unrealistic simulation of unity. The realities of the situation after divorce compel the realization that the child's quality of life and style of life are provided by the custodial parent. That the interests of the child are closely interwoven with those of the custodial parent is consistent with psychological studies of children of divorced or separated parents.

. . .

Historically, relocation was not looked upon favorably by our courts.... [I]n *Cooper* [*v. Cooper*, 491 A.2d 606 (N.J. 1984)] we held that:

When removal is challenged under N.J. Stat. Ann. § 9:2–2, we hold that to establish sufficient cause for the removal, *the custodial parent initially must show that there is a real advantage to that parent in the move* and that the move is not inimical to the best interests of the children.... It is only after the custodial parent establishes these threshold requirements that the court should consider, based on evidence presented by both parties, visitation and other factors to determine whether the custodial parent has sufficient cause to permit removal under the statute.

Over time, there has been a shift in relocation law across the country. That shift has resulted from several factors: the mobility of the population, advances in technology, the notion that what is good for the custodial parent is good for the children of the divorce, and a renewed recognition that "[t]he custodial parent who bears the burden and responsibility for the child is entitled, to the greatest possible extent, to the same freedom to seek a better life for herself or himself and the children as enjoyed by the noncustodial parent."

Thus, in *Holder v. Polanski*, 544 A.2d 852, 855 (N.J. 1988), where we addressed the liberty interests of custodial parents and the fundamental inequity that emerges out of a scheme that holds a custodial parent hostage in this state while allowing a noncustodial parent complete freedom of movement, we said:

> As men and women approach parity, the question arises when a custodial mother wants to move from one state to another, why not? Until today, our response has included the requirement that the custodial parent establish, among other things, a real advantage to that parent from the move. We now modify that requirement and hold that a custodial parent may move with the children of the marriage to another state as long as the move does not interfere with the best interests of the children or the visitation rights of the noncustodial parent.

Because the case law following *Holder* was in disarray regarding the initial burden of proof, the burden of going forward, the ultimate burden of proof, and the elements to be considered in determining whether the move would be "inimical" to the interests of the child, we detailed the proper approach in *Baures*.

. . .

[I]n a removal case the movant must prove "a good faith reason for the move and that the child will not suffer from it." To assist in that analysis, we set forth a twelve-factor metric for deciding whether removal is warranted under that two-part test:

> (1) the reasons given for the move; (2) the reasons given for the opposition; (3) the past history of dealings between the parties insofar as it bears on the reasons advanced by both parties for supporting and opposing the move; (4) whether the child will receive educational, health and leisure opportunities at least equal to what is available here; (5) any special needs or talents of the child that require accommodation and whether such accommodation or its equivalent is available in the new location; (6) whether a visitation and communication schedule can be developed that will allow the noncustodial parent to maintain a full and continuous relationship with the child; (7) the likelihood that the custodial parent will continue to foster the child's relationship with the noncustodial parent if the move is allowed; (8) the effect of the move on extended family relationships here and in the new location; (9) if the

child is of age, his or her preference; (10) whether the child is entering his or her senior year in high school at which point he or she should generally not be moved until graduation without his or her consent; (11) whether the noncustodial parent has the ability to relocate; (12) any other factor bearing on the child's interest.

Obviously, not all factors will apply in every case and, to the extent that factors are applicable, all may not have equal relevance.

We also made clear in *Baures* that a mere change in parenting time would not be sufficient to bar a move. Indeed, as we had said in *Cooper,* the advantages of the move should not be sacrificed solely to maintain the "same" visitation schedule where a reasonable alternative visitation scheme is available.

Procedurally, the first step of the removal test considers the type of parenting arrangement between the parties and whether the matter is actually an application for a change in custody as opposed to a removal case. For example, a removal motion by a party in a case where the children rotate between houses, with each parent assuming full parental responsibility half of the time, is clearly an application to change the custodial status which cannot be maintained from a distance. In contrast, an application by a custodial parent to move away in a case in which the noncustodial parent sees the children once or twice a week and is not seeking to change that state of affairs, is a removal motion. . . . [W]hether the motion should be viewed through the *Baures* prism or as one for custody will depend on the facts.

The distinction between custody and removal is important in terms of the burden of proof. A custody case is squarely dependent on what is in the child's best interests. In a removal case,

> the parents' interests take on importance. However, although the parties often do not seem to realize it, the conflict in a removal case is not purely between the parents' needs and desires. Rather, it is a conflict based on the extent to which those needs and desires can be viewed as intertwined with the child's interests. *Cooper,* and more particularly, *Holder,* recognize that subtlety by according special respect to the liberty interests of the custodial parent to seek happiness and fulfillment because that parent's happiness and fulfillment enure to the child's benefit in the new family unit. At the same time those cases underscore the importance of the child's relationship with the noncustodial parent and require a visitation schedule sufficient to support and nurture that relationship. The critical path to a removal disposition therefore is not necessarily the one that satisfies one parent or even splits the difference between the parents, but the one that will not cause detriment to the child.

The harm standard, which is deeply rooted in our removal jurisprudence, is necessary in a traditional removal setting because of the real-life consequences of the application of a pure best-interests standard. Practically speaking, that standard would always, or nearly always, break in favor of keeping the child in proximity to two fit parents, thus chaining the custodial parent, who bears the laboring oar in child rearing, to New Jersey, while permitting the noncustodial parent free movement. It was that scenario that *Cooper, Holder,* and *Baures* recognized and addressed, prioritizing the right of the custodial parent to self-determination by permitting a good faith move that is not inimical to the child's interest. There is no need for such prioritization where the parties equally share in the daily burdens of child rearing.

Once the parties' status is determined and the case is denominated as one involving removal, the burden of production rests initially on the movant to make out a prima facie showing on the good faith and harm to the child prongs, which typically requires a "visitation proposal." That burden "is not a particularly onerous one":

> It will be met, for example, by a custodial parent who shows that he is seeking to move closer to a large extended family that can help him raise his child; that the child will have educational, health and leisure opportunities at least equal to that which is available here, and that he has thought out a visitation schedule that will allow the child to maintain his or her relationship with the noncustodial parent.

Should the moving party meet the burden of production, the noncustodial parent must then "produce evidence opposing the move as either not in good faith or inimical to the child's interest." Problems, in the form of detriment to the child, with regard to changed visitation may prove particularly important. Further:

> Although children are generally resilient and can adapt to removal so long as their relationship with the noncustodial parent is fully sustained through a new visitation scheme, the noncustodial parent remains free to adduce evidence that for particular reasons, and in light of the unique facts surrounding his or her relationship with the child, such a conclusion should not be drawn. . . .

Once that evidence is produced, the custodial parent may adduce further evidence or may rest. Either way, the ultimate burden of proving both good faith and that the children will not be harmed by the move remains with the party seeking to relocate. That is the backdrop for our inquiry.

· · ·

The Appellate Division concluded that the trial court made several significant errors in its *Baures* analysis, requiring reversal of the order denying removal. In particular, the appellate panel found that the trial court erred in: (1) failing to apply the "good faith" standard of *Baures;* (2) failing to recognize that that standard was satisfied; and (3) concluding that Leary's "emotional instability" was supported by admissible evidence in the record.

We have carefully reviewed this record in light of the appropriate legal standards and have determined that those conclusions are unassailable. Indeed, although the trial court properly credited the importance of Morgan's role in the girls' lives, it did not apply the good faith standard; did not recognize that that standard was satisfied by the reasons Leary advanced for the move; and permitted evidence of non-testifying experts it had previously ruled inadmissible to affect its judgment regarding Leary's mental state. Whether the Appellate Division should have entered an order of its own permitting Leary to move, or remanded the matter to the trial court to decide the case anew under the correct legal standards, is debatable. However, we need not join that debate because at this point, a full remand is in order.

Four years have elapsed since the evidence was adduced before the trial court. Enormous changes in the parties' lives have occurred. Leary's engagement is off. Mambro will not be supporting the family and Leary will not be a stay-at-home mother. Thus, two of the three pediments on which Leary's proposal to move was based no longer exist. Further, the girls are now twelve and nine, respectively. Anna has a legal right to express a preference regarding the move. Both girls are likely more fully ensconced in school, extra-curricular activities, and in community life with family and friends. Morgan has remarried and now has a son—the girls' new half-brother. Moreover, by this time we assume that the parties' participation in the children's day-to-day lives has reached an angle of repose, the precise details of which are not before us. Under the circumstances, a remand that does not take those changes into account is inadequate.

Indeed, there is abundant support for the proposition that a remand in a removal case should be sufficiently broad in scope to permit consideration of the "living record." As we noted in *Baures*, "with the passage of time, the evidence adduced in the earlier proceedings may have changed." Likewise, in *Cooper*, where we remanded for consideration under a new rule of law, we permitted the parties to present new evidence:

> Since we recognize that the circumstances of the parties have changed in the year that has elapsed since the original hearing on this motion, on remand both parties may supplement the record with any information that may be pertinent to the trial judge's determination of this case.

That is not to suggest that the ticking clock alone will justify a reversal and a full remand in every case. To the contrary, it is the substantive changes in the parties' lives that take place during the passage of time that are the focus. Each case is fact sensitive. On the facts before us, so many dramatic changes have occurred that the broader remedy is justified. At the hearing, all of the *Baures* factors that are relevant should be addressed and updated psychological evaluations should be ordered, if appropriate. The hearing should take place expeditiously.

The judgment of the Appellate Division is affirmed and modified. We affirm the court's conclusion that Morgan did not establish *de facto* shared custody and that the trial court's prohibition against relocation required reversal. We also affirm the order of remand, but modify the scope of the remand order to account for present circumstances in accordance with the principles to which we have adverted.

Linda D. Elrod, *National and International Momentum Builds for More Child Focus in Relocation Disputes*

44 Fam. L.Q. 341, 341–44, 351–57, 359–63 (2010).

Relocation cases are ... the "San Andreas fault"[3] of family law. When one parent attempts to move a child a significant distance from the other parent, the child's relationship with each parent changes in quality and quantity.[4] These "no-win" cases are occurring with increasing frequency, create enormous tensions for parents and their children, and burden the legal system and the judges who have to decide them. A potential relocation can generate conflict in cases where there had been none before, reopen old wounds in others, or exacerbate an already highly-conflicted situation. Requests for moves within a state or country perplex decision-makers, but

---

3. *Patrick Parkinson, Judy Cashmore, & Judi Single, The Need for Reality Testing in Relocation Cases,* 44 Fam. L.Q. 1, 1 (2010).

4. *See* William G. Austin & Jonathan W. Gould, *Exploring Three Functions in Child Custody Evaluation for the Relocation Case: Prediction, Investigation, and Making Recommendations for a Long–Distance Parenting Plan,* 3 J. Child Custody 63, 99 (2006) (noting that long distances leave a child outside the "dynamic sphere of influence" of the absent parent, changing the nature of their relationship).

international relocation requests add other logistical, economic, and enforcement obstacles.

Predicting the result of relocation disputes remains difficult because they are so intensely fact-driven. Neither the laws in the United States nor the laws of most other countries provide enough guidance to encourage settlement and dissuade litigation. While decisions are difficult even when one parent has sole custody, today's requests present enormous dilemmas when joint and shared parenting arrangements are becoming the norm. The outcome of any given case depends upon the existence of a statute or case precedent making it easy or difficult for a parent to relocate with a child, the type of parenting arrangement that currently exists, and, perhaps most importantly, the attitude of the trial judge who exercises broad discretion and is rarely reversed on appeal. Complicating the situation is that relocation cases have become part of the "gender" wars, as fathers' rights advocates who feel fathers are usually the left-behind parent battle feminists' groups who support a custodial mother's desire to relocate. In addition, mental health professionals are weighing in on appropriate considerations.[15]

Absent the ability to predict the outcome, the parties engage in expensive, emotionally-charged and time-consuming litigation. As one parent's freedom of movement and "new life" opportunities bump against the other parent's interest in maintaining a meaningful parental relationship, the child can become embroiled in a protracted battle between the parents. Although some of the research on the effects of relocation on children has been contradictory and sometimes confusing, nearly all of the existing research confirms that children suffer harm from being involved in high-conflict situations.[18]

. . .

II.   National and International Attempts at Developing Relocation Guidelines

[I]n 1997, the American Academy of Matrimonial Lawyers promulgated the *Model Act on Relocation* which had twenty-two sections, mandated notice of a move, offered three options for presumptions and the burden of proof, listed eight factors, and provided remedies. A few years later, the American Law Institute's *Principles of the Law of Family Dissolution* also provided for notice and adopted a position generally favoring a child's relocation with a primary caretaker parent. The Joint Editorial Board on Uniform Family Laws of the Uniform Law Commission (ULC) suggested that a Uniform

---

15.   *Compare* Judith S. Wallerstein & Tony J. Tanke, *To Move or Not to Move—Psychological and Legal Considerations in the Relocation of Children Following Divorce*, 30 FAM. L.Q. 305 (1996) *with* Richard A. Warshak, *Social Science and Children's Best Interests in Relocation Cases: Burgess revisited*, 34 FAM. L.Q. 83 (2000) *and* Sanford L. Braver, Ira M. Ellman & William V. Fabricius, *Relocation of Children After Divorce and Children's Best Interests: New Evidence and Legal Considerations*, 17 J. FAM PSYCH 206 (2003) (suggesting harm to children from move of either parent, but criticized for both methodology and conclusions). *See also* Joan B. Kelly & Michael Lamb, *Developmental Issues in Relocation Cases Involving Young Children: When, whether and How?*, 17(2) J. FAM. PSYCH. 193 (2003); William G. Austin, *Relocation Law and the Threshold of Harm: Integrating Legal and Behavioral Perspectives*, 34 FAM. L.Q. 63 (2000) (suggesting use of a risk assessment scale).

18.   JANET JOHNSTON, VIVIENNE ROSEBY, & KATHRYN KUEHNLE, IN THE NAME OF THE CHILD: A DEVELOPMENTAL APPROACH TO UNDERSTANDING AND HELPING CHILDREN OF CONFLICTED AND VIOLENT DIVORCE 5–6 (2d ed. 2009) (noting the level and intensity of parental conflict is thought to be the most important factor in a child's postdivorce adjustment and the single best predictor of a poor outcome); CARLA B. GARRITY & MITCHELL A. BARIS, CAUGHT IN THE MIDDLE: PROTECTING THE CHILDREN OF HIGH-CONFLICT DIVORCE 19 (1994); Paul R. Amato & Bruce Keith, *Parental Divorce and the Well-being of Children: A Meta–Analysis*, 110 PSYCHOL. BULL. 26 (1991).

Relocation Act would be helpful to states. The ULC set up a drafting committee. After one preliminary meeting and one draft, a letter terminating the project in February 2009, stated:

> ... given that the various interest groups are contentious and the states have adopted varying approaches on how to deal with the issue of relocation of children, the members of the Scope and Program Committee and Executive Committees were concerned that any act drafted by the ULC on this subject, no matter how much an advancement in the law, would not be enacted in a significant number of states.

Even though these prior models were not widely adopted, each helped to move the discussion forward....

. . .

IV. Lack of Uniformity in State, National, or International Laws

[L]ack of uniformity begins with defining what constitutes a relocation.... Thirty seven states have specific relocation statutes, whereas others rely on the general modification of custody provisions. States and countries differ on whether, when, and how notice is required; whether a contemplated move is a change of circumstances; the proper presumptions or burdens of proof to consider; and the appropriate factors to consider. The lack of uniformity can lead to a lack of predictability, which can lead to litigation.

A. *Notice Requirements*

In the absence of safety issues, common sense dictates that a parent planning to move provide some notice to the other parent. At least half of the states do require the moving parent to give notice or to obtain either the consent of the other parent or a judge. The time for giving notice varies considerably from thirty to ninety days (one state) with sixty days (nine states) being the most common. The form, contents and manner of notice also vary. Many states require that the notice be sent by certified mail and include (1) the intended date of the relocation; (2) the address of the intended new residence, if known; (3) the specific reasons for the intended relocation; and (4) a proposal for how custodial responsibility should be modified, if necessary, in light of the intended move. If notice is given and the nonmoving parent either agrees to the move or fails to object to the move, generally the moving parent may relocate. States are divided as to what happens when a parent fails to give the proper notice.[60]

. . .

B. *Move as Change of Circumstances*

Generally, modification of an existing custody order requires the person seeking to change custody to prove that there has been a material change of circumstances and that modification is in the best interests of the child. Whether the relocation case gets a hearing may depend on whether the move is a change of circumstances. Usually, a proposed move is a change if

---

60. *Compare In re* Marriage of Grippin, 186 P.3d 852 (Kan. Ct. App. 2008) (finding that custody should not be changed in retaliation for the mother not giving the proper statutory notice) *with* Frances v. Frances, 266 S.W.3d 754 (Ky. 2008) (changing custody to father where mother moved to Iowa without notice to father and child had close ties to father and extended family).

the parents share custody or if the move is a certain number of miles away from the current residence. . . .

. . .

C. Presumptions and Burdens of Proof

Many jurisdictions are still struggling with complex approaches to presumptions for or against relocation and the burden of proof. . . .

. . .

In 1996, a New York case led the way toward abolishing presumptions for or against a parent's relocation, saying:

> It serves neither the interests of the children nor the ends of justice to view relocation cases through prisms of presumptions and threshold tests that artificially skew the analysis in favor of one outcome or another. Courts should be free to consider and give appropriate weight to all of the factors that may be relevant. . . .[77]

The clear trend in the United States seems to be to abandon presumptions and to adopt a "best interests of the child" test that requires both parents to prove that their position is in the child's best interests. The neutral best interests appears to be gaining traction as the standard for international relocations also. . . .

A world without presumptions requires judges to make a best-interest-of-the-child determination on a case-by-case basis. Some lament that after decades of use, the "best interest" standard remains vague and vulnerable to judges using their own values to make decisions. The argument is that because decisions are based on the circumstances of each case, clearly defining and uniformly applying "best interests" is difficult. While this makes predictability challenging, the best interest standard is flexible and adaptable to each child's particular circumstance. If children are truly the focus of the relocation analysis, the key then is to provide judges with weighted, prioritized, child-focused factors. In addition, an attorney for the child, mental health professional, or court service officers can assist judges with relevant information to make the best interest determination.

D. The Growing Lists of Factors to Guide Decision Makers

[I]n an attempt to make relocation decisions more consistent, legislatures and courts have set out increasingly long lists of factors to assist judges in evaluating the appropriateness of a move.[83] The 1976 New Jersey *D'Onofrio* case[84] recognized that the existence of a new family unit post-divorce and set out as factors: (1) the prospective advantages of the move in improving the custodial parent's and the child's quality of life; (2) the integrity of the custodial parent's motive for relocation; (3) the integrity of the noncustodial parent's motives for opposing the move; and (4) whether there is a realistic

---

77. Tropea v. Tropea, 665 N.E.2d 145, 151 (N.Y. 1996).

83. *See* ALA. CODE § 30–3–169.3(a)(1) (2009) (listing seventeen factors); COLO. REV. STAT. § 14–10–129 (2009) (listing nine factors, but incorporating by reference the general custody statute that has eleven factors); Dupre v. Dupre, 857 A.2d 242 (R.I. 2004) (setting out factors, but incorporating custody factors in Pettinato v. Pettinato, 582 A.2d 909 (R.I. 1990)).

84. D'Onofrio v. D'Onofrio, 365 A.2d 27 (N.J. Super. Ct. Ch. Div. 1976), *affirmed* 365 A.2d 716 (N.J. Super. Ct. App. Div. 1976) (allowing mother to move to her native town in South Carolina where she had extended family, higher paying job, and lower cost of living and father had refused to keep children overnight). *See In re* Marriage of Eckert, 518 N.E.2d 1041 (Ill. 1988) (using New Jersey factors).

opportunity for visitation that can provide an adequate basis for preserving and fostering the noncustodial parent's relationship with the child if relocation is allowed.

. . .

In analyzing the factors, most courts have adopted a two-step process. The relocating parent generally must demonstrate a good reason for the move. If a good reason exists, the issue becomes whether the move is in the best interests of the child.

Because of the potential geographical and emotional disruptions for a child, courts are reluctant to allow a move based on a whim. Most relocating parents have more than one reason. The ALI Principles section 2.17(4)(a)(ii) summarized what courts have found to be valid reasons for a relocation:

> (1) to be close to significant family or other sources of support;
>
> (2) to address significant health problems;
>
> (3) to protect the safety of the child or another member of the child's household from a significant risk of harm;
>
> (4) to pursue a significant employment or educational opportunity;
>
> (5) to be with one's spouse or domestic partner who lives in, or is pursuing a significant opportunity in, the new location;
>
> (6) to significantly improve the family's quality of life.

If there is no firm job offer, no new spouse, or no improvement of the child's well-being, courts often find the reasons insufficient. A moving parent who has a history of interfering with the other parent's relationship with the child may find relocation denied because of the potential difficulty in enforcing the contact order once the parent is far away.

Courts have also been interested in the integrity of the nonmoving parent's motives for opposing the move. If a parent has been actively parenting, he or she wants to maintain the frequent contact and for the child to remain near extended family and the community. A parent who has not been paying child or spousal support may be objecting to the child's relocation to secure a financial advantage. An abusive parent may be trying to punish, control, or hurt the former partner. A parent who has sporadically exercised parenting time in the past or is using the child as a pawn in a power struggle with the other parent may not have pure motives, and little basis, for opposing the relocation.

Courts have allowed moves when convinced that the move will genuinely improve the quality of life for the child and primary residential parent. For many years, courts favored relocation as in the best interest of the child and a sole custodial parent, usually the mother. Social science data supported courts in finding that the most important consideration was to maintain the primary parenting relationship. . . .

As joint physical residency and shared parenting have become the norm for many postdivorce or never-married families, there are two primary caregivers—two actively-involved, loving parents. The New Jersey Supreme Court noted that different standards should apply in shared parenting situations:

> [The normal removal inquiry] is entirely inapplicable to a case in which the noncustodial parent shares physical custody either de facto or de jure. . . . In those circumstances, the removal application effectively

constitutes a motion for change in custody and will be governed initially by a changed circumstances inquiry.[107]

If the parents share substantial time with their child, in the absence of violence or extremely high conflict, a growing number of social scientists believe that it is usually in the child's best interests to maintain meaningful relationships with both parents.[108] Even if the parents share parenting, however, the mere fact that the nonmoving parent's access may be more difficult or diminished in time will not keep a court from allowing a move if it is in the child's best interests.... On the other hand, where the move has the potential to disrupt the child's life, not only now, but in the future, courts are more willing to not allow the child to move and change residential placement.

Generally, the moving parent must show that a new parenting plan can provide realistic opportunities for sufficient parenting time to allow the nonmoving parent and the child to maintain a close relationship. The travel burdens should be mainly on the parents, not the child. In addition, parties need to realistically assess the costs of relocation (when added to the costs of litigation), which will often include not only transportation but also lodging and food for several days. The moving parent must convince the court that he or she will comply with the new arrangements. While modern technology and virtual visitation may be able to mitigate some of the potential stresses on the relationship between the child and the nonresidential parent, they cannot replace a parent and child's ability to hug each other. Some courts have required parents to purchase technologically advanced computer systems to allow the child to maintain contact.

F. VISITATION

UNIFORM MARRIAGE AND DIVORCE ACT

(1973).

Section 407   Visitation

(a) A parent not granted custody of the child is entitled to reasonable visitation rights unless the court finds, after a hearing, that visitation would endanger seriously the child's physical, mental, moral, or emotional health.

(b) The court may modify an order granting or denying visitation rights whenever modification would serve the best interest of the child; but the court shall not restrict a parent's visitation rights unless it finds that the visitation would endanger seriously the child's physical, mental, moral, or emotional health.

COMMENT

With two important exceptions, this section states the traditional rule for visitation rights. The general rule implies a "best interest of the child"

---

107.   Baures v. Lewis, 770 A.2d 214, 229 (N.J. 2001).

108.   *See* Kelly & Lamb, *Development Issues, supra* note 15; Paul R. Amato & Joan G. Gilbreth, *Nonresidential Fathers and Children's Well-Being: A Meta-Analysis*, 61 J. MARRIAGE & FAM. 557 (1999) (summarizing sixty-seven studies and finding that the qualify of father-child interaction was more important than frequency); Richard Warshak, *Social Science and Children's Best Interests in Relocation Cases*: Burgess Revisited, 34 FAM. L.Q. 83, 84, 92 (2000) (citing studies showing correlation between child's success and stronger father-child relationships).

standard. Although the judge should never compel the noncustodial parent to visit the child, visitation rights should be arranged to an extent and in a fashion which suits the child's interest rather than the interest of either the custodial or noncustodial parent. The empirical data on post-divorce living arrangements suggests that, if the judge can arrange visitation with a minimum of contest, most parties will eventually reach an accommodation and the bitterness accompanying the divorce will gradually fade. The section does make clear, however, that the judge must hold a hearing and make an extraordinary finding to deprive the noncustodial parent of all visitation rights. To preclude visitation completely, the judge must find that visitation would endanger "seriously the child's physical, mental, moral, or emotional health." These words are intended to mesh with other uniform legislation. *See* UNIFORM JUVENILE COURT ACT, Section 47. Although the standard is necessarily somewhat vague, it was deliberately chosen to indicate its stringency when compared to the "best interest" standard traditionally applied to this problem. The special standard was chosen to prevent the denial of visitation to noncustodial parent on the basis of moral judgments about parental behavior which have no relevance to the parent's interest in or capacity to maintain a close and benign relationship to the child. The same onerous standard is applicable when the custodial parent tries to have the noncustodial parent's visitation privileges restricted or eliminated.

Eldridge v. Eldridge

Supreme Court of Tennessee, 2001.
42 S.W.3d 82.

■ HOLDER, J.

We granted review of this child visitation case to determine whether the trial court abused its discretion in ordering unrestricted overnight visitation with the mother. The Court of Appeals held that the trial court had abused its discretion and imposed restrictions prohibiting the presence of the mother's lesbian partner during overnight visitation. We hold that the record does not support a finding of an abuse of discretion. Accordingly, we reverse the judgment of the Court of Appeals.

Anthony and Julia Eldridge were divorced in 1992. The couple agreed to joint custody of their minor daughters, Andrea and Taylor, who were ages eight and nine respectively. Two years later, a dispute arose regarding Ms. Eldridge's visitation rights. Ms. Eldridge, who is engaged in a live-in homosexual relationship with Lisa Franklin, moved the court to establish a visitation schedule. In response, Mr. Eldridge moved for sole custody of the children.

In July 1995, the Court awarded sole custody of the children to Mr. Eldridge. The court also appointed a Special Master, Dr. James Granger, Head of the East Tennessee University Division of Child and Adolescent Psychiatry, to counsel the parties and their children and make recommendations to the court regarding visitation. Dr. Granger's written final report and testimony reflected that counseling was unsuccessful. An agreement as to visitation was not reached.

Upon Mr. Eldridge's motion, the trial court appointed a guardian ad litem ("GAL") for both children. The GAL concluded that regular visitation with the mother was essential and recommended regular visitation with standard visitation every other weekend. The first few weekend visitations were recommended to be limited to Saturday morning through Sunday evening and eventually to be extended to Friday through Sunday.

In September 1996, the trial court ordered overnight visitation with Taylor every other Saturday night through Sunday. Eight months later, Ms. Eldridge moved the court to extend Taylor's overnight visitation to include Friday nights, holidays and summer vacation. Ms. Eldridge also moved that another Special Master be appointed. Mr. Eldridge opposed expanding Ms. Eldridge's visitation rights.

In September 1997, the trial court approved an agreement reached by the parties. The agreement provided for a visitation schedule and appointment of Dr. Judy Millington, a counselor at Church Circle Counseling Center, as Special Master. The court's order provided that Dr. Millington's written recommendations were to take effect immediately without further order of the court. Dr. Millington recommended to the court that Ms. Eldridge's overnight visitation be expanded. Various disputes regarding visitation continued.

A hearing was held in October 1998 to resolve the visitation issue. In November 1998, the trial court entered an order adopting Dr. Millington's recommendations and permitting Ms. Eldridge unrestricted overnight visitation with Taylor. The Court of Appeals reversed, finding that the trial court abused its discretion in failing to prohibit Taylor's overnight visitation with Ms. Eldridge while Ms. Franklin was present in the home. One judge dissented. We granted review.

. . .

In reviewing the trial court's visitation order for an abuse of discretion, the child's welfare is given "paramount consideration," and "the right of the noncustodial parent to reasonable visitation is clearly favored." Nevertheless, the noncustodial parent's visitation "may be limited, or eliminated, if there is definite evidence that to permit . . . the right would jeopardize the child, in either a physical or moral sense."

Under the abuse of discretion standard, a trial court's ruling "will be upheld so long as reasonable minds can disagree as to propriety of the decision made." *State v. Scott*, 33 S.W.3d 746, 752 (Tenn. 2000). . . .

Mr. Eldridge challenges the trial court's visitation order on grounds that Ms. Franklin should not be present during Taylor's overnight visitation with Ms. Eldridge. The Court of Appeals held that "the trial court abused its discretion by not prohibiting Ms. Franklin's presence during the court-ordered overnight visitation." To cure this abuse of discretion, it modified the trial court's visitation order by prohibiting Lisa Franklin's presence during Taylor's overnight visitation with her mother.

The Court of Appeals' opinion makes clear that the court did "not rely on the fact that Ms. Eldridge is a lesbian" in modifying the trial court's order. The court fails to state, however, what it did rely upon. The Court of Appeals did not identify any legal or factual error by the trial court that might constitute an abuse of discretion. It also failed to establish how the ordered modification would cure the trial court's supposed error. The court offered that "the courts of Tennessee commonly place reasonable restrictions on the visitation rights of heterosexual parents who engage in sexual activity with partners with whom they are not married." Mere observation that restrictions have been imposed in past cases does nothing, however, to reveal why the trial court in this case abused its discretion in permitting unrestricted overnight visitation.

The Court of Appeals cited *Dailey v. Dailey*, 635 S.W.2d 391 (Tenn. Ct. App. 1982), as having "addressed the issue raised by Mr. Eldridge." In *Dailey*, the Court of Appeals upheld the trial court's decision to modify a custody order to shift custody from the mother, a homosexual, to the father. The court also, sua sponte, modified the trial court's visitation order to prohibit the visitation in the home where the mother lived with her lesbian partner or from having the child in the presence of any lesbian partner.

. . .

The record in *Dailey* established that the noncustodial parent engaged in overt, lascivious, sexual conduct in the presence of her five-year-old, mentally and physically handicapped child. Certainly, this is the type of "definite evidence" that unrestricted visitation "would jeopardize the child, in either a physical or moral sense" that might constitute a finding of an abuse of discretion.

. . .

The Court of Appeals in this case held that "the facts of this case do not rise to the level of harmful behavior displayed by the mother in *Dailey*." This statement indicates either: (1) that the court held *Dailey* to be inapplicable; or (2) that the court found at least some conduct by Ms. Eldridge similar to that in *Dailey*. The court's recitation of the facts shows no conduct by Ms. Eldridge that might arguably be construed as similar to that of the mother in *Dailey*, and our independent review of the record reveals none. The only similarity between this case and *Dailey* is that the mother is homosexual. As the Court of Appeals affirmatively stated that it did not rely on Ms. Eldridge's homosexuality in modifying the trial court's order, we can only infer that the Court of Appeals found *Dailey* to be completely irrelevant to this case. We agree.

The Court of Appeals' failure to state a basis for its decision leaves us little insight as to what facts in the record show the trial court abused its discretion. Our own review of the record shows that Ms. Eldridge and Ms. Franklin offered substantial testimony regarding their relationship and living arrangement. At the time of the hearing, they had been together for nearly five years. They live in the same home but had slept in separate bedrooms for three months prior to the hearing. Ms. Franklin provides all the financial support for the home. Ms. Eldridge is not a lessor of the home. They have a monogamous relationship but have not been sexually intimate in over a year. Ms. Franklin characterized them as "best friends, roommates." They make no expression of "physical emotion or physical contact" when Taylor is in the home. Taylor has her own bedroom in the home. Ms. Franklin testified that she had a good relationship with Taylor.

Mr. Eldridge and his wife, Chantal Eldridge, testified that unrestricted overnight visitation has a deleterious effect on Taylor. Mr. Eldridge testified that allowing Ms. Franklin to be present during overnight visitation would set a bad example for Taylor. He tries to teach Taylor to live by the Bible and that unmarried persons should not cohabit. He also testified that Taylor, based on her own sense of morality, believed that homosexuality and extramarital relationships were wrong. He testified that Taylor does not want Ms. Franklin present during visitation and that Taylor has many questions about Ms. Eldridge's and Ms. Franklin's relationship. Mr. Eldridge did not believe that Taylor would be physically harmed during overnight visitation. He was, however, concerned about her emotional well-being.

Chantal Eldridge testified that Taylor is visibly upset before leaving to spend the night with her mother. She was unsure what produced Taylor's response but opined that Taylor might miss her, Mr. Eldridge, and their children. Ms. Eldridge, however, testified that Taylor refuses to come into her house only until Taylor is certain her father has left. Then, Taylor enters the home and is very comfortable, eating and playing normally. As the time to return to her father approaches, however, Taylor paces, cries, and worries. Taylor makes efforts to hide the fact that she has eaten or enjoyed herself at Ms. Eldridge's home. Larry Davis, Ms. Eldridge's brother-in-law, offered testimony that supported this contention. He stated that during one of his family's visits with Ms. Eldridge, Taylor was playing outside with him and his children and acting normally. In the last hour before Mr. Eldridge came to pick her up, however, Taylor became withdrawn, refused to come outside, and would not associate with anyone in the home.

Dr. Millington testified that Taylor wants to love and please both of her parents. This conflict causes Taylor to lie to her father about having fun while visiting with her mother. Dr. Millington had observed no adverse or detrimental effects on Taylor resulting from overnight visitation with Ms. Eldridge in Ms. Franklin's presence. Dr. Millington stated, however, that Taylor has admitted to being somewhat uncomfortable during overnight visitation in Ms. Franklin's presence. Dr. Millington observed that Taylor's behavior around Ms. Eldridge was very positive and opined that increased visitation would further encourage their relationship.

In her June 30, 1997 report, Dr. Millington suggested that Taylor's overnight visitation every other weekend should be extended from one night to two. Dr. Millington expressed in an addendum to her report that interaction with Lisa appears (from videotapes viewed) to have no deleterious effects on Taylor at present.... Although Taylor most likely will have difficulty with her mother's orientation in the future, I don't know whether it will make a difference having had Lisa there versus not there. Taylor seems comfortable with Lisa now.

In that same document, Dr. Millington opined that "on the continuum the best for Taylor ... would be to have visitation without Lisa present, because the sexual orientation and modeling behavior issues become less obvious and so less of an issue parent-to-child in the future than it otherwise might be."

In her deposition of June 30, 1997, Dr. Millington stated that although overnight visits generally might be stressful for a child, she was not sure that Ms. Franklin was the source of Taylor's stress. Upon question about what would be the "ideal situation" regarding visitation, she testified that "the very best situation, which would probably be for the girls to see [Ms. Eldridge] just completely by herself, but I don't know how practical that is." At the October 1998 hearing, Dr. Millington ultimately was noncommittal on the issue of overnight visits.

> . . .

The trial court evaluated and resolved this competing testimony and held that overnight visitation without restriction was appropriate. Mr. Eldridge claims on appeal that prohibiting overnight visitation while Ms. Franklin is present is a reasonable way to resolve his concerns and would constitute a minimal inconvenience to Ms. Eldridge. His argument, however, is one to be made in the trial court, not on appeal.

It is not the function of appellate courts to tweak a visitation order in the hopes of achieving a more reasonable result than the trial court. Appellate courts correct errors. When no error in the trial court's ruling is evident from the record, the trial court's ruling must stand. . . .

. . .

As a general proposition, we agree that in an appropriate case a trial court may impose restrictions on a child's overnight visitation in the presence of non-spouses. The procedural posture of the case at bar is markedly different. In this case, the appellate court, in spite of the deference to which the trial court is entitled, has displaced the trial court's ruling and imposed a restriction that was considered and rejected by the trial court. Justification for that action must be found in the record and, preferably, be developed in the appellate court's opinion. We find no justification in this record.

. . .

The record does not show that Taylor is in moral crisis because of Ms. Franklin's presence during overnight visitation. At most, it appears that Taylor, like many children of divorce, is caught in the crossfire of parental acrimony. It is argued as a general proposition of morality that a parent's unwed love interest should not be present during overnight visitation with the child. A trial court's acceptance of that proposition, taking into account all the facts and circumstances, may give rise to a reasonable conclusion that overnight visitation should be restricted. Nevertheless, that proposition does not in all cases foreclose the possibility of the trial court reaching a reasonable alternative conclusion. In the absence of any evidence of harm beyond the mere unsubstantiated predictions of a vying parent, the trial court's ruling in this case cannot be said to be unreasonable. The evidence adduced in this case supports a reasonable conclusion that unrestricted overnight visitation was in Taylor's best interests. Accordingly, on this record, there was no abuse of discretion by the trial court.

NOTE

In *Boswell v. Boswelll*, 721 A.2d 662 (Md. 1998), the trial court had restricted the father's visitation rights by prohibiting visitation where his same-sex partner or "anyone having homosexual tendencies or such persuasions, male or female, or . . . anyone that the father may be living with in a non-marital relationship" was present. *Id.* at 665. The Court of Appeals of Maryland held that visitation should be based on the best interests of the child and should be restricted only "upon a showing of actual or potential harm to the child resulting from contact with the non-marital partner." *Id.* at 679. The court found that presence of the father's same-sex partner posed no actual or potential harm and the young child's preference to see his father alone should not be considered because the child did not possess the requisite maturity to make a reasoned decision regarding visitation. The court noted that "[l]earning to cope with new adults and the disrupting effects of visitation schedules are the unavoidable consequences of divorce," *Boswell*, 721 A.2d at 679 (quoting *Robinson v. Robinson*, 615 A.2d 1190, 1192 (Md. 1992)).

Zummo v. Zummo

Superior Court of Pennsylvania, 1990.
574 A.2d 1130.

■ KELLY, J.

In this case we are asked to determine whether an order prohibiting a father from taking his children to religious services "contrary to the Jewish faith" during periods of lawful custody or visitation violated the father's constitutional rights, or constituted an abuse of discretion. We find that, under the facts of the instant case, the father's constitutional rights were violated, the trial court's discretion was abused, and the restriction challenged cannot be sustained. We vacate the restriction imposed.

We are also called upon to determine whether the father may be directed to present the children at Synagogue for Sunday School during his periods of weekend visitation. We affirm this part of the trial court's order.

The facts and procedural history of the case were set forth by the trial court in its opinion as follows:

> Pamela S. Zummo (mother) and David S. Zummo (father) were married on December 17, 1978, separated August 1987, and divorced April 19, 1988. Three children were born of this marriage, namely Adam, age eight; Rachael, age four; and Daniel, age three. Mother was raised a Jew and has *actively* practiced her faith since childhood. Father was raised Roman Catholic but had attended Catholic services only *sporadically*. Prior to their marriage, mother and father discussed their religious differences and *agreed that any children would be raised in the Jewish faith.*

> During the marriage, the Zummo family participated fully in the life of the Jewish faith and community. They became members of the Norristown Community Jewish Center in 1983, celebrated Sabbath every Friday night and attended all of the high holiday services as well. In addition, mother and father participated in a social couples' group at their Synagogue and joined B'nai B'rith. All three of the children were formally given Hebrew names.

> Before the parties separated, the children attended no religious services outside the Jewish faith. Adam will begin preparing for his Bar Mitzvah this fall. Customary instruction would require attendance at two classes each week after school, participation in Saturday services and attendance at Sunday School. This training will culminate in Adam's Bar Mitzvah at age thirteen. Rachael will begin her formal Jewish education and training this fall at Sunday School.

> Since separation, father has refused to arrange for Adam's attendance to Sunday School while exercising visitation rights on alternate weekends. Father also wishes to take the children to *occasional* Roman Catholic services as he sees fit. Father suggests the children would benefit from a bi-cultural upbringing and should therefore be exposed to the religion of each parent. Mother opposes visitation by father to the extent it disrupts the formal Jewish training of the children. She further opposes exposing the children to a second religion which would confuse and disorient them. Mother filed a divorce complaint on July 6, 1987, which included a count seeking confirmation of her custody of the children. *The parties have since agreed to share legal custody.* They have also agreed that *Mother should have primary physical custody subject so father's partial physical custody on alternating weekends,* as well as certain holidays and vacation periods. To this end, the parties submitted a Stipulation and Agreement setting forth the nature and timing of father's partial physical custody. By virtue of the agreement, *the hearing and this Court's Order concerned itself only with the issues of to what extent father should be obligated to see to the attendance of the children at Jewish services during his*

visitation periods and whether father should be permitted to take the children to Roman Catholic senates to the extent he attends on his visitation weekends. Subsequent to hearing, it was determined that Adam's Saturday classes could be made up during the week so as not to interfere with father's visitation. . . .

. . .

The trial court applied the best interests standard to the facts presented, and concluded that restrictions upon the father's right to expose his children to his religious beliefs were permissible and appropriate. . . .

Pre–Divorce Religious Training Agreements

. . .

[The court held that the agreement between the parents regarding the children's religious training was unenforceable] . . . We note that the authorities establish several persuasive grounds upon which to deny legal effect to such agreements:

1) such agreements are generally too vague to demonstrate a meeting of minds, or to provide an adequate basis for objective enforcement;

2) enforcement of such an agreement would promote a particular religion, serve little or no secular purpose, and would excessively entangle the courts in religious matters; and,

3) enforcement would be contrary to a public policy embodied in the First Establishment and Free Exercise Clauses (as well as their state equivalents) that parents be free to doubt, question, and change their beliefs, and that they be free to instruct their children in accordance with those beliefs.

. . .

Perceived Probability of Harmful Effects From Exposure to "Inconsistent" Religions

The trial court's principal justification [for prohibiting the father from taking the children to Catholic services] was the perceived risk of harm to the children arising from their exposure to Catholicism. The trial court concluded that, "to expose the children to a competing religion after so assiduously grounding them in the tenets of Judaism would unfairly confuse and disorient them and quite possibly vitiate the benefits flowing from either religion."

The vast majority of courts addressing this issue, . . . have concluded that each parent must be free to provide religious exposure and instruction, as that parent sees fit, during any and all period of legal custody or visitation without restriction, unless the challenged beliefs or conduct of the parent are demonstrated to present a substantial threat of present or future, physical or emotional harm to the child in absence of the proposed restriction. We find the reasoning expressed in these cases to be persuasive, and adopt the standard stated above as applicable in this Commonwealth.

Applying this standard, courts have rejected speculation by parents and by experts as to potential future emotional harm to a *particular* child based upon the assumption that such exposure is *generally* harmful. Likewise, parental attributions of current child disturbances or distress as the result of a religious conflict, rather than the divorce generally or other causes, have similarly been rejected.

. . .

We hold that in order to justify restrictions upon parent's rights to inculcate religious beliefs in their children, the party seeking the restriction must demonstrate by competent evidence that the belief or practice of the party to be restricted actually presents a substantial threat of present or future physical or emotional harm to the particular child or children involved in absence of the proposed restriction, and that the restriction is the least intrusive means adequate to prevent the specified harm. Because the evidence presented in this case was wholly insufficient to meet this standard, Clause 6 of the Order of May 6. 1988, forbidding the father to take his children to religious services "contrary to the Jewish faith," must be vacated.

Obligations to Take Children to Religious Services

The trial court found "little if any" distinction between prohibiting the father's affirmative act of taking his children to Catholic services and its direction that the father present the children at the Synagogue for Sunday School. We, on the other hand, find a material and controlling distinction; and consequently, affirm that part of the order requiring the father to present his children at the Synagogue for Sunday School.

Both parents have rights to inculcate religious beliefs in their children. Accordingly, the trial court may constitutionally accommodate the mother's rights with a directive of the type imposed here, which essentially carves out a time period each Sunday during which the mother has the right to custody and control of the children.

. . .

While such provisions generally may be affirmed if they do not otherwise restrict the inculcation of religious beliefs, doubts, or disbeliefs by either parent, we emphasize the constitutional prerequisite of "benign neutrality" towards *both* parent's religious viewpoints. If, for example, the court entered an order which granted a Christian parent custody or visitation on all Christian holy days, but denied similar custody or visitation to the other parent on his or her Jewish holy days (without an adequate basis to encroach on the parent's right to expose the child to that parent's religious viewpoint as described supra), such a provision might constitute an impermissible restriction on religious and parental rights, and a violation of the Establishment Clause, albeit an indirect one.

On the other hand, a parent's right to inculcate religious beliefs in his or her child would not provide a compelling reason to justify the denial of the other parent's right to maintain a meaningful parental relationship with his or her children. If the court must choose between meaningful visitation and the full benefits of a desired program of religious indoctrination, the religious indoctrination must yield to the greater interest in preserving the parent-child relationship.

Here, despite the father's argument to the contrary, we find that adequate accommodation of the father's visitation right was made. The Saturday religion classes desired by the mother will be made up on weeknights. Moreover, the mother has indicated willingness to allow the father reasonable weeknight visitation to compensate for the portion of Sunday taken up by the mother's chosen religious indoctrination for her children. The mother's cooperation on this point is noteworthy and commendable.

We find Clause 5 of the order directing the father to present the children at Synagogue for Sunday School to be severable and distingishable from Clause 6 which forbids the father to take the children t religious services contrary to the Jewish faith. We affirm Clause 5 of the order.

Troxel v. Granville

Supreme Court of the United States, 2000.
530 U.S. 57, 120 S.Ct. 2054, 147 L.Ed.2d 49.

[The opinion is printed at page 384 *supra*].

NOTE

An analysis of visitation rights post-*Troxel* concludes

the lack of a majority, the multiplicity of opinions, and the confusion characterizing each opinion have provided fertile ground for diverse and even contradictory interpretations of *Troxel*. Indeed, non-parental visitation cases attempting to follow the *Troxel* precedent are mixed and confused. Courts in different states have interpreted *Troxel* differently and even within states, variant understandings of *Troxel* have led to contradictory rulings as to the constitutionality of state statutes. *Troxel* has also proven a rich vein for extensive academic attempts to discern the case's meaning and implications. Not surprisingly, these scholarly analyses also offer contradictory readings of the case and its various opinions. In many respects, *Troxel* seems to have only triggered further doubts regarding non-parents' visitation rights. The confusion exposed in *Troxel* is exacerbated by the perplexity surrounding the meaning of legal parenthood.

Ayelet Blecher–Prigat, *Rethinking Visitation: From a Parental To a Relational Right*, 16 DUKE J. GENDER L. & POL'Y 1, 11 (2009).

The element of a grandparent visitation scheme most often deemed essential to constitutionality is the presumption that a fit parent's decision concerning visitation is in the best interest of the child. *See, e.g., Santi v. Santi*, 633 N.W.2d 312 (Iowa 2001); *State Department of Social and Rehabilitation Services v. Paillet*, 16 P.3d 962 (Kan. 2001); *Lulay v. Lulay*, 739 N.E.2d 521 (Ill. 2000).

G. STEPPARENTS

In re Marriage of DePalma

Colorado Court of Appeals, 2007.
176 P.3d 829.

■ GRAHAM, JUDGE.

In this post-dissolution of marriage proceeding, Melissa Ann DePalma (mother) appeals from orders permitting P. Jon DePalma (father) to exercise his parenting time rights during his military deployment by having his current wife care for the children in his home during his parenting time.

Father and mother are the parents of two children. In May 2002, they agreed to a parenting plan providing, among other things, that the children would be in father's care two evenings a week and every other weekend, that they would be in mother's care at all other times, and that if either parent was unavailable during his or her designated parenting time, that parent would offer the other parent the right of first refusal for the care of the children. When their marriage was dissolved in June 2002, the parenting plan was incorporated into the decree.

Father is an airline pilot and an Air Force Reserve pilot. Before he remarried in 2004, he and mother coordinated their parenting time each month to take his schedule into account. When he was deployed by the Air Force, mother exercised all parenting time.

After father remarried, he was again deployed to Iraq. During this deployment, the children spent one night and one evening per week in the care of father's new wife (stepmother). The remainder of the parenting time was exercised by mother. In January 2006, facing another deployment, father requested that parental responsibilities be modified to allow the children to spend equal time with each parent. He also requested that the parenting time schedule remain in effect when he was stationed in Iraq. He asserted that this would be in the children's best interests because it would allow them to maintain their normal schedule and their bonded relationship with stepmother and their stepbrother. Mother opposed this motion, arguing that father was impermissibly attempting to establish parental rights for his new wife that the new wife could not have obtained in her own right, and that mother should not be required to decrease her parenting time in favor of a nonparent.

An initial hearing was held in April 2006, followed by a second hearing in May. After considering the parties' arguments, the court determined that the presumption that a natural parent has the right to control the upbringing of a child is rebuttable; that the best interests of the children must be considered in determining whether the presumption has been rebutted; and that in the case before the court, the court was required to consider the relationship between the children and the stepparent as well as father's rights.

An additional hearing was held in June 2006. After considering the testimony of both parents, the stepmother, and the child and family investigator, the court determined that father could decide to have stepmother care for the children during his parenting time and that in doing so, he was presumed to be acting in the best interests of the children. The court further found that allowing father to designate stepmother as the children's caregiver during his absence did not modify the parties' parenting plan, as the children would remain in mother's care at all times except during father's parenting time, nor did it grant parenting time to stepmother. The court concluded that the right of first refusal set forth in the parenting plan did not require that father offer the children to mother while he was deployed, and that imposing such a requirement would interfere with father's parenting time. Accordingly, the court ordered that the children should be in the care of stepmother during father's parenting time as he had requested.

Mother now appeals from these orders.

.   .   .

We first address mother's argument that the trial court failed to accord her the presumption that she had the first and prior right to parenting time of the children, and the presumption that, as a fit natural parent, she acted in the best interests of the children. We are not persuaded that the court failed to accord mother the benefit of any applicable presumption.

In determining a custodial dispute between a parent and a nonparent, Colorado courts recognize a presumption that a biological parent has a first and prior right to the custody of his or her child. Colorado courts also recognize a presumption that a fit parent acts in the best interests of his or her children.

Here, the court expressly recognized that a parent has "a presumptive right to control the upbringing of a child," and that there is a presumption that a natural parent can make the decisions concerning the children. The court ultimately concluded that father could make the decision to have stepmother care for the children during his parenting time, noting that because parental unfitness had not been alleged, father was presumed to act in the best interests of the children.

We are not persuaded that the trial court failed to accord mother the benefit of the presumptions to which she was entitled as one of the children's biological parents.

We note that from the beginning, the trial court treated this matter as a dispute between two fit parents regarding the arrangements for the care of the children during father's parenting time, rather than a dispute between a nonparent seeking parenting time and a parent opposing it. We are not persuaded that the court erred in doing so. Stepmother never requested parenting time in her own right, and we are aware of no authority for the proposition that a parent's request that a stepparent or other nonparent be permitted to provide care for a child should be imputed to the nonparent and treated as a request by the nonparent for parenting time.

Because the dispute was between mother and father, and not between mother and stepmother, the presumption that a parent has a "first and prior" right to the custody of his or her child was not implicated, and there was no need for the court to comment upon the presumption that a parent's right to custody is superior to that of a nonparent.

Because the dispute was between mother and father, the court did not err in according the presumption that a fit parent acts in the best interests of the children to father as well as to mother. As the courts of several other jurisdictions have found, when two fit parents disagree, the court must weigh the wishes of both to determine what is in the child's best interests.

Because the dispute concerned father's parenting time and father's determination that it would be in the best interests of the children to allow them to maintain their relationship with their stepmother and stepbrother by maintaining the usual parenting time schedule during his deployment, we conclude that the court did not err by considering first the presumption that father was acting in the best interests of the children, and determining that the issue of stepmother's care of the children was resolved when that presumption was not rebutted by mother. The presumption that mother, too, was acting in the best interests of the children, was addressed by the court when it acknowledged mother's concern that parental rights should not be extended to stepmother, and resolved the issue by stating explicitly that the court did not intend to grant parenting time or parenting responsibility to stepmother. By addressing her concern in this manner, the court acknowledged that her concern was reasonable and that she also was acting in the best interests of the children in bringing it to the court's attention.

We next consider mother's argument that the trial court erred in denying her legal objection to father's motion to modify parenting time. We construe this as an argument that the trial court effectively granted parenting time to stepmother when it granted father's motion, and, thus, entered an order that violated mother's constitutional right to the care, custody, and control of the children. We do not agree with this argument.

We begin our analysis by observing that the trial court expressly stated in its June 8, 2006, order that "[t]he court is not granting any parenting time or parenting responsibility to [stepmother]." Indeed, the orders entered by the court do not grant stepmother any rights at all. Her "right" to parenting time is in reality only a potential obligation, if she chooses to accept it, to care for the children during father's parenting time. It is father's right to ask her to do so, and if he does not, the orders entered by the court do not grant her the right to see the children or care for them. In addition, stepmother has no right to make decisions for the children, as that authority is shared exclusively by mother and father, with day-to-day decision-making allocated to mother during father's deployments.

Because the orders from which mother appeals do not provide step-mother with any legal rights, this case is distinguishable from cases in which a parent has attempted to delegate his or her parental rights to a nonparent, or has requested that the court do so, without regard to the availability of a fit, natural parent who already possesses parental rights and is prepared to assume the responsibility for the child.

Mother's argument that the trial court erred in extending "special rights" to stepmother and that the court should have required stepmother to petition for parenting time is also unpersuasive.

Stepmother did not seek parental rights, and father did not ask that such rights be extended to her. Rather, father requested only that stepmother be permitted to care for the children in his home during his absence. As mother acknowledges, parents routinely entrust their children to the care of teachers, family, and daycare providers during their parenting time. Although mother suggests that there is a substantive difference between leaving a child with a nonparent on a short-term basis and doing so for an extended period, she has not cited any authority in support of this proposition or explained why she believes this to be true. Nor has she explained why the entrustment of children to the care of a nonparent over a longer period necessarily requires the extension of parental rights to the nonparent.

Finally, we reject mother's argument that the trial court erred in failing to make specific findings regarding the best interests of the children.

Under § 14–10–129(1)(a)(I), C.R.S. 2006, with certain exceptions not applicable here, a court may make or modify an order granting or denying parenting time rights whenever such order or modification would serve the best interests of the child.

Here, mother did not dispute that it was in the children's best interests to maintain a relationship with their stepmother and stepbrother, and she did not contend that the children's visits with them were harmful. She specifically agreed that father was a fit parent and that he should have joint decision-making responsibility for the children. She testified that she thought that it was "very important" that the children continue to spend time with father's family, including stepmother, and that she felt that "[t]he more people who love them, the better." When asked about the reason for her opposition to father's proposal that stepmother be permitted to care for the children during his deployment, mother stated that she felt that it diminished her rights as a parent, and that it was "not anything against [stepmother] as a person, or as a parent." Thus, the court could reasonably conclude that both parents agreed it was in the best interests of the children to continue their relationship with stepmother and that they disagreed only as to whether father's proposal improperly extended parental rights to stepmother.

. . .

The orders are affirmed.

Simons by & Through Simons v. Gisvold

Supreme Court of North Dakota, 1994.
519 N.W.2d 585.

■ SANDSTROM, JUSTICE.

For as long as she could remember, 9–year–old Jessica Simons, her father Bruce, and his wife Debra had lived together as a family. While Bruce worked at his job, Debra stayed home and cared for Jessica. In 1993, Bruce died of cancer.

Both Debra Simons, Jessica's "psychological parent," and Joelle Gisvold, Jessica's natural mother, divorced from Bruce shortly after the birth, sought custody. The guardian ad litem recommended Jessica's best interests would be served if she continued to live with Debra.

The district court found the natural mother, although having given up custody of Jessica, had maintained a loving, caring relationship with Jessica. The district court found both the natural mother and the "psychological parent" to be good and decent people: morally fit; able to meet Jessica's physical, emotional and educational needs; and capable and disposed to give her love, affection and guidance.

The district court concluded Joelle Gisvold should be given custody of Jessica because the natural parent has a paramount right to custody when the child would not sustain serious harm or detriment.

Debra Simons appeals, urging, in the exceptional circumstances where there is a "psychological parent," the best interests of the child should prevail, with no preference for a natural parent.

Concluding the district court applied the correct law, we affirm.

Jessica was born in July 1983. When Jessica's natural father, Bruce Simons, and Joelle were divorced in May 1984, Bruce was awarded custody of Jessica and Joelle was granted liberal visitation privileges. In 1986, Bruce married Debra, and they resided in Fargo with Jessica until Bruce died from cancer in 1993. Joelle also remarried, and she currently resides with her husband in Galesburg. Bruce left no will or other document expressing his preference as to Jessica's custody after his death.

Joelle filed a motion requesting the district court award her custody of Jessica. Joelle alleged Bruce's death constituted a material change in circumstances and she, as Jessica's natural mother, is entitled to custody of Jessica. Debra responded she is entitled to custody of Jessica because she had become Jessica's psychological parent during the nearly eight years she, Bruce, and Jessica lived together as a family.

In addition to finding both Debra and Joelle to be fit, able and willing to be good parents, the district court made the following findings of fact. Both Debra and Joelle could provide a permanent family unit, and a stable, satisfactory environment. Joelle had exercised her visitation rights and maintained a good relationship with Jessica. Jessica, who had not been asked for nor expressed a preference, expressed love and affection for each, referring to both as "mom." Jessica will not sustain serious harm or detriment to her welfare if she is removed from her home in Fargo and placed in Joelle's custody.

The trial court awarded Joelle custody of Jessica with visitation rights for Debra. Debra then filed this appeal.

[I]n matters of child custody, the district court is vested substantial discretion. On appeal, the district court's custody decision fact finding will not be set aside unless it is clearly erroneous. . . .

Parents generally have the right to the custody and companionship of their children superior to that of any other person. This right is not absolute. We recently noted, "parental rights do not spring full-blown from the biological connection between parent and child. They require relationships more enduring." Parental rights may be forfeited because of unfitness or abandonment. . . .

When a psychological parent and a natural parent each seek a court ordered award of custody, the natural parent's paramount right to custody prevails unless the court finds it in the child's best interest to award custody to the psychological parent to prevent serious harm or detriment to the welfare of the child.

The circumstances of this case are distinguishable from those cases where custody has been awarded to a psychological parent, rather than the natural parent. Unlike here, the children in those cases had not established a significant bond or relationship with the natural parent. Also, there was evidence in those cases the children would suffer serious harm or detriment if they were removed from the home of the psychological parent and placed with the natural parent. Here, Jessica has a close relationship and strong bond with her natural mother, and there is no evidence Jessica will suffer harm or detriment by being placed in Joelle's custody. Both natural and psychological parent are good people who are fit, willing, and able to parent. Under the facts of this case, we are not convinced the trial court's custody disposition is clearly erroneous.

Edwards v. Edwards

Supreme Court of North Dakota, 2010.
777 N.W.2d 606.

■ SANDSTROM, JUSTICE

Katherine Edwards appeals a district court judgment awarding Robert Edwards visitation and certain legal custody rights with K.A.E., Katherine Edwards' daughter and Robert Edwards' stepdaughter, as part of a divorce action. We affirm in part and reverse in part.

Katherine and Robert Edwards first married in "1989 or 1990." They divorced in September 1996. In December 1996, Katherine Edwards gave birth to K.A.E., whose biological father is not Robert Edwards. In September 1997, Katherine and Robert Edwards married for the second time. They had twins together in 2001. K.A.E. has lived with Katherine and Robert Edwards since shortly after her birth and has minimal contact with her biological father.

Katherine and Robert Edwards divorced again in 2008. As part of the divorce action, the district court gave Robert Edwards visitation rights with K.A.E. The district court also gave Robert Edwards certain rights and duties with regard to K.A.E. While the district court did not refer to the rights and duties as legal custody rights but instead stated they were "rights and duties which go along with Robert's visitation privileges," they are in effect certain legal custody rights, or "decisionmaking responsibility" under the current N.D. Cent Code ch. 14–09. The district court awarded Robert and Katherine Edwards the right to participate on an equal basis in making major decisions concerning K.A.E.'s upbringing, including her education, health care, and religious training; the right to mutually discuss and develop a workable agreement concerning the education of K.A.E. (and the duty to keep each other informed of the names and addresses of the schools attended by K.A.E.); the right to attend educational conferences concerning K.A.E.; the right to have reasonable access to K.A.E. by written, telephonic, and electronic means; and the right to obtain necessary medical, psychological, dental, and other health care services for K.A.E. The district court also conferred on Robert and Katherine Edwards the duties to inform each other as soon as reasonably possible of a serious accident or serious illness for which K.A.E. receives health care treatment and to immediately inform each other of a change in residential telephone number and address. The district court stated that during times when Robert and Katherine Edwards are unable to agree on an appropriate course of action for decisions concerning K.A.E., Katherine Edwards, as primary physical custodian, will make the ultimate decision. The district court also ordered that all rights and duties of Robert Edwards are subservient to those of K.A.E.'s biological father.

Katherine Edwards appeals, arguing the district court clearly erred by awarding Robert Edwards visitation and custodial rights with K.A.E. without first finding Robert Edwards was a psychological parent and without finding such an order was necessary to prevent serious detriment to the welfare of K.A.E. Katherine Edwards also argues the district court did not have jurisdiction to adjudicate visitation and custodial rights of K.A.E. as part of the divorce, because jurisdiction over parties and their children as part of a divorce proceeding is limited to children of the marriage.

. . .

A district court's determinations on visitation are findings of fact, which will not be reversed on appeal unless they are clearly erroneous. Similarly, a district court's award of custody is treated as a finding of fact and will not be reversed unless clearly erroneous. A finding of fact is clearly erroneous if it is induced by an erroneous view of the law, if there is no evidence to support it, or if, although there is some evidence to support it, on the entire evidence we are left with a definite and firm conviction a mistake has been made.

Katherine Edwards first contends the district court did not have jurisdiction to decide legal custody and visitation of K.A.E. as part of the divorce, because Robert Edwards is not K.A.E.'s biological father. This Court has held, however, that in a divorce proceeding, an award of custody may be made to a third party if exceptional circumstances require that such a custody disposition be made. *See Worden v. Worden*, 434 N.W.2d 341, 342 (N.D. 1989) (reversing an award of custody to a child's stepfather as part of a divorce, because the stepfather's presence in the child's life was "short-lived and sporadic"); *Hust v. Hust*, 295 N.W.2d 316, 318–19 (N.D. 1980) (reversing an award of custody to a child's grandparents as part of a divorce, because the district court failed to find exceptional circumstances justifying the award). *Hamers v. Guttormson*, 610 N.W.2d 758 (N.D. 2000), though not a divorce action, clearly laid out the exceptional circumstances framework. In that case, we stated:

> It is well-settled that parents have a paramount and constitutional right to the custody and companionship of their children superior to that of any other person. That right, however, is not absolute, and in custody disputes between a natural parent and a third party exceptional circumstances may require, in the child's best interests to prevent serious harm or detriment to the child, that the child be placed in the custody of a third party rather than with the natural parent. While this Court has not attempted to narrowly define or circumscribe the exceptional circumstances which must exist . . . , each case in which such a placement has been upheld by this Court has involved a child who has been in the actual physical custody of the third party for a sufficient period of time to develop a psychological parent relationship with that third party.

Hamers, 610 N.W.2d 758, 759–60 (citations omitted). A maxim of jurisprudence provides, "The greater contains the less." N.D. Cent. Code § 31–11–05(27). Thus, because custody may be awarded to a third party in exceptional circumstances in order to prevent serious harm or detriment to a child, visitation may also be awarded under those conditions.

In *Worden*, we noted that in each case in which custody to a third party rather than to a natural parent has been upheld, the child has been in the actual physical custody of the third party for a sufficient period in which to develop a "psychological parent" relationship with that party. *Worden*, 434 N.W.2d at 342–43. Katherine Edwards contends the district court erred when it failed to decide whether Robert Edwards was a psychological parent. K.A.E. has lived with Katherine and Robert Edwards for nearly her entire life. The district court found that she has had only minimal contact with her biological father, and that Robert Edwards "is truly the only 'father' [she] has ever known." The district court found Robert Edwards has loved and cared for K.A.E. in the same manner he has for the twins, and has provided for all of her needs. The district court found:

> In arriving at its decision to allow Robert to have visitation with [K.A.E.], the Court finds it unnecessary to attach any label-such as "psychological parent"—to the role Robert has played in [K.A.E.'s] life, essentially from the moment of her birth. *See, e.g., Mansukhani v. Pailing*, 318 N.W.2d 748 (N.D. 1982); *Gardebring v. Rizzo*, 269 N.W.2d 104 (N.D. 1978); *In Interest of D.G.*, 246 N.W.2d 892 (N.D. 1976). To reiterate, Robert has always been [K.A.E.'s] *father*, in every sense of the word-and there was no evidence presented to the Court that her natural father . . . has any intentions of supplanting Robert in that role.

Though the district court did not label Robert Edwards a "psychological parent," it made a finding at least as great as a psychological parent when it found he has always been her "father, in every sense of the word." [T]he court did not use the words "exceptional circumstances," but the effect of its findings is nonetheless that completely cutting K.A.E. off from "the only 'father' [she] has ever known" would likely cause her serious harm and detriment. In light of these exceptional circumstances, it was not clearly erroneous for the district court to award Robert Edwards visitation with K.A.E. The legislature has also recognized the relationship that arises between stepparent and stepchild. Section 14–09–09 of the North Dakota Century Code requires a stepparent to support a stepchild for as long as the stepchild is a part of the stepparent's family.

Our holding here does not mean that visitation should be awarded to all stepparents in a divorce, but rather that in some cases exceptional circumstances may require, in a child's best interests and in order to prevent serious harm or detriment to the child, that the child should have visitation with a third party.

In addition to visitation, the district court also gave Robert Edwards certain rights and duties with regard to K.A.E. While the district court did not refer to the rights and duties as legal custody rights but instead stated they were "rights and duties which go along with Robert's visitation privileges," they are effectively legal custody rights, or "decisionmaking responsibility" under the current N.D. CENT. CODE ch. 14–09. The district court awarded Robert and Katherine Edwards the right to participate on an equal basis in making major decisions concerning K.A.E.'s upbringing. . . . The district court also conferred on Robert and Katherine Edwards the duties to inform each other as soon as reasonably possible of a serious accident or serious illness for which K.A.E. receives health care treatment and to immediately inform each other of a change in residential telephone number and address. The district court ordered that when Robert and Katherine Edwards are unable to agree on an appropriate course of action for decisions concerning K.A.E., Katherine Edwards, as primary physical custodian, will make the ultimate decision.

The district court awarded Robert Edwards joint legal custody and visitation with the twins, but awarded him only visitation privileges with K.A.E. While some of the rights and duties the district court awarded to Robert Edwards concerning K.A.E. are reasonable and relate to visitation, others are decisionmaking authority. We affirm those related to visitation and communication, including the right to reasonable access to K.A.E. by written, telephonic, and electronic means; the right to obtain emergency medical, psychological, dental, and other health care services for K.A.E.; the duty to inform Katherine Edwards as soon as reasonably possible of a serious accident or serious illness for which K.A.E. receives health care treatment; and the duty to immediately inform Katherine Edwards of a change in residential telephone number and address. We reverse the other rights granted to Robert Edwards, including the right to participate on an equal basis in making major decisions concerning K.A.E.'s upbringing, including her education, health care, and religious training; the right to mutually discuss and develop a workable agreement with Katherine Edwards concerning the education of K.A.E.; and the right to attend educational conferences concerning K.A.E. Additionally, we affirm the duties of Katherine Edwards to keep Robert Edwards informed of the names and addresses of the schools attended by K.A.E.; to inform Robert Edwards as soon as reasonably possible of a serious accident or serious illness for which K.A.E. receives treatment; and to immediately inform Robert Edwards of a change in residential telephone number and address.

. . .

We affirm the district court's award to Robert Edwards of visitation with K.A.E. We reverse the district court's award of decisionmaking authority to Robert Edwards.

NOTE

The law surrounding stepparent claims for visitation and custody of stepchildren varies substantially by state. *See* Susan L. Pollet, *Still a Patchwork Quilt: A Nationwide*

Survey of State Laws Regarding Stepparent Rights and Obligations, 48 FAM. CT. REV. 528 (2010); Margaret M. Mahoney, *Stepparents As Third Parties in Relation to Their Stepchildren*, 40 FAM. L.Q. 81, 85, 103 (2006):

> [T]he traditional common law rule establishes custody and visitation rights exclusively for legal parents, and generally denies standing to stepparents and other third parties to seek judicial visitation orders. The denial of legal recognition to the stepparent in this context enhances the authority of the custodial parent to make decisions for the child, including decisions about access to other persons. This traditional rule continues as the default rule governing stepfamily visitation disputes in some jurisdictions.
>
> In recent decades, a number of state courts and legislatures have broken with this tradition by establishing the right to petition for judicial visitation orders for certain categories of nonparents, including stepparents. The third-party visitation laws attempt to balance the interests of the parent and the child associated with parental authority, against the competing interests arising out of the child's established relationships with other family members.

See also McAllister v. McAllister, 779 N.W.2d 652, 662 (N.D. 2010) (granting stepfather reasonable visitation because of his status as psychological parent and his strong relationship with the child); *Schaffer v. Schaffer*, 884 N.E.2d 423, 424 (Ind. Ct. App. 2008) (holding that parental presumption does not apply to modification of visitation rights and refusing to terminate stepfather's visitation rights without a showing that termination in child's best interest). Many states, however, continue to reject standing for stepparents. *See Strauss v. Tuschman*, 216 P.3d 370, 373 (Utah Ct. App. 2009) (holding that stepfather did not have standing to seek visitation with his former stepchild because the child's mother had terminated his standing *in loco parentis*); *In the Interest of C.T.G.*, 179 P.3d 213, 225 (Colo. Ct. App. 2007) (terminating stepfather's visitation rights because there was no "evidence showing 'special circumstances' that would justify his indefinite visitation with the child over [the biological mother's] objections"). *Pruitt v. Payne*, 14 So. 3d 806, 811 (Miss. Ct. App. 2009) (denying stepfather visitation absent a showing that the biological father was unfit and holding that statute granting visitation to grandparents did not apply to stepparents).

As a general rule, stepparent claims for custody are denied. Some courts have granted custody to stepparents under certain circumstances in order to protect the best interests of the child. *See e.g. In the Interest of R.T.K.*, 324 S.W.3d 896, 905 (Tex. App. 2010), *rev. den.* (June 10, 2011) (awarding custody to stepmother after biological father's death to keep the child "in the only home he has known"); *Mace v. Mace*, 45 A.D.3d 1193 (N.Y. 2007) (awarding custody to the stepfather where the biological father had failed to attempt to develop a meaningful relationship with the child); *Charles v. Stehlik*, 744 A.2d 1255, 1259 (Pa. 2000) (granting a stepfather's petition for sole custody of the child over a competing claim made by the biological father at the biological mother's death because the stepfather's relationship with the child was that of a "day-to-day father").

H.   UNMARRIED COUPLES

Smith v. Gordon

Supreme Court of Delaware, 2009.
968 A.2d 1.

■ HOLLAND, JUSTICE

The respondent-appellant, Lacey M. Smith ("Smith"), appeals from a final judgment entered by the Family Court. The Family Court held that the petitioner-appellee, Charlene M. Gordon ("Gordon"), had standing as a parent to petition for custody of Smith's adopted daughter, A.N.S. Gordon argued that she is a *legal* parent under the Uniform Parentage Act of

Delaware ("DUPA") and that she is also a *de facto* parent. The Family Court concluded that, although Gordon did not qualify as a *legal* parent of the child under the DUPA, Gordon was a *de facto* parent and entitled to the same status as a legal parent for purposes of the standing required to file a petition for custody. The Family Court then granted the parties joint legal and physical custody of A.N.S.

In this appeal, Smith argues that the Family Court erred when it held that a *de facto* parent has standing as a parent to petition for child custody under title 13, section 721(a) of the Delaware Code. She also argues that, even if Gordon did have standing as a *de facto* parent to petition for custody, the Family Court erred when it granted Gordon joint custody because Smith did not consent to Gordon forming a relationship with the child....

We have concluded that a *de facto* parent does not have standing as a parent to file a petition for custody under title 13, section 721(a). Therefore, the judgment of the Family Court must be reversed.

Gordon and Smith are two women who met on August 23, 1994, and became involved in a romantic relationship. Gordon moved into Smith's home in February 1995 and lived there until May 2, 2004. On various occasions, the parties met with a financial advisor. They discussed the possibility of executing joint wills with an attorney, but never did so. They were beneficiaries of one another's life insurance policies. In 2004, they opened a joint account to process their joint bills.

Smith and Gordon did not have a commitment ceremony, but were recognized by friends and family as a long-term committed couple. They celebrated August 23 as their anniversary date. Early in their relationship, they briefly discussed having children, but serious conversation on the subject was deferred for several years.

After Smith and Gordon had been together for five years, they felt they had established a "strong relationship" and wanted to have a baby. After failed attempts for Smith to have a child via artificial insemination ("AI") and in vitro fertilization ("IVF"), the couple decided to adopt a child from a foreign country. Because the law of Kazakhstan did not permit two women to adopt the same child, they decided that Smith would be the adoptive parent. Gordon participated in the adoption process and accompanied Smith to Kazakhstan for the adoption in March 2003, but only Smith legally adopted the child, A.N.S.

Gordon took paid adoption leave from her employer and stayed home with A.N.S. for nearly two months. When Gordon's leave ended, she returned to work and Smith began to work from home so that she could stay home with A.N.S. Gordon enrolled A.N.S. as her dependent under the employee benefit plan so that A.N.S. would have medical, dental and vision coverage as well as spending accounts for health care and dependent care. The parties shared the expenses to care for and support A.N.S.

In June 2003, Smith and Gordon met with an attorney to discuss Gordon adopting A.N.S. They left the meeting with the understanding that Gordon would have to care for the child for one year in order for the Family Court to permit the adoption. Gordon did not pursue formal adoption after she had lived with A.N.S. for more than one year.

The testimony regarding the termination of Smith's and Gordon's relationship is disputed. There is no dispute, however, that on May 2, 2004, Smith and Gordon broke up, and Gordon moved out of the house at Smith's request. Smith permitted Gordon to see A.N.S. periodically until June 6, 2004.

On June 22, 2004, Gordon filed a petition for custody of A.N.S. in the Family Court. In that petition, she alleged that she and Smith intended that both would function as the parents of an adopted child and understood that only one person could initially adopt the child. She further alleged that the parties anticipated that Gordon would become a second adoptive parent, that Gordon was a co-parent of A.N.S., and that A.N.S. now calls Gordon "Mommy."

On July 6, 2004, Gordon filed a motion for a temporary visitation order. Smith filed a motion to dismiss on the same day. Gordon had no contact with A.N.S. from June 6, 2004, until August 13, 2004, when the parties stipulated to a temporary consent visitation order permitting Gordon visitation without prejudice to Smith's motion to dismiss the custody petition.

On July 22, 2005, Gordon filed a motion to amend her petition for custody, requesting permission to include a request for a determination of parentage under the DUPA in addition to her assertion of her right to seek custody/visitation as a *de facto* parent. In a response filed August 4, 2005, Smith denied that Gordon had standing to bring an action for adjudication under the DUPA because Gordon lacks a biological tie to A.N.S. On September 6, 2005, the Family Court granted Gordon's motion to amend her petition to include a determination of parentage.

. . .

[T]he Family Court determined that Gordon had standing to petition for custody as a *de facto* parent and denied Smith's motion to dismiss. The Family Court found that for the purpose of section 721(a), a "parent" is not restricted to an individual who is a biological or adoptive parent, or who has established a legal parent-child relationship under the DUPA but also includes an individual who has established a relationship with a child as a *de facto* parent. On March 30, 2007, the Family Court granted Gordon joint legal and physical custody of A.N.S.

Upon appeal from the Family Court, this Court reviews the facts and the law, as well as the inferences and deductions made by the Family Court judge. Findings of fact will not be disturbed unless they are clearly wrong and justice requires that they be overturned. . . .

. . .

Someone who is not a parent may petition for and be awarded custody only if the child is dependent or neglected and the Family Court determines that it is in the child's best interests not to be placed in the custody of the parent. Gordon does not contend that A.N.S. is dependent or neglected. Therefore, Gordon's standing to petition for custody of A.N.S. depends on Gordon's status as a parent.

There is no definition of parent in Delaware's child custody statute. To determine Gordon's parental status, the Family Court looked to the DUPA because it "applies to determinations of parentage in this State." The DUPA defines "parent" as "an individual who has established a parent-child relationship." A "parent-child relationship" is "the *legal* relationship between a child and a parent of the child." The DUPA provides that a parent-child relationship may be established as follows:

(a) The mother-child relationship is established between a woman and a child by:

> (1) The woman's having given birth to the child;
>
> (2) An adjudication of the woman's maternity; or
>
> (3) Adoption of the child by the woman.

(b) The father-child relationship is established between a man and a child by:

> (1) An unrebutted presumption of the man's paternity of the child [ ];
>
> (2) An effective acknowledgement of paternity by the man ... unless the acknowledgement has been rescinded or successfully challenged;
>
> (3) An adjudication of the man's paternity;
>
> (4) Adoption of the child by the man; or
>
> (5) The man's having consented to an assisted reproduction by a woman ... which resulted in the birth of the child.

. . .

The Family Court is authorized to adjudicate parentage under the DUPA. Section 8–610 lists "child custody or visitation" as a proceeding in which "parentage *may* be determined." A woman whose maternity of the child is to be adjudicated can therefore seek an adjudication of parentage and custody in the same proceeding. The Family Court would have to first adjudicate the woman a parent of the child and then determine whether to give her custody of the child.

There was no adjudication of Gordon's maternity in any prior matter in this State. Gordon's petition for custody, however, contained a request for an adjudication of her maternity under the DUPA. Despite Gordon's arguments, the Family Court found that she could not establish a parent-child relationship under the DUPA.

The Family Court concluded that Gordon did not qualify as a *legal* parent under any determination of parentage in the DUPA ... because she was neither the biological nor adoptive mother. Reading the DUPA in gender neutral terms, the Family Court also explained that Gordon could not establish a parent-child relationship under section 8–201(b)(1), which provides that the father-child relationship may be established by "[a]n unrebutted presumption of the man's paternity of the child under § 8–204," because Gordon could not meet any of the criteria for establishing a presumption of paternity. Under section 8–204(a)(5), "A man is presumed to be the father of a child if ... [f]or the 1st 2 years of the child's life, he resided in the same household with the child and openly held out the child as his own." The Family Court explained that Gordon failed to meet the requirements of section 8–204(a)(5) because, "even if the Court were to consider the first two years of A.N.S.'s life to be the first two years *after* her adoption rather than immediately following her birth, Gordon only lived in the same household with A.N.S. for approximately thirteen months, not the required two years."

The Family Court's reading of section 8–204(a)(5) appears to be a reasonable, gender-neutral interpretation. Therefore, had Gordon resided with A.N.S. for at least two years after the adoption and held A.N.S. out as her child during that time, she apparently would have been able to establish a *legal* parent-child relationship under sections 8–201(b)(1) and 8–204(a)(5) of the DUPA regardless of her status as a *de facto* parent. However, the undisputed record reflects that Gordon only lived with A.N.S. for about thirteen months.

The Family Court determined that the DUPA's requirement for a *"legal* relationship between a child and a parent of the child" was not the exclusive means of establishing a "parent-child relationship" for purposes of petitioning for custody under title 13, section 721(a) of the Delaware Code. It determined that *de facto* parent status was also a means of qualifying as a "parent" under section 721(a). The Family Court held that, for purposes of title 13, section 721(a), a "parent" includes not only a biological parent, an adoptive parent and a person who has established a *legal* parent-child relationship under the DUPA, but also a person who has established that he or she is a *de facto* parent.

The Family Court then applied the five-part test for establishing *de facto* parent status that the Family Court, in *In re Hart*, originally adopted from the Wisconsin Supreme Court.[35] In *Hart*, the Family Court held that *de facto* parent status is established if the *de facto* parent:

(1) has the support and consent of the parent who fostered the formation and establishment of a parent-like relationship with the child;

(2) has assumed the obligations of parenthood by taking significant responsibility for the child's care, education and development-including the child's support, without the expectation of financial compensation;

(3) has acted in a parental role for a length of time sufficient to have established a bonded and dependent relationship that is parental in nature;

(4) has helped to shape the child's daily routine by addressing developmental needs, disciplining the child, providing for the child's education and medical care and serving as a moral guide;

(5) has on a day to day basis, through interaction, companionship, interplay and mutuality, fulfilled the child's needs for a psychological adult who helped fulfill the child's needs to be loved, valued, appreciated and received as an essential person by the adult who cares for him or her.

In re Hart, 806 A.2d at 1187–88 (citing *In re H.S.H.–K.*, 533 N.W.2d 419, 435–36 (1995)).

The Family Court also relied on *S.S. v. E.M.S.*, 2004 WL 3245935 (Del. Fam. Ct. 2004), which followed the reasoning of the New Jersey Supreme Court in *V.C. v. M.J.B.*, 748 A.2d 539 (2000). The New Jersey Supreme Court held that a psychological (*de facto*) parent is a parent for the purpose of petitioning for joint custody and visitation. In *S.S. v. E.M.S.*, the Family Court concluded that "once the non-biological parent is determined to be a '*de facto*' parent, they stand in parity with the legal parent and have standing

---

35. In re Hart, 806 A.2d 1179 (Del. Fam. Ct. 2001). The Family Court held that an unmarried person can adopt his or her partner's adoptive child in a "second-parent" adoption if that person qualifies as a *de facto* parent and has the consent of the adoptive parent. A "second-parent" adoption is similar to a "stepparent" adoption and does not affect the legal rights of the adoptive parent. The Family Court adopted the five-part test for determining whether someone qualifies as a *de facto* parent for purposes of consensual, "second-parent" adoption from the Wisconsin Supreme Court. *Id.* at 1187–88 (citing In re Custody of H.S.H.–K., 533 N.W.2d 419, 435–36 (Wisc. 1995)).

to petition [the Family] Court for custody of the children pursuant to [title 13, section 721]." *Id.* at 5. In this case, the Family Court concluded that Gordon qualified as a *de facto* parent. Therefore, it held that Gordon had standing as a parent to seek custody of A.N.S. under section 721(a).

The National Conference of Commissioners on Uniform State Laws ("NCCUSL") promulgated the first version of the UNIFORM PARENTAGE ACT ("UPA") in 1973 following a law review article about the unequal legal treatment of illegitimate children for child support and inheritance purposes. The UPA intended to identify "two legal parents for both marital and non-marital children," and was mostly concerned with asserting the rights of children born out of wedlock in a civil paternity action against their fathers. The Act also provided a right to bring a maternity action in those rare cases where the identity of the biological mother might be disputed.

In 1988, in response to the increasing use of assisted reproduction and surrogacy agreements, the NCCUSL promulgated the UNIFORM STATUS OF CHILDREN OF ASSISTED CONCEPTION ACT ("USCACA") for establishing the legal parents of children born as a result of assisted reproduction. The UNIFORM PUTATIVE AND UNKNOWN FATHERS ACT ("UPUFA") followed with procedures for identifying putative and unknown fathers and for terminating their parental rights.

The UPA was revised in 2000. The revised Act "continues to serve the purposes of the 1973 UNIFORM PARENTAGE ACT, particularly the purpose of identifying fathers so that child support obligations may be ordered." It also incorporates the 1988 USCACA and UPUFA, and takes account of new technology that makes it possible to identify a father by genetic testing.

The UPA was amended further in 2002, to address concerns that the 2000 revisions "did not adequately treat a child of unmarried parents equally with a child of married parents." In the 2000 revisions, a husband who consented to his wife's assisted reproduction was the legal father of the resulting child, even though he was not the biological father. A couple who intended to become the parents of a child born as a result of a surrogacy agreement had to be married. In the 2002 amendments, "husband" and "wife" were changed to "man" and "woman" to account for unmarried couples and avoid treating children of unmarried parents differently. Because of the wording, however, a child born to an unmarried same-sex couple as a result of assisted reproduction could not have two legal parents.

The requirements for establishing maternity and paternity under the American Law Institute ("ALI") are markedly different from the requirements for qualifying as a parent under the UPA. Commentators consider the ALI PRINCIPLES to provide the most expansive definition of parental rights. The American Law Institute's Principles of the Law of Family Dissolution ("ALI Principles") define "parent" as a "legal parent," "parent by estoppel" or "*de facto* parent."

All three types of "parents" have standing under the ALI PRINCIPLES to seek "parenting time," i.e., custody. A "legal parent" is someone who currently would be identified as a parent under state law. A "parent by estoppel" is someone who has lived with the child and assumed full parental duties on a permanent basis with the legal parents' consent but is not otherwise recognized under existing law. A "*de facto* parent" is someone who, for at least two years, has lived with the child and provided care and nurturance on an equal level with the legal parents, either with the legal parents' consent or in response to the legal parents' failure to act as parents to the child.

The ALI explains that other individuals such as a stepparent or nonmarital partner of the legal parent may function as a parent and be recognized as a *de facto* parent "under a strict set of criteria designed to test the individual's level of commitment and involvement in the child's life." The ALI's requirements for a *de facto* parent are rigid "to avoid unnecessary and inappropriate intrusion into the relationships between legal parents and their children." We note, however, that even under the expansive ALI standards, Gordon would not qualify as a *de facto* parent because she did not live with A.N.S. for at least two years.

The foregoing discussion reflects that the UPA provides a more narrow scope of who may be adjudicated a parent than does the ALI PRINCIPLES. The ALI PRINCIPLES were known when the UPA was amended in 2002. Nevertheless, the 2002 UPA does not recognize the status of *de facto* parent. It has been noted that, "[w]hile the UPA made some strides to address changing avenues to parentage, [for example, surrogate parenting and assisted reproduction], it inevitably did not contemplate nor address every conceivable family constellation" and fails to address directly *de facto* parenthood. *In re Parentage of L.B.*, 122 P.3d 161, 166 n. 5 (Wash. 2005) (citations omitted).

A 2007 law review article also notes the UPA's omissions.[67] The author writes that the drafters of the revised UPA chose to leave a child born to a same-sex couple as a result of assisted reproduction with only one parent, "despite the fact that the same scientific, social, and legal arguments that convinced the [NCCUSL] to recognize both parents of non-marital children in the 1973 UPA existed in support of recognizing both parents of children conceived through [assisted reproduction] and born to same-sex couples in the [revised] UPA."[68] Similarly, as we already noted, a child adopted by only one partner in a same-sex relationship has only one parent under the UPA even if both partners function as her parents. The UPA has developed without same-sex couples in mind.

The Delaware General Assembly enacted the DUPA in 1983. It was adopted from the 1973 UPA. In 1992, the Delaware Supreme Court held that the DUPA was not the exclusive way to determine paternity. This Court explained in *Blake v. Myrks*, 606 A.2d 748, 751 (Del. 1992), that the DUPA was ambiguous and inconsistent as to whether it was intended to be exclusive. One section of the 1983 DUPA provided that the parent-child relationship between a child and his or her natural father "*may* be established in accordance with this chapter," which suggested the DUPA was not exclusive. Another section suggested that the DUPA was exclusive. It provided that a court order as to whether a parent-child relationship exists "*is determinative for all purposes.*" In *Blake*, this Court concluded: "In the absence of clear language to the contrary, this Court will not interpret the [DUPA] as revoking the Family Court's ability to determine paternity in accordance with procedures established before the statute's enactment." *Blake*, 606 A.2d at 751 n. 3.

In 2004, the Delaware General Assembly repealed the 1983 DUPA and enacted a new statute to reflect the 2000 revisions and 2002 amendments to the UPA. The new DUPA superseded the prior statute. It also superseded the *Blake* case, which interpreted the prior statute as nonexclusive. The 2004 DUPA unambiguously provides that it "applies to determination of parentage in this state."

---

67. Mary Patricia Byrn, *From Right to Wrong: A Critique of the 2000 Uniform Parentage Act*, 16 U.C.L.A. WOMEN'S L.J. 163 (2007).

68. *Id.* at 166.

Several jurisdictions have statutes that courts have interpreted to permit *de facto* parents to petition for custody, visitation, an allocation of parental rights or similar orders. In states where statutes have not specifically recognized *de facto* parents, some courts have found that individuals with the status of *de facto* parent, or other similar status, have standing to petition for child custody or visitation, or have child support obligations. For example, in *V.C. v. M.J.B.*, 748 A.2d 539 (N.J. 2000), the New Jersey Supreme Court recognized a psychological (*de facto*) parent as a "parent" with standing to petition for custody or visitation, but not joint custody under the facts of that case.

In one state, Washington, which adopted the revised UPA, its highest court recognized the status of *de facto* parent under the common law as a means of determining parentage, in addition to, and apart from, the UPA as adopted by that state. *In re Parentage of L.B.*, 122 P.3d at 173–174. The Washington Supreme Court concluded that, although Washington's version of the UPA "fails to contemplate all potential scenarios which may arise in the ever-changing and evolving notion of familial relations," the statute's "fail[ure] to speak to a specific situation" did not preclude "the availability of potential redress" under the common law. *Id.* at 176. In reaching that conclusion, the Washington Supreme Court stated:

> Reason and common sense support recognizing the existence of *de facto* parents and according them the rights and responsibilities which attach to parents in this state. We adapt our common law today to fill the interstices that our current legislative enactment fails to cover in a manner consistent with our laws and stated legislative policy.
>
> . . .
>
> We thus hold that henceforth in Washington, a *de facto* parent stands in legal parity with an otherwise legal parent, whether biological, adoptive, or otherwise. As such, recognition of a person as a child's *de facto* parent necessarily "authorizes [a] court to consider an award of parental rights and responsibilities . . . based on its determination of the best interest of the child."

Id. at 176–77.

Family relationships in Delaware are highly regulated by statute. Title 13 of the Delaware Code, entitled "Domestic Relations," governs, among other things, marriage, divorce, domestic violence, child custody, child support, and adoption. The DUPA, which is also part of title 13, was adopted from the UPA.

Section 8–103 explains the scope of the DUPA. Subsection (a) provides unambiguously that the DUPA "applies to determinations of parentage in this State." Although the DUPA "does not create, enlarge, or diminish parental rights or duties under other law of this State," the DUPA, like the revised UPA, does not include the *de facto* parent doctrine.

The *de facto* parent doctrine was known in 2004 when the General Assembly enacted the new DUPA not only because the ALI Principles were extant, but, also because the Family Court had embraced the doctrine in the child adoption context.[93] Nevertheless, the General Assembly did not include or recognize the doctrine in the new statute. Instead, the DUPA unambigu-

---

93. In re Hart, 806 A.2d 1179, 1187–89 (Del. Fam. Ct. 2001) (holding that an unmarried person can adopt his or her partner's adopted child in a "second-parent" adoption if he or she meets the *de facto* parent test and has the consent of the adoptive parent) (citing In re H.S.H.–K., 193 Wis.2d 649, 533 N.W.2d 419, 435–46 (Wisc. 1995)).

ously defines the "parent-child relationship" as "the *legal* relationship between a child and the parent of the child."

The Delaware General Assembly adopted detailed legislation that does not include *de facto* parent in the definition of parent. The Delaware General Assembly's declination to include a *de facto* parent in any Delaware statute was not inadvertent. The Delaware judiciary cannot now independently confer upon a *de facto* parent the same status as a *legal* parent either as a matter of statutory construction or common law. Where the General Assembly enacts a comprehensive statutory scheme that reflects a public policy unambiguously to define the parent-child relationship as a *legal* relationship, any modifications in that policy must be made by the legislature.

For example, if *de facto* parent status is recognized by statute, the General Assembly would decide, *inter alia*, whether the *de facto* parent must reside with the child for "a significant period of time not less than two years" or "for a length of time sufficient to have established a bonded and dependent relationship that is parental in nature." At least two other provisions in the DUPA require a person seeking to establish a parent-child relationship to have resided with the child for at least *two years* and to have held out the child as his or her own during that time: section 8–204(a)(5) and section 8–704(b). Therefore, if *de facto* parent were recognized by statute, it seems that the General Assembly would be more likely to enact the two-year ALI approach than to follow the *de facto* parent bonding test adopted by the Family Court in *In re Hart* and applied in this case to a thirteen-month relationship. *In re Hart*, 806 A.2d 1179, 1187 (Del. Fam. Ct. 2001).

Title 13, section 721 of the Delaware Code distinguishes between parents and an "other person." Those distinctions governing who can petition for custody reflect the policy of protecting legal parents from the intrusions of third parties. Even the ALI Principles recognize the need for such limitations, and acknowledge that "[t]he requirements for becoming a *de facto* parent are strict, to avoid unnecessary and inappropriate intrusion into the relationship between legal parents and their children."

A person who does not qualify as a legal parent has no standing to petition for custody of a child unless the child is dependent or neglected and a consideration of the best interests of the child lead the Family Court to determine that the child should not be placed in the custody of the legal parent. Gordon is not a legal parent, nor can she establish that A.N.S. is dependent or neglected and that it would be in A.N.S.'s best interests not to place A.N.S. in the custody of her adoptive mother. Therefore, we hold that Gordon does not have standing to seek custody under section 721(a).

This case involved a dispute between unmarried same-sex former partners. The issues presented in this appeal are not limited to unmarried same-sex partners and could arise in a variety of other circumstances. Providing relief in such situations, however, is a public policy decision for the General Assembly to make.

The judgments of the Family Court are reversed. This matter is remanded for further proceedings in accordance with this opinion.

NOTES

1. In 2009, the Delaware General Assembly amended the Delaware Uniform Parentage Act to include *de facto* parent within the statutory definition of parent. DEL. CODE

Ann. tit. 13, § 8–201(a)(4). The Supreme Court of Delaware has upheld the constitutionality of the amendment. *Smith v. Guest*, 16 A.3d 920, 933 (Del. 2011).

2. An increasing number of courts have been willing to recognize parental rights for persons who do not meet statutory definitions of "parent." *See, e.g., In re Carvin*, 122 P.3d 161 (Wash. 2005) (finding that non-biological, non-adoptive parent has standing to petition for status as *de facto* parent where legal parent consented to and fostered the parent-child relationship); *C.E.W v. D.E.W.*, 845 A.2d 1146 (Me. 2004) (stating that a finding of *de facto* parentage for non-biological, non-adoptive parent authorizes consideration of award of parental rights and responsibilities in best interests of child); *In re Interest of E.L.M.C.*, 100 P.3d 546 (Colo. Ct. App. 2004), *cert. denied*, 100 P.3d 546 (allocating parental responsibilities to psychological parent against the wishes of adoptive parent did not violate adoptive parent's constitutional rights where adoptive parent fostered relationship and where there was risk of emotional harm to child); *In re Bonfield*, 780 N.E.2d 241 (Ohio 2002) (holding that while same-sex partner was not a parent under meaning of statute, juvenile court could determine custody in best interest of the child); *T.B. v. L.R.M.* 786 A.2d 913 (Pa. 2001) (holding that former same-sex partner had standing *in loco parentis* to seek visitation where she assumed parental status and duties with consent of biological parent); *Rubano v. DiCenzo*, 759 A.2d 959 (R.I. 2000) (holding that constitutional rights of biological parent to prevent third parties from exercising parental rights over her child are not absolute where best interests of the child are at stake and that she is estopped by her conduct from objecting to the non-biological parent's court-ordered visitation).

Some courts, however, have refused to do so. *See, e.g., Jones v. Barlow*, 154 P.3d 808 (Utah 2007) (holding that former domestic partner lacked standing to seek visitation under doctrine of *in loco parentis* after legal parent terminated the relationship); *White v. White*, 293 S.W.3d 1 (Mo. Ct. App. 2009) (holding that former same-sex partner lacks standing *in loco parentis* to seek joint legal and physical custody after legal parent ended the relationship).

K.B. v. J.R.

Supreme Court of New York, 2009.
26 Misc.3d 465.

■ Morgenstern, J.

[P]etitioner and Respondent began living together in the first months of 1998 and on August 28, 1998, the parties were married in the state of New York. It is not disputed that the parties were aware and discussed the fact that the Petitioner was born a woman but lived as a man since he was a teenager. On June 8, 1998 the Petitioner legally changed his name from Cassandra to KB. Since the age of 15 Petitioner adopted the hair style, clothing, demeanor and name of a man. In addition, the Petitioner received hormone treatments to effectuate a fully masculine appearance. Petitioner plans to undergo gender re-assignment surgery in the future.

The Respondent stated that "despite knowing KB was born a female JR agreed to marry KB. The couple filled out the marriage certificate together." The Respondent contends that the first year of marriage was happy and that in the beginning of the second year the Petitioner became physically abusive. (1999). After four years of marriage the Respondent agreed to conceive a child through artificial insemination with the Petitioner despite this alleged continued abuse. In 2001 the parties agreed that the mother would undergo artificial insemination and the parties selected a sperm donor whose characteristics and interests matched those of the Petitioner. The parties collaborated, contributed and supported the artificial insemination process. The Petitioner signed the consent form for the Respondent to be inseminated. The procedure had to be repeated three times before it resulted in a pregnancy which concluded with the birth of the subject child, KB Jr., on June 13, 2002. The parties submitted a Birth Certificate which reflected that the Petitioner was the father of the child and that the Respondent was the mother of the subject child. According to the parties, the child was born premature and had to remain in the hospital for over one month after his birth. A letter, dated September 20, 2007, written by Dr. Pinyavat described KJ Jr. as a "five year old child born premature and asthmatic." The child has been diagnosed as having asthma, but the parties disagree whether the condition is aggravated by the consumption of dairy products.

On June 7, 2002, the Respondent received a note from the hospital which stated, "Ms. JR, a married patient, will be hospitalized at St. John's Queens Hospital for an unknown number of days and/or weeks." On June 25, 2002 the hospital prepared a letter which stated, "This is to certify Mr. KB, father of KB Jr., was at St. John's Queens Hospital to bring his child home. The infant was discharged today after a lengthy hospital stay." It is undisputed that the Petitioner financially supported the family for approximately six months while the Respondent took a leave of absence from her employment to care for the infant. The medical and school records of the child reflect that the Petitioner is the father of the child. According to the Petitioner, the Respondent eventually returned to work, worked long hours and spent days away from the marital residence for her employment while Petitioner would provide daily care for the child. Sometime after May of 2006 the parties became estranged. It is undisputed that the Respondent left the marital home in May of 2006 and left the child in the physical custody of the Petitioner.

Although the Respondent failed to file a Petition in Family Court for a Temporary Order of Protection, the Respondent alleged that she was forced to leave the residence due to the domestic violence perpetrated by the Petitioner. The Petitioner alleged that Respondent left the residence to move into the apartment of another man. The Respondent further alleged that she left the marital residence on August 3, 2007 to escape the abuse and that the Petitioner picked up the child from the babysitter without her knowledge. The Respondent never explained why she left the child with the Petitioner when she did not intend to return to the marital residence.

The parties filed cross-petitions for custody of KB Jr. . . . The Respondent stated in her cross-petition that it would be in the best interest of the child if custody of the child was awarded to her since the Petitioner is actually a woman. In Respondent's affirmation it is alleged that Petitioner committed acts of domestic violence against her while they lived together and that she feared for the safety of the child. In Respondent's custody petition she stated that the Petitioner was "actually a woman" and therefore the marriage was "invalid".

On August 6, 2007, the same day the Cross Petition for Custody was filed, the Respondent filed a Family Offense petition against the Petitioner alleging that he threatened her with a knife. On August 24, 2007, in Kings County Family Court, Hon. Helene D. Sacco ordered that the child remain in the temporary custody of the Petitioner and directed that the Respondent be granted visitation every Sunday. On September 28, 2007, the Respondent made an application seeking the transfer of temporary custody of the child since the Petitioner was actually a woman and the child was conceived by artificial insemination. The Family Court declined to hear argument on that application since a proceeding regarding the validity of a marriage could properly be determined only by the Supreme Court.

A Court Order of Investigation (COI) was conducted by the Administration for Children's Services. The Respondent acknowledged to the CPS investigator that the parties agreed to have a child and agreed to use artificial insemination in order to have a child.

The Respondent also acknowledged that she knowingly entered into a relationship with the Petitioner and willingly entered into a fraudulent marriage despite the fact that the Petitioner is biologically a woman. The parties openly lived together as husband and wife for four years before KB Jr. was born. The Respondent never objected that KB Jr. acknowledged the Petitioner as his father and she allowed the child to call the Petitioner "Dad" without admonition. According to the attorney for the child, KB Jr. has steadfastly referred to the Petitioner as his father and the Respondent as his mother. "During my numerous interviews with ... the child has never wavered in his view that Ms. JR is his mother and Mr. KB is his father." The parties attempted to settle the custody and visitation issues concerning KB Jr. while the Petitioner exercised temporary custody and the court granted expanded visitation to the Respondent. On December 23, 2007 during a visitation exchange the Respondent alleged that the Petitioner threatened her in violation of a temporary order of protection and the Petitioner was arrested.

On January 8, 2008 the proceedings were transferred to IDV–2 in Kings County Supreme Court. On March 21, 2008 the Respondent initiated a contested matrimonial proceeding in Supreme Court entitled *JR v. KB* which was transferred to this Court. On May 5, 2008, in the matrimonial proceeding, this Court continued the temporary order of custody of the child to the Petitioner. At the same time, the Petitioner reported that Respondent repeatedly gave the subject child food containing dairy products which aggravated his asthma and neglected to give him his asthma medication as prescribed. The child reported to his attorney, that, at times, he shared the Respondent's bed with her boyfriend. On July 21, 2008, the parties consented to the issuance of a declaratory judgment in the matrimonial proceeding which adjudged the marriage to be void. Subsequent to the resolution of the matrimonial proceeding, the child reported to his attorney that there was an increased use of derogatory language by the Respondent about the Petitioner. The Petitioner alleged that the Respondent used vulgar epithets to refer to the Petitioner when speaking to the subject child including "bitch", "fucking bitch" and "fucking idiot".

On August 8, 2008 the child made an allegation to his attorney of excessive corporal punishment by the Respondent which was reported to the Court. The child described, to his attorney, that he was struck with a belt on the genitals and on the buttocks by the Respondent. On August 14, 2008 the temporary order of visitation was suspended. Visitation with the Respondent was reinstated after further investigation and a series of supervised visits.

On June 16, 2009 the Respondent made an application to transfer custody of the child pending a fact-finding hearing. The request was based on an allegation that the Petitioner failed to provide the child with medical care and for violation of the Court direction that Petitioner cooperate to assure that Respondent would see the child on his birthday although it occurred during Petitioner's parenting time.

[T]he Respondent contends that a proceeding for custody of the subject child cannot be maintained by the Petitioner since he is not biologically related to KB Jr. and could never have been legally married to the

Respondent, therefore, he did not have standing to file a petition for custody or visitation. . . .

The Court of Appeals has held that a non-parent lacked . . . standing to seek the custody of a child over the objection of the parent absent a showing of abandonment, unfitness, neglect, extended disruption in custody or other equivalent that demonstrated "extraordinary circumstances" which would affect the welfare of a child. *Bennett v. Jeffreys*, 356 N.E.2d 277 (N.Y. 1976). . . . Once such extraordinary circumstances are found the court may make a determination on what would be in the best interests of the child. Separation of the mother from the child is one example of extraordinary circumstances. . . . Psychological bonding between a non biological parent and a child has resulted in a court finding that extraordinary circumstances do exist which allowed the non biological party to petition a court for custody of a child. *See, Doe v. Doe*, 399 N.Y.S.2d 977 (N.Y. Sup. Ct. 1977). Extraordinary circumstances may be found even in the absence of a finding of unfitness by the biological parent. If removal from the custody of a non-parent would cause "significant emotional injury" since a strong bond developed between a child and the non-biological parent the possibility of that injury would justify a finding of extraordinary circumstances. *Curry v. Ashby*, 517 N.Y.S.2d 990 (App.Div. 1987).

In the case at bar, the proceedings reflect that KB Jr. has a strong emotional and psychological bond with the Petitioner and, in fact, the Petitioner is the only father that the child has known. This situation was created with the active cooperation of the Respondent when the parties entered into the "marriage". The Petitioner and Respondent lived as husband and wife for at least eight years, executed a marriage certificate, completed an artificial insemination consent form, filed a birth certificate which identified the Petitioner as father of the child, and encouraged KB Jr. to accurately and without qualification address and consider the Petitioner as his father for more than six years.

. . .

The circumstances presented, in the case at bar, reflect an "unfortunate" disruption of custody of the biological parent over an extended period time, the voluntary abdication of physical custody and parenting responsibility by the biological parent under the color of the law since the conception of the child, and . . . credible allegations of inappropriate parenting decisions by the biological parent which together amount to sufficient compelling circumstances to apply the doctrine of equitable estoppel to the analysis of the total circumstances of the dispute. These circumstances alone support a finding of exceptional circumstances in the case.

The Appellate Division has stated that "a psychological bond . . . is insufficient, *standing alone* (emphasis added), to establish extraordinary circumstances that would overcome the established right of a legal parent to chose with whom her child may associate." "Equitable considerations that arise when a man has been held out by a child's biological mother as the child's biological father in birth and baptismal certificates or in judicial proceedings (citations omitted) are not present when a boyfriend, stepfather or same-sex partner of an adoptive or biological mother seeks visitation or custody of the legal mother's child (citations omitted)." *Matter of Behrens v. Rimland*, 822 N.Y.S.2d 285 (App.Div. 2006). In the case at bar, the Petitioner, the legal father at the time of conception and birth of the subject child, is seeking standing to petition for visitation and custody even though the marriage is null and void.

The case at bar is factually distinguishable from *Behrens* in significant ways. In this case, the Petitioner petitioned for custody while the parties were still married, Petitioner was the legal parent of the subject child at conception and birth and the Respondent gave the Petitioner full parenting authority over the subject child for almost six years before raising any objection to the arrangement. The Petitioner acquired his status as husband to Respondent and father to KB Jr. for more than six years only because of the active cooperation of the Respondent for more than nine years. The Respondent now seeks to prevent the Petitioner from having any relationship with the subject child who has only known one person, the Petitioner, as his father for more than six years. In addition, the Respondent never explained why when she left the marital residence she left the child in the actual physical custody of the Petitioner between July and August of 2007 (Family Court and Supreme Court granted temporary custody to Petitioner), why she made no effort to set aside the marriage until March 21, 2008, although she alleged the parties were estranged and why she made no issue of the standing of Petitioner until he was granted temporary custody of the subject child in Family Court.... In the case at bar, the Respondent is seeking to prevent the Petitioner from being able to petition for custody or visitation although Respondent was complicit in the fraud that engendered the current litigation. These parties cooperated during the artificial insemination of the Respondent and the Respondent gave the Petitioner the parental power to raise the child as his son for more than six years without the Respondent raising any objection. The fact is that this unimpaired active parenting by the Petitioner was encouraged by the biological mother without complaint for six years. This alone is an extraordinary circumstance. In addition, during the pendency of the instant proceedings the Court granted temporary custody to the Petitioner before the marriage was adjudged null and void because of child safety allegations from when the child visited the Respondent. The Respondent failed to explain why she waited to petition for custody, why she failed to exercise her exclusive right of parenthood with the child (as biological parent of the child) or why she encouraged the child to develop a father-son relationship with Petitioner over the course of the child's entire life....

An abrupt termination of the father-son relationship which Petitioner and Respondent together created would "put the child in a situation where his welfare could be affected drastically and thus an extraordinary circumstance exists requiring inquiry into the child's best interests." *Boyles v. Boyles,* 466 N.Y.S.2d 762 (App.Div. 1983). In the case at bar, the Respondent through her words and deeds held out the Petitioner as the father of the child. In addition, the subject child is now seven years old and the additional years of relationship has dramatically increased the potential for a traumatic effect on the subject child if that father-son relationship with the Petitioner would be terminated.

.   .   .

The exact quantum of evidence needed by a petitioner to establish extraordinary circumstances may not be clearly or exactly measured but "the length of time the child has lived with the nonparent, the quality of the relationship and the length of time the biological parent allowed such custody to continue without trying to assume the primarily parental role," certainly should be factors to be considered. *See Matter of Bennor v. Hewson,* 849 N.Y.S.2d 727 (App.Div. 2008).

In the case at bar, the child has known the Petitioner as his father for his entire life and the Petitioner has had temporary custody of the child throughout all of the proceedings. The Respondent did not raise the issue of the biological status of Petitioner in the proceedings and, in fact, hid it from the child and the rest of the world until the Petitioner filed a Petition for Custody of the child. The Respondent never sought exclusive parental responsibility for the child until the child was five years old although it is undisputed that she is the biological parent of the child. However, the Petitioner, the non-biological parent, enjoyed legal status as husband to the Respondent and as father to the child through conception, birth and until the child was more than six years old when the marriage was declared null and void. It is not in dispute that the child has a strong emotional and psychological bond with his father despite the fact there is no biological relationship with the child. Dr. Carlin reported that Petitioner "responded sensitively and appropriately" when questioned about any situations or problems that may arise regarding raising KB Jr. . . .

The Petitioner contends that the animus that now exists between the parties "blinds her to the effect the demand for custody will have on the child . . . [T]he Respondent again fails to recognize or chooses to ignore how her depriving the Child of the relationship with his father and the father's family would not simply devastate the Child, but might cause him harm extending well beyond childhood . . . creating a greater risk for him psychologically."

In the case at bar, the fact that the Petitioner is biologically a woman is irrelevant to the question of whether there are exceptional circumstances to grant Petitioner standing to petition for custody. One factor relevant to a determination of whether extraordinary circumstances are present is the psychological bonding between the child and non-biological party. *Matter of Michael G.B. v. Angela L.B.*, 642 N.Y.S.2d 452 (App.Div. 1996). The abdication of parental responsibility by the natural parent of the child to a non-biological party may establish extraordinary circumstances. *Bisignano v. Walz*, 563 N.Y.S.2d 938 (App.Div. 1990). The possible psychological harm of a change in custody from an uncle to the children's father is sufficient to establish the existence of extraordinary circumstances. *See Matter of Scott L. v. Bruce N.*, 513 N.Y.S.2d 121 (App.Div. 1987). A psychological bond is usually insufficient to establish sufficient extraordinary circumstances for a non-biological party to be granted standing to seek custody or visitation. *See Matter of Esposito v. Shannon*, 823 N.Y.S.2d 159 (App.Div. 2006). However in the case at bar there is much more than a psychological bond between the Petitioner and the subject child. The Respondent consented and encouraged the Petitioner to share a full parental role in the child's life from birth until August 6, 2007 when the Respondent declared that the Petitioner was "actually a woman" although the parties were still "married". At times during the marriage, the Respondent abdicated all parental responsibilities for the subject child to the Petitioner. The Respondent did not seek an immediate change in custody of the subject child until August 6, 2007 in her cross-petition for custody.

The Court holds that based on the statements of the parties contained in their affidavits, the reports submitted, and the Court's observations of the demeanor and conduct of the parties in court that Petitioner has sustained his burden of proof to establish extraordinary circumstances are present to grant standing to proceed with a petition for custody. The Court hereby finds that there are extraordinary circumstances present based on the facts of the case, as presented in the record, and furthermore there are additional equitable considerations present that were created by both of the parties who entered into the marriage. The Respondent should be equitably estopped from challenging the standing of the Petitioner to seek custody since Respondent perpetrated the fraud and derived benefits from it until she raised it in the matrimonial action. The Respondent admitted that she entered the relationship with full knowledge that the Petitioner was biologically a woman. The Respondent agreed and married the Petitioner. The Respondent received benefits as the wife of the Petitioner. The Respondent agreed and collaborated freely with the Petitioner in the decision to have a child by artificial insemination. The Petitioner signed the consent form as the husband to the Respondent which was needed to commence the procedure. The Respondent freely divided parenting responsibilities with her "husband" for almost six years and fostered a close father-son relationship between the child and the Petitioner.

The Court holds that the Respondent abdicated her parenting authority to the Petitioner and actively encouraged the creation of a father-son relationship between the Petitioner and the subject child. In fact, the Respondent does not dispute that a close father-son relationship bonds the Petitioner and subject child together at this time. The finding of extraordinary circumstances is based on the credible allegations made by the Petitioner which are supported by the record, the reports from ACS, the Lincoln hearing, the statements of the parties and the observation of the demeanor of the parties.

For the foregoing reasons it is hereby

ORDERED and ADJUDGED that there are sufficient facts to establish extraordinary circumstances to allow the Petitioner to petition for custody of the subject child; and it is further

ORDERED and ADJUDGED that there are sufficient circumstances to move the Court to apply the doctrine of equitable estoppel to estop the Respondent from raising the issue of standing of this individual application under the totality of the circumstances.

AMERICAN LAW INSTITUTE, PRINCIPLES OF THE LAW OF FAMILY DISSOLUTION

(2002).

Section 203 Definitions

For purposes of this Chapter, the following definitions apply.

(1) Unless otherwise specified, a *parent* is either a legal parent, a parent by estoppel, or a de facto parent.

(a) A *legal parent* is an individual who is defined as a parent under other state law.

(b) A *parent by estoppel* is an individual who, though not a legal parent,

(i) is obligated to pay child support . . . or

(ii) lived with the child for at least two years and

(A) over that period had a reasonable, good faith belief that he was the child's biological father, based on marriage to the mother or on the actions or representations of the mother, and fully accepted parental responsibilities consistent with that belief, and

(B) if some time thereafter that belief no longer existed, continued to make reasonable, good-faith efforts to accept responsibilities as the child's father; or

(iii) lived with the child since the child's birth, holding out and accepting full and permanent responsibilities as parent, as part of a prior co-parenting agreement with the child's legal parent (or, if there are two legal parents, both parents) to raise a child together each with full parental rights and responsibilities, when the court finds that recognition of the individual as a parent is in the child's best interests; or

(iv) lived with the child for at least two years, holding out and accepting full and permanent responsibilities as a parent, pursuant to an agreement with the child's parent (or, if there are two legal parents, both parents), when the court finds that recognition of the individual as a parent is in the child's best interests.

(c) A *de facto parent* is an individual other than a legal parent or a parent by estoppel who, for a significant period of time not less than two years,

(i) lived with the child and,

(ii) for reasons primarily other than financial compensation, and with the agreement of a legal parent to form a parent-child relationship, or as a result of a complete failure or inability of any legal parent to perform caretaking functions,

(A) regularly performed a majority of the caretaking functions for the child, or

(B) regularly performed a share of caretaking functions at least as great as that of the parent with whom the child primarily lived.

. . .

(5) *Caretaking functions* are tasks that involve interaction with the child or that direct, arrange, and supervise the interaction and care provided by others. Caretaking functions include but are not limited to all of the following:

(a) satisfying the nutritional needs of the child, managing the child's bedtime and wake-up routines, caring for the child when sick or injured, being attentive to the child's personal hygiene needs including washing, grooming, and dressing, playing with the child and arranging for recreation, protecting the child's physical safety, and providing transportation;

(b) directing the child's various developmental needs, including the acquisition of motor and language skills, toilet training, self-confidence, and maturation;

(c) providing discipline, giving instruction in manners, assigning and supervising chores, and performing other tasks that attend to the child's needs for behavioral control and self-restraint;

(d) arranging for the child's education, including remedial or special services appropriate to the child's needs and interests, communicating with teachers and counselors, and supervising homework;

(e) helping the child to develop and maintain appropriate interpersonal relationships with peers, siblings, and other family members;

(f) arranging for health-care providers, medical follow-up, and home health care;

(g) providing moral and ethical guidance;

(h) arranging alternative care by a family member, babysitter, or other child-care provider or facility, including investigation of alternatives, communication with providers, and supervision of care.

COMMENTS

. . .

C.   De facto parent. . . . The requirements for becoming a de facto parent are strict, to avoid unnecessary and inappropriate intrusion into the relationships between legal parents and their children. The individual must have lived with the child for a significant period of time (not less than two years), and acted in the role of a parent for reasons primarily other than financial compensation. The legal parent or parents must have agreed to the arrangement, or it must have arisen because of a complete failure or inability of any legal parent to perform caretaking functions. In addition, the individual must have functioned as a parent either by (a) having performed the majority of caretaking functions for the child, or (b) having performed a share of caretaking functions that is equal to or greater than the share assumed by the legal parent with whom the child primarily lives.

. . .

Section 2.18.   Allocations of Responsibility to Individuals Other Than Legal Parents

(1) The court should allocate responsibility to a legal parent, a parent by estoppel, or a de facto parent. . . . in accordance with the same standards [set forth in other sections of the Principles], except that

(a) it should not allocate the majority of custodial responsibility to a de facto parent over the objection of a legal parent or a parent by estoppel who is fit and willing to assume the majority of custodial responsibility unless

(i) the legal parent or parent by estoppel has not been performing a reasonable share of parenting functions . . . or

(ii) the available alternatives would cause harm to the child; and

(b) it should limit or deny an allocation otherwise to be made if, in light of the number of other individuals to be allocated responsibility, the allocation would be impractical in light of the objectives of this Chapter.

I.   ENFORCEMENT

1.   TORT LAW

Khalifa v. Shannon

Court of Appeals of Maryland, 2008.
945 A.2d 1244.

■ BATTAGLIA, J.

The issue in this case is whether a cause of action for intentional interference with custody and visitation rights is sustainable by a father,

Michael Shannon, against his former wife, Nermeen Khalifa Shannon, and her mother, Afaf Nassar Khalifa ("Appellants"), both of whom fled to Egypt with the couple's two minor children, who remain there. Appellants moved to dismiss the father's complaint, arguing that interference with custody and visitation rights is not a cognizable cause of action in Maryland, and alternatively, that even if Maryland recognizes the tort, the Complaint fails to allege a loss of the children's services, which is a required element. The trial court disagreed, and after a trial, the jury awarded $3,017,500 in compensatory and punitive damages. Appellants noted an appeal to the Court of Special Appeals, and prior to any proceedings in that court, we issued a writ of certiorari on our own initiative ... to address the following issues:

I. Did the trial court commit reversible error when it denied the defendant-appellants' motion to dismiss Count One of the Complaint by recognizing the tort of interference with custody and visitation rights of children?

. . .

III. Did the trial court commit reversible error when it denied the defendant-appellants' motion for a new trial, and/or for remittur, because the punitive damages awarded by the jury were grossly excessive and there was no evidence on the record of defendant-appellants' ability to pay?

. . .

Michael Shannon initiated the instant civil suit against his ex-wife, Nermeen Khalifa Shannon, her mother, Afaf Nassar Khalifa, her father, Mohammed Osama Khalifa, and her older sister, Dahlia Khalifa, in March of 2004. The Complaint contained four counts: Count I, Interference with Custody and Visitation Rights of Children; Count II, Civil Conspiracy; Count III, Loss of Society of Children; and Count IV, False Imprisonment, with the following factual allegations:

8.   Mr. Shannon married Defendant Nermeen Khalifa Shannon on March 3, 1996.

9.   Adam Osama Shannon was born on February 9, 1997.

10.   Jason Osama Kalifa [sic] was born on January 10, 2001.

11.   Mr. Shannon and defendant Nermmen Khalifa Shannon separated in January 2000.

12.   In February 2001 this Court entered a consent order that granted Mr. Shannon custody of Adam; and Nermeen custody of Jason.

13.   Each parent also had visitation rights with their non-custodial child.

14.   On August 18, 2001, Defendant Afaf Nassar Khalifa flew to Washington, D.C. from Egypt and stayed with Nermeen Shannon in her apartment.

15.   Mr. Shannon agreed that both boys could visit a cousin in Brooklyn, New York with Defendants, Nermeen Khalifa Shannon and Afaf Nassar Khalifa, as long as the boys were returned to him by Sunday night, August 26, 2001.

16.   The boys were not returned to Maryland.

17.   The Defendants had previously and calculatedly arranged to put the boys on an airplane to Egypt.

18.   The Defendants did put the boys on an airplane to Egypt and Mr. Shannon has not seen his American sons since August 2001.

19.   Defendant, Afaf Nassar Khalifa was extradited to Maryland.

20.   Defendant, Afaf Nassar Khalifa was sentenced to a ten-year prison term. That sentence was later revised to a three-year sentence.

21.   The abductions and kidnapping [sic] of the children are ongoing.

. . .

23.   At the time of the abductions. Mr. Shannon was legally entitled to custody of Adam and visitation with Jason.

24.   The Defendants intentionally interfered, and continue to interfere with Mr. Shannon's custody and custody [sic] and visitations rights by abducting the children to Egypt and refusing to return them.

25.   The Defendants intentionally interfered, and continue to interfere with Mr. Shannon's custody and visitation rights by knowingly and intentionally refusing to allow Mr. Shannon to see or communicate in any manner with his sons.

26.   As a result of the Defendants' ongoing and continuing intentional interference with Mr. Shannon's custody and visitation rights, Mr. Shannon has suffered damages.

. . .

The case went to trial in December of 2006. At the close of argument, the court dismissed the false imprisonment and loss of society counts. After deliberating over the remaining counts of interference with custody and visitation rights and civil conspiracy and completing a special verdict form, the jury awarded Shannon $17,500 in attorney fees and costs; $500,000 in compensatory damages against each defendant; $900,000 in punitive damages against Afaf Nassar Khalifa and $1,100,000 in punitive damages against Nermeen Khalifa Shannon. Appellants moved for a judgment notwithstanding the verdict, a new trial, and for remittur, arguing grossly excessive damages, all of which the Circuit Court denied. Appellants noted their appeal to the Court of the Special Appeals, and we issued a writ of certiorari prior to any proceedings in the intermediate appellate court.

Appellants contend that the Circuit Court erred when it denied their Motion to Dismiss the Complaint for failure to state a claim upon which relief can be granted, because Maryland does not recognize the tort of interference with custody and visitation. Appellants alternatively posit that if Maryland recognizes the tort of interference with custody and visitation, the lower court erred when it refused to dismiss the complaint for failure to state a claim because a parent must plead and prove a child's services to maintain the cause of action, which did not occur in the present case, and also contend that if this Court accepts Comment d to the RESTATEMENT (SECOND) OF TORTS § 700 (1977), which states that the loss of service element is not necessary, it will be creating new law, which cannot apply retroactively. Appellants, further, contend that the jury's punitive damage award was excessive, because Shannon "placed no evidence whatsoever on the record of [Appellants'] ability to pay $900,000 and $1,100,000 in punitive damages, respectively;" because the punitive damage award "far exceeded [the $5,000] maximum monetary fine imposed by the Maryland Family Law Article for the same conduct;" and because the punitive damage award is not commensurate with other punitive awards in the State.

. . .

This Court apparently first explicitly recognized the torts of abduction of a child from a parent and harboring in *Baumgartner v. Eigenbrot*, 60 A. 601 (Md. 1905). In *Baumgartner*, an aunt, who had legal guardianship over a teenage girl, sued a husband and wife with whom the girl had chosen to live, alleging that they had abducted the child and harbored her after she had been so abducted. The complaint specifically alleged that defendants abducted and knowingly deprived the aunt of the young woman, that the aunt "became greatly attached to her," and that the aunt "derived great comfort from [the child's] society as she grew to be larger," thereby incurring non-economic losses. *Id.* at 601. The trial judge had directed a verdict because of insufficiency of the evidence, and we affirmed, opining that the evidence was not sufficient to meet the elements of abduction and harboring, which we declared were tortious acts. . . .

. . .

Our acknowledgment of the torts of abduction and of harboring in *Baumgartner*, furthermore, was consistent with substantial authority from many of our sister states, who also were original American colonies, facing the same question. In what appears to be the earliest known and most frequently cited American case on abduction, the South Carolina Court of Law in *Kirkpatrick v. Lockhart*, 4 S.C.L. (2 Brev.) 276 (1809), held that a father could sustain an abduction action not only for his son and heir, but for the abduction of any one of his children. . . .

In total, the torts of abduction and harboring have been recognized in at least eight of the other original American colonies. What we glean from these cases, and in particular those cases discussing the English common law, is that the torts of abduction and harboring existed in England prior to 1776, and that, therefore, we adopted them as part of our common law under Article V of the Maryland Declaration of Rights, which states in pertinent part that "the Inhabitants of Maryland are entitled to the Common Law of England . . . according to the course of that Law, and to the benefit of the English statutes as existed on the Fourth day of July, seventeen hundred and seventy-six."

Nevertheless, this Court was not called upon to address whether abduction and harboring could be the basis of a cause of action for interference with parent-child relations until *Hixon v. Buchberger*, 507 A.2d 607 (Md. 1986), when asked to confront the question of whether, under the common law of Maryland, a cause of action exists, or ought to be recognized, for money damages resulting from the intentional tortious interference by a non-custodial third-party with the visitation rights of a parent. Hixon was the noncustodial parent of a child born out of wedlock who complained of interference with his relationship with the child by the mother's fiancé, Buchberger, who allegedly made belligerent statements to him in the child's presence, made it physically difficult "at times" for Hixon to take the child with him, and intended "to supplant Hixon in the child's mind as the child's father"; Hixon never alleged that he was physically prevented from taking the child. Based on these allegations, the trial judge dismissed the complaint for failure to state a claim upon which relief can be granted.

In responding to the question posed to this Court by *Hixon*, Judge Lawrence F. Rodowsky, writing for this Court, analyzed the various causes of

action that could have been implicated by the factual averments and concluded that Hixon's allegations were insufficient to sustain a cause of action for
assault, battery or the intentional infliction of emotional distress:

> While Hixon's point is that Buchberger's conduct is a tort for which
> money damages will lie, Hixon does not allege that the interference
> constituted an assault or a battery. The complaint does not undertake to
> describe conduct which is " 'so outrageous in character, and so extreme
> in degree, as to go beyond all possible bounds of decency, and to be
> regarded as atrocious, and utterly intolerable in a civilized community,' "
> *Harris v. Jones,* 380 A.2d 611, 614 (Md. 1977) (quoting RESTATEMENT
> (SECOND) OF TORTS § 46 comment *d* (1965)), and Hixon does not argue
> that Buchberger committed an intentional infliction of emotional dis-
> tress.

> . . .

He continued the discussion with citation to the primary cases upon
which Hixon relied, one being *Ruffalo v. United States,* 590 F.Supp. 706
(W.D.Mo. 1984), in which a mother sued the government for tortious
interference with the parent-child relationship when the government suddenly removed her child with his father and placed both in the Witness
Protection Program in violation of her ongoing visitation rights. The mother
alleged that she had habitually seen her child after school each day, that on
the day of removal her child simply disappeared, and that she lost all contact
with the child for nearly four years. Over the government's contentions that
Missouri did not recognize a tort for interference with a parent's visitation
rights, the United States District Court Judge determined that under state
law a parent with either custody or visitation rights could pursue a cause of
action for interference with the parent-child relationship. *Id.* at 713. *See also
Raftery v. Scott,* 756 F.2d 335 (4th Cir. 1985), (in which the United States
Court of Appeals for the Fourth Circuit affirmed a money judgment in favor
of a non-custodial father for the intentional infliction of emotional distress
when the child's mother moved from New York to Virginia with the child,
and the father did not discover the child's whereabouts for over four years);
L.S.J. v. E.B., 672 S.W.2d 937 (Ky. Ct. App. 1984) (permitting a noncustodial mother to counterclaim for damages for tortious interference when
a child's foster parents brought an action to terminate the mother's parental
rights in violation of the foster parent's agreement with the governing state
agency); *Bartanus v. Lis,* 480 A.2d 1178 (Pa. Sup. Ct. 1984) (allowing damages
for intentional infliction of emotional distress based on wrongful enticement
and harboring of a child away from the parent.)

After elucidating the possible causes of action and discussing these cases,
we concluded that Hixon failed to state a claim upon which relief can be
granted because Hixon's factual allegations were insufficient, when juxta-
posed against those allegations determined to be sufficient in other cases
involving the tort of interference with parent-child relations.

In concluding that Hixon's allegations were insufficient when compared
to "the more substantial interferences presented in many of the cases relied
upon by Hixon," we not only recognized that the tort of interference with
parent-child relations was extant, but also defined the elements and applied
them to the factual allegations.

In the present case, Shannon's Complaint is sufficient to have survived a
motion to dismiss. He alleged that the Appellants abducted and harbored his
children in knowing interference with his custody right, when to obtain his

consent they led him to believe that they were taking the boys to New York "to visit relatives" and would return them on Sunday, August 26, 2001, but in reality, they intentionally and "calculatedly" had planned to, and did, abduct the boys and harbor them in Egypt. Shannon also averred that he was entitled to custody of the boys at the time when they were abducted and harbored because he had been granted legal custody of Adam and because with respect to Jason, he had a specific visitation planned for the night of August 26, 2001, and a right to ongoing visitation with him thereafter. Assuming the truth of all well-pleaded, relevant, and material facts in the complaint and any reasonable inferences that can be drawn therefrom, we conclude that Shannon sufficiently alleged the elements of the tort of interference with parent-child relations and that the trial court did not err when denying the motion to dismiss for failure to state a claim upon which relief can be granted.

Whether a parent must allege economic loss of the child's services to maintain an action for the interference with parent-child relations when the parent has custody and visitation rights regarding the children at the time the suit was brought is the next issue that we address. Although this Court's discussion in *Hixon* may have given the impression that loss of economic services was a mandatory element of the substantive tort of abduction, a focused analysis reveals that loss of services has never been an element of the tort itself, but rather, arose from common law pleading requirements in force in England, and Maryland, the latter at least until 1870....

. . .

The third issue in this case relating to the tort of interference with parent-child relations involves who can bring the cause of action; Michael Shannon was the custodial parent of Adam but also the visitation parent of Jason at the time of the abduction in 2001 and throughout the ongoing harboring. A parent with custodial rights clearly can initiate a cause of action for interference with parents-child relations. The question of whether a visitation parent can sue for the tort and receive damages necessarily was addressed in *Hixon,* in which the relevant question before us was whether, under the common law of Maryland, a cause of action exists (or ought to be recognized) for money damages resulting from the intentional tortious interference by a non-custodial third-party with the visitation rights of a parent....

[In *Hixon,*] we distinguished minor interferences with visitation from more substantial ones and held that Hixon failed to state a claim upon which relief can be granted because the interferences alleged fell short of the more substantial interferences complained of in *Ruffalo* and the other cases upon which Hixon relied.

Accordingly, by dismissing Hixon's complaint as insufficient, we determined that Maryland recognizes a cause of action for interference with visitation rights so long as the alleged interference is not minor. *Id.*

Clearly, the Complaint in the present case alleges a major and substantial interference with visitation rights because Shannon stated that he has been deprived of his right to visitation from August 26, 2001, to the present. To be sure, the allegations of the abduction and harboring of Jason since August 26, 2001, are precisely the type of substantial interference contemplated by *Hixon.* The trial court, therefore, did not err in denying the motion to dismiss. In reaching this conclusion, however, we emphasize our admonition in *Hixon* that allegations of less than a major or substantial interference with visitation rights will not suffice to state a cause of action.

Appellants also challenge the trial court's dismissal of their post-trial motions, arguing that the jury's punitive damage award was excessive. In determining whether an award of punitive damages is appropriate, we have recognized that "[t]he factors limiting the size of punitive damages awards ... are principles of law," *Bowden v. Caldor, Inc.*, 710 A.2d 267, 288 (Md. 1998), and "decisions on matters of law ... are reviewed *de novo.*" *Renbaum v. Custom Holding, Inc.*, 871 A.2d 554, 563 (Md. 2005); *Davis v. Slater*, 861 A.2d 78, 80–81 (Md. 2004) (interpretations of the Maryland Code and the Maryland Rules are reviewed *de novo*); *Nesbit v. Gov't Employees Ins. Co.*, 854 A.2d 879, 883 (Md. 2004) (interpretations of Maryland statutory and case law are conducted under a *de novo* review).

We generally review punitive damages in light of nine, non-exclusive, legal principles articulated by Judge John C. Eldridge, speaking on behalf of this Court in *Bowden*, 710 A.2d at 278–85. Seven of the nine *Bowden* factors are relevant to the instant review: (1) the defendant's ability to pay; (2) the relationship of the award to statutorily imposed criminal fines; (3) the amount of the award in comparison to other final punitive damage awards in the jurisdiction and, in particular, in somewhat comparable cases; (4) the gravity of the defendant's conduct; (5) the deterrent value of the award both with respect to the defendant and the general public; (6) whether compensatory damages, including litigation expenses, sufficiently compensate the plaintiff, and (7) whether a reasonable relationship exists between compensatory and punitive damages....

. . .

The Appellants ... argue that an award totaling $2,000,000 in punitive damages and $1,017,500 in compensatory damages cannot stand because there was no evidence at all on this record of their ability to pay damages. Their assertion, however, that there is nothing whatsoever in the record to provide a "guidepost" for determining their ability to pay punitive damages is rebuffed by Michael Shannon's uncontroverted testimony on direct examination:

Q   ... Where does Afaf Khalifa maintain different residences?

A   I stayed for four days at a beach house with Spanish marble in Al–Alemein on the Mediterranean coast. She told me it was valued at three million dollars. They have apartments in Alexandria, [Egypt] which is also on the Mediterranean coast about 50 miles to the east. We stayed there for one night. They have a 400–acre farm home, a farm in Giza with a three-story farmhouse that grows mangos and plantains and other vegetables and it's worked.

They also have a chalet outside Zurich, Switzerland. On the way to Egypt we stopped there for two days. It's in Coor, south of Zurich. They own a chalet there. And I've been to a home they own in San Marcos, California, just north of San Diego on the coast. So, I've been in six properties that they own.

Q   How many cars to your personal knowledge have you seen at those residences?

. . .

A   At the one in Al–Almein, there were two Mercedes and then four cars were kept at the Heliopolis complex.

Although the likelihood that the damages will bankrupt Appellants is a relevant consideration, we do not require Shannon to prove that appellants can pay nor do we require him to prove that the referenced properties were titled under their names. Shannon's uncontroverted testimony concerning the Khalifas' wealth is sufficient to conclude that the jury's $2,000,000 award is neither disproportionate nor excessive with respect to the Khalifa's ability to pay.

．．．

We also conclude that the final four *Bowden* factors, the gravity of the defendant's conduct, the deterrent value of the award both with respect to the defendant and the general public, whether compensatory damages, including litigation expenses, sufficiently compensate the plaintiff, and whether a reasonable relationship exists between compensatory and punitive damages, justify the imposition of $1,100,000 and $900,000 in punitive damages. First, the evidence shows that Appellants activity is particularly heinous. In 2001, Appellants told Shannon that they were taking his sons Adam and Jason to New York and that they would return them thereafter; in reality, they put the young boys on a plane for Egypt, never to return. It is clear from the record that Appellants consciously and knowingly have deprived a father of the love and comfort of his two children for an extended period of time.

There is no evidence, furthermore, that Appellants have taken any action to rectify the situation. Rather, Appellants have done quite the opposite, because as each day passes, Shannon is deprived of contact with the boys, who are now eleven and eight. We view Appellants' ongoing harboring of Shannon's children in Egypt as an aggravating factor, and a high punitive award is appropriate to deter others from engaging in similar conduct. Evidence of the ongoing absence of the children also indicates to us that Shannon will never be fully compensated for the loss of society and companionship that he has suffered at the hands of the Appellants.

In light of all of the factors, we conclude that the punitive damage award is neither excessive nor disproportionate.

2.   CRIMINAL LIABILITY

United States v. Amer

United States Court of Appeals, Second Circuit, 1997.
110 F.3d 873.

■ NEWMAN, CHIEF JUDGE.

This appeal concerns several issues arising from a conviction for violation of the International Parental Kidnapping Crime Act ("IPKCA" or "the Act"), 18 U.S.C. § 1204. The IPKCA bars a parent from removing a child from the United States or retaining outside the United States a child who has been in the United States, with the intent to obstruct the other parent's right to physical custody. We have not previously considered this statute. The specific questions raised are (i) whether the IPKCA is unconstitutionally vague, (ii) whether it is overbroad in intruding upon the free exercise of religion, (iii) whether it incorporates the affirmative defenses found in the Hague Convention on the Civil Aspects of International Parental Child

Abduction ("Hague Convention"), (iv) whether the sentencing court properly imposed, as a condition of the convicted defendant's term of supervised release, a requirement that the defendant return the still-retained children to the United States, and (v) whether the sentencing court properly applied a three-level enhancement for substantial interference with the administration of justice.

These issues of first impression arise on an appeal by Ahmed Amer from the March 14, 1996, judgment of the District Court for the Eastern District of New York (Carol Bagley Amon, Judge), convicting him, after a jury trial, of one count of international parental kidnapping in violation of the IPKCA and sentencing him to twenty-four months' imprisonment and a one-year term of supervised release with the special condition that he effect the return of the abducted children to the United States. We affirm.

Ahmed Amer ("Ahmed") and Mona Amer ("Mona"), Egyptian citizens and adherents of the Islamic faith, were married in Egypt in 1980. Four years later, while still in Egypt, Mona gave birth to the couple's first child, a boy named Amachmud. In 1985, Ahmed, seeking employment, left his wife and newborn son in Egypt and moved to the United States. Ahmed eventually settled in Queens, New York.

In 1987, Mona and Amachmud joined Ahmed in Queens. Mona stayed home to take care of the child while Ahmed worked as a cook in various diners in the city. In 1989, the couple had another child, a girl named Maha. In 1991, the couple's third child, a son named Omar, was born.

The two children born in the United States, Maha and Omar, became American citizens upon their birth. In 1991, Ahmed became a naturalized United States citizen, though he continued to retain his Egyptian citizenship. Mona obtained permanent resident alien status in this country the following year. Also in 1992, the entire Amer family returned to Egypt for a one-month visit, which was the only time that anyone in the family returned to Egypt prior to the episode on which the indictment is based.

During the early 1990s, the Amers' marriage began to deteriorate. Ahmed and Mona quarreled frequently over Ahmed's bigamous marriage to another woman, Mona's decision to work outside the home, and her decision to apply for welfare. Ahmed regularly abused Mona both verbally and physically. In April 1994, Mona asked Ahmed to leave the family apartment. He obliged and moved into a friend's apartment. The couple did not, however, divorce or become legally separated. The three children remained with Mona at the Queens home. No formal custody arrangement was made. Ahmed visited the children whenever he wished, usually once each week. During this period, Mona supported herself with public assistance and loans from friends.

Although he was no longer living in the family home, Ahmed continued to abuse Mona when he saw her. He also began to try to persuade her to move back to Egypt with him, suggesting that the children would receive a better education there and that the family would benefit from living among close relatives. Although Mona at one point appeared to agree, she eventually told Ahmed that neither she nor the children would return to Egypt. Ahmed threatened to kill Mona for her refusal, but she would not agree to leave the United States or to allow him to take the children from this country.

On January 27, 1995, Ahmed came to the family apartment in Queens to have dinner with Mona and the children. After dinner, Mona left the house to do some shopping. When she returned two hours later, Ahmed and the children were gone. The next morning Mona learned that Ahmed had taken the children to Egypt. Mona has not seen her children since that time.

Records from Egypt Air showed that on the evening of January 27th, Ahmed and the three children boarded a flight from JFK Airport to Egypt. After arriving in Egypt, Ahmed took the children to his mother's home, which is about ten minutes from the home of Mona's parents. The children visited with Mona's parents a few days after their arrival in Egypt. Amachmud, Maha, and Omar continue to reside in Egypt with Ahmed's mother.

In February 1995, Mona filed a complaint in Queens Family Court seeking custody of the children. The court awarded her full legal custody of the three children and issued a warrant for Ahmed's arrest. At around the same time, Ahmed obtained an order from an Egyptian court compelling Mona to return to the "conjugal home" in Egypt. After Mona failed to return to Egypt within three months, the Egyptian court in May 1995 awarded Ahmed custody of the three children. Additionally, Mona no longer has custody rights to twelve-year-old Amachmud under Egyptian law, which provides that a mother loses all rights to her male child when he reaches the age of ten.

In June 1995, Ahmed left the children in his mother's care and returned to the United States. He was apprehended the following month in New Jersey. The eventual indictment, issued in the Eastern District of New York, charged that "[o]n or about and between January 27, 1995 and August 4, 1995, . . . the defendant Ahmed Amer did knowingly and intentionally remove and retain children who had been in the United States, to wit [Amachmud] Amer, Maha Amer and Omar Amer, outside the United States with the intent to obstruct the lawful exercise of parental rights," in violation of the IPKCA. Ahmed was convicted by a jury on the sole count of the indictment. Judge Amon imposed a sentence of twenty-four months' imprisonment and a one-year term of supervised release, with the special condition that Ahmed effect the return of the three children to the United States. At the time of this appeal, the children remain in Egypt.

The IPKCA was enacted in December 1993, but has apparently been sparingly used. We have found no published decision of a federal court construing this statute. The IPKCA provides, in relevant part:

(a) Whoever removes a child from the United States or retains a child (who has been in the United States) outside the United States with intent to obstruct the lawful exercise of parental rights shall be fined under this title or imprisoned not more than 3 years, or both.

(b) As used in this section—

(1) the term "child" means a person who has not attained the age of 16 years; and

(2) the term "parental rights", with respect to a child, means the right to physical custody of the child—

(A) whether joint or sole (and includes visiting rights); and

(B) whether arising by operation of law, court order, or legally binding agreement of the parties.

18 U.S.C. § 1204.

. . .

Ahmed contends that the District Court erred when it refused to permit him to argue in his defense that he was justified in removing and retaining the children in Egypt under the Hague Convention. The Convention, he asserts, affords him a defense where "there is a grave risk that [the children's] return would expose the child[ren] to physical or psychological harm or otherwise place the child[ren] in an intolerable situation." This risk, he argues, arises from Mona's allegedly neglectful care. Ahmed also contends that the Hague Convention allows him to argue in his defense that the children's return would not be "permitted by the fundamental principles of [Egyptian law] relating to the protection of human rights and fundamental freedoms," which allegedly do not permit Muslim children to be denied their right to an Islamic upbringing. Hague Convention, arts. 13(b) & 20. The District Court denied Ahmed's request because it found that the three affirmative defenses specifically set forth in section 1204(c) of the Act are the only ones available to a defendant facing an IPKCA prosecution:

(c) It shall be an affirmative defense under this section that—

(1) the defendant acted within the provisions of a valid court order granting the defendant legal custody or visitation rights and that order was obtained pursuant to the Uniform Child Custody Jurisdiction Act and was in effect at the time of the offense;

(2) the defendant was fleeing an incidence or pattern of domestic violence;

(3) the defendant had physical custody of the child pursuant to a court order granting legal custody or visitation rights and failed to return the child as a result of circumstances beyond the defendant's control, and the defendant notified or made reasonable attempts to notify the other parent or lawful custodian of the child of such circumstances within 24 hours after the visitation period had expired and returned the child as soon as possible.

18 U.S.C. § 1204(c). Since Ahmed did not qualify under any of these subsections, the Court ruled that he could not argue that he was justified in removing and retaining the children because, among other things, Mona was a poor parent or because Egyptian human rights laws protected the right of Islamic children to a proper religious education.

. . .

The Hague Convention, which was drafted in 1980 and, as of May 1995, had been ratified by forty-one nations, was adopted in order "to protect children internationally from the harmful effects of their wrongful removal or retention and to establish procedures to ensure their prompt return to the State of their habitual residence, as well as to secure protection for rights of access." Hague Convention, preamble. It created a previously unavailable civil remedy for the return of abducted children, whereby the left-behind parent can request the designated "Central Authority" of the state in which the abducted child is retained to locate the child, institute proceedings to effect its return, assist in administrative technicalities, and generally aid in the amicable resolution of the kidnapping situation.

. . .

Because the Convention does not apply when children habitually resident in the United States (and who are often American citizens) are abducted from this country and retained in a non-contracting country, the perception arose that something was needed to deter parents from removing and retaining their children in these "safe haven" countries, and thus to close the gap left open by the unfortunate fact that few countries have signed on to the Convention. As the IPKCA's legislative history shows, it was against this backdrop that the Act was enacted:

> There is an international civil mechanism relating to these cases, the Hague Convention ..., for which Congress passed implementing legislation in 1988. As a result of this convention, the signatories will recognize the custody decrees of other signatories, thereby facilitating the return of abducted children. *However, most countries are not signatories to the Convention, thus leaving individual countries to take whatever legal unilateral action they can to obtain the return of abducted children.*
>
> *Creating a federal felony offense responds to these problems....*

House Report at 3, 1993 U.S.C.C.A.N. at 2421 (emphasis added). Nonetheless, Congress continued to believe that the civil mechanism of the Hague Convention, when available, was the preferred route for resolving the complex and difficult problems surrounding international child abductions. It thus provided a "Sense of Congress" resolution to accompany the Act:

> It is the sense of the Congress that, inasmuch as use of the procedures under the Hague Convention ... has resulted in the return of many children, *those procedures, in circumstances in which they are applicable, should be the option of first choice* for a parent who seeks the return of a child who has been removed from the parent.

Pub. L. No. 103–173, § 2(b), 107 Stat. 1998 (1993) (emphasis added).... In that spirit, section 1204(d) of the IPKCA provides that the Act "does not detract from the Hague Convention." 18 U.S.C. § 1204(d).

Construing the IPKCA against this background, we conclude that rejecting Hague Convention defenses in Ahmed's prosecution does not "detract from" the Convention. In the first place, Egypt, the country to which the Amer children have been removed and in which they are currently being retained, is not a signatory to the Convention. Second, because the civil mechanism of the Convention is therefore unavailable to Mona to effect the return of her children, the United States' criminal prosecution of Ahmed for the abduction and retention of the children under the IPKCA cannot in any way "detract from" the Hague Convention within the meaning of section 1204(d), and, indeed, perfectly fulfills the "enforcement-gap-closing" function for which the IPKCA was partially enacted. Although it might be a close question whether a defendant should be permitted to raise Hague Convention defenses when, for instance, there is a parallel or ongoing civil proceeding under the Convention and its implementing legislation, we do not need to decide that question in this case. The District Court acted properly in restricting Ahmed to the three available affirmative defenses found in section 1204(c) of the Act.

Ahmed next objects to the District Court's imposition of the following special condition of supervised release: "[T]he defendant [must] effect the return of the children to the United States to Mona Amer." He contends that (a) the District Court exceeded its authority under the Sentencing Guidelines provisions concerning appropriate conditions of supervised release, (b) this condition is inconsistent with the Sentencing Commission's intent that the abducting parent not be punished for the length or duration of his retention of the children, (c) re-imprisonment following a violation of the condition would constitute double jeopardy, (d) the condition is impossible to meet, and (e) the condition violates the Egyptian court order granting Ahmed custody over the children. We discuss each objection in turn.

(a) *Guidelines limitations.* Ahmed contends that the "return" condition exceeds the sentencing court's authority under 18 U.S.C. § 3583 and U.S.S.G. § 5D1.3(b). Although sentencing courts have "broad discretion to tailor conditions of supervised release to the goals and purposes outlined in § 5D1.3(b)," this provision does not provide sentencing courts with "untrammelled discretion" in this regard. Specifically, section 5D1.3(b) provides:

> The court may impose other conditions of supervised release, to the extent that such conditions are reasonably related to (1) the nature and circumstances of the offense and the history and characteristics of the defendant, and (2) the need for the sentence imposed to afford adequate deterrence to criminal conduct, to protect the public from further crimes of the defendant, and to provide the defendant with needed educational or vocational training, medical care, or other correctional treatment in the most effective manner.

This Circuit has ruled that "despite the continuous use of the ... conjunctive 'and' in § 5D1.3(b), taking into account the authorizing statutes, a condition may be imposed if it is reasonably related to any one or more of the specified factors."

The "return" condition is obviously closely related to "the nature and circumstances of the offense" of child abduction and "the history and characteristics" of Ahmed. Indeed, it is difficult to imagine a condition more closely tailored to the crime and the criminal in question than this one. Moreover, the requirement that Ahmed return the children serves the goal of general deterrence. As the District Court put it,

> It seems that often in cases such as this, a vindictive parent may be willing to possibly face a modest prison term in order to keep the children from the spouse. But if the parent recognizes that the Court has a legal mechanism to additionally order the return of the children, then recognizing that may well serve as an additional deterrent.

The condition also serves the function of specific deterrence. It deters Ahmed both from committing the offense of the unlawful retention of the children in Egypt after his release from prison, and from attempting to kidnap his children again after they have been returned to the United States.

. . .

The judgment of the District Court is affirmed.

3. CHANGE OF CUSTODY

Doe v. Doe

Supreme Court of Idaho, 2010.
239 P.3d 774.

■ EISMANN, CHIEF JUSTICE.

This is an appeal from an order modifying the custody provisions in a divorce decree on the ground that Mother was engaging in a pattern of dysfunctional behavior showing that she was completely irrational with regard to sharing custody of their child with Father and that Mother's behavior was negatively impacting the child's relationship with Father. We affirm the order of the magistrate court.

. . .

John Doe I (Father) and Jane Doe I (Mother) were married on August 30, 2003, but they separated about four months later. They have a son who was born in March of 2004. On November 5, 2004, Father filed for divorce, and the divorce decree was entered on September 9, 2005. The parties were granted joint legal and physical custody of their son, with Mother being granted primary physical custody. Father was to have "the right to actual physical custody of said child at such times and in such a way as to assure said child a frequent and continuing contact with both parties, in order that each of said parties might foster and preserve the parent-child relationship."

On June 27, 2007, Father filed a motion to modify the decree to grant him sole legal custody and primary physical custody of the parties' son on the ground that Mother had engaged in a pattern of denying him access to the child. The motion was tried during six days from August 27 to December 12, 2008. After post-trial briefing by the parties, on February 13, 2009, the Magistrate entered findings of fact and an order granting Father's motion.

Based upon Mother's course of conduct since the divorce, the magistrate found: "It must be said that she is completely irrational on the subject of sharing this child with his father. She seems strangely unaware of the inconvenience and difficulty which her actions cause to others, and of the damage which these behaviors can do to her child." Noting that Mother continued attempting to deny Father access to their son while the motion to amend the decree was pending, even up to a week or two before the trial started, the magistrate wrote that he "is not persuaded that [Mother] understands her dysfunctional role in these problems; or has, at present, the maturity to change it." The magistrate concluded that the best chance for the parties' son to be raised by mature adults was for Father to have primary physical custody. Father had remarried in April 2006.

After denying Mother's motion for reconsideration, the court entered an order on April 16, 2009, modifying the divorce decree by granting Father sole legal custody and primary physical custody of the parties' son. The order also set forth the specific times that Mother would have physical custody. Mother requested permission to appeal directly to this Court, and we granted that motion. She then timely filed a notice of appeal.

. . .

"Once a custodial order is entered, the party seeking to modify it must first demonstrate that a material and substantial change of circumstances has occurred since the entry of the last custodial order." *Brownson v. Allen,* 995 P.2d 830, 832–33 (Idaho 2000). The trial court must base its decision regarding custody on the best interests of the child. IDAHO CODE ANN. § 32–717(1); *King v. King,* 50 P.3d 453, 459–60 (Idaho 2002). "[T]he determination of whether to modify child custody is left to the sound discretion of the trial court, and this Court will not attempt to substitute its judgment and discretion for that of the trial court except in cases where the record reflects a clear abuse of discretion." *Levin v. Levin,* 836 P.2d 529, 532 (Idaho 1992).

. . .

Mother characterizes the decision changing custody as merely punishing her because the parties could not get along. In making that argument, she quotes from *Kalousek v. Kalousek*, 293 P.2d 953, 957 (Idaho 1956), wherein we stated: "Custody of children in divorce cases must always be determined upon the basis of the welfare of the children. It cannot be used as a means of punishment or reward of either parent." Mother contends, "The yardstick for determining custody is, and should be, the welfare and best interests of the child. Once [sic] looks in vain in this record for any substantial evidence [the child's] welfare is being directly and systematically harmed by either of these parents and their squabbling."

In *Kalousek*, the trial court changed custody of the parties' twelve-year-old daughter from the mother to the father because the mother, who lived in Utah, had failed to deliver the child to the father in Idaho for his three-month summer visitation. The trial court found that mother had done so for the purpose of alienating the child's affections for her father. During the hearing on the motion to change custody, the child testified that she did not want to live with her father. This Court held that mother's conduct in that case did not warrant transferring custody to the father because there was no showing that the child's welfare was adversely affected by mother's conduct. *Id.*

. . .

In 1980, the [Idaho] legislature amended and renumbered the [child custody] statute so that it provided as follows, "In an action for divorce the court may, before and after judgment, give such direction for the custody, care and education of the children of the marriage as may seem necessary or proper in the best interests of the children. . . ." *Id.* Although the statute has since been amended, it still provides that the custody determination, including any modification, shall be "as may seem necessary or proper in the best interests of the children." Idaho Code Ann. § 32–717(1).

Thus, the issue is whether there is substantial and competent evidence to support the magistrate's conclusion that changing physical custody was in the child's best interests. In this case, there was evidence that Mother's conduct was directly affecting the child's relationship with Father. . . .

Shortly after their son was born, Father would call to arrange times with Mother when he could visit their son. When he would arrive for the scheduled visitation, Mother and their son would be gone. Father then tried dropping by unannounced for visitations, but that understandably annoyed Mother and her parents, with whom she was living.

Father filed for divorce, and the parties agreed to a child custody arrangement, with the assistance of a clinical social worker. The times that Father was to have physical custody were not specified, but were to be determined by agreement with Mother. Father started having physical custody on Saturdays, and then it expanded to Saturdays and Sundays, but not overnight. When their son reached age two and one-half, Father had visitation every other weekend, including overnight on Saturday. Mother would bring their son to Father's residence in Twin Falls on Friday evenings, and Father would return the child to Mother's residence near Burley on Sunday. Although Father was generally able to exercise his visitation rights, Mother engaged in various types of conduct, in their son's presence, that simply amounted to harassment.

Mother's conduct included falsely telling Father that he could not exercise visitation because their son was sick and, at another time, falsely telling Father that she had to take the child to the emergency room after picking him up from Father's house. Once, she told Father that the time for visitation had to be changed because she was getting married and moving across the state. Two days later, she told him that her fiancé had been killed in a car accident. The entire story was false, and at trial she lied about having made those statements, even though they had been recorded by Father. She also called the police, falsely claiming that Father had harassed her and yelled at her when he picked up their son for visitation. Because Father had begun recording some of his contacts with Mother, he was able to show the officer that Mother's allegations were false. When Mother would not allow Father to have their son at a family reunion that included members of Father's family who had come from other states and from Mexico, Father drove some family members past Mother's house so they could at least see the child, who was playing outside. Mother responded by attempting to obtain a domestic violence protection order against Father. Another time, Mother and Father agreed that Father could return their son from visitation at 7:00 p.m. At about 6:00 p.m., she called Father and told him she had changed her mind and demanded that the child be returned immediately. Father agreed to do so, and as he was driving to Mother's residence with the child Mother called the police to report that Father had not returned the child at the time stated in the custody order. After Father remarried, Mother refused several times to drop the child off at Father's home because he was not physically present and Mother refused to leave the child with his stepmother. One of the times, Father was in the bathroom, but Mother would not believe the stepmother when she said that was where Father was. At other times, Father was not yet home from work.

The above incidents are a sample of Mother's behavior. There were also numerous incidents of Father calling to talk with Mother, and her responding by hanging up the telephone or by simply putting it down and walking away. When Mother would have a telephone conversation with Father, she was very argumentative. Many of these incidents occurred in the presence of the parties' son. When Father would try to talk to Mother when she brought their son to Father's house, she would not respond but merely walk away. After driving a ways down the street, she would often telephone Father and begin arguing with him.

The parties stipulated to an order appointing as the court's custodial expert a clinical social worker who had been doing child custody evaluations for about twenty-five years. She submitted a written report and recommendations and was called by Mother as a witness. The custodial expert testified that Mother was demanding, arbitrary, and capricious in front of the parties' son and that he had begun mimicking her. Mother was pulling the child into her drama, and her conduct was "seriously unhealthy" for the child regarding his relationship with Father. In Mother's presence, the child would refer to Father by his first name, rather than by "Daddy," and would not show affection to Father. Once Mother would leave, the child's conduct changed. He wanted Father and stepmother to hold him and became very comfortable. The expert stated that the current relationship was very detrimental to the child and if he remained in Mother's home, he would not grow up feeling like he could love both parents. In her written report, the expert concluded, "[Mother's] behaviors demonstrate she cannot handle the responsibilities of primary custodian as they relate to noninterference with the father's relationship with the child. This is having a detrimental effect on the child." The magistrate did not conclude that Father was faultless or that he handled the situations perfectly, but it found that "the problem clearly lies mostly with [Mother's] immaturity."

The magistrate did not change custody simply because the parties could not get along. There was substantial evidence that Mother's behavior was contrary to the child's best interests. Although the magistrate did not expressly state that the change in custody was in the child's best interests, such a finding is implicit in the magistrate's written decision.... [T]he magistrate began by writing, "In decisions concerning the custody of children, the welfare and best interests of the child is of paramount importance." The magistrate found, "It must be said that [Mother] is completely irrational on the subject of sharing this child with his father. She seems strangely unaware of the inconvenience and difficulty which her actions cause to others, and of the damage which these behaviors can do to her child." The magistrate wrote that "children should be raised by mature adults" and concluded that the child's "best chance for such a parent-child relationship is at present in the home of his father." Finally, the magistrate found that "stability for this child will be promoted by primary residence with his father." The magistrate did not err in concluding that changing physical custody was in the child's best interests.

. . .

We affirm the order of the magistrate court. We award costs, including attorney fees, to respondent.

4. SEPARATION OF VISITATION RIGHTS AND CHILD SUPPORT

Farmer v. Farmer

Court of Appeals of Indiana, Fifth District, 2000.
735 N.E.2d 285.

■ BARNES, JUDGE.

Farmer and his former wife, Susan Farmer a/k/a/ Susan Feliciano, have a thirteen-year-old daughter. Feliciano has custody of the child. On July 1, 1999, the parties appeared on all pending matters, including Feliciano's Petition for Rule to Show Cause for failing to pay child support and Farmer's Petition to Modify Visitation. A few weeks later, the trial court entered a contempt citation and visitation order.

. . .

Farmer contends that portions of the trial court's amended order are erroneous because it intermingles the issues of visitation [and] child support. Specifically, Farmer contends that the trial court abused its discretion by conditioning his visitation rights upon the payment of child support.... Farmer also argues that the trial court abused its discretion because it threatens to revoke his suspended sentence, which was imposed for failing to pay child support, if he does not comply with visitation.

. . .

The problems with the amended order are two-fold. First, the trial court impermissibly conditions Farmer's visitation rights upon the payment of child support. This court has held numerous times that a parent may not interfere with visitation when the non-custodial parent fails to pay support. Similarly, we have held that a parent may not withhold child support payments even though the other parent interferes with visitation rights. The facts of these cases are somewhat distinguishable because they involve situations where one parent withheld child support when the other parent refused to permit visitation or where one parent withheld visitation when the other parent failed to pay support. None of those cases address a situation where the court threatened to terminate visitation rights if a parent did not pay child support. Despite these distinctions, however, the underlying principle espoused by those cases is still applicable to the case before us. Visitation rights and child support are separate issues, not to be commingled. A court cannot condition visitation upon the payment of child support if a custodial parent is not entitled to do so.

In so holding, we do not dispute the trial court's use of discretion in visitation matters and recognize its authority to restrict or terminate visitation rights of a parent under certain circumstances. Indiana Code Section 31–17–4–2 states:

> The court may modify an order granting or denying visitation rights whenever modification would serve the best interests of the child. However, a court shall not restrict a parent's rights unless the court finds that the visitation might endanger the child's physical health or significantly impair the child's emotional development.

Here, the trial court stated in its findings that "in the event that [Farmer] fails to . . . pay all sums required by this Order for current support . . . the Court finds that any further visitation by [Farmer] would endanger the child's physical health or significantly impair the child's emotional development and will vacate its Order with respect to visitation." However, the trial court provides no other findings or rationale to support its conclusion that the failure to pay child support would cause further visitation to endanger the child's physical health or significantly impair her emotional development. Notwithstanding the trial court's statutory authority to restrict or terminate visitation altogether upon a showing that the visitation endangers the child or impairs her emotional development, no such showing was made by the trial court in its amended order. Although we do not condone a non-custodial parent's failure to pay child support, visitation rights cannot be "automatically" terminated as a result of this failure. Consequently, the trial court improperly restricted Farmer's visitation rights by conditioning them upon the continued payment of support without the proper showing with respect to the physical and emotional well-being of the child.

Second, the trial court threatens to revoke Farmer's suspended sentence, which was ordered for failing to pay child support, if he does not continue visitation with his daughter. In particular, the trial court suspended Farmer's 180–day sentence as long as he "diligently schedules and exercises visitation" and "continues to visit with the parties' child without again terminating regular visitation."

We recognize that it is within the discretion of the trial court to hold an individual in contempt for willfully disobeying a court order. We also acknowledge that contempt is available to assist in the enforcement of child support orders and judgments, which is why the trial court held Farmer in contempt here. However, the trial court's amended order goes beyond its original contempt citation for Farmer's failure to pay support and even beyond its threat to revoke his suspended sentence if he fails to make all of his future child support payments. The trial court's threat with respect to Farmer's suspended sentence crosses into the realm of his visitation rights. We find no authority or policy permitting the trial court to make this leap.

Indiana has long recognized that the right of parents to visit their children is a sacred and precious privilege that should be enjoyed by non-custodial parents. Numerous cases have examined the trial court's discretion to find a parent in contempt for failing to comply with visitation orders. In those cases, the parent who failed to comply with the order was interfering with the other parent's ability to exercise visitation rights. In other words, those cases involve one parent's frustration of the other's visitation rights.

Unlike those cases, however, the case before us presents an unusual situation in which we are faced with a trial court's attempt to force a parent to visit a child and threat to imprison him for failing to do so. Although parents clearly have a statutory duty to support their children, no such duty requires them to visit or maintain a relationship with their children if they choose not to do so. The statute governing visitation states, "A parent not granted custody of the child is entitled to reasonable visitation rights...." IND. CODE § 31–17–4–1. As the statute states, visitation is an entitlement to the non-custodial parent, not an obligation. Farmer contends that "If a person chooses not to exercise [his] privilege or entitlement, [he] should not be sanctioned." Although we find it disturbing that a parent would not want to visit his child, we are forced to agree with Farmer's proposition, particularly in this case where the suspended sentence was originally imposed for failing to pay child support. Not only are child support and visitation separate issues that should not be commingled, but we do not believe that a parent should be forced to visit his child under threat of imprisonment.[2]

Although we understand the trial court's attempt to coerce Farmer into complying with the visitation and child support terms set forth in the amended order in an effort to safeguard the well-being of the parties' daughter, we believe it is improper for the trial court to intermingle Farmer's visitation rights with his obligation to pay child support and attorney fees. We reverse the trial court's amended order to the extent it conditions visitation rights and the suspended sentence upon the payment of the attorney fee judgment. We further reverse the amended order to the extent it conditions Farmer's visitation upon his payment of support and to the extent it conditions his suspended sentence on his continued exercise of visitation with his daughter. In all other respects, we affirm the amended order and remand for further proceedings consistent with this opinion.

---

2. We note, however, that Farmer's failure to exercise his visitation may result in the curtailment and ultimately the termination of the visitation to protect the well-being of the child.

CHAPTER 9

PROPERTY, ALIMONY, AND CHILD SUPPORT AWARDS

Marriage encourages interdependency between spouses, not only emotional, but also financial. Spouses commonly combine their labor, income, and assets for mutual use and consumption. As long as a marriage is ongoing, its financial aspects often remain obscured. But they quickly come to the fore at the moment of divorce. Defining what a fair disentanglement of the spouses' financial affairs entails has been a challenging task for courts. This process may involve resolving disputes ranging from property distribution to alimony and child support.

Modern divorce law generally seeks to distribute assets equitably between divorcing spouses and, with the exception of child support, send them on their separate ways without further financial entanglement. Most couples, however, have little or no property available to divide at divorce.[1] This creates a challenge for courts that seek to make equitable economic arrangements at divorce. One response has been to increase the amount of property deemed marital, rather than separate, in order to maximize the assets available for distribution between the parties. In some cases, this has required courts to push the boundaries of property law. Doing so has expanded the types of assets available for distribution, but there are limits on property law's ability to accommodate dependent spouses' claims at divorce.

Most courts, for example, have stopped short of characterizing a spouse's increase in earning capacity as a marital asset, even though the future streams of income generated by such capacity may be the only "asset" available for division. By contrast, courts have typically taken earning capacity into consideration for alimony awards, treating a spouse's ability to pay as one of the primary considerations when the other spouse is in need of alimony. As a practical matter, therefore, awarding alimony is the most common—if inadequate—response to the typical dearth of marital assets available for distribution at divorce. This has led to efforts to formulate a coherent theory of obligation for a practice that has never had one. As the section on alimony discusses, courts awarding alimony rarely have articulated coherent bases for their awards.

In practice, the line between property and alimony awards is often blurred. A court may conclude that a divorcing spouse is entitled to a certain share of assets regardless of future need. This is consistent with the concept of a traditional property interest. The spouse who must provide these assets, however, may be able to do so only over time in the form of periodic payments. In these cases, the entitlement resembles an alimony award.

---

1. After the 2008 financial crisis, many couples were left with nothing more than a mortgage balance larger than their equity to divide between themselves, which seems to have led many to postpone divorce proceedings. *See* Mary Pilon, *Amid Downturn, Divorce and Infidelity Decrease*, WALL ST. J. BLOGS (Aug. 31, 2010, 12:52 PM ET), http://blogs.wsj.com/economics/2010/08/31/amid-downturn-divorce-and-infidelity-decrease/.

Furthermore, courts attempting to do financial justice between the parties may look to both tangible assets and future earnings as sources for accomplishing this objective.

Finally, statutes governing child support, required by the federal government, have imposed greater restraints on the discretion of judges. Although states vary in the theories of obligation that they adopt, each has established guidelines that specify the presumptive amount of child support that must be awarded. Judges must justify any departure from these guidelines.

The steady expansion of marital property categories, the persistence of alimony awards despite the lack of a coherent justification for them, and the increased certainty and collectability of child support payments are reactions to the pressure of the financial losses and risks that result from divorce. In a country where families, rather than the state, are principally responsible for individual welfare, the tendency is to expand and strengthen familial responsibility rather than to let the public internalize the costs. This characteristic of the law has led some commentators to describe family law as a regime of private insurance or private welfare.[2]

As you read the materials in this Chapter, take note of the implicit principles that animate statutes and court decisions dealing with property division, alimony, and child support. Ask yourself if it is possible to formulate a coherent and explicit foundation for each.

A. PROPERTY DIVISION

1. BACKGROUND TO MARITAL PROPERTY REGIMES

As described in Chapter 3, most states have marital property systems derived from common law, while nine states follow principles of community property. The commonly-asserted Spanish influence of community property systems in the United States is indirect. Arizona, California, Nevada, New Mexico, and Texas were part of Mexico until about the middle of the nineteenth century (Texas proclaimed its independence in 1836), which is where the Spanish influence is derived from.[3] Louisiana, by contrast, was mostly influenced by French civil law, while Washington and Idaho seem to have copied their systems from the other community property states. Wisconsin did not adopt its community property system until 1986.[4] Common law and community property systems began to converge in the last part of the twentieth century towards principles of equitable distribution of—usually—marital property.

---

2. *See* Anne L. Alstott, *Private Tragedies? Family Law as Social Insurance*, 4 HARV. L. & POL'Y REV. 3 (2010); Janet Halley, *What Is Family Law?: A Genealogy Part I*, 23 YALE J.L. & HUMAN. 1, 5–6 (2011).

3. Charles Sumner Lobingier, *The Marital Community: Its Origin and Diffusion*, 14 A.B.A. J. 211, 215–17 (1928). It seems that in most of these states there was a period of confusion or even struggle as to the applicability of community property, which was later settled through legislative acts. *See* M. R. Kirkwood, *Historical Background and Objectives of the Law of Community Property in the Pacific Coast States*, 11 WASH. L. REV. & ST. B. J. 1, 3–5 (1936).

4. Kelly M. Cannon, *Beyond the "Black Hole"—A Historical Perspective on Understanding the Non–Legislative History of Washington Community Property Law*, 39 GONZ. L. REV. 7, 10–12 (2004) (with brief history of community property systems in the U.S.).

The main principles of the common law system are derived from the common law of England, where marriage had been a central way in which property changed hands. For males, it was one of the main ways to acquire or retain property and therefore status (as aptly illustrated by the woes of the non-propertied female characters of Jane Austen). Under the principle of coverture, a wife's personal property (with minor exceptions) became the husband's. He also acquired the right to manage her real estate under his estate or freehold *jure uxoris*. This right to manage included the right to rents and profits from her property, as well as the right to place a lien on the property for debts incurred during the marriage. The underlying idea was that as the only one burdened with a legal duty of support, the husband should be able to use the wife's property to sustain the family. When the husband was profligate, however, the system merely provided a windfall for the husband.

This system of separate properties encumbered by the husband's rights under common law was followed by a majority of American states. Beginning in 1839, most common law states adopted Married Women's Property Acts (MWPA), which allowed married women to hold their own property free and clear from any of the husband's traditional interests at common law. But this only protected the property a woman brought into the marriage or acquired during the marriage through her labor outside the home. It did not create any rights to property accumulated during the marriage by her spouse, and therefore all that a court needed to do upon divorce was return property to its owner based on title. The system's harshness was evident by the middle of the twentieth century, as divorce rates increased and more homemakers found themselves divorced, unemployable, and without any title to the assets accumulated during the marriage. Courts began to apply equitable remedies, such as the application of constructive or resulting trusts, in favor of the wife against property titled in the husband's name.

Equitable remedies, however, were only a partial solution. They were mostly applied when there was evidence of an agreement between the spouses about specific property or where the wife's contribution to the husband's material betterment was considered to go above and beyond her standard marital duties. The latter scenario typically encompassed a wife who, in addition to her homemaking duties, had worked on the husband's business or farm. This still left traditional homemakers susceptible to economic dislocation at divorce. Most common law states starting in the 1970s adopted equitable distribution statutes to address this problem. The statutes replaced the patchwork of limited equitable remedies against specific property with a generalized right to have an *equitable portion* of all or most property accumulated during the marriage by either spouse. Equitable distribution statutes borrow principles from the community property system, but apply them only at divorce, which is why equitable distribution in common law states has been described as a system of deferred community property.

Community property systems distinguish between the property that each spouse possessed before marriage and the property that either spouse accumulated during marriage (except by gift or inheritance). The former remains the separate property of the titled spouse, while the latter becomes part of the community, which is split—traditionally in half—between the spouses upon divorce or death. Despite its more egalitarian underlying principles, community property systems were also characterized by gender inequality in the rights of use and management. In practice, they often reached results similar to common law states, at least while the marriage lasted. If the marriage was dissolved by divorce, however, the splitting of the community property provided more protection, especially to homemakers.

The last forty years have been characterized by a convergence of community property and common law principles of divorce towards equitable distribution. Common law states adopted community property law distinctions through equitable distribution statutes that divided marital property upon divorce. At the same time, the majority of community property states moved away from splitting community property equally; instead they require courts to effectuate an equitable distribution of community property (California, Louisiana, and New Mexico still require equal division).

UNIFORM MARRIAGE AND DIVORCE ACT

(1973).

Section 307. Disposition of Property: Alternative A

(a) In a proceeding for dissolution of a marriage, [or] legal separation, . . . the court, without regard to marital misconduct, shall, and in a proceeding for legal separation may, finally equitably apportion between the parties the property and assets belonging to either or both however and whenever acquired, and whether the title thereto is in the name of the husband or wife or both. In making apportionment the court shall consider the duration of the marriage, any prior marriage of either party, any antenuptial agreement of the parties, the age, health, station, occupation, amount and sources of income, vocational skills, employability, estate, liabilities, and needs of each of the parties, custodial provisions, whether the apportionment is in lieu of or in addition to maintenance, and the opportunity of each for future acquisition of capital assets and income. The court shall also consider the contribution or dissipation of each party in the acquisition, preservation, depreciation, or appreciation in value of the respective estates, and as the contribution of a spouse as a homemaker or to the family unit.

. . .

Section 307. Disposition of Property: Alternative B

In a proceeding for dissolution of the marriage, [or] legal separation, . . . the court shall assign each spouse's separate property to that spouse. It also shall divide community property, without regard to marital misconduct, in just proportions after considering all relevant factors including:

(1) contribution of each spouse to acquisition of the marital property, including contribution of a spouse as homemaker;

(2) value of the property set apart to each spouse;

(3) duration of the marriage; and

(4) economic circumstances of each spouse when the division of property is to become effective, including the desirability of awarding the family home or the right to live therein for a reasonable period to the spouse having custody of any children.

COMMENT

Alternative A, which is the alternative recommended generally for adoption, proceeds upon the principle that all the property of the spouses, however acquired, should be regarded as assets of the married couple, available for distribution among them, upon consideration of the various factors enumerated in subsection (a)....

. . .

Alternative B was included because a number of Commissioners from community property states represented that their jurisdictions would not wish to substitute, for their own systems, the great hotchpot of assets created by Alternative A, preferring to adhere to the distinction between community property and separate property, and providing for the distribution of that property alone....

NOTES

1. Alternative B of the Uniform Marriage and Divorce Act (UMDA) § 307 was adopted to reflect the practice in community property states of distinguishing between individual and marital property at divorce. The majority of common law states today also follow this practice. States that follow some version of Alternative A are known as "kitchen sink" or "hotchpot" systems, because they include every piece held by either spouse at the time of divorce in the "pot" to be distributed. At the distribution stage, however, "hotchpot" systems also make distinctions based on how and when a piece of property was acquired, in order to distribute equitably between the spouses on the basis of contribution. Finally, there are some states that follow a mixed system. They distinguish between marital and separate property as in Alternative B, but allow the distribution of separate property at divorce if equity so requires.

2. The community property system is said to have originated with the customs of the Germanic tribes that invaded Europe in the Middle Ages. A universal community property system that includes all of the spouses' assets—much like the "hotchpot"—and which operates from the moment of marriage rather than at the moment of divorce is currently only in effect in the Netherlands, even though spouses can now contract out of these default rules. *See* Katharina Boele-Woelki et al., Comm'n on European Family Law, National Report: Netherlands (2008), *available at* http://www.ceflonline.net/Reports/pdf3/Netherlands.pdf. Some countries in continental Europe follow a community of the acquests system (France, Italy, parts of Spain), which resembles a limited version of the community property system of Texas. Many others follow a system of either deferred community property, which is more like the equitable distribution systems in place in the majority of the United States, or separate property coupled with a settlement clause meant to equalize the difference between the spouses' acquisitions during marriage (Germany, Norway, Sweden, Greece). *See* Branka Rešetar, *Matrimonial Property in Europe: A Link Between Sociology and Family Law*, 12.3 Electronic J. of Comp. L. 1 (Dec. 2008), http://www.ejcl.org/123/art123–4.pdf; Walter Pintens, *Europeanisation of Family Law*, *in* Perspectives for the Unification and Harmonisation of Family Law in Europe 3, 9–12 (Katharina Boele–Woelki ed., 2003).

2. The Problem of Characterization in Equitable Distribution

a. WHAT IS *MARITAL* PROPERTY?

American Law Institute, Principles of the Law of Family Dissolution

(2002).

Section 4.03.   Definition of Marital and Separate Property

(1) Property acquired during marriage is marital property, except as otherwise expressly provided in this Chapter.

(2) Inheritances, including bequests and devises, and gifts from third parties, are the separate property of the acquiring spouse even if acquired during marriage.

(3) Property received in exchange for separate property is separate property even if acquired during marriage.

. . .

(6) Property acquired during a relationship between the spouses that immediately preceded their marriage, and which was a domestic-partner relationship as defined by § 6.03, is treated as if it were acquired during the marriage.

NOTES

1. The American Law Institute (ALI) is an independent organization comprised of lawyers, judges, and law professors. It publishes Restatements of the Law, Model Statutes, and Principles, whose purpose is sometimes to clarify and restate the law and sometimes to promote law reform. Its 2002 PRINCIPLES OF THE LAW OF FAMILY DISSOLUTION were the ALI's first intervention in the field of family law. The PRINCIPLES have engendered a lot of academic debate but have had little influence on legislatures or courts. *See* Michael R. Clisham & Robin Fretwell Wilson, *American Law Institute's Principles of the Law of Family Dissolution, Eight Years After Adoption: Guiding Principles or Obligatory Footnote?*, 42 FAM. L.Q. 573, 576 (2008). For further discussion of the ALI *see supra* Chapter 8, Section E.4.

2. Section 4.03 of the PRINCIPLES is typical of the definitions commonly found in equitable distribution statutes. Most equitable distribution states use this temporal criterion to define marital property, and also commonly exclude inheritances and gifts to either spouse from the marital "pot."

3. What if one of the spouses gives a gift to the other spouse? Should it be considered marital property? What if relatives give a gift jointly to both spouses? What if one spouse changes the title of a house she owned before marriage to include her husband as joint tenant? Should that be considered a gift? Should it be considered a gift to the husband's separate estate or to the marital estate?

Definitions of marital property in equitable distribution states commonly include the temporal criterion cited above as the starting point. When a spouse's separate property appreciates in value over the course of the marriage, however, courts need to decide whether to characterize any increase in value as separate or as marital. A common practice drawn from the experience of community property states is to distinguish between *active* and *passive* increases. An active increase is any increase in value of separate property that is attributable either to the expenditure of marital capital (capital acquired by either or both spouses during marriage) or to marital labor (labor performed by either or both spouses during marriage). A passive increase is any increase attributable to market forces or the efforts of third parties outside the marriage. *See, e.g. Rogers v. Rogers*, 405 S.E.2d 235 (W. Va. 1991). An active increase in the value of separate property is treated as marital property, while a passive increase is treated as separate. The case that follows illustrates the adoption of this principle by an equitable distribution state.

Innerbichler v. Innerbichler

Court of Special Appeals of Maryland, 2000.
132 Md. App. 207, 752 A.2d 291.

■ HOLLANDER, JUDGE.

This appeal arises from the dissolution of the marriage of Nicholas R. Innerbichler, appellant, and Carole Jean Innerbichler, appellee. After more than fourteen years of marriage, the parties were granted a divorce by the Circuit Court for Prince George's County, pursuant to an order dated July 27, 1998, and modified on January 13, 1999. Two aspects of the court's orders are at the heart of this appeal: 1) the monetary award to appellee, in the amount of $2,581,864.75, which was based, in part, on the court's determination that the appreciation in value of appellant's 51% ownership interest in Technical and Management Services Corporation ("TAMSCO") constituted marital property; and 2) the court's award to appellee of monthly alimony of $8000.00 for five years, followed by indefinite monthly alimony of $6,000.00.

Appellant noted a timely appeal to this Court, posing several questions for our consideration, which we have rephrased slightly:

I. Did the trial court err in granting the monetary award to appellee by:

A. Improperly finding that the increase in value in TAMSCO was marital property?

. . .

The parties were married on January 21, 1984, when Mr. Innerbichler (the "Husband") was 41 years old and appellee (the "Wife") was 33. Although appellant had been married twice before, it was appellee's first marriage. The parties have one child, Michelle Nicole, who was born on May 1, 1986. Appellant also has three adult children from prior marriages.

In 1995, after eleven years of marriage, the Husband moved out of the marital home. On September 12, 1995, he filed a Complaint for Limited Divorce, and the Wife filed a countersuit, seeking an absolute divorce on the ground of adultery. Her suit was later amended in court to include a two year separation as an additional ground for divorce.

. . .

At the time of trial, appellant was 55 years old and resided with his paramour in a home that he purchased for about $600,000.00 and financed with a mortgage and a loan from his business. Appellee was a 47–year–old high school graduate who had completed one semester of college. The trial culminated in a divorce based on the parties' separation of two years. . . .

In October 1982, more than one year prior to the parties' marriage, appellant co-founded TAMSCO with his friend and colleague, William Bilawa. At the time, appellant was employed by Lockheed Corporation, and remained employed there until June 1983; in the evenings, appellant worked for TAMSCO. The company provides technical and management services to agencies of the federal government and to the private sector in various disciplines, including program management, integrated logistics support, software development, and data management. At the relevant time, appellant owned 51% of TAMSCO and Bilawa owned a 49% interest in the company.

When TAMSCO was founded, appellant was married to Barbara Innerbichler ("Barbara"). In 1983, as part of his divorce settlement with Barbara, appellant claimed that he waived his interest in the home that they occupied, allegedly worth about $300,000.00, in exchange for Barbara's agreement to waive her claim to TAMSCO, which appellant contends was worth at least as much as the home.

In June 1983, about six months before appellant's marriage to appellee, appellant submitted an application on behalf of TAMSCO to the United States Small Business Administration ("SBA") to obtain "8(a) certification." According to appellant, who is an Hispanic American, the "8(a) program" was established during the Nixon years to assist small businesses owned and controlled by socially and economically disadvantaged persons. . . .

Appellee insists that TAMSCO was in its "embryonic stages" when the parties were first married. Ample evidence was presented at trial showing that TAMSCO was in its fledgling stage of development at the time of the marriage.

. . .

On April 14, 1984, some 83 days after the parties' marriage, TAMSCO obtained the desired 8(a) certification. It is undisputed that the 8(a) program enabled TAMSCO to obtain lucrative sole source government contracts, the first of which was awarded to TAMSCO in September 1984. TAMSCO grew rapidly after the award of the 8(a) certification. For fiscal year 1983, the company reported approximately $52,000.00 in revenues, and $188,000.00 in revenues for fiscal year 1984. By the end of fiscal year 1992, TAMSCO had been awarded contracts totaling $356,439,719. For 1995, TAMSCO generated revenues of $46 million and employed over 500 people. In 1996, TAMSCO earned $47,000,000.00 in revenues, followed by $51,000,000.00 for fiscal year 1997.

From 1984 through 1989, approximately 85% of TAMSCO's work related to 8(a) contracts, and from 1989 until 1993, approximately 75% of TAMSCO's work derived from those contracts. When TAMSCO left the SBA's 8(a) program in 1993, it had already received approximately $356,000,000.00 in 8(a) revenue. By the time of the divorce trial, however, TAMSCO was no longer eligible to participate in the SBA's 8(a) program, although it still had residual 8(a) business. According to appellant, because TAMSCO could no longer "pursue contracts in a non-competitive market-place," its business position had declined. Nevertheless, at the time of trial, appellant was earning in excess of $650,000.00 in annual salary.

Although appellant concedes that most of TAMSCO's lucrative contracts were obtained and performed after his marriage to appellee, he maintains that neither TAMSCO nor the post-marriage appreciation in the company's value constituted marital property. He argues that the company was created before the marriage and its success was directly linked to an Army contract awarded prior to the marriage. Appellant points out that, in October 1993, while the 8(a) application was still pending, TAMSCO was notified that it had "won" a non–8(a) contract with the Army, worth in excess of one million dollars. Thus, he claims that over 97% of TAMSCO's government contracts were "traceable to contracts won at the company's inception and prior to the marriage." . . . Although the Army contract was "awarded" on January 1, 1984, shortly before the parties' marriage, performance of the Army contract did not begin until the summer of 1984, after the parties were married.

. . .

On July 27, 1998, the court . . . granted a monetary award to the Wife in the amount of $2,880,000.00 [in addition to alimony].

The monetary award was based largely on the court's determination as to TAMSCO's value. The court expressly indicated that it found the testimony of the Wife's expert as to TAMSCO's value "more persuasive" than appellant's expert. Based on the opinion of the Wife's expert, the court concluded that TAMSCO had a fair market value of $8.3 million. The court also determined that appellant's 51% ownership interest in TAMSCO was worth $4,233,000.00, and that appellant's pre-marital interest in TAMSCO was worth $153,000.00.

Additionally, the court found that the post-marriage "increase in value of TAMSCO is marital," and that "the Husband's share (51%) of the increased value of TAMSCO stock is marital," because TAMSCO's "success is attributable to a large degree to the work efforts of the Husband throughout the marriage." The court explained: "He was the president of the company and was more responsible for the mission and rating of TAMSCO than his partner. He made the ultimate decisions on the contracts and was actively involved in making presentations to the early contracting parties which generated the value of TAMSCO." The judge also relied on an informal action of TAMSCO's Board of Directors in July 1988, which acknowledged that "without [appellant] and his personal efforts, the contracts, the past corporate growth and financial stability would not have been realized by the corporation." Further, the court observed that TAMSCO earned less than $60,000.00 before the marriage, and that most of the "contracts which formed the basis of TAMSCO's value were entered into after the marriage."

. . .

Following post-trial motions, the court entered a revised order on January 28, 1999, in which it concluded that the total marital value of TAMSCO was $4,080,000.00. Further, it determined that the total value of marital assets, including TAMSCO, equaled $5,576,280.50. Exclusive of TAMSCO, the court found that appellee had $74,653.00 in property titled to her, appellant had property worth $1,367,991.50 titled to him, and the parties had $53,636.00 in joint property. After awarding appellee $104,804.50 as her share of appellant's pension, the court recalculated the monetary award and reduced it to $2,581,864.75. The court then ordered appellant to make full payment of that sum over a five year period, without interest. Of that sum, $430,310.79 was due by July 27, 1999.

. . .

Title 8 of the Family Law Article of the Maryland Code provides for the equitable distribution of marital property. "'Marital Property' means the property, however titled, acquired by 1 or both parties during the marriage." F.L. § 8–201(e)(1). Pursuant to F.L. § 8–201(e)(3), marital property does not include property that is:

> (i) acquired before the marriage;

> (ii) acquired by inheritance or gift from a third party;

> (iii) excluded by valid agreement; or

> (iv) directly traceable to any of these sources.

Property that is initially non-marital can become marital, however. Moreover, the party who asserts a marital interest in property bears the burden of producing evidence as to the identity of the property. Conversely, "[t]he party seeking to demonstrate that particular property acquired during the marriage is nonmarital must trace the property to a nonmarital source."

If a property interest cannot be traced to a nonmarital source, it is considered marital property.

. . .

When a party petitions for a monetary award, the trial court must first follow a three-step procedure. First, for each disputed item of property, the court must determine whether it is marital or nonmarital. Second, the court must determine the value of all marital property. Third, the court must decide if the division of marital property according to title will be unfair; if so, the court *may* make a monetary award to rectify any inequity "created by the way in which property acquired during marriage happened to be titled." In doing so, the court must consider the statutory factors contained in F.L. § 8–205(b). [These are:]

. . .

(1) the contributions, monetary and nonmonetary, of each party to the well-being of the family;

(2) the value of all property interests of each party;

(3) the economic circumstances of each party at the time the award is to be made;

(4) the circumstances that contributed to the estrangement of the parties;

(5) the duration of the marriage;

(6) the age of each party;

(7) the physical and mental condition of each party;

(8) how and when specific marital property or interest in the pension, retirement, profit sharing, or deferred compensation plan, was acquired, including the effort expended by each party in accumulating the marital property or the interest in the pension, retirement, profit sharing, or deferred compensation plan, or both;

(9) the contribution by either party of property described in § 8–201(e)(3) of this subtitle to the acquisition of real property held by the parties as tenants by the entirety;

(10) any award of alimony and any award or other provision that the court has made with respect to family use personal property or the family home; and

(11) any other factor that the court considers necessary or appropriate to consider in order to arrive at a fair and equitable monetary award or transfer of an interest in the pension, retirement, profit sharing, or deferred compensation plan, or both.

. . .

As we previously observed, appellant contends that the court erred in finding that TAMSCO constituted marital property. He argues that "TAMSCO was brought into the marriage as an established, flourishing nonmarital asset. By the time the parties married, the ground work had already been laid to make TAMSCO a success." In addition, the Husband quarrels with the court's decision to attribute the appreciation of TAMSCO solely to his efforts. He maintains that TAMSCO's growth was the result of the efforts of many people as well as several other factors, such as the thriving defense industry. In his view, "this is a classic case of being in the right place at the right time." Moreover, appellant complains that the court should not have treated 51% of the appreciation as marital property, merely because he owned 51% of the company. Appellant asserts that the court was required to ascertain the precise portion of TAMSCO's increase in value for which appellant was responsible, and that only the portion attributable to his work efforts could qualify as marital property.

The court was not clearly erroneous in rejecting appellant's claim that TAMSCO was entirely non-marital property. Although it is undisputed that TAMSCO was created before the marriage, the evidence that we summarized earlier supported the court's conclusion that TAMSCO's value soared after the marriage. For example, when TAMSCO submitted its application for SBA 8(a) certification in June 1983, it had only completed a $13,000.00 contract and a $6,000.00 contract, and a $131,000.00 contract was in progress. Moreover, TAMSCO owned little in the way of tangible property. At the time of the marriage, the business had only two full-time employees and operated from Bilawa's kitchen. TAMSCO received its 8(a) certification after the marriage, and all of the 8(a) contracts were performed during the marriage. By the time TAMSCO graduated from the SBA Section 8(a) program in 1993, it had received over $356,000,000.00 in Section 8(a) revenue, placing it among the top 10 such firms nationally.

Appellant also challenges the court's decision to treat all of the appreciation as marital property. He relies on the court's own acknowledgment that appellant was merely responsible, "to a large degree" (and thus not entirely), for the increased value. On the other hand, appellant also seems to suggest that the court miscalculated the monetary award, because it did not find that all of the appreciation was marital property.

We are of the view that the court found that all of TAMSCO's appreciation constituted marital property, and it attributed all of the appreciation to appellant's work efforts. After comparing the financial status of TAMSCO before and after the marriage, the court focused on the extent of appellant's role in the corporation and his work efforts on behalf of TAMSCO, concluding that "*the increase* in value of TAMSCO is marital. . . ." (Emphasis added). Significantly, the court did not qualify its statement by saying words to the effect that *some* of the increase or *part* of the increase in value is marital. The common sense construction of the court's pronouncement is that it determined that *all* of the appreciation was marital.

Moreover, notwithstanding the court's statement that appellant was responsible "to a large degree" for TAMSCO's success, we are satisfied that the court did not err, on the record before it, when it attributed all of the appreciation to appellant's efforts for purposes of calculating the monetary award. It follows that the court did not err by failing to assign a specific percentage of responsibility to appellant in achieving that corporate growth.

. . .

. . . [W]e pause to question whether the court truly could have ascertained, with either genuine accuracy, mathematical certainty, or scientific precision, the exact extent to which appellant's efforts led to TAMSCO's success. Although we acknowledge that it is rare for one person singularly to wear all hats in the operation of a complex, technical, multi-million dollar business enterprise such as TAMSCO, one person can function in a capacity critical to a company's growth and development. Here, the court was clearly satisfied from the evidence that appellant was the driving force in TAMSCO's huge financial growth. It is equally apparent that, because of appellant's vital and instrumental role in TAMSCO's success, the court did not assign to appellant an arbitrary percentage of responsibility for the increased corporate value.

In determining the marital or non-marital character of disputed property that has its origins as non-marital property, the cases distinguish between passive ownership and increases in value resulting from the active efforts of the owner-spouse. In *Mount v. Mount*, 59 Md. App. 538, 549–50, 476 A.2d 1175 (1984), we recognized that there are various ways in which property that increases in value may become marital. We said:

> Property can produce other property in many different ways. In some instances, it may require active intervention and management by the owner or some assistance by the owner's spouse; in other instances, non-marital property can accrete or produce income without any effort at all on the part of the owner or the owner's spouse. In either case, all, some, or none of the income or accretion generated by or from the initial property may be used for family purposes. . . .

> . . .

. . . [W]e are satisfied that the record clearly supports the court's decision to treat all of TAMSCO's appreciation as marital; TAMSCO's value soared after the marriage, while the Husband was at the helm and shepherded TAMSCO's growth. Despite the Husband's assertion that the corporate success resulted from the efforts of others and from a variety of factors not related to his skills, such as "the expanding defense industry during the Reagan administration . . . ," the court, as fact-finder, was not compelled to accept appellant's version of events.

Although the trial court attributed the entire appreciation to appellant's efforts, appellant only owned 51% of TAMSCO. Therefore, the court properly concluded that only 51% of that appreciation, corresponding to appellant's ownership interest, constituted marital property for purposes of a monetary award. After subtracting the premarital value of TAMSCO ($153,000.00), the court multiplied the value of TAMSCO by 51% to determine the value of appellant's ownership interest in the company. The court then allocated half of that value (i.e., 1/2 of 51% of the appreciation) to the Wife's monetary award. . . .

In this case, the court considered the statutory factors under F.L. § 8–205(b) in fashioning the monetary award. For example, the judge also found that appellant "was responsible for the estrangement of the parties by committing adultery during the marriage and later deserting [appellee]." In addition, the court considered that appellant had "spent large amounts of marital property during the separation on his life style and gambling." Moreover, the court was mindful that appellant had invested a substantial amount of marital funds in SeaMats and TRAMS, even though the court did not include these investments as marital property. Under the circumstances of this case, we perceive neither error nor abuse of discretion by the court in evenly dividing the marital portion of TAMSCO.

NOTES

1. How much of the increase in value of the business did the court characterize as marital? How much did the husband retain as his separate property? The ALI PRINCIPLES propose the following system for apportioning any enhancement in value of separate property, which is based on the practice of several equitable distribution states:

> Section 4.05. Enhancement of Separate Property by Marital Labor
>
> (1) A portion of any increase in the value of separate property is marital property whenever either spouse has devoted substantial time during marriage to the property's management or preservation.
>
> (2) The increase in value of separate property over the course of the marriage is measured by the difference between the market value of the property when acquired, or at the beginning of the marriage, if later, and the market value of the property when sold, or at the end of the marriage, if sooner.
>
> (3) The portion of the increase in value that is marital property under Paragraph (1) is the difference between the actual amount by which the property has increased in value, and the amount by which capital of the same value would have increased over the same time period if invested in assets of relative safety requiring little management.

How does this approach compare with the *Innerbichler* court's solution?

2. The problem of active appreciation has commonly arisen in cases where one spouse owns a pre-marital, separate stock portfolio, whose value appreciates during marriage. Is the hiring of an investment advisor to manage the account enough to constitute active participation? Generally courts have held that it is not, but each of these cases is intensely fact-specific. *See, e.g, Baker v. Baker,* 753 N.W.2d 644, 653 (Minn. 2008) (court rejected the idea that advisor was agent whose efforts should be credited to the spouse, holding that "only the financial and nonfinancial efforts of the spouses themselves are relevant to the assessment of marital effort").

Holman v. Holman

Missouri Court of Appeals, Southern District, Division Two, 2007.
228 S.W.3d 628.

■ PER CURIAM.

Appellant William Hill Holman ("Husband") appeals the trial court's judgment dissolving his marriage to Respondent LaVonne Carol Holman ("Wife")....

. . .

... [T]he record reveals the parties were married on October 20, 1991, and separated on November 4, 2004. There were no children born of the marriage....

. . .

At the time of the parties' marriage, Husband owned a house ("the Farmhouse") on thirty acres, but was not living at that location because his ex-wife resided there. When Husband's former wife vacated the Farmhouse in May of 1992, Husband and Wife began remodeling it. A portion of the proceeds from the sale of [another marital] house were used by the parties to remodel the Farmhouse. Wife testified that when she and Husband took possession of the Farmhouse it "wasn't livable" and they "gutted it." Wife testified the parties spent $90,000.00 remodeling the Farmhouse. She stated the parties took out a loan for the remodeling, the amount of which is not clearly revealed by the record. Wife testified without objection that the Farmhouse was valued at $54,640.00 when the parties began remodeling it shortly after Husband's ex-wife vacated the home. Wife also stated that after the remodeling, the Farmhouse was appraised at the time of trial for

$185,000.00, and she valued the marital interest in the Farmhouse at $130,360.00, being the difference in the value of $54,640.00 prior to remodeling and the value of $185,000.00 after remodeling.

Wife also testified the parties borrowed $75,000.00 to construct a commercial building ("the Commercial Building") on real property ("the Commercial Property") Husband inherited during the course of the marriage when his father passed away in 1997. According to Wife, Husband made all of the payments on the loan for the Commercial Building out of their joint account. She testified ... that at the time Husband inherited the Commercial Property the value of the "bare land" was $30,000.00. Wife also testified the parties spent $62,000.00 on the Commercial Building together with $5,600.00 constructing a parking lot adjacent to it. She stated the parties received rental income from the Commercial Building and that she opened a business in the newly constructed Commercial Building. Wife also related she purchased fixtures for her business with $15,000.00 of her own money and the fixtures were then sold with the business. Wife also testified she placed the money she received from selling the business into her separate account to pay for her "living expenses" and "personal needs."

Wife also stated the Commercial Building and Commercial Property were appraised shortly before trial at $127,000.00. Wife opined that the value of the marital interest in the Commercial Building and Commercial Property was $97,000.00, that is $127,000.00 for the Commercial Property plus the Commercial Building minus $30,000.00 for the "bare land" inherited by Husband.

. . .

At the close of all the evidence, the trial court found ... Wife had acquired a marital interest "in real property titled in [Husband's] name;" found Wife's nonmarital property to be valued at $89,223.00 and valued Husband's nonmarital property at $624,799.00; and found there was an unequal division of marital property, such that Wife was entitled to a judgment against Husband in the amount of $203,832.67 to equalize the distribution of marital property. This appeal by Husband followed.

. . .

In his first point relied on Husband asserts ... the Commercial Property and Commercial Building should have been deemed separate property because the Commercial Property was inherited by Husband from his father; all of the funds used to improve the Commercial Property and construct the Commercial Building "came from Husband's separate funds;" and "[w]hile Wife did invest $15,000.00 in buying fixtures for her business that was located in the [C]ommercial [B]uilding, she recovered these funds when she later sold the fixtures along with her business."

In his second point on appeal, Husband asserts the trial court erred in finding that the value of the Commercial Property and Commercial Building, set in at $97,000.00 by the trial court, was marital property. He maintains such a finding by the trial court was in error because the Commercial Property was inherited by him and never titled in Wife's name; the value of the Commercial Property at the time of his inheritance was $62,000.00; and the fair market value of the property after the construction of the Commercial Building was $127,000.00, which was only an increase in value of $65,000.00.

Husband also maintains, as previously set out, that Wife's contribution to the construction of the Commercial Building was, if anything, only $15,000.00, "while the remaining cost was financed by a $75,000.00 loan paid exclusively from the rental income from the property, and therefore under the "source of funds rule" the marital portion of the $65,000.00 increase in value ... was only 16.7 [percent] of the increase or $10,855.00."

... "Generally, any property acquired by a spouse prior to marriage is that spouse's separate property upon dissolution of the marriage." "However, any 'increase in the value of separate property can constitute marital property if marital assets or labor contributed to acquiring that increase.' " ... "In determining if property is marital or separate, courts follow the 'source of funds rule.' " As explained in *In re Marriage of Herr*, 705 S.W.2d 619, 623–24 (Mo.App. 1986):

> under the source of funds rule, when property is acquired by an expenditure of both nonmarital and marital property, the property is characterized as part nonmarital and part marital. Thus, a spouse contributing nonmarital property is entitled to an interest in the property in the ratio of the nonmarital investment to the total nonmarital and marital investment in the property. The remaining property is characterized as marital and its value is subject to equitable distribution. Thus the spouse who contributed nonmarital funds, and the marital unit that contributed marital funds each receive a proportional and fair return on their investment.

Herr, 705 S.W.2d at 625, set forth the formula to be used as:

$$\frac{\text{nonmarital}}{\text{property}} = \frac{\text{nonmarital contribution}}{\text{total contribution}} \quad \text{x} \quad \text{equity}$$

$$\frac{\text{marital}}{\text{property}} = \frac{\text{marital contribution}}{\text{total contribution}} \quad \text{x} \quad \text{equity}$$

Returning to the instant case, both parties agree the real property upon which the Commercial Building was constructed was inherited by Husband from his father and, as such, is clearly Husband's separate property. At issue is the *increase in value* to the Commercial Property and how that increase should be distributed. In this connection, we observe that "[t]he source of funds rule does not cause the entire increase in value of separate property accruing during a marriage to be marital property irrespective of the source of that increase."

Wife acknowledges the correctness of Husband's assertions that, given the circumstances of this case, the mere fact that the loan for the construction of the Commercial Building was taken out in both of their names does not instantly convert it to marital property. Rather, Wife's assertion is that it is not the loan which created a marital interest but "the construction and payment of the loan with income generated during the marriage which established a marital interest in the property." In this connection she is correct. ...

Wife testified the Commercial Property upon which the Commercial Building was constructed was worth $30,000.00 at the time it was inherited by Husband in 1997 when Husband's father died; that the parties took out a $75,000.00 loan to construct the Commercial Building; and the entirety of the Commercial Building and Commercial Property was valued prior to trial at $127,000.00. She testified the loan was paid from the rental income received from the lease of space in the Commercial Building, including rental income paid by her for leasing space for her own business. It is clear that the trial court accepted the evidence tendered by Wife relating to the Commercial Building and Commercial Property. "An appellate court assumes a trial court believed the testimony consistent with its judgment." *In re Marriage of Heirigs*, 34 S.W.3d 835, 841 (Mo.App.2000).

While the trial court was correct in its determination that the value of the "bare land" of the Commercial Property at the time of inheritance by Husband was $30,000.00 and that the undisputed value of the Commercial Property and Commercial Building at the time of trial was $127,000.00, it erred in its determination that the value of the "marital portion" subject to division between the parties was $97,000.00. This is because "a spouse contributing nonmarital property is entitled to an interest in the property in the ratio of the nonmarital investment to the total nonmarital and marital investment in the property." *Brooks*, 911 S.W.2d at 633.

Applying the formula set out in *Brooks*, 911 S.W.2d at 633, and *Herr*, 705 S.W.2d at 625, we make the following calculations in determining the correct value of Husband's "nonmarital property" and the value of the "marital property" pursuant to the source of funds rule, as follows:

$$\text{nonmarital property} = \frac{\$30,000 \text{ (nonmarital)}}{\$30,000 + \$75,000 \text{ (marital)} = \$105,000 \text{ (total)}} \times \$127,000 \text{ equity}$$

$$\text{marital property} = \frac{\$75,000 \text{ (marital)}}{\$30,000 \text{ (nonmarital)} + 75,000 = \$105,000 \text{ (total)}} \times \$127,000 \text{ equity}$$

Accordingly, the ratio of the nonmarital investment by Husband to the total nonmarital and marital investment in the property yields 28.57142% of the equity, hence the value of Husband's nonmarital interest in the property is $36,285.70 (28.57142% x $127,000.00). Thus, the value of the marital interest in the property is $90,714.30 (71.42858% x $127,000.00). Therefore, the trial court's judgment must be amended to reflect an increase in the value of Husband's nonmarital property from $18,000.00 to $36,285.70 and a concomitant reduction in the value of Wife's share of the marital property subject to division. Point One is denied. . . .

In his fourth point relied on, Husband essentially states the trial court erred in finding the marital portion of the Farmhouse was $130,360.00. . . .

As previously related, Wife testified that shortly after Husband's ex-wife vacated "the home", i.e., the Farmhouse, it was valued at $54,640.00 and the fair market value of the Farmhouse at the time of trial was $185,000.00. Wife testified the parties spent about $90,000.00 remodeling the Farmhouse. Both parties agreed they each expended time and labor in the remodeling process in addition to the aforementioned sums of money.

It is clear that in the instant matter the increase in value to the Farmhouse resulted *in part* from the expenditure of marital assets. Wife was entitled to a marital interest in that increased value. As with the increase in the value of the Commercial Property upon which the Commercial Building was constructed, the parties took out a loan together to remodel the Farmhouse, and all of the payments on that loan were made during the marriage from their joint checking account into which funds earned by marital, rental income and marital earnings had been placed. Additionally, while neither spouse was specific as to the extent of each party's individual labor on the Farmhouse, there was testimony that Wife as well as Husband expended their respective labor in the remodeling process.

In its division of property, the trial court found the Farmhouse was Husband's separate property; that his "nonmarital portion" of the property was valued at $54,640.00; and that the fair market value of the property was $185,000.00. . . .

However, we disagree with the trial court's determination that the value of the "marital portion" of the Farmhouse is $130,360.00. Once more applying the source of funds formula, we make the following calculations, to-wit:

$$\text{nonmarital property} = \frac{\$54,640 \text{ (nonmarital)}}{\$54,640 + \$90,000 \text{ (marital)} = \$144,640 \text{ (total)}} \times \$185,000 \text{ equity}$$

$$\text{marital property} = \frac{\$90,000 \text{ (marital)}}{\$54,640 \text{ (nonmarital)} + 90,000 = \$144,640 \text{ (total)}} \times \$185,000 \text{ equity}$$

Accordingly, the ratio of the nonmarital investment by Husband to the total of the nonmarital and marital investment in the property yields $69,886.60 (37.77654% x $185,000.00), and the value of the marital interest in the property is $115,113.38 (62.22345% x $185,000.00). Therefore, the trial court's judgment must be amended to reflect an increase in the value of Husband's nonmarital property from $54,640.00 to $69,886.60, and a concomitant reduction in the value of Wife's share of the marital property subject to division. . . .

. . .

. . . As so modified, the judgment of the trial court is affirmed.

NOTES

1. Property inherited by a spouse is commonly categorized as his or her separate property. Why does the court reject Mr. Holman's argument that the commercial property he inherited from his father should be deemed separate? Why does the court of appeals think the trial court was wrong in its calculation of the marital portion of the property? Answer the same questions for the Farmhouse.

2. The source of funds theory adopted by the court essentially creates a category of mixed property. The property is separate in proportion to the separate contributions to its acquisition and marital in proportion to the marital contributions to its acquisition. This rule is favored by most equitable distribution states shaped by the common law tradition. Some community property states have followed two other approaches when dealing with property whose value has increased partly through marital funds or labor: inception of title and the transmutation approach.

The inception of title method decides the characterization of the property at the moment the property was first acquired. If the property was acquired as separate it remains titled as separate. Contributions by either spouse to the increase in value during the marriage, made in capital or labor, are reimbursed either to the separate estate or to the community. In the first case, which occurs if the premarital separate efforts of the titled spouse are largely responsible for the increase, the community is reimbursed for the fair value of community capital or labor invested in the separate property minus any compensation already received. This is known as the Van Camp rule from the California decision first adopting it. *Van Camp v. Van Camp*, 199 P. 885 (Cal. App. 1921). In the latter, which occurs if the increase is largely attributable to the efforts of the spouse during marriage, the separate estate of the titled spouse is reimbursed for the capital or labor invested in the separate property plus a fair return for the investment based on annual rate of return. The remainder of the value is community. This is known as the Pereira rule from the California case adopting it. *Pereira v. Pereira*, 103 P. 488 (Cal. 1909). The title to the property itself however, remains separate.

The transmutation of property approach recharacterizes separate property as community whenever there is contribution of community labor or capital in the increase of value of the separate property. Usually, transmutation requires the expenditure of substantial community labor or capital. The separate estate of the spouse whose property has been transmuted is reimbursed for the initial investment along with a fair return. Transmutation also occurs if the spouse intended to change the nature of the property from separate to community. Changes in the way property is titled, from separate to joint, for example, are usually taken as evidence of intent to transmute.

Hence, inception of title and transmutation are the mirror images of each other in terms of how they title the property. In terms of the distribution of the property's value, however, both methods can yield similar results in some cases.

3. In *Holman*, both properties were paid off entirely using marital funds, so that total equity was equal to the value of the house. The more common scenario is one in which a spouse's separate property is acquired with a mortgage, which is then paid down to some extent during the marriage using marital funds. Assume for example, that before marriage one of the spouses acquires a house worth $260,000 using a down payment of $75,000 and a mortgage of $185,000. The value of the house at trial is calculated to be $351,000. During the marriage the spouses paid down the mortgage from $185,000 to $177,000 using marital funds. This is a classic case where the net equity in a property increases partly due to marital efforts and partly due to market forces. The source of funds rule would apportion this increase in proportion to the contributions of the separate and marital estates. How would you apply the *Holman* source of funds rule?

Some courts would not apply the source of funds rule in such cases at all. In *Kaaa v. Kaaa*, 9 So. 3d 756 (Fla. Dist. Ct. App. 2009), for example, one of the spouses had bought a home prior to marriage, which the couple subsequently lived in. The District Court of Appeal of Florida (second district), awarded all of the value of the home to the spouse who had initially bought it. The court reimbursed the marital estate only for marital contributions to the mortgage plus the value of certain improvements that were made using marital funds. Because the value of the house had greatly appreciated during the marriage, the marital estate was deprived of a stake in this appreciation. This is essentially the same as applying the inception of title rule, using the Van Camp method (*see supra* note 2). *Kaaa* was reversed by the Supreme Court of Florida, 58 So. 3d 867 (Fla. 2010), which held instead that if the market-driven (therefore *passive*) appreciation in value happened during the marriage, while a mortgage was being paid down using marital funds, and the non-titled spouse contributed to the upkeep of the home through his labor, the *entire value of the appreciation* was marital.

4. In *Innerbichler*, the court held that value of TAMSCO increased largely because of the efforts of the spouse who owned the business. In a minority of cases, courts have held that for the increase in value of separate property to benefit the marital estate, it needs to have increased due to the active efforts of the non-titled spouse. What is the reasoning behind this rule? Does it make sense? In several of these jurisdictions, a homemaker's services will not suffice as active participation in the increase of value of the other spouse's separate property. Consider for example the court's reasoning in the following case:

> The wife's contention that her services and efforts as a homemaker, traveling companion and entertainer were contributions made to the enhancement of the stock's value has no merit, as she made no substantial financial contributions to the business nor were her personal contributions sufficiently extensive to warrant additional compensation by sharing in the husband's separate property

Hoffmann v. Hoffmann, 676 S.W.2d 817, 826 (Mo. 1984). How would Mrs. Innerbichler have fared under this rule? Is it fair?

5. How would the *Innerbichler* court decide the case if it were following the source of funds rule? The inception of title rule? The transmutation rule? Which one of these three approaches is the doctrine of active appreciation closest to?

6. How would the *Holman* court split the value of the Commercial Property and the Farmhouse if it were following inception of title or transmutation?

7. A very common problem at the end of a marriage is the splitting of the balance in separate bank accounts. Joint accounts are created with the purpose of co-ownership and are easily classified as marital. Separate accounts however present a problem, especially when a spouse has continued depositing his or her salary and other income in a pre-marital, separate account. Because a spouse's wages during marriage are considered marital, depositing them in a separate account commingles separate and marital funds, with the result that the entire balance in the account may end up being considered marital. Drawing from the experience of community property regimes, courts will allow spouses to trace funds, so as to distinguish between marital and separate funds, but this is a very complicated process that often ends with the judicial assumption that commingling of funds transmutes separate into marital property. *See, e.g.*, *Thomson v. Thomson*, 661 S.E.2d 130, 137 (S.C. Ct. App. 2008) ("[p]roperty which is nonmarital at the time of its acquisition may be transmuted into marital property . . . if it becomes so commingled with marital property as to be untraceable") (internal quotation marks and citation omitted).

b.   WHAT IS MARITAL *PROPERTY*?

Once legislatures adopted equitable distribution statutes, courts began running into recurring interpretation problems. Could intangible assets count as property? Under pressure to make sure former spouses did not end up on welfare, most courts today have overcome theoretical objections based on the nature of property and regularly include intangible assets such as pension rights and business goodwill in their definition of property. The following cases review some of the most important categories of intangible assets that are categorized as property for the purposes of equitable distribution upon divorce.

1. PENSIONS AND OTHER DEFERRED INCOME

Laing v. Laing

Supreme Court of Alaska, 1987.
741 P.2d 649.

■ COMPTON, J.

This appeal challenges a marital property division.... We affirm the trial court's findings and conclusions except with regard to its disposition of the husband's nonvested pension, which we conclude cannot be presently divided. We remand the case with instructions that the trial court redetermine the property division in a manner consistent with this opinion.

Kenneth and Marla Laing were married on November 16, 1964. At the time of the marriage, Marla lived in her own furnished home, the equity in which was approximately $15,000. She also had benefits from her first husband's death which amounted to approximately $10,000 and a two-year old car worth approximately $500. Throughout their twenty-year marriage, Marla was responsible for most of the housework and child care, even during approximately ten years she was employed outside the home.

Kenneth apparently had no substantial assets at the time of the marriage. He was employed all but a few months during the marriage.

At the time of divorce, Marla was 49 years old and employed as a dental office receptionist/clerk. She earned $18,750 gross income the year before trial. Kenneth was 50 years old and had been employed at Union Chemicals (now UNOCAL) for seven and a half years. The trial court found that he had earned approximately $40,000 by August 1985; his income in 1984 was $61,471.43.

The parties stipulated to the value of most of the marital assets. The only items in dispute were certain household goods not at issue in this appeal.

. . .

The trial court awarded Kenneth his pension with a present value of $27,000 and awarded Marla offsetting marital assets. Kenneth challenges the award on the grounds that there was insufficient evidence to support the $27,000 figure and that Marla's share should not have been awarded in a lump sum. We first address the issue whether the trial court properly characterized Kenneth's nonvested pension as marital property.

. . .

Alaska ... follows the majority rule that "vested" pension and retirement benefits are subject to division by a divorce court. Whether the majority rule can also be applied with regard to Kenneth's *nonvested*[8] pension rights is a question of first impression in Alaska. Jurisdictions are split on this issue. Those in which nonvested pensions are held not to be divisible marital property rely primarily on the notion that such interests are too speculative and cannot be said to constitute a property right. *See, e.g., Wilson v. Wilson*, 409 N.E.2d 1169, 1178 (Ind.App.1980); *Ratcliff v. Ratcliff*, 586 S.W.2d 292, 293 (Ky.App.1979).

The trend, however, is to consider pensions as marital property regardless of whether they have vested.

Supporting this trend is the reasoning that the contingent nature of a nonvested pension presents simply a valuation problem, not bearing on the non-employee spouse's entitlement to a just share of the marital assets. Pension benefits are generally viewed as deferred compensation for services rendered and the employee spouse's right thereto is a contractual right. [*In re Marriage of*] *Brown*, 544 P.2d [561]at 565 [(Cal. 1976)]. "The fact that a contractual right is contingent upon future events does not degrade that right to an expectancy." *Brown*, 544 P.2d at 566 n. 8.

. . .

We are persuaded that the contingencies that may prevent the employee spouse from ever collecting his or her nonvested pension should not bar the non-employee spouse from recovering a share if the pension is in fact paid out. Indeed, a contrary rule would frustrate the statutory command that Alaska courts effect a "just division of the marital assets." AS 25.24.160(a)(4). This obviously requires that the trial court consider the financial circumstances of each party. It would be wholly inconsistent with this policy to ignore the existence of so substantial an asset as a party's pension rights. In this regard, we adopt the rule representing the current trend and recognize nonvested pension rights as a marital asset.

---

8. The term "nonvested" is used here to mean that if Kenneth's employment were to terminate immediately he would be entitled to no future retirement or pension benefits. The term is not used, as some courts have done, to indicate merely that the pension rights have not matured. When a pension or retirement benefits plan is vested but not matured, an employee is absolutely entitled to benefits, though he is not entitled to actual payments until some future date.

The trial court assigned a present value of $27,000 to Kenneth's pension, awarded it to him and awarded Marla offsetting assets. Kenneth asserts that there was insufficient evidence to support the present value figure adopted by the trial court. . . .

Courts have used two primary methods of valuing and dividing pension benefits, whether vested or nonvested, upon divorce: the present value approach and the reserved jurisdiction approach.[9]

In the present value approach, a court faced with a nonvested pension factors the contingencies to collection into a "reduced to present value" calculation. A similar reduction to present value can easily be obtained for a vested pension. The court determines a fraction of the present value representing the marital contribution to the accrued pension benefits. The numerator of this fraction is the number of years the pension has accrued during the marriage; the denominator is the total number of years during which the employee spouse's pension has accrued.[11] Once this calculation is complete, the court may award the pension interest to the employee spouse and give the non-employee spouse an offsetting amount of other assets.

Citing the goal that a property settlement should provide a final resolution of a divorcing couple's financial affairs, a number of courts have stated that the present value approach is preferred where a present value can be attached to the pension and where there exist other marital assets sufficient to satisfy the non-employee spouse's claim without undue hardship on the employee spouse.

We nonetheless find this method unacceptable. Since the non-employee spouse receives his or her share in a lump sum at the time of the divorce, the method unfairly places all risk of possible forfeiture on the employee spouse. While the probability of forfeiture is supposedly factored in to reduce the present value amount determined at the time of the divorce, it is clear that the non-employee spouse has taken only a reduction in the amount of the award whereas the employee spouse loses the entire amount awarded to the non-employee spouse in the event of forfeiture. We find this approach to be inherently unfair.

In the other scheme used by the courts for valuation and division of a pension, the reserved jurisdiction approach, the trial court retains jurisdiction and orders the employee spouse to pay to the former spouse a fraction of each pension payment actually received.[12] This scheme more evenly allocates the risk of forfeiture between the parties, although it also runs counter to our expressed preference for finalizing a couple's financial affairs as soon as possible.

However, reserving jurisdiction does not necessarily mean that a protracted pay-out to the former spouse will follow vesting. Once vesting occurs, that portion of the pension which is marital property can be calculated as of the time of the divorce. The non-employee spouse's share of this figure may,

---

9. A third possible method of division is to award the non-employee spouse a percentage of the employee spouse's contribution to the plan plus interest. We reject this method because it ignores employer contributions which, to the extent they were made during marriage, ought to be considered a marital asset.

11. In this case, Kenneth's entire term of employment with UNOCAL occurred during the marriage.

12. This court recently adopted a variation on this method in a case in which the employee spouse could have begun collecting benefits but desired to continue working. We simply ordered him to pay his wife a monthly amount equivalent to what she would have received if he retired.

in appropriate cases, be payable in a lump sum or in installments which do not particularly have to be keyed to the time that the pension benefits are actually received.

We are persuaded that reserving jurisdiction more closely parallels the societal goals of retirement benefits generally—that is, to provide financial security to participants. A present lump sum award to the non-employee spouse calculated on a pension which has not vested does not necessarily promote this purpose. The fact is that nonvested pensions are sometimes forfeited, often for reasons which properly should be within the power of the employee to decide, and sometimes for reasons which are entirely beyond the control of the employee. There is no reliable way to factor the contingency of forfeiture into a present value calculation. Thus, we are willing to accept a degree of continued financial entanglement insofar as that may be necessary to effect a just division of nonvested pension rights.

We adopt the following approach for dividing nonvested pension rights after divorce. First, because the nonvested pension may, by definition, be forfeited in its entirety, it should not be considered when the trial court makes the initial property division at the time of the divorce. If and when the employee spouse's pension rights vest and if the parties are unable to reach an agreement on their own, the non-employee spouse may at any time thereafter seek an order dividing the pension. This is to be done in the same manner as if the pension had been vested at the time of the divorce. Realistically, there is such a variety of pension plan designs that it is impossible to develop any one detailed formula that will produce an equitable result in every instance. Once the pension has vested, the trial court can determine whether the present value or the retained jurisdiction approach is appropriate in a given case and adapt that approach to the specific circumstances presented.

As one possible resolution, we direct the trial court on remand to investigate the applicability of the Retirement Equity Act of 1984 (REACT), Pub.L. No. 98–397, 98 Stat. 1426 (1984). REACT applies to retirement benefit plans covered by the Employee Retirement Income Security Act of 1974 (ERISA), Pub.L. No. 93–406, 88 Stat. 829 (1974). The record does not indicate whether Kenneth's UNOCAL pension was such a plan. Under REACT, a "qualified domestic relations order" (QDRO) can be filed with the administrator of the employee spouse's pension plan. 29 U.S.C. 1056(d)(3). If and when the employee spouse's pension vests and matures, the plan administrator makes appropriate payments directly to the non-employee former spouse in accordance with the QDRO. 29 U.S.C. 1056(d)(3)(A).

REACT thus solves the problem of continuing financial entanglement between former spouses. Moreover, because payments are made directly by the plan, the non-employee spouse is sure to receive the payments to which he or she is entitled.[13] In certain circumstances, REACT allows the non-employee spouse to convert his or her share of the benefits to pay status independently of the employee spouse. 29 U.S.C. § 1056(d)(3)(E).[14]

---

13. It is important to note that REACT affects only the method by which a non-employee spouse may *collect* ERISA pension benefits. The fact and amount of his or her entitlement to the former spouse's pension is determined by state law. 29 U.S.C. § 1056(d)(3)(B)

14. Similar provisions for direct payment of retirement benefits to employees' former spouses exist with regard to military and federal civil service retirement benefit plans....

It thus appears that only in rare circumstances would the QDRO solution be unavailable.

We reverse and remand for a reevaluation of Kenneth's nonvested pension. If Kenneth's UNOCAL plan is not covered by ERISA, we direct the trial court to retain jurisdiction so that an appropriate division may be made if and when Kenneth's pension becomes vested.

NOTES

1. Today, the vast majority of courts consider unvested pensions to be marital property if they accrued during the marriage. Suppose that Kenneth had worked for UNOCAL before, as well as during, the marriage. How would the court recalculate the portion of the pension that could be classified as a marital asset?

2. Defined contribution plans, in which an individual account is created for each employee and is disbursed to the employee upon retirement, are easier to divide through the present value method. By contrast, defined benefit plans, which entitle the retiree to a certain amount of monthly benefits upon retirement, are usually divided by a court order that entitles the non-employee spouse to a certain percentage of these monthly benefits. As noted in *Laing*, when a plan is covered by ERISA, the plan administrator can be made to pay directly to the non-employee spouse through a Qualified Domestic Relations Order (QDRO). QDROs have become increasingly common, as they allow for the financial disentanglement of the former spouses. Qualified orders are also available for plans not covered by ERISA.

3. Just as in *Laing*, courts have found that contract rights accrued during marriage constitute marital property even if their payout is deferred, as opposed to interests that are mere expectancies. Even though distinguishing between the two has proven complicated, the general thrust of the cases has been towards a constant expansion of the pool of possible marital assets.

The idea is that any asset, right, entitlement, or benefit accrued during the marriage should be characterized as marital property and distributed equitably. In *Niroo v. Niroo*, 545 A.2d 35 (Md. 1988), for instance, the Court of Appeals of Maryland had to decide whether future renewal commissions on insurance policies sold by the husband during the marriage would be classified as marital property. The court rejected the husband's argument that in order to secure the renewal commission he would have to service the accounts with labor expended post-divorce and emphasized instead that the contractual right to the renewal commissions had been secured during his marriage, which meant the commissions could be classified as marital property. *Id.* at 39–41. Recently, the Tennessee Supreme Court addressed the issue of whether a $17 million attorney fee that was received by an attorney-husband several months after the wife filed for divorce was a marital asset. *Larsen–Ball v. Ball*, 301 S.W.3d 228 (Tenn. 2010). The court held that "marital property includes all property owned as of the date of filing of the complaint for divorce or acquired up to the date of the final divorce hearing." *Id.* at 233. Because the husband acquired the fee almost a year before the final hearing, the fee was marital. *Id.*

Courts have even started considering accrued vacation and leave time. In *In re Marriage of Cardona & Castro*, No. 09CA1996, 2010 WL 5013737, at *3 (Colo. Ct. App., Dec. 9, 2010), the husband had accumulated accrued vacation and leave time, valued at $23,232. The trial court had ordered the husband to pay half the amount to the wife. *Id.* Accrued vacation and leave time would only be payable to the husband upon retirement if the time had remained unused. *See id.* In a case of first impression, the appeals court concluded that the interest was too uncertain to be considered "property subject to distribution on dissolution." *Id.* at *3–*5. Other jurisdictions have concluded the opposite. *See, e.g., Forrester v. Forrester*, 953 A.2d 175, 186–88 (Del. 2008) (husband's accumulated compensatory time could be converted to cash at any time; therefore it was deemed to be an acquired property right that could be included in the marital estate).

4. Social Security benefits are not considered divisible assets at divorce because, contrary to pensions, they are not contractual rights but a form of social insurance. Federal law explicitly preempts division of social security benefits as part of equitable division at divorce. *See* 42 U.S.C. § 407 (2006). In *Forrester v. Forrester*, 953 A.2d 175, 180, 184–85 (Del. 2008), the court affirmed that Social Security benefits cannot be considered marital assets but held that pensions awarded to substitute for Social Security benefits can be. Other jurisdictions have held that because Social Security benefits themselves are not divisible, neither should pensions in lieu of Social Security be. *See, e.g., Kohler v. Kohler*, 118 P.3d 621 (Ariz. Ct. App. 2005).

II. HUMAN CAPITAL AND OTHER INTANGIBLE ASSETS

Postema v. Postema

Court of Appeals of Michigan, 1991.
189 Mich. App. 89, 471 N.W.2d 912.

■ MAHER, PRESIDING JUDGE.

The defendant appeals and the plaintiff cross appeals from the property distribution provisions of a February 3, 1989, judgment of divorce. The primary issue concerns the valuation of defendant's law degree and whether the trial court erred in finding the law degree to be a marital asset. We affirm in part and remand.

Plaintiff and defendant were married on August 11, 1984. At the time of their marriage, defendant was employed as a cost accountant and plaintiff was working as a licensed practical nurse and attending school in pursuit of an associate's degree in nursing so that she could become a registered nurse. It was the plan of the parties when they married that defendant would enroll in law school and that plaintiff would postpone her schooling and work full-time to support them while defendant attended school. Accordingly, shortly after the marriage, the parties moved from Grand Rapids to the Detroit area, where they stayed from September 1984 until May 1987 while defendant attended Wayne State University Law School. In furtherance of the parties' plan, plaintiff obtained a full-time job at an area hospital, earning approximately $53,000 during the period defendant was in law school. Plaintiff also assumed the primary responsibility of maintaining the household, doing all cooking and cleaning, and running all errands. Though defendant did not work at all during his first year in law school, he later worked as a law clerk, full-time during the summers following his first and second years in law school and then part-time during his second and part of his third years. In all, defendant earned approximately $12,000 from clerking. The parties' earnings were used primarily for their support, while defendant's education was financed mostly through student loans totaling $15,000.

Defendant proved to be a successful law student and wrote for the school's law review. After defendant graduated in May 1987, the parties moved back to the Grand Rapids area, where defendant accepted a position as an associate attorney with a local law firm at a starting annual salary of $41,000. The following September, plaintiff resumed classes in pursuit of her associate's degree in nursing. In November 1987, however, the parties separated. Despite the separation, plaintiff continued her classes and eventually received her associate's degree in May 1988, although she had to support herself during that period by working full-time at a local hospital.

. . .

The trial court found that the breakdown of the marriage was primarily the fault of defendant, and announced it had considered this fact in its property distribution. After awarding each of the parties their respective automobiles, the trial court awarded plaintiff specific household goods and bank funds totaling $5,000, while awarding defendant specific goods and funds totaling $3,000. Defendant was also held solely responsible for repayment of $14,000 in student loans. Finally, the trial court determined that defendant's law degree was a marital asset subject to distribution. The court valued the degree at $80,000, and awarded plaintiff, as her share of the degree, $32,000 on the basis that this amount would equalize the parties' respective distributive shares. The court ordered this obligation to be paid off in monthly installments of $371.55 or more, at seven percent interest, until fully paid. The court did not award either party alimony.

Defendant now appeals and plaintiff cross appeals as of right. . . .

The goal of a trial court with respect to the division of the marital estate is a fair and equitable distribution under all of the circumstances. The division is not governed by any rigid rules or mathematical formula and need not be equal. The primary question is what is fair. On review, this Court is required to accept the trial court's factual findings unless those findings are clearly erroneous.

I. THE LAW DEGREE

Panels of this Court have expressed different views concerning the treatment, characterization, and valuation of an advanced degree in a divorce situation. Nevertheless, most panels have agreed that *fairness* dictates that a spouse who did not earn an advanced degree be compensated whenever the advanced degree is the end product of a *concerted family effort* involving mutual sacrifice and effort by both spouses.

. . .

A. The Concerted Family Effort.

. . .

. . . [T]he concept "concerted family effort" stresses the fact that it is not the existence of an advanced degree itself that gives rise to an equitable claim for compensation, but rather the fact of the degree being the end product of the mutual sacrifice, effort, and contribution of both parties as part of a larger, long-range plan intended to benefit the family as a whole. The concept is premised, in part, on the fact that the attainment of an advanced degree is a prolonged undertaking involving considerable expenditure of time, effort, and money, as well as other sacrifices. Where such an undertaking is pursued as part of a concerted family effort, both spouses expect to be compensated for their respective sacrifices, efforts, and contributions by eventually sharing in the fruits of the degree. Where, however, the parties' relationship ends in divorce, such a sharing is impossible. Although the degree holder will always have the degree to show for the efforts, the nonstudent spouse is left with nothing. Therefore, a remedy consistent with fairness and equity requires that an attempt be made to at least return financially to the nonstudent spouse the value of what that spouse contributed toward attainment of the degree.

Generally, the existence of a concerted family effort will be reflected in many ways. For instance, it is reflected not only through a spouse's tangible efforts and financial contributions associated with working and supporting the mate while the mate pursues the advanced degree, but also through other intangible, nonpecuniary efforts and contributions, such as where a spouse increases the share of the daily tasks, child-rearing responsibilities, or other details of household and family management undertaken in order to provide the mate with the necessary time and energy to study and attend classes. A concerted family effort is also exemplified by the fact that both spouses typically share in the emotional and psychological burdens of the educational experience. For the nonstudent spouse, these burdens may be experienced either directly, such as through the presence of increased tension within the household, or indirectly, such as where the spouse shares vicariously in the stress of the educational experience. Finally, the attainment of an advanced degree during marriage is usually accompanied by considerable sacrifice on the part of both spouses. For the nonstudent spouse, such sacrifice may be reflected by a change in life style during the educational process, the availability of less time to pursue personal interests, or even a decision to either give up or temporarily postpone one's own educational or career pursuits as part of the larger, long-range plan designed to benefit the family as a whole.

Turning now to the instant case, the facts show that plaintiff temporarily postponed her pursuit of an associate's degree in nursing, moved with defendant to the Detroit area so that he could attend law school, and then worked full-time to support herself and defendant while defendant attended classes. This was all done as part of a larger plan to benefit both parties as a whole. Plaintiff, in addition to being the primary financial provider while defendant attended school, wherein she accounted for approximately eighty percent of the parties' total financial support, also bore primary responsibility for the daily household tasks. Moreover, the stress of the law school experience was certainly experienced by both parties, as reflected by the fact that defendant repeatedly blamed his inappropriate behavior toward plaintiff on the stress of law school, and by plaintiff's testimony explaining that her whole life revolved around her trying not to agitate defendant.

We conclude, therefore, that defendant's law degree was clearly the end product of a concerted family effort giving rise to an equitable claim for compensation in favor of plaintiff in recognition of her unrewarded sacrifices, efforts, and contributions toward attainment of the degree.

B. Characterization of a Claim for Compensation Involving an Advanced Degree

Despite the common recognition among panels of this Court that a spouse who did not obtain an advanced degree should be compensated whenever the degree is the end product of a concerted family effort, panels are in disagreement over the appropriate manner in which a claim for compensation should be considered. While some panels have characterized an advanced degree as a marital asset subject to property division, other panels have held that an advanced degree is more properly considered as a factor in awarding alimony.

After reviewing the various decisions addressing the issue and taking into consideration the underlying principles upon which an award of compensation for an advanced degree is premised, we reject the view holding that an advanced degree is more properly considered as a factor in awarding alimony.

. . .

In rejecting the alimony approach, we first recognize that the basic purpose of paying alimony is to assist in the other spouse's support. Unlike alimony, however, the principles underlying an award of compensation based on the attainment of an advanced degree are neither rooted in nor based on notions of support. Rather, as noted previously, entitlement to compensation stems from the recognition that where a degree is the end product of a concerted family effort, fairness and equity will not permit the degree holder to reap the benefits of the degree without compensating the other spouse for unrewarded sacrifices, efforts, and contributions toward attainment of the degree. Thus, where a concerted family effort is involved, a spouse's entitlement to compensation constitutes a recognized right; it is not dependent upon factors related to the need for support. Therefore, we do not find that an award of alimony is the appropriate means for awarding compensation.

Moreover, . . . an award in terms of alimony may unfairly jeopardize a spouse's recognized right to compensation because a trial court has broad discretion in deciding whether to grant alimony, because an award of alimony is dependent on factors different from those related to the division of marital property, and because, pursuant to M.C.L. § 552.13; M.S.A. § 25.93, alimony may be terminated if the spouse receiving it remarries. Regarding this latter observation, we agree with the panel in *Lewis,* 181 Mich.App. p. 6, 448 N.W.2d 735, which stated: "Because the value of an advanced degree does not 'evaporate' upon the nondegree-earning spouse's remarriage, we do not find an award of alimony a satisfactory method of recognizing that spouse's efforts toward earning the degree." Furthermore, we note that it is often the case that a nonstudent spouse will already have demonstrated the ability of self-support by virtue of having supported the degree-earning spouse through graduate school. While such fact would ordinarily militate against an award of alimony, we do not believe it should operate to deprive the nonstudent spouse of a recognized right to be compensated for unrewarded sacrifices, efforts, and contributions toward attainment of the degree.

Finally, contrary to the observations in *Graham, supra,* we do not believe that the consideration of an advanced degree when making the property distribution would be improper merely because a degree cannot be characterized as "property" in the classic sense. Rather, we agree with *Woodworth,* . . . 126 Mich.App. p. 263, 337 N.W.2d 332, that "whether or not an advanced degree can physically or metaphysically be defined as 'property' is beside the point[;] [c]ourts must instead focus on the most equitable solution to dissolving the marriage and dividing among the respective parties what they have." . . .

We conclude, therefore, that where an advanced degree is the end product of a concerted family effort, involving the mutual sacrifice, effort, and contribution of both spouses, there arises a "marital asset" subject to distribution, wherein the interest of the nonstudent spouse consists of an "equitable claim" regarding the degree.

C.   Valuation

. . .

Woodworth, supra, 126 Mich.App. pp. 268–269, 337 N.W.2d 332, discussed two methods of compensating a nonstudent spouse for an interest in an advanced degree: (1) awarding a percentage share of the present value of the future earnings attributable to the degree, or (2) restitution. The first method focuses on the degree's present value by attempting to estimate what the person holding the degree is likely to make in a particular job market and subtracting therefrom what that person would probably have earned without the degree. According to *Woodworth*, the nonstudent spouse should then be awarded a percentage share of this value after considering (1) the length of the marriage after the degree was obtained, (2) the sources and extent of financial support given to the degreeholder during the years in school, and (3) the overall division of the parties' marital property. The second method is less involved, because it focuses on the cost of obtaining the degree.

In this case, plaintiff presented an expert who, using the present value method discussed in *Woodworth*, valued defendant's law degree at $230,000.... Using essentially the same formula, but with modifications to the underlying assumptions, defendant presented his own valuations of $15,000, $46,000, and $79,500. The trial court ultimately valued defendant's law degree at $80,000, and then, after determining that the remainder of the property distribution resulted in plaintiff receiving a net amount of $5,000, but defendant having a deficit of $11,000, awarded plaintiff $32,000 as her share of the degree, noting that such an award would equalize the parties' respective distributive shares.

It is difficult to tell from the record how the trial court arrived at its initial $80,000 valuation figure. Further, while we certainly agree that plaintiff is entitled to be compensated for her unrewarded sacrifices, efforts, and contributions toward the attainment of defendant's law degree, our review of the record reveals that the trial court's ultimate award of $32,000 failed to account for several relevant and applicable considerations. Accordingly, we conclude that the appropriate remedy in this case is to remand to the trial court for revaluation of plaintiff's "equitable claim" in light of this opinion. On remand, we do not believe that the present value method discussed in *Woodworth*, and purportedly used by plaintiff's expert, is an appropriate means by which to evaluate plaintiff's equitable claim involving the degree. Such a method emphasizes the notion that a nonstudent spouse possesses some sort of pecuniary interest in the degree itself. We believe such a notion misconstrues the underlying premise upon which an award of compensation involving an advanced degree is based. As we have attempted to explain throughout this opinion, an award of compensation is premised upon equitable considerations, wherein the goal is to attempt to financially return to the nonstudent spouse what that spouse contributed toward attainment of the degree. Because such an award is not premised upon the notion that a nonstudent spouse possesses an interest in the degree itself, we do not believe the actual value of the degree is a relevant consideration. In this respect, we agree with the following observations made in *Krause, supra*, 177 Mich.App. pp. 197–198, 441 N.W.2d 66:

. . .

> The trial court must focus solely on what is necessary to compensate defendant for the burdens on her or the sacrifices made by her so that plaintiff could pursue his degree.

> ... [W]e emphasize that the focus of an award involving an advanced degree is not to reimburse the nonstudent spouse for "loss of expectations" over what the degree might potentially have produced, but to reimburse that spouse for unrewarded sacrifices, efforts, and contributions toward attainment of the degree on the ground that it would be equitable to do so *in view of the fact* that that spouse will not be sharing in the fruits of the degree.

. . .

In our view, any valuation of a nonstudent spouse's equitable claim involving an advanced degree involves a two-step analysis. First, an examination of the sacrifices, efforts, and contributions of the nonstudent spouse toward attainment of the degree. Second, given such sacrifices, efforts, and contributions, a determination of what remedy or means of compensation would most equitably compensate the nonstudent spouse under the facts of the case. In this regard, we agree with *Woodworth* that the length of the marriage after the degree was obtained, the sources and extent of financial support given to the degree holder during the years in school, and the overall division of the parties' marital property are all relevant considerations in valuing a nonstudent spouse's equitable claim involving an advanced degree upon divorce.

Where, for instance, the parties remain married for a substantial period of time after an advanced degree is obtained, fairness suggests that the value of an equitable claim would not be as great, inasmuch as the nonstudent spouse will already have been rewarded, in part, for efforts contributed by virtue of having already shared, in part, in the fruits of the degree. Similarly, where the extent of support or assistance provided by the nonstudent spouse, financial or otherwise, is not significant, or where such assistance comes primarily from outside sources for which the nonstudent spouse was not responsible or is not liable, fairness and equity would also suggest that the value of an equitable claim would not be as great.

Furthermore, an equitable remedy may be exemplified in different ways. For example, as this Court recognized in *Krause, supra*, 177 Mich.App. pp. 197–198, 441 N.W.2d 66: "[I]f [the nonstudent spouse] wishes to pursue [an] education or take other similar steps to improve . . . employability or income earning potential, it is reasonable and equitable to require the [degree-holding spouse] to assist . . . in those endeavors." Thus, in this type of situation, an award consistent with fairness and equity would be one which requires the degree-earning spouse to provide assistance, in the form of financial support, equivalent to that provided by the nonstudent spouse during the marriage.

Where, however, a nonstudent spouse does not wish to further pursue an education, then perhaps equity would best be served by an award reimbursing the spouse for the amount of financial assistance provided toward attainment of the degree, while also recognizing the other intangible, nonpecuniary sacrifices made and efforts expended.

Ultimately, however, the goal is to arrive at a remedy which, consistent with fairness and equity, will compensate the nonstudent spouse for unrewarded sacrifices, efforts, and contributions toward the degree. Thus, in reviewing such a claim on appeal, the ultimate inquiry is whether the remedy or decision of the trial court was a fair and equitable one under the facts of the case, given the sacrifices, efforts, and contributions of the nonstudent spouse toward the degree.

We note in this case that the parties separated shortly after defendant attained his law degree. Thus, plaintiff received little reward, if any, for her sacrifices, efforts, and contributions toward defendant's degree. Further, while defendant did contribute some financial support during the degree-earning period, it was plaintiff who accounted for the vast majority of it, approximately eighty percent. Moreover, while defendant certainly worked hard in obtaining his degree, it is abundantly clear from the record that plaintiff's nonpecuniary efforts and contributions toward the degree were indeed significant also, and that she certainly endured many hardships and sacrifices as a result of her participation in the law school experience. We also note that while plaintiff did ultimately further her own career objectives in the manner she chose, she was required to do so on her own and did not have nearly the same benefits, financial or otherwise, that defendant had while he attended school. Defendant was, however, primarily responsible for the actual cost of his education, which was financed mostly through student loans for which he remains solely responsible. These are just some of the factors which were not discussed by the trial court, but yet are relevant to the valuation of plaintiff's equitable claim involving the degree. Therefore, these factors shall be considered by the trial court on remand.

After valuing plaintiff's equitable claim, the trial court may order that the amount determined to be due be payable in monthly installments over a fixed period of time.... Finally, we believe it would be in order to allow the parties the opportunity to present new evidence on the issue of valuation in light of this opinion.

NOTE

Note that even though the *Postema* court holds the degree to be the result of concerted family effort, it does not distribute a percentage of the present value of the degree itself. Why is that? See by contrast *O'Brien v. O'Brien*, 489 N.E.2d 712 (N.Y. 1985). Courts in a majority of states have held that educational degrees do not constitute marital property. For example, in *In re Marriage of Graham*, 574 P.2d 75 (Colo. 1978), the court held that the husband's degree in business administration was not marital property, despite the fact that he obtained the degree while his wife was earning approximately 70 percent of the marital income.

Elkus v. Elkus

Supreme Court of New York, Appellate Division, First Department, 1991.
169 A.D.2d 134, 572 N.Y.S.2d 901.

■ ROSENBERGER, J.

In this matrimonial action, the plaintiff, Frederica von Stade Elkus, moved for an order determining, prior to trial, whether her career and/or celebrity status constituted marital property subject to equitable distribution. The parties have already stipulated to mutual judgments of divorce terminating their 17–year marriage and to joint custody of their two minor children. The trial on the remaining economic issues has been stayed pending the outcome of this appeal from the order of the Supreme Court, which had determined that the enhanced value of the plaintiff's career and/or celebrity status was not marital property subject to equitable distribution. Contrary to the conclusion reached by the Supreme Court, we find that to the extent the defendant's contributions and efforts led to an increase in the value of the plaintiff's career, this appreciation was a product of the marital partnership, and, therefore, marital property subject to equitable distribution.

At the time of her marriage to the defendant on February 9, 1973, the plaintiff had just embarked on her career, performing minor roles with the Metropolitan Opera Company. During the course of the marriage, the plaintiff's career succeeded dramatically and her income rose accordingly. In the first year of the marriage, she earned $2,250. In 1989, she earned $621,878. She is now a celebrated artist with the Metropolitan Opera, as well as an international recording artist, concert and television performer. She has garnered numerous awards, and has performed for the President of the United States.

During the marriage, the defendant traveled with the plaintiff throughout the world, attending and critiquing her performances and rehearsals, and photographed her for album covers and magazine articles. The defendant was also the plaintiff's voice coach and teacher for 10 years of the marriage. He states that he sacrificed his own career as a singer and teacher to devote himself to the plaintiff's career and to the lives of their young children, and that his efforts enabled the plaintiff to become one of the most celebrated opera singers in the world. Since the plaintiff's career and/or celebrity status increased in value during the marriage due in part to his contributions, the defendant contends that he is entitled to equitable distribution of this marital property.

The Supreme Court disagreed, refusing to extend the holding in *O'Brien v[.] O'Brien* (66 N[.]Y[.]2d 576) in which the Court of Appeals determined that a medical license constituted marital property subject to equitable distribution, to the plaintiff's career as an opera singer. The court found that since the defendant enjoyed a substantial life-style during the marriage and since he would be sufficiently compensated through distribution of the parties' other assets, the plaintiff's career was not marital property.

... The plaintiff maintains that since her career and celebrity status are not licensed, are not entities which are owned like a business, nor are protected interests which are subject to due process of law, they are not marital property. In our view, neither the Domestic Relations Law, nor relevant case law, allows for such a limited interpretation of the term marital property.

Domestic Relations Law § 236(B)(1)(c) broadly defines marital property as property acquired during the marriage "regardless of the form in which title is held". In enacting the Equitable Distribution Law, the Legislature created a radical change in the traditional method of distributing property upon the dissolution of a marriage. By broadly defining the term "marital property," it intended to give effect to the "economic partnership" concept of the marriage relationship. It then left it to the courts to determine what interests constitute marital property.

Things of value acquired during marriage are marital property even though they may fall outside the scope of traditional property concepts. The statutory definition of marital property does not mandate that it be an asset with an exchange value or be salable, assignable or transferable. The property may be tangible or intangible.

Medical licenses have been held to enhance the earning capacity of their holders, so as to enable the other spouse who made direct or indirect contributions to their acquisition, to share their value as part of equitable distribution. A Medical Board certification, a law degree, an accounting degree, a podiatry practice, the licensing and certification of a physician's assistant, a Masters degree in teaching, and a fellowship in the Society of Actuaries have also been held to constitute marital property.

Although the plaintiff's career, unlike that of the husband in *O'Brien (supra)*, is not licensed, the *O'Brien* court did not restrict its holding to professions requiring a license or degree. In reaching its conclusion that a medical license constitutes marital property, the *O'Brien* court referred to the language contained in Domestic Relations Law § 236 which provides that in making an equitable distribution of marital property, "the court shall consider:

> (6) any equitable claim to, interest in, or direct or indirect contribution made to the acquisition of such marital property by the party not having title, including joint efforts or expenditures and contributions and services as a spouse, parent, wage earner and homemaker, and to the career or career potential of the other party ..."

... (Domestic Relations Law § 236[B][5][d][6] [emphasis added]).

The court also cited section 236[B][5][e] which provides that where, equitable distribution of marital property is appropriate, but "the distribution of an interest in a business, corporation or profession would be contrary to law", the court shall make a distributive award in lieu of an actual distribution of the property.

The Court of Appeals' analysis of the statute is equally applicable here. "The words mean exactly what they say: that an interest in a profession or professional career potential is marital property which may be represented by direct or indirect contributions of the non-title-holding spouse, including financial contributions and nonfinancial contributions made by caring for the home and family" (*O'Brien v. O'Brien, supra, at 584*). Nothing in the statute or the *O'Brien* decision supports the plaintiff's contention that her career and/or celebrity status are not marital property. The purpose behind the enactment of the legislation was to prevent inequities which previously occurred upon the dissolution of a marriage. Any attempt to limit marital property to professions which are licensed would only serve to discriminate against the spouses of those engaged in other areas of employment. Such a distinction would fail to carry out the premise upon which equitable distribution is based, i.e., that a marriage is an economic partnership to which both parties contribute, as spouse, parent, wage earner or homemaker.

. . .

... [T]here is tremendous potential for financial gain from the commercial exploitation of famous personalities. While the plaintiff insists that she will never be asked to endorse a product, this is simply speculation. More and more opportunities have presented themselves to her as her fame increased. They will continue to present themselves to her as she continues to advance in her career. The career of the plaintiff is unique, in that she has risen to the top in a field where success is rarely achieved.

. . .

... We agree with the courts that have considered the issue, that the enhanced skills of an artist such as the plaintiff, albeit growing from an innate talent, which have enabled her to become an exceptional earner, may be valued as marital property subject to equitable distribution.

The plaintiff additionally contends that her career is not marital property because she had already become successful prior to her marriage to the defendant. As noted, *supra*, during the first year of marriage, the plaintiff earned $2,250. By 1989, her earnings had increased more than 275 fold. Further, in *Price v. Price*[, 503 N.E.2d 684 (N.Y. 1986)] (*supra*, at 11), the Court of Appeals held that "under the Equitable Distribution Law an increase in the value of separate property of one spouse, occurring during the marriage and prior to the commencement of matrimonial proceedings, which is due in part to the indirect contributions or efforts of the other spouse as homemaker and parent, should be considered marital property."

In this case, it cannot be overlooked that the defendant's contributions to plaintiff's career were direct and concrete, going far beyond child care and the like, which he also provided.

While it is true that the plaintiff was born with talent, and, while she had already been hired by the Metropolitan Opera at the time of her marriage to the defendant, her career, at this time, was only in the initial stages of development. During the course of the marriage, the defendant's active involvement in the plaintiff's career, in teaching, coaching, and critiquing her, as well as in caring for their children, clearly contributed to the increase in its value. Accordingly, to the extent the appreciation in the plaintiff's career was due to the defendant's efforts and contributions, this appreciation constitutes marital property.

In sum, we find that it is the nature and extent of the contribution by the spouse seeking equitable distribution, rather than the nature of the career, whether licensed or otherwise, that should determine the status of the enterprise as marital property.

NOTES

1. The courts in both *Postema* and *Elkus* concluded that a spouse who helps the other enhance his or her earning power has a property interest in the income resulting from that enhancement. Why, then, did each court calculate the value of that interest differently? Which is more consistent with the concept of enhanced earning capacity as property?

2. How would a homemaker have fared under the *Elkus* test of contribution?

3. Courts that refuse to distribute the value of increased earning capacity usually appeal to the notion that increased earning capacity is a personal attribute. For example, examine the reasoning of the following appeals court:

> In undertaking the statutory allocation of marital assets, the trial judge included, apparently as a separate item of property, defendant's earning capacity. The opinion states:
>
>> His ability (earning capacity) is an amorphous asset of this marriage in the absence of other assets. It consists of natural ability, undergraduate and post-graduate education, marriage to the daughter of a man of high standing and lucrative income in the area of his professional activity, entree to his office and ultimate partnership, subsequent management of the firm, with advancement in the esteem of his professional peers. (123 N.J.Super. at 568, 304 A.2d at 204)
>
> We agree with defendant's contention that a person's earning capacity, even where its development has been aided and enhanced by the other spouse, as is here the case, should not be recognized as a separate, particular item of property within the meaning of N.J.S.A. 2A:34–23. Potential earning capacity is doubtless a factor to be considered by a trial judge in determining what distribution will be 'equitable' and it is even more obviously relevant upon the issue of alimony. But it should not be deemed property as such within the meaning of the statute.

Stern v. Stern, 331 A.2d 257, 260 (N.J. 1975). If increased earning capacity is the result of common marital effort, should the marital estate also be burdened with losses of earning capacity when these occur?

4. Contribution to the increase of earning capacity may be taken into consideration as a factor in equitable distribution rather than as a marital asset to be distributed. This makes no difference, of course, if there is not much property to distribute in the first place. In addition, earning capacity is usually included in the list of equitable factors for property distribution regardless of a spouse's contribution to such increase. *See, e.g., Lorenz v. Lorenz*, 729 N.W.2d 692 (N.D. 2007).

Wilson v. Wilson

Supreme Court of Appeals of West Virginia, 2010.
227 W. Va. 157, 706 S.E.2d 354.

■ WORKMAN, JUSTICE:

. . .

Mr. Wilson and Ms. Wilson (collectively, "the parties") were married in 1990 and separated on May 31, 2005. They had no children as part of the marriage. Both parties were involved in aspects of real estate development prior to and during their marriage. In 1993, the parties formed Hunter Company of West Virginia (hereinafter, "Hunter") to conduct real estate development; each party separately owned one half of the stock. Both parties agree that Hunter is a highly successful business which generated a net income to the parties of nearly $12 million in 2004, and more than $5 million in 2005.

Beginning in 1993, Hunter was chosen by National Land Partners (hereinafter, "NLP") to manage real estate development projects in West Virginia, which was accomplished through successive Management Agreements. . . . The agreement between Hunter and NLP provides that Hunter is an independent contractor. Hunter does not own any of the real estate involved in any of the projects as NLP buys the real estate through one of its wholly-owned subsidiaries. NLP also utilizes Inland Management, another one of its wholly-owned subsidiaries, to employ the people who work for NLP, to provide all of the accounting services for the projects, and for other services associated with the financial aspects of completing a project.

Under the Management Agreement, Hunter's duties are to identify property that would qualify for development, and complete due diligence and feasibility studies to determine if NLP should purchase the property. If NLP purchases the property, Hunter then conducts engineering and design work, obtains all permits and subdivision approval, and oversees the construction of the infrastructure. Upon completion of the road system and utilities, Hunter then hires a sales force, conducts advertising, marketing, and other promotions, sells all of the building lots, and oversees the closings of properties with the attorneys. Under the Management Agreement, typically at the end of the project, Hunter is paid a manager fee which is defined as any "net profit" remaining after twelve-and-one-half-percent of the gross sales are paid to NLP and all other expenses are paid. If NLP's preferential payment of twelve-and-one-half-percent exceeds the total net profit, Hunter receives no compensation.

On June 1, 2005, Ms. Wilson filed for divorce. . . . [T]he sole issue in contention that was litigated before the family court was the valuation of Hunter's manager fees on the projects that existed at the date of separation for purposes of equitable distribution. . . .

. . .

On November 21, 2008, the family court entered a final order and adopted the valuation of the manager fees as opined by Mr. Apple [i.e. Ms Wilson's expert], and concluded that Hunter possessed "enterprise goodwill," which was subject to equitable distribution. In doing so, the family court concluded that the evidence supported a finding that the Management Agreement between Hunter and NLP created independent value of Hunter separate and apart from the abilities and skills of Mr. Wilson, and that Hunter would continue to have value beyond its existing accounts and physical assets even if Mr. Wilson were dead.... The family court then ordered Mr. Wilson to pay Ms. Wilson the additional sum of $4,914,582.50 and awarded judgment in that amount.

Mr. Wilson thereafter filed a motion for reconsideration with the family court which was denied on December 23, 2008. Mr. Wilson then filed an appeal with the Circuit Court of Berkeley County. On March 25, 2009, the circuit court reversed the final order of the family court. The circuit court reversed the family court's finding that Hunter's manager fees were valued at $8,927,957.00 at the time of separation and found that such fees were actually a negative $(2,196,915.00)....

. . .

... Thereafter, Ms. Wilson filed an appeal with this Court.

. . .

In her first argument, Ms. Wilson states that the circuit court committed reversible error by misapplying this Court's holding in *May v. May*, 589 S.E.2d 536 ([W.Va.] 2003), on the issue of enterprise goodwill....

In *May*, this Court recognized that businesses possess an intangible asset known as "goodwill." "Goodwill" may be defined generally as

[T]he advantage or benefit, which is acquired by an establishment, beyond the mere value of the capital stock, funds, or property employed therein, in consequence of general public patronage and encouragement, which it receives from constant or habitual customers, on account of its local position, or common celebrity, or reputation for skill or affluence, or punctuality, or from other accidental circumstances or necessities, or even from ancient partialities or prejudices.

Essentially, goodwill is " 'the favor which the management of a business has won from the public, and probability that old customers will continue their patronage.' " Further, marketable "[g]oodwill associated with a business is an asset distributable upon dissolution of a marriage." However, "[w]here no market exists for goodwill, it should be considered to have no value."

The *May* Court explained that "[e]ssentially, there are two types of goodwill recognized by courts in divorce litigation: enterprise goodwill (also called commercial or professional goodwill) and personal goodwill...." *Id*. Ultimately, the *May* Court concluded that enterprise goodwill was marital property subject to equitable distribution. The Court explained that

[e]nterprise goodwill attaches to a business entity and is associated separately from the reputation of the owners. Product names, business locations, and skilled labor forces are common examples of enterprise goodwill. The asset has a determinable value because the enterprise goodwill of an ongoing business will transfer upon sale of the business to a willing buyer.

In contrast,

[P]ersonal goodwill is associated with individuals. It is that part of increased earning capacity that results from the reputation, knowledge and skills of individual people. Accordingly, the goodwill of a service business, such as a professional practice, consists largely of personal goodwill.

. . .

In determining that enterprise goodwill was subject to equitable distribution, the *May* Court explained that " '[T]he majority of states [24] differentiate between "enterprise goodwill," ... and "personal goodwill[.]" ' " (Citation omitted.) 589 S.E.2d at 545. The *May* Court noted that one of the leading cases discussing and adopting the distinction between personal goodwill and enterprise goodwill is the decision in *Yoon v. Yoon,* 711 N.E.2d 1265 (Ind.1999). In *Yoon,* the wife was granted a divorce from her husband. In granting the divorce the trial court assigned a value of $2,519,366.00 to the husband's medical practice. This figure included a value for goodwill. The husband appealed to a mid-level appellate court. There, the valuation was upheld. The husband then appealed to the state Supreme Court. In addressing the issue of goodwill, the Indiana Supreme Court stated:

> Goodwill has been described as the value of a business or practice that exceeds the combined value of the net assets used in the business. Goodwill in a professional practice may be attributable to the business enterprise itself by virtue of its existing arrangements with suppliers, customers or others, and its anticipated future customer base due to factors attributable to the business. It may also be attributable to the individual owner's personal skill, training or reputation. This distinction is sometimes reflected in the use of the term "enterprise goodwill," as opposed to "personal goodwill."

> Enterprise goodwill is an asset of the business and accordingly is property that is divisible in a dissolution to the extent that it inheres in the business, independent of any single individual's personal efforts and will outlast any person's involvement in the business. It is not necessarily marketable in the sense that there is a ready and easily priced market for it, but it is in general transferrable to others and has a value to others.

> . . .

> In contrast, the goodwill that depends on the continued presence of a particular individual is a personal asset, and any value that attaches to a business as a result of this "personal goodwill" represents nothing more than the future earning capacity of the individual and is not divisible. Professional goodwill as a divisible marital asset has received a variety of treatments in different jurisdictions, some distinguishing divisible enterprise goodwill from nondivisible personal goodwill and some not.

> Accordingly, we join the states that exclude goodwill based on the personal attributes of the individual from the marital estate.

> [B]efore including the goodwill of a self-employed business or professional practice in a marital estate, a court must determine that the goodwill is attributable to the business as opposed to the owner as an individual. If attributable to the individual, it is not a divisible asset and is properly considered only as future earning capacity that may affect the relative property division.

Yoon, 711 N.E.2d at 1268–69 (citations omitted).

Following an extensive discussion, the *May* Court held ... that " '[e]nterprise goodwill' is an asset of the business and may be attributed to a business by virtue of its existing arrangements with suppliers, customers or others, and its anticipated future customer base due to factors attributable to the business." ... [T]he *May* Court explained that " '[p]ersonal goodwill' is a personal asset that depends on the continued presence of a particular individual and may be attributed to the individual owner's personal skill, training or reputation." Finally, . . . the *May* Court held that:

> In determining whether goodwill should be valued for purposes of equitable distribution, courts must look to the precise nature of that goodwill. Personal goodwill, which is intrinsically tied to the attributes and/or skills of an individual, is not subject to equitable distribution. On the other hand, enterprise goodwill, which is wholly attributable to the business itself, is subject to equitable distribution.

Upon a thorough review of the record and consideration of the relevant case law, this Court finds that the circuit court did not abuse its discretion in concluding that Hunter only has personal goodwill which is not subject to equitable distribution. In that regard, the circuit court concluded that the contractual provisions in the management agreements between NLP and Hunter amounted to insufficient evidence to establish that Hunter possesses enterprise goodwill. In particular, the circuit court found that the portion of the management agreement providing for a continuing income stream to Hunter in the event of Mr. Wilson's death was "nothing more than a method of payment to [Hunter] for Mr. Wilson's progress upon his death or incapacity." The circuit court also found that Hunter only has one employee—Mr. Wilson and that his personal services were the basis for the management agreements with NLP.

In this appeal, Ms. Wilson argues that Hunter has enterprise goodwill because it employs a highly skilled workforce and the circuit court erred when it concluded that Mr. Wilson is Hunter's only employee. According to Ms. Wilson, Hunter uses the skills of twenty to twenty-five highly compensated employees. Mr. Wilson, however, maintains that the aforementioned employees are not employees of Hunter, but are employees of NLP.

In support of her contention that Hunter has many employees, Ms. Wilson relies upon the testimony of her expert witness, Mr. Apple, which was also the basis for the family court's conclusion that Hunter has enterprise goodwill. . . .

. . .

While Ms. Wilson is correct in her assertion there was a dispute regarding the number of employees employed by Hunter, the evidence in the record supports the circuit court's conclusion that Hunter has only one employee—Mr. Wilson. In that regard, the evidence presented below showed that Hunter did not produce or provide a single check to any "employee," other than Mr. Wilson himself. . . . Hunter is not free to hire anyone to be a part of any of the projects, nor can it independently set their salaries, without the express permission of NLP. . . . In consideration of all of the above, the circuit court did not error in finding that employees were not employees of Hunter.

Ms. Wilson also argues that Hunter possesses enterprise goodwill based upon a future income stream to Hunter in the event of Mr. Wilson's death or incapacitation. . . . As previously noted, the circuit court determined that such provision merely provided a method for payment to Hunter for Mr. Wilson's work in progress in the event of his death or incapacitation.

Contrary to Ms. Wilson's assertions, the evidence of record overwhelmingly supports a conclusion that Hunter only has personal goodwill. For example, it is undisputed that Mr. Wilson had a long relationship with the principals of NLP going back to the 1980s. Moreover, Mr. Murray explained that Mr. Wilson's association with NLP was based upon "a long record of performance in projects that Harry Patt[e]n [President of NLP] has been associated with, and when we formed National Land Partners, [Mr. Wilson] was the logical person to manage our projects."

. . .

This Court has also considered Ms. Wilson's argument that Hunter has enterprise value based upon the product names associated with Hunter for the various construction projects under construction, the amounts spent on advertising those projects, and her contention that Hunter has seven business locations. With regard to the business locations, the circuit court found that the evidence of record supports the conclusion that Hunter only owns one business location. The remaining properties are owned in the entirety by an NLP subsidiary and the only association that Hunter has with those locations is in utilizing them in the management of each particular project. Moreover, upon completion of a project, Hunter's use of that particular business location ceases to exist. With regard to the advertising campaigns for the various projects, the circuit court correctly found that it is undisputed in the record that such advertising and promotional expenses are costs of the project paid exclusively by NLP and not Hunter. While Ms. Wilson claims that she may have helped design some of the ads, Mr. Murray explained, "[NLP] take[s] care of all the marketing [at NLP's home office in Massachusetts], we place classified ads, TV commercials, radio commercials, anything that's needed to market the project. We develop that in Massachusetts and take care of the . . . the [sic] placement." Likewise, none of the advertising campaigns actually advertised Hunter. Instead, as the circuit court explained, they advertised particular projects such as The Point or Ashton Woods. Based upon these facts, Ms. Wilson's argument that the circuit court erred is without merit.

In consideration of all of the above, it is clear that any goodwill attributable to Hunter is exclusively personal goodwill. . . .

NOTES

1.   If goodwill has been accumulating during a marriage, such as a degree, or fame in *Elkus*, why should it not be distributable?

2.   Recently, courts have had to dispose of "assets" even more personal than human capital. An Oregon court decided that the contractual rights to the disposition of frozen embryos deriving from a couple's agreement with an IVF clinic could properly be considered "personal property" to be equitably distributed. *In re Marriage of Dahl & Angle*, 194 P.3d 834, 839 (Or. Ct. App. 2008). The court noted:

> We acknowledge that there is some inherent awkwardness in describing these contractual rights as "personal property". . . . However, we nonetheless conclude that the right to possess or dispose of the frozen embryos is personal property that is subject to a "just and proper" division under ORS 107.105.

Id. The court further decided that a court order directing the clinic to destroy the frozen pre-embryos per the terms of the agreement but against the husband's objections was a "just and proper" division. *Id.* at 842. On the disposition of frozen pre-embryos generally, *see supra* Chapter 6, Section D.1.

The question of the value of cosmetic surgery and whether it can be included in the marital estate has recently made its appearance in the court dockets. In *Isaacson v. Isaacson*, 777 N.W.2d 886 (N.D. 2010), Erik Isaacson sought to include Traci Isaacson's cosmetic surgery as a marital asset. The court noted:

> Erik Isaacson argues the district court improperly excluded the value of breast implants from the marital estate because doing so allowed Traci Isaacson

to spend marital assets on property she would keep after the divorce.... Here, the parties' . . . property and debt listing indicated to the district court that Erik Isaacson considered Traci Isaacson's breast implants to be personal property worth $5,500.

Citing cases from Hawaii, Delaware and Kentucky, Erik Isaacson invites us to hold that breast implants are a marital asset, the value of which are [sic] subject to distribution in the division of the marital estate. We decline Erik Isaacson's invitation because the cases he cited are neither controlling nor persuasive.

. . .

At the beginning of the divorce hearing, the district court reviewed the . . . property and debt listing submitted by the parties. Without objection or comment from either party, the court removed breast implants from the list and admonished Erik Isaacson for wasting the court's time. There was no subsequent discussion or argument whether the breast implants are marital assets or, if they were found to be assets, what their value should be. Erik Isaacson did not argue that the expenditure of funds to obtain the breast implants was a dissipation of marital assets, nor did he present the district court with any reason why breast implants should be considered a marital asset. Absent a timely objection, absent these arguments, and because the cases cited on appeal are unrelated to this case, the district did not err by excluding breast implants as a marital asset.

Id. at 891–92. Before deciding whether the value of the breast implants could potentially be included as marital debt or as dissipation of the marital estate read the relevant cases *infra*.

III. MARITAL DEBT

Rice v. Rice

Supreme Court of Kentucky, 2011.
336 S.W.3d 66.

■ Opinion of the Court by JUSTICE NOBLE.

. . .

Jackie Rice, Appellee, and Carolyn Rice, Appellant, were married on February 22, 1966, and were divorced on March 14, 2008, after forty-two years of marriage. At the time of the divorce, there were no minor children, but one adult child, Darrin, plays a significant role in the sole issue before the Court. In the divorce decree, the trial court held that credit card debt in the amount of $65,000 was marital, and assigned half the debt to each party.

However, this debt was incurred over a four-year period, primarily by the adult son, Darrin, with the permission and some degree of knowledge of his father, Jackie. Carolyn, on the other hand, did not know of the credit cards' existence, nor that Darrin was being allowed to use the cards. Indeed, some of the cards were obtained by using another family member's name, with Jackie making the payments. Carolyn was kept in the dark about this until Damn's [sic] bill collectors started calling her home in Greenup County, Kentucky, about debts he had incurred in Florida.

Jackie testified at trial that he began helping Darrin after his home in Florida was damaged by a hurricane. However, it is notable that he did not, as he admitted, tell Carolyn about this help. In fact, Jackie obtained multiple credit cards for his son and, in his testimony at trial, exhibited a somewhat cavalier attitude about helping Darrin get "a little old credit card" even after Carolyn learned of the large debt and demanded he stop. At some point,

Darrin changed the billing address so the statement would come directly to him, but Jackie admitted to continuing to make the payments on the cards and assisting Darrin surreptitiously with other debt such as co-signing for the purchase of a van and making all the payments on it even after it was completely destroyed by fire. Since Darrin had allowed the insurance to lapse, it was a total loss.

Carolyn did not discover the enormity of the debt until she retired from her eight-dollar-an-hour job, and was home to take the debt collectors' calls and check into the paperwork. When Jackie and Darrin persisted with additional debt, she filed for divorce.

The trial court determined that the debt was marital, and divided it equally between the parties. The Court of Appeals affirmed, with Judge Combs dissenting. To address the question of the nature of the debt and whether there was an obligation of both parties to pay the debt incurred for an adult child without the knowledge and consent of one of the parties, this Court granted discretionary review.

Questions of whether property or debt is marital or nonmarital are left to the sound discretion of the trial court, as is the equitable division of any marital property, and will be reviewed for abuse of discretion, namely, "whether the decision was arbitrary, unreasonable, unfair, or unsupported by sound legal principles." KRS 403.190 creates a presumption that property acquired during the marriage is marital property; that presumption is rebuttable by showing a lack of any marital contribution or purpose. However, the statute does not create a presumption in regard to debt, though as a practical matter, the assignment of debts acquired during the marriage speaks to whether a debt is marital or nonmarital, and is reviewed for abuse of discretion. *Neidlinger v. Neidlinger*, 52 S.W.3d 513 (Ky.2001); *Bodie v. Bodie*, 590 S.W.2d 895 (Ky.App.1979). The burden of proving that a debt is marital is upon the party that incurred it and now claims it is marital.

The *Neidlinger* case is this Court's latest discussion on the assignment of debt incurred during the marriage. It establishes a logical analysis as to who has the burden of proving that a debt is marital and what factors should be considered. As the Court of Appeals had established in *Bodie*, the nature of a debt must be determined by looking at who participated in the making of the debt, and who received the benefits of the debt. Thus this Court enunciated four factors in *Neidlinger* that give a clear basis for determining the nature of a debt as either marital or nonmarital: (1) Was the debt incurred for the purchase of marital property? (2) Was the debt necessary to maintain and support the family? (3) What was the extent and participation of each party in incurring or benefitting from the debt? and (4) What are the economic circumstances of the parties after divorce to allow for payment of the debt? *Neidlinger*, 52 S.W.3d at 523.

The question presented by this case is whether debt acquired for the benefit of an adult child, without the other parent's knowledge or consent, is nonetheless a marital debt subject to equitable division because of the "implied" benefits a parent receives from helping his or her child. If the answer to this question is yes, then one parent could choose, for example, to acquire debt to send a child to an Ivy League school, even after emancipation, without consent of the other parent, and the debt would be marital. If divorce later occurred, that debt, being marital, would be subject to assignment in whole or in part, depending on the equities, to the protesting parent. Modern disputes are more often of this type rather than the case before the Court, but the analysis is the same. This thinking would expand the concept of "family support" beyond any existing law and beyond the age of emancipation set by the legislature.

In this case, it is uncontroverted that the debt was not incurred for the purchase of marital property, and that Carolyn not only did not participate in making the debt, she was kept completely unaware of it until some years later. It is also clear, based on the award of maintenance to her, that Carolyn does not have personal assets sufficient to provide for her own support, let alone pay off this unknown debt. But the majority at the Court of Appeals appears to have taken an expansive view of the factor of family support and maintenance.

At the time Jackie began giving financial assistance and credit cards, his son Darrin was 38 years old and long emancipated. He was living with a family of his own in Florida. And while natural parental care and sympathy would be aroused by a child at any age having his home damaged by a hurricane and finding himself out of work, there is no *legal* obligation to support emancipated children. Certainly, the parents could make a joint decision to give such a large gift to their son, or even a small gift individually, but it is undisputed that Carolyn did not participate in the gifting decisions in this case. And it may be that Jackie intended only relatively small gifts at the beginning. But much as a gambler loses control over his gambling addiction, Jackie lost control over the expenditures as time went by. To this family of modest means, the sum of $65,000.00 in debt can be staggering, especially when compared to what could be purchased such as automobiles, medical care, and even a significant down payment on a home. Jackie and Carolyn have worked and raised six children, only two of whom were their biological children. As competent adults, the law puts the burden of being self-supporting on the adult children. If in generosity parents choose to help their children beyond the legal age, that is their sound prerogative; it is not an obligation.

Here, the situation is especially egregious because the gift at issue is *debt*, which binds the obligor into the future. As such, it has a totally different character than a consensual gift of property or money that is gone when given. Debt in this case is an encumbrance into the parties' old age. The question should be parsed to ask what a party is *legally obligated* to pay. As one who is not a party to the credit card contract, Carolyn could not be made to pay this debt through normal legal process. On what equitable grounds could a Family Court require her to pay half of it? Without some nexus to the debt other than being married to the person who made the debt, such as knowledge, consent, or receiving a direct benefit from the debt, there is no fairness in saddling Carolyn with this unanticipated debt after divorce, when there is no longer a marital purpose of any kind.

Jackie has not advanced any convincing arguments as to why this debt should be marital. More importantly, it is clear that none of the *Neidlinger* factors apply to support finding the debt to be marital. Thus, the trial court abused its discretion in so finding. Having so found, it naturally follows that the trial court further abused its discretion by assigning any of the debt to Carolyn.

Because none of the *Neidlinger* factors favored assigning to Carolyn a debt that she did not consent to nor receive any benefit from at this late stage in life, the trial court's decision to do so was unreasonable, unfair and unsupported by sound legal principles. Parents should not be required to buy their children's good will, and if they do, they must do so by choice rather than being compelled to it. There is no sound reason to expand longstanding law, which has been set by the legislature, to broaden "family support" to make one parent obligated for debt caused by gifts to an adult child created by the other parent alone.

By the same analysis, no parent is required by law to be the "best" parent. Perhaps the "best" parent would choose to face bankruptcy himself rather than see his child suffer or need something at any age. Or perhaps the "best" parent is one who requires his adult children to live life's lessons as they come, with self-sufficiency. Such a debate is philosophical—or moral or ethical—rather than legal, and is not the province of law when the law has been clearly stated by the legislature and our common law to chart a specific course. Lacking a legal obligation to support a competent adult child, Carolyn may not be made to pay debt incurred for that support without her knowledge, consent and benefit.

For the foregoing reasons, the Court of Appeals is reversed, and this case is remanded to the trial court for proceedings consistent with this opinion.

NOTES

1. Many courts inferred their authority to divide debt from the equitable distribution statutes, most of which did not include any clear provision on debt. *See* Margaret M. Mahoney, *The Equitable Distribution of Debt*, 79 UMKC LAW. REV. 445, 451–55 (2010). Some legislatures eventually made it part of the statutory requirements. *See, e.g., Gilliam v. McGrady*, 691 S.E.2d 797, 799–800 (Va. 2010) (discussing the relevant Virginia statute). For an example of when this authority is not permissive, *see Smith v. Emery–Smith*, 941 N.E.2d 1233, 1240 (Ohio Ct. App. 2010) (remanding case for reconsideration of distribution of property because trial court erred by not taking into account the marital debt when it initially divided the property).

2. Compare the *Rice* approach with the approach to marital debt in the following case:

> [T]he *Mondelli* analysis ... requires a trial court to engage in a preliminary determination of whether debt incurred during a marriage is marital or separate based on a "joint benefit" test. We believe that such a test would create substantial confusion and difficulty in determining what debts would meet the standard. For example, if one spouse incurs debt during the marriage to purchase a new automobile, would the purchase be for the joint benefit of both parties? If the automobile was used to drive children to school, would that change the result? The "joint benefit" test would require trial courts to go through a difficult and unnecessary inquiry, and we decline to adopt it.
>
> ... We now hold that "marital debts" are all debts incurred by either or both spouses during the course of the marriage up to the date of the final divorce hearing.

Alford v. Alford, 120 S.W.3d 810, 813 (Tenn. 2003). The court proceeded to consider the following factors in deciding how to distribute the marital debt: "(1) the debt's purpose; (2) which party incurred the debt; (3) which party benefitted from incurring the debt; and (4) which party is best able to repay the debt." *Id.* at 814. How is this different from the *Rice* approach? Which one is better? Other courts will allow spouses to argue against a prima facie showing of the debt's character. As one court stated,

> Section 20–3–620(B)(13) creates a rebuttable presumption that a debt of either spouse incurred prior to the beginning of marital litigation is a marital debt and must be factored in the totality of equitable apportionment. When the debt is incurred before marital litigation begins, the burden of proving a debt is nonmarital rests upon the party who makes such an assertion.

Grumbos v. Grumbos, 710 S.E.2d 76, 83 (S.C. Ct. App. 2011). Alternatively, there may be no statutory presumption regarding the character of debts. *See Gilliam v. McGrady*, 691 S.E.2d 797, 800 (Va. 2010).

3. The question of characterization is distinct from the question of distribution. On the broad discretionary powers of a court to divide debt *see, e.g., Hackett v. Hackett*, 643 S.W.2d 560 (Ark. 1982). That court noted:

> [I]t would be unrealistic for a chancellor to refuse to consider debts of the parties in deciding a divorce case. But that does not mean the chancellor must divide the debts. He may leave the parties as he found them, obligated individually or jointly to the creditor who is not ordinarily a party to a divorce and cannot therefore be bound by an order regarding the parties' debts.

Id. at 562. *See also Williams v. Williams*, 108 S.W.3d 629, 638 (Ark. Ct App. 2003) (finding the statutory mandate that marital property be divided equally unless such division is inequitable is not applicable to division of marital debts and that "[i]t is not error to determine that debts should be allocated … on the basis of their relative ability to pay"); *Pruitt v. Pruitt*, 697 S.E.2d 702, 710 (S.C. Ct. App. 2010) (" 'Basically the same rules of fairness and equity [that] apply to the equitable division of marital property also apply to the division of marital debts.' " (alteration in original) (citation omitted)). Note that most courts will not allocate the value of the net marital estate (after deducting debt from assets). Instead courts will usually allocate debt separately from assets.

In some instances, the court's broad discretionary powers will lead it to examine property and debts acquired before the marriage, when deciding how to equitably distribute the marital estate. In *Barnett v. Barnett*, 238 P.3d 594, 600 (Alaska 2010), for instance, the court noted that "[c]ourts may look to property acquired before the marriage when the balancing of the equities between the parties requires it." Nonetheless, it held that "courtship" debts that the husband incurred by traveling to Belarus and sponsoring the wife's immigration were erroneously characterized as marital. *Id.* at 599–600.

3.   THE PROBLEM OF FAIRNESS: WHAT IS EQUITABLE?

Adams v. Adams

Court of Civil Appeals of Alabama, 2000.
778 So. 2d 825.

■ CRAWLEY, JUDGE.

Annie Adams appeals from a judgment divorcing her and Lewis Adams, her husband of 41 years. She argues that the circuit court inequitably divided the marital property. We agree, and we therefore reverse the judgment of the circuit court and remand for that court to reconsider the division of property.

The wife is 59 years old and in good health. She lives with the parties' only child, a 37–year–old unmarried daughter. Neither the wife nor the daughter is employed. The parties agree that the daughter has "emotional problems," that she has always lived with her parents, and that she has never been employed. With the exception of several short-term or seasonal jobs, such as Christmas employment at a local department store, the wife was not employed during the marriage. When she married, she had a high school diploma. Between 1988 and 1990, she earned three degrees: two associate degrees (one in general education and one in retail merchandising) and a bachelor's degree in personnel management.

The husband is 62 years old and in poor health. After having cardiac-bypass surgery, he retired in 1994 from the Monsanto Corporation, where he had been employed for over 30 years. The husband testified that, after his retirement, he set up an investment account at A.G. Edwards & Sons and that he intended that he, his wife, and his daughter would live on the interest from that account during his retirement. The parties were separated for a year before the divorce. At the time of the separation, the A.G. Edwards account balance was approximately $426,000. At the time of the divorce, the account balance was $367,542. The parties agree that the net monthly income from the investment account is $1,960. The husband testified that he will receive an additional $1,200 per month in Social Security benefits when he reaches age 65. It is undisputed that, during the parties' one-year separation, the husband voluntarily deposited $1,000 per month in a checking account for the wife. It is also undisputed that the wife routinely overdrew that account in the amount of $500 to $700 every month.

The wife was awarded the marital home and an adjoining lot, together valued at between $50,000 and $56,000. She was also awarded all the furnishings of the home, valued at $2,000. The husband was ordered to pay the $3,000 mortgage indebtedness on the marital home, at a monthly payment of $155. The wife was awarded two vehicles valued at $3,000 each; the husband was awarded two vehicles valued at $3,500 and $3,000. The husband was awarded stocks worth $17,800 and the investment account totalling $367,542. The husband was ordered to pay the wife periodic alimony of $600 per month for three years and then $750 per month thereafter. The husband was also ordered to provide health insurance for the wife through a COBRA plan for as long as the law allowed.

The trial court awarded the wife assets totalling approximately $64,-000—or 16% of the marital property—and awarded the husband assets totalling approximately $385,000—or 84% of the marital property. The husband argues that the award represents the trial court's recognition that the wife is financially irresponsible and that she cannot be trusted not to squander the parties' joint assets. The husband maintains, therefore, that the trial court did not abuse its discretion by declining to award the wife any portion of the investment account. We reject the husband's argument.

> In a divorce action, a property settlement is made giving each spouse the value of their *interest in the marriage*. Each spouse has a right, even a property right in this.

Pattillo v. Pattillo, 414 So.2d 915, 917 (Ala.1982). What each spouse may do with his or her share of the marital property after the marriage is over may be relevant to, but should not be decisive of, the issue of how to divide the property.

> When making ... a division of property, the court should consider several factors, including the future prospects of the parties; their ages, health, and stations in life; the length of their marriage; the source, value and type of property owned; the standard of living to which the parties have become accustomed during the marriage and the potential for maintaining that standard; and, in appropriate situations, the conduct of the parties with reference to the cause of the divorce. *Johnson v. Johnson*, 565 So.2d 629 (Ala.Civ.App.1989). Each case must be determined on its own facts and circumstances. The division of property does not have to be equal, but must be equitable. *Id.*

Bolton v. Bolton, 720 So.2d 929, 930 (Ala.Civ.App.1998). A property division is final after 30 days from the judgment of divorce. Unlike an award of periodic alimony, a division of marital property cannot be modified upon a showing of changed circumstances.

In *Henderson v. Henderson*, [Ms. 2981092, February 18, 2000] 800 So.2d 595 (Ala.Civ.App.2000), this court reversed a trial court's division of marital property, holding that "it is inequitable to deny the wife [who was unemployed and who did not have a retirement plan of her own] a portion of the husband's retirement benefits after 34 years of marriage." In the present case, the wife also has no retirement plan or Social Security account of her own.

. . .

To the extent that the trial court determined that the wife was not entitled to any portion of the parties' investment account because she would likely squander those assets, the trial court misapplied the law of marital property. The trial court has discretion to consider a party's financial management skills as a factor in fashioning a marital property award, but it does not have discretion to deny a party an equitable share of the marital assets solely on the basis that, in its opinion, the party will likely mismanage the assets. We hold that the property award to the wife is so disproportionate as to be inequitable and that it constitutes an abuse of discretion. We therefore reverse the judgment of the circuit court and remand the cause with directions that that court make an equitable division of the marital property.

NOTES

1. Equitable distribution statutes typically include a list of factors to be considered, many of which are similar to those cited in *Adams*. The factors are not weighted, which means there is considerable variation in the application of the factors not only between different states, but also between similar cases before the same court.

2. As the court notes, equitable does not mean equal. Some states have statutes that require equal division, however, unless equity demands otherwise. The relevant Arkansas statute, for instance, provides that "[a]ll marital property shall be distributed one-half (½) to each party unless the court finds such a division to be inequitable." ARK. CODE ANN. § 9–12–315(a)(1) (2009). A few other courts have interpreted their statutes to require equal distribution, which can nonetheless be challenged. *See, e.g., Luedke v. Luedke*, 487 N.E.2d 133 (Ind. 1985). Some commentators have argued that there is a developing trend towards equal division even though discretion remains the distinguishing characteristic of equitable distribution. *See* JOHN DEWITT GREGORY, JANET LEACH RICHARDS, & SHERYL WOLF, PROPERTY DIVISION IN DIVORCE PROCEEDINGS: A FIFTY STATE GUIDE § 11.03, at 24 (Supp. 2004).

3. Many equitable distribution statutes were adopted to soften the harshness of the common law system's penchant for leaving homemakers without assets simply because at the end of a long marriage they had little property titled in their name. Many such statutes therefore mention the contributions of a homemaker as a factor in equitable distribution. The Tennessee Code, for instance, provides that " 'substantial contribution' may include, but not be limited to, the direct or indirect contribution of a spouse as homemaker, wage earner, parent or family financial manager, together with such other factors as the court having jurisdiction thereof may determine." TENN. CODE ANN. § 36–4–121(b)(1)(D) (2010). After passage of such equitable distribution statutes, some courts tried to measure the value of such contribution by calculating the replacement cost of homemaker services, but the trend is towards assuming that a homemaker's contributions were equal in value to the financial contributions of the breadwinning spouse. *See, e.g., Hoebelheinrich v. Hoebelheinrich*, 600 S.E.2d 152, 156–57 (Va. Ct. App. 2004) (court affirmed equal split of husband's medical practice, where "husband and wife . . . separated [after] twenty-two years[, and] . . . husband and wife agreed that wife would stay home to raise their children and care for the home. They had four children, and wife raised them well. . . ."). This is merely a presumption, however, and courts have regularly deviated from it. Just as a divorce court can scrutinize spouses' long-term financial contributions, it can do the same with their long-term contributions as homemakers. It is not uncommon, for instance, to see a court deviate from an equal award if the homemaking services were not delivered personally, but mostly through hired help. *See, e.g., Pfeifer v. Pfeifer*, 938 P.2d 684 (Mont. 1997).

Finan v. Finan

Supreme Court of Connecticut, 2008.
287 Conn. 491, 949 A.2d 468.

■ NORCOTT, J.

The principal issue in this certified appeal requires us to answer the question, which was left unanswered in our recent decision in *Gershman v. Gershman*, 286 Conn. 341, 350–51 n. 10 (2008), of whether a trial court fashioning financial orders in dissolution cases may consider a party's pre-separation dissipation of marital assets. The plaintiff, Meredith Finan, ... asks this court ... to determine whether trial courts should consider both preseparation [sic] and postseparation [sic] dissipation of marital assets when fashioning financial orders....

The Appellate Court decision sets forth the following facts and procedural history. "The parties married on September 11, 1982, and, at the time of the trial, had three children, of which two were minors. The court rendered judgment dissolving the marriage on March 11, 2005. The court found that the marriage had broken down irretrievably without attributing fault to either party as to the cause of the breakdown.

"The court entered orders regarding property distribution, alimony, child support and other miscellaneous matters. As part of the dissolution decree, the court ordered the defendant to pay to the plaintiff 'unallocated alimony and child support in equal semimonthly installments on the first and fifteenth of each month, the annual sum of $95,000 based on his base salary of $225,000.'"

The plaintiff appealed the trial court's judgment to the Appellate Court, claiming, inter alia, that the trial court "improperly refused to admit into evidence a report detailing the defendant's preseparation [sic] dissipation of marital assets ... [and] that the court failed to consider evidence that the defendant dissipated marital assets by spending large sums of money prior to the parties' separation." ... The Appellate Court declined to review the plaintiff's claim pertaining to this ruling.... This certified appeal followed.

. . .

In *Gershman v. Gershman, supra*, 286 Conn. at 351, we recently concluded that "dissipation in the marital dissolution context requires financial misconduct involving marital assets, such as intentional waste or a selfish financial impropriety, coupled with a purpose unrelated to the marriage." We now address the question left unanswered in *Gershman*, namely, whether a temporal element is an essential component of dissipation. *See id.*, at 350–51 n. 10. More specifically, we must determine whether transactions that occur prior to the physical separation of spouses may constitute dissipation of marital assets for purposes of equitable property distribution under § 46b–81. As this issue is a matter of first impression for Connecticut's appellate courts, it presents a question of law subject to plenary review.

We begin by examining the language of the relevant statute. Section 46b–81 provides in relevant part: "(a) At the time of entering a decree annulling or dissolving a marriage or for legal separation pursuant to a complaint under section 46b–45, the Superior Court may assign to either the husband or wife all or any part of the estate of the other.... (c) In fixing the nature and value of the property ... to be assigned ... [t]he court shall also consider the contribution of each of the parties in the acquisition, *preservation* or appreciation in value of their respective estates." (Emphasis added.)

As the term "preservation" is not defined in the statute, "GENERAL STATUTES § 1–1(a) requires that we construe the term in accordance with the commonly approved usage of the language ... [and, therefore] it is appropriate to look to the common understanding of the term as expressed in a dictionary." (Citation omitted; internal quotation marks omitted.) The definition of "preserve" in the American Heritage Dictionary of the English Language (4th Ed. 2000) is "[t]o maintain in safety from injury, peril, or harm; protect...." "Dissipation," on the other hand, is defined as "[w]asteful expenditure or consumption...." Id. Under the common usage of the terms, "dissipation" is the financial antithesis of "preservation." More specifically, a party that dissipates assets detracts from the preservation of those assets. Accordingly, Connecticut trial courts have the statutory authority, under § 46b–81, to consider a spouse's dissipation of marital assets when determining the nature and value of property to be assigned to each respective spouse. The language of § 46b–81 does not, however, expressly provide any temporal limitation on a court's consideration of marital asset dissipation. Furthermore, after review, we are unable to extrapolate any meaningful guidance from the relationship of § 46b–81 to other statutes, its legislative history or its underlying policy, with regard to whether the legislature intended to limit a court's consideration of dissipation to actions occurring within a prescribed time period. Accordingly, our resolution of this issue requires us to address a gap in the statute.

A review of case law in other jurisdictions reveals that the majority of our sister states allow trial courts to consider a spouse's dissipation of marital assets, that occurs *prior* to the spouses' physical separation, in determining the allocation of assets to each respective spouse. We agree with the majority of our sister states, and conclude, therefore, that trial courts are permitted to consider, when determining the allocation of assets between spouses in a dissolution proceeding, whether a spouse's actions that occur *prior* to the spouses' physical separation constitute the dissipation of marital assets.

Several of the states that allow courts to recognize preseparation [sic] dissipation also require, however, that the actions constituting dissipation must occur either: (1) in contemplation of divorce or separation; or (2) when the marriage was in serious jeopardy or undergoing an irretrievable breakdown. At least three rationales have been offered for why courts have adopted the foregoing temporal restrictions. For instance, "it has been argued that without a breakdown test [or some equivalent test], every expenditure and economic decision made during the marriage can be questioned, and the courts would become auditing agencies for every failed marriage." L. Becker, *Conduct of a Spouse That Dissipates Property Available for Equitable Property Distribution: A Suggested Analysis*, 52 OHIO ST. L.J. 95, 108 (1991). "It has also been suggested that the breakdown test appropriately draws the line between, on the one hand, the right of a spouse to be protected against improper expenditures by the other spouse and, on the other hand, the right of a spouse to manage and control property owned solely by that spouse." L. Becker, *supra*, at 108, citing *Booth v. Booth*, 7

Va.App. 22, 27–28, 371 S.E.2d 569 (1988) ("at least until the parties contemplate divorce, each is free to spend marital funds"). Furthermore, the temporal restrictions better assist courts in determining the impropriety of a spouse's actions, namely, whether the actions were carried out, at least in part, to deprive the other spouse of assets that would otherwise be available for equitable division by the court. In addition, it has been noted that, when imposing temporal limitations on when trial courts may consider acts of dissipation, courts should remain cognizant of the fact that "depletion [of assets] in anticipation of divorce is not limited to depletion after the date of separation or after the completion of the marital breakdown. Many spouses begin divorce planning before actual separation, when the marital breakdown is not yet complete." B. Turner, Equitable Distribution of Property (2004 Sup.) p. 865.

We are persuaded by the foregoing rationales for adopting temporal limitations, with regard to the trial court's consideration of *when* the alleged dissipative actions of a spouse occurs. Accordingly, we conclude that, in order for a transaction to constitute dissipation of marital assets for purposes of equitable distribution under § 46b–81, it must occur either: (1) in contemplation of divorce or separation; or (2) while the marriage is in serious jeopardy or is undergoing an irretrievable breakdown. Trial courts are not precluded from considering preseparation [sic] dissipation, therefore, so long as the transactions constituting dissipation occur within the foregoing temporal framework.

. . . Accordingly, a new trial is required.

NOTES

1. A majority of states do not permit consideration of marital misconduct for purposes of equitable distribution, unless the misconduct has an economic impact on the marriage. Dissipation of assets for purposes outside the scope of the marriage is the form of economic misconduct most commonly recognized by courts.

2. Many dissipation cases involve a one-time financial waste towards the end of the marriage or separation. Sometimes, however, courts are faced with the effects of a spouse's long-term bad spending habits or profligacy. Even though courts are reluctant to become the ex-post accountants of a marriage, a spouse's net negative financial contribution to a marriage will usually be taken into consideration. In *Bragg v. Bragg*, 553 S.E.2d 251 (S.C. Ct. App. 2001) the court held:

> In this case, we find the family court's award to Wife of 35% of the marital estate fair and equitable. Husband earned a substantially higher income than Wife, and Wife's exuberant charging habits and calculated attempts to conceal her spending from Husband negatively affected the parties' finances. Therefore, we cannot conclude the family court placed undue weight on Wife's financial misconduct in reaching its equitable apportionment decision.

Id. at 255. Bad financial decisions, however, will usually not qualify. For instance, in *Long v. Long*, No. M2006–02526–COA–R3–CL, 2008 WL 2649645 (Tenn. Ct. App., July 3, 2008), a husband asked his wife to approve sale of their stock, which he felt would decrease in value. She refused and the stock price subsequently fell. A Tennessee court of appeals declined to characterize the wife's refusal to sell as dissipation.

> With benefit of hindsight, we see that Husband's prediction that the value of the BSF stock could drop was correct. Wife, however, was not required to be clairvoyant or to simply accept Husband's investment advice. Had the stock been sold and the value thereafter rose dramatically, would this amount to dissipation by Husband? In explaining her refusal to sell the BSF stock, Wife testified that she considered the stock to be a long-term investment, and there is no evidence

indicating that Wife's refusal to sell was intended to deplete a marital asset, or that it was a careless wasting of marital property. Husband's argument is without merit.

Id. at *9.

Tucker v. Tucker

Missouri Court of Appeals, Eastern District, Division Four, 1991.
806 S.W.2d 758.

■ SMITH, PRESIDING JUDGE.

. . .

The parties were married in June, 1981 and separated in July, 1988. One child, Nichole, was born of the marriage. In April and May, 1988, husband's sister, Sharon, was dying of terminal cancer. Wife spent considerable time in her sister-in-law's home assisting the family. Sharon died in late May, 1988. In July, wife went to Texas to assist the family of husband's brother when the wife in that family went into a hospital, apparently as a result of her involvement in assisting Sharon and her family and the strain of Sharon's death and several other family deaths. Sharon's widower, Dennis Babor, also went to Texas during this same period although not with Donna. They returned to Missouri together. Husband, who had received reports from Texas of involvement between wife and Babor, confronted wife on her return from Texas. Husband testified that wife indicated her preference for Babor over husband. Husband filed for dissolution the next day. Husband produced witnesses who testified to observing wife and Babor hugging and kissing passionately on occasions prior to husband and wife's separation. Wife denied any sexual relationship with Babor prior to separation and testified that any hugging and kissing were attempts to comfort Babor after the loss of his wife. The trial court found wife guilty of marital misconduct presumably based on the contacts with Babor although the nature of the misconduct was not specified in the decree. The court did find this misconduct "directly contributed to the dissolution of the marriage."

The marital assets of the parties were limited. The major assets were $12,000 equity in the family home and a four to five thousand dollar interest to husband's pension and retirement plan with his employer. The evidence concerning the pension plan did not establish that it met the requirements necessary for it to be considered divisible marital property. Two motor vehicles with a total equity value of $50, bank accounts of nominal amounts, and home furnishings and clothing constituted the remainder of the marital property. The decree awarded husband the home, title to his pension and retirement plan, both motor vehicles, all bank accounts in his name, all household furnishings and appliances contained in the marital home, and his clothing, jewelry and personal effects. Wife received her clothing, jewelry and personal effects, bank accounts in her name, and all household furnishings and appliances in her possession. The effect of the decree was to award husband virtually all the marital property and a washing machine which the parties agreed wife had inherited from her grandmother. No maintenance was asked for or was awarded to either party.

. . .

. . . [C]ounsel for husband prepared and the court signed the decree containing the distribution previously set forth. Husband justifies the court's action in giving husband almost all the marital property solely upon the misconduct of the wife.

The division of marital property need not be equal but it must be just. We addressed the function of the "conduct of the parties" statutory factor (§ 452.330.1(4) R.S.Mo.1986) in *Burtscher v. Burtscher*, 563 S.W.2d 526 (Mo. App.1978). We noted first that marital misconduct should not serve as a basis for ordering excessive maintenance against, or inadequate marital property to, the offending spouse. *Id.* [1–3]. We then set forth the circumstances in which the conduct factor became relevant:

> We believe the conduct factor becomes important when the conduct of one party to the marriage is such that it throws upon the other party marital burdens beyond the norms to be expected in the marital relationship. The thrust of the dissolution law is to treat the marriage as a partnership to which each spouse presumably contributes equally. When the misconduct of one party changes that balance so that the other party must assume more than his or her share of the partnership load it is appropriate that such misconduct should affect the distribution of the property of that partnership. It is logical that if one party to the partnership has, because of the other's misconduct, contributed more to the partnership, he or she should receive a greater portion of the partnership assets. *Id.*

Nothing in the record here demonstrates the above type of misconduct. The evidence indicates the wife contributed equally throughout the marriage to the partnership. Her misconduct, if it occurred, (and we defer to the trial court in that regard) occurred no earlier than the last two months of the marriage. The misconduct was serious and presumably caused the breakup of the marriage but that alone does not destroy the right of the wife to share in the marital assets. Husband did not suggest in his testimony that he believed wife should receive nothing in the way of marital assets. To the contrary, his testimony suggests that he believed wife was entitled to half of the equity in the home. While it is true, as he suggests in his brief, that he did not specifically state that, it is also true that he implied it and certainly did not affirmatively disavow it. The court erred in its division of marital property.

. . .

We are authorized to enter the decree that should have been entered by the trial court. Rule 84.14. Accordingly, the decree is modified to provide that wife, in addition to the property awarded in the decree, shall receive from husband as her share of the home equity, $6,000, to be paid in equal monthly principal installments over a period of six years with full or partial prepayment authorized at any time. Each installment to bear interest on the remaining principal balance at the rate of 9% per annum. Washing machine is awarded to wife as her separate property. As modified the judgment is affirmed.

NOTES

1. Despite the adoption of no-fault grounds, some twenty-one states allow the consideration of marital misconduct other than dissipation for the purposes of equitable distribution. *See* Brett R. Turner, *The Role of Marital Misconduct in Dividing Property upon Divorce*, 15 No. 7 DIVORCE LITIG. 117 (2003). Some states do so by express statutory reference to the spouses' conduct, or through the concept of contribution to the marriage as a factor in equitable distribution, or through a reference to "any other relevant factors" in a list of factors to be taken into consideration. In all jurisdictions that allow consideration of marital misconduct for the purposes of equitable distribution, such conduct is only one among many factors to be considered. Justifying a property award solely on the basis of marital misconduct can therefore be deemed reversible error.

2. As in *Tucker*, most jurisdictions that allow consideration of marital misconduct require behavior that has placed an extra burden on the non-offending spouse or on the marriage more generally. Proof of this burden is a requirement. In *Ballard v. Ballard*, 77 S.W.3d 112 (Mo. Ct. App. 2002), for instance, the Missouri Court of Appeals held that even though the husband had fathered a child outside of marriage, had paid child support using marital funds, and had brought home the child to live with him and the wife for a year and a half, the wife had not argued or proven that such misconduct had placed a burden on her. Some courts require that the misconduct be at the root of the breakdown of the marriage. For example, in *Wells v. Wells*, 567 So.2d 361 (Ala. Civ. App. 1990), the court held that the husband's adultery was unrelated to marital breakdown, therefore the award of 65 percent of marital assets to him was not error. In Texas, courts interpreted *Young v. Young*, 609 S.W.2d 758 (Tex. 1980), to mean that unless a divorce was granted on the basis of fault, courts should not take fault into consideration when distributing community property. The underlying fear was that otherwise courts would need to deal with "every bicker, nag and pout." *Id.* at 762. *See, e.g., Phillips v. Phillips*, 75 S.W.3d 564, 572 (Tex. Ct. App. 2002). This interpretation was challenged in a later case, in which the court ruled that fault could be considered in the division of property regardless of the grounds for divorce. *See In re Marriage of Brown*, 187 S.W.3d 143, 146 (Tex. Ct. App. 2006).

Several jurisdictions require a certain threshold or gravity of misconduct for fault to be considered in property distribution. New York courts for example regularly hold that only egregious fault that shocks the conscience may be considered in equitable distribution. As one court noted:

> That is so because marital fault is inconsistent with the underlying assumption that a marriage is in part an economic partnership and upon its dissolution the parties are entitled to a fair share of the marital estate, because fault will usually be difficult to assign and because introduction of the issue may involve the courts in time-consuming procedural maneuvers relating to collateral issues.

O'Brien v. O'Brien, 489 N.E.2d 712, 719 (N.Y. 1985). What do you think about the court's reasoning? New York became the last state to allow a no-fault ground for divorce in 2010. Does this change what you think about the court's reasoning?

3. If both parties are equally guilty of marital misconduct then a court might not take their misconduct into consideration. *See Sinopole v. Sinopole*, 871 S.W.2d 46 (Mo. Ct. App. 1993) (both spouses had allegedly committed adultery, hence trial court did not err in giving misconduct no weight in property division).

B.   ALIMONY

Mary Kay Kisthardt, *Re-thinking Alimony: The AAML's Considerations for Calculating Alimony, Spousal Support or Maintenance*

21 J. AM. ACAD. MATRIM. LAW. 61, 65–69 (2008).

III.   In Search of a Rationale

A.   The Traditional Theory of Alimony

The initial rationale for alimony or support had its origins in the English common law system. Historically there were two remedies from the bonds of marriage. Although an absolute divorce was theoretically possible, it required an act of Parliament and was therefore hardly ever used. More commonly a plea was made for a separation from bed and board (mensa et thoro). This action available from the ecclesiastical courts constituted a legal separation as absolute divorce was prohibited under canon law. A husband who secured such a divorce retained the right to control his wife's property and the corresponding duty to support his wife. Even after Parliament authorized the courts to grant absolute divorces, the concept of alimony remained. The initial rationale appeared be premised [sic] on the fact that women gave up their property rights at marriage and after the marriage ended they were without the means to support themselves. The original award of alimony was similar to the wife's claim of dower, and courts used the traditional one-third of the property standard so instead of one-third of the estate at the husband's death she would receive one-third of the income of her husband at the time of the divorce. The concept of alimony came across the Atlantic with the founding of the colonies but seemingly without a corresponding rationale.

The introduction of the Married Women's Property Acts changed the ability of women to retain property, but alimony remained. It appears that at least one rationale was based on contract theories because, for many courts, the role of fault played a significant role. Alimony then became damages for breach of the marital contract reflected in the fact that in most states it was only available to the innocent and injured spouse. The measure of damages often approximated the standard of living the wife would have enjoyed but for her husband's breach. Alternatively it represented compensatory damages for tortious conduct.

B.   The Beginning of the "Modern Era"

In the 1970's the economic picture of spouses at divorce began to change. Many states adopted principles of equitable distribution allowing for property acquired during the marriage to be divided between the spouses regardless of how it was titled. This allowed economically dependent spouses to retain assets that were previously unavailable to them. Property division was used to address the inequities. These statutes resulted in decreasing spousal support awards.

In addition, women, who were historically the economically dependent spouses, joined the workforce in increasing numbers. The previous assumption that women would be unable to support themselves through employment gave way to the idea that dependence could no longer be used as a rationale for alimony. However, the practical reality of women's financial dependency remained in many marriages.

With the advent of no-fault divorce, alimony also lost its punitive rationale. The Uniform Marriage and Divorce Act (UMDA) changed the character of these awards to one that was almost exclusively needs based and at the same time gave spousal support a new name: maintenance. Maintenance was only available to the spouse who had an inability to meet his or her reasonable needs through appropriate employment. The marital standard of living was only one of six factors relied upon in making awards under the UMDA, where the focus was now on "self-support" even if it was at a substantially lower level than existed during the marriage. In addition, when awards were made they were generally only for a short term, sufficient to allow the dependent spouse to become "self-supporting." This spousal support reform often left wives, who were frequently the financially dependent spouses in long term marriages, without permanent support.

Maintenance was sometimes awarded for "rehabilitative" purposes such as providing income for the time it takes the recipient to acquire skills or education necessary to become self-supporting. Short term transitional awards were used to make a spouse economically self sufficient as soon as possible.

1.   TYPES OF ALIMONY

a.   NEED AND ABILITY TO PAY

Hodge v. Hodge

Supreme Court of Pennsylvania, 1986.
513 Pa. 264, 520 A.2d 15.

■ ZAPPALA, JUSTICE.

We granted cross-petitions for allowance of appeal to determine whether or not a medical license is "marital property" under our Divorce Code and whether the award of alimony was proper. . . .

[The parties married in 1967. Between 1971 and 1977, Mr. Hodge underwent medical training in Mexico and the U.S. Mrs. Hodge remained in the U.S. during his first year of school, working to support Dr. Hodge's studies and caring for the couple's daughter. She and their daughter joined Dr. Hodge in Mexico for the next three years of his training there. After a residency program in the U.S., Dr. Hodge received his medical license in February 1977. On August 27, 1977, Dr. Hodge told his wife that he did not want to continue their marital relationship. An action in divorce by Mrs. Hodge remained dormant until March 1981, when Dr. Hodge filed his own action. On October 9, 1981, a divorce decree was entered. The court rejected Mrs. Hodge's claim that the medical license was "marital property" and awarded her alimony of $100 per week for fourteen years. The Superior Court affirmed after both parties appealed. The Supreme Court of Pennsylvania granted allocatur.]

[In Part I, the Court rejects marital property theory of the medical license.]

PART II

Next, Dr. Hodge argues it was improper to award Mrs. Hodge alimony for fourteen years. Section 501(a) states:

(a) The court may allow alimony, as it deems reasonable, to either party, only if it finds that the party seeking alimony:

(1) lacks sufficient property, including but not limited to any property distributed pursuant to Chapter 4, to provide for his or her reasonable needs; and

(2) is unable to support himself or herself through appropriate employment.

Subsection (b) lists the factors to be considered in determining whether alimony is necessary and in determining the nature, duration and amount of any such award.

In awarding Mrs. Hodge fourteen years of alimony, the trial court adopted the special master's conclusion that the "only remaining method which our law allows by which economic responsibility can be equitably adjusted under such circumstances is to impose an order of alimony upon plaintiff for the benefit of defendant." (R. 16a). The trial court stated that this "equitable adjustment (is) needed in order to place some economic responsibility on the plaintiff for the defendant's sacrifices made during the marriage." (Slip opinion p. 27). Superior Court affirmed finding no abuse of discretion on the part of the trial court. We cannot agree.

Although the Divorce Code was adopted with the intent to "effectuate economic justice", 23 P.S. § 102(a)(6), we cannot ignore that alimony was intended to be based on "actual need and ability to pay." *Id.* This is clear from reading sections 501(a)(1) and (2) and 501(c). The primary purpose of alimony is to provide one spouse with sufficient income to obtain the necessities of life, not to punish the other spouse. Any alimony order must be based on need. Although both parents have an equal duty to support their children, the fact that one parent is a student and not contributing support for the children does not result in a future claim by the other spouse for the unpaid past support. Therefore, the purpose of alimony under our statute is rehabilitation not reimbursement. As Judge Wieand has astutely stated:

> The duty of support is imposed by rule of law on both spouses. Compliance with this legal duty does not result in unjust enrichment to the other. Marriage is for better or worse. It is not entered with a conscious intent that at some future time there will be an accounting of and reimbursement for moneys contributed to the support of the family. To inject such a concept would, in my judgment, have far-reaching and unfortunate consequences. If I am correct in my view regarding the duty of spousal support, then it is difficult to perceive good reason for creating an exception which would reimburse a spouse for support contributed while the other is attending an institution of higher learning or otherwise obtaining advanced training.

Accordingly, after a spouse has established a need for alimony, the court may then take into consideration those expenses incurred in excess of the traditional support obligation (i.e., tuition, books, fees, etc.), in determining an alimony award.

How then should the factors listed in section 501(b) be applied to section 501(a)? In applying section 501(b), the trial court must keep in mind the purpose of alimony, i.e., to provide support when there exists a lack of sufficient property and appropriate employment to provide for reasonable needs. Since section 501(b) sets forth factors to be considered in determining whether alimony is necessary and in determining the amount, duration and manner of payment, it is clear that certain factors are only relevant to a determination of entitlement while others are relevant to the amount, duration and manner of payment. Thus, when a trial court considers these enumerated factors in determining whether alimony is appropriate, the court must keep in mind the purpose of alimony as set forth in section 501(a) in evaluating whether a certain factor is relevant. A factor may be important in determining the duration of alimony a spouse should receive, but be irrelevant in making the initial determination of whether that spouse is entitled to alimony at all. To interpret section 501 otherwise would virtually eliminate the introductory language of section 501(b), that "[i]n determining whether alimony is necessary," the court must consider the factors enumerated therein. 23 P.S. § 501(b).

Applying this reasoning to the present appeal, it is evident that both the special master and the lower courts applied section 501 incorrectly in determining the award of alimony. Both the special master and the trial court attempted to effectuate economic equality through the use of alimony.

Although an honorable attempt to compensate the wife for lack of marital property, it clearly was improper. Since the alimony award was based upon an erroneous application of the statute, this matter should be remanded to the trial court for a redetermination of the issue of alimony. On remand, the trial court must first determine whether Mrs. Hodge is entitled to alimony, keeping in mind that alimony is intended to rehabilitate a spouse not to provide a source of economic equalization, before determining an appropriate amount and duration.

. . .

NOTE

What are the acceptable bases according to the court for awarding alimony? How would the fact that Mrs. Hodge had worked part-time to support the family affect the court's appraisal of "need"?

b. STANDARD OF LIVING

Lorenz v. Lorenz

Supreme Court of New York, Appellate Division, 2009.
63 A.D.3d 1361, 881 N.Y.S.2d 208.

■ SPAIN, J.

Appeal from a judgment of the Supreme Court (Work, J.), entered June 19, 2008 in Ulster County, ordering, among other things, equitable distribution of the parties' marital property, upon a decision of the court.

In October 2006, after more than 33 years of marriage, plaintiff commenced this divorce action. There are two emancipated children of the marriage. After a bench trial, at which time both parties were 54 years of age, Supreme Court, among other things, equally distributed the marital property and awarded maintenance to plaintiff in the amount of $500 per week, retroactive to September 4, 2007 and until such time as plaintiff can draw full Social Security benefits, apparently when she becomes 66. Defendant appeals.

The principal issues raised by defendant on appeal focus on Supreme Court's award of maintenance. Initially, defendant asserts that the court abused its discretion in awarding maintenance because plaintiff is capable of being self-supporting and, in the alternative, that the amount and duration were excessive. In maintenance determinations "the amount of earnings necessary to enable the recipient to become self-supporting must be determined with some reference to the standard of living of the parties, as well as the earning capacity of each party; and these factors carry more weight in a marriage of long duration" (*Garvey v. Garvey*, 223 A.D.2d 968, 970, 636 N.Y.S.2d 893 [1996]). Here, in fashioning its award, the court considered each of the relevant statutory factors (*see* Domestic Relations Law § 236[B][6]), including the parties' incomes, their future earning capacity, and the long duration of the marriage.

The testimony of the parties and their 2006 joint income tax returns provide ample record proof to support Supreme Court's conclusion that defendant's annual income was in excess of $100,000 and plaintiff's income was upwards of $20,000. Whereas defendant is in good health, plaintiff has a back problem—which recently required surgery—and a heart arrhythmia ailment, each of which impacts negatively on her future earning capacity as a self-employed hairdresser. While defendant was building his skills and a lucrative career, plaintiff was devoting a good portion of her time and talent tending to the needs of their children and attending to the family's domestic needs. Indeed, although the purpose of maintenance is to provide temporary support while the recipient develops the skills and experience necessary to become self-sufficient, self-sufficiency "is not always possible", and we find ample record evidence to support the court's conclusion that plaintiff's potential to become self-sufficient was very low. Moreover, the fact that plaintiff will eventually obtain her share of the marital assets is not a bar to an appropriate period of maintenance, especially where, as here, Supreme Court did not favor plaintiff in its 50–50 distribution of the marital property.

Further, we find that the amount of the maintenance award is within defendant's means and appropriately crafted to meet plaintiff's needs, providing some assurance that she will be able to maintain their predivorce standard of living. Supreme Court found that plaintiff will now be required to pay for her own health insurance, estimated to cost between $350 and $500 per month, and, in the likely event she will not be able to purchase defendant's half of the marital residence, she will have to find a new place to live. The court also considered defendant's ability to deduct his maintenance payments from his income taxes. On this record, we cannot say that the amount set by the court of $500 per week was an abuse of discretion.

NOTE

What are the factors that the court considers in deciding to affirm the alimony award? What role should the "marital standard of living" play in an award of alimony?

c. REIMBURSEMENT

In re Marriage of Probasco

Supreme Court of Iowa, 2004.
676 N.W.2d 179.

■ LAVORATO, CHIEF JUSTICE.

. . .

I. Background Facts and Proceedings.

Ralane and Craig met in 1983. At the time both were attending Morningside College. Eventually they developed an intimate relationship, resulting in the birth of their child, Kally, on October 30, 1985. . . .

. . .

The parties formally married on February 12, 1991. However, for purposes of this action, they stipulated that they have been married since November 1985. Neither party brought property of appreciable value into the marriage.

In May 1986, Craig graduated from college with a Bachelor's degree in business administration. His grade point average was 2.52. Ralane graduated in December 1986 also with a Bachelor's degree in business administration. Her grade point average was 3.71. Neither party contributed to the education of the other, and both intended to pursue careers in business.

Following his graduation, Craig began working for New York Life Insurance Company as a salesperson. Following her graduation, Ralane worked in the home, caring for the children. She also handled all of the household finances and assisted Craig in keeping track of his business with New York Life.

Throughout 1987 and 1988, the parties lived primarily on borrowed money from a number of sources because Craig's income from New York Life was low. Ralane continued to work in the home, caring for the children, handling family finances, and preparing reports for Craig's insurance work.

In 1989, because Craig was without a driver's license, Ralane had to drive Craig to his business appointments. Craig's income that year was $5,118.

It was at this time that the parties thought about opening a restaurant. They were looking for a family-type restaurant and began considering a Perkins franchise. Craig focused his efforts on the acquisition and development of such a franchise. Ralane worked for the Census Bureau in 1990 and eventually landed a permanent position with Wilson Trailer of Sioux City in January 1991. She also assisted Craig in the evenings on the Perkins franchise project. Because Craig's insurance income was substantially reduced, the family had to rely on Ralane's income over the next four years.

. . .

When the restaurant opened, Ralane continued her employment with Wilson Trailer to maintain health insurance for the family. In the beginning, Craig and Ralane used their home for an office. In January 1994, Ralane terminated her employment with Wilson Trailer and became accounts payable coordinator at the restaurant. Her initial salary was $18,000 per year and that later increased to $32,000 per year. The business was so successful that it became the highest volume Perkins in the system with annual sales in excess of $3,800,000.

Ralane worked in the restaurant from January 1994 through late October 1998, when the serious marital problems the parties had been experiencing came to a head. After October 1998, Ralane no longer worked in the restaurant.

In March 1999, Craig filed this dissolution of marriage action. At the time the parties were living in a home they had purchased in 1986 with a loan of $60,000. . . . The parties agreed that Ralane should move. She located a house she liked. Craig borrowed $160,000 to purchase the home for her and had the property deeded to her without any encumbrance.

. . .

Following a trial on property and alimony issues, the district court dissolved the marriage, awarded Ralane alimony, and divided the property and debts.

. . .

In his cross-appeal, Craig challenged the district court's award of reimbursement alimony of $60,000 per year for thirteen years.

. . .

Craig filed an application for further review challenging the court of appeals decision on the reimbursement alimony issue. We granted the application.

. . .

III. Property Division.

Before addressing the reimbursement alimony issue, we think it would helpful to put things in perspective. To do so, we need to show how the court divided the parties' net worth in the marital assets.

. . .

The court found that CGP, Inc. had a fair market value of $1,282,051. Craig's sixty percent interest, the court found, was therefore $769,000.

Regarding Probasco Properties, the court found it had a fair market value of $1,960,000. After deducting the $537,000 debt against Probasco Properties, the court found Craig's fifty percent interest had a fair market value of $711,500.

. . .

. . . . In sum, Ralane received net assets of $801,082, and Craig received net assets of $716,070.

In addition to the property award, the district court awarded Ralane reimbursement alimony of $60,000 per year for thirteen years payable on the first day of April of each year commencing in 2001.

The court also awarded Ralane attorney fees totaling $20,000 and expert witness fees totaling $5000.

IV. Reimbursement Alimony.

As mentioned, the district court awarded Ralane reimbursement alimony in the amount of $60,000 per year for thirteen years. The court gave the following rationale for the award:

> The alimony award is compensation for Ralane's contribution to Craig's obtaining the downtown Perkins franchise, which, like a professional license, is an ongoing benefit to Craig, which Ralane reasonably relied on as a benefit to her future but for the interruption of this dissolution.
>
> Craig's gross income is approximately $238,000 per year and is not likely to decrease but is likely to increase given the persistent success of his downtown Perkins franchise. The evidence shows Craig's tax rate is around thirty-two percent (percentage of income paid on taxes). At the time of trial, Craig's income is a result of the success of the downtown Perkins restaurant because the Eastgate and Norfolk properties were not yet producing income to Craig. This income will no longer be shared by Ralane because of the dissolution and the granting of the downtown franchise to Craig.
>
> Because the lease on the downtown restaurant will be at least for another 12 years, the Court concludes that reimbursement alimony should be paid to Ralane for 13 years and payable in the amount of $60,000 each year and payable on the 1st day of April of each year commencing in 2001.

For reasons that follow, we agree with Craig that the district court's award of reimbursement alimony under the facts of this case is contrary to our case law.

The purposes of property division and alimony are not the same. Property division is based on each spouse's "right to 'a just and equitable share of the property accumulated as the result of their joint efforts.'" (citation omitted). Alimony "is a stipend to a spouse in lieu of the other spouse's legal obligation for support." IOWA CODE section 598.21(3)(c)(Supp.1999) authorizes a court to consider the property division in connection with a request for alimony.

This court recognizes three different types of alimony. Traditional alimony "is payable for life or so long as a spouse is incapable of self-support."

Rehabilitative alimony is "a way of supporting an economically dependent spouse through a limited period of re-education or retraining following divorce, thereby creating incentive and opportunity for that spouse to become self-supporting." The goal of rehabilitative alimony is self-sufficiency and for that reason "such an award may be limited or extended depending on the realistic needs of the economically dependent spouse."

Reimbursement alimony was first denominated as such in *Francis*. *In re Marriage of Francis*, 442 N.W.2d 59, 64 (Iowa 1989). The concept is an outgrowth of our decision in *In re Marriage of Horstmann*, 263 N.W.2d 885 (Iowa 1978). In that case, this court held that an advanced degree or professional license is not in and of itself an asset for property division purposes. However, the court in *Horstmann* further held that the future earning capacity flowing from such a degree or license is a factor to be considered in the division of property and the award of alimony. IOWA CODE section 598.21(3)(e) authorizes a court to consider the earning capacity of each party on the question of property division.

In *Francis*, the husband was just completing his education as a physician at the time of the dissolution trial. We characterized the case as an "advanced degree/divorce decree" dissolution of marriage action. The issue as framed on appeal was this: "What compensation, if any, should [the wife] receive for her contribution to [the husband's] increased earning capacity due to his education received during the marriage?" We ultimately affirmed an award of reimbursement alimony in the amount of $100,000. In doing so, we offered the following rationale for reimbursement alimony and what it was designed to do:

> As previously stated in this opinion, alimony has traditionally taken the place of support that would have been provided had the marriage continued. A calculation of future earning capacity, in a case like the present one, essentially represents a value placed on the income to be derived from the advanced degree achieved during the marriage. The amount that would have been the student spouse's contribution to the future support of the parties is logically tied, if not wholly determined by, future earning capacity. Thus the court's duty to look at the future earning capacity of the spouses tracks more closely with a concern for loss of anticipated support, reimbursable through alimony, than through division of as-yet-unrealized tangible assets.

> The alimony of which we speak is designed to give the "supporting" spouse a stake in the "student" spouse's future earning capacity, in exchange for recognizable contributions to the source of that income—

the student's advanced education. As such, it is to be clearly distinguished from "rehabilitative" or "permanent" alimony.

Id. at 63.

In *Francis*, we also described the circumstances under which reimbursement alimony should be awarded:

> We are persuaded that the trial court neither misapplied legal doctrine nor erroneously misconstrued the evidence so as to compensate [the wife] far beyond her contribution to the marriage, as [the husband] suggests. We conclude, however, that for marriages of short duration which are devoted almost entirely to the educational advancement of one spouse and yield the accumulation of few tangible assets, alimony—rehabilitative, reimbursement, or a combination of the two—rather than an award of property, furnishes a fairer and more logical means of achieving the equity sought under *Horstmann* and its progeny.

Id. at 62.

We then determined that reimbursement alimony should not be subject to modification or termination until full compensation is achieved because such alimony

> is predicated upon economic sacrifices made by one spouse during the marriage that directly enhance the future earning capacity of the other.... Similar to a property award, but based on future earning capacity rather than a division of tangible assets, it should be fixed at the time of the decree. In recognition of the personal nature of the award and the current tax laws, however, a spouse's obligation to pay reimbursement alimony must terminate upon the recipient's death.

Id. at 64.

The facts here militate against an award of reimbursement alimony. The marriage was not one of short duration devoted almost entirely to the educational advancement of one spouse. To the contrary, both parties obtained their degrees and neither contributed to the education of the other.

Although Ralane may not have pursued her career in business as much as she may have liked, she nevertheless was active in the job market during the marriage. In fact, for a time she was active in the operation of the downtown Perkins restaurant. She learned all of the job positions in the restaurant and helped set up an accounting procedure to manage cash flow. So her career skills are not outdated. Moreover, the district court found Ralane "is a very competent and business-minded person with great opportunity for career success in the business community. She has the appropriate people skills and pays attention to detail." Given these facts, we can hardly say that she sacrificed for the benefit of Craig's earning capacity.

This is not a case where the parties have little or no net worth resulting in a case where the "supporting" spouse receives little or nothing by way of a property settlement whereas the other spouse has a substantial earning capacity. The parties had significant assets to balance the equities without the need for an award of reimbursement alimony. Ralane leaves the marriage with a net worth in excess of $800,000 compared with a net worth of $716,070 for Craig. Additionally, Ralane will be receiving 8.052 in interest on $580,250—her share of the net worth of the business and real estate. In short, Ralane has her degree, her skills, an unencumbered home and car, and a property award in excess of $800,000 with very little debt. We agree with Craig that Ralane has been compensated for her contributions.

The district court awarded reimbursement alimony because the court believed that Craig has acquired an asset that will produce income for him in the future and Ralane has no such asset. This reasoning ignores that the valuation of the business took into consideration the future earnings of CGP, Inc. and the future rents paid to Probasco Properties. It also ignores the risk that Craig assumes in continuing the business operation. As Craig points out, Ralane has been awarded one-half of the current value of those assets. We agree with Craig that the award of reimbursement alimony in these circumstances amounts to a duplicative award. Moreover, an award of reimbursement alimony in these circumstances effectively means that Ralane would be entitled to future income regardless of whether the business and real estate remain profitable, a result that hardly seems equitable.

We note, however, that in his application for further review, Craig suggests that "[p]erhaps Ralane would be entitled to one or two years of financial support (rehabilitative alimony) while she is getting back into the workforce." At oral argument, counsel for Craig suggested that to accomplish this we might order that Ralane keep the payments Craig has already made on the reimbursement alimony award. We think the suggestion is a good one and we adopt it.

. . .

We remand to allow the district court to modify its decree consistent with this opinion.

NOTES

1. What are the differences between the types of alimony the court discusses? What is the underlying theory for reimbursement alimony? Is it an entitlement stemming from a partnership theory of marriage? Or is it contractual? Why does the court not award it in this case?

2. Joan Williams has argued that framing the alimony question in terms of redistributing future income that belongs to the breadwinner is misleading, because the breadwinner's salary reflects the joint efforts of the spouses. More specifically, Williams argues that it is the services of the homemaker that enable the breadwinner to perform in the market as an "ideal worker"—that is as a worker with no care responsibilities for dependents—allowing him to command a higher wage. The same arrangement marginalizes the homemaker by reducing her earning capacity. Joan Williams, *Is Coverture Dead? Beyond A New Theory of Alimony*, 82 Geo. L.J. 2227, 2229–30 (1994). She goes on to observe:

> The ideal-worker's salary ... reflects the work of two adults: the ideal-worker's market labor and the marginalized-caregiver's unpaid labor.... Of course the husband owns his wage vis a vis his employer, but this does not determine whether he owns it vis a vis his family.

Id. at 2229. Under this theory, a spouse's earning capacity is the product of the marriage, regardless of whether his earning capacity was enhanced during the marriage. His salary belongs to the marriage because he was only able to command it thanks to the flow of domestic services from the homemaker. If it weren't for the homemaker, the breadwinner would need to spend time, money, and attention to either buy or provide the homemaker's services himself. What do you think about this argument?

3. A number of courts have recognized reimbursement alimony when one spouse helped the other enhance their earning capacity (especially by supporting them through school), and a majority of courts recognize some form of restitution or other compensation in such cases. *See generally* William M. Howard, Annotation, *Spouse's*

Professional Degree or License as Marital Property for Purposes of Alimony, Support, or Property Settlement, 3 A.L.R.6TH 447 (2005 & Supp. 2011).

d. FAULT

Dykman v. Dykman

Court of Appeals of Arkansas, 2007.
98 Ark. App. 145, 253 S.W.3d 23.

■ JOHN MAUZY PITTMAN, CHIEF JUDGE.

This is an appeal from a divorce decree. The appellant is a doctor of psychology and the appellee is a psychiatrist. Appellant is eighty-five years of age and appellee is fifty-two. The only issue on appeal is whether the trial court's award of alimony to appellee was proper in light of appellant's advanced age. We affirm.

A grant of alimony is an issue within the sound discretion of the chancellor that will not be disturbed on appeal absent an abuse of discretion. Although many factors are considered in setting the amount of alimony, the primary factors are the need of one spouse and the ability of the other spouse to pay. Ordinarily, fault or marital misconduct is not a factor in an award of alimony. However, fault and misconduct will be considered when it meaningfully relates to need or ability to pay.

Here there was evidence that appellee was employed for several years by a consulting firm in Dallas and delivered much of her considerable earnings to appellant, in amounts up to $12,000 per month, with the express understanding that he would use these funds for marital purposes, such as reduction of debt on the parties' real property. There was also evidence that, during this time, appellant was planning to divorce appellee and assume an open relationship with one or more young women, to whom he gave substantial gifts of automobiles, clothing from Victoria's Secret, other gifts paid for with marital assets, and several checks for many thousands of dollars.

An exhibit titled "Cash and ATM Withdrawals by Roscoe Dykman and Checks to Chinese Women" shows scores of checks were regularly written between 1999 and 2002, most of which are in the range of several hundred dollars at weekly or biweekly intervals. Other checks are for exceptional amounts, including an automobile purchased for Chenghua Wang in 1999, a check in the amount of $7000 to Chenghua Wang in 2000, checks to Chenghua Wang for $1500 and $1000 in 2001, and a check to Ling Ling Zhang in 2002 in the amount of $11,000. Appellant denied that his relationship with these women was anything other than platonic and asserted that the checks were merely short-term loans. However, his testimony is belied by the following letter written by appellant in 2001:

> Dear Lingling,
>
> This may be the last letter I ever write you, but there are some things I need to say. First, trust is a two-way street, my trust in you and your trust in me. Neither of these conditions were met in our relationship and they could have been had things been taken one step at a time. I needed to get to know you over a period of several months and you needed to get to know me over the same length of time. No one goes out and gets a divorce and marries someone else without knowing them. I thought that as I got to know you better that our relationship would

improve in the same way that my relationship with Chenghua improved. But even that did not last. She wanted to have children and I did not.

A few words about my wife. I have told you the kind of relation we have. She is just company sometimes and nothing more. I will divorce her once her court case is settled. I will be called as a witness in this settlement, mainly to testify to the fact that her disability has ruined our relationship.... I will continue to see her once in a while until the divorce is finalized (no sex). She believes that I will not leave her even though I have told her I intend to do this. I have spent millions of dollars on her and on property that both of us own jointly. A divorce at this moment, and I have thought about doing it, would result in a huge financial loss. It is important that she gets her practice up and going again before the final papers are filed.

In addition to using marital assets to fund his extramarital affairs rather than pay debt on marital property, appellant forged appellee's signature to obtain a second mortgage on one of their properties without her knowledge. He also fraudulently forged appellee's name to tax returns.

The evidence that appellant placed a snake in a box on appellee's driveway with a note saying "Die Bitch" is evidence of fault that cannot properly be considered in an award of alimony. Likewise, appellant's moral fault for his extramarital liaisons is not a legitimate consideration in an award of alimony. However, we think that appellant's diversion of marital funds to these young women, meaningfully relates to appellee's need for alimony because appellee had a right to believe her substantial monetary contributions to the marriage were being employed for marital purposes instead of funding appellant's courtship of several young women through lavish gifts. As a result of this diversion of marital funds, appellee does not have available the marital assets that she believed were being paid for by her contributions. Instead, at a time when she is attempting to establish a psychiatric practice, appellee faces bankruptcy.

Appellee's attempt to establish her own psychiatric practice, rather than working as an employee, was engendered by a vocal impairment; appellee sustained an injury in 1999 that caused neurological damage and dsyphonia [sic], a disorder causing speech to be interrupted, strained, or garbled. She was subsequently terminated from her employment. Appellee's injury makes her tire easily when talking, and her speech becomes progressively more difficult to understand as she tires. The trial judge expressly found that appellee's speech was difficult to understand, limiting her ability to practice psychiatry. Her endurance is limited, and we think her plan to establish her own practice in order to control the amount and type of work that she does in light of her injury is a reasonable one. Appellee testified that she currently has no income but that she anticipates that her psychiatric practice will become self-supporting within a short period of time. Here, appellant's financial misconduct directly relates to appellee's need, and we think that it can properly be considered in awarding alimony. Finally, with regard to appellant's argument that it is unfair to order "an eighty-five year old gentleman" to pay alimony in an amount that would require him to seek further employment, we note that appellant was employed at the time of the hearing and that the $1023 in monthly alimony awarded was well within his ability to pay. Although appellant testified that his job was being terminated and that he would be unable to find another at his advanced age, we think that appellant has demonstrated that he retains a considerable amount of vigor and ability, and the alimony award is subject to revision in the event of changed circumstances.

Affirmed.

NOTES

1. How does marital misconduct figure in the court's decision on alimony?

2. About twenty-eight jurisdictions allow consideration of marital misconduct in awarding alimony, and it can often be any type of misconduct and not merely economic dissipation. *See* Linda D. Elrod & Robert G. Spector, *A Review of the Year in Family Law: Looking at Interjurisdictional Recognition*, 43 FAM. L.Q. 923, 972 chart 1 (2010). Some states make lack of fault a condition for establishing an alimony claim, which means that alimony is precluded if fault is established. In *Guillory v. Guillory*, for instance, the wife was accused of being intemperate, locking her husband outside the home when he came back late, and leaving the marital home for days at a time without notification or contact. 7 So. 3d 144, 148 (La. Ct. App. 2009). Because the relevant statute required that the spouse requesting spousal support be faultless, her request for periodic support was rejected. *Id.*

2. MODIFICATION

Schwarz v. Schwarz

Appellate Court of Connecticut, 2010.
124 Conn. App. 472, 5 A.3d 548.

■ BEACH, J.

The defendant, Alan L. Schwarz, appeals from the judgment of the trial court granting both his motion and the motion filed by the plaintiff, Majella W. Schwarz, for modification of alimony and increasing his alimony obligation from $2000 per week to $2175 per week. The defendant claims that the court improperly (1) found a substantial change in his financial circumstances and (2) increased the plaintiff's award of alimony after finding that he had met his burden with regard to his motion to modify alimony on the basis of the change in the plaintiff's financial circumstances caused by her living with another person. We disagree, and, accordingly, affirm the judgment of the trial court.

The record reveals the following facts. The parties' twenty-nine year marriage was dissolved on February 23, 2005. At the time of dissolution, the parties filed a separation agreement, which was incorporated by reference into the dissolution decree. Paragraph three of the agreement provided that the defendant shall pay alimony to the plaintiff in the amount of $2000 per week until the death of either party or the plaintiff's remarriage. It also specifically stated that "[a]limony shall be subject to section 46b–86(b) of the CONNECTICUT GENERAL STATUTES."

. . .

The defendant claims that the court erred when it found that the increase in his income constituted a substantial change in circumstances warranting a modification of his alimony obligation. We disagree.

. . .

The plaintiff . . . claimed that there was a substantial change in circumstances due to a substantial increase in the cost of her health insurance coverage. The parties' separation agreement contemplated the plaintiff's need for health insurance and, accordingly, provided that the defendant would pay for the plaintiff's COBRA coverage for three years. When the defendant stopped paying for the plaintiff's COBRA coverage in 2008, the plaintiff procured insurance coverage by working at the golf pro shop for the man with whom she was living. The plaintiff's cohabiting partner testified that due to circumstances beyond his control, the golf pro shop could no longer pay for the plaintiff's health insurance. As a result, the plaintiff anticipated paying approximately $15,000 per year for her health insurance.

. . .

"Trial courts have broad discretion in deciding motions for modification.... Modification of alimony, after the date of a dissolution judgment, is governed by GENERAL STATUTES § 46b–86.... When ... the disputed issue is alimony, the applicable provision of the statute is § 46b–86(a), which provides that a final order for alimony may be modified by the trial court upon a showing of a substantial change in the circumstances of either party.... The party seeking modification bears the burden of showing the existence of a substantial change in the circumstances.... The change may be in the circumstances of either party.... The date of the most recent prior proceeding in which an alimony order was entered is the appropriate date to use in determining whether a significant change in circumstances warrants a modification of an alimony award...."

. . .

Here, the court found that the defendant's gross income had increased from $373,620 to $450,000 per year and that his net income had increased from $265,980 to $301,756 per year. These figures represented an increase in his gross income of 20 percent and an increase in his net income of over 13 percent. "[T]he increase need not be termed 'dramatic' or 'startling' so long as it is found to be a substantial change in circumstances." This finding alone is a sufficient basis for a finding of a substantial change in circumstances. We conclude that the court applied the correct legal standard and did not abuse its discretion in determining that a substantial change in circumstances had occurred.

The defendant next claims that the court improperly increased the plaintiff's award of alimony after concluding that he had met his burden with regard to his motion to modify alimony based on the change in the plaintiff's financial situation caused by her living with another person. The defendant appears to claim that a court, as a matter of law, cannot increase the amount of alimony after finding that the party receiving alimony was living with another person, as contemplated in § 46b–86(b). The defendant appears additionally to claim that even if the court had the statutory authority to increase alimony in these circumstances, it abused its discretion in this case. We disagree.

The court summarized its factual findings regarding the plaintiff's living arrangements as follows.

> Prior to the dissolution on February 23, 2005, the plaintiff had moved out of the marital residence and had purchased a three bedroom house located at 142 Colin Hill Drive, Meriden. Some time in 2006, the plaintiff began residing with Arthur 'Tex' Kane on a permanent basis. In addition to living together at the Meriden residence, they lived from January through March at the plaintiff's home in Port St. Lucie, Florida. A judicial pretrial was conducted in January, and, shortly thereafter,

Kane moved out of the Meriden home but traveled with the plaintiff to the Florida home. The plaintiff testified that once in Florida, Kane 'stayed with a friend' and did not stay in the Florida home. Throughout their cohabitation, the plaintiff paid for the expenses of both homes. She paid the utilities, taxes, telephone, heat, etc., and Kane paid for expenses 'outside of the home,' dinners, entertainment, etc. She testified that she never asked him to contribute to any of the household expenses and that she did not want him to contribute, as the bills were in her name and [were] her responsibility. She stated that she did not want to be dependent on anyone for money, and if Kane gave her money, it might increase her income and she could possibly live beyond her means. This was her 'conscious decision' not to accept any money from Kane. She does not accept the fact that she is dependent on someone else for money—her [former spouse].

The plaintiff is a registered nurse, and has an additional certification as an [advanced practice registered nurse]. She stopped working as a nurse practitioner in June, 2002, and does sporadic work for the Wallingford board of education. Her income from that job has not varied much since the date of dissolution, as her financial affidavit filed on February 23, 2005, and the financial affidavit filed on April 7, 2009, indicate essentially the same gross and net income from the board of education. She has several chronic and serious health issues. She suffered from ulcerative colitis when she was in her twenties, and after the birth of her third son, had a total colectomy. She also has a spinal condition, causing her difficulty in doing routine chores, such as getting dressed. Her most serious condition, however, is leukemia, which was diagnosed in May, 2003, prior to the dissolution. Currently she is treating it with a chemotherapy drug [that] she takes on a daily basis. The side effects of nausea and diarrhea are particularly grueling, given the fact she is without a colon. Although the leukemia is in a chronic stage at the present time, it could progress into an acute situation, which would make it difficult to control, and may be fatal. The [separation] agreement provided that the plaintiff would receive COBRA benefits for her medical insurance and [that] the defendant would pay for those benefits for three years. When the benefits expired, the plaintiff began to work at Kane's golf shop as a bookkeeper, so that she would be able to obtain insurance, under an arrangement that the plaintiff would do the books, record keeping, etc., and Kane would pay for her health insurance, which was approximately $600 to $700 per month. That insurance expired in May, 2009, due to a change beyond Kane's control, and her new coverage will cost approximately $15,000 per year, or approximately $300 per week.

Kane is a golf pro at a golf course in Meriden and has been the head pro for the last five years. The defendant issued a subpoena for certain records, and tax returns, but Kane did not comply. His gross income from all sources of his employment is approximately $200,000—'maybe a little more.' He is paid by the town, leases golf carts, gives golf lessons, sells equipment and receives some of his income by way of cash. In addition, while he is in Florida with the plaintiff, he also does some teaching of golf. His 2007 tax return indicates business income of $8858 and gambling winnings of $108,638. He acknowledged that he began living with the plaintiff on a full-time basis in the spring of 2006, both while in Connecticut and in Florida. He testified that he does not pay her anything by way of rent but pays for their evenings out, and that amounts to approximately five nights out a week, spending approximately $30 to $60 per night, all with cash. He has no recollection of any conversations with the plaintiff about payment of rent or any other living expenses. Currently, he is living in a hotel while an apartment he intends to rent is being renovated. It was his idea that [the plaintiff] work for him, handling his books, and he would pay for her health insurance but would pay no salary. Since he can no longer offer her health insurance, he will pay her $15 per hour for the work she does for him, which amounts to approximately $180 per month, substantially less than payments he was making on her behalf for the health insurance. Kane testified that he moved out because it was causing [the plaintiff] undue stress due to the defendant's filing of the motion for modification. He did provide her a great deal of assistance while living with her, helping with her medical conditions and issues. It is uncontroverted that but for the defendant's filing of the motion for modification, Kane and the plaintiff would still be living together.

The defendant argues that the court erred when it found that he had met his burden of proof under § 46b–86(b) but then failed to reduce his alimony payments accordingly. . . .

. . .

Section 46b–86(b) provides: "In an action for divorce, dissolution of marriage, legal separation or annulment brought by a husband or wife, in which a final judgment has been entered providing for the payment of periodic alimony by one party to the other, the Superior Court *may*, in its discretion and upon notice and hearing, modify such judgment and suspend, reduce or terminate the payment of periodic alimony upon a showing that the party receiving the periodic alimony is living with another person under circumstances which the court finds should result in the modification, suspension, reduction or termination of alimony because the living arrangements cause such a change of circumstances as to alter the financial needs of that party." (Emphasis added.)

The court found, and the parties do not dispute, that for purposes of § 46b–86(b) the plaintiff was living with Kane. The court also found that the plaintiff's financial circumstances had changed as a result of her living arrangement with Kane. The issue in this case is whether the court may, in its discretion, increase the plaintiff's alimony on the basis of her motion to increase alimony in accordance with § 46b–86(a) despite the defendant's motion to reduce or to terminate alimony based on § 46b–86(b). We conclude that in the circumstances of this case, the court did not abuse its discretion in increasing the plaintiff's alimony after finding that the defendant had met his burden under § 46b–86(b), because it also found that the plaintiff had met her burden with regard to § 46b–86(a).

We previously have held that once a party has met his or her burden under either § 46b–86(a) or (b), the court then should apply the factors of § 46b–82 to fashion a new alimony award. . . . In light of the court's decision that both of the parties' motions should be granted, it therefore was free to fashion an alimony award under either § 46b–86(a) or (b). Section 46b–86(b) does not require a court to reduce alimony if a party proves that the other party's financial circumstances have changed as a result of his or her choice to live with another person. In addition, there is no language in § 46b–86(b) to preclude the party who is receiving alimony from pursuing a motion to increase alimony.

Having determined that the court was permitted in these circumstances to increase the plaintiff's alimony, we now turn to the defendant's claim that the court abused its discretion by increasing the alimony under these facts....

The court concluded that its finding that the parties' financial circumstances significantly had changed pursuant to § 46b–86(a) warranted an increase in alimony. It first found that the financial needs of the plaintiff had increased but that the increase in her financial needs was being met mostly by Kane. It also found that she now needed to pay for health insurance. The court subsequently found that, as the defendant's income had increased, it was equitable for him to pay a portion of the plaintiff's increased need. The court also took into account the fact that the plaintiff's needs were not as high as she had claimed, because of her living arrangements with Kane, but that despite Kane's contributions to her financial circumstances, she still was in need of additional alimony. Accordingly, the court increased the plaintiff's alimony award on the basis of these findings. In light of its findings, we conclude that the court applied the law correctly and did not abuse its discretion in increasing the plaintiff's alimony by $175 per week.

The judgment is affirmed.

■ Flynn, J., dissenting.

The majority holds that where a trial court grants a party's motion to terminate or to reduce alimony such that, at a minimum, alimony must accordingly be terminated or reduced, the court may simultaneously grant an opposing motion to increase alimony. Because I believe that these actions are inherently inconsistent and, further, would vitiate the purpose of General Statutes § 46b–86(b), I cannot agree with the majority. Therefore, I respectfully dissent.

If a party remarries after divorce, the remarriage terminates the alimony such a party receives. Human nature being what it is, some parties who had been divorced entered cohabiting relationships rather than remarrying, to avoid termination of alimony received from a former spouse. To avoid such arrangements which took unjust advantage of a former spouse, the legislature enacted a reform in adopting § 46b–86(b). Subsection (b) "is a separate and independent statutory basis for the modification of alimony...." It is a distinct statutory basis for such modifications from § 46b–86(a), which authorizes modifications for other reasons. "Section 46b–86(b) was enacted to correct the injustice of making a party pay alimony when his or her ex-spouse is living with a person of the opposite sex, without marrying, to prevent the loss of support." It consists of two prongs. First, the divorced party receiving the alimony must have commenced living with another person, and, second, the former spouse's financial needs have been altered and decreased because of the cohabitation.

... This appeal is before us because after the defendant filed a § 46b–86(b) motion because the plaintiff was living with another man and her financial needs had been altered, the plaintiff filed a § 46b–86(a) motion to increase her alimony because the defendant's income had increased. The court, after having granted the defendant's subsection (b) motion, nonetheless granted the plaintiff's motion to increase alimony based on this increase in the defendant's income.

This last action is inconsistent with the first. If a divorced former spouse is found to be living with another person and her needs are altered and diminished, but said former spouse can avoid a diminution or decrease in alimony simply by the expedient of making a motion to increase alimony because the former spouse is making more money than at the time of the dissolution, then the legislature's attempt in enacting § 46b–86(b) to remedy the unjust taking advantage of a former spouse, would be of no force or effect. I therefore would conclude that the increase in alimony ordered pursuant to § 46b–86(a) was an abuse of discretion under the facts that the court found and would reverse that judgment. The defendant ex-husband has suffered an injustice where, in order to avoid alimony termination, the plaintiff entered a relationship with another person without benefit of marriage, and then, after termination or modification should have occurred, he suffered an increase in alimony because his income had increased.

NOTES

1. Most state statutes and case law provide that alimony terminates upon the remarriage or cohabitation of the recipient spouse. Questions often arise when spouses have a settlement agreement which provides for alimony without specifying whether alimony will terminate upon remarriage and cohabitation or not. *See, e.g., Artman v. Hoy*, 257 S.W.3d 864 (Ark. 2007) (holding that when the spouses agreed to alimony for a ten year term without any more specification, the termination on remarriage rule of the relevant statute did not apply). *But see Messer v. Messer*, 134 S.W.3d 570 (Ky. 2004).

Because the underlying idea is that remarriage or cohabitation mean that the former spouse is now dependent on someone else, or that in the very least his/her living costs have been reduced, some courts will not automatically terminate alimony, unless there is proof that the alimony recipient is no longer in need or is cohabiting "as a husband and wife." *See, e.g, Myers v. Myers*, 231 P.3d 815 (Utah Ct. App. 2010) (court of appeals reversed the trial court's termination of alimony due to the recipient's cohabitation because all of the hallmarks of a husband-wife relationship, such as shared meals and expenses, were missing).

By contrast, a Missouri court of appeals found that there was a changed condition that justified a modification to husband's maintenance payments where an ex-wife lived with her life partner. *Schuchard v. Schuchard*, 292 S.W.3d 498, 500 (Mo. Ct. App. 2009). The ex-wife and a woman shared a residence and four bank accounts. *Id.* The court reached "the unavoidable conclusion that Wife has benefited financially from substantial and continuing support from [life partner]." *Id.* The contribution of her partner's salary reduced the ex-wife's need for the husband's financial support. *Id.* at 501. On the treatment of same-sex cohabitation for the purposes of ending alimony *see* Jill Bornstein, Note, *At a Cross–Road: Anti–Same–Sex Marriage Policies and Principles of Equity: The Effect of Same–Sex Cohabitation on Alimony Payments to an Ex–Spouse*, 84 CHI.-KENT L. REV. 1027 (2010).

2. Should a former spouse's voluntary decrease in income qualify as a substantial change in circumstances for purposes of alimony modification? In *Parnell v. Parnell*, 239 P.3d 216, 218 (Okla. Civ. App. 2010), the husband had taken a substantially lower-paying job after his wife filed for divorce. Even though the case was about setting alimony for the first time, the court's reasoning applies in modification cases as well. The court held that "[w]hen a spouse deliberately refuses to use his best efforts to obtain employment, or intentionally becomes under-employed to thwart his spouse or former spouse's effort to obtain his financial assistance in transitioning to a separate life, equity may justify imputing income to him." *Id.* at 221. Under the facts of the case, imputing income to the husband was not an error. *Id.*

The Supreme Judicial Court of Massachusetts upheld a trial judge's decision to reduce, but not terminate, a husband's alimony obligation when he voluntarily retired at a customary retirement age. *Pierce v. Pierce*, 916 N.E.2d 330 (Mass. 2009). The court observed:

In determining a fair balance of sacrifice between the parties, the judge may credit that the support provider has good faith, persuasive reasons for selecting employment paying less than his or her potential earning capacity. People often prefer careers that may not maximize their lifestyle income, and divorce should not entirely deprive an individual of this freedom. But these considerations must be balanced against a provider's obligation to support the former spouse....

... Just as a support provider will naturally ask himself whether *he* or *she* can afford now to retire or to reduce his or her workload to part-time employment, a judge deciding a complaint to modify an alimony judgment must ask whether the supporting spouse *and* the recipient spouse can afford the supporting spouse's retirement at that time. If the answer is, "No," the judge in her discretion must determine a fair balance of sacrifice between the wants and needs of the two parties. This may include ensuring that the supporting spouse is willing to assume an appropriate portion of the shared financial burden that will result from his or her decision to retire.

Id. at 341–42.

3. THE FUTURE OF ALIMONY

Mary Kay Kisthardt, *Re-thinking Alimony: The AAML's Considerations for Calculating Alimony, Spousal Support or Maintenance*

21 J. AM. ACAD. MATRIM. LAW. 61, 64–65, 69–81 (2008).

... Alimony statutes vary significantly from state to state with some authorizing payments in a wide variety of situations and others restricting it to very narrow circumstances. But in almost all states judges are given a great deal of discretion with the result that these awards are rarely overturned. Because of an inability to come to a consensus regarding the underlying rationale for alimony, legislatures often include a long list of factors for judges to consider. One commentator found over sixty factors mentioned in the fifty states. Unfortunately there are often internal inconsistencies in the factors and no state provides a priority ranking. Judges struggle with how to apply a myriad of factors to reach a fair result. Statutory criteria, with no rules for their application, then result in a "pathological effect on the settlement process by which most divorces are handled."

Without a reliable method of prediction, clients are often uncertain about whether to assume the risk of trial. This situation may present the greatest challenge for women who often do not have the financial resources to fund protracted litigation with an uncertain outcome. A study in Maryland found that courts made very few alimony awards even though a majority of the marriages studied had lasted more than ten years and at the time of the divorce the average income of the husbands was almost double that of the wives. What was striking was the number of cases in which the economically dependent spouse did not seek an award. The authors concluded that this was due in large part to the reluctance to expend money on litigation costs without the likelihood of any beneficial result.

. . .

C. 1990's Reforms

In response to the denial of long term awards for those most in need of them, the "second wave" of reform took place in the 1990's and expanded the factors justifying an award beyond "need." This new legislation encouraged courts to base awards more on the unique facts of a case and less on broad assumptions about need and the obligation to become self-supporting in spite of the loss of earning capacity that often occurs in long term marriages. The use of vocational experts to measure earning capacity became more widespread and there were attempts to quantify the value of various aspects of homemaker services as part of a support award.

As a result of the frustration in developing a cohesive theory of alimony that would in turn lead to more consistent awards, many commentators turned to an analysis premised on compensation for loss of human capital by virtue of non-market work engaged in by the claimant during the marriage. In the human capital view, a claim for post-divorce support is based on an economic analysis that assumes that during a marriage the parties are engaged in a search for economic efficiency. These models assume that in addition to income generation, the parties also value child-rearing, and the development of income producing skills and abilities. Rational economic decisionmaking guides the parties in choices that will maximize the ability of the partnership to realize the largest gains. In most instances since women are less likely to command as high a wage in the job market, the efficiency model would lead to a decision that the non-market tasks be assumed by her. While this results in an economically satisfactory arrangement during the marriage, it often means that at divorce the non-market spouse will be disadvantaged if there is insufficient compensation for the efforts that were devoted to the partnership.

Several commentators have chosen to use this analysis as the basis for arriving at "compensation." For instance, Prof. Ira Mark Ellman would allow compensation for loss of earning capacity as a result of decisions made during the marriage.[49] The measure of the award is based on the claimant's earning capacity at the end of the marriage compared to what it would have been had the claimant remained single, thus the "marriage cost" that should be compensated. This compensation is only available if the claimants' "sacrifice" of development of human capital assets is economically rational, with the exception of child care because it is based on traditional values. There need not be a corresponding gain to the non-sacrificing spouse.

Another theory based on compensation for efforts during the marriage that seeks not to focus on losses but on unrealized gain is Prof. Robert Kirkman Collins' theory of "marital residuals."[51] It is based on the premise that during the marriage efforts were made by both spouses to maximize gains for the partnership and that at divorce there are residual economic benefits that flow from those efforts. He analogizes this to a partner in a law firm receiving compensation for "works in progress" for the efforts that were already expended but for which the benefits have not yet been fully realized. The compensation for the marriage partners should be a sharing of the post-dissolution income that was due in part to the efforts expended during the marriage. The length of income sharing is dependent on the duration of the marriage when joint efforts were expended and reduces over time, becoming an increasingly smaller percentage of the parties' post-divorce differences in income. In this way it captures both the needs rationale by focusing on the differences in income and the value of prior contributions as a function of the number of years of joint contribution.

Another theory for deciding an alimony award based on contribution for acquisition of career assets has been proposed by Marshall Willick. He

---

49. Ira Mark Ellman, *The Theory of Alimony*, 77 CAL. L. REV. 1, 42–49 (1989).

51. [Robert Kirkman Collins, *The Theory of Marital Residuals: Applying an Income Adjustment Calculus to the Enigma of Alimony*, 24 HARV. WOMEN'S L.J. 23, 49–50 (2001).]

suggests that there are generally both separate contributions (natural ability) and marital contributions to the career asset that "could be weighted and attributed as separate or marital contributions to the future income stream."[55] At that point the duration of the income could be calculated using market data and factors relevant to the present case. The income from the career asset is then divided as each partner shares in its value. When it no longer has a value (for instance at retirement), the alimony would cease.

D. The ALI Principles

In response to the problems highlighted above, the ALI in its Principles recommends the setting of presumptions or guidelines. The ALI focuses on spousal payments as compensation for economic losses that one of the spouses incurred as a result of the marriage. The ALI guidelines are premised on the assumption that when a marriage is dissolved there are usually losses associated with it such as lost employment opportunities or opportunities to acquire education or training that lead to disparities in post-divorce earning capacities. The ALI takes the position that these losses, to the extent they are reflected in a difference in incomes at the time of dissolution, should be shared by the partners. The Principles assume a loss of earning capacity when one parent has been the primary caregiver of the children. They also make provisions for compensation for losses in short term marriages where sacrifices by one spouse leave that spouse with a lower standard of living than he or she enjoyed prior to the marriage. Finally, under the Principles, compensation could be awarded based on a loss of a return on an investment in human capital (where one spouse has supported the other through school). This would be most important in the vast majority of states that do not recognize enhanced earning capacity or a degree or license as a divisible marital partnership asset. In setting the amount and duration, the ALI recommends a formula that is based on a specified percentage of the difference in the spouses' post-divorce income for a period of time that is dependent on the length of the marriage.

E. Guidelines

While the ALI chose to focus on both the substantive rationale for alimony as well as a guideline approach to ensuring some predictability, increasing numbers of jurisdictions have chosen to focus primarily on the prediction problem by turning to mathematical formulas or guidelines. In almost all instances these guidelines are intended to be used as a starting point for discussion and do not constitute a presumption. Most guidelines are confined to temporary or pendente lite awards and are the result of local, not state-wide adoption.

In California, the Santa Clara guidelines were initially adopted in 1977. They were eventually adopted by many counties in the state. The Santa Clara formula is used to calculate both the amount and the duration of an award. In a simplified form the amount of temporary support is computed by taking 40 percent of the net income of the payor, minus 50 percent of the net income of the payee, adjusted for tax consequences. If there is child support, temporary spousal or partner support is calculated on net income not allocated to child support and/or child-related expenses. The temporary spousal support calculations apply these assumptions. The duration factor is based on the length of the marriage. For marriages under ten years, the award should be one half of the months the parties were married. Between

---

55. Marshal Willick, *In Search of a Coherent Theoretical Model for Alimony*, 15 Nev. Law. 40, 42 (Apr. 2007).

ten and twenty years the award gradually increase [sic] until it hits a maximum of the number of months married.

As is the case with most mathematical formulas, the resulting amount must be adjusted by incorporating deviations necessary to achieve a fair result. In California these include additional payments that the payor is making for the children's benefit, such as education, whether the payor is assuming a greater portion of the marital debt and whether either of the parties is underemployed.

In Arizona, the Maricopa County Family Court published guidelines that are based on the ALI recommendations. They are designed to apply to marriages that lasted over five years and in which the payee's income is no more than 75 percent of the payor's. The guideline amount is determined by multiplying the difference between the parties' post-dissolution income by a marital duration factor. The duration factor equals the number of years of marriage times .015 with a maximum of .50. Initially the committee chose a duration factor of .6 times the number of years married. However after an empirical study revealed a correlation of only .21 between those cases under the guidelines and 160 actual cases, the committee revised its recommendation with respect to duration. The guideline duration now reflects not a single number but a range of years. It is calculated as between .3 and .5 of the number of years married.

Pennsylvania has gone a step further by taking alimony factors and incorporating them into actual monetary guidelines that are statutorily mandated in temporary alimony situations. First a determination must be made that alimony is necessary based on the statutory factors. Once this is established, a temporary award is made pursuant to statewide guidelines. The guideline is based on the reasonable needs of the spouse seeking support and the ability to pay of the supporting spouse. Net income is used and the earning capacities of the spouses are considered. The guidelines are income driven and do not contemplate consideration of individual "reasonable needs." Deviations are permitted for special circumstances, but the court is required to specify in writing the reasons for a deviation.

[The author summarizes alimony formulas used in Michigan, New Mexico, and Fairfax County, VA.]

IV.   The American Academy of Matrimonial Lawyers' Considerations

The AAML ALI Commission worked for over two years gathering data and soliciting input from Academy members prior to making its final report. After reviewing the ALI position the Commission rejected the substantive changes in the law that the ALI proposed—i.e., moving to a compensatory rationale for spousal support. The Commission sought not to make recommendations for changes in the substantive law but rather to come up with a tool that its members could use in any jurisdiction.

With this in mind, the Commission conducted an extensive review of the guidelines being used in jurisdictions throughout the country. Like the New Mexico committee, the Commission wished to provide a simplified formula that could be used as a starting point in negotiations. The common denominators in all the guidelines reviewed were income of the spouses and duration of the marriage. These two factors therefore became the focus of the AAML Considerations. The amount is be calculated [sic] by taking 30 percent of the payor's gross income minus 20 percent of the payee's gross income. The additional limitation is that the alimony amount, so calculated, when added to the gross income of the payee, shall not result in the recipient receiving in excess of 40 percent of the combined gross income of the parties. To test whether the formula would yield results similar to those applying other guidelines a common hypothetical was used and support amounts were calculated using the proposed AAML Considerations and seven other guidelines currently in use or proposed. The result was that the amounts arrived at using the AAML Considerations were well within the norm.

Recognizing that certain circumstance would render an award based solely on the Considerations unfair, the Commission also included factors that would suggest a deviation. Deviations may be justified when a spouse is the primary caretaker of a dependent minor or a disabled adult child; when a spouse has pre-existing court-ordered support obligations; when a spouse is complying with court-ordered payment of debts or other obligations (including uninsured or unreimbursed medical expenses); when a spouse has unusual needs, or has received a disproportionate share of the marital estate or where there are unusual tax consequences. An additional deviation factor allows consideration of those instances where the application of the formula would result in an award that is inequitable. Finally, a respect for private ordering is honored by the inclusion of an exception for the parties' agreement to an alternative amount.

... One result of the discussion was the addition of two deviation factors: one considers the age and health of the spouses; the other focuses on those situations where a spouse has given up a career, a career opportunity or otherwise supported the career of the other spouse. The Board of Governors then approved the Report.

V. Conclusion

The proposed Considerations are designed to be used in conjunction with state statutes that first determine eligibility for an award. They are not intended to replace existing state public policy regarding eligibility for an award. In addition, the factors that are listed as deviations are intended to address the considerations for setting an amount and duration of an award found in most states' statutes. These recommendations are ones that the Commission hopes Academy members can utilize in advocating for a fair result for their clients.

Appendix A

The AAML Commission Recommendations

Adopted by Board of Governors

March 9, 2007

. . .

The recommendations are:

Amount:

Unless one of the deviation factors listed below applies, a spousal support award should be calculated by taking 30% of the payor's gross income minus 20% of the payee's gross income the alimony amount, so calculated, however, when added to the gross income of the payee shall not result in the recipient receiving in excess of 40% of the combined gross income of the parties.

Length:

Unless one of the deviation factors listed below applies, the duration of the award is arrived at by multiplying the length of the marriage by the following factors: 0–3 years (.3); 3–10 (.5); 10–20 years (.75), over 20 years, permanent alimony.

"Gross Income" is defined by a state's definition of gross income under the child support guidelines, including actual and imputed income.

The spousal support payment is calculated before child support is determined.

This method of spousal support calculation does not apply to cases in which the combined gross income of the parties exceeds $1,000,000 a year.

Deviation factors:

The following circumstances may require an adjustment to the recommended amount or duration:

1) A spouse is the primary caretaker of a dependent minor or a disabled adult child;

2) A spouse has pre-existing court-ordered support obligations;

3) A spouse is complying with court-ordered payment of debts or other obligations (including uninsured or unreimbursed medical expenses);

4) A spouse has unusual needs;

5) A spouse's age or health;

6) A spouse has given up a career, a career opportunity or otherwise supported the career of the other spouse;

7) A spouse has received a disproportionate share of the marital estate;

8) There are unusual tax consequences;

9) Other circumstances that make application of these considerations inequitable;

10) The parties have agreed otherwise.

. . .

NOTES

1. In *Boemio v. Boemio*, 994 A.2d 911, 922 (Md. 2010), the Court of Appeals of Maryland upheld a trial court's alimony award, which was challenged by the obligor husband on the basis that the court had relied on the AAML's guidelines instead of on the appropriate statutory factors. The Court of Appeals held that the trial court did not err in consulting the AAML guidelines because it had first applied the appropriate Maryland statutory factors.

2. Massachusetts is a latecomer to the trend of limiting alimony. On September 26, 2011, Governor Deval Patrick signed a law that sets specific limits on the number of years alimony may be awarded based on the marriage's duration, although the courts retain discretion to order indefinite alimony for marriages lasting longer than 20 years. The new law also terminates alimony upon the retirement of the payor or the remarriage/cohabitation of the payee, and limits "rehabilitative alimony" payments to 5 years. *See* H.3617, 187th Gen. Ct. (Mass. 2011).

Some think the law is a much needed reform for overburdened elderly payors, while others worry that it will disadvantage women who take time off to raise children. *See* Jess Bidgood, *Alimony in Massachusetts Gets Overhaul, With Limits*, N.Y. TIMES (Sept. 26, 2011), http://www.nytimes.com/2011/09/27/us/massachusetts-curbs-lifetime-alimony-payments.html.

C. EVALUATING DIVORCE AWARDS

Despite the fact that property and alimony formally are two distinct bases for awards, in practice the line between the two can become blurred. Courts seeking to divide a couple's wealth fairly must confront the fact that most spouses have relatively little property available to distribute at divorce. Doing justice between the parties thus may require providing entitlements both to tangible assets and to a future stream of income. These may resemble property and alimony, respectively. Essentially, however, the court is seeking to fashion a combination of entitlements that will achieve a fair distribution of wealth between the parties.

This leads naturally to the question: what principle or principles should guide this attempt to do economic justice at divorce? From the material in this Chapter, we can extract at least five possibilities: marital fault, need, status, rehabilitation, and contribution.

If we examine the five principles closely, we will see that each leads us in a different direction—sometimes dramatically so. Furthermore, if we examine the factors that courts are instructed by legislatures to consider in decisions about property division and alimony, we will see that those factors instruct courts to rely on different principles. These statutes therefore point judges simultaneously in different directions. As you read the material below, consider whether legislatures should attempt to use a single principle to guide financial awards at divorce. If so, what should it be? If not, how should a court reconcile principles that point to different outcomes?

1. THE MARITAL FAULT PRINCIPLE

Using the allocation of assets to punish the spouse who caused the marital breakup is perhaps the oldest guiding principle. Fault is alive and well, moreover, in many jurisdictions today. Even in California, the state that initiated the American no-fault revolution in 1970, marital behavior, specifically abuse, is still admissible in child custody determinations.[5] Many states that have adopted no-fault divorce grounds, moreover, permit evidence of marital misconduct to be weighed in the allocation of assets at divorce.[6]

A major drawback of this principle is that it is not easily translated into cash. How much is adultery worth? $1,000? Half the accumulated property of the marriage? If both spouses commit adultery, should their actions cancel out the relevance of marital fault when the property is divided? Because marital misconduct is typically only one in a list of statutory factors, it is difficult to determine how much weight courts actually give to it.

2. THE NEED PRINCIPLE

According to this principle, a spouse is entitled to be supported after the marriage ends at a level the covers his or her basic needs. The principle's most obvious virtue from society's viewpoint is that it requires the ex-spouse, rather than taxpayers, to pay for the support of the recipient. At the same time, the need principle requires an explanation of why responsibility should

---

5. CAL. FAM. CODE § 3011 (West 2004).

6. *E.g.*, MO. ANN. STAT. § 452.335 (West 2003).

be assigned to an ex-spouse, rather than society as a whole, especially after relatively brief marriages. In addition, the need principle may foster the ongoing dependence of one ex-spouse on another for an indefinite time after divorce. Under this principle, the allocation of assets should not depend on the length of the marriage. Alimony guided by this principle should end only when the need ends, that is, when the dependent spouse remarries, dies, or becomes self-supporting.

3.   THE STATUS PRINCIPLE

The status principle directs courts to ensure at divorce that the less affluent spouse continues to enjoy the same standard of living that he or she had during the marriage. This principle is embraced in § 5.04 of the ALI PRINCIPLES, which provides that in lengthy marriages the law should recognize the less affluent spouse's "expectation of continuing to enjoy a standard of living that has been sustained by the other spouse's income." Although the ALI envisions the status principle as benefiting only the long-time homemaker whose income at divorce is considerably less than that of her spouse, the status principle can be used as the basis for an award in any divorce.

One possible appeal of the status principle is that it vindicates the notion that marriage is a serious commitment in which the parties pledge to take one another "for richer or poorer." With respect to long marriages in particular, it reflects the idea that, as the Comment to ALI § 5.04 puts it, "[t]o leave the financially dependent spouse in a long marriage without a remedy would facilitate exploitation of the trusting spouse and discourage domestic investment by the nervous one."

On the other hand, an award based on the status principle resembles an award of expectation damages for breach of contract, which leaves the financially dependent spouse in the same position as she would occupy had the marital contract continued in force. In an era of no-fault divorce, is it appropriate to conceptualize divorce as a breach of contract? With nearly half of marriages ending in divorce, can any spouse reasonably expect that his or her marriage will continue indefinitely? Finally, at least in briefer marriages, might reliance on the status principle result in what economists call "moral hazard?" That is, would it make a financially dependent spouse indifferent between continuing the marriage or seeking a divorce—thus actually undermining marital commitment?

4.   THE REHABILITATION PRINCIPLE

According to this principle, the goal of divorce awards should be to enable the financially dependent spouse to acquire sufficient earning capacity to support himself or herself. If "sufficient" earning capacity is defined as enough to meet basic needs, this principle is similar to the need principle. Enabling the recipient to obtain additional education or training, however, may result in an increase in earning power that provides more than mere subsistence.

The rehabilitation principle differs from the need principle in that its implicit premise is that support should be for a temporary, rather than indefinite, period of time. If earning capacity is defined more expansively as enough to sustain the marital standard of living, rehabilitation resembles the status principle. In this case, rehabilitation still would reflect the assumption that support should be temporary, but the period of time would be longer than if earning capacity were defined in terms of basic needs.

Rehabilitation is appealing in its effort to ensure that spouses are at least able to be self-supporting after divorce. It also is consistent with the "clean break" philosophy in that it attempts to end the need for ongoing financial duties after divorce. In some divorces, however, a spouse charged with a financial obligation may claim that the marriage is not responsible for the other spouse's low earning capacity. It would therefore be unfair to require the higher-earning spouse to compensate the other spouse for failing to enhance his or her earning power. Potential recipients also may criticize the rehabilitation principle for not taking into account all of the contributions and sacrifices made during marriage.

5. THE CONTRIBUTION PRINCIPLE

The contribution principle is rooted in the idea that spouses pool their efforts during the marriage for their mutual benefit. On this view, when the marriage ends each spouse has earned certain benefits to which he or she is entitled. Financial awards at divorce thus should seek to compensate spouses for their efforts, regardless of need. Alimony should end only when the entitlement is paid off.

There are at least four different ways to calculate how assets should be divided under the contribution principle.

a. RESTITUTION OR THE MARKET VALUE OF SERVICES APPROACH

Restitution attempts to return to the spouse what he or she contributed to the marriage. A court might, for instance, calculate the market value of domestic services actually performed by the spouse, as well as the amount of earnings he or she contributed to the household.

One drawback of the restitution approach is that many of the services performed in the home have been traditionally undervalued by the job market. The result might be an unrealistically low estimate of the value of the domestic contributions that a spouse has made. The duration of the marriage also will affect the calculation. On the one hand, the longer the marriage, the greater the contributions it is likely that the spouse has made. At the same time, however, the spouse has received benefits from those contributions in the form of enjoyment of the marital standard of living.

b. COMPENSATION FOR FORGONE OPPORTUNITIES APPROACH

We might conceptualize a spouse's contributions not only as the services and income that he or she has provided, but as the earning power that he or she has forgone. One way to compute this is to estimate what the spouse's earning capacity would be had he or she stayed full-time in the labor market during the marriage. Subtracting his or her actual earning power at divorce from this figure, discounted to present value, would represent the reduction in earning power caused by the marriage.

A major difficulty with this approach is that it may require excessive speculation. If the spouse failed to complete his or her education, for instance, it may be extremely hard to determine what his or her earning power would have been. Would he or she have completed college? Law school? Would he or she have been first in her class? It is hard to know how life might have been different if a person had not married, much less to determine the economic consequences of each of the different paths he or she may have taken. In addition to this problem, the opportunity cost approach may end up rewarding highly educated homemakers a lot more than it would homemakers with less education, even when they have rendered essentially the same services.

ALI § 5.05 proposes a way to compensate a spouse for lost earning power that avoids the need for such speculation. The ALI adopts a conclusive presumption that a spouse who has been the primary caregiver for children during marriage has suffered a reduction in earning power. It presumes that the amount of that reduction is the difference in earning capacity between the two spouses at divorce. The ALI PRINCIPLES acknowledge that, among other things, this approach is intended to preserve incentives for one spouse to assume the main responsibility for childrearing. Some argue, however, that the price of avoiding speculation and creating incentives is a willingness to accept unfair awards in a certain percentage of cases.

c.   ENHANCED EARNING CAPACITY APPROACH

Another way to value a spouse's contributions is to determine whether he or she enhanced the earning power of the other spouse. A marriage in which one spouse works to support both of them and to put the other spouse through school is an example of this scenario. In such cases, the present value of the difference in lifetime earnings made possible by these contributions should be shared between the divorcing spouses. This approach focuses on compensating the spouse for the gain that he or she expected from his or her contributions, rather than the amount actually expended.

Determining what is a fair share is a major uncertainty with this approach. How should the contribution by the supporting spouse be compared to the effort of the spouse who works in the job market? Furthermore, how feasible is it to calculate future earnings that are attributable to a degree? If there is no degree involved, how plausible is it to posit that certain career moves during marriage will result in a specific amount of future earnings? Does an award based on this principle effectively prevent the obligated spouse from ever taking a less remunerative job for personal reasons?

d.   PARTNERSHIP APPROACH

Under this approach, all assets acquired during the marriage should be divided equally, on the ground that this best reflects widely held understandings of what marriage involves. In addition, this principle avoids the need to engage in speculative calculations, and values equally the contributions that each spouse makes regardless of the form that they take.

Some contend that treating an increase in earning power as an asset acquired during marriage is faithful to the partnership principle. It is at least analytically possible, however, to distinguish the selection of a distribution principle from the determination of what constitutes a marital asset.

Take note that the five principles often are mutually exclusive. For instance, a woman who was married for only six weeks, but who contracted a disabling disease might be entitled to a fairly large sum of alimony under the need principle, but little under the contribution principle.

Now that we have identified five possible principles on which to base financial awards at divorce, consider the factors that property division and alimony statutes instruct a court to take into account. Under both alternatives of UMDA § 307, for instance, in dividing property the first factor listed is the *contribution of each spouse to acquiring marital property, including the provision of homemaker services.* This factor reflects the contribution principle, but does not specify which approach to valuing contribution the court should take.

The second factor is *the value of each spouse's separate property.* This could lead the judge to rely on any of the principles. The judge might attempt to divide marital property so that combined separate and marital property ensured that each spouse would be able to meet basic needs; that each spouse would be able to approximate the marital standard of living; that the financially dependent spouse received enough to rehabilitate her earning power; that each spouse received compensation for the contributions that he or she made to the acquisition of marital assets; or that all marital property be divided equally, which might or might not include increased earning power.

The third factor, *the duration of the marriage,* seems most relevant to the status principle. As the ALI suggests, the longer the marriage, the fairer it seems that a spouse should not lose the standard of living to which he or she has become accustomed. In addition, a court could treat the length of the marriage as relevant in determining the extent to which a spouse has been compensated for her contributions by enjoying an enhanced marital standard of living.

Finally, directing the court to consider *the economic circumstances of each spouse* appears to direct the judge to focus on relative, rather than absolute, financial condition. This suggests reliance on the contribution principle. The contribution principle would attempt to ensure that neither spouse would enjoy an unfair gain or suffer an unfair loss from participation in the marriage. It also suggests the need principle, ensuring that neither spouse is left destitute if the other can afford to support them.

If we turn to the list of factors relevant to alimony, we see the same mixture of principles. UMDA § 308, for instance, conditions alimony on a finding that a spouse *lacks sufficient property to provide for reasonable needs,* and is *unable to support herself through employment* or is the custodian of a child and work outside the home is infeasible. This signals that need is a prerequisite for receipt of alimony, based on a standard of basic necessities.

If this prerequisite is satisfied, the statute lists six factors that a court may consider. The first is *the financial resources of the party seeking* alimony, his or her *ability to meet his or her needs independently,* and the extent to which a provision for support of a child living with the party includes *a sum for that party as custodian.* This factor asks the court to consider just how needy the spouse is. What resources does he or she have to meet his or her own needs, taking into account the needs that may arise because he or she has custody of a child? The second factor is the time necessary for the spouse to acquire enough *education or training to obtain appropriate employment.* This factor reflects reliance on the rehabilitation principle. The third factor, *the standard of living during the marriage,* suggests that the judge should rely on the status principle in making an alimony award.

The fourth factor is *the duration of the marriage.* As under the property division statute, this factor is relevant under the status principle, and also may be taken into account under the contribution principle in determining whether a spouse has been compensated during the marriage for his or her contributions. The *age and physical and emotional condition* of the spouse directs attention to need. Finally, the ability of the obligor spouse to meet his needs indicates that any financial awards should be limited to those that do not jeopardize basic necessities for the obligor.

Faced with factors that invoke so many different principles, with no guidance on which should have priority, what's a judge to do? On the one hand, one might argue that justice is not a unitary concept, but requires flexible reliance on multiple considerations. A certain amount of unpredictability is the price we pay for being able to tailor compensation to the circumstances of divorcing spouses. On the other hand, is it really plausible to contend that such a system reflects the rule of law, as opposed to virtually unfettered judicial discretion? Should it not be possible to identify a small number of principles on which there is consensus, so as to provide more consistency and predictability? As this section should make clear, that task requires not only that we ask what we want from divorce, but what it means to be married.

Alicia Brokars Kelly, *Rehabilitating Partnership Marriage as a Theory of Wealth Distribution at Divorce: In Recognition of a Shared Life*

19 Wis. Women's L.J. 141 (2004).

Consider the possible answers that might be offered by a person who knows nothing about legal doctrines in family law if we asked the question: what do you think it means to say that marriage is a partnership? Predictably, a common response would emphasize extensive sharing between spouses. A common cultural understanding of the concept is that partnership marriage means working together and sharing your life in a multitude of ways with your partner. Joint labor ("working together") and sharing more generally are central. . . .

The principles of joint labor and pervasive sharing that are core to the cultural meaning of partnership are paralleled in modern family law theory. It is overwhelmingly the cultural meaning of the term that has been (at least rhetorically) embraced in contemporary law governing marriage and divorce. . . . In law, partnership theory views marriage as a sharing venture and specifically recognizes that both spouses make vital financial and non-financial contributions. Non-financial contributions are said to be fully credited, so that a spouse who provides home labor, such as a spouse who stays at home to provide care for children, has provided valuable resources to the family just as the spouse who provides income from the paid labor market has. Joint spousal efforts mean that assets are jointly, not individually, owned. As a result, upon divorce, the assets produced by the efforts of either spouse belong to the marital partnership. Each spouse is entitled to share in the marital estate because each participated in its acquisition. Under this view, economic resources are apportioned not based on need or status, but because they have been jointly earned.

. . .

Although contemporary marital property systems have widely adopted the rhetoric of partnership marriage, many of its current constructions in law are distortions or only partial, and therefore incomplete, applications of its underlying principles. In some instances, legal decision makers reject the logic of the theory altogether, betraying its basic principles. . . .

. . .

. . . Judges, empowered to measure contribution, have (whether consciously or not) systematically devalued the contributions of women, particularly home labor. Statutory requirements to consider homemaker contributions have not been effective. . . .

. . .

A closer examination is revealing. The conclusion in nearly all career asset cases is that the supporting spouse has made, at best, only minimal contributions. But what of the facts of the cases that suggest quite the opposite? Case after case describes the supporting spouse as having sacrificed much, including forgone income of the enhanced spouse, or her own career, and, as having contributed extensive resources for the good of the family unit, including direct economic support for education, food and shelter, homemaking services and primary care for children. . . . While it is not surprising that the marketplace (which has long disadvantaged women) does not value these marital investments, it is appalling that modern marital law adopts this same view. Of course, a view of marriage as a partnership that recognizes the equal dignity and value of each spouse's contribution to the marriage would lead to an opposite conclusion: that earning capacity enhanced during marriage is jointly acquired and therefore jointly owned.

. . .

Under modern marital property regimes, legal decision makers face an impracticable task. In the absence of bright line rules, among a list of other factors, judges are asked to identify the respective contributions of each spouse over the length of the marriage and then determine their relative value. How can any person get an accurate view inside a marriage that lasted perhaps many, many years to retrospectively account for the breadth, kinds, and relative value of the innumerable contributions each spouse makes to a marriage?

. . .

Even assuming we could identify discrete contributions, how do you compare and value things like changing diapers against mowing the lawn? As Lee Starnes asks:

Does ten hours of vacuumuing [sic] equal ten hours of watching a little league baseball game? Ten hours of cleaning bathrooms? Ten hours of helping children with homework? Ten hours of painting a bedroom? And what of the husband who was a more efficient grocery shopper than his wife, or the wife who more efficiently vacuumed the house?

. . .

The law does not need to measure contribution in this way. Contributions can be legally recognized and protected by granting an entitlement to wealth without undertaking a strict cost-benefit analysis. Partnership theory does not require the retrospective accounting that modern law sometimes reflects. Although contribution is a core concept, so is equality. The theory *assumes* that each partner has made valuable contributions to the marriage and thus supports the conclusion of equal ownership.

. . .

... [P]artnership theory ... concludes that whatever wealth is produced during marriage is the product of the partners' joint labor, even if the kind of labor each spouse performs is different. This joint acquisition norm is based on sharing and interdependent behavior thought to characterize marriage. We don't look for a direct link with traditional property, like a bank account. Instead, we assume accumulated wealth was produced from a host of efforts and decisions by the spouses as to which resources to consume and which to save and invest in. This joint allocation of resources is the basis for sharing its results. For the same reason, the direct link question is the wrong one when thinking about an earnings stream. Under the theory of marriage as a partnership, as long as wealth (whatever its form) is produced during marriage, it is jointly owned. In fact, divorce law readily treats earnings received during marriage as jointly owned without the need for any showing that her labor contributed to his wages (or vice versa).

. . .

Consider [a scenario in which the husband is a dentist and his wife a hygienist]. [T]he spouses share a life for 23 years and at the end of the marriage she earns $22,000 from her employment and he $110,000 from his. It is entirely reasonable to assume that sharing a life as a couple powerfully influenced the path of both spouses' lives. Specifically, a logical conclusion is that an influential reason for why she is, at the end of the marriage, still a hygienist is because within the context of the parties' marriage, that role contributed to the couple's joint welfare. She is a hygienist because that is what made sense for the couple's lives together and likewise, enhancing his profession as a dentist also made sense in the context of their marriage. We can be reasonably confident of this because ... research demonstrates that spouses generally think of themselves as a unit (although, of course there is not a complete unity of interest) and make major decisions accordingly. The marriage then, although surely not the only factor, nonetheless shaped each partner's life in crucial ways and pervasively contributed to the financial situation each faces at divorce....

. . .

... [I]n crucial ways, conduct in marriage [thus] creates the financial situation each spouse confronts at divorce. Accordingly, we need to reconstruct our thinking about "causation" in partnership marriage. Specifically, the law should assume that the economic circumstances faced by each spouse are, in important part, *caused* by conduct and choices made jointly in marriage. The theory of partnership marriage then demands that there should be shared (not widely disparate) results while the results endure....

. . .

... The notion of contribution then must be made purposefully explicit.

... First (consistent with the original tenets of partnership theory) contribution must be understood to include a host of benefits and sacrifices given by spousal partners to the *marriage as a whole*. As a result, searching for a direct causal link between one spouse's specific conduct and a particular addition to wealth is inappropriate because it fails to recognize collaborative roles in marriage—that each spouse is contributing to the marriage in their own way, and in many cases, in very different ways than the other spouse. Instead, because both spouses have contributed, partnership marriage assumes that any benefits (or disadvantages) that stem from marriage *were jointly produced*. [Second], home-based contributions and market-based contributions must both be recognized as valuable to the family's joint welfare by giving rise to *a legal entitlement* (a property right) to share in whatever wealth is produced during marriage. Absent a legal entitlement, some contributions can wrongly be ignored. And, as I will argue below, home labor and market labor should be treated as equally valuable. [Third], spouses contribute not only to the acquisition of traditional property such as a house and a bank account, but they pervasively invest in and contribute to career development and enhanced earning power (often primarily in one spouse), which is just another form of wealth that is particularly important in modern families. Contribution then must give rise to an *entitlement to property whatever its form*, including enhanced earning power. Partnership marriage thus provides a basis for claims to income sharing (alimony) in addition to traditional property....

. . .

... A presumption of contribution within marriage and that the marriage crucially shaped each spouse's economic status would clarify the basis for mutual entitlements to wealth at divorce and would justly extend the application of partnership theory to income streams as well as traditional property.

But should we assume equal contribution? Unequal contribution? Or should we leave the issue to the adversarial process and let divorcing spouses and judges decide on a case-by-case basis who contributed more and how (which is more or less what happens now)....

A presumption of equal division is desirable and appropriate for a number of reasons. Importantly, a recognition in law that both spouses make contributions that are equally valuable emphasizes the equal human dignity of each person in the marriage. Specifically, home labor should be accorded equal status to market labor, emphasizing that work at home—disproportionately performed by women—must be accorded the same respect and value within marriage as market work. Equality then, is more than just a method of division; it has both real and symbolic power.

. . .

Next, equal division is desirable because, as a practical matter, it is very difficult to get an accurate and reliable record of the various kinds and qualities of contributions each partner makes over the length of a marriage.... It would be ... difficult to come up with general agreement on an inclusive list of *all* the varying kinds of contributions spouses make to a marriage.... In addition to the problem of identifying contributions, there is the impossible dilemma of valuing them. How can we possibly quantify and qualify things like emotional support? Inevitable and undoubtedly pervasive flaws would result. The likely unreliability of this process and lack of consensus on how to go about it argues strongly against doing it.

. . .

It appears that married couples themselves do not precisely count and measure *individual* contributions and instead accept their collaborative roles as generally equitable. The focus is on mutuality of contribution and a generalized sense of reciprocity appears to be enough to satisfy most spouses. As the best approximation we have for doing equity then, a presumption of equality would most closely correspond to the dominant understandings and perspectives of spousal partners about relative contributions in marriage.

. . .

What should be considered "marital wealth" to which the parties have a claim? Partnership theory dictates that any asset that has been affected by marital conduct ought to be included. Clearly, traditional assets that have accumulated during marriage should be divisible, based on a presumption of mutual contribution to the marriage. Modern property regimes already reflect this principle of partnership marriage. Additionally, . . . human capital, the most important kind of wealth for most families, must be recognized as property. Here, current law betrays the partnership ideal and wrongly excludes these assets.

Next, does the partnership ideal support the usual distinction in contemporary law between marital property and separate property? That depends on whether the separate assets have been affected by marital conduct or whether marital assets and conduct have been affected by the existence of separate property. To the extent that separate property has been influenced by the marriage or has itself influenced marital conduct, then these effects should be shared at divorce.

. . .

However, devising a sensible methodology for sharing the effects of marriage on human capital is a difficult challenge. Because of its nature, human capital investments cannot be accurately disaggregated. Additionally, measuring human capital losses that occur either because market skills and experience are diminished during marriage or because they are not "grown" during marriage by new and increasing investments in market work would require wholly unfounded and unreliable speculations about who the spouses would have become if they had never married or had children.

. . . Taking into account the nature of conduct in marriage, the best we can do is come up with a sensible compromise for identifying and dividing the impact of changes in human capital that predictably occur during marriage.

Thus, . . . I support the adoption of income sharing for a period of time after divorce. . . . [A]n entitlement to share income acknowledges that marriage merges spouses' economic lives and has long lasting economic consequences, particularly on earning power. Moreover, sharing income is also consistent with the expectations couples commonly have when they arrange their life together. For the same reasons that underpin the equal division of traditional property, income sharing for the relevant period must also be equal.

How long should income be shared? In formulating specific rules, there are a number of appealing proposals already in the literature that, in important ways, the theory of partnership marriage would support. Jana Singer, who has also supported the partnership approach to marriage, suggests one year of income sharing for every two years of marriage. Similarly, the ALI Principles advocate a fractional approach to income sharing related to marital duration. Although a rough compromise of many variables, I endorse this kind of an approach because it takes into account *both increases and losses* in earning capacity and shares the financial benefits and burdens that accrue from sharing a life together. . . . At the same time, the rule of one for two or a similar fraction of marital length recognizes that marital decisions strongly shape respective financial outcomes at divorce, but that the marriage is *not* completely responsible. . . .

As I have suggested, in terms of methodology for implementing partnership theory, I recommend a formulaic approach rather than a case by case approach to wealth division. . . . I believe clear rules that are fairly easy to apply, enhance predictability, and minimize costs are best. . . .

NOTES

1. Do you agree that the partnership theory as Professor Kelly describes it reflects the expectations of most married couples?

2. Is it possible to subscribe to partnership theory without accepting the claim that human capital is a marital asset?

Anne L. Alstott, *Private Tragedies? Family Law as Social Insurance*

4 Harv. L. & Pol'y Rev. 3, 3–17 (2010).

Family law is full of private tragedy. Case after case pits one family member against another in a zero-sum struggle for resources. Spouses battle over limited assets; parents clash over child support; and children fight each other for resources when parental income is stretched across multiple families. Bad choices and bad luck, it seems, precipitate calamity; and there is little that the law can do when families self-destruct amidst unemployment, poverty, mental illness, disability, substance abuse, domestic violence, child neglect, and other problems.

By legal tradition, family law is private law: it governs relationships between individuals, rather than between individuals and the state. On this view, family law, like other forms of private law, exists primarily to foster private order. On this view, family law should implement individuals' intentions—and should not redistribute risk and resources according to some public ideal. As private law, then, family law's core mission is to resolve disputes among family members when private order breaks down. Accordingly, functional families should have little to do with the law; they manage their own affairs without legal supervision. Dysfunctional families, by contrast, involve the law in inevitable tragedy. Once affective bonds have frayed and private order has failed, the courts must resolve disputes as best they can, and all too often any decision will harm one party or the other.

This Essay argues that this view of family law rests on an exaggerated distinction between private and public. Family law is more than a mechanism for implementing private preferences and resolving disputes when private order breaks down. Instead, family law forms part of a larger system of public law—a social insurance system that allocates the risk of life events like disability, family breakup, mental illness, substance abuse, and parental poverty. Family law does not simply pick up the pieces when individuals make bad choices or suffer bad luck. Instead, the law creates distributive rules that help determine which choices are bad ones and whose bad luck carries ruinous consequences. Taking this view, it is not just the dysfunctional who live in law's domain: successful families flourish amidst legal rules that protect some from life's risks while leaving others vulnerable.

Put another way, family law rules that establish financial relationships and liability between individuals constitute a form of social insurance: the rules of family law supplement those of familiar public programs, like Social Security and Temporary Assistance to Needy Families (TANF), that address life risks including poverty, unemployment, and disability. For instance, family law confers a legal right to care and to financial support based on formalized marriage, biological and adoptive parenthood, and certain kinds of recognized and rewarded behavior during marriage. Social insurance in the United States also adopts categorical protections; and while these vary across programs, distinctions may reflect formal marital status, paid-employment history, and income level. The categories and their consequences may differ in the two regimes, but both systems of law adopt normative classifications that recognize some relationships (and not others) and protect against some risks (and not others). Further, both systems of law can be understood as distributing risks ex ante, rather than simply addressing failure ex post.

One apparent difference between the obviously *public* realm of social insurance and the purportedly *private* sphere of family law lies in the redistributive power of the two types of law. Family law typically limits support obligations to a small class of related people: it imposes alimony obligations on spouses and support duties on parents or children. And family law does not have access to the state's taxing power, no matter how great a spouse's or child's need. By contrast, social insurance deliberately uses the power of the state to effect broad redistribution—taxing workers, income earners, and consumers for the legal benefit of third parties.

But this difference too is often overstated. Some family law rules use state power to impose lasting obligations on people who are affective or literal strangers, who believe themselves to have contracted around responsibility, or who are actively hostile to one another. Think about the child support obligations of an estranged parent or a divorced stepparent, filial responsibility laws that tax children with the support of their aged parents, or alimony imposed on long-divorced spouses. One scholar has proposed a child support assurance plan that would blend the two regimes, expanding family law's mandate to include a claim on public funds if needed. At the same time, some social insurance programs do not redistribute among individuals. They may simply extract a fee for services or regulate the purchase of certain goods, or they may create an intrapersonal obligation of an individual to her (older) self or to her own family. Think about private accounts proposed to replace Social Security or mandated benefits like family leave that may reduce workers' own wages.

In this Essay, I begin to integrate family law and social insurance, with the goal of gaining a better understanding of both regimes and their relationship to each other. To make the discussion concrete, I consider two cases—one involving spousal support and disability and the other involving child support for multiple families—and I demonstrate that they illustrate two points of overlap in family law and social insurance. First, both cases illustrate the interdependence of financial entitlements in family law and in social welfare. Both legal regimes make assumptions about the other and about the existence of family financial support and care. And the two regimes operate together to determine who suffers financial disaster when families break up and when disability and poverty strike.

Second, both cases demonstrate that a range of changes in family law, social welfare law, or other elements of law could alter the distribution of life's risks—and thus the likelihood and consequences of apparently private tragedies. For example, scholars have debated whether child support should be imposed on parents alone or shared by the state. A social insurance analysis challenges the binary distinction (parent/state) and opens up new possibilities ranging from small income taxes on extended family members to taxation of the child's own (adult) earnings.

To be sure, present family law and social insurance address different, if sometimes co-occurring, life risks. Family law governs disruptions in what I term "affective life"—the realm of life including formalized family bonds of marriage and parenthood, as well as less formal but still important emotional relationships including cohabitation and potentially even friendship. By contrast, social insurance addresses disruptions in working life—disability, unemployment, retirement, and low wages. It might seem, then, that the two bodies of law are distinct enough to occupy separate analytic categories.

But one agenda of this Essay is to challenge the split embodied in current law between large scale, ex ante, public protections for working life and smaller scale, ex post, purportedly private protections for affective life. Put another way, I want to frame as problematic the fact that conventional social insurance takes work disruption—and only work disruption—as its subject. The risks of working life are, indeed, major risks in a capitalist society. But an engagement with family law helps remind us that a wider range of risks can threaten adults' well-being and children's development. Disruptions in affective life can also threaten economic security and individual development: divorce, parental exit, and parental dysfunction, for instance, can lead to calamity just as surely as unemployment and disability.

My point, then, is that once we understand social insurance as the use of law to address, in a deliberate way, the major risks of life, then the focus of present programs on the risks of paid employment begins to seem oddly narrow. A first step, which I take here, is to show how family law operates— despite its traditional private-law label—as social insurance for affective life....

.   .   .

I.   In re Marriage of Wilson: Spousal Support and Disability

Spousal support (alimony) offers one divorced spouse a legal claim for continued financial support from the other. A California case, *In Re Marriage of Wilson*, illustrates the interplay of spousal support with Social Security disability and shows how changing family law rules, social insurance entitlements, or other legal regimes might alter the seemingly zero-sum, private tragedy of the Wilson marriage.

A.   The Tragedy: Divorce and Disability

Tom and Elma Wilson married in 1976, when he was thirty-six and she was thirty-eight. Their marriage lasted a little less than six years. Four years into the marriage, in 1980, Elma fell and suffered severe brain damage and deficits in social judgment, common sense, and social intelligence. She could no longer work, and doctors predicted that the damage would be permanent. They divorced in 1982, and Tom paid Elma alimony of $500 per month. Together with $436 per month in Social Security disability benefits, Elma could just make ends meet.

But after paying spousal support for more than four years, Tom had had enough. He sued to stop paying alimony, and Elma contested. Their dispute, *Wilson v. Wilson*, exemplifies the kind of private tragedy family law routinely encounters. The trial court, and then the appellate court, faced a zero-sum game. Relieving Tom of his support obligation would leave the disabled Elma in need and with no capacity to support herself. But continuing Tom's support obligation would limit his capacity to make a fresh start in life. (Note that in *Wilson* and in this Essay, the technical term "spousal support" means legally mandated, post-separation or post-divorce payments; the term does not refer to the financial support offered to a spouse in an intact marriage.)

According to the trial court, *Wilson* posed a conflict between two lines of family law doctrine. On the one hand, the law treats marriage as a serious obligation with lasting consequences. Spouses are understood to be part of an economic community, so that a needy (former) spouse has a legitimate claim on a prosperous one, even after divorce. Of the eight factors to be weighed in spousal support cases under California law at the time, six of them implemented this principle of need: the factors gave weight to Elma's disability, her age, her employment prospects; and to Tom's greater earnings and assets, and his higher living standard. On the other hand, the court noted, the law does permit marital dissolution, and implicit in that decision must be a principle that at some point marital obligations cease so that each spouse may get on with his or her life.

The trial court asked, "[A]t what point in time does the obligation to assist Mrs. Wilson become one of society's as distinguished from an obligation that is Mr. Wilson's?" and found "that it is society's at this point in time." The appellate court found that the trial court had not abused its discretion in balancing the equities and finding "under these circumstances the obligation to assist Elma should shift from Tom to society."

The appellate court mentioned, in passing, that Elma received $436 per month in "Social Security" benefits. The reference, presumably, is to Social Security Disability Insurance (SSDI), which is payable to workers with a substantial work history. In 1986, when *Wilson* terminated Tom's support obligation, the federal poverty threshold for one person was $5,360. With Tom's support, Elma lived modestly but sustainably at about 200% of the official poverty line. Without Tom's support, Elma's $436 per month ($5,232 per year) would leave her below the official poverty line, a living standard that represents dire economic distress.

Wilson remains good law, although its application to particular cases is uncertain given the multi-factor determinations necessary. A subsequent California case declined to read *Wilson* as establishing a broad public policy against long-term spousal support. In that case, the appellate court reversed a trial court order terminating spousal support for a functionally disabled, fifty-nine-year-old woman after a marriage of nine years. The court cautioned that the *Wilson* holding should be considered in the specific context of the marriage at issue and called for a careful weighing of all the factors in each case.

Wilson takes place against the backdrop of legal reforms intended to protect displaced homemakers. These spouses, typically wives, spent years rearing children and subordinating their careers (if any) to ensure that their husbands could work full-time and develop their own careers. Upon divorce, these often middle-aged women found themselves at a disadvantage in the labor market, and yet, at one point, the doctrine of spousal support called for them to become self-supporting on the theory that the dissolution of a marriage properly leaves each party to subsist solely on his or her own earning power. In effect, the limitation of spousal support permitted the husbands to retain most of the value of their own earnings while consigning the wives to live on their own wages—typically at a far lower standard of living than they had while married.

In response to criticism by scholars, lawmakers, and others, the law of spousal support developed, albeit unevenly, to incorporate protections for the displaced homemaker. We can see these protections in *Wilson*, where the court acknowledged the protections accorded to longer marriages, those with children, and those in which one spouse sacrificed for the other.

The irony, of course, is that the court in *Wilson* not only found these protections inapplicable to Elma but also made use of them to terminate her spousal support. Drawing a contrast to the long-married, self-sacrificing, good mother protected by the law, the appellate court described the Wilson partnership as "a childless marriage of short duration" and referred to Elma as "a middle aged bartender with adult children." In the next sentence, the court implied that Elma did little to accommodate Tom, again drawing an implicit contrast with the family-centered homemaker who leaves her job: "[Elma's] lifestyle was established [at the time of the marriage and did not change thereafter]."

Wilson thus poses hard questions about the nature of marriage: Should the law presume that all marriages create solemn, life-long obligations? Or should the law, in effect, recognize a lesser category of companionate marriage, signaled by middle-aged entry and childlessness, and accommodated by the law with an easier-come, easier-go set of obligations?

At first glance, *Wilson* represents a classic private tragedy. The law of spousal support presents the courts with a zero-sum game: they can protect the needy Elma, but only by yoking Tom to a long-term financial burden that would limit his life options and deny him, perhaps, the ability to marry again.

The courts, then, must harm one party or the other, and perhaps for that reason, both the trial and appellate opinions adopt language that emphasizes Elma's (risky) choices and bad luck: she is a "middle-aged bartender" with adult children whose father is no longer in the picture. Her bad luck—or perhaps her "drunken stupor"—left her with brain damage. At the same time, the courts implicitly treat Tom's (better) choices and luck as equally private and personally owned. Elma did not, says the court, make sacrifices to further Tom's career; nor did they have children together. In the end, the courts resolve the private tragedy by appealing to public law. Tom's private obligation to Elma, the courts find, has come to an end, and so Elma must become a state responsibility, a public charge.

But a closer look at the legal context of *Wilson* reveals how Tom's and Elma's choices and luck occurred amidst two social insurance systems—the law of marriage and the Social Security program. We do not always think of legal marriage as a form of social insurance, and of course marriage represents more than that. Still, the financial support and in-kind care obligations that attend marriage (as well as those that persist following divorce) represent a significant potential resource for people with disabilities. The scope of marital obligation is clearly the issue presented in *Wilson*, and the trial court addressed it head-on: in the court's view, Elma had exhausted the social insurance entitlement accruing to her particular marriage and would now become the state's responsibility.

But the decision in *Wilson* likely did not qualify Elma for any additional state support—despite her dire situation. Social Security disability insurance is categorical, meaning that only those suffering severe work disability can qualify, and those who return to employment can no longer claim benefits. But the program is not income-tested, meaning that benefits do not rise if the beneficiary's income drops. Thus, Elma's monthly cash benefit was determined by her own earnings and work history, and it would not increase if her other sources of income disappeared.

Supplemental Security Income (SSI) is a means-tested program that can supplement Social Security disability benefits, but it assists only those in extreme poverty. While SSDI provides a benefit based solely on past earnings (and thus is paid without regard to current income), SSI is means-tested and paid only to those in the direst financial circumstances. In 1982, Elma would most likely have been ineligible for SSI, which, during this period, provided maximum benefits for a single person amounting to less than seventy-five percent of the individual poverty line.

Strikingly, then, and despite the court's rhetoric, the denial of spousal support in Elma's situation did not impose any additional responsibility on the state. Instead, the decision left Elma to live in dire poverty, subsisting on her SSDI income alone, unless she could marry again or prevail upon her adult children for assistance.

Another striking feature of the family law/social insurance system is that spousal support following divorce is frankly redistributive in a way that social insurance may not be. Tom's spousal support represented redistribution from a better-off individual to a worse-off one, and it took place between two now-unrelated people hostile to each other. But Elma's SSDI benefit to some degree represented a return of her own earlier payroll tax contributions, which purchased retirement savings and an insurance contract against disability. To be sure, Social Security does redistribute income by giving lower-wage workers a relative bargain compared to a purely actuarial insurance premium. Still, Elma's public benefits had a substantial private component—just as if she were drawing down savings or had purchased private disability insurance.

B. Spousal Support as Social Insurance

Putting family law and social welfare law together, we can see that the nominally private tragedy of *Wilson* occurred amidst two legal sources of social insurance: a family-law entitlement to spousal support and a public entitlement to Social Security. Stepping back from *Wilson* to generalize, Table 1 depicts the combined family law/social welfare system for adults who develop disabilities. The table describes the individual's legally enforceable rights (and omits consideration of voluntary financial support and care by affective partners, children, and others).

Table 1: Family Law and Social Insurance Provision for Adults (Up to Age Sixty–Two) With Disabilities.

	Potential Benefits	Potential Risks
Married	• Individual's spouse has unlimited, though minimally enforceable, obligation of support. • SSDI provides benefits based on the individual's own work history. • SSDI may provide additional benefits to the spouse if the spouse is rearing the working individual's young children.	• Spouse's income is low or spouse withholds support or care (within legal boundaries). • Individual has no young children, eliminating SSDI spousal benefit. • Individual is poor but not poor enough to qualify for SSI.

	Potential Benefits	Potential Risks
Divorced; Performed Child–Rearing Work	• Spouse may have extended obligation of support following divorce. • SSDI provides benefits based on the individual's own work history.	• Former spouse's income too low for spousal support award. • Low SSDI payments due to individual's low earnings or intermittent work history. • Individual is poor but not poor enough to qualify for SSI.
Divorced; Never Performed Child–Rearing Work	• Spouse may have time-limited obligation of support following divorce. • SSDI provides benefits based on the individual's own work history.	• Former spouse's income too low for spousal support award. • Spousal support not awarded or terminates. • Low SSDI payments due to individual's low earnings or intermittent work history. • Individual is poor but not poor enough to qualify for SSI.
Never Married	• SSDI provides benefits based on the individual's own work history.	• No legal claim for support from any former partners, except for palimony claims. • Low SSDI payments due to individual's low earnings or intermittent work history. • Individual is poor but not poor enough to qualify for SSI.

Elma Wilson fell into one of the most vulnerable categories: she was divorced after a short-term, childless marriage. Her work and earnings history qualified her for a modest SSDI benefit, so she was luckier than those with lower earnings or a sporadic work record. And Tom's middle-class earnings supported an award of spousal support for nearly five years. Taken together, Elma's spousal support of $500 per month plus her Social Security of $436 per month gave her $11,232 per year, or just above 200% of the poverty line and less than half the median income. Still, even that income left Elma at a far lower standard of living than middle-class Tom, whose $38,400 income put him at over 700% of the poverty line and at 150% of the median income of $24,897. The termination of spousal support left Elma in severe economic distress—below the poverty line.

Treating family law as social insurance may seem to gloss over legal and substantive differences in the two regimes. After all, Tom is Elma's ex-husband, not a stranger; he is supporting his former life partner, not paying taxes to the state. But these distinctions—like most legal dualisms—are overstated. The law mandated Tom's obligations, just as it sets the terms of taxation. After the divorce, Tom was in some sense a stranger to Elma—he no longer had day-to-day obligations toward her. And both he and the courts framed his spousal support very much as an income "tax"—a financial burden calibrated by Tom's income to pay for someone else's benefit. The court ultimately concluded that the tax on Tom weighed too heavily and should be spread more widely. On Elma's side, as we have seen, her seemingly public benefits had a substantial private component, since SSDI reflects payroll tax contributions as well as state subsidies (and the amount of the subsidy varies from positive to negative—some people receive less, in actuarial terms, than if they had purchased a private insurance policy).

On the benefits side, we can also analyze spousal support in the same terms we would use for a social insurance program. Table 2 compares spousal support and SSDI along six dimensions.

Table 2: Comparing Spousal Support and SSDI.

	Spousal Support	SSDI
Categorical	• Formal marriage. • Lengthy marriage. • Childcare or other sacrifice of earning power.	• Permanent, severe disability. • Work history.
Work Test	• Support may be reduced or eliminated if employable.	• Benefits cease if employable.
Means Test	• Need for support taken into account along with earnings capability.	• No.
Eligibility Determination	• Individualized determination by a judge (unless a negotiated contract is valid).	• Individualized disability determination by caseworkers and an Administrative Law Judge.
Time Limit	• Yes, particularly if a short marriage, if no children, and if no demonstrable sacrifice to build the spouse's earning power.	• No.
Conditional on an Ex–Spouse's Income	• Yes.	• No.

Table 2 suggests substantial similarities. Both spousal support and SSDI are legally enforceable entitlements, not voluntary transfers. Both are categorical programs with individualized eligibility determinations. Both terminate support when the recipient is—or could be—self-supporting through employment. In the end, both family law and Social Security provide cash transfers that may meet the needs of people with disabilities—or fall short of meeting need, depending on the circumstances.

One important legal distinction between the two regimes does not appear in Table 2. Spousal support can be negotiated, either before the marriage in a prenuptial agreement or at divorce in a separation agreement. Depending on state law, the substantive terms of the agreement, and the situation of the parties, these private agreements may be enforceable, which is to say they can negate application of the default rules applied in *Wilson*. By contrast, SSDI taxes are mandatory for nearly all U.S. workers, and there is no opportunity for customization by contract. This formal difference is probably less significant than it may first appear, however, to the extent that the parties bargain in the shadow of the baseline entitlements set by the law.

The conventional distinction between private and public benefits may rest on the entries in the last column on the right. An individual's entitlement to spousal support depends on the ex-spouse's income, while the entitlement to SSDI does not. To be sure, the distinction is not entirely crisp. If an ex-spouse is sufficiently well-off, his income is not a major limitation on the claimant's benefit. And not all social welfare programs are entitlements: block grants, for instance, may deny services to eligible individuals simply because government funding falls short of demand.

Still, in the ordinary range of cases, the distinction has some bite: if the ex-spouse is poor, even the most deserving claimant for spousal support will walk away with nothing. Put another way, the family law portion of the social insurance system awards entitlements of varying "credit quality"—those formally married to rich partners have AAA-quality claims, while others have financially contingent entitlements.

The two systems of social insurance—family law and Social Security— each take account of the other, but the legal mechanisms are different. Family courts generally may (or must) take need into account in determining spousal support, as in *Wilson*; and so Elma's SSDI entitlement would tend to reduce her spousal support, all else equal. But, just as in *Wilson*, when the entitlement to spousal support ends, the spouse's level of income becomes irrelevant. The *Wilson* decision left Elma below the federal poverty line—a measure social scientists view as representing dire poverty. The court does not mention the poverty level, nor does it recognize that living below the poverty line likely means severe deprivation. Instead, the appellate court endorses the trial court's conclusion that Elma's well-being is now the state's obligation—without giving much consideration to the content of that obligation.

By contrast, SSDI benefits are set without a means test for the recipient and so do not explicitly take account of other income. Implicitly, however, SSDI sets benefits for some workers low enough that, to escape poverty, beneficiaries functionally must maintain or form a family relationship—or make a successful claim on an ex-spouse.

To summarize, the law creates a combined system of social insurance that distributes the risk of disability in a distinctive way: all else equal, high-earning workers with intact marriages (or divorces after long-term, child-rearing marriages) to high earners receive the largest benefits awards. Low-earning workers (without children) whose marriages dissolve fare less well, and low-earning, never-married workers have the fewest legal protections.

Analyzed from an ex ante perspective, Elma Wilson was vulnerable long before her fall in 1980. Given her marital situation, her child-rearing situation, and her earnings, she faced substantial financial risk if divorce or disability struck. Had her low wages been connected to child-rearing duties or a long marriage, she could have fared better in the family-law portion of the system (qualifying for long-term spousal support). And had her earnings been higher, she could have fared better in the public, SSDI portion of the system (qualifying for higher benefits).

Perhaps it is not surprising that high-income people with long-term marriages and traditional gender roles fare best under both family law and Social Security. The law often perpetuates privilege and reproduces underlying inequalities. Still, an integrated view of family law and SSDI helps us see the extent to which the social insurance system as a whole mitigates—or fails to mitigate—the risks created by marriage and the labor market.

Both family law and Social Security allocate the consequences of life risks amidst other legal structures that entrench privilege and vulnerability.

Consider two elements of U.S. law that we often take for granted. First, U.S. labor and employment laws influenced Elma's work history and working conditions. Bartending tends to pay relatively low wages and provide few benefits; thus, Elma apparently was left without access to the *third* portion of the U.S. social insurance system—private insurance benefits for disability and retirement. We sometimes speak of the labor market as if it exists in some natural space outside law. But economists know that the law structures market interactions. Thus, there are multiple possible forms of a "free" labor market, corresponding to an array of possible legal-institutional choices about matters like collective bargaining and legal mandates for wages, working conditions, fringe benefits, and so on.

Second, Elma's disability and marital breakup occurred amidst a legal context that required her—and nearly everyone else—to purchase most goods in the marketplace at prices set by the market. Housing, food, clothing, and transportation all had to be funded after the *Wilson* ruling out of Elma's $436 per month SSDI benefit. We have already seen that Elma was unlikely to qualify for SSI, and without children she could not collect federally sponsored welfare benefits (then called Aid to Families with Dependent Children (AFDC), and now called TANF). The major supplemental benefit she would receive was Medicare, which would, after a waiting period, pay for a major portion (though not all) of Elma's medical care.

C.   Legal Reforms: Family Law and Beyond

Armed with this map of family law, SSDI, and other legal structures, we can now see at least four entry points for legal reforms. Changes in family law, in Social Security, in labor markets, and in the distribution of primary goods could all change the tragic nature of the court's choice in *Wilson* by altering the ex ante distribution of the risks of disability and/or marital dissolution. To be sure, I have not—and will not here—offer a normative argument that would support any specific reform, or indeed any reform at all. My goal here is not to prescribe the proper form of the social insurance system; rather, I mean only to offer options for discussion that illustrate some counterintuitive legal choices.

Family law represents one avenue for reform. In response to *Wilson*, the courts or legislatures might mandate longer-lasting obligations for spousal support when severe disability and extreme need combine. Instead of distinguishing between child-rearing marriages, on the one hand, and companionate marriages, on the other, the law might—contrary to the approach the court adopted in *Wilson*—treat all marriages as an explicit form of social insurance against disability, with marital obligations lasting for a lengthy, even permanent, time after divorce.

This direction for legal reform would, of course, mark a major change in the present understanding of marriage and divorce. At present, divorce offers a fresh start, with the exception being long-term, child-rearing marriages with one spouse shouldering the care work and sacrificing market opportunities. Changing the result in *Wilson* would usher in a new approach, and one that raises many questions. At present, the United States has a high degree of serial monogamy, with a high rate of divorce and remarriage. Extending the alimony obligation could stand at odds with that cultural pattern, tying ex-spouses together financially for the long term. And of course, there is the deeper normative question: *should* marriage involve long-term income insurance by each spouse to the other? Operational questions arise as well: Should very short marriages be excepted? Should spouses be permitted to opt out via prenuptial agreements?

I do not offer here a concrete proposal for legal reform. Instead, my limited point at this stage is that we can conceive of such a change in social-insurance terms. An extended alimony obligation would award a longer-term, means-tested benefit to the ex-spouse suffering a disability, funded by an income "tax" on her former spouse.

D. CHILD SUPPORT

1. INTRODUCTION

As a general rule, parents are responsible for child support until a child reaches majority. Originally, the duty to support was the father's only, and it was symmetrical to his right to demand services from the child. This legal practice complemented the social practice of extensively using children as young as six years old as household labor, sometimes even renting them out through apprenticeships.[1] During the nineteenth century, however, middle-class children were withdrawn from the market and placed instead in schools. At the same time, divorcing mothers were for the first time given preference over the fathers for the custody of their children. Under the pressure of increased numbers of children becoming a public burden, courts practically invented the father's legal duty to support his minor children, and states criminalized the failure to pay child support when this led children to poor relief.[2] Unlike other western nations where the state often undertakes to support every child at some basic level, child support in the United States from its origins has been a private obligation, initially of the father and eventually of both parents equally.

During the twentieth century, courts had to adjudicate an increasing number of child support cases as the number of divorces rose. The 1973 version of the UMDA provides an example of the factors that courts considered relevant in setting a child support obligation.

UNIFORM MARRIAGE AND DIVORCE ACT

(1973).

Section 309. Child Support

In a proceeding for dissolution of marriage, legal separation, maintenance, or child support, the court may order either or both parents owing a duty of support to a child to pay an amount reasonable or necessary for his support, without regard to marital misconduct, after considering all relevant factors including:

(1) the financial resources of the child;

(2) the financial resources of the custodial parent;

(3) the standard of living the child would have enjoyed had the marriage not been dissolved;

---

1. *See* MARY ANN MASON, FROM FATHER'S PROPERTY TO CHILDREN'S RIGHTS: THE HISTORY OF CHILD CUSTODY IN THE UNITED STATES 6–7 (1994).

2. *See* Drew D. Hansen, Note, *The American Invention of Child Support: Dependency and Punishment in Early American Child Support Law*, 108 YALE L.J. 1123, 1129–47 (1999) (describing the shift in treatment of children, in custody preferences, and in the necessity of support obligations).

(4) the physical and emotional condition of the child and his educational needs; and

(5) the financial resources and needs of the noncustodial parent.

As with spousal support, these factors were not weighted and produced results that were highly variable and unpredictable not only between different states but also between different courts within a single state.[3] Critiques of the inequities produced by such variability and pressure for better enforcement of child support obligations against "deadbeat dads"—especially those with children on welfare—eventually led to the adoption of child support guidelines. Minimum standards for the guidelines were set by federal regulation.

45 C.F.R. § 302.56. Guidelines for setting child support awards

(2010).

. . .

(c) The guidelines . . . must at a minimum:

(1) Take into consideration all earnings and income of the noncustodial parent;

(2) Be based on specific descriptive and numeric criteria and result in a computation of the support obligation; and

(3) Address how the parents will provide for the child(ren)'s health care needs. . . .

. . .

(e) The State must review, and revise, if appropriate, the guidelines . . . at least once every four years to ensure that their application results in the determination of appropriate child support award amounts.

(f) . . . [T]he State must provide that there shall be a rebuttable presumption, in any judicial or administrative proceeding for the award of child support, that the amount of the award which would result from the application of the guidelines . . . is the correct amount of child support to be awarded.

(g) A written finding or specific finding . . . that the application of the guidelines . . . would be unjust or inappropriate in a particular case shall be sufficient to rebut the presumption in that case, as determined under criteria established by the State. Such criteria must take into consideration the best interests of the child. . . .

(h) As part of the review of a State's guidelines . . ., a State must consider economic data on the cost of raising children and analyze case data . . . on the application of, and deviations from, the guidelines. The analysis of the data must be used in the State's review of the guidelines to ensure that deviations from the guidelines are limited.

---

3. *See* Lucy Marsh Yee, *What Really Happens in Child Support Cases: An Empirical Study of Establishment and Enforcement of Child Support Orders in the Denver District Court*, 57 DENV. L.J. 21 (1979–1980).

2.   CHILD SUPPORT GUIDELINES

There are two main models of Child Support Guidelines currently in use. The income shares model is used by a majority of states. The percentage of income model is used in about seven states. A third model, known as the Melson formula after the judge who came up with its basic elements, is in use in Delaware, Hawaii, and Montana.

a.   THE INCOME SHARES MODEL

There are two basic ideas behind the income shares model. First, a child of divorce should be supported at the same level as in an intact family. Second, both parents should be contributing to child support. To implement the first idea, income shares models calculate child support on the basis of survey data about what percentage of their overall income intact families spend on their children. To simplify, income shares guidelines directly translate these percentages into a basic child support obligation for different combined income levels via Child Support Guideline tables, such as the one below. To implement the second idea, income shares models add both parents' incomes to calculate a combined income, *as if* the parties were still living in one household, and then prorate the resulting basic child support obligation between the parents, based on their proportionate contribution to combined income.

The table below is drawn from Louisiana's statutory guidelines. LA. REV. STAT. ANN. § 9:315.19 (West 2008 & Supp. 2011).

Combined Adjusted Monthly Gross Income	One Child	Two Children (Total)	Three Children (Total)	Four Children (Total)	Five Children (Total)	Six Children (Total)
0–600.00	100	100	100	100	100	100
700.00	136	138	139	141	142	144
800.00	174	206	208	211	213	215
900.00	189	274	277	280	283	286
1,000.00	203	315	339	342	346	350
2,000.00	378	549	655	737	805	865
3,000.00	548	801	939	1023	1126	1224
4,000.00	696	1026	1206	1343	1477	1605
5,000.00	826	1206	1412	1577	1735	1886
10,000.00	1269	1808	2097	2343	2577	2801
20,000.00	1891	2663	3052	3409	3750	4076

For example, assume that two divorced parents each have a monthly income (as defined by the statute) of $2,500. They have two children. Assume that there are no other deductions or expenses. First, determine their combined income, which is $5,000. Determine the monthly support obligation from the table above based on combined income and number of children. It is $1,206. Finally, determine the noncustodial (obligor) parent's prorated share. In this case, it is fifty percent because that parent earns half of the combined income. Therefore, the presumed obligation is $603.

NOTES

1. Note that as income goes up, the percentage of income families spend on their children goes down. The income shares model incorporates this fact by reducing the percentage of the parents' combined income imposed for child support as the level of income rises. This is one of the income shares advantages over the percentage of obligor model, which usually retains the same percentage regardless of level of income. Laura W. Morgan, Child Support Guidelines: Interpretation and Application § 1.03, at 20.2, 22–23 (1996 & Supp. 2010).

2.   As noted above, the guideline amounts are calculated on the basis of survey data, which look at *marginal* expenditures. Professor Ira Mark Ellman and his co-author Tara O'Toole Ellman have argued that it is important to understand that marginal expenditures on children are not the same as child costs. In order to calculate marginal expenditures on children, researchers calculate the additional amounts that a couple with a certain number of children would have to spend as compared to a childless couple. This means that certain fixed costs, such as rent or transportation, will not count in the calculation (except to the extent that a bigger apartment or a different car is needed to cover the needs of the couple with child/ren) regardless of whether there was an actual benefit conferred on the child. Ellman and Ellman have argued that this method yields guideline amounts that may be sub-optimal and seriously underestimate the needs of children of divorced parents, who, contrary to an intact family, have to maintain two different households. *See* Ira Mark Ellman & Tara O'Toole Ellman, *The Theory of Child Support*, 45 Harv. J. on Legis. 107, 118 (2008) ("marginal analysis of child expenditures marginalizes children").

3.   When one parent has physical custody and the other visitation, incomes shares guidelines usually assume that the custodial parent is already spending his or her child support obligation directly on the child. The non-custodial parent then owes the custodial parent the amount determined through the guidelines. When parents have a more complicated arrangement, such as split custody, some income shares models provide adjustments of the child support obligation based on how much time a parent spends as the physical custodian of the child.

For example, Michigan adjusts the base child support obligation by a "parental time offset" that takes into account each parent's obligation and the number of nights the child stays with each parent. *See* State Court Administrative Office, Family Services Division, Friend of the Court Bureau, 2008 Michigan Child Support Formula Manual 3.03, *available at* http://courts.michigan.gov/scao/services/focb/mcsf.htm (last visited Aug. 25, 2011) [hereinafter 2008 MCSF]. The manual states that the offset should generally apply in all support determinations. 2008 MCSF 3.03(B).

4.   Over time, income shares formulas have incorporated various deductions from available income, as well as add-ons and exclusions to account for various contingencies and to avoid the need to deviate from the presumptive guideline award. For example, Michigan first determines the parents' net incomes, which includes all income after allowable deductions and adjustments. 2008 MCSF 2.01(A). Subject to certain rules, allowable deductions include alimony or spousal support that a parent pays to a person who is not the other parent, actual income taxes, mandatory payments required for employment, and some life insurance premiums. *See* 2008 MCSF 2.07. A base child support obligation is calculated, but other expenses may be added on for ordinary and extraordinary medical expenses, health care coverage, and child care. *See* 2008 MCSF 3.01.

b.   PERCENTAGE OF OBLIGOR INCOME MODEL

The percentage of income model sets the child support obligation based only on the non-custodial parent's level of income and the number of children. The custodial parent is assumed to be already spending part of their own income on the child or children who live in the household. Despite appearances, both income shares and percentage of income models arrive at almost identical child support obligations when it comes to middle incomes, with differences accentuated at the low and high income levels.[1]

---

1.   Laura W. Morgan, Child Support Guidelines: Interpretation and Application § 1.03, at 26–27 (1996 & Supp. 2005).

The following table is from the Mississippi guidelines. MISS CODE ANN. § 43–19–101 (2009).

Number of Children Due Support	Percentage of Adjusted Gross Income That Should be Awarded for Support
1	14%
2	20%
3	22%
4	24%
5 or more	26%

For example, assume that two divorced parents each have a monthly income (as defined by the statute) of $2,500. They have two children. Assume that there are no other deductions or expenses. Looking at the table, the percentage of the noncustodial parent's income that should go towards support is twenty percent. Multiplying this twenty percent by that parent's monthly income yields the presumed monthly support obligation of $500.

NOTE

Many of the percentage of obligor's income models have been criticized because they fail to make adjustments for such things as extraordinary medical care costs, childcare, and/or joint or split custody. These models then have to take some of these factors into account as a deviation, rather than incorporate them into the presumptive amount, which detracts from the goal of judicial certainty. *See* LAURA W. MORGAN CHILD SUPPORT GUIDELINES: INTERPRETATION AND APPLICATION § 1.03, at 22–23 (1996 & Supp. 2002).

c. THE MELSON FORMULA

The Melson formula is known to be the most fact-specific of the three models in use, but also the one that entails the most steps and calculations, which is why it has not been widely adopted. There are three underlying principles to the Melson formula. First, every parent should be allowed to retain the minimum amount that is necessary for their own basic needs and the continuation of their employment. Second, until every child's basic needs are covered, parents should not be allowed to retain more than the minimum amount necessary for their own basic needs. Third, if income is enough to cover the basic needs of both parents and their dependents, children should be able to share in the additional income and higher standard of living of their parents.[2]

To implement these principles, the Melson formula begins by calculating the net income of each parent. This usually excludes income tax and certain other expenses such as pre-existing child support obligations. The next step is to calculate the minimum reserve needed for each parent's own basic needs and subtract that from net income. The Melson formula then proceeds to calculate a basic child support need based on the parents' combined net incomes. At this step, the Melson formula includes reasonable childcare and health insurance costs in its calculation of this basic child support need, which is considered one of its advantages. After the basic child support need

---

2. For a description of the main elements of the Melson formula *see* Dalton v. Clanton, 559 A.2d 1197, 1203–04 (Del. 1989).

has been calculated it is subtracted from the parents combined available net income. If there is income left after this operation, the formula applies a percentage to the remaining combined income in order to calculate a standard of living adjustment (SOLA). The basic child support need and SOLA are added to provide the total child support obligation, which is then divided between the parents in proportion to their contribution to combined income—much like the income shares formula.

3.   APPLYING THE GUIDELINES

a.   WHAT COUNTS AS INCOME?

The following example from Colorado illustrates the expansive definition of income typically contained in the statutory guidelines:

COLO. REV. STAT. ANN. § 14–10–115

(West 2005 & Supp. 2010).

. . .

(3) Definitions. As used in this section, unless the context otherwise requires:

(a) "Adjusted gross income" means gross income, as specified in subsection (5) of this section, less preexisting child support obligations and less alimony or maintenance actually paid by a parent.

(b) "Combined gross income" means the combined monthly adjusted gross incomes of both parents.

(c) "Income" means the actual gross income of a parent, if employed to full capacity, or potential income, if unemployed or underemployed. Gross income of each parent shall be determined according to subsection (5) of this section.

. . .

(5) Determination of income. (a) For the purposes of the child support guidelines and schedule of basic child support obligations specified in this section, the gross income of each parent shall be determined according to the following guidelines:

(I) "Gross income" includes income from any source, except as otherwise provided in subparagraph (II) of this paragraph (a), and includes, but is not limited to:

(A) Income from salaries;

(B) Wages, including tips declared by the individual for purposes of reporting to the federal internal revenue service or tips imputed to bring the employee's gross earnings to the minimum wage for the number of hours worked, whichever is greater;

(C) Commissions;

(D) Payments received as an independent contractor for labor or services;

(E) Bonuses;

(F) Dividends;

(G) Severance pay;

(H) Pensions and retirement benefits, including but not limited to those paid pursuant to articles 51, 54, 54.5, and 54.6 of title 24, C.R.S., and article 30 of title 31, C.R.S.;

(I) Royalties;

(J) Rents;

(K) Interest;

(L) Trust income;

(M) Annuities;

(N) Capital gains;

(O) Any moneys drawn by a self-employed individual for personal use;

(P) Social security benefits, including social security benefits actually received by a parent as a result of the disability of that parent or as the result of the death of the minor child's stepparent but not including social security benefits received by a minor child or on behalf of a minor child as a result of the death or disability of a stepparent of the child;

(Q) Workers' compensation benefits;

(R) Unemployment insurance benefits;

(S) Disability insurance benefits;

(T) Funds held in or payable from any health, accident, disability, or casualty insurance to the extent that such insurance replaces wages or provides income in lieu of wages;

(U) Monetary gifts;

(V) Monetary prizes, excluding lottery winnings not required by the rules of the Colorado lottery commission to be paid only at the lottery office;

(W) Taxable distributions from general partnerships, limited partnerships, closely held corporations, or limited liability companies;

(X) Expense reimbursements or in-kind payments received by a parent in the course of employment, self-employment, or operation of a business if they are significant and reduce personal living expenses;

(Y) Alimony or maintenance received; and

(Z) Overtime pay, only if the overtime is required by the employer as a condition of employment.

(II) "Gross income" does not include:

(A) Child support payments received;

(B) Benefits received from means-tested public assistance programs, including but not limited to assistance provided under the Colorado works program, as described in part 7 of article 2 of title 26, C.R.S., supplemental security income, food stamps, and general assistance;

(C) Income from additional jobs that result in the employment of the obligor more than forty hours per week or more than what would otherwise be considered to be full-time employment; and

(D) Social security benefits received by the minor children, or on behalf of the minor children, as a result of the death or disability of a stepparent are not to be included as income for the minor children for the determination of child support.

. . .

(b)(I) If a parent is voluntarily unemployed or underemployed, child support shall be calculated based on a determination of potential income; except that a determination of potential income shall not be made for a parent who is physically or mentally incapacitated or is caring for a child under the age of thirty months for whom the parents owe a joint legal responsibility or for an incarcerated parent sentenced to one year or more.

. . .

(III) For the purposes of this section, a parent shall not be deemed "underemployed" if:

(A) The employment is temporary and is reasonably intended to result in higher income within the foreseeable future; or

(B) The employment is a good faith career choice that is not intended to deprive a child of support and does not unreasonably reduce the support available to a child; or

(C) The parent is enrolled in an educational program that is reasonably intended to result in a degree or certification within a reasonable period of time and that will result in a higher income, so long as the educational program is a good faith career choice that is not intended to deprive the child of support and that does not unreasonably reduce the support available to a child.

. . .

NOTES

1. Some states base their guidelines on net rather than gross income. For a table listing which states use net versus gross *see* Jane C. Venohr & Robert G. Williams, *The Implementation and Periodic Review of State Child Support Guidelines*, 33 FAM. L.Q. 7, 11 tbl. 1 (1999).

2. The incarceration exception of 5(b)(I) of COLO. REV. STAT. ANN § 14–10–115 (West 2005 & Supp. 2010) is not included in every statute. In fact some courts have held that incarceration is a voluntary decrease in income that does not warrant an exemption from imputing income to the incarcerated obligor. *See, e.g., Richardson v. Ballard*, 681 N.E.2d 507, 508 (Ohio Ct. App. 1996) (incarceration was due to criminal conduct; therefore it was voluntary and did not justify a modification of a child support order); *Commonwealth ex rel. Marshall v. Marshall*, 15 S.W.3d 396, 401 (Ky. Ct. App. 2000) (incarceration results from a voluntary act and does not excuse a child support obligation). *But see In re Marriage of Smith*, 108 Cal. Rptr.2d 537, 544–45 (Cal. Ct. App. 2001) ("if [a parent] does not have an opportunity to work, whether in prison or not, the earning capacity test is not satisfied and cannot be used to determine his child support payments") (internal quotes and citation omitted).

The following case discusses the different tests that courts have used to decide whether to impute income to a parent who has voluntarily chosen to be unemployed or underemployed.

Little v. Little

Supreme Court of Arizona, En Banc, 1999.
193 Ariz. 518, 975 P.2d 108.

■ McGREGOR, JUSTICE.

In this opinion, we consider the standard courts should apply in determining whether a non-custodial parent's voluntary decision to leave his or her employment to become a full-time student constitutes a sufficient change in circumstances to warrant a downward modification of the parent's child support obligation.

The parties divorced in November 1995. The court ordered appellant Billy L. Little, Jr., an Air Force lieutenant, to pay $1,186 per month for the support of his two young children. In August 1996, appellant resigned his commission in the Air Force, a position that paid $48,000 in yearly salary plus benefits, and chose to enroll as a full-time student at Arizona State University College of Law rather than to seek employment.

Upon leaving the Air Force, appellant petitioned the court to reduce his child support obligation to $239 per month. The trial court concluded that appellant had failed to prove a substantial and continuing change of circumstances in accordance with ARIZONA REVISED STATUTES (A.R.S.) §§ 25–327.A and 25–503.F, and denied his request for modification. The trial court specifically found that appellant voluntarily left his employment to further his own ambition; that he failed to consider the needs of his children when he made that decision; and that to reduce his child support obligation would be to his children's immediate detriment and their previously established needs. The trial court did reduce appellant's child support obligation to $972 per month on the ground that appellee Lisa L. Little had acquired a higher paying job.

The court of appeals, applying a good faith test to determine whether appellant acted reasonably in voluntarily leaving his employment, held that the trial court abused its discretion in finding that appellant's decision to terminate his employment and pursue a law degree was unreasonable. Because we hold that a court, rather than rely upon a good faith test, must balance a number of factors to determine whether to modify a child support order to reflect a substantial and continuing change of circumstances, we vacate the opinion of the court of appeals and affirm the decision of the trial court.

The decision to modify an award of child support rests within the sound discretion of the trial court and, absent an abuse of that discretion, will not be disturbed on appeal. . . .

Arizona's law governing modification of child support orders, codified at A.R.S. §§ 25–327.A and 25–503.F, states that a court should modify a child support order only if a parent shows a substantial, continuing change of circumstances. Guidelines adopted by this court provide procedural guidance in applying the substantive law. According to the Guidelines, when a parent is unemployed or working below his or her full earning potential, a trial court calculating the appropriate child support payment may impute income to that parent, up to full earning capacity, if the parent's earnings are reduced voluntarily and not for reasonable cause. The Guidelines also state that the trial court may elect not to impute income to a parent if he or she is enrolled in reasonable occupational training that will establish basic skills or is reasonably calculated to enhance earning capacity. Significantly, both the governing statute and the Guidelines recognize that a parent's child support obligation is paramount to all other financial obligations, and that a parent has a legal duty to support his or her biological and adopted children.

. . .

A number of other jurisdictions have considered the issue that confronts us. Courts in sister jurisdictions have applied one of three tests to determine whether to modify a child support order when a parent voluntarily terminates his or her employment. The first of these tests, the good faith test, "considers the actual earnings of a party rather than his earning capacity, so long as" he or she acted in good faith and not "primarily for the purpose of avoiding a support obligation" when he or she terminated employment. The second test, designated the strict rule test, "disregards any income reduction produced by voluntary conduct and . . . looks at the earning capacity of a party in fashioning a support obligation." The third test, referred to as the intermediate test, balances various factors to determine "whether to use actual income or earning capacity in making a support determination." Each of the tests evidences its own strengths and weaknesses, and each reflects the public policy of its adopting jurisdiction.

Other jurisdictions have detected three fundamental flaws in the good faith test, which assigns the highest value to the obligor parent's individual freedom of choice. First, the test erroneously "assumes that a divorced or separated party to a support proceeding will continue to make decisions in the best overall interest of the family unit," when often, in fact, the party will not. Second, the test fails to attach sufficient importance to a parent's existing obligation to support his or her children. As one court explained, the good faith test allows a parent to be "free to retire, take a vow of poverty, write poetry, or hawk roses in an airport, if he or she sees fit," provided only that his or her motivation for acting is not to shirk a child support obligation. Third, once the party seeking a downward modification provides a seemingly good faith reason for leaving employment, the burden of proof often shifts to the party opposing the reduction to then show that the reason given is merely a sham. Even if the burden of proof does not shift, the trial court is still left with the difficult task of evaluating a party's subjective motivation. While all those factors influence our decision to reject the good faith test, we regard the primary shortcoming of the good faith test as being its focus upon the parent's motivation for leaving employment rather than upon the parent's responsibility to his or her children and the effect of the parent's decision on the best interests of the children.

The strict rule test also contains a fatal flaw. This test is too inflexible because it considers only one factor, the parent's earning capacity, in determining whether to modify a child support order when a parent voluntarily leaves employment. We decline to adopt the strict rule test because it allows no consideration of the parent's individual freedom or of the economic benefits that can result to both parent and children from additional training or education.

We reject both these extreme approaches and instead adopt an intermediate balancing test that considers a number of factors. . . .

Arizona law prescribes that "the obligation to pay child support is primary and other financial obligations are secondary." A.R.S. § 25–501.C. Thus, the paramount factor a trial court must consider in determining whether a voluntary change in employment constitutes a substantial and continuing change in circumstances sufficient to justify a child support modification is the financial impact of the parent's decision on the child or children the support order protects. If a reduction in child support due to a non-custodial parent's voluntary decision to change his or her employment status places a child in financial peril, then the court generally should not permit a downward modification.

In many instances, the impact on the children will not be so severe as to place the children in peril. In those circumstances, courts must consider the overall reasonableness of a parent's voluntary decision to terminate employment and return to school. The answers to several questions will provide relevant information. The court should ask whether the parent's current educational level and physical capacity provide him or her with the ability to find suitable work in the marketplace. If so, the decision to leave employment is less reasonable. In contrast, answers to other questions make the parent's decision to leave employment more reasonable. If the additional training is likely to increase the parent's earning potential, the decision is more likely to be found reasonable. The court should also consider the length of the parent's proposed educational program, because it matters whether the children are young enough to benefit from the parent's increased future income. The court also should inquire whether the parent is able to finance his or her child support obligation while in school through other resources such as student loans or part-time employment. Finally, the court should consider whether the parent's decision is made in good faith, as a decision to forego employment and return to school usually will not be reasonable or made in good faith if the parent acts to avoid a child support obligation.

. . .

We believe the balancing test described above comports not only with Arizona's public policy, but also with a national policy trend that favors strictly enforcing child support obligations. . . .

. . .

Applying the balancing test to the facts involved here, we conclude that the trial court did not abuse its discretion when it refused appellant's request for a downward modification of his child support obligation. First, the negative impact of the requested reduction on appellant's children, had the trial court granted it, would have been substantial. The trial court found that such a reduction "would be to the children's immediate detriment and their previously established needs." The record also reveals that appellee earns only $1,040 per month in salary. This income places the Little family well below the 1998 federal poverty level. Without their father's support, appellant's children would face significant economic hardship. Second, appellant holds Bachelor of Arts and Master of Business Administration degrees. Appellant, by asking the trial court to assume he will earn more money when he completes law school than he could have earned in the private business sector, invited the court to engage in speculation. Therefore, while appellant's children are young enough to benefit from any increased income their father earns, the speculative nature of the increase justified giving this factor minimal weight. Third, the record does not reflect that appellant, upon leaving the Air Force, even attempted to obtain suitable employment in the Phoenix metropolitan area that would have allowed him to be close to his children and fulfill his financial obligations to them. Fourth, appellant has been able to finance his law school education and most of his child support obligation through student loans. Nothing in the record suggests that appellant is unable to obtain part-time employment to fulfill the remainder of his child support obligation. Finally, the trial court specifically found that appellant failed to act in good faith and instead endeavored to further his own ambition when he chose to forego employment and become a full-time student. Thus, the trial court did not abuse its discretion when it determined that appellant failed to act in his children's best interests when he voluntarily left full-time employment to enroll in law school.

We realize that the "responsibilities of begetting a family many times raise havoc with dreams. Nevertheless, the duty [to support one's children] persists, with full authority in the State to enforce it." We therefore vacate the opinion of the court of appeals and affirm the decision of the trial court.

NOTE

Interpreting the Colorado Child Support Guidelines referenced *supra*, the court in *In re Marriage of Bregar*, 952 P.2d 783, 784–85 (Colo. App. 1997) held that the father was voluntarily underemployed and imputed to him the income he had made as a lawyer in 1992, despite the fact that he was thereafter fired, made significantly less money as a solo practitioner in 1993, and testified that he made no money as a lawyer in 1994. The court rejected the father's argument that his choice to start a cattle ranch fell under the "good faith" exception because it was a childhood dream of his and that no alternative employment as a lawyer was currently available to him. *Id.* at 784–86. Other courts have also confirmed that a voluntary diminution of income for the purposes of seeking further education will not justify downward modification of child support. *See, e.g., Arnold v. Arnold*, 177 P.3d 89 (Utah Ct. App. 2008).

Kraisinger v. Kraisinger

Superior Court of Pennsylvania, 2007.
2007 Pa. Super. 197, 928 A.2d 333.

■ Opinion by TAMILIA, J.

. . .

The record reveals the following pertinent factual and procedural history. The parties married in January 1989 and had four children before wife filed for divorce on October 25, 2001. On April 20, 2002, the parties entered into a marriage settlement agreement which was incorporated with, but did not merge into, the May 15, 2002, Divorce Decree.

The parties' agreement encompassed such issues as property settlement, custody, and support. . . .

Despite the parties' agreement, on February 8, 2005, wife filed for additional child support. . . .

Pursuant to *Roberts*[*v. Furst*, 561 A.2d 802 (Pa. Super. Ct. 1989)], the hearing officer considered whether the agreement was made without fraud and coercion, fair and reasonable, and did not prejudice the children's welfare. She determined there was no fraud or coercion. She further determined husband was paying $2,000 per month in child support ($500 per child). She also concluded that the $2,393.45 per month husband was paying for the mortgage must also be considered child support since the parties' agreement stated that wife waived the right to seek additional child support because of the amount husband agreed to pay for the mortgage. Since the hearing officer concluded husband was paying more than he would be required to pay under the support guidelines, she determined the agreement was fair and reasonable and did not prejudice the welfare of the children.

The court considered the parties' exceptions to the hearing officer's recommendations.... The court remanded to the hearing officer for recalculation of support based upon the new guidelines in effect. Ultimately, the court directed husband to pay support as set forth above.

. . .

Husband ... asserts the court erred in applying the nurturing parent doctrine and in failing to impute an earning capacity to wife when fashioning the support Order.

In appropriate cases the earning capacity of a parent who elects to stay home with a young child need not be considered when calculating support. This nurturing parent doctrine excuses the parent from contributing support. *Kelly v. Kelly*, 633 A.2d 218, 220 ([Pa. Super. Ct.]1993).

> The nurturing parent doctrine ... recognizes that a custodial parent who stays at home and cares for a child does, in fact, support the child. In determining whether to expect a nurturing parent to seek employment, the trial court must balance factors such as the age and maturity of the child, the availability and adequacy of others who might assist the custodial parent, and the adequacy of available financial resources if the parent does remain at home.

Doherty[v. Doherty],[859 A.2d 811 (Pa. Super. Ct. 2004)] ... at 813.

The hearing officer reviewed the testimony, including that of husband's vocational expert, and relied upon the nurturing parent doctrine to establish wife's income at $0 per month. She noted that the parties made a conscious decision to allow wife to stay home while they were together and concluded that wife should be afforded the opportunity to do the same until the parties' youngest child is in school full-time. The hearing officer found husband's vocational expert to be credible but acknowledged that on cross-examination, she admitted she had not considered the fact that wife has four children. The hearing officer found this to be relevant, particularly because the youngest child did not yet attend school full-time. The trial court considered the evidence and the hearing officer's rational and affirmed the application of the doctrine.

Husband alleges this was error since wife worked when the parties were together and had two infant children, and alleges she was employed until they had four young children. He emphasizes that the youngest child was then attending half-day kindergarten. He further contends that he can provide daycare at no cost in his own facility.

We emphasize ... that the hearing officer recommended that wife be afforded the opportunity to stay at home with the youngest child *until the child is in school full-time.* Thus, husband may certainly seek to revisit the issue when all of the children are in school full-time. We note that the youngest child, Owen, is approximately 7 ½ years of age and presumably is now in school full-time. As the parties apparently agreed wife should stay home with the children while they were together, (at least when there were four young children), we can discern no reason to disturb the finding that the youngest child should receive that same benefit until the child is in school full-time. We also note that wife may not have been providing financial support to the children as a result of the court's holding, the courts recognize, by the application of the nurturing parent doctrine, that she nonetheless was supporting the children.

We find that the hearing officer's and trial court's conclusions were not reached as the result of partiality, prejudice, bias, or ill-will nor was the law overridden or the judgment exercised manifestly unreasonable as the hearing officer and trial court considered and weighed all of the factors necessary for application of the nurturing parent doctrine. Accordingly, we must affirm but reiterate that as the youngest child is now of school age, husband is free to revisit the issue of child support in light of mother's earning capacity.

. . .

NOTES

1. Pennsylvania courts apply the nurturing parent doctrine even in cases where the children being nurtured are not mutual. *See, e.g., Bender v. Bender*, 444 A.2d 124 (Pa. Super. Ct. 1982). Only Pennsylvania has a formal "nurturing parent" doctrine but many states will consider several factors before imputing income to a stay-at-home parent for the purposes of calculating their child support obligation. For example, look at the reasoning of the court in *Stanton v. Abbey*:

> What constitutes "appropriate circumstances" [for imputing income] will depend on the facts and must be determined on a case-by-case basis. We have previously mentioned factors that other courts have found helpful in making this determination. Among additional factors that a trial court should consider are: (1) the age, maturity, health, and number of children in the home; (2) the custodial parent's employment history, including recency of employment and earnings, as well as the availability of suitable employment; (3) the age and health of the custodial parent; (4) the availability of appropriate child-care givers; (5) the relationship between the expense of child-care givers and the net income the custodial parent would receive; (6) the cost, if any, for transportation, suitable clothing, and other items required for the custodial parent to have the imputed employment; (7) the custodial parent's motivation or reasons for being at home; and (8) the adequacy of available resources if the custodial parent remains at home.

874 S.W.2d 493, 499 (Mo. Ct. App. 1994). Some states' guidelines have a built-in exception from imputing income to a parent who is staying home with a child of up to a certain age. *See, e.g.*, MD. CODE ANN., FAM. LAW § 12–204(b)(2) (LexisNexis 2006 & Supp. 2010) (child up to two years); N.M. STAT. § 40–4–11.1(C)(1) (2006 & Supp. 2011) (child up to six years).

2. 42 U.S.C. § 607 (2006 & Supp. 2009) determines eligibility criteria that states receiving federal funding for Temporary Assistance for Needy Families (TANF) need to satisfy. With certain exceptions, each TANF recipient is required to be engaged in a work activity for a certain number of hours per week. In a two-parent household receiving federally funded child-care benefits, the parents need to be engaged in work activities that amount to 55 hours per week. In a household headed by a single parent the TANF recipient needs to be engaged in work activities for at least 20 hours per week. States may at their discretion establish an exemption from the work requirement if there is a child up to twelve months old in the single parent household. A single parent may also be exempt from work requirements until the child reaches the age of six, but only if there is no appropriate and affordable child care in the area, which includes informal child care arrangements with a relative. The predecessor program to TANF, Aid to Families with Dependent Children (AFDC), provided that a recipient of aid with a child less than three years old did not need to register for job training programs before receiving benefits.

b. DEVIATION FROM THE GUIDELINES

I. COURT DISCRETION GENERALLY

Schmidt v. Schmidt

Supreme Court of South Dakota, 1989.
444 N.W.2d 367.

■ SABERS, JUSTICE.

Mother appeals a change in custody of the eldest of three boys to Father. Father appeals the requirement that he pay $250 monthly child support for two boys.

Father and Mother were divorced on July 13, 1984. They had three children during the marriage; David, Randy, and Michael. By stipulation, Father and Mother agreed that Mother would receive custody of the three boys. Custody was not contested at the divorce hearing, and Father appeared without counsel. Mother presented evidence in the form of testimony and exhibits. The trial court awarded custody of the three boys to Mother. As provided in the stipulation, Father was ordered to pay $375 monthly child support.

Following the divorce, Father continued to farm near Flandreau, South Dakota. Mother lived in Brookings, South Dakota, where she worked at Minnesota Mining & Manufacturing (3M). On June 3, 1988, Father made a motion to modify the child custody and support provisions in the divorce decree. Father requested custody of the oldest, David, and that all three boys be permitted to reside with him during the summer months. The motion further requested that child support obligations be modified accordingly. A hearing was held on the motion on July 25, 1988.

David was fourteen at the time of the hearing. Father introduced evidence showing that David enjoyed the farm and preferred to live with Father. On the farm, David did chores and repair work on an old car. According to Father's testimony, Randy, age eleven, and Michael, age nine, also enjoyed the farm.

. . .

On September 12, 1988, the trial court amended the original divorce decree and gave Father custody of David. The decree was also modified to permit all three boys to live with Father during the summer months, with the exception of three weeks when all three would be with Mother. Father's monthly child support was reduced to $250 and reduced further to $125 during the summer months when all three boys stay with Father. Mother appeals the custody change and denial of attorney fees. Father appeals the amount of child support. We affirm the change of custody and denial of attorney fees and reverse and remand on child support.

. . .

After granting Father custody of David, the court modified Father's monthly child support obligation. The court determined Father's child support under the guidelines in SDCL 25–7–7 by cancelling out one child with each parent, leaving Mother with an additional child. The court then considered Father's child support for one child under the guidelines. Father's net monthly income at the time of the hearing was $1,250. Accordingly, the court set Father's monthly child support at $250. Father claims this was error. He claims that the court should have compared the amount of child support Father would pay for two children under the guidelines against the amount of child support Mother would pay for one child and subtract the difference to determine Father's support.

We agree with Father in part. SDCL 25–7–7 provides that "The child support obligation shall be established in accordance with the obligor's net income and number of children affected[.]" Following the change of custody, Father was obligated to pay support for two children based on his net monthly income of $1,250. Mother was obligated to pay support for one child based on her net monthly income of $1,582. Since Mother's net monthly income exceeded Father's, her child support obligation for one nearly cancels out Father's child support obligation for two under the guidelines.[2] Mother argues that such a formula may lead to absurd results.[3] However, SDCL 25–7–7 does not permit deviation from the guidelines absent specific findings. Thus, the trial court erred in its calculation of child support. We reverse and remand for the trial court to reconsider child support in accordance with this opinion. We note, however, this may provide inadequate support for the boys. Father's farm occupation provides certain necessities, such as housing, utilities, transportation, etc. which would otherwise be personal expenses. On remand, the trial court may look to the record and make additional specific findings which may support deviations from the child support guidelines and provide adequate support.

Affirmed in part, reversed and remanded in part.

. . .

■ HENDERSON, JUSTICE (concurring in part, concurring in result in part, dissenting in part).

On the change of custody issue, I concur in the result. . . .

. . .

As one peruses and ponders upon the majority's child support dissertation, one fancies a trip with Alice through Wonderland. Wonderland is the world of child support, resulting from this State's charting a course, thrusting rigidity upon trial courts, in an effort to follow the United States Congress, which required no such mandated rigidity. The rigidity of the guidelines turns logic on its head.

In the past I have sought, through numerous writings, to academically advance that judges cannot decide child support by formulas and tables. When tables are used, judgment flees. As I have written in the past, judges are not "schedule-automatons." *Peterson v. Peterson*, 434 N.W.2d 732, 739–741 (S.D.1989) (Henderson, J., concurring in part, concurring in result in

---

2. Under the guidelines, Father's obligation for two children with his net monthly income of $1,250 would be between $360 to $390 monthly. Mother's obligation for one child with her net monthly income of $1,582 would be at least $330 monthly. Subtracting the difference, Father would owe child support of approximately $30 to $60 monthly.

3. Assume a mother with custody of five children and a net monthly income of $1,500, and father with a net monthly income of $1,000. Father would pay approximately $350 per month child support to the mother under the guidelines. However, if the father were to gain custody of one child he would no longer pay any child support for the four children in mother's custody. In fact, the mother would be required to pay $20 per month for support of the one child in the father's custody. While such a result appears inequitable, such a result *is* required under the current guidelines in the absence of specific findings supporting deviations. In this context, it is important to note that the guidelines in SDCL 25–7–7 have been replaced with new guidelines effective July 1, 1989.

part). In my previous writings, I have argued that the abuse of discretion test is not only the primary but solid scope of review test—not whether the guidelines have or have not been followed in the particular set of facts before the trial judge. We are substituting, with these guidelines and decisions thereunder, at least to date, something of inferior value. If we in the law are substituting a new concept, it should be something of greater value. We should continue to consider the needs of the child, the ability to pay by the parent, and, essentially, the trial judge's abuse or non-abuse of his discretion in setting child support. In doing so, we, in the judiciary, retain our independence; we also vault a known, Equity, forged through the centuries in jurisprudence, over an unknown substitute of legislative dogmatism. . . .

. . .

Presently, the states are in fear so the guidelines are born. In time, this mechanical jurisprudence shall disappear because of its despisement [sic] by those who are called upon to administer them. A bond, now established to create these guidelines, is created by a chain of governmental obligation. Fear is the cement which holds the chain unbroken. Unquestionably, many prisoners of this chain will be held captive until reason and courage overcome fear and fad.

. . . [T]he federal Child Support Enforcement Amendments of 1984 (Pub.L. No. 98–378) required States to establish guidelines, but Congress provided that the guidelines "need not be binding upon such judges or other officials." 42 U.S.C. § 667(b). On October 13, 1988, Congress changed its mandate by deleting the quoted wording and substituted the following:

> There shall be a rebuttable presumption, in any judicial or administrative proceeding for the award of child support, that the amount of the award which would result from the guidelines is the correct amount of child support to be awarded. A written finding or specific finding on the record that the application of the guidelines would be unjust or inappropriate in a particular case as determined under criteria established by the State, shall be sufficient to rebut the presumption in that case.

Pub.L. 100–485, Title I, Subtitle A, § 103, 102 Stat. 2346 (1988) (effective October 13, 1989). Deviation from the guidelines, where their application is unjust, is apt, as trial courts in these cases are sitting in equity. Do we see some sunshine of common sense beginning to evolve?

The 1989 State Legislature, in extensively revising SDCL ch. 25–7, has now provided, effective July 1, 1989, that deviation from that chapter's guidelines may be made, *inter alia,* for "any financial condition of either parent which would make application of the schedule inequitable." The way appears open, under the new law, for any trial court of this State to return to adjudication of child support issues based "on the realities of the domestic situation before it" as in *State ex rel. Larsgaard v. Larsgaard,* 298 N.W.2d 381, 384 (S.D.1980). May the sunshine illuminate the Lady of Equity.

Under the rules of equity, I would affirm the trial court's award of child support on the ground that there was no abuse of discretion. The majority opinion, while reversing the trial court's award for failure to strictly follow guidelines, simultaneously instructs the trial court to sift through the record seeking an excuse to deviate from the guidelines noting, at footnote 3, the absurdity of such guidelines.

II. RICH FAMILIES

Smith v. Smith

Court of Civil Appeals of Oklahoma, Division No. 1, 2002.
67 P.3d 351.

■ Opinion by KENNETH L. BUETTNER, JUDGE.

Defendant/Appellant Stephen Michael Smith (Father) appeals from the trial court's order modifying Father's child support obligation. Plaintiff/Appellee Judith Ann Smith (Mother) sought an increase in child support payments from Father based on changes in the parties' incomes as well as the expenses of the minor child. The trial court increased Father's child support obligation from $460 per month to $4,300 per month.... Because we find the evidence supports the trial court's decision to modify child support, we affirm. However, we find the trial court abused its discretion in setting the monthly child support obligation far beyond the amount prescribed by the child support guidelines. We therefore modify the amount ordered to be paid as child support in the trial court's modification order....

Mother and Father were married in 1981. Their only child was born August 11, 1984. The parties were divorced in 1988, and the decree awarded custody to Mother, granted visitation to Father, and ordered Father to pay $460 per month as child support. The decree had not been modified before Mother filed her motion to modify child support May 31, 2001, which led to this appeal.

. . .

Trial was held July 11, 2001. The trial court entered its order modifying child support July 31, 2001. In its order, the trial court noted that the parties had stipulated that a substantial and material change of circumstances had occurred since the entry of the decree, which justified a modification of child support. The court also noted that the parties' combined incomes exceeded $15,000 per month, requiring the court to determine child support pursuant to 43 O.S.Supp.2000 § 119(B).

The court ordered Father to pay $4,300 per month as child support beginning June 1, 2001, "until the minor child reaches the age of 18 or through the age of 18, so long as the child is regularly and continuously attending high school." The court ordered Mother to maintain the child on her employer-sponsored health, dental and vision insurance, but ordered Father to pay 88% of the cost of such insurance. Father was also ordered to pay 88% of any uninsured health costs of the child. The child support computation was attached to the order.

. . .

Father asserts that the instant case involves a question of first impression. Father alleges that the trial court in this modification proceeding extended the pre-divorce standard of living consideration to the determination of modified support. Father argues that Mother asserted that the minor child was deprived because Father's income had increased dramatically. Father argues that actually the child enjoyed a very good lifestyle before the modification, due to Mother's income and due to Father's voluntary payment of double his original $460 child support obligation as well as some other expenses of the child. Father argues the trial court erred in modifying child support to an amount above the "statutory cap."

Father notes that 43 O.S.Supp.2000 § 119(B) provides that in the event the parents' combined gross monthly income exceeds $15,000, the child support shall be the amount due under the guidelines for income of $15,000 (the amount at which the guidelines are capped) "and an additional amount determined by the court." The guidelines in effect at the time of the modification proceedings provided for the total monthly child support for one child of parents with combined monthly income of $15,000 to be $1,372, which is 9.15% of $15,000.

The child support computation attached to the order modifying child support lists Father's monthly income as $46,015 and Mother's monthly income as $6,419. Accordingly, the combined gross monthly income of the parties was $52,434. It is clear from the child support computation attached to the modification order that the trial court multiplied that amount by 9.15% to calculate that the child support amount would be $4,797 under the guidelines. Father's percentage share of 88% of $4,797 would be $4,220. To that amount, the trial court added 88% of the child's monthly health insurance premium, $78, and rounded that number to $4,300, which was the amount of child support Father was ordered to pay in the modification order.

Father urges that the trial court should not have simply extrapolated the amount due under the guidelines for the parties' incomes in this case. We note one commentary which urges that a simple mathematical extrapolation is not a well-received method of determining the support amount in cases involving parents with very high incomes. *See* Hogan, *Child Support in High Income Cases*, 17 J. Am. Acad. Matrim. Law[.]349, 351 (2001). That article noted that at least some consideration should be given to the child's actual needs, which may include consideration of the child's lifestyle. *Id.*

A review of the child support table found at 43 O.S.Supp.2000 § 119(A) reveals that as the parents' combined gross income increases, the proportion of that income which is designated for child support decreases. This is due in part to the fact that a child's needs, both essential and lifestyle-related, do not inherently increase regardless of the amount of income. This has been referred to as the "three pony rule," which is that no child needs three ponies, no matter that the parents might easily afford to provide them. 17 J. Am. Acad. Matrim. Law[.] 349, 351. That article noted that, in the case of parents with very high incomes, determining child support on the basis of a simple percentage of income used to determine child support at a lower income level may result in such an exorbitant child support award that it effectively results in a redistribution of the wealthy parent's estate, rather than simply providing support for the child consistent with the child's reasonable needs. *Id.*

At least two Oklahoma cases have addressed deviating from the child support guidelines as a result of the parents' combined gross monthly income exceeding the guidelines cap. *Archer v. Archer*, 813 P.2d 1059[(Okla. Civ. App. 1991)], involved an appeal from the original decree of divorce. The evidence in *Archer* was that the husband's income was at least $18,500 per month. The trial court determined that the high income was an extraordinary circumstance which excused compliance with the child support guidelines. The trial court ordered the husband to pay $900 per month per child, for a total monthly obligation of $2,700. In his appeal, the husband argued that the trial court could only exceed the maximum amount provided by the guidelines if "exceptional needs" were shown. The *Archer* court explained that child support in high income cases must be determined on a case by case basis, with the minimum support award being the capped amount under the guidelines. The court explained that the trial court is not limited to considering the child's bare bone needs, but may also consider the payor parent's affluent lifestyle in determining the proper amount of support. The court noted that the husband's share of the total child support would be 80% and that, based on the amount the husband was ordered to pay, the total child support amount would have been $3,375. The court noted that the evidence presented showed that the children had a monthly need of $3,669, and therefore concluded that the amount awarded was not against the clear weight of the evidence.

A year later the Oklahoma Supreme Court addressed this issue in the case of *Mocnik v. Mocnik*, 838 P.2d 500[(Okla. 1992)]. In *Mocnik*, the trial court ordered the husband to pay child support of $2,000 per month, while the wife presented evidence that the children's expenses were over $4,700 per month. On appeal, the court noted that the parties' joint monthly income was $19,543. The court noted that the top amount of child support in the guidelines equaled 13.52% of income and the court multiplied that percentage by $19,543 and concluded that a proper child support amount would be $2,642.21, and that the husband owed 91% of that amount, or $2,404.41. The court approved the trial court's reduced award of $2,000 per month based on the extensive visitation awarded to the husband. The court affirmed the amount awarded as child support.

However, the *Mocnik* court's method of multiplying the parties' monthly income by the percentage of income used at the top bracket of the guidelines fails to consider the methodology of the guidelines. As explained above, as income increases, the percentage of income directed to child support decreases. A more accurate method of calculating child support for income amounts beyond the guidelines chart is to consider the decreasing percentage of income for each bracket as income rises. This would recognize that at some point, child support for each additional $1000 in income approaches zero. In this case, even if the percentage for the highest bracket of income (4%) is applied to income exceeding $15,000 per month, the result is total support of $2,869 per month. Absent other considerations, the trial court would have been justified in using this amount as an extrapolation of the guidelines.

Mother submitted an exhibit detailing the child's monthly expenses which totaled $3,355.90 per month. A child's reasonable living expenses could justify a child support award in excess of an extrapolation for income exceeding the guidelines. However, we find it was an abuse of the trial court's discretion to award child support in an amount greater than even the liberal amount of expenses of the child asserted by Mother. We therefore modify the child support calculations. Using the living expenses submitted by Mother, $3,355.90, Father's 88% share of that amount is $2,953.19 per month. Any greater amount would simply be a transfer of wealth from Father to Mother.

. . .

NOTES

1. Only a minority of states provide a special formula for calculating child support at the highest income levels. Most guidelines posit that child support should be provided at the highest guideline amount, with deviations based on the specific needs of the child, or that the court should determine the needs of the child and base its decision without reference to the guidelines altogether. *See, e.g., McGowin v. McGowin*, 991 So.2d 735, 743 (Ala. Civ. App. 2008) (when combined income of both parents exceeds uppermost limit of guidelines, it is abuse of discretion to award only highest guideline amount even though children's higher needs and obligor parent's ability to pay have been proven). *See generally* Laura W. Morgan, Child Support Guidelines: Interpretation and Application § 4.07, at 40.1–65 (1996 & Supp. 2006, 2009 & 2010).

2. Compare the *Smith* court's approach to the following:

'[N]ecessaries,' and 'luxuries' are relative matters....

Children of wealthy parents are entitled to the educational advantages of travel, private lessons in music, drama, swimming, horseback riding, and other activities in which they show interest and ability. They are entitled to the best medical care, good clothes, and familiarity with good restaurants, good hotels, good shows, and good camps. It is possible that a child with nothing more than a house to shelter him, a coat to keep him warm and sufficient food to keep him healthy will be happier and more successful than a child who has all the 'advantages,' but most parents strive and sacrifice to give their children 'advantages' which cost money.

A wealthy father has a legal duty to give his children the 'advantages' which his financial status indicates to be reasonable.

Hecht v. Hecht, 150 A.2d 139, 143 (Pa. Super. Ct. 1959).

3. What role should the standard of living the children enjoyed during the marriage play in the determination of an appropriate child support award? Should the custodial parent enjoy support on the basis of the children's standard of living? Is it possible to distinguish between the two? Consider the court's reasoning in the following case:

The family court also heard testimony about the standard of living the children would have enjoyed if the marriage had not been dissolved, and the financial resources and needs of the children. During the marriage, the children had nannies and the family had expensive homes in Scottsdale and Tucson. Mother's expert, Michael Black, testified that in 2004, before the separation, the family incurred approximately $13,476 per month in expenses for the "children's benefit of lifestyle." Black also stated that from February through March 2005, after the separation, Mother's average monthly living expenses for the children was $5,271, but that their lifestyle with Mother after the separation was "certainly less than the previous lifestyle" and "there [had] been a substantial reduction in lifestyle with the current child support."

Mother testified about the different lifestyles the children would experience between her home and Father's home due to Father's substantially higher level of income. Mother explained the children's lifestyle was not "being duplicated in both homes" because "we don't get to travel and resort live, like we used [to], or what they get to do presently. We are—we obviously don't live in the same home, or [have] the same cars." She stated her "surroundings" and "furniture" were not comparable to Father's. Mother testified Father took their children to "Hotel Del for weekends at a time, on sailboats that he's renting, yachts, you know, all kinds of elaborate things. So I guess whatever they get to do with daddy, I'd like to just one time [a] year get to do it with mommy." She further stated she wanted the lifestyles to be "[c]omparable, not exact."

This evidence showing the different lifestyles the children would experience at Mother's and Father's homes supports the family court's finding "the emotional needs of the children would be impacted by the moves back and forth between the parents [sic] houses if the mother does not get additional child support."

Labine v. Labine, No. 1 CA–CV 07–0367, 2009 WL 1262960, at *5–*6 (Ariz. Ct. App., May 7, 2009).

III. POOR FAMILIES

Rose on Behalf of Clancy v. Moody

Court of Appeals of New York, 1993.
83 N.Y.2d 65, 607 N.Y.S.2d 906, 629 N.E.2d 378.

■ BELLACOSA, JUDGE.

Respondent mother has custody of two of her children and subsists on Social Services financial aid. Family Court rejected petitioner Oswego County Social Services Commissioner's objections to the Hearing Examiner's findings and determination that the respondent mother's child support obligation for her third, noncustodial child was $0. The Commissioner and intervenor Attorney–General of the State of New York appeal as of right on constitutional grounds from the Appellate Division's order affirming Family Court. They argue that New York's Family Court Act § 413(1)(g), which conclusively fixes a minimum $25 per month floor in all cases, is not preemptively nullified by any conflict with Federal law 42 U.S.C. § 667, which mandates a rebuttable presumption in all such instances. We disagree and affirm the determination of both lower courts in favor of the respondent indigent mother.

Where a Federal statute facially clashes with a State statute, the Federal statute must triumph. New York State's Family Court Act § 413(1)(g) creates an irrebuttable presumption imposing, in cases like this one, a $25 per month floor on all child support obligations up to an accumulated debt of $500. Thus, it flatly contradicts the enabling legislation, 42 U.S.C. § 667, that commands an opportunity in all cases to rebut and drop the support award floor to $0, when impoverished circumstances so dictate.

Respondent has three children. At the commencement of this proceeding, her two-year-old twins lived with her; her first born, Robert, age 4, lived with his grandmother. He is, thus, a noncustodial child for purposes of section 413(1)(g) of the Family Court Act. The mother and her children are entirely dependent upon the Department of Social Services for financial living assistance.

In January 1991, the Oswego County Department of Social Services filed a petition for support against the mother on behalf of the grandmother and the noncustodial child, Robert. The Family Court Hearing Examiner found against the Commissioner and directed an award of $0 per month in child support against the mother for Robert. The mother's income, pursuant to Family Court Act § 413(1)(b)(5), was determined to be $0 annually. Her basic child support obligation under the formula of the Child Support Standards Act was 17% of $0, which, of course, equals $0. He further determined that even though $0 is less than the poverty level, application of the New York State guidelines nevertheless would mandate a minimum child support obligation against her in the sum of $25 per month (Family Ct.Act § 413[1][g]). The Hearing Examiner concluded that application of the mandatory minimum monthly award would be unjust and inappropriate, since the mother and her two custodial children were themselves recipients of public assistance.

Family Court upheld the findings of fact and the determination of the Hearing Examiner. The Appellate Division unanimously concluded that the Federal Child Support Enforcement Act prohibits a State from creating a "conclusive presumption that $25 is the correct amount of child support to be awarded, regardless of the parent's means and circumstances" While it agreed with Family Court that the imposition of an uncollectible support figure would be unjust and inappropriate, it added that the conclusively mandated minimum award was also preempted by Federal law.

The County and intervenor assert a constitutional basis to support the appeal as of right. They argue that Family Court Act § 413(1)(g) avoids the constitutional preemption conflict of an irrebuttable mandatory minimum of $25 per month as an obligation of child support against any noncustodial parent, because the figure is a justifiable, albeit pro forma, public policy message, not a true collectible obligation. 42 U.S.C. § 667(b)(2) provides that the amount of an award under State child support guidelines shall be presumed correct, subject to rebuttable criteria established by the State which allow noncustodial parents to show inability to pay. By establishing an irrebuttable minimum of $25, even though concededly uncollectible and solely "to send a uniform public policy message," the State treads on the Federal mandate which gives a noncustodial parent the right to rebut any presumed support amount, all the way down to zero, by showing inability to pay. Thus, while a substantial constitutional question is directly involved in this appeal, we resolve the issue against the appellants.

New York participates in the Federally funded reimbursement program designed to foster child support payments from noncustodial parents. The program promulgates national standards and guidelines. Pursuant to Federal statute, each participating State is required to adopt State-wide guidelines in connection with child support awards as a condition for the State's receipt of Federal funds under 42 U.S.C. §§ 654 and 655. New York has, thus, subjected itself to full compliance with the national regime by accepting Federal funds, a factor the dissent does not take cognizance of or credit.

Section 103(a) of the United States Family Support Act of 1988 (amending 42 U.S.C. § 667 [entitled "State guidelines for child support awards"]) states in pertinent part:

> (2) There shall be a rebuttable presumption, in any judicial or administrative proceeding for the award of child support, that the amount of the award which would result from the application of such guidelines is the correct amount of child support to be awarded. A written finding or specific finding on the record that the application of the guidelines would be unjust or inappropriate in a particular case, as determined under criteria established by the State, shall be sufficient to rebut the presumption in that case (42 U.S.C. § 667[b]).

The New York State Legislature in 1989 enacted the Child Support Standards Act (L.1989, ch. 567, amending Family Ct.Act art. 4 *et seq.*) pursuant to the enabling United States Family Support Act. The New York implementation opens with a provision that parents with sufficient means or ability to acquire such means shall be required to pay child support pursuant to the established guidelines (Family Ct.Act § 413[1][a]).

Section 413(1)(c) of the Family Court Act provides for application of guidelines based on a pro rata share of a certain percentage of the combined parental income. "Income", defined at section 413(1)(b)(5), does not include public assistance. The respondent mother's circumstances are such that her entire income is derived from public assistance. Thus, for purposes of the Family Court Act, she has $0 income. Family Court Act § 413(1)(f) prescribes factors for deciding whether a guideline award is "unjust or inappropriate," and details the criteria or factors that should provide a basis to rebut the presumptive guidelines. For example, the financial resources of the custodial and noncustodial parent and those of the child are pertinent (Family Ct.Act § 413[1][f][1]). Also relevant are the financial needs of any children of the noncustodial parent not subject to the particular support proceeding. A comparative resources analysis of the respective support needs of the custodial children and the noncustodial child who is the subject of the proceeding is also appropriate (Family Ct.Act § 413[1][f][8]).

In this case, the mother has satisfied one unassailable criterion to overcome the presumption that would require her to be obligated for support of her noncustodial son (*see*, Family Ct. Act § 413[1] [f]). She is indigent and needs Social Services financial assistance for herself and her twin custodial children. Since she has nothing, she can pay nothing. For a judicial decree to declare that she, nevertheless, owes what she cannot realistically or legally pay is not only unjust and inappropriate, it is a legal pretense. The Family Court Act paradigm erects a facial, not implied, contradiction because the proviso in section 413(1)(g), that even where a guideline award is rebutted as unjust or inappropriate it must still result in a minimum award of no less than $25 per month. The prescribed national norms expressly provide for a substantively different mechanism.

Family Court Act § 413(1)(g) states in pertinent part:

Where the court finds that the non-custodial parent's pro rata share of the basic child support obligation is unjust or inappropriate, the court shall order the non-custodial parent to pay such amount of child support as the court finds just and appropriate, and the court shall set forth, in a written order, the factors it considered; the amount of each party's pro rata share of the basic child support obligation; and the reasons that the court did not order the basic child support obligation ... *In no instance shall the court order child support below twenty-five dollars per month.* Where the non-custodial parent's income is less than or equal to the poverty income guidelines amount for a single person as reported by the federal department of health and human services, unpaid child support arrears in excess of five hundred dollars shall not accrue (emphasis added).

Family Court observed that "[t]o require her to pay $25.00 per month in support towards her noncustodial child lowers her current monthly [public assistance] cash allotment from $126.00 to $101.00, a substantial percentage decrease, and, arguably a penalty per se for being a public charge." Since New York otherwise immunizes public assistance recipients from levy and execution of judgments against them, including judgments for child support, the appellants' sought-after decree of a support obligation would be a mere showpiece.

Appellants also advocate that the interoperative effect of Family Court Act § 413(1)(g) with Social Services Law § 137 clearly and manifestly excuses a chargeable parent without income, such as the respondent mother here, from any real payment obligation to any child. This position highlights the insurmountable problems of their argument that Family Court Act § 413(1)(g) may be de facto harmonized with its Federal source statute, while de jure contradicting it on its face and in its inevitable application.

The Appellate Division affirmed in this case, stating because 42 U.S.C. § 667(b)(2) "directly prohibits a State from enacting child support guidelines which permit no rebuttal of the amount awarded, we conclude that the provision in Family Court Act § 413(1)(g) mandating a $25 minimum award is preempted under the Supremacy Clause". We agree with that Court that this is "directly prohibit[ed]," and that a perfunctory, legally noncollectible judicial order of support is not authorized and would send wrong messages. It would degrade the value and integrity of the judicial decree, and it would unjustly and unaccountably brand the respondent parent a deadbeat.

Appellants' argument that Family Court abused its discretion is unavailing. So, too, is their claim that despite the fact that any percent of zero will inevitably equal zero, Family Court Act § 413(1)(g) somehow constitutionally survives. The New York scheme cannot support a de jure irrebuttable presumption for the mandatory imposition of a minimum $25 per month statement of obligation against an indigent noncustodial parent.

The order of the Appellate Division should be affirmed, with costs.

■ LEVINE, JUDGE (dissenting) [on the basis that court did not meet exacting standard for federal pre-emption].

NOTE

When parental income is below the minimum amount provided for in the guidelines, about twenty states provide for a presumptive minimum award of $50 that can be lowered in the discretion of the court in five states. LAURA MORGAN, CHILD SUPPORT GUIDELINES: INTERPRETATION AND ANALYSIS § 4.07, at 66–67, 68–70 tbl.4–8 (1996 & Supp. 2010).

c.   COLLEGE EDUCATION

Solomon v. Findley

Supreme Court of Arizona, En Banc, 1991.
167 Ariz. 409, 808 P.2d 294.

■ CAMERON, JUSTICE.

Defendant, Lloyd Talbott Findley (Findley), petitioned for review of the court of appeals' opinion allowing plaintiffs, Wilma Cornell Solomon and Adrienne Michelle Findley (Solomon), to pursue their claim for post-majority educational support in contract, rather than by enforcement of the dissolution decree. . . .

. . .

On January 8, 1976, Solomon and Findley filed a joint petition for dissolution of marriage. The petition, which the parties filed *in propria persona*, contained the following provision:

> Husband also agrees to provide educational funds to the best of his ability for said minor child through college or until child reaches age of 25 whichever comes first.

On January 30, 1976, at a hearing with Findley absent, the decree was entered by default. The divorce court approved the agreement, including the educational support provision, and incorporated it into the decree.

Solomon first sought to enforce the decree by filing an order to show cause, alleging failure to provide educational funds to Adrienne, their daughter, as the decree required. The divorce court denied the relief requested because Adrienne was beyond the age of minority and the court therefore lacked jurisdiction. Solomon then filed a breach of contract action. The trial court granted Findley's motion to dismiss, finding that "the doctrine of merger applied in the judgment and that plaintiffs' claim stemmed from the judgment."

Solomon appealed arguing that there had been no merger because there was no language showing an intent to merge and no finding by the court or order pursuant to statute.

Findley argued that any agreement between the parties was merged into the dissolution decree. He urged that the obligation to perform the agreement ended when Adrienne reached majority because the divorce court, in a dissolution action, lacks jurisdiction to adjudicate the question of liability for child support beyond the age of majority.

. . .

Several states have addressed this issue and have reached different solutions. In a leading case from the Tennessee Supreme Court, a property settlement agreement imposed an obligation upon the husband to pay all future educational expenses of the children beyond the high school level. *Penland v. Penland*, 521 S.W.2d 222, 223 (Tenn. 1975). As such, the agreement constituted a contractual obligation outside the scope of the legal duty of support during minority. The Tennessee Supreme Court stated:

> Paragraph 2(c) of the contractual agreement between the Penlands makes no reference, direct or indirect, to age, minority or majority. It imposes an obligation to pay all future educational expenses beyond high school level. Being without any limitation, it necessarily envisioned continuance of the obligation beyond age 21, the age of majority at the time the agreement was entered into.

> We hold that paragraph 2(c) is a contractual obligation outside the scope of the legal duty of support during minority, and retained its contractual nature, although incorporated in the final decree of divorce. Mrs. Penland or the daughters are entitled to enforce said obligation by the obtaining of a money judgment, from time to time, as the obligation matures, and for the enforcement thereof by execution as provided by law.

Similarly, the Arkansas Supreme Court noted that when a husband entered into an improvident agreement, this was not grounds for relief and the agreement could be independently enforceable in a court of law. *Armstrong v. Armstrong*, 454 S.W.2d 660, 663 ([Ark.]1970). In *Armstrong*, the husband agreed to pay alimony to the wife for life or until she remarried, and to provide support for the daughter for so long as she was enrolled in school and not employed. The court could not have ordered these provisions and, therefore, the parties must have made a separate and independently enforceable contract.

The Georgia Supreme Court, taking another approach, allowed a wife to enforce a post-majority support agreement by contempt. *McClain v. McClain*, 221 S.E.2d 561, 563–64 ([Ga.]1975). In *McClain*, a husband agreed to provide child support until each child reached 21, and further agreed to provide a college education for each child. The court found significant differences between a decree rendered under the law and a contract entered into between husband and wife, which is incorporated into a decree. The court stated that "[w]here parties separate and by contract, as here, settle the right of their minor children for support and maintenance and such contract is approved by the trial judge and made part of a final divorce decree, the trial court will enforce the contract as made by them."

In *Gaddis v. Gaddis*, 314 N.E.2d 627 ([Ill. App. Ct.]1974) an Illinois appeals court took a similar position. The settlement agreement in *Gaddis* provided that the husband would continue child support payments past majority if the children were attending college, and that the husband would be responsible for tuition, books, and board. The court refused to allow the husband to modify the decree, thereby relieving himself of this obligation. The court noted that the husband was not attempting to relieve himself of his support obligation when he entered into the property settlement agreement, but rather that he contracted to do more than the law required. The court noted further that in divorce proceedings the parties often will promise whatever they can in order to obtain a divorce, and then later try to scale down these promises. The court in *Gaddis* stated that "when the parties voluntarily enter into a property settlement whereby each gives consideration for the promises of the other, the resulting contract will be enforced by the trial court." The agreement is enforced to provide stability in negotiations between the parties, and to prevent one party from being penalized due to the other party's failure to comply.

Although respectable authority allows a court to enforce an agreement for post-majority support by way of contempt in the divorce court, we believe that the better rule is the contract for post-majority support should be enforced in a separate contract action. We reach this conclusion because the divorce court only has jurisdiction to enforce child support provisions until the child reaches majority. Because the divorce court did not have authority to enforce the post-majority educational support provision, that portion of the contract did not merge into the dissolution decree, but rather retained its independent nature enforceable as a contract claim.

. . .

The court of appeals' decision is approved, and the case is remanded to the trial court for proceedings consistent with this opinion.

Curtis v. Kline

Supreme Court of Pennsylvania, 1995.
542 Pa. 249, 666 A.2d 265.

■ ZAPPALA, JUSTICE

In *Blue v. Blue*, 616 A.2d 628 ([Pa.]1992), we declined to recognize a duty requiring a parent to provide college educational support because no such legal duty had been imposed by the General Assembly or developed by our case law. As a result of our *Blue* decision, the legislature promulgated Act 62 of 1993. Section 3 of the Act states:

> (a) General rule.—... a court may order either or both parents who are separated, divorced, unmarried or otherwise subject to an existing support obligation to provide equitably for educational costs of their child whether an application for this support is made before or after the child has reached 18 years of age.

23 PA.C.S.§ 4327(a).

The issue now before us is whether the Act violates the equal protection clause of the Fourteenth Amendment of the United States Constitution. The Court of Common Pleas of Chester County held that it did, resulting in this direct appeal.

The relevant facts are not in dispute. Appellee is the father of Jason, Amber and Rebecca. On July 12, 1991, an order of court for support was entered on behalf of Appellee's children. On March 2, 1993, Appellee filed a petition to terminate his support obligation as to Amber, a student at

Kutztown University, and Jason, a student at West Chester University. After Act 62 was promulgated, Appellee was granted leave to include a constitutional challenge to the Act as a basis for seeking relief from post-secondary educational support.

. . .

The equal protection clause of the Fourteenth Amendment of the United States Constitution in pertinent part provides:

> No State shall . . . deprive any person of life, liberty, or property, without due process of law; nor deny to any person within its jurisdiction the equal protection of the laws.

. . .

. . . Act 62 must be upheld if there exists any rational basis for the prescribed classification. It is in this context that we review the Act's creation of a duty, and more significantly a legal mechanism for enforcement of that duty, limited to situations of separated, divorced, or unmarried parents and their children.

In applying the rational basis test, we have adopted a two-step analysis. First, we must determine whether the challenged statute seeks to promote any legitimate state interest or public value. If so, we must next determine whether the classification adopted in the legislation is reasonably related to accomplishing that articulated state interest or interests.

The preamble to Act 62 sets forth the legislature's intention "to codify the decision of the Superior Court in the case of *Ulmer v. Sommerville*, . . . and the subsequent line of cases interpreting *Ulmer* prior to the decision of the Pennsylvania Supreme Court in *Blue v. Blue* . . . ." (Citations omitted). It also states:

> Further, the General Assembly finds that it has a rational and legitimate governmental interest in requiring some parental financial assistance for a higher education for children of parents who are separated, divorced, unmarried or otherwise subject to an existing support obligation.

This latter statement begs the question of whether the legislature actually has a legitimate interest in treating children of separated, divorced, or unmarried parents differently than children of married parents with respect to the costs of post-secondary education.

. . .

Act 62 classifies young adults according to the marital status of their parents, establishing for one group an action to obtain a benefit enforceable by court order that is not available to the other group. The relevant category under consideration is children in need of funds for a post-secondary education. The Act divides these persons, similarly situated with respect to their need for assistance, into groups according to the marital status of their parents, i.e., children of divorced/separated/never-married parents and children of intact families.

It will not do to argue that this classification is rationally related to the legitimate governmental purpose of obviating difficulties encountered by those in non-intact families who want parental financial assistance for post-secondary education, because such a statement of the governmental purpose assumes the validity of the classification. Recognizing that within the category of young adults in need of financial help to attend college there are some having a parent or parents unwilling to provide such help, the question remains whether the authority of the state may be selectively applied to empower only those from non-intact families to compel such help. We hold that it may not. In the absence of an entitlement on the part of any individual to post-secondary education, or a generally applicable requirement that parents assist their adult children in obtaining such an education, we perceive no rational basis for the state government to provide only certain adult citizens with legal means to overcome the difficulties they encounter in pursuing that end.

It is not inconceivable that in today's society a divorced parent, e.g., a father, could have two children, one born of a first marriage and not residing with him and the other born of a second marriage and still residing with him. Under Act 62, such a father could be required to provide post-secondary educational support for the first child but not the second, even to the extent that the second child would be required to forego a college education. Further, a child over the age of 18, of a woman whose husband had died would have no action against the mother to recover costs of a post-secondary education, but a child over the age of 18, of a woman who never married, who married and divorced, or even who was only separated from her husband when he died would be able to maintain such an action. These are but two examples demonstrating the arbitrariness of the classification adopted in Act 62.

In *LeClair v. LeClair*, 624 A.2d 1350 ([N.H.]1993), the New Hampshire Supreme Court was faced with the issue of the constitutionality of a state statute regarding post-secondary educational support. Initially, it must be noted that the Court decided this appeal based upon the New Hampshire constitution even though the appellant contended that the statute denied him equal protection under both the federal and state constitution.

The underlying premise upon which the New Hampshire Supreme Court undertook its constitutional analysis of the post-secondary educational support scheme was that the legislation created two classifications: married parents and divorced parents. The object of the legislation was to protect children of divorced parents from being unjustly deprived of opportunities they would otherwise have had if their parents had not divorced. The statute was promulgated to ensure that children of divorced families are not deprived of educational opportunities solely because their families are no longer intact. The result is a heightened judicial involvement in the financial and personal lives of divorced families with children that is not necessary with intact families with children. The New Hampshire Supreme Court concluded that because of the unique problems of divorced families, the legislature could rationally conclude that absent judicial involvement, children of divorced families may be less likely than children of intact families to receive post-secondary educational support from both parents.

With all due respect to our sister state, we must reject the New Hampshire Supreme Court's analysis in *LeClair*. The discriminatory classification adopted by our legislature is not focused on the parents but rather the children. The question is whether similarly situated young adults, i.e. those in need of financial assistance, may be treated differently.

Ultimately, we can conceive of no rational reason why those similarly situated with respect to needing funds for college education, should be treated unequally. Accordingly, we agree with the common pleas court and conclude that Act 62 is unconstitutional.

. . .

■ MONTEMURO, JUSTICE, dissenting.

I must dissent.

As the Majority correctly points out, the rational basis test to determine whether a statute is constitutional requires, first, a determination of whether the challenged legislation seeks to promote any legitimate state interest. It must then be decided whether the statute bears a reasonable relationship to the intended objective.... The Majority challenges not merely the means of execution, but the legitimacy of the government interest which the statute is expressly designed to promote.

Act 62 is directed at furthering the education of the citizens of this Commonwealth. It operates on the assumption that divorce necessarily involves a disadvantage to the children of broken families, and is intended to assure that children who are thus disadvantaged by the divorce or separation of their parents are not deprived of the opportunity to acquire post secondary school education. In effect, it attempts to maintain the children of divorce in the same position they would have been in had their parents' marriage remained intact. The Act is not intended to, nor does it, place a premium on the rights of children of divorce while devaluing the same rights for children from intact marriage. It merely recognizes that, in general, divorce has a deleterious effect upon children, which should, insofar as is possible, be redressed. Thus while constitutional principles permit this intended result, a "difference in fact or opinion" recognized by the Legislature as within its purview, the Majority has declared that, at least for college age children, the distinction between the children of broken families and those of intact families simply does not exist.

In rejecting the authenticity of the premise underlying the statute, the Majority also challenges the validity of the legislative interest. It contends that the expressed intention of the statute "will not do" because the Legislature actually has no legitimate interest in treating children of broken marriages differently than children of intact marriages. The Majority theorizes that since the children of intact families may be no less in need of funds for purposes of higher education, they are situated similarly to children of divorced or separated parents, and any distinction between them is inconsequential.

.   .   .

It has also been widely acknowledged that among the negative effects of divorce on children are those which concern higher education.... Whether because they lose concern for their children's welfare, or out of animosity toward the custodial parent, non-custodial parents frequently become reluctant to provide financial support for any purpose, but are particularly determined to avoid the costs of a college education. Then the custodial parent, who typically has less money than the non-custodial parent, most often becomes the de facto bearer of most, if not all, of the burden of educational expenses, even where the non-custodial parent possesses both resources and background which would inure to the child's benefit were the parents still married. Such parents, are, in addition, even less inclined to assist with the educational expenses of daughters than of sons.

The courts addressing the issue have uniformly decided that equal protection is not offended by an attempt to equalize the disparate situation faced by children of divorce. Only the means are different. Those facing challenges to a statutory provision have all found that the differences between married and divorced parents establishes the necessity to discriminate between the classes. Others, in examining judge-made law found an extended dependency justified court intervention. They all, however, delegated to the court the authority to determine the propriety of an award.

In *LeClair v. LeClair*, 624 A.2d 1350 ([N.H.]1993), the New Hampshire Supreme Court recognized and addressed the very concerns toward which Act 62 is directed—the disadvantage wrought on children by divorce of their parents, and the necessity for court intervention to protect them from the consequences of this disadvantage. The New Hampshire statute, RSA 458:20, codified decisions in which the New Hampshire Supreme Court had recognized the jurisdiction of the superior court to order divorced parents, consistent with their means, to contribute toward the educational expenses of their college age children. Challengers of the statute bore the burden of showing that the court had committed an abuse of discretion, and that the order was "improper and unfair." The equal protection argument focused on the parents, finding them similarly situated with respect to the issue. However, the Majority here states that because the focus of Act 62 is the treatment of children, the marital status of their parents is irrelevant.

This argument is specious, since *any* child support legislation necessarily involves the marital status of the parents. Intact families do not suffer intervention by the courts unless their children are abused or neglected. Recognition of the need for legislative or judicial action to require support for children of broken families is irrefutable, as the continuing governmental efforts to improve collection of support attest. It is unrealistic to conclude, as the Majority does, that merely because children are in need of funds for college rather than subsistence, the effect of their parents marital status has magically altered, and that enforcement of an obligation is no longer necessary.

What must be remembered, and what the Majority fails to explore, is that Act 62 does not make mandatory the directive to pay child support for college. Section 4327(e) lists standards to assist the court in determining whether or not support is appropriate. Unless these criteria are, in the estimation of the court, met by the parties, no liability exists.

The problem lies with the nature of the liability, which is, quite simply, a moral duty, circumstantially prescribed. Under Act 62, it is owed only by parents who are subject to an existing support obligation, that is, they have acknowledged either voluntarily through contract, or involuntarily through the necessity of court order that a financial responsibility to pay for their children's upkeep exists. The court has thus already become involved to the extent of entering an order, or there exists another legal mechanism, e.g., separation agreement, through which enforcement can be accomplished and contribution monitored. In intact families, absent abuse or neglect, no such initial intervention has occurred, and the court has no forum in which to enforce a duty imposed on these parents. Moreover, limitations have been placed on the ability to control children's education by legislative fiat. Thus intervention in the form of a statute requiring parents of an intact marriage to finance their children's college education would indeed infringe upon the constitutional/privacy right of the parties.

While it does not necessarily follow that in all cases children of divorce are deprived of parental support for college, or that the reverse is true and all children of intact families are provided with the necessary encouragement and finances, children whose parents are still married most often continue to receive support past majority. Equal protection does not demand that every permutation be addressed separately, what is sought is equality not uniformity.

NOTES

1. Most states require support only until the child reaches the age of majority and most define majority as age eighteen or nineteen. In the minority of states where majority is defined as twenty-one, some courts may order child support for college expenses, while others are limited to high school education. Most states allow private agreements between divorcing spouses on college education. These however, have repeatedly run into enforcement problems. In *Hawkins v. Gilbo*, 663 A.2d 9 (Me. 1995), the Supreme Judicial Court of Maine held that a promisee mother's failure to join her college student child (who was the third party donee beneficiary of a tuition contract) severely limited the damages she could recover from her ex-husband. The court explained the dilemma as follows:

> If the promisee has no economic interest in the performance, as in many cases involving gift promises, the ordinary remedy for breach of contract is an inadequate remedy, since only nominal damages can be recovered. Thus without joining Keith, Nancy could have brought an action for specific enforcement of the contract and for her actual damages, but not for damages suffered by Keith. Moreover, absent a showing that she was obligated to pay for Keith's education, her actual damages would be limited to nominal damages.

Id. at 11 (internal quotation marks and citation omitted). *See also Noble v. Fisher*, 894 P.2d 118, 123 (Idaho 1995) (declaring that children and not their mother have standing as third party beneficiaries to enforce the tuition provision in a property settlement); *Mattocks v. Matus*, 466 S.E.2d 840, 842 (Ga. 1996) (holding father's contractual obligation to support college student ceased when child left school and did not resume when the child decided to enroll again).

2. In *Stanton v. Stanton*, 421 U.S. 7 (1975), a father had agreed to pay child support for his son and daughter until both reached their "majority." The Supreme Court held that the relevant Utah statute (which provided that minority lasts until twenty-one for males but only eighteen for females) violated the Equal Protection Clause, explaining:

> If a specified age of minority is required for the boy in order to assure him parental support while he attains his education and training, so, too, it is for girls. To distinguish between the two is self-serving: if the female is not to be supported so long as the male, she hardly can be expected to attend school as long as he does, and bringing her education to an end earlier coincides with the role-typing society has long imposed.

Id. at 15. On remand, an award of child support for the daughter was granted by the trial court but overturned on appeal to the Utah Supreme Court. 552 P.2d 112 (Utah 1976). This Utah decision was voided by the Supreme Court, 429 U.S. 501 (1977), for failure to deal with the discrimination issue presented by the case. On remand, the Supreme Court of Utah decided that both males and females would be considered emancipated at age eighteen because the statute had been amended. 564 P.2d 303 (Utah 1977).

3. In *Johnson v. Louis*, 654 N.W.2d 886 (Iowa 2002), the Supreme Court of Iowa held that it was not a violation of Equal Protection to allow postsecondary child support for children of divorced parents, but not for children of unmarried parents. The court explained:

> As we recognized in *In re Marriage of Vrban*, 293 N.W.2d 198, 202 (Iowa 1980), the benefited class of children have had the attributes of a legally recognized parental relationship taken from them by court decree. The educational benefit is a quid pro quo for the loss of stability resulting from divorce. Children like Jared, whose parents never sought State involvement to formalize or dissolve their relationships, are not similarly situated. They cannot claim the

loss of stability such change in status brings. And, while they may rightfully claim a similarly vulnerable status insofar as furthering their education, we deem the classification drawn by the legislature to be rational, not arbitrary, and thus not constitutionally infirm.

Id. at 891. What do you think of the court's reasoning?

4. Most jurisdictions impose a continued obligation of child support past the age of majority if the child has a disability that pre-existed its majority. *See* Sande L. Buhai, *Parental Support of Adult Children with Disabilities*, 91 Minn. L. Rev. 710, 723–24, 730–31 (2007). About nineteen jurisdictions impose a duty to continued support of a disabled child past the age of majority, regardless of when the disability came about. *Id.* at 730–31. Nine states follow the common law rule, which does not impose a continued duty of support past majority regardless of a child's disability. *Id.* at 722–23. Should families or the state be held responsible for the maintenance of disabled adults?

d. WHO IS RESPONSIBLE FOR CHILD SUPPORT?

Miller v. Miller

Supreme Court of New Jersey, 1984.
97 N.J. 154, 478 A.2d 351.

■ The opinion of the Court was delivered by GARIBALDI, J.

Today we must decide whether a stepparent can be equitably estopped from denying the duty to provide child support for minor stepchildren after divorcing their natural parent. If equitable estoppel does apply to stepparents' situation, we must also decide what evidence must be presented to establish a cause of action for child support.

Gladys Miller married Jay Miller on December 16, 1972. No children were born of their marriage. During the couple's marriage Gladys' two daughters by her prior marriage lived with the Millers. Gladys and Jay separated on December 12, 1979. In February, 1980, Gladys filed a Verified Complaint seeking dissolution of the Millers' marriage. Although Jay was not the natural or adoptive father of Gladys' daughters, Gladys sought child support from Jay for her children. In her complaint, she alleged that by his actions, Jay had induced the girls to rely on him as their natural father, to their emotional and financial detriment. By so doing, he had prevented and cut off the girls' relationship with their natural father. Therefore, she claimed he was equitably estopped from denying a duty to pay child support. Jay claimed that although he stood *in loco parentis* to the children during his marriage, he was merely their stepfather and any legal relationship he had with the children terminated with his divorce from their mother.

The trial court agreed with Gladys. It held that Jay was equitably estopped from denying his duty to support the girls, and required him to pay child support of $75 per week per child. The trial court based its holding primarily on the concept of "emotional bonding." Jay, by his actions, had knowingly and intentionally fostered a *bona fide* parental relationship with the girls, so that in their minds he became their father. Therefore, he could not avoid the financial obligations flowing from that relationship.

The Appellate Division affirmed the trial court's judgment, primarily because it found that Jay had actively interfered with the normal relationship between the girls and their natural father to the girls' emotional and financial detriment. We granted certification.

We conclude that in appropriate cases *pendente lite* and permanent support obligations may be imposed on a stepparent on the basis of equitable estoppel. In this case, we hold that the facts established at trial are sufficient to impose a *pendente lite* award but are not sufficient to indicate whether a permanent support obligation should be imposed. We therefore reverse and remand this case to the trial court for further findings of fact and a determination consistent with this opinion.

Prior to her marriage to Jay, Gladys was married to Ralph Febre. Two children were born of that marriage: Michelle, born July, 1963, and Suzette, born July, 1966. Shortly after Suzette's birth in 1966, Gladys separated from Ralph; she divorced him in 1969.

The essential facts concerning Ralph's support of his children are undisputed. Although there was no support provision in the divorce agreement, Ralph continued to support Gladys and the children after the couple's separation until he went to prison on a narcotics charge in 1968. Immediately before going to prison, Ralph gave Gladys $5,000 for the support of his daughters. While he was in prison and after he was released, he continued to express his concern for his children.

[Gladys married Jay in 1972, while Ralph was in prison. During the Millers' marriage, Jay developed a loving relationship with the two girls and supported them financially.]

The Appellate Division found from the testimony, and for the purpose of this appeal we find, that

> upon Ralph's release from jail he attempted to visit his children but defendant [Jay] strenuously opposed any visitation and, in fact, prohibited it. He rejected all offers of Ralph to contribute to the support of his children and tore up a check tendered for that purpose. Ralph desisted from further attempts at visitation or payment of support.

Jay contends that the loving relationship he developed with the girls was not sufficient to impose a financial obligation on him to continue to support the girls after his separation from their mother. He claims that upon the termination of his marriage to their mother, his financial obligation to the girls ceased.

New Jersey has no statutory requirement imposing a duty of support on a stepparent for his or her spouse's children by a former marriage. Nor did the common law impose a legal obligation on a stepparent to support the children of his or her spouse by another party. Such an obligation arises by a voluntary assumption on the part of the stepparent to support the children. This *in loco parentis* relationship exists when a stepparent receives a child into the family home under circumstances giving rise to a presumption that he or she will assume responsibility to maintain, rear, and educate the child. The relationship, however,

> exists only so long as the parties thereto, namely the surrogate parent and/or the child, desire that it exist. In that regard, the *in loco parentis* status differs from natural parenthood or adoption. The latter two permanently affix rights and duties, while the former affixed rights and duties temporary in nature.

Thus, in most cases, when a stepparent who stands *in loco parentis* to a stepchild divorces that child's natural parent, the *in loco parentis* relationship is deemed terminated and any obligation of support the stepparent has assumed terminates.

Despite the general rule that an *in loco parentis* relationship terminates upon the intent of the stepparent, courts in certain cases have held that a stepparent's duty to support a spouse's children extends beyond the dissolution of their marriage. In most of these cases the courts have relied on principles of equitable estoppel or implied contract to impose a continuing obligation of child support on a stepparent after he or she divorces the children's natural parent.

The burden of proof of a claim based on principles of equitable estoppel is clearly on the party asserting estoppel. To establish a claim of equitable estoppel, the claiming party must show that the alleged conduct was done, or representation was made, intentionally or under such circumstances that it was both natural and probable that it would induce action. Further, the conduct must be relied on, and the relying party must act so as to change his or her position to his or her detriment.

. . .

Today, we decide that in appropriate cases, a permanent support obligation may be imposed on a stepparent on the basis of equitable estoppel, but that this doctrine should be applied with caution. Voluntary support by a stepparent should not be discouraged.

It is essential, however, that, in the interim period between the spouse's separation and the trial court's decision on permanent child support, the children have a source of support. We therefore find that if, in a motion for *pendente lite* child support, the natural parent demonstrates that he or she is not receiving support for the children from their other natural parent and establishes by affidavit that the stepparent's conduct actively interfered with the children's support by their natural parent, so that *pendente lite* support may not be obtained from the natural parent, the children should be awarded *pendente lite* support from the stepparent. By permitting a spouse to get interim support for the children, we alleviate any immediate hardship to the children caused by the breakup of a marriage in which a stepparent is the sole or major source of support for the family. Such interim support order should remain in force until circumstances justify a modification of the Order or the court makes its final determination.

To be entitled to permanent child support, Gladys, as the party alleging equitable estoppel, has the burden to prove that Jay's conduct established the three prerequisites to equitable estoppel—representation, reliance, and detriment. We recognize that there can be many forms of misrepresentation. We do not agree with those courts that have held that for equitable estoppel to apply the children must believe that the stepparent is their natural parent. Such a requirement would unduly limit this cause of action to those cases in which the stepparent appeared on the scene when the children were infants. We do believe, however, that for equitable estoppel to apply the stepparent must have made some representation of support to either the children or the natural parent as to his or her responsibilities in his or her relationship with them.

With respect to the reliance element of equitable estoppel Gladys contends that Jay's actions induced the girls to rely on him emotionally and financially, while he deliberately alienated the children from their natural father's emotional and financial support. It is undisputed that Jay, while living with Gladys, developed a loving relationship with the girls, and that the girls relied on him for emotional support. However, no court has ever applied equitable estoppel to force a husband to support the children of his divorced spouse merely because he developed a close relationship with the children, nurtured them into a family unit with himself as the father, and had the children call him "daddy." We decline to be the first to set such a precedent.

We specifically determine that the development of "emotional bonding" as set forth by the trial court is not sufficient to invoke the doctrine of equitable estoppel in stepparent cases. As stated previously, to hold otherwise would create enormous policy difficulties. A stepparent who tried to create a warm family atmosphere with his or her stepchildren would be penalized by being forced to pay support for them in the event of a divorce. At the same time, a stepparent who refused to have anything to do with his or her stepchildren beyond supporting them would be rewarded by not having to pay support in the event of a divorce.

To prove equitable estoppel, the custodial parent has the burden to establish not only representation of support and reliance but also detriment, *i.e.*, that the children will suffer future financial detriment as a result of the stepparent's representation or conduct that caused the children to be cut off from their natural parent's financial support. Matrimonial cases are extremely fact-sensitive because each case involves a unique set of interpersonal relationships. The burden of establishing economic detriment depends on the facts of the particular case.

For example, at the final hearing if the custodial parent demonstrates that he or she (1) does not know the whereabouts of the natural parent; (2) cannot locate the other natural parent; or (3) cannot secure jurisdiction over the natural parent for valid legal reasons, and that the natural parent's unavailability is due to the actions of the stepparent, a trial court could hold that the stepparent is equitably estopped from denying his or her duty to support the children.

If, as in the present case, the wife knows where the natural father is, she has the burden to bring him before the court and to seek child support from him. Once in court the burden is on the natural father to show why he should not, in equity, be required to pay child support for his children. If the court finds that the natural father should not be required to pay child support due to the stepfather's conduct, the natural father having relied thereon and having placed himself in such a position that he is unable to meet that obligation, the stepparent should be responsible for the children's continued support. This, of course, is subject to modification or change whenever the natural father can meet his obligation. We have, in countless situations, recognized that changed circumstances should be reflected in changed obligations regardless of earlier commitments.

We emphasize, however, that the natural parent should always be considered the primary recourse for child support because society and its current laws assume that the natural parent will support his or her child. It is only when a stepparent by his or her conduct actively interferes with the children's support from their natural parent that he or she may be equitably estopped from denying his or her duty to support the children.... If a stepparent marries a divorced parent who is not receiving any child support, or if during their marriage the natural parent stops paying child support without interference from the stepparent, the stepparent does not thereby inherit the permanent support obligations of the nonpaying natural parent. The stepparent must take positive action interfering with the natural parent's support obligation to be bound. Further, if the stepparent paid *pendente lite* or permanent support, he or she may have a claim for reimbursement against the natural parent.

In applying this rule to the present case, the trial court must decide whether the two girls, both of whom were in their late teens when this action arose, incurred any detriment as to their *future* support by their previous reliance on their stepfather for support. To decide that the girls have incurred such detriment, the court must find that Jay's conduct interfered with Ralph's present duty to support them.

In concluding this issue, we hold that in appropriate cases, the doctrine of equitable estoppel may be invoked to impose on a stepparent the duty to support a stepchild after a divorce from the child's natural parent. But we admonish that the doctrine be invoked cautiously. Here, Jay should be required to pay child support during the pendency of this litigation since Gladys has satisfied the requirements that we have set down for a motion for *pendente lite* child support. However, to obtain permanent support Gladys must prove at the trial that the facts support the application of the equitable estoppel doctrine. We therefore reverse the Appellate Division's judgment and remand to the trial court for a determination of the facts necessary to decide this issue in accordance with this opinion.

. . .

■ HANDLER, J., concurring in part and dissenting in part.

Equity may insist that a stepfather accept a continuing obligation to support his minor stepchildren upon the termination by divorce of his marriage to their mother. I firmly believe that this is an appropriate case to recognize that defendant be required, under principles of equitable estoppel, to continue to provide child support for his minor stepchildren. In my opinion, the record discloses sufficient facts to call for the imposition of such an obligation. I would therefore affirm the judgment of the Appellate Division.

. . .

Equitable estoppel is a doctrine that is designed to bring an uniquely individualized controversy to a just and fair disposition, taking into account the special and particular relationship and course of dealing between the parties. The doctrine, well understood in its classic definition, requires of one party a representation, and of the other party expected, consequential, and detrimental reliance. Equitable estoppel may be appropriate in any equitable cause of action or defense. In this case, its application is especially compelling because children are involved. Consequently, the doctrine, in this setting, requires a somewhat broader conceptualization.

In the matrimonial context, when the rights and interests of innocent children are at stake, we should consider in applying the doctrine of equitable estoppel whether there was a course of conduct that, in its cumulative impact, was tantamount to a representation made by one party with the expectation that other persons would rely on this conduct, and whether, as a natural and probable consequence, such persons did in fact reasonably rely, resulting in a detriment to them. That detriment—the disadvantage or change of position—can occur because of the actor's subsequent repudiation of his or her conduct and disavowal of the expectations engendered by that conduct.

. . .

In this case, the gravamen of plaintiff's complaint is, and the evidence presented shows, that by a pronounced and purposeful course of conduct, defendant induced his stepdaughters to rely on him as their father and as their sole source of paternal sustenance and support. Further, in so doing, he frustrated and cut off the girls' relationship with their natural father. There is little question that when defendant terminated his marriage and ended his familial relationship with his wife and his stepdaughters, he left the children at a substantial financial disadvantage. In effect, he repudiated his prior course of conduct and disavowed the expectations he himself created. I am satisfied that the record meets plaintiff's evidential burden to demonstrate that defendant equitably should be estopped from disclaiming a continuing duty to support these children.

. . .

I agree with the Court that the love between defendant and the stepchildren is not the pivotal consideration. The gist of the equitable cause of action here is rooted in the fact that defendant affirmatively established himself as the sole or primary supporter of the family and zealously deprived his stepchildren of the support they were otherwise entitled to secure from their natural father. Nevertheless, parental love may be a relevant factor to be weighed in making the equitable assessment. Thus, if this emotional bonding with the stepfather has contributed to or exacerbated the alienation of the children from their natural father and, as important, has served to discourage the natural father from maintaining a full parental relationship with his own children, it may have a material bearing on his failure to support his children.

Here, it is undisputed that throughout the seven years that plaintiff and defendant lived together, defendant developed a loving relationship with the two girls. . . .

. . .

In sum, I would find that when a stepparent walks away from his marital family, regardless of spousal fault, after a marriage characterized by a course of conduct on his part that has resulted in the cutting off of financial assistance from the natural parent, the stepparent should remain provisionally responsible for the family's continued support. The responsibility is provisional because, as a matrimonial obligation, it is of course subject to modification or change. Changed circumstances may always be addressed by changing obligations, regardless of how fair these were when first imposed. The support obligation, equitably imposed on the stepfather in this case, need not endure indefinitely and does not eliminate or supersede the natural father's legal obligation to support his own children. Therefore, either party should be required, or given the opportunity, to assert this obligation against the natural father. The trial court should be vested with the discretion to determine the circumstances under which it would be appropriate or necessary to shift the responsibility for child support to the natural father. However, unless and until the natural father can be brought back into the picture, equitable estoppel should prevent the stepfather from passing the buck—literally. In no event should the stepchildren be left holding an empty bag.

NOTES

1. *Miller* reflects the general consensus on the obligations of a stepparent for child support. *See, e.g., In the Matter of Glaude & Fogg,* 855 A.2d 494 (N.H. 2004); *W. v. W.,* 779 A.2d 716 (Conn. 2001).

2. In a more recent case, a New Jersey court applied the *Miller* test to the situation of a psychological parent, where no biological father was known:

> [T]his court holds that the *Miller* test is applicable to the within matter, i.e. where the biological father is unknown and the only "father" available is a psychological father. Although the *Miller* case involved a stepparent situation, a broader reading of the case indicates that it applies where there is one natural parent and the other "while absent, may still be available." Although R.K. has not acted as a stepfather because the parties were never married, he has acted as, and this court holds that he is, a psychological parent to T.K.

Monmouth County Div. of Soc. Servs. v. R.K., 757 A.2d 319, 327 (N.J. Super. Ct. Ch. Div. 2000).

e. MODIFICATION

Ainsworth v. Ainsworth

Supreme Court of Vermont, 1990.
154 Vt. 103, 574 A.2d 772.

■ DOOLEY, JUSTICE.

This action for modification of child support calls upon us to interpret Vermont's recently enacted child support guidelines law, 15 V.S.A. §§ 650–663. Specifically at issue is whether expenses for a second family should enter into the determination of child support for the preexisting family. Although the trial court decided that defendant, Reginald Ainsworth, did not have a duty to support his stepson under 15 V.S.A. § 296, it held, pursuant to § 659, that a child support order based on the guidelines sought by plaintiff, Julie Ann Ainsworth, on her behalf and on behalf of the two children of the parties, would be inequitable and ordered him to pay them less than what would be required under the guidelines. Plaintiff appealed and we reverse and remand.

The parties were divorced on April 30, 1986. They stipulated then that defendant was to pay child support in the amount of $35 per week for each of their two children for a total of $70 per week. Mr. Ainsworth remarried on August 15, 1987, and established a new home with his wife and her son at that time. On September 21, 1987, plaintiff filed a motion for modification pursuant to 15 V.S.A. § 660,[1] seeking increased support in an amount to be determined under the guidelines mandated by the statute that was effective on April 1, 1987. . . .

. . .

In order to fully and logically analyze the issues presented by plaintiff's appeal, we will recategorize the issues from those used by the trial court into three questions: (1) whether the trial court may deviate from child support amounts calculated under the guidelines when defendant is supporting children in a second family; (2) if the answer to the first question is yes, whether the power to deviate applies if the children in the second family are

---

1. Section 660 provides in part:

(a) On motion of either parent . . . and upon a showing of a real, substantial and unanticipated change of circumstances, the court may annul, vary or modify a child support order, whether or not the order is based upon a stipulation or agreement.

(b) A child support order, including an order in effect prior to adoption of the support guideline, which varies more than 15 percent from the amounts required to be paid under the support guideline, shall be considered a real, substantial and unanticipated change of circumstances.

stepchildren and not natural children; and (3) if the answer to the first two questions is yes, whether the actual order in this case was within the discretion of the trial court....

. . .

In Vermont, the guideline amounts are established by rule of the Secretary of Human Services. Under the guideline regulations, a basic support amount for the children is derived from tables based solely on the total gross income of the parents and the number of children. *See* 15 V.S.A. § 653(1) ("Basic support obligation" defined as guideline amount unless court finds that amount inequitable and establishes a different amount). The next step is to calculate a "total support obligation" by adding expenditures in two categories to the basic support amount: (1) the amount of child care costs reasonably incurred by a parent as a result of employment or employment related education; and (2) extraordinary medical or education expenses. Once the total support obligation is calculated, the amount is divided between the parents "in proportion to their respective gross incomes." In this calculation, as well as in the derivation of the basic support amount from the tables, a broad definition of gross income is used. There are, however, three exclusions from income in reaching the "gross incomes" recognized by the statute: (1) the amount of "preexisting spousal maintenance or child support obligations actually paid;" (2) amounts received from means tested public assistance programs; and (3) the actual cost of providing adequate health insurance coverage for the involved children.

Except as set forth above, the actual expenditures of the parents are not relevant to the guideline calculation. Thus, the guideline calculation for a noncustodial parent with a large mortgage payment would be the same as for a noncustodial parent with a low rent payment as long as both have the same income.

The total support obligation calculated under the guideline is "presumed to be the amount of child support needed," upon which the noncustodial parent's obligation is calculated. However, if the court finds that a child support order based on the guidelines "would be inequitable," the court may establish support after considering all relevant factors. The statute contains a noninclusive list of factors to be considered.

The first question we face is whether the trial court can find an order based on the guidelines "inequitable" because of the expenses of supporting another child when the support obligation for that other child did not preexist the one for the child or children included in the guideline calculation. We believe that the trial court has this power.

We start with the wording chosen by the Legislature to describe when the court should deviate from the guidelines. The term "equitable" normally means "[j]ust; conformable to the principles of justice and right." *Black's Law Dictionary* 482 (5th ed. 1979). Thus, the use of the term "inequitable" must give the trial court authority to look at whether a guideline-based amount is just under the circumstances....

While the wording chosen by the Legislature makes clear that it intended to give trial courts discretion to ensure support awards are just, this is an area where we must be careful to define the nature and scope of that discretion so that it is not used to create inequity or to undermine the standardization that the Legislature intended. If we allow the trial courts to consider any variation in the needs of the children or the living situation or expenses of the parents, we would return to the preguideline law where a wide range of support amounts was permissible in almost every case. In short, the "escape valve" of § 659 would eat up the rule and destroy the predictability of amounts and the maintenance of the standard of living of the children that are the desired results of a guideline system.

Our examination of the statutory scheme demonstrates, however, that this case involves the type of situation where the Legislature intended that the court exercise discretion consistent with the policies of the act. That intent is demonstrated by the exclusion from gross income of certain support payments. While the drafting is not a model of clarity, we conclude that the exclusion covers amounts being paid pursuant to preexisting support orders.

It is important to analyze what is covered by the exclusion and what is not. First, as we construe the legislative intent, it requires that there be an actual support order. Second, it requires that the order, not merely the obligation, be preexisting at the time the calculation is made. Third, it requires that payments be made on the order.

The limits of the second requirement are particularly important. It shows that the Legislature was primarily concerned about the timing of the orders. If a noncustodial parent is subject to two child support orders, the amount paid under the first order is always deductible under § 653(5)(E)(i) from that parent's income in determining the amount of the second order, even though the child covered by the second order might have been born before the child covered by the first order.

There are practical reasons why the Legislature created a rule allowing a parent to deduct the expenses of other support obligations only in limited circumstances. They are explained in *People in Interest of C.D.*, 767 P.2d [809,]at 811–12 [(Colo. Ct. App. 1988)], in describing the identical Colorado rule:

> Inherent in the statutory scheme is a legislative recognition that child support obligations which have been previously imposed by a court have been determined to be both necessary and reasonable in amount in proper judicial proceedings. Non-ordered support obligations, on the other hand, have not been judicially scrutinized either as to their necessity or their reasonableness, and the General Assembly accordingly has not provided for automatic income adjustments based upon those obligations, whether or not they are actually paid.
>
> . . .

It would be unfair, however, to consider amounts paid under existing support obligations only when they are the subject of court orders. By allowing consideration of payments made to discharge support obligations in instances where they have been scrutinized by a court and can be fit within mathematical formulas and allowing courts to deviate from support amounts calculated under the guidelines when such amounts are "inequitable," the Legislature must have intended that the courts use their discretion to consider the expenses connected with second families. The use of discretion in this area prevents the guideline system from being wholly arbitrary.

In reaching the conclusion that the court could consider the expenses of supporting other families under § 659, we also rely on the fact that the courts in Colorado, the state with a guideline system closest to that adopted in Vermont,[3] have reached the same conclusion. The Colorado courts have

---

3. Colorado and Vermont use an income-share approach to setting guidelines. *See* Robert Williams, *Guidelines for Setting Levels of Child Support Orders*, 21 Fam.L.Q. at 291. As noted earlier,

held that support obligations to other dependents may be evaluated in determining the extent to which a deviation from the guidelines is necessary to avoid an "inequitable" support order. . . .

For the above reasons, we answer the first question in this case in the affirmative. The trial court may, under § 659, find that calculating a support order based on the guidelines would be inequitable because of a parent's expenses in supporting other dependents.

The second question is whether the court's discretion under § 659 extends to situations where the expenses are for the support of a second wife and a stepchild. . . .

The trial court found no obligation of support in this case because the statutory support obligation of stepparents is limited to situations where the financial resources of the natural parents are inadequate to provide the child with a reasonable subsistence. Although the stepparent support statute, 15 V.S.A. § 296, contains the language cited, it also states that the duty it imposes is "coextensive" with the duty to support a natural child. Therefore, we disagree with the trial court and find that the statute creates a general obligation of support.

Neither the trial court nor the parties have raised any question about the defendant's obligation to support his second wife. The general obligation to support spouses extends to defendant's second spouse. *See* 15 V.S.A. § 291.

Having decided that the trial court could find the application of the guidelines to be inequitable in this case, we must address whether the court properly exercised its discretion in setting a support amount. We emphasize here that the fact that the court finds the application of guidelines to be "inequitable" in a particular case does not mean that it must automatically order a substantially lower support amount. . . . The use of § 659 means only that the special circumstances of the case make it inappropriate to determine a support amount based *solely* on the mathematical calculations involved in the guidelines. Instead, the court must consider all "relevant factors," including eight specific ones itemized in the statute. It may be that an evaluation of these factors will lead to a support award as high as that calculated under the guidelines.

It is particularly important to emphasize that consideration of a case under § 659 does not necessarily mean a lower support amount in second-family cases. We have held that a change in financial circumstances "resulting from a deliberate and voluntary act, absent a sufficient reason for the sacrificing of income," will not support a modification of a child support order. . . .

The voluntary nature of second-family obligations is not the only consideration in establishing the child support order under § 659. . . . We agree with the trial court in this case that the financial resources of the new spouse of the parent is also a relevant consideration. A parent should not be able to rely on second-family expenses without consideration of second-family income and resources.

We have held with respect to the custody statute, when the Legislature itemized certain factors to be considered in determining parental rights and

---

Colorado has adopted an exclusion from income for the amount of preexisting child support obligations actually paid. Colorado also allows a deviation from the guidelines where their application would be inequitable. *See* COLO.REV.STAT.ANN. § 14–10–115(3)(a).

responsibilities, that the court's findings must show that it took each of the statutory factors into consideration. . . .

The findings and conclusions here are incomplete and much too sketchy to meet the above requirements. The court had evidence from both parties on their income and expenses. The evidence from the defendant showed a high level of consumer debt connected with the purchase of a house and furnishings for his new family. Although the court found that defendant's new spouse had "financial resources as represented by her education and former work experience," it apparently considered her to have no potential income when it set the support amount. In any event, the court never specified how, based on the evidence and its findings, it arrived at the figure of $90 per week as the new child support amount. Nor can we conclude that the court considered all the factors specified in § 659(a)(1)–(8) and considered the extent to which the defendant's expenses were voluntarily incurred in the face of his obligation to the children of his first marriage.

Because the findings and conclusions do not specify the reasons for the amount of support awarded and show consideration of the statutory factors, we must reverse and remand for a new hearing.

. . .

■ MORSE, JUSTICE, dissenting.

. . .

In adopting the new child support statute, the legislature stated its purpose as follows:

> The legislature . . . finds and declares as public policy that parents have the responsibility to provide child support and that child support orders should reflect the true costs of raising children and approximate insofar as possible *the standard of living the child would have enjoyed had the marriage not been dissolved.*

15 V.S.A. § 650 (emphasis added). . . . The priority is clear. Children come first. Their living standard should not drop "insofar as possible."

. . .

While I agree with most of what is said in the Court's opinion, I do not construe § 659, which permits deviations from the guidelines "[i]f the court finds that a child support order based on the support guidelines would be inequitable," to allow a deviation on this record. The Court's holding today will lead to irrational results, rendering the child support law less effective and fair; indeed, it undermines the explicit purpose of the legislation. If defendant's new house and furnishings came before his children, he would *not* be honoring his "responsibility to provide child support [where] child support orders should reflect the true costs of raising children," § 650, and the children's needs would *not* be met by "the parents in proportion to their respective gross incomes," § 656.

In light of the legislation as a whole and its evident purpose, § 659 must be given a more narrow reading. The trial court's discretion to deviate from the legislative scheme is constrained. The determination of inequitability cannot be supported by the sorts of facts already considered in arriving at the support guideline figure. As stated above, that figure depends on what parents "ordinarily spend on their children," an amount that necessarily reflects their other ordinary expenses. The legislature therefore did not intend that ordinary expenses incurred by the noncustodial parent could support a finding that a guideline-based order would be inequitable. Only *extraordinary* expenses can justify a departure from the guidelines. This record reveals no extraordinary expenses. What they might be should be left to subsequent cases.

. . .

I am not of the view that defendant has no obligation to support his stepson. I would hold only that any such obligation must not be subtracted from his gross income in calculating the guideline child support figure. In this sense defendant's obligation to his stepchild is no different than his obligation to pay taxes. He may have a legal duty to pay both, but neither enters into the calculation of his child support obligation under the statutory guidelines.

It may be useful to compare the situation of a parent who is subject to a child support order stemming from a *former* marriage. In such a case, the earlier child support obligations, if actually paid, may reduce the parent's obligations to the children of the second marriage under the new statutory framework. *See* 15 V.S.A. § 653(5)(E)(i). Children of the second marriage receive diminished support relative to children of the first marriage. The legislature had to choose where to place the inevitable hardship—all things being equal—resulting from the assumption of second-family responsibilities. It chose to keep child support, as dictated by the guidelines in the usual case, intact for children who were already the beneficiaries of a child support order. This is as it should be. The decision to assume added familial responsibilities should include an evaluation of the added cost, without factoring in a reduction in support to children of the divorce to help finance the second family. In short, the Court's decision today reduces the cost equation at the expense of children of divorce.

I would not fashion a per se rule. Expenses for children in a second family in some instances might well warrant a departure from the guidelines. It is not necessary to broaden discretion under § 659(a)'s inequitability standard, however, to, in the words of the Court, "prevent[ ] the guideline system from being wholly arbitrary." . . .

. . .

Under today's ruling, determination of child support is subject in large measure to the vagaries of individual judgment as to what is fair, given all the facts and circumstances of each case. The guidelines, however, are designed to give child support determinations a measure of predictability and equality and to reduce litigation. They are intended to ensure that like cases will be treated alike by judges who do not think alike in this area of subjective value judgments. If the guidelines are circumvented under the "equitable" rubric of § 659(a), we will return to the inequities, waste and drain of preguideline litigation. Exceptions to the guidelines should not be based on a judge's opinion of the fairness of the guidelines per se or upon voluntary undertakings by a party to establish and support a second family with funds that would otherwise go to support existing children. This policy may not appear romantic, but it reflects the pragmatic belief that new obligations should not be created or assumed at the expense of existing ones.

Accordingly, I would reverse and remand for an order setting child support at $141 per week.

NOTES

1. Following the *Ainsworth* decision, the Vermont legislature amended its guidelines to include the possibility of a gross income adjustment for additional dependents that are not the subject of a court order. *See* VT. STAT. ANN. tit. 15, § 656a(b) (2002) ("[i]n any proceeding to establish or modify child support, the total child support obligation for the children who are the subject of the support order shall be adjusted if a parent is also responsible for the support of additional dependents who are not the subject of the support order."). In *Miller v. Miller*, 882 A.2d 1196, 1199 (Vt. 2005), the Supreme Court of Vermont held that this adjustment was only available to custodial parents of additional children, who were presumed to be spending the guideline amount directly on the supported children.

2. As a general rule, guidelines allow the deduction from income of child support amounts owed by the parent under a pre-existing child support order. *See, e.g.,* COLO. REV. STAT. ANN. § 14–10–115 (6)(a) (West 2005 & Supp. 2010). If there is a prior child but no pre-existing court order, some states will still allow a *deduction* from income for support that is actually being provided. *See, e.g., Miller v. Miller, supra* note 1; *Lacy v. Arvin*, 780 A.2d 1180 (Md. Ct. App. 2001) (support provided pursuant to previous agreement but without court order justified deduction). Some states will allow the support provided without a court order to be considered as a reason *to deviate* downward from the guideline amount. *See, e.g.,* VA. CODE ANN. § 20–108.1(B)(1) (2008 & Supp. 2011). When it comes to children from a subsequent relationship, most states will allow support to such children to be considered as a *deviation* factor but not necessarily as a deduction from available income. Why do you think that is?

3. Note that in *Ainsworth* the father sought to defend against an application for an increase of his child support obligation by asking for his second family expenses to be taken into consideration as a deviation factor. Many states will only allow consideration of subsequent child expenses when the obligor is defending against upward modification, but not when she is herself seeking to modify her initial child support obligation. *See, e.g., Ameen v. Ameen*, 84 P.3d 802, 804 (Okla. Civ. App. 2003).

4. CHILD SUPPORT ENFORCEMENT

A survey published by the U.S. Census Bureau estimated that as of spring 2008 over one quarter of the 82.8 million children living in families in the United States lived with a custodial parent while the other parent lived elsewhere. This amounted to an estimated 13.7 million custodial parents. The majority of these parents, 82.6 percent, were mothers. Almost 25 percent of custodial parents and their children were estimated to have incomes in 2007 below the poverty level. That figure was almost twice the national rate. TIMOTHY S. GRALL, U.S. CENSUS BUREAU, U.S. DEP'T. OF COMMERCE, P60–237, CUSTODIAL MOTHERS AND FATHERS AND THEIR CHILD SUPPORT: 2007 (2009), *available at* http://www.census.gov/prod/2009pubs/p60–237.pdf.

Only 54 percent of custodial parents (7.4 million) had an agreement or award for child support from the noncustodial parent. The majority (6.8 million) were reported as having been established by a court or government entity. The proportion of custodial mothers with awards or agreements was greater than that proportion for custodial fathers. Of these 7.4 million custodial parents, 6.4 million were due to receive child support payments for their children in 2007. Only 46.8 percent of parents due support received the full amount, while 29.5 percent received partial payment, and 23.7 percent received nothing at all. There was no statistical difference between the proportions of mothers versus fathers who received full support. The annual average amount due was $5,350, while the average amount received was $3,350. *Id.*

Compare the figures for 1999, when there were approximately 13.5 million parents with children under 21 years of age whose other parent was not present in the household. Of these custodial parents, over 7.9 million (58.7 percent) had a child support award or agreement, and almost 6.8 million were due to receive payments for their children. Of the 6.8 million, 45.1 percent received the full amount, 28.6 percent received partial payment, and 26.3 received nothing at all. The average amount due was $5,917, and the average amount received was $3,473. *Id.* (citing the 1999 statistics in 2007 dollars).

Nationally, child support payments due for 2007, as reported to the Census Bureau, amounted to $34.1 billion. The total child support payments received was reported to be only $21.4 billion, a shortfall of $12.7 billion or 62.7 percent. *Id.*

Children deserve and need emotional and financial support from both their parents. Many custodial parents require assistance in establishing and enforcing support obligations owed to their children. The materials below discuss some of the measures that have been adopted to increase compliance with child support obligations, as well as some of the critiques of the enforcement mechanisms that have emerged.

Elizabeth G. Patterson, *Civil Contempt and the Indigent Child Support Obligor: The Silent Return of Debtor's Prison*

18 CORNELL J.L. & PUB. POL'Y 95, 99–100 (2008).

In fashioning the child support enforcement program, the federal focus was on creating a relentlessly effective system for collecting as much accrued child support debt as possible from absent parents. The federal requirements address every aspect of the process of identifying and locating absent parents, and establishing and enforcing the support obligation. Welfare eligibility is conditioned on identification of the father (in the case of female applicants) and cooperation with efforts to obtain support from the absent parent. Judicial proceedings for determining paternity and ordering payment of child support have been replaced with administrative proceedings. Consistency and accuracy of these determinations are to be assured by reliance on genetic testing to establish paternity and the use of child support guidelines that apply a mathematical formula to calculate the amount of the support award.

Once the order is in place, collection of the required support is facilitated through a broad array of mechanisms created or mandated by federal law. A vast network of automated systems provides the child support agency with information on obligors' bank accounts, tax filings, and assets, as well as means for effecting automated seizures of certain assets, including tax refunds. Wage withholding is mandatory in all cases where child support enforcement is being handled by the agency. Employers can be identified through interlinked automated state and national "new hire" directories, to which employers must report information on each newly hired employee.

If insufficient funds are obtained through wage withholding and seizure of assets, a variety of coercive mechanisms are available to try to induce payment by the obligor. These include the revocation of occupational, driver's, and other licenses; the denial of passports; and reporting of delinquent obligors to consumer reporting agencies.

The federal statute also provides for interstate cooperation in enforcement efforts and creates state and federal "Parent Locate" systems with access to records of departments of corrections, employment security commissions, utility companies, the postal service, the military, and other entities with extensive records on members of the public.

. . .

The cases below discuss some of the constitutional challenges that have been raised in relationship to the federal and state child support enforcement mechanisms.

Eunique v. Powell

U.S. Court of Appeals for the Ninth Circuit, 2002.
302 F.3d 971.

■ FERNANDEZ, CIRCUIT JUDGE.

Eudene Eunique was denied a passport because she was severely in arrears on her child support payments. She brought an action for declaratory and injunctive relief on the theory that the statute and regulation authorizing that denial were unconstitutional. The district granted summary judgment against her, and she appealed. We affirm.

When Eunique's marriage was dissolved, her husband was awarded custody of the children, and she was ordered to pay child support. She failed to pay the ordered amounts, and by 1998 she was in arrears in an amount over $20,000. Thereafter, the arrearage continued to grow. Despite the fact that she is unable or unwilling to pay her child support obligations, she desires to travel internationally for both business and pleasure, including visiting a sister in Mexico.

Eunique applied for a passport, but by that time California had certified to the Secretary of Health and Human Services that she owed "arrearages of child support in an amount exceeding $5,000." 42 U.S.C. § 652(k)....

The Secretary of Health and Human Services received that certification and was required by law to transmit it "to the Secretary of State for action." That was accomplished here. The law then directed that "the Secretary of State shall, upon certification ..., refuse to issue a passport to" the individual in question. 42 U.S.C. § 652(k)(2). The regulations adopted by the Secretary of State ... track[] the statutory language....

As a result of the statutory and regulatory requirements, Eunique was denied a passport. In her view, that denial was unconstitutional, so this action ensued. The district court ruled against her and she appeals.

. . .

Eunique argues that there is an insufficient connection between her breach of the duty to pay for the support of her children, and the government's interference with her right to international travel. Thus, she argues, her constitutional rights have been violated. We disagree.

Eunique asserts that she has a constitutional right to international travel, which is so fundamental that it can be restricted for only the most important reasons, and by a narrowly tailored statute. It is undoubtedly true that there is a constitutional right to international travel. However, as the Supreme Court has said, "the right of international travel has been considered to be no more than an aspect of the liberty protected by the Due Process Clause of the Fifth Amendment. As such this right, the Court has held, can be regulated within the bounds of due process." In that respect, it differs from "[t]he constitutional right of interstate travel [which] is virtually unqualified." The difference means that we do not apply strict scrutiny to restrictions on international travel rights that do not implicate First Amendment concerns.

At an early point in the development of Supreme Court jurisprudence in this area, the Court seemed to suggest that restrictions upon travel must be looked upon with a jaded eye. However, it was then dealing with a law which touched on First Amendment concerns because it keyed on mere association. The Court has not been as troubled in cases which do not directly involve those concerns. Rather, as I see it, the Court has suggested that rational basis review should be applied.

When confronted with legislation which denied Supplemental Security Income benefits to people who were outside of the country, the Court commented that legislation which was said to infringe the right to international travel was "not to be judged by the same standard applied to laws that penalized the right to interstate travel." "It is enough," said the Court, "if the provision is rationally based." I recognize that because the SSI statute did not directly regulate passports, *Califano* is not directly applicable here, but it indicates that the Court does not apply the restrictive form of review advocated by Eunique. . . .

. . . In *Freedom to Travel Campaign v. Newcomb*, 82 F.3d 1431, 1439 (9th Cir. 1996), we held that, "given the lesser importance of . . . freedom to travel abroad, the Government need only advance a rational, or at most an important, reason for imposing the ban." The District of Columbia Circuit has read the Supreme Court tea leaves in the same way. As it has noted, "international travel is no more than an aspect of liberty that is subject to reasonable government regulation within the bounds of due process, whereas interstate travel is a fundamental right subject to a more exacting standard." *Hutchins v. Dist. of Columbia*, 188 F.3d 531, 537 (D.C. Cir. 1999). Because, as I see it, rational basis review is the proper standard, the statute is constitutional if there is a " 'reasonable fit' between governmental purpose . . . and the means chosen to advance that purpose." . . .

The statute easily passes that test. There can be no doubt that the failure of parents to support their children is recognized by our society as a serious offense against morals and welfare. It "is in violation of important social duties [and is] subversive of good order." It is the very kind of problem that the legislature can address.

Moreover, the economic problems caused by parents who fail to provide support for their children are both well known and widespread. They can be exacerbated when the non-paying parent is out of the state, as, of course, a parent traveling internationally must be. Indeed, even within the United States itself, the problem is serious. . . . [I]nternational travel by what our society often calls "deadbeat parents" presents even more difficulties because the United States cannot easily reach them once they have left the country.

. . .

All of this not only illustrates the rationality of Congress's goal, but also demonstrates its rational connection to the passport denial in question. Surely it makes sense to assure that those who do not pay their child support obligations remain within the country, where they can be reached by our processes in an at least relatively easy way. Notably, even when the Court iterated the constitutional right to travel in *Kent*, 357 U.S. at 127, it, without disapproval, took notice of a long-standing policy of denying passports to those who were "trying to escape the toils of the law" or "engaging in conduct which would violate the laws of the United States." A person who fails to pay child support may well attempt to escape the toils of the law by going abroad, and may even be violating the laws of the United States.

Moreover, if a parent, like Eunique, truly wishes to partake of the joys and benefits of international travel, § 652(k) does have the effect of focusing that person's mind on a more important concern—the need to support one's children first. It doubtless encourages parents to do their duty to family. In short, the statute passes rational basis review with flying colors. The Second Circuit, by the way, agrees with our conclusion.

Eunique has failed to live up to a most basic civic and even moral responsibility: the provision of support to her own children. Yet she has brought this action because she feels that her right to the pleasures and benefits of international travel has been improperly curtailed. Unfortunately for her, Congress has decreed that her duties to her children must take precedence over her international travel plans. It has ordered her priorities for her.

We hold that, without violating Eunique's Fifth Amendment freedom to travel internationally, Congress (and the State Department) can refuse to let her have a passport as long as she remains in substantial arrears on her child support obligations. . . .

.   .   .

■ KLEINFELD, CIRCUIT JUDGE, dissenting.

I respectfully dissent.

Judge Fernandez's opinion would hold that "rational basis review is the proper standard" for testing restrictions on a person's right to leave the United States. The right to leave one's country is too important to be subject to abridgment on so permissive a standard. The practical effect of consigning the right to travel to this lowly category of constitutional protection is to grant Congress plenary power to restrict it. . . .

. . . In this case, unlike those in which the Supreme Court has upheld restrictions on travel, the government has not offered a foreign policy or national security justification for the restriction, the government has not narrowly tailored the restriction to its purpose, and the apparent purpose of the restriction is to penalize past misconduct rather than to restrict travel as such. Thus the travel ban in this case is unconstitutional under controlling Supreme Court precedent. That Court can revise its approach if it so decides, but we can't.

The right to leave is among the most important of all human rights. . . . Magna Carta established that subjects had a right to leave the kingdom and return. The exceptions to the right to travel abroad in Magna Carta were for "those imprisoned or outlawed" and for "a short period in time of war," a public policy reason relating to national security.

. . . In Europe in the 1930s and 1940s, for many citizens emigration or not meant life or death.

Ms. Eunique got caught by part of the "deadbeat dads" law, and cannot get a passport, because she has not been paying her ex-husband the $175 per month per child in child support that she agreed to pay when she divorced him. She was then in law school and "had thought that all lawyers earned a lot of money," but "things have not turned out as I expected." She has earned negligible net income from her law practice. She says that a Peruvian–American friend has invited her to go to Peru to meet relatives who have a law firm there, and has suggested that her trip "could open up opportunities for the law firm to hire me when they need legal work in California." Ms. Eunique is plainly derelict in her duty to pay child support, and was properly denied a passport, if the statute and regulation are constitutional.

The Supreme Court has dealt with three kinds of interference with the right to travel abroad: bans on travel by specific classes of persons; bans on travel to specific countries; and residency requirements for government benefits that incidentally burden persons who travel abroad. The Court has held that incidental burdens on permitted travel need only have a rational basis, but has subjected restrictions on travel itself to much greater scrutiny. The Court has not formally stated the constitutional test, but its elements are clear. Travel restrictions must be justified by an important or compelling government interest and must be narrowly tailored to that end. Travel bans aimed at specific individuals or classes of individuals must be more narrowly tailored than bans aimed at specific countries.

The statute and regulation in this case impose a direct restriction on travel, rather than an incidental burden, and must meet a higher standard of scrutiny than rational basis. They do not restrict travel *to* a specific country or region for reasons of national security or foreign policy.... Instead, they restrict travel by a specific class of people *from* their own country. The Supreme Court has upheld such restrictions when a person's activities threaten national security or foreign policy, ... and has suggested that bans on travel by people "participating in illegal conduct, trying to escape the toils of the law, promoting passport frauds, or otherwise engaging in conduct which would violate the laws of the United States" would also be proper. Had Eunique been held in contempt and ordered to stay in the United States and purge it, she might be "trying to escape the toils of the law" by traveling abroad. But the statute and regulation in this case only require that she be a debtor, not a fugitive, and so far as the record shows, that is all she is.

. . .

... Judge Fernandez's opinion suggests that "it makes sense to assure that those who do not pay their child support obligations remain within the country." But the statute and regulation do not do require people to remain within the country. Someone fleeing the country to avoid collection attempts may flee to Mexico, Canada, and a number of other countries without a passport....

The passport ban is also overbroad because ... it does not take into account individual reasons that might support a passport. For example, travel abroad would, in some businesses (importing) and some lines of professional work, be necessary to earning the money with which the parent would be able to pay child support. And it does not allow for considerations that would bear on the risk of a person traveling abroad to evade child support obligations. Were it tailored to avoiding such flight, then posting of security, owning assets fixed in the United States, or having a job or business in the United States could be considered in determining whether to issue a passport, just as they would be in a bail application....

If Ms. Eunique were a murderer who had done her time, she could get a passport. But a person delinquent in paying child support is punished by denial of a passport. All debtors should pay their debts. Debts for child support have special moral force. But that does not justify tossing away a constitutional liberty so important that it has been a constant of Anglo–American law since Magna Carta, and of civilized thought since Plato. . . .

. . .

. . . [T]he right to leave one's country is a very important guarantor of freedom (and in some countries, of life). That right is too important to let the government take it away as punishment to advance a government policy just because it is important. . . .

. . . [T]he scheme upheld does not provide a carefully tailored means of enforcing important legal objectives, just an unrelated and ineffective burden on an arbitrarily selected subset of people who don't do what they're supposed to do. Our liberty matters too much for that.

State v. Talty

Supreme Court of Ohio, 2004.
103 Ohio St.3d 177, 814 N.E.2d 1201.

■ MOYER, C.J.

. . .

On February 27, 2002, the Medina County Grand Jury indicted Talty on two counts of nonsupport in violation of R.C. 2919.21(A)(2) or (B), a fifth-degree felony. After initially pleading not guilty, Talty changed his plea to no contest. The trial court accepted Talty' no-contest plea and found him guilty of both counts of nonsupport in violation of R.C. 2919.21(B).

Prior to sentencing, the trial court ordered each party to brief "whether or not the Court can lawfully order that, as a condition of his supervision by the Adult Probation Department, the defendant may not impregnate a woman while under supervision." The American Civil Liberties Union of Ohio Foundation filed a motion for leave to file an amicus brief, which the trial court granted. The parties and the ACLU thereafter filed briefs on the constitutionality of an antiprocreation sanction.

In a journal entry dated September 6, 2002, the trial court sentenced Talty to community control for five years under nonresidential sanctions in the form of the general supervision and control of the Adult Probation Department. As a condition of that community control, the trial court ordered Talty to "make all reasonable efforts to avoid conceiving another child." The court additionally stated, "What those efforts are are up to [Talty], that is not for me to say; I am not mandating what he does, only that he has to make reasonable efforts to do so."

. . .

. . . [T]he court of appeals held that the condition was constitutional and affirmed the judgment of the trial court.

. . .

This appeal requires us to consider the validity of a community-control sanction that ordered a defendant to "make all reasonable efforts to avoid conceiving another child" during a five-year probationary period. It is undisputed that the right to procreate is considered fundamental under the United States Constitution, *see Skinner v. Oklahoma* (1942), 316 U.S. 535, 541, and that the trial court's order in this case infringes that right. The issue on appeal is whether that infringement is permissible when imposed upon a probationer who has been convicted of nonsupport.

. . .

. . . [A] trial court's discretion in imposing probationary conditions is not limitless. . . .

. . . [C]ourts must "consider whether the condition (1) is reasonably related to rehabilitating the offender, (2) has some relationship to the crime of which the offender was convicted, and (3) relates to conduct which is criminal or reasonably related to future criminality and serves the statutory ends of probation." *Jones,* 49 Ohio St.3d at 53, 550 N.E.2d 469.

In addition . . . probation conditions "cannot be overly broad so as to unnecessarily impinge upon the probationer's liberty." . . .

. . .

Talty asserts that his community-control order is overbroad because there was no opportunity to have the antiprocreation condition lifted if he became current on his child-support payments. The government counters that other states have applied a test similar to *Jones* and upheld "virtually identical" conditions. Specifically, the state points to *State v. Oakley* (2001), 245 Wis.2d 447, 629 N.W.2d 200, in which the Wisconsin Supreme Court upheld an antiprocreation condition imposed upon a father who had been convicted of intentionally refusing to pay child support.

Significantly, however, the antiprocreation condition in *Oakley* included the stipulation that the court would terminate the condition if the defendant could prove to the court that he had supported his children. The Wisconsin Supreme Court considered this portion of the order critical, stating that "the condition is not overly broad because it does not eliminate Oakley's ability to exercise his constitutional right to procreate. He can satisfy the condition of probation by making efforts to support his children as required by law."

Unlike the facts in *Oakley,* the trial court in the instant case did not allow for suspending the procreation ban if Talty fulfilled his child-support obligations. Indeed, the trial court cited Talty's rehabilitation and the avoidance of future violations as the reasons for imposing the condition. In view of these objects, however, the antiprocreation condition is, by any objective measure, overbroad; it restricts Talty's right to procreate without providing a mechanism by which the prohibition can be lifted if the relevant conduct should change.

Although we do not determine whether a mechanism that allowed the antiprocreation condition to be lifted would have rendered the condition valid under *Jones,* such a mechanism would have been, at the very least, an easy alternative that would have better accommodated Talty's procreation rights at de minimis costs to the legitimate probationary interests of rehabilitation and avoiding future criminality. Nor can the condition be considered valid merely because the trial court *could* modify the order if Talty became current on his child-support payments. Our review of a condition of community control is limited, as it must be, to what the sentencing order says and not what a trial court might later modify it to say.

Further, we reject the argument that the antiprocreation order is valid because Talty could have been incarcerated but for the trial judge's "act of grace" and that, if incarcerated, he would have been denied conjugal visits. Although it is true that probationers, like incarcerated persons, do not enjoy the absolute liberty to which every citizen is entitled, the United States Supreme Court has rejected the "act of grace" doctrine. Thus, the fact that the state might have incarcerated a defendant does not, in itself, justify a lesser intrusion of his or her rights.

Our rejection of the "act of grace" theory is predicated on the undisputed proposition that infringements of constitutional rights must be tailored to specific government interests, and these interests may differ depending on whether the defendant is incarcerated or whether the defendant is sentenced to community control. Thus, a prisoner who is convicted of a crime wholly unrelated to procreation (say, burglary) may nonetheless be denied conjugal visits—arguably an infringement of the right to procreate—because, for example, the regulation is reasonably related to the legitimate government interest of maintaining the security of the prison. For the same crime (burglary), however, a probationer may not be denied the right to procreate on the basis of the same government interest—maintaining the security of a prison—because the probationer is not in prison. It follows, therefore, that a legitimate *penological* interest may be different from a legitimate *probationary* interest, thus rendering unsound the notion that the government may withhold from a probationer any right that it could withhold from a prisoner.

Finally, a decision that upheld a condition on an "act of grace" theory would be incompatible with the three-part test that we adopted in *Jones,* 49 Ohio St.3d at 53, 550 N.E.2d 469. For if a trial judge could deny to a probationer any right that a prison official could deny to an inmate, then a condition of community control need not be related to the rehabilitation of the defendant, the administration of justice, or the prevention of future criminality. Rather, the condition need only infringe the rights of a probationer as much as or less than a prison regulation may infringe those of an inmate. This proposition, if not implicitly rejected in *Jones,* was expressly rejected in *Gagnon,* 411 U.S. at 782, 93 S.Ct. 1756, 36 L.Ed.2d 656, fn. 4. Hence, in addition to the reality that the government has different interests in imposing community-control sanctions than it does in administering prisons—and thus probationers may retain certain liberties that inmates do not—we reject the "act of grace" doctrine as being contrary to our precedent.

For the foregoing reasons, we hold that the antiprocreation order is overbroad under *Jones,* 49 Ohio St.3d at 52, 550 N.E.2d 469, and vacate that portion of the trial court's sentencing order. Given our disposition, we need not address Talty's constitutional and remaining nonconstitutional challenges to the antiprocreation condition. Accordingly, we reverse the judgment of the court of appeals and remand the cause to the trial court for resentencing.

Judgment reversed.

■ PFEIFER, J., dissenting.

According to the trial court's journal entry dated September 6, 2002, defendant Sean Talty "is a 30–year–old male who has fathered six or seven children. (The evidence was unclear as to the exact number of children.) Two children were conceived during a marriage: Heather Talty and Shyann Talty. The Defendant owes child support arrears for those children in the amount of $28,044.79, as of June 21, 2002. He has one child, Courtney

Hunter, for whom he owes child support in the amount of $10,642.51 as of June 21, 2002.

"The Defendant also has two children by the woman with whom he is currently living and has two children by other women, one of whom lives in Butler County, and he possibly has a child living in Dayton, Ohio."

In a prior child-support action in domestic relations court, a journal entry stated that Talty had refused to provide any support for his children for more than two years. The court found that Talty "never paid" toward his child-support obligations even though he was aware of them. Based in part on these facts, the court found Talty to be in contempt of his support obligations, threatened him with incarceration, and stated that Talty was "disrespectful and antagonizing." On January 9, 2001, Talty was again found in contempt for failure to fulfill his support obligations, this time under a different support order.

In the criminal case now before us, the trial court found Talty guilty of two counts of felony nonsupport of dependents, in violation of R.C. 2929.21(B), and sentenced him, among other things, to "make all reasonable efforts to avoid conceiving another child." Talty asserts that that part of the sentencing violates his constitutional right to procreate. For the following reasons, I disagree, and I therefore dissent from the majority opinion.

The majority ultimately concludes that the trial judge's community-control condition is overbroad, based on this court's decision in *State v. Jones* (1990), 49 Ohio St.3d 51, 550 N.E.2d 469. I am not persuaded that *Jones*, which addressed conditions of probation pursuant to former R.C. 2951.02, applies to this case, which addresses conditions of community control pursuant to R.C. 2929.15. For one thing, R.C. 2929.15 was enacted several years after *Jones* was decided. Although community control is in large measure the functional equivalent of probation, the drafting of the two statutes is markedly different. I prefer to address R.C. 2929.15, the community-control statute, which must have been enacted for a reason, as separate from probation.

Pursuant to R.C. 2929.15(A)(1), a trial court may impose residential, nonresidential, and financial sanctions, and "may impose any other conditions of release under a community control sanction that the court considers appropriate." When imposing community-control sanctions for a felony, the trial court "shall be guided by the overriding purposes of felony sentencing," which are "to protect the public from future crime by the offender and others and to punish the offender." R.C. 2929.11(A). To achieve those purposes, the sentencing court "shall consider the need for incapacitating the offender, deterring the offender and others from future crime, [and] rehabilitating the offender." R.C. 2929.11(A). Sanctions imposed by trial courts must be "reasonably calculated to achieve the two overriding purposes of felony sentencing ..., commensurate with and not demeaning to the seriousness of the offender's conduct and its impact upon the victim, and consistent with sentences imposed for similar crimes committed by similar offenders." R.C. 2929.11(B). The General Assembly has thus charged trial courts with tempering the possibly draconian results of excessive focus on the overriding purposes of punishment and public protection by considering reasonableness, proportionality, and consistency.

Talty was ordered to "make all reasonable efforts" to avoid fathering another child. I consider this sanction appropriate, or reasonable, and proportionate, under the egregious circumstances of this case because the sanction relates directly to the crime of which Talty was convicted and is tailored to prevent even more instances of felony nonsupport. Given Talty's propensity to sire children, the antiprocreation condition must also be considered in the nature of punishment. These considerations are remarkably similar to the second and third parts of the *Jones* test, but as noted, I am applying the current statutory framework, not the *Jones* test. Part one of the *Jones* test is even mentioned in the current statutory framework, though as a mere consideration. In short, I believe that the sanction was imposed in compliance with the current statutory framework.

Next, I turn to the merits as addressed by the majority opinion. The majority opinion held that "the antiprocreation order is overbroad." As the majority clearly states, overbreadth in this context is not constitutional overbreadth, which can be invoked only when the Free Speech Clause of the First Amendment to the United States Constitution is implicated. Rather, overbreadth in this context is more in the nature of a reasonableness argument. *See* R.C. 2929.11(B) (sentence must be reasonably calculated to achieve the two overriding purposes of felony sentencing).

The majority states that the antiprocreation condition is overbroad because "it restricts Talty's right to procreate without providing a mechanism by which the prohibition can be lifted if the relevant conduct should change." To the contrary, R.C. 2929.15(C) provides that "[i]f an offender, for a significant period of time, fulfills the conditions of a sanction imposed pursuant to section 2929.16, 2929.17 or 2929.18 of the Revised Code in an exemplary manner, the court may reduce the period of time under the sanction or impose a less restrictive sanction." The community-control statute provides the very mechanism the majority criticizes the trial court for omitting. Further, the trial court ordered Talty to make only "reasonable efforts," stating, "What those efforts are are up to him, that is not for me to say; I am not mandating what he does, only that he has to make reasonable efforts to do so." The language of the antiprocreation condition is reasonable, not excessively rigid or absolute. I conclude that the antiprocreation condition is not overbroad.

Next, I turn to constitutional considerations. As the majority states, "the right to procreate is considered fundamental under the United States Constitution." . . . In Ohio, persons on parole enjoy only the " 'conditional liberty properly dependent on observance of special parole restrictions.' " The same is true of community control. Like federal courts that have reviewed similar issues, I do not believe that felons subject to community control are entitled to strict scrutiny even for the deprivation of fundamental rights. *See, also, State v. Oakley* (2001), 245 Wis.2d 447, 629 N.W.2d 200; and *Commonwealth v. Power* (1995), 420 Mass. 410, 650 N.E.2d 87. *But see People v. Pointer* (1984), 151 Cal.App.3d 1128, 199 Cal.Rptr. 357. I would apply a reasonableness test to community-control sanctions that interfere with fundamental rights, for the same reasons that the Wisconsin Supreme Court gave for applying a reasonableness test to probation: "[I]f probation conditions were subject to strict scrutiny, it would necessarily follow that the more severe punitive sanction of incarceration, which deprives an individual of the right to be free from physical restraint and infringes upon various other fundamental rights, likewise would be subject to strict scrutiny analysis. [The position in favor of strict scrutiny] is either illogical in that it requires strict scrutiny for conditions of probation that infringe upon fundamental rights but not for the more restrictive alternative of incarceration, or it is unworkable in that it demands the State meet the heavy burden of strict scrutiny whenever it is confronted with someone who has violated the law." (Citation omitted.) *Oakley*, 245 Wis.2d at 464, 629 N.W.2d 200, fn. 23.

Applying the words of the Wisconsin court to this case, I conclude that "in light of [Talty's] ongoing victimization of his ... children and extraordinarily troubling record manifesting his disregard for the law, this [antiprocreation] condition—imposed on a convicted felon facing the far more restrictive and punitive sanction of prison—is not overly broad and is reasonably related to [Talty's] rehabilitation. Simply put, because [Talty] was convicted of [nonsupport of a dependent]—a felony in [Ohio]—and could have been imprisoned ..., which would have eliminated his right to procreate altogether during [the term of his imprisonment], this [community control] condition, which infringes on his right to procreate during his term of [community control], is not invalid under these facts."

... In this case, Talty has had due process. He even had an extra opportunity to specifically address the antiprocreation condition. Talty is not being deprived of a constitutional right without due process; he is being deprived of a constitutional right because he is a convicted felon, because the crime for which he was convicted directly related to the constitutional right, because he exercised the constitutional right irresponsibly, and because the deprivation of the constitutional right will make it less likely for him to commit again the offense of which he was convicted.

One last comment: the likely outcome of the majority opinion is that the trial judge will add a provision enabling the sanction to be lifted and then Talty will appeal the new sanction. In the interests of judicial economy, the majority should address the merits at this stage, as I have done. I dissent.

NOTE

On remand, the conditions of Mr. Talty's probation came again before the trial court. This time, the judge held that an anti-procreation condition could not be imposed because Mr. Talty had in the meantime gotten married to his girlfriend and such a condition would violate his constitutional right to marriage. *See* Elizabeth M. Bux, *The Unwelcome Cohort: When the Sentencing Judge Invades Your Bedroom*, 85 NOTRE DAME L. REV. 745, 748 (2010).

Turner v. Rogers

Supreme Court of the United States, 2011.
___ U.S. ___, 131 S.Ct. 2507, 180 L.Ed.2d 452.

■ JUSTICE BREYER delivered the opinion of the Court.

South Carolina's Family Court enforces its child support orders by threatening with incarceration for civil contempt those who are (1) subject to a child support order, (2) able to comply with that order, but (3) fail to do so. We must decide whether the Fourteenth Amendment's Due Process Clause requires the State to provide counsel (at a civil contempt hearing) to an *indigent* person potentially faced with such incarceration. We conclude that where as here the custodial parent (entitled to receive the support) is unrepresented by counsel, the State need not provide counsel to the noncustodial parent (required to provide the support). But we attach an important caveat, namely, that the State must nonetheless have in place alternative procedures that assure a fundamentally fair determination of the critical incarceration-related question, whether the supporting parent is able to comply with the support order.

South Carolina family courts enforce their child support orders in part through civil contempt proceedings. Each month the family court clerk reviews outstanding child support orders, identifies those in which the supporting parent has fallen more than five days behind, and sends that parent an order to "show cause" why he should not be held in contempt.... At the hearing that parent may demonstrate that he is not in contempt, say, by showing that he is not able to make the required payments. If he fails to make the required showing, the court may hold him in civil contempt. And it may require that he be imprisoned unless and until he purges himself of contempt by making the required child support payments (but not for more than one year regardless).

In June 2003 a South Carolina family court entered an order, which (as amended) required petitioner, Michael Turner, to pay $51.73 per week to respondent, Rebecca Rogers, to help support their child. (Rogers' father, Larry Price, currently has custody of the child and is also a respondent before this Court.) Over the next three years, Turner repeatedly failed to pay the amount due and was held in contempt on five occasions. The first four times he was sentenced to 90 days' imprisonment, but he ultimately paid the amount due (twice without being jailed, twice after spending two or three days in custody). The fifth time he did not pay but completed a 6–month sentence.

After his release in 2006 Turner remained in arrears. On March 27, 2006, the clerk issued a new "show cause" order. And after an initial postponement due to Turner's failure to appear, Turner's civil contempt hearing took place on January 3, 2008. Turner and Rogers were present, each without representation by counsel.

The hearing was brief. The court clerk said that Turner was $5,728.76 behind in his payments. The judge asked Turner if there was "anything you want to say." Turner replied,

> "Well, when I first got out, I got back on dope. I done meth, smoked pot and everything else, and I paid a little bit here and there. And, when I finally did get to working, I broke my back, back in September. I filed for disability and SSI. And, I didn't get straightened out off the dope until I broke my back and laid up for two months. And, now I'm off the dope and everything. I just hope that you give me a chance. I don't know what else to say. I mean, I know I done wrong, and I should have been paying and helping her, and I'm sorry. I mean, dope had a hold to me."

The judge then said, "[o]kay," and asked Rogers if she had anything to say. After a brief discussion of federal benefits, the judge stated,

> "If there's nothing else, this will be the Order of the Court. I find the Defendant in willful contempt. I'm [going to] sentence him to twelve months in the Oconee County Detention Center. He may purge himself of the contempt and avoid the sentence by having a zero balance on or before his release. I've also placed a lien on any SSI or other benefits."

The judge added that Turner would not receive good-time or work credits, but "[i]f you've got a job, I'll make you eligible for work release." When Turner asked why he could not receive good-time or work credits, the judge said, "[b]ecause that's my ruling."

The court made no express finding concerning Turner's ability to pay his arrearage (though Turner's wife had voluntarily submitted a copy of Turner's application for disability benefits). Nor did the judge ask any followup [sic] questions or otherwise address the ability-to-pay issue. After the hearing, the judge filled out a prewritten form titled "Order for Contempt of Court," which included the statement:

> Defendant (was) (was not) gainfully employed and/or (had) (did not have) the ability to make these support payments when due.

But the judge left this statement as is without indicating whether Turner was able to make support payments.

While serving his 12–month sentence, Turner, with the help of *pro bono* counsel, appealed. He claimed that the Federal Constitution entitled him to counsel at his contempt hearing. The South Carolina Supreme Court decided Turner's appeal after he had completed his sentence. And it rejected his "right to counsel" claim. . . .

Turner sought certiorari. In light of differences among state courts (and some federal courts) on the applicability of a "right to counsel" in civil contempt proceedings enforcing child support orders, we granted the writ.

. . .

We must decide whether the Due Process Clause grants an indigent defendant, such as Turner, a right to state-appointed counsel at a civil contempt proceeding, which may lead to his incarceration. This Court's precedents provide no definitive answer to that question. This Court has long held that the Sixth Amendment grants an indigent defendant the right to state-appointed counsel in a *criminal* case. . . .

But the Sixth Amendment does not govern civil cases. Civil contempt differs from criminal contempt in that it seeks only to "coerc[e] the defendant to do" what a court had previously ordered him to do. A court may not impose punishment "in a civil contempt proceeding when it is clearly established that the alleged contemnor is unable to comply with the terms of the order." *Hicks v. Feiock,* 485 U.S. 624, 638, n. 9 (1988). And once a civil contemnor complies with the underlying order, he is purged of the contempt and is free. *Id.,* at 633 (he "carr[ies] the keys of [his] prison in [his] own pockets").

Consequently, the Court has made clear (in a case not involving the right to counsel) that, where civil contempt is at issue, the Fourteenth Amendment's Due Process Clause allows a State to provide fewer procedural protections than in a criminal case.

. . .

Civil contempt proceedings in child support cases constitute one part of a highly complex system designed to assure a noncustodial parent's regular payment of funds typically necessary for the support of his children. Often the family receives welfare support from a state-administered federal program, and the State then seeks reimbursement from the noncustodial parent. Other times the custodial parent (often the mother, but sometimes the father, a grandparent, or another person with custody) does not receive government benefits and is entitled to receive the support payments herself.

The Federal Government has created an elaborate procedural mechanism designed to help both the government and custodial parents to secure the payments to which they are entitled. These systems often rely upon wage withholding, expedited procedures for modifying and enforcing child support orders, and automated data processing. But sometimes States will use contempt orders to ensure that the custodial parent receives support payments or the government receives reimbursement. Although some experts have criticized this last-mentioned procedure, and the Federal Government believes that "the routine use of contempt for non-payment of child support is likely to be an ineffective strategy," the Government also tells us that "coercive enforcement remedies, such as contempt, have a role to play." South Carolina, which relies heavily on contempt proceedings, agrees that they are an important tool.

We here consider an indigent's right to paid counsel at such a contempt proceeding. It is a civil proceeding. And we consequently determine the "specific dictates of due process" by examining the "distinct factors" that this Court has previously found useful in deciding what specific safeguards the Constitution's Due Process Clause requires in order to make a civil proceeding fundamentally fair. As relevant here those factors include (1) the nature of "the private interest that will be affected," (2) the comparative "risk" of an "erroneous deprivation" of that interest with and without "additional or substitute procedural safeguards," and (3) the nature and magnitude of any countervailing interest in not providing "additional or substitute procedural requirement [s]."

The "private interest that will be affected" argues strongly for the right to counsel that Turner advocates. That interest consists of an indigent defendant's loss of personal liberty through imprisonment. The interest in securing that freedom, the freedom "from bodily restraint," lies "at the core of the liberty protected by the Due Process Clause." . . .

Given the importance of the interest at stake, it is obviously important to assure accurate decisionmaking in respect to the key "ability to pay" question. Moreover, the fact that ability to comply marks a dividing line between civil and criminal contempt, reinforces the need for accuracy. That is because an incorrect decision (wrongly classifying the contempt proceeding as civil) can increase the risk of wrongful incarceration by depriving the defendant of the procedural protections (including counsel) that the Constitution would demand in a criminal proceeding. And since 70% of child support arrears nationwide are owed by parents with either no reported income or income of $10,000 per year or less, the issue of ability to pay may arise fairly often. *See* E. Sorensen, L. Sousa, & S. Schaner, *Assessing Child Support Arrears in Nine Large States and the Nation* 22 (2007) (prepared by The Urban Institute), online at http://aspe.hhs.gov/hsp/07/assessing-CS-debt/report.pdf (as visited June 16, 2011, and available in Clerk of Court's case file).

. . .

. . . [W]e find three related considerations that, when taken together, argue strongly against the Due Process Clause requiring the State to provide indigents with counsel in every proceeding of the kind before us.

First, the critical question likely at issue in these cases concerns, as we have said, the defendant's ability to pay. That question is often closely related to the question of the defendant's indigence. But when the right procedures are in place, indigence can be a question that in many—but not all—cases is sufficiently straightforward to warrant determination *prior* to providing a defendant with counsel, even in a criminal case. Federal law, for example, requires a criminal defendant to provide information showing that he is indigent, and therefore entitled to state-funded counsel, *before* he can receive that assistance. *See* 18 U.S.C. § 3006A(b).

Second, sometimes, as here, the person opposing the defendant at the hearing is not the government represented by counsel but the custodial parent *un* represented [sic] by counsel. The custodial parent, perhaps a woman with custody of one or more children, may be relatively poor, unemployed, and unable to afford counsel. Yet she may have encouraged the court to enforce its order through contempt. She may be able to provide the court with significant information. And the proceeding is ultimately for her benefit.

A requirement that the State provide counsel to the noncustodial parent in these cases could create an asymmetry of representation that would "alter significantly the nature of the proceeding." Doing so could mean a degree of formality or delay that would unduly slow payment to those immediately in need. And, perhaps more important for present purposes, doing so could make the proceedings *less* fair overall, increasing the risk of a decision that would erroneously deprive a family of the support it is entitled to receive. The needs of such families play an important role in our analysis.

Third, as the Solicitor General points out, there is available a set of "substitute procedural safeguards," which, if employed together, can significantly reduce the risk of an erroneous deprivation of liberty. They can do so, moreover, without incurring some of the drawbacks inherent in recognizing an automatic right to counsel. Those safeguards include (1) notice to the defendant that his "ability to pay" is a critical issue in the contempt proceeding; (2) the use of a form (or the equivalent) to elicit relevant financial information; (3) an opportunity at the hearing for the defendant to respond to statements and questions about his financial status, (*e.g.*, those triggered by his responses on the form); and (4) an express finding by the court that the defendant has the ability to pay. In presenting these alternatives, the Government draws upon considerable experience in helping to manage statutorily mandated federal-state efforts to enforce child support orders. It does not claim that they are the only possible alternatives, and this Court's cases suggest, for example, that sometimes assistance other than purely legal assistance (here, say, that of a neutral social worker) can prove constitutionally sufficient. But the Government does claim that these alternatives can assure the "fundamental fairness" of the proceeding even where the State does not pay for counsel for an indigent defendant.

While recognizing the strength of Turner's arguments, we ultimately believe that the three considerations we have just discussed must carry the day. In our view, a categorical right to counsel in proceedings of the kind before us would carry with it disadvantages (in the form of unfairness and delay) that, in terms of ultimate fairness, would deprive it of significant superiority over the alternatives that we have mentioned. We consequently hold that the Due Process Clause does not *automatically* require the provision of counsel at civil contempt proceedings to an indigent individual who is subject to a child support order, even if that individual faces incarceration (for up to a year). In particular, that Clause does not require the provision of counsel where the opposing parent or other custodian (to whom support funds are owed) is not represented by counsel and the State provides alternative procedural safeguards equivalent to those we have mentioned (adequate notice of the importance of ability to pay, fair opportunity to present, and to dispute, relevant information, and court findings).

We do not address civil contempt proceedings where the underlying child support payment is owed to the State, for example, for reimbursement of welfare funds paid to the parent with custody. Those proceedings more closely resemble debt-collection proceedings. The government is likely to have counsel or some other competent representative. And this kind of proceeding is not before us. Neither do we address what due process requires in an unusually complex case where a defendant "can fairly be represented only by a trained advocate."

The record indicates that Turner received neither counsel nor the benefit of alternative procedures like those we have described. He did not receive clear notice that his ability to pay would constitute the critical question in his civil contempt proceeding. No one provided him with a form (or the equivalent) designed to elicit information about his financial circumstances. The court did not find that Turner was able to pay his arrearage, but instead left the relevant "finding" section of the contempt order blank. The court nonetheless found Turner in contempt and ordered him incarcerated. Under these circumstances Turner's incarceration violated the Due Process Clause.

We vacate the judgment of the South Carolina Supreme Court and remand the case for further proceedings not inconsistent with this opinion.

It is so ordered.

■ JUSTICE THOMAS, with whom JUSTICE SCALIA joins, and with whom THE CHIEF JUSTICE and JUSTICE ALITO join [in part], dissenting.

. . .

The majority agrees that the Constitution does not entitle Turner to appointed counsel. But at the invitation of the Federal Government as *amicus curiae,* the majority holds that his contempt hearing violated the Due Process Clause for an entirely different reason, which the parties have never raised: The family court's procedures "were inadequate to ensure an accurate determination of [Turner's] present ability to pay." Brief for United States as *Amicus Curiae* 19 (capitalization and boldface type deleted); *see ante,* at 2519–2520. I would not reach this issue.

. . .

The majority errs in moving beyond the question that was litigated below, decided by the state courts, petitioned to this Court, and argued by the parties here, to resolve a question raised exclusively in the Federal Government's *amicus* brief. In some cases, the Court properly affirms a lower court's judgment on an alternative ground or accepts the persuasive argument of an *amicus* on a question that the parties have raised. But it transforms a case entirely to vacate a state court's judgment based on an alternative constitutional ground advanced only by an *amicus* and outside the question on which the petitioner sought (and this Court granted) review.

. . .

For the reasons explained ..., I would not engage in the majority's balancing analysis. But there is yet another reason not to undertake the *Mathews v. Eldridge* balancing test here. That test weighs an individual's interest against that of the Government. It does not account for the interests of the child and custodial parent, who is usually the child's mother. But their interests are the very reason for the child support obligation and the civil contempt proceedings that enforce it.

When fathers fail in their duty to pay child support, children suffer....

The interests of children and mothers who depend on child support are notoriously difficult to protect....

That some fathers subject to a child support agreement report little or no income "does not mean they do not have the ability to pay any child support." Rather, many "deadbeat dads" "opt to work in the underground economy" to "shield their earnings from child support enforcement efforts." To avoid attempts to garnish their wages or otherwise enforce the support obligation, "deadbeats" quit their jobs, jump from job to job, become self-employed, work under the table, or engage in illegal activity.

Because of the difficulties in collecting payment through traditional enforcement mechanisms, many States also use civil contempt proceedings to coerce "deadbeats" into paying what they owe. The States that use civil contempt with the threat of detention find it a "highly effective" tool for collecting child support when nothing else works. For example, Virginia, which uses civil contempt as "a last resort," reports that in 2010 "deadbeats" paid approximately $13 million "either before a court hearing to avoid a contempt finding or after a court hearing to purge the contempt finding." Other States confirm that the mere threat of imprisonment is often quite effective because most contemners "will pay . . . rather than go to jail."

This case illustrates the point. After the family court imposed Turner's weekly support obligation in June 2003, he made no payments until the court held him in contempt three months later, whereupon he paid over $1,000 to avoid confinement. Three more times, Turner refused to pay until the family court held him in contempt—then paid in short order.

Although I think that the majority's analytical framework does not account for the interests that children and mothers have in effective and flexible methods to secure payment, I do not pass on the wisdom of the majority's preferred procedures. Nor do I address the wisdom of the State's decision to use certain methods of enforcement. Whether "deadbeat dads" should be threatened with incarceration is a policy judgment for state and federal lawmakers, as is the entire question of government involvement in the area of child support. This and other repercussions of the shift away from the nuclear family are ultimately the business of the policymaking branches.

. . .

I would affirm the judgment of the South Carolina Supreme Court because the Due Process Clause does not provide a right to appointed counsel in civil contempt hearings that may lead to incarceration. As that is the only issue properly before the Court, I respectfully dissent.

NOTES

1. The trial judge's nonchalant approach to the question of Mr. Turner's ability to pay raises the question, as the Supreme Court noted, of the legitimacy of civil contempt as an enforcement mechanism against the very poor. For an argument that the use of civil contempt has created a system of unjustified incarcerations of the indigent, *see* Elizabeth G. Patterson, *Civil Contempt and the Indigent Child Support Obligor: The Silent Return of Debtor's Prison*, 18 CORNELL J.L. & PUB. POL'Y 95 (2008). In addition, there is some indication that the current system may be creating a vicious circle of incarceration, inability to pay, and re-incarceration. According to one scholar, the ease with which courts establish child support arrears, in combination with the policy of imputing income to parents, awarding support through default proceedings, and a high yearly interest rate, has created a situation in which indigent parents are slammed with thousands of dollars in child support with very little concern for their actual ability to pay. *See* Ann Cammett, *Deadbeats, Deadbrokes, and*

Prisoners, 18 GEO. J. ON POVERTY L. & POL'Y 127, 141–45 (2011). In the case of incarcerated parents, a large child support order is likely to lead them into the underground economy after release, in an effort either to earn more than minimum wage, or to avoid formal garnishment mechanisms. *Id*. at 145. Either way, child support payment becomes less likely, while the chances for re-incarceration increase. *Id*.

2.   Some states have adopted a naming and shaming approach to "deadbeat parents." The website of the Virginia Department of Social Services, for example, provides photographs and information on some of the most wanted "child support evaders." Against the background of a sketch of three peaceful houses the following words flash by: "Think you know what a child support evader looks like? They could be the person next door." Pictures of the evaders then appear along with their name, child support owed, last known address, and occupation. The word "FOUND" is written in red across some of the pictures. *See Child Support Most Wanted*, VA. DEP'T OF SOCIAL SERVS., http://www.dss.virginia.gov/family/dcse/2008_most_wanted/index.html (last visited Sept. 1, 2011).

CHAPTER 10

FAMILY LAW JURISDICTION, RECOGNITION, AND CHOICE OF LAW

Questions of jurisdiction have long posed challenges for family lawyers. For one thing, the rules of jurisdiction that apply to divorce are different from those that govern alimony or child custody. Because there is no national law of marriage and divorce in the United States, there are also often recognition and choice-of-law problems to resolve as family members move to different states. The choice-of-law issues have become even more complex now that a growing number of families have members who live in other countries, not just other states.

Traditional choice-of-law principles do not apply in divorce cases. In adjudicating a tort action involving an accident that occurred in New York and parties who were New York residents when the accident occurred, for example, a Nevada court would apply New York law. But in adjudicating a divorce involving a couple who had lived their entire married life in New York, a Nevada court would apply Nevada divorce law. Jurisdictional principles, in other words, sometimes do the work of traditional choice-of-law principles in divorce litigation. Jurisdiction, for this reason, is a frequent point of contention.

The jurisdictional complexity of family law is exacerbated by the fact that the federal courts have created a domestic relations exception to federal diversity jurisdiction; the exception prevents litigants from using federal courts to resolve conflicting family decisions from courts in different states. A spate of recent federal statutes has brought some relief to these jurisdictional and choice-of-law problems, but the statutes also pose new questions of their own.

A. RECOGNITION OF MARRIAGE

Wilson v. Ake

United States District Court for the Middle District of Florida, 2005.
354 F.Supp.2d 1298.

■ MOODY, J.

Plaintiffs Nancy Wilson and Paula Schoenwether allege that they are a lesbian couple who reside together in the Middle District of Florida. According to the Complaint, Plaintiffs were legally married in the State of Massachusetts and possess a valid marriage license from that State. Plaintiffs allege that they personally presented their Massachusetts marriage license to a Deputy Clerk at the Clerk of the Circuit Court's Office in Hillsborough County, Florida, asking for "acceptance of the valid and legal Massachusetts marriage license." Plaintiffs allege that "their demand was refused by Defendant Ake, whose Deputy Clerk stated that according to Federal and Florida law, the Clerk is not allowed to recognize, for marriage purposes, the Massachusetts marriage license, because Federal and Florida law prohibit such recognition."

Plaintiffs have filed a Complaint for Declaratory Judgment asking this Court to declare the Federal Defense of Marriage Act ("DOMA"), 1 U.S.C. § 7; 28 U.S.C. § 1738C,[1] and Florida Statutes § 741.212,[2] unconstitutional and to enjoin their enforcement. Plaintiffs have sued, in their official capacities, Richard L. Ake, Clerk of the Circuit Court in Hillsborough County, Florida, and United States Attorney General John Ashcroft.

Plaintiffs allege that the two statutes violate the Full Faith and Credit Clause, the Due Process clause of the Fourteenth Amendment, the Equal Protection Clause of the Fourteenth Amendment, the Privileges and Immunities Clause, and the Commerce Clause of the United States Constitution.

Plaintiffs assert that Florida is required to recognize Plaintiffs' valid Massachusetts marriage license because DOMA exceeds Congress' power under the Full Faith and Credit Clause. Plaintiffs also argue that twelve United States Supreme Court cases (which Plaintiffs label "The Dynamite Dozen"), beginning with *Brown v. Board of Education*, 347 U.S. 483 (1954), and ending with *Lawrence v. Texas*, 539 U.S. 558 (2003), demonstrate a recent trend by the United States Supreme Court to expand "the fundamental liberty of personal autonomy in connection with one's intimate affairs and family relations." Plaintiffs urge this Court to expand on "The Dynamite Dozen" by finding that the right to enter into a same-sex marriage is protected by the Constitution.

---

1. The Defense of Marriage Act ("DOMA") provides:

[Section 2] No State, territory, or possession of the United States, or Indian tribe, shall be required to give effect to any public act, record, or judicial proceeding of any other State, territory, possession, or tribe respecting a relationship between persons of the same sex that is treated as a marriage under the laws of such other State, territory, possession, or tribe, or a right or claim arising from such relationship.

28 U.S.C. § 1738C.

. . .

[Section 3] In determining the meaning of any Act of Congress, or of any ruling, regulation, or interpretation of the various administrative bureaus and agencies of the United States, the word "marriage" means only a legal union between one man and one woman as husband and wife, and the word "spouse" refers only to a person of the opposite sex who is a husband or a wife.

1 U.S.C. § 7.

2. [FLA. STAT. § 741.212], Marriages between persons of the same sex, provides:

(1) Marriages between persons of the same sex entered into in any jurisdiction, whether within or outside the State of Florida, the United States, or any other jurisdiction, either domestic or foreign, or any other place or location, or relationships between persons of the same sex which are treated as marriages in any jurisdiction, whether within or outside the State of Florida, the United States, or any other jurisdiction, either domestic or foreign, or any other place or location, are not recognized for any purpose in this state.

(2) The state, its agencies, and its political subdivisions may not give effect to any public act, record, or judicial proceeding of any state, territory, possession, or tribe of the United States or of any other jurisdiction, either domestic or foreign, or any other place or location respecting either a marriage or relationship not recognized under subsection (1) or a claim arising from such a marriage or relationship.

(3) For purposes of interpreting any state statute or rule, the term "marriage" means only a legal union between one man and one woman as husband and wife, and the term "spouse" applies only to a member of such a union.

Defendant Ashcroft has moved to dismiss Plaintiffs' Complaint ... on the grounds that the Complaint fails to state a claim upon which relief can be granted....

. . .

Plaintiffs' Complaint asserts that DOMA conflicts with the Constitution's Full Faith and Credit Clause. Article IV, Section I of the Constitution provides:

> Full Faith and Credit shall be given in each State to the public Acts, Records, and Judicial Proceedings of every other State; And the Congress may by general Laws prescribe the Manner in which such Acts, Records and Proceedings shall be proved, and the Effect thereof.

Plaintiffs argue that "[o]nce Massachusetts sanctioned legal same-gender marriage, all other states should be constitutionally required to uphold the validity of the marriage." Plaintiffs believe that the differences in individuals' rights to enter into same-sex marriages among the States, such as Florida and Massachusetts, is exactly what the Full Faith and Credit Clause prohibits. They also assert that DOMA is beyond the scope of Congress' legislative power under the Full Faith and Credit Clause because Congress may only regulate what effect a law may have, it may not dictate that the law has no effect at all.

This Court disagrees with Plaintiff's interpretation of the Full Faith and Credit Clause. Congress' actions in adopting DOMA are exactly what the Framers envisioned when they created the Full Faith and Credit Clause. DOMA is an example of Congress exercising its powers under the Full Faith and Credit Clause to determine the effect that "any public act, record, or judicial proceeding of any other State, territory, possession, or tribe respecting a relationship between persons of the same sex that is treated as a marriage" has on the other States. Congress' actions are an appropriate exercise of its power to regulate conflicts between the laws of two different States, in this case, conflicts over the validity of same-sex marriages.

Adopting Plaintiffs' rigid and literal interpretation of the Full Faith and Credit would create a license for a single State to create national policy. The Supreme Court has clearly established that "the Full Faith and Credit Clause does not require a State to apply another State's law in violation of its own legitimate public policy." [*Nevada v. Hall*, 440 U.S. 410, 422, 423–24 (1979) ("Full Faith and Credit does not ... enable one state to legislate for the other or to project its laws across state lines so as to preclude the other from prescribing for itself the legal consequences of acts within it.")] Florida is not required to recognize or apply Massachusetts' same-sex marriage law because it clearly conflicts with Florida's legitimate public policy of opposing same-sex marriage.

The United States argues that this Court is bound by the United States Supreme Court's decision in *Baker v. Nelson*, 191 N.W.2d 185 (Minn. 1971). In *Baker v. Nelson*, two adult males' application for a marriage license was denied by the Clerk of the Hennepin County District Court because the petitioners were of the same sex. The plaintiffs, following the quashing of a writ of mandamus directing the clerk to issue a marriage license, appealed to the Minnesota Supreme Court. Plaintiffs argued that Minnesota Statute § 517.08, which did not authorize marriage between persons of the same sex, violated the First, Eighth, Ninth and Fourteenth Amendments of the United States Constitution. The Minnesota Supreme Court rejected plaintiffs' assertion that "the right to marry without regard to the sex of the parties is a fundamental right of all persons" and held that § 517.08 did not violate the Due Process Clause or Equal Protection Clause.

The plaintiffs then appealed the Minnesota Supreme Court's ruling to the United States Supreme Court pursuant to 28 U.S.C. § 1257(2).[7] Under 28 U.S.C. § 1257(2), the Supreme Court had no discretion to refuse to adjudicate the case on its merits. *Hicks v. Miranda*, 422 U.S. 332, 344 (1975). The Supreme Court dismissed the appeal "for want of a substantial federal question."

Plaintiffs assert that *Baker v. Nelson* is not binding upon this Court because the Supreme Court did not issue a written opinion and because the case was decided thirty-two years ago, before the "current civil rights revolution." This Court disagrees. A dismissal for lack of a substantial federal question constitutes an adjudication on the merits that is binding on lower federal courts. As Justice White noted, the Court was "not obligated to grant the case plenary consideration . . . but [the Court was] required to deal with its merits."

Although *Baker v. Nelson* is over thirty years old, the decision addressed the same issues presented in this action and this Court is bound to follow the Supreme Court's decision.

The Supreme Court's holding in *Lawrence* does not alter the dispositive effect of *Baker*. The Supreme Court has not explicitly or implicitly overturned its holding in *Baker* or provided the lower courts, including this Court, with any reason to believe that the holding is invalid today. Accordingly, *Baker v. Nelson* is binding precedent upon this Court and Plaintiffs' case against Attorney General Ashcroft must be dismissed.

Recent Eleventh Circuit precedent also constrains this Court to rule contrary to Plaintiffs' position. Plaintiffs argue that their right to marry someone of the same sex is a fundamental right that is guaranteed by the Fourteenth Amendment's Due Process Clause. . . .

The Supreme Court has defined fundamental rights as those liberties that are "implicit in the concept of ordered liberty, such that neither liberty nor justice would exist if they were sacrificed." The Court observed that the Due Process clause "specially protects those fundamental rights and liberties which are, objectively, 'deeply rooted in this Nation's history and tradition.' "

Although the Supreme Court has held that marriage is a fundamental right, no federal court has recognized that this right includes the right to marry a person of the same sex. Plaintiffs urge this Court to interpret the Supreme Court's decision in *Lawrence v. Texas* as establishing a fundamental right to private sexual intimacy. Plaintiffs argue that this Court should expand the fundamental right recognized in *Lawrence* to include same-sex marriages.

· · ·

---

7. At the time, 28 U.S.C. § 1257(2) provided:

Final judgments or decrees rendered by the highest court of a State in which a decision could be had, may be reviewed by the Supreme Court as follows:

(2) by appeal, where is drawn in question the validity of a statute of any state on the ground of its being repugnant to the Constitution, treaties or laws of the United States, and the decision is in favor of its validity.

This appeal as of right was eliminated by the Supreme Court Case Selections Act (Public Law 100–352), which became law on June 27, 1988.

But the Supreme Court's decision in *Lawrence* cannot be interpreted as creating a fundamental right to same-sex marriage. First, the Eleventh Circuit disagrees with Plaintiffs' assertion that *Lawrence* created a fundamental right in private sexual intimacy and this Court must follow the holdings of the Eleventh Circuit. *See Lofton v. Sec'y of Dept. of Children and Family Servs.*, 358 F.3d 804, 817 (11th Cir.) ("We conclude that it is a strained and ultimately incorrect reading of *Lawrence* to interpret it to announce a new fundamental right."); *Williams v. Attorney Gen. of Ala.*, 378 F.3d 1232, 1238 (11th Cir. 2004). The Court in *Lawrence* did not find private sexual conduct between consenting adults to be a fundamental right. *Lawrence*, 539 U.S. at 586 (Scalia, J., dissenting) ("nowhere does the Court's opinion declare that homosexual sodomy is a 'fundamental right' under the Due Process Clause; nor does it subject the Texas law to the standard of review that would be appropriate (strict scrutiny) if homosexual sodomy *were* a 'fundamental right.' "). Rather, the Court determined that the Texas statute failed under the rational basis analysis.

Second, the majority in *Lawrence* was explicitly clear that its holding did not extend to the issue of same-sex marriage, stating that the case "does not involve whether the government must give formal recognition to any relationship that homosexual persons seek to enter". It is disingenuous to argue that the Supreme Court's precise language in *Lawrence* established a fundamental right to enter into a same-sex marriage.

Moreover, this Court is not inclined to elevate the ability to marry someone of the same sex to a fundamental right. Although the Court recognizes the importance of a heterosexual or homosexual individual's choice of a partner, not all important decisions are protected fundamental rights. . . .

The Eleventh Circuit has also noted that once a right is elevated to a fundamental right, it is "effectively removed from the hands of the people and placed into the guardianship of unelected judges. We are particularly mindful of this fact in the delicate area of morals legislation." *Williams*[v. AG], 378 F.3d [1232,]1250 [(11th Cir. 2004)]. "Of course, the Court may in due course expand *Lawrence's* precedent . . . but for us preemptively to take that step would exceed our mandate as a lower court." *Williams*, 378 F.3d at 1238; *see also Lofton*, 358 F.3d at 827 (the "legislature is the proper forum for this debate, and we do not sit as a superlegislature 'to award by judicial decree what was not achievable by political consensus.' ") (quoting *Thomasson v. Perry*, 80 F.3d 915, 923 (4th Cir. 1996)). Therefore, the Court finds that the right to marry a person of the same sex is not a fundamental right under the Constitution.

Plaintiffs also argue that this Court should apply strict scrutiny in determining the constitutionality of DOMA because it violates the Equal Protection Clause of the Fourteenth Amendment.[11] The Eleventh Circuit has held that homosexuality is not a suspect class that would require subjecting DOMA to strict scrutiny under the Equal Protection Clause of the Fourteenth Amendment or the equal protection component of the Fifth Amendment's Due Process Clause. Moreover, DOMA does not discriminate on the basis of sex because it treats women and men equally. Therefore this Court

---

11. The Court again notes that the Fourteenth Amendment only applies to the states and that Plaintiffs' equal protection claims should have been brought pursuant to the equal protection component of the Due Process Clause of the Fifth Amendment.

must apply rational basis review to its equal protection analysis of the constitutionality of DOMA.

. . .

The United States asserts that DOMA is rationally related to two legitimate governmental interests. First, the government argues that DOMA fosters the development of relationships that are optimal for procreation, thereby encouraging the "stable generational continuity of the United States." DOMA allegedly furthers this interest by permitting the states to deny recognition to same-sex marriages performed elsewhere and by adopting the traditional definition of marriage for purposes of federal statutes. Second, DOMA "encourage[s] the creation of stable relationships that facilitate the rearing of children by both of their biological parents." The government argues that these stable relationships encourage the creation of stable families that are well suited to nurturing and raising children.

Plaintiffs offer little to rebut the government's argument that DOMA is rationally related to the government's proffered legitimate interests. Rather, Plaintiffs repeatedly urge the Court to apply the more rigid strict scrutiny analysis.

Although this Court does not express an opinion on the validity of the government's proffered legitimate interests, it is bound by the Eleventh Circuit's holding that encouraging the raising of children in homes consisting of a married mother and father is a legitimate state interest. DOMA is rationally related to this interest. Moreover, Plaintiffs have failed to satisfy their burden of establishing that DOMA fails rational basis review. *See Lofton*, 358 F.3d at 818–19.[12] Accordingly, the United States' motion to dismiss is granted.

NOTES

1. *Wilson v. Ake* involved Section 2 of DOMA. On February 23, 2011, Attorney General Holder wrote a letter to the leaders of Congress explaining why the administration considers Section 3 of DOMA to be unconstitutional. The letter is summarized at page 120, *supra*. Do the arguments in the Holder letter apply to Section 2 as well?

2. For additional analysis of whether DOMA is constitutional, *see generally* Robert C. Farrell, *The Two Versions of Rational Basis Review and Same–Sex Relationships*, 86 WASH. L. REV. 281, 324–29 (2011) (describing two bases of constitutional review of DOMA under Equal Protection); Mark P. Strasser, *Defending Marriage in Light of the Moreno– Cleburne–Romer–Lawrence Jurisprudence: Why DOMA Cannot Pass Muster after Lawrence*, 38 CREIGHTON L. REV. 421 (2005) (declaring both sections of DOMA unconstitutional on "several grounds, which range from federalism concerns to equal protection"); Andrew Koppelman, *Dumb and DOMA: Why the Defense of Marriage Act Is Unconstitutional*, 83 IOWA L. REV. 1 (1997) (asserting that both provisions of DOMA are "facially invalid"). Although most scholars have argued that DOMA is unconstitutional, Rosen defends it as an instance of "congressional participation in the process of defining our country's constitutional culture." Mark D. Rosen, *Why the Defense of Marriage Act Is Not (Yet?) Unconstitutional: Lawrence, Full Faith and Credit, and the Many Societal Actors that Determine What the Constitution Requires*, 90 MINN. L. REV. 915, 920 (2006).

---

12. Moreover, despite Justice Scalia's fears in *Lawrence*, the Eleventh Circuit has recently reiterated that the "furtherance of public morality [is] a legitimate state interest." *Williams*, 378 F.3d at 1238 n.8. "One would expect the Supreme Court to be manifestly more specific and articulate than it was in *Lawrence* if now such a traditional and significant jurisprudential principal has been jettisoned wholesale (with all due respect to Justice Scalia's ominous dissent notwithstanding)." *Id.*

B.   DIVORCE JURISDICTION

Sosna v. Iowa

Supreme Court of the United States, 1975.
419 U.S. 393, 95 S.Ct. 553, 42 L.Ed.2d 532.

[The opinion is printed at page 752 *supra*.]

NOTE

With the adoption of no-fault divorce grounds in all fifty states, the subject of recognition of other states' divorce decrees has become less important. The matter was so contentious in earlier years that the Supreme Court issued two rulings on one divorce: *Williams v. North Carolina*, 317 U.S. 287 (1942) (*Williams I*), and *Williams v. North Carolina*, 325 U.S. 226 (1945) (*Williams II*). *Williams I* held that the Full Faith and Credit Clause requires all states to give full faith and credit to *ex parte* divorce decrees. *Williams II* clarified that states may withhold full faith and credit if they determine that the spouse who obtained the foreign divorce was not properly domiciled in the other state. The cases involved Mr. Williams, a storekeeper in Granite Falls, North Carolina (population 2,147), who eloped with the wife of his clerk. Both showed up in Las Vegas, checked into a motel and six weeks later filed for divorce. As soon as the last divorce was granted, they were married and returned to North Carolina, where they set up housekeeping in Pineola (population 306) "where they were very well spoken of by the witness who testified as to their living together". *See* Lawrence Powell, *And Repent at Leisure*, 58 HARV. L. REV. 930 (1945). Williams and his new wife were later tried and convicted of bigamous cohabitation by North Carolina and sentenced to a term of years in prison. Their conviction was overturned by the Supreme Court in *Williams I*. Undaunted, North Carolina retried Mr. and Mrs. Williams. This time the jury was charged that if they had gone to Nevada "simply and solely for the purpose of obtaining" a divorce, then they had not acquired new domiciles in Nevada. In *Williams II*, their convictions were upheld.

During the five years between the Nevada divorces and the second Supreme Court decision, one of the stay-at-home spouses died and the other obtained a North Carolina divorce. Thus when the Supreme Court affirmed their convictions for bigamous cohabitation in *Williams II*, neither was married to their first spouse. After the Supreme Court decision in *Williams II*, North Carolina permitted the Williams to undergo another marriage ceremony and paroled both immediately thereafter. Neither served a single day in jail. *See* Powell, *supra*.

Ankenbrandt v. Richards

Supreme Court of the United States, 1992.
504 U.S. 689, 112 S.Ct. 2206, 119 L.Ed.2d 468.

■ JUSTICE WHITE delivered the opinion of the Court.

This case presents the issue whether the federal courts have jurisdiction or should abstain in a case involving alleged torts committed by the former husband of petitioner and his female companion against petitioner's children, when the sole basis for federal jurisdiction is the diversity-of-citizenship provision of 28 U.S.C. § 1332.

Petitioner Carol Ankenbrandt, a citizen of Missouri, brought this lawsuit on September 26, 1989, on behalf of her daughters L. R. and S. R. against respondents Jon A. Richards and Debra Kesler, citizens of Louisiana, in the

United States District Court for the Eastern District of Louisiana. Alleging federal jurisdiction based on the diversity-of-citizenship provision of § 1332, Ankenbrandt's complaint sought monetary damages for alleged sexual and physical abuse of the children committed by Richards and Kesler. Richards is the divorced father of the children and Kesler his female companion. On December 10, 1990, the District Court granted respondents' motion to dismiss this lawsuit. Citing *In re Burrus*, 136 U.S. 586, 593–94 (1890), for the proposition that "the whole subject of the domestic relations of husband and wife, parent and child, belongs to the laws of the States and not to the laws of the United States," the court concluded that this case fell within what has become known as the "domestic relations" exception to diversity jurisdiction, and that it lacked jurisdiction over the case. . . .

. . .

The domestic relations exception upon which the courts below relied to decline jurisdiction has been invoked often by the lower federal courts. The seeming authority for doing so originally stemmed from the announcement in *Barber v. Barber*, 62 U.S. 582 (1859), that the federal courts have no jurisdiction over suits for divorce or the allowance of alimony. In that case, the Court heard a suit in equity brought by a wife (by her next friend) in Federal District Court pursuant to diversity jurisdiction against her former husband. She sought to enforce a decree from a New York state court, which had granted a divorce and awarded her alimony. The former husband thereupon moved to Wisconsin to place himself beyond the New York courts' jurisdiction so that the divorce decree there could not be enforced against him; he then sued for divorce in a Wisconsin court, representing to that court that his wife had abandoned him and failing to disclose the existence of the New York decree. In a suit brought by the former wife in Wisconsin Federal District Court, the former husband alleged that the court lacked jurisdiction. The court accepted jurisdiction and gave judgment for the divorced wife.

On appeal, it was argued that the District Court lacked jurisdiction on two grounds: first, that there was no diversity of citizenship because although divorced, the wife's citizenship necessarily remained that of her former husband; and second, that the whole subject of divorce and alimony, including a suit to enforce an alimony decree, was exclusively ecclesiastical at the time of the adoption of the Constitution and that the Constitution therefore placed the whole subject of divorce and alimony beyond the jurisdiction of the United States courts. Over the dissent of three Justices, the Court rejected both arguments. After an exhaustive survey of the authorities, the Court concluded that a divorced wife could acquire a citizenship separate from that of her former husband and that a suit to enforce an alimony decree rested within the federal courts' equity jurisdiction. The Court reached these conclusions after summarily dismissing the former husband's contention that the case involved a subject matter outside the federal courts' jurisdiction. In so stating, however, the Court also announced the following limitation on federal jurisdiction:

> Our first remark is—and we wish it to be remembered—that this is not a suit asking the court for the allowance of alimony. That has been done by a court of competent jurisdiction. The court in Wisconsin was asked to interfere to prevent that decree from being defeated by fraud.

> We disclaim altogether any jurisdiction in the courts of the United States upon the subject of divorce, or for the allowance of alimony,

either as an original proceeding in chancery or as an incident to divorce *a vinculo*, or to one from bed and board.

Barber, supra, at 584.

. . .

The statements disclaiming jurisdiction over divorce and alimony decree suits, though technically dicta, formed the basis for excluding "domestic relations" cases from the jurisdiction of the lower federal courts, a jurisdictional limitation those courts have recognized ever since. The *Barber* Court, however, cited no authority and did not discuss the foundation for its announcement. Since that time, the Court has dealt only occasionally with the domestic relations limitation on federal-court jurisdiction, and it has never addressed the basis for such a limitation. Because we are unwilling to cast aside an understood rule that has been recognized for nearly a century and a half, we feel compelled to explain why we will continue to recognize this limitation on federal jurisdiction.

[A]n examination of Article III, *Barber* itself, and our cases since *Barber* makes clear that the Constitution does not exclude domestic relations cases from the jurisdiction otherwise granted by statute to the federal courts.

Article III, § 2, of the Constitution provides in pertinent part:

The judicial Power shall extend to all Cases, in Law and Equity, arising under this Constitution, the Laws of the United States, and Treaties made, or which shall be made, under their Authority;—to all Cases affecting Ambassadors, other public Ministers and Consuls;—to all Cases of admiralty and maritime Jurisdiction;—to Controversies to which the United States shall be a Party;—to Controversies between two or more States;—between a State and Citizens of another State;—between Citizens of different States;—between Citizens of the same State claiming Land under Grants of different States, and between a State, or the Citizens thereof, and foreign States, Citizens or Subjects.

. . .

That Article III, § 2, does not mandate the exclusion of domestic relations cases from federal-court jurisdiction, however, does not mean that such courts necessarily must retain and exercise jurisdiction over such cases. Other constitutional provisions explain why this is so. Article I, § 8, cl. 9, for example, authorizes Congress "to constitute Tribunals inferior to the supreme Court" and Article III, § 1, states that "the judicial Power of the United States, shall be vested in one supreme Court, and in such inferior Courts as the Congress may from time to time ordain and establish." The Court's cases state the rule that "if inferior federal courts were created, [Congress was not] required to invest them with all the jurisdiction it was authorized to bestow under Art. III." *Palmore v. United States*, 411 U.S. 389, 401 (1973).

This position has held constant since at least 1845, when the Court stated that "the judicial power of the United States . . . is (except in enumerated instances, applicable exclusively to this Court) dependent for its distribution and organization, and for the modes of its exercise, entirely upon the action of Congress, who possess the sole power of creating the tribunals (inferior to the Supreme Court) . . . and of investing them with jurisdiction either limited, concurrent, or exclusive, and of withholding jurisdiction from them in the exact degrees and character which to Congress may seem proper for the public good." *Cary* v. *Curtis*, 44 U.S. 236, 245 (1845). We thus turn our attention to the relevant jurisdictional statutes.

The Judiciary Act of 1789 provided that "the circuit courts shall have original cognizance, concurrent with the courts of the several States, of *all suits of a civil nature at common law or in equity, where the matter in dispute exceeds,* exclusive of costs, the sum or value of *five hundred dollars,* and ... an alien is a party, or the suit is *between a citizen of the State where the suit is brought, and a citizen of another State.*" The defining phrase, "all suits of a civil nature at common law or in equity," remained a key element of statutory provisions demarcating the terms of diversity jurisdiction until 1948, when Congress amended the diversity jurisdiction provision to eliminate this phrase and replace in its stead the term "all civil actions."

The *Barber* majority itself did not expressly refer to the diversity statute's use of the limitation on "suits of a civil nature at common law or in equity." The dissenters in *Barber,* however, implicitly made such a reference, for they suggested that the federal courts had no power over certain domestic relations actions because the court of chancery lacked authority to issue divorce and alimony decrees. Stating that "the origin and the extent of [the federal courts'] jurisdiction must be sought in the laws of the United States, and in the settled rules and principles by which those laws have bound them," the dissenters contended that "as the jurisdiction of the chancery in England does not extend to or embrace the subjects of divorce and alimony, and as the jurisdiction of the courts of the United States in chancery is bounded by that of the chancery in England, all power or cognizance with respect to those subjects by the courts of the United States *in chancery* is equally excluded." *Barber,* 62 U.S. at 605 (Daniel, J., dissenting). Hence, in the dissenters' view, a suit seeking such relief would not fall within the statutory language "all suits of a civil nature at common law or in equity." Because the *Barber* Court did not disagree with this reason for accepting the jurisdictional limitation over the issuance of divorce and alimony decrees, it may be inferred fairly that the jurisdictional limitation recognized by the Court rested on this statutory basis and that the disagreement between the Court and the dissenters thus centered only on the extent of the limitation.

[W]e ... are content to rest our conclusion that a domestic relations exception exists as a matter of statutory construction not on the accuracy of the historical justifications on which it was seemingly based, but rather on Congress' apparent acceptance of this construction of the diversity jurisdiction provisions in the years prior to 1948, when the statute limited jurisdiction to "suits of a civil nature at common law or in equity." As the court in *Phillips, Nizer, Benjamin, Krim & Ballon* v. *Rosenstiel,* 490 F.2d 509, 514 (2d Cir. 1973), observed: "More than a century has elapsed since the *Barber* dictum without any intimation of Congressional dissatisfaction.... Whatever Article III may or may not permit, we thus accept the *Barber* dictum as a correct interpretation of the Congressional grant." Considerations of *stare decisis* have particular strength in this context, where "the legislative power is implicated, and Congress remains free to alter what we have done." *Patterson* v. *McLean Credit Union,* 491 U.S. 164, 172–73 (1989).

When Congress amended the diversity statute in 1948 to replace the law/equity distinction with the phrase "all civil actions," we presume Congress did so with full cognizance of the Court's nearly century-long interpretation of the prior statutes, which had construed the statutory diversity jurisdiction to contain an exception for certain domestic relations matters. With respect to the 1948 amendment, the Court has previously stated that "no changes of law or policy are to be presumed from changes of language in the revision unless an intent to make such changes is clearly expressed." *Fourco Glass Co. v. Transmirra Products Corp.*, 353 U.S. 222, 227 (1957). With respect to such a longstanding and well-known construction of the diversity statute, and where Congress made substantive changes to the statute in other respects, *see* 28 U.S.C. § 1332 note, we presume, absent any indication that Congress intended to alter this exception, that Congress "adopted that interpretation" when it reenacted the diversity statute.

In the more than 100 years since this Court laid the seeds for the development of the domestic relations exception, the lower federal courts have applied it in a variety of circumstances. Many of these applications go well beyond the circumscribed situations posed by *Barber* and its progeny. *Barber* itself disclaimed federal jurisdiction over a narrow range of domestic relations issues involving the granting of a divorce and a decree of alimony, and stated the limits on federal court power to intervene prior to the rendering of such orders:

> It is, that when a court of competent jurisdiction over the subject-matter and the parties decrees a divorce, and alimony to the wife as its incident, and is unable of itself to enforce the decree summarily upon the husband, that courts of equity will interfere to prevent the decree from being defeated by fraud. The interference, however, is limited to cases in which alimony has been decreed; then only to the extent of what is due, and always to cases in which no appeal is pending from the decree for the divorce or for alimony.

[*Barber*, 62 U.S.] at 591.

The *Barber* Court thus did not intend to strip the federal courts of authority to hear cases arising from the domestic relations of persons unless they seek the granting or modification of a divorce or alimony decree. The holding of the case itself sanctioned the exercise of federal jurisdiction over the enforcement of an alimony decree that had been properly obtained in a state court of competent jurisdiction. Contrary to the *Barber* dissenters' position, the enforcement of such validly obtained orders does not "regulate the domestic relations of society" and produce an "inquisitorial authority" in which federal tribunals "enter the habitations and even into the chambers and nurseries of private families, and inquire into and pronounce upon the morals and habits and affections or antipathies of the members of every household." *Id.* at 602 (Daniel, J., dissenting). And from the conclusion that the federal courts lacked jurisdiction to issue divorce and alimony decrees, there was no dissent.

Subsequently, this Court expanded the domestic relations exception to include decrees in child custody cases. In a child custody case brought pursuant to a writ of habeas corpus, for instance, the Court held void a writ issued by a Federal District Court to restore a child to the custody of the father. "As to the right to the control and possession of this child, as it is contested by its father and its grandfather, it is one in regard to which neither the Congress of the United States nor any authority of the United States has any special jurisdiction." *In re Burrus*, 136 U.S. 586, 594 (1890).

Although *In re Burrus* technically did not involve a construction of the diversity statute, as we understand *Barber* to have done, its statement that "the whole subject of the domestic relations of husband and wife, parent and child, belongs to the laws of the States and not to the laws of the United States," has been interpreted by the federal courts to apply with equal vigor in suits brought pursuant to diversity jurisdiction. This application is consistent with *Barber*'s directive to limit federal courts' exercise of diversity jurisdiction over suits for divorce and alimony decrees. We conclude, therefore, that the domestic relations exception, as articulated by this Court since *Barber*, divests the federal courts of power to issue divorce, alimony, and child custody decrees. Given the long passage of time without any expression of congressional dissatisfaction, we have no trouble today reaffirming the validity of the exception as it pertains to divorce and alimony decrees and child custody orders.

Not only is our conclusion rooted in respect for this long-held understanding, it is also supported by sound policy considerations. Issuance of decrees of this type not infrequently involves retention of jurisdiction by the court and deployment of social workers to monitor compliance. As a matter of judicial economy, state courts are more eminently suited to work of this type than are federal courts, which lack the close association with state and local government organizations dedicated to handling issues that arise out of conflicts over divorce, alimony, and child custody decrees. Moreover, as a matter of judicial expertise, it makes far more sense to retain the rule that federal courts lack power to issue these types of decrees because of the special proficiency developed by state tribunals over the past century and a half in handling issues that arise in the granting of such decrees.

By concluding, as we do, that the domestic relations exception encompasses only cases involving the issuance of a divorce, alimony, or child custody decree, we necessarily find that the Court of Appeals erred by affirming the District Court's invocation of this exception. This lawsuit in no way seeks such a decree; rather, it alleges that respondents Richards and Kesler committed torts against L. R. and S. R. Ankenbrandt's children by Richards. Federal subject-matter jurisdiction pursuant to § 1332 thus is proper in this case. . . .

NOTES

1. Are you persuaded by the court's argument that federal courts lack the special proficiency needed to handle divorce, alimony, and custody cases? Consider the alternative explanation provided by Judith Resnik, *"Naturally" Without Gender: Women, Jurisdiction and the Federal Courts*, 66 N.Y.U. L. REV. 1682, 1749 (1991):

> Women and the families they sometimes inhabit are not only assumed to be outside the federal courts, they also are assumed not to be related to the "national issues" to which the federal judiciary is to devote its interests. Jurisdictional lines have not been drawn according to the laws of nature but by men, who today are seeking to confirm their prestige as members of the most important judiciary in the country. Individual problems move lower on the federal courts' agenda. Dealing with women—in and out of families, arguing about federal statutory rights of relatively small value—is not how they want to frame their job. As a consequence, while present—in federal statutory, administrative, common, and constitutional law—the interaction between federal courts and women is not a subject of discussion. And, when possible, federal courts divest themselves of "family issues."

2. Given the existence of the domestic relations exception, why did the Supreme Court hear and decide *Orr v. Orr*, a case discussed in Chapter 3, which involved a request for alimony?

3. In *Marshall v. Marshall*, 547 U.S. 293, 308 (2006), the Court reaffirmed its position in *Ankenbrandt* by stating "only 'divorce, alimony, and child custody decrees' remain outside federal jurisdictional bounds." *Marshall*, 547 U.S. at 308. Despite the Supreme Court's discussions in *Ankenbrandt* and *Marshall*, lower federal courts have varied in their treatment of the domestic relations exception. *See* Meredith Johnson Harbach, *Is the Family a Federal Question?*, 66 WASH. & LEE L. REV. 131, 142 (2009).

Some federal courts dismiss family-law-related cases by denying subject matter jurisdiction under the domestic relations exception. This approach is particularly common in the Second and Seventh Circuits. *See* Harbach, *supra*, at 146–47; *McKnight v. Middleton*, 699 F.Supp.2d 507, 519–20 (E.D.N.Y. 2010). In other circuits, courts dismiss these cases by using abstention, *see* Harbach, *supra*, at 149–52, or other avoidance doctrines, Harbach, *supra*, at 152–54.

C.   CUSTODY JURISDICTION

1.   INTERSTATE CUSTODY DISPUTES

The mobility of people in the United States has increased the likelihood that the courts of more than one state may be asked to decide disputes involving custody or visitation. The Full Faith and Credit Clause of the U.S. Constitution requires states to give full faith and credit to, among other things, the final judgments of other states. Custody decrees, however, are *not* regarded as final judgments because the state court issuing the decree retains jurisdiction to modify it in the best interest of the child until he or she is eighteen. The Parental Kidnapping Prevention Act (PKPA) is a federal statute that addresses the problem of conflicting state custody decisions by requiring states to give full faith and credit to the custody decrees of other states.

If there is no outstanding custody decree from another state, a court must determine if it has jurisdiction to entertain a custody petition. Today almost every state makes that determination according to the Uniform Child Custody Jurisdiction and Enforcement Act of 1997 (UCCJEA). Forty-nine states, the District of Columbia, Guam, and the U.S. Virgin Islands have adopted the UCCJEA.[1] Under the UCCJEA, the child's "home state" has "exclusive [and] continuing jurisdiction" for child custody litigation. The "home state" is defined as the state where the child has lived with a parent for six consecutive months prior to the commencement of the proceeding (or since birth for children younger than six months). If the child has not lived in any state for at least six months, then a court in a state may exercise exclusive jurisdiction over custody if it determines the child has (1) "significant connections" with the state and at least one parent lives in that state, and (2) the court has access to "substantial evidence concerning the child's care, protection, training, and personal relationships."

For instance, Jason lives in Alabama with his mother and father for three years. If the mother moves to Tennessee, but Jason stays in Alabama, then Tennessee will not have jurisdiction to determine custody over Jason. Alabama is the only state that can determine custody at this point.

The second basis for jurisdiction under the UCCJEA is when a child and a parent have a "significant connection" with a state AND there is "substantial evidence" in that state with respect to the appropriate care for the child. For example, Jane lives with her mother and father in Ohio for five years. Her parents split up and she and her mother move to Wisconsin for four months, Indiana for three months, and Florida for three months. Jane's mother has a job in Florida and Jane has enrolled in school there and is taking dance classes after school. Jane's father continues to live in Ohio.

---

1.   A bill is pending in Massachusetts to adopt the UCCJEA.

No state court in this instance is authorized to exercise home state jurisdiction, because Jane has been gone from Ohio for more than six months and has not lived in another state for six months.

Do Jane and her mother have a "significant connection" to Florida? If her mother's job and Jane's schooling are intended to be permanent, they may. Is there "substantial evidence" available in Florida about the appropriate care for Jane? There could be, because a Florida court might be in a position to evaluate Jane's education and caregiving arrangements, as well as her mother's schedule. Jane's father, however, might argue that Jane still has a significant connection to Ohio since he lives there, and his claim would be even stronger if, for instance, either or both sets of grandparents lived in Ohio. Such information also could suggest that substantial evidence about the best custody arrangement for Jane is available in Ohio.

Once a custody determination is made by a court with jurisdiction under the UCCJEA, a court of another state does not have authority to modify the determination, unless the state with jurisdiction determines that it does not have jurisdiction, or a state court determines that the child and parents no longer reside in the state which currently has jurisdiction.

If Jason's father has custody of Jason in Alabama, and Jason visits his mother in Tennessee for the summer, his mom cannot go to the Tennessee courts and attempt to modify custody—Alabama has continuing jurisdiction.

Foster v. Wolkowitz

Supreme Court of Michigan, 2010.
785 N.W.2d 59.

■ YOUNG, J.

At issue in this case is whether the statutorily required presumptive award of custody given to a mother when an acknowledgment of parentage (AOP) is executed pursuant to the Acknowledgment of Parentage Act serves as an "initial custody determination" under the Uniform Child–Custody Jurisdiction and Enforcement Act (UCCJEA)....

Plaintiff and defendant are the biological parents of M., born October 12, 2006. Plaintiff and defendant cohabitated but never married. The parties moved from Illinois to Michigan months before M. was born in Michigan. On January 25, 2007, plaintiff and defendant executed and filed an AOP naming defendant as the child's father and establishing paternity.

In April 2007, the parties and the child returned to Illinois and continued to reside together. Plaintiff attended college and worked, while defendant attended law school. Both parties had Illinois driver's licenses, and M. received state health insurance that required Illinois residency. During the time that the family resided in Illinois, plaintiff regularly returned to Michigan with the child for extended visits with Michigan family members.

In May 2008, the relationship between the parties ended, and plaintiff and the child returned to Michigan to live with plaintiff's parents. Five days after returning to Michigan, plaintiff filed a paternity action in the Monroe Circuit Court. On June 4, 2008, defendant filed a custody action in Illinois.

On July 7, 2008, a telephone conference was held between the judges from the Michigan and Illinois courts, as well as the parties, to discuss which state had home-state jurisdiction under the UCCJEA. Defendant argued that

Illinois had jurisdiction under the UCCJEA. Plaintiff argued that Michigan should exercise jurisdiction because the child was residing with plaintiff in Michigan, plaintiff's petition had been filed first, and both plaintiff and the child had significant ties to Michigan. Both the Illinois and Michigan judges expressed initial agreement that jurisdiction should lie in Michigan, but also agreed that an evidentiary hearing should be held in Michigan in order to determine which state had home-state jurisdiction.

After adjournments, discovery, and failed settlement attempts, the jurisdictional hearing was conducted on January 6, 2009. The AOP was entered into evidence in the court record for the first time at this hearing. On February 17, 2009, the trial court entered a five-page "decision and order regarding jurisdiction." The court ruled that Michigan had jurisdiction to hear the case because, by executing an AOP, the parents "consent[ed] to the jurisdiction of Michigan specifically on the issues of custody, support and parenting time." Furthermore, because an AOP granted "initial custody" of a minor to the mother, the judge reasoned that the "UCCJEA would not be invoked" because the "grant of initial custody was already made by the parents who voluntarily invoked the Acknowledgment of Parentage law."[1]

Subsequently, a trial was held to determine custody. After taking testimony from a number of witnesses, the trial court . . . award[ed] joint legal custody to both parties, and physical custody to the plaintiff. Defendant was awarded parenting time, and a child support order was entered.

Defendant appealed the order of custody. On September 15, 2009, the Court of Appeals affirmed the trial court's exercise of jurisdiction, "albeit for a different reason."

. . .

This case involves the requirements of the UCCJEA and the interplay between the UCCJEA and the Acknowledgment of Parentage Act. Issues of statutory construction are questions of law reviewed de novo. Additionally, in the absence of any factual dispute, whether Michigan may exercise home-state jurisdiction under the UCCJEA is a question of law reviewed de novo.

The Acknowledgment of Parentage Act provides a voluntary means for both parents, acting together, to establish paternity of a child born out of wedlock. An AOP is "valid and effective" when the unwed parents complete the form, sign it, and have their signatures notarized. A validly executed AOP establishes paternity and may provide the "basis for court ordered child support, custody, or parenting time without further adjudication under the paternity act...."

> After a mother and father sign an acknowledgment of parentage, the mother has *initial custody* of the minor child, *without prejudice to the determination of either parent's custodial rights*, until otherwise determined by the court or otherwise agreed upon by the parties in writing and acknowledged by the court. This grant of initial custody to the mother *shall not*, by itself, *affect the rights of either parent* in a proceeding to seek a court order for custody or parenting time.

Lastly, parents who execute an AOP agree to consent to the "general, *personal* jurisdiction" of Michigan courts "regarding the issues of the support, custody, and parenting time of the child."

---

1. On March 3, 2009, after the Michigan court held that Michigan had jurisdiction over the case, the Illinois circuit court entered an order transferring the case to Michigan and dismissing defendant's Illinois case with prejudice.

The UCCJEA governs interstate child custody disputes. At issue in this case is [the section of the UCCJEA] which governs a state court's authority to make an "initial child-custody determination." That provision states:

(1) Except as otherwise provided in section 204,[15] a court of this state has jurisdiction to make an initial child-custody determination *only* in the following situations:

(a) This state is the *home state* of the child on the date of the commencement of the proceeding, or was the home state of the child within 6 months before the commencement of the proceeding and the child is absent from this state but a parent or person acting as a parent continues to live in this state.

(b) A court of another state does not have jurisdiction under subdivision (a), or a court of the home state of the child has *declined to exercise jurisdiction* on the ground that this state is the more appropriate forum under section 207 or 208, and the court finds both of the following:

(*i*) The child and the child's parents, or the child and at least 1 parent or a person acting as a parent, have a significant connection with this state other than mere physical presence.

(*ii*) Substantial evidence is available in this state concerning the child's care, protection, training, and personal relationships.

.   .   .

(3) Physical presence of, or personal jurisdiction over, a party or a child is neither necessary nor sufficient to make a child-custody determination.

The UCCJEA also defines statutory terms that are critical to our resolution of this case. Of note, a "child-custody determination" is defined as "a judgment, decree, or *other court order* providing for legal custody, physical custody, or parenting time with respect to a child. Child-custody determination includes a permanent, temporary, initial, and modification order. Child-custody determination *does not* include an order relating to child support or other monetary obligation of an individual." Additionally, the child's "home state" is defined as the state in which a child lived with a parent *"for at least 6 consecutive months immediately before the commencement of a child-custody proceeding."*

The Court of Appeals in this case held that an AOP, executed pursuant to the Acknowledgment of Parentage Act, operated as an initial custody determination for the purposes of the UCCJEA. It is true that the plain language of the Acknowledgment of Parentage Act effectively conditions the parents' ability to execute an AOP on their willingness to allow the mother to be granted "initial custody of the minor child. . . ." While this grant of initial custody occurs by operation of law when the parties stipulate to the child's paternity, the statutory language also makes clear that the initial grant of custody creates no impediment should either parent wish to seek a judicial determination of custodial rights. [The Acknowledgement of Parentage Act] indicates that the grant of initial custody is *"without prejudice* to the determination of either parent's custodial rights" and that the grant of initial custody "shall not, by itself, *affect the rights of either parent* in a proceeding to *seek a*

---

15. [The UCCJEA] permits a state to exercise "temporary emergency jurisdiction" when a child has been abandoned or it is necessary to protect the child on an emergency basis because the child, his siblings, or his parent is "subjected to or threatened with mistreatment or abuse." The temporary emergency orders remain in effect until an order is obtained from the state court having proper jurisdiction under the UCCJEA.

court order for custody or parenting time." Thus, nothing in the plain language of the [statute] equates the execution of an AOP to a judicial determination regarding custody; rather, the statutory language leads to the opposite conclusion.

An AOP is not issued or entered by *any* court, nor is it in the form of a "judgment, decree, or other court order...." Rather, the parental stipulation is filed in the executive branch with the State Registrar and kept in a specific parentage registry. The judicial branch has absolutely no involvement in the execution of an AOP. Indeed, the involvement of the judicial branch occurs, if ever, only *after* the AOP has been filed, as the acknowledgment serves as the "basis for court ordered child support, custody, or parenting time without further adjudication under the paternity act...." Simply put, the initial grant of custody to the mother required under the Acknowledgment of Parentage Act is not an "initial child-custody determination" under the UCCJEA, and the Court of Appeals erred by concluding otherwise.

It is true that the Acknowledgment of Parentage Act requires, as a condition of executing an AOP, that parents consent "to the general, personal jurisdiction" of Michigan courts regarding "the issues of the support, custody, and parenting time...." However, jurisdiction over a *person* has never been synonymous with jurisdiction over a *case*, and the parties' consent to personal jurisdiction provides no support for the conclusion that Michigan has home-state jurisdiction under the UCCJEA. The plain language of the UCCJEA indicates that it provides "the *exclusive* jurisdictional basis for making a child-custody determination." Merely having personal jurisdiction over a party or child is insufficient to make a child custody determination. Therefore, the consent to personal jurisdiction required by the Acknowledgment of Parentage Act provides no basis for Michigan to exert home-state jurisdiction pursuant to the UCCJEA.

The record reveals that the child's home state for the purposes of the UCCJEA is the state of Illinois, because that is the state in which the child resided "for at least 6 consecutive months immediately before the commencement of a child-custody proceeding." Plaintiff argues that, despite the fact that the state of Illinois has home-state jurisdiction, the state of Michigan is a more convenient forum for the resolution of the custody dispute. However, under the UCCJEA, it is the *home state* that must decide whether to "decline to exercise its jurisdiction" because "it determines" that "it is an inconvenient forum" and that "a court of another state is a more appropriate forum." Thus, while plaintiff presents persuasive arguments supporting the conclusion that Michigan is the more appropriate forum in which to resolve the interstate custody dispute, these arguments are best directed to the Illinois court.

The Court of Appeals erred by concluding that the presumptive award of custody given to a mother when an AOP is executed pursuant to the Acknowledgment of Parentage Act serves as an "initial custody determination" under the UCCJEA. We therefore reverse the judgment of the Court of Appeals and remand this matter to the Monroe Circuit Court for further proceedings consistent with this opinion.

Thompson v. Thompson

United States Supreme Court, 1988.
484 U.S. 174, 108 S.Ct. 513, 98 L.Ed.2d 512.

■ JUSTICE MARSHALL delivered the opinion of the Court.

We granted certiorari in this case to determine whether the Parental Kidnaping Prevention Act of 1980, 28 U.S.C. § 1738A, furnishes an implied cause of action in federal court to determine which of two conflicting state custody decisions is valid.

. . .

The Parental Kidnaping Prevention Act (PKPA or Act) imposes a duty on the States to enforce a child custody determination entered by a court of a sister State if the determination is consistent with the provisions of the Act. In order for a state court's custody decree to be consistent with the provisions of the Act, the State must have jurisdiction under its own local law and one of five conditions set out in § 1738A(c)(2) must be met. . . . Once a State exercises jurisdiction consistently with the provisions of the Act, no other State may exercise concurrent jurisdiction over the custody dispute, § 1738A(g), even if it would have been empowered to take jurisdiction in the first instance,[2] and all States must accord full faith and credit to the first State's ensuing custody decree.

As the legislative scheme suggests, and as Congress explicitly specified, one of the chief purposes of the PKPA is to "avoid jurisdictional competition and conflict between State courts." This case arises out of a jurisdictional stalemate that came to pass notwithstanding the strictures of the Act. In July 1978, respondent Susan Clay (then Susan Thompson) filed a petition in Los Angeles Superior Court asking the court to dissolve her marriage to petitioner David Thompson and seeking custody of the couple's infant son, Matthew. The court initially awarded the parents joint custody of Matthew, but that arrangement became infeasible when respondent decided to move from California to Louisiana to take a job. The court then entered an order providing that respondent would have sole custody of Matthew once she left for Louisiana. This state of affairs was to remain in effect until the court investigator submitted a report on custody, after which the court intended to make a more studied custody determination.

Respondent and Matthew moved to Louisiana in December of 1980. Three months later, respondent filed a petition in Louisiana state court for enforcement of the California custody decree, judgment of custody, and modification of petitioner's visitation privileges. By order dated April 7, 1981, the Louisiana court granted the petition and awarded sole custody of Matthew to respondent. Two months later, however, the California court, having received and reviewed its investigator's report, entered an order awarding sole custody of Matthew to petitioner. Thus arose the current impasse.

In August 1983, petitioner brought this action in the District Court for the Central District of California. Petitioner requested an order declaring the Louisiana decree invalid and the California decree valid, and enjoining the enforcement of the Louisiana decree. Petitioner did not attempt to enforce the California decree in a Louisiana state court before he filed suit in federal court. The District Court granted respondent's motion to dismiss the complaint for lack of subject matter and personal jurisdiction. The Court of Appeals for the Ninth Circuit affirmed. . . . We granted *certiorari*, 479 U.S. 1063 (1987), and we now affirm.

. . .

---

2. The sole exception to this constraint occurs where the first State either has lost jurisdiction or has declined to exercise continuing jurisdiction. *See* § 1738A(f).

In determining whether to infer a private cause of action from a federal statute, our focal point is Congress' intent in enacting the statute. As guides to discerning that intent, we have relied on the four factors set out in *Cort v. Ash, see* 422 U.S. 66, 78 (1975), along with other tools of statutory construction. Our focus on congressional intent does not mean that we require evidence that Members of Congress, in enacting the statute, actually had in mind the creation of a private cause of action. The implied cause of action doctrine would be a virtual dead letter were it limited to correcting drafting errors when Congress simply forgot to codify its evident intention to provide a cause of action. Rather, as an *implied* cause of action doctrine suggests, "the legislative history of a statute that does not expressly create or deny a private remedy will typically be equally silent or ambiguous on the question." We therefore have recognized that Congress' "intent may appear implicitly in the language or structure of the statute, or in the circumstances of its enactment." . . . In this case, the essential predicate for implication of a private remedy plainly does not exist. None of the factors that have guided our inquiry in this difficult area points in favor of inferring a private cause of action. Indeed, the context, language, and legislative history of the PKPA all point sharply away from the remedy petitioner urges us to infer.

We examine initially the context of the PKPA with an eye toward determining Congress' perception of the law that it was shaping or reshaping. At the time Congress passed the PKPA, custody orders held a peculiar status under the full faith and credit doctrine, which requires each State to give effect to the judicial proceedings of other States, *see* U.S. CONST., art. IV, § 1; 28 U.S.C. § 1738. The anomaly traces to the fact that custody orders characteristically are subject to modification as required by the best interests of the child. As a consequence, some courts doubted whether custody orders were sufficiently "final" to trigger full faith and credit requirements, and this Court had declined expressly to settle the question. Even if custody orders were subject to full faith and credit requirements, the Full Faith and Credit Clause obliges States only to accord the same force to judgments as would be accorded by the courts of the State in which the judgment was entered. Because courts entering custody orders generally retain the power to modify them, courts in other States were no less entitled to change the terms of custody according to their own views of the child's best interest. For these reasons, a parent who lost a custody battle in one State had an incentive to kidnap the child and move to another State to relitigate the issue. This circumstance contributed to widespread jurisdictional deadlocks like this one, and more importantly, to a national epidemic of parental kidnaping. At the time the PKPA was enacted, sponsors of the Act estimated that between 25,000 and 100,000 children were kidnaped by parents who had been unable to obtain custody in a legal forum.

A number of States joined in an effort to avoid these jurisdictional conflicts by adopting the Uniform Child Custody Jurisdiction Act (UCCJA), 9 U.L.A. §§ 1–28 (1979). . . . The project foundered, however, because a number of States refused to enact the UCCJA while others enacted it with modifications. In the absence of uniform national standards for allocating and enforcing custody determinations, noncustodial parents still had reason to snatch their children and petition the courts of any of a number of haven States for sole custody.

The context of the PKPA therefore suggests that the principal problem Congress was seeking to remedy was the inapplicability of full faith and credit requirements to custody determinations. Statements made when the Act was introduced in Congress forcefully confirm that suggestion. The sponsors and supporters of the Act continually indicated that the purpose of the PKPA was to provide for nationwide enforcement of custody orders made in accordance with the terms of the UCCJA. As Deputy Attorney General Michel testified:

. . .

> In essence [the PKPA] would impose on States a Federal duty, under enumerated standards derived from the UCCJA, to give full faith and credit to the custody decrees of other States. Such legislation would, in effect, amount to Federal adoption of key provisions of the UCCJA for all States and would eliminate the incentive for one parent to remove a minor child to another jurisdiction.

The significance of Congress' full faith and credit approach to the problem of child snatching is that the Full Faith and Credit Clause, in either its constitutional or statutory incarnations, does not give rise to an implied federal cause of action. Rather, the clause "only prescribes a rule by which courts, Federal and state, are to be guided when a question arises in the progress of a pending suit as to the faith and credit to be given by the court to the public acts, records, and judicial proceedings of a State other than that in which the court is sitting." Because Congress' chief aim in enacting the PKPA was to extend the requirements of the Full Faith and Credit Clause to custody determinations, the Act is most naturally construed to furnish a rule of decision for courts to use in adjudicating custody disputes and not to create an entirely new cause of action. It thus is not compatible with the purpose and context of the legislative scheme to infer a private cause of action. *See Cort v. Ash*, 422 U.S. at 78.

The language and placement of the statute reinforce this conclusion. The PKPA, 28 U.S.C. § 1738A, is an addendum to the full faith and credit statute, 28 U.S.C. § 1738. This fact alone is strong proof that the Act is intended to have the same operative effect as the full faith and credit statute. . . . As for the language of the Act, it is addressed entirely to States and state courts. Unlike statutes that explicitly confer a right on a specified class of persons, the PKPA is a mandate directed to state courts to respect the custody decrees of sister States. . . .

Finally, the legislative history of the PKPA provides unusually clear indication that Congress did not intend the federal courts to play the enforcement role that petitioner urges.

. . .

In sum, the context, language, and history of the PKPA together make out a conclusive case against inferring a cause of action in federal court to determine which of two conflicting state custody decrees is valid. Against this impressive evidence, petitioner relies primarily on the argument that failure to infer a cause of action would render the PKPA nugatory. We note, as a preliminary response, that ultimate review remains available in this Court for truly intractable jurisdictional deadlocks. In addition, the unspoken presumption in petitioner's argument is that the States are either unable or unwilling to enforce the provisions of the Act. This is a presumption we are not prepared, and more importantly, Congress was not prepared, to indulge. State courts faithfully administer the Full Faith and Credit Clause every day; now that Congress has extended full faith and credit requirements to child custody orders, we can think of no reason why the courts' administration of federal law in custody disputes will be any less vigilant. Should state courts prove as obstinate as petitioner predicts, Congress may choose to revisit the issue. But any more radical approach to the problem will have to await further legislative action; we "will not engraft a remedy on a statute, no matter how salutary, that Congress did not intend to provide."

The judgment of the Court of Appeals is affirmed.

2. INTERNATIONAL CUSTODY DISPUTES

Abbott v. Abbott

Supreme Court of the United States, 2010.
___ U.S. ___, 130 S.Ct. 1983, 176 L.Ed.2d 789.

■ JUSTICE KENNEDY delivered the opinion of the Court.

This case presents . . . a question of interpretation under the Hague Convention on the Civil Aspects of International Child Abduction (Convention). The United States is a contracting state to the Convention; and Congress has implemented its provisions through the International Child Abduction Remedies Act (ICARA). The Convention provides that a child abducted in violation of "rights of custody" must be returned to the child's country of habitual residence, unless certain exceptions apply. The question is whether a parent has a "righ[t] of custody" by reason of that parent's *ne exeat* right: the authority to consent before the other parent may take the child to another country.

Timothy Abbott and Jacquelyn Vaye Abbott married in England in 1992. He is a British citizen, and she is a citizen of the United States. Mr. Abbott's astronomy profession took the couple to Hawaii, where their son A.J. A. was born in 1995. The Abbotts moved to La Serena, Chile, in 2002. There was marital discord, and the parents separated in March 2003. The Chilean courts granted the mother daily care and control of the child, while awarding the father "direct and regular" visitation rights, including visitation every other weekend and for the whole month of February each year.

Chilean law conferred upon Mr. Abbott what is commonly known as a *ne exeat* right: a right to consent before Ms. Abbott could take A.J. A. out of Chile. After Mr. Abbott obtained a British passport for A.J. A., Ms. Abbott grew concerned that Mr. Abbott would take the boy to Britain. She sought and obtained a "*ne exeat* of the minor" order from the Chilean family court, prohibiting the boy from being taken out of Chile.

In August 2005, while proceedings before the Chilean court were pending, the mother removed the boy from Chile without permission from either the father or the court. A private investigator located the mother and the child in Texas. In February 2006, the mother filed for divorce in Texas state court. Part of the relief she sought was a modification of the father's rights, including full power in her to determine the boy's place of residence and an order limiting the father to supervised visitation in Texas. This litigation remains pending.

Mr. Abbott brought an action in Texas state court, asking for visitation rights and an order requiring Ms. Abbott to show cause why the court should not allow Mr. Abbott to return to Chile with A.J. A. In February 2006, the court denied Mr. Abbott's requested relief but granted him "liberal periods of possession" of A.J. A. throughout February 2006, provided Mr. Abbott remained in Texas.

In May 2006, Mr. Abbott filed the instant action in the United States District Court for the Western District of Texas. He sought an order requiring his son's return to Chile pursuant to the Convention and enforcement provisions of the ICARA. In July 2007, after holding a bench trial during which only Mr. Abbott testified, the District Court denied relief. The court held that the father's *ne exeat* right did not constitute a right of custody under the Convention and, as a result, that the return remedy was not authorized.

The United States Court of Appeals for the Fifth Circuit affirmed on the same rationale. The court held the father possessed no rights of custody under the Convention because his *ne exeat* right was only "a veto right over his son's departure from Chile." The court expressed substantial agreement with the Court of Appeals for the Second Circuit in *Croll v. Croll,* 229 F.3d 133 (2d Cir. 2000). Relying on American dictionary definitions of "custody" and noting that *ne exeat* rights cannot be " 'actually exercised' " within the meaning of the Convention, *Croll* held that *ne exeat* rights are not rights of custody. A dissenting opinion in *Croll* was filed by then-Judge Sotomayor. The dissent maintained that a *ne exeat* right is a right of custody because it "provides a parent with decisionmaking authority regarding a child's international relocation."

. . .

The Convention was adopted in 1980 in response to the problem of international child abductions during domestic disputes. The Convention seeks "to secure the prompt return of children wrongfully removed to or retained in any Contracting State," and "to ensure that rights of custody and of access under the law of one Contracting State are effectively respected in the other Contracting States."

The provisions of the Convention of most relevance at the outset of this discussion are as follows:

Article 3: The removal or the retention of the child is to be considered wrongful where–

a. it is in breach of rights of custody attributed to a person, an institution or any other body, either jointly or alone, under the law of the State in which the child was habitually resident immediately before the removal or retention; and

b. at the time of removal or retention those rights were actually exercised, either jointly or alone, or would have been so exercised but for the removal or retention.

. . .

Article 5: For the purposes of this Convention–

a. 'rights of custody' shall include rights relating to the care of the person of the child and, in particular, the right to determine the child's place of residence;

b. 'rights of access' shall include the right to take a child for a limited period of time to a place other than the child's habitual residence.

. . .

Article 12: Where a child has been wrongfully removed or retained in terms of Article 3 . . . the authority concerned shall order the return of the child forthwith.

The Convention's central operating feature is the return remedy. When a child under the age of 16 has been wrongfully removed or retained, the country to which the child has been brought must "order the return of the child forthwith," unless certain exceptions apply. A removal is "wrongful" where the child was removed in violation of "rights of custody." The Convention defines "rights of custody" to "include rights relating to the care of the person of the child and, in particular, the right to determine the child's place of residence." A return remedy does not alter the pre-abduction allocation of custody rights but leaves custodial decisions to the courts of the country of habitual residence. The Convention also recognizes "rights of access," but offers no return remedy for a breach of those rights.

The United States has implemented the Convention through the [International Child Abduction Remedies Act] ICARA. The statute authorizes a person who seeks a child's return to file a petition in state or federal court and instructs that the court "shall decide the case in accordance with the Convention." 42 U.S.C. §§ 11603(a), (b), (d). If the child in question has been "wrongfully removed or retained within the meaning of the Convention," the child shall be "promptly returned," unless an exception is applicable. § 11601(a)(4).

As the parties agree, the Convention applies to this dispute. A.J. A. is under 16 years old; he was a habitual resident of Chile; and both Chile and the United States are contracting states. The question is whether A.J. A. was "wrongfully removed" from Chile, in other words, whether he was removed in violation of a right of custody.... [T]he Court determines that Mr. Abbott's *ne exeat* right is a right of custody under the Convention.

"The interpretation of a treaty, like the interpretation of a statute, begins with its text." *Medellín v. Texas*, 552 U.S. 491, 506 (2008). This Court consults Chilean law to determine the content of Mr. Abbott's right, while following the Convention's text and structure to decide whether the right at issue is a "righ[t] of custody."

Chilean law granted Mr. Abbott a joint right to decide his child's country of residence, otherwise known as a *ne exeat* right. [A provision of Minors Law] provides that "[o]nce the court has decreed" that one of the parents has visitation rights, that parent's "authorization ... shall also be required" before the child may be taken out of the country, subject to court override only where authorization "cannot be granted or is denied without good reason." Mr. Abbott has "direct and regular" visitation rights and it follows from Chilean law, that he has a shared right to determine his son's country of residence under this provision.

 . . .

The Convention defines "rights of custody" to "include rights relating to the care of the person of the child and, in particular, the right to determine the child's place of residence." Mr. Abbott's *ne exeat* right gives him both the joint "right to determine the child's place of residence" and joint "rights relating to the care of the person of the child."

Mr. Abbott's joint right to decide A.J. A.'s country of residence allows him to "determine the child's place of residence." The phrase "place of residence" encompasses the child's country of residence, especially in light of the Convention's explicit purpose to prevent wrongful removal across international borders.

Mr. Abbott's joint right to determine A.J. A.'s country of residence also gives him "rights relating to the care of the person of the child." Few decisions are as significant as the language the child speaks, the identity he finds, or the culture and traditions she will come to absorb. These factors, so essential to self-definition, are linked in an inextricable way to the child's country of residence. One need only consider the different childhoods an adolescent will experience if he or she grows up in the United States, Chile, Germany, or North Korea, to understand how choosing a child's country of residence is a right "relating to the care of the person of the child." The Court of Appeals described Mr. Abbott's right to take part in making this decision as a mere "veto;" but even by that truncated description, the father has an essential role in deciding the boy's country of residence. For example, Mr. Abbott could condition his consent to a change in country on A.J. A.'s moving to a city outside Chile where Mr. Abbott could obtain an astronomy position, thus allowing the father to have continued contact with the boy.

That a *ne exeat* right does not fit within traditional notions of physical custody is beside the point. The Convention defines "rights of custody," and it is that definition that a court must consult. And, in any case, our own legal system has adopted conceptions of custody that accord with the Convention's broad definition. Joint legal custody, in which one parent cares for the child while the other has joint decisionmaking authority concerning the child's welfare, has become increasingly common. *See* [Jana B.] Singer, *Dispute Resolution and the Postdivorce Family: Implications of a Paradigm Shift*, 47 FAMILY CT. REV. 363, 366 (2009) ("[A] recent study of child custody outcomes in North Carolina indicated that almost 70% of all custody resolutions included joint legal custody, as did over 90% of all mediated custody agreements"); E. MACCOBY & R. MNOOKIN, DIVIDING THE CHILD: SOCIAL AND LEGAL DILEMMAS OF CUSTODY 107 (1992) ("[F]or 79% of our entire sample, the [California] divorce decree provided for joint legal custody"); *see generally* [Linda D.] Elrod, *Reforming the System to Protect Children in High Conflict Custody Cases*, 28 WM. MITCHELL L. REV. 495, 505–08 (2001).

. . .

The Court of Appeals' conclusion that a breach of a *ne exeat* right does not give rise to a return remedy would render the Convention meaningless in many cases where it is most needed. The Convention provides a return remedy when a parent takes a child across international borders in violation of a right of custody. The Convention provides no return remedy when a parent removes a child in violation of a right of access but requires contracting states "to promote the peaceful enjoyment of access rights." But unlike rights of access, *ne exeat* rights can only be honored with a return remedy because these rights depend on the child's location being the country of habitual residence.

. . .

This Court's conclusion that Mr. Abbott possesses a right of custody under the Convention is supported and informed by the State Department's view on the issue. The United States has endorsed the view that *ne exeat* rights are rights of custody. In its brief before this Court the United States advises that "the Department of State, whose Office of Children's Issues serves as the Central Authority for the United States under the Convention, has long understood the Convention as including *ne exeat* rights among the protected 'rights of custody.'" Brief for United States as *Amicus Curiae* 21; *see Sumitomo Shoji America, Inc. v. Avagliano*, 457 U.S. 176, 184–85, n. 10 (1982) (deferring to the Executive's interpretation of a treaty as memorialized in a brief before this Court). It is well settled that the Executive Branch's interpretation of a treaty "is entitled to great weight." There is no reason to doubt that this well-established canon of deference is appropriate here. . . .

[The Court cites other contracting states' decisions holding that *ne exeat* rights were rights of custody. The United Kingdom, Israel, Austria, South Africa, and Germany have all found them to be rights of custody. The Canadian courts have a more restrictive view, and the French courts are divided on the issue.]

. . .

The Convention is based on the principle that the best interests of the child are well served when decisions regarding custody rights are made in the country of habitual residence. Ordering a return remedy does not alter the existing allocation of custody rights, but does allow the courts of the home country to decide what is in the child's best interests. It is the Convention's premise that courts in contracting states will make this determination in a responsible manner.

Custody decisions are often difficult. Judges must strive always to avoid a common tendency to prefer their own society and culture, a tendency that ought not interfere with objective consideration of all the factors that should be weighed in determining the best interests of the child. This judicial neutrality is presumed from the mandate of the Convention, which affirms that the contracting states are "[f]irmly convinced that the interests of children are of paramount importance in matters relating to their custody." International law serves a high purpose when it underwrites the determination by nations to rely upon their domestic courts to enforce just laws by legitimate and fair proceedings.

To interpret the Convention to permit an abducting parent to avoid a return remedy, even when the other parent holds a *ne exeat* right, would run counter to the Convention's purpose of deterring child abductions by parents who attempt to find a friendlier forum for deciding custodial disputes. Ms. Abbott removed A.J. A. from Chile while Mr. Abbott's request to enhance his relationship with his son was still pending before Chilean courts. After she landed in Texas, the mother asked the state court to diminish or eliminate the father's custodial and visitation rights. The Convention should not be interpreted to permit a parent to select which country will adjudicate these questions by bringing the child to a different country, in violation of a *ne exeat* right. Denying a return remedy for the violation of such rights would "legitimize the very action—removal of the child—that the home country, through its custody order [or other provision of law], sought to prevent" and would allow "parents to undermine the very purpose of the Convention." *Croll*, 229 F.3d at 147 (Sotomayor, J., dissenting). This Court should be most reluctant to adopt an interpretation that gives an abducting parent an advantage by coming here to avoid a return remedy that is granted, for instance, in the United Kingdom, Israel, Germany, and South Africa.

. . .

The judgment of the Court of Appeals is reversed, and the case is remanded for further proceedings consistent with this opinion.

■ Justice Stevens, with whom Justice Thomas and Justice Breyer join, dissenting.

Petitioner Timothy Abbott, the father of A.J. A., has no authority to decide whether his son undergoes a particular medical procedure; whether his son attends a school field trip; whether and in what manner his son has a religious upbringing; or whether his son can play a videogame before he completes his homework. These are all rights and responsibilities of A.J. A.'s mother, respondent Jacquelyn Abbott. It is she who received sole custody, or "daily care and control," of A.J. A. when the expatriate couple divorced while living in Chile in 2004. Mr. Abbott possesses only visitation rights. [Justice Stevens concludes that because Mr. Abbott had minimal control over his son's day-to-day life, his *ne exeat* right did not create a right to custody under the Convention.]

NOTE

After the Supreme Court's decision in *Abbott*, the Fifth Circuit remanded the case to the federal district court for further proceedings. On December 2 and 6, 2010, Judge Lee Yeakel presided over remand hearings regarding two new allegations in Ms. Abbott's answer: (1) that A.J. A. would be subject to a risk of harm if returned to Chile; and (2) that A.J. A. did not want to return to Chile. On June 6, 2011, before the district court made its decision, A.J. A. turned 16, and was no longer subject to the provisions of the Hague Convention. As a result, Ms. Abbott has filed a motion for judgment on the pleadings, while Mr. Abbott claims that the court lacks jurisdiction because the case is now moot.

Charalambous v. Charalambous

United States Court of Appeals, First Circuit, 2010.
627 F.3d 462.

Before LYNCH, CHIEF JUDGE, LIPEZ AND HOWARD, CIRCUIT JUDGES.

■ PER CURIAM.

Savvas Charalambous filed a petition for the return of his two children, A.C. and N.C., to Cyprus pursuant to the Hague Convention on the Civil Aspects of International Child Abduction, which was implemented by the International Child Abduction Remedies Act (ICARA). The children were removed in June 2010 from Cyprus, their country of habitual residence, to the United States by their mother, Elizabeth R. Charalambous. She did not return the children to Cyprus before September 2010 as she had represented she would. She defended against the petition primarily on the ground that returning the children would expose them to a grave risk of harm, an exception to return under Article (b) of the Convention.

Following a two-day evidentiary hearing, the district court held that there was not clear and convincing evidence of a grave risk of harm to the children, and that the Convention required their return. The court ordered the children placed in their father's custody.... [T]his court stayed the removal of the children pending the outcome of respondent's appeal, but expedited the appeal....

We now lift the stay, and affirm, finding no error of law by the district court and holding that its findings and conclusions are well supported. We order that the children be placed in the custody of the father no later than December 9, 2010 at 12:00 p.m. for their return to Cyprus, and we return jurisdiction to the district court should any further orders be necessary to secure enforcement.

. . .

Savvas, a citizen of Cyprus, married Elizabeth, a citizen of the United States, in a civil ceremony in Virginia in 1996, and again in a religious ceremony in Cyprus in 1998. The couple has resided in Limassol, Cyprus since December 1997, save for a few months in 2004 during which Elizabeth and Savvas briefly separated and Elizabeth returned on her own to her parents' home in Maine. They have two children: N.C., born in 2002, and A.C., born in 2008.

On June 18, 2010, Elizabeth, N.C. and A.C. departed Cyprus for a summer visit to Elizabeth's family in Maine. Elizabeth had purchased return tickets to Cyprus, and Savvas expected Elizabeth and the children to return in August 2010.

By July 2010, Savvas came to believe Elizabeth would not return to Cyprus with the children. . . . These beliefs were confirmed when Elizabeth informed Savvas on July 23, 2010, that she and the children would not be returning as planned. Consequently, on July 26, 2010, Savvas filed an application for return of his children under the Hague Convention with the Central Authority in Cyprus. Savvas then filed a petition in the District of Maine on September 3, 2010, alleging that Elizabeth had wrongfully retained N.C. and A.C. in the United States, and seeking the return of the children to Cyprus pursuant to the Hague Convention and ICARA.

The district court promptly held an evidentiary hearing on October 6 and 7, 2010. . . . The court concluded that Elizabeth had wrongfully retained the children in Maine and that Elizabeth had failed to prove either that Savvas had consented or acquiesced to the retention or that the children faced a grave risk of physical or psychological harm if they were returned to Cyprus.[1]

. . .

This appeal followed, accompanied by an Emergency Motion to Stay Judgment of the District Court. We granted the Motion to Stay on October 28, 2010. . . .

. . .

The Hague Convention was enacted to "secure the prompt return of children wrongfully removed to or retained in any Contracting State" and to "ensure that rights of custody and of access under the law of one Contracting State are effectively respected in the other Contracting States." Hague Convention, art. 1; *see also Abbott v. Abbott*, 130 S.Ct. 1983, 1989 (2010). The Convention establishes a strong presumption favoring return of a wrongfully removed child, and is "based on the principle that the best interests of the child are well served when decisions regarding custody rights are made in the country of habitual residence." The Hague Convention is generally intended to restore the status quo before the removal and to prevent a parent from engaging in international forum shopping. We interpret the Convention's text mindful of these purposes.

Children who have been wrongfully retained outside of their country of habitual residence must be expeditiously returned, unless the respondent can prove one of the defenses provided for by the Convention. In the district court, Elizabeth invoked the Article (b) defense that returning N.C. and A.C. to Cyprus would create a "grave risk" of "physical or psychological harm" or "otherwise place the child[ren] in an intolerable situation." Specifically, she alleged a grave risk of such harm existed based on the children having been physically, sexually or psychologically abused by Savvas and his mother. She also argued that returning to Cyprus would place her own safety at risk, thus

---

1.   The court determined that Cyprus was the children's country of habitual residence.

causing her children psychological harm.[3] The district court rejected Elizabeth's argument based on its findings of fact.

. . .

The only questions on appeal are (1) whether the district court erred in its interpretation of the Hague Convention concerning any psychological harm to the children that returning them to Cyprus could cause, and (2) whether it was clearly erroneous for the district court to conclude that Elizabeth had not demonstrated that any spousal abuse would create a grave risk to the children.

Under Article (b), "grave" means a more than serious risk, but it need not be an immediate risk. Elizabeth bears the burden of establishing the existence of such a grave risk by clear and convincing evidence. The district court's conclusion that she failed to meet her burden is not in error and is strongly supported by the record.

Elizabeth argues that the district court made an error of law and asserts that the court only considered physical harm, sexual abuse, and spousal abuse, and overlooked the question of "psychological harm," a term used in Article (b).

The argument flatly ignores the fact that the district court made an express finding that Elizabeth had failed to meet her burden of showing psychological harm: "Respondent has not shown by clear and convincing evidence that returning the Children to Cyprus will expose them to physical *or psychological harm* or otherwise place them in an intolerable situation."

. . .

The district court was highly attuned to the psychological well-being of N.C. and A.C., and to the risks presented to the children's emotional well-being. The district court also explicitly considered the forms of psychological harm that Elizabeth identifies: the risks that returning N.C. and A.C. to Cyprus might force them to witness future spousal abuse (they had not witnessed any before), or force their separation from their mother should Elizabeth choose not to return to Cyprus. The finding that she had failed to meet her burden of showing grave risk of psychological harm to the children is amply supported.

On appeal, Elizabeth also argues the district court failed to adequately consider the risk that, if returned to Cyprus, N.C. will be less likely to get the psychological treatment she believes he needs. She says that treatment is unavailable, citing that there are only three therapists specializing in the treatment of children in Limassol, and that Savvas's extended family will prevent N.C. from obtaining the psychological services he requires.[6] The district court explicitly considered "the . . . evidence relating to the influence of the Charalambous family in Cyprus," and concluded that "the total weight of the evidence does not present a clear and convincing case of grave risk." "The Article (b) defense may not be used 'as a vehicle to litigate (or relitigate) the child's best interests.' "

---

3. Before the district court, Elizabeth also invoked the defense, which the court rejected, that Savvas "had consented to or subsequently acquiesced in the removal or retention" of the children in the United States.

6. It is not at all clear why the family would be motivated to deny psychological services if N.C. were in need of them.

The Second Circuit's decision in *Blondin v. Dubois*, 238 F.3d 153 (2d Cir. 2001), does not help Elizabeth. That decision was based on a diagnosis that the children's post-traumatic stress disorder would recur if they were returned to their home country, not the relative availability of resources in each country. The court expressly rejected the argument, made here by Elizabeth, that the grave risk exception prevents "return to a home where money is in short supply, or where educational or other opportunities are more limited than in the requested State."[7]

The relevant inquiry is not whether there would be a grave risk of harm to Elizabeth if she returned to Cyprus; rather, the grave risk inquiry goes to the children. *See Abbott*, 130 S.Ct. 1983, 1997 (2010).... Elizabeth failed to draw a connection establishing, by clear and convincing evidence, that any risk to her constituted a grave risk to the children.

The district court found that "Elizabeth was subjected to some verbal and emotional abuse and that there was one incident of physical abuse" which "did not require any medical treatment."[8] The court further determined that "the record does not reflect that N.C. and A.C. have witnessed their father being abusive toward their mother." In light of these findings, the court reasoned it could not conclude "the Children would suffer from psychological harm or be placed in an intolerable situation based on spousal abuse if they are returned."

Elizabeth argues the district court's findings are clearly erroneous. We disagree. The record supports the district court's conclusion that there was only one act of physical abuse, an incident in April 2010 in which Savvas braced Elizabeth against a wall during an argument and held his hand next to her face. Elizabeth does not specify any other incidents that the district court overlooked. The record also supports the district court's conclusion that neither N.C. nor A.C. witnessed any act of physical abuse, which further suggests the lack of grave risk to the children. Further, Elizabeth has avowed not to return to Cyprus due to her subjective personal fears; if she does not return that removes any risk of the children witnessing any future abusive acts in Cyprus.

In view of the district court's well supported findings, there is no grave risk to the children under Article (b) associated with any potential future abuse of their mother.

Finally, Elizabeth argues that the district court failed to consider the impact that returning the children to Cyprus without their mother would have on them, given her stated choice to remain in the United States regardless. She focuses on evidence of the "extraordinary attachment" between the children and their mother.

---

7. The court further explained:

In other words, at one end of the spectrum are those situations where repatriation might cause inconvenience or hardship, eliminate certain educational or economic opportunities, or not comport with the child's preferences; at the other end of the spectrum are those situations in which the child faces a real risk of being hurt, physically or psychologically, as a result of repatriation. The former do not constitute a grave risk of harm under Article 13(b); the latter do.

8. The district court made these findings having credited all of Elizabeth's testimony. But the court noted that both Elizabeth and Savvas lacked credibility in certain respects. The record also reflects that Elizabeth did not consider herself a victim of domestic abuse while in Cyprus and that she did not seek protection under Cyprus's domestic abuse laws. We do not enter the parties' dispute over the effectiveness of such laws.

The district court supportably found that Elizabeth's stated refusal to return to Cyprus was based upon "her subjective perception of a threat" that was "not corroborated by other evidence in the record." Regardless, the court weighed the consequences of Elizabeth choosing not to return to Cyprus, and concluded that "the alternative of allowing these children to remain wrongfully retained in this country is equally likely to traumatize the children." Elizabeth offers no argument on appeal as to why that is not so. The district court correctly concluded that "the impact of any loss of contact with the Mother is something that must be resolved by the courts of the Children's habitual residence." We point out that Elizabeth is free, in the courts of Cyprus, to seek custody of the children and such other orders as may become necessary as to the children.

We affirm the judgment entered by the district court on October 12, 2010. We find no error in the district court's Findings of Fact and Conclusions of Law, and we approve all aspects of the district court's orders pertaining to removal.

D.   PROPERTY, ALIMONY, AND CHILD SUPPORT JURISDICTION

1.   PROPERTY AND DIVISIBLE DIVORCE

Vanderbilt v. Vanderbilt

Supreme Court of the United States, 1957.
354 U.S. 416, 77 S.Ct. 1360, 1 L.Ed.2d 1456.

■ JUSTICE BLACK delivered the opinion of the Court.

Cornelius Vanderbilt, Jr., petitioner, and Patricia Vanderbilt, respondent, were married in 1948. They separated in 1952 while living in California. The wife moved to New York where she has resided since February 1953. In March of that year the husband filed suit for divorce in Nevada. This proceeding culminated, in June 1953, with a decree of final divorce which provided that both husband and wife were "freed and released from the bonds of matrimony and all the duties and obligations thereof...." The wife was not served with process in Nevada and did not appear before the divorce court.

In April 1954, Mrs. Vanderbilt instituted an action in a New York court praying for separation from petitioner and for alimony. The New York court did not have personal jurisdiction over him, but in order to satisfy his obligations, if any, to Mrs. Vanderbilt, it sequestered his property within the State. He appeared specially and, among other defenses to the action, contended that the Full Faith and Credit Clause of the United States Constitution compelled the New York court to treat the Nevada divorce as having ended the marriage and as having destroyed any duty of support which he owed the respondent. While the New York court found the Nevada decree valid and held that it had effectively dissolved the marriage, it nevertheless entered an order, under § 1170–b of the New York Civil Practice Act, directing petitioner to make designated support payments to respondent. The New York Court of Appeals upheld the support order. Petitioner then applied to this Court for certiorari contending that § 1170–b, as applied, is unconstitutional because it contravenes the Full Faith and Credit Clause....

In *Estin v. Estin*, 334 U.S. 541 (1948), this Court decided that a Nevada divorce court, which had no personal jurisdiction over the wife, had no power to terminate a husband's obligation to provide her support as required in a pre-existing New York separation decree. The factor which distinguishes the present case from *Estin* is that here the wife's right to support had not been reduced to judgment prior to the husband's *ex parte* divorce. In our opinion this difference is not material on the question before us. Since the wife was not subject to its jurisdiction, the Nevada divorce court had no power to extinguish any right which she had under the law of New York to financial support from her husband. It has long been the constitutional rule that a court cannot adjudicate a personal claim or obligation unless it has jurisdiction over the person of the defendant. Here, the Nevada divorce court was as powerless to cut off the wife's support right as it would have been to order the husband to pay alimony if the wife had brought the divorce action and he had not been subject to the divorce court's jurisdiction. Therefore, the Nevada decree, to the extent it purported to affect the wife's right to support, was void and the Full Faith and Credit Clause did not obligate New York to give it recognition.

NOTE

One of the difficult issues left unresolved by the opinion in *Vanderbilt* is what law governs the property rights of the stay-at-home spouse: that of the domicile at the time of divorce, or of the forum (if the two are different). The generally accepted view is that the determining law is that of the stay-at-home spouse's domicile at the time of divorce. *See Loeb v. Loeb*, 152 N.E.2d 36 (N.Y. 1958); *Lewis v. Lewis*, 317 P.2d 987 (Calif. 1957); *see generally* Note, *Long–Arm Jurisdiction in Alimony and Custody Cases*, 73 COLUM. L. REV. 289, 293 (1975). *See also Manfrini v. Manfrini*, 346 A.2d 430 (N.J.Super.A.D. 1975), where the court held that full faith and credit would be granted to a decision of the New York Supreme Court providing the husband a divorce because of the wife's adultery, and denying alimony to the wife because of her misconduct. The wife had moved into their summer home in New Jersey, where she was served personally with notice of the New York action. Apparently in an effort to avail herself of the more favorable New Jersey law, she chose to default in the New York action.

2.   FOREIGN V. DOMESTIC LAW ON MARITAL PROPERTY

Aleem v. Aleem

Maryland Court of Special Appeals, 2007.
931 A.2d 1123.

[This opinion is printed at page 17, *supra*.]

3.   CHILD SUPPORT

a.   LONG–ARM JURISDICTION

Kulko v. Superior Court of California

United States Supreme Court, 1978.
436 U.S. 84, 98 S.Ct. 1690, 56 L.Ed.2d 132.

■ JUSTICE MARSHALL delivered the opinion of the Court.

The issue before us is whether, in this action for child support, the California state courts may exercise in personam jurisdiction over a nonresident, nondomiciliary parent of minor children domiciled within the State. For reasons set forth below, we hold that the exercise of such jurisdiction would violate the Due Process Clause of the Fourteenth Amendment.

Appellant Ezra Kulko married appellee Sharon Kulko Horn in 1959, during appellant's three-day stopover in California en route from a military base in Texas to a tour of duty in Korea. At the time of this marriage, both parties were domiciled in and residents of New York State. Immediately following the marriage, Sharon Kulko returned to New York, as did appellant after his tour of duty. Their first child, Darwin, was born to the Kulkos in New York in 1961, and a year later their second child, Ilsa, was born, also in New York. The Kulkos and their two children resided together as a family in New York City continuously until March 1972, when the Kulkos separated.

Following the separation, Sharon Kulko moved to San Francisco, Cal[ifornia]. A written separation agreement was drawn up in New York; in September 1972, Sharon Kulko flew to New York City in order to sign this agreement. The agreement provided, *inter alia*, that the children would remain with their father during the school year but would spend their Christmas, Easter, and summer vacations with their mother. While Sharon Kulko waived any claim for her own support or maintenance, Ezra Kulko agreed to pay his wife $3,000 per year in child support for the periods when the children were in her care, custody, and control. Immediately after execution of the separation agreement, Sharon Kulko flew to Haiti and procured a divorce there; the divorce decree incorporated the terms of the agreement. She then returned to California, where she remarried and took the name Horn.

The children resided with appellant during the school year and with their mother on vacations, as provided by the separation agreement, until December 1973. At this time, just before Ilsa was to leave New York to spend Christmas vacation with her mother, she told her father that she wanted to remain in California after her vacation. Appellant bought his daughter a one-way plane ticket, and Ilsa left, taking her clothing with her. Ilsa then commenced living in California with her mother during the school year and spending vacations with her father. In January 1976, appellant's other child, Darwin, called his mother from New York and advised her that he wanted to live with her in California. Unbeknownst to appellant, appellee Horn sent a plane ticket to her son, which he used to fly to California where he took up residence with his mother and sister.

Less than one month after Darwin's arrival in California, appellee Horn commenced this action against appellant in the California Superior Court. She sought to establish the Haitian divorce decree as a California judgment; to modify the judgment so as to award her full custody of the children; and to increase appellant's child-support obligations.

Appellant appeared specially and moved to quash service of the summons on the ground that he was not a resident of California and lacked sufficient "minimum contacts" with the State under *International Shoe Co. v. Washington*, 326 U.S. 310, 316 (1945), to warrant the State's assertion of personal jurisdiction over him.

The trial court summarily denied the motion to quash, and appellant sought review in the California Court of Appeal by petition for a writ of mandate. Appellant did not contest the court's jurisdiction for purposes of the custody determination, but, with respect to the claim for increased support, he renewed his argument that the California courts lacked personal jurisdiction over him. The appellate court affirmed the denial of appellant's motion to quash, reasoning that, by consenting to his children's living in California, appellant had "caused an effect in [the] state" warranting the exercise of jurisdiction over him.

The California Supreme Court granted appellant's petition for review, and in a 4–2 decision sustained the rulings of the lower state courts.

. . .

The Due Process Clause of the Fourteenth Amendment operates as a limitation on the jurisdiction of state courts to enter judgments affecting rights or interests of nonresident defendants. It has long been the rule that a valid judgment imposing a personal obligation or duty in favor of the plaintiff may be entered only by a court having jurisdiction over the person of the defendant. The existence of personal jurisdiction, in turn, depends upon the presence of reasonable notice to the defendant that an action has been brought, and a sufficient connection between the defendant and the forum State to make it fair to require defense of the action in the forum. In this case, appellant does not dispute the adequacy of the notice that he received, but contends that his connection with the State of California is too attenuated, under the standards implicit in the Due Process Clause of the Constitution, to justify imposing upon him the burden and inconvenience of defense in California.

The parties are in agreement that the constitutional standard for determining whether the State may enter a binding judgment against appellant here is that set forth in this Court's opinion in *International Shoe*: that a defendant "have certain minimum contacts with [the forum State] such that the maintenance of the suit does not offend 'traditional notions of fair play and substantial justice.'" While the interests of the forum State and of the plaintiff in proceeding with the cause in the plaintiff's forum of choice are, of course, to be considered, an essential criterion in all cases is whether the "quality and nature" of the defendant's activity is such that it is "reasonable" and "fair" to require him to conduct his defense in that State.

. . . [W]e believe that the California Supreme Court's application of the minimum-contacts test in this case represents an unwarranted extension of *International Shoe* and would, if sustained, sanction a result that is neither fair, just, nor reasonable.

. . .

The "purposeful act" that the California Supreme Court believed . . . warrant[ed] the exercise of personal jurisdiction over appellant in California was his "actively and fully [consenting] to Ilsa living in California for the school year . . . and . . . [sending] her to California for that purpose." We cannot accept the proposition that appellant's acquiescence in Ilsa's desire to live with her mother conferred jurisdiction over appellant in the California courts in this action. A father who agrees, in the interests of family harmony and his children's preferences, to allow them to spend more time in California than was required under a separation agreement can hardly be said to have "purposefully availed himself" of the "benefits and protections" of California's laws.

Nor can we agree with the assertion of the court below that the exercise of *in personam* jurisdiction here was warranted by the financial benefit appellant derived from his daughter's presence in California for nine months of the year. This argument rests on the premise that, while appellant's liability for support payments remained unchanged, his yearly expenses for supporting the child in New York decreased. But this circumstance, even if true, does not support California's assertion of jurisdiction here. Any diminution in appellant's household costs resulted, not from the child's presence in California, but rather from her absence from appellant's home. . . . Any ultimate financial advantage to appellant thus results not from the child's presence in California, but from appellee's failure earlier to seek an increase in payments under the separation agreement. The argument below to the contrary, in our view, confuses the question of appellant's liability with that of the proper forum in which to determine that liability.

. . .

The circumstances in this case clearly render "unreasonable" California's assertion of personal jurisdiction. There is no claim that appellant has visited physical injury on either property or persons within the State of California. The cause of action herein asserted arises, not from the defendant's commercial transactions in interstate commerce, but rather from his personal, domestic relations. It thus cannot be said that appellant has sought a commercial benefit from solicitation of business from a resident of California that could reasonably render him liable to suit in state court; appellant's activities cannot fairly be analogized to an insurer's sending an insurance contract and premium notices into the State to an insured resident of the State. Furthermore, the controversy between the parties arises from a separation that occurred in the State of New York; appellee Horn seeks modification of a contract that was negotiated in New York and that she flew to New York to sign. . . . [T]he instant action involves an agreement that was entered into with virtually no connection with the forum State.

Finally, basic considerations of fairness point decisively in favor of appellant's State of domicile as the proper forum for adjudication of this case, whatever the merits of appellee's underlying claim. It is appellant who has remained in the State of the marital domicile, whereas it is appellee who has moved across the continent. Appellant has at all times resided in New York State, and, until the separation and appellee's move to California, his entire family resided there as well. As noted above, appellant did no more than acquiesce in the stated preference of one of his children to live with her mother in California. This single act is surely not one that a reasonable parent would expect to result in the substantial financial burden and personal strain of litigating a child-support suit in a forum 3,000 miles away, and we therefore see no basis on which it can be said that appellant could reasonably have anticipated being "haled before a [California] court." To make jurisdiction in a case such as this turn on whether appellant bought his daughter her ticket or instead unsuccessfully sought to prevent her departure would impose an unreasonable burden on family relations, and one wholly unjustified by the "quality and nature" of appellant's activities in or relating to the State of California.

. . .

. . . [T]he mere act of sending a child to California to live with her mother is not a commercial act and connotes no intent to obtain or expectancy of receiving a corresponding benefit in the State that would make fair the assertion of that State's judicial jurisdiction.

Accordingly, we conclude that the appellant's motion to quash service, on the ground of lack of personal jurisdiction, was erroneously denied by the California courts. The judgment of the California Supreme Court is, therefore, [r]eversed.

Rosemarie T. Ring, *Personal Jurisdiction and Child Support: Establishing the Parent–Child Relationship as Minimum Contacts*

89 CALIF. L. REV. 1125, 1139–45 (2001).

The Court's holding in *Kulko* not only [limited] the authority of state courts to assert jurisdiction over nonresident parents under existing long-arm statutes, but severely limited how legislatures could approach the problem in the future. Because the parent-child relationship was not a relevant basis for asserting jurisdiction, purposeful availment became the focus of courts and legislatures seeking to hold nonresident parents responsible for the financial support of their minor children. Accordingly, state courts struggled to find purposeful availment by analogizing the child support obligation to obligations arising out of relationships based on contractual arrangements or tortious conduct. In addition, legislatures enacted new long-arm statutes incorporating acts of purposeful availment considered to be especially relevant in the context of child support actions. Despite these efforts, courts and legislatures continue to struggle as they are forced to disregard the parent-child relationship in favor of finding some act of purposeful availment in order to navigate the barriers created by *Kulko*. Indeed, upon closer examination, these efforts confirm that the rule announced in Kulko is untenable and ought to be overruled.

1. Lower Courts Struggling to Find Purposeful Availment under Existing Long–Arm Statutes

State legislatures authorize the exercise of state power over nonresidents by enacting long-arm statutes. Thus, all assertions of personal jurisdiction must satisfy the forum state's long-arm statute and comport with due process. While many states authorize their courts to exercise personal jurisdiction over nonresident defendants on any basis that is constitutionally permissible, others allow courts to assert jurisdiction based on specific acts or circumstances, such as tortious conduct by a nonresident defendant causing injury within the state. Following *Kulko*, courts attempted to assert jurisdiction over nonresident parents under both types of long-arm statutes by identifying various acts of purposeful availment related to the parent-child relationship.

Long-arm statutes based on specific acts or circumstances typically allow states to assert jurisdiction based on a nonresident's business transactions or tortious conduct. Although these statutes were designed to protect state citizens in interstate business transactions and to allow recovery for physical injuries resulting from torts committed by nonresidents, following *Kulko* courts employed "judicial creativity" in extending these provisions to child support actions. Unfortunately, because an existing divorce decree or child support order is required to assert jurisdiction under these statutes, this approach is limited in its ability to address the problems created by *Kulko* in establishing child support orders in cases involving a nonresident parent.

Under "transacting business" long-arm statutes, courts typically assert jurisdiction based on the existence of a separation or divorce agreement with a "substantial connection" to the forum state. Relying on the separation or divorce agreement, the court is able to treat the dispute as a contract case from which the support obligation arises. This approach obscures the real significance of the dispute as being primarily concerned with the activities of the nonresident parent as opposed to an obligation arising out of the parent-child relationship. Moreover, it is only available to resident parents whose divorce or separation agreement has been entered into in the forum state. It does nothing to aid parents who have left the state of marital domicile, as in *Kulko*.

Courts have also relied on "tortious conduct" long-arm statutes in asserting personal jurisdiction over nonresident parents. Some courts have construed "tortious conduct" provisions broadly to include failure to support a minor child. For example, in *In re Custody of Miller* [548 P.2d 542 (Wash. 1976)], the Washington Supreme Court held that "the failure of a parent to support his or her children constitutes a tort" within the meaning of the long-arm statute. Unfortunately, this case is an exception to the rule. Most courts require an existing support order before finding that the nonresident defendant is in violation of a duty or has engaged in tortious conduct, reasoning that in the absence of a valid court order no duty has been violated because no support amount has been set. As a result, long-arm statutes based on tortious conduct can usually only be used to enforce existing orders.

In addition to their limited applicability, "tortious conduct" long-arm statutes can take a variety of forms, introducing unnecessary confusion into a court's analysis. Some statutes explicitly include tortious acts that occur outside the forum state but have effects inside the state. Others limit their application to torts occurring within the forum state. Still others distinguish between acts and omissions occurring both within and without the forum state. As a result, in determining whether they may assert personal jurisdiction over a nonresident parent in a particular case, courts may have to determine where the failure to support occurs. In addition, they may be required to decide whether the failure to support is an act or an omission. While the custodial parent is likely to argue that the failure to support is an act occurring in the child's state of residence, the nonresident parent is likely to argue that it is an omission occurring in the nonresident parent's state of residence. Thus, before courts can even consider the child support obligation at issue, they must spend considerable time and effort in working through the above intricacies of long-arm statutes based on tortious conduct.

Both "transacting business" and "tortious conduct" long-arm statutes are of limited use to courts seeking to assert personal jurisdiction over a nonresident parent. Unless the nonresident parent has entered into a divorce agreement in the forum state, there is no act of purposeful availment. Likewise, even if a court is willing to find that the nonresident parent's failure to support the child constitutes an act of purposeful availment, it is of limited use unless there is an existing child support order. In addition to the limited applicability of these long-arm statutes, both approaches focus on the nonresident parent's activities to the total exclusion of the parent-child relationship. The obligation to financially support one's child does not arise out of the activities of a nonresident parent in relation to the state in which the child resides. The parent-child relationship is the source of that obligation and should be the focus of the court's inquiry.

At the other end of the spectrum, some states enact long-arm statutes allowing state courts to assert jurisdiction on any basis not inconsistent with the demands of due process. Kulko's extension of the purposeful availment requirement to child support actions also severely limited the reach of long-arm statutes authorizing the exercise of jurisdiction "on any basis not inconsistent with the Constitution of this state of or the United States." By its holding, *Kulko* required courts to disregard the parent-child relationship. Thus, even courts presumably given the greatest degree of latitude in asserting jurisdiction were limited by *Kulko*.

2.   Limiting Legislative Efforts to Respond to Issues of Personal Jurisdiction in the Context of Child Support Actions

The holding in *Kulko* not only served as a barrier to courts asserting personal jurisdiction under existing long-arm statutes, but also dictated how legislatures could approach the problem in the future. While courts have struggled to find acts of purposeful availment comparable to a breach of contract or tortious conduct, legislatures have endeavored to enact new long-arm statutes specifically designed to confer jurisdiction based on activities held to constitute minimum contacts in actions for child support. However, despite these efforts *Kulko's* purposeful availment requirement remains a barrier to real change.

These specialized statutes do offer some benefit over traditional long-arm statutes in that they clearly indicate the legislature's intent to assert jurisdiction over nonresident parents in child support actions. However, courts are still forced to disregard the parent-child relationship in assessing minimum contacts. Instead, courts must find some act of purposeful availment by analyzing issues such as whether a child is present in the forum state as a result of the actions of the defendant or whether the defendant engaged in sexual intercourse in the state that may have resulted in the conception of the child who is the subject of the child support action.

One act of purposeful availment identified in these specialized long-arm statutes is where the child resides in the forum state because of the acts or directives of the nonresident parent. In *Franklin v. Commonwealth* [497 S.E.2d 881 (Va. Ct. App. 1998)], a case in which a mother and her two children had relocated to Virginia after the nonresident defendant abused and finally expelled them from their home, a Virginia appellate court held that it could assert personal jurisdiction over the nonresident father because the children had become residents of Virginia "as a result of his acts." Although the defendant did not contest the fact that he had abused and expelled his family from their home, he argued that he had not purposefully availed himself of the benefits and protections of the forum state because he had not specifically directed them to relocate to Virginia. The court dismissed this argument, stating that to allow [a] husband to escape his support obligations merely because he failed to dictate the specific destination when he ordered his family to leave the marital home would frustrate the purpose of the legislature ... to create an economical and expedient means of enforcing support orders for parties located in different states.

The court distinguished cases in which other courts declined to exercise jurisdiction over nonresident fathers under similar long-arm provisions by stating that in each of those cases "the children resided in [the forum state] after their mother chose to move out of state without any urging from their fathers."

This distinction has no basis in reality and is an example of why forcing courts to show purposeful availment in the context of an action for child support is inappropriate. As dictated by *Kulko*, unless a court can point to some act of purposeful availment, there can be no basis for finding minimum contacts. Under this logic, it is significantly more difficult for a mother who leaves an abusive husband of her own volition, as opposed to being ordered out of the home by her abuser, to obtain personal jurisdiction over him should she and her children move to another state.

A nonresident parent's act of sexual intercourse in the forum state, where the act may have resulted in conception of a child who is the subject of the action, is another act of purposeful availment often identified in specialized long-arm statutes. In *Phillips v. Fallen* [No. WD 55199, 1999 WL 50159 (Jan. 26, 1999)], a Missouri appellate court upheld the validity of a support order issued by a Washington court asserting personal jurisdiction over a nonresident defendant where he had "not overcome adequately [the resident mother's] averment that the couple had sexual intercourse in Washington which may have resulted in their child's conception." The defendant father acknowledged visiting Washington with the plaintiff mother around Thanksgiving 1982, but contended that he "did not remember" having sexual intercourse and that "the child's conception could not have occurred during the couple's visit to Washington."

Relying on a medical dictionary and the mother's medical records, the court held that the Washington court had not erred in asserting personal jurisdiction over the nonresident father. While the medical records suggest that the child was born prematurely by approximately three weeks, these records were not authenticated, and [defendant] did not present any medical testimony supporting his interpretation of them. We discern no basis for concluding that the decision erred in rejecting *Phillips'* interpretation. The child was born 271 days after Thanksgiving 1982. A normal gestational period is 280 days, but a range of 250 to 310 days is not abnormal.

In struggling to find some act of purposeful availment, rather than focusing on the parent-child relationship and the child support obligation arising from it, the court spent the majority of its opinion analyzing the definition of a normal gestational period.

The *Phillips* case is yet another example of how requiring purposeful availment in the context of actions for child support can distort the true nature of the child support obligation and require courts to engage in meaningless analysis. When and where a nonresident parent engaged in sexual intercourse is a private matter and should be irrelevant in child support actions once paternity has been established. Thus, even under long-arm statutes specifically designed to confer jurisdiction in child support actions, *Kulko's* focus on purposeful availment obscures the real significance of the child support obligation. Courts and legislatures are forced to spend time analyzing the nonresident parent's activities in relation to the forum state, rather than focusing on the parent-child relationship as the source of the obligation.

Bergaust v. Flaherty

Court of Appeals of Virginia, 2011.
703 S.E.2d 248.

■ HUMPHREYS, J.

Jane Louise Bergaust ("Bergaust") appeals the Fairfax County Circuit Court's dismissal of her petition for child support. Bergaust alleges the circuit court erred in finding it did not have personal jurisdiction over the appellee, Edward Flaherty ("Flaherty"). For the reasons that follow, we affirm the circuit court.

In June of 1994, Bergaust traveled to Giverny, France, just outside of Paris, to visit her mother during the opening of the American Museum. While there, Bergaust met Flaherty, an American filmmaker then living in Paris, who was hired to film the event.... They cultivated "an unusual connection."

Flaherty kept in touch with Bergaust after she returned to her home in Virginia.... Over the next 18 months, the relationship continued to develop. Bergaust returned to France on December 1, 1995 to visit Flaherty. During her visit, Bergaust stayed at Flaherty's apartment. She also shared his bed. Bergaust returned to Virginia a few days before Christmas. Shortly thereafter, she discovered she was pregnant.

Because she had not had sexual intercourse with any other person, Bergaust called Flaherty and explained that the baby was his. Although Flaherty was "a little bit shocked," he said he would do whatever Bergaust wanted to do and he promised to support her "in any way that he possibly could." Flaherty called Bergaust at least twice a week during her pregnancy, and from the very first conversation he acknowledged his paternity.... [H]e consistently referred to the forthcoming child as "our baby."

Bergaust's daughter, C.B., was born in Arlington, Virginia, on August 1, 1996. Bergaust immediately called Flaherty to tell him the news. Flaherty was "elated." ... After that, Flaherty called Bergaust at least twice a week to talk about the baby. During these early conversations, Flaherty expressly referred to C.B. as "our daughter." In March of 1997, when C.B. was about seven months old, Flaherty came to Virginia for a visit. He wanted to see Bergaust and C.B. Flaherty arrived at Bergaust's house in McLean at around noon and stayed until around five. During this visit, Flaherty held C.B. and played with her. Bergaust later testified that Flaherty was "enamored with" C.B. He "couldn't get over her beauty, and he was just absolutely enchanted with her." This visit was memorialized in pictures.

Upon the conclusion of his visit, Flaherty returned to France. He initially continued to call Bergaust "once every two weeks or so," but then the frequency of his phone calls decreased over time. Flaherty last phoned Bergaust on August 1, 1997, C.B.'s first birthday. Bergaust, who by that time had not heard from Flaherty in several months, expressed her anger and irritation over Flaherty's lack of involvement in C.B.'s life. Flaherty ended the call; he never called again.

In the summer of 2008, C.B., who was then almost twelve years old, was watching a documentary on television in which Flaherty appeared. C.B. recognized Flaherty from the photographs taken of his visit to McLean in 1997. She expressed her excitement at seeing her father to Bergaust. Bergaust did some research on the film and was able to ascertain Flaherty's current address in France.

On March 16, 2009, Bergaust filed a Uniform Support Petition in the Fairfax County Juvenile and Domestic Relations District Court (J & DRC), seeking establishment of paternity and child support. Flaherty defended the action on the ground that the J & DRC lacked personal jurisdiction over him. The J & DRC agreed with Flaherty and, on June 2, 2009, granted Flaherty's motion to dismiss.

On June 11, 2009, Bergaust appealed the J & DRC's dismissal of her petition to the circuit court. Flaherty again moved to dismiss the case for lack of personal jurisdiction. After briefing and oral argument, the circuit court denied Flaherty's motion and found that it did have personal jurisdiction over Flaherty. The case, then, proceeded to trial. Because Flaherty refused to cooperate with discovery, he was prohibited from objecting to Bergaust's evidence at trial and from presenting any evidence on his own behalf. Flaherty did not attend the trial.

Upon the conclusion of the evidence, the circuit court re-visited the issue of personal jurisdiction. The court allowed the parties to submit additional briefs and then issued a letter opinion, dated March 3, 2010, in which it found the circuit court did not have personal jurisdiction over Flaherty. The circuit court held that Flaherty's contacts with Virginia did not satisfy Virginia's long arm statute or otherwise comport with due process.

Bergaust's sole assertion on appeal is that the circuit court erred in finding it did not have personal jurisdiction over Flaherty. . . .

"It is well settled that a plaintiff is not entitled to 'a judgment *in personam* to extra-territorial effect if it be made to appear that it was rendered without jurisdiction over the person sought to be bound.'" *Harrel v. Preston*, 421 S.E.2d 676, 677 (Va. App. 1992) (quoting *May v. Anderson*, 345 U.S. 528 (1953)). To obtain the requisite personal jurisdiction over an out-of-state defendant in a claim for child support, the record must clearly indicate "'at a minimum, a connection to Virginia that is recognized by Virginia's long-arm statute.'" "The purpose of our 'long arm statute' is to assert jurisdiction, to the extent permissible under the Due Process Clause of the Constitution of the United States, over nonresidents who engage in some purposeful activity in Virginia." Such purposeful activity includes any "single act by a nonresident" giving "rise to a cause of action" in our courts.

To that end, [VA. CODE ANN.] § 8.01–328.1(A)(8), the statutory provision governing long arm control over child support matters, provides in pertinent part,

A court may exercise personal jurisdiction over a person, who acts directly or by an agent, as to a cause of action arising from the person's:

. . .

Having . . . (iii) shown by personal conduct in this Commonwealth, as alleged by affidavit, that the person conceived or fathered a child in this Commonwealth[.]

In adopting [VA. CODE ANN.] § 8.01–328.1, "the legislature evinced a policy of extending the jurisdiction of its courts to the maximum extent permitted" by due process. . . . Once the long arm statute is satisfied, the question simply becomes "whether the defendant has sufficient 'minimum contacts with [the forum] such that the maintenance of the suit does not offend traditional notions of fair play and substantial justice.'"

If Flaherty, in fact, "conceived or fathered" a child in this Commonwealth, he is within reach of Virginia's long arm statute. Thus, the resolution of this case turns on the meaning of the phrase "conceived or fathered" in [VA. CODE ANN.] § 8.01–328.1(A)(8)(iii). The circuit court adopted the definition of those two words advanced by Flaherty, and found that the "plain, common and ordinary meaning of the term 'fathered' used in [VA. CODE ANN.] § 8.01–328 is to beget or to procreate as the father; whereas the term 'conceived' refers to the act of the mother becoming pregnant." The circuit court concluded that the General Assembly intended a gender specific definition to each term and treated them as synonyms. Essentially, the circuit court construed the definition of the terms "conceived" and "fathered" to mean Bergaust's act of becoming pregnant and Flaherty's act of making her pregnant. The circuit court then found that since Bergaust literally became pregnant in France, Flaherty was beyond the reach of Virginia's long arm statute because he did not, in the words of the statute, "father[ ] a child in this Commonwealth." Accordingly, the court held that personal jurisdiction "does not lie under [[VA. CODE ANN.] § 8.01–328.1(A)(8)(iii)]."

Bergaust asserts the court's gender specific interpretation of the phrase "conceived or fathered" amounts to plain error. Bergaust suggests instead that the word "conceived" means the act of getting pregnant (since conception cannot occur without the participation of both a male and a female) and the word "fathered" means the acknowledgment of paternity. Bergaust concedes the act of conception took place in France. She simply maintains that because Flaherty acknowledged his parentage of C.B. while in Virginia, the circuit court erred in finding it could not exercise personal jurisdiction over him for purposes of Bergaust's child support petition. Flaherty, on the other hand, maintains the circuit court correctly interpreted the statute in gender specific, synonymous terms, and reasons that Virginia's long arm statute extends only to persons who actually conceive a child here in the Commonwealth. We agree with the argument advanced by Flaherty.

. . .

[I]n this case, because the terms "conceived" and "fathered" are not defined statutorily, we must afford the terms their plain and ordinary meaning. To "conceive" means "to become pregnant with: be with (child or young)," or "to beget." The verb "fathered" means "to make oneself the father of: beget." Thus, it is clear that the plain meaning of the words "conceived" and "fathered" refer to the act of procreation. Indeed, the word "beget" means "to procreate as the father: sire," or "to give birth to: breed." To "procreate" means "to produce (offspring) by generation: beget, propagate, generate, [or] reproduce."

It is true, as Bergaust contends, that one plain and ordinary meaning of the verb "fathered" includes "to make oneself the father or author of by acknowledgment." However, if the General Assembly intended by the Commonwealth's long arm statute to include the mere acknowledgment of parentage by a nonresident, it presumably would have included the word "mothered" along with "conceived or fathered," in order to encompass the non-custodial mother of a child living in this Commonwealth. . . .

This is not to say that Bergaust's argument is entirely without merit. Indeed, in rendering child support decisions, the first inquiry involves identification of the parents. Courts making such decisions normally know the identity of the mother, because she gave birth to the child; but often we can only ascertain the identity of the father by the fact that he has publicly held himself out as the father. While the act of conceiving a child elsewhere may ultimately give rise to a father's presence, and perhaps even his acknowledgment of paternity, in the Commonwealth, we conclude that, given the words it chose, the General Assembly intended the long arm statute to apply only to both parties responsible for actually conceiving a child in Virginia.

. . .

For the foregoing reasons, we hold the circuit court did not err in finding it did not have personal jurisdiction over Flaherty under Virginia's long arm statute, [VA. CODE ANN.] § 8.01–328.1(A)(8)(iii). We further hold that because the circuit court did not have personal jurisdiction over Flaherty under the long arm statute, we need not decide whether Flaherty maintained sufficient minimum contacts with Virginia justifying the exercise of jurisdiction over him under the Due Process Clause of the United States Constitution. We, thus, affirm the judgment of the circuit court.

b. UNIFORM INTERSTATE FAMILY SUPPORT ACT

Hamilton v. Hamilton

Supreme Court of Indiana, 2009.
914 N.E.2d 747.

■ BOEHM, J.

This case involves a Florida child support order registered for enforcement in Indiana pursuant to the Uniform Interstate Family Support Act. The Indiana trial court issued a contempt order requiring the father to pay less than the full amount of the Florida support obligation to avoid incarceration. We hold that the trial court's order did not impermissibly modify the foreign judgment.

Richard and Suzanne Hamilton were granted a divorce in Florida in July 2005. The Florida divorce judgment awarded Suzanne physical custody of the couple's two children and required Richard to pay support in the amount of $1,473 per month. The judgment also required Richard to pay a $3,619 arrearage in support from the time the couple separated in March 2005.

Richard did not fulfill his child support responsibilities, and by January 2006 he owed a total of $11,879. Suzanne sought enforcement of Richard's support obligation by filing a motion for contempt in the Florida court. Richard did not appear at the hearing on Suzanne's motion, and on January 13, 2006, the Florida court held Richard in contempt. The Florida court found Richard had the ability to pay Suzanne but had willfully failed to do so, and sentenced him to 170 days in jail unless he tendered $7,500 within twenty days. The court also set up a payment schedule for Richard to satisfy the balance of the arrearages and the ongoing support obligation.

Suzanne and the children remained Florida residents, but at some point Richard moved to Evansville in Vanderburgh County, Indiana where he lived with his parents. Suzanne sought enforcement of the Florida orders by registering the Florida support judgment and contempt order in Vanderburgh Superior Court. The Indiana court ruled that the child support judgment was a properly registered foreign order entitled to full faith and credit. The court also extended full faith and credit to the findings and conclusions in the Florida contempt order, "except as to its judgment that the Husband is ordered incarcerated in the [county] jail for a time of 170 days." The court concluded that remedies for contempt are discretionary and do not bind responding tribunals. Although the Indiana court found Richard in contempt, it stayed the jail sentence if Richard tendered $3,750 and made monthly payments of $1,250. In a separate order entered November 10, 2006, the court established Richard's arrearages at $20,466.50.

Richard struggled to meet his monthly obligations, and Suzanne soon sought relief through a writ of bodily attachment. On March 29, 2007, the Indiana trial court ordered Richard to serve 170 days in the county jail, but stayed the sentence contingent upon Richard's paying Suzanne $1,000, obtaining full-time employment, and executing a wage assignment in an amount specified by the Indiana Child Support Guidelines or $150 per week, whichever was greater.

In May 2007, Suzanne again sought to hold Richard in contempt for failure to meet the conditions of the court's orders. Richard testified that he had met the three conditions imposed by the March 29 order, and the court found no contempt. In November 2007, Suzanne again asked the court to find Richard in contempt and asked for larger monthly payments and more aggressive enforcement of the Florida support order. At the hearing on this motion, Richard testified that he was working between thirty and fifty hours per week and earning $7 per hour. Financial exhibits reflected that he was paying an average of $150 per week in support. On March 4, 2008, the trial court ruled that Richard was not in contempt of the Indiana orders.

The first issue is whether the trial court's March 4 judgment constituted a modification of the original Florida support order that would violate either the Full Faith and Credit Clause or the Supremacy Clause of the Constitution of the United States. This is an issue of law which we review *de novo*.

Article IV, Section 1 of the United States Constitution provides that "Full Faith and Credit shall be given in each State to the public Acts, Records, and judicial Proceedings of every other State. And the Congress may by general Laws prescribe the Manner in which such Acts, Records and Proceedings shall be proved, and the Effect thereof." In 1994, Congress exercised its Article IV authority to "prescribe . . . the Effect" of state court support orders by enacting the Full Faith and Credit for Child Support Orders Act (FFCCSOA). 28 U.S.C. § 1738B. FFCCSOA provides that a state which first issues a support order retains continuing, exclusive jurisdiction over the judgment subject to exceptions not relevant here. Under the Supremacy Clause of the United States Constitution, the provisions of FFCCSOA are binding on the states and supersede any inconsistent provisions of state law.

State legislatures also addressed this issue in the same general time-frame. . . . The National Conference of Commissioners on Uniform State Laws first adopted the Uniform Interstate Family Support Act (UIFSA) in 1992. Amended versions were promulgated in 1996 and 2001, and UIFSA has now been adopted in one version or another by all fifty states. Indiana has enacted the 1996 version. IND. CODE §§ 31–18–1–1 to –9–4 (2004).

The rather odd circumstance that the two statutes occupy the same legal space is apparently an accident of history. As one scholar explains:

> The rationale for promulgating both a uniform law . . . and a federal statute, FFCCSOA, that accomplish essentially the same objective is somewhat elusive. Many states began enacting UIFSA after the National Conference of Commissioners on Uniform State Laws approved UIFSA in 1992. Some child support advocates, however, worried that piece-meal, state-by-state adoption of UIFSA would delay receipt of the intended benefits by interstate obligees. In addition, . . . UIFSA supporters believed that the "uniform law" would become anything but uniform.
>
> Congress ultimately adopted two solutions to the threat of non-uniform state law. First, FFCCSOA required states to accord full faith and credit to another state's child support order under most circumstances. Second, Congress recently required every state to pass UIFSA without alteration.

Patricia Wick Hatamyar, *Critical Applications and Proposals for Improvement of the Uniform Interstate Family Support Act and the Full Faith and Credit for Child Support Orders Act,* 71 ST. JOHN'S L. REV. 1, 6–7 (1997).

It has been observed that FFCCSOA and UIFSA are "virtually identical." The two are not precisely the same, however, and "where UIFSA is silent, the FFCCSOA may help fill any gaps." The two statutes are to be viewed as complementary and duplicative, not contradictory. As we recently held, the FFCCSOA does not preempt the UIFSA.

The stated objective of both UIFSA and FFCCSOA is to create a national regime in which only a single support order is effective at any given time. UIFSA's cornerstone provision is:

> As long as one of the individual parties or the child continues to reside in the issuing State [in this case Florida], and as long as the parties do not agree to the contrary, the issuing tribunal has continuing, exclusive jurisdiction over its [child-support] order—which in practical terms means that it may modify its order.

As a corollary, a responding state, in this case Indiana, "shall recognize and enforce, but may not modify, a registered order if the issuing tribunal had jurisdiction." UIFSA does not expressly define "modify," but FFCCSOA defines the term as "a change in a child support order that affects the amount, scope, or duration of the order and modifies, replaces, supersedes, or otherwise is made subsequent to the child support order." Suzanne contends that the Vanderburgh Superior Court orders impermissibly modified the Florida support order. Richard responds that the orders were proper enforcement mechanisms that UIFSA and FFCCSOA leave to the discretion of the Indiana courts. For the reasons explained below, we agree with Richard.

The Full Faith and Credit Clause "generally requires every State to give to a judgment at least the *res judicata* effect which the judgment would be accorded in the state which rendered it." *Durfee v. Duke*, 375 U.S. 106, 109 (1963). This "does not mean that States must adopt the practices of other States regarding the time, manner, and mechanisms for enforcing judgments. Enforcement measures do not travel with the sister state judgment as preclusive effects do; such measures remain subject to the evenhanded control of forum law." *Baker v. General Motors Corp.*, 522 U.S. 222, 235 (1998). . . .

[T]he commentary to UIFSA makes clear that "the power to enforce the order of the issuing State is not 'exclusive' with that State. Rather, on request one or more responding States may also exercise authority to enforce the order of the issuing State." Several provisions of UIFSA reflect respect for the enforcement procedures of the responding state. And UIFSA includes a lengthy list of actions a responding state court "may" take to enforce an order.

In this case, the Florida court issued the $1,473 per month support judgment. Suzanne and her children remained Florida residents, and the parties never agreed to grant modification jurisdiction to another tribunal. Florida therefore retained continuing, exclusive jurisdiction over the original order. Indiana became a "responding" state when Suzanne registered the support order and requested that it be enforced by the Vanderburgh court. Indiana acquired authority to enforce the judgment but not to modify it. The Indiana trial court then issued a series of orders acknowledging Richard's obligation and arrearages but ultimately permitting Richard to avoid incarceration if he paid $150 per week through a wage assignment. The issue, as the Court of Appeals aptly framed it, is whether the trial court's orders constituted valid enforcement or impermissible modification of the original Florida support judgment.

We agree with the Court of Appeals that the trial court's contempt orders were valid enforcement mechanisms. The trial court gave full faith and credit to the Florida support order and did not alter "the amount, scope, or duration" of Richard's $1,473–per–month obligation. The arrearages continue to accrue in accordance with the Florida order. To be sure, the trial court issued a contempt order requiring Richard to pay only $150 per month to avoid incarceration. But as a responding tribunal, the Vanderburgh Superior court had discretion to "specify[ ] the amount and the manner of compliance" with the original support order, and to fashion a remedy that would most effectively compel payment. The UIFSA enforcement options are permissive, not compulsory, and contemplate that not all enforcement mechanisms will demand 100 cents on every dollar owed.

Just as the trial court's order is consistent with UIFSA, it also meets the requirements of the Federal Constitution. We are obligated to give the Florida order the same effect it would receive in a Florida court. But we are directed to no principle of Florida law that mandates imprisonment for contempt for violation of a support order, or precludes orders that attempt to maximize compliance in light of realistic prospects of payment. To the contrary, Florida, like any sensible jurisdiction, recognizes that some flexibility in enforcement is in the interest of the affected child.

Suzanne cites *Reis v. Zimmer*, 263 A.D.2d 136 (N.Y. App. Div. 1999), *amended*, 270 A.D.2d 968 (N.Y. App. Div. 2000), and *Walker v. Amos*, 746 N.E.2d 642 (Ohio Ct. App. 2000). . . .

. . .

Neither *Reis* nor *Walker* has any application to this case. In *Reis*, the trial court reallocated support money that would have gone directly to the children, and diverted it to the father's expenses in visiting and communicating. And in *Walker*, the trial court suspended the support obligation entirely, which both halted payments and reduced the amount of any accumulating arrearages. Here, by contrast, the trial court did not divert, suspend, or otherwise alter Richard's support responsibilities. Arrearages continue to accrue as provided in the Florida order. The trial court is entitled to fashion its order in a manner best designed to encourage compliance. Its refusal to find Richard in contempt if the conditions are met is a valid enforcement mechanism.

For the reasons stated, we hold that the trial court's contempt orders did not modify the Florida support judgment in violation of UIFSA or FFCCSOA, and are consistent with the requirements of the Full Faith and Credit Clause.

CHAPTER 11

PRIVATE ORDERING

A. INTRODUCTION TO PRIVATE ORDERING

Brian Bix, *Private Ordering and Family Law*

23 J. AM. ACAD. MATRIM. LAW. 249, 249, 251–59 (2010).

Until recently in American family law (and the family law of most countries), private arrangements to alter the legal rules surrounding family status were rarely enforced. There was, of course, "private ordering" of a basic sort: e.g., one chose whether to marry or not, and whom to marry; but once one married, the legally enforceable rules of marriage, the ability to exit through divorce or annulment, the financial obligations upon divorce, and so on, were all set by the state, which might also limit the power of the parties to distribute their own property upon death, as with a spouse's "statutory share." Similarly with parenthood: one could choose whether to have (and whether to adopt) children, but once one was a parent, one's obligations and rights were set by the state, which would also determine the limited circumstances and set terms under which one could surrender parental rights to a child.

Much has changed in recent decades, with American states increasingly allowing different types of private ordering in a range of different family law areas. One can speak of premarital agreements, marital agreements, separation agreements, open adoption agreements, co-parenting agreements, agreements on the disposition of frozen embryos, and agreements to arbitrate disputes arising out of any of the above agreements. . . .

I. General Justifications for State Enforcement of Private Ordering

. . .

The basic idea behind private ordering—whether under the rubric of contract, capitalism or family—is that individuals know better than do other people (including those in government) what is in their own best interests. On one level, this is the justification against paternalistic intervention by government (as in John Stuart Mill's "harm principle," from his *On Liberty*.)[5] On a more general level, it is an argument for the value of liberty.

Certainly, it would seem strange to think that government bureaucracies know more than a given person does about what sort of domestic arrangements would best suit that person's interests and needs. Just as we would not have government tell people whether to marry or whom, whether to have children or how many, it seems but a small step to say that individuals should have comparable freedom to select or modify some of the terms of their domestic ties.

---

5. JOHN STUART MILL, ON LIBERTY (1869); the "harm principle" is discussed in chapter 4 of Mill's text.

A different, but overlapping point relates to the value of autonomy to living a good life—a point most famously articulated by the German philosopher Immanuel Kant, but which has its roots, in different ways, in the classical Greek philosophers and in a variety of religious traditions. It is not merely doing the right things, but also that the things we do are due to our own choices, that is important. Living a good life is not merely doing the right things, but also choosing to do the right things. "Autonomy" means self-governance, and we can only be said to be governing our lives in any significant sense when we have a variety of tenable choices, and can make un-coerced choices among them. Thus, to the extent that the state offers a variety of institutional options, or allows individuals, through express agreement, to alter the terms of the options offered, individuals are given greater governance over their own lives.

Arguments of autonomy often overlap with arguments about consent: e.g., within contract law (that purported paradigm of private ordering), about the extent to which provisions should be enforced because the parties have assented to the provisions. In the context of contract scholarship, this raises the question of the extent to which "consent" to most agreements is "full consent" (morally significant consent), an issue that also, obviously, arises in the private ordering of domestic relations, whether such "ordering" has been done through written contracts or in other ways. Limitations or distortions of consent can become an argument against the state enforcement of private arrangements.

In American legal scholarship generally, the economic analysis of law (the "law and economics" school) is ascendant, though its influence is perhaps less in family law than in most other areas. Where some scholars might speak of autonomy (as in the previous section), law and economics theorists would speak in terms of efficiency. Private ordering is efficient (increases overall social wealth[11]) because, as discussed earlier, individuals are best placed to know their own preferences; thus, objects and services are likely to end up with individuals or entities that value them more if voluntary transactions are allowed, and individual commitments are enforced.

II.   Justifications for Limits on the State Enforcement of Private Ordering

A.   Public Policy

One standard justification for the regulation of private transactions is the public interest: there are reasons for public (governmental) promotion of transactions that work to the general benefit, and for placing burdens upon, or prohibiting outright, transactions that work against the general benefit.

The prior paragraph is an argument that sounds purely consequentialist—that we should compare the benefits of authorizing and perhaps enforcing private ordering against the costs that these particular kinds of ordering might cause. Alternatively, some arguments about regulating or prohibiting certain categories of private ordering are better understood in a more deontological way: that these transactions are (or at least are viewed as being, by some significant portion of the population) simply wrong, and should be discouraged or prohibited even if bad consequences cannot be quantified.

---

11.   More precisely, "efficiency" is often equated with Kaldor–Hicks efficiency, or more generally with "wealth maximization" (where "wealth" is understood very broadly). *See, e.g.,* Richard A. Posner, The Economics of Justice 31–115 (1981); Jules L. Coleman, Markets, Morals and the Law 67–132 (1988).

In the past, marriage was considered sufficiently important both for individuals and for society that significant legal and social penalties were imposed on those who sought to maintain relationships, cohabit, or raise children outside of marriage, and to impose significant penalties also on children born to such unions. This is no longer the case. From a different ideological perspective, some commentators would today have the state, in the interest of both individuals and society, strongly encourage equality within the family. (Of course, "strong encouragement" still leaves room for private ordering, in a way that the coercive social and legal sanctions of prior generations did not.)

B. Externalities (Third–Party Effects)

Even those most opposed to paternalistic governmental interference with private arrangements (like John Stuart Mill, or a wide range of contemporary economic theorists) concede the need for government regulation when those private arrangements directly and significantly harm third parties. In the case of agreements between intimates, the obvious vulnerable third parties are (minor) children. There are voluminous claims from social commentators and social scientists that unconventional family forms are unstable, and end up harming children born to such arrangements....

Additionally, many of these same social scientists and commentators would list a different category of third-party effects: (negative) effects upon society generally, that purportedly come from "broken-down" families, and the like.

In the context of domestic agreements, many observers at the opposite end of the ideological spectrum have raised gender equity concerns, arguing that the enforcement of certain kinds of agreements in this area tends systematically to work against the interests of women.[20]

C. Bounded Rationality

If the general argument for private ordering is that private arrangements should be enforced because people are generally in the best position to determine what is in their best interests, then the circumstances when that is no longer the case would be the situations where "the greatest good of the greatest number" would point towards non-enforcement. This, of course, is the general justification for the significant limits on enforcement for agreements entered by those who are under-age or mentally incompetent. Additionally, when a party is coerced or defrauded, one would say that this party has not really chosen, has not really assented. This is the grounding for other doctrinal defenses to enforcement of agreements in contract law, like misrepresentation, duress and undue influence. One might also add the doctrinal category of "fiduciary relationships," dealings with trusted friends and advisors, where those in a situation of trust must show full disclosure and the substantive fairness of the agreement's terms before a court will enforce an agreement.

Beyond these relatively straightforward situations, there are also categories of circumstances where individuals are thought to be insufficiently self-protective due to basic limitations on the way (most) people reason. There

---

20. *See, e.g.,* Gail Frommer Brod, *Premarital Agreements and Gender Justice,* 6 YALE J.L. & FEMINISM 229 (1994); Judith T. Younger, *Lovers' Contracts in the Courts: Forsaking the Minimum Decencies,* 13 WM. & MARY J. WOMEN & L. 349 (2007). Thus, those who are hostile towards the enforcement of premarital agreements might welcome the enforcement of (e.g.) co-parenting agreements, and vice versa.

are standard limitations, heuristics, and irrationalities that cause us to be insufficiently self-protective when dealing with high-pressure door-to-door salespeople, when selecting pension plans, or when considering post-employment restrictions in an employment agreement. The common law of contract has developed rules which regulate enforcement in some of these cases, and legislatures and administrative agencies have created consumer protection rules and regulations for many others.

The relevance of this to private ordering in domestic relations is that it has been widely argued that certain kinds of arrangements among intimates reflect situations where people will be less likely to understand their own interests or to protect them. Problems of bounded rationality and the absence of knowing consent have been noted even for the decision to get married. Premarital agreements are standardly considered an even stronger case of bounded rationality. A standard narrative for premarital agreements is that one party was motivated to ask for such an agreement by a bad experience he or she (usually he) had with a prior divorce; the other partner, however, often is marrying for the first time (and may thus have no experience with divorce), and is being asked to think seriously about a waiver of rights at divorce at a time when he or she (usually she) is fully in love, and assuming that this union will last forever. Of course, being asked to sign a document about what happens at divorce and being asked to waive one's rights may be an effective way to shake someone out of romantic idealistic notions about love (and about one's partner); but the fact is that most people are poor at thinking well about events in the distant future, especially if it involves contingencies contrary to our optimistic assumptions.

In some ways, these domestic agreements may be superior to their conventional commercial analogues in relation to concerns about assent and rationality. First, agreements are far more likely to be negotiated, term by term, in a premarital or marital agreement than in a consumer purchase from a large company (usually executed on a standardized form). Second, in the closest analogue to a premarital agreement, an employment contract with a post-termination restrictive covenant, the potential employee's focus is clearly on the primary terms and conditions of employment, and the employee is far less likely to focus on the post-termination provisions. By contrast, in a premarital agreement, there are usually no provisions to distract a contracting party from the rights he or she is waiving; the whole focus of the agreement is on the waiver of rights.

D. Exploitation

        . . .

"Exploitation" most often comes up as a possible complaint when one of the parties is desperately poor and the other has significantly more resources, and where the transaction involves either an activity that could be characterized as degrading or as expressing a significant imbalance of power between the parties. One example within family law . . . is surrogacy, where critics of surrogacy agreements (and sometimes also of gamete donation) claim that the private ordering there is "exploitative." Less frequently, one might also hear a similar complaint about premarital agreements creating one-sided property arrangements in a marriage or a non-marital cohabitation (at least where palimony or similar claims do not apply).

NOTE

Henry Sumner Maine, writing in 1861, is best known for noticing the growing role of contracts in society. As you read part of his essay, consider whether you think his description is accurate, and, if so, whether the movement to contract is a good thing for society?:

> The movement of progressive societies has been uniform in one respect. Through all of its course it has been distinguished by the gradual dissolution of family dependency, and the growth of individual obligation in its place. The Individual is steadily substituted for the Family, as the unit of which civil laws take account. The advance has been accomplished at varying rates of celerity, and there are societies not absolutely stationary in which the collapse of the ancient organization can only be perceived by careful study of the phenomena they present. But, whatever its pace, the change has not been subject to reach or recoil, and apparent retardation will be found to have been occasioned through the absorption of archaic ideas and customs from some entirely foreign source. Nor is it difficult to see what is the tie between man and man which replaces by degrees those forms of reciprocity in rights and duties which have their origin in the Family. It is Contract. Starting, as from one terminus of history, from a condition of society in which all the relations of Persons are summed up in the relations of Family, we seem to have steadily moved towards a phase of the social order in which all these relations arise from the free agreement of Individuals. In Western Europe the progress achieved in this direction has been considerable.... The apparent exceptions are exceptions of that stamp which illustrate the rule. The child before years of discretion, the orphan under guardianship, the adjudged lunatic, have all their capacities and incapacities regulated by the Law of Persons. But why? The reason is differently expressed in the conventional language of the different systems, but in substance it is stated to the same effect by all. The great majority of Jurists are constant to the principle that the classes of person just mentioned are subject to extrinsic control on the single ground that they do not possess the faculty of forming a judgment on their own interests; in other words, that they are wanting in the first essential of an engagement by Contract.
>
> The word Status may be usefully employed to construct a formula expressing the law of progress thus indicated.... [W]e may say that the movement of the progressive societies has hitherto been a movement from Status to Contract.

HENRY SUMNER MAINE, ANCIENT LAW 139–41 (1861).

Maynard v. Hill

Supreme Court of the United States, 1888.
125 U.S. 190, 8 S.Ct. 723, 31 L.Ed. 654.

Marriage, as creating the most important relation in life, as having more to do with the morals and civilization of a people than any other institution, has always been subject to the control of the legislature. That body prescribes the age at which parties may contract to marry, the procedure or form essential to constitute marriage, the duties and obligations it creates, its effects upon the property rights of both, present and prospective, and the acts which may constitute grounds for its dissolution.

. . .

It is also to be observed that, whilst marriage is often termed by text writers and in decisions of courts a civil contract—generally to indicate that it must be founded upon the agreement of the parties, and does not require any religious ceremony for its solemnization—it is something more than a mere contract. The consent of the parties is of course essential to its existence, but when the contract to marry is executed by the marriage, a relation between the parties is created which they cannot change. Other contracts may be modified, restricted, or enlarged, or entirely released upon the consent of the parties. Not so with marriage. The relation once formed, the law steps in and holds the parties to various obligations and liabilities. It is an institution, in the maintenance of which in its purity the public is deeply interested, for it is the foundation of the family and of society, without which there would be neither civilization nor progress. This view is well expressed by the Supreme Court of Maine in *Adams v. Palmer*, 51 Me. 480, 483 (1863). Said that court, speaking by Chief Justice Appleton:

> When the contracting parties have entered into the married state, they have not so much entered into a contract as into a new relation, the rights, duties, and obligations of which rest not upon their agreement, but upon the general law of the State, statutory or common, which defines and prescribes those rights, duties, and obligations. They are of law, not contract. It was of contract that the relation should be established, but, being established, the power of the parties as to its extent or duration is at an end. Their rights under it are determined by the will of the sovereign, as evidenced by law. They can neither be modified nor changed by any agreement of parties. It is a relation for life, and the parties cannot terminate it at any shorter period by virtue of any contract they may make. The reciprocal rights arising from this relation, so long as it continues, are such as the law determines from time to time, and none other.... It is not, then, a contract within the meaning of the clause of the Constitution which prohibits the impairing the obligation of contracts. It is, rather, a social relation, like that of parent and child, the obligations of which arise not from the consent of concurring minds, but are the creation of the law itself; a relation the most important, as affecting the happiness of individuals, the first step from barbarism to incipient civilization, the purest tie of social life and the true basis of human progress.

And the Chief Justice cites in support of this view the cases of *Maguire v. Maguire*, 37 Ky. 181, 183 (1838), and *Ditson v. Ditson*, 4 R.I. 87, 101 (1856). In the first of these the Supreme Court of Kentucky said that marriage was more than a contract; that it was the most elementary and useful of all the social relations, was regulated and controlled by the sovereign power of the state, and could not, like mere contracts, be dissolved by the mutual consent of the contracting parties, but might be abrogated by the sovereign will whenever the public good, or justice to both parties, or either of the parties, would thereby be subserved; that being more than a contract, and depending especially upon the sovereign will, it was not embraced by the constitutional inhibition of legislative acts impairing the obligation of contracts. In the second case the Supreme Court of Rhode Island said that "marriage, in the sense in which it is dealt with by a decree of divorce, is not a contract, but one of the domestic relations. In strictness, though formed by contract, it signifies the relation of husband and wife, deriving both its rights and duties from a source higher than any contract of which the parties are capable, and as to these uncontrollable by any contract which they can make. When formed, this relation is no more a contract than 'fatherhood' or 'sonship' is a contract."

NOTE

The decision in *Maynard v. Hill*, came twenty-seven years after Henry Sumner Maine's book. Does the decision mean that he was wrong, or merely ahead of his time?

Robert Mnookin and Lewis Kornhauser, *Bargaining in the Shadow of the Law: The Case of Divorce*

88 YALE L.J. 950, 951, 954–57 (1979).

Available evidence concerning how divorce proceedings actually work suggests that a reexamination from the perspective of private ordering is timely. "Typically, the parties do not go to court at all, until they have worked matters out and are ready for the rubber stamp." Both in the United States and in England, the overwhelming majority of divorcing couples resolve distributional questions concerning marital property, alimony, child support, and custody without bringing any contested issue to court for adjudication.

The parties' power to determine the consequences of divorce depends on the presence of children. When the divorcing couple has no children, the law generally recognizes the power of the parties upon separation or divorce to make their own arrangements concerning marital property and alimony. . . .

In families with minor children, existing law imposes substantial doctrinal constraints. For those allocational decisions that directly affect children—that is, child support, custody, and visitation—parents lack the formal power to make their own law. Judges, exercising the state's *parens patriae power, are said to have responsibility to determine who should have custody and on what conditions.* Private agreements concerning these matters are possible and common, but agreements cannot bind the court, which, as a matter of official dogma, is said to have an independent responsibility for determining what arrangement best serves the child's welfare. Thus, the court has the power to reject a parental agreement and order some other level of child support or some other custodial arrangement it believes to be more desirable.

. . .

On the other hand, available evidence on how the legal system processes undisputed divorce cases involving minor children suggests that parents actually have broad powers to make their own deals. Typically, separation agreements are rubber stamped even in cases involving children.

. . .

The parents' broad discretion is not surprising for several reasons. First, getting information is difficult when there is no dispute. The state usually has very limited resources for a thorough and independent investigation of the family's circumstances. Furthermore, parents may be unwilling to provide damaging information that may upset their agreed arrangements. Second, the applicable legal standards are extremely vague and give judges very little guidance as to what circumstances justify overriding a parental decision. Finally, there are obvious limitations on a court's practical power to control the parents once they leave the courtroom. For all these reasons, it is not surprising that most courts behave as if their function in the divorce process is *dispute settlement, not child protection.* When there is no dispute, busy judges or registrars are typically quite willing to rubber stamp a private agreement, in order to conserve resources for disputed cases.

[T]here are obvious and substantial savings when a couple can resolve distributional consequences of divorce without resort to courtroom adjudication. The financial cost of litigation, both private and public, is minimized. The pain of a formal adversary proceeding is avoided. Recent psychological studies indicate that children benefit when parents agree on custodial arrangements. Moreover, a negotiated agreement allows the parties to avoid the risks and uncertainties of litigation, which may involve all-or-nothing consequences. Given the substantial delays that often characterize contested judicial proceedings, agreement can often save time and allow each spouse to proceed with his or her life. Finally, a consensual solution is by definition more likely to be consistent with the preferences of each spouse, and acceptable over time, than would a result imposed by a court.

. . .

Legal doctrine separates the potential consequences of divorce into four distributional questions: (1) how should the couple's property—the stock of existing wealth owned separately or together—be divided? (marital property law); (2) what ongoing claims should each spouse have on the future earnings of the other (alimony law); (3) what on-going claims should a child have for a share of the earnings or wealth of each of his parents? (child-support law); and (4) how should the responsibilities and opportunities of child rearing be divided in the future? (child-custody and visitation law).

[Examining the bargaining from the perspective of spouses who are negotiating their own divorce settlements suggests that] the money and custody issues are inextricably linked.

CUSTODY

[B]y varying the time the child spends with each parent, and by assigning particular child-rearing tasks to one parent or the other, a divorce settlement may divide prerogatives in many different ways. At the extreme, one parent may be entirely responsible for the child all the time, with the other spouse spending no time with the child. Or, divorcing parents may agree to share child-rearing responsibilities equally after divorce through joint custody. For example, the child may live with each parent one-half of the time, with the parents together deciding where and how the child should be educated, who the pediatrician should be, etc. Between these extremes, many other alternatives are often possible.

THE RELATIONSHIP OF CUSTODY AND MONEY

. . .

[T]o a considerable degree, it is possible to reduce the concerns of divorce bargaining into two elements: money and custody. From a bargaining perspective, even these two elements are inextricably linked for two reasons: over some range of alternatives, each parent may be willing to exchange custodial rights and obligations for income or wealth, and parents may tie support duties to custodial prerogatives as a means of enforcing their rights without resort to court.

Economic analysis suggests that a parent may, over some range, trade custodial rights for money. Although this notion may offend some, a contrary assertion would mean that a parent with full custody would accept no sum of money in exchange for slightly less custody, even if the parent were extremely poor. Faced with such alternatives, most parents would prefer to see the child a bit less and be able to give the child better housing, more food, more education, better health care, and some luxuries. Suggesting the possibility of such trade-offs does *not mean that the parent would be willing to relinquish all time with the child for a sufficiently large sum of money.* Indeed, with a minimum level of resources, a parent may have a parallel minimum of custodial rights for the reduction of which no additional payment, however large, could be adequate compensation.

The negotiating process itself provides many opportunities for the parties to link money and custody issues. The most obvious opportunity exists in the context of enforcement of support or visitation. The legal system does not permit these connections in most states: in a suit brought to collect overdue support payments, a father cannot defend on the ground that his ex-wife did not permit visitation. Nor have courts permitted a custodial parent to cut off visitation because of a failure to pay support. Nevertheless, it is often time-consuming and expensive to enforce promises in court. There can be substantial advantages, therefore, from the perspective of one or both bargainers, in having piecemeal bargains that spread support payments over time and, as a practical matter, link the custody issue (especially visitation) with the financial issues. If a father who values visitation fails to make support payments, then, quite apart from the mother's ability to enforce his promise in court (which may often be too slow and expensive to be effective), the mother may believe that she can retaliate by informally cutting off the father's visitation or making it more difficult. Even though this tactic has no legal validity, it is nevertheless likely to be faster, cheaper, and more effective than court enforcement. Similarly, a father may believe that his ability to cut off support will ensure that the mother will keep her word concerning visitation.

HOW LEGAL RULES CREATE BARGAINING ENDOWMENTS

Divorcing parents do not bargain over the division of family wealth and custodial prerogatives in a vacuum; they bargain in the shadow of the law. The legal rules governing alimony, child support, marital property, and custody give each parent certain claims based on what each would get if the case went to trial. In other words, the outcome that the law will impose if no agreement is reached gives each parent certain bargaining chips—an endowment of sorts.

A simplified example may be illustrative. Assume that in disputed custody cases the law flatly provided that all mothers had the right to custody of minor children and that all fathers only had the right to visitation two weekends a month. Absent some contrary agreement acceptable to both parents, a court would order this arrangement. Assume further that the legal rules relating to marital property, alimony, and child support gave the mother some determinate share of the family's economic resources. In negotiations under this regime, neither spouse would ever consent to a division that left him or her worse off than if he or she insisted on going to court. The range of negotiated outcomes would be limited to those that leave both parents as well off as they would be in the absence of a bargain.

If private ordering were allowed, we would not necessarily expect parents to split custody and money the way a judge would if they failed to agree. The father might well negotiate for more child-time and the mother for less. This result might occur either because the father made the mother better off by giving her additional money to compensate her for accepting less child-time, or because the mother found custody burdensome and considered herself better off with less custody. Indeed, she might agree to accept less money, or even to pay the father, if he agreed to relieve her of some child-rearing responsibilities. In all events, because the parents' tastes with regard to the trade-offs between money and child-time may differ, it will often be possible for the parties to negotiate some outcome that makes both better off than they would be if they simply accepted the result a court would impose.

PRIVATE ORDERING AGAINST A BACKDROP OF UNCERTAINTY

Legal rules are generally not as simple or straightforward as is suggested by the last example. Often, the outcome in court is far from certain, with any number of outcomes possible. Indeed, existing legal standards governing custody, alimony, child support, and marital property are all striking for their lack of precision and thus provide a bargaining backdrop clouded by uncertainty.

. . .

Analyzing the effects of uncertainty on bargaining is an extremely complicated task. It is apparent, however, that the effects in any particular case will depend in part on the attitudes of the two spouses toward risk—what economists call "risk preferences." This can be illustrated by considering a mechanism suggested in BEYOND THE BEST INTERESTS OF THE CHILD[66] FOR RESOLVING CUSTODY DISPUTES BETWEEN EQUALLY ACCEPTABLE SPOUSES: they would draw straws, with the winner getting full custodial rights and the loser none.

Because drawing straws, like flipping a coin, gives each parent a fifty percent chance of receiving full custody, economic theory suggests that for each parent the "expected" outcome is half-custody. We cannot, however, simply assume that each parent will bargain as if receiving half of the child's time were certain. Attitudes toward risk may be defined by asking a parent to compare two alternatives: (1) a certainty of having one-half of the child's time; or (2) a gamble in which the "expected" or average outcome is one-half of the child's time. By definition, a parent who treats these alternatives as equally desirable is risk-neutral. A parent who would accept a certain outcome of less than half-custody in order to avoid the gamble—the chance of losing the coin flip and receiving no custody—is risk-averse. Other parents may be risk preferrers: they would rather take the gamble and have a fifty percent chance of winning full custody than accept the certain outcome of split custody.

STRATEGIC BEHAVIOR

The actual bargain that is struck through negotiations—indeed, whether a bargain is struck at all—depends on the negotiation process. During this process, each party transmits information about his or her own preferences to the other. This information may be accurate or intentionally inaccurate; each party may promise, threaten, or bluff. Parties may intentionally exaggerate their chances of winning in court in the hope of persuading the other side to accept less. Or they may threaten to impose substantial transaction costs—economic or psychological—on the other side. In short, there are a variety of ways in which the parties may engage in strategic behavior during the bargaining process.

Opportunities for strategic behavior exist because the parties often will not know with certainty (1) the other side's true preferences with regard to the allocational outcomes; and (2) the other spouse's preferences or attitudes towards risk; and (3) what the outcome in court will be, or even what the actual odds in court are. Although parents may know a great deal about each other's preferences for money and children, complete knowledge of the other spouse's attitudes is unlikely.

---

66. J. GOLDSTEIN, A. FREUD & A. SOLNIT, BEYOND THE BEST INTERESTS OF THE CHILD (1973).

How do the parties and their representatives actually behave during the process? Two alternative models are suggested by the literature: (1) a *Strategic Model, which would characterize the process as* "a relatively norm-free process centered on the transmutation of underlying bargaining strength into agreement by the exercise of power, horse-trading, threat, and bluff"; and (2) a *Norm–Centered Model, which would characterize the process by elements normally associated with adjudication—the parties and their representatives would invoke rules, cite precedents, and engage in reasoned elaboration.* Anecdotal observation suggests that each model captures part of the flavor of the process. The parties and their representatives do make appeals to legal and social norms in negotiation, but they frequently threaten and bluff as well.

Given the advantages of negotiated settlements, why do divorcing spouses ever require courtroom adjudication of their disputes? There are a variety of reasons why some divorce cases will be litigated:

1. *Spite.* One or both parties may be motivated in substantial measure by a desire to punish the other spouse, rather than simply to increase their own net worth.

2. *Distaste for Negotiation.* Even though it costs more, one or both parties may prefer the adjudicative process (with third-party decision) to any process that requires a voluntary agreement with the other spouse. Face-to-face contact may be extremely distasteful, and the parties may not be able to negotiate—even with lawyers acting as intermediaries—because of distrust or distaste.

3. *Calling the Bluff—The Breakdown of Negotiations.* If the parties get heavily engaged in strategic behavior and get carried away with making threats, a courtroom battle may result, despite both parties' preference for a settlement. Negotiations may resemble a game of "chicken" in which two teenagers set their cars on a collision course to see who turns first. Some crack-ups may result.

4. *Uncertainty and Risk Preferences.* The exact odds for any given outcome in court are unknown, and it has been suggested that litigants typically overestimate their chances of winning. To the extent that one or both of the parties typically overestimate their chances of winning, more cases will be litigated than in a world in which the outcome is uncertain but the odds are known. In any event, when the outcome is uncertain, settlement prospects depend on the risk preferences of the two spouses.

5. *No Middle Ground.* If the object of dispute cannot be divided into small enough increments—whether because of the law, the practical circumstances, or the nature of the subject at issue—there may be no middle ground on which to strike a feasible compromise. Optimal bargaining occurs when, in economic terminology, nothing is indivisible.

These points can be illustrated through a simple example. Assume a divorcing couple has no children and the only issue is how they will divide 100 shares of stock worth $10,000. Let us further assume that it would cost each spouse $1,000 to have a court decide this issue, and that each spouse must pay his own litigation costs.

If the outcome in court were entirely certain, would the parties ever litigate? Suppose it were clear that a court would inevitably award one-half of the stock to each spouse because it would be characterized as community property. If the issue were litigated, each spouse would end up with only $4,000. A spouse would therefore never accept a settlement offer of less than $4,000. One might expect that the parties would normally simply settle for

$5,000, and save the costs of litigation. Taking the issue to court would substitute an expensive mode of dispute resolution—adjudication—for a cheaper mode—negotiation.

Even when the outcome in court is certain, litigation is still possible. A spouse might engage in strategic behavior and threaten to litigate in order to get more than half. Suppose the husband threatened to litigate unless the wife agreed to accept a settlement of $4,500. The wife might accept $4,500 but only if she believed the threat. She would know with proper legal advice that her husband would only end up with $4,000 if he litigated. Therefore the threat ordinarily would not be credible. She might call his bluff and tell him to sue. If the wife were convinced, however, that her husband was motivated by spite and in fact preferred to litigate rather than accept less than $5,500, she might accept $4,500. If the outcome in court is certain, then, absent spite, strategic behavior, or a distaste for negotiations, adjudication should not generally occur; litigation would impose an expensive mode of dispute settlement when a less expensive alternative could achieve the same result.

What about cases in which the result in court is uncertain? Assume, for example, that there is a fifty percent chance that the husband will get all $10,000, and a fifty percent chance that the wife will get all $10,000. Settlement in these circumstances obviously depends on the risk preferences of the two spouses. If both are risk-neutral, then both will negotiate the same way as they would if they knew for certain that a court would award each of them $5,000—the "expected" value of the litigation in this case.

To the extent that the parties are both risk-averse—each is prepared to accept less than $5,000 to avoid the risks of litigation—the parties have a broader range of possible settlements that both would prefer to the risks of litigation. This may facilitate agreement.

Conversely, if both parties are risk preferrers—each prefers the gamble to an offer of the expected value of $5,000—all cases are likely to be litigated. When one party is a risk preferrer and the other is risk-averse, it is difficult to predict the effect on the rate of litigation. In any negotiated outcome, a risk preferrer will have an advantage over the party who is risk-averse.

NOTE

Courts are authorized to scrutinize parental agreements dealing with custody more stringently than agreements on matters that concern other aspects of separation or divorce. Thus, a court may reject a custody agreement not only on standard contract grounds such as lack of voluntariness, but on the ground that it is not in the best interest of the child. *See, e.g.,* OHIO REV. CODE ANN. § 3109.04(D)(1)(a)(i) (2011); WIS. STAT. ANN. § 767.11(12)(a) (2000). Some states, however, require a court to adopt a custody agreement unless it makes findings on the record that support a conclusion that the agreement is not in the child's best interest. *See, e.g.,* Mass. Ann. Laws ch. 208, § 31 (2000). In Michigan, the court must determine by "clear and convincing evidence" that the custody arrangement is not in the best interest of the child. MICH. COMP. LAWS ANN. § 722.27a(2) (2001).

Reporter's Notes to the AMERICAN LAW INSTITUTE'S PRINCIPLES OF THE LAW OF FAMILY DISSOLUTION, however, declare, "Despite judicial rhetoric about the reviewability of [custody] agreements, agreements are rarely rejected on any grounds." AMERICAN LAW INSTITUTE, PRINCIPLES OF THE LAW OF FAMILY DISSOLUTION, Chapter 2, Topic 2, § 2.06, Reporter's Notes, comment a, at 163 (2002). The ALI recommends that a court accept the provisions of a plan agreed to by the parents unless it is not knowing or voluntary, or it would be harmful to the child. ALI PRINCIPLES, § 2.06(1).

B.   ORDERING BY PRIVATE CONTRACT

1.   PREMARITAL CONTRACTS

Edwardson v. Edwardson

Supreme Court of Kentucky, 1990.
798 S.W.2d 941.

■ LAMBERT, JUSTICE.

Almost seventy-five years ago this Court declared "the law will not permit parties contemplating marriage to enter into a contract providing for, and looking to, future separation after marriage." *Stratton v. Wilson*, 185 S.W. 522, 523 (Ky. 1916).... This Court granted appellant's motion for discretionary review to reconsider the position taken in *Stratton*....

Prior to their marriage to each other, both parties had been married previously. In the divorce decree dissolving her prior marriage, appellant was awarded the sum of seventy-five dollars ($75.00) per week as maintenance, the payment of which was to be terminated upon her remarriage. Appellant and appellee executed an agreement prior to the time their marriage was solemnized which contained, *inter alia,* the following provision:

> In the event that the marriage of the parties shall be dissolved or the parties become legally separated, to the extent permitted under Kentucky law or the state of residence where said action is filed, the Party of the First Part shall receive SEVENTY–FIVE DOLLARS ($75.00) per week as maintenance (alimony) from the Party of the Second Part for her life, or until her remarriage. Furthermore, Party of the Second Part shall maintain medical/hospitalization insurance for the Party of the First Part for her life or her remarriage, which insurance program shall have benefits substantially similar to those presently held by the Party of the First Part through the ROTHROCK INSURANCE SERVICE. Other than as provided in this paragraph, neither party shall have any obligation to the other for alimony or support, and neither party shall have any claim against the property of the other nor any claim thereto by reason of the marriage or the manner or cause thereto by reason of the marriage or the manner or cause of dissolution thereof, it being the intent hereof that the parties, each having adequate separate estates on the date of marriage, shall each retain their separate estates, any increase in the value thereof and accretions thereto, free of any and all claims or interest in property or other rights which may come into existence or arise by reason of the marriage of the parties hereto, except as stated herein.

After about two and a half years of marital turbulence, the parties finally separated. In the divorce action which followed, appellant sought enforcement of the agreement. Enforcement was denied in the trial court and on appeal the judgment of the trial court was affirmed....

[T]he ... issue before the Court is whether any antenuptial agreement which contemplates divorce and provides for the payment of maintenance and the disposition of property upon subsequent dissolution of the marriage is enforceable.

. . .

In unmistakable terms, the Court in *Stratton* held the portion of the agreement which provided for payment of alimony in the event of separation or divorce to be void. The decision was based on the view that such an agreement was destabilizing to the marital relationship and might promote or encourage marital breakup.

It is an indisputable fact that since rendition of our decision in *Stratton*, the incidence of divorce in Kentucky has followed the national experience and risen steadily. Further, the Kentucky General Assembly has abandoned the fault-based system of allowing dissolution of marriage which prevailed prior to 1972 and adopted portions of the Uniform Marriage and Divorce Act which is substantially a "no-fault" marriage dissolution system. A legislative determination has been made that abandoning the necessity of proving fault would, *inter alia*, "[s]trengthen and preserve the integrity of marriage and safeguard family relationships." KY. REV. STAT. ANN. § 403.110(1). While the rising incidence of divorce and the existence of profound legislative changes do not *per se* render the *Stratton* rule invalid, neither do they support its continuation. . . .

A number of other jurisdictions have confronted the question before this Court and abandoned or modified the prohibition against enforcement of antenuptial agreements which contemplate divorce. In a leading decision, *Posner v. Posner*, 233 So. 2d 381 (Fla. 1970), the Supreme Court of Florida reviewed a number of authorities and noted a "clearly discernible" trend in favor of enforcing antenuptial agreements. The Court observed that in some circumstances, the existence of an antenuptial agreement might actually promote the continuation of marriage rather than its dissolution and further noted the widespread enforcement of antenuptial agreements to settle property rights upon the death of a spouse. Abandoning its prior rule, the Court held that such agreements should no longer be void *ab initio*, but should be measured by the stringent standards prescribed in *Del Vecchio v. Del Vecchio*, 143 So. 2d 17 (Fla. 1962), for agreements which settle property rights on the death of a spouse, and the additional requirement that it not appear the agreement promoted procurement of the divorce. In another leading case, *Scherer v. Scherer*, 292 S.E.2d 662 (Ga. 1982), the Supreme Court of Georgia overruled its prior decisions holding antenuptial agreements in contemplation of divorce invalid. As grounds for its decision, the Court recognized that divorce is a commonplace fact of life, that state law and public policy permit married persons to obtain divorces, and the absence of empirical evidence to show that antenuptial agreements in contemplation of divorce actually encourage or incite divorce. . . .

While the foregoing cases present differing factual circumstances and subtle differences in the legal issues addressed and answered, a common theme may be found throughout. The notion that divorce is promoted by an antenuptial agreement which contemplates such a possibility has been rejected and the right of parties to enter into appropriate agreements has been upheld. We concur with this view.

Finally, we observe that the legal status of marriage partners is vastly different today than it was when *Stratton v. Wilson* was decided. At that time the Nineteenth Amendment to the Constitution of the United States had not yet been ratified, married women's property acts were not yet in existence or were in their infancy, and in general the status of women in this society was decidedly second class. In 1916 it may have been entirely logical to restrict the nature of agreements available to persons contemplating marriage in an effort to avoid marital instability. Subsequent changes in society and seventy-five years of experience have rendered such restrictions inappropriate. . . .

. . .

The first limitation upon parties to an antenuptial agreement is the requirement of full disclosure. Before parties should be bound by agreements which affect their substantial rights upon dissolution of marriage, it should appear that the agreement was free of any material omission or misrepresentation. The second limitation to be observed is that the agreement must not be unconscionable at the time enforcement is sought. Regardless of the terms of the agreement and regardless of the subsequent acquisition or loss of assets, at the time enforcement is sought, the court should be satisfied that the agreement is not unconscionable.[2] Upon a finding of unconscionability, the trial court entertaining such an action may modify the parties' agreement to satisfy the necessary standard, but should otherwise give effect to the agreement as nearly as possible providing the agreement was not procured by fraud or duress.

While it may go without saying, we observe that antenuptial agreements may apply only to disposition of property and maintenance. Questions of child support, child custody and visitation are not subject to such agreements; and unless the parties otherwise agree, non-marital property retains its character as such.

We recognize that this opinion may raise a number of questions. No effort has been made to write a comprehensive treatise which answers all the questions likely to arise. The ingenuity of persons contemplating marriage to fashion unusual agreements, particularly with the assistance of counsel, cannot be overestimated. We will observe the tradition whereby the law develops on a case by case basis. It should be recognized, however, that trial courts have been vested with broad discretion to modify or invalidate antenuptial agreements. Parties and their counsel should be admonished to refrain from entering into agreements lacking mutuality and without a rational basis. Courts reviewing antenuptial agreements and faced with a claim of unconscionability should not overlook the wisdom, which is fully applicable to both spouses, expressed in this Court's decision rendered in *Clark v. Clark*, 192 S.W.2d 968, 970 (Ky. 1946):

> A separation agreement will be closely scrutinized by a court of equity, ... It must appear that the husband exercised the utmost good faith; that there was a full disclosure of all material facts, including the husband's circumstances and any other fact which might affect the terms of the contract; and that the provisions made in the agreement ... were fair, reasonable, just, equitable, and adequate in view of the conditions and circumstances of the parties....

For the reasons stated, we reverse and remand this cause to the Jefferson Circuit Court for further proceedings consistent herewith.

Simeone v. Simeone

Supreme Court of Pennsylvania, 1990.
581 A.2d 162.

■ FLAHERTY, JUSTICE.

At issue in this appeal is the validity of a prenuptial agreement executed between the appellant, Catherine E. Walsh Simeone, and the appellee,

---

2. Upon review of a post-nuptial separation agreement entered into pursuant to KRS 403.180, the trial court must determine whether the agreement is unconscionable. A number of Kentucky decisions have addressed the construction of this term and we need not attempt further refinement in this opinion. The concept of unconscionability is familiar to circuit courts by virtue of KRS 403.180 and KRS 403.250.

Frederick A. Simeone. At the time of their marriage, in 1975, appellant was a twenty-three year old nurse and appellee was a thirty-nine year old neurosurgeon. Appellee had an income of approximately $90,000 per year, and appellant was unemployed. Appellee also had assets worth approximately $300,000. On the eve of the parties' wedding, appellee's attorney presented appellant with a prenuptial agreement to be signed. Appellant, without the benefit of counsel, signed the agreement. Appellee's attorney had not advised appellant regarding any legal rights that the agreement surrendered. The parties are in disagreement as to whether appellant knew in advance of that date that such an agreement would be presented for signature. Appellant denies having had such knowledge and claims to have signed under adverse circumstances, which, she contends, provide a basis for declaring it void.

The agreement limited appellant to support payments of $200 per week in the event of separation or divorce, subject to a maximum total payment of $25,000. The parties separated in 1982, and, in 1984, divorce proceedings were commenced. Between 1982 and 1984 appellee made payments which satisfied the $25,000 limit. In 1985, appellant filed a claim for alimony *pendente lite*. A master's report upheld the validity of the prenuptial agreement and denied this claim. Exceptions to the master's report were dismissed by the Court of Common Pleas of Philadelphia County. The Superior Court affirmed.

We granted allowance of appeal because uncertainty was expressed by the Superior Court regarding the meaning of our plurality decision in *Estate of Geyer*, 533 A.2d 423 (Pa. 1987) (Opinion Announcing Judgment of the Court). The Superior Court viewed *Geyer* as permitting a prenuptial agreement to be upheld if it *either* made a reasonable provision for the spouse *or* was entered after a full and fair disclosure of the general financial positions of the parties and the statutory rights being relinquished. Appellant contends that this interpretation of *Geyer* is in error insofar as it requires disclosure of statutory rights *only* in cases where there has not been made a reasonable provision for the spouse. Inasmuch as the courts below held that the provision made for appellant was a reasonable one, appellant's efforts to overturn the agreement have focused upon an assertion that there was an inadequate disclosure of statutory rights. Appellant continues to assert, however, that the payments provided in the agreement were less than reasonable.

The statutory rights in question are those relating to alimony *pendente lite*.... [The present agreement expressly stated] that alimony *pendente lite* was being relinquished. It also recited that appellant "has been informed and understands" that, were it not for the agreement, appellant's obligation to pay alimony *pendente lite* "might, as a matter of law, exceed the amount provided." Hence, appellant's claim is not that the agreement failed to disclose the particular right affected, but rather that she was not adequately informed with respect to the nature of alimony *pendente lite*.

. . .

There is no longer validity in the implicit presumption that supplied the basis for *Geyer* and similar earlier decisions. Such decisions rested upon a belief that spouses are of unequal status and that women are not knowledgeable enough to understand the nature of contracts that they enter. Society has advanced, however, to the point where women are no longer regarded as the "weaker" party in marriage, or in society generally. Indeed, the stereotype that women serve as homemakers while men work as breadwinners is no longer viable. Quite often today both spouses are income earners. Nor is there viability in the presumption that women are uninformed, uneducated, and readily subjected to unfair advantage in marital agreements. Indeed, women nowadays quite often have substantial education, financial awareness, income, and assets.

Accordingly, the law has advanced to recognize the equal status of men and women in our society. *See, e.g.,* PA. CONST. art. 1, § 28 (constitutional prohibition of sex discrimination in laws of the Commonwealth). Paternalistic presumptions and protections that arose to shelter women from the inferiorities and incapacities which they were perceived as having in earlier times have, appropriately, been discarded. It would be inconsistent, therefore, to perpetuate the standards governing prenuptial agreements that were described in *Geyer* and similar decisions, as these reflected a paternalistic approach that is now insupportable.

Further, *Geyer* and its predecessors embodied substantial departures from traditional rules of contract law, to the extent that they allowed consideration of the knowledge of the contracting parties and reasonableness of their bargain as factors governing whether to uphold an agreement. Traditional principles of contract law provide perfectly adequate remedies where contracts are procured through fraud, misrepresentation, or duress. Consideration of other factors, such as the knowledge of the parties and the reasonableness of their bargain, is inappropriate. Prenuptial agreements are contracts, and, as such, should be evaluated under the same criteria as are applicable to other types of contracts. Absent fraud, misrepresentation, or duress, spouses should be bound by the terms of their agreements.

Contracting parties are normally bound by their agreements, without regard to whether the terms thereof were read and fully understood and irrespective of whether the agreements embodied reasonable or good bargains. Based upon these principles, the terms of the present prenuptial agreement must be regarded as binding, without regard to whether the terms were fully understood by appellant. *Ignorantia non excusat.*

Accordingly, we find no merit in a contention raised by appellant that the agreement should be declared void on the ground that she did not consult with independent legal counsel. To impose a *per se* requirement that parties entering a prenuptial agreement must obtain independent legal counsel would be contrary to traditional principles of contract law, and would constitute a paternalistic and unwarranted interference with the parties' freedom to enter contracts.

Further, the reasonableness of a prenuptial bargain is not a proper subject for judicial review. *Geyer* and earlier decisions required that, at least where there had been an inadequate disclosure made by the parties, the bargain must have been reasonable at its inception. Some have even suggested that prenuptial agreements should be examined with regard to whether their terms remain reasonable at the time of dissolution of the parties' marriage.

By invoking inquiries into reasonableness, however, the functioning and reliability of prenuptial agreements is severely undermined. Parties would not have entered such agreements, and, indeed, might not have entered their marriages, if they did not expect their agreements to be strictly enforced. If parties viewed an agreement as reasonable at the time of its inception, as evidenced by their having signed the agreement, they should be foreclosed from later trying to evade its terms by asserting that it was not in fact reasonable. Pertinently, the present agreement contained a clause reciting that "each of the parties considers this agreement fair, just and reasonable...."

Further, everyone who enters a long-term agreement knows that circumstances can change during its term, so that what initially appeared desirable might prove to be an unfavorable bargain. Such are the risks that contracting parties routinely assume. Certainly, the possibilities of illness, birth of children, reliance upon a spouse, career change, financial gain or loss, and numerous other events that can occur in the course of a marriage cannot be regarded as unforeseeable. If parties choose not to address such matters in their prenuptial agreements, they must be regarded as having contracted to bear the risk of events that alter the value of their bargains.

We are reluctant to interfere with the power of persons contemplating marriage to agree upon, and to act in reliance upon, what *they* regard as an acceptable distribution scheme for their property. A court should not ignore the parties' expressed intent by proceeding to determine whether a prenuptial agreement was, in the court's view, reasonable at the time of its inception or the time of divorce. These are exactly the sorts of judicial determinations that such agreements are designed to avoid. Rare indeed is the agreement that is beyond possible challenge when reasonableness is placed at issue. Parties can routinely assert some lack of fairness relating to the inception of the agreement, thereby placing the validity of the agreement at risk. And if reasonableness at the time of divorce were to be taken into account ... [e]very change in circumstance, foreseeable or not, and substantial or not, might be asserted as a basis for finding that an agreement is no longer reasonable.

In discarding the approach of *Geyer* ... we do not depart from the longstanding principle that a full and fair disclosure of the financial positions of the parties is required. Absent this disclosure, a material misrepresentation in the inducement for entering a prenuptial agreement may be asserted. Parties to these agreements do not quite deal at arm's length, but rather at the time the contract is entered into stand in a relation of mutual confidence and trust that calls for disclosure of their financial resources. It is well settled that this disclosure need not be exact, so long as it is "full and fair." In essence therefore, the duty of disclosure under these circumstances is consistent with traditional principles of contract law.

If an agreement provides that full disclosure has been made, a presumption of full disclosure arises. If a spouse attempts to rebut this presumption through an assertion of fraud or misrepresentation then this presumption can be rebutted if it is proven by clear and convincing evidence.

The present agreement recited that full disclosure had been made, and included a list of appellee's assets totaling approximately $300,000. Appellant contends that this list understated by roughly $183,000 the value of a classic car collection which appellee had included at a value of $200,000. The master ... found that appellant failed to prove by clear and convincing evidence that the value of the collection had been understated. The courts below affirmed that finding. We have examined the record and find ample basis for concluding that the value of the car collection was fully disclosed. Appellee offered expert witnesses who testified to a value of approximately $200,000. Further, appellee's disclosure included numerous cars that appellee did not even own but which he merely hoped to inherit from his mother at some time in the future. Appellant's contention is plainly without merit.

Appellant's final contention is that the agreement was executed under conditions of duress in that it was presented to her at 5 p.m. on the eve of her wedding, a time when she could not seek counsel without the trauma, expense, and embarrassment of postponing the wedding. The master found this claim not credible. The courts below affirmed that finding, upon an ample evidentiary basis.

Although appellant testified that she did not discover until the eve of her wedding that there was going to be a prenuptial agreement, testimony from a number of other witnesses was to the contrary. Appellee testified that, although the final version of the agreement was indeed presented to appellant on the eve of the wedding, he had engaged in several discussions with appellant regarding the contents of the agreement during the six month period preceding that date. . . . [A]nother witness confirmed that, during the months preceding the wedding, appellant participated in several discussions of prenuptial agreements. [T]he legal counsel who prepared the agreement for appellee testified that, prior to the eve of the wedding, changes were made in the agreement to increase the sums payable to appellant in the event of separation or divorce. He also stated that he was present when the agreement was signed and that appellant expressed absolutely no reluctance about signing. It should be noted, too, that during the months when the agreement was being discussed appellant had more than sufficient time to consult with independent legal counsel if she had so desired. Under these circumstances, there was plainly no error in finding that appellant failed to prove duress.

Hence, the courts below properly held that the present agreement is valid and enforceable. Appellant is barred, therefore, from receiving alimony *pendente lite.*

Order affirmed.

■ PAPADAKOS, JUSTICE, concurring.

Although I continue to adhere to the principles enunciated in *Estate of Geyer*, 533 A.2d 423 (Pa. 1987), I concur in the result because the facts fully support the existence of a valid and enforceable agreement between the parties and any suggestion of duress is totally negated by the facts. The full and fair disclosure, as well as the lack of unfairness and inequity, standards reiterated in *Geyer* are supported by the facts in this case so that I can concur in the result.

However, I cannot join the opinion authored by Mr. Justice Flaherty, because, it must be clear to all readers, it contains a number of unnecessary and unwarranted declarations regarding the "equality" of women. Mr. Justice Flaherty believes that, with the hard-fought victory of the Equal Rights Amendment in Pennsylvania, all vestiges of inequality between the sexes have been erased and women are now treated equally under the law. I fear my colleague does not live in the real world. If I did not know him better I would think that his statements smack of male chauvinism, an attitude that "you women asked for it, now live with it." If you want to know about equality of women, just ask them about comparable wages for comparable work. Just ask them about sexual harassment in the workplace. Just ask them about the sexual discrimination in the Executive Suites of big business. And the list of discrimination based on sex goes on and on.

I view prenuptial agreements as being in the nature of contracts of adhesion with one party generally having greater authority than the other who deals in a subservient role. I believe the law protects the subservient party, regardless of that party's sex, to insure equal protection and treatment under the law.

The present case does not involve the broader issues to which the gratuitous declarations in question are addressed, and it is injudicious to offer declarations in a case which does not involve those issues. Especially when those declarations are inconsistent with reality.

NOTES

1. Although marriage contracts contemplating separation or divorce were not accepted by American courts before 1970, marriage contracts contemplating termination of the marriage by death were common as early as the seventeenth century. Consider the marriage contract of John French and Eleanor Veazie:

> A covenant of marriage being purposed and intended between John French and Eleanor Veazie of Braintree in New England, made and concluded this eighth day of July, Anno Domini one thousand six hundred and eighty three, doe witness that the said John French doth preengage unto the said Eleanor Veazie not to meddle with or take into his hand any part of her estate wherein she is invested by her former husband William Veazie or any otherwise, nor any wise weakening her right or claim to the same. The said John French doth hereby engage and covenant to pay to the said Eleanor Veazie after my decease four pounds per annum, annually, to be paid each year immediately insuing after the said John French's decease, by his lawful Administrators, Executors or Assigns, at her dwelling house, the specie of which payment shall be paid in cord wood, porke, beefe, malt or corne proportionably of each at price current. And that shee the said Eleanor Veazie shall have, hold, possess and enjoy the new end of the dwelling house, in which the said French now dwelleth with the cellar appertaining, during the time of her widowhood. But the four pound annuity to bee and continue to her and her heirs or assigns during the terme of her natural life. To the true performance whereof the said John French doth hereunto set hand this eighth day of July Anno Domini one thousand six hundred eighty three. Before signing. And she shall have apples what she pleases for spending and a place for a garden plot.
>
> Signed and concluded on before us
> John French
> Samuel Tompson
> Ben Tompson

AMERICA'S FAMILIES: A DOCUMENTARY HISTORY 70–72 (Donald M. Scott & Bernard Wishy eds. 1982).

> Compare the 1855 agreement between Henry Blackwell and Lucy Stone:

> While acknowledging our mutual affection by publicly assuming the relationship of husband and wife, yet in justice to ourselves and a great principle, we deem it a duty to declare that this act on our part implies no sanction of, nor promise of voluntary obedience to such of the present laws of marriage, as refuse to recognize the wife as an independent, rational being, while they confer upon the husband an injurious and unnatural superiority, investing him with legal powers which no honorable man would exercise, and which no man should possess.

> We protest especially against the laws which give to the husband:

> 1. The custody of the wife's person.

> 2. The exclusive control and guardianship of their children.

> 3. The sole ownership of her personal property, and use of her real estate, unless previously settled upon her, or placed in the hands of trustees, as in the case of minors, lunatics, and idiots.

> 4. The absolute right to the product of her industry.

5. Also against laws which give to the widower so much larger and more permanent an interest in the property of his deceased wife, than they give to the widow in that of the deceased husband.

6. Finally, against the whole system by which "the legal existence of the wife is suspended during marriage," so that in most States, she neither has a legal part in the choice of her residence, nor can she make a will, nor sue or be sued in her own name, nor inherit property.

We believe that personal independence and equal human rights can never be forfeited, except for crime; that marriage should be an equal and permanent partnership, and so recognized by law; that until it is so recognized, married partners should provide against the radical injustice of present laws, by every means in their power.

We believe that where domestic difficulties arise, no appeal should be made to legal tribunals under existing laws, but that all difficulties should be submitted to the equitable adjustment of arbitrators mutually chosen.

Thus reverencing law, we enter our protest against rules and customs which are unworthy of the name, since they violate justice, the essence of law.

(Signed) Henry B. Blackwell

Lucy Stone

2. Consider the contracts proposed by Lenore Weitzman in *Legal Regulation of Marriage: Tradition and Change*, 62 CAL. L. REV. 1169, 1278–84 (1974). Which provisions, if any, are enforceable in court?

1. TRADITIONAL MARRIAGE—PARTNERSHIP OF DOCTOR AND HOUSEWIFE

David, a medical student, and Nancy, an aspiring dancer, agree to a contract under which Nancy will give up her potential career as a dancer and support David through medical school in return for a comfortable life as a doctor's wife and a guarantee of financial compensation if the relationship dissolves.

a. Aims and expectations

Both parties want to state their goals and future expectations at the time this contract is signed. Nancy is entering into the relationship with the expectation that she will enjoy the usual benefits of being a doctor's wife. In return for the assurance of a future in which she will be supported in comfort, she is willing to give up her dancing career and to support David until he completes his internship. While she supports David she realizes that she will have to work hard and make do with very little money. Further, she realizes that David's studies will be very time-consuming, and that he will be less than an ideal companion. Since she will be making a very significant contribution toward David's career, she expects to have a future interest in it. Once David becomes a doctor she will enjoy the social benefits of being a doctor's wife. Nancy expects to have a beautiful home and summer home, expensive clothing, vacations in Europe, child care and private schools for her children, and a housekeeper.

David understands that Nancy's efforts will make it possible for him to obtain his medical education in a fairly comfortable fashion. Her support will ensure that he will not have to drop out of school to earn money and he will not have to spend any time on part-time jobs or housework. He will be able to devote all his time to his studies. In return, he wants to guarantee Nancy a share in his future career.

Both parties feel that they are making a life-time contract and are building a community from which they will both benefit. Both parties feel that they are equal partners in this community and that income, property, and other gains that may accrue to the income-earning partner are the result of the joint efforts of both parties—and therefore belong equally to both parties.

b. Property

Any property of the parties shall be jointly owned as community property. Nancy will manage and control the community property and will take care of all other household business matters.

c. Support

Nancy will work as a secretary in order to support David until he has finished medical school and an internship. David will support the family from then on; he will take a (paying) residency, or begin to practice medicine. Nancy will not work outside the home after David's career has commenced.

d. Domicile

The location of the family domicile will be decided by David; the main consideration in making such a decision will be the best interests of David's career.

e. Name

Both parties will use David's surname.

f. Housekeeping responsibilities

Nancy will be responsible for maintaining the household with the assistance of a full-time housekeeper.

g. Birth control

Since the most efficient contraceptives currently available are female contraceptives, Nancy will assume the responsibility for birth control for the present. However, if a male oral contraceptive or other safe and effective male contraceptive is perfected, David agrees to use it.

h. Other responsibilities

Nancy agrees to further David's career by entertaining, serving on medical auxiliary committees, and maintaining good social relations with other doctors' wives. She will also participate actively in church and country club activities in order to maintain good contacts with potential patients and physicians. David agrees to accompany Nancy to the ballet at least once a month. He also agrees to schedule at least two two-week vacations with her each year, at least one of them in Europe.

i. Children

Children will be postponed until David's education is completed. If Nancy should become pregnant prior to that time, she will have an abortion. Nancy will have full responsibility for the care of the children; financial responsibility will be assumed by David.

j. Termination

This partnership may be dissolved by either party, at will, upon six months notice to the other party.

If this partnership is terminated by either party prior to the completion of David's education, Nancy's obligation to support him will cease. Moreover, once David's career is begun, he will have the obligation of supporting Nancy at the rate of $12,000 a year (1974 rate to be adjusted for inflation and cost of living) for as many years as she supported him. If necessary, David will secure a loan to repay Nancy for her support. If Nancy prefers a lump sum settlement equal to the value of this support, David will arrange a loan to provide it. Both parties agree to treat Nancy's original support of David as a loan of the value specified above. David's obligation to repay this loan has the standing of any other legal debt.

If the partnership is terminated after David's career has begun, Nancy will be entitled to one-fourth of his net income for as many years as the partnership lasted. David will purchase insurance or a bond to guarantee this payment. It is agreed that this payment is not alimony, and that it shall be continued unmodified regardless of her earning capacity or remarriage. The parties consider this Nancy's reimbursement for helping David's career. It is agreed that her efforts will have helped to make his success possible and he will therefore owe her this compensation.

David also agrees to pay Nancy the fixed sum of $15,000 if their marriage terminates within 15 years, as liquidated damages for the pain and suffering she will experience from the change in her expectations and life plans.

David also agrees to pay for Nancy's medical expenses or to provide her with adequate insurance at the rate of one year of coverage for every year of marriage. It is explicitly agreed that psychiatric and dental bills be included in the above.

Community property will be divided equally upon termination. If there are children, Nancy will have custody of the children. David will have full responsibility for their support, as well as the responsibility for compensating Nancy for her services in caring for them (at the then current rate for private nurses). Suitable visiting arrangements will be made.

k.   Death

Both parties agree to make wills stipulating the other partner the sole legatee. After termination of this agreement this obligation will not continue; however, David is obliged to make sure any continuing support obligations toward Nancy and the children are reflected in his will.

2.   YOUNG, DUAL–CAREER, PROFESSIONAL COUPLE

Susan, an aspiring lawyer, and Peter, an aspiring social worker, have devised the following contract to maximize both career opportunities and their personal relationship.

a.   Educational and living expenses

Susan and Peter decide that they will take turns going to school, so that the nonstudent partner can support the other until he or she receives a degree. Because Susan will earn more money as an attorney, they decide that they will maximize their joint income if Susan goes to school first. They therefore agree that Peter will be solely responsible for Susan's educational expenses and support for three full years. Susan will assume these same responsibilities for the following two years. If their partnership should dissolve at any time during these first five years, their contract stipulates that each shall have the following financial obligations to the other: (1) If dissolution occurs during the first three years, Peter will pay Susan's remaining tuition (which may be up to three full years' tuition in graduate school) and pay her $4,200 a year for living expenses. (2) Thereafter, Susan will pay Peter's remaining tuition (up to two full years of tuition in a school of social work) and pay him $4,200 a year in living expenses. All living expenses will be paid at the rate of $350 a month. This amount will be tied to the cost-of-living index to allow for automatic increases.

b.   Domicile

Susan and Peter agree to maintain a joint domicile for the first five years of their relationship, location to be determined by the student partner to maximize educational opportunity.

After the first five years, Susan and Peter will make decisions regarding domicile jointly, with no presumption that the career of either is of greater importance in making the decision. However, if they cannot agree on where to live, the decision will be Susan's—for a period of three years. Peter will then have the right to choose the location for the following three years. They will continue to rotate the domicile decision on a three-year basis. As both parties realize that their career opportunities may not coincide with this prearranged schedule, they may decide to exchange the right of decision for any given period or make another equitable agreement which would then be incorporated into this contract. Further, both parties will always retain the option of establishing a temporary separate residence, at their own expense, if this is necessary for their careers.

c.   Property

During the first five years all income and property, excluding gifts and inheritances, shall be considered community property. The income-earning partner shall have sole responsibility for its management and control.

After the first five years an inventory will be taken of all community property. Thereafter each party's earnings, as well as any gifts or bequests or the income from any property held, shall be her or his separate property. Neither party will have any rights in any present or future property of the other. A list will be kept of all household items in order to keep track of their ownership; in the event Susan and Peter decide to make a joint purchase, this will be noted on the list. Any joint purchase of items of value over $100 will be covered by a separate agreement concerning its ownership. Each party will manage and control her or his separate property, and will maintain a separate bank account.

d. Household expenses

(This part of the agreement shall go into effect five years hence.)

Household expenses will consist of rent, utilities, food, and housekeeping expenses. Susan and Peter will each contribute 50 percent of their gross income to household expenses. Their contributions will be made in monthly installments of equal amounts, and placed in a joint checking account. Responsibility for the joint account and for paying the above expenses will be rotated, with each having this responsibility for a three-month period. Each partner will be responsible for his or her own cleaning expenses, and for food and entertainment outside of the household. Each will maintain a separate car and a separate phone and will take care of these expenses separately. If money in the joint account is not exhausted by household expenses, it may be used for joint leisure activities.

Both parties recognize that Susan's income is likely to be higher than Peter's and that 50 percent of her income will allow her more money for separate expenses. The parties therefore agree to review this arrangement six months after it goes into effect. If it seems that the arrangement places an unfair burden on Peter, they will change the second line above to read: Each party's contribution to household expenses shall be as follows: Susan shall contribute 55 percent of her gross income; Peter shall contribute 40 percent of his gross income.

e. Housekeeping responsibilities

Housework will be shared equally. All necessary tasks will be divided into two categories. On even-numbered months Susan will be responsible for category 1 and Peter for category 2; and vice versa on odd-numbered months. Each party will do her or his own cooking and clean up afterwards for breakfast and lunch, as well as keeping her or his own study clean. Dinner cooking and clean up will be considered part of the housework to be rotated as specified above. In the event that one party neglects to perform any task, the other party can perform it and charge the nonperforming partner $15 per hour for his or her labor, or agree to be repaid in kind.

f. Sexual relations

Sexual relations are subject to the consent of both parties. Responsibility for birth control will be shared equally. Susan will have this responsibility for the first six months of the year, Peter for the second six months.

g. Surname

Both parties will retain their own surnames.

h. Children

While the parties have decided to have two children at some time in the future, birth control will be practiced until a decision to have a child has been reached. Since the parties believe that a woman should have control over her own body, the decision of whether or not to terminate an accidental pregnancy before then shall be Susan's alone. If Susan decides to have an abortion, the party who had responsibility for birth control the month that conception occurred will bear the cost of the abortion. This will include expenses not covered by insurance, and any other expenses or loss of pay incurred by Susan. However, if Susan decides to have the child and Peter does not agree, Susan will bear full financial and social responsibility for the child. In that event, Susan also agrees to compensate Peter should he be required to support the child. If the parties agree to have a child and Susan changes her mind after conception has occurred, she will pay for the abortion. If Peter changes his mind after conception has occurred and Susan agrees to an abortion, he will pay for it. If she does not agree, Peter will share the social and financial responsibility for the child, just as if he had not changed his mind.

When the parties decide to have a child, the following provisions will apply: Susan and Peter will assume equal financial responsibility for the child. This will include the medical expenses connected with the birth of the child as well as any other expenses incurred in preparation for the child. If it is necessary for Susan to take time off from work in connection with her pregnancy or with the birth of the child, Peter will pay her one-half of his salary to compensate for the loss. If either party has to take time off from work to care for the child, the other party will repay that party with one-half of his or her salary. All child-care, medical, and educational expenses will be shared equally.

Since Peter expects to become a psychiatric social worker specializing in pre-school children, he will have the primary child-care responsibility. He will take a paternity leave after the birth in order to care for the child full-time, until day-care arrangements can be made. Susan will compensate him at the rate of one-half of her salary. Responsibility for caring for the child on evenings and weekends will be divided equally.

Any children will take the hyphenated surname of both parties.

i. Dissolution

If there are children, both parties agree to submit to at least one conciliation session prior to termination. In addition, if a decision to dissolve the partnership is made, both parties agree to submit to binding arbitration if they are unable to reach a mutual decision regarding the issues of child custody, child support, and property division. A list of mutually agreeable arbitrators is attached to this agreement. While both agree that custody should be determined according to the best interests of the child, a presumption exists in favor of Peter, since he will have had superior training in the rearing of children. Each party agrees to assume half of the financial burden of caring for the child.

If there are no children, this household agreement can be terminated by either party for any reason upon giving the other party 60 days' notice in writing. Upon separation, each party will take his or her separate property and any jointly owned property will be divided equally. Neither party will have any financial or other responsibility toward the other after separation and division of property.

3. The Uniform Premarital Agreement Act, approved by the American Bar Association in 1984, provides in pertinent part:

§ 1. Definitions

As used in this Act:

(1) "Premarital agreement" means an agreement between prospective spouses made in contemplation of marriage and to be effective upon marriage.

(2) "Property" means an interest, present or future, legal or equitable, vested or contingent, in real or personal property, including income and earnings.

§ 2. Formalities

A premarital agreement must be in writing and signed by both parties. It is enforceable without consideration.

§ 3. Content

(a) Parties to a premarital agreement may contract with respect to:

(1) the rights and obligations of each of the parties in any of the property of either or both of them whenever and wherever acquired or located;

(2) the right to buy, sell, use, transfer, exchange, abandon, lease, consume, expend, assign, create a security interest in, mortgage, encumber, dispose of, or otherwise manage and control property;

(3) the disposition of property upon separation, marital dissolution, death, or the occurrence or nonoccurrence of any other event;

(4) the modification or elimination of spousal support;

(5) the making of a will, trust, or other arrangement to carry out the provisions of the agreement;

(6) the ownership rights in and disposition of the death benefit from a life insurance policy;

(7) the choice of law governing the construction of the agreement; and

(8) any other matter, including their personal rights and obligations, not in violation of public policy or a statute imposing a criminal penalty.

(b) The right of a child to support may not be adversely affected by a premarital agreement.

§ 4. Effect of Marriage

A premarital agreement becomes effective upon marriage.

§ 5. Amendment, Revocation

After marriage, a premarital agreement may be amended or revoked only by a written agreement signed by the parties. The amended agreement or the revocation is enforceable without consideration.

§ 6. Enforcement

(a) A premarital agreement is not enforceable if the party against whom enforcement is sought proves that:

(1) that party did not execute the agreement voluntarily; or

(2) the agreement was unconscionable when it was executed and, before execution of the agreement, that party:

(i) was not provided a fair and reasonable disclosure of the property or financial obligations of the other party;

(ii) did not voluntarily and expressly waive, in writing, any right to disclosure of the property or financial obligations of the other party beyond the disclosure provided; and

(iii) did not have, or reasonably could not have had, an adequate knowledge of the property or financial obligations of the other party.

(b) If a provision of a premarital agreement modifies or eliminates spousal support and that modification or elimination causes one party to the agreement to be eligible for support under a program of public assistance at the time of separation or marital dissolution, a court, notwithstanding the terms of the agreement, may require the other party to provide support to the extent necessary to avoid that eligibility.

(c) An issue of unconscionability of a premarital agreement shall be decided by the court as a matter of law.

4. As of 2010, twenty-six states and the District of Columbia had adopted the Uniform Premarital Agreement Act. UNIF. PREMARITAL AGREEMENT ACT, REFERENCES & ANNOTATIONS, 9C U.L.A. 35 (Table of Jurisdictions Wherein Act Has Been Adopted).

5. Should marriage contracts be encouraged even if they will not be enforced by the courts? Consider Karl Fleischmann, *Marriage by Contract: Defining the Terms of Relationship*, 8 FAM. L.Q. 27, 31 (1974):

The most traditional sort of marriage counseling involves the attempt to resolve disputes between people whose marriages have become troubled. But before a marriage reaches the stage where it is in serious trouble there will usually be a period during which conflicts are arising but go unresolved. These conflicts may be generated by problems peculiar to the marriage or may be significantly involved with the change in value structure presently taking place in the United States: wives becoming uncertain about the role they should play in their marriage, older spouses seeking the sexual freedom of the young.

If there were an established and recognized opportunity for married couples to discuss with professional assistance the sources of conflict between them with the hope of resolving them by contract, such disputes might be more easily and frequently resolved.

If Fleischman correctly describes a major purpose of such contracts, should they be drafted by lawyers or professionals trained in therapy or counseling?

2.   SEPARATION AGREEMENTS

A growing percentage of divorces involve separation agreements between the parties. These agreements are submitted to the court and may be incorporated into the divorce decree. Separation agreements are entered into in contemplation of divorce, and thus differ from pre-marital contracts that purport to determine the consequences if the couple ever divorces. As you read the material in this section, consider whether courts should review separation agreements as they do any other contract, or should they provide a more searching review. Should couples be able by contract to preclude courts from retaining jurisdiction to entertain later requests for modification of the custody and financial arrangements made at the time of divorce?

UNIFORM MARRIAGE AND DIVORCE ACT

(1970).

Section 306.   Separation Agreement

(a) To promote amicable settlement of disputes between parties to a marriage attendant upon their separation or the dissolution of their marriage, the parties may enter into a written separation agreement containing provisions for disposition of any property owned by either of them, maintenance of either of them, and support, custody, and visitation of their children.

(b) In a proceeding for dissolution of marriage or for legal separation, the terms of the separation agreement, except those providing for the support, custody, and visitation of children, are binding upon the court unless it finds, after considering the economic circumstances of the parties and any other relevant evidence produced by the parties, on their own motion or on request of the court, that the separation agreement is unconscionable.

(c) If the court finds the separation agreement unconscionable, it may request the parties to submit a revised separation agreement or may make orders for the disposition of property, maintenance, and support.

(d) If the court finds that the separation agreement is not unconscionable as to disposition of property or maintenance, and not unsatisfactory as to support:

(1) unless the separation agreement provides to the contrary, its terms shall be set forth in the decree of dissolution or legal separation and the parties shall be ordered to perform them, or

(2) if the separation agreement provides that its terms shall not be set forth in the decree, the decree shall identify the separation agreement and state that the court has found the terms not unconscionable.

(e) Terms of the agreement set forth in the decree are enforceable by all remedies available for enforcement of a judgment, including contempt, and are enforceable as contract terms.

(f) Except for terms concerning the support, custody, or visitation of children, the decree may expressly preclude or limit modification of terms set forth in the decree if the separation agreement so provides. Otherwise, terms of a separation agreement set forth in the decree are automatically modified by modification of the decree.

COMMENT

An important aspect of the effort to reduce the adversary trappings of marital dissolution is the attempt, made by Section 306, to encourage the parties to reach an amicable disposition of the financial and other incidents of their marriage. This section entirely reverses the older view that property settlement agreements are against public policy because they tend to promote divorce. Rather, when a marriage has broken down irretrievably, public policy will be served by allowing the parties to plan their future by agreeing upon a disposition of their property, their maintenance, and the support, custody, and visitation of their children.

Subsection (b) undergirds the freedom allowed the parties by making clear that the terms of the agreement respecting maintenance and property disposition are binding upon the court unless those terms are found to be unconscionable. The standard of unconscionability is used in commercial law, where its meaning includes protection against one-sidedness, oppression, or unfair surprise and in contract law. It has been used in cases respecting divorce settlements or awards. Hence the act does not introduce a novel standard unknown to the law. In the context of negotiations between spouses as to the financial incidents of their marriage, the standard includes protection against overreaching, concealment of assets, and sharp dealing not consistent with, the obligations of marital partners to deal fairly with each other.

In order to determine whether the agreement is unconscionable, the court may look to the economic circumstances of the parties resulting from the agreement, and any other relevant evidence such as the conditions under which the agreement was made, including the knowledge of the other party. If the court finds the agreement not unconscionable, its terms respecting property division and maintenance may not be altered by the court at the hearing.

The terms of the agreement respecting support, custody, and visitation of children are not binding upon the court even if these terms are not unconscionable. The court should perform its duty to provide for the children by careful examination of the agreement as to these terms in light of the standards established by Section 309 for support and by Part IV for custody and visitation.

Subsection (c) envisages that, if the court finds the agreement unconscionable, it will afford the parties the opportunity to negotiate further. If they are unable to arrive at an agreement that is not unconscionable, the court, on motion of either party, may decide the issues of property disposition, support, and maintenance in light of the standards established in Sections 307 through 309. The court's power to make orders for the custody and visitation of the children is set forth in Part IV.

Subsection (d) permits the parties, in drawing the separation agreement, to choose whether its terms shall or shall not be set forth in the decree. In the former event, the provisions of subsection (e), making these terms enforceable through the remedies available for the enforcement of a judgment, but retaining also the enforceability of them as contract terms, apply.... There still remains a place for agreements the terms of which are not set forth in the decree, if the parties prefer that it retain the status of a private contract, only. In this instance, the remedies for the enforcement of a judgment will not be available, but the court's determination, in the decree, that the terms are not unconscionable, under the ordinary rules of res adjudicata, will prevent a later successful claim of unconscionability. Such an agreement, unless its terms expressly so permit, will not be modifiable as to economic matters. Other subjects, relating to the children, by subsection (b) do not bind the Court.

Subsection (f) allows the parties to agree that their provisions as to maintenance and property division will not be modifiable or can be modified only in accordance with the terms of the agreement, even though those terms are included in the decree. If the court finds that these are not unconscionable, it may include them in its decree. The effect of including in the decree a provision precluding or limiting modification of the terms respecting maintenance or property division is to make the decree nonmodifiable or modifiable only in the limited way as to those terms. Subsection (f) thus permits the parties to agree that their future arrangements may not be altered except in accord with their agreement. Such an agreement maximizes the advantages of careful future planning and eliminates uncertainties based on the fear of subsequent motions to increase or decrease the obligations of the parties. However, as stated in the subsection, this does not apply to provisions for the support, custody, or visitation of children.

Duffy v. Duffy

Court of Appeals of the District of Columbia, 2005.
881 A.2d 630.

■ Ruiz, Associate Judge.

Appellant challenges the trial court's enforcement of the parties' separation agreement as part of its Judgment of Absolute Divorce. The trial court found that the agreement, which was contained in a letter signed by both parties, was complete and unambiguous on its face, and that the parties had demonstrated an intention to be bound by it. Consequently, the trial court found that the agreement is an enforceable contract, and required appellant to provide appellee with an accounting of the child support that was in arrears under the terms of the separation agreement, pay the outstanding amount within thirty days, and continue to pay child support in the amount provided for in the separation agreement. Finding no error in the trial court's judgment, we affirm.

The parties were married in Grand Rapids, Michigan on December 29, 1977. They adopted a daughter, born on September 19, 1995, who began residing with them on September 21, 1995. In 1998, appellant decided he wanted to separate from his wife. During their separation, the parties worked together to sell their marital home, divide the proceeds, pay their various debts, and distribute their personal property.

. . .

In an effort to save time and attorney's fees, the parties negotiated an agreement on the terms of their divorce, which the appellee reduced to writing in the form of a letter addressed to her attorney, whom the parties agreed would then prepare a formal agreement incorporating the terms they agreed upon for review by appellant's lawyer. . . . On May 12, 2001, both parties read over the letter drafted by appellee and signed it (hereinafter referred to as the "Letter").

Soon after, counsel for appellee prepared a Marital Settlement Agreement (hereinafter referred to as the "Draft Agreement") incorporating the terms set out in the Letter, and sent it to appellant on May 23, 2001.[1] Although appellant did not execute the Draft Agreement, the parties abided by the terms set out in the Letter from May 2001, when the Letter was signed, until November 2002, when appellant unilaterally reduced his child support payment from the $5000 per month provided for in the Letter, to $2000 per month.

. . .

The law in this jurisdiction encourages the use of separation agreements to settle the financial affairs of spouses who intend to divorce. This policy is based on the notion that the parties are in a better position than the court to determine what is fair and reasonable in their circumstances. In the absence of fraud, duress, concealment or overreaching, a separation agreement is presumptively valid and binding no matter how ill-advised a party may have been in executing it.

. . .

During trial and on appeal appellant has expressed concern that the Letter does not address what would happen to his child support obligation in the event he lost his job, or had other financial constraints. Although provision for future contingencies could well have been part of the parties' agreement,[12] it is not a necessary component for enforceability because, to be complete, a contract need only be sufficiently definite so that the parties can be reasonably certain as to how they are to perform. However, even without an express provision in the Letter for modification of child support to take into account changes in appellant's financial situation, appellant would not be precluded from seeking relief from the court should a change in his circumstances adversely affect his ability to pay child support.

The standard for granting a modification to child support specified in a settlement agreement depends on whether the agreement was merged into the court's judgment, or incorporated by reference. The trial court has

---

1. It appears that appellant was not represented by counsel at the time. In her letter to appellant enclosing the Draft Agreement, appellee's counsel advised appellant that she did not represent him and that he had a right to be represented by an attorney and should consult one if he had any questions or concerns about the Draft Agreement she had prepared.

12. We note, for example, that the Letter states that "Joan would also like a clause that states that amount [of child support] will be adjusted annually to reflect the then current Consumer Price Index." This statement reflects that although some contingencies were considered, the parties did not incorporate them in their agreement.

limited authority to alter a child support provision in a separation agreement that is incorporated, but not merged, into an order of divorce, due to the "presumption that 'a child support agreement negotiated between two parents is adequate to meet the child's foreseeable needs, and that at the time of the agreement the best interests of the child were a paramount consideration.'" A trial court may modify such an agreement only upon a showing of "(1) a change in circumstances which was unforeseen at the time the agreement was entered and (2) that the change is both substantial and material to the welfare and best interests of the children." "However, a change in the parents' financial circumstances alone 'cannot provide the basis for modifying a contract between the parties.'" As a result, a trial court may increase a child support payment provided in a settlement agreement if there arises an unforeseen change in circumstances that is substantial and material to the interests of the child, but it may not decrease such a child support agreement simply because the payor's financial circumstances have declined, or the child support payment subsequently proves to exceed the child's needs.

. . .

[I]n order to have the court reduce the child support provided in a settlement agreement incorporated by the court, a payor would therefore have to avail himself of a contract theory that would relieve him of the burden of such performance, e.g., contract defenses such as "fraud, duress, concealment, or overreaching," "frustration of performance" either due to "strict impossibility," or "impracticability due to extreme or unreasonable difficulty or expense." Thus, if the appellant were to become unexpectedly disabled and, as a result, his finances suffered significantly, the court could reduce or excuse the child support obligation only if it were impossible or impracticable for appellant to make child support payments at the stipulated amount.

Where a settlement agreement is merged into the trial court's order, on the other hand, the binding force of the amount of child support is not based on the contractual obligation arising from an agreement between the parties, but on the authority of the court's order. The court's order is guided by the child support guidelines established by statute. Consequently, where a settlement agreement on child support is merged into the court's order, the court has discretion to modify its own order based on a showing by either party of a material change in the circumstances of either the child or the parents. A parent seeking relief from an onerous child support payment need then only show a "substantial or material change of circumstances," that would support a significantly different amount of child support under the guidelines. D.C. Code § 16–916.01(o)(3) (establishing presumption that modification is warranted if current circumstances would vary child support "by 15% or more" under the guidelines).

A settlement agreement is merged, and not merely incorporated into a court order, where "the agreement was adopted by the court as its own determination of the proper disposition of the rights and property between the parties." The trial court's order in this case did not make an independent assessment of the needs of the child, but only determined the enforceability of the terms contained in the Letter. The Letter, for its part, did not specify how the parties wanted the court to treat their agreement in the order granting the divorce. We note, however, that in ordering that "the plaintiff shall pay child support in accordance with the May 12, 2001 letter agreement," the court also required that the amount of child support be "adjusted in accordance with the consumer price index," an adjustment that had not been agreed to in the Letter. *See supra* note 12. Thus, there is a question whether the trial court in this case merged the settlement agreement into its order, or incorporated it by reference.

Though other jurisdictions have enunciated criteria for determining whether a settlement agreement has been merged or incorporated into an order of divorce, we have not had occasion to do so thus far. Nor do we need to decide it at the present juncture in this case, as appellant is not presently claiming a change in circumstances as a basis for modification. We note, moreover, appellee's concession in her brief and at oral argument that the standard for merged agreements would apply in this case were appellant to claim at some future date that changes in his employment situation, income, or other responsibilities require modification of his child support obligation under the trial court's order.[13] Although the trial court would not necessarily be bound by the parties' interpretation of its order, their agreement on the standard for modification of child support would be an important, if not definitive, consideration.

The record in this case shows a serious, sustained effort by mature adults seeking to come to a reasonable agreement about their property and, most important, their continuing responsibility to and relationship with their child. Appellant may now regret that he entered into an agreement without first seeking the advice of counsel, or he may think, after the passage of time, that he should not have agreed to the terms contained in the Letter. These doubts do not negate that the Letter is complete as to the essential terms of the parties' divorce, and that appellant's course of conduct for over a year—from signing the Letter, to abiding by its terms, to stating in his e-mail communications his desire that any formalized agreement incorporate the terms in the Letter—demonstrates his intent to be bound by the conditions set forth in that agreement.

For the foregoing reasons the trial court's Judgment of Absolute Divorce enforcing the terms of the separation agreement is affirmed.

Toni v. Toni

Supreme Court of North Dakota, 2001.
636 N.W.2d 396.

■ VANDEWALLE, C.J.

Sheila A. Toni appealed from an order denying her motion to modify a divorce decree under N.D. CENT. CODE § 14–05–24. In the motion Sheila Toni asked the trial court to modify a spousal support award granted in a divorce judgment which incorporated her agreement with Conrad R. Toni to divest the court of jurisdiction to modify the amount and term of spousal support set forth in the agreement. We conclude the parties' agreement, which was found by the court in the divorce action to be "fair, just and equitable," is enforceable under North Dakota law and divested the court of jurisdiction to modify the spousal support award. We therefore affirm.

Conrad and Sheila Toni were married from July 9, 1971, until May 10, 1999. The couple had three children during the marriage, and one of them

---

13. Contrary to appellee's representations on appeal, the Draft Agreement prepared by appellee's counsel provided that it would not be merged into the court's order, and the appellee's counter-complaint similarly requested that the Letter be incorporated, but not merged, into the judgment of divorce.

was a minor at the time of the divorce. Both parties are employed in Fargo: Conrad as a urologist, and Sheila as a clerk at Barnes & Noble Bookstore.

Before their divorce was granted, the parties entered into a "Custody and Property Settlement Agreement" which comprehensively addressed all divorce issues. The agreement stated that, although Conrad had been represented by counsel, Sheila "has not been represented by counsel and has been informed that Maureen Holman does not represent her interests in this matter but has not sought such independent counsel and enters into this custody and property settlement agreement of her own free will." The agreement also stated, "both parties agree that each has made a full disclosure to the other of all assets and liabilities and is satisfied that this custody and property settlement agreement is fair and equitable," and "each party has entered into this custody and property settlement agreement intending it to be a full and final settlement of all claims of every kind, nature, and description which either party may have or claim to have, now or in the future, against the other and, except as is expressly provided herein to the contrary, each is released from all further liability of any kind, nature or description whatsoever to the other."

The agreement provided for "joint physical custody" of the couple's minor daughter.

... The agreement divided the parties' real property, stocks and retirement accounts, but did not disclose the value of those assets. The agreement also contained the following provision on spousal support:

> Commencing May 1, 1999, Conrad shall pay to Sheila the sum of $5,000 per month as and for spousal support. Said payments will continue on the first day of each month thereafter until the death of either party, Sheila's remarriage, or until the payment due on April 1, 2002 has been made. It is intended that the spousal support payable to Sheila shall be included in Sheila's gross income for income tax purposes and shall be deductible by Conrad. The court shall be divested of jurisdiction to modify in any manner whatsoever the amount and term of the spousal support awarded to Sheila immediately upon entry of the judgment and decree herein. The court shall retain jurisdiction to enforce Conrad's obligation to pay spousal support to Sheila.

At the divorce hearing, Conrad appeared with his attorney, but Sheila, who had admitted service of the summons and complaint, did not personally appear. The trial court granted the divorce and, finding the parties' agreement to be "a fair, just and equitable settlement," incorporated its provisions into the divorce decree.

In November 2000, Sheila moved under N.D. CENT. CODE § 14–05–24 to modify the spousal support award. Sheila claimed in an affidavit that Conrad earned $14,000 per month in "take-home pay" when they married and she believed he continued to earn a "similar" amount per month, while she earns $1,000 per month working full-time as a clerk at Barnes & Noble Bookstore. Sheila further alleged, although income from assets she received in the divorce had paid her about $2,700 per month, the "return on those assets this year has been almost nothing." Sheila estimated her monthly expenses to be $5,340.... Sheila ... stayed home with the children during her marriage to Conrad rather than pursuing her own career. Sheila also stated:

> I met Bob Boman after I separated from my husband. I had agreed to a reduced three-year term for spousal support because Dr. Boman was in

his residency following medical school. Once he finished, we had agreed that he would pay the family expenses. Conrad and I had decided to divorce in August and I met Bob in October. Bob and I planned to marry after the divorce. Bob and I are no longer together and I do not receive any money from him.

The parties agreed to submit to the trial court the sole issue whether the provision of the parties' agreement divesting the court of jurisdiction to modify spousal support was valid under North Dakota law, and to stay any proceedings on the merits of the motion to modify the spousal support award. The trial court dismissed Sheila's motion, ruling "the parties entered into a binding contract which was incorporated into the judgment and . . . the court now lacks jurisdiction to modify spousal support."

We assume, for purposes of argument only, that Sheila's claims of lowered investment yields and a failed relationship are sufficient to constitute a material change of circumstances to support a motion to modify spousal support. . . . The legal question in this case is whether the parties' divorce stipulation regarding spousal support can divest the trial court of its statutory authority to modify the amount and duration of support. . . .

Under N.D. Cent. Code § 14–05–24, the trial court generally retains continuing jurisdiction to modify spousal support, child support, and child custody upon a showing of changed circumstances. . . . This Court has construed the statute, however, to not allow a trial court continuing jurisdiction to modify a final property distribution, . . . and we have held when a trial court makes no initial award of spousal support and fails to expressly reserve jurisdiction over the issue, the court subsequently lacks jurisdiction to award spousal support. . . . Sheila argues N.D. Cent. Code § 14–05–24 gives a trial court the unconditional right to modify a spousal support award, regardless of any agreement by divorcing parties purporting to divest the court of that power.

We encourage peaceful settlements of disputes in divorce matters. . . . It is the promotion of the strong public policy favoring prompt and peaceful resolution of divorce disputes that generates a judicial bias in favor of the adoption of a stipulated agreement of the parties. . . . We have also noted a person may waive "all rights and privileges to which a person is legally entitled, whether secured by contract, conferred by statute, or guaranteed by the constitution, provided such rights and privileges rest in the individual who has waived them and are intended for his benefit." . . .

[W]e have encouraged spousal support awards based on agreements between the divorcing parties, and noted those agreements "should be changed only with great reluctance by the trial court." . . . Although this Court has often said a spousal support award based on an agreement between the parties can be modified upon a showing of material change of circumstances, . . . we have not been confronted with a contractual settlement clause, adopted by the trial court and incorporated into the divorce decree, attempting to divest the court of its continuing jurisdiction to modify the amount and term of the spousal support award.

Jurisdictions differ over their treatment of agreements between divorcing couples seeking to limit a court's ability to modify spousal support arrangements. . . . Some jurisdictions, by statute, specifically allow parties to enter into nonmodifiable spousal support agreements. . . . Other jurisdictions, by statute, specifically prohibit nonmodifiable spousal support agreements. . . .

Several jurisdictions, by judicial decision, have allowed contractual waivers of the right to seek spousal support modification.... Other jurisdictions, through court decisions, have disallowed contractual waivers of the right to seek modification of spousal support....

We think the reasoning of the current trend of jurisdictions which allow divorcing couples to agree to make spousal support nonmodifiable is persuasive.

This result is consistent with our prior caselaw on spousal support. In [*Becker v. Becker*, 262 N.W.2d 478, 484 (N.D. 1978)], this Court held, unless a trial court makes an initial award of spousal support or expressly reserves jurisdiction over the issue, the court lacks jurisdiction under N.D. CENT. CODE § 14–05–24 to subsequently modify its decision and award spousal support. The original divorce decree in *Becker* stated, " 'neither party shall pay alimony to the other,' " and that language was incorporated from the parties' stipulation and property settlement agreement found to be "fair and equitable" by the trial court. *Id.* at 480, 484. This Court ruled the contract provision was unambiguous, and the "parties are bound by their contract provision for no alimony even if the court is not." *Id.* at 484. We see no valid distinction between a stipulation to waive all spousal support at the time of the initial divorce decree and a waiver of future modification. If a spouse can waive all right to spousal support, it logically follows that a spouse can waive the right to modification....

Section 14–05–24, N.D. CENT. CODE, does not expressly prohibit nonmodification agreements. If the legislature intended to prevent parties from entering into nonmodifiable spousal support agreements, it could have expressly prohibited them.... We recognize there can be no waiver of statutory rights if the waiver would be against public policy.... However, we do not believe allowing parties to agree that spousal support is nonmodifiable violates the public policy of this state.

Our case law invalidating parental divorce stipulations prohibiting or limiting a court's modification powers over child support is governed by public policy principles entirely different from those present when reviewing an agreement concerning spousal support. While a spousal support agreement "serves primarily to determine the interests of the contracting parties themselves," a child support agreement "directly affects the interests of the children of the marriage, who have the most at stake as a result of such an agreement but who have the least ability to protect their interests." ... "Put simply, the parties to a [spousal support] agreement are both grown-ups, free to bargain with their own legal rights." ... Freedom to contract on terms not specifically prohibited by statute ... is the major public policy question presented here.

Permitting parties to determine the future modifiability of their spousal support agreements maximizes the advantages of careful future planning and eliminates uncertainties based on the fear of subsequent motions to increase or decrease the obligations of the parties. In [*Staple v. Staple*, 616 N.W.2d 219, 228 (Mich. App. 2000)], the court relied on public policy reasons identified by the American Academy of Matrimonial Lawyers (AAML) for validating agreements to waive future modification of spousal support awards:

The AAML comments that "recognizing and enforcing" the parties' waiver of modification "does no violence to public policy, and is consistent with the reasonable expectancy interests of the parties." The AAML also offers five public policy reasons why courts should enforce duly executed nonmodifiable alimony arrangements: (1) Nonmodifiable agreements enable parties to structure package settlements, in which alimony, asset divisions, attorney fees, postsecondary tuition for children, and related matters are all coordinated in a single, mutually acceptable agreement; (2) finality of divorce provisions allows predictability for parties planning their postdivorce lives; (3) finality fosters judicial economy; (4) finality and predictability lower the cost of divorce for both parties; (5) enforcing agreed-upon provisions for alimony will encourage increased compliance with agreements by parties who know that their agreements can and will be enforced by the court.

Nullifying waivers of future spousal support modifications would discourage the settlement of divorce cases, . . . contrary to our public policy favoring peaceful settlements of disputes in divorce matters. . . . We conclude agreements by divorcing parties to make spousal support nonmodifiable and which are adopted by the trial court do not violate N.D. Cent. Code § 14–05–24 or public policy.

The parties' agreement in this case is not ambiguous, but is clear and unequivocal: "The court shall be divested of jurisdiction to modify in any manner whatsoever the amount and term of the spousal support awarded to Sheila immediately upon entry of the judgment and decree herein." Similar stipulations have been enforced in other jurisdictions. . . . Sheila acknowledged full disclosure of assets and liabilities; Conrad's attorney did not represent her, she did not obtain counsel, and entered into the agreement "of her own free will;" and the agreement is "fair and equitable" and is intended "to be a full and final settlement of all claims of every kind . . ." The divorce court found the agreement to be "a fair, just and equitable settlement" of the parties' divorce action and incorporated the provisions of the agreement into the divorce decree. We conclude the trial court correctly ruled it had no jurisdiction under N.D. Cent. Code § 14–05–24 to entertain Sheila's motion to modify the spousal support award.

. . .

■ Maring, J., dissenting.

[T]he principle of finality has never applied to spousal support or child support. If parties need finality and freedom to agree to a definitive spousal support, then we should not modify their agreement for any reason. Parties, however, should not be able to bind themselves in advance to an amount and duration regardless of what circumstances arise because the right to seek modification of a judgment for spousal support is not only given for the protection of persons obligated to pay and the persons who are entitled to support, but also for the benefit of society. If a spouse becomes destitute, then society will bear the burden of support.

Sidden v. Mailman

Court of Appeals of North Carolina, 2000.
529 S.E.2d 266.

■ Greene, J.

Judy Ann Sidden (Plaintiff) appeals from an order and judgment upholding the validity of a "Contract of Separation and Property Settlement" (the Agreement) between Plaintiff and Richard Bernard Mailman (Defendant) (collectively, the parties).

. . .

The parties separated on or about 15 August 1996, at which time Defendant moved out of the marital home. At that time Plaintiff told Defendant she was "tired of fighting," he could "have it all," and to "draw up what [he thought was] fair" and she would sign it. Defendant prepared a listing of the parties' assets and liabilities, which did not include Defendant's North Carolina State Employees' Retirement Account (State Retirement Account), worth $158,100.00. Defendant testified this was an inadvertent omission.

On 1 September 1996, the parties met, reviewed, and discussed the listing, and then signed a one-page informal document which outlined the terms of a separation agreement. On 9 September 1996, Defendant retained attorney Wayne Hadler (Hadler) to prepare a final separation agreement, the Agreement at issue in this case. The Agreement formalized the terms of the one-page informal agreement the parties had previously signed, and the Agreement was executed and acknowledged before a notary by the parties on 10 September 1996 at Hadler's office.

At trial, Hadler who holds a Master's degree in Social Work and previously worked for twelve years as a social worker for the Alamance County Mental Health Department, testified he did not see anything about Plaintiff's appearance, demeanor, or behavior that would indicate she was confused or lacked the capacity to enter into the Agreement. Hadler informed Plaintiff he was representing Defendant and could not give her any legal advice, and he encouraged her to have the Agreement reviewed by separate counsel. Hadler explained to Plaintiff she could take as much time as she needed to review the Agreement, and he left her in the conference room of his office to allow her time to review the Agreement in privacy. Although Plaintiff was in regular consultation with her business attorneys and an accountant from July 1996 to October 1996, she chose not to have an attorney review the Agreement.

After the parties executed the Agreement, Plaintiff directed Defendant to immediately take her to a bank so she could receive the funds due her under the terms of the Agreement. Defendant followed Plaintiff's directions, and the parties have fully performed and complied with the terms of the Agreement.

Defendant testified at trial that several months after the Agreement's execution he came across a statement of his State Retirement Account. Realizing he had inadvertently omitted the State Retirement Account from his listing of assets and from the Agreement, Defendant telephoned Plaintiff to inquire whether she wanted to discuss the State Retirement Account and whether any adjustment should be made to the Agreement. Defendant testified Plaintiff responded she was "going to get more out of [him] than that," and their conversation ended.

Plaintiff testified at trial that she was suffering from hypo-mania and was psychotic and out of touch with reality from the spring of 1996 throughout the events surrounding the execution of the Agreement until her 20 January 1997 admittance into the UNC Memorial Hospital, where she was placed under a suicide watch. In April of 1995, Plaintiff was seeing a psychiatrist, Thomas N. Stephenson, M.D. (Dr. Stephenson), as an individual patient. Dr. Stephenson diagnosed Plaintiff as suffering from depression and anxiety and prescribed an anti-depressant, Zoloft, for Plaintiff. In May of 1996, before the execution of the Agreement, Dr. Stephenson saw Plaintiff for the last time. Dr. Stephenson found Plaintiff was "continuing to do well," but the problems with her husband were continuing.

Dr. Stephenson testified Zoloft can induce hypo-mania. Plaintiff's expert in psychiatry, Jeffrey J. Fahs, M.D. (Dr. Fahs), defined hypo-mania as a psychiatric condition that is a milder form of mania which is marked by grandiosity, a decreased need for sleep, loquaciousness, and involvement in activities that have a high potential for painful consequences like foolish business investments or buying sprees. Dr. Stephenson saw Plaintiff again on 13 September 1996, and at that time, he thought her judgment was impaired but she was not manic.

Dr. Fahs testified he examined Plaintiff on 10 March 1997 and reviewed her records and summary of treatment. Dr. Fahs opined Plaintiff had exhibited symptoms of a mood disorder that included depression, mania, and hypo-mania. Dr. Fahs testified Plaintiff "may have had a cognitive understanding" she was signing the Agreement, but she could not truly appreciate the consequences of signing it. Dr. Fahs also stated Zoloft can cause mania or hypo-mania, and mania impairs judgment.

. . .

The issues are whether: (I) the evidence supports the trial court's finding that Plaintiff's "mental state . . . was not . . . impaired" at the time the Agreement was executed; (II) the evidence supports the trial court's findings that Plaintiff signed the Agreement "of her own free and voluntary will . . . without . . . coercion"; [and] (III) Plaintiff alleged and offered evidence of fraud as a basis to set aside the Agreement. . . .

Separation and/or property settlement agreements are contracts and as such are subject to rescission on the grounds of (1) lack of mental capacity, (2) mistake, (3) fraud, (4) duress, or (5) undue influence. . . . Furthermore, these contracts are not enforceable if their terms are unconscionable. . . .

A claim for fraud may be based "on an affirmative misrepresentation of a material fact or a failure to disclose a material fact relating to a transaction which the parties had a duty to disclose." . . . A duty to disclose arises where: (1) "a fiduciary relationship exists between the parties to the transaction"; (2) there is no fiduciary relationship and "a party has taken affirmative steps to conceal material facts from the other"; and (3) there is no fiduciary relationship and "one party has knowledge of a latent defect in the subject matter of the negotiations about which the other party is both ignorant and unable to discover through reasonable diligence." . . . A husband and wife, unless they have separated and become adversaries negotiating over the terms of a separation and/or property settlement agreement, are in a fiduciary relationship. . . .

A claim that an agreement is unconscionable "requires a determination that the agreement is both substantively and procedurally unconscionable." . . . Procedural deficiencies involve "bargaining naughtiness," . . . "such as deception or a refusal to bargain over contract terms," 8 SAMUEL WILLISTON, A TREATISE ON THE LAW OF CONTRACTS § 18:10, at 57 (Richard A. Lord ed., 4th ed. 1998). The failure of a husband and/or a wife to accurately disclose his or her assets and debts in negotiating a separation and/or a property agreement can constitute procedural unconscionability, even if the failure to disclose does not constitute fraud. . . . Substantive unconscionability involves the "inequality of the bargain." . . .

Mental Capacity

Plaintiff first argues she was mentally incompetent at the time she signed the Agreement, and the trial court thus erred in refusing to rescind the Agreement on this basis. We disagree.

. . .

The record to this Court reveals conflicting evidence regarding Plaintiff's mental state at the time she executed the Agreement: there is evidence Plaintiff did not have the capacity to enter into a contract because she was under a drug induced mania that impaired her judgment; there is also evidence Plaintiff had the capacity to contract; Hadler did not see anything about Plaintiff's behavior or appearance which would indicate she lacked the capacity to contract at the Agreement's execution; and Dr. Dawkins did not notice any signs that Plaintiff was mentally impaired shortly after the Agreement was executed. Furthermore, Plaintiff directed Defendant take her to a bank so she could receive the money due her under the Agreement, thus, demonstrating she understood the nature of the act she was engaged in and its consequences.

The trial court resolved this conflict of evidence in favor of Defendant, and thus, did not err in refusing to rescind the Agreement on the ground of Plaintiff's lack of capacity to contract.

Undue Influence

Plaintiff argues the Agreement must be rescinded because Defendant exercised undue influence over her decision to sign the Agreement. We disagree.

. . .

The parties executed an informal agreement two weeks after their separation and the formal Agreement was executed two weeks later. At the time of the formal execution, Plaintiff was told by Defendant's attorney she could have an attorney review the Agreement before she signed it and she was given time to review the Agreement, in private, in Hadler's office. Plaintiff chose to sign the Agreement without the advice of an attorney, even though she had a business attorney and an accountant who regularly represented her in her psychotherapy practice. The trial court, thus, did not err in refusing to rescind the Agreement on the ground of undue influence.

Fraud

The trial court found Plaintiff "did not plead . . . breach of fiduciary duty in her Complaint nor did she offer any evidence of same."

. . .

Plaintiff offered evidence that she and her husband, the Defendant, soon after separating and before their divorce, informally agreed to the distribution of their marital assets and debts. This informal agreement was reduced to writing by Defendant's attorney and was signed by both parties. At some point after the execution of the Agreement, Plaintiff learned Defendant had failed to disclose the existence of his State Retirement Account, having a value of $158,100.00.

This evidence is some evidence Defendant failed to disclose a material fact to Plaintiff at a time when the parties were in a fiduciary relationship.

The trial court, thus, erred in finding Plaintiff had not presented "any evidence" of a breach of a fiduciary relationship.

Because the trial court found Plaintiff had not alleged breach of fiduciary duty and had not offered any evidence on this issue, that court made no findings or conclusions on this issue. This was error and remand must be had to the trial court. On remand, the trial court must enter findings and conclusions, based on the evidence in this record, on the breach of fiduciary duty issue.

NOTE

On remand, the trial court determined that "the facts surrounding the parties' marriage, including the time between their separation and the signing of the Agreement, were insufficient to establish a confidential relationship giving rise to a fiduciary duty," and that the "plaintiff effectively waived any duty of disclosure defendant may have owed to her" by refusing to participate in the disclosure process. *Sidden v. Mailman*, 563 S.E.2d 55, 58 (N.C. Ct. App. 2002), *cert. denied*, 577 S.E.2d 888 (2003). The trial court held, and the Court of Appeals affirmed that "[t]hese actions establish that the value of defendant's state retirement account was not material to plaintiff's decision to sign the Agreement; rather, plaintiff's decision was based on her desire to finalize her separation from defendant." 563 S.E.2d at 58–59.

Kelley v. Kelley

Supreme Court of Virginia, 1994.
449 S.E.2d 55.

■ Stephenson, J.

In this appeal, we decide (1) whether a provision of a property settlement agreement, which was ratified, affirmed, and incorporated by reference into a divorce decree, is void and, if so, (2) whether the decree may be attacked and vacated after it has become final.

On April 29, 1985, David Allen Kelley (Husband) and Marilyn Gibson Kelley (Wife) executed a property settlement agreement (the Agreement). On September 23, 1985, the trial court (the Circuit Court of the City of Roanoke) entered a divorce decree which ratified, affirmed, and incorporated by reference the Agreement.

The Agreement contained the following provision:

> The parties hereto agree, in consideration of Husband relinquishing all of his equity in the jointly-owned marital home, that Husband shall never be responsible for payment of child support. The [Wife] covenants and agrees never to file a petition in any Court requesting that [Husband] be placed under a child support Order because [Wife] has accepted all of [Husband's] equity in lieu of requesting child support.

> In the event [Wife] should ever petition any Court of competent jurisdiction for support and maintenance of [the children], and should a Court grant any such child support award, the said [Wife] hereby covenants and agrees to pay directly to [Husband], any amount of support that he is directed to pay to any party. In other words, [Wife] is agreeing to hold harmless [Husband] from the payment of any amount of child support, regardless of the circumstances under which he is paying same.

Pursuant to the Agreement, the Husband conveyed his equity in the marital home, valued at $40,000, to the Wife. For approximately six years thereafter, the Husband paid nothing toward the support of his children; the Wife, alone, supported them.

In late 1990, the Husband petitioned the trial court for definite periods of visitation with his children, and the Wife petitioned the court to require the Husband to pay child support. The Husband countered with a motion requesting the court to order the Wife to reimburse him for any amount of child support he was required to pay.

The trial court ordered the Husband to pay support and denied the Husband's motion, ruling that the indemnification and reimbursement provision of the Agreement was null and void. The Husband appealed from the trial court's judgment to the Court of Appeals. The Husband did not challenge the ordered child support, but contended that the trial court erred in holding that the indemnification and reimbursement provision of the Agreement was void and unenforceable.

The Court of Appeals, upon rehearing en banc, reversed the trial court's judgment, concluding that the trial court lacked jurisdiction to alter the terms of the Agreement or decree.... We awarded the Wife an appeal from the judgment of the Court of Appeals, concluding that the case involves a matter of significant precedential value....

Both parents owe a duty of support to their minor children.... A divorce court retains continuing jurisdiction to change or modify its decree relating to the maintenance and support of minor children.... Consequently, parents cannot contract away their children's rights to support nor can a court be precluded by agreement from exercising its power to decree child support.

In the present case, the parties agreed that the "Husband shall never be responsible for payment of child support." The Wife agreed "never to file a petition in any court" requesting support for the children. The Wife covenanted that, if a court ordered the Husband to pay child support, she would reimburse the Husband for all sums paid by him. She further agreed to hold the Husband harmless for any amount of child support he was required to pay.

Clearly, the parties contracted away the Husband's legal duty to support his children and, in effect, placed upon the Wife the sole duty of support. Additionally, the Wife's ability to contribute to the support of the children was adversely affected. Thus, the children's rights to receive support from both parents were substantially abridged, and the court's power to decree support was diminished. We hold, therefore, that the challenged provision of the Agreement is null and void because it is violative of clearly established law.

Next, we consider whether the trial court had jurisdiction to declare the provision null and void. The Court of Appeals ruled that the trial court lacked jurisdiction. Citing Rule 1:1, the Court of Appeals held that "after the expiration of twenty-one days immediately following the entry of the 1985 divorce decree, except to modify the amount of child support, the trial court lacked jurisdiction to alter the terms of the [Agreement] or the decree."

The Court of Appeals relied largely upon *Rook v. Rook*, 353 S.E.2d 756 (Va. 1987). In *Rook*, a married couple executed a property settlement agreement prior to the filing of a suit for divorce. Thereafter, the agreement was ratified, affirmed, and incorporated by reference into a divorce decree.

In a subsequent contempt proceeding for failure to comply with the terms of the decree, the husband contended that the agreement was void as against public policy, asserting that its purpose was to facilitate a divorce. We held, in *Rook*, that the challenge to the agreement's validity should have been made before the divorce decree was entered or within 21 days thereafter.

The present case is distinguishable from *Rook* because it involves the rights of children to support and maintenance. These rights, as previously noted, cannot be impinged by contract, and any contract purporting to do so is facially illegal and void.

In the present case, the subject provision of the Agreement was ratified, affirmed, and incorporated by reference into the divorce decree and, therefore, "shall be deemed for all purposes to be a term of the decree." Code § 20–109.1. Consequently, that portion of the decree that relates to the void provision is, itself, void.

It is firmly established that a void judgment may be attacked and vacated in any court at any time, directly or collaterally.... Therefore, the trial court had jurisdiction to declare the provision void and unenforceable.

Accordingly, we will reverse the judgment of the Court of Appeals, affirm the trial court's ruling, and enter final judgment for the Wife.

3.   MARITAL CONTRACTS

Ansin v. Craven–Ansin

Supreme Judicial Court of Massachusetts, 2010.
929 N.E.2d 955.

■ MARSHALL, C.J.

We granted direct appellate review in this divorce proceeding to determine whether so-called "postnuptial" or "marital" agreements are contrary to public policy and, if not, whether the marital agreement at issue is enforceable.[1] The dispute is between Kenneth S. Ansin (husband) and Cheryl A. Craven–Ansin (wife) concerning the validity of their 2004 written agreement "settling all rights and obligations arising from their marital relationship" in the event of a divorce. Two years after the agreement was executed, in November, 2006, the husband filed a complaint for divorce, and sought to enforce the terms of the agreement. At the time of the complaint, the parties had been married for twenty-one years and had two sons.

A judge in the Probate and Family Court upheld the agreement, finding that it was negotiated by independent counsel for each party, was not the product of fraud or duress, and was based on full financial disclosures by the husband, and that the terms of the agreement were fair and reasonable at the time of execution and at the time of divorce. Judgment entered enforc-

---

1. A "postnuptial" or "marital" agreement is an "agreement between spouses who plan to continue their marriage that alters or confirms the legal rights and obligations that would otherwise arise under ... [the] law governing marital dissolution." AMERICAN LAW INSTITUTE. PRINCIPLES OF THE LAW OF FAMILY DISSOLUTION: ANALYSIS AND RECOMMENDATIONS § 7.01(1)(b) (2002) (ALI PRINCIPLES OF FAMILY DISSOLUTION). *See* Fogg v. Fogg, 567 N.E.2d 921, 922 (1991) (same). Consistent with the ALI, we adopt the term "premarital" agreement for what is often termed a prenuptial or antenuptial agreement, and the term "marital" agreement for what is often termed a postnuptial agreement. *See* ALI PRINCIPLES OF FAMILY DISSOLUTION, *supra* at § 7.01(1)(a) and (b).

ing the marital agreement. The wife appealed, and we granted both parties' applications for direct appellate review.[2] We now affirm.

We recite the facts as found by the judge, all of which are supported by the record.

[A]t the time of the execution of the marital agreement in 2004, the value of the combined assets of the husband and wife was approximately $19 million. One of the assets, now at issue, is the husband's interest in certain trusts and business entities established by his grandfather, currently managed by his uncle. The assets of these various entities are substantial real estate holdings in Florida.[3] The husband's interest in the Florida real estate is passive; he was not involved in the management of the properties, and did not have or exercise control over the sale or other disposition of the properties. During the course of the marriage, the husband received, and the wife was aware of, distributions from his interest in the Florida real estate. The timing and amount of the distributions was unpredictable, and varied widely, as the wife knew.

During the course of their marriage the couple retained RINET Company LLC (RINET) to provide financial advice to them and to prepare their joint tax returns.... Because the husband's interest in the Florida real estate was "fractional" and "non-controlling," and because "speculation" is "inherent in any attempt to assign any values to such interests," there was no attempt by RINET to assign concrete values to these assets. Rather, on the reports prepared by RINET, the husband's interest in the Florida real estate was given a "placeholder" value of $4 million to $5 million (the amount varied from time to time), of which the wife was well aware. The wife understood that the husband's principal objective in executing a marital agreement was to protect his interest in the Florida real estate in the event of a divorce.

[T]he parties were married in July, 1985. The execution of their marital agreement nineteen years later was precipitated by marital problems that began toward the end of 2003. At the time the couple sought the assistance of a marriage counselor. In early 2004, the husband informed his wife that he "needed" her to sign an agreement if their marriage was to continue. He testified that his "uncertainty" about the wife's commitment to their relationship was the reason for this request. It caused the wife a "great deal of stress"; she told her husband that she would not sign any such agreement, and that discussion of the issue made her "physically ill." The parties separated, as it turned out for some six weeks. While the parties were separated, the husband promised his wife that he would recommit to the marriage if she would sign a marital agreement. She agreed to do so, she said, in an attempt to preserve the marriage and the family....

In April, 2004, they began negotiating the terms of the agreement.... Each retained counsel. The judge's detailed description of the negotiations depicts back-and-forth discussions between counsel for the wife and counsel for the husband, during which the wife negotiated terms more favorable to her.... The judge found that in the course of the negotiations the wife was "fully informed" of the marital assets, and that she was "satisfied" with the

---

2. In September, 2008, the proceedings having been bifurcated, a judgment of divorce nisi was entered on the grounds that the parties' marriage was irretrievably broken down. The judgment became absolute in December, 2008. The wife neither sought to stay, nor appealed from, that judgment.

3. We shall refer to the husband's interests in the trusts and business entities owned by his family as the husband's interest in Florida real estate.

disclosures made by the husband with respect to the Florida real estate, which included the financial summaries prepared by RINET that used the "placeholder" values. Finally, with the assistance of their respective counsel, the parties reached an agreement; it was signed in July, 2004.

We briefly summarize key provisions of the marital agreement. The agreement sets forth the parties' intent that, in the event of a divorce, the terms of the agreement are to be "valid and enforceable" against them, and "limit the rights" that "otherwise arise by reason of their marriage." The agreement recites that the parties are aware of the rights to which they may be entitled under Massachusetts law, that each has retained independent legal counsel, and that each executed the agreement "freely and voluntarily." The agreement states that the parties are "aware of the other's income," warrants that each has been provided with "all information requested by the other," and affirms that each "waives his or her rights to further inquiry, discovery and investigation." The agreement further recites that each is "fully satisfied" that the agreement "will promote marital harmony" and "will ensure the treatment of Husband's property to which the parties agreed before their marriage and since their separation."

As for the distribution of property in the event of a divorce, the agreement states that the wife "disclaims any and all interest she now has or ever may have" in the husband's interest in the Florida real estate and other marital assets. The husband agreed to pay the wife $5 million, and thirty per cent of the appreciation of all marital property held by the couple from the time of the agreement to the time of the divorce. The agreement provides that the wife could remain in the marital home for one year after any divorce, with the husband paying all reasonable expenses of that household. The husband agreed to pay for the wife's medical insurance until her death or remarriage, and he agreed to maintain a life insurance policy to the exclusive benefit of the wife in the amount of $2.5 million while the parties remained married.

[O]n execution of the marital agreement, the relationship between the husband and wife took on, in the judge's words, a "light and optimistic tone" and both were "looking forward to strengthening their marriage." . . . However, in August, 2004, the parties had a discussion that "led the [w]ife to believe that their marriage was over." The husband had not decided to divorce his wife, and the judge credited his testimony that he was "unwilling" to abandon the marriage at that time.

In response to their marital difficulties, the parties again considered separating, but decided not to do so at least until their younger son graduated from high school. They remained living together from August, 2004, until June, 2005, engaged in an intimate relationship, and "attempted to preserve the appearance of their marriage." . . .

Meanwhile, the husband applied for and was accepted to Harvard University's Kennedy School of Government; his decision to enroll as a student there was not supported by his wife. The wife began to increase her consumption of alcohol, leading to more arguments with her husband. In June, 2005, at the wife's request, the husband moved out of the house. He did not file for divorce at that time, believing that while things looked "grim," filing for divorce would have been the "ultimate declaration" that his marriage was over. After separating from her husband, the wife maintained contact with their RINET financial advisor, inquiring on multiple occasions what the value of any payment to her would be under the terms of the marital agreement. In 2006 the wife became involved in a serious relationship with another man. In February of that year, the wife informed the husband that "one of us has to be strong enough to take the steps to bring closure to our relationship." . . . In November, 2006, the husband filed a petition for divorce.

Whether a marital agreement should be recognized in Massachusetts is a long-deferred question of first impression. Consistent with the majority of States to address the issue, *see Bratton v. Bratton*, 136 S.W.3d 595, 599–600 (Tenn. 2004), we conclude that such agreements may be enforced. *See e.g., Matter of Estate of Harber*, 449 P.2d 7, 14 (Ariz. 1969); *Casto v. Casto*, 508 So. 2d 330, 333 (Fla. 1987); *Lipic v. Lipic*, 103 S.W.3d 144, 149 (Mo. Ct. App. 2003); *Matter of Estate of Gab*, 364 N.W.2d 924, 925 (S.D. 1985).[7] Our decision is consistent with our established recognition that a marital relationship need not vitiate contractual rights between the parties. We have, for example, recognized the validity of premarital agreements, *Osborne v. Osborne*, 428 N.E.2d 810, 815 (Mass. 1981), and separation agreements, *Knox v. Remick*, 358 N.E.2d 432, 435 (Mass. 1976), reasoning that it was important to respect the parties' "freedom to contract" and that such agreements may serve a "useful function" in permitting the parties to arrange their financial affairs "as they best see fit." *DeMatteo v. DeMatteo*, 762 N.E.2d 797, 808 (Mass. 2002) (concerning premarital agreements). *See Osborne v. Osborne, supra* ("no reason not to allow persons about to enter into a marriage the freedom to settle their rights in the event their marriage should prove unsuccessful"). . . .

The wife argues that marital agreements are different in kind and should be declared void against public policy because they are "innately coercive," "usually" arise when the marriage is already failing, and may "encourage" divorce. The wife provides no support for, and we reject, any assumption that marital agreements are typically executed amid threats of divorce or induced by illusory promises of remaining in a failing marriage. Marital contracts are not the product of classic arm's-length bargaining, but that does not make them necessarily coercive. Such contracts may inhibit the dissolution of a marriage, or may protect the interests of third parties such as children from a prior relationship. In any event, a marital agreement will always be reviewed by a judge to ensure that coercion or fraud played no part in its execution.

A marital agreement stands on a different footing from both a premarital and a separation agreement.[8] Before marriage, the parties have greater freedom to reject an unsatisfactory premarital contract. *See* C.P. KINDREGAN, JR., & M.L. INKER, FAMILY LAW AND PRACTICE § 50:15 (3d ed. 2002) (hereinafter Kindregan & Inker) (agreement made in expectation of marriage "radically"

---

7. Several States have enacted statutes that permit the enforcement of marital agreements. *See, e.g.*, Tibbs v. Anderson, 580 So. 2d 1337, 1339 (Ala. 1991); Boudreaux v. Boudreaux, 745 So. 2d 61, 63 (La. Ct. App. 1999); Button v. Button, 131 Wis. 2d 84, 87–88, 388 N.W.2d 546 (1986). *But see* OHIO REV. CODE ANN. § 3103.06 (West 2005) ("A husband and wife cannot, by any contract with each other, alter their legal relations, except that they may agree to an immediate separation and make provisions for the support of either of them and their children during the separation"). Many States have not addressed the issue. We are aware of no jurisdiction that has declined to enforce such agreements unless required to do so by statute.

8. The ALI takes the position that "the principles applicable to marital and premarital agreements are the same" and suggests, as some States have done, applying substantially the same standards for enforcing both types of agreements. ALI Principles of Family Dissolution, *supra* at § 7.01 Reporter's Notes to comment e, citing Reese v. Reese, 984 P.2d 987 (Utah 1999). While we draw on some aspects of the ALI's suggestions on how to evaluate marital agreements, we conclude that the principles applicable to premarital and marital agreements are not the same in all respects.

different situation from "that which faces a spouse attempting to save a long existing family relationship to which she has committed her best years"); *Pacelli v. Pacelli*, 725 A.2d 56, 59 (N.J. App. Div. 1999) (wife faced more difficult choice "than the bride who is presented with a demand for a pre-nuptial agreement" because cost "would have been the destruction of a family and the stigma of a failed marriage"). *See also* AMERICAN LAW INSTITUTE, PRINCIPLES OF FAMILY DISSOLUTION: ANALYSIS AND RECOMMENDATIONS § 7.01 comment e (2002) ("opportunities for hard dealing may be greater" with marital contracts than with premarital contracts).

A separation agreement, in turn, is negotiated when a marriage has failed and the spouses "intend a permanent separation or marital dissolution." The family unit will no longer be kept intact, and the parties may look to their own future economic interests. The circumstances surrounding marital agreements in contrast are "pregnant with the opportunity for one party to use the threat of dissolution 'to bargain themselves into positions of advantage.'" *Pacelli v. Pacelli, supra* at 195 (quoting *Mathie v. Mathie*, 363 P.2d 779, 783 (Utah 1961)).

For these reasons, we join many other States in concluding that marital agreements must be carefully scrutinized. *See, e.g., Casto v. Casto*, 508 So. 2d 330, 334 (Fla. 1987) (court "must recognize that parties to a marriage are not dealing at arm's length, and, consequently, trial judges must carefully examine the circumstances to determine the validity of [marital] agreements"); *Matter of Estate of Gab*, 364 N.W.2d 924, 925–26 (S.D. 1985), citing *Matter of Estate of Harber*, 449 P.2d 7 (Ariz. 1969) (because of "confidential relationship" existing between husband and wife, marital agreements "are subjected to close scrutiny by the courts to insure that they are fair and equitable"); *Bratton v. Bratton*, 136 S.W.3d 595, 601 (Tenn. 2004) (same). *See also* ALI PRINCIPLES OF FAMILY DISSOLUTION, *supra* at § 7.01 Reporter's Notes to comment e ("the problems presented by the two kinds of agreements [premarital and marital] are different, which has led some states to adopt different rules" for each).

Before a marital agreement is sanctioned by a court, careful scrutiny by the judge should determine at a minimum whether (1) each party has had an opportunity to obtain separate legal counsel of each party's own choosing;[9] (2) there was fraud or coercion in obtaining the agreement; (3) all assets were fully disclosed by both parties before the agreement was executed; (4) each spouse knowingly and explicitly agreed in writing to waive the right to a judicial equitable division of assets and all marital rights in the event of a divorce; and (5) the terms of the agreement are fair and reasonable at the time of execution and at the time of divorce.[10] Where one spouse challenges

---

9. We do not require, as do some other States, that a marital agreement will be enforceable only if each spouse is represented by separate counsel. *See, e.g.,* MINN. STAT. ANN. § 519.11(1a)(c) (West 2006) ("A postnuptial contract or settlement is valid and enforceable only if at the time of its execution each spouse is represented by separate legal counsel"). Reliance on the advice of experienced, independent legal counsel, however, will go a long way toward ensuring the enforceability of an agreement. *Cf.* ALI Principles of Family Dissolution, *supra* at § 7.04 (marital agreement "rebuttably presumed" to satisfy showing that contesting party's consent was "informed and not obtained under duress" if parties were "advised to obtain independent legal counsel, and had reasonable opportunity to do so before the agreement's execution"). Here it is undisputed that both parties to this agreement not only had the opportunity to, but did, obtain separate legal counsel.

10. The wife argues that she did not receive "sufficient" consideration because the financial components of the agreements were "far less" than she was "already entitled to receive" on divorce. In this case, and likely would be in any case, this is in essence an argument that the marital agreement was not fair and reasonable. Because the marital agreement was

the enforceability of the agreement, the spouse seeking to enforce the agreement shall bear the burden of satisfying these criteria. *See* ALI PRINCIPLES OF FAMILY DISSOLUTION, *supra* at § 7.04 (2) ("A party seeking to enforce an agreement must show that the other party's consent to it was informed and not obtained under duress").

We now elaborate on those points as they apply to the marital agreement here.

[A]s with contracts generally, marital agreements are not enforceable if tainted by fraud or coercion. We agree with those States that have held that the spouse seeking to enforce a marital agreement, in contrast to the enforcement of contracts generally, must establish that the other spouse's consent was not obtained through coercion or fraud. *See, e.g., Matter of Estate of Harber, supra* at 88 (where marital agreement challenged on grounds of fraud or coercion, it is other party's "burden to prove by clear and convincing evidence that the agreement was not fraudulent or coerced").[11] *See also* ALI Principles of Family Dissolution, *supra* at § 7.04 comment b (burden shifting reflects appropriate "heightened scrutiny" of bargaining process leading to marital agreements as compared with bargaining process leading to commercial contracts). . . .

Even though the judge in this case did not utilize a burden-shifting analysis, we see no reason to question her ultimate finding that the marital agreement was not the product of coercion or fraud. The agreement was the product of lengthy negotiations between the parties, each represented by separate, experienced counsel. The wife's attorney testified that, consistent with the instructions of her client, she intended to negotiate an enforceable marital agreement. A vigorous exchange ensued with the husband's counsel in which she was able to negotiate significant gains for the wife. The evidence is clear that the wife made an informed, voluntary choice to sign the agreement.[13]

As to fraud, the wife argues that the husband misrepresented his intention to stay in the marriage in order to induce her to sign the agreement. The judge found to the contrary, and her findings are fully supported by the evidence. For example, after the agreement had been signed, the husband worked "hard" in the areas the wife "felt needed improvement." The couple traveled together extensively. They purchased and substantially renovated a new house together. It was not until over two years later, after the wife had asked the husband to leave the marital home and after she had become involved with another man, that the husband filed for divorce.[14] A judge should be careful to ensure that the contesting spouse

---

supported by consideration, we need not consider whether a marital agreement needs to be supported by consideration. *See* ALI Principles of Dissolution, *supra* at § 7.01 (4) (consideration not required to create enforceable marital agreement).

11. We do not agree with the Arizona court, *see* Matter of Estate of Harber, 449 P.2d 7, 16 (Ariz. 1969), that the burden must be satisfied by "clear and convincing" evidence. *See* ALI PRINCIPLES OF FAMILY DISSOLUTION, *supra* at § 7.04 comment b (shift burden of proof to spouse seeking to enforce agreement, but not suggesting proof by clear and convincing evidence).

13. The wife suggests that because the parties' younger son suffers from an illness, she was pressured into signing the agreement to preserve her son's "happiness and stability." The judge made no findings concerning the son's illness or its effect on the wife's decision to sign the marital agreement. The wife made no request for additional findings on those points, and we do not consider them. It may be that in some circumstances evidence that a spouse agrees to a marital agreement because of concern for the illness of a child and evidence that the child will be harmed by a divorce will be sufficient to establish coercion or duress.

14. The wife testified at trial . . . several weeks after the agreement was signed, the parties had a counselor, as well as their son's physician, to consider a separation that would be the least

has not been misled in any way by a spouse that at the time seems committed. We are confident that the judge did so in this case.

[W]e have explained with respect to premarital agreements that "[f]ull and fair" disclosure of each party's financial circumstances is a "significant aspect" of the parties' obligation to deal with each other fairly "because they stand in a confidential relationship with each other" and must have such information in order to make an informed decision about the terms of the agreement. *DeMatteo v. DeMatteo*, 762 N.E.2d 797, 806 (Mass. 2002). The obligation is greater with respect to marital agreements because each spouse owes a duty of absolute fidelity to the other. *See Krapf v. Krapf*, 786 N.E.2d 318, 323 (Mass. 2003) (spouses "stand as fiduciaries to each other, and will be held to the highest standards of good faith and fair dealing in the performance of their contractual obligations"). Because a marital agreement is consummated without the safeguards attendant to divorce proceedings, such as court-ordered disclosures, *see* Rule 401 (a) of the Supplemental Rules of the Probate Court, Mass. Ann. Laws Court Rules, at 1133 (Lexis Nexis 2008–2009), and discovery, enforcement of a marital agreement can occur only when a judge finds that there was a full disclosure of all assets of both spouses, whether jointly or separately held. The requirement of full disclosure may be satisfied if "prior to signing the agreement the party seeking to enforce it provided the other party with a written statement accurately listing (i) his or her significant assets, and their total approximate market value; (ii) his or her approximate annual income ... and (iii) any significant future acquisitions, or changes in income, to which the party has a current legal entitlement, or which the party reasonably expects to realize" in the near future. ALI PRINCIPLES OF FAMILY DISSOLUTION, *supra* at § 7.04(5).[15] The disclosure need not be exact, but must approximate the value of the assets.

We agree with the judge that the disclosures here were sufficient to meet this rigorous standard. The wife argues that the husband undervalued his interest in the Florida real estate, and that he committed a breach of the warranty in the agreement that such disclosures were "accurate and truthful." The facts as found by the judge belie this claim.[16] During the marriage

---

disruptive for him. The wife argues that the judge erred in not allowing her to testify concerning the contents of this conversation, which she claims would have shown that the husband did not intend to stay in the marriage when he asked her to sign the agreement. The judge excluded her testimony on the grounds of "spousal disqualification." That evidentiary rule provides that "a witness shall not testify as to private conversations with a spouse occurring during their marriage," see § 504(b) (2010), but recognize Mass. G. Evid. as an exception for proceedings "arising out of or involving a contract between spouses," *id.* at § 504(b)(2)(A). We question whether the evidence should have been excluded, given the exception to the spousal disqualification rule. Even if the ruling was erroneous, however, it was harmless. There was ample other evidence to support the judge's finding that the husband did not fraudulently induce the wife to sign the agreement.

15. The ALI PRINCIPLES OF FAMILY DISSOLUTION, *supra* at § 7.04(5), specifies that the spouse seeking to enforce the agreement must have disclosed his income for "each of the preceding three years" and any significant future acquisitions or changes in income that the party "reasonably expects to realize within three years of the agreement's execution." We need not determine whether a three-year period is appropriate in this case because the wife was aware of the couple's marital assets and income, and participated regularly in meetings with the couple's financial advisor throughout the marriage. *See* ALI PRINCIPLES OF FAMILY DISSOLUTION, *supra* at § 7.04(5) comment g (evidence that contesting spouse has knowledge of all other spouse's assets independent of any written disclosures will satisfy requirement of disclosure).

16. The judge held a separate hearing to receive evidence as to the husband's and the wife's finances, in connection with which each spouse was required to submit financial statements, and each was able to cross-examine the other as to the information in these statements. The judge found that the husband's financial statement was a "true, accurate and complete" representation of his financial affairs. In contrast, the judge found that the wife's statements

the wife was aware of her husband's interest in a "significant amount" of real estate in Florida, that the precise value of that interest was uncertain and speculative, that there was limited information available concerning the real estate, and that the $4 million to $5 million value assigned to those interests by RINET was a "placeholder." During the negotiation of the agreement, the wife provided her attorney with a December 31, 2003, summary of the parties' net worth prepared by RINET, and the husband provided a similar June 30, 2004, report. Each summary contained the "placeholder" value, stating that the Florida properties had an "[a]nticipated" value of $5 million. While she was negotiating the marital agreement, the wife had access to the couple's financial advisor, with whom she previously had regularly met, and her own independent counsel to assist her in making any inquiries about the "placeholder" value that she felt was required. The judge found that the wife was "satisfied" with the disclosures, accepting that the available information about the properties was necessarily limited. Information about the Florida real estate was not, in the judge's words, "a strong point of contention between the parties."

The wife acknowledged when she executed the marital agreement that she had "been provided with all information requested," that she was "afforded sufficient opportunity to inquire and investigate further financial circumstances" of her husband, and that she waived her "rights to further inquiry." There is nothing in the record to suggest that those representations were inaccurate.

[B]y the terms of their agreement, the husband and wife agreed that they intended the marital agreement to limit their rights in the event of divorce, and that the agreement should govern "in lieu of and in full discharge and satisfaction of the rights which otherwise arise by reason of their marriage." As we explained in the context of premarital agreements, waiver is "important because it underscores that each party is exercising a meaningful choice when he or she agrees to give up certain rights." *DeMatteo v. DeMatteo*, 762 N.E.2d 797, 808 (Mass. 2002). In determining whether there was a meaningful waiver of rights, a judge should consider "whether each party was represented by independent counsel, the adequacy of the time to review the agreement, the parties' understanding of the terms of the agreement and their effect, and a party's understanding of his or her rights in the absence of an agreement." Here, the wife was represented by independent counsel, who represented her over the course of several weeks as the terms of the agreement were negotiated. The wife affirmed in writing that she understood the rights she was waiving, and she does not claim that she did not understand any terms of the agreement. The evidence supports the conclusion that the wife's waiver was meaningful.

[W]e turn finally to the requirement that a marital agreement contain terms that are "fair and reasonable" at the time of execution and at the time of divorce. We do not accept the husband's suggestion that the standard applicable to marital agreements should be the same as the one applicable to premarital agreements.[19] As the wife points out, a marital agreement more

_____

were not an "accurate" picture of her financial affairs because, among other things, she failed to list interest income on over $1 million in brokerage account investments.

19.   We adopted a more deferential standard of review for premarital agreements in part because when "terms of a proposed antenuptial agreement are unsatisfactory, a party is free not to marry." DeMatteo v. DeMatteo, 762 N.E.2d 797 (Mass. 2002). One party, perhaps having significant family wealth, may decline to enter the marriage unless he or she can protect these assets in the event of a divorce. Consequently, a premarital agreement may provide that on divorce there will be great inequality accorded to each party. For a spouse to relinquish

closely resembles a separation agreement. The statutory rights and obligations conferred by marriage are not potential benefits for a divorcing spouse but an integral aspect of the marriage itself. The Legislature has required that the relinquishment of marital rights be assessed in light of the factors set forth in Mass. Gen. Laws ch. 208, § 34. In *DeMatteo v. DeMatteo, supra* at 33, we noted that "it is entirely appropriate" that the judge consider the factors set forth in Mass. Gen. Laws ch. 208, § 34, in evaluating a separation agreement; the "separation agreement is, after all, a substitute for the independent application by a judge" of the equitable division of parties' property as mandated by the Legislature. Similar considerations inform our view of the enforceability of marital agreements, with this additional observation: parties to a marital agreement do not bargain as freely as separating spouses may do. Because a marital agreement is executed when the parties do not contemplate divorce and when they owe absolute fidelity to each other, the heightened scrutiny to which we made reference earlier applies in this context as well.

In evaluating whether a marital agreement is fair and reasonable at the time of execution, a judge should accordingly consider the entire context in which the agreement was reached, allowing greater latitude for agreements reached where each party is represented by separate counsel of their own choosing. A judge may consider "the magnitude of the disparity between the outcome under the agreement and the outcome under otherwise prevailing legal principles," whether "the purpose of the agreement was to benefit or protect the interests of third parties (such as the children from a prior relationship)," and "the impact of the agreement's enforcement upon the children of the parties." Other factors may include the length of the marriage, the motives of the contracting spouses, their respective bargaining positions, the circumstances giving rise to the marital agreement, the degree of the pressure, if any, experienced by the contesting spouse, and other circumstances the judge finds relevant.

Viewed at the time of execution, we agree with the judge that the marital agreement at issue here was fair and reasonable. As noted earlier, the wife was represented by experienced, independent counsel throughout the negotiations. In the event of a divorce, the wife was to receive a substantial fixed sum payment from her husband. If the marital estate appreciated in value after execution of the agreement, she would receive, in addition, a percentage of the increase in value; she did not forgo the fixed payment if the marital assets, including the husband's interest in the Florida real estate, declined substantially. There is no basis to the wife's claim that the judge "ignore[d]" the husband's "legal obligation of disclosure of value" of the Florida real estate. As we discussed in detail earlier, the basis of the valuation was known to and accepted by the wife and her lawyer. We see no reason to disturb the judge's ruling on this point.

In determining whether a marital agreement is fair and reasonable at the time of divorce, a judge will be able to satisfy the searching inquiry we require by examining the same factors employed for evaluating a separation agreement. Thus, a judge may consider, among other factors: "(1) the nature and substance of the objecting party's complaint; (2) the financial and property division provisions of the agreement as a whole; (3) the context in which the negotiations took place; (4) the complexity of the issues involved; (5) the background and knowledge of the parties; (6) the experience and

---

statutorily proscribed marital rights to significant assets necessarily requires a more searching inquiry as to whether an agreement is "fair and reasonable."

ability of counsel; (7) the need for and availability of experts to assist the parties and counsel; and (8) the mandatory and, if the judge deems it appropriate, the discretionary factors set forth in Mass. Gen. Laws ch. 208, § 34"[20] (footnotes omitted). *Dominick v. Dominick, supra.* As with a judge's evaluation of separation agreements, the § 34 factors are not determinative; the judge is not required to "divine" what judgment she would likely enter had the case been litigated in the absence of an agreement. Rather, she considers only whether the agreement is "fair and reasonable" when considered in light of the factors we have identified and any other relevant circumstances.

The gravamen of the wife's complaint is that she will be left with a disproportionately small percentage of the couple's marital assets. A marital agreement need not provide for an equal distribution of assets, as long as a judge has concluded that the agreement is fair and reasonable. In her careful and detailed findings, the judge considered the factors set forth in Mass. Gen. Laws ch. § 208, § 34, as well as many of the other factors we have just detailed. The wife points to no material change between the time she, on the advice of counsel, executed the marital agreement and the husband's petition for divorce in 2006. We again see no reason to conclude that the judge was erroneous in her conclusion.

Enforcement of a marital agreement is not contrary to public policy. We agree with the judge in the Probate and Family Court that the marital agreement in this case should be specifically enforced.

C.   ALTERNATIVE DISPUTE RESOLUTION

1.   ARBITRATION

Johnson v. Johnson

Supreme Court of New Jersey, 2010.
9 A.3d 1003.

■ JUSTICE LONG delivered the opinion of the Court.

Recently, in *Fawzy v. Fawzy*, 973 A.2d 347 (2009), we held that the constitutional guarantee of parental autonomy includes the right of parents to choose arbitration as the forum in which to resolve their disputes over child custody and parenting time. *Id.* at 350. In that case, we set forth the prerequisites for an enforceable arbitration agreement and the methodology by which an arbitration award in the child custody setting may be judicially reviewed. [W]e declared, in recognition of our *parens patriae* authority, that in addition to the remedies provided in the Arbitration Act, an arbitrator's award is subject to judicial review if a party establishes that the award threatens harm to a child. To ensure a basis on which to evaluate a claim of harm, we required that a record of all documentary evidence be kept;

---

20.   In relevant part, Mass. Gen. Laws ch. 208, § 34, provides that a judge "shall consider the length of the marriage, the conduct of the parties during the marriage, the age, health, station, occupation, amount and sources of income, vocational skills, employability, estate, liabilities and needs of each of the parties and the opportunity of each for future acquisition of capital assets and income.... [T]he court shall also consider the present and future needs of the dependent children of the marriage. The court may also consider the contribution of each of the parties in the acquisition, preservation or appreciation in value of their respective estates and the contribution of each of the parties as a homemaker to the family unit."

testimony be recorded verbatim; and that an award, including findings of fact and conclusions of law, issue.

The case before us was not decided under the Arbitration Act, but under the New Jersey Alternative Procedure for Dispute Resolution Act (APDRA), N.J. STAT. ANN. 2A:23A–1 to–19, which conforms in many respects to the procedures we set forth in *Fawzy*. The trial judge ruled that the record was adequate for review and confirmed the arbitration award. However, because of the absence of a verbatim transcript, the Appellate Division reversed the trial judge's confirmation order and remanded the matter for a plenary hearing.

We now reverse. . . . The purpose behind *Fawzy*'s procedural safeguards was to assure a basis upon which meaningful judicial review of an arbitration award can occur in a case in which harm to a child is claimed. . . .

In this case, the arbitrator produced a complete record of all evidence he considered, a detailed recapitulation of every interview and observation he conducted, a full explanation of the underpinnings of the award, and a separate opinion on reconsideration. That satisfies the spirit of *Fawzy* and constitutes an acceptable substitute for a verbatim transcript.

. . . David Johnson and Molly V.G.B. Johnson were married on October 26, 1994, and divorced on August 16, 2005. Two children were born during the marriage: Amelia, on February 9, 2001, and Elsie, on January 30, 2003. In May 2005, the couple separated; Ms. Johnson elected to move out of the marital home and ceded residential custody of the children to Mr. Johnson. From May 2005 until November 2005, Ms. Johnson spent parenting time at the marital residence while she lived in an apartment with roommates. When she purchased her current home, the children began to spend time with her there.

The final judgment of divorce incorporated a May 24, 2005, property settlement agreement, which provided that the parties would share joint legal custody of the children and that Mr. Johnson would continue as the residential custodial parent. . . .

Following the divorce, the parties encountered difficulties with the parenting schedule and thereafter consented to resolving those issues in arbitration. Pursuant to a consent order, the parties chose to be governed by the APDRA. Their agreement was extremely thorough and explained what the parties viewed as the issue and how they intended the APDRA to operate. The agreement began by identifying the issue:

> The parties are the parents of AMELIA JOHNSON, age six, and ELSIE JOHNSON age four. For several years [they] have experienced on-going difficulties in resolving differing parenting approaches and Parenting Time Schedules that will advance their children's best interests.

The agreement went on to detail the parties' expectations regarding how the case was to be conducted:

> To resolve parenting differences and Parenting Time scheduling issue[s] *in futuro*, the parties have agreed to utilize the Arbitration services of MARK WHITE, Ph.D. . . . [I]t is envisaged that Dr. WHITE shall initially meet with the parties and counsel; and thereafter meet with both parties on one or more occasions as he shall deem necessary in his sole discretion. Dr. WHITE shall receive position papers of the parties which may be prepared with the assistance of and prepared by their attorneys. The position papers may include examples of the difficulties the parties have faced, citing examples, findings of facts that are request-

ed to be made by Dr. WHITE, as well as [the] law of the State of New Jersey applicable to such facts. Dr. WHITE will observe the children in the presence of the parents. With this input and without the necessity of taking formal testimony of the parties in the presence of their attorneys, it is anticipated that Dr. WHITE will have sufficient information to craft a decision intend[ed] to resolve the parenting issues and scheduling issues that currently [exist]. It is not envisaged that Dr. WHITE will require formal Arbitration in the presence of both parties and counsel to make findings of fact in this case; although he shall have the power and authority to do so, in his sound discretion. It is required that Dr. WHITE create a scheduling calendar, with the intent of limiting future parenting schedule controversy to a minimum. The fact that testimony of the parties in each other's presence and counsel's presence was not adduced by the Arbitrator/Umpire shall not constitute a good cause grounds for reversing the Arbitration Award.

In addition, the agreement vested the arbitrator with the duty to make findings of relevant material facts and legal determinations; provided that the arbitrator would make an award on all submitted issues in accordance with applicable principles of New Jersey substantive law, as required by N.J. Stat. Ann. 2A:23A–12(e); afforded a right to file a motion for reconsideration of the award and for modification, pursuant to N.J. Stat. Ann. 2A:23A–12(d); limited the parties' right to appeal to the issue of whether the arbitrator properly applied the law to the factual findings and issues presented for resolution; and specified that there would be no transcript of proceedings and that the detailed findings of the arbitrator would constitute the record, as supplemented by the written certified statements submitted by the parties prior to arbitration. The agreement was explicit that testimony outside a party's or counsel's presence would not constitute good cause grounds for reversing any award. Finally, the parties waived their rights to a trial on the merits and preserved the right to appeal the award within the constraints of the APDRA.

As anticipated by the agreement, over the course of several months the arbitrator conducted various interviews.... In addition, he observed the children in both home settings and reviewed their school records.

In April 2008, the arbitrator issued his award. At the outset, he detailed the parties' proposals, which were not vastly different from what was in effect at the time:

Proposal of Mr. Johnson

> The children would be at the home of Mr. Johnson Sunday night through Friday afternoon, and every other weekend. Alternation of parenting time during the two extended winter and spring breaks from school. Alternation of holidays. One week vacation with each parent. Sunday evening overnights with Ms. Johnson before all Monday holidays when the children are off from school. Children to be returned by noon Monday. Dinner with Ms. Johnson one night during the week, to be scheduled "based upon the best arrangement factoring everyone's schedule."

> · · ·

Proposal of Ms. Johnson

> The weekend the children are with Ms. Johnson should be extended to include Sunday overnights, and then drop off at schools Monday mornings. Scheduling of activities for the children only upon mutual

consent of both parents. Pick up of the children from schools on Thursdays.

The arbitrator then recounted the substance of every interview and observation he undertook, including a particularized recitation of the parties' claims about their different approaches to parenting and the problems with scheduling transitions. Mr. Johnson, who remains angry at his former wife over the divorce, contended that she is unreliable and frequently late picking up the children; that she tends to drop the children off without remembering to bring their things; ... that they are not ready for school on mornings after they stay with their mother; that they eat snacks at her house before dinner at his house; that Ms. Johnson creates emotionally dramatic transfers; ... and that she has issues with boundaries (for example, she allows the girls to sleep with her) that cause problems in his home....

Ms. Johnson countered that her former husband is rigid; has excessive control over the children's schedules; arranges activities during her parenting time; and that he has otherwise decreased the amount of time the children spend with her. She further claimed that he over schedules the children (e.g., dance, violin, swimming, T-ball, soccer), and that there is poor communication between the parties in that Mr. Johnson fails to convey essential information to her and verbally attacks her when the subject of increased parenting time comes up.

Ms. Johnson also contended that ... the children benefit from the less structured, more creative environment at her home ... and that he does not consult her on scheduled activities. Following that interview, Ms. Johnson sent the arbitrator a long letter reiterating all of her concerns, in particular, that her former husband's actions have the effect of "marginalizing" her....

The home visits, according to the arbitrator, were uneventful—with both homes, though very different, fully appropriate for the girls. The arbitrator perceived the girls as well-adjusted, but affected by the parenting conflicts and the amount of moving around required.

. . .

The arbitrator concluded that both parties are decent, well-intentioned, non-pathological parents and that the children are positively developing in their care. He proceeded to evaluate the case in terms of how the parties' behavior imposed on their daughters' experiences. He noted that it was his "fervent hope" that his involvement would "result in the prevention of escalation of the family system factors that could elevate the probability of [the girls] developing psychological symptoms later in their childhoods."

To accomplish that goal, the arbitrator stated that Ms. Johnson needed to accept responsibility for leaving the marriage and for her lackadaisical approach, evidenced by her tardiness and inefficiency which prevented a "more robust co-parenting alliance," and that Mr. Johnson needed to confront and resolve his anger towards Ms. Johnson over the divorce. In addition, the arbitrator reasoned that the children were too young to experience so many transitions, particularly in light of the "intrinsic tension" between their parents and the "dissimilarity of the home cultures." Accordingly, he set forth a decision "[i]n the hope that both parties will accept [the provisions] in the child-protective spirit in which they are offered."

With a view toward carrying out what the parties had commissioned him to do—"create a scheduling calendar, with the intent of limiting future parenting schedule controversy to a minimum," the arbitrator increased the amount of uninterrupted weekly time the children spent with Mr. Johnson, but extended the weekend and holiday time spent with Ms. Johnson. Specifically, the arbitrator expanded Ms. Johnson's weekends with the children to Sunday overnights and limited her weekday overnights to Wednesdays only. He compensated for the time that the girls lost with their mother by providing her with a majority of three-day, four-overnight weekends and additional time during school vacations.

In addition, he referred Ms. Johnson to a neuropsychologist for an evaluation for Attention Deficit Hyperactivity Disorder based upon her "time management and attentional difficulties." He also referred Mr. Johnson to counseling for his unresolved emotions related to the divorce. Specifically addressing Ms. Johnson's concern that the children were overly programmed, the arbitrator limited them to one scheduled activity in a given season.

The award left open Ms. Johnson's request for expanded time with the children to be reconsidered after she had undergone her evaluation and demonstrated that Amelia could attend school for three consecutive months without receiving a tardy notice. The decision also permitted future meetings between the arbitrator and the parties starting around October 1, 2008, to consider further modifications.

Ms. Johnson filed a motion for reconsideration of the entire decision or clarification of the extent of her vacation time custody. The gravamen of the motion was that she did not "feel as though [her] viewpoints and concerns were considered...." In response, the arbitrator prepared an eleven-point decision in which he reaffirmed his conclusion that both parents are well-intentioned and deeply invested in their children's welfare....

. . .

The arbitrator explained that changes in the schedule were based on the children's needs rather than any conclusion about Ms. Johnson's ability to parent. It was his explicit intention "to prevent the post-divorce version of the Johnsons' inability to collaboratively solve problems from metastasizing to a level that will represent a pathogenic risk to their beautiful daughters." The arbitrator stated that divorce and remarriage "necessitates the need to more clearly establish boundaries between Mom's house and Dad's house."

As an addendum to the decision, the arbitrator delayed implementation of the new schedule from the original decision because "stresses attendant to changing Amelia's schedule so late in the school year" outweighed the benefits of implementation. The arbitrator remained open to meeting with the parents prior to the start of the next school year to rebalance the children's time at each home and determine the advisability of a parent coordinator. He observed that the "ultimate goal ... was to foster good faith in their post-divorce parenting alliance. Otherwise, a more adversarial and conflict-enhancing option would have been selected for resolution of their custody/visitation issues." He noted that such a climate of cooperation would be of immeasurable value to the girls' psychological development.

In July 2008, Ms. Johnson sought the arbitrator's removal based on the Appellate Division's decision in *Fawzy v. Fawzy*, 948 A.2d 709 (N.J. Super. Ct. App. Div. 2008), which had held that parties cannot agree to binding arbitration in a custody matter. In response, Mr. Johnson filed a motion to confirm the arbitrator's decision. Ms. Johnson filed a cross-motion requesting modification of the parenting time schedule or a plenary hearing to determine custody and parenting time.

[A]fter a hearing, [the trial court judge] confirmed the arbitrator's award....

Ms. Johnson appealed. Meanwhile, we issued our opinion in *Fawzy*. Based on *Fawzy*, the appellate panel reversed the trial court decision and remanded the case for a plenary hearing because the procedural requirements set forth in *Fawzy* were not satisfied. In particular, because there was no verbatim record of testimony, the panel concluded that the trial court had no basis on which to evaluate the threat of harm to the children or confirm the award. The panel determined that this case was not distinguishable from *Fawzy*, which involved the Arbitration Act, and not the APDRA, because the acts "are similar" and "neither is immune to public policy concerns." We granted Mr. Johnson's petition for certification.

The parties differ essentially over the applicability of *Fawzy* to this APDRA arbitration; over whether, if applicable, *Fawzy* requires reversal on the basis of the absence of a verbatim transcript; and over whether Ms. Johnson's claims of harm were sufficient to trigger substantive judicial review.

We begin with a recap of *Fawzy*. On the day that their divorce trial was to occur, the Fawzys agreed to binding arbitration and selected the recently-appointed guardian ad litem to serve as the arbitrator on all issues. *Fawzy*, 973 A.2d at 350. In the parties' interim arbitration order, they agreed to be governed by the Arbitration Act.

Between the time that the arbitration proceedings began and the taking of testimony, Mr. Fawzy filed an order to show cause seeking to restrain the arbitrator from deciding any parenting-time or custody issues on the grounds that our prior decision in *Faherty v. Faherty*, 477 A.2d 1257 (N.J. 1984), precluded arbitration of such issues. He further claimed that he had been rushed into agreeing to arbitrate, and had done so because he believed he would be viewed as uncooperative otherwise. The judge denied the application. Thereafter, the arbitrator awarded the parties joint legal custody and designated Mrs. Fawzy as the primary residential parent....

Mr. Fawzy appealed, arguing that permitting parties to submit custody issues to binding arbitration deprives the court of exercising its *parens patriae* jurisdiction to protect children's best interests. The Appellate Division agreed, reversed the trial court's ruling, and remanded the case for a plenary hearing on the custody and parenting-time issues. On certification, we affirmed that judgment, although on different grounds.

In *Fawzy* we recognized the benefits of arbitration in the family law setting and, in particular, the potential to "minimize the harmful effects of divorce litigation on both children and parents." We further noted the wide-ranging scholarly support for such arbitration that had developed since the issue was left open in *Faherty*.

In ruling, we reaffirmed the constitutional right to parental autonomy in child-rearing:

> Deference to parental autonomy means that the State does not second-guess parental decision making or interfere with the shared opinion of parents regarding how a child should be raised. Nor does it impose its own notion of a child's best interests on a family. Rather, the State permits to stand unchallenged parental judgments that it might not have made or that could be characterized as unwise. That is because parental autonomy includes the "freedom to decide wrongly."

Id. at 358.

At the same time, we recognized that "[t]he right of parents to the care and custody of their children is not absolute," *id.* at 474, 973 A.2d 347 (quoting *V.C. v. M.J.B.*, 748 A.2d 539, 548 (N.J. 2000)), and that "the state has an obligation, under the *parens patriae* doctrine, to intervene where it is necessary to prevent harm to a child." *Fawzy*, at 362 (footnote omitted). As we said in *Moriarty v. Bradt*, 827 A.2d 203, 222 (N.J. 2003), "interference with parental autonomy will be tolerated only to avoid harm to the health or welfare of a child." Indeed, that harm standard "is a constitutional necessity because a parent's right to family privacy and autonomy are at issue." *Id.* at 224. In short, potential harm to a child is the constitutional imperative that allows the State to intervene into the otherwise private and protected realm of parent-child relations. With that as a backdrop, we concluded that

> [T]he bundle of rights that the notion of parental autonomy sweeps in includes the right to decide how issues of custody and parenting time will be resolved. Indeed, we have no hesitation in concluding that, just as parents "choose" to decide issues of custody and parenting time among themselves without court intervention, they may opt to sidestep the judicial process and submit their dispute to an arbitrator whom they have chosen.

Fawzy, 973 A.2d at 360.

We then turned to the standard of review of a child custody arbitration award and concluded that

> [W]here no harm to the child is threatened, there is no justification for the infringement on the parents' choice to be bound by the arbitrator's decision. In the absence of a claim of harm, the parties are limited to the remedies provided in the Arbitration Act. On the contrary, where harm is claimed and a prima facie case advanced, the court must determine the harm issue. If no finding of harm ensues, the award will only be subject to review under the Arbitration Act standard. If there is a finding of harm, the presumption in favor of the parents' choice of arbitration will be overcome and it will fall to the court to decide what is in the child's best interests.

However, we expressed concern in *Fawzy* over the court's ability to intervene, where necessary, to prevent harm to the child,

> [I]n light of the fact that the Arbitration Act does not require a full record to be kept of arbitration proceedings. Nor does it compel the recordation of testimony or a statement by the arbitrator of his findings and conclusions beyond the issuance of an award, N.J. STAT. ANN. 2A:23B–19(a), although parties are free to agree upon other procedures, *see* N.J. STAT. ANN. 2A:23B–4.

Id. at 362.

Because of that, and because we determined that an empty record, like the one before us in *Fawzy*, could provide no basis for a harm review, we said:

> We therefore direct that when parties in a dissolution proceeding agree to arbitrate their dispute, the general rules governing the conduct of arbitration shall apply, N.J. STAT. ANN. 2A:23B–1 to–32. However, in respect of child-custody and parenting-time issues only, a record of all documentary evidence shall be kept; all testimony shall be recorded verbatim; and the arbitrator shall state in writing or otherwise record his or her findings of fact and conclusions of law with a focus on the best-interests standard. It is only upon such a record that an evaluation of

the threat of harm can take place without an entirely new trial. Any arbitration award regarding child-custody and parenting-time issues that results from procedures other than those that we have mandated will be subject to vacation upon motion.

We then set forth the minimum elements of an agreement to arbitrate a child custody dispute, including that it

[M]ust be in writing or recorded in accordance with the requirements of N.J. STAT. ANN. 2A:23B–1. In addition, it must state in clear and unmistakable language: (1) that the parties understand their entitlement to a judicial adjudication of their dispute and are willing to waive that right; (2) that the parties are aware of the limited circumstances under which a challenge to the arbitration award may be advanced and agree to those limitations; (3) that the parties have had sufficient time to consider the implications of their decision to arbitrate; and (4) that the parties have entered into the arbitration agreement freely and voluntarily, after due consideration of the consequences of doing so.

Because the record in *Fawzy* was inadequate to assure that the parties fully understood the consequences of removing their custody dispute from the judicial arena into binding arbitration, we affirmed the decision of the appellate panel that had reversed the arbitration award and remanded for a new trial.

As a matter of practice, *Fawzy* plays out this way: When a child custody or parenting time arbitration award issues, one party will ordinarily move for confirmation. If there is no challenge, the award will be confirmed. If there is a challenge that does not implicate harm to the child, the award is subject to review under the limited standards in the relevant arbitration statute or as agreed by the parties. If a party advances the claim that the arbitration award will harm the child, the trial judge must determine whether a prima facie case has been established. In other words, is there evidence which if not controverted, would prove harm? If that question is answered in the negative, for example, where a claim of harm is insubstantial or frivolous (e.g., not enough summer vacation), the only review available will be that provided in the relevant arbitration act or as otherwise agreed. If, on the other hand, the claim is one that, if proved, would implicate harm to the child, the judge must determine if the arbitration record is an adequate basis for review. If it is, the judge will evaluate the harm claim and, if there is a finding of harm, the parents' choice of arbitration will be overcome and it will fall to the judge to decide what is in the children's best interests. If the arbitration record is insufficient, the judge will be required to conduct a plenary hearing. That is the backdrop for our inquiry.

We turn first to Mr. Johnson's contention that *Fawzy* was intended to apply to Arbitration Act proceedings and not those conducted under AP-DRA, a notion with which we disagree. To be sure, there are differences between the Acts....

. . .

Despite those differences, we are in agreement with the Appellate Division that the procedures we put in place in *Fawzy* to assure an adequate record against which to test a child custody arbitration award are applicable to all child custody arbitrations, whether conducted under the Arbitration Act, APDRA, or some other agreed-upon methodology. As we have said, the parents' constitutional right to decide how to resolve their child-rearing disputes must give way to our constitutional duty to protect children from harm. Thus, where a prima facie claim of harm is advanced, our substantive review is compelled. That review can only take place on a full record. That is the principle of *Fawzy* and it is applicable regardless of the statute under which the arbitration is conducted. The issue is the existence of a record that is sufficient to permit judicial review.

Because there was no record whatsoever in *Fawzy*, no review could take place. That is not the case here. Here, the arbitrator did exactly what was anticipated by the parties and, in accordance with the provisions of the APDRA, created a full record of what transpired. In crafting his award, he gave a complete recitation of what the parties told him and what he heard and saw during his observations. His opinions, both on the original award and on reconsideration, were painstakingly detailed and, like the trial judge, we have absolutely no reservation in declaring the record he created as adequate to review the arbitration award.

In the final analysis, whether an arbitration is conducted under the Arbitration Act or APDRA is not the issue of consequence. What matters is the state of the record. Obviously, a verbatim transcript of a trial-type hearing will satisfy *Fawzy*, assuming the other requirements of that case are met. However, where, as here, the arbitrator creates a detailed record for review, the award can be confirmed without verbatim transcription. It goes without saying that it would behoove any arbitrator tasked with resolving a child custody or parenting-time issue to prepare a record, at least as detailed as the one we have approved today. Such preparation will avoid a judicial replay of the entire matter in the event of a substantial claim of harm.

We turn, finally, to Mr. Johnson's contention that Ms. Johnson's claim of harm was insufficient to tee up the issue of entitlement to judicial review. We agree. For that conclusion, we hearken back to our directive in *Fawzy*:

> Mere disagreement with the arbitrator's decision obviously will not satisfy the harm standard. The threat of harm is a significantly higher burden than a best-interests analysis. Although each case is unique and fact intensive, by way of example, in a case of two fit parents, a party's challenge to an arbitrator's custody award because she would be "better" is not a claim of harm. Nor will the contention that a particular parenting-time schedule did not include enough summer vacation time be sufficient to pass muster. To the contrary, a party's claim that the arbitrator granted custody to a parent with serious substance abuse issues or a debilitating mental illness could raise the specter of harm. Obviously, evidential support establishing a prima facie case of harm will be required in order to trigger a hearing. Where the hearing yields a finding of harm, the court must set aside the arbitration award and decide the case anew, using the best-interests test.

Fawzy, 973 A.2d at 361–62.

Here, neither party raised any real claim of unfitness. They agreed that there was "a lot of love in both homes and consistency between the homes in parenting, relative to a sense of respect, the importance of getting work done and manners." The issue was always parenting style, not capacity, and the arbitrator's commission was to create a schedule that would minimize conflicts and problems in the face of such different parenting styles. His new schedule was nothing more than a tweaking of an agreed-upon parenting time schedule to minimize disruption for the children. Simply put, that does not begin to approach a showing of harm sufficient to warrant judicial inquiry beyond what is provided in the APDRA.

One final note. Our holding that Ms. Johnson's contentions fell short of triggering a substantive judicial review of the arbitration award is without prejudice to her pursuing an application for expanded parenting time as anticipated in the arbitrator's award. Much has transpired since the award issued in April 2008. The girls are growing up and how the parties have fared with the parenting time schedule during the interim period should be factored into any revised award. Either party may request such reconsideration.

For the foregoing reasons, the judgment of the Appellate Division is reversed and the order of the trial judge confirming the arbitration award is reinstated.

2.   MEDIATION

Ronald S. Granberg & Sarah A. Cavassa, *Private Ordering and Alternative Dispute Resolution*

23 J. AM. ACAD. MATRIM. LAW. 287 (2010).

Alternative dispute resolution in family law is on the rise nationally, and with good reason. The ability to determine one's own fate, the de-escalation of a charged emotional environment and the privacy gained through avoidance of public litigation are all excellent reasons for taking a less traditional path. When minor children are involved, these litigation alternatives can help parties become more responsible parents. By making affirmative adult decisions about their pre- and post-judgment issues rather than leaving choices to the judicial officer, parents empower themselves to privately order their own lives, and effectively reinforce their roles as problem-solving adults.

Divorcing spouses are better informed about their own needs, goals, patterns, predilections and fears than any judge could be. If the parties reach an agreement (provided they do so with reasonably-equal bargaining power) their agreement will be superior to any judicially-imposed ruling.

For better or worse, few mandatory national standards exist for private ordering ADR in family law. The American Bar Association's Section of Dispute Resolution was established in 1993. The ABA provides that a family law attorney-mediator should be "qualified by training, experience, and temperament."

In 2001, the ABA House of Delegates approved the Model Standards of Practice for Family and Divorce Mediation, produced by the Association of Family and Conciliation Courts. The Model Standards endorse individual freedom, stating: "Self-determination is the fundamental principle of family mediation. The mediation process relies upon the ability of participants to make their own voluntary and informed decisions." The Model Standards have been adopted by the Academy of Family Mediators, a voluntary professional organization, but are not mandatory to any group.

Similarly, the Ethical Standards of Professional Responsibility, approved by the Society of Professionals in Dispute Resolution (now known as the Association for Conflict Resolution), provide guidelines for a neutral in various types of dispute, but those standards are also voluntary. The key points of the standards include disclosures to parties, duty of impartiality, full disclosure between parties, confidentiality, roles of parties and consulting attorneys, and understanding termination of mediation.

... We now turn to samples of approaches to mediation regulation in four states.

A. California's Approach to Private Ordering

Mediation is only lightly regulated in California. Sections of the California Evidence Code address confidentiality of mediation and admissibility of documents created for or in mediation. Mediation is confidential, and no evidence of statements made during the course of mediation is admissible in court. This confidentiality extends to writings made in the course of mediation. However, no writing that would otherwise be admissible becomes inadmissible solely due to its introduction in mediation.

No legal requirements specify how a mediation must occur. Although the mediator role is commonly performed by an attorney or retired judge, no specific qualifications are required for a mediator—any person may act as a mediator, so long as that person is agreed upon by the parties.

. . .

There are, however, some limitations on private ordering, intended to protect third parties. Except in unusual cases, child support orders must be calculated within the statewide child support guidelines. Parents cannot contract away or impair the child's right to support. Similarly, the court maintains jurisdiction to determine custody and visitation in the best interests of minor children. The parties cannot divest the court of this jurisdiction, despite a private ordering attempting to do so. These safeguards are designed to protect children from unwise decisions of their parents.

Other than the protection of the child's best interests in regards to support, custody and visitation, California provides few limitations in private ordering. Competent adults are generally free to resolve their disputes as they desire, to their own benefit or at their own detriment.

B. New York's Approach to Private Ordering

New York's approach to private ordering is similar to California's. Parties to a family law proceeding may mediate, arbitrate, or choose another method of dispute resolution. However, certain types of decisions are subject to judicial review to make certain third parties are not being adversely affected.

The New York Constitution provides: "nor shall any divorce be granted otherwise than by due judicial proceedings," which means (as is true in all other states) that only the court can grant a divorce. Although parties are free to elect their method of resolution, all settlement agreements that are incorporated into the final resolution must be submitted to the court as necessary components of the divorce documents required for entry of dissolution.

Parties divorcing in New York have freedom to determine the division of their property without oversight, but issues affecting parenting and support are reviewed. Decisions regarding child support must be calculated under the statewide guidelines, and are subject to judicial review. All child support awards agreed to outside court are subject to review.

Child custody and visitation issues may not be arbitrated. Further, the court cannot delegate its authority to determine issues of custody and visitation. A decision by the parties regarding spousal support will not be judicially upheld if it would make a spouse a public charge, or if it is unfair and unreasonable or unconscionable. This protects both the would-be supported spouse and the public fisc.

Mediation in New York is designed by the parties who elect to engage in the process. As in California, "there are no specific statutory requirements for private party mediation in the matrimonial field." Unlike California, no explicit statutory or case-made confidentiality protections exist in private mediation. The parties can contract to make their mediation confidential, but in the absence of such agreement, the content of a mediation is admissible in court.

. . .

New York provides for an early settlement panel and an early neutral evaluation, a confidential, non-binding process in which a neutral third party or panel listens to an abbreviated presentation and provides an evaluation of strengths and weaknesses in an effort to foster settlement. These methods, although not dispositive of the case, can assist parties in reaching a fair and efficient settlement, without the many costs (financial, emotional, judicial, etc.) of extensive litigation.

The New York Office of Court Administration funds and oversees Community Dispute Resolution Centers ("CDRC"), some of which provide free or low cost family law alternative dispute resolution. Unlike private mediation, a CDRC mediator must be qualified by 25 hours of training in conflict resolution, and CDRC mediation is confidential and not subject to disclosure in judicial proceedings. In addition, New York has set guidelines establishing qualifications for mediators and evaluators serving on court rosters.

Private ordering is promoted in New York, but with the recognition that people can be damaged by unfair agreements. To prevent unfair agreements affecting the parties to the action or third parties, New York has instituted a review process. Where the issues of custody, visitation, child support, or spousal support are concerned, the court retains jurisdiction to approve or deny an agreement or arbitration award.

C.   Illinois' Approach to Private Ordering

Parties divorcing in Illinois may enter into an agreement regarding property division, spousal support, child support, child custody and visitation. The terms of the agreement, except for child support, custody and visitation, are binding unless the court finds them unconscionable. Child support, custody and visitation agreements are not binding if they are not in the best interests of the child. Similar to both California and New York, the law of Illinois seeks to protect the children of the relationship from bad agreements.

In regards to mediation, the parties may elect to engage in that process if they desire. However, where good cause is shown, the court may prohibit mediation that requires parties to meet without counsel. The court may also order mediation to assist in custody determinations or as part of a visitation enforcement proceeding.

Although the Illinois General Assembly has discussed a "Mediator Certification Act," none has been passed and there are currently no mediator requirements. The only requirement regarding mediation is that the process be confidential.

. . .

While private ordering has long been discussed, and in many cases encouraged, in Illinois the field remains largely unregulated. Parties can elect whomever they desire as a mediator and may be free to engage in other processes. However, the court again recognizes that third parties may be affected by private agreements, and retains jurisdiction to review decisions on child support, custody and visitation.

D. Texas' Approach to Private Ordering

Texas has a well-established policy for alternative dispute resolution. Mediation, arbitration, and several other options are presented in the Civil Practice Code. The legislature expresses its position clearly:

> It is the policy of this state to encourage the peaceable resolution of disputes, with special consideration given to disputes involving the parent-child relationship, including the mediation of issues involving conservatorship, possession, and support of children, and the early settlement of pending litigation through voluntary settlement proce-dures. Despite its policy of supporting private ordering, Texas, like California, New York and Illinois, recognizes that rubber-stamping all agreements would not serve justice. The court can decline to enter judgment on an agreement if a party has been a victim of family violence which affected that person's ability to make decisions, or if the agreement is not in a child's best interest.

Mediation has more statutory involvement in Texas than in the other three states discussed above. A person appointed by the court as a mediator must have 40 hours' classroom training in a court-approved dispute resolu-tion program and 24 additional hours in family dynamics, child development and family law, or be otherwise qualified by legal or professional training.

Parties may voluntarily agree to mediation without any court involve-ment, or the court may refer parties to mediation by the parties' written agreement or sua sponte. An exception to the court's power to order mediation is if domestic violence has occurred and the victim spouse objects to mediation on the basis of that violence. This does not mean that there cannot be mediation, but provisions for safety must be made prior to the mediation taking place. Mediation communications are confidential and cannot be disclosed, unless specifically admissible under another rule of law, similar to California and New York regulations.

. . .

Similar to New York's early settlement panels, Texas provides for mini-trials and moderated settlement conferences, which are conducted under agreement of the parties. In a mini-trial, each party presents its case to an impartial third party who then makes a non-binding advisory opinion (unless the parties agree that it is binding and enter into a written settlement agreement). In a moderated settlement conference, a neutral panel makes a non-binding, advisory opinion. The goal of such evaluation is to encourage settlement by demonstrating to the parties a likely trial outcome. Additional-ly, provisions for any or all of the aforementioned alternative disputes resolution methods may be incorporated in a collaborative law case.

. . .

V. Parenting the Parents

. . . When divorcing parties present a judge with a settlement agreement they have signed, should the judge simply rubber stamp it? What duty does the government have to assure fair (and not merely consensual) resolution of divorces? Although these issues exist irrespective of whether ADR played a role in the creation of the agreement, the rise in mediation and collaborative practice has greatly increased the numbers of agreed-upon documents being filed by divorcing parties.

The doctrine of *parens patriae* (literally: 'parent of his or her country') refers to a government's protection of persons unable to protect themselves. If law is a parent, the parenting duties of the family law department judge far exceed the parenting duties of judges sitting in other departments.

As divorcing spouses, valuing freedom, address their relations with one another, courts must decide daily the extent to which litigants should govern themselves versus the extent to which government should "protect" litigants from their ill-advised decisions. Freedom instructs to allow willing persons to resolve their family law disputes with as much autonomy as possible.

Private ordering is vetoed every time a bench officer refuses to approve a mediated settlement agreement. The two primary logical justifications for the exercise of judicial veto power are: first, because the parties' settlement adversely impacts a third party, and second, because unequal bargaining power has resulted in an unfair settlement.

One of the unique characteristics of family law is the considerable extent to which the litigants' decisions impact lives of third parties. Of course, the "third parties" most at risk from unwise divorce decisions are the parties' minor children. Another example of third party impact is the spouse who was intimidated into waiving necessary spousal support and ends up a burden on a creditor or a welfare budget.

The U.S. Supreme Court has described America as a "government resting on . . . the protection of the weak against the strong."[59] When the "weak one" is an innocent child, few would question the occasional necessity for governmental intervention. If an abused parent has been browbeaten into relinquishing physical custody of a child to the abuser, law must veto the parties' agreement to protect the child.

But when the "weak one" is a divorce litigant who has agreed to an unfavorable property division, "protection of the weak against the strong" goes by a less flattering name: paternalism. In contrast to the above child custody example, in which the parties' settlement adversely impacted a third party, in this example the only justification for disallowing private ordering would be the unfair settlement. The reviewing court would have to reach beyond ordinary contract principles to invalidate such a property settlement agreement.

Contract law is grounded in the theory that people mean what they say and should be forced to perform their promises. The very purpose of contract law is to hold folks to their bad decisions—no one needs to be sued to complete a profitable transaction.

Of course, public policy considerations impose limits on enforceability of some contracts. Employers must pay minimum wage and tenants cannot contract away habitable housing. But normally an agreement is enforceable unless the party seeking to avoid it establishes a contract defense such as incapacity, menace, fraud or undue influence. One must live with the results of a decision freely (albeit foolishly) made. Liberty carries consequences.

---

59.   Halter v. Nebraska, 205 U.S. 34, 43 (1907)

Some jurists contend that, even where rights of third parties are not affected, divorce litigants deserve special protection from disadvantageous agreements. Freedom/protection policy considerations inevitably consider the skill sets that domestic litigants bring to their negotiating tables. One party may be highly educated and a savvy negotiator, while the other party is neither. Consider a wife who has a high IQ, strong social skills, a Ph.D. in Economics, and is a ferocious bargainer. Her husband has a below-average IQ, weak social skills, little education, and a desire to avoid conflict at all costs. The husband will have no remedy in contract law if the wife prevails on every issue in their marital termination agreement negotiation.

Negotiating imbalances can be exacerbated in the family law setting, which often finds people at the most distraught point in their lives. Their marriage, the world they have built for themselves, and the futures they have envisioned have failed. Their financial resources are stretched and their relationships with their children are strained. They find themselves unable to understand their place in the world. In this vulnerable emotional state, not all persons are capable of making good decisions about their long-term futures.

Divorce judges commonly have wide discretion in deciding whether to adopt as a court judgment an agreement reached by the parties: an Illinois judge can reject a property agreement that he or she considers unconsciona-ble and a New York judge can reject a spousal support agreement that he or she considers unfair. Liberal standards of review permit judicial consider-ation of factors far beyond traditional contract defenses.

A history of physical abuse is an extreme example of unequal bargaining positions. Above-mentioned disparities in intelligence and education can be factors. One party may be prepared for trial—financially, emotionally, and in terms of risk tolerance—while the other party is unprepared for trial on all three fronts. One party (the "leavee") may be reeling from recent revela-tions, such as marital infidelity and abandonment, while the other party (the "leaver") coolly executes a well-planned strategy. One party may have a negotiating weak point that the other party identifies and intentionally exploits.

As experienced family law practitioners know, even if an emotionally-distraught litigant is represented by competent legal counsel, bargaining parity cannot be assured.

VI.   Piercing the Contractual Veil

Although a judicial officer with broad discretion to decide whether to approve a divorce stipulation can consider many factors, including unfair-ness of the agreement and inequalities in the parties' respective bargaining powers, applying those factors can be difficult. An agreement's unfairness is seldom apparent, and unequal bargaining positions of the parties are even less frequently apparent on the face of the document. Also, what appears to be an unjust resolution in one area of the agreement can turn out to be fair when viewed in light of other settlement terms. Reasonable settlements can come in a wide variety.

If a bench officer suspects a stipulated agreement is so unfair as to lie beyond the realm of reasonable settlements, he or she can inquire further into the matter by, for example, requiring the submission of additional documentation or by conducting a hearing at which testimony is taken regarding the effects of the agreement. But how is the bench officer to know, from the face of the agreement, that it is unfair enough to warrant further inquiry?

The adversarial system of justice is designed to bring all relevant matters to the attention of the court. But once parties have signed their agreement and submitted it for approval, the system is no longer adversarial or, if it is, the adversaries have changed to: the parties (now working together) versus the reviewing court. The parties' shared goal is to win a judicial imprimatur, and they will draft their agreement with that goal in mind.

Some portions of a submitted divorce agreement are susceptible of judicial review, while other portions are not. In states with formulaic child support guidelines, the judicial officer can review income levels and other factors for assurance that the support amounts have been calculated correctly. No state has formulaic child custody guidelines, however, because custody decisions depend on so many variables. Thus, the most important issue before the court—child custody—is all too often the issue regarding which the reviewing court is given the least amount of data. Because an unfair agreement can appear fair, the reviewing court is seldom able to "pierce the contractual veil."

. . .

VIII.   Conclusion

Under "no fault" laws, spouses have the right to end their marriage without having to convince a judge that they should be allowed to do so. Although government involvement in divorce litigation has thus diminished, the involvement remains substantial. A litigant who requires an order, judgment or decree always needs a judicial officer's signature.

California, New York, Illinois and Texas all permit private ordering ADR in domestic relations cases. All four states find themselves walking the line between freedom and paternalism, and seeking an appropriate balance.

. . .

All four states encourage mediation regarding all divorce issues. Mediation is helpful in resolving cases and furthers private ordering but how can a busy judge, holding dozens of stipulated agreements awaiting signature, be expected to conduct an insightful review of settlement terms? The answer is that he or she cannot—a reviewing judge sees only what lies inside the "four corners" of the settlement agreement and both settling parties are motivated to draft the agreement in such a manner that no indication of coercion or unfairness will appear.

Ironically, mediation private ordering is implemented out of procedural necessity, if not out of philosophical choice, and a divorce litigant's freedom to settle foolishly is respected by practical default, if not by jurisprudential decision.

Under what standard should a judge reject a settlement agreement? We believe that a reviewing court should do so only in an extreme case where rejection appears necessary to prevent manifest injustice, such as where wife/mother has apparently waived financial support from husband/father in trade for child custody. We believe that when rejection has occurred, a hearing should be conducted at which the parties are permitted to explain their motivations and intentions regarding the agreement.

Parties are more familiar with their needs and concerns than a bench officer can be, and are in a better position to make informed choices. A settlement that appears unworkable on its surface may properly serve its parties, and their children, for reasons that aren't apparent. Parties are more likely to comply with their own agreements than with judicial pronouncements. Mediation private ordering through should be the rule, and a rejected settlement agreement a rare exception.

Ferguson v. Ferguson

District Court of Appeal of Florida, Third District, 2011.
54 So.3d 553.

■ SHEPHERD, J.

This is an appeal from an order voiding a provision of a mediated marital settlement agreement as a result of changes in the economy. Based upon the bedrock principle of contract law—applicable as well to marital settlement agreements—that bad deals are as enforceable in the law as good deals, we reverse the order under review.

The mediated marital settlement agreement in this case was signed and the final judgment of dissolution entered on August 8, 2008. The paragraph of the agreement which gives rise to this action reads as follows:

18. REAL PROPERTY:

(A) The parties are owners as tenants by the entirety real property located at ... and referred to as the marital residence. The approximately [sic] market value is $950,000.00 and there is currently one mortgage on the home of approximately $603,000.00.

(B) In consideration the Husband shall pay to the Wife the sum of $185,000.00 within sixty (60) days from the execution of this agreement.

(C) Said refinancing shall take place within 120 days from the execution of this agreement. The Husband shall be solely responsible for all of the expenses associated with the refinancing.

(C) [sic] Simultaneously with the execution of the agreement the Wife shall execute and deliver unto the Husband, a Quit–Claim Deed transferring all of her right, title and interest in and to the above described property together with all fixtures located therein to him and said property shall thereupon become his sole property and he shall be entitled to a quiet and peaceful enjoyment of said property including any and all utility deposits in connection therewith. Said Quit–Claim Deed shall be held in escrow by the Husband's counsel to be given to the closing agent at the time of the refinancing.

(D) The Husband shall indemnify and hold harmless the Wife from any and all property taxes, assessments, insurance payments, repair expenses, maintenance expenses, utility bills and all other expenses concerning said real property after the Wife vacates the marital home.

(E) If the Husband fails to refinance the home to release to the Wife within 120 days, then the home shall be immediately placed for sale with a licensed realtor to be agreed upon solely by Husband. The net proceeds of the sale shall be the sole property of the Husband.

(F) The parties agree that the Wife shall be able to reside in the marital residence with the minor child once the Temporary Certificate of Occupancy has been issued by the city of Palmetto Bay. While the Wife is occupying the marital home, she shall be responsible for the utilities during the period of time of her occupancy. The marital home is to be returned to the Husband upon the conclusion of the occupancy period absent normal wear and tear. The Husband shall give to the Wife reasonable notice when he will be going to the marital home and access to the home cannot be unreasonably denied.

(G) The Wife shall vacate the marital home thirty days after she receives the $185,000.00 as her equalization payment for the marital home and the $5,500.00 in child support arrears minus one half of the net proceeds from the sale of the mobile home.

Although not a candidate for a future style manual, the agreement is unambiguous. Subsection (C) obligated the former wife to execute and deposit a quitclaim deed in escrow with the former husband's counsel upon execution of the marital settlement agreement, which she did. Subsection (B) required the former husband to pay the former wife an "equalization payment" of $185,000 (subject to minor adjustments) within sixty days of the date the agreement was executed. Subsection (C) requires the former husband to refinance the home within 120 days of the agreement's execution. The plain language of the agreement establishes that its object was (1) to bring about an unconditional payment of $185,000 to the former wife; (2) achieve an ownership transfer of the property to the former husband; and (3) relieve the former wife of any further financial responsibility for the property contemporaneously with the transfer. Notably, the couple, in paragraph (E) of the agreement, anticipated the possibility of one future circumstance, the failure of the former husband to refinance the property within 120 days of the execution of the agreement. In that circumstance, the parties agreed the property immediately would be placed for sale, with the net proceeds going to the former husband. It cannot be gainsaid that the couple's mutual understanding of the value of the property influenced the negotiation.

Shortly after August 8, 2008, and apparently unanticipated by the former husband, the Florida real estate market entered into one of its periodic downward adjustments, for which it has become famous since the time of the Great Depression. The former husband neither paid his former wife the approximate $185,000 equalization payment nor tried to refinance the house. Instead, he unilaterally sought to list the house for sale with a realtor, but the former wife, who has lived in the home with the parties' minor child, has not cooperated.

Rather, the former wife filed a motion for contempt and enforcement of paragraph eighteen, specifically for the payment of $185,000 and the refinancing of the house. The former husband filed a motion requesting the trial court to order the former wife to cooperate with the sale of the home pursuant to the parties' agreement. In his motion, the former husband stated, "Due to the real estate market conditions, the former husband has not been able to refinance the former marital home solely under his name and thus has not been able to pay the monies owed to the former wife pursuant to the parties' agreement."

After hearing arguments on the motions, the trial court declared paragraph eighteen "to be an impossibility of performance due to changes in the economy and therefore void." The court further ordered the former wife to vacate the home, that the home be appraised, and finally that it immediately be listed for sale with the net proceeds divided between the parties. The former wife appeals.

The former husband advances the preliminary complaint that the former wife has not brought forward an adequate appellate record for our review. *See Applegate v. Barnett Bank of Tallahassee*, 377 So. 2d 1150, 1152 (Fla. 1979). He complains specifically that the record lacks a transcript or approved statement of the proceedings from which emanated the orders under review. The record in this case is sparse. The absence of a transcript of a hearing can be fatal to an appellant, especially if the hearing was an evidentiary hearing. However, it is not a rule absolute in an appellate proceeding that the appellant must present a transcript of the proceeding below. For example, an appellate court may, as we now do, reverse a trial court order if there exists reversible error on the face of the order or judgment. In this case, we find the trial court reversibly erred by voiding paragraph eighteen of the mediated marital settlement agreement for impossibility of performance due to changes in the economy.

A marital settlement agreement entered into by the parties and ratified by a final judgment is a contract, subject to the laws of contract. *See Andersen Windows, Inc. v. Hochberg*, 997 So. 2d 1212, 1213 (Fla. Dist. Ct. App. 2008); *Delissio v. Delissio*, 821 So. 2d 350, 353 (Fla. Dist. Ct. App. 2002). Because of the central importance placed upon the enforceability of contracts in our culture, the defense of impossibility (and its cousins, impracticability and frustration of purpose) must therefore be applied with great caution if the contingency was foreseeable at the inception of the agreement. *Home Design Ctr.–Joint Venture v. Cnty. Appliances of Naples, Inc.*, 563 So. 2d 767, 769–70 (Fla. Dist. Ct. App. 1990). As further developed by Professor Williston in his treatise,

> The important question [in an impossibility inquiry] is whether an unanticipated circumstance has made performance of the promise vitally different from what should reasonably have been within the contemplation of both parties when they entered into the contract. If so, the risk should not fairly be thrown upon the promisor.

6 WILLISTON, CONTRACTS (Rev. ed.) § 1931 (1938).

In this case, the decline in the real estate market shortly after the Former Husband signed the marital settlement agreement, while marked and unfortunate, was not the sort of unanticipated circumstance that falls within the purview of the doctrine of impossibility. Economic downturns and other market shifts do not truly constitute unanticipated circumstances in a market-based economy. The assignment of this risk before a final closing of the transaction between the parties was therefore among those for which a reasonably prudent person, represented by counsel, might have provided. A trial court is not authorized to intervene to ameliorate a hardship that a promisor, such as the former husband in this case, could have thus avoided. *McCutcheon v. Tracy*, 928 So. 2d 364, 364 (Fla. Dist. Ct. App. 2006) ("[A] court may not deviate from the terms of a voluntary contract either to achieve what it might think is a more appropriate result or 'to relieve the parties from the apparent hardship of an improvident bargain.' ") (quoting *Beach Resort Hotel Corp. v. Wieder*, 79 So. 2d 659, 663 (Fla. 1955)).

In addition, the former husband cannot sidestep the consequence of his failure to include such a provision with the argument that the lack of such a provision renders this otherwise unambiguous agreement ambiguous. *See Life Ins. Co. of N. Am. v. Cichowlas*, 659 So. 2d 1333, 1338 (Fla. Dist. Ct. App. 1995) ("[W]here a contract is simply silent as to a particular matter, that is, its language neither expressly nor by reasonable implication indicates that the parties intended to contract with respect to the matter, the court should not, under the guise of construction, impose contractual rights and duties on the parties which they themselves omitted."). The former husband is bound to the agreement he struck.

Accordingly, the trial court was obligated to enforce the mediated marital settlement agreement as voluntarily agreed upon by the parties. The former wife is entitled to a judgment against the former husband for the $185,000 equalization payment after any adjustments required by the marital settlement agreement.[1] If the marital residence has a temporary certificate of occupancy, the former wife and child shall be entitled to occupy the house consistent with the terms of the marital settlement agreement until such time as the equalization amount is paid or the house is sold. The marital residence should be listed for sale with a real estate agent chosen by the former husband, who shall be contractually entitled to receive the net proceeds of the sale, as provided in the marital settlement agreement.

Reversed and remanded for further proceedings consistent with this opinion.

NOTE

There is a substantial body of literature on the advantages and disadvantages of using mediation in divorce proceedings. *See, e.g.,* DIVORCE MEDIATION: THEORY AND PRACTICE (Jay Folberg & Ann Milne, eds. 1988); Connie Beck & Bruce Sales, *A Critical Reappraisal of Divorce Mediation and Policy*, 6 PSYCHOL. PUB. POL'Y 989 (2000); Jaime Abraham, *Divorce Mediation–Limiting the Profession to Family/Matrimonial Lawyers*, 10 CARDOZO J. CONFLICT RESOL. 241 (2008); Peter A. Dillon & Robert E. Emery, *Divorce Mediation and Resolution of Child Custody Disputes: Long–Term Effects* 66 AM. J. ORTHOPSYCHIATRY 131 (1996); Robert E. Emery, David Sbarra, & Tara Grover, *Divorce Mediation: Research and Reflections*, 43 FAM. CT. REV. 22 (2005); Colleen N. Kotyk, *Tearing Down the House: Weakening the Foundations of Divorce Mediation Brick by Brick*, 6 WM. & MARY BILL OF RTS. J. 227 (1997); Mary G. Marcus, Walter Marcus, Nancy A. Stillwell, & Neville Doherty, *To Mediate or Not to Mediate: Financial Outcomes in Mediated Versus Adversarial Divorces*, 17 MEDIATION Q. 143 (1999); Dennis P. Saccuzzo, *Controversies in Divorce Mediation*, 79 N.D. L. REV. 425 (2003); Nancy Ver Steegh, *Yes, No, and Maybe: Informed Decision Making About Divorce Mediation in the Presence of Domestic Violence*, 9 WM. & MARY J. OF WOMEN & L. 161 (2003) Laurel Wheeler, *Mandatory Family Mediation and Domestic Violence*, 26 S. ILL. U. L.J. 559 (2002).

3.   COLLABORATIVE LAWYERING

Regina A. DeMeo, History of Collaborative Divorce
(2011).

John F. Kennedy once said, "let us never negotiate out of fear, but let us never fear to negotiate."[1] With this very goal in mind, in the late 1980's, Stuart Webb, a family law attorney in Minneapolis, Minnesota, developed a dispute resolution model that would promote cooperation between lawyers focused on settling their client's family issues, without having those discussions tainted by the pressure of litigation by imposing as a prerequisite to engaging in the Collaborative Divorce process that both attorneys and their

---

1. The former husband's agreement to pay is not enforceable by contempt at this stage of the proceeding. *See* Braswell v. Braswell, 881 So. 2d 1193, 1198 (Fla. D.Ct. App.). However, if the former wife occupies the marital home, she must pay the utilities as required by the agreement and, of course, cooperate in any effort to sell the property.

1. Inaugural Address, Jan. 20, 1961.

clients sign an agreement not to go to court. In the event that the Collaborative Process fails to help the parties reach an agreement, the attorneys are disqualified from assisting their clients with litigation. This unique feature of the Collaborative process allows the attorneys and their clients to speak freely about their concerns and brainstorm creative settlement options after they have gathered all the relevant information.

Lawyers from Minneapolis presented the idea of Collaborative Divorce at a national conference in the early 1990's, and by 1994, family lawyers in Northern California had started practicing Collaborative Law. At the same time, psychologists Peggy Thompson and Rodney Nurse were working with a group of lawyers and financial professionals to develop an interdisciplinary team model to help couples address in tandem their financial, legal, and emotional issues arising from a separation and/or divorce. Pauline Tesler, an attorney in California, introduced the Collaborative law idea to Dr. Thompson's group, and eventually they designed the concept of an interdisciplinary Collaborative Team approach.[2]

In 1999, a dedicated group of Collaborative professionals in California formed the American Institute of Collaborative Professionals ("AICP"), a non-profit organization. The group's vision was to share resources and host regular networking events for like-minded Collaborative professionals, so that they could discuss what they were learning through their case experiences. In May of 1999, the AICP hosted its first annual forum in Oakland, California. In 2001, recognizing that the Collaborative movement was growing outside the United States, the organization was renamed the International Academy of Collaborative Professionals ("IACP") and tasked with the broader mission of assisting Collaborative practitioners throughout the world.[3]

IACP now has over 4,000 members in 24 countries. It is estimated that there are 22,000 Collaboratively-trained lawyers worldwide.[4] The organization's mission is to promote Collaborative Practice throughout the world by (i) establishing practice standards; (ii) providing educational resources and media materials for professionals interested in this evolving conflict resolution method; (iii) hosting training seminars and networking events that highlight new trends; and (iv) helping local practice groups develop and share pertinent information. Ms. Talia Katz has been IACP's Executive Director since 2005. Although the organization's headquarters is located in Phoenix, Arizona, the Board and Standing Committee members are spread throughout the world and remain connected through regular telephone bridges. IACP's goal is to act as a resource for all local practice groups and individual practitioners by making model agreements and educational material available on the website, coordinating monthly telephone bridges, disseminating on a bi-monthly basis an e-newsletter the "Collaborative Connection," distributing a scholarly Journal "The Collaborative Review" three times a year, and hosting annual Forums.

With the assistance of IACP, local practice groups have formed in various regions and countries. The local groups are responsible for recruiting new professionals interested in offering the Collaborative option to their clients. Local groups are self-governed—each group determines its own

---

2. *See* History of International Academy of Collaborative Professionals, http://www.collaborativepractice.com.

3. *Id.*

4. Telephone interview by Regina A. DeMeo with Talia Katz, Exec. Dir., IACP (Jan. 5, 2011).

organizational structure and the criteria for membership, and many develop their own form agreements and practice protocols with the goal of standardizing the message and method in which information is delivered to clients in a particular region.

When there are multiple local practice groups in a concentrated area, these groups tend to coordinate educational programs and networking events for like-minded Collaborative Professionals. These groups often pool their resources to create websites and develop materials that will provide information to the public about the process and the local professionals trained to assist in Collaborative cases. As public awareness has increased in the United States, various local jurisdictions have issued ethics opinions approving of this limited representation practice of law. Various well-known law schools are teaching students about this alternative to litigation, and the media is increasingly covering the spread of this movement.[5]

In an effort to promote standard practice guidelines and address the myriad of concerns related to sufficient notice to clients about the disqualification provision, privileges and confidentiality waivers inherent in this legal process, which limits the scope of the attorney's representation as counselor and advocate, the Uniform Law Commission, which is compromised of appointees from the governor of each state, drafted the Uniform Collaborative Law Act ("UCLA").[6] The Commission intends to seek approval of the ABA Board of Governors in 2011; in the meantime, several states and the District of Columbia are considering its enactment. The UCLA has passed in Utah and Nevada, and many Collaborative practice groups are working together with the IACP to ensure the enactment in other jurisdictions.[7]

Pauline H. Tesler, *Collaborative Family Law*

4 Pepp. Disp. Resol. L.J. 317, 319–21, 326–32 (2004).

The core element that distinguishes a collaborative law representation from "friendly negotiations" and other lawyer-facilitated efforts to settle divorce-related disputes is that in collaborative law, the representation begins with the clients and lawyers signing a binding agreement (referred to as a "participation agreement" or "collaborative stipulation") that prohibits those lawyers from ever participating in contested court proceedings on behalf of those clients. With that core element, the case is a collaborative law case, and without it, no matter how cordial or cooperative the lawyers and parties may be in their behavior, attitudes and intention to reach agreement, the case is not a collaborative law case. The term "collaborative law" is not just a synonym for "nice," or "cooperative." It refers to a specifically-defined model for dispute resolution, the essential element of which is that the lawyers are disqualified contractually from ever representing those clients against one another in court proceedings.

It is that unique element that gives collaborative law its considerable power to guide clients to acceptable settlements while building vigorous assistance of legal counsel into the heart of the process. Experienced collaborative practitioners who have come to this work from a background as family law litigators believe that in the face of apparent impasses in settlement

---

5. Regina A. DeMeo, *The Expanding Role of Collaborative Family Law, in* Understanding Collaborative Family Law 19 (2011).

6. The Collaborative Rev. 4 (Summer 2010)

7. *Id.*

negotiations, lawyers who are not contractually barred from taking the issue to court tend to decide too quickly that the issue should be taken to a third party for resolution. By temperament, lawyers tend to be impatient and result oriented. Moreover, trial practice is generally the most lucrative work for lawyers. Thus, the reasoning goes, internal and external factors coincide in favor of inducing traditional litigation-matrix lawyers to abort negotiations in the face of impasse where court is an option. In collaborative practice, however, such a decision will terminate the involvement of those lawyers in the case, and for that reason, collaborative lawyers operate within a significant external incentive to remain longer at the negotiating table working with their clients to find a way through the impasse. With the contractual disqualification from going to court, the risk of failure becomes distributed to the lawyers as well as the clients. With this element, lawyers as well as clients are highly motivated by the procedural "carrots and sticks" built into the model to remain at the negotiating table in the face of apparent impasse far longer than in any other mode of lawyer-facilitated family law dispute resolution. This is sometimes expressed as: collaborative practice liberates the problem solver within.

.   .   .

Collaborative Law Differs Greatly From Conventional Settlement Negotiations

On first hearing about collaborative law, traditional family law attorneys often remark that it's nothing new, "I've been doing it for years, I just don't call it that. After all, I settle more than 90% of my cases." Family law cases do overwhelmingly settle short of a full trial on the merits, but these are settlements fashioned in the shadow of the law, with the [possibility of] litigation shaping the representation from the first attorney-client contact. Often, family law litigators settle cases these cases virtually, if not literally, on the courthouse steps, after expenditure of enormous emotional and financial resources on pendente lite motions and discovery. The settlement may be on the eve of trial, supervised by a settlement conference judge who applies evaluative pressure on parties and counsel in the interests of lightening the court's docket.

The movement of a case from first interview to settlement in this kind of litigation-[oriented] settlement practice is shaped from the start by the limitations and demands inherent in court rules and legal restrictions on the family court's jurisdiction and exercise of discretion. From the start, a "litigation-oriented" attorney excludes from consideration much of what the new client considers most troubling about the divorce situation, because the court lacks the power to make effective orders about wounded feelings and the nagging annoyances that angry or vengeful spouses can inflict upon one another below the threshold of a court's power or willingness to act.

The job of the lawyer in this kind of representation is to shape and pare the facts of the client's situation into a story, a theory of the case that will enable the lawyer to "win big" on the client's behalf. To do this, the lawyer will ignore or deem irrelevant many parts of the client's story, and will emphasize or exaggerate others. From the first interview, the lawyer typically uses leading, closed-ended questions to spot issues that lie within the court's jurisdiction to resolve and develop goals, strategies, and tactics for successful outcomes. Sometimes, custody and support motions are prepared in the course of the first interview, and the client—who may be highly anxious and driven by fear, grief, or other primitive emotion—may be asked to sign inflammatory declarations under penalty of perjury then or soon afterward, for maximum tactical and strategic advantage in the litigation process. "Hurry up and wait" is the normal pace in litigation: hurry to meet arbitrary court deadlines, wait for the court calendar to have space to attend to client needs. Always, the norm of third party judicial resolution is the template that shapes development of goals, sharing of information, advocacy of positions, and pacing of resolution.

. . .

In many ways, the real interests of divorcing parties get lost in the process of bringing a litigation-driven case to settlement. The focus, in these settlements, is on the immediate divorce-related financial and custody provisions of the divorce judgment. Limited or no attention is given to the interests and needs of the post-divorce restructured family, either in the sense of positive planning for healthy long term family restructuring and change, or in the sense of minimizing the destructive impacts of the divorce process itself on economic interests of family members and on possibilities for effective parenting of children after the divorce. In most U.S. jurisdictions, litigated court proceedings and files (including those of cases that ultimately settle) are open to the public and all vestiges of privacy are lost, at the same time that matters formerly decided privately by the couple are handed placed under the control of disinterested and busy professionals.

. . .

The [collaborative] process invites maximum client involvement and control over outcome, while maximizing privacy and creativity. The participation agreements signed at the outset commit all participants to good faith bargaining, voluntary full disclosures, interest-based bargaining, inclusion of relational and long term interests in the identification of clients' goals and strategies. The role of the lawyer is redefined in collaborative practice, as advocate for achieving the long-term enlightened interests of the client, rather than zealous advocate for goals and strategies identified by clients possessed by transient states of diminished capacity associated with the trauma of divorce. The disqualification of all professionals from participation in litigation between these clients has the effect of keeping both lawyers and clients at the negotiating table in the face of apparent impasse much longer than is typically the case in conventional settlement negotiations, where resort to the local judge to resolve impasses is a comfortable and familiar option on the dispute resolution menu that litigation attorneys carry in their mental armory. For collaborative lawyers, deciding to see what the local judge can do with an apparent impasse is identical to a decision to cease participating in the case. Unlike litigation attorneys, collaborative lawyers share the risk of failure in collaboration with their clients. Collaborative lawyers see these features of the collaborative law model as powerful aids to creative conflict resolution—as the means for liberating the effective problem solver trapped within litigating lawyers.

Collaborative Law Resembles But Differs in Important Ways from Mediation

While collaborative law builds upon important conflict resolution skills and understandings developed in the field of mediation, collaborative law differs from mediation in important ways. First and foremost, collaborative lawyers are advocates, not neutrals. They work within all professional ethics and standards of practice for lawyers and are a licensed profession. They owe a primary duty to their own clients. But, this duty is reframed not as the duty to zealously advocate for whatever fear-driven objective the client might grasp for during the course of recovering from loss of a marriage, but rather the duty to work with the client to help him or her achieve the goal nearly all clients say they want—the "good divorce," speedy, economical, respectful, individualized, and protective of children—in a process specifically tailored to help the client be able to realize that goal. This means that collaborative lawyers undertake much more than either a conventional lawyer or a mediator considers to be part of the job description: to educate clients, help them work from positions to interests, remove them from the negotiating table when they are too upset to think clearly, counsel them when they behave in self-defeating or bad faith ways, and assist them to recalibrate back to the high intentions identified at the start of the collaborative retention. Moreover, collaborative lawyers generally agree to protocols for practice whereby they will withdraw from representing a client who hides information, stonewalls, misrepresents, or otherwise misuses the collaborative process.

Where clients in mediation may occupy an uneven playing field, collaborative law builds in advocacy and legal advice into the heart of the process. Where neutral mediators may encounter great difficulty working with clients who subvert the process (whether intentionally or otherwise) while still maintaining neutrality, collaborative lawyers take on as part of their agreed job description the responsibility to work with such clients until they can return to the table willing and able to engage in effective good faith negotiations.

Finally, the structure of the collaborative legal model itself seems to offer more wattage of focused dispute resolution power than is generally available in family law mediation. Family law mediation often takes place as a three-way process, including the two divorcing spouses and one neutral mediator; lawyers for the parties, if they are involved at all, participate from their own offices, not in the mediation room. Even when consulting attorneys for the parties participate directly in the mediation, they participate not as designated conflict resolution professionals working explicitly toward settlement, but rather as conventional legal counsel who provide advice and representation in an adversarial model in which the decision to terminate mediation and take the matter to court is readily available and without built-in disincentives. Only in collaborative practice is the option-generating and negotiating process conducted by two trained legal advocates committed to consensual dispute resolution and skilled in interest-based bargaining who share a commitment to help clients stay on the high road and discover common ground for solutions. Because these advocates, who have every incentive to continue working toward settlement, meet in "real time" around a table with the clients who are expert in the facts and interests associated with the case, and everyone can hear and respond to the ideas of all the other participants in the conversation, the creative "out of the box" lateral thinking power available at the negotiating table to help clients reach agreement is considerably amplified as compared to single-neutral mediation.

Interdisciplinary Collaborative Practice

During the early 1990's, at the same time that lawyers were developing and extending collaborative legal practice, a parallel model called collaborative divorce emerged among a certain segment of mental health professionals experienced working in the court system on the custody battles of high conflict divorcing couples. These psychologists, social workers, and counselors mediated at the courthouse, and conducted the child custody evaluations used in trials and court-annexed settlement conferences to provide recommendations and rationales about which parent was more deserving of custody of the children. These professionals came to see that their evaluation reports, though intended to serve the best interests of children, were further polarizing the already-conflicted parents and decreasing their ability to provide effective post-divorce parenting for children.

[T]he collaborative law model, developing simultaneously and separately among family law attorneys, was the final component of an approach that now offers integrated virtual professional teams to divorcing spouses in many communities across the U.S. and Canada. These teams include: two collaborative lawyers, two divorce coaches (who must be licensed mental health professionals experienced in divorce work), a child specialist, and a financial neutral. These professionals are trained in the psychodynamics of divorce and healthy family restructuring as well as effective communication skills, conflict resolution skills, and interdisciplinary collaboration.

. . .

Where clients have the intention, but not the emotional or intellectual ability, to work effectively with their collaborative lawyers in legal negotiations, this interdisciplinary model can provide the additional resources needed for couple to realize their intention of having a "good divorce." For such clients, paradoxically, paying to bring in the necessary range of professional resources typically results in a divorce that costs less than it would have if they had been represented solely by collaborative lawyers, without the interdisciplinary team. . . . Like collaborative lawyers, all interdisciplinary collaborative divorce professionals sign contractual agreements with their clients that bar them from ever participating in contested court proceedings between the parties.

NOTE

The National Conference of Commissioners on Uniform State Law completed a model Collaborative Law Act in 2009, which was revised and supplemented by Uniform Collaborative Law Rules in 2010. The act has been adopted in Nevada, Texas, and Utah.

ABA Committee on Ethics and Professional Responsibility Formal Opinion 07–447: Ethical Considerations in Collaborative Law Practice

Aug. 9, 2007.

In this opinion, we analyze the implications of the Model Rules on collaborative law practice. Collaborative law is a type of alternative dispute resolution in which the parties and their lawyers commit to work cooperatively to reach a settlement. It had its roots in, and shares many attributes of, the mediation process. Participants focus on the interests of both clients, gather sufficient information to insure that decisions are made with full knowledge, develop a full range of options, and then choose options that best meet the needs of the parties. The parties structure a mutually acceptable written resolution of all issues without court involvement. The product of the process is then submitted to the court as a final decree. The structure creates a problem-solving atmosphere with a focus on interest-based negotiation and client empowerment.[3] Since its creation in Minnesota in 1990, collaborative practice has spread rapidly throughout the United States and into Canada, Australia, and Western Europe. Numerous established collaborative law organizations develop local practice protocols, train practitioners, reach out to the public, and build referral networks. On its website, the International Academy of Collaborative Professionals describes its mission as fostering professional excellence in conflict resolution by protecting the essentials of collaborative practice, expanding collaborative practice worldwide, and providing a central resource for education, networking, and standards of practice.[6] Although there are several models of collaborative practice, all of them share the same core elements that are set out in a contract between the clients and their lawyers (often referred to as a "four-way" agreement). In that agreement, the parties commit to negotiating a mutually acceptable settlement without court intervention, to engaging in open communication and information sharing, and to creating shared solutions that meet the needs of both clients. To ensure the commitment of the lawyers to the collaborative process, the four-way agreement also includes a requirement that, if the process breaks down, the lawyers will withdraw from representing their respective clients and will not handle any subsequent court proceedings. Several state bar opinions have analyzed collaborative practice and, with one exception, have concluded that it is not inherently inconsistent with the Model Rules.[7] Most authorities treat collaborative law practice as a species of limited scope representation and discuss the duties of lawyers in those situations, including communication, competence, diligence, and confidentiality. However, even those opinions are guarded, and caution that collaborative practice carries with it a potential for significant ethical difficulties.

As explained herein, we agree that collaborative law practice and the provisions of the four-way agreement represent a permissible limited scope representation under Model Rule 1.2, with the concomitant duties of competence, diligence, and communication. We reject the suggestion that collaborative law practice sets up a non-waivable conflict under Rule 1.7(a)(2).

Rule 1.2(c) permits a lawyer to limit the scope of a representation so long as the limitation is reasonable under the circumstances and the client gives informed consent. Nothing in the Rule or its Comment suggest that limiting a representation to a collaborative effort to reach a settlement is per

---

3. *See generally* Sherri Goren Slovin, "The Basics of Collaborative Family Law: A Divorce Paradigm Shift," 18 AMER. J. OF FAMILY LAW 74 (Summer 2004), available at http://www.mediate. com/pfriendly.cfm?id=1684.

6. *See* http://www.collaborativepractice.com/t2.asp?T=Mission.

7. Colorado Bar Ass'n Eth. Op. 115 (Feb. 24, 2007), "Ethical Considerations in the Collaborative and Cooperative Law Contexts," available at http://www.cobar.org/group/display. cfm?GenID=10159 & EntityID=ceth, is the only opinion to conclude that a non-consentable conflict arises in collaborative practice. Other state authorities analyze the disqualification obligation under Rules 1.2, 1.16, or 5.6. *See e.g.*, Kentucky Bar Ass'n Op. E–425 (June 2005), Participation in the "Collaborative Law" Process, available at http://www.kybar.org/documents/ ethics_opinions/kba_e–425.pdf; New Jersey Adv. Comm. on Prof'l Eth. Op. 699 (Dec. 12, 2005), "Collaborative Law," available at http://lawlibrary.rutgers.edu/ethicsdecisions/acpe/acp699_1. html; North Carolina State Bar Ass'n 2002 Formal Eth. Op. 1 (Apr. 19, 2002), "Participation in Collaborative Resolution Process Requiring Lawyer to Agree to Limit Future Court Representation," available at http://www.ncbar.com/ethics/ethics.asp?page=2 & from=4/ 2002 & to=4/2002; Pennsylvania Bar Ass'n Comm. on Legal Eth. & Prof'l Resp. Inf. Op. 2004–24 (May 11, 2004), available at http://www.collaborativelaw.us/articles/Ethics_Opinion_Penn_CL_2004. pdf. Several states have special rules for collaborative law practice. *See, e.g.*, CAL. FAM. § 2013 (West 2007); N.C. GEN. STAT. § 50–70 to 50–79 (2006); TEX. FAM. CODE ANN. §§ 6.603 & 153.0072 (Vernon 2005).

se unreasonable. On the contrary, comment [6] provides that "[a] limited representation may be appropriate because the client has limited objectives for the representation. In addition, the terms upon which representation is undertaken may exclude specific means that might otherwise be used to accomplish the client's objectives."

Obtaining the client's informed consent requires that the lawyer communicate adequate information and explanation about the material risks of and reasonably available alternatives to the limited representation. The lawyer must provide adequate information about the rules or contractual terms governing the collaborative process, its advantages and disadvantages, and the alternatives. The lawyer also must assure that the client understands that, if the collaborative law procedure does not result in settlement of the dispute and litigation is the only recourse, the collaborative lawyer must withdraw and the parties must retain new lawyers to prepare the matter for trial.

INDEX

References are to Pages

†